Occupational Outlook Handbook

2006-07 Edition

U.S. Department of Labor
Elaine L. Chao, Secretary

U.S. Bureau of Labor Statistics
Kathleen Utgoff, Commissioner

February 2006

Bulletin 2600

For Reference

Not to be taken from this room

U.S. GOVERNMENT OFFICIAL EDITION NOTICE

Legal Status and Use of Trademarks, Logos and Seals

The seal of the U.S. Bureau of Labor Statistics (BLS) authenticates this publication as the Official U.S. Government edition of the *BLS Occupational Outlook Handbook*, a nationally recognized source of career information describing the job duties, working conditions, training requirements, earnings, and job prospects in a wide variety of occupations.

Under the provisions of 15 U.S.C § 1125 and 18 U.S.C. § 709, the unauthorized use of this seal is prohibited and subject to civil and criminal penalties including fines and imprisonment.

Use of ISBN Prefix

This is the Official U.S. Government edition of this publication and is herein identified to certify its authenticity. Use of the 0-16 ISBN prefix is for U.S. Government Printing Office Official Editions only. The Superintendent of Documents of the U.S. Government Printing Office requests that any reprinted edition be labeled clearly as a copy of the authentic work with a new ISBN.

ISBN 0-16-072941-6

9 780160 729416

90000

Suggested citation: U.S. Bureau of Labor Statistics, U.S. Department of Labor, *Occupational Outlook Handbook, 2006-07 Edition*, Bulletin 2600. Superintendent of Documents, U.S. Government Printing Office, Washington, DC 2006.

For sale by the Superintendent of Documents, U.S. Government Printing Office
Internet: bookstore.gpo.gov   Phone: toll free (866) 512-1800;   DC area (202) 512-1800
Fax: (202) 512-2250 Mail: Stop SSOP, Washington, DC 20402-0001

ISBN 0-16-072941-6

Acknowledgments

The Bureau of Labor Statistics produced the *Handbook* under the general guidance and direction of Mike Pilot, Chief, Division of Occupational Outlook, Office of Occupational Statistics and Employment Projections. Chester C. Levine and Jon Q. Sargent, Managers of Occupational Outlook Studies, provided planning and day-to-day direction.

Supervisors overseeing the research and preparation of material were Douglas Braddock, Theresa Cosca, Arlene K. Dohm, and Terry Schau. Occupational analysts who contributed material were Andrew D. Alpert, Sadie Blanchard, Hall Dillon, Tamara Dillon, Thomas DiVincenzo, Diana Gehlhaus, Henry T. Kasper, Jonathan Kelinson, Jill Lacey, William Lawhorn, C. Brett Lockard, Kevin M. McCarron, Roger J. Moncarz, Michelle Murillo, Gregory Niemesh, Brian Roberts, Lynn Shniper, Patricia Tate, Dave Terkanian, Nicholas Terrell, Michael Wolf, Benjamin Wright, and Ian Wyatt.

Editorial work was provided by Edith Baker, Monica Gabor, Lori Pastro, and Allison Tarmann, under the supervision of Mary K. Rieg. Word processing support was provided by Monique Smith and Beverly A. Williams. Computer programming support was provided by David S. Frank and Erik A. Savisaar. The cover and other art were designed by Bruce Boyd. T. Alan Lacey also contributed art.

Photographs were taken by Shawn Moore, Department of Labor Photographic Services, Barry Gardner; Kevin Kennedy; Freddie Lieberman; Doug Sonders; and James Tkatch. The Bureau of Labor Statistics also wishes to express its appreciation for the cooperation and assistance of the many organizations and individuals who either contributed photographs or made their facilities available to photographers working for or under contract to the U.S. Department of Labor. Situations portrayed in the photographs may not be free of every possible safety or health hazard. Depiction of company or trade name in no way constitutes endorsement by the Department of Labor.

Note

Many trade associations, professional societies, unions, industrial organizations, and government agencies provide career information that is valuable to counselors and jobseekers. For the convenience of *Handbook* users, some of these organizations and, in some cases, their Internet addresses are listed at the end of each occupational statement. Although these references were carefully compiled, the Bureau of Labor Statistics has neither authority nor facilities for investigating the organizations or the information or publications that may be sent in response to a request and cannot guarantee the accuracy of such information. The listing of an organization, therefore, does not constitute in any way an endorsement or recommendation by the Bureau either of the organization and its activities or of the information it may supply. Each organization has sole responsibility for whatever information it may issue.

The *Handbook* describes the job outlook over a projected 10-year period for occupations across the Nation; consequently, short-term labor market fluctuations and regional differences in job outlook generally are not discussed. Similarly, the *Handbook* provides a general, composite description of jobs and cannot be expected to reflect work situations in specific establishments or localities. The *Handbook*, therefore, is not intended and should not be used as a guide for determining wages, hours of work, the right of a particular union to represent workers, appropriate bargaining units, or formal job evaluation systems. Nor should earnings data in the *Handbook* be used to compute future loss of earnings in adjudication proceedings involving work injuries or accidental deaths.

Material in this publication is in the public domain and, with appropriate credit, may be reproduced without permission. Comments about the contents of this publication and suggestions for improving it are welcome. Please address them to Chief, Division of Occupational Outlook, Office of Occupational Statistics and Employment Projections, Bureau of Labor Statistics, U.S. Department of Labor, 2 Massachusetts Ave. NE, Room 2135, Washington, DC 20212. Phone: **(202) 691-5700.** FAX: **(202) 691-5745.** E-mail: *oohinfo@bls.gov.* Addtional information is available on the Internet: **http://www.bls.gov/oco.** Information in the *Handbook* is available to sensory impaired individuals upon request. Voice telephone: **(202) 691-5200;** Federal Relay Service: **(800) 877-8339.**

Contents

Special Features

Tomorrow's Jobs 001
Sources of Career Information 009
Sources of Education, Training, and Financial
    Aid 014
Finding a Job and Evaluating a Job Offer 017
Occupational Information Included in the
    Handbook 022
Data for Occupations Not Studied in Detail 661
Assumptions and Methods Used in Preparing
    Employment Projections 674
Occupational Information Network Coverage 676
Index 684

Occupational Coverage

Management, business, and financial occupations

Management occupations
Administrative services managers 025
Advertising, marketing, promotions, public relations, and sales
    managers 027
Computer and information systems managers 030
Construction managers 032
Education administrators 034
Engineering and natural sciences managers 038
Farmers, ranchers, and agricultural managers 040
Financial managers 042
Food service managers 045
Funeral directors 048
Human resources, training, and labor relations managers and
    specialists 050
Industrial production managers 054
Lodging managers 056
Medical and health services managers 059
Property, real estate, and community association managers 061
Purchasing managers, buyers, and purchasing agents 064
Top executives 067

Business and financial operations occupations
Accountants and auditors 070
Appraisers and assessors of real estate 074
Budget analysts 077
Claims adjusters, appraisers, examiners, and investigators 080
Cost estimators 083
Financial analysts and personal financial advisors 085
Insurance underwriters 088
Loan officers 090
Management analysts 092
Meeting and convention planners 095
Tax examiners, collectors, and revenue agents 098

Professional and related occupations

Computer and mathematical occupations
Actuaries 102
Computer programmers 104

Computer scientists and database administrators 107
Computer software engineers 111
Computer support specialists and systems administrators 113
Computer systems analysts 116
Mathematicians 119
Operations research analysts 121
Statisticians 123

Architects, surveyors, and cartographers
Architects, except landscape and naval 125
Landscape architects 128
Surveyors, cartographers, photogrammetrists, and surveying
    technicians 130

Engineers 133

Drafters and engineering technicians
Drafters 141
Engineering technicians 144

Life scientists
Agricultural and food scientists 147
Biological scientists 150
Conservation scientists and foresters 153
Medical scientists 156

Physical scientists
Atmospheric scientists 159
Chemists and materials scientists 162
Environmental scientists and hydrologists 164
Geoscientists 167
Physicists and astronomers 170

Social scientists and related occupations
Economists 173
Market and survey researchers 175
Psychologists 177
Urban and regional planners 180
Social scientists, other 182

Science technicians 185

Community and social services occupations
Counselors 189
Probation officers and correctional treatment specialists 192
Social and human service assistants 194
Social workers 196

Legal occupations
Court reporters 199
Judges, magistrates, and other judicial workers 201
Lawyers 204
Paralegals and legal assistants 207

Education, training, library, and museum occupations
Archivists, curators, and museum technicians 210
Instructional coordinators 213
Librarians 214
Library technicians 217
Teacher assistants 219
Teachers—adult literacy and remedial education 221
Teachers—postsecondary 223
Teachers—preschool, kindergarten, elementary, middle, and
    secondary 227
Teachers—self-enrichment education 231
Teachers—special education 232

Art and design occupations
Artists and related workers 235
Commercial and industrial designers 238
Fashion designers 240
Floral designers 242

Graphic designers.. 243
Interior designers 245

Entertainers and performers, sports and related occupations
Actors, producers, and directors 249
Athletes, coaches, umpires, and related workers....... 252
Dancers and choreographers................................ 255
Musicians, singers, and related workers.............. 257

Media and communication-related occupations
Announcers 259
Broadcast and sound engineering technicians and radio
    operators.. 261
Interpreters and translators................................. 263
News analysts, reporters, and correspondents 267
Photographers 269
Public relations specialists 271
Television, video, and motion picture camera operators and
    editors 274
Writers and editors... 275

Health diagnosing and treating practitioners
Audiologists.. 278
Chiropractors.. 280
Dentists 282
Dietitians and nutritionists 284
Occupational therapists....................................... 285
Optometrists.. 287
Pharmacists 289
Physical therapists.. 292
Physician assistants.. 293
Physicians and surgeons 295
Podiatrists... 298
Radiation therapists.. 300
Recreational therapists.. 302
Registered nurses 303
Respiratory therapists... 307
Speech-language pathologists.............................. 309
Veterinarians 311

Health technologists and technicians
Athletic trainers 314
Cardiovascular technologists and technicians 316
Clinical laboratory technologists and technicians 318
Dental hygienists.. 320
Diagnostic medical sonographers 322
Emergency medical technicians and paramedics 324
Licensed practical and licensed vocational nurses 326
Medical records and health information technicians 328
Nuclear medicine technologists........................... 330
Occupational health and safety specialists and technicians.......... 331
Opticians, dispensing 334
Pharmacy technicians.. 336
Radiologic technologists and technicians 337
Surgical technologists 339
Veterinary technologists and technicians.............. 341

Service occupations

Healthcare support occupations
Dental assistants... 343
Massage therapists 344
Medical assistants 347
Medical transcriptionists..................................... 348
Nursing, psychiatric, and home health aides 350
Occupational therapist assistants and aides 353
Pharmacy aides 354
Physical therapist assistants and aides 356

Protective service occupations
Correctional officers... 357
Fire fighting occupations..................................... 359

Police and detectives... 362
Private detectives and investigators..................... 366
Security guards and gaming surveillance officers 368

Food preparation and serving related occupations
Chefs, cooks, and food preparation workers......... 371
Food and beverage serving and related workers...... 374

Building and grounds cleaning and maintenance occupations
Building cleaning workers 378
Grounds maintenance workers.............................. 380
Pest control workers.. 382

Personal care and service occupations
Animal care and service workers......................... 384
Barbers, cosmetologists, and other personal appearance
    workers.. 387
Child care workers.. 389
Fitness workers 392
Flight attendants... 394
Gaming services occupations............................... 397
Personal and home care aides 399
Recreation workers... 400

Sales and related occupations
Advertising sales agents...................................... 403
Cashiers.. 405
Counter and rental clerks 407
Demonstrators, product promoters, and models 408
Insurance sales agents 411
Real estate brokers and sales agents 414
Retail salespersons... 417
Sales engineers... 419
Sales representatives, wholesale and manufacturing 421
Sales worker supervisors..................................... 423
Securities, commodities, and financial services sales agents........ 426
Travel agents 429

Office and administrative support occupations

Financial clerks
Bill and account collectors.................................. 431
Billing and posting clerks and machine operators 432
Bookkeeping, accounting, and auditing clerks 434
Gaming cage workers 435
Payroll and timekeeping clerks............................ 437
Procurement clerks... 438
Tellers.. 440

Information and record clerks
Brokerage clerks 441
Credit authorizers, checkers, and clerks 442
Customer service representatives......................... 444
File clerks... 447
Hotel, motel, and resort desk clerks.................... 448
Human resources assistants, except payroll and timekeeping 449
Interviewers.. 451
Library assistants, clerical................................... 453
Order clerks.. 454
Receptionists and information clerks................... 455
Reservation and transportation ticket agents and travel clerks..... 457

Material recording, scheduling, dispatching, and distributing occupations
Cargo and freight agents 459
Couriers and messengers..................................... 460
Dispatchers... 461
Meter readers, utilities 463
Postal Service workers.. 464
Production, planning, and expediting clerks.......... 466
Shipping, receiving, and traffic clerks 467

Stock clerks and order fillers.. 469
Weighers, measurers, checkers, and samplers, recordkeeping 470

Other office and administrative support occupations
Communications equipment operators 471
Computer operators... 473
Data entry and information processing workers 475
Desktop publishers.. 477
Office and administrative support worker supervisors and
    managers.. 479
Office clerks, general 481
Secretaries and administrative assistants 482

Farming, fishing, and forestry occupations

Agricultural workers 485
Fishers and fishing vessel operators.......................... 487
Forest, conservation, and logging workers 490

Construction trades and related workers

Boilermakers... 494
Brickmasons, blockmasons, and stonemasons.............. 495
Carpenters 497
Carpet, floor, and tile installers and finishers............. 499
Cement masons, concrete finishers, segmental pavers, and
    terrazzo workers... 502
Construction and building inspectors......................... 504
Construction equipment operators............................. 507
Construction laborers 509
Drywall installers, ceiling tile installers, and tapers 511
Electricians... 513
Elevator installers and repairers............................... 516
Glaziers 517
Hazardous materials removal workers 519
Insulation workers.. 522
Painters and paperhangers...................................... 523
Pipelayers, plumbers, pipefitters, and steamfitters........ 525
Plasterers and stucco masons 528
Roofers.. 530
Sheet metal workers.. 531
Structural and reinforcing iron and metal workers 534

Installation, maintenance, and repair occupations

**Electrical and electronic equipment mechanics, installers,
and repairers**
Computer, automated teller, and office machine repairers............ 536
Electrical and electronics installers and repairers......... 538
Electronic home entertainment equipment installers and
    repairers 540
Radio and telecommunications equipment installers and
    repairers 542

**Vehicle and mobile equipment mechanics, installers, and
repairers**
Aircraft and avionics equipment mechanics and service
    technicians 544
Automotive body and related repairers....................... 547
Automotive service technicians and mechanics 549
Diesel service technicians and mechanics 552

Heavy vehicle and mobile equipment service technicians and
    mechanics 555
Small engine mechanics... 558

Other installation, maintenance, and repair occupations
Coin, vending, and amusement machine servicers and repairers....... 560
Heating, air-conditioning, and refrigeration mechanics and
    installers.. 562
Home appliance repairers 565
Industrial machinery mechanics and maintenance workers........ 567
Line installers and repairers.................................... 569
Maintenance and repair workers, general 572
Millwrights... 573
Precision instrument and equipment repairers.............. 575

Production occupations

Assemblers and fabricators 579
Food processing occupations 581
Metal workers and plastic workers
Computer control programmers and operators 585
Machinists... 587
Machine setters, operators, and tenders—metal and plastic 589
Tool and die makers 592
Welding, soldering, and brazing workers.................... 594
Printing occupations
Bookbinders and bindery workers 596
Prepress technicians and workers 598
Printing machine operators 600
Textile, apparel, and furnishings occupations 602
Woodworkers 606
Plant and system operators
Power plant operators, distributors, and dispatchers 608
Stationary engineers and boiler operators................... 610
Water and liquid waste treatment plant and system operators...... 612
Other production occupations
Inspectors, testers, sorters, samplers, and weighers 614
Jewelers and precious stone and metal workers 616
Medical, dental, and ophthalmic laboratory technicians 619
Painting and coating workers, except construction and
    maintenance.. 622
Photographic process workers and processing machine operators 625
Semiconductor processors 626

Transportation and material moving occupations

Air transportation occupations
Aircraft pilots and flight engineers 629
Air traffic controllers.. 632
Motor vehicle operators
Bus drivers 634
Taxi drivers and chauffeurs..................................... 637
Truck drivers and driver/sales workers...................... 640
Rail transportation occupations 644
Water transportation occupations 647
Material moving occupations 650

Job Opportunities in the Armed Forces 653

Additional Information About the 2004-14 Projections

Readers interested in more information about the projections; about the methods and assumptions that underlie them; or about details on economic growth, the labor force, or industry and occupational employment, should consult the November 2005 *Monthly Labor Review,* or the Winter 2005-06 *Occupational Outlook Quarterly.*

For more information about employment change, job openings, earnings, unemployment rates, and training requirements by occupation, consult *Occupational Projections and Training Data, 2006-07 Edition,* BLS Bulletin 2602.

For occupational information from an industry perspective, including discussions of some occupations and career paths that the *Occupational Outlook Handbook* does not cover, consult the *Career Guide to Industries, 2006-07 Edition,* BLS Bulletin 2601.

Tomorrow's Jobs

Making informed career decisions requires reliable information about opportunities in the future. Opportunities result from the relationships between the population, labor force, and the demand for goods and services.

Population ultimately limits the size of the labor force—individuals working or looking for work—which constrains how much can be produced. Demand for various goods and services determines employment in the industries providing them. Occupational employment opportunities, in turn, result from demand for skills needed within specific industries. Opportunities for medical assistants and other healthcare occupations, for example, have surged in response to rapid growth in demand for health services.

Examining the past and projecting changes in these relationships is the foundation of the Occupational Outlook Program. This chapter presents highlights of Bureau of Labor Statistics projections of the labor force and occupational and industry employment that can help to guide your career plans. Sources of detailed information about the projections appear on page viii.

Population

Population trends affect employment opportunities in a number of ways. Changes in population influence the demand for goods and services. For example, a growing and aging population has increased the demand for health services. Equally important, population changes produce corresponding changes in the size and demographic composition of the labor force.

The U.S. civilian noninstitutional population is expected to increase by 23.9 million over the 2004-14 period, at a slower rate of growth than during both the 1994-2004 and 1984-94 periods (chart 1). Continued growth will mean more consumers of goods and services, spurring demand for workers in a wide range of occupations and industries. The effects of population growth on various occupations will differ. The differences are partially accounted for by the age distribution of the future population.

The youth population, aged 16 to 24, will grow 2.9 percent over the 2004-14 period. As the baby boomers continue to age, the group aged 55 to 64 will increase by 36 percent or 10.4 million persons, more than any other group. The group aged 35 to 44 will decrease in size, reflecting the birth dearth following the baby boom generation.

Minorities and immigrants will constitute a larger share of the U.S. population in 2014. The number of Hispanics is projected to continue to grow much faster than those of all other racial and ethnic groups.

Labor force

Population is the single most important factor in determining the size and composition of the labor force—that is, people who are either working or looking for work. The civilian labor force is projected to increase by 14.7 million, or 10 percent, to 162.1 million over the 2004-14 period.

The U.S. workforce will become more diverse by 2014. White, non-Hispanic persons will continue to make up a decreasing share of the labor force, falling from 70 percent in 2004 to 65.6 percent in 2014 (chart 2). However, despite relatively slow growth, white, non-Hispanics will remain the largest group in the labor force in 2014. Asians are projected to account for an increasing share of the labor force by 2014, growing from 4.3 to 5.1 percent. Hispanics are projected be the fastest growing of the four labor force groups, growing by 33.7 percent. By 2014, Hispanics will continue to constitute a larger proportion of the labor force than will blacks, whose share will grow from 11.3 percent to 12.0 percent.

The numbers of men and women in the labor force will grow, but the number of women will grow at a faster rate than the number of men. The male labor force is projected to grow by 9.1 percent from 2004 to 2014, compared with 10.9 percent for

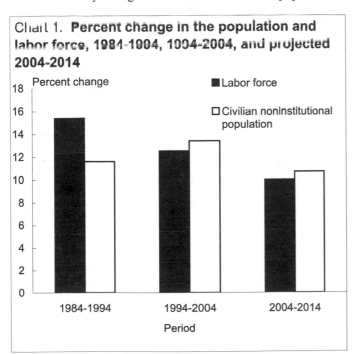

Chart 1. **Percent change in the population and labor force, 1984-1994, 1994-2004, and projected 2004-2014**

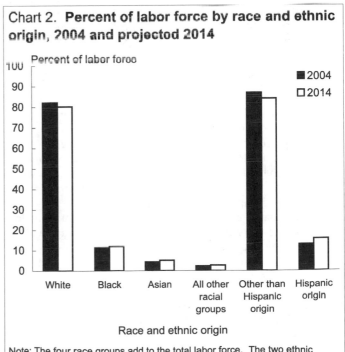

Chart 2. **Percent of labor force by race and ethnic origin, 2004 and projected 2014**

Note: The four race groups add to the total labor force. The two ethnic origin groups also add to the total labor force. Hispanics may be of any race.

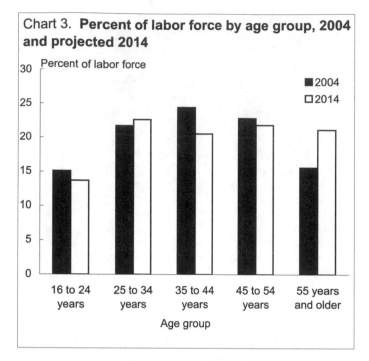

Chart 3. Percent of labor force by age group, 2004 and projected 2014

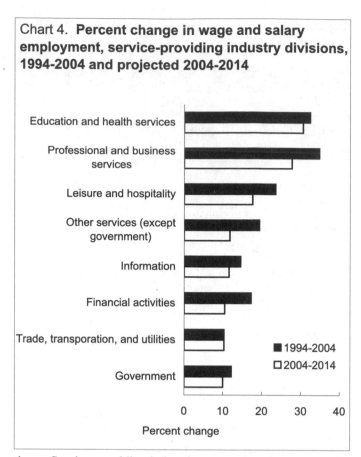

Chart 4. Percent change in wage and salary employment, service-providing industry divisions, 1994-2004 and projected 2004-2014

women. As a result, men's share of the labor force is expected to decrease from 53.6 to 53.2 percent, while women's share is expected to increase from 46.4 to 46.8 percent.

The youth labor force, aged 16 to 24, is expected to slightly decrease its share of the labor force to 13.7 percent by 2014. The primary working age group, between 25 and 54 years old, is projected to decline from 69.3 percent of the labor force in 2004 to 65.2 percent by 2014. Workers 55 and older, on the other hand, are projected to increase from 15.6 percent to 21.2 percent of the labor force between 2004 and 2014, due to the aging of the baby-boom generation (chart 3).

Employment

Total employment is expected to increase from 145.6 million in 2004 to 164.5 million in 2014, or by 13 percent. The 18.9 million jobs that will be added by 2014 will not be evenly distributed across major industrial and occupational groups. Changes in consumer demand, technology, and many other factors will contribute to the continually changing employment structure in the U.S. economy.

The following two sections examine projected employment change from both industrial and occupational perspectives. The industrial profile is discussed in terms of primary wage and salary employment. Primary employment excludes secondary jobs for those who hold multiple jobs. The exception is employment in agriculture, which includes self-employed and unpaid family workers in addition to wage and salary workers.

The occupational profile is viewed in terms of total employment—including primary and secondary jobs for wage and salary, self-employed, and unpaid family workers. Of the nearly 146 million jobs in the U.S. economy in 2004, wage and salary workers accounted for 133.5 million; self-employed workers accounted for 12.1 million; and unpaid family workers accounted for about 141,000. Secondary employment accounted for 1.7 million jobs. Self-employed workers held 9 out of 10 secondary jobs; wage and salary workers held most of the remainder.

Industry

Service-providing industries. The long-term shift from goods-producing to service-providing employment is expected to con-

tinue. Service-providing industries are expected to account for approximately 18.7 million of the 18.9 million new wage and salary jobs generated over the 2004-14 period (chart 4).

Education and health services. This industry supersector is projected to grow faster, 30.6 percent, and add more jobs than any other industry supersector. About 3 out of every 10 new jobs created in the U.S. economy will be in either the healthcare and social assistance or private educational services sectors.

Healthcare and social assistance—including private hospitals, nursing and residential care facilities, and individual and family services—will grow by 30.3 percent and add 4.3 million new jobs. Employment growth will be driven by increasing demand for healthcare and social assistance because of an aging population and longer life expectancies. Also, as more women enter the labor force, demand for childcare services is expected to grow.

Private educational services will grow by 32.5 percent and add 898,000 new jobs through 2014. Rising student enrollments at all levels of education will create demand for educational services.

Professional and business services. This industry supersector, which includes some of the fastest growing industries in the U.S. economy, will grow by 27.8 percent and add more than 4.5 million new jobs.

Employment in administrative and support and waste management and remediation services will grow by 31 percent and add 2.5 million new jobs to the economy by 2014. The fastest growing industry in this sector will be employment services, which will grow by 45.5 percent and will contribute almost two-thirds of all new jobs in administrative and support and waste management and remediation services. Employment services ranks among the fastest growing industries in the Nation and is expected to be among those that provide the most new jobs.

Employment in professional, scientific, and technical services will grow by 28.4 percent and add 1.9 million new jobs by 2014.

Employment in computer systems design and related services will grow by 39.5 percent and add almost one-fourth of all new jobs in professional, scientific, and technical services. Employment growth will be driven by the increasing reliance of businesses on information technology and the continuing importance of maintaining system and network security. Management, scientific, and technical consulting services also will grow very rapidly, by 60.5 percent, spurred by the increased use of new technology and computer software and the growing complexity of business.

Management of companies and enterprises will grow by 10.6 percent and add 182,000 new jobs.

Information. Employment in the information supersector is expected to increase by 11.6 percent, adding 364,000 jobs by 2014. Information contains some of the fast-growing computer-related industries such as software publishers; Internet publishing and broadcasting; and Internet service providers, Web search portals, and data processing services. Employment in these industries is expected to grow by 67.6 percent, 43.5 percent, and 27.8 percent, respectively. The information supersector also includes telecommunications, broadcasting, and newspaper, periodical, book, and directory publishers. Increased demand for residential and business land-line and wireless services, cable service, high-speed Internet connections, and software will fuel job growth among these industries.

Leisure and hospitality. Overall employment will grow by 17.7 percent. Arts, entertainment, and recreation will grow by 25 percent and add 460,000 new jobs by 2014. Most of these new job openings will come from the amusement, gambling, and recreation sector. Job growth will stem from public participation in arts, entertainment, and recreation activities—reflecting increasing incomes, leisure time, and awareness of the health benefits of physical fitness.

Accommodation and food services is expected to grow by 16.5 percent and add 1.8 million new jobs through 2014. Job growth will be concentrated in food services and drinking places, reflecting increases in population, dual-income families, and dining sophistication.

Trade, transportation, and utilities. Overall employment in this industry supersector will grow by 10.3 percent between 2004 and 2014. Transportation and warehousing is expected to increase by 506,000 jobs, or by 11.9 percent through 2014. Truck transportation will grow by 9.6 percent, adding 129,000 new jobs, while rail transportation is projected to decline. The warehousing and storage sector is projected to grow rapidly at 24.8 percent, adding 138,000 jobs. Demand for truck transportation and warehousing services will expand as many manufacturers concentrate on their core competencies and contract out their product transportation and storage functions.

Employment in retail trade is expected to increase by 11 percent, from 15 million to 16.7 million. Increases in population, personal income, and leisure time will contribute to employment growth in this industry, as consumers demand more goods. Wholesale trade is expected to increase by 8.4 percent, growing from 5.7 million to 6.1 million jobs.

Employment in utilities is projected to decrease by 1.3 percent through 2014. Despite increased output, employment in electric power generation, transmission, and distribution and natural gas distribution is expected to decline through 2014 due to improved technology that increases worker productivity. However, employment in water, sewage, and other systems is expected to increase 21 percent by 2014. Jobs are not easily eliminated by technological gains in this industry because water treatment and waste disposal are very labor-intensive activities.

Financial activities. Employment is projected to grow 10.5 percent over the 2004-14 period. Real estate and rental and leasing is expected to grow by 16.9 percent and add 353,000 jobs by 2014. Growth will be due, in part, to increased demand for housing as the population grows. The fastest growing industry in the financial activities supersector will be activities related to real estate, which will grow by 32.1 percent, reflecting the housing boom that persists throughout most of the Nation.

Finance and insurance is expected to increase by 496,000 jobs, or 8.3 percent, by 2014. Employment in securities, commodity contracts, and other financial investments and related activities is expected to grow 15.8 percent by 2014, reflecting the increased number of baby boomers in their peak savings years, the growth of tax-favorable retirement plans, and the globalization of the securities markets. Employment in credit intermediation and related services, including banks, will grow by 5.4 percent and add about one-third of all new jobs within finance and insurance. Insurance carriers and related activities is expected to grow by 9.5 percent and add 215,000 new jobs by 2014. The number of jobs within agencies, brokerages, and other insurance related activities is expected to grow about 19.4 percent, as many insurance carriers downsize their sales staffs and as agents set up their own businesses.

Government. Between 2004 and 2014, government employment, including that in public education and hospitals, is expected to increase by 10 percent, from 21.6 million to 23.8 million jobs. Growth in government employment will be fueled by growth in State and local educational services and the shift of responsibilities from the Federal Government to the State and local governments. Local government educational services is projected to increase 10 percent, adding 783,000 jobs. State government educational services is projected to grow by 19.6 percent, adding 442,000 jobs. Federal Government employment, including the Postal Service, is expected to increase by only 1.6 percent as the Federal Government continues to contract out many government jobs to private companies.

Other services (except government). Employment will grow by 14 percent. More than 1 out of every 4 new jobs in this supersector will be in religious organizations, which is expected to grow by 11.9 percent. Other automotive repair and maintenance will be the fastest growing industry at 30.7 percent. Also included among other services is personal care services, which is expected to increase by 19.5 percent

Goods-producing industries. Employment in the goods-producing industries has been relatively stagnant since the early 1980s. Overall, this sector is expected to decline 0.4 percent over the 2004-14 period. Although employment is expected to decline or increase more slowly than in the service-providing industries, projected growth among goods-producing industries varies considerably (chart 5).

Construction. Employment in construction is expected to increase by 11.4 percent, from 7 million to 7.8 million. Demand for new housing and an increase in road, bridge, and tunnel construction will account for the bulk of job growth in this supersector.

Manufacturing. Employment change in manufacturing will vary by individual industry, but overall employment in this supersector will decline by 5.4 percent or 777,000 jobs. For example, employment in transportation equipment manufacturing is expected to grow by 95,000 jobs. Due to an aging population and increasing life expectancies, pharmaceutical and medicine manufacturing is expected to grow by 26.1 percent and add 76,000 jobs through 2014. However, productivity gains, job automation, and international competition will adversely affect

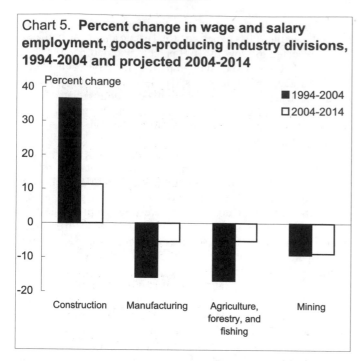

Chart 5. **Percent change in wage and salary employment, goods-producing industry divisions, 1994-2004 and projected 2004-2014**

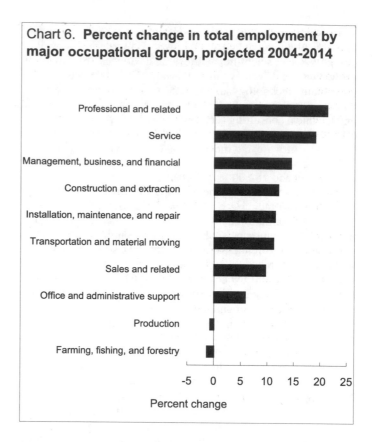

Chart 6. **Percent change in total employment by major occupational group, projected 2004-2014**

employment in many other manufacturing industries. Employment in textile mills and apparel manufacturing will decline by 119,000 and 170,000 jobs, respectively. Employment in computer and electronic product manufacturing also will decline by 94,000 jobs through 2014.

Agriculture, forestry, fishing, and hunting. Overall employment in agriculture, forestry, fishing, and hunting is expected to decrease by 5.2 percent. Employment is expected to continue to decline due to advancements in technology. The only industry within this supersector expected to grow is support activities for agriculture and forestry, which includes farm labor contractors and farm management services. This industry is expected to grow by 18.2 percent and add 19,000 new jobs.

Mining. Employment in mining is expected to decrease 8.8 percent, or by some 46,000 jobs, by 2014. Employment in coal mining and metal ore mining is expected to decline by 23.3 percent and 29.3 percent, respectively. Employment in oil and gas extraction also is projected to decline by 13.1 percent through 2014. Employment decreases in these industries are attributable mainly to technology gains that boost worker productivity, growing international competition, restricted access to Federal lands, and strict environmental regulations that require cleaning of burning fuels.

Occupation

Expansion of service-providing industries is expected to continue, creating demand for many occupations. However, projected job growth varies among major occupational groups (chart 6).

Professional and related occupations. Professional and related occupations will grow the fastest and add more new jobs than any other major occupational group. Over the 2004-14 period, a 21.2 percent increase in the number of professional and related jobs is projected, which translates into 6 million new jobs. Professional and related workers perform a wide variety of duties, and are employed throughout private industry and government. About three-quarters of the job growth will come from three groups of professional occupations—computer and mathematical occupations, healthcare practitioners and technical occupations, and education, training, and library occupations—which will add 4.5 million jobs combined.

Service occupations. Service workers perform services for the public. Employment in service occupations is projected to increase by 5.3 million, or 19 percent, the second largest numerical gain and second highest rate of growth among the major occupational groups. Food preparation and serving related occupations are expected to add the most jobs among the service occupations, 1.7 million by 2014. However, healthcare support occupations are expected to grow the fastest, 33.3 percent, adding 1.2 million new jobs.

Management, business, and financial occupations. Workers in management, business, and financial occupations plan and direct the activities of business, government, and other organizations. Their employment is expected to increase by 2.2 million, or 14.4 percent, by 2014. Among managers, the numbers of preschool and childcare center/program educational administrators and of computer and information systems managers will grow the fastest, by 27.9 percent and 25.9 percent, respectively. General and operations managers will add the most new jobs, 308,000, by 2014. Farmers and ranchers are the only workers in this major occupational group whose numbers are expected to decline, losing 155,000 jobs. Among business and financial occupations, accountants and auditors and management analysts will add the most jobs, 386,000 combined. Employment, recruitment, and placement specialists and personal financial advisors will be the fastest growing occupations in this group, with job increases of 30.5 percent and 25.9 percent, respectively.

Construction and extraction occupations. Construction and extraction workers construct new residential and commercial buildings, and also work in mines, quarries, and oil and gas fields. Employment of these workers is expected to grow 12 percent, adding 931,000 new jobs. Construction trades and related workers will account for more than three-fourths of these new jobs, 699,000, by 2014. Many extraction occupations will decline, reflecting overall employment losses in the mining and oil and gas extraction industries.

Installation, maintenance, and repair occupations. Workers in installation, maintenance, and repair occupations install new equipment and maintain and repair older equipment. These occupations will add 657,000 jobs by 2014, growing by 11.4 percent. Automotive service technicians and mechanics and general maintenance and repair workers will account for half of all new installation, maintenance, and repair jobs. The fastest growth rate will be among security and fire alarm systems installers, an occupation that is expected to grow 21.7 percent over the 2004-14 period.

Transportation and material moving occupations. Transportation and material moving workers transport people and materials by land, sea, or air. The number of these workers should grow 11.1 percent, accounting for 1.1 million additional jobs by 2014. Among transportation occupations, motor vehicle operators will add the most jobs, 629,000. Material moving occupations will grow 8.3 percent and will add 405,000 jobs. Rail transportation occupations are the only group in which employment is projected to decline, by 1.1 percent, through 2014.

Sales and related occupations. Sales and related workers transfer goods and services among businesses and consumers. Sales and related occupations are expected to add 1.5 million new jobs by 2014, growing by 9.6 percent. The majority of these jobs will be among retail salespersons and cashiers, occupations that will add 849,000 jobs combined.

Office and administrative support occupations. Office and administrative support workers perform the day-to-day activities of the office, such as preparing and filing documents, dealing with the public, and distributing information. Employment in these occupations is expected to grow by 5.8 percent, adding 1.4 million new jobs by 2014. Customer service representatives will add the most new jobs, 471,000. Desktop publishers will be among the fastest growing occupations in this group, increasing by 23.2 percent over the decade. However, due to rising productivity and increased automation, office and administrative support occupations also account for 11 of the 20 occupations with the largest employment declines.

Farming, fishing, and forestry occupations. Farming, fishing, and forestry workers cultivate plants, breed and raise livestock, and catch animals. These occupations will decline 1.3 percent and lose 13,000 jobs by 2014. Agricultural workers, including farmworkers and laborers, accounted for the overwhelming majority of new jobs in this group. The number of fishing and hunting workers is expected to decline, by 16.6, percent, while the number of logging workers is expected to increase by less than 1 percent.

Production occupations. Production workers are employed mainly in manufacturing, where they assemble goods and operate plants. Production occupations are expected to decline less than 1 percent, losing 79,000 jobs by 2014. Jobs will be created for many production occupations, including food processing workers, machinists, and welders, cutters, solderers, and brazers. Textile, apparel, and furnishings occupations, as well as assemblers and fabricators, will account for much of the job losses among production occupations.

Among all occupations in the economy, computer and healthcare occupations are expected to grow the fastest over the projection period (chart 7). In fact, healthcare occupations make up 12 of the 20 fastest growing occupations, while computer occupations account for 5 out of the 20 fastest growing occupations in the economy. In addition to high growth rates, these 17 computer and healthcare occupations combined will add more than 1.8 million new jobs. High growth rates among computer and healthcare occupations reflect projected

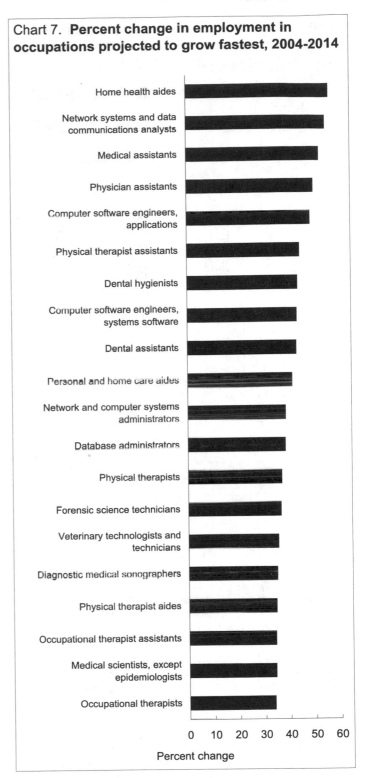

Chart 7. **Percent change in employment in occupations projected to grow fastest, 2004-2014**

rapid growth in the computer and data processing and health services industries.

The 20 occupations listed in chart 8 will account for more than one-third of all new jobs, 7.1 million combined, over the 2004-14 period. The occupations with the largest numerical increases cover a wider range of occupational categories than do those occupations with the fastest growth rates. Health occupations will account for some of these increases in employment, as well as occupations in education, sales, transportation, office and administrative support, and food service. Many of these occupations are very large, and will create more new jobs than will those with high growth rates. Only 3 out of the 20 fastest

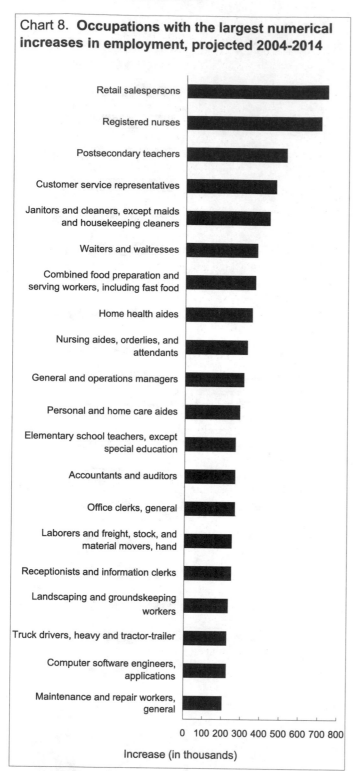

Chart 8. Occupations with the largest numerical increases in employment, projected 2004-2014

Retail salespersons

Registered nurses

Postsecondary teachers

Customer service representatives

Janitors and cleaners, except maids and housekeeping cleaners

Waiters and waitresses

Combined food preparation and serving workers, including fast food

Home health aides

Nursing aides, orderlies, and attendants

General and operations managers

Personal and home care aides

Elementary school teachers, except special education

Accountants and auditors

Office clerks, general

Laborers and freight, stock, and material movers, hand

Receptionists and information clerks

Landscaping and groundskeeping workers

Truck drivers, heavy and tractor-trailer

Computer software engineers, applications

Maintenance and repair workers, general

0   100 200 300 400 500 600 700 800

Increase (in thousands)

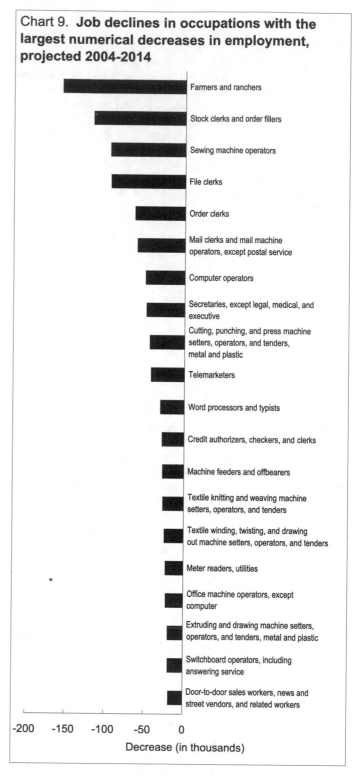

Chart 9. Job declines in occupations with the largest numerical decreases in employment, projected 2004-2014

Farmers and ranchers

Stock clerks and order fillers

Sewing machine operators

File clerks

Order clerks

Mail clerks and mail machine operators, except postal service

Computer operators

Secretaries, except legal, medical, and executive

Cutting, punching, and press machine setters, operators, and tenders, metal and plastic

Telemarketers

Word processors and typists

Credit authorizers, checkers, and clerks

Machine feeders and offbearers

Textile knitting and weaving machine setters, operators, and tenders

Textile winding, twisting, and drawing out machine setters, operators, and tenders

Meter readers, utilities

Office machine operators, except computer

Extruding and drawing machine setters, operators, and tenders, metal and plastic

Switchboard operators, including answering service

Door-to-door sales workers, news and street vendors, and related workers

-200   -150   -100   -50   0

Decrease (in thousands)

growing occupations—home health aides, personal and home care aides, and computer software application engineers—also are projected to be among the 20 occupations with the largest numerical increases in employment.

Declining occupational employment stems from declining industry employment, technological advancements, changes in business practices, and other factors. For example, increased productivity and farm consolidations are expected to result in a decline of 155,000 farmers and ranchers over the 2004-14 period (chart 9). The majority of the 20 occupations with the largest numerical decreases are office and administrative support and production occupations, which are affected by increasing plant

and factory automation and the implementation of office technology that reduces the needs for these workers. For example, employment of word processors and typists is expected to decline due to the proliferation of personal computers, which allows other workers to perform duties formerly assigned to word processors and typists.

Education and training

Among the 20 fastest growing occupations, a bachelor's or associate degree is the most significant source of postsecondary education or training for 12 of them—network systems and data communications analysts; physician assistants; computer soft-

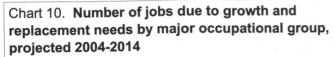

Chart 10. **Number of jobs due to growth and replacement needs by major occupational group, projected 2004-2014**

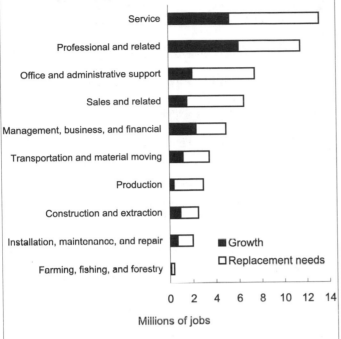

occupations with the largest numerical decreases. Table 1 lists the fastest growing occupations and occupations projected to have the largest numerical increases in employment between 2004 and 2014, by level of postsecondary education or training.

Total job openings

Job openings stem from both employment growth and replacement needs (chart 10). Replacement needs arise as workers leave occupations. Some transfer to other occupations while others retire, return to school, or quit to assume household responsibilities. Replacement needs are projected to account for more than 60 percent of the approximately 55 million job openings between 2004 and 2014. Thus, even occupations projected to experience slower than average growth or to decline in employment still may offer many job openings.

Professional and related occupations are projected to grow faster and add more jobs than any other major occupational group, with 6 million new jobs by 2014. Three-fourths of the job growth in professional and related occupations is expected among computer and mathematical occupations; healthcare practitioners and technical occupations; and education, training, and library occupations. With 5.5 million job openings due to replacement needs, professional and related occupations are the only major group projected to generate more openings from job growth than from replacement needs.

Service occupations are projected to have the largest number of total job openings, 13.2 million, reflecting high replacement needs. A large number of replacements will be necessary as young workers leave food preparation and service occupations. Replacement needs generally are greatest in the largest occupations and in those with relatively low pay or limited training requirements.

Office automation will significantly affect many individual office and administrative support occupations. Overall, these occupations are projected to grow more slowly than average, while some are projected to decline. Office and administrative support occupations are projected to create 7.5 million job openings over the 2004-14 period, ranking third behind service and professional and related occupations.

Farming, fishing, and forestry occupations are projected to have the fewest job openings, approximately 286,000. Because job growth is expected to be slow, and levels of retirement and job turnover high, more than 95 percent of these projected job openings are due to replacement needs.

ware engineers, applications; physical therapist assistants; dental hygienists; computer software engineers, systems software; network and computer systems administrators; database administrators; forensic science technicians; veterinary technologists and technicians; diagnostic medical sonographers; and occupational therapists assistants. On-the-job training is the most significant source of postsecondary education or training for another 5 of the 20 fastest growing occupations—physical therapist aides, medical assistants, home health aides, dental assistants, and personal and home care aides. In contrast, on-the-job training is the most significant source of postsecondary education or training for 13 of the 20 occupations with the largest numerical increases; 6 of these 20 occupations have an associate or higher degree as the most significant source of postsecondary education or training. On-the-job training also is the most significant source of postsecondary education or training for all 20 of the

Table 1. Fastest growing occupations and occupations projected to have the largest numerical increases in employment between 2004 and 2014, by level of postsecondary education or training

Fastest growing occupations	Postsecondary education or training level	Occupations having the largest numerical job growth
	First-professional degree	
Pharmacists		Physicians and surgeons
Physicians and surgeons		Lawyers
Chiropractors		Pharmacists
Optometrists		Dentists
Veterinarians		Chiropractors
	Doctoral degree	
Medical scientists, except epidemiologists		Postsecondary teachers
Postsecondary teachers		Clinical, counseling, and school psychologists
Computer and information scientists, research		Medical scientists, except epidemiologists
Biochemists and biophysicists		Computer and information scientists, research
Clinical, counseling, and school psychologists		Biochemists and biophysicists
	Master's degree	
Physical therapists		Physical therapists
Occupational therapists		Clergy
Hydrologists		Educational, vocational, and school counselors
Substance abuse and behavioral disorder counselors		Instructional coordinators
Instructional coordinators		Rehabilitation counselors
	Bachelor's or higher degree, plus work experience	
Education administrators, preschool and child care center/program		General and operations managers
Computer and information systems managers		Management analysts
Training and development managers		Financial managers
Actuaries		Computer and information systems managers
Medical and health services managers		Sales managers
	Bachelor's degree	
Network systems and data communications analysts		Elementary school teachers, except special education
Physician assistants		Accountants and auditors
Computer software engineers, applications		Computer software engineers, applications
Computer software engineers, systems software		Computer systems analysts
Network and computer systems administrators		Secondary school teachers, except special and vocational education
	Associate degree	
Physical therapist assistant		Registered nurses
Dental hygienists		Computer support specialists
Forensic science technicians		Dental hygienists
Veterinary technologists and technicians		Paralegals and legal assistants
Diagnostic medical sonographers		Medical records and health information technicians
	Postsecondary vocational award	
Preschool teachers, except special education		Nursing aides, orderlies, and attendants
Surgical technologists		Preschool teachers, except special education
Gaming dealers		Automotive service technicians and mechanics
Emergency medical technicians and paramedics		Licensed practical and licensed vocational nurses
Fitness trainers and aerobics instructors		Hairdressers, hairstylists, and cosmetologists
	Work experience in a related occupation	
Self-enrichment education teachers		First-line supervisors/managers of food preparation and serving workers
Emergency management specialists		First-line supervisors/managers of office and administrative support workers
Gaming managers		First-line supervisors/managers of construction trades and extraction workers
Construction and building inspectors		Self-enrichment education teachers
First-line supervisors/managers of fire fighting and prevention workers		First-line supervisors/managers of retail sales workers
	Long-term on-the-job training	
Fire fighters		Carpenters
Tile and marble setters		Cooks, restaurant
Athletes and sports competitors		Police and sheriff's patrol officers
Coaches and scouts		Plumbers, pipefitters, and steamfitters
Interpreters and translators		Electricians
	Moderate-term on-the-job training	
Medical assistants		Customer service representatives
Dental assistants		Truck drivers, heavy and tractor-trailer
Hazardous materials removal workers		Maintenance and repair workers, general
Social and human service assistants		Medical assistants
Residential advisors		Executive secretaries and administrative assistants
	Short-term on-the-job training	
Home health aides		Retail salespersons
Personal and home care aides		Janitors and cleaners, except maids and housekeeping cleaners
Physical therapist aides		Waiters and waitresses
Amusement and recreation attendants		Combined food preparation and serving workers, including fast food
Occupational therapist aides		Home health aides

Sources of Career Information

This section identifies some major sources of information on careers. These sources are meant to be used in addition to those listed at the end of each *Handbook* statement, and may provide additional information.

Career information

Like any major decision, selecting a career involves a lot of fact finding. Fortunately, some of the best informational resources are easily accessible. You should assess career guidance materials carefully. Information that seems out of date or glamorizes an occupation—overstates its earnings or exaggerates the demand for workers, for example—should be evaluated with skepticism. Gathering as much information as possible will help you make a more informed decision.

People you know. One of the best resources can be those you know, such as friends and family. They may answer some questions about a particular occupation or put you in touch with someone who has some experience in the field. This personal networking can be invaluable in evaluating an occupation or an employer. These people will be able to tell you about their specific duties and training, as well as what they did or did not like about a job. People who have worked in an occupation locally also may be able to recommend and get you in touch with specific employers.

Local libraries. Libraries can be an invaluable source of information. Since most areas have libraries, they can be a convenient place to look for information. Also, for those who do not otherwise have access to the Internet or e-mail, many libraries provide this access.

Libraries may have information on job openings, locally and nationally; potential contacts within occupations or industries; colleges and financial aid; vocational training; individual businesses or careers; and writing résumés. Libraries frequently have subscriptions to various trade magazines that can provide information on occupations and industries. These sources often have references to organizations which can provide additional information about training and employment opportunities. Your local library also may have video materials.

If you need help getting started or finding a resource, ask your librarian for assistance.

Professional societies, trade groups, and labor unions. These groups have information on an occupation or various related occupations with which they are associated or which they actively represent. This information may cover training requirements, earnings, and listings of local employers. These groups may train members or potential members themselves, or may be able to put you in contact with organizations or individuals who perform such training.

Each occupational statement in the *Handbook* concludes with a section on sources of additional information, which lists organizations that may be contacted for more information. Another valuable source for finding organizations associated with occupations is *The Encyclopedia of Associations*, an annual publication that lists trade associations, professional societies, labor unions, and fraternal and patriotic organizations.

Employers. This is the primary source of information on specific jobs. Employers may post lists of job openings and application requirements, including the exact training and experience required, starting wages and benefits, and advancement opportunities and career paths.

Postsecondary institutions. Colleges, universities, and other postsecondary institutions may put a lot of effort into helping place their graduates in good jobs, because the success of their graduates may indicate the quality of their institution and affect their ability to attract new students. Postsecondary institutions frequently have career centers with libraries of information on different careers, listings of related jobs, and alumni contacts in various professions. Career centers frequently employ career counselors who generally provide their services only to their students and alumni. Career centers can help you build your résumé, find internships and co-ops which can lead to full-time positions, and tailor your course selection or program to make you a more attractive job applicant.

Guidance and career counselors. Counselors can help you make choices about which careers might suit you best. Counselors can help you determine what occupations suit your skills by testing your aptitude for various types of work, and determining your strengths and interests. Counselors can help you evaluate your options and search for a job in your field or help you select a new field altogether. They can also help you determine which educational or training institutions best fit your goals, and find ways to finance them. Some counselors offer other services such as interview coaching, résumé building, and help in filling out various forms. Counselors in secondary schools and postsecondary institutions may arrange guest speakers, field trips, or job fairs.

Common places where guidance and career counselors are employed include:

● High school guidance offices
● College career planning and placement offices
● Placement offices in private vocational or technical schools and institutions
● Vocational rehabilitation agencies
● Counseling services offered by community organizations
● Private counseling agencies and private practices
● State employment service offices

When using a private counselor, check to see if the counselor is experienced. One way to do so is to ask people who have used their services in the past. The National Board of Certified Counselors and Affiliates is an institution which accredits career counselors. To verify the credentials of a career counselor and to find a career counselor in your area, contact:

➤ National Board for Certified Counselor and Affiliates, 3 Terrace Way, Suite D, Greensboro, NC 27403-3660. Internet: **http://www.nbcc.org/cfind**

Internet resources. With the growing popularity of the Internet, a wide verity of career information has become easily accessible. Many online resources include job listings, résumé posting services, and information on job fairs, training, and local wages. Many of the resources listed elsewhere in this section have Internet sites that include valuable information on potential careers. Since no single source contains all information on an occupation, field, or employer, you will likely need to use a variety of sources.

When using Internet resources, be sure that the organization is a credible, established source of information on the particular occupation. Individual companies may include job listings on their Web sites, and may include information about required credentials, wages and benefits, and the job's location. Contact information, such as whom to call or where to send a résumé, is typically included.

Some sources exist primarily as a Web service. These services often have information on specific jobs, and can greatly aid in the job hunting process. Some commercial sites offer these services, as do Federal, State, and some local governments. *Career OneStop*, a joint program by the Department of Labor and the States as well as local agencies, provides these services free of charge.

Online Sources from the Department of Labor. A major portion of the U.S. Department of Labor's Labor Market Information System is the Career OneStop site. This site includes:

- *America's Job Bank* allows you to search over a million job openings listed with State employment agencies.
- *America's Career InfoNet* provides data on employment growth and wages by occupation; the knowledge, skills, and abilities required by an occupation; and links to employers.
- *America's Service Locator* is a comprehensive database of career centers and information on unemployment benefits, job training, youth programs, seminars, educational opportunities, and disabled or older worker programs.

Career OneStop, along with the National Tollfree Helpline (877-USA-JOBS) and the local One-Stop Career Centers in each State, combine to provide a wide range of workforce assistance and resources:

➤ Career OneStop. Internet: **http://www.careeronestop.org**

Use the O*NET numbers at the start of each *Handbook* statement to find more information on specific occupations:

➤ O*NET Online. Internet: **http://www.onetcenter.org**

Provided in collaboration with the U.S. Department of Education, *Career Voyages* has information on certain high-demand occupations:

➤ Career Voyages. Internet: **http://www.careervoyages.org**

The Department of Labor's Bureau of Labor Statistics publishes a wide range of labor market information, from regional wages for specific occupations to statistics on National, State, and area employment.

➤ Bureau of Labor Statistics. Internet: **http://www.bls.gov**

While the *Handbook* discusses careers from an occupational perspective, a companion publication—*Career Guide to Industries*—discusses careers from an industry perspective. The *Career Guide* is also available at your local career center and library:

➤ *Career Guide to Industries*. Internet: **http://www.bls.gov/oco/cg/home.htm**

For information on occupational wages:

➤ Wage Data. Internet: **http://www.bls.gov/bls/blswage.htm**

For information on training, workers' rights, and job listings:

➤ Education and Training Administration. Internet: **http://www.doleta.gov/jobseekers**

Organizations for specific groups. Some organizations provide information designed to help specific groups of people. Consult directories in your library's reference center or a career guidance office for information on additional organizations associated with specific groups.

Disabled workers:
State counseling, training, and placement services for those with disabilities are available from:

➤ State Vocational Rehabilitation Agency. Internet: **http://www.ed.gov/Programs/EROD**

Information on employment opportunities, transportation, and other considerations for people with all types of disabilities is available from:

➤ National Organization on Disability, 910 Sixteenth St. NW., Suite 600, Washington, DC 20006. Telephone: (202) 293-5960. TTY: (202) 293-5968. Internet: **http://www.nod.org/economic**

For information on making accommodations in the work place for people with disabilities:

➤ Job Accommodation Network (JAN), P.O. Box 6080, Morgantown, WV 26506. Internet: **http://www.jan.wvu.edu**

A comprehensive Federal Web site of disability-related resources is accessible at: **http://www.disabilityinfo.gov**

Blind workers:
Information on the free national reference and referral service for the blind can be obtained by contacting:

➤ National Federation of the Blind, Job Opportunities for the Blind (JOB), 1800 Johnson St., Baltimore, MD 21230. Telephone: (410) 659-9314. Internet: **http://www.nfb.org**

Older workers:

➤ National Council on the Aging, 300 D St. SW., Suite 801, Washington, DC 20024. Telephone: (202) 479-1200. Internet: **http://www.ncoa.org**

➤ National Caucus and Center on Black Aged, Inc., Senior Employment Programs, 1220 L St. NW., Suite 800, Washington, DC 20005. Telephone: (202) 637-8400. Fax: (202) 347-0895. Internet: **http://www.ncba-aged.org**

Veterans:
Contact the nearest regional office of the U.S. Department of Labor's Veterans Employment and Training Service or:

➤ Credentialing Opportunities Online (COOL), which explains how Army soldiers can meet civilian certification and license requirements related to their Military Occupational Specialty (MOS). Internet: **http://www.cool.army.mil/index.htm**

Women:

➤ Department of Labor, Women's Bureau, 200 Constitution Ave. NW., Washington, DC 20210. Telephone: (800) 827-5335. Internet: **http://www.dol.gov/wb**

Federal laws, executive orders, and selected Federal grant programs bar discrimination in employment based on race, color, religion, sex, national origin, age, and handicap. Information on how to file a charge of discrimination is available from U.S. Equal Employment Opportunity Commission offices around the country. Their addresses and telephone numbers are listed in telephone directories under:

➤ U.S. Government, EEOC. Telephone: (800) 669-4000. TTY: (800) 669-6820. Internet: **http://www.eeoc.gov**

Office of Personnel Management. Information on obtaining civilian positions within the Federal Government is available from the U.S. Office of Personnel Management through USA Jobs, the Federal Government's official employment information system. This resource for locating and applying for job opportunities can be accessed through the Internet or through an interactive voice response telephone system at (703) 724-1850 or TDD (978) 461-8404. These numbers are not tollfree, and charges may result.

➤ USA Jobs: **http://www.usajobs.opm.gov**

Military. The military employs and has information on hundreds of occupations. Information is available on the Montgomery G.I. Bill, which provides money for school and educational debt repayments. Information on military service can be provided by your local recruiting office. Also see the *Handbook* statement on Job Opportunities in the Armed Forces. For more information on careers in the military:

➤ Today's Military. Internet: **http://www.todaysmilitary.com**

State Sources. Most States have career information delivery systems (CIDS), which may be found in secondary and post-secondary institutions, as well as libraries, job training sites, vocational-technical schools, and employment offices. A wide range of information is provided, from employment opportunities to unemployment insurance claims.

Whereas the *Handbook* provides information for occupations on a national level, each State has detailed information on occupations and labor markets within their respective jurisdictions. State occupational projections are available at: **http://www.projectionscentral.com**

Alabama
Director, Labor Market Information Division, Alabama Department of Industrial Relations, 649 Monroe St., Room 422, Montgomery, AL 36131. Telephone: (334) 242-8859. Internet: **http://dir.alabama.gov**

Alaska
Chief, Research and Analysis Section, Department of Labor and Workforce Development, P.O. Box 25501, Juneau, AK 99802-5501. Telephone: (907) 465-4518. Internet: **http://almis.labor.state.ak.us**

Arizona
Research Administrator, Arizona Department of Economic Security, P.O. Box 6123 SC 733A, Phoenix, AZ 85005-6123. Telephone: (602) 542-5984. Internet: **http://www.workforce.az.gov**

Arkansas
Division Chief, Labor Market Information, Department of Workforce Services, P.O. Box 2981, Little Rock, AR 72203-2981. Telephone: (501) 682-3198. Internet: **http://www.arkansas.gov/esd**

California
Chief, State of California Employment Development Department, Labor Market Information Division, P.O. Box 826880, Sacramento, CA 94280-0001. Telephone: (916) 262-2160. Internet: **http://www.calmis.cahwnet.gov**

Colorado
Director, Labor Market Information, Colorado Department of Labor and Employment, 633 17th St., Suite 600, Denver, CO 80202-3660. Telephone: (303) 318-8850. Internet: **http://www.coworkforce.com/lmi**

Connecticut
Director, Office of Research, Connecticut Department of Labor, 200 Folly Brook Blvd., Wethersfield, CT 06109-1114. Telephone: (860) 263-6275. Internet: **http://www.ctdol.state.ct.us/lmi**

Delaware
Chief, Office of Occupational and Labor Market Information, Department of Labor, 4425 N. Market St.-Fox Valley Annex, Wilmington, DE 19809-1307. Telephone: (302) 761-8069. Internet: **http://www.delawareworks.com/oolmi/welcome.shtml**

District of Columbia
Chief, Office of Labor Market Research and Information, 64 New York Ave. NE., Suite 3035, Washington, D.C. 20002. Telephone: (202) 671-1633. Internet: **http://www.does.dc.gov/does**

Florida
Director, Labor Market Statistics, Agency for Workforce Innovation, MSC G-020, 107 E. Madison St., Tallahassee, FL 32399-4111. Telephone: (850) 245-7205. Internet: **http://www.labormarketinfo.com**

Georgia
Director, Workforce Information and Analysis, Room 300, Department of Labor, 223 Courtland St., CWC Building, Atlanta, GA 30303. Telephone: (404) 232-3875. Internet: **http://www.dol.state.ga.us/em/get_labor_market_information.htm**

Guam
Chief Economist, Guam Department of Labor, P.O. Box 9970, Tamuning, Guam 96931. Telephone: (671) 475-7062.

Hawaii
Chief, Research and Statistics Office, Department of Labor and Industrial Relations, 830 Punchbowl St., Room 304, Honolulu, HI 96813. Telephone: (808) 586-8999. Internet: **http://www.hiwi.org**

Idaho
Chief, Research and Analysis Bureau, Department of Commerce and Labor, 317 West Main St., Boise, ID 83735-0670. Telephone: (208) 332-3570. Internet: **http://lmi.idaho.gov**

Illinois
Deputy Director of Workforce and Career Information, Illinois Department of Employment Security, Economic Information and Analysis Division, 33 S. State St., 9th Floor, Chicago, IL 60603. Telephone: (312) 793-2316. Internet: **http://lmi.ides.state.il.us**

Indiana
Director, Research and Analysis—Indiana Workforce Development, SE 211, 10 North Senate Ave., Indianapolis, IN 46204-2277. Telephone: (317) 232-7460. Internet: **http://www.in.gov/dwd**

Iowa
Policy and Information Division, Iowa Workforce Development, 1000 East Grand Ave., Des Moines, IA 50319-0209. Telephone: (515) 281-6642. Internet: **http://www.iowaworkforce.org/lmi**

Kansas
Director, Kansas Department of Labor, Labor Market Information Services, 401 SW Topeka Blvd., Topeka, KS 66603-3182. Telephone: (785) 296-5058. Internet:**http://laborstats.dol.ks.gov**

Kentucky
Research and Statistics Branch, Office of Employment and Training, 275 East Main St.—Mail Stop 2-WG, Frankfort, KY 40621. Telephone: (502) 564-7976. Internet: **http://www.workforcekentucky.ky.gov**

Louisiana
Director, Research and Statistics Division, Department of Labor, 1001 North 23rd St., Baton Rouge, LA 70804-9094. Telephone: (225) 342-3141. Internet: **http://www.laworks.net**

Maine
Director, Labor Market Information Services Division, Maine Department of Labor, 19 Union St., Augusta, ME 04332. Telephone: (207) 287-2271. Internet: **http://www.state.me.us/labor/lmis/index.html**

Maryland
Maryland Department of Labor Licensing and Regulation, Office of Labor Market Analysis and Information, Room 316, 1100 N. Eutaw, Baltimore, MD 21201. Telephone: (410) 767-2250. Internet: **http://www.dllr.state.md.us/lmi/index.htm**

Massachusetts
Assistant Director of Economic Research, Massachusetts Division of Unemployment Assistance, 19 Staniford St., Boston, MA 02421. Telephone: (617) 626-6556. Internet: **http://www.detma.org/LMIdataprog.htm**

Michigan
Director, Bureau of Labor Market Information and Strategic Initiatives, Department of Labor and Economic Growth, 3032 West Grand Blvd., Suite 9-100, Detroit, MI 48202. Telephone: (313) 456-3100. Internet: **http://www.michlmi.org**

Minnesota
Research Director, Department of Employment and Economic Development, Labor Market Information Office, 1st National Bank Building, 332 Minnesota St., Suite E200, St. Paul, MN 55101-1351. Telephone: (651) 296-6545. Internet: **http://www.deed.state.mn.us/lmi**

Mississippi
Chief, Labor Market Information Division, Mississippi Department of Employment Security, 1235 Echelon Pkwy., Jackson, MS 39213. Telephone: (601) 321-6262. Internet: **http://mdes.ms.gov**

Missouri
LMI Research Manager, Missouri Economic Research and Information Center, P.O. Box 3150, Jefferson City, MO 65101-3150. Telephone: (573) 751-3637. Internet: **http://www.missourieconomy.org**

Montana
Research and Analysis Bureau, P.O. Box 1728, Helena, MT 59624. Telephone: (406) 444-2430. Internet: **http://www.ourfactsyourfuture.org**

Nebraska
Administrator, Nebraska Workforce Development—Labor Market Information, Nebraska Department of Labor, P.O. Box 4600, Lincoln, NE 68509-4600. Telephone: (402) 471-2600. Internet: **http://www.dol.state.ne.us/nelmi.htm**

Nevada
Chief, Research and Analysis, Department of Employment Training and Rehabilitation, 500 East Third St., Carson City, NV 89713-0020. Telephone: (775) 684-0387. Internet: **http://www.detr.state.nv.us/lmi/index.htm**

New Hampshire
Director, Economic and Labor Market Information Bureau, New Hampshire Employment Security, 32 South Main St., Concord, NH 03301-4857. Telephone: (603) 228-4123. Internet: **http://www.nhes.state.nh.us/elmi**

New Jersey
Director, Division of Labor Market and Demographic Research, Department of Labor and Workforce Development, P.O. Box 388, Trenton, NJ 08625-0388. Telephone: (609) 984-2593. Internet: **http://www.state.nj.us/labor/lra**

New Mexico
Research Chief, New Mexico Department of Labor , Economic Research and Analysis, 501 Mountain Road NE., Albuquerque, NM 87102. Telephone: (505) 222-4684. Internet: **http://www.dol.state.nm.us/dol_lmif.html**

New York
Director, Research and Statistics, New York State Department of Labor, State Office Campus, Room 400, Albany, NY 12240. Telephone: (518) 457-3805. Internet: **http://www.labor.state.ny.us/workforceindustrydata/index.asp**

North Carolina
Director, Labor Market Information Division, Employment Security Commission, 700 Wade Ave., Raleigh, NC 27605. Telephone: (919) 733-2936. Internet: **http://www.ncesc.com**

North Dakota
Labor Market Information Manager, Job Service North Dakota, P.O. Box 5507, Bismarck, ND 58506-5507. Telephone: (701) 328-3136. Internet: **http://www.jobsnd.com/data/index.html**

Ohio
Director, Bureau of Labor Market Information, Office of Workforce Development, Ohio Department of Job and Family Services, 4300 Kimberly Pkwy., Columbus, OH 43232. Telephone: (614) 752-9494. Internet: **http://www.ohioworkforceinformer.org**

Oklahoma
Labor Market Information, Oklahoma Employment Security Commission, P.O. Box 52003, Oklahoma City, OK 73152. Telephone: (405) 557-7221. Internet: **http://www.oesc.state.ok.us/lmi/default.htm**

Oregon
Oregon Employment Department, Attention: Research Division, Room 207, 875 Union St. NE., Salem, OR 97311. Telephone: (503) 947-1200. Internet: **http://www.qualityinfo.org/olmisj/OlmisZine**

Pennsylvania
Director, Center for Workforce Information & Analysis, Pennsylvania Department of Labor and Industry, 220 Labor and Industry Building, Seventh and Forster Sts., Harrisburg, PA 17121. Telephone: (877) 493-3282. Internet: **http://www.paworkstats.state.pa.us**

Puerto Rico
Economist, Labor Market Information Office, P.O. Box 195540, San Juan, Puerto Rico 00919-5540. Telephone: (787) 754-5347. Internet: **http://www.net-empleopr.org /almis23/index.jsp**

Rhode Island
Assistant Director, Labor Market Information, Rhode Island Department of Labor and Training, 1511 Pontiac Ave., Cranston, RI 02920. Telephone: (401) 462-8767. Internet: **http://www.dlt.ri.gov/lmi**

South Carolina
Director, Labor Market Information Department, South Carolina Employment Security Commission, 631 Hampton St., Columbia, SC 29202. Telephone: (803) 737-2660. Internet: **http://www.sces.org/lmi/index.asp**

South Dakota
Director, Labor Market Information Center, Department of Labor, 420 S. Roosevelt St., Aberdeen, SD 57402-4730. Telephone: (605) 626-2314. Internet: **http://www.state.sd.us/dol/lmic/index.htm**

Tennessee
Director, Research and Statistics Division, Department of Labor and Workforce Development, 500 James Robertson Pkwy., 11th Floor, Nashville, TN 37245-1000. Telephone: (615) 741-2284. Internet: **http://www.state.tn.us/labor-wfd/lmi.htm**

Texas
Labor Market Information, Texas Workforce Commission, 9001 North IH-35, Suite 103A, Austin, TX 75753. Telephone: (512) 491-4800. Internet: **http://www.tracer2.com**

Utah
Director of Workforce Information, Utah Department of Workforce Services, 140 East 300 South, Salt Lake City, UT 84111. Telephone: (801) 526-9401. Internet: **http://jobs.utah.gov/opencms/wi**

Vermont
Chief, Research and Analysis, Vermont Department of Labor, P.O. Box 488, Montpelier, VT 05601-0488. Telephone: (802) 828-4202. Internet: **http://www.labor.vermont.gov**

Virgin Islands
Chief, Bureau of Labor Statistics, Department of Labor, P.O. Box 303359, St Thomas, VI 00803-3359. Telephone: (340) 776-3700. Internet: **http://www.vidol.gov**

Virginia
Director, Economic Information Services, Virginia Employment Commission, 703 East Main St., Room 327, Richmond, VA 23218. Telephone: (804) 786-5496. Internet: **http://velma.virtuallmi.com**

Washington
Director, Labor Market and Economic Analysis, Washington Employment Security Department, P.O. Box 9046, Olympia, WA 98507-9046. Telephone: (360) 438-4804. Internet: **http://www.workforceexplorer.com**

West Virginia
WORKFORCE West Virginia, Research, Information and Analysis Division, 112 California Ave., Charleston, WV 25303-0112. Telephone: (304) 558-2660. Internet: **http://www.wvbep.org/bep/lmi**

Wisconsin
Director, Bureau of Workforce Information, Department of Workforce Development, 201 E. Washington Ave., Madison, WI 53702. Telephone: (608) 266-8212. Internet: **http://worknet.wisconsin.gov/worknet**

Wyoming
Manager, Research and Planning, Wyoming Department of Employment, P.O. Box 2760, Casper, WY 82602-2760. Telephone: (307) 473-3807.Internet: **http://doe.state.wy.us/lmi**

Sources of Education, Training, and Financial Aid

Education can open doors for those looking to start a new career or change specialty within their current occupation. This section outlines some major sources of education and training required to enter many occupations, as well as some ways to finance the education or training.

For information on the specific training and educational requirements for a particular occupation, and what training is typically provided by an employer, consult the Training, Other Qualifications, and Advancement section of the appropriate *Handbook* statement.

Sources of Education and Training

Four-year colleges and universities. These institutions provide detailed information on theory and practice for a wide variety of subjects. Colleges and universities can provide one with the knowledge and background necessary to be successful in many fields. They also can help to place students in cooperative education programs—often called "co-ops"—or internships. Co-ops and internships are short-term jobs with firms related to one's field of study that lead to college credit. In co-ops and internships, students learn the specifics of a job while making valuable contacts that can lead to a permanent position.

For more information on colleges and universities, go to your local library, consult your high school guidance counselor, or contact individual colleges. Also check with your State's higher education agency. A list of these agencies is available on the Internet: **http://wdcrobcolp01.ed.gov/Programs/EROD**.

Junior and community colleges. Junior and community colleges offer a mixture of programs that lead to associate degrees and training certificates. Community colleges tend to be less expensive than 4-year colleges and universities. They typically are more willing to accommodate part-time students, and their programs are more tailored to the needs of local employers. Many have an open admissions policy, and often these institutions offer weekend and night classes.

Many community colleges form partnerships with local businesses that allow students to gain job-specific training. For students who may not be able to enroll in a college or university because of their academic record, limited finances, or distance from such an institution, junior or community colleges are often used as a place to earn credits that can be applied toward a degree at a 4-year college. Junior and community colleges also are noted for their extensive role in continuing and adult education.

For more information on junior and community colleges, go to your local library, consult your high school guidance counselor, or contact individual schools. Also check with your State's higher education agency. A list of these agencies is available on the Internet: **http://wdcrobcolp01.ed.gov/Programs/EROD**.

Vocational and trade schools. These institutions train people in specific trades. They offer courses designed to provide hands-on experience. Vocational and trade schools tend to concentrate on trades, services, and other types of skilled work.

Vocational and trade schools frequently engage students in real-world projects, allowing them to apply field methods while learning theory in classrooms. Graduates of vocational and trade schools have an advantage over informally trained or self-trained job seekers because graduates have an independent organization certifying that they have the knowledge, skills, and abilities necessary to perform the duties of a particular occupation. These schools also help students to acquire any license or other credentials needed to enter the job market.

For more information on vocational and trade schools, go to your local library, consult your high school guidance counselor, or contact individual schools. Also check with your State's director of vocational-technical education. A list of State directors of vocational-technical education is available on the Internet: **http://wdcrobcolp01.ed.gov/Programs/EROD**.

Apprenticeships. An apprenticeship provides work experience as well as education and training for those entering certain occupations. Apprenticeships are offered by sponsors, who employ and train the apprentice. The apprentice follows a training course under close supervision and receives some formal education to learn the theory related to the job.

Apprenticeships are a way for inexperienced people to become skilled workers. Apprenticeships are an agreement between the apprentice and the sponsor and generally last between 1 and 4 years. Some apprenticeships allow the apprentice to earn an associate degree. An *Apprenticeship Completion Certificate* is granted to those completing programs. This certificate is administered by federally approved State agencies.

Information on apprenticeships is available from the Office of Apprenticeship Training, Employer, and Labor Services on the Internet: **http://www.doleta.gov/atels_bat**. For assistance finding an apprenticeship program, go to: **http://www.doleta.gov/atels_bat/fndprgm.cfm**.

Professional societies, trade associations, and labor unions. These groups are made up of people with common interests, usually in related occupations or industries. The groups frequently are able to provide training, access to training through their affiliates, or information on acceptable sources of training for their field. If licensing or certification is required, they also may be able to assist you in meeting those requirements.

For a listing of professional societies, trade associations, and labor unions related to an occupation, check the Sources of Additional Information section at the end of that occupational statement in the *Handbook*.

Employers. Many employers provide on-the-job training. On-the-job training can range from spending a few minutes watching another employee demonstrate a task to participating in formal training programs that may last for several months. In some jobs, employees may continually undergo training to stay up to date with new developments and technologies, or to add new skills.

Military. The United States Armed Forces trains and employs people in more than 4,100 different occupations. For more information, see the *Handbook* statement on "Job Opportunities in The Armed Forces." For detailed answers to specific questions, contact your local recruiting office. Valuable resources also are available on the Internet: **http://www.todaysmilitary.com.**

Sources of Financial Aid

Many people fund their education or training through financial aid or tuition assistance programs. Federal student aid comes in three forms—grants, work-study programs, and loans. All Federal student aid applicants must first fill out a Frcc Application for Federal Student Aid (FAFSA), which provides a Student Aid Report (SAR) and eligibility rating. Forms must be submitted to desired institutions of study, which determine the amount of aid you will receive.

For information on applying for Federal financial aid, visit the FAFSA Internet site: **http://www.fafsa.ed.gov.**

A U.S. Department of Education publication describing Federal financial aid programs, called *The Student Guide*, is available at: **http://www.studentaid.ed.gov/students/publications/ student_guide/index.html**.

Information on Federal programs is available from: **http://www.studentaid.ed.gov** and **www.students.gov**.

Information on State programs is available from your State's higher education agency. A list of these agencies is available at: **http://wdcrobcolp01.ed.gov/Programs/EROD**.

Grants. A grant is money which is given to a student or the institution they are attending in order to pay for their education or training and any associated expenses. Grants are typically given on the basis of financial need. Grants are considered gifts and are not paid back. Federal grants are almost exclusively for undergraduate students. They include Pell Grants, which can be worth up to $4,050 annually, and Federal Supplemental Educational Opportunity Grants (FSEOG), which can be worth up to $4,000 annually. Priority for FSEOG awards is given to those who have also received the Pell Grant and have exceptional financial need.

Additional information on grants is available on the Internet: **http://www.studentaid.ed.gov**.

Information also is available from your State Higher Education agency. A list of these agencies is available at: **http://wdcrobcolp01.ed.gov/Programs/EROD**.

Federal Work-Study program. The Federal Work-Study program is offered at most institutions and consists of Federal sponsorship of a student who works part time at the institution he or she is attending. The money a student earns through this program goes directly toward the cost of attending the institution. There are no set minimum or maximum amounts for this type of aid, although, on average, a student can expect to earn about $2,000 per school year.

For additional information on work-study opportunities offered, check with individual institutions. General information on the Federal Work-Study program is available at: **http://www.studentaid.ed.gov/students/publications/ student_guide/2005-2006/english/types-fed-workstudy.htm**.

Scholarships. A scholarship is a sum of money donated to a student to help pay for his or her education or training and any associated costs. Scholarships can range from small amounts up to the full cost of schooling. They are based on financial need, academic merit, athletic ability, or a wide variety of other criteria set by the organizations that provide the scholarships. Frequently, students must meet minimum academic requirements to be considered for a scholarship. Other qualifying requirements—such as intended major field of study, heritage, or group membership—may be added by the organization providing the scholarship.

Scholarships can be provided by a wide variety of institutions, including educational institutions, State and local governments, private associations, social groups, and individuals. There are no federally awarded scholarships based on academic merit. Most large scholarships are awarded to students by the institution they plan to attend. Students who have received State scholarships and plan to attend a school in another State should check with their State to see if the scholarship can be transferred.

Information on scholarships is typically available from high school guidance counselors and local libraries. Additional scholarship information is available from State higher education agencies. A list of these agencies is available at: **http://wdcrobcolp01.cd.gov/Programs/EROD**. The College Board has information on available scholarships at: **http://www.collegeboard.com/pay**.

Student loans. Many institutions, both public and private, provide low-interest loans to students and their parents or guardians. The Federal Government also provides several types of student loans based on the applicant's level of financial need. The amount of money a student can receive in loans varies by the distributing institution and depends on whether the student is claimed by a parent or guardian as a dependent. Since the process of applying for a loan may take several months, it is a good idea to start applying for Federal student loans well in advance.

The available Federal loan programs can accommodate prospective undergraduate, graduate, vocational, and disabled students. Federal loans can be distributed through the school that the student is attending, from the Federal Government directly, or from a third-party private lender or bank. Perkins loans are distributed through the school the student is attending. Loans coming from the Federal Government directly from the William D. Ford Federal Direct Loan Program are dispersed by the Department of Education. Third-party loans through a private lender or bank are from the Federal Family Education Loan (FFEL) program. For all federally funded loans, payments are made to the institution that originally dispersed the funds.

For those with financial need, Federal Perkins loans and both Direct and FFEL-subsidized Stafford loans are available. Perkins loans have no minimum amount, but they are capped at $4,000 per year for undergraduates and $6,000 per year for graduate students. Subsidized Stafford loans can range in value from $2,625 to $8,500 per year and can increase as a student completes more years of undergraduate, graduate, or professional education. Interest rates remain at a flat 5 percent for all Perkins loans, while rates can fluctuate up to 8.25 percent for subsidized Stafford loans. Those with Perkins loans are not responsible for starting to repay the loan until they have been out of school for 9 months. Those with subsidized Stafford loans must begin payments within 6 to 9 months of leaving school but are not charged monthly interest while in school.

For those who do not demonstrate financial need, Direct and FFEL-unsubsidized Stafford Loans and Federal Parent Loans for Students (PLUS) are available. Unsubsidized Stafford loans can range in value from $2,625 to $18,500 per year. PLUS loans are capped at the cost of attendance. With Federal unsubsidized Stafford Loans, interest payments start almost immediately and can be paid monthly or accrued until the completion of studies. The latter option results in a larger total loan cost but may be more convenient for some students. With PLUS loans, the parent must pay interest and principal payments while the student is enrolled in school and must continue payments after completion. Check with your lender for available repayment schedules. Typically, students have 10 years to repay Perkins loans and from 10 to 30 years for unsubsidized Stafford loans.

Subsidized and unsubsidized Stafford loans are only available to students who are enrolled in an academic program at least half time. As with any loan, be sure to investigate different lenders, and understand what your loan contract requires of you before agreeing to any loan. Check with established financial institutions to compare the terms of available private student loans.

Comparisons of the various types of loans are available on the Internet: **http://www.studentaid.ed.gov/students/publications/ student_guide/index.html**.

The College Board has information on available loans at: **http://www.collegeboard.com/pay**.

Employer tuition support programs. Some employers offer tuition assistance programs as part of their employee benefits package. The terms of these programs depend on the firm and can vary by the type and amount of training subsidized, as well as by eligibility requirements. Consult your human resources department for information on tuition support programs offered by your employer.

Military tuition support programs. The United States Armed Forces offer various tuition assistance and loan repayment programs for military personnel. See the *Handbook* statement on "Job Opportunities in the Armed Forces" for more information. Also go to: **http://www.todaysmilitary.com/app/tm/get/collegehelp/support**.

Finding a Job and Evaluating a Job Offer

Finding information on available jobs

It often takes months of time and effort to find a job that matches your qualifications and desires. Actively pursuing multiple leads will maximize your search efforts and reduce the time it takes you to find employment. This means devoting as much time as you can to your job search. If you are unemployed, treat your job search like a full-time job, waking up early and working a full day. If you are working or in school, it is still important to devote time every day to your job search.

Inform people you know that you are looking for a job. Read the classified ads. Use the Internet, including general job search sites, special interest sites, company Web sites, and trade and professional association Web sites. Directly contact employers in which you are interested, even if they are not advertising a job opening. You may also wish to consult State employment service offices and to consider private employment agencies.

Where to learn about job openings

Personal contacts
School career planning and placement offices
Employers
Classified ads
—National and local newspapers
—Professional journals
—Trade magazines
Internet networks and resources
State employment service offices
Federal Government
Professional associations
Labor unions
Private employment agencies and career consultants
Community agencies

Job search methods

Personal contacts. Eighty percent of available jobs are never advertised, and over half of all employees get their jobs through networking, according to BH Careers International. Therefore, the people you know—friends, family, neighbors, acquaintances, teachers, and former coworkers—are some of the most effective resources for your job search. The network of people that you know and the people that they know can lead to information about specific job openings that are not publicly posted. To develop new contacts, join student, community, or professional organizations.

School career planning and placement offices. High school and college placement offices help their students and alumni find jobs. They allow recruiters to use their facilities for interviews or career fairs. Placement offices usually have a list of part-time, temporary, and summer jobs offered on campus. They also may have lists of jobs for regional, nonprofit, and government organizations. In addition to linking you to potential employers, career planning offices usually provide career counseling, career testing, and job search advice. Some have career resource libraries; host workshops on job search strategy, resume writing, letter writing, and effective interviewing; critique drafts of resumes; conduct mock interviews; and sponsor job fairs.

Employers. Through your library and Internet research, develop a list of potential employers in your desired career field. Employer Web sites often contain lists of job openings. Web sites and business directories can provide you with information on how to apply for a position or whom to contact. Even if no open positions are posted, do not hesitate to contact the employer and the relevant department. Set up an interview with someone working in the same area in which you wish to work. Ask them how they got started, what they like and dislike about the work, what type of qualifications are necessary for the job, and what type of personality succeeds in that position. Even if they don't have a position available, they may be able to put you in contact with other people who might hire you, and they can keep you in mind if a position opens up. Make sure to send them your resume and a cover letter. If you are able to obtain an interview, be sure to send a thank-you note. Directly contacting employers is one of the most successful means of job hunting.

Classified ads. The "Help Wanted" ads in newspapers list numerous jobs. You should realize, however, that many other job openings are not listed, and that the classified ads sometimes do not give all of the important information. They may offer little or no description of the job, working conditions, or pay. Some ads do not identify the employer. They may simply give a post office box to which you can mail your resume, making follow-up inquiries very difficult. Some ads offer out-of-town jobs; others advertise employment agencies rather than actual employment opportunities.

When using classified ads, keep the following in mind:

- Do not rely solely on the classifieds to find a job; follow other leads as well.
- Answer ads promptly, because openings may be filled quickly, even before the ad stops appearing in the paper.
- Read the ads every day, particularly the Sunday edition, which usually includes the most listings.
- Beware of "no experience necessary" ads. These ads often signal low wages, poor working conditions, or commission work.
- Keep a record of all ads to which you have responded, including the specific skills, educational background, and personal qualifications required for the position.

Internet networks and resources. The Internet is an invaluable resource. Use it to find advice on conducting your job search more effectively; to search for a job; to research prospective employers; and to communicate with people who can help you with your job search. No single Web site will contain all the information available on employment or career opportunities, so in addition to the Web sites listed below, use a search engine to find what you need. The different types of sites that may be useful include general career advice sites, job search sites, company Web sites, trade and professional association Web sites, and forums. Internet forums, also called message boards, are online discussion groups where anyone may post and read messages. Use forums specific to your profession or to career-related topics to post questions or messages and to read about other peoples' job searches or career experiences.

In job databases, remember that job listings may be posted by field or discipline, so begin your search using keywords. Some Web sites provide national or local classified listings and allow job seekers to post their resumes online. When searching employment databases on the Internet, it usually is possible to send your resume to an employer by e-mail or to post it online.

CareerOneStop is a database consisting of three separate career resource tools. It can be accessed on the Internet at: **http://www.CareerOneStop.org**, or by telephone at: (877) 348-0502. Alternatively, each resource tool can be accessed directly at its own Internet address.

America's Job Bank allows you to search through a database of more than 1 million jobs nationwide, create and post your resume online, and set up an automated job search. The database contains a wide range of mostly full-time private sector jobs that are available all over the country. Job seekers can access America's Job Bank at: **http://www.ajb.org**.

America's Career InfoNet provides information on educational, licensing, and certification requirements for different occupations by State. It also provides information on wages, cost of living, and employment trends, and helps job seekers identify their skills and write resumes and cover letters. Job seekers can access America's Career InfoNet at: **http://www.acinet.org**.

America's Service Locator provides listings of local employment service offices which help job seekers find jobs and help employers find qualified workers at no cost to either. At the State employment service office, an interviewer will determine if you are "job ready" or if you need help from counseling and testing services to assess your occupational aptitudes and interests and to help you choose and prepare for a career. After you are "job ready," you may examine available job listings and select openings that interest you. A staff member can then describe the job openings in detail and arrange for interviews with prospective employers. Job seekers can access *America's Service* Locator at: **http://www.servicelocator.org**. A list of offices is also in the State government telephone listings under "Job Service" or "Employment."

Using Internet Resources to Plan your Future, a U.S. Department of Labor publication, offers advice on organizing your Internet job search. It is primarily intended to provide instruction for job seekers on how to use the Internet to their best advantage, but recruiters and other career service industry professionals will find information here to help them also. *How to Use the Internet in your Job Search*; *The Job Search Process*; and the *Career-Related Pages*, other U.S. Department of Labor Internet publications, each discusses specific steps that job seekers can follow to identify employment opportunities. Included are daily tips and hints, plus a large database of links and job search engines. Check with your State employment service office, or order a copy of these and other publications from the U.S. Government Printing Office's Superintendent of Documents. Telephone: (202) 512-1800. Internet: **http://bookstore.gpo.gov** or **http://www.doleta.gov**.

State employment service offices. The State employment service, sometimes called the Job Service, operates in coordination with the U.S. Department of Labor's Employment and Training Administration. Local offices, found nationwide, help job seekers to find jobs and help employers to find qualified workers at no cost to either. To find the office nearest you, look in the State government telephone listings under "Job Service" or "Employment."

Job matching and referral. At the State employment service office, an interviewer will determine if you are "job ready" or if you need help from counseling and testing services to assess your occupational aptitudes and interests and to help you choose and prepare for a career. After you are "job ready," you may examine available job listings and select openings that interest you. A staff member can then describe the job openings in detail and arrange for interviews with prospective employers.

Services for special groups. By law, veterans are entitled to priority for job placement at State employment service centers. If you are a veteran, a veterans' employment representative can inform you of available assistance and help you to deal with problems.

State employment service offices refer people to opportunities available under the Workforce Investment Act (WIA) of 1998. WIA reforms Federal employment, adult education, and vocational rehabilitation programs to create an integrated, "one-stop" system of workforce investment and education activities for adults and youths. Services are provided to employers and job seekers, including adults, dislocated workers, and youths. WIA's primary purpose is to increase the employment, retention, skills, and earnings of participants. These programs help to prepare people to participate in the State's workforce, increase their employment and earnings potential, improve their educational and occupational skills, and reduce their dependency on welfare, which will improve the quality of the workforce and enhance the productivity and competitiveness of the Nation's economy.

Federal Government. Information on obtaining a position with the Federal Government is available from the U.S. Office of Personnel Management (OPM) through USAJOBS, the Federal Government's official employment information system. This resource for locating and applying for job opportunities can be accessed through the Internet at **http://www.usajobs.opm.gov** or through an interactive voice response telephone system at (703) 724-1850 or TDD (978) 461-8404. These numbers are not tollfree, and charges may result.

Professional associations. Many professions have associations that offer employment information, including career planning, educational programs, job listings, and job placement. To use these services, associations usually require that you be a member; information can be obtained directly from an association through the Internet, by telephone, or by mail.

Labor unions. Labor unions provide various employment services to members, including apprenticeship programs that teach a specific trade or skill. Contact the appropriate labor union or State apprenticeship council for more information.

Private employment agencies and career consultants. These agencies can be helpful, but they may charge you for their services. Most operate on a commission basis, with the fee dependent upon a percentage of the salary paid to a successful applicant. You or the hiring company will pay the fee. Find out the exact cost and who is responsible for paying associated fees before using the service.

Although employment agencies can help you save time and contact employers who otherwise might be difficult to locate, the costs may outweigh the benefits if you are responsible for the fee. Contacting employers directly often will generate the same type of leads that a private employment agency will provide. Consider any guarantees that the agency offers when determining if the service is worth the cost.

Community agencies. Many nonprofit organizations, including religious institutions and vocational rehabilitation agencies, offer counseling, career development, and job placement services, generally targeted to a particular group, such as women, youths, minorities, ex-offenders, or older workers.

Applying for a job

Resumes and application forms. Resumes and application forms are two ways to provide employers with written evidence of your qualifications and skills. Generally, the same information appears on both the resume and the application form, but the way in which it is presented differs. Some employers prefer a resume and others require an application form. The accompanying box presents the basic information you should include in your resume.

There are many ways of organizing a resume; choose the format that best showcases your skills and experience. It may be helpful to look for examples on the Internet or in books at your local library or bookstore. Typically, an employer has a very limited amount of time to review your resume. It is important to make sure it is clear and concise and highlights your skills and experiences effectively through the use of formatting, ordering, and headings.

Many employers scan resumes into databases, which they then search for specific keywords or phrases. The keywords are usually nouns referring to experience, education, personal characteristics, or industry buzz words. Identify keywords by reading the job description and qualifications; use the same words in your resume that are used in the job ad. For example, if the job description includes customer service tasks, use the words "customer service" on your resume. Scanners sometimes misread paper resumes, which could mean some of your keywords don't get into the database. So, if you know that your resume will be scanned, and you have the option, e-mail an electronic version. If you must submit a paper resume, make it scannable by using a simple font and avoiding underlines, italics, and graphics. It is also a good idea to send a traditionally formatted resume along with your scannable resume, with a note on each marking its purpose.

What usually goes into a resume

- Name, address, e-mail address, and telephone number.
- Employment objective. State the type of work or specific job you are seeking.
- Education, including school name and address, dates of attendance, major, and highest grade completed or degree awarded. Consider including any courses or areas of focus that might be relevant to the position.
- Experience, paid and volunteer. For each job, include the job title, name and location of employer, and dates of employment. Briefly describe your job duties.
- Special skills, computer skills, proficiency in foreign languages, achievements, and membership in organizations.
- References, only when requested.
- Keep it short; only one page for less experienced applicants.
- Avoid long paragraphs; use bullets to highlight key skills and accomplishments.
- Have several people review your resume for any spelling or grammatical errors.
- Print it on high quality paper.

When you fill out an application form, make sure you fill it out completely and follow all instructions. Do not omit any requested information and make sure that the information you provide is correct.

Cover letters. A cover letter is sent with a resume or application form, as a way of introducing yourself to prospective employers. As with your resume, it may be helpful to look for examples on the Internet or in books at your local library or bookstore, but be sure not to copy letters directly from other sources. Your cover letter should be original, capture the employer's attention, follow a business letter format, and usually should include the following information:

- Name and address of the specific person to whom the letter is addressed.
- Reason for your interest in the company or position.
- Your main qualifications for the position.
- Request for an interview.
- Your home and work telephone numbers.

If you send a scannable resume, you should also include a scannable cover letter, which is created similarly to a scannable resume, by avoiding graphics, fancy fonts, italics, and underlines.

Interviewing. An interview gives you the opportunity to showcase your qualifications to an employer, so it pays to be well prepared. The information in the accompanying box provides some helpful hints.

Job interview tips

Preparation:
Learn about the organization.
Have a specific job or jobs in mind.
Review your qualifications for the job.
Prepare answers to broad questions about yourself.
Review your resume.
Practice an interview with a friend or relative.
Arrive before the scheduled time of your interview.

Personal appearance:
Be well groomed.
Dress appropriately.
Do not chew gum or smoke.

The interview:
Relax and answer each question concisely.
Respond promptly.
Use good manners.
Learn the name of your interviewer and greet him or her with a firm handshake.
Use proper English—avoid slang.
Be cooperative and enthusiastic.
Use body language to show interest.
Ask questions about the position and the organization, but avoid questions whose answers can easily be found on the company Web site. Also avoid asking questions about salary and benefits unless a job offer is made.
Thank the interviewer when you leave and, as a follow-up, in writing.

Test (if employer gives one):
Listen closely to instructions.
Read each question carefully.
Write legibly and clearly.
Budget your time wisely and don't dwell on one question.

Information to bring to an interview:
Social Security card.
Government-issued identification (driver's license).
Resume. Although not all employers require applicants to bring a resume, you should be able to furnish the interviewer information about your education, training, and previous-employment.
References. Employers typically require three references. Get permission before using anyone as a reference. Make sure that they will give you a good reference. Try to avoid using relatives as references.
Transcripts. Employers may require an official copy of transcripts to verify grades, coursework, dates of attendance, and highest grade completed or degree awarded.

Evaluating a job offer

Once you receive a job offer, you are faced with a difficult decision and must evaluate the offer carefully. Fortunately, most organizations will not expect you to accept or reject an offer immediately.

There are many issues to consider when assessing a job offer. Will the organization be a good place to work? Will the job be interesting? Are there opportunities for advancement? Is the salary fair? Does the employer offer good benefits? If you have not already figured out exactly what you want, the following discussion may help you to develop a set of criteria for judging job offers, whether you are starting a career, reentering the labor force after a long absence, or planning a career change.

The organization. Background information on an organization can help you to decide whether it is a good place for you to work. Factors to consider include the organization's business or activity, financial condition, age, size, and location.

You generally can get background information on an organization, particularly a large organization, on its Internet site or by telephoning its public relations office. A public company's annual report to the stockholders tells about its corporate philosophy, history, products or services, goals, and financial status. Most government agencies can furnish reports that describe their programs and missions. Press releases, company newsletters or magazines, and recruitment brochures also can be useful. Ask the organization for any other items that might interest a prospective employee. If possible, speak to current or former employees of the organization.

Background information on the organization may be available at your public or school library. If you cannot get an annual report, check the library for reference directories that may provide basic facts about the company, such as earnings, products and services, and number of employees. Some directories widely available in libraries either in print or as online databases include:

- *Dun & Bradstreet's Million Dollar Directory*
- *Standard and Poor's Register of Corporations*
- *Mergent's Industry Review (formerly Moody's Industrial Manual)*
- *Thomas Register of American Manufacturers*
- *Ward's Business Directory*

Stories about an organization in magazines and newspapers can tell a great deal about its successes, failures, and plans for the future. You can identify articles on a company by looking under its name in periodical or computerized indexes in libraries. However, it probably will not be useful to look back more than 2 or 3 years.

The library also may have government publications that present projections of growth for the industry in which the organization is classified. Long-term projections of employment and output for detailed industries, covering the entire U.S. economy, are developed by the Bureau of Labor Statistics and revised every 2 years. See the November 2005 *Monthly Labor Review* for the most recent projections, covering the 2004-14 period, on the Internet at: **http://www.bls.gov/opub/mlr/mlrhome.htm**. Trade magazines also may include articles on the trends for specific industries.

Career centers at colleges and universities often have information on employers that is not available in libraries. Ask a career center representative how to find out about a particular organization.

Does the organization's business or activity match your own interests and beliefs?
It is easier to apply yourself to the work if you are enthusiastic about what the organization does.

How will the size of the organization affect you?
Large firms generally offer a greater variety of training programs and career paths, more managerial levels for advancement, and better employee benefits than do small firms. Large employers also may have more advanced technologies. However, many jobs in large firms tend to be highly specialized.

Jobs in small firms may offer broader authority and responsibility, a closer working relationship with top management, and a chance to clearly see your contribution to the success of the organization.

Should you work for a relatively new organization or one that is well established?
New businesses have a high failure rate, but for many people, the excitement of helping to create a company and the potential for sharing in its success more than offset the risk of job loss. However, it may be just as exciting and rewarding to work for a young firm that already has a foothold on success.

Does it make a difference if the company is private or public?
An individual or a family may control a privately owned company and key jobs may be reserved for relatives and friends. A board of directors responsible to the stockholders controls a publicly owned company and key jobs usually are open to anyone.

Is the organization in an industry with favorable long-term prospects?
The most successful firms tend to be in industries that are growing rapidly.

Nature of the job. Even if everything else about the job is attractive, you will be unhappy if you dislike the day-to-day work. Determining in advance whether you will like the work may be difficult. However, the more you find out about the job before accepting or rejecting the offer, the more likely you are to make the right choice. Actually working in the industry and, if possible, for the company would provide considerable insight. You can gain work experience through part-time, temporary, or summer jobs, or through internship or work-study programs while in school, all of which can lead to permanent job offers.

Where is the job located?
If the job is in another section of the country, you need to consider the cost of living, the availability of housing and transportation, and the quality of educational and recreational facilities in that section of the country. Even if the job location is in your area, you should consider the time and expense of commuting.

Does the work match your interests and make good use of your skills?
The duties and responsibilities of the job should be explained in enough detail to answer this question.

How important is the job in this company?
An explanation of where you fit in the organization and how you are supposed to contribute to its overall objectives should give you an idea of the job's importance.

Are you comfortable with the hours?
Most jobs involve regular hours—for example, 40 hours a week, during the day, Monday through Friday. Other jobs require night, weekend, or holiday work. In addition, some jobs routinely require overtime to meet deadlines or sales or production goals, or to better serve customers. Consider the effect that the work hours will have on your personal life.

How long do most people who enter this job stay with the company?
High turnover can mean dissatisfaction with the nature of the work or something else about the job.

Opportunities offered by employers. A good job offers you opportunities to learn new skills, increase your earnings, and rise to positions of greater authority, responsibility, and prestige. A lack of opportunities can dampen interest in the work and result in frustration and boredom.

The company should have a training plan for you. What valuable new skills does the company plan to teach you?

The employer should give you some idea of promotion possibilities within the organization. What is the next step on the career ladder? If you have to wait for a job to become vacant before you can be promoted, how long does this usually take? When opportunities for advancement do arise, will you compete with applicants from outside the company? Can you apply for jobs for which you qualify elsewhere within the organization, or is mobility within the firm limited?

Salaries and benefits. Wait for the employer to introduce these subjects. Some companies will not talk about pay until they have decided to hire you. In order to know if their offer is reasonable, you need a rough estimate of what the job should pay. You may have to go to several sources for this information. Try to find family, friends, or acquaintances who recently were hired in similar jobs. Ask your teachers and the staff in placement offices about starting pay for graduates with your qualifications. Help-wanted ads in newspapers sometimes give salary ranges for similar positions. Check the library or your school's career center for salary surveys such as those conducted by the National Association of Colleges and Employers or various professional associations.

If you are considering the salary and benefits for a job in another geographic area, make allowances for differences in the cost of living, which may be significantly higher in a large metropolitan area than in a smaller city, town, or rural area.

You also should learn the organization's policy regarding overtime. Depending on the job, you may or may not be exempt from laws requiring the employer to compensate you for overtime. Find out how many hours you will be expected to work each week and whether you receive overtime pay or compensatory time off for working more than the specified number of hours in a week.

Also take into account that the starting salary is just that—the start. Your salary should be reviewed on a regular basis; many organizations do it every year. How much can you expect to earn after 1, 2, or 3 or more years? An employer cannot be specific about the amount of pay if it includes commissions and bonuses.

Benefits also can add a lot to your base pay, but they vary widely. Find out exactly what the benefit package includes and how much of the cost you must bear.

National, State, and metropolitan area data from the Bureau's National Compensation Survey are available from:

➤ Bureau of Labor Statistics, Office of Compensation Levels and Trends, 2 Massachusetts Ave. NE., Room 4175, Washington, DC 20212-0001. Telephone: (202) 691-6199. Internet: **http://www.bls.gov/ncs**.

Data on earnings by detailed occupation from the Occupational Employment Statistics (OES) Survey are available from:

➤ Bureau of Labor Statistics, Office of Occupational Statistics and Employment Projections, 2 Massachusetts Ave. NE., Room 2135, Washington, DC 20212-0001. Telephone: (202) 691-6569. Internet: **http://www.bls.gov/oes**.

Occupational Information Included in the *Handbook*

The *Occupational Outlook Handbook* is best used as a reference; it is not meant to be read from cover to cover. Instead, start by looking at the table of contents, in which related occupations are grouped in clusters, or look in the alphabetical index in the back of the *Handbook* for specific occupations that interest you. For any occupation that seems interesting, use the *Handbook* to learn about the type of work that is performed in the occupation, the working conditions, the education and training requirements, the possibilities for advancement, earnings in the occupation, the job outlook, and related occupations. Each occupational statement in the *Handbook* follows a standard format, making it easier for you to compare occupations.

Three previous sections—"Tomorrow's Jobs," "Sources of Career Information," and "Sources of Education, Training, and Financial Aid"—highlight the forces that are likely to determine employment opportunities in industries and occupations through the year 2014 and indicate where to obtain additional information. The current section is an overview of how the occupational statements are developed and organized. It highlights information presented in each section of a *Handbook* statement, explains the source of the information, gives examples of specific occupations in some cases, and offers some hints on how to interpret the information provided.

Unless otherwise noted, the source of employment and earnings data presented in the *Handbook* is the Bureau of Labor Statistics. Nearly all *Handbook* statements cite employment and earnings data from the Occupational Employment Statistics (OES) survey. Some statements include data from outside sources. OES data may be used to compare earnings among occupations; however, outside data may not be used in this manner, because characteristics of these data vary widely.

About those numbers at the beginning of each statement

The numbers in parentheses that appear just below the title of every detailed occupational statement are from the Occupational Information Network (O*NET)—a system used by State employment service offices to classify applicants and job openings, and by some career information centers and libraries to file occupational information.

You can use O*NET to search for occupations that match your skills, or you may search by keyword or O*NET code. For each occupation, O*NET reports information about different aspects of the job, including tasks performed, knowledge, skills, abilities, and work activities. It also lists interests, work styles, such as independence, and work values, such as achievement, that are well suited to the occupation. O*NET ranks and scores the descriptors in each category by their importance to the occupation.

Occupational Information Network Coverage, a section beginning on page 676, cross-references O*NET codes to occupations covered in the *Handbook*. O*NET codes are based on the 2000 Standard Occupational Classification (SOC) system. You can access O*NET on the Internet at **http://www.online.onetcenter.org.**

Significant Points

This section highlights key occupational characteristics discussed in the statement.

Nature of the Work

This section discusses what workers do on the job, what tools and equipment they use, and how closely they are supervised. Individual job duties may vary by industry or employer. For instance, workers in larger firms tend to be more specialized, whereas those in smaller firms often have a wider variety of duties. Most occupations have several levels of skills and responsibilities through which workers may progress. Beginners may start as trainees performing routine tasks under close supervision. Experienced workers usually undertake more difficult tasks and are expected to perform with less supervision.

Some statements mention common alternative job titles or occupational specialties. For example, the statement on accountants and auditors discusses a few specialties, such as public accountants, management accountants, and internal auditors. Some statements—such as that on advertising, marketing, promotions, public relations, and sales managers—discuss titles or specialties that are detailed OES survey occupations. For these occupations, such as sales managers or marketing managers, separate employment projections are developed and their O*NET codes appear at the beginning of the statement.

Information in this section may be updated for several reasons. One is the emergence of occupational specialties. For instance, webmasters—who are responsible for the technical aspects of operating a Web site—constitute a specialty within computer scientists and database administrators. Information also may be updated due to changing technology that affects the way in which a job is performed. For example, the Internet allows purchasers to acquire supplies with a click of the mouse, saving time and money. Furthermore, job duties may be affected by modifications to business practices, such as organizational restructuring or changes in response to government regulations. An example is paralegals and legal assistants, who are increasingly being utilized by law firms in order to lower costs and increase the efficiency and quality of legal services.

Many sources are consulted in researching changes to the nature of the work section or any other section of a *Handbook* statement. Usual sources include articles in newspapers, magazines, and professional journals. Useful information also appears on the Web sites of professional associations, unions, and trade groups. Information found on the Internet or in periodicals is verified through interviews with individuals employed in the occupation, professional associations, unions, and others with occupational knowledge, such as university professors and counselors in career centers.

Working Conditions

This section identifies the typical hours worked, the workplace environment, physical activities and susceptibility to injury, special equipment, and the extent of travel required. In many occupations, people work regular business hours—40 hours a week, Monday through Friday—but many do not. For example, waiters and waitresses often work evenings and weekends.

The work setting can range from a hospital, to a mall, to an offshore oil rig. Truck drivers might be susceptible to injury, while paramedics have high job-related stress. Semiconductor processors may wear protective clothing or equipment, some construction laborers do physically demanding work, and top executives may travel frequently.

Information on various worker characteristics, such as the average number of hours worked per week, is obtained from the Current Population Survey (CPS)—a survey of households conducted by the U.S. Census Bureau for BLS.

Training, Other Qualifications, and Advancement

After knowing what a job is all about, it is important to understand how to prepare for it. This section describes the most significant sources of education and training, including the education or training preferred by employers, the typical length of training, and the possibilities for advancement. Job skills sometimes are acquired through high school, informal on-the-job training, formal training (including apprenticeships), the U.S. Armed Forces, home study, hobbies, or previous work experience. For example, sales experience is particularly important for many sales jobs. Many professional jobs, on the other hand, require formal postsecondary education—postsecondary vocational or technical training, or college, postgraduate, or professional education.

In addition to training requirements, the *Handbook* mentions desirable skills, aptitudes, and personal characteristics. For example, meeting and convention planners must have excellent interpersonal skills, organizational skills, attention to detail, and the ability to work under pressure. For some entry-level jobs, personal characteristics are more important than formal training. Employers generally seek people who read, write, and speak well; compute accurately; think logically; learn quickly; get along with others; and demonstrate dependability.

Some occupations require certification or licensing for entry, advancement, or independent practice. Certification or licensing usually requires completing courses and passing examinations. Some occupations have numerous professional credentials granted by different organizations. In this case, the most widely recognized organizations are listed in the *Handbook*.

Many occupations increasingly are requiring workers to participate in continuing education or training in relevant skills, either to keep up with the changes in their occupation or to improve their advancement opportunities.

Some statements list the number of training programs. For example, the statement on pharmacists indicates the number of colleges of pharmacy accredited by the American Council on Pharmaceutical Education. The minimum requirements for Federal Government employment cited in some statements are based on standards set by the U.S. Office of Personnel Management.

Revisions to the training section may focus on changes in educational, certification, or licensing requirements, such as an increase in the number of hours of required training or in the number of States requiring a license. Information also is updated if new skills are needed to complete the job, such as those arising from the adoption of new technology.

Information in this section comes from personal interviews with individuals employed in the occupation, Web sites, published training materials, and interviews with the organizations that grant degrees, certifications, or licenses, or are otherwise associated with the occupation.

Employment

This section reports the number of jobs that the occupation provided in 2004, the key industries in which those jobs were found, and the number or proportion of self-employed workers in the occupation, if significant. Self-employed workers accounted for about 8 percent of the workforce in 2004; however, they were concentrated in a small number of occupations, such as farmers

and ranchers, childcare workers, lawyers, health practitioners, and the construction trades.

BLS develops the National Employment Matrix, which presents current and projected employment for 336 detailed industries and 754 detailed occupations over the 2004–14 period. Data in the matrix come primarily from the OES survey, which reports employment of wage and salary workers for each occupation in almost all industries. The CPS survey provides information on the total number of self-employed and unpaid family workers in each occupation. The CPS also provides employment data on agriculture and private households. The Office of Personnel Management (OPM) furnishes employment data on Federal Government workers.

Because total employment in each occupation combines data from several different sources, employment numbers cited in the *Handbook* often differ from employment data provided by the OES, CPS, and other employment surveys. This may be a source of confusion for some readers.

When significant, the geographic distribution of jobs and the proportion of part-time workers (those working less than 35 hours a week) are mentioned, reflecting CPS data. On the basis of OES survey data, some *Handbook* statements, such as those on textile, apparel, and furnishings occupations, list States that employ substantial numbers of workers in the occupation.

Job Outlook

In planning for the future, it is important to consider potential job opportunities. This section describes the factors that will result in employment growth or decline. Projecting occupational employment is the final step in the employment projections process. (A more detailed description of the projections process is discussed in the *Handbook* section entitled "Assumptions and Methods Used in Preparing Employment Projections.") The job outlook section reflects the occupational projections in the National Employment Matrix. Each occupation is assigned a descriptive phrase based on its projected percent change in employment over the 2004–14 period. This phrase describes the occupation's projected employment change relative to the projected average employment change for all occupations combined. (These phrases are listed at the end of this section.)

Many factors are examined in developing employment projections and updating the job outlook section. One is job growth or decline in industries that employ a significant percentage of workers in the occupation. If workers are concentrated in an industry that is growing rapidly, their employment will likely also grow rapidly. For example, the growing need for business expertise is fueling demand for consulting services. Hence, management, scientific, and technical consulting services is projected to be among the fastest growing industries through 2014. Projected rapid growth in this industry helps to spur faster than average growth in employment of management analysts.

Demographic changes, which affect what services are required, can influence occupational growth or decline. For example, an aging population demands more health care workers, from registered nurses to pharmacists.

Technological change is another key factor. New technology can either create new job opportunities or eliminate jobs by making workers obsolete. The Internet has increased the demand for workers in the computer and information technology fields, such as computer support specialists and systems administrators. However, the Internet also has adversely affected travel agents, because many people now book tickets, hotels, and rental cars online.

Another factor affecting job growth or decline is changes in business practices, such as restructuring businesses or outsourcing (contracting out) work. Corporate restructuring has made many organizations "flatter," resulting in fewer middle management positions. Also, in the past few years, insurance carriers have been outsourcing sales and claims adjuster jobs to large, 24-hour call centers in order to reduce costs. Jobs in some occupations, such as computer programmers and customer service representatives, have been "offshored"—moved to low-wage foreign countries.

The substitution of one product or service for another can affect employment projections. For example, consumption of plastic products has grown as they have been substituted for metal goods in consumer and manufactured products in recent years. The process is likely to continue and should result in stronger demand for machine operators in plastics than in metal.

Competition from foreign trade usually has a negative impact on employment in an occupation. Often, foreign manufacturers can produce goods more cheaply than they can be produced in the United States, and the cost savings can be passed on in the form of lower prices with which U.S. manufacturers cannot compete. Increased international competition is a major reason for the decline in employment among textile, apparel, and furnishings workers.

In some cases, the *Handbook* mentions that an occupation is likely to provide numerous job openings or, in others, that an occupation likely will have relatively few openings. This information reflects the projected change in employment, as well as replacement needs. Large occupations that have high turnover, such as food and beverage serving occupations, generally provide the most job openings—reflecting the need to replace workers who transfer to other occupations or who stop working.

Some *Handbook* statements discuss the relationship between the number of job seekers and the number of job openings. (The phrases used to describe that relationship appear at the end of this section.) In some occupations, there is a rough balance between job seekers and job openings, resulting in good opportunities. In other occupations, employers may report difficulty finding qualified applicants, resulting in excellent job opportunities. Still other occupations are characterized by a surplus of applicants, leading to keen competition for jobs. On the one hand, because many young people who have the educational and personal qualifications necessary to learn tool and die making may prefer to attend college or may not wish to enter production occupations, employers report an insufficient number of entrants to fill all job openings for tool and die makers and some other production occupations. On the other hand, glamorous or potentially high-paying occupations, such as actors or musicians, generally have surpluses of job seekers. Variation in job opportunities by industry, educational attainment, size of firm, or geographic location also may be discussed. Even in crowded occupations, job openings do exist. Good students or highly qualified individuals should not be deterred from undertaking training for, or seeking entry into, those occupations.

Earnings

This section discusses typical earnings and how workers are compensated—by means of annual salaries, hourly wages, commissions, piece rates, tips, or bonuses. Within every occupation, earnings vary by experience, responsibility, performance, tenure, and geographic area. Almost every statement in the *Handbook* contains 2004 OES-survey earnings data for wage and salary workers. Information on earnings in the major industries in which the occupation is employed, also supplied by the OES survey, may be given as well.

In addition to presenting earnings data from the OES survey, some statements contain additional earnings data from non-BLS sources. Starting and average salaries of Federal workers are based on 2005 data from the U.S. Office of Personnel Management. The National Association of Colleges and Employers supplies information on average salary offers in 2005 for students

graduating with a bachelor's, master's, or Ph.D. degree in certain fields. A few statements contain additional earnings information from other sources, such as unions, professional associations, and private companies. These data sources are cited in the text.

Benefits account for a significant portion of total compensation costs to employers. Benefits such as paid vacation, health insurance, and sick leave may not be mentioned, because they are so widespread. In some occupational statements, the absence of these traditional benefits is pointed out. Although not as common as traditional benefits, flexible hours and profit-sharing plans may be offered to attract and retain highly qualified workers. Less common benefits also include childcare, tuition for dependents, housing assistance, summers off, and free or discounted merchandise or services. For certain occupations, the percentage of workers affiliated with a union is listed. These data come from the CPS survey.

Related Occupations

Occupations involving similar duties, skills, interests, education, and training are listed.

Sources of Additional Information

No single publication can describe all aspects of an occupation. Thus, the *Handbook* lists the mailing addresses of associations, government agencies, unions, and other organizations that can provide occupational information. In some cases, toll free telephone numbers and Internet addresses also are listed. Free or relatively inexpensive publications offering more information may be mentioned; some of these publications also may be available in libraries, in school career centers, in guidance offices, or on the Internet. Most of the organizations listed in this section were sources of information on the nature of the work, training, and job outlook discussed in the *Handbook*.

For additional sources of information, also read the earlier chapters, "Sources of Career Information" and "Sources of Information on Education, Training, and Financial Aid."

Key phrases in the *Handbook*

This box explains how to interpret the key phrases used to describe projected changes in employment. It also explains the terms used to describe the relationship between the number of job openings and the number of job seekers. The description of this relationship in a particular occupation reflects the knowledge and judgment of economists in the BLS Office of Occupational Statistics and Employment Projections.

Changing employment between 2004 and 2014

If the statement reads:	Employment is projected to:
Grow much faster than average	increase 27 percent or more
Grow faster than average	increase 18 to 26 percent
Grow about as fast as average	increase 9 to 17 percent
Grow more slowly than average	increase 0 to 8 percent
Decline	decrease any amount

Opportunities and competition for jobs

If the statement reads:	Job openings compared with job seekers may be:
Very good to excellent opportunities	More numerous
Good or favorable opportunities	In rough balance
May face, or can expect, keen competition	Fewer

Management, Business, and Financial Occupations

Management Occupations

Administrative Services Managers

(O*NET 11-3011.00)

Significant Points

- Applicants will face keen competition because of the substantial supply of competent, experienced workers seeking managerial jobs.

- Administrative services managers work throughout private industry and government and have a wide range of responsibilities, experience, earnings, and education.

- Administrative services managers should be analytical, detail-oriented, flexible, decisive, and have good communication skills.

Nature of the Work

Administrative services managers perform a broad range of duties in virtually every sector of the economy. They coordinate and direct support services to organizations as diverse as insurance companies, computer manufacturers, and government offices. These workers manage the many services that allow organizations to operate efficiently, such as secretarial and reception, administration, payroll, conference planning and travel, information and data processing, mail, materials scheduling and distribution, printing and reproduction, records management, telecommunications management, security, parking, and personal property procurement, supply, and disposal.

Specific duties for these managers vary by degree of responsibility and authority. First-line administrative services managers directly supervise a staff that performs various support services. Mid-level managers, on the other hand, develop departmental plans, set goals and deadlines, implement procedures to improve productivity and customer service, and define the responsibilities of supervisory-level managers. Some mid-level administrative services managers oversee first-line supervisors from various departments, including the clerical staff. Mid-level managers also may be involved in the hiring and dismissal of employees, but they generally have no role in the formulation of personnel policy. Some of these managers advance to upper level positions, such as vice president of administrative services, which are discussed in the *Handbook* statement on top executives.

In small organizations, a single administrative services manager may oversee all support services. In larger ones, however, first-line administrative services managers often report to mid-level managers who, in turn, report to owners or top-level managers. As the size of the firm increases, administrative services managers are more likely to specialize in specific support activities. For example, some administrative services managers work primarily as office managers, contract administrators, or unclaimed property officers. In many cases, the duties of these administrative services managers are similar to those of other managers and supervisors, some of which are discussed in other *Handbook* statements.

The nature of managerial jobs varies as significantly as the range of administrative services required by organizations. For example, administrative services managers who work as contract administrators oversee the preparation, analysis, negotiation, and review of contracts related to the purchase or sale of equipment, materials, supplies, products, or services. In addition, some administrative services managers acquire, distribute, and store supplies, while others dispose of surplus property or oversee the disposal of unclaimed property.

Administrative services managers who work as facility managers plan, design, and manage buildings and grounds in addition to people. This task requires integrating the principles of business administration, architecture, and behavioral and engineering science. Although the specific tasks assigned to facility managers vary substantially depending on the organization, the duties fall into several categories, relating to operations and maintenance, real estate, project planning and management, communication, finance, quality assessment, facility function, technology integration, and management of human and environmental factors. Tasks within these broad categories may include space and workplace planning, budgeting, purchase and sale of real estate, lease management, renovations, or architectural planning and design. Facility managers may suggest and oversee renovation projects for a variety of reasons, ranging from improving efficiency to ensuring that facilities meet government regulations and environmental, health, and security standards. Additionally, facility managers continually monitor the facility to ensure that it remains safe, secure, and well-maintained. Often, the facility

Administrative services managers supervise a staff that performs various support services.

manager is responsible for directing staff, including maintenance, grounds, and custodial workers.

Working Conditions

Administrative services managers generally work in comfortable offices. Managers involved in contract administration and personal property procurement, use, and disposal may travel between their home office, branch offices, vendors' offices, and property sales sites. Also, facility managers who are responsible for the design of workspaces may spend time at construction sites and may travel between different facilities while monitoring the work of maintenance, grounds, and custodial staffs. However, new technology has increased the number of managers who telecommute from home or other offices, and teleconferencing has reduced the need for travel.

Most administrative services managers work a standard 40-hour week. However, uncompensated overtime frequently is required to resolve problems and meet deadlines. Facility managers often are "on call" to address a variety of problems that can arise in a facility during nonwork hours.

Training, Other Qualifications, and Advancement

Educational requirements for these managers vary widely, depending on the size and complexity of the organization. In small organizations, experience may be the only requirement needed to enter a position as office manager. When an opening in administrative services management occurs, the office manager may be promoted to the position based on past performance. In large organizations, however, administrative services managers normally are hired from outside and each position has formal education and experience requirements. Some administrative services managers have advanced degrees.

Specific requirements vary by job responsibility. For first-line administrative services managers of secretarial, mailroom, and related support activities, many employers prefer an associate degree in business or management, although a high school diploma may suffice when combined with appropriate experience. For managers of audiovisual, graphics, and other technical activities, postsecondary technical school training is preferred. Managers of highly complex services, such as contract administration, generally need at least a bachelor's degree in business, human resources, or finance. Regardless of major, the curriculum should include courses in office technology, accounting, business mathematics, computer applications, human resources, and business law. Most facility managers have an undergraduate or graduate degree in engineering, architecture, construction management, business administration, or facility management. Many have a background in real estate, construction, or interior design, in addition to managerial experience.

Whatever the manager's educational background, it must be accompanied by related work experience reflecting demonstrated ability. For this reason, many administrative services managers have advanced through the ranks of their organization, acquiring work experience in various administrative positions before assuming first-line supervisory duties. All managers who oversee departmental supervisors should be familiar with office procedures and equipment. Managers of personal property acquisition and disposal need experience in purchasing and sales, and knowledge of a variety of supplies, machinery, and equipment. Managers concerned with supply, inventory, and distribution should be experienced in receiving, warehousing, packaging, shipping, transportation, and related operations. Contract administrators may have worked as contract specialists, cost analysts, or procurement specialists. Managers of unclaimed property often have experience in insurance claims analysis and records management.

Persons interested in becoming administrative services managers should have good communication skills and be able to establish effective working relationships with many different people, ranging from managers, supervisors, and professionals, to clerks and blue-collar workers. They should be analytical, detail-oriented, flexible, and decisive. They must be able to coordinate several activities at once, quickly analyze and resolve specific problems, and cope with deadlines.

Most administrative services managers in small organizations advance by moving to other management positions or to a larger organization. Advancement is easier in large firms that employ several levels of administrative services managers. Attainment of the Certified Manager (CM) designation offered by the Institute of Certified Professional Managers (ICPM), through education, work experience, and successful completion of examinations, can enhance a manager's advancement potential. In addition, a master's degree in business administration or a related field enhances a first-level manager's opportunities to advance to a mid-level management position, such as director of administrative services, and eventually to a top-level management position, such as executive vice president for administrative services. Those with enough money and experience can establish their own management consulting firm.

Advancement of facility managers is based on the practices and size of individual companies. Some facility managers transfer from other departments within the organization or work their way up from technical positions. Others advance through a progression of facility management positions that offer additional responsibilities. Completion of the competency-based professional certification program offered by the International Facility Management Association can give prospective candidates an advantage. In order to qualify for this Certified Facility Manager (CFM) designation, applicants must meet certain educational and experience requirements. People entering the profession also may obtain the Facility Management Professional (FMP) credential, a stepping stone to the CFM.

Employment

Administrative services managers held about 268,000 jobs in 2004. About 80 percent worked in service-providing industries, including Federal, State, and local government; health care; financial services; professional, scientific, and technical services; administrative and support services; and education. Most of the remaining managers worked in wholesale and retail trade, in management of companies and enterprises, or in manufacturing.

Job Outlook

Employment of administrative services managers is projected to grow about as fast as the average for all occupations through 2014. Like persons seeking other managerial positions, applicants will face keen competition because there will be more competent, experienced workers seeking jobs than there will be positions available. However, demand should be strong for facility managers because businesses increasingly are realizing the importance of maintaining, securing, and efficiently operating their facilities, which are very large investments for most organizations. Administrative services managers employed in management services and management consulting also should be in demand, as public and private organizations continue to streamline and, in some cases, contract out administrative services functions in an effort to cut costs.

At the same time, continuing corporate restructuring and increasing utilization of office technology should result in a flatter organizational structure with fewer levels of management, reducing the need for some middle management positions. This should adversely affect administrative services managers who oversee first-line mangers. However, the effects of these changes on employment should be less severe for administrative services managers, who have a wide range of responsibilities, than for other middle managers who specialize in certain functions. In addition to new administrative services management jobs created over the 2004-14 projection period, many job openings will stem from the need to replace workers who transfer to other jobs, retire, or leave the occupation for other reasons.

Earnings

Earnings of administrative services managers vary greatly depending on the employer, the specialty, and the geographic area. In general, however, median annual earnings of administrative services managers in May 2004 were $60,290. The middle 50 percent earned between $42,680 and $83,510. The lowest 10 percent earned less than $31,120, and the highest 10 percent earned more than $110,270. Median annual earnings in the industries employing the largest numbers of these managers in May 2004 were:

Management of companies and enterprises	$71,870
Elementary and secondary schools	65,850
Colleges, universities, and professional schools	61,020
Local government	59,380
State government	55,500

In the Federal Government, industrial specialists in nonsupervisory, supervisory, and managerial positions averaged $69,802 a year in 2005. Corresponding averages were $69,211 for facility operations services managers, $67,185 for industrial property managers, $63,614 for property disposal specialists, $67,855 for administrative officers, and $60,370 for support services administrators.

Related Occupations

Administrative services managers direct and coordinate support services and oversee the purchase, use, and disposal of personal property. Occupations with similar functions include office and administrative support worker supervisors and managers; cost estimators; property, real estate, and community association managers; purchasing managers, buyers, and purchasing agents; and top executives.

Sources of Additional Information

For information about careers and education and degree programs in facility management, as well as the Certified Facility Manager designation, contact:
➤ International Facility Management Association, 1 East Greenway Plaza, Suite 1100, Houston, TX 77046-0194. Internet: **http://www.ifma.org**

General information regarding facility management and a list of facility management education and degree programs may be obtained from:
➤ Association of Higher Education Facilities Officers, 1643 Prince St., Alexandria, VA 22314-2818. Internet: **http://www.appa.org**

For information about the Certified Manager (CM) designation, contact:
➤ Institute of Certified Professional Managers, James Madison University, MSC 5504, Harrisonburg, VA 22807.

Advertising, Marketing, Promotions, Public Relations, and Sales Managers

(O*NET 11-2011.00, 11-2021.00, 11-2022.00, 11-2031.00)

Significant Points

● Keen competition for jobs is expected.

● College graduates with related experience, a high level of creativity, strong communication skills, and computer skills should have the best job opportunities.

● High earnings, substantial travel, and long hours, including evenings and weekends, are common.

Nature of the Work

The objective of any firm is to market and sell its products or services profitably. In small firms, the owner or chief executive officer might assume all advertising, promotions, marketing, sales, and public relations responsibilities. In large firms, which may offer numerous products and services nationally or even worldwide, an executive vice president directs overall advertising, promotions, marketing, sales, and public relations policies. (Executive vice presidents are included in the *Handbook* statement on top executives.) Advertising, marketing, promotions, public relations, and sales managers coordinate the market research, marketing strategy, sales, advertising, promotion, pricing, product development, and public relations activities.

Advertising managers oversee advertising and promotion staffs, which usually are small, except in the largest firms. In a small firm, managers may serve as liaisons between the firm and the advertising or promotion agency to which many advertising or promotional functions are contracted out. In larger firms, advertising managers oversee in-house account, creative, and media services departments. The *account executive* manages the account services department, assesses the need for advertising, and, in advertising agencies, maintains the accounts of clients. The creative services department develops the subject matter and presentation of advertising. The *creative director* oversees the copy chief, art director, and associated staff. The *media director* oversees planning groups that select the communication media—for example, radio, television, newspapers, magazines, the Internet, or outdoor signs—to disseminate the advertising.

Promotions managers supervise staffs of promotion specialists. These managers direct promotion programs that combine advertising with purchase incentives to increase sales. In an effort to establish closer contact with purchasers—dealers, distributors, or consumers—promotion programs may use direct mail, telemarketing, television or radio advertising, catalogs, exhibits, inserts in newspapers, Internet advertisements or Web sites, in-store displays or product endorsements, and special events. Purchasing incentives may include discounts, samples, gifts, rebates, coupons, sweepstakes, and contests.

Marketing managers develop the firm's marketing strategy in detail. With the help of subordinates, including *product development managers* and *market research managers,* they estimate the demand for products and services offered by the firm and its competitors. In addition, they identify potential markets—for example, business firms, wholesalers, retailers, government, or the general public. Marketing managers develop pricing strategy to help firms maximize profits and market share while ensuring that the firm's customers are satisfied. In collaboration with sales, product development, and other managers, they monitor trends that indicate the need for new products and services, and they oversee product development. Marketing managers work with advertising and promotion managers to promote the firm's products and services and to attract potential users.

Public relations managers supervise public relations specialists. (See the *Handbook* statement on public relations specialists.) These managers direct publicity programs to a targeted audience. They often specialize in a specific area, such as crisis management, or in a specific industry, such as health care. They use every available communication medium to maintain the support of the specific group upon whom their organization's success depends, such as consumers, stockholders, or the general public. For example, public relations managers may clarify or justify the firm's point of view on health or environmental issues to community or special-interest groups.

Public relations managers also evaluate advertising and promotion programs for compatibility with public relations efforts and

Advertising, marketing, promotions, public relations, and sales managers have a wide range of educational backgrounds.

serve as the eyes and ears of top management. They observe social, economic, and political trends that might ultimately affect the firm, and they make recommendations to enhance the firm's image on the basis of those trends.

Public relations managers may confer with labor relations managers to produce internal company communications—such as newsletters about employee-management relations—and with financial managers to produce company reports. They assist company executives in drafting speeches, arranging interviews, and maintaining other forms of public contact; oversee company archives; and respond to requests for information. In addition, some of these managers handle special events, such as the sponsorship of races, parties introducing new products, or other activities that the firm supports in order to gain public attention through the press without advertising directly.

Sales managers direct the firm's sales program. They assign sales territories, set goals, and establish training programs for the sales representatives. (See the *Handbook* statement on sales representatives, wholesale and manufacturing.) Sales managers advise the sales representatives on ways to improve their sales performance. In large, multiproduct firms, they oversee regional and local sales managers and their staffs. Sales managers maintain contact with dealers and distributors. They analyze sales statistics gathered by their staffs to determine sales potential and inventory requirements and to monitor customers' preferences. Such information is vital in the development of products and the maximization of profits.

Working Conditions
Advertising, marketing, promotions, public relations, and sales managers work in offices close to those of top managers. Long hours, including evenings and weekends, are common. In 2004, about two-thirds of advertising, marketing, and public relations managers worked more than 40 hours a week. Working under pressure is unavoidable when schedules change and problems arise, but deadlines and goals must still be met.

Substantial travel may be involved. For example, attendance at meetings sponsored by associations or industries often is mandatory. Sales managers travel to national, regional, and local offices and to the offices of various dealers and distributors. Advertising and promotions managers may travel to meet with clients or representatives of communications media. At times, public relations managers travel to meet with special-interest groups or government

officials. Job transfers between headquarters and regional offices are common, particularly among sales managers.

Training, Advancement, and Other Qualifications
A wide range of educational backgrounds is suitable for entry into advertising, marketing, promotions, public relations, and sales managerial jobs, but many employers prefer those with experience in related occupations plus a broad liberal arts background. A bachelor's degree in sociology, psychology, literature, journalism, or philosophy, among other subjects, is acceptable. However, requirements vary, depending upon the particular job.

For marketing, sales, and promotions management positions, some employers prefer a bachelor's or master's degree in business administration with an emphasis on marketing. Courses in business law, economics, accounting, finance, mathematics, and statistics are advantageous. In highly technical industries, such as computer and electronics manufacturing, a bachelor's degree in engineering or science, combined with a master's degree in business administration, is preferred.

For advertising management positions, some employers prefer a bachelor's degree in advertising or journalism. A course of study should include marketing, consumer behavior, market research, sales, communication methods and technology, and visual arts—for example, art history and photography.

For public relations management positions, some employers prefer a bachelor's or master's degree in public relations or journalism. The applicant's curriculum should include courses in advertising, business administration, public affairs, public speaking, political science, and creative and technical writing.

For all these specialties, courses in management and the completion of an internship while the candidate is in school are highly recommended. Familiarity with word-processing and database applications also is important for many positions. Computer skills are vital because marketing, product promotion, and advertising on the Internet are increasingly common. Also, the ability to communicate in a foreign language may open up employment opportunities in many rapidly growing areas around the country, especially cities with large Spanish-speaking populations.

Most advertising, marketing, promotions, public relations, and sales management positions are filled by promoting experienced staff or related professional personnel. For example, many managers are former sales representatives, purchasing agents, buyers, or product, advertising, promotions, or public relations specialists. In small firms, where the number of positions is limited, advancement to a management position usually comes slowly. In large firms, promotion may occur more quickly.

Although experience, ability, and leadership are emphasized for promotion, advancement can be accelerated by participation in management training programs conducted by larger firms. Many firms also provide their employees with continuing education opportunities—either in-house or at local colleges and universities—and encourage employee participation in seminars and conferences, often held by professional societies. In collaboration with colleges and universities, numerous marketing and related associations sponsor national or local management training programs. Course subjects include brand and product management, international marketing, sales management evaluation, telemarketing and direct sales, interactive marketing, promotion, marketing communication, market research, organizational communication, and data-processing systems procedures and management. Many firms pay all or part of the cost for employees who successfully complete courses.

Some associations offer certification programs for these managers. Certification—an indication of competence and achievement—is particularly important in a competitive job market. While relatively few advertising, marketing, promotions, public relations, and sales managers currently are certified, the number of managers who seek certification is expected to grow. Today, there are numerous management certification programs based on education and job performance. In addition, The Public Relations Society of America offers a certification program for public relations practitioners based on years of experience and performance on an examination.

Persons interested in becoming advertising, marketing, promotions, public relations, and sales managers should be mature, creative, highly motivated, resistant to stress, flexible, and decisive. The ability to communicate persuasively, both orally and in writing, with other managers, staff, and the public is vital. These managers also need tact, good judgment, and exceptional ability to establish and maintain effective personal relationships with supervisory and professional staff members and client firms.

Because of the importance and high visibility of their jobs, advertising, marketing, promotions, public relations, and sales managers often are prime candidates for advancement to the highest ranks. Well-trained, experienced, and successful managers may be promoted to higher positions in their own or another firm; some become top executives. Managers with extensive experience and sufficient capital may open their own businesses.

Employment

Advertising, marketing, promotions, public relations, and sales managers held about 646,000 jobs in 2004. The following tabulation shows the distribution of jobs by occupational specialty:

Sales managers	337,000
Marketing managers	188,000
Advertising and promotions managers	64,000
Public relations managers	58,000

These managers were found in virtually every industry. Sales managers held almost half of the jobs; most were employed in wholesale and retail trade, and finance and insurance industries. Marketing managers held more than fourth of the jobs; the professional, scientific, and technical services industries employed almost one-third of marketing managers. About one-fourth of advertising and promotions managers worked in the professional, scientific, and technical services industries, and the, information industries, including advertising and related services, and publishing industries. Most public relations managers were employed in service-providing industries, such as professional, scientific, and technical services, finance and insurance, health care and social assistance, and educational services.

Job Outlook

Advertising, marketing, promotions, public relations, and sales manager jobs are highly coveted and will be sought by other managers or highly experienced professionals, resulting in keen competition. College graduates with related experience, a high level of creativity, and strong communication skills should have the best job opportunities. In particular, employers will seek those who have the computer skills to conduct advertising, marketing, promotions, public relations, and sales activities on the Internet.

Employment of advertising, marketing, promotions, public relations, and sales managers is expected to increase faster than the average for all occupations through 2014, spurred by intense domestic and global competition in products and services offered to consumers. However, projected employment growth varies by industry. For example, employment is projected to grow much faster than average in scientific, professional, and related services, such as computer systems design and related services, and in advertising and related services, as businesses increasingly hire contractors for these services instead of additional full-time staff. By contrast, a decline in employment is expected in many manufacturing industries.

Earnings

Median annual earnings in May 2004 were $63,610 for advertising and promotions managers, $87,640 for marketing managers, $84,220 sales managers, and $70,000 for public relations managers.

Median annual earnings of advertising and promotions managers in May 2004 in the advertising and related services industry were $89,570.

Median annual earnings in the industries employing the largest numbers of marketing managers in May 2004 were as follows:

Computer systems design and related services	$107,030
Management of companies and enterprises	98,700
Insurance carriers	86,810
Architectural, engineering, and related services	83,610
Depository credit intermediation	76,450

Median annual earnings in the industries employing the largest numbers of sales managers in May 2004 were as follows:

Computer systems design and related services	$119,140
Wholesale electronic markets and agents and brokers	101,930
Automobile dealers	97,460
Management of companies and enterprises	95,410
Machinery, equipment, and supplies merchant wholesalers	84,680

According to a National Association of Colleges and Employers survey, starting salaries for marketing majors graduating in 2005 averaged $33,873; starting salaries for advertising majors averaged $31,340.

Salary levels vary substantially, depending upon the level of managerial responsibility, length of service, education, size of firm, location, and industry. For example, manufacturing firms usually pay these managers higher salaries than do nonmanufacturing firms. For sales managers, the size of their sales territory is another important determinant of salary. Many managers earn bonuses equal to 10 percent or more of their salaries.

Related Occupations

Advertising, marketing, promotions, public relations, and sales managers direct the sale of products and services offered by their firms and the communication of information about their firms' activities. Other workers involved with advertising, marketing, promotions, public relations, and sales include actors, producers, and directors; advertising sales agents; artists and related workers; demonstrators, product promoters, and models; market and survey researchers; public relations specialists; sales representatives, wholesale and manufacturing; and writers and editors.

Sources of Additional Information

For information about careers in advertising management, contact:

➤ American Association of Advertising Agencies, 405 Lexington Ave., New York, NY 10174-1801. Internet: **http://www.aaaa.org**

Information about careers and professional certification in public relations management is available from:

➤ Public Relations Society of America, 33 Maiden Lane, New York, NY 10038-5150. Internet: **http://www.prsa.org**

Computer and Information Systems Managers

(O*NET 11-3021.00)

Significant Points

- Employment of computer and information systems managers is expected to grow faster than the average for all occupations through the year 2014.

- Many managers possess advanced technical knowledge gained from working in a computer occupation.

- Job opportunities will be best for applicants with computer-related work experience; a master's degree in business administration (MBA) with technology as a core component, or a management information systems degree; and strong communication and administrative skills.

Computer and information systems managers plan, coordinate, and direct the computing resources of firms.

Nature of the Work

How and when companies and organizations use technology are critical to remaining competitive. Computer and information systems managers play a vital role in the technological direction of their organizations. They do everything from constructing the business plan to overseeing network security to directing Internet operations.

Computer and information systems managers plan, coordinate, and direct research and facilitate the computer-related activities of firms. They help determine both technical and business goals in consultation with top management and make detailed plans for the accomplishment of these goals. For example, working with their staff, they may develop the overall concepts and requirements of a new product or service, or may identify how an organization's computing capabilities can effectively aid project management.

Computer and information systems managers direct the work of systems analysts, computer programmers, support specialists, and other computer-related workers. These managers plan and coordinate activities such as installation and upgrading of hardware and software, programming and systems design, development of computer networks, and implementation of Internet and intranet sites. They are increasingly involved with the upkeep, maintenance, and security of networks. They analyze the computer and information needs of their organizations from an operational and strategic perspective and determine immediate and long-range personnel and equipment requirements. They assign and review the work of their subordinates and stay abreast of the latest technology to ensure the organization does not lag behind competitors.

The duties of computer and information systems managers vary with their specific titles. *Chief technology officers*, for example, evaluate the newest and most innovative technologies and determine how these can help their organizations. The chief technology officer, who often reports to the organization's chief information officer, manages and plans technical standards and tends to the daily information technology issues of the firm. (Chief information officers are covered in a separate *Handbook* statement on top executives.) Because of the rapid pace of technological change, chief technology officers must constantly be on the lookout for developments that could benefit their organizations. They are responsible for demonstrating to a company how information technology can be used as a competitive tool that not only cuts costs, but also increases revenue and maintains or increases competitive advantage.

Management information systems (MIS) directors manage information systems and computing resources for their organizations. They also may work under the chief information officer and plan and direct the work of subordinate information technology employees. These managers oversee a variety of user services such as an organization's help desk, which employees can call with questions or problems. MIS directors also may make hardware and software upgrade recommendations based on their experience with an organization's technology. Helping ensure the availability, continuity, and security of data and information technology services is the primary responsibility of these workers.

Project managers develop requirements, budgets, and schedules for their firms' information technology projects. They coordinate such projects from development through implementation, working with internal and external clients, vendors, consultants, and computer specialists. These managers are increasingly involved in projects that upgrade the information security of an organization.

LAN/WAN (local area network/wide area network) *managers* provide a variety of services, from design to administration of the local area network, which connects staff within an organization. These managers direct the network and its computing environment, including hardware, systems software, applications software, and all other computer-related configurations.

Computer and information systems managers need strong communication skills. They coordinate the activities of their unit with those of other units or organizations. They confer with top executives; financial, production, marketing, and other managers; and contractors and equipment and materials suppliers.

Working Conditions

Computer and information systems managers spend most of their time in an office. Most work at least 40 hours a week and may have to work evenings and weekends to meet deadlines or solve unexpected problems. Some computer and information systems managers may experience considerable pressure in meeting technical goals within short timeframes or tight budgets. As networks continue to expand and more work is done remotely, computer and information systems managers have to communicate with and oversee offsite employees using modems, laptops, e-mail, and the Internet.

Like other workers who sit continuously in front of a keyboard, computer and information systems managers are susceptible to eyestrain, back discomfort, and hand and wrist problems such as carpal tunnel syndrome.

Training, Other Qualifications, and Advancement

Advanced technical knowledge is essential for computer and information systems managers, who must understand and guide the work of their subordinates yet also explain the work in nontechnical terms to senior managers and potential customers. Therefore, many computer and information systems managers have experience in a computer occupation such as systems analyst; other managers may have worked as a computer support specialist, programmer, or other information technology professional.

A bachelor's degree usually is required for management positions, although employers often prefer a graduate degree, especially an MBA with technology as a core component. This degree differs from a traditional MBA in that there is a heavy emphasis on information technology in addition to the standard business curriculum. This preparation is becoming important because more computer and information systems managers are making important technology decisions as well as business decisions for their organizations. Some universities specialize in offering degrees in management information systems, which blend technical core subjects with business, accounting, and communications courses. A few computer and information systems managers attain their positions with only an associate degree, but they must have sufficient experience and must have acquired additional skills on the job. To aid their professional advancement, though, many managers with an associate degree eventually earn a bachelor's or master's degree while working.

Computer and information systems managers need a broad range of skills. Employers want managers who have experience with the specific software or technology used on the job, as well as a background in either consulting or business management. The expansion of electronic commerce has elevated the importance of business insight; many computer and information systems managers are called on to make important business decisions. Managers need a keen understanding of people, management processes, and customers' needs.

Computer and information systems managers must possess strong interpersonal, communication, and leadership skills because they are required to interact not only with their staff, but also with other people inside and outside their organizations. They also must possess team skills to work on group projects and other collaborative efforts. Computer and information systems managers increasingly interact with persons outside their organizations, reflecting their emerging role as vital parts of their firms' executive teams.

Computer and information systems managers may advance to progressively higher leadership positions in their field. Some may become managers in nontechnical areas such as marketing, human resources, or sales. In high-technology firms, managers in nontechnical areas often must possess the same specialized knowledge as do managers in technical areas.

Employment

Computer and information systems managers held about 280,000 jobs in 2004. About 9 in 10 computer managers worked in service-providing industries, mainly in computer systems design and related services. This industry provides services related to the commercial use of computers on a contract basis, including custom computer programming services; computer systems integration design services; computer facilities management services, including computer systems or data-processing facilities support services; and other computer-related services, such as disaster recovery services and software installation. Other large employers include insurance and financial firms, government agencies, and manufacturers.

Job Outlook

Employment of computer and information systems managers is expected to grow faster than the average for all occupations through the year 2014. Technological advancements will boost the employment of computer-related workers; as a result, the demand for managers to direct these workers also will increase. In addition, job openings will result from the need to replace managers who retire or move into other occupations. Opportunities for obtaining a management position will be best for those with computer-related work experience; an MBA with technology as a core component, or a management information systems degree; and strong communication and administrative skills.

Despite the downturn in the technology sector in the early part of the decade, the outlook for computer and information systems managers remains strong. To remain competitive, firms will continue to install sophisticated computer networks and set up more complex Internet and intranet sites. Keeping a computer network running smoothly is essential to almost every organization. Firms will be more willing to hire managers who can accomplish that.

Similarly, the security of computer networks will continue to increase in importance as more business is conducted over the Internet. The security of the Nation's entire electronic infrastructure has come under renewed scrutiny in light of recent threats. Organizations need to understand how their systems are vulnerable and how to protect their infrastructure and Internet sites from hackers, viruses, and other acts of cyberterrorism. The emergence of cybersecurity as a key issue facing most organizations should lead to strong growth for computer managers. Firms will increasingly hire cybersecurity experts to fill key leadership roles in their information technology departments because the integrity of their computing environments is of utmost concern. As a result, there will be a high demand for managers proficient in computer security issues.

With the explosive growth of electronic commerce and the capacity of the Internet to create new relationships with customers, the role of computer and information systems managers will continue to evolve. Persons in these jobs will become increasingly vital to their companies. The expansion of the wireless Internet will spur the need for computer and information systems managers with both business savvy and technical proficiency.

Opportunities for those who wish to become computer and information systems managers should be closely related to the growth of the occupations they supervise and the industries in which they are found. (See the statements on computer programmers, computer software engineers, computer support specialists and systems administrators, computer systems analysts, and computer scientists and database administrators elsewhere in the *Handbook*.)

Earnings

Earnings for computer and information systems managers vary by specialty and level of responsibility. Median annual earnings of these managers in May 2004 were $92,570. The middle 50 percent earned between $71,650 and $118,330. Median annual earnings in the industries employing the largest numbers of computer and information systems managers in May 2004 were as follows:

Software publishers	$107,870
Computer systems design and related services	103,850
Management of companies and enterprises	99,880
Insurance carriers	97,900
Depository credit intermediation	86,450

According to Robert Half International, a professional staffing and consulting services firm, average starting salaries in 2005 for high-level information technology managers ranged from

$80,250 to $112,250. According to a 2005 survey by the National Association of Colleges and Employers, starting salary offers for those with an MBA, a technical undergraduate degree, and 1 year or less of experience averaged $52,300; for those with a master's degree in management information systems/business data processing, the starting salary averaged $56,909.

In addition, computer and information systems managers, especially those at higher levels, often receive more employment-related benefits—such as expense accounts, stock option plans, and bonuses—than do nonmanagerial workers in their organizations.

Related Occupations

The work of computer and information systems managers is closely related to that of computer programmers, computer software engineers, computer systems analysts, computer scientists and database administrators, and computer support specialists and systems administrators. Computer and information systems managers also have some high-level responsibilities similar to those of top executives.

Sources of Additional Information

For information about a career as a computer and information systems manager, contact the sources of additional information for the various computer occupations discussed elsewhere in the *Handbook*.

Construction Managers

(O*NET 11-9021.00)

Significant Points

- Construction managers must be available—often 24 hours a day—to deal with delays, bad weather, or emergencies at the jobsite.

- Employers prefer individuals who combine construction industry work experience with a bachelor's degree in construction science, construction management, or civil engineering.

- Excellent employment opportunities are expected as the increasing complexity of many construction projects requires more managers to oversee them.

Nature of the Work

Construction managers plan, direct, and coordinate a wide variety of construction projects, including the building of all types of residential, commercial, and industrial structures, roads, bridges, wastewater treatment plants, and schools and hospitals. Construction managers may oversee an entire project or just part of a project and, although they usually play no direct role in the actual construction of a structure, they typically schedule and coordinate all design and construction processes, including the selection, hiring, and oversight of specialty trade contractors.

Construction managers are salaried or self-employed managers who oversee construction supervisors and workers. They often go by the job titles program manager, constructor, construction superintendent, project engineer, project manager, construction supervisor, general contractor, or similar designations. Construction managers may be owners or salaried employees of a construction management or contracting firm, or may work under contract or as a salaried employee of the property owner, developer, or contracting firm overseeing the construction project.

Construction managers coordinate and supervise the construction process from the conceptual development stage through final construction, making sure that the project gets done on time and within budget. They often work with owners, engineers, architects, and others who are involved in the construction process. Given the designs for buildings, roads, bridges, or other projects, construction managers oversee the planning, scheduling, and implementation of the project to execute those designs.

Large construction projects, such as an office building or industrial complex, are often too complicated for one person to manage. Therefore, these projects are divided into many segments: Site preparation, including land clearing and earth moving; sewage systems; landscaping and road construction; building construction, including excavation and laying of foundations and erection of the structural framework, floors, walls, and roofs; and building systems, including fire-protection, electrical, plumbing, air-conditioning, and heating. Construction managers may be in charge of one or more of these activities.

Construction managers evaluate and help determine appropriate construction delivery systems and the most cost-effective plan and schedule for completing the project. They divide all required construction site activities into logical steps, budgeting the time required to meet established deadlines. This may require sophisticated estimating and scheduling techniques and use of computers with specialized software. (See the section on cost estimators elsewhere in the *Handbook*.)

Construction managers oversee the selection of general contractors and trade contractors to complete specific pieces of the project—which could include everything from structural metalworking and plumbing to painting and carpet installation. Construction managers determine the labor requirements and, in some cases, supervise or monitor the hiring and dismissal of workers. They oversee the performance of all trade contractors and are responsible for ensuring that all work is completed on schedule.

Construction managers direct and monitor the progress of construction activities, sometimes through construction supervisors or other construction managers. They oversee the delivery and use of materials, tools, and equipment; and the quality of construction, worker productivity, and safety. They are responsible for obtaining all necessary permits and licenses and, depending upon the contractual arrangements, direct or monitor compliance with building and safety codes and other regulations. And they continually track and control construction costs to avoid cost overruns. They may direct

Construction managers diagnose construction-related problems and determine the most cost-effective method to solve them.

the work of several subordinates, such as assistant managers or superintendents, field engineers, or crew supervisors.

Working Conditions

Construction managers work out of a main office from which the overall construction project is monitored, or out of a field office at the construction site. Advances in telecommunications and Internet access allow construction managers to be onsite without being out of contact of the main office. Management decisions regarding daily construction activities generally are made at the jobsite. Managers may travel extensively when the construction site is not close to their main office or when they are responsible for activities at two or more sites. Management of overseas construction projects usually entails temporary residence in another country.

Construction managers may be "on call"—often 24 hours a day—to deal with delays, the effects of bad weather, or emergencies at the site. Most work more than a standard 40-hour week because construction may proceed around-the-clock. They may have to work this type of schedule for days, even weeks, to meet special project deadlines, especially if there are delays.

Although the work usually is not considered inherently dangerous, construction managers must be careful while performing onsite services.

Training, Other Qualifications, and Advancement

Persons interested in becoming a construction manager need a solid background in building science, business and management, as well as related work experience within the construction industry. They need to understand contracts, plans, and specifications, and to be knowledgeable about construction methods, materials, and regulations. Familiarity with computers and software programs for job costing, online collaboration, scheduling, and estimating also is important. The ability to converse fluently in Spanish is also an asset because Spanish is the first language of many workers in the construction industry.

Construction managers should be flexible and work effectively in a fast-paced environment. They should be decisive and work well under pressure, particularly when faced with unexpected occurrences or delays. The ability to coordinate several major activities at once, while analyzing and resolving specific problems, is essential, as is an understanding of engineering, architectural, and other construction drawings. Good oral and written communication skills also are important, as are leadership skills. Managers must be able to establish a good working relationship with many different people, including owners, other managers, designers, supervisors, and craftworkers.

For construction manager jobs, employers increasingly prefer to hire individuals with a bachelor's degree in construction science, construction management, or civil engineering, as well as industry work experience. Practical industry experience is very important, whether it is acquired through an internship, a cooperative education program, or work experience in a trade or another job in the industry. Traditionally, persons advanced to construction management positions after having substantial experience as construction craftworkers—carpenters, masons, plumbers, or electricians, for example—or after having worked as construction supervisors or as owners of independent specialty contracting firms, overseeing workers in one or more construction trades. However, as construction processes become increasingly complex, employers are placing a growing importance on postsecondary education.

Many colleges and universities offer 4-year degree programs in construction management, construction science, and construction engineering. These programs include courses in project control and development, site planning, design, construction methods, construction materials, value analysis, cost estimating, scheduling,

contract administration, accounting, business and financial management, safety, building codes and standards, inspection procedures, engineering and architectural sciences, mathematics, statistics, and information technology. Graduates from 4-year degree programs usually are hired as assistants to project managers, field engineers, schedulers, or cost estimators. An increasing number of graduates in related fields—engineering or architecture, for example—also enter construction management, often after acquiring substantial experience on construction projects or after completing graduate studies in construction management or building science.

Several colleges and universities offer a master's degree program in construction management or construction science. Master's degree recipients, especially those with work experience in construction, typically become construction managers in very large construction or construction management companies. Often, individuals who hold a bachelor's degree in an unrelated field seek a master's degree in construction management or construction science in order to work in the construction industry. Some construction managers obtain a master's degree in business administration or finance to further their career prospects. Doctoral degree recipients usually become college professors or conduct research.

Many individuals also attend training and educational programs sponsored by industry associations, often in collaboration with postsecondary institutions. A number of 2-year colleges throughout the country offer construction management or construction technology programs.

There is a growing movement towards certification of construction managers to ensure that a construction manager has a certain body of knowledge, abilities, and experience. Although certification is not required to work in the construction industry, voluntary certification can be valuable because it provides evidence of competence and experience. Both the American Institute of Constructors (AIC) and the Construction Management Association of America (CMAA) have established voluntary certification programs for construction managers. Requirements combine written examinations with verification of education and professional experience. AIC awards the Associate Constructor (AC) and Certified Professional Constructor (CPC) designations to candidates who meet its requirements and pass the appropriate construction examinations. CMAA awards the Certified Construction Manager (CCM) designation to practitioners who meet its requirements through work performed in a construction management organization and by passing a technical examination. Applicants for the CMAA certification also must complete a self-study course that covers a broad range of topics central to construction management, including the professional role of a construction manager, legal issues, and allocation of risk.

Advancement opportunities for construction managers vary depending upon an individual's performance and the size and type of company for which they work. Within large firms, managers may eventually become top-level managers or executives. Highly experienced individuals may become independent consultants; some serve as expert witnesses in court or as arbitrators in disputes. Those with the required capital may establish their own construction management services, specialty contracting, or general contracting firm.

Employment

Construction managers held 431,000 jobs in 2004. Over half were self-employed, many as owners of general or specialty trade construction firms. Most of the rest were employed in the construction industry, 13 percent by specialty trade contractors—for example, plumbing, heating and air-conditioning and electrical contractors—and 18 percent by general building contractors. Others were employed by architectural, engineering, and related services firms and by local governments.

Job Outlook

Excellent employment opportunities for construction managers are expected through 2014 because the number of job openings will exceed the number of qualified individuals seeking to enter the occupation. This situation is expected to continue even as college construction management programs expand to meet the current high demand for graduates. The construction industry often does not attract sufficient numbers of qualified job seekers because it is often seen as having poor working conditions.

Employment of construction managers is projected to increase about as fast as the average for all occupations through 2014. In addition to job openings arising from employment growth, many additional openings should result annually from the need to replace workers who transfer to other occupations or who retire or leave the labor force for other reasons. More construction managers will be needed as the level of construction activity continues to grow. In addition, opportunities will increase for construction managers to start their own firms. However, employment of construction managers can be sensitive to the short-term nature of many projects and to cyclical fluctuations in construction activity.

The increasing complexity of construction projects is boosting the demand for management-level personnel within the construction industry. Sophisticated technology and the proliferation of laws setting standards for buildings and construction materials, worker safety, energy efficiency, and environmental protection have further complicated the construction process. Advances in building materials and construction methods; the need to replace portions the Nation's infrastructure; and the growing number of multipurpose buildings and energy-efficient structures will further add to the demand for more construction managers. More opportunities for construction managers also will result from the need for greater cost control and financial management of projects and to oversee the numerous subcontractors being employed.

Prospects for individuals seeking construction manager jobs in construction management, architectural and engineering services, and construction contracting firms should be best for persons who have a bachelor's or higher degree in construction science, construction management, or civil engineering—but also practical experience working in construction. Employers will increasingly prefer applicants with college degrees, previous construction work experience, including internships, and a strong background in building technology.

Earnings

Earnings of salaried construction managers and self-employed independent construction contractors vary depending upon the size and nature of the construction project, its geographic location, and economic conditions. In addition to typical benefits, many salaried construction managers receive benefits such as bonuses and use of company motor vehicles.

Median annual earnings of construction managers in May 2004 were $69,870. The middle 50 percent earned between $53,430 and $92,350. The lowest paid 10 percent earned less than $42,120, and the highest paid 10 percent earned more than $126,330. Median annual earnings in the industries employing the largest numbers of construction managers in 2004 were as follows:

Building equipment contractors	$72,560
Nonresidential building construction	71,700
Other specialty trade contractors	68,110
Residential building construction	67,190
Foundation, structure, and building exterior contractors	64,250

According to a July 2005 salary survey by the National Association of Colleges and Employers, candidates with a bachelor's degree in construction science/management received job offers averaging $42,923 a year.

Related Occupations

Construction managers participate in the conceptual development of a construction project and oversee its organization, scheduling, and implementation. Other workers who perform similar functions include architects, except landscape and naval; civil engineers; cost estimators; landscape architects; and engineering and natural sciences managers.

Sources of Information

For information about constructor certification, contact:
➤ American Institute of Constructors, 717 Princess St., Alexandria, VA 22314. Internet: **http://www.constructorcertification.org** or **http://www.aicnet.org**

For information about construction management and construction manager certification, contact:
➤ Construction Management Association of America, 7918 Jones Branch Dr., Suite 540, McLean, VA 22102-3307. Internet: **http://www.cmaanet.org**

Information on accredited construction science and management educational programs and accreditation requirements is available from:
➤ American Council for Construction Education, 1717 North Loop 1604 E, Ste 320, San Antonio, TX 78232 Internet: **http://www.acce-hq.org**
➤ National Center for Construction Education and Research, P.O. Box 141104, Gainesville, FL 32614. Internet: **http://www.nccer.org**

Education Administrators

(O*NET 11-9031.00, 11-9032.00, 11-9033.00, 11-9039.99)

Significant Points

● Many jobs require a master's or doctoral degree and experience in a related occupation, such as a teacher or admissions counselor.

● Strong interpersonal and communication skills are essential because much of an administrator's job involves working and collaborating with others.

● Excellent opportunities are expected since a large proportion of education administrators is expected to retire over the next 10 years.

Nature of the Work

Smooth operation of an educational institution requires competent administrators. *Education administrators* provide instructional leadership as well as manage the day-to-day activities in schools, preschools, daycare centers, and colleges and universities. They also direct the educational programs of businesses, correctional institutions, museums, and job training and community service organizations. (College presidents and school superintendents are covered in the *Handbook* statement on general managers and top executives.) Education administrators set educational standards and goals and establish the policies and procedures to carry them out. They also supervise managers, support staff, teachers, counselors, librarians, coaches, and others. They develop academic programs; monitor students' educational progress; train and motivate teachers and other staff; manage career counseling and other student services; administer recordkeeping; prepare budgets; handle relations with parents, prospective and current students, employers, and the community; and perform many other duties. In an organization such as a small daycare center, one administrator may handle all these functions. In universities or large school systems, responsibilities are divided among many administrators, each with a specific function.

Educational administrators who manage elementary, middle, and secondary schools are called *principals*. They set the academic tone and hire, evaluate, and help improve the skills of teachers and other staff. Principals confer with staff to advise, explain, or answer procedural questions. They visit classrooms, observe teaching methods, review instructional objectives, and examine learning materials. They actively work with teachers to develop and maintain high curriculum standards, develop mission statements, and set performance goals and objectives. Principals must use clear, objective guidelines for teacher appraisals, because pay often is based on performance ratings.

Principals also meet and interact with other administrators, students, parents, and representatives of community organizations. Decision-making authority has increasingly shifted from school district central offices to individual schools. School principals have greater flexibility in setting school policies and goals, but when making administrative decisions they must pay attention to the concerns of parents, teachers, and other members of the community.

Principals prepare budgets and reports on various subjects, including finances and attendance, and oversee the requisition and allocation of supplies. As school budgets become tighter, many principals have become more involved in public relations and fundraising to secure financial support for their schools from local businesses and the community.

Principals must take an active role to ensure that students meet national, State, and local academic standards. Many principals develop school/business partnerships and school-to-work transition programs for students. Increasingly, principals must be sensitive to the needs of the rising number of non-English speaking and culturally diverse students. In some areas growing enrollments also are a cause for concern because they are leading to overcrowding at many schools. When addressing problems of inadequate resources, administrators serve as advocates for the building of new schools or the repair of existing ones. During summer months, principals are responsible for planning for the upcoming year, overseeing summer school, participating in workshops for teachers and administrators, supervising building repairs and improvements, and working to be sure the school has adequate staff for the school year.

Schools continue to be involved with students' emotional welfare as well as their academic achievement. As a result, principals face responsibilities outside the academic realm. For example, in response to the growing numbers of dual-income and single-parent families and teenage parents, schools have established before- and after-school childcare programs or family resource centers, which also may offer parenting classes and social service referrals. With the help of community organizations, some principals have established programs to combat increases in crime, drug and alcohol abuse, and sexually transmitted diseases among students.

Assistant principals aid the principal in the overall administration of the school. Some assistant principals hold this position for several years to prepare for advancement to principal jobs; others are career assistant principals. They are primarily responsible for scheduling student classes, ordering textbooks and supplies, and coordinating transportation, custodial, cafeteria, and other support services. They usually handle student discipline and attendance problems, social and recreational programs, and health and safety matters. They also may counsel students on personal, educational, or vocational matters. With the advent of site-based management, assistant principals are playing a greater role in ensuring the academic

success of students by helping to develop new curriculums, evaluating teachers, and dealing with school-community relations—responsibilities previously assumed solely by the principal. The number of assistant principals that a school employs may vary, depending on the number of students.

Administrators in school district central offices oversee public schools under their jurisdiction. This group includes those who direct subject-area programs such as English, music, vocational education, special education, and mathematics. They supervise instructional coordinators and curriculum specialists, and work with them to evaluate curriculums and teaching techniques and improve them. (Instructional coordinators are covered elsewhere in the *Handbook*.) Administrators also may oversee career counseling programs and testing that measures students' abilities and helps to place them in appropriate classes. Others may also direct programs such as school psychology, athletics, curriculum and instruction, and professional development. With site-based management, administrators have transferred primary responsibility for many of these programs to the principals, assistant principals, teachers, instructional coordinators, and other staff in the schools.

In preschools and childcare centers, education administrators are the director or supervisor of the school or center. Their job is similar to that of other school administrators in that they oversee daily activities and operation of the schools, hire and develop staff, and make sure that the school meets required regulations.

In colleges and universities, *provosts* also known as *chief academic officers* assist presidents, make faculty appointments and tenure decisions, develop budgets, and establish academic policies and programs. With the assistance of *academic deans and deans of faculty*, they also direct and coordinate the activities of deans of individual colleges and chairpersons of academic departments. Fundraising is the chief responsibility of the *director of development* and also is becoming an essential part of the job for all administrators.

College or university department heads or *chairpersons* are in charge of departments that specialize in particular fields of study, such as English, biological science, or mathematics. In addition to teaching, they coordinate schedules of classes and teaching assignments; propose budgets; recruit, interview, and hire applicants for teaching positions; evaluate faculty members; encourage faculty development; serve on committees; and perform other administrative duties. In overseeing their departments, chairpersons must consider and balance the concerns of faculty, administrators, and students.

Education administrators manage the day-to-day operations of schools.

Higher education administrators also direct and coordinate the provision of student services. *Vice presidents of student affairs or student life, deans of students*, and *directors of student services* may direct and coordinate admissions, foreign student services, health and counseling services, career services, financial aid, and housing and residential life, as well as social, recreational, and related programs. In small colleges, they may counsel students. In larger colleges and universities, separate administrators may handle each of these services. *Registrars* are custodians of students' records. They register students, record grades, prepare student transcripts, evaluate academic records, assess and collect tuition and fees, plan and implement commencement, oversee the preparation of college catalogs and schedules of classes, and analyze enrollment and demographic statistics. *Directors of admissions* manage the process of recruiting, evaluating, and admitting students, and work closely with *financial aid directors*, who oversee scholarship, fellowship, and loan programs. Registrars and admissions officers at most institutions need computer skills because they use electronic student information systems. For example, for those whose institutions present college catalogs, schedules, and other information on the Internet, knowledge of online resources, imaging, and other computer skills is important. *Athletic directors* plan and direct intramural and intercollegiate athletic activities, seeing to publicity for athletic events, preparation of budgets, and supervision of coaches. Other increasingly important administrators direct public relations, distance learning, and technology.

Working Conditions

Education administrators hold leadership positions with significant responsibility. Most find working with students extremely rewarding, but as the responsibilities of administrators have increased in recent years, so has the stress. Coordinating and interacting with faculty, parents, students, community members, business leaders, and State and local policymakers can be fast-paced and stimulating, but also stressful and demanding. Principals and assistant principals, whose varied duties include discipline, may find working with difficult students to be challenging. They are also increasingly being held accountable for ensuring that their schools meet recently imposed State and Federal guidelines for student performance and teacher qualifications.

Many education administrators work more than 40 hours a week, often including school activities at night and on weekends. Most administrators work 11 or 12 months out of the year. Some jobs include travel.

Training, Other Qualifications, and Advancement

Most education administrators begin their careers in related occupations, often as teachers, and prepare for advancement into education administration by completing a master's or doctoral degree. Because of the diversity of duties and levels of responsibility, their educational backgrounds and experience vary considerably. Principals, assistant principals, central office administrators, academic deans, and preschool directors usually have held teaching positions before moving into administration. Some teachers move directly into principal positions; others first become assistant principals, or gain experience in other administrative jobs at either the school or district level in positions such as department head, curriculum specialist, or subject matter advisor. In some cases, administrators move up from related staff jobs such as recruiter, school counselor, librarian, residence hall director, or financial aid or admissions counselor.

To be considered for education administrator positions, workers must first prove themselves in their current jobs. In evaluating candidates, supervisors look for leadership, determination, confidence, innovativeness, and motivation. The ability to make sound decisions

and to organize and coordinate work efficiently is essential. Because much of an administrator's job involves interacting with others—such as students, parents, teachers, and the community— a person in such a position must have strong interpersonal skills and be an effective communicator and motivator. Knowledge of leadership principles and practices, gained through work experience and formal education, is important. A familiarity with computer technology is a necessity for principals, who are required to gather information and coordinate technical resources for their students, teachers, and classrooms.

In most public schools, principals, assistant principals, and school district administrators need a master's degree in education administration or educational leadership. Some principals and central office administrators have a doctorate or specialized degree in education administration. Most States require principals to be licensed as school administrators. License requirements vary by State, but nearly all States require either a master's degree or some other graduate-level training. Some States also require candidates for licensure to pass a test. Increasingly, on-the-job training, often with a mentor, is required or recommended for new school leaders. Some States require administrators to take continuing education courses to keep their license, thus ensuring that administrators have the most up-to-date skills. The number and types of courses required to maintain licensure vary by State. In private schools, which are not subject to State licensure requirements, some principals and assistant principals hold only a bachelor's degree, but the majority have a master's or doctoral degree.

Educational requirements for administrators of preschools and childcare centers vary depending on the setting of the program and the State of employment. Administrators who oversee preschool programs in public schools are often required to have at least a bachelor's degree. Child care directors are generally not required to have a degree; however, most States require a general preschool education credential, such as the Child Development Associate credential (CDA) sponsored by the Council for Professional Recognition, or a credential specifically designed for administrators. The National Child Care Association, offers a National Administration Credential, which some recent college graduates voluntarily earn to better qualify for positions as child care center directors.

Academic deans and chairpersons usually have a doctorate in their specialty. Most have held a professorship in their department before advancing. Admissions, student affairs, and financial aid directors and registrars sometimes start in related staff jobs with bachelor's degrees—any field usually is acceptable—and obtain advanced degrees in college student affairs, counseling, or higher education administration. A Ph.D. or Ed.D. usually is necessary for top student affairs positions. Computer literacy and a background in accounting or statistics may be assets in admissions, records, and financial work.

Advanced degrees in higher education administration, educational leadership, and college student affairs are offered in many colleges and universities. Education administration degree programs include courses in school leadership, school law, school finance and budgeting, curriculum development and evaluation, research design and data analysis, community relations, politics in education, and counseling. The National Council for Accreditation of Teacher Education and the Educational Leadership Constituent Council accredit programs designed for elementary and secondary school administrators. While completion of an accredited program is not required, it may assist in fulfilling licensure requirements.

Education administrators advance through promotion to more responsible administrative positions or by transferring to more responsible positions at larger schools or systems. They also may become superintendents of school systems or presidents of educational institutions.

Employment

Education administrators held about 442,000 jobs in 2004. Of these, 58,000 were preschool or child care administrators, 225,000 were elementary or secondary school administrators, and 132,000 were postsecondary administrators. About 2 in 10 worked for private education institutions, and 6 in 10 worked for State and local governments, mainly in schools, colleges and universities, and departments of education. Less than 4 percent were self-employed. The rest worked in child daycare centers, religious organizations, job training centers, and businesses and other organizations that provided training for their employees.

Job Outlook

Employment of education administrators is projected to grow as fast as the average for all occupations through 2014. As education and training take on greater importance in everyone's lives, the need for people to administer education programs will grow. Job opportunities for many of these positions should also be excellent because a large proportion of education administrators are expected to retire over the next 10 years.

Enrollments of school-age children are the primary factor determining the demand for education administrators. Enrollment of students in elementary and secondary schools is expected to grow slowly over the next decade, which will limit the growth of principals and other administrators in these schools. However, preschool and childcare center administrators are expected to experience substantial growth as enrollments in formal child care programs continue to expand as fewer private households care for young children. Additionally, as more States begin implementing public preschool programs, more preschool directors will be needed. The number of postsecondary school students is projected to grow more rapidly than other student populations, creating significant demand for administrators at that level. Opportunities may vary by geographical area, as enrollments are expected to increase the fastest in the West and South, where the population is growing, and to decline or remain stable in the Northeast and the Midwest. School administrators also are in greater demand in rural and urban areas, where pay is generally lower than in the suburbs.

Principals and assistant principals should have very favorable job prospects. A sharp increase in responsibilities in recent years has made the job more stressful, and has discouraged some teachers from taking positions in administration. Principals are now being held more accountable for the performance of students and teachers, while at the same time they are required to adhere to a growing number of government regulations. In addition, overcrowded classrooms, safety issues, budgetary concerns, and teacher shortages in some areas all are creating additional stress for administrators. Many teachers feel the higher pay of administrators is not high enough to compensate for the greater responsibilities.

Job prospects also are expected to be favorable for college and university administrators, particularly those seeking nonacademic positions. Public colleges and universities may be subject to funding shortfalls during economic downturns, but increasing enrollments over the projection period will require that institutions replace the large numbers of administrators who retire, and even hire additional administrators. In addition, a significant portion of growth will stem from growth in the private and for-profit segments of higher education. Many of these schools cater to working adults who might not ordinarily participate in postsecondary education. These schools allow students to earn a degree, receive job-specific training, or update their skills in a convenient manner, such as through part-time programs or distance learning. As the number of these schools continues to grow, more administrators will be needed to oversee them.

While competition among faculty for prestigious positions as academic deans and department heads is likely to remain keen, fewer applicants are expected for nonacademic administrative jobs, such as director of admissions or student affairs. Furthermore, many people are discouraged from seeking administrator jobs by the requirement that they have a master's or doctoral degree in education administration—as well as by the opportunity to earn higher salaries in other occupations.

Earnings

In May 2004, elementary and secondary school administrators had median annual earnings of $74,190; postsecondary school administrators had median annual earnings of $68,340, while preschool and childcare center administrators earned a median of $35,730 per year. Salaries of education administrators depend on several factors, including the location and enrollment level in the school or school district. According to a survey of public schools, conducted by the Educational Research Service, average salaries for principals and assistant principals in the 2004-05 school year were as follows:

Principals:
Senior high school	$82,225
Jr. high/middle school	78,160
Elementary school	74,062

Assistant principals:
Senior high school	$68,945
Jr. high/middle school	66,319
Elementary school	63,398

According to the College and University Professional Association for Human Resources, median annual salaries for selected administrators in higher education in 2004-05 were as follows:

Chief academic officer	$127,066

Academic deans:
Business	$120,460
Arts and sciences	110,412
Graduate programs	109,309
Education	107,660
Nursing	100,314
Health-related professions	100,185
Continuing education	91,800
Occupational or vocational education	79,845

Other administrators:
Chief development officer	$114,400
Dean of students	75,245
Director, student financial aid	63,130
Registrar	61,953
Director, student activities	45,636

Benefits for education administrators are generally very good. Many get 4 or 5 weeks vacation every year and have generous health and pension packages. Many colleges and universities offer free tuition to employees and their families.

Related Occupations

Education administrators apply organizational and leadership skills to provide services to individuals. Workers in related occupations include administrative services managers; office and administrative support worker supervisors and managers; and human resource, training, and labor relations managers and specialists. Education administrators also work with students and have backgrounds similar to those of counselors; librarians; instructional coordinators; teachers—preschool, kindergarten, elementary, middle, and secondary; and teachers—postsecondary.

Sources of Additional Information

For information on principals, contact:

➤ The National Association of Elementary School Principals, 1615 Duke St., Alexandria, VA 22314-3483. Internet: **http://www.naesp.org**

➤ The National Association of Secondary School Principals, 1904 Association Drive, Reston, VA 20191-1537. Internet: **http://www.nassp.org**

For a list of nationally recognized programs in elementary and secondary educational administration, contact:

➤ The Educational Leadership Constituent Council, 1904 Association Drive, Reston, VA 20191. Internet:
http://www.npbea.org/ELCC/index.html

For information on collegiate registrars and admissions officers, contact:

➤ American Association of Collegiate Registrars and Admissions Officers, One Dupont Circle NW., Suite 520, Washington, DC 20036-1171. Internet: **http://www.aacrao.org**

For information on professional development and graduate programs for college student affairs administrators, contact:

➤ NASPA, Student Affairs Administrators in Higher Education, 1875 Connecticut Ave. NW., Suite 418, Washington, DC 20009. Internet: **http://www.naspa.org**

Engineering and Natural Sciences Managers

(O*NET 11-9041.00, 11-9121.00)

Significant Points

● Most engineering and natural sciences managers have previous experience as engineers, scientists, or mathematicians.

● Projected employment growth for engineering and natural sciences managers should be closely related to growth in employment of the engineers and scientists they supervise and of the industries in which they are found.

● Opportunities will be best for workers with strong communication and business management skills.

Nature of the Work

Engineering and natural sciences managers plan, coordinate, and direct research, design, and production activities. They may supervise engineers, scientists, and technicians, along with support personnel. These managers use their knowledge of engineering and natural sciences to oversee a variety of activities. They determine scientific and technical goals within broad outlines provided by top executives, who are discussed elsewhere in the *Handbook*. These goals may include improving manufacturing processes, advancing scientific research, or developing new products. Managers make detailed plans to accomplish these goals. For example, they may develop the overall concepts of a new product or identify technical problems preventing the completion of a project.

To perform effectively, they also must acquire knowledge of administrative procedures, such as budgeting, hiring, and supervision. These managers propose budgets for projects and programs and determine staff, training, and equipment needs. They hire and assign scientists, engineers, and support personnel to carry out specific parts of each project. They also supervise the work of these employees, review their output, and establish administrative procedures and policies—including environmental standards, for example.

In addition, these managers use communication skills extensively. They spend a great deal of time coordinating the activities of their unit with those of other units or organizations. They confer with higher levels of management; with financial, production, marketing, and other managers; and with contractors and equipment and materials suppliers.

Engineering managers may supervise people who design and develop machinery, products, systems, and processes, or they may direct and coordinate production, operations, quality assurance, testing, or maintenance in industrial plants. Many are plant engineers, who direct and coordinate the design, installation, operation, and maintenance of equipment and machinery in industrial plants. Others manage research and development teams that produce new products and processes or improve existing ones.

Natural sciences managers oversee the work of life and physical scientists (including agricultural scientists, chemists, biologists, geologists, medical scientists, and physicists). These managers direct research and development projects and coordinate activities such as testing, quality control, and production. They may work on basic research projects or on commercial activities. Science managers sometimes conduct their own research in addition to managing the work of others.

Working Conditions

Engineering and natural sciences managers spend most of their time in an office. Some managers, however, also may work in laboratories, where they may be exposed to the same conditions as research scientists, or in industrial plants, where they may be exposed to the same conditions as production workers. Most managers work at least 40 hours a week and may work much longer on occasion to meet project deadlines. Some may experience considerable pressure to meet technical or scientific goals on a short deadline or within a tight budget.

Training, Other Qualifications, and Advancement

Strong technical knowledge is essential for engineering and natural sciences managers, who must understand and guide the work of their subordinates and explain the work in nontechnical terms to senior management and potential customers. Therefore, these management positions usually require work experience and formal education as an engineer, scientist, or mathematician.

Engineering and natural sciences managers must have people skills to effectively coordinate work on the many aspects of each project.

Most engineering managers begin their careers as engineers, after completing a bachelor's degree in the field. To advance to higher level positions, engineers generally must assume management responsibility. To fill management positions, employers seek engineers who possess administrative and communication skills in addition to technical knowledge in their specialty. Many engineers gain these skills by obtaining a master's degree in engineering management or a master's degree in business administration (MBA). Employers often pay for such training. In large firms, some courses required in these degree programs may be offered onsite. Typically, engineers who prefer to manage in technical areas pursue a master's degree in engineering management, while those interested in nontechnical management earn an MBA.

Many science managers begin their careers as scientists, such as chemists, biologists, geologists, or mathematicians. Most scientists or mathematicians engaged in basic research have a Ph.D.; some in applied research and other activities may have a bachelor's or master's degree. Science managers must be specialists in the work they supervise. In addition, employers prefer managers with good communication and administrative skills. Graduate programs allow scientists to augment their undergraduate training with instruction in other fields, such as management or computer technology. Given the rapid pace of scientific developments, science managers must continuously upgrade their knowledge.

Engineering and natural sciences managers may advance to progressively higher leadership positions within their discipline. Some may become managers in nontechnical areas such as marketing, human resources, or sales. In high technology firms, managers in nontechnical areas often must possess the same specialized knowledge as do managers in technical areas. For example, employers in an engineering firm may prefer to hire experienced engineers as sales workers because the complex services offered by the firm can be marketed only by someone with specialized engineering knowledge. Such sales workers could eventually advance to jobs as sales managers.

Employment

Engineering and natural sciences managers held about 233,000 jobs in 2004. About 27 percent worked in professional, scientific, and technical services industries, primarily for firms providing architectural, engineering, and related services; computer systems design and related services; and scientific research and development services. Manufacturing industries employed 37 percent of engineering and natural sciences managers. Manufacturing industries with the largest employment include those producing computer and electronic equipment; transportation equipment, including aerospace products and parts; chemicals, including pharmaceuticals; and machinery manufacturing. Other large employers include government agencies and telecommunications and utilities companies.

Job Outlook

Employment of engineering and natural sciences managers is expected to grow about as fast as the average for all occupations through the year 2014—in line with projected employment growth in engineering and most sciences. However, many additional jobs will result from the need to replace managers who retire or move into other occupations. Opportunities for obtaining a management position will be best for workers with advanced technical knowledge and strong communication skills. Because engineering and natural sciences managers are involved in their firms' financial, production, and marketing activities, business management skills are also important.

Projected employment growth for engineering and natural sciences managers should be closely related to the growth of the occupations they supervise and of the industries in which they are found. For example, opportunities for managers should be better in rapidly growing areas of engineering—such as environmental and biomedical engineering—than in more slowly growing areas, such as nuclear and aerospace engineering. (See the statements on engineers and on life and physical scientists elsewhere in the *Handbook*.) In addition, many employers are finding it more efficient to contract engineering and science management services to outside companies and consultants, creating good opportunities for managers in management services and management, scientific, and technical consulting firms.

Earnings

Earnings for engineering and natural sciences managers vary by specialty and by level of responsibility. Median annual earnings of engineering managers were $97,630 in May 2004. The middle 50 percent earned between $78,820 and $121,090. Median annual earnings in the industries employing the largest numbers of engineering managers in May 2004 were:

Semiconductor and other electronic component manufacturing	$116,400
Navigational, measuring, electromedical, and control instruments manufacturing	107,160
Aerospace product and parts manufacturing	103,570
Federal government	97,000
Architectural, engineering, and related services	96,020

Median annual earnings of natural sciences managers were $88,660 in May 2004. The middle 50 percent earned between $64,550 and $118,210. Median annual earnings in the industries employing the largest numbers of natural sciences managers in May 2004 were:

Scientific research and development services	$106,530
Federal government	81,460

A survey of manufacturing firms, conducted by Abbot, Langer & Associates, found that engineering department managers and superintendents earned a median annual income of $89,232 in 2004, while research and development managers earned $90,377.

In addition, engineering and natural sciences managers, especially those at higher levels, often receive more benefits—such as expense accounts, stock option plans, and bonuses—than do nonmanagerial workers in their organizations.

Related Occupations

The work of engineering and natural sciences managers is closely related to that of engineers; mathematicians; and physical and life scientists, including agricultural and food scientists, atmospheric scientists, biological scientists, conservation scientists and foresters, chemists and materials scientists, environmental scientists and hydrologists, geoscientists, medical scientists, and physicists and astronomers. It also is related to the work of other managers, especially top executives.

Sources of Additional Information

For information about a career as an engineering and natural sciences manager, contact the sources of additional information for engineers, life scientists, and physical scientists that are listed at the end of statements on these occupations elsewhere in the *Handbook*.

Farmers, Ranchers, and Agricultural Managers

(O*NET 11-9011.01, 11-9011.02, 11-9011.03, 11-9012.00)

Significant Points

● Modern farming requires knowledge of new developments in agriculture, as well as work experience acquired through growing up on a farm or through postsecondary education.

● Overall employment is projected to decline because of increasing productivity and consolidation of farms.

● Horticulture and organic farming will provide better employment opportunities.

● Small-scale farming is a major growth area and offers the best opportunity for entering the occupation.

Nature of the Work

American farmers, ranchers, and agricultural managers direct the activities of one of the world's largest and most productive agricultural sectors. They produce enough food and fiber to meet the needs of the United States and for export.

Farmers and ranchers own and operate mainly family-owned farms. They also may lease land from a landowner and operate it as a working farm. The type of farm they operate determines their specific tasks. On crop farms—farms growing grain, cotton, other fibers, fruit, and vegetables—farmers are responsible for preparing, tilling, planting, fertilizing, cultivating, spraying, and harvesting. After the harvest, they make sure that the crops are properly packaged, stored, or marketed. Livestock, dairy, and poultry farmers must feed and care for the animals and keep barns, pens, coops, and other farm buildings clean and in good condition. They also plan and oversee breeding and marketing activities. Horticultural specialty farmers oversee the production of ornamental plants, nursery products—such as flowers, bulbs, shrubbery, and sod—and fruits and vegetables grown in greenhouses. Aquaculture farmers raise fish and shellfish in marine, brackish, or fresh water, usually in ponds, floating net pens, raceways, or recirculating systems. They stock, feed, protect, and otherwise manage aquatic life sold for consumption or used for recreational fishing.

Responsibilities of farmers and ranchers range from caring for livestock, to operating machinery, to maintaining equipment and facilities. The size of the farm or ranch often determines which of these tasks farmers and ranchers will handle themselves. Operators of small farms usually perform all tasks, physical and administrative. They keep records for management and tax purposes, service machinery, maintain buildings, and grow vegetables and raise animals. Operators of large farms, by contrast, have employees who help with the physical work that small-farm operators do themselves. Although employment on most farms is limited to the farmer and one or two family workers or hired employees, some large farms have 100 or more full-time and seasonal workers. Some of these employees are in nonfarm occupations, working as truck drivers, sales representatives, bookkeepers, and computer specialists.

Agricultural managers manage the day-to-day activities of one or more farms, ranches, nurseries, timber tracts, greenhouses, and other agricultural establishments for farmers, absentee landowners, or corporations. Their duties and responsibilities vary widely, but focus on the business aspects of running a farm. On small farms, they may oversee the entire operation; on larger farms, they may oversee a single activity, such as marketing. Agricultural managers usually do not perform production activities; instead, they hire and supervise farm and livestock workers, who perform most of the daily production tasks. In these cases, managers may establish output goals; determine financial constraints; monitor production and marketing; hire, assign, and supervise workers; determine crop transportation and storage requirements; and oversee maintenance of the property and equipment.

Farmers, ranchers, and agricultural managers make many managerial decisions. Farm output and income are strongly influenced by the weather, disease, fluctuations in prices of domestic and foreign farm products, and Federal farm programs. In crop production operations, farmers and managers usually determine the best time to plant seed, apply fertilizer and chemicals, and harvest and market the crops. They use different strategies to protect themselves from unpredictable changes in the markets for agricultural products. Many farmers and managers carefully plan the combination of crops they grow, so that if the price of one crop drops, they will have sufficient income from another crop to make up for the loss. While most farm output is sold directly to food-processing companies, some farmers—particularly operators of smaller farms—may choose to sell their goods directly through farmers' markets or may use cooperatives to reduce their financial risk and to gain a larger share of the retail dollar. For example, in community-supported agriculture (CSA), cooperatives sell shares of a harvest to consumers prior to the planting season, thus freeing the farmer from having to bear all the financial risks and ensuring the farmer a market for the produce of the coming season.

Farmers, ranchers, and agricultural managers also negotiate with banks and other credit lenders to get the best financing deals for their equipment, livestock, and seed. They also must keep abreast of constantly changing prices for their products and manage the risk of fluctuating prices. Those who plan ahead may be able to store their crops or keep their livestock to take advantage of higher prices later in the year. Those who participate in the risky futures market, where contracts on future production of agricultural goods are bought and sold, can minimize the risk of sudden price changes by buying futures contracts which guarantee that they will get at least a certain price for their agricultural goods when they are ready to sell.

Like other businesses, farming operations have become more complex in recent years, so many farmers use computers to keep financial and inventory records. They also use computer databases and spreadsheets to manage breeding, dairy, and other farm operations.

Many farmers work part time on small farms.

Working Conditions

The work of full-time farmers, ranchers, and agricultural managers is often strenuous; work hours are frequently long, and they rarely have days off during the planting, growing, and harvesting seasons. Nevertheless, for those who enter farming or ranching, the disadvantages are counterbalanced by the quality of life in a rural area, working outdoors, being self-employed, and making a living off the land. Farmers and farm managers on crop farms usually work from sunrise to sunset during the planting and harvesting seasons. The rest of the year, they plan next season's crops, market their output, and repair machinery.

On livestock-producing farms and ranches, work goes on throughout the year. Animals, unless they are grazing, must be fed and watered every day, and dairy cows must be milked two or three times a day. Many livestock and dairy farmers monitor and attend to the health of their herds, which may include assisting in the birthing of animals. Such farmers rarely get the chance to get away, unless they hire an assistant or arrange for a temporary substitute.

Farmers who grow produce and perishables have different demands on their time. For example, organic farmers must maintain cover crops during the cold months, thus keeping them occupied with farming beyond the typical growing season.

Farmwork also can be hazardous. Tractors and other farm machinery can cause serious injury, and workers must be constantly alert on the job. The proper operation of equipment and handling of chemicals are necessary to avoid accidents, safeguard one's health, and protect the environment.

On very large farms, farmers spend substantial time meeting with farm managers or farm supervisors in charge of various activities. Professional farm managers overseeing several farms may divide their time between traveling to meet farmers or landowners and planning the farm operations in their offices. As farming practices and agricultural technology become more sophisticated, farmers and farm managers are spending more time in offices and at computers, where they electronically manage many aspects of their businesses. Some farmers also spend time at conferences exchanging information, particularly during the winter months.

Training, Other Qualifications, and Advancement

Growing up on a family farm and participating in agricultural programs for young people, such as the National FFA Organization or the 4-H youth educational programs, are important sources of training for those interested in pursuing agriculture as a career. However, modern farming requires increasingly complex scientific, business, and financial decisions, so postsecondary education in agriculture is important even for people who were raised on farms.

The completion of a 2-year degree, or better, a 4-year bachelor's degree program in a college of agriculture, is becoming increasingly important for farm managers and for farmers and ranchers who expect to make a living at farming. A degree in business or farm management with a concentration in agriculture is important, but even after obtaining formal education, novices may need to spend time working under an experienced farmer to learn how to put into practice the skills learned through academic training. A small number of farms offer, on a formal basis, apprenticeships to help young people acquire such practical skills.

Students should select the college most appropriate to their specific interests and location. All State university systems have at least one land-grant college or university with a school of agriculture. Common programs of study include agronomy, dairy science, agricultural economics and business, horticulture, crop and fruit science, and animal science. For students interested in aquaculture, formal programs also are available and include coursework in fisheries biology, fish culture, hatchery management

and maintenance, and hydrology. Whatever one's interest, the college curriculum should include courses in agricultural production, marketing, and economics.

Agricultural managers can enhance their professional status through voluntary certification as an Accredited Farm Manager (AFM) by the American Society of Farm Managers and Rural Appraisers. Accreditation requires several years of farm management experience, the appropriate academic background—a bachelor's degree or, preferably, a master's degree in a field of agricultural science—and the passing of courses and examinations relating to the business, financial, and legal aspects of farm and ranch management.

Farmers, ranchers, and agricultural managers need to keep abreast of continuing advances in agricultural methods both in the United States and abroad, as well as monitor changes in governmental regulations that may affect methods or markets for particular crops. Besides print journals that inform the agricultural community, the spread of the Internet allows quick access to the latest developments in areas such as agricultural marketing, legal arrangements, and growing crops, vegetables, and livestock. Electronic mail, online journals, and newsletters from agricultural organizations also speed the exchange of information directly between farming associations and individual farmers.

Farmers, ranchers, and agricultural managers also must have enough technical knowledge of crops, growing conditions, and plant diseases to make decisions that ensure the successful operation of their farms. A rudimentary knowledge of veterinary science, as well as animal husbandry, is important for livestock and dairy farmers. Knowledge of the relationship between farm operations—for example, the use of pesticides—and environmental conditions is essential. Mechanical aptitude and the ability to work with tools of all kinds also are valuable skills for a small-farm operator, who often maintains and repairs machinery or farm structures.

Farmers, ranchers, and agricultural managers need the managerial skills necessary to organize and operate a business. A basic knowledge of accounting and bookkeeping is essential in keeping financial records, while knowledge of sources of credit is vital for buying seed, fertilizer, and other inputs necessary for planting. It also is necessary to be familiar with complex safety regulations and requirements of governmental agricultural support programs. Computer skills are becoming increasingly important, especially on large farms, where computers are widely used for recordkeeping and business analysis. For example, some farmers, ranchers, and agricultural managers use personal computers to access the Internet to get the latest information on prices of farm products and other agricultural news. In addition, skills in personnel management, communication, and conflict resolution are equally important in the operation of a farm or ranch business.

Employment

Farmers, ranchers, and agricultural managers held nearly 1.3 million jobs in 2004. About 83 percent were self-employed. Most farmers, ranchers, and agricultural managers oversee crop production activities, while others manage livestock and dairy production. Most farmers and ranchers operate small farms on a part-time basis.

The soil, topography of the land, and climate often determine the type of farming and ranching done in a particular area. California, Texas, Iowa, Nebraska, and Kansas are the leading agricultural States.

Job Outlook

Market pressures and low prices for many agricultural goods will cause more farms to go out of business over the 2004–14 period. The complexity of modern farming and keen competition among farmers leave little room for the marginally successful farmer. Therefore, the long-term trend toward the consolidation of farms into fewer and larger ones is expected to continue over the 2004–14 period and result in a continued decline in employment of self-employed farmers and ranchers and slower-than-average growth in employment of salaried agricultural managers. As land, machinery, seed, and chemicals become more expensive, only well-capitalized farmers and corporations will be able to acquire many of the farms that become available. The larger, more productive farms are better able to withstand the adverse effects of climate and price fluctuations upon farm output and income. Larger farms also may have advantages in obtaining government subsidies and payments as these payments are usually based on per-unit production.

In addition, the agriculture sector continues to produce more with fewer workers. Increasing productivity in the U.S. agriculture industry is expected to allow greater domestic consumption needs and export requirements to be met with fewer farmers, ranchers, and agricultural managers overall. The overwhelming majority of job openings for self-employed farmers and ranchers will result from the need to replace farmers who retire or leave the occupation for economic or other reasons.

Despite the expected continued consolidation of farmland and the projected decline in overall employment of farmers, ranchers, and agricultural managers, an increasing number of small-scale farmers have developed successful market niches that involve personalized, direct contact with their customers. Many are finding opportunities in organic food production, as more consumers demand food grown without pesticides or chemicals. Others use farmers' markets that cater directly to urban and suburban consumers, allowing the farmers to capture a greater share of consumers' food dollars. Some small-scale farmers belong to collectively owned marketing cooperatives that process and sell their product. Other farmers participate in community-supported agriculture cooperatives that allow consumers to directly buy a share of the farmer's harvest.

Aquaculture may continue to provide some new employment opportunities over the 2004–14 period. New concerns about over-fishing and the depletion of the stock of some wild fish species will likely lead to more restrictions on deep-sea fishing, even as public demand for the consumption of seafood continues to grow. This demand has spurred the growth of aquaculture farms that raise selected aquatic species—such as shrimp, salmon, trout and catfish— in pens or ponds. Aquaculture's presence even in landlocked States has increased as farmers attempt to diversify and cater to the growing demand for fish by consumers. In addition, growing demand for horticulture products, such as flowers, ornamentals, trees, shrubs, and other nonedibles, is expected to produce better employment opportunities for greenhouse and nursery farmers and managers.

Earnings

Incomes of farmers and ranchers vary greatly from year to year because prices of farm products fluctuate with weather conditions and other factors influencing the quantity and quality of farm output and the demand for those products. A farm that shows a large profit one year may show a loss the following year. According to the U.S. Department of Agriculture, the average net cash farm business income for farm operator households in 2004 was $15,603. This figure, however, does not reflect that farmers often receive government subsidies or other payments that supplement their incomes and reduce some of the risk of farming. Additionally, most farmers—primarily operators of small farms—have income from off-farm business activities or careers, often greater than that of their farm income.

Full-time, salaried farm managers had median weekly earnings of $621 in 2004. The middle half earned between $464 and $890.

The highest paid 10 percent earned more than $1,264, and the lowest paid 10 percent earned less than $350.

Farmers and self-employed farm managers make their own provisions for benefits. As members of farm organizations, they may derive benefits such as group discounts on health and life insurance premiums.

Related Occupations

Farmers, ranchers, and agricultural managers strive to improve the quality of agricultural products and the efficiency of farms. Others whose work is related to agricultural products include agricultural engineers, agricultural and food scientists, agricultural workers, and purchasing agents and buyers of farm products.

Sources of Additional Information

For general information about farming and agricultural occupations, contact either of the following organizations:
➤ Center for Rural Affairs, P.O. Box 406, Walthill, NE 68067. Internet: **http://www.cfra.org**
➤ National FFA Organization, The National FFA Center, Attention Career Information Requests, P.O. Box 68690, Indianapolis, IN 46268-0960. Internet: **http://www.ffa.org**

For information about certification as an accredited farm manager, contact:
➤ American Society of Farm Managers and Rural Appraisers, 950 Cherry St., Suite 508, Denver, CO 80222. Internet: **http://www.asfmra.org**

For information on the USDA's program to help small farmers get started, contact:
➤ Small Farm Program, U.S. Department of Agriculture, Cooperative State, Research, Education, and Extension Service, Stop 2220, Washington, DC 20250-2220. Internet: **http://www.csrees.usda.gov/nea/ag_systems/part/smallfarms_part_directory.html**

For information on aquaculture, diversified agriculture, education, training, or community-supported agriculture, contact either of the following organizations:
➤ Alternative Farming System Information Center (AFSIC), National Agricultural Library USDA, 10301 Baltimore Ave., Room 132, Beltsville, MD 20705-2351. Internet: **http://www.nal.usda.gov/afsic**
➤ Appropriate Technology Transfer for Rural Areas (ATTRA), the National Sustainable Agriculture Information Service, P.O. Box 3657, Fayetteville, AR 72702. Internet: **http://www.attra.ncat.org**

Financial Managers

(O*NET 11-3031.01, 11-3031.02)

Significant Points

- About 3 out of 10 work in finance and insurance industries.

- A bachelor's degree in finance, accounting, or a related field is the minimum academic preparation, but many employers increasingly seek graduates with a master's degree in business administration, economics, finance, or risk management.

- Experience may be more important than formal education for some financial manager positions—most notably, branch managers in banks.

- Jobseekers are likely to face competition.

Nature of the Work

Almost every firm, government agency, and other type of organization has one or more financial managers who oversee the preparation of financial reports, direct investment activities, and implement cash management strategies. Because computers are increasingly used to record and organize data, many financial managers are spending more time developing strategies and implementing the long-term goals of their organization.

The duties of financial managers vary with their specific titles, which include controller, treasurer or finance officer, credit manager, cash manager, and risk and insurance manager. *Controllers* direct the preparation of financial reports that summarize and forecast the organization's financial position, such as income statements, balance sheets, and analyses of future earnings or expenses. Controllers also are in charge of preparing special reports required by regulatory authorities. Often, controllers oversee the accounting, audit, and budget departments. *Treasurers* and *finance officers* direct the organization's financial goals, objectives, and budgets. They oversee the investment of funds, manage associated risks, supervise cash management activities, execute capital-raising strategies to support a firm's expansion, and deal with mergers and acquisitions. *Credit managers* oversee the firm's issuance of credit, establishing credit-rating criteria, determining credit ceilings, and monitoring the collections of past-due accounts. Managers specializing in international finance develop financial and accounting systems for the banking transactions of multinational organizations.

Cash managers monitor and control the flow of cash receipts and disbursements to meet the business and investment needs of the firm. For example, cash flow projections are needed to determine whether loans must be obtained to meet cash requirements or whether surplus cash should be invested in interest-bearing instruments. *Risk* and *insurance managers* oversee programs to minimize risks and losses that might arise from financial transactions and business operations undertaken by the institution. They also manage the organization's insurance budget.

Financial institutions, such as commercial banks, savings and loan associations, credit unions, and mortgage and finance companies, employ additional financial managers who oversee various functions, such as lending, trusts, mortgages, and investments, or programs, including sales, operations, or electronic financial services. These managers may be required to solicit business, authorize loans, and direct the investment of funds, always adhering to Federal and State laws and regulations. (Chief financial officers and other executives are included with top executives elsewhere in the *Handbook*.)

Branch managers of financial institutions administer and manage all of the functions of a branch office, which may include hiring personnel, approving loans and lines of credit, establishing a rapport with the community to attract business, and assisting customers with account problems. The trend is for branch mangers to become more oriented toward sales and marketing. It is important that they have substantial knowledge about all types of products that the bank sells. Financial managers who work for financial institutions must keep abreast of the rapidly growing array of financial services and products.

In addition to carrying out the preceding general duties, all financial managers perform tasks unique to their organization or industry. For example, government financial managers must be experts on the government appropriations and budgeting processes, whereas health care financial managers must be knowledgeable about issues surrounding health care financing. Moreover, financial managers must be aware of special tax laws and regulations that affect their industry.

Financial managers play an increasingly important role in mergers and consolidations and in global expansion and related financing. These areas require extensive, specialized knowledge on the part of the financial manager to reduce risks and maximize profit. Financial managers increasingly are hired on a temporary basis to advise senior managers on these and other matters. In fact, some small firms contract out all their accounting and financial functions to companies that provide such services.

Financial managers oversee the preparation of financial reports and investment activities.

The role of the financial manager, particularly in business, is changing in response to technological advances that have significantly reduced the amount of time it takes to produce financial reports. Financial managers now perform more data analysis and use it to offer senior managers ideas on how to maximize profits. They often work on teams, acting as business advisors to top management. Financial managers need to keep abreast of the latest computer technology in order to increase the efficiency of their firm's financial operations.

Working Conditions
Working in comfortable offices, often close to top managers and to departments that develop the financial data those managers need, financial managers typically have direct access to state-of-the-art computer systems and information services. They commonly work long hours, often up to 50 or 60 per week. Financial managers generally are required to attend meetings of financial and economic associations and may travel to visit subsidiary firms or to meet customers.

Training, Other Qualifications, and Advancement
A bachelor's degree in finance, accounting, economics, or business administration is the minimum academic preparation for financial managers. However, many employers now seek graduates with a master's degree, preferably in business administration, economics, finance, or risk management. These academic programs develop analytical skills and provide knowledge of the latest financial analysis methods and technology.

Experience may be more important than formal education for some financial manager positions—most notably, branch managers in banks. Banks typically fill branch manager positions by promoting experienced loan officers and other professionals who excel at their jobs. Other financial managers may enter the profession through formal management training programs offered by the company. The American Institute of Banking, which is affiliated with the American Bankers Association, sponsors educational and training programs for bank officers through a wide range of banking schools and educational conferences.

Continuing education is vital to financial managers, who must cope with the growing complexity of global trade, changes in Federal and State laws and regulations, and the proliferation of new and complex financial instruments. Firms often provide opportunities for workers to broaden their knowledge and skills by encouraging them to take graduate courses at colleges and universities or attend conferences related to their specialty. Financial management, banking, and credit union associations, often in cooperation with colleges and universities, sponsor numerous national and local training programs. Persons enrolled prepare extensively at home and then attend sessions on subjects such as accounting management, budget management, corporate cash management, financial analysis, international banking, and information systems. Many firms pay all or part of the costs for employees who successfully complete courses. Although experience, ability, and leadership are emphasized for promotion, advancement may be accelerated by this type of special study.

In some cases, financial managers also may broaden their skills and exhibit their competency by attaining professional certification. Many different associations offer professional certification programs. For example, the CFA Institute confers the Chartered Financial Analyst designation on investment professionals who have a bachelor's degree, pass three sequential examinations, and meet work experience requirements. The Association for Financial Professionals (AFP) confers the Certified Cash Manager credential to those who pass a computer-based exam and have a minimum of 2 years of relevant experience. The Institute of Management Accountants offers a Certified in Financial Management designation to members with a bachelor's degree, with at least 2 years of work experience, and who pass the institute's four-part examination and fulfill continuing education requirements. Also, financial managers who specialize in accounting may earn the Certified Public Accountant (CPA) or Certified Management Accountant (CMA) designation. (See accountants and auditors elsewhere in the *Handbook*.)

Candidates for financial management positions need a broad range of skills. Interpersonal skills are important because these jobs involve managing people and working as part of a team to solve problems. Financial managers must have excellent communication skills to explain complex financial data. Because financial managers work extensively with various departments in their firm, a broad overview of the business is essential.

Financial managers should be creative thinkers and problem-solvers, applying their analytical skills to business. They must be comfortable with the latest computer technology. Financial operations are increasingly being affected by the global economy, so financial managers must have knowledge of international finance. Proficiency in a foreign language also may be important.

Because financial management is critical to efficient business operations, well-trained, experienced financial managers who display a strong grasp of the operations of various departments within their organization are prime candidates for promotion to top management positions. Some financial managers transfer to closely related positions in other industries. Those with extensive experience and access to sufficient capital may start their own consulting firms.

Employment

Financial managers held about 528,000 jobs in 2004. Although they can be found in every industry, approximately 3 out of 10 are employed by finance and insurance establishments, such as banks, savings institutions, finance companies, credit unions, insurance carriers, and securities dealers. About 1 in 10 works for Federal, State, or local government.

Job Outlook

Employment of financial managers is expected to grow about as fast as the average for all occupations through 2014. The increasing need for financial expertise as a result of regulatory reforms and the expansion of the economy will drive job growth over the next decade. As the economy expands, both the growth of established companies and the creation of new businesses will spur demand for financial managers. However, mergers, acquisitions, and corporate downsizing are likely to restrict the employment growth to some extent.

As in other managerial occupations, jobseekers are likely to face competition, because the number of job openings is expected to be less than the number of applicants. Candidates with expertise in accounting and finance—particularly those with a master's degree—should enjoy the best job prospects. Strong computer skills and knowledge of international finance are important; so are excellent communication skills, because financial management jobs involve working on strategic planning teams. In addition, a good knowledge of compliance procedures is essential because of the many regulatory changes instituted in recent years.

Over the short term, employment growth in this occupation may slow or even reverse due to economic downturns, during which companies are more likely to close departments or even go out of business—decreasing the need for financial managers.

The banking industry will continue to consolidate, although at a slower rate than in previous years. In spite of this trend, employment of bank branch managers is expected to increase, because banks are refocusing on the importance of their existing branches and are creating new branches to service a growing population. As banks expand the range of products and services they offer to include insurance and investment products, branch managers with knowledge in these areas will be needed. As a result, candidates who are licensed to sell insurance or securities will have the most favorable prospects. (See the *Handbook* statements on insurance sales agents; and securities, commodities, and financial services sales agents.)

The long-run prospects for financial managers in the securities and commodities industry should be favorable, because more people will be needed to handle increasingly complex financial transactions and manage a growing amount of investments. Financial managers also will be needed to handle mergers and acquisitions, raise capital, and assess global financial transactions. Risk managers, who assess risks for insurance and investment purposes, also will be in demand.

Some companies may hire financial managers on a temporary basis, to see the organization through a short-term crisis or to offer suggestions for boosting profits. Other companies may contract out all accounting and financial operations. Even in these cases, however, financial managers may be needed to oversee the contracts.

Computer technology has reduced the amount of time and the staff required to produce financial reports. As a result, forecasting earnings, profits, and costs and generating ideas and creative ways to increase profitability will become a major role of corporate financial managers over the next decade. Financial managers who are familiar with computer software that can assist them in this role will be needed.

Earnings

Median annual earnings of financial managers were $81,880 in May 2004. The middle 50 percent earned between $59,490 and $112,320. Median annual earnings in the industries employing the largest numbers of financial managers in 2004 were as follows:

Securities and commodity contracts intermediation and brokerage	$129,770
Management of companies and enterprises	97,730
Nondepository credit intermediation	88,870
Local government	67,260
Depository credit intermediation	64,530

According to a 2005 survey by Robert Half International, a staffing services firm specializing in accounting and finance professionals, directors of finance earned between $78,500 and $178,250, and corporate controllers earned between $61,250 and $147,250.

A 2004 survey of manufacturing firms conducted by Abbot, Langer, and Associates, Inc., a human resources management consulting firm, reported the following median annual incomes: chief corporate financial officers, $130,000; corporate controllers, $86,150; cost accounting managers, $67,161; and general accounting managers, $64,100.

Large organizations often pay more than small ones, and salary levels also can depend on the type of industry and location. Many financial managers in both public and private industry receive additional compensation in the form of bonuses, which, like salaries, vary substantially by size of firm. Deferred compensation in the form of stock options is becoming more common, especially for senior-level executives.

Related Occupations
Financial managers combine formal education with experience in one or more areas of finance, such as asset management, lending, credit operations, securities investment, or insurance risk and loss control. Workers in other occupations requiring similar training and skills include accountants and auditors; budget analysts; financial analysts and personal financial advisors; insurance sales agents; insurance underwriters; loan officers; securities, commodities, and financial services sales agents; and real estate brokers and sales agents.

Sources of Additional Information
For information about careers and certification in financial management, contact:
➤ Financial Management Association International, College of Business Administration, University of South Florida, Tampa, FL 33620-5500. Internet: **http://www.fma.org**

For information about careers in financial and treasury management and the Certified Cash Manager program, contact:
➤ Association for Financial Professionals, 7315 Wisconsin Ave., Suite 600 West, Bethesda, MD 20814. Internet: **http://www.afponline.org**

For information about the Chartered Financial Analyst program, contact:
➤ CFA Institute, P.O. Box 3668, 560 Ray Hunt Dr., Charlottesville, VA 22903-0668. Internet: **http://www.cfainstitute.org**

For information on the Financial Risk Manager program, contact:
➤ Global Association of Risk Professionals, 100 Pavonia Ave., Suite 405, Jersey City, NJ 07310.

For information about the Certified in Financial Management designation, contact:
➤ Institute of Management Accountants, 10 Paragon Dr., Montvale, NJ, 07645-1718 Internet: **http://www.imanet.org**

Food Service Managers
(O*NET 11-9051.00)

Significant Points

● Experience as food and beverage preparation and service workers is essential for promotion into managerial positions, however, applicants with a college degree in restaurant and institutional food service management should have the best job opportunities.

● Many new food service manager jobs will arise in the food services and drinking places industry as the number of establishments increases along with the population.

● Job opportunities for salaried food service managers should be better than for self-employed managers because more restaurant managers will be employed by regional or national restaurant chains to run their establishments.

Nature of the Work
Food service managers are responsible for the daily operations of restaurants and other establishments that prepare and serve meals and beverages to customers. Besides coordinating activities among various departments, such as kitchen, dining room, and banquet operations, food service managers ensure that customers are satisfied with their dining experience. In addition, they oversee the inventory and ordering of food, equipment, and supplies and arrange for the routine maintenance and upkeep of the restaurant, its equipment, and facilities. Managers generally are responsible for all of the administrative and human-resource functions of running the business, including recruiting new employees and monitoring employee performance and training.

In most full-service restaurants and institutional food service facilities, the management team consists of a *general manager*, one or more *assistant managers*, and *an executive chef*. The executive chef is responsible for all food preparation activities, including running kitchen operations, planning menus, and maintaining quality standards for food service. In limited-service eating places, such as sandwich shops, coffee bars, or fast-food establishments, managers, not executive chefs, are responsible for supervising routine food preparation operations. Assistant managers in full-service facilities generally oversee service in the dining rooms and banquet areas. In larger restaurants and fast-food or other food service facilities that serve meals daily and maintain longer hours, individual assistant managers may supervise different shifts of workers. In smaller restaurants, formal titles may be less important, and one person may undertake the work of one or more food service positions. For example, the executive chef also may be the general manager or even sometimes an owner. (For additional information on these other workers, see material on top executives and chefs, cooks, and food preparation workers elsewhere in the *Handbook*.)

One of the most important tasks of food service managers is assisting executive chefs as they select successful menu items. This task varies by establishment depending on the seasonality of menu items, the frequency with which restaurants change their menus, and the introduction of daily or weekly specials. Many restaurants rarely change their menus while others make frequent alterations. Managers or executive chefs select menu items, taking into account the likely number of customers and the past popularity of dishes. Other issues considered when planning a menu include whether there was any unserved food left over from prior meals that should not be wasted, the need for variety, and the seasonal availability of foods. Managers or executive chefs analyze the recipes of the dishes to determine food, labor, and overhead costs and to assign prices to various dishes. Menus must be developed far enough in advance that supplies can be ordered and received in time.

Managers or executive chefs estimate food needs, place orders with distributors, and schedule the delivery of fresh food and supplies. They plan for routine services or deliveries, such as linen services or the heavy cleaning of dining rooms or kitchen equipment, to occur during slow times or when the dining room is closed. Managers also arrange for equipment maintenance and repairs, and coordinate a variety of services such as waste removal and pest control. Managers or executive chefs receive deliveries and check the contents against order records. They inspect the quality of fresh meats, poultry, fish, fruits, vegetables, and baked goods to ensure that expectations are met. They meet with representatives from restaurant supply companies and place orders to replenish stocks of tableware, linens, paper products, cleaning supplies, cooking utensils, and furniture and fixtures.

Managers must be good communicators. They need to speak well, often in several languages, with a diverse clientele and staff. They must motivate employees to work as a team, to ensure that food and service meet appropriate standards. Managers also must ensure that written supply orders are clear and unambiguous.

Managers interview, hire, train, and, when necessary, fire employees. Retaining good employees is a major challenge facing food service managers. Managers recruit employees at career fairs, contact schools that offer academic programs in hospitality or culinary arts, and arrange for newspaper advertising to attract additional applicants. Managers oversee the training of new employees and explain the establishment's policies and practices. They schedule work hours, making sure that enough workers are present to cover each shift. If employees are unable to work, managers may have to call in alternates to cover for them or fill in themselves when needed. Some managers may help with cooking, clearing tables, or other tasks when the restaurant becomes extremely busy.

Food service managers ensure that diners are served properly and in a timely manner. They investigate and resolve customers' complaints about food quality or service. They monitor orders in the kitchen to determine where backups may occur, and they work with the chef to remedy any delays in service. Managers direct the cleaning of the dining areas and the washing of tableware, kitchen utensils, and equipment to comply with company and government sanitation standards. Managers also monitor the actions of their employees and patrons on a continual basis to ensure the personal safety of everyone. They make sure that health and safety standards and local liquor regulations are obeyed.

In addition to their regular duties, food service managers perform a variety of administrative assignments, such as keeping employee work records, preparing the payroll, and completing paperwork to comply with licensing laws and reporting requirements of tax, wage and hour, unemployment compensation, and Social Security laws. Some of this work may be delegated to an assistant manager or bookkeeper, or it may be contracted out, but most general managers retain responsibility for the accuracy of business records. Managers also maintain records of supply and equipment purchases and ensure that accounts with suppliers are paid.

Technology influences the jobs of food service managers in many ways, enhancing efficiency and productivity. Many restaurants use computers to track orders, inventory, and the seating of patrons. Point-of-service (POS) systems allow servers to key in a customer's order, either at the table, using a hand-held device, or from a computer terminal in the dining room, and send the order to the kitchen instantaneously so preparation can begin. The same system totals and prints checks, functions as a cash register, connects to credit card authorizers, and tracks sales. To minimize food costs and spoilage, many managers use inventory-tracking software to compare the record of sales from the POS with a record of the current inventory. Some establishments enter an inventory of standard ingredients and suppliers into their POS system. When supplies of particular ingredients run low, they can be ordered directly from the supplier using preprogrammed information. Computers also allow restaurant and food service managers to keep track of employee schedules and paychecks more efficiently.

Food service managers use the Internet to track industry news, find recipes, conduct market research, purchase supplies or equipment, recruit employees, and train staff. Internet access also makes service to customers more efficient. Many restaurants maintain Web sites that include menus and online promotions, provide information about the restaurant's location, and offer patrons the option to make a reservation.

Managers tally the cash and charge receipts received and balance them against the record of sales. They are responsible for depositing the day's receipts at the bank or securing them in a safe place. Finally, managers are responsible for locking up the establishment, checking that ovens, grills, and lights are off, and switching on alarm systems.

Food service managers schedule employees to assure adequate staffing.

Working Conditions

Food service managers are among the first to arrive in the morning and the last to leave at night. Long hours—12 to 15 per day, 50 or more per week, and sometimes 7 days a week—are common. Managers of institutional food service facilities, such as school, factory, or office cafeterias, work more regular hours because the operating hours of these establishments usually conform to the operating hours of the business or facility they serve. However, hours for many managers are unpredictable.

Managers should be calm, flexible, and able to work through emergencies, such as a fire or flood, in order to ensure everyone's safety. Managers also should be able to fill in for absent workers on short notice. Managers often experience the pressures of simultaneously coordinating a wide range of activities. When problems occur, it is the manager's responsibility to resolve them with minimal disruption to customers. The job can be hectic, and dealing with irate customers or uncooperative employees can be stressful.

Managers also may experience the typical minor injuries of other restaurant workers, such as muscle aches, cuts, or burns. They might endure physical discomfort from moving tables or chairs to accommodate large parties, receiving and storing daily supplies from vendors, or making minor repairs to furniture or equipment.

Training, Other Qualifications, and Advancement

Experience in the food services industry, whether as a full-time waiter or waitress or as a part-time or seasonal counter attendant, is essential training for a food services manger. Many food service management companies and national or regional restaurant chains recruit management trainees from 2- and 4-year college hospitality management programs which require internships and real-life experience to graduate. Some restaurant chains prefer to hire people with degrees in restaurant and institutional food service management, but they often hire graduates with degrees in other fields who have demonstrated experience, interest and aptitude. Many restaurant and food service manager positions—particularly self-service and fast-food—are filled by promoting experienced food and beverage preparation and service workers. Waiters, waitresses, chefs, and fast-food workers demonstrating potential for handling increased responsibility sometimes advance to assistant manager or management trainee jobs. Executive chefs need extensive experience working as chefs, and general managers need prior restaurant experience, usually as assistant managers.

A bachelor's degree in restaurant and food service management provides particularly strong preparation for a career in this occupation. Almost 1,000 colleges and universities offer 4-year programs in restaurant and hospitality management or institutional food service management; a growing number of university programs offer graduate degrees in hospitality management or similar fields. For those not interested in pursuing a 4-year degree, community and junior colleges, technical institutes, and other institutions offer programs in the field leading to an associate degree or other formal certification. Both 2- and 4-year programs provide instruction in subjects such as nutrition, sanitation, and food planning and preparation, as well as accounting, business law and management, and computer science. Some programs combine classroom and laboratory study with internships providing on-the-job experience. In addition, many educational institutions offer culinary programs in food preparation. Such training can lead to a career as a cook or chef and provide a foundation for advancement to an executive chef position. Many larger food service operations will provide, or offer to pay for, technical training, such as computer or business courses, so that employees can acquire the business skills necessary to read a spreadsheet or understand the concepts and practices of running a business. Generally, this requires a long-term commitment on the employee's part to both the employer and to the profession.

Most restaurant chains and food service management companies have rigorous training programs for management positions. Through a combination of classroom and on-the-job training, trainees receive instruction and gain work experience in all aspects of the operation of a restaurant or institutional food service facility. Areas include food preparation, nutrition, sanitation, security, company policies and procedures, personnel management, recordkeeping, and preparation of reports. Training on use of the restaurant's computer system is increasingly important as well. Usually, after 6 months or a year, trainees receive their first permanent assignment as an assistant manager.

Most employers emphasize personal qualities when hiring managers. For example, self-discipline, initiative, and leadership ability are essential. Managers must be able to solve problems and concentrate on details. They need good communication skills to deal with customers and suppliers, as well as to motivate and direct their staff. A neat and clean appearance is important, because managers must convey self-confidence and show respect in dealing with the public. Becasuse food service management can be physically demanding, good health and stamina are important.

The certified Foodservice Management Professional (FMP) designation is a measure of professional achievement for food service managers. Although not a requirement for employment or advancement in the occupation, voluntary certification provides recognition of professional competence, particularly for managers who acquired their skills largely on the job. The National Restaurant Association Educational Foundation awards the FMP designation to managers who achieve a qualifying score on a written examination, complete a series of courses that cover a range of food service management topics, and meet standards of work experience in the field.

Willingness to relocate often is essential for advancement to positions with greater responsibility. Managers typically advance to larger establishments or regional management positions within restaurant chains. Some eventually open their own food service establishments.

Employment

Food service managers held about 371,000 jobs in 2004. Most managers were salaried, but more than 40 per cent were self-employed in independent restaurants or other small food service establishments. About 70 percent of all salaried jobs for food service managers were in full-service restaurants or limited-service eating places, such as fast-food restaurants and cafeterias. Other salaried jobs were in drinking places (alcoholic beverages) and in special food services—an industry that includes food service contractors who supply food services at institutional, governmental, commercial, or industrial locations. A small number of salaried jobs were in traveler accommodation (hotels); educational services; amusement, gambling, and recreation industries; nursing care facilities; and hospitals. Jobs are located throughout the country, with large cities and tourist areas providing more opportunities for full-service dining positions.

Job Outlook

Employment of food service managers is expected to grow about as fast as the average for all occupations through 2014. In addition to job openings arising out of employment growth, the need to replace managers who transfer to other occupations or stop working will create many job opportunities. Although practical experience is an integral part of finding a food service management position, applicants with a degree in restaurant, hospitality or institutional food service management will have an edge; those with higher-level degrees should have the best opportunities.

Projected employment growth varies by industry. Most new jobs will arise in full-service restaurants and limited-service eating places as the number of these establishments increase along with the population. Manager jobs in special food services, an industry that includes food service contractors, will increase as hotels, schools, healthcare facilities, and other businesses contract out their food services to firms in this industry. Food service manager jobs still are expected to increase in hotels, schools, and health-care facilities, but growth will be slowed as contracting out becomes more common.

Job opportunities should be better for salaried managers than for self-employed managers. More new restaurants are affiliated with national or regional chains than are independently owned and operated. As this trend continues, fewer owners will manage restaurants themselves, and more restaurant managers will be employed by larger companies to run individual establishments.

Earnings

Median annual earnings of salaried food service managers were $39,610 in May 2004. The middle 50 percent earned between $31,010 and $51,460. The lowest 10 percent earned less than $24,500, and the highest 10 percent earned more than $68,860.

Median annual earnings in the industries employing the largest numbers of food service managers in May 2004 were as follows:

Traveler accommodation	$43,660
Special food services	43,530
Full-service restaurants	41,490
Limited-service eating places	36,400
Elementary and secondary schools	36,290

In addition to receiving typical benefits, most salaried food service managers are provided free meals and the opportunity for additional training, depending on their length of service. Some food service managers, especially those in full-service restaurants, may earn bonuses depending on sales volume or revenue.

Related Occupations

Food service managers direct the activities of a hospitality-industry business and provide a service to customers. Other managers and supervisors in hospitality-oriented businesses include gaming managers, lodging managers, sales worker supervisors, and first-line supervisors or managers of food preparation and serving workers.

Sources of Additional Information

Information about a career as a food service manager, 2- and 4-year college programs in restaurant and food service management, and certification as a Foodservice Management Professional is available from:

➤ National Restaurant Association Educational Foundation, 175 West Jackson Blvd., Suite 1500, Chicago, IL 60604-2702. Internet: **http://www.nraef.org**

General information on hospitality careers may be obtained from:

➤ The International Council on Hotel, Restaurant, and Institutional Education, 2613 North Parham Rd., 2nd Floor, Richmond, VA 23294. Internet: **http://www.chrie.org**

Additional information about job opportunities in food service management may be obtained from local employers and from local offices of State employment services agencies.

Funeral Directors

(O*NET 11-9061.00)

Significant Points

● Job opportunities should be good, particularly for those who also embalm; however, mortuary science graduates may have to relocate to find jobs.

● Funeral directors are licensed by their State.

● Advancement opportunities generally are best in larger funeral homes.

Nature of the Work

Funeral practices and rites vary greatly among cultures and religions. Although the U.S. population is diverse, funeral practices usually share some common elements—removing the deceased to a mortuary; preparing the remains; performing a ceremony that honors the deceased and addresses the spiritual needs of the family; and carrying out final disposition of the remains. Funeral directors arrange and direct these tasks for grieving families.

Funeral directors also are called morticians or undertakers. This career may not appeal to everyone, but those who work as funeral directors take great pride in their ability to provide efficient and appropriate services.

Funeral directors arrange the details and handle the logistics of funerals. They interview the family to learn what family members desire with regard to the nature of the funeral, the clergy members or other persons who will officiate, and the final disposition of the remains. Sometimes, the deceased leaves detailed instructions for his or her own funeral. Together with the family, funeral directors establish the location, dates, and times of wakes, memorial services, and burials. They arrange for a hearse to carry the body to the funeral home or mortuary. They also comfort the family and friends of the deceased.

Funeral directors also prepare obituary notices and have them placed in newspapers, arrange for pallbearers and clergy, schedule the opening and closing of a grave with a representative of the cemetery, decorate and prepare the sites of all services, and provide transportation for the remains, mourners, and flowers between sites. They also direct preparation and shipment of remains for out-of-State burial.

Most funeral directors also are trained, licensed, and practicing embalmers. Embalming is a sanitary, cosmetic, and preservative process through which the body is prepared for interment. If more than 24 hours elapse between death and interment, State laws usually require that the remains be refrigerated or embalmed.

When embalming a body, funeral directors wash the body with germicidal soap and replace the blood with embalming fluid to preserve the tissues. They may reshape and reconstruct disfigured or maimed bodies using materials such as clay, cotton, plaster of paris, and wax. They also may apply cosmetics to provide a natural appearance, dress the body and place it in a casket. Funeral directors maintain records such as embalming reports and itemized lists of clothing or valuables delivered with the body. In large funeral homes, an embalming staff of two or more, plus several apprentices, may be employed.

Funeral services may take place in a home, house of worship, or funeral home, or at the gravesite or crematory. Services may be nonreligious, but because they often reflect the religion of the family, funeral directors must be familiar with the funeral and burial customs of many faiths, ethnic groups, and fraternal organizations. For example, members of some religions seldom have the deceased embalmed or cremated.

Burial in a casket is the most common method of disposing of remains in this country, although entombment also occurs. Cremation, which is the burning of the body in a special furnace, is increasingly selected because it can be less expensive and is becoming more appealing. Memorial services can be held anywhere, and at any time, sometimes months later when all relatives and friends can get together. Even when the remains are cremated, many people still want a funeral service.

A funeral service followed by cremation need not be any different from a funeral service followed by a burial. Usually, cremated remains are placed in some type of permanent receptacle, or urn, before being committed to a final resting place. The urn may be buried, placed in an indoor or outdoor mausoleum or columbarium, or interred in a special urn garden that many cemeteries provide for cremated remains.

Funeral directors handle the paperwork involved with the person's death, such as submitting papers to State authorities so that a formal death certificate may be issued and copies distributed to the heirs. They may help family members apply for veterans' burial benefits, and they notify the Social Security Administration of the death. Also, funeral directors may apply for the transfer of any pensions, insurance policies, or annuities on behalf of survivors.

Funeral directors also work with those who want to plan their own funerals in advance. This provides peace of mind by ensuring that the client's wishes will be taken care of in a way that is satisfying to the client and to the client's survivors.

Most funeral homes are small, family-run businesses, and the funeral directors are either owner-operators or employees of the operation. Funeral directors, therefore, are responsible for the success and the profitability of their businesses. Directors keep records of expenses, purchases, and services rendered; prepare and send invoices for services; prepare and submit reports for unemployment insurance; prepare Federal, State, and local tax forms; and prepare itemized bills for customers. Funeral directors increasingly are using computers for billing, bookkeeping, and marketing. Some are beginning to use the Internet to communicate with clients who are planning their funerals in advance, or to assist them by developing electronic obituaries and guestbooks. Directors strive to foster a cooperative spirit and friendly attitude among employees and a compassionate demeanor toward the families. Increasingly, funeral directors also are involved in helping individuals adapt to changes in their lives following a death, through aftercare services or support-group activities.

Most funeral homes have a chapel, one or more viewing rooms, a casket-selection room, and a preparation room. Many also have a crematory on the premises. Equipment may include a hearse, a flower car, limousines, and sometimes an ambulance. Funeral homes usually stock a selection of caskets and urns for families to purchase or rent.

Working Conditions

Funeral directors often work long, irregular hours, and the occupation can be highly stressful. Many are on call at all hours because they may be needed to remove remains in the middle of the night. Shiftwork sometimes is necessary because funeral home hours include evenings and weekends. In smaller funeral homes, working hours vary, but in larger homes employees usually work 8 hours a day, 5 or 6 days a week.

Funeral directors occasionally come into contact with the remains of persons who had contagious diseases, but the possibility of infection is remote if strict health regulations are followed.

To show proper respect and consideration for the families and the dead, funeral directors must dress appropriately. The profession usually requires short, neat haircuts and trim beards, if any, for men. Suits and ties for men and dresses for women are customary for a conservative look.

Training, Other Qualifications, and Advancement

Funeral directors are licensed in all States. Licensing laws vary from State to State, but most require applicants to be 21 years old, have 2

Funeral directors explain burial options and arrange details of funerals with clients.

years of formal education that includes studies in mortuary science, serve a 1-year apprenticeship, and pass a qualifying examination. After becoming licensed, new funeral directors may join the staff of a funeral home. Funeral directors who embalm must be licensed in all States, and some States license only those who embalm. In States that have separate licensing requirements, most people in the field obtain both licenses. Persons interested in a career as a funeral director should contact their State licensing board for specific requirements.

College programs in mortuary science usually last from 2 to 4 years. The American Board of Funeral Service Education accredits about 50 mortuary science programs. A few community and junior colleges offer 2-year programs, and a few colleges and universities offer both 2-year and 4-year programs. Mortuary science programs include courses in anatomy, physiology, pathology, embalming techniques, restorative art, business management, accounting and use of computers in funeral home management, and client services. They also include courses in the social sciences and in legal, ethical, and regulatory subjects such as psychology, grief counseling, oral and written communication, funeral service law, business law, and ethics.

Many State and national associations offer continuing education programs designed for licensed funeral directors. These programs address issues in communications, counseling, and management. More than 30 States have requirements that funeral directors receive continuing education credits to maintain their licenses.

Apprenticeships must be completed under the direction of an experienced and licensed funeral director. Depending on State regulations, apprenticeships last from 1 to 3 years and may be served before, during, or after mortuary school. Apprenticeships provide practical experience in all facets of the funeral service, from embalming to transporting remains.

State board licensing examinations vary, but they usually consist of written and oral parts and include a demonstration of practical skills. Persons who want to work in another State may have to pass the examination for that State; however, some States have reciprocity arrangements and will grant licenses to funeral directors from another State without further examination.

High school students can start preparing for a career as a funeral director by taking courses in biology and chemistry and participating in public speaking or debate clubs. Part-time or summer jobs in funeral homes consist mostly of maintenance and cleanup tasks, such as washing and polishing limousines and hearses, but these tasks can help students become familiar with the operation of funeral homes.

Important personal traits for funeral directors are composure, tact, and the ability to communicate easily with the public. Funeral directors also should have the desire and ability to comfort people in a time of sorrow.

Advancement opportunities generally are best in larger funeral homes. Funeral directors may earn promotions to higher paying positions such as branch manager or general manager. Some directors eventually acquire enough money and experience to establish their own funeral home businesses.

Employment

Funeral directors held about 30,000 jobs in 2004. Twenty percent were self-employed. Nearly all worked in the death care services industry.

Job Outlook

Employment opportunities for funeral directors are expected to be good, particularly for those who also embalm. However, mortuary science graduates may have to relocate to find jobs.

Employment of funeral directors is projected to increase more slowly than the average for all occupations through the year 2014, reflecting slow growth in the death care services industry, where funeral directors are employed. The need to replace funeral directors who retire or leave the occupation for other reasons will account for more job openings than will employment growth. Funeral directors are older, on average, than workers in most other occupations and should be retiring in greater numbers between 2004 and 2014. In addition, some funeral directors leave the profession because of the long and irregular hours.

Earnings

Median annual earnings for funeral directors were $45,960 in May 2004. The middle 50 percent earned between $35,880 and $60,860. The lowest 10 percent earned less than $26,470 and the top 10 percent earned more than $85,910.

Salaries of funeral directors depend on the number of years of experience in funeral service, the number of services performed, the number of facilities operated, the area of the country, the size of the community, and the level of formal education. Funeral directors in large cities earn more than their counterparts in small towns and rural areas.

Related Occupations

The job of a funeral director requires tact, discretion, and compassion when dealing with grieving people. Others who need these qualities include social workers, psychologists, physicians and surgeons, and other health practitioners involved in diagnosis and treatment.

Sources of Additional Information

For a list of accredited mortuary science programs and information on the funeral service profession, write to:
➤ The National Funeral Directors Association, 13625 Bishop's Dr., Brookfield, WI 53005. Internet: **http://www.nfda.org**

For information about college programs in mortuary science, scholarships, and funeral service as a career, contact:
➤ The American Board of Funeral Service Education, 38 Florida Ave., Portland, ME 04103. Internet: **http://www.abfse.org/index.html**

For information on specific State licensing requirements, contact the State's licensing board.

Human Resources, Training, and Labor Relations Managers and Specialists

(O*NET 11-3040.00, 11-3041.00, 11-3042.00, 11-3049.99, 13-1071.01, 13-1071.02, 13-1072.00, 13-1073.00, 13-1079.99)

Significant Points

● In filling entry-level jobs, many employers seek college graduates who have majored in human resources, human resources administration, or industrial and labor relations; other employers look for college graduates with a technical or business background or a well-rounded liberal arts education.

● For many specialized jobs, previous experience is an asset; for more advanced positions, including those of managers, arbitrators, and mediators, it is essential.

● Keen competition for jobs is expected because of the plentiful supply of qualified college graduates and experienced workers.

Nature of the Work

Attracting the most qualified employees and matching them to the jobs for which they are best suited is significant for the success of any organization. However, many enterprises are too large to permit close contact between top management and employees. Human resources, training, and labor relations managers and specialists provide this connection. In the past, these workers have been associated with performing the administrative function of an organization, such as handling employee benefits questions or recruiting, interviewing, and hiring new staff in accordance with policies and requirements that have been established in conjunction with top management. Today's human resources workers manage these tasks and, increasingly, consult top executives regarding strategic planning. They have moved from behind-the-scenes staff work to leading the company in suggesting and changing policies. Senior management is recognizing the significance of the human resources department to their financial success.

In an effort to enhance morale and productivity, limit job turnover, and help organizations increase performance and improve business results, they also help their firms effectively use employee skills, provide training and development opportunities to improve those skills, and increase employees' satisfaction with their jobs and working conditions. Although some jobs in the human resources field require only limited contact with people outside the office, dealing with people is an important part of the job.

In a small organization, a *human resources generalist* may handle all aspects of human resources work, and thus require an extensive range of knowledge. The responsibilities of human resources generalists can vary widely, depending on their employer's needs. In a large corporation, the top human resources executive usually develops and manages human resources programs and policies. (Executives are included in the *Handbook* statement on top executives.) These policies usually are implemented by a director or manager of human resources and, in some cases, a director of industrial relations.

The *director of human resources* may supervise several departments, each headed by an experienced manager who most likely specializes in one human resources activity, such as employment, compensation, benefits, training and development, or employee relations.

Employment and placement managers supervise the hiring and separation of employees and supervise various workers, including equal employment opportunity specialists and recruitment specialists. *Employment, recruitment,* and *placement specialists* recruit and place workers.

Recruiters maintain contacts within the community and may travel considerably, often to college campuses, to search for promising job applicants. Recruiters screen, interview, and occasionally test applicants. They also may check references and extend job offers. These workers must be thoroughly familiar with the organization and its human resources policies in order to discuss wages, working conditions, and promotional opportunities with prospective employees. They also must keep informed about equal employment opportunity (EEO) and affirmative action guidelines and laws, such as the Americans with Disabilities Act.

EEO officers, representatives, or *affirmative action coordinators* handle EEO matters in large organizations. They investigate and resolve EEO grievances, examine corporate practices for possible violations, and compile and submit EEO statistical reports.

Employer relations representatives, who usually work in government agencies, maintain working relationships with local employers and promote the use of public employment programs and services. Similarly, *employment interviewers*—whose many job titles include *human resources consultants, human resources development specialists*, and *human resources coordinators*—help to match employers with qualified jobseekers.

Compensation, benefits, and job analysis specialists conduct programs for employers and may specialize in specific areas such as position classifications or pensions. *Job analysts*, occasionally called *position classifiers*, collect and examine detailed information about job duties in order to prepare job descriptions. These descriptions explain the duties, training, and skills that each job requires. Whenever a large organization introduces a new job or reviews existing jobs, it calls upon the expert knowledge of the job analyst.

Occupational analysts conduct research, usually in large firms. They are concerned with occupational classification systems and study the effects of industry and occupational trends upon worker relationships. They may serve as technical liaison between the firm and other firms, government, and labor unions.

Establishing and maintaining a firm's pay system is the principal job of the *compensation manager*. Assisted by staff specialists, compensation managers devise ways to ensure fair and equitable pay rates. They may conduct surveys to see how their firm's rates compare with others and to see that the firm's pay scale complies with changing laws and regulations. In addition, compensation managers often manage their firm's performance evaluation system, and they may design reward systems such as pay-for-performance plans.

Employee benefits managers and specialists manage the company's employee benefits program, notably its health insurance and pension plans. Expertise in designing and administering benefits programs continues to take on importance as employer-provided benefits account for a growing proportion of overall compensation costs, and as benefit plans increase in number and complexity. For example, pension benefits might include savings and thrift, profit-sharing, and stock ownership plans; health benefits might include long-term catastrophic illness insurance and dental insurance. Familiarity with health benefits is a top priority for employee benefits managers and specialists, as more firms struggle to cope with the rising cost of health care for employees and retirees. In addition to health insurance and pension coverage, some firms offer employees life and accidental death and dismemberment insurance, disability insurance, and relatively new benefits designed to meet the needs of a changing workforce, such as parental leave, child and elder care, long-term nursing home care insurance, employee assistance and wellness programs, and flexible benefits plans. Benefits managers must keep abreast of changing Federal and State regulations and legislation that may affect employee benefits.

Employee assistance plan managers, also called *employee welfare managers*, are responsible for a wide array of programs covering occupational safety and health standards and practices; health promotion and physical fitness, medical examinations, and minor health treatment, such as first aid; plant security; publications; food service and recreation activities; carpooling and transportation programs, such as transit subsidies; employee suggestion systems; child care and elder care; and counseling services. Child care and elder care are increasingly significant because of growth in the number of dual-income households and the elderly population. Counseling may help employees deal with emotional disorders, alcoholism, or marital, family, consumer, legal, and financial problems. Some employers offer career counseling as well. In large firms, certain programs, such as those dealing with security and safety, may be in separate departments headed by other managers.

Training and development managers and specialists conduct and supervise training and development programs for employees. Increasingly, management recognizes that training offers a way of developing skills, enhancing productivity and quality of work, and

building worker loyalty to the firm, and most importantly, increasing individual and organizational performance to achieve business results. While training is widely accepted as an employee benefit and a method of improving employee morale, enhancing employee skills has become a business imperative. Increasingly, managers and leaders realize that the key to business growth and success is through developing the skills and knowledge of its workforce.

Other factors involved in determining whether training is needed include the complexity of the work environment, the rapid pace of organizational and technological change, and the growing number of jobs in fields that constantly generate new knowledge, and thus, require new skills. In addition, advances in learning theory have provided insights into how adults learn, and how training can be organized most effectively for them.

Training managers provide worker training either in the classroom or onsite. This includes setting up teaching materials prior to the class, involving the class, and issuing completion certificates at the end of the class. They have the responsibility for the entire learning process, and its environment, to ensure that the course meets its objectives and is measured and evaluated to understand how learning impacts business results.

Training specialists plan, organize, and direct a wide range of training activities. Trainers respond to corporate and worker service requests. They consult with onsite supervisors regarding available performance improvement services and conduct orientation sessions and arrange on-the-job training for new employees. They help all employees maintain and improve their job skills, and possibly prepare for jobs requiring greater skill. They help supervisors improve their interpersonal skills in order to deal effectively with employees. They may set up individualized training plans to strengthen an employee's existing skills or teach new ones. Training specialists in some companies set up leadership or executive development programs among employees in lower level positions. These programs are designed to develop leaders to replace those leaving the organization and as part of a succession plan. Trainers also lead programs to assist employees with job transitions as a result of mergers and acquisitions, as well as technological changes. In government-supported training programs, training specialists function as case managers. They first assess the training needs of clients and then guide them through the most appropriate training method. After training, clients may either be referred to employer relations representatives or receive job placement assistance.

Planning and program development is an essential part of the training specialist's job. In order to identify and assess training needs within the firm, trainers may confer with managers and supervisors or conduct surveys. They also evaluate training effectiveness to ensure that the training employees receive, helps the organization meet its strategic business goals and achieve results.

Depending on the size, goals, and nature of the organization, trainers may differ considerably in their responsibilities and in the methods they use. Training methods include on-the-job training; operating schools that duplicate shop conditions for trainees prior to putting them on the shop floor; apprenticeship training; classroom training; and electronic learning, which may involve interactive Internet-based training, multimedia programs, distance learning, satellite training, other computer-aided instructional technologies, videos, simulators, conferences, and workshops.

An organization's *director of industrial relations* forms labor policy, oversees industrial labor relations, negotiates collective bargaining agreements, and coordinates grievance procedures to handle complaints resulting from management disputes with unionized employees. The director of industrial relations also advises and collaborates with the director of human resources, other managers, and members of their staff, because all aspects of human resources policy—such as wages, benefits, pensions, and work practices—may be involved in drawing up a new or revised union contract.

Labor relations managers and their staffs implement industrial labor relations programs. Labor relations specialists prepare information for management to use during collective bargaining agreement negotiations, a process that requires the specialist to be familiar with economic and wage data and to have extensive knowledge of labor law and collective bargaining trends. The labor relations staff interprets and administers the contract with respect to grievances, wages and salaries, employee welfare, health care, pensions, union and management practices, and other contractual stipulations. As union membership continues to decline in most industries, industrial relations personnel are working more often with employees who are not members of a labor union.

Dispute resolution—attaining tacit or contractual agreements—has become increasingly significant as parties to a dispute attempt to avoid costly litigation, strikes, or other disruptions. Dispute resolution also has become more complex, involving employees, management, unions, other firms, and government agencies. Specialists involved in dispute resolution must be highly knowledgeable and experienced, and often report to the director of industrial relations. *Conciliators*, or *mediators*, advise and counsel labor and management to prevent and, when necessary, resolve disputes over labor agreements or other labor relations issues. *Arbitrators*, occasionally called umpires or referees, decide disputes that bind both labor and management to specific terms and conditions of labor contracts. Labor relations specialists who work for unions perform many of the same functions on behalf of the union and its members.

Other emerging specialties include *international human resources managers*, who handle human resources issues related to a company's foreign operations; and *human resources information system specialists*, who develop and apply computer programs to process human resources information, match job seekers with job openings, and handle other human resources matters.

Working Conditions

Human resources work usually takes place in clean, pleasant, and comfortable office settings. Arbitrators and mediators may work out of their homes. Many human resources, training, and labor relations managers and specialists work a standard 35- to 40-hour week. However, longer hours might be necessary for some workers—for example, labor relations managers and specialists, arbitrators, and mediators—when contract agreements are being prepared and negotiated.

Human resources workers handle employee benefits, recruiting, interviewing, and hiring and training personnel.

Although most human resources, training, and labor relations managers and specialists work in the office, some travel extensively. For example, recruiters regularly attend professional meetings and visit college campuses to interview prospective employees; arbitrators and mediators often must travel to the site chosen for negotiations.

Training, Other Qualifications, and Advancement

The educational backgrounds of human resources, training, and labor relations managers and specialists vary considerably because of the diversity of duties and levels of responsibility. In filling entry-level jobs, many employers seek college graduates who have majored in human resources, human resources administration, or industrial and labor relations. Other employers look for college graduates with a technical or business background or a well-rounded liberal arts education.

Many colleges and universities have programs leading to a degree in personnel, human resources, or labor relations. Some offer degree programs in human resources administration or human resources management, training and development, or compensation and benefits. Depending on the school, courses leading to a career in human resources management may be found in departments of business administration, education, instructional technology, organizational development, human services, communication, or public administration, or within a separate human resources institution or department.

Because an interdisciplinary background is appropriate in this field, a combination of courses in the social sciences, business, and behavioral sciences is useful. Some jobs may require a more technical or specialized background in engineering, science, finance, or law, for example. Most prospective human resources specialists should take courses in compensation, recruitment, training and development, and performance appraisal, as well as courses in principles of management, organizational structure, and industrial psychology. Other relevant courses include business administration, public administration, psychology, sociology, political science, economics, and statistics. Courses in labor law, collective bargaining, labor economics, labor history, and industrial psychology also provide a valuable background for the prospective labor relations specialist. As in many other fields, knowledge of computers and information systems also is useful.

An advanced degree is increasingly important for some jobs. Many labor relations jobs require graduate study in industrial or labor relations. A strong background in industrial relations and law is highly desirable for contract negotiators, mediators, and arbitrators; in fact, many people in these specialties are lawyers. A background in law also is desirable for employee benefits managers and others who must interpret the growing number of laws and regulations. A master's degree in human resources, labor relations, or in business administration with a concentration in human resources management is highly recommended for those seeking general and top management positions.

For many specialized jobs in the human resources field, previous experience is an asset; for more advanced positions, including those of managers as well as arbitrators and mediators, it is essential. Many employers prefer entry-level workers who have gained some experience through an internship or work-study program while in school. Human resources administration and human resources development require the ability to work with individuals as well as a commitment to organizational goals. This field also demands other skills that people may develop elsewhere—using computers, selling, teaching, supervising, and volunteering, among others. The field offers clerical workers opportunities for advancement to professional positions. Responsible positions occasionally are filled by experienced individuals from other fields, including business, government, education, social services administration, and the military.

The human resources field demands a range of personal qualities and skills. Human resources, training, and labor relations managers and specialists must speak and write effectively. The growing diversity of the workforce requires that they work with or supervise people with various cultural backgrounds, levels of education, and experience. They must be able to cope with conflicting points of view, function under pressure, and demonstrate discretion, integrity, fair-mindedness, and a persuasive, congenial personality.

The duties given to entry-level workers will vary, depending on whether the new workers have a degree in human resource management, have completed an internship, or have some other type of human resources-related experience. Entry-level employees commonly learn the profession by performing administrative duties—helping to enter data into computer systems, compiling employee handbooks, researching information for a supervisor, or answering the phone and handling routine questions. Entry-level workers often enter formal or on-the-job training programs in which they learn how to classify jobs, interview applicants, or administer employee benefits. They then are assigned to specific areas in the human resources department to gain experience. Later, they may advance to a managerial position, supervising a major element of the human resources program—compensation or training, for example.

Exceptional human resources workers may be promoted to director of human resources or industrial relations, which can eventually lead to a top managerial or executive position. Others may join a consulting firm or open their own business. A Ph.D. is an asset for teaching, writing, or consulting work.

Most organizations specializing in human resources offer classes intended to enhance the marketable skills of their members. Some organizations offer certification programs, which are signs of competence and can enhance one's advancement opportunities. For example, the International Foundation of Employee Benefit Plans confers a designation to persons who complete a series of college-level courses and pass exams covering employee benefit plans. The American Society for Training & Development Certification Institute offers certification; it requires passing a knowledge-based exam and successful work product. The Society for Human Resource Management has two levels of certification; both require experience and a passing score on a comprehensive exam.

Employment

Human resources, training, and labor relations managers and specialists held about 820,000 jobs in 2004. The following tabulation shows the distribution of jobs by occupational specialty:

Training and development specialists	216,000
Employment, recruitment, and placement specialists	182,000
Human resources, training, and labor relations specialists, all other	166,000
Human resources managers	157,000
Compensation, benefits, and job analysis specialist	99,000

Human resources, training, and labor relations managers and specialists were employed in virtually every industry. About 21,000 specialists were self-employed, working as consultants to public and private employers.

The private sector accounted for more than 8 out of 10 salaried jobs, including 11 percent in administrative and support services; 9 percent in professional, scientific, and technical services; 9 percent in manufacturing; 9 percent in health care and social assistance; and 9 percent in finance and insurance firms.

Government employed 17 percent of human resources managers and specialists. They handled the recruitment, interviewing, job classification, training, salary administration, benefits, employee relations, and other matters related to the Nation's public employees.

Job Outlook

The abundant supply of qualified college graduates and experienced workers should create keen competition for jobs. Overall employment of human resources, training, and labor relations managers and specialists is expected to grow faster than the average for all occupations through 2014. In addition to openings due to growth, many job openings will arise from the need to replace workers who transfer to other occupations or leave the labor force.

Legislation and court rulings setting standards in various areas—occupational safety and health, equal employment opportunity, wages, health care, pensions, and family leave, among others—will increase demand for human resources, training, and labor relations experts. Rising health care costs should continue to spur demand for specialists to develop creative compensation and benefits packages that firms can offer prospective employees. Employment of labor relations staff, including arbitrators and mediators, should grow as firms become more involved in labor relations, and attempt to resolve potentially costly labor-management disputes out of court. Additional job growth may stem from increasing demand for specialists in international human resources management and human resources information systems.

Demand may be particularly strong for certain specialists. For example, employers are expected to devote greater resources to job-specific training programs in response to the increasing complexity of many jobs, the aging of the workforce, and technological advances that can leave employees with obsolete skills. This should result in strong demand for training and development specialists. In addition, increasing efforts throughout industry to recruit and retain quality employees should create many jobs for employment, recruitment, and placement specialists.

Among industries, firms involved in management, consulting, and employment services should offer many job opportunities, as businesses increasingly contract out human resources functions or hire human resources specialists on a temporary basis in order to deal with the increasing cost and complexity of training and development programs. Demand also should increase in firms that develop and administer complex employee benefits and compensation packages for other organizations.

Demand for human resources, training, and labor relations managers and specialists also are governed by the staffing needs of the firms for which they work. A rapidly expanding business is likely to hire additional human resources workers—either as permanent employees or consultants—while a business that has experienced a merger or a reduction in its workforce will require fewer human resources workers. Also, as human resources management becomes increasingly important to the success of an organization, some small and medium-size businesses that do not have a human resources department may assign employees various human resources duties together with other unrelated responsibilities. In any particular firm, the size and the job duties of the human resources staff are determined by the firm's organizational philosophy and goals, skills of its workforce, pace of technological change, government regulations, collective bargaining agreements, standards of professional practice, and labor market conditions.

Job growth could be limited by the widespread use of computerized human resources information systems that make workers more productive. Like that of other workers, employment of human resources, training, and labor relations managers and specialists, particularly in larger firms, may be adversely affected by corporate downsizing, restructuring, and mergers.

Earnings

Annual salary rates for human resources workers vary according to occupation, level of experience, training, location, and size of the firm, and whether they are union members.

Median annual earnings of compensation and benefits managers were $66,530 in May 2004. The middle 50 percent earned between $49,970 and $89,340. The lowest 10 percent earned less than $39,250, and the highest 10 percent earned more than $118,880. In May 2004, median annual earnings were $ 81,080 in the Management companies and enterprises' industry.

Median annual earnings of training and development managers were $67,460 in May 2004. The middle 50 percent earned between $49,060 and $91,020. The lowest 10 percent earned less than $36,430, and the highest 10 percent earned more than $119,580.

Median annual earnings of human resources managers, all other were $81,810 in May 2004. The middle 50 percent earned between $62,080 and $106,440. The lowest 10 percent earned less than $48,060, and the highest 10 percent earned more than $136,600. In May 2004, median annual earnings were $92,590, in the Management companies and enterprises' industry.

Median annual earnings of employment, recruitment, and placement specialists were $41,190 in May 2004. The middle 50 percent earned between $31,820 and $55,540. The lowest 10 percent earned less than $25,690, and the highest 10 percent earned more than $76,230. In May 2004, median annual earnings in the industries employing the largest numbers of employment, recruitment, and placement specialists were:

Management, scientific, and technical consulting services	$52,800
Management of companies and enterprises	46,780
Local government	40,540
Employment services	37,780
State government	35,390

Median annual earnings of compensation, benefits, and job analysis specialists were $47,490 in May 2004. The middle 50 percent earned between $37,050 and $59,860. The lowest 10 percent earned less than $30,030, and the highest 10 percent earned more than $74,650. In May 2004, median annual earnings in the industries employing the largest numbers of compensation, benefits, and job analysis specialists were:

Local government	$51,430
Management of companies and enterprises	50,970
State government	39,150

Median annual earnings of training and development specialists were $44,570 in May 2004. The middle 50 percent earned between $33,530 and $58,750. The lowest 10 percent earned less than $25,800, and the highest 10 percent earned more than $74,650. In May 2004, median annual earnings in the industries employing the largest numbers of training and development specialists were:

Management of companies and enterprises	$49,540
Insurance carriers	47,300
Local government	45,320
State government	41,770
Federal Government	38,930

According to a 2005 salary survey conducted by the National Association of Colleges and Employers, bachelor's degree candidates majoring in human resources, including labor relations, received starting offers averaging $36,967 a year.

The average salary for human resources managers employed by the Federal Government was $71,232 in 2005; for employee relations specialists, $84,847; for labor relations specialists, $93,895; and for employee development specialists, $80,958. Salaries were slightly higher in areas where the prevailing local pay level was higher. There are no formal entry-level requirements for managerial positions. Applicants must possess a suitable combination of educational attainment, experience, and record of accomplishment.

Related Occupations

All human resources occupations are closely related. Other workers with skills and expertise in interpersonal relations include counselors, education administrators, public relations specialists, lawyers, psychologists, social and human service assistants, and social workers.

Sources of Additional Information

For information about human resource management careers and certification, contact:
➤ Society for Human Resource Management, 1800 Duke St., Alexandria, VA 22314. Internet: **http://www.shrm.org**

For information about careers in employee training and development and certification, contact:
➤ American Society for Training &Development, 1640 King St., Box 1443, Alexandria, VA 22313-2043. Internet: **http://www.astd.org**

For information about careers and certification in employee compensation and benefits, contact:
➤ International Foundation of Employee Benefit Plans, 18700 W. Bluemound Rd., P.O. Box 69, Brookfield, WI 53008-0069. Internet: **http://www.ifebp.org**
➤ World at Work, 14040 N. Northsight Blvd., Scottsdale, AZ 85260. Internet: **http://www.worldatwork.org**

For information about academic programs in labor and employment relations, write to:
➤ Labor and Employment Relations Association, University of Illinois at Urbana-Champaign, 121 Labor and Industrial Relations Bldg., 504 E. Armory Ave., Champaign, IL 61820. Internet:**http://www.lera.uiuc.edu**

Information about human resources careers in the health care industry is available from:
➤ American Society for Healthcare Human Resources Administration, One North Franklin, 31st Floor, Chicago, IL 60606. Internet: **http://www.ashhra.org**

Industrial Production Managers

(O*NET 11-3051.00)

Significant Points

● While there is no standard preparation, a college degree is helpful.

● Applicants with a college degree in industrial engineering, management, or business administration, and particularly those with an undergraduate engineering degree and a master's degree in business administration or industrial management, enjoy the best job prospects.

● Employment of industrial production managers is expected to grow more slowly than average as overall employment in manufacturing declines; however, because production managers are so essential to the efficient operation of a plant, they have not been as affected by efforts to flatten management structures.

Nature of the Work

Industrial production managers plan, direct, and coordinate the production activities required to produce millions of goods every year in the United States. They make sure that production proceeds smoothly and stays within budget. Depending on the size of the manufacturing plant, industrial production managers may oversee the entire plant or just one area.

One of the main responsibilities of the industrial production manager is to oversee the production process, reducing costs wherever possible and making sure products are produced on time and are of good quality. They do this by analyzing the plant's personnel and capital resources to select the best way of meeting the production goals. Industrial production managers may determine which machines will be used, whether new machines need to be purchased, whether overtime or extra shifts are necessary, and what the sequence of production will be. They monitor the production run to make sure that it stays on schedule and correct any problems that may arise.

Part of an industrial production manager's job is to come up with ways to make the production process more efficient. In recent years, traditional mass assembly lines have given way to "lean" production techniques, which gives managers more flexibility. In a traditional assembly line, each worker is responsible for only a small portion of the assembly, repeating that task on every product. Lean production employs teams to build and assemble products in stations or cells, so rather than specializing in a specific task, workers are capable of performing all jobs within a team. Without the constraints of the traditional assembly line, industrial production managers can more easily change production levels and staffing on different product lines to minimize inventory levels and more quickly react to changing customer demands.

Industrial production managers also monitor product standards and implement quality control programs. They make sure the finished product meets a certain level of quality, and if not, they try to find out what the problem is and find a solution. While traditional quality control programs reacted only to problems that reached a certain significant level, newer management techniques and programs, such as ISO 9000, Total Quality Management (TQM), or Six Sigma, emphasize continuous quality improvement. If the problem relates to the quality of work performed in the plant, the manager may implement better training programs or reorganize the manufacturing process, often based upon the suggestions of employee teams. If the cause is substandard materials or parts from outside suppliers, the industrial production manager may work with the supplier to improve their quality.

Industrial production managers work closely with the other managers of the firm to implement the company's policies and goals. They also must work with the financial departments in order to come up with a budget and spending plan. In particular, though, production managers work most closely with the heads of sales, procurement, and logistics. Sales managers relay the client's needs and the price the client is willing to pay to the production department, which must then fulfill the order. The logistics, or distribution department, handles the delivery of the goods, which often needs to be coordinated with the production department. The procurement department orders the supplies that the production department needs to make its products. It is also responsible for making sure that the inventories of supplies are maintained at their optimal levels in order for production to proceed without interruption. A breakdown in communications between the production manager and the procurement department can cause slowdowns and a failure to meet production schedules. Just-in-time production techniques have reduced inventory levels, making constant communication among the manager, suppliers, and procurement departments even more important.

Industrial production managers supervise all aspects of production.

Industrial production managers must keep abreast of new technology that can be used in the production process. They must be computer savvy as computers increasingly play an integral role in the manufacturing process and in the coordination among departments, suppliers, and clients.

Working Conditions

Most industrial production managers divide their time between production areas and their offices. While in the production area, they must follow established health and safety practices and wear the required protective clothing and equipment. The time in the office, which often is located near production areas, usually is spent meeting with subordinates or other department managers, analyzing production data, and writing and reviewing reports.

Most industrial production managers work more than 40 hours a week, especially when production deadlines must be met. In facilities that operate around-the-clock, managers often work late shifts and may be called at any hour to deal with emergencies. This could mean going to the plant to resolve the problem, regardless of the hour, and staying until the situation is under control. Dealing with production workers as well as superiors when working under the pressure of production deadlines or emergency situations can be stressful. Corporate restructuring has eliminated levels of management and support staff, thus shifting more responsibilities to production managers and compounding this stress.

Training, Other Qualifications, and Advancement

Because of the diversity of manufacturing operations and job requirements, there is no standard preparation for this occupation. Some employers require a college degree, while other employers train promising apprentices or workers. However, most employers would prefer a college degree, even for those who have worked their way up through the ranks. Many industrial production managers have a college degree in business administration, management, industrial technology, or industrial engineering. Some are former production-line supervisors who have been promoted and have taken employer-sponsored training classes. Although many employers prefer candidates with a business or engineering background, some companies hire well-rounded liberal arts graduates, who are willing to spend time in a production-related job.

As production operations become more sophisticated, increasing numbers of employers are looking for candidates with graduate degrees in industrial management or business administration.

Combined with an undergraduate degree in engineering, either of these graduate degrees is considered particularly good preparation. Managers who do not have graduate degrees often take courses in decision sciences, which provide them with techniques and statistical formulas that can be used to maximize efficiency and improve quality. Companies also are placing greater importance on a candidate's interpersonal skills. Because the job requires the ability to compromise, persuade, and negotiate, successful production managers must be well-rounded and have excellent communication skills.

Those who enter the field directly from college or graduate school often are unfamiliar with the firm's production process. As a result, they may spend their first few months in the company's training program. These programs familiarize trainees with the production process, company policies, and the requirements of the job. In larger companies, they also may include assignments to other departments, such as purchasing and accounting. A number of companies hire college graduates as first-line supervisors and later promote them.

Some industrial production managers have worked their way up through the ranks, perhaps after having worked as first-line supervisors. These workers already have an intimate knowledge of the production process and the firm's organization. To be selected for promotion, workers can expand their skills by obtaining a college degree, demonstrating leadership qualities, or by taking company-sponsored management and communication courses.

In addition to formal training, industrial production managers must keep informed of new production technologies and management practices. Many belong to professional organizations and attend trade shows at which new equipment is displayed; they also attend industry conferences and conventions at which changes in production methods and technological advances are discussed. Some take courses to become certified in various quality and management systems.

Industrial production managers with a proven record of superior performance may advance to plant manager or vice president for manufacturing. Others transfer to jobs with more responsibilities at larger firms. Opportunities also exist for managers to become consultants. (For more information, see the statement on management analysts elsewhere in the *Handbook*.)

Employment

Industrial production managers held about 160,000 jobs in 2004. Almost all are employed in manufacturing industries, including the plastics product manufacturing, printing and related support activities, motor vehicle parts manufacturing, and semiconductor and other electronic component manufacturing industries. Production managers work in all parts of the country, but jobs are most plentiful in areas where manufacturing is concentrated.

Job Outlook

Employment of industrial production managers is expected to grow more slowly than the average for all occupations through 2014, as overall employment in manufacturing declines. As more manufacturing plants move abroad and others are able to produce more with fewer people, there will be less need for industrial production managers. Also, new computerized machines are better able to control quality. However, because production managers are so essential to the efficient operation of a plant, they have not been as affected by efforts to flatten management structures. Nevertheless, this trend has led production managers to assume more responsibilities and has limited the creation of more employment opportunities.

Despite slow growth, a number of jobs are expected to open due to the need to replace workers who will retire or who will transfer to other occupations. Applicants with a college degree in industrial engineering, management, or business administration, and particularly

those with an undergraduate engineering degree and a master's degree in business administration or industrial management, will enjoy the best job prospects. Employers also are likely to seek candidates who have excellent communication skills, related work experience, and who are personable, flexible, and eager to enhance their knowledge and skills through ongoing training.

Productivity gains that are occurring throughout the manufacturing sector will also impact industrial production managers. With the increasing use of computers for scheduling, planning, and coordination among departments, their work is made much easier. In addition, more emphasis on quality in the production process has redistributed some of the production manager's oversight responsibilities to supervisors and workers on the production line.

Earnings

Median annual earnings for industrial production managers were $73,000 in May 2004. The middle 50 percent earned between $55,700 and $94,850. The lowest 10 percent earned less than $43,660, and the highest 10 percent earned more than $123,010. Median annual earnings in the manufacturing industries employing the largest numbers of industrial production managers in May 2004 were:

Management of companies and enterprises	$90,140
Motor vehicle parts manufacturing	76,490
Printing and related support activities	69,210
Plastics product manufacturing	66,880

Related Occupations

Industrial production managers oversee production staff and equipment, ensure that production goals and quality standards are being met, and implement company policies. Other managerial occupations with similar responsibilities are general and operations managers, construction managers, and sales managers. Occupations requiring comparable training and problem-solving skills are engineers, management analysts, and operations research analysts.

Sources of Additional Information

For more information on industrial production management, contact local manufacturers or schools with programs in industrial management.

Lodging Managers

(O*NET 11-9081.00)

Significant Points

- Long hours, including night and weekend work, are common.

- Employment is projected to grow about as fast as the average for all occupations.

- College graduates with degrees in hotel or hospitality management should have the best job opportunities.

Nature of the Work

A comfortable room, good food, and a helpful staff can make being away from home an enjoyable experience for both vacationing families and business travelers. While most lodging managers work in traditional hotels and motels, some work in other lodging establishments, such as camps, inns, boardinghouses, dude ranches, and recreational resorts. In full-service hotels, lodging managers help their guests have a pleasant stay by providing many of the comforts of home, including cable television, fitness equipment, and voice mail, as well as specialized services such as health spas. For business travelers, lodging managers often schedule available meeting rooms and electronic equipment, including slide projectors and fax machines.

Lodging managers are responsible for keeping their establishments efficient and profitable. In a small establishment with a limited staff, the manager may oversee all aspects of operations. However, large hotels may employ hundreds of workers, and the general manager usually is aided by a number of assistant managers assigned to the various departments of the operation. In hotels of every size, managerial duties vary significantly by job title.

General managers have overall responsibility for the operation of the hotel. Within guidelines established by the owners of the hotel or executives of the hotel chain, the general manager sets room rates, allocates funds to departments, approves expenditures, and ensures expected standards for guest service, decor, housekeeping, food quality, and banquet operations. Managers who work for chains also may organize and staff a newly built hotel, refurbish an older hotel, or reorganize a hotel or motel that is not operating successfully. In order to fill entry-level service and clerical jobs in hotels, some managers attend career fairs.

Resident or hotel managers are responsible for the day-to-day operations of the property. In larger properties, more than one of these managers may assist the general manager, frequently dividing responsibilities between the food and beverage operations and the rooms or lodging services. At least one manager, either the general manager or a hotel manager, is on call 24 hours a day to resolve problems or emergencies.

Assistant managers help run the day-to-day operations of the hotel. In large hotels, they may be responsible for activities such as personnel, accounting, office administration, marketing and sales, purchasing, security, maintenance, and pool, spa, or recreational facilities. In smaller hotels, these duties may be combined into one position. Assistant managers may adjust charges on a hotel guest's bill when a manager is unavailable.

An *Executive Committee* made up of a hotel's senior managers advises the general manager, assists in setting hotel policy, coordinates services that cross departmental boundaries, and collaborates on efforts to ensure consistent and efficient guest services throughout the hotel. The Committee may be comprised of the department heads for housekeeping, front office, food and beverage, security, sales and public relations, meetings and conventions, engineering and building maintenance, and human resources. Executive committee members bring a different perspective of guest service to the total management objective reflecting the unique expertise and training of their positions.

Executive housekeepers ensure that guest rooms, meeting and banquet rooms, and public areas are clean, orderly, and well maintained. They also train, schedule, and supervise the work of housekeepers, inspect rooms, and order cleaning supplies.

Front office managers coordinate reservations and room assignments, as well as train and direct the hotel's front desk staff. They ensure that guests are treated courteously, complaints and problems are resolved, and requests for special services are carried out. Front office managers may adjust charges posted on a customer's bill.

Convention services managers coordinate the activities of various departments in larger hotels to accommodate meetings, conventions, and special events. They meet with representatives of groups or organizations to plan the number of rooms to reserve, the desired configuration of the meeting space, and banquet services. During the meeting or event, they resolve unexpected problems and monitor activities to ensure that hotel operations conform to the expectations of the group.

Food and beverage managers oversee all food service operations maintained by the hotel. They coordinate menus with the Executive Chef for the hotel's restaurants, lounges, and room service operations. They supervise the ordering of food and supplies, direct service and maintenance contracts within the kitchens and dining areas, and manage food service budgets.

Catering managers arrange for food service in a hotel's meeting and convention rooms. They coordinate menus and costs for banquets, parties, and events with meeting and convention planners or individual clients. They coordinate staffing needs and arrange schedules with kitchen personnel to ensure appropriate food service.

Sales or marketing directors and *public relations directors* oversee the advertising and promotion of hotel operations and functions, including lodging and dining specials and special events, such as holiday or seasonal specials. They direct the efforts of their staff to purchase advertising and market their property to organizations or groups seeking a venue for conferences, conventions, business meetings, trade shows, and special events. They also coordinate media relations and answer questions from the press.

Human resources directors manage the personnel functions of a hotel, ensuring that all accounting, payroll, and employee relations matters are handled in compliance with hotel policy and applicable laws. They also oversee hiring practices and standards and ensure that training and promotion programs reflect appropriate employee development guidelines.

Finance (or revenue) directors monitor room sales and reservations. In addition to overseeing accounting and cash-flow matters at the hotel, they also project occupancy levels, decide which rooms to discount and when to offer rate specials.

Computers are used extensively by lodging managers and their assistants to keep track of guests' bills, reservations, room assignments, meetings, and special events. In addition, computers are used to order food, beverages, and supplies, as well as to prepare reports for hotel owners and top-level managers. Managers work with computer specialists to ensure that the hotel's computer system functions properly. Should the hotel's computer system fail, managers must continue to meet the needs of hotel guests and staff.

Working Conditions
Because hotels are open around the clock, night and weekend work is common. Many lodging managers work more than 40 hours per week,

Lodging managers ensure that the work of all departments meets guests' expectations.

and may be called back to work at any time. Some managers of resort properties or other hotels where much of the business is seasonal have other duties on the property during the off-season or find work at other hotels or in other areas.

Lodging managers experience the pressures of coordinating a wide range of activities. At larger hotels, they also carry the burden of managing a large staff and finding a way to satisfy guest needs while maintaining positive attitudes and employee morale. Conventions and large groups of tourists may present unusual problems or require extended work hours. Moreover, dealing with irate guests can be stressful. The job can be particularly hectic for front office managers during check-in and check-out times. Computer failures can further complicate processing and add to frustration levels.

Training, Other Qualifications, and Advancement

Hotels increasingly emphasize specialized training. Postsecondary training in hotel, restaurant, or hospitality management is preferred for most hotel management positions; however, a college liberal arts degree may be sufficient when coupled with related hotel experience or business education. Internships or part-time or summer work experience in a hotel are an asset to students seeking a career in hotel management. The experience gained and the contacts made with employers can greatly benefit students after graduation. Most degree programs include work-study opportunities.

Community colleges, junior colleges, and many universities offer certificate or degree programs in hotel, restaurant, or hospitality management leading to an associate, bachelor, or graduate degree. Technical institutes, vocational and trade schools, and other academic institutions also offer courses leading to formal recognition in hospitality management. In total, more than 800 educational facilities provide academic training for would-be lodging managers. Hotel management programs include instruction in hotel administration, accounting, economics, marketing, housekeeping, food service management and catering, and hotel maintenance engineering. Computer training also is an integral part of hotel management training, due to the widespread use of computers in reservations, billing, and housekeeping management.

More than 450 high schools in 45 States offer the Lodging Management Program created by the Educational Institute of the American Hotel and Lodging Association. This two-year program offered to high school juniors and seniors teaches management principles and leads to a professional certification called the "Certified Rooms Division Specialist." Many colleges and universities grant participants credit towards a post-secondary degree in hotel management.

Lodging managers must be able to get along with many different types of people, even in stressful situations. They must be able to solve problems and concentrate on details. Initiative, self-discipline, effective communication skills, and the ability to organize and direct the work of others also are essential for managers at all levels.

Persons wishing to make a career in the hospitality industry may be promoted into a management trainee position sponsored by the hotel or a hotel chain's corporate parent. Typically, trainees work as assistant managers and may rotate assignments among the hotel's departments—front office, housekeeping, or food and beverage—to gain a wide range of experiences. Relocation to another property may be required to help round out the experience and to help grow a trainee into the position.

Work experience in the hospitality industry at any level or in any segment, including summer jobs or part-time work in a hotel or restaurant, is good background for entering hotel management. Most employers require a bachelor's degree with some education in business and computer literacy, while some prefer a master's degree for hotel management positions. However, employees who demonstrate

leadership potential and possess sufficient length or breadth of experience may be invited to participate in a management training program and advance to hotel management positions without the education beyond high school.

Large hotel and motel chains may offer better opportunities for advancement than small, independently owned establishments, but relocation every several years often is necessary for advancement. The large chains have more extensive career ladder programs and offer managers the opportunity to transfer to another hotel or motel in the chain or to the central office. Career advancement can be accelerated by the completion of certification programs offered by various associations. These programs usually require a combination of course work, examinations, and experience. For example, outstanding lodging managers may advance to higher level manager positions. (For more information, see the material on top executives elsewhere in the *Handbook*.)

Employment

Lodging managers held about 58,000 jobs in 2004. Self-employed managers—primarily owners of small hotels, motels, and inns—held about 45 percent of these jobs. Companies that manage hotels and motels under contract employed many managers.

Job Outlook

Employment of lodging managers is expected to grow about as fast as the average for all occupations through 2014. Additional job openings are expected to occur as experienced managers transfer to other occupations or leave the labor force, in part because of the long hours and stressful working conditions. Job opportunities are expected to be best for persons with college degrees in hotel or hospitality management.

Renewed business travel and domestic and foreign tourism will drive employment growth of lodging managers in full-service hotels. The numbers of economy-class rooms and extended-stay hotels also are expected to increase to accommodate leisure travelers and bargain-conscious guests. An increasing range of lodging accommodations is available to travelers, from economy hotels which offer clean, comfortable rooms and front desk services without costly extras such as restaurants and room service, to luxury and boutique inns that offer sumptuous furnishings and personal services. The accommodation industry is expected to continue to consolidate as lodging chains acquire independently owned establishments or undertake their operation on a contract basis. The increasing number of extended-stay hotels will moderate growth of manager jobs because these properties usually have fewer departments and require fewer managers. Also, these establishments often do not require a manager to be available 24 hours a day, instead assigning front desk clerks on duty at night some of the responsibilities previously reserved for managers.

Additional demand for managers is expected in suite hotels, because some guests—especially business customers—are willing to pay higher prices for rooms with kitchens and suites that provide the space needed to conduct small meetings. In addition, large full-service hotels—offering restaurants, fitness centers, large meeting rooms, and play areas for children, among other amenities—will continue to provide many trainee and managerial opportunities.

Earnings

Median annual earnings of lodging managers were $37,660 in May 2004. The middle 50 percent earned between $28,640 and $51,030. The lowest 10 percent earned less than $22,680, while the highest 10 percent earned more than $72,160. Median annual earnings for lodging managers in traveler accommodations were $37,420.

Salaries of lodging managers vary greatly according to their responsibilities and the segment of the hotel industry in which they are employed, as well as the location and region where the hotel is located. Managers may earn bonuses of up to 25 percent of their basic salary in some hotels and also may be furnished with meals, parking, laundry, and other services. In addition to providing typical benefits, some hotels offer profit-sharing plans and educational assistance to their employees.

Related Occupations

Other occupations concerned with organizing and directing a business in which customer service is the cornerstone of their success include food service managers, gaming managers, sales worker supervisors, and property, real estate, and community association managers.

Sources of Additional Information

For information on careers and scholarships in hotel management, contact

➤ American Hotel and Lodging Association, 1201 New York Ave. NW., Suite 600, Washington, DC 20005-3931.

Information on careers in the lodging industry and professional development and training programs may be obtained from:

➤ Educational Institute of the American Hotel and Lodging Association, 800 N. Magnolia Ave., Suite 1800, Orlando, FL 32853-1126. Internet: **http://www.ei-ahla.org**

For information on educational programs in hotel and restaurant management, including correspondence courses, write to:

➤ International Council on Hotel, Restaurant, and Institutional Education, 2613 North Parham Rd., 2nd Floor, Richmond, VA 23294-4442. Internet: **http://www.chrie.org**

Medical and Health Services Managers

(O*NET 11-9111.00)

Significant Points

- Rapid employment growth is projected; job opportunities will be especially good in offices of health practitioners, general medical and surgical hospitals, home health care services, and outpatient care centers.

- Applicants with work experience in health care and strong business and management skills likely will have the best opportunities.

- Earnings are high, but long work hours are common.

- A master's degree is the standard credential for most positions, although a bachelor's degree is adequate for some entry-level positions in smaller facilities and in health information management.

Nature of the Work

Health care is a business and, like every other business, it needs good management to keep it running smoothly. Medical and health services managers, also referred to as *health care executives* or *health care administrators*, plan, direct, coordinate, and supervise the delivery of health care. Medical and health services managers include specialists and generalists. Specialists are in charge of specific clinical departments or services, while generalists manage or help manage an entire facility or system.

The structure and financing of health care are changing rapidly. Future medical and health services managers must be pre-

pared to deal with evolving integrated health care delivery systems, technological innovations, an increasingly complex regulatory environment, restructuring of work, and an increased focus on preventive care. They will be called on to improve efficiency in health care facilities and the quality of the health care provided. Increasingly, medical and health services managers will work in organizations in which they must optimize efficiency of a variety of related services—for example, those ranging from inpatient care to outpatient followup care.

Large facilities usually have several assistant administrators to aid the top administrator and to handle daily decisions. Assistant administrators may direct activities in clinical areas such as nursing, surgery, therapy, medical records, or health information. (Managers in nonhealth areas, such as administrative services, computer and information systems, finance, and human resources, are not included in this statement. For information about them, see the statements on management occupations elsewhere in the *Handbook*.)

In smaller facilities, top administrators handle more of the details of daily operations. For example, many nursing home administrators manage personnel, finances, facility operations, and admissions and also have a larger role in resident care.

Clinical managers have training or experience in a specific clinical area and, accordingly, have more specific responsibilities than do generalists. For example, directors of physical therapy are experienced physical therapists, and most health information and medical record administrators have a bachelor's degree in health information or medical record administration. Clinical managers establish and implement policies, objectives, and procedures for their departments; evaluate personnel and work; develop reports and budgets; and coordinate activities with other managers.

Health information managers are responsible for the maintenance and security of all patient records. Recent regulations enacted by the Federal Government require that all health care providers maintain electronic patient records and that these records be secure. As a result, health information managers must keep up with current computer and software technology and with legislative requirements and developments. In addition, as patient data become more frequently used for quality management and in medical research, health information managers ensure that databases are complete, accurate, and available only to authorized personnel.

In group medical practices, managers work closely with physicians. Whereas an office manager might handle business affairs in

Medical and health services managers frequently oversee personnel matters, billing and collection, budgeting, and the procurement of supplies.

small medical groups, leaving policy decisions to the physicians themselves, larger groups usually employ a full-time administrator to help formulate business strategies and coordinate day-to-day business.

A small group of 10 to 15 physicians might employ 1 administrator to oversee personnel matters, billing and collection, budgeting, planning, equipment outlays, and patient flow. A large practice of 40 to 50 physicians might have a chief administrator and several assistants, each responsible for different areas.

Medical and health services managers in managed care settings perform functions similar to those of their counterparts in large group practices, except that they could have larger staffs to manage. In addition, they might do more community outreach and preventive care than do managers of a group practice.

Some medical and health services managers oversee the activities of a number of facilities in health systems. Such systems might contain both inpatient and outpatient facilities and offer a wide range of patient services.

Working Conditions
Most medical and health services managers work long hours. Facilities such as nursing care facilities and hospitals operate around the clock, and administrators and managers may be called at all hours to deal with problems. They also may travel to attend meetings or inspect satellite facilities.

Some managers work in comfortable, private offices; others share space with other managers or staff. They may spend considerable time walking, to consult with coworkers.

Training, Other Qualifications, and Advancement
Medical and health services managers must be familiar with management principles and practices. A master's degree in health services administration, long-term care administration, health sciences, public health, public administration, or business administration is the standard credential for most generalist positions in this field. However, a bachelor's degree is adequate for some entry-level positions in smaller facilities, at the departmental level within health care organizations, and in health information management. Physicians' offices and some other facilities may substitute on-the-job experience for formal education.

Bachelor's, master's, and doctoral degree programs in health administration are offered by colleges; universities; and schools of public health, medicine, allied health, public administration, and business administration. In 2005, 70 schools had accredited programs leading to the master's degree in health services administration, according to the Commission on Accreditation of Healthcare Management Education.

For persons seeking to become heads of clinical departments, a degree in the appropriate field and work experience may be sufficient early in their career. However, a master's degree in health services administration or a related field might be required to advance. For example, nursing service administrators usually are chosen from among supervisory registered nurses with administrative abilities and graduate degrees in nursing or health services administration.

Health information managers require a bachelor's degree from an accredited program and a Registered Health Information Administrator (RHIA) certification from the American Health Information Management Association. In 2005, there were 45 accredited bachelor's programs in health information management according to the Commission on Accreditation for Health Informatics and Information Management Education.

Some graduate programs seek students with undergraduate degrees in business or health administration; however, many graduate programs prefer students with a liberal arts or health profession background. Candidates with previous work experience in health care also may have an advantage. Competition for entry into these programs is keen, and applicants need above-average grades to gain admission. Graduate programs usually last between 2 and 3 years. They may include up to 1 year of supervised administrative experience and coursework in areas such as hospital organization and management, marketing, accounting and budgeting, human resources administration, strategic planning, law and ethics, biostatistics or epidemiology, health economics, and health information systems. Some programs allow students to specialize in one type of facility—hospitals, nursing care facilities, mental health facilities, or medical groups. Other programs encourage a generalist approach to health administration education.

New graduates with master's degrees in health services administration may start as department managers or as staff. The level of the starting position varies with the experience of the applicant and the size of the organization. Hospitals and other health facilities offer postgraduate residencies and fellowships, which usually are staff positions. Graduates from master's degree programs also take jobs in large medical group practices, clinics, mental health facilities, nursing care corporations, and consulting firms.

Graduates with bachelor's degrees in health administration usually begin as administrative assistants or assistant department heads in larger hospitals. They also may begin as department heads or assistant administrators in small hospitals or nursing care facilities.

All States and the District of Columbia require nursing care facility administrators to have a bachelor's degree, pass a licensing examination, complete a State-approved training program, and pursue continuing education. Some States also require licenses for administrators in assisted living facilities. A license is not required in other areas of medical and health services management.

Medical and health services managers often are responsible for millions of dollars' worth of facilities and equipment and hundreds of employees. To make effective decisions, they need to be open to different opinions and good at analyzing contradictory information. They must understand finance and information systems and be able to interpret data. Motivating others to implement their decisions requires strong leadership abilities. Tact, diplomacy, flexibility, and communication skills are essential because medical and health services managers spend most of their time interacting with others.

Medical and health services managers advance by moving into more responsible and higher paying positions, such as assistant or associate administrator, department head, or CEO, or by moving to larger facilities. Some experienced managers also may become consultants or professors of health care management.

Employment
Medical and health services managers held about 248,000 jobs in 2004. About 30 percent worked in private hospitals, and another 16 percent worked in offices of physicians or in nursing care facilities. The remainder worked mostly in home health care services, Federal Government health care facilities, ambulatory facilities run by State and local governments, outpatient care centers, insurance carriers, and community care facilities for the elderly.

Job Outlook
Employment of medical and health services managers is expected to grow faster than the average for all occupations through 2014, as the health care industry continues to expand and diversify. Job opportunities will be especially good in offices of health practitioners, general medical and surgical hospitals, home health care services, and outpatient care centers. Applicants with work experience in the health care field and strong business and management skills should have the best opportunities. Competition for jobs at the highest management levels will be keen because of the high pay and prestige.

Managers in all settings will be needed to improve quality and efficiency of health care while controlling costs, as insurance companies and Medicare demand higher levels of accountability. Managers also will be needed to computerize patient records and to ensure their security as required by law. Additional demand for managers will stem from the need to recruit workers and increase employee retention, to comply with changing regulations, to implement new technology, and to help improve the health of their communities by emphasizing preventive care.

Hospitals will continue to employ the most medical and health services managers over the 2004-14 projection period. However, the number of new jobs created is expected to increase at a slower rate in hospitals than in many other industries because of the growing utilization of clinics and other outpatient care sites. Despite relatively slow employment growth, a large number of new jobs will be created because of the industry's large size. Medical and health services managers with experience in large facilities will enjoy the best job opportunities, as hospitals become larger and more complex.

Employment will grow fastest in practitioners' offices and in home health care agencies. Many services previously provided in hospitals will continue to shift to these sectors, especially as medical technologies improve. Demand in medical group practice management will grow as medical group practices become larger and more complex. Managers with specialized experience in a particular field, such as reimbursement, should have good opportunities.

Medical and health services managers also will be employed by health care management companies that provide management services to hospitals and other organizations, as well as to specific departments such as emergency, information management systems, managed care contract negotiations, and physician recruiting.

Earnings
Median annual earnings of medical and health services managers were $67,430 in May 2004. The middle 50 percent earned between $52,530 and $88,210. The lowest 10 percent earned less than $41,450, and the highest 10 percent earned more than $117,990. Median annual earnings in the industries employing the largest numbers of medical and health services managers in May 2004 were as follows:

Federal Government	$87,200
General medical and surgical hospitals	71,280
Offices of physicians	61,320
Nursing care facilities	60,940
Home health care services	60,320

Earnings of medical and health services managers vary by type and size of the facility, as well as by level of responsibility. For example, the Medical Group Management Association reported that, in 2004, median salaries for administrators were $72,875 in practices with 6 or fewer physicians, $95,766 in practices with 7 to 25 physicians, and $132,955 in practices with 26 or more physicians.

According to a survey by *Modern Healthcare* magazine, median annual compensation in 2004 for hospital administrators of selected clinical departments was $76,800 in respiratory care, $81,100 in physical therapy, $87,700 in home health care, $88,800 in laboratory services, $90,200 in long-term care, $93,500 in medical imaging/diagnostic radiology, $94,400 in rehabilitation services, $95,200 in cancer treatment facilities, $96,200 in cardiology, $102,800 in nursing services, and $113,200 in pharmacies. Salaries also varied according to size of facility and geographic region.

According to a survey by the Professional Association of Health Care Office Management, total 2004 median compensation for office managers in specialty physicians' practices was $72,047 in

gastroenterology, $66,946 in dermatology, $66,207 in cardiology, $64,543 in ophthalmology, $63,801 in obstetrics and gynecology, $62,545 in orthopedics, $58,595 in pediatrics, $52,211 in internal medicine, $50,924 in psychiatry, and $50,049 in family practice.

Related Occupations
Medical and health services managers have training or experience in both health and management. Other occupations requiring knowledge of both fields are insurance underwriters and social and community service managers.

Sources of Additional Information
Information about undergraduate and graduate academic programs in this field is available from:
➤ Association of University Programs in Health Administration, 2000 North 14th St., Suite 780, Arlington, VA 22201. Internet: **http://www.aupha.org**

For a list of accredited graduate programs in medical and health services administration, contact:
➤ Commission on Accreditation of Healthcare Management Education, 2000 North 14th St., Suite 780, Arlington, VA 22201. Internet: **http://www.cahmeweb.org**

For information about career opportunities in health care management, contact:
➤ American College of Healthcare Executives, One N. Franklin St., Suite 1700, Chicago, IL 60606-4425. Internet: **http://www.healthmanagementcareers.org**

For information about career opportunities in long term care administration, contact:
➤ American College of Health Care Administrators, 300 N. Lee St., Suite 301, Alexandria, VA 22314. Internet:**http://www.achca.org**

For information about career opportunities in medical group practices and ambulatory care management, contact:
➤ Medical Group Management Association, 104 Inverness Terrace East, Englewood, CO 80112-5306. Internet: **http://www.mgma.org**

For information about medical and health care office managers, contact:
➤ Professional Association of Health Care Office Management, 461 East Ten Mile Rd., Pensacola, FL 32534-9712.

For information about career opportunities in health information management, contact:
➤ American Health Information Management Association, 233 N. Michigan Ave., Suite 2150, Chicago, IL 60601-5800. Internet:**http://www.ahima.org**

Property, Real Estate, and Community Association Managers

(O*NET 11-9141.00)

Significant Points
● Opportunities should be best for those with college degrees in business administration, real estate, or related fields and with professional designations.

● Good speaking, writing, computer, and financial skills, as well as an ability to tactfully deal with people, are essential.

● More than half of property, real estate, and community association managers are self-employed.

Nature of the Work
Buildings can be homes, stores, or offices to those who use them. To businesses and investors, properly managed real estate is a source of income and profits; to homeowners, it is a way to preserve and enhance resale values. Property, real estate, and community

association managers maintain and increase the value of real estate investments. *Property and real estate managers* oversee the performance of income-producing commercial or residential properties and ensure that real estate investments achieve their expected revenues. *Community association managers* manage the common property and services of condominiums, cooperatives, and planned communities through their homeowners' or community associations.

When owners of apartments, office buildings, or retail or industrial properties lack the time or expertise needed for the day-to-day management of their real estate investments or homeowners' associations, they often hire a property or real estate manager or a community association manager. The manager is employed either directly by the owner or indirectly through a contract with a property management firm.

Generally, property and real estate managers handle the financial operations of the property, ensuring that rent is collected and that mortgages, taxes, insurance premiums, payroll, and maintenance bills are paid on time. In community associations, although homeowners pay no rent and pay their own real estate taxes and mortgages, community association managers must collect association dues. Some property managers, called *asset property managers*, supervise the preparation of financial statements and periodically report to the owners on the status of the property, occupancy rates, expiration dates of leases, and other matters.

Often, property managers negotiate contracts for janitorial, security, groundskeeping, trash removal, and other services. When contracts are awarded competitively, managers solicit bids from several contractors and advise the owners on which bid to accept. They monitor the performance of contractors and investigate and resolve complaints from residents and tenants when services are not properly provided. Managers also purchase supplies and equipment for the property and make arrangements with specialists for repairs that cannot be handled by regular property maintenance staff.

In addition to fulfilling these duties, property managers must understand and comply with provisions of legislation, such as the Americans with Disabilities Act and the Federal Fair Housing Amendment Act, as well as local fair housing laws. They must ensure that their renting and advertising practices are not discriminatory and that the property itself complies with all of the local, State, and Federal regulations and building codes.

Onsite property managers are responsible for the day-to-day operations of a single property, such as an office building, a shopping center, a community association, or an apartment complex. To ensure that the property is safe and properly maintained, onsite managers routinely inspect the grounds, facilities, and equipment to determine whether repairs or maintenance is needed. In handling requests for repairs or trying to resolve complaints they meet not only with current residents, but also with prospective residents or tenants to show vacant apartments or office space. Onsite managers also are responsible for enforcing the terms of rental or lease agreements, such as rent collection, parking and pet restrictions, and termination-of-lease procedures. Other important duties of onsite managers include keeping accurate, up-to-date records of income and expenditures from property operations and submitting regular expense reports to the asset property manager or owners.

Property managers who do not work onsite act as a liaison between the onsite manager and the owner. They also market vacant space to prospective tenants through the use of a leasing agent or by advertising or other means, and they establish rental rates in accordance with prevailing local economic conditions.

Some property and real estate managers, often called *real estate asset managers*, act as the property owners' agent and adviser for the property. They plan and direct the purchase, development, and disposition of real estate on behalf of the business and investors.

These managers focus on long-term strategic financial planning, rather than on day-to-day operations of the property.

In deciding to acquire property, real estate asset managers take several factors into consideration, such as property values, taxes, zoning, population growth, transportation, and traffic volume and patterns. Once a site is selected, they negotiate contracts for the purchase or lease of the property, securing the most beneficial terms. Real estate asset managers review their company's real estate holdings periodically and identify properties that are no longer financially profitable. They then negotiate the sale of, or terminate the lease on, such properties.

In many respects, the work of community association managers parallels that of property managers. They collect monthly assessments, prepare financial statements and budgets, negotiate with contractors, and help to resolve complaints. In other respects, however, the work of these managers differs from that of other residential property and real estate managers. Community association managers interact with homeowners and other residents on a daily basis. Hired by the volunteer board of directors of the association, they administer the daily affairs, and oversee the maintenance, of property and facilities that the homeowners own and use jointly through the association. They also assist the board and owners in complying with association and government rules and regulations.

Some associations encompass thousands of homes and employ their own onsite staff and managers. In addition to administering the associations' financial records and budget, managers may be

Property, real estate, and community association managers are responsible for landscaping and parking areas.

responsible for the operation of community pools, golf courses, and community centers and for the maintenance of landscaping and parking areas. Community association managers also may meet with the elected boards of directors to discuss and resolve legal issues or disputes that may affect the owners, as well as to review any proposed changes or improvements by homeowners to their properties, to make sure that they comply with community guidelines.

Working Conditions

The offices of most property, real estate, and community association managers are clean, modern, and well lighted. However, many managers spend a major portion of their time away from their desks. Onsite managers in particular may spend a large portion of their workday away from their offices, visiting the building engineer, showing apartments, checking on the janitorial and maintenance staff, or investigating problems reported by tenants. Property and real estate managers frequently visit the properties they oversee, sometimes on a daily basis when contractors are doing major repair or renovation work. Real estate asset managers may spend time away from home while traveling to company real estate holdings or searching for properties to acquire.

Property, real estate, and community association managers often must attend evening meetings with residents, property owners, community association boards of directors, or civic groups. Not surprisingly, many managers put in long workweeks, especially before financial and tax reports are due and before board and annual meetings. Some apartment managers are required to live in the apartment complexes where they work so that they are available to handle any emergency that occurs, even when they are off duty. They usually receive compensatory time off for working nights or weekends. Many apartment managers receive time off during the week so that they are available on weekends to show apartments to prospective residents.

Training, Other Qualifications, and Advancement

Most employers prefer to hire college graduates for property management positions. Entrants with degrees in business administration, accounting, finance, real estate, public administration, or related fields are preferred, but those with degrees in the liberal arts also may qualify. Good speaking, writing, computer, and financial skills, as well as an ability to deal tactfully with people, are essential in all areas of property management.

Many people enter property management as onsite managers of apartment buildings, office complexes, or community associations or as employees of property management firms or community association management companies. As they acquire experience working under the direction of a property manager, they may advance to positions greater responsibility at larger properties. Those who excel as onsite managers often transfer to assistant property manager positions, in which they can acquire experience handling a broad range of property management responsibilities.

Previous employment as a real estate sales agent may be an asset to onsite managers because it provides experience that is useful in showing apartments or office space. In the past, those with backgrounds in building maintenance have advanced to onsite manager positions on the strength of their knowledge of building mechanical systems, but this path is becoming less common as employers place greater emphasis on administrative, financial, and communication abilities for managerial jobs.

Although many people entering jobs such as assistant property manager do so by having previously gained onsite management experience, employers increasingly are hiring inexperienced college graduates with bachelor's or master's degrees in business administration, accounting, finance, or real estate for these positions. Assistants

work closely with a property manager and learn how to prepare budgets, analyze insurance coverage and risk options, market property to prospective tenants, and collect overdue rent payments. In time, many assistants advance to property manager positions.

The responsibilities and compensation of property, real estate, and community association managers increase as these workers manage more and larger properties. Most property managers, often called portfolio managers, are responsible for several properties at a time. As their careers advance, they gradually are entrusted with larger properties that are more complex to manage. Many specialize in the management of one type of property, such as apartments, office buildings, condominiums, cooperatives, homeowners associations, or retail properties. Managers who excel at marketing properties to tenants might specialize in managing new properties, while those who are particularly knowledgeable about buildings and their mechanical systems might specialize in the management of older properties requiring renovation or more frequent repairs. Some experienced managers open their own property management firms.

Persons most commonly enter real estate asset manager jobs by transferring from positions as property managers or real estate brokers. Real estate asset managers must be good negotiators, adept at persuading and handling people, and good at analyzing data in order to assess the fair-market value of property or its development potential. Resourcefulness and creativity in arranging financing are essential for managers who specialize in land development.

Many employers encourage attendance at short-term formal training programs conducted by various professional and trade associations that are active in the real estate field. Employers send managers to these programs to improve their management skills and expand their knowledge of specialized subjects, such as the operation and maintenance of building mechanical systems, the enhancement of property values, insurance and risk management, personnel management, business and real estate law, community association risks and liabilities, tenant relations, communications, accounting and financial concepts, and reserve funding. Managers also participate in these programs to prepare themselves for positions of greater responsibility in property management. The completion of these programs, related job experience, and a satisfactory score on a written examination leads to certification, or the formal award of a professional designation, by the sponsoring association. (Some organizations offering such programs are listed as sources of additional information at the end of this statement.) In addition to seeking these qualifications, some associations require their members to adhere to a specific code of ethics. In a few States, community association managers must be licensed.

Managers of public housing subsidized by the Federal Government are required to be certified, but many property, real estate, and community association managers who work with all types of property choose to earn a professional designation voluntarily, because it represents formal recognition of their achievements and status in the occupation. Real estate asset managers who buy or sell property are required to be licensed by the State in which they practice.

Employment

Property, real estate, and community association managers held about 361,000 jobs in 2004. More that one-third worked for real estate agents and brokers, lessors of real estate, or property management firms. Others worked for real estate development companies, government agencies that manage public buildings, and corporations with extensive holdings of commercial properties. More than half of property, real estate, and community association managers were self-employed.

Job Outlook

Employment of property, real estate, and community association managers is projected to increase about as fast as the average for all occupations through the year 2014. In addition to job growth, a number of openings are expected to occur as managers transfer to other occupations or leave the labor force. Opportunities should be best for those with a college degree in business administration, real estate, or a related field and for those who attain a professional designation.

Job growth among onsite property managers in commercial real estate is expected to accompany the projected expansion of the real estate and rental and leasing industry. An increase in the Nation's stock of apartments, houses, and offices also should require more property managers. Developments of new homes increasingly are being organized with community or homeowners' associations that provide community services and oversee jointly owned common areas requiring professional management. To help properties become more profitable or to enhance the resale values of homes, more commercial and residential property owners are expected to place their investments in the hands of professional managers.

The changing demographic composition of the population also should create more jobs for property, real estate, and community association managers. The number of older people will grow during the 2004–14 projection period, increasing the need for various types of suitable housing, such as assisted-living facilities and retirement communities. Accordingly, demand will rise for property and real estate managers to operate these facilities—especially those individuals who have a background in the operation and administrative aspects of running a health unit.

Earnings

Median annual earnings of salaried property, real estate, and community association managers were $39,980 in May 2004. The middle 50 percent earned between $27,190 and $59,360 a year. The lowest 10 percent earned less than $18,510, and the highest 10 percent earned more than $89,840 a year. Median annual earnings of salaried property, real estate, and community association managers in the largest industries that employed them in 2004 were as follows:

Local government	$51,980
Offices of real estate agents and brokers	40,000
Activities related to real estate	38,370
Lessors of real estate	34,300

Many resident apartment managers and onsite association managers receive the use of an apartment as part of their compensation package. Managers often are reimbursed for the use of their personal vehicles, and managers employed in land development often receive a small percentage of ownership in the projects that they develop.

Related Occupations

Property, real estate, and community association managers plan, organize, staff, and manage the real estate operations of businesses. Workers who perform similar functions in other fields include administrative services managers, education administrators, food service managers, lodging managers, medical and health services managers, real estate brokers and sales agents, and urban and regional planners.

Sources of Additional Information

For information about education and careers in property management, as well as information about professional designation and certification programs in both residential and commercial property management, contact:

➤ Institute of Real Estate Management, 430 N. Michigan Ave., Chicago, IL 60611. Internet: **http://www.irem.org**

For information on careers and certification programs in commercial property management, contact:

➤ Building Owners and Managers Institute, 1521 Ritchie Hwy., Arnold, MD 21012. Internet: **http://www.bomi-edu.org**

For information on careers and professional designation and certification programs in residential property management and community association management, contact:

➤ Community Associations Institute, 225 Reinekers Ln., Suite 300, Alexandria, VA 22314. Internet: **http://www.caionline.org**

➤ National Board of Certification for Community Association Managers, 225 Reinekers Lane, Suite 310, Alexandria, VA 22314. Internet: **http://www.nbccam.org**

Purchasing Managers, Buyers, and Purchasing Agents

(O*NET 11-3061.00, 13-1021.00, 13-1022.00, 13-1023.00)

Significant Points

- Forty-three percent are employed in wholesale trade or manufacturing establishments.

- Some firms promote qualified employees to these positions, while other employers recruit college graduates; regardless of academic preparation, new employees need 1 to 5 years to learn the specifics of their employer's business.

- Overall employment growth is expected to be slower than average.

- Opportunities should be best for those with a college degree.

Nature of the Work

Purchasing managers, buyers, and purchasing agents make up a key component of a firm's supply chain. They buy the goods and services the company or institution needs to either resell to customers or for the establishment's own use. *Wholesale and retail buyers* purchase goods for resale, such as clothing or electronics and *purchasing agents* buy goods and services for use by their own company or organization such as raw materials for manufacturing or office supplies. *Purchasing agents and buyers of farm products* purchase goods such as grain, Christmas trees, and tobacco for further processing or resale. Purchasing professionals consider price, quality, availability, reliability, and technical support when choosing suppliers and merchandise. They try to get the best deal for their company, meaning the highest quality goods and services at the lowest possible cost to their companies. In order to accomplish these tasks successfully, purchasing managers, buyers, and purchasing agents study sales records and inventory levels of current stock, identify foreign and domestic suppliers, and keep abreast of changes affecting both the supply of, and demand for, needed products and materials.

In large industrial organizations, a distinction often is drawn between the work of a buyer or purchasing agent and that of a *purchasing manager*. Purchasing agents commonly focus on routine purchasing tasks, often specializing in a commodity or group of related commodities, such as steel, lumber, cotton, grains, fabricated metal products, or petroleum products. Purchasing agents usually track market conditions, price trends, and futures markets. Purchasing managers usually handle the more complex or critical purchases and may supervise a group of purchasing agents handling other goods and services. Whether a person is titled purchasing manager, buyer, or purchasing agent depends more on specific industry and employer practices than on specific job duties.

Purchasing specialists employed by government agencies or manufacturing firms usually are called purchasing directors, managers, or agents; or contract specialists. These workers acquire materials, parts, machines, supplies, services, and other inputs to the production of a final product. Some purchasing managers specialize in negotiating and supervising supply contracts, and are called contract or supply managers. Purchasing agents and managers obtain items ranging from raw materials, fabricated parts, machinery, and office supplies to construction services and airline tickets. Often, purchasing specialists in government place solicitations for services and accept bids and offers through the Internet. Government purchasing agents and managers must follow strict laws and regulations in their work, in order to avoid any appearance of impropriety. To be effective, purchasing specialists must have a working technical knowledge of the goods or services to be purchased.

Purchasing specialists who buy finished goods for resale are employed by wholesale and retail establishments, where they commonly are known as buyers or merchandise managers. Wholesale and retail buyers are an integral part of a complex system of distribution and merchandising that caters to the vast array of consumer needs and desires. Wholesale buyers purchase goods directly from manufacturers or from other wholesale firms for resale to retail firms, commercial establishments, institutions, and other organizations. In retail firms, buyers purchase goods from wholesale firms or directly from manufacturers for resale to the public. Buyers largely determine which products their establishment will sell. Therefore, it is essential that they have the ability to predict what will appeal to consumers. They must constantly stay informed of the latest trends, because failure to do so could jeopardize profits and the reputation of their company. They keep track of inventories and sales levels through computer software that is linked to the store's cash registers. Buyers also follow ads in newspapers and other media to check competitors' sales activities, and they watch general economic conditions to anticipate consumer buying patterns. Buyers working for large and medium-sized firms usually specialize in acquiring one or two lines of merchandise, whereas buyers working for small stores may purchase the establishment's complete inventory.

The use of private-label merchandise and the consolidation of buying departments have increased the responsibilities of retail buyers. Private-label merchandise, produced for a particular retailer, requires buyers to work closely with vendors to develop and obtain the desired product. The downsizing and consolidation of buying departments increases the demands placed on buyers because, although the amount of work remains unchanged, there are fewer people to accomplish it. The result is an increase in the workloads and levels of responsibility for all.

Many merchandise managers assist in the planning and implementation of sales promotion programs. Working with merchandise executives, they determine the nature of the sale and purchase items accordingly. Merchandise managers may work with advertising personnel to create an ad campaign. For example, they may determine in which media the advertisement will be placed—newspapers, direct mail, television, or some combination of all three. In addition, merchandise managers often visit the selling floor to ensure that goods are properly displayed. Buyers stay in constant contact with store and department managers to find out what products are selling well and which items the customers are demanding to be added to the product line. Often, assistant buyers are responsible for placing orders and checking shipments.

Evaluating suppliers is one of the most critical functions of a purchasing manager, buyer, or purchasing agent. Many firms now run on a lean manufacturing schedule and use just-in-time inventories so any delays in the supply chain can shut down production and cost the firm its customers and reputation. Purchasing professionals use many resources to find out all they can about potential suppliers. The Internet has become an effective tool in searching catalogs, trade journals, and industry and company publications, and directories. Purchasing professionals will attend meetings, trade shows, and conferences to learn of new industry trends and make contacts with suppliers. Purchasing managers, agents, and buyers will usually interview prospective suppliers and visit their plants and distribution centers to asses their capabilities. It is important to make certain that the supplier is capable of delivering the desired goods or services on time, in the correct quantities without sacrificing quality. Once all of the necessary information on suppliers is gathered, orders are placed and contracts are awarded to those suppliers who meet the purchaser's needs. Most of the transaction process is now automated using electronic purchasing systems that link the supplier and firms together through the Internet.

Purchasing professionals can gain instant access to the specifications for thousands of commodities, inventory records, and their customers' purchase records to avoid overpaying for goods and to avoid shortages of popular goods or surpluses of goods that do not sell as well. These systems permit faster selection, customization, and ordering of products, and they allow buyers to concentrate on the qualitative and analytical aspects of the job. Long-term contracts are an important strategy of purchasing professionals because it allows purchasers to consolidate their supply bases around fewer suppliers. In today's global economy purchasing managers, buyers, and purchasing agents should expect to deal with foreign suppliers which may require travel to other countries and to be familiar with other cultures and languages.

Changing business practices have altered the traditional roles of purchasing or supply management specialists in many industries. For example, manufacturing companies increasingly involve workers in this occupation at most stages of product development because of their ability to forecast a part's or material's cost, availability, and suitability for its intended purpose. Furthermore, potential problems with the supply of materials may be avoided by consulting the purchasing department in the early stages of product design.

Purchasing specialists often work closely with other employees in their own organization when deciding on purchases, an arrangement

Purchasing managers, buyers, and purchasing agents are a key link in a firm's supply chain.

sometimes called team buying. For example, before submitting an order, they may discuss the design of custom-made products with company design engineers, talk about problems involving the quality of purchased goods with quality assurance engineers and production supervisors, or mention shipment problems to managers in the receiving department.

Working Conditions

Most purchasing managers, buyers, and purchasing agents work in comfortable offices. They frequently work more than the standard 40-hour week, because of special sales, conferences, or production deadlines. Evening and weekend work also is common, before holiday and back-to-school seasons for those working in retail trade. Consequently, many retail firms discourage the use of vacation time during peak periods.

Buyers and merchandise managers often work under great pressure. Because wholesale and retail stores are so competitive, buyers need physical stamina to keep up with the fast-paced nature of their work.

Many purchasing managers, buyers, and purchasing agents travel at least several days a month. Purchasers for worldwide manufacturing companies and large retailers, as well as buyers of high fashion, may travel outside the United States.

Training, Other Qualifications, and Advancement

Qualified persons may begin as trainees, purchasing clerks, expediters, junior buyers, or assistant buyers. Retail and wholesale firms prefer to hire applicants who have a college degree and who are familiar with the merchandise they sell and with wholesaling and retailing practices. Some retail firms promote qualified employees to assistant buyer positions; others recruit and train college graduates as assistant buyers. Most employers use a combination of methods.

Educational requirements tend to vary with the size of the organization. Large stores and distributors prefer applicants who have completed a bachelor's degree program with a business emphasis. Many manufacturing firms put yet a greater emphasis on formal training, preferring applicants with a bachelor's or master's degree in engineering, business, economics, or one of the applied sciences. A master's degree is essential for advancement to many top-level purchasing manager jobs.

Regardless of academic preparation, new employees must learn the specifics of their employers' business. Training periods vary in length, with most lasting 1 to 5 years. In wholesale and retail establishments, most trainees begin by selling merchandise, supervising sales workers, checking invoices on material received, and keeping track of stock. As they progress, retail trainees are given increased buying-related responsibilities.

In manufacturing, new purchasing employees often are enrolled in company training programs and spend a considerable amount of time learning about their firm's operations and purchasing practices. They work with experienced purchasers to learn about commodities, prices, suppliers, and markets. In addition, they may be assigned to the production planning department to learn about the material requirements system and the inventory system the company uses to keep production and replenishment functions working smoothly.

Purchasing managers, buyers, and purchasing agents must know how to use both word processing and spreadsheet software, as well as the Internet. Other important qualities include the ability to analyze technical data in suppliers' proposals; good communication, negotiation, and mathematical skills; knowledge of supply-chain management; and the ability to perform financial analyses.

Persons who wish to become wholesale or retail buyers should be good at planning and decisionmaking and have an interest in merchandising. Anticipating consumer preferences and ensuring that goods are in stock when they are needed requires resourcefulness, good judgment, and self-confidence. Buyers must be able to make decisions quickly and to take risks. Marketing skills and the ability to identify products that will sell also are very important. Employers often look for leadership ability, too, because buyers spend a large portion of their time supervising assistant buyers and dealing with manufacturers' representatives and store executives.

Experienced buyers may advance by moving to a department that manages a larger volume or by becoming a merchandise manager. Others may go to work in sales for a manufacturer or wholesaler.

An experienced purchasing agent or buyer may become an assistant purchasing manager in charge of a group of purchasing professionals before advancing to purchasing manager, supply manager, or director of materials management. At the top levels, duties may overlap with other management functions, such as production, planning, logistics, and marketing.

Regardless of industry, continuing education is essential for advancement. Many purchasers participate in seminars offered by professional societies and take college courses in supply management. Professional certification is becoming increasingly important, especially for those just entering the occupation.

In private industry, recognized marks of experience and professional competence are the Accredited Purchasing Practitioner (APP) and Certified Purchasing Manager (CPM) designations, conferred by the Institute for Supply Management, and the Certified Purchasing Professional (CPP) and Certified Professional Purchasing Manager (CPPM) designations, conferred by the American Purchasing Society. In Federal, State, and local government, the indications of professional competence are Certified Professional Public Buyer (CPPB) and Certified Public Purchasing Officer (CPPO), conferred by the National Institute of Governmental Purchasing. Most of these certifications are awarded only after work-related experience and education requirements are met, and written or oral exams are successfully completed.

Employment

Purchasing managers, buyers, and purchasing agents held about 520,000 jobs in 2004. Forty-three percent worked in the wholesale trade and manufacturing industries, and another twelve percent worked in retail trade. The remainder worked mostly in service establishments, such as hospitals, or different levels of government. A small number were self-employed.

The following tabulation shows the distribution of employment by occupational specialty:

Purchasing agents, except wholesale, retail, and farm products .. 273,000
Wholesale and retail buyers, except farm products 156,000
Purchasing managers 75,000
Purchasing agents and buyers, farm products 16,000

Job Outlook

Overall employment of purchasing managers, buyers, and purchasing agents is expected to grow slower than the average for all occupations through the year 2014. Offsetting some declines for purchasing workers in the manufacturing sector will be increases in the services sector. Companies in the services sector, which have typically made purchases on an ad hoc basis, are beginning to realize that centralized purchasing offices may be more efficient. Also, many purchasing agents are now charged with procuring services that were traditionally done in-house in the past, such as computer and IT (information technology) support in addition to traditionally contracted services such as advertising. Demand for purchasing workers will be limited by improving software, which has eliminated much of the paperwork involved in ordering and procuring supplies, and also by the growing number of purchases being made electronically through the internet and electronic data interchange (EDI). Despite slower-than-average growth, some job openings will result from the need to replace workers who transfer to other occupations or leave the labor force.

Employment of purchasing managers is expected to grow more slowly than average. The use of the Internet to conduct electronic commerce has made information easier to obtain, thus increasing the productivity of purchasing managers. The Internet also allows both large and small companies to bid on contracts. Exclusive supply contracts and long-term contracting have allowed companies to negotiate with fewer suppliers less frequently.

Employment of wholesale and retail buyers, except farm products, also is projected to grow more slowly than average. In the retail industry, mergers and acquisitions have caused buying departments to consolidate. In addition, larger retail stores are eliminating local buying departments and centralizing them at their headquarters.

Employment of purchasing agents, except wholesale, retail, and farm products, is expected to increase more slowly than average, limited by the increased globalization of the U.S. economy. As more materials and supplies come from abroad, firms have begun to outsource more of their purchasing duties to foreign purchasing agents who are located closer to the foreign suppliers of goods and materials they will need. This trend is expected to continue, but it will likely be limited to routine transactions with complex and critical purchases still being handled in-house.

Finally, employment of purchasing agents and buyers, farm products, also is projected to increase more slowly than average, as overall growth in agricultural industries decreases and retailers in the grocery-related industries consolidate.

Persons who have a bachelor's degree in business should have the best chance of obtaining a buyer position in wholesale or retail trade or within government. A bachelor's degree, combined with industry experience and knowledge of a technical field, will be an advantage for those interested in working for a manufacturing or industrial company. Government agencies and larger companies usually require a master's degree in business or public administration for top-level purchasing positions.

Earnings
Median annual earnings of purchasing managers were $72,450 in May 2004. The middle 50 percent earned between $54,150 and $94,970 a year. The lowest 10 percent earned less than $41,300, and the highest 10 percent earned more than $121,600 a year.

Median annual earnings for purchasing agents and buyers, farm products were $43,720 in May 2004. The middle 50 percent earned between $33,100 and $59,420 a year. The lowest 10 percent earned less than $25,260, and the highest 10 percent earned more than $82,330 a year.

Median annual earnings for wholesale and retail buyers, except farm products, were $42,230 in May 2004. The middle 50 percent earned between $31,550 and $57,010 a year. The lowest 10 percent earned less than $24,380, and the highest 10 percent earned more than $79,340 a year. Median annual earnings in the industries employing the largest numbers of wholesale and retail buyers, except farm products, in May 2004 were:

Management of companies and enterprises	$49,770
Grocery and related product wholesalers	43,910
Wholesale electronic markets and agents and brokers	43,860
Building material and supplies dealers	35,850
Grocery stores	32,790

Median annual earnings for purchasing agents, except wholesale, retail, and farm products, were $47,680 in May 2004. The middle

50 percent earned between $36,760 and $62,600 a year. The lowest 10 percent earned less than $29,640, and the highest 10 percent earned more than $79,710 a year. Median annual earnings in the industries employing the largest numbers of purchasing agents, except of wholesale, retail, and farm products, in May 2004 were:

Federal executive branch and United States Postal Service	$63,940
Aerospace product and parts manufacturing	55,820
Management of companies and enterprises	53,750
Local government	44,730
General medical and surgical hospitals	37,090

Purchasing managers, buyers, and purchasing agents receive the same benefits package as other workers, including vacations, sick leave, life and health insurance, and pension plans. In addition to receiving standard benefits, retail buyers often earn cash bonuses based on their performance and may receive discounts on merchandise bought from their employer.

Related Occupations
Workers in other occupations who need a knowledge of marketing and the ability to assess consumer demand include those in advertising, marketing, promotions, public relations, and sales managers; food service managers; insurance sales agents; lodging managers; sales engineers; and sales representatives, wholesale and manufacturing.

Sources of Additional Information
Further information about education, training, employment, and certification for purchasing careers is available from:
➤ American Purchasing Society, North Island Center, Suite 203, 8 East Galena Blvd., Aurora, IL 60506.
➤ Institute for Supply Management, P.O. Box 22160, Tempe, AZ 85285-2160. Internet: **http://www.ism.ws**
➤ National Institute of Governmental Purchasing, Inc., 151 Spring St., Suite 300, Herndon, VA 20170-5223. Internet: **http://www.nigp.org**

Top Executives

(O*NET 11-1011.01, 11-1011.02, 11-1021.00)

Significant Points

● Keen competition is expected because the prestige and high pay attract a large number of qualified applicants.

● Top executives are among the highest paid workers; however, long hours, considerable travel, and intense pressure to succeed are common.

● The formal education and experience of top executives vary as widely as the nature of their responsibilities.

Nature of the Work
All organizations have specific goals and objectives that they strive to meet. Top executives devise strategies and formulate policies to ensure that these objectives are met. Although they have a wide range of titles—such as chief executive officer, chief operating officer, board chair, president, vice president, school superintendent, county administrator, or tax commissioner—all formulate policies and direct the operations of businesses and corporations, public sector organizations, nonprofit institutions, and other organizations.

A corporation's goals and policies are established by the *chief executive officer* in collaboration with other top executives, who are overseen by a board of directors. In a large corporation, the chief executive officer meets frequently with subordinate executives to ensure that operations are conducted in accordance with these policies. The chief executive officer of a corporation retains overall accountability; however, a *chief operating officer* may be delegated several responsibilities, including the authority to oversee executives who direct the activities of various departments and implement the organization's policies on a day-to-day basis. In publicly held and nonprofit corporations, the board of directors ultimately is accountable for the success or failure of the enterprise, and the chief executive officer reports to the board.

The nature of other high-level executives' responsibilities depends on the size of the organization. In large organizations, the duties of such executives are highly specialized. Some managers, for instance, are responsible for the overall performance of one aspect of the organization, such as manufacturing, marketing, sales, purchasing, finance, personnel, training, administrative services, computer and information systems, property management, transportation, or legal services. (Some of these and other management occupations are discussed elsewhere in this section of the *Handbook*.)

In smaller organizations, such as independent retail stores or small manufacturers, a partner, owner, or general manager often is responsible for purchasing, hiring, training, quality control, and day-to-day supervisory duties.

Chief financial officers direct the organization's financial goals, objectives, and budgets. They oversee the investment of funds and manage associated risks, supervise cash management activities, execute capital-raising strategies to support a firm's expansion, and deal with mergers and acquisitions.

Chief information officers are responsible for the overall technological direction of their organizations. They are increasingly involved in the strategic business plan of a firm as part of the executive team. To perform effectively, they also need knowledge of administrative procedures, such as budgeting, hiring, and supervision. These managers propose budgets for projects and programs and make decisions on staff training and equipment purchases. They hire and assign computer specialists, information technology workers, and support personnel to carry out specific parts of the projects. They supervise the work of these employees, review their output, and establish administrative procedures and policies. Chief information officers also provide organizations with the vision to master information technology as a competitive tool.

Chief executives have overall responsibility for the operation of their organizations. Working with executive staff, they set goals and arrange programs to attain these goals. Executives also appoint department heads, who manage the employees who carry out programs. Chief executives also oversee budgets and ensure that resources are used properly and that programs are carried out as planned.

Chief executive officers carry out a number of other important functions, such as meeting with staff and board members to determine the level of support for proposed programs. In addition, they often nominate citizens to boards and commissions, encourage business investment, and promote economic development in their communities. To do all of these varied tasks effectively, chief executives rely on a staff of highly skilled personnel. Executives who control small companies, however, often do this work by themselves.

General and operations managers plan, direct, or coordinate the operations of companies or public and private sector organizations. Their duties include formulating policies, managing daily operations, and planning the use of materials and human resources, but are too diverse and general in nature to be classified in any one area of management or administration, such

Top executives devise strategies and formulate policies to ensure that objectives are met.

as personnel, purchasing, or administrative services. In some organizations, the duties of general and operations managers may overlap the duties of chief executive officers.

In addition to being responsible for the operational success of a company, top executives also are increasingly being held accountable for the accuracy of their financial reporting, particularly among publicly traded companies. For example, recently enacted legislation contains provisions for corporate governance, internal control, and financial reporting.

Working Conditions

Top executives typically have spacious offices and numerous support staff. General managers in large firms or nonprofit organizations usually have comfortable offices close to those of the top executives to whom they report. Long hours, including evenings and weekends, are standard for most top executives and general managers, although their schedules may be flexible.

Substantial travel between international, national, regional, and local offices to monitor operations and meet with customers, staff, and other executives often is required of managers and executives. Many managers and executives also attend meetings and conferences sponsored by various associations. The conferences provide an opportunity to meet with prospective donors, customers, contractors, or government officials and allow managers and executives to keep abreast of technological and managerial innovations.

In large organizations, job transfers between local offices or subsidiaries are common for persons on the executive career track. Top executives are under intense pressure to succeed; depending on the organization, this may mean earning higher profits, providing better service, or attaining fundraising and charitable goals. Executives in charge of poorly performing organizations or departments usually find their jobs in jeopardy.

Training, Other Qualifications, and Advancement

The formal education and experience of top executives vary as widely as the nature of their responsibilities. Many top executives have a bachelor's or higher degree in business administration or liberal arts. College presidents typically have a doctorate in the field in which they originally taught, and school superintendents often have a master's degree in education administration. (For information on lower-level managers in educational services, see the *Handbook* statement on education administrators.) A brokerage office manager needs a strong background in securities and finance, and department store executives generally have extensive experience in retail trade.

Some top executives in the public sector have a background in public administration or liberal arts. Others might have a background related to their jobs. For example, a health commissioner might have a graduate degree in health services administration or business administration. (For information on lower-level managers in health services, see the *Handbook* statement on medical and health services managers.)

Many top executive positions are filled from within the organization by promoting experienced, lower-level managers when an opening occurs. In industries such as retail trade or transportation, for instance, it is possible for individuals without a college degree to work their way up within the company and become managers. However, many companies prefer that their top executives have specialized backgrounds and, therefore, hire individuals who have been managers in other organizations.

Top executives must have highly developed personal skills. An analytical mind able to quickly assess large amounts of information and data is very important, as is the ability to consider and evaluate the relationships between numerous factors. Top executives also must be able to communicate clearly and persuasively. Other qualities critical for managerial success include leadership, self-confidence, motivation, decisiveness, flexibility, sound business judgment, and determination.

Advancement may be accelerated by participation in company training programs that impart a broader knowledge of company policy and operations. Managers also can help their careers by becoming familiar with the latest developments in management techniques at national or local training programs sponsored by various industry and trade associations. Managers who have experience in a particular field, such as accounting or engineering, may attend executive development programs to facilitate their promotion to an even higher level. Participation in conferences and seminars can expand knowledge of national and international issues influencing the organization and can help the participants develop a network of useful contacts.

General managers may advance to a top executive position, such as executive vice president, in their own firm or they may take a corresponding position in another firm. They may even advance to peak corporate positions such as chief operating officer or chief executive officer. Chief executive officers often become members of the board of directors of one or more firms, typically as a director of their own firm and often as chair of its board of directors. Some top executives establish their own firms or become independent consultants.

Employment

Top executives held about 2.3 million jobs in 2004. Employment by detailed occupation was distributed as follows:

General and operations managers	1,807,000
Chief executives	444,000
Legislators	66,000

Top executives are found in every industry, but service-providing industries, including government, employ 8 out of 10.

Job Outlook

Keen competition is expected for top executive positions because the prestige and high pay attract a large number of qualified applicants. Because this is a large occupation, numerous openings will occur each year as executives transfer to other positions, start

their own businesses, or retire. However, many executives who leave their jobs transfer to other executive positions, a pattern that tends to limit the number of job openings for new entrants.

Experienced managers whose accomplishments reflect strong leadership qualities and the ability to improve the efficiency or competitive position of an organization will have the best opportunities. In an increasingly global economy, experience in international economics, marketing, information systems, and knowledge of several languages also may be beneficial.

Employment of top executives—including chief executives and general and operations managers—is expected to grow about as fast as the average for all occupations through 2014. Because top managers are essential to the success of any organization, their jobs are unlikely to be automated or to be eliminated through corporate restructuring—trends that are expected to adversely affect employment of lower-level managers. Projected employment growth of top executives over the 2004-14 period varies by industry. For example, employment growth is expected to be much faster than average in professional, scientific, and technical services and in administrative and support services. However, employment is projected to decline in some manufacturing industries.

Earnings

Top executives are among the highest paid workers in the U.S. economy. However, salary levels vary substantially depending on the level of managerial responsibility; length of service; and type, size, and location of the firm. For example, a top manager in a very large corporation can earn significantly more than a counterpart in a small firm.

Median annual earnings of general and operations managers in May 2004 were $77,420. The middle 50 percent earned between $52,420 and $118,310. Because the specific responsibilities of general and operations managers vary significantly within industries, earnings also tend to vary considerably. Median annual earnings in the industries employing the largest numbers of general and operations managers in May 2004 were:

Computer systems design and related services	$117,730
Management of companies and enterprises	99,670
Building equipment contractors	83,080
Depository credit intermediation	76,060
Local government	68,590

Median annual earnings of chief executives in May 2004 were $140,350; although chief executives in some industries earned considerably more.

Salaries vary substantially by type and level of responsibilities and by industry. According to a 2005 survey by Abbott, Langer, and Associates, the median income of chief executive officers in the nonprofit sector was $88,006 in 2005, but some of the highest paid made more than $700,000.

In addition to salaries, total compensation often includes stock options, dividends, and other performance bonuses. The use of executive dining rooms and company aircraft and cars, expense allowances, and company-paid insurance premiums and physical examinations also are among benefits commonly enjoyed by top executives in private industry. A number of chief executive officers also are provided with company-paid club memberships and other amenities.

Related Occupations

Top executives plan, organize, direct, control, and coordinate the operations of an organization and its major departments or programs. The members of the board of directors and lower-level managers also are involved in these activities. Many other management occupations have similar responsibilities; however, they are concentrated in specific industries or are responsible for a specific department within an organization. A few examples are administrative services managers; education administrators; financial managers; food service managers; and advertising, marketing, promotions, public relations, and sales managers. Legislators oversee their staffs and help set public policies in Federal, State, and local governments.

Sources of Additional Information

For a variety of information on top executives, including educational programs, certification programs, and job listings, contact:

➤ American Management Association, 1601 Broadway, 6th Floor, New York, NY 10019. Internet: **http://www.amanet.org**
➤ International Public Management Association for Human Resources, 1617 Duke St., Alexandria, VA 22314. Internet: **http://www.ipma-hr.org**
➤ National Management Association, 2210 Arbor Blvd., Dayton, OH 45439. Internet: **http://www.nma1.org**

For information on executive financial management careers and certification, contact:

➤ Financial Executives International, 200 Campus Dr., P.O. Box 674, Florham Park, NJ 07932-0674. Internet:**http://www.fei.org**
➤ Financial Management Association International, College of Business Administration, University of South Florida, 4202 East Fowler Ave., BSN 3331, Tampa, FL 33620-5500. Internet:**http://www.fma.org**

Business and Financial Operations Occupations

Accountants and Auditors

(O*NET 13-2011.01, 13-2011.02)

Significant Points

- Most jobs require at least a bachelor's degree in accounting or a related field.

- Overall job opportunities should be favorable; jobseekers who obtain professional recognition through certification or licensure, a master's degree, proficiency in accounting and auditing computer software, or specialized expertise will have the best opportunities

- An increase in the number of businesses, changing financial laws and regulations, and greater scrutiny of company finances will drive faster-than-average growth of accountants and auditors.

Nature of the Work

Accountants and auditors help to ensure that the Nation's firms are run efficiently, its public records kept accurately, and its taxes paid properly and on time. They perform these vital functions by offering an increasingly wide array of business and accounting services, including public, management, and government accounting, as well as internal auditing, to their clients. Beyond carrying out the fundamental tasks of the occupation—preparing, analyzing, and verifying financial documents in order to provide information to clients—many accountants now are required to possess a wide range of knowledge and skills. Accountants and auditors are broadening the services they offer to include budget analysis, financial and investment planning, information technology consulting, and limited legal services.

Specific job duties vary widely among the four major fields of accounting: *public, management, and government accounting and internal auditing.*

Public accountants perform a broad range of accounting, auditing, tax, and consulting activities for their clients, which may be corporations, governments, nonprofit organizations, or individuals. For example, some public accountants concentrate on tax matters, such as advising companies about the tax advantages and disadvantages of certain business decisions and preparing individual income tax returns. Others offer advice in areas such as compensation or employee health care benefits, the design of accounting and data-processing systems, and the selection of controls to safeguard assets. Still others audit clients' financial statements and inform investors and authorities that the statements have been correctly prepared and reported. Public accountants, many of whom are Certified Public Accountants (CPAs), generally have their own businesses or work for public accounting firms.

Some public accountants specialize in forensic accounting—investigating and interpreting white-collar crimes such as securities fraud and embezzlement, bankruptcies and contract disputes, and other complex and possibly criminal financial transactions, including money laundering by organized criminals. Forensic accountants combine their knowledge of accounting and finance with law and investigative techniques in order to determine whether an activity is illegal. Many forensic accountants work closely with law enforcement personnel and lawyers during investigations and often appear as expert witnesses during trials.

In response to recent accounting scandals, new Federal legislation restricts the nonauditing services that public accountants can provide to clients. If an accounting firm audits a client's financial statements, that same firm cannot provide advice on human resources, technology, investment banking, or legal matters, although accountants may still advise on tax issues, such as establishing a tax shelter. Accountants may still advise other clients in these areas or may provide advice within their own firm.

Management accountants—also called cost, managerial, industrial, corporate, or private accountants—record and analyze the financial information of the companies for which they work. Among their other responsibilities are budgeting, performance evaluation, cost management, and asset management. Usually, management accountants are part of executive teams involved in strategic planning or the development of new products. They analyze and interpret the financial information that corporate executives need in order to make sound business decisions. They also prepare financial reports for other groups, including stockholders, creditors, regulatory agencies, and tax authorities. Within accounting departments, management accountants may work in various areas, including financial analysis, planning and budgeting, and cost accounting.

Government accountants and auditors work in the public sector, maintaining and examining the records of government agencies and auditing private businesses and individuals whose activities are subject to government regulations or taxation. Accountants employed by Federal, State, and local governments guarantee that revenues are received and expenditures are made in accordance with laws and regulations. Those employed by the Federal Government may work as Internal Revenue Service agents or in financial management, financial institution examination, or budget analysis and administration.

Internal auditors verify the accuracy of their organization's internal records and check for mismanagement, waste, or fraud. Internal auditing is an increasingly important area of accounting and auditing.

Internal auditors examine and evaluate their firms' financial and information systems, management procedures, and internal controls to ensure that records are accurate and controls are adequate to protect against fraud and waste. They also review company operations, evaluating their efficiency, effectiveness, and compliance with corporate policies and procedures, laws, and government regulations. There are many types of highly specialized auditors, such as electronic data-processing, environmental, engineering, legal, insurance premium, bank, and health care auditors. As computer systems make information timelier, internal auditors help managers to base their decisions on actual data, rather than personal observation. Internal auditors also may recommend controls for their organization's computer system, to ensure the reliability of the system and the integrity of the data.

Computers are rapidly changing the nature of the work of most accountants and auditors. With the aid of special software packages, accountants summarize transactions in standard formats used by financial records and organize data in special formats employed in financial analysis. These accounting packages greatly reduce the amount of tedious manual work associated with data management and recordkeeping. Computers enable accountants and auditors to be more mobile and to use their clients' computer systems to extract information from databases and the Internet. As a result, a growing number of accountants and auditors with extensive computer skills are specializing in correcting problems with software or in developing software to meet unique data management and analytical needs. Accountants also are beginning to perform more technical duties, such as implementing, controlling, and auditing systems and networks, developing technology plans, and analyzing and devising budgets.

Increasingly, accountants also are assuming the role of a personal financial advisor. They not only provide clients with accounting and tax help, but also help them develop personal budgets, manage assets and investments, plan for retirement, and recognize and reduce their exposure to risks. This role is a response to clients' demands for a single trustworthy individual or firm to meet all of their financial needs. However, accountants are restricted from providing these services to clients whose financial statements they also prepare. (See financial analysts and personal financial advisors elsewhere in the *Handbook*.)

Working Conditions

Most accountants and auditors work in a typical office setting. Self-employed accountants may be able to do part of their work at home. Accountants and auditors employed by public accounting firms and government agencies may travel frequently to perform audits at branches of their firm, clients' places of business, or government facilities.

Most accountants and auditors generally work a standard 40-hour week, but many work longer hours, particularly if they are self-employed and have numerous clients. Tax specialists often work long hours during the tax season.

Training, Other Qualifications, and Advancement

Most accountant and auditor positions require at least a bachelor's degree in accounting or a related field. Beginning accounting and auditing positions in the Federal Government, for example, usually require 4 years of college (including 24 semester hours in accounting or auditing) or an equivalent combination of education and experience. Some employers prefer applicants with a master's degree in accounting, or with a master's degree in business administration with a concentration in accounting.

Previous experience in accounting or auditing can help an applicant get a job. Many colleges offer students an opportunity to gain experience through summer or part-time internship programs conducted by public accounting or business firms. In addition, practical knowledge of computers and their applications in accounting and internal auditing is a great asset for jobseekers in the accounting field.

Professional recognition through certification or licensure provides a distinct advantage in the job market. CPAs are licensed by a State Board of Accountancy. The vast majority of States require CPA candidates to be college graduates, but a few States substitute a number of years of public accounting experience for a college degree.

As of early 2005, on the basis of recommendations made by the American Institute of Certified Public Accountants (AICPA), 42 States and the District of Columbia required CPA candidates to complete 150 semester hours of college coursework—an additional 30 hours beyond the usual 4-year bachelor's degree. Another five States have adopted similar legislation that will become effective between 2006 and 2009. Colorado, Delaware, New Hampshire, and Vermont are the only States that do not require 150 semester hours. In response to this trend, many schools have altered their curricula accordingly, with most programs offering master's degrees as part of the 150 hours, so prospective accounting majors should carefully research accounting curricula and the requirements of any States in which they hope to become licensed.

All States use the four-part Uniform CPA Examination prepared by the AICPA. The 2-day CPA examination is rigorous, and only about one-quarter of those who take it each year pass every part they attempt. Candidates are not required to pass all four parts at once, but most States require candidates to pass at least two parts for partial credit and to complete all four sections within a certain period. The CPA exam is now computerized and is offered quarterly at various testing centers throughout the United States. Most States also require applicants for a CPA certificate to have some accounting experience.

The AICPA also offers members with valid CPA certificates the option to receive any or all of the Accredited in Business Valuation (ABV), Certified Information Technology Professional (CITP),

Accountants and auditors prepare, analyze, and verify financial information for individuals and businesses.

or Personal Financial Specialist (PFS) designations. CPA's with these designations may claim a certain level of expertise in the nontraditional areas in which accountants are practicing ever more frequently. The ABV designation requires a written exam, as well as the completion of a minimum of 10 business valuation projects that demonstrate a candidate's experience and competence. The CITP requires payment of a fee, a written statement of intent, and the achievement of a set number of points awarded for business experience and education. Those who do not meet the required number of points may substitute a written exam. Candidates for the PFS designation also must achieve a certain level of points, based on experience and education, and must pass a written exam and submit references.

Nearly all States require CPAs and other public accountants to complete a certain number of hours of continuing professional education before their licenses can be renewed. The professional associations representing accountants sponsor numerous courses, seminars, group study programs, and other forms of continuing education.

Accountants and auditors also can seek to obtain other forms of credentials from professional societies on a voluntary basis. Voluntary certification can attest to professional competence in a specialized field of accounting and auditing. It also can certify that a recognized level of professional competence has been achieved by accountants and auditors who have acquired some skills on the job, without the formal education or public accounting work experience needed to meet the rigorous standards required to take the CPA examination.

The Institute of Management Accountants (IMA) confers the Certified Management Accountant (CMA) designation upon applicants who complete a bachelor's degree or who attain a minimum score or higher on specified graduate school entrance exams. Applicants, who must have worked at least 2 years in management accounting, also must pass a four-part examination, agree to meet continuing education requirements, and comply with standards of professional conduct. The CMA exam provides an in-depth measure of competence in areas such as financial statement analysis, working-capital policy, capital structure, valuation issues, and risk management. The CMA program is administered by the Institute of Certified Management Accountants, an affiliate of the IMA.

Graduates from accredited colleges and universities who have worked for 2 years as internal auditors and have passed a four-part examination may earn the Certified Internal Auditor (CIA) designation from the Institute of Internal Auditors (IIA). The IIA recently implemented three new specialty designations: Certification in Control Self-Assessment (CCSA), Certified Government Auditing Professional (CGAP), and Certified Financial Services Auditor (CFSA). Requirements are similar to those of the CIA. The Information Systems Audit and Control Association confers the Certified Information Systems Auditor (CISA) designation upon candidates who pass an examination and have 5 years of experience auditing information systems. Auditing or data-processing experience and a college education may be substituted for up to 2 years of work experience in this program. Accountants and auditors may hold multiple designations. For instance, an internal auditor might be a CPA, CIA, and CISA.

The Accreditation Council for Accountancy and Taxation, a satellite organization of the National Society of Public Accountants, confers four designations—Accredited Business Accountant (ABA), Accredited Tax Advisor (ATA), Accredited Tax Preparer (ATP) and Elder Care Specialist (ECS)—on accountants specializing in tax preparation for small and medium-sized businesses. Candidates for the ABA must pass an exam; candidates for the ATA, ATP, and ECS

must complete the required coursework and pass an exam. Often, a practitioner will hold multiple licenses and designations.

The Association of Government Accountants grants the Certified Government Financial Manager (CGFM) designation for accountants, auditors, and other government financial personnel at the Federal, State, and local levels. Candidates must have a minimum of a bachelor's degree, 24 hours of study in financial management, and 2 years' experience in government and must pass a series of three exams. The exams cover topics in governmental environment; governmental accounting, financial reporting, and budgeting; and financial management and control.

Persons planning a career in accounting should have an aptitude for mathematics and be able to analyze, compare, and interpret facts and figures quickly. They must be able to clearly communicate the results of their work to clients and managers both verbally and in writing. Accountants and auditors must be good at working with people, as well as with business systems and computers. At a minimum, accountants should be familiar with basic accounting software packages. Because financial decisions are made on the basis of their statements and services, accountants and auditors should have high standards of integrity.

Capable accountants and auditors may advance rapidly; those having inadequate academic preparation may be assigned routine jobs and find promotion difficult. Many graduates of junior colleges or business or correspondence schools, as well as bookkeepers and accounting clerks who meet the education and experience requirements set by their employers, can obtain junior accounting positions and advance to positions with more responsibilities by demonstrating their accounting skills on the job.

Beginning public accountants usually start by assisting with work for several clients. They may advance to positions with more responsibility in 1 or 2 years and to senior positions within another few years. Those who excel may become supervisors, managers, or partners; open their own public accounting firm; or transfer to executive positions in management accounting or internal auditing in private firms.

Management accountants often start as cost accountants, junior internal auditors, or trainees for other accounting positions. As they rise through the organization, they may advance to accounting manager, chief cost accountant, budget director, or manager of internal auditing. Some become controllers, treasurers, financial vice presidents, chief financial officers, or corporation presidents. Many senior corporation executives have a background in accounting, internal auditing, or finance.

In general, public accountants, management accountants, and internal auditors have much occupational mobility. Practitioners often shift into management accounting or internal auditing from public accounting, or between internal auditing and management accounting. It is less common for accountants and auditors to move from either management accounting or internal auditing into public accounting.

Employment

Accountants and auditors held about 1.2 million jobs in 2004. They worked throughout private industry and government, but 1 out of 4 wage and salary accountants worked for accounting, tax preparation, bookkeeping, and payroll services firms. Approximately 1 out of 10 accountants or auditors was self-employed.

Many accountants and auditors are unlicensed management accountants, internal auditors, or government accountants and auditors; however, a large number are licensed CPAs. Most accountants and auditors work in urban areas, where public accounting firms and central or regional offices of businesses are concentrated.

Some individuals with backgrounds in accounting and auditing are full-time college and university faculty; others teach part time while working as self-employed accountants or as accountants for private industry or government. (See teachers—postsecondary elsewhere in the *Handbook*.)

Job Outlook

Employment of accountants and auditors is expected to grow faster than the average for all occupations through the year 2014. An increase in the number of businesses, changing financial laws and regulations, and increased scrutiny of company finances will drive growth. In addition to openings resulting from growth, the need to replace accountants and auditors who retire or transfer to other occupations will produce numerous job openings in this large occupation.

As the economy grows, the number of business establishments will increase, requiring more accountants and auditors to set up books, prepare taxes, and provide management advice. As these businesses grow, the volume and complexity of information developed by accountants and auditors regarding costs, expenditures, and taxes will increase as well. An increased need for accountants and auditors will arise from changes in legislation related to taxes, financial reporting standards, business investments, mergers, and other financial events. The growth of international business also has led to more demand for accounting expertise and services related to international trade and accounting rules, as well as to international mergers and acquisitions. These trends should create more jobs for accountants and auditors.

As a result of accounting scandals at several large corporate companies, Congress passed legislation in an effort to curb corporate accounting fraud. This legislation requires public companies to maintain well-functioning internal controls to ensure the accuracy and reliability of their financial reporting. It also holds the company's chief executive personally responsible for falsely reporting financial information.

These changes should lead to increased scrutiny of company finances and accounting procedures and should create opportunities for accountants and auditors, particularly CPAs, to audit financial records more thoroughly. In order to ensure that finances comply with the law before public accountants conduct audits, management accountants and internal auditors increasingly will be needed to discover and eliminate fraud. Also, in an effort to make government agencies more efficient and accountable, demand for government accountants should increase.

Increased awareness of financial crimes such as embezzlement, bribery, and securities fraud will increase the demand for forensic accountants, to detect illegal financial activity by individuals, companies, and organized crime rings. Computer technology has made these crimes easier to commit, and they are on the rise. At the same time, the development of new computer software and electronic surveillance technology has made tracking down financial criminals easier, thus increasing the ease with which, and likelihood that, forensic accountants will discover their crimes. As success rates of investigations grow, demand also will grow for forensic accountants.

The changing role of accountants and auditors also will spur job growth, although this growth will be limited as a result of financial scandals. In response to demand, some accountants were offering more financial management and consulting services as they assumed a greater advisory role and developed more sophisticated accounting systems. Because Federal legislation now prohibits accountants from providing nontraditional services to clients whose books they audit, opportunities for accountants to offer such services could be limited. However, accountants will still be able to advise on other financial matters for clients that are not publicly traded companies and for nonaudit clients, but growth in these areas will be slower than in the past. Also, due to the increasing popularity of tax preparation firms and computer software, accountants will shift away from tax

preparation. As computer programs continue to simplify some accounting-related tasks, clerical staff will increasingly handle many routine calculations.

Overall, job opportunities for accountants and auditors should be favorable. After most States instituted the 150-hour rule for CPAs, enrollment in accounting programs declined; however, enrollment is slowly beginning to grow again as more students become attracted to the profession because of the attention from the accounting scandals. Those who earn a CPA should have excellent job prospects. However, many accounting graduates are instead pursuing other certifications, such as the CMA and CIA, so job prospects may not be as favorable in management accounting and internal auditing as in public accounting. Regardless of specialty, accountants and auditors who have earned professional recognition through certification or licensure should have the best job prospects. Applicants with a master's degree in accounting, or a master's degree in business administration with a concentration in accounting, also will have an advantage. In the aftermath of the accounting scandals, professional certification is even more important in order to ensure that accountants' credentials and ethics are sound.

Proficiency in accounting and auditing computer software, or expertise in specialized areas such as international business, specific industries, or current legislation, may be helpful in landing certain accounting and auditing jobs. In addition, employers increasingly are seeking applicants with strong interpersonal and communication skills. Because many accountants work on teams with others from different backgrounds, they must be able to communicate accounting and financial information clearly and concisely. Regardless of one's qualifications, however, competition will remain keen for the most prestigious jobs in major accounting and business firms.

Earnings

Median annual wage and salary earnings of accountants and auditors were $50,770 in May 2004. The middle half of the occupation earned between $39,890 and $66,900. The top 10 percent of accountants and auditors earned more than $88,610, and the bottom 10 percent earned less than $32,320. In May 2004, median annual earnings in the industries employing the largest numbers of accountants and auditors were as follows:

Federal executive branch and United States Postal Service	$56,900
Accounting, tax preparation, bookkeeping and payroll services	53,870
Management of companies and enterprises	52,260
Local government	47,440
State government	43,400

According to a salary survey conducted by the National Association of Colleges and Employers, bachelor's degree candidates in accounting received starting offers averaging $43,269 a year in 2005; master's degree candidates in accounting were offered $46,251 initially.

According to a 2005 salary survey conducted by Robert Half International, a staffing services firm specializing in accounting and finance, accountants and auditors with up to 1 year of experience earned between $28,250 and $45,000 a year. Those with 1 to 3 years of experience earned between $33,000 and $52,000. Senior accountants and auditors earned between $40,750 and $69,750, managers between $48,000 and $90,000, and directors of accounting and auditing between $64,750 and $200,750. The variation in salaries reflects differences in size of firm, location, level of education, and professional credentials.

In the Federal Government, the starting annual salary for junior accountants and auditors was $24,677 in 2005. Candidates who had a superior academic record might start at $30,567, while applicants with a master's degree or 2 years of professional experience usually began at $37,390. Beginning salaries were slightly higher in selected areas where the prevailing local pay level was higher. Accountants employed by the Federal Government in nonsupervisory, supervisory, and managerial positions averaged $74,907 a year in 2005; auditors averaged $78,890.

Related Occupations

Accountants and auditors design internal control systems and analyze financial data. Others for whom training in accounting is valuable include budget analysts; cost estimators; loan officers; financial analysts and personal financial advisors; tax examiners, collectors, and revenue agents; bill and account collectors; and bookkeeping, accounting, and auditing clerks. Recently, accountants have assumed the role of management analysts and are involved in the design, implementation, and maintenance of accounting software systems. Others who perform similar work include computer programmers, computer software engineers, and computer support specialists and systems administrators.

Sources of Additional Information

Information on accredited accounting programs can be obtained from:

➤ AACSB International—Association to Advance Collegiate Schools of Business, 777 South Harbour Island Blvd., Suite 750, Tampa FL 33602-5730. Internet: **http://www.aacsb.edu/accreditation/AccreditedMembers.asp**

Information about careers in certified public accounting and CPA standards and examinations may be obtained from:

➤ American Institute of Certified Public Accountants, 1211 Avenue of the Americas, New York, NY 10036. Internet: **http://www.aicpa.org**

Information on CPA licensure requirements by State may be obtained from:

➤ National Association of State Boards of Accountancy, 150 Fourth Ave. North, Suite 700, Nashville, TN 37219-2417. Internet: **http://www.nasba.org**

Information on careers in management accounting and the CMA designation may be obtained from:

➤ Institute of Management Accountants, 10 Paragon Dr., Montvale, NJ 07645-1718. Internet: **http://www.imanet.org**

Information on the Accredited in Accountancy, Accredited Business Accountant, Accredited Tax Advisor, or Accredited Tax Preparer designation may be obtained from:

➤ Accreditation Council for Accountancy and Taxation, 1010 North Fairfax St., Alexandria, VA 22314.-1574 Internet: **http://www.acatcredentials.org**

Information on careers in internal auditing and the CIA designation may be obtained from:

➤ The Institute of Internal Auditors, 247 Maitland Ave., Altamonte Springs, FL 32701-4201. Internet: **http://www.theiia.org**

Information on careers in information systems auditing and the CISA designation may be obtained from:

➤ Information Systems Audit and Control Association, 3701 Algonquin Rd., Suite 1010, Rolling Meadows, IL 60008. Internet: **http://www.isaca.org**

Information on careers in government accounting and the CGFM designation may be obtained from:

➤ Association of Government Accountants, 2208 Mount Vernon Ave., Alexandria, VA 22301. Internet: **http://www.agacgfm.org**

Information on obtaining positions as an accountant or auditor with the Federal Government is available from the Office of Personnel Management through USAJOBS, the Federal Government's official employment information system. This resource for locating and applying for job opportunities can be accessed through the Internet at **http://www.usajobs.opm.gov** or through an interactive voice response telephone system at (703) 724-1850 or TDD (978) 461-8404. These numbers are not tollfree, and charges may result.

Appraisers and Assessors of Real Estate

(O*NET 13-2021.01 and 13-2021.02)

Significant Points

● Appraisers and assessors must meet licensing and/or certification requirements which vary by State, but generally include specific training requirements, a period of work as a trainee, and passing one or more examinations.

● Although no specific degree is required to enter the occupation, most have at least a bachelor's degree.

● Nearly 4 out of 10 are self-employed; salaried assessors worked primarily in local government, while salaried appraisers worked mainly for real estate firms.

● Employment is expected to grow faster than average.

Nature of the Work

Appraisers and assessors of real estate estimate the value of real property for a variety of purposes, such as to assess property tax, to determine a sales price, or to determine the amount of a mortgage that might be granted on a property. They may be called on to determine the value of any type of real estate, ranging from farmland to a major shopping center, although they often specialize in appraising or assessing only a certain type of real estate such as residential buildings or commercial properties. Assessors determine the value of all properties in a locality for property tax purposes whereas appraisers appraise properties one at a time for a variety of purposes, such as to determine what a good sale price would be for a home or to settle an estate or aid in a divorce settlement.

Valuations of all types of real property are conducted using similar methods, regardless of the type of property or who employs the appraiser or assessor. Appraisers and assessors work in localities they are familiar with so they have a knowledge of any environmental or other concerns that may affect the value of a property. They note any unique characteristics of the property and of the surrounding area, such as a specific architectural style of a building or a major highway located next to the parcel. They also take into account additional aspects of a property like the condition of the foundation and roof of a building or any renovations that may have been done. Additionally, they may take pictures to document a certain room or feature, in addition to taking pictures of the exterior of the building. After visiting the property, the appraiser or assessor will determine the fair value of the property by taking into consideration such things as comparable home sales, lease records, location, previous appraisals, and income potential. They will then put all of their research and observations together in a detailed report, stating not only the value of the parcel but the precise reasoning and methodology of how they arrived at the estimate.

Appraisers have independent clients and focus solely on valuing one property at a time. They primarily work on a client-to-client basis, and make appraisals for a variety of reasons. Real property appraisers often specialize by the type of real estate they appraise, such as residential properties, golf courses, or strip malls. In general, commercial appraisers have the ability to appraise any real property but may generally only appraise property used for commercial purposes, such as stores or hotels. Residential appraisers focus on appraising homes or other residences and only value those that house 1 to 4 families. Other appraisers have a general practice and value any type of real property.

Assessors predominately work for local governments and are responsible for valuing properties so a tax formula can be used to assess property taxes. Unlike appraisers, assessors value entire neighborhoods using mass appraisal techniques to value all the homes in a local neighborhood at one time. Although they do not usually focus on a single property they may assess a single property if the property owner challenges the assessment. They may use a computer-programmed automated valuation model specifically developed for their assigned jurisdictions. In most jurisdictions the entire community must be revalued annually or every few years. Depending on the size of the jurisdiction and the number of staff in an assessor's office, an appraisal firm, often called a revaluation firm, may do much of the work of valuing the properties in the jurisdiction. These results are then officially certified by the assessor.

When properties are reassessed, assessors issue notices of assessments and taxes that each property owner must pay. Assessors must be current on tax assessment procedures and must be able to defend their property assessments, either to the owner directly or at a public hearing, as accurate, since assessors are also responsible for dealing with tax payers who want to contest their assigned property taxes. Assessors also keep a database of every parcel in their jurisdiction labeling the property owner, issued tax assessment, and size of the property, as well as property maps of the jurisdiction that detail the property distribution of the jurisdiction.

Appraisers and assessors write a detailed report of each appraisal. Writing these reports has become faster and easier through the use of laptop computers, allowing them to access data and write at least some of the report on-site. Another computer technology which has impacted this occupation are electronic maps, made by assessor's offices, of a given jurisdiction and its respective property distribution. Appraisers and assessors use these maps to obtain an accurate perspective on the property and buildings surrounding a property. Digital cameras are also commonly used to document the physical appearance of a building or land at the time of appraisal, and the pictures are also used in the documentation of the report.

Working Conditions

Appraisers and assessors spend much of their time researching and writing reports. However, with the advancement of computers and other technologies, such as wireless Internet, time spent in the office has decreased as research can now be done in less time or on-site or at home. Records that once required a visit to a courthouse or city hall can often be found online. This has especially affected

Many real estate appraisers take pictures to document the property in their valuation reports.

self-employed appraisers, often called independent fee appraisers, who make their own office hours, allowing them to spend much more time on-site doing research and less time in their office. Time spent on-site versus in the office also depends on the specialty. For example, residential appraisers tend to spend less time on office work than commercial appraisers, who could spend up to several weeks for one site analyzing documents and writing reports. Appraisers who work for private institutions generally spend most of their time inside the office, making on-site visits when necessary.

Independent fee appraisers tend to work more than a standard 40 hour work week, in addition to working evenings and weekends writing reports. On-site visits usually occur during daylight hours, and according to the client's schedule. Assessors and privately employed appraisers, on the other hand, usually work a standard 40-hour work week. Occasionally they work an evening or Saturday, to speak with a concerned tax payer, for example.

Appraisers and assessors usually conduct on-site appraisal work alone. Their office may consist of just themselves or a small support staff.

Training, Other Qualifications, and Advancement

The requirements that must be met to become a fully qualified appraiser or assessor are complex and vary for appraisers and assessors, by State, and sometimes by the value or type of property to be assessed or appraised. In general, both appraisers and assessors must meet licensing and/or certification requirements which include specific training requirements, a period of work as a trainee, and passing one or more examination. Therefore it is essential that prospective appraisers and assessors check with their State governments to determine the specific education and experience required in their State. There also are additional certifications or association designations that are helpful for advancement as well as continuing education requirements.

Although there are currently no formal degree requirements to become an appraiser or assessor, the majority of practicing appraisers and assessors have at least a bachelor's degree, sometimes in a related field such as economics, finance, or real estate. The specific training courses necessary, however, are not commonly available as part of most bachelor's programs and must be taken separately, usually at community colleges or through appraisal related or assessor-related organizations.

A Federal law requires that any appraiser involved in a Federally-related transaction with a loan amount of $250,000 or more must have a State-issued license or certification. All States also are required to conform to the licensing and certification requirements established by The Appraisal Foundation, a Congressionally-approved organization dedicated to this purpose. The Appraisal Foundation requires that appraisers pass a Foundation-approved State examination as well as meet education and experience requirements. The education requirements include a course and examination on the Uniform Standards of Professional Appraisal Practice (USPAP) set forth by The Appraisal Foundation.

Although Federal standards do not require an appraisal license for those appraisers valuing real property with loan amounts of less than $250,000, many States require any practicing appraiser to obtain a license or certification, regardless of transaction value. In addition, many States have different, more stringent requirements for licensure than The Appraisal Foundation.

The qualifications necessary to become an assessor also vary by State but often are similar to the requirements for becoming an appraiser. In most States, the qualifications are established by a State assessor board that sets education and experience requirements that must be met to obtain a certificate to practice as an assessor. A few States have no State-wide requirements; in these States standards are set by each locality.

The State-issued appraiser licenses currently available are the State Certified General Real Property Appraiser license, which allows an appraiser to value any type of real property regardless of value, and the State Certified Residential Real Property Appraiser license, which allows an appraiser to value any residential unit of 1 to 4 families regardless of value. An additional license, which is recommended or used by many States is the State Licensed Appraiser license, which permits its holder to appraise commercial property up to $250,000 and 1 to 4 family residential units worth up to $1 million.

In most States, those working on their appraiser requirements for licensure are classified as a "trainee." Some of these States have their own training programs while others use the recommended program of the Appraisal Foundation. This program requires 75 hours of specified appraisal education, 15 of which must be on the USPAP, before applying for a trainee position. The number of additional courses one must take while a trainee depends on the State requirements for the license they wish to obtain. For the State Licensed Appraiser license, which is available or required in a majority of States, the candidate must obtain 90 education hours, 15 of which must be on the USPAP, and 2,000 hours of on-the-job training. For the State Certified Residential Appraiser and State Certified General Appraiser licenses, the required education hours are much more rigorous. In addition, the candidate must pass an examination. Commencing in 2008, individuals wishing to become State certified appraisers will need to either possess a college degree or complete a specified number of hours in certain college-level courses.

States mandating assessor certification have requirements similar to those for appraisers. Some States also have more than one level of certification. All candidates must attend State-approved schools and facilities and take basic appraisal courses. Although appraisers value one property at a time while an assessor values many, the methods and techniques used are the same, so the main courses assessors take are the same as those for appraisers. In addition, there is usually a set level of experience hours that must be obtained and all assessor candidates in these States must pass an examination. In some States, assessors must abide by the USPAP standards and are strongly encouraged to follow these standards in most other States. For those States not requiring certificates, the hiring assessor's office will usually require the candidate to also take basic appraisal courses, and at the end of their on-the-job training the candidate often will have accrued sufficient experience hours to meet the requirements for appraisal licenses or certificates. Many assessors also possess a State appraisal license.

Obtaining on-the-job training is an essential part of becoming a fully qualified assessor or appraiser and is required for obtaining a license or certification. Although in the past many appraisers obtained this experience working in financial institutions or real estate offices, a new trend for candidates is to get their initial experience in the office of an independent fee appraiser. Assessors tend to start out in an assessor's office that is willing to provide on-the-job training, although smaller municipalities are unable to provide this experience. An alternate source of experience for aspiring assessors is through a revaluation firm.

For both appraisers and assessors, continuing education is necessary to maintaining a license or certification. The minimum continuing education requirement for appraisers, as set by The Appraisal Foundation, is 14 hours per year. A State-approved course also must be taken on the USPAP every two years. Some States have further requirements. Continuing education can be obtained in any State-approved school or facility, as well as recognized seminars and conferences held by associations or related organizations. Assessors must also fulfill a continuing education requirement in most States, but the amount varies by State.

Appraisers and assessors must possess good analytical skills, mathematical skills, and the ability to pay attention to detail. They also must work well with people and alone. Since they will work with the public, politeness is a must, along with the ability to listen and thoroughly answer any questions about their work.

Many appraisers and assessors choose to become a designated member of a regional or Nationally recognized appraisal or assessor association. Designations are particularly useful in States or types of practices where a license is not mandatory or a certificate has not been established. Designations are another way for an appraiser or assessor to establish themselves in the profession, and are recognizable credentials to show employers a higher level of education and experience. Obtaining a designation often requires much more training and experience than the minimum licensing requirements of The Appraisal Foundation, and usually are awarded after 5 to 10 years of experience. Many appraisers and assessors start with getting their license or certificate and work their way up to a designation. Many appraisal associations have a membership category specifically for trainees, who then can receive full membership after licensure. Since States differ greatly on the requirements to become an assessor, licensure is not necessarily required for membership or designations; however, the imposed designation qualifications tend to be very stringent.

Advancement within the occupation comes with experience. The higher the level of appraiser licensure, for example, the higher the fees an independent fee appraiser may charge. Staying in one particular region or focusing on one type of appraising specialty will also help to establish one's business, reputation, and expertise. Assessors often have a career progression within their office, starting as a trainee and eventually ending up as a senior appraiser or supervisor.

Employment

In 2004, appraisers and assessors of real estate held about 102,000 jobs. Most appraisers and assessors work full-time. Nearly 4 out of 10 are self-employed; virtually all are appraisers. Employment is concentrated in areas with high levels of real estate activity, such as major metropolitan areas. Assessors are more uniformly spread throughout the country than appraisers because every locality has at least one assessor.

About 1 out of 4 worked in local government; almost all were assessors. Another 1 out of 4, mainly appraisers, worked for real estate firms, while a relatively small number worked for financial institutions, such as banks and credit unions.

Most independent fee appraisers' offices are relatively small, consisting of either just themselves or a small staff. However, private institutions such as banks and mortgage broker offices may employ several appraisers in one office. The size of the office employing assessors depends on the size of the local government; in some States assessments are by counties whereas in other States assessments are made by municipalities or other local governments. Therefore a county assessor's office probably would employ more assessors than a small town, which may only employ a single assessor.

Job Outlook

Employment of appraisers and assessors of real estate is expected to grow faster than the average for all occupations over the 2004–14 period. Employment of appraisers will grow with increases in the level of real estate activity and employment of assessors will grow with the increase in the amount of real property to be assessed. However, employment will be held down to a certain extent by productivity increases brought about by the increased use of computers and other technologies, which make for faster valuations and allow appraisers to take on more customers and each assessor to assess more properties. In addition to growth openings, there should be numerous openings due to the need to replace the many appraisers and assessors who are expected to retire or decrease their working hours over the projection period.

Employment opportunities should be best in areas with active real estate markets, such as the East and West coasts and major cities and suburbs. Although opportunities for established appraisers and assessors are expected to be good in these areas, those wishing to enter the occupation may have difficulty locating a training position because increasingly traditional sources of training positions prefer not to take on new trainees.

Appraisers may find the best opportunities as independent fee appraisers because the banks and other financial institutions that, in the past, employed a significant number of appraisers are increasingly contracting out to independent fee appraisers to make loan appraisals on a case-by-case basis, decreasing their need to have appraisers on staff. The increased use of automated valuation models to conduct appraisals for loan and mortgage purposes has also shifted work out of the financial sector.

The cyclical nature of the real estate market will also have a large effect on the future of appraisers, especially those who appraise residential properties. In times of recession, fewer people buy or sell real estate, causing a decrease in the demand for appraisers. However, during a downturn in the residential real estate market appraisers often are able to switch specialties and appraise other types of properties.

Because assessors are needed in every local or State jurisdiction to make assessments for property tax purposes regardless of the state of the local economy, assessors are less affected by fluctuations in the economy and real estate market than appraisers.

Earnings

Median annual earnings of appraisers and assessors of real estate were $43,390 in May 2004. The middle 50 percent earned between $30,820 and $60,110. The lowest 10 percent earned less than $22,300 and the highest 10 percent earned more than $81,240. Median annual earnings of those working for local governments were $38,940. Median annual earnings of those working for real estate firms were $46,330. Generally, those working in urban and coastal regions earned more than those working in rural locations.

Related Occupations

Other occupations that involve the inspection of real estate include construction and building inspectors, real estate brokers and sales agents, and urban and regional planners. Appraisers and assessors must also place a monetary value on properties. Occupations also involved in valuing items include claims adjusters, appraisers, examiners and investigators, as well as cost estimators.

Sources of Additional Information

For more information on licensure requirements, contact:
➤ Appraisal Foundation, 1029 Vermont Ave. NW., Suite 900, Washington DC, 20005-3517. Internet: **http://www.appraisalfoundation.org**

For more information on appraisers of real estate, contact:
➤ Appraisal Institute, 550 W. Van Buren St., Suite 1000, Chicago, IL 60607. Internet: **http://www.appraisalinstitute.org**
➤ National Association of Real Estate Appraisers, 1224 North Nokomis NE., Alexandria, MN 56308. Internet: **http://www.iami.org/narea/home.cfm**
➤ American Society of Appraisers, 555 Herndon Pkwy., Suite 125, Herndon, VA 20170. Internet: **http://www.appraisers.org**

For more information on assessors of real estate, contact:
➤ International Association of Assessing Officers, 314 W 10th St., Kansas City, MO 64105. Internet: **http://www.iaao.org**

Budget Analysts

(O*NET 13-2031.00)

Significant Points

● Competition for jobs is expected.

● Although a bachelor's degree generally is the minimum educational requirement, many employers prefer or require a master's degree.

● About 52 percent of all budget analysts work in Federal, State, and local governments.

Nature of the Work

Deciding how to efficiently distribute limited financial resources is an important challenge in all organizations. In most large and complex organizations, this task would be nearly impossible without budget analysts. These workers play the primary role in the development, analysis, and execution of budgets, which are used to allocate current resources and estimate future financial requirements. Without effective budget analysis and feedback about budgetary problems, many private and public organizations could become bankrupt.

Budget analysts can be found in private industry, nonprofit organizations, and the public sector. In private sector firms, a budget analyst examines budgets and seeks new ways to improve efficiency and increase profits. Although analysts working in nonprofit and governmental organizations usually are not concerned with profits, they still try to find the most efficient distribution of funds and other resources among various departments and programs.

Budget analysts have many responsibilities in these organizations, but their primary task is providing advice and technical assistance in the preparation of annual budgets. At the beginning of each budget cycle, managers and department heads submit proposed operational and financial plans to budget analysts for review. These plans outline prospective programs, including proposed funding increases and new initiatives, estimated costs and expenses, and capital expenditures needed to finance these programs.

Analysts examine the budget estimates or proposals for completeness; accuracy; and conformance with established procedures, regulations, and organizational objectives. Sometimes, they employ cost-benefit analysis to review financial requests, assess program tradeoffs, and explore alternative funding methods. They also examine past and current budgets and research economic and financial developments that affect the organization's spending. This process enables analysts to evaluate proposals in terms of the organization's priorities and financial resources.

After the initial review process, budget analysts consolidate individual departmental budgets into operating and capital budget summaries. These summaries contain comments and statements that support or argue against funding requests. Budget summaries then are submitted to senior management, or, as is often the case in local and State governments, to appointed or elected officials. Budget analysts then help the chief operating officer, agency head, or other top managers analyze the proposed plan and devise possible alternatives if the projected results are unsatisfactory. The final decision to approve the budget, however, usually is made by the organization head in a private firm or by elected officials in government, such as the State legislature.

Throughout the remainder of the year, analysts periodically monitor the budget by reviewing reports and accounting records to determine if allocated funds have been spent as specified.

Budget analysts play the primary role in the development, analysis, and execution of budgets.

Working Conditions

Budget analysts usually work in a comfortable office setting. Long hours are common among these workers, especially during the initial development and midyear and final reviews of budgets. The pressures of deadlines and tight work schedules during these periods can be stressful, and analysts usually are required to work more than the routine 40 hours a week.

Budget analysts spend the majority of their time working independently, compiling and analyzing data and preparing budget proposals. Nevertheless, their schedules sometimes are interrupted by special budget requests, meetings, and training sessions. Some budget analysts travel to obtain budget details and explanations of various programs from coworkers, or to personally verify funding allocation.

Training, Other Qualifications, and Advancement

Private firms and government agencies generally require candidates for budget analyst positions to have at least a bachelor's degree, but many prefer or require a master's degree. Within the Federal Government, a bachelor's degree in any field is sufficient for an entry-level budget analyst position, but, again, master's degrees are preferred. State and local governments have varying requirements, but a bachelor's degree in one of many areas—accounting, finance, business, public administration, economics, statistics, political science, or sociology—may qualify one for employment. Many States, especially larger, more urban States, require a master's degree. Sometimes a degree in a field closely related to that of the employing industry or organization, such as engineering, may be preferred. Some firms prefer candidates with a degree in business because business courses emphasize quantitative and analytical skills. Many government employers prefer candidates with strong analytic and policy analysis backgrounds that may be obtained through such majors as political science, economics, public administration, or public finance. Occasionally, budget-related or finance-related work experience can be substituted for formal education.

Because developing a budget involves manipulating numbers and requires strong analytical skills, courses in statistics or accounting are helpful, regardless of the prospective budget analyst's major field of study. Financial analysis is automated in almost every organization and, therefore, familiarity with word-processing programs and with financial software packages used in budget analysis often is required. Software packages commonly used by budget analysts include electronic spreadsheet, database, and graphics programs. Employers usually prefer candidates who already possess these computer skills.

Those seeking a career as a budget analyst also must be able to work under strict time constraints. Strong oral and written communication skills are essential for analysts because they must prepare, present, and defend budget proposals to decision makers.

In addition, budget analysts, along with all other financial officers, must abide by strict ethical standards. Integrity, objectivity, and confidentiality are all important to budget analysis, and budget analysts must avoid any personal conflicts of interest.

Entry-level budget analysts may receive some formal training when they begin their jobs, but most employers feel that the best training is obtained by working through one complete budget cycle. During the cycle, which typically is 1 year, analysts become familiar with the various steps involved in the budgeting process. The Federal Government, on the other hand, offers extensive on-the-job and classroom training for entry-level trainees. In addition to on-the-job training, budget analysts are encouraged to participate in various professional development classes throughout their careers.

If deviations appear between the approved budget and actual performance, budget analysts may write a report providing reasons for the variations, along with recommendations for new or revised budget procedures. To avoid or alleviate deficits, budget analysts may recommend program cuts or reallocation of excess funds. They also inform program managers and others within their organization of the status and availability of funds in different budget accounts. Before any changes are made to an existing program, or before a new one is implemented, a budget analyst must assess the program's efficiency and effectiveness. Analysts also may be involved in long-range planning activities such as projecting future budget needs.

The amount of data and information that budget analysts are able to analyze has greatly increased through the use of computerized financial software programs. The analysts also make extensive use of spreadsheet, database, and word-processing software.

Budget analysts have seen their role broadened as limited funding has led to downsizing and restructuring throughout private industry and government. Not only do they develop guidelines and policies governing the formulation and maintenance of the budget, but they also measure organizational performance, assess the effects of various programs and policies on the budget, and help draft budget-related legislation. In addition, budget analysts sometimes conduct training sessions for company or government agency personnel regarding new budget procedures.

Some government budget analysts employed at the Federal, State, or local level may earn the Certified Government Financial Manager (CGFM) designation granted by the Association of Government Accountants. Other government financial officers also may earn this designation. To do so, candidates must have a minimum of a bachelor's degree, 24 hours of study in financial management, and 2 years of government work experience in financial management. They also must pass a series of three exams that cover topics on the organization and structure of government; governmental accounting, financial reporting, and budgeting; and financial management and control. To maintain the CGFM designation, individuals must complete 80 hours of continuing professional education every 2 years.

Budget analysts start their careers with limited responsibilities. In the Federal Government, for example, beginning budget analysts compare projected costs with prior expenditures, consolidate and enter data prepared by others, and assist higher grade analysts by doing research. As analysts progress in their careers, they begin to develop and formulate budget estimates and justification statements, perform detailed analyses of budget requests, write statements supporting funding requests, advise program managers and others on the status and availability of funds for various budget activities, and present and defend budget proposals to senior managers.

Beginning analysts usually work under close supervision. Capable entry-level analysts can be promoted to intermediate-level positions within 1 to 2 years, and then to senior positions within a few more years. Progressing to higher levels means added budgetary responsibility, and can lead to a supervisory role. Because of the importance and high visibility of their jobs, senior budget analysts are prime candidates for promotion to management positions in various parts of their organizations, or with other organizations with which they have worked.

Employment
Budget analysts held 58,000 jobs throughout private industry and government in 2004. Federal, State, and local governments are major employers, accounting for 52 percent of budget analyst jobs. About 23 percent worked for the Federal Government. Many other budget analysts worked in manufacturing, financial services, or management services. Other employers include schools and hospitals.

Job Outlook
Competition for budget analyst jobs is expected over the 2004-14 projection period. Candidates with a master's degree should have the best job opportunities. Familiarity with computer financial software packages also should enhance a jobseeker's employment prospects.

Employment of budget analysts is expected to grow about as fast as the average for all occupations through 2014. Employment growth will be driven by the continuing demand for sound financial analysis in both the public and the private sectors. In addition to employment growth, many job openings will result from the need to replace experienced budget analysts who transfer to other occupations or leave the labor force.

The increasing efficiency of computer applications used in budget analysis has increased worker productivity by enabling analysts to process more data in less time. However, because budget analysts now have much more data available to them, their jobs are becoming more complicated. In addition, as businesses and other organizations become more complex and specialized, budget planning and financial control will demand greater attention. These factors should offset any adverse effects of computer applications on employment of budget analysts.

In coming years, all types of organizations will continue to rely heavily on budget analysts to develop and analyze budgets. Because of the importance of financial analysis performed by budget analysts, employment of these workers should remain relatively unaffected by any downsizing in the Nation's workplaces. In addition, budget analysts usually are less subject to layoffs than are many other workers during economic downturns because financial and budget reports must be completed during periods of both economic growth and slowdowns.

Earnings
Salaries of budget analysts vary widely by experience, education, and employer. Median annual earnings of budget analysts in May 2004 were $56,040. The middle 50 percent earned between $45,170 and $70,530. The lowest 10 percent earned less than $36,850, and the highest 10 percent earned more than $87,380. Median annual earnings in the industries employing the largest numbers of budget analysts in May 2004 were:

Federal Government	$61,640
Local government	52,520
State government	51,870

According to a 2005 survey conducted by Robert Half International—a staffing services firm specializing in accounting and finance—starting salaries of financial, budget, treasury, and cost analysts in small companies ranged from $29,750 to $36,250. In large companies, starting salaries ranged from $33,500 to $40,000.

In the Federal Government, budget analysts usually started as trainees earning $24,677 or $30,567 year in 2005. Candidates with a master's degree began at $37,390. Beginning salaries were slightly higher in areas where the prevailing local pay level was higher. The average annual salary in 2005 for budget analysts employed by the Federal Government in nonsupervisory, supervisory, and managerial positions was $67,767.

Related Occupations
Budget analysts analyze and interpret financial data, make recommendations for the future, and assist in the implementation of new ideas and financial strategies. Other workers who have similar duties include accountants and auditors, cost estimators, economists, financial analysts and personal financial advisors, financial managers, loan counselors and officers, and management analysts.

Sources of Additional Information
Information about career opportunities as a budget analyst may be available from your State or local employment service.

Information on careers in government financial management and the CGFM designation may be obtained from:
➤ Association of Government Accountants, 2208 Mount Vernon Ave., Alexandria, VA 22301. Internet: **http://www.agacgfm.org**

Information on careers in budget analysis at the State government level may be obtained from:
➤ National Association of State Budget Officers, Hall of the States Building, Suite 642, 444 North Capitol St. NW., Washington, DC 20001-1511. Internet: **http://www.nasbo.org**

Information on obtaining positions as occupational health and safety specialists and technicians with the Federal Government is available from the Office of Personnel Management through USAJOBS, the Federal Government's official employment information system. This resource for locating and applying for job opportunities can be accessed through the Internet at **http://www.usajobs.opm.gov** or through an interactive voice response telephone system at (703) 724-1850 or TDD (978) 461-8404. These numbers are not tollfree, and charges may result.

Claims Adjusters, Appraisers, Examiners, and Investigators

(O*NET 13-1031.01, 13-1031.02, 13-1032.00)

Significant Points

- Adjusters and examiners investigate insurance claims, negotiate settlements, and authorize payments; appraisers assess the cost or value of an insured item; investigators deal with claims about which there is a question of liability and where fraud or criminal activity is suspected.

- Licensing and continuing education requirements vary by State.

- College graduates have the best opportunities; competition will be keen for jobs as investigators, because this occupation attracts many qualified people.

Nature of the Work

Individuals and businesses purchase insurance policies to protect against monetary losses. In the event of a loss, policyholders submit claims, or requests for payment, seeking compensation for their loss. Adjusters, appraisers, examiners, and investigators work primarily for property and casualty insurance companies, for whom they handle a wide variety of claims alleging property damage, liability, or bodily injury. Their main role is to investigate the claims, negotiate settlements, and authorize payments to claimants, all the while mindful not to violate the claimant's rights under Federal and State privacy laws. They must determine whether the customer's insurance policy covers the loss and how much of the loss should be paid to the claimant. Although many adjusters, appraisers, examiners, and investigators have overlapping functions and may even perform the same job, the insurance industry generally assigns specific roles to each of these claims workers.

Adjusters plan and schedule the work required to process a claim that would follow, for example, an automobile accident or damage to one's home caused by a storm. They investigate claims by interviewing the claimant and witnesses, consulting police and hospital records, and inspecting property damage to determine the extent of the company's liability. Adjusters may consult with other professionals, such as accountants, architects, construction workers, engineers, lawyers, and physicians, who can offer a more expert evaluation of a claim. The information gathered, including photographs and written or audio-taped or video-taped statements, is set down in a report that is then used to evaluate the associated claim. When the policyholder's claim is legitimate, the claims adjuster negotiates with the claimant and settles the claim. When claims are contested, adjusters will work with attorneys and expert witnesses to defend the insurer's position.

Many companies centralize claims adjustment in a claims center, where the cost of repair is determined and a check is issued immediately. More complex cases, usually involving bodily injury, are referred to senior adjusters. Some adjusters work with multiple types of insurance; however, most specialize in homeowner claims, business losses, automotive damage, or workers' compensation.

Claimants can opt not to rely on the services of their insurance company's adjuster and may instead choose to hire a public adjuster. These workers assist clients in preparing and presenting claims to insurance companies and in trying to negotiate a fair settlement. They perform the same services as adjusters who work

directly for companies; however, they work in the best interests of the client, rather than the insurance company.

Claims examiners within property and casualty insurance firms may have duties similar to those of an adjuster, but often their primary job is to review the claims submitted in order to ensure that proper guidelines have been followed. They may assist adjusters with complex and complicated claims or when a disaster suddenly greatly increases the volume of claims. Most claims examiners work for life or health insurance companies. In health insurance companies, examiners review health-related claims to see whether costs are reasonable on the basis of the diagnosis. The examiners are provided with guides that supply information on the average period of disability, the expected treatments, and the average hospital stay, for patients with the various ailments for which a claim may be submitted. Examiners check claim applications for completeness and accuracy, interview medical specialists, and consult policy files to verify the information reported in a claim. Examiners will then either authorize the appropriate payment or refer the claim to an investigator for a more thorough review. Claims examiners usually specialize in group or individual insurance plans and in hospital, dental, or prescription drug claims.

In life insurance, claims examiners review the causes of death, particularly in the case of an accident, because most life insurance policies pay additional benefits if a death is accidental. Claims examiners also may review new applications for life insurance to make sure that the applicants have no serious illnesses that would make them a high risk to insure and thus disqualify them from obtaining insurance.

Another occupation that plays an important role in the accurate settlement of claims is that of the *appraiser*, whose role is to assess the cost or value of an insured item. The majority of appraisers employed by insurance companies and independent adjusting firms are *auto damage appraisers*. These appraisers inspect damaged vehicles after an accident and estimate the cost of repairs. This information is then relayed to the adjuster, who incorporates the appraisal into the settlement. Auto damage appraisers are valued by insurance companies because they can provide an unbiased judgment of repair costs. Otherwise, the companies would have to rely on auto mechanics' estimates, which might be unreasonably high.

Many claims adjusters and auto damage appraisers are equipped with laptop computers from which they can download the necessary forms and files from insurance company databases. Many adjusters and appraisers use digital cameras, which allow photographs of the damage to be sent to the company via the Internet. Many also input information about the damage directly into their computers, where software programs produce estimates of damage on standard forms. These new technologies allow for faster and more efficient processing of claims.

When adjusters or examiners suspect fraud, they refer the claim to an investigator. *Insurance investigators* in an insurance company's special investigative unit handle claims in which the company suspects fraudulent or criminal activity, such as arson, falsified workers' disability claims, staged accidents, or unnecessary medical treatments. The severity of insurance fraud cases can vary greatly, from claimants simply overstating the damage to a vehicle to complicated fraud rings responsible for many claimants and supported by dishonest doctors, lawyers, and even insurance personnel.

Investigators usually start with a database search to obtain background information on claimants and witnesses. Investigators can access certain personal information and identify Social Security numbers, aliases, driver's license numbers, addresses, phone numbers, criminal records, and past claims histories to establish whether a claimant has ever attempted insurance fraud. Then, investigators may visit claimants and witnesses to obtain a recorded statement,

After evaluating insurance claims, claims adjusters report their findings and make recommendations.

take photographs, and inspect facilities, such as doctors' offices, to determine whether the doctors have a proper license. Investigators often consult with legal counsel and can be expert witnesses in court cases.

Often, investigators also perform surveillance work. For example, in a case involving fraudulent workers' compensation claims, an investigator may covertly observe the claimant for several days or even weeks. If the investigator observes the subject performing an activity that is ruled out by injuries stated in a workers' compensation claim, the investigator will take video or still photographs to document the activity and report it to the insurance company.

Working Conditions
Working environments of claims adjusters, appraisers, examiners, and investigators vary greatly. Most claims examiners employed by life and health insurance companies work a standard 5-day, 40-hour week in a typical office environment. Many claims adjusters and auto damage appraisers, however, often work outside the office, inspecting damaged buildings and automobiles. Adjusters who inspect damaged buildings must be wary of potential hazards such as collapsed roofs and floors, as well as weakened structures.

In general, adjusters are able to arrange their work schedules to accommodate evening and weekend appointments with clients. This accommodation sometimes results in adjusters working irregular schedules or more than 40 hours a week, especially when they have a lot of claims to investigate. Some report to the office every morning to get their assignments, while others simply call in from home and spend their days traveling to claim sites. New technology, such as laptop computers and cellular telephones, is making telecommuting easier for claims adjusters and auto damage appraisers. Many adjusters work inside their office only a few hours a week, while others conduct their business entirely out of their home and automobile. Occasionally, experienced adjusters must be away from home for days—for example, when they travel to the scene of a disaster such as a tornado, hurricane, or flood—to work with local adjusters and government officials. Adjusters often are called

to work in the event of such emergencies and may have to work 50 or 60 hours a week until all claims are resolved.

Insurance investigators often work irregular hours because of the need to conduct surveillance and contact people who are not available during normal working hours. Early morning, evening, and weekend work is common. Some days, investigators will spend all day in the office, searching databases, making telephone calls, and writing reports. Other times, they may be away, performing surveillance activities or interviewing witnesses. Some of the work can involve confrontation with claimants and others involved in a case, so the job can be stressful and dangerous.

Training, Other Qualifications, and Advancement
Training and entry requirements vary widely for claims adjusters, appraisers, examiners, and investigators. Although many in these occupations do not have a college degree, most companies prefer to hire college graduates. No specific college major is recommended, but a variety of backgrounds can be an asset. A claims adjuster who, for example, has a business or an accounting background might specialize in claims of financial loss due to strikes, breakdowns of equipment, or damage to merchandise. College training in architecture or engineering is helpful in adjusting industrial claims, such as those involving damage from fires or other accidents. Some claims adjusters and examiners apply expertise acquired through specialized professional training to adjust claims. A legal background can be beneficial to someone handling workers' compensation and product liability cases. A medical background is useful for those examiners working on medical and life insurance claims.

Because they often work closely with claimants, witnesses, and other insurance professionals, claims adjusters and examiners must be able to communicate effectively with others. Knowledge of computer applications also is extremely helpful. In addition, a valid driver's license and a good driving record are required for workers for whom travel is an important aspect of their job. Some companies require applicants to pass a series of written aptitude tests designed to measure their communication, analytical, and general mathematical skills.

Licensing requirements for these workers vary by State. Some States have very few requirements, while others require either the completion of prelicensing education or a satisfactory score on a licensing exam. Fulfilling the requirements for earning a voluntary professional designation may, in some cases, be substituted for completing the exam. In some States, claims adjusters employed by insurance companies can work under the company license and need not become licensed themselves. Separate or additional requirements may apply for public adjusters. For example, some States require public adjusters to file a surety bond.

Continuing education in claims is very important for claims adjusters, appraisers, examiners, and investigators, because Federal and State laws and court decisions affect how claims are handled or who is covered by insurance policies. Also, examiners working on life and health claims must be familiar with new medical procedures and prescription drugs. Some States that require licensing also require a certain number of continuing education credits per year in order to renew the license. These credits can be obtained from a number of sources. Many companies offer training sessions to inform their employees of industry changes. A number of schools and associations give courses and seminars on various topics having to with claims. Correspondence courses via the Internet are making long-distance learning possible. Workers also can earn continuing education credits by writing articles for claims publications or by giving lectures and presentations. In addition, numerous adjusters and examiners choose to earn professional certifications and designations for independent recognition of their professional expertise. Although requirements for these designations vary, many entail at least 5 to 10 years of experience in the claims field and the successful completion of an examination; in addition, a certain number of continuing education credits must be earned each year to retain the designation.

For auto damage appraiser jobs, insurance companies and independent adjusting firms typically prefer to hire persons with experience as an estimator for, or manager of, an auto body repair shop. An appraiser must know how to repair vehicles in order to identify and estimate damage, and technical skills are essential. While auto damage appraisers do not require a college education, most companies prefer to hire persons with formal training. Many vocational colleges offer 2-year programs in auto body repair on how to estimate and repair damaged vehicles. Some States require auto damage appraisers to be licensed, and certification also may be required or preferred. Basic computer skills are an important qualification for many auto damage appraiser positions. As with adjusters and examiners, continuing education is important because of the continual introduction of new car models and repair techniques.

Most insurance companies prefer to hire former law enforcement officers or private investigators as insurance investigators. Many experienced claims adjusters or examiners also become investigators. Licensing requirements vary among States. Most employers look for individuals with ingenuity who are persistent and assertive. Investigators should not be afraid of confrontation, should communicate well, and should be able to think on their feet. Good interviewing and interrogation skills also are important and usually are acquired in earlier careers in law enforcement.

Beginning claims adjusters, appraisers, examiners, and investigators work on small claims under the supervision of an experienced worker. As they learn more about claims investigation and settlement, they are assigned larger, more complex claims. Trainees are promoted as they demonstrate competence in handling assignments and progress in their coursework. Employees who demonstrate competence in claims work or administrative skills may be promoted to more responsible managerial or administrative jobs. Similarly, claims investigators may rise to supervisor or manager of the investigations department. Once they achieve a certain level of expertise, many choose to start their own independent adjusting or auto damage appraising firms.

Employment

Adjusters, appraisers, examiners, and investigators held about 263,000 jobs in 2004. Only 5 percent of these jobs were held by auto damage insurance appraisers. Insurance carriers, agencies, brokerages, and related industries, such as private claims adjusting companies, employed more than 8 out of 10 claims adjusters, appraisers, examiners, and investigators. Relatively few adjusters, appraisers, examiners, and investigators were self-employed.

Job Outlook

Employment of claims adjusters, appraisers, examiners, and investigators is expected to grow about as fast as the average for all occupations over the 2004–14 period. College graduates have the best opportunities. Numerous job openings also will result from the need to replace workers who transfer to other occupations or leave the labor force.

Many insurance carriers are downsizing their claims staff in an effort to contain costs. Larger companies are relying more on customer service representatives in call centers to handle the recording of the necessary details of the claim, allowing adjusters to spend more of their time investigating claims. New technology is reducing the amount of time it takes for an adjuster to complete a claim, thereby increasing the number of claims that one adjuster can handle. However, as long as more insurance policies are being sold to accommodate a growing population, there will be a need for adjusters, appraisers, examiners, and investigators. Further, as the elderly population increases, there will be a greater need for health care, resulting in more health insurance claims.

Despite recent gains in productivity resulting from technological advances, these jobs are not easily automated. Adjusters still are needed to contact policyholders, inspect damaged property, and consult with experts. Although the number of claims in litigation and the number and complexity of insurance fraud cases are expected to increase over the next decade, demand for insurance investigators is not expected to grow significantly, because technology such as the Internet, which reduces the amount of time it takes to perform background checks, will allow investigators to handle more cases. Competition for investigator jobs will remain keen because the occupation attracts many qualified people, including retirees from law enforcement and military careers, as well as experienced claims adjusters and examiners who choose to get their investigator license.

As with claims adjusters, examiners, and investigators, employment of auto damage appraisers should grow about as fast as the average for all occupations. Insurance companies and agents continue to sell growing numbers of auto insurance policies, leading to more claims being filed that require the attention of an auto damage appraiser. The work of this occupation is not easily automated, because most appraisals require an onsite inspection. However, employment growth will be limited by downsizing in the insurance industry and by the implementation of new technology that is making auto damage appraisers more efficient. In addition, some insurance companies are opening their own repair facilities, which may reduce the need for auto damage appraisers.

Earnings

Earnings of claims adjusters, appraisers, examiners, and investigators vary significantly. Median annual earnings were $44,220 in May 2004. The middle 50 percent earned between $33,900 and $57,410. The lowest 10 percent earned less than $27,220, and the highest 10 percent earned more than $72,620.

Many claims adjusters, especially those who work for insurance companies, receive additional bonuses or benefits as part of their job. Adjusters often are furnished a laptop computer, a cellular telephone, and a company car or are reimbursed for the use of their own vehicle for business purposes.

Median annual earnings of auto damage insurance appraisers were $45,330 in May 2004. The middle 50 percent earned between $37,210 and $54,280. The lowest 10 percent earned less than $29,550, and the highest 10 percent earned more than $63,220.

Related Occupations

Property-casualty insurance adjusters and life and health insurance examiners must determine the validity of a claim and negotiate a settlement. They also are responsible for determining how much to reimburse the client. Occupations similar to those of claims adjusters, appraisers, examiners, and investigators include cost estimators; bill and account collectors; medical records and health information technicians; billing and posting clerks; credit authorizers, checkers, and clerks; and bookkeeping, accounting, and auditing clerks. In determining the validity of a claim, insurance adjusters must inspect the damage in order to assess the magnitude of the loss. Workers who perform similar duties include fire inspectors and investigators and construction and building inspectors.

To ensure that company practices and procedures are followed, property and casualty examiners review insurance claims to which a claims adjuster has already proposed a settlement. Others in occupations that review documents for accuracy and compliance with a given set of rules and regulations are tax examiners and revenue agents, as well as accountants and auditors.

Insurance investigators detect and investigate fraudulent claims and criminal activity. Their work is similar to that of private detectives and investigators.

Like automotive body and related repairers and automotive service technicians and mechanics, auto damage appraisers must be familiar with the structure and functions of various automobiles and their parts.

Sources of Additional Information

General information about a career as a claims adjuster, appraiser, examiner, or investigator is available from the home offices of many insurance companies.

Information about licensing requirements for claims adjusters may be obtained from the department of insurance in each State.

For information about professional designation and training programs, contact any of the following organizations:

➤ American Institute for Chartered Property Casualty Underwriters and the Insurance Institute of America, 720 Providence Rd., P.O. Box 3016, Malvern, PA 19355–0716. Internet: **http://www.aicpcu.org**
➤ American College, 270 South Bryn Mawr Ave., Bryn Mawr, PA 19010–2196. Internet: **http://www.theamericancollege.edu**
➤ International Claim Association, 1255 23rd St. N.W., Washington, DC 20037. Internet: **http://www.claim.org**

Information on careers in auto damage appraising can be obtained from:

➤ Independent Automotive Damage Appraisers Association, P.O. Box 12291 Columbus, GA 31917–2291. Internet: **http://www.iada.org**

Cost Estimators

(O*NET 13-1051.00)

Significant Points

- More than half of all cost estimators work in the construction industry, and another 17 percent are employed in manufacturing industries.

- Growth of the construction industry will account for most new jobs.

- In construction and manufacturing, job prospects should be best for those with industry work experience and a bachelor's degree in a related field.

Nature of the Work

Accurately forecasting the cost of future projects is vital to the survival of any business. Cost estimators develop the cost information that business owners or managers need to make a bid for a contract or to decide whether a proposed new product will be profitable. They also determine which endeavors are making a profit.

Regardless of the industry in which they work, estimators compile and analyze data on all of the factors that can influence costs—such as materials, labor, location, and special machinery requirements, including computer hardware and software. Job duties vary widely depending on the type and size of the project.

The methods and motivations for estimating costs can differ greatly by industry. On a construction project, for example, the estimating process begins with the decision to submit a bid. After reviewing various preliminary drawings and specifications, the estimator visits the site of the proposed project. The estimator needs to gather information on access to the site and the availability of

electricity, water, and other services, as well as on surface topography and drainage. The information developed during the site visit usually is recorded in a signed report that is included in the final project estimate.

After the site visit, the estimator determines the quantity of materials and labor the firm will need to furnish. This process, called the quantity survey or "takeoff," involves completing standard estimating forms, filling in dimensions, numbers of units, and other information. A cost estimator working for a general contractor, for example, estimates the costs of all of the items that the contractor must provide. Although subcontractors estimate their costs as part of their own bidding process, the general contractor's cost estimator often analyzes bids made by subcontractors as well. Also during the takeoff process, the estimator must make decisions concerning equipment needs, the sequence of operations, the size of the crew required, and physical constraints at the site. Allowances for wasted materials, inclement weather, shipping delays, and other factors that may increase costs also must be incorporated in the estimate.

On completion of the quantity surveys, the estimator prepares a cost summary for the entire project, including the costs of labor, equipment, materials, subcontracts, overhead, taxes, insurance, markup, and any other costs that may affect the project. The chief estimator then prepares the bid proposal for submission to the owner.

Construction cost estimators also may be employed by the project's architect or owner to estimate costs or to track actual costs relative to bid specifications as the project develops. In large construction companies employing more than one estimator, it is common practice for estimators to specialize. For example, one may estimate only electrical work and another may concentrate on excavation, concrete, and forms.

In manufacturing and other firms, cost estimators usually are assigned to the engineering, cost, or pricing department. The estimator's goal in manufacturing is to accurately estimate the costs associated with making products. The job may begin when management requests an estimate of the costs associated with a major redesign of an existing product or the development of a new product or production process. When estimating the cost of developing a new product, for example, the estimator works with engineers, first reviewing blueprints or conceptual drawings to determine the machining operations, tools, gauges, and materials that would be required for the job. The estimator then prepares a parts list and determines whether it is more efficient to produce or to purchase the parts. To do this, the estimator must initiate inquiries for price information from potential suppliers. The next step is to determine the cost of manufacturing each component of the product. Some high-technology products require a considerable amount of computer programming during the design phase. The cost of software development is one of the fastest growing and most difficult activities to estimate. As a result, some cost estimators now specialize in estimating only computer software development and related costs.

The cost estimator then prepares time-phase charts and learning curves. Time-phase charts indicate the time required for tool design and fabrication, tool "debugging"—finding and correcting all problems—manufacturing of parts, assembly, and testing. Learning curves graphically represent the rate at which the performance of workers producing parts for the new product improves with practice. These curves are commonly called "cost reduction" curves, because many problems—such as engineering changes, rework, shortages of parts, and lack of operator skills—diminish as the number of units produced increases, resulting in lower unit costs.

Using all of this information, the estimator then calculates the standard labor hours necessary to produce a specified number of units. Standard labor hours are then converted to dollar values, to which are added factors for waste, overhead, and profit to yield the unit cost in dollars. The estimator then compares the cost of purchasing parts with the firm's cost of manufacturing them to determine which is cheaper.

Computers play an integral role in cost estimation, because estimating often involves complex mathematical calculations and requires advanced mathematical techniques. For example, to undertake a parametric analysis (a process used to estimate project costs on a per unit basis, subject to the specific requirements of a project), cost estimators use a computer database containing information on the costs and conditions of many other similar projects. Although computers cannot be used for the entire estimating process, they can relieve estimators of much of the drudgery associated with routine, repetitive, and time-consuming calculations. Computer word-processing and spreadsheet software is used to produce all of the necessary documentation for cost-estimation results, leaving estimators more time to study and analyze projects.

Operations research, production control, cost, and price analysts who work for government agencies may do significant amounts of cost estimating in the course of their regular duties. In addition, the duties of construction managers may include estimating costs. (For more information, see the statements on operations research analysts and construction managers elsewhere in the *Handbook*.)

Working Conditions

Although estimators spend most of their time in an office, construction estimators must make visits to project worksites that can be dusty, dirty, and occasionally hazardous. Likewise, estimators in manufacturing

Cost estimators compile and analyze data on all factors that can influence the costs involved in a project.

must spend time on the factory floor, where it also can be noisy and dirty. In some industries, frequent travel between a firm's headquarters and its subsidiaries or subcontractors may be required.

Although estimators normally work a 40-hour week, overtime is common. Cost estimators often work under pressure and stress, especially when facing bid deadlines. Inaccurate estimating can cause a firm to lose a bid or to lose money on a job that was not accurately estimated.

Training, Other Qualifications, and Advancement

Job entry requirements for cost estimators vary by industry. In the construction industry, employers increasingly prefer individuals with a degree in building construction, construction management, construction science, engineering, or architecture. However, most construction estimators also have considerable construction experience, gained through work in the industry, internships, or cooperative education programs. Applicants with a thorough knowledge of construction materials, costs, and procedures in areas ranging from heavy construction to electrical work, plumbing systems, or masonry work have a competitive edge.

In manufacturing industries, employers prefer to hire individuals with a degree in engineering, physical science, operations research, mathematics, or statistics; or in accounting, finance, business, economics, or a related subject. In most industries, great emphasis is placed on experience involving quantitative techniques.

Cost estimators should have an aptitude for mathematics; be able to quickly analyze, compare, and interpret detailed but sometimes poorly defined information; and be able to make sound and accurate judgments based on this information. Assertiveness and self-confidence in presenting and supporting one's conclusions are important, as are strong communications and interpersonal skills, because estimators may work as part of a project team alongside managers, owners, engineers, and design professionals. Cost estimators also need knowledge of computers, including word-processing and spreadsheet packages. In some instances, familiarity with special estimation software or programming skills also may be required.

Regardless of their background, estimators receive much training on the job, because every company has its own way of handling estimates. Working with an experienced estimator, newcomers become familiar with each step in the process. Those with no experience reading construction specifications or blueprints first learn that aspect of the work. Then they may accompany an experienced estimator to the construction site or shop floor, where they observe the work being done, take measurements, or perform other routine tasks. As they become more knowledgeable, estimators learn how to tabulate quantities and dimensions from drawings and how to select the appropriate prices for materials.

For most estimators, advancement takes the form of higher pay and prestige. Some move into management positions, such as project manager for a construction firm or manager of the industrial engineering department for a manufacturer. Others may go into business for themselves as consultants, providing estimating services for a fee to government or to construction or manufacturing firms.

Many colleges and universities include cost estimating as part of bachelor's and associate's degree curriculums in civil engineering, industrial engineering, and construction management or construction engineering technology. In addition, cost estimating is a significant part of many master's degree programs in construction science or construction management. Organizations representing cost estimators, such as the Association for the Advancement of Cost Engineering (AACE International) and the Society of Cost Estimating and Analysis (SCEA), also sponsor educational and professional development programs. These programs help students, estimators-in-training, and experienced estimators stay abreast of changes affecting the profession. Specialized courses and programs in cost-estimating techniques and procedures also are offered by many technical schools, community colleges, and universities.

Voluntary certification can be valuable to cost estimators because it provides professional recognition of the estimator's competence and experience. In some instances, individual employers may even require professional certification for employment. Both AACE International and SCEA administer certification programs. To become certified, estimators usually must have between 2 and 8 years of estimating experience and must pass an examination. In addition, certification requirements may include the publication of at least one article or paper in the field.

Employment

Cost estimators held about 198,000 jobs in 2004. About 58 percent of estimators were in the construction industry, and another 17 percent were employed in manufacturing. The remainder worked in a wide range of other industries.

Cost estimators work throughout the country, usually in or near major industrial, commercial, and government centers and in cities and suburban areas undergoing rapid change or development.

Job Outlook

Overall employment of cost estimators is expected to grow faster than average for all occupations through the year 2014. In addition to openings created by growth, some job openings will arise from the need to replace workers who transfer to other occupations or leave the labor force. In construction and manufacturing—the primary employers of cost estimators—job prospects should be best for those with industry work experience and a bachelor's degree in a related field.

Employment growth in the construction industry, in which most cost estimators are employed, will account for most new jobs in this occupation. Construction and repair of highways, streets, and bridges, as well as construction of more subway systems, airports, water and sewage systems, and electric power plants and transmission lines, will stimulate demand for many more cost estimators. Similarly, increasing population and changing demographics will boost demand for residential construction and remodeling and school construction and repair, spurring demand for more cost estimators. As the population ages, the demand for nursing and extended-care facilities will increase. Job prospects in construction should be best for cost estimators who have a degree in construction management or in construction science, engineering, or architecture and who have practical experience in various phases of construction or in a specialty craft area.

Employment of cost estimators also will grow in manufacturing, but not as fast as in construction, as firms continue to use cost estimators to identify and control operating costs. Experienced estimators with degrees in engineering, science, mathematics, business administration, or economics should have the best job prospects in manufacturing.

Earnings

Salaries of cost estimators vary widely by experience, education, size of firm, and industry. Median annual earnings of cost estimators in May 2004 were $49,940. The middle 50 percent earned between $38,420 and $65,620. The lowest 10 percent earned less than $30,240, and the highest 10 percent earned more than $84,870. Median annual earnings in the industries employing the largest numbers of cost estimators in May 2004 were:

Nonresidential building construction	$56,570
Building equipment contractors	53,310
Residential building construction	49,830
Foundation, structure, and building exterior contractors	49,500
Building finishing contractors	47,980

College graduates with degrees in fields that provide a strong background in cost estimating, such as engineering or construction management, could start at a higher level. According to a July 2005 salary survey by the National Association of Colleges and Employers, those with bachelor's degrees in construction science/management received job offers averaging $42,923 a year.

Related Occupations

Other workers who quantitatively analyze information include accountants and auditors; budget analysts; claims adjusters, appraisers, examiners, and investigators; economists; financial analysts and personal financial advisors; insurance underwriters; loan counselors and officers; market and survey researchers; and operations research analysts. In addition, the duties of industrial production managers and construction managers also may involve analyzing costs.

Sources of Additional Information

Information about career opportunities, certification, educational programs, and cost-estimating techniques may be obtained from the following organizations:
➤ Association for the Advancement of Cost Engineering (AACE International), 209 Prairie Ave., Suite 100, Morgantown, WV 26501. Internet: **http://www.aacei.org**
➤ Society of Cost Estimating and Analysis, 101 S. Whiting St., Suite 201, Alexandria, VA 22304. Internet: **http://www.sceaonline.net**

Financial Analysts and Personal Financial Advisors

(O*NET 13-2051.00, 13-2052.00)

Significant Points

- A college degree and good interpersonal skills are among the most important qualifications for these workers.

- Although both occupations will benefit from an increase in investing by individuals, personal financial advisors will benefit more.

- Financial analysts and personal financial advisors who have earned a professional designation are expected to have the best opportunities; competition is anticipated to be keen for highly lucrative positions in investment banking.

- About 4 out of 10 personal financial advisors are self-employed.

Nature of the Work

Financial analysts and personal financial advisors provide analysis and guidance to businesses and individuals to help them with their investment decisions. Both types of specialists gather financial information, analyze it, and make recommendations to their clients. However, their job duties differ because of the type of investment information they provide and the clients for whom they work. *Financial analysts* assess the economic performance of companies and industries for firms and institutions with money to invest. *Personal financial advisors* generally assess the financial needs of individuals, offering them a wide range of options.

Financial analysts, also called *securities analysts* and *investment analysts*, work for banks, insurance companies, mutual and pension funds, securities firms, and other businesses, helping these companies or their clients make investment decisions. Financial analysts read company financial statements and analyze commodity prices, sales, costs, expenses, and tax rates in order to determine a company's value and to project its future earnings. They often meet with company officials to gain a better insight into the firm's prospects and to determine its managerial effectiveness. Usually, financial analysts study an entire industry, assessing current trends in business practices, products, and industry competition. They must keep abreast of new regulations or policies that may affect the industry, as well as monitor the economy to determine its effect on earnings.

Financial analysts use spreadsheet and statistical software packages to analyze financial data, spot trends, and develop forecasts. On the basis of their results, they write reports and make presentations, usually making recommendations to buy or sell a particular investment or security. Senior analysts may even be the ones who decide to buy or sell if they are responsible for managing the company's or client's assets. Other analysts use the data they find to measure the financial risks associated with making a particular investment decision.

Financial analysts in investment banking departments of securities or banking firms often work in teams, analyzing the future prospects of companies that want to sell shares to the public for the first time. They also ensure that the forms and written materials necessary for compliance with Securities and Exchange Commission regulations are accurate and complete. They may make presentations to prospective investors about the merits of investing in the new company. Financial analysts also work in mergers and acquisitions departments, preparing analyses on the costs and benefits of a proposed merger or takeover.

Some financial analysts, called *ratings analysts*, evaluate the ability of companies or governments that issue bonds to repay their debts. On the basis of their evaluation, a management team assigns a rating to a company's or government's bonds. Other financial analysts perform budget, cost, and credit analysis as part of their responsibilities.

Personal financial advisors, also called *financial planners* or *financial consultants*, use their knowledge of investments, tax laws, and insurance to recommend financial options to individuals in accordance with the individual's short-term and long-term goals. Some of the issues that planners address are retirement and estate planning, funding for college, and general investment options. While most planners offer advice on a wide range of topics, some specialize in areas such as retirement and estate planning or risk management.

An advisor's work begins with a consultation with the client, from whom the advisor obtains information on the client's finances and financial goals. The advisor then develops a comprehensive financial plan that identifies problem areas, makes recommendations for improvement, and selects appropriate investments compatible with the client's goals, attitude toward risk, and expectation or need for a return on the investment. Sometimes this plan is written, but more often it is in the form of verbal advice. Financial advisors usually meet with established clients at least once a year to update them on potential investments and to determine whether the clients have been through any life changes—such as marriage, disability, or retirement—that might affect their financial goals. Financial advisors also answer questions from clients regarding changes in benefit plans or the consequences of a change in their jobs or careers. A large part of the success of financial planners depends on their ability to educate their clients about risks and various possible scenarios so that the clients don't harbor unrealistic expectations.

Some advisors buy and sell financial products, such as mutual funds or insurance, or refer clients to other companies for products

Financial analysts research and analyze financial data, helping managers make sound decisions.

and services—for example, the preparation of taxes or wills. A number of advisors take on the responsibility of managing the clients' investments for them.

Finding clients and building a customer base is one of the most important of a financial advisor's job, because referrals from satisfied clients are an important source of new business. Many advisors also contact potential clients by giving seminars or lectures or meet clients through business and social contacts.

Working Conditions

Financial analysts and personal financial advisors usually work indoors in safe, comfortable offices or their own homes. Many of these workers enjoy the challenge of helping firms or people make financial decisions. However, financial analysts may face long hours, frequent travel to visit companies and talk to potential investors, and the pressure of deadlines. Much of their research must be done after office hours, because their day is filled with telephone calls and meetings. Personal financial advisors usually work standard business hours, but they also schedule meetings with clients in the evenings or on weekends. Many teach evening classes or hold seminars in order to bring in more clients.

Training, Other Qualifications, and Advancement

A college education is required for financial analysts and is strongly preferred for personal financial advisors. Most companies require financial analysts to have at least a bachelor's degree in business administration, accounting, statistics, or finance. Coursework in statistics, economics, and business is required, and knowledge of accounting policies and procedures, corporate budgeting, and financial analysis methods is recommended. A master's degree in business administration is desirable. Advanced courses in options pricing or bond valuation and knowledge of risk management also are suggested.

Employers usually do not require a specific field of study for personal financial advisors, but a bachelor's degree in accounting, finance, economics, business, mathematics, or law provides good preparation for the occupation. Courses in investments, taxes, estate planning, and risk management also are helpful. Programs in financial planning are becoming more widely available in colleges and universities. Working for a broker-dealer is a good way to gain experience that can help individuals pass the security license exams needed to practice financial planning. Individuals who start out as independent financial planners may find it more difficult to build their client base, and they often start by servicing their family members and friends. However, many financial planners enter the field after working in a related occupation, such as accountant; auditor; insurance sales agent; lawyer, or securities, commodities, and financial services sales agent.

Mathematical, computer, analytical, and problem-solving skills are essential qualifications for financial analysts and personal financial advisors. Good communication skills also are necessary, because these workers must present complex financial concepts and strategies in easy-to-understand language to clients and other professionals. Self-confidence, maturity, and the ability to work independently are important as well. Financial analysts must be detail oriented, motivated to seek out obscure information, and familiar with the workings of the economy, tax laws, and money markets. Strong interpersonal skills and sales ability are crucial to the success of both financial analysts and personal financial advisors.

Although not required for financial analysts or personal financial advisors to practice, certification can enhance one's professional standing and is strongly recommended by many employers. Financial analysts may receive the Chartered Financial Analyst (CFA) designation, sponsored by the CFA Institute To qualify for this designation, applicants need a bachelor's degree and 3 years of work experience in a related field and must pass a series of three examinations. These essay exams, administered once a year for 3 years, cover subjects such as accounting, economics, securities analysis, financial markets and instruments, corporate finance, asset valuation, and portfolio management. Personal financial advisors may obtain the Certified Financial Planner credential, often referred to as CFP (R), demonstrating extensive training and competency in financial planning. This certification, issued by the Certified Financial Planner Board of Standards, requires relevant experience, the completion of education requirements, passing a comprehensive examination, and adherence to an enforceable code of ethics. The CFP (R) exams test the candidate's knowledge of the financial planning process, insurance and risk management, employee benefits planning, taxes and retirement planning, and investment and estate planning. The exam has been revised in recent years. Candidates are now required to have a working knowledge of debt management, planning liability, emergency fund reserves, and statistical modeling. It may take from 2 to 3 years of study to complete these programs.

Personal financial advisors also may obtain the Chartered Financial Consultant (ChFC) designation, issued by the American College in Bryn Mawr, Pennsylvania, which requires experience and the completion of an eight-course program of study. The ChFC designation and other professional designations have continuing education requirements.

A license is not required to work as a personal financial advisor, but advisors who sell stocks, bonds, mutual funds, insurance, or real estate may need licenses to perform these additional services. Also, if legal advice is provided, a license to practice law may be required. Financial advisors who do not offer these additional services often refer clients to those who are qualified to provide them.

Financial analysts may advance by becoming portfolio managers or financial managers, directing the investment portfolios of their companies or of clients. Personal financial advisors who work in firms also may move into managerial positions, but most advisors advance by accumulating clients and managing more assets.

Employment

Financial analysts and personal financial advisors held 355,000 jobs in 2004, of which financial analysts held 197,000. Many financial analysts work at the headquarters of large financial companies, several of which are based in New York City. More than 4 out of 10 financial analysts work for finance and insurance industries, including securities and commodity brokers, banks and credit institutions, and insurance carriers. Others worked throughout private industry and government.

Personal financial advisors held 158,000 jobs in 2004. Much like financial analysts, more than half work for finance and insurance industries, including securities and commodity brokers, banks, insurance carriers, and financial investment firms. However, 4 out of 10 personal financial advisors are self-employed, operating small investment advisory firms, usually in urban areas.

Job Outlook

Overall employment of financial analysts and personal financial advisors is expected to increase faster than the average for all occupations through 2014, resulting from increased investment by businesses and individuals. Personal financial advisors will benefit even more than financial analysts as baby boomers save for retirement and as a generally better educated and wealthier population requires investment advice. In addition, people are living longer and must plan to finance more years of retirement. The globalization of the securities markets also will increase the need for analysts and advisors to help investors make financial choices. Financial analysts and personal financial advisors who have earned a professional designation are expected to have the best opportunities.

Deregulation of the financial services industry is expected to spur demand for financial analysts and personal financial advisors. In recent years, banks, insurance companies, and brokerage firms have been allowed to broaden their financial services. Many firms are adding investment advice to their list of services and are expected to increase their hiring of personal financial advisors. Many banks are entering the securities brokerage and investment banking fields and will increasingly need the skills of financial analysts.

Employment of personal financial advisors is projected to grow faster than the average for all occupations. The rapid expansion of self-directed retirement plans, such as 401(k) plans, is expected to continue. As the number and complexity of investments rises, more individuals will look to financial advisors to help manage their money.

Employment of financial analysts is expected to grow about as fast as the average for all occupations. As the number of mutual funds and the amount of assets invested in the funds increase, mutual fund companies will need increased numbers of financial analysts to recommend which financial products the funds should buy or sell.

Financial analysts also will be needed in the investment banking field, where they help companies raise money and work on corporate mergers and acquisitions. However, growth in demand for financial analysts to do company research has been, and will continue to be, constrained by regulations that require investment firms to separate research from investment banking. As a result, firms have eliminated research jobs in an effort to contain the costs of implementing these regulations.

Demand for financial analysts in investment banking fluctuates because investment banking is sensitive to changes in the stock market. In addition, further consolidation in the finance industries may eliminate some financial analyst positions, dampening overall employment growth somewhat. Competition is expected to be keen for these highly lucrative positions, with many more applicants than jobs.

Earnings

Median annual earnings of financial analysts were $61,910 in May 2004. The middle 50 percent earned between $47,410 and $82,730. The lowest 10 percent earned less than $37,580, and the highest 10 percent earned more than $113,490. Median annual earnings in the industries employing the largest numbers of financial analysts in 2004 were as follows:

Other financial investment activities	$74,580
Securities and commodity contracts intermediation and brokerage	67,730
Management of companies and enterprises	62,890
Insurance carriers	58,120
Depository credit intermediation	56,860

Median annual earnings of personal financial advisors were $62,700 in May 2004. The middle 50 percent earned between $41,860 and $108,280. Median annual earnings in the industries employing the largest number of personal financial advisors in 2004 were as follows:

Other financial investment activities	$78,350
Securities and commodity contracts intermediation and brokerage	63,310
Depository credit intermediation	57,180
Agencies, brokerages, and other insurance related activities	56,950

Many financial analysts receive a bonus in addition to their salary, and the bonus can add substantially to their earnings. Usually, the bonus is based on how well their predictions compare to the actual performance of a benchmark investment. Personal financial advisors who work for financial services firms are generally paid a salary plus bonus. Advisors who work for financial investment or planning firms or who are self-employed either charge hourly fees for their services or charge one set fee for a comprehensive plan, based on its complexity. Advisors who manage a client's assets may charge a percentage of those assets. Advisors generally receive commissions for financial products they sell, in addition to charging a fee.

Related Occupations

Other jobs requiring expertise in finance and investment or in the sale of financial products include accountants and auditors; financial managers; insurance sales agents; real estate brokers and sales agents; and securities, commodities, and financial services sales agents.

Sources of Additional Information

For information on a career in financial planning, contact:
➤ The Financial Planning Association, 4100 E. Mississippi Ave., Suite 400, Denver, CO 80246-3053. Internet: **http://www.fpanet.org**

For information about the Certified Financial Planner (CFP) (R) certification, contact:
➤ Certified Financial Planner Board of Standards, Inc., 1670 Broadway, Suite 600, Denver, CO 80202-4809. Internet: **http://www.cfp.net/become**

For information about the Chartered Financial Consultant (ChFC) designation, contact:
➤ The American College, 270 South Bryn Mawr Ave., Bryn Mawr, PA 19010. Internet: **http://www.amercoll.edu**

For information on a career as a financial analyst, contact either of the following organizations:
➤ American Academy of Financial Management, 2 Canal St., Suite 2317, New Orleans, LA 70130. Internet: **http://www.financialanalyst.org**
➤ CFA Institute, P.O. Box 3668, 560 Ray C. Hunt Dr., Charlottesville, VA 22903. Internet: **http://www.cfainstitute.org**

Insurance Underwriters

(O*NET 13-2053.00)

Significant Points

- Most large insurance companies prefer college graduates who have a degree in business administration or finance with courses in accounting; however, a bachelor's degree in any field—plus courses in business law and accounting—may be sufficient to qualify.

- Continuing education is necessary for advancement.

- Employment is expected to grow more slowly than average as the continuing spread of underwriting software increases worker productivity.

- Job opportunities should be best for those with a background in finance and strong computer and communication skills.

Nature of the Work

Insurance companies protect individuals and organizations from financial loss by assuming billions of dollars in risk each year. Underwriters are needed to identify and calculate the risk of loss from policyholders, establish appropriate premium rates, and write policies that cover this risk. An insurance company may lose business to competitors if the underwriter appraises risks too conservatively, or it may have to pay excessive claims if the underwriting actions are too liberal.

With the aid of computers, underwriters analyze information in insurance applications to determine whether a risk is acceptable and will not result in a loss. Applications often are supplemented with reports from loss-control consultants, medical reports, reports from data vendors, and actuarial studies. Underwriters then must decide whether to issue the policy and, if so, the appropriate premium to charge. In making this determination, underwriters serve as the main link between the insurance carrier and the insurance agent. On occasion, they accompany sales agents to make presentations to prospective clients.

Technology plays an important role in an underwriter's job. Underwriters use computer applications called "smart systems" to manage risks more efficiently and accurately. These systems automatically analyze and rate insurance applications, recommend acceptance or denial of the risk, and adjust the premium rate in accordance with the risk. With these systems, underwriters are better equipped to make sound decisions and avoid excessive losses.

The Internet also has affected the work of underwriters. Many insurance carriers' computer systems are now linked to different databases on the Internet that allow immediate access to information—such as driving records—necessary in determining a potential client's risk. This kind of access reduces the amount of time and paperwork necessary for an underwriter to complete a risk assessment.

Most underwriters specialize in one of three major categories of insurance: life, health, and property and casualty. Life and health insurance underwriters may further specialize in group or individual policies.

Property and casualty underwriters usually specialize in either commercial or personal insurance and then by type of risk insured, as in fire, homeowners', automobile, marine, or liability insurance, or workers' compensation. In cases where casualty companies

Insurance underwriters review insurance applications and determine the appropriate premium to charge a customer.

provide insurance through a single "package" policy covering various types of risks, the underwriter must be familiar with different lines of insurance. For business insurance, the underwriter often must be able to evaluate the firm's entire operation in appraising its application for insurance.

An increasing proportion of insurance sales, particularly in life and health insurance, is being made through group contracts. A standard group policy insures everyone in a specified group through a single contract at a standard premium rate. The group underwriter analyzes the overall composition of the group to ensure that the total risk is not excessive. Another type of group policy provides members of a group—a labor union, for example—with individual policies reflecting their needs. These usually are casualty policies, such as those covering automobiles. The casualty underwriter analyzes the application of each group member and makes individual appraisals. Some group underwriters meet with union or employer representatives to discuss the types of policies available to their group.

Working Conditions
Underwriters have desk jobs that require no unusual physical activity. Their offices usually are comfortable and pleasant. Although underwriters typically work a standard 40-hour week, more are working longer hours due to the downsizing of many insurance companies. Most underwriters are based in a home or regional branch office, but they occasionally attend meetings away from home for several days. Construction and marine underwriters frequently travel to inspect worksites and assess risks.

Training, Other Qualifications, and Advancement
For entry-level underwriting jobs, most large insurance companies prefer college graduates who have a degree in business administration or finance with courses or experience in accounting. However, a bachelor's degree in almost any field—plus courses in business law and accounting—provides a good general background and may be sufficient to qualify an individual. Because computers are an integral part of most underwriters' jobs, computer skills are essential.

New employees usually start as underwriter trainees or assistant underwriters. They may help collect information on applicants and evaluate routine applications under the supervision of an experienced risk analyst. Property and casualty trainees study claims files to become familiar with factors associated with certain types of losses. Many larger insurers offer work-study training programs, lasting from a few months to a year. As trainees gain experience, they are assigned policy applications that are more complex and cover greater risks. Analyzing and processing these applications efficiently requires the use of computers.

Underwriting can be a satisfying career for people who enjoy analyzing information and paying attention to detail. In addition, underwriters must possess good judgment in order to make sound decisions. Excellent communication and interpersonal skills also are essential, as much of the underwriter's work involves dealing with agents and other insurance professionals.

Continuing education is necessary for advancement. Insurance companies usually pay tuition for underwriting courses that their trainees complete; some also offer salary incentives. Independent-study programs for experienced property and casualty underwriters are available as well. The Insurance Institute of America offers both a program called "Introduction to Underwriting" for beginning underwriters, and the specialty designation of Associate in Commercial Underwriting (ACU), a formal step in developing a career in underwriting business insurance policies. Those interested in developing a career underwriting personal insurance policies may earn the Associate in Personal Insurance (API) designation. To earn either the ACU or API designation, underwriters complete a series of courses and examinations that generally last 1 to 2 years.

The American Institute for Chartered Property Casualty Underwriters (AICPCU) awards the Chartered Property and Casualty Underwriter (CPCU) designation, the final stage of development for an underwriter. Earning the CPCU designation requires passing 10 exams, meeting a requirement of at least 3 years of insurance experience, and abiding by the AICPCU's code of professional ethics. Exams cover risk management; insurance operations and regulations, business and insurance law, and financial management and financial institutions. In conjunction with the Insurance Institute of America, the AICPCU offers 22 insurance-related educational programs, including associate designation programs in claims underwriting, risk management, and reinsurance. The American College offers the Chartered Life Underwriter (CLU) designation and the Registered Health Underwriter (RHU) designation for all life and health insurance professionals.

Experienced underwriters who complete courses of study may advance to senior underwriter or underwriting manager positions. Some underwriting managers are promoted to senior managerial jobs. Some employers require a master's degree to achieve this level. Other underwriters are attracted to the earnings potential of sales and, therefore, obtain State licenses to sell insurance and related financial products as agents or brokers.

Employment
Insurance underwriters held about 101,000 jobs in 2004. Approximately 2 out of 3 underwriters work for insurance carriers. Most of the remaining underwriters work in insurance agencies or for organizations that offer insurance services to insurance companies and policyholders. A small number of underwriters work in agencies owned and operated by banks, mortgage companies, and real estate firms.

Most underwriters are based in the insurance company's home office, but some, mainly in the property and casualty area, work out of regional branch offices of the insurance company. These underwriters usually have the authority to underwrite most risks and determine an appropriate rating without consulting the home office.

Job Outlook

Employment of underwriters is expected to grow more slowly than the average for all occupations through 2014. Underwriting software will continue to make workers more productive; however, because computer software does not do away with the need for human skills, employment will increase as economic and population growth result in increased insurance needs by businesses and individuals. Job opportunities should be best for those with a background in finance and strong computer and communication skills. In addition to openings arising from some job growth, openings will be created by the need to replace underwriters who transfer to another job or leave the occupation.

Insurance carriers always are assessing new risks and offering policies to meet changing circumstances. Underwriters are needed particularly in the area of product development, where they assess risks and set the premiums for new lines of insurance. One new line of insurance being offered by life insurance carriers that may provide job opportunities for underwriters is long-term care insurance.

Demand for underwriters also is expected to improve as insurance carriers try to restore profitability to make up for an unusually large number of underwriting losses in recent years. As the carriers' returns on their investments have declined, insurers are placing more emphasis on underwriting to generate revenues. This renewed interest in underwriting should result in job opportunities for underwriters.

Because insurance is considered a necessity for people and businesses, there will always be a need for underwriters—a profession that is less subject to recession and layoffs than other fields.

Earnings

Median annual earnings of insurance underwriters were $48,550 in May 2004. The middle 50 percent earned between $37,490 and $65,450 a year. The lowest 10 percent earned less than $30,410, while the highest 10 percent earned more than $86,110. Median annual earnings of underwriters working with insurance carriers were $49,280, while earnings of these in agencies, brokerages, and other insurance related activities were $46,750.

Insurance companies usually provide better-than-average benefits, including retirement plans and employer-financed group life and health insurance.

Related Occupations

Underwriters make decisions on the basis of financial and statistical data. Other workers with the same type of responsibility include accountants and auditors, actuaries, budget analysts, cost estimators, financial analysts and personal financial advisors, financial managers, loan officers, and credit analysts. Other related jobs in the insurance industry include insurance sales agents and claims adjusters, appraisers, examiners, and investigators.

Sources of Additional Information

Information about a career as an insurance underwriter is available from the home offices of many insurance companies.

Information about the property-casualty insurance field can be obtained by contacting:

➤ Insurance Information Institute, 110 William St., New York, NY 10038. Internet: http://www.iii.org

Information on careers in the life insurance field can be obtained from:

➤ LIMRA International, P.O. Box 203, Hartford, CT 06141.

Information on the underwriting function and the CPCU and AU designations can be obtained from:

➤ American Institute for Chartered Property and Casualty Underwriters and Insurance Institute of America, 720 Providence Rd., P.O. Box 3016, Malvern, PA 19355-0716. Internet: http://www.aicpcu.org

Information on the CLU and RHU designations can be obtained from:

➤ American College, 270 South Bryn Mawr Ave., Bryn Mawr, PA 19010-2196. Internet: http://www.theamericancollege.edu

Loan Officers

(O*NET 13-2072.00)

Significant Points

● About 9 out of 10 loan officers work for commercial banks, savings institutions, credit unions, and related financial institutions.

● Loan officer positions generally require a bachelor's degree in finance, economics, or a related field; training or experience in banking, lending, or sales is advantageous.

● Slower-than-average employment growth is expected despite rising demand for loans, because technology is making for simpler and faster processing and approval of loans.

● Earnings often fluctuate with the number of loans generated, rising substantially when the economy is good and interest rates are low.

Nature of the Work

For many individuals, taking out a loan may be the only way to afford a house, car, or college education. For businesses, loans likewise are essential to start many companies, purchase inventory, or invest in capital equipment. *Loan officers* facilitate this lending by finding potential clients and assisting them in applying for loans. Loan officers also gather personal information about clients and businesses to ensure that an informed decision is made regarding the creditworthiness of the borrower and the probability of repayment. Loan officers may provide guidance to prospective loan applicants who have problems qualifying for traditional loans. The guidance may include determining the most appropriate type of loan for a particular customer and explaining specific requirements and restrictions associated with the loan.

Loan officers usually specialize in commercial, consumer, or mortgage loans. Commercial or business loans help companies pay for new equipment or expand operations; consumer loans include home equity, automobile, and personal loans; mortgage loans are made to purchase real estate or to refinance an existing mortgage. As banks and other financial institutions begin to offer new types of loans and a growing variety of financial services, loan officers will have to keep abreast of these new product lines so that they can meet their customers' needs.

In many instances, loan officers act as salespeople. Commercial loan officers, for example, contact firms to determine their needs for loans. If a firm is seeking new funds, the loan officer will try to persuade the company to obtain the loan from his or her institution. Similarly, mortgage loan officers develop relationships with commercial and residential real estate agencies so that, when an individual or firm buys a property, the real estate agent might recommend contacting a specific loan officer for financing.

Once the initial contact has been made, loan officers guide clients through the process of applying for a loan. The process begins with a formal meeting or telephone call with a prospective client, during which the loan officer obtains basic information about the purpose of the loan and explains the different types of loans and credit terms that are available to the applicant. Loan officers answer questions about the process and sometimes assist clients in filling out the application.

After a client completes the application, the loan officer begins the process of analyzing and verifying the information on the application to determine the client's creditworthiness. Often, loan officers can quickly access the client's credit history by computer and obtain a credit "score," representing a software program's assessment of the client's creditworthiness. In cases a credit history is not available or in which unusual financial circumstances are present, the loan officer may request additional financial information from the client or, in the case of commercial loans, copies of the company's financial statements. With this information, loan officers who specialize in evaluating a client's creditworthiness—often called loan underwriters—may conduct a financial analysis or other risk assessment. Loan officers include such information and their written comments in a loan file, which is used to analyze whether the prospective loan meets the lending institution's requirements. Loan officers then decide, in consultation with their managers, whether to grant the loan. If the loan is approved, a repayment schedule is arranged with the client.

A loan may be approved that would otherwise be denied if the customer can provide the lender with appropriate collateral—property pledged as security for the repayment of the loan. For example, when lending money for a college education, a bank may insist that borrowers offer their home as collateral. If the borrowers should ever default on the loan, the home would be seized under court order and sold to raise the necessary money.

Some loan officers, referred to as. *loan collection officers*, contact borrowers with delinquent loan accounts to help them find a method of repayment in order to avoid their defaulting on the loan. If a repayment plan cannot be developed, the loan collection officer initiates collateral liquidation, in which the lender seizes the collateral used to secure the loan—a home or car, for example—and sells it to repay the loan.

Working Conditions
Working as a loan officer usually involves considerable travel. For example, commercial and mortgage loan officers frequently work away from their offices and rely on laptop computers, cellular telephones, and pagers to keep in contact with their employ-

Loan officers guide clients through the loan application process.

ers and clients. Mortgage loan officers often work out of their home or car, visiting offices or homes of clients to complete loan applications. Commercial loan officers sometimes travel to other cities to prepare complex loan agreements. Consumer loan officers, however, are likely to spend most of their time in an office.

Most loan officers work a standard 40-hour week, but many work longer, depending on the number of clients and the demand for loans. Mortgage loan officers can work especially long hours, because they are free to take on as many customers as they choose. Loan officers usually carry a heavy caseload and sometimes cannot accept new clients until they complete current cases. They are especially busy when interest rates are low, a condition that triggers a surge in loan applications.

Training, Other Qualifications, and Advancement
Loan officer positions generally require a bachelor's degree in finance, economics, or a related field. Banking, lending, or sales experience is highly valued by employers. Most employers also prefer applicants who are familiar with computers and their applications in banking. Loan officers without college degrees usually advance to their positions from other jobs in an organization after acquiring several years of work experience in various other occupations, such as teller or customer service representative. Personal qualities such as sales ability, good interpersonal and communication skills, and a strong desire to succeed also are important qualities for loan officers.

There are currently no specific licensing requirements for loan officers working in banks or credit unions. Training and licensing requirements for loan officers who work in mortgage banks or brokerages vary by State.

Various banking-related associations and private schools offer courses and programs for students interested in lending, as well as for experienced loan officers who want to keep their skills current. For example, the Bank Administration Institute, an affiliate of the American Banker's Association, offers the Loan Review Certificate Program for persons who review and approve loans. This program enhances the quality of reviews and improves the early detection of deteriorating loans, thereby contributing to the safety and soundness of the loan portfolio. The Certified Mortgage Banker (CMB) designation demonstrates the holder's superior knowledge, understanding, and competency in real estate finance. The Mortgage Bankers Association offers three CMB designations: residential, commerce, and master's. To obtain the CMB, the candidate must have 3 years of experience, earn educational credits, and pass an exam. Completion of these courses and programs generally enhances one's employment and advancement opportunities.

Persons planning a career as a loan officer should be capable of developing effective working relationships with others, confident in their abilities, and highly motivated. For public relations purposes, loan officers must be willing to attend community events as representatives of their employer.

Capable loan officers may advance to larger branches of the firm or to managerial positions, while less capable workers—and those having weak academic preparation—could be assigned to smaller branches and might find promotion difficult without obtaining training to upgrade their skills. Advancement beyond a loan officer position usually includes supervising other loan officers and clerical staff.

Employment
Loan officers held about 291,000 jobs in 2004. About 9 out of 10 loan officers were employed by commercial banks, savings institutions, credit unions, and related financial institutions. Loan officers are employed throughout the Nation, but most work in urban and

suburban areas. At some banks, particularly in rural areas, the branch or assistant manager often handles the loan application process.

Job Outlook

Employment of loan officers is projected to increase more slowly than the average for all occupations through 2014. College graduates and those with banking, lending, or sales experience should have the best job prospects. Employment growth stemming from economic expansion and population increases—factors that generate demand for loans—will be partially offset by increased automation that speeds lending processes and by the growing use of the Internet to apply for and obtain loans. Job opportunities for loan officers are influenced by the volume of applications, which is determined largely interest rates and by the overall level of economic activity. However, besides openings arising from growth, additional job openings will result from the need to replace workers who retire or otherwise leave the occupation permanently.

The use of credit scoring has made the loan evaluation process much simpler than in the past and even unnecessary in some cases. Credit scoring allows loan officers—particularly loan underwriters—to evaluate many more loans in much less time, thus increasing the loan officer's efficiency. In addition, the mortgage application process has become highly automated and standardized, a simplification that has enabled online mortgage loan vendors to offer their services over the Internet. Online vendors accept loan applications from customers over the Internet and determine which lenders have the best interest rates for particular loans. With this knowledge, customers can go directly to the lending institution, thereby bypassing mortgage loan brokers. Shopping for loans on the Internet is expected to become more common in the future, especially for mortgages, thereby reducing demand for loan officers.

Although loans remain a major source of revenue for banks, demand for new loans fluctuates and affects the income and employment opportunities of loan officers. An upswing in the economy or a decline in interest rates often results in a surge in real estate buying and mortgage refinancing, requiring loan officers to work long hours processing applications and inducing lenders to hire additional loan officers, who often are paid by commission on the value of the loans they place. When the real estate market slows, loan officers often suffer a decline in earnings and may even be subject to layoffs. The same applies to commercial loan officers, whose workloads increase during good economic times as companies seek to invest more in their businesses. In difficult economic conditions, an increase in the number of delinquent loans results in more demand for loan collection officers.

Earnings

Median annual earnings of loan officers were $48,830 in May 2004. The middle 50 percent earned between $35,360 and $69,160. The lowest 10 percent earned less than $27,580 while the top 10 percent earned more than $98,280. Median annual earnings in the industries employing the largest numbers of loan officers in 2004 were as follows:

Activities related to credit intermediation	$54,180
Management of companies and enterprises	51,670
Nondepository credit intermediation	49,930
Depository credit intermediation	44,460

The form of compensation for loan officers varies. Most are paid a commission that is based on the number of loans they originate. In this way, commissions are used to motivate loan officers to bring in more loans. Some institutions pay only salaries, while others pay their loan officers a salary plus a commission or bonus based on the number of loans originated. Banks and other lenders sometimes of-

fer their loan officers free checking privileges and somewhat lower interest rates on personal loans.

According to a salary survey conducted by Robert Half International, a staffing services firm specializing in accounting and finance, mortgage loan officers earned between $30,000 and $100,000 in 2005, consumer loan officers with 1 to 3 years of experience earned between $30,000 and $35,000, and commercial loan officers with 1 to 3 years of experience made between $45,500 and $70,000. Commercial loan officers with more than 3 years of experience made between $61,750 and $100,000, and consumer loan officers earned between $25,500 and $50,000. Earnings of loan officers with graduate degrees or professional certifications are higher. Loan officers who are paid on a commission basis usually earn more than those on salary only, and those who work for smaller banks generally earn less than those employed by larger institutions.

Related Occupations

Loan officers help people manage financial assets and secure loans. Occupations that involve similar functions include those of securities, commodities, and financial services sales agents; financial analysts and personal financial advisors; real estate brokers and sales agents; insurance underwriters; insurance sales agents; and loan counselors.

Sources of Additional Information

Information about a career as a mortgage loan officer can be obtained from:

➤ Mortgage Bankers Association, 1919 Pennsylvania Ave. NW., Washington, DC 20006. Internet: **http://www.mortgagebankers.org**

State bankers' associations can furnish specific information about job opportunities in their State. Also, individual banks can supply information about job openings and the activities, responsibilities, and preferred qualifications of their loan officers.

Management Analysts

(O*NET 13-1111.00)

Significant Points

- Despite fast employment growth, keen competition is expected for jobs; opportunities should be best for those with a graduate degree, specific industry expertise, and a talent for salesmanship and public relations.

- About 29 percent, more than 3 times the average for all occupations, are self-employed.

- Most positions in private industry require a master's degree and additional years of specialized experience; a bachelor's degree is sufficient for entry-level government jobs.

Nature of the Work

As business becomes more complex, the Nation's firms are continually faced with new challenges. Firms increasingly rely on management analysts to help them remain competitive amidst these changes. Management analysts, often referred to as *management consultants* in private industry, analyze and propose ways to improve an organization's structure, efficiency, or profits. For example, a small but rapidly growing company that needs help improving the system of control over inventories and expenses may decide to employ a consultant who is an expert in just-in-time inventory management. In another case, a large company that has recently acquired a new division may hire management analysts to help reorganize the corporate structure and eliminate duplicate or nonessential jobs. In recent years, information technology and electronic commerce have provided new opportunities for management analysts. Companies hire consultants to develop strategies for entering and remaining competitive in the new electronic marketplace. (For information on computer specialists working in consulting, see the following statements elsewhere in the *Handbook*: Computer software engineers; systems analysts, computer scientists, and database administrators; and computer programmers.)

Firms providing management analysis range in size from a single practitioner to large international organizations employing thousands of consultants. Some analysts and consultants specialize in a specific industry, such as health care or telecommunications, while others specialize by type of business function, such as human resources, marketing, logistics, or information systems. In government, management analysts tend to specialize by type of agency. The work of management analysts and consultants varies with each client or employer, and from project to project. Some projects require a team of consultants, each specializing in one area. In other projects, consultants work independently with the organization's managers. In all cases, analysts and consultants collect, review, and analyze information in order to make recommendations to managers.

Both public and private organizations use consultants for a variety of reasons. Some lack the internal resources needed to handle a project, while others need a consultant's expertise to determine what resources will be required and what problems may be encountered if they pursue a particular opportunity. To retain a consultant, a company first solicits proposals from a number of consulting firms specializing in the area in which it needs assistance. These proposals include the estimated cost and scope of the project, staffing requirements, references from a number of previous clients, and a completion deadline. The company then selects the proposal that best suits its needs.

After obtaining an assignment or contract, management analysts first define the nature and extent of the problem. During this phase, they analyze relevant data—which may include annual revenues, employment, or expenditures—and interview managers and employees while observing their operations. The analyst or consultant then develops solutions to the problem. While preparing their recommendations, they take into account the nature of the organization, the relationship it has with others in the industry, and its internal organization and culture. Insight into the problem often is gained by building and solving mathematical models.

Once they have decided on a course of action, consultants report their findings and recommendations to the client. These suggestions usually are submitted in writing, but oral presentations regarding findings also are common. For some projects, management analysts are retained to help implement the suggestions they have made.

Like their private-sector colleagues, management analysts in government agencies try to increase efficiency and worker productivity, and to control costs. For example, if an agency is planning to purchase personal computers, it must first determine which type to buy, given its budget and data-processing needs. In this case, management analysts would assess the prices and characteristics of various machines and determine which ones best meet the agency's needs. Analysts may manage contracts for a wide range of goods and services to ensure quality performance and to prevent cost overruns.

Working Conditions
Management analysts usually divide their time between their offices and the client's site. In either situation, much of an analyst's time is

Management analysts analyze and propose ways to improve an organization's structure, efficiency, or profits.

spent indoors in clean, well-lit offices. Because they must spend a significant portion of their time with clients, analysts travel frequently.

Analysts and consultants generally work at least 40 hours a week. Uncompensated overtime is common, especially when project deadlines are approaching. Analysts may experience a great deal of stress as a result of trying to meet a client's demands, often on a tight schedule.

Self-employed consultants can set their workload and hours and work at home. On the other hand, their livelihood depends on their ability to maintain and expand their client base. Salaried consultants also must impress potential clients to get and keep clients for their company.

Training, Other Qualifications, and Advancement
Educational requirements for entry-level jobs in this field vary widely between private industry and government. Most employers in private industry generally seek individuals with a master's degree in business administration or a related discipline. Some employers also require additional years of experience in the field or industry in which the worker plans to consult, in addition to a master's degree. Some will hire workers with a bachelor's degree as a research analyst or associate. Research analysts usually need to pursue a master's degree in order to advance to a consulting position. Most government agencies hire people with a bachelor's degree and no pertinent work experience for entry-level management analyst positions.

Few universities or colleges offer formal programs of study in management consulting; however, many fields of study provide a suitable educational background for this occupation because of the wide range of areas addressed by management analysts. Common educational backgrounds include most academic programs in business and management, such as accounting and marketing, as well as economics, computer and information sciences, and engineering. In addition to the appropriate formal education, most entrants to this occupation have years of experience in management, human resources, information technology, or other specialties. Analysts also routinely attend conferences to keep abreast of current developments in their field.

Management analysts often work with minimal supervision, so they need to be self-motivated and disciplined. Analytical skills, the ability to get along with a wide range of people, strong oral and written communication skills, good judgment, time management skills, and creativity are other desirable qualities. The ability to work in teams also is an important attribute as consulting teams become more common.

As consultants gain experience, they often become solely responsible for a specific project, taking on more responsibility and managing their own hours. At the senior level, consultants may supervise teams working on more complex projects and become more involved in seeking out new business. Those with exceptional skills may eventually become a partner in the firm. Others with entrepreneurial ambition may open their own firm.

A high percentage of management consultants are self-employed, partly because business startup costs are low. Self-employed consultants also can share office space, administrative help, and other resources with other self-employed consultants or small consulting firms, thus reducing overhead costs. Since many small consulting firms fail each year because of lack of managerial expertise and clients, persons interested in opening their own firm must have good organizational and marketing skills and several years of consulting experience.

The Institute of Management Consultants USA, Inc. (IMC USA) offers a wide range of professional development programs and resources, such as meetings and workshops, which can be helpful for management consultants. The IMC USA also offers the Certified Management Consultant (CMC) designation to those who meet minimum levels of education and experience, submit client reviews, and pass an interview and exam covering the IMC USA's Code of Ethics. Management consultants with a CMC designation must be recertified every 3 years. Certification is not mandatory for management consultants, but it may give a jobseeker a competitive advantage.

Employment

Management analysts held about 605,000 jobs in 2004. About 29 percent of these workers, more than 3 times the average for all occupations, were self-employed. Management analysts are found throughout the country, but employment is concentrated in large metropolitan areas. Management analyst jobs are found in a wide range of industries, including management, scientific, and technical consulting firms; computer systems design and related services firms; and Federal, State, and local governments. The majority of those working for the Federal Government are in the U.S. Department of Defense.

Job Outlook

Despite projected rapid employment growth, keen competition is expected for jobs as management analysts. The pool of applicants from which employers can draw is quite large since analysts can come from very diverse educational backgrounds. Furthermore, the independent and challenging nature of the work, combined with high earnings potential, makes this occupation attractive to many. Job opportunities are expected to be best for those with a graduate degree, specific industry expertise, and a talent for salesmanship and public relations.

Employment of management analysts is expected to grow faster than the average for all occupations through 2014, as industry and government increasingly rely on outside expertise to improve the performance of their organizations. Job growth is projected in very large consulting firms with international expertise and in smaller consulting firms that specialize in specific areas, such as biotechnology, health care, information technology, human resources, engineering, and marketing. Growth in the number of individual practitioners may be hindered by increasing use of consulting teams, that can expedite solutions to a variety of different issues and problems within an organization.

Employment growth of management analysts has been driven by a number of changes in the business environment that have forced firms to take a closer look at their operations. These changes include developments in information technology and the growth of electronic commerce. Traditional companies hire analysts to help design intranets or company Web sites, or to establish online businesses. New Internet startup companies hire analysts not only to design Web sites but also to advise them in more traditional business practices, such as pricing strategies, marketing, and inventory and human resource management. In order to offer clients better quality and a wider variety of services, consulting firms are partnering with traditional computer software and technology firms. Also, many computer firms are developing consulting practices of their own in order to take advantage of this expanding market. Although information technology consulting should remain one of the fastest growing consulting areas, the volatility of the computer services industry necessitates that the most successful management analysts have knowledge of traditional business practices in addition to computer applications, systems integration, Web design, and management skills.

The growth of international business also has contributed to an increase in demand for management analysts. As U.S. firms expand their business abroad, many will hire management analysts to help them form the right strategy for entering the market; to advise them on legal matters pertaining to specific countries; or to help them with organizational, administrative, and other issues, especially if the U.S. company is involved in a partnership or merger with a local firm. These trends provide management analysts with more opportunities to travel or work abroad but also require them to have a more comprehensive knowledge of international business and foreign cultures and languages.

Furthermore, as international and domestic markets have become more competitive, firms have needed to use resources more efficiently. Management analysts increasingly are sought to help reduce costs, streamline operations, and develop marketing strategies. As this process continues and businesses downsize, even more opportunities will be created for analysts to perform duties that previously were handled internally. Finally, more management analysts also will be needed in the public sector, as Federal, State, and local government agencies seek ways to become more efficient.

Though management consultants are continually expanding their services, employment growth could be hampered by increasing competition for clients from occupations that do not traditionally perform consulting work, such as accountants, financial analysts, lawyers, and computer systems analysts. Furthermore, economic downturns also can have adverse effects on employment for some management consultants. In these times, businesses look to cut costs, and consultants may be considered an excess expense. On the other hand, some consultants might experience an increase in work during recessions because they advise businesses on how to cut costs and remain profitable.

Earnings

Salaries for management analysts vary widely by years of experience and education, geographic location, sector of expertise, and size of employer. Generally, management analysts employed in large firms or in metropolitan areas have the highest salaries. Median annual wage and salary earnings of management analysts in May 2004 were $63,450. The middle 50 percent earned between $48,340 and $86,650. The lowest 10 percent earned less than $37,680, and the highest 10 percent earned more than $120,220. Median annual earnings in the industries employing the largest numbers of management analysts in May 2004 were:

Management, scientific, and technical consulting services	$72,480
Federal Government	72,440
Computer systems design and related services	69,800
Management of companies and enterprises	59,420
State government	48,070

According to the Association of Management Consulting Firms, typical earnings in 2004—including bonuses and profit sharing—averaged $52,482 for research associates in member firms; $65,066 for entry-level consultants; $89,116 for management consultants; $123,305 for senior consultants; $191,664 for junior partners; and $317,339 for senior partners. Only the most experienced workers in highly successful management consulting firms earn these top salaries.

Salaried management analysts usually receive common benefits, such as health and life insurance, a retirement plan, vacation, and sick leave, as well as less common benefits, such as profit sharing and bonuses for outstanding work. In addition, all travel expenses usually are reimbursed by the employer. Self-employed consultants have to maintain their own office and provide their own benefits.

Related Occupations

Management analysts collect, review, and analyze data; make recommendations; and implement their ideas. Occupations with similar duties include accountants and auditors; budget analysts; cost estimators; financial analysts and personal financial advisors; operations research analysts; economists; and market and survey researchers. Some management analysts specialize in information technology and work with computers, as do computer systems analysts and computer scientists and database administrators. Most management analysts also have managerial experience similar to that of administrative services managers; advertising, marketing, promotions, public relations, and sales managers; financial managers; human resources, training, and labor relations managers and specialists; and top executives.

Sources of Additional Information

Information about career opportunities in management consulting is available from:

➤ Association of Management Consulting Firms, 380 Lexington Ave., Suite 1700, New York, NY 10168. Internet: **http://www.amcf.org**

Information about the Certified Management Consultant designation can be obtained from:

➤ Institute of Management Consultants USA, Inc., 2025 M St. NW., Suite 800, Washington, DC 20036. Internet: **http://www.imcusa.org**

Information on obtaining a management analyst position with the Federal Government is available from the Office of Personnel Management (OPM) through USAJOBS, the Federal Government's official employment information system. This resource for locating and applying for job opportunities can be accessed through the Internet at **http://www.usajobs.opm.gov** or through an interactive voice response telephone system at (703) 724-1850 or TDD (978) 461-8404. These numbers are not tollfree, and charges may result.

Meeting and Convention Planners

(O*NET 13-1121.00)

Significant Points

● Planners often work long hours in the period prior to and during a meeting or convention, and extensive travel may be required.

● Employment is expected to grow faster than average.

● Opportunities will be best for individuals with a bachelor's degree and some meeting planning experience.

Nature of the Work

Meetings and conventions bring people together for a common purpose, and meeting and convention planners work to ensure that this purpose is achieved seamlessly. Meeting planners coordinate every detail of meetings and conventions, from the speakers and meeting location to arranging for printed materials and audio-visual equipment. Meeting and convention planners work for nonprofit organizations, professional and similar associations, hotels, corporations, and government. Some organizations have internal meeting planning staffs, and others hire independent meeting and convention planning firms to organize their events.

The first step in planning a meeting or convention is determining the purpose, message, or impression that the sponsoring organization wants to communicate. Planners increasingly focus on how meetings impact the goals of their organizations; for example, they may survey prospective attendees to find out what motivates them and how they learn best. Planners then choose speakers, entertainment, and content, and arrange the program to present the organization's information in the most effective way.

Meeting and convention planners search for prospective meeting sites, which may be hotels, convention centers, or conference centers. They issue requests for proposals—documents that state the meeting dates and outline their needs for the meeting or convention, including meeting and exhibit space, lodging, food and beverages, telecommunications, audio-visual requirements, transportation, and any other necessities—to all the sites in which they are interested. The establishments respond with proposals describing what space and services they can supply, and at what prices. Meeting and convention planners review these proposals and either make recommendations to top management or choose the site themselves.

Once the location is selected, meeting and convention planners arrange support services, coordinate needs with the facility, prepare the site staff for the meeting, and set up all forms of electronic communication needed for the meeting or convention, such as e-mail, voice mail, video, and online communication.

Meeting logistics, the management of the details of meetings and conventions, such as labor and materials, is another major component of the job. Planners register attendees and issue name badges, coordinate lodging reservations, and arrange transportation. They make sure that all necessary supplies are ordered and transported to the meeting site on time, that meeting rooms are equipped with sufficient seating and audio-visual equipment, that all exhibits and booths are set up properly, and that all materials are printed. They also make sure that the meeting adheres to fire and labor regulations and oversee food and beverage distribution.

There also is a financial management component of the work. Planners negotiate contracts with facilities and suppliers. These contracts, which have become increasingly complex, are often drawn up more than a year in advance of the meeting or convention. Contracts may include clauses requiring the planner to book a certain number of rooms for meeting attendees and imposing penalties if the rooms are not filled. Therefore, it is important that the planner is able to closely estimate how many people will attend the meeting, based on previous meeting attendance and current circumstances. Planners must also oversee the finances of meetings and conventions. They are given overall budgets by their organizations and must create a detailed budget, forecasting what each aspect of the event will cost. Additionally, some planners oversee meetings that contribute significantly to their organization's operating budget and must ensure the meeting meets income goals.

An increasingly important part of the work is measuring how well the meeting's purpose was achieved, and planners begin this measurement as they outline the meeting's goals. Planners set their own specific goals after learning an organization's goals for a meeting or convention. They choose objectives for which success is measurable and define what will constitute achievement of each goal. The most obvious way to gauge their success is to have attendees fill out surveys about their experiences at the event. Planners can ask specific questions about what the attendees learned, how well organized the meeting or convention appeared, and how they felt about the overall experience. If the purpose of a meeting or convention is publicity, a good measure of success would be how much press coverage the event received. A more precise measurement of meeting success, and one that is gaining importance, is return on investment. Planners compare the costs and benefits of an event and show whether it was worthwhile to the organization. For example, if a company holds a meeting to motivate its employees and improve company morale, the planner might track employee turnover before and after the meeting.

An important part of all these different functions of meeting professionals is establishing and maintaining relationships. Meeting and convention planners interact with a variety of people and must communicate effectively. They must understand their organization's goals for the meeting or convention, be able to communicate their needs clearly to meeting site staff and other suppliers, maintain contact with many different people, and inform people about changes as they occur.

Some aspects of the work vary by the type of organization for which planners work. Those who work for associations must market their meetings to association members, convincing members that attending the meeting is worth their time and expense. Marketing is usually less important for corporate meeting planners because employees are generally required to attend company meetings. Corporate planners usually have shorter time frames in which to prepare their meetings. Planners who work in Federal, State, and local governments must learn how to operate within established government procedures, such as procedures and rules for procuring materials and booking lodging for government employees.

Convention service managers, meeting professionals who work in hotels, convention centers, and similar establishments, act as liaisons between the meeting facility and association, corporate, or government planners. They present food service options to outside planners, coordinate special requests, suggest hotel services based on the planners' budgets, and otherwise help outside planners present effective meetings and conventions in their facilities.

Meeting planners in small organizations perform a wider range of duties, with perhaps one person coordinating an entire meeting. These planners usually need to multi-task even more than planners in larger organizations.

In large organizations or those that sponsor large meetings or conventions, meeting professionals are more likely to specialize in a particular aspect of meeting planning. Some specialties are conference coordinators, who handle most of the meeting logis-

Meeting and covention planners spend most of their time in offices, but during meetings and conventions they work on-site.

tics; registrars, who handle advance registration and payment, name badges, and the set-up of on-site registration; and education planners, who coordinate the meeting content, including speakers and topics. In organizations that hold very large or complex meetings, there may be several senior positions, such as manager of registration, education seminar coordinator, or conference services director, with the entire meeting planning department headed by a department director.

Working Conditions
The work of meeting and convention planners may be considered either stressful or energizing, but there is no question that it is fast-paced and demanding. Planners oversee multiple operations at one time, face numerous deadlines, and orchestrate the activities of several different groups of people. Meeting and convention planners spend the majority of their time in offices; but during meetings, they work on-site at the hotel, convention center, or other meeting location. They travel regularly to attend meetings and to visit prospective meeting sites. The extent of travel depends upon the type of organization for which the planner works. Local and regional organizations require mostly regional travel, while national and international organizations require travel to more distant locales, including travel abroad. Working hours can be long and irregular, with planners working more than 40 hours per week in the time leading up to a meeting and fewer hours after finishing a large meeting. During meetings or conventions, planners may work very long days, possibly starting as early as 5:00 a.m. and working until midnight. They are sometimes required to work on weekends.

Some physical activity is required, including long hours of standing and walking, and some lifting and carrying of boxes of materials, exhibits, or supplies. Planners work with the public and with workers from diverse backgrounds. They may get to travel to beautiful hotels and interesting places and meet speakers and meeting attendees from around the world, and they usually enjoy a high level of autonomy.

Training, Other Qualifications, and Advancement
Meeting and convention planners can qualify for their jobs through a variety of methods. Many migrate into the occupation from other occupations when they are given meeting planning duties in addition to their other duties. For example, an administrative assistant may begin planning small meetings and

gradually move into a full-time position as a meeting and convention planner. Others with a variety of educational or work backgrounds may seek out meeting and convention planning positions. Although there are some certification programs and college and university courses in meeting and convention planning available, a large proportion of the skills needed is learned on the job and through experience.

Many employers prefer a person with a bachelor's degree, but this is not always required. The proportion with a bachelor's degree is increasing because the work and responsibilities are becoming more complex, causing employers to prefer workers with more formal education. Planners have backgrounds in a variety of disciplines, but some useful undergraduate majors are marketing, public relations, communications, business, and hotel or hospitality management. A few schools offer courses or degree programs in meeting and event management. Individuals who have studied hospitality management may start out with greater responsibilities than those with other academic backgrounds. Because formal education is increasingly important, those who enter the occupation may enhance their professional standing by enrolling in meeting planning courses offered by professional meeting and convention planning organizations, colleges, or universities.

Others enter the occupation after working in hotel sales or as marketing or catering coordinators. These are effective ways to learn about meeting and convention planning because these hotel personnel work with numerous meeting planners, participate in negotiations for hotel services, and witness many different meetings. Workers who enter the occupation in these ways often start at a higher level than those with bachelor's degrees and no experience.

Meeting and convention planners must have excellent written and verbal communications skills and interpersonal skills. They must be detail-oriented with excellent organizational skills, and they must be able to multi-task, meet tight deadlines, and maintain composure under pressure in a fast-paced environment. Quantitative and analytic skills are needed to formulate and follow budgets and to understand and negotiate contracts. The ability to speak multiple languages is a plus, since some planners must communicate with meeting attendees and speakers from around the world. They also need computer skills, such as the ability to use financial and registration software and the Internet. In the course of their careers, planners may work in a number of different, unrelated industries, and they must be able to learn independently about each new industry so they can coordinate programs that address the industry's important issues.

Entry-level planners, depending upon their education, generally begin by performing small tasks under the supervision of senior meeting professionals. For example, they may issue requests for proposals and discuss the resulting proposals with higher level planners. They also may assist in registration, review of contracts, or the creation of meeting timelines, schedules, or objectives. They may start by planning small meetings, such as committee meetings. Those who start at small organizations have the opportunity to learn more quickly, since they will be required to take on a larger number of tasks.

To advance in this occupation, planners must volunteer to take on more responsibility and find new and better ways of doing things in their organizations. The most important factors are demonstrated skill on the job, determination, and gaining the respect of others within the organization. Advancement based solely on education is uncommon. On the other hand, education may improve work performance, and therefore may be an important factor in career development.

As meeting and convention planners prove themselves, they are given greater responsibilities. This may mean taking on a wider range of duties or moving to another planning specialty to gain experience in that area before moving to a higher level. For example, a planner may be promoted from conference coordinator, with responsibility for meeting logistics, to program coordinator, with responsibility for booking speakers and formatting the meeting's program. The next step up may be meeting manager, who supervises all parts of the meeting, and then director of meetings, and then possibly department director of meetings and education. Another path for promotion is to move from a small organization to a larger one, taking on responsibility for larger meetings and conventions.

At least two universities offer bachelor's degrees with majors in meetings management. Additionally, meeting and convention planning continuing education programs are offered by a few universities and colleges. These programs are designed for career development of meeting professionals as well as for people wishing to enter the occupation. Some programs may require 40 to more than 100 classroom hours during a period of one semester to two years for a certificate of completion.

The Convention Industry Council offers the Certified Meeting Professional (CMP) credential, a voluntary certification for meeting and convention planners. Although the CMP is not required, it is widely recognized in the industry and may help in career advancement. In order to qualify, candidates must have a minimum of three years of meeting management experience, full-time employment in a meeting management capacity, and proof of accountability for successfully completed meetings. Those who qualify must then pass an examination that covers topics such as adult learning, financial management, facilities and services, logistics, and meeting programs.

With significant experience, meeting planners may become independent meeting consultants, advance to vice presidents or executive directors of associations, or start their own meeting planning firms.

Employment
Meeting and convention planners held about 43,000 jobs in 2004. About 30 percent worked for religious, grantmaking, civic, professional, and similar organizations; 17 percent worked for hotels and other accommodation establishments; 9 percent worked for public and private schools, colleges, universities, and training centers; 6 percent worked for governments; and 6 percent were self-employed. The rest were employed by convention and trade show organizing firms and in other industries as corporate meeting and convention planners.

Job Outlook
Employment of meeting and convention planners is expected to grow faster than the average for all occupations over the 2004-14 period, due to growth of business, the increasing globalization of the economy, and increasing use of electronic forms of communication to bring people together. There will also be some job openings that arise due to the need to replace workers who leave the workforce or transfer to other occupations. Opportunities will be best for individuals with a bachelor's degree and some meeting planning experience.

As businesses and organizations become increasingly international, meetings and conventions become even more important. In organizations that span the country or the globe, the periodic meeting is increasingly the only time the organization can bring all of its members together. Despite the proliferation of alternative forms of communication, such as e-mail, videoconferencing, and the Web, face-to-face interaction is still a necessity. In fact, new forms of communication foster interaction and connect individuals and groups that previously would not have collaborated. By increasing the number of human connections, electronic forms of communication actually increase the demand for meetings, which may offer the only opportunity for these people to interact in person.

Industries that are experiencing high growth tend to experience corresponding growth in meetings and conferences. For example, the medical and pharmaceutical sectors in particular, because of their high growth and their knowledge-intensive natures, will experience large increases in meeting activity. However, these increases will spur employment growth of meeting professionals in medical and pharmaceutical associations rather than in the industries directly. Professional associations hold conferences and conventions that offer the continuing education, training, and opportunities to exchange ideas that are vital to medical and pharmaceutical professionals. Unlike workers in some occupations, meeting and convention planners can often change industries relatively easily, so they often are able to move to different industries in response to the growth or declines in particular sectors of the economy.

Partly because of bioterrorism and homeland security issues, Government agencies are now holding more meetings than ever. Private security and insurance companies also have increased their meeting activity. Because the Government increasingly outsources its non-core functions, this increased activity may spur demand for independent meeting consultants or workers in private meeting planning firms rather than increasing employment of Government meeting planners.

Demand for corporate meeting planners is highly susceptible to business cycle fluctuations since meetings are usually among the first expenses to be cut when budgets are tight. For associations, fluctuations are less pronounced because meetings are generally a source of revenue rather than an expense. However, since fewer people are able to attend association meetings during recessions, associations often reduce their meeting staffs as well. Associations for industries such as health care, in which meeting attendance is required for professionals to maintain their licensure, are the least likely to experience cutbacks during downturns in the economy.

Earnings

Median annual earnings of meeting and convention planners in May 2004 were $39,620. The middle 50 percent earned between $31,180 and $50,790. The lowest 10 percent earned less than $24,660, and the highest 10 percent earned more than $65,060. In May 2004, median annual earnings in the industries employing the largest numbers of meeting and convention planners were as follows:

Business, professional, labor, political, and similar
   organizations $43,100
Traveler accommodation... 36,440

Related Occupations

Meeting and convention planners work to communicate a particular message or impression about an organization, as do public relations specialists. They coordinate the activities of several operations to create a service for large numbers of people, using organizational, logistical, communication, budgeting, and interpersonal skills. Food service managers use the same skills for similar purposes. Like meeting and convention planners, producers and directors coordinate a range of activities to produce a television show or movie, negotiate contracts, and communicate with a wide variety of people. Travel agents also use similar skills, such as interacting with many people and coordinating travel arrangements, including hotel accommodations, transportation, and advice on destinations.

Sources of Additional Information

For information about meeting planner certification, contact:
➤ Convention Industry Council, 8201 Greensboro Dr., Suite 300, McLean, VA 22102. Internet: **http://www.conventionindustry.org**

For information about internships and on-campus student meeting planning organizations, contact:
➤ Professional Convention Management Association, 2301 S. Lake Shore Dr., Suite 1001, Chicago, IL 60616-1419. Internet: **http://www.pcma.org**

For information about meeting planning education, entering the profession, and career paths, contact:
➤ Meeting Professionals International, 3030 LBJ Fwy., Suite 1700, Dallas, TX 75244-5903. Internet: **http://www.mpiweb.org**

Tax Examiners, Collectors, and Revenue Agents

(O*NET 13-2081.00)

Significant Points

- Tax examiners, collectors, and revenue agents work for Federal, State, and local governments.

- A bachelor's degree in accounting is becoming the standard source of training; in State and local government, less formal education or work experience may be sufficient.

- Employment is expected to grow more slowly than average.

- Because of the relatively small number of openings, jobseekers can expect to face competition; workers with knowledge of tax laws and experience working with complex tax issues will have the best opportunities.

Nature of the Work

Taxes are one of the certainties of life, and as long as governments collect taxes, there will be jobs for tax examiners, collectors, and revenue agents. By reviewing tax returns, conducting audits, identifying taxes payable, and collecting overdue tax dollars, these workers ensure that governments obtain revenues from businesses and citizens.

Tax examiners do similar work whether they are employed at the Federal, State, or local government level. They review filed tax returns for accuracy and determine whether tax credits and deductions are allowed by law. Because many States assess individual income taxes based on the taxpayer's reported Federal adjusted gross income, tax examiners working for the Federal Government report any adjustments or corrections they make to the States. State tax examiners then determine whether the adjustments affect the taxpayer's State tax liability. At the local level, tax examiners often have additional duties, but an integral part of the work still includes the need to determine the factual basis for claims for refunds.

Tax examiners usually deal with the simplest tax returns—those filed by individual taxpayers with few deductions or those filed by small businesses. At the entry level, many tax examiners perform clerical duties, such as reviewing tax returns and entering them into a computer system for processing. If there is a problem, tax examiners may contact the taxpayer to resolve it.

Tax examiners also review returns for accuracy, checking taxpayers' math and making sure that the amounts that they report match those reported from other sources, such as employers and banks. In addition, examiners verify that Social Security numbers match names and that taxpayers have correctly interpreted the instructions on tax forms.

Much of a tax examiner's job involves making sure that tax credits and deductions claimed by taxpayers are legitimate. Tax examiners contact taxpayers by mail or telephone to address discrepancies and request supporting documentation. They may notify taxpayers of any overpayment or underpayment and either issue a refund or request further payment. If a taxpayer owes additional taxes, tax examiners adjust the total amount by assessing fees, interest, and penalties and notify the taxpayer of the total liability. Although most tax examiners deal with uncomplicated returns, some may work in more complex tax areas, such as pensions or business net operating losses.

Revenue agents specialize in tax-related accounting work for the U.S. Internal Revenue Service (IRS) and for equivalent agencies in State and local governments. Like tax examiners, they audit returns for accuracy. However, revenue agents handle complicated income, sales, and excise tax returns of businesses and large corporations. As a result, their work differs in a number of ways from that of tax examiners.

Entry-level Federal revenue agents usually audit tax returns of small businesses whose market specializations are similar. As they develop expertise in an industry, such as construction, retail sales, or finance, insurance, and real estate, revenue agents work with tax returns of larger corporations.

Many experienced revenue agents specialize; for example, they may focus exclusively on multinational businesses. But all revenue agents working for the Federal Government must keep abreast of the lengthy, complex, and frequently changing tax code. Computer technology has simplified the research process, allowing revenue agents Internet access to relevant legal bulletins, IRS notices, and tax-related court decisions. Revenue agents are increasingly using computers to analyze data and identify trends that help to pinpoint tax offenders.

At the State level, revenue agents have duties similar to those of their counterparts in the Federal Government. State revenue agents use revenue adjustment reports forwarded by the IRS to determine whether adjustments made by Federal revenue agents affect a taxpayer's taxable income in the eyes of the States. In addition, State agents consider the sales and income taxes for their own States.

At the local level, revenue agents have varying titles and duties, but they still perform field audits or office audits of financial records for business firms. In some cases, local revenue agents also examine financial records of individuals. These local agents, like their State counterparts, rely on the information contained in Federal tax returns. However, local agents also must be knowledgeable enough to apply local tax laws regarding income, utility fees, or school taxes.

Collectors, also called revenue officers in the IRS, deal with delinquent accounts. The process of collecting a delinquent account starts with the revenue agent or tax examiner sending a report to the taxpayer. If the taxpayer makes no effort to resolve the delinquent account, the case is assigned to a collector. When a collector takes a case, he or she first sends the taxpayer a notice. The collector then works with the taxpayer on how to settle the debt.

In cases in which taxpayers fail to file a tax return, Federal collectors may request that the IRS prepare the return on a taxpayer's behalf. In other instances, collectors are responsible for verifying claims that delinquent taxpayers cannot pay their taxes. They investigate these claims by researching court information on the status of liens, mortgages, or financial statements; locating assets through third parties, such as neighbors or local departments of motor vehicles; and requesting legal summonses for other records. Ultimately, collectors must decide whether the IRS should take a lien—a claim on an asset such as a bank account, real estate, or an automobile—to settle a debt. Collectors also have the discretion to garnish wages—that is, take a portion of earned wages—to collect taxes owed.

Tax examiners, collectors, and revenue agents review tax returns, conduct audits, and collect overdue taxes.

A big part of a collector's job at the Federal level is imposing and following up on delinquent taxpayers' payment deadlines. For each case file, collectors must maintain records, including contacts, telephone numbers, and actions taken.

Like tax examiners and revenue agents, collectors use computers to maintain files. Computer technology also gives collectors access to data to help them identify high-risk debtors—those who are unlikely to pay or are likely to flee.

Collectors at the IRS usually work independently. However, they call on experts when tax examiners or revenue agents find fraudulent returns, or when the seizure of a property will involve complex legal steps.

At the State level, collectors decide whether to take action on the basis of their own States' tax returns. Collection work may be handled over the telephone or turned over to a collector who specializes in obtaining settlements. These collectors contact people directly and have the authority to issue subpoenas and request seizures of property. At the local levels, collectors have less power than their State and Federal counterparts. Although they can start the processes leading to the seizure of property and garnishment of wages, they must go through the local court system.

Working Conditions

Tax examiners, collectors, and revenue agents generally work a 40-hour week, although some overtime might be needed during the tax season. State and local tax examiners, who may review sales, gasoline, and cigarette taxes instead of handling tax returns, may have a steadier workload year-round. Stress can result from the need to work under a deadline in checking returns and evaluating taxpayer claims. Collectors also must face the unpleasant task of confronting delinquent taxpayers.

Tax examiners, collectors, and revenue agents work in clean, well-lighted offices, either in cubicles or at desks. Sometimes travel is necessary. Revenue agents at both the Federal and State levels spend a significant portion of their time in the offices of private firms, accessing tax-related records. Some agents may be permanently stationed in the offices of large corporations with complicated tax structures. Agents at the local level usually work in city halls or municipal buildings. Collectors travel to local courthouses, county and municipal seats of government, businesses, and taxpayers' homes to look up records, search for assets, and settle delinquent accounts.

Training, Other Qualifications, and Advancement

Tax examiners, collectors, and revenue agents work with confidential financial and personal information; therefore, trustworthiness is crucial for maintaining the confidentiality of individuals and businesses. Applicants for Federal Government jobs must submit to a background investigation.

A degree in accounting is becoming the standard source of training for tax examiners, collectors, and revenue agents. A bachelor's degree generally is required for employment with the Federal Government. In State and local governments, prospective workers may be able to enter the occupation with an associate's degree in accounting or with a combination of related tax and accounting work experience and some college-level business classes. For more advanced entry-level positions, applicants must have a bachelor's degree; demonstrate specialized experience working with tax records, tax laws and regulations, documents, financial accounts, or similar records; or have some combination of postsecondary education and specialized experience.

Tax examiners must be able to understand fundamental tax regulations and procedures, pay attention to detail, and cope well with deadlines. After they are hired, tax examiners receive some formal training. In addition, annual employer-provided updates keep tax examiners current with changes in procedures and regulations.

Revenue agents need strong analytical, organizational, and time management skills. They also must be able to work independently, because they spend so much time away from their home office, and they must keep current with changes in the tax code and laws. Newly hired revenue agents expand their accounting knowledge and remain up to date by consulting auditing manuals and other sources for detailed information about individual industries. Employers also continually offer training in new auditing techniques and tax-related issues and court decisions.

Collectors need good interpersonal and communication skills because they deal directly with the public and because their reports are scrutinized when the IRS must legally justify attempts to seize assets. They also must be able to act independently and to exercise good judgment in deciding when and how to collect a debt. Applicants for collector jobs need experience demonstrating knowledge of business and financial practices or knowledge of credit operations and collection of delinquent accounts.

Entry-level collectors receive formal and on-the-job training under an instructor's guidance before working independently. Collectors usually complete initial training by the end of their second year of service, but may receive advanced technical instruction as they gain seniority and take on more difficult cases. Also, collectors are encouraged to continue their professional education by attending meetings to exchange information about how changes in tax laws affect collection methods.

Advancement potential within Federal, State, and local agencies varies for tax examiners, revenue agents, and collectors. For related jobs outside government, experienced workers can take a licensing exam administered by the Federal Government to become enrolled agents—nongovernment tax professionals authorized to represent taxpayers before the IRS.

As revenue agents gain experience, they may specialize in an industry, work with larger corporations, and cover increasingly complex tax returns. Some revenue agents also specialize in assisting in criminal investigations, auditing the books of known or suspected criminals such as drug dealers or money launderers. Some agents work with grand juries to help secure indictments. Others become international agents, assessing taxes on companies with subsidiaries abroad.

Collectors who demonstrate leadership skills and a thorough knowledge of collection activities may advance to supervisory or managerial collector positions, in which they oversee the activities of other collectors. It is only these higher level supervisors and managers who may authorize the more serious actions against individuals and businesses. The more complex collection attempts, which usually are directed at larger businesses, are reserved for collectors at these higher levels.

Employment

In 2004, tax examiners, revenue agents, and collectors held about 76,000 jobs at all levels of government. About half worked for the Federal Government, 3 out of 10 for State governments, and the remainder in local governments. Among those employed by the IRS, tax examiners and revenue agents predominate because of the need to examine or audit tax returns. Collectors make up a smaller proportion, because most disputed tax liabilities do not require enforced collection.

Job Outlook

Employment of tax examiners, collectors, and revenue agents is projected to grow more slowly than the average for all occupations during the 2004-14 projection period. Because of the relatively small number of openings, jobseekers can expect to face competition.

Demand for tax examiners, revenue agents, and tax collectors will stem from changes in government policy toward tax enforcement and from growth in the number of businesses. The Federal Government is expected to increase its tax enforcement efforts. Also, new technology and information sharing among tax agencies make it easier for agencies to pinpoint potential offenders, increasing the number of cases for audit and collection. These two factors should increase the demand for revenue agents and tax collectors. The IRS plans to streamline its tax examination and collections process, and both State and Federal tax agencies are turning their enforcement focus to higher income taxpayers and businesses, which file more complicated tax returns. Because of these shifts, workers with knowledge of tax laws and experience working with complex tax issues will have the best opportunities.

Several factors may limit the growth of these occupations. Because much of the simpler work done by tax examiners, collectors, and revenue agents is now computerized, productivity has increased, limiting the need for more workers. The work of tax examiners is especially well suited to automation, adversely affecting demand for these workers in particular. In addition, more than 40 States and many local tax agencies contract out their tax collection functions to private-sector collection agencies in order to reduce costs, and this trend is likely to continue. In 2005, the IRS received Congressional approval to begin outsourcing tax collection. IRS outsourcing will dampen growth in employment of revenue officers but is not expected to affect employment of revenue agents.

Employment at the State and local levels may fluctuate with the overall state of the economy. When the economy is contracting, State and local governments are likely to freeze hiring and lay off workers in response to budgetary constraints. Opportunities at the Federal level will reflect the tightening or relaxation of budget constraints imposed on the IRS, the primary employer of these workers.

Earnings

In May 2004, median annual earnings for all tax examiners, collectors, and revenue agents were $43,490. The middle 50 percent earned between $32,520 and $62,570. The bottom 10 percent earned less than $25,120, and the top 10 percent earned more than $81,240.

However, median earnings vary considerably, depending on the level of government. At the Federal level, May 2004 median annual earnings for tax examiners were $52,830; at the State level, they were $41,920; and at the local level, they were $31,310. Earnings also vary by occupational specialty. For example, in the Federal Government in 2005, tax examiners earned an average of $36,963, revenue agents earned $81,417, and tax specialists earned $54,364.

Related Occupations

Tax examiners, collectors, and revenue agents analyze and interpret financial data. Occupations with similar responsibilities include accountants and auditors, budget analysts, cost estimators, financial analysts and personal financial advisors, financial managers, and loan officers.

Sources of Additional Information

Information on obtaining positions as tax examiners, collectors, or revenue agents with the Federal Government is available from the Office of Personnel Management through USAJOBS, the Federal Government's official employment information system. This resource for locating and applying for job opportunities can be accessed through the Internet at **http://www.usajobs.opm.gov** or through an interactive voice response telephone system at (703) 724-1850 or TDD (978) 461-8404. These numbers are not tollfree, and charges may result.

State or local government personnel offices can provide information about tax examiner, collector, or revenue agent jobs at those levels of government.

For information about careers at the Internal Revenue Service, contact:
➤ Internal Revenue Service, 1111 Constitution Ave. NW., Washington, D.C. 20224. Internet: **http://www.jobs.irs.gov/index.html**

Actuaries

(O*NET 15-2011.00)

Significant Points

- A strong background in mathematics is essential; actuaries must pass a series of examinations to gain full professional status.

- About 6 out of 10 actuaries are employed in the insurance industry.

- Employment opportunities should remain good for those who qualify, because the stringent qualifying examination system restricts the number of candidates.

Nature of the Work

One of the main functions of actuaries is to help businesses assess the risk of certain events occurring and to formulate policies that minimize the cost of that risk. For this reason, actuaries are essential to the insurance industry. Actuaries assemble and analyze data to estimate the probability and likely cost of the occurrence of an event such as death, sickness, injury, disability, or loss of property. Actuaries also address financial questions, including those involving the level of pension contributions required to produce a certain retirement income and the way in which a company should invest resources to maximize its return on investments in light of potential risk. Using their broad knowledge of statistics, finance, and business, actuaries help design insurance policies, pension plans, and other financial strategies in a manner which will help ensure that the plans are maintained on a sound financial basis.

Most actuaries are employed in the insurance industry, specializing in life and health insurance or property and casualty insurance. They produce probability tables which determine the likelihood that a potential future event will generate a claim. From these tables, they estimate the amount a company can expect to pay in claims. For example, property and casualty actuaries calculate the expected amount payable in claims resulting from automobile accidents, an amount that varies with the insured person's age, sex, driving history, type of car, and other factors. Actuaries ensure that the price, or premium, charged for such insurance will enable the company to cover claims and other expenses. The premium must be profitable, yet competitive with other insurance companies. Within the life and health insurance fields, actuaries are helping to develop long-term-care insurance and annuity policies, the latter a growing investment tool for many individuals.

Actuaries in other financial services industries manage credit and price corporate security offerings. They also devise new investment tools to help their firms compete with other financial services companies. Pension actuaries working under the provisions of the Employee Retirement Income Security Act (ERISA) of 1974 evaluate pension plans covered by that Act and report on the plans' financial soundness to participants, sponsors, and Federal regulators. Actuaries working in government help manage social programs such as Social Security and Medicare.

Actuaries may play a role in determining company policy and may need to explain complex technical matters to company executives, government officials, shareholders, policyholders, or the public in general. They may testify before public agencies on proposed legislation affecting their businesses or explain changes in contract provisions to customers. They also may help companies develop plans to enter new lines of business or new geographic markets with existing lines of business by forecasting demand in competitive settings.

Both staff actuaries employed by businesses and consulting actuaries provide advice to clients on a contract basis. The duties of most consulting actuaries are similar to those of other actuaries. For example, some may evaluate company pension plans by calculating the future value of employee and employer contributions and determining whether the amounts are sufficient to meet the future needs of retirees. Others help companies reduce their insurance costs by lowering the level of risk the companies assume. For instance, they may provide advice on how to lessen the risk of injury on the job, which will lower worker's compensation costs. Consulting actuaries sometimes testify in court regarding the value of the potential lifetime earnings of a person who is disabled or killed in an accident, the

Actuaries need a strong background in mathematics.

current value of future pension benefits (in divorce cases), or other values arrived at by complex calculations. Many consulting actuaries work in reinsurance, a field in which one insurance company arranges to share a large prospective liability policy with another insurance company in exchange for a percentage of the premium.

Working Conditions

Actuaries have desk jobs, and their offices usually are comfortable and pleasant. They often work at least 40 hours a week. Some actuaries —particularly consulting actuaries—may travel to meet with clients. Consulting actuaries also may experience more erratic employment and be expected to work more than 40 hours per week.

Employment

Actuaries held about 18,000 jobs in 2004, with 6 out of 10 employed in the insurance industry. A growing number of actuaries work for firms providing a variety of corporate services, especially management and public relations, or for firms offering consulting services. A relatively small number of actuaries are employed by security and commodity brokers or by government agencies.

Training, Other Qualifications, and Advancement

Actuaries need a strong background in mathematics. Applicants for beginning actuarial jobs usually have a bachelor's degree in mathematics, actuarial science, statistics, or a business-related discipline such as economics, finance, or accounting. About 100 colleges and universities offer an actuarial science program, and most offer a degree in mathematics, statistics, economics, or finance. Some companies hire applicants without specifying a major, provided that the applicant has a working knowledge of mathematics, including calculus, probability, and statistics, and has demonstrated this knowledge by passing one or two actuarial exams required for professional designation. Courses in economics, accounting, finance, and insurance also are useful. Companies increasingly prefer well-rounded individuals who, in addition to having acquired a strong technical background, have some training in liberal arts and business and possess strong communication skills.

In addition to knowledge of mathematics, computer skills are becoming increasingly important. Actuaries should be able to develop and use spreadsheets and databases, as well as standard statistical analysis software. Knowledge of computer programming languages, such as Visual Basic, also is useful.

Two professional societies sponsor programs leading to full professional status in their specialty. The Society of Actuaries (SOA) administers a series of actuarial examinations in the life insurance, health benefits systems, retirement systems, and finance and investment fields. The Casualty Actuarial Society (CAS) gives a series of examinations in the property and casualty field, which includes fire, accident, medical malpractice, worker's compensation, and personal injury liability.

The first four exams in the SOA and CAS examination series are jointly sponsored by the two societies and cover the same material. For this reason, students do not need to commit themselves to a specialty until they have taken the initial examinations, which test an individual's competence in probability, calculus, statistics, and other branches of mathematics. The first few examinations help students evaluate their potential as actuaries. Many prospective actuaries begin taking the exams in college with the help of self-study guides and courses. Those who pass one or more examinations have better opportunities for employment at higher starting salaries than those who do not.

After graduating from college, most prospective actuaries gain on-the job experience at an insurance company or consulting firm, while at the same time working to complete the examination process. Actuaries are encouraged to finish the entire series of examinations as soon as possible, advancing first to the Associate level (with an ASA or ACAS designation) and then to the Fellowship level (FSA or FCAS designation). Advanced topics in the casualty field include investment and assets, dynamic financial analysis, and valuation of insurance. Candidates in the SOA examination series must choose a specialty—group and health benefits, individual life and annuities, pensions, investments, or finance. Examinations are given twice a year, in the spring and the fall. Although many companies allot time to their employees for study, home study is required to pass the examinations, and many actuaries study for months to prepare for each examination. It is likewise common for employers to pay the hundreds of dollars for examination fees and study materials. Most actuaries reach the Associate level within 4 to 6 years and the Fellowship level a few years later.

Specific requirements apply to pension actuaries, who verify the financial status of defined benefit pension plans for the Federal Government. These actuaries must be enrolled by the Joint Board of the U.S. Treasury Department and the U.S. Department of Labor for the Enrollment of Actuaries. To qualify for enrollment, applicants must meet certain experience and examination requirements, as stipulated by the Board.

To perform their duties effectively, actuaries must keep up with current economic and social trends and legislation, as well as with health, business, finance, and economic developments that could affect insurance or investment practices. Good communication and interpersonal skills also are important, particularly for prospective consulting actuaries.

Beginning actuaries often rotate among different jobs in an organization to learn various actuarial operations and phases of insurance work, such as marketing, underwriting, and product development. At first, they prepare data for actuarial projects or perform other simple tasks. As they gain experience, actuaries may supervise clerks, prepare correspondence, draft reports, and conduct research. They may move from one company to another early in their careers as they advance to higher positions.

Advancement depends largely on job performance and the number of actuarial examinations passed. Actuaries with a broad knowledge of the insurance, pension, investment, or employee benefits fields can rise to administrative and executive positions in their companies. Actuaries with supervisory ability may advance to management positions in other areas, such as underwriting, accounting, data processing, marketing, and advertising. Some actuaries assume college and university faculty positions. (See the statement on teachers—postsecondary elsewhere in the *Handbook*.)

Job Outlook

Employment of actuaries is expected to grow faster than the average for all occupations through 2014. Employment opportunities should remain good for those who qualify, because the stringent qualifying examination system restricts the number of candidates. Employment growth in the insurance industry is expected to continue at a stable pace, while more significant job growth is likely in some other industries. In addition, a small number of jobs will open up each year to replace actuaries who leave the occupation to retire or who find new jobs.

Steady demand by the insurance industry—the largest employer of actuaries—should ensure the creation of new actuary jobs in this key industry over the projection period. Actuaries will continue to be needed to develop, price, and evaluate a variety of insurance products and calculate the costs of new risks. Although employment of actuaries in life insurance had begun to decline recently, the growing popularity of annuities, a financial product offered primarily by life insurance companies, has resulted in some job growth in this specialty. Also, new actuarial positions have been created in property-casualty insurance to analyze evolving risks, such as terrorism.

Some new employment opportunities for actuaries should also become available in the health care field as health care issues and Medicare reform continue to receive growing attention. Increased regulation of managed health care companies and the desire to contain health care costs will continue to provide job opportunities for actuaries, who will also be needed to evaluate the risks associated with new medical issues, such as genetic testing and the impact of new diseases. Others in this field are involved in drafting health care legislation.

A significant proportion of new actuaries will find employment with consulting firms. Companies that may not find it cost effective to hire their own actuaries are increasingly hiring consulting actuaries to analyze various risks. Other areas with notable growth prospects are information services and accounting services. Also, because actuarial skills are increasingly seen as useful to other industries that deal with risk, such as the airline and the banking industries, additional job openings may be created in these industries.

The best job prospects for entry-level positions will be for those candidates who have passed at least one or two of the initial actuarial exams. Candidates with additional knowledge or experience, such as those who possess computer programming skills, will be particularly attractive to employers. Most jobs in this occupation are located in urban areas, but opportunities vary by geographic location. States in which actuary jobs are concentrated include Illinois, New Jersey, New York, and Connecticut.

Earnings

Median annual earnings of actuaries were $76,340 in May 2004. The middle 50 percent earned between $54,770 and $107,650.

According to the National Association of Colleges and Employers, annual starting salaries for graduates with a bachelor's degree in actuarial science averaged $52,741 in 2005.

Insurance companies and consulting firms give merit increases to actuaries as they gain experience and pass examinations. Some companies also offer cash bonuses for each professional designation achieved.

Related Occupations

Actuaries need a strong background in mathematics, statistics, and related fields. Other workers whose jobs involve related skills include accountants and auditors, budget analysts, economists, market and survey researchers, financial analysts and personal financial advisors, insurance underwriters, mathematicians, and statisticians.

Sources of Additional Information

Career information on actuaries specializing in pensions is available from:
➤ American Society of Pension Actuaries, 4245 N. Fairfax Dr., Suite 750, Arlington, VA 22203. Internet: **http://www.aspa.org**

For information about actuarial careers in life and health insurance, employee benefits and pensions, and finance and investments, contact:
➤ Society of Actuaries (SOA), 475 N. Martingale Rd., Suite 600, Schaumburg, IL 60173-2226. Internet: **http://www.soa.org**

For information about actuarial careers in property and casualty insurance, contact:
➤ Casualty Actuarial Society (CAS), 1100 N. Glebe Rd., Suite 600, Arlington, VA 222010425. Internet: **http://www.casact.org**

The SOA and CAS jointly sponsor a Web site for those interested in pursuing an actuarial career. Internet: **http://www.BeAnActuary.org**

For general information on a career as an actuary, contact:
➤ American Academy of Actuaries, 1100 17th St. NW., 7th Floor, Washington, DC 20036. Internet: **http://www.actuary.org**

Computer Programmers

(O*NET 15-1021.00)

Significant Points

- Sixty-seven percent of computer programmers held a college or higher degree in 2004; nearly half held a bachelor's degree, and about 1 in 5 held a graduate degree.

- Employment is expected to grow much more slowly than that for other computer specialists.

- Prospects likely will be best for college graduates with knowledge of a variety of programming languages and tools; those with less formal education or its equivalent in work experience are apt to face strong competition for programming jobs.

Nature of the Work

Computer programmers write, test, and maintain the detailed instructions, called programs, that computers must follow to perform their functions. Programmers also conceive, design, and test logical structures for solving problems by computer. Many technical innovations in programming—advanced computing technologies and sophisticated new languages and programming tools—have redefined the role of a programmer and elevated much of the programming work done today. Job titles and descriptions may vary, depending on the organization. In this occupational statement, *computer programmers* are individuals whose main job function is programming; this group has a wide range of responsibilities and educational backgrounds.

Computer programs tell the computer what to do—which information to identify and access, how to process it, and what equipment to use. Programs vary widely depending on the type of information to be accessed or generated. For example, the instructions involved in updating financial records are very different from those required to duplicate conditions on an aircraft for pilots training in a flight simulator. Although simple programs can be written in a few hours, programs that use complex mathematical formulas whose solutions can only be approximated or that draw data from many existing systems may require more than a year of work. In most cases, several programmers work together as a team under a senior programmer's supervision.

Programmers write programs according to the specifications determined primarily by computer software engineers and systems analysts. (Separate statements on computer software engineers and on computer systems analysts appear elsewhere in the *Handbook*) After the design process is complete, it is the job of the programmer to convert that design into a logical series of instructions that the computer can follow. The programmer codes these instructions in a conventional programming language such as COBOL; an artificial intelligence language such as Prolog; or one of the most advanced object-oriented languages, such as Java, C++, or ACTOR. Different programming languages are used depending on the purpose of the program. COBOL, for example, is commonly used for business applications, whereas Fortran (short for "formula translation") is used in science and engineering. C++ is widely used for both scientific and business applications. Extensible Markup Language (XML) has become a popular programming tool for Web programmers, along with J2EE (Java 2 Platform). Programmers generally know more than one programming language and, because many languages are similar, they often can learn new languages relatively easily. In practice, programmers often are referred to by the language they know, such as Java programmers, or by the type of function they perform or environment in which they work—for example, database programmers, mainframe programmers, or Web programmers.

Many programmers update, repair, modify, and expand existing programs. When making changes to a section of code, called a routine, programmers need to make other users aware of the task that the routine is to perform. They do this by inserting comments in the coded instructions so that others can understand the program. Many programmers use computer-assisted software engineering (CASE) tools to automate much of the coding process. These tools enable a programmer to concentrate on writing the unique parts of the program, because the tools automate various pieces of the program being built. CASE tools generate whole sections of code automatically, rather than line by line. Programmers also use libraries of basic code that can be modified or customized for a specific application. This approach yields more reliable and consistent programs and increases programmers' productivity by eliminating some routine steps.

Programmers test a program by running it to ensure that the instructions are correct and that the program produces the desired outcome. If errors do occur, the programmer must make the appropriate change and recheck the program until it produces the correct results. This process is called testing and debugging. Programmers may continue to fix these problems throughout the life of a program. Programmers working in a mainframe environment, which involves a large centralized computer, may prepare instructions for a computer operator who will run the program. (A separate statement on computer operators appears elsewhere in the *Handbook*) Programmers also may contribute to a manual for persons who will be using the program.

Computer programmers often are grouped into two broad types—applications programmers and systems programmers. *Applications programmers* write programs to handle a specific job, such as a program to track inventory within an organization. They also may revise existing packaged software or customize generic applications which are frequently purchased from vendors. *Systems programmers*, in contrast, write programs to maintain and control computer systems software, such as operating systems, networked systems, and database systems. These workers make changes in the instructions that determine how the network, workstations, and central processing unit of the system handle the various jobs they have been given and how they communicate with peripheral equipment such as terminals, printers, and disk drives. Because of their knowledge of the entire computer system, systems programmers often help applications programmers determine the source of problems that may occur with their programs.

Programmers in software development companies may work directly with experts from various fields to create software—either programs designed for specific clients or packaged software for general use—ranging from games and educational software to programs for desktop publishing and financial planning. Programming of packaged software constitutes one of the most rapidly growing segments of the computer services industry.

In some organizations, particularly small ones, workers commonly known as *programmer-analysts* are responsible for both the systems analysis and the actual programming work. (A more detailed description of the work of programmer-analysts is presented in the statement on computer systems analysts elsewhere in the *Handbook*.) Advanced programming languages and new object-oriented programming capabilities are increasing the efficiency and productivity of both programmers and users. The transition from a mainframe environment to one that is based primarily on personal computers (PCs) has blurred the once rigid distinction between the programmer and the user. Increasingly, adept end users are taking over many of the tasks previously performed by programmers. For example, the growing use of packaged software, such as spreadsheet and database management software packages, allows users to write simple programs to access data and perform calculations.

Working Conditions

Programmers generally work in offices in comfortable surroundings. Many programmers may work long hours or weekends to meet deadlines or fix critical problems that occur during off hours. Telecommuting is becoming common for a wide range of computer professionals, including computer programmers. As computer networks expand, more programmers are able to make corrections or fix problems remotely using modems, e-mail, and the Internet to connect to a customer's computer.

Like other workers who spend long periods in front of a computer terminal typing at a keyboard, programmers are susceptible to eyestrain, back discomfort, and hand and wrist problems such as carpal tunnel syndrome.

Training, Other Qualifications, and Advancement

Although there are many training paths available for programmers, mainly because employers' needs are so varied, the level of education and experience employers seek has been rising due to the growing number of qualified applicants and the specialization involved with most programming tasks. Bachelor's degrees are commonly required, although some programmers may qualify for certain jobs with 2-year degrees or certificates. The associate degree is a widely used

Computer programmers tell the computer what to do.

entry-level credential for prospective computer programmers. Most community colleges and many independent technical institutes and proprietary schools offer an associate degree in computer science or a related information technology field.

Employers primarily are interested in programming knowledge, and computer programmers can become certified in a programming language such as C++ or Java. College graduates who are interested in changing careers or developing an area of expertise also may return to a 2-year community college or technical school for additional training. In the absence of a degree, substantial specialized experience or expertise may be needed. Even when hiring programmers with a degree, employers appear to place more emphasis on previous experience.

Some computer programmers hold a college degree in computer science, mathematics, or information systems, whereas others have taken special courses in computer programming to supplement their degree in a field such as accounting, inventory control, or another area of business. As the level of education and training required by employers continues to rise, the proportion of programmers with a college degree should increase in the future. As indicated by the following tabulation, more than two-thirds of computer programmers had a bachelor's or higher degree in 2004.

	Percent
High school graduate or less	8.3
Some college, no degree	14.1
Associate degree	10.2
Bachelor's degree	49.1
Graduate degree	18.3

Required skills vary from job to job, but the demand for various skills generally is driven by changes in technology. Employers using computers for scientific or engineering applications usually prefer college graduates who have degrees in computer or information science, mathematics, engineering, or the physical sciences. Graduate degrees in related fields are required for some jobs. Employers who use computers for business applications prefer to hire people who have had college courses in management information systems and business and who possess strong programming skills. Although knowledge of traditional languages still is important, employers are placing increasing emphasis on newer, object-oriented programming languages and tools such as C++ and Java. Additionally, employers are seeking persons familiar with fourth-generation and fifth-generation languages that involve graphic user interface and systems programming. Employers also prefer applicants who have general business skills and experience related to the operations of the firm. Students can improve their employment prospects by participating in a college work-study program or by undertaking an internship.

Most systems programmers hold a 4-year degree in computer science. Extensive knowledge of a variety of operating systems is essential for such workers. This includes being able to configure an operating system to work with different types of hardware and having the skills needed to adapt the operating system to best meet the needs of a particular organization. Systems programmers also must be able to work with database systems, such as DB2, Oracle, or Sybase.

When hiring programmers, employers look for people with the necessary programming skills who can think logically and pay close attention to detail. The job calls for patience, persistence, and the ability to work on exacting analytical work, especially under pressure. Ingenuity and creativity are particularly important when programmers design solutions and test their work for potential failures. The ability to work with abstract concepts and to do technical analysis is especially important for systems programmers because they work with the software that controls the computer's operation. Because programmers are expected to work in teams and

interact directly with users, employers want programmers who are able to communicate with nontechnical personnel.

Entry-level or junior programmers may work alone on simple assignments after some initial instruction, or they may be assigned to work on a team with more experienced programmers. Either way, beginning programmers generally must work under close supervision. Because technology changes so rapidly, programmers must continuously update their knowledge and skills by taking courses sponsored by their employer or by software vendors, or offered through local community colleges and universities.

For skilled workers who keep up to date with the latest technology, the prospects for advancement are good. In large organizations, programmers may be promoted to lead programmer and be given supervisory responsibilities. Some applications programmers may move into systems programming after they gain experience and take courses in systems software. With general business experience, programmers may become programmer-analysts or systems analysts or be promoted to managerial positions. Other programmers, with specialized knowledge and experience with a language or operating system, may work in research and development for multimedia or Internet technology and may even become computer software engineers. As employers increasingly contract with outside firms to do programming jobs, more opportunities should arise for experienced programmers with expertise in a specific area to work as consultants.

Certification is a way to demonstrate a level of competence, and may provide a jobseeker with a competitive advantage. In addition to language-specific certificates that a programmer can obtain, product vendors or software firms also offer certification and may require professionals who work with their products to be certified. Voluntary certification also is available through various other organizations.

Employment

Computer programmers held about 455,000 jobs in 2004. Programmers are employed in almost every industry, but the largest concentration is in computer systems design and related services. Large numbers of programmers also work for telecommunications companies, software publishers, financial institutions, insurance carriers, educational institutions, and government agencies.

Many computer programmers are employed on a temporary or contract basis or work as independent consultants, providing companies expertise with new programming languages or specialized areas of application. Rather than hiring programmers as permanent employees and then laying them off after a job is completed, employers can contract with temporary help agencies, with consulting firms, or with programmers themselves. A marketing firm, for example, may require programming services only to write and debug the software necessary to get a new customer database running. Bringing in an independent contractor or consultant with experience in a new or advanced programming language enables the firm to complete the job without having to retrain existing workers. Such jobs may last anywhere from several weeks to a year or longer. There were 25,000 self-employed computer programmers in 2004.

Job Outlook

As programming tasks become increasingly sophisticated and additional levels of skill and experience are demanded by employers, graduates of 2-year programs and people with less than a 2-year degree or its equivalent in work experience will face strong competition for programming jobs. Competition for entry-level positions, however, also can affect applicants with a bachelor's degree. Prospects should be best for college graduates with knowledge of, and experience working with, a variety of programming languages and tools—including C++ and other object-oriented languages such as Java, as well as newer, domain-specific languages that apply to computer networking, database management, and Internet application development. Obtaining vendor-specific or language-specific certification also can provide a competitive edge. Because demand fluctuates with employers' needs, jobseekers should keep up to date with the latest skills and technologies. Individuals who want to become programmers can enhance their prospects by combining the appropriate formal training with practical work experience.

Employment of programmers is expected to grow more slowly than the average for all occupations through the year 2014. Sophisticated computer software now has the capability to write basic code, eliminating the need for many programmers to do this routine work. The consolidation and centralization of systems and applications, developments in packaged software, advances in programming languages and tools, and the growing ability of users to design, write, and implement more of their own programs mean that more of the programming functions can be transferred from programmers to other types of information workers, such as computer software engineers.

Another factor limiting growth in employment is the outsourcing of these jobs to other countries. Computer programmers can perform their job function from anywhere in the world and can digitally transmit their programs to any location via e-mail. Programmers are at a much higher risk of having their jobs outsourced abroad than are workers involved in more complex and sophisticated information technology functions, such as software engineering, because computer programming has become an international language, requiring little localized or specialized knowledge. Additionally, the work of computer programmers can be routinized, once knowledge of a particular programming language is mastered.

Nevertheless, employers will continue to need programmers who have strong technical skills and who understand an employer's business and its programming requirements. This means that programmers will have to keep abreast of changing programming languages and techniques. Given the importance of networking and the expansion of client/server, Web-based, and wireless environments, organizations will look for programmers who can support data communications and help implement electronic commerce and intranet strategies. Demand for programmers with strong object-oriented programming capabilities and technical specialization in areas such as client/server programming, wireless applications, multimedia technology, and graphic user interface likely will stem from the expansion of intranets, extranets, and Internet applications. Programmers also will be needed to create and maintain expert systems and embed these technologies in more products. Finally, a growing emphasis on cybersecurity will lead to increased demand for programmers who are familiar with digital security issues and skilled in using appropriate security technology.

Jobs for both systems and applications programmers should be most plentiful in data-processing service firms, software houses, and computer consulting businesses. These types of establishments are part of computer systems design and related services and software publishers, which are projected to be among the fastest growing industries in the economy over the 2004-14 period. As organizations attempt to control costs and keep up with changing technology, they will need programmers to assist in conversions to new computer languages and systems. In addition, numerous job openings will result from the need to replace programmers who leave the labor force or transfer to other occupations such as manager or systems analyst.

Earnings
Median annual earnings of computer programmers were $62,890 in May 2004. The middle 50 percent earned between $47,580 and $81,280 a year. The lowest 10 percent earned less than $36,470; the highest 10 percent earned more than $99,610. Median annual earnings in the industries employing the largest numbers of computer programmers in May 2004 are shown below:

Software publishers	$73,060
Computer systems design and related services	67,600
Data processing, hosting, and related services	64,540
Insurance carriers	62,990
Management of companies and enterprises	62,160

According to the National Association of Colleges and Employers, starting salary offers for graduates with a bachelor's degree in computer science averaged $50,820 a year in 2005.

According to Robert Half International, a firm providing specialized staffing services, average annual starting salaries in 2005 ranged from $52,500 to $83,250 for applications development programmers/analysts, and from $55,000 to $88,250 for software developers. Average starting salaries for mainframe systems programmers ranged from $50,250 to $67,500 in 2005.

Related Occupations
Other professional workers who deal extensively with data include computer software engineers; computer scientists and database administrators; computer systems analysts; statisticians; mathematicians; engineers; and operations research analysts.

Sources of Additional Information
State employment service offices can provide information about job openings for computer programmers. Municipal chambers of commerce are an additional source of information on an area's largest employers.

Further information about computer careers is available from:
➤ Association for Computing Machinery, 1515 Broadway, New York, NY 10036. Internet: **http://www.acm.org**
➤ Institute of Electrical and Electronics Engineers Computer Society, Headquarters Office, 1730 Massachusetts Ave. NW., Washington, DC 20036-1992. Internet: **http://www.computer.org**
➤ National Workforce Center for Emerging Technologies, 3000 Landerholm Circle SE., Bellevue, WA 98007. Internet: **http://www.nwcet.org**

Computer Scientists and Database Administrators
(O*NET 15-1011.00, 15-1061.00, 15-1081.00, 15-1099.99)

Significant Points
● Education requirements range from an associate degree to a doctoral degree.

● Employment is expected to increase much faster than the average as organizations continue to adopt increasingly sophisticated technologies.

● Job prospects are favorable.

Nature of the Work
The rapid spread of computers and information technology has generated a need for highly trained workers proficient in various job functions. These workers—computer scientists, database administrators, and network systems and data communication analysts—include a wide range of computer specialists. Job tasks and occupational titles used to describe these workers evolve rapidly, reflecting new areas of specialization or changes in technology, as well as the preferences and practices of employers.

Computer scientists work as theorists, researchers, or inventors. Their jobs are distinguished by the higher level of theoretical expertise and innovation they apply to complex problems and the creation or application of new technology. Those employed by academic institutions work in areas ranging from complexity theory to hardware to programming-language design. Some work on multidisciplinary projects, such as developing and advancing uses of virtual reality, extending human-computer interaction, or designing robots. Their counterparts in private industry work in areas such as applying theory; developing specialized languages or information technologies; or designing programming tools, knowledge-based systems, or even computer games.

With the Internet and electronic business generating large volumes of data, there is a growing need to be able to store, manage, and extract data effectively. *Database administrators* work with database management systems software and determine ways to organize and store data. They identify user requirements, set up computer databases, and test and coordinate modifications to the computer database systems. An organization's database administrator ensures the performance of the system, understands the platform on which the database runs, and adds new users to the system. Because they also may design and implement system security, database administrators often plan and coordinate security measures. With the volume of sensitive data generated every second growing rapidly, data integrity, backup systems, and database security have become increasingly important aspects of the job of database administrators.

Database administrators determine ways to organize and store data.

Because networks are configured in many ways, *network systems and data communications analysts* are needed to design, test, and evaluate systems such as local area networks (LANs), wide area networks (WANs), the Internet, intranets, and other data communications systems. Systems can range from a connection between two offices in the same building to globally distributed networks, voice mail, and e-mail systems of a multinational organization. Network systems and data communications analysts perform network modeling, analysis, and planning; they also may research related products and make necessary hardware and software recommendations. *Telecommunications specialists* focus on the interaction between computer and communications equipment. These workers design voice and data communication systems, supervise the installation of the systems, and provide maintenance and other services to clients after the systems are installed.

The growth of the Internet and the expansion of the World Wide Web (the graphical portion of the Internet) have generated a variety of occupations related to the design, development, and maintenance of Web sites and their servers. For example, *webmasters* are responsible for all technical aspects of a Web site, including performance issues such as speed of access, and for approving the content of the site. *Internet developers* or *Web developers*, also called *Web designers*, are responsible for day-to-day site creation and design.

Working Conditions

Computer scientists and database administrators normally work in offices or laboratories in comfortable surroundings. They usually work about 40 hours a week—the same as many other professional or office workers do. However, evening or weekend work may be necessary to meet deadlines or solve specific problems. With the technology available today, telecommuting is common for computer professionals. As networks expand, more work can be done from remote locations through modems, laptops, electronic mail, and the Internet.

Like other workers who spend long periods in front of a computer terminal typing on a keyboard, computer scientists and database administrators are susceptible to eyestrain, back discomfort, and hand and wrist problems such as carpal tunnel syndrome or cumulative trauma disorder.

Training, Other Qualifications, and Advancement

Rapidly changing technology requires an increasing level of skill and education on the part of employees. Companies look for professionals with an ever-broader background and range of skills, including not only technical knowledge, but also communication and other interpersonal skills. While there is no universally accepted way to prepare for a job as a network systems analyst, computer scientist, or database administrator, most employers place a premium on some formal college education. A bachelor's degree is a prerequisite for many jobs; however, some jobs may require only a 2-year degree. Relevant work experience also is very important. For more technically complex jobs, persons with graduate degrees are preferred.

For database administrator positions, many employers seek applicants who have a bachelor's degree in computer science, information science, or management information systems (MIS). MIS programs usually are part of the business school or college and differ considerably from computer science programs, emphasizing business and management-oriented coursework and business computing courses. Employers increasingly seek individuals with a master's degree in business administration (MBA), with a concentration in information systems, as more firms move their business to the Internet. For some network systems and data communication analysts, such as webmasters, an associate degree or certificate is sufficient, although more advanced positions might require a computer-related bachelor's degree. For computer and information scientists, a doctoral degree generally is required because of the highly technical nature of their work.

Despite employers' preference for those with technical degrees, persons with degrees in a variety of majors find employment in these occupations. The level of education and the type of training that employers require depend on their needs. One factor affecting these needs is changes in technology. Employers often scramble to find workers capable of implementing new technologies. Workers with formal education or experience in information security, for example, are in demand because of the growing need for their skills and services. Employers also look for workers skilled in wireless technologies as wireless networks and applications have spread into many firms and organizations.

Most community colleges and many independent technical institutes and proprietary schools offer an associate's degree in computer science or a related information technology field. Many of these programs may be geared more toward meeting the needs of local businesses and are more occupation specific than are 4-year degree programs. Some jobs may be better suited to the level of training that such programs offer. Employers usually look for people who have broad knowledge and experience related to computer systems and technologies, strong problem-solving and analytical skills, and good interpersonal skills. Courses in computer science or systems design offer good preparation for a job in these computer occupations. For jobs in a business environment, employers usually want systems analysts to have business management or closely related skills, while a background in the physical sciences, applied mathematics, or engineering is preferred for work in scientifically oriented organizations. Art or graphic design skills may be desirable for webmasters or Web developers.

Jobseekers can enhance their employment opportunities by participating in internship or co-op programs offered through their schools. Because many people develop advanced computer skills in a noncomputer occupation and then transfer those skills to a computer occupation, a background in the industry in which the person's job is located, such as financial services, banking, or accounting, can be important. Others have taken computer science courses to supplement their study in fields such as accounting, inventory control, or other business areas.

Computer scientists and database administrators must be able to think logically and have good communication skills. Because they often deal with a number of tasks simultaneously, the ability to concentrate and pay close attention to detail is important. Although these computer specialists sometimes work independently, they frequently work in teams on large projects. They must be able to communicate effectively with computer personnel, such as programmers and managers, as well as with users or other staff who may have no technical computer background.

Computer scientists employed in private industry may advance into managerial or project leadership positions. Those employed in academic institutions can become heads of research departments or published authorities in their field. Database administrators may advance into managerial positions, such as chief technology officer, on the basis of their experience managing data and enforcing security. Computer specialists with work experience and considerable expertise in a particular subject or a certain application may find lucrative opportunities as independent consultants or may choose to start their own computer consulting firms.

Technological advances come so rapidly in the computer field that continuous study is necessary to keep one's skills up to date. Employers, hardware and software vendors, colleges and universities, and private training institutions offer continuing education. Additional training may come from professional development seminars offered by professional computing societies.

Certification is a way to demonstrate a level of competence in a particular field. Some product vendors or software firms offer certification and require professionals who work with their products to be certified. Many employers regard these certifications as the industry standard. For example, one method of acquiring enough knowledge to get a job as a database administrator is to become certified in a specific type of database management. Voluntary certification also is available through various organizations associated with computer specialists. Professional certification may afford a jobseeker a competitive advantage.

Employment

Computer scientists and database administrators held about 507,000 jobs in 2004, including about 66,000 who were self-employed. Employment was distributed among the detailed occupations as follows:

Network systems and data communication analysts	231,000
Database administrators	104,000
Computer and information scientists, research	22,000
Computer specialists, all other	149,000

Although they are increasingly employed in every sector of the economy, the greatest concentration of these workers is in the computer systems design and related services industry. Firms in this industry provide services related to the commercial use of computers on a contract basis, including custom computer programming services; computer systems integration design services; computer facilities management services, including computer systems or data processing facilities support services for clients; and other computer-related services, such as disaster recovery services and software installation. Many computer scientists and database administrators are employed by Internet service providers; Web search portals; and data processing, hosting, and related services firms. Others work for government, manufacturers of computer and electronic products, insurance companies, financial institutions, and universities.

A growing number of computer specialists, such as network and data communications analysts, are employed on a temporary or contract basis; many of these individuals are self-employed, working independently as contractors or consultants. For example, a company installing a new computer system may need the services of several network systems and data communication analysts just to get the system running. Because not all of the analysts would be needed once the system is functioning, the company might contract for such employees with a temporary help agency or a consulting firm or with the network systems analysts themselves. Such jobs may last from several months to 2 years or more. This growing practice enables companies to bring in people with the exact skills they need to complete a particular project, rather than having to spend time or money training or retraining existing workers. Often, experienced consultants then train a company's in-house staff as a project develops.

Job Outlook

Computer scientists and database administrators should continue to enjoy favorable job prospects. As technology becomes more sophisticated and complex, however, employers demand a higher level of skill and expertise from their employees. Individuals with an advanced degree in computer science or computer engineering or with an MBA with a concentration in information systems should enjoy favorable employment prospects. College graduates with a bachelor's degree in computer science, computer engineering, information science, or MIS also should enjoy favorable prospects, particularly if they have supplemented their formal education with practical experience. Because employers continue to seek computer specialists who can combine strong technical skills with good interpersonal and business skills, graduates with degrees in fields other than computer science who have had courses in computer programming, systems analysis, and other information technology areas also should continue to find jobs in these computer fields. In fact, individuals with the right experience and training can work in these computer occupations regardless of their college major or level of formal education.

Computer scientists and database administrators are expected to be among the fastest growing occupations through 2014. Employment of these computer specialists is expected to grow much faster than the average for all occupations as organizations continue to adopt and integrate increasingly sophisticated technologies. Job increases will be driven by very rapid growth in computer systems design and related services, which is projected to be one of the fastest growing industries in the U.S. economy. Job growth will not be as rapid as during the previous decade, however, as the information technology sector begins to mature and as routine work is increasingly outsourced overseas. In addition to growth, many job openings will arise annually from the need to replace workers who move into managerial positions or other occupations or who leave the labor force.

The demand for networking to facilitate the sharing of information, the expansion of client–server environments, and the need for computer specialists to use their knowledge and skills in a problem-solving capacity will be major factors in the rising demand for computer scientists and database administrators. Moreover, falling prices of computer hardware and software should continue to induce more businesses to expand their computerized operations and integrate new technologies into them. To maintain a competitive edge and operate more efficiently, firms will keep demanding computer specialists who are knowledgeable about the latest technologies and are able to apply them to meet the needs of businesses.

Increasingly, more sophisticated and complex technology is being implemented across all organizations, fueling demand for computer scientists and database administrators. There is growing demand for network systems and data communication analysts to help firms maximize their efficiency with available technology. Expansion of electronic commerce—doing business on the Internet—and the continuing need to build and maintain databases that store critical information on customers, inventory, and projects are fueling demand for database administrators familiar with the latest technology. Also, the increasing importance placed on cybersecurity—the protection of electronic information—will result in a need for workers skilled in information security.

The development of new technologies usually leads to demand for various kinds of workers. The expanding integration of Internet technologies into businesses, for example, has resulted in a growing need for specialists who can develop and support Internet and intranet applications. The growth of electronic commerce means that more establishments use the Internet to conduct their business online. The introduction of the wireless Internet, known as WiFi, creates new systems to be analyzed and new data to be administered. The spread of such new technologies translates into a need for information technology professionals who can help organizations use technology to communicate with employees, clients, and consumers. Explosive growth in these areas also is expected to fuel demand for specialists who are knowledgeable about network, data, and communications security.

Earnings

Median annual earnings of computer and information scientists, research, were $85,190 in May 2004. The middle 50 percent earned between $64,860 and $108,440. The lowest 10 percent earned less than $48,930, and the highest 10 percent earned more than $132,700. Median annual earnings of computer and information scientists employed in computer systems design and related services in May 2004 were $85,530.

Median annual earnings of database administrators were $60,650 in May 2004. The middle 50 percent earned between $44,490 and $81,140. The lowest 10 percent earned less than $33,380, and the highest 10 percent earned more than $97,450. In May 2004, median annual earnings of database administrators employed in computer systems design and related services were $70,530, and for those in management of companies and enterprises, earnings were $65,990.

Median annual earnings of network systems and data communication analysts were $60,600 in May 2004. The middle 50 percent earned between $46,480 and $78,060. The lowest 10 percent earned less than $36,260, and the highest 10 percent earned more than $95,040. Median annual earnings in the industries employing the largest numbers of network systems and data communications analysts in May 2004 are shown below:

Wired telecommunications carriers	$65,130
Insurance carriers	64,660
Management of companies and enterprises	64,170
Computer systems design and related services	63,910
Local government	52,300

Median annual earnings of all other computer specialists were $59,480 in May 2004. Median annual earnings of all other computer specialists employed in computer systems design and related services were $57,430, and, for those in management of companies and enterprises, earnings were $68,590 in May 2004.

According to the National Association of Colleges and Employers, starting offers for graduates with a doctoral degree in computer science averaged $93,050 in 2005. Starting offers averaged $50,820 for graduates with a bachelor's degree in computer science; $46,189 for those with a degree in computer systems analysis; $44,417 for those with a degree in management information systems; and $44,775 for those with a degree in information sciences and systems.

According to Robert Half International, a firm providing specialized staffing services, starting salaries in 2005 ranged from $67,750 to $95,500 for database administrators. Salaries for networking and Internet-related occupations ranged from $47,000 to $68,500 for LAN administrators and from $51,750 to $74,520 for web developers. Starting salaries for information security professionals ranged from $63,750 to $93,000 in 2005.

Related Occupations

Others who work with large amounts of data are computer programmers, computer software engineers, computer and information systems managers, engineers, mathematicians, and statisticians.

Sources of Additional Information

Further information about computer careers is available from:
➤ Association for Computing Machinery (ACM), 1515 Broadway, New York, NY 10036. Internet: **http://www.acm.org**
➤ Institute of Electrical and Electronics Engineers Computer Society, Headquarters Office, 1730 Massachusetts Ave. NW., Washington, DC 20036-1992. Internet: **http://www.computer.org**
➤ National Workforce Center for Emerging Technologies, 3000 Landerholm Circle SE., Bellevue, WA 98007. Internet: **http://www.nwcet.org**

Computer Software Engineers

(O*NET 15-1031.00, 15-1032.00)

Significant Points

- Computer software engineers are projected to be one of the fastest growing occupations over the 2004-14 period.

- Very good opportunities are expected for college graduates with at least a bachelor's degree in computer engineering or computer science and with practical work experience.

- Computer software engineers must continually strive to acquire new skills in conjunction with the rapid changes that are occurring in computer technology.

Nature of the Work

The explosive impact of computers and information technology on our everyday lives has generated a need to design and develop new computer software systems and to incorporate new technologies into a rapidly growing range of applications. The tasks performed by workers known as computer software engineers evolve quickly, reflecting new areas of specialization or changes in technology, as well as the preferences and practices of employers. Computer software engineers apply the principles and techniques of computer science, engineering, and mathematical analysis to the design, development, testing, and evaluation of the software and systems that enable computers to perform their many applications. (A separate statement on computer hardware engineers appears elsewhere in the *Handbook*)

Software engineers working in applications or systems development analyze users' needs and design, construct, test, and maintain computer applications software or systems. Software engineers can be involved in the design and development of many types of software, including software for operating systems and network distribution, and compilers, which convert programs for execution on a computer. In programming, or coding, software engineers instruct a computer, line by line, how to perform a function. They also solve technical problems that arise. Software engineers must possess strong programming skills, but are more concerned with developing algorithms and analyzing and solving programming problems than with actually writing code. (A separate statement on computer programmers appears elsewhere in the *Handbook*)

Computer applications software engineers analyze users' needs and design, construct, and maintain general computer applications software or specialized utility programs. These workers use different programming languages, depending on the purpose of the program. The programming languages most often used are C, C++, and Java, with Fortran and COBOL used less commonly. Some software engineers develop both packaged systems and systems software or create customized applications.

Computer systems software engineers coordinate the construction and maintenance of a company's computer systems and plan their future growth. Working with the company, they coordinate each department's computer needs—ordering, inventory, billing, and payroll recordkeeping, for example—and make suggestions about its technical direction. They also might set up the company's intranets—networks that link computers within the organization and ease communication among the various departments.

Systems software engineers work for companies that configure, implement, and install complete computer systems. These workers may be members of the marketing or sales staff, serving as the primary technical resource for sales workers and customers. They also may be involved in product sales and in providing their customers with continuing technical support. Since the selling of complex computer systems often requires substantial customization for the purchaser's organization, software engineers help to explain the requirements necessary for installing and operating the new system in the purchaser's computing environment. In addition, systems software engineers are responsible for ensuring security across the systems they are configuring.

Computer software engineers often work as part of a team that designs new hardware, software, and systems. A core team may comprise engineering, marketing, manufacturing, and design people, who work together until the product is released. .

Working Conditions

Computer software engineers normally work in well-lighted and comfortable offices or laboratories in which computer equipment is located. Most software engineers work at least 40 hours a week; however, due to the project-oriented nature of the work, they also may have to work evenings or weekends to meet deadlines or solve unexpected technical problems. Like other workers who sit for hours at a computer, typing on a keyboard, software engineers are susceptible to eyestrain, back discomfort, and hand and wrist problems such as carpal tunnel syndrome.

Computer software engineers develop, design, and modify computer applications and systems.

As they strive to improve software for users, many computer software engineers interact with customers and coworkers. Computer software engineers who are employed by software vendors and consulting firms, for example, spend much of their time away from their offices, frequently traveling overnight to meet with customers. They call on customers in businesses ranging from manufacturing plants to financial institutions.

As networks expand, software engineers may be able to use modems, laptops, e-mail, and the Internet to provide more technical support and other services from their main office, connecting to a customer's computer remotely to identify and correct developing problems.

Training, Other Qualifications, and Advancement

Most employers prefer to hire persons who have at least a bachelor's degree and broad knowledge of, and experience with, a variety of computer systems and technologies. The usual degree concentration for applications software engineers is computer science or software engineering; for systems software engineers, it is computer science or computer information systems. Graduate degrees are preferred for some of the more complex jobs.

Academic programs in software engineering emphasize software and may be offered as a degree option or in conjunction with computer science degrees. Increasing emphasis on computer security suggests that software engineers with advanced degrees that include mathematics and systems design will be sought after by software developers, government agencies, and consulting firms specializing in information assurance and security. Students seeking software engineering jobs enhance their employment opportunities by participating in internship or co-op programs offered through their schools. These experiences provide the students with broad knowledge and experience, making them more attractive candidates to employers. Inexperienced college graduates may be hired by large computer and consulting firms that train new employees in intensive, company-based programs. In many firms, new hires are mentored, and their mentors have an input into the performance evaluations of these new employees.

For systems software engineering jobs that require workers who have a college degree, a bachelor's degree in computer science or computer information systems is typical. For systems engineering jobs that place less emphasis on workers having a computer-related degree, computer training programs leading to certification are offered by systems software vendors. Nonetheless, most training authorities feel that program certification alone is not sufficient for the majority of software engineering jobs.

Persons interested in jobs as computer software engineers must have strong problem-solving and analytical skills. They also must be able to communicate effectively with team members, other staff, and the customers they meet. Because they often deal with a number of tasks simultaneously, they must be able to concentrate and pay close attention to detail.

As is the case with most occupations, advancement opportunities for computer software engineers increase with experience. Entry-level computer software engineers are likely to test and verify ongoing designs. As they become more experienced, they may become involved in designing and developing software. Eventually, they may advance to become a project manager, manager of information systems, or chief information officer. Some computer software engineers with several years of experience or expertise find lucrative opportunities working as systems designers or independent consultants or starting their own computer consulting firms.

As technological advances in the computer field continue, employers demand new skills. Computer software engineers must continually strive to acquire such skills if they wish to remain in this extremely dynamic field. For example, computer software engineers interested in working for a bank should have some expertise in finance as they integrate new technologies into the computer system of the bank. To help them keep up with the changing technology, continuing education and professional development seminars are offered by employers, software vendors, colleges and universities, private training institutions, and professional computing societies.

Employment

Computer software engineers held about 800,000 jobs in 2004. Approximately 460,000 were computer applications software engineers, and around 340,000 were computer systems software engineers. Although they are employed in most industries, the largest concentration of computer software engineers—almost 30 percent—are in computer systems design and related services. Many computer software engineers also work for establishments in other industries, such as software publishers, government agencies, manufacturers of computers and related electronic equipment, and management of companies and enterprises.

Employers of computer software engineers range from startup companies to established industry leaders. The proliferation of Internet, e-mail, and other communications systems is expanding electronics to engineering firms that are traditionally associated with unrelated disciplines. Engineering firms specializing in building bridges and powerplants, for example, hire computer software engineers to design and develop new geographic data systems and automated drafting systems. Communications firms need computer software engineers to tap into growth in the personal communications market. Major communications companies have many job openings for both computer software applications engineers and computer systems engineers.

An increasing number of computer software engineers are employed on a temporary or contract basis, with many being self-employed, working independently as consultants. Some consultants work for firms that specialize in developing and maintaining client companies' Web sites and intranets. About 23,000 computer software engineers were self-employed in 2004.

Job Outlook

Computer software engineers are projected to be one of the fastest-growing occupations from 2004 to 2014. Rapid employment growth in the computer systems design and related services industry, which employs the greatest number of computer software engineers, should result in very good opportunities for those college graduates with at least a bachelor's degree in computer engineering or computer science and practical experience working with computers. Employers will continue to seek computer professionals with strong programming, systems analysis, interpersonal, and business skills. With the software industry beginning to mature, however, and with routine software engineering work being increasingly outsourced overseas, job growth will not be as rapid as during the previous decade.

Employment of computer software engineers is expected to increase much faster than the average for all occupations, as businesses and other organizations adopt and integrate new technologies and seek to maximize the efficiency of their computer systems. Competition among businesses will continue to create an incentive for increasingly sophisticated technological innovations, and organizations will need more computer software engineers to implement these changes. In addition to jobs created through employment growth, many job openings will result annually from the need to replace workers who move into managerial positions, transfer to other occupations, or leave the labor force.

Demand for computer software engineers will increase as computer networking continues to grow. For example, the expanding integration of Internet technologies and the explosive growth in electronic commerce—doing business on the Internet—have resulted in rising demand for computer software engineers who can develop Internet, intranet, and World Wide Web applications. Likewise, expanding electronic data-processing systems in business, telecommunications, government, and other settings continue to become more sophisticated and complex. Growing numbers of systems software engineers will be needed to implement, safeguard, and update systems and resolve problems. Consulting opportunities for computer software engineers also should continue to grow as businesses seek help to manage, upgrade, and customize their increasingly complicated computer systems.

New growth areas will continue to arise from rapidly evolving technologies. The increasing uses of the Internet, the proliferation of Web sites, and mobile technology such as the wireless Internet have created a demand for a wide variety of new products. As individuals and businesses rely more on hand-held computers and wireless networks, it will be necessary to integrate current computer systems with this new, more mobile technology. Also, information security concerns have given rise to new software needs. Concerns over "cyber security" should result in businesses and government continuing to invest heavily in software that protects their networks and vital electronic infrastructure from attack. The expansion of this technology in the next 10 years will lead to an increased need for computer engineers to design and develop the software and systems to run these new applications and integrate them into older systems.

As with other information technology jobs, employment growth of computer software engineers may be tempered somewhat as more software development is contracted out abroad. Firms may look to cut costs by shifting operations to lower wage foreign countries with highly educated workers who have strong technical skills. At the same time, jobs in software engineering are less prone to being sent abroad compared with jobs in other computer specialties, because the occupation requires innovation and intense research and development.

Earnings

Median annual earnings of computer applications software engineers who worked full time in May 2004 were about $74,980. The middle 50 percent earned between $59,130 and $92,130. The lowest 10 percent earned less than $46,520, and the highest 10 percent earned more than $113,830. Median annual earnings in the industries employing the largest numbers of computer applications software engineers in May 2004 were as follows:

Software publishers	$79,930
Management, scientific, and technical consulting services	78,460
Computer systems design and related services	76,910
Management of companies and enterprises	70,520
Insurance carriers	68,440

Median annual earnings of computer systems software engineers who worked full time in May 2004 were about $79,740. The middle 50 percent earned between $63,150 and $98,220. The lowest 10 percent earned less than $50,420, and the highest 10 percent earned more than $118,350. Median annual earnings in the industries employing the largest numbers of computer systems software engineers in May 2004 are as follows:

Scientific research and development services	$91,390
Computer and peripheral equipment manufacturing	87,800
Software publishers	83,670
Computer systems design and related services	79,950
Wired telecommunications carriers	74,370

According to the National Association of Colleges and Employers, starting salary offers for graduates with a bachelor's degree in computer engineering averaged $52,464 in 2005; offers for those with a master's degree averaged $60,354. Starting salary offers for graduates with a bachelor's degree in computer science averaged $50,820.

According to Robert Half International, starting salaries for software engineers in software development ranged from $63,250 to $92,750 in 2005. For network engineers, starting salaries in 2005 ranged from $61,250 to $88,250.

Related Occupations

Other workers who use mathematics and logic extensively include computer systems analysts, computer scientists and database administrators, computer programmers, computer hardware engineers, computer support specialists and systems administrators, engineers, statisticians, mathematicians, and actuaries.

Sources of Additional Information

Additional information on a career in computer software engineering is available from the following organizations:
➤ Association for Computing Machinery (ACM), 1515 Broadway, New York, NY 10036. Internet: **http://www.acm.org**
➤ Institute of Electronics and Electrical Engineers Computer Society, Headquarters Office, 1730 Massachusetts Ave. N.W., Washington, DC 20036-1992. Internet: **http://www.computer.org**
➤ National Workforce Center for Emerging Technologies, 3000 Landerholm Circle S.E., Bellevue, WA 98007. Internet: **http://www.nwcet.org**

Computer Support Specialists and Systems Administrators

(O*NET 15-1041.00, 15-1071.00)

Significant Points

● Rapid job growth is projected over the 2004–14 period.

● There are many paths of entry to these occupations.

● Job prospects should be best for college graduates who are up to date with the latest skills and technologies; certifications and practical experience are essential for persons without degrees.

Nature of the Work

In the last decade, computers have become an integral part of everyday life, used for a variety of reasons at home, in the workplace, and at schools. Of course, almost every computer user encounters a problem occasionally, whether it is the disaster of a crashing hard drive or the annoyance of a forgotten password. The explosive use of computers has created a high demand for specialists to provide advice to users, as well as for day-to-day administration, maintenance, and support of computer systems and networks.

Computer support specialists provide technical assistance, support, and advice to customers and other users. This occupational group includes *technical support specialists* and *help-desk technicians*. These troubleshooters interpret problems and provide technical support for hardware, software, and systems. They answer telephone calls, analyze problems by using automated diagnostic programs, and resolve recurring difficulties. Support specialists may work either within a company that uses computer systems or directly for a computer hardware or software vendor. Increasingly, these specialists work for help-desk or support services firms, for which they provide computer support to clients on a contract basis.

Technical support specialists answer telephone calls from their organizations' computer users and may run automatic diagnostics programs to resolve problems. Working on monitors, keyboards, printers, and mice, they install, modify, clean, and repair computer hardware and software. They also may write training manuals and train computer users in how to use new computer hardware and software. In addition, technical support specialists oversee the daily performance of their company's computer systems and evaluate software programs with regard to their usefulness.

Help-desk technicians assist computer users with the inevitable hardware and software questions that are not addressed in a product's instruction manual. Help-desk technicians field telephone calls and e-mail messages from customers who are seeking guidance on technical problems. In responding to these requests for guidance, help-desk technicians must listen carefully to the customer, ask questions to diagnose the nature of the problem, and then patiently walk the customer through the problem-solving steps.

Help-desk technicians deal directly with customer issues, and companies value them as a source of feedback on their products. These technicians are consulted for information about what gives customers the most trouble, as well as other customer concerns. Most computer support specialists start out at the help desk.

Network administrators and *computer systems administrators* design, install, and support an organization's local-area network (LAN), wide-area network (WAN), network segment, Internet, or intranet system. They provide day-to-day onsite administrative support for software users in a variety of work environments, including professional offices, small businesses, government, and large corporations. They maintain network hardware and software, analyze problems, and monitor the network to ensure its availability to system users. These workers gather data to identify customer needs and then use the information to identify, interpret, and evaluate system and network requirements. Administrators also may plan, coordinate, and implement network security measures.

Systems administrators are the information technology employees responsible for the efficient use of networks by organizations. They ensure that the design of an organization's computer site allows all of the components, including computers, the network, and software, to fit together and work properly. Furthermore, they monitor and adjust the performance of existing networks and continually survey the current computer site to determine future network needs.

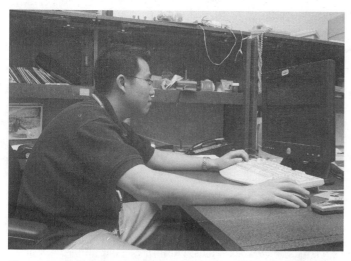

Computer support specialists often run automatic diagnostics programs to resolve problems.

Administrators also troubleshoot problems reported by users and by automated network monitoring systems and make recommendations for enhancements in the implementation of future servers and networks.

In some organizations, *computer security specialists* may plan, coordinate, and implement the organization's information security. These workers may be called upon to educate users about computer security, install security software, monitor the network for security breaches, respond to cyber attacks, and, in some cases, gather data and evidence to be used in prosecuting cyber crime. The responsibilities of computer security specialists has increased in recent years as there has been a large increase in the number of cyber attacks on data and networks. This and other growing specialty occupations reflect an increasing emphasis on client-server applications, the expansion of Internet and intranet applications, and the demand for more end-user support.

Working Conditions
Computer support specialists and systems administrators normally work in well-lighted, comfortable offices or computer laboratories. They usually work about 40 hours a week, but that may include being "on call" via pager or telephone for rotating evening or weekend work if the employer requires computer support over extended hours. Overtime may be necessary when unexpected technical problems arise. Like other workers who type on a keyboard for long periods, computer support specialists and systems administrators are susceptible to eyestrain, back discomfort, and hand and wrist problems such as carpal tunnel syndrome.

Due to the heavy emphasis on helping all types of computer users, computer support specialists and systems administrators constantly interact with customers and fellow employees as they answer questions and give valuable advice. Those who work as consultants are away from their offices much of the time, sometimes spending months working in a client's office.

As computer networks expand, more computer support specialists and systems administrators may be able to connect to a customer's computer remotely, using modems, laptops, e-mail, and the Internet, to provide technical support to computer users. This capability would reduce or eliminate travel to the customer's workplace. Systems administrators also can administer and configure networks and servers remotely, although this practice is not as common as it is among computer support specialists.

Training, Other Qualifications, and Advancement
Due to the wide range of skills required, there are many paths of entry to a job as a computer support specialist or systems administrator. While there is no universally accepted way to prepare for a job as a computer support specialist, many employers prefer to hire persons with some formal college education. A bachelor's degree in computer science or information systems is a prerequisite for some jobs; however, other jobs may require only a computer-related associate's degree. For systems administrators, many employers seek applicants with bachelor's degrees, although not necessarily in a computer-related field.

A number of companies are becoming more flexible about requiring a college degree for support positions. However, certification and practical experience demonstrating these skills will be essential for applicants without a degree. The completion of a certification training program, offered by a variety of vendors and product makers, may help some people to qualify for entry-level positions. Relevant computer experience may substitute for formal education.

Beginning computer support specialists usually work for organizations that deal directly with customers or in-house users. Then they may advance into more responsible positions in which they use what they have learned from customers to improve the design and efficiency of future products. Job promotions usually depend more on performance than on formal education. Eventually, some computer support specialists become applications developers, designing products rather than assisting users. Computer support specialists at hardware and software companies often enjoy great upward mobility; advancement sometimes comes within months of one's initial employment.

Entry-level network and computer systems administrators are involved in routine maintenance and monitoring of computer systems, typically working behind the scenes in an organization. After gaining experience and expertise, they often are able to advance into more senior-level positions, in which they take on more responsibilities. For example, senior network and computer systems administrators may present recommendations to management on matters related to a company's network. They also may translate the needs of an organization into a set of technical requirements based on the available technology. As with support specialists, administrators may become software engineers, actually involved in the designing of the system or network and not just its day-to-day administration.

Persons interested in becoming a computer support specialist or systems administrator must have strong problem-solving, analytical, and communication skills, because troubleshooting and helping others are vital parts of the job. The constant interaction with other computer personnel, customers, and employees requires computer support specialists and systems administrators to communicate effectively on paper, via e-mail, or in person. Strong writing skills are useful in preparing manuals for employees and customers.

As technology continues to improve, computer support specialists and systems administrators must keep their skills current and acquire new ones. Many continuing education programs are provided by employers, hardware and software vendors, colleges and universities, and private training institutions. Professional development seminars offered by computing services firms also can enhance one's skills and advancement opportunities.

Employment

Computer support specialists and systems administrators held about 797,000 jobs in 2004. Of these, approximately 518,000 were computer support specialists and around 278,000 were network and computer systems administrators. Although they worked in a wide range of industries, about 23 percent of all computer support specialists and systems administrators were employed in professional, scientific, and technical services industries, principally computer systems design and related services. Other organizations that employed substantial numbers of these workers include administrative and support services companies, banks, government agencies, insurance companies, educational institutions, and wholesale and retail vendors of computers, office equipment, appliances, and home electronic equipment. Many computer support specialists worked for manufacturers of computers, semiconductors, and other electronic components.

Employers of computer support specialists and systems administrators range from startup companies to established industry leaders. With the continued development of the Internet, telecommunications, and e-mail, industries not typically associated with computers—such as construction—increasingly need computer workers. Small and large firms across all industries are expanding or developing computer systems, creating an immediate need for computer support specialists and systems administrators.

Job Outlook

Job prospects should be best for college graduates who are up to date with the latest skills and technologies, particularly if they have supplemented their formal education with some relevant work experience. Employers will continue to seek computer specialists who possess a strong background in fundamental computer skills combined with good interpersonal and communication skills. Due to the demand for computer support specialists and systems administrators over the next decade, those who have strong computer skills, but do not have a bachelor's degree, should continue to qualify for some entry-level positions. However, certifications and practical experience are essential for persons without degrees.

Employment of computer support specialists is expected to increase faster than the average for all occupations through 2014, as organizations continue to adopt increasingly sophisticated technology and integrate it into their systems. Job growth will continue to be driven by the ongoing expansion of the computer system design and related services industry, which is projected to remain one of the fastest-growing industries in the U.S. economy. Growth will not be as explosive as during the previous decade, however, as the information technology industry matures and some of these jobs are increasingly outsourced overseas.

Job growth among computer support specialists reflects the rapid pace of improved technology. As computers and software become more complex, support specialists will be needed to provide technical assistance to customers and other users. New mobile technologies, such as the wireless Internet, will continue to create a demand for these workers to familiarize and educate computer users. Consulting opportunities for computer support specialists also should continue to grow as businesses increasingly need help managing, upgrading, and customizing ever more complex computer systems. However, growth in employment of support specialists may be tempered somewhat as firms continue to cut costs by shifting more routine work abroad to countries where workers are highly skilled and labor costs are lower. Physical location is not as important for computer support specialists as it is for others, because these workers can provide assistance remotely and support services can be provided around the clock.

Employment of systems administrators is expected to increase much faster than the average for all occupations as firms continue to invest heavily in securing computer networks. Companies are looking for workers who are knowledgeable about the function and administration of networks. Such employees have become increasingly hard to find as systems administration has moved from being a separate function within corporations to one that forms a crucial element of business in an increasingly high-technology economy. Also, demand for computer security specialists will grow as businesses and government continue to invest heavily in "cyber security," protecting vital computer networks and electronic infrastructures from attack. The information security field is expected to generate many opportunities over the next decade as firms across all industries place a high priority on safeguarding their data and systems.

The growth of electronic commerce means that more establishments use the Internet to conduct their business online. This growth translates into a need for information technology specialists who can help organizations use technology to communicate with employees, clients, and consumers. Growth in these areas also is expected to fuel demand for specialists who are knowledgeable about network, data, and communications security.

Earnings

Median annual earnings of computer support specialists were $40,430 in May 2004. The middle 50 percent earned between $30,980 and $53,010. The lowest 10 percent earned less than $24,190, and the highest 10 percent earned more than $69,110. Median annual earnings in the industries employing the largest numbers of computer support specialists in May 2004 were as follows:

Software publishers	$44,890
Management of companies and enterprises	42,780
Computer systems design and related services	42,750
Colleges, universities, and professional schools	37,940
Elementary and secondary schools	35,500

Median annual earnings of network and computer systems administrators were $58,190 in May 2004. The middle 50 percent earned between $46,260 and $73,620. The lowest 10 percent earned less than $37,100, and the highest 10 percent earned more than $91,300. Median annual earnings in the industries employing the largest numbers of network and computer systems administrators in May 2004 were as follows:

Wired telecommunications carriers	$65,120
Computer systems design and related services	63,710
Management of companies and enterprises	61,600
Elementary and secondary schools	51,420
Colleges, universities, and professional schools	51,170

According to Robert Half International, starting salaries in 2005 ranged from $26,250 to $53,750 for help-desk and technical support staff and from $44,500 to $63,250 for more senior technical support specialists. For systems administrators, starting salaries in 2005 ranged from $47,250 to $70,500.

Related Occupations

Other computer specialists include computer programmers, computer software engineers, computer systems analysts, and computer scientists and database administrators.

Sources of Additional Information

For additional information about a career as a computer support specialist, contact the following organizations:
➤ Association of Computer Support Specialists., 333 Mamaroneck Ave., # 129, White Plains, NY 10605. Internet: **http://www.acss.org**
➤ Association of Support Professionals, 122 Barnard Ave., Watertown, MA 02472.

For additional information about a career as a systems administrator, contact:
➤ System Administrators Guild, 2560 9th St., Suite 215, Berkeley, CA 94710. Internet: **http://www.sage.org**

Further information about computer careers is available from:
➤ National Workforce Center for Emerging Technologies, 3000 Landerholm Circle SE., Bellevue, WA 98007. Internet: **http://www.nwcet.org**

Computer Systems Analysts

(O*NET 15-1051.00)

Significant Points

● Employers generally prefer applicants who have at least a bachelor's degree in computer science, information science, or management information systems (MIS).

● Employment is expected to increase much faster than the average as organizations continue to adopt increasingly sophisticated technologies.

● Job prospects are favorable.

Nature of the Work

All organizations rely on computer and information technology to conduct business and operate more efficiently. The rapid spread of technology across all industries has generated a need for highly trained workers to help organizations incorporate new technologies. The tasks performed by workers known as computer systems analysts evolve rapidly, reflecting new areas of specialization or changes in technology, as well as the preferences and practices of employers.

Computer systems analysts solve computer problems and apply computer technology to meet the individual needs of an organization. They help an organization to realize the maximum benefit from its investment in equipment, personnel, and business processes. Systems analysts may plan and develop new computer systems or devise ways to apply existing systems' resources to additional operations. They may design new systems, including both hardware and software, or add a new software application to harness more of the computer's power. Most systems analysts work with specific types of systems—for example, business, accounting, or financial systems, or scientific and engineering systems—that vary with the kind of organization. Some systems analysts also are known as *systems developers* or *systems architects*

Systems analysts begin an assignment by discussing the systems problem with managers and users to determine its exact nature. Defining the goals of the system and dividing the solutions into individual steps and separate procedures, systems analysts use techniques such as structured analysis, data modeling, information engineering, mathematical model building, sampling, and cost accounting to plan the system. They specify the inputs to be accessed by the system, design the processing steps, and format the output to meet users' needs. They also may prepare cost-benefit and return-on-investment analyses to help management decide whether implementing the proposed technology will be financially feasible.

When a system is accepted, systems analysts determine what computer hardware and software will be needed to set the system up. They coordinate tests and observe the initial use of the system to ensure that it performs as planned. They prepare specifications, flow charts, and process diagrams for computer programmers to follow; then, they work with programmers to "debug," or eliminate, errors from the system. Systems analysts who do more in-depth testing of products may be referred to as *software quality assurance analysts* In addition to running tests, these individuals diagnose problems, recommend solutions, and determine whether program requirements have been met.

In some organizations, *programmer-analysts* design and update the software that runs a computer. Because they are responsible for both programming and systems analysis, these workers must be proficient in both areas. (A separate statement on computer programmers appears elsewhere in the *Handbook*) As this dual proficiency becomes more commonplace, these analysts are increasingly working with databases, object-oriented programming languages, as well as client–server applications development and multimedia and Internet technology.

One obstacle associated with expanding computer use is the need for different computer systems to communicate with each other. Because of the importance of maintaining up-to-date information—accounting records, sales figures, or budget projections, for example—systems analysts work on making the computer systems within an organization, or among organizations, compatible so that information can be shared among them. Many systems analysts are involved with "networking," connecting all the computers internally—in an individual office, department, or establishment—or externally, because many organizations rely on e-mail or the Internet. A primary goal of networking is to allow users to retrieve data from a mainframe computer or a server and use it on their desktop computer. Systems analysts must design the hardware and

Computer systems analysts help organizations get the most out of available technology.

software to allow the free exchange of data, custom applications, and the computer power to process it all. For example, analysts are called upon to ensure the compatibility of computing systems between and among businesses to facilitate electronic commerce.

Working Conditions

Computer systems analysts work in offices or laboratories in comfortable surroundings. They usually work about 40 hours a week—the same as many other professional or office workers do. However, evening or weekend work may be necessary to meet deadlines or solve specific problems. Given the technology available today, telecommuting is common for computer professionals. As networks expand, more work can be done from remote locations through modems, laptops, electronic mail, and the Internet.

Like other workers who spend long periods in front of a computer terminal typing on a keyboard, computer systems analysts are susceptible to eyestrain, back discomfort, and hand and wrist problems such as carpal tunnel syndrome or cumulative trauma disorder.

Training, Other Qualifications, and Advancement

Rapidly changing technology requires an increasing level of skill and education on the part of employees. Companies increasingly look for professionals with a broad background and range of skills, including not only technical knowledge, but also communication and other interpersonal skills. This shift from requiring workers to possess solely sound technical knowledge emphasizes workers who can handle various responsibilities. While there is no universally accepted way to prepare for a job as a systems analyst, most employers place a premium on some formal college education. Relevant work experience also is very important. For more technically complex jobs, persons with graduate degrees are preferred.

Many employers seek applicants who have at least a bachelor's degree in computer science, information science, or management information systems (MIS). MIS programs usually are part of the business school or college and differ considerably from computer science programs, emphasizing business and management-oriented course work and business computing courses. Employers are increasingly seeking individuals with a master's degree in business administration (MBA), with a concentration in information systems, as more firms move their business to the Internet.

Despite employers' preference for those with technical degrees, persons with degrees in a variety of majors find employment as system analysts. The level of education and type of training that employers require depend on their needs. One factor affecting these needs is changes in technology. Employers often scramble to find workers capable of implementing "hot" new technologies such as the wireless Internet. Those workers with formal education or experience in information security, for example, are in demand because of the growing need for their skills and services. Another factor driving employers' needs is the timeframe during which a project must be completed.

Employers usually look for people who have broad knowledge and experience related to computer systems and technologies, strong problem-solving and analytical skills, and good interpersonal skills. Courses in computer science or systems design offer good preparation for a job in these computer occupations. For jobs in a business environment, employers usually want systems analysts to have business management or closely related skills, while a background in the physical sciences, applied mathematics, or engineering is preferred for work in scientifically oriented organizations.

Job seekers can enhance their employment opportunities by participating in internship or co-op programs offered through their schools. Because many people develop advanced computer skills in a non-computer-related occupation and then transfer those skills to a computer occupation, a background in the industry in which the person's job is located, such as financial services, banking, or accounting, can be important. Others have taken computer science courses to supplement their study in fields such as accounting, inventory control, or other business areas.

Computer systems analysts must be able to think logically and have good communication skills. Because they often deal with a number of tasks simultaneously, the ability to concentrate and pay close attention to detail is important. Although these workers sometimes work independently, they frequently work in teams on large projects. They must be able to communicate effectively with computer personnel, such as programmers and managers, as well as with users or other staff who may have no technical computer background.

Systems analysts may be promoted to senior or lead systems analyst. Those who show leadership ability also can become project managers or advance into management positions such as manager of information systems or chief information officer. Workers with work experience and considerable expertise in a particular subject or a certain application may find lucrative opportunities as independent consultants or may choose to start their own computer consulting firms.

Technological advances come so rapidly in the computer field that continuous study is necessary to keep one's skills up to date. Employers, hardware and software vendors, colleges and universities, and private training institutions offer continuing education.

Additional training may come from professional development seminars offered by professional computing societies.

Employment

Computer systems analysts held about 487,000 jobs in 2004; about 28,000 were self-employed.

Although they are increasingly employed in every sector of the economy, the greatest concentration of these workers is in the computer systems design and related services industry. Firms in this industry provide services related to the commercial use of computers on a contract basis, including custom computer programming services; computer systems integration design services; computer facilities management services, including computer systems or data processing facilities support services for clients; and other computer services, such as disaster recovery services and software installation. Computer systems analysts are also employed by governments, insurance companies, financial institutions, Internet service providers, data processing services firms, and universities.

A growing number of systems analysts are employed on a temporary or contract basis; many of these individuals are self-employed, working independently as contractors or consultants. For example, a company installing a new computer system may need the services of several systems analysts just to get the system running. Because not all of the analysts would be needed once the system is functioning, the company might contract for such employees with a temporary help agency or a consulting firm or with the systems analysts themselves. Such jobs may last from several months up to 2 years or more. This growing practice enables companies to bring in people with the exact skills the firm needs to complete a particular project, rather than having to spend time or money training or retraining existing workers. Often, experienced consultants then train a company's in-house staff as a project develops.

Job Outlook

Employment of computer systems analysts is expected to grow much faster than the average for all occupations through the year 2014 as organizations continue to adopt and integrate increasingly sophisticated technologies. Job increases will be driven by very rapid growth in computer system design and related services, which is projected to be among the fastest growing industries in the U.S. economy. In addition, many job openings will arise annually from the need to replace workers who move into managerial positions or other occupations or who leave the labor force. Job growth will not be as rapid as during the previous decade, however, as the information technology sector begins to mature and as routine work is increasingly outsourced to lower-wage foreign countries.

Workers in the occupation should enjoy favorable job prospects. The demand for networking to facilitate the sharing of information, the expansion of client–server environments, and the need for computer specialists to use their knowledge and skills in a problem-solving capacity will be major factors in the rising demand for computer systems analysts. Moreover, falling prices of computer hardware and software should continue to induce more businesses to expand their computerized operations and integrate new technologies into them. In order to maintain a competitive edge and operate more efficiently, firms will keep demanding system analysts who are knowledgeable about the latest technologies and are able to apply them to meet the needs of businesses.

Increasingly, more sophisticated and complex technology is being implemented across all organizations, which should fuel the demand for these computer occupations. There is a growing demand for system analysts to help firms maximize their efficiency with available technology. Expansion of electronic commerce—doing business on the Internet—and the continuing need to build and maintain databases that store critical information on customers, inventory, and projects are fueling demand for database administrators familiar with the latest technology. Also, the increasing importance being placed on "cybersecurity"—the protection of electronic information—will result in a need for workers skilled in information security.

The development of new technologies usually leads to demand for various kinds of workers. The expanding integration of Internet technologies into businesses, for example, has resulted in a growing need for specialists who can develop and support Internet and intranet applications. The growth of electronic commerce means that more establishments use the Internet to conduct their business online. The introduction of the wireless Internet, known as WiFi, creates new systems to be analyzed. The spread of such new technologies translates into a need for information technology professionals who can help organizations use technology to communicate with employees, clients, and consumers. Explosive growth in these areas also is expected to fuel demand for analysts who are knowledgeable about network, data, and communications security.

As technology becomes more sophisticated and complex, employers demand a higher level of skill and expertise from their employees. Individuals with an advanced degree in computer science or computer engineering, or with an MBA with a concentration in information systems, should enjoy favorable employment prospects. College graduates with a bachelor's degree in computer science, computer engineering, information science, or MIS also should enjoy favorable prospects for employment, particularly if they have supplemented their formal education with practical experience. Because employers continue to seek computer specialists who can combine strong technical skills with good interpersonal and business skills, graduates with non-computer-science degrees, but who have had courses in computer programming, systems analysis, and other information technology subjects, also should continue to find jobs in computer fields. In fact, individuals with the right experience and training can work in computer occupations regardless of their college major or level of formal education.

Earnings

Median annual earnings of computer systems analysts were $66,460 in May 2004. The middle 50 percent earned between $52,400 and $82,980 a year. The lowest 10 percent earned less than $41,730, and the highest 10 percent earned more than $99,180. Median annual earnings in the industries employing the largest numbers of computer systems analysts in May 2004 were:

Federal Government	$71,770
Computer systems design and related services	69,560
Management of companies and enterprises	67,230
Insurance carriers	66,840
State government	57,040

According to the National Association of Colleges and Employers, starting offers for graduates with a master's degree in computer science averaged $62,727 in 2005. Starting offers averaged $50,820 for graduates with a bachelor's degree in computer science; $46,189 for those with a degree in computer systems analysis; $44,417for those with a degree in management information systems; and $44,775 for those with a degree in information sciences and systems.

According to Robert Half International, starting salaries for systems analysts ranged from $61,500 to $82,500 in 2005.

Related Occupations

Other workers who use computers extensively, and who use logic and creativity to solve business and technical problems, include computer programmers, computer software engineers, computer and information systems managers, engineers, mathematicians, statisticians, operations research analysts, management analysts, and actuaries.

Sources of Additional Information
Further information about computer careers is available from:
➤ Association for Computing Machinery (ACM), 1515 Broadway, New York, NY 10036. Internet: **http://www.acm.org**
➤ Institute of Electrical and Electronics Engineers Computer Society, Headquarters Office, 1730 Massachusetts Ave. NW., Washington, DC 20036-1992. Internet: **http://www.computer.org**
➤ National Workforce Center for Emerging Technologies, 3000 Landerholm Circle SE., Bellevue, WA 98007. Internet: **http://www.nwcet.org**

Mathematicians

(O*NET 15-2021.00)

Significant Points

- A Ph.D. degree in mathematics usually is the minimum educational requirement, except in the Federal Government.

- The number of jobs with the title "mathematician" is declining as the workforce becomes increasingly specialized; competition will be keen for the limited number of available jobs.

- Master's and Ph.D. degree holders with a strong background in mathematics and a related field, such as computer science or engineering, should have better employment opportunities in related occupations.

Nature of the Work
Mathematics is one of the oldest and most fundamental sciences. Mathematicians use mathematical theory, computational techniques, algorithms, and the latest computer technology to solve economic, scientific, engineering, physics, and business problems. The work of mathematicians falls into two broad classes—theoretical (pure) mathematics and applied mathematics. These classes, however, are not sharply defined and often overlap.

Theoretical mathematicians advance mathematical knowledge by developing new principles and recognizing previously unknown relationships between existing principles of mathematics. Although these workers seek to increase basic knowledge without necessarily considering its practical use, such pure and abstract knowledge has been instrumental in producing or furthering many scientific and engineering achievements. Many theoretical mathematicians are employed as university faculty, dividing their time between teaching and conducting research. (See the statement on teachers—postsecondary elsewhere in the *Handbook*.)

Applied mathematicians, on the other hand, use theories and techniques, such as mathematical modeling and computational methods, to formulate and solve practical problems in business, government, and engineering and in the physical, life, and social sciences. For example, they may analyze the most efficient way to schedule airline routes between cities, the effects and safety of new drugs, the aerodynamic characteristics of an experimental automobile, or the cost-effectiveness of alternative manufacturing processes. Applied mathematicians working in industrial research and development may develop or enhance mathematical methods when solving a difficult problem. Some mathematicians, called cryptanalysts, analyze and decipher encryption systems designed to transmit military, political, financial, or law enforcement-related information in code.

Applied mathematicians start with a practical problem, envision the separate elements of the process under consideration, and then reduce the elements to mathematical variables. They often use computers to analyze relationships among the variables and solve complex problems by developing models with alternative solutions.

Much of the work in applied mathematics is done by individuals with titles other than mathematician. In fact, because mathematics is the foundation on which so many other academic disciplines are built, the number of workers using mathematical techniques is much greater than the number formally designated as mathematicians. For example, engineers, computer scientists, physicists, and economists are among those who use mathematics extensively. Some professionals, including statisticians, actuaries, and operations research analysts, actually are specialists in a particular branch of mathematics. Frequently, applied mathematicians are required to collaborate with other workers in their organizations to achieve common solutions to problems. (For more information, see the statements on actuaries, operations research analysts, and statisticians elsewhere in the *Handbook*.)

Working Conditions
Mathematicians usually work in comfortable offices. They often are part of interdisciplinary teams that may include economists, engineers, computer scientists, physicists, technicians, and others. Deadlines, overtime work, special requests for information or analysis, and prolonged travel to attend seminars or conferences may be part of their jobs. Mathematicians who work in academia usually have a mix of teaching and research responsibilities. These mathematicians may conduct research alone or in close collaboration with other mathematicians. Collaborators may work together at the same institution or from different locations, using technology such as e-mail to communicate. Mathematicians in academia also may be aided by graduate students.

Training, Other Qualifications, and Advancement
A Ph.D. degree in mathematics usually is the minimum educational requirement for prospective mathematicians, except in the Federal Government. In the Federal Government, entry-level job candidates usually must have a 4-year degree with a major in mathematics or a 4-year degree with the equivalent of a mathematics major—24 semester hours of mathematics courses.

In private industry, candidates for mathematician jobs typically need a Ph.D., although there may be opportunities for those with a master's degree. Most of the positions designated for mathematicians

Mathematicians sometimes collaborate to solve problems.

are in research and development laboratories, as part of technical teams. In such settings, mathematicians engage either in basic research on pure mathematical principles or in applied research on developing or improving specific products or processes. The majority of those with a bachelor's or master's degree in mathematics who work in private industry do so not as mathematicians but in related fields such as computer science, where they have titles such as computer programmer, systems analyst, or systems engineer.

A bachelor's degree in mathematics is offered by most colleges and universities. Mathematics courses usually required for this degree include calculus, differential equations, and linear and abstract algebra. Additional courses might include probability theory and statistics, mathematical analysis, numerical analysis, topology, discrete mathematics, and mathematical logic. Many colleges and universities urge or require students majoring in mathematics to take courses in a field that is closely related to mathematics, such as computer science, engineering, life science, physical science, or economics. A double major in mathematics and another related discipline is particularly desirable to many employers. High school students who are prospective college mathematics majors should take as many mathematics courses as possible while in high school.

In 2004, about 200 colleges and universities offered a master's degree as the highest degree in either pure or applied mathematics; about 200 offered a Ph.D. degree in pure or applied mathematics. In graduate school, students conduct research and take advanced courses, usually specializing in a subfield of mathematics.

For jobs in applied mathematics, training in the field in which the mathematics will be used is very important. Mathematics is used extensively in physics, actuarial science, statistics, engineering, and operations research. Computer science, business and industrial management, economics, finance, chemistry, geology, life sciences, and behavioral sciences are likewise dependent on applied mathematics. Mathematicians also should have substantial knowledge of computer programming, because most complex mathematical computation and much mathematical modeling are done on a computer.

Mathematicians need good reasoning ability and persistence to identify, analyze, and apply basic principles to technical problems. Communication skills also are important, as mathematicians must be able to interact and discuss proposed solutions with people who may not have extensive knowledge of mathematics.

Employment
Mathematicians held about 2,500 jobs in 2004. Many people with mathematical backgrounds also worked in other occupations. For example, about 53,000 persons held positions as postsecondary mathematical science teachers in 2004.

Many mathematicians work for Federal or State governments. The U.S. Department of Defense is the primary Federal employer, accounting for about three-fourths of the mathematicians employed by the Federal Government. Many of the other mathematicians employed by the Federal Government work for the National Aeronautics and Space Administration (NASA). In the private sector, major employers include scientific research and development services and management, scientific, and technical consulting services. Some mathematicians also work for software publishers, insurance companies, and in aerospace or pharmaceutical manufacturing.

Job Outlook
Employment of mathematicians is expected to decline through 2014, reflecting the reduction in the number of jobs with the title "mathematician." As a result, competition is expected to be keen for the limited number of jobs as mathematicians. Master's and Ph.D. degree holders with a strong background in mathematics and a related discipline, such as engineering or computer science,

should have the best opportunities. Many of these workers have job titles that reflect their occupation, such as systems analyst, rather than the title mathematician, reflecting their primary educational background.

Advancements in technology usually lead to expanding applications of mathematics, and more workers with knowledge of mathematics will be required in the future. However, jobs in industry and government often require advanced knowledge of related scientific disciplines in addition to mathematics. The most common fields in which mathematicians study and find work are computer science and software development, physics, engineering, and operations research. More mathematicians also are becoming involved in financial analysis. Mathematicians must compete for jobs, however, with people who have degrees in these other disciplines. The most successful jobseekers will be able to apply mathematical theory to real-world problems and will possess good communication, teamwork, and computer skills.

Private industry jobs require at least a master's degree in mathematics or in a related field. Bachelor's degree holders in mathematics usually are not qualified for most jobs, and many seek advanced degrees in mathematics or a related discipline. However, bachelor's degree holders who meet State certification requirements may become primary or secondary school mathematics teachers. (For additional information, see the statement on teachers—preschool, kindergarten, elementary, middle, and secondary elsewhere in the *Handbook*.)

Holders of a master's degree in mathematics will face very strong competition for jobs in theoretical research. Because the number of Ph.D. degrees awarded in mathematics continues to exceed the number of university positions available, many of these graduates will need to find employment in industry and government.

Earnings
Median annual earnings of mathematicians were $81,240 in May 2004. The middle 50 percent earned between $60,050 and $101,360. The lowest 10 percent had earnings of less than $43,160, while the highest 10 percent earned over $120,900.

In early 2005, the average annual salary for mathematicians employed by the Federal Government in supervisory, nonsupervisory, and managerial positions was $88,194; that for mathematical statisticians was $91,446; and for cryptanalysts the average was $70,774.

Related Occupations
Other occupations that require extensive knowledge of mathematics or, in some cases, a degree in mathematics include actuaries, statisticians, computer programmers, computer systems analysts, computer scientists and database administrators, computer software engineers, and operations research analysts. A strong background in mathematics also facilitates employment as teachers—post secondary; teachers—preschool, kindergarten, elementary, middle, and secondary; engineers; economists; market and survey researchers; financial analysts and personal financial advisors; and physicists and astronomers.

Sources of Additional Information
For more information about careers and training in mathematics, especially for doctoral-level employment, contact:
➤ American Mathematical Society, 201 Charles St., Providence, RI 02904-2294. Internet: **http://www.ams.org**

For specific information on careers in applied mathematics, contact:
➤ Society for Industrial and Applied Mathematics, 3600 University City Science Center, Philadelphia, PA 19104-2688. Internet: **http:// www.siam.org**

Information on obtaining positions as mathematicians with the Federal Government is available from the Office of Personnel Management through USAJOBS, the Federal Government's official employment information system. This resource for locating and applying for job opportunities can be accessed through the Internet at **http://www.usajobs.opm.gov** or through an interactive voice response telephone system at (703) 724-1850 or TDD (978) 461-8404. These numbers are not tollfree, and charges may result.

Operations Research Analysts

(O*NET 15-2031.00)

Significant Points

- Employers generally prefer applicants with at least a master's degree in operations research or management science, or a closely related field such as computer science, engineering, business, mathematics, or information systems.

- Employment growth is projected to be slower than average, reflecting slow growth in the number of jobs with the title "operations research analyst."

- Individuals with a master's or Ph.D. degree in management science, operations research, or equivalent should have good job opportunities as operations research analysts or in closely related occupations, such as systems analysts, computer scientists, or management analysts.

Nature of the Work

"Operations research" and "management science" are terms that are used interchangeably to describe the discipline of applying advanced analytical techniques to help make better decisions and to solve problems. The procedures of operations research have been used effectively during wartime in areas such as deploying radar, searching for enemy submarines, and getting supplies to where they were needed most. New analytical methods have been developed, and numerous peacetime applications have emerged, leading to the use of operations research in many industries and occupations.

The prevalence of operations research in the Nation's economy reflects the growing complexity of managing large organizations that require the effective use of money, materials, equipment, and people. Operations research analysts help determine better ways to coordinate these elements by applying analytical methods from mathematics, science, and engineering. Analysts often find multiple possible solutions for meeting the particular goals of a project. These potential solutions are then presented to managers, who choose the course of action that they perceive to be best for the organization.

Operations research analysts often have one area of specialization, such as working in the transportation or the financial services industry, but the issues and industries in which operations research can be used are many. In general, operations research analysts may be involved in top-level strategizing, planning, forecasting, allocating resources, measuring performance, scheduling, designing production facilities and systems, managing the supply chain, pricing, coordinating transportation and distribution, or analyzing large databases.

The duties of the operations research analyst vary according to the structure and management of the employer's or client's organization. Some firms centralize operations research in one department; others use operations research in each division. Operations research analysts also may work closely with senior managers to identify and solve a variety of problems. Some organizations contract with consulting firms to provide operations research services. Economists, computer systems analysts, mathematicians, industrial engineers, and others may apply operations research techniques to address problems in their respective fields. (These occupations are discussed elsewhere in the *Handbook*.)

Regardless of the type or structure of the client organization, operations research entails following a standard set of procedures and conducting analysis to help managers improve performance. Managers begin the process by describing the symptoms of a problem to the analyst, who then formally defines the problem. For example, an operations research analyst for an auto manufacturer may be asked to determine the best inventory level for each of the parts needed on a production line and to ascertain the optimal number of windshields to be kept in stock. Too many windshields would be wasteful and expensive, whereas too few could result in an unintended halt in production.

Operations research analysts study such problems, breaking them into their components. Analysts then gather information about each of the components from a variety of sources. To determine the optimal inventory, for example, operations research analysts might talk with engineers about production levels, discuss purchasing arrangements with buyers, and examine storage-cost data provided by the accounting department.

With the relevant information in hand, the analyst determines the most appropriate analytical technique. Techniques used may include Monte Carlo simulation, linear and nonlinear programming, dynamic programming, queuing and other stochastic-process models, Markov decision processes, econometric methods, data envelopment analysis, neural networks, expert systems, decision analysis, and the analytic hierarchy process. Nearly all of these techniques involve the construction of a mathematical model that attempts to describe the system being studied. The use of models enables the analyst to explicitly describe the different components and clarify the relationships among them. The descriptions can be altered to examine what may happen to the system under different circumstances. In most cases, a computer program is developed to numerically evaluate the model.

Usually the model chosen is modified and run repeatedly to obtain different solutions. A model for airline flight scheduling, for example, might stipulate such things as connecting cities,

Operations research analysts use computers to perform in-depth analyses of problems in many fields.

the amount of fuel required to fly the routes, projected levels of passenger demand, varying ticket and fuel prices, pilot scheduling, and maintenance costs. By assessing different possible schedules, the analyst is able to determine the best flight schedule consistent with particular assumptions.

Based on the results of the analysis, the operations research analyst presents recommendations to managers. The analyst may need to modify and rerun the computer program to consider different assumptions before presenting the final recommendation. Once managers reach a decision, the analyst usually works with others in the organization to ensure the plan's successful implementation.

Working Conditions

Operations research analysts generally work regular hours in an office environment. However, because they work on projects that are of immediate interest to top managers, operations research analysts often are under pressure to meet deadlines and may work more than a 40-hour week.

Training, Other Qualifications, and Advancement

Employers generally prefer applicants with at least a master's degree in operations research or a closely related field, such as computer science, engineering, business, mathematics, information systems, or management science, coupled with a bachelor's degree in computer science or a quantitative discipline such as economics, mathematics, or statistics. Dual graduate degrees in operations research and computer science are especially attractive to employers. Operations research analysts must be able to think logically, use computers proficiently, work well with people, and demonstrate good oral and written communication skills.

In addition to supporting formal education in one manner or another, employers often sponsor training for experienced workers, helping them keep up with new developments in operations research techniques and computer science. Some analysts attend advanced university classes on these subjects at their employer's expense.

Computers are the most important tools used by operations research analysts for performing in-depth analysis. As a result, training and experience in programming are required. Analysts typically need to be proficient in database collection and management, programming, and the development and use of sophisticated software packages.

Beginning analysts usually perform routine work under the supervision of more experienced analysts. As the novices gain knowledge and experience, they are assigned more complex tasks and are given greater autonomy to design models and solve problems. Operations research analysts can advance by assuming positions as technical specialists or supervisors. Analysts also gain valuable insights into the industry or field in which they specialize and may assume higher level nontechnical managerial or administrative positions. Operations research analysts with significant experience may become consultants, and some may even open their own consulting practices.

Employment

Operations research analysts held about 58,000 jobs in 2004. Major employers include computer systems design firms; insurance carriers and other financial institutions; telecommunications companies; management, scientific, and technical consulting services firms; and Federal, State, and local governments. More than 4 out of 5 operations research analysts in the Federal Government work for the Department of Defense, and many in private industry work directly or indirectly on national defense.

Job Outlook

Employment of operations research analysts is expected to grow more slowly than the average for all occupations through 2014, reflecting slow growth in the number of jobs with the title "operations research analyst." Job opportunities in operations research should be good, however, because organizations throughout the economy will strive to improve their productivity, effectiveness, and competitiveness and because of the extensive availability of data, computers, and software. Many jobs in operations research have other titles, such as operations analyst, management analyst, systems analyst, and computer scientist. Individuals who hold a master's or Ph.D. degree in operations research, management science, or a closely related field should find good job opportunities because the number of openings generated by employment growth and the need to replace those leaving the occupation is expected to exceed the number of persons graduating with these credentials.

Organizations face pressure today from growing domestic and international competition and must work to make their operations as effective as possible. As a result, businesses increasingly will rely on operations research analysts to optimize profits by improving productivity and reducing costs. As new technology is introduced into the marketplace, operations research analysts will be needed to determine how to utilize the technology in the best way.

Opportunities for operations research analysts exist in almost every industry because of the diversity of applications for their work. As businesses and government agencies continue to contract out jobs to cut costs, opportunities for operations research analysts will be best in management, scientific, and technical consulting firms. Opportunities in the military will exist as well, but will depend on the size of future military budgets. Military leaders will rely on operations research analysts to test and evaluate the accuracy and effectiveness of new weapons systems and strategies. (See the *Handbook* statement on job opportunities in the Armed Forces.)

Earnings

Median annual earnings of operations research analysts were $60,190 in May 2004. The middle 50 percent earned between $45,640 and $78,420. The lowest 10 percent had earnings of less than $36,180, while the highest 10 percent earned more than $95,990.

The average annual salary for operations research analysts in the Federal Government in nonsupervisory, supervisory, and managerial positions was $89,882 in 2005.

Related Occupations

Operations research analysts apply advanced analytical methods to large, complicated problems. Workers in other occupations that stress advanced analysis include computer systems analysts, computer scientists and database administrators, computer programmers, engineers, mathematicians, statisticians, economists, and market and survey researchers. Because its goal is improved organizational effectiveness, operations research also is closely allied to managerial occupations such as computer and information systems managers, and management analysts.

Sources of Additional Information

Information on career opportunities for operations research analysts is available from:

➤ Institute for Operations Research and the Management Sciences, 7240 Parkway Dr., Suite 310, Hanover, MD 21076. Internet: **http://www.informs.org**

For information on operations research careers in the Armed Forces and the U.S. Department of Defense, contact:

➤ Military Operations Research Society, 1703 N. Beauregard St., Suite 450, Alexandria, VA 22311. Internet: **http://www.mors.org**

Information on obtaining positions as operations research analysts with the Federal Government is available from the Office of Personnel Management through USAJOBS, the Federal Government's official employment information system. This resource for locating and applying for job opportunities can be accessed through the Internet at **http://www.usajobs.opm.gov** or through an interactive voice response telephone system at (703) 724-1850 or TDD (978) 461-8404. These numbers are not tollfree, and charges may result.

Statisticians

(O*NET 15-2041.00)

Significant Points

- About 41 percent of statisticians work for Federal, State, and local governments; other employers include scientific research and development services and finance and insurance firms.

- A master's degree in statistics or mathematics is the minimum educational requirement for most jobs as a statistician.

- Employment of statisticians is projected to grow more slowly than average because many jobs that require a degree in statistics will not carry the title "statistician."

- Individuals with a degree in statistics should have favorable job opportunities in a variety of disciplines.

Nature of the Work

Statistics is the scientific application of mathematical principles to the collection, analysis, and presentation of numerical data. Statisticians contribute to scientific inquiry by applying their mathematical and statistical knowledge to the design of surveys and experiments; the collection, processing, and analysis of data; and the interpretation of the results. Statisticians may apply their knowledge of statistical methods to a variety of subject areas, such as biology, economics, engineering, medicine, public health, psychology, marketing, education, and sports. Many economic, social, political, and military decisions cannot be made without statistical techniques, such as the design of experiments to gain Federal approval of a newly manufactured drug.

One technique that is especially useful to statisticians is sampling—obtaining information about a population of people or group of things by surveying a small portion of the total. For example, to determine the size of the audience for particular programs, television-rating services survey only a few thousand families, rather than all viewers. Statisticians decide where and how to gather the data, determine the type and size of the sample group, and develop the survey questionnaire or reporting form. They also prepare instructions for workers who will collect and tabulate the data. Finally, statisticians analyze, interpret, and summarize the data using computer software.

In business and industry, statisticians play an important role in quality control and in product development and improvement. In an automobile company, for example, statisticians might design experiments to determine the failure time of engines exposed to extreme weather conditions by running individual engines until failure and breakdown. Working for a pharmaceutical company, statisticians might develop and evaluate the results of clinical trials to determine the safety and effectiveness of new medications. And, at a computer software firm, statisticians might help construct new statistical software packages to analyze data more accurately and efficiently. In addition to product development and testing, some statisticians also are involved in deciding what products to manufacture, how much to charge for them, and to whom the products should be marketed. Statisticians also may manage assets and liabilities, determining the risks and returns of certain investments.

Statisticians also are employed by nearly every government agency. Some government statisticians develop surveys that measure population growth, consumer prices, or unemployment. Other statisticians work for scientific, environmental, and agricultural agencies and may help determine the level of pesticides in drinking water, the number of endangered species living in a particular area, or the number of people afflicted with a particular disease. Statisticians also are employed in national defense agencies, determining the accuracy of new weapons and the likely effectiveness of defense strategies.

Because statistical specialists are employed in so many work areas, specialists who use statistics often have different professional designations. For example, a person using statistical methods to analyze economic data may have the title econometrician, while statisticians in public health and medicine may hold titles such as biostatistician, biometrician, or epidemiologist.

Working Conditions

Statisticians usually work regular hours in comfortable offices. Some statisticians travel to provide advice on research projects, supervise and set up surveys, or gather statistical data. While advanced communications devices such as e-mail and teleconferencing are making it easier for statisticians to work with clients in different areas, there still are situations that require the statistician to be present, such as during meetings or while gathering data. Some in this occupation may have duties that vary widely, such as designing experiments or performing fieldwork in various communities. Statisticians who work in academia generally have a mix of teaching and research responsibilities.

Training, Other Qualifications, and Advancement

Although employment opportunities exist for individuals with a bachelor's degree, a master's degree in statistics or mathematics is usually the minimum educational requirement for most statistician jobs. Research and academic positions in institutions of higher education, for example, require at least a master's degree, and usually a Ph.D.,

Statisticians usually work in offices, though they may travel to consult with clients, supervise or set up surveys, or gather statistical data.

in statistics. Beginning positions in industrial research often require a master's degree combined with several years of experience.

The training required for employment as an entry-level statistician in the Federal Government, however, is a bachelor's degree, including at least 15 semester hours of statistics or a combination of 15 hours of mathematics and statistics, if at least 6 semester hours are in statistics. Qualifying as a mathematical statistician in the Federal Government requires 24 semester hours of mathematics and statistics, with a minimum of 6 semester hours in statistics and 12 semester hours in an area of advanced mathematics, such as calculus, differential equations, or vector analysis.

In 2004, approximately 230 universities offered a degree program in statistics, biostatistics, or mathematics. Many other schools also offered graduate-level courses in applied statistics for students majoring in biology, business, economics, education, engineering, psychology, and other fields. Acceptance into graduate statistics programs does not require an undergraduate degree in statistics, although good training in mathematics is essential.

Many schools also offered degrees in mathematics, operations research, and other fields that include a sufficient number of courses in statistics to qualify graduates for some entry-level positions with the Federal Government. Required subjects for statistics majors include differential and integral calculus, statistical methods, mathematical modeling, and probability theory. Additional courses that undergraduates should take include linear algebra, design and analysis of experiments, applied multivariate analysis, and mathematical statistics.

Because computers are used extensively for statistical applications, a strong background in computer science is highly recommended. For positions involving quality and productivity improvement, training in engineering or physical science is useful. A background in biological, chemical, or health science is important for positions involving the preparation and testing of pharmaceutical or agricultural products. Courses in economics and business administration are helpful for many jobs in market research, business analysis, and forecasting.

Good communications skills are important for prospective statisticians in industry, who often need to explain technical matters to persons without statistical expertise. An understanding of business and the economy also is valuable for those who plan to work in private industry.

Beginning statisticians generally are supervised by an experienced statistician. With experience, they may advance to positions with more technical responsibility and, in some cases, supervisory duties. However, opportunities for promotion are greater for persons with advanced degrees. Master's and Ph.D. degree holders usually enjoy independence in their work and may become qualified to engage in research; develop statistical methods; or, after a number of years of experience in a particular area, become statistical consultants.

Employment

Statisticians held about 19,000 jobs in 2004. Twenty percent of these jobs were in the Federal Government, where statisticians were concentrated in the Departments of Commerce, Agriculture, and Health and Human Services. Another 20 percent were found in State and local governments, including State colleges and universities. Most of the remaining jobs were in private industry, especially in scientific research and development services, insurance carriers, and pharmaceutical and medicine manufacturing. In addition, many professionals with a background in statistics were among the 53,000 postsecondary mathematical science teachers. (See the statement on teachers—postsecondary elsewhere in the *Handbook*.)

Job Outlook

Employment of statisticians is projected to grow more slowly than the average for all occupations over the 2004-14 period, because many jobs that require a degree in statistics will not carry the title "statistician." However, job opportunities should remain favorable for individuals with a degree in statistics. For example, many jobs involve the analysis and interpretation of data from economics, biological science, psychology, computer software engineering, and other disciplines. Despite the limited number of jobs resulting from growth, a number of openings will become available as statisticians transfer to other occupations or retire or leave the workforce for other reasons.

The use of statistics is widespread and growing. Among graduates with a master's degree in statistics, those with a strong background in an allied field, such as finance, biology, engineering, or computer science, should have the best prospects of finding jobs related to their field of study. Federal agencies will hire statisticians in many fields, including demography, agriculture, consumer and producer surveys, Social Security, health care, and environmental quality. Because the Federal Government is one of the few employers that considers a bachelor's degree an adequate entry-level qualification, competition for entry-level positions in the Federal Government is expected to be strong for persons just meeting the minimum qualifications for statisticians. Those who meet State certification requirements may become high school statistics teachers. (For additional information, see the statement on teachers—preschool, kindergarten, elementary, middle, and secondary elsewhere in the *Handbook*.)

Manufacturing firms will hire statisticians with master's and doctoral degrees for quality control of various products, including pharmaceuticals, motor vehicles, aircraft, chemicals, and food. For example, pharmaceutical firms will employ statisticians to assess the effectiveness and safety of new drugs, to decide whether to market them, and to make sure they comply with federal standards. To address global product competition, motor vehicle manufacturers will need statisticians to improve the quality of automobiles, trucks, and their components by developing and testing new designs. Statisticians with knowledge of engineering and the physical sciences will find jobs in research and development, working with teams of scientists and engineers to help improve design and production processes to ensure consistent quality of newly developed products. Many statisticians also will find opportunities developing statistical software for computer software manufacturing firms.

Firms will rely heavily on workers with a background in statistics to forecast sales, analyze business conditions, and help to solve management problems to maximize profits. In addition, consulting firms increasingly will offer sophisticated statistical services to other businesses. Because of the widespread use of computers in this field and the growing number of widely used software packages, statisticians in all industries should have good computer programming skills and knowledge of statistical software.

Earnings

Median annual earnings of statisticians were $58,620 in May 2004. The middle 50 percent earned between $42,770 and $80,690. The lowest 10 percent earned less than $32,870, while the highest 10 percent earned more than $100,500.

The average annual salary for statisticians in the Federal Government in nonsupervisory, supervisory, and managerial positions was $81,262 in 2005, while mathematical statisticians averaged $91,446. According to a 2005 survey by the National Association of Colleges and Employers, starting salary offers for mathematics/statistics graduates with a bachelor's degree averaged $43,448 a year.

Related Occupations

People in a wide range of occupations work with statistics. Among these are actuaries, mathematicians, operations research analysts, computer scientists and database administrators, computer systems analysts, computer programmers, computer software engineers, engineers, economists, market and survey researchers, and financial analysts and personal financial advisors. Some statisticians also work as secondary or postsecondary teachers.

Sources of Additional Information

For information about career opportunities in statistics, contact:
➤ American Statistical Association, 1429 Duke St., Alexandria, VA 22314-3415. Internet: **http://www.amstat.org**

For more information on doctoral-level careers and training in mathematics, a field closely related to statistics, contact:
➤ American Mathematical Society, 201 Charles St., Providence, RI 02904-2213. Internet: **http://www.ams.org**

Information on obtaining positions as statisticians with the Federal Government is available from the Office of Personnel Management through USAJOBS, the Federal Government's official employment information system. This resource for locating and applying for job opportunities can be accessed through the Internet at **http://www.usajobs.opm.gov** or through an interactive voice response telephone system at (703) 724-1850 or TDD (978) 461-8404. These numbers are not tollfree, and charges may result.

Architects, Surveyors, and Cartographers

Architects, Except Landscape and Naval

(O*NET 17-1011.00)

Significant Points

- About 1 in 4 architects was self-employed—more than three times the proportion for all professional and related occupations.

- Licensing requirements include a professional degree in architecture, 3 years of practical work training, and passing all divisions of the Architect Registration Examination.

- Architecture graduates may face competition, especially for jobs in the most prestigious firms; opportunities will be best for those with experience working for a firm while still in school and for those with knowledge of computer-aided design and drafting technology.

Nature of the Work

People need places in which to live, work, play, learn, worship, meet, govern, shop, and eat. These places may be private or public; indoors or outdoors; or rooms, buildings, or complexes, and together, they make up neighborhoods, towns, suburbs, and cities. *Architects*—licensed professionals trained in the art and science of building design—transform these needs into concepts and then develop the concepts into images and plans of buildings that can be constructed by others.

Architects design the overall aesthetic and look of buildings and other structures, but the design of a building involves far more than its appearance. Buildings also must be functional, safe, and economical and must suit the needs of the people who use them. Architects consider all these factors when they design buildings and other structures.

Architects provide professional services to individuals and organizations planning a construction project. They may be involved in all phases of development, from the initial discussion with the client through the entire construction process. Their duties require specific skills—designing, engineering, managing, supervising, and communicating with clients and builders. Architects spend a great deal of time explaining their ideas to clients, construction contrac-

tors, and others. Successful architects must be able to communicate their unique vision persuasively.

The architect and client discuss the objectives, requirements, and budget of a project. In some cases, architects provide various predesign services—conducting feasibility and environmental impact studies, selecting a site, or specifying the requirements the design must meet. For example, they may determine space requirements by researching the numbers and types of potential users of a building. The architect then prepares drawings and a report presenting ideas for the client to review.

After discussing and agreeing on the initial proposal, architects develop final construction plans that show the building's appearance and details for its construction. Accompanying these plans are drawings of the structural system; air-conditioning, heating, and ventilating systems; electrical systems; communications systems; plumbing; and, possibly, site and landscape plans. The plans also specify the building materials and, in some cases, the interior furnishings. In developing designs, architects follow building codes, zoning laws, fire regulations, and other ordinances, such as those requiring easy access by disabled persons. Throughout the planning stage, they make necessary changes. Computer-aided design and drafting (CADD) technology has replaced traditional paper and pencil as the most common method for creating design and construction drawings. Continual revision of plans on the basis of client needs and budget constraints is often necessary.

Architects may also assist clients in obtaining construction bids, selecting contractors, and negotiating construction contracts. As construction proceeds, they may visit building sites to make sure that contractors follow the design, adhere to the schedule, use the specified materials, and meet work quality standards. The job is not complete until all construction is finished, required tests are conducted, and construction costs are paid. Sometimes, architects also provide postconstruction services, such as facilities management. They advise on energy efficiency measures, evaluate how well the building design adapts to the needs of occupants, and make necessary improvements.

Architects design a wide variety of buildings, such as office and apartment buildings, schools, churches, factories, hospitals, houses, and airport terminals. They also design complexes such as urban centers, college campuses, industrial parks, and entire communities. In addition, they may advise on the selection of building sites, prepare cost analysis and land-use studies, and do long-range planning for land development.

Architects sometimes specialize in one phase of work. Some specialize in the design of one type of building—for example, hospitals, schools, or housing. Others focus on planning and predesign services or construction management and do minimal design work. They often work with engineers, urban planners, interior designers, landscape architects, and other professionals. In fact, architects spend a great deal of their time coordinating information from, and the work of, others engaged in the same project. Many architects—particularly at larger firms—use the Internet and e-mail to update designs and communicate changes efficiently. Architects also use the Internet to research product specifications and government regulations.

Working Conditions

Architects usually work in a comfortable environment. Most of their time is spent in offices consulting with clients, developing reports and drawings, and working with other architects and engineers. However, they often visit construction sites to review the progress of projects. Although most architects work approximately 40 hours per week, they often have to work nights and weekends to meet deadlines.

Training, Other Qualifications, and Advancement

All States and the District of Columbia require individuals to be licensed (registered) before they may call themselves architects and contract to provide architectural services. During this time between graduation and becoming licensed, architecture school graduates generally work in the field under supervision of a licensed architect who takes legal responsibility for all work. Licensing requirements include a professional degree in architecture, a period of practical

Architects often produce scale models of their designs.

training or internship, and a passing score on all divisions of the Architect Registration Examination (ARE).

In most States, the professional degree in architecture must be from one of the 113 schools of architecture that have degree programs accredited by the National Architectural Accrediting Board (NAAB). However, State architectural registration boards set their own standards, so graduation from a non-NAAB-accredited program may meet the educational requirement for licensing in a few States. Three types of professional degrees in architecture are available through colleges and universities. The majority of all architectural degrees are from 5-year Bachelor of Architecture programs, intended for students entering university-level studies from high school or with no previous architectural training. In addition, a number of schools offer a 2-year Master of Architecture program for students with a preprofessional undergraduate degree in architecture or a related area, or a 3- or 4-year Master of Architecture program for students with a degree in another discipline.

The choice of degree depends upon each individual's preference and educational background. Prospective architecture students should consider the available options before committing to a program. For example, although the 5-year Bachelor of Architecture program offers the fastest route to the professional degree, courses are specialized, and if the student does not complete the program, transferring to a program offered by another discipline may be difficult. A typical program includes courses in architectural history and theory, building design, structures, technology, construction methods, professional practice, math, physical sciences, and liberal arts. Central to most architectural programs is the design studio, where students put into practice the skills and concepts learned in the classroom. During the final semester of many programs, students devote their studio time to creating an architectural project from beginning to end, culminating in a three-dimensional model of their design.

Many schools of architecture also offer postprofessional degrees for those who already have a bachelor's or master's degree in architecture or other areas. Although graduate education beyond the professional degree is not required for practicing architects, it may be for research, teaching, and certain specialties.

Architects must be able to communicate their ideas visually to their clients. Artistic and drawing ability is helpful, but not essential, to such communication. More important are a visual orientation and the ability to conceptualize and understand spatial relationships. Good communication skills, the ability to work independently or as part of a team, and creativity are important qualities for anyone interested in becoming an architect. Computer literacy also is required for writing specifications, for two- and three-dimensional drafting, and for financial management. Knowledge of CADD is essential and has become a critical tool for architects. Most schools now teach students CADD programs and methods that adhere to the National CAD Standards.

All State architectural registration boards require architecture graduates to complete a training period—usually 3 years—before they may sit for the ARE, the third and final requirement for becoming licensed. Every State, with the exception of Arizona, has adopted the training standards established by the Intern Development Program, a branch of the American Institute of Architects and the National Council of Architectural Registration Boards (NCARB). These standards stipulate broad and diversified training under the supervision of a licensed architect over a 3-year period. Most new graduates complete their training period by working as interns at architectural firms. Some States allow a portion of the training to occur in the offices of related professionals, such as engineers or general contractors. Architecture students who complete internships in architectural firms while still in school can count some of that time toward the required 3-year training period.

Interns in architectural firms may assist in the design of one part of a project, help prepare architectural documents or drawings, build models, or prepare construction drawings on CADD. Interns also may research building codes and materials or write specifications for building materials, installation criteria, the quality of finishes, and other, related details.

After completing their on-the-job training period, interns are eligible to sit for the ARE. The examination tests a candidate's knowledge, skills, and ability to provide the various services required in the design and construction of buildings. The test is broken down into 9 divisions consisting of either multiple choice or graphical questions; States give candidates an eligibility period for completion of all divisions of the exam that varies by State. Candidates who pass the ARE and meet all standards established by their State Board become licensed to practice in that State.

Most States require some form of continuing education to maintain a license, and many others are expected to adopt mandatory continuing education. Requirements vary by State, but usually involve the completion of a certain number of credits annually or biennially through workshops, formal university classes, conferences, self-study courses, or other sources.

A growing number of architects voluntarily seek certification by the NCARB, which can facilitate an individual's becoming licensed to practice in additional States. This practice is known as "reciprocity." Certification is awarded after independent verification of the candidate's educational transcripts, employment record, and professional references. Certification is the primary requirement for reciprocity of licensing among State Boards that are NCARB members. In 2004, approximately one-third of all licensed architects had NCARB certification.

After becoming licensed and gaining experience, architects take on increasingly responsible duties, eventually managing entire projects. In large firms, architects may advance to supervisory or managerial positions. Some architects become partners in established firms, while others set up their own practices. Graduates with degrees in architecture also enter related fields, such as graphic, interior, or industrial design; urban planning; real estate development; civil engineering; and construction management.

Employment

Architects held about 129,000 jobs in 2004. Approximately 3 out of 5 jobs were in the architectural, engineering, and related services industry—mostly in architectural firms with fewer than five workers. A small number worked for residential and nonresidential building construction firms and for government agencies responsible for housing, community planning, or construction of government buildings, such as the U.S. Departments of Defense and Interior, and the General Services Administration. About 1 in 4 architects was self-employed.

Job Outlook

Employment of architects is expected to grow about as fast the average for all occupations through 2014. Besides employment growth, additional job openings will arise from the need to replace the many architects who are nearing retirement, and others who transfer to other occupations or stop working for other reasons. Internship opportunities for new architectural students are expected to be good over the next decade, but more students are graduating with architectural degrees and some competition for entry-level jobs can be anticipated. Competition will be especially keen for jobs at the most prestigious architectural firms as prospective architects try to build their reputation. Prospective architects who have had internships while in school will have an advantage in obtaining intern positions after graduation.

Employment of architects is strongly tied to the activity of the construction industry. Strong growth is expected to come from nonresidential construction as demand for commercial space increases. Residential construction, buoyed by low interest rates, is also expected to grow as more and more people become homeowners. If interest rates rise significantly, this sector may see a falloff in home building.

Current demographic trends also support an increase in demand for architects. As the population of Sunbelt States continues to grow, the people living there will need new places to live and work. As the population continues to live longer and baby-boomers begin to retire there will be a need for more healthcare facilities, nursing homes, and retirement communities. In education, buildings at all levels are getting older and class sizes are getting larger. This will require many school districts and universities to build new facilities and renovate existing ones.

Some types of construction are sensitive to cyclical changes in the economy. Architects seeking design projects for office and retail construction will face especially strong competition for jobs or clients during recessions, and layoffs may ensue in less successful firms. Those involved in the design of institutional buildings, such as schools, hospitals, nursing homes, and correctional facilities, will be less affected by fluctuations in the economy. Residential construction makes up a small portion of work for architects, so major changes in the housing market would not be as significant as fluctuations in the nonresidential market.

Despite good overall job opportunities some architects may not fare as well as others. The profession is geographically sensitive and some parts of the Nation may have fewer new building projects than others. Also, many firms specialize in specific buildings, such as hospitals or office towers, and demand for these buildings may vary by region. Architects may find it increasingly necessary to gain reciprocity in order to compete for the best jobs and projects in other States.

In recent years, some architecture firms have outsourced to architecture firms overseas the drafting of construction documents for large-scale commercial and residential projects. This trend is expected to continue and may have a negative impact on employment growth for lower level architects and interns who would normally gain experience by producing these drawings. However, most firms will keep design services in-house, and opportunities will be best for those architects that are able to distinguish themselves from others with their creativity.

Earnings

Median annual earnings of wage and salary architects were $60,300 in May 2004. The middle 50 percent earned between $46,690 and $79,230. The lowest 10 percent earned less than $38,060, and the highest 10 percent earned more than $99,800. Those just starting their internships can expect to earn considerably less.

Earnings of partners in established architectural firms may fluctuate because of changing business conditions. Some architects may have difficulty establishing their own practices and may go through a period when their expenses are greater than their income, requiring substantial financial resources.

Related Occupations

Architects design buildings and related structures. Construction managers, like architects, also plan and coordinate activities concerned with the construction and maintenance of buildings and facilities. Others who engage in similar work are landscape architects, civil engineers, urban and regional planners, and designers, including interior designers, commercial and industrial designers, and graphic designers.

Sources of Additional Information

Head:Information about education and careers in architecture can be obtained from:

➤ The American Institute of Architects, 1735 New York Ave. NW., Washington, DC 20006. Internet: **http://www.aia.org**

➤ Intern Development Program, National Council of Architectural Registration Boards, Suite 1100K, 1801 K Street NW., Washington, D.C. 20006-1310. Internet: **http://www.ncarb.org**

Landscape Architects

(O*NET 17-1012.00)

Significant Points

● More than 26 percent of all landscape architects are self-employed—more than 3 times the proportion for all professionals.

● A bachelor's degree in landscape architecture is the minimum requirement for entry-level jobs; many employers prefer to hire landscape architects who also have completed at least one internship.

● Landscape architect jobs are expected to increase due to a growing demand for incorporating natural elements into man-made environments, along with the need to meet a wide array of environmental restrictions.

Nature of the Work

Everyone enjoys attractively designed residential areas, public parks and playgrounds, college campuses, shopping centers, golf courses, parkways, and industrial parks. Landscape architects design these areas so that they are not only functional, but also beautiful, and compatible with the natural environment. They plan the location of buildings, roads, and walkways, and the arrangement of flowers, shrubs, and trees.

Landscape architects work for many types of organizations—from real estate development firms starting new projects to municipalities constructing airports or parks—and they often are involved with the development of a site from its conception. Working with architects, surveyors, and engineers, landscape architects help determine the best arrangement of roads and buildings. They also collaborate with environmental scientists, foresters, and other professionals to find the best way to conserve or restore natural resources. Once these decisions are made, landscape architects create detailed plans indicating new topography, vegetation, walkways, and other landscaping details, such as fountains and decorative features.

In planning a site, landscape architects first consider the nature and purpose of the project and the funds available. They analyze the natural elements of the site, such as the climate, soil, slope of the land, drainage, and vegetation; observe where sunlight falls on the site at different times of the day and examine the site from various angles; and assess the effect of existing buildings, roads, walkways, and utilities on the project.

After studying and analyzing the site, landscape architects prepare a preliminary design. To account for the needs of the client as well as the conditions at the site, they frequently make changes before a final design is approved. They also take into account any local, State, or Federal regulations, such as those protecting wetlands or historic resources. In preparing designs, computer-aided design (CAD) has become an essential tool for most landscape architects. Many landscape architects also use video simulation to help clients envision the proposed ideas and plans. For larger scale site planning, landscape architects also use geographic information systems technology, a computer mapping system.

Throughout all phases of the planning and design, landscape architects consult with other professionals, such as civil engineers, hydrologists, or architects, involved in the project. Once the design is complete, they prepare a proposal for the client. They produce detailed plans of the site, including written reports, sketches, models, photographs, land-use studies, and cost estimates, and submit them for approval by the client and by regulatory agencies. When the plans are approved, landscape architects prepare working drawings showing all existing and proposed features. They also outline in detail the methods of construction and draw up a list of necessary materials. Landscape architects then mainly monitor the implementation of their design, with general contractors or landscape contractors usually directing the actual construction of the site and installation of plantings.

Some landscape architects work on a variety of projects. Others specialize in a particular area, such as residential development, street and highway beautification, waterfront improvement projects, parks and playgrounds, or shopping centers. Still others work in regional planning and resource management; feasibility, environmental impact, and cost studies; or site construction. Increasingly, landscape architects are becoming involved with projects in environmental remediation, such as preservation and restoration of wetlands or abatement of stormwater run-off in new developments. Historic landscape preservation and restoration is another important area where landscape architects are increasingly playing an important role.

Most landscape architects do at least some residential work, but relatively few limit their practice to individual homeowners. Residential landscape design projects usually are too small to provide suitable income compared with larger commercial or multiunit residential projects. Some nurseries offer residential landscape design services, but these services often are performed by design professionals with fewer formal credentials such as landscape designers, or by others with training and experience in related areas.

Landscape architects who work for government agencies do site and landscape design for government buildings, parks, and other public lands, as well as park and recreation planning in national parks and forests. In addition, they prepare environmental impact statements and studies on environmental issues such as public land-use planning. Some restore degraded land, such as mines or landfills. Other landscape architects use their skills in traffic-calming, the "art" of slowing traffic down through use of traffic design, enhancement of the physical environment, and greater attention to aesthetics.

Working Conditions

Landscape architects spend most of their time in offices creating plans and designs, preparing models and cost estimates, doing research, or attending meetings with clients and other professionals involved in a design or planning project. The remainder of their time is spent at the site. During the design and planning stage, landscape architects visit and analyze the site to verify that the design can be incorporated into the landscape. After the plans and specifications are completed, they may spend additional time at the site observing or supervising the construction. Those who work in large national or regional firms may spend considerably more time out of the office traveling to sites away from the local area.

Salaried employees in both government and landscape architectural firms usually work regular hours; however, they may work overtime to meet a project deadline. Hours of self-employed landscape architects vary depending on the demands of the projects on which they are working.

Landscape architects spend much time in the office, reviewing plans of the site.

Training, Other Qualifications, and Advancement

A bachelor's or master's degree in landscape architecture usually is necessary for entry into the profession. A bachelor's degree in landscape architecture takes 4 or 5 years to complete. There also are two types of accredited master's degree programs. The most common type of master's degree is a 3-year first professional degree program designed for students with an undergraduate degree in another discipline. The second type of master's degree is a 2-year second professional degree program for students who have a bachelor's degree in landscape architecture and who wish to teach or specialize in some aspect of landscape architecture, such as regional planning or golf course design.

In 2004, 59 colleges and universities offered 77 undergraduate and graduate programs in landscape architecture that were accredited by the Landscape Architecture Accreditation Board of the American Society of Landscape Architects. College courses required in these programs usually include technical subjects such as surveying, landscape design and construction, landscape ecology, site design, and urban and regional planning. Other courses include history of landscape architecture, plant and soil science, geology, professional practice, and general management. The design studio is another important aspect of many landscape architecture curriculums. Whenever possible, students are assigned real projects, providing them with valuable hands-on experience. While working on these projects, students become more proficient in the use of computer-aided design, geographic information systems, and video simulation.

In 2004, 47 States required landscape architects to be licensed or registered. Licensing is based on the Landscape Architect Registration Examination (L.A.R.E.), sponsored by the Council of Landscape Architectural Registration Boards and administered in two portions, graphic and multiple choice. Each portion of the testing is conducted over two days. Admission to the exam usually requires a degree from an accredited school plus 1 to 4 years of work experience under the supervision of a registered landscape architect, although standards vary from State to State. Currently, 14 States require that a State examination be passed in addition to the L.A.R.E. to satisfy registration requirements. State examinations, which usually are 1 hour in length and completed at the end of the L.A.R.E., focus on laws, environmental regulations, plants, soils, climate, and any other characteristics unique to the State.

Because State requirements for licensure are not uniform, landscape architects may not find it easy to transfer their registration from one State to another. However, those who meet the national standards of graduating from an accredited program, serving 3 years of internship under the supervision of a registered landscape architect, and passing the L.A.R.E. can satisfy requirements in most States. Through this means, a landscape architect can obtain certification from the Council of Landscape Architectural Registration Boards, and so gain reciprocity (the right to work) in other States.

In the Federal Government, candidates for entry positions should have a bachelor's or master's degree in landscape architecture. The Federal Government does not require its landscape architects to be licensed.

Persons planning a career in landscape architecture should appreciate nature, enjoy working with their hands, and possess strong analytical skills. Creative vision and artistic talent also are desirable qualities. Good oral communication skills are essential; landscape architects must be able to convey their ideas to other professionals and clients, and to make presentations before large groups. Strong writing skills also are valuable, as is knowledge of computer applications of all kinds, including word processing, desktop publishing, and spreadsheets. Landscape architects use these tools to develop presentations, proposals, reports, and land impact studies for clients, colleagues, and superiors. The ability to draft and design using CAD software is essential. Many employers recommend that prospective landscape architects complete at least one summer internship with a landscape architecture firm in order to gain an understanding of the day-to-day operations of a small business, including how to win clients, generate fees, and work within a budget.

In States where licensure is required, new hires may be called "apprentices" or "intern landscape architects" until they become licensed. Their duties vary depending on the type and size of the employing firm. They may do project research or prepare working drawings, construction documents, or base maps of the area to be landscaped. Some are allowed to participate in the actual design of a project. However, interns must perform all work under the supervision of a licensed landscape architect. Additionally, all drawings and specifications must be signed and sealed by the licensed landscape architect, who takes legal responsibility for the work. After gaining experience and becoming licensed, landscape architects usually can carry a design through all stages of development. After several years, they may become project managers, taking on the responsibility for meeting schedules and budgets, in addition to overseeing the project design. Later, they may become associates or partners of a firm, with a proprietary interest in the business.

Many landscape architects are self-employed because start-up costs, after an initial investment in CAD software, are relatively low. Self-discipline, business acumen, and good marketing skills are important qualities for those who choose to open their own business. Even with these qualities, however, some may struggle while building a client base.

Those with landscape architecture training also qualify for jobs closely related to landscape architecture, and may, after gaining some experience, become construction supervisors, land or environmental planners, or landscape consultants.

Employment

Landscape architects held about 25,000 jobs in 2004. Almost 6 out of 10 workers were employed in firms that provide architectural, landscape architectural, engineering, and landscaping services. State and local governments were the next largest employers. About 1 out of 4 landscape architects was self-employed.

Employment of landscape architects is concentrated in urban and suburban areas throughout the country; some landscape architects work in rural areas, particularly those employed by the Federal Government to plan and design parks and recreation areas.

Job Outlook

Employment of landscape architects is expected to increase faster than the average for all occupations through the year 2014. In addition to growth, the need to replace landscape architects who retire or leave the labor force will produce some additional job openings. Employment will grow because the expertise of landscape architects will be highly sought after in the planning and development of new residential, commercial, and other types of construction to meet the needs of a growing population. With land costs rising and the public desiring more beautiful spaces, the importance of good site planning and landscape design is growing. In addition, new demands to manage stormwater run-off in both existing and new landscapes, combined with the growing need to manage water resources in the Western States, should cause increased demand for this occupation's services.

New construction also is increasingly contingent upon compliance with environmental regulations, zoning laws, and water restrictions, which will spur demand for landscape architects to help plan sites that meet these requirements and integrate new structures with the natural environment in the least disruptive way. Landscape architects also will be increasingly involved in preserving and restoring wetlands and other environmentally sensitive sites.

Continuation of the Transportation Equity Act for the Twenty-First Century also is expected to spur employment for landscape architects, particularly through State and local governments. This Act, known as TEA-21, provides funds for surface transportation and transit programs, such as interstate highway construction and maintenance and environment-friendly pedestrian and bicycle trails.

In addition to the work related to new development and construction, landscape architects are expected to be involved in historic preservation, land reclamation, and refurbishment of existing sites. They are also doing more residential design work as households spend more on landscaping than in the past. Because landscape architects can work on many different types of projects, they may have an easier time than other design professionals finding employment when traditional construction slows down. Opportunities will vary from year to year, and by geographic region, depending on local economic conditions. During a recession, when real estate sales and construction slow down, landscape architects may face greater competition for jobs and sometimes layoffs.

New graduates can expect to face competition for jobs in the largest and most prestigious landscape architecture firms, but should face good job opportunities overall as demand increases, while the number of graduates of landscape architecture holds steady or only

goes up slightly. Opportunities will be best for landscape architects who develop strong technical skills—such as computer design—and communication skills, as well as knowledge of environmental codes and regulations. Those with additional training or experience in urban planning increase their opportunities for employment in landscape architecture firms that specialize in site planning as well as landscape design. Many employers prefer to hire entry-level landscape architects who have internship experience, which significantly reduces the amount of on-the-job training required.

Earnings

In May 2004, median annual earnings for landscape architects were $53,120. The middle 50 percent earned between $40,930 and $70,400. The lowest 10 percent earned less than $32,390 and the highest 10 percent earned over $90,850. Architectural, engineering, and related services employed more landscape architects than any other group of industries, and there the median annual earnings were $51,670 in May 2004.

In 2005, the average annual salary for all landscape architects in the Federal Government in nonsupervisory, supervisory, and managerial positions was $74,508.

Because many landscape architects work for small firms or are self-employed, benefits tend to be less generous than those provided to workers in large organizations.

Related Occupations

Landscape architects use their knowledge of design, construction, land-use planning, and environmental issues to develop a landscape project. Others whose work requires similar skills are architects, except landscape and naval; surveyors, cartographers, photogrammetrists, and surveying technicians; civil engineers; and urban and regional planners. Landscape architects also must know how to grow and use plants in the landscape. Some conservation scientists and foresters and biological scientists study plants in general and do related work, while environmental scientists and geoscientists work in the area of environmental remediation.

Sources of Additional Information

Additional information, including a list of colleges and universities offering accredited programs in landscape architecture, is available from:
➤ American Society of Landscape Architects, Career Information, 636 Eye St. NW., Washington, DC 20001-3736. Internet: **http://www.asla.org**

General information on registration or licensing requirements is available from:
➤ Council of Landscape Architectural Registration Boards, 144 Church Street NW., Suite 201, Vienna, VA 22180-4550. Internet: **http://www.clarb.org**

Surveyors, Cartographers, Photogrammetrists, and Surveying Technicians

(O*NET 17-1021.00, 17-1022.00, 17-3031.01, 17-3031.02)

Significant Points

● About 2 out of 3 jobs were in architectural, engineering, and related services.

● Opportunities will be best for surveyors, cartographers, and photogrammetrists who have a bachelor's degree and strong technical skills.

● Applicants for jobs as technicians may face competition.

Nature of the Work

Surveyors, cartographers, and photogrammetrists are responsible for measuring and mapping the earth's surface. Traditionally, surveyors establish official land, airspace, and water boundaries. They write descriptions of land for deeds, leases, and other legal documents; define airspace for airports; and take measurements of construction and mineral sites. Other surveyors provide data relevant to the shape, contour, location, elevation, or dimension of land or land features. *Cartographers* compile geographic, political, and cultural information and prepare maps of large areas. *Photogrammetrists* measure and analyze aerial photographs that are subsequently used to prepare detailed maps and drawings. Surveying and mapping technicians assist these professionals in their duties by collecting data in the field and using it to calculate mapmaking information for use in performing computations and computer-aided drafting.

Surveyors measure distances, directions, and angles between points and elevations of points, lines, and contours on, above, and below the earth's surface. In the field they select known survey reference points, and determine the precise location of important features in the survey area. Surveyors research legal records, look for evidence of previous boundaries, and analyze the data to determine the location of boundary lines. They also record the results of surveys, verify the accuracy of data, and prepare plots, maps, and reports. Surveyors who establish boundaries must be licensed by the State in which they work. Surveyors are sometimes called to provide expert testimony in court cases concerning matters pertaining to surveying.

Cartographers measure, map, and chart the earth's surface. Their work involves everything from performing geographical research and compiling data to actually producing maps. Cartographers collect, analyze, and interpret both spatial data—such as latitude, longitude, elevation, and distance—and nonspatial data—for example, population density, land-use patterns, annual precipitation levels, and demographic characteristics. Their maps may give both physical and social characteristics of the land. They prepare maps in either digital or graphic form, using information provided by geodetic surveys, aerial photographs, and satellite data.

Photogrammetrists prepare detailed maps and drawings from aerial photographs, usually of areas that are inaccessible, difficult, or more costly to survey by other methods. *Map editors* develop and verify the contents of maps, using aerial photographs and other reference sources. Some States require photogrammetrists to be licensed as surveyors.

Some surveyors perform specialized functions closer to those of cartographers than to those of traditional surveyors. For example, *geodetic surveyors* use high-accuracy techniques, including satellite observations (remote sensing), to measure large areas of the earth's surface. *Geophysical prospecting surveyors* mark sites for subsurface exploration, usually in relation to petroleum. *Marine or hydrographic surveyors* survey harbors, rivers, and other bodies of water to determine shorelines, the topography of the bottom, water depth, and other features.

There is more to surveying and cartography than meets the eye. Chains, transits, theodolites, and plumb lines have given way to cutting-edge technology such as the Global Positioning System (GPS), laptops, and robotic total stations as the preferred tools of surveyors. Advanced computer software known as Geographic Information Systems (GIS) have become an invaluable tool to both surveyors and cartographers.

Surveyors are able to use GPS to locate reference points with a high degree of precision. To use this system, a surveyor places a satellite signal receiver—a small instrument mounted on a tripod—on a desired point, and another receiver on a point for which the geographic position is known. The receiver simultaneously collects information from several satellites to establish a precise

position. The receiver also can be placed in a vehicle for tracing out road systems. Because receivers now come in different sizes and shapes, and because the cost of receivers has fallen, much more surveying work can be done with GPS. Surveyors then must interpret and check the results produced by the new technology.

Fieldwork is done by a survey party that gathers the information needed by the surveyor. A typical survey party consists of a party chief and one or more surveying technicians and helpers. The party chief, who may be either a surveyor or a senior surveying technician, leads day-to-day work activities. Surveying technicians assist the party chief by adjusting and operating surveying instruments, such as the total station, which measures and records angles and distances simultaneously. Surveying technicians or assistants position and hold the vertical rods, or targets, that the operator sights on to measure angles, distances, or elevations. In addition, they may hold measuring tapes, if electronic distance-measuring equipment is not used. Surveying technicians compile notes, make sketches, and enter the data obtained from surveying instruments into computers either in the field or at the office. Survey parties also may include laborers or helpers who perform less skilled duties, such as clearing brush from sight lines, driving stakes, or carrying equipment.

GIS software is capable of assembling, integrating, analyzing, and displaying data identified according to location and compiled from previous surveys and mappings. GIS software has become an important tool of both surveyors and cartographers. A GIS typically is used to handle maps which combine information that is useful for environmental studies, geology, engineering, planning, business marketing, and other disciplines. As more of these systems are developed, a new type of mapping scientist is emerging from the older specialties of photogrammetrist and cartographer; the *geographic information specialist* combines the functions of mapping science and surveying into a broader field concerned with the collection and analysis of geographic data.

Working Conditions

Surveyors and surveying technicians usually work an 8-hour day, 5 days a week, and may spend a lot of time outdoors. Sometimes they work

Knowledge of GIS and GPS technologies will enhance one's employment prospects.

longer hours during the summer, when weather and light conditions are most suitable for fieldwork. Seasonal demands for longer hours are related to demand for specific surveying services. For example, construction-related work may be limited during times of inclement weather and aerial photography is most effective when the leaves are off the trees.

Surveyors and technicians engage in active, sometimes strenuous, work. They often stand for long periods, walk considerable distances, and climb hills with heavy packs of instruments and other equipment. They also can be exposed to all types of weather. Traveling is sometimes part of the job, and land surveyors and technicians may commute long distances, stay away from home overnight, or temporarily relocate near a survey site.

Although surveyors can spend considerable time indoors while planning surveys, searching court records for deed information, analyzing data, and preparing reports and maps, cartographers and photogrammetrists spend virtually all of their time in offices using computers and seldom visit the sites they are mapping.

Training, Other Qualifications, and Advancement

Most people prepare for a career as a licensed surveyor by combining postsecondary school courses in surveying with extensive on-the-job training. However, as technology advances, a 4-year college degree is increasingly becoming a prerequisite. A number of universities now offer 4-year programs leading to a bachelor's degree in surveying. Junior and community colleges, technical institutes, and vocational schools offer 1-year, 2-year, and 3-year programs in both surveying and surveying technology.

All 50 States and all U.S. territories license surveyors. For licensure, most State licensing boards require that individuals pass a written examination given by the National Council of Examiners for Engineering and Surveying (NCEES). Most States also require surveyors to pass a written examination prepared by the State licensing board. In addition, candidates must meet varying standards of formal education and work experience in the field.

In the past, many with little formal training in surveying started as members of survey crews and worked their way up to become licensed surveyors. Currently, the route to licensure is most often a combination of 4 years of college, followed by passage of the Fundamentals of Surveying Exam. After passing this exam, most candidates continue to work under the supervision of an experienced surveyor for another 4 years and then take the Principles and Practice of Surveyors Exam for licensure. Specific requirements for training and education vary among the States. An increasing number of States require a bachelor's degree in surveying or in a closely related field, such as civil engineering or forestry (with courses in surveying), regardless of the number of years of experience. Some States require the degree to be from a school accredited by the Accreditation Board for Engineering and Technology (ABET). Many States also have a continuing education requirement.

High school students interested in surveying should take courses in algebra, geometry, trigonometry, drafting, mechanical drawing, and computer science. High school graduates with no formal training in surveying usually start as apprentices. Beginners with postsecondary school training in surveying usually can start as technicians or assistants. With on-the-job experience and formal training in surveying—either in an institutional program or from a correspondence school—workers may advance to senior survey technician, then to party chief, and, in some cases, to licensed surveyor (depending on State licensing requirements). However, it is becoming increasingly difficult to gain licensure without a formal education in surveying.

The National Society of Professional Surveyors, a member organization of the American Congress on Surveying and Mapping, has a voluntary certification program for surveying technicians.

Technicians are certified at four levels requiring progressive amounts of experience, in addition to the passing of written examinations. Although not required for State licensure, many employers require certification for promotion to positions with greater responsibilities.

Surveyors should have the ability to visualize objects, distances, sizes, and abstract forms. They must work with precision and accuracy, because mistakes can be costly. Members of a survey party must be in good physical condition, because they work outdoors and often carry equipment over difficult terrain. They need good eyesight, coordination, and hearing to communicate verbally and manually (using hand signals). Surveying is a cooperative operation, so good interpersonal skills and the ability to work as part of a team are important. Good office skills also are essential, because surveyors must be able to research old deeds and other legal papers and prepare reports that document their work.

Cartographers and photogrammetrists usually have a bachelor's degree in cartography, geography or a related field such as surveying, engineering, forestry, or a physical science. Although it is possible to enter these positions through previous experience as a photogrammetric or cartographic technician, nowadays most cartographic and photogrammetric technicians have had some specialized postsecondary school training. With the development of GIS, cartographers and photogrammetrists need additional education and stronger technical skills—including more experience with computers—than in the past.

The American Society for Photogrammetry and Remote Sensing has a voluntary certification program for photogrammetrists. To qualify for this professional distinction, individuals must meet work experience standards and pass an oral or a written examination.

Employment

Surveyors, cartographers, photogrammetrists, and surveying technicians held about 131,000 jobs in 2004. The following tabulation shows the distribution of employment by occupational specialty:

Surveying and mapping technicians 65,000
Surveyors 56,000
Cartographers and photogrammetrists 11,000

The architectural, engineering, and related services industry—including firms that provided surveying and mapping services to other industries on a contract basis—provided 2 out of 3 jobs for these workers. Federal, State, and local governmental agencies provided almost 1 in 6 jobs. Major Federal Government employers are the U.S. Geological Survey (USGS), the Bureau of Land Management (BLM), the National Geodetic Survey, and the Army Corps of Engineers. Most surveyors in State and local government work for highway departments or urban planning and redevelopment agencies. Construction, mining and utility companies also employ surveyors, cartographers, photogrammetrists, and surveying technicians. Only a small number were self-employed in 2004.

Job Outlook

Overall employment of surveyors, cartographers, photogrammetrists, and surveying technicians is expected to grow about as fast as the average for all occupations through the year 2014. The widespread availability and use of advanced technologies, such as GPS, GIS, and remote sensing, will continue to increase both the accuracy and productivity of these workers, limiting job growth to some extent. However, job openings will continue to arise from the need to replace workers who transfer to other occupations or who leave the labor force altogether. Many of the workers in these occupations are approaching retirement age.

Opportunities for surveyors, cartographers, and photogrammetrists should remain concentrated in architectural, engineering, and related services firms. Areas such as urban planning, emergency preparedness, and natural resource exploration and mapping also should provide employment growth, particularly with regard to producing maps for the management of emergencies and updating maps with the newly available technology. However, employment may fluctuate from year to year as a function of construction activity or with mapping needs for land and resource management.

Opportunities should be stronger for professional surveyors than for surveying and mapping technicians. Advancements in technology, such as total stations and GPS, have made surveying parties smaller than they were in the past. Opportunities for technicians should be available in basic GIS-related data-entry work. However, many persons possess the basic skills needed to qualify for these jobs, so applicants for technician jobs may face competition.

As technologies become more complex, opportunities will be best for surveyors, cartographers, and photogrammetrists who have a bachelor's degree and strong technical skills. Increasing demand for geographic data, as opposed to traditional surveying services, will mean better opportunities for cartographers and photogrammetrists who are involved in the development and use of geographic and land information systems. New technologies, such as GPS and GIS, also may enhance employment opportunities for surveyors, and for surveying technicians who have the educational background and who have acquired technical skills that enable them to work with the new systems. At the same time, upgraded licensing requirements will continue to limit opportunities for professional advancement for those without a bachelor's degree.

Earnings
Median annual earnings of cartographers and photogrammetrists were $46,080 in May 2004. The middle 50 percent earned between $35,160 and $59,830. The lowest 10 percent earned less than $28,210 and the highest 10 percent earned more than $74,440.

Median annual earnings of surveyors were $42,980 in May 2004. The middle 50 percent earned between $31,940 and $57,190. The lowest 10 percent earned less than $24,640 and the highest 10 percent earned more than $71,640. Median hourly earnings of surveyors employed in architectural, engineering, and related services were $41,710 in May 2004.

Median annual earnings of surveying and mapping technicians were $30,380 in May 2004. The middle 50 percent earned between $23,600 and $40,100. The lowest 10 percent earned less than $19,140, and the highest 10 percent earned more than $51,070. Median annual earnings of surveying and mapping technicians employed in architectural, engineering, and related services were $28,610 in May 2004, while those employed by local governments had median annual earnings of $34,810.

Related Occupations
Surveying is related to the work of civil engineers, architects, and landscape architects because an accurate survey is the first step in land development and construction projects. Cartography and geodetic surveying are related to the work of environmental scientists and geoscientists, who study the earth's internal composition, surface, and atmosphere. Cartography also is related to the work of geographers and urban and regional planners, who study and decide how the earth's surface is to be used.

Sources of Additional Information
For career information on surveyors, cartographers, photogrammetrists, and surveying technicians, contact:
➤ American Congress on Surveying and Mapping, Suite 403, 6 Montgomery Village Ave., Gaithersburg, MD 20879. Internet: **http://www.acsm.net**

Information about career opportunities, licensure requirements, and the surveying technician certification program is available from:
➤ National Society of Professional Surveyors, Suite 403, 6 Montgomery Village Ave., Gaithersburg, MD 20879. Internet: **http://www.acsm.net/nsps**

For information on a career as a geodetic surveyor, contact:
➤ American Association of Geodetic Surveying (AAGS), Suite 403, 6 Montgomery Village Ave., Gaithersburg, MD 20879. Internet: **http://www.acsm.net/aags**

General information on careers in photogrammetry and remote sensing is available from:
➤ ASPRS, Imaging and Geospatial Information Society, 5410 Grosvenor Ln., Suite 210, Bethesda, MD 20814-2160. Internet: **http://www.asprs.org**

Engineers

(O*NET 17-2011.00, 17-2021.00, 17-2031.00, 17-2041.00, 17-2051.00, 17-2061.00, 17-2071.00, 17-2072.00, 17-2081.00, 17-2111.01, 17-2111.02, 17-2111.03, 17-2112.00, 17-2121.01, 17-2121.02, 17-2131.00, 17-2141.00, 17-2151.00, 17-2161.00, 17-2171.00, 17-2199.99)

Significant Points
● Overall job opportunities in engineering are expected to be good, but will vary by specialty.
● A bachelor's degree is required for most entry-level jobs.
● Starting salaries are significantly higher than those of college graduates in other fields.
● Continuing education is critical for engineers wishing to enhance their value to employers as technology evolves.

Nature of the Work
Engineers apply the principles of science and mathematics to develop economical solutions to technical problems. Their work is the link between perceived social needs and commercial applications.

Engineers consider many factors when developing a new product. For example, in developing an industrial robot, engineers precisely specify the functional requirements; design and test the robot's components; integrate the components to produce the final design; and evaluate the design's overall effectiveness, cost, reliability, and safety. This process applies to the development of many different products, such as chemicals, computers, gas turbines, helicopters, and toys.

In addition to design and development, many engineers work in testing, production, or maintenance. These engineers supervise production in factories, determine the causes of component failure, and test manufactured products to maintain quality. They also estimate the time and cost to complete projects. Some move into engineering management or into sales. In sales, an engineering background enables them to discuss technical aspects and assist in product planning, installation, and use. Supervisory engineers are responsible for major components or entire projects. (See the statements on sales engineers and engineering and natural sciences managers elsewhere in the *Handbook*.)

Engineers use computers extensively to produce and analyze designs; to simulate and test how a machine, structure, or system operates; and to generate specifications for parts. Many engineers also use computers to monitor product quality and control process efficiency. The field of nanotechnology, which involves the creation of high-performance materials and components by integrating atoms and molecules, also is introducing entirely new principles to the design process.

Most engineers specialize. This section provides details on the 17 engineering specialties covered in the Federal Government's Standard Occupational Classification system and on engineering in general. Numerous specialties are recognized by professional societies, and the major branches of engineering have numerous subdivisions. Some examples include structural and transportation engineering, which are subdivisions of civil engineering; and ceramic, metallurgical, and polymer engineering, which are subdivisions of materials engineering. Engineers also may specialize in one industry, such as motor vehicles, or in one type of technology, such as turbines or semiconductor materials.

● **Aerospace engineers** design, develop, and test aircraft, spacecraft, and missiles and supervise the manufacture of these products. Those who work with aircraft are called *aeronautical engineers,* and those working specifically with spacecraft are *astronautical engineers.* Aerospace engineers develop new technologies for use in aviation, defense systems, and space exploration, often specializing in areas such as structural design, guidance, navigation and control, instrumentation and communication, or production methods. They also may specialize in a particular type of aerospace product, such as commercial aircraft, military fighter jets, helicopters, spacecraft, or missiles and rockets, and may become experts

Engineers use computer models to develop and test new designs.

in aerodynamics, thermodynamics, celestial mechanics, propulsion, acoustics, or guidance and control systems.

● **Agricultural engineers** apply knowledge of engineering technology and science to agriculture and the efficient use of biological resources. (See biological scientists and agricultural and food scientists elsewhere in the *Handbook*.) They design agricultural machinery and equipment and agricultural structures. Some specialize in areas such as power systems and machinery design; structures and environment engineering; and food and bioprocess engineering. They develop ways to conserve soil and water and to improve the processing of agricultural products. Agricultural engineers often work in research and development, production, sales, or management.

● **Biomedical engineers** develop devices and procedures that solve medical and health-related problems by combining their knowledge of biology and medicine with engineering principles and practices. Many do research, along with life scientists, chemists, and medical scientists, to develop and evaluate systems and products such as artificial organs, prostheses (artificial devices that replace missing body parts), instrumentation, medical information systems, and health management and care delivery systems. (See biological scientists, medical scientists, and chemists and materials scientists elsewhere in the *Handbook*.) Biomedical engineers may also design devices used in various medical procedures, imaging systems such as magnetic resonance imaging (MRI), and devices for automating insulin injections or controlling body functions. Most engineers in this specialty need a sound background in another engineering specialty, such as mechanical or electronics engineering, in addition to specialized biomedical training. Some specialties within biomedical engineering include biomaterials, biomechanics, medical imaging, rehabilitation engineering, and orthopedic engineering.

● **Chemical engineers** apply the principles of chemistry to solve problems involving the production or use of chemicals and biochemicals. They design equipment and processes for large-scale chemical manufacturing, plan and test methods of manufacturing products and treating byproducts, and supervise production. Chemical engineers also work in a variety of manufacturing industries other than chemical manufacturing, such as those producing energy, electronics, food, clothing, and paper. They also work in healthcare, biotechnology, and business services. Chemical engineers apply principles of chemistry, physics, mathematics, and mechanical and electrical engineering. (See chemists and materials scientists, physicists and astronomers, and mathematicians elsewhere in the *Handbook*.) Some may specialize in a particular chemical process, such as oxidation or polymerization. Others specialize in a particular field, such as materials science, or in the development of specific products. They must be aware of all aspects of chemicals manufacturing and how the manufacturing process affects the environment and the safety of workers and consumers.

● **Civil engineers** design and supervise the construction of roads, buildings, airports, tunnels, dams, bridges, and water supply and sewage systems. They must consider many factors in the design process, from the construction costs and expected lifetime of a project to government regulations and potential environmental hazards such as earthquakes. Civil engineering, considered one of the oldest engineering disciplines, encompasses many specialties. The major specialties are structural, water resources, construction, environmental, transportation, and geotechnical engineering. Many civil engineers hold supervisory or administrative positions, from supervisor of a construction site to city engineer. Others may work in design, construction, research, and teaching.

● **Computer hardware engineers** research, design, develop, test, and oversee the installation of computer hardware and supervise its manufacture and installation. Hardware refers to computer chips, circuit boards, computer systems, and related equipment such as keyboards, modems, and printers. (Computer software engineers—often simply called computer engineers—design and develop the software systems that control computers. These workers are covered elsewhere in the *Handbook*.) The work of computer hardware engineers is very similar to that of electronics engineers, but, unlike electronics engineers, computer hardware engineers work exclusively with computers and computer-related equipment. The rapid advances in computer technology are largely a result of the research, development, and design efforts of computer hardware engineers.

● **Electrical engineers** design, develop, test, and supervise the manufacture of electrical equipment. Some of this equipment includes electric motors; machinery controls, lighting, and wiring in buildings; automobiles; aircraft; radar and navigation systems; and power-generating, -controlling, and transmission devices used by electric utilities. Although the terms "electrical" and "electronics" engineering often are used interchangeably in academia and industry, electrical engineers have traditionally focused on the generation and supply of power, whereas electronics engineers have worked on applications of electricity to control systems or signal processing. Electrical engineers specialize in areas such as power systems engineering or electrical equipment manufacturing.

● **Electronics engineers, except computer**, are responsible for a wide range of technologies, from portable music players to the global positioning system (GPS), which can continuously provide the location of a vehicle. Electronics engineers design, develop, test, and supervise the manufacture of electronic equipment such as broadcast and communications systems. Many electronics engineers also work in areas closely related to computers. However, engineers whose work is related exclusively to computer hardware are considered computer hardware engineers. Electronics engineers specialize in areas such as communications, signal processing, and control systems or have a specialty within one of these areas—industrial robot control systems or aviation electronics, for example.

● **Environmental engineers** develop solutions to environmental problems using the principles of biology and chemistry. They are involved in water and air pollution control, recycling, waste disposal, and public health issues. Environmental engineers conduct hazardous-waste management studies in which they evaluate the significance of the hazard, advise on treatment and containment, and develop regulations to prevent mishaps. They design municipal water supply and industrial wastewater treatment systems. They conduct research on the environmental impact of proposed construction projects, analyze scientific data, and perform quality-control checks. Environmental engineers are concerned with local and worldwide environmental issues. They study and attempt to minimize the effects of acid rain, global warming, automobile emissions, and ozone depletion. They may also be involved in the protection of wildlife. Many environmental engineers work as consultants, helping their clients to comply with regulations and to clean up hazardous sites.

● **Health and safety engineers, except mining safety engineers and inspectors**, promote worksite or product safety by applying knowledge of industrial processes and mechanical, chemical, and human performance principles. Using this specialized knowledge, they identify and measure potential hazards to people or property, such as the risk of fires or the dangers involved in the handling of toxic chemicals. Health and safety engineers develop procedures and designs to reduce the risk of injury or damage. Some work in manufacturing industries to ensure the designs of new products do not create unnecessary hazards. They must be able to anticipate, recognize, and evaluate hazardous conditions, as well as develop hazard control methods.

● **Industrial engineers** determine the most effective ways to use the basic factors of production—people, machines, materials, information, and energy—to make a product or to provide a service. They are mostly concerned with increasing productivity through the management of people, methods of business organization, and technology. To solve organizational, production, and related problems efficiently, industrial engineers carefully study the product requirements, use mathematical methods to meet those requirements, and design manufacturing and information systems. They develop management control systems to aid in financial planning and cost analysis, and design production planning and control systems to coordinate activities and ensure product quality. They also design or improve systems for the physical distribution of goods and services, as well as determine the most efficient plant locations. Industrial engineers develop wage and salary administration systems and job evaluation programs. Many industrial engineers move into management positions because the work is closely related to the work of managers.

● **Marine engineers and naval architects** are involved in the design, construction, and maintenance of ships, boats, and related equipment. They design and supervise the construction of everything from aircraft carriers to submarines, and from sailboats to tankers. Naval architects work on the basic design of ships, including hull form and stability. Marine engineers work on the propulsion, steering, and other systems of ships. Marine engineers and naval architects apply knowledge from a range of fields to the entire design and production process of all water vehicles. Workers who operate or supervise the operation of marine machinery on ships and other vessels also may be called marine engineers or, more frequently, ship engineers. (These workers are covered under water transportation occupations elsewhere in the *Handbook*.)

● **Materials engineers** are involved in the development, processing, and testing of the materials used to create a range of products, from computer chips and television screens to golf clubs and snow skis. They work with metals, ceramics, plastics, semiconductors, and composites to create new materials that meet certain mechanical, electrical, and chemical requirements. They also are involved in selecting materials for new applications. Materials engineers have developed the ability to create and then study materials at an atomic level, using advanced processes to replicate the characteristics of materials and their components with computers. Most materials engineers specialize in a particular material. For example,

Collaboration speeds design work and introduces novel approaches to problems.

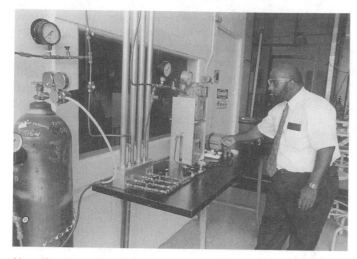

Not all engineering work is done at a desk; many engineers spend part of their time in laboratories and factories.

metallurgical engineers specialize in metals such as steel, and ceramic engineers develop ceramic materials and the processes for making ceramic materials into useful products such as glassware or fiber optic communication lines.

● **Mechanical engineers** research, develop, design, manufacture, and test tools, engines, machines, and other mechanical devices. They work on power-producing machines such as electric generators, internal combustion engines, and steam and gas turbines, as well as power-using machines such as refrigeration and air-conditioning equipment, machine tools, material handling systems, elevators and escalators, industrial production equipment, and robots used in manufacturing. Mechanical engineers also design tools that other engineers need for their work. Mechanical engineering is one of the broadest engineering disciplines. Mechanical engineers may work in production operations in manufacturing or agriculture, maintenance, or technical sales; many are administrators or managers.

● **Mining and geological engineers, including mining safety engineers**, find, extract, and prepare coal, metals, and minerals for use by manufacturing industries and utilities. They design open-pit and underground mines, supervise the construction of mine shafts and tunnels in underground operations, and devise methods for transporting minerals to processing plants. Mining engineers are responsible for the safe, economical, and environmentally sound operation of mines. Some mining engineers work with geologists and metallurgical engineers to locate and appraise new ore deposits. Others develop new mining equipment or direct mineral- processing operations that separate minerals from the dirt, rock, and other materials with which they are mixed. Mining engineers frequently specialize in the mining of one mineral or metal, such as coal or gold. With increased emphasis on protecting the environment, many mining engineers work to solve problems related to land reclamation and water and air pollution. Mining safety engineers use their knowledge of mine design and practices to ensure the safety of workers and to comply with State and Federal safety regulations. They inspect walls and roof surfaces, monitor air quality, and examine mining equipment for compliance with safety practices.

● **Nuclear engineers** research and develop the processes, instruments, and systems used to derive benefits from nuclear energy and radiation. They design, develop, monitor, and operate nuclear plants to generate power. They may work on the nuclear fuel cycle—the production, handling, and use of nuclear fuel and the safe disposal of waste produced by the generation of nuclear energy—or on the development of fusion energy. Some specialize in the development of nuclear power sources for spacecraft; others find industrial and medical uses for radioactive materials, as in equipment used to diagnose and treat medical problems.

● **Petroleum engineers** search the world for reservoirs containing oil or natural gas. Once these resources are discovered, petroleum engineers work with geologists and other specialists to understand the geologic formation and properties of the rock containing the reservoir, determine the drilling methods to be used, and monitor drilling and production operations. They design equipment and processes to achieve the maximum profitable recovery of oil and gas. Because only a small proportion of oil and gas in a reservoir flows out under natural forces, petroleum engineers develop and use various enhanced recovery methods. These include injecting water, chemicals, gases, or steam into an oil reservoir to force out more of the oil and doing computer-controlled drilling or fracturing to connect a larger area of a reservoir to a single well. Because even the best techniques in use today recover only a portion of the oil and gas in a reservoir, petroleum engineers research and develop technology and methods to increase recovery and lower the cost of drilling and production operations.

Working Conditions
Most engineers work in office buildings, laboratories, or industrial plants. Others may spend time outdoors at construction sites and

Engineering work requires strong math skills and attention to detail.

oil and gas exploration and production sites, where they monitor or direct operations or solve onsite problems. Some engineers travel extensively to plants or worksites.

Many engineers work a standard 40-hour week. At times, deadlines or design standards may bring extra pressure to a job, requiring engineers to work longer hours.

Training, Other Qualifications, and Advancement

A bachelor's degree in engineering is required for almost all entry-level engineering jobs. College graduates with a degree in a physical science or mathematics occasionally may qualify for some engineering jobs, especially in specialties in high demand. Most engineering degrees are granted in electrical, electronics, mechanical, or civil engineering. However, engineers trained in one branch may work in related branches. For example, many aerospace engineers have training in mechanical engineering. This flexibility allows employers to meet staffing needs in new technologies and specialties in which engineers may be in short supply. It also allows engineers to shift to fields with better employment prospects or to those that more closely match their interests.

Most engineering programs involve a concentration of study in an engineering specialty, along with courses in both mathematics and the physical and life sciences. General courses not directly related to engineering, such as those in the social sciences or humanities, are often a required component of programs. Many programs also include courses in general engineering. A design course, sometimes accompanied by a computer or laboratory class or both, is part of the curriculum of most programs.

In addition to the standard engineering degree, many colleges offer 2- or 4-year degree programs in engineering technology. These programs, which usually include various hands-on laboratory classes that focus on current issues in the application of engineering principles, prepare students for practical design and production work, rather than for jobs that require more theoretical and scientific knowledge. Graduates of 4-year technology programs may get jobs similar to those obtained by graduates with a bachelor's degree in engineering. Engineering technology graduates, however, are not qualified to register as professional engineers under the same terms as graduates with degrees in engineering. Some employers regard technology program graduates as having skills between those of a technician and an engineer.

Graduate training is essential for engineering faculty positions and many research and development programs, but is not required for the majority of entry-level engineering jobs. Many engineers obtain graduate degrees in engineering or business administration to learn new technology and broaden their education. Many high-level executives in government and industry began their careers as engineers.

About 360 colleges and universities offer bachelor's degree programs in engineering that are accredited by the Accreditation Board for Engineering and Technology (ABET), Inc. and about 230 colleges offer accredited programs in engineering technology. ABET accreditation is based on an examination of an engineering program's student achievement, program improvement, faculty, curriculum, facilities, and institutional commitment to certain principles of quality and ethics. Although most institutions offer programs in the major branches of engineering, only a few offer programs in the smaller specialties. Also, programs of the same title may vary in content. For example, some programs emphasize industrial practices, preparing students for a job in industry, whereas others are more theoretical and are designed to prepare students for graduate work. Therefore, students should investigate curriculums and check accreditations carefully before selecting a college.

Admissions requirements for undergraduate engineering schools include a solid background in mathematics (algebra, geometry, trigonometry, and calculus) and science (biology, chemistry, and physics), with courses in English, social studies, and humanities. Bachelor's degree programs in engineering typically are designed to last 4 years, but many students find that it takes between 4 and 5 years to complete their studies. In a typical 4-year college curriculum, the first 2 years are spent studying mathematics, basic sciences, introductory engineering, humanities, and social sciences. In the last 2 years, most courses are in engineering, usually with a concentration in one specialty. Some programs offer a general engineering curriculum; students then specialize on the job or in graduate school.

Some engineering schools and 2-year colleges have agreements whereby the 2-year college provides the initial engineering education, and the engineering school automatically admits students for their last 2 years. In addition, a few engineering schools have arrangements that allow students who spend 3 years in a liberal arts college studying pre-engineering subjects and 2 years in an engineering school studying core subjects to receive a bachelor's degree from each school. Some colleges and universities offer 5-year master's degree programs. Some 5-year or even 6-year cooperative plans combine classroom study and practical work, permitting students to gain valuable experience and to finance part of their education.

All 50 States and the District of Columbia require licensure for engineers who offer their services directly to the public. Engineers who are licensed are called professional engineers (PE). This licensure generally requires a degree from an ABET-accredited engineering program, 4 years of relevant work experience, and successful completion of a State examination. Recent graduates can start the licensing process by taking the examination in two stages. The initial Fundamentals of Engineering (FE) examination can be taken upon graduation. Engineers who pass this examination commonly are called engineers in training (EIT) or engineer interns (EI). After acquiring suitable work experience, EITs can take the second examination, the Principles and Practice of Engineering exam. Several States have imposed mandatory continuing education requirements for relicensure. Most States recognize licensure from other States, provided that the manner in which the initial license was obtained meets or exceeds their own licensure requirements. Many civil, electrical, mechanical, and chemical engineers are licensed PEs. Independent of licensure, various certification programs are offered by professional organizations to demonstrate competency in specific fields of engineering.

Engineers should be creative, inquisitive, analytical, and detail oriented. They should be able to work as part of a team and to communicate well, both orally and in writing. Communication abilities are important because engineers often interact with specialists in a wide range of fields outside engineering.

Beginning engineering graduates usually work under the supervision of experienced engineers and, in large companies, also may receive formal classroom or seminar-type training. As new engineers gain knowledge and experience, they are assigned more difficult projects with greater independence to develop designs, solve problems, and make decisions. Engineers may advance to become technical specialists or to supervise a staff or team of engineers and technicians. Some may eventually become engineering managers or enter other managerial or sales jobs. (See the statements under management and business and financial operations occupations and under sales and related occupations elsewhere in the *Handbook*.)

Employment

In 2004 engineers held 1.4 million jobs. The distribution of employment by engineering specialty is as follows:

Specialty	Employment	Percent
Total, all engineers	1,449,000	100
Civil	237,000	16.4
Mechanical	226,000	15.6
Industrial	177,000	12.2
Electrical	156,000	10.8
Electronics, except computer	143,000	9.9
Computer hardware	77,000	5.3
Aerospace	76,000	5.2
Environmental	49,000	3.4
Chemical	31,000	2.1
Health and safety, except mining safety	27,000	1.8
Materials	21,000	1.5
Nuclear	17,000	1.2
Petroleum	16,000	1.1
Biomedical	9,700	0.7
Marine engineers and naval architects	6,800	0.5
Mining and geological, including mining safety	5,200	0.4
Agricultural	3,400	0.2
All other engineers	172,000	11.8

About 555,000 engineering jobs were found in manufacturing industries, and another 378,000 wage and salary jobs were in the professional, scientific, and technical services sector, primarily in architectural, engineering, and related services and in scientific research and development services. Many engineers also worked in the construction and transportation, telecommunications, and utilities industries.

Federal, State, and local governments employed about 194,000 engineers in 2004. About 91,000 of these were in the Federal Government, mainly in the U.S. Departments of Defense, Transportation, Agriculture, Interior, and Energy and in the National Aeronautics and Space Administration. Most engineers in State and local government agencies worked in highway and public works departments. In 2004, about 41,000 engineers were self-employed, many as consultants.

Engineers are employed in every State, in small and large cities and in rural areas. Some branches of engineering are concentrated in particular industries and geographic areas—for example, petroleum engineering jobs tend to be located in areas with sizable petroleum deposits, such as Texas, Louisiana, Oklahoma, Alaska, and California. Others, such as civil engineering, are widely dispersed, and engineers in these fields often move from place to place to work on different projects.

Engineers are employed in every major industry. The industries employing the most engineers in each specialty are given in table 1, along with the percent of occupational employment in the industry.

Job Outlook

Overall engineering employment is expected to grow about as fast as the average for all occupations over the 2004-14 period. Engineers have traditionally been concentrated in slow-growing manufacturing industries, in which they will continue to be needed to design, build, test, and improve manufactured products. However, increasing employment of engineers in faster growing service industries should generate most of the employment growth. Overall job opportunities in engineering are expected to be favorable because the number of engineering graduates should be in rough balance with the number of job openings over this period. However, job outlook varies by specialty, as discussed later in this section.

Competitive pressures and advancing technology will force companies to improve and update product designs and to optimize their manufacturing processes. Employers will rely on engineers to further increase productivity as investment in plant and equipment increases to expand output of goods and services. New technologies continue to improve the design process, enabling engineers to produce and analyze various product designs much more rapidly than in the past. Unlike in other fields, however, technological advances are not expected to limit employment opportunities substantially, because they will permit the development of new products and processes.

There are many well-trained, often English-speaking engineers available around the world willing to work at much lower salaries than are U.S. engineers. The rise of the Internet has made it relatively easy for much of the engineering work previously done by engineers in this country to be done by engineers in other countries, a factor that will tend to hold down employment growth. Even so, the need for onsite engineers to interact with other employees and with clients will remain.

Compared with most other workers, a smaller proportion of engineers leave their jobs each year. Nevertheless, many job openings will arise from replacement needs, reflecting the large size of this profession. Numerous job openings will be created by engineers who transfer to management, sales, or other professional occupations; additional openings will arise as engineers retire or leave the labor force for other reasons.

Many engineers work on long-term research and development projects or in other activities that continue even during economic slowdowns. In industries such as electronics and aerospace, however, large cutbacks in defense expenditures and in government funding for research and development have resulted in significant layoffs of engineers in the past. The trend toward contracting for engineering work with engineering services firms, both domestic and foreign, has had the same result.

It is important for engineers, as it is for those working in other technical and scientific occupations, to continue their education throughout their

Table 1.   Percent concentration of engineering specialty employment in key industries, 2004

Specialty	Industry	Percent
Aerospace	Aerospace product and parts manufacturing	59.6
Agricultural	State and local government	22.6
Biomedical	Scientific research and development services	18.7
	Pharmaceutical and medicine manufacturing	15.6
Chemical	Chemical manufacturing	27.8
	Architectural, engineering, and related services	16.3
Civil	Architectural, engineering, and related services	46.0
Computer hardware	Computer and electronic product manufacturing	43.2
	Computer systems design and related services	15.0
Electrical	Architectural, engineering, and related services	19.6
	Navigational, measuring, electromedical, and control instruments manufacturing	10.8
Electronics, except computer	Telecommunications	17.5
	Federal government	14.4
Environmental	Architectural, engineering, and related services	28.9
	State and local government	19.6
Health and safety, except mining safety	State and local government	12.4
Industrial	Machinery manufacturing	7.8
	Motor vehicle parts manufacturing	7.1
Marine engineers and naval architects	Architectural, engineering, and related services	34.5
Materials	Computer and electronic product manufacturing	14.3
Mechanical	Architectural, engineering, and related services	18.1
	Machinery manufacturing	13.4
Mining and geological, including mining safety	Mining	49.9
Nuclear	Electric power generation, transmission and distribution	36.1
Petroleum	Oil and gas extraction	47.4

careers because much of their value to their employer depends on their knowledge of the latest technology. Engineers in high-technology areas, such as advanced electronics or information technology, may find that technical knowledge can become outdated rapidly. By keeping current in their field, engineers are able to deliver the best solutions and greatest value to their employers. Engineers who have not kept current in their field may find themselves passed over for promotions or vulnerable to layoffs.

The following section discusses job outlook by engineering specialty.

● **Aerospace engineers** are expected to have slower-than-average growth in employment over the projection period. Although increases in the number and scope of military aerospace projects likely will generate new jobs, increased efficiency will limit the number of new jobs in the design and production of commercial aircraft. Even with slow growth, the employment outlook for aerospace engineers through 2014 appears favorable: the number of degrees granted in aerospace engineering declined for many years because of a perceived lack of opportunities in this field, and, although this trend is reversing, new graduates continue to be needed to replace aerospace engineers who retire or leave the occupation for other reasons.

● **Agricultural engineers** are expected to have employment growth about as fast as the average for all occupations through 2014. The growing interest in worldwide standardization of agricultural equipment should result in increased employment of agricultural engineers. Job opportunities also should result from the need to feed a growing population, develop more efficient agricultural production, and conserve resources.

● **Biomedical engineers** are expected to have employment growth that is much faster than the average for all occupations through 2014. The aging of the population and the focus on health issues will drive demand for better medical devices and equipment designed by biomedical engineers. Along with the demand for more sophisticated medical equipment and procedures, an increased concern for cost-effectiveness will boost demand for biomedical engineers, particularly in pharmaceutical manufacturing and related industries. However, because of the growing interest in this field, the number of degrees granted in biomedical engineering has increased greatly. Biomedical engineers, particularly those with only a bachelor's degree, may face competition for jobs. Unlike the case for many other engineering specialties, a graduate degree is recommended or required for many entry-level jobs.

● **Chemical engineers** are expected to have employment growth about as fast as the average for all occupations though 2014. Although overall employment in the chemical manufacturing industry is expected to decline, chemical companies will continue to research and develop new chemicals and more efficient processes to increase output of existing chemicals. Among manufacturing industries, pharmaceuticals may provide the best opportunities for jobseekers. However, most employment growth for chemical engineers will be in service industries such as scientific research and development services, particularly in energy and the developing fields of biotechnology and nanotechnology.

● **Civil engineers** are expected to see average employment growth through 2014. Spurred by general population growth and an increased emphasis on infrastructure security, more civil engineers will be needed to design and construct safe and higher capacity transportation, water supply, and pollution control systems, as well as large buildings and building complexes. They also will be needed to repair or replace existing roads, bridges, and other public structures. Because construction and related industries—including those providing design services—employ many civil engineers, employment opportunities will vary by geographic area and may decrease during economic slowdowns, when construction often is curtailed.

● **Computer hardware engineers** are expected to have average employment growth through 2014. Although the use of information technology continues to expand rapidly, the manufacture of computer hardware is expected to be adversely affected by intense foreign competition. As computer and semiconductor manufacturing contract out more of their engineering needs, much of the growth in employment should occur in the computer systems design and related services industry. However, use of foreign computer hardware engineering services also will serve to limit job growth. Computer engineers should still have favorable employment opportunities, as the number of new entrants is expected to be in balance with demand.

● **Electrical engineers** should have favorable employment opportunities. The number of job openings resulting from employment growth and from the need to replace electrical engineers who transfer to other occupations or leave the labor force is expected to be in rough balance with the supply of graduates. Employment of electrical engineers is expected to increase about as fast as the average for all occupations through 2014. Although international competition and the use of engineering services performed in other countries may limit employment growth, strong demand for electrical devices such as giant electric power generators or wireless phone transmitters should boost growth. Prospects should be particularly good for electrical engineers working in engineering services firms providing technical expertise to other companies on specific projects.

● **Electronics engineers, except computer**, should have good job opportunities, and employment is expected to increase about as fast as the average for all occupations through 2014. Although rising demand for electronic goods—including advanced communications equipment, defense-related electronic equipment, medical electronics, and consumer products—should continue to increase employment, foreign competition in electronic products development and the use of engineering services performed in other countries will act to limit employment growth. Job growth is expected to be fastest in service-providing industries—particularly consulting firms that provide expertise in electronics engineering.

● **Environmental engineers** should have favorable job opportunities. Employment of environmental engineers is expected to increase much faster than the average for all occupations through 2014. More environmental engineers will be needed to comply with environmental regulations and to develop methods of cleaning up existing hazards. A shift in emphasis toward preventing problems rather than controlling those that already exist, as well as increasing public health concerns, also will spur demand for environmental engineers. Even though employment of environmental engineers should be less affected by economic conditions than that of most other types of engineers, a significant economic downturn could reduce the emphasis on environmental protection, reducing environmental engineers' job opportunities.

● **Health and safety engineers, except mining safety engineers and inspectors**, are projected to experience average employment growth through 2014. Because the main function of health and safety engineers is to make products and production processes as safe as possible, their services should be in demand as concern for health and safety within work environments increases. As new technologies for production or processing are developed, health and safety engineers will be needed to ensure their safety.

● **Industrial engineers** are expected to have employment growth about as fast as the average for all occupations through 2014. As firms seek to reduce costs and increase productivity, they increasingly will turn to industrial engineers to develop more efficient processes to reduce costs, delays, and waste. Because their work is similar to that done in management occupations, many industrial engineers leave the occupation to become managers. Many openings will be created by the need to replace industrial engineers who transfer to other occupations or leave the labor force.

● **Marine engineers and naval architects** likely will experience employment growth that is slower than the average for all occupations. Strong demand for naval vessels and for yachts and other small craft should more than offset the long-term decline in the domestic design and construction of large oceangoing vessels. There should be good prospects for marine engineers and naval architects because of growth in employment, the need to replace workers who retire or take other jobs, and the limited number of students pursuing careers in this occupation.

● **Materials engineers, including mining safety engineers**, are expected to have employment growth about as fast as the average for all occupations through 2014. Although many of the manufacturing industries in which materials engineers are concentrated are expected to experience declining employment, materials engineers still will be needed to develop new materials for electronics, biotechnology, and plastics products. Growth should be particularly strong for materials engineers working on nanomaterials and biomaterials. As manufacturing firms contract for their materials engineering needs, employment growth is expected in professional, scientific, and technical services industries.

● **Mechanical engineers** are projected to have an average rate of employment growth through 2014. Although total employment in manufacturing industries—in which employment of mechanical engineers is concentrated—is expected to decline, employment of mechanical engineers in manufacturing should increase as the demand for improved machinery and machine tools grows and as industrial machinery and processes become increasingly complex. Also, emerging technologies in biotechnology, materials science, and nanotechnology will create new job opportunities for mechanical engineers. Additional opportunities for mechanical engineers will arise because the skills acquired through earning a degree in mechanical engineering often can be applied in other engineering specialties.

● **Mining and geological engineers, including mining safety engineers**, are expected to have good employment opportunities, despite a projected decline in employment. Many mining engineers currently employed are approaching retirement age, a factor that should create some job openings over the 2004-14 period. In addition, relatively few schools offer mining engineering programs, and the small number of yearly graduates is not expected to increase substantially. Favorable job opportunities also may be available worldwide as mining operations around the world recruit graduates of U.S. mining engineering programs. As a result, some graduates may travel frequently or even live abroad. Employment of mining and geological engineers, including mining safety engineers, is projected to decline through 2014, primarily because most of the industries in which mining engineers are concentrated—such as coal, metal, and copper mining—are expected to experience declines in employment.

● **Nuclear engineers** are expected to have good opportunities because the small number of nuclear engineering graduates is likely to be in rough balance with the number of job openings. Employment of nuclear engineers is expected to grow more slowly than the average for all occupations through 2014. Most openings will result from the need to replace nuclear engineers who transfer to other occupations or leave the labor force. Although no commercial nuclear powerplants have been built in the United States for many years, nuclear engineers will be needed to operate existing plants. In addition, nuclear engineers may be needed to research and develop future nuclear power sources. They also will be needed to work in defense-related areas, to develop nuclear medical technology, and to improve and enforce waste management and safety standards.

● **Petroleum engineers** are expected to have a decline in employment through 2014 because most of the potential petroleum-producing areas in the United States already have been explored. Even so, favorable opportunities are expected for petroleum engineers because the number of job openings is likely to exceed the relatively small number of graduates. All job openings should result from the need to replace petroleum engineers who transfer to other occupations or leave the labor force. Petroleum engineers work around the world and, in fact, the best employment opportunities may be in other countries. Many foreign employers seek U.S.-trained petroleum engineers, and many U.S. employers maintain overseas branches.

Earnings

Earnings for engineers vary significantly by specialty, industry, and education. Even so, as a group, engineers earn some of the highest average starting salaries among those holding bachelor's degrees. The following tabulation shows average starting salary offers for engineers, according to a 2005 survey by the National Association of Colleges and Employers.

Curriculum	Bachelor's	Master's	Ph.D.
Aerospace/aeronautical/			
astronautical	$50,993	$62,930	$72,529
Agricultural	46,172	53,022	—
Bioengineering and biomedical	48,503	59,667	—
Chemical	53,813	57,260	79,591
Civil	43,679	48,050	59,710
Computer	52,464	60,354	69,625
Electrical/electronics and			
communications	51,888	64,416	80,206
Environmental/environmental health	47,384	—	—
Industrial/manufacturing	49,567	56,561	85,000
Materials	50,982	—	—
Mechanical	50,236	59,880	68,299
Mining and mineral	48,643	—	—
Nuclear	51,182	58,814	—
Petroleum	61,516	58,000	—

Variation in median earnings and in the earnings distributions for engineers in the various branches of engineering also is significant. For engineers in specialties covered in this statement, earnings distributions by percentile in May 2004 are shown in the following tabulation.

Specialty	Lowest 10%	Lowest 25%	Median	Highest 25%	Highest 10%
Aerospace	$52,820	$64,380	$79,100	$94,900	$113,520
Agricultural	37,680	43,270	56,520	77,740	90,410
Biomedical	41,260	51,620	67,690	86,400	107,530
Chemical	49,030	60,920	76,770	94,740	115,180
Civil	42,610	51,430	64,230	79,920	94,660
Computer hardware	50,490	63,730	81,150	102,100	123,560
Electrical	47,310	57,540	71,610	88,400	108,070
Electronics, except					
computer	49,120	60,280	75,770	92,870	112,200
Environmental	40,620	50,740	66,480	83,690	100,050
Health and safety, except					
mining safety	39,930	49,900	63,730	79,500	92,870
Industrial	42,450	52,210	65,020	79,830	93,950
Marine engineers and					
naval architects	43,790	54,530	72,040	89,900	109,190
Materials	44,130	53,510	67,110	83,830	101,120
Mechanical	43,900	53,070	66,320	82,380	97,850
Mining and geological,					
including mining					
safety	39,700	50,500	64,690	83,050	103,790
Nuclear	61,790	73,340	84,880	100,220	118,870
Petroleum	48,260	65,350	88,500	113,180	140,800

In the Federal Government, mean annual salaries for engineers ranged from $100,059 in ceramic engineering to $70,086 in agricultural engineering in 2005.

Related Occupations

Engineers apply the principles of physical science and mathematics in their work. Other workers who use scientific and mathematical principles include architects, except landscape and naval; engineering and natural sciences managers; computer and information systems managers; computer programmers; computer software engineers; mathematicians; drafters; engineering technicians; sales engineers; science technicians; and physical and life scientists, including agricultural and food scientists, biological scientists, conservation scientists and foresters, atmospheric scientists, chemists and materials scientists, environmental scientists and hydrologists, geoscientists, and physicists and astronomers.

Sources of Additional Information

Information about careers in engineering is available from:

➤ JETS, 1420 King St., Suite 405, Alexandria, VA 22314-2794. Internet: **http://www.jets.org**

Information on ABET-accredited engineering programs is available from:

➤ Accreditation Board for Engineering and Technology, Inc., 111 Market Place, Suite 1050, Baltimore, MD 21202-4012. Internet: **http://www.abet.org**

Those interested in information on the Professional Engineer licensure should contact:

➤ National Society of Professional Engineers, 1420 King St., Alexandria, VA 22314-2794. Internet: **http://www.nspe.org**

➤ National Council of Examiners for Engineering and Surveying, P.O. Box 1686, Clemson, SC 29633-1686. Internet: **http://www.ncees.org**

Information on general engineering education and career resources is available from:

➤ American Society for Engineering Education, 1818 N St. NW., Suite 600, Washington, DC 20036-2479. Internet: **http://www.asee.org**

Information on obtaining positions as engineers with the Federal Government is available from the Office of Personnel Management through USAJOBS, the Federal Government's official employment information system. This resource for locating and applying for job opportunities can be accessed through the Internet at **http://www.usajobs.opm.gov** or through an interactive voice response telephone system at (703) 724-1850 or TDD (978) 461-8404. These numbers are not tollfree, and charges may result.

For more detailed information on an engineering specialty, contact societies representing the individual branches of engineering. Each can provide information about careers in the particular branch.

Aerospace engineers

➤ Aerospace Industries Association, 1000 Wilson Blvd., Suite 1700, Arlington, VA 22209-3901. Internet: **http://www.aia-aerospace.org**

➤ American Institute of Aeronautics and Astronautics, Inc., 1801 Alexander Bell Dr., Suite 500, Reston, VA 20191-4344. Internet: **http://www.aiaa.org**

Agricultural engineers

➤ American Society of Agricultural and Biological Engineers, 2950 Niles Rd., St. Joseph, MI 49085-9659. Internet: **http://www.asabe.org**

Biomedical engineers

➤ Biomedical Engineering Society, 8401 Corporate Dr., Suite 225, Landover, MD 20785-2224. Internet: **http://www.bmes.org**

Chemical engineers

➤ American Institute of Chemical Engineers, 3 Park Ave., New York, NY 10016-5991. Internet: **http://www.aiche.org**

➤ American Chemical Society, Department of Career Services, 1155 16th St. NW., Washington, DC 20036. Internet: **http://www.chemistry.org/portal/Chemistry**

Civil engineers

➤ American Society of Civil Engineers, 1801 Alexander Bell Dr., Reston, VA 20191-4400. Internet: **http://www.asce.org**

Computer hardware engineers

➤ IEEE Computer Society, 1730 Massachusetts Ave. NW., Washington, DC 20036-1992. Internet: **http://www.computer.org**

Electrical and electronics engineers

➤ Institute of Electrical and Electronics Engineers–USA, 1828 L St. NW., Suite 1202, Washington, DC 20036. Internet: **http://www.ieeeusa.org**

Environmental engineers

➤ American Academy of Environmental Engineers, 130 Holiday Court, Suite 100, Annapolis, MD 21401. Internet: **http://www.aaee.net**

Health and safety engineers

➤ American Society of Safety Engineers, 1800 E Oakton St., Des Plaines, IL 60018. Internet: **http://www.asse.org**

➤ Board of Certified Safety Professionals, 208 Burwash Ave., Savoy, IL 61874. Internet: **http://www.bcsp.org**

Industrial engineers

➤ Institute of Industrial Engineers, 3577 Parkway Lane, Suite 200, Norcross, GA 30092. Internet: **http://www.iienet.org**

Materials engineers

➤ The Minerals, Metals, & Materials Society, 184 Thorn Hill Rd., Warrendale, PA 15086-7514. Internet: **http://www.tms.org**

➤ ASM International, 9639 Kinsman Rd., Materials Park, OH 44073-0002. Internet: **http://www.asminternational.org**

Mechanical engineers

➤ The American Society of Mechanical Engineers, 3 Park Ave., New York, NY 10016-5990. Internet: **http://www.asme.org**

➤ American Society of Heating, Refrigerating, and Air-Conditioning Engineers, Inc., 1791 Tullie Circle NE., Atlanta, GA 30329. Internet: **http://www.ashrae.org**

➤ Society of Automotive Engineers, 400 Commonwealth Dr., Warrendale, PA 15096-0001. Internet: **http://www.sae.org**

Marine engineers and naval architects

➤ Society of Naval Architects and Marine Engineers, 601 Pavonia Ave., Jersey City, NJ 07306. Internet: **http://www.sname.org**

Mining and geological engineers, including mining safety engineers

➤ The Society for Mining, Metallurgy, and Exploration, Inc., 8307 Shaffer Parkway, Littleton, CO 80127-4102. Internet: **http://www.smenet.org**

Nuclear engineers

➤ American Nuclear Society, 555 North Kensington Ave., LaGrange Park, IL 60526. Internet: **http://www.ans.org**

Petroleum engineers

➤ Society of Petroleum Engineers, P.O. Box 833836, Richardson, TX 75083-3836. Internet: **http://www.spe.org**

Drafters and Engineering Technicians

Drafters

(O*NET 17-3011.01, 17-3011.02, 17-3012.01, 17-3012.02, 17-3013.00)

Significant Points

● The type and quality of postsecondary drafting programs vary considerably; prospective students should be careful in selecting a program.

● Employment is projected to grow more slowly than average.

● Opportunities should be best for individuals with at least 2 years of postsecondary training in drafting and considerable skill and experience using computer-aided design and drafting (CADD) systems.

● Demand for drafters varies by specialty and depends on the needs of local industry, particularly architectural and engineering services and manufacturing.

Nature of the Work

Drafters prepare technical drawings and plans used by production and construction workers to build everything from manufactured products such as toys, toasters, industrial machinery, and spacecraft to structures such as houses, office buildings, and oil and gas pipelines. Drafters' drawings provide visual guidelines; show the technical details of the products and structures; and specify dimensions, materials, and procedures. Drafters fill in technical details using drawings, rough sketches, specifications, codes, and calculations previously made by engineers, surveyors, architects, or scientists. For example, drafters use their knowledge of standardized building techniques to draw in the details of a structure. Some use their knowledge of engineering and manufacturing theory and standards to draw the parts of a machine to determine design elements, such as the numbers and kinds of fasteners needed to assemble the machine. Drafters use technical handbooks, tables, calculators, and computers to complete their work.

Traditionally, drafters sat at drawing boards and used pencils, pens, compasses, protractors, triangles, and other drafting devices to prepare a drawing manually. Most drafters now use CADD systems to prepare drawings. Consequently, some drafters may be referred to as *CADD operators*. CADD systems employ computers to create and store drawings electronically that can then be viewed, printed, or programmed directly into automated manufacturing systems. These systems also permit drafters to quickly prepare variations of a design. Although drafters use CADD extensively, it is only a tool. Persons who produce technical drawings with CADD still function as drafters and need the knowledge of traditional drafters, in addition to CADD skills. Despite the nearly universal use of CADD systems, manual drafting and sketching still are used in certain applications.

Drafting work has many specialties, and titles may denote a particular discipline of design or drafting.

Aeronautical drafters prepare engineering drawings detailing plans and specifications used in the manufacture of aircraft, missiles, and related parts.

Architectural drafters draw architectural and structural features of buildings and other structures. These workers may specialize in a type of structure, such as residential or commercial, or in a kind of material used, such as reinforced concrete, masonry, steel, or timber.

Civil drafters prepare drawings and topographical and relief maps used in major construction or civil engineering projects, such as highways, bridges, pipelines, flood control projects, and water and sewage systems.

Electrical drafters prepare wiring and layout diagrams used by workers who erect, install, and repair electrical equipment and wiring in communication centers, powerplants, electrical distribution systems, and buildings.

Electronics drafters draw wiring diagrams, circuit board assembly diagrams, schematics, and layout drawings used in the manufacture, installation, and repair of electronic devices and components.

Mechanical drafters prepare drawings showing the detail and assembly of a wide variety of machinery and mechanical devices, indicating dimensions, fastening methods, and other requirements.

Process piping or pipeline drafters prepare drawings used in the layout, construction, and operation of oil and gas fields, refineries, chemical plants, and process piping systems.

Drafters produce the detailed technical drawings necessary for construction or manufacturing.

Working Conditions

Most drafters work a standard 40-hour week; only a small number work part time. Drafters usually work in comfortable offices furnished to accommodate their tasks. They may sit at adjustable drawing boards or drafting tables when doing manual drawings, although most drafters work at computer terminals much of the time. Because they spend long periods in front of computer terminals doing detailed work, drafters may be susceptible to eyestrain, back discomfort, and hand and wrist problems.

Training, Other Qualifications, and Advancement

Employers prefer applicants who have completed postsecondary school training in drafting, training that is offered by technical institutes, community colleges, and some 4-year colleges and universities. Employers are most interested in applicants with well-developed drafting and mechanical drawing skills; knowledge of drafting standards, mathematics, science, and engineering technology; and a solid background in CADD techniques. In addition, communication and problem-solving skills are important.

Training and coursework differ somewhat within the drafting specialties. The initial training for each specialty is similar. All incorporate math and communication skills, for example, but coursework relating to the specialty varies. In an electronics drafting program, for example, students learn how to depict electronic components and circuits in drawings.

Many types of publicly and privately operated schools provide some form of training in drafting. Because the kind and quality of programs vary considerably, prospective students should be careful in selecting a program. They should contact prospective employers regarding their preferences and ask schools to provide information about the kinds of jobs that are obtained by the school's graduates, the types and conditions of the instructional facilities and equipment, and the faculty's qualifications.

Technical institutes offer intensive technical training, but less general education than do junior and community colleges. Certificates or diplomas based on the completion of a certain number of course hours may be awarded. Many technical institutes offer 2-year associate degree programs, which are similar to, or part of, the programs offered by community colleges or State university systems. Their programs vary considerably in both length and type of courses offered. Some area vocational-technical schools are postsecondary public institutions that serve local students and emphasize the type of training preferred by local employers. Many offer introductory drafting instruction. Most require a high school diploma or its equivalent for admission. Other technical institutes are run by private, often for-profit, organizations sometimes called proprietary schools.

Community colleges offer curricula similar to those in technical institutes but include more courses on theory and liberal arts. Often, there is little or no difference between technical institute and community college programs. However, courses taken at community colleges are more likely than those given at technical institutes to be accepted for credit at 4-year colleges. After completing a 2-year associate degree program, graduates may obtain jobs as drafters or continue their education in a related field at 4-year colleges. Most 4-year colleges usually do not offer training in drafting, but college courses in engineering, architecture, and mathematics are useful for obtaining a job as a drafter.

Technical training obtained in the Armed Forces also can be applied in civilian drafting jobs. Some additional training may be necessary, depending on the technical area or military specialty.

The American Design Drafting Association (ADDA) has established a certification program for drafters. Although employers usually do not require drafters to be certified, certification demonstrates an understanding of nationally recognized practices and standards of knowledge. Individuals who wish to become certified must pass the Drafter Certification Test, which is administered periodically at ADDA-authorized sites. Applicants are tested on their knowledge and understanding of basic drafting concepts, such as geometric construction, working drawings, and architectural terms and standards.

Individuals planning careers in drafting should take courses in mathematics, science, computer technology, design, and computer graphics, as well as any high school drafting courses available. Mechanical ability and visual aptitude are important. Prospective drafters should be able to draw well and perform detailed work accurately and neatly. Artistic ability is helpful in some specialized fields, as is knowledge of manufacturing and construction methods. In addition, prospective drafters should have good interpersonal skills because they work closely with engineers, surveyors, architects, and other professionals and, sometimes, with customers.

Entry-level or junior drafters usually do routine work under close supervision. After gaining experience, they may become intermediate drafters and progress to more difficult work with less supervision. At the intermediate level, they may need to exercise more judgment and perform calculations when preparing and modifying drawings. Drafters may eventually advance to senior drafter, designer, or supervisor. Many employers pay for continuing education, and, with appropriate college degrees, drafters may go on to become engineering technicians, engineers, or architects.

Employment
Drafters held about 254,000 jobs in 2004. Architectural and civil drafters held 43 percent of all jobs for drafters, mechanical drafters held about 32 percent of all jobs, and about 15percent of jobs were held by electrical and electronics drafters.

About 44 percent of all jobs for drafters were in architectural, engineering, and related services firms that design construction projects or do other engineering work on a contract basis for other industries. Another 27 percent of jobs were in manufacturing industries such as machinery manufacturing, including metalworking and other general machinery; fabricated metal products manufacturing, including architectural and structural metals; computer and electronic products manufacturing, including navigational, measuring, electromedical, and control instruments; and transportation equipment manufacturing, including aerospace products and parts manufacturing, as well as ship and boat building. Most of the rest were employed in construction, government, wholesale trade, utilities, and employment services. Approximately 6 percent were self-employed in 2004.

Job Outlook
Employment of drafters is expected to grow more slowly than the average for all occupations through 2014. Industrial growth and increasingly complex design problems associated with new products and manufacturing processes will increase the demand for drafting services. Further, drafters are beginning to break out of the traditional drafting role and do work traditionally performed by engineers and architects, thus also increasing demand for drafters. However, drafters tend to be concentrated in slowly growing or declining manufacturing industries. CADD systems that are more powerful and easier to use also should limit demand for lesser skilled drafters as simple tasks are increasingly done quickly and easily by other drafters or other technical professionals, resulting in slower-than-average overall employment growth. Because some drafting work can be done in other locations using the Internet to send CADD files

internationally, the offshoring of some drafting jobs also should dampen growth. Most job openings are expected to arise from the need to replace drafters who transfer to other occupations, leave the labor force, or retire.

Opportunities should be best for individuals with at least 2 years of postsecondary training in a drafting program that provides strong technical skills, as well as considerable experience with CADD systems. CADD has increased the complexity of drafting applications while enhancing the productivity of drafters. It also has enhanced the nature of drafting by creating more possibilities for design and drafting. As technology continues to advance, employers will look for drafters with a strong background in fundamental drafting principles, a high level of technical sophistication, and the ability to apply their knowledge to a broader range of responsibilities.

While growth is expected to be greatest for mechanical, architectural, and civil drafters, demand for particular drafting specialties varies throughout the country because employment usually is contingent on the needs of local industry. Employment of drafters remains highly concentrated in industries that are sensitive to cyclical changes in the economy, primarily manufacturing industries. During recessions, drafters may be laid off. However, a growing number of drafters should continue to find employment on a temporary or contract basis as more companies turn to the employment services industry to meet their changing needs.

Earnings
Drafters' earnings vary by specialty, location, and level of responsibility. Median annual earnings of architectural and civil drafters were $39,190 in May 2004. The middle 50 percent earned between $31,460 and $47,800. The lowest 10 percent earned less than $25,670, and the highest 10 percent earned more than $57,670. Median annual earnings for architectural and civil drafters in architectural, engineering, and related services were $38,760.

Median annual earnings of mechanical drafters were $43,000 in May 2004. The middle 50 percent earned between $34,090 and $54,240. The lowest 10 percent earned less than $27,490, and the highest 10 percent earned more than $67,650. Median annual earnings for mechanical drafters in architectural, engineering, and related services were $44,560.

Median annual earnings of electrical and electronics drafters were $43,180 in May 2004. The middle 50 percent earned between $33,920 and $56,110. The lowest 10 percent earned less than $27,600, and the highest 10 percent earned more than $72,050. In architectural, engineering, and related services, median annual earnings for electrical and electronics drafters were $42,200.

Related Occupations
Other workers who prepare or analyze detailed drawings and make precise calculations and measurements include architects, except landscape and naval; landscape architects; commercial and industrial designers; engineers; engineering technicians; science technicians; and surveyors, cartographers, photogrammetrists, and surveying technicians.

Sources of Additional Information
Information on schools offering programs in drafting and related fields is available from:
➤ Accrediting Commission of Career Schools and Colleges of Technology, 2101 Wilson Blvd., Suite 302, Arlington, VA 22201. Internet: **http://www.accsct.org**
Information about certification is available from:
➤ American Design Drafting Association, 105 E. Main St., Newbern, TN 38059. Internet: **http://www.adda.org**

Engineering Technicians

(O*NET 17-3021.00, 17-3022.00, 17-3023.01, 17-3023.02, 17-3023.03, 17-3024.00, 17-3025.00, 17-3026.00, 17-3027.00, 17-3029.99)

Significant Points

- Because the type and quality of training programs vary considerably, prospective students should carefully investigate training programs before enrolling.

- Electrical and electronic engineering technicians make up 34 percent of all engineering technicians.

- Employment of engineering technicians often is influenced by the same local and national economic conditions that affect engineers; as a result, job outlook varies with industry and specialization.

- Opportunities will be best for individuals with an associate degree or extensive job training in engineering technology.

Nature of the Work

Engineering technicians use the principles and theories of science, engineering, and mathematics to solve technical problems in research and development, manufacturing, sales, construction, inspection, and maintenance. Their work is more limited in scope and application-oriented than that of scientists and engineers. Many engineering technicians assist engineers and scientists, especially in research and development. Others work in quality control, inspecting products and processes, conducting tests, or collecting data. In manufacturing, they may assist in product design, development, or production. Although many workers who repair or maintain various types of electrical, electronic, or mechanical equipment are called technicians, these workers are covered in the *Handbook* section on installation, maintenance, and repair occupations.

Engineering technicians who work in research and development build or set up equipment; prepare and conduct experiments; collect data; calculate or record results; and help engineers or scientists in other ways, such as making prototype versions of newly designed equipment. They also assist in design work, often using computer-aided design and drafting (CADD) equipment.

Most engineering technicians specialize, learning skills and working in the same disciplines as engineers. Occupational titles, therefore, tend to reflect engineering specialties. Some branches of engineering technology for which there are accredited programs of study are not covered in detail in the *Handbook,* such as chemical engineering technology (the development of new chemical products and processes) and bioengineering technology (the development and implementation of biomedical equipment).

Aerospace engineering and operations technicians construct, test, and maintain aircraft and space vehicles. They may calibrate test equipment and determine causes of equipment malfunctions. Using computer and communications systems, aerospace engineering and operations technicians often record and interpret test data.

Civil engineering technicians help civil engineers plan and build highways, buildings, bridges, dams, wastewater treatment systems, and other structures, as well as do related research. Some estimate construction costs and specify materials to be used, and some may even prepare drawings or perform land-surveying duties. Others may set up and monitor instruments used to study traffic conditions. (Cost estimators; drafters; and surveyors, cartographers, photogrammetrists, and surveying technicians are covered elsewhere in the *Handbook.*)

Electrical and electronics engineering technicians help design, develop, test, and manufacture electrical and electronic equipment such as communication equipment; radar, industrial, and medical monitoring or control devices; navigational equipment; and computers. They may work in product evaluation and testing, using measuring and diagnostic devices to adjust, test, and repair equipment. (Workers whose jobs are limited to repairing electrical and electronic equipment, who often are referred to as electronics technicians, are included with electrical and electronics installers and repairers elsewhere in the *Handbook.*)

Electromechanical engineering technicians combine fundamental principles of mechanical engineering technology with knowledge of electrical and electronic circuits to design, develop, test, and manufacture electrical and computer-controlled mechanical systems. Their work often overlaps that of both electrical and electronics engineering technicians and mechanical engineering technicians.

Environmental engineering technicians work closely with environmental engineers and scientists in developing methods and devices used in the prevention, control, or correction of environmental hazards. They inspect and maintain equipment related to air pollution and recycling. Some inspect water and wastewater treatment systems to ensure that pollution control requirements are met.

Industrial engineering technicians study the efficient use of personnel, materials, and machines in factories, stores, repair shops, and offices. They prepare layouts of machinery and equipment, plan the flow of work, make statistical studies, and analyze production costs.

Mechanical engineering technicians help engineers design, develop, test, and manufacture industrial machinery, consumer

Engineering technicians assist engineering staff in aspects of design, development, and testing.

products, and other equipment. They may assist in product tests—for example, by setting up instrumentation for auto crash tests. They may make sketches and rough layouts, record and analyze data, make calculations and estimates, and report on their findings. When planning production, mechanical engineering technicians prepare layouts and drawings of the assembly process and of parts to be manufactured. They estimate labor costs, equipment life, and plant space. Some test and inspect machines and equipment or work with engineers to eliminate production problems.

Working Conditions

Most engineering technicians work at least 40 hours a week in laboratories, offices, manufacturing or industrial plants, or on construction sites. Some may be exposed to hazards from equipment, chemicals, or toxic materials.

Training, Other Qualifications, and Advancement

Although it may be possible to qualify for certain engineering technician jobs without formal training, most employers prefer to hire someone with at least a 2-year associate degree in engineering technology. Training is available at technical institutes, community colleges, extension divisions of colleges and universities, public and private vocational-technical schools, and in the Armed Forces. Persons with college courses in science, engineering, and mathematics may qualify for some positions but may need additional specialized training and experience. Although employers usually do not require engineering technicians to be certified, such certification may provide jobseekers a competitive advantage.

Prospective engineering technicians should take as many high school science and math courses as possible to prepare for postsecondary programs in engineering technology. Most 2-year associate degree programs accredited by the Technology Accreditation Commission of the Accreditation Board for Engineering and Technology (ABET) require, at a minimum, college algebra and trigonometry and one or two basic science courses. Depending on the specialty, more math or science may be required. About 230 colleges offer ABET-accredited programs in engineering technology.

The type of technical courses required also depends on the specialty. For example, prospective mechanical engineering technicians may take courses in fluid mechanics, thermodynamics, and mechanical design; electrical engineering technicians may need classes in electrical circuits, microprocessors, and digital electronics; and those preparing to work in environmental engineering technology need courses in environmental regulations and safe handling of hazardous materials.

Because many engineering technicians assist in design work, creativity is desirable. Because these workers often are part of a team of engineers and other technicians, good communication skills and the ability to work well with others also are important.

Engineering technicians usually begin by performing routine duties under the close supervision of an experienced technician, technologist, engineer, or scientist. As they gain experience, they are given more difficult assignments with only general supervision. Some engineering technicians eventually become supervisors.

Many publicly and privately operated schools provide technical training, but the type and quality of training vary considerably. Therefore, prospective students should be careful in selecting a program. They should ascertain prospective employers' preferences and ask schools to provide information about the kinds of jobs obtained by program graduates, about instructional facilities and equipment, and about faculty qualifications. Graduates of ABET-accredited programs usually are recognized as having achieved an acceptable level of competence in the mathematics, science, and technical courses required for this occupation.

Technical institutes offer intensive technical training through application and practice, but they provide less theory and general education than do community colleges. Many technical institutes offer 2-year associate degree programs and are similar to or part of a community college or State university system. Other technical institutes are run by private, often for-profit organizations, sometimes called proprietary schools. Their programs vary considerably in length and types of courses offered, although some are 2-year associate degree programs.

Community colleges offer curriculums that are similar to those in technical institutes but include more theory and liberal arts. There may be little or no difference between programs at technical institutes and community colleges, as both offer associate degrees. After completing the 2-year program, some graduates get jobs as engineering technicians, whereas others continue their education at 4-year colleges. However, there is a difference between an associate degree in pre-engineering and one in engineering technology. Students who enroll in a 2-year pre-engineering program may find it very difficult to find work as an engineering technician if they decide not to enter a 4-year engineering program, because pre-engineering programs usually focus less on hands-on applications and more on academic preparatory work. Conversely, graduates of 2-year engineering technology programs may not receive credit for some of the courses they have taken if they choose to transfer to a 4-year engineering program. Colleges with these 4-year programs usually do not offer engineering technician training, but college courses in science, engineering, and mathematics are useful for obtaining a job as an engineering technician. Many 4-year colleges offer bachelor's degrees in engineering technology, but graduates of these programs often are hired to work as technologists or applied engineers, not technicians.

Area vocational-technical schools, another source of technical training, include postsecondary public institutions that serve local students and emphasize training needed by local employers. Most require a high school diploma or its equivalent for admission.

Other training in technical areas may be obtained in the Armed Forces. Many military technical training programs are highly regarded by employers. However, skills acquired in military programs are often narrowly focused and may be of limited applicability in civilian industry, which often requires broader training. Therefore, some additional training may be needed, depending on the acquired skills and the kind of job.

The National Institute for Certification in Engineering Technologies has established a voluntary certification program for engineering technicians. Certification is available at various levels, each level combining a written examination in 1 of about 30 specialties with a certain amount of job-related experience, a supervisory evaluation, and a recommendation.

Employment

Engineering technicians held 532,000 jobs in 2004. About a third were electrical and electronics engineering technicians, as indicated by the following tabulation.

Electrical and electronic engineering technicians	182,000
Civil engineering technicians	94,000
Industrial engineering technicians	69,000
Mechanical engineering technicians	48,000
Environmental engineering technicians	20,000
Electro-mechanical technicians	19,000
Aerospace engineering and operations technicians	9,500
Engineering technicians, except drafters, all other	91,000

About 36 percent of all engineering technicians worked in manufacturing, mainly in the computer and electronic equipment, transportation equipment, and machinery manufacturing industries. Another 22 percent worked in professional, scientific, and technical service industries, mostly in engineering or business services companies that do engineering work on contract for government, manufacturing firms, or other organizations.

In 2004, the Federal Government employed 37,000 engineering technicians. State governments employed 39,000, and local governments employed 27,000.

Job Outlook

Opportunities will be best for individuals with an associate degree or extensive job training in engineering technology. As technology becomes more sophisticated, employers will continue to look for technicians who are skilled in new technology and require a minimum of additional job training. An increase in the number of jobs related to public health and safety should create job opportunities for engineering technicians with the appropriate training and certification.

Overall employment of engineering technicians is expected to increase about as fast as the average for all occupations through 2014. Competitive pressures will force companies to improve and update manufacturing facilities and product designs, resulting in more jobs for engineering technicians. In addition to growth, many job openings will stem from the need to replace technicians who retire or leave the labor force.

Growth of engineering technician employment in some design functions may be dampened by increasing globalization of the development process. To reduce costs and speed project completion, some companies may relocate part of their development operations to facilities overseas, impacting both engineers and the engineering technicians that support them—particularly in electronics and computer-related areas. However, much of the work of engineering technicians requires on-site presence, so demand for engineering technicians within the US should continue to grow.

Because engineering technicians work closely with engineers, employment of engineering technicians is often influenced by the same local and national economic conditions that affect engineers. As a result, the employment outlook varies with industry and specialization. Growth in the largest specialty—electrical and electronics engineering technicians—is expected to be about as fast as the average, while employment of environmental engineering technicians is expected to grow faster than average to meet the environmental demands of an ever-growing population.

Earnings

Median annual earnings in May 2004 of engineering technicians by specialty are shown in the following tabulation.

Aerospace engineering and operations technicians	$52,500
Electrical and electronic engineering technicians	46,310
Industrial engineering technicians	43,590
Mechanical engineering technicians	43,400
Electro-mechanical technicians	41,440
Environmental engineering technicians	38,550
Civil engineering technicians	38,480

Median annual earnings of electrical and electronics engineering technicians were $46,310 in May 2004. The middle 50 percent earned between $36,290 and $55,750. The lowest 10 percent earned less than $29,000, and the highest 10 percent earned more than $67,900. Median annual earnings in the industries employing the largest numbers of electrical and electronics engineering technicians in May 2004 are shown below.

Federal Government	$64,160
Wired telecommunications carriers	51,250
Architectural, engineering, and related services	44,800
Navigational, measuring, electromedical, and control instruments manufacturing	42,780
Semiconductor and other electronic component manufacturing	41,300

Median annual earnings of civil engineering technicians were $38,480 in May 2004. The middle 50 percent earned between $29,880 and $48,590. The lowest 10 percent earned less than $24,180, and the highest 10 percent earned more than $57,550. Median annual earnings in the industries employing the largest numbers of civil engineering technicians in May 2004 are shown below.

Local government	$43,700
Architectural, engineering, and related services	37,470
State government	35,970

In May 2004, the average annual salary for aerospace engineering and operations technicians in the aerospace products and parts manufacturing industry was $52,250, and the average annual salary for environmental engineering technicians in the architectural, engineering, and related services industry was $36,530. The average annual salary for industrial engineering technicians in the semiconductor and other electronic component manufacturing industry was $40,020. In the architectural, engineering, and related services industry, the average annual salary for mechanical engineering technicians was $43,190.

Related Occupations

Engineering technicians apply scientific and engineering principles usually acquired in postsecondary programs below the baccalaureate level. Similar occupations include science technicians; drafters; surveyors, cartographers, photogrammetrists, and surveying technicians; and broadcast and sound engineering technicians and radio operators.

Sources of Additional Information

For information about careers in engineering technology, contact:
➤ JETS (Junior Engineering Technical Society)-Guidance, 1420 King St., Suite 405, Alexandria, VA 22314-2794. Internet: **http://www.jets.org**

Information on ABET-accredited engineering technology programs is available from:
➤ Accreditation Board for Engineering and Technology, Inc., 111 Market Plc., Suite 1050, Baltimore, MD 21202-4012. Internet: **http://www.abet.org**

Information on certification of engineering technicians, as well as job and career information, is available from:
➤ National Institute for Certification in Engineering Technologies, 1420 King St., Alexandria, VA 22314-2794. Internet: **http://www.nicet.org**

Life Scientists

Agricultural and Food Scientists

(O*NET 19-1011.00, 19-1012.00, 19-1013.01, 19-1013.02)

Significant Points

- About 1 in 4 agricultural and food scientists work for Federal, State, or local governments.

- A bachelor's degree in agricultural science is sufficient for some jobs in applied research; a master's or Ph.D. degree is required for basic research or teaching.

- Over 1 in 3 agricultural and food scientists are self-employed.

Nature of the Work

The work of agricultural and food scientists plays an important part in maintaining the Nation's food supply by ensuring agricultural productivity and the safety of the food supply. Agricultural scientists study farm crops and animals, and develop ways of improving their quantity and quality. They look for ways to improve crop yield with less labor, control pests and weeds more safely and effectively, and conserve soil and water. They research methods of converting raw agricultural commodities into attractive and healthy food products for consumers.

Agricultural science is closely related to biological science, and agricultural scientists use the principles of biology, chemistry, physics, mathematics, and other sciences to solve problems in agriculture. They often work with biological scientists on basic biological research and on applying to agriculture the advances in knowledge brought about by biotechnology.

In the past two decades, rapid advances in basic biological knowledge related to genetics spurred growth in the field of biotechnology. Some agricultural and food scientists use this technology to manipulate the genetic material of plants and crops, attempting to make organisms more productive or resistant to disease. These advances in biotechnology have opened up research opportunities in many areas of agricultural and food science, including commercial applications in agriculture, environmental remediation, and the food industry. Another emerging technology expected to affect agriculture is nanotechnology—a future molecular manufacturing technology which promises to revolutionize methods of manufacturing and distribution in many industries.

Many agricultural scientists work in basic or applied research and development. Others manage or administer research and development programs, or manage marketing or production operations in companies that produce food products or agricultural chemicals, supplies, and machinery. Some agricultural scientists are consultants to business firms, private clients, or government.

Depending on the agricultural or food scientist's area of specialization, the nature of the work performed varies.

Food science. Food scientists and technologists usually work in the food processing industry, universities, or the Federal Government, and help to meet consumer demand for food products that are healthful, safe, palatable, and convenient. To do this, they use their knowledge of chemistry, physics, engineering, microbiology, biotechnology, and other sciences to develop new or better ways of preserving, processing, packaging, storing, and delivering foods. Some food scientists engage in basic research, discovering new food sources; analyzing food content to determine levels of vitamins, fat, sugar, or protein; or searching for substitutes for harmful or undesirable additives, such as nitrites. They also develop ways to process, preserve, package, or store food according to industry and government regulations. Traditional food processing research into functions involving baking, blanching, canning, drying, evaporation, and pasteurization will continue to be conducted and will find new applications. Other food scientists enforce government regulations, inspecting food processing areas and ensuring that sanitation, safety, quality, and waste management standards are met. Food technologists generally work in product development, applying the findings from food science research to the selection, preservation, processing, packaging, distribution, and use of safe, nutritious, and wholesome food.

Plant science. Agronomy, crop science, entomology, and plant breeding are included in plant science. Scientists in these disciplines study plants and their growth in soils, helping producers of food, feed, and fiber crops to continue to feed a growing population while conserving natural resources and maintaining the environment. Agronomists and crop scientists not only help increase productivity, but also study ways to improve the nutritional value of crops and the quality of seed, often through biotechnology. Some crop scientists study the breeding, physiology, and management of crops and use genetic engineering to develop crops resistant to pests and drought. Entomologists conduct research to develop new technologies to control or eliminate pests in infested areas and to prevent the spread of harmful pests to new areas, as well as technologies that are compatible with the environment. They also conduct research or engage in oversight activities aimed at halting the spread of insect-borne disease.

Soil science. Soil scientists study the chemical, physical, biological, and mineralogical composition of soils as they relate to plant or crop growth. They also study the responses of various soil types to fertilizers, tillage practices, and crop rotation. Many soil scientists who work for the Federal Government conduct soil surveys, classifying and mapping soils. They provide information and recommendations to farmers and other landowners regarding the best use of land, plant growth, and methods to avoid or correct problems such as erosion. They may also consult with engineers and other technical personnel working on construction projects about the effects of, and solutions to, soil problems. Because soil science is closely related to environmental science, persons trained in soil science also apply their knowledge to ensure environmental quality and effective land use.

Animal science. Animal scientists work to develop better, more efficient ways of producing and processing meat, poultry, eggs, and milk. Dairy scientists, poultry scientists, animal breeders, and other scientists in related fields study the genetics, nutrition, reproduction, growth, and development of domestic farm animals. Some animal scientists inspect and grade livestock food products, purchase livestock, or work in technical sales or marketing. As extension agents or consultants, animal scientists advise agricultural producers on how to upgrade animal housing facilities properly, lower mortality rates, handle waste matter, or increase production of animal products, such as milk or eggs.

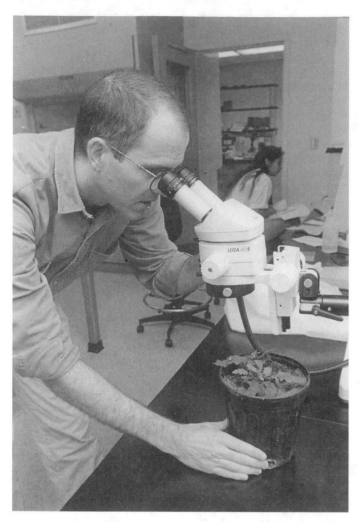

A bachelor's degree in agricultural science is sufficient for some jobs as an agricultural or food scientist in applied research; a master's or Ph.D. degree is required for basic research or teaching.

Working Conditions

Agricultural scientists involved in management or basic research tend to work regular hours in offices and laboratories. The work environment for those engaged in applied research or product development varies, depending on the discipline of agricultural science and on the type of employer. For example, food scientists in private industry may work in test kitchens while investigating new processing techniques. Animal scientists working for Federal, State, or university research stations may spend part of their time at dairies, farrowing houses, feedlots, or farm animal facilities, or outdoors conducting research associated with livestock. Soil and crop scientists also spend time outdoors conducting research on farms and agricultural research stations. Entomologists work in laboratories, insectories, or agricultural research stations, and also may spend time outdoors studying or collecting insects in their natural habitat.

Training, Other Qualifications, and Advancement

Training requirements for agricultural scientists depend on their specialty and on the type of work they perform. A bachelor's degree in agricultural science is sufficient for some jobs in applied research or for assisting in basic research, but a master's or doctoral degree is required for basic research. A Ph.D. in agricultural science usually is needed for college teaching and for advancement to administrative research positions. Degrees

in related sciences such as biology, chemistry, or physics or in related engineering specialties also may qualify persons for some agricultural science jobs.

All States have a land-grant college that offers agricultural science degrees. Many other colleges and universities also offer agricultural science degrees or some agricultural science courses. However, not every school offers all specialties. A typical undergraduate agricultural science curriculum includes communications, mathematics, economics, business, and physical and life sciences courses, in addition to a wide variety of technical agricultural science courses. For prospective animal scientists, these technical agricultural science courses might include animal breeding, reproductive physiology, nutrition, and meats and muscle biology. Graduate students typically specialize in a subfield of agricultural science, such as animal breeding and genetics, crop science, or horticulture science, depending on their interest and the kind of work they wish to do. For example, those interested in doing genetic and biotechnological research in the food industry need to develop a strong background in life and physical sciences, such as cell and molecular biology, microbiology, and inorganic and organic chemistry. However, students normally need not specialize at the undergraduate level. In fact, undergraduates who are broadly trained have greater flexibility when changing jobs than if they had narrowly defined their interests.

Students preparing as food scientists take courses such as food chemistry, food analysis, food microbiology, food engineering, and food processing operations. Those preparing as crop or soil scientists take courses in plant pathology, soil chemistry, entomology, plant physiology, and biochemistry, among others. Advanced degree programs include classroom and fieldwork, laboratory research, and a thesis or dissertation based on independent research.

Agricultural and food scientists should be able to work independently or as part of a team and be able to communicate clearly and concisely, both orally and in writing. Most of these scientists also need an understanding of basic business principles, and the ability to apply basic statistical techniques. Employers increasingly prefer job applicants who are able to apply computer skills to determine solutions to problems, to collect and analyze data, and to control various processes.

The American Society of Agronomy offers certification programs in crop science, agronomy, crop advising, soil science, plant pathology, and weed science. To become certified, applicants must pass designated examinations and have at least 2 years of experience with at least a bachelor's degree in agriculture or 4 years of experience with no degree. To become a certified crop advisor, however, candidates do not need a degree.

Agricultural scientists who have advanced degrees usually begin in research or teaching. With experience, they may advance to jobs such as supervisors of research programs or managers of other agriculture-related activities.

Employment

Agricultural and food scientists held about 30,000 jobs in 2004. In addition, several thousand persons held agricultural science faculty positions in colleges and universities. (See the statement on postsecondary teachers elsewhere in the *Handbook*.)

About 1 in 4 salaried agricultural and food scientists work for Federal, State, or local governments. One out of 7 worked for State governments at State agricultural colleges or agricultural research stations. Another one out of 10 worked for the Federal Government in 2004, mostly in the U.S. Department of Agriculture. Some worked for agricultural service companies; others worked for commercial research and development laboratories, seed companies, pharmaceutical companies, wholesale distributors, and food products companies. About 10,000 agricultural scientists were self-employed in 2004, mainly as consultants.

Job Outlook

Employment of agricultural and food scientists is expected to grow about as fast as the average for all occupations through 2014. Past agricultural research has resulted in the development of higher yielding crops, crops with better resistance to pests and plant pathogens, and chemically based fertilizers and pesticides. Research is still necessary, particularly as insects and diseases continue to adapt to pesticides and as soil fertility and water quality continue to need improvement, resulting in job opportunities in biotechnology. Agricultural scientists are using new avenues of research in biotechnology to develop plants and food crops that require less fertilizer, fewer pesticides and herbicides, and even less water for growth. Emerging biotechnologies and nanotechnologies will play an increasingly larger role in creating more plentiful global food supplies.

Biotechnological research will continue to offer possibilities for the development of new food products. This research will allow agricultural and food scientists to develop techniques to detect and control food pathogens, and should lead to better understanding of other infectious agents in foods.

Agricultural scientists will be needed to balance increased agricultural output with protection and preservation of soil, water, and ecosystems. They will increasingly encourage the practice of "sustainable agriculture" by developing and implementing plans to manage pests, crops, soil fertility and erosion, and animal waste in ways that reduce the use of harmful chemicals and do little damage to farms and the natural environment.

Further studies at scientific research and development services firms will result in more job opportunities for food scientists and technologists. This research will be stimulated by a heightened public focus on diet, health, changes in food safety, and biosecurity—preventing the introduction of infectious agents, such as foot and mouth disease into a herd of animals. Increasing demand for these workers also will stem from issues such as a growing world population, availability and cost of usable water, shrinking natural resources including the loss of arable land, and deforestation, environmental pollution, and climate change.

Graduates with a bachelor's degree should find work in a variety of fields, mostly in the private sector, although many of the positions may be related to agricultural or food science rather than as an agricultural or food scientist. A bachelor's degree in agricultural science is useful for managerial jobs in businesses that deal with ranchers and farmers, such as feed, fertilizer, seed, and farm equipment manufacturers; retailers or wholesalers; and farm credit institutions. In some cases, persons with a 4-year degree can provide consulting services or work in sales and marketing—promoting high-demand products such as organic foods. Bachelor's degree holders also can work in some applied research and product development positions under the guidance of a Ph.D. scientist, but usually only in certain subfields, such as food science and technology. The Federal Government hires bachelor's degree holders to work as soil scientists. Four-year degrees also may help persons enter occupations such as farmer, or farm or ranch manager; cooperative extension service agent; agricultural products inspector; or purchasing or sales agent for agricultural commodity or farm supply companies.

Opportunities may be better for those with a master's degree, particularly for graduates seeking applied research positions in a laboratory. Master's degree candidates also can seek to become a certified crop advisor, helping farmers better manage their crops. Those with a Ph.D. in agricultural and food science will experience the best opportunities, especially in basic research and teaching positions at colleges and universities as retirements of faculty are expected to accelerate during the projection period.

Fewer opportunities for agricultural and food scientists are expected in the Federal government, mostly because of budgetary cutbacks at the U.S. Department of Agriculture.

Employment of agricultural and food scientists is relatively stable during periods of economic recession. Layoffs are less likely among agricultural and food scientists than in some other occupations because food is a staple item and its demand fluctuates very little with economic activity.

Earnings

Median annual earnings of food scientists and technologists were $50,840 in May 2004. The middle 50 percent earned between $36,450 and $72,510. The lowest 10 percent earned less than $28,410, and the highest 10 percent earned more than $91,300. Median annual earnings of soil and plant scientists were $51,200 in May 2004. The middle 50 percent earned between $37,890 and $69,120. The lowest 10 percent earned less than $30,660, and the highest 10 percent earned more than $88,840. In May 2004, median annual earnings of animal scientists were $49,920.

The average Federal salary for employees in nonsupervisory, supervisory, and managerial positions in 2005 was $87,025 in animal science and $73,573 in agronomy.

According to the National Association of Colleges and Employers, beginning salary offers in 2005 for graduates with a bachelor's degree in animal sciences averaged $30,614 a year; plant sciences, $31,649 a year; and in other agricultural sciences, $36,189 a year.

Related Occupations

The work of agricultural scientists is closely related to that of other scientists, including biological scientists, chemists, and conservation scientists and foresters. It also is related to the work of managers of agricultural production, such as farmers, ranchers, and agricultural managers. Certain specialties of agricultural science also are related to other occupations. For example, the work of animal scientists is related to the work of veterinarians, and horticulturists perform duties similar to duties of landscape architects.

Sources of Additional Information

Agricultural career brochures are available from:
➤ American Society of Agronomy, Crop Science Society of America, Soil Science Society of America, 677 S. Segoe Rd., Madison, WI 53711-1086. Internet: **http://www.agronomy.org**

Information on careers in agricultural science is available from:
➤ Food and Agricultural Careers for Tomorrow, Purdue University, 1140 Agricultural Administration Bldg., West Lafayette, IN 47907-1140.

Information on acquiring a job as an agricultural scientist with the Federal Government is available from the Office of Personnel Management through USAJOBS, the Federal Government's official employment information system. This resource for locating and applying for job opportunities can be accessed through the Internet at **http://www.usajobs.opm.gov** or through an interactive voice response telephone system at (703) 724-1850 or TDD (978) 461-8404. These numbers are not tollfree, and charges may result.

Biological Scientists

(O*NET 19-1020.01, 19-1021.01, 19-1021.02, 19-1022.00, 19-1023.00, 19-1029.99)

Significant Points

- A Ph.D. degree usually is required for independent research, but a master's degree is sufficient for some jobs in applied research or product development; a bachelor's degree is adequate for some nonresearch jobs.

- Doctoral degree holders face competition for basic research positions; holders of bachelor's or master's degrees in biological science can expect better opportunities in nonresearch positions.

- Biotechnological research and development will continue to drive employment growth.

Nature of the Work

Biological scientists study living organisms and their relationship to their environment. They research problems dealing with life processes and living organisms. Most specialize in some area of biology, such as zoology (the study of animals) or microbiology (the study of microscopic organisms). (Medical scientists, whose work is closely related to that of biological scientists, are discussed elsewhere in the *Handbook*.)

Many biological scientists work in research and development. Some conduct basic research to advance knowledge of living organisms, including viruses, bacteria, and other infectious agents. Basic biological research continues to provide the building blocks necessary to develop solutions to human health problems and to preserve and repair the natural environment. Biological scientists mostly work independently in private industry, university, or government laboratories, often exploring new areas of research or expanding on specialized research started in graduate school. Those who are not wage and salary workers in private industry typically submit grant proposals to obtain funding for their projects. Colleges and universities, private industry, and Federal Government agencies such as the National Institutes of Health and the National Science Foundation contribute to the support of scientists whose research proposals are determined to be financially feasible and to have the potential to advance new ideas or processes.

Biological scientists who work in applied research or product development use knowledge provided by basic research to develop new drugs, treatments, and medical diagnostic tests; increase crop yields; and protect and clean up the environment by developing new biofuels. They usually have less autonomy than basic researchers to choose the emphasis of their research, relying instead on market-driven directions based on their firms' products and goals. Because biological scientists doing applied research and product development in private industry may be required to describe their research plans or results to nonscientists who are in a position to veto or approve their ideas, they must understand the potential cost of their work and its impact on business. Scientists often work in teams, interacting with engineers, scientists of other disciplines, business managers, and technicians. Some biological scientists also work with customers or suppliers and manage budgets.

Those who conduct research usually work in laboratories and use electron microscopes, computers, thermal cyclers, and a wide variety of other equipment. Some conduct experiments using laboratory animals or greenhouse plants. This is particularly true of botanists, physiologists, and zoologists. For some biological scientists, research also is performed outside of laboratories. For example, a botanist might do research in tropical rain forests to see what plants grow there, or an ecologist might study how a forest area recovers after a fire. Some marine biologists also work outdoors, often on research vessels from which they study various marine organisms such as marine plankton or fish.

Some biological scientists work in managerial or administrative positions, usually after spending some time doing research and learning about a particular firm, agency, or project. They may plan and administer programs for testing foods and drugs, for example, or direct activities at zoos or botanical gardens. Some work as consultants to businesses or to government agencies.

Recent advances in biotechnology and information technology are transforming the industries in which biological scientists work. In the 1980s, swift advances in basic biological knowledge related to genetics and molecules spurred growth in the field of biotechnology. Biological scientists using this technology manipulate the genetic material of animals or plants, attempting to make organisms more productive or resistant to disease. Research using biotechnology techniques, such as recombining DNA, has led to the production of important substances, including human insulin and growth hormone. Many other substances not previously available in large quantities are starting to be produced by biotechnological means; some may be useful in treating cancer and other diseases. Today, many biological scientists are involved in biotechnology. Those who work on the Human Genome Project isolate genes and determine their function. This work continues to lead to the discovery of the genes associated with specific diseases and inherited traits, such as certain types of cancer or obesity. These advances in biotechnology have created research opportunities in almost all areas of biology, with commercial applications in the food industry, agriculture, and environmental remediation, and in other emerging areas such as DNA fingerprinting.

Most biological scientists are further classified by the type of organism they study or by the specific activity they perform, although recent advances in the understanding of basic life processes at the molecular and cellular levels have blurred some traditional classifications.

Aquatic biologists study micro-organisms, plants, and animals living in water. *Marine biologists* study salt water organisms, and *limnologists* study fresh water organisms. Much of the work of marine biology centers on molecular biology, the study of the biochemical processes that take place inside living cells. Marine biologists sometimes are mistakenly called oceanographers, but oceanography is the study of the physical characteristics of oceans and the ocean

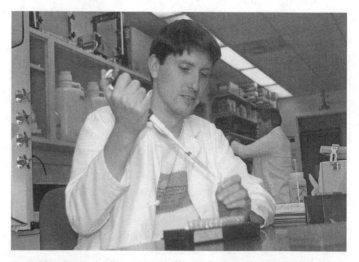

Biotechnological research and development will continue to drive employment growth of biological scientists.

floor. (See the *Handbook* statements on environmental scientists and hydrologists and on geoscientists.)

Biochemists study the chemical composition of living things. They analyze the complex chemical combinations and reactions involved in metabolism, reproduction, growth, and heredity. Biochemists and molecular biologists do most of their work in biotechnology, which involves understanding the complex chemistry of life.

Botanists study plants and their environment. Some study all aspects of plant life, including algae, fungi, lichens, mosses, ferns, conifers, and flowering plants; others specialize in areas such as identification and classification of plants, the structure and function of plant parts, the biochemistry of plant processes, the causes and cures of plant diseases, the interaction of plants with other organisms and the environment, and the geological record of plants.

Microbiologists investigate the growth and characteristics of microscopic organisms such as bacteria, algae, or fungi. Most microbiologists specialize in environmental, food, agricultural, or industrial microbiology; virology (the study of viruses); immunology (the study of mechanisms that fight infections); or bioinformatics (the process of integrating molecular biology and information science). Many microbiologists use biotechnology to advance knowledge of cell reproduction and human disease.

Physiologists study life functions of plants and animals, both in the whole organism and at the cellular or molecular level, under normal and abnormal conditions. Physiologists often specialize in functions such as growth, reproduction, photosynthesis, respiration, or movement, or in the physiology of a certain area or system of the organism.

Biophysicists study the application of principles of physics, such as electrical and mechanical energy and related phenomena, to living cells and organisms.

Zoologists and wildlife biologists study animals and wildlife— their origin, behavior, diseases, and life processes. Some experiment with live animals in controlled or natural surroundings, while others dissect dead animals to study their structure. Zoologists and wildlife biologists also may collect and analyze biological data to determine the environmental effects of current and potential use of land and water areas. Zoologists usually are identified by the animal group studied—ornithologists (birds), mammalogists (mammals), herpetologists (reptiles), and ichthyologists (fish).

Ecologists study the relationships among organisms and between organisms and their environments, examining the effects of population size, pollutants, rainfall, temperature, and altitude. Using knowledge of various scientific disciplines, ecologists may collect, study, and report data on the quality of air, food, soil, and water.

Agricultural and food scientists, sometimes referred to as biological scientists, are discussed elsewhere in the *Handbook*.

Working Conditions

Biological scientists usually work regular hours in offices or laboratories and usually are not exposed to unsafe or unhealthy conditions. Those who work with dangerous organisms or toxic substances in the laboratory must follow strict safety procedures to avoid contamination. Many biological scientists such as botanists, ecologists, and zoologists take field trips that involve strenuous physical activity and primitive living conditions. Biological scientists in the field may work in warm or cold climates, in all kinds of weather. In their research, they may dig, chip with a hammer, scoop with a net, and carry equipment in a backpack. They also may climb, stand, kneel, or dive.

Marine biologists encounter a variety of working conditions. Some marine biologists work in laboratories; others work on research ships. Marine biologists who work underwater must practice safe diving while working around sharp coral reefs and hazardous marine life. Although some marine biologists obtain their specimens from the sea, many still spend a good deal of their time in laboratories and offices, conducting tests, running experiments, recording results, and compiling data.

Some biological scientists depend on grant money to support their research. They may be under pressure to meet deadlines and to conform to rigid grant-writing specifications when preparing proposals to seek new or extended funding.

Training, Other Qualifications, and Advancement

A Ph.D. degree usually is necessary for independent research, industrial research, and college teaching, as well as for advancement to administrative positions. A master's degree is sufficient for some jobs in basic research, applied research or product development, management, or inspection; it also may qualify one to work as a research technician or as a teacher in an aquarium. The bachelor's degree is adequate for some nonresearch jobs. For example, some graduates with a bachelor's degree start as biological scientists in testing and inspection or get jobs related to biological science, such as technical sales or service representatives. In some cases, graduates with a bachelor's degree are able to work in a laboratory environment on their own projects, but this is unusual. Some may work as research assistants, whereas others become biological laboratory technicians or, with courses in education, high school biology teachers. (See the statements elsewhere in the *Handbook* on clinical laboratory technologists and technicians; science technicians; and teachers—preschool, kindergarten, elementary, middle, and secondary.) Many with a bachelor's degree in biology enter medical, dental, veterinary, or other health profession schools.

In addition to required courses in chemistry and biology, undergraduate biological science majors usually study allied disciplines such as mathematics, physics, engineering, and computer science. Computer courses are essential because employers prefer job applicants who are able to apply computer skills to modeling and simulation tasks and to operate computerized laboratory equipment, particularly in emerging fields such as bioinformatics. Those interested in studying the environment also should take courses in environmental studies and become familiar with current legislation and regulations. Prospective biological scientists who hope to work as marine biologists should have at least a bachelor's degree in a biological or marine science. However, students should not overspecialize in undergraduate study, as knowledge of marine biology often is acquired in graduate study. Most colleges and universities offer bachelor's degrees in biological science, and many offer advanced degrees. Curriculums for advanced degrees often emphasize a subfield such as microbiology or botany, but not all universities offer all curriculums. Larger universities frequently have separate departments specializing in different areas of biological science. For example, a program in botany might cover agronomy, horticulture, or plant pathology. Advanced degree programs include classroom and fieldwork, laboratory research, and a thesis or dissertation.

Biological scientists with a Ph.D. often take temporary postdoctoral research positions that provide specialized research experience. Postdoctoral positions may offer the opportunity to publish research findings. A solid record of published research is essential in obtaining a permanent position involving basic research, especially for those seeking a permanent college or university faculty position. In private industry, some may become managers or administrators within the field of biology; others leave biology for nontechnical managerial, administrative, or sales jobs.

Biological scientists should be able to work independently or as part of a team and be able to communicate clearly and concisely, both orally and in writing. Those in private industry, especially those who aspire to management or administrative positions, should possess strong business and communication skills and be familiar with regulatory issues and marketing and management techniques. Those doing field research in remote areas must have physical stamina. Biological scientists also must have patience and self-discipline to conduct long and detailed research projects.

Employment

Biological scientists held about 77,000 jobs in 2004. Slightly more than half of all biological scientists were employed by Federal, State, and local governments. Federal biological scientists worked mainly for the U.S. Departments of Agriculture, Interior, and Defense and for the National Institutes of Health. Most of the rest worked in scientific research and testing laboratories, the pharmaceutical and medicine manufacturing industry, or hospitals.

In addition, many biological scientists held biology faculty positions in colleges and universities. (See the statement on teachers—postsecondary elsewhere in the *Handbook*.)

Job Outlook

Employment of biological scientists is projected to grow about as fast as the average for all occupations over the 2004-14 period, as biotechnological research and development continues to drive job growth. However, doctoral degree holders face competition for basic research positions. The Federal Government funds much basic research and development, including many areas of medical research that relate to biological science. Recent budget increases at the National Institutes of Health have led to large increases in Federal basic research and development expenditures, with research grants growing both in number and in dollar amount. Nevertheless, the increase in expenditures is expected to slow significantly over the 2004-14 projection period, resulting in a highly competitive environment for winning and renewing research grants. Furthermore, should the number of advanced degrees awarded continue to grow, applicants for research grants are likely to face even more competition. Currently, about 1 in 3 grant proposals are approved for long-term research projects. In addition, applied research positions in private industry may become more difficult to obtain if increasing numbers of scientists seek jobs in private industry because of the competitive job market for independent research positions in universities and for college and university faculty.

Opportunities for those with a bachelor's or master's degree in biological science are expected to be better. The number of science-related jobs in sales, marketing, and research management for which non-Ph.D.s usually qualify is expected to exceed the number of independent research positions. Non-Ph.D.s also may fill positions as science or engineering technicians or as medical health technologists and technicians. Some may become high school biology teachers.

Biological scientists enjoyed very rapid gains in employment between the mid-1980s and mid-1990s— reflecting, in part, increased staffing requirements in new biotechnology companies. Employment growth should slow somewhat, along with a slowdown in the number of new biotechnology firms; some existing firms will merge or be absorbed by larger biotechnology or pharmaceutical firms. Also, some companies are expected to conduct an increasing amount of research in other lower-wage countries, further limiting employment growth. However, much of the basic biological research done in recent years has resulted in new knowledge, including the isolation and identification of genes. Biological scientists will be needed to take this knowledge to the next stage, which is understanding how certain genes function within an entire organism, so that gene therapies can be developed to treat diseases. Even pharmaceutical and other firms not solely engaged in biotechnology use biotechnology techniques extensively, spur-

ring employment increases for biological scientists. For example, biological scientists are continuing to help farmers increase crop yields by pinpointing genes that can help crops such as wheat grow worldwide in areas that currently are hostile to the crop. Expected expansion of research related to health issues such as AIDS, cancer, and Alzheimer's disease also should create more jobs for these scientists. In addition, efforts to discover new and improved ways to clean up and preserve the environment will continue to add to job growth. More biological scientists will be needed to determine the environmental impact of industry and government actions and to prevent or correct environmental problems such as the negative effects of pesticide use. Some biological scientists will find opportunities in environmental regulatory agencies; others will use their expertise to advise lawmakers on legislation to save environmentally sensitive areas. There will continue to be demand for biological scientists specializing in botany, zoology, and marine biology, but opportunities will be limited because of the small size of these fields. New industrial applications of biotechnology, such as changing how companies make ethanol for transportation fuel, also will spur demand for biological scientists.

Marine biology, despite its attractiveness as a career, is a very small specialty within biological science. Prospective marine biology students should be aware that those who would like to enter this specialty far outnumber the very few openings that occur each year for the type of glamorous research jobs that many would like to obtain. Almost all marine biologists who do basic research have a Ph.D.

Biological scientists are less likely to lose their jobs during recessions than are those in many other occupations because many are employed on long-term research projects. However, an economic downturn could influence the amount of money allocated to new research and development efforts, particularly in areas of risky or innovative research. An economic downturn also could limit the possibility of extension or renewal of existing projects.

Earnings

Median annual earnings of biochemists and biophysicists were $68,950 in May 2004. The middle 50 percent earned between $49,430 and $88,540. The lowest 10 percent earned less than $38,710, and the highest 10 percent earned more than $110,660. Median annual earnings of microbiologists were $54,840 in May 2004. The middle 50 percent earned between $41,000 and $74,260. The lowest 10 percent earned less than $32,630, and the highest 10 percent earned more than $101,720. Median annual earnings of zoologists and wildlife biologists were $50,330 in May 2004. The middle 50 percent earned between $39,150 and $63,800. The lowest 10 percent earned less than $31,450, and the highest 10 percent earned more than $81,200. Median annual earnings of biochemists and biophysicists employed in scientific research and development services were $73,900 in May 2004.

According to the National Association of Colleges and Employers, beginning salary offers in July 2005 averaged $31,258 a year for bachelor's degree recipients in biological and life sciences.

In the Federal Government in 2005, general biological scientists in nonsupervisory, supervisory, and managerial positions earned an average salary of $69,908; microbiologists, $80,798; ecologists, $72,021; physiologists, $93,208; geneticists, $85,170; zoologists, $101,601; and botanists, $62,207.

Related Occupations

Many other occupations deal with living organisms and require a level of training similar to that of biological scientists. These include medical scientists, agricultural and food scientists, and conservation scientists and foresters, as well as health occupations such as physicians and surgeons, dentists, and veterinarians.

Sources of Additional Information

For information on careers in the biological sciences, contact:

➤ American Institute of Biological Sciences, 1444 I St. NW., Suite 200, Washington, DC 20005. Internet: **http://www.aibs.org**

For information on careers in biochemistry or biological sciences, contact:

➤ Federation of American Societies for Experimental Biology, 9650 Rockville Pike, Bethesda, MD 20814. Internet: **http://www.faseb.org**

For a brochure titled *Careers in Botany,* contact:

➤ The Botanical Society of America, 4475 Castleman Ave., P.O. Box 299, St. Louis, MI 63166. Internet: **http://www.botany.org**

For information on careers in microbiology, contact:

➤ American Society for Microbiology, Career Information–Education Department, 1752 N St. NW., Washington, DC 20036. Internet: **http://www.asm.org**

Information on obtaining a biological scientist position with the Federal Government is available from the Office of Personnel Management through USAJOBS, the Federal Government's official employment information system. This resource for locating and applying for job opportunities can be accessed through the Internet at **http://www.usajobs.opm.gov** or through an interactive voice response telephone system at (703) 724-1850 or TDD (978) 461-8404. These numbers are not tollfree, and charges may result.

Conservation Scientists and Foresters

(O*NET 19-1031.01, 19-1031.02, 19-1031.03, 19-1032.00)

Significant Points

● About two thirds of salaried conservation scientists and foresters work for Federal, State, or local governments.

● A bachelor's degree in forestry, range management, or a related discipline is the minimum educational requirement.

● Slower than average job growth is projected; most new jobs will be in State and local governments and in private sector forestry and conservation consulting.

Nature of the Work

Forests and rangelands supply wood products, livestock forage, minerals, and water; serve as sites for recreational activities; and provide habitats for wildlife. Conservation scientists and foresters manage their use and development and help to protect these and other natural resources, and for this reason are becoming known as natural resource managers.

Foresters manage forested lands for a variety of purposes. Those working in private industry may manage company-owned forest land or procure timber from private landowners. Company forests usually are managed to produce a sustainable supply of wood for company mills. *Procurement foresters* contact local forest owners and gain permission to take inventory of the type, amount, and location of all standing timber on the property, a process known as timber cruising. These foresters then appraise the timber's worth, negotiate its purchase, and draw up a contract for procurement. Next, they subcontract with loggers or pulpwood cutters for tree removal and aid in laying out roads to access the timber. Throughout the process, foresters maintain close contact with the subcontractor's workers and the landowner to ensure that the work meets the landowner's requirements, as well as Federal, State, and local environmental specifications. Forestry consultants often act as agents for forest owners, monitoring the growth of the timber on the owners' property and negotiating timber sales with industrial procurement foresters.

Foresters, referred to as *land management foresters,* work for both government and private industry and manage and protect the forests and supervise harvests. These foresters supervise the planting and growing of new trees, called regeneration. They choose and direct the preparation of the site using controlled burning, bulldozers, or herbicides to clear weeds, brush, and logging debris. They advise on the type, number, and placement of trees to be planted. Foresters then monitor the seedlings to ensure healthy growth and to determine the best time for harvesting. If they detect signs of disease or harmful insects, they consult with specialists in forest pest management to decide on the best course of treatment. They may also design campgrounds and recreation areas on public lands.

Throughout the forest management and procurement processes, foresters consider the economics as well as the environmental impact on natural resources. To do this, they determine how to conserve wildlife habitats, creek beds, water quality, and soil stability, and how best to comply with environmental regulations. Foresters must balance the desire to conserve forested ecosystems for future generations with the need to use forest resources for recreational or economic purposes.

Foresters use a number of tools to perform their jobs. Clinometers measure the height of trees; diameter tapes measure the diameter; and increment borers and bark gauges measure the growth of trees so that timber volumes can be computed and growth rates estimated. Remote sensing (aerial photographs and other imagery taken from airplanes and satellites) and Geographic Information Systems (GIS) data often are used for mapping large forest areas and for detecting widespread trends of forest and land use. Once the map is generated, the data are digitized to create a computerized inventory of information required to manage the forest land and its resources. Moreover, hand-held computers, Global Positioning Systems (GPS), and World Wide Web-based applications are used extensively.

Conservation scientists manage, improve, and protect the country's natural resources. They work with the landowners and Federal, State, and local governments to devise ways to use and improve the land without damaging the environment. Although conservation scientists mainly advise farmers, farm managers, and ranchers on ways they can improve their land for agricultural purposes and to control erosion, a growing number are advising landowners and governments on recreational uses for the land.

Two of the more common conservation scientists are range managers and soil conservationists. *Range managers,* also called *range conservationists, range ecologists,* or *range scientists,* study, manage, improve, and protect rangelands to maximize their use without damaging the environment. Rangelands cover hundreds of millions of acres of the United States, mostly in Western States and Alaska. They contain many natural resources, including grass and shrubs for animal grazing, wildlife habitats, water from vast watersheds, recreation facilities, and valuable mineral and energy resources. Range managers may inventory soils, plants, and animals, develop resource management plans, help to restore degraded ecosystems, or assist in managing a ranch. For example, they may help ranchers attain optimum livestock production by determining the number and kind of animals to graze, the grazing system to use, and the best season for grazing. At the same time, however, range managers maintain soil stability and vegetation for other uses such as wildlife habitats and outdoor recreation. They also plan and implement revegetation of disturbed sites.

Soil and water conservationists provide technical assistance to farmers, ranchers, forest managers, State and local agencies, and others concerned with the conservation of soil, water, and related natural resources. They develop programs for private landowners designed to make the most productive use of land without damaging it. Soil conservationists also assist landowners by visiting areas with erosion problems, finding the source of the problem, and

Conservation scientists and foresters collect data on stands of trees.

helping landowners and managers develop management practices to combat it. Water conservationists also assist private landowners and Federal, State, and local governments by advising on a broad range of natural resource topics—specifically, issues of water quality, preserving water supplies, groundwater contamination, and management and conservation of water resources.

Conservation scientists and foresters often specialize in one area, such as wildlife management, urban forestry, pest management, native species, or forest economics.

Working Conditions

Working conditions vary considerably. Although some of the work is solitary, foresters and conservation scientists also deal regularly with landowners, loggers, forestry technicians and aides, farmers, ranchers, government officials, special interest groups, and the public in general. Some foresters and conservation scientists work regular hours in offices or labs. Others may split their time between fieldwork and office work, while independent consultants and especially new, less experienced workers spend the majority of their time outdoors overseeing or participating in hands-on work.

The work can be physically demanding. Some conservation scientists and foresters work outdoors in all types of weather, sometimes in isolated areas, and consequently may need to walk long distances through densely wooded land to carry out their work. Foresters also may work long hours fighting fires. Conservation scientists often

are called to prevent erosion after a forest fire, and they provide emergency help after floods, mudslides, and tropical storms.

Training, Other Qualifications, and Advancement

A bachelor's degree in forestry, biology, natural resource management, environmental sciences, or a related discipline is the minimum educational requirement for careers in forestry or conservation science. In the Federal Government, a combination of experience and appropriate education occasionally may substitute for a 4-year forestry degree, but job competition makes this difficult. Foresters who wish to perform specialized research or teach should have an advanced degree, preferably a Ph.D.

Seventeen States have mandatory licensing and/or voluntary registration requirements that a forester must meet in order to acquire the title "professional forester" and practice forestry in the State. Of those 17 States, 9 have mandatory licensing; 8 have mandatory registration. Both licensing and registration requirements usually entail completing a 4-year degree in forestry and several years of forestry work experience. Candidates pursuing licensing also may be required to pass a comprehensive written exam.

Most land-grant colleges and universities offer a bachelor's or higher degree in forestry. The Society of American Foresters accredits about 48 such programs throughout the country. Curriculums stress four components: Forest ecology and biology, measurement of forest resources, management of forest resources, and public policy. Students should balance general science courses such as ecology, biology, tree physiology, taxonomy, and soil formation with technical forestry courses, such as forest inventory or wildlife habitat assessment, remote sensing, land surveying, GPS technology, integrated forest resource management, silviculture, and forest protection. In addition mathematics, statistics, and computer science courses also are recommended. Many forestry curriculums include advanced computer applications such as GIS and resource assessment programs. Courses in resource policy and administration, specifically forest economics and business administration, supplement the student's scientific and technical knowledge. Forestry curriculums increasingly include courses on best management practices, wetlands analysis, and sustainability and regulatory issues in response to the growing focus on protecting forested lands during timber harvesting operations. Prospective foresters should have a strong grasp of Federal, State, and local policy issues and of increasingly numerous and complex environmental regulations that affect many forestry-related activities. Many colleges require students to complete a field session either in a camp operated by the college or in a cooperative work-study program with a Federal or State agency or with private industry. All schools encourage students to take summer jobs that provide experience in forestry or conservation work.

Conservation scientists generally hold a minimum of a bachelor's degree in fields such as: ecology, natural resource management, agriculture, biology, environmental science, or related field. A master's or Ph.D. degree is usually required for teaching and research positions.

Range managers usually have a degree in range management or range science. Nine colleges and universities offer degrees in range management that are accredited by the Society of Range Management. More than forty other schools offer course work in range science or in a closely related discipline offering a range management or range science option. Specialized range management courses combine plant, animal, and soil sciences with principles of ecology and resource management. Desirable electives include economics, statistics, forestry, hydrology, agronomy, wildlife, animal husbandry, computer science, and recreation. Selection of a minor in range management, such as wildlife ecology, watershed management, animal science, or agricultural economics, can often enhance qualifications for certain types of employment.

The Society for Range Management offers two types of certification: one as a certified professional in rangeland management (CPRM) and another as a certified range management Consultant. Candidates seeking certification must have at least a bachelor's degree in range science or a closely related field, have a minimum of 6 years of full-time work experience, and pass a comprehensive written exam.

The Society of American Foresters has a Certified Forester Program. To become certified through this program, a candidate must graduate with at least a bachelor's degree from a forestry program accredited by the Society, or from a forestry program that, though not accredited by the Society, is substantially equivalent. In addition, the candidate must have five years of qualifying professional experience and pass an examination.

Additionally, a graduate with the proper coursework in college can seek certification as a wetland scientist through the Society of Wetland Scientists, and certification as a professional wildlife biologist through the Wildlife Society.

Very few colleges and universities offer degrees in soil conservation. Most soil conservationists have degrees in environmental studies, agronomy, general agriculture, hydrology, or crop or soil science; a few have degrees in related fields such as wildlife biology, forestry, and range management. Programs of study usually include 30 semester hours in natural resources or agriculture, including at least 3 hours in soil science.

In addition to meeting the demands of forestry and conservation research and analysis, foresters and conservation scientists generally must enjoy working outdoors, be able to tolerate extensive walking and other types of physical exertion, and be willing to move to where the jobs are. They also must work well with people and have good communication skills.

Recent forestry and conservation scientist graduates usually work under the supervision of experienced foresters or scientists. After gaining experience, they may advance to more responsible positions. In the Federal Government, most entry-level foresters work in forest resource management. An experienced Federal forester may supervise a ranger district, and may advance to forest supervisor, to regional forester, or to a top administrative position in the national headquarters. In private industry, foresters start by learning the practical and administrative aspects of the business and acquiring comprehensive technical training. They are then introduced to contract writing, timber harvesting, and decisionmaking. Some foresters work their way up to top managerial positions within their companies. Foresters in management usually leave the fieldwork behind, spending more of their time in an office, working with teams to develop management plans and supervising others. After gaining several years of experience, some foresters may become consulting foresters, working alone or with one or several partners. They contract with State or local governments, private landowners, private industry, or other forestry consulting groups.

Soil conservationists usually begin working within one county or conservation district and, with experience, may advance to the area, State, regional, or national level. Also, soil conservationists can transfer to related occupations, such as farm or ranch management advisor or land appraiser.

Employment
Conservation scientists and foresters held about 32,000 jobs in 2004. More than 1 in 3 workers were employed by the Federal Government, mostly in the U.S. Departments of Agriculture (USDA) and Interior. Foresters were concentrated in the USDA's Forest Service; soil conservationists were employed primarily in the USDA's Natural Resource Conservation Service. Most range managers worked in the U.S. Department of the Interior's Bureau of Land Management, the Natural Resource Conservation Service, or the Forest Service. Another 21 percent of conservation scientists and foresters worked for State governments, and about 11 percent worked for local governments. The remainder worked in private industry, mainly in support activities for agriculture and forestry or in wood product manufacturing. Some were self-employed as consultants for private landowners, Federal and State governments, and forestry-related businesses.

Although conservation scientists and foresters work in every State, employment of foresters is concentrated in the Western and Southeastern States, where many national and private forests and parks, and most of the lumber and pulpwood-producing forests, are located. Range managers work almost entirely in the Western States, where most of the rangeland is located. Soil conservationists, on the other hand, are employed in almost every county in the country. Besides the jobs described above, some foresters and conservation scientists held faculty positions in colleges and universities. (See the section on teachers—postsecondary elsewhere in the *Handbook*.)

Job Outlook
Employment of conservation scientists and foresters is expected to increase more slowly than the average for all occupations through 2014. Growth should be strongest in private sector consulting firms. Demand will be spurred by a continuing emphasis on environmental protection, responsible land management, and water-related issues. Growing interest in developing private lands and forests for recreational purposes will generate additional jobs for foresters and conservation scientists. Fire prevention is another area of growth for these two occupations.

Job opportunities for conservation scientists will arise because government regulations, such as those regarding the management of storm water and coastlines, have created demand for persons knowledgeable about runoff and erosion on farms and in cities and suburbs. Soil and water quality experts will be needed as States design initiatives to improve water resources by preventing pollution by agricultural producers and industrial plants.

Overall employment of conservation scientists and foresters is expected to decline slightly in Federal Government, mostly because of budgetary constraints and the trend among all levels of government toward contracting these functions out to private consulting firms. Also, Federal land management agencies, such as the USDA Forest Service, have de-emphasized their timber programs and increasingly focused on wildlife, recreation, and sustaining ecosystems, thereby spurring demand for other life and social scientists rather than for foresters. However, departures of foresters who retire or leave the Government for other reasons will result in many job openings. Additionally, State governments are expected to increase their hiring of conservation scientists and foresters as their budgetary situations improve. A small number of new jobs will result from the need for range and soil conservationists to provide technical assistance to owners of grazing land through the Natural Resource Conservation Service.

Foresters involved with timber harvesting will find good opportunities in the Southeast, where much forested land is privately owned. However, the recent opening of public lands, especially in the West, to commercial activity will also help the outlook for foresters. Salaried foresters working for private industry—such as paper companies, sawmills, and pulpwood mills—and consulting foresters will be needed to provide technical assistance and management plans to landowners.

Scientific research and development services have increased their hiring of conservation scientists and foresters in recent years in response to demand for professionals to prepare environmental impact statements and erosion and sediment control plans, monitor water quality near logging sites, and advise on tree harvesting practices required by Federal, State, or local regulations. Hiring in these firms should continue during the 2004-14 period.

Earnings

Median annual earnings of conservation scientists in May 2004 were $52,480. The middle 50 percent earned between $39,660 and $65,550. The lowest 10 percent earned less than $30,740, and the highest 10 percent earned more than $78,470.

Median annual earnings of foresters in 2004 were $48,230. The middle 50 percent earned between $37,260 and $60,500. The lowest 10 percent earned less than $29,770, and the highest 10 percent earned more than $72,050.

In 2005, most bachelor's degree graduates entering the Federal Government as foresters, range managers, or soil conservationists started at $24,677 or $30,567, depending on academic achievement. Those with a master's degree could start at $37,390 or $45,239. Holders of doctorates could start at $54,221. Beginning salaries were slightly higher in selected areas where the prevailing local pay level was higher. In 2005, the average Federal salary for foresters in nonsupervisory, supervisory, and managerial positions was $63,492; for soil conservationists, $60,671; and for rangeland managers, $58,162.

According to the National Association of Colleges and Employers, graduates with a bachelor's degree in conservation and renewable natural resources received an average starting salary offer of $27,950 in 2005.

In private industry, starting salaries for students with a bachelor's degree were comparable with starting salaries in the Federal Government, but starting salaries in State and local governments were usually lower.

Conservation scientists and foresters who work for Federal, State, and local governments and large private firms generally receive more generous benefits than do those working for smaller firms.

Related Occupations

Conservation scientists and foresters manage, develop, and protect natural resources. Other workers with similar responsibilities include environmental engineers; agricultural and food scientists; biological scientists; environmental scientists and geoscientists; and farmers, ranchers, and agricultural managers.

Sources of Additional Information

For information about the forestry profession and lists of schools offering education in forestry, send a self-addressed, stamped business envelope to:

➤ Society of American Foresters, 5400 Grosvenor Lane, Bethesda, MD 20814-2198. Internet: **http://www.safnet.org**

Information about a career as a range manager, as well as a list of schools offering training, is available from:

➤ Society for Range Management, 445 Union Blvd., Suite 230, Lakewood, CO 80228-1259. Internet: **http://www.rangelands.org**

For information on certification as a professional wildlife biologist, contact:

➤ The Wildlife Society, 5410 Grosvenor Lane, Suite 200, Bethesda, MD 20814-2197. Internet: **http://www.wildlife.org/certification/index.cfm**

Information on obtaining a position as a conservation scientist or forester with the Federal Government is available from the Office of Personnel Management (OPM) through USAJOBS, the Federal Government's official employment information system. This resource for locating and applying for job opportunities can be accessed through the Internet at **http://www.usajobs.opm.gov** or through an interactive voice response telephone system at (703) 724-1850 or TDD (978) 461-8404. These numbers are not toll free, and charges may result.

Medical Scientists

(O*NET 19-1041.00, 19-1042.00)

Significant Points

- Most medical scientists work in research and development.

- Most medical scientists need a Ph.D. degree in a biological science; however, epidemiologists typically require a master's degree in public health or, in some cases, a Ph.D. or medical degree.

- Despite projected rapid job growth, competition is expected for most positions.

Nature of the Work

Medical scientists research human diseases in order to improve human health. Most medical scientists conduct biomedical research and development to advance knowledge of life processes and living organisms, including viruses, bacteria, and other infectious agents. Past research has resulted in advances in diagnosis, treatment, and prevention of many diseases. Basic medical research continues to provide the building blocks necessary to develop solutions to human health problems, such as vaccines and medicines. Medical scientists also engage in clinical investigation, technical writing, drug application review, patent examination, and related activities.

Medical scientists study biological systems to understand the causes of disease and other health problems and to develop treatments and research tools and techniques, many of which have medical applications. These scientists try to identify changes in a cell or in chromosomes that signal the development of medical problems, such as different types of cancer. For example, medical scientists involved in cancer research may formulate a combination of drugs that will lessen the effects of the disease. Medical scientists who are also physicians can administer these drugs to patients in clinical trials, monitor their reactions, and observe the results. Those who are not physicians normally collaborate with a physician who deals directly with patients. Medical scientists examine the results of clinical trials and, if necessary, adjust the dosage levels to reduce negative side effects or to try to induce even better results. In addition to developing treatments for health problems, medical scientists attempt to discover ways to prevent health problems, for example, by affirming the link between smoking and lung cancer or between alcoholism and liver disease.

Many medical scientists work independently in private industry, university, or government laboratories, often exploring new areas of research or expanding on specialized research that they began in graduate school. Medical scientists working in colleges and universities, hospitals, and nonprofit medical research organizations typically submit grant proposals to obtain funding for their projects. Colleges and universities, private industry, and Federal Government agencies, such as the National Institutes of Health and the National Science Foundation, contribute greatly to the support of scientists whose research proposals are determined to be financially feasible and to have the potential to advance new ideas or processes.

Medical scientists who work in applied research or product development use knowledge discovered through basic research to develop new drugs and medical treatments. They usually have less autonomy than basic medical researchers to choose the emphasis of their research, relying instead on market-driven forces arising from their firm's products and goals. Medical scientists doing applied research and product development in private industry may be required to express their research plans or results to nonscientists who are in a position to reject or approve their ideas; thus, they must understand the impact of their work on business. Scientists increasingly work as part of teams, interacting with engineers, scientists of other disciplines, business managers, and technicians.

Medical scientists who conduct research usually work in laboratories and use electron microscopes, computers, thermal cyclers, or a wide variety of other equipment. Some may work directly with individual patients or larger groups as they administer drugs and monitor and observe the patients during clinical trials. Medical scientists who are also physicians may administer gene therapy to human patients, draw blood, excise tissue, or perform other invasive procedures.

Some medical scientists work in managerial, consulting, or administrative positions, usually after spending some time doing research and learning about the firm, agency, or project. In the 1980s, swift advances in basic medical knowledge related to genetics and molecules spurred growth in the field of biotechnology. Medical scientists using this technology manipulate the genetic material of animals, attempting to make organisms more productive or resistant to disease. Research using biotechnology techniques, such as recombining DNA, has led to the discovery of important drugs, including human insulin and growth hormone. Many other substances not previously available in large quantities are now produced by biotechnological means; some may one day be useful in treating diseases such as Parkinson's or Alzheimer's. Today, many medical scientists are involved in the science of genetic engineering—isolating, identifying, and sequencing human genes and then determining their function. This work continues to lead to the discovery of the genes associated with specific diseases and inherited traits, such as certain types of cancer or obesity. These advances in biotechnology have opened up research opportunities in almost all areas of medical science.

Some medical scientists specialize in epidemiology. This branch of medical science investigates and describes the determinants of disease, disability, and other health outcomes and develops the means for prevention and control. Epidemiologists may study many different diseases, such as tuberculosis, influenza, or cholera, often focusing on epidemics.

Most medical scientists need a Ph.D. in a biological science.

Epidemiologists can be separated into two groups—research and clinical. Research epidemiologists conduct research in an effort to eradicate or control infectious diseases that affect the entire body, such as AIDS or typhus. Others may focus only on localized infections of the brain, lungs, or digestive tract, for example. Research epidemiologists work at colleges and universities, schools of public health, medical schools, and research and development services firms. For example, Federal Government agencies, such as the U.S. Department of Defense, may contract with a research firm's epidemiologists to evaluate the incidence of malaria in certain parts of the world. While some perform consulting services, other research epidemiologists may work as college and university faculty.

Clinical epidemiologists work primarily in consulting roles at hospitals, informing the medical staff of infectious outbreaks and providing containment solutions. These epidemiologists sometimes are referred to as infection control professionals, and some of them are also physicians. Epidemiologists who are not physicians often collaborate with physicians to find ways to contain diseases and outbreaks. In addition to traditional duties of studying and controlling diseases, clinical epidemiologists also may be required to develop standards and guidelines for the treatment and control of communicable diseases. Some clinical epidemiologists may work in outpatient settings.

Working Conditions
Medical scientists typically work regular hours in offices or laboratories and usually are not exposed to unsafe or unhealthy conditions. However, those scientists who work with dangerous organisms or toxic substances in the laboratory must follow strict safety procedures to avoid contamination. Medical scientists also spend time working in clinics and hospitals administering drugs and treatments to patients in clinical trials. On occasion, epidemiologists may be required to work evenings and weekends to attend meetings and hearings for medical investigations.

Some medical scientists depend on grant money to support their research. They may be under pressure to meet deadlines and to conform to rigid grant-writing specifications when preparing proposals to seek new or extended funding.

Training, Other Qualifications, and Advancement
A Ph.D. degree in a biological science is the minimum education required for most prospective medical scientists, except epidemiologists, because the work of medical scientists is almost entirely research oriented. A Ph.D. degree qualifies one to do research on basic life processes or on particular medical problems or diseases and to analyze and interpret the results of experiments on patients. Some medical scientists obtain a medical degree instead of a Ph.D., but may not be licensed physicians because they have not taken the State licensing examination or completed a residency program, typically because they prefer research to clinical practice. Medical scientists who administer drug or gene therapy to human patients, or who otherwise interact medically with patients—drawing blood, excising tissue, or performing other invasive procedures—must be licensed physicians. To be licensed, physicians must graduate from an accredited medical school, pass a licensing examination, and complete 1 to 7 years of graduate medical education. (See physicians and surgeons elsewhere in the *Handbook*.) It is particularly helpful for medical scientists to earn both Ph.D. and medical degrees.

Students planning careers as medical scientists should have a bachelor's degree in a biological science. In addition to required courses in chemistry and biology, undergraduates should study allied disciplines, such as mathematics, engineering, physics, and computer science, or courses in their field of interest. Once they have completed undergraduate studies, they can then select a specialty area for their advanced degree, such as cytology, bioinformatics, genomics, or pathology. In addition to formal education, medical scientists usually spend several years in a postdoctoral position before they apply for permanent jobs. Postdoctoral work provides valuable laboratory experience, including experience in specific processes and techniques such as gene splicing, which is transferable to other research projects. In some institutions, the postdoctoral position can lead to a permanent job.

Medical scientists should be able to work independently or as part of a team and be able to communicate clearly and concisely, both orally and in writing. Those in private industry, especially those who aspire to consulting and administrative positions, should possess strong communication skills so that they can provide instruction and advice to physicians and other health care professionals.

The minimum educational requirement for epidemiology is a master's degree from a school of public health. Some jobs require a Ph.D. or medical degree, depending on the work performed. Epidemiologists who work in hospitals and health care centers often must have a medical degree with specific training in infectious diseases. Currently, about 140 infectious disease training programs exist in 42 States. Some employees in research epidemiology positions are required to be licensed physicians because they must administer drugs in clinical trials.

Epidemiologists who perform laboratory tests often require the knowledge and expertise of a licensed physician in order to administer drugs to patients in clinical trials. Epidemiologists who are not physicians frequently work closely with one.

Few students select epidemiology for undergraduate study. Undergraduates, nonetheless, should study biological sciences and should have a solid background in chemistry, mathematics, and computer science. Once a student is prepared for graduate studies, he or she can choose a specialty within epidemiology. For example, those interested in studying environmental epidemiology should focus on environmental coursework, such as water pollution, air pollution, or pesticide use. The core work of environmental studies includes toxicology and molecular biology, and students may continue with advanced coursework in environmental or occupational epidemiology. Other specialty areas that students can pursue include infectious process, infection control precautions, surveillance methodology, and outbreak investigation. Some epidemiologists begin their careers in other health care occupations, such as registered nurse and medical technologist.

The Association for Professionals in Infection Control and Epidemiology (APIC) offers continuing-education courses and certification programs in infection prevention and control and applied epidemiology. To become certified as an infection control professional, applicants are required by a certified board to pass an examination for a one-time fee. Certification is recommended for those seeking advancement and for those seeking to continually upgrade their knowledge in a rapidly evolving field.

Employment

Medical scientists held about 77,000 jobs in 2004. Epidemiologists accounted for only 4,800 of that total. In addition, many medical scientists held faculty positions in colleges and universities, but they are classified as college or university faculty. (See teachers—postsecondary elsewhere in the *Handbook.*)

About 24 percent of medical scientists were employed in government; 24 percent were employed in scientific research and development services firms ; 14 percent were employed in pharmaceutical and medicine manufacturing; 9 percent were employed in private hospitals; and most of the remainder were employed in private educational services and ambulatory health care services.

Among epidemiologists, 50 percent were employed in government; 23 percent were employed in management, scientific, and technical consulting services; 12 percent were employed in scientific research and development services; and 8 percent were employed in private hospitals.

Job Outlook

Employment of medical scientists is expected to grow much faster than the average for all occupations through 2014. Despite projected rapid job growth, doctoral degree holders can expect to face considerable competition for basic research positions. The Federal Government funds much basic research and development, including many areas of medical research. Recent budget increases at the National Institutes of Health have led to large increases in Federal basic research and development expenditures, with the number of grants awarded to researchers growing in number and dollar amount. However, the increase in expenditures is expected to slow significantly over the 2004-14 projection period, resulting in a highly competitive environment for winning and renewing research grants. In addition, if the number of advanced degrees awarded continues to grow, applicants are likely to face even more competition.

Medical scientists enjoyed rapid gains in employment between the mid-1980s and mid-1990s—reflecting, in part, increased staffing requirements in new biotechnology companies. Job growth should be dampened somewhat as increases in the number of new biotechnology firms slow down and as existing firms merge or are absorbed by larger, more established biotechnology or pharmaceutical firms. Also, some companies are expected to conduct an increasing amount of research in other lower-wage countries, further limiting employment growth. However, much of the basic medical research done in recent years has resulted in new knowledge, including the isolation and identification of new genes. Medical scientists will be needed to take this knowledge to the next stage—understanding how certain genes function within an entire organism—so that gene therapies can be developed to treat diseases. Even pharmaceutical and other firms not solely engaged in biotechnology are expected to increasingly use biotechnology techniques, thus creating employment for medical scientists.

Expected expansion in research related to health issues such as AIDS, cancer, and Alzheimer's disease, along with treating growing threats such as the increase in antibiotic resistance, also should result in employment growth. Moreover, environmental conditions such as overcrowding and the increasing frequency of international travel will tend to spread existing diseases and give rise to new ones. Medical scientists will continue to be needed because they greatly contribute to the development of many treatments and medicines that improve human health.

Opportunities in epidemiology also should be highly competitive, as the number of available positions remains limited. However, an increasing focus on monitoring patients at hospitals and health care centers to ensure positive patient outcomes will contribute to job growth. In addition, a heightened awareness of bioterrorism and rare, but infectious diseases such as West Nile Virus or severe acute respiratory syndrome (SARS) should spur demand for these workers. As hospitals enhance their infection control programs, many will seek to boost the quality and quantity of their staff. Besides job openings due to employment growth, additional openings will result as workers leave the labor force or transfer to other occupations.

Medical scientists and some epidemiologists are less likely to lose their jobs during recessions than are those in many other occupations because they are employed on long-term research projects. However, a recession could influence the amount of money allocated to new research and development, particularly in areas of risky or innovative medical research. A recession also could limit extensions or renewals of existing projects.

Earnings

Median annual earnings of medical scientists, except epidemiologists, were $61,320 in May 2004. The middle 50 percent of these workers earned between $44,120 and $86,830. The lowest 10 percent earned less than $33,030, and the highest 10 percent earned more than $114,360. Median annual earnings in the industries employing the largest numbers of medical scientists in May 2004 were:

Pharmaceutical and medicine manufacturing	$76,800
Scientific research and development services	65,110
General medical and surgical hospitals	55,410
Colleges, universities, and professional schools	45,600

Median annual earnings of epidemiologists were $54,800 in May 2004. The middle 50 percent earned between $45,320 and $67,160. The lowest 10 percent earned less than $36,130, and the highest 10 percent earned more than $82,310.

Related Occupations

Many other occupations deal with living organisms and require a level of training similar to that of medical scientists. These occupations include biological scientists, agricultural and food scientists, and health occupations such as physicians and surgeons, dentists, and veterinarians.

Sources of Additional Information

For a brochure entitled *Is a Career in the Pharmaceutical Sciences Right for Me?*, contact:
➤ American Association of Pharmaceutical Scientists (AAPS), 2107 Wilson Blvd., Suite 700, Arlington, VA 22201.

For a career brochure entitled *A Million and One,* contact:
➤ American Society for Microbiology, Career Information—Education Department, 1752 N St. NW., Washington, DC 20036-2804. Internet: **http://www.asm.org**

For information on infectious diseases training programs, contact:
➤ Infectious Diseases Society of America, Guide to Training Programs, 66 Canal Center Plaza, Suite 600, Alexandria, VA 22314. Internet: **http://www.idsociety.org**

Information on obtaining a medical scientist position with the Federal Government is available from the Office of Personnel Management through USAJOBS, the Federal Government's official employment information system. This resource for locating and applying for job opportunities can be accessed through the Internet at **http://www.usajobs.opm.gov** or through an interactive voice response telephone system at (703) 724-1850 or TDD (978) 461-8404. These numbers are not tollfree, and charges may result.

Physical Scientists

Atmospheric Scientists

(O*NET 19-2021.00)

Significant Points

- 4 in 10 atmospheric scientists work for the Federal Government, the largest employer of these workers.

- A bachelor's degree in meteorology, or in a closely related field with courses in meteorology, is the minimum educational requirement; a master's degree is necessary for some positions, and a doctoral degree (Ph.D.) is required for most basic research positions.

- Job opportunities are expected to be better in private industry than in the Federal Government; opportunities in broadcasting, however, are rare and highly competitive.

Nature of the Work

Atmospheric science is the study of the atmosphere—the blanket of air covering the Earth. Atmospheric scientists, commonly called *meteorologists*, study the atmosphere's physical characteristics, motions, and processes, and the way in which these factors affect the rest of our environment. The best known application of this knowledge is forecasting the weather. In addition to predicting the weather, atmospheric scientists attempt to identify and interpret climate trends, understand past weather, and analyze today's weather. Weather information and meteorological research are also applied in air-pollution control, agriculture, forestry, air and sea transportation, defense, and the study of possible trends in the Earth's climate, such as global warming, droughts, and ozone depletion.

Atmospheric scientists who forecast the weather, known professionally as *operational meteorologists*, are the largest group of specialists. They study information on air pressure, temperature, humidity, and wind velocity; and they apply physical and mathematical relationships to make short-range and long-range weather forecasts. Their data come from weather satellites, radars, sensors, and stations in many parts of the world. Meteorologists use sophisticated computer models of the world's atmosphere to make long-term, short-term, and local-area forecasts. More accurate instruments for measuring and observing weather conditions, as well as high-speed computers to process and analyze weather data, have revolutionized weather forecasting. Using satellite data, climate theory, and sophisticated computer models of the world's atmosphere, meteorologists can more effectively interpret the results of these models to make local-area weather predictions. These forecasts inform not only the general public, but also those who need accurate weather information for both economic and safety reasons, such as the shipping, air transportation, agriculture, fishing, forestry, and utilities industries.

The use of weather balloons, launched a few times a day to measure wind, temperature, and humidity in the upper atmosphere, is currently supplemented by sophisticated atmospheric monitoring equipment that transmits data as frequently as every few minutes. Doppler radar, for example, can detect airflow patterns in violent storm systems—allowing forecasters to better predict thunderstorms, flash floods, tornadoes, and other hazardous winds, and to monitor the direction and intensity of storms.

Some atmospheric scientists work in research. *Physical meteorologists*, for example, study the atmosphere's chemical and physical properties; the transmission of light, sound, and radio waves; and the transfer of energy in the atmosphere. They also study factors affecting the formation of clouds, rain, and snow; the dispersal of air pollutants over urban areas; and other weather phenomena, such as the mechanics of severe storms. *Synoptic meteorologists* develop new tools for weather forecasting using computers and sophisticated mathematical models of atmospheric activity. *Climatologists* study climatic variations spanning hundreds or even millions of years. They also may collect, analyze, and interpret past records of wind, rainfall, sunshine, and temperature in specific areas or

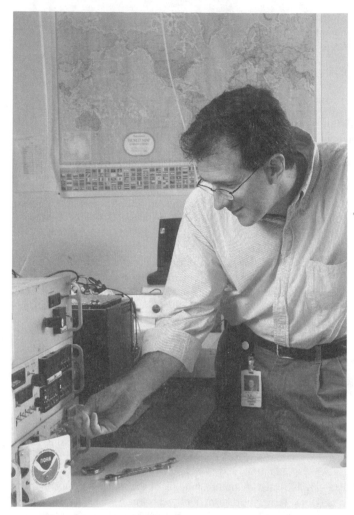

Because most weather stations operate around the clock 7 days a week, jobs in such facilities usually involve night, weekend, and holiday work.

regions. Their studies are used to design buildings, plan heating and cooling systems, and aid in effective land use and agricultural production. Environmental problems, such as pollution and shortages of fresh water, have widened the scope of the meteorological profession. *Environmental meteorologists* study these problems and may evaluate and report on air quality for environmental impact statements. Other research meteorologists examine the most effective ways to control or diminish air pollution.

Working Conditions

Most weather stations operate around the clock, 7 days a week. Jobs in such facilities usually involve night, weekend, and holiday work, often with rotating shifts. During weather emergencies, such as hurricanes, operational meteorologists may work overtime. Operational meteorologists also are often under pressure to meet forecast deadlines. Weather stations are found everywhere—at airports, in or near cities, and in isolated and remote areas. Some atmospheric scientists also spend time observing weather conditions and collecting data from aircraft. Weather forecasters who work for radio or television stations broadcast their reports from station studios, and may work evenings and weekends. Meteorologists in smaller weather offices often work alone; in larger ones, they work as part of a team. Meteorologists who are not involved in forecasting tasks work regular hours, usually in offices. Those who work for private consulting firms or for companies analyzing

and monitoring emissions to improve air quality usually work with other scientists or engineers; fieldwork and travel may be common for these workers.

Training, Other Qualifications, and Advancement

A bachelor's degree in meteorology or atmospheric science, or in a closely related field with courses in meteorology, usually is the minimum educational requirement for an entry-level position as an atmospheric scientist.

The preferred educational requirement for entry-level meteorologists in the Federal Government is a bachelor's degree—not necessarily in meteorology—with at least 24 semester hours of meteorology courses, including 6 hours in the analysis and prediction of weather systems, 6 hours of atmospheric dynamics and thermodynamics, 3 hours of physical meteorology, and 2 hours of remote sensing of the atmosphere or instrumentation. Other required courses include 3 semester hours of ordinary differential equations, 6 hours of college physics, and at least 9 hours of courses appropriate for a physical science major—such as statistics, chemistry, physical oceanography, physical climatology, physical hydrology, radiative transfer, aeronomy, advanced thermodynamics, advanced electricity and magnetism, light and optics, and computer science. Sometimes, a combination of education and appropriate experience may be substituted for a degree.

Although positions in operational meteorology are available for those with only a bachelor's degree, obtaining a second bachelor's degree or a master's degree enhances employment opportunities, pay, and advancement potential. A master's degree usually is necessary for conducting applied research and development, and a Ph.D. is required for most basic research positions. Students planning on a career in research and development do not necessarily need to major in atmospheric science or meteorology as an undergraduate. In fact, a bachelor's degree in mathematics, physics, or engineering provides excellent preparation for graduate study in atmospheric science.

Because atmospheric science is a small field, relatively few colleges and universities offer degrees in meteorology or atmospheric science, although many departments of physics, earth science, geography, and geophysics offer atmospheric science and related courses. In 2005, the American Meteorological Society (AMS) approved approximately 100 undergraduate and graduate atmospheric science programs. Many of these programs combine the study of meteorology with another field, such as agriculture, hydrology, oceanography, engineering, or physics. For example, hydrometeorology is the blending of hydrology (the science of Earth's water) and meteorology, and is the field concerned with the effect of precipitation on the hydrologic cycle and the environment.

Prospective students should make certain that courses required by the National Weather Service and other employers are offered at the college they are considering. Computer science courses, additional meteorology courses, a strong background in mathematics and physics, and good communication skills are important to prospective employers.

Students should also take courses in subjects that are most relevant to their desired area of specialization. For example, those who wish to become broadcast meteorologists for radio or television stations should develop excellent communication skills through courses in speech, journalism, and related fields. Students interested in air quality work should take courses in chemistry and supplement their technical training with coursework in policy or government affairs. Prospective meteorologists seeking opportunities at weather consulting firms should possess knowledge of business, statistics, and economics, as an increasing emphasis is being placed on long-range seasonal forecasting to assist businesses.

Beginning atmospheric scientists often do routine data collection, computation, or analysis, and some basic forecasting. Entry-level operational meteorologists in the Federal Government usually are placed in intern positions for training and experience. During this period, they learn about the Weather Service's forecasting equipment and procedures, and rotate to different offices to learn about various weather systems. After completing the training period, they are assigned to a permanent duty station. Experienced meteorologists may advance to supervisory or administrative jobs, or may handle more complex forecasting jobs. After several years of experience, some meteorologists establish their own weather consulting services.

AMS offers professional certification of consulting meteorologists, administered by a Board of Certified Consulting Meteorologists. Applicants must meet formal education requirements (but not necessarily have a college degree), pass an examination to demonstrate thorough meteorological knowledge, have a minimum of 5 years of experience or a combination of experience plus an advanced degree, and provide character references from fellow professionals. In addition, AMS also offers professional certification for broadcast meteorologists.

Employment

Atmospheric scientists held about 7,400 jobs in 2004. The Federal Government was the largest single employer of civilian meteorologists, accounting for about 2,900. The National Oceanic and Atmospheric Administration (NOAA) employed most Federal meteorologists in National Weather Service stations throughout the Nation; the remainder of NOAA's meteorologists worked mainly in research and development or management. The U.S. Department of Defense employed several hundred civilian meteorologists. Others worked for professional, scientific, and technical services firms, including private weather consulting services; radio and television broadcasting; air carriers; and State government.

Although several hundred people teach atmospheric science and related courses in college and university departments of meteorology or atmospheric science, physics, earth science, or geophysics, these individuals are classified as college or university faculty, rather than atmospheric scientists. (See the statement on postsecondary teachers elsewhere in the *Handbook*.)

In addition to civilian meteorologists, hundreds of Armed Forces members are involved in forecasting and other meteorological work. (See the statement on job opportunities in the Armed Forces elsewhere in the *Handbook*.)

Job Outlook

Employment of atmospheric scientists is projected to increase about as fast as average for all occupations through 2014. The National Weather Service has completed an extensive modernization of its weather forecasting equipment and finished all hiring of meteorologists needed to staff the upgraded stations, however. The Service has no plans to increase the number of weather stations or the number of meteorologists in existing stations. Employment of meteorologists in other Federal agencies is expected to remain stable.

In private industry, on the other hand, job opportunities for atmospheric scientists are expected to be better than in the Federal Government over the 2004-14 period. As research leads to continuing improvements in weather forecasting, demand should grow for private weather consulting firms to provide more

detailed information than has formerly been available, especially to climate-sensitive industries. Farmers, commodity investors, radio and television stations, and utilities, transportation, and construction firms can greatly benefit from additional weather information more closely targeted to their needs than the general information provided by the National Weather Service. Additionally, research on seasonal and other long-range forecasting is yielding positive results, which should spur demand for more atmospheric scientists to interpret these forecasts and advise climate-sensitive industries. However, because many customers for private weather services are in industries sensitive to fluctuations in the economy, the sales and growth of private weather services depend on the health of the economy.

There will continue to be demand for atmospheric scientists to analyze and monitor the dispersion of pollutants into the air to ensure compliance with Federal environmental regulations, but related employment increases are expected to be small. Efforts toward making and improving global weather observations also could have a positive impact on employment. Opportunities in broadcasting are rare and highly competitive, however, making for very few job openings in this industry. Prospects for academic positions may improve. While a competitive job market will continue to exist for independent research positions in universities and for college and university faculty, opportunities are expected to be better than in the past as an increasing number of faculty are expected to retire through the projection period.

Earnings

Median annual earnings of atmospheric scientists in May 2004 were $70,100. The middle 50 percent earned between $48,880 and $86,610. The lowest 10 percent earned less than $34,590, and the highest 10 percent earned more than $106,020.

The average salary for meteorologists in nonsupervisory, supervisory, and managerial positions employed by the Federal Government was about $80,499 in 2005. Meteorologists in the Federal Government with a bachelor's degree and no experience received a starting salary of $27,955 or $34,544, depending on their college grades. Those with a master's degree could start at $42,090 or $54,393, and those with a Ph.D. could begin at $70,280. Beginning salaries for all degree levels are slightly higher in areas of the country where the prevailing local pay level is higher.

Related Occupations

Workers in other occupations concerned with the physical environment include environmental scientists and geoscientists, physicists and astronomers, mathematicians, and civil, chemical, and environmental engineers.

Sources of Additional Information

Information about careers in meteorology and a listing of colleges and universities offering meteorology programs is provided by the American Meteorological Society on the Internet at: **http://www.ametsoc.org/AMS**.

Information on obtaining a position as a meteorologist with the Federal Government is available from the Office of Personnel Management through USAJOBS, the Federal Government's official employment information system. This resource for locating and applying for job opportunities can be accessed through the Internet at **http://www.usajobs.opm.gov** or through an interactive voice response telephone system at (703) 724-1850 or TDD (978) 461-8404. These numbers are not tollfree, and charges may result.

Chemists and Materials Scientists

(O*NET 19-2031.00, 19-2032.00)

Significant Points

- A bachelor's degree in chemistry or a related discipline is the minimum educational requirement; however, many research jobs require a master's degree, or more often a Ph.D.

- Slower-than-average growth in employment is projected.

- Job growth will be concentrated in pharmaceutical and medicine manufacturing companies and in professional, scientific, and technical services firms.

- Graduates with a bachelor's degree will have opportunities at smaller research organizations; those with a master's degree, and particularly those with a Ph.D., will enjoy better opportunities at larger pharmaceutical and biotechnology firms.

Nature of the Work

Everything in the environment, whether naturally occurring or of human design, is composed of chemicals. Chemists and materials scientists search for and use new knowledge about chemicals. Chemical research has led to the discovery and development of new and improved synthetic fibers, paints, adhesives, drugs, cosmetics, electronic components, lubricants, and thousands of other products. Chemists and materials scientists also develop processes such as improved oil refining and petrochemical processing that save energy and reduce pollution. Research on the chemistry of living things spurs advances in medicine, agriculture, food processing, and other fields.

Materials scientists study the structures and chemical properties of various materials to develop new products or enhance existing ones. They also determine ways to strengthen or combine materials or develop new materials for use in a variety of products. Materials science encompasses the natural and synthetic materials used in a wide range of products and structures, from airplanes, cars, and bridges to clothing and household goods. Companies whose products are made of metals, ceramics, and rubber employ most materials scientists. Other applications of materials science include studies of superconducting materials, graphite materials, integrated-circuit chips, and fuel cells. Materials scientists, applying chemistry and physics, study all aspects of these materials. Chemistry plays an increasingly dominant role in materials science because it provides information about the structure and composition of materials. Materials scientists often specialize in specific areas such as ceramics or metals.

Many chemists and materials scientists work in research and development (R&D). In basic research, they investigate properties, composition, and structure of matter and the laws that govern the combination of elements and reactions of substances. In applied R&D, they create new products and processes or improve existing ones, often using knowledge gained from basic research. For example, synthetic rubber and plastics resulted from research on small molecules uniting to form large ones, a process called polymerization. R&D chemists and materials scientists use computers and a wide variety of sophisticated laboratory instrumentation for modeling and simulation in their work.

The use of computers to analyze complex data has allowed chemists and materials scientists to practice combinatorial chemistry. This technique makes and tests large quantities of chemical compounds simultaneously to find those with certain desired properties. Combinatorial chemistry has allowed chemists to produce thousands of compounds more quickly and inexpensively than was formerly possible and assisted in the completion of the sequencing of human genes. Today, specialty chemists, such as medicinal and organic chemists, are working with life scientists to translate this knowledge into new drugs.

Chemists also work in production and quality control in chemical manufacturing plants. They prepare instructions for plant workers that specify ingredients, mixing times, and temperatures for each stage in the process. They also monitor automated processes to ensure proper product yield and test samples of raw materials or finished products to ensure that they meet industry and government standards, including regulations governing pollution. Chemists report and document test results and analyze those results in hopes of improving existing theories or developing new test methods.

Chemists often specialize. *Analytical chemists* determine the structure, composition, and nature of substances by examining and identifying their various elements or compounds. These chemists are absolutely crucial to the pharmaceutical industry because pharmaceutical companies need to know the identity of compounds that they hope to turn into drugs. Furthermore, analytical chemists study the relations and interactions of the parts of compounds and develop analytical techniques. They also identify the presence and concentration of chemical pollutants in air, water, and soil. *Organic chemists* study the chemistry of the vast number of carbon compounds that make up all living things. Organic chemists who synthesize elements or simple compounds to create new compounds or substances that have different properties and applications have developed many commercial products, such as drugs, plastics, and elastomers (elastic substances similar to rubber). *Inorganic chemists* study compounds consisting mainly of elements other than carbon, such as those in electronic components. *Physical* and *theoretical chemists* study the physical characteristics of atoms and molecules and the theoretical properties of matter and investigate how chemical reactions work. Their research may result in new and better energy sources. *Macromolecular chemists* study the behavior of atoms and molecules. *Medicinal chemists* study the structural properties of compounds intended for applications to human medicine. *Materials chemists* study and develop new materials to improve existing products or make new ones. In fact, virtually all chemists are involved in this quest in one way or another. Developments in the field of chemistry that involve life sciences will expand, resulting in more interaction among biologists, engineers, computer specialists, and chemists. (*Biochemists*, whose work encompasses both biology and chemistry, are discussed in the *Handbook* statement on biological scientists.)

Working Conditions

Chemists and materials scientists usually work regular hours in offices and laboratories. R&D chemists and materials scientists spend much time in laboratories but also work in offices when they do theoretical research or plan, record, and report on their lab research. Although some laboratories are small, others are large enough to incorporate prototype chemical manufacturing facilities as well as advanced equipment for chemists. In addition to working in a laboratory, materials scientists also work with engineers and processing specialists in industrial manufacturing facilities. After a material is sold, materials scientists often help customers tailor the material to suit their needs. Chemists do some of their work in a chemical plant or outdoors—while gathering water samples to test for pollutants, for example. Some chemists are exposed to health or safety hazards when handling certain chemicals, but there is little risk if proper procedures are followed.

Training, Other Qualifications, and Advancement

A bachelor's degree in chemistry or a related discipline usually is the minimum educational requirement for entry-level chemist jobs. However, many research jobs require a master's degree, or more often a Ph.D. While some materials scientists hold a degree in materials science, a bachelor's degree in chemistry, physics, or electrical engineering also is accepted. Many R&D jobs require a Ph.D. in materials science or a related science.

Many colleges and universities offer degree programs in chemistry. In 2005, the American Chemical Society (ACS) approved 631 bachelor's, 308 master's, and 192 doctoral degree programs. In addition to these schools, several hundred colleges and universities also offer advanced degree programs in chemistry. The number of colleges that offer a degree program in materials science is small but gradually increasing.

Students planning careers as chemists and materials scientists should take courses in science and mathematics, should like working with their hands building scientific apparatus and performing laboratory experiments, and should like computer modeling. Perseverance, curiosity, and the ability to concentrate on detail and to work independently are essential. Interaction among specialists in this field is increasing, especially for specialty chemists in drug development. One type of chemist often relies on the findings of another type of chemist. For example, an organic chemist must understand findings on the identity of compounds prepared by an analytical chemist.

In addition to required courses in analytical, inorganic, organic, and physical chemistry, undergraduate chemistry majors usually study biological sciences; mathematics; physics; and increasingly, computer science. Computer courses are essential because employ-

ers prefer job applicants who are able to apply computer skills to modeling and simulation tasks and operate computerized laboratory equipment. This is increasingly important as combinatorial chemistry and high-throughput screening (HTS)—the ability to enhance processing capacity—techniques are more widely applied. Those interested in the environmental field also should take courses in environmental studies and become familiar with current legislation and regulations. Specific courses should include atmospheric chemistry, water chemistry, soil chemistry, and energy. Courses in statistics are useful because both chemists and materials scientists need the ability to apply basic statistical techniques.

Because R&D chemists and materials scientists are increasingly expected to work on interdisciplinary teams, some understanding of other disciplines, including business and marketing or economics, is desirable, along with leadership ability and good oral and written communication skills. Experience, either in academic laboratories or through internships, fellowships, or work-study programs in industry, also is useful. Some employers of research chemists, particularly in the pharmaceutical industry, prefer to hire individuals with several years of postdoctoral experience.

Graduate students typically specialize in a subfield of chemistry, such as analytical chemistry or polymer chemistry, depending on their interests and the kind of work they wish to do. For example, those interested in doing drug research in the pharmaceutical industry usually develop a strong background in medicinal or synthetic organic chemistry. However, students normally need not specialize at the undergraduate level. In fact, undergraduates who are broadly trained have more flexibility when job hunting or changing jobs than if they have narrowly defined their interests. Most employers provide new graduates additional training or education.

In government or industry, beginning chemists with a bachelor's degree work in quality control, perform analytical testing, or assist senior chemists in R&D laboratories. Many employers prefer chemists and materials scientists with a Ph.D., or at least a master's degree, to lead basic and applied research. Chemists who hold a Ph.D. and have previous industrial experience may be particularly attractive to employers because such people are more likely to understand the complex regulations that apply to the pharmaceutical industry. Within materials science, a broad background in various sciences is preferred. This broad base may be obtained through degrees in physics, engineering, or chemistry. While many companies prefer hiring Ph.D.s, some may employ materials scientists with bachelor's and master's degrees.

Employment

Chemists and materials scientists held about 90,000 jobs in 2004. About 43 percent of all chemists and material scientists are employed in manufacturing firms—mostly in the chemical manufacturing industry, which includes firms that produce plastics and synthetic materials, drugs, soaps and cleaners, pesticides and fertilizers, paint, industrial organic chemicals, and other chemical products. About 15 percent of chemists and material scientists work in scientific research and development services; 12 percent work in architectural, engineering, and related services. In addition, thousands of people with a background in chemistry and materials science hold teaching positions in high schools and in colleges and universities. (See the statements on teachers—postsecondary, and teachers—preschool, kindergarten, elementary, middle, and secondary elsewhere in the *Handbook*.)

Chemists and materials scientists are employed in all parts of the country, but they are mainly concentrated in large industrial areas.

Job Outlook

Employment of chemists is expected to grow more slowly than the average rate for all occupations through 2014. Job growth will be concentrated in pharmaceutical and medicine manufacturing and in

Many research jobs as chemists require at least a master's degree, or more often a Ph.D.

professional, scientific, and technical services firms. Employment in the nonpharmaceutical segments of the chemical industry, a major employer of chemists, is expected to decline over the projection period. Consequently, new chemists at all levels may experience competition for jobs in these segments, including basic chemical manufacturing and synthetic materials. Graduates with a bachelor's degree may find science-related jobs in sales, marketing, and middle management. Some become chemical technicians or technologists or high school chemistry teachers. In addition, bachelor's degree holders are increasingly finding assistant research positions at smaller research organizations. Graduates with a master's degree, and particularly those with a Ph.D., will enjoy better opportunities at larger pharmaceutical and biotechnology firms. Furthermore, those with an advanced degree will continue to fill most senior research and upper management positions, although applicants are likely to experience competition for these jobs.

Within the chemical industry, job opportunities are expected to be most plentiful in pharmaceutical and biotechnology firms. Biotechnological research, including studies of human genes, continues to offer possibilities for the development of new drugs and products to combat illnesses and diseases that have previously been unresponsive to treatments derived by traditional chemical processes. Stronger competition among drug companies and an aging population are contributing to the need for new drugs.

Employment in the remaining segments of the chemical industry is expected to decline as companies downsize. To control costs, most chemical companies, including many large pharmaceutical and biotechnology companies, will increasingly turn to scientific R&D services firms to perform specialized research and other work formerly done by in-house chemists. Also, some companies are expected to conduct an increasing amount of research in other lower-wage countries, further limiting employment growth. As a result, these firms will experience healthy growth. Despite downsizing, some job openings will result from the need to replace chemists who retire or otherwise leave the labor force, although not all positions will be filled. Quality control will continue to be an important issue in chemical manufacturing and other industries that use chemicals in their manufacturing processes.

Chemists also will be needed to develop and improve the technologies and processes used to produce chemicals for all purposes, and to monitor and measure air and water pollutants to ensure compliance with local, State, and Federal environmental regulations. Environmental research will offer many new opportunities for chemists and materials scientists. To satisfy public concerns and to comply with government regulations, the chemical industry will continue to invest billions of dollars each year in technology that reduces pollution and cleans up existing wastesites. Chemists also are needed to find ways to use less energy and to discover alternative sources of energy.

During periods of economic recession, layoffs of chemists may occur—especially in the industrial chemicals industry. Layoffs are less likely in the pharmaceutical industry, where long development cycles generally overshadow short-term economic effects. The traditional chemical industry, however, provides many raw materials to the auto manufacturing and construction industries, both of which are vulnerable to temporary slowdowns during recessions.

Earnings
Median annual earnings of chemists in May 2004 were $56,060. The middle 50 percent earned between $41,900 and $76,080. The lowest 10 percent earned less than $33,170, and the highest 10 percent earned more than $98,010. Median annual earnings of materials scientists in May 2004 were $72,390. The middle 50 percent earned between $53,350 and $92,340. The lowest 10 percent earned

less than $40,030, and the highest 10 percent earned more than $113,460. Median annual earnings in the industries employing the largest numbers of chemists in May 2004 are shown below:

Federal Government	$80,550
Scientific research and development services	62,460
Pharmaceutical and medicine manufacturing	57,050
Architectural, engineering, and related services	42,370

The ACS reports that in 2004 the median salary of all of its members with a bachelor's degree was $62,000; for those with a master's degree, it was $72,300; and for those with a Ph.D., it was $91,600. The median salary was highest for those working in private industry and lowest for those in academia. According to an ACS survey of recent graduates, inexperienced chemistry graduates with a bachelor's degree earned a median starting salary of $32,500 in October 2004; those with a master's degree earned a median salary of $43,600; and those with a Ph.D. had median earnings of $65,000. Among bachelor's degree graduates, those who had completed internships or had other work experience while in school commanded the highest starting salaries.

In 2005, chemists in nonsupervisory, supervisory, and managerial positions in the Federal Government averaged $83,777 a year.

Related Occupations
The research and analysis conducted by chemists and materials scientists is closely related to work done by agricultural and food scientists, biological scientists, medical scientists, chemical engineers, materials engineers, physicists, and science technicians.

Sources of Additional Information
General information on career opportunities and earnings for chemists is available from:
➤ American Chemical Society, Education Division, 1155 16th St. NW., Washington, DC 20036. Internet: http://www.acs.org

Information on obtaining a position as a chemist with the Federal Government is available from the Office of Personnel Management through USAJOBS, the Federal Government's official employment information system. This resource for locating and applying for job opportunities can be accessed through the Internet at http://www.usajobs.opm.gov or through an interactive voice response telephone system at (703) 724-1850 or TDD (978) 461-8404. These numbers are not tollfree, and charges may result.

Environmental Scientists and Hydrologists

(O*NET 19-2041.00, 19-2043.00)

Significant Points

- Environmental scientists and hydrologists often split their work between offices, laboratories, and field sites.

- Federal, State, and local governments employ over half of all environmental scientists and hydrologists.

- Although a bachelor's degree in an earth science is adequate for a few entry-level jobs, employers increasingly prefer a master's degree; a Ph.D. degree is required for most high-level research or college teaching positions.

- The strongest job growth should be in private-sector consulting firms.

Nature of the Work

Environmental scientists and hydrologists use their knowledge of the physical makeup and history of the Earth to protect the environment, study the properties of underground and surface waters, locate water and energy resources, predict water-related geologic hazards, and offer environmental site assessments and advice on indoor air quality and hazardous-waste-site remediation.

Environmental scientists conduct research to identify and abate or eliminate sources of pollutants or hazards that affect people, wildlife, and their environments. These workers analyze and report measurements or observations of air, food, water, soil, and other sources and make recommendations on how best to clean and preserve the environment. Understanding the issues involved in protecting the environment—degradation, conservation, recycling, and replenishment—is central to the work of environmental scientists, who often use their skills and knowledge to design and monitor waste disposal sites, preserve water supplies, and reclaim contaminated land and water to comply with Federal environmental regulations.

Many environmental scientists do work and have training that is similar to other physical or life scientists, but is applied to environmental areas. Many specialize in some specific area, such as environmental ecology and conservation, environmental chemistry, environmental biology, or fisheries science. Most environmental scientists are further classified by the specific activity they perform, although recent advances in the understanding of basic life processes within the ecosystem have blurred some traditional classifications. For example, *environmental ecologists* study the relationships between organisms and their environments and the effects of influences such as population size, pollutants, rainfall, temperature, and altitude. Utilizing their knowledge of various scientific disciplines, they may collect, study, and report data on air, food, soil, and water. *Ecological modelers* study ecosystems, the control of environmental pollution, and the management of resources. These environmental scientists may use mathematical modeling, systems analysis, thermodynamics, and computer techniques. *Environmental chemists* may study the toxicity of various chemicals—how those chemicals affect plants, animals, and people.

Hydrologists study the quantity, distribution, circulation, and physical properties of underground and surface waters. Often, they specialize in either underground water or surface water. They examine the form and intensity of precipitation, its rate of infiltration into the soil, its movement through the earth, and its return to the ocean and atmosphere. Hydrologists use sophisticated techniques and instruments. For example, they may use remote sensing technology, data assimilation, and numerical modeling to monitor the change in regional and global water cycles. Some surface-water hydrologists use sensitive stream-measuring devices to assess flow rates and the quality of water. The work hydrologists do is particularly important in flood control and environmental preservation, including groundwater decontamination.

Many environmental scientists and hydrologists work at consulting firms, advising and helping businesses and government agencies comply with environmental policy, particularly with regard to ground-water decontamination and flood control. Environmental scientists and hydrologists at consulting firms are generally hired to solve problems. Most firms fall into two categories: large multidisciplinary engineering companies, the largest of which may employ more than 15,000 workers, and small niche firms that may employ fewer than 50 workers. When entering the field, prospects should consider the type of firm and the scope of the projects it undertakes. In larger firms, environmental scientists are more likely to engage in large, long-term projects in which their role will mesh with those of workers in other scientific disciplines. In smaller specialty firms, however, they may be responsible for many skills

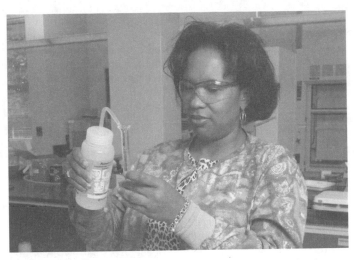

Environmental scientists conduct research to identify and reduce or eliminate sources of pollutants or hazards that affect people, wildlife, and their environments.

beyond traditional environmental disciplines, such as working with environmental laws and regulations, making environmental risk assessments, writing technical proposals, giving presentations to managers and regulators, and working with other specialists on a variety of issues, including engineering remediation.

Environmental scientists who determine policy may help identify how human behavior can be modified in the future to avoid such problems as ground water contamination and depletion of the ozone layer. Some environmental scientists work in managerial positions, usually after spending some time performing research or learning about environmental laws and regulations. (Information on geoscientists, whose work is closely related to that of environmental scientists and hydrologists, is located elsewhere in the *Handbook*.)

Working Conditions

Most entry-level environmental scientists and hydrologists spend the majority of their time in the field, while more experienced workers generally devote more of their time to office or laboratory work. Many beginning hydrologists and some environmental scientists, such as environmental ecologists and environmental chemists, often take field trips that involve physical activity. Environmental scientists and hydrologists in the field may work in warm or cold climates, in all kinds of weather. In their research, they may dig or chip with a hammer, scoop with a net, come in contact with water, and carry equipment in a backpack. Travel often is required to meet with prospective clients or investors. Those in laboratories may conduct tests, run experiments, record results, and compile data.

Environmental scientists and hydrologists in research positions with the Federal Government or in colleges and universities frequently are required to design programs and write grant proposals in order to continue their data collection and research. Environmental scientists and hydrologists in consulting jobs face similar pressures to market their skills and write proposals so that they will have steady work. Occasionally, those who write technical reports to business clients and regulators may be under pressure to meet deadlines.

Training, Other Qualifications, and Advancement

A bachelor's degree is adequate for a few entry-level positions, but environmental scientists are increasingly needing a master's degree in a natural science. A master's degree also is the minimum educational requirement for most entry-level applied research positions in private industry, in State and Federal agencies, and at State geological surveys.

A doctoral degree is necessary for college teaching and most high-level research positions.

Many environmental scientists earn degrees in life science, chemistry, geology, geophysics, atmospheric science, or physics and then, either through further education or through their research interests and work experience, apply their education to environmental areas. Others earn a degree in environmental science. A bachelor's degree in environmental science offers an interdisciplinary approach to the natural sciences, with an emphasis on biology, chemistry, and geology. In addition, undergraduate environmental science majors should focus on data analysis and physical geography, particularly if they are interested in studying pollution abatement, water resources, or ecosystem protection, restoration, or management. Understanding the geochemistry of inorganic compounds is becoming increasingly important in developing remediation goals. Those students interested in working in the environmental or regulatory fields, either in environmental consulting firms or for Federal or State governments, should take courses in hydrology, hazardous-waste management, environmental legislation, chemistry, fluid mechanics, and geologic logging. An understanding of environmental regulations and government permit issues also is valuable for those planning to work in mining and oil and gas extraction.

Students interested in the field of hydrology should take courses in the physical sciences, geophysics, chemistry, engineering science, soil science, mathematics, aquatic biology, atmospheric science, geology, oceanography, hydrogeology, and the management or conservation of water resources. In some cases, graduates with a bachelor's degree in a hydrologic science are qualified for positions in environmental consulting and planning regarding water quality or wastewater treatment. Curricula for advanced degrees often emphasize the natural sciences, but not all universities offer all curricula.

The American Institute of Hydrology offers certification programs in professional hydrology. Certification is recommended for those seeking advancement and for those seeking to upgrade their knowledge.

For environmental scientists and hydrologists who enter the field of consulting, courses in business, finance, marketing, or economics may be useful. In addition, combining environmental science training with other disciplines such as engineering, or a technical degree coupled with a master's degree in business administration, qualifies these scientists for the widest range of jobs. Environmental scientists and hydrologists also should have some knowledge of the potential liabilities associated with some environmental work.

Computer skills are essential for prospective environmental scientists and hydrologists. Students who have some experience with computer modeling, data analysis and integration, digital mapping, remote sensing, and geographic information systems will be the most prepared to enter the job market. A knowledge of the Geographic Information System (GIS) and Global Positioning System (GPS)—a locator system that uses satellites—is vital.

Environmental scientists and hydrologists must have excellent interpersonal skills, because they usually work as part of a team with other scientists, engineers, and technicians. Strong oral and written communication skills also are essential, because writing technical reports and research proposals and communicating technical and research results to company managers, regulators, and the public are important aspects of the work. Those involved in fieldwork must have physical stamina.

Environmental scientists and hydrologists often begin their careers in field exploration or, occasionally, as research assistants or technicians in laboratories or offices. They are given more difficult assignments as they gain experience. Eventually, they may be promoted to project leader, program manager, or some other management and research position.

Because international work is becoming increasingly pervasive, knowledge of a second language can be a valuable skill to employers.

Employment

Environmental scientists and hydrologists held about 81,000 jobs in 2004. Jobs for hydrologists accounted for only 10 percent of the total. Many more individuals held environmental science faculty positions in colleges and universities, but they are classified as college and university faculty. (See the statement on teachers—postsecondary elsewhere in the *Handbook*.)

About 44 percent of environmental scientists were employed in State and local governments; 15 percent in management, scientific, and technical consulting services; 14 percent in architectural, engineering and related services; and 8 percent in the Federal Government. About 5 percent were self-employed.

Among hydrologists, 22 percent were employed in architectural, engineering, and related services, and 18 percent worked for management, scientific, and technical consulting services. In 2004, the Federal Government employed about 2,500 hydrologists, mostly within the U.S. Department of the Interior for the U.S. Geological Survey (USGS) and within the U.S. Department of Defense. Another 15 percent worked for State agencies, such as State geological surveys and State departments of conservation. About 5 percent of hydrologists were self-employed, most as consultants to industry or government.

Job Outlook

Employment of environmental scientists is expected to grow about as fast as the average for all occupations through 2014, while employment of hydrologists should grow much faster than the average. Job growth for environmental scientists and hydrologists should be strongest at private-sector consulting firms. Demand for environmental scientists and hydrologists will be spurred largely by public policy, which will oblige companies and organizations to comply with complex environmental laws and regulations, particularly those regarding ground-water decontamination, clean air, and flood control.

Job opportunities also will be spurred by a continued general awareness regarding the need to monitor the quality of the environment, to interpret the impact of human actions on terrestrial and aquatic ecosystems, and to develop strategies for restoring ecosystems.

Many environmental scientists and hydrologists work in consulting. Consulting firms have hired these scientists to advise and help businesses and government comply with new regulations on issues related to underground tanks, land disposal areas, and other hazardous-waste-management facilities. Currently, environmental consulting is maturing and evolving from investigations to remediation and engineering solutions. At the same time, the regulatory climate is evolving from a rigid structure to a more flexible risk-based approach. These factors, coupled with new Federal and State initiatives that integrate environmental activities into the business process itself, will result in a greater focus on waste minimization, resource recovery, pollution prevention, and the consideration of environmental effects during product development. This shift in focus from reactive solutions to preventive management will provide many new opportunities for environmental scientists and hydrologists in consulting roles.

Some opportunities are expected for environmental scientists at State geological surveys, stemming from the need to conduct environmental site assessments for local governments to help improve the flow of railroad and automobile traffic in urban areas. In addition, environmental scientists will be needed to help planners and communities develop and construct buildings, transportation corridors, and utilities that protect water resources and reflect efficient and beneficial land use.

Opportunities will be better for hydrologists as the population increases and moves to more environmentally sensitive locations. For example, as people increasingly migrate toward coastal regions, hydrologists will be needed to assess building sites for potential geologic hazards and to mitigate the effects of natural hazards such as floods and landslides. Hydrologists also will be needed to conduct research on hazardous-waste sites in order to determine the impact of hazardous pollutants on soil and ground water so that engineers can design remediation systems. Demand is growing for hydrologists who understand both the scientific and engineering aspects of waste remediation. As States design initiatives to improve water resources by preventing pollution, there should be opportunities for hydrologists in State government. Increased government regulations, such as those regarding the management of storm water, and issues related to water conservation, deteriorating coastal environments, and rising sea levels also will stimulate employment growth for these workers.

Federal and State geological surveys depend to a large extent on the public climate and the current budget. Thus, job security for environmental scientists and hydrologists within a State survey may be cyclical. During periods of economic recession, layoffs of environmental scientists and hydrologists may occur in consulting firms; layoffs are much less likely in government.

Earnings

Median annual earnings of environmental scientists were $51,080 in May 2004. The middle 50 percent earned between $39,100 and $67,360. The lowest 10 percent earned less than $31,610, and the highest 10 percent earned more than $85,940.

Median annual earnings of hydrologists were $61,510 in May 2004, with the middle 50 percent earning between $47,080 and $77,910, the lowest 10 percent earning less than $38,580, and the highest 10 percent earning more than $94,460.

Median annual earnings in the industries employing the largest number of environmental scientists in May 2004 were as follows:

Federal Government	$73,530
Management, scientific, and technical consulting services	51,190
Architectural, engineering, and related services	49,160
Local government	48,870
State government	46,850

According to the National Association of Colleges and Employers, beginning salary offers in July 2005 for graduates with bachelor's degrees in a environmental science averaged $31,366 a year.

In 2005, the Federal Government's average salary for hydrologists in managerial, supervisory, and nonsupervisory positions was $77,182.

Related Occupations

Environmental scientists and hydrologists perform investigations for the purpose of abating or eliminating sources of pollutants or hazards that affect the environment or some population—plant, animal, or human. Many other occupations deal with preserving or researching the natural environment, including conservation scientists and foresters, atmospheric scientists, and some biological scientists and science and engineering technicians. Environmental scientists and hydrologists have extensive training in physical sciences, and many apply their knowledge of chemistry, physics, biology, and mathematics to explain certain phenomena closely related to the work of geoscientists.

Using their qualitative and quantitative problem-solving skills, physicists; chemists; engineers; mathematicians; surveyors, cartographers, photogrammetrists, and surveying technicians; computer systems analysts; and computer scientists and database administrators may perform similar work in environment-related activities.

Sources of Additional Information

Information on training and career opportunities for environmental scientists is available from:
➤ American Geological Institute, 4220 King St., Alexandria, VA 22302-1502. Internet: **http://www.agiweb.org**

For information on careers in hydrology, contact:
➤ American Institute of Hydrology, 300 Village Green Circle, Suite #201, Smyrna, GA 30080. Internet: **http://www.aihydro.org**

For career information and a list of education and training programs in oceanography and related fields, contact:
➤ Marine Technology Society, 5565 Sterrett Place, Suite 108, Columbia, MD 21004. Internet: **http://www.mtsociety.org**

Information on obtaining a position as a hydrologist or an environmental protection specialist with the Federal Government is available from the Office of Personnel Management through USAJOBS, the Federal Government's official employment information system. This resource for locating and applying for job opportunities can be accessed through the Internet at **http://www.usajobs.opm.gov** or through an interactive voice response telephone system at (703) 724-1850 or TDD (978) 461-8404. These numbers are not tollfree, and charges may result.

Geoscientists

(O*NET 19-2041.00, 19-2042.01, 19-2043.00)

Significant Points

- Work at remote field sites is common.
- Federal, State, and local governments employ 24 percent of all geoscientists.
- A master's degree is usually the minimum educational requirement; a Ph.D. degree is required for most high-level research and college teaching positions.
- Although employment of geoscientists is expected to grow more slowly than average, good job opportunities are expected in most areas of geoscience.

Nature of the Work

Geoscientists study the composition, structure, and other physical aspects of the Earth. With the use of sophisticated instruments and by analyzing the composition of the earth and water, geoscientists study the Earth's geologic past and present. Many geoscientists are involved in searching for adequate supplies of natural resources such as groundwater, metals, and petroleum, while others work closely with environmental and other scientists in preserving and cleaning up the environment.

Geoscientists usually study, and are subsequently classified into, one of several closely related fields of geoscience. *Geologists* study the composition, processes, and history of the Earth. They try to find out how rocks were formed and what has happened to them since their formation. They also study the evolution of life by analyzing plant and animal fossils. *Geophysicists* use the principles of physics, mathematics, and chemistry to study not only the Earth's surface, but also its internal composition; ground and surface waters; atmosphere; oceans; and magnetic, electrical, and gravitational forces.

Oceanographers use their knowledge of geology and geophysics, in addition to biology and chemistry, to study the world's oceans and coastal waters. They study the motion and circulation of the ocean waters; the physical and chemical properties of the oceans; and how these properties affect coastal areas, climate, and weather. Oceanographers are further broken down according to their areas of expertise. For example, *physical oceanographers* study the tides, waves, currents, temperatures, density, and salinity of the ocean. They examine the interaction of various forms of energy, such as light, radar, sound, heat, and wind, with the sea, in addition to investigating the relationship between the sea, weather, and climate. *Chemical oceanographers* study the distribution of chemical compounds and chemical interactions that occur in the ocean and on the sea floor. They may investigate how pollution affects the chemistry of the ocean. *Geological and geophysical oceanographers* study the topographic features and the physical makeup of the ocean floor. Their knowledge can help companies find oil and gas off coastal waters. (*Biological oceanographers,* often called marine biologists, study the distribution and migration patterns of the many diverse forms of sea life in the ocean, but because they are considered biological scientists, they are not covered in this statement on geoscientists. See the statement on biological scientists elsewhere in the *Handbook.*)

Geoscientists can spend a large part of their time in the field, identifying and examining rocks, studying information collected by remote sensing instruments in satellites, conducting geological surveys, constructing field maps, and using instruments to measure the Earth's gravity and magnetic field. For example, they often perform seismic studies, which involve bouncing energy waves off buried layers of rock, to search for oil and gas or to understand the structure of the subsurface layers. Seismic signals generated by an earthquake are used to determine the earthquake's location and intensity. In laboratories, geologists and geophysicists examine the chemical and physical properties of specimens. They study fossil remains of animal and plant life or experiment with the flow of water and oil through rocks.

Numerous specialties that further differentiate the type of work geoscientists do fall under the two major disciplines of geology and geophysics. For example, *petroleum geologists* map the subsurface of the ocean or land as they explore the terrain for oil and gas deposits. They use sophisticated geophysical instrumentation and computers to interpret geological information. *Engineering geologists* apply geologic principles to the fields of civil and environmental engineering, offering advice on major construction projects and assisting in environmental remediation and natural hazard-reduction projects. *Mineralogists* analyze and classify minerals and precious stones according to their composition and structure. They study the environment surrounding rocks in order to find new mineral resources. *Sedimentologists* study the nature, origin, distribution, and alteration of sediments, such as sand, silt, and mud. These sediments may contain oil, gas, coal, and many other mineral deposits. Paleontologists study fossils found in geological formations to trace the evolution of plant and animal life and the geologic history of the Earth. *Stratigraphers* examine the formation and layering of rocks to understand the environment in which they were formed. *Volcanologists* investigate volcanoes and volcanic phenomena to try to predict the potential for future eruptions and hazards to human health and welfare. *Glacial geologists* study the physical properties and movement of glaciers and ice sheets. *Geochemists* study the nature and distribution of chemical elements in groundwater and earth materials.

Geophysicists specialize in areas such as geodesy, seismology, and magnetic geophysics. *Geodesists* study the Earth's

size, shape, gravitational field, tides, polar motion, and rotation. *Seismologists* interpret data from seismographs and other geophysical instruments to detect earthquakes and locate earthquake-related faults. *Geomagnetists* measure the Earth's magnetic field and use measurements taken over the past few centuries to devise theoretical models that explain the Earth's origin. *Paleomagnetists* interpret fossil magnetization in rocks and sediments from the continents and oceans to record the spreading of the sea floor, the wandering of the continents, and the many reversals of polarity that the Earth's magnetic field has undergone through time. Other geophysicists study atmospheric sciences and space physics. (See the statement on atmospheric scientists, and physicists and astronomers, elsewhere in the *Handbook.*)

Working Conditions

Some geoscientists spend the majority of their time in an office, but many others divide their time between fieldwork and office or laboratory work. Work at remote field sites is common. Many geoscientists, such as volcanologists, often take field trips that involve physical activity. Geoscientists in the field may work in warm or cold climates and in all kinds of weather. In their research, they may dig or chip with a hammer, scoop with a net, and carry equipment in a backpack. Oceanographers may spend considerable time at sea on academic research ships. Fieldwork often requires working long hours. Geologists frequently travel to remote field

Due to the relatively low number of qualified geoscience graduates and the large number of expected retirements, opportunities are expected to be good in most areas of geoscience.

sites by helicopter or four-wheel-drive vehicles and cover large areas on foot. An increasing number of exploration geologists and geophysicists work in foreign countries, sometimes in remote areas and under difficult conditions. Travel often is required to meet with prospective clients or investors.

Geoscientists in research positions with the Federal Government or in colleges and universities frequently are required to design programs and write grant proposals in order to continue their data collection and research. Geoscientists in consulting jobs face similar pressures to market their skills and write proposals so that they will have steady work.

Training, Other Qualifications, and Advancement

A bachelor's degree is adequate for a few entry-level positions, but most geoscientists need at least a master's degree in general geology or earth science. A master's degree also is the minimum educational requirement for most entry-level research positions in private industry, Federal agencies, and State geological surveys. A Ph.D. degree is necessary for most high-level research and college teaching positions.

Many colleges and universities offer a bachelor's or higher degree in a geoscience. In 2005, more than 100 universities offered accredited bachelor's degree programs in geoscience, about 80 universities had master's degree programs, and about 60 offered doctoral degree programs.

Traditional geoscience courses emphasizing classical geologic methods and topics (such as mineralogy, petrology, paleontology, stratigraphy, and structural geology) are important for all geoscientists. Persons studying physics, chemistry, biology, mathematics, engineering, or computer science may also qualify for some geoscience positions if their course work includes study in geology or natural sciences.

Computer skills are essential for prospective geoscientists; students who have experience with computer modeling, data analysis and integration, digital mapping, remote sensing, and geographic information systems will be the most prepared entering the job market. A knowledge of the Global Information System (GIS) and Global Positioning System (GPS)—a locator system that uses satellites—has also become essential. Some employers seek applicants with field experience, so a summer internship may be beneficial to prospective geoscientists.

Geoscientists must have excellent interpersonal skills, because they usually work as part of a team with other geoscientists and with environmental scientists, engineers, and technicians. Strong oral and written communication skills also are important, because writing technical reports and research proposals, as well as communicating research results to others, are important aspects of the work. Because many jobs require foreign travel, knowledge of a second language is becoming an important attribute to employers. Geoscientists must be inquisitive, be able to think logically, and be capable of complex analytical thinking, including spatial visualization and the ability to develop comprehensive conclusions often from sparse data. Those involved in fieldwork must have physical stamina.

Geoscientists often begin their careers in field exploration or as research assistants or technicians in laboratories or offices. They are given more difficult assignments as they gain experience. Eventually, they may be promoted to project leader, program manager, or some other management or research position.

Employment

Geoscientists held about 28,000 jobs in 2004. Many more individuals held geoscience faculty positions in colleges and universities, but they are classified as college and university faculty. (See the statement on teachers—postsecondary elsewhere in the *Handbook*.)

About 25 percent of geoscientists were employed in architectural, engineering, and related services, and 20 percent worked for oil and gas extraction companies. In 2004, State agencies such as State geological surveys and State departments of conservation employed about 3,600 geoscientists. Another 2,900 worked for the Federal Government, including geologists, geophysicists, and oceanographers, mostly within the U.S. Department of the Interior for the U.S. Geological Survey (USGS) and within the U.S. Department of Defense. About 5 percent of geoscientists were self-employed, most as consultants to industry or government.

Job Outlook

Although employment growth will vary by occupational specialty, overall employment of geoscientists is expected to grow more slowly than the average for all occupations through 2014. However, due to the relatively low number of qualified geoscience graduates and the large number of expected retirements, opportunities are expected to be good in most areas of geoscience.

Graduates with a master's degree may have the best opportunities. Those with a Ph.D. who wish to become college and university faculty or to do advanced research may face competition. There are few openings for graduates with only a bachelor's degree in geoscience, but these graduates may find excellent opportunities as high school science teachers. They also can become science technicians, or enter a wide variety of related occupations.

Few opportunities for geoscientists are expected in Federal and State Government, mostly because of budgetary constraints at key agencies, such as the USGS, and the trend among governments toward contracting out to consulting firms. However, departures of geoscientists who retire or leave the Government for other reasons will result in some job openings over the next decade. A small number of new jobs will result from the need for oceanographers to conduct research for the military or for Federal agencies such as the National Oceanic and Atmospheric Administration (NOAA) on issues related to maintaining healthy and productive oceans.

Many geoscientists work in the exploration and production of oil and gas. Historically, employment of petroleum geologists, geophysicists, and some other geoscientists has been cyclical and affected considerably by the price of oil and gas. When prices were low, oil and gas producers curtailed exploration activities and laid off geologists. When prices were higher, companies had the funds and incentive to renew exploration efforts and hire geoscientists in larger numbers. In recent years, a growing worldwide demand for oil and gas and for new exploration and recovery techniques—particularly in deep water and previously inaccessible sites in Alaska and the Gulf of Mexico—has returned some stability to the petroleum industry. Growth in this area, though, will be limited due to increasing efficiencies in finding oil and gas. Geoscientists who speak a foreign language and who are willing to work abroad should enjoy the best opportunities, as the need for energy, construction materials, and a broad range of geoscience expertise grows in developing nations.

Job growth is expected within management, scientific, and technical consulting services. Demand will be spurred by a continuing emphasis on the need for energy, environmental protection, responsible land management, and water-related issues. Management, scientific, and technical consulting services have increased their hiring of many geoscientists in recent years due to increased government contracting, and also in response to demand for professionals to provide technical assistance and management plans to corporations. Moreover, many of these workers will be needed to monitor the quality of the environment, including aquatic ecosystems, issues related to water conservation, deteriorating coastal environments, and rising sea levels—all of which will stimulate employment growth of geoscientists.

An expected increase in highway building and other infrastructure projects will be a source of jobs for engineering geologists.

During periods of economic recession, geoscientists may be laid off. Especially vulnerable to layoffs are those in consulting and, to a lesser extent, workers in Government. Employment for those working in the production of oil and gas, however, will largely be dictated by the cyclical nature of the energy sector and changes in government policy.

Earnings

Median annual earnings of geoscientists were $68,730 in May 2004. The middle 50 percent earned between $49,260 and $98,380; the lowest 10 percent earned less than $37,700, the highest 10 percent more than $130,750.

According to the National Association of Colleges and Employers, beginning salary offers in July 2005 for graduates with bachelor's degrees in geology and related sciences averaged $39,365 a year.

In 2005, the Federal Government's average salary for managerial, supervisory, and nonsupervisory positions was $83,178 for geologists, $94,836 for geophysicists, and $87,007 for oceanographers.

The petroleum, mineral, and mining industries are vulnerable to recessions and to changes in oil and gas prices, among other factors, and usually release workers when exploration and drilling slow down. Consequently, they offer higher salaries, but less job security, than other industries.

Related Occupations

Many geoscientists work in the petroleum and natural-gas industry, an industry that also employs numerous other workers whose jobs deal with the scientific and technical aspects of the exploration and extraction of petroleum and natural gas. Among these other workers are engineering technicians, science technicians, petroleum engineers, surveyors, cartographers, photogrammetrists, and surveying technicians. Also, some physicists, chemists, atmospheric scientists, biological scientists, and environmental scientists—as well as mathematicians, computer systems analysts, database administrators, and computer scientists—perform related work both in the exploration and extraction of petroleum and natural gas and in activities having to do with the environment.

Sources of Additional Information

Information on training and career opportunities for geologists is available from either of the following organizations:
➤ American Geological Institute, 4220 King St., Alexandria, VA 22302-1502. Internet: **http://www.agiweb.org**
➤ American Association of Petroleum Geologists, P.O. Box 979, Tulsa, OK 74101. Internet: **http://www.aapg.org**

Information on oceanography and related fields is available from:
➤ Marine Technology Society, 5565 Sterrett Place, Suite 108, Columbia, MD 21004. Internet: **http://www.mtsociety.org**

Information on obtaining a position as a geologist, geophysicist, or oceanographer with the Federal Government is available from the Office of Personnel Management through USAJOBS, the Federal Government's official employment information system. This resource for locating and applying for job opportunities can be accessed through the Internet at **http://www.usajobs.opm.gov** or through an interactive voice response telephone system at (703) 724-1850 or TDD (978) 461-8404. These numbers are not tollfree, and charges may result.

Physicists and Astronomers

(O*NET 19-2011.00, 19-2012.00)

Significant Points

- Scientific research and development services firms and the Federal Government employ 3 out of 5 physicists and astronomers.
- Most jobs are in basic research and development, usually requiring a doctoral degree; master's degree holders qualify for many jobs in applied research and development, while bachelor's degree holders often qualify as technicians, research assistants, or other types of jobs.
- Employment is expected to grow more slowly than average.
- Competition for jobs is expected; however, graduates with a physics or astronomy degree at any level will find their knowledge of science and mathematics useful for entry to many other occupations.

Nature of the Work

Physicists explore and identify basic principles and laws governing motion and gravitation, the macroscopic and microscopic behavior of gases, and the structure and behavior of matter, the generation and transfer between energy, and the interaction of matter and energy. Some physicists use these principles in theoretical areas, such as the nature of time and the origin of the universe; others apply their knowledge of physics to practical areas, such as the development of advanced materials, electronic and optical devices, and medical equipment.

Physicists design and perform experiments with lasers, particle accelerators, telescopes, mass spectrometers, and other equipment. On the basis of their observations and analysis, they attempt to discover and explain laws describing the forces of nature, such as gravity, electromagnetism, and nuclear interactions. Physicists also find ways to apply physical laws and theories to problems in nuclear energy, electronics, optics, materials, communications, aerospace technology, and medical instrumentation.

Astronomy is sometimes considered a subfield of physics. *Astronomers* use the principles of physics and mathematics to learn about the fundamental nature of the universe, including the sun, moon, planets, stars, and galaxies. They also apply their knowledge to solve problems in navigation, space flight, and satellite communications and to develop the instrumentation and techniques used to observe and collect astronomical data.

Most physicists work in research and development. Some do basic research to increase scientific knowledge. Physicists who conduct applied research build upon the discoveries made through basic research and work to develop new devices, products, and processes. For example, basic research in solid-state physics led to the development of transistors and, then, integrated circuits used in computers.

Physicists also design research equipment, which often has additional unanticipated uses. For example, lasers are used in surgery, microwave devices function in ovens, and measuring instruments can analyze blood or the chemical content of foods. A small number of physicists work in inspection, testing, quality control and other production-related jobs in industry.

Much physics research is done in small or medium-sized laboratories. However, experiments in plasma, nuclear, and high-energy physics, as well as in some other areas of physics, require extremely large, expensive equipment, such as particle accelerators. Physicists in these subfields often work in large teams. Although physics research may require extensive experimentation in laboratories, research physicists still spend time in offices planning, recording, analyzing, and reporting on research.

Almost all astronomers do research. Some are theoreticians, working on the laws governing the structure and evolution of astronomical objects. Others analyze large quantities of data gathered by observatories and satellites and write scientific papers or reports on their findings. Some astronomers actually operate large space- or ground-based telescopes, usually as part of a team. However, astronomers may spend only a few weeks each year making observations with optical telescopes, radio telescopes, and other instruments. For many years, satellites and other space-based instruments, such as the Hubble space telescope, have provided prodigious amounts of astronomical data. New technology resulting in improvements in analytical techniques and instruments, such as computers and optical telescopes and mounts, is leading to a resurgence in ground-based research. A small number of astronomers work in museums housing planetariums. These astronomers develop and revise programs presented to the public and may direct planetarium operations.

Physicists generally specialize in one of many subfields: elementary particle physics, nuclear physics, atomic and molecular physics, physics of condensed matter (solid-state physics), optics, acoustics, space physics, plasma physics, or the physics of fluids. Some specialize in a subdivision of one of these subfields. For example, within condensed-matter physics, specialties include superconductivity, crystallography, and semiconductors. However, all physics involves the same fundamental principles, so specialties may overlap, and physicists may switch from one subfield to another. Also, growing numbers of physicists work in interdisciplinary fields, such as biophysics, chemical physics, and geophysics.

Working Conditions

Physicists often work regular hours in laboratories and offices. At times, however, those who are deeply involved in research may work long or irregular hours. Most do not encounter unusual hazards in their work. Some physicists temporarily work away from home at national or international facilities with unique equipment, such as particle accelerators. Astronomers who make observations with ground-based telescopes may spend long periods in observatories; this work usually involves travel to remote locations and may require long hours, including night work.

Physicists design and perform experiments with lasers, particle accelerators, telescopes, mass spectrometers, and other equipment.

Physicists and astronomers whose work depends on grant money often are under pressure to write grant proposals to keep their work funded.

Training, Other Qualifications, and Advancement

Because most jobs are in basic research and development, a doctoral degree is the usual educational requirement for physicists and astronomers. Additional experience and training in a postdoctoral research appointment, although not required, is important for physicists and astronomers aspiring to permanent positions in basic research in universities and government laboratories. Many physics and astronomy Ph.D. holders ultimately teach at the college or university level.

Master's degree holders usually do not qualify for basic research positions, but do qualify for many kinds of jobs requiring a physics background, including positions in manufacturing and applied research and development. Increasingly, many master's degree programs are specifically preparing students for physics-related research and development that does not require a Ph.D. degree. These programs teach students specific research skills that can be used in private-industry jobs. In addition, a master's degree coupled with State certification usually qualifies one for teaching jobs in high schools or at 2-year colleges.

Those with bachelor's degrees in physics are rarely qualified to fill positions in research or in teaching at the college level. They are, however, usually qualified to work as technicians or research assistants in engineering-related areas, in software development and other scientific fields, or in setting up computer networks and sophisticated laboratory equipment. Increasingly, some may qualify for applied research jobs in private industry or take on nontraditional physics roles, often in computer science, such as a systems analyst or database administrator. Some become science teachers in secondary schools. Holders of a bachelor's or master's degree in astronomy often enter an unrelated field. In addition, they are qualified to work in planetariums running science shows, to assist astronomers doing research, and to operate space-based and ground-based telescopes and other astronomical instrumentation. (See the statements on engineers, geoscientists, computer programmers, computer scientists and database administrators, computer software engineers, and computer systems analysts elsewhere in the *Handbook*.)

About 510 colleges and universities offer a bachelor's degree in physics. Undergraduate programs provide a broad background in the natural sciences and mathematics. Typical physics courses include electromagnetism, optics, thermodynamics, atomic physics, and quantum mechanics.

Approximately 185 colleges and universities have departments offering Ph.D. degrees in physics; an additional 68 colleges offer a master's as their highest degree in physics. Graduate students usually concentrate in a subfield of physics, such as elementary particles or condensed matter. Many begin studying for their doctorate immediately after receiving their bachelor's degree.

About 80 universities grant degrees in astronomy, either through an astronomy, physics, or combined physics-astronomy department. Currently, about 40 departments are combined with the physics department and the same number are administered separately. With fewer than 40 doctoral programs in astronomy, applicants face considerable competition for available slots. Those planning a career in the subject should have a very strong physics background. In fact, an undergraduate degree in either physics or astronomy is excellent preparation, followed by a Ph.D. in astronomy.

Mathematical ability, problem-solving and analytical skills, an inquisitive mind, imagination, and initiative are important traits for anyone planning a career in physics or astronomy. Prospective physicists who hope to work in industrial laboratories applying physics knowledge to practical problems should broaden their educational background to include courses outside of physics, such as economics, information technology, and business management. Good oral and written communication skills also are important because many physicists work as part of a team, write research papers or proposals, or have contact with clients or customers with nonphysics backgrounds.

Many physics and astronomy Ph.D. holders begin their careers in a postdoctoral research position, in which they may work with experienced physicists as they continue to learn about their specialty and develop ideas and results to be used in later work. Initial work may be under the close supervision of senior scientists. After some experience, physicists perform increasingly complex tasks and work more independently. Those who develop new products or processes sometimes form their own companies or join new firms to exploit their own ideas. Experience, either in academic laboratories or through internships, fellowships, or work-study programs in industry, also is useful. Some employers of research physicists, particularly in the information technology industry, prefer to hire individuals with several years of postdoctoral experience.

Employment

Physicists and astronomers held about 16,000 jobs in 2004. Jobs for astronomers accounted for only 5 percent of the total. About 33 percent of physicists and astronomers worked for scientific research and development services firms. The Federal Government employed 25 percent, mostly in the U.S. Department of Defense, but also in the National Aeronautics and Space Administration (NASA) and in the U.S. Departments of Commerce, Health and Human Services, and Energy. Other physicists and astronomers worked in colleges and universities in nonfaculty, usually research, positions, or for State governments, information technology companies, pharmaceutical and medicine manufacturing companies, or electronic equipment manufacturers.

In 2004, many physicists and astronomers held faculty positions in colleges and universities. (See the statement on teachers—postsecondary elsewhere in the *Handbook*.)

Although physicists and astronomers are employed in all parts of the country, most work in areas in which universities, large research and development laboratories, or observatories are located.

Job Outlook

Employment of physicists and astronomers is expected to grow more slowly than the average for all occupations through 2014. Federal research expenditures are the major source of physics-related and astronomy-related research funds, especially for basic research. Although these expenditures are expected to increase over the 2004–14 projection period, resulting in some growth in employment and opportunities, the limited science research funds available still will result in competition for basic research jobs among Ph.D. holders. The need to replace physicists and astronomers who retire or otherwise leave the occupation permanently will account for most expected job openings.

Although research and development expenditures in private industry will continue to grow, many research laboratories in private industry are expected to continue to reduce basic research, which includes much physics research, in favor of applied or manufacturing research and product and software development. Nevertheless, persons with a physics background continue to be in demand in the areas of information technology, semiconductor technology, and other applied sciences. This trend is expected to continue; however, many of the new workers will have job titles such as computer software engineer, computer programmer, or systems analyst or developer, rather than physicist.

Throughout the 1990s, the number of doctorates granted in physics was much greater than the number of job openings for physicists, resulting in keen competition, particularly for research positions in colleges and universities and in research and development centers. Recent increases in undergraduate physics enrollments, however, may lead to growth in enrollments in graduate physics programs, so that toward the end of the projection period, there may be an increase in the number of doctoral degrees granted that will intensify the competition for job openings.

Opportunities may be more numerous for those with a master's degree, particularly graduates from programs preparing students for applied research and development, product design, and manufacturing positions in private industry. Many of these positions, however, will have titles other than physicist, such as engineer or computer scientist.

Persons with only a bachelor's degree in physics or astronomy are not qualified to enter most physicist or astronomer research jobs, but may qualify for a wide range of positions related to engineering, mathematics, computer science, environmental science, and, for those with the appropriate background, some nonscience fields, such as finance. Those who meet State certification requirements can become high school physics teachers, an occupation in strong demand in many school districts. Most States require new teachers to obtain a master's degree in education within a certain time. (See the statement on teachers—preschool, kindergarten, elementary, middle, and secondary elsewhere in the *Handbook*.) Despite competition for traditional physics and astronomy research jobs, graduates with a physics or astronomy degree at any level will find their knowledge of science and mathematics useful for entry into many other occupations.

Earnings

Median annual earnings of physicists were $87,450 in May 2004. The middle 50 percent earned between $66,590 and $109,420. The lowest 10 percent earned less than $49,450, and the highest 10 percent earned more than $132,780.

Median annual earnings of astronomers were $97,320 in May 2004. The middle 50 percent earned between $66,190 and $120,350, the lowest 10 percent less than $43,410, and the highest 10 percent more than $137,860.

According to a 2005 National Association of Colleges and Employers survey, the average annual starting salary offer to physics doctoral degree candidates was $56,070.

The American Institute of Physics reported a median annual salary of $104,000 in 2004 for its full-time members with Ph.D.'s (excluding those in postdoctoral positions); the median was $94,000 for those with master's degrees and $72,000 for bachelor's degree holders. Those working in temporary postdoctoral positions earned significantly less.

The average annual salary for physicists employed by the Federal Government was $104,917 in 2005; for astronomy and space scientists, it was $110,195.

Related Occupations

The work of physicists and astronomers relates closely to that of engineers, chemists and materials scientists, atmospheric scientists, environmental scientists, geoscientists, computer systems analysts, computer scientists and database administrators, computer programmers, and mathematicians.

Sources of Additional Information

General information on career opportunities in physics is available from the following organizations:

➤ American Institute of Physics, Career Services Division and Education and Employment Division, One Physics Ellipse, College Park, MD 20740-3843. Internet: **http://www.aip.org**

➤ The American Physical Society, One Physics Ellipse, College Park, MD 20740-3844. Internet: **http://www.aps.org**

Social Scientists and Related Occupations

Economists

(O*NET 19-3011.00)

Significant Points

- Slower than average job growth is expected as firms increasingly employ workers to perform more specialized tasks with titles that reflect the specific duties of the job rather than the general title of economist.

- Job seekers with a background in economics should have good opportunities, although some of these opportunities will be in related occupations.

- Candidates who hold a master's or Ph.D. degree in economics will have the best employment prospects and advancement opportunities.

- Quantitative skills are important in all economics specialties.

Nature of the Work

Economists study how society distributes scarce resources, such as land, labor, raw materials, and machinery, to produce goods and services. They conduct research, collect and analyze data, monitor economic trends, and develop forecasts. They research issues such as energy costs, inflation, interest rates, exchange rates, business cycles, taxes, or employment levels.

Economists devise methods and procedures for obtaining the data they need. For example, sampling techniques may be used to conduct a survey, and various mathematical modeling techniques may be used to develop forecasts. Preparing reports, including tables and charts, on research results is an important part of an economist's job. Presenting economic and statistical concepts in a clear and meaningful way is particularly important for economists whose research is directed toward making policies for an organization. Some economists also might perform economic analysis for the media.

Many economists specialize in a particular area of economics, although general knowledge of basic economic principles is useful in each area. *Microeconomists* study the supply and demand decisions of individuals and firms, such as how profits can be maximized and how much of a good or service consumers will demand at a certain price. *Industrial economists* or *organizational economists* study the market structure of particular industries in terms of the number of competitors within those industries and examine the market decisions of competitive firms and monopolies. These economists also may be concerned with antitrust policy and its impact on market structure. *Macroeconomists* study historical trends in the whole economy and forecast future trends in areas such as unemployment, inflation, economic growth, productivity, and investment. Closely related to macroeconomists are *monetary economists* or *financial economists*, who study the money and banking system and the effects of changing interest rates. *International economists* study international financial markets, exchange rates, and the effects of various trade policies such as tariffs. *Labor economists* or *demographic economists* study the supply and demand for labor and the determination of wages. These economists also try to explain the reasons for unemployment and the effects of changing demographic trends, such as an aging population and increasing immigration, on labor markets. *Public finance economists* are involved primarily in studying the role of the government in the economy and the effects of tax cuts, budget deficits, and welfare policies. *Econometricians* investigate all areas of economics and use mathematical techniques such as calculus, game theory, and regression analysis to formulate economic models that help to explain economic relationships and that are used to develop forecasts related to the nature and length of business cycles, the effects of a specific rate of inflation on the economy, the effects of tax legislation on unemployment levels, and other economic phenomena. Many economists have applied these fundamental areas of economics to specific applications such as health, education, agriculture, urban and regional economics, law, history, energy, and the environment.

Most economists are concerned with practical applications of economic policy and work for a variety of organizations. Economists working for corporations are involved primarily in microeconomic issues, such as forecasting consumer demand and sales of the firm's products. Some analyze their competitors' growth and market share and advise their company on how to handle the competition. Others monitor legislation passed by Congress, such as environmental and worker safety regulations, and assess its impact on their business. Corporations with many international branches or subsidiaries might employ economists to monitor the economic situations in countries where they do business or to provide a risk assessment of a country into which the company might expand.

Economists working in economic consulting or research firms may perform the same tasks as economists working for corporations. Economists in consulting firms also perform much of the macroeconomic analysis and forecasting that is conducted in the United States. These economists collect data on various indicators, maintain databases, analyze historical trends, and develop models to forecast growth, inflation, unemployment, or interest rates. Their analyses and forecasts are frequently published in newspapers and journal articles.

Another large employer of economists is the government. Economists in the Federal Government administer most of the surveys and collect the majority of the economic data characterizing the United States. For example, economists in the U.S. Department of Commerce

Preparing reports, including tables and charts, on research results is an important part of an economist's job.

collect and analyze data on the production, distribution, and consumption of commodities produced in the United States and overseas, while economists employed by the U.S. Department of Labor collect and analyze data on the domestic economy, including data on prices, wages, employment, productivity, and safety and health. Economists who work for government agencies also assess economic conditions in the United States or abroad in order to estimate the economic effects of specific changes in legislation or public policy. Government economists advise policy makers in areas such as telecommunications deregulation, Social Security revamping, the effects of tax cuts on the budget deficit, and the effectiveness of imposing tariffs on imported steel. An economist working in State or local government might analyze data on the growth of school-age or prison populations, and on employment and unemployment rates, in order to project future spending needs.

Working Conditions

Economists have structured work schedules. They often work alone, writing reports, preparing statistical charts, and using computers, but they also may be an integral part of a research team. Most work under pressure of deadlines and tight schedules, which may require overtime. Their routine may be interrupted by special requests for data and by the need to attend meetings or conferences. Frequent travel may be necessary.

Training, Other Qualifications, and Advancement

A master's or Ph.D. degree in economics is required for many private-sector economist jobs and for advancement to more responsible positions. Economics includes numerous specialties at the graduate level, such as advanced economic theory, econometrics, international economics, and labor economics. Students should select graduate schools that are strong in specialties in which they are interested. Undergraduate economics majors can choose from a variety of courses, ranging from microeconomics, macroeconomics, and econometrics to more philosophical courses, such as the history of economic thought. Because of the importance of quantitative skills to economists, courses in mathematics, statistics, econometrics, sampling theory and survey design, and computer science are extremely helpful. Some schools help graduate students find internships or part-time employment in government agencies, economic consulting or research firms, or financial institutions prior to graduation.

In the Federal Government, candidates for entry-level economist positions must have a bachelor's degree with a minimum of 21 semester hours of economics and 3 hours of statistics, accounting, or calculus.

Whether working in government, industry, research organizations, or consulting firms, economists with a bachelor's degree usually qualify for most entry-level positions as a research assistant, for administrative or management trainee positions, or for various sales jobs. A master's degree usually is required to qualify for more responsible research and administrative positions. Many businesses, research and consulting firms, and government agencies seek individuals who have strong computer and quantitative skills and can perform complex research. A Ph.D. is necessary for top economist positions in many organizations. Many corporation and government executives have a strong background in economics.

A master's degree usually is the minimum requirement for a job as an instructor in a junior or community college. In most colleges and universities, however, a Ph.D. is necessary for appointment as an instructor. A Ph.D. and extensive publications in academic journals are required for a professorship, tenure, and promotion.

Aspiring economists should gain experience gathering and analyzing data, conducting interviews or surveys, and writing reports on their findings while in college. This experience can prove invaluable later in obtaining a full-time position in the field, because much of

the economist's work, especially in the beginning, may center on these duties. With experience, economists eventually are assigned their own research projects. Related job experience, such as work as a stock or bond trader, might be advantageous.

Those considering careers as economists should be able to pay attention to details, because much time is spent on precise data analysis. Patience and persistence are necessary qualities, given that economists must spend long hours on independent study and problem solving. Good communication skills also are useful, as economists must be able to present their findings, both orally and in writing, in a clear, concise manner.

Employment

Economists held about 13,000 jobs in 2004. Government employed 58 percent of economists, in a wide range of government agencies, with 34 percent in Federal government and 24 percent in State and local government. The U.S. Departments of Labor, Agriculture, and State are the largest Federal employers of economists. The remaining jobs were spread throughout private industry, particularly in scientific research and development services and management, scientific, and technical consulting services. A number of economists combine a full-time job in government, academia, or business with part-time or consulting work in another setting.

Employment of economists is concentrated in large cities. Some work abroad for companies with major international operations, for U.S. Government agencies, and for international organizations, such as the World Bank, International Monetary Fund, and United Nations.

In addition to the previously mentioned jobs, economists hold faculty positions in colleges and universities. Economics faculties have flexible work schedules and may divide their time among teaching, research, consulting, and administration. (See the statement on teachers—postsecondary elsewhere in the *Handbook*.)

Job Outlook

Employment of economists is expected to grow more slowly than the average for all occupations through 2014. Employment growth should be the fastest in private industry, especially in management, scientific, and technical consulting services. Rising demand for economic analysis in virtually every industry should stem from the growing complexity of the global economy, the effects of competition on businesses, and increased reliance on quantitative methods for analyzing and forecasting business, sales, and other economic trends. Some corporations choose to hire economic consultants to fill these needs, rather than keeping an economist on staff. This practice should result in more economists being employed in consulting services. However, job growth will be limited as firms increasingly employ workers to perform more specialized tasks with titles that reflect the specific duties of the job instead of the general title of economist. In addition, few new jobs are expected in government, but the need to replace experienced workers who transfer to other occupations or who retire or leave the labor force for other reasons will lead to job openings for economists across all industries in which they are employed.

Individuals with a background in economics should have job opportunities, although some of these opportunities will be in related occupations. As firms increasingly employ workers to perform more specialized tasks, the best opportunities for individuals with backgrounds in economics are expected to be in positions that have titles other than economist. Some examples of job titles often held by those with an economics background are financial analyst, market analyst, public policy consultant, researcher or research assistant, and econometrician.

A master's or Ph.D. degree, coupled with a strong background in economic theory, mathematics, statistics, and econometrics, provides the basis for acquiring any specialty within the economics field. Economists who are skilled in quantitative techniques and their application to economic modeling and forecasting, and who also have good communications skills, should have the best job opportunities. Like those in many other disciplines, however, Ph.D. holders are likely to face keen competition for tenured teaching positions in colleges and universities.

Bachelor's degree holders may face competition for the limited number of economist positions for which they qualify. However, they will qualify for a number of other positions in which they can take advantage of their economic knowledge by conducting research, developing surveys, or analyzing data. Many graduates with bachelor's degrees will find jobs in industry and business as management or sales trainees or as administrative assistants. Bachelor's degree holders with good quantitative skills and a strong background in mathematics, statistics, survey design, and computer science also may be hired by private firms as researchers. Some will find jobs in government.

Candidates who meet State certification requirements may become high school economics teachers. The demand for secondary school economics teachers is expected to grow, as economics becomes an increasingly important and popular course. (See the statement on teachers—preschool, kindergarten, elementary, middle, and secondary elsewhere in the *Handbook*.)

Earnings
Median annual wage and salary earnings of economists were $72,780 in May 2004. The middle 50 percent earned between $53,650 and $96,240. The lowest 10 percent earned less than $41,040, and the highest 10 percent earned more than $129,170.

The Federal Government recognizes education and experience in certifying applicants for entry-level positions. The starting salary for economists having a bachelor's degree was about $24,667 a year in 2005; however, those with superior academic records could begin at $30,567. Those having a master's degree could qualify for positions at an annual salary of $37,390. Those with a Ph.D. could begin at $45,239, while some individuals with experience and an advanced degree could start at $54,221. Starting salaries were slightly higher in selected geographical areas where the prevailing local pay was higher. The average annual salary for economists employed by the Federal Government was $89,441 a year in 2005.

Related Occupations
Economists are concerned with understanding and interpreting financial matters, among other subjects. Other occupations in this area include accountants and auditors; actuaries; budget analysts; financial analysts and personal financial advisors; financial managers; insurance underwriters; loan officers; and purchasing managers, buyers, and purchasing agents. Other occupations involved in market research and data collection are management analysts and market and survey researchers.

Sources of Additional Information
For information on careers in business economics, contact:
➤ National Association for Business Economics, 1233 20th St. NW., Suite 505, Washington, DC 20036.

Information on obtaining positions as economists with the Federal Government is available from the Office of Personnel Management through USAJOBS, the Federal Government's official employment information system. This resource for locating and applying for job opportunities can be accessed through the Internet at **http://www.usajobs.opm.gov** or through an interactive voice response telephone system at (703) 724-1850 or TDD (978) 461-8404. These numbers are not tollfree, and charges may result.

Market and Survey Researchers
(O*NET 19-3021.00, 19-3022.00)

Significant Points
● Market and survey researchers need at least a bachelor's degree, but a master's degree may be required for employment; continuing education also is important.

● Employment is expected to grow faster than average.

● Job opportunities should be best for those with a master's or Ph.D. degree in marketing or a related field and strong quantitative skills.

Nature of the Work
Market, or *marketing, research analysts* are concerned with the potential sales of a product or service. Gathering statistical data on competitors and examining prices, sales, and methods of marketing and distribution, they analyze data on past sales to predict future sales. Market research analysts devise methods and procedures for obtaining the data they need. Often, they design telephone, mail, or Internet surveys to assess consumer preferences. They conduct some surveys as personal interviews, going door-to-door, leading focus group discussions, or setting up booths in public places such as shopping malls. Trained interviewers usually conduct the surveys under the market research analyst's direction.

After compiling and evaluating the data, market research analysts make recommendations to their client or employer on the basis of their findings. They provide a company's management with information needed to make decisions on the promotion, distribution, design, and pricing of products or services. The information also may be used to determine the advisability of adding new lines of merchandise, opening new branches, or otherwise diversifying the company's operations. Market research analysts also might develop advertising brochures and commercials, sales plans, and product promotions such as rebates and giveaways.

Survey researchers design and conduct surveys for a variety of clients, such as corporations, government agencies, political candidates, and providers of various services. The surveys collect information that is used for performing research, making fiscal or policy decisions, measuring the effectiveness of those decisions, or improving customer satisfaction. Analysts may conduct opinion research to determine public attitudes on various issues; the research results may help political or business leaders and others assess public support for their electoral prospects or social policies. Like market research analysts, survey researchers may use a variety of mediums to conduct surveys, such as the Internet, personal or telephone interviews, or questionnaires sent through the mail. They also may supervise interviewers who conduct surveys in person or over the telephone.

Survey researchers design surveys in many different formats, depending upon the scope of their research and the method of collection. Interview surveys, for example, are common because they can increase participation rates. Survey researchers may consult with economists, statisticians, market research analysts, or other data users in order to design surveys. They also may present survey results to clients.

Working Conditions
Market and survey researchers generally have structured work schedules. Some often work alone, writing reports, preparing statistical charts, and using computers, but they also may be an integral

Market and survey researchers often use surveys to assess consumer preferences.

part of a research team. Market researchers who conduct personal interviews have frequent contact with the public. Most work under pressure of deadlines and tight schedules, which may require overtime. Their routine may be interrupted by special requests for data, as well as by the need to attend meetings or conferences. Travel may be necessary.

Training, Other Qualifications, and Advancement

A bachelor's degree is the minimum educational requirement for many market and survey research jobs. However, a master's degree may be required, especially for technical positions, and increases opportunities for advancement to more responsible positions. Also, continuing education is important in order to keep current with the latest methods of developing, conducting, and analyzing surveys and other data. Market and survey researchers may earn advanced degrees in business administration, marketing, statistics, communications, or some closely related discipline. Some schools help graduate students find internships or part-time employment in government agencies, consulting firms, financial institutions, or marketing research firms prior to graduation.

In addition to completing courses in business, marketing, and consumer behavior, prospective market and survey researchers should take other liberal arts and social science courses, including economics, psychology, English, and sociology. Because of the importance of quantitative skills to market and survey researchers, courses in mathematics, statistics, sampling theory and survey design, and computer science are extremely helpful. Many corporation and government executives have a strong background in marketing.

A master's degree is usually the minimum educational requirement for a job as a marketing or survey research instructor in junior and community colleges. In most colleges and universities, however, a Ph.D. is necessary for appointment as an instructor. A Ph.D. and extensive publications in academic journals are required for a professorship, tenure, and promotion.

While in college, aspiring market and survey researchers should gain experience gathering and analyzing data, conducting interviews or surveys, and writing reports on their findings. This experience can prove invaluable later in obtaining a full-time position in the field, because much of the initial work may center on these duties. With experience, market and survey researchers eventually are assigned their own research projects.

Much of the market and survey researcher's time is spent on precise data analysis, so those considering careers in the occupation should be able to pay attention to detail. Patience and persistence are necessary qualities because these workers must spend long hours on independent study and problem solving. At the same time, they must work well with others: often, market and survey researchers oversee interviews of a wide variety of individuals. Communication skills are important, too, because researchers must be able to present their findings both orally and in writing, in a clear, concise manner.

While certification currently is not required for market and survey researchers, the Marketing Research Association (MRA) offers a certification program for professional researchers. Certification is based on education and experience requirements, as well as on continuing education.

Employment

Market and survey researchers held about 212,000 jobs in 2004, most of which—190,000—were held by market research analysts. Because of the applicability of market research to many industries, market research analysts are employed throughout the economy. The industries that employ the largest number of market research analysts were management of companies and enterprises; management, scientific, and technical consulting services; insurance carriers; credit intermediation and related activities; computer systems design and related services; marketing research and public opinion polling; software publishers; professional and commercial equipment and supplies merchant wholesalers; securities and commodity contracts intermediation and brokerage; and advertising and related services.

Survey researchers held about 22,000 jobs in 2004. Survey researchers were employed mainly by professional, scientific, and technical services firms, especially in market research and public opinion polling; scientific research and development services; and management, scientific, and technical consulting services. State government also provided many jobs for survey researchers.

A number of market and survey researchers combine a full-time job in government, academia, or business with part-time or consulting work in another setting. About nine percent of market and survey researchers are self-employed.

Besides holding the previously mentioned jobs, many market and survey researchers held faculty positions in colleges and universities. Marketing faculties have flexible work schedules and may divide their time among teaching, research, consulting, and administration. (See the statement on teachers—postsecondary elsewhere in the *Handbook*.)

Job Outlook

Employment of market and survey researchers is expected to grow faster than the average for all occupations through 2014. Many job openings are likely to result from the need to replace experienced workers who transfer to other occupations or who retire or leave the labor force for other reasons.

Job opportunities should be best for those with a master's or Ph.D. degree in marketing or a related field and strong quantitative skills. Bachelor's degree holders may face competition, as many positions, especially the more technical ones, require a master's or higher degree. Among bachelor's degree holders, those with good quantitative skills, including a strong background in mathematics, statistics, survey design, and computer science, will have the best opportunities. Ph.D. degree holders in marketing and related fields should have a range of opportunities in industry and consulting firms. Like those in many other disciplines, however, Ph.D. holders probably will face keen competition for tenured teaching positions in colleges and universities.

Demand for market research analysts should be strong because of an increasingly competitive economy. Marketing research provides organizations valuable feedback from purchasers, allowing companies to evaluate consumer satisfaction and plan more effectively for the future. As companies seek to expand their market and as consumers become better informed, the need for marketing professionals will increase. In addition, as globalization of the marketplace continues, market researchers will increasingly be utilized to analyze foreign markets and competition for goods and services.

Market research analysts should have the best opportunities in consulting firms and marketing research firms as companies find it more profitable to contract for market research services rather than support their own marketing department. Increasingly, market research analysts not only are collecting and analyzing information, but also are helping clients implement the analysts' ideas and recommendations. Other organizations, including computer systems design companies, software publishers, financial services organizations, health care institutions, advertising firms, and insurance companies, may offer job opportunities for market research analysts. Survey researchers will be needed to meet the growing demand for market and opinion research as an increasingly competitive economy requires businesses to allocate advertising funds more effectively and efficiently.

Earnings

Median annual earnings of market research analysts in May 2004 were $56,140. The middle 50 percent earned between $40,510 and $79,990. The lowest 10 percent earned less than $30,890, and the highest 10 percent earned more than $105,870. Median annual earnings in the industries employing the largest numbers of market research analysts in May 2004 were:

Management of companies and enterprises	$58,440
Computer systems design and related services	58,100
Insurance carriers	51,030
Other professional, scientific, and technical services	50,950
Management, scientific, and technical consulting services	49,080

Median annual earnings of survey researchers in May 2004 were $26,490. The middle 50 percent earned between $17,920 and $41,390. The lowest 10 percent earned less than $15,330, and the highest 10 percent earned more than $56,740. Median annual earnings of survey researchers in other professional, scientific, and technical services were $22,880.

Related Occupations

Market and survey researchers perform research to find out how well the market receives products or services. Such research may include planning, implementing, and analyzing surveys to determine the needs and preferences of people. Other jobs using these skills include economists, psychologists, sociologists, statisticians, and urban and regional planners.

Sources of Additional Information

For information about careers and certification in market research, contact:

➤ Marketing Research Association, 110 National Dr., Glastonbury, CT 06033. Internet: **http://www.mra-net.org**

For information about careers in survey research, contact:

➤ Council of American Survey Research Organizations, 170 North Country Rd., Suite 4, Port Jefferson, NY 11777. Internet: **http://www.casro.org**

Psychologists

(O*NET 19-3031.01, 19-3031.02, 19-3031.03, 19-3032.00, 19-3039.99)

Significant Points

● About 4 out of 10 psychologists are self-employed, compared with less than 1 out of 10 among all professional workers.

● Most specialists, including clinical and counseling psychologists, need a doctoral degree; school psychologists need an educational specialist degree, and industrial-organizational psychologists need a master's degree.

● Competition for admission to graduate psychology programs is keen.

● Overall employment of psychologists is expected to grow faster than the average for all occupations through 2014.

Nature of the Work

Psychologists study the human mind and human behavior. Research psychologists investigate the physical, cognitive, emotional, or social aspects of human behavior. Psychologists in health service provider fields provide mental health care in hospitals, clinics, schools, or private settings. Psychologists employed in applied settings, such as business, industry, government, or nonprofits, provide training, conduct research, design systems, and act as advocates for psychology.

Like other social scientists, psychologists formulate hypotheses and collect data to test their validity. Research methods vary with the topic under study. Psychologists sometimes gather information through controlled laboratory experiments or by administering personality, performance, aptitude, or intelligence tests. Other methods include observation, interviews, questionnaires, clinical studies, and surveys.

Psychologists apply their knowledge to a wide range of endeavors, including health and human services, management, education, law, and sports. In addition to working in a variety of settings, psychologists usually specialize in one of a number of different areas.

Clinical psychologists—who constitute the largest specialty—work most often in counseling centers, independent or group practices, hospitals, or clinics. They help mentally and emotionally disturbed clients adjust to life and may assist medical and surgical patients in dealing with illnesses or injuries. Some clinical psychologists work in physical rehabilitation settings, treating patients with spinal cord injuries, chronic pain or illness, stroke, arthritis, and neurological conditions. Others help people deal with times of personal crisis, such as divorce or the death of a loved one.

Clinical psychologists often interview patients and give diagnostic tests. They may provide individual, family, or group psychotherapy and may design and implement behavior modification programs. Some clinical psychologists collaborate with physicians and other specialists to develop and implement treatment and intervention programs that patients can understand and comply with. Other clinical psychologists work in universities and medical schools, where they train graduate students in the delivery of mental health and behavioral medicine services. Some administer community mental health programs.

Areas of specialization within clinical psychology include health psychology, neuropsychology, and geropsychology. *Health psychologists* promote good health through health maintenance counseling programs designed to help people achieve goals, such as stopping smoking or losing weight. *Neuropsychologists* study the relation between the brain and behavior. They often work in stroke and head injury programs. *Geropsychologists* deal with the special problems faced by the elderly. The emergence and growth of these specialties reflects the increasing participation of psychologists in providing direct services to special patient populations.

Often, clinical psychologists will consult with other medical personnel regarding the best treatment for patients, especially treatment that includes medication. Clinical psychologists generally are not permitted to prescribe medication to treat patients; only psychiatrists and other medical doctors may prescribe certain medications. (See the statement on physicians and surgeons elsewhere in the *Handbook*.) However, two States—Louisiana and New Mexico—currently allow clinical psychologists to prescribe medication with some limitations, and similar proposals have been made in other States.

Counseling psychologists use various techniques, including interviewing and testing, to advise people on how to deal with problems of everyday living. They work in settings such as university counseling centers, hospitals, and individual or group practices. (See also the statements on counselors and social workers elsewhere in the *Handbook*.)

School psychologists work with students in elementary and secondary schools. They collaborate with teachers, parents, and school personnel to create safe, healthy, and supportive learning environments for all students; address students' learning and behavior problems; improve classroom management strategies or parenting skills; counter substance abuse; assess students with learning disabilities and gifted and talented students to help determine the best way to educate them; and improve teaching, learning, and socialization strategies. They also may evaluate the effectiveness of academic programs, prevention programs, behavior management procedures, and other services provided in the school setting.

Industrial-organizational psychologists apply psychological principles and research methods to the workplace in the interest of improving productivity and the quality of worklife. They also are involved in research on management and marketing problems. They screen, train and counsel applicants for jobs, as well as perform organizational development and analysis. An industrial psychologist might work with management to reorganize the work setting in order to improve productivity or quality of life in the workplace. Industrial psychologists frequently act as consultants, brought in by management to solve a particular problem.

Developmental psychologists study the physiological, cognitive, and social development that takes place throughout life. Some specialize in behavior during infancy, childhood, and adolescence, or changes that occur during maturity or old age. Developmental psychologists also may study developmental disabilities and their effects. Increasingly, research is developing ways to help elderly people remain independent as long as possible.

Social psychologists examine people's interactions with others and with the social environment. They work in organizational consultation, marketing research, systems design, or other applied psychology fields. Prominent areas of study include group behavior, leadership, attitudes, and perception.

Experimental or *research psychologists* work in university and private research centers and in business, nonprofit, and governmental organizations. They study the behavior of both human beings and animals, such as rats, monkeys, and pigeons. Prominent areas of study in experimental research include motivation, thought, attention, learning and memory, sensory and perceptual processes, effects of substance abuse, and genetic and neurological factors affecting behavior.

Working Conditions

A psychologist's subfield and place of employment determine his or her working conditions. Clinical, school, and counseling

Psychologists who deal directly with patients must be emotionally stable, mature, and able to deal effectively with people.

psychologists in private practice have their own offices and set their own hours. However, they often offer evening and weekend hours to accommodate their clients. Those employed in hospitals, nursing homes, and other health care facilities may work shifts that include evenings and weekends, while those who work in schools and clinics generally work regular hours.

Psychologists employed as faculty by colleges and universities divide their time between teaching and research and also may have administrative responsibilities; many have part-time consulting practices. Most psychologists in government and industry have structured schedules.

Increasingly, many psychologists are working as part of a team, consulting with other psychologists and professionals. Many experience pressures because of deadlines, tight schedules, and overtime. Their routine may be interrupted frequently. Travel may be required in order to attend conferences or conduct research.

Training, Other Qualifications, and Advancement

A doctoral degree usually is required for employment as an independent licensed clinical or counseling psychologist. Psychologists with a Ph.D. qualify for a wide range of teaching, research, clinical, and counseling positions in universities, health care services, elementary and secondary schools, private industry, and government. Psychologists with a Doctor of Psychology (Psy.D.) degree usually work in clinical positions or in private practices, but they also sometime teach, conduct research, or carry out administrative responsibilities.

A doctoral degree generally requires 5 to 7 years of graduate study. The Ph.D. degree culminates in a dissertation based on original research. Courses in quantitative research methods, which include the use of computer-based analysis, are an integral part of graduate study and are necessary to complete the dissertation. The Psy.D. may be based on practical work and examinations rather than a dissertation. In clinical or counseling psychology, the requirements for the doctoral degree include at least a 1-year internship.

A specialist degree is required in most States for an individual to work as a school psychologist, although a few States still credential school psychologists with master's degrees. A specialist (Ed.S.)

degree in school psychology requires a minimum of 3 years of full-time graduate study (at least 60 graduate semester hours) and a 1-year internship. Because their professional practice addresses educational and mental health components of students' development, school psychologists' training includes coursework in both education and psychology.

Persons with a master's degree in psychology may work as industrial-organizational psychologists. They also may work as psychological assistants under the supervision of doctoral-level psychologists and may conduct research or psychological evaluations. A master's degree in psychology requires at least 2 years of full-time graduate study. Requirements usually include practical experience in an applied setting and a master's thesis based on an original research project.

Competition for admission to graduate psychology programs is keen. Some universities require applicants to have an undergraduate major in psychology. Others prefer only coursework in basic psychology with courses in the biological, physical, and social sciences and in statistics and mathematics.

A bachelor's degree in psychology qualifies a person to assist psychologists and other professionals in community mental health centers, vocational rehabilitation offices, and correctional programs. Bachelor's degree holders may work as research or administrative assistants for psychologists. Some work as technicians in related fields, such as marketing research. Many find employment in other areas, such as sales or business management.

In the Federal Government, candidates having at least 24 semester hours in psychology and one course in statistics qualify for entry-level positions. However, competition for these jobs is keen because this is one of the few areas in which one can work as a psychologist without an advanced degree.

The American Psychological Association (APA) presently accredits doctoral training programs in clinical, counseling, and school psychology, as well as accrediting institutions that provide internships for doctoral students in school, clinical, and counseling psychology. The National Association of School Psychologists, with the assistance of the National Council for Accreditation of Teacher Education, also is involved in the accreditation of advanced degree programs in school psychology.

Psychologists in independent practice or those who offer any type of patient care—including clinical, counseling, and school psychologists—must meet certification or licensing requirements in all States and the District of Columbia. Licensing laws vary by State and by type of position and require licensed or certified psychologists to limit their practice to areas in which they have developed professional competence through training and experience. Clinical and counseling psychologists usually require a doctorate in psychology, the completion of an approved internship, and 1 to 2 years of professional experience. In addition, all States require that applicants pass an examination. Most State licensing boards administer a standardized test, and many supplement that with additional oral or essay questions. Some States require continuing education for renewal of the license.

The National Association of School Psychologists (NASP) awards the Nationally Certified School Psychologist (NCSP) designation, which recognizes professional competency in school psychology at a national, rather than State, level. Currently, 26 States recognize the NCSP and allow those with the certification to transfer credentials from one State to another without taking a new certification exam. In States that recognize the NCSP, the requirements for certification or licensure and those for the NCSP often are the same or similar. Requirements for the NCSP include the completion of 60 graduate semester hours in school psychology; a 1,200-hour internship, 600 hours of which must be completed

in a school setting; and a passing score on the National School Psychology Examination.

The American Board of Professional Psychology (ABPP) recognizes professional achievement by awarding specialty certification, primarily in clinical psychology, clinical neuropsychology, and counseling, forensic, industrial-organizational, and school psychology. Candidates for ABPP certification need a doctorate in psychology, postdoctoral training in their specialty, five years of experience, professional endorsements, and a passing grade on an examination.

Aspiring psychologists who are interested in direct patient care must be emotionally stable, mature, and able to deal effectively with people. Sensitivity, compassion, good communication skills, and the ability to lead and inspire others are particularly important qualities for persons wishing to do clinical work and counseling. Research psychologists should be able to do detailed work both independently and as part of a team. Patience and perseverance are vital qualities, because achieving results in the psychological treatment of patients or in research may take a long time.

Employment

Psychologists held about 179,000 jobs in 2004. Educational institutions employed about 1 out of 4 psychologists in positions other than teaching, such as counseling, testing, research, and administration. Almost 2 out of 10 were employed in health care, primarily in offices of mental health practitioners, physicians' offices, outpatient mental health and substance abuse centers, and private hospitals. Government agencies at the State and local levels employed psychologists in public hospitals, clinics, correctional facilities, and other settings.

After several years of experience, some psychologists—usually those with doctoral degrees—enter private practice or set up private research or consulting firms. About 4 out of 10 psychologists were self-employed in 2004, compared with less than 1 out of 10 among all professional workers.

In addition to the previously mentioned jobs, many psychologists held faculty positions at colleges and universities and as high school psychology teachers. (See the statements on teachers—postsecondary and teachers—preschool, kindergarten, elementary, middle, and secondary elsewhere in the *Handbook*.)

Job Outlook

Employment of psychologists is expected to grow faster than the average for all occupations through 2014, because of increased demand for psychological services in schools, hospitals, social service agencies, mental health centers, substance abuse treatment clinics, consulting firms, and private companies.

Among the specialties in this field, school psychologists—especially those with a specialist degree or higher—may enjoy the best job opportunities. Growing awareness of how students' mental health and behavioral problems, such as bullying, affect learning is increasing demand for school psychologists to offer student counseling and mental health services. Clinical and counseling psychologists will be needed to help people deal with depression and other mental disorders, marriage and family problems, job stress, and addiction. The rise in health care costs associated with unhealthy lifestyles, such as smoking, alcoholism, and obesity, has made prevention and treatment more critical. An increase in the number of employee assistance programs, which help workers deal with personal problems, also should spur job growth in clinical and counseling specialties. Industrial-organizational psychologists will be in demand to help to boost worker productivity and retention rates in a wide range of businesses. Industrial-organizational psychologists will help companies deal with issues such as workplace diversity and antidiscrimination policies. Companies also will use psychologists' expertise in survey design, analysis, and research to develop tools for marketing evaluation and statistical analysis.

Demand should be particularly strong for persons holding doctorates from leading universities in applied specialties—such as counseling, health, and school psychology. Psychologists with extensive training in quantitative research methods and computer science may have a competitive edge over applicants without background.

Master's degree holders in fields other than industrial-organizational psychology will face keen competition for jobs, because of the limited number of positions that require only a master's degree. Master's degree holders may find jobs as psychological assistants or counselors, providing mental health services under the direct supervision of a licensed psychologist. Still others may find jobs involving research and data collection and analysis in universities, government, or private companies.

Opportunities directly related to psychology will be limited for bachelor's degree holders. Some may find jobs as assistants in rehabilitation centers or in other jobs involving data collection and analysis. Those who meet State certification requirements may become high school psychology teachers.

Earnings

Median annual earnings of wage and salary clinical, counseling, and school psychologists in May 2004 were $54,950. The middle 50 percent earned between $41,850 and $71,880. The lowest 10 percent earned less than $32,280, and the highest 10 percent earned more than $92,250. Median annual earnings in the industries employing the largest numbers of clinical, counseling, and school psychologists in May 2004 were:

Offices of other health practitioners	$64,460
Elementary and secondary schools	58,360
Outpatient care centers	46,850
Individual and family services	42,640

Median annual earnings of wage and salary industrial-organizational psychologists in May 2004 were $71,400. The middle 50 percent earned between $56,880 and $93,210. The lowest 10 percent earned less than $45,620, and the highest 10 percent earned more than $125,560.

Related Occupations

Psychologists are trained to conduct research and teach, evaluate, counsel, and advise individuals and groups with special needs. Others who do this kind of work include clergy, counselors, physicians and surgeons, social workers, sociologists, and special education teachers.

Sources of Additional Information

For information on careers, educational requirements, financial assistance, and licensing in all fields of psychology, contact:

➤ American Psychological Association, Research Office and Education Directorate, 750 1st St. N.E., Washington, DC 20002-4242. Internet: **http://www.apa.org/students**

For information on careers, educational requirements, certification, and licensing of school psychologists, contact:

➤ National Association of School Psychologists, 4340 East West Hwy., Suite 402, Bethesda, MD 20814. Internet: **http://www.nasponline.org**

Information about State licensing requirements is available from:

➤ Association of State and Provincial Psychology Boards, P.O. Box 241245, Montgomery, AL 36124-1245. Internet: **http://www.asppb.org**

Information about psychology specialty certifications is available from:

➤ American Board of Professional Psychology, Inc., 300 Drayton St., 3rd Floor, Savannah, GA 31401. Internet: **http://www.abpp.org**

Urban and Regional Planners

(O*NET 19-3051.00)

Significant Points

● Local governments employ 7 out of 10 urban and regional planners.

● Most entry-level jobs require a master's degree; bachelor's degree holders may find some entry-level positions, but advancement opportunities are limited.

● Most new jobs will be in affluent, rapidly growing urban and suburban communities.

Nature of the Work

Planners develop long- and short-term plans to use land for the growth and revitalization of urban, suburban, and rural communities, while helping local officials make decisions concerning social, economic, and environmental problems. Because local governments employ the majority of urban and regional planners, they often are referred to as community, regional, or city planners.

Planners promote the best use of a community's land and resources for residential, commercial, institutional, and recreational purposes. Planners may be involved in various other activities, including making decisions relating to establishing alternative public transportation systems, developing resources, and protecting ecologically sensitive regions. Urban and regional planners address issues such as traffic congestion, air pollution, and the effects of growth and change on a community. They may formulate plans relating to the construction of new school buildings, public housing, or other kinds of infrastructure. Some planners are involved in environmental issues ranging from pollution control to wetland preservation, forest conservation, and the location of new landfills. Planners also may be involved in drafting legislation on environmental, social, and economic issues, such as sheltering the homeless, planning a new park, or meeting the demand for new correctional facilities.

Planners examine proposed community facilities, such as schools, to be sure that these facilities will meet the changing demands placed upon them over time. They keep abreast of economic and legal issues involved in zoning codes, building codes, and environmental regulations. They ensure that builders and developers follow these codes and regulations. Planners also deal with land-use issues created by population movements. For example, as suburban growth and economic development create more new jobs outside cities, the need for public transportation that enables workers to get to those jobs increases. In response, planners develop transportation models and explain their details to planning boards and the general public.

Before preparing plans for community development, planners report on the current use of land for residential, business, and community purposes. Their reports include information on the location and capacity of streets, highways, airports, water and sewer lines, schools, libraries, and cultural and recreational sites. They also provide data on the types of industries in the community, the characteristics of the population, and employment and economic trends. Using this information, along with input from citizens' advisory committees, planners design the layout of land uses for buildings and other facilities, such as subway lines and stations. Planners prepare reports showing how their programs can be carried out and what they will cost.

Planners use computers to record and analyze information and to prepare reports and recommendations for government executives and others. Computer databases, spreadsheets, and analytical techniques are utilized to project program costs and forecast future trends in employment, housing, transportation, or population. Computerized geographic information systems enable planners to map land areas, to overlay maps with geographic variables such as population density, and to combine or manipulate geographic information to produce alternative plans for land use or development.

Urban and regional planners often confer with land developers, civic leaders, and public officials and may function as mediators in community disputes, presenting alternatives that are acceptable to opposing parties. Planners may prepare material for community relations programs, speak at civic meetings, and appear before legislative committees and elected officials to explain and defend their proposals.

In large organizations, planners usually specialize in a single area, such as transportation, demography, housing, historic preservation, urban design, environmental and regulatory issues, or economic development. In small organizations, planners do various kinds of planning.

Working Conditions

Urban and regional planners often travel to inspect the features of land under consideration for development or regulation, including its current use and the types of structures on it. Some local government planners involved in site development inspections spend most of their time in the field. Although most planners have a scheduled 40-hour workweek, they frequently attend evening or weekend meetings or public hearings with citizens' groups. Planners may experience the pressure of deadlines and tight work schedules, as well as political pressure generated by interest groups affected by proposals related to urban development and land use.

Training, Other Qualifications, and Advancement

For jobs as urban and regional planners, employers prefer workers who have advanced training. Most entry-level jobs in Federal, State, and local government agencies require a master's degree from an accredited program in urban or regional planning or a master's degree in a related field, such as urban design

Urban and regional planners develop plans to use land for the growth and revitalization of communities.

or geography. A bachelor's degree from an accredited planning program, coupled with a master's degree in architecture, landscape architecture, or civil engineering, is good preparation for entry-level planning jobs in various areas, including urban design, transportation, and the environment. A master's degree from an accredited planning program provides the best training for a wide range of planning fields. Although graduates from one of the limited number of accredited bachelor's degree programs qualify for some entry-level positions, their advancement opportunities often are limited, unless they acquire an advanced degree.

Courses in related disciplines, such as architecture, law, earth sciences, demography, economics, finance, health administration, geographic information systems, and management, are highly recommended. Because familiarity with computer models and statistical techniques is important, courses in statistics and computer science also are recommended.

In 2005, 68 colleges and universities offered an accredited master's degree program, and 15 offered an accredited bachelor's degree program, in urban or regional planning. Accreditation for these programs is from the Planning Accreditation Board, which consists of representatives of the American Institute of Certified Planners, the American Planning Association, and the Association of Collegiate Schools of Planning. Most graduate programs in planning require a minimum of 2 years of study.

Specializations most commonly offered by planning schools are environmental planning, land use and comprehensive planning, economic development, housing, historic preservation, and social planning. Other popular offerings include community development, transportation, and urban design. Graduate students spend considerable time in studios, workshops, and laboratory courses, learning to analyze and solve planning problems. They often are required to work in a planning office part time or during the summer. Local government planning offices frequently offer students internships, providing experience that proves invaluable in obtaining a full-time planning position after graduation.

The American Institute of Certified Planners, a professional institute within the American Planning Association, grants certification to individuals who have the appropriate combination of education and professional experience and who pass an examination. Certification may be helpful for promotion.

Planners must be able to think in terms of spatial relationships and visualize the effects of their plans and designs. They should be flexible and be able to reconcile different viewpoints and make constructive policy recommendations. The ability to communicate effectively, both orally and in writing, is necessary for anyone interested in this field.

After a few years of experience, planners may advance to assignments requiring a high degree of independent judgment, such as designing the physical layout of a large development or recommending policy and budget options. Some public-sector planners are promoted to community planning director and spend a great deal of time meeting with officials, speaking to civic groups, and supervising a staff. Further advancement occurs through a transfer to a larger jurisdiction with more complex problems and greater responsibilities or into related occupations, such as director of community or economic development.

Employment

Urban and regional planners held about 32,000 jobs in 2004. About 7 out of 10 were employed by local governments. Companies involved with architectural, engineering, and related services, as well as management, scientific, and technical consulting services, employ an increasing proportion of planners in the private sector. Others are employed in State government agencies dealing with housing, transportation, or environmental protection, and a small number work for the Federal Government.

Job Outlook

Employment of urban and regional planners is expected to grow about as fast as the average for all occupations through 2014. Employment growth will be driven by the need for State and local governments to provide public services such as regulation of commercial development, the environment, transportation, housing, and land use and development for an expanding population. Nongovernmental initiatives dealing with historic preservation and redevelopment will provide additional openings. Some job openings also will arise from the need to replace experienced planners who transfer to other occupations, retire, or leave the labor force for other reasons. Graduates with a master's degree from an accredited program should have an advantage in the job market.

Most new jobs for urban and regional planners will be in local government, as planners will be needed to address an array of problems associated with population growth, especially in affluent, rapidly expanding communities. For example, new housing developments require roads, sewer systems, fire stations, schools, libraries, and recreation facilities that must be planned for in the midst of a consideration of budgetary constraints. Small-town chambers of commerce, economic development authorities, and tourism bureaus may hire planners, preferably with some background in marketing and public relations.

The fastest job growth for urban and regional planners will occur in the private sector, primarily in professional, scientific, and technical services. For example, planners may be employed by these firms to help design security measures for a building that meet a desired security level, but that also are subtle and blend in with the surrounding area. However, because the private sector employs fewer than 2 out of 10 urban and regional planners, not as many new jobs will be created in the private sector as in government.

Earnings

Median annual earnings of urban and regional planners were $53,450 in May 2004. The middle 50 percent earned between $41,950 and $67,530. The lowest 10 percent earned less than $33,840, and the highest 10 percent earned more than $82,610. Median annual earnings in local government, the industry employing the largest number of urban and regional planners, were $52,520.

Related Occupations

Urban and regional planners develop plans for the growth of urban, suburban, and rural communities. Others whose work is similar include architects, civil engineers, environmental engineers, landscape architects, and geographers.

Sources of Additional Information

Information on careers, salaries, and certification in urban and regional planning is available from:

➤ American Planning Association, 1776 Massachusetts Ave. N.W., Washington, DC 20036-1904. Internet: **http://www.planning.org**

Information on accredited urban and regional planning programs is available from:

➤ Association of Collegiate Schools of Planning, 6311 Mallard Trace, Tallahassee, FL 32312. Internet: **http://www.acsp.org**

Social Scientists, Other

(O*NET 19-3041.00, 19-3091.01, 19-3091.02, 19-3092.00, 19-3093.00, 19-3094.00)

Significant Points

● About half worked for Federal, State, and local governments, mostly for the Federal Government.

● The educational attainment of social scientists is among the highest of all occupations.

● Anthropologists and archaeologists will experience average growth, but slower-than-average employment growth is expected for geographers, historians, political scientists, and sociologists because they enjoy fewer opportunities outside of government and academic settings.

● Competition for jobs will remain keen for all specialties because many of these social scientists compete for jobs with other workers, such as psychologists, statisticians, and market and survey researchers.

Nature of the Work

The major social science occupations covered in this statement include anthropologists, archaeologists, geographers, historians, political scientists, and sociologists. (Economists, market and survey researchers, psychologists, and urban and regional planners are covered elsewhere in the *Handbook*.)

Social scientists study all aspects of society—from past events and achievements to human behavior and relationships among groups. Their research provides insights that help us understand different ways in which individuals and groups make decisions, exercise power, and respond to change. Through their studies and analyses, social scientists suggest solutions to social, business, personal, governmental, and environmental problems.

Research is a major activity of many social scientists, who use a variety of methods to assemble facts and construct theories. Applied research usually is designed to produce information that will enable people to make better decisions or manage their affairs more effectively. Collecting information takes many forms, including interviews and questionnaires to gather demographic and opinion data; living and working among the population being studied; performing field investigations; analyzing historical records and documents; experimenting with human or animal subjects in a laboratory; and preparing and interpreting maps and computer graphics. The work of specialists in social science varies greatly, although specialists in one field may find that their research overlaps work being conducted in another discipline.

Anthropologists study the origin and the physical, social, and cultural development and behavior of humans. They may examine the way of life, archaeological remains, language, or physical characteristics of people in various parts of the world. Some compare the customs, values, and social patterns of different cultures. Anthropologists usually concentrate in sociocultural anthropology, archaeology, linguistics, or biophysical anthropology. Sociocultural anthropologists study the customs, cultures, and social lives of groups in settings that range from unindustrialized societies to modern urban centers. Linguistic anthropologists investigate the role of, and changes to, language over time in various cultures. Biophysical anthropologists research the evolution of the human body, look for the earliest evidences of human life, and analyze how culture and biology influence one another. Physical anthropologists examine human remains found at archaeological sites in order to understand population demographics and factors that affected these populations, such as nutrition and disease.

Archaeologists examine and recover material evidence, such as the ruins of buildings, tools, pottery, and other objects remaining from past human cultures in order to determine the chronology, history, customs, and living habits of earlier civilizations. Most anthropologists and archaeologists specialize in a particular region of the world.

Geographers analyze distributions of physical and cultural phenomena on local, regional, continental, and global scales. Economic geographers study the distribution of resources and economic activities. Political geographers are concerned with the relationship of geography to political phenomena, whereas cultural geographers study the geography of cultural phenomena. Physical geographers examine variations in climate, vegetation, soil, and landforms and their implications for human activity. Urban and transportation geographers study cities and metropolitan areas, while regional geographers study the physical, economic, political, and cultural characteristics of regions ranging in size from a congressional district to entire continents. Medical geographers investigate health care delivery systems, epidemiology (the study of the causes and control of epidemics), and the effect of the environment on health. Most geographers use geographic information systems (GIS) technology to assist with their work. For example, they may use GIS to create computerized maps that can track information such as population growth, traffic patterns, environmental hazards, natural resources, and weather patterns, after which they use the information to advise governments on the development of houses, roads, or landfills.

Historians research, analyze, and interpret the past. They use many sources of information in their research, including government and institutional records, newspapers and other periodicals, photographs, interviews, films, and unpublished manuscripts such as personal diaries and letters. Historians usually specialize in a country or region, a particular period, or a particular field, such as social, intellectual, cultural, political, or diplomatic history. Biographers collect detailed information on individuals. Other historians help study and preserve archival materials, artifacts, and historic buildings and sites.

Political scientists study the origin, development, and operation of political systems and public policy. They conduct research on a wide range of subjects, such as relations between the United States and other countries, the institutions and political life of nations, the politics of small towns or a major metropolis, and the decisions of the U.S. Supreme Court. Studying topics such as public opinion, political decision making, ideology, and public policy, they analyze the structure and operation of governments, as well as various political entities. Depending on the topic, a political scientist might conduct a public-opinion survey, analyze election results or public documents, or interview public officials.

Sociologists study society and social behavior by examining the groups and social institutions people form, as well as various social, religious, political, and business organizations. They also study the behavior of, and interaction among, groups, trace their origin and growth, and analyze the influence of group activities on individual members. Sociologists are concerned with the characteristics of social groups, organizations, and institutions; the ways individuals are affected by each other and by the groups to which they belong; and the effect of social traits such as gender, age, or race on a person's daily life. The results of sociological research aid educators, lawmakers, administrators, and others who are interested in resolving social problems and formulating public policy.

Most sociologists work in one or more specialties, such as social organization, stratification, and mobility; racial and ethnic relations; education; the family; social psychology; urban, rural, political, and comparative sociology; gender relations; demography; gerontology; criminology; and sociological practice.

Working Conditions

Most social scientists have regular hours. Generally working behind a desk, either alone or in collaboration with other social scientists, they read and write research articles or reports. Many experience the pressures of writing and publishing, as well as those associated with deadlines and tight schedules. Sometimes they must work overtime, for which they usually are not compensated. Social scientists often work as an integral part of a research team, among whose members good communications skills are important. Travel may be necessary to collect information or attend meetings. Social scientists on foreign assignment must adjust to unfamiliar cultures, climates, and languages.

Some social scientists do fieldwork. For example, anthropologists, archaeologists, and geographers may travel to remote areas, live among the people they study, learn their languages, and stay for long periods at the site of their investigations. They may work under rugged conditions, and their work may involve strenuous physical exertion.

Social scientists employed by colleges and universities usually have flexible work schedules, often dividing their time among teaching, research, writing, consulting, and administrative responsibilities.

Training, Other Qualifications, and Advancement

The educational attainment of social scientists is among the highest of all occupations. The Ph.D. or an equivalent degree is a minimum requirement for most positions in colleges and universities and is important for advancement to many top-level nonacademic research and administrative posts. Graduates with master's degrees in applied specialties usually have better opportunities outside of colleges and universities, although the situation varies by field. Graduates with a master's degree in a social science may qualify for teaching positions in community colleges. Bachelor's degree holders have limited opportunities and, in most social science occupations, do not qualify for "professional" positions. The bachelor's degree does, however, provide a suitable background for many different kinds of entry-level jobs, such as research assistant, administrative aide, or management or sales trainee. With the addition of sufficient education courses, social science graduates also can qualify for teaching positions in secondary and elementary schools.

Social scientists often read and write research articles or reports.

Training in statistics and mathematics is essential for many social scientists. Mathematical and quantitative research methods increasingly are being used in geography, political science, and other fields. The ability to utilize computers for research purposes is mandatory in most disciplines. Most geographers—and increasing numbers of archaeologists— also will need to be familiar with GIS technology.

Many social science students find that internships or field experience is beneficial. Numerous local museums, historical societies, government agencies, and other organizations offer internships or volunteer research opportunities. Archaeological field schools instruct future anthropologists, archaeologists, and historians in how to excavate, record, and interpret historical sites.

Depending on their jobs, social scientists may need a wide range of personal characteristics. Intellectual curiosity and creativity are fundamental personal traits, because social scientists constantly seek new information about people, things, and ideas. The ability to think logically and methodically is important to a political scientist comparing, for example, the merits of various forms of government. Objectivity, having an open mind, and systematic work habits are important in all kinds of social science research. Perseverance is essential for an anthropologist, who might have to spend years studying artifacts from an ancient civilization before making a final analysis and interpretation. Excellent written and oral communication skills also are necessary for all these professionals.

Employment

Social scientists held about 18,000 jobs in 2004. Many worked as researchers, administrators, and counselors for a wide range of employers. About half worked for Federal, State, and local governments, mostly in the Federal Government. Other employers included scientific research and development services; management, scientific, and technical consulting services; business, professional, labor, political, and similar organizations; and architectural, engineering, and related firms.

Many individuals with training in a social science discipline teach in colleges and universities and in secondary and elementary schools. (For more information, see teachers—postsecondary and teachers—preschool, kindergarten, elementary, middle, and secondary elsewhere in the *Handbook.*) The proportion of social scientists who teach varies by specialty: for example, the academic world usually is a more important source of jobs for graduates in history than for graduates in most other social science fields.

Job Outlook

Overall employment of social scientists is expected to grow more slowly than the average for all occupations through 2014. However, projected growth rates vary by specialty. Anthropologists and archaeologists will experience average employment growth. Employment of geographers, historians, political scientists, and sociologists will grow more slowly than average, mainly because these workers enjoy fewer opportunities outside of government and academic settings.

Competition will remain keen for social science positions. Many jobs in policy, research, or marketing for which social scientists qualify are not advertised exclusively as social scientist positions. Because of the wide range of skills and knowledge possessed by the social scientists discussed in this *Handbook* statement, many compete for jobs with other workers, such as market and survey researchers, psychologists, engineers, urban and regional planners, and statisticians.

A few social scientists will find opportunities as university faculty, although competition for these jobs also will remain keen. Usually, there are more graduates than available faculty positions, although retirements among faculty are expected to rise in the next few years. The growing importance and popularity of social science subjects in secondary schools is strengthening the demand for social science teachers at that level.

Anthropologists and archaeologists will see the majority of their employment growth in the management, scientific, and technical consulting services industry. Anthropologists who work as consultants often apply anthropological knowledge and methods to problems ranging from economic development issues to forensics. Also, as construction projects increase, archaeologists will be needed to perform preliminary excavations in order to preserve historical sites and artifacts.

Geographers will have opportunities to utilize their skills to advise government, real estate developers, utilities, and telecommunications firms on where to build new roads, buildings, power plants, and cable lines. Geographers also will advise on environmental matters, such as where to build a landfill or preserve wetland habitats. Geographers with a background in GIS will find numerous job opportunities applying GIS technology in nontraditional areas, such as emergency assistance, where GIS can track locations of ambulances, police, and fire rescue units and their proximity to the emergency. Workers in these jobs may not necessarily be called "geographers", but instead may be referred to by a different title, such as "GIS analyst" or "GIS specialist." GIS technology also will be utilized in areas of growing importance, such as homeland security and defense.

Historians, political scientists, and sociologists will find jobs in policy or research. Historians may find opportunities with historic preservation societies as public interest in preserving and restoring historical sites increases. Political scientists will be able to utilize their knowledge of political institutions to further the interests of nonprofit, political lobbying, and social organizations. Sociologists may find work conducting policy research for consulting firms and nonprofit organizations, and their knowledge of society and social behavior may be used by a variety of companies in product development, marketing, and advertising. Job growth will be very slow in the Federal Government, a key employer of social scientists.

Earnings

In May 2004, anthropologists and archaeologists had median annual earnings of $43,890; geographers, $58,970; historians, $44,490; political scientists, $86,750; and sociologists, $57,870.

In the Federal Government, social scientists with a bachelor's degree and no experience could start at a yearly salary of $24,677 or $30,567 in 2005, depending on their college records. Those with a master's degree could start at $37,390, and those with a Ph.D. degree could begin at $45,239, while some individuals with experience and an advanced degree could start at $54,221. Beginning salaries were slightly higher in selected areas of the country where the prevailing local pay level was higher.

Related Occupations

Social scientists' duties and training outlined in this statement are similar to those of other occupations covered elsewhere in the *Handbook*, including other social science occupations: economists, market and survey researchers, psychologists, and urban and regional planners. Many social scientists conduct surveys, study social problems, teach, and work in museums, performing tasks similar to those of statisticians; counselors; social workers; teachers—postsecondary; teachers—preschool, kindergarten, elementary, middle, and secondary; and archivists, curators, and museum technicians.

Political scientists are concerned with the function of government, including the legal system, as are lawyers; paralegals and legal assistants; and judges, magistrates, and other judicial workers. Many political scientists analyze and report on current events, much as do news analysts, reporters, and correspondents.

Along with conservation scientists and foresters, atmospheric scientists, and environmental scientists and hydrologists, geographers are concerned with the earth's environment and natural resources. Geographers also use GIS computer technology to make maps. Other occupations with similar duties are surveyors, cartographers, photogrammetrists, and surveying technicians; computer systems analysts; and computer scientists and database administrators.

Sources of Additional Information

Detailed information about economists, market and survey researchers, psychologists, and urban and regional planners is presented elsewhere in the *Handbook*.

For information about careers in anthropology, contact:
➤ American Anthropological Association, 2200 Wilson Blvd., Suite 600, Arlington, VA 22201. Internet: **http://www.aaanet.org**

For information about careers in archaeology, contact:

➤ Society for American Archaeology, 900 2nd St. N.E., Suite 12, Washington, DC 20002-3560. Internet: **http://www.saa.org**
➤ Archaeological Institute of America, 656 Beacon St., 6th Floor, Boston, MA 02215-2006. Internet: **http://www.archaeological.org**

For information about careers in geography, contact:
➤ Association of American Geographers, 1710 16th St. N.W., Washington, DC 20009-3198. Internet: **http://www.aag.org**

Information on careers for historians is available from:
➤ American Historical Association, 400 A St. S.E., Washington, DC 20003-3889. Internet: **http://www.historians.org**

For information about careers in political science, contact:
➤ American Political Science Association, 1527 New Hampshire Ave. N.W., Washington, DC 20036-1206. Internet: **http://www.apsanet.org**
➤ National Association of Schools of Public Affairs and Administration, 1120 G St. N.W., Suite 730, Washington, DC 20005-3869. Internet: **http://www.naspaa.org**

Information about careers in sociology is available from:
➤ American Sociological Association, 1307 New York Ave. N.W., Suite 700, Washington, DC 20005-4712. Internet: **http://www.asanet.org**

Science Technicians

(O*NET 19-4011.01, 19-4011.02, 19-4021.00, 19-4031.00, 19-4041.01, 19-4041.02, 19-4051.01, 19-4051.02, 19-4091.00, 19-4092.00, 19-4093.00)

Significant Points

- Science technicians in production jobs can be employed on day, evening, or night shifts; some other technicians work outdoors, sometimes in remote locations.

- Many employers prefer applicants who have at least 2 years of specialized training or an associate's degree.

- Projected job growth varies among occupational specialties; for example, forensic science technicians will grow much faster than average, while chemical technicians will grow more slowly than average.

- Job opportunities are expected to be best for graduates of applied science technology programs.

Nature of the Work

Science technicians use the principles and theories of science and mathematics to solve problems in research and development and to help invent and improve products and processes. However, their jobs are more practically oriented than those of scientists. Technicians set up, operate, and maintain laboratory instruments, monitor experiments, make observations, calculate and record results, and often develop conclusions. They must keep detailed logs of all of their work-related activities. Those who perform production work monitor manufacturing processes and may be involved in ensuring quality by testing products for proper proportions of ingredients, for purity, or for strength and durability.

As laboratory instrumentation and procedures have become more complex, the role of science technicians in research and development has expanded. In addition to performing routine tasks, many technicians now develop and adapt laboratory procedures to achieve the best results, interpret data, and devise solutions to problems, under the direction of scientists. Moreover, technicians must master the laboratory equipment, so that they can adjust settings when necessary and recognize when equipment is malfunctioning.

The increasing use of robotics to perform many routine tasks has freed technicians to operate more sophisticated laboratory equipment. Science technicians make extensive use of computers, computer-interfaced equipment, robotics, and high-technology industrial applications, such as biological engineering.

Most science technicians specialize, learning skills and working in the same disciplines in which scientists work. Occupational titles, therefore, tend to follow the same structure as those for scientists. *Agricultural technicians* work with agricultural scientists in food, fiber, and animal research, production, and processing. Some conduct tests and experiments to improve the yield and quality of crops or to increase the resistance of plants and animals to disease, insects, or other hazards. Other agricultural technicians breed animals for the purpose of investigating nutrition. *Food science technicians* assist food scientists and technologists in research and development, production technology, and quality control. For example, food science technicians may conduct tests on food additives and preservatives to ensure compliance with Food and Drug Administration regulations regarding color, texture, and nutrients. These technicians analyze, record, and compile test results; order supplies to maintain laboratory inventory; and clean and sterilize laboratory equipment.

Biological technicians work with biologists studying living organisms. Many assist scientists who conduct medical research—helping to find a cure for cancer or AIDS, for example. Those who work in pharmaceutical companies help develop and manufacture medicinal and pharmaceutical preparations. Those working in the field of microbiology generally work as laboratory assistants, studying living organisms and infectious agents. Biological technicians also analyze organic substances, such as blood, food, and drugs, and some examine evidence in a forensic science laboratory. Biological technicians working in biotechnology laboratories use the knowledge and techniques gained from basic research by scientists, including gene splicing and recombinant DNA, and apply them in product development.

Chemical technicians work with chemists and chemical engineers, developing and using chemicals and related products and equipment. Generally, there are two types of chemical technicians: research and development technicians who work in experimental laboratories and process control technicians who work in manufacturing or other industrial plants. Many research and development chemical technicians conduct a variety of laboratory procedures, from routine process control to complex research projects. For example, they may collect and analyze samples of air and water to monitor pollution levels, or they may produce compounds through complex organic synthesis. Most process technicians work in manufacturing, testing packaging for design, integrity of materials, and environmental acceptability. Often, process technicians who work in plants also focus on quality assurance, monitoring product quality or production processes and developing new production techniques. A few work in shipping to provide technical support and expertise for these functions.

Environmental science and protection technicians perform laboratory and field tests to monitor environmental resources and determine the contaminants and sources of pollution in the environment. They may collect samples for testing or be involved in abating, controlling, or remediating sources of environmental pollution. Some are responsible for waste management operations, control and management of hazardous materials inventory, or general activities involving regulatory compliance. Many environmental science technicians employed at private consulting firms work directly under the supervision of an environmental scientist.

Forensic science technicians investigate crimes by collecting and analyzing physical evidence. Often, they specialize in areas such as DNA analysis or firearm examination, performing tests on weapons or on substances such as fiber, glass, hair, tissue, and body fluids to determine their significance to the investigation. Proper collection and storage methods are important to protect the evidence. Forensic science technicians also prepare reports to document their findings and the laboratory techniques used, and they may provide information and expert opinion to investigators. When criminal cases come to trial, forensic science technicians often give testimony, as expert witnesses, on specific laboratory findings by identifying and classifying substances, materials, and other evidence collected at the scene of a crime. Some forensic science technicians work closely with other experts or technicians. For example, a forensic science technician may consult either a medical expert about the exact time and cause of a death or a technician who specializes in DNA typing in hopes of matching a DNA type to a suspect.

Forest and conservation technicians compile data on the size, content, and condition of forest land tracts. These workers usually work in a forest under the supervision of a forester, conducting specific tasks such as measuring timber, supervising harvesting operations, assisting in roadbuilding operations, and locating property lines and features. They also may gather basic information, such as data on species and populations of trees, disease and insect damage, tree seedling mortality, and conditions that may pose a fire hazard. In addition, forest and conservation technicians train and lead forest and conservation workers in seasonal activities, such as planting tree seedlings, putting out forest fires, and maintaining recreational facilities. Increasing numbers of forest and conservation technicians work in urban forestry—the study of individual trees in cities—and other nontraditional specialties, rather than in forests or rural areas.

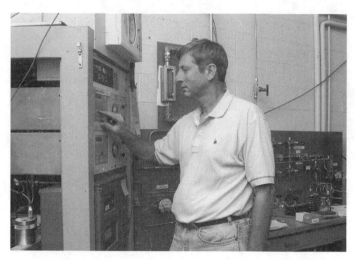

Many employers prefer science technicians who have at least 2 years of specialized training or an associate degree.

Geological and petroleum technicians measure and record physical and geologic conditions in oil or gas wells, using advanced instruments lowered into the wells or analyzing the mud from the wells. In oil and gas exploration, these technicians collect and examine geological data or use scanning electron microscopes to test geological samples to determine their petroleum content and their mineral and element composition. Some petroleum technicians, called *scouts*, collect information about oil and gas well-drilling operations, geological and geophysical prospecting, and land or lease contracts.

Nuclear technicians operate nuclear test and research equipment, monitor radiation, and assist nuclear engineers and physicists in research. Some also operate remote control equipment to manipulate radioactive materials or materials to be exposed to radioactivity.

Other science technicians collect weather information or assist oceanographers.

Working Conditions

Science technicians work under a wide variety of conditions. Most work indoors, usually in laboratories, and have regular hours. Some occasionally work irregular hours to monitor experiments that cannot be completed during regular working hours. Production technicians often work in 8-hour shifts around the clock. Others, such as agricultural, forest and conservation, geological and petroleum, and environmental science and protection technicians, perform much of their work outdoors, sometimes in remote locations.

Some science technicians may be exposed to hazards from equipment, chemicals, or toxic materials. Chemical technicians sometimes work with toxic chemicals or radioactive isotopes, nuclear technicians may be exposed to radiation, and biological technicians sometimes work with disease-causing organisms or radioactive agents. Forensic science technicians often are exposed to human body fluids and firearms. However, these working conditions pose little risk if proper safety procedures are followed. For forensic science technicians, collecting evidence from crime scenes can be distressing and unpleasant.

Training, Other Qualifications, and Advancement

There are several ways to qualify for a job as a science technician. Many employers prefer applicants who have at least 2 years of specialized training or an associate's degree in applied science or science-related technology. Because employers' preferences vary, however, some science technicians have a bachelor's degree in chemistry, biology, or forensic science or have taken several science and math courses at 4-year colleges.

Many technical and community colleges offer associate's degrees in a specific technology or a more general education in science and mathematics. A number of 2-year associate's degree programs are designed to provide easy transfer to a 4-year college or university. Technical institutes usually offer technician training, but provide less theory and general education than do technical or community colleges. The length of programs at technical institutes varies, although 1-year certificate programs and 2-year associate's degree programs are common.

Approximately 20 colleges or universities offer a bachelor's degree program in forensic science; about another 20 schools offer a bachelor-of-science degree in chemistry, biochemistry, or genetic engineering with an emphasis on forensic science or criminology; a few additional schools offer a bachelor-of-science degree with an emphasis in a specialty area, such as criminology, pathology, jurisprudence, investigation, odontology, toxicology, or forensic accounting. In contrast to some other science technician positions that require only a 2-year degree, forensic science positions usually require a 4-year degree to work in the field. Knowledge and understanding of legal procedures also can be helpful. Prospective forestry and conservation technicians can choose from more than 20 associate's degree programs in forest technology accredited by the Society of American Foresters.

Most chemical process technicians have a 2-year degree, usually an associate's degree in process technology, although in some cases a high school diploma is sufficient. These workers usually receive additional on-the-job training. Entry-level workers whose college training encompasses extensive hands-on experience with a variety of diagnostic laboratory equipment generally require less on-the-job training. Those with a high school diploma typically begin work as trainees under the direct supervision of a more experienced process technician. Many with only a high school diploma eventually earn a 2-year degree in process technology, often paid for by their employer.

Some schools offer cooperative-education or internship programs, allowing students the opportunity to work at a local company or some other workplace while attending classes during alternate terms. Participation in such programs can significantly enhance a student's employment prospects.

Persons interested in careers as science technicians should take as many high school science and math courses as possible. Science courses taken beyond high school, in an associate's or bachelor's degree program, should be laboratory oriented, with an emphasis on bench skills. A solid background in applied basic chemistry, physics, and math is vital. Because computers often are used in research and development laboratories, technicians should have strong computer skills, especially in computer modeling. Communication skills also are important: technicians often are required to report their findings both orally and in writing. In addition, technicians should be able to work well with others, because teamwork is common. Organizational ability, an eye for detail, and skill in interpreting scientific results are important as well. A high mechanical aptitude, attention to detail, and analytical thinking are all important characteristics of science technicians.

Prospective science technicians can acquire good career preparation through 2-year formal training programs that combine the teaching of scientific principles and theory with practical hands-on application in a laboratory setting with up-to-date equipment. Graduates of 4-year bachelor's degree programs in

science who have considerable experience in laboratory-based courses, have completed internships, or have held summer jobs in laboratories also are well qualified for science technician positions and are preferred by some employers. However, those with a bachelor's degree who accept technician jobs generally cannot find employment that uses their more advanced academic education.

Technicians usually begin work as trainees in routine positions under the direct supervision of a scientist or a more experienced technician. Job candidates whose training or educational background encompasses extensive hands-on experience with a variety of laboratory equipment, including computers and related equipment, usually require a short period of on-the-job training. As they gain experience, technicians take on more responsibility and carry out assignments under only general supervision, and some eventually become supervisors. However, technicians employed at universities often have their fortunes tied to those of particular professors; when those professors retire or leave, these technicians face uncertain employment prospects.

Employment

Science technicians held about 324,000 jobs in 2004. As indicated by the following tabulation, chemical and biological technicians accounted for 39 percent of all jobs:

Biological technicians	64,000
Chemical technicians	62,000
Forest and conservation technicians	33,000
Environmental science and protection technicians, including health	31,000
Agricultural and food science technicians	23,000
Geological and petroleum technicians	11,000
Forensic science technicians	9,800
Nuclear technicians	7,300

Chemical technicians held jobs in a wide range of manufacturing and service-providing industries. Thirty-five percent worked in chemical manufacturing and another 26 percent worked in professional, scientific, or technical services firms. About 27 percent of biological technicians also worked in professional, scientific, or technical services firms; most other biological technicians worked in pharmaceutical and medicine manufacturing or for Federal, State, or local governments. Significant numbers of environmental science and protection technicians also worked for State and local governments and professional, scientific, and technical services firms. About 75 percent of forest and conservation technicians held jobs in the Federal Government; another 13 percent worked for State governments. Around 18 percent of agricultural and food science technicians worked for food-processing companies; most of the rest worked for scientific research and development services firms and State governments. Approximately 23 percent of all geological and petroleum technicians worked for oil and gas extraction companies, and forensic science technicians worked primarily for State and local governments.

Job Outlook

Job opportunities are expected to be best for graduates of applied science technology programs who are well trained on equipment used in industrial and government laboratories and production facilities. As the instrumentation and techniques used in industrial research, development, and production become increasingly more complex, employers are seeking individuals with highly developed technical and communication skills.

Overall employment of science technicians is expected to increase about as fast as the average for all occupations through the year 2014. The continued growth of scientific and medical research—particularly research related to biotechnology—as well as the development and production of technical products should stimulate demand for science technicians in many industries. The increase in the number of biological technicians will be about as fast as average, as the growing number of agricultural and medicinal products developed with the use of biotechnology techniques will boost demand for these workers. Also, stronger competition among pharmaceutical companies and an aging population are expected to contribute to the need for innovative and improved drugs, further spurring demand for biological technicians. The fastest employment growth of biological technicians should occur in the pharmaceutical and medicine manufacturing industry and educational services.

Job growth for chemical technicians is projected to be slower than average. The chemical manufacturing industry, the major employer of chemical technicians, is anticipated to experience a decline in overall employment as companies downsize and turn to outside contractors to provide specialized services. Some of these contractors will be in other lower-wage countries, further limiting employment growth. Job opportunities are expected to be more plentiful in pharmaceutical and medicine manufacturing as the public continues to demand newer and better pharmaceuticals. To meet this demand, pharmaceutical manufacturing firms are expected to continue to devote money to research and development, either through in-house teams or, increasingly, by contracting to professional, scientific, and technical services firms, spurring employment growth of chemical technicians in that industry. An increasing focus on quality assurance will require a greater number of process technicians, further stimulating demand for these workers.

Employment of environmental science and protection technicians should grow about as fast as the average; these workers will be needed to help regulate waste products; to collect air, water, and soil samples for measuring levels of pollutants; to monitor compliance with environmental regulations; and to clean up contaminated sites.

Limited demand for forest and conservation technicians within the Federal Government will lead to slower-than-average growth in this occupation, due to general downsizing and continued reductions in timber management on Federal lands. Opportunities at State and local governments within specialties such as urban forestry and geographic information systems (GIS)—a locator system that uses satellites—may, however, provide some new jobs. In addition, an increased emphasis on specific conservation issues, such as environmental protection, preservation of water resources, and control of exotic and invasive pests, may provide some employment opportunities. Few opportunities will be available in the private sector.

Employment of agricultural and food science technicians is projected to grow about as fast as the average. Best opportunities will be in specific segments of the food-processing industry and in agricultural biotechnology, specifically in scientific research and development services. Research—particularly biotechnological research—will be necessary as it becomes increasingly important to balance greater agricultural output with protection and preservation of soil, water, and the ecosystem. In particular, research will be needed to combat insects and diseases as they further adapt to pesticides and as soil fertility and water quality continue to need improvement. State and local government also should provide many opportunities due both to projected increases in employment and as the need to replace retiring workers is expected to accelerate.

Jobs for forensic science technicians are expected to increase much faster than average. Crime scene technicians who work for State Public Safety Departments should experience favorable employment prospects. Jobseekers with a 4-year degree in a forensic science will enjoy much better opportunities than those with only a 2-year degree.

Slower-than-average employment growth is expected for geological and petroleum technicians because employment in the oil and gas extraction and mining industries, among the largest employers of geological and petroleum technicians, is expected to decline. Due to a lack of qualified candidates, however, prospective jobseekers should experience little competition for positions, especially in energy-related fields. Job opportunities also will be favorable in professional, scientific, and technical services firms because geological and petroleum technicians will be needed to assist environmental scientists and geoscientists as they provide consultation services for companies regarding environmental policy and Federal Government mandates, such as those requiring lower sulfur emissions.

Along with opportunities created by growth, many job openings should arise from the need to replace technicians who retire or leave the labor force for other reasons. During periods of economic recession, science technicians may be laid off.

Earnings

Median hourly earnings of science technicians in May 2004 were as follows:

Nuclear technicians	$28.46
Forensic science technicians	21.16
Geological and petroleum technicians	19.35
Chemical technicians	18.35
Environmental science and protection technicians, including health	16.99
Biological technicians	15.97
Agricultural and food science technicians	14.29
Forest and conservation technicians	13.14

In 2005, the average annual salary in nonsupervisory, supervisory, and managerial positions in the Federal Government was $38,443 for biological science technicians; $50,264 for physical science technicians; $62,854 for geodetic technicians; $48,238 for hydrologic technicians; and $58,725 for meteorological technicians.

Related Occupations

Other technicians who apply scientific principles at a level usually acquired in 2-year associate's degree programs include engineering technicians, broadcast and sound engineering technicians and radio operators, drafters, and health technologists and technicians, especially clinical laboratory technologists and technicians, diagnostic medical sonographers, and radiologic technologists and technicians.

Sources of Additional Information

For information about a career as a chemical technician, contact:
➤ American Chemical Society, Education Division, Career Publications, 1155 16th St. NW., Washington, DC 20036. Internet: **http://www.acs.org**

For career information and a list of undergraduate, graduate, and doctoral programs in forensic sciences, contact:
➤ American Academy of Forensic Sciences, P.O. Box 669, Colorado Springs, CO, 80901. Internet: **http://www.aafs.org**

For general information on forestry technicians and a list of schools offering education in forestry, send a self-addressed, stamped business envelope to:
➤ Society of American Foresters, 5400 Grosvenor Ln., Bethesda, MD 20814. Internet: **http://www.safnet.org**

Community and Social Services Occupations

Counselors

(O*NET 21-1011.00, 21-1012.00, 21-1013.00, 21-1014.00, 21-1015.00, 21-1019.99)

Significant Points

- School counselors must be certified, and other counselors must be licensed to practice in all but two States.
- A master's degree generally is needed to become a licensed counselor.
- Job opportunities for counselors should be very good because job openings are expected to exceed the number of graduates from counseling programs.
- State and local governments employ about 4 in 10 counselors, and the health services industry employs most of the others.

Nature of the Work

Counselors assist people with personal, family, educational, mental health, and career decisions and problems. Their duties depend on the individuals they serve and on the settings in which they work.

Educational, vocational, and school counselors provide individuals and groups with career and educational counseling. In school settings—elementary through postsecondary—they usually are called school counselors, and they work with students, including those with academic and social development problems and those with special needs. They advocate for students and work with other individuals and organizations to promote the academic, career, personal, and social development of children and youths. School counselors help students evaluate their abilities, interests, talents, and personality characteristics in order to develop realistic academic and career goals. Counselors use interviews, counseling sessions, interest and aptitude assessment tests, and other methods to evaluate and advise students. They also operate career information centers and career education programs. High school counselors advise students regarding college majors, admission requirements, entrance exams, financial aid, trade or technical schools, and apprenticeship programs. They help students develop job search skills, such as resume writing and interviewing techniques. College career planning and placement counselors assist alumni or students with career development and job-hunting techniques.

Elementary school counselors observe younger children during classroom and play activities and confer with their teachers and parents to evaluate the children's strengths, problems, or special needs. In conjunction with teachers and administrators, they make sure that the curriculum addresses both the academic and the emotional development needs of students. Elementary school counselors do less vocational and academic counseling than do secondary school counselors.

School counselors at all levels help students to understand and deal with social, behavioral, and personal problems. These counselors emphasize preventive and developmental counseling to provide students with the life skills needed to deal with problems before they occur and to enhance students' personal, social, and academic growth. Counselors provide special services, including alcohol and drug prevention programs and conflict resolution classes. They also

try to identify cases of domestic abuse and other family problems that can affect a student's development. Counselors interact with students individually, in small groups, or with entire classes. They consult and collaborate with parents, teachers, school administrators, school psychologists, medical professionals, and social workers in order to develop and implement strategies to help students be successful in the education system.

Vocational counselors who provide mainly career counseling outside the school setting are also referred to as *employment counselors* or *career counselors*. Their chief focus is helping individuals with career decisions. Vocational counselors explore and evaluate the client's education, training, work history, interests, skills, and personality traits, and arrange for aptitude and achievement tests to assist the client in making career decisions. They also work with individuals to develop their job-search skills, and they assist clients in locating and applying for jobs. In addition, career counselors provide support to persons experiencing job loss, job stress, or other career transition issues.

Rehabilitation counselors help people deal with the personal, social, and vocational effects of disabilities. They counsel people with disabilities resulting from birth defects, illness or disease, accidents, or the stress of daily life. They evaluate the strengths and limitations of individuals, provide personal and vocational counseling, and arrange for medical care, vocational training, and job placement. Rehabilitation counselors interview both individuals with disabilities and their families, evaluate school and medical reports, and confer and plan with physicians, psychologists, occupational therapists, and employers to determine the capabilities and skills of the individual. Conferring with the client, they develop a rehabilitation program that often includes training to help the person develop job skills. Rehabilitation counselors also work toward increasing the client's capacity to live independently.

Mental health counselors work with individuals, families, and groups to address and treat mental and emotional disorders and to promote optimum mental health. They are trained in a variety of therapeutic techniques used to address a wide range of issues, including depression, addiction and substance abuse, suicidal impulses, stress management, problems with self-esteem, issues associated with aging, job and career concerns, educational decisions, issues related to mental and emotional health, and family, parenting, and marital or other relationship problems. Mental health counselors often work closely with other mental health specialists, such as psychiatrists, psychologists, clinical social workers, psychiatric nurses, and school counselors. (Information on physicians and surgeons, psychologists, registered nurses, and social workers appears elsewhere in the *Handbook*.)

Substance abuse and behavioral disorder counselors help people who have problems with alcohol, drugs, gambling, and eating disorders. They counsel individuals who are addicted to drugs, helping them to identify behaviors and problems related to their addiction. They also conduct programs aimed at preventing addictions from occurring in the first place. These counselors hold sessions designed for individuals, families, or groups.

Marriage and family therapists apply principles, methods, and therapeutic techniques to individuals, families, couples, or organizations in order to resolve emotional conflicts. In doing so, they modify people's perceptions and behaviors, enhance communication and understanding among family members, and help to prevent family and individual crises. Marriage and family therapists also may engage in psychotherapy of a nonmedical nature, make appropriate referrals to psychiatric resources, perform research, and teach courses about human development and interpersonal relationships.

Other counseling specialties include gerontological, multicultural, and genetic counseling. A gerontological counselor provides services to elderly persons and their families when they face changing lifestyles as they grow older. A multicultural counselor helps employers adjust to an increasingly diverse workforce. Genetic counselors provide information and support to families who have members with birth defects or genetic disorders and to families who may be at risk for a variety of inherited conditions. These counselors identify families at risk, investigate the problem that is present in the family, interpret information about the disorder, analyze inheritance patterns and risks of recurrence, and review available options with the family.

Working Conditions
Some school counselors work the traditional 9- to 10-month school year with a 2- to 3-month vacation, but increasing numbers, especially those working in middle and high schools, are employed on 11-month or full-year contracts. They usually work the same hours as teachers, but may travel more frequently to attend conferences and conventions. College career planning and placement counselors work long and irregular hours during student recruiting periods.

Rehabilitation counselors usually work a standard 40-hour week. Self-employed counselors and those working in mental health and community agencies, such as substance abuse and behavioral disorder counselors, frequently work evenings in order to counsel clients who work during the day. Both mental health counselors and marriage and family therapists also often work flexible hours to accommodate families in crisis or working couples who must have evening or weekend appointments.

Counselors must possess high physical and emotional energy to handle the array of problems that they address. Dealing daily with these problems can cause stress. Although the risk of litigation is relatively low, it is still prudent for counselors in all fields to hold some form of personal liability insurance. Because privacy is essential for confidential and frank discussions with clients, counselors usually have private offices.

Training, Other Qualifications, and Advancement
All States require school counselors to hold a State school counseling certification and to have completed at least some graduate course

Counselors help people with personal, family, educational, mental health, and career decisions and problems.

work; most require the completion of a master's degree. Some States require public school counselors to have both counseling and teaching certificates and to have had some teaching experience before receiving certification. For counselors based outside of schools, 48 States and the District of Columbia have some form of counselor licensure that governs their practice of counseling. Requirements typically include the completion of a master's degree in counseling, the accumulation of 2 years or 3,000 hours of supervised clinical experience beyond the master's degree level, the passage of a State-recognized exam, adherence to ethical codes and standards, and the completion of annual continuing education requirements.

Counselors must be aware of educational and training requirements that are often very detailed and that vary by area and by counseling specialty. Prospective counselors should check with State and local governments, employers, and national voluntary certification organizations in order to determine which requirements apply.

As mentioned, a master's degree is typically required to be licensed as a counselor. A bachelor's degree often qualifies a person to work as a counseling aide, rehabilitation aide, or social service worker. Some States require counselors in public employment to have a master's degree; others accept a bachelor's degree with appropriate counseling courses. Counselor education programs in colleges and universities usually are found in departments of education or psychology. Fields of study include college student affairs, elementary or secondary school counseling, education, gerontological counseling, marriage and family counseling, substance abuse counseling, rehabilitation counseling, agency or community counseling, clinical mental health counseling, counseling psychology, career counseling, and related fields. Courses are grouped into eight core areas: Human growth and development, social and cultural diversity, relationships, group work, career development, assessment, research and program evaluation, and professional identity. In an accredited master's degree program, 48 to 60 semester hours of graduate study, including a period of supervised clinical experience in counseling, are required.

Graduate programs in career, community, gerontological, mental health, school, student affairs, and marriage and family counseling are accredited by the Council for Accreditation of Counseling and Related Educational Programs (CACREP). While completion of a CACREP-accredited program is not necessary to become a counselor, it makes it easier to fulfill the requirements for State licensing. Another organization, the Council on Rehabilitation Education (CORE), accredits graduate programs in rehabilitation counseling. Accredited master's degree programs include a minimum of 2 years of full-time study, including 600 hours of supervised clinical internship experience.

Some counselors elect to be nationally certified by the National Board for Certified Counselors, Inc. (NBCC), which grants the general practice credential "National Certified Counselor." To be certified, a counselor must hold a master's degree with a concentration in counseling from a regionally accredited college or university; must have at least 2 years of supervised field experience in a counseling setting (graduates from counselor education programs accredited by CACREP are exempted); must provide two professional endorsements, one of which must be from a recent supervisor; and must have a passing score on the NBCC's National Counselor Examination for Licensure and Certification (NCE). This national certification is voluntary and is distinct from State licensing. However, in some States, those who pass the national exam are exempted from taking a State certification exam. NBCC also offers specialty certifications in school, clinical mental health, and addiction counseling, which supplement the national certified counselor designation. These specialty certifications require passage of a supplemental exam. To maintain their certification, counselors retake and pass the NCE or complete 100 credit hours of acceptable continuing education every 5 years.

Another organization, the Commission on Rehabilitation Counselor Certification, offers voluntary national certification for rehabilitation counselors. Some employers may require rehabilitation counselors to be nationally certified. To become certified, rehabilitation counselors usually must graduate from an accredited educational program, complete an internship, and pass a written examination. (Certification requirements vary according to an applicant's educational history. Employment experience, for example, is required for those with a counseling degree in a specialty other than rehabilitation.) After meeting these requirements, candidates are designated "Certified Rehabilitation Counselors." To maintain their certification, counselors must successfully retake the certification exam or complete 100 credit hours of acceptable continuing education every 5 years.

Other counseling organizations also offer certification in particular counseling specialties. Usually, becoming certified is voluntary, but having certification may enhance one's job prospects.

Some employers provide training for newly hired counselors. Others may offer time off or provide help with tuition if it is needed to complete a graduate degree. Counselors must participate in graduate studies, workshops, and personal studies to maintain their certificates and licenses.

Persons interested in counseling should have a strong desire to help others and should possess the ability to inspire respect, trust, and confidence. They should be able to work independently or as part of a team. Counselors must follow the code of ethics associated with their respective certifications and licenses.

Prospects for advancement vary by counseling field. School counselors can move to a larger school; become directors or supervisors of counseling, guidance, or pupil personnel services; or, usually with further graduate education, become counselor educators, counseling psychologists, or school administrators. (Psychologists and education administrators are covered elsewhere in the *Handbook*.) Some counselors choose to work for a State's department of education. For marriage and family therapists, doctoral education in family therapy emphasizes the training of supervisors, teachers, researchers, and clinicians in the discipline.

Counselors can become supervisors or administrators in their agencies. Some counselors move into research, consulting, or college teaching or go into private or group practice.

Employment

Counselors held about 601,000 jobs in 2004. Employment was distributed among the counseling specialties as follows:

Educational, vocational, and school counselors 248,000
Rehabilitation counselors.. 131,000
Mental health counselors 96,000
Substance abuse and behavioral disorder counselors 76,000
Marriage and family therapists 24,000
Counselors, all other 25,000

Educational, vocational, and school counselors work primarily in elementary and secondary schools and colleges and universities. Other types of counselors work in a wide variety of public and private establishments, including healthcare facilities; job training, career development, and vocational rehabilitation centers; social agencies; correctional institutions; and residential care facilities, such as halfway houses for criminal offenders and group homes for children, the elderly, and the disabled. Some sub-

stance abuse and behavioral disorder counselors work in therapeutic communities where addicts live while undergoing treatment. Counselors also work in organizations engaged in community improvement and social change, drug and alcohol rehabilitation programs, and State and local government agencies. A growing number of counselors are self-employed and work in group practices or private practice, due in part to new laws allowing counselors to be paid for their services by insurance companies and to the growing recognition that counselors are well-trained, effective professionals.

Job Outlook

Overall employment of counselors is expected to grow faster than the average for all occupations through 2014. In addition, numerous job openings will occur as many counselors retire or leave the profession. While job prospects will vary with location and specialization, opportunities generally should be very good because the number of job openings that arise should exceed the number of graduates of counseling programs. Rehabilitation counselors and substance abuse and behavioral disorder counselors, in particular, should experience excellent prospects.

Employment of school counselors is expected to grow with increases in student enrollments at postsecondary schools and colleges and as more States require elementary schools to employ counselors. Expansion of the responsibilities of school counselors should also lead to increases in their employment. For example, counselors are becoming more involved in crisis and preventive counseling, helping students deal with issues ranging from drug and alcohol abuse to death and suicide. Although schools and governments realize the value of counselors in helping their students to achieve academic success, budget constraints at every school level will dampen job growth of school counselors. However, Federal grants and subsidies may help to offset tight budgets and allow the reduction in student-to-counselor ratios to continue. Job prospects should be more favorable in rural and inner-city schools.

Demand for vocational or career counselors should grow as multiple job and career changes become common for workers and as workers become increasingly aware of the counselors' services. In addition, State and local governments will employ growing numbers of counselors to assist beneficiaries of welfare programs who exhaust their eligibility and must find jobs. Other opportunities for employment counselors will arise in private job-training centers that provide training and other services to laid-off workers and others seeking to acquire new skills or new careers.

Demand is expected to be strong for substance abuse and behavioral disorder counselors because drug offenders are increasingly being sent to treatment programs rather than to jail. Mental health counselors will be needed to staff statewide networks that are being established to improve services for children and adolescents with serious emotional disturbances and for their family members. Under managed care systems, insurance companies are increasingly providing for reimbursement of counselors as a less costly alternative to psychiatrists and psychologists.

The number of people who will need rehabilitation counseling is expected to grow as advances in medical technology allow more people to survive injury or illness and live independently again. In addition, legislation requiring equal employment rights for people with disabilities will spur demand for counselors, who not only help these people make a transition into the workforce but also help companies to comply with the law.

Employment of mental health counselors and marriage and family therapists will grow as more people become comfortable with seeking professional help for a variety of health, personal, and family problems. Employers are also increasingly offering employee assistance programs that provide mental health and alcohol and drug abuse counseling. More people are expected to use these services as society focuses on ways of developing mental well-being, such as controlling stress associated with job and family responsibilities.

Earnings
Median annual earnings of educational, vocational, and school counselors in May 2004 were $45,570. The middle 50 percent earned between $34,530 and $58,400. The lowest 10 percent earned less than $26,260, and the highest 10 percent earned more than $72,390. School counselors can earn additional income working summers in the school system or in other jobs. Median annual earnings in the industries employing the largest numbers of educational, vocational, and school counselors in 2004 were as follows:

Elementary and secondary schools	$51,160
Junior colleges	45,730
Colleges, universities, and professional schools	39,110
Individual and family services	30,240
Vocational rehabilitation services	27,800

Median annual earnings of substance abuse and behavioral disorder counselors in May 2004 were $32,130. The middle 50 percent earned between $25,840 and $40,130. The lowest 10 percent earned less than $21,060, and the highest 10 percent earned more than $49,600.

Median annual earnings of mental health counselors in May 2004 were $32,960. The middle 50 percent earned between $25,660 and $43,370. The lowest 10 percent earned less than $20,880, and the highest 10 percent earned more than $55,810.

Median annual earnings of rehabilitation counselors in May 2004 were $27,870. The middle 50 percent earned between $22,110 and $36,120. The lowest 10 percent earned less than $18,560, and the highest 10 percent earned more than $48,130.

For substance abuse, mental health, and rehabilitation counselors, government employers generally pay the highest wages, followed by hospitals and social service agencies. Residential care facilities often pay the lowest wages.

Median annual earnings of marriage and family therapists in May 2004 were $38,980. The middle 50 percent earned between $30,260 and $49,990. The lowest 10 percent earned less than $23,460, and the highest 10 percent earned more than $65,080. Median annual earnings in May 2004 were $33,620 in individual and family social services, the industry employing the largest number of marriage and family therapists.

Self-employed counselors who have well-established practices, as well as counselors employed in group practices, usually have the highest earnings.

Related Occupations
Counselors help people evaluate their interests, abilities, and disabilities and deal with personal, social, academic, and career problems. Others who help people in similar ways include teachers, social and human service assistants, social workers, psychologists, physicians and surgeons, registered nurses, members of the clergy, occupational therapists, and human resources, training, and labor relations managers and specialists.

Sources of Additional Information
For general information about counseling, as well as information on specialties such as college, mental health, rehabilitation, multicultural, career, marriage and family, and gerontological counseling, contact:
➤ American Counseling Association, 5999 Stevenson Ave., Alexandria, VA 22304-3300. Internet: **http://www.counseling.org**

For information on school counselors, contact:
➤ American School Counselors Association, 1101 King St., Suite 625, Alexandria, VA 22314. Internet: **http://www.schoolcounselor.org**

For information on accredited counseling and related training programs, contact:
➤ Council for Accreditation of Counseling and Related Educational Programs, American Counseling Association, 5999 Stevenson Ave., 4th floor, Alexandria, VA 22304. Internet: **http://www.cacrep.org**

For information on national certification requirements for counselors, contact:
➤ National Board for Certified Counselors, Inc., 3 Terrace Way, Suite D, Greensboro, NC 27403-3660. Internet: **http://www.nbcc.org**

State departments of education can supply information on those colleges and universities offering guidance and counseling training that meets State certification and licensure requirements.

State employment service offices have information about job opportunities and entrance requirements for counselors.

Probation Officers and Correctional Treatment Specialists

(O*NET 21-1092.00)

Significant Points

● State and local governments employ most workers.

● A bachelor's degree in social work, criminal justice, or a related field usually is required.

● Employment growth, which is projected to be about as fast as average, depends on government funding.

Nature of the Work
Many people who are convicted of crimes are placed on probation instead of being sent to prison. During probation, offenders must stay out of trouble and meet various other requirements. *Probation officers*, who are called community supervision officers in some States, supervise people who have been placed on probation. *Correctional treatment specialists*, who may also be known as case managers, counsel and create rehabilitation plans for offenders to follow when they are no longer in prison or on parole.

Parole officers and *pretrial services officers* perform many of the same duties that probation officers perform. The difference is that parole officers supervise offenders who have been released from prison, whereas probation officers work with those who are sentenced to probation instead of prison. In some States, the jobs of parole and probation officers are combined. Pretrial services officers conduct pretrial investigations, the findings of which help determine whether suspects should be released before their trial. When suspects are released before their trial, pretrial services officers supervise them to make sure they adhere to the terms of their release and that they show up for trial. Occasionally, in the Federal courts system, probation officers perform the functions of pretrial services officers.

Probation officers supervise offenders on probation or parole through personal contact with the offenders and their families. Instead of requiring offenders to meet officers in their offices, many officers meet offenders in their homes and at their places of employment or therapy. Probation and parole agencies also seek the assistance of community organizations, such as religious institutions, neighborhood groups, and local residents, to monitor the behavior of many offenders. Some offenders are required to wear an electronic device so that probation officers can monitor their location and movements. Probation officers may arrange for offenders to get substance abuse rehabilitation or job training. Probation officers usually work with either adults or juveniles exclusively. Only in small, usually rural, jurisdictions do probation officers counsel both adults and juveniles.

Probation officers also spend much of their time working for the courts. They investigate the backgrounds of the accused, write presentence reports, and recommend sentences. They review sentencing recommendations with offenders and their families before submitting them to the court. Probation officers may be required to testify in court as to their findings and recommendations. They also attend hearings to update the court on offenders' efforts at rehabilitation and compliance with the terms of their sentences.

Correctional treatment specialists work in jails, prisons, or parole or probation agencies. In jails and prisons, they evaluate the progress of inmates. They also work with inmates, probation officers, and other agencies to develop parole and release plans. Their case reports are provided to the appropriate parole board when their clients are eligible for release. In addition, they plan education and training programs to improve offenders' job skills and provide them with coping, anger management, and drug and sexual abuse counseling either individually or in groups. They usually write treatment plans and summaries for each client. Correctional treatment specialists working in parole and probation agencies perform many of the same duties as their counterparts who work in correctional institutions.

The number of cases a probation officer or correctional treatment specialist handles at one time depends on the needs of offenders and the risks they pose. Higher risk offenders and those who need more counseling usually command more of the officer's time and resources. Caseload size also varies by agency jurisdiction. Consequently, officers may handle from 20 to more than 100 active cases at a time.

Computers, telephones, and fax machines enable the officers to handle the caseload. Probation officers may telecommute from

Probation officers attend court hearings, testify, and make sentencing recommendations.

their homes. Other technological advancements, such as electronic monitoring devices and drug screening, also have assisted probation officers and correctional treatment specialists in supervising and counseling offenders.

Working Conditions
Probation officers and correctional treatment specialists work with criminal offenders, some of whom may be dangerous. In the course of supervising offenders, they usually interact with many other individuals, such as family members and friends of their clients, who may be angry, upset, or difficult to work with. Workers may be assigned to fieldwork in high- crime areas or in institutions where there is a risk of violence or communicable disease. Probation officers and correctional treatment specialists are required to meet many court-imposed deadlines, which contribute to heavy workloads.

In addition, extensive travel and fieldwork may be required to meet with offenders who are on probation or parole. Workers may be required to carry a firearm or other weapon for protection. They generally work a 40-hour week, but some may work longer. They may be on call 24 hours a day to supervise and assist offenders at any time. They also may be required to collect and transport urine samples of offenders for drug testing. All of these factors make for a stressful work environment. Although the high stress levels can make these jobs very difficult at times, this work also can be very rewarding. Many workers obtain personal satisfaction from counseling members of their community and helping them become productive citizens.

Training, Other Qualifications, and Advancement
Background qualifications for probation officers and correctional treatment specialists vary by State, but a bachelor's degree in social work, criminal justice, or a related field is usually required. Some employers require previous experience or a master's degree in criminal justice, social work, psychology, or a related field.

Applicants usually are administered written, oral, psychological, and physical examinations. Most probation officers and some correctional treatment specialists are required to complete a training program sponsored by their State government or the Federal Government, after which a certification test may be required.

Prospective probation officers or correctional treatment specialists should be in good physical and emotional condition. Most agencies require applicants to be at least 21 years old and, for Federal employment, not older than 37. Those convicted of felonies may not be eligible for employment in this occupation. Familiarity with the use of computers often is required due to the increasing use of computer technology in probation and parole work. Candidates also should be knowledgeable about laws and regulations pertaining to corrections. Probation officers and correctional treatment specialists should have strong writing skills because they are required to prepare many reports.

Most probation officers and correctional treatment specialists work as trainees or on a probationary period for up to a year before being offered a permanent position. A typical agency has several levels of probation and parole officers and correctional treatment specialists, as well as supervisors. A graduate degree, such as a master's degree in criminal justice, social work, or psychology, may be helpful for advancement.

Employment
Probation officers and correctional treatment specialists held about 93,000 jobs in 2004. Most jobs are in State or local

governments. In some States, the State government employs all probation officers and correctional treatment specialists; in other States, local governments are the only employers. In still other States, both levels of government employ these workers. Jobs are more plentiful in urban areas. Probation officers and correctional treatment specialists who work for the Federal Government are employed by the U.S. courts and by the U.S. Department of Justice's Bureau of Prisons.

Job Outlook

Employment of probation officers and correctional treatment specialists is projected to grow about as fast as the average for all occupations through 2014. In addition to openings due to growth, many openings will be created by replacement needs, especially openings due to the large number of these workers who are expected to retire. This occupation is not attractive to some potential entrants due to relatively low earnings, heavy workloads, and high stress.

Mandatory sentencing guidelines calling for longer sentences and reduced parole for inmates have resulted in a large increase in the prison population. However, mandatory sentencing guidelines are being reconsidered in many States because of budgetary constraints, court decisions, and doubts about the guidelines' effectiveness. Instead, there may be more emphasis in many States on rehabilitation and alternate forms of punishment, such as probation, spurring demand for probation and parole officers and correctional treatment specialists. However, the job outlook depends primarily on the amount of government funding that is allocated to corrections, and especially to probation systems. Although community supervision is far less expensive than keeping offenders in prison, a change in political trends toward more imprisonment and away from community supervision could result in reduced employment opportunities.

Earnings

Median annual earnings of probation officers and correctional treatment specialists in May 2004 were $39,600. The middle 50 percent earned between $31,500 and $52,100. The lowest 10 percent earned less than $26,310, and the highest 10 percent earned more than $66,660. In May 2004, median annual earnings for probation officers and correctional treatment specialists employed in State government were $39,810; those employed in local government earned $40,560. Higher wages tend to be found in urban areas.

Related Occupations

Probation officers and correctional treatment specialists counsel criminal offenders while they are in prison or on parole. Other occupations that involve similar responsibilities include social workers, social and human service assistants, and counselors.

Probation officers and correctional treatment specialists also play a major role in maintaining public safety. Other occupations related to corrections and law enforcement include police and detectives, correctional officers, and firefighting occupations.

Sources of Additional Information

For information about criminal justice job opportunities in your area, contact your State's department of corrections, criminal justice, or probation.

Further information about probation officers and correctional treatment specialists is available from:

➤ American Probation and Parole Association, P.O. Box 11910, Lexington, KY 40578. Internet: http://www.appa-net.org

Social and Human Service Assistants

(O*NET 21-1093.00)

Significant Points

- While a bachelor's degree usually is not required, employers increasingly seek individuals with relevant work experience or education beyond high school.

- Employment is projected to grow much faster than average.

- Job opportunities should be excellent, particularly for applicants with appropriate postsecondary education, but pay is low.

Nature of the Work

Social and human service assistant is a generic term for people with a wide array of job titles, including human service worker, case management aide, social work assistant, community support worker, mental health aide, community outreach worker, life skill counselor, or gerontology aide. They usually work under the direction of workers from a variety of fields, such as nursing, psychiatry, psychology, rehabilitative or physical therapy, or social work. The amount of responsibility and supervision they are given varies a great deal. Some have little direct supervision; others work under close direction.

Social and human service assistants provide direct and indirect client services to ensure that individuals in their care reach their maximum level of functioning. They assess clients' needs, establish their eligibility for benefits and services such as food stamps, Medicaid, or welfare, and help to obtain them. They also arrange for transportation and escorts, if necessary, and provide emotional support. Social and human service assistants monitor and keep case records on clients and report progress to supervisors and case managers.

Social and human service assistants play a variety of roles in a community. They may organize and lead group activities, assist clients in need of counseling or crisis intervention, or administer a food bank or emergency fuel program. In halfway houses, group homes, and government-supported housing programs, they assist adults who need supervision with personal hygiene and daily living skills. They review clients' records, ensure that they take correct doses of medication, talk with family members, and confer with medical personnel and other caregivers to gain better insight into clients' backgrounds and needs. Social and human service assistants also provide emotional support and help clients become involved in their own well-being, in community recreation programs, and in other activities.

In psychiatric hospitals, rehabilitation programs, and outpatient clinics, social and human service assistants work with professional care providers, such as psychiatrists, psychologists, and social workers, to help clients master everyday living skills, communicate more effectively, and get along better with others. They support the client's participation in a treatment plan, such as individual or group counseling or occupational therapy.

Working Conditions

Working conditions of social and human service assistants vary. Some work in offices, clinics, and hospitals, while others work in group homes, shelters, sheltered workshops, and day programs. Many work under close supervision, while others work much of the time on their own, such as those who spend their time in the field visiting clients. Sometimes visiting clients can be dangerous even though most agencies do everything they can to ensure

Social and human service assistants provide client services to ensure that individuals in their care function as well as possible.

their workers' safety. Most work a 40-hour week, although some work in the evening and on weekends.

The work, while satisfying, can be emotionally draining. Understaffing and relatively low pay may add to the pressure. Turnover is reported to be high, especially among workers without academic preparation for this field.

Training, Other Qualifications, and Advancement

While a bachelor's degree usually is not required for entry into this occupation, employers increasingly seek individuals with relevant work experience or education beyond high school. Certificates or associate degrees in subjects such as social work, human services, gerontology, or one of the social or behavioral sciences meet most employers' requirements. Some jobs may require a bachelor's or master's degree in human services or a related field such as counseling, rehabilitation, or social work.

Human services degree programs have a core curriculum that trains students to observe patients and record information, conduct patient interviews, implement treatment plans, employ problem-solving techniques, handle crisis intervention matters, and use proper case management and referral procedures. General education courses in liberal arts, sciences, and the humanities also are part of the curriculum. Most programs offer the opportunity to take specialized courses related to addictions, gerontology, child protection, and other areas. Many degree programs require completion of a supervised internship.

Educational attainment often influences the kind of work employees may be assigned and the degree of responsibility that may be entrusted to them. For example, workers with no more than a high school education are likely to receive extensive on-the-job training to work in direct-care services, while employees with a college degree might be assigned to do supportive counseling, coordinate program activities, or manage a group home. Social and human service assistants with proven leadership ability, either from previous experience or as a volunteer in the field, often have greater autonomy in their work. Regardless of the academic or work background of employees, most employers provide some form of inservice training, such as seminars and workshops, to their employees.

There may be additional hiring requirements in group homes. For example, employers may require employees to have a valid driver's license or to submit to a criminal background investigation.

Employers try to select applicants who have a strong desire to help others, have effective communication skills, a strong sense of responsibility, and the ability to manage time effectively. Many human services jobs involve direct contact with people who are vulnerable to exploitation or mistreatment; therefore, patience, understanding, and a strong desire to help others are highly valued characteristics.

Formal education almost always is necessary for advancement. In general, advancement requires a bachelor's or master's degree in human services, counseling, rehabilitation, social work, or a related field. Typically, advancement brings case management, supervision, and administration roles.

Employment

Social and human service assistants held about 352,000 jobs in 2004. More than half worked in the health care and social assistance industries. One in three were employed by State and local governments, primarily in public welfare agencies and facilities for mentally disabled and developmentally challenged individuals.

Job Outlook

Job opportunities for social and human service assistants are expected to be excellent, particularly for applicants with appropriate postsecondary education. The number of social and human service assistants is projected to grow much faster than the average for all occupations between 2004 and 2014—ranking the occupation among the most rapidly growing. Many additional job opportunities will arise from the need to replace workers who advance into new positions, retire, or leave the workforce for other reasons. There will be more competition for jobs in urban areas than in rural areas, but qualified applicants should have little difficulty finding employment. Faced with rapid growth in the demand for social and human services many employers increasingly rely on social and human service assistants to undertake greater responsibility for delivering services to clients.

Opportunities are expected to be good in private social service agencies, which provide such services as adult day care and meal delivery programs. Employment in private agencies will grow as State and local governments continue to contract out services to the private sector in an effort to cut costs. Demand for social services will expand with the growing elderly population, who are more likely to need these services. In addition, more social and human service assistants will be needed to provide services to pregnant teenagers, the homeless, the mentally disabled and developmentally challenged, and substance abusers. Some private agencies have been employing more social and human service assistants in place of social workers, who are more educated and, thus, more highly paid.

Job training programs also are expected to require additional social and human service assistants. As social welfare policies shift focus from benefit-based programs to work-based initiatives there will be more demand for people to teach job skills to the people who are new to, or returning to, the workforce.

Residential care establishments should face increased pressures to respond to the needs of the mentally and physically disabled. Many of these patients have been deinstitutionalized and lack the knowledge or the ability to care for themselves. Also, more community-based programs and supportive independent-living sites are expected to be established to house and assist the homeless and the mentally and physically disabled. As substance abusers are increasingly being sent to treatment programs instead of prison, employment of social and human service assistants in substance abuse treatment programs also will grow.

The number of jobs for social and human service assistants in local governments will grow but not as fast as employment for social and human service assistants in other industries. Employment in the public sector may fluctuate with the level of funding provided by

State and local governments. Also, some State and local governments are contracting out selected social services to private agencies in order to save money.

Earnings

Median annual earnings of social and human service assistants were $24,270 in May 2004. The middle 50 percent earned between $19,220 and $30,900. The top 10 percent earned more than $39,620, while the lowest 10 percent earned less than $15,480.

Median annual earnings in the industries employing the largest numbers of social and human service assistants in May 2004 were:

State government $29,270
Local government 28,230
Individual and family services...................................... 23,400
Vocational rehabilitation services 21,770
Residential mental retardation, mental health and
    substance abuse facilities 20,410

Related Occupations

Workers in other occupations that require skills similar to those of social and human service assistants include social workers; clergy; counselors; child care workers; occupational therapist assistants and aides; physical therapist assistants and aides; and nursing, psychiatric, and home health aides.

Sources of Additional Information

Information on academic programs in human services may be found in most directories of 2-year and 4-year colleges, available at libraries or career counseling centers.

For information on programs and careers in human services, contact:

➤ National Organization for Human Services, 5601 Brodie Lane, Suite 620-215, Austin, TX 78745. Internet: **http://www.nohse.org**
➤ Council for Standards in Human Services Education, Harrisburg Area Community College, Human Services Program, One HACC Dr., Harrisburg, PA 17110-2999. Internet: **http://www.cshse.org**

Information on job openings may be available from State employment service offices or directly from city, county, or State departments of health, mental health and mental retardation, and human resources.

Social Workers

(O*NET 21-1021.00, 21-1022.00, 21-1023.00, 21-1029.99)

Significant Points

● About 9 out of 10 jobs were in health care and social assistance industries, as well as State and local government agencies.

● While a bachelor's degree is the minimum requirement, a master's degree in social work or a related field has become the standard for many positions.

● Employment is projected to grow faster than average.

● Competition for jobs is expected in cities, but opportunities should be good in rural areas.

Nature of the Work

Social work is a profession for those with a strong desire to help improve people's lives. Social workers help people function the best way they can in their environment, deal with their relationships, and solve personal and family problems. Social workers often see clients who face a life-threatening disease or a social problem, such as inadequate housing, unemployment, a serious illness, a disability, or substance abuse. Social workers also assist families that have serious domestic conflicts, sometimes involving child or spousal abuse.

Social workers often provide social services in health-related settings that now are governed by managed care organizations. To contain costs, these organizations emphasize short-term intervention, ambulatory and community-based care, and greater decentralization of services.

Most social workers specialize. Although some conduct research or are involved in planning or policy development, most social workers prefer an area of practice in which they interact with clients.

Child, family, and school social workers provide social services and assistance to improve the social and psychological functioning of children and their families and to maximize the family well-being and academic functioning of children. Some social workers assist single parents, arrange adoptions, or help find foster homes for neglected, abandoned, or abused children. In schools, they address such problems as teenage pregnancy, misbehavior, and truancy and advise teachers on how to cope with problem students. Increasingly, school social workers are teaching workshops to an entire class. Some social workers specialize in services for senior citizens, running support groups for family caregivers or for the adult children of aging parents, advising elderly people or family members about choices in areas such as housing, transportation, and long-term care, and coordinating and monitoring these services. Through employee assistance programs, they may help workers cope with job-related pressures or with personal problems that affect the quality of their work. Child, family, and school social workers typically work for individual and family services agencies, schools, or State or local governments. These social workers may be known as child welfare social workers, family services social workers, child protective services social workers, occupational social workers, or gerontology social workers.

Medical and public health social workers provide persons, families, or vulnerable populations with the psychosocial support needed to cope with chronic, acute, or terminal illnesses, such as Alzheimer's disease, cancer, or AIDS. They also advise family caregivers, counsel patients, and help plan for patients' needs after discharge by arranging for at-home services, from meals-on-wheels to oxygen equipment. Some work on interdisciplinary teams that evaluate certain kinds of patients—geriatric or organ transplant patients, for example. Medical and public health social workers may work for hospitals, nursing and personal care facilities, individual and family services agencies, or local governments.

Mental health and substance abuse social workers assess and treat individuals with mental illness or substance abuse problems, including abuse of alcohol, tobacco, or other drugs. Such services include individual and group therapy, outreach, crisis intervention, social rehabilitation, and training in skills of everyday living. They also may help plan for supportive services to ease patients' return to the community. Mental health and substance abuse social workers are likely to work in hospitals, substance abuse treatment centers, individual and family services agencies, or local governments. These social workers may be known as clinical social workers. (Counselors and psychologists, who may provide similar services, are discussed elsewhere in the *Handbook*.)

Other types of social workers include social work planners and policymakers, who develop programs to address such issues as child abuse, homelessness, substance abuse, poverty, and violence. These workers research and analyze policies, programs, and regulations. They identify social problems and suggest legislative and other solutions. They may help raise funds or write grants to support these programs.

Social workers often see clients who face inadequate housing, unemployment, serious illness, disability, or substance abuse.

Working Conditions

Full-time social workers usually work a standard 40-hour week; however, some occasionally work evenings and weekends to meet with clients, attend community meetings, and handle emergencies. Some, particularly in voluntary nonprofit agencies, work part time. Social workers usually spend most of their time in an office or residential facility, but also may travel locally to visit clients, meet with service providers, or attend meetings. Some may use one of several offices within a local area in which to meet with clients. The work, while satisfying, can be emotionally draining. Understaffing and large caseloads add to the pressure in some agencies. To tend to patient care or client needs, many hospitals and long-term care facilities are employing social workers on teams with a broad mix of occupations, including clinical specialists, registered nurses, and health aides.

Training, Other Qualifications, and Advancement

A bachelor's degree in social work (BSW) degree is the most common minimum requirement to qualify for a job as a social worker; however, majors in psychology, sociology, and related fields may qualify for some entry-level jobs, especially in small community agencies. Although a bachelor's degree is sufficient for entry into the field, an advanced degree has become the standard for many positions. A master's degree in social work (MSW) is typically required for positions in health settings and is required for clinical work as well. Some jobs in public and private agencies also may require an advanced degree, such as a master's degree in social services policy or administration. Supervisory, administrative, and staff training positions usually require an advanced degree. College and university teaching positions and most research appointments normally require a doctorate in social work (DSW or Ph.D.).

As of 2004, the Council on Social Work Education (CSWE) accredited 442 BSW programs and 168 MSW programs. The Group for the Advancement of Doctoral Education (GADE) listed 80 doctoral programs in social work (DSW or Ph.D.). BSW programs prepare graduates for direct service positions, such as caseworker, and include courses in social work values and ethics, dealing with a culturally diverse clientele, at-risk populations, promotion of social and economic justice, human behavior and the social environment, social welfare policy and services, social work practice, social research methods, and field education. Accredited BSW programs require a minimum of 400 hours of supervised field experience.

Master's degree programs prepare graduates for work in their chosen field of concentration and continue to develop the skills required to perform clinical assessments, manage large caseloads, take on supervisory roles, and explore new ways of drawing upon social services to meet the needs of clients. Master's programs last 2 years and include a minimum of 900 hours of supervised field instruction, or internship. A part-time program may take 4 years. Entry into a master's program does not require a bachelor's degree in social work, but courses in psychology, biology, sociology, economics, political science, and social work are recommended. In addition, a second language can be very helpful. Most master's programs offer advanced standing for those with a bachelor's degree from an accredited social work program.

All States and the District of Columbia have licensing, certification, or registration requirements regarding social work practice and the use of professional titles. Although standards for licensing vary by State, a growing number of States are placing greater emphasis on communications skills, professional ethics, and sensitivity to cultural diversity issues. Most States require two years (3,000 hours) of supervised clinical experience for licensure of clinical social workers. In addition, the National Association of Social Workers (NASW) offers voluntary credentials. Social workers with an MSW may be eligible for the Academy of Certified Social Workers (ACSW), the Qualified Clinical Social Worker (QCSW), or the Diplomate in Clinical Social Work (DCSW) credential, based on their professional experience. Credentials are particularly important for those in private practice; some health insurance providers require social workers to have them in order to be reimbursed for services.

Social workers should be emotionally mature, objective, and sensitive to people and their problems. They must be able to handle responsibility, work independently, and maintain good working relationships with clients and coworkers. Volunteer or paid jobs as a social work aide offer ways of testing one's interest in this field.

Advancement to supervisor, program manager, assistant director, or executive director of a social service agency or department is possible, but usually requires an advanced degree and related work experience. Other career options for social workers include teaching, research, and consulting. Some of these workers also help formulate government policies by analyzing and advocating policy positions in government agencies, in research institutions, and on legislators' staffs.

Some social workers go into private practice. Most private practitioners are clinical social workers who provide psychotherapy, usually paid for through health insurance or by the client themselves. Private practitioners must have at least a master's degree and a period of supervised work experience. A network of contacts for referrals also is essential. Many private practitioners split their time between working for an agency or hospital and working in their private practice. They may continue to hold a position at a hospital or agency in order to receive health and life insurance.

Employment

Social workers held about 562,000 jobs in 2004. About 9 out of 10 jobs were in health care and social assistance industries, as well as State and local government agencies, primarily in departments of health and human services. Although most social workers are employed in cities or suburbs, some work in rural areas. The following tabulation shows 2004 employment by type of social worker:

Child, family, and school social workers	272,000
Mental health and substance abuse social workers	116,000
Medical and public health social workers	110,000
Social workers, all other	64,000

Job Outlook

Competition for social worker jobs is expected in cities, where demand for services often is highest and training programs for social workers are prevalent. However, opportunities should be good in rural areas, which often find it difficult to attract and retain qualified staff. By specialty, job prospects may be best for those social workers with a background in gerontology and substance abuse treatment.

Employment of social workers is expected to increase faster than the average for all occupations through 2014. The rapidly growing elderly population and the aging baby boom generation will create greater demand for health and social services, resulting in particularly rapid job growth among gerontology social workers. Many job openings also will stem from the need to replace social workers who leave the occupation.

As hospitals continue to limit the length of patient stays, the demand for social workers in hospitals will grow more slowly than in other areas. Because hospitals are releasing patients earlier than in the past, social worker employment in home health care services is growing. However, the expanding senior population is an even larger factor. Employment opportunities for social workers with backgrounds in gerontology should be good in the growing numbers of assisted-living and senior-living communities. The expanding senior population also will spur demand for social workers in nursing homes, long-term care facilities, and hospices.

Strong demand is expected for substance abuse social workers over the 2004–14 projection period. Substance abusers are increasingly being placed into treatment programs instead of being sentenced to prison. Because of the increasing numbers of individuals sentenced to prison or probation who are substance abusers, correctional systems are increasingly requiring substance abuse treatment as a condition added to their sentencing or probation. As this trend grows, demand will increase for treatment programs and social workers to assist abusers on the road to recovery.

Employment of social workers in private social service agencies also will increase. However, agencies increasingly will restructure services and hire more lower paid social and human service assistants instead of social workers. Employment in State and local government agencies may grow somewhat in response to increasing needs for public welfare, family services, and child protection services; however, many of these services will be contracted out to private agencies. Employment levels in public and private social services agencies may fluctuate, depending on need and government funding levels.

Employment of school social workers also is expected to grow as expanded efforts to respond to rising student enrollments and continued emphasis on integrating disabled children into the general school population lead to more jobs. There could be competition for school social work jobs in some areas because of the limited number of openings. The availability of Federal, State and local funding will be a major factor in determining the actual job growth in schools.

Opportunities for social workers in private practice will expand, but growth may be somewhat hindered by restrictions that managed care organizations put on mental health services. The growing popularity of employee assistance programs is expected to spur demand for private practitioners, some of whom provide social work services to corporations on a contractual basis. However, the popularity of employee assistance programs will fluctuate with the business cycle, because businesses are not likely to offer these services during recessions.

Earnings

Median annual earnings of child, family, and school social workers were $34,820 in May 2004. The middle 50 percent earned between $27,840 and $45,140. The lowest 10 percent earned less than $23,130, and the top 10 percent earned more than $57,860. Median annual earnings in the industries employing the largest numbers of child, family, and school social workers in May 2004 were:

Elementary and secondary schools	$44,300
Local government	40,620
State government	35,070
Individual and family services	30,680
Other residential care facilities	30,550

Median annual earnings of medical and public health social workers were $40,080 in May 2004. The middle 50 percent earned between $31,620 and $50,080. The lowest 10 percent earned less than $25,390, and the top 10 percent earned more than $58,740. Median annual earnings in the industries employing the largest numbers of medical and public health social workers in May 2004 were:

General medical and surgical hospitals	$44,920
Home health care services	42,710
Local government	39,390
Nursing care facilities	35,680
Individual and family services	32,100

Median annual earnings of mental health and substance abuse social workers were $33,920 in May 2004. The middle 50 percent earned between $26,730 and $43,430. The lowest 10 percent earned less than $21,590, and the top 10 percent earned more than $54,180. Median annual earnings in the industries employing the largest numbers of mental health and substance abuse social workers in May 2004 were:

Psychiatric and substance abuse hospitals	$36,170
Local government	35,720
Outpatient care centers	33,220
Individual and family services	32,810
Residential mental retardation, mental health and substance abuse facilities	29,110

Median annual earnings of social workers, all other were $39,440 in May 2004. The middle 50 percent earned between $30,350 and $51,530. The lowest 10 percent earned less than $24,080, and the top 10 percent earned more than $62,720. Median annual earnings in the industries employing the largest numbers of social workers, all other in May 2004 were:

Local government	$42,570
State government	40,940
Individual and family services	32,280

About 1 out of 5 social workers is a member of a union. Many belong to the union associated with their place of employment.

Related Occupations

Through direct counseling or referral to other services, social workers help people solve a range of personal problems. Workers in occupations with similar duties include the clergy, counselors, probation officers and correctional treatment specialists, psychologists, and social and human services assistants.

Sources of Additional Information

For information about career opportunities in social work and voluntary credentials for social workers, contact:

➤ National Association of Social Workers, 750 First St. N.E., Suite 700, Washington, DC 20002-4241. Internet: **http://www.socialworkers.org**

For a listing of accredited social work programs, contact:

➤ Council on Social Work Education, 1725 Duke St., Suite 500, Alexandria, VA 22314-3457. Internet: **http://www.cswe.org**

Information on licensing requirements and testing procedures for each State may be obtained from State licensing authorities, or from:

➤ Association of Social Work Boards, 400 South Ridge Pkwy., Suite B, Culpeper, VA 22701. Internet: **http://www.aswb.org**

Legal Occupations

Court Reporters

(O*NET 23-2091.00)

Significant Points

- Job prospects are expected to be excellent as job openings continue to outnumber jobseekers.

- Demand for real-time and broadcast captioning and translating will spur employment growth.

- The amount of training required to become a court reporter varies with the type of reporting chosen.

- Job opportunities should be best for those with certification.

Nature of the Work

Court reporters typically create verbatim transcripts of speeches, conversations, legal proceedings, meetings, and other events when written accounts of spoken words are necessary for correspondence, records, or legal proof. Court reporters play a critical role not only in judicial proceedings, but also at every meeting where the spoken word must be preserved as a written transcript. They are responsible for ensuring a complete, accurate, and secure legal record. In addition to preparing and protecting the legal record, many court reporters assist judges and trial attorneys in a variety of ways, such as organizing and searching for information in the official record or making suggestions to judges and attorneys regarding courtroom administration and procedure. Increasingly, court reporters are providing closed-captioning and real-time translating services to the deaf and hard-of-hearing community.

There are several methods of court reporting. The most common method is called stenographic. Using a stenotype machine, stenotypists document all statements made in official proceedings. The machine allows them to press multiple keys at a time to record combinations of letters representing sounds, words, or phrases. These symbols are electronically recorded and then translated and displayed as text in a process called computer-aided transcription. Real-time court reporting is another method of court reporting, wherein stenotype machines used for real-time captioning are linked directly to the computer. As the reporter keys in the symbols, they instantly appear as text on the screen. This process, called Communications Access Realtime Translation (CART), is used in courts, in classrooms, at meetings, and for closed captioning for the hearing-impaired on television.

Electronic reporting refers to the use of audio equipment to record court proceedings. The court reporter monitors the process, takes notes to identify speakers, and listens to the recording to ensure clarity and quality. The equipment used may include analog tape recorders or digital equipment. Electronic reporters and transcribers often are responsible for producing a subsequent written transcript of the recorded proceeding.

Another method of court reporting is called voice writing. Using the voice-writing method, a court reporter speaks directly into a voice silencer—a hand-held mask containing a microphone. As the reporter repeats the testimony into the recorder, the mask prevents the reporter from being heard during testimony. Voice writers record everything that is said by judges, witnesses, attorneys, and other parties to a proceeding, including gestures and emotional reactions.

Regardless of the method used, accuracy in court reporting is crucial because the court reporter is the only person creating an official transcript. In a judicial setting, for example, appeals often depend on the court reporter's transcript.

Some voice writers produce a transcript in real time, using computer speech recognition technology. Other voice writers prefer to translate their voice files after the proceeding is over, or they transcribe the files manually, without using speech recognition at all. In any event, speech recognition-enabled voice writers pursue not only court reporting careers, but also careers as closed captioners, CART reporters for hearing-impaired individuals, and Internet streaming text providers or caption providers.

Court reporters who use either the stenographic or voice-writing method are responsible for a number of duties both before and after transcribing events. First, they must create and maintain the computer dictionary that they use to translate stenographic strokes or voice files into written text. They may customize the dictionary

Court reporters prepare written transcripts, make copies, and provide information from the transcripts to courts, counsels, parties, and the public.

with parts of words, entire words, or terminology specific to the proceeding, program, or event—such as a religious service—they plan to transcribe. After documenting proceedings, court reporters must edit their CAT translation for correct grammar, for accurate identification of proper names and places, and to ensure that the record or testimony is discernible. They usually prepare written transcripts, make copies, and provide information from the transcript to courts, counsels, parties, and the public on request. Court reporters also develop procedures for easy storage and retrieval of all stenographic notes and voice files in paper or digital format.

Although many court reporters record official proceedings in the courtroom, others work outside the courtroom. For example, they may take depositions for attorneys in offices and document proceedings of meetings, conventions, and other private activities. Still others capture the proceedings taking place in government agencies at all levels, from the U.S. Congress to State and local governing bodies. Court reporters who specialize in captioning live television programming for people with hearing loss are commonly known as stenocaptioners. They work for television networks or cable stations, captioning news, emergency broadcasts, sporting events, and other programming. With CART and broadcast captioning, the level of understanding gained by a person with hearing loss depends entirely on the skill of the stenocaptioner. In an emergency, such as a tornado or a hurricane, people's safety may depend on the accuracy of information provided in the form of captioning.

Working Conditions
The majority of court reporters work in comfortable settings, such as offices of attorneys, courtrooms, legislatures, and conventions. An increasing number of court reporters work from home-based offices as independent contractors, or freelancers.

Work in this occupation presents few hazards, although sitting in the same position for long periods can be tiring, and workers can suffer wrist, back, neck, or eye strain. Workers also risk repetitive stress injuries such as carpal tunnel syndrome. In addition, the pressure to be accurate and fast can be stressful.

Many official court reporters work a standard 40-hour week. Self-employed court reporters, or freelancers, usually work flexible hours, including part time, evenings, and weekends, or they may be on call.

Training, Other Qualifications, and Advancement
The amount of training required to become a court reporter varies with the type of reporting chosen. It usually takes less than a year to become a voice writer, while electronic reporters and transcribers learn their skills on the job. In contrast, the average length of time it takes to become a stenotypist is 33 months. Training is offered by about 160 postsecondary vocational and technical schools and colleges. The National Court Reporters Association (NCRA) has approved about 70 programs, all of which offer courses in stenotype computer-aided transcription and real-time reporting. NCRA-approved programs require students to capture a minimum of 225 words per minute, a requirement for Federal Government employment as well.

Some States require court reporters to be notary publics. Others require the Certified Court Reporter (CCR) designation, for which a reporter must pass a State test administered by a board of examiners. The NCRA confers the entry-level designation Registered Professional Reporter (RPR) upon those who pass a four-part examination and participate in mandatory continuing education programs. Although voluntary, the designation is recognized as a mark of distinction in the field. A reporter may obtain additional certifications that demonstrate higher levels of competency, such as Registered Merit Reporter (RMR) or

Registered Diplomate Reporter (RDR). The RDR is the highest level of certification available to court reporters. To earn it, a court reporter must either have 5 consecutive years of experience as an RMR or be an RMR and hold a 4-year bachelor's degree.

The NCRA also offers the designations Certified Realtime Reporter (CRR), Certified Broadcast Captioner (CBC), and Certified CART Provider (CCP). These designations promote and recognize competence in instantaneously converting the spoken word into the written word.

Some States require voice writers to pass a test and to earn State licensure. As a substitute for State licensure, the National Verbatim Reporters Association offers three national certifications to voice writers: Certified Verbatim Reporter (CVR), the Certificate of Merit (CM), and Real-Time Verbatim Reporter (RVR). Earning these certifications is sufficient to be licensed in States where the voice method of court reporting is permitted. To get the CM or RVR, one must first earn the CVR. Candidates for the CVR must pass a written test covering spelling, punctuation, vocabulary, legal and medical terminology, and also must pass three 5-minute dictation and transcription examinations that test for speed, accuracy, and silence. Passing the CM exam requires high levels of speed, knowledge, and accuracy. The RVR measures the candidate's skill at real-time transcription. To retain these certifications, the voice writer must obtain continuing education credits. Credits are given for voice writer education courses, continuing legal education courses, and college courses.

The American Association of Electronic Reporters and Transcribers (AAERT) certifies electronic court reporters. Certification is voluntary and includes a written and a practical examination. To be eligible to take the exams, candidates must have at least 2 years of court reporting or transcribing experience, must be eligible for notary public commissions in their States, and must have completed high school. AAERT offers three types of certificates—Certified Electronic Court Reporter (CER), Certified Electronic Court Transcriber (CET), and Certified Electronic Court Reporter and Transcriber (CERT). Some employers may require electronic court reporters and transcribers to obtain certificates once they are eligible.

In addition to possessing speed and accuracy, court reporters must have excellent listening skills, as well as good English grammar, vocabulary, and punctuation skills. Voice writers must learn to listen and speak simultaneously and very quickly, while also identifying speakers and describing peripheral activities in the courtroom or deposition room. They must be aware of business practices and current events as well as the correct spelling of names of people, places, and events that may be mentioned in a broadcast or in court proceedings. For those who work in courtrooms, an expert knowledge of legal terminology and criminal and appellate procedure is essential. Because capturing proceedings requires the use of computerized stenography or speech recognition equipment, court reporters must be knowledgeable about computer hardware and software applications.

With experience and education, court reporters can advance to administrative and management, consulting, or teaching positions.

Employment
Court reporters held about 18,000 jobs in 2004. About 60 percent worked for State and local governments, a reflection of the large number of court reporters working in courts, legislatures, and various agencies. Most of the remaining wage and salary workers worked for court reporting agencies. Around 13 percent of court reporters were self-employed.

Job Outlook
Job opportunities for court reporters are expected to be excellent as job openings continue to outnumber jobseekers. Court reporters with certification should have the best job opportunities. The favorable job

market reflects the fact that fewer people are entering this profession, particularly as stenographic typists.

Employment of court reporters is projected to grow about as fast as the average for all occupations through 2014. Demand for court reporter services will be spurred by the continuing need for accurate transcription of proceedings in courts and in pretrial depositions, and by the growing need to create captions for live or prerecorded television and to provide other real-time translating services for the deaf and hard-of-hearing community. Voice writers have become more widely accepted because of the difficulty in attracting workers and as the accuracy of speech recognition technology improves. Still, many courts allow only stenotypists to perform court reporting duties; as a result, demand for these highly skilled reporters will remain high.

Federal legislation mandates that, by 2006, all new television programming must be captioned for the deaf and hard-of-hearing. In addition, the Americans with Disabilities Act gives deaf and hard-of-hearing students in colleges and universities the right to request access to real-time translation in their classes. Both of these factors are expected to increase demand for court reporters to provide real-time captioning and CART services. Although these services forgo transcripts and differ from traditional court reporting, which uses computer-aided transcription to turn spoken words into permanent text, they require the same skills that court reporters learn in their training.

Despite increasing numbers of civil and criminal cases, budget constraints are expected to limit the ability of Federal, State, and local courts to expand, thereby also limiting the demand for traditional court reporting services in courtrooms and other legal venues. Further, because of the difficulty in attracting workers and in efforts to control costs, many courtrooms have installed tape recorders that are maintained by electronic court reporters and transcribers to record court proceedings. However, courts use electronic reporters and transcribers only in a limited capacity, and court reporters will continue to be used in felony trials and other proceedings. Despite the use of audiotape and videotape technology, court reporters can quickly turn spoken words into readable, searchable, permanent text, and they will continue to be needed to produce written legal transcripts and proceedings for publication.

Earnings
Court reporters had median annual earnings of $42,920 in May 2004. The middle 50 percent earned between $30,680 and $60,760. The lowest paid 10 percent earned less than $23,690, and the highest paid 10 percent earned more than $80,300. Median annual earnings in May 2004 were $41,070 for court reporters working in local government.

Both compensation and compensation methods for court reporters vary with the type of reporting job, the experience of the individual reporter, the level of certification achieved, and the region of the country. Official court reporters earn a salary and a per-page fee for transcripts. Many salaried court reporters supplement their income by doing freelance work. Freelance court reporters are paid per job and receive a per-page fee for transcripts. CART providers are paid by the hour. Stenocaptioners receive a salary and benefits if they work as employees of a captioning company; stenocaptioners working as independent contractors are paid by the hour.

Related Occupations
Workers in several other occupations type, record information, and process paperwork. Among these are secretaries and administrative assistants; medical transcriptionists; data entry and information processing workers; receptionists and information clerks; and human resources assistants, except payroll and timekeeping. Other workers who provide legal support include paralegals and legal assistants.

Sources of Additional Information
State employment service offices can provide information about job openings for court reporters. For information about careers, training, and certification in court reporting, contact:
➤ National Court Reporters Association, 8224 Old Courthouse Rd., Vienna, VA 22182. Internet: **http://www.ncraonline.org**
➤ United States Court Reporters Association, P.O. Box 465, Chicago, IL 60690-0465. Internet: **http://www.uscra.org**
➤ National Verbatim Reporters Association, 207 Third Ave., Hattiesburg, MS 39401. Internet: **http://www.nvra.org**
➤ American Association of Electronic Reporters and Transcribers, 23812 Rock Circle, Bothell, WA 98021-8573. Internet: **http://www.aaert.org**

Judges, Magistrates, and Other Judicial Workers

(O*NET 23-1021.00, 23-1022.00, 23-1023.00)

Significant Points

● A bachelor's degree and work experience are the minimum requirements for a judgeship or magistrate position, but most workers filling these positions also have law degrees.

● Overall employment is projected to grow about as fast as the average, but varies by occupational specialty.

● Judges and magistrates are expected encounter competition for jobs because of the prestige associated with serving on the bench.

Nature of the Work
Judges, magistrates, and other judicial workers apply the law and oversee the legal process in courts according to local, State, and Federal statutes. They preside over cases concerning every aspect of society, from traffic offenses to disputes over the management of professional sports to issues concerning the rights of huge corporations. All judicial workers must ensure that trials and hearings are conducted fairly and that the court safeguards the legal rights of all parties involved.

The most visible responsibility of judges is presiding over trials or hearings and listening as attorneys represent the parties present. Judges rule on the admissibility of evidence and the methods of conducting testimony, and they may be called on to settle disputes between opposing attorneys. Also, they ensure that rules and procedures are followed, and, if unusual circumstances arise for which standard procedures have not been established, judges interpret the law to determine the manner in which the trial will proceed.

Judges often hold pretrial hearings for cases. They listen to allegations and determine whether the evidence presented merits a trial. In criminal cases, judges may decide that persons charged with crimes should be held in jail pending trial, or they may set conditions for their release. In civil cases, they occasionally impose restrictions on the parties until a trial is held.

In many trials, juries are selected to decide guilt or innocence in criminal cases or liability and compensation in civil cases. Judges instruct juries on applicable laws, direct them to deduce the facts from the evidence presented, and hear their verdict. When the law does not require a jury trial or when the parties waive their right to a jury, judges decide cases. In such instances, the judge determines guilt in criminal cases and imposes sentences; in civil cases, the judge awards relief—such as compensation for damages—to the parties to the lawsuit, called litigants. Judges also work outside the courtroom in their chambers or private offices. There, judges read documents on pleadings and motions, research legal issues, write opinions, and oversee the court's operations. In some jurisdictions, judges also manage the courts' administrative and clerical staff.

Judges' duties vary according to the extent of their jurisdictions and powers. *General trial court judges* of the Federal and State court systems have jurisdiction over any case in their system. They usually try civil cases transcending the jurisdiction of lower courts and all cases involving felony offenses. Federal and State *appellate court judges*, although few in number, have the power to overrule decisions made by trial court or *administrative law judges*; appellate court judges exercise their power if they determine that legal errors were made in a case or if legal precedent does not support the judgment of the lower court. Appellate court judges rule on a small number of cases and rarely have direct contact with litigants. Instead, they usually base their decisions on lower court records and on lawyers' written and oral arguments.

Many State court judges preside in courts whose jurisdiction is limited by law to certain types of cases. A variety of titles are assigned to these judges; among the most common are *municipal court judge, county court judge, magistrate*, and *justice of the peace*. Traffic violations, misdemeanors, small-claims cases, and pretrial hearings constitute the bulk of the work of State court judges, but some States allow these judges to handle cases involving domestic relations, probate, contracts, and other selected areas of the law.

Administrative law judges, sometimes called *hearing officers or adjudicators*, are employed by government agencies to make determinations for administrative agencies. These judges make decisions, for example, on a person's eligibility for various Social Security or workers' compensation benefits, on protection of the environment, on the enforcement of health and safety regulations, on employment discrimination, and on compliance with economic regulatory requirements.

Arbitration, mediation, and conciliation—collectively called appropriate dispute resolution (ADR)—are alternative processes that can be used to settle disputes between parties. All ADR hearings are private and confidential, and the processes are less formal than a court trial. If no settlement is reached through ADR, no statements made during the proceedings are admissible as evidence in any subsequent litigation.

There are two types of arbitration—compulsory and voluntary. During compulsory arbitration, opposing parties submit their dispute to one or more impartial persons, called arbitrators, for a final and non-binding decision. Either party may reject the ruling and request a trial in court. Voluntary arbitration is a process in which opposing parties choose one or more arbitrators to hear their dispute and submit a final, binding decision. Arbitrators usually are attorneys or business persons with expertise in a particular field. The parties identify, in advance, the issues to be resolved by arbitration, the scope of the relief to be awarded, and many of the procedural aspects of the process.

Mediation, or neutral evaluation, involves an attempt by the parties to resolve their dispute with the aid of a neutral third party. This process generally is used when the parties wish to preserve their relationship. A mediator may offer suggestions, but resolution of the dispute rests with the parties themselves. Mediation proceedings also are confidential and private. If the parties are unable to reach a settlement, they are free to pursue other options. The parties usually decide in advance how they will contribute to the cost of mediation. However, many mediators volunteer their services, or they may be court staff. Courts ask that voluntary mediators provide their services at the lowest possible rate and that parties split the cost. Depending on the type of case, court-referred community mediation centers may charge a small fee to the parties involved in mediation.

Conciliation, or facilitation, is similar to mediation. The conciliator's role is to guide the parties to a settlement. The parties must decide

Judges must ensure that trials and hearings are conducted fairly and that the court safeguards the legal rights of all parties involved.

in advance whether they will be bound by the conciliator's recommendations; they generally share equally in the cost of the conciliation.

Working Conditions
Judges, magistrates, and other judicial workers do most of their work in offices, law libraries, and courtrooms. Work in these occupations presents few hazards, although sitting in the same position in the courtroom for long periods can be tiring. Most judges wear robes when they are in a courtroom. Judges typically work a standard 40-hour week, but many work more than 50 hours per week. Some judges with limited jurisdiction are employed part time and divide their time between their judicial responsibilities and other careers.

Arbitrators, mediators, and conciliators usually work in private offices or meeting rooms; no public record is made of the proceedings.

Training, Other Qualifications, and Advancement
A bachelor's degree and work experience usually constitute the minimum requirements for a judgeship or magistrate position. A number of lawyers become judges, and most judges have first been lawyers. In fact, Federal and State judges usually are required to be lawyers. About 40 States allow nonlawyers to hold limited-jurisdiction judgeships, but opportunities are better for those with law experience. Federal administrative law judges must be lawyers and pass a competitive examination administered by the U.S. Office of Personnel Management. Some State administrative law judges and other hearing officials are not required to be lawyers.

Federal administrative law judges are appointed by various Federal agencies, with virtually lifetime tenure. Federal magistrate judges are appointed by district judges—the life-tenured Federal judges of district courts—to serve in a U.S. district court for 8 years. A part-time Federal magistrate judge's term of office is 4 years. Some State judges are appointed, but the remainder are elected in partisan or nonpartisan State elections. Many State and local judges serve fixed renewable terms ranging from 4 or 6 years for some trial court judgeships to as long as 14 years or even life for other trial or appellate court judgeships. Judicial nominating commissions, composed of members of the bar and the public, are used to screen candidates for judgeships in many States and for some Federal judgeships.

All States have some type of orientation for newly elected or appointed judges. The Federal Judicial Center, American Bar Association, National Judicial College, and National Center for State Courts provide judicial education and training for judges and other judicial-branch personnel. General and continuing education courses usually last from a few days to 3 weeks in length. More than half of all States, as well as Puerto Rico, require judges to enroll in continuing education courses while serving on the bench.

Training and education requirements for arbitrators, mediators, and conciliators differ from those for judges. Mediators who practice in State-funded or court-funded mediation programs usually must meet specific training or experience standards, which vary by State and court. In most States, individuals who offer private mediation services do not need a license, certification, or specific coursework; however, many private mediators and most of those affiliated with mediation organizations and programs have completed mediation training and agreed to comply with certain ethical standards. For example, the American Arbitration Association (AAA) requires mediators listed on its mediation panel to complete an AAA training course, receive recommendations from the trainers, and complete an apprenticeship.

Training for arbitrators, mediators, and conciliators is available through independent mediation programs, national and local mediation membership organizations, and postsecondary schools. In 2004, 16 colleges or universities in the United States offered master's degrees in dispute resolution or conflict management, and 2 offered doctoral degrees. Many more schools offer conflict-management specializations within other degree programs. Degrees in public policy, law, and related fields also provide good background for prospective arbitrators, mediators, and conciliators.

Employment

Judges, magistrates, and other judicial workers held 47,000 jobs in 2004. Judges, magistrates, and magistrate judges held 27,000 jobs, all in State and local governments. Administrative law judges, adjudicators, and hearing officers held about 16,000 jobs; 52 percent in State governments, 29 percent Federal Government, and 20 percent in local governments. Arbitrators, mediators, and conciliators held another 5,200 jobs. Approximately 40 percent worked for State and local governments. The remainder worked for labor organizations, law offices, insurance carriers, and other private companies and for organizations that specialize in providing dispute resolution services.

Job Outlook

Overall employment of judges, magistrates, and other judicial workers is projected to about as fast at the average for all occupations through 2014. Budgetary pressures at all levels of government will hold down the hiring of judges, despite rising caseloads, particularly in Federal courts. Most job openings will arise as judges retire. However, additional openings will occur when new judgeships are authorized by law or when judges are elevated to higher judicial offices.

Public concerns about crime and safety, as well as a public willingness to go to court to settle disputes, should spur demand for judges. Both the quantity and the complexity of judges' work have increased because of developments in information technology, medical science, electronic commerce, and globalization. The prestige associated with serving on the bench will ensure continued competition for judge and magistrate positions. However, a growing number of judges and candidates for judgeships are choosing to forgo the bench and work in the private sector, where pay is significantly higher. This movement may lessen the competition somewhat. Becoming a judge often is difficult because judicial candidates must compete with other qualified people and because they frequently must gain political support to be elected or appointed, and getting that support can be expensive.

Employment of arbitrators, mediators, and conciliators is expected to grow about as fast as the average for all occupations through 2014. Many individuals and businesses try to avoid litigation, which can involve lengthy delays, high costs, unwanted publicity, and ill will. Arbitration and other alternatives to litigation usually are faster, less expensive, and more conclusive, spurring demand for the services of arbitrators, mediators, and conciliators. Administrative law judges also are expected to experience average growth in employment.

Earnings

Judges, magistrate judges, and magistrates had median annual earnings of $93,070 in May 2004. The middle 50 percent earned between $54,140 and $124,400. The top 10 percent earned more than $141,750, while the bottom 10 percent earned less than $29,920. Median annual earnings in the industries employing the largest numbers of judges, magistrate judges, and magistrates in May 2004 were $111,810 in State government and $65,800 in local government. Administrative law judges, adjudicators, and hearing officers earned a median of $68,930, and arbitrators, mediators, and conciliators earned a median of $54,760.

In the Federal court system, the Chief Justice of the U.S. Supreme Court earned $208,100 in 2005, and the Associate Justices earned $199,200. Federal court of appeals judges earned $171,800 a year, while district court judges had salaries of $162,100, as did judges in the Court of Federal Claims and the Court of International Trade. Federal judges with limited jurisdiction, such as magistrates and bankruptcy court judges, had salaries of $149,132.

According to a 2004 survey by the National Center for State Courts, salaries of chief justices of State high courts averaged $130,461 and ranged from $95,000 to $191,483. Annual salaries of associate justices of the State highest courts averaged $126,159 and ranged from $95,000 to $175,575. Salaries of State intermediate appellate court judges averaged $122,682 and ranged from $94,212 to $164,604. Salaries of State judges of general jurisdiction trial courts averaged $113,504 and ranged from $88,164 to $158,100.

Most salaried judges are provided health, life, and dental insurance; pension plans; judicial immunity protection; expense accounts; vacation, holiday, and sick leave; and contributions to retirement plans made on their behalf. In many States, judicial compensation committees, which make recommendations on the amount of salary increases, determine judicial salaries. States without commissions have statutes that regulate judicial salaries, link judicial salaries to the increases in pay for Federal judges, or adjust annual pay according to the change in the Consumer Price Index, calculated by the U.S. Bureau of Labor Statistics.

Related Occupations

Legal training and mediation skills are useful to those in many other occupations, including counselors; lawyers; paralegals and legal assistants; title examiners, abstractors, and searchers; law clerks; and detectives and criminal investigators.

Sources of Additional Information

Information on judges, magistrates, and other judicial workers may be obtained from:
➤ National Center for State Courts, 300 Newport Ave., Williamsburg, VA 23185-4147. Internet: **http://www.ncsconline.org**

Information on arbitrators, mediators, and conciliators may be obtained from:
➤ American Arbitration Association, 335 Madison Ave., Floor 10, New York, NY 10017-4605. Internet: **http://www.adr.org**

Lawyers

(O*NET 23-1011.00)

Significant Points

- Competition for job openings should be keen because of the large number of students graduating from law school each year.

- Formal requirements to become a lawyer generally include a 4-year college degree, 3 years of law school, and passing a written bar examination; however, some requirements may vary by State.

- Competition for admission to most law schools is intense.

- About 3 out of 4 lawyers practiced privately, either as partners in law firms or in solo practices.

Nature of the Work

The legal system affects nearly every aspect of our society, from buying a home to crossing the street. Lawyers form the backbone of this vital system, linking it to society in numerous ways. For that reason, they hold positions of great responsibility and are obligated to adhere to a strict code of ethics.

Lawyers, also called *attorneys*, act as both advocates and advisors in our society. As advocates, they represent one of the parties in criminal and civil trials by presenting evidence and arguing in court to support their client. As advisors, lawyers counsel their clients concerning their legal rights and obligations and suggest particular courses of action in business and personal matters. Whether acting as an advocate or an advisor, all attorneys research the intent of laws and judicial decisions and apply the law to the specific circumstances faced by their client.

The more detailed aspects of a lawyer's job depend upon his or her field of specialization and position. Although all lawyers are licensed to represent parties in court, some appear in court more frequently than others. Trial lawyers, who specialize in trial work, must be able to think quickly and speak with ease and authority. In addition, familiarity with courtroom rules and strategy is particularly important in trial work. Still, trial lawyers spend the majority of their time outside the courtroom, conducting research, interviewing clients and witnesses, and handling other details in preparation for a trial.

Lawyers may specialize in a number of areas, such as bankruptcy, probate, international, or elder law. Those specializing in environmental law, for example, may represent interest groups, waste disposal companies, or construction firms in their dealings with the U.S. Environmental Protection Agency (EPA) and other Federal and State agencies. These lawyers help clients prepare and file for licenses and applications for approval before certain activities may occur. In addition, they represent clients' interests in administrative adjudications.

Some lawyers specialize in the growing field of intellectual property, helping to protect clients' claims to copyrights, artwork under contract, product designs, and computer programs. Still other lawyers advise insurance companies about the legality of insurance transactions, guiding the company in writing insurance policies to conform with the law and to protect the companies from unwarranted claims. When claims are filed against insurance companies, these attorneys review the claims and represent the companies in court.

Most lawyers are in private practice, concentrating on criminal or civil law. In criminal law, lawyers represent individuals who have been charged with crimes and argue their cases in courts of law. Attorneys dealing with civil law assist clients with litigation, wills, trusts, contracts, mortgages, titles, and leases. Other lawyers handle only public-interest cases—civil or criminal—which may have an impact extending well beyond the individual client.

Lawyers are sometimes employed full time by a single client. If the client is a corporation, the lawyer is known as "house counsel" and usually advises the company concerning legal issues related to its business activities. These issues might involve patents, government regulations, contracts with other companies, property interests, or collective bargaining agreements with unions.

A significant number of attorneys are employed at the various levels of government. Lawyers who work for State attorneys general, prosecutors, public defenders, and courts play a key role in the criminal justice system. At the Federal level, attorneys investigate cases for the U.S. Department of Justice and other agencies. Government lawyers also help develop programs, draft and interpret laws and legislation, establish enforcement procedures, and argue civil and criminal cases on behalf of the government.

Other lawyers work for legal aid societies—private, nonprofit organizations established to serve disadvantaged people. These lawyers generally handle civil, rather than criminal, cases. A relatively small number of trained attorneys work in law schools. Most are faculty members who specialize in one or more subjects; however, some serve as administrators. Others work full time in nonacademic settings and teach part time. (For additional information, see the *Handbook* section on teachers—postsecondary.)

Lawyers are increasingly using various forms of technology to perform their varied tasks more efficiently. Although all lawyers continue to use law libraries to prepare cases, some supplement conventional printed sources with computer sources, such as the Internet and legal databases. Software is used to search this legal literature automatically and to identify legal texts relevant to a specific case. In litigation involving many supporting documents, lawyers may use computers to organize and index material. Lawyers also utilize electronic filing, videoconferencing, and voice-recognition technology to share information more effectively with other parties involved in a case.

Working Conditions

Lawyers do most of their work in offices, law libraries, and courtrooms. They sometimes meet in clients' homes or places of business and, when necessary, in hospitals or prisons. They may travel to attend meetings, gather evidence, and appear before courts, legislative bodies, and other authorities.

Lawyers research the intent of the laws and judicial decisions and apply the law to the specific circumstances faced by their client.

Salaried lawyers usually have structured work schedules. Lawyers who are in private practice may work irregular hours while conducting research, conferring with clients, or preparing briefs during nonoffice hours. Lawyers often work long hours, and of those who regularly work full time, about half work 50 hours or more per week. They may face particularly heavy pressure when a case is being tried. Preparation for court includes keeping abreast of the latest laws and judicial decisions.

Although legal work generally is not seasonal, the work of tax lawyers and other specialists may be an exception. Because lawyers in private practice often can determine their own workload and the point at which they will retire, many stay in practice well beyond the usual retirement age.

Training, Other Qualifications, and Advancement

To practice law in the courts of any State or other jurisdiction, a person must be licensed, or admitted to its bar, under rules established by the jurisdiction's highest court. All States require that applicants for admission to the bar pass a written bar examination; most States also require applicants to pass a separate written ethics examination. Lawyers who have been admitted to the bar in one State occasionally may be admitted to the bar in another without taking an examination if they meet the latter jurisdiction's standards of good moral character and a specified period of legal experience. In most cases, however, lawyers must pass the bar examination in each State in which they plan to practice. Federal courts and agencies set their own qualifications for those practicing before or in them.

To qualify for the bar examination in most States, an applicant usually must earn a college degree and graduate from a law school accredited by the American Bar Association (ABA) or the proper State authorities. ABA accreditation signifies that the law school—particularly its library and faculty—meets certain standards developed to promote quality legal education. As of 2005, there were 191 ABA-accredited law schools; others were approved by State authorities only. With certain exceptions, graduates of schools not approved by the ABA are restricted to taking the bar examination and practicing in the State or other jurisdiction in which the school is located; most of these schools are in California. In 2005, seven States—California, Maine, New York, Vermont, Virginia, Washington, and Wyoming—accepted the study of law in a law office as qualification for taking the bar examination; three jurisdictions—California, the District of Columbia, and New Mexico—now accept the study of law by correspondence. Several States require registration and approval of students by the State Board of Law Examiners, either before the students enter law school or during their early years of legal study.

Although there is no nationwide bar examination, 48 States, the District of Columbia, Guam, the Northern Mariana Islands, Puerto Rico, and the Virgin Islands require the 6-hour Multistate Bar Examination (MBE) as part of the overall bar examination; the MBE is not required in Louisiana or Washington. The MBE covers a broad range of issues, and sometimes a locally prepared State bar examination is given in addition to it. The 3-hour Multistate Essay Examination (MEE) is used as part of the bar examination in several States. States vary in their use of MBE and MEE scores.

Many States also require Multistate Performance Testing (MPT) to test the practical skills of beginning lawyers. Requirements vary by State, although the test usually is taken at the same time as the bar exam and is a one-time requirement.

The required college and law school education usually takes 7 years of full-time study after high school—4 years of undergraduate study, followed by 3 years of law school. Law school applicants must have a bachelor's degree to qualify for admission. To meet the needs of students who can attend only part time, a number of law schools have night or part-time divisions, which usually require 4 years of study; about 1 in 10 graduates from ABA-approved schools attended part time.

Although there is no recommended "prelaw" major, prospective lawyers should develop proficiency in writing and speaking, reading, researching, analyzing, and thinking logically—skills needed to succeed both in law school and in the profession. Regardless of major, a multidisciplinary background is recommended. Courses in English, foreign languages, public speaking, government, philosophy, history, economics, mathematics, and computer science, among others, are useful. Students interested in a particular aspect of law may find related courses helpful. For example, prospective patent lawyers need a strong background in engineering or science, and future tax lawyers must have extensive knowledge of accounting.

Acceptance by most law schools depends on the applicant's ability to demonstrate an aptitude for the study of law, usually through good undergraduate grades, the Law School Admission Test (LSAT), the quality of the applicant's undergraduate school, any prior work experience, and sometimes, a personal interview. However, law schools vary in the weight they place on each of these and other factors.

All law schools approved by the ABA require applicants to take the LSAT. Nearly all law schools require applicants to have certified transcripts sent to the Law School Data Assembly Service, which then submits the applicants' LSAT scores and their standardized records of college grades to the law schools of their choice. Both this service and the LSAT are administered by the Law School Admission Council. Competition for admission to many law schools—especially the most prestigious ones—generally is intense, with the number of applicants greatly exceeding the number that can be admitted.

During the first year or year and a half of law school, students usually study core courses, such as constitutional law, contracts, property law, torts, civil procedure, and legal writing. In the remaining time, they may elect specialized courses in fields such as tax, labor, or corporate law. Law students often acquire practical experience by participating in school-sponsored legal clinic activities; in the school's moot court competitions, in which students conduct appellate arguments; in practice trials under the supervision of experienced lawyers and judges; and through research and writing on legal issues for the school's law journal.

A number of law schools have clinical programs in which students gain legal experience through practice trials and projects under the supervision of practicing lawyers and law school faculty. Law school clinical programs might include work in legal aid clinics, for example, or on the staff of legislative committees. Part-time or summer clerkships in law firms, government agencies, and corporate legal departments also provide valuable experience. Such training can lead directly to a job after graduation and can help students decide what kind of practice best suits them. Clerkships also may be an important source of financial aid.

In 2004, law school graduates in 52 jurisdictions were required to pass the Multistate Professional Responsibility Examination (MPRE), which tests their knowledge of the ABA codes on professional responsibility and judicial conduct. In some States, the MPRE may be taken during law school, usually after completing a course on legal ethics.

Law school graduates receive the degree of *juris doctor* (J.D.) as the first professional degree. Advanced law degrees may be desirable for those planning to specialize, research, or teach. Some law students pursue joint degree programs, which usually require an additional semester or year of study. Joint degree programs are offered in a number of areas, including law and business administration or public administration.

After graduation, lawyers must keep informed about legal and nonlegal developments that affect their practices. Currently, 40 States and jurisdictions mandate continuing legal education (CLE). Many law schools and State and local bar associations provide continuing education courses that help lawyers stay abreast of recent developments. Some States allow CLE credits to be obtained through participation in seminars on the Internet.

The practice of law involves a great deal of responsibility. Individuals planning careers in law should like to work with people and be able to win the respect and confidence of their clients, associates, and the public. Perseverance, creativity, and reasoning ability also are essential to lawyers, who often analyze complex cases and handle new and unique legal problems.

Most beginning lawyers start in salaried positions. Newly hired salaried attorneys usually start as associates and work with more experienced lawyers or judges. After several years of gaining more responsibilities, some lawyers are admitted to partnership in their firm or go into practice for themselves. Some experienced lawyers are nominated or elected to judgeships. (See the section on judges, magistrates, and other judicial workers elsewhere in the *Handbook*.) Others become full-time law school faculty or administrators; a growing number of these lawyers have advanced degrees in other fields as well.

Some attorneys use their legal training in administrative or managerial positions in various departments of large corporations. A transfer from a corporation's legal department to another department often is viewed as a way to gain administrative experience and rise in the ranks of management.

Employment

Lawyers held about 735,000 jobs in 2004. Approximately 3 out of 4 lawyers practiced privately, either as partners in law firms or in solo practices. Most salaried lawyers held positions in government or with corporations or nonprofit organizations. The greatest number of lawyers working in government were employed at the local level. In the Federal Government, lawyers work for many different agencies, but are concentrated in the Departments of Justice, Treasury, and Defense. Many salaried lawyers working outside of government are employed as house counsel by public utilities, banks, insurance companies, real estate agencies, manufacturing firms, and other business firms and nonprofit organizations. Some also have part-time independent practices, while others work part time as lawyers and full time in another occupation.

Job Outlook

Employment of lawyers is expected to grow about as fast as the average for all occupations through 2014, primarily as a result of growth in the population and in the general level of business activities. Job growth among lawyers also will result from increasing demand for legal services in such areas as health care, intellectual property, venture capital, energy, elder, antitrust, and environmental law. In addition, the wider availability and affordability of legal clinics should result in increased use of legal services by middle-income people. However, growth in demand for lawyers will be limited as businesses, in an effort to reduce costs, increasingly use large accounting firms and paralegals to perform some of the same functions that lawyers do. For example, accounting firms may provide employee-benefit counseling, process documents, or handle various other services previously performed by a law firm. Also, mediation and dispute resolution increasingly are being used as alternatives to litigation.

Competition for job openings should continue to be keen because of the large number of students graduating from law school each year. Graduates with superior academic records from highly regarded law schools will have the best job opportunities. Perhaps as a result of competition for attorney positions, lawyers are increasingly finding work in nontraditional areas for which legal training is an asset, but not normally a requirement—for example, administrative, managerial, and business positions in banks, insurance firms, real estate companies, government agencies, and other organizations. Employment opportunities are expected to continue to arise in these organizations at a growing rate.

As in the past, some graduates may have to accept positions in areas outside of their field of interest or for which they feel overqualified. Some recent law school graduates who have been unable to find permanent positions are turning to the growing number of temporary staffing firms that place attorneys in short-term jobs until they are able to secure full-time positions. This service allows companies to hire lawyers on an "as-needed" basis and permits beginning lawyers to develop practical skills while looking for permanent positions.

Because of the keen competition for jobs, a law graduate's geographic mobility and work experience assume greater importance. The willingness to relocate may be an advantage in getting a job, but to be licensed in another State, a lawyer may have to take an additional State bar examination. In addition, employers are increasingly seeking graduates who have advanced law degrees and experience in a specialty, such as tax, patent, or admiralty law.

Employment growth for lawyers will continue to be concentrated in salaried jobs, as businesses and all levels of government employ a growing number of staff attorneys and as employment in the legal services industry grows. Most salaried positions are in urban areas where government agencies, law firms, and big corporations are concentrated. The number of self-employed lawyers is expected to decrease slowly, reflecting the difficulty of establishing a profitable new practice in the face of competition from larger, established law firms. Moreover, the growing complexity of law, which encourages specialization, along with the cost of maintaining up-to-date legal research materials, favors larger firms.

For lawyers who wish to work independently, establishing a new practice will probably be easiest in small towns and expanding suburban areas. In such communities, competition from larger, established law firms is likely to be less keen than in big cities, and new lawyers may find it easier to become known to potential clients.

Some lawyers are adversely affected by cyclical swings in the economy. During recessions, demand declines for some discretionary legal services, such as planning estates, drafting wills, and handling real estate transactions. Also, corporations are less likely to litigate cases when declining sales and profits result in budgetary restrictions. Some corporations and law firms will not hire new attorneys until business improves, and these establishments may even cut staff to contain costs. Several factors, however, mitigate the overall impact of recessions on lawyers; during recessions, for example, individuals and corporations face other legal problems, such as bankruptcies, foreclosures, and divorces requiring legal action.

Earnings

Lawyers In May 2004, the median annual earnings of all lawyers were $94,930. The middle half of the occupation earned between $64,620 and $143,620. Median annual earnings in the industries employing the largest numbers of lawyers in May 2004 were as follows:

Management of companies and enterprises	$126,250
Federal Government	108,090
Legal services	99,580
Local government	73,410
State government	70,280

Median salaries of lawyers 9 months after graduation from law school in 2004 varied by type of work, as indicated in table 1.

Table 1. Median salaries of lawyers 9 months after graduation, 2004

All graduates	$55,000
Type of work	
Private practice	80,000
Business/industry	60,000
Judicial clerkship and government	44,700
Academe	40,000

Source: *National Association of Law Placement*

Salaries of experienced attorneys vary widely according to the type, size, and location of their employer. Lawyers who own their own practices usually earn less than those who are partners in law firms. Lawyers starting their own practice may need to work part time in other occupations to supplement their income until their practice is well established.

Most salaried lawyers are provided health and life insurance, and contributions are made to retirement plans on their behalf. Lawyers who practice independently are covered only if they arrange and pay for such benefits themselves.

Related Occupations

Legal training is necessary in many other occupations, including paralegals and legal assistants; law clerks; title examiners, abstractors, and searchers; and judges, magistrates, and other judicial workers.

Sources of Additional Information

Information on law schools and a career in law may be obtained from the following organizations:
➤ American Bar Association, 321 North Clark St., Chicago, IL 60610. Internet: **http://www.abanet.org**
➤ National Association for Law Placement, 1025 Connecticut Ave. NW., Suite 1110, Washington, DC 20036. Internet: **http://www.nalp.org**

Information on the LSAT, the Law School Data Assembly Service, the law school application process, and financial aid available to law students may be obtained from:
➤ Law School Admission Council, P.O. Box 40, Newtown, PA 18940. Internet: **http://www.lsac.org**

Information on obtaining positions as lawyers with the Federal Government is available from the Office of Personnel Management through USAJOBS, the Federal Government's official employment information system. This resource for locating and applying for job opportunities can be accessed through the Internet at **http://www.usajobs.opm.gov** or through an interactive voice response telephone system at (703) 724-1850 or TDD (978) 461-8404. These numbers are not tollfree, and charges may result.

The requirements for admission to the bar in a particular State or other jurisdiction also may be obtained at the State capital, from the clerk of the Supreme Court, or from the administrator of the State Board of Bar Examiners.

Paralegals and Legal Assistants

(O*NET 23-2011.00)

Significant Points

- About 7 out of 10 work for law firms; others work for corporate legal departments and government agencies.

- Most entrants have an associate's degree in paralegal studies, or a bachelor's degree coupled with a certificate in paralegal studies.

- Employment is projected to grow much faster than average, as employers try to reduce costs by hiring paralegals to perform tasks formerly carried out by lawyers.

- Competition for jobs should continue; experienced, formally trained paralegals should have the best employment opportunities.

Nature of the Work

While lawyers assume ultimate responsibility for legal work, they often delegate many of their tasks to paralegals. In fact, paralegals—also called legal assistants—are continuing to assume a growing range of tasks in the Nation's legal offices and perform many of the same tasks as lawyers. Nevertheless, they are still explicitly prohibited from carrying out duties that are considered to be the practice of law, such as setting legal fees, giving legal advice, and presenting cases in court.

One of a paralegal's most important tasks is helping lawyers prepare for closings, hearings, trials, and corporate meetings. Paralegals investigate the facts of cases and ensure that all relevant information is considered. They also identify appropriate laws, judicial decisions, legal articles, and other materials that are relevant to assigned cases. After they analyze and organize the information, paralegals may prepare written reports that attorneys use in determining how cases should be handled. Should attorneys decide to file lawsuits on behalf of clients, paralegals may help prepare the legal arguments, draft pleadings and motions to be filed with the court, obtain affidavits, and assist attorneys during trials. Paralegals also organize and track files of all important case documents and make them available and easily accessible to attorneys.

In addition to this preparatory work, paralegals perform a number of other vital functions. For example, they help draft contracts, mortgages, separation agreements, and instruments of trust. They also may assist in preparing tax returns and planning estates. Some paralegals coordinate the activities of other law office employees and maintain financial office records. Various additional tasks may differ, depending on the employer.

Paralegals are found in all types of organizations, but most are employed by law firms, corporate legal departments, and various government offices. In these organizations, they can work in many different areas of the law, including litigation, personal injury, corporate law, criminal law, employee benefits, intellectual property, labor law, bankruptcy, immigration, family law, and real estate. As the law has become more complex, paralegals have responded by becoming more specialized. Within specialties, functions often are broken down further so that paralegals may deal with a specific area. For example, paralegals specializing in labor law may concentrate exclusively on employee benefits.

The duties of paralegals also differ widely with the type of organization in which they are employed. Paralegals who work for corporations often assist attorneys with employee contracts, shareholder agreements, stock-option plans, and employee benefit plans. They also may help prepare and file annual financial reports, maintain corporate minutes' record resolutions, and prepare forms to secure loans for the corporation. Paralegals often monitor and review government regulations to ensure that the corporation is aware of new requirements and is operating within the law. Increasingly, experienced paralegals are assuming additional supervisory responsibilities such as overseeing team projects and serving as a communications link between the team and the corporation.

The duties of paralegals who work in the public sector usually vary within each agency. In general, paralegals analyze legal material for internal use, maintain reference files, conduct research for attorneys, and collect and analyze evidence for agency hearings. They may prepare informative or explanatory material on laws, agency regulations, and agency policy for general use by the agency and the public. Paralegals employed in community legal-service projects help the poor, the aged, and others who are in need of legal assistance. They file forms, conduct research, prepare documents, and, when authorized by law, may represent clients at administrative hearings.

Paralegals in small and medium-size law firms usually perform a variety of duties that require a general knowledge of the law. For example, they may research judicial decisions on improper police arrests or help prepare a mortgage contract. Paralegals employed by large law firms, government agencies, and corporations, however, are more likely to specialize in one aspect of the law.

Familiarity with computers use and technical knowledge have become essential to paralegal work. Computer software packages and the Internet are used to search legal literature stored in computer databases and on CD-ROM. In litigation involving many supporting documents, paralegals usually use computer databases to retrieve, organize, and index various materials. Imaging software allows paralegals to scan documents directly into a database, while billing programs help them to track hours billed to clients. Computer software packages also are used to perform tax computations and explore the consequences of various tax strategies for clients.

Paralegals prepare written reports that attorneys use in determining how cases should be handled.

Working Conditions

Paralegals employed by corporations and government usually work a standard 40-hour week. Although most paralegals work year round, some are temporarily employed during busy times of the year and then are released when the workload diminishes. Paralegals who work for law firms sometimes work very long hours when they are under pressure to meet deadlines. Some law firms reward such loyalty with bonuses and additional time off.

These workers handle many routine assignments, particularly when they are inexperienced. As they gain experience, paralegals usually assume more varied tasks with additional responsibility. Paralegals do most of their work at desks in offices and law libraries. Occasionally, they travel to gather information and perform other duties.

Training, Other Qualifications, and Advancement

There are several ways to become a paralegal. The most common is through a community college paralegal program that leads to an associate's degree. The other common method of entry, mainly for those who already have a college degree, is through a program that leads to a certification in paralegal studies. A small number of schools also offer bachelor's and master's degrees in paralegal studies. Some employers train paralegals on the job, hiring college graduates with no legal experience or promoting experienced legal secretaries. Other entrants have experience in a technical field that is useful to law firms, such as a background in tax preparation for tax and estate practice or in criminal justice, nursing, or health administration for personal injury practice.

An estimated 1,000 colleges and universities, law schools, and proprietary schools offer formal paralegal training programs. Approximately 260 paralegal programs are approved by the American Bar Association (ABA). Although many programs do not require such approval, graduation from an ABA-approved program can enhance one's employment opportunities. The requirements for admission to these programs vary. Some require certain college courses or a bachelor's degree, others accept high school graduates or those with legal experience, and a few schools require standardized tests and personal interviews.

Paralegal programs include 2-year associate degree's programs, 4-year bachelor's degree programs, and certificate programs that can take only a few months to complete. Most certificate programs provide intensive and, in some cases, specialized paralegal training for individuals who already hold college degrees, while associate's and bachelor's degree programs usually combine paralegal training with courses in other academic subjects. The quality of paralegal training programs varies; the better programs usually include job placement services. Programs generally offer courses introducing students to the legal applications of computers, including how to perform legal research on the Internet. Many paralegal training programs also offer an internship in which students gain practical experience by working for several months in a private law firm, the office of a public defender or attorney general, a bank, a corporate legal department, a legal aid organization, or a government agency. Experience gained in internships is an asset when one is seeking a job after graduation. Prospective students should examine the experiences of recent graduates before enrolling in a paralegal program.

Although most employers do not require certification, earning a voluntary certificate from a professional society may offer advantages in the labor market. The National Association of Legal Assistants (NALA), for example, has established standards for certification requiring various combinations of education and experience. Paralegals who meet these standards are eligible to take a 2-day examination, given three times each year at several regional testing centers. Those who pass this examination may use the Certified Legal Assistant (CLA) designation. The NALA also offers an advanced paralegal certification for those who want to specialize in other areas of the law. In addition, the Paralegal Advanced Competency Exam, administered through the National Federation of Paralegal Associations, offers professional recognition to paralegals with a bachelor's degree and at least 2 years of experience. Those who pass this examination may use the Registered Paralegal (RP) designation.

Paralegals must be able to document and present their findings and opinions to their supervising attorney. They need to understand legal terminology and have good research and investigative skills. Familiarity with the operation and applications of computers in legal research and litigation support also is important. Paralegals should stay informed of new developments in the laws that affect their area of practice. Participation in continuing legal education seminars allows paralegals to maintain and expand their knowledge of the law.

Because paralegals frequently deal with the public, they should be courteous and uphold the ethical standards of the legal profession. The National Association of Legal Assistants, the National Federation of Paralegal Associations, and a few States have established ethical guidelines for paralegals to follow.

Paralegals usually are given more responsibilities and require less supervision as they gain work experience. Experienced paralegals who work in large law firms, corporate legal departments, or government agencies may supervise and delegate assignments to other paralegals and clerical staff. Advancement opportunities also include promotion to managerial and other law-related positions within the firm or corporate legal department. However, some paralegals find it easier to move to another law firm when seeking increased responsibility or advancement.

Employment

Paralegals and legal assistants held about 224,000 jobs in 2004. Private law firms employed 7 out of 10 paralegals and legal assistants; most of the remainder worked for corporate legal departments and various levels of government. Within the Federal Government, the U.S. Department of Justice is the largest employer, followed by the Social Security Administration and the U.S. Department of the Treasury. A small number of paralegals own their own businesses and work as freelance legal assistants, contracting their services to attorneys or corporate legal departments.

Job Outlook

Employment for paralegals and legal assistants is projected to grow much faster than the average for all occupations through 2014. Employers are trying to reduce costs and increase the availability and efficiency of legal services by hiring paralegals to perform tasks formerly carried out by lawyers. Besides new jobs created by employment growth, additional job openings will arise as people leave the occupation. Despite projections of rapid employment growth, competition for jobs should continue as many people seek to go into this profession; however, experienced, formally trained paralegals should have the best employment opportunities.

Private law firms will continue to be the largest employers of paralegals, but a growing array of other organizations, such as corporate legal departments, insurance companies, real estate and title insurance firms, and banks hire paralegals. Corporations in particular are boosting their in-house legal departments to cut costs. Demand for paralegals also is expected to grow as an ex-

panding population increasingly requires legal services, especially in areas such as intellectual property, health care, international law, elder issues, criminal law, and environmental law. Paralegals who specialize in areas such as real estate, bankruptcy, medical malpractice, and product liability should have ample employment opportunities. The growth of prepaid legal plans also should contribute to the demand for legal services. Paralegal employment is expected to increase as organizations presently employing paralegals assign them a growing range of tasks and as paralegals are increasingly employed in small and medium-size establishments. A growing number of experienced paralegals are expected to establish their own businesses.

Job opportunities for paralegals will expand in the public sector as well. Community legal-service programs, which provide assistance to the poor, elderly, minorities, and middle-income families, will employ additional paralegals to minimize expenses and serve the most people. Federal, State, and local government agencies, consumer organizations, and the courts also should continue to hire paralegals in increasing numbers.

To a limited extent, paralegal jobs are affected by the business cycle. During recessions, demand declines for some discretionary legal services, such as planning estates, drafting wills, and handling real estate transactions. Corporations are less inclined to initiate certain types of litigation when falling sales and profits lead to fiscal belt tightening. As a result, full-time paralegals employed in offices adversely affected by a recession may be laid off or have their work hours reduced. However, during recessions, corporations and individuals are more likely to face other problems that require legal assistance, such as bankruptcies, foreclosures, and divorces. Paralegals, who provide many of the same legal services as lawyers at a lower cost, tend to fare relatively better in difficult economic conditions.

Earnings

Earnings of paralegals and legal assistants vary greatly. Salaries depend on education, training, experience, the type and size of employer, and the geographic location of the job. In general, paralegals who work for large law firms or in large metropolitan areas earn more than those who work for smaller firms or in less populated regions. In addition to earning a salary, many paralegals receive bonuses. In May 2004, full-time wage and salary paralegals and legal assistants had median annual earnings, including bonuses, of $39,130. The middle 50 percent earned between $31,040 and $49,950. The top 10 percent earned more than $61,390, while the bottom 10 percent earned less than $25,360. Median annual earnings in the industries employing the largest numbers of paralegals in May 2004 were as follows:

Federal Government	$59,370
Local government	38,260
Legal services	37,870
State government	34,910

Related Occupations

Among the other occupations that call for a specialized understanding of the law and the legal system, but do not require the extensive training of a lawyer, are law clerks; title examiners, abstractors, and searchers; claims adjusters, appraisers, examiners, and investigators; and occupational health and safety specialists and technicians.

Sources of Additional Information

General information on a career as a paralegal can be obtained from:

➤ Standing Committee on Paralegals, American Bar Association, 321 North Clark St., Chicago, IL 60610. Internet: **http://www.abanet.org/legalservices/paralegals**

For information on the Certified Legal Assistant exam, schools that offer training programs in a specific State, and standards and guidelines for paralegals, contact:
➤ National Association of Legal Assistants, Inc., 1516 South Boston St., Suite 200, Tulsa, OK 74119. Internet: **http://www.nala.org**

Information on a career as a paralegal, schools that offer training programs, job postings for paralegals, the Paralegal Advanced Competency Exam, and local paralegal associations can be obtained from:
➤ National Federation of Paralegal Associations, 2517 Eastlake Ave. East, Suite 200, Seattle, WA 98102. Internet: **http://www.paralegals.org**

Information on paralegal training programs, including the pamphlet *How to Choose a Paralegal Education Program*, may be obtained from:
➤ American Association for Paralegal Education, 19 Mantua Rd., Mt. Royal, NJ 08061. Internet: **http://www.aafpe.org**

Information on obtaining positions as paralegals and legal assistants with the Federal Government is available from the Office of Personnel Management through USAJOBS, the Federal Government's official employment information system. This resource for locating and applying for job opportunities can be accessed through the Internet at **http://www.usajobs.opm.gov** or through an interactive voice response telephone system at (703) 724-1850 or TDD (978) 461-8404. These numbers are not tollfree, and charges may result.

Education, Training, Library, and Museum Occupations

Archivists, Curators, and Museum Technicians

(O*NET 25-4011.00, 25-4012.00, 25-4013.00)

Significant Points

● Most worked in museums, historical sites, and similar institutions; educational institutions; or in Federal, State, or local government.

● A graduate degree and related work experience generally are required.

● Keen competition is expected for most jobs because qualified applicants generally outnumber job openings.

Nature of the Work

Archivists, curators, and museum technicians acquire and preserve important documents and other valuable items for permanent storage or display. They work for museums, governments, zoos, colleges and universities, corporations, and other institutions that require experts to preserve important records. They also describe, catalogue, analyze, exhibit, and maintain valuable objects and collections for the benefit of researchers and the public. These documents and collections may include works of art, transcripts of meetings, coins and stamps, living and preserved plants and animals, and historic objects, buildings, and sites.

Archivists and curators plan and oversee the arrangement, cataloguing, and exhibition of collections and, along with technicians and conservators, maintain collections. Archivists and curators may coordinate educational and public outreach programs, such as tours, workshops, lectures, and classes, and may work with the boards of institutions to administer plans and policies. They also may research topics or items relevant to their collections. Although some duties of archivists and curators are similar, the types of items they deal with differ: curators usually handle objects with cultural, biological, or historical significance, such as sculptures, textiles, and paintings, while archivists handle mainly records and documents that are retained because of their importance and potential value in the future.

Archivists collect, organize, and maintain control over a wide range of information deemed important enough for permanent safekeeping. This information takes many forms: photographs, films, video and sound recordings, computer tapes, and video and optical disks, as well as more traditional paper records, letters, and documents. Archivists work for a variety of organizations, including government agencies, museums, historical societies, corporations, and educational institutions that use or generate records of great potential value to researchers, exhibitors, genealogists, and others who would benefit from having access to original source material.

Archivists maintain records in accordance with accepted standards and practices that ensure the long-term preservation and easy retrieval of the documents. Records may be saved on any medium, including paper, film, videotape, audiotape, electronic disk, or computer. They also may be copied onto some other format to protect the original and to make the records more accessible to researchers who use them. As various storage media evolve, archivists must keep abreast of technological advances in electronic information storage.

Archivists often specialize in an area of history or technology so they can more accurately determine which records in that area qualify for retention and should become part of the archives. Archivists also may work with specialized forms of records, such as manuscripts, electronic records, photographs, cartographic records, motion pictures, and sound recordings.

Computers are increasingly being used to generate and maintain archival records. Professional standards for the use of computers in handling archival records are still evolving. Expanding computer capabilities that allow more records to be stored and exhibited electronically have transformed, and are expected to continue to transform, many aspects of archival collections.

Curators administer the affairs of museums, zoos, aquariums, botanical gardens, nature centers, and historic sites. The head curator of the museum is usually called the *museum director*. Curators direct the acquisition, storage, and exhibition of collections, including negotiating and authorizing the purchase, sale, exchange, or loan of collections. They are also responsible for authenticating, evaluating, and categorizing the specimens in a collection. Curators oversee and help conduct the institution's research projects and related educational programs. Today, an increasing part of a curator's duties involves fundraising and promotion, which may include the writing and reviewing of grant proposals, journal articles, and publicity materials, as well as attendance at meetings, conventions, and civic events.

Most curators specialize in a particular field, such as botany, art, paleontology, or history. Those working in large institutions may be highly specialized. A large natural-history museum, for example, would employ separate curators for its collections of birds, fishes, insects, and mammals. Some curators maintain their collections, others do research, and others perform administrative tasks.

In small institutions with only one or a few curators, one curator may be responsible for a number of tasks, from maintaining collections to directing the affairs of the museum.

Conservators manage, care for, preserve, treat, and document works of art, artifacts, and specimens—work that may require substantial historical, scientific, and archaeological research. They use x rays, chemical testing, microscopes, special lights, and other laboratory equipment and techniques to examine objects and determine their condition, their need for treatment or restoration, and the appropriate method for preserving them. Conservators document their findings and treat items to minimize their deterioration or to restore them to their original state. Conservators usually specialize in a particular material or group of objects, such as documents and books, paintings, decorative arts, textiles, metals, or architectural material.

Museum technicians assist curators by performing various preparatory and maintenance tasks on museum items. Some museum technicians also may assist curators with research. Archives technicians help archivists organize, maintain, and provide access to historical documentary materials.

Working Conditions

The working conditions of archivists and curators vary. Some spend most of their time working with the public, providing reference assistance and educational services. Others perform research or process records, which often means working alone or in offices with only a few people. Those who restore and install exhibits or

Archivists organize and maintain documents such as photographs, manuscripts, and letters.

work with bulky, heavy record containers may lift objects, climb, or stretch. Those in zoos, botanical gardens, and other outdoor museums and historic sites frequently walk great distances.

Curators who work in large institutions may travel extensively to evaluate potential additions to the collection, organize exhibitions, and conduct research in their area of expertise. However, travel is rare for curators employed in small institutions.

Training, Other Qualifications, and Advancement

Employment as an archivist, conservator, or curator usually requires graduate education and related work experience. While completing their formal education, many archivists and curators work in archives or museums to gain the "hands-on" experience that many employers seek.

Although archivists earn a variety of undergraduate degrees, a graduate degree in history or library science, with courses in archival science, is preferred by most employers. Also, a few institutions now offer master's degrees in archival studies. Some positions may require knowledge of the discipline related to the collection, such as business or medicine. Many colleges and universities offer courses or practical training in archival science as part of their history, library science, or other curriculum. The Academy of Certified Archivists offers voluntary certification for archivists. The designation "Certified Archivist" is obtained by those with at least a master's degree and a year of appropriate archival experience. The certification process requires candidates to pass a written examination, and they must renew their certification periodically.

Archivists need research and analytical ability to understand the content of documents and the context in which they were created and to decipher deteriorated or poor-quality printed matter, handwritten manuscripts, photographs, or films. A background in preservation management is often required of archivists because they are responsible for taking proper care of their records. Archivists also must be able to organize large amounts of information and write clear instructions for its retrieval and use. In addition, computer skills and the ability to work with electronic records and databases are very important. Because electronic records are becoming the prevalent form of recordkeeping, and archivists must create searchable databases, a knowledge of Web technology is increasingly being required.

Many archives, including one-person shops, are very small and have limited opportunities for promotion. Archivists typically advance by transferring to a larger unit that has supervisory positions. A doctorate in history, library science, or a related field may be needed for some advanced positions, such as director of a State archive.

For employment as a curator, most museums require a master's degree in an appropriate discipline of the museum's specialty—art, history, or archaeology—or in museum studies. Many employers prefer a doctoral degree, particularly for curators in natural history or science museums. Earning two graduate degrees—in museum studies (museology) and a specialized subject—gives a candidate a distinct advantage in this competitive job market. In small museums, curatorial positions may be available to individuals with a bachelor's degree. For some positions, an internship of full-time museum work supplemented by courses in museum practices is needed.

Curatorial positions often require knowledge in a number of fields. For historic and artistic conservation, courses in chemistry, physics, and art are desirable. Because curators—particularly those in small museums—may have administrative and managerial responsibilities, courses in business administration, public relations, marketing, and fundraising also are recommended. Like archivists, curators need computer skills and the ability to work with electronic databases. Many curators are responsible for posting information on the Internet, so they also need to be familiar with digital imaging, scanning technology, and copyright law.

Curators must be flexible because of their wide variety of duties, among which are the design and presentation of exhibits. In small museums, curators need manual dexterity to build exhibits or restore objects. Leadership ability and business skills are important for museum directors, while marketing skills are valuable in increasing museum attendance and fundraising.

In large museums, curators may advance through several levels of responsibility, eventually becoming the museum director. Curators in smaller museums often advance to larger ones. Individual research and publications are important for advancement in larger institutions.

When hiring conservators, employers look for a master's degree in conservation or in a closely related field, together with substantial experience. There are only a few graduate programs in museum conservation techniques in the United States. Competition for entry to these programs is keen; to qualify, a student must have a background in chemistry, archaeology or studio art, and art history, as well as work experience. For some programs, knowledge of a foreign language also is helpful. Conservation apprenticeships or internships as an undergraduate can enhance one's admission prospects. Graduate programs last 2 to 4 years, the latter years of which include internship training. A few individuals enter conservation through apprenticeships with museums, nonprofit organizations, and conservators in private practice. Apprenticeships should be supplemented with courses in chemistry, studio art, and history. Apprenticeship training, although accepted, is a more difficult route into the conservation profession.

Museum technicians usually need a bachelor's degree in an appropriate discipline of the museum's specialty, training in museum studies, or previous experience working in museums, particularly in the design of exhibits. Similarly, archives technicians usually need a bachelor's degree in library science or history, or relevant work experience. Technician positions often serve as a steppingstone for individuals interested in archival and curatorial work. Except in small museums, a master's degree is needed for advancement.

Relatively few schools grant a bachelor's degree in museum studies. More common are undergraduate minors or tracks of study that are part of an undergraduate degree in a related field, such as art history, history, or archaeology. Students interested in further study may obtain a master's degree in museum studies, offered in colleges and universities throughout the country. However, many employers feel that, while museum studies are helpful, a thorough knowledge of the museum's specialty and museum work experience are more important.

Continuing education, which enables archivists, curators, and museum technicians to keep up with developments in the field, is available through meetings, conferences, and workshops sponsored by archival, historical, and museum associations. Some larger organizations, such as the National Archives, offer such training in-house.

Employment

Archivists, curators, and museum technicians held about 27,000 jobs in 2004. About 34 percent were employed in museums, historical sites, and similar institutions, and 16 percent worked for State and private educational institutions, mainly college and university libraries. Nearly 28 percent worked in Federal, State, and local government, excluding educational institutions. Most Federal archivists work for the National Archives and Records Administration; others manage military archives in the U.S. Department of Defense. Most Federal Government curators work at the Smithsonian Institution, in the military museums of the Department of Defense, and in archaeological and other museums and historic sites managed by the U.S. Department of the Interior. All State governments have archival or historical-record sections employing archivists. State and local governments also have numerous historical museums, parks, libraries, and zoos employing curators.

Some large corporations that have archives or record centers employ archivists to manage the growing volume of records created or maintained as required by law or necessary to the firms' operations. Religious and fraternal organizations, professional associations, conservation organizations, major private collectors, and research firms also employ archivists and curators.

Conservators may work under contract to treat particular items, rather than as regular employees of a museum or other institution. These conservators may work on their own as private contractors, or they may work as an employee of a conservation laboratory or regional conservation center that contracts their services to museums.

Job Outlook

Keen competition is expected for most jobs as archivists, curators, and museum technicians because qualified applicants generally outnumber job openings. Graduates with highly specialized training, such as master's degrees in both library science and history, with a concentration in archives or records management and extensive computer skills, should have the best opportunities for jobs as archivists. A curator job also is attractive to many people, and many applicants have the necessary training and knowledge of the subject, but there are only a few openings. Consequently, candidates may have to work part time, as an intern, or even as a volunteer assistant curator or research associate after completing their formal education. Substantial work experience in collection management, research, exhibit design, or restoration, as well as database management skills, will be necessary for permanent status.

The job outlook for conservators may be more favorable, particularly for graduates of conservation programs. However, competition is stiff for the limited number of openings in these programs, and applicants need a technical background. Conservation program graduates with knowledge of a foreign language and a willingness to relocate will have an advantage over less qualified candidates.

Employment of archivists, curators, and museum technicians is expected to increase about as fast as the average for all occupations through 2014. Jobs are expected to grow as public and private organizations emphasize establishing archives and organizing records and information and as public interest in science, art, history, and technology increases. Museum and zoo attendance has experienced a drop in recent years because of a weak economy, but the long-term trend has been a rise in attendance, and this trend is expected to continue. There is healthy public and private support for and interest in museums, which will generate demand for archivists, curators, and museum technicians. However, museums and other cultural institutions can be subject to cuts in funding during recessions or periods of budget tightening, reducing demand for these workers. Although the rate of turnover among archivists and curators is relatively low, the need to replace workers who leave the occupation or stop working will create some additional job openings.

Earnings

Median annual earnings of archivists in May 2004 were $36,470. The middle 50 percent earned between $28,900 and $46,480. The lowest 10 percent earned less than $21,780, and the highest 10 percent earned more than $61,260. Median annual earnings of curators in May 2004 were $43,620. The middle 50 percent earned between $32,790 and $58,280. The lowest 10 percent earned less than $25,360, and the highest 10 percent earned more than $77,490. Median annual earnings of museum technicians and conservators in May 2004 were $31,820. The middle 50 percent earned between $23,770 and $43,020. The lowest 10 percent earned less than $18,210, and the highest 10 percent earned more than $58,260.

In 2005, the average annual salary for archivists in the Federal Government in nonsupervisory, supervisory, and managerial positions was $75,876; for museum curators, $76,126; for museum specialists and technicians, $55,291; and for archives technicians, $41,347.

Related Occupations

The skills that archivists, curators, and museum technicians use in preserving, organizing, and displaying objects or information of historical interest are shared by artists and related workers; librarians; and anthropologists and archeologists, historians, and other social scientists.

Sources of Additional Information

For information on archivists and on schools offering courses in archival studies, contact:

➤ Society of American Archivists, 527 South Wells St., 5th floor, Chicago, IL 60607-3922. Internet: **http://www.archivists.org**

For general information about careers as a curator and schools offering courses in museum studies, contact:

➤ American Association of Museums, 1575 Eye St. NW., Suite 400, Washington, DC 20005. Internet: **http://www.aam-us.org**

For information about careers and education programs in conservation and preservation, contact:

➤ American Institute for Conservation of Historic and Artistic Works, 1717 K St. NW., Suite 200, Washington, DC 20006. Internet: **http://aic.stanford.edu**

For information about archivists and archivist certification, contact:

➤ Academy of Certified Archivists, 48 Howard St., Albany, NY 12207. Internet: **http://www.certifiedarchivists.org**

For information about government archivists, contact:

➤ National Association of Government Archivists and Records Administrators, 48 Howard St., Albany, NY 12207. Internet: **http://www.nagara.org**

Information on obtaining positions as archivists, curators, and museum technicians with the Federal Government is available from the Office of Personnel Management through USAJOBS, the Federal Government's official employment information system. This resource for locating and applying for job opportunities can be accessed through the Internet at **http://www.usajobs.opm.gov** or through an interactive voice response telephone system at (703) 724-1850 or TDD (978) 461-8404. These numbers are not tollfree, and charges may result.

Instructional Coordinators

(O*NET 25-9031.00)

Significant Points

● Many instructional coordinators have experience as teachers or education administrators.

● A bachelor's degree is the minimum educational requirement, but a graduate degree is preferred.

● The need to meet new educational standards will create more demand for instructional coordinators to train teachers and develop new materials.

Nature of the Work

Instructional coordinators, also known as curriculum specialists, staff development specialists, or directors of instructional material, play a large role in improving the quality of education in the classroom. They develop curricula, select textbooks and other materials, train teachers, and assess educational programs in terms of quality and adherence to regulations and standards. They also assist in implementing new technology in the classroom. Instructional coordinators often specialize in specific subjects, such as reading, language arts, mathematics, or social studies.

Instructional coordinators evaluate how well a school or training program's curriculum, or plan of study, meets students' needs. They research teaching methods and techniques and develop procedures to determine whether program goals are being met. To aid in their evaluation, they may meet with members of educational committees and advisory groups to learn about subjects—English, history, or mathematics, for example—and to relate curriculum materials to these subjects, to students' needs, and to occupations for which these subjects are good preparation. They also may develop questionnaires and interview school staff about the curriculum. Based on their research and observations of instructional practice, they recommend instruction and curriculum improvements.

Another duty some instructional coordinators have is to review textbooks, software, and other educational materials and make recommendations on purchases. They monitor materials ordered and the ways in which teachers use them in the classroom. They also supervise workers who catalogue, distribute, and maintain a school's educational materials and equipment.

Instructional coordinators develop effective ways to use technology to enhance student learning. They monitor the introduction of new technology, including the Internet, into a school's curriculum. In addition, instructional coordinators might recommend installing educational computer software, such as interactive books and exercises designed to enhance student literacy and develop math skills. Instructional coordinators may invite experts—such as computer hardware, software, and library or media specialists—into the classroom to help integrate technological materials into a school's curriculum.

Many instructional coordinators plan and provide onsite education for teachers and administrators. They may train teachers about the use of materials and equipment or help them to improve their skills. Instructional coordinators also mentor new teachers and train experienced ones in the latest instructional methods. This role becomes especially important when a school district introduces new content, program innovations, or a different organizational structure. For example, when a State or school district introduces standards or tests that must be met by students in order to pass to the next grade, instructional coordinators often must advise teachers on the content of the standards and provide instruction on implementing the standards in the classroom.

Instructional coordinators work with teachers and administrators to develop new curricula and methods of teaching.

Working Conditions

Instructional coordinators, including those employed by school districts, often work year round, usually in offices or classrooms. Some spend much of their time traveling between schools meeting with teachers and administrators. The opportunity to shape and improve instructional curricula and work in an academic environment can be satisfying. However, some instructional coordinators find the work stressful because the occupation requires continual accountability to school administrators and it is not uncommon for people in this occupation to work long hours.

Training, Other Qualifications, and Advancement

The minimum educational requirement for instructional coordinators is a bachelor's degree, usually in education. Most employers, however, prefer candidates with a master's or higher degree. State licensing is necessary for instructional coordinators in public school systems, although specific requirements vary by State. In some States, a teaching license is needed, while in others instructional coordinators need an education administrator license. Instructional coordinators should have training in curriculum development and instruction, or in the specific field for which they are responsible, such as mathematics or history. Instructional coordinators must have a good understanding of how to teach specific groups of students, in addition to expertise in developing educational materials. As a result, many persons transfer into instructional coordinator jobs after working for several years as teachers. Work experience in an education administrator position, such as principal or assistant principal, also can be beneficial.

Helpful college courses may include those in curriculum development and evaluation, instructional approaches, or research design, which teaches how to create and implement research studies to determine the effectiveness of a given method of instruction or curriculum, or to measure and improve student performance. Moreover, instructional coordinators usually are required to take continuing education courses to keep their skills current. Topics for continuing education courses may include teacher evaluation techniques, curriculum training, new teacher induction, consulting and teacher support, and observation and analysis of teaching.

Instructional coordinators must be able to make sound decisions about curriculum options and to organize and coordinate work efficiently. They should have strong interpersonal and communication skills. Familiarity with computer technology also is important for instructional coordinators, who are increasingly involved in gathering and coordinating technical information for students and teachers.

Depending on experience and educational attainment, instructional coordinators may advance to higher administrative positions in a school system, or to management or executive positions in private industry.

Employment

Instructional coordinators held about 117,000 jobs in 2004. More than 2 in 5 worked for local governments, mainly in public schools and school district offices. One in 5 worked in private education, primarily in private elementary, secondary, and postsecondary schools and educational consulting firms. About 1 in 5 worked for State governments in public colleges and universities or State departments of education. The remainder worked mostly in the following industries: Individual and family services; child day care services; scientific research and development services; and management, scientific, and technical consulting services.

Job Outlook

Employment of instructional coordinators is expected to grow much faster than the average for all occupations through the year 2014. Over the next decade, instructional coordinators will be instrumental in developing new curricula to meet the demands of a changing society and in training the teacher workforce. Although budget constraints may limit employment growth to some extent, a continuing emphasis on improving the quality of education is expected to result in an increasing demand for these workers. Also, as an increased emphasis on accountability at all levels of government causes more schools to focus on improving educational quality and student performance, growing numbers of coordinators will be needed to incorporate the standards into existing curricula and make sure teachers and administrators are informed of the changes. Opportunities are expected to be best for those who specialize in subject areas that have been targeted for improvement by the No Child Left Behind Act—namely, reading, math, and science.

Instructional coordinators also will be needed to provide classes on using technology in the classroom, to keep teachers up-to-date on changes in their fields, and to demonstrate new teaching techniques. Additional job growth for instructional coordinators will stem from the increasing emphasis on lifelong learning and on programs for students with special needs, including those for whom English is a second language. These students often require more educational resources and consolidated planning and management within the educational system.

Earnings

Median annual earnings of instructional coordinators in May 2004 were $48,790. The middle 50 percent earned between $35,940 and $65,040. The lowest 10 percent earned less than $27,300, and the highest 10 percent earned more than $81,210.

Related Occupations

Instructional coordinators are professionals involved in education and training and development, which requires organizational, administrative, teaching, research, and communication skills. Occupations with similar characteristics include preschool, kindergarten, elementary, middle, and secondary school teachers; postsecondary teachers; education administrators; counselors; and human resources, training, and labor relations managers and specialists.

Sources of Additional Information

Information on requirements and job opportunities for instructional coordinators is available from local school systems and State departments of education.

Librarians

(O*NET 25-4021.00)

Significant Points

- A master's degree in library science usually is required; special librarians may need an additional graduate or professional degree.

- A large number of retirements in the next decade is expected to result in many job openings for librarians to replace those who leave.

- Librarians increasingly use information technology to perform research, classify materials, and help students and library patrons seek information.

Nature of the Work

The traditional concept of a library is being redefined from a place to access paper records or books to one that also houses the most advanced media, including CD-ROM, the Internet, virtual libraries, and remote access to a wide range of resources. Consequently, librarians, or information professionals, increasingly are combining traditional duties with tasks involving quickly changing technology. Librarians assist people in finding information and using it effectively for personal and professional purposes. Librarians must have knowledge of a wide variety of scholarly and public information sources and must follow trends related to publishing, computers, and the media in order to oversee the selection and organization of library materials. Librarians manage staff and develop and direct information programs and systems for the public, to ensure that information is organized in a manner that meets users' needs.

Most librarian positions incorporate three aspects of library work: User services, technical services, and administrative services. Still, even librarians specializing in one of these areas have other responsibilities. Librarians in user services, such as reference and children's librarians, work with patrons to help them find the information they need. The job involves analyzing users' needs to determine what information is appropriate, as well as searching for, acquiring, and providing the information. The job also includes an instructional role, such as showing users how to access information. For example, librarians commonly help users navigate the Internet so they can search for relevant information efficiently. Librarians in technical services, such as acquisitions and cataloguing, acquire and prepare materials for use and often do not deal directly with the public. Librarians in administrative services oversee the management and planning of libraries: negotiate contracts for services, materials, and equipment; supervise library employees; perform public-relations and fundraising duties; prepare budgets; and direct activities to ensure that everything functions properly.

In small libraries or information centers, librarians usually handle all aspects of the work. They read book reviews, publishers' announcements, and catalogues to keep up with current literature and other available resources, and they select and purchase materials from publishers, wholesalers, and distributors. Librarians prepare new materials by classifying them by subject matter and describe books and other library materials to make them easy to find. Librarians supervise assistants, who prepare cards, computer records, or other access tools that direct users to resources. In large libraries, librarians often specialize in a single area, such as acquisitions, cataloguing, bibliography, reference, special collections, or administration. Teamwork is increasingly important to ensure quality service to the public.

Librarians also compile lists of books, periodicals, articles, and audiovisual materials on particular subjects; analyze collections; and recommend materials. They collect and organize books, pamphlets, manuscripts, and other materials in a specific field, such as rare books, genealogy, or music. In addition, they coordinate programs such as storytelling for children and literacy skills and book talks for adults, conduct classes, publicize services, provide reference help, write grants, and oversee other administrative matters.

Librarians are classified according to the type of library in which they work: A public library; school library media center; college, university, or other academic library; or special library. Some librarians work with specific groups, such as children, young adults, adults, or the disadvantaged. In school library media centers, librarians—often called school media specialists—help teachers develop curricula, acquire materials for classroom instruction, and sometimes team teach.

Librarians also work in information centers or libraries maintained by government agencies, corporations, law firms, advertising agencies, museums, professional associations, unions, medical centers, hospitals, religious organizations, and research laboratories. They acquire and arrange an organization's information resources, which usually are limited to subjects of special interest to the organization. These special librarians can provide vital information services by preparing abstracts and indexes of current periodicals, organizing bibliographies, or analyzing background information and preparing reports on areas of particular interest. For example, a special librarian working for a corporation could provide the sales department with information on competitors or new developments affecting the field. A medical librarian may provide information about new medical treatments, clinical trials, and standard procedures to health professionals, patients, consumers, and corporations. Government document librarians, who work for government agencies and depository libraries in each of the States, preserve government publications, records, and other documents that make up a historical record of government actions.

Many libraries have access to remote databases and maintain their own computerized databases. The widespread use of automation in libraries makes database-searching skills important to librarians. Librarians develop and index databases and help train users to develop searching skills for the information they need. Some libraries are forming consortiums with other libraries to allow patrons to access a wider range of databases and to submit information requests to several libraries simultaneously. The Internet also has greatly expanded the amount of available reference information. Librarians must be aware of how to use these resources in order to locate information.

Librarians with computer and information systems skills can work as automated-systems librarians, planning and operating computer systems, and as information architects, designing information storage and retrieval systems and developing procedures for collecting, organizing, interpreting, and classifying information. These librarians analyze and plan for future information needs. (See the section on computer scientists and database administrators elsewhere in the *Handbook*.) The increasing use of automated information systems is enabling librarians to focus on administrative and budgeting responsibilities, grant writing, and specialized research requests, while delegating more technical and user services responsibilities to technicians. (See the section on library technicians elsewhere in the *Handbook*.)

More and more, librarians are applying their information management and research skills to arenas outside of libraries—for

Librarians provide research assistance to patrons and help them to find needed resources.

example, database development, reference tool development, information systems, publishing, Internet coordination, marketing, web content management and design, and training of database users. Entrepreneurial librarians sometimes start their own consulting practices, acting as freelance librarians or information brokers and providing services to other libraries, businesses, or government agencies.

Working Conditions

Librarians spend a significant portion of time at their desks or in front of computer terminals; extended work at video display terminals can cause eyestrain and headaches. Assisting users in obtaining information or books for their jobs, homework, or recreational reading can be challenging and satisfying, but working with users under deadlines can be demanding and stressful. Some librarians lift and carry books, and some climb ladders to reach high stacks, although most modern libraries have readily accessible stacks. Librarians in small organizations sometimes shelve books themselves.

More than 2 out of 10 librarians work part time. Public and college librarians often work weekends and evenings, as well as some holidays. School librarians usually have the same workday and vacation schedules as classroom teachers. Special librarians usually work normal business hours, but in fast-paced industries—such as advertising or legal services—they can work longer hours when needed.

Training, Other Qualifications, and Advancement

A master's degree in library science (MLS) is necessary for librarian positions in most public, academic, and special libraries and in some school libraries. The Federal Government requires that the librarians it employs have an MLS or the equivalent in education and experience. Many colleges and universities offer MLS programs, but employers often prefer graduates of the approximately 56 schools accredited by the American Library Association. Most MLS programs require a bachelor's degree, but no specific undergraduate program is required.

Most MLS programs take one year to complete; some take two. A typical graduate program includes courses in the foundations of library and information science, including the history of books and printing, intellectual freedom and censorship, and the role of libraries and information in society. Other basic courses cover the selection and processing of materials, the organization of information, reference tools and strategies, and user services. Courses are adapted to educate librarians to use new resources brought about by advancing technology, such as online reference systems, Internet search methods, and automated circulation systems. Course options can include resources for children or young adults; classification, cataloguing, indexing, and abstracting; library administration; and library automation. Computer-related course work is an increasingly important part of an MLS degree. Some programs offer interdisciplinary degrees combining technical courses in information science with traditional training in library science.

The MLS degree provides general preparation for library work, but some individuals specialize in a particular area, such as reference, technical services, or children's services. A Ph.D. degree in library and information science is advantageous for a college teaching position or for a top administrative job in a college or university library or large library system.

In addition to an MLS degree, most special librarians supplement their education with knowledge of the field in which they are specializing, sometimes earning a master's, doctoral, or professional degree in the subject. Areas of specialization include medicine, law, business, engineering, and the natural and social sciences. For example, a librarian working for a law firm may also be a licensed attorney, holding both library science and law degrees, while medical librarians should have a strong background in the sciences. In some jobs, knowledge of a foreign language is needed.

States generally have certification requirements for librarians in public schools and local libraries, though there are wide variations among States. Many require school librarians, often called library media specialists, to be certified as teachers in addition to having courses in library science. An MLS is needed in some States, often with a library media specialization, while in others a master's in education with a specialty in school library media or educational media is needed. Twenty-four States also require certification of librarians employed in local library systems, while several others have voluntary certification guidelines.

Librarians participate in continuing education and training, once they are on the job, in order to keep abreast of new information systems brought about by changing technology.

Experienced librarians can advance to administrative positions, such as department head, library director, or chief information officer.

Employment

Librarians held about 159,000 jobs in 2004. Most worked in school and academic libraries, but one-fourth worked in public libraries. The remainder worked in special libraries or as information professionals for companies and other organizations.

Job Outlook

Employment of librarians is expected to grow more slowly than the average for all occupations over the 2004–14 period. However, job opportunities are expected to be very good because a large number of librarians are expected to retire in the coming decade. More than 3 in 5 librarians are aged 45 or older and will become eligible for retirement in the next 10 years, which will result in many job openings. Also, the number of people going into this profession has fallen in recent years, resulting in more jobs than applicants in some cases.

Growth in the number of librarians will be limited by government budget constraints and the increasing use of computerized information storage and retrieval systems. Both will result in the hiring of fewer librarians and the replacement of librarians with less costly library technicians and assistants. Computerized systems make cataloguing easier, allowing library technicians to perform the work. In addition, many libraries are equipped for users to access library computers directly from their homes or offices. That way, users can bypass librarians altogether and conduct research on their own. However, librarians will still be needed to manage staff, help users develop database-searching techniques, address complicated reference requests, and define users' needs.

Jobs for librarians outside traditional settings will grow the fastest over the decade. Nontraditional librarian jobs include working as information brokers and working for private corporations, nonprofit organizations, and consulting firms. Many companies are turning to librarians because of their research and organizational skills and their knowledge of computer databases and library automation systems. Librarians can review vast amounts of information and analyze, evaluate, and organize it according to a company's specific needs. Librarians also are hired by organizations to set up information on the Internet. Librarians working in these settings may be classified as systems analysts, database specialists and trainers, webmasters or web developers, or local area network (LAN) coordinators.

Earnings

Salaries of librarians vary according to the individual's qualifications and the type, size, and location of the library. Librarians with primarily administrative duties often have greater earnings. Median annual earnings of librarians in May 2004 were $45,900. The middle 50 percent earned between $36,980 and $56,960. The lowest 10 percent earned less than $28,930, and the highest 10 percent earned more than $70,200. Median annual earnings in the industries employing the largest numbers of librarians in May 2004 were as follows:

Colleges, universities, and professional schools	$47,830
Elementary and secondary schools	47,580
Local government	42,500
Other information services	40,000

The average annual salary for all librarians in the Federal Government in nonsupervisory, supervisory, and managerial positions was $74,630 in 2005.

About three in ten librarians are a member of a union or are covered under a union contract.

Related Occupations

Librarians play an important role in the transfer of knowledge and ideas by providing people with access to the information they need and want. Jobs requiring similar analytical, organizational, and communication skills include archivists, curators, and museum technicians; and computer and information scientists, research. School librarians have many duties similar to those of school teachers. Librarians are increasingly storing, cataloguing, and accessing information with computers. Other jobs that use similar computer skills include systems analysts, computer scientists, and database administrators.

Sources of Additional Information

For information on a career as a librarian and information on accredited library education programs and scholarships, contact:
➤ American Library Association, Office for Human Resource Development and Recruitment, 50 East Huron St., Chicago, IL 60611. Internet: **http://www.ala.org**

For information on a career as a special librarian, contact:
➤ Special Libraries Association,331 South Patrick St., Alexandria, VA 22314. Internet: **http://www.sla.org**

For information on a career as a law librarian, scholarship information, and a list of ALA-accredited schools offering programs in law librarianship, contact:
➤ American Association of Law Libraries, 53 West Jackson Blvd., Suite 940, Chicago, IL 60604. Internet: **http://www.aallnet.org**

For information on employment opportunities for health sciences librarians and for scholarship information, credentialing information, and a list of MLA-accredited schools offering programs in health sciences librarianship, contact:
➤ Medical Library Association, 65 East Wacker Place , Suite 1900, Chicago, IL 60601. Internet: **http://www.mlanet.org**

Information concerning requirements and application procedures for positions in the Library of Congress can be obtained directly from:
➤ Human Resources Office, Library of Congress, 101 Independence Ave. SE., Washington, DC 20540-2231. Internet: **http://www.loc.gov/hr**

State library agencies can furnish information on scholarships available through their offices, requirements for certification, and general information about career prospects in the particular State of interest. Several of these agencies maintain job hot lines reporting openings for librarians.

State departments of education can furnish information on certification requirements and job opportunities for school librarians.

Library Technicians

(O*NET 25-4031.00)

Significant Points

- Training requirements range from a high school diploma to an associate degree, but computer skills are necessary for all workers.

- Increasing use of computerized circulation and information systems should continue to spur job growth, but many libraries' budget constraints should moderate growth.

- Employment should grow rapidly in special libraries because growing numbers of professionals and other workers use those libraries.

Nature of the Work

Library technicians both help librarians acquire, prepare, and organize material and assist users in finding information. Library technicians usually work under the supervision of a librarian, although they work independently in certain situations. Technicians in small libraries handle a range of duties; those in large libraries usually specialize. As libraries increasingly use new technologies—such as CD-ROM, the Internet, virtual libraries, and automated databases—the duties of library technicians will expand and evolve accordingly. Library technicians are assuming greater responsibilities, in some cases taking on tasks previously performed by librarians. (See the section on librarians elsewhere in the *Handbook*.)

Depending on the employer, library technicians can have other titles, such as library technical assistant or media aide. Library technicians direct library users to standard references, organize and maintain periodicals, prepare volumes for binding, handle interlibrary loan requests, prepare invoices, perform routine cataloguing and coding of library materials, retrieve information from computer databases, and supervise support staff.

The widespread use of computerized information storage and retrieval systems has resulted in technicians handling technical services—such as entering catalogue information into the library's computer—that were once performed by librarians. Technicians assist with customizing databases. In addition, technicians instruct patrons in how to use computer systems to access data. The increased automation of recordkeeping has reduced the amount of clerical work performed by library technicians. Many libraries now offer self-service registration and circulation areas with computers, decreasing the time library technicians spend manually recording and inputting records.

Some library technicians operate and maintain audiovisual equipment, such as projectors, tape and CD players, and DVD and videocassette players, and assist users with microfilm or microfiche readers. They also design posters, bulletin boards, or displays.

Library technicians in school libraries encourage and teach students to use the library and media center. They also help teachers obtain instructional materials, and they assist students with special assignments. Some work in special libraries maintained by government agencies, corporations, law firms, advertising agencies, museums, professional societies, medical centers, and research laboratories, where they conduct literature searches, compile bibliographies, and prepare abstracts, usually on subjects of particular interest to the organization.

To extend library services to more patrons, many libraries operate bookmobiles, often run by library technicians. The technicians take trucks stocked with books, or bookmobiles, to designated sites on a regular schedule, frequently stopping at shopping centers, apartment complexes, schools, and nursing homes. Bookmobiles also may be used to extend library service to patrons living in remote areas. Depending on local conditions, the technicians may operate a bookmobile alone or may be accompanied by another library employee.

Library technicians who drive bookmobiles are responsible for answering patrons' questions, receiving and checking out books, collecting fines, maintaining the book collection, shelving materials, and occasionally operating audiovisual equipment to show slides or films. They participate, and may assist, in planning programs sponsored by the library, such as reader advisory programs, used-book sales, or outreach programs. Technicians who drive the bookmobile keep track of their mileage, the materials lent out, and the amount of fines collected. In some areas, they are responsible for maintenance of the vehicle and any photocopiers or other equipment in it. They record statistics on circulation and the number of people visiting the bookmobile. Technicians also may record requests for special items from the main library and arrange for the materials to be mailed or delivered to a patron during the next scheduled visit. Many bookmobiles are equipped with personal computers and CD-ROM systems linked to the main library system, allowing technicians to reserve or locate books immediately. Some bookmobiles now offer Internet access to users.

Working Conditions

Technicians answer questions and provide assistance to library users. Those who prepare library materials sit at desks or computer terminals for long periods and can develop headaches or eyestrain from working with the terminals. Some duties, like calculating circulation statistics, can be repetitive and boring. Others, such as performing computer searches with the use of local and regional library networks and cooperatives, can be interesting and challenging. Library technicians may lift and carry books, climb ladders to reach high stacks, and bend low to shelve books on bottom shelves.

Library technicians in school libraries work regular school hours. Those in public libraries and college and university (academic) libraries also work weekends, evenings and some holidays. Library technicians in special libraries usually work normal business hours, although they often work overtime as well.

The schedules of library technicians who drive bookmobiles depend on the size of the area being served. Some bookmobiles operate

Library technicians assist patrons with routine requests and handle the circulation of library materials.

every day, while others go only on certain days. Some bookmobiles operate in the evenings and weekends, to give patrons as much access to the library as possible. Because library technicians who operate bookmobiles may be the only link some people have to the library, much of their work consists of helping the public. They may assist handicapped or elderly patrons to the bookmobile or shovel snow to ensure their safety. They may enter hospitals or nursing homes to deliver books to patrons who are bedridden.

Training, Other Qualifications, and Advancement

Training requirements for library technicians vary widely, ranging from a high school diploma to specialized postsecondary training. Some employers hire individuals with work experience or other training; others train inexperienced workers on the job. Many employers prefer to hire technicians who have an associate degree or some other postsecondary training. Given the rapid spread of automation in libraries, computer skills are a necessity, with knowledge of databases, library automation systems, online library systems, online public access systems, and circulation systems particularly valuable. Many bookmobile drivers are required to have a commercial driver's license.

Some community colleges offer an associate degree or certificate programs designed for library technicians. Programs include both liberal arts and library-related study. Students learn about library and media organization and operation, as well as how to order, process, catalogue, locate, and circulate library materials and work with library automation. Libraries and associations offer continuing education courses to keep technicians abreast of new developments in the field.

Library technicians usually advance by assuming added responsibilities. For example, technicians often start at the circulation desk, checking books in and out. After gaining experience, they may become responsible for storing and verifying information. As they advance, they may become involved in budget and personnel matters in their departments. Some library technicians advance to supervisory positions and are in charge of the day-to-day operation of their departments.

Employment

Library technicians held about 122,000 jobs in 2004; almost half worked in county or municipal public libraries. Most of the rest worked in school or academic libraries, while some worked in special libraries for health and legal services. The Federal Government employs library technicians primarily at the U.S. Department of Defense and the U.S. Library of Congress.

Job Outlook

Employment of library technicians is expected to grow about as fast as the average for all occupations through 2014. In addition to jobs opening up through employment growth, some job openings will result from the need to replace library technicians who transfer to other fields or leave the labor force.

The increasing use of library automation is expected to continue to spur job growth among library technicians. Computerized information systems have simplified certain tasks, such as descriptive cataloguing, which can now be handled by technicians instead of librarians. For example, technicians now can easily retrieve information from a central database and store it in the library's computer. Although efforts to contain costs could dampen employment growth of library technicians in school, public, and college and university libraries, cost containment efforts could also result in hiring more library technicians than librarians. Growth in the number of professionals and other workers who use special libraries should result in good job opportunities for library technicians in those settings.

Earnings

Median annual earnings of library technicians in May 2004 were $24,940. The middle 50 percent earned between $18,640 and $32,600. The lowest 10 percent earned less than $14,760, and the highest 10 percent earned more than $40,730. Median annual earnings in the industries employing the largest numbers of library technicians in May 2004 were as follows:

Colleges, universities, and professional schools	$28,940
Local government	23,560
Other information services	22,550
Elementary and secondary schools	22,510

Salaries of library technicians in the Federal Government averaged $39,647 in 2005.

Related Occupations

Library technicians perform organizational and administrative duties. Workers in other occupations with similar duties include library assistants, clerical; information and record clerks; and medical records and health information technicians.

Sources of Additional Information

For information on training programs for library/media technical assistants, write to:

➤ American Library Association, Office for Human Resource Development and Recruitment, 50 East Huron St., Chicago, IL 60611. Internet: **http://www.ala.org**

Information concerning requirements and application procedures for positions in the Library of Congress can be obtained directly from:

➤ Human Resources Office, Library of Congress, 101 Independence Ave. SE., Washington, DC 20540-2231. Internet: **http://www.loc.gov/hr**

State library agencies can furnish information on requirements for technicians and general information about career prospects in the State. Several of these agencies maintain job hot lines reporting openings for library technicians.

State departments of education can furnish information on requirements and job opportunities for school library technicians.

Teacher Assistants

(O*NET 25-9041.00)

Significant Points

● About 4 in 10 teacher assistants work part time.

● Educational requirements range from a high school diploma to some college training.

● Workers with experience in helping special education students, or who can speak a foreign language, will be especially in demand.

Nature of the Work

Teacher assistants provide instructional and clerical support for classroom teachers, allowing teachers more time for lesson planning and teaching. Teacher assistants tutor and assist children in learning class material using the teacher's lesson plans, providing students with individualized attention. Teacher assistants also supervise students in the cafeteria, schoolyard, and hallways, or on field trips. They record grades, set up equipment, and help prepare materials for instruction. Teacher assistants also are called teacher aides or instructional aides. Some assistants refer to themselves as paraeducators or paraprofessionals.

Some teacher assistants perform exclusively noninstructional or clerical tasks, such as monitoring nonacademic settings. Playground and lunchroom attendants are examples of such assistants. Most teacher assistants, however, perform a combination of instructional and clerical duties. They generally provide instructional reinforcement to children, under the direction and guidance of teachers. They work with students individually or in small groups—listening while students read, reviewing or reinforcing class lessons, or helping them find information for reports. At the secondary school level, teacher assistants often specialize in a certain subject, such as math or science. Teacher assistants often take charge of special projects and prepare equipment or exhibits, such as for a science demonstration. Some assistants work in computer laboratories, helping students using computers and educational software programs.

In addition to instructing, assisting, and supervising students, teacher assistants grade tests and papers, check homework, keep health and attendance records, do typing and filing, and duplicate materials. They also stock supplies, operate audiovisual equipment, and keep classroom equipment in order.

Many teacher assistants work extensively with special education students. As schools become more inclusive, integrating special education students into general education classrooms, teacher assistants in both general education and special education classrooms increasingly assist students with disabilities. Teacher assistants attend to a disabled student's physical needs, including feeding, teaching good grooming habits, or assisting students riding the schoolbus. They also provide personal attention to students with other special needs, such as those who speak English as a second language, or those who need remedial education. Teacher assistants help assess a student's progress by observing performance and recording relevant data.

While the majority of teacher assistants work in primary and secondary educational settings, others work in preschools and other child care centers. Often one or two assistants will work with a lead teacher in order to better provide the individual attention that young children require. In addition to assisting in educational instruction, they also supervise the children at play and assist in feeding and other basic care activities.

Teacher assistants work with small groups of students to help them learn skills such as reading comprehension.

Teacher assistants also work with infants and toddlers who have developmental delays or other disabilities. Under the guidance of a teacher or therapist, teacher assistants perform exercises or play games to help the child develop physically and behaviorally. Some teacher assistants work with young adults to help them obtain a job or to apply for community services for the disabled.

Working Conditions

Approximately 4 in 10 teacher assistants work part time. However, even among full-time workers, about 16 percent work less than 40 hours per week. Most assistants who provide educational instruction work the traditional 9- to 10-month school year. Teacher assistants work in a variety of settings—including preschools, child care centers, and religious and community centers, where they work with young adults—but most work in classrooms in elementary, middle, and secondary schools. They also work outdoors supervising recess when weather allows, and they spend much of their time standing, walking, or kneeling.

Seeing students develop and gain appreciation of the joy of learning can be very rewarding. However, working closely with students can be both physically and emotionally tiring. Teacher assistants who work with special education students often perform more strenuous tasks, including lifting, as they help students with their daily routine. Those who perform clerical work may tire of administrative duties, such as copying materials or typing.

Training, Other Qualifications, and Advancement

Educational requirements for teacher assistants vary by State or school district and range from a high school diploma to some college training, although employers increasingly prefer applicants with some college training. Teacher assistants with instructional responsibilities usually require more training than do those who do not perform teaching tasks. Federal regulations require teacher assistants with instructional responsibilities in Title I schools—those with a large proportion of students from low-income households—to meet one of three requirements: hold a 2-year or higher degree, have a minimum of 2 years of college, or pass a rigorous State or local assessment. Many schools also require previous experience in working with children and a valid driver's license. Some schools may require the applicant to pass a background check.

A number of 2-year and community colleges offer associate degree or certificate programs that prepare graduates to work as teacher assistants. However, most teacher assistants receive on-the-job training. Those who tutor and review lessons with students must have a thorough understanding of class materials and instructional methods, and should be familiar with the organization and operation of a school. Teacher assistants also must know how to operate audiovisual equipment, keep records, and prepare instructional materials, as well as have adequate computer skills.

Teacher assistants should enjoy working with children from a wide range of cultural backgrounds, and be able to handle classroom situations with fairness and patience. Teacher assistants also must demonstrate initiative and a willingness to follow a teacher's directions. They must have good writing skills and be able to communicate effectively with students and teachers. Teacher assistants who speak a second language, especially Spanish, are in great demand for communicating with growing numbers of students and parents whose primary language is not English.

Advancement for teacher assistants—usually in the form of higher earnings or increased responsibility—comes primarily with experience or additional education. Some school districts provide time away from the job or tuition reimbursement so that teacher assistants can earn their bachelor's degrees and pursue licensed teaching positions. In return for tuition reimbursement, assistants are often required to teach a certain length of time for the school district.

Employment

Teacher assistants held almost 1.3 million jobs in 2004. Nearly 3 in 4 worked for State and local government education institutions, mostly at the preschool and elementary school level. Private schools, child care centers, and religious organizations employed most of the rest.

Job Outlook

Employment of teacher assistants is expected to grow about as fast as the average for all occupations through 2014. In addition to job openings stemming from employment growth, numerous openings will arise as assistants leave their jobs and must be replaced. Many assistant jobs require limited formal education and offer relatively low pay so each year many transfer to other occupations or leave the labor force to assume family responsibilities, to return to school, or for other reasons.

School enrollments are projected to increase only slowly over the next decade, but special education students and students for whom English is not their first language—the student populations for which teacher assistants are most needed—are expected to grow faster and increase as a share of the total school-age population. Legislation that requires students with disabilities and non-native English speakers to receive an education "equal" to that of other students, will continue to generate jobs for teacher assistants to accommodate these students' special needs. Children with special needs require much personal attention, and special education teachers, as well as general education teachers with special education students, rely heavily on teacher assistants.

The greater focus on quality and accountability that has been placed on education in recent years also is likely to lead to an increased demand for teacher assistants. Growing numbers of teacher assistants may be needed to help teachers prepare students for standardized testing and to provide extra assistance to students who perform poorly on standardized tests. This growth may be moderated, however, as schools are encouraged to allocate resources to hiring more full teachers for instructional purposes. An increasing number of after-school programs and summer programs also will create new opportunities for teacher assistants.

Opportunities for teacher assistant jobs are expected to be best for persons with at least 2 years of formal education after high school. Persons who can speak a foreign language should be in particular demand in school systems with large numbers of students whose families do not speak English at home. Demand is expected to vary by region of the country. Areas in which the population and school enrollments are expected to grow faster, such as many communities in the South and West, should have rapid growth in the demand for teacher assistants.

Earnings

Median annual earnings of teacher assistants in May 2004 were $19,410. The middle 50 percent earned between $15,410 and $24,320. The lowest 10 percent earned less than $13,010, and the highest 10 percent earned more than $29,220.

Full-time workers usually receive health coverage and other benefits. Teacher assistants who work part time ordinarily do not receive benefits.

In 2004, about 3 out of 10 teacher assistants belonged to unions—mainly the American Federation of Teachers and the National Education Association—which bargain with school systems over wages, hours, and the terms and conditions of employment.

Related Occupations

Teacher assistants who instruct children have duties similar to those of preschool, kindergarten, elementary, middle, and secondary school teachers, as well as special education teachers. However, teacher assistants do not have the same level of responsibility or training. The support activities of teacher assistants and their educational backgrounds are similar to those of childcare workers, library technicians, and library assistants. Teacher assistants who work with children with disabilities perform many of the same functions as occupational therapy assistants and aides.

Sources of Additional Information

For information on teacher assistants, including training and certification, contact:

➤ American Federation of Teachers, Paraprofessional and School Related Personnel Division, 555 New Jersey Ave. NW., Washington, DC 20001. Internet: **http://www.aft.org/psrp/index.htm**

➤ National Education Association, Educational Support Personnel Division, 1201 16th Street, NW., Washington, DC 20036. Internet: **http://www.nea.org/esphome/**

For information on a career as a teacher assistant, contact:

➤ National Resource Center for Paraprofessionals, 6526 Old Main Hill, Utah State University, Logan, UT 84322. Internet: **http://www.nrcpara.org**

Human resource departments of school systems, school administrators, and State departments of education also can provide details about employment opportunities and required qualifications for teacher assistant jobs.

Teachers—Adult Literacy and Remedial Education

(O*NET 25-3011.00)

Significant Points

- Many adult literacy and remedial education teachers work part time and receive no benefits; unpaid volunteers also teach these subjects.

- Most programs require teachers to have at least a bachelor's degree; a public school teaching license is required for public programs in some States.

- Opportunities for teachers of English as a second language are expected to be very good because their classes should be in demand by the increasing number of residents with limited English skills.

Nature of the Work

Adult literacy and remedial education teachers instruct adults and out-of-school youths in reading, writing, speaking English, and performing elementary mathematical calculations—basic skills that equip them to solve problems well enough to become active participants in our society, to hold a job, and to further their education. The instruction provided by these teachers can be divided into three principle categories: *remedial or adult basic education (ABE)* is geared toward adults whose skills are either at or below an eighth-grade level; *adult secondary education (ASE)* is geared towards students who wish to obtain their General Educational Development (GED) certificate or other high school equivalency credential; and *English literacy* instruction for adults with limited proficiency in English. Traditionally, the students in these adult education classes have been primarily those who did not graduate high school or who passed through school without acquiring the knowledge needed to meet their educational goals or to participate fully in today's high-skill society. Increasingly, however, students in these classes are immigrants or other people whose native language is not English.

Adult literacy teachers use role-playing and problem-solving exercises to help students learn.

Educators who work with adult English-language learners are usually called *teachers of English as a second language (ESL)* or *teachers of English to speakers of other languages (ESOL)*.

Remedial education teachers, more commonly called adult basic education teachers, teach basic academic courses in mathematics, languages, history, reading, writing, science, and other areas, using instructional methods geared toward adult learning. They teach these subjects to students 16 years of age and older who demonstrate the need to increase their skills in one or more of the subject areas mentioned. Classes are taught to appeal to a variety of learning styles and usually include large-group, small-group, and one-on-one instruction. Because the students often are at different proficiency levels for different subjects, adult basic education teachers must make individual assessments of each student's abilities beforehand. In many programs, the assessment is used to develop an individualized education plan for each student. Teachers are required to evaluate students periodically to determine their progress and potential for advancement to the next level.

Teachers in remedial or adult basic education may have to assist students in acquiring effective study skills and the self-confidence they need to reenter an academic environment. Teachers also may encounter students with a learning or physical disability that requires additional expertise. Teachers should possess an understanding of how to help these students achieve their goals, but they also may need to have the knowledge to detect challenges their students may have and provide them with access to a broader system of additional services that are required to address their challenges.

For students who wish to get a GED credential in order to get a job or qualify for postsecondary education, adult secondary education, or GED, teachers provide help in acquiring the necessary knowledge and skills to pass the test. The GED tests students in subject areas such as reading, writing, mathematics, science, and social studies, while at the same time measuring students' communication, information-processing, problem-solving, and critical-thinking skills. The emphasis in class is on acquiring the knowledge needed to pass the GED test, as well as preparing students for success in further educational endeavors.

ESOL teachers help adults to speak, listen, read, and write in English, often in the context of real-life situations to promote learning. More advanced students may concentrate on writing and conversational skills or focus on learning more academic or job-related communication skills. ESOL teachers teach adults who possess a wide range of cultures and abilities and who speak a variety of languages. Some of their students have a college degree and many advance quickly through the program owing to a variety of factors, such as their age, previous language experience, educational background, and native language. Others may need additional time due to these same factors. Because the teacher and students often do not share a common language, creativity is an important part of fostering communication in the classroom and achieving learning goals.

All adult literacy and remedial teachers must prepare lessons beforehand, do any related paperwork, and stay current in their fields. Attendance for students is mostly voluntary and course work is rarely graded. Many teachers also must learn the latest uses for computers in the classroom, as computers are increasingly being used to supplement instruction in basic skills and in teaching ESOL.

Working Conditions

A large number of adult literacy and remedial education teachers work part time. Some have several part-time teaching assignments or work full time in addition to their part-time teaching job. Classes for adults are held on days and at times that best accommodate students who may have a job or family responsibilities.

Because many of these teachers work with adult students, they do not encounter some of the behavioral or social problems sometimes found with younger students. Adults attend by choice, are highly motivated, and bring years of experience to the classroom—attributes that can make teaching these students rewarding and satisfying. However, many adult education programs are located in cramped facilities that lack modern amenities, which can be frustrating for teachers.

Training, Other Qualifications, and Advancement

Requirements for teaching adult literacy and basic and secondary education vary by State and by program. Programs that are run by State and local governments require high accountability to student achievement standards. Most States require teachers in these programs to have some form of credential; the most common are a public school teacher license, an adult education credential, or both. However, programs in States that do not have these requirements still generally require that adult education teachers have at least a bachelor's degree and, preferably, a master's degree. Teaching experience, especially with adults, also is preferred or required. Those programs run by private religious, community, or volunteer organizations generally develop standards based on their own needs and organizational goals, but generally also require paid teachers to have at least a bachelor's degree. Volunteers usually do not need a bachelor's degree, but often must attend a training program before they are allowed to work with students.

Most programs recommend that adult literacy and basic and secondary education teachers take classes or workshops on teaching adults, using technology to teach, working with learners from a variety of cultures, and teaching adults with learning disabilities. ESOL teachers also should have courses or training in second-language acquisition theory and linguistics. In addition, knowledge of the citizenship and naturalization process may be useful. Knowledge of a second language is not necessary to teach ESOL students, but can be helpful in understanding the students' perspectives. GED teachers should know what is required to pass the GED and be able to instruct students in the subject matter. Training for literacy volunteers usually consists of instruction in effective teaching practices, needs assessment, lesson planning, the selection of appropriate instructional materials, characteristics of adult learners, and cross-cultural awareness.

Adult education and literacy teachers must have the ability to work with students who come from a variety of cultural, educational, and economic backgrounds. They must be understanding and respectful of their students' circumstances and be familiar with their concerns. All teachers, both paid and volunteer, should be able to communicate well and motivate their students.

Professional development among adult education and literacy teachers varies widely. Both part-time and full-time teachers are expected to participate in ongoing professional development activities in order to keep current on new developments in the field and to enhance skills already acquired. Each State's professional development system reflects the unique needs and organizational structure of that State. Attendance by teachers at professional development workshops and other activities is often outlined in State or local policy. Some teachers are able to access professional development activities through alternative delivery systems such as the Internet or distance learning.

Opportunities for advancement for adult education and literacy teachers again vary from State to State and program to program. Some part-time teachers are able to move into full-time teaching positions or program administrator positions, such as coordinator or director, when such vacancies occur. Others may decide to use their classroom experience to move into policy work at a nonprofit organization or with the local, State, or Federal government or to perform research.

Employment

Teachers of adult literacy and remedial education held about 98,000 jobs in 2004. About 1 in 3 was self-employed. Many additional teachers worked as unpaid volunteers. Many of the jobs are federally funded, with additional funds coming from State and local governments. State and local governments employ the majority of these teachers, who work in adult learning centers, libraries, community colleges, juvenile detention centers, and corrections institutions, among other places. Others work for private educational institutions and for social service organizations, such as job-training or residential care facilities.

Job Outlook

Opportunities for jobs as adult literacy and remedial education teachers are expected to be favorable. Employment is expected to grow as fast as the average for all occupations through 2014, and a large number of job openings is expected due to the need to replace people who leave the occupation or retire.

As employers increasingly require a more literate workforce, workers' demand for adult literacy, basic education, and secondary education classes is expected to grow. Significant employment growth is anticipated especially for ESOL teachers, who will be needed by the increasing number of immigrants and other residents living in this country that need to learn, or improve, their English skills. In addition, greater proportions of these groups are expected to take ESOL classes. Demand for ESOL teachers will be greatest in States that have large populations of residents who have limited English skills—such as California, Florida, Texas, and New York,. However, many other parts of the Nation have begun to attract large numbers of immigrants, making good opportunities in this field widely available.

The demand for adult literacy and basic and secondary education often fluctuates with the economy. When the economy is good and workers are hard to find, employers relax their standards and hire workers without a degree or GED or good proficiency in English. As the economy softens, employers can be more selective, and more students may find that they need additional education to get a job. In addition, adult education classes often are subject to changes in funding levels, which can cause the number of teaching jobs to fluctuate from year to year. In particular, budget pressures may limit Federal funding of adult education, which may cause programs to rely more on volunteers if other organizations and governments do not make up the difference. Other factors such as immigration policies and the relative prosperity of the United States compared with other countries also may have an impact on the number of immigrants entering this country and, consequently, on the demand for ESOL teachers.

Earnings

Median hourly earnings of adult literacy and remedial education teachers were $18.74 in May 2004. The middle 50 percent earned between $14.07 and $25.49. The lowest 10 percent earned less than $10.57, and the highest 10 percent earned more than $34.94. Part-time adult literacy and remedial education instructors are usually paid by the hour or for each class that they teach, and receive few or no benefits. Full-time teachers are generally paid a salary and

In addition to their teaching duties, many postsecondary teachers conduct original research in their field of study.

receive health insurance and other benefits if they work for a school system or government.

Related Occupations

The work of adult literacy and remedial education teachers is closely related to that of other types of teachers, especially preschool, kindergarten, elementary school, middle school, and secondary school teachers. In addition, adult literacy and basic and secondary education teachers require a wide variety of skills and aptitudes. Not only must they be able to teach and motivate students (including, at times, those with learning disabilities), but they also must often take on roles as advisers and mentors. Workers in other occupations that require these aptitudes include special-education teachers, counselors, and social workers.

Sources of Additional Information

Information on adult literacy, basic and secondary education programs, and teacher certification requirements is available from State departments of education, local school districts, and literacy resource centers. Information also may be obtained through local religious and charitable organizations.

For information on adult education and family literacy programs, contact

➤ The U.S. Department of Education, Office of Vocational and Adult Education, Potomac Center Plaza, 400 Maryland Ave. SW., Washington, DC 20202. Internet: **http://www.ed.gov/about/offices/list/ovae/index.html**

For information on teaching English as a second language, contact

➤ The Center for Adult English Language Acquisition, 4646 40th St. NW., Washington, DC 20016. Internet: **http://www.cal.org/caela**

Teachers—Postsecondary

(O*NET 25-1011.00, 25-1021.00, 25-1022.00, 25-1031.00, 25-1032.00, 25-1041.00, 25-1042.00, 25-1043.00, 25-1051.00, 25-1052.00, 25-1053.00, 25-1054.00, 25-1061.00, 25-1062.00, 25-1063.00, 25-1064.00, 25-1065.00, 25-1066.00, 25-1067.00, 25-1069.99, 25-1071.00, 25-1072.00, 25-1081.00, 25-1082.00, 25-1111.00, 25-1112.00, 25-1113.00, 25-1121.00, 25-1122.00, 25-1123.00, 25-1124.00, 25-1125.00, 25-1126.00, 25-1191.00, 25-1192.00, 25-1193.00, 25-1194.00, 25-1199.99)

Significant Points

● Opportunities for postsecondary teaching jobs are expected to be good, but many new openings will be for part-time or non-tenure-track positions.

● Prospects for teaching jobs will be better and earnings higher in academic fields in which many qualified teachers opt for nonacademic careers, such as health specialties, business, and computer science, for example.

● Educational qualifications for postsecondary teacher jobs range from expertise in a particular field to a Ph.D, depending on the subject being taught and the type of educational institution.

Nature of the Work

Postsecondary teachers instruct students in a wide variety of academic and vocational subjects beyond the high school level that may lead to a degree or to improvement in one's knowledge or career skills. These teachers include college and university faculty, postsecondary career and technical education teachers, and graduate teaching assistants.

College and university faculty make up the majority of postsecondary teachers. They teach and advise more than 16 million full- and part-time college students and perform a significant part of our Nation's research. Faculty also keep up with new developments in their field and may consult with government, business, nonprofit, and community organizations.

Faculty usually are organized into departments or divisions, based on academic subject or field. They usually teach several different related courses in their subject—algebra, calculus, and statistics, for example. They may instruct undergraduate or graduate students, or both. College and university faculty may give lectures to several hundred students in large halls, lead small seminars, or supervise students in laboratories. They prepare lectures, exercises, and laboratory experiments; grade exams and papers; and advise and work with students individually. In universities, they also supervise graduate students' teaching and research. College faculty work with an increasingly varied student population made up of growing shares of part-time, older, and culturally and racially diverse students.

Faculty keep abreast of developments in their field by reading current literature, talking with colleagues, and participating in professional conferences. They may also do their own research to expand knowledge in their field. They may perform experiments; collect and analyze data; and examine original documents, literature, and other source material. From this process, they arrive at conclusions, and publish their findings in scholarly journals, books, and electronic media.

Most college and university faculty extensively use computer technology, including the Internet; e-mail; CD-ROMS; and software programs, such as statistical packages. They may use computers in the classroom as teaching aids and may post course content, class notes, class schedules, and other information on the Internet. The use of e-mail, chat rooms, and other techniques has greatly improved communications between students and teachers and among students

Some faculty use the Internet to teach courses to students at remote sites. These so-called "distance learning" courses are an increasingly popular option for non-traditional students such as working adults. While more convenient for students, faculty who teach these courses must be able to adapt existing courses to make them successful online or design a new course that takes advantage of the format.

Most faculty members serve on academic or administrative committees that deal with the policies of their institution, departmental matters, academic issues, curricula, budgets, equipment purchases, and hiring. Some work with student and community organizations. Department chairpersons are faculty members who usually teach some courses but have heavier administrative responsibilities.

The proportion of time spent on research, teaching, administrative, and other duties varies by individual circumstance and type of institution. Faculty members at universities normally spend a significant part of their time doing research; those in 4-year colleges, somewhat less; and those in 2-year colleges, relatively little. The teaching load, however, often is heavier in 2-year colleges and somewhat lighter at 4-year institutions. Full professors at all types of institutions usually spend a larger portion of their time conducting research than do assistant professors, instructors, and lecturers.

In addition to traditional 2- and 4-year institutions, an increasing number of faculty work in alternative schools or in programs that are aimed at providing career-related education for working adults. Courses are usually offered online or on nights and weekends. Faculty at these programs generally work part time and are only responsible for teaching, with little to no administrative and research responsibilities.

Postsecondary vocational education teachers, also known as *postsecondary career and technical education teachers*, provide instruction for occupations that require specialized training, but may not require a 4-year degree, such as welder, dental hygienist, x-ray technician, auto mechanic, and cosmetologist. Classes often are taught in an industrial or laboratory setting where students are provided hands-on experience. For example, welding instructors show students various welding techniques and essential safety practices, watch them use tools and equipment, and have them repeat procedures until they meet the specific standards required by the trade. Increasingly, career and technical education teachers are integrating academic and vocational curriculums so that students obtain a variety of skills that can be applied to the "real world."

Career and technical education teachers have many of the same responsibilities that other college and university faculty have. They must prepare lessons, grade papers, attend faculty meetings, and keep abreast of developments in their field. Career and technical education teachers at community colleges and career and technical schools also often play a key role in students' transition from school to work by helping to establish internship programs for students and by facilitating contact between students and prospective employers.

Graduate teaching assistants, often referred to as *graduate TAs*, assist faculty, department chairs, or other professional staff at colleges and universities by performing teaching or teaching-related duties. In addition to their work responsibilities, assistants have their own school commitments, as they are also students who are working towards earning a graduate degree, such as a Ph.D. Some teaching assistants have full responsibility for teaching a course—usually one that is introductory in nature—which can include preparation of lectures and exams, and assigning final grades to students. Others provide assistance to faculty members, which may consist of a variety of tasks such as grading papers, monitoring exams, holding office hours or help-sessions for students, conducting laboratory sessions, or administering quizzes to the class. Teaching assistants generally meet initially with the faculty member whom they are going to assist in order to determine exactly what is expected of them, as each faculty member may have his or her own needs. For example, some faculty members prefer assistants to sit in on classes, while others assign them other tasks to do during class time. Graduate teaching assistants may work one-on-one with a faculty member or, for large classes, they may be one of several assistants.

Working Conditions
Postsecondary teachers who work full time usually have flexible schedules. They must be present for classes, usually 12 to 16 hours per week, and for faculty and committee meetings. Most establish regular office hours for student consultations, usually 3 to 6 hours per week. Otherwise, teachers are free to decide when and where they will work, and how much time to devote to course preparation, grading, study, research, graduate student supervision, and other activities.

Some teach night and weekend classes. This is particularly true for teachers at 2-year community colleges or institutions with large enrollments of older students who have full-time jobs or family responsibilities. Most colleges and universities require teachers to work 9 months of the year, which allows them the time to teach additional courses, do research, travel, or pursue nonacademic interests during the summer and school holidays. Colleges and universities usually have funds to support research or other professional development needs of full time faculty, including travel to conferences and research sites.

About 3 out of 10 college and university faculty worked part time in 2004. Some part-timers, known as "adjunct faculty," have primary jobs outside of academia—in government, private industry, or nonprofit research—and teach "on the side." Others prefer to work part-time hours or seek full-time jobs but are unable to obtain them due to intense competition for available openings. Some work part time in more than one institution. Some adjunct faculty are not qualified for tenure-track positions because they lack a doctoral degree.

University faculty may experience a conflict between their responsibilities to teach students and the pressure to do research and publish their findings. This may be a particular problem for young faculty seeking advancement in 4-year research universities. Also, recent cutbacks in support workers and the hiring of more part-time faculty have put a greater administrative burden on full-time faculty. Requirements to teach online classes also have added greatly to the workloads of postsecondary teachers. Many find that developing the courses to put online, plus learning how to operate the technology and answering large amounts of e-mail, is very time-consuming.

Graduate TAs usually have flexibility in their work schedules like college and university faculty, but they also must spend a considerable amount of time pursuing their own academic coursework and studies. The number of hours that TAs work varies, depending on their assignments. Work may be stressful, particularly when assistants are given full responsibility for teaching a class; however, these types of positions allow graduate students the opportunity to gain valuable teaching experience. This experience is especially helpful for those graduate teaching assistants who seek to become faculty members at colleges and universities after completing their degree.

Training, Other Qualifications, and Advancement
The education and training required of postsecondary teachers varies widely, depending on the subject taught and educational institution employing them. Educational requirements for teachers are generally the highest at 4-year research universities while experience and expertise in a related occupation is the principal qualification at career and technical institutes.

Postsecondary teachers should communicate and relate well with students, enjoy working with them, and be able to motivate them. They should have inquiring and analytical minds, and a strong desire to pursue and disseminate knowledge. Additionally, they must be self-motivated and able to work in an environment in which they receive little direct supervision.

Training requirements for postsecondary career and technical education teachers vary by State and by subject. In general, teachers need a bachelor's or higher degree, plus at least 3 years of work experience in their field. In some fields, a license or certificate that demonstrates one's qualifications may be all that is required. Teachers update their skills through continuing education, in order to maintain certification. They must also maintain ongoing dialogue with businesses to determine the most current skills needed in the workplace.

Four-year colleges and universities usually consider doctoral degree holders for full-time, tenure-track positions, but may hire master's degree holders or doctoral candidates for certain disciplines, such as the arts, or for part-time and temporary jobs. Most college and university faculty are in four academic ranks—professor, associate professor, assistant professor, and instructor. These positions usually are considered to be tenure-track positions. Most faculty members are hired as instructors or assistant professors. A smaller number of additional faculty members, called lecturers, are usually employed on contracts for a single academic term and are not on the tenure track.

In 2-year colleges, master's degree holders fill most full-time positions. However, in certain fields where there may be more applicants than available jobs, institutions can be more selective in their hiring practices. In these fields, Master's degree holders may

be passed over in favor of candidates holding Ph.Ds. Many 2-year institutions increasingly prefer job applicants to have some teaching experience or experience with distance learning. Preference also may be given to those holding dual master's degrees, especially at smaller institutions, because they can teach more subjects.

Schools and programs that provide education and training for working adults generally hire people who are experienced in the field to teach part time. A master's degree is also usually required.

Doctoral programs take an average of 6 years of full-time study beyond the bachelor's degree, including time spent completing a master's degree and a dissertation. Some programs, such as those in the humanities, may take longer to complete; others, such as those in engineering, usually are shorter. Candidates specialize in a subfield of a discipline—for example, organic chemistry, counseling psychology, or European history—but also take courses covering the entire discipline. Programs typically include 20 or more increasingly specialized courses and seminars plus comprehensive examinations on all major areas of the field. Candidates also must complete a dissertation—a written report on original research in the candidate's major field of study. The dissertation sets forth an original hypothesis or proposes a model and tests it. Students in the natural sciences and engineering usually do laboratory work; in the humanities, they study original documents and other published material. The dissertation is done under the guidance of one or more faculty advisors and usually takes 1 or 2 years of full-time work.

Some students, particularly those who studied in the natural sciences, spend additional years after earning their degree on postdoctoral research and study before taking a faculty position. Some Ph.D.s are able to extend postdoctoral appointments, or take new ones, if they are unable to find a faculty job. Most of these appointments offer a nominal salary.

Obtaining a position as a graduate teaching assistant is a good way to gain college teaching experience. To qualify, candidates must be enrolled in a graduate school program. In addition, some colleges and universities require teaching assistants to attend classes or take some training prior to being given responsibility for a course.

Although graduate teaching assistants usually work at the institution and in the department where they are earning their degree, teaching or internship positions for graduate students at institutions that do not grant a graduate degree have become more common in recent years. For example, a program called Preparing Future Faculty, administered by the Association of American Colleges and Universities and the Council of Graduate Schools, has led to the creation of many now-independent programs that offer graduate students at research universities the opportunity to work as teaching assistants at other types of institutions, such as liberal arts or community colleges. Working with a mentor, the graduate students teach classes and learn how to improve their teaching techniques. They may attend faculty and committee meetings, develop a curriculum, and learn how to balance the teaching, research, and administrative roles that faculty play. These programs provide valuable learning opportunities for graduate students interested in teaching at the postsecondary level, and also help to make these students aware of the differences among the various types of institutions at which they may someday work.

For faculty, a major step in the traditional academic career is attaining tenure. New tenure-track faculty usually are hired as instructors or assistant professors, and must serve a period—usually 7 years—under term contracts. At the end of the period, their record of teaching, research, and overall contribution to the institution is reviewed; tenure is granted if the review is favorable. Those denied tenure usually must leave the institution. Tenured professors cannot be fired without just cause and due process. Tenure protects the faculty's academic freedom—the ability to teach and conduct research without fear of being fired for advocating controversial or unpopular ideas. It also gives both faculty and institutions the stability needed for effective research and teaching, and provides financial security for faculty. Some institutions have adopted post-tenure review policies to encourage ongoing evaluation of tenured faculty.

The number of tenure-track positions is declining as institutions seek flexibility in dealing with financial matters and changing student interests. Institutions rely more heavily on limited term contracts and part-time, or adjunct, faculty, thus shrinking the total pool of tenured faculty. Limited-term contracts—typically 2- to 5 years, may be terminated or extended when they expire, but generally do not lead to the granting of tenure. In addition, some institutions have limited the percentage of faculty who can be tenured.

For most postsecondary teachers, advancement involves a move into administrative and managerial positions, such as departmental chairperson, dean, and president. At 4-year institutions, such advancement requires a doctoral degree. At 2-year colleges, a doctorate is helpful but not usually required, except for advancement to some top administrative positions. (Deans and departmental chairpersons are covered in the *Handbook* statement on education administrators, while college presidents are included in the *Handbook* statement on top executives.)

Employment

Postsecondary teachers held nearly 1.6 million jobs in 2004. Most were employed in public and private 4-year colleges and universities and in 2-year community colleges. Other postsecondary teachers are employed by schools and institutes that specialize in training people in a specific field, such as technology centers or culinary schools, or work for businesses that provide professional development courses to employees of companies. Some career and technical education teachers work for State and local governments and job training facilities. The following tabulation shows postsecondary teaching jobs in specialties having 20,000 or more jobs in 2004:

Health specialties teachers	150,000
Graduate teaching assistants	143,000
Vocational education teachers	127,000
Business teachers	85,000
Art, drama, and music teachers	78,000
Biological science teachers	76,000
English language and literature teachers	69,000
Education teachers	60,000
Mathematical science teachers	53,000
Computer science teachers	45,000
Engineering teachers	42,000
Nursing instructors and teachers	41,000
Psychology teachers	37,000
Foreign language and literature teachers	27,000
Communications teachers	26,000
History teachers	24,000
Chemistry teachers	23,000
Philosophy and religion teachers	23,000

Job Outlook

Overall, employment of postsecondary teachers is expected to grow much faster than the average for all occupations through 2014. A significant proportion of these new jobs will be part-time positions. Job opportunities are generally expected to be very good—although they will vary somewhat from field to field—as numerous openings for all types of postsecondary teachers result from retirements of current postsecondary teachers and continued increases in student enrollments.

Projected growth in college and university enrollment over the next decade stems mainly from the expected increase in the population of 18- to 24-year-olds, who constitute the majority of students at postsecondary institutions, and from the increasing number of high school graduates who choose to attend these institutions. Adults returning to college to enhance their career prospects or to update their skills also will continue to create new opportunities for postsecondary teachers, particularly at community colleges and for-profit institutions that cater to working adults. However, many postsecondary educational institutions receive a significant portion of their funding from State and local governments, so expansion of public higher education will be limited by State and local budgets. Nevertheless, in addition to growth in enrollments, the need to replace the large numbers of postsecondary teachers who are likely to retire over the next decade will also create a significant number of openings. Many postsecondary teachers were hired in the late 1960s and the 1970s to teach members of the baby boom generation, and they are expected to retire in growing numbers in the years ahead.

Ph.D. recipients seeking jobs as postsecondary teachers will experience favorable job prospects over the next decade. While competition will remain tight for tenure-track positions at 4-year colleges and universities, there will be a considerable number of part-time or renewable, term appointments at these institutions and positions at community colleges available to them. Opportunities for master's degree holders are also expected to be favorable, as community colleges and other institutions that employ them, such as professional career education programs, are expected to experience considerable growth.

Opportunities for graduate teaching assistants are expected to be very good due to prospects for much higher undergraduate enrollments coupled with more modest graduate enrollment increases. Constituting almost 9 percent of all postsecondary teachers, graduate teaching assistants play an integral role in the postsecondary education system, and they are expected to continue to do so in the future.

One of the main reasons why students attend postsecondary institutions is to prepare themselves for careers, so the best job prospects for postsecondary teachers are likely to be in fields where job growth is expected to be strong over the next decade. These will include fields such as business, health specialties, nursing, and biological sciences. Community colleges and other institutions offering career and technical education have been among the most rapidly growing, and these institutions are expected to offer some of the best opportunities for postsecondary teachers.

Earnings

Median annual earnings of all postsecondary teachers in May 2004 were $51,800. The middle 50 percent earned between $36,590 and $72,490. The lowest 10 percent earned less than $25,460, and the highest 10 percent earned more than $99,980.

Earnings for college faculty vary according to rank and type of institution, geographic area, and field. According to a 2004-05 survey by the American Association of University Professors, salaries for full-time faculty averaged $68,505. By rank, the average was $91,548 for professors, $65,113 for associate professors, $54,571 for assistant professors, $39,899 for instructors, and $45,647 for lecturers. Faculty in 4-year institutions earn higher salaries, on average, than do those in 2-year schools. In 2004-05, faculty salaries averaged $79,342 in private independent institutions, $66,851 in public institutions, and $61,103 in religiously affiliated private colleges and universities. In fields with high-paying nonacademic alternatives—medicine, law, engineering, and business, among others—earnings exceed these averages. In others fields—such as the humanities and education—they are lower.

Many faculty members have significant earnings in addition to their base salary, from consulting, teaching additional courses, research, writing for publication, or other employment. In addition, many college and university faculty enjoy some unique benefits, including access to campus facilities, tuition waivers for dependents, housing and travel allowances, and paid sabbatical leaves. Part-time faculty usually have fewer benefits than full-time faculty.

Earnings for postsecondary career and technical education teachers vary widely by subject, academic credentials, experience, and region of the country. Part-time instructors usually receive few benefits.

Related Occupations

Postsecondary teaching requires the ability to communicate ideas well, motivate students, and be creative. Workers in other occupations that require these skills are teachers—preschool, kindergarten, elementary, middle, and secondary; education administrators; librarians; counselors; writers and editors; public relations specialists; and management analysts. Faculty research activities often are similar to those of scientists, as well as to those of managers and administrators in industry, government, and nonprofit research organizations.

Sources of Additional Information

Professional societies related to a field of study often provide information on academic and nonacademic employment opportunities. Names and addresses of many of these societies appear in statements elsewhere in the *Handbook*.

Special publications on higher education, such as *The Chronicle of Higher Education*, list specific employment opportunities for faculty. These publications are available in libraries.

For information on the Preparing Future Faculty program, contact:

➤ Council of Graduate Schools, One Dupont Circle, NW, Suite 430, Washington, DC 20036-1173. Internet: **http://www.preparing-faculty.org**

For information on postsecondary career and technical education teaching positions, contact State departments of career and technical education. General information on adult and career and technical education is available from:

➤ Association for Career and Technical Education, 1410 King St., Alexandria, VA 22314. Internet: **http://www.acteonline.org**

Teachers—Preschool, Kindergarten, Elementary, Middle, and Secondary

(O*NET 25-2011.00, 25-2012.00, 25-2021.00, 25-2022.00, 25-2023.00, 25 2031.00, 25-2032.00)

Significant Points

- Public school teachers must have at least a bachelor's degree, complete an approved teacher education program, and be licensed.

- Many States offer alternative licensing programs to attract people into teaching, especially for hard-to-fill positions.

- Excellent job opportunities are expected as retirements, especially among secondary school teachers, outweigh slowing enrollment growth; opportunities will vary by geographic area and subject taught.

Nature of the Work

Teachers act as facilitators or coaches, using interactive discussions and "hands-on" approaches to help students learn and apply concepts in subjects such as science, mathematics, or English. They utilize

In addition to core subjects, teachers instruct students in fields such as photography and painting.

"props" or "manipulatives" to help children understand abstract concepts, solve problems, and develop critical thought processes. For example, they teach the concepts of numbers or of addition and subtraction by playing board games. As the children get older, the teachers use more sophisticated materials, such as science apparatus, cameras, or computers.

To encourage collaboration in solving problems, students are increasingly working in groups to discuss and solve problems together. Preparing students for the future workforce is a major stimulus generating changes in education. To be prepared, students must be able to interact with others, adapt to new technology, and think through problems logically. Teachers provide the tools and the environment for their students to develop these skills.

Preschool, kindergarten, and elementary school teachers play a vital role in the development of children. What children learn and experience during their early years can shape their views of themselves and the world and can affect their later success or failure in school, work, and their personal lives. Preschool, kindergarten, and elementary school teachers introduce children to mathematics, language, science, and social studies. They use games, music, artwork, films, books, computers, and other tools to teach basic skills.

Preschool children learn mainly through play and interactive activities. *Preschool teachers* capitalize on children's play to further language and vocabulary development (using storytelling, rhyming games, and acting games), improve social skills (having the children work together to build a neighborhood in a sandbox), and introduce scientific and mathematical concepts (showing the children how to balance and count blocks when building a bridge or how to mix colors when painting). Thus, a less structured approach, including small-group lessons, one-on-one instruction, and learning through creative activities such as art, dance, and music, is adopted to teach preschool children. Play and hands-on teaching also are used by *kindergarten teachers*, but academics begin to take priority in kindergarten classrooms. Letter recognition, phonics, numbers, and awareness of nature and science, introduced at the preschool level, are taught primarily in kindergarten.

Most *elementary school teachers* instruct one class of children in several subjects. In some schools, two or more teachers work as a team and are jointly responsible for a group of students in at least one subject. In other schools, a teacher may teach one special subject—usually music, art, reading, science, arithmetic, or physical education—to a number of classes. A small but growing number of teachers instruct multilevel classrooms, with students at several different learning levels.

Middle school teachers and *secondary school teachers* help students delve more deeply into subjects introduced in elementary school and expose them to more information about the world. Middle and secondary school teachers specialize in a specific subject, such as English, Spanish, mathematics, history, or biology. They also can teach subjects that are career oriented. *Vocational education teachers*, also referred to as career and technical or career-technology teachers, instruct and train students to work in a wide variety of fields, such as healthcare, business, auto repair, communications, and, increasingly, technology. They often teach courses that are in high demand by area employers, who may provide input into the curriculum and offer internships to students. Many vocational teachers play an active role in building and overseeing these partnerships. Additional responsibilities of middle and secondary school teachers may include career guidance and job placement, as well as follow-ups with students after graduation. (Special education teachers—who instruct elementary and secondary school students who have a variety of disabilities—are discussed separately in this section of the *Handbook*.)

Computers play an integral role in the education teachers provide. Resources such as educational software and the Internet expose students to a vast range of experiences and promote interactive learning. Through the Internet, students can communicate with other students anywhere in the world, allowing them to share experiences and differing viewpoints. Students also use the Internet for individual research projects and to gather information. Computers are used in other classroom activities as well, from solving math problems to learning English as a second language. Teachers also may use computers to record grades and perform other administrative and clerical duties. They must continually update their skills so that they can instruct and use the latest technology in the classroom.

Teachers often work with students from varied ethnic, racial, and religious backgrounds. With growing minority populations in most parts of the country, it is important for teachers to work effectively with a diverse student population. Accordingly, some schools offer training to help teachers enhance their awareness and understanding of different cultures. Teachers may also include multicultural programming in their lesson plans, to address the needs of all students, regardless of their cultural background.

Teachers design classroom presentations to meet students' needs and abilities. They also work with students individually. Teachers plan, evaluate, and assign lessons; prepare, administer, and grade tests; listen to oral presentations; and maintain classroom discipline. They observe and evaluate a student's performance and potential and increasingly are asked to use new assessment methods. For example, teachers may examine a portfolio of a student's artwork or writing in order to judge the student's overall progress. They then can provide additional assistance in areas in which a student needs help. Teachers also grade papers, prepare report cards, and meet with parents and school staff to discuss a student's academic progress or personal problems.

In addition to conducting classroom activities, teachers oversee study halls and homerooms, supervise extracurricular activities, and accompany students on field trips. They may identify students with physical or mental problems and refer the students to the proper authorities. Secondary school teachers occasionally assist students

in choosing courses, colleges, and careers. Teachers also participate in education conferences and workshops.

In recent years, site-based management, which allows teachers and parents to participate actively in management decisions regarding school operations, has gained popularity. In many schools, teachers are increasingly involved in making decisions regarding the budget, personnel, textbooks, curriculum design, and teaching methods.

Working Conditions

Seeing students develop new skills and gain an appreciation of knowledge and learning can be very rewarding. However, teaching may be frustrating when one is dealing with unmotivated or disrespectful students. Occasionally, teachers must cope with unruly behavior and violence in the schools. Teachers may experience stress in dealing with large classes, heavy workloads, or old schools that are run down and lack many modern amenities. Accountability standards also may increase stress levels, with teachers expected to produce students who are able to exhibit satisfactory performance on standardized tests in core subjects. Many teachers, particularly in public schools, are also frustrated by the lack of control they have over what they are required to teach.

Teachers in private schools generally enjoy smaller class sizes and more control over establishing the curriculum and setting standards for performance and discipline. Their students also tend to be more motivated, since private schools can be selective in their admissions processes.

Teachers are sometimes isolated from their colleagues because they work alone in a classroom of students. However, some schools allow teachers to work in teams and with mentors to enhance their professional development.

Including school duties performed outside the classroom, many teachers work more than 40 hours a week. Part-time schedules are more common among preschool and kindergarten teachers. Although some school districts have gone to all-day kindergartens, most kindergarten teachers still teach two kindergarten classes a day. Most teachers work the traditional 10-month school year with a 2-month vacation during the summer. During the vacation break, those on the 10-month schedule may teach in summer sessions, take other jobs, travel, or pursue personal interests. Many enroll in college courses or workshops to conti chedule typically work 8 weeks, are on vacation for 1 week, and have a 5-week midwinter break. Preschool teachers working in day care settings often work year round.

Most States have tenure laws that prevent public school teachers from being fired without just cause and due process. Teachers may obtain tenure after they have satisfactorily completed a probationary period of teaching, normally 3 years. Tenure does not absolutely guarantee a job, but it does provide some security.

Training, Other Qualifications, and Advancement

All 50 States and the District of Columbia require public school teachers to be licensed. Licensure is not required for teachers in private schools in most States. Usually licensure is granted by the State Board of Education or a licensure advisory committee. Teachers may be licensed to teach the early childhood grades (usually preschool through grade 3); the elementary grades (grades 1 through 6 or 8); the middle grades (grades 5 through 8); a secondary-education subject area (usually grades 7 through 12); or a special subject, such as reading or music (usually grades kindergarten through 12).

Requirements for regular licenses to teach kindergarten through grade 12 vary by State. However, all States require general education teachers to have a bachelor's degree and to have completed an approved teacher training program with a prescribed number of subject and education credits, as well as supervised practice teaching. Some States also require technology training and the attainment of a minimum grade point average. A number of States require that teachers obtain a master's degree in education within a specified period after they begin teaching.

Almost all States require applicants for a teacher's license to be tested for competency in basic skills, such as reading and writing, and in teaching. Almost all also require the teacher to exhibit proficiency in his or her subject. Many school systems are presently moving toward implementing performance-based systems for licensure, which usually require a teacher to demonstrate satisfactory teaching performance over an extended period in order to obtain a provisional license, in addition to passing an examination in their subject. Most States require continuing education for renewal of the teacher's license. Many States have reciprocity agreements that make it easier for teachers licensed in one State to become licensed in another.

Many States also offer alternative licensure programs for teachers who have a bachelor's degree in the subject they will teach, but who lack the necessary education courses required for a regular license. Many of these alternative licensure programs are designed to ease shortages of teachers of certain subjects, such as mathematics and science. Other programs provide teachers for urban and rural schools that have difficulty filling positions with teachers from traditional licensure programs. Alternative licensure programs are intended to attract people into teaching who do not fulfill traditional licensing standards, including recent college graduates who did not complete education programs and those changing from another career to teaching. In some programs, individuals begin teaching quickly under provisional licensure. After working under the close supervision of experienced educators for 1 or 2 years while taking education courses outside school hours, they receive regular licensure if they have progressed satisfactorily. In other programs, college graduates who do not meet licensure requirements take only those courses that they lack and then become licensed. This approach may take 1 or 2 semesters of full-time study. States may issue emergency licenses to individuals who do not meet the requirements for a regular license when schools cannot attract enough qualified teachers to fill positions. Teachers who need to be licensed may enter programs that grant a master's degree in education, as well as a license.

In many States, vocational teachers have many of the same requirements for teaching as their academic counterparts. However, because knowledge and experience in a particular field are important criteria for the job, some States will license vocational education teachers without a bachelor's degree, provided they can demonstrate expertise in their field. A minimum number of hours in education courses may also be required.

Licensing requirements for preschool teachers also vary by State. Requirements for public preschool teachers are generally more stringent than those for private preschool teachers. Some States require a bachelor's degree in early childhood education, while others require an associate's degree, and still others require certification by a nationally recognized authority. The Child Development Associate (CDA) credential, the most common type of certification, requires a mix of classroom training and experience working with children, along with an independent assessment of an individual's competence.

Private schools are generally exempt from meeting State licensing standards. For secondary school teacher jobs, they prefer candidates who have a bachelor's degree in the subject they intend to teach, or in childhood education for elementary school teachers. They seek candidates among recent college graduates as well as from those who have established careers in other fields. Private schools associated with religious institutions also desire candidates who share the values that are important to the institution.

In some cases, teachers of kindergarten through high school may attain professional certification in order to demonstrate competency beyond that required for a license. The National Board for Professional Teaching Standards offers a voluntary national certification. To become nationally accredited, experienced teachers must prove their aptitude by compiling a portfolio showing their work in the classroom and by passing a written assessment and evaluation of their teaching knowledge. Currently, teachers may become certified in a variety of areas, on the basis of the age of the students and, in some cases, the subject taught. For example, teachers may obtain a certificate for teaching English language arts to early adolescents (aged 11 to 15), or they may become certified as early childhood generalists. All States recognize national certification, and many States and school districts provide special benefits to teachers holding such certification. Benefits typically include higher salaries and reimbursement for continuing education and certification fees. In addition, many States allow nationally certified teachers to carry a license from one State to another.

The National Council for Accreditation of Teacher Education currently accredits teacher education programs across the United States. Graduation from an accredited program is not necessary to become a teacher, but it does make it easier to fulfill licensure requirements. Generally, 4-year colleges require students to wait until their sophomore year before applying for admission to teacher education programs. Traditional education programs for kindergarten and elementary school teachers include courses—designed specifically for those preparing to teach—in mathematics, physical science, social science, music, art, and literature, as well as prescribed professional education courses, such as philosophy of education, psychology of learning, and teaching methods. Aspiring secondary school teachers most often major in the subject they plan to teach while also taking a program of study in teacher preparation. Teacher education programs are now required to include classes in the use of computers and other technologies in order to maintain their accreditation. Most programs require students to perform a student-teaching internship.

Many States now offer professional development schools—partnerships between universities and elementary or secondary schools. Students enter these 1-year programs after completion of their bachelor's degree. Professional development schools merge theory with practice and allow the student to experience a year of teaching firsthand, under professional guidance.

In addition to being knowledgeable in their subject, teachers must have the ability to communicate, inspire trust and confidence, and motivate students, as well as understand the students' educational and emotional needs. Teachers must be able to recognize and respond to individual and cultural differences in students and employ different teaching methods that will result in higher student achievement. They should be organized, dependable, patient, and creative. Teachers also must be able to work cooperatively and communicate effectively with other teachers, support staff, parents, and members of the community.

With additional preparation, teachers may move into positions as school librarians, reading specialists, instructional coordinators, or guidance counselors. Teachers may become administrators or supervisors, although the number of these positions is limited and competition can be intense. In some systems, highly qualified, experienced teachers can become senior or mentor teachers, with higher pay and additional responsibilities. They guide and assist less experienced teachers while keeping most of their own teaching responsibilities. Preschool teachers usually work their way up from assistant teacher, to teacher, to lead teacher—who may be responsible for the instruction of several classes—and, finally, to director of the center. Preschool teachers with a bachelor's degree frequently are qualified to teach kindergarten through grade 3 as well. Teaching at these higher grades often results in higher pay.

Employment

Preschool, kindergarten, elementary school, middle school, and secondary school teachers, except special education, held about 3.8 million jobs in 2004. Of the teachers in those jobs, about 1.5 million are elementary school teachers, 1.1 million are secondary school teachers, 628,000 are middle school teachers, 431,000 are preschool teachers, and 171,000 are kindergarten teachers. The majority work in local government educational services. About 10 percent work for private schools. Preschool teachers, except special education, are most often employed in child daycare services (61 percent), religious organizations (12 percent), local government educational services (9 percent), and private educational services (7 percent). Employment of teachers is geographically distributed much the same as the population.

Job Outlook

Job opportunities for teachers over the next 10 years will vary from good to excellent, depending on the locality, grade level, and subject taught. Most job openings will result from the need to replace the large number of teachers who are expected to retire over the 2004-14 period. Also, many beginning teachers decide to leave teaching after a year or two—especially those employed in poor, urban schools—creating additional job openings for teachers. Shortages of qualified teachers will likely continue, resulting in competition among some localities, with schools luring teachers from other States and districts with bonuses and higher pay.

Through 2014, overall student enrollments in elementary, middle, and secondary schools—a key factor in the demand for teachers—are expected to rise more slowly than in the past as children of the baby boom generation leave the school system. This will cause employment to grow as fast as the average for teachers from kindergarten through the secondary grades. Projected enrollments will vary by region. Fast-growing States in the West—particularly California, Idaho, Hawaii, Alaska, Utah, and New Mexico—will experience the largest enrollment increases. Enrollments in the South will increase at a more modest rate than in recent years, while those in the Northeast and Midwest are expected to hold relatively steady or decline. Teachers who are geographically mobile and who obtain licensure in more than one subject should have a distinct advantage in finding a job.

The job market for teachers also continues to vary by school location and by subject taught. Job prospects should be better in inner cities and rural areas than in suburban districts. Many inner cities—often characterized by overcrowded, ill-equipped schools and higher-than-average poverty rates—and rural areas—characterized by their remote location and relatively low salaries—have difficulty attracting and retaining enough teachers. Currently, many school districts have difficulty hiring qualified teachers in some subject areas—most often mathematics, science (especially chemistry and physics), bilingual education, and foreign languages. Increasing enrollments of minorities, coupled with a shortage of minority teachers, should cause efforts to recruit minority teachers to intensify. Also, the number of non-English-speaking students will continue to grow, creating demand for bilingual teachers and for those who teach English as a second language. Specialties that have an adequate number of qualified teachers include general elementary education, physical education, and social studies. Qualified vocational teachers also are currently in demand in a variety of fields at both the middle school and secondary school levels.

The number of teachers employed is dependent as well on State and local expenditures for education and on the enactment of leg-

islation to increase the quality and scope of public education. At the Federal level, there has been a large increase in funding for education, particularly for the hiring of qualified teachers in lower income areas. Also, some States are instituting programs to improve early childhood education, such as offering full day kindergarten and universal preschool. These last two programs, along with projected higher enrollment growth for preschool age children, will create many new jobs for preschool teachers, which are expected to grow much faster than the average for all occupations.

The supply of teachers is expected to increase in response to reports of improved job prospects, better pay, more teacher involvement in school policy, and greater public interest in education. In recent years, the total number of bachelor's and master's degrees granted in education has increased steadily. Because of a shortage of teachers in certain locations, and in anticipation of the loss of a number of teachers to retirement, many States have implemented policies that will encourage more students to become teachers. In addition, more teachers may be drawn from a reserve pool of career changers, substitute teachers, and teachers completing alternative certification programs.

Earnings

Median annual earnings of kindergarten, elementary, middle, and secondary school teachers ranged from $41,400 to $45,920 in May 2004; the lowest 10 percent earned $26,730 to $31,180; the top 10 percent earned $66,240 to $71,370. Median earnings for preschool teachers were $20,980.

According to the American Federation of Teachers, beginning teachers with a bachelor's degree earned an average of $31,704 in the 2003–04 school year. The estimated average salary of all public elementary and secondary school teachers in the 2003–04 school year was $46,597. Private school teachers generally earn less than public school teachers, but may be given other benefits, such as free or subsidized housing.

In 2004, more than half of all elementary, middle, and secondary school teachers belonged to unions—mainly the American Federation of Teachers and the National Education Association—that bargain with school systems over wages, hours, and other terms and conditions of employment. Fewer preschool and kindergarten teachers were union members—about 17 percent in 2004.

Teachers can boost their salary in a number of ways. In some schools, teachers receive extra pay for coaching sports and working with students in extracurricular activities. Getting a master's degree or national certification often results in a raise in pay, as does acting as a mentor. Some teachers earn extra income during the summer by teaching summer school or performing other jobs in the school system.

Related Occupations

Preschool, kindergarten, elementary school, middle school, and secondary school teaching requires a variety of skills and aptitudes, including a talent for working with children; organizational, administrative, and recordkeeping abilities; research and communication skills; the power to influence, motivate, and train others; patience; and creativity. Workers in other occupations requiring some of these aptitudes include teachers—postsecondary; counselors; teacher assistants; education administrators; librarians; child care workers; public relations specialists; social workers; and athletes, coaches, umpires, and related workers.

Sources of Additional Information

Information on licensure or certification requirements and approved teacher training institutions is available from local school systems and State departments of education.

Information on the teaching profession and on how to become a teacher can be obtained from:
➤ Recruiting New Teachers, Inc., 385 Concord Ave., Suite 103, Belmont, MA 02478. Internet: **http://www.recruitingteachers.org**

Information on teachers' unions and education-related issues may be obtained from the following sources:
➤ American Federation of Teachers, 555 New Jersey Ave. NW., Washington, DC 20001.
➤ National Education Association, 1201 16th St. NW., Washington, DC 20036.

A list of institutions with accredited teacher education programs can be obtained from:
➤ National Council for Accreditation of Teacher Education, 2010 Massachusetts Ave. NW., Suite 500, Washington, DC 20036-1023. Internet: **http://www.ncate.org**

Information on alternative certification programs can be obtained from:
➤ National Center for Alternative Certification, 1901 Pennsylvania Ave NW, Suite 201, Washington, DC 20006. Internet: **http://www.teach-now.org**

For information on vocational education and vocational education teachers, contact:
➤ Association for Career and Technical Education, 1410 King St., Alexandria, VA 22314. Internet: **http://www.acteonline.org**

For information on careers in educating children and issues affecting preschool teachers, contact either of the following organizations:
➤ National Association for the Education of Young Children, 1509 16th St. NW., Washington, DC 20036. Internet: **http://www.naeyc.org**
➤ Council for Professional Recognition, 2460 16th St. NW., Washington, DC 20009-3575. Internet: **http://www.cdacouncil.org**

Teachers—Self-Enrichment Education

(O*NET 25-3021.00)

Significant Points

● Part-time jobs, a lack of benefits, and self-employed workers are relatively common among self-enrichment teachers.

● Teachers should have knowledge and enthusiasm for their subject, but little formal training is required.

● Demand for self-enrichment courses is expected to rise as more people embrace lifelong learning and as growth continues in the numbers of retirees, who have more free time to take classes.

Nature of the Work

Self-enrichment teachers provide instruction in a wide variety of subjects that students take for personal enrichment or self-improvement. Some teach a series of classes that provide students with useful life skills, such as cooking, personal finance, and time management classes. Others provide group instruction intended solely for recreation, such as photography, pottery, and painting courses. Many others provide one-on-one instruction in a variety of subjects, including dance, singing, or playing a musical instrument. The instruction self-enrichment teachers provide seldom leads to a particular degree and attendance is voluntary, but dedicated, talented students sometimes go on to careers in the arts. Teachers who conduct courses on academic subjects in a non-academic setting, such as literature, foreign language, and history courses, are also included in this occupation.

A self-enrichment teacher instructs a class in gardening.

Self-enrichment teachers provide instruction on a wide range of subjects, so they may have styles and methods of instruction that differ greatly. Most self-enrichment classes are relatively informal and not demanding of instructors. Some classes, such as pottery or sewing, may be largely hands-on, with the instructor demonstrating methods or techniques for the class, observing students as they attempt to do it themselves, and pointing out mistakes to students and offering suggestions to improve techniques. Other classes, such as those involving financial planning or religion and spirituality, may be more similar to a lecture in nature or rely more heavily on group discussions. Self-enrichment teachers may also teach classes offered through religious institutions, such as marriage preparation or classes in religion for children.

Many of the classes that self-enrichment educators teach are shorter in duration than classes taken for academic credit; some finish in 1 or 2 days to several weeks. These brief classes tend to be introductory in nature and generally focus on only one topic—for example, a cooking class that teaches students how to make bread. Some self-enrichment classes introduce children and youths to activities such as piano or drama, and may be designed to last anywhere from 1 week to several months.

Many self-enrichment teachers provide one-on-one lessons to students. The instructor may only work with the student for an hour or two a week, but direct the student what they should practice in the interim until their next lesson. Many instructors work with the same students on a weekly basis for years and derive satisfaction from observing them mature and gain expertise. The most talented students may go on to paid careers as craft artists, painters, sculptors, dancers, singers, or musicians.

All self-enrichment teachers must prepare lessons beforehand and stay current in their fields. Many self-enrichment teachers are self employed and provide instruction as a business. As such, they must collect any fees or tuition and keep records of students whose accounts are prepaid or in arrears. Although not a requirement for most types of classes, teachers may use computers and other modern technologies in their instruction or to maintain business records.

Working Conditions

Few self-enrichment education teachers are full time salaried workers. Most either work part time or are self-employed. Some have several part-time teaching assignments, but it is most common for teachers to have a full time job in another occupation, often related to the subject that they teach, in addition to their part-time teaching job. Although jobs in this occupation are primarily part time and pay is low, most teachers enjoy their work because it gives them the opportunity to share a subject they enjoy with others.

Many classes for adults are held in the evenings and on weekends in order to accommodate students who have a job or family responsibilities. Similarly, self-enrichment classes for children are usually held after school, on weekends, or during school vacations.

Students in self-enrichment programs attend by choice so they tend to be highly motivated and eager to learn. Students also often bring unique experiences of their own to classes, which can make teaching these students rewarding and satisfying. Self-enrichment teachers must have a great deal of patience, however, particularly when working with young children.

Training, Other Qualifications, and Advancement

The main qualification for self-enrichment teachers is expertise in their subject area, but requirements may vary greatly with both the type of class taught and the place of employment. In some cases, a portfolio of one's work may be required. For example, to secure a job teaching a photography course, an applicant would need to show examples of previous work. Some self-enrichment teachers are trained educators or other professionals who teach enrichment classes in their spare time. In many self-enrichment fields, however, instructors are simply experienced in the field, and want to share that experience with others.

In some disciplines, such as art or music, specific teacher training programs are available. Prospective dance teachers, for example, may complete programs that prepare them to instruct any number of types of dance—from ballroom dancing to ballet. In addition to knowledge of their subject, self-enrichment teachers should have good speaking skills and a talent for making the subject interesting. Patience and the ability to explain and instruct students at a basic level are important as well, particularly when one is working with children.

Opportunities for advancement in this profession are limited. Some part-time teachers are able to move into full-time teaching positions or program administrator positions, such as coordinator or director, when such vacancies occur. Experienced teachers may mentor new instructors.

Employment

Teachers of self-enrichment education held about 253,000 jobs in 2004. About 3 in 10 were self-employed. The largest numbers of teachers were employed by public and private educational institutions, religious organizations, and providers of social assistance and amusement and recreation services.

Job Outlook

Employment of self-enrichment education teachers is expected to grow faster than the average for all occupations through 2014. A large number of job openings is expected, due to both the growth of the occupation as well as to many existing teachers retiring or leaving their jobs for other reasons. New opportunities arise constantly in this occupation because many self-enrichment education jobs are short term and are often held as a second job.

The need for self-enrichment teachers is expected to grow as more people embrace lifelong learning and as course offerings expand. Self-enrichment education will also grow as a result of demographic changes. Retirees are one of the larger groups of par-

ticipants in self-enrichment education because they have more time for classes, and as the baby boomers begin to retire, demand for self-enrichment education should grow. At the same time, the children of the baby boomer will be entering the age range of another large group of participants, young adults–who often are single and participate for the social as well as the educational experience.

Teachers who are knowledgeable in subjects that are not easily researched on the Internet and those that benefit from hands-on experiences, such as cooking, crafts, and the arts, will be in greater demand. Classes on self-improvement, personal finance, and computer and internet-related subjects are also expected to be popular.

Earnings

Median hourly earnings of self-enrichment teachers were $14.85 in May 2004. The middle 50 percent earned between $10.39 and $20.80. The lowest 10 percent earned less than $7.90, and the highest 10 percent earned more than $28.85. Self-enrichment teachers are generally paid by the hour or for each class that they teach.

Part-time instructors are usually paid for each class that they teach, and receive few benefits. Full-time teachers are generally paid a salary and may receive health insurance and other benefits..

Related Occupations

The work of self-enrichment teachers is closely related to that of other types of teachers, especially preschool, kindergarten, elementary school, middle school, and secondary school teachers. Self-enrichment teachers also teach a wide variety of subjects that may be related to the work done by those in many other occupations, such as dancers and choreographers; artists and related workers; musicians, singers, and related workers; recreation workers; and athletes, coaches, umpires, and related workers.

Sources of Additional Information

For information on employment of self-enrichment teachers, contact schools or local companies that offer self-enrichment programs.

Teachers—Special Education

(O*NET 25-2041.00, 25-2042.00, 25-2043.00)

Significant Points

- All States require teachers to be licensed; licensing requires the completion of a teacher training program and at least a bachelor's degree, though many States require a master's degree.

- Excellent job prospects are expected due to rising enrollments of special education students and reported shortages of qualified teachers.

- Many States offer alternative licensure programs to attract people to these jobs who do not have the qualifications to become teachers under normal procedures.

Nature of the Work

Special education teachers work with children and youths who have a variety of disabilities. A small number of special education teachers work with students with mental retardation or autism, primarily teaching them life skills and basic literacy. However, the majority of special education teachers work with children with mild to moderate disabilities, using the general education curriculum, or modifying it, to meet the child's individual needs. Most special education teachers

Special education teachers help provide instruction customized to the needs of students with disabilities.

instruct students at the elementary, middle, and secondary school level, although some teachers work with infants and toddlers.

The various types of disabilities that qualify individuals for special education programs include specific learning disabilities, speech or language impairments, mental retardation, emotional disturbance, multiple disabilities, hearing impairments, orthopedic impairments, visual impairments, autism, combined deafness and blindness, traumatic brain injury, and other health impairments. Students are classified under one of the categories, and special education teachers are prepared to work with specific groups. Early identification of a child with special needs is an important part of a special education teacher's job. Early intervention is essential in educating children with disabilities.

Special education teachers use various techniques to promote learning. Depending on the disability, teaching methods can include individualized instruction, problem-solving assignments, and small-group work. When students need special accommodations in order to take a test, special education teachers see that appropriate ones are provided, such as having the questions read orally or lengthening the time allowed to take the test.

Special education teachers help to develop an Individualized Education Program (IEP) for each special education student. The IEP sets personalized goals for each student and is tailored to the student's individual needs and ability. When appropriate, the program includes a transition plan outlining specific steps to prepare students with disabilities for middle school or high school or, in the case of older students, a job or postsecondary study. Teachers review the IEP with the student's parents, school administrators, and the student's general education teacher. Teachers work closely with parents to inform them of their child's progress and suggest techniques to promote learning at home.

Special education teachers design and teach appropriate curricula, assign work geared toward each student's needs and abilities, and grade papers and homework assignments. They are involved in the students' behavioral, social, and academic development, helping the students develop emotionally, feel comfortable in social situations, and be aware of socially acceptable behavior. Preparing special education students for daily life after graduation also is an important aspect of the job. Teachers provide students with career counseling or help them learn routine skills, such as balancing a checkbook.

As schools become more inclusive, special education teachers and general education teachers are increasingly working together in general education classrooms. Special education teachers help general educators adapt curriculum materials and teaching techniques to meet the needs of students with disabilities. They coordinate the work of teachers, teacher assistants, and related personnel, such as therapists and social workers, to meet the individualized needs of the student within inclusive special education programs. A large part of a special education teacher's job involves interacting with others. Special education teachers communicate frequently with parents, social workers, school psychologists, occupational and physical therapists, school administrators, and other teachers.

Special education teachers work in a variety of settings. Some have their own classrooms and teach only special education students; others work as special education resource teachers and offer individualized help to students in general education classrooms; still others teach together with general education teachers in classes composed of both general and special education students. Some teachers work with special education students for several hours a day in a resource room, separate from their general education classroom. Considerably fewer special education teachers work in residential facilities or tutor students in homebound or hospital environments.

Special education teachers who work with infants usually travel to the child's home to work with the child and his or her parents. Many of these infants have medical problems that slow or preclude normal development. Special education teachers show parents techniques and activities designed to stimulate the infant and encourage the growth and development of the child's skills. Toddlers usually receive their services at a preschool where special education teachers help them develop social, self-help, motor, language, and cognitive skills, often through the use of play.

Technology is playing an increasingly important role in special education. Teachers use specialized equipment such as computers with synthesized speech, interactive educational software programs, and audiotapes to assist children.

Working Conditions

Special education teachers enjoy the challenge of working with students with disabilities and the opportunity to establish meaningful relationships with them. Although helping these students can be highly rewarding, the work also can be emotionally and physically draining. Many special education teachers are under considerable stress due to heavy workloads and administrative tasks. They must produce a substantial amount of paperwork documenting each student's progress and work under the threat of litigation against the school or district by students' parents if correct procedures are not followed or if the parents feel that their child is not receiving an adequate education, although recent legislation that has been passed is intended to reduce the burden of paperwork and the threat of litigation. The physical and emotional demands of the job cause some special education teachers to leave the occupation.

Some schools offer year-round education for special education students, but most special education teachers work only the traditional 10-month school year.

Training, Other Qualifications, and Advancement

All 50 States and the District of Columbia require special education teachers to be licensed. The State board of education or a licensure advisory committee usually grants licenses, and licensure varies by State. In some States, special education teachers receive a general education credential to teach kindergarten through grade 12. These teachers then train in a specialty, such as learning disabilities or behavioral disorders. Many States offer general special education licenses across a variety of disability categories, while others license several different specialties within special education.

For traditional licensing, all States require a bachelor's degree and the completion of an approved teacher preparation program with a prescribed number of subject and education credits and supervised practice teaching. However, many States require a master's degree in special education, involving at least 1 year of additional course work, including a specialization, beyond the bachelor's degree. Often a prospective teacher must pass a professional assessment test as well. Some States have reciprocity agreements allowing special education teachers to transfer their licenses from one State to another, but many others still require that experienced teachers reapply and pass licensing requirements to work in the State.

Many states also offer alternative routes to licensing, since there are not enough graduates from education programs to meet the needs of most schools. Alternative licensure programs are intended to attract people into teaching who do not fulfill traditional licensing standards, including recent college graduates who did not complete education programs and those changing from another career to teaching. Requirements vary by State, but generally require holding a bachelor's degree, successfully accomplishing a period of supervised preparation and induction, and passing an assessment test. In some programs, individuals begin teaching quickly under a provisional license and can obtain a regular license after teaching under the supervision of licensed teachers for a period of 1 to 2 years and completing required education courses.

Many colleges and universities across the United States offer programs in special education at the undergraduate, master's, and doctoral degree levels. Special education teachers usually undergo longer periods of training than do general education teachers. Most bachelor's degree programs are 4-year programs that include general and specialized courses in special education. However, an increasing number of institutions are requiring a 5th year or other graduate-level preparation. Among the courses offered are educational psychology, legal issues of special education, and child growth and development; programs also include courses imparting knowledge and skills needed for teaching students with disabilities. Some programs require specialization, while others offer generalized special education degrees or a course of study in several specialized areas. The last year of the program usually is spent student teaching in a classroom supervised by a certified teacher.

Special education teachers must be patient, able to motivate students, understanding of their students' special needs, and accepting of differences in others. Teachers must be creative and apply different types of teaching methods to reach students who are having difficulty learning. Communication and cooperation are essential skills, because special education teachers spend a great deal of time interacting with others, including students, parents, and school faculty and administrators.

Special education teachers can advance to become supervisors or administrators. They may also earn advanced degrees and become instructors in colleges that prepare others to teach special education. In some school systems, highly experienced teachers can become mentors to less experienced ones, providing guidance to those teachers while maintaining a light teaching load.

Employment

Special education teachers held a total of about 441,000 jobs in 2004. A great majority, about 90 percent, work in public schools. Another 6 percent work at private schools. Almost half work in elementary schools. A few worked for individual and social assistance agencies or residential facilities, or in homebound or hospital environments.

Job Outlook

Employment of special education teachers is expected to increase faster than the average for all occupations through 2014. Although student enrollments are expected to grow only slowly, additional positions for these workers will be created by continued increases in

the number of special education students needing services, by legislation emphasizing training and employment for individuals with disabilities, and by educational reforms requiring higher standards for graduation. In addition to job openings resulting from growth, a large number of openings will result from the need to replace special education teachers who switch to teaching general education, change careers altogether, or retire. At the same time, many school districts report difficulty finding sufficient numbers of qualified teachers. As a result, special education teachers should have excellent job prospects.

The job outlook varies by geographic area and specialty. Although most areas of the country report difficulty finding qualified applicants, positions in inner cities and rural areas usually are more plentiful than job openings in suburban or wealthy urban areas. Student populations, in general, also are expected to increase more rapidly in certain parts of the country, such as the South and West, resulting in increased demand for special education teachers in those regions. In addition, job opportunities may be better in certain specialties—such as teachers who work with children with multiple disabilities or severe disabilities like autism—because of large increases in the enrollment of special education students classified under those categories. Legislation encouraging early intervention and special education for infants, toddlers, and preschoolers has created a need for early childhood special education teachers. Bilingual special education teachers and those with multicultural experience also are needed to work with an increasingly diverse student population.

The number of students requiring special education services has grown steadily in recent years as improvements in identification has allowed learning disabilities to be diagnosed at earlier ages. In addition, medical advances have resulted in more children surviving serious accidents or illnesses, but with impairments that require special accommodations. The percentage of foreign-born special education students also is expected to grow, as teachers become more adept in recognizing learning disabilities in that population. Finally, more parents are expected to seek special services for those of their children who have difficulty meeting the new, higher standards required of students.

Earnings

Median annual earnings in May 2004 of special education teachers who worked primarily in preschools, kindergartens, and elementary schools were $43,570. The middle 50 percent earned between $35,340 and $55,350. The lowest 10 percent earned less than $29,880, and the highest 10 percent earned more than $68,660.

Median annual earnings in May 2004 of middle school special education teachers were $44,160. The middle 50 percent earned between $35,650 and $57,070. The lowest 10 percent earned less than $30,230, and the highest 10 percent earned more than $74,230.

Median annual earnings in May 2004 of special education teachers who worked primarily in secondary schools were $45,700. The middle 50 percent earned between $36,920 and $59,340. The lowest 10 percent earned less than $30,860, and the highest 10 percent earned more than $73,190.

In 2004, about 62 percent of special education teachers belonged to unions—mainly the American Federation of Teachers and the National Education Association—that bargain with school systems over wages, hours, and the terms and conditions of employment.

In most schools, teachers receive extra pay for coaching sports and working with students in extracurricular activities. Some teachers earn extra income during the summer, working in the school system or in other jobs.

Related Occupations

Special education teachers work with students who have disabilities and special needs. Other occupations involved with the identification, evaluation, and development of students with disabilities include psychologists, social workers, speech-language pathologists, audiologists, counselors, teacher assistants, occupational therapists, recreational therapists, and teachers—preschool, kindergarten, elementary, middle, and secondary.

Sources of Additional Information
For information on professions related to early intervention and education for children with disabilities, listings of schools with special education training programs, information on teacher cer-

tification, and general information on related personnel issues, contact:

➤ The Council for Exceptional Children, 1110 N. Glebe Road, Suite 300, Arlington, VA 22201-5704. Internet: **http://www.cec.sped.org**
➤ National Center for Special Education Personnel & Related Service Providers, National Association of State Directors of Special Education, 1800 Diagonal Road, Suite 320, Alexandria, VA 22314. Internet: **http://www.personnelcenter.org**

To learn more about the special education teacher certification and licensing requirements in individual States, contact the State's department of education.

Art and Design Occupations

Artists and Related Workers

(O*NET 27-1011.00, 27-1012.00, 27-1013.01, 27-1013.02, 27-1013.03, 27-1013.04, 27-1014.00)

Significant Points

- About 63 percent of artists and related workers are self-employed.

- Keen competition is expected for both salaried jobs and freelance work; the number of qualified workers exceeds the number of available openings because the arts attract many talented people with creative ability.

- Artists usually develop their skills through a bachelor's degree program or other postsecondary training in art or design.

- Earnings for self-employed artists vary widely; some well-established artists earn more than salaried artists, while others find it difficult to rely solely on income earned from selling art.

Nature of the Work
Artists create art to communicate ideas, thoughts, or feelings. They use a variety of methods—painting, sculpting, or illustration—and an assortment of materials, including oils, watercolors, acrylics, pastels, pencils, pen and ink, plaster, clay, and computers. Artists' works may be realistic, stylized, or abstract and may depict objects, people, nature, or events.

Artists generally fall into one of four categories. *Art directors* formulate design concepts and presentation approaches for visual communications media. *Craft artists* create or reproduce handmade objects for sale or exhibition. *Fine artists*, including *painters, sculptors, and illustrators* create original artwork, using a variety of media and techniques. *Multi-media artists and animators* create special effects, animation, or other visual images on film, on video, or with computers or other electronic media. (Designers, including graphic designers, are discussed elsewhere in the *Handbook*.)

Art directors develop design concepts and review material that is to appear in periodicals, newspapers, and other printed or digital media. They decide how best to present the information visually, so that it is eye catching, appealing, and organized. Art directors decide which photographs or artwork to use and oversee the layout design and production of the printed material. They may direct workers engaged in artwork, layout design, and copywriting.

Craft artists hand-make a wide variety of objects that are sold either in their own studios, in retail outlets, or at arts-and-crafts

shows. Some craft artists may display their works in galleries and museums. Craft artists work with many different materials—ceramics, glass, textiles, wood, metal, and paper—to create unique pieces of art, such as pottery, stained glass, quilts, tapestries, lace, candles, and clothing. Many craft artists also use fine-art techniques—for example, painting, sketching, and printing—to add finishing touches to their art.

Fine artists typically display their work in museums, commercial art galleries, corporate collections, and private homes. Some of their artwork may be commissioned (done on request from clients), but most is sold by the artist or through private art galleries or dealers. The gallery and the artist predetermine how much each will earn from the sale. Only the most successful fine artists are able to support themselves solely through the sale of their works. Most fine artists have at least one other job to support their art careers. Some work in museums or art galleries as fine-arts directors or as curators, planning and setting up art exhibits. A few artists work as art critics for newspapers or magazines or as consultants to foundations or institutional collectors. Other artists teach art classes or conduct workshops in schools or in their own studios. Some artists also hold full-time or part-time jobs unrelated to the art field and pursue fine art as a hobby or second career.

Usually, fine artists specialize in one or two art forms, such as painting, illustrating, sketching, sculpting, printmaking, and restoring. *Painters, illustrators, cartoonists, and sketch artists* work with two-dimensional art forms, using shading, perspective, and color to produce realistic scenes or abstractions.

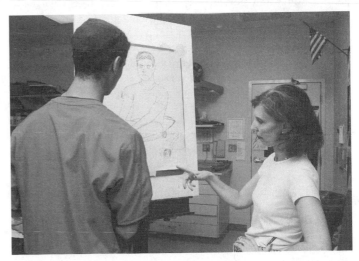

Some artists teach classes or conduct workshops in schools or in their own studios.

Illustrators typically create pictures for books, magazines, and other publications and for commercial products such as textiles, wrapping paper, stationery, greeting cards, and calendars. Increasingly, illustrators are working in digital format, preparing work directly on a computer.

Medical and *scientific illustrators* combine drawing skills with knowledge of biology or other sciences. Medical illustrators draw illustrations of human anatomy and surgical procedures. Scientific illustrators draw illustrations of animal and plant life, atomic and molecular structures, and geologic and planetary formations. The illustrations are used in medical and scientific publications and in audiovisual presentations for teaching purposes. Medical illustrators also work for lawyers, producing exhibits for court cases.

Cartoonists draw political, advertising, social, and sports cartoons. Some cartoonists work with others who create the idea or story and write the captions. Most cartoonists have comic, critical, or dramatic talents in addition to drawing skills.

Sketch artists create likenesses of subjects with pencil, charcoal, or pastels. Sketches are used by law enforcement agencies to assist in identifying suspects, by the news media to depict courtroom scenes, and by individual patrons for their own enjoyment.

Sculptors design three-dimensional artworks, either by molding and joining materials such as clay, glass, wire, plastic, fabric, or metal or by cutting and carving forms from a block of plaster, wood, or stone. Some sculptors combine various materials to create mixed-media installations. Some incorporate light, sound, and motion into their works.

Printmakers create printed images from designs cut or etched into wood, stone, or metal. After creating the design, the artist inks the surface of the woodblock, stone, or plate and uses a printing press to roll the image onto paper or fabric. Some make prints by pressing the inked surface onto paper by hand or by graphically encoding and processing data, using a computer. The digitized images are then printed on paper with the use of a computer printer.

Painting restorers preserve and restore damaged and faded paintings. They apply solvents and cleaning agents to clean the surfaces of the paintings, they reconstruct or retouch damaged areas, and they apply preservatives to protect the paintings. Restoration is highly detailed work and usually is reserved for experts in the field.

Multi-media artists and animators work primarily in motion picture and video industries, advertising, and computer systems design services. They draw by hand and use computers to create the large series of pictures that form the animated images or special effects seen in movies, television programs, and computer games. Some draw storyboards for television commercials, movies, and animated features. Storyboards present television commercials in a series of scenes similar to a comic strip and allow an advertising agency to evaluate commercials proposed by the company doing the advertising. Storyboards also serve as guides to placing actors and cameras on the television or motion picture set and to other details that need to be taken care of during the production of commercials.

Working Conditions

Many artists work in fine- or commercial-art studios located in office buildings, warehouses, or lofts. Others work in private studios in their homes. Some fine artists share studio space, where they also may exhibit their work. Studio surroundings usually are well lighted and ventilated; however, fine artists may be exposed to fumes from glue, paint, ink, and other materials and to dust or other residue from filings, splattered paint, or spilled fluids. Artists who sit at drafting tables or who use computers for extended periods may experience back pain, eyestrain, or fatigue.

Artists employed by publishing companies, advertising agencies, and design firms generally work a standard workweek. During busy periods, they may work overtime to meet deadlines. Self-employed artists can set their own hours, but may spend much time and effort selling their artwork to potential customers or clients and building a reputation.

Training, Other Qualifications, and Advancement

Postsecondary training is recommended for all artist specialties. Although formal training is not strictly required, it is very difficult to become skilled enough to make a living without some training. Many colleges and universities offer programs leading to the bachelor's or master's degree in fine arts. Courses usually include core subjects such as English, social science, and natural science, in addition to art history and studio art.

Independent schools of art and design also offer postsecondary studio training in the craft, fine, and multi-media arts leading to a certificate in the specialty or to an associate's or bachelor's degree in fine arts. Typically, these programs focus more intensively on studio work than do the academic programs in a university setting. The National Association of Schools of Art and Design accredits about 250 postsecondary institutions with programs in art and design; most award a degree in art.

Formal educational programs in art also provide training in computer techniques. Computers are used widely in the visual arts, and knowledge and training in computer graphics and other visual display software are critical elements of many jobs in these fields.

Medical illustrators must have both a demonstrated artistic ability and a detailed knowledge of living organisms, surgical and medical procedures, and human and animal anatomy. A bachelor's degree combining art and premedical courses usually is required. However, most medical illustrators also choose to pursue a master's degree in medical illustration. This degree is offered in five accredited schools in the United States.

Art directors usually begin as entry-level artists in advertising, publishing, design, and motion picture production firms. Artists are promoted to art director after demonstrating artistic and leadership abilities. Some art schools offer coursework in art direction as part of postsecondary training. Depending on the scope of their responsibilities, some art directors also may pursue a degree in art administration, which teaches nonartistic skills such as project management and communication.

Those who want to teach fine arts at public elementary or secondary schools must have a teaching certificate in addition to a bachelor's degree. An advanced degree in fine arts or arts administration is necessary for management or administrative positions in government or in foundations or for teaching in colleges and universities. (See the statements for teachers—postsecondary; and teachers—preschool, kindergarten, elementary, middle, and secondary school elsewhere in the *Handbook*.)

Evidence of appropriate talent and skill, displayed in an artist's portfolio, is an important factor used by art directors, clients, and others in deciding whether to hire an individual or to contract out work. The portfolio is a collection of handmade, computer-generated, photographic, or printed samples of the artist's best work. Assembling a successful portfolio requires skills usually developed through postsecondary training in art or visual communications. Internships also provide excellent opportunities for artists to develop and enhance their portfolios.

Artists hired by firms often start with relatively routine work. While doing this work, however, they may observe and practice their skills on the side. Many artists freelance on a part-time basis while continuing to hold a full-time job until they are established. Others freelance part time while still in school, to develop experience and to build a portfolio of published work.

Freelance artists try to develop a set of clients who regularly contract for work. Some freelance artists are widely recognized for their skill in specialties such as cartooning or children's book illustration. These artists may earn high incomes and can choose the type of work they do.

Craft and fine artists advance professionally as their work circulates and as they establish a reputation for a particular style. Many of the most successful artists continually develop new ideas, and their work often evolves over time.

Employment

Artists held about 208,000 jobs in 2004. Sixty-three percent were self-employed. Employment was distributed as follows:

Multi-media artists and animators	94,000
Art directors	71,000
Fine artists, including painters, sculptors, and illustrators	29,000
Artists and related workers, all other	8,500
Craft artists	6,100

Of the artists who were not self-employed, many worked in advertising and related services; newspaper, periodical, book, and software publishers; motion picture and video industries; specialized design services; and computer systems design and related services. Some self-employed artists offered their services to advertising agencies, design firms, publishing houses, and other businesses on a contract or freelance basis.

Job Outlook

Employment of artists and related workers is expected to grow about as fast as the average for all occupations through the year 2014. However, the competition for jobs is expected to be keen for both salaried and freelance jobs in all specialties, because the number of qualified workers exceeds the number of available openings. Also, because the arts attract many talented people with creative ability, the number of aspiring artists continues to grow. Employers in all industries should be able to choose from among the most qualified candidates.

Art directors work in a variety of industries, such as advertising, public relations, publishing, and design firms. Despite an expanding number of opportunities, they should experience keen competition for the available openings.

Craft and fine artists work mostly on a freelance or commission basis and may find it difficult to earn a living solely by selling their artwork. Only the most successful craft and fine artists receive major commissions for their work. Competition among artists for the privilege of being shown in galleries is expected to remain acute, and grants from sponsors such as private foundations, State and local arts councils, and the National Endowment for the Arts should remain competitive. Nonetheless, studios, galleries, and individual clients are always on the lookout for artists who display outstanding talent, creativity, and style. Among craft and fine artists, talented individuals who have developed a mastery of artistic techniques and skills will have the best job prospects.

The growth in computer graphics packages and stock art Web sites is making it easier for writers, publishers, and art directors to create their own illustrations. As the use of this technology grows, there will be fewer opportunities for illustrators. One exception is the small number of medical illustrators, who will be in greater demand to illustrate journal articles and books as medical research continues to grow.

Salaried cartoonists will have fewer job opportunities because many newspapers and magazines are increasingly relying on freelance work. In addition, many cartoonists are opting to post their work on political Web sites and online publications. As online posting of cartoons increases, many are creating animated or interactive images to satisfy readers' demands for more sophisticated cartoons.

Multi-media artists and animators should have better job opportunities than other artists, but still will experience competition. Demand for these workers will increase as consumers continue to demand more realistic video games, movie and television special effects, and 3D animated movies. Additional job openings will arise from an increasing demand for Web site development and for computer graphics adaptation from the growing number of mobile technologies. Job opportunities for animators of lower-technology, two-dimensional television cartoons could be hampered as these jobs continue to be outsourced overseas.

Earnings

Median annual earnings of salaried art directors were $63,840 in May 2004. The middle 50 percent earned between $47,890 and $88,120. The lowest 10 percent earned less than $35,500, and the highest 10 percent earned more than $123,320. Median annual earnings were $66,900 in advertising and related services.

Median annual earnings of salaried craft artists were $23,520 in May 2004. The middle 50 percent earned between $17,950 and $32,980. The lowest 10 percent earned less than $14,740, and the highest 10 percent earned more than $44,490.

Median annual earnings of salaried fine artists, including painters, sculptors, and illustrators, were $38,060 in May 2004. The middle 50 percent earned between $25,990 and $51,730. The lowest 10 percent earned less than $17,390, and the highest 10 percent earned more than $68,860. According to the Association of Medical Illustrators, the median earnings in 2005 for salaried medical illustrators were $59,000.

Median annual earnings of salaried multi-media artists and animators were $50,360 in May 2004. The middle 50 percent earned between $37,980 and $70,730. The lowest 10 percent earned less than $29,030, and the highest 10 percent earned more than $94,260. Median annual earnings were $67,390 in motion picture and video industries and $46,810 in advertising and related services.

Earnings for self-employed artists vary widely. Some charge only a nominal fee while they gain experience and build a reputation for their work. Others, such as well-established freelance fine artists and illustrators, can earn more than salaried artists. Many, however, find it difficult to rely solely on income earned from selling paintings or other works of art. Like other self-employed workers, freelance artists must provide their own benefits.

Related Occupations

Other workers who apply art skills include architects, except landscape and naval; archivists, curators, and museum technicians; commercial and industrial designers; fashion designers; floral designers; graphic designers; interior designers; jewelers and precious stone and metal workers; landscape architects; photographers; and woodworkers. Some workers who use computers extensively, including computer software engineers and desktop publishers, may require art skills.

Sources of Additional Information

For general information about art and design and a list of accredited college-level programs, contact:
➤ National Association of Schools of Art and Design, 11250 Roger Bacon Dr., Suite 21, Reston, VA 20190-5248. Internet: **http://nasad.arts-accredit.org**

For information on careers in the craft arts and for a list of schools and workshops, contact:
➤ American Craft Council Library, 72 Spring St., 6th Floor, New York, NY 10012-4019. Internet: **http://www.craftcouncil.org**

For information on careers in illustration, contact:
➤ Society of Illustrators, 128 E. 63rd St., New York, NY 10021-7303. Internet: **http://www.societyillustrators.org**

For information on careers in medical illustration, contact:
➤ Association of Medical Illustrators, 245 First St., Suite 1800, Cambridge, MA 02142. Internet: **http://www.ami.org**

For information on workshops, scholarships, internships, and competitions for art students interested in advertising careers, contact:
➤ Art Directors Club, 106 W. 29th St., New York, NY 10001. Internet: **http://www.adcglobal.org**

Commercial and Industrial Designers

(O*NET 27-1021.00)

Significant Points

- Commercial and industrial designers usually work closely with engineers, materials scientists, marketing and corporate strategy staff, cost estimators, and accountants.

- About 1 out of 3 are self-employed.

- A bachelor's degree in industrial design, architecture, or engineering is required for entry-level positions; however, many commercial and industrial designers choose to pursue a master's degree in either industrial design or business administration.

- Keen competition is expected for most jobs because many qualified individuals are attracted to careers in this field; those with strong backgrounds in engineering and computer-aided design, as well as extensive business expertise, will have the best prospects.

Nature of the Work

Commercial and industrial designers combine the fields of art, business, and engineering to design the products used every day by businesses and consumers. These designers are responsible for the style, function, quality, and safety of most manufactured goods. Usually these designers will specialize in one particular product category. Some specialties include automobiles and other transportation vehicles, appliances, technology goods, medical equipment, furniture, toys, tools and construction equipment, and housewares.

The first steps in developing a new design, or altering an existing one, are to determine the requirements of the client, the ultimate function for which the design is intended, and its appeal to customers or users. When creating a new design, designers often begin by researching the product user or the context in which the product will be used, and desired product characteristics, such as size, shape, weight, color, materials used, cost, ease of use, fit, and safety. Designers gather this information by meeting with clients, conducting market research, reading design and consumer publications, attending trade shows, and visiting potential users, suppliers and manufacturers.

Designers then prepare conceptual sketches or diagrams—by hand or with the aid of a computer—to illustrate the vision for the design. After conducting research and consulting with a creative director or other members of the product development team, designers then create detailed sketches or renderings. Many designers use computer-aided design (CAD) tools to create and better visualize the final product. Computer models allow ease and flexibility in

Most commercial and industrial designers use computer-aided industrial design software to prepare conceptual product diagrams.

exploring a greater number of design alternatives, thus reducing design costs and cutting the time it takes to deliver a product to market. Industrial designers who work for manufacturing firms also use computer-aided industrial design (CAID) tools to create designs and machine-readable instructions that communicate with automated production tools. Often, designers will create physical models out of clay, wood, and other materials to give clients a better idea of what the finished product will look like.

Designers then present the designs and prototypes to their client or managers and incorporate any changes and suggestions. Designers also will work with engineers, accountants, and cost estimators to determine if the product could be made safer, easier to assemble or use, or cheaper to manufacture. Designers also may participate in usability and safety tests with prototypes in order to make further adjustments to the design before it goes to manufacturing.

Commercial and industrial designers also work with marketing staff to develop plans to best market the new product or design to consumers. Increasingly, designers are working with corporate strategy staff to ensure that their designs fit into the company's business plan and strategic vision. This involves designing new products that accurately reflect the company's image and values. It also involves identifying and designing products that best fit consumers' needs before a competitor markets a similar product. Increasingly, designers must focus on creating innovative products in addition to considering the style and technical aspects of the product.

Working Conditions

Working conditions and places of employment vary. Designers employed by manufacturing establishments, large corporations, or design firms generally work regular hours in well-lighted and comfortable settings. Designers in smaller design consulting firms, or those who freelance, may work on a contract, or job, basis. They frequently adjust their workday to suit their clients' schedules and deadlines, meeting with the clients during evening or weekend hours when necessary. Consultants and self-employed designers tend to work longer hours and in smaller, more congested, environments. Additional hours may be required in order to meet deadlines.

Designers may transact business in their own offices or studios or in clients' homes or offices. They also may travel to other locations, such as testing facilities, design centers, clients' exhibit sites, user's homes or workplaces, and manufacturing facilities. With the increased speed and sophistication of computers and advanced communications networks, designers may form international design teams, serve a geographically more dispersed clientele, research design alternatives by using information on the Internet, and purchase supplies electronically.

Training, Other Qualifications, and Advancement

A bachelor's degree in industrial design, architecture, or engineering is required for most entry-level commercial and industrial design positions. Many candidates in industrial design also pursue a master's degree in order to increase their employment opportunities. Creativity and technical knowledge are crucial in this occupation. People in this field also must have a strong sense of the esthetic—an eye for color and detail and a sense of balance and proportion. Designers must understand the technical aspects of how the product functions. Despite the advancement of computer-aided design, sketching ability remains an important advantage. A good portfolio—a collection of examples of a person's best work—often is the deciding factor in getting a job.

Bachelor's of fine arts or bachelor's of science degrees in industrial design are granted at many colleges and universities, and in private art and design schools. Baccalaureate curriculum includes principles of design, sketching, computer-aided design, industrial materials and processes, manufacturing methods, and some coursework in engineering, physical science, mathematics, psychology, and anthropology. Many programs also include internships in design or manufacturing firms.

Commercial and industrial designers also may pursue a master's degree in industrial design. With the growing emphasis on strategic design and how products fit into the overall business plan, an increasing number of designers are pursing a master's degree in business administration in order to gain valuable business skills. Also, a growing number of professionals in other industries, such as marketing and information technology, are entering the industrial design field by pursuing advanced degrees in design.

The National Association of Schools of Art and Design accredits about 250 postsecondary institutions with programs in art and design. Approximately 45 of these schools award a degree in industrial design. Many schools require the successful completion of 1 year of basic art and design courses before formal entry into a bachelor's degree program. Applicants also may be required to submit sketches and other examples of their artistic ability.

Employers increasingly expect new designers to be familiar with computer-aided design software as a design tool. Designers must also be creative, imaginative, and persistent and must be able to communicate their ideas in writing, visually, and verbally. Because tastes in style can change quickly, designers need to be well read, open to new ideas and influences, and quick to react to changing trends. Problem-solving skills and the ability to work independently and under pressure also are important traits. People in this field need self-discipline to start projects on their own, to budget their time, and to meet deadlines and production schedules.

As strategic design becomes more important, employers will seek designers with project management skills and knowledge of accounting, marketing, quality assurance, purchasing, and strategic planning. Good business sense and sales ability also are important, especially for those who freelance or run their own business.

Beginning commercial and industrial designers usually receive on-the-job training and normally need 1 to 3 years of training before they can advance to higher level positions. Experienced designers in large firms may advance to chief designer, design department head, or other supervisory positions. Some designers leave the occupation to become teachers in design schools or in colleges and universities. Many faculty members continue to consult privately or operate small design studios to complement their classroom activities. Some experienced designers open their own design firms.

Employment

Commercial and industrial designers held about 49,000 jobs in 2004. About 1 out of 3 were self-employed. About 13 percent of designers were employed in either engineering or specialized design services firms. Manufacturing companies employed the rest of commercial and industrial designers, with the largest number employed in aerospace products and parts manufacturing.

Job Outlook

Employment of commercial and industrial designers is expected to grow about as fast as the average for all occupations through 2014. Employment growth will arise from an expanding economy and from an increase in consumer and business demand for new or upgraded products. However, competition for jobs will be keen because many talented individuals are attracted to the design field. The best job opportunities will be in specialized design firms which are used by manufacturers to design products or parts of products. Designers with strong backgrounds in engineering and computer-aided design, as well as extensive business expertise, may have the best prospects.

Increasing demand for commercial and industrial designers will stem from the continued emphasis on the quality and safety of products, the increasing demand for new products that are easy and comfortable to use, and the development of high-technology products in consumer electronics, medicine, transportation, and other fields. However, employment can be affected by fluctuations in the economy. For example, during periods of economic downturns, companies may cut research and development spending, including new product development.

Increasingly, manufacturers have been outsourcing design work to design services firms in order to cut costs and to find the most qualified design talent. Additionally, some companies use design firms located overseas, especially for design of high-technology products. These overseas design firms are located closer to their suppliers, which reduces the time it takes to design and sell a product—an important consideration when technology is changing quickly. Offshoring of design work, particularly for high-technology products, could continue to have a negative impact on domestic employment of commercial and industrial designers.

Despite the increase in design work performed overseas, most design jobs—particularly jobs not related to high-technology product design—will still remain in the U.S. because design is essential to a firm's success, and firms will want to retain control over the design process. As the demand for design work becomes more consumer-driven, designers also will need to closely monitor, and react to, changing customer demands. Designers will increasingly have to come up with innovative new products in order to stay competitive. Domestic designers also will be required to work with marketing and strategic planning staffs to design products that will be more usable and appealing to consumers and that accurately define a company's image and brand.

Earnings

Median annual earnings for commercial and industrial designers were $52,310 in May 2004. The middle 50 percent earned between $39,130 and $68,980. The lowest 10 percent earned less than $29,080, and the highest 10 percent earned more than $86,250.

Related Occupations

Workers in other art and design occupations include artists and related workers; fashion designers; floral designers; graphic designers; and interior designers. Some other occupations that require computer-aided design skills are architects, except landscape and naval; computer software engineers; desktop publishers; drafters; and engineers.

Sources of Additional Information

For general career information on commercial and industrial design, contact:

➤ Industrial Designers Society of America, 45195 Business Court, Suite 250, Dulles, VA 20166-6717. Internet: **http://www.idsa.org**

For general information about art and design and a list of accredited college-level programs, contact:

➤ National Association of Schools of Art and Design, 11250 Roger Bacon Dr., Suite 21, Reston, VA 20190-5248. Internet: **http://nasad.arts-accredit.org**

Fashion Designers

(O*NET 27-1022.00,)

Significant Points

● In 2004, two-thirds of salaried fashion designers were employed in either New York or California.

● Employers seek designers with a 2- or 4-year degree who are knowledgeable about textiles, fabrics, ornamentation, and fashion trends.

● Job competition is expected to be keen as many designers are attracted to the creativity and glamour associated with the occupation, while relatively few job openings arise.

● More than 1 out of 4 are self-employed.

Nature of the Work

Fashion designers help create the billions of clothing articles, shoes, and accessories purchased every year by consumers. Designers study fashion trends, sketch designs of clothing and accessories, select colors and fabrics, and oversee the final production of their designs. Clothing designers create and help produce men's, women's, and children's apparel, including casual wear, suits, sportswear, formalwear, outerwear, maternity, and intimate apparel. *Footwear designers* help create and produce different styles of shoes and boots. *Accessory designers* help create and produce items that add the finishing touches to an outfit, such as handbags, belts, scarves, hats, hosiery, and eyewear. (The work of jewelers and precious stone and metal workers is described elsewhere in the *Handbook*.) Some fashion designers specialize in clothing, footwear, or accessory design, while others create designs in all three fashion categories.

The design process from initial design inception to final production takes between 18 and 24 months. The first step in creating a design is researching fashion trends and making predictions of future trends. Some designers conduct their own research, while others rely on trend reports published by fashion industry trade groups. Trend reports indicate what styles, colors, and fabrics will be popular for a particular season in the future. Textile manufacturers use these trend reports to begin designing fabrics and patterns while fashion designers begin to sketch preliminary designs. Designers will then visit manufacturers or trade shows to procure samples of fabrics and decide which fabrics to use with which designs.

Once designs and fabrics are chosen, a prototype of the article using cheaper materials is created and then worn by a model to see what adjustments to the design need to be made. During this time, designers usually will narrow down their choices of which designs to offer for sale. After the final adjustments and selections have been made, samples of the article using the actual materials are sewn, and then marketed to clothing retailers. Many designs are shown at fashion and trade shows a few times a year. Retailers will then place orders for certain items, which are then manufactured and distributed to stores.

Most fashion designers travel several times a year to trade shows in order to view new fabric and other material samples.

Computer-aided design (CAD) is increasingly being used in the fashion design industry. While most designers initially sketch designs by hand, a growing number also translate these hand sketches to the computer. CAD allows designers to view designs of clothing on virtual models and in various colors and shapes, thus saving time by requiring fewer adjustments of prototypes and samples later.

Depending on the size of the design firm and level of experience, fashion designers may have varying levels of involvement in different aspects of design and production. In large design firms, fashion designers often are the lead designers who are responsible for creating the designs, choosing the colors and fabrics, and overseeing technical designers who turn the designs into a final product. They are responsible for creating the prototypes and patterns and work with the manufacturers and suppliers during the production stages. Large design houses also employ their own patternmakers, tailors, and sewers who create the master patterns for the design and sew the prototypes and samples. Designers working in small firms, or those new to the job, usually perform most of the technical, patternmaking, and sewing tasks in addition to designing the clothing. (The work of pattern makers, hand sewers, and tailors is covered in the statement on textile, apparel, and furnishings occupations elsewhere in the *Handbook*).

Fashion designers working for apparel wholesalers or manufacturers create designs for the mass market. These designs are manufactured in various sizes and colors. A small number of high-fashion (haute couture) designers are self-employed and create custom designs for individual clients, usually at very high prices. Other high-fashion designers sell their designs in their own retail stores or cater to specialty stores or high-fashion department stores. These designers create a mixture of original garments and those that follow established fashion trends.

Some fashion designers specialize in costume design for performing arts, motion picture, and television productions. The work of costume designers is similar to other fashion designers. Costume designers perform extensive research into the styles worn during the period in which the performance takes place, or work with directors to select appropriate attire for performances. They make sketches of designs, select fabric and other materials, and oversee the production of the costumes. They also must stay within the costume budget for the particular production.

Working Conditions

Fashion designers employed by manufacturing establishments, wholesalers, or design firms generally work regular hours in well-lighted and comfortable settings. Designers who freelance generally work on a contract, or job, basis. They frequently adjust their workday to suit their clients' schedules and deadlines, meeting with the clients during evening or weekend hours when necessary. Freelance designers tend to work longer hours and in smaller, more congested, environments, and are under pressure to please clients and to find new ones in order to maintain a steady income. Regardless of their work setting, all fashion designers occasionally work long hours to meet production deadlines or prepare for fashion shows.

The global nature of the fashion business requires constant communication with suppliers, manufacturers, and customers all over the United States and the world. Most fashion designers travel several times a year to trade and fashion shows in order to learn about the latest fashion trends. Designers also may travel frequently to meet with fabric and materials suppliers and with manufacturers who produce the final apparel products.

Training, Other Qualifications, and Advancement

In fashion design, employers seek individuals with a 2-year or 4-year degree who are knowledgeable about textiles, fabrics, ornamentation, and fashion trends. Designers must have a strong sense of the esthetic—an eye for color and detail, a sense of balance and proportion, and an appreciation for beauty. Fashion designers also need excellent communication and problem-solving skills. Despite the advancement of computer-aided design, sketching ability remains an important advantage in fashion design. A good portfolio—a collection of examples of a person's best work—often is the deciding factor in getting a job.

Bachelor's of fine arts and associate degree programs in fashion design are offered at many colleges, universities, and private art and design schools. Some fashion designers also combine a fashion design degree with a business, marketing, or fashion merchandising degree, especially those who want to run their own business or retail store. Basic coursework includes color, textiles, sewing and tailoring, pattern making, fashion history, CAD, and design of different types of clothing such as menswear or footwear. Coursework in human anatomy, mathematics, and psychology also is useful.

The National Association of Schools of Art and Design accredits approximately 250 postsecondary institutions with programs in art and design. Most of these schools award degrees in fashion design. Many schools do not allow formal entry into a program until a student has successfully completed basic art and design courses. Applicants usually have to submit sketches and other examples of their artistic ability.

In addition to creativity and sketching ability, fashion designers also need to have sewing and patternmaking skills, even if they do not perform these tasks themselves. Designers need to be able to understand these skills so they can give proper instructions as to how the garment should be constructed. Fashion designers also need strong sales and presentation skills in order to persuade clients to purchase their designs. Good teamwork and communication skills also are necessary because of the increasingly international nature of the business that requires constant contact with suppliers, manufacturers, and buyers around the world.

Aspiring fashion designers can learn these necessary skills through internships with design or manufacturing firms. Some designers also gain valuable experience working in retail stores, as personal stylists, or as custom tailors. Such experience can help designers gain sales and marketing skills while learning what styles and fabrics look good on different people. Designers also can gain exposure to potential employers by entering their designs in student or amateur contests. Because of the global nature of the fashion industry, experience in one of the international fashion centers, such as Milan or Paris, can be useful.

Beginning fashion designers usually start out as pattern makers or sketching assistants for more experienced designers before they can advance to higher level positions. Experienced designers may advance to chief designer, design department head, or other supervisory position. Some designers may start their own design company, or sell their designs in their own retail stores. A few of the most successful designers can work for high-fashion design houses that offer personalized design services to wealthy clients.

Employment

Fashion designers held about 17,000 jobs in 2004. More than 1 out of 4 were self-employed. About 25 percent of fashion designers worked for apparel and piece goods merchant wholesalers. Another 15 percent worked in cut and sew apparel manufacturing. The remainder worked for corporate offices involved in the management of companies and enterprises, clothing stores, performing arts companies, specialized design services firms, textile and textile product mills, and footwear and accessories manufacturers.

Employment of fashion designers tends to be concentrated in regional fashion centers. In 2004, two-thirds of salaried fashion designers were employed in either New York or California.

Job Outlook

Job competition is expected be keen as many designers are attracted to the creativity and glamour associated with the occupation, while relatively few job openings arise because of low job turnover and a small number of new openings created every year. Employment of fashion designers is projected to grow more slowly than the average for all occupations through 2014. Employment declines in cut and sew apparel manufacturing are projected to offset increases in apparel wholesalers.

Employment growth for fashion designers will stem from a growing population demanding more clothing, footwear, and accessories. Demand is increasing for stylish clothing that is affordable, especially among middle income consumers. The best job opportunities will be in design firms that design mass market clothing sold in department stores and retail chain stores, such as apparel wholesale firms. Few employment opportunities are expected in design firms that cater to high-end department stores and specialty boutiques as demand for expensive, high-fashion design declines relative to other luxury goods and services.

Job opportunities in cut and sew manufacturing will continue to decline as apparel is increasingly manufactured overseas. However, employment of fashion designers in this industry will not decline as fast as other occupations because firms are more likely to keep design work in-house.

Earnings

Median annual earnings for fashion designers were $55,840 in May 2004. The middle 50 percent earned between $38,800 and $77,580. The lowest 10 percent earned less than $27,970, and the highest 10 percent earned more than $112,840.

Earnings in fashion design can vary widely based on the employer and years of experience. Starting salaries in fashion design tend to be very low until designers are established in the industry. Salaried fashion designers usually earn higher and more stable incomes than self-employed or freelance designers. However, a few of the most successful self-employed fashion designers may earn many times the salary of the highest paid salaried designers. Self-employed fashion designers must provide their own benefits and retirement.

Related Occupations

Workers in other art and design occupations include artists and related workers, commercial and industrial designers, floral designers, graphic designers, and interior designers. Jewelers and precious stone and metal workers also design wearable accessories. Other common occupations in the fashion industry include demonstrators, product promoters, and models; photographers; purchasing managers, buyers, and purchasing agents; retail salespersons; and textile, apparel, and furnishings occupations.

Sources of Additional Information

For general information about art and design and a list of accredited college-level programs, contact:

➤ National Association of Schools of Art and Design, 11250 Roger Bacon Dr., Suite 21, Reston, VA 20190-5248. Internet: **http://nasad.arts-accredit.org**

For general information about careers in fashion design, contact:

➤ Fashion Group International, 8 West 40th St., 7th Floor, New York, NY 10018. Internet: **http://www.fgi.org**

Floral designers

(O*NET 27-1023.00)

Significant Points

● Job opportunities should be good because of relatively high replacement needs stemming from low starting pay and limited advancement opportunities.

● Floral design is the only design specialty that does not require formal postsecondary training.

● Many floral designers work long hours on weekends and holidays, filling orders and setting up decorations for weddings and other events.

● About 1 out of 3 is self-employed.

Nature of the Work

Floral designers, or florists, cut live, dried, or silk flowers and other greenery and arrange them into displays of various sizes and shapes. They design these displays by selecting flowers, containers, and ribbons and arranging them into bouquets, corsages, centerpieces of tables, wreaths, and the like for weddings, funerals, holidays, and other special occasions. Some floral designers also utilize accessories such as balloons, candles, toys, candy, and gift baskets as part of their displays.

Job duties can vary by type of employment setting. Most floral designers work in small independent floral shops that specialize in custom orders and also handle large orders for weddings, caterers, or interior designers. Floral designers may meet with customers to discuss the arrangement or work from a written order. They note the occasion, the customer's preferences, the price of the order, the time the floral display or plant is to be ready, and the place to which it is to be delivered. For special occasions, floral designers usually will help set up floral decorations. Floral designers also will prearrange a few displays to have available for walk-in customers or last-minute orders. Some floral designers also assist interior designers in creating live or silk displays for hotels, restaurants, and private residences.

Some florists work in the floral departments of grocery stores or for Internet florists, which specialize in creating prearranged floral decorations and bouquets. These floral retailers also may fill small custom orders for special occasions and funerals, but some grocery store florists do not deliver to clients or handle large custom orders. Florists who work for wholesale flower distributors assist in the selection of different types of flowers and greenery to purchase and sell to retail florists. Wholesale floral designers also select flowers for displays that they use as examples for retail florists.

A significant portion of a floral designer's job is arranging flowers and other greenery into custom displays for special occasions.

Self-employed floral designers must handle the various aspects of running their own businesses, such as selecting and purchasing flowers, hiring and supervising staff, and maintaining financial records. Self-employed designers also may run gift shops or wedding consultation businesses in addition to providing floral design services. Some conduct design workshops for amateur gardeners or others with an interest in floral design.

Working Conditions

Most floral designers work in comfortable, well-lit spaces in retail outlets or at home, although working outdoors is sometimes required. Designers also may frequently make short trips delivering flowers, setting up arrangements for special events, and procuring flowers and other supplies.

Floral designers have frequent contact with customers and must work to satisfy their demands, including last-minute holiday and funeral orders. Because many flowers are perishable, most orders cannot be completed too far in advance. As a result, some designers often work long hours before and during holidays. Some also work nights and weekends to complete large orders for weddings and other special events.

Floral designers may suffer muscle strain from long periods of standing and from repeated finger and arm movements required to make floral arrangements. They are susceptible to back strain from lifting and carrying heavy flower arrangements. Designers also may suffer allergic reactions to certain types of pollen when working with flowers. In addition, they frequently use sharp objects—scissors, knives, and metal wire—that can cause injuries if handled improperly.

Training, Other Qualifications, and Advancement

Floral design is the only design occupation that does not require formal postsecondary training; most floral designers learn their skills on the job. Employers generally look for high school graduates who have creativity, a flair for arranging flower, and a desire to learn. Many florists gain their initial experience working as cashiers or delivery people in retail floral stores. The completion of formal design training, however, is an asset for floral designers, particularly those interested in advancing to chief floral designer or in opening their own businesses.

Private floral schools, vocational schools, and community colleges award certificates in floral design. These programs generally require a high school diploma for admission and last from several weeks to 1 year. Floral design courses teach the basics of arranging flowers—the different types of flowers there are, their color and texture, cutting and taping techniques, tying bows and ribbons, proper handling and care of flowers, floral trends, and pricing.

Some floral designers also may choose to attend an associate's or bachelor's degree program at a community college or university. Some programs offer formal degrees in floral design, while others offer degrees in floriculture, horticulture, or ornamental horticulture, which can prepare students for a career in floral design. In addition to floral design courses, these programs teach courses in botany, chemistry, hydrology, microbiology, pesticides, and soil management.

Since many floral designers manage their own business, additional courses in business, accounting, marketing, and computer technology can be helpful.

The American Institute of Floral Designers offers an accreditation examination as an indication of professional achievement in floral design. The exam consists of a written part covering floral terminology and an onsite floral-arranging test in which candidates have 4 hours to complete five floral designs. The five categories of floral designs are funeral tributes, table arrangements, wedding arrangements, wearable flowers, and in one category of the candidate's choosing.

Floral designers must be creative, service oriented, and able to communicate their ideas visually and verbally. Because trends in floral design change quickly, designers must be open to new ideas and react quickly to changing trends. Problem-solving skills and the ability to work independently and under pressure also are important traits. Individuals in this field need self-discipline to budget their time and meet deadlines.

Advancement in the floral field is limited. After a few years of on-the-job training, designers can either advance to a supervisory position or open their own floral shop.

Employment

Floral designers held about 98,000 jobs in 2004. Approximately 1 out of 3 was self-employed. Almost half of all floral designers worked in florist shops. Another 8 percent worked in the floral departments of grocery stores. Others were employed by miscellaneous nondurable goods merchant wholesalers, other general merchandise stores, and in lawn and garden equipment and supply stores.

Job Outlook

Employment of floral designers is expected to grow about as fast as the average for all occupations through 2014. Job opportunities should be good because of the relatively high replacement needs in retail florists that result from comparatively low starting pay and limited opportunities for advancement.

The demand for floral designers will continue to grow as flower sales increase as a result of the increasing population and lavishness of weddings and other special events that require floral decorations. As disposable incomes rise, more people also desire fresh flowers in their homes and offices. Increased spending on interior design also is creating demand for stylish artificial arrangements for homes and businesses.

Opportunities should be available in grocery store and Internet floral shops as sales of floral arrangements from these outlets grow. The prearranged displays and gifts available in these stores appeal to consumers because of the convenience and because of prices that are lower than can be found in independent floral shops.

As mass marketers capture more of the small flower orders, independent floral shops are increasingly finding themselves under pressure to remain profitable. Many independent shops have added online ordering systems in order to compete with Internet florists. Others are trying to distinguish their services by specializing in certain areas of floral design or by combining floral design with event planning and interior design services. Some florists also are adding holiday decorating services in which they will set up decorations for businesses and residences.

Few job opportunities are expected in floral wholesalers, primarily because an increasing number of shops are purchasing flowers and supplies directly from growers in order to cut costs. In addition, the growth of e-commerce in the floral industry will make it easier for retail florists to locate their own suppliers.

Earnings

Median annual earnings for wage and salary floral designers were $20,450 in May 2004. The middle 50 percent earned between $16,670 and $25,610. The lowest 10 percent earned less than $14,360, and the highest 10 percent earned more than $32,370. Median annual earnings were $22,520 in grocery stores and $20,110 in florists.

Related Occupations

Other art and design occupations include artists and related workers, commercial and industrial designers, fashion designers, graphic designers, and interior designers. Landscape architects also create designs involving plants and flowers. Other occupations that work directly with plants and flowers include soil and plant scientists; and farm workers and laborers, crop, nursery, and greenhouse.

Sources of Additional Information

For information about careers in floral design, contact:
➤ American Institute of Floral Designers, 720 Light St., Baltimore, MD 21230. Internet:**http://www.aifd.org**
➤ Society of American Florists, 1601 Duke St., Alexandria, VA 22314. Internet: **http://www.safnow.org**

Graphic Designers

(O*NET 27 1024.00)

Significant Points

- Among the five design occupations, graphic designers are expected to have the most new jobs through 2014; however, job seekers are expected to face keen competition for available positions.

- Graphic designers with Web site design and animation experience will have the best opportunities.

- A bachelor's degree is required for most entry-level positions; however, an associate degree may be sufficient for technical positions.

- About 3 out of 10 designers are self-employed; many do freelance work in addition to holding a salaried job in design or in another occupation.

Nature of the Work

Graphic designers—or graphic artists—plan, analyze, and create visual solutions to communications problems. They decide the most effective way of getting a message across in print, electronic, and film media using a variety of methods such as color, type, illustration, photography, animation, and various print and layout techniques. Graphic designers develop the overall layout and production design of magazines, newspapers, journals, corporate reports, and other publications. They also produce promotional displays, packaging, and marketing brochures for products and services, design distinctive logos for products and businesses, and develop signs and signage systems—called environmental graphics—for business and government. An increasing number of graphic designers also are developing material for Internet Web pages, interactive media, and multimedia projects. Graphic designers also may produce the credits that appear before and after television programs and movies.

Graphic designers frequently use graphics and layout software to assist in their designs.

The first step in developing a new graphic design is to determine the needs of the client, the message the design should portray, and its appeal to customers or users. Graphic designers consider cognitive, cultural, physical, and social factors in planning and executing designs for the target audience. Designers gather relevant information by meeting with clients, creative or art directors, and by performing their own research. Identifying the needs of consumers is becoming increasingly important for graphic designers as the scope of their work continues to focus on creating corporate communication strategies in addition to technical design and layout work.

Graphic designers prepare sketches or layouts—by hand or with the aid of a computer—to illustrate the vision for the design. They select colors, sound, artwork, photography, animation, style of type, and other visual elements for the design. Designers also select the size and arrangement of the different elements on the page or screen. They also may create graphs and charts from data for use in publications, and often consult with copywriters on any text that may accompany the visual part of the design. Designers then present the completed design to their clients or art or creative director for approval. In printing and publishing firms, graphic designers also may assist the printers by selecting the type of paper and ink for the publication and reviewing the mock-up design for errors before final publication.

Graphic designers use a variety of graphics and layout computer software to assist in their designs. Designers creating Web pages or other interactive media designs also will use computer animation and programming packages. Computer software programs allow ease and flexibility in exploring a greater number of design alternatives, thus reducing design costs and cutting the time it takes to deliver a product to market.

Graphic designers sometimes supervise assistants who carry out their creations. Designers who run their own businesses also may devote a considerable amount of time to developing new business contacts, examining equipment and space needs, and performing administrative tasks, such as reviewing catalogues and ordering samples. The need for up-to-date computer and communications equipment is an ongoing consideration for graphic designers.

Working Conditions

Working conditions and places of employment vary. Graphic designers employed by large advertising, publishing, or design firms generally work regular hours in well-lighted and comfortable settings. Designers in smaller design consulting firms, or those who freelance, generally work on a contract, or job, basis. They frequently adjust their workday to suit their clients' schedules and deadlines. Consultants

and self-employed designers tend to work longer hours and in smaller, more congested, environments.

Designers may transact business in their own offices or studios or in clients' offices. Designers who are paid by the assignment are under pressure to please clients and to find new ones in order to maintain a steady income. All designers sometimes face frustration when their designs are rejected or when their work is not as creative as they wish. Graphic designers may work evenings or weekends to meet production schedules, especially in the printing and publishing industries where deadlines are shorter and more frequent.

Training, Other Qualifications, and Advancement

A bachelor's degree is required for most entry-level and advanced graphic design positions; although some entry-level technical positions may only require an associate degree. In addition to postsecondary training in graphic design, creativity, and communication and problem-solving skills are crucial. Graphic designers also need to be familiar with computer graphics and design software. A good portfolio—a collection of examples of a person's best work—often is the deciding factor in getting a job.

Bachelor's of fine arts degree programs in graphic design are offered at many colleges, universities, and private design schools. The curriculum includes studio art, principles of design, computerized design, commercial graphics production, printing techniques, and Web site design. In addition to design courses, a liberal arts education or a program that includes courses in art history, writing, psychology, sociology, foreign languages and cultural studies, marketing, and business are useful in helping designers work effectively with the content of their work. Graphic designers must effectively communicate complex subjects to a variety of audiences. Increasingly, clients rely on graphic designers to develop the content and the context of the message in addition to performing technical layout work.

Associate degrees and certificates in graphic design also are available from 2- and 3-year professional schools. These programs usually focus on the technical aspects of graphic design and include very few liberal arts courses. Graduates of 2-year programs normally qualify as assistants to graphic designers or for positions requiring technical skills only. Individuals who wish to pursue a career in graphic design—and who already possess a bachelor's degree in another field—can complete a 2-year or 3-year program in graphic design to learn the technical requirements.

The National Association of Schools of Art and Design accredits about 250 postsecondary institutions with programs in art and design. Most of these schools award a degree in graphic design. Many schools do not allow formal entry into a bachelor's degree program until a student has successfully finished a year of basic art and design courses. Applicants may be required to submit sketches and other examples of their artistic ability.

Increasingly, employers expect new graphic designers to be familiar with computer graphics and design software. Graphic designers must continually keep up to date with the development of new and updated software, usually either on their own or through software training programs.

Graphic designers also must be creative and able to communicate their ideas in writing, visually, and verbally. Because consumer tastes can change quickly, designers need to be well read, open to new ideas and influences, and quick to react to changing trends. Problem-solving skills, paying attention to detail, and the ability to work independently and under pressure also are important traits. People in this field need self-discipline to start projects on their own, to budget their time, and to meet deadlines and production schedules. Good business sense and sales ability also are important, especially for those who freelance or run their own business.

Beginning graphic designers usually receive on-the-job training and normally need 1 to 3 years of training before they can advance to higher level positions. Experienced graphic designers in large firms may advance to chief designer, art or creative director, or other supervisory positions. Some designers leave the occupation to become teachers in design schools or in colleges and universities. Many faculty members continue to consult privately or operate small design studios to complement their classroom activities. Some experienced designers open their own firms or choose to specialize in one area of graphic design.

Employment

Graphic designers held about 228,000 jobs in 2004. About 7 out of 10 were wage and salary designers. Most worked in specialized design services; advertising and related services; printing and related support activities; or newspaper, periodical, book, and directory publishers. Other graphic designers produced computer graphics for computer systems design firms or motion picture production firms. A small number of designers also worked in engineering services or for management, scientific, and technical consulting firms.

About 3 out of 10 designers were self-employed. Many did freelance work—full time or part time—in addition to holding a salaried job in design or in another occupation.

Job Outlook

Employment of graphic designers is expected to grow about as fast as the average for all occupations through the year 2014, as demand for graphic design continues to increase from advertisers, publishers, and computer design firms. Among the five different design occupations, graphic designers will have the most new jobs. However, graphic designers are expected to face keen competition for available positions. Many talented individuals are attracted to careers as graphic designers. Individuals with a bachelor's degree and knowledge of computer design software, particularly those with Web site design and animation experience, will have the best opportunities.

Demand for graphic designers should increase because of the rapidly expanding market for Web-based information and expansion of the video entertainment market, including television, movies, video, and made-for-Internet outlets. Graphic designers with Web site design and animation experience will especially be needed as demand for design projects increase for interactive media—Web sites, video games, cellular telephones, personal digital assistants (PDAs), and other technology. Demand for graphic designers also will increase as advertising firms create print and Web marketing and promotional materials for a growing number of products and services.

In recent years, some computer, printing, and publishing firms have outsourced basic layout and design work to design firms overseas. This trend is expected to continue and may have a negative impact on employment growth for lower level, technical graphic design workers. However, most higher-level graphic design jobs will remain in the U.S. and will focus on developing communication strategies, called strategic design, for clients and firms in order for them to gain competitive advantages in the market. Strategic design work requires close proximity to the consumer in order to identify and target their needs and interests. Graphic designers with a broad liberal arts education and experience in marketing and business management will be best suited for these positions.

Earnings

Median annual earnings for graphic designers were $38,030 in May 2004. The middle 50 percent earned between $29,360 and $50,840. The lowest 10 percent earned less than $23,220, and the highest 10 percent earned more than $65,940. Median annual earnings in the industries employing the largest numbers of graphic designers were:

Architectural, engineering, and related services	$42,740
Specialized design services	41,620
Advertising and related services	40,010
Printing and related support activities	32,830
Newspaper, periodical, book, and directory publishers	32,390

The American Institute of Graphic Arts reported 2005 median annual total cash compensation for graphic designers according to level of responsibility. Entry-level designers earned a median salary of $32,000 in 2005, while staff-level graphic designers earned $42,500. Senior designers, who may supervise junior staff or have some decision-making authority that reflects their knowledge of graphic design, earned $56,000. Solo designers, who freelanced or worked under contract to another company, reported median earnings of $60,000. Design directors, the creative heads of design firms or in-house corporate design departments, earned $90,000. Graphic designers with ownership or partnership interests in a firm or who were principals of the firm in some other capacity earned $100,000.

Related Occupations

Workers in other occupations in the art and design field include artists and related workers; commercial and industrial designers; fashion designers; floral designers; and interior designers. Other occupations that require computer-aided design skills include computer software engineers, drafters, and desktop publishers. Other occupations involved in the design, layout, and copy of publications include advertising, marketing, promotions, public relations, and sales managers; photographers; writers and editors; and prepress technicians and workers.

Sources of Additional Information

For general information about art and design and a list of accredited college-level programs, contact:
➤ National Association of Schools of Art and Design, 11250 Roger Bacon Dr., Suite 21, Reston, VA 20190-5248. Internet: **http://nasad.arts-accredit.org**

For information about graphic, communication, or interaction design careers, contact:
➤ American Institute of Graphic Arts, 164 Fifth Ave., New York, NY 10010. Internet: **http://www.aiga.org**

For information on workshops, scholarships, internships, and competitions for graphic design students interested in advertising careers, contact:
➤ Art Directors Club, 106 West 29th St., New York, NY 10001. Internet: **http://www.adcglobal.org**

Interior designers

(O*NET 27-1025.00)

Significant Points

- Keen competition is expected for jobs in interior design because many talented individuals are attracted to careers as interior designers.

- Individuals with little or no formal training in interior design, as well as those lacking creativity and perseverance, will find it very difficult to establish and maintain a career in this occupation.

- About 3 out of 10 are self-employed.

- Postsecondary education—especially a bachelor's degree—is recommended for entry-level positions in interior design; licensure is required in 23 States, the District of Columbia, and Puerto Rico.

Interior designers look at many fabric and paint samples in order to choose an appropriate design.

Nature of the Work

Interior designers draw upon many disciplines to enhance the function, safety, and aesthetics of interior spaces. Interior designers are concerned with how different colors, textures, furniture, lighting, and space work together to meet the needs of a building's occupants. Designers are involved in planning the interior spaces of almost all buildings—offices, airport terminals, theaters, shopping malls, restaurants, hotels, schools, hospitals, and private residences. Designers help to improve these spaces in order to boost office productivity, increase sales, attract a more affluent clientele, provide a more relaxing hospital stay, or increase the building's market value.

Traditionally, most interior designers focused on decorating: choosing a style and color palette and then selecting appropriate furniture, floor and window coverings, artwork, and lighting. However, an increasing number of designers are becoming more involved in designing architectural detailing, such as crown molding and built-in bookshelves, or planning layouts of buildings undergoing renovation, including helping to determine the location of windows, stairways, escalators, and walkways. Interior designers must be able to read blueprints, understand building and fire codes, and know how to make the space accessible to the disabled. Designers frequently collaborate with architects, electricians, and building contractors to ensure that their designs are safe and meet construction requirements.

Despite the varied building spaces interior designers work with, almost all projects follow the same design process. The first step in developing a new design is to determine the needs of the client, known as programming. The designer usually will meet face-to-face with the client in order to find out how the space will be used and to get an idea of the client's design preferences and budget. For example, the designer might inquire about a family's cooking habits if the family is remodeling a kitchen or ask about a store or restaurant's target customer in order to pick an appropriate design. The designer also will visit the space and take inventory of the existing furniture and equipment as well as identify the any potential design problems and the positive attributes of the space.

Following the initial meeting with the client, the designer will formulate a design plan and estimate the costs on the basis of the client's goals and budget. Today, designs often are created with the use of computer-aided design (CAD), which provides a more detailed layout and also allows for easier corrections than sketches made by hand. Once the designer has completed the proposed design, he or she will present it to the client and make revisions on the basis of the client's input.

When a design concept has been finalized, the designer will begin specifying the materials, finishes, and furnishings required, such as furniture, lighting, flooring, wall covering, and artwork. In addition, depending on the complexity of the project, the designer will need to prepare drawings and submit them for architectural review and approval by a construction inspector to ensure that the design meets all applicable building codes. If a project requires any structural work, the designer will need to work with an architect or engineer for that part of the project. Most designs also will require the hiring of contractors to do such technical work as lighting, plumbing, or electrical wiring. When necessary, the designer will choose qualified contractors and write up work contracts.

Finally, the designer will develop a timeline for the project and ensure that it is completed on time, including coordinating the work schedules of contractors if necessary. The designer will oversee the installation of the design elements, and after the project is complete, the designer, together with the client, will pay follow-up visits to the building site to ensure that the client is satisfied with the final product. If the client is not satisfied, the designer will make all necessary corrections.

Designers who work as in-store designers for furniture or home and garden stores offer their design services in addition to selling the store's merchandise. In-store designers provide services similar to those offered by other interior designers, such as selecting a style and color scheme that fits the client's needs or finding suitable accessories and lighting. However, in-store designers rarely visit their clients' spaces and are limited in using only a particular store's products.

Interior designers sometimes supervise assistants who carry out their creations and perform administrative tasks, such as reviewing catalogues and ordering samples. Designers who run their own businesses also may devote a considerable amount of time meeting with clients and contractors, developing new business contacts, examining equipment and space needs, and attending to business matters.

Although most interior designers do many kinds of projects, some specialize in one area of interior design. Some specialize in the type of building space—usually residential or commercial—while others specialize in a certain design element or type of client, such as health care facilities. The most common specialties of this kind are lighting, kitchen and bath, and closet designs. However, designers can specialize in almost any area of design, including acoustics and noise abatement, security, electronics and home theaters, home spas, and indoor gardens.

Three areas of design that are becoming increasingly popular are ergonomic design elder design, and environmental—or green—design. Ergonomic design involves designing work spaces and furniture that emphasize good posture and minimize muscle strain on the body. Elder design involves planning interior space to aid in the movement of the elderly and disabled, such as widening passageways to accommodate wheelchairs. Green design involves selecting furniture and carpets that are free of chemicals and hypoallergenic and selecting construction materials that are energy efficient or are made from renewable resources.

Working Conditions

Working conditions and places of employment vary. Interior designers employed by large corporations or design firms generally work regular hours in well-lighted and comfortable settings. Designers in smaller design consulting firms or those who freelance generally work on a contract, or job, basis. They frequently adjust their workday to suit their clients' schedules and deadlines, meeting with the clients during evening or weekend hours when necessary. Consultants and self-employed designers tend to work longer hours and in smaller, more congested environments.

Interior designers may work under stress to meet deadlines, stay on budget, and please clients. Self-employed designers also are under pressure to find new clients in order to maintain a steady income.

Designers may transact business in their own offices or studios or in clients' homes or offices. They also may travel to other locations, such as showrooms, design centers, clients' exhibit sites, and manufacturing facilities. With the increased speed and sophistication of computers and advanced communications networks, designers may form international design teams, serve a geographically more dispersed clientele, research design alternatives by using information on the Internet, and purchase supplies electronically, all with the aid of a computer in their workplace or studio.

Training, Other Qualifications, and Advancement

Postsecondary education—especially a bachelor's degree—is recommended for entry-level positions in interior design. In addition, 24 States, the District of Columbia, and Puerto Rico register or license interior designers. Following formal training, graduates usually enter a 1-year to 3-year apprenticeship to gain experience before taking a national licensing exam or joining a professional association. Designers in States that do not require the exam may opt to take it as proof of their qualifications. The National Council administers the licensing exam for Interior Design Qualification (NCIDQ). To be eligible to take the exam, applicants must have at least 6 years of combined education and experience in interior design, of which at least 2 years constitute postsecondary education in design. Once candidates have passed the qualifying exam, they are granted the title of Certified, Registered, or Licensed Interior Designer, depending on the State. Continuing education is required in order to maintain one's licensure.

Training programs are available from professional design schools or from colleges and universities and usually take 2 to 4 years to complete. Graduates of 2-year and 3-year programs are awarded certificates or associate's degrees in interior design and normally qualify as assistants to interior designers upon graduation. Graduates with bachelor's degrees usually qualify for entry into a formal design apprenticeship program. Basic course-

work includes computer-aided design (CAD), drawing, perspective, spatial planning, color and fabrics, furniture design, architecture, ergonomics, ethics, and psychology.

The National Association of Schools of Art and Design accredits approximately 250 postsecondary institutions with programs in art and design. Most of these schools award a degree in interior design. Applicants may be required to submit sketches and other examples of their artistic ability.

The Foundation for Interior Design Education Research also accredits interior design programs that lead to a bachelor's degree. In 2005, there were 137 accredited bachelor's degree programs in interior design in the United States, located primarily in schools of art, architecture, and home economics.

After the completion of formal training, interior designers will enter a 1-year to 3-year apprenticeship to gain experience before taking a licensing exam. Most apprentices work in design or architecture firms under the strict supervision of an experienced designer. Apprentices also may choose to gain experience working as an in-store designer in furniture stores. The NCIDQ offers the Interior Design Experience Program (IDEP), which helps entry-level interior designers gain valuable work experience by supervising work experience and offering mentoring services and workshops to new designers.

Following the apprenticeship, designers will take the national licensing exam or choose to become members of a professional association. Because registration or licensure is not mandatory in all States, membership in a professional association is an indication of an interior designer's qualifications and professional standing. The American Society of Interior Designers (ASID) is the largest professional association for interior designers in the United States. Interior designers can qualify for membership with at least a 2-year or higher degree and work experience.

In addition to national licensure and membership in a professional association, optional certifications in kitchen and bath design are available from the National Kitchen and Bath Association. The association offers three different levels of certification for kitchen and bath designers, each completed through training seminars that culminate in certification exams.

Employers increasingly prefer interior designers who are familiar with CAD software. Interior designers also increasingly need to know the basics of architecture and engineering in order to ensure that their designs meet building safety codes.

In addition to possessing technical knowledge, interior designers must be creative, imaginative, and persistent and must be able to communicate their ideas in writing, visually, and verbally. Because tastes in style can change quickly, designers need to be well read, open to new ideas and influences, and quick to react to changing trends. Problem-solving skills and the ability to work independently and under pressure are important traits. People in this field need self-discipline to start projects on their own, to budget their time, and to meet deadlines and production schedules. Good business sense and sales ability also are important, especially for those who freelance or run their own business.

Beginning interior designers receive on-the-job training and normally need 1 to 3 years of training before they can advance to higher level positions. Experienced designers in large firms may advance to chief designer, design department head, or some other supervisory position. Some experienced designers open their own firms or decide to specialize in one aspect of interior design. Other designers leave the occupation to become teachers in schools of design or in colleges and universities. Many faculty members continue to consult privately or operate small design studios to complement their classroom activities.

Employment

Interior designers held about 65,000 jobs in 2004. Approximately 3 out of 10 were self-employed. About 2 out of 10 wage and salary interior designers worked in specialized design services. Another 1 out of 10 worked in architectural and landscape architectural services. The remaining of interior designers provided design services in furniture and home-furnishing stores, building material and supplies dealers, and residential building construction companies. Many interior designers also performed freelance work in addition to holding a salaried job in interior design or another occupation.

Job Outlook

Employment of interior designers is expected to grow about as fast as the average for all occupations through 2014. Economic expansion, growing homeowner wealth, and an increased interest in interior design will increase demand for designers. However, interior designers are expected to face keen competition for available positions because many talented individuals are attracted to this profession. Individuals with little or no formal training in interior design, as well as those lacking creativity and perseverance, will find it very difficult to establish and maintain a career in this occupation.

As the economy grows, more private businesses and consumers will request the services of interior designers. However, design services are considered a luxury expense and may be subject to fluctuations in the economy. For example, decreases in consumer and business income and spending caused by a slow economy can have a detrimental effect on employment of interior designers. Nevertheless, demand from the health care industry is expected to be especially high because of an anticipated increase in demand for facilities that will accommodate the aging population. Designers will be needed to make these facilities as comfortable and homelike as possible for patients. Demand from businesses in the hospitality industry—hotels, resorts, and restaurants—also is expected to be high because of an expected increase in tourism.

Recent increases in homeowner wealth and the growing popularity of home improvement television programs have increased demand for residential design services. Homeowners increasingly have been using the equity in their homes to finance new additions, remodel aging kitchens and bathrooms, and update the general décor of the home. Many homeowners also have requested design help in adding year-round outdoor living spaces.

Growth in home improvement television programs and discount furniture stores has spurred a trend in do-it-yourself design, which could hamper employment growth of designers. However, some clients will still hire designers for a few initial consultations, but then will purchase and install the design elements themselves.

Some interior designers are choosing to specialize in one design element in order to create a niche for themselves in an increasingly competitive market. The demand for kitchen and bath design is growing in response to the increasing demand for home remodeling. Designs utilizing the latest technology, such as home theaters, state-of-the-art conference facilities, and security systems are expected to be especially popular. In addition, demand for home spas, indoor gardens, and outdoor living spaces are expected to continue to increase.

Extensive knowledge of ergonomics and green design are expected to be in demand. Ergonomic design has gained in popularity with the growth in the elderly population and workplace safety requirements. The public's growing awareness of environmental quality and the growing number of individuals with allergies and asthma are expected to increase the demand for green design.

Earnings

Median annual earnings for interior designers were $40,670 in May 2004. The middle 50 percent earned between $30,890 and $53,790. The lowest 10 percent earned less than $23,440, and the highest 10 percent earned more than $71,220. Median annual earnings in the industries employing the largest numbers of interior designers in May 2004 were as follows:

Architectural, engineering, and related services	$44,740
Specialized design services	42,000
Furniture stores	37,750

Interior design salaries vary widely with the specialty, type of employer, number of years of experience, and reputation of the individuals. Among salaried interior designers, those in large specialized design and architectural firms tend to earn higher and more stable salaries. Interior designers working in retail stores usually earn a commission, which can be irregular.

For residential design projects, self-employed interior designers and those working in smaller firms usually earn a per-hour consulting fee, plus a percentage of the total cost of furniture, lighting, artwork, and other design elements. For commercial projects, they might charge a per-hour consulting fee, charge by the square footage, or charge a flat fee for the whole project. Also, designers who use specialty contractors usually earn a percentage of the contractor's earnings on the project in return for hiring the contractor. Self-employed designers must provide their own benefits.

Related Occupations

Workers in other occupations who design or arrange objects to enhance their appearance and function include architects, except landscape and naval; artists and related workers; commercial and industrial designers; fashion designers; floral designers; graphic designers; and landscape architects.

Sources of Additional Information

For information on degrees, continuing education, and licensure programs in interior design and interior design research, contact:

➤ American Society of Interior Designers, 608 Massachusetts Ave. N.E., Washington, DC 20002-6006. Internet: **http://www.asid.org**

For a list of schools with accredited bachelor's degree programs in interior design, contact:

➤ Foundation for Interior Design Education Research, 146 Monroe Center N.W., Suite 1318, Grand Rapids, MI 49503-2822. Internet: **http://www.fider.org**

For general information about art and design and a list of accredited college-level programs, contact:

➤ National Association of Schools of Art and Design, 11250 Roger Bacon Dr., Suite 21, Reston, VA 20190-5248. Internet: **http://nasad.arts-accredit.org**

For information on State licensing requirements and exams, and the Interior Design Experience Program, contact:

➤ National Council for Interior Design Qualification, 1200 18th St. NW., Suite 1001, Washington, DC 20036-2506. Internet: **http://www.ncidq.org**

For information on careers, continuing education, and certification programs in the interior design specialty of residential kitchen and bath design, contact:

➤ National Kitchen and Bath Association, 687 Willow Grove St., Hackettstown, NJ 07840. Internet: **http://www.nkba.org/student**

Entertainers and Performers, Sports and Related Occupations

Actors, Producers, and Directors

(O*NET 27-2011.00, 27-2012.01, 27-2012.02, 27-2012.03, 27-2012.04, 27-2012.05)

Significant Points

- Actors endure long periods of unemployment, intense competition for roles, and frequent rejections in auditions.

- Formal training through a university or acting conservatory is typical; however, many actors, producers, and directors find work on the basis of their experience and talent alone.

- Because earnings for actors are erratic, many supplement their incomes by holding jobs in other fields.

Actors, producers, and directors work together, often for very long hours, to get the scene done right.

Nature of the Work

Actors, producers, and directors express ideas and create images in theater, film, radio, television, and other performing arts media. They interpret a writer's script to entertain, inform, or instruct an audience. Although the most famous actors, producers, and directors work in film, network television, or theater in New York or Los Angeles, far more work in local or regional television studios, theaters, or film production companies preparing advertising, public-relations, or independent, small-scale movie productions.

Actors perform in stage, radio, television, video, or motion picture productions. They also work in cabarets, nightclubs, theme parks, commercials, and "industrial" films produced for training and educational purposes. Most actors struggle to find steady work; only a few ever achieve recognition as stars. Some well-known, experienced performers may be cast in supporting roles. Others work as "extras," with no lines to deliver, or make brief, cameo appearances, speaking only one or two lines. Some actors do voiceover and narration work for advertisements, animated features, books on tape, and other electronic media, including computer games. They also teach in high school or university drama departments, acting conservatories, or public programs.

Producers are entrepreneurs, overseeing the business and financial decisions of a motion picture, made-for-television feature, or stage production. They select scripts, approve the development of ideas for the production, arrange financing, and determine the size and cost of the endeavor. Producers hire or approve the selection of directors, principal cast members, and key production staff members. They also negotiate contracts with artistic and design personnel in accordance with collective bargaining agreements and guarantee payment of salaries, rent, and other expenses. Television and radio producers determine which programs, episodes, or news segments get aired. They may research material, write scripts, and oversee the production of individual pieces. Producers in any medium coordinate the activities of writers, directors, managers, and agents to ensure that each project stays on schedule and within budget.

Directors are responsible for the creative decisions of a production. They interpret scripts, express concepts to set and costume designers, audition and select cast members, conduct rehearsals, and direct the work of cast and crew. They approve the design elements of a production, including the sets, costumes, choreography, and music. Assistant directors cue the performers and technicians to make entrances or to make light, sound, or set changes.

Working Conditions

Actors, producers, and directors work under constant pressure. Many face stress from the continual need to find their next job. To succeed, actors, producers, and directors need patience and commitment to their craft. Actors strive to deliver flawless performances, often while working under undesirable and unpleasant conditions. Producers and directors organize rehearsals and meet with writers, designers, financial backers, and production technicians. They experience stress not only from these activities, but also from the need to adhere to budgets, union work rules, and production schedules.

Acting assignments typically are short term—ranging from 1 day to a few months—which means that actors frequently experience long periods of unemployment between jobs. The uncertain nature of the work results in unpredictable earnings and intense competition for even the lowest paid jobs. Often, actors, producers, and directors must hold other jobs in order to sustain a living.

When performing, actors typically work long, irregular hours. For example, stage actors may perform one show at night while rehearsing another during the day. They also might travel with a show when it tours the country. Movie actors may work on location, sometimes under adverse weather conditions, and may spend considerable time in their trailers or dressing rooms waiting to perform their scenes. Actors who perform in a television series often appear on camera with little preparation time, because scripts tend to be revised frequently or even written moments before taping. Those who appear live or before a studio audience must be able to handle impromptu situations and calmly ad lib, or substitute, lines when necessary.

Evening and weekend work is a regular part of a stage actor's life. On weekends, more than one performance may be held per day. Actors and directors working on movies or television programs—especially those who shoot on location—may work in the early morning or late evening hours to film night scenes or tape scenes inside public facilities outside of normal business hours.

Actors should be in good physical condition and have the necessary stamina and coordination to move about theater stages and large movie and television studio lots. They also need to maneuver about complex technical sets while staying in character and projecting their voices audibly. Actors must be fit to endure heat from stage or studio lights and the weight of heavy costumes. Producers and directors ensure the safety of actors by conducting extra rehearsals on the set so that the actors can learn the layout of set pieces and props, by allowing time for warmups and stretching exercises to guard against physical and vocal injuries, and by providing an adequate number of breaks to prevent heat exhaustion and dehydration.

Training, Other Qualifications, and Advancement

Persons who become actors, producers, and directors follow many paths. Employers generally look for people with the creative instincts, innate talent, and intellectual capacity to perform. Actors should possess a passion for performing and enjoy entertaining others. Most aspiring actors participate in high school and college plays, work in college radio stations, or perform with local community theater groups. Local and regional theater experience and work in summer stock, on cruise lines, or in theme parks helps many young actors hone their skills and earn qualifying credits toward membership in one of the actors' unions. Union membership and work experience in smaller communities may lead to work in larger cities, notably New York or Los Angeles. In television and film, actors and directors typically start in smaller television markets or with independent movie production companies and then work their way up to larger media markets and major studio productions. Intense competition, however, can be expected at each level, because ever more applicants will be vying for increasingly fewer numbers of available positions.

Formal dramatic training, either through an acting conservatory or a university program, generally is necessary, but some people successfully enter the field without it. Most people studying for a bachelor's degree take courses in radio and television broadcasting, communications, film, theater, drama, or dramatic literature. Many continue their academic training and receive a Master of Fine Arts (MFA) degree. Advanced curricula may include courses in stage speech and movement, directing, playwriting, and design, as well as intensive acting workshops. The National Association of Schools of Theatre accredits 135 programs in theater arts. A few people go into acting following successful careers in other fields, such as broadcasting or announcing.

Actors, regardless of experience level, may pursue workshop training through acting conservatories or mentoring by a drama coach. Actors also research roles so that they can grasp concepts quickly during rehearsals and understand the story's setting and background. Sometimes actors learn a foreign language or train with a dialect coach to develop an accent to make their characters more realistic.

Actors need talent, creativity, and training that will enable them to portray different characters. Because competition for parts is fierce, versatility and a wide range of related performance skills, such as singing, dancing, skating, juggling, or miming are especially useful. Experience in horseback riding, fencing, or stage combat also can lift some actors above the average and get them noticed by producers and directors. Actors must have poise, stage presence, the capability to affect an audience, and the ability to follow direction. Modeling experience also may be helpful. Physical appearance, such as possessing the right size, weight, or features, often is a deciding factor in being selected for particular roles.

Many professional actors rely on agents or managers to find work, negotiate contracts, and plan their careers. Agents generally earn a percentage of the pay specified in an actor's contract. Other actors rely solely on attending open auditions for parts. Trade publications list the times, dates, and locations of these auditions.

To become a movie extra, one usually must be listed by a casting agency, such as Central Casting, a no-fee agency that supplies extras to the major movie studios in Hollywood. Applicants are accepted only when the numbers of persons of a particular type on the list—for example, athletic young women, old men, or small children—falls below the foreseeable need. In recent years, only a very small proportion of applicants have succeeded in being listed.

There are no specific training requirements for producers. They come from many different backgrounds. Talent, experience, and business acumen are important determinants of success for producers. Actors, writers, film editors, and business managers commonly enter the field. Also, many people who start out as actors move into directing, while some directors might try their hand at acting. Producers often start in a theatrical management office, working for a press agent, managing director, or business manager. Some start in a performing arts union or service organization. Others work behind the scenes with successful directors, serve on boards of directors, or promote their own projects. No formal training exists for producers; however, a growing number of colleges and universities now offer degree programs in arts management and in managing nonprofits.

As the reputations and box-office draw of actors, producers, and directors grow, they might work on bigger budget productions, on network or syndicated broadcasts, or in more prestigious theaters. Actors may advance to lead roles and receive star billing. A few actors move into acting-related jobs, such as drama coaches or directors of stage, television, radio, or motion picture productions. Some teach drama privately or in colleges and universities.

Employment

In 2004, actors, producers, and directors held about 157,000 jobs, primarily in motion picture and video, performing arts, and broadcast industries. Because many others were between jobs, the total number of actors, producers, and directors available for work was higher. Employment in the theater, and other performing arts companies, is cyclical—higher in the fall and spring seasons—and concentrated in New York and other major cities with large commercial houses for musicals and touring productions. Also, many cities support established professional regional theaters that operate on a seasonal or year-round basis. About one-fourth of actors, producers, and directors were self-employed.

Actors, producers, and directors may find work in summer festivals, on cruise lines, and in theme parks. Many smaller, nonprofit professional companies, such as repertory companies, dinner theaters, and theaters affiliated with drama schools, acting conservatories, and universities, provide employment opportunities for local amateur talent and professional entertainers. Auditions typically are held in New York for many productions across the country and for shows that go on the road.

Employment in motion pictures and in films for television is centered in New York and Hollywood. However, small studios are located throughout the country. Many films are shot on location and may employ local professional and nonprofessional actors. In television, opportunities are concentrated in the network centers of New York and Los Angeles, but cable television services and local television stations around the country also employ many actors, producers, and directors.

A growing number of actors and other entertainers appear on the payrolls of firms who do accounting and payroll work. Frequently film production companies will hire actors through casting agencies or contract out their payroll services to accounting firms. Similarly, many actors arrange with a company in this industry to collect their pay from producers or entrepreneurs; make the appropriate deductions for taxes, union dues, and benefits payments; and pay them their net earnings for each job. The result of these increasingly more common payroll arrangements is that many actors appear to be working for accounting offices, rather than for the theatrical production companies or studios where they actually perform.

Job Outlook

Employment of actors, producers, and directors is expected to grow about as fast as the average for all occupations through 2014. Although a growing number of people will aspire to enter these professions, many will leave the field early because the work—when it is available—is hard, the hours are long, and the pay is low. Competition for jobs will be stiff, in part because the large number of highly trained and talented actors auditioning for roles generally exceeds the number of parts that become available. Only performers with the most stamina and talent will find regular employment.

Expanding cable and satellite television operations, increasing production and distribution of major studio and independent films, and continued growth and development of interactive media, such as direct-for-Web movies and videos, should increase demand for actors, producers, and directors. However, greater emphasis on national, rather than local, entertainment productions may restrict employment opportunities in the broadcasting industry.

Venues for live entertainment, such as Broadway and Off-Broadway theaters, touring productions, and repertory theaters in many major metropolitan areas, as well as theme parks and resorts, are expected to offer many job opportunities. However, prospects in these venues are more variable, because they fluctuate with economic conditions.

Earnings

Median hourly earnings of actors were $11.28 in May 2004. The middle 50 percent earned between $7.75 and $30.76. The lowest 10 percent earned less than $6.63, and the highest 10 percent earned more than $56.48. Median annual earnings were $15.20 in performing arts companies and $9.27 in motion picture and video industries. Annual earnings data for actors were not available because of the wide variation in the number of hours worked by actors and the short-term nature of many jobs, which may last for 1 day or 1 week; it is extremely rare for actors to have guaranteed employment that exceeded 3 to 6 months.

Minimum salaries, hours of work, and other conditions of employment are covered in collective bargaining agreements between the producers and the unions representing workers. The Actors' Equity Association (Equity) represents stage actors; the Screen Actors Guild (SAG) covers actors in motion pictures, including television, commercials, and films; and the American Federation of Television and Radio Artists (AFTRA) represents television and radio studio performers. Some actors who regularly work in several media find it advantageous to join multiple unions, while SAG and AFTRA may share jurisdiction for work in additional areas, such as the production of training or educational films not slated for broadcast, television commercial work, and interactive media. While these unions generally determine minimum salaries, any actor or director may negotiate for a salary higher than the minimum.

Under terms of a joint SAG and AFTRA contract covering all unionized workers, motion picture and television actors with speaking parts earned a minimum daily rate of $716 or $2,483 for a 5-day week as of October 1, 2005. Actors also receive contributions to their health and pension plans and additional compensation for reruns and foreign telecasts of the productions in which they appear.

According to Equity, the minimum weekly salary for actors in Broadway productions as of June 30, 2005 was $1,422. Actors in Off-Broadway theaters received minimums ranging from $493 to $857 a week as of October 23, 2005, depending on the seating capacity of the theater. Regional theaters that operate under an Equity agreement pay actors $531 to $800 per week. For touring productions, actors receive an additional $777 per week for living expenses ($819 per week in higher cost cities). New terms were negotiated under an "experimental touring program" provision for lower budget musicals that tour to smaller cities or that perform for fewer performances at each stop. In an effort to increase the number of paid workweeks while on tour, actors may be paid less than the full production rate for touring shows in exchange for higher per diems and profit participation.

Some well-known actors—stars—earn well above the minimum; their salaries are many times the figures cited, creating the false impression that all actors are highly paid. For example, of the nearly 100,000 SAG members, only about 50 might be considered stars. The average income that SAG members earn from acting—less than $5,000 a year—is low because employment is sporadic. Therefore, most actors must supplement their incomes by holding jobs in other occupations.

Many actors who work more than a qualifying number of days, or weeks per year or earn over a set minimum pay, are covered by a union health, welfare, and pension fund, which includes hospitalization insurance to which employers contribute. Under some employment conditions, Equity and AFTRA members receive paid vacations and sick leave.

Median annual earnings of salaried producers and directors were $52,840 in May 2004. The middle 50 percent earned between $35,550 and $87,980. Median annual earnings were $75,200 in motion picture and video industries and $43,890 in radio and television broadcasting.

Many stage directors belong to the Society of Stage Directors and Choreographers (SSDC), and film and television directors belong to the Directors Guild of America. Earnings of stage directors vary greatly. According to the SSDC, summer theaters offer compensation, including "royalties" (based on the number of performances), usually ranging from $2,500 to $8,000 for a 3- to 4-week run. Directing a production at a dinner theater generally will pay less than directing one at a summer theater, but has more potential for generating income from royalties. Regional theaters may hire directors for longer periods, increasing compensation accordingly. The highest-paid directors work on Broadway and commonly earn $50,000 per show. However, they also receive payment in the form of royalties—a negotiated percentage of gross box office receipts—that can exceed their contract fee for long-running box office successes.

Stage producers seldom get a set fee; instead, they get a percentage of a show's earnings or ticket sales.

Related Occupations

People who work in performing arts occupations that may require acting skills include announcers; dancers and choreographers; and musicians, singers, and related workers. Others working in film- and theater-related occupations are makeup artists, theatrical and performance; fashion designers; set and exhibit designers; and writers and authors. Producers share many responsibilities with those who work as top executives.

Sources of Additional Information

For general information about theater arts and a list of accredited college-level programs, contact:

➤ National Association of Schools of Theater, 11250 Roger Bacon Dr., Suite 21, Reston, VA 20190. Internet: **http://nast.arts-accredit.org**

For general information on actors, producers, and directors, contact any of the following organizations:

➤ Actors Equity Association, 165 West 46th St., New York, NY 10036. Internet: **http://www.actorsequity.org**

➤ Screen Actors Guild, 5757 Wilshire Blvd., Los Angeles, CA 90036-3600. Internet: **http://www.sag.org**
➤ American Federation of Television and Radio Artists—Screen Actors Guild, 4340 East-West Hwy., Suite 204, Bethesda, MD 20814-4411. Internet: **http://www.aftra.org** or **http://www.sag.org**

Athletes, Coaches, Umpires, and Related Workers

(O*NET 27-2021.00, 27-2022.00, 27-2023.00)

Significant Points

● Work hours are often irregular; travel may be extensive.

● Career-ending injuries are always a risk for athletes.

● Job opportunities will be best for part-time coaches, sports instructors, umpires, referees, and sports officials in high schools, sports clubs, and other settings.

● Competition for professional athlete jobs will continue to be extremely intense; athletes who seek to compete professionally must have extraordinary talent, desire, and dedication to training.

Nature of the Work

We are a nation of sports fans and sports players. Some of those who participate in amateur sports dream of becoming paid professional athletes, coaches, or sports officials, but very few beat the long and daunting odds of making a full-time living from professional athletics. Those athletes who do make it to professional levels find that careers are short and jobs are insecure. Even though the chances of employment as a professional athlete are slim, there are many opportunities for at least a part-time job as a coach, instructor, referee, or umpire in amateur athletics or in high school, college, or university sports.

Athletes and *sports competitors* compete in organized, officiated sports events to entertain spectators. When playing a game, athletes are required to understand the strategies of their game while obeying the rules and regulations of the sport. The events in which they compete include both team sports—such as baseball, basketball, football, hockey, and soccer—and individual sports—such as golf, tennis, and bowling. The level of play varies from unpaid high school athletics to professional sports, in which the best from around the world compete in events broadcast on international television.

Being an athlete involves more than competing in athletic events. Athletes spend many hours each day practicing skills and improving teamwork under the guidance of a coach or a sports instructor. They view videotapes to critique their own performances and techniques and to learn their opponents' tendencies and weaknesses to gain a competitive advantage. Some athletes work regularly with strength trainers to gain muscle and stamina and to prevent injury. Many athletes push their bodies to the limit during both practice and play, so career-ending injury always is a risk; even minor injuries may put a player at risk of replacement. Because competition at all levels is extremely intense and job security is always precarious, many athletes train year round to maintain excellent form and technique and peak physical condition. Very little downtime from the sport exists at the professional level. Athletes also must conform to regimented diets during their sports season to supplement any physical training program.

Coaches organize amateur and professional athletes and teach them the fundamentals of individual and team sports. (In individual sports, *instructors* sometimes may fill this role.) Coaches train ath-

Coaches manage their teams during practice and competition and instill good sportsmanship.

letes for competition by holding practice sessions to perform drills that improve the athletes' form, technique, skills, and stamina. Along with refining athletes' individual skills, coaches are responsible for instilling good sportsmanship, a competitive spirit, and teamwork and for managing their teams during both practice sessions and competitions. Before competition, coaches evaluate or scout the opposing team to determine game strategies and practice specific plays. During competition, coaches may call specific plays intended to surprise or overpower the opponent, and they may substitute players for optimum team chemistry and success. Coaches' additional tasks may include selecting, storing, issuing, and taking inventory of equipment, materials, and supplies.

Many coaches in high schools are primarily teachers of academic subjects who supplement their income by coaching part time. (For more information on high school teachers, see the statement on teachers—preschool, kindergarten, elementary, middle, and secondary, elsewhere in the *Handbook*.) College coaches consider coaching a full-time discipline and may be away from home frequently as they travel to scout and recruit prospective players.

Sports instructors teach professional and nonprofessional athletes individually. They organize, instruct, train, and lead athletes in indoor and outdoor sports such as bowling, tennis, golf, and swimming. Because activities are as diverse as weight lifting, gymnastics, scuba diving, and karate, instructors tend to specialize in one or a few activities. Like coaches, sports instructors also may hold daily practice sessions and be responsible for any needed equipment and supplies. Using their knowledge of their sport and of physiology, they determine the type and level of difficulty of exercises, prescribe specific drills, and correct athletes' techniques. Some instructors also teach and demonstrate the use of training apparatus, such as trampolines or weights, for correcting athletes' weaknesses and enhancing their conditioning. As coaches do, sports instructors evaluate the athlete and the athlete's opponents to devise a competitive game strategy.

Coaches and sports instructors sometimes differ in their approaches to athletes because of the focus of their work. For example, while coaches manage the team during a game to optimize its chance for victory, sports instructors—such as those who work for professional tennis players—often are not permitted to instruct their athletes during competition. Sports instructors spend more of their time with athletes working one-on-one, which permits them to design customized training programs for each individual. Motivating athletes to play hard challenges most coaches and sports instructors but is vital for the athlete's success. Many coaches and instructors derive great satisfaction working with children or young adults, helping them to learn new physical and social skills, improve their physical condition, and achieve success in their sport.

Umpires, referees, and other sports officials officiate at competitive athletic and sporting events. They observe the play, detect infractions of rules, and impose penalties established by the rules and regulations of the various sports. Umpires, referees, and sports officials anticipate play and position themselves to best see the action, assess the situation, and determine any violations. Some sports officials, such as boxing referees, may work independently, while others such as umpires work in groups. Regardless of the sport, the job is highly stressful because officials are often required to make a decision in a split second, sometimes resulting in strong disagreement among competitors, coaches, and spectators.

Professional *scouts* evaluate the skills of both amateur and professional athletes to determine talent and potential. As a sports intelligence agent, the scout's primary duty is to seek out top athletic candidates for the team he or she represents. At the professional level, scouts typically work for scouting organizations or as freelance scouts. In locating new talent, scouts perform their work in secrecy so as not to "tip off" their opponents about their interest in certain players. At the college level, the head scout often is an assistant coach, although freelance scouts may aid colleges by reporting to coaches about exceptional players. Scouts at this level seek talented high school athletes by reading newspapers, contacting high school coaches and alumni, attending high school games, and studying videotapes of prospects' performances. They also evaluate potential players' background and personal characteristics, such as motivation and discipline, by talking to the players' coaches, parents, and teachers.

Working Conditions
Irregular work hours are the trademark of the athlete. They also are common for coaches, umpires, referees, and other sports officials. People in these occupations often work Saturdays, Sundays, evenings, and holidays. Athletes and full-time coaches usually work more than 40 hours a week for several months during the sports season, if not most of the year. Some coaches in educational institutions may coach more than one sport, particularly in high schools.

Athletes, coaches, and sports officials who participate in competitions that are held outdoors may be exposed to all weather conditions of the season; those involved in events that are held indoors tend to work in climate-controlled comfort, often in arenas, enclosed stadiums, or gymnasiums. Athletes, coaches, and some sports officials frequently travel to sporting events by bus or airplane. Scouts also travel extensively in locating talent, often by automobile.

Umpires, referees, and other sports officials regularly encounter verbal abuse by fans, coaches, and athletes. The officials also face possible physical assault and, increasingly, lawsuits from injured athletes based on their officiating decisions.

Training, Other Qualifications, and Advancement
Education and training requirements for athletes, coaches, umpires, and related workers vary greatly by the level and type of sport. Regardless of the sport or occupation, jobs require immense overall knowledge of the game, usually acquired through years of experience at lower levels. Athletes usually begin competing in their sports while in elementary or middle school, and continue through high school and sometimes college. They play in amateur tournaments and on high school and college teams, where the best attract the attention of professional scouts. Most schools require that participating athletes maintain specific academic standards to remain eligible to play. Becoming a professional athlete is the culmination

of years of effort. Athletes who seek to compete professionally must have extraordinary talent, desire, and dedication to training.

For high school coaching and sports instructor jobs, schools usually prefer to hire teachers willing to take on the jobs part time. If no one suitable is found, schools hire someone from outside. Some entry-level positions for coaches or instructors require only experience derived as a participant in the sport or activity. Many coaches begin their careers as assistant coaches to gain the knowledge and experience needed to become a head coach. Head coaches at large schools that strive to compete at the highest levels of a sport require substantial experience as a head coach at another school or as an assistant coach. To reach the ranks of professional coaching, a person usually needs years of coaching experience and a winning record in the lower ranks.

Head coaches at public secondary schools and sports instructors at all levels usually must have a bachelor's degree. (For information on teachers, including those specializing in physical education, see the section on teachers—preschool, kindergarten, elementary, middle, and secondary elsewhere in the *Handbook*.) Those who are not teachers must meet State requirements for certification to become a head coach. Certification, however, may not be required for coaching and sports instructor jobs in private schools. Degree programs specifically related to coaching include exercise and sports science, physiology, kinesiology, nutrition and fitness, physical education, and sports medicine.

For those interested in becoming a tennis, golf, karate, or other kind of instructor, certification is highly desirable. Often, one must be at least 18 years old and certified in cardiopulmonary resuscitation (CPR). There are many certifying organizations specific to the various sports, and their training requirements vary. Participation in a clinic, camp, or school usually is required for certification. Part-time workers and those in smaller facilities are less likely to need formal education or training.

For example, there are two organizations that certify tennis instructors and coaches—the Professional Tennis Registry, an international organization, and the U.S. Professional Tennis Association. Both organizations offer three levels of certification, but the requirements are slightly different. Each level of certification is based on the candidate's National Tennis Rating Program rating, teaching experience, and score on the organization's written and practical certifying exams. There are also minimum age requirements for each level.

Each sport has specific requirements for umpires, referees, and other sports officials. Umpires, referees, and other sports officials often begin their careers by volunteering for intramural, community, and recreational league competitions. To officiate at high school athletic events, officials must register with the State agency that oversees high school athletics and pass an exam on the rules of the particular game. For college refereeing, candidates must be certified by an officiating school and be evaluated during a probationary period. Some larger college sports conferences require officials to have certification and other qualifications, such as residence in or near the conference boundaries, along with several years of experience officiating at high school, community college, or other college conference games.

Standards are even more stringent for officials in professional sports. Whereas umpires for high school baseball need a high school diploma or its equivalent, 20/20 vision, and quick reflexes, those seeking to officiate at minor or major league games must attend professional umpire training school. Currently, there are two schools whose curriculums have been approved by the Professional Baseball Umpires Corporation for training. Top graduates are selected for further evaluation while officiating in a rookie minor league. Umpires then usually need 8 to 10 years of experience in various minor leagues before being considered for major league jobs. Becoming an official for professional football also is competitive, as candidates must have at least 10 years of officiating experience, with 5 of them at a collegiate varsity or minor professional level. For the National Football League (NFL), prospective trainees are interviewed by clinical psychologists to determine levels of intelligence and ability to handle extremely stressful situations. In addition, the NFL's security department conducts thorough background checks. Potential candidates are likely to be interviewed by a panel from the NFL officiating department and are given a comprehensive examination on the rules of the sport.

Scouting jobs require experience playing a sport at the college or professional level that makes it possible to spot young players who possess extraordinary athletic ability and skills. Most beginning scouting jobs are as part-time talent spotters in a particular area or region. Hard work and a record of success often lead to full-time jobs responsible for bigger territories. Some scouts advance to scouting director jobs or various administrative positions in sports.

Athletes, coaches, umpires, and related workers must relate well to others and possess good communication and leadership skills. Coaches also must be resourceful and flexible to successfully instruct and motivate individuals and groups of athletes.

Employment

Athletes, coaches, umpires, and related workers held about 212,000 jobs in 2004. Coaches and scouts held 178,000 jobs; athletes, 17,000; and umpires, referees, and other sports officials, 16,000. Nearly 37 percent of athletes, coaches, umpires, and related workers worked part time, while 20 percent maintained variable schedules. Many sports officials and coaches receive such small and irregular payments for their services— occasional officiating at club games, for example—that they may not consider themselves employed in these occupations, even part time.

Among those employed in wage and salary jobs, 30 percent held jobs in private educational services. About 15 percent worked in amusement, gambling, and recreation industries, including golf and tennis clubs, gymnasiums, health clubs, judo and karate schools, riding stables, swim clubs, and other sports and recreation facilities. Another 9 percent worked in the spectator sports industry.

About 1 out of 4 workers in this occupation was self-employed, earning prize money or fees for lessons, scouting, or officiating assignments. Many other coaches and sports officials, although technically not self-employed, have such irregular or tenuous working arrangements that their working conditions resemble those of self-employment.

Job Outlook

Employment of athletes, coaches, umpires, and related workers is expected to increase faster than the average for all occupations through the year 2014. Employment will grow as the general public continues to participate in organized sports for entertainment, recreation, and physical conditioning. Increasing participation in organized sports by girls and women will boost demand for coaches, umpires, and related workers. Job growth also will be driven by the increasing number of baby boomers approaching retirement, during which they are expected to participate more and require instruction in leisure activities such as golf and tennis. The large number of children of baby boomers also will be active participants in high school and college athletics and will require coaches and instructors.

Employment of coaches and instructors also will increase with expansion of school and college athletic programs and growing demand for private sports instruction. Sports-related job growth within education also will be driven by the decisions of local school

boards. Population growth dictates the construction of additional schools, particularly in the expanding suburbs, but funding for athletic programs often is cut first when budgets become tight. Still, the popularity of team sports often enables shortfalls to be offset somewhat by assistance from fundraisers, booster clubs, and parents. Persons who are State-certified to teach academic subjects in addition to physical education are likely to have the best prospects for obtaining coaching and instructor jobs. The need to replace the many high school coaches who change occupations or leave the labor force entirely also will provide some coaching opportunities.

Competition for professional athlete jobs will continue to be extremely intense. Opportunities to make a living as a professional in individual sports such as golf or tennis may grow as new tournaments are established and as prize money distributed to participants increases. Because most professional athletes' careers last only a few years due to debilitating injuries and age, annual turnover in these jobs is high, creating some job opportunities. However, the talented young men and women who dream of becoming sports superstars greatly outnumber and will compete aggressively for these openings.

Opportunities should be best for persons seeking part-time umpire, referee, and other sports official jobs at the high school level. Competition is expected for higher paying jobs at the college level and will be even greater for jobs in professional sports. Competition should be very keen for jobs as scouts, particularly for professional teams, because the number of available positions is limited.

Earnings

Median annual earnings of athletes were $48,310 in May 2004. However, the highest paid professional athletes earn much more.

Median annual earnings of umpires and related workers were $21,260 in May 2004. The middle 50 percent earned between $16,870 and $31,390. The lowest paid 10 percent earned less than $14,160, and the highest paid 10 percent earned more than $44,140.

In May 2004, median annual earnings of coaches and scouts were $26,350. The middle 50 percent earned between $17,230 and $40,460. The lowest paid 10 percent earned less than $13,320, and the highest paid 10 percent earned more than $57,800. However, the highest paid professional coaches earn much more. Median annual earnings in the industries employing the largest numbers of coaches and scouts in May 2004 are shown below:

Colleges, universities, and professional schools	$36,610
Other amusement and recreation industries	26,340
Other schools and instruction	22,560
Elementary and secondary schools	21,970
Civic and social organizations	19,020

Earnings vary by level of education, certification, and geographic region. Some instructors and coaches are paid a salary, while others may be paid by the hour, per session, or based on the number of participants.

Related Occupations

Athletes and coaches use their extensive knowledge of physiology and sports to instruct, inform, and encourage sports participants. Other workers with similar duties include dietitians and nutritionists; physical therapists; recreation workers; fitness workers; recreational therapists; and teachers—preschool, kindergarten, elementary, middle, and secondary.

Sources of Additional Information

For information about sports officiating for team and individual sports, contact:

➤ National Association of Sports Officials, 2017 Lathrop Ave., Racine, WI 53405. Internet: **http://www.naso.org**

For more information about certification of tennis instructors and coaches, contact:

➤ Professional Tennis Registry, P.O. Box 4739, Hilton Head Island, SC 29938. Internet: **http://www.ptrtennis.org**

➤ U.S. Professional Tennis Association, 3535 Briarpark Dr., Suite One, Houston, TX 77042. Internet: **http://www.uspta.org**

Dancers and Choreographers

(O*NET 27-2031.00, 27-2032.00)

Significant Points

● Many dancers stop performing by their late thirties, but some remain in the field as choreographers, dance teachers, or artistic directors.

● Most dancers begin formal training at an early age—between 5 and 15—and many have their first professional audition by age 17 or 18.

● Dancers and choreographers face intense competition; only the most talented find regular work.

Nature of the Work

From ancient times to the present, dancers have expressed ideas, stories, and rhythm with their bodies. They use a variety of dance forms that allow free movement and self-expression, including classical ballet, modern dance, and culturally specific dance styles. Many dancers combine performance work with teaching or choreography.

Dancers perform in a variety of settings, such as musical productions, and may present folk, ethnic, tap, jazz, and other popular kinds of dance. They also perform in opera, musical theater, television, movies, music videos, and commercials, in which they also may sing and act. Dancers most often perform as part of a group, although a few top artists perform solo.

Dancers work with choreographers, who create original dances and develop new interpretations of existing dances. Because few dance routines are written down, choreographers instruct performers at rehearsals to achieve the desired effect. In addition, choreographers usually are involved in auditioning performers.

Working Conditions

Dance is strenuous. Many dancers stop performing by their late thirties because of the physical demands on the body. However, some continue to work in the field as choreographers, dance teachers and coaches, or artistic directors. Others move into administrative positions, such as company managers. A few celebrated dancers, however, continue performing even beyond the age of 50.

Daily rehearsals require very long hours. Many dance companies tour for part of the year to supplement a limited performance schedule at home. Dancers who perform in musical productions and other family entertainment spend much of their time on the road; others work in nightclubs or on cruise ships. Most dance performances are in the evening, whereas rehearsals and practice take place during the day. As a result, dancers often work very long and late hours. Generally, dancers and choreographers work in modern and temperature-controlled facilities; however, some studios may be older and less comfortable.

Training, Other Qualifications, and Advancement

Training varies with the type of dance and is a continuous part of all dancers' careers. Many dancers and dance instructors believe

Dancers must be fit and limber to endure the physical demands of their work.

that dancers should start with a good foundation in classical dance before selecting a particular dance style. Ballet training for women usually begins at 5 to 8 years of age with a private teacher or through an independent ballet school. Serious training traditionally begins between the ages of 10 and 12. Men often begin their ballet training between the ages of 10 and 15. Students who demonstrate potential in their early teens may seek out more intensive and advanced professional training. At about this time, students should begin to focus their training on a particular style and decide whether to pursue additional training through a dance company's school or a college dance program. Leading dance school companies often have summer training programs from which they select candidates for admission to their regular full-time training programs. Formal training for modern and culturally specific dancers often begins later than training in ballet; however, many folk dance forms are taught to very young children. Many dancers have their first professional auditions by age 17 or 18.

Training is an important component of professional dancers' careers. Dancers normally spend 8 hours a day in class and rehearsal, keeping their bodies in shape and preparing for performances. Their daily training period includes time to warm up and cool down before and after classes and rehearsals.

Because of the strenuous and time-consuming training required, some dancers view formal education as secondary. However, a broad, general education including music, literature, history, and the visual arts is helpful in the interpretation of dramatic episodes, ideas, and feelings. Dancers sometimes conduct research to learn more about the part they are playing.

Many colleges and universities award bachelor's or master's degrees in dance, typically through departments of dance, theater, or fine arts. The National Association of Schools of Dance accredits about 60 programs in dance. Many programs concentrate on modern dance, but some also offer courses in jazz, culturally specific, ballet, or classical techniques; dance composition, history, and criticism; and movement analysis.

A college education is not essential to obtaining employment as a professional dancer; however, many dancers obtain degrees in unrelated fields to prepare themselves for careers after dance. The completion of a college program in dance and education is essential to qualify to teach dance in college, high school, or elementary school. Colleges and conservatories sometimes require graduate degrees but may accept performance experience. A college background is not necessary, however, for teaching dance or choreography in local recreational programs. Studio schools prefer teachers to have experience as performers.

Because of the rigorous practice schedules of most dancers, self-discipline, patience, perseverance, and a devotion to dance are essential for success in the field. Dancers also must possess good problem-solving skills and an ability to work with people. Good health and physical stamina also are necessary attributes. Above all, dancers must have flexibility, agility, coordination, grace, a sense of rhythm, a feeling for music, and a creative ability to express themselves through movement.

Because dancers typically perform as members of an ensemble made up of other dancers, musicians, and directors or choreographers, they must be able to function as part of a team. They also should be highly motivated and prepared to face the anxiety of intermittent employment and rejections when auditioning for work. For dancers, advancement takes the form of a growing reputation, more frequent work, bigger and better roles, and higher pay. Some dancers may take on added responsibilities, such as by becoming a dance captain in musical theater or ballet master/ballet mistress in concert dance companies, by leading rehearsals, or by working with less experienced dancers in the absence of the choreographer.

Choreographers typically are experienced dancers with years of practice working in the theater. Through their performance as dancers, they develop reputations that often lead to opportunities to choreograph productions.

Employment

Professional dancers and choreographers held about 38,000 jobs in 2004. Many others were between engagements, so that the total number of people available for work as dancers over the course of the year was greater. Dancers and choreographers worked in a variety of industries, such as private educational services, which includes dance studios and schools, as well as colleges and universities; food services and drinking establishments; performing arts companies, which includes dance, theater, and opera companies; and amusement and recreation venues, such as casinos and theme parks. Over one-fifth of dancers and choreographers were self-employed.

Most major cities serve as home to major dance companies; however, many smaller communities across the Nation also support home-grown, full-time professional dance companies.

Job Outlook

Dancers and choreographers face intense competition for jobs. Only the most talented find regular employment.

Employment of dancers and choreographers is expected to grow about as fast as the average for all occupations through 2014. The public's continued interest in dance will sustain larger dance companies, but funding from public and private organizations is not expected to keep pace with rising production costs. For many small and midsize organizations, the result will be fewer performances and more limited employment opportunities. Although job openings will arise each year because dancers and choreographers retire or leave the occupation for other reasons, the number of applicants will continue to vastly exceed the number of job openings.

National dance companies likely will continue to provide jobs in this field. Opera companies and dance groups affiliated with colleges and universities and with television and motion pictures also will offer some opportunities. Moreover, the growing popularity of dance for recreational and fitness purposes has resulted in increased opportunities to teach dance. Finally, music video channels will provide opportunities for both dancers and choreographers.

Earnings

Median hourly earnings of dancers were $8.54 in May 2004. The middle 50 percent earned between $6.71 and $15.62. The lowest

10 percent earned less than $5.87, and the highest 10 percent earned more than $21.59. Annual earnings data for dancers were not available, because of the wide variation in the number of hours worked by dancers and the short-term nature of many jobs—which may last for 1 day or 1 week—made it extremely rare for dancers to have guaranteed employment that exceeded 3 to 6 months. Median hourly earnings in the industries employing the largest number of dancers were as follows:

Other schools and instruction	$14.94
Performing arts companies	14.82
Drinking places, alcoholic beverages	6.78
Other amusement and recreation industries	7.68

Median annual earnings of salaried choreographers were $33,670 in May 2004. The middle 50 percent earned between $21,530 and $48,940. The lowest 10 percent earned less than $14,980, and the highest 10 percent earned more than $68,190. Median annual earnings were $34,090 in "other schools and instruction," a North American Industry Classification System category that includes dance studios and schools.

Dancers who were on tour usually received an additional allowance for room and board, as well as extra compensation for overtime. Earnings from dancing are usually low because employment is part year and irregular. Dancers often supplement their income by working as guest artists with other dance companies, teaching dance, or taking jobs unrelated to the field.

Earnings of dancers at many of the largest companies and in commercial settings are governed by union contracts. Dancers in the major opera ballet, classical ballet, and modern dance corps belong to the American Guild of Musical Artists, Inc. of the AFL-CIO; those who appear on live or videotaped television programs belong to the American Federation of Television and Radio Artists; those who perform in films and on television belong to the Screen Actors Guild; and those in musical theater are members of the Actors' Equity Association. The unions and producers sign basic agreements specifying minimum salary rates, hours of work, benefits, and other conditions of employment. However, the contract each dancer signs with the producer of the show may be more favorable than the basic agreement.

Most salaried dancers and choreographers covered by union contracts receive some paid sick leave and various health and pension benefits, including extended sick pay and family-leave benefits provided by their unions. Employers contribute toward these benefits. Dancers and choreographers not covered by union contracts usually do not enjoy such benefits.

Related Occupations

People who work in other performing arts occupations include actors, producers, and directors and musicians, singers, and related workers. Those directly involved in the production of dance programs include set and exhibit designers; fashion designers; and barbers, cosmetologists, and other personal appearance workers. Like dancers, athletes, coaches, umpires, and related workers need strength, flexibility, and agility.

Sources of Additional Information

For general information about dance and a list of accredited college-level programs, contact:

➤ National Association of Schools of Dance, 11250 Roger Bacon Dr., Suite 21, Reston, VA 20190. Internet: http://nasd.arts-accredit.org

For information about dance and dance companies, contact:

➤ Dance/USA, 1156 15th St., NW., Suite 820, Washington, DC 20005. Internet: www.danceusa.org

Musicians, Singers, and Related Workers

(O*NET 27-2041.01, 27-2041.02, 27-2041.03, 27-2042.01, 27-2042.02)

Significant Points

- Part-time schedules and intermittent unemployment are common; many musicians supplement their income with earnings from other sources.

- Aspiring musicians begin studying an instrument or training their voices at an early age.

- Competition for jobs is keen; those who can play several instruments and perform a wide range of musical styles should enjoy the best job prospects.

Nature of the Work

Musicians, singers, and related workers play musical instruments, sing, compose or arrange music, or conduct groups in instrumental or vocal performances. They may perform solo or as part of a group. Musicians, singers, and related workers entertain live audiences in nightclubs, concert halls, and theaters featuring opera, musical theater, or dance. Many of these entertainers play for live audiences; others perform exclusively for recording or production studios. Regardless of the setting, musicians, singers, and related workers spend considerable time practicing, alone and with their bands, orchestras, or other musical ensembles.

Musicians often gain their reputation or professional standing by exhibiting a high level of professionalism and proficiency in a particular kind of music or performance. However, those who learn several related instruments and who can perform equally well in several musical styles have better employment opportunities. Instrumental musicians, for example, may play in a symphony orchestra, rock group, or jazz combo one night, appear in another ensemble the next, and work in a studio band the following day. Some play a variety of string, brass, woodwind, or percussion instruments or electronic synthesizers.

Singers interpret music and text, using their knowledge of voice production, melody, and harmony. They sing character parts or perform in their own individual style. Singers are often classified according to their voice range—soprano, contralto, tenor, baritone, or bass—or by the type of music they sing, such as opera, rock, popular, folk, rap, or country and western.

Music directors conduct, direct, plan, and lead instrumental or vocal performances by musical groups, such as orchestras, choirs, and glee clubs. *Conductors* lead instrumental music groups, such as symphony orchestras, dance bands, show bands, and various popular ensembles. These leaders audition and select musicians, choose the music most appropriate for their talents and abilities, and direct rehearsals and performances. Choral directors lead choirs and glee clubs, sometimes working with a band or an orchestra conductor. Directors audition and select singers and lead them at rehearsals and performances to achieve harmony, rhythm, tempo, shading, and other desired musical effects.

Composers create original music such as symphonies, operas, sonatas, radio and television jingles, film scores, and popular songs. They transcribe ideas into musical notation, using harmony, rhythm, melody, and tonal structure. Although most composers and songwriters practice their craft on instruments and transcribe the notes with pen and paper, some use computer software to compose and edit their music.

Musicians and singers perform in a variety of settings, inlcuding concert halls, nightclubs, and outdoor venues.

Arrangers transcribe and adapt musical compositions to a particular style for orchestras, bands, choral groups, or individuals. Components of music—including tempo, volume, and the mix of instruments needed—are arranged to express the composer's message. While some arrangers write directly into a musical composition, others use computer software to make changes.

Working Conditions

Musicians typically perform at night and on weekends. They spend much additional time practicing or in rehearsal. Full-time musicians with long-term employment contracts, such as those with symphony orchestras or television and film production companies, enjoy steady work and less travel. Nightclub, solo, or recital musicians frequently travel to perform in a variety of local settings and may tour nationally or internationally. Because many musicians find only part-time or intermittent work, experiencing unemployment between engagements, they often supplement their income with other types of jobs. The stress of constantly looking for work leads many musicians to accept permanent, full-time jobs in other occupations, while working only part time as musicians.

Most instrumental musicians work closely with a variety of other people, including their colleagues, agents, employers, sponsors, and audiences. Although they usually work indoors, some perform outdoors for parades, concerts, and festivals. In some nightclubs and restaurants, smoke and odors may be present, and lighting and ventilation may be poor.

Training, Other Qualifications, and Advancement

Aspiring musicians begin studying an instrument at an early age. They may gain valuable experience playing in a school or community band or an orchestra or with a group of friends. Singers usually start training when their voices mature. Participation in school musicals or choirs often provides good early training and experience.

Musicians need extensive and prolonged training and practice to acquire the necessary skills, knowledge, and ability to interpret music at a professional level. Like other artists, musicians and singers continually strive to stretch themselves—exploring different forms of music. Formal training may be obtained through private study with an accomplished musician, in a college or university music program, or in a music conservatory. For university or conservatory study, an audition generally is necessary. The National Association of Schools of Music accredits more than 600 college-level programs in music. Courses typically include music theory, music interpretation, composition, conducting, and performance in a particular instrument or in voice. Music directors, composers, conductors, and arrangers need considerable related work experience or advanced training in these subjects.

Many colleges, universities, and music conservatories grant bachelor's or higher degrees in music. A master's or doctoral degree usually is required to teach advanced music courses in colleges and universities; a bachelor's degree may be sufficient to teach basic courses. A degree in music education qualifies graduates for a State certificate to teach music in public elementary or secondary schools. Musicians who do not meet public school music education requirements may teach in private schools and recreation associations or instruct individual students in private sessions.

Musicians must be knowledgeable about a broad range of musical styles but keenly aware of the form that interests them most. Having a broader range of interest, knowledge, and training can help expand employment opportunities and musical abilities. Voice training and private instrumental lessons, taken especially when the individual is young, also help develop technique and enhance one's performance.

Young persons considering careers in music should have musical talent, versatility, creativity, poise, and a good stage presence. Because quality performance requires constant study and practice, self-discipline is vital. To sustain a career as a musician or singer, performers must achieve a level performing excellence and be counted on to be on their game whenever they perform. Moreover, musicians who play in concerts or in nightclubs and those who tour must have physical stamina to endure frequent travel and an irregular performance schedule. Because musicians and singers always must make their performances look effortless, preparation and practice are important. Musicians and singers also must be prepared to face the anxiety of intermittent employment and of rejection when auditioning for work.

Advancement for musicians usually means becoming better known, finding work more easily, and performing for higher earnings. Successful musicians often rely on agents or managers to find them performing engagements, negotiate contracts, and develop their careers.

Employment

Musicians, singers, and related workers held about 249,000 jobs in 2004. Around 40 percent worked part time; almost half were self-employed. Many found jobs in cities in which entertainment and recording activities are concentrated, such as New York, Los Angeles, Las Vegas, Chicago, and Nashville.

Musicians, singers, and related workers are employed in a variety of settings. Of those who earn a wage or salary, almost two-thirds were employed by religious organizations and almost one-fourth by performing arts companies such as professional orchestras, small chamber music groups, opera companies, musical theater companies, and ballet troupes. Musicians and singers also perform in nightclubs and restaurants and for weddings and other events. Well-known musicians and groups may perform in concerts, appear on radio and television broadcasts, and make recordings and music videos. The Armed Forces also offer careers in their bands and smaller musical groups.

Job Outlook

Competition for jobs for musicians, singers, and related workers is expected to be keen. The vast number of persons with the desire to perform will continue to greatly exceed the number of openings. Talent alone is no guarantee of success: many people start out to become musicians or singers but leave the profession because they find the work difficult, the discipline demanding, and the long periods of intermittent unemployment unendurable.

Overall employment of musicians, singers, and related workers is expected to grow about as fast as the average for all occupations through 2014. Most new wage and salary jobs for musicians will arise in religious organizations. Slower-than-average growth is expected for self-employed musicians, who generally perform in nightclubs, concert tours, and other venues. Growth in demand for musicians will generate a number of job opportunities, and many openings also will arise from the need to replace those who leave the field each year because they are unable to make a living solely as musicians or for other reasons.

Earnings

Median hourly earnings of musicians and singers were $17.85 in May 2004. The middle 50 percent earned between $9.68 and $30.75. The lowest 10 percent earned less than $6.47, and the highest 10 percent earned more than $53.59. Median hourly earnings were $20.70 in performing arts companies and $12.17 in religious organizations. Annual earnings data for musicians and singers were not available, because of the wide variation in the number of hours worked by musicians and singers and the short-term nature of many jobs, which may last for 1 day or 1 week; it is extremely rare for musicians and singers to have guaranteed employment that exceeds 3 to 6 months.

Median annual earnings of salaried music directors and composers were $34,570 in May 2004. The middle 50 percent earned between $24,040 and $51,770. The lowest 10 percent earned less than $15,960, and the highest 10 percent earned more than $75,380.

Yearly earnings typically reflect the number of gigs a freelance musician or singer played or the number of hours and weeks of salaried contract work, in addition to a performer's professional reputation and setting: performers who can fill large concert halls, arenas, or outdoor stadiums generally command higher pay than those who perform in local clubs. Soloists or headliners usually receive higher earnings than band members or opening acts. The most successful musicians earn performance or recording fees that far exceed the median earnings.

According to the American Federation of Musicians, weekly minimum salaries in major orchestras ranged from about $700 to $2,080 during the 2004–05 performing season. Each orchestra works out a separate contract with its local union, but individual musicians may negotiate higher salaries. Top orchestras have a season ranging from 24 to 52 weeks, with 18 orchestras reporting 52-week contracts. In regional orchestras, minimum salaries are often less because fewer performances are scheduled. Regional orchestra musicians often are paid for their services, without any guarantee of future employment. Community orchestras often have even more limited levels of funding and offer salaries that are much lower for seasons of shorter duration.

Although musicians employed by some symphony orchestras work under master wage agreements, which guarantee a season's work up to 52 weeks, many other musicians face relatively long periods of unemployment between jobs. Even when employed, many musicians and singers work part time in unrelated occupations. Thus, their earnings usually are lower than earnings in many other occupations. Moreover, because they may not work steadily for one employer, some performers cannot qualify for unemployment compensation, and few have typical benefits such as sick leave or paid vacations. For these reasons, many musicians give private lessons or take jobs unrelated to music to supplement their earnings as performers.

Many musicians belong to a local of the American Federation of Musicians. Professional singers who perform live often belong to a branch of the American Guild of Musical Artists; those who record for the broadcast industries may belong to the American Federation of Television and Radio Artists.

Related Occupations

Musical instrument repairers and tuners (part of precision instrument and equipment repairers) require technical knowledge of musical instruments. Others whose work involves the performing arts include actors, producers, and directors; announcers; and dancers and choreographers.

Sources of Additional Information

For general information about music and music teacher education and a list of accredited college-level programs, contact:
➤ National Association of Schools of Music, 11250 Roger Bacon Dr., Suite 21, Reston, VA 20190. Internet: **http://nasm.arts-accredit.org**

Media and Communication-Related Occupations

Announcers

(O*NET 27-3011.00, 27-3012.00)

Significant Points

- Competition for announcer jobs will continue to be keen.

- Jobs at small stations usually have low pay, but offer the best opportunities for inexperienced announcers.

- Related work experience at a campus radio station or as an intern at a commercial station can be helpful in breaking into the occupation.

- Employment is projected to decline.

Nature of the Work

Announcers in radio and television perform a variety of tasks on and off the air. They announce station program information, such as program schedules and station breaks for commercials, or public service information, and they introduce and close programs. Announcers read prepared scripts or ad lib commentary on the air, as they present news, sports, the weather, time, and commercials. If a written script is required, they may do the research and writing. Announcers also interview guests and moderate panels or discussions. Some provide commentary for the audience during sporting events, at parades, and on other occasions. Announcers often are well known to radio and television audiences and may make promotional appearances and do remote broadcasts for their stations.

Radio announcers who broadcast music often are called *disc jockeys (DJs)*. Some DJs specialize in one kind of music, announcing selections as they air them. Most DJs do not select much of the music they play (although they often did so in the past); instead, they follow schedules of commercials, talk, and music provided to them by management. While on the air, DJs comment on the music, weather, and traffic. They may take requests from listeners, interview guests, and manage listener contests.

Newscasters, or *anchors*, work at large stations and specialize in news, sports, or weather. (See the related statement on news analysts, reporters, and correspondents elsewhere in the *Handbook*.) *Show hosts* may specialize in a certain area of interest, such as politics, personal finance, sports, or health. They contribute to the preparation of the program's content, interview guests, and discuss issues with viewers, listeners, or the studio audience.

Announcers at smaller stations may cover all of these areas and tend to have more off-air duties as well. They may operate the control board, monitor the transmitter, sell commercial time to advertisers, keep a log of the station's daily programming, and produce advertisements and other recorded material. Advances in technology make it possible for announcers to do some work previously performed by broadcast technicians. At many music stations, the announcer is simultaneously responsible both for

Announcers at radio and television stations provide information to their audiences, including station programming information and public service announcements.

announcing and for operating the control board, which is used to broadcast programming, commercials, and public-service announcements according to the station's schedule. (See the statement on broadcast and sound engineering technicians and radio operators elsewhere in the *Handbook*.) Public radio and television announcers are involved in station fundraising efforts.

Changes in technology have led to more remote operation of stations. Several stations in different locations of the same region may be operated from one office. Some stations operate overnight without any staff, playing programming from a satellite feed or using programming that was recorded earlier, including segments from announcers.

Public address system announcers provide information to the audience at sporting, performing arts, and other events. Some

DJs announce and play music at clubs, dances, restaurants, and weddings. They generally have their own equipment with which to produce announcements and other material, and they rent their services out on a job-by-job basis.

Announcers frequently participate in community activities. Sports announcers, for example, may serve as masters of ceremonies at sports club banquets or may greet customers at openings of sporting goods stores.

Working Conditions

Announcers usually work in well-lighted, air-conditioned, sound-proof studios. The broadcast day is long for radio and TV stations—many are on the air 24 hours a day—so announcers can expect to work unusual hours. Many present early-morning shows, when most people are getting ready for work or commuting, while others do late-night programs. The shifts, however, may not be as varied as in the past because new technology is allowing stations to prerecord programs and air them at a later time, especially for the overnight hours.

Announcers often work within tight schedules, which can be physically and mentally stressful. For many announcers, the intangible rewards—creative work, many personal contacts, and the satisfaction of becoming widely known—far outweigh the disadvantages of irregular and often unpredictable hours, work pressures, and disrupted personal lives.

Training, Other Qualifications, and Advancement

Entry into this occupation is highly competitive. Formal training in broadcasting from a college, a technical school, or a private broadcasting school is valuable. These programs prepare students to work with emerging technologies, a skill that is becoming increasingly important. Many announcers have a bachelor's degree in a major such as communications, broadcasting, or journalism. Station officials pay particular attention to taped auditions that show an applicant's delivery and—in television—appearance and style in commercials, news reports, and interviews. Those hired by television stations usually start out as production assistants, researchers, or reporters and are given a chance to move into announcing if they show an aptitude for "on-air" work. A beginner's chance of landing an on-air job is remote. The best chances for an on-air job for inexperienced announcers may be as a substitute for a familiar announcer at a small radio station or on the late-night shift at a larger station. In radio, newcomers usually start out taping interviews and operating equipment.

Announcers usually begin at a station in a small community and, if they are qualified, may move to a better paying job in a large city. They also may advance by hosting a regular program as a disc jockey, sportscaster, or other specialist. Competition for employment by networks is particularly intense, and employers look for college graduates with at least several years of successful announcing experience.

Announcers must have a pleasant and well-controlled voice, good timing, excellent pronunciation, and correct grammar. College broadcasting programs offer courses, such as voice and diction, to help students improve their vocal qualities. Television announcers need a neat, pleasing appearance as well. Knowledge of theater, sports, music, business, politics, and other subjects likely to be covered in broadcasts improves one's chances for success. Announcers should be capable of using computers, editing equipment, and other broadcast-related devices because new advances in technology allow more of these responsibilities to be incorporated into an announcer's work. Announcers also need strong writing skills, because they normally write their own material. In addition, they should be able to ad lib all or part of a show and to work under tight deadlines. The most successful announcers attract a large audience by combining a pleasing personality and voice with an appealing style.

High school and college courses in English, public speaking, drama, foreign languages, and computer science are valuable, and hobbies such as sports and music are additional assets. Students may gain valuable experience at campus radio or TV facilities and at commercial stations while serving as interns. Paid or unpaid internships provide students with hands-on training and the chance to establish contacts in the industry. Unpaid interns often receive college credit and are allowed to observe and assist station employees. Although the Fair Labor Standards Act limits the amount of work that unpaid interns may perform in a station, unpaid internships are more common than paid internships. Unpaid internships sometimes lead to paid internships, however, which are valuable because interns do work ordinarily performed by regular employees and may even go on the air.

Individuals considering enrolling in a broadcasting school should contact personnel managers of radio and television stations, as well as broadcasting trade organizations, to determine the school's reputation for producing suitably trained candidates.

Employment

Announcers held about 69,000 jobs in 2004. About 57 percent were employed in broadcasting. Another 27 percent were self-employed freelance announcers who sold their services for individual assignments to networks and stations, to advertising agencies and other independent producers, or to sponsors of local events. About 30 percent of all announcers worked part time.

Job Outlook

Competition for jobs as announcers will be keen because the broadcasting field attracts many more jobseekers than there are jobs. Small radio stations are more inclined to hire beginners, but the pay is low. Applicants who have completed internships and those with related work experience usually receive preference for available positions. Because competition for ratings is so intense in major metropolitan areas, large stations will continue to seek announcers who have proven that they can attract and retain a sizable audience. Announcers who are knowledgeable about business, consumer, and health news also may have an advantage over others. While subject-matter specialization is more common at large stations and the networks, many small stations also encourage it.

Employment of announcers is projected to decline through 2014 because of the lack of growth in the number of new radio and television stations and the consolidation of existing stations. Some job openings will arise from the need to replace those who transfer to other kinds of work or leave the labor force. In some cases, announcers leave the field because they cannot advance to better paying jobs. Changes in station ownership, format, and ratings frequently cause periods of unemployment for many announcers.

Increasing consolidation of radio and television stations, the advent of new technology, and growth of alternative media sources, such as cable television and satellite radio, will contribute to the expected decline in employment of announcers. Consolidation among broadcasting companies may lead to an increased use of syndicated programming and programs originating outside a station's viewing or listening area. Digital technology is increasing the productivity of announcers, reducing the time required to edit material or perform other off-air technical and production work.

Earnings

Salaries in broadcasting vary widely, but generally are relatively low, except for announcers who work for large stations in major markets or for networks. Earnings are higher in television than in radio and higher in commercial broadcasting than in public broadcasting.

Median hourly earnings of wage and salary radio and television announcers in May 2004 were $10.64. The middle 50 percent earned between $7.43 and $16.81. The lowest 10 percent earned less than $6.16, and the highest 10 percent earned more than $27.61. Median hourly earnings of radio and television announcers were $10.49 in the radio and television broadcasting industry.

Median hourly earnings of wage and salary public address and other system announcers in May 2004 were $10.56. The middle 50 percent earned between $7.72 and $16.24. The lowest 10 percent earned less than $6.33 and the highest 10 percent earned more than $23.90.

Related Occupations

The success of announcers depends upon how well they communicate. Others who must be skilled at oral communication include news analysts, reporters, and correspondents; interpreters and translators; salespersons and those in related occupations; and public-relations specialists. Many announcers also must entertain their audience, so their work is similar to other entertainment-related occupations, such as actors, producers, and directors; and musicians, singers, and related workers. Some announcers write their own material, as do writers and editors. Announcers perform a variety of duties, including some technical operations, as do broadcast and sound engineering technicians and radio operators.

Sources of Additional Information

General information on the broadcasting industry, in which many announcers are employed, is available from:

➤ National Association of Broadcasters, 1771 N St. NW., Washington, DC 20036. Internet: **http://www.nab.org**

Broadcast and Sound Engineering Technicians and Radio Operators

(O*NET 27-4011.00, 27-4012.00, 27-4013.00, 27-4014.00)

Significant Points

- Job applicants will face keen competition for jobs in major metropolitan areas, where pay generally is higher; prospects are expected to be better in small cities and towns.

- Technical school, community college, or college training in broadcast technology, electronics, or computer networking provides the best preparation.

- About 30 percent work in broadcasting, mainly for radio and television stations, and 17 percent work in the motion picture, video, and sound recording industries.

- Evening, weekend, and holiday work is common.

Nature of the Work

Broadcast and sound engineering technicians and radio operators set up, operate, and maintain a wide variety of electrical and electronic equipment involved in almost any radio or television broadcast, concert, play, musical recording, television show, or movie. With such a range of work, there are many specialized occupations within the field.

Audio and video equipment technicians set up and operate audio and video equipment, including microphones, sound speakers, video

Broadcast and sound engineering technicians and radio operators operate a wide variety of electrical and electronic equipment.

screens, projectors, video monitors, recording equipment, connecting wires and cables, sound and mixing boards, and related electronic equipment for concerts, sports events, meetings and conventions, presentations, and news conferences. They also may set up and operate associated spotlights and other custom lighting systems.

Broadcast technicians set up, operate, and maintain equipment that regulates the signal strength, clarity, and range of sounds and colors of radio or television broadcasts. These technicians also operate control panels to select the source of the material. Technicians may switch from one camera or studio to another, from film to live programming, or from network to local programming.

Sound engineering technicians operate machines and equipment to record, synchronize, mix, or reproduce music, voices, or sound effects in recording studios, sporting arenas, theater productions, or movie and video productions.

Radio operators mainly receive and transmit communications using a variety of tools. These workers also repair equipment, using such devices as electronic testing equipment, handtools, and power tools. One of their major duties is to help to maintain communication systems in good condition.

The transition to digital recording, editing, and broadcasting has greatly changed the work of broadcast and sound engineering technicians and radio operators. Software on desktop computers has replaced specialized electronic equipment in many recording and editing functions. Most radio and television stations have replaced videotapes and audiotapes with computer hard drives and other computer data storage systems. Computer networks linked to specialized equipment dominate modern broadcasting. This transition has forced technicians to learn computer networking and software skills. (See the statement on computer support specialists and systems administrators elsewhere in the *Handbook*.)

Broadcast and sound engineering technicians and radio operators perform a variety of duties in small stations. In large stations and at the networks, technicians are more specialized, although job assignments may change from day to day. The terms "operator," "engineer," and "technician" often are used interchangeably to describe these jobs. Workers in these positions may monitor and log outgoing signals and operate transmitters; set up, adjust, service, and repair electronic broadcasting equipment; and regulate fidelity, brightness, contrast, volume, and sound quality of television broadcasts.

Technicians also work in program production. *Recording engineers* operate and maintain video and sound recording equipment. They may operate equipment designed to produce special effects, such as the illusions of a bolt of lightning or a police siren. *Sound mixers* or *re-recording mixers* produce soundtracks for movies or television programs. After filming or recording is complete, these workers may use a process called "dubbing" to insert sounds. *Field technicians* set up and operate portable transmission equipment outside the studio. Because television news coverage requires so much electronic equipment and the technology is changing so rapidly, many stations assign technicians exclusively to news.

Chief engineers, transmission engineers, and *broadcast field supervisors* oversee other technicians and maintain broadcasting equipment.

Working Conditions

Broadcast and sound engineering technicians and radio operators generally work indoors in pleasant surroundings. However, those who broadcast news and other programs from locations outside the studio may work outdoors in all types of weather. Technicians doing maintenance may climb poles or antenna towers, while those setting up equipment do heavy lifting.

Technicians at large stations and the networks usually work a 40-hour week under great pressure to meet broadcast deadlines, and may occasionally work overtime. Technicians at small stations routinely work more than 40 hours a week. Evening, weekend, and holiday work is usual because most stations are on the air 18 to 24 hours a day, 7 days a week. Even though a technician may not be on duty when the station is broadcasting, some technicians may be on call during nonwork hours; these workers must handle any problems that occur when they are on call.

Technicians who work on motion pictures may be on a tight schedule and may work long hours to meet contractual deadlines.

Training, Other Qualifications, and Advancement

The best way to prepare for a broadcast and sound engineering technician job is to obtain technical school, community college, or college training in broadcast technology, electronics, or computer networking. In the motion picture industry, people are hired as apprentice editorial assistants and work their way up to more skilled jobs. Employers in the motion picture industry usually hire experienced freelance technicians on a picture-by-picture basis. Reputation and determination are important in getting jobs.

When starting out, broadcast and sound engineering technicians learn skills on the job from experienced technicians and supervisors. These beginners often start their careers in small stations and, once experienced, move on to larger ones. Large stations usually hire only technicians with experience. Experienced technicians can become supervisory technicians or chief engineers. A college degree in engineering is needed in order to become chief engineer at a large television station. Many employers pay tuition and expenses for courses or seminars to help technicians keep abreast of developments in the field.

Audio and video equipment technicians generally need a high school diploma. Many recent entrants have a community college degree or other forms of postsecondary degrees, although they are not always required. These technicians may substitute on-the-job training for formal education requirements. Working in a studio as an assistant is a great way of gaining experience and knowledge.

Radio operators usually are not required to complete any formal training. This is an entry-level position that generally requires on-the-job training.

Licensing is not required for broadcast technicians. However, certification by the Society of Broadcast Engineers is a mark of competence and experience. The certificate is issued to experienced technicians who pass an examination.

Prospective technicians should take high school courses in math, physics, and electronics. Building electronic equipment from hobby kits and operating a "ham," or amateur, radio are good experience, as is working in college radio and television stations.

Broadcast and sound engineering technicians and radio operators must have manual dexterity and an aptitude for working with electrical, electronic, and mechanical systems and equipment.

Employment

Broadcast and sound engineering technicians and radio operators held about 95,000 jobs in 2004. Their employment was distributed among the following detailed occupations:

Audio and video equipment technicians	46,000
Broadcast technicians	34,000
Sound engineering technicians	13,000
Radio operators	2,000

About 30 percent worked in broadcasting (except Internet) and 17 percent worked in the motion picture, video, and sound recording industries. About 7 percent were self-employed. Television stations employ, on average, many more technicians than radio stations. Some technicians are employed in other industries, producing employee communications, sales, and training programs. Technician jobs in television and radio are located in virtually all cities; jobs in radio also are found in many small towns. The highest paying and most specialized jobs are concentrated in New York City, Los Angeles, Chicago, and Washington, DC—the originating centers for most network or news programs. Motion picture production jobs are concentrated in Los Angeles and New York City.

Job Outlook

People seeking entry-level jobs as technicians in broadcasting are expected to face keen competition in major metropolitan areas, where pay generally is higher and the number of qualified jobseekers typically exceeds the number of openings. Prospects for entry-level positions are expected to be better in small cities and towns for beginners with appropriate training.

Overall employment of broadcast and sound engineering technicians and radio operators is expected to grow about as fast as the average for all occupations through the year 2014. Job growth in radio and television broadcasting will be limited by consolidation of ownership of radio and television stations and by labor-saving technical advances, such as computer-controlled programming and remotely controlled transmitters. The Federal Communications Commission (FCC) is required to examine its media ownership rules quadrennially. Thus, the rules can change periodically. In 2005, FCC regulations stated that a single owner could own up to eight radio stations in a single large market and that a single owner could not own television stations that would reach more than 39 percent of households. Revisions to these rules have been passed by the FCC, but have not been implemented because of legal challenges. When broader common ownership is allowed, stations often are consolidated and operated from a single location, reducing employment because one or a few technicians can provide support to multiple stations. Technicians who know how to install transmitters will be in demand as television stations install digital transmitters. Although most television stations are broadcasting in both analog and digital formats and plan to switch entirely to digital, radio stations are only beginning to broadcast digital signals.

Employment of broadcast and sound engineering technicians in the cable and pay television portion of the broadcasting industry is expected to grow as the range of products and services expands, including cable Internet access and video-on-demand. Employment of these workers in the motion picture industry is expected to grow rapidly. However, job prospects are expected to remain competitive because of the large number of people who are attracted by the glamour of working in motion pictures.

Projected job growth varies among detailed occupations in this field. Employment of audio and video equipment technicians and sound engineering technicians is expected to grow faster than the average for all occupations. Not only will these workers have to set up audio and video equipment, but they will have to maintain and repair it as well. Employment of broadcast technicians is expected to grow about as fast as the average for all occupations through 2014, as advancements in technology enhance the capabilities of technicians to produce higher quality radio and television programming. Employment of radio operators, on the other hand, is projected to decline as more stations control programming and operate transmitters remotely.

In addition to employment growth, job openings also will result from the need to replace experienced technicians who leave this field. Some of these workers leave for other jobs that require knowledge of electronics, such as computer repairer or industrial machinery repairer.

Earnings

Television stations usually pay higher salaries than radio stations; commercial broadcasting usually pays more than public broadcasting; and stations in large markets pay more than those in small markets.

Median annual earnings of audio and video equipment technicians in May 2004 were $32,570. The middle 50 percent earned between $24,180 and $44,290. The lowest 10 percent earned less than $19,110, and the highest 10 percent earned more than $58,620. Median annual earnings in motion picture and video industries, which employed the largest number of audio and video equipment technicians, were $33,670.

Median annual earnings of broadcast technicians in May 2004 were $28,010. The middle 50 percent earned between $19,240 and $42,760. The lowest 10 percent earned less than $14,960, and the highest 10 percent earned more than $62,850. Median annual earnings in radio and television broadcasting, which employed the largest number of broadcast technicians, were $25,220.

Median annual earnings of sound engineering technicians in May 2004 were $38,110. The middle 50 percent earned between $25,470 and $56,320. The lowest 10 percent earned less than $19,180, and the highest 10 percent earned more than $80,450.

Median annual earnings of radio operators in May 2004 were $32,720. The middle 50 percent earned between $23,960 and $43,850. The lowest 10 percent earned less than $17,960, and the highest 10 percent earned more than $57,420.

Related Occupations

Broadcast and sound engineering technicians and radio operators need the electronics training necessary to operate technical equipment, and they generally complete specialized postsecondary programs. Occupations with similar characteristics include engineering technicians, science technicians, and electrical and electronics installers and repairers. Broadcast and sound engineering technicians also may operate computer networks, as do computer

support specialists and systems administrators. Broadcast technicians on some live radio and television programs screen incoming calls; these workers have responsibilities similar to those of communications equipment operators.

Sources of Additional Information

For career information and links to employment resources, contact:
➤ National Association of Broadcasters, 1771 N St. NW., Washington, DC 20036. Internet: **http://www.nab.org**

For information on certification, contact:
➤ Society of Broadcast Engineers, 9247 North Meridian St., Suite 305, Indianapolis, IN 46260. Internet: **http://www.sbe.org**

For information on audio and video equipment technicians, contact:
➤ InfoComm International, 11242 Waples Mill Rd., Suite 200, Fairfax, VA 22030. Internet: **http://www.infocomm.org**

Interpreters and Translators

(O*NET 27-3091.00)

Significant Points

● 15 percent of these workers are self-employed.

● Work is often sporadic, and many interpreters and translators work part time.

● Although training requirements can vary, most interpreters and translators have a bachelor's degree.

● Job outlook varies by specialty and language combination.

Nature of the Work

Interpreters and translators enable the cross cultural communication necessary in today's society by converting one language into another. However, these language specialists do more than simply translate words—they relay concepts and ideas between languages. They must thoroughly understand the subject matter in which they work so that they are able to convert information from one language, known as the source language, into another, the target language. In addition, they must remain sensitive to the cultures associated with their languages of expertise.

Interpreters and translators are often discussed together because they share some common traits. For example, both need a special ability, known as language combination. This enables them to be

Interpreters help people who speak, read, and write different languages communicate.

fluent in at least two languages—a native, or active, language and a secondary, or passive, language; a small number of interpreters and translators are fluent in two or more passive languages. Their active language is the one that they know best and into which they interpret or translate, and their passive language is one of which they have nearly perfect knowledge.

Although some people do both, interpretation and translation are different professions. Each requires a distinct set of skills and aptitudes, and most people are better suited for one or the other. While interpreters often work into and from both languages, translators generally work only into their active language.

Interpreters convert one spoken language into another—or, in the case of sign-language interpreters, between spoken communication and sign language. This requires interpreters to pay attention carefully, understand what is communicated in both languages, and express thoughts and ideas clearly. Strong research and analytical skills, mental dexterity, and an exceptional memory also are important.

The first part of an interpreter's work begins before arriving at the jobsite. The interpreter must become familiar with the subject matter that the speakers will discuss, a task that may involve research to create a list of common words and phrases associated with the topic. Next, the interpreter usually travels to the location where his or her services are needed. Physical presence may not be required for some work, such as telephone interpretation. But it is usually important that the interpreter see the communicators in order to hear and observe the person speaking and to relay the message to the other party.

There are two types of interpretation: simultaneous and consecutive. Simultaneous interpretation requires interpreters to listen and speak (or sign) at the same time. In simultaneous interpretation, the interpreter begins to convey a sentence being spoken while the speaker is still talking. Ideally, simultaneous interpreters should be so familiar with a subject that they are able to anticipate the end of the speaker's sentence. Because they need a high degree of concentration, simultaneous interpreters work in pairs, with each interpreting for 20- to 30-minute segments. This type of interpretation is required at international conferences and is sometimes used in the courts.

In contrast to simultaneous interpretation's immediacy, consecutive interpretation begins only after the speaker has verbalized a group of words or sentences. Consecutive interpreters often take notes while listening to the speakers, so they must develop some type of note-taking or shorthand system. This form of interpretation is used most often for person-to-person communication, during which the interpreter sits near both parties.

Translators convert written materials from one language into another. They must have excellent writing and analytical ability. And because the documents that they translate must be as flawless as possible, they also need good editing skills.

Translators' assignments may vary in length, writing style, and subject matter. When they first receive text to convert into another language, translators usually read it in its entirety to get an idea of the subject. Next, they identify and look up any unfamiliar words. Multiple additional readings are usually needed before translators begin to actually write and finalize the translation. Translators also might do additional research on the subject matter if they are unclear about anything in the text. They consult with the text's originator or issuing agency to clarify unclear or unfamiliar ideas, words, or acronyms.

Translating involves more than replacing a word with its equivalent in another language; sentences and ideas must be manipulated to flow with the same coherence as those in the source document so that the translation reads as though it originated in the target language. Translators also must bear in mind any cultural references that may need to be explained to the intended audience, such as colloquialisms, slang, and other expressions that do not translate

literally. Some subjects may be more difficult than others to translate because words or passages may have multiple meanings that make several translations possible. Not surprisingly, translated work often goes through multiple revisions before final text is submitted.

The way in which translators do their jobs has changed with advancements in technology. Today, nearly all translation work is done on a computer, and most assignments are received and submitted electronically. This enables translators to work from almost anywhere, and a large percentage of them work from home. The Internet provides advanced research capabilities and valuable language resources, such as specialized dictionaries and glossaries. In some cases, use of machine-assisted translation—including memory tools that provide comparisons of previous translations with current work—helps save time and reduce repetition.

The services of interpreters and translators are needed in a number of subject areas. While these workers may not completely specialize in a particular field or industry, many do focus on one area of expertise. Some of the most common areas are described below; however, interpreters and translators also may work in a variety of other areas, including business, social services, or entertainment.

Conference interpreters work at conferences that involve non-English-speaking attendees. This work includes international business and diplomacy, although conference interpreters also may interpret for any organization that works with foreign language speakers. Employers prefer high-level interpreters who have the ability to translate from at least two passive languages into one active (native) language—for example, the ability to interpret from Spanish and French into English. For some positions, such as those with the United Nations, this qualification is mandatory.

Much of the interpreting performed at conferences is simultaneous; however, at some meetings with a small number of attendees, consecutive interpreting also may be used. Usually, interpreters sit in soundproof booths, listening to the speakers through headphones and interpreting into a microphone what is said. The interpreted speech is then relayed to the listener through headsets. When interpreting is needed for only one or two people, the interpreter generally sits behind or next to the attendee and whispers a translation of the proceedings.

Guide or escort interpreters accompany either U.S. visitors abroad or foreign visitors in the United States to ensure that they are able to communicate during their stay. These specialists interpret on a variety of subjects, both on an informal basis and on a professional level. Most of their interpretation is consecutive, and work is generally shared by two interpreters when the assignment requires more than an 8-hour day. Frequent travel, often for days or weeks at a time, is common, an aspect of the job that some find particularly appealing.

Judiciary interpreters and translators help people appearing in court who are unable or unwilling to communicate in English. These workers must remain detached from the content of their work and not alter or modify the meaning or tone of what is said. Legal translators must be thoroughly familiar with the language and functions of the U.S. judicial system, as well as other countries' legal systems. Court interpreters work in a variety of legal settings, such as attorney-client meetings, preliminary hearings, depositions, trials, and arraignments. Success as a court interpreter requires an understanding of both legal terminology and colloquial language. In addition to interpreting what is said, court interpreters also may be required to translate written documents and read them aloud, also known as sight translation.

Literary translators adapt written literature from one language into another. They may translate any number of documents, including journal articles, books, poetry, and short stories. Literary translation is related to creative writing; literary translators must create a new text in the target language that reproduces the content and style of the original. Whenever possible, literary translators work closely with authors in order to best capture their intended meanings and literary characteristics.

This type of work often is done as a sideline by university professors; however, opportunities exist for well-established literary translators. As is the case with writers, finding a publisher and maintaining a network of contacts in the publishing industry is a critical part of the job. Most aspiring literary translators begin by submitting a short sample of their work, in the hope that it will be printed and give them recognition. For example, after receiving permission from the author, they might submit to a publishing house a previously unpublished short work, such as a poem or essay.

Localization translators constitute a relatively recent and rapidly expanding specialty. Localization involves the complete adaptation of a product for use in a different language and culture. At its earlier stages, this work dealt primarily with software localization, but the specialty has expanded to include the adaptation of Internet sites and products in manufacturing and other business sectors.

Translators working in localization need a solid grasp of the languages to be translated, a thorough understanding of technical concepts and vocabulary, and a high degree of knowledge about the intended target audience or users of the product. The goal of these specialists is for the product to appear as if it were originally manufactured in the country where it will be sold and supported. Because software often is involved, it is not uncommon for people who work in this area of translation to have a strong background in computer science or computer-related work experience.

Providing language services to health care patients with limited English proficiency is the realm of *medical interpreters and translators*. Medical interpreters help patients to communicate with doctors, nurses, and other medical staff. Translators working in this specialty primarily convert patient materials and informational brochures, issued by hospitals and medical facilities, into the desired language. Medical interpreters need a strong grasp of medical and colloquial terminology in both languages, along with cultural sensitivity regarding how the patient receives the information. They must remain detached but aware of the patient's feelings and pain.

Sign language interpreters facilitate communication between people who are deaf or hard of hearing and people who can hear. Sign language interpreters must be fluent in English and in American Sign Language (ASL), which combines signing, finger spelling, and specific body language. ASL has its own grammatical rules, sentence structure, idioms, historical contexts, and cultural nuances. Sign language interpreting, like foreign language interpreting, involves more than simply replacing a word of spoken English with a sign representing that word.

Most sign language interpreters either interpret, aiding communication between English and ASL, or transliterate, facilitating communication between English and contact signing—a form of signing that uses a more English language-based word order. Some interpreters specialize in oral interpreting for deaf or hard of hearing persons who lip-read instead of sign. Other specialties include tactile signing, which is interpreting for persons who are blind as well as deaf by making manual signs into a person's hands; cued speech; and signing exact English.

Self-employed and freelance interpreters and translators need general business skills to successfully manage their finances and careers. They must set prices for their work, bill customers, keep financial records, and market their services to attract new business and build their client base.

Working Conditions

Working environments of interpreters and translators vary. Interpreters work in a variety of settings, such as hospitals, courtrooms, and conference centers. They are required to travel to the site—whether it is in a neighboring town or on the other side of the world—where their services are needed. Interpreters who work over the telephone generally work on call, often in call centers in urban areas, and keep to a standard 5-day, 40-hour workweek. Interpreters for deaf students in schools usually work in a school setting for 9 months out of the year. Translators usually work alone, and they must frequently perform under pressure of deadlines and tight schedules. Many translators choose to work at home; however, technology allows translators to work from virtually anywhere.

Because many interpreters and translators freelance, their schedules are often erratic, with extensive periods of no work interspersed with others requiring long, irregular hours. For those who freelance, a significant amount of time must be dedicated to looking for jobs. In addition, freelancers must manage their own finances, and payment for their services may not always be prompt. Freelancing, however, offers variety and flexibility, and allows many workers to choose which jobs to accept or decline.

The number of work-related accidents in these occupations is relatively low. The work can be stressful and exhausting, and translation can be lonesome or dull. However, interpreters and translators may use their irregular schedules to pursue other interests, such as traveling, dabbling in a hobby, or working a second job. Many interpreters and translators enjoy what they do and value the ability to control their schedules and workloads.

Training, Other Qualifications, and Advancement

The educational backgrounds of interpreters and translators vary. Knowing a language in addition to a native language is essential. Although it is not necessary to have been raised bilingual to succeed, many interpreters and translators grew up speaking two languages.

In high school, students can prepare for these careers by taking a broad range of courses that include English writing and comprehension, foreign languages, and basic computer proficiency. Other helpful pursuits include spending time abroad, engaging in comparable forms of direct contact with foreign cultures, and reading extensively on a variety of subjects in English and at least one other language.

Beyond high school, there are many educational options. Although a bachelor's degree is often required, interpreters and translators note that it is acceptable to major in something other than a language. However, specialized training in how to do the work is generally required. A number of formal programs in interpreting and translation are available at colleges nationwide and through nonuniversity training programs, conferences, and courses. Many people who work as conference interpreters or in more technical areas—such as localization, engineering, or finance—have master's degrees, while those working in the community as court or medical interpreters or translators are more likely to complete job-specific training programs.

There is currently no universal form of certification required of all interpreters and translators in the United States, but there are a variety of different tests that workers can voluntarily take to demonstrate proficiency. The American Translators Association provides accreditation in more than 24 language combinations for its members; other options include a certification program offered by The Translators and Interpreters Guild. Many interpreters are not certified. Federal courts have certification for Spanish, Navajo, and Haitian Creole interpreters, and many State and municipal courts offer their own forms of certification. The National Association of Judiciary Interpreters and Translators also offers certification for court interpreting.

The U.S. Department of State has a three-test series for interpreters, including simple consecutive interpreting (for escort work), simultaneous interpreting (for court or seminar work), and conference-level interpreting (for international conferences). These tests are not referred to directly as certification, but successful completion often indicates that a person has an adequate level of skill to work in the field.

The National Association of the Deaf and the Registry of Interpreters for the Deaf (RID) jointly offer certification for general sign interpreters. In addition, RID offers specialty tests in legal interpreting, speech reading, and deaf-to-deaf interpreting—which includes interpreting between deaf speakers with different native languages and from ASL to tactile signing.

Experience is an essential part of a successful career in either interpreting or translation. In fact, many agencies or companies use only the services of people who have worked in the field for 3 to 5 years or who have a degree in translation studies or both.

A good way for translators to learn firsthand about the profession is to start out working in-house for a company; however, such jobs are not very numerous. Persons seeking to enter interpreter or translator jobs should begin by getting experience whatever way they can—even if it means doing informal or unpaid work. All translation can be used as examples for potential clients, even translation done as practice. Mentoring relationships and internships are other ways to build skills and confidence. Escort interpreting may offer an opportunity for inexperienced candidates to work alongside a more seasoned interpreter. Interpreters might also find it easier to break into areas with particularly high demand for language services, such as court or medical interpretation. Once interpreters and translators have gained sufficient experience, they may then move up to more difficult or prestigious assignments, may seek certification, may be given editorial responsibility, or may eventually manage or start their own translation agency.

Employment

Interpreters and translators held about 31,000 jobs in 2004. However, the actual number of interpreters and translators is probably significantly higher because many work in the occupation only sporadically. Interpreters and translators are employed in a variety of industries, reflecting the diversity of employment options in the field. About 9,900 worked in public and private educational institutions, such as schools, colleges, and universities. About 4,100 worked in health care, many of which worked for hospitals. Another 3,400 worked in other areas of government, such as Federal, State and local courts. Other employers of interpreters and translators include publishing companies, telephone companies, airlines, and interpreting and translating agencies.

About 4,600 interpreters and translators are self-employed. To find work, these interpreters and translators may submit resumes to many different employment agencies, and then wait to be contacted when an agency matches their skills with a job. After establishing a few regular clients, interpreters and translators may receive enough work from a few clients to stay busy, and they often hear of subsequent jobs by word of mouth or through referrals from existing clients. Many who freelance in the occupation work only part time, relying on other sources of income to supplement earnings from interpreting or translation.

Job Outlook

Employment of interpreters and translators is projected to increase faster than the average for all occupations over the 2004-14 period, reflecting strong growth in the industries employing interpreters and translators. Higher demand for interpreters and translators in recent years has resulted directly from the broadening of international ties and the increase in the number of foreign language speakers in the United States. Both of these trends are expected to continue, contributing to relatively rapid growth in the number of jobs for interpreters

and translators. Demand will remain strong for translators of the languages referred to as "PFIGS"—Portuguese, French, Italian, German, and Spanish—and the principal Asian languages—Chinese, Japanese, and Korean. In addition, current events and changing political environments, often difficult to foresee, will increase the need for persons who can work with other languages. For example, homeland security needs are expected to drive increasing demand for interpreters and translators of Middle Eastern and North African languages, primarily in Federal Government agencies.

Technology has made the work of interpreters and translators easier. However, technology is not likely to have a negative impact on employment of interpreters and translators because such innovations are incapable of producing work comparable with work produced by these professionals.

Urban areas, especially those in California and New York, and Washington, DC, provide the largest numbers of employment possibilities, especially for interpreters; however, as the immigrant population spreads into more rural areas, jobs in smaller communities will become more widely available.

Job prospects for interpreters and translators vary by specialty. In particular, there should be strong demand for specialists in localization, driven by imports and exports, the expansion of the Internet, and demand in other technical areas, such as medicine or law. Rapid employment growth among interpreters and translators in health services industries will be fueled by the implementation of relatively recent guidelines regarding compliance with Title VI of the Civil Rights Act, which require all health care providers receiving Federal aid to provide language services to non-English speakers. Similarly, the Americans with Disabilities Act and other laws, such as the Rehabilitation Act, mandate that, in certain situations, an interpreter must be available for people who are deaf or hard of hearing. Given the shortage of interpreters and translators meeting the desired skill level of employers, interpreters for the deaf will continue to have favorable employment prospects. On the other hand, job growth is expected to be limited for both conference interpreters and literary translators.

Earnings

Salaried interpreters and translators had median hourly earnings of $16.28 in May 2004. The middle 50 percent earned between $12.40 and $21.09. The lowest 10 percent earned less than $9.67, and the highest 10 percent earned more than $27.45.

Earnings depend on language, subject matter, skill, experience, education, certification, and type of employer, and salaries of interpreters and translators can vary widely. Interpreters and translators with language skills for which there is a greater demand, or for which there are relatively few people with the skills, often have higher earnings. Interpreters and translators with specialized expertise, such as those working in software localization, also generally command higher rates. Individuals classified as language specialists for the Federal Government earned an average of $71,625 annually in 2005. Limited information suggests that some highly skilled interpreters and translators—for example, high-level conference interpreters—working full time can earn more than $100,000 annually.

For those who are not salaried, earnings may fluctuate, depending on the availability of work. Furthermore, freelancers do not have any employer-paid benefits. Freelance interpreters usually earn an hourly rate, whereas translators who freelance typically earn a rate per word or per hour.

Related Occupations

Interpreters and translators use their multilingual skills, as do teachers of languages. These include teachers—preschool, kindergarten, elementary, middle, and secondary; teachers—postsecondary; teachers—special education; teachers—adult literacy and remedial education; and teachers—self-enrichment education. The work of interpreters, particularly guide or escort interpreters, can be likened to that of tour and travel guides, in that they accompany individuals or groups on tours or to places of interest.

The work of translators is similar to that of writers and editors, in that they communicate information and ideas through the written word and prepare texts for publication or dissemination. Furthermore, interpreters or translators working in a legal or health care environment are required to have a knowledge of terms and concepts that is similar to that of professionals working in these fields, such as court reporters or medical transcriptionists.

Sources of Additional Information

Organizations dedicated to these professions can provide valuable advice and guidance for people interested in learning more about interpretation and translation. The language services division of local hospitals or courthouses also may have information about available opportunities.

For general career information, contact the organizations listed below:

➤ American Translators Association, 225 Reinekers Ln., Suite 590, Alexandria, VA 22314. Internet: **http://www.atanet.org**
➤ The Translators and Interpreters Guild, 962 Wayne Avenue, Suite 500, Silver Spring, MD 20910. Internet: **http://www.ttig.org**
➤ U.S. Department of State, Office of Language Services, Suite 1400 SA-1, Department of State, Washington, DC 20520.

For more detailed information by specialty, contact the association affiliated with that subject area:

➤ National Association of Judiciary Interpreters and Translators, 603 Stewart St., Suite 610, Seattle, WA 98101. Internet: **http://www.najit.org**
➤ American Literary Translators Association, The University of Texas at Dallas, Box 830688 Mail Station JO51, Richardson, TX 75083-0688. Internet: **http://www.literarytranslators.org**
➤ Localization Industry Standards Association, 7 Route du Monastère-CH-1173, Féchy, Switzerland. Internet: **http://www.lisa.org**
➤ Registry of Interpreters for the Deaf, 333 Commerce St., Alexandria, VA 22314. Internet: **http://www.rid.org**

News Analysts, Reporters, and Correspondents

(O*NET 27-3021.00, 27-3022.00)

Significant Points

● Competition will be keen for jobs at large metropolitan and national newspapers, broadcast stations, and magazines; most entry-level openings arise at small broadcast stations and publications.

● Most employers prefer individuals with a bachelor's degree in journalism or mass communications and experience gained at school newspapers or broadcasting stations or through internships with news organizations.

● Jobs often involve irregular hours, night and weekend work, and pressure to meet deadlines.

● Slower than average employment growth is expected.

Nature of the Work

News analysts, reporters, and correspondents gather information, prepare stories, and make broadcasts that inform us about local, State, national, and international events; present points of view on current issues; and report on the actions of public officials, corporate executives, interest groups, and others who exercise power.

News analysts, reporters, and correspondents examine and interpret news from a variety of sources.

News analysts—also called *newscasters* or *news anchors*—examine, interpret, and broadcast news received from various sources. News anchors present news stories and introduce videotaped news or live transmissions from on-the-scene reporters. Newscasters at large stations and networks usually specialize in a particular type of news, such as sports or weather. *Weathercasters*, also called weather reporters, report current and forecasted weather conditions. They gather information from national satellite weather services, wire services, and local and regional weather bureaus. Some weathercasters are trained meteorologists and can develop their own weather forecasts. (See the statement on atmospheric scientists elsewhere in the *Handbook*.) *Sportscasters* select, write, and deliver sports news. This may include interviews with sports personalities and coverage of games and other sporting events. *News correspondents* report on news occurring in the large U.S. and foreign cities where they are stationed.

In covering a story, *reporters* investigate leads and news tips, look at documents, observe events at the scene, and interview people. Reporters take notes and also may take photographs or shoot videos. At their office, they organize the material, determine the focus or emphasis, write their stories, and edit accompanying video material. Many reporters enter information or write stories using laptop computers and electronically submit the material to their offices from remote locations. In some cases, *newswriters* write a story from information collected and submitted by reporters. Radio and television reporters often compose stories and report "live" from the scene. At times, they later tape an introduction to or commentary on their story in the studio. Some journalists also interpret the news or offer opinions to readers, viewers, or listeners. In this role, they are called *commentators* or *columnists*.

General-assignment reporters write about newsworthy occurrences—such as accidents, political rallies, visits of celebrities, or business closings—as assigned. Large newspapers and radio and television stations assign reporters to gather news about specific topics, such as crime or education. Some reporters specialize in fields such as health, politics, foreign affairs, sports, theater, consumer affairs, social events, science, business, or religion. Investigative reporters cover stories that may take many days or weeks of information gathering. Some publications use teams of reporters instead of assigning each reporter one specific topic, allowing reporters to cover a greater variety of stories. News teams may include reporters, editors, graphic artists, and photographers working together to complete a story. Reporters on small publications cover all aspects of the news. They take photographs, write headlines, lay out pages, edit wire-service stories, and write editorials. Some also solicit advertisements, sell subscriptions, and perform general office work.

Working Conditions

The work of news analysts, reporters, and correspondents is usually hectic. They are under great pressure to meet deadlines. Broadcasts sometimes are aired with little or no time for preparation. Some news analysts, reporters, and correspondents work in comfortable, private offices; others work in large rooms filled with the sound of keyboards and computer printers, as well as the voices of other reporters. Curious onlookers, police, or other emergency workers can distract those reporting from the scene for radio and television. Covering wars, political uprisings, fires, floods, and similar events is often dangerous.

Working hours vary. Reporters on morning papers often work from late afternoon until midnight. Radio and television reporters usually are assigned to a day or evening shift. Magazine reporters usually work during the day.

Reporters sometimes have to change their work hours to meet a deadline or to follow late-breaking developments. Their work demands long hours, irregular schedules, and some travel. Because many stations and networks are on the air 24 hours a day, newscasters can expect to work unusual hours.

Training, Other Qualifications, and Advancement

Most employers prefer individuals with a bachelor's degree in journalism or mass communications, but some hire graduates with other majors. They look for experience at school newspapers or broadcasting stations, and internships with news organizations. Large-city newspapers and stations also may prefer candidates with a degree in a subject-matter specialty such as economics, political science, or business. Some large newspapers and broadcasters may hire only experienced reporters.

More than 1,200 institutions offer programs in communications, journalism, and related programs. In 2004, 104 of these were accredited by the Accrediting Council on Education in Journalism and Mass Communications. About three-fourths of the courses in a typical curriculum are in liberal arts; the remaining courses are in journalism. Examples of journalism courses are introductory mass media, basic reporting and copy editing, history of journalism, and press law and ethics. Students planning a career in broadcasting take courses in radio and television news and production. Those planning newspaper or magazine careers usually specialize in news-editorial journalism. To create stories for online media, they need to learn to use computer software to combine online story text with audio and video elements and graphics.

Some schools also offer a master's or Ph.D. degree in journalism. Some graduate programs are intended primarily as preparation for news careers, while others prepare journalism teachers, researchers and theorists, and advertising and public relations workers. A graduate degree may help those looking to advance.

High school courses in English, journalism, and social studies provide a good foundation for college programs. Useful college liberal arts courses include English with an emphasis on writing, sociology, political science, economics, history, and psychology. Courses in computer science, business, and speech are useful as well. Fluency in a foreign language is necessary in some jobs.

Reporters typically need more than good word-processing skills. Computer graphics and desktop-publishing skills also are useful. Computer-assisted reporting involves the use of computers to analyze data in search of a story. This technique and the interpretation of the results require computer skills and familiarity with databases. Knowledge of news photography also is valuable for

entry-level positions, which sometimes combine the responsibilities of a reporter with those of a camera operator or photographer.

Employers report that practical experience is the most important part of education and training. Upon graduation many students already have gained much practical experience through part-time or summer jobs or through internships with news organizations. Most newspapers, magazines, and broadcast news organizations offer reporting and editing internships. Work on high school and college newspapers, at broadcasting stations, or on community papers or U.S. Armed Forces publications also provides practical training. In addition, journalism scholarships, fellowships, and assistantships awarded to college journalism students by universities, newspapers, foundations, and professional organizations are helpful. Experience as a stringer or freelancer—a part-time reporter who is paid only for stories printed—is advantageous.

Reporters should be dedicated to providing accurate and impartial news. Accuracy is important, both to serve the public and because untrue or libelous statements can lead to lawsuits. A nose for news, persistence, initiative, poise, resourcefulness, a good memory, and physical stamina are important, as is the emotional stability to deal with pressing deadlines, irregular hours, and dangerous assignments. Broadcast reporters and news analysts must be comfortable on camera. All reporters must be at ease in unfamiliar places and with a variety of people. Positions involving on-air work require a pleasant voice and appearance.

Most reporters start at small publications or broadcast stations as general assignment reporters or copy editors. They are usually assigned to cover court proceedings and civic and club meetings, summarize speeches, and write obituaries. With experience, they report more difficult assignments or specialize in a particular field. Large publications and stations hire few recent graduates; as a rule, they require new reporters to have several years of experience.

Some news analysts and reporters can advance by moving to larger newspapers or stations. A few experienced reporters become columnists, correspondents, writers, announcers, or public relations specialists. Others become editors in print journalism or program managers in broadcast journalism, who supervise reporters. Some eventually become broadcasting or publishing industry managers.

Employment

News analysts, reporters, and correspondents held about 64,000 jobs in 2004. About 61 percent worked for newspaper, periodical, book, and directory publishers. Another 25 percent worked in radio and television broadcasting. About 7 percent of news analysts, reporters, and correspondents were self-employed.

Job Outlook

Competition will continue to be keen for jobs on large metropolitan and national newspapers, broadcast stations and networks, and magazines. Most job opportunities will be with small-town and suburban newspapers and radio and television stations. Talented writers who can handle highly specialized scientific or technical subjects have an advantage. Also, newspapers increasingly are hiring stringers and freelancers.

Journalism graduates have the background for work in closely related fields such as advertising and public relations, and many take jobs in these fields. Other graduates accept sales, managerial, or other nonmedia positions.

Employment of news analysts, reporters, and correspondents is expected to grow more slowly than the average for all occupations through the year 2014. Many factors will contribute to the limited job growth in this occupation. Consolidation and convergence should continue in the publishing and broadcasting industries. As a result, companies will be better able to allocate their news analysts, reporters, and correspondents to cover news stories. Constantly improving technology also is allowing workers to do their jobs more efficiently, another factor that will limit the number of workers needed to cover a story or certain type of news. However, the continued demand for news will create some job opportunities. For example, some job growth likely will occur in newer media areas, such as online newspapers and magazines. Job openings also will result from the need to replace workers who leave their occupations permanently; some news analysts, reporters, and correspondents find the work too stressful and hectic or do not like the lifestyle, and transfer to other occupations.

The number of job openings in the newspaper and broadcasting industries—in which news analysts, reporters, and correspondents are employed—is sensitive to economic ups and downs because these industries depend on advertising revenue.

Earnings

Salaries for news analysts, reporters, and correspondents vary widely. Median annual earnings of reporters and correspondents were $31,320 in May 2004. The middle 50 percent earned between $22,900 and $47,860. The lowest 10 percent earned less than $18,470, and the highest 10 percent earned more than $68,250. Median annual earnings of reporters and correspondents were $30,070 in newspaper, periodical, book, and directory publishers and $34,050 in radio and television broadcasting.

Median annual earnings of broadcast news analysts were $36,980 in May 2004. The middle 50 percent earned between $25,560 and $68,440. The lowest 10 percent earned less than $19,040, and the highest 10 percent earned more than $122,800. Median annual earnings of broadcast news analysts were $37,840 in radio and television broadcasting.

Related Occupations

News analysts, reporters, and correspondents must write clearly and effectively to succeed in their profession. Others for whom good writing ability is essential include writers and editors and public relations specialists. Many news analysts, reporters, and correspondents also must communicate information orally. Others for whom oral communication skills are important are announcers, interpreters and translators, those in sales and related occupations, and teachers.

Sources of Additional Information

For information on broadcasting education and scholarship resources, contact:

➤ National Association of Broadcasters, 1771 N St. NW., Washington, DC 20036. Internet: **http://www.nab.org**

Information on careers in journalism, colleges and universities offering degree programs in journalism or communications, and journalism scholarships and internships may be obtained from:

➤ Dow Jones Newspaper Fund, Inc., P.O. Box 300, Princeton, NJ 08543-0300.

Information on union wage rates for newspaper and magazine reporters is available from:

➤ Newspaper Guild, Research and Information Department, 501 Third St. NW., Suite 250, Washington, DC 20001.

For a list of schools with accredited programs in journalism and mass communications, send a stamped, self-addressed envelope to:

➤ Accrediting Council on Education in Journalism and Mass Communications, University of Kansas School of Journalism and Mass Communications, Stauffer-Flint Hall, 1435 Jayhawk Blvd., Lawrence, KS 66045. Internet: **http://www.ku.edu/~acejmc/STUDENT/STUDENT.SHTML**

Names and locations of newspapers and a list of schools and departments of journalism are published in the *Editor and Publisher International Year Book*, available in most public libraries and newspaper offices.

Photographers

(O*NET 27-4021.01, 27-4021.02)

Significant Points

- Competition for jobs is expected to be keen because the work is attractive to many people.

- Technical expertise, a "good eye," imagination, and creativity are essential.

- More than half of all photographers are self-employed; the most successful are adept at operating a business and able to take advantage of opportunities provided by rapidly changing technologies.

Nature of the Work

Photographers produce and preserve images that paint a picture, tell a story, or record an event. To create commercial-quality photographs, photographers need both technical expertise and creativity. Producing a successful picture requires choosing and presenting a subject to achieve a particular effect, and selecting the appropriate equipment. For example, photographers may enhance the subject's appearance with natural or artificial light, shoot the subject from an interesting angle, draw attention to a particular aspect of the subject by blurring the background, or use various lenses to produce desired levels of detail at various distances from the subject.

Today, most photographers use digital cameras instead of traditional silver-halide film cameras, although some photographers use both types, depending on their own preference and the nature of the assignment. Regardless of the camera they use, photographers also employ an array of other equipment—from lenses, filters, and tripods to flash attachments and specially constructed lighting equipment—to improve the quality of their work.

Digital cameras capture images electronically, allowing them to be edited on a computer. Images can be stored on portable memory devices such as compact disks (CDs) or on smaller "minipocket" storage devices such as flash disks, which are small memory cards used in digital cameras. Once the raw image has been transferred to a computer, photographers can use processing software to crop or modify the image and enhance it through color correction and other specialized effects. As soon as a photographer has finished editing the image, it can be sent anywhere in the world over the Internet.

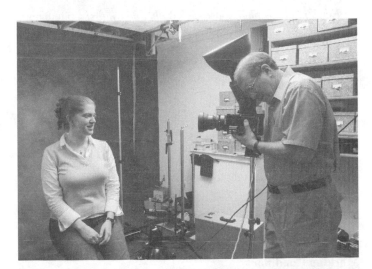

Portrait photographers need both technical skill and artistic creativity.

Photographers also can create electronic portfolios of their work and display them on their own webpage, allowing them to reach prospective customers directly. Digital technology also allows the production of larger, more colorful, and more accurate prints or images for use in advertising, photographic art, and scientific research. Photographers who process their own digital images need to have computers, high-quality printers, and editing software, as well as the technical knowledge to use these tools effectively.

Photographers who use cameras with silver-halide film often send their film to laboratories for processing. Color film requires expensive equipment and exacting conditions for correct processing and printing. (See the statement on photographic process workers and processing machine operators elsewhere in the *Handbook*.) Other photographers develop and print their own photographs using their own fully equipped darkroom, especially if they use black and white film or seek to achieve special effects. Photographers who do their own film developing must invest in additional developing and printing equipment and acquire the technical skills to operate it.

Some photographers specialize in areas such as portrait, commercial and industrial, scientific, news, or fine arts photography. *Portrait photographers* take pictures of individuals or groups of people and often work in their own studios. Some specialize in weddings, religious ceremonies, or school photographs and may work on location. Portrait photographers who own and operate their own business have many responsibilities in addition to taking pictures. They must arrange for advertising, schedule appointments, set and adjust equipment, purchase supplies, keep records, bill customers, pay bills, and—if they have employees—hire, train, and direct their workers. Many also process their own images, design albums, and mount and frame the finished photographs.

Commercial and industrial photographers take pictures of various subjects, such as buildings, models, merchandise, artifacts, and landscapes. These photographs are used in a variety of media, including books, reports, advertisements, and catalogs. Industrial photographers often take pictures of equipment, machinery, products, workers, and company officials. The pictures are used for various purposes—for example, analysis of engineering projects, publicity, or records of equipment development or deployment, such as placement of an offshore oil rig. This photography frequently is done on location.

Scientific photographers take images of a variety of subjects to illustrate or record scientific or medical data or phenomena, using knowledge of scientific procedures. They typically possess additional knowledge in areas such as engineering, medicine, biology, or chemistry.

News photographers, also called *photojournalists*, photograph newsworthy people, places, and sporting, political, and community events for newspapers, journals, magazines, or television.

Fine arts photographers sell their photographs as fine artwork. In addition to technical proficiency, fine arts photographers need artistic talent and creativity.

Self-employed, or freelance, photographers usually specialize in one of the above fields. In addition to carrying out assignments under direct contract with clients, they may license the use of their photographs through stock-photo agencies or market their work directly to the public. Stock-photo agencies sell magazines and other customers the right to use photographs, and pay the photographer a commission. These agencies require an application from the photographer and a sizable portfolio of pictures. Once accepted, photographers usually are required to submit a large number of new photographs each year.

Working Conditions

Working conditions for photographers vary considerably. Photographers employed in government and advertising studios usually work a 5-day, 40-hour week. On the other hand, news photographers often work long, irregular hours and must be available to work on short notice. Many photographers work part time or on variable schedules. Most photographers spend only a small portion of their work schedule actually taking photographs. Their most common activities are editing images on a computer—if they use a digital camera—and looking for new business—if they are self-employed.

Portrait photographers usually work in their own studios but also may travel to take photographs at the client's location, such as a school, a company office, or a private home. News and commercial photographers frequently travel locally, stay overnight on assignments, or travel to distant places for long periods.

Some photographers work in uncomfortable or even dangerous surroundings, especially news photographers covering accidents, natural disasters, civil unrest, or military conflicts. Many photographers must wait long hours in all kinds of weather for an event to take place and stand or walk for long periods while carrying heavy equipment. News photographers often work under strict deadlines.

Self-employment allows for greater autonomy, freedom of expression, and flexible scheduling. However, income can be uncertain and the continuous, time consuming search for new clients can be stressful. Some self-employed photographers hire assistants who help seek out new business.

Employment

Photographers held about 129,000 jobs in 2004. More than half were self-employed, a much higher proportion than for most occupations. Some self-employed photographers have contracts with advertising agencies, magazine publishers, or other businesses to do individual projects for a set fee, while others operate portrait studios or provide photographs to stock-photo agencies.

Most salaried photographers work in portrait or commercial photography studios; most of the others work for newspapers, magazines, and advertising agencies. Photographers work in all areas of the country, but most are employed in metropolitan areas.

Training, Other Qualifications, and Advancement

Employers usually seek applicants with a "good eye," imagination, and creativity, as well as a good technical understanding of photography. Entry-level positions in photojournalism or in industrial or scientific photography generally require a college degree in photography or in a field related to the industry in which the photographer seeks employment. Freelance and portrait photographers need technical proficiency, gained through either a degree program, vocational training, or extensive photography experience.

Photography courses are offered by many universities, community and junior colleges, vocational-technical institutes, and private trade and technical schools. Basic courses in photography cover equipment, processes, and techniques. Bachelor's degree programs, especially those including business courses, provide a well-rounded education. Art schools offer useful training in design and composition.

Individuals interested in a career in photography should try to develop contacts in the field by subscribing to photographic newsletters and magazines; joining camera clubs; and seeking summer or part-time employment in camera stores, newspapers, or photo studios.

Photographers may start out as assistants to experienced photographers. Assistants acquire the technical knowledge needed to be a successful photographer and also learn other skills necessary to run a portrait or commercial photography business. Freelance photographers also should develop an individual style of photography to differentiate themselves from the competition. Some photographers enter the field by submitting unsolicited a portfolio of photographs to magazines and to art directors at advertising agencies; for freelance photographers, a good portfolio is critical.

Photographers need good eyesight, artistic ability, and good hand-eye coordination. They should be patient, accurate, and detail-oriented. Photographers should be able to work well with others, as they frequently deal with clients, graphic designers, and advertising and publishing specialists. Photographers need to know how to use computer software programs and applications that allow them to prepare and edit images, and those who market directly to clients should be familiar with using the Internet to display their work.

Portrait photographers need the ability to help people relax in front of the camera. Commercial and fine arts photographers must be imaginative and original. News photographers must not only be good with a camera, but also understand the story behind an event so that their pictures match the story. They must be decisive in recognizing a potentially good photograph and act quickly to capture it.

Photographers who operate their own business, or freelance, need business skills as well as talent. These individuals must know how to prepare a business plan; submit bids; write contracts; keep financial records; market their work; hire models, if needed; get permission to shoot on locations that normally are not open to the public; obtain releases to use photographs of people; license and price photographs; and secure copyright protection for their work. To protect their rights and their work, self-employed photographers require basic knowledge of licensing and copyright laws, as well as knowledge of contracts and negotiation procedures.

After several years of experience, magazine and news photographers may advance to photography or picture editor positions. Some photographers teach at technical schools, film schools, or universities.

Job Outlook

Photographers can expect keen competition for job openings because the work is attractive to many people. The number of individuals interested in positions as commercial and news photographers usually is much greater than the number of openings. Those who succeed in landing a salaried job or attracting enough work to earn a living by freelancing are likely to be adept at operating a business and to be among the most creative, able to find and exploit the new opportunities available from rapidly changing technologies. Related work experience, job-related training, or some unique skill or talent—such as a background in computers or electronics—also are beneficial to prospective photographers.

Employment of photographers is expected to increase about as fast as the average for all occupations through 2014. Demand for portrait photographers should increase as the population grows. Growth of Internet versions of magazines, journals, and newspapers will require increasing numbers of commercial photographers to provide digital images. The Internet also should make it easier for freelancers to market directly to their customers, increasing opportunities for self-employment.

Job growth, however, will be constrained somewhat by the widespread use of digital photography and the falling price of digital equipment. Improvements in digital technology reduce barriers of entry into this profession and allow more individual consumers and businesses to produce, store, and access photographic images on their own. Declines in the newspaper industry also will reduce demand for photographers to provide still images for print. Salaried jobs in particular may be difficult to find as more companies contract with freelancers rather than hire their own photographers.

Earnings

Median annual earnings of salaried photographers were $26,080 in May 2004. The middle 50 percent earned between $18,380

and $37,370. The lowest 10 percent earned less than $15,000, and the highest 10 percent earned more than $54,180. Median annual earnings in the industries employing the largest numbers of salaried photographers were $32,800 for newspapers and periodicals and $23,100 for other professional, scientific, and technical services.

Salaried photographers—more of whom work full time—tend to earn more than those who are self-employed. Because most freelance and portrait photographers purchase their own equipment, they incur considerable expense acquiring and maintaining cameras and accessories. Unlike news and commercial photographers, few fine arts photographers are successful enough to support themselves solely through their art.

Related Occupations

Other occupations requiring artistic talent and creativity include architects, except landscape and naval; artists and related workers; commercial and industrial designers, fashion designers, and graphic designers; and television, video, and motion picture camera operators and editors. Photojournalists are often required to cover news stories much the same as news analysts, reporters, and correspondents. The processing work that photographers do on computers is similar to the work of prepress technicians and workers and desktop publishers.

Sources of Additional Information

Career information on photography is available from:
➤ Professional Photographers of America, Inc., 229 Peachtree St. NE., Suite 2200, Atlanta, GA 30303. Internet: **http://www.ppa.com**
➤ National Press Photographers Association, Inc., 3200 Croasdaile Dr., Suite 306, Durham, NC 27705. Internet: **http://www.nppa.org**
➤ American Society of Media Photographers, Inc., 150 North Second St., Philadelphia, PA 19106. Internet: **http://www.asmp.org**

Public Relations Specialists

(O*NET 27-3031.00)

Significant Points

- Although employment is projected to grow faster than average, keen competition is expected for entry-level jobs.

- Opportunities should be best for college graduates who combine a degree in public relations, journalism, or another communications-related field with a public relations internship or other related work experience.

- Creativity, initiative, and the ability to communicate effectively are essential.

Nature of the Work

An organization's reputation, profitability, and even its continued existence can depend on the degree to which its targeted "publics" support its goals and policies. Public relations specialists—also referred to as communications specialists and media specialists, among other titles—serve as advocates for businesses, nonprofit associations, universities, hospitals, and other organizations, and build and maintain positive relationships with the public. As managers recognize the importance of good public relations to the success of their organizations, they increasingly rely on public relations specialists for advice on the strategy and policy of such programs.

Public relations specialists handle organizational functions such as media, community, consumer, industry, and governmental relations; political campaigns; interest-group representation;

Public relations specialists serve as advocates for businesses, nonprofit associations, universities, hospitals, and other organizations.

conflict mediation; and employee and investor relations. They do more than "tell the organization's story." They must understand the attitudes and concerns of community, consumer, employee, and public interest groups and establish and maintain cooperative relationships with them and with representatives from print and broadcast journalism.

Public relations specialists draft press releases and contact people in the media who might print or broadcast their material. Many radio or television special reports, newspaper stories, and magazine articles start at the desks of public relations specialists. Sometimes the subject is an organization and its policies toward its employees or its role in the community. Often the subject is a public issue, such as health, energy, or the environment, and what an organization does to advance that issue.

Public relations specialists also arrange and conduct programs to keep up contact between organization representatives and the public. For example, they set up speaking engagements and often prepare speeches for company officials. These media specialists represent employers at community projects; make film, slide, or other visual presentations at meetings and school assemblies; and plan conventions. In addition, they are responsible for preparing annual reports and writing proposals for various projects.

In government, public relations specialists—who may be called press secretaries, information officers, public affairs specialists, or communication specialists—keep the public informed about the activities of agencies and officials. For example, public affairs specialists in the U.S. Department of State keep the public informed of travel advisories and of U.S. positions on foreign issues. A press secretary for a member of Congress keeps constituents aware of the representative's accomplishments.

In large organizations, the key public relations executive, who often is a vice president, may develop overall plans and policies with other executives. In addition, public relations departments employ public relations specialists to write, research, prepare materials, maintain contacts, and respond to inquiries.

People who handle publicity for an individual or who direct public relations for a small organization may deal with all aspects of the job. They contact people, plan and research, and prepare materials for distribution. They also may handle advertising or sales promotion work to support marketing efforts.

Working Conditions

Some public relations specialists work a standard 35- to 40-hour week, but unpaid overtime is common. Occasionally, they must be at the job or on call around the clock, especially if there is an emergency or crisis. Public relations offices are busy places; work schedules can be irregular and frequently interrupted. Schedules often have to be rearranged so that workers can meet deadlines, deliver speeches, attend meetings and community activities, and travel.

Training, Other Qualifications, and Advancement

There are no defined standards for entry into a public relations career. A college degree combined with public relations experience, usually gained through an internship, is considered excellent preparation for public relations work; in fact, internships are becoming vital to obtaining employment. The ability to communicate effectively is essential. Many entry-level public relations specialists have a college major in public relations, journalism, advertising, or communication. Some firms seek college graduates who have worked in electronic or print journalism. Other employers seek applicants with demonstrated communication skills and training or experience in a field related to the firm's business—information technology, health, science, engineering, sales, or finance, for example.

Many colleges and universities offer bachelor's and postsecondary degrees in public relations, usually in a journalism or communications department. In addition, many other colleges offer at least one course in this field. A common public relations sequence includes courses in public relations principles and techniques; public relations management and administration, including organizational development; writing, emphasizing news releases, proposals, annual reports, scripts, speeches, and related items; visual communications, including desktop publishing and computer graphics; and research, emphasizing social science research and survey design and implementation. Courses in advertising, journalism, business administration, finance, political science, psychology, sociology, and creative writing also are helpful. Specialties are offered in public relations for business, government, and nonprofit organizations.

Many colleges help students gain part-time internships in public relations that provide valuable experience and training. Membership in local chapters of the Public Relations Student Society of America (affiliated with the Public Relations Society of America) or in student chapters of the International Association of Business Communicators provides an opportunity for students to exchange views with public relations specialists and to make professional contacts that may help them find a job in the field. A portfolio of published articles, television or radio programs, slide presentations, and other work is an asset in finding a job. Writing for a school publication or television or radio station provides valuable experience and material for one's portfolio.

Creativity, initiative, good judgment, and the ability to communicate thoughts clearly and simply are essential in this occupation. Decision-making, problem-solving, and research skills also are important. People who choose public relations as a career need an outgoing personality, self-confidence, an understanding of human psychology, and an enthusiasm for motivating people. They should be competitive, yet able to function as part of a team and open to new ideas.

Some organizations, particularly those with large public relations staffs, have formal training programs for new employees. In smaller organizations, new employees work under the guidance of experienced staff members. Beginners often maintain files of material about company activities, scan newspapers and magazines for appropriate articles to clip, and assemble information for speeches and pamphlets. They also may answer calls from the press and the public, work on invitation lists and details for press conferences, or escort visitors and clients. After gaining experience, they write news releases, speeches, and articles for publication or plan and carry out public relations programs. Public relations specialists in smaller firms usually get all-around experience, whereas those in larger firms tend to be more specialized.

The Universal Accreditation Board accredits public relations specialists who are members of the Public Relations Society of America and who participate in the Examination for Accreditation in Public Relations process. This process includes both a readiness review and an examination, which are designed for candidates who have at least 5 years of full-time work or teaching experience in public relations and who have earned a bachelor's degree in a communications-related field. The readiness review includes a written submission by each candidate, a portfolio review, and dialogue between the candidate and a three-member panel. Candidates who successfully advance through readiness review and pass the computer-based examination earn the Accredited in Public Relations (APR) designation.

The International Association of Business Communicators (IABC) also has an accreditation program for professionals in the communications field, including public relations specialists. Those who meet all the requirements of the program earn the Accredited Business Communicator (ABC) designation. Candidates must have at least 5 years of experience and a bachelor's degree in a communications field and must pass written and oral examinations. They also must submit a portfolio of work samples demonstrating involvement in a range of communications projects and a thorough understanding of communications planning.

Employers may consider professional recognition through accreditation as a sign of competence in this field, which could be especially helpful in a competitive job market.

Promotion to supervisory jobs may come to public relations specialists who show that they can handle more demanding assignments. In public relations firms, a beginner might be hired as a research assistant or account coordinator and be promoted to account executive, senior account executive, account manager, and eventually vice president. A similar career path is followed in corporate public relations, although the titles may differ. Some experienced public relations specialists start their own consulting firms. (For more information on public relations managers, see the *Handbook* statement on advertising, marketing, promotions, public relations, and sales managers.)

Employment

Public relations specialists held about 188,000 jobs in 2004. Public relations specialists are concentrated in service-providing industries such as advertising and related services; health care and social assistance; educational services; and government. Others worked for communications firms, financial institutions, and government agencies.

Public relations specialists are concentrated in large cities, where press services and other communications facilities are readily available and many businesses and trade associations have their headquarters. Many public relations consulting firms, for example, are in New York, Los Angeles, San Francisco, Chicago, and Washington, DC. There is a trend, however, for public relations jobs to be dispersed throughout the Nation, closer to clients.

Job Outlook

Keen competition likely will continue for entry-level public relations jobs, as the number of qualified applicants is expected to exceed the number of job openings. Many people are attracted to this profession because of the high profile nature of the work. Opportunities should be best for college graduates who combine a degree in journalism, public relations, advertising, or another communications-related field with a public relations internship or other related work experience. Applicants without the appropriate educational background or work experience will face the toughest obstacles.

Employment of public relations specialists is expected to grow faster than average for all occupations through 2014. The need for good public relations in an increasingly competitive business environment should spur demand for public relations specialists in organizations of all types and sizes. The value of a company is measured not just by its balance sheet, but also by the strength of its relationships with those on whom it depends for its success. With the increasing demand for corporate accountability, more emphasis will be placed on improving the image of the client, as well as on building public confidence.

Employment in public relations firms should grow as firms hire contractors to provide public relations services rather than support full-time staff. In addition to those arising from employment growth, job opportunities should result from the need to replace public relations specialists who leave the occupation.

Earnings

Median annual earnings for salaried public relations specialists were $43,830 in May 2004. The middle 50 percent earned between $32,970 and $59,360; the lowest 10 percent earned less than $25,750, and the top 10 percent earned more than $81,120. Median annual earnings in the industries employing the largest numbers of public relations specialists in May 2004 were:

Advertising and related services	$50,450
Management of companies and enterprises	47,330
Business, professional, labor, political, and similar organizations	45,400
Local government	44,550
Colleges, universities, and professional schools	39,610

Related Occupations

Public relations specialists create favorable attitudes among various organizations, interest groups, and the public through effective communication. Other workers with similar jobs include advertising, marketing, promotions, public relations, and sales managers; demonstrators, product promoters, and models; news analysts, reporters, and correspondents; lawyers; market and survey researchers; sales representatives, wholesale and manufacturing; and police and detectives involved in community relations.

Sources of Additional Information

A comprehensive directory of schools offering degree programs, a sequence of study in public relations, a brochure on careers in public relations, and a $5 brochure entitled *Where Shall I Go to Study Advertising and Public Relations?* are available from:
➤ Public Relations Society of America, Inc., 33 Maiden Lane, New York, NY 10038-5150. Internet: **http://www.prsa.org**

For information on accreditation for public relations professionals and the IABC Student Web site, contact:
➤ International Association of Business Communicators, One Hallidie Plaza, Suite 600, San Francisco, CA 94102.

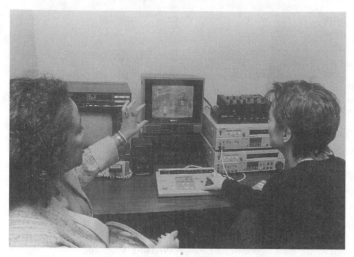

Film and video editors edit soundtracks, film, and video for the motion picture, cable, and broadcast television industries.

Television, Video, and Motion Picture Camera Operators and Editors

(O*NET 27-4031.00, 27-4032.00)

Significant Points

- Workers acquire their skills through on-the-job or formal postsecondary training.

- Technical expertise, a good eye, imagination, and creativity are essential.

- Keen competition for job openings is expected because many talented peopled are attracted to the field.

Nature of the Work

Television, video, and motion picture camera operators produce images that tell a story, inform or entertain an audience, or record an event. *Film and video editors* edit soundtracks, film, and video for the motion picture, cable, and broadcast television industries. Some camera operators do their own editing.

Making commercial-quality movies and video programs requires technical expertise and creativity. Producing successful images requires choosing and presenting interesting material, selecting appropriate equipment, and applying a good eye and a steady hand to ensure smooth, natural movement of the camera.

Camera operators use television, video, or motion picture cameras to shoot a wide range of material, including television series, studio programs, news and sporting events, music videos, motion pictures, documentaries, and training sessions. Some camera operators film or videotape private ceremonies and special events, such as weddings and conference program sessions. Those who record images on videotape are often called *videographers*. Many are employed by independent television stations; local affiliate stations of television networks; large cable and television networks; or smaller, independent production companies. *Studio camera operators* work in a broadcast studio and usually videotape their subjects from a fixed position. *News camera operators*, also called *electronic news gathering (ENG) operators*, work as part of a reporting team, following newsworthy events as they unfold. To capture live events, they must anticipate the action and act quickly. ENG operators sometimes edit raw footage on the spot for relay to a television affiliate for broadcast.

Camera operators employed in the entertainment field use motion picture cameras to film movies, television programs, and commercials. Those who film motion pictures also are known as *cinematographers*. Some specialize in filming cartoons or special effects. Cinematographers may be an integral part of the action, using cameras in any of several different mounts. For example, the camera operator can be stationary and shoot whatever passes in front of the lens, or the camera can be mounted on a track, with the camera operator responsible for shooting the scene from different angles or directions. Wider use of digital cameras has enhanced the number of angles and the clarity that a camera operator can provide. Other camera operators sit on cranes and follow the action while crane operators move them into position. *Steadicam operators* mount a harness and carry the camera on their shoulders to provide a clear picture while they move about the action. Camera operators who work in the entertainment field often meet with directors, actors, editors, and camera assistants to discuss ways of filming, editing, and improving scenes.

Working Conditions

Working conditions for camera operators and editors vary considerably. Those employed by television and cable networks and advertising agencies usually work a 5-day, 40-hour week; however, they may work longer hours to meet production schedules. ENG operators often work long, irregular hours and must be available to work on short notice. Camera operators and editors working in motion picture production also may work long, irregular hours.

ENG operators and those who cover major events, such as conventions or sporting events, frequently travel locally and stay overnight or travel to distant places for longer periods. Camera operators filming television programs or motion pictures may travel to film on location.

Some camera operators—especially ENG operators covering accidents, natural disasters, civil unrest, or military conflicts—work in uncomfortable or even dangerous surroundings. Many camera operators must wait long hours in all kinds of weather for an event to take place and must stand or walk for long periods while carrying heavy equipment. ENG operators often work under strict deadlines.

Training, Other Qualifications, and Advancement

Employers usually seek applicants with a good eye, imagination, and creativity, as well as a good technical understanding of how the camera operates. Television, video, and motion picture camera operators and editors usually acquire their skills through on-the-job training or formal postsecondary training at vocational schools, colleges, universities, or photographic institutes. Formal education may be required for some positions.

Many universities, community and junior colleges, vocational-technical institutes, and private trade and technical schools offer courses in camera operation and videography. Basic courses cover equipment, processes, and techniques. Bachelor's degree programs, especially those including business courses, provide a well-rounded education. Film schools also may provide training on the artistic or aesthetic aspects of filmmaking.

Individuals interested in camera operations should subscribe to videographic newsletters and magazines, join audio-video clubs, and seek summer or part-time employment in cable and television networks, motion picture studios, or camera and video stores.

Camera operators in entry-level jobs learn to set up lights, cameras, and other equipment. They may receive routine assignments requiring adjustments to their cameras or decisions on what subject matter to capture. Camera operators in the film and television industries usually are hired for a project on the basis of recommendations from individuals such as producers, directors of photography, and camera assistants from previous projects or through interviews with the producer. ENG and studio camera operators who work for television affiliates usually start in small markets to gain experience.

Camera operators need good eyesight, artistic ability, and hand-eye coordination. They should be patient, accurate, and detail oriented. Camera operators also should have good communication skills and, if needed, the ability to hold a camera by hand for extended periods.

Camera operators who run their own businesses, or freelance, need business skills as well as talent. These individuals must know how to submit bids, write contracts, get permission to shoot on locations that normally are not open to the public, obtain releases to use film or tape of people, price their services, secure copyright protection for their work, and keep financial records.

With experience, operators may advance to more demanding assignments or to positions with larger or network television stations. Advancement for ENG operators may mean moving to larger media markets. Other camera operators and editors may become directors of photography for movie studios, advertising agencies, or television programs. Some teach at technical schools, film schools, or universities.

Employment

Television, video, and motion picture camera operators held about 28,000 jobs in 2004, and film and video editors held about 20,000. Many are employed by independent television stations, local affiliate stations of television networks or broadcast groups, large cable and television networks, or smaller independent production companies. About 1 in 5 camera operators were self-employed. Some self-employed camera operators contracted with television networks, documentary or independent filmmakers, advertising agencies, or trade show or convention sponsors to work on individual projects for a set fee, often at a daily rate.

Most of the salaried camera operators were employed by television broadcasting stations or motion picture studios. More than half of the salaried film and video editors worked for motion picture studios. Most camera operators and editors worked in large metropolitan areas.

Job Outlook

Television, video, and motion picture camera operators and editors can expect keen competition for job openings because the work is attractive to many people. The number of individuals interested in positions as videographers and movie camera operators usually is much greater than the number of openings. Those who succeed in landing a salaried job or attracting enough work to earn a living by freelancing are likely to be the most creative and highly motivated people, able to adapt to rapidly changing technologies and adept at operating a business. Related work experience or job-related training also can benefit prospective camera operators.

Employment of camera operators and editors is expected to grow about as fast as the average for all occupations through 2014. Rapid expansion of the entertainment market, especially motion picture production and distribution, will spur growth of camera operators. In addition, computer and Internet services will provide new outlets for interactive productions. Growth will be tempered, however, by the increased off-shore production of motion pictures. Camera operators will be needed to film made-for-the-Internet broadcasts, such as live music videos, digital movies, sports features, and general information or entertainment programming. These images can be delivered directly into the home either on compact discs or as streaming video over the Internet. Job growth in radio and television broadcasting will be tempered by the use of robocams and Parkervision systems for studio broadcasts; cameras in these systems are automated and under the control of a single person working either on the studio floor or in a director's booth.

Earnings

Median annual earnings for television, video, and motion picture camera operators were $37,610 in May 2004. The middle 50 percent earned between $22,640 and $56,400. The lowest 10 percent earned less than $15,730, and the highest 10 percent earned more than $76,100. Median annual earnings were $48,900 in the motion picture and video industries and $29,560 in radio and television broadcasting.

Median annual earnings for film and video editors were $43,590 in May 2004. The middle 50 percent earned between $29,310 and $63,890. The lowest 10 percent earned less than $21,710, and the highest 10 percent earned more than $93,950. Median annual earnings were $44,710 in the motion picture and video industries, which employed the largest numbers of film and video editors.

Many camera operators who work in film or video are freelancers, whose earnings tend to fluctuate each year. Because most freelance camera operators purchase their own equipment, they incur considerable expense acquiring and maintaining cameras and accessories. Some camera operators belong to unions, including the International Alliance of Theatrical Stage Employees and the National Association of Broadcast Employees and Technicians.

Related Occupations

Related arts and media occupations include artists and related workers, broadcast and sound engineering technicians, and radio operators, designers, and photographers.

Sources of Additional Information

For information about careers as a camera operator, contact:
➤ International Cinematographer's Guild, 80 Eighth Avenue, 14th Floor, New York, NY 10011.
➤ National Association of Broadcast Employees and Technicians, 501 Third Street, NW., 6th floor, Washington, DC 20001. Internet: **http://www.nabetcwa.org/**

Information about career and employment opportunities for camera operators and film and video editors also is available from local offices of State employment service agencies, local offices of the relevant trade unions, and local television and film production companies that employ these workers.

Writers and Editors

(O*NET 27-3041.00, 27-3042.00, 27-3043.01, 27-3043.02, 27-3043.03, 27-3043.04)

Significant Points

- Most jobs in this occupation require a college degree in communications, journalism, or English, although a degree in a technical subject may be useful for technical-writing positions.

- The outlook for most writing and editing jobs is expected to be competitive because many people are attracted to the occupation.

- Online publications and services are growing in number and sophistication, spurring the demand for writers and editors, especially those with Web experience.

Nature of the Work

Communicating through the written word, writers and editors generally fall into one of three categories. *Writers and authors* develop

Writers and editors typically conduct library research before writing their stories.

original fiction and nonfiction for books, magazines, trade journals, online publications, company newsletters, radio and television broadcasts, motion pictures, and advertisements. (*Reporters and correspondents*, who collect and analyze facts about newsworthy events, are described elsewhere in the *Handbook*.) *Editors* examine proposals and select material for publication or broadcast. They review and revise a writer's work for publication or dissemination. *Technical writers* develop technical materials, such as equipment manuals, appendixes, or operating and maintenance instructions. They also may assist in layout work.

Most writers and editors have at least a basic familiarity with technology, regularly using personal computers, desktop or electronic publishing systems, scanners, and other electronic communications equipment. Many writers prepare material directly for the Internet. For example, they may write for electronic newspapers or magazines, create short fiction or poetry, or produce technical documentation that is available only online. Also, they may write text for Web sites. These writers should be knowledgeable about graphic design, page layout, and multimedia software. In addition, they should be familiar with interactive technologies of the Web so that they can blend text, graphics, and sound together.

Writers—especially of nonfiction—are expected to establish their credibility with editors and readers through strong research and the use of appropriate sources and citations. Sustaining high ethical standards and meeting publication deadlines are essential.

Creative writers, poets, and lyricists, including novelists, playwrights, and screenwriters, create original works—such as prose, poems, plays, and song lyrics—for publication or performance. Some works may be commissioned by a sponsor; others may be written for hire (on the basis of the completion of a draft or an outline).

Nonfiction writers either propose a topic or are assigned one, often by an editor or publisher. They gather information about the topic through personal observation, library and Internet research, and interviews. Writers then select the material they want to use, organize it, and use the written word to express ideas and convey information. Writers also revise or rewrite sections, searching for the best organization or the right phrasing. *Copy writers* prepare advertising copy for use by publication or broadcast media or to promote the sale of goods and services. *Newsletter writers* produce information for distribution to association memberships, corporate employees, organizational clients, or the public.

Freelance writers sell their work to publishers, publication enterprises, manufacturing firms, public relations departments, or advertising agencies. Sometimes, they contract with publishers to write a book or an article. Others may be hired to complete specific assignments, such as writing about a new product or technique.

Bloggers write for the Internet. Most bloggers write personal reflections on a subject of close personal or professional interest. Some blogs take the form of a personal diary; others read like reports from the field—first-hand, subjective accounts of an event or an activity. Most blogs are written for recreational reasons with little expectation of earning a fee; however, some blogs promote a business or support a cause and may generate interest or income through other activities.

Editors review, rewrite, and edit the work of writers. They may also do original writing. An editor's responsibilities vary with the employer and type and level of editorial position held. Editorial duties may include planning the content of books, technical journals, trade magazines, and other general-interest publications. Editors also decide what material will appeal to readers, review and edit drafts of books and articles, offer comments to improve the work, and suggest possible titles. In addition, they may oversee the production of the publications. In the book-publishing industry, an editor's primary responsibility is to review proposals for books and decide whether to buy the publication rights from the author.

Major newspapers and newsmagazines usually employ several types of editors. The *executive editor* oversees *assistant editors*, who have responsibility for particular subjects, such as local news, international news, feature stories, or sports. Executive editors generally have the final say about what stories are published and how they are covered. The *managing editor* usually is responsible for the daily operation of the news department. *Assignment editors* determine which reporters will cover a given story. *Copy editors* mostly review and edit a reporter's copy for accuracy, content, grammar, and style.

In smaller organizations, such as small daily or weekly newspapers or the membership or publications departments of nonprofit or similar organizations, a single editor may do everything or share responsibility with only a few other people. Executive and managing editors typically hire writers, reporters, and other employees. They also plan budgets and negotiate contracts with freelance writers, sometimes called "stringers" in the news industry. In broadcasting companies, *program directors* have similar responsibilities.

Editors and program directors often have assistants, many of whom hold entry-level jobs. These assistants, such as copy editors and *production assistants*, review copy for errors in grammar, punctuation, and spelling and check the copy for readability, style, and agreement with editorial policy. They suggest revisions, such as changing words and rearranging sentences, to improve clarity or accuracy. They also carry out research for writers and verify facts, dates, and statistics. Production assistants arrange page layouts of articles, photographs, and advertising; compose headlines; and prepare copy for printing. *Publication assistants* who work for publishing houses may read and evaluate manuscripts submitted by freelance writers, proofread printers' galleys, and answer letters about published material. Production assistants on small newspapers or in radio stations compile articles available from wire services or the Internet, answer phones, and make photocopies.

Technical writers put technical information into easily understandable language. They prepare operating and maintenance manuals, catalogs, parts lists, assembly instructions, sales promotion materials, and project proposals. Many technical writers work with engineers on technical subject matters to prepare written interpretations of engineering and design specifications and other information for a general readership. Technical writers also may serve as part of a team conducting usability studies to help improve the design of a product that still is in the prototype stage. They plan and edit technical materials and oversee the preparation of illustrations, photographs, diagrams, and charts.

Science and medical writers prepare a range of formal documents presenting detailed information on the physical or medical sciences. They convey research findings for scientific or medical professions and organize information for advertising or public relations needs. Many writers work with researchers on technical subjects to prepare written interpretations of data and other information for a general readership.

Working Conditions

Some writers and editors work in comfortable, private offices; others work in noisy rooms filled with the sound of keyboards and computer printers, as well as the voices of other writers tracking down information over the telephone. The search for information sometimes requires that writers travel to diverse workplaces, such as factories, offices, or laboratories, but many find their material through telephone interviews, the library, and the Internet.

Advances in electronic communications have changed the work environment for many writers. Laptop computers and wireless communications technologies allow growing numbers of writers to work from home and even on the road. The ability to e-mail, transmit, and download stories, research, or editorial review materials using the Internet allows writers and editors greater flexibility in where and how they complete assignments.

Some writers keep regular office hours, either to maintain contact with sources and editors or to establish a writing routine, but most writers set their own hours. Many writers, especially freelance writers, are paid per assignment; therefore, they work any number of hours necessary to meet a deadline. As a result, writers must be willing to work evenings, nights, or weekends to produce a piece acceptable to an editor or client by the publication deadline. Those who prepare morning or weekend publications and broadcasts also may regularly work nights and weekends.

While many freelance writers enjoy running their own businesses and the advantages of working flexible hours, most routinely face the pressures of juggling multiple projects with competing demands and the continual need to find new work in order to earn a living. Deadline pressures and long, erratic work hours—often part of the daily routine in these jobs—may cause stress, fatigue, or burnout; use of computers for extended periods may cause some individuals to experience back pain, eyestrain, or fatigue.

Training, Other Qualifications, and Advancement

A college degree generally is required for a position as a writer or editor. Although some employers look for a broad liberal arts background, most prefer to hire people with degrees in communications, journalism, or English. For those who specialize in a particular area, such as fashion, business, or law, additional background in the chosen field is expected. Knowledge of a second language is helpful for some positions.

Increasingly, technical writing requires a degree in, or some knowledge about, a specialized field—for example, engineering, business, or one of the sciences. In many cases, people with good writing skills can acquire specialized knowledge on the job. Some transfer from jobs as technicians, scientists, or engineers. Others begin as research assistants or as trainees in a technical information department, develop technical communication skills, and then assume writing duties.

Writers and editors must be able to express ideas clearly and logically and should love to write. Creativity, curiosity, a broad range of knowledge, self-motivation, and perseverance also are valuable. Writers and editors must demonstrate good judgment and a strong sense of ethics in deciding what material to publish. Editors also need tact and the ability to guide and encourage others in their work.

For some jobs, the ability to concentrate amid confusion and to work under pressure is essential. Familiarity with electronic publishing, graphics, and video production equipment increasingly is needed. Use of electronic and wireless communications equipment to send e-mail, transmit work, and review copy often is necessary. Online newspapers and magazines require knowledge of computer software used to combine online text with graphics, audio, video, and animation.

High school and college newspapers, literary magazines, community newspapers, and radio and television stations all provide valuable, but sometimes unpaid, practical writing experience. Many magazines, newspapers, and broadcast stations have internships for students. Interns write short pieces, conduct research and interviews, and learn about the publishing or broadcasting business.

In small firms, beginning writers and editors hired as assistants may actually begin writing or editing material right away. Opportunities for advancement can be limited, however. Many writers look for work on a short-term, project-by-project basis. Many small or not-for-profit organizations either do not have enough regular work or cannot afford to employ writers on a full-time basis. However, they routinely contract out work to freelance writers.

In larger businesses, jobs usually are more formally structured. Beginners generally do research, fact checking, or copy editing. Advancement to full-scale writing or editing assignments may occur more slowly for newer writers and editors in larger organizations than for employees of smaller companies. Advancement often is more predictable, though, coming with the assignment of more important articles.

Advancement for freelancers often means working on larger, more complex projects for more money. Building a reputation and establishing a track record for meeting deadlines also makes it easier to get future assignments, as does instituting long-term freelance relationships with the same publications.

The growing popularity of blogs could allow some writers to get their work read; a few well-written blogs may garner some recognition for the author and may lead to a few paid pieces in other print or electronic publications. However, most bloggers do not earn much money writing their blogs.

Employment

Writers and editors held about 320,000 jobs in 2004. More than one-third were self-employed. Writers and authors held about 142,000 jobs; editors, about 127,000 jobs; and technical writers, about 50,000 jobs. About one-half of the salaried jobs for writers and editors were in the information sector, which includes newspaper, periodical, book, and directory publishers; radio and television broadcasting; software publishers; motion picture and sound-recording industries; Internet service providers, Web search portals, and data-processing services; and Internet publishing and broadcasting. Substantial numbers also worked in advertising and related services, computer systems design and related services, and public and private educational services. Other salaried writers and editors worked in computer and electronic product manufacturing; government agencies; religious organizations; and business, professional, labor, political, and similar organizations.

Jobs with major book publishers, magazines, broadcasting companies, advertising agencies, and public relations firms are concentrated in New York, Chicago, Los Angeles, Boston, Philadelphia, and San Francisco; however, many writers work elsewhere and travel regularly to meet with personnel at the headquarters. Jobs with newspapers, business and professional journals, and technical and trade magazines are more widely dispersed throughout the country.

Thousands of other individuals work as freelance writers, earning some income from their articles, books, and, less commonly, television and movie scripts. Most support themselves with income derived from other sources.

Job Outlook

Employment of writers and editors is expected to grow about as fast as the average for all occupations through the year 2014. The outlook for most writing and editing jobs is expected to be competitive because many people with writing or journalism training are attracted to the occupation.

Employment of salaried writers and editors for newspapers, periodicals, book publishers, and nonprofit organizations is expected to increase as demand grows for these publications. Magazines and other periodicals increasingly are developing market niches, appealing to readers with special interests. Businesses and organizations are developing newsletters and websites, and more companies are experimenting with publishing materials directly on the Internet. Online publications and services are growing in number and sophistication, spurring the demand for writers and editors, especially those with Web experience. Advertising and public relations agencies, which also are growing, should be another source of new jobs.

Opportunities should be best for technical writers and those with training in a specialized field. Demand for technical writers and writers with expertise in areas such as law, medicine, or economics is expected to increase because of the continuing expansion of scientific and technical information and the need to communicate it to others. Legal, scientific, and technological developments and discoveries generate demand for people to interpret technical information for a more general audience. Rapid growth and change in the high-technology and electronics industries result in a greater need for people to write users' guides, instruction manuals, and training materials. This work requires people who not only are technically skilled as writers, but also are familiar with the subject area.

In addition to job openings created by employment growth, some openings will arise as experienced workers retire, transfer to other occupations, or leave the labor force. Replacement needs are relatively high in this occupation; many freelancers leave because they cannot earn enough money.

Earnings

Median annual earnings for salaried writers and authors were $44,350 in May 2004. The middle 50 percent earned between $31,720 and $62,930. The lowest 10 percent earned less than $23,330, and the highest 10 percent earned more than $91,260. Median annual earnings were $54,410 in advertising and related services and $37,010 in newspaper, periodical, book, and directory publishers.

Median annual earnings for salaried editors were $43,890 in May 2004. The middle 50 percent earned between $33,130 and $58,850. The lowest 10 percent earned less than $25,780, and the highest 10 percent earned more than $80,020. Median annual earnings of those working for newspaper, periodical, book, and directory publishers were $43,620.

Median annual earnings for salaried technical writers were $53,490 in May 2004. The middle 50 percent earned between $41,440 and $68,980. The lowest 10 percent earned less than $32,490, and the highest 10 percent earned more than $86,780. Median annual earnings in computer systems design and related services were $54,710.

According to the Society for Technical Communication, the median annual salary for entry level technical writers was $42,500 in 2004. The median annual salary for midlevel nonsupervisory technical writers was $51,500, and for senior nonsupervisory technical writers, $66,000.

Related Occupations

Writers and editors communicate ideas and information. Other communications occupations include announcers; interpreters and translators; news analysts, reporters, and correspondents; and public relations specialists.

Sources of Additional Information

For information on careers in technical writing, contact:
➤ Society for Technical Communication, Inc., 901 N. Stuart St., Suite 904, Arlington, VA 22203. Internet: **www.stc.org**

Health Diagnosing and Treating Practitioners

Audiologists

(O*NET 29-1121.00)

Significant Points

● Employment growth will be spurred by the expanding population in older age groups that are prone to medical conditions that result in hearing problems.

● More than half worked in health care facilities; many others were employed by educational services.

● A master's degree in audiology has been the standard credential; however, a clinical doctoral degree is becoming more common for new entrants and is expected to become the new standard for the profession.

Nature of the Work

Audiologists work with people who have hearing, balance, and related ear problems. They examine individuals of all ages and identify those with the symptoms of hearing loss and other auditory, balance, and related sensory and neural problems. They then assess the nature and extent of the problems and help the individuals manage them. Using audiometers, computers, and other testing devices, they measure the loudness at which a person begins to hear sounds, the ability to distinguish between sounds, and the impact of hearing loss on an individual's daily life. In addition, audiologists use computer equipment to evaluate and diagnose balance disorders. Audiologists interpret these results and may coordinate them with medical, educational, and psychological information to make a diagnosis and determine a course of treatment.

Hearing disorders can result from a variety of causes including trauma at birth, viral infections, genetic disorders, exposure to loud noise, certain medications, or aging. Treatment may include examining and cleaning the ear canal, fitting and dispensing hearing aids, and fitting and programming cochlear implants. Audiologic treatment also includes counseling on adjusting to hearing loss, training on the use of hearing instruments, and teaching communication strategies for use in a variety of environments. For example, they may provide instruction in listening strategies. Audiologists also may recommend, fit, and dispense personal or large area amplification systems and alerting devices.

In audiology (hearing) clinics, audiologists may independently develop and carry out treatment programs. They keep records on the initial evaluation, progress, and discharge of patients. In other settings, audiologists may work with other health and education providers as part of a team in planning and implementing services for children and adults, from birth to old age. Audiologists who diagnose and treat balance disorders often work in collaboration with physicians, and physical and occupational therapists.

Some audiologists specialize in work with the elderly, children, or hearing-impaired individuals who need special treatment programs. Others develop and implement ways to protect workers' hearing from on-the-job injuries. They measure noise levels in workplaces and conduct hearing protection programs in factories, as well as in schools and communities.

Audiologists who work in private practice also manage the business aspects of running an office, such as developing a patient base, hiring employees, keeping records, and ordering equipment and supplies.

A few audiologists conduct research on types of—and treatment for—hearing, balance, and related disorders. Others design and develop equipment or techniques for diagnosing and treating these disorders.

Working Conditions
Audiologists usually work at a desk or table in clean, comfortable surroundings. The job is not physically demanding but does require attention to detail and intense concentration. The emotional needs of patients and their families may be demanding. Most full-time audiologists work about 40 hours per week, which may include weekends and evenings to meet the needs of patients. Some work part time. Those who work on a contract basis may spend a substantial amount of time traveling between facilities.

Training, Other Qualifications, and Advancement
Audiologists are regulated in 49 States; all require that individuals have at least a master's degree in audiology. However, a clinical doctoral degree is expected to become the new standard, and several States are currently in the process of changing their regulations to require the Doctor of Audiology (Au.D.) degree or equivalent. A passing score on the national examination on audiology offered through the Praxis Series of the Educational Testing Service also

Audiologists diagnose and treat patients with hearing or balance problems.

is needed. Other requirements typically are 300 to 375 hours of supervised clinical experience and 9 months of postgraduate professional clinical experience. Forty-one States have continuing education requirements for licensure renewal. An additional examination and license is required in order to dispense hearing aids in some States. Medicaid, Medicare, and private health insurers generally require practitioners to be licensed to qualify for reimbursement.

In 2005, there were 24 master's degree programs and 62 clinical doctoral programs offered at accredited colleges and universities. Graduation from an accredited program may be required to obtain a license. Requirements for admission to programs in audiology include courses in English, mathematics, physics, chemistry, biology, psychology, and communication. Graduate course work in audiology includes anatomy; physiology; physics; genetics; normal and abnormal communication development; auditory, balance, and neural systems assessment and treatment; diagnosis and treatment; pharmacology; and ethics.

Audiologists can acquire the Certificate of Clinical Competence in Audiology (CCC-A) offered by the American Speech-Language-Hearing Association. To earn a CCC, a person must have a graduate degree and 375 hours of supervised clinical experience, complete a 36-week postgraduate clinical fellowship, and pass the Praxis Series examination in audiology, administered by the Educational Testing Service. According to the American Speech-Language-Hearing Association, as of 2007, audiologists will need to have a bachelor's degree and complete 75 hours of credit toward a doctoral degree in order to seek certification. As of 2012, audiologists will have to earn a doctoral degree in order to be certified.

Audiologists may also be certified through the American Board of Audiology. Applicants must earn a master's or doctoral degree in audiology from a regionally accredited college or university, achieve a passing score on a national examination in audiology, and demonstrate that they have completed a minimum of 2,000 hours of mentored professional practice in a two-year period with a qualified audiologist. Certificants must apply for renewal every three years. They must demonstrate that they have earned 45 hours of approved continuing education within the three-year period. Beginning in 2007, all applicants must earn a doctoral degree in audiology.

Audiologists should be able to effectively communicate diagnostic test results, diagnoses, and proposed treatments in a manner easily understood by their patients. They must be able to approach problems objectively and provide support to patients and their families. Because a patient's progress may be slow, patience, compassion, and good listening skills are necessary.

Employment
Audiologists held about 10,000 jobs in 2004. More than half of all jobs were in offices of physicians or other health practitioners, including audiologists; in hospitals; and in outpatient care centers. About 1 in 7 jobs was in educational services, including elementary and secondary schools. Other jobs for audiologists were in health and personal care stores, including hearing aid stores; scientific research and development services; and State and local governments.

A small number of audiologists were self-employed in private practice. They provided hearing health care services in their own offices or worked under contract for schools, health care facilities, or other establishments.

Job Outlook
Employment of audiologists is expected to grow about as fast as the average for all occupations through the year 2014. Because

hearing loss is strongly associated with aging, rapid growth in older population groups will cause the number of persons with hearing and balance impairments to increase markedly. Medical advances are also improving the survival rate of premature infants and trauma victims, who then need assessment and possible treatment. Greater awareness of the importance of early identification and diagnosis of hearing disorders in infants also will increase employment. Most States now require that all newborns be screened for hearing loss and receive appropriate early intervention services.

Employment in educational services will increase along with growth in elementary and secondary school enrollments, including enrollment of special education students. The number of audiologists in private practice will rise due to the increasing demand for direct services to individuals as well as increasing use of contract services by hospitals, schools, and nursing care facilities.

Growth in employment of audiologists will be moderated by limitations on insurance reimbursements for the services they provide. Additionally, increased educational requirements may limit the pool of workers entering the profession and any resulting higher salaries may cause doctors to hire more lower paid ear technicians to perform the functions that audiologists held in doctor's offices. Only a few job openings for audiologists will arise from the need to replace those who leave the occupation, because the occupation is small.

Earnings
Median annual earnings of audiologists were $51,470 in May 2004. The middle 50 percent earned between $42,160 and $62,210. The lowest 10 percent earned less than $34,990, and the highest 10 percent earned more than $75,990.

According to a 2004 survey by the American Speech-Language-Hearing Association, the median annual salary for full-time certified audiologists who worked on a calendar-year basis, generally 11 or 12 months annually, was $56,000. For those who worked on an academic-year basis, usually 9 or 10 months annually, the median annual salary was $53,000. The median starting salary for certified audiologists with one to three years of experience was $45,000 on a calendar-year basis.

Related Occupations
Audiologists specialize in the prevention, diagnosis, and treatment of hearing problems. Workers in related occupations include occupational therapists, optometrists, physical therapists, psychologists, recreational therapists, rehabilitation counselors, and speech-language pathologists.

Sources of Additional Information
State licensing boards can provide information on licensure requirements. State departments of education can supply information on certification requirements for those who wish to work in public schools.

General information on careers in audiology is available from:
➤ American Academy of Audiology, 11730 Plaza America Dr., Suite 300, Reston, VA 20190. Internet: **http://www.audiology.org**

Career information, a description of the CCC-A credential, and a listing of accredited graduate programs, is available from:
➤ American Speech-Language-Hearing Association, 10801 Rockville Pike, Rockville, MD 20852. Internet: **http://www.asha.org**

Information on American Board of Audiology certification is available from:
➤ American Board of Audiology, 11730 Plaza America Dr., Suite 300, Reston, VA 20190. Internet: **http://www.americanboardofaudiology.org**

Chiropractors

(O*NET 29-1011.00)

Significant Points

- Job prospects should be good; employment is expected to increase faster than average as consumer demand for alternative health care grows.

- Chiropractors must be licensed, requiring 2 to 4 years of undergraduate education, the completion of a 4-year chiropractic college course, and passing scores on national and State examinations.

- About 58 percent of chiropractors are self-employed.

- Earnings are relatively low in the beginning, but increase as the practice grows.

Nature of the Work
Chiropractors, also known as *doctors of chiropractic* or *chiropractic physicians*, diagnose and treat patients whose health problems are associated with the body's muscular, nervous, and skeletal systems, especially the spine. Chiropractors believe that interference with these systems impairs the body's normal functions and lowers its resistance to disease. They also hold that spinal or vertebral dysfunction alters many important body functions by affecting the nervous system and that skeletal imbalance through joint or articular dysfunction, especially in the spine, can cause pain.

The chiropractic approach to health care is holistic, stressing the patient's overall health and wellness. It recognizes that many factors affect health, including exercise, diet, rest, environment, and heredity. Chiropractors provide natural, drugless, nonsurgical health treatments and rely on the body's inherent recuperative abilities. They also recommend changes in lifestyle—in eating, exercise, and sleeping habits, for example—to their patients. When appropriate, chiropractors consult with and refer patients to other health practitioners.

Like other health practitioners, chiropractors follow a standard routine to secure the information they need for diagnosis and treatment. They take the patient's medical history; conduct physical, neurological, and orthopedic examinations; and may order laboratory tests. X rays and other diagnostic images are important tools because of the chiropractor's emphasis on the spine and its proper function. Chiropractors also employ a postural and spinal analysis common to chiropractic diagnosis.

In cases in which difficulties can be traced to the involvement of musculoskeletal structures, chiropractors manually adjust the spinal column. Some chiropractors use water, light, massage, ultrasound, electric, acupuncture, and heat therapy. They also may apply supports such as straps, tapes, and braces. Chiropractors counsel patients about wellness concepts such as nutrition, exercise, changes in lifestyle, and stress management, but do not prescribe drugs or perform surgery.

Some chiropractors specialize in sports injuries, neurology, orthopedics, pediatrics, nutrition, internal disorders, or diagnostic imaging.

Many chiropractors are solo or group practitioners who also have the administrative responsibilities of running a practice. In larger offices, chiropractors delegate these tasks to office managers and chiropractic assistants. Chiropractors in private practice are responsible for developing a patient base, hiring employees, and keeping records.

Working Conditions
Chiropractors work in clean, comfortable offices. Their average workweek is about 40 hours, although longer hours are not

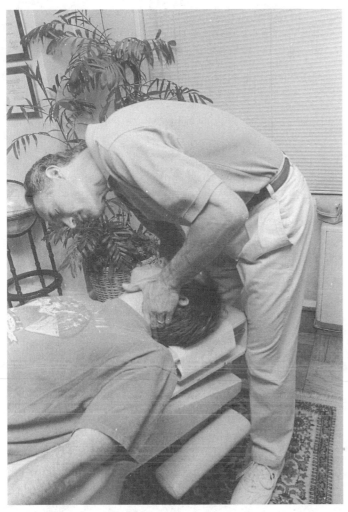

Chiropractors provide natural, drugless, nonsurgical health treatments to patients, including spinal adjustments.

uncommon. Solo practitioners set their own hours, but may work evenings or weekends to accommodate patients.

Like other health practitioners, chiropractors are sometimes on their feet for long periods. Chiropractors who take x rays must employ appropriate precautions against the dangers of repeated exposure to radiation.

Training, Other Qualifications, and Advancement

All States and the District of Columbia regulate the practice of chiropractic and grant licenses to chiropractors who meet the educational and examination requirements established by the State. Chiropractors can practice only in States where they are licensed. Some States have agreements permitting chiropractors licensed in one State to obtain a license in another without further examination, provided that their educational, examination, and practice credentials meet State specifications.

Most State boards require at least 2 years of undergraduate education; an increasing number are requiring a 4-year bachelor's degree. All boards require the completion of a 4-year program at an accredited chiropractic college leading to the Doctor of Chiropractic degree.

For licensure, most State boards recognize either all or part of the four-part test administered by the National Board of Chiropractic Examiners. State examinations may supplement the National Board tests, depending on State requirements. All States except New Jersey require the completion of a specified number of hours of continuing education each year in order to maintain licensure. Chiropractic

associations and accredited chiropractic programs and institutions offer continuing education programs.

In 2005, 15 chiropractic programs and 2 chiropractic institutions in the United States were accredited by the Council on Chiropractic Education. Applicants are required to have at least 90 semester hours of undergraduate study leading toward a bachelor's degree, including courses in English, the social sciences or humanities, organic and inorganic chemistry, biology, physics, and psychology. Many applicants have a bachelor's degree, which may eventually become the minimum entry requirement. Several chiropractic colleges offer prechiropractic study, as well as a bachelor's degree program. Recognition of prechiropractic education offered by chiropractic colleges varies among the State boards.

Chiropractic programs require a minimum of 4,200 hours of combined classroom, laboratory, and clinical experience. During the first 2 years, most chiropractic programs emphasize classroom and laboratory work in basic science subjects such as anatomy, physiology, public health, microbiology, pathology, and biochemistry. The last 2 years stress courses in manipulation and spinal adjustment and provide clinical experience in physical and laboratory diagnosis, neurology, orthopedics, geriatrics, physiotherapy, and nutrition. Chiropractic programs and institutions grant the degree of Doctor of Chiropractic.

Chiropractic colleges also offer Postdoctoral training in orthopedics, neurology, sports injuries, nutrition, rehabilitation, radiology, industrial consulting, family practice, pediatrics, and applied chiropractic sciences. Once such training is complete, chiropractors may take specialty exams leading to "diplomate" status in a given specialty. Exams are administered by specialty chiropractic associations.

Chiropractic requires keen observation to detect physical abnormalities. It also takes considerable manual dexterity, but not unusual strength or endurance, to perform adjustments. Chiropractors should be able to work independently and handle responsibility. As in other health-related occupations, empathy, understanding, and the desire to help others are good qualities for dealing effectively with patients.

Newly licensed chiropractors can set up a new practice, purchase an established one, or enter into partnership with an established practitioner. They also may take a salaried position with an established chiropractor, a group practice, or a health care facility.

Employment

Chiropractors held about 53,000 jobs in 2004. Approximately 58 percent of chiropractors are self-employed. Most chiropractors are in solo practice, although some are in group practice or work for other chiropractors. A small number teach, conduct research at chiropractic institutions, or work in hospitals and clinics.

Many chiropractors are located in small communities. However, there still often are geographic imbalances in the distribution of chiropractors, in part because many establish practices close to one of the few chiropractic institutions.

Job Outlook

Job prospects are expected to be good for persons who enter the practice of chiropractic. Employment of chiropractors is expected to grow faster than the average for all occupations through the year 2014 as consumer demand for alternative health care grows. Because chiropractors emphasize the importance of healthy lifestyles and do not prescribe drugs or perform surgery, chiropractic care is appealing to many health-conscious Americans. Chiropractic treatment of the back, neck, extremities, and joints has become more accepted as a result of research and changing attitudes about alternative, noninvasive health care practices. The rapidly expanding older population, with its increased likelihood of mechanical and structural problems, also will increase demand for chiropractors.

Demand for chiropractic treatment, however, is related as well to the ability of patients to pay, either directly or through health insurance. Although more insurance plans now cover chiropractic services, the extent of such coverage varies among plans. Increasingly, chiropractors must educate communities about the benefits of chiropractic care in order to establish a successful practice.

In this occupation, replacement needs arise almost entirely from retirements. Chiropractors usually remain in the occupation until they retire; few transfer to other occupations. Establishing a new practice will be easiest in areas with a low concentration of chiropractors.

Earnings

Median annual earnings of salaried chiropractors were $69,910 in May 2004. The middle 50 percent earned between $46,710 and $118,280 a year.

In 2005, the mean salary for chiropractors was $104,363, according to a survey conducted by *Chiropractic Economics* magazine.

In chiropractic, as in other types of independent practice, earnings are relatively low in the beginning and increase as the practice grows. Geographic location and the characteristics and qualifications of the practitioner also may influence earnings. Self-employed chiropractors must provide their own health insurance and retirement.

Related Occupations

Chiropractors treat patients and work to prevent bodily disorders and injuries. So do athletic trainers, massage therapists, occupational therapists, physical therapists, physicians and surgeons, podiatrists, and veterinarians.

Sources of Additional Information

General information on a career as a chiropractor is available from the following organizations:

➤ American Chiropractic Association, 1701 Clarendon Blvd., Arlington, VA 22209. Internet: **http://www.acatoday.org**

➤ International Chiropractors Association, 1110 North Glebe Rd., Suite 1000, Arlington, VA 22201. Internet: **http://www.chiropractic.org**

For a list of chiropractic programs and institutions, as well as general information on chiropractic education, contact:

➤ Council on Chiropractic Education, 8049 North 85th Way, Scottsdale, AZ 85258-4321. Internet: **http://www.cce-usa.org**

For information on State education and licensure requirements, contact:

➤ Federation of Chiropractic Licensing Boards, 5401 W. 10th St., Suite 101, Greeley, CO 80634-4400. Internet: **http://www.fclb.org**

For more information on the national chiropractic licensing exam, contact:

➤ National Board of Chiropractic Examiners, 901 54th Ave., Suite 101, Greeley, CO 80634-4400. Internet: **http://www.nbce.org**

For information on admission requirements to a specific chiropractic college, as well as scholarship and loan information, contact the college's admissions office.

Dentists

(O*NET 29-1021.00, 29-1022.00, 29-1023.00, 29-1024.00, 29-1029.99)

Significant Points

● Most dentists are solo practitioners.

● Dentists usually complete at least 8 years of education beyond high school.

● Employment is projected to grow about as fast as average, and most job openings will result from the need to replace the large number of dentists expected to retire.

● Job prospects should be good.

Nature of the Work

Dentists diagnose, prevent, and treat problems with teeth or mouth tissue. They remove decay, fill cavities, examine x rays, place protective plastic sealants on children's teeth, straighten teeth, and repair fractured teeth. They also perform corrective surgery on gums and supporting bones to treat gum diseases. Dentists extract teeth and make models and measurements for dentures to replace missing teeth. They provide instruction on diet, brushing, flossing, the use of fluorides, and other aspects of dental care. They also administer anesthetics and write prescriptions for antibiotics and other medications.

Dentists use a variety of equipment, including x-ray machines; drills; and instruments such as mouth mirrors, probes, forceps, brushes, and scalpels. They wear masks, gloves, and safety glasses to protect themselves and their patients from infectious diseases.

Dentists in private practice oversee a variety of administrative tasks, including bookkeeping and buying equipment and supplies. They may employ and supervise dental hygienists, dental assistants, dental laboratory technicians, and receptionists. (These occupations are described elsewhere in the *Handbook*.)

Most dentists are general practitioners, handling a variety of dental needs. Other dentists practice in any of nine specialty areas. *Orthodontists,* the largest group of specialists, straighten teeth by applying pressure to the teeth with braces or retainers. The next largest group, *oral and maxillofacial surgeons*, operates on the mouth and jaws. The remainder may specialize as *pediatric dentists* (focusing on dentistry for children); *periodontists* (treating gums and bone supporting the teeth); *prosthodontists* (replacing missing teeth with permanent fixtures, such as crowns and bridges, or with removable fixtures such as dentures); *endodontists* (performing root canal therapy); *public health dentists* (promoting good dental health and preventing dental diseases within the community); *oral pathologists* (studying oral diseases); or *oral and maxillofacial radiologists* (diagnosing diseases in the head and neck through the use of imaging technologies).

Working Conditions

Most dentists work 4 or 5 days a week. Some work evenings and weekends to meet their patients' needs. Most full-time dentists work between 35 and 40 hours a week, but others work more. Initially, dentists may work more hours as they establish their practice. Experienced dentists often work fewer hours. Many continue in part-time practice well beyond the usual retirement age.

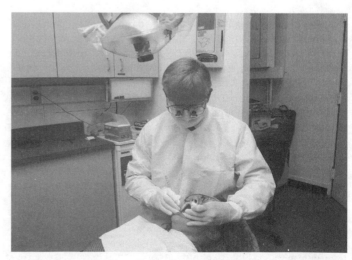

Dentists use a variety of instruments such as mouth mirrors, probes, forceps, brushes, and scalpels.

Most dentists are solo practitioners, meaning that they own their own businesses and work alone or with a small staff. Some dentists have partners, and a few work for other dentists as associate dentists.

Training, Other Qualifications, and Advancement

All 50 States and the District of Columbia require dentists to be licensed. To qualify for a license in most States, candidates must graduate from 1 of the 56 dental schools accredited by the American Dental Association's (ADA's) Commission on Dental Accreditation in 2004, and then must pass written and practical examinations. Candidates may fulfill the written part of the State licensing requirements by passing the National Board Dental Examinations. Individual States or regional testing agencies administer the written or practical examinations.

Dental schools require a minimum of 2 years of college-level predental education, regardless of the major chosen. However, most dental students have at least a bachelor's degree. Predental education emphasizes coursework in science, and many applicants to dental school major in a science such as biology or chemistry, while other applicants major in another subject and take many science courses as well. A few applicants are accepted to dental school after 2 or 3 years of college and complete their bachelor's degree while attending dental school.

All dental schools require applicants to take the Dental Admissions Test (DAT). When selecting students, schools consider scores earned on the DAT, applicants' grade point averages, and information gathered through recommendations and interviews. Competition for admission to dental school is keen.

Dental school usually lasts 4 academic years. Studies begin with classroom instruction and laboratory work in basic sciences, including anatomy, microbiology, biochemistry, and physiology. Beginning courses in clinical sciences, including laboratory techniques, also are provided at this time. During the last 2 years, students treat patients, usually in dental clinics, under the supervision of licensed dentists. Most dental schools award the degree of Doctor of Dental Surgery (DDS). The rest award an equivalent degree, Doctor of Dental Medicine (DMD).

Some dental school graduates work for established dentists as associates for 1 to 2 years to gain experience and save money to equip an office of their own. Most dental school graduates, however, purchase an established practice or open a new one immediately after graduation.

In 2004, 17 States licensed or certified dentists who intended to practice in a specialty area. Requirements include 2 to 4 years of postgraduate education and, in some cases, the completion of a special State examination. Most State licenses permit dentists to engage in both general and specialized practice. Dentists who want to teach or conduct research usually spend an additional 2 to 5 years in advanced dental training, in programs operated by dental schools or hospitals. According to the ADA, each year about 12 percent of new graduates enroll in postgraduate training programs to prepare for a dental specialty.

Dentistry requires diagnostic ability and manual skills. Dentists should have good visual memory, excellent judgment regarding space and shape, a high degree of manual dexterity, and scientific ability. Good business sense, self-discipline, and good communication skills are helpful for success in private practice. High school and college students who want to become dentists should take courses in biology, chemistry, physics, health, and mathematics.

Employment

Dentists held about 150,000 jobs in 2004. Employment was distributed among general practitioners and specialists as follows:

Dentists, general	128,000
Orthodontists	10,000
Oral and maxillofacial surgeons	6,000
Prosthodontists	1,000
Dentists, all other specialists	5,000

About one third of dentists were self-employed and not incorporated. Almost all dentists work in private practice. According to ADA, 78 percent of dentists in private practice are sole proprietors, and 14 percent belong to a partnership. A few salaried dentists work in hospitals and offices of physicians.

Job Outlook

Employment of dentists is projected to grow about as fast as the average for all occupations through 2014. Although employment growth will provide some job opportunities, most jobs will result from the need to replace the large number of dentists expected to retire. Job prospects should be good as new dentists take over established practices or start their own.

Demand for dental care should grow substantially through 2014. As members of the baby-boom generation advance into middle age, a large number will need complicated dental work, such as bridges. In addition, elderly people are more likely to retain their teeth than were their predecessors, so they will require much more care than in the past. The younger generation will continue to need preventive checkups despite treatments such as fluoridation of the water supply, which decreases the incidence of tooth decay. However, employment of dentists is not expected to grow as rapidly as the demand for dental services. As their practices expand, dentists are likely to hire more dental hygienists and dental assistants to handle routine services.

Dentists will increasingly provide care and instruction aimed at preventing the loss of teeth, rather than simply providing treatments such as fillings. Improvements in dental technology also will allow dentists to offer more effective and less painful treatment to their patients.

Earnings

Median annual earnings of salaried dentists were $129,920 in May 2004. Earnings vary according to number of years in practice, location, hours worked, and specialty.

Self-employed dentists in private practice tend to earn more than do salaried dentists, and a relatively large proportion of dentists is self-employed. Like other business owners, these dentists must provide their own health insurance, life insurance, and retirement benefits.

Related Occupations

Dentists examine, diagnose, prevent, and treat diseases and abnormalities. Chiropractors, optometrists, physicians and surgeons, podiatrists, psychologists, and veterinarians do related work.

Sources of Additional Information

For information on dentistry as a career, a list of accredited dental schools, and a list of State boards of dental examiners, contact:
➤ American Dental Association, Commission on Dental Accreditation, 211 E. Chicago Ave., Chicago, IL 60611. Internet: **http://www.ada.org**

For information on admission to dental schools, contact:
➤ American Dental Education Association, 1400 K St., NW., Suite 1100, Washington, DC 20005. Internet: **http://www.adea.org**

Persons interested in practicing dentistry should obtain the requirements for licensure from the board of dental examiners of the State in which they plan to work.

To obtain information on scholarships, grants, and loans, including Federal financial aid, prospective dental students should contact the office of student financial aid at the schools to which they apply.

Dietitians and Nutritionists

(O*NET 29-1031.00)

Significant Points

- Most jobs are in hospitals, nursing care facilities, and offices of physicians or other health practitioners.

- Dietitians and nutritionists need at least a bachelor's degree in dietetics, foods and nutrition, food service systems management, or a related area.

- Faster than average employment growth is expected; however, growth may be constrained if employers substitute other workers for dietitians and if limitations are placed on insurance reimbursement for dietetic services.

- Those who have specialized training in renal or diabetic diets or have a master's degree should experience good employment opportunities.

Nature of the Work

Dietitians and nutritionists plan food and nutrition programs and supervise the preparation and serving of meals. They help to prevent and treat illnesses by promoting healthy eating habits and recommending dietary modifications, such as the use of less salt for those with high blood pressure or the reduction of fat and sugar intake for those who are overweight.

Dietitians manage food service systems for institutions such as hospitals and schools, promote sound eating habits through education, and conduct research. Major areas of practice include clinical, community, management, and consultant dietetics.

Clinical dietitians provide nutritional services for patients in institutions such as hospitals and nursing care facilities. They assess patients' nutritional needs, develop and implement nutrition programs, and evaluate and report the results. They also confer with doctors and other health care professionals to coordinate medical and nutritional needs. Some clinical dietitians specialize in the management of overweight patients or in the care of critically ill or renal (kidney) and diabetic patients. In addition, clinical dietitians in nursing care facilities, small hospitals, or correctional facilities may manage the food service department.

Community dietitians counsel individuals and groups on nutritional practices designed to prevent disease and promote health. Working in places such as public health clinics, home health agencies, and health maintenance organizations, community dietitians evaluate individual needs, develop nutritional care plans, and instruct individuals and their families. Dietitians working in home health agencies provide instruction on grocery shopping and food preparation to the elderly, individuals with special needs, and children.

Increased public interest in nutrition has led to job opportunities in food manufacturing, advertising, and marketing. In these areas, dietitians analyze foods, prepare literature for distribution, or report on issues such as the nutritional content of recipes, dietary fiber, or vitamin supplements.

Management dietitians oversee large-scale meal planning and preparation in health care facilities, company cafeterias, prisons, and schools. They hire, train, and direct other dietitians and food service workers; budget for and purchase food, equipment, and supplies; enforce sanitary and safety regulations; and prepare records and reports.

Consultant dietitians work under contract with health care facilities or in their own private practice. They perform nutrition screenings for

Dietitians and nutritionists work with clients to plan food and nutrition programs to reach the client's health goals.

their clients and offer advice on diet-related concerns such as weight loss and cholesterol reduction. Some work for wellness programs, sports teams, supermarkets, and other nutrition-related businesses. They may consult with food service managers, providing expertise in sanitation, safety procedures, menu development, budgeting, and planning.

Working Conditions

Most full-time dietitians and nutritionists work a regular 40-hour week, although some work weekends. About 1 in 4 worked part time in 2004.

Dietitians and nutritionists usually work in clean, well-lighted, and well-ventilated areas. However, some dietitians work in warm, congested kitchens. Many dietitians and nutritionists are on their feet for much of the workday.

Training, Other Qualifications, and Advancement

High school students interested in becoming a dietitian or nutritionist should take courses in biology, chemistry, mathematics, health, and communications. Dietitians and nutritionists need at least a bachelor's degree in dietetics, foods and nutrition, food service systems management, or a related area. College students in these majors take courses in foods, nutrition, institution management, chemistry, biochemistry, biology, microbiology, and physiology. Other suggested courses include business, mathematics, statistics, computer science, psychology, sociology, and economics.

Of the 46 States and jurisdictions with laws governing dietetics, 31 require licensure, 14 require certification, and 1 requires registration. Requirements vary by State. As a result, interested candidates should determine the requirements of the State in which they want to work before sitting for any exam. Although not required, the Commission on Dietetic Registration of the American Dietetic Association (ADA) awards the Registered Dietitian credential to those who pass an exam after completing their academic coursework and supervised experience.

As of 2004, there were about 227 bachelor's and master's degree programs approved by the ADA's Commission on Accreditation for Dietetics Education (CADE).

Supervised practice experience can be acquired in two ways. The first requires the completion of a CADE-accredited program. As of 2004, there were more than 50 accredited programs, which combined academic and supervised practice experience and generally lasted 4 to 5 years. The second option requires the completion of 900 hours of supervised practice experience in any of the 265 CADE-accredited internships. These internships may be full-time programs lasting 6 to 12 months or part-time programs lasting 2 years. To maintain a registered dietitian status, at least 75 credit hours in approved continuing education classes are required every 5 years.

Students interested in research, advanced clinical positions, or public health may need an advanced degree.

Experienced dietitians may advance to management positions, such as assistant director, associate director, or director of a dietetic department, or may become self-employed. Some dietitians specialize in areas such as renal, diabetic, cardiovascular, or pediatric dietetics. Others may leave the occupation to become sales representatives for equipment, pharmaceutical, or food manufacturers.

Employment

Dietitians and nutritionists held about 50,000 jobs in 2004. More than half of all jobs were in hospitals, nursing care facilities, outpatient care centers, or offices of physicians and other health practitioners. State and local government agencies provided about 1 job in 5—mostly in correctional facilities, health departments, and other public-health-related areas. Some dietitians and nutritionists were employed in special food services, an industry made up of firms providing food services on contract to facilities such as colleges and universities, airlines, correctional facilities, and company cafeterias. Other jobs were in public and private educational services, community care facilities for the elderly (which includes assisted-living facilities), individual and family services, home health care services, and the Federal Government—mostly in the U.S. Department of Veterans Affairs.

Some dietitians were self-employed, working as consultants to facilities such as hospitals and nursing care facilities or providing dietary counseling to individuals.

Job Outlook

Employment of dietitians is expected to grow faster than the average for all occupations through 2014 as a result of increasing emphasis on disease prevention through improved dietary habits. A growing and aging population will boost the demand for meals and nutritional counseling in hospitals, residential care facilities, schools, prisons, community health programs, and home health care agencies. Public interest in nutrition and increased emphasis on health education and prudent lifestyles also will spur demand, especially in management. In addition to employment growth, job openings will result from the need to replace experienced workers who leave the occupation.

The number of dietitian positions in nursing care facilities and in State government hospitals is expected to decline, as these establishments continue to contract with outside agencies for food services. However, employment is expected to grow rapidly in contract providers of food services, in outpatient care centers, and in offices of physicians and other health practitioners. With increased public awareness of obesity and diabetes, Medicare coverage may be expanded to include medical nutrition therapy for renal and diabetic patients. As a result, dietitians that have specialized training in renal or diabetic diets or have a master's degree should experience good employment opportunities.

Employment growth for dietitians and nutritionists may be constrained if some employers substitute other workers, such as health educators, food service managers, and dietetic technicians. Growth also may be curbed by limitations on insurance reimbursement for dietetic services.

Earnings

Median annual earnings of dietitians and nutritionists were $43,630 in May 2004. The middle 50 percent earned between $35,940 and $53,370. The lowest 10 percent earned less than $27,500, and the highest 10 percent earned more than $63,760. In May 2004, median annual earnings in general medical and surgical hospitals, the industry employing the largest number of dietitians and nutritionists, were $44,050.

According to the American Dietetic Association, median annualized wages for registered dietitians in 2005 varied by practice area as follows: $53,800 in consultation and business; $60,000 in food and nutrition management; $60,200 in education and research; $48,800 in clinical nutrition/ambulatory care; $50,000 in clinical nutrition/long-term care; $44,800 in community nutrition; and $45,000 in clinical nutrition/acute care. Salaries also vary by years in practice, education level, geographic region, and size of the community.

Related Occupations

Workers in other occupations who may apply the principles of dietetics include food service managers, health educators, dietetic technicians, and registered nurses.

Sources of Additional Information

For a list of academic programs, scholarships, and other information about dietetics, contact:
➤ The American Dietetic Association, 120 South Riverside Plaza, Suite 2000, Chicago, IL 60606-6995. Internet: **http://www.eatright.org**

Occupational Therapists

(O*NET 29-1122.00)

Significant Points

- Employment is projected to increase much faster than the average, as rapid growth in the number of middle-aged and elderly individuals increases the demand for therapeutic services.

- Beginning in 2007, a master's degree or higher in occupational therapy will be the minimum educational requirement.

- Occupational therapists are increasingly taking on supervisory roles, allowing assistants and aides to work more closely with clients under the guidance of a therapist, in an effort to reduce the cost of therapy.

- More than a quarter of occupational therapists work part time.

Nature of the Work

Occupational therapists (OTs) help people improve their ability to perform tasks in their daily living and working environments. They work with individuals who have conditions that are mentally, physically, developmentally, or emotionally disabling. They also help them to develop, recover, or maintain daily living and work skills. Occupational therapists help clients not only to improve their basic motor functions and reasoning abilities, but also to compensate for permanent loss of function. Their goal is to help clients have independent, productive, and satisfying lives.

Occupational therapists assist clients in performing activities of all types, ranging from using a computer to caring for daily needs such as dressing, cooking, and eating. Physical exercises may be used to increase strength and dexterity, while other activities may be chosen to improve visual acuity and the ability to discern patterns. For example, a client with short-term memory loss might be encouraged to make lists to aid recall, and a person with coordination problems might be assigned exercises to improve hand-eye coordination. Occupational therapists also use computer programs to help clients improve decisionmaking, abstract-reasoning, problem-solving, and perceptual skills, as well as memory, sequencing, and coordination—all of which are important for independent living.

Therapists instruct those with permanent disabilities, such as spinal cord injuries, cerebral palsy, or muscular dystrophy, in the use of adaptive equipment, including wheelchairs, orthotics, and aids for eating and dressing. They also design or make special equipment needed at home or at work. Therapists develop computer-aided adaptive equipment and teach clients with severe limitations how to use that equipment in order to communicate better and control various aspects of their environment.

Some occupational therapists treat individuals whose ability to function in a work environment has been impaired. These practitioners arrange employment, evaluate the work environment, plan work activities, and assess the client's progress. Therapists also may collaborate with the client and the employer to modify the work environment so that the work can be successfully completed.

Occupational therapists may work exclusively with individuals in a particular age group or with particular disabilities. In schools, for example, they evaluate children's abilities, recommend and provide therapy, modify classroom equipment, and help children participate as fully as possible in school programs and activities. A therapist may work with children individually, lead small groups in the classroom, consult with a teacher, or serve on a curriculum or other administrative committee. Early intervention therapy services are provided to infants and toddlers who have, or at the risking of having, developmental delays. Specific therapies may include facilitating the use of the hands, promoting skills for listening and following directions, fostering social play skills, or teaching dressing and grooming skills.

Occupational therapy also is beneficial to the elderly population. Therapists help the elderly lead more productive, active, and independent lives through a variety of methods, including the use of adaptive equipment. Therapists with specialized training in driver rehabilitation assess an individual's ability to drive using both clinical and on-the-road tests. The evaluations allow the therapist to make recommendations for adaptive equipment, training to prolong driving independence, and alternative transportation options. Occupational therapists also work with the client to asses the home for hazards and to identify environmental factors that contribute to falls.

Occupational therapists in mental health settings treat individuals who are mentally ill, mentally retarded, or emotionally disturbed. To treat these problems, therapists choose activities that help people learn to engage in and cope with daily life. Activities include time management skills, budgeting, shopping, homemaking, and the use of public transportation. Occupational therapists also may work with individuals who are dealing with alcoholism, drug abuse, depression, eating disorders, or stress-related disorders.

Assessing and recording a client's activities and progress is an important part of an occupational therapist's job. Accurate records are essential for evaluating clients, for billing, and for reporting to physicians and other health care providers.

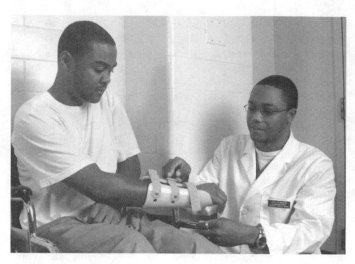

Occupational therapists help people improve their ability to perform tasks in their daily living and working environments.

Working Conditions

Occupational therapists in hospitals and other health care and community settings usually work a 40-hour week. Those in schools may participate in meetings and other activities during and after the school day. In 2004, more than a quarter of occupational therapists worked part time.

In large rehabilitation centers, therapists may work in spacious rooms equipped with machines, tools, and other devices generating noise. The work can be tiring, because therapists are on their feet much of the time. Those providing home health care services may spend time driving from appointment to appointment. Therapists also face hazards such as back strain from lifting and moving clients and equipment.

Therapists increasingly are taking on supervisory roles. Because of rising health care costs, third-party payers are beginning to encourage occupational therapist assistants and aides to take more hands-on responsibility. By having assistants and aides work more closely with clients under the guidance of a therapist, the cost of therapy should decline.

Training, Other Qualifications, and Advancement

Currently, a bachelor's degree in occupational therapy is the minimum requirement for entry into the field. Beginning in 2007, however, a master's degree or higher will be the minimum educational requirement. As a result, students in bachelor's-level programs must complete their coursework and fieldwork before 2007. All States, Puerto Rico, Guam, and the District of Columbia regulate the practice of occupational therapy. To obtain a license, applicants must graduate from an accredited educational program and pass a national certification examination. Those who pass the exam are awarded the title "Occupational Therapist Registered (OTR)." Some States have additional requirements for therapists who work in schools or early intervention programs. These requirements may include education-related classes, an education practice certificate, or early intervention certification requirements.

In 2005, 122 master's degree programs offered entry-level education, 65 programs offered a combined bachelor's and master's degree, and 5 offered an entry-level doctoral degree. Most schools have full-time programs, although a growing number are offering weekend or part-time programs as well. Bachelor's degree programs in occupational therapy are no longer offered because of the requirement for a master's degree or higher beginning in 2007. In addition, post baccalaureate certificate programs for students with a degree other than occupational therapy are no longer offered.

Occupational therapy coursework includes the physical, biological, and behavioral sciences and the application of occupational therapy theory and skills. The completion of 6 months of supervised fieldwork also is required.

Persons considering this profession should take high school courses in biology, chemistry, physics, health, art, and the social sciences. College admissions offices also look favorably at paid or volunteer experience in the health care field. Relevant undergraduate majors include biology, psychology, sociology, anthropology, liberal arts, and anatomy.

Occupational therapists need patience and strong interpersonal skills to inspire trust and respect in their clients. Patience is necessary because many clients may not show rapid improvement. Ingenuity and imagination in adapting activities to individual needs are assets. Those working in home health care services must be able to adapt to a variety of settings.

Employment

Occupational therapists held about 92,000 jobs in 2004. About 1 in 10 occupational therapists held more than one job. The largest number of jobs were in hospitals. Other major employers were offices of other health practitioners (including offices of occupational therapists), public and private educational services, and nursing care facilities. Some occupational therapists were employed by home health care services, outpatient care centers, offices of physicians, individual and family services, community care facilities for the elderly, and government agencies.

A small number of occupational therapists were self-employed in private practice. These practitioners saw clients referred by physicians or other health professionals or provided contract or consulting services to nursing care facilities, schools, adult day care programs, and home health care agencies.

Job Outlook

Employment of occupational therapists is expected to increase much faster than the average for all occupations through 2014. The impact of proposed Federal legislation imposing limits on reimbursement for therapy services may adversely affect the job market for occupational therapists in the short run. However, over the long run, the demand for occupational therapists should continue to rise as a result of growth in the number of individuals with disabilities or limited function who require therapy services. The baby-boom generation's movement into middle age, a period when the incidence of heart attack and stroke increases, will spur demand for therapeutic services. Growth in the population 75 years and older—an age group that suffers from high incidences of disabling conditions—also will increase demand for therapeutic services. Driver rehabilitation and fall-prevention training for the elderly are emerging practice areas for occupational therapy. In addition, medical advances now enable more patients with critical problems to survive—patients who ultimately may need extensive therapy.

Hospitals will continue to employ a large number of occupational therapists to provide therapy services to acutely ill inpatients. Hospitals also will need occupational therapists to staff their outpatient rehabilitation programs.

Employment growth in schools will result from the expansion of the school-age population, the extension of services for disabled students, and an increasing prevalence of sensory disorders in children. Therapists will be needed to help children with disabilities prepare to enter special education programs.

Earnings

Median annual earnings of occupational therapists were $54,660 in May 2004. The middle 50 percent earned between $45,690 and $67,010. The lowest 10 percent earned less than $37,430, and the highest 10 percent earned more than $81,600. Median annual earnings in the industries employing the largest numbers of occupational therapists in May 2004 were:

Home health care services	$58,720
Offices of other health practitioners	56,620
Nursing care facilities	56,570
General medical and surgical hospitals	55,710
Elementary and secondary schools	48,580

Related Occupations

Occupational therapists use specialized knowledge to help individuals perform daily living skills and achieve maximum independence. Other workers performing similar duties include audiologists, chiropractors, physical therapists, recreational therapists, rehabilitation counselors, respiratory therapists, and speech-language pathologists.

Sources of Additional Information

For more information on occupational therapy as a career, contact:
➤ American Occupational Therapy Association, 4720 Montgomery Lane, Bethesda, MD 20824-1220. Internet: **http://www.aota.org**

For information regarding the requirements to practice as an occupational therapist in schools, contact the appropriate occupational therapy regulatory agency for your State.

Optometrists

(O*NET 29-1041.00)

Significant Points

- Admission to optometry school is competitive.

- To be licensed, optometrists must earn a Doctor of Optometry degree from an accredited optometry school and pass a written National Board exam and a clinical examination.

- Employment is expected to grow faster than average in response to the vision care needs of a growing and aging population.

Nature of the Work

Optometrists, also known as *doctors of optometry*, or *ODs*, provide most primary vision care. They examine people's eyes to diagnose vision problems and eye diseases, and they test patients' visual acuity, depth and color perception, and ability to focus and coordinate the eyes. Optometrists prescribe eyeglasses and contact lenses and provide vision therapy and low-vision rehabilitation. Optometrists analyze test results and develop a treatment plan. They administer drugs to patients to aid in the diagnosis of vision problems and prescribe drugs to treat some eye diseases. Optometrists often provide preoperative and postoperative care to cataract patients, as well as to patients who have had laser vision correction or other eye surgery. They also diagnose conditions caused by systemic diseases such as diabetes and high blood pressure, referring patients to other health practitioners as needed.

Optometrists should not be confused with *ophthalmologists* or *dispensing opticians*. *Ophthalmologists* are physicians who perform eye surgery, as well as diagnose and treat eye diseases and injuries. Like optometrists, they also examine eyes and prescribe eyeglasses and contact lenses. *Dispensing opticians* fit and adjust eyeglasses and, in some States, may fit contact lenses according to

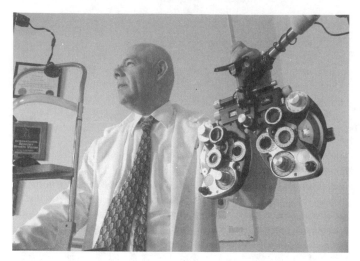

The Doctor of Optometry degree requires the completion of a 4-year program at an accredited optometry school.

prescriptions written by ophthalmologists or optometrists. (See the sections on *physicians and surgeons*; and *opticians, dispensing*, elsewhere in the *Handbook*.)

Most optometrists are in general practice. Some specialize in work with the elderly, children, or partially sighted persons who need specialized visual devices. Others develop and implement ways to protect workers' eyes from on-the-job strain or injury. Some specialize in contact lenses, sports vision, or vision therapy. A few teach optometry, perform research, or consult.

Most optometrists are private practitioners who also handle the business aspects of running an office, such as developing a patient base, hiring employees, keeping paper and electronic records, and ordering equipment and supplies. Optometrists who operate franchise optical stores also may have some of these duties.

Working Conditions

Optometrists work in places—usually their own offices—that are clean, well lighted, and comfortable. Most full-time optometrists work about 40 hours a week. Many work weekends and evenings to suit the needs of patients. Emergency calls, once uncommon, have increased with the passage of therapeutic-drug laws expanding optometrists' ability to prescribe medications.

Training, Other Qualifications, and Advancement

All States and the District of Columbia require that optometrists be licensed. Applicants for a license must have a Doctor of Optometry degree from an accredited optometry school and must pass both a written National Board examination and a National, regional, or State clinical board examination. The written and clinical examinations of the National Board of Examiners in Optometry usually are taken during the student's academic career. Many States also require applicants to pass an examination on relevant State laws. Licenses are renewed every 1 to 3 years and, in all States, continuing education credits are needed for renewal.

The Doctor of Optometry degree requires the completion of a 4-year program at an accredited optometry school, preceded by at least 3 years of preoptometric study at an accredited college or university. Most optometry students hold a bachelor's or higher degree. In 2004, 17 U.S. schools and colleges of optometry offered programs accredited by the Accreditation Council on Optometric Education of the American Optometric Association.

Requirements for admission to schools of optometry include courses in English, mathematics, physics, chemistry, and biology. A few schools also require or recommend courses in psychology,

history, sociology, speech, or business. Because a strong background in science is important, many applicants to optometry school major in a science such as biology or chemistry, while other applicants major in another subject and take many science courses offering laboratory experience. Applicants must take the Optometry Admissions Test, which measures academic ability and scientific comprehension. Admission to optometry school is competitive. As a result, most applicants take the test after their sophomore or junior year, allowing them an opportunity to take the test again and raise their score. A few applicants are accepted to optometry school after 3 years of college and complete their bachelor's degree while attending optometry school.

Optometry programs include classroom and laboratory study of health and visual sciences, as well as clinical training in the diagnosis and treatment of eye disorders. Courses in pharmacology, optics, vision science, biochemistry, and systemic disease are included.

Business ability, self-discipline, and the ability to deal tactfully with patients are important for success. The work of optometrists requires attention to detail and manual dexterity.

Optometrists wishing to teach or conduct research may study for a master's or Ph.D. degree in visual science, physiological optics, neurophysiology, public health, health administration, health information and communication, or health education. One-year postgraduate clinical residency programs are available for optometrists who wish to obtain advanced clinical competence. Specialty areas for residency programs include family practice optometry, pediatric optometry, geriatric optometry, vision therapy and rehabilitation, low-vision rehabilitation, cornea and contact lenses, refractive and ocular surgery, primary eye care optometry, and ocular disease.

Employment

Optometrists held about 34,000 jobs in 2004. The number of jobs is greater than the number of practicing optometrists because some optometrists hold two or more jobs. For example, an optometrist may have a private practice but also work in another practice, in a clinic, or in a vision care center. According to the American Optometric Association, about three-fourths of practicing optometrists are in private practice. Although many practice alone, optometrists increasingly are in a partnership or group practice.

Salaried jobs for optometrists were primarily in offices of optometrists; offices of physicians, including ophthalmologists; and health and personal care stores, including optical goods stores. A few salaried jobs for optometrists were in hospitals, the Federal government, or outpatient care centers including health maintenance organizations. Almost one third of optometrists were self-employed and not incorporated.

Job Outlook

Employment of optometrists is expected to grow faster than average for all occupations through 2014, in response to the vision care needs of a growing and aging population. As baby boomers age, they will be more likely to visit optometrists and ophthalmologists because of the onset of vision problems in middle age, including those resulting from the extensive use of computers. The demand for optometric services also will increase because of growth in the oldest age group, with its increased likelihood of cataracts, glaucoma, diabetes, and hypertension. Greater recognition of the importance of vision care, along with rising personal incomes and growth in employee vision care plans, also will spur job growth.

Employment of optometrists would grow more rapidly were it not for anticipated productivity gains that will allow each optometrist to see more patients. These expected gains stem from greater use of optometric assistants and other support personnel, who will reduce the amount of time optometrists need with each patient. Also, laser surgery that can correct some vision problems is available, and although optometrists still will be needed to provide preoperative and postoperative care for laser surgery patients, patients who successfully undergo this surgery may not require optometrists to prescribe glasses or contacts for several years.

In addition to growth, the need to replace optometrists who retire or leave the occupation for another reason will create employment opportunities.

Earnings

Median annual earnings of salaried optometrists were $88,410 in May 2004. The middle 50 percent earned between $63,840 and $118,320. Median annual earnings of salaried optometrists in May 2004 were $87,430 in offices of optometrists. Salaried optometrists tend to earn more initially than do optometrists who set up their own practices. In the long run, however, those in private practice usually earn more.

According to the American Optometric Association, median net annual income for all optometrists, including the self-employed, was $114,000 in 2004. The middle 50 percent earned between $84,000 and $166,000.

Related Occupations

Other workers who apply scientific knowledge to prevent, diagnose, and treat disorders and injuries are chiropractors, dentists, physicians and surgeons, psychologists, podiatrists, and veterinarians.

Sources of Additional Information

For information on optometry as a career and a list of accredited optometric institutions of education, contact:
➤ Association of Schools and Colleges of Optometry, 6110 Executive Blvd., Suite 510, Rockville, MD 20852. Internet: **http:// www.opted.org**

Additional career information is available from:
➤ American Optometric Association, Educational Services, 243 North Lindbergh Blvd., St. Louis, MO 63141. Internet: **http://www.aoanet.org**

The board of optometry in each State can supply information on licensing requirements.

For information on specific admission requirements and sources of financial aid, contact the admissions officers of individual optometry schools.

Pharmacists

(O*NET 29-1051.00)

Significant Points

- Very good employment opportunities are expected for pharmacists.

- Earnings are high, but some pharmacists work long hours, nights, weekends, and holidays.

- Pharmacists are becoming more involved in making decisions regarding drug therapy and in counseling patients.

- A license is required; the prospective pharmacist must graduate from an accredited college of pharmacy and pass a State examination.

Nature of the Work

Pharmacists distribute drugs prescribed by physicians and other health practitioners and provide information to patients about medications and their use. They advise physicians and other health practitioners on the selection, dosages, interactions, and side effects of medications. Pharmacists also monitor the health and progress of patients in response to drug therapy to ensure the safe and effective use of medication. Pharmacists must understand the use, clinical effects, and composition of drugs, including their chemical, biological, and physical properties. Compounding—the actual mixing of ingredients to form powders, tablets, capsules, ointments, and solutions—is a small part of a pharmacist's practice, because most medicines are produced by pharmaceutical companies in a standard dosage and drug delivery form. Most pharmacists work in a community setting, such as a retail drugstore, or in a health care facility, such as a hospital, nursing home, mental health institution, or neighborhood health clinic.

Pharmacists in community and retail pharmacies counsel patients and answer questions about prescription drugs, including questions regarding possible side effects or interactions among various drugs. They provide information about over-the-counter drugs and make recommendations after talking with the patient. They also may give advice about the patient's diet, exercise, or stress management or about durable medical equipment and home health care supplies. In addition, they also may complete third-party insurance forms and other paperwork. Those who own or manage community pharmacies may sell non-health-related merchandise, hire and supervise personnel, and oversee the general operation of the pharmacy. Some community pharmacists provide specialized services to help patients manage conditions such as diabetes, asthma, smoking cessation, or high blood pressure. Some community pharmacists also are trained to administer vaccinations.

Pharmacists in health care facilities dispense medications and advise the medical staff on the selection and effects of drugs. They may make sterile solutions to be administered intravenously. They also assess, plan, and monitor drug programs or regimens. Pharmacists counsel hospitalized patients on the use of drugs and on their use at home when the patients are discharged. Pharmacists also may evaluate drug-use patterns and outcomes for patients in hospitals or managed care organizations.

Pharmacists who work in home health care monitor drug therapy and prepare infusions—solutions that are injected into patients—and other medications for use in the home.

Some pharmacists specialize in specific drug therapy areas, such as intravenous nutrition support, oncology (cancer), nuclear pharmacy (used for chemotherapy), geriatric pharmacy, and psychopharmacotherapy (the treatment of mental disorders by means of drugs).

Most pharmacists keep confidential computerized records of patients' drug therapies to prevent harmful drug interactions. Pharmacists are responsible for the accuracy of every prescription that is filled, but they often rely upon pharmacy technicians and pharmacy aides to assist them in the dispensing process. Thus, the pharmacist may delegate prescription-filling and administrative tasks and supervise their completion. Pharmacists also frequently oversee pharmacy students serving as interns in preparation for graduation and licensure.

Increasingly, pharmacists are pursuing nontraditional pharmacy work. Some are involved in research for pharmaceutical manufacturers, developing new drugs and therapies and testing their effects on people. Others work in marketing or sales, providing expertise to clients on a drug's use, effectiveness, and possible side effects. Some pharmacists work for health insurance companies, developing pharmacy benefit packages and carrying out cost-benefit analyses on certain drugs. Other pharmacists work for the government, public health care services, the armed services, and pharmacy associations. Finally, some pharmacists are employed full time or part time as college faculty, teaching classes and performing research in a wide range of areas.

Pharmacists are becoming more involved in making decisions regarding drug therapy and in counseling patients.

Working Conditions

Pharmacists work in clean, well-lighted, and well-ventilated areas. Many pharmacists spend most of their workday on their feet. When working with sterile or dangerous pharmaceutical products, pharmacists wear gloves and masks and work with other special protective equipment. Many community and hospital pharmacies are open for extended hours or around the clock, so pharmacists may work nights, weekends, and holidays. Consultant pharmacists may travel to nursing homes or other facilities to monitor patients' drug therapy.

About 21 percent of pharmacists worked part time in 2004. Most full-time salaried pharmacists worked approximately 40 hours a week. Some, including many self-employed pharmacists, worked more than 50 hours a week.

Training, Other Qualifications, and Advancement

A license to practice pharmacy is required in all States, the District of Columbia, and all U.S. territories. To obtain a license, the prospective pharmacist must graduate from a college of pharmacy that is accredited by the Accreditation Council for Pharmacy Education (ACPE) and pass an examination. All States require the North American Pharmacist Licensure Exam (NAPLEX), which tests pharmacy skills and knowledge, and 43 states and the District of Columbia require the Multistate Pharmacy Jurisprudence Exam (MPJE), which tests pharmacy law. Both exams are administered by the National Association of Boards of Pharmacy. Pharmacists in the eight states that do not require the MJPE must pass a state-specific exam that is similar to the MJPE. In addition to the NAPLEX and MPJE, some States require additional exams unique to their State. All States except California currently grant a license without extensive reexamination to qualified pharmacists who already are licensed by another State. In Florida, reexamination is not required if a pharmacist has passed the NAPLEX and MPJE within 12 years of his or her application for a license transfer. Many pharmacists are licensed to practice in more than one State. Most States require continuing education for license renewal. Persons interested in a career as a pharmacist should check with individual State boards of pharmacy for details on examination requirements, license renewal requirements, and license transfer procedures.

In 2004, 89 colleges of pharmacy were accredited to confer degrees by the Accreditation Council for Pharmacy Education. Pharmacy programs grant the degree of Doctor of Pharmacy (Pharm.D.), which requires at least 6 years of postsecondary study and the passing of a State board of pharmacy's licensure examination. Courses offered at colleges of pharmacy are designed to teach students about all aspects of drug therapy. In addition, schools teach students how to communicate with patients and other health care providers about drug information and patient care. Students also learn professional ethics, how to develop and manage medication distribution systems, and concepts of public health. In addition to receiving classroom instruction, students in Pharm.D. programs spend about one-forth of their time learning in a variety of pharmacy practice settings under the supervision of licensed pharmacists. The Pharm.D. degree has replaced the Bachelor of Pharmacy (B.Pharm.) degree, which is no longer being awarded.

The Pharm.D. is a 4-year program that requires at least 2 years of college study prior to admittance, although most applicants have completed 3 years. Entry requirements usually include courses in mathematics and natural sciences, such as chemistry, biology, and physics, as well as courses in the humanities and social sciences. Approximately two-thirds of all colleges require applicants to take the Pharmacy College Admissions Test (PCAT).

In 2003, the American Association of Colleges of Pharmacy (AACP) launched the Pharmacy College Application Service, known as PharmCAS, for students who are interested in applying to schools and colleges of pharmacy. This centralized service allows applicants to use a single Web-based application and one set of transcripts to apply to multiple schools of pharmacy. A total of 43 schools participated in 2003.

In the 2003–04 academic year, 67 colleges of pharmacy awarded the master-of-science degree or the Ph.D. degree. Both degrees are awarded after the completion of a Pharm.D. degree and are designed for those who want more laboratory and research experience. Many master's and Ph.D. degree holders do research for a drug company or teach at a university. Other options for pharmacy graduates who are interested in further training include 1-year or 2-year residency programs or fellowships. Pharmacy residencies are postgraduate training programs in pharmacy practice and usually require the completion of a research study. There currently are more than 700 residency training programs nationwide. Pharmacy fellowships are highly individualized programs that are designed to prepare participants to work in a specialized area of pharmacy, such clinical practice or research laboratories. Some pharmacists who run their own pharmacy obtain a master's degree in business administration (MBA). Others may obtain a degree in public administration or public health.

Areas of graduate study include pharmaceutics and pharmaceutical chemistry (physical and chemical properties of drugs and dosage forms), pharmacology (effects of drugs on the body), toxicology and pharmacy administration.

Prospective pharmacists should have scientific aptitude, good communication skills, and a desire to help others. They also must be conscientious and pay close attention to detail, because the decisions they make affect human lives.

In community pharmacies, pharmacists usually begin at the staff level. In independent pharmacies, after they gain experience and secure the necessary capital, some become owners or part owners of pharmacies. Pharmacists in chain drugstores may be promoted to pharmacy supervisor or manager at the store level, then to manager at the district or regional level, and later to an executive position within the chain's headquarters.

Hospital pharmacists may advance to supervisory or administrative positions. Pharmacists in the pharmaceutical industry may advance in marketing, sales, research, quality control, production, packaging, or other areas.

Employment

Pharmacists held about 230,000 jobs in 2004. About 61 percent work in community pharmacies that are either independently owned or part of a drugstore chain, grocery store, department store, or mass merchandiser. Most community pharmacists are salaried employees, but some are self-employed owners. About 24 percent of salaried pharmacists work in hospitals. Others work in clinics, mail-order pharmacies, pharmaceutical wholesalers, home health care agencies, or the Federal Government.

Job Outlook

Very good employment opportunities are expected for pharmacists over the 2004–14 period because the number of job openings created by employment growth and the need to replace pharmacists who leave the occupation or retire are expected to exceed the number of degrees granted in pharmacy. Enrollments in pharmacy programs are rising as more students are attracted by high salaries and good job prospects. Despite this increase in enrollments, job openings should still be more numerous than those seeking employment.

Employment of pharmacists is expected to grow faster than the average for all occupations through the year 2014, because of the increasing demand for pharmaceuticals, particularly from the growing elderly population. The increasing numbers of middle-aged and elderly people—who use more prescription drugs than younger people—will continue to spur demand for pharmacists in all employment settings. Other factors likely to increase the demand for pharmacists include scientific advances that will make more drug products available, new developments in genome research and medication distribution systems, increasingly sophisticated consumers seeking more information about drugs, and coverage of prescription drugs by a greater number of health insurance plans and Medicare.

Community pharmacies are taking steps to manage an increasing volume of prescriptions. Automation of drug dispensing and greater employment of pharmacy technicians and pharmacy aides will help these establishments to dispense more prescriptions.

With its emphasis on cost control, managed care encourages the use of lower cost prescription drug distributors, such as mail-order firms and online pharmacies, for purchases of certain medications. Prescriptions ordered through the mail and via the Internet are filled in a central location and shipped to the patient at a lower cost. Mail-order and online pharmacies typically use automated technology to dispense medication and employ fewer pharmacists. If the utilization of mail-order pharmacies increases rapidly, job growth among pharmacists could be limited.

Employment of pharmacists will not grow as fast in hospitals as in other industries, because hospitals are reducing inpatient stays, downsizing, and consolidating departments. The number of outpatient surgeries is increasing, so more patients are being discharged and purchasing their medications through retail, supermarket, or mail-order pharmacies, rather than through hospitals. An aging population means that more pharmacy services will be required in nursing homes, assisted-living facilities, and home care settings. The most rapid job growth among pharmacists is expected in these 3 settings.

New opportunities are emerging for pharmacists in managed care organizations where they analyze trends and patterns in medication use, and in pharmacoeconomics—the cost and benefit analysis of different drug therapies. Opportunities also are emerging for pharmacists

trained in research and disease management—the development of new methods for curing and controlling diseases. Pharmacists also are finding jobs in research and development and in sales and marketing for pharmaceutical manufacturing firms. New breakthroughs in biotechnology will increase the potential for drugs to treat diseases and expand the opportunities for pharmacists to conduct research and sell medications. In addition, pharmacists are finding employment opportunities in pharmacy informatics, which uses information technology to improve patient care.

Job opportunities for pharmacists in patient care will arise as cost-conscious insurers and health systems continue to emphasize the role of pharmacists in primary and preventive health care. Health insurance companies realize that the expense of using medication to treat diseases and various health conditions often is considerably less than the costs for patients whose conditions go untreated. Pharmacists also can reduce the expenses resulting from unexpected complications due to allergic reactions or interactions among medications.

Earnings

Median annual wage and salary earnings of pharmacists in May 2004 were $84,900. The middle 50 percent earned between $75,720 and $94,850 a year. The lowest 10 percent earned less than $61,200, and the highest 10 percent earned more than $109,850 a year. Median annual earnings in the industries employing the largest numbers of pharmacists in May 2004 were:

Department stores	$86,720
Grocery stores	85,680
Health and personal care stores	85,380
General medical and surgical hospitals	84,560
Other general merchandise stores	84,170

Related Occupations

Pharmacy technicians and pharmacy aides also work in pharmacies. Persons in other professions who may work with pharmaceutical compounds include biological scientists, medical scientists, and chemists and materials scientists. Increasingly, pharmacists are involved in patient care and therapy, work that they have in common with physicians and surgeons.

Sources of Additional Information

For information on pharmacy as a career, preprofessional and professional requirements, programs offered by colleges of pharmacy, and student financial aid, contact:

➤ American Association of Colleges of Pharmacy, 1426 Prince St., Alexandria, VA 22314. Internet: **http://www.aacp.org**

General information on careers in pharmacy is available from:

➤ American Society of Health-System Pharmacists, 7272 Wisconsin Ave., Bethesda, MD 20814. Internet: **http://www.ashp.org**

➤ National Association of Chain Drug Stores, 413 N. Lee St., P.O. Box 1417-D49, Alexandria, VA 22313-1480. Internet: **http://www.nacds.org**

➤ Academy of Managed Care Pharmacy, 100 North Pitt St., Suite 400, Alexandria, VA 22314. Internet: **http://www.amcp.org**

➤ American Pharmacists Association, 2215 Constitution Ave. N.W., Washington, DC 20037-2985. Internet: **http://www.aphanet.org**

Information on the North American Pharmacist Licensure Exam (NAPLEX) and the Multistate Pharmacy Jurisprudence Exam (MPJE) is available from:

➤ National Association of Boards of Pharmacy, 1600 Feehanville Dr., Mount Prospect, IL 60056. Internet: **http://www.nabp.net**

State licensure requirements are available from each State's board of pharmacy. Information on specific college entrance requirements, curriculums, and financial aid is available from any college of pharmacy.

Physical Therapists

(O*NET 29-1123.00)

Significant Points

- Employment is expected to increase much faster than the average, as growth in the number of individuals with disabilities or limited functioning spurs demand for therapy services.

- Job opportunities should be particularly good in acute hospital, rehabilitation, and orthopedic settings.

- After graduating from an accredited physical therapist educational program, therapists must pass a licensure exam before they can practice.

- Nearly 6 out of 10 physical therapists work in hospitals or in offices of physical therapists.

Nature of the Work

Physical therapists provide services that help restore function, improve mobility, relieve pain, and prevent or limit permanent physical disabilities of patients suffering from injuries or disease. They restore, maintain, and promote overall fitness and health. Their patients include accident victims and individuals with disabling conditions such as low-back pain, arthritis, heart disease, fractures, head injuries, and cerebral palsy.

Therapists examine patients' medical histories and then test and measure the patients' strength, range of motion, balance and coordination, posture, muscle performance, respiration, and motor function. They also determine patients' ability to be independent and reintegrate into the community or workplace after injury or illness. Next, physical therapists develop plans describing a treatment strategy, its purpose, and its anticipated outcome. Physical therapist assistants, under the direction and supervision of a physical therapist, may be involved in implementing treatment plans with patients. Physical therapist aides perform routine support tasks, as directed by the therapist. (*Physical therapist assistants and aides* are discussed elsewhere in the *Handbook*.)

Treatment often includes exercise for patients who have been immobilized and lack flexibility, strength, or endurance. Physical therapists encourage patients to use their own muscles to increase their flexibility and range of motion before finally advancing to other exercises that improve strength, balance, coordination, and endurance. The goal is to improve how an individual functions at work and at home.

Physical therapists also use electrical stimulation, hot packs or cold compresses, and ultrasound to relieve pain and reduce swelling. They may use traction or deep-tissue massage to relieve pain. Therapists also teach patients to use assistive and adaptive devices, such as crutches, prostheses, and wheelchairs. They also may show patients exercises to do at home to expedite their recovery.

As treatment continues, physical therapists document the patient's progress, conduct periodic examinations, and modify treatments when necessary. Besides tracking the patient's progress, such documentation identifies areas requiring more or less attention.

Physical therapists often consult and practice with a variety of other professionals, such as physicians, dentists, nurses, educators, social workers, occupational therapists, speech-language pathologists, and audiologists.

Some physical therapists treat a wide range of ailments; others specialize in areas such as pediatrics, geriatrics, orthopedics, sports medicine, neurology, and cardiopulmonary physical therapy.

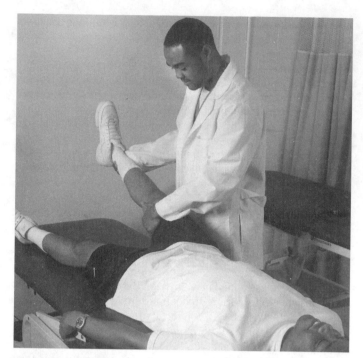

Physical therapists use traction or deep-tissue massage to relieve pain.

Working Conditions

Physical therapists practice in hospitals, clinics, and private offices that have specially equipped facilities, or they treat patients in hospital rooms, homes, or schools.

In 2004, most full-time physical therapists worked a 40-hour week; some worked evenings and weekends to fit their patients' schedules. About 1 in 4 physical therapists worked part time. The job can be physically demanding because therapists often have to stoop, kneel, crouch, lift, and stand for long periods. In addition, physical therapists move heavy equipment and lift patients or help them turn, stand, or walk.

Training, Other Qualifications, and Advancement

All States require physical therapists to pass a licensure exam before they can practice, after graduating from an accredited physical therapist educational program.

According to the American Physical Therapy Association, there were 205 accredited physical therapist programs in 2004. Of the accredited programs, 94 offered master's degrees, and 111 offered doctoral degrees. All physical therapist programs seeking accreditation are required to offer degrees at the master's degree level and above, in accordance with the Commission on Accreditation in Physical Therapy Education.

Physical therapist programs start with basic science courses such as biology, chemistry, and physics and then introduce specialized courses, including biomechanics, neuroanatomy, human growth and development, manifestations of disease, examination techniques, and therapeutic procedures. Besides getting classroom and laboratory instruction, students receive supervised clinical experience. Among the courses that are useful when one applies to a physical therapist educational program are anatomy, biology, chemistry, social science, mathematics, and physics. Before granting admission, many professional education programs require experience as a volunteer in a physical therapy department of a hospital or clinic. For high school students, volunteering with the school athletic trainer is a good way to gain experience.

Physical therapists should have strong interpersonal skills in order to be able to educate patients about their physical therapy treatments. Physical therapists also should be compassionate and possess a desire to help patients. Similar traits are needed to interact with the patient's family.

Physical therapists are expected to continue their professional development by participating in continuing education courses and workshops. In fact, a number of States require continuing education as a condition of maintaining licensure.

Employment

Physical therapists held about 155,000 jobs in 2004. The number of jobs is greater than the number of practicing physical therapists, because some physical therapists hold two or more jobs. For example, some may work in a private practice, but also work part time in another health care facility.

Nearly 6 out of 10 physical therapists worked in hospitals or in offices of physical therapists. Other jobs were in home health care services, nursing care facilities, outpatient care centers, and offices of physicians.

Some physical therapists were self-employed in private practices, seeing individual patients and contracting to provide services in hospitals, rehabilitation centers, nursing care facilities, home health care agencies, adult day care programs, and schools. Physical therapists also teach in academic institutions and conduct research.

Job Outlook

Employment of physical therapists is expected to grow much faster than the average for all occupations through 2014. The impact of proposed Federal legislation imposing limits on reimbursement for therapy services may adversely affect the short-term job outlook for physical therapists. However, over the long run, the demand for physical therapists should continue to rise as growth in the number of individuals with disabilities or limited function spurs demand for therapy services. Job opportunities should be particularly good in acute hospital, rehabilitation, and orthopedic settings, because the elderly receive the most treatment in these settings. The growing elderly population is particularly vulnerable to chronic and debilitating conditions that require therapeutic services. Also, the baby-boom generation is entering the prime age for heart attacks and strokes, increasing the demand for cardiac and physical rehabilitation. Further, young people will need physical therapy as technological advances save the lives of a larger proportion of newborns with severe birth defects.

Future medical developments also should permit a higher percentage of trauma victims to survive, creating additional demand for rehabilitative care. In addition, growth may result from advances in medical technology that could permit the treatment of more disabling conditions.

Widespread interest in health promotion also should increase demand for physical therapy services. A growing number of employers are using physical therapists to evaluate worksites, develop exercise programs, and teach safe work habits to employees in the hope of reducing injuries in the workplace.

Earnings

Median annual earnings of physical therapists were $60,180 in May 2004. The middle 50 percent earned between $50,330 and $71,760. The lowest 10 percent earned less than $42,010, and the highest 10 percent earned more than $88,580. Median annual earnings in the industries employing the largest numbers of physical therapists in May 2004 were:

Home health care services	$64,650
Nursing care facilities	61,720
Offices of physicians	61,270
General medical and surgical hospitals	60,350
Offices of other health practitioners	60,130

Related Occupations

Physical therapists rehabilitate persons with physical disabilities. Others who work in the rehabilitation field include audiologists, chiropractors, occupational therapists, recreational therapists, rehabilitation counselors, respiratory therapists, and speech-language pathologists.

Sources of Additional Information

Additional career information and a list of accredited educational programs in physical therapy are available from:
➤ American Physical Therapy Association, 1111 North Fairfax St., Alexandria, VA 22314-1488. Internet: **http://www.apta.org**

Physician Assistants

(O*NET 29-1071.00)

Significant Points

- Physician assistant programs usually last at least 2 years; admission requirements vary by program, but many require at least 2 years of college and some health care experience.

- All States require physician assistants to complete an accredited education program and to pass a national exam in order to obtain a license.

- Physician assistants rank among the fastest growing occupations, as physicians and health care institutions increasingly utilize physician assistants in order to contain costs.

- Job opportunities should be good, particularly in rural and inner city clinics.

Nature of the Work

Physician assistants (PAs) practice medicine under the supervision of physicians and surgeons. They should not be confused with medical assistants, who perform routine clinical and clerical tasks. (Medical assistants are discussed elsewhere in the *Handbook*.) PAs are formally trained to provide diagnostic, therapeutic, and preventive health care services, as delegated by a physician. Working as members of the health care team, they take medical histories, examine and treat patients, order and interpret laboratory tests and x rays, and make diagnoses. They also treat minor injuries, by suturing, splinting, and casting. PAs record progress notes, instruct and counsel patients, and order or carry out therapy. In 48 States and the District of Columbia, physician assistants may prescribe medications. PAs also may have managerial duties. Some order medical supplies or equipment and supervise technicians and assistants.

Physician assistants work under the supervision of a physician. However, PAs may be the principal care providers in rural or inner city clinics, where a physician is present for only 1 or 2 days each week. In such cases, the PA confers with the supervising physician and other medical professionals as needed and as required by law. PAs also may make house calls or go to hospitals and nursing care facilities to check on patients, after which they report back to the physician.

The duties of physician assistants are determined by the supervising physician and by State law. Aspiring PAs should investigate the laws and regulations in the States in which they wish to practice.

Many PAs work in primary care specialties, such as general internal medicine, pediatrics, and family medicine. Other specialty areas include general and thoracic surgery, emergency medicine, orthopedics, and geriatrics. PAs specializing in surgery provide preoperative and postoperative care and may work as first or second assistants during major surgery.

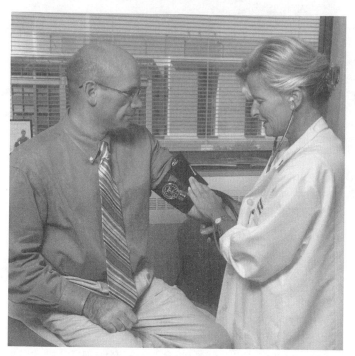

Physician assistants may be the principal care providers in rural or inner city clinics, where a physician is present for only 1 or 2 days each week.

Working Conditions

Although PAs usually work in a comfortable, well-lighted environment, those in surgery often stand for long periods, and others do considerable walking. Schedules vary according to the practice setting, and often depend on the hours of the supervising physician. The workweek of hospital-based PAs may include weekends, nights, or early morning hospital rounds to visit patients. These workers also may be on call. PAs in clinics usually work a 40-hour week.

Training, Other Qualifications, and Advancement

All States require that PAs complete an accredited, formal education program and pass a National exam to obtain a license. PA programs usually last at least 2 years and are full time. Most programs are in schools of allied health, academic health centers, medical schools, or 4-year colleges; a few are in community colleges, the military, or hospitals. Many accredited PA programs have clinical teaching affiliations with medical schools.

In 2005, more than 135 education programs for physician assistants were accredited or provisionally accredited by the American Academy of Physician Assistants. More than 90 of these programs offered the option of a master's degree, and the rest offered either a bachelor's degree or an associate degree. Most applicants to PA educational programs already have a bachelor's degree.

Admission requirements vary, but many programs require 2 years of college and some work experience in the health care field. Students should take courses in biology, English, chemistry, mathematics, psychology, and the social sciences. Many PAs have prior experience as registered nurses, while others come from varied backgrounds, including military corpsman/medics and allied health occupations such as respiratory therapists, physical therapists, and emergency medical technicians and paramedics.

PA education includes classroom instruction in biochemistry, pathology, human anatomy, physiology, microbiology, clinical pharmacology, clinical medicine, geriatric and home health care, disease prevention, and medical ethics. Students obtain supervised clinical training in several areas, including family medicine, internal medicine, surgery, prenatal care and gynecology, geriatrics, emergency medicine, psychiatry, and pediatrics. Sometimes, PA students serve one or more of these "rotations" under the supervision of a physician who is seeking to hire a PA. The rotations often lead to permanent employment.

All States and the District of Columbia have legislation governing the qualifications or practice of physician assistants. All jurisdictions require physician assistants to pass the Physician Assistant National Certifying Examination, administered by the National Commission on Certification of Physician Assistants (NCCPA) and open only to graduates of accredited PA education programs. Only those successfully completing the examination may use the credential "Physician Assistant-Certified." In order to remain certified, PAs must complete 100 hours of continuing medical education every 2 years. Every 6 years, they must pass a recertification examination or complete an alternative program combining learning experiences and a take-home examination.

Some PAs pursue additional education in a specialty such as surgery, neonatology, or emergency medicine. PA postgraduate educational programs are available in areas such as internal medicine, rural primary care, emergency medicine, surgery, pediatrics, neonatology, and occupational medicine. Candidates must be graduates of an accredited program and be certified by the NCCPA.

Physician assistants need leadership skills, self-confidence, and emotional stability. They must be willing to continue studying throughout their career to keep up with medical advances.

As they attain greater clinical knowledge and experience, PAs can advance to added responsibilities and higher earnings. However, by the very nature of the profession, clinically practicing PAs always are supervised by physicians.

Employment

Physician assistants held about 62,000 jobs in 2004. The number of jobs is greater than the number of practicing PAs because some hold two or more jobs. For example, some PAs work with a supervising physician, but also work in another practice, clinic, or hospital. According to the American Academy of Physician Assistants, about 15 percent of actively practicing PAs worked in more than one clinical job concurrently in 2004.

More than half of jobs for PAs were in the offices of physicians. About a quarter were in hospitals, public or private. The rest were mostly in outpatient care centers, including health maintenance organizations; the Federal Government; and public or private colleges, universities, and professional schools. A few were self-employed.

Job Outlook

Employment of PAs is expected to grow much faster than the average for all occupations through the year 2014, ranking among the fastest growing occupations, due to anticipated expansion of the health care industry and an emphasis on cost containment, resulting in increasing utilization of PAs by physicians and health care institutions.

Physicians and institutions are expected to employ more PAs to provide primary care and to assist with medical and surgical procedures because PAs are cost-effective and productive members of the health care team. Physician assistants can relieve physicians of routine duties and procedures. Telemedicine—using technology to facilitate interactive consultations between physicians and physician assistants—also will expand the use of physician assistants. Job opportunities for PAs should be good, particularly in rural and inner city clinics, because those settings have difficulty attracting physicians.

Besides the traditional office-based setting, PAs should find a growing number of jobs in institutional settings such as hospitals, academic medical centers, public clinics, and prisons. Additional PAs may be needed to augment medical staffing in inpatient teaching hospital settings as the number of hours physician residents are permitted to work is reduced, encouraging hospitals to use PAs to supply some physician resident services. Opportunities will be best in States that allow PAs a wider scope of practice.

Earnings

Median annual earnings of physician assistants were $69,410 in May 2004. The middle 50 percent earned between $57,110 and $83,560. The lowest 10 percent earned less than $37,320, and the highest 10 percent earned more than $94,880. Median annual earnings of physician assistants in 2004 were $70,310 in general medical and surgical hospitals and $69,210 in offices of physicians.

According to the American Academy of Physician Assistants, median income for physician assistants in full-time clinical practice in 2004 was $74,264; median income for first-year graduates was $64,536. Income varies by specialty, practice setting, geographical location, and years of experience. Employers often pay for their employees' liability insurance, registration fees with the Drug Enforcement Administration, State licensing fees, and credentialing fees.

Related Occupations

Other health care workers who provide direct patient care that requires a similar level of skill and training include audiologists, occupational therapists, physical therapists, registered nurses, and speech-language pathologists.

Sources of Additional Information

For information on a career as a physician assistant, including a list of accredited programs, contact:
➤ American Academy of Physician Assistants Information Center, 950 North Washington St., Alexandria, VA 22314-1552. Internet: http://www.aapa.org

For eligibility requirements and a description of the Physician Assistant National Certifying Examination, contact:
➤ National Commission on Certification of Physician Assistants, Inc., 12000 Findley Rd., Suite 200, Duluth, GA 30097. Internet: http://www.nccpa.net

Physicians and Surgeons

(O*NET 29-1061.00, 29-1062.00, 29-1063.00, 29-1064.00, 29-1065.00, 29-1066.00, 29-1067.00, 29-1069.99)

Significant Points

- Many physicians and surgeons work long, irregular hours; over one-third of full-time physicians worked 60 or more hours a week in 2004.

- Formal education and training requirements are among the most demanding of any occupation, but earnings are among the highest.

- Job opportunities should be very good, particularly in rural and low-income areas.

- New physicians are much less likely to enter solo practice and more likely to work as salaried employees of group medical practices, clinics, hospitals, or health networks.

Nature of the Work

Physicians and surgeons serve a fundamental role in our society and have an effect upon all our lives. They diagnose illnesses and prescribe and administer treatment for people suffering from injury or disease. Physicians examine patients, obtain medical histories, and order, perform, and interpret diagnostic tests. They counsel patients on diet, hygiene, and preventive health care.

There are two types of physicians: M.D.—Doctor of Medicine—and D.O.—Doctor of Osteopathic Medicine. M.D.s also are known as allopathic physicians. While both M.D.s and D.O.s may use all accepted methods of treatment, including drugs and surgery, D.O.s place special emphasis on the body's musculoskeletal system, preventive medicine, and holistic patient care. D.O.s are more likely than M.D.s to be primary care specialists although they can be found in all specialties. About half of D.O.s practice general or family medicine, general internal medicine, or general pediatrics.

Physicians work in one or more of several specialties, including, but not limited to, anesthesiology, family and general medicine, general internal medicine, general pediatrics, obstetrics and gynecology, psychiatry, and surgery.

Anesthesiologists. Anesthesiologists focus on the care of surgical patients and pain relief. Like other physicians, they evaluate and treat patients and direct the efforts of those on their staffs. Anesthesiologists confer with other physicians and surgeons about appropriate treatments and procedures before, during, and after operations. These critical care specialists are responsible for maintenance of the patient's vital life functions—heart rate, body temperature, blood pressure, breathing—through continual monitoring and assessment during surgery. They often work outside of the operating room, providing pain relief in the intensive care unit, during labor and delivery, and for those who suffer from chronic pain.

Family and general practitioners. Family and general practitioners are often the first point of contact for people seeking health care, acting as the traditional family doctor. They assess and treat a wide range of conditions, ailments, and injuries, from sinus and respiratory infections to broken bones and scrapes. Family and general practitioners typically have a patient base of regular, long-term visitors. Patients with more serious conditions are referred to specialists or other health care facilities for more intensive care.

General internists. General internists diagnose and provide nonsurgical treatment for diseases and injuries of internal organ systems. They provide care mainly for adults who have a wide range of problems associated with the internal organs, such as the stomach, kidneys, liver, and digestive tract. Internists use a variety of diagnostic techniques to treat patients through medication or hospitalization. Like general practitioners, general internists are commonly looked upon as primary care specialists. They have patients referred to them by other specialists, in turn referring patients to those and yet other specialists when more complex care is required.

General pediatricians. Providing care from birth to early adulthood, pediatricians are concerned with the health of infants, children, and teenagers. They specialize in the diagnosis and treatment of a variety of ailments specific to young people and track their patients' growth to adulthood. Like most physicians, pediatricians work with different health care workers, such as nurses and other physicians, to assess and treat children with various ailments, such as muscular dystrophy. Most of the work of pediatricians, however, involves treating day-to-day illnesses that are common to children—minor injuries, infectious diseases, and immunizations—much as a general practitioner treats adults. Some pediatricians specialize in serious medical conditions and pediatric surgery, treating autoimmune disorders or serious chronic ailments.

Obstetricians and gynecologists. Obstetricians and gynecologists (ob/gyns) are specialists whose focus is women's health.

They are responsible for general medical care for women, but also provide care related to pregnancy and the reproductive system. Like general practitioners, ob/gyns are concerned with the prevention, diagnosis, and treatment of general health problems, but they focus on ailments specific to the female anatomy, such as breast and cervical cancer, urinary tract and pelvic disorders, and hormonal disorders. Ob/gyns also specialize in childbirth, treating and counseling women throughout their pregnancy, from giving prenatal diagnoses to delivery and postpartum care. Ob/gyns track the health of, and treat, both mother and fetus as the pregnancy progresses.

Psychiatrists. Psychiatrists are the primary caregivers in the area of mental health. They assess and treat mental illnesses through a combination of psychotherapy, psychoanalysis, hospitalization, and medication. Psychotherapy involves regular discussions with patients about their problems; the psychiatrist helps them find solutions through changes in their behavioral patterns, the exploration of their past experiences, and group and family therapy sessions. Psychoanalysis involves long-term psychotherapy and counseling for patients. In many cases, medications are administered to correct chemical imbalances that may be causing emotional problems. Psychiatrists may also administer electroconvulsive therapy to those of their patients who do not respond to, or who cannot take, medications.

Surgeons. Surgeons are physicians who specialize in the treatment of injury, disease, and deformity through operations. Using a variety of instruments, and with patients under general or local anesthesia, a surgeon corrects physical deformities, repairs bone and tissue after injuries, or performs preventive surgeries on patients with debilitating diseases or disorders. Although a large number perform general surgery, many surgeons choose to specialize in a specific area. One of the most prevalent specialties is orthopedic surgery: the treatment of the musculoskeletal system. Others include neurological surgery (treatment of the brain and nervous system), cardiovascular surgery, otolaryngology (treatment of the ear, nose, and throat), and plastic or reconstructive surgery. Like primary care

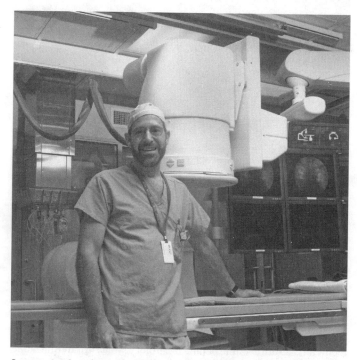

Increasingly, physicians are practicing in groups or health care organizations that provide backup coverage and allow for more time off.

and other specialist physicians, surgeons also examine patients, perform and interpret diagnostic tests, and counsel patients on preventive health care.

A number of other medical specialists, including allergists, cardiologists, dermatologists, emergency physicians, gastroenterologists, ophthalmologists, pathologists, and radiologists, also work in clinics, hospitals, and private offices.

Working Conditions
Many physicians—primarily general and family practitioners, general internists, pediatricians, ob/gyns, and psychiatrists—work in small private offices or clinics, often assisted by a small staff of nurses and other administrative personnel. Increasingly, physicians are practicing in groups or health care organizations that provide backup coverage and allow for more time off. These physicians often work as part of a team coordinating care for a population of patients; they are less independent than solo practitioners of the past.

Surgeons and anesthesiologists typically work in well-lighted, sterile environments while performing surgery and often stand for long periods. Most work in hospitals or in surgical outpatient centers. Many physicians and surgeons work long, irregular hours. Over one-third of full-time physicians and surgeons worked 60 hours or more a week in 2004. Only 8 percent of all physicians and surgeons worked part-time, compared with 16 percent for all occupations. Physicians and surgeons must travel frequently between office and hospital to care for their patients. Those who are on call deal with many patients' concerns over the phone and may make emergency visits to hospitals or nursing homes.

Training and Other Qualifications
Formal education and training requirements for physicians are among the most demanding of any occupation—4 years of undergraduate school, 4 years of medical school, and 3 to 8 years of internship and residency, depending on the specialty selected. A few medical schools offer combined undergraduate and medical school programs that last 6 rather than the customary 8 years.

Premedical students must complete undergraduate work in physics, biology, mathematics, English, and inorganic and organic chemistry. Students also take courses in the humanities and the social sciences. Some students volunteer at local hospitals or clinics to gain practical experience in the health professions.

The minimum educational requirement for entry into a medical school is 3 years of college; most applicants, however, have at least a bachelor's degree, and many have advanced degrees. There are 146 medical schools in the United States—126 teach allopathic medicine and award a Doctor of Medicine (M.D.) degree; 20 teach osteopathic medicine and award the Doctor of Osteopathic Medicine (D.O.) degree. Acceptance to medical school is highly competitive. Applicants must submit transcripts, scores from the Medical College Admission Test, and letters of recommendation. Schools also consider an applicant's character, personality, leadership qualities, and participation in extracurricular activities. Most schools require an interview with members of the admissions committee.

Students spend most of the first 2 years of medical school in laboratories and classrooms, taking courses such as anatomy, biochemistry, physiology, pharmacology, psychology, microbiology, pathology, medical ethics, and laws governing medicine. They also learn to take medical histories, examine patients, and diagnose illnesses. During their last 2 years, students work with patients under the supervision of experienced physicians in hospitals and clinics, learning acute, chronic, preventive, and rehabilitative care. Through rotations in internal medicine, family practice, obstetrics and gynecology, pediatrics, psychiatry, and surgery, they gain experience in the diagnosis and treatment of illness.

Following medical school, almost all M.D.s enter a residency—graduate medical education in a specialty that takes the form of paid on-the-job training, usually in a hospital. Most D.O.s serve a 12-month rotating internship after graduation and before entering a residency, which may last 2 to 6 years.

All States, the District of Columbia, and U.S. territories license physicians. To be licensed, physicians must graduate from an accredited medical school, pass a licensing examination, and complete 1 to 7 years of graduate medical education. Although physicians licensed in one State usually can get a license to practice in another without further examination, some States limit reciprocity. Graduates of foreign medical schools generally can qualify for licensure after passing an examination and completing a U.S. residency.

M.D.s and D.O.s seeking board certification in a specialty may spend up to 7 years in residency training, depending on the specialty. A final examination immediately after residency or after 1 or 2 years of practice also is necessary for certification by a member board of the American Board of Medical Specialists (ABMS) or the American Osteopathic Association (AOA). The ABMS represents 24 specialty boards, ranging from allergy and immunology to urology. The AOA has approved 18 specialty boards, ranging from anesthesiology to surgery. For certification in a subspecialty, physicians usually need another 1 to 2 years of residency.

A physician's training is costly. According to the Association of American Medical Colleges, in 2004 more than 80 percent of medical school graduates were in debt for educational expenses.

People who wish to become physicians must have a desire to serve patients, be self-motivated, and be able to survive the pressures and long hours of medical education and practice. Physicians also must have a good bedside manner, emotional stability, and the ability to make decisions in emergencies. Prospective physicians must be willing to study throughout their career in order to keep up with medical advances.

Employment

Physicians and surgeons held about 567,000 jobs in 2004; approximately 1 out of 7 was self-employed and not incorporated. About 60 percent of salaried physicians and surgeons were in office of physicians, and 16 percent were employed by private hospitals. Others practiced in Federal, State, and local governments, including hospitals, colleges, universities, and professional schools; private colleges, universities, and professional schools; and outpatient care centers.

According to the American Medical Association (AMA), in 2003 about 2 out 5 physicians in patient care were in primary care, but not in a subspecialty of primary care (table 1).

Table 1. Percent distribution of physicians by specialty, 2003

	Percent
Total	100.0
Primary care	40.8
Family medicine and general practice	12.8
Internal medicine	15.1
Obstetrics & gynecology	5.3
Pediatrics	7.6
Specialties	59.2
Anesthesiology	5.4
Psychiatry	5.4
Surgical specialties, selected	14.6
All other specialties	33.9

SOURCE: *American Medical Association, Physician Characteristics and Distribution in the US, 2005.*

A growing number of physicians are partners or salaried employees of group practices. Organized as clinics or as associations of physicians, medical groups can afford expensive medical equipment and realize other business advantages.

According to the AMA, the New England and Middle Atlantic States have the highest ratio of physicians to population; the South Central and Mountain States have the lowest. D.O.s are more likely than M.D.s to practice in small cities and towns and in rural areas. M.D.s tend to locate in urban areas, close to hospital and education centers.

Job Outlook

Employment of physicians and surgeons is projected to grow faster than the average for all occupations through the year 2014 due to continued expansion of health care industries. The growing and aging population will drive overall growth in the demand for physician services, as consumers continue to demand high levels of care using the latest technologies, diagnostic tests, and therapies. In addition to employment growth, job openings will result from the need to replace physicians and surgeons who retire over the 2004-14 period.

Demand for physicians' services is highly sensitive to changes in consumer preferences, health care reimbursement policies, and legislation. For example, if changes to health coverage result in consumers facing higher out-of-pocket costs, they may demand fewer physician services. Demand for physician services may also be tempered by patients relying more on other health care providers—such as physician assistants, nurse practitioners, optometrists, and nurse anesthetists—for some health care services. In addition, new technologies will increase physician productivity. Telemedicine will allow physicians to treat patients or consult with other providers remotely. Increasing use of electronic medical records, test and prescription orders, billing, and scheduling will also improve physician productivity.

Opportunities for individuals interested in becoming physicians and surgeons are expected to be very good. Reports of shortages in some specialties or geographic areas should attract new entrants, encouraging schools to expand programs and hospitals to expand available residency slots. However, because physician training is so lengthy, employment change happens gradually. In the short term, to meet increased demand, experienced physicians may work longer hours, delay retirement, or take measures to increase productivity, such as using more support staff to provide services. Opportunities should be particularly good in rural and low-income areas, because some physicians find these areas unattractive due to less control over work hours, isolation from medical colleagues, or other reasons.

Unlike their predecessors, newly trained physicians face radically different choices of where and how to practice. New physicians are much less likely to enter solo practice and more likely to take salaried jobs in group medical practices, clinics, and health networks.

Earnings

Earnings of physicians and surgeons are among the highest of any occupation. According to the Medical Group Management Association's Physician Compensation and Production Survey, median total compensation for physicians in 2004 varied by specialty, as shown in table 2. Total compensation for physicians reflects the amount reported as direct compensation for tax purposes, plus all voluntary salary reductions. Salary, bonus and/or incentive payments, research stipends, honoraria, and distribution of profits were included in total compensation.

Table 2. Median total compensation of physicians by specialty, 2004

	Less than two years in specialty	Over one year in specialty
Anesthesiology	$259,948	$321,686
Surgery: General	228,839	282,504
Obstetrics/gynecology: General	203,270	247,348
Psychiatry: General	173,922	180,000
Internal medicine: General	141,912	166,420
Pediatrics: General	132,953	161,331
Family practice (without obstetrics)	137,119	156,011

SOURCE: *Medical Group Management Association, Physician Compensation and Production Report, 2005.*

Self-employed physicians—those who own or are part owners of their medical practice—generally have higher median incomes than salaried physicians. Earnings vary according to number of years in practice, geographic region, hours worked, and skill, personality, and professional reputation. Self-employed physicians and surgeons must provide for their own health insurance and retirement.

Related Occupations

Physicians work to prevent, diagnose, and treat diseases, disorders, and injuries. Other health care practitioners who need similar skills and who exercise critical judgment include chiropractors, dentists, optometrists, physician assistants, podiatrists, registered nurses, and veterinarians.

Sources of Additional Information

For a list of medical schools and residency programs, as well as general information on premedical education, financial aid, and medicine as a career, contact:

➤ Association of American Medical Colleges, Section for Student Services, 2450 N St. NW., Washington, DC 20037-1126. Internet: **http://www.aamc.org**

➤ American Association of Colleges of Osteopathic Medicine, 5550 Friendship Blvd., Suite 310, Chevy Chase, MD 20815-7231. Internet: **http://www.aacom.org**

For general information on physicians, contact:

➤ American Medical Association, 515 N. State St., Chicago, IL 60610. Internet: **http://www.ama-assn.org**

➤ American Osteopathic Association, Division of Communications, 142 East Ontario St., Chicago, IL 60611. Internet: **http://www.osteopathic.org**

For information about various medical specialties, contact:

➤ American Board of Medical Specialties, 1007 Church St., Suite 404, Evanston, IL 60201-5913. Internet: **http://www.abms.org**

➤ American Society of Anesthesiologists, 520 N. Northwest Hwy., Park Ridge, IL 60068-2573. Internet: **http://www.asahq.org**

➤ American Academy of Family Physicians, Resident Student Activities Department, 11400 Tomahawk Creek Pkwy., Leawood, KS 66211-2672. Internet: **http://fmignet.aafp.org**

➤ American College of Physicians, 190 North Independence Mall West, Philadelphia, PA 19106. Internet: **http://www.acponline.org**

➤ American College of Obstetricians and Gynecologists, 409 12th St. SW., P.O. Box 96920, Washington, DC 20090-6920. Internet: **http://www.acog.org**

➤ American Academy of Pediatrics, 141 Northwest Point Blvd., Elk Grove Village, IL 60007-1098. Internet: **http://www.aap.org**

➤ American Psychiatric Association, 1000 Wilson Blvd., Suite 1825, Arlington, VA 22209-3901. Internet: **http://www.psych.org**

➤ American College of Surgeons, Division of Education, 633 North Saint Clair St., Chicago, IL 60611-3211. Internet: **http://www.facs.org**

Information on Federal scholarships and loans is available from the directors of student financial aid at schools of medicine. Information on licensing is available from State boards of examiners.

Podiatrists

(O*NET 29-1081.00)

Significant Points

● Despite increasing demand for podiatric care, job openings for podiatrists are expected to be limited because the occupation is small and most podiatrists remain in it until they retire.

● Opportunities for newly trained podiatrists will be better in group medical practices, clinics, and health networks than in traditional, solo practices.

● Podiatrists need a State license that requires the completion of at least 90 hours of undergraduate study; a 4-year post-graduate program at a college of podiatric medicine; and, in most States, a postdoctoral residency program lasting at least 2 years.

● Podiatrists enjoy very high earnings.

Nature of the Work

Americans spend a great deal of time on their feet. As the Nation becomes more active across all age groups, the need for foot care will become increasingly important to maintaining a healthy lifestyle.

The human foot is a complex structure. It contains 26 bones—plus muscles, nerves, ligaments, and blood vessels—and is designed for balance and mobility. The 52 bones in the feet make up about one-fourth of all the bones in the human body. Podiatrists, also known as *doctors of podiatric medicine* (DPMs), diagnose and treat disorders, diseases, and injuries of the foot and lower leg.

Podiatrists treat corns, calluses, ingrown toenails, bunions, heel spurs, and arch problems; ankle and foot injuries, deformities, and infections; and foot complaints associated with diseases such as diabetes. To treat these problems, podiatrists prescribe drugs, order physical therapy, set fractures, and perform surgery. They also fit corrective inserts called orthotics, design plaster casts and strappings to correct deformities, and design custom-made shoes. Podiatrists may use a force plate or scanner to help design the orthotics: patients walk across a plate connected to a computer that "reads" their feet, picking up pressure points and weight distribution. From the computer readout, podiatrists order the correct design or recommend another kind of treatment.

To diagnose a foot problem, podiatrists also order x rays and laboratory tests. The foot may be the first area to show signs of serious conditions such as arthritis, diabetes, and heart disease. For example, patients with diabetes are prone to foot ulcers and infections due to poor circulation. Podiatrists consult with and refer patients to other health practitioners when they detect symptoms of these disorders.

Most podiatrists have a solo practice, although more are forming group practices with other podiatrists or health practitioners. Some specialize in surgery, orthopedics, primary care, or public health. Besides these board-certified specialties, podiatrists may practice other specialties, such as sports medicine, pediatrics, dermatology, radiology, geriatrics, or diabetic foot care.

Podiatrists who are in private practice are responsible for running a small business. They may hire employees, order supplies, and keep records, among other tasks. In addition, some educate the community on the benefits of foot care through speaking engagements and advertising.

Podiatrists diagnose and treat disorders of the feet and ankles.

Working Conditions

Podiatrists usually work in their own offices. They also may spend time visiting patients in nursing homes or performing surgery at hospitals or ambulatory surgical centers, but usually have fewer afterhours emergencies than other doctors have. Those with private practices set their own hours, but may work evenings and weekends to accommodate their patients.

Training, Other Qualifications, and Advancement

All States and the District of Columbia require a license for the practice of podiatric medicine. Each State defines its own licensing requirements, although many States grant reciprocity to podiatrists who are licensed in another State. Applicants for licensure must be graduates of an accredited college of podiatric medicine and must pass written and oral examinations. Some States permit applicants to substitute the examination of the National Board of Podiatric Medical Examiners, given in the second and fourth years of podiatric medical college, for part or all of the written State examination. Most States also require the completion of a postdoctoral residency program of at least 2 years and continuing education for license renewal.

Prerequisites for admission to a college of podiatric medicine include the completion of at least 90 semester hours of undergraduate study, an acceptable grade point average, and suitable scores on the Medical College Admission Test (some colleges also may accept the Dental Admission Test or the Graduate Record Exam). All of the colleges require 8 semester hours each of biology, inorganic chemistry, organic chemistry, and physics, as well as 6 hours of English. The science courses should be those designed for premedical students. Potential podiatric medical students also are evaluated on the basis of extracurricular and community activities, personal interviews, and letters of recommendation. About 95 percent of podiatric students have at least a bachelor's degree.

In 2005, there were seven colleges of podiatric medicine accredited by the Council on Podiatric Medical Education. Colleges of podiatric medicine offer a 4-year program whose core curriculum is similar to that in other schools of medicine. During the first 2 years, students receive classroom instruction in basic sciences, including anatomy, chemistry, pathology, and pharmacology. Third- and fourth-year students have clinical rotations in private practices, hospitals, and clinics. During these rotations, they learn how to take general and podiatric histories, perform routine physical examinations, interpret tests and findings, make diagnoses, and perform therapeutic procedures. Graduates receive the degree of Doctor of Podiatric Medicine (DPM).

Most graduates complete a hospital-based residency program after receiving a DPM. Residency programs last from 2 to 4 years. Residents receive advanced training in podiatric medicine and surgery and serve clinical rotations in anesthesiology, internal medicine, pathology, radiology, emergency medicine, and orthopedic and general surgery. Residencies lasting more than 1 year provide more extensive training in specialty areas.

There are a number of certifying boards for the podiatric specialties of orthopedics, primary medicine, and surgery. Certification means that the DPM meets higher standards than those required for licensure. Each board requires advanced training, the completion of written and oral examinations, and experience as a practicing podiatrist. Most managed-care organizations prefer board-certified podiatrists.

People planning a career in podiatry should have scientific aptitude, manual dexterity, interpersonal skills, and good business sense.

Podiatrists may advance to become professors at colleges of podiatric medicine, department chiefs in hospitals, or general health administrators.

Employment

Podiatrists held about 10,000 jobs in 2004. About 23 percent of podiatrists are self-employed. Most podiatrists were solo practitioners, although more are entering group practices with other podiatrists or other health practitioners. Solo practitioners primarily were unincorporated self-employed workers, although some also were incorporated wage and salary workers in offices of other health practitioners. Other podiatrists are employed in hospitals and by the Federal Government.

Job Outlook

Employment of podiatrists is expected to grow about as fast as the average for all occupations through 2014. More people will turn to podiatrists for foot care because of the rising number of injuries sustained by a more active and increasingly older population. Additional job openings will result from podiatrists who retire from the occupation, particularly members of the baby-boom generation. However, relatively few job openings from this source are expected because the occupation is small and most podiatrists remain in it until they retire.

Medicare and most private health insurance programs cover acute medical and surgical foot services, as well as diagnostic x rays and leg braces. Details of such coverage vary among plans. However, routine foot care, including the removal of corns and calluses, ordinarily is not covered unless the patient has a systemic condition that has resulted in severe circulatory problems or areas of desensitization in the legs or feet. Like dental services, podiatric care is often discretionary and, therefore, more dependent on disposable income than some other medical services.

Employment of podiatrists would grow even faster were it not for continued emphasis on controlling the costs of specialty health care. Insurers will balance the cost of sending patients to podiatrists against the cost and availability of substitute practitioners, such as physicians and physical therapists. Opportunities will be better for board-certified podiatrists, because many managed-care organizations require board certification. Opportunities for newly trained podiatrists will be better in group medical practices, clinics, and health networks than in traditional solo practices. Establishing a practice will be most difficult in the areas surrounding colleges of podiatric medicine, where podiatrists are concentrated.

Earnings
Podiatrists enjoy very high earnings. Median annual earnings of salaried podiatrists were $94,400 in 2004. Additionally, a survey by *Podiatry Management Magazine* reported median net income of $113,000 in 2004. Podiatrists in partnerships tended to earn higher net incomes than those in solo practice. Self-employed podiatrists must provide for their own health insurance and retirement.

Related Occupations
Other workers who apply medical knowledge to prevent, diagnose, and treat lower body muscle and bone disorders and injuries include athletic trainers, chiropractors, massage therapists, occupational therapists, physical therapists, and physicians and surgeons. Workers who specialize in developing orthopedic shoe inserts, braces, and prosthetic limbs are orthotists and prosthetists.

Sources of Additional Information
For information on a career in podiatric medicine, contact:
➤ American Podiatric Medical Association, 9312 Old Georgetown Rd., Bethesda, MD 20814-1621. Internet: **http://www.apma.org**

Information on the colleges of podiatric medicine and their entrance requirements, curricula, and student financial aid is available from:
➤ American Association of Colleges of Podiatric Medicine, 15850 Crabbs Branch Way, Suite 320, Rockville, MD 20855-2622. Internet: **http://www.aacpm.org**

Radiation Therapists

(O*NET 29-1124.00)

Significant Points

- Good job opportunities are expected; applicants who are certified and who possess a bachelor's or an associate degree or a certificate in radiation therapy should have the best prospects.

- Employment is projected to grow faster than average.

- Radiation therapists need good communication skills because their work involves a great deal of patient interaction.

Nature of the Work
Radiation therapy is the use of radiation to treat cancer in the human body. As part of a medical radiation oncology team, radiation therapists use machines—called linear accelerators—to administer radiation treatment to patients. Linear accelerators, used in a procedure called external beam therapy, project high-energy x-rays at targeted cancer cells. As the x-rays collide with human tissue, they produce highly energized ions that can shrink and eliminate cancerous tumors. Radiation therapy sometimes is used as the sole treatment for cancer, but usually is used in conjunction with chemotherapy or surgery.

The first step in the radiation treatment process is called simulation. During simulation, a radiation therapist uses an x-ray imaging machine to pinpoint the location of the tumor. The therapist also may use a computerized tomography or CT scan to help determine how best to direct the radiation to minimize damage to healthy tissue. The therapist then positions the patient and adjusts the linear accelerator so that, during treatment, radiation exposure is concentrated on the tumor cells. The radiation therapist then develops a treatment plan in conjunction with a radiation oncologist (a physician who specializes in therapeutic radiology), and a dosimetrist (a technician who calculates the dose of radiation that will be used for treatment). The therapist later explains the treatment plan to the patient and answers any questions that the patient may have.

After simulation, the radiation therapist positions the patient and adjusts the linear accelerator to mirror the conditions that were established in simulation. Then the therapist leaves the room to administer the radiation treatment. From a separate room that is protected from the x-ray radiation, the therapist operates the linear accelerator and monitors the patient's condition through a TV monitor and an intercom system. Treatment can take anywhere from 10 to 30 minutes and is usually administered once a day, 5 days a week, for a period of 2 to 9 weeks.

During the treatment phase, the radiation therapist monitors the patient's physical condition to determine if any adverse side effects are taking place. In addition, the therapist must be aware of the patient's emotional condition. Because many patients are under stress, and are emotionally fragile, it is important for the therapist to maintain a positive attitude and provide emotional support. Radiation therapists also must keep detailed records of their patients' treatments. These records include information such as the dose of radiation used for each treatment, the total amount of radiation used to date, the area treated, and the patient's reactions. Radiation oncologists and dosimetrists review these records to ensure that the treatment plan is working, to monitor the amount of radiation exposure that the patient has received, and to keep unwanted side effects to a minimum.

Radiation therapists also assist medical radiation physicists, who keep the linear accelerator working. Because radiation therapists often work alone during the treatment phase, they need to be able to check the linear accelerator for problems and make any adjustments that are needed. Therapists also may assist dosimetrists, who calculate the amount of radiation for each treatment. Therapists may perform the routine aspects of this process, called dosimetry, which involves complex mathematical computations.

Working Conditions
Radiation therapists work in hospitals or in cancer treatment centers. These places are clean, well lighted, and well ventilated. Therapists do a considerable amount of lifting and must be able to help disabled patients get on and off treatment tables. Therapists also work on their feet most of the time. Therapists generally work 40 hours a week, and, unlike other health care occupations, they normally work only during the day. However, because radiation therapy emergencies do occur, some therapists are required to be on call and may have to work outside of their normal hours.

Because they work around radioactive materials, radiation therapists take great care to ensure that they are not exposed to

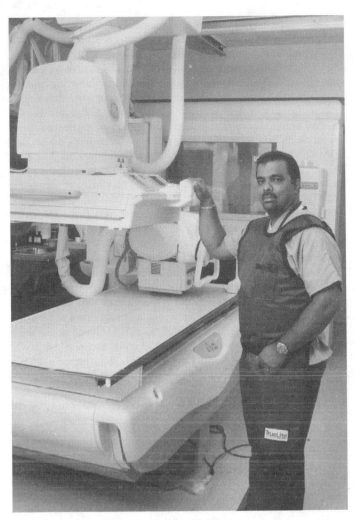

Radiation therapists use machines called linear accelerators to administer radiation treatment to patients.

dangerous levels of radiation. Following standard safety procedures can prevent overexposure.

Training, Other Qualifications, and Advancement

Employers generally require applicants to complete an associate or a bachelor's degree program in radiation therapy. Individuals also may become qualified by completing an associate or a bachelor's degree program in radiography, which is the study of radiological imaging, and then completing a 12-month certificate program in radiation therapy. Radiation therapy programs have core courses on radiation therapy procedures and the scientific theories behind these procedures. In addition, such programs often include courses on human anatomy, human physiology, physics, algebra, precalculus, writing, public speaking, computer science, and research methodology.

Some States require that radiation therapists be licensed by a State accrediting board. Some States, as well as many employers, also require that radiation therapists be certified by the American Registry of Radiologic Technologists (ARRT). In order to become ARRT-certified, an applicant needs to complete an accredited radiation therapy program, adhere to ARRT ethical standards, and pass the ARRT certification examination. In 2005 there were 94 accredited radiation therapy programs. While enrolled in an accredited radiation therapy program, students who wish to become ARRT-certified must take classes that are related to the subject matter of the certification examination. The certification examination

covers radiation protection and quality assurance, clinical concepts in radiation oncology, treatment planning, treatment delivery, and patient care and education. Candidates also must demonstrate competency in several clinical practices, which include patient care activities; simulation procedures; dosimetry calculations; fabrication of beam modification devices; low-volume, high-risk procedures; and radiation treatment procedures.

AART certification is valid for 1 year, after which therapists must renew their certification. Requirements for renewal include abiding by the ARRT ethical standards, paying the annual dues, and satisfying the continuing education requirements. Continuing education requirements must be met every 2 years and include either the completion of 24 credits of radiation therapy-related courses or the successful attainment of ARRT certification in a discipline other than radiation therapy. Renewed certification, however, may not be required by all States or employers that require initial certification.

Individuals interested in becoming radiation therapists should be psychologically capable of working with cancer patients. They should be caring and empathetic because they work with patients who are ill and under stress. Individuals also need good communication skills because their work involves a great deal of patient interaction. They should be able to keep accurate, detailed records. They also should be physically fit because they work on their feet for long periods and lift and move disabled patients.

Experienced radiation therapists may advance to manage radiation therapy programs in treatment centers or other health care facilities. Managers generally continue to treat patients while taking on management responsibilities. Other advancement opportunities include teaching, technical sales, and research. With additional training and certification, therapists also can become dosimetrists, who use complex mathematical formulas to calculate proper radiation doses.

Employment

Radiation therapists held about 15,000 jobs in 2004. About 84 percent worked in the health care industry, primarily in hospitals and in physicians' offices. Another 13 percent worked for State and local governments.

Job Outlook

Good job opportunities are expected. Applicants who are certified and who possess a bachelor's or an associate degree or a certificate in radiation therapy should have the best prospects.

Employment of radiation therapists is projected to grow faster than the average for all occupations during the 2004-14 period. As the U.S. population grows and ages, demand will increase for radiation treatment. As radiation technology advances, radiation treatment will be prescribed for an increasing proportion of cancer patients. In addition to new jobs created over the projection period, a number of job openings will result as experienced radiation therapists retire or leave the occupation for other reasons.

Earnings

The median annual earnings of radiation therapists in May 2004 were $57,700. The middle 50 percent earned between $47,380 and $69,650. The lowest 10 percent earned less than $38,550, and the highest 10 percent earned more than $83,340. Some employers also reimburse their employees for the cost of continuing education.

Related Occupations

Radiation therapists use advanced machinery to administer medical treatment to patients. Other occupations that perform similar duties include radiation technologists and technicians, diagnostic medical sonographers, nuclear medicine technicians, dental hygienists, respiratory therapists, physical therapy assistants and aides, registered nurses, and physicians and surgeons.

Besides radiation therapists, occupations that build relationships with patients and provide them with emotional support include nursing, psychiatric, and home health aides; counselors; psychologists; social workers; and social and human service assistants.

Sources of Additional Information

Information on certification by the American Registry of Radiologic Technologists and on accredited radiation therapy programs may be obtained from:

➤ American Registry of Radiologic Technologists, 1255 Northland Dr., St. Paul, Minnesota 55120-1155. Internet: **http://www.arrt.org/web**

Information on careers in radiation therapy may be obtained from:

➤ American Society of Radiologic Technologists, 15000 Central Ave., SE., Albuquerque, NM 87123-3917. Internet: **http://www.asrt.org**

Recreational Therapists

(O*NET 29-1125.00)

Significant Points

● Overall employment of recreational therapists is expected to grow more slowly than the average for all occupations, but employment of therapists who work in community care facilities for the elderly and in residential mental retardation, mental health, and substance abuse facilities should grow faster than the average.

● Opportunities should be best for persons with a bachelor's degree in therapeutic recreation, or in recreation with a concentration in therapeutic recreation.

● Recreational therapists should be comfortable working with persons who are ill or who have disabilities.

Nature of the Work

Recreational therapists, also referred to as *therapeutic recreation specialists*, provide treatment services and recreation activities to individuals with disabilities or illnesses. Using a variety of techniques, including arts and crafts, animals, sports, games, dance and movement, drama, music, and community outings, therapists treat and maintain the physical, mental, and emotional well-being of their clients. Therapists help individuals reduce depression, stress, and anxiety; recover basic motor functioning and reasoning abilities; build confidence; and socialize effectively so that they can enjoy greater independence, as well as reduce or eliminate the effects of their illness or disability. In addition, therapists help integrate people with disabilities into the community by teaching them how to use community resources and recreational activities. Recreational therapists should not be confused with recreation workers, who organize recreational activities primarily for enjoyment. (Recreation workers are discussed elsewhere in the *Handbook*.)

In acute health care settings, such as hospitals and rehabilitation centers, recreational therapists treat and rehabilitate individuals with specific health conditions, usually in conjunction or collaboration with physicians, nurses, psychologists, social workers, and physical and occupational therapists. In long-term and residential care facilities, recreational therapists use leisure activities—especially structured group programs—to improve and maintain their clients' general health and well-being. They also may provide interventions

to prevent the client from suffering further medical problems and complications related to illnesses and disabilities.

Recreational therapists assess clients on the basis of information the therapists learn from standardized assessments, observations, medical records, the medical staff, the clients' families, and the clients themselves. They then develop and carry out therapeutic interventions consistent with the clients' needs and interests. For example, clients who are isolated from others or who have limited social skills may be encouraged to play games with others, and right-handed persons with right-side paralysis may be instructed in how to adapt to using their unaffected left side to throw a ball or swing a racket. Recreational therapists may instruct patients in relaxation techniques to reduce stress and tension, stretching and limbering exercises, proper body mechanics for participation in recreational activities, pacing and energy conservation techniques, and individual as well as team activities. In addition, therapists observe and document a patient's participation, reactions, and progress.

Community-based recreational therapists may work in park and recreation departments, special-education programs for school districts, or programs for older adults and people with disabilities. Included in the last group are programs and facilities such as assisted-living, adult day care, and substance abuse rehabilitation centers. In these programs, therapists use interventions to develop specific skills, while providing opportunities for exercise, mental stimulation, creativity, and fun. Although most therapists are employed in other areas, those who work in schools help counselors, teachers, and parents address the special needs of students, including easing disabled students' transition into adult life.

Working Conditions

Recreational therapists provide services in special activity rooms, but also plan activities and prepare documentation in offices. When working with clients during community integration programs, they may travel locally to instruct the clients regarding the accessibility of public transportation and other public areas, such as parks, playgrounds, swimming pools, restaurants, and theaters.

Therapists often lift and carry equipment, as well as lead recreational activities. Recreational therapists generally work a 40-hour week that may include some evenings, weekends, and holidays.

Training, Other Qualifications, and Advancement

A bachelor's degree in therapeutic recreation, or in recreation with a concentration in therapeutic recreation, is the usual requirement for

Using a variety of techniques, including games, recreational therapists treat clients and maintain their well-being.

entry-level positions. Persons may qualify for paraprofessional positions with an associate degree in therapeutic recreation or a health care related field. An associate degree in recreational therapy; training in art, drama, or music therapy; or qualifying work experience may be sufficient for activity director positions in nursing homes.

Approximately 150 programs prepare students to become recreational therapists. Most offer bachelor's degrees, although some also offer associate, master's, or doctoral degrees. Programs include courses in assessment, treatment and program planning, intervention design, and evaluation. Students also study human anatomy, physiology, abnormal psychology, medical and psychiatric terminology, characteristics of illnesses and disabilities, professional ethics, and the use of assistive devices and technology.

Although certification is usually voluntary, most employers prefer to hire candidates who are certified therapeutic recreation specialists. The National Council for Therapeutic Recreation Certification is the certificatory agency. To become certified, specialists must have a bachelor's degree, pass a written certification examination, and complete an internship of at least 480 hours. Additional requirements apply in order to maintain certification and to recertify. Some States require licensure or certification to practice recreational therapy.

Recreational therapists should be comfortable working with persons who are ill or who have disabilities. Therapists must be patient, tactful, and persuasive when working with people who have a variety of special needs. Ingenuity, a sense of humor, and imagination are needed to adapt activities to individual needs, and good physical coordination is necessary to demonstrate or participate in recreational activities.

Therapists may advance to supervisory or administrative positions. Some teach, conduct research, or consult for health or social services agencies.

Employment

Recreational therapists held about 24,000 jobs in 2004. About 6 out of 10 were in nursing care facilities and hospitals. Others worked in State and local government agencies and in community care facilities for the elderly, including assisted-living facilities. The rest worked primarily in residential mental retardation, mental health, and substance abuse facilities; individual and family services; Federal Government agencies; educational services; and outpatient care centers. Only a small number of therapists were self-employed, generally contracting with long-term care facilities or community agencies to develop and oversee programs.

Job Outlook

Overall employment of recreational therapists is expected to grow more slowly than the average for all occupations through the year 2014. In nursing care facilities—the largest industry employing recreational therapists—employment will grow slightly faster than the occupation as a whole as the number of older adults continues to grow. Employment is expected to decline, however, in hospitals as services shift to outpatient settings and employers emphasize cost containment. Fast employment growth is expected in the residential and outpatient settings that serve disabled persons, the elderly, or those diagnosed with mental retardation, mental illness, or substance abuse problems. Among these settings are community care facilities for the elderly (including assisted-living facilities); residential mental retardation, mental health, and substance abuse facilities; and facilities that provide individual and family services (such as day care centers for disabled persons and the elderly). Opportunities should be best for persons with a bachelor's degree in therapeutic recreation or in recreation with an option in therapeutic recreation. Opportunities

also should be good for therapists who hold specialized certifications, for example, in, aquatic therapy, meditation, or crisis intervention.

Health care facilities will support a growing number of jobs in adult day care and outpatient programs offering short-term mental health and alcohol or drug abuse services. Rehabilitation, home health care, and transitional programs will provide additional jobs.

The rapidly growing number of older adults is expected to spur job growth for recreational therapy professionals and paraprofessionals in assisted-living facilities, adult day care programs, and other social assistance agencies. Continued growth also is expected in community residential care facilities, as well as in day care programs for individuals with disabilities.

Earnings

Median annual earnings of recreational therapists were $32,900 in May 2004. The middle 50 percent earned between $25,520 and $42,130. The lowest 10 percent earned less than $20,130, and the highest 10 percent earned more than $51,800. In May 2004, median annual earnings for recreational therapists were $28,130 in nursing care facilities.

Related Occupations

Recreational therapists primarily design activities to help people with disabilities lead more fulfilling and independent lives. Other workers who have similar jobs are occupational therapists, physical therapists, recreation workers, and rehabilitation counselors.

Sources of Additional Information

For information on how to order materials describing careers and academic programs in recreational therapy, contact:

➤ American Therapeutic Recreation Association, 1414 Prince St., Suite 204, Alexandria, VA 22314-2853. Internet: http://www.atra-tr.org
➤ National Therapeutic Recreation Society, 22377 Belmont Ridge Rd., Ashburn, VA 20148-4501. Internet: http://www.nrpa.org/content/default.aspx?documentid=530

Information on certification may be obtained from:

➤ National Council for Therapeutic Recreation Certification, 7 Elmwood Dr., New City, NY 10956. Internet: http://www.nctrc.org

Registered Nurses

(O*NET 29-1111.00)

Significant Points

● Registered nurses constitute the largest health care occupation, with 2.4 million jobs.

● About 3 out of 5 jobs are in hospitals.

● The three major educational paths to registered nursing are a bachelor's degree, an associate degree, and a diploma from an approved nursing program.

● Registered nurses are projected to create the second largest number of new jobs among all occupations; job opportunities in most specialties and employment settings are expected to be excellent, with some employers reporting difficulty in attracting and retaining enough RNs.

Nature of the Work

Registered nurses (RNs), regardless of specialty or work setting, perform basic duties that include treating patients, educating patients and the public about various medical conditions, and providing advice and emotional support to patients' family members. RNs record patients' medical histories and symptoms, help to perform diagnostic tests and analyze results, operate medical machinery, administer treatment and medications, and help with patient follow-up and rehabilitation.

RNs teach patients and their families how to manage their illness or injury, including post-treatment home care needs, diet and exercise programs, and self-administration of medication and physical therapy. Some RNs also are trained to provide grief counseling to family members of critically ill patients. RNs work to promote general health by educating the public on various warning signs and symptoms of disease and where to go for help. RNs also might run general health screening or immunization clinics, blood drives, and public seminars on various conditions.

RNs can specialize in one or more patient care specialties. The most common specialties can be divided into roughly four categories—by work setting or type of treatment; disease, ailment, or condition; organ or body system type; or population. RNs may combine specialties from more than one area—for example, pediatric oncology or cardiac emergency—depending on personal interest and employer needs.

RNs may specialize by work setting or by type of care provided. For example, *ambulatory care nurses* treat patients with a variety of illnesses and injuries on an outpatient basis, either in physicians' offices or in clinics. Some ambulatory care nurses are involved in telehealth, providing care and advice through electronic communications media such as videoconferencing or the Internet. *Critical care nurses* work in critical or intensive care hospital units and provide care to patients with cardiovascular, respiratory, or pulmonary failure. *Emergency*, or *trauma, nurses* work in hospital emergency departments and treat patients with life-threatening conditions caused by accidents, heart attacks, and strokes. Some emergency nurses are flight nurses, who provide medical care to patients who must be flown by helicopter to the nearest medical facility. *Holistic nurses* provide care such as acupuncture, massage and aroma therapy, and biofeedback, which are meant to treat patients' mental and spiritual health in addition to their physical health. *Home health care nurses* provide at-home care for patients who are recovering from surgery, accidents, and childbirth. *Hospice and palliative care nurses* provide care for, and help ease the pain of, terminally ill patients outside of hospitals. *Infusion nurses* administer medications, fluids, and blood to patients through injections into patients' veins. *Long- term care nurses* provide medical services on a recurring basis to patients with chronic physical or mental disorders. *Medical-surgical nurses* provide basic medical care to a variety of patients in all health settings. *Occupational health nurses* provide treatment for job-related injuries and illnesses and help employers to detect workplace hazards and implement health and safety standards. *Perianesthesia nurses* provide preoperative and postoperative care to patients undergoing anesthesia during surgery. *Perioperative nurses* assist surgeons by selecting and handling instruments, controlling bleeding, and suturing incisions. Some of these nurses also can specialize in plastic and reconstructive surgery. *Psychiatric nurses* treat patients with personality and mood disorders. *Radiologic nurses* provide care to patients undergoing diagnostic radiation procedures such as ultrasounds and magnetic resonance imaging. *Rehabilitation nurses* care for patients with temporary and permanent disabilities. *Transplant nurses* care for both transplant recipients and living donors and monitor signs of organ rejection.

RNs specializing in a particular disease, ailment, or condition are employed in virtually all work settings, including physicians' offices, outpatient treatment facilities, home health care agencies, and hospitals. For instance, *addictions nurses* treat patients seeking help with alcohol, drug, and tobacco addictions. *Developmental disabilities nurses* provide care for patients with physical, mental, or behavioral disabilities; care may include help with feeding, controlling bodily functions, and sitting or standing independently. *Diabetes management nurses* help diabetics to manage their disease by teaching them proper nutrition and showing them how to test blood sugar levels and administer insulin injections. *Genetics nurses* provide early detection screenings and treatment of patients with genetic disorders, including cystic fibrosis and Huntington's disease. *HIV/AIDS nurses* care for patients diagnosed with HIV and AIDS. *Oncology nurses* care for patients with various types of cancer and may administer radiation and chemotherapies. Finally, *wound, ostomy, and continence nurses* treat patients with wounds caused by traumatic injury, ulcers, or arterial disease; provide postoperative care for patients with openings that allow for alternative methods of bodily waste elimination; and treat patients with urinary and fecal incontinence.

RNs specializing in treatment of a particular organ or body system usually are employed in specialty physicians' offices or outpatient care facilities, although some are employed in hospital specialty or critical care units. For example, *cardiac and vascular nurses* treat patients with coronary heart disease and those who have had heart surgery, providing services such as postoperative rehabilitation. *Dermatology nurses* treat patients with disorders of the skin, such as skin cancer and psoriasis. *Gastroenterology nurses* treat patients with digestive and intestinal disorders, including ulcers, acid reflux disease, and abdominal bleeding. Some nurses in this field also specialize in endoscopic procedures, which look inside the gastrointestinal tract using a tube equipped with a light and a camera that can capture images of diseased tissue. *Gynecology nurses* provide care to women with disorders of the reproductive system, including endometriosis, cancer, and sexually transmitted diseases. *Nephrology nurses* care for patients with kidney disease caused by diabetes, hypertension, or substance abuse. *Neuroscience nurses* care for patients with dysfunctions of the nervous system, including brain and spinal cord injuries and seizures. *Ophthalmic nurses* provide care to patients with disorders of the eyes, including blindness and glaucoma, and to patients undergoing eye surgery. *Orthopedic nurses* care for patients with muscular and skeletal problems, including arthritis, bone fractures, and muscular dystrophy. *Otorhinolaryngology nurses* care for patients with ear, nose, and throat disorders, such as cleft palates, allergies, and sinus disorders. *Respiratory nurses* provide care to patients with respiratory disorders such as asthma, tuberculosis, and cystic fibrosis. *Urology nurses* care for patients with disorders of the kidneys, urinary tract, and male reproductive organs, including infections, kidney and bladder stones, and cancers.

Finally, RNs may specialize by providing preventive and acute care in all health care settings to various segments of the population, including newborns (neonatology), children and adolescents (pediatrics), adults, and the elderly (gerontology or geriatrics). RNs also may provide basic health care to patients outside of health care settings in such venues as including correctional facilities, schools, summer camps, and the military. Some RNs travel around the United States and abroad providing care to patients in areas with shortages of medical professionals.

Most RNs work as staff nurses, providing critical health care services along with physicians, surgeons, and other health care practitioners. However, some RNs choose to become advanced practice nurses, who often are considered primary health care practitioners and work independently or in collaboration with physicians. For example, *clinical nurse specialists* provide direct patient care and expert consultations in one of many of the nursing specialties listed above. *Nurse anesthetists* administer anesthesia, monitor patient's vital signs during surgery, and provide post-anesthesia care. *Nurse midwives* provide primary care to women, including gynecological exams, family planning advice, prenatal care, assistance in labor and delivery, and neonatal care. *Nurse practitioners* provide basic preventive health care to patients, and increasingly serve as primary and specialty care providers in mainly medically underserved areas. The most common areas of specialty for nurse practitioners are family practice, adult practice, women's health, pediatrics, acute care, and gerontology; however, there are many other specialties. In most States, advanced practice nurses can prescribe medications.

Some nurses have jobs that require little or no direct patient contact. Most of these positions still require an active RN license. *Case managers* ensure that all of the medical needs of patients with severe injuries and illnesses are met, including the type, location, and duration of treatment. *Forensics nurses* combine nursing with law enforcement by treating and investigating victims of sexual assault, child abuse, or accidental death. *Infection control nurses* identify, track, and control infectious outbreaks in health care facilities; develop methods of outbreak prevention and biological terrorism responses; and staff immunization clinics. *Legal nurse consultants* assist lawyers in medical cases by interviewing patients and witnesses, organizing medical records, determining damages and costs, locating evidence, and educating lawyers about medical issues. *Nurse administrators* supervise nursing staff, establish work schedules and budgets, and maintain medical supply inventories. *Nurse educators* teach student nurses and also provide continuing education for RNs. *Nurse informaticists* collect, store, and analyze nursing data in order to improve efficiency, reduce risk, and improve patient care. RNs also may work as health care consultants, public policy advisors, pharmaceutical and medical supply researchers and salespersons, and medical writers and editors.

Working Conditions

Most RNs work in well-lighted, comfortable health care facilities. Home health and public health nurses travel to patients' homes, schools, community centers, and other sites. RNs may spend considerable time walking and standing. Patients in hospitals and nursing care facilities require 24-hour care; consequently, nurses in these institutions may work nights, weekends, and holidays. RNs also may be on call—available to work on short notice. Nurses who work in office settings are more likely to work regular business hours. About 23 percent of RNs worked part time in 2004, and 7 percent held more than one job.

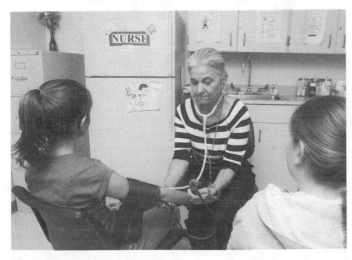

Working as a school nurse is one of many specialties practiced by registered nurses.

Nursing has its hazards, especially in hospitals, nursing care facilities, and clinics, where nurses may care for individuals with infectious diseases. RNs must observe rigid, standardized guidelines to guard against disease and other dangers, such as those posed by radiation, accidental needle sticks, chemicals used to sterilize instruments, and anesthetics. In addition, they are vulnerable to back injury when moving patients, shocks from electrical equipment, and hazards posed by compressed gases. RNs who work with critically ill patients also may suffer emotional strain from observing patient suffering and from close personal contact with patients' families.

Training, Other Qualifications, and Advancement

In all States and the District of Columbia, students must graduate from an approved nursing program and pass a national licensing examination, known as the NCLEX-RN, in order to obtain a nursing license. Nurses may be licensed in more than one State, either by examination or by the endorsement of a license issued by another State. Currently 18 States participate in the Nurse Licensure Compact Agreement, which allows nurses to practice in member States without recertifying. All States require periodic renewal of licenses, which may involve continuing education.

There are three major educational paths to registered nursing: A bachelor's of science degree in nursing (BSN), an associate degree in nursing (ADN), and a diploma. BSN programs, offered by colleges and universities, take about 4 years to complete. In 2004, 674 nursing programs offered degrees at the bachelor's level. ADN programs, offered by community and junior colleges, take about 2 to 3 years to complete. About 846 RN programs in 2004 granted associate degrees. Diploma programs, administered in hospitals, last about 3 years. Only 69 programs offered diplomas in 2004. Generally, licensed graduates of any of the three types of educational programs qualify for entry-level positions as staff nurses.

Many RNs with an ADN or diploma later enter bachelor's programs to prepare for a broader scope of nursing practice. Often, they can find a staff nurse position and then take advantage of tuition reimbursement benefits to work toward a BSN by completing an RN-to-BSN program. In 2004, there were 600 RN-to-BSN programs in the United States. Accelerated master's degree programs in nursing also are available. These programs combine 1 year of an accelerated BSN program with 2 years of graduate study. In 2004, there were 137 RN-to-MSN programs.

Accelerated BSN programs also are available for individuals who have a bachelor's or higher degree in another field and who are interested in moving into nursing. In 2004, more than 165 of these programs were available. Accelerated BSN programs last 12 to 18 months and provide the fastest route to a BSN for individuals who already hold a degree.

Individuals considering nursing should carefully weigh the advantages and disadvantages of enrolling in a BSN program, because, if they do, their advancement opportunities usually are broader. In fact, some career paths are open only to nurses with a bachelor's or master's degree. A bachelor's degree often is necessary for administrative positions and is a prerequisite for admission to graduate nursing programs in research, consulting, and teaching, and all four advanced practice nursing specialties—clinical nurse specialists, nurse anesthetists, nurse midwives, and nurse practitioners. Individuals who complete a bachelor's receive more training in areas such as communication, leadership, and critical thinking, all of which are becoming more important as nursing care becomes more complex. Additionally, bachelor's degree programs offer more clinical experience in nonhospital settings. In 2004, 417 nursing schools offered master's degrees, 93 offered doctoral degrees, and 46 offered accelerated BSN-to-doctoral programs.

All four advanced practice nursing specialties require at least a master's degree. Most programs last about 2 years and require a BSN degree and some programs require at least 1 to 2 years of clinical experience as an RN for admission. In 2004, there were 329 master's and post-master's programs offered for nurse practitioners, 218 master's and post-master's programs for clinical nurse specialists, 92 programs for nurse anesthetists, and 45 programs for nurse midwives. Upon completion of a program, most advanced practice nurses become nationally certified in their area of specialty. In some States, certification in a specialty is required in order to practice that specialty.

All nursing education programs include classroom instruction and supervised clinical experience in hospitals and other health care facilities. Students take courses in anatomy, physiology, microbiology, chemistry, nutrition, psychology and other behavioral sciences, and nursing. Coursework also includes the liberal arts for ADN and BSN students.

Supervised clinical experience is provided in hospital departments such as pediatrics, psychiatry, maternity, and surgery. A growing number of programs include clinical experience in nursing care facilities, public health departments, home health agencies, and ambulatory clinics.

Nurses should be caring, sympathetic, responsible, and detail oriented. They must be able to direct or supervise others, correctly assess patients' conditions, and determine when consultation is required. They need emotional stability to cope with human suffering, emergencies, and other stresses.

Some RNs start their careers as licensed practical nurses or nursing aides, and then go back to school to receive their RN degree. Most RNs begin as staff nurses, and with experience and good performance often are promoted to more responsible positions. In management, nurses can advance to assistant head nurse or head nurse and, from there, to assistant director, director, and vice president. Increasingly, management-level nursing positions require a graduate or an advanced degree in nursing or health services administration. They also require leadership, negotiation skills, and good judgment.

Some nurses move into the business side of health care. Their nursing expertise and experience on a health care team equip them to manage ambulatory, acute, home-based, and chronic care. Employers—including hospitals, insurance companies, pharmaceutical manufacturers, and managed care organizations, among others—need RNs for health planning and development, marketing, consulting, policy development, and quality assurance. Other nurses work as college and university faculty or conduct research.

Foreign-educated nurses wishing to work in the United States must obtain a work visa. Applicants are required to undergo a review of their education and licensing credentials and pass a nursing certification and English proficiency exam, both conducted by the Commission on Graduates of Foreign Nursing Schools. (The commission is an immigration-neutral, nonprofit organization that is recognized internationally as an authority on credentials evaluation in the health care field.) Applicants from Australia, Canada (except Quebec), Ireland, New Zealand, and the United Kingdom are exempt from the language proficiency exam. In addition to these national requirements, most States have their own requirements.

Employment

As the largest health care occupation, registered nurses held about 2.4 million jobs in 2004. About 3 out of 5 jobs were in hospitals, in inpatient and outpatient departments. Others worked in offices of physicians, nursing care facilities, home health care services, employment services, government agencies, and outpatient care centers. The remainder worked mostly in social assistance agencies and educational services, public and private. About 1 in 4 RNs worked part time.

Job Outlook

Job opportunities for RNs in all specialties are expected to be excellent. Employment of registered nurses is expected to grow much faster than the average for all occupations through 2014, and, because the occupation is very large, many new jobs will result. In fact, registered nurses are projected to create the second largest number of new jobs among all occupations. Thousands of job openings also will result from the need to replace experienced nurses who leave the occupation, especially as the median age of the registered nurse population continues to rise.

Much faster-than-average growth will be driven by technological advances in patient care, which permit a greater number of medical problems to be treated, and by an increasing emphasis on preventive care. In addition, the number of older people, who are much more likely than younger people to need nursing care, is projected to grow rapidly.

Employers in some parts of the country and in certain employment settings are reporting difficulty in attracting and retaining an adequate number of RNs, primarily because of an aging RN workforce and a lack of younger workers to fill positions. Enrollments in nursing programs at all levels have increased more rapidly in the past couple of years as students seek jobs with stable employment. However, many qualified applicants are being turned away because of a shortage of nursing faculty to teach classes. The need for nursing faculty will only increase as a large number of instructors nears retirement. Many employers also are relying on foreign-educated nurses to fill open positions.

Even though employment opportunities for all nursing specialties are expected to be excellent, they can vary by employment setting. For example, employment is expected to grow more slowly in hospitals—which comprise health care's largest industry—than in most other health care industries. While the intensity of nursing care is likely to increase, requiring more nurses per patient, the number of inpatients (those who remain in the hospital for more than 24 hours) is not likely to grow by much. Patients are being discharged earlier, and more procedures are being done on an outpatient basis, both inside and outside hospitals. Rapid growth is expected in hospital outpatient facilities, such as those providing same-day surgery, rehabilitation, and chemotherapy.

Despite the slower employment growth in hospitals, job opportunities should still be excellent because of the relatively high turnover of hospital nurses. RNs working in hospitals frequently work overtime and night and weekend shifts and also treat seriously ill and injured patients, all of which can contribute to stress and burnout. Hospital departments in which these working conditions occur most frequently—critical care units, emergency departments, and operating rooms—generally will have more job openings than other departments.

To attract and retain qualified nurses, hospitals may offer signing bonuses, family-friendly work schedules, or subsidized training. A growing number of hospitals also are experimenting with online bidding to fill open shifts, in which nurses can volunteer to fill open shifts at premium wages. This can decrease the amount of mandatory overtime that nurses are required to work.

More and more sophisticated procedures, once performed only in hospitals, are being performed in physicians' offices and in outpatient care centers, such as freestanding ambulatory surgical and emergency centers. Accordingly, employment is expected to grow much faster than average in these places as health care in general expands. However, RNs may face greater competition for these positions because they generally offer regular working hours and more comfortable working environments.

Employment in nursing care facilities is expected to grow faster than average because of increases in the number of elderly, many of whom require long-term care. In addition, the financial pressure on hospitals to discharge patients as soon as possible should produce more admissions to nursing care facilities. Job growth also is expected in units that provide specialized long-term rehabilitation for stroke and head injury patients, as well as units that treat Alzheimer's victims.

Employment in home health care is expected to increase rapidly in response to the growing number of older persons with functional disabilities, consumer preference for care in the home, and technological advances that make it possible to bring increasingly complex treatments into the home. The type of care demanded will require nurses who are able to perform complex procedures.

Generally, RNs with at least a bachelor's degree will have better job prospects than those without a bachelor's. In addition, all four advanced practice specialties—clinical nurse specialists, nurse practitioners, midwives, and anesthetists—will be in high demand, particularly in medically underserved areas such as inner cities and rural areas. Relative to physicians, these RNs increasingly serve as lower-cost primary care providers.

Earnings

Median annual earnings of registered nurses were $52,330 in May 2004. The middle 50 percent earned between $43,370 and $63,360. The lowest 10 percent earned less than $37,300, and the highest 10 percent earned more than $74,760. Median annual earnings in the industries employing the largest numbers of registered nurses in May 2004 were as follows:

Employment services	$63,170
General medical and surgical hospitals	53,450
Home health care services	48,990
Offices of physicians	48,250
Nursing care facilities	48,220

Many employers offer flexible work schedules, child care, educational benefits, and bonuses.

Related Occupations

Workers in other health care occupations with responsibilities and duties related to those of registered nurses are cardiovascular technologists and technicians; diagnostic medical sonographers; dietitians and nutritionists; emergency medical technicians and paramedics; licensed practical and licensed vocational nurses; massage therapists; medical and health services managers; nursing, psychiatric, and home health aides; occupational therapists; physical therapists; physician assistants; physicians and surgeons; radiologic technologists and technicians; respiratory therapists; and surgical technologists.

Sources of Additional Information

For information on a career as a registered nurse and nursing education, contact:
➤ National League for Nursing, 61 Broadway, New York, NY 10006. Internet: http:// www.nln.org

For information on nursing career options, financial aid, and listings of BSN, graduate, and accelerated nursing programs, contact:
➤ American Association of Colleges of Nursing, 1 Dupont Circle NW., Suite 530, Washington, DC 20036. Internet: http://www.aacn.nche.edu

For additional information on registered nurses, including credentialing, contact:
➤ American Nurses Association, 8515 Georgia Ave., Suite 400, Silver Spring, MD 20910. Internet: http://nursingworld.org

For information on the NCLEX-RN exam and a list of individual States' boards of nursing, contact:
➤ National Council of State Boards of Nursing, 111 E. Wacker Dr., Suite 2900, Chicago, IL 60611. Internet: http://www.ncsbn.org

For information on obtaining U.S. certification and work visas for foreign-educated nurses, contact:
➤ Commission on Graduates of Foreign Nursing Schools, 3600 Market St., Suite 400, Philadelphia, PA 19104. Internet: http://www.cgfns.org

For a list of accredited clinical nurse specialist programs, contact:
➤ National Association of Clinical Nurse Specialists, 2090 Linglestown Rd., Suite 107, Harrisburg, PA 17110. Internet: http://www.nacns.org/student/

For information on nurse anesthetists, including a list of accredited programs, contact:
➤ American Association of Nurse Anesthetists, 222 Prospect Ave., Park Ridge, IL 60068.

For information on nurse midwives, including a list of accredited programs, contact:
➤ American College of Nurse-Midwives, 8403 Colesville Rd., Suite 1550, Silver Spring, MD 20910. Internet: http://www.midwife.org

For information on nurse practitioners, including a list of accredited programs, contact:
➤ American Academy of Nurse Practitioners, P.O. Box 12846, Austin, TX 78711. Internet: http://www.aanp.org

Respiratory Therapists

(O*NET 29-1126.00, 29-2054.00)

Significant Points

● Job opportunities will be very good, especially for therapists with cardiopulmonary care skills or experience working with infants.

● All States (except Alaska and Hawaii), the District of Columbia, and Puerto Rico require respiratory therapists to obtain a license.

● Hospitals will continue to employ the vast majority of respiratory therapists, but a growing number of therapists will work in other settings.

Nature of the Work

Respiratory therapists and *respiratory therapy technicians*—also known as respiratory care practitioners—evaluate, treat, and care for patients with breathing or other cardiopulmonary disorders. Practicing under the direction of a physician, respiratory therapists assume primary responsibility for all respiratory care therapeutic treatments and diagnostic procedures, including the supervision of respiratory therapy technicians. Respiratory therapy technicians follow specific, well-defined respiratory care procedures under the direction of respiratory therapists and physicians. In clinical practice, many of the daily duties of therapists and technicians overlap; furthermore, the two have the same education and training requirements. However, therapists generally have greater responsibility than technicians. For example, respiratory therapists will consult with physicians and other health care staff to help develop and modify individual patient care plans. Respiratory therapists also are more likely to provide complex therapy requiring considerable independent judgment, such as caring for patients on life support in intensive-care units of hospitals. In this *Handbook* statement, the term *respiratory therapists* includes both respiratory therapists and respiratory therapy technicians.

Respiratory therapists evaluate and treat all types of patients, ranging from premature infants whose lungs are not fully developed to elderly people whose lungs are diseased. Respiratory therapists provide temporary relief to patients with chronic asthma or emphysema, as well as emergency care to patients who are victims of a heart attack, stroke, drowning, or shock.

To evaluate patients, respiratory therapists interview them, perform limited physical examinations, and conduct diagnostic tests. For example, respiratory therapists test patients' breathing capacity and determine the concentration of oxygen and other gases in patients' blood. They also measure patients' pH, which indicates the acidity or alkalinity of the blood. To evaluate a patient's lung capacity, respiratory therapists have the patient breathe into an instrument that measures the volume and flow of oxygen during inhalation and exhalation. By comparing the reading with the norm for the patient's age, height, weight, and sex, respiratory therapists can provide information that helps determine whether the patient has any lung deficiencies. To analyze oxygen, carbon dioxide, and pH levels, therapists draw an arterial blood sample, place it in a blood gas analyzer, and relay the results to a physician, who then may make treatment decisions.

To treat patients, respiratory therapists use oxygen or oxygen mixtures, chest physiotherapy, and aerosol medications. When a patient has difficulty getting enough oxygen into his or her blood, therapists increase the patient's concentration of oxygen by placing an oxygen mask or nasal cannula on the patient and set the oxygen flow at the level prescribed by a physician. Therapists also connect patients who cannot breathe on their own to ventilators that deliver pressurized oxygen into the lungs. The therapists insert a tube into the patient's trachea, or windpipe; connect the tube to the ventilator; and set the rate, volume, and oxygen concentration of the oxygen mixture entering the patient's lungs.

Therapists perform regular assessments of patients and equipment. If the patient appears to be having difficulty breathing or if the oxygen, carbon dioxide, or pH level of the blood is abnormal, therapists change the ventilator setting according to the doctor's orders or check the equipment for mechanical problems. In home care, therapists teach patients and their families to use ventilators and other life-support systems. In addition, therapists visit patients several times a month to inspect and clean equipment and to ensure its proper use. Therapists also make emergency visits if equipment problems arise.

Respiratory therapists perform chest physiotherapy on patients to remove mucus from their lungs and make it easier for them to breathe. For example, during surgery, anesthesia depresses respiration, so chest physiotherapy may be prescribed to help get the patient's lungs back to normal and to prevent congestion. Chest physiotherapy also helps patients suffering from lung diseases, such as cystic fibrosis, that cause mucus to collect in the lungs. Therapists

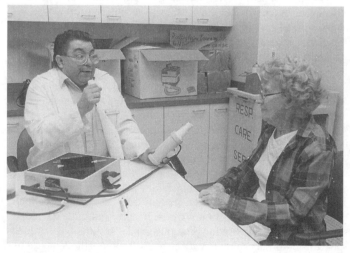

Respiratory therapists conduct diagnostic tests on patients with breathing and cardiopulmonary disorders.

place patients in positions that help drain mucus, and then vibrate the patients' rib cages and instruct the patients to cough.

Respiratory therapists also administer aerosols—liquid medications suspended in a gas that forms a mist which is inhaled—and teach patients how to inhale the aerosol properly to ensure its effectiveness.

In some hospitals, therapists perform tasks that fall outside their traditional role. Therapists' tasks are expanding into areas such as pulmonary rehabilitation, smoking cessation counseling, disease prevention, case management, and polysomnography—the diagnosis of breathing disorders during sleep, such as apnea. Respiratory therapists also increasingly treat critical care patients, either as part of surface and air transport teams or as part of rapid-response teams in hospitals.

Working Conditions
Respiratory therapists generally work between 35 and 40 hours a week. Because hospitals operate around the clock, therapists may work evenings, nights, or weekends. They spend long periods standing and walking between patients' rooms. In an emergency, therapists work under a great deal of stress. Respiratory therapists employed in home health care must travel frequently to the homes of patients.

Respiratory therapists are trained to work with hazardous gases stored under pressure. Adherence to safety precautions and regular maintenance and testing of equipment minimize the risk of injury. As in many other health occupations, respiratory therapists run the risk of catching an infectious disease, but carefully following proper procedures minimizes this risk.

Training, Other Qualifications, and Advancement
Formal training is necessary for entry into this field. Training is offered at the postsecondary level by colleges and universities, medical schools, vocational-technical institutes, and the Armed Forces. An associate's degree is required for entry into the field. Most programs award associate's or bachelor's degrees and prepare graduates for jobs as advanced respiratory therapists. A limited number of associate's degree programs lead to jobs as entry-level respiratory therapists. According to the Commission on Accreditation of Allied Health Education Programs (CAAHEP), 51 entry-level and 329 advanced respiratory therapy programs were accredited in the United States, including Puerto Rico, in 2005.

Among the areas of study in respiratory therapy are human anatomy and physiology, pathophysiology, chemistry, physics, microbiology, pharmacology, and mathematics. Other courses deal with therapeutic and diagnostic procedures and tests, equipment, patient assessment, cardiopulmonary resuscitation, the application of clinical practice guidelines, patient care outside of hospitals, cardiac and pulmonary rehabilitation, respiratory health promotion and disease prevention, and medical recordkeeping and reimbursement.

The National Board for Respiratory Care (NBRC) offers certification and registration to graduates of programs accredited by CAAHEP or the Committee on Accreditation for Respiratory Care (CoARC). Two credentials are awarded to respiratory therapists who satisfy the requirements: Registered Respiratory Therapist (RRT) and Certified Respiratory Therapist (CRT). Graduates from accredited entry-level or advanced-level programs in respiratory therapy may take the CRT examination. CRTs who were graduated from advanced-level programs and who meet additional experience requirements can take two separate examinations leading to the award of the RRT credential.

All States (except Alaska and Hawaii), the District of Columbia, and Puerto Rico require respiratory therapists to obtain a license. Passing the CRT exam qualifies respiratory therapists for

State licenses. Also, most employers require respiratory therapists to maintain a cardiopulmonary resuscitation (CPR) certification. Supervisory positions and intensive-care specialties usually require the RRT or at least RRT eligibility.

Therapists should be sensitive to patients' physical and psychological needs. Respiratory care practitioners must pay attention to detail, follow instructions, and work as part of a team. In addition, operating advanced equipment requires proficiency with computers.

High school students interested in a career in respiratory care should take courses in health, biology, mathematics, chemistry, and physics. Respiratory care involves basic mathematical problem solving and an understanding of chemical and physical principles. For example, respiratory care workers must be able to compute dosages of medication and calculate gas concentrations.

Respiratory therapists advance in clinical practice by moving from general care to the care of critically ill patients who have significant problems in other organ systems, such as the heart or kidneys. Respiratory therapists, especially those with bachelor's or master's degrees, also may advance to supervisory or managerial positions in a respiratory therapy department. Respiratory therapists in home health care and equipment rental firms may become branch managers. Some respiratory therapists advance by moving into teaching positions.

Employment

Respiratory therapists held about 118,000 jobs in 2004. More than 4 out of 5 jobs were in hospital departments of respiratory care, anesthesiology, or pulmonary medicine. Most of the remaining jobs were in offices of physicians or other health practitioners, consumer-goods rental firms that supply respiratory equipment for home use, nursing care facilities, and home health care services. Holding a second job is relatively common for respiratory therapists. About 13 percent held another job, compared with 5 percent of workers in all occupations.

Job Outlook

Job opportunities are expected to be very good, especially for respiratory therapists with cardiopulmonary care skills or experience working with infants. Employment of respiratory therapists is expected to increase faster than the average for all occupations through the year 2014, because of substantial growth in the numbers of the middle-aged and elderly population—a development that will heighten the incidence of cardiopulmonary disease—and because of the expanding role of respiratory therapists in the early detection of pulmonary disorders, case management, disease prevention, and emergency care.

Older Americans suffer most from respiratory ailments and cardiopulmonary diseases such as pneumonia, chronic bronchitis, emphysema, and heart disease. As their numbers increase, the need for respiratory therapists will increase as well. In addition, advances in inhalable medications and in the treatment of lung transplant patients, heart attack and accident victims, and premature infants (many of whom are dependent on a ventilator during part of their treatment) will increase the demand for the services of respiratory care practitioners.

Although hospitals will continue to employ the vast majority of therapists, a growing number can expect to work outside of hospitals in home health care services, offices of physicians or other health practitioners, or consumer-goods rental firms.

Earnings

Median annual earnings of respiratory therapists were $43,140 in May 2004. The middle 50 percent earned between $37,650 and $50,860. The lowest 10 percent earned less than $32,220, and the highest 10 percent earned more than $57,580. In general medical and surgical hospitals, median annual earnings of respiratory therapists were $43,140 in May 2004.

Median annual earnings of respiratory therapy technicians were $36,740 in May 2004. The middle 50 percent earned between $30,490 and $43,830. The lowest 10 percent earned less than $24,640, and the highest 10 percent earned more than $52,280. Median annual earnings of respiratory therapy technicians employed in general medical and surgical hospitals were $36,990 in May 2004.

Related Occupations

Under the supervision of a physician, respiratory therapists administer respiratory care and life support to patients with heart and lung difficulties. Other workers who care for, treat, or train people to improve their physical condition include registered nurses, occupational therapists, physical therapists, and radiation therapists.

Sources of Additional Information

Information concerning a career in respiratory care is available from:

➤ American Association for Respiratory Care, 9425 N. MacArthur Blvd., Suite 100, Irving, TX 75063-4706. Internet: **http://www.aarc.org**

For a list of accredited educational programs for respiratory care practitioners, contact either of the following organizations:
➤ Commission on Accreditation for Allied Health Education Programs, 35 East Wacker Dr., Suite 1970., Chicago, IL 60601. Internet: **http://www.caahep.org**

Information on gaining credentials in respiratory care and a list of State licensing agencies can be obtained from:
➤ National Board for Respiratory Care, Inc., 8310 Nieman Rd., Lenexa, KS 66214-1579. Internet: **http://www.nbrc.org**

Speech-Language Pathologists

(O*NET 29-1127.00)

Significant Points

- About half work in educational services, and most others were employed by health care and social assistance facilities.

- A master's degree in speech-language pathology is the standard credential required for licensing in most States.

- Employment is expected to grow because the expanding population in older age groups is prone to medical conditions that result in speech, language, and swallowing problems.

- Excellent job opportunities are expected.

Nature of the Work

Speech-language pathologists, sometimes called *speech therapists*, assess, diagnose, treat, and help to prevent speech, language, cognitive-communication, voice, swallowing, fluency, and other related disorders.

Speech-language pathologists work with people who cannot produce speech sounds, or cannot produce them clearly; those with speech rhythm and fluency problems, such as stuttering; people with voice disorders, such as inappropriate pitch or harsh voice; those with problems understanding and producing language; those who wish to improve their communication skills by modifying an accent; and those with cognitive communication impairments, such as attention, memory, and problem solving disorders. They also work with people who have swallowing difficulties.

Speech, language, and swallowing difficulties can result from a variety of causes including stroke, brain injury or deterioration, developmental delays or disorders, learning disabilities, cerebral palsy, cleft palate, voice pathology, mental retardation, hearing loss, or emotional problems. Problems can be congenital, developmental, or acquired. Speech-language pathologists use qualitative and quantitative assessment methods, including standardized tests, as well as special instruments, to analyze and diagnose the nature and extent of speech, language, and swallowing impairments. Speech-language pathologists develop an individualized plan of care, tailored to each patient's needs. For individuals with little or no speech capability, speech-language pathologists may select augmentative or alternative communication methods, including automated devices and sign language, and teach their use. They teach these individuals how to make sounds, improve their voices, or increase their oral or written language skills to communicate more effectively. They also teach individuals how to strengthen muscles or use compensatory strategies to swallow without choking or inhaling food or liquid. Speech-language pathologists help patients develop, or recover, reliable communication and swallowing skills so patients can fulfill their educational, vocational, and social roles.

Speech-language pathologists keep records on the initial evaluation, progress, and discharge of clients. This helps pinpoint problems, tracks client progress, and justifies the cost of treatment when applying for reimbursement. They counsel individuals and their families concerning communication disorders and how to cope with the stress and misunderstanding that often accompany them. They also work with family members to recognize and change behavior patterns that impede communication and treatment and show them communication-enhancing techniques to use at home.

Most speech-language pathologists provide direct clinical services to individuals with communication or swallowing disorders. In medical facilities, they may perform their job in conjunction with physicians, social workers, psychologists, and other therapists. Speech-language pathologists in schools collaborate with teachers, special educators, interpreters, other school personnel, and parents to develop and implement individual or group programs, provide counseling, and support classroom activities. Some speech-language pathologists conduct research on how people communicate. Others design and develop equipment or techniques for diagnosing and treating speech problems.

Working Conditions

Speech-language pathologists usually work at a desk or table in clean comfortable surroundings. In medical settings, they may work at the patient's bedside and assist in positioning the patient. In school settings they may work with students in an office or classroom. Some deliver services in the client's home. While the job is not physically demanding, it requires attention to detail and intense concentration. The emotional needs of clients and their families may be demanding. Most full-time speech-language pathologists work 40 hours per week; about 1 in 5 work part time. Those who work on a contract basis may spend a substantial amount of time traveling between facilities.

Training, Other Qualifications, and Advancement

In 2005, 47 States required speech-language pathologists to be licensed if they worked in a health care setting, and all States required a master's degree or equivalent. A passing score on the national examination on speech-language pathology, offered through the Praxis Series of the Educational Testing Service, is needed as well. Other requirements typically are 300 to 375 hours of supervised clinical experience and 9 months of postgraduate professional clinical experience. Forty-one States have continuing education requirements for licensure renewal. Medicaid, Medicare, and private health insurers generally require a practitioner to be licensed to qualify for reimbursement.

Only 11 States require this same license to practice in the public schools. The other States issue a teaching license or certificate that typically requires a master's degree from an approved college or university. Some States will grant a temporary teaching license or certificate to bachelor's degree applicants, but a master's degree must be earned in 3 to 5 years. A few States grant a full teacher's certificate or license to bachelor's degree applicants.

In 2004, 239 colleges and universities offered graduate programs in speech-language pathology that are accredited by the Council on Academic Accreditation in Audiology and Speech-Language Pathology. While graduation from an accredited program is not always required to become a speech-language pathologist, it may be helpful in obtaining a license or may be required to obtain a license in some States. Courses cover the anatomy, physiology, and the development of the areas of the body involved in speech, language, and swallowing; the nature of disorders; acoustics; and psychological aspects of communication. Graduate students also learn to evaluate and treat speech, language, and swallowing disorders and receive supervised clinical training in communication disorders.

Speech-language pathologists can acquire the Certificate of Clinical Competence in Speech-Language Pathology (CCC-SLP) offered by the American Speech-Language-Hearing Association. To earn a CCC, a person must have a graduate degree and 400 hours of supervised clinical experience, complete a 36-week postgraduate clinical fellowship, and pass the Praxis Series examination in speech-language pathology administered by the Educational Testing Service (ETS).

Speech-language pathologists should be able to effectively communicate diagnostic test results, diagnoses, and proposed treatment in a manner easily understood by their patients and their families. They must

About half of speech-language pathologists work in schools, helping students with communication-related disorders.

be able to approach problems objectively and be supportive. Because a patient's progress may be slow, patience, compassion, and good listening skills are necessary.

As speech-language pathologists gain clinical experience and engage in continuing professional education, many develop expertise with certain populations, such as preschoolers and adolescents, or disorders, such as aphasia and learning disabilities. Some may obtain board recognition in a specialty area, such as child language, fluency, or feeding and swallowing. Experienced clinicians may become mentors or supervisors of other therapists or be promoted to administrative positions.

Employment

Speech-language pathologists held about 96,000 jobs in 2004. About half were employed in educational services, primarily in preschools and elementary and secondary schools. Others were employed in hospitals; offices of other health practitioners, including speech-language pathologists; nursing care facilities; home health care services; individual and family services; outpatient care centers; and child day care centers.

A few speech-language pathologists are self-employed in private practice. They contract to provide services in schools, offices of physicians, hospitals, or nursing care facilities, or work as consultants to industry.

Job Outlook

Employment of speech-language pathologists is expected to grow about as fast as the average for all occupations through the year 2014. As the members of the baby boom generation continue to age, the possibility of neurological disorders and associated speech, language, and swallowing impairments increases. Medical advances are also improving the survival rate of premature infants and trauma and stroke victims, who then need assessment and possible treatment. An increased emphasis also has been placed on early identification of speech and language problems in young children. The combination of growth in the occupation and an expected increase in retirements over the coming years should create excellent job opportunities for speech-language pathologists. Opportunities should be particularly favorable for those with the ability to speak a second language, such as Spanish.

In health care facilities, restrictions on reimbursement for therapy services may limit the growth of speech-language pathologists in the near term. However, over the long run, the demand for therapists should continue to rise as growth in the number of individuals with disabilities or limited function spurs demand for therapy services.

Employment in educational services will increase along with growth in elementary and secondary school enrollments, including enrollment of special education students. Federal law guarantees special education and related services to all eligible children with disabilities. Greater awareness of the importance of early identification and diagnosis of speech and language disorders will also increase employment.

The number of speech-language pathologists in private practice will rise due to the increasing use of contract services by hospitals, schools, and nursing care facilities.

Earnings

Median annual earnings of speech-language pathologists were $52,410 in May 2004. The middle 50 percent earned between $42,090 and $65,750. The lowest 10 percent earned less than $34,720, and the highest 10 percent earned more than $82,420. Median annual earnings in the industries employing the largest numbers of speech-language pathologists in May 2004 were:

Offices of other health practitioners	$57,240
General medical and surgical hospitals	55,900
Elementary and secondary schools	48,320

According to a 2003 survey by the American Speech-Language-Hearing Association, the median annual salary for full-time certified speech-language pathologists who worked on a calendar-year basis, generally 11 or 12 months annually, was $48,000. Certified speech-language pathologists who worked 25 or fewer hours per week had a median hourly salary of $40.00. Starting salaries for certified speech-language pathologists with one to three years of experience were $42,000 for those who worked on a calendar-year. According to a 2004 survey by the American Speech-Language-Hearing Association, the median annual salary for speech-language pathologists in schools was $50,000 for those employed on an academic year basis (usually 9 or 10 months).

Related Occupations

Speech-language pathologists specialize in the prevention, diagnosis, and treatment of speech and language problems. Workers in related occupations include audiologists, occupational therapists, optometrists, physical therapists, psychologists, and recreational therapists. Speech-language pathologists in school systems often work closely with special education teachers in assisting students with disabilities.

Sources of Additional Information

State licensing boards can provide information on licensure requirements. State departments of education can supply information on certification requirements for those who wish to work in public schools.

For information on careers in speech-language pathology, a description of the CCC-SLP credential, and a listing of accredited graduate programs in speech-language pathology, contact:

➤ American Speech-Language-Hearing Association, 10801 Rockville Pike, Rockville, MD 20852. Internet: **http://www.asha.org**

Veterinarians

(O*NET 29-1131.00)

Significant Points

- Veterinarians should have an affinity for animals and the ability to get along with their owners.

- Graduation from an accredited college of veterinary medicine and a State license are required.

- Competition for admission to veterinary school is keen; however, graduates should have very good job opportunities.

- About 1 out of 5 veterinarians was self-employed; self-employed veterinarians usually have to work hard and long to build a sufficient client base.

Nature of the Work

Veterinarians play a major role in the healthcare of pets, livestock, and zoo, sporting, and laboratory animals. Some veterinarians use their skills to protect humans against diseases carried by animals and conduct clinical research on human and animal health problems. Others work in basic research, broadening the scope of fundamental theoretical knowledge, and in applied research, developing new ways to use knowledge.

Most veterinarians perform clinical work in private practices. More than 50 percent of these veterinarians predominately, or exclusively treat small animals. Small-animal practitioners usually care for companion animals, such as dogs and cats, but also treat birds, reptiles, rabbits, and other animals that can be kept as pets. About one-fourth of all veterinarians work in mixed animal practices, where they see pigs, goats, sheep, and some nondomestic animals in addition to companion animals. Veterinarians in clinical practice diagnose animal health problems; vaccinate against diseases, such as distemper and rabies; medicate animals suffering from infections or illnesses; treat and dress wounds; set fractures; perform surgery; and advise owners about animal feeding, behavior, and breeding.

A small number of private-practice veterinarians work exclusively with large animals, mostly horses or cows; some also care for various kinds of food animals. These veterinarians usually drive to farms or ranches to provide veterinary services for herds or individual animals. Much of this work involves preventive care to maintain the health of the animals. These veterinarians test for and vaccinate against diseases and consult with farm or ranch owners and managers regarding animal production, feeding, and housing issues. They also treat and dress wounds, set fractures, and perform surgery, including cesarean sections on birthing animals. Veterinarians euthanize animals when necessary. Other veterinarians care for zoo, aquarium, or laboratory animals.

Employment opportunities for veterinarians are expected to be very good, but competition to veterinary school is keen.

Veterinarians who treat animals use medical equipment such as stethoscopes, surgical instruments, and diagnostic equipment, including radiographic and ultrasound equipment. Veterinarians working in research use a full range of sophisticated laboratory equipment.

Veterinarians can contribute to human as well as animal health. A number of veterinarians work with physicians and scientists as they research ways to prevent and treat various human health problems. For example, veterinarians contributed greatly in conquering malaria and yellow fever, solved the mystery of botulism, produced an anticoagulant used to treat some people with heart disease, and defined and developed surgical techniques for humans, such as hip and knee joint replacements and limb and organ transplants. Today, some determine the effects of drug therapies, antibiotics, or new surgical techniques by testing them on animals.

Some veterinarians are involved in food safety at various levels. Veterinarians who are livestock inspectors check animals for transmissible diseases, advise owners on the treatment of their animals and may quarantine animals. Veterinarians who are meat, poultry, or egg product inspectors examine slaughtering and processing plants, check live animals and carcasses for disease, and enforce government regulations regarding food purity and sanitation.

Working Conditions

Veterinarians often work long hours. Those in group practices may take turns being on call for evening, night, or weekend work; solo practitioners may work extended and weekend hours, responding to emergencies or squeezing in unexpected appointments. The work setting often can be noisy.

Veterinarians in large-animal practice spend time driving between their office and farms or ranches. They work outdoors in all kinds of weather and may have to treat animals or perform surgery under unsanitary conditions. When working with animals that are frightened or in pain, veterinarians risk being bitten, kicked, or scratched.

Veterinarians working in nonclinical areas, such as public health and research, have working conditions similar to those of other professionals in those lines of work. In these cases, veterinarians enjoy clean, well-lit offices or laboratories and spend much of their time dealing with people rather than animals.

Training, Other Qualifications, and Advancement

Prospective veterinarians must graduate with a Doctor of Veterinary Medicine (D.V.M. or V.M.D.) degree from a 4-year program at an accredited college of veterinary medicine and must obtain a license to practice. There are 28 colleges in 26 States that meet accreditation standards set by the Council on Education of the American Veterinary Medical Association (AVMA). The prerequisites for admission vary. Many of these colleges do not require a bachelor's degree for entrance, but all require a significant number of credit hours—ranging from 45 to 90 semester hours—at the undergraduate level. However, most of the students admitted have completed an undergraduate program. Applicants without a bachelor's degree face a difficult task gaining admittance.

Preveterinary courses emphasize the sciences. Veterinary medical colleges typically require classes in organic and inorganic chemistry, physics, biochemistry, general biology, animal biology, animal nutrition, genetics, vertebrate embryology, cellular biology, microbiology, zoology, and systemic physiology. Some programs require calculus; some require only statistics, college algebra and trigonometry, or precalculus. Most veterinary medical colleges also require core courses, including some in English or literature, the social sciences, and the humanities. Increasingly, courses in practice management and career development are becoming a standard part of the curriculum, to provide a foundation of general business knowledge for new graduates.

In addition to satisfying preveterinary course requirements, applicants must submit test scores from the Graduate Record Examination (GRE), the Veterinary College Admission Test (VCAT), or the Medical College Admission Test (MCAT), depending on the preference of the college to which they are applying. Currently, 22 schools require the GRE, 4 require the VCAT, and 2 accept the MCAT.

In admittance decisions, some veterinary medical colleges place heavy consideration on a candidate's veterinary and animal experience. Formal experience, such as work with veterinarians or scientists in clinics, agribusiness, research, or some area of health science, is particularly advantageous. Less formal experience, such as working with animals on a farm or ranch or at a stable or animal shelter, also is helpful. Students must demonstrate ambition and an eagerness to work with animals.

There is keen competition for admission to veterinary school. The number of accredited veterinary colleges has remained largely the same since 1983, whereas the number of applicants has risen significantly. Only about 1 in 3 applicants was accepted in 2004. AVMA-recognized veterinary specialties—such as pathology, internal medicine, dentistry, nutrition, ophthalmology, surgery, radiology, preventive medicine, and laboratory animal medicine—are usually in the form of a 2-year internship. Interns receive a small salary but usually find that their internship experience leads to a higher beginning salary, relative to those of other starting veterinarians. Veterinarians who seek board certification in a specialty also must complete a 3- to 4-year residency program that provides intensive training in specialties such as internal medicine, oncology, radiology, surgery, dermatology, anesthesiology, neurology, cardiology, ophthalmology, and exotic small-animal medicine.

All States and the District of Columbia require that veterinarians be licensed before they can practice. The only exemptions are for veterinarians working for some Federal agencies and some State governments. Licensing is controlled by the States and is not strictly uniform, although all States require the successful completion of the D.V.M. degree—or equivalent education—and a passing grade on a national board examination. The Educational Commission for Foreign Veterinary Graduates (ECFVG) grants certification to individuals trained outside the United States who demonstrate that they meet specified requirements for the English language and for clinical proficiency. ECFVG certification fulfills the educational requirement for licensure in all States. Applicants for licensure satisfy the examination requirement by passing the North American Veterinary Licensing Exam (NAVLE), an 8-hour computer-based examination consisting of 360 multiple-choice questions covering all aspects of veterinary medicine. Administered by the National Board of Veterinary Medical Examiners (NBVME), the NAVLE includes visual materials designed to test diagnostic skills and constituting 10 percent of the total examination.

The majority of States also require candidates to pass a State jurisprudence examination covering State laws and regulations. Some States do additional testing on clinical competency as well. There are few reciprocal agreements between States, making it difficult for a veterinarian to practice in a different State without first taking that State's examination.

Nearly all States have continuing education requirements for licensed veterinarians. Requirements differ by State and may involve attending a class or otherwise demonstrating knowledge of recent medical and veterinary advances.

Most veterinarians begin as employees in established practices. Despite the substantial financial investment in equipment, office space, and staff, many veterinarians with experience set up their own practice or purchase an established one.

Newly trained veterinarians can become U.S. Government meat and poultry inspectors, disease-control workers, animal welfare and safety workers, epidemiologists, research assistants, or commissioned officers in the U.S. Public Health Service or various branches of the U.S. Armed Forces. A State license may be required.

Prospective veterinarians must have good manual dexterity. They should have an affinity for animals and the ability to get along with their owners, especially pet owners, who tend to form a strong bond with their pet. Veterinarians who intend to go into private practice should possess excellent communication and business skills, because they will need to manage their practice and employees successfully and promote, market, and sell their services.

Employment

Veterinarians held about 61,000 jobs in 2004. About 1 out of 5 veterinarians was self-employed in a solo or group practice. Most others were salaried employees of another veterinary practice. The Federal Government employed about 1,200 civilian veterinarians, chiefly in the U.S. Departments of Agriculture, Health and Human Services, and, increasingly, Homeland Security. Other employers of veterinarians are State and local governments, colleges of veterinary medicine, medical schools, research laboratories, animal food companies, and pharmaceutical companies. A few veterinarians work for zoos, but most veterinarians caring for zoo animals are private practitioners who contract with the zoos to provide services, usually on a part-time basis.

In addition, many veterinarians hold veterinary faculty positions in colleges and universities. (See the statement on teachers—postsecondary elsewhere in the *Handbook*.)

Job Outlook

Employment of veterinarians is expected to increase as fast as the average for all occupations over the 2004–14 projection period. Despite this average growth, very good job opportunities are expected because the 28 schools of veterinary medicine, even at full capacity, result in a limited number of graduates each year. However, as mentioned earlier, there is keen competition for admission to veterinary school. As pets are increasingly viewed as a member of the family, pet owners will be more willing to spend on advanced veterinary medical care, creating further demand for veterinarians.

Most veterinarians practice in animal hospitals or clinics and care primarily for companion animals. Recent trends indicate particularly strong interest in cats as pets. Faster growth of the cat population is expected to increase the demand for feline medicine and veterinary services, while demand for veterinary care for dogs should continue to grow at a more modest pace.

Pet owners are becoming more aware of the availability of advanced care and are more willing to pay for intensive veterinary care than in the past because many pet owners are more affluent and because they consider their pet part of the family. More pet owners even purchase pet insurance, increasing the likelihood that a considerable amount of money will be spent on veterinary care for their pets. More pet owners also will take advantage of nontraditional veterinary services, such as preventive dental care.

New graduates continue to be attracted to companion-animal medicine because they prefer to deal with pets and to live and work near heavily populated areas. This situation will not necessarily limit the ability of veterinarians to find employment or to set up and maintain a practice in a particular area. Rather, beginning veterinarians may take positions requiring evening or weekend work to accommodate the extended hours of operation that many practices are offering. Some veterinarians take salaried positions in retail stores offering veterinary services. Self-employed veterinarians usually have to work hard and long to build a sufficient client base.

The number of jobs for large-animal veterinarians is likely to grow more slowly than that for veterinarians in private practice who care for companion animals. Nevertheless, job prospects may be better for veterinarians who specialize in farm animals than for companion-animal practitioners because of low earnings in the former specialty and because many veterinarians do not want to work in rural or isolated areas.

Continued support for public health and food safety, national disease control programs, and biomedical research on human health problems will contribute to the demand for veterinarians, although positions in these areas of interest are few in number. Homeland security also may provide opportunities for veterinarians involved in efforts to minimize animal diseases and prevent them from entering the country. Veterinarians with training in food safety, animal health and welfare, and public health and epidemiology should have the best opportunities for a career in the Federal Government.

Earnings

Median annual earnings of veterinarians were $66,590 in May 2004. The middle 50 percent earned between $51,420 and $88,060. The lowest 10 percent earned less than $39,020, and the highest 10 percent earned more than $118,430.

According to a survey by the American Veterinary Medical Association, average starting salaries of veterinary medical college graduates in 2004 varied by type of practice as follows:

Small animals, predominantly	$50,878
Small animals, exclusively	50,703
Large animals, exclusively	50,403
Private clinical practice	49,635
Large animals, predominantly	48,529
Mixed animals	47,704
Equine (horses)	38,628

The average annual salary for veterinarians in the Federal Government in nonsupervisory, supervisory, and managerial positions was $78,769 in 2005.

Related Occupations

Veterinarians prevent, diagnose, and treat diseases, disorders, and injuries in animals. Those who do similar work for humans include chiropractors, dentists, optometrists, physicians and surgeons, and podiatrists. Veterinarians have extensive training in physical and life sciences, and some do scientific and medical research, similar to the work of biological scientists and medical scientists.

Animal care and service workers and veterinary technologists and technicians work extensively with animals. Like veterinarians, they must have patience and feel comfortable with animals. However, the level of training required for these occupations is substantially less than that needed by veterinarians.

Sources of Additional Information

For additional information on careers in veterinary medicine, a list of U.S. schools and colleges of veterinary medicine, and accreditation policies, send a letter-size, self-addressed, stamped envelope to:
➤ American Veterinary Medical Association, 1931 N. Meacham Rd., Suite 100, Schaumburg, IL 60173-4360. Internet: **http://www.avma.org**

For information on veterinary education, write to:
➤ Association of American Veterinary Medical Colleges, 1101 Vermont Ave. N.W., Suite 710, Washington, DC 20005. Internet: **http://www.aavmc.org**

For information on scholarships, grants, and loans, contact the financial aid officer at the veterinary schools to which you wish to apply.

Information on obtaining a veterinary position with the Federal Government is available from the Office of Personnel Management through USAJOBS, the Federal Government's official employment information system. This resource for locating and applying for job opportunities can be accessed through the Internet at **http://www.usajobs.opm.gov** or through an interactive voice response telephone system at (703) 724-1850 or TDD (978) 461-8404. These numbers are not tollfree, and charges may result.

Health Technologists and Technicians

Athletic Trainers

(O*NET 29-9091.00)

Significant Points

- Job prospects should be good in the health care industry; however, competition is expected for positions with sports teams.

- Long hours, sometimes including nights and weekends, are common.

- About one-third of athletic trainers work in health care.

- About 7 out of 10 athletic trainers have a master's or higher degree.

Nature of the Work

Athletic trainers help prevent and treat injuries for people of all ages. Their clients include everyone from professional athletes to industrial workers. Recognized by the American Medical Association as allied health professionals, athletic trainers specialize in the prevention, assessment, treatment, and rehabilitation of musculoskeletal injuries. Athletic trainers are often one of the first heath care providers on the scene when injuries occur, and therefore must be able to recognize, evaluate, and assess injuries and provide immediate care when needed. They also are heavily involved in the rehabilitation and reconditioning of injuries.

Athletic trainers often help prevent injuries by advising on the proper use of equipment and applying protective or injury-preventive devices such as tape, bandages, and braces. Injury prevention also often includes educating people on what they should do to avoid putting themselves at risk for injuries. Athletic trainers should not be confused with fitness trainers or personal trainers, who are not health care workers, but rather train people to become physically fit. (Fitness workers are discussed elsewhere in the *Handbook*.)

Athletic trainers work under the supervision of a licensed physician, and in cooperation with other health care providers. The level of medical supervision varies, depending upon the setting. Some athletic trainers meet with the team physician or consulting physician once or twice a week; others interact with a physician every day. The extent of the supervision ranges from discussing specific injuries and treatment options with a physician to performing evaluations and treatments as directed by a physician.

Athletic trainers also may have administrative responsibilities. These may include regular meetings with an athletic director or other administrative officer to deal with budgets, purchasing, policy implementation, and other business-related issues.

Athletic trainers are heavily involved in the rehabilitation and reconditioning of injuries.

Working Conditions

The work of athletic trainers requires frequent interaction with others. This includes consulting with physicians as well as frequent contact with athletes and patients to discuss and administer treatments, rehabilitation programs, injury-preventive practices, and other health-related issues. Many athletic trainers work indoors most of the time; others, especially those in some sports-related jobs, spend much of their time working outdoors. The job also might require standing for long periods, working with medical equipment or machinery, and being able to walk, run, kneel, crouch, stoop, or crawl. Some travel may be required.

Schedules vary by work setting. Athletic trainers in nonsports settings generally have an established schedule with nights and weekends off; the number of hours differs by employer, but usually are about 40 to 50 hours per week. Trainers working in hospitals and clinics spend part of their time working at other locations on an outreach basis. Most commonly, those outreach programs include secondary schools, colleges, and commercial business locations. Athletic trainers in sports settings, however, deal with schedules that are longer and more variable. These trainers must be present for team practices and games, which often are on evenings and weekends, and their schedules can change on short notice when games and practices have to be rescheduled. As a result, athletic trainers in sports settings regularly may have to work 6 or 7 days per week, including late hours.

In high schools, athletic trainers who also teach may work at least 60 to 70 hours a week. In NCAA Division I colleges and universities, athletic trainers generally work with one team; when that team's sport is in season, working at least 50 to 60 hours a week is common. Athletic trainers in smaller colleges and universities often work with several teams and have teaching responsibilities. During the off-season, a 40-hour to 50-hour work week may be normal in most settings. Athletic trainers for professional sports teams generally work the most hours per week. During training camps, practices, and competitions, they may be required to work up to 12 hours a day.

There is some stress involved with being an athletic trainer, as there is with most health-related occupations. Athletic trainers are responsible for their clients' health, and sometimes have to make quick decisions that could affect the health or career of their clients. Athletics trainers also can be affected by the pressure to win that is typical of competitive sports teams.

Training, Other Qualifications, and Advancement

A bachelor's degree from an accredited college or university is required for almost all jobs as an athletic trainer. In 2004, there were more than 300 accredited programs nationwide. Students in these programs are educated both in the classroom and in clinical settings. Formal education includes many science and health-related courses, such as human anatomy, physiology, nutrition, and biomechanics.

A bachelor's degree with a major in athletic training from an accredited program is part of the requirement for becoming certified by the Board of Certification (BOC). In addition, a successful candidate for board certification must pass an examination that includes written questions and practical applications. To retain certification, credential holders must continue taking medical-related courses and adhere to standards of practice. In the 43 States with athletic trainer licensure or registration or both in 2004, BOC certification was required.

According to the National Athletic Trainers Association, 70 percent of athletic trainers have a master's or doctoral degree. Athletic trainers may need a master's or higher degree to be eligible for some positions, especially those in colleges and universities, and to increase their advancement opportunities. Because some positions in high schools involve teaching along with athletic trainer responsibilities, a teaching certificate or license could be required.

There are a number ways in which athletic trainers can advance or move into related positions. Assistant athletic trainers may become head athletic trainers and, eventually, athletic directors. Athletic trainers might also enter a physician group practice and assume a management role. Some athletic trainers move into sales and marketing positions, using their athletic trainer expertise to sell medical and athletic equipment.

Because all athletic trainers deal directly with a variety of people, they need good social and communication skills. They should be able to manage difficult situations and the stress associated with them—for example, when disagreements arise with coaches, clients, or parents regarding suggested treatment. Athletic trainers also should be organized, be able to manage time wisely, be inquisitive, and have a strong desire to help people.

Employment

Athletic trainers held about 15,000 jobs in 2004 and are found in every part of the country. Most athletic trainer jobs are related to sports, although many also work in nonsports settings. About one-third of athletic trainers worked in health care, including jobs in hospitals, offices of physicians, and offices of other health practitioners. Another one-third were found in public and private educational services, primarily in colleges, universities, and high schools. About 20 percent worked in fitness and recreational sports centers.

Job Outlook

Employment of athletic trainers is expected to grow much faster than the average for all occupations through 2014. Job growth will be concentrated in health care industry settings, such as ambulatory heath care services and hospitals. Growth in sports-related positions will be somewhat slower, as most professional sports clubs and colleges, universities, and professional schools already have complete athletic training staffs. Job prospects should be good for people looking for a position in the health care industry. Athletic trainers looking for a position with a sports team, however, may face competition.

The demand for health care should grow dramatically as the result of advances in technology, increasing emphasis on preventive care, and an increasing number of older people who are more likely to need medical care. Athletic trainers will benefit from this expansion, because they provide a cost-effective way to increase the number of health professionals in an office or other setting. Also, employers increasingly emphasize sports medicine, in which an immediate responder, such as an athletic trainer, is on site to help prevent injuries and provide immediate treatment for any injuries that do occur. Athletic trainers' increased licensure requirements and regulation has led to a greater acceptance of their role as qualified health care providers. As a result, third-party reimbursement is expected to continue to grow for athletic training services. As athletic trainers continue to expand their services, more employers are expected to use these workers to realize the cost savings that can be achieved by providing health care in-house. Settings outside the sports world, especially those that focus on health care, are expected to experience fast employment growth among athletic trainers over the next decade. Continuing efforts to have an athletic trainer in every high school reflect concern for student-athletes' health as well as efforts to provide more funding for schools, and may lead to growth in the number of athletic trainers employed in high schools.

Turnover among athletic trainers is limited. When dealing with sports teams, there is a tendency to want to continue to work with the same coaches, administrators, and players when a good working relationship already exists. Because of relatively low worker turnover, the settings with the best job prospects will be the ones that are expected to grow most quickly, primarily positions in heath care settings. There will also be opportunities in elementary and secondary schools as more positions are created. Some of these positions also will require teaching responsibilities. There will be more competition for positions within colleges, universities, and professional schools as well as professional sports clubs. The occupation is expected to continue to change over the next decade including more administrative responsibilities, adapting to new technology, and working with larger populations, and job seekers must be able to adapt to these changes.

Earnings

Most athletic trainers work in full-time positions, and typically receive benefits. The salary of an athletic trainer depends on experience and job responsibilities, and varies by job setting. Median annual earnings of athletic trainers were $33,940 in May 2004. The middle 50 percent earned between $27,140 and $42,380. The lowest 10 percent earned less than $20,770, while the top 10 percent earned more than $53,760. Also, many employers pay for some of the continuing education required of ATCs, although the amount covered varies from employer to employer.

Related Occupations

The American Medical Association recognizes athletic trainers as allied health professionals. They work under the direction of physicians and provide immediate care for injuries. Also, they provide education and advice on the prevention of injuries and work closely with injured patients to rehabilitate and recondition injuries, often through therapy. Other occupations that may require similar responsibilities include emergency medical technicians and paramedics, physical therapists, physician assistants, registered nurses, licensed practical and licensed vocational nurses, recreational therapists, occupational therapists, and respiratory therapists.

There also are opportunities for athletic trainers to join the military, although they would not be classified as an athletic trainer. Enlisted soldiers and officers who are athletic trainers are usually placed in another program in which their skills are useful, such as health educator or training specialist. (For information on military careers, see the *Handbook* statement on job opportunities in the armed forces.)

Sources of Additional Information

For further information on careers in athletic training, contact:
➤ National Athletic Trainers' Association, 2952 Stemmons Freeway, Dallas, TX 75247. Internet: **http://www.nata.org**

For further information on certification, contact:
➤ Board of Certification, Inc., 4223 South 143rd Circle, Omaha, NE 68137. Internet: **http://www.bocatc.org**

Cardiovascular Technologists and Technicians

(O*NET 29-2031.00)

Significant Points

- About 3 out of 4 jobs were in hospitals.

- The vast majority of cardiovascular technologists and technicians complete a 2-year junior or community college program.

- Employment will grow much faster than the average, but the number of job openings created will be low because the occupation is small.

- Employment of most specialties will grow, but fewer EKG technicians will be needed.

Nature of the Work

Cardiovascular technologists and technicians assist physicians in diagnosing and treating cardiac (heart) and peripheral vascular (blood vessel) ailments. Cardiovascular technologists may specialize in any of three areas of practice: invasive cardiology, echocardiography, and vascular technology. Cardiovascular technicians who specialize in electrocardiograms (EKGs), stress testing, and Holter monitors are known as *cardiographic technicians*, or *EKG technicians*.

Cardiovascular technologists specializing in invasive procedures are called *cardiology technologists*. They assist physicians with cardiac catheterization procedures in which a small tube, or catheter, is threaded through a patient's artery from a spot on the patient's groin to the heart. The procedure can determine whether a blockage exists in the blood vessels that supply the heart muscle. The procedure also can help to diagnose other problems. Part of the procedure may involve balloon angioplasty, which can be used to treat blockages of blood vessels or heart valves without the need for heart surgery. Cardiology technologists assist physicians as they insert a catheter with a balloon on the end to the point of the obstruction.

Technologists prepare patients for cardiac catheterization and balloon angioplasty by first positioning them on an examining table and then shaving, cleaning, and administering anesthesia to the top of their leg near the groin. During the procedures, they monitor patients' blood pressure and heart rate with EKG equipment and notify the physician if something appears to be wrong. Technologists also may prepare and monitor patients during open-heart surgery and during the insertion of pacemakers and stents that open up blockages in arteries to the heart and major blood vessels.

Cardiovascular technologists who specialize in echocardiography or vascular technology often run noninvasive tests using ultrasound instrumentation, such as Doppler ultrasound. Tests are called "noninvasive" if they do not require the insertion of probes or other instruments into the patient's body. The ultrasound instrumentation transmits high-frequency sound waves into areas of the patient's body and then processes reflected echoes of the sound waves to form an image. Technologists view the ultrasound image on a screen and may record the image on videotape or photograph it for interpretation and diagnosis by a physician. As the instrument scans the image, technologists check the image on the screen for subtle differences between healthy and diseased areas, decide which images to include in the report to the physician, and judge whether the images are satisfactory for diagnostic purposes. They also explain the procedure to patients, record any additional medical history the patient relates, select appropriate equipment settings, and change the patient's position as necessary. (See the statement on diagnostic medical sonographers elsewhere in the *Handbook* to learn more about other sonographers.)

Those who assist physicians in the diagnosis of disorders affecting the circulation are known as *vascular technologists* or *vascular sonographers*. They perform a medical history, evaluate pulses and assess blood flow in arteries and veins by listening to the vascular flow sounds for abnormalities. Then they perform a noninvasive procedure using ultrasound instrumentation to record vascular information such as vascular blood flow, blood pressure, changes in limb volume, oxygen saturation, cerebral circulation, peripheral circulation, and abdominal circulation. Many of these tests are performed during or immediately after surgery.

Technologists who use ultrasound to examine the heart chambers, valves, and vessels are referred to as *cardiac sonographers*, or *echocardiographers*. They use ultrasound instrumentation to create images called echocardiograms. An echocardiogram may be performed while the patient is either resting or physically active. Technologists may administer medication to physically active patients to assess their heart function. Cardiac sonographers also may assist physicians who perform transesophageal echocardiography, which involves placing a tube in the patient's esophagus to obtain ultrasound images.

Cardiovascular technicians who obtain EKGs are known as *electrocardiograph* (or *EKG*) *technicians*. To take a basic EKG, which traces electrical impulses transmitted by the heart, technicians attach electrodes to the patient's chest, arms, and legs, and then manipulate switches on an EKG machine to obtain a reading. An EKG is printed out for interpretation by the physician. This test is done before most kinds of surgery or as part of a routine physical examination, especially on persons who have reached middle age or who have a history of cardiovascular problems.

EKG technicians with advanced training perform Holter monitor and stress testing. For Holter monitoring, technicians place electrodes on the patient's chest and attach a portable EKG monitor to the patient's belt. Following 24 or more hours of normal activity by the patient, the technician removes a tape from the monitor and places it in a scanner. After checking the quality of the recorded impulses on an electronic screen, the technician usually prints the information from the tape for analysis by a physician. Physicians use the output from the scanner to diagnose heart ailments, such as heart rhythm abnormalities or problems with pacemakers.

For a treadmill stress test, EKG technicians document the patient's medical history, explain the procedure, connect the patient to an EKG monitor, and obtain a baseline reading and resting blood pressure. Next, they monitor the heart's performance while the patient is walking on a treadmill, gradually increasing the treadmill's speed to observe the effect of increased exertion. Like vascular technologists and cardiac sonographers, cardiographic technicians who perform EKG, Holter monitor, and stress tests are known as "noninvasive" technicians.

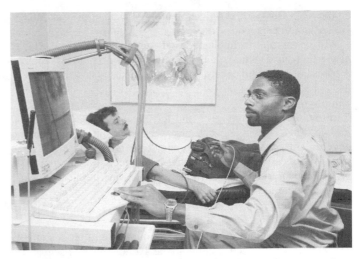
Cardiovascular technologists use ultrasound technology to produce images for diagnosis.

Some cardiovascular technologists and technicians schedule appointments, type doctors' interpretations, maintain patient files, and care for equipment.

Working Conditions
Technologists and technicians generally work a 5-day, 40-hour week that may include weekends. Those in catheterization laboratories tend to work longer hours and may work evenings. They also may be on call during the night and on weekends.

Cardiovascular technologists and technicians spend a lot of time walking and standing. Heavy lifting may be involved to move equipment or transfer patients. These workers wear heavy protective aprons while conducting some procedures. Those who work in catheterization laboratories may face stressful working conditions because they are in close contact with patients with serious heart ailments. For example, some patients may encounter complications that have life-or-death implications.

Training, Other Qualifications, and Advancement
Although a few cardiovascular technologists, vascular technologists, and cardiac sonographers are currently trained on the job, most receive training in 2- to 4-year programs. The majority of technologists complete a 2-year junior or community college program, but 4-year programs are increasingly available. The first year is dedicated to core courses and is followed by a year of specialized instruction in either invasive, noninvasive cardiovascular, or noninvasive vascular technology. Those who are qualified in an allied health profession need to complete only the year of specialized instruction.

Graduates of the 33 programs accredited by the Joint Review Committee on Education in Cardiovascular Technology are eligible to obtain professional certification in cardiac catheterization, echocardiography, vascular ultrasound, and cardiographic techniques from Cardiovascular Credentialing International. Cardiac sonographers and vascular technologists also may obtain certification from the American Registry of Diagnostic Medical Sonographers.

Most EKG technicians are trained on the job by an EKG supervisor or a cardiologist. On-the-job training usually lasts about 8 to 16 weeks. Most employers prefer to train people already in the health care field—nursing aides, for example. Some EKG technicians are students enrolled in 2-year programs to become technologists, working part time to gain experience and make contact with employers. One-year certification programs exist for basic EKGs, Holter monitoring, and stress testing.

Cardiovascular technologists and technicians must be reliable, have mechanical aptitude, and be able to follow detailed instructions. A pleasant, relaxed manner for putting patients at ease is an asset.

Employment

Cardiovascular technologists and technicians held about 45,000 jobs in 2004. About 3 out 4 jobs were in hospitals (private and government), primarily in cardiology departments. The remaining jobs were mostly in offices of physicians, including cardiologists or in medical and diagnostic laboratories, including diagnostic imaging centers.

Job Outlook

Employment of cardiovascular technologists and technicians is expected to grow much faster than the average for all occupations through the year 2014. Growth will occur as the population ages, because older people have a higher incidence of heart problems and use more diagnostic imaging. Employment of vascular technologists and echocardiographers will grow as advances in vascular technology and sonography reduce the need for more costly and invasive procedures. However, fewer EKG technicians will be needed, as hospitals train nursing aides and others to perform basic EKG procedures. Individuals trained in Holter monitoring and stress testing are expected to have more favorable job prospects than are those who can perform only a basic EKG.

Some job openings for cardiovascular technologists and technicians will arise from replacement needs as individuals transfer to other jobs or leave the labor force. However, job growth and replacement needs will produce relatively few job openings because the occupation is small.

Earnings

Median annual earnings of cardiovascular technologists and technicians were $38,690 in May 2004. The middle 50 percent earned between $27,890 and $50,130. The lowest 10 percent earned less than $21,790, and the highest 10 percent earned more than $59,000. Median annual earnings of cardiovascular technologists and technicians in May 2004 were $36,890 in offices of physicians and $38,150 in general medical and surgical hospitals.

Related Occupations

Cardiovascular technologists and technicians operate sophisticated equipment that helps physicians and other health practitioners to diagnose and treat patients. So do diagnostic medical sonographers, nuclear medicine technologists, radiation therapists, radiologic technologists and technicians, and respiratory therapists.

Sources of Additional Information

For general information about a career in cardiovascular technology, contact:
➤ Alliance of Cardiovascular Professionals, Thalia Landing Offices, Bldg. 2, 4356 Bonney Rd., Suite 103, Virginia Beach, VA 23452-1200. Internet: **http://www.acp-online.org**

For a list of accredited programs in cardiovascular technology, contact:
➤ Committee on Accreditation for Allied Health Education Programs, 39 East Wacker Dr., Chicago, IL 60601. Internet: **http://www.caahep.org**
➤ Joint Review Committee on Education in Cardiovascular Technology, 1248 Harwood Rd., Bedford, TX 76021.

For information on vascular technology, contact:
➤ Society for Vascular Ultrasound, 4601 Presidents Dr., Suite 260, Lanham, MD 20706-4381. Internet: **http://www.svunet.org**

For information on echocardiography, contact:
➤ American Society of Echocardiography, 1500 Sunday Dr., Suite 102, Raleigh, NC 27607. Internet: **http://www.asecho.org**

For information regarding registration and certification, contact:
➤ Cardiovascular Credentialing International, 1500 Sunday Dr., Suite 102, Raleigh, NC 27607. Internet: **http://www.cci-online.org**
➤ American Registry of Diagnostic Medical Sonographers, 51 Monroe St., Plaza East One, Rockville, MD 20850-2400. Internet: **http://www.ardms.org**

Clinical Laboratory Technologists and Technicians

(O*NET 29-2011.00, 29-2012.00)

Significant Points

● Faster than average employment growth is expected as the volume of laboratory tests continues to increase with both population growth and the development of new types of tests.

● Clinical laboratory technologists usually have a bachelor's degree with a major in medical technology or in one of the life sciences; clinical laboratory technicians generally need either an associate degree or a certificate.

● Job opportunities are expected to be excellent.

Nature of the Work

Clinical laboratory testing plays a crucial role in the detection, diagnosis, and treatment of disease. Clinical laboratory technologists, also referred to as clinical laboratory scientists or medical technologists, and clinical laboratory technicians, also known as medical technicians or medical laboratory technicians, perform most of these tests.

Clinical laboratory personnel examine and analyze body fluids, and cells. They look for bacteria, parasites, and other microorganisms; analyze the chemical content of fluids; match blood for transfusions; and test for drug levels in the blood to show how a patient is responding to treatment. Technologists also prepare specimens for examination, count cells, and look for abnormal cells in blood and body fluids. They use automated equipment and computerized instruments capable of performing a number of tests simultaneously, as well as microscopes, cell counters, and other sophisticated laboratory equipment. Then they analyze the results and relay them to physicians. With increasing automation and the use of computer technology, the work of technologists and technicians has become less hands-on and more analytical.

The complexity of tests performed, the level of judgment needed, and the amount of responsibility workers assume depend largely on the amount of education and experience they have.

Clinical laboratory technologists perform complex chemical, biological, hematological, immunologic, microscopic, and bacteriological tests. Technologists microscopically examine blood and other body fluids. They make cultures of body fluid and tissue samples, to determine the presence of bacteria, fungi, parasites, or other microorganisms. Clinical laboratory technologists analyze samples for chemical content or a chemical reaction and determine concentrations of compounds such as blood glucose and cholesterol levels. They also type and cross match blood samples for transfusions.

Clinical laboratory technologists evaluate test results, develop and modify procedures, and establish and monitor programs, to ensure the accuracy of tests. Some technologists supervise clinical laboratory technicians.

Technologists in small laboratories perform many types of tests, whereas those in large laboratories generally specialize. Technologists who prepare specimens and analyze the chemical and hormonal contents of body fluids are called clinical chemistry technologists. Those who examine and identify bacteria and other microorganisms are microbiology technologists. Blood bank technologists, or immunohematology technologists, collect, type, and prepare blood and its components for transfusions. Immunology technologists examine elements of the human immune system and its response to foreign bodies. Cytotechnologists prepare slides of body cells and examine these cells microscopically for abnormalities that may signal the beginning of a cancerous growth. Molecular biology technologists perform complex protein and nucleic acid testing on cell samples.

Clinical laboratory technicians perform less complex tests and laboratory procedures than technologists perform. Technicians may prepare specimens and operate automated analyzers, for example, or they may perform manual tests in accordance with detailed instructions. Like technologists, they may work in several areas of the clinical laboratory or specialize in just one. Histotechnicians cut and stain tissue specimens for microscopic examination by pathologists, and phlebotomists collect blood samples. They usually work under the supervision of medical and clinical laboratory technologists or laboratory managers.

Working Conditions

Hours and other working conditions of clinical laboratory technologists and technicians vary with the size and type of employment setting. In large hospitals or in independent laboratories that operate continuously, personnel usually work the day, evening, or night shift and may work weekends and holidays. Laboratory personnel in small facilities may work on rotating shifts, rather than on a regular shift. In some facilities, laboratory personnel are on call several nights a week or on weekends, in case of an emergency.

Clinical laboratory personnel are trained to work with infectious specimens. When proper methods of infection control and sterilization

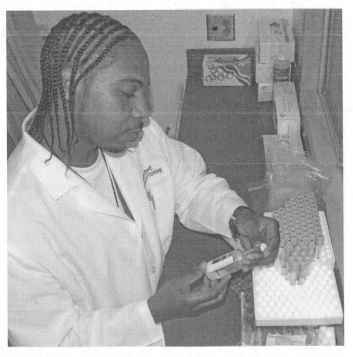

Clinical laboratory technicians may prepare specimens, operate automated analyzers, or perform manual tests in accordance with detailed instructions.

are followed, few hazards exist. Protective masks, gloves, and goggles are often necessary to ensure the safety of laboratory personnel.

Laboratories usually are well lighted and clean; however, specimens, solutions, and reagents used in the laboratory sometimes produce fumes. Laboratory workers may spend a great deal of time on their feet.

Training, Other Qualifications, and Advancement

The usual requirement for an entry-level position as a clinical laboratory technologist is a bachelor's degree with a major in medical technology or in one of the life sciences; although it is possible to qualify through a combination of education, on-the-job, and specialized training. Universities and hospitals offer medical technology programs.

Bachelor's degree programs in medical technology include courses in chemistry, biological sciences, microbiology, mathematics, and statistics, as well as specialized courses devoted to knowledge and skills used in the clinical laboratory. Many programs also offer or require courses in management, business, and computer applications. The Clinical Laboratory Improvement Act requires technologists who perform highly complex tests to have at least an associate degree.

Medical and clinical laboratory technicians generally have either an associate degree from a community or junior college or a certificate from a hospital, a vocational or technical school, or one of the U.S. Armed Forces. A few technicians learn their skills on the job.

The National Accrediting Agency for Clinical Laboratory Sciences (NAACLS) fully accredits 469 programs for medical and clinical laboratory technologists, medical and clinical laboratory technicians, histotechnologists and histotechnicians, cytogenetic technologists, and diagnostic molecular scientists. NAACLS also approves 57 programs in phlebotomy and clinical assisting. Other nationally recognized accrediting agencies that accredit specific areas for clinical laboratory workers include the Commission on Accreditation of Allied Health Education Programs and the Accrediting Bureau of Health Education Schools.

Some States require laboratory personnel to be licensed or registered. Information on licensure is available from State departments of health or boards of occupational licensing. Certification is a voluntary process by which a nongovernmental organization, such as a professional society or certifying agency, grants recognition to an individual whose professional competence meets prescribed standards. Widely accepted by employers in the health care industry, certification is a prerequisite for most jobs and often is necessary for advancement. Agencies certifying medical and clinical laboratory technologists and technicians include the Board of Registry of the American Society for Clinical Pathology, the American Medical Technologists, the National Credentialing Agency for Laboratory Personnel, and the Board of Registry of the American Association of Bioanalysts. These agencies have different requirements for certification and different organizational sponsors.

Clinical laboratory personnel need good analytical judgment and the ability to work under pressure. Close attention to detail is essential, because small differences or changes in test substances or numerical readouts can be crucial for patient care. Manual dexterity and normal color vision are highly desirable. With the widespread use of automated laboratory equipment, computer skills are important. In addition, technologists in particular are expected to be good at problem solving.

Technologists may advance to supervisory positions in laboratory work or may become chief medical or clinical laboratory technologists or laboratory managers in hospitals. Manufacturers of home diagnostic testing kits and laboratory equipment and supplies seek experienced technologists to work in product development, marketing, and sales. A graduate degree in medical technology, one of the biological sciences, chemistry, management, or education usually speeds advancement. A doctorate is needed to become a laboratory director; however, Federal regulation allows directors of moderately complex laboratories to have either a master's degree or a bachelor's degree, combined with the appropriate amount of training and experience. Technicians can become technologists through additional education and experience.

Employment

Clinical laboratory technologists and technicians held about 302,000 jobs in 2004. More than half of jobs were in hospitals. Most of the remaining jobs were in offices of physicians and in medical and diagnostic laboratories. A small proportion was in educational services and in all other ambulatory health care services.

Job Outlook

Job opportunities are expected to be excellent, because the number of job openings is expected to continue to exceed the number of job seekers. Employment of clinical laboratory workers is expected to grow faster than the average for all occupations through the year 2014, as the volume of laboratory tests continues to increase with both population growth and the development of new types of tests.

Technological advances will continue to have two opposing effects on employment. On the one hand, new, increasingly powerful diagnostic tests will encourage additional testing and spur employment. On the other hand, research and development efforts targeted at simplifying routine testing procedures may enhance the ability of nonlaboratory personnel—physicians and patients in particular—to perform tests now conducted in laboratories. Although hospitals are expected to continue to be the major employer of clinical laboratory workers, employment is expected to grow faster in medical and diagnostic laboratories, offices of physicians, and all other ambulatory health care services.

Although significant, job growth will not be the only source of opportunities. As in most occupations, many openings will result from the need to replace workers who transfer to other occupations, retire, or stop working for some other reason.

Earnings

Median annual earnings of medical and clinical laboratory technologists were $45,730 in May 2004. The middle 50 percent earned between $38,740 and $54,310. The lowest 10 percent earned less than $32,240, and the highest 10 percent earned more than $63,120. Median annual earnings in the industries employing the largest numbers of medical and clinical laboratory technologists in May 2004 were as follows:

General medical and surgical hospitals... $46,020
Medical and diagnostic laboratories 45,840
Offices of physicians.. 41,070

Median annual earnings of medical and clinical laboratory technicians were $30,840 in May 2004. The middle 50 percent earned between $24,890 and $37,770. The lowest 10 percent earned less than $20,410, and the highest 10 percent earned more than $45,680. Median annual earnings in the industries employing the largest numbers of medical and clinical laboratory technicians in May 2004 were as follows:

Colleges, universities, and professional schools......................... $32,410
General medical and surgical hospitals....................................... 31,830
Offices of physicians.. 29,620
Medical and diagnostic laboratories 29,220
Other ambulatory health care services.. 28,130

According to the American Society for Clinical Pathology, median hourly wages of staff clinical laboratory technologists and technicians in 2003 varied by specialty and laboratory type as follows:

	Hospital	Private clinic	Physician office laboratory
Cytotechnoligist	$24.70	$24.07	$25.66
Histotechnologist	19.88	19.22	20.50
Medical technologist.......................	20.40	19.00	18.00
Histotechnician	16.97	16.13	20.00
Medical laboratory technician.........	16.12	15.00	14.75
Phlebotomist	11.13	10.57	10.50

Related Occupations

Clinical laboratory technologists and technicians analyze body fluids, tissue, and other substances, using a variety of tests. Similar or related procedures are performed by chemists and materials scientists, science technicians, and veterinary technologists and technicians.

Sources of Additional Information

For a list of accredited and approved educational programs for clinical laboratory personnel, contact:
➤ National Accrediting Agency for Clinical Laboratory Sciences, 8410 W. Bryn Mawr Ave., Suite 670, Chicago, IL 60631. Internet: **http://www.naacls.org**

Information on certification is available from:
➤ American Association of Bioanalysts, Board of Registry, 906 Olive St., Suite 1200, St. Louis, MO 63101-1434. Internet: **http://www.aab.org**
➤ American Medical Technologists, 710 Higgins Rd., Park Ridge, IL 60068.
➤ American Society for Clinical Pathology, 2100 West Harrison St., Chicago, IL 60612. Internet: **http://www.ascp.org**
➤ National Credentialing Agency for Laboratory Personnel, P.O. Box 15945, Lenexa, KS 66285. Internet: **http://www.nca-info.org**

Additional career information is available from:
➤ American Association of Blood Banks, 8101 Glenbrook Rd., Bethesda, MD 20814-2749. Internet: **http://www.aabb.org**
➤ American Society for Clinical Laboratory Science, 6701 Democracy Blvd., Suite 300, Bethesda, MD 20817. Internet: **http://www.ascls.org**
➤ American Society for Cytopathology, 400 West 9th St., Suite 201, Wilmington, DE 19801. Internet: **http://www.cytopathology.org**
➤ Clinical Laboratory Management Association, 989 Old Eagle School Rd., Suite 815, Wayne, PA 19087. Internet: **http://www.clma.org**

Dental Hygienists

(O*NET 29-2021.00)

Significant Points

● Most dental hygiene programs grant an associate degree; others offer a certificate, a bachelor's degree, or a master's degree.

● Dental hygienists rank among the fastest growing occupations.

● Job prospects are expected to remain excellent.

● More than half work part time, and flexible scheduling is a distinctive feature of this job.

Nature of the Work

Dental hygienists remove soft and hard deposits from teeth, teach patients how to practice good oral hygiene, and provide other preventive dental care. Hygienists examine patients' teeth and gums, recording the presence of diseases or abnormalities. They remove calculus, stains, and plaque from teeth; perform root planing as a periodontal therapy; take and develop dental x rays; and apply cavity-preventive agents such as fluorides and pit and fissure sealants. In some States, hygienists administer anesthetics; place and carve filling materials, temporary fillings, and periodontal dressings; remove sutures; and smooth and polish metal restorations. Although hygienists may not diagnose diseases, they can prepare clinical and laboratory diagnostic tests for the dentist to interpret. Hygienists sometimes work chairside with the dentist during treatment.

Dental hygienists also help patients develop and maintain good oral health. For example, they may explain the relationship between diet and oral health or inform patients how to select toothbrushes and show them how to brush and floss their teeth.

Dental hygienists use hand and rotary instruments and ultrasonics to clean and polish teeth, x-ray machines to take dental pictures, syringes with needles to administer local anesthetics, and models of teeth to explain oral hygiene.

Working Conditions

Flexible scheduling is a distinctive feature of this job. Full-time, part-time, evening, and weekend schedules are widely available. Dentists frequently hire hygienists to work only 2 or 3 days a week, so hygienists may hold jobs in more than one dental office.

Dental hygienists work in clean, well-lighted offices. Important health safeguards include strict adherence to proper radiological procedures, and the use of appropriate protective devices when administering anesthetic gas. Dental hygienists also wear safety glasses, surgical masks, and gloves to protect themselves and patients from infectious diseases.

Training, Other Qualifications, and Advancement

Dental hygienists must be licensed by the State in which they practice. To qualify for licensure in nearly all States, a candidate

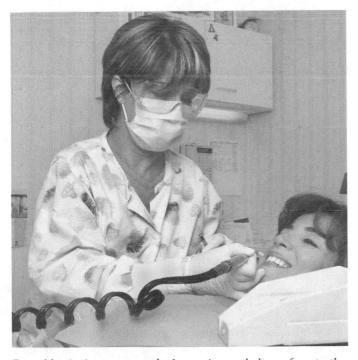

Dental hygienists remove calculus, stains, and plaque from teeth.

must graduate from an accredited dental hygiene school and pass both a written and clinical examination. The American Dental Association's Joint Commission on National Dental Examinations administers the written examination, which is accepted by all States and the District of Columbia. State or regional testing agencies administer the clinical examination. In addition, most States require an examination on the legal aspects of dental hygiene practice. Alabama allows candidates to take its examinations if they have been trained through a State-regulated on-the-job program in a dentist's office.

In 2004, the Commission on Dental Accreditation accredited 266 programs in dental hygiene. Most dental hygiene programs grant an associate degree, although some also offer a certificate, a bachelor's degree, or a master's degree. A minimum of an associate degree or certificate in dental hygiene is generally required for practice in a private dental office. A bachelor's or master's degree usually is required for research, teaching, or clinical practice in public or school health programs.

A high school diploma and college entrance test scores are usually required for admission to a dental hygiene program. Also, some dental hygiene programs prefer applicants who have completed at least 1 year of college. Requirements vary from one school to another. Schools offer laboratory, clinical, and classroom instruction in subjects such as anatomy, physiology, chemistry, microbiology, pharmacology, nutrition, radiography, histology (the study of tissue structure), periodontology (the study of gum diseases), pathology, dental materials, clinical dental hygiene, and social and behavioral sciences.

Dental hygienists should work well with others and must have good manual dexterity, because they use dental instruments within a patient's mouth, with little room for error. High school students interested in becoming a dental hygienist should take courses in biology, chemistry, and mathematics.

Employment

Dental hygienists held about 158,000 jobs in 2004. Because multiple job holding is common in this field, the number of jobs exceeds the number of hygienists. More than half of all dental hygienists worked part time—less than 35 hours a week.

Almost all jobs for dental hygienists were in offices of dentists. A very small number worked for employment services or in offices of physicians.

Job Outlook

Employment of dental hygienists is expected to grow much faster than the average for all occupations through 2014, ranking among the fastest growing occupations, in response to increasing demand for dental care and the greater utilization of hygienists to perform services previously performed by dentists. Job prospects are expected to remain excellent.

Population growth and greater retention of natural teeth will stimulate demand for dental hygienists. Older dentists, who have been less likely to employ dental hygienists, are leaving the occupation and will be replaced by recent graduates, who are more likely to employ one or even two hygienists. In addition, as dentists' workloads increase, they are expected to hire more hygienists to perform preventive dental care, such as cleaning, so that they may devote their own time to more profitable procedures.

Earnings

Median hourly earnings of dental hygienists were $28.05 in May 2004. The middle 50 percent earned between $22.72 and $33.82 an hour. The lowest 10 percent earned less than $18.05, and the highest 10 percent earned more than $40.70 an hour.

Earnings vary by geographic location, employment setting, and years of experience. Dental hygienists may be paid on an hourly, daily, salary, or commission basis.

Benefits vary substantially by practice setting and may be contingent upon full-time employment. According to the American Dental Association (ADA), almost all full-time dental hygienists employed by private practitioners received paid vacation. The ADA also found that 9 out of 10 full-time and part-time dental hygienists received dental coverage. Dental hygienists who work for school systems, public health agencies, the Federal Government, or State agencies usually have substantial benefits.

Related Occupations
Other workers supporting health practitioners in an office setting include dental assistants, medical assistants, occupational therapist assistants and aides, physical therapist assistants and aides, physician assistants, and registered nurses.

Sources of Additional Information
For information on a career in dental hygiene, including educational requirements, contact:
➤ Division of Education, American Dental Hygienists Association, 444 N. Michigan Ave., Suite 3400, Chicago, IL 60611. Internet: **http://www.adha.org**

For information about accredited programs and educational requirements, contact:
➤ Commission on Dental Accreditation, American Dental Association, 211 E. Chicago Ave., Suite 1814, Chicago, IL 60611. Internet: **http://www.ada.org**

The State Board of Dental Examiners in each State can supply information on licensing requirements.

Diagnostic Medical Sonographers

(O*NET 29-2032.00)

Significant Points

● Job opportunities should be favorable, as sonography becomes an increasingly attractive alternative to radiologic procedures.

● About 6 out of 10 sonographers were employed by hospitals, and most of the rest worked in offices of physicians or in medical and diagnostic laboratories, including diagnostic imaging centers.

● Sonographers may train in hospitals, vocational-technical institutions, colleges and universities, and the Armed Forces.

Nature of the Work
Diagnostic imaging embraces several procedures that aid in diagnosing ailments. Besides the familiar xray, another common diagnostic imaging method is magnetic resonance imaging, which uses giant magnets that create radio waves, rather than radiation, to form an image. Not all imaging technologies use ionizing radiation or radio waves, however. Sonography, or ultrasonography, is the use of sound waves to generate an image for the assessment and diagnosis of various medical conditions. Sonography usually is associated with obstetrics and the use of ultrasound imaging during pregnancy, but this technology has many other applications in the diagnosis and treatment of medical conditions.

Diagnostic medical sonographers, also known as *ultrasonographers*, use special equipment to direct nonionizing, high frequency sound waves into areas of the patient's body. Sonographers operate the equipment, which collects reflected echoes and forms an image that may be videotaped, transmitted, or photographed for interpretation and diagnosis by a physician.

Sonographers begin by explaining the procedure to the patient and recording any medical history that may be relevant to the condition being viewed. They then select appropriate equipment settings and direct the patient to move into positions that will provide the best view. To perform the exam, sonographers use a transducer, which transmits sound waves in a cone- or rectangle-shaped beam. Although techniques vary with the area being examined, sonographers usually spread a special gel on the skin to aid the transmission of sound waves.

Viewing the screen during the scan, sonographers look for subtle visual cues that contrast healthy areas with unhealthy ones. They decide whether the images are satisfactory for diagnostic purposes and select which ones to show to the physician. Sonographers take measurements, calculate values, and analyze the results in preliminary reports for the physicians.

Diagnostic medical sonographers may specialize in obstetric and gynecologic sonography (the female reproductive system), abdominal sonography (the liver, kidneys, gallbladder, spleen, and pancreas), neurosonography (the brain), or breast sonography. In addition, sonographers may specialize in vascular technology or echocardiography. (Vascular technologists and echocardiographers are covered in the *Handbook* statement on cardiovascular technologists and technicians.)

Obstetric and gynecologic sonographers specialize in the study of the female reproductive system. Included in the discipline is one of the more well-known uses of sonography: examining the fetus of a pregnant woman to track the baby's growth and health.

Abdominal sonographers inspect a patient's abdominal cavity to help diagnose and treat conditions primarily involving the gallbladder, bile ducts, kidneys, liver, pancreas, and spleen. Abdominal sonographers also are able to scan parts of the chest, although studies of the heart using sonography usually are done by echocardiographers.

Neurosonographers focus on the nervous system, including the brain. In neonatal care, neurosonographers study and diagnose neurological and nervous system disorders in premature infants. They also may scan blood vessels to check for abnormalities indicating a stroke in infants diagnosed with sickle-cell anemia. Like other sonographers, neurosonographers operate transducers to perform the sonogram, but use frequencies and beam shapes different from those used by obstetric and abdominal sonographers.

Breast sonographers use sonography to study the disease in breasts. Sonography aids mammography in the detection of breast cancer. Breast sonography can also track tumors, blood supply conditions, and assist in the accurate biopsy of breast tissue. Breast sonographers use high-frequency transducers, made exclusively to study breast tissue.

In addition to working directly with patients, diagnostic medical sonographers keep patient records and adjust and maintain equipment. They also may prepare work schedules, evaluate equipment purchases, or manage a sonography or diagnostic imaging department.

Working Conditions
Most full-time sonographers work about 40 hours a week. Hospital-based sonographers may have evening and weekend hours and times when they are on call and must be ready to report to work on short notice.

Sonographers typically work in healthcare facilities that are clean and well lighted. Some travel to patients in large vans equipped with sophisticated diagnostic equipment. A growing number of

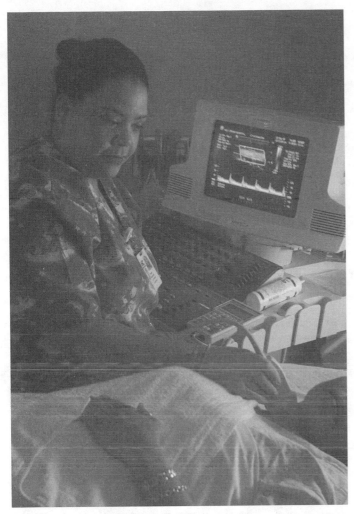

Using ultrasound equipment, a diagnostic medical sonographer creates an image of a patient's throat.

sonographers work as contract employees and may perform tests at a number of different hospitals. Sonographers are on their feet for long periods and may have to lift or turn disabled patients. They work at diagnostic imaging machines, but also may perform some procedures at patients' bedsides.

Training, Other Qualifications, and Advancement

There are several avenues for entry into the field of diagnostic medical sonography. Sonographers may train in hospitals, vocational-technical institutions, colleges and universities, and the Armed Forces. Some training programs prefer applicants with a background in science or experience in other healthcare professions, but also will consider high school graduates with courses in mathematics and science, as well as applicants with liberal arts backgrounds.

Colleges and universities offer formal training in both 2- and 4-year programs, culminating in an associate or a bachelor's degree. Two-year programs are most prevalent. Course work includes classes in anatomy, physiology, instrumentation, basic physics, patient care, and medical ethics. The Commission on Accreditation for Allied Health Education Programs accredits most formal training programs—132 programs in 2005.

Some healthcare workers, such as obstetric nurses and radiologic technologists, increase their marketability by seeking training in fields such as sonography. This usually requires completion of an additional 1-year program that may result in a certificate. In addi-

tion, sonographers specializing in one particular discipline often seek competency in others; for example, obstetric sonographers might seek training in abdominal sonography to broaden their opportunities.

Although no State requires licensure in diagnostic medical sonography, organizations such as the American Registry for Diagnostic Medical Sonography (ARDMS) certify the competency of sonographers through registration. Because registration provides an independent, objective measure of an individual's professional standing, many employers prefer to hire registered sonographers. Registration with ARDMS requires passing a general physical principles and instrumentation examination, in addition to passing an exam in a specialty such as obstetric and gynecologic sonography, abdominal sonography, or neurosonography. To keep their registration current, sonographers must complete continuing education to stay abreast of technological advances related to the occupation.

Sonographers need good communication and interpersonal skills because they must be able to explain technical procedures and results to their patients, some of whom may be nervous about the exam or the problems it may reveal. Sonographers also should have a background in mathematics and science.

Employment

Diagnostic medical sonographers held about 42,000 jobs in 2004. About 6 out of 10 sonographer jobs were in hospitals—public and private. Most of the rest were in offices of physicians or in medical and diagnostic laboratories, including diagnostic imaging centers

Job Outlook

Employment of diagnostic medical sonographers is expected to grow much faster than the average for all occupations through 2014 as the population grows and ages, increasing the demand for diagnostic imaging and therapeutic technology. In addition to job openings from growth, some job openings will arise from the need to replace sonographers who leave the occupation permanently.

Opportunities should be favorable because sonography is becoming an increasingly attractive alternative to radiologic procedures, as patients seek safer treatment methods. Unlike most diagnostic imaging methods, sonography does not involve radiation, so harmful side effects and complications from repeated use are rarer for both the patient and the sonographer. Sonographic technology is expected to evolve rapidly and to spawn many new sonography procedures, such as 3D- and 4D-sonography for use in obstetric and ophthalmologic diagnosis. However, high costs may limit the rate at which some promising new technologies are adopted.

Hospitals will remain the principal employer of diagnostic medical sonographers. However, employment is expected to grow more rapidly in offices of physicians and in medical and diagnostic laboratories, including diagnostic imaging centers. Healthcare facilities such as these are expected to grow very rapidly through 2014 because of the strong shift toward outpatient care, encouraged by third-party payers and made possible by technological advances that permit more procedures to be performed outside the hospital.

Earnings

Median annual earnings of diagnostic medical sonographers were $52,490 in May 2004. The middle 50 percent earned between $44,720 and $61,360 a year. The lowest 10 percent earned less than $37,800, and the highest 10 percent earned more than $72,230. Median annual earnings of diagnostic medical sonographers in May 2004 were $53,790 in offices of physicians and $51,860 in general medical and surgical hospitals.

Related Occupations

Diagnostic medical sonographers operate sophisticated equipment to help physicians and other health practitioners diagnose and treat patients. Workers in related occupations include cardiovascular technologists and technicians, clinical laboratory technologists and technicians, nuclear medicine technologists, radiologic technologists and technicians, and respiratory therapists.

Sources of Additional Information

For information on a career as a diagnostic medical sonographer, contact:

➤ Society of Diagnostic Medical Sonography, 2745 Dallas Pkwy., Suite 350, Plano, TX 75093-8730. Internet: **http://www.sdms.org**

For information on becoming a registered diagnostic medical sonographer, contact:

➤ American Registry for Diagnostic Medical Sonography, 51 Monroe St., Plaza East 1, Rockville, MD 20850-2400. Internet: **http://www.ardms.org**

For a current list of accredited education programs in diagnostic medical sonography, contact:

➤ Joint Review Committee on Education in Diagnostic Medical Sonography, 2025 Woodlane Dr., St. Paul, MN 55125-2998. Internet: **http://www.jrcdms.org**

➤ Commission on Accreditation for Allied Health Education Programs, 35 East Wacker Dr., Suite1970, Chicago, IL 60601. Internet: **http://www.caahep.org**

Emergency Medical Technicians and Paramedics

(O*NET 29-2041.00)

Significant Points

- Because emergency services function 24 hours a day, emergency medical technicians and paramedics have irregular working hours.

- Emergency medical technicians and paramedics need formal training and certification, but requirements vary by State.

- Employment is projected to grow much faster than average as paid emergency medical technician positions replace unpaid volunteers.

- Competition will be greater for jobs in local fire, police, and rescue squad departments than in private ambulance services; opportunities will be best for those who have advanced certification.

Nature of the Work

People's lives often depend on the quick reaction and competent care of emergency medical technicians (EMTs) and paramedics—EMTs with additional advanced training to perform more difficult prehospital medical procedures. Incidents as varied as automobile accidents, heart attacks, drownings, childbirth, and gunshot wounds all require immediate medical attention. EMTs and paramedics provide this vital attention as they care for and transport the sick or injured to a medical facility.

In an emergency, EMTs and paramedics typically are dispatched to the scene by a 911 operator, and often work with police and fire department personnel. (Police and detectives and firefighting occupations are discussed elsewhere in the *Handbook*.) Once they arrive, they determine the nature and extent of the patient's condition while trying to ascertain whether the patient has pre-existing medical problems. Following strict rules and guidelines, they give appropriate emergency care and, when necessary, transport the patient. Some paramedics are trained to treat patients with minor injuries on the scene of an accident or at their home without transporting them to a medical facility. Emergency treatment for more complicated problems is carried out under the direction of medical doctors by radio preceding or during transport.

EMTs and paramedics may use special equipment, such as backboards, to immobilize patients before placing them on stretchers and securing them in the ambulance for transport to a medical facility. Usually, one EMT or paramedic drives while the other monitors the patient's vital signs and gives additional care as needed. Some EMTs work as part of the flight crew of helicopters that transport critically ill or injured patients to hospital trauma centers.

At the medical facility, EMTs and paramedics help transfer patients to the emergency department, report their observations and actions to emergency room staff, and may provide additional emergency treatment. After each run, EMTs and paramedics replace used supplies and check equipment. If a transported patient had a contagious disease, EMTs and paramedics decontaminate the interior of the ambulance and report cases to the proper authorities.

Beyond these general duties, the specific responsibilities of EMTs and paramedics depend on their level of qualification and training. To determine this, the National Registry of Emergency Medical Technicians (NREMT) registers emergency medical service (EMS) providers at four levels: First Responder, EMT-Basic, EMT-Intermediate, and EMT-Paramedic. Some States, however, do their own certification and use numeric ratings from 1 to 4 to distinguish levels of proficiency.

The lowest-level workers—First Responders—are trained to provide basic emergency medical care because they tend to be the first persons to arrive at the scene of an incident. Many firefighters, police officers, and other emergency workers have this level of training. The EMT-Basic, also known as EMT-1, represents the first component of the emergency medical technician system. An EMT-1 is trained to care for patients at the scene of an accident and while transporting patients by ambulance to the hospital under medical direction. The EMT-1 has the emergency skills to assess a patient's condition and manage respiratory, cardiac, and trauma emergencies.

The EMT-Intermediate (EMT-2 and EMT-3) has more advanced training that allows the administration of intravenous fluids, the use of manual defibrillators to give lifesaving shocks to a stopped heart, and the application of advanced airway techniques and equipment to assist patients experiencing respiratory emergencies. EMT-Paramedics (EMT-4) provide the most extensive prehospital care. In addition to carrying out the procedures already described, paramedics may administer drugs orally and intravenously, interpret electrocardiograms (EKGs), perform endotracheal intubations, and use monitors and other complex equipment.

Working Conditions

EMTs and paramedics work both indoors and outdoors, in all types of weather. They are required to do considerable kneeling, bending, and heavy lifting. These workers risk noise-induced hearing loss from sirens and back injuries from lifting patients. In addition, EMTs and paramedics may be exposed to diseases such as hepatitis-B and AIDS, as well as violence from drug overdose victims or mentally unstable patients. The work is not only physically strenuous, but can be stressful, sometimes involving life-or-death situations and suffering patients. Nonetheless, many people find

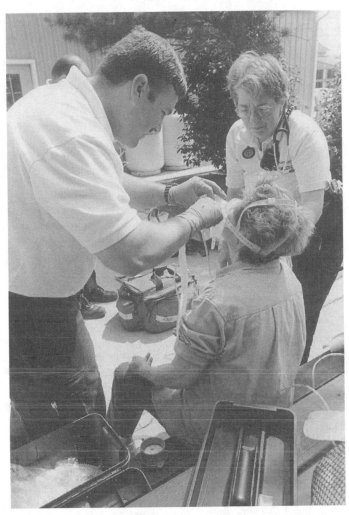

Emergency medical technicians provide medical care to patients at the scene of an emergency.

the work exciting and challenging and enjoy the opportunity to help others.

EMTs and paramedics employed by fire departments work about 50 hours a week. Those employed by hospitals frequently work between 45 and 60 hours a week, and those in private ambulance services, between 45 and 50 hours. Some of these workers, especially those in police and fire departments, are on call for extended periods. Because emergency services function 24 hours a day, EMTs and paramedics have irregular working hours.

Training, Other Qualifications, and Advancement

Formal training and certification is needed to become an EMT or paramedic. A high school diploma is typically required to enter a formal training program. Some programs offer an associate degree along with the formal EMT training. All 50 States have a certification procedure. In most States and the District of Columbia, registration with the NREMT is required at some or all levels of certification. Other States administer their own certification examination or provide the option of taking the NREMT examination. To maintain certification, EMTs and paramedics must reregister, usually every 2 years. In order to reregister, an individual must be working as an EMT or paramedic and meet a continuing education requirement.

Training is offered at progressive levels: EMT-Basic, also known as EMT-1; EMT-Intermediate, or EMT-2 and EMT-3; and EMT-

Paramedic, or EMT-4. EMT-Basic coursework typically emphasizes emergency skills, such as managing respiratory, trauma, and cardiac emergencies, and patient assessment. Formal courses are often combined with time in an emergency room or ambulance. The program also provides instruction and practice in dealing with bleeding, fractures, airway obstruction, cardiac arrest, and emergency childbirth. Students learn how to use and maintain common emergency equipment, such as backboards, suction devices, splints, oxygen delivery systems, and stretchers. Graduates of approved EMT basic training programs who pass a written and practical examination administered by the State certifying agency or the NREMT earn the title "Registered EMT-Basic." The course also is a prerequisite for EMT-Intermediate and EMT-Paramedic training.

EMT-Intermediate training requirements vary from State to State. Applicants can opt to receive training in EMT-Shock Trauma, wherein the caregiver learns to start intravenous fluids and give certain medications, or in EMT-Cardiac, which includes learning heart rhythms and administering advanced medications. Training commonly includes 35 to 55 hours of additional instruction beyond EMT-Basic coursework, and covers patient assessment as well as the use of advanced airway devices and intravenous fluids. Prerequisites for taking the EMT-Intermediate examination include registration as an EMT-Basic, required classroom work, and a specified amount of clinical experience.

The most advanced level of training for this occupation is EMT-Paramedic. At this level, the caregiver receives additional training in body function and learns more advanced skills. The Technology program usually lasts up to 2 years and results in an associate degree in applied science. Such education prepares the graduate to take the NREMT examination and become certified as an EMT-Paramedic. Extensive related coursework and clinical and field experience is required. Because of the longer training requirement, almost all EMT-Paramedics are in paid positions, rather than being volunteers. Refresher courses and continuing education are available for EMTs and paramedics at all levels.

EMTs and paramedics should be emotionally stable, have good dexterity, agility, and physical coordination, and be able to lift and carry heavy loads. They also need good eyesight (corrective lenses may be used) with accurate color vision.

Advancement beyond the EMT-Paramedic level usually means leaving fieldwork. An EMT-Paramedic can become a supervisor, operations manager, administrative director, or executive director of emergency services. Some EMTs and paramedics become instructors, dispatchers, or physician assistants, while others move into sales or marketing of emergency medical equipment. A number of people become EMTs and paramedics to assess their interest in health care, and then decide to return to school and become registered nurses, physicians, or other health workers.

Employment

EMTs and paramedics held about 192,000 jobs in 2004. Most career EMTs and paramedics work in metropolitan areas. Volunteer EMTs and paramedics are more common in small cities, towns, and rural areas. These individuals volunteer for fire departments, emergency medical services (EMS), or hospitals, and may respond to only a few calls for service per month or may answer the majority of calls, especially in smaller communities. EMTs and paramedics work closely with firefighters, who often are certified as EMTs as well and act as first responders. A large number of EMTs or paramedics belong to a union.

Full-time and part-time paid EMTs and paramedics were employed in a number of industries. About 4 out of 10 worked as employees of private ambulance services. About 3 out of 10 worked in local government for fire departments, public ambulance services, and EMS. Another 2 out of 10 were found in hospitals, working full time within the medical facility or responding to calls in ambulances or helicopters to transport critically ill or injured patients. The remainder worked in various industries providing emergency services.

Job Outlook

Employment of emergency medical technicians and paramedics is expected to grow much faster than the average for all occupations through 2014, as full-time paid EMTs and paramedics replace unpaid volunteers. As population and urbanization increase, and as a large segment of the population—aging baby boomers—becomes more likely to have medical emergencies, demand will increase for EMTs and paramedics. There will still be demand for part-time, volunteer EMTs and paramedics in rural areas and smaller metropolitan areas. In addition to jobs arising from growth, openings will occur because of replacement needs; turnover is relatively high in this occupation because of the limited potential for advancement and the modest pay and benefits in private-sector jobs.

Job opportunities should be best in private ambulance services. Competition will be greater for jobs in local government, including fire, police, and independent third-service rescue squad departments, in which salaries and benefits tend to be slightly better. EMTs and paramedics who have advanced certifications, such as EMT-Intermediate and EMT-Paramedic, should enjoy the most favorable job prospects as clients and patients demand higher levels of care before arriving at the hospital.

Earnings

Earnings of EMTs and paramedics depend on the employment setting and geographic location as well as the individual's training and experience. Median annual earnings of EMTs and paramedics were $25,310 in May 2004. The middle 50 percent earned between $19,970 and $33,210. The lowest 10 percent earned less than $16,090, and the highest 10 percent earned more than $43,240. Median annual earnings in the industries employing the largest numbers of EMTs and paramedics in May 2004 were:

Local government	$27,710
General medical and surgical hospitals	26,590
Other ambulatory health care services	23,130

Those in emergency medical services who are part of fire or police departments receive the same benefits as firefighters or police officers. For example, many are covered by pension plans that provide retirement at half pay after 20 or 25 years of service or if the worker is disabled in the line of duty.

Related Occupations

Other workers in occupations that require quick and level-headed reactions to life-or-death situations are air traffic controllers, firefighting occupations, physician assistants, police and detectives, and registered nurses.

Sources of Additional Information

General information about emergency medical technicians and paramedics is available from:

➤ National Association of Emergency Medical Technicians, P.O. Box 1400, Clinton, MS 39060-1400. Internet: **http://www.naemt.org**
➤ National Registry of Emergency Medical Technicians, Rocco V. Morando Bldg., 6610 Busch Blvd., P.O. Box 29233, Columbus, OH 43229. Internet: **http://www.nremt.org**
➤ National Highway Transportation Safety Administration, EMS Division, 400 7th St. SW., NTS-14, Washington, DC 20590. Internet: **http://nhtsa.gov/portal/site/nhtsa/menuitem.2a0771e91315babbbf30811060008a0c/**

Licensed Practical and Licensed Vocational Nurses

(O*NET 29-2061.00)

Significant Points

- Training lasting about 1 year is available in about 1,200 State-approved programs, mostly in vocational or technical schools.

- Applicants for jobs in hospitals may face competition as the number of hospital jobs for licensed practical nurses declines; however, rapid employment growth is projected in other health care industries, with the best job opportunities occurring in nursing care facilities and in home health care services.

- Replacement needs will be a major source of job openings, as many workers leave the occupation permanently.

Nature of the Work

Licensed practical nurses (LPNs), or licensed vocational nurses (LVNs), care for the sick, injured, convalescent, and disabled under the direction of physicians and registered nurses. (The work of physicians and surgeons and of registered nurses is described elsewhere in the *Handbook*.)

Most LPNs provide basic bedside care, taking vital signs such as temperature, blood pressure, pulse, and respiration. They also prepare and give injections and enemas, monitor catheters, apply dressings, treat bedsores, and give alcohol rubs and massages. LPNs monitor their patients and report adverse reactions to medications or treatments. They collect samples for testing, perform routine laboratory tests, feed patients, and record food and fluid intake and output. To help keep patients comfortable, LPNs assist with bathing, dressing, and personal hygiene. In States where the law allows, they may administer prescribed medicines or start intravenous fluids. Some LPNs help to deliver, care for, and feed infants. Experienced LPNs may supervise nursing assistants and aides.

In addition to providing routine bedside care, LPNs in nursing care facilities help to evaluate residents' needs, develop care plans, and supervise the care provided by nursing aides. In

Licensed practical nurses often stand for long periods and help patients move into bed, stand, or walk.

doctors' offices and clinics, they also may make appointments, keep records, and perform other clerical duties. LPNs who work in private homes may prepare meals and teach family members simple nursing tasks.

Working Conditions

Most licensed practical nurses in hospitals and nursing care facilities work a 40-hour week, but because patients need round-the-clock care, some work nights, weekends, and holidays. They often stand for long periods and help patients move in bed, stand, or walk.

LPNs may face hazards from caustic chemicals, radiation, and infectious diseases such as hepatitis. They are subject to back injuries when moving patients and shock from electrical equipment. They often must deal with the stress of heavy workloads. In addition, the patients they care for may be confused, irrational, agitated, or uncooperative.

Training, Other Qualifications, and Advancement

All States and the District of Columbia require LPNs to pass a licensing examination, known as the NCLEX-PN, after completing a State-approved practical nursing program. A high school diploma or its equivalent usually is required for entry, although some programs accept candidates without a diploma, and some are designed as part of a high school curriculum.

In 2004, approximately 1,200 State-approved programs provided training in practical nursing. Most training programs are available from technical and vocational schools, or from community and junior colleges. Other programs are available through high schools, hospitals, and colleges and universities.

Most practical nursing programs last about 1 year and include both classroom study and supervised clinical practice (patient care). Classroom study covers basic nursing concepts and patient care-related subjects, including anatomy, physiology, medical-surgical nursing, pediatrics, obstetrics, psychiatric nursing, the administration of drugs, nutrition, and first aid. Clinical practice usually is in a hospital, but sometimes includes other settings.

In some employment settings, such as nursing homes, LPNs can advance to become charge nurses who oversee the work of other LPNs and of nursing aides. Some LPNs also choose to become registered nurses through numerous LPN-to-RN training programs.

LPNs should have a caring, sympathetic nature. They should be emotionally stable because working with the sick and injured can be stressful. They also should have keen observational, decision-making, and communication skills. As part of a health care team, they must be able to follow orders and work under close supervision.

Employment

Licensed practical nurses held about 726,000 jobs in 2004. About 27 percent of LPNs worked in hospitals, 25 percent in nursing care facilities, and another 12 percent in offices of physicians. Others worked for home health care services; employment services; community care facilities for the elderly; public and private educational services; outpatient care centers; and Federal, State, and local government agencies. About 1 in 5 worked part time.

Job Outlook

Employment of LPNs is expected to grow about as fast as the average for all occupations through 2014 in response to the long-term care needs of an increasing elderly population and the general growth of health care services. Replacement needs will be a ma-

jor source of job openings, as many workers leave the occupation permanently. Applicants for jobs in hospitals may face competition as the number of hospital jobs for LPNs declines; however, rapid employment growth is projected in other health care industries, with the best job opportunities occurring in nursing care facilities and in home health care services.

Employment of LPNs in hospitals is expected to continue to decline. Sophisticated procedures once performed only in hospitals are being performed in physicians' offices and in outpatient care centers such as ambulatory surgical and emergency medical centers, largely because of advances in technology. Consequently, employment of LPNs in most health care industries outside the traditional hospital setting is projected to grow faster than average.

Employment of LPNs is expected to grow much faster than average in home health care services. Home health care agencies also will offer the most new jobs for LPNs because of an increasing number of older persons with functional disabilities, consumer preference for care in the home, and technological advances that make it possible to bring increasingly complex treatments into the home.

Employment of LPNs in nursing care facilities is expected to grow about as fast as average because of the growing number of aged and disabled persons in need of long-term care. In addition, LPNs in nursing care facilities will be needed to care for the increasing number of patients who have been discharged from the hospital but who have not recovered enough to return home. However, changes in consumer preferences towards less restrictive and more cost-effective care from assisted living facilities and home health care agencies will limit employment growth.

Earnings

Median annual earnings of licensed practical nurses were $33,970 in May 2004. The middle 50 percent earned between $28,830 and $40,670. The lowest 10 percent earned less than $24,480, and the highest 10 percent earned more than $46,270. Median annual earnings in the industries employing the largest numbers of licensed practical nurses in May 2004 were:

Employment services	$41,550
Nursing care facilities	35,460
Home health care services	35,180
General medical and surgical hospitals	32,570
Offices of physicians	30,400

Related Occupations

LPNs work closely with people while helping them. So do emergency medical technicians and paramedics; medical assistants; nursing, psychiatric, and home health aides; registered nurses; social and human service assistants; and surgical technologists.

Sources of Additional Information

For information about practical nursing, contact any of the following organizations:
➤ National Association for Practical Nurse Education and Service, Inc., P.O. Box 25647, Alexandria, VA 22313. Internet: **http:// www.napnes.org**
➤ National League for Nursing, 61 Broadway, New York, NY 10006. Internet: **http:// www.nln.org**
➤ National Federation of Licensed Practical Nurses, Inc., 605 Poole Dr., Garner, NC 27529. Internet: **http://www.nflpn.org**

Information on the NCLEX-PN licensing exam is available from:
➤ National Council of State Boards of Nursing, 111 East Wacker Dr., Suite 2900, Chicago, IL 60611. Internet: **http://www.ncsbn.org**

A list of State-approved LPN programs is available from individual State boards of nursing.

Medical Records and Health Information Technicians

(O*NET 29-2071.00)

Significant Points

- Employment is expected to grow much faster than average.
- Job prospects should be very good; technicians with a strong background in medical coding will be in particularly high demand.
- Entrants usually have an associate degree; courses include anatomy, physiology, medical terminology, statistics, and computer science.
- This is one of the few health occupations in which there is little or no direct contact with patients.

Nature of the Work

Every time a patient receives health care, a record is maintained of the observations, medical or surgical interventions, and treatment outcomes. This record includes information that the patient provides concerning his or her symptoms and medical history, the results of examinations, reports of x rays and laboratory tests, diagnoses, and treatment plans. Medical records and health information technicians organize and evaluate these records for completeness and accuracy.

Technicians assemble patients' health information. They make sure that patients' initial medical charts are complete, that all forms are completed and properly identified and signed, and that all necessary information is in the computer. They regularly communicate with physicians and other health care professionals to clarify diagnoses or to obtain additional information.

Some medical records and health information technicians specialize in coding patients' medical information for insurance purposes. Technicians who specialize in coding are called *health information coders, medical record coders, coder/abstractors*, or *coding specialists*. These technicians assign a code to each diagnosis and procedure. They consult classification manuals and also rely on their knowledge of disease processes. Technicians then use computer software to assign the patient to one of several hundred "diagnosis-related groups," or DRGs. The DRG determines the amount for which the hospital will be reimbursed if the patient is covered by Medicare or other insurance programs using the DRG system. In addition to the DRG system, coders use other coding systems, such as those geared toward ambulatory settings or long-term care.

Some technicians also use computer programs to tabulate and analyze data to improve patient care, control costs, provide documentation for use in legal actions, respond to surveys, or use in research studies. For example, *cancer* (or tumor) *registrars* maintain facility, regional, and national databases of cancer patients. Registrars review patient records and pathology reports, assign codes for the diagnosis and treatment of different cancers and selected benign tumors. Registrars conduct annual followups on all patients in the registry to track their treatment, survival, and recovery. Physicians and public health organizations then use this information to calculate survivor rates and success rates of various types of treatment, locate geographic areas with high incidences of certain cancers, and identify potential participants for clinical drug trials. Cancer registry data also is used by public health officials to target areas for the allocation of resources to provide intervention and screening.

Medical records and health information technicians ensure that patient records are complete and accurate.

Medical records and health information technicians' duties vary with the size of the facility where they work. In large to medium-sized facilities, technicians might specialize in one aspect of health information or might supervise health information clerks and transcriptionists while a medical records and health information administrator manages the department. (See the statement on medical and health services managers elsewhere in the *Handbook*.) In small facilities, a credentialed medical records and health information technician sometimes manages the department.

Working Conditions

Medical records and health information technicians usually work a 40-hour week. Some overtime may be required. In hospitals—where health information departments often are open 24 hours a day, 7 days a week—technicians may work day, evening, and night shifts.

Medical records and health information technicians work in pleasant and comfortable offices. This is one of the few health occupations in which there is little or no direct contact with patients. Because accuracy is essential in their jobs, technicians must pay close attention to detail. Technicians who work at computer monitors for prolonged periods must guard against eyestrain and muscle pain.

Training, Other Qualifications, and Advancement

Medical records and health information technicians entering the field usually have an associate degree from a community or junior college. In addition to general education, coursework includes medical terminology, anatomy and physiology, legal aspects of health information, coding and abstraction of data, statistics, database management, quality improvement methods, and computer science. Applicants can improve their chances of admission into a program by taking biology, chemistry, health, and computer science courses in high school.

Hospitals sometimes advance promising health information clerks to jobs as medical records and health information technicians, although this practice may be less common in the future. Advancement usually requires 2 to 4 years of job experience and completion of a hospital's in-house training program.

Most employers prefer to hire Registered Health Information Technicians (RHIT), who must pass a written examination offered by the American Health Information Management Association (AHIMA). To take the examination, a person must graduate from a 2-year associate degree program accredited by the Commission on Accreditation for Health Informatics and Information Management Education (CAHIIM). Technicians trained in non-CAHIIM-accredited programs or trained on the job are not eligible to take the examination. In 2005, CAHIIM accredited 184 programs for health information technicians.

Experienced medical records and health information technicians usually advance in one of two ways—by specializing or managing. Many senior technicians specialize in coding, particularly Medicare coding, or in cancer registry. Most coding and registry skills are learned on the job. Some schools offer certificates in coding as part of the associate degree program for health information technicians, although there are no formal degree programs in coding. For cancer registry, there were 11 formal 2-year certificate programs in 2005 approved by the National Cancer Registrars Association (NCRA). Some schools and employers offer intensive 1- to 2-week training programs in either coding or cancer registry. Once coders and registrars gain some on-the-job experience, many choose to become certified. Certifications in coding are available either from AHIMA or from the American Academy of Professional Coders. Certification in cancer registry is available from the NCRA.

In large medical records and health information departments, experienced technicians may advance to section supervisor, overseeing the work of the coding, correspondence, or discharge sections, for example. Senior technicians with RHIT credentials may become director or assistant director of a medical records and health information department in a small facility. However, in larger institutions, the director usually is an administrator with a bachelor's degree in medical records and health information administration.

Employment
Medical records and health information technicians held about 159,000 jobs in 2004. About 2 out of 5 jobs were in hospitals. The rest were mostly in offices of physicians, nursing care facilities, outpatient care centers, and home health care services. Insurance firms that deal in health matters employ a small number of health information technicians to tabulate and analyze health information. Public health departments also hire technicians to supervise data collection from health care institutions and to assist in research.

Job Outlook
Job prospects should be very good. Employment of medical records and health information technicians is expected to grow much faster than the average for all occupations through 2014 because of rapid growth in the number of medical tests, treatments, and procedures that will be increasingly scrutinized by health

insurance companies, regulators, courts, and consumers. Also, technicians will be needed to enter patient information into computer databases to comply with Federal legislation mandating the use of electronic patient records.

Although employment growth in hospitals will not keep pace with growth in other health care industries, many new jobs will, nevertheless, be created. The majority of new jobs is expected in offices of physicians as a result of increasing demand for detailed records, especially in large group practices. Rapid growth also is expected in home health care services, outpatient care centers, and nursing and residential care facilities. Additional job openings will result from the need to replace technicians who retire or leave the occupation permanently.

Technicians with a strong background in medical coding will be in particularly high demand. Changing government regulations and the growth of managed care have increased the amount of paperwork involved in filing insurance claims. Additionally, health care facilities are having difficulty attracting qualified workers, primarily because of the lack of both formal training programs and sufficient resources to provide on-the-job training for coders. Job opportunities may be especially good for coders employed through temporary help agencies or by professional services firms.

Some cancer registrars may have difficulty finding open positions in their geographic area because of a limited number of registrars employed by health care facilities and low job turnover. However, when a position does become vacant, qualified cancer registrars have excellent prospects because of the limited number of trained registrars available for employment.

Earnings
Median annual earnings of medical records and health information technicians were $25,590 in 2004. The middle 50 percent earned between $20,650 and $32,990. The lowest 10 percent earned less than $17,720, and the highest 10 percent earned more than $41,760. Median annual earnings in the industries employing the largest numbers of medical records and health information technicians in 2004 were as follows:

General medical and surgical hospitals	$26,640
Nursing care facilities	26,330
Outpatient care centers	23,070
Offices of physicians	22,130

Related Occupations
Medical records and health information technicians need a strong clinical background to analyze the contents of medical records. Other workers who need knowledge of medical terminology, anatomy, and physiology but have little or no direct contact with patients include medical secretaries and medical transcriptionists.

Sources of Additional Information
Information on careers in medical records and health information technology, including a list of programs accredited by CAHIIM, is available from:
➤ American Health Information Management Association, 233 N. Michigan Ave., Suite 2150, Chicago, IL 60601-5800. Internet: **http://www.ahima.org**

Information on training and certification for medical coders is available from:
➤ American Academy of Professional Coders, P.O. Box 45855, Salt Lake City, UT 84145-0855.

Information on a career as a cancer registrar is available from:
➤ National Cancer Registrars Association, 1340 Braddock Pl., #203, Alexandria, VA 22314. Internet: **http://www.ncra-usa.org**

Nuclear Medicine Technologists

(O*NET 29-2033.00)

Significant Points

- About 7 out of 10 work in hospitals.

- Nuclear medicine technology programs range in length from 1 to 4 years and lead to a certificate, an associate degree, or a bachelor's degree.

- Faster than average growth will arise from an increase in the number of middle-aged and elderly persons, who are the primary users of diagnostic procedures.

- The number of job openings each year will be relatively low because the occupation is small; technologists who also are trained in other diagnostic methods, such as radiologic technology or diagnostic medical sonography, will have the best prospects.

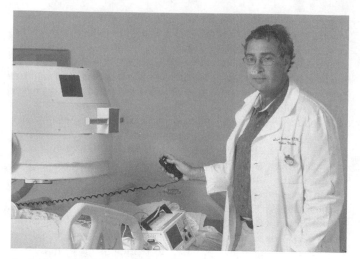

A nuclear medicine technologist prepares a patient prior to a scan.

Nature of the Work

Diagnostic imaging embraces several procedures that aid in diagnosing ailments, the most familiar being the x ray. Another increasingly common diagnostic imaging method, called magnetic resonance imaging (MRI), uses giant magnets and radio waves, rather than radiation, to create an image. In nuclear medicine, radionuclides—unstable atoms that emit radiation spontaneously—are used to diagnose and treat disease. Radionuclides are purified and compounded to form radiopharmaceuticals. Nuclear medicine technologists administer radiopharmaceuticals to patients and then monitor the characteristics and functions of tissues or organs in which the drugs localize. Abnormal areas show higher-than-expected or lower-than-expected concentrations of radioactivity. Nuclear medicine differs from other diagnostic imaging technologies because it determines the presence of disease on the basis of biological changes rather than changes in organ structure.

Nuclear medicine technologists operate cameras that detect and map the radioactive drug in a patient's body to create diagnostic images. After explaining test procedures to patients, technologists prepare a dosage of the radiopharmaceutical and administer it by mouth, injection, inhalation, or other means. They position patients and start a gamma scintillation camera, or "scanner," which creates images of the distribution of a radiopharmaceutical as it localizes in, and emits signals from, the patient's body. The images are produced on a computer screen or on film for a physician to interpret.

When preparing radiopharmaceuticals, technologists adhere to safety standards that keep the radiation dose to workers and patients as low as possible. Technologists keep patient records and record the amount and type of radionuclides that they receive, use, and discard.

Radiologic technologists and technicians, diagnostic medical sonographers, and cardiovascular technologists and technicians also operate diagnostic imaging equipment, but their equipment creates images by means of a different technology. (See the statements on these occupations elsewhere in the *Handbook*.)

Nuclear medicine technologists also perform radioimmunoassay studies that assess the behavior of a radioactive substance inside the body. For example, technologists may add radioactive substances to blood or serum to determine levels of hormones or of therapeutic drugs in the body. Most nuclear medicine studies, such as cardiac function studies, are processed with the aid of a computer.

Working Conditions

Nuclear medicine technologists generally work a 40-hour week, perhaps including evening or weekend hours, in departments that operate on an extended schedule. Opportunities for part-time and shift work also are available. In addition, technologists in hospitals may have on-call duty on a rotational basis.

Physical stamina is important because technologists are on their feet much of the day and may lift or turn disabled patients.

Although the potential for radiation exposure exists in this field, it is kept to a minimum by the use of shielded syringes, gloves, and other protective devices and by adherence to strict radiation safety guidelines. The amount of radiation in a nuclear medicine procedure is comparable to that received during a diagnostic x-ray procedure. Technologists also wear badges that measure radiation levels. Because of safety programs, badge measurements rarely exceed established safety levels.

Training, Other Qualifications, and Advancement

Many employers and an increasing number of States require certification or licensure. Aspiring nuclear medicine technologists should check the requirements of the State in which they plan to work. Certification is available from the American Registry of Radiologic Technologists and from the Nuclear Medicine Technology Certification Board. Some workers receive certification from both agencies. Nuclear medicine technologists must meet the minimum Federal standards on the administration of radioactive drugs and the operation of radiation detection equipment.

Nuclear medicine technology programs range in length from 1 to 4 years and lead to a certificate, an associate degree, or a bachelor's degree. Generally, certificate programs are offered in hospitals, associate degree programs in community colleges, and bachelor's degree programs in 4-year colleges and universities. Courses cover the physical sciences, biological effects of radiation exposure, radiation protection and procedures, the use of radiopharmaceuticals, imaging techniques, and computer applications.

One-year certificate programs are for health professionals who already posses an associate degree—especially radiologic technologists and diagnostic medical sonographers—but who wish to specialize in nuclear medicine. The programs also attract medical technologists, registered nurses, and others who wish to change fields or specialize. Others interested in nuclear medicine technology have three options: a 2-year certificate program, a 2-year associate degree program, or a 4-year bachelor's degree program.

The Joint Review Committee on Education Programs in Nuclear Medicine Technology accredits most formal training programs in nuclear medicine technology. In 2005, there were 100 accredited programs in the continental United States and Puerto Rico.

Nuclear medicine technologists should be sensitive to patients' physical and psychological needs. They must pay attention to detail, follow instructions, and work as part of a team. In addition, operating complicated equipment requires mechanical ability and manual dexterity.

Technologists may advance to supervisor, then to chief technologist, and, finally, to department administrator or director. Some technologists specialize in a clinical area such as nuclear cardiology or computer analysis or leave patient care to take positions in research laboratories. Some become instructors in, or directors of, nuclear medicine technology programs, a step that usually requires a bachelor's or master's degree in the subject. Others leave the occupation to work as sales or training representatives for medical equipment and radiopharmaceutical manufacturing firms or as radiation safety officers in regulatory agencies or hospitals.

Employment

Nuclear medicine technologists held about 18,000 jobs in 2004. About 7 out of 10 were in hospitals—private and government. Most of the rest were in offices of physicians or in medical and diagnostic laboratories, including diagnostic imaging centers.

Job Outlook

Employment of nuclear medicine technologists is expected to grow faster than the average for all occupations through the year 2014. Growth will arise from technological advancement, the development of new nuclear medicine treatments, and an increase in the number of middle-aged and older persons, who are the primary users of diagnostic procedures, including nuclear medicine tests. However, the number of openings each year will be relatively low because the occupation is small. Technologists who also are trained in other diagnostic methods, such as radiologic technology or diagnostic medical sonography, will have the best prospects.

Technological innovations may increase the diagnostic uses of nuclear medicine. One example is the use of radiopharmaceuticals in combination with monoclonal antibodies to detect cancer at far earlier stages than is customary today and without resorting to surgery. Another is the use of radionuclides to examine the heart's ability to pump blood. New nuclear medical imaging technologies, including positron emission tomography (PET) and single photon emission computed tomography (SPECT), are expected to be used increasingly and to contribute further to employment growth. The wider use of nuclear medical imaging to observe metabolic and biochemical changes during neurology, cardiology, and oncology procedures also will spur demand for nuclear medicine technologists.

Nonetheless, cost considerations will affect the speed with which new applications of nuclear medicine grow. Some promising nuclear medicine procedures, such as positron emission tomography, are extremely costly, and hospitals contemplating these procedures will have to consider equipment costs, reimbursement policies, and the number of potential users.

Earnings

Median annual earnings of nuclear medicine technologists were $56,450 in May 2004. The middle 50 percent earned between $48,720 and $67,460. The lowest 10 percent earned less than $41,800, and the highest 10 percent earned more than $80,300. Median annual earnings of nuclear medicine technologists in May 2004 were $54,920 in general medical and surgical hospitals.

Related Occupations

Nuclear medical technologists operate sophisticated equipment to help physicians and other health practitioners diagnose and treat patients. Cardiovascular technologists and technicians, clinical laboratory technologists and technicians, diagnostic medical sonographers, radiation therapists, radiologic technologists and technicians, and respiratory therapists perform similar functions.

Sources of Additional Information

Additional information on a career as a nuclear medicine technologist is available from:
➤ Society of Nuclear Medicine Technologists, 1850 Samuel Morse Dr., Reston, VA 20190-5316. Internet: **http://www.snm.org**

For career information, send a stamped, self-addressed, business-size envelope with your request to:
➤ American Society of Radiologic Technologists, 15000 Central Ave. S.E., Albuquerque, NM 87123-3917. Internet: **http://www.asrt.org**

For a list of accredited programs in nuclear medicine technology, write to:
➤ Joint Review Committee on Educational Programs in Nuclear Medicine Technology, 1716 Black Point Rd., P.O. Box 1149, Polson, MT 59860-1149. Internet: **http://www.jrcnmt.org**

Information on certification is available from:
➤ American Registry of Radiologic Technologists, 1255 Northland Dr., St. Paul, MN 55120-1155. Internet: **http://www.arrt.org**
➤ Nuclear Medicine Technology Certification Board, 2970 Clairmont Rd., Suite 935, Atlanta, GA 30329-4421. Internet: **http://www.nmtcb.org**

Occupational Health and Safety Specialists and Technicians

(O*NET 29-9011.00, 29-9012.00)

Significant Points

- About 2 out of 5 specialists worked in Federal, State, and local government agencies that enforce rules on safety, health, and the environment.

- Many employers, including the Federal Government, require a bachelor's degree in occupational health, safety, or a related field for some specialist positions.

- Projected average employment growth reflects a balance of continuing public demand for a safe and healthy work environment against the desire for smaller government and fewer regulations.

Nature of the Work

Occupational health and safety specialists and technicians, also known as *safety and health practitioners* or *occupational health and safety inspectors*, help prevent harm to workers, property, the environment, and the general public. They promote occupational health and safety within organizations in many ways, such as by advising management on how to increase worker productivity through raising morale and reducing absenteeism, turnover, and equipment downtime while securing savings on insurance premiums, workers' compensation benefits, and litigation expenses. (Industrial engineers, including health and safety, have similar goals. See the section on engineers elsewhere in the *Handbook*.)

Occupational health and safety specialists analyze work environments and design programs to control, eliminate, and prevent disease or injury caused by chemical, physical, radiological, and biological agents or ergonomic factors that involve the impact of equipment design on a worker's comfort or fatigue. They may conduct inspections and inform the management of a business which areas may not be in compliance with State and Federal laws or employer policies, in order to gain their support for addressing these areas. They advise management on the cost and effectiveness of safety and health programs.

Occupational health and safety technicians collect data on work environments for analysis by occupational health and safety specialists. Usually working under the supervision of specialists, they help implement and evaluate programs designed to limit risks to workers.

The specific responsibilities of occupational health and safety specialists and technicians vary by industry, workplace, and types of hazards affecting employees. In most settings, they initially focus on identifying hazardous conditions and practices. Sometimes they develop methods to predict hazards from experience, historical data, workplace analysis, and other information sources. Then they identify potential hazards in systems, equipment, products, facilities, or processes planned for use in the future. For example, they might uncover patterns in injury data that implicate a specific cause such as system failure, human error, incomplete or faulty decision making, or a weakness in existing policies or practices. After reviewing the causes or effects of hazards, they evaluate the probability and severity of accidents or exposures to hazardous materials that may result. Then they identify where controls need to be implemented to reduce or eliminate hazards and advise if a new program or practice is required. As necessary, they conduct training sessions for management, supervisors, and workers on health and safety practices and regulations to promote an understanding of a new or existing process. After implementation, they may monitor and evaluate the program's progress, making additional suggestions when needed.

To ensure the machinery and equipment meet appropriate safety regulations, occupational health and safety specialists and technicians may examine and test machinery and equipment, such as lifting devices, machine guards, or scaffolding. They may check that personal protective equipment, such as masks, respirators, protective eyewear, or hardhats, is being used in workplaces according to regulations. They also check that hazardous materials are stored correctly. They test and identify work areas for potential accident and health hazards, such as toxic vapors, mold, mildew, and explosive gas-air mixtures, and help implement appropriate control measures, such as adjustments to ventilation systems. Their survey of the workplace might involve talking with workers and observing their work, as well as inspecting elements in their work environment, such as lighting, tools, and equipment.

To measure and control hazardous substances, such as the noise or radiation levels, occupational health and safety specialists and technicians prepare and calibrate scientific equipment. They must properly collect and handle samples of dust, gases, vapors, and other potentially toxic materials to ensure personal safety and accurate test results.

If an injury or illness occurs, occupational health and safety specialists and technicians help investigate unsafe working conditions, study possible causes, and recommend remedial action. Some occupational health and safety specialists and technicians assist with the rehabilitation of workers after accidents and injuries, and make sure they return to work successfully.

Frequent communication with management may be necessary to report on the status of occupational health and safety programs. Consultation with engineers or physicians also may be required.

Occupational health and safety specialists and technicians prepare reports including accident reports, Occupational Safety and Health Administration record-keeping forms, observations, analysis of contaminants, and recommendations for control and correction of hazards. They may prepare documents to be used in legal proceedings and give testimony in court proceedings. Those who develop expertise in certain areas may develop occupational health and safety systems, including policies, procedures, and manuals.

Specialists and technicians that concentrate in particular areas include environmental protection officers, ergonomists, health physicists, industrial hygienists, and mine examiners. Environmental protection officers evaluate and coordinate programs that impact the environment, such as the storage and handling of hazardous waste or monitoring the

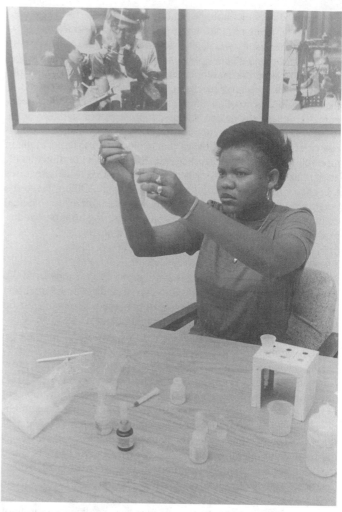

Occupational health and safety specialists and technicians must properly collect and handle samples of dust, gases, vapors, and other potentially toxic materials to ensure accurate test results.

cleanup of contaminated soil or water. Ergonomists help ensure that the work environment allows employees to maximize their comfort, safety, and productivity. Health physicists help protect people and the environment from hazardous radiation exposure by monitoring the manufacture, handling, and disposal of radioactive material. Industrial hygienists examine the workplace for health hazards, such as worker exposure to lead, asbestos, pesticides, or communicable diseases. Mine examiners are technicians who inspect mines for proper air flow and health hazards such as the buildup of methane or other noxious gases.

Working Conditions

Occupational health and safety specialists and technicians work with many different people in a variety of environments. Their jobs often involve considerable fieldwork, and some travel frequently. Many occupational health and safety specialists and technicians work long and often irregular hours.

Occupational health and safety specialists and technicians may be exposed to many of the same physically strenuous conditions and hazards as industrial employees, and the work may be performed in unpleasant, stressful, and dangerous working conditions. They may find themselves in an adversarial role if the management of an organization disagrees with the recommendations for ensuring a safe working environment.

Training, Other Qualifications, and Advancement

All occupational health and safety specialists and technicians are trained in the applicable laws or inspection procedures through some combination of classroom and on-the-job training. Awards and degrees in programs related to occupational safety and health include 1-year certificates, associate degrees, bachelor's degrees, and graduate degrees. The Accreditation Board for Engineering and Technology (ABET) accredits health physics, industrial hygiene, and safety programs, in addition to engineering programs. Many employers, including the Federal Government, require a bachelor's degree in occupational health, safety, or a related field, such as engineering, biology, or chemistry, for some specialist positions. Many industrial hygiene programs result in a master's degree. Experience as an occupational health and safety professional is also a prerequisite for many positions. Advancement to senior specialist positions is likely to require an advanced degree and substantial experience in several areas of practice.

In general, people who want to enter this occupation should be responsible and like detailed work. Occupational health and safety specialists and technicians should be able to communicate well. Recommended high school courses include English, mathematics, chemistry, biology, and physics.

Certification is available through the Board of Certified Safety Professionals (BCSP) and the American Board of Industrial Hygiene (ABIH). The BCSP offers the Certified Safety Professional (CSP) credential, while the ABIH offers the Certified Industrial Hygienist (CIH) and Certified Associate Industrial Hygienist (CAIH) credentials. Also, the Council on Certification of Health, Environmental, and Safety Technologists, a joint effort between the BCSP and ABIH, awards the Occupational Health and Safety Technologist (OHST) and Construction Health and Safety Technician (CHST) credentials. Requirements for the OHST and CHST credentials are less stringent than those for the CSP, CIH, or CAIH credentials. Once education and experience requirements have been met, certification may be obtained through an examination. Continuing education is required for recertification. Although voluntary, many employers encourage certification.

Federal Government occupational health and safety specialists and technicians whose job performance is satisfactory advance through their career ladder to a specified full-performance level. For positions above this level, usually supervisory positions, advancement is competitive and based on agency needs and individual merit. Advancement opportunities in State and local governments and the private sector are often similar to those in the Federal Government.

Research or related teaching positions at the college level require advanced education.

Employment

Occupational health and safety specialists held about 40,000 jobs in 2004. While the majority of jobs were spread throughout the private sector, about 2 out of 5 specialists worked for government agencies. Local governments employed 19 percent, State governments employed 18 percent, and the Federal Government employed 4 percent. Other occupational health and safety specialists were employed in manufacturing firms; private general medical and surgical hospitals; management, scientific, and technical consulting services; management of companies and enterprises; support activities for mining; research and development in the physical, engineering, and life sciences; private colleges, universities, and professional schools; and electric power generation, transmission, and distribution. Some were self-employed.

Occupational health and safety technicians held about 12,000 jobs in 2004. Nearly 3 out of 10 technicians worked in government agencies. Local governments employed 13 percent, State governments employed 7 percent, and the Federal Government employed 9 percent. Other occupational health and safety technicians were employed in manufacturing firms; private general medical and surgical hospitals; private colleges, universities, and professional schools; employment services; management, scientific, and technical consulting services; testing laboratories

for architectural, engineering, and related services; research and development in the physical, engineering, and life sciences; and electric power generation, transmission, and distribution.

Within the Federal Government, most jobs are as Occupational Safety and Health Administration (OSHA) inspectors, who enforce U.S. Department of Labor regulations that ensure adequate safety principles, practices, and techniques are applied in workplaces. Employers may be fined for violation of OSHA standards. Within the U.S. Department of Health and Human Services, occupational health and safety specialists working for the National Institute of Occupational Safety and Health (NIOSH) provide private companies with an avenue to evaluate the health and safety of their employees without the risk of being fined. Most large government agencies also employ occupational health and safety specialists and technicians who work to protect agency employees.

Most private companies either employ their own occupational health and safety personnel or contract with occupational health and safety professionals to ensure the safety of their workers and compliance with Federal, State, and local government agencies that enforce rules on safety, health, and the environment.

Job Outlook

Employment of occupational health and safety specialists and technicians is expected to grow about as fast as the average for all occupations through 2014, reflecting a balance of continuing public demand for a safe and healthy work environment against the desire for smaller government and fewer regulations. Since the September 11, 2001 attacks, emergency preparedness has become a greater focus for the public and private sectors, and for occupational health and safety specialists and technicians. Additional job openings will arise from the need to replace those who transfer to other occupations, retire, or leave for other reasons. In private industry, employment growth will reflect industry growth and the continuing self-enforcement of government and company regulations and policies.

Employment of occupational health and safety specialists and technicians in the private sector is somewhat affected by general economic fluctuations. Federal, State, and local governments, which employ about 2 out of 5 of all specialists and technicians, provide considerable job security; workers are less likely to be affected by changes in the economy.

Earnings

Median annual earnings of occupational health and safety specialists were $51,570 in May 2004. The middle 50 percent earned between $39,580 and $65,370. The lowest 10 percent earned less than $30,590, and the highest 10 percent earned more than $79,530. Median annual earnings of occupational health and safety specialists in May 2004 were $48,710 in local government and $44,400 in State government.

Median annual earnings of occupational health and safety technicians were $42,130 in May 2004. The middle 50 percent earned between $29,900 and $56,640. The lowest 10 percent earned less than $22,860, and the highest 10 percent earned more than $70,460.

Most occupational health and safety specialists and technicians work in large private firms or for Federal, State, and local governments, most of which generally offer more generous benefits than smaller firms.

Related Occupations

Occupational health and safety specialists and technicians help to ensure that laws and regulations are obeyed. Others who enforce laws and regulations include agricultural inspectors, construction and building inspectors, correctional officers, financial examiners, fire inspectors, police and detectives, and transportation inspectors.

Sources of Additional Information

Information about jobs in Federal, State, and local governments and in private industry is available from State employment service offices.

For information on a career as an industrial hygienist, including a list of colleges and universities offering industrial hygiene and related degrees, contact:

➤ American Industrial Hygiene Association, 2700 Prosperity Ave., Suite 250, Fairfax, VA 22031. Internet: **http://www.aiha.org**

For information on the Certified Industrial Hygienist or Certified Associate Industrial Hygienist credential, contact:

➤ American Board of Industrial Hygiene, 6015 West St. Joseph Hwy., Suite 102, Lansing, MI 48917. Internet: **http://www.abih.org**

For more information on professions in safety, a comprehensive list of colleges and universities offering safety and related degrees, and applications for scholarships, contact:

➤ American Society of Safety Engineers, 1800 E Oakton St., Des Plaines, IL 60018. Internet: **http://www.asse.org**

For more information on professions in safety, a list of programs in safety and related academic fields, and the Certified Safety Professional credential, contact:

➤ Board of Certified Safety Professionals, 208 Burwash Ave., Savoy, IL 61874. Internet: **http://www.bcsp.org**

For information on the Occupational Health and Safety Technologist and Construction Health and Safety Technician credentials, contact:

➤ Council on Certification of Health, Environmental, and Safety Technologists, 208 Burwash Ave., Savoy, IL 61874. Internet: **http://www.cchest.org**

For information on a career as a health physicist, contact:

➤ Health Physics Society, 1313 Dolley Madison Blvd., Suite 402, McLean, VA 22101. Internet: **http://www.hps.org**

For additional career information, contact:

➤ U.S. Department of Health and Human Services, Center for Disease Control and Prevention, National Institute of Occupational Safety and Health, Hubert H. Humphrey Bldg., 200 Independence Ave. SW., Room 715H, Washington, DC 20201. Internet: **http://www.cdc.gov/niosh**

➤ U.S. Department of Labor, Occupational Safety and Health Administration, Office of Communication, 200 Constitution Ave. NW., Washington, DC 20210. Internet: **http://www.osha.gov**

Information on obtaining positions as occupational health and safety specialists and technicians with the Federal Government is available from the Office of Personnel Management through USA-JOBS, the Federal Government's official employment information system. This resource for locating and applying for job opportunities can be accessed through the Internet at **http://www.usajobs.opm.gov** or through an interactive voice response telephone system at (703) 724-1850 or TDD (978) 461-8404. These numbers are not tollfree, and charges may result.

Opticians, Dispensing

(O*NET 29-2081.00)

Significant Points

● Most dispensing opticians receive training on the job or through apprenticeships lasting 2 or more years; however, some employers seek graduates of postsecondary training programs in opticianry.

● About 20 States require a license.

● Projected average employment growth reflects the steady demand for corrective lenses and eyeglass frames that are in fashion.

Nature of Work

Dispensing opticians fit eyeglasses and contact lenses, following prescriptions written by ophthalmologists or optometrists. (The work of optometrists is described in a statement elsewhere in the *Handbook*. See the statement on physicians and surgeons for information about ophthalmologists.)

Dispensing opticians examine written prescriptions to determine the specifications of lenses. They recommend eyeglass frames, lenses, and lens coatings after considering the prescription and the customer's occupation, habits, and facial features. Dispensing opticians measure clients' eyes, including the distance between the centers of the pupils and the distance between the ocular surface and the lens. For customers without prescriptions, dispensing opticians may use a focimeter to record eyeglass measurements in order to duplicate the eyeglasses. They also may obtain a customer's previous record to re-make eyeglasses or contact lenses, or they may verify a prescription with the examining optometrist or ophthalmologist.

Dispensing opticians prepare work orders that give ophthalmic laboratory technicians information needed to grind and insert lenses into a frame. The work order includes prescriptions for lenses and information on their size, material, color, and style. Some dispensing opticians grind and insert lenses themselves. After the glasses are made, dispensing opticians verify that the lenses have been ground to specifications. Then they may reshape or bend the frame, by hand or using pliers, so that the eyeglasses fit the customer properly and comfortably. Some also fix, adjust, and refit broken frames. They instruct clients about adapting to, wearing, or caring for eyeglasses.

Some dispensing opticians, after additional education and training, specialize in fitting contacts, artificial eyes, or cosmetic shells to cover blemished eyes.

To fit contact lenses, dispensing opticians measure the shape and size of the eye, select the type of contact lens material, and prepare work orders specifying the prescription and lens size. Fitting contact lenses requires considerable skill, care, and patience. Dispensing opticians observe customers' eyes, corneas, lids, and contact lenses with specialized instruments and microscopes. During several follow-up visits, opticians teach proper insertion, removal, and care of contact lenses. Opticians do all this to ensure that the fit is correct.

Dispensing opticians keep records on customers' prescriptions, work orders, and payments; track inventory and sales; and perform other administrative duties.

Dispensing opticians deal directly with the public, so they should be tactful, pleasant, and communicate well.

Working Conditions

Dispensing opticians work indoors in attractive, well-lighted, and well-ventilated surroundings. They may work in medical offices or small stores where customers are served one at a time. Some work in large stores where several dispensing opticians serve a number of customers at once. Opticians spend a fair amount of time on their feet. If they prepare lenses, they need to take precautions against the hazards associated with glass cutting, chemicals, and machinery.

Most dispensing opticians work about 40 hours a week, although a few work longer hours. Those in retail stores may work evenings and weekends. Some work part time.

Training, Other Qualifications, and Advancement

Employers usually hire individuals with no background as an optician or as an ophthalmic laboratory technician. (See the statement on ophthalmic laboratory technicians elsewhere in the *Handbook*.) The employers then provide the required training. Most dispensing opticians receive training on the job or through apprenticeships lasting 2 or more years. Some employers, however, seek people with postsecondary training in the field.

Knowledge of physics, basic anatomy, algebra, and trigonometry as well as experience with computers are particularly valuable, because training usually includes instruction in optical mathematics, optical physics, and the use of precision measuring instruments and other machinery and tools. Dispensing opticians deal directly with the public, so they should be tactful, pleasant, and communicate well. Manual dexterity and the ability to do precision work are essential.

Large employers usually offer structured apprenticeship programs; small employers provide more informal, on-the-job training. About 20 States require dispensing opticians to be licensed. States may require individuals to pass one or more of the following for licensure: a State practical examination, a State written examination, and certification examinations offered by the American Board of Opticianry (ABO) and the National Contact Lens Examiners (NCLE). To qualify for the examinations, States often require applicants to complete postsecondary training or work from 2 to 4 years as apprentices. Continuing education is commonly required for licensure renewal. Information about specific licensing requirements is available from the State board of occupational licensing. Apprenticeships or formal training programs are offered in other States as well.

Apprentices receive technical training and learn office management and sales. Under the supervision of an experienced optician, optometrist, or ophthalmologist, apprentices work directly with patients, fitting eyeglasses and contact lenses.

Formal training in the field is offered in community colleges and a few colleges and universities. In 2004, the Commission on Opticianry Accreditation accredited 24 programs that awarded 2-year associate degrees. There also are shorter programs of 1 year or less. Some States that offer a license to dispensing opticians allow graduates to take the licensure exam immediately upon graduation; others require a few months to a year of experience.

Dispensing opticians may apply to the ABO and the NCLE for certification of their skills. All applicants age 18 or older with a high school diploma or equivalent are eligible for the exam; however, some States licensing boards have additional eligibility requirements. Certification must be renewed every 3 years through continuing education. Those licensed in States where licensure renewal requirements include continuing education credits may use proof of their renewed State license to meet the recertification requirements of the ABO. Likewise, the NCLE will accept proof of renewal from any State that has contact lens requirements.

Many experienced dispensing opticians open their own optical stores. Others become managers of optical stores or sales representatives for wholesalers or manufacturers of eyeglasses or lenses.

Employment

Dispensing opticians held about 66,000 jobs in 2004. Nearly one-third worked in health and personal care stores, including optical goods stores. Many of these stores offer one-stop shopping. Customers may have their eyes examined, choose frames, and have glasses made on the spot. About 30 percent of dispensing opticians worked in offices of other health practitioners, including offices of optometrists. Over 10 percent worked in offices of physicians, including ophthalmologists who sell glasses directly to patients. Some work in optical departments of department stores or other general merchandise stores, such as warehouse clubs and superstores. Nearly 6 percent are self-employed and run their own unincorporated businesses.

Job Outlook

Employment of dispensing opticians is expected to increase about as fast as the average for all occupations through 2014 as demand grows for corrective lenses. The number of middle-aged and elderly persons is projected to increase rapidly. Middle age is a time when many individuals use corrective lenses for the first time, and elderly persons generally require more vision care than others. Fashion also influences demand. Frames come in a growing variety of styles and colors—encouraging people to buy more than one pair.

Increasing awareness of laser surgery that corrects some vision problems will have an impact on demand for eyewear. Although the surgery remains relatively more expensive than eyewear, patients who successfully undergo this surgery may not require glasses or contact lenses for several years.

The need to replace those who leave the occupation will result in additional job openings. Nevertheless, the number of job openings will be limited because the occupation is small. Dispensing opticians are vulnerable to changes in the business cycle, because eyewear purchases often can be deferred for a time.

Earnings

Median annual earnings of dispensing opticians were $27,950 in May 2004. The middle 50 percent earned between $21,360 and $35,940. The lowest 10 percent earned less than $17,390, and the highest 10 percent earned more than $45,340. Median annual earnings in the industries employing the largest numbers of dispensing opticians in May 2004 were:

Health and personal care stores	$30,890
Offices of physicians	30,560
Offices of other health practitioners	26,970

Related Occupations

Other workers who deal with customers and perform delicate work include jewelers and precious stone and metal workers, locksmiths and safe repairers, orthotists and prosthetists, and precision instrument and equipment repairers.

Sources of Additional Information

For general information about opticians and a list of home-study programs, seminars, and review materials, contact:
➤ National Academy of Opticianry, 8401 Corporate Dr., Suite 605, Landover, MD 20785. Telephone (tollfree): 800-229-4828. Internet: **http://www.nao.org**

For a list of accredited programs in opticianry, contact:
➤ Commission on Opticianry Accreditation, 8665 Sudley Rd., #341, Manassas, VA 20110.

To learn about voluntary certification for opticians who fit eyeglasses, as well as a list of State licensing boards for opticians, contact:
➤ American Board of Opticianry, 6506 Loisdale Rd., Suite 209, Springfield, VA 22150. Internet: **http://www.abo.org**

For information on voluntary certification for dispensing opticians who fit contact lenses, contact:

➤ National Contact Lens Examiners, 6506 Loisdale Rd., Suite 209, Springfield, VA 22150. Internet: **http://www.abo-ncle.org/**

Pharmacy Technicians

(O*NET 29-2052.00)

Significant Points

- Job opportunities are expected to be good for full-time and part-time work, especially for those with certification or previous work experience.

- Many technicians work evenings, weekends, and holidays.

- About 7 out of 10 of jobs were in retail pharmacies, grocery stores, department stores, or mass retailers.

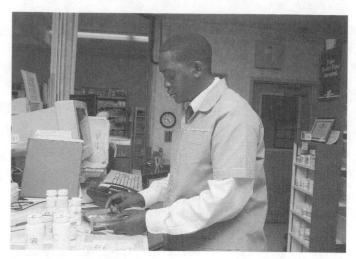

Pharmacy technicians help licensed pharmacists provide medication and other health care products to patients.

Nature of the Work

Pharmacy technicians help licensed pharmacists provide medication and other health care products to patients. Technicians usually perform routine tasks to help prepare prescribed medication for patients, such as counting tablets and labeling bottles. Technicians refer any questions regarding prescriptions, drug information, or health matters to a *pharmacist.* (See the statement on pharmacists elsewhere in the *Handbook.*)

Pharmacy aides work closely with pharmacy technicians. They often are clerks or cashiers who primarily answer telephones, handle money, stock shelves, and perform other clerical duties. (See the statement on pharmacy aides elsewhere in the *Handbook.*) Pharmacy technicians usually perform more complex tasks than do pharmacy aides, although in some States their duties and job titles may overlap.

Pharmacy technicians who work in retail or mail-order pharmacies have varying responsibilities, depending on State rules and regulations. Technicians receive written prescriptions or requests for prescription refills from patients. They also may receive prescriptions sent electronically from the doctor's office. They must verify that the information on the prescription is complete and accurate. To prepare the prescription, technicians must retrieve, count, pour, weigh, measure, and sometimes mix the medication. Then, they prepare the prescription labels, select the type of prescription container, and affix the prescription and auxiliary labels to the container. Once the prescription is filled, technicians price and file the prescription, which must be checked by a pharmacist before it is given to the patient. Technicians may establish and maintain patient profiles, prepare insurance claim forms, and stock and take inventory of prescription and over-the-counter medications.

In hospitals, nursing homes, and assisted-living facilities, technicians have added responsibilities, including reading patients' charts and preparing and delivering the medicine to patients. Still, the pharmacist must check the order before it is delivered to the patient. The technician then copies the information about the prescribed medication onto the patient's profile. Technicians also may assemble a 24-hour supply of medicine for every patient. They package and label each dose separately. The packages are then placed in the medicine cabinets of patients until the supervising pharmacist checks them for accuracy. The packages are then given to the patients.

Working Conditions

Pharmacy technicians work in clean, organized, well-lighted, and well-ventilated areas. Most of their workday is spent on their feet. They may be required to lift heavy boxes or to use stepladders to retrieve supplies from high shelves.

Technicians work the same hours that pharmacists work. These may include evenings, nights, weekends, and holidays, particularly in facilities, such as hospitals and retail pharmacies, that are open 24 hours a day. As their seniority increases, technicians often acquire increased control over the hours they work. There are many opportunities for part-time work in both retail and hospital settings.

Training, Other Qualifications, and Advancement

Although most pharmacy technicians receive informal on-the-job training, employers favor those who have completed formal training and certification. However, there are currently few State and no Federal requirements for formal training or certification of pharmacy technicians. Employers who have insufficient resources to give on-the-job training often seek formally educated pharmacy technicians. Formal education programs and certification emphasize the technician's interest in and dedication to the work. In addition to the military, some hospitals, proprietary schools, vocational or technical colleges, and community colleges offer formal education programs.

Formal pharmacy technician education programs require classroom and laboratory work in a variety of areas, including medical and pharmaceutical terminology, pharmaceutical calculations, pharmacy recordkeeping, pharmaceutical techniques, and pharmacy law and ethics. Technicians also are required to learn medication names, actions, uses, and doses. Many training programs include internships, in which students gain hands-on experience in actual pharmacies. Students receive a diploma, a certificate, or an associate's degree, depending on the program.

Prospective pharmacy technicians with experience working as an aide in a community pharmacy or volunteering in a hospital may have an advantage. Employers also prefer applicants with strong customer service and communication skills, as well as those with experience managing inventories, counting tablets, measuring dosages, and using computers. Technicians entering the field need strong mathematics, spelling, and reading skills. A background in chemistry, English, and health education also may be beneficial. Some technicians are hired without formal training, but under the condition that they obtain certification within a specified period to retain their employment.

The Pharmacy Technician Certification Board administers the National Pharmacy Technician Certification Examination. This exam is voluntary in most States and displays the competency of the individual to act as a pharmacy technician. However, more States and employers are requiring certification as reliance on pharmacy technicians grows. Eligible candidates must have a high school diploma or

GED and no felony convictions, and those who pass the exam earn the title of Certified Pharmacy Technician (CPhT). The exam is offered several times per year at various locations nationally. Employers—often pharmacists—know that individuals who pass the exam have a standardized body of knowledge and skills. Many employers also will reimburse the costs of the exam as an incentive for certification.

Certified technicians must be recertified every 2 years. Technicians must complete 20 contact hours of pharmacy-related topics within the 2-year certification period to become eligible for recertification. Contact hours are awarded for on-the-job training, attending lectures, and college coursework. At least 1 contact hour must be in pharmacy law. Contact hours can be earned from several different sources, including pharmacy associations, pharmacy colleges, and pharmacy technician training programs. Up to 10 contact hours can be earned when the technician is employed under the direct supervision and instruction of a pharmacist.

Successful pharmacy technicians are alert, observant, organized, dedicated, and responsible. They should be willing and able to take directions. They must be precise; details are sometimes a matter of life and death. Although a pharmacist must check and approve all their work, they should be able to work independently without constant instruction from the pharmacist. Candidates interested in becoming pharmacy technicians cannot have prior records of drug or substance abuse.

Strong interpersonal and communication skills are needed because pharmacy technicians interact daily with patients, coworkers, and health care professionals. Teamwork is very important because technicians often are required to work with pharmacists, aides, and other technicians.

Employment

Pharmacy technicians held about 258,000 jobs in 2004. About 7 out of 10 jobs were in retail pharmacies, either independently owned or part of a drugstore chain, grocery store, department store, or mass retailer. About 2 out of 10 jobs were in hospitals and a small proportion was in mail-order and Internet pharmacies, clinics, pharmaceutical wholesalers, and the Federal Government.

Job Outlook

Good job opportunities are expected for full-time and part-time work, especially for technicians with formal training or previous experience. Job openings for pharmacy technicians will result from the expansion of retail pharmacies and other employment settings and from the need to replace workers who transfer to other occupations or leave the labor force.

Employment of pharmacy technicians is expected to grow much faster than the average for all occupations through 2014 because as the population grows and ages, demand for pharmaceuticals will increase dramatically. The increased number of middle-aged and elderly people—who use more prescription drugs than younger people—will spur demand for technicians in all practice settings. With advances in science, more medications are becoming available to treat a greater number of conditions.

In addition, cost-conscious insurers, pharmacies, and health systems will continue to expand the role of technicians. As a result, pharmacy technicians will assume responsibility for some of the more routine tasks previously performed by pharmacists. Pharmacy technicians also will need to learn and master new pharmacy technology as it emerges. For example, robotic machines are being increasingly used to dispense medicine into containers; technicians must oversee the machines, stock the bins, and label the containers. Thus, while automation is increasingly incorporated into the job, it will not necessarily reduce the need for technicians.

Almost all States have legislated the maximum number of technicians who can safely work under a pharmacist at one time. In some States, technicians have assumed more medication-dispensing duties as pharmacists have become more involved in patient care, resulting in more technicians per pharmacist. Changes in these laws could directly affect employment.

Earnings

Median hourly earnings of wage and salary pharmacy technicians in May 2004 were $11.37. The middle 50 percent earned between $9.40 and $13.85. The lowest 10 percent earned less than $7.96, and the highest 10 percent earned more than $16.61. Median hourly earnings in the industries employing the largest numbers of pharmacy technicians in May 2004 were:

General medical and surgical hospitals	$12.93
Grocery stores	11.77
Other general merchandise stores	11.11
Department stores	10.56
Health and personal care stores	10.51

Certified technicians may earn more. Shift differentials for working evenings or weekends also can increase earnings. Some technicians belong to unions representing hospital or grocery store workers.

Related Occupations

This occupation is most closely related to pharmacists and pharmacy aides. Workers in other medical support occupations include dental assistants, licensed practical and licensed vocational nurses, medical transcriptionists, medical records and health information technicians, occupational therapist assistants and aides, physical therapist assistants and aides, and surgical technologists.

Sources of Additional Information

For information on the Certified Pharmacy Technician designation, contact:

➤ Pharmacy Technician Certification Board, 2215 Constitution Ave. NW., Washington DC 20037-2985. Internet: **http://www.ptcb.org**

For a list of accredited pharmacy technician training programs, contact:

➤ American Society of Health-System Pharmacists, 7272 Wisconsin Ave., Bethesda, MD 20814. Internet: **http://www.ashp.org**

For pharmacy technician career information, contact:

➤ National Pharmacy Technician Association, P.O. Box 683148, Houston, TX 77268. Internet: **http://www.pharmacytechnician.org**

Radiologic Technologists and Technicians

(O*NET 29-2034.01, 29-2034.02)

Significant Points

● Job opportunities are expected to be favorable; some employers report difficulty hiring sufficient numbers of radiologic technologists and technicians.

● Formal training programs in radiography range in length from 1 to 4 years and lead to a certificate, an associate degree, or a bachelor's degree.

● Although hospitals will remain the primary employer, a greater number of new jobs will be found in physicians' offices and diagnostic imaging centers.

Nature of the Work

Radiologic technologists and technicians take x rays and administer nonradioactive materials into patients' bloodstreams for diagnostic purposes.

Some specialize in diagnostic imaging technologies, such as computerized tomography (CT) and magnetic resonance imaging (MRI).

In addition to radiologic technologists and technicians, others who conduct diagnostic imaging procedures include cardiovascular technologists and technicians, diagnostic medical sonographers, and nuclear medicine technologists. (Each is discussed elsewhere in the *Handbook*.)

Radiologic technologists and technicians, also referred to as *radiographers*, produce x-ray films (radiographs) of parts of the human body for use in diagnosing medical problems. They prepare patients for radiologic examinations by explaining the procedure, removing articles such as jewelry, through which x rays cannot pass, and positioning patients so that the parts of the body can be appropriately radiographed. To prevent unnecessary exposure to radiation, these workers surround the exposed area with radiation protection devices, such as lead shields, or limit the size of the x-ray beam. Radiographers position radiographic equipment at the correct angle and height over the appropriate area of a patient's body. Using instruments similar to a measuring tape, they may measure the thickness of the section to be radiographed and set controls on the x-ray machine to produce radiographs of the appropriate density, detail, and contrast. They place the x-ray film under the part of the patient's body to be examined and make the exposure. They then remove the film and develop it.

Experienced radiographers may perform more complex imaging procedures. For fluoroscopies, radiographers prepare a solution of contrast medium for the patient to drink, allowing the radiologist (a physician who interprets radiographs) to see soft tissues in the body. Some radiographers, called *CT technologists*, operate CT scanners to produce cross-sectional images of patients. Radiographers who operate machines that use strong magnets and radio waves, rather than radiation, to create an image are called *MRI technologists*.

Radiologic technologists and technicians must follow physicians' orders precisely and conform to regulations concerning the use of radiation to protect themselves, their patients, and their coworkers from unnecessary exposure.

In addition to preparing patients and operating equipment, radiologic technologists and technicians keep patient records and adjust and maintain equipment. They also may prepare work schedules, evaluate purchases of equipment, or manage a radiology department.

Working Conditions

Most full-time radiologic technologists and technicians work about 40 hours a week. They may, however, have evening, weekend, or on-call hours. Opportunities for part-time and shift work also are available.

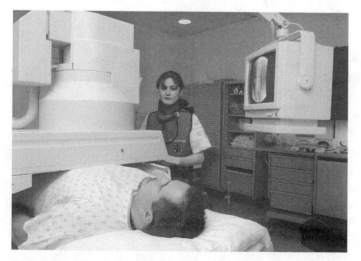

Radiologic technologists use advanced imaging technology to create diagnostic images for interpretation by a physician.

Physical stamina is important, because technologists and technicians are on their feet for long periods and may lift or turn disabled patients. Technologists and technicians work at diagnostic machines, but also may perform some procedures at patients' bedsides. Some travel to patients in large vans equipped with sophisticated diagnostic equipment.

Although radiation hazards exist in this occupation, they are minimized by the use of lead aprons, gloves, and other shielding devices, as well as by instruments monitoring exposure to radiation. Technologists and technicians wear badges measuring radiation levels in the radiation area, and detailed records are kept on their cumulative lifetime dose.

Training, Other Qualifications, and Advancement

Preparation for this profession is offered in hospitals, colleges and universities, vocational-technical institutes, and the U.S. Armed Forces. Hospitals, which employ most radiologic technologists and technicians, prefer to hire those with formal training.

Formal training programs in radiography range in length from 1 to 4 years and lead to a certificate, an associate degree, or a bachelor's degree. Two-year associate degree programs are most prevalent.

Some 1-year certificate programs are available for experienced radiographers or individuals from other health occupations, such as medical technologists and registered nurses, who want to change fields or specialize in CT or MRI. A bachelor's or master's degree in one of the radiologic technologies is desirable for supervisory, administrative, or teaching positions.

The Joint Review Committee on Education in Radiologic Technology accredits most formal training programs for the field. The committee accredited 606 radiography programs in 2005. Radiography programs require, at a minimum, a high school diploma or the equivalent. High school courses in mathematics, physics, chemistry, and biology are helpful. The programs provide both classroom and clinical instruction in anatomy and physiology, patient care procedures, radiation physics, radiation protection, principles of imaging, medical terminology, positioning of patients, medical ethics, radiobiology, and pathology.

Federal legislation protects the public from the hazards of unnecessary exposure to medical and dental radiation by ensuring that operators of radiologic equipment are properly trained. Under this legislation, the Federal Government sets voluntary standards that the States may use for accrediting training programs and certifying individuals who engage in medical or dental radiography.

In 2005, 38 States certified radiologic technologists and technicians. Certification, which is voluntary, is offered by the American Registry of Radiologic Technologists. To be eligible for certification, technologists generally must graduate from an accredited program and pass an examination. Many employers prefer to hire certified radiographers. To be recertified, radiographers must complete 24 hours of continuing education every two years.

Radiologic technologists and technicians should be sensitive to patients' physical and psychological needs. They must pay attention to detail, follow instructions, and work as part of a team. In addition, operating complicated equipment requires mechanical ability and manual dexterity.

With experience and additional training, staff technologists may become specialists, performing CT scanning, angiography, and magnetic resonance imaging. Experienced technologists also may be promoted to supervisor, chief radiologic technologist, and, ultimately, department administrator or director. Depending on the institution, courses or a master's degree in business or health administration may be necessary for the director's position. Some technologists progress by leaving the occupation to become instructors or directors in radiologic technology programs; others take jobs as sales representatives or instructors with equipment manufacturers.

Employment

Radiologic technologists and technicians held about 182,000 jobs in 2004. More than half of all jobs were in hospitals. Most of the rest were in offices of physicians; medical and diagnostic laboratories, including diagnostic imaging centers; and outpatient care centers.

Job Outlook

Job opportunities are expected to be favorable. Some employers report difficulty hiring sufficient numbers of radiologic technologists and technicians. Imbalances between the demand for, and supply of, radiologic technologists and technicians should spur efforts to attract and retain qualified workers, such as improved compensation and working conditions. Radiologic technologists who also are experienced in more complex diagnostic imaging procedures, such as CT and MRI, will have better employment opportunities, brought about as employers seek to control costs by using multi-skilled employees.

Employment of radiologic technologists and technicians is expected to grow faster than the average for all occupations through 2014, as the population grows and ages, increasing the demand for diagnostic imaging. Although healthcare providers are enthusiastic about the clinical benefits of new technologies, the extent to which they are adopted depends largely on cost and reimbursement considerations. For example, digital imaging technology can improve the quality of the images and the efficiency of the procedure, but remains expensive. Some promising new technologies may not come into widespread use because they are too expensive and third-party payers may not be willing to pay for their use.

Hospitals will remain the principal employer of radiologic technologists and technicians. However, a greater number of new jobs will be found in offices of physicians and diagnostic imaging centers. Health facilities such as these are expected to grow rapidly through 2014, due to the strong shift toward outpatient care, encouraged by third-party payers and made possible by technological advances that permit more procedures to be performed outside the hospital. Some job openings also will arise from the need to replace technologists and technicians who leave the occupation.

Earnings

Median annual earnings of radiologic technologists and technicians were $43,350 in May 2004. The middle 50 percent earned between $36,170 and $52,430. The lowest 10 percent earned less than $30,020, and the highest 10 percent earned more than $60,210. Median annual earnings in the industries employing the largest numbers of radiologic technologists and technicians in May 2004 were:

Medical and diagnostic laboratories	$46,620
General medical and surgical hospitals	43,960
Offices of physicians	40,290

Related Occupations

Radiologic technologists and technicians operate sophisticated equipment to help physicians, dentists, and other health practitioners diagnose and treat patients. Workers in related occupations include cardiovascular technologists and technicians, clinical laboratory technologists and technicians, diagnostic medical sonographers, nuclear medicine technologists, radiation therapists, and respiratory therapists.

Sources of Additional Information

For career information, send a stamped, self-addressed business-size envelope with your request to:
➤ American Society of Radiologic Technologists, 15000 Central Ave. S.E., Albuquerque, NM 87123-3917. Internet: **http://www.asrt.org**

For the current list of accredited education programs in radiography, write to:
➤ Joint Review Committee on Education in Radiologic Technology, 20 N. Wacker Dr., Suite 2850, Chicago, IL 60606-3182. Internet: **http://www.jrcert.org**

For information on certification, contact:
➤ American Registry of Radiologic Technologists, 1255 Northland Dr., St. Paul, MN 55120-1155. Internet: **http://www.arrt.org**

Surgical Technologists

(O*NET 29-2055.00)

Significant Points

● Employment is expected to grow much faster than the average for all occupations through the year 2014.

● Job opportunities are expected to be good.

● Training programs last 9 to 24 months and lead to a certificate, diploma, or associate degree.

● Hospitals will continue to be the primary employer, although much faster employment growth is expected in offices of physicians and in outpatient care centers, including ambulatory surgical centers.

Nature of the Work

Surgical technologists, also called scrubs and surgical or operating room technicians, assist in surgical operations under the supervision of surgeons, registered nurses, or other surgical personnel. Surgical technologists are members of operating room teams, which most commonly include surgeons, anesthesiologists, and circulating nurses. Before an operation, surgical technologists help prepare the operating room by setting up surgical instruments and equipment, sterile drapes, and sterile solutions. They assemble both sterile and nonsterile equipment, as well as adjust and check it to ensure it is working properly. Technologists also get patients ready for surgery by washing, shaving, and disinfecting incision sites. They transport patients to the operating room, help position them on the operating table, and cover them with sterile surgical "drapes." Technologists also observe patients' vital signs, check charts, and assist the surgical team with putting on sterile gowns and gloves.

During surgery, technologists pass instruments and other sterile supplies to surgeons and surgeon assistants. They may hold retractors, cut sutures, and help count sponges, needles, supplies, and instruments. Surgical technologists help prepare, care for, and dispose of specimens taken for laboratory analysis and help apply dressings. Some operate sterilizers, lights, or suction machines, and help operate diagnostic equipment.

After an operation, surgical technologists may help transfer patients to the recovery room and clean and restock the operating room.

Working Conditions

Surgical technologists work in clean, well-lighted, cool environments. They must stand for long periods and remain alert during operations. At times they may be exposed to communicable diseases and unpleasant sights, odors, and materials.

Most surgical technologists work a regular 40-hour week, although they may be on call or work nights, weekends, and holidays on a rotating basis.

Training, Other Qualifications, and Advancement

Surgical technologists receive their training in formal programs offered by community and junior colleges, vocational schools, universities,

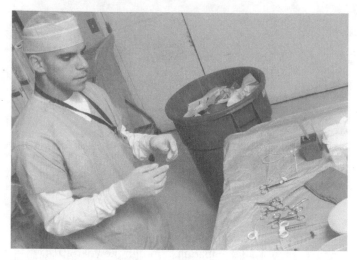

Before an operation, surgical technologists help prepare the operating room by setting up surgical instruments and equipment, sterile drapes, and sterile solutions.

hospitals, and the military. In 2005, the Commission on Accreditation of Allied Health Education Programs (CAAHEP) recognized more than 400 accredited programs. Programs last from 9 to 24 months and lead to a certificate, diploma, or associate degree. High school graduation normally is required for admission. Recommended high school courses include health, biology, chemistry, and mathematics.

Programs provide classroom education and supervised clinical experience. Students take courses in anatomy, physiology, microbiology, pharmacology, professional ethics, and medical terminology. Other studies cover the care and safety of patients during surgery, sterile techniques, and surgical procedures. Students also learn to sterilize instruments; prevent and control infection; and handle special drugs, solutions, supplies, and equipment.

Most employers prefer to hire certified technologists. Technologists may obtain voluntary professional certification from the Liaison Council on Certification for the Surgical Technologist by graduating from a CAAHEP-accredited program and passing a national certification examination. They may then use the Certified Surgical Technologist (CST) designation. Continuing education or reexamination is required to maintain certification, which must be renewed every 4 years.

Certification also may be obtained from the National Center for Competency Testing. To qualify to take the exam, candidates follow one of three paths: complete an accredited training program; undergo a 2-year hospital on-the-job training program; or acquire seven years of experience working in the field. After passing the exam, individuals may use the designation Tech in Surgery-Certified, TS-C (NCCT). This certification may be renewed every 5 years through either continuing education or reexamination.

Surgical technologists need manual dexterity to handle instruments quickly. They also must be conscientious, orderly, and emotionally stable to handle the demands of the operating room environment. Technologists must respond quickly and must be familiar with operating procedures in order to have instruments ready for surgeons without having to be told. They are expected to keep abreast of new developments in the field.

Technologists advance by specializing in a particular area of surgery, such as neurosurgery or open heart surgery. They also may work as circulating technologists. A circulating technologist is the "unsterile" member of the surgical team who prepares patients; helps with anesthesia; obtains and opens packages for the "sterile" persons to remove the sterile contents during the procedure; interviews the patient before surgery; keeps a written account of the surgical procedure; and answers the surgeon's questions about the patient during the surgery. With additional training, some technologists advance to first assistants, who help with retracting, sponging, suturing, cauterizing bleeders, and closing and treating wounds. Some surgical technologists manage central supply departments in hospitals, or take positions with insurance companies, sterile supply services, and operating equipment firms.

Employment

Surgical technologists held about 84,000 jobs in 2004. About 7 out of 10 jobs for surgical technologists were in hospitals, mainly in operating and delivery rooms. Other jobs were in offices of physicians or dentists who perform outpatient surgery and in outpatient care centers, including ambulatory surgical centers. A few, known as private scrubs, are employed directly by surgeons who have special surgical teams, like those for liver transplants.

Job Outlook

Employment of surgical technologists is expected to grow much faster than the average for all occupations through the year 2014 as the volume of surgery increases. Job opportunities are expected to be good. The number of surgical procedures is expected to rise as the population grows and ages. The number of older people, including the baby boom generation, who generally require more surgical procedures, will account for a larger portion of the general population. Technological advances, such as fiber optics and laser technology, will permit an increasing number of new surgical procedures to be performed and also will allow surgical technologists to assist with a greater number of procedures.

Hospitals will continue to be the primary employer of surgical technologists, although much faster employment growth is expected in offices of physicians and in outpatient care centers, including ambulatory surgical centers.

Earnings

Median annual earnings of surgical technologists were $34,010 in May 2004. The middle 50 percent earned between $28,560 and $40,750. The lowest 10 percent earned less than $23,940, and the highest 10 percent earned more than $45,990. Median hourly earnings in the industries employing the largest numbers of surgical technologists in May 2004 were:

Offices of dentists	$37,510
Offices of physicians	36,570
General medical and surgical hospitals	33,130

Related Occupations

Other health occupations requiring approximately 1 year of training after high school include dental assistants, licensed practical and licensed vocational nurses, clinical laboratory technologists and technicians, and medical assistants.

Sources of Additional Information

For additional information on a career as a surgical technologist and a list of CAAHEP-accredited programs, contact:
➤ Association of Surgical Technologists, 6 West Dry Creek Circle, Littleton, CO 80120. Internet: **http://www.ast.org**

For information on becoming a Certified Surgical Technologist, contact:
➤ Liaison Council on Certification for the Surgical Technologist, 6 West Dry Creek Circle, Suite 100, Littleton, CO 80120. Internet: **http://www.lcc-st.org**

For information on becoming a Tech in Surgery-Certified, contact:
➤ National Center for Competency Testing, 7007 College Blvd., Suite 250, Overland Park, KS 66211.

Veterinary Technologists and Technicians

(O*NET 29-2056.00)

Significant Points

- Animal lovers get satisfaction in this occupation, but aspects of the work can be unpleasant, physically and emotionally demanding, and sometimes dangerous.

- Entrants generally complete a 2-year or 4-year veterinary technology program and must pass a State examination.

- Employment is expected to grow much faster than average.

- Keen competition is expected for jobs in zoos.

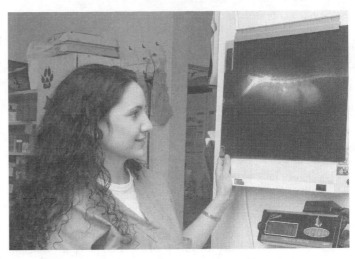

Veterinary technologists and technicians often assist veterinarians by taking x rays.

Nature of the Work

Owners of pets and other animals today expect state-of-the-art veterinary care. To provide this service, veterinarians use the skills of veterinary technologists and technicians, who perform many of the same duties for a veterinarian that a nurse would for a physician, including routine laboratory and clinical procedures. Although specific job duties vary by employer, there often is little difference between the tasks carried out by technicians and by technologists, despite some differences in formal education and training. As a result, most workers in this occupation are called technicians.

Veterinary technologists and technicians typically conduct clinical work in a private practice under the supervision of a veterinarian—often performing various medical tests along with treating and diagnosing medical conditions and diseases in animals. For example, they may perform laboratory tests such as urinalysis and blood counts, assist with dental prophylaxis, prepare tissue samples, take blood samples, or assist veterinarians in a variety of tests and analyses in which they often utilize various items of medical equipment, such as test tubes and diagnostic equipment. While most of these duties are performed in a laboratory setting, many are not. For example, some veterinary technicians obtain and record patients' case histories, expose and develop x rays, and provide specialized nursing care. In addition, experienced veterinary technicians may discuss a pet's condition with its owners and train new clinic personnel. Veterinary technologists and technicians assisting small-animal practitioners usually care for companion animals, such as cats and dogs, but can perform a variety of duties with mice, rats, sheep, pigs, cattle, monkeys, birds, fish, and frogs. Very few veterinary technologists work in mixed animal practices where they care for both small companion animals and larger, nondomestic animals.

Besides working in private clinics and animal hospitals, veterinary technologists and technicians may work in research facilities, where they may administer medications orally or topically, prepare samples for laboratory examinations, and record information on an animal's genealogy, diet, weight, medications, food intake, and clinical signs of pain and distress. Some may be required to sterilize laboratory and surgical equipment and provide routine postoperative care. At research facilities, veterinary technologists typically work under the guidance of veterinarians, physicians, and other laboratory technicians. Some veterinary technologists vaccinate newly admitted animals and occasionally are required to euthanize seriously ill, severely injured, or unwanted animals.

While the goal of most veterinary technologists and technicians is to promote animal health, some contribute to human health as well. Veterinary technologists occasionally assist veterinarians as they work with other scientists in medical-related fields such as gene therapy and cloning. Some find opportunities in biomedical research, wildlife medicine, the military, livestock management, or pharmaceutical sales.

Working Conditions

People who love animals get satisfaction from working with and helping them. However, some of the work may be unpleasant, physically and emotionally demanding, and sometimes dangerous. At times, veterinary technicians must clean cages and lift, hold, or restrain animals, risking exposure to bites or scratches. These workers must take precautions when treating animals with germicides or insecticides. The work setting can be noisy.

Veterinary technologists and technicians who witness abused animals or who euthanize unwanted, aged, or hopelessly injured animals may experience emotional stress. Those working for humane societies and animal shelters often deal with the public, some of whom might react with hostility to any implication that the owners are neglecting or abusing their pets. Such workers must maintain a calm and professional demeanor while they enforce the laws regarding animal care. In some animal hospitals, research facilities, and animal shelters, a veterinary technician is on duty 24 hours a day, which means that some may work night shifts. Most full-time veterinary technologists and technicians work about 40 hours a week, although some work 50 or more hours a week.

Training, Other Qualifications, and Advancement

There are primarily two levels of education and training for entry to this occupation: a 2-year program for veterinary technicians and a 4-year program for veterinary technologists. Most entry-level veterinary technicians have a 2-year degree, usually an associate's degree, from an accredited community college program in veterinary technology in which courses are taught in clinical and laboratory settings using live animals. About 15 colleges offer veterinary technology programs that are longer and that culminate in a 4-year bachelor's degree in veterinary technology. These 4-year colleges, in addition to some vocational schools, also offer 2-year programs in laboratory animal science. Approximately 5 schools offer distance learning.

In 2004, 116 veterinary technology programs in 43 States were accredited by the American Veterinary Medical Association (AVMA). Graduation from an AVMA-accredited veterinary technology program allows students to take the credentialing exam in any

State in the country. Each State regulates veterinary technicians and technologists differently; however, all States require them to pass a credentialing exam following coursework. Passing the State exam assures the public that the technician or technologist has sufficient knowledge to work in a veterinary clinic or hospital. Candidates are tested for competency through an examination that includes oral, written, and practical portions and that is regulated by the State Board of Veterinary Examiners or the appropriate State agency. Depending on the State, candidates may become registered, licensed, or certified. Most States, however, use the National Veterinary Technician (NVT) exam. Prospects usually can have their passing scores transferred from one State to another, so long as both States utilize the same exam.

Employers recommend American Association for Laboratory Animal Science (AALAS) certification for those seeking employment in a research facility. AALAS offers certification for three levels of technician competence, with a focus on three principal areas—animal husbandry, facility management, and animal health and welfare. Those who wish to become certified must satisfy a combination of education and experience requirements prior to taking an exam. Work experience must be directly related to the maintenance, health, and well-being of laboratory animals and must be gained in a laboratory animal facility as defined by AALAS. Candidates who meet the necessary criteria can begin pursuing the desired certification on the basis of their qualifications. The lowest level of certification is Assistant Laboratory Animal Technician (ALAT), the second level is Laboratory Animal Technician (LAT), and the highest level of certification is Laboratory Animal Technologist (LATG). The examination consists of multiple-choice questions and is longer and more difficult for higher levels of certification, ranging from 2 hours for the ALAT to 3 hours for the LATG.

Persons interested in careers as veterinary technologists and technicians should take as many high school science, biology, and math courses as possible. Science courses taken beyond high school, in an associate's or bachelor's degree program, should emphasize practical skills in a clinical or laboratory setting. Because veterinary technologists and technicians often deal with pet owners, communication skills are very important. In addition, technologists and technicians should be able to work well with others, because teamwork with veterinarians is common. Organizational ability and the ability to pay attention to detail also are important.

Technologists and technicians usually begin work as trainees in routine positions under the direct supervision of a veterinarian. Entry-level workers whose training or educational background encompasses extensive hands-on experience with a variety of laboratory equipment, including diagnostic and medical equipment, usually require a shorter period of on-the-job training. As they gain experience, technologists and technicians take on more responsibility and carry out more assignments under only general veterinary supervision. Some eventually may become supervisors.

Employment

Veterinary technologists and technicians held about 60,000 jobs in 2004. Most worked in veterinary services. The remainder worked in boarding kennels, animal shelters, stables, grooming salons, zoos, and local, State, and Federal agencies.

Job Outlook

Employment of veterinary technologists and technicians is expected to grow much faster than the average for all occupations through the year 2014. Job openings also will stem from the need to replace veterinary technologists and technicians who leave the occupation over the 2004–14 period. Keen competition is expected for veterinary technologist and technician jobs in zoos, due to expected slow growth in zoo capacity, low turnover among workers, the limited number of positions, and the fact that the occupation attracts many candidates.

Pet owners are becoming more affluent and more willing to pay for advanced care because many of them consider their pet to be part of the family. This growing affluence and view of pets will spur employment growth for veterinary technologists and technicians. The number of dogs used as companion pets, which also drives employment growth, is expected to increase more slowly during the projection period than in the previous decade. However, the rapidly growing number of cats utilized as companion pets is expected to boost the demand for feline medicine and services, offsetting any reduced demand for veterinary care for dogs. The availability of advanced veterinary services, such as preventive dental care and surgical procedures, may provide opportunities for workers specializing in those areas. Biomedical facilities, diagnostic laboratories, wildlife facilities, humane societies, animal control facilities, drug or food manufacturing companies, and food safety inspection facilities will provide additional jobs for veterinary technologists and technicians. Furthermore, demand for these workers will stem from the desire to replace veterinary assistants with more highly skilled technicians and technologists in animal clinics and hospitals, shelters, kennels, and humane societies.

Employment of veterinary technicians and technologists is relatively stable during periods of economic recession. Layoffs are less likely to occur among veterinary technologists and technicians than in some other occupations because animals will continue to require medical care.

Earnings

Median hourly earnings of veterinary technologists and technicians were $11.99 in May 2004. The middle 50 percent earned between $9.88 and $14.56. The bottom 10 percent earned less than $8.51, and the top 10 percent earned more than $17.12.

Related Occupations

Others who work extensively with animals include animal care and service workers, veterinary assistants, and laboratory animal caretakers. Like veterinary technologists and technicians, they must have patience and feel comfortable with animals. However, the level of training required for these occupations is less than that needed by veterinary technologists and technicians. Veterinarians, who need much more formal education, also work extensively with animals, preventing, diagnosing, and treating their diseases, disorders, and injuries.

Sources of Additional Information

For information on certification as a laboratory animal technician or technologist, contact:
➤ American Association for Laboratory Animal Science, 9190 Crestwyn Hills Dr., Memphis, TN 38125. Internet: **http://www.aalas.org**

For information on careers in veterinary medicine and a listing of AVMA-accredited veterinary technology programs, contact:
➤ American Veterinary Medical Assocation, 1931 N. Meacham Rd., Suite 100, Schaumburg, IL 60173-4360. Internet: **http://www.avma.org**

Dental Assistants

(O*NET 31-9091.00)

Significant Points

- Job prospects should be excellent.

- Dentists are expected to hire more assistants to perform routine tasks so that they may devote their own time to more complex procedures.

- Most assistants learn their skills on the job, although an increasing number are trained in dental-assisting programs; most programs take 1 year or less to complete.

Nature of the Work

Dental assistants perform a variety of patient care, office, and laboratory duties. They work chairside as dentists examine and treat patients. They make patients as comfortable as possible in the dental chair, prepare them for treatment, and obtain their dental records. Assistants hand instruments and materials to dentists and keep patients' mouths dry and clear by using suction or other devices. Assistants also sterilize and disinfect instruments and equipment, prepare trays of instruments for dental procedures, and instruct patients on postoperative and general oral health care.

Some dental assistants prepare materials for impressions and restorations, take dental x rays, and process x-ray film as directed by a dentist. They also may remove sutures, apply topical anesthetics

to gums or cavity-preventive agents to teeth, remove excess cement used in the filling process, and place rubber dams on the teeth to isolate them for individual treatment.

Those with laboratory duties make casts of the teeth and mouth from impressions, clean and polish removable appliances, and make temporary crowns. Dental assistants with office duties schedule and confirm appointments, receive patients, keep treatment records, send bills, receive payments, and order dental supplies and materials.

Dental assistants should not be confused with dental hygienists, who are licensed to perform different clinical tasks. (See the statement on dental hygienists elsewhere in the *Handbook*.)

Working Conditions

Dental assistants work in a well-lighted, clean environment. Their work area usually is near the dental chair so that they can arrange instruments, materials, and medication and hand them to the dentist when needed. Dental assistants must wear gloves, masks, eyewear, and protective clothing to protect themselves and their patients from infectious diseases. Assistants also follow safety procedures to minimize the risks associated with the use of x-ray machines.

About half of dental assistants have a 35- to 40-hour workweek, which may include work on Saturdays or evenings.

Training, Other Qualifications, and Advancement

Most assistants learn their skills on the job, although an increasing number are trained in dental-assisting programs offered by community and junior colleges, trade schools, technical institutes, or the Armed Forces. Assistants must be a second pair of hands for a dentist; therefore, dentists look for people who are reliable, work well with others, and have good manual dexterity. High school students interested in a career as a dental assistant should take courses in biology, chemistry, health, and office practices.

The Commission on Dental Accreditation within the American Dental Association (ADA) approved 265 dental-assisting training programs in 2005. Programs include classroom, laboratory, and preclinical instruction in dental-assisting skills and related theory. In addition, students gain practical experience in dental schools, clinics, or dental offices. Most programs take 1 year or less to complete and lead to a certificate or diploma. Two-year programs offered in community and junior colleges lead to an associate degree. All programs require a high school diploma or its equivalent, and some require science or computer-related courses for admission. A number of private vocational schools offer 4-month to 6-month courses in dental assisting, but the Commission on Dental Accreditation does not accredit these programs.

Most States regulate the duties that dental assistants are allowed to perform through licensure or registration. Licensure or registration may require passing a written or practical examination. States offering licensure or registration have a variety of schools offering courses—approximately 10 to 12 months in length—that meet their State's requirements. Other States require dental assistants to complete State-approved education courses of 4 to 12 hours in length. Some States offer registration of other dental assisting credentials with little or no education required. Some States require continuing education to maintain licensure or registration. A few States allow dental assistants to perform any function delegated to them by the dentist.

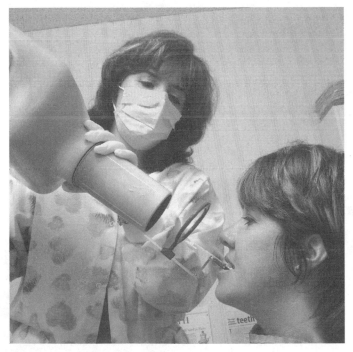

About 2 out of 5 dental assistants work part time, sometimes in more than one dental office.

Individual States have adopted different standards for dental assistants who perform certain advanced duties, such as radiological procedures. Completion of the Radiation Health and Safety examination offered by the Dental Assisting National Board (DANB) meets those standards in more than 30 States. Some States require completion of a State-approved course in radiology as well.

Certification is available through DANB and is recognized or required in more than 30 States. Other organizations offer registration, most often at the State level. Certification is an acknowledgment of an assistant's qualifications and professional competence and may be an asset when one is seeking employment. candidates may qualify to take the DANB certification examination by graduating from an ADA-accredited dental assisting education program or by having 2 years of full-time, or 4 years of part-time, experience as a dental assistant. In addition, applicants must have current certification in cardiopulmonary resuscitation. For annual recertification, individuals must earn continuing education credits.

Without further education, advancement opportunities are limited. Some dental assistants become office managers, dental-assisting instructors, or dental product sales representatives. Others go back to school to become dental hygienists. For many, this entry-level occupation provides basic training and experience and serves as a steppingstone to more highly skilled and higher paying jobs.

Employment

Dental assistants held about 267,000 jobs in 2004. Almost all jobs for dental assistants were in offices of dentists. A small number of jobs were in the Federal, State, and local governments or in offices of physicians. About 2 out of 5 dental assistants worked part time, sometimes in more than one dental office.

Job Outlook

Job prospects for dental assistants should be excellent. Employment is expected to grow much faster than the average for all occupations through the year 2014. In fact, dental assistants is expected to be one of the fastest growing occupations over the 2004-14 projection period.

In addition to job openings due to employment growth, numerous job openings will arise out of the need to replace assistants who transfer to other occupations, retire, or leave for other reasons. Many opportunities are for entry-level positions offering on-the-job training.

Population growth and greater retention of natural teeth by middle-aged and older people will fuel demand for dental services. Older dentists, who have been less likely to employ assistants, are leaving the occupation and will be replaced by recent graduates, who are more likely to use one or even two assistants. In addition, as dentists' workloads increase, they are expected to hire more assistants to perform routine tasks, so that they may devote their own time to more complex procedures.

Earnings

Median hourly earnings of dental assistants were $13.62 in May 2004. The middle 50 percent earned between $11.06 and $16.65 an hour. The lowest 10 percent earned less than $9.11, and the highest 10 percent earned more than $19.97 an hour.

Benefits vary substantially by practice setting and may be contingent upon full-time employment. According to the American Dental Association (ADA), almost all full-time dental assistants employed by private practitioners received paid vacation time. The ADA also found that 9 out of 10 full-time and part-time dental assistants received dental coverage.

Related Occupations

Other workers supporting health practitioners include medical assistants, occupational therapist assistants and aides, pharmacy aides, pharmacy technicians, and physical therapist assistants and aides.

Sources of Additional Information

Information about career opportunities and accredited dental assistant programs is available from:
➤ Commission on Dental Accreditation, American Dental Association, 211 East Chicago Ave., Suite 1814, Chicago, IL 60611. Internet: **http://www.ada.org**

For information on becoming a Certified Dental Assistant and a list of State boards of dentistry, contact:
➤ Dental Assisting National Board, Inc., 676 North Saint Clair St., Suite 1880, Chicago, IL 60611. Internet: **http://www.danb.org**

For more information on a career as a dental assistant and general information about continuing education, contact:
➤ American Dental Assistants Association, 35 East Wacker Dr., Suite 1730, Chicago, IL 60601. Internet: **http://www.dentalassistant.org**

For more information about continuing education courses, contact:
➤ National Association of Dental Assistants, 900 South Washington St., Suite G-13, Falls Church, VA 22046.

Massage Therapists

(O*NET 31-9011.00)

Significant Points

● Employment is expected to grow faster than average over the 2004-2014 period as more people learn about the benefits of massage therapy.

● Many States require formal training and a national certification in order to practice massage therapy.

● This occupation contains a large number of part-time and self-employed workers.

Nature of the Work

Many physicians have been recommending massage therapy for years. Nearly 2,400 years. The medical benefits of "friction" were first documented in Western culture by the Greek physician Hippocrates around 400 BC. Today, massage therapy is being used as a means of treating painful ailments, decompressing tired and overworked muscles, reducing stress, rehabilitating sports injuries, and promoting general health. This is accomplished by manipulating a client's soft tissues in order to improve the body's circulation and remove waste products from the muscles.

While massage therapy is done for medical benefit, a massage can be given to simply relax or rejuvenate the person being massaged. It is important to note that this type of massage is not intended for a medical purpose, and provides medical value only through general stress reduction and increased energy levels. Massage therapy, on the other hand, is practiced by thoroughly trained individuals who provide specialized care with their client's medical health in mind.

Massage therapists can specialize in over 80 different types of massage, called modalities. Swedish massage, deep tissue massage, reflexology, acupressure, sports massage, and neuromuscular massage are just a few of the many approaches to massage therapy. Most massage therapists specialize in several modalities, which require different techniques. Some use exaggerated strokes ranging the length of a body part, while others use quick, percussion-like strokes with a cupped or closed hand. A massage can be as long as two hours or as short as five or ten minutes. Usually, the type of massage therapists give depends on the client's needs and the client's physical condition. For example, they use special techniques for elderly clients that they would not use for athletes, and they would use approaches for clients with injuries that would not be appropriate for clients seeking relaxation. There are also some forms of massage that are given solely to one type of client, for example prenatal massage and infant massage.

Massage therapists work by appointment. Before beginning a massage therapy session, therapists conduct an informal interview with the client to find out about the person's medical history and desired results from the massage. This gives therapists a chance to discuss which techniques could be beneficial to the client and which could be harmful. Because massage therapists tend to specialize in only a few areas of massage, customers will often be referred or seek a therapist with a certain type of massage in mind. Based on the person's goals, ailments, medical history, and stress- or pain-related problem areas, a massage therapist will conclude whether a massage would be harmful, and if not, move forward with the session while concentrating on any areas of particular discomfort to the client. While giving the massage, therapists alter their approach or concentrate on a particular area as necessary.

Many modalities of massage therapy use massage oils, lotions, or creams to massage and rub the client's muscles. Most massage therapists, particularly those who are self-employed, supply their own table or chair, sheets, pillows, and body lotions or oils. Most modalities of massage require clients to be covered in a sheet or blanket, and require clients to be undressed or to wear loose-fitting clothing. The therapist only exposes the body part on which he or she is currently massaging. Some types of massage are done without oils or lotions and are performed with the client fully-clothed.

Massage can be a delicate issue for some clients, and those clients may indicate that they are comfortable with contact only in specified areas. For this reason—and also for general purpose business risks—about half of all massage therapists have liability insurance, either through a professional association membership or through other insurance carriers.

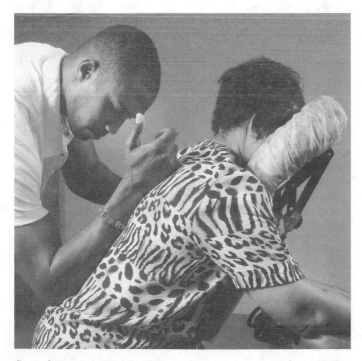

Seated massage is just one type of therapy used by massage therapists.

Massage therapists must develop a rapport with their clients if repeat customers are to be secured. Because those who seek a therapist tend to make regular visits, developing a loyal clientele is an important part of becoming successful.

Working Conditions

Massage therapists work in an array of settings both private and public: private offices, studios, hospitals, nursing homes, fitness centers, sports medicine facilities, airports, and shopping malls, for example. Some massage therapists also travel to clients' homes or offices to provide a massage. It is not uncommon for full-time massage therapists to divide their time among several different settings, depending on the clients and locations scheduled.

Most massage therapists give massages in dimly lit settings. Using candles and/or incense is not uncommon. Ambient or other calm, soothing music is often played. The dim lighting, smells, and background noise are meant to put clients at ease. On the other hand, when visiting a client's office, a massage therapist may not have those amenities. The working conditions depend heavily on a therapist's location and what the client wants.

Because massage is physically demanding, massage therapists can succumb to injury if the proper technique is not used. Repetitive motion problems and fatigue from standing for extended periods of time are most common. This risk can be limited by use of good technique, proper spacing between sessions, exercise, and in many cases by the therapists themselves receiving a massage on a regular basis.

Because of the physical nature of the work and time needed in between sessions, massage therapists typically give massages less than 40 hours per week. Therapists who give massages anywhere from 15 to 30 hours per week usually consider themselves to be full-time workers.

Training, Other Qualifications, and Advancement

Training standards and requirements for massage therapists vary greatly by State and locality. In 2004, 33 States and the District of Columbia had passed laws regulating massage therapy in some way. Most of the boards governing massage therapy in these States require practicing massage therapists to complete a formal education program and pass the national certification examination or a State exam. Some State regulations require that therapists keep up on their knowledge and technique through continuing education. It is best to check information on licensing, certification, and accreditation on a State-by-State basis.

There are roughly 1,300 massage therapy postsecondary schools, college programs, and training programs throughout the country. Massage therapy programs generally cover subjects such as anatomy; physiology, the study of organs and tissues; kinesiology, the study of motion and body mechanics; business; ethics; as well as hands-on practice of massage techniques. Most formal training programs require an application and some require an in-person interview. Training programs may concentrate on certain modalities of massage. Several programs also provide alumni services such as post-graduate job placement and continuing educational services. Both full- and part-time programs are available.

These programs vary in accreditation. Massage therapy training programs are generally accredited by a State board or other accrediting agency. Of the many massage therapy programs in the country, about 300 are accredited by a State board or department of education-certified accrediting agency. In States that regulate massage therapy, graduation from an approved school or training program is usually required in order to practice massage therapy.

After completion of a training program, many massage therapists opt to take the national certification examination for therapeutic massage and bodywork. This exam is administered by the National Certification Board for Therapeutic Massage and Bodywork (NCBTMB), which has eligibility requirements of its own. Several States require that a massage therapist pass this test in order to practice massage therapy. In States that require massage therapy program accreditation, an exam candidate must graduate from a State-licensed training institute with at least 500 hours of training or submit a portfolio of training experience for NCBTMB review; in locations that do not require accredited training programs, this is unnecessary. After the applicant is approved for testing, the applicant may schedule a test time at a local testing center. Tests are available six or seven days a week, depending on the test site, and are entirely computer based with multiple choice questions. The exam covers six areas of content: general knowledge of the body systems; detailed knowledge of anatomy, physiology and kinesiology; pathology; therapeutic massage assessment; therapeutic massage application; and professional standards, ethics, business and legal practices.

When a therapist passes the national certification exam for therapeutic massage and bodywork, he or she can use the recognized national credential: Nationally Certified in Therapeutic Massage and Bodywork (NCTMB). The credential must be renewed every four years. In order to remain certified, a therapist must perform at least 200 hours of therapeutic massage during the four year period, and complete a minimum of 48 credit hours of continuing education. In 2005, the NCBTMB introduced a new national certification test and corresponding professional credential. These are the national certification exam for therapeutic massage and the Nationally Certified in Therapeutic Massage (NCTM) credential. The new test covers the same topics as the traditional national certification exam, but covers fewer modalities of massage therapy. Recognition of this new national certification varies by State.

Many of the national, State, and local requirements coincide. States that require the national credential also require accredited training programs to comply with NCBTMB standards of training. Professional associations require that a professional member graduate from a training program that meets NCBTMB standards, have a State license, and/or have a national certification from the NCBTMB. Actual requirements differ on a State-by-State basis.

Because of the nature of massage therapy, opportunities for advancement are limited. However, with increased experience and an expanding client base, there are opportunities for therapists to increase client fees, and therefore income. Both strong communication skills and a friendly, empathetic personality are extremely helpful qualities for fostering a trusting relationship with clients and in turn, expanding one's client base. In addition, those who are well organized and have an entrepreneurial spirit may even go into business for themselves. Self-employed massage therapists with a large client base have the highest earnings.

Employment

Massage therapists held about 97,000 jobs in 2004. About two-thirds were self-employed. Of those self-employed, most owned their own business, and the rest worked as independent contractors. Others found employment in salons and spas; the offices of physicians and chiropractors; fitness and recreational sports centers; and hotels. About three-quarters of all massage therapists worked part-time or had variable schedules, although as mentioned earlier many massage therapists who work 15 to 30 hours per week consider themselves to be full-time workers.

Job Outlook

Employment for massage therapists is expected to increase faster than average over the period from 2004 to 2014 as more people learn about the benefits of massage therapy. In States that regulate massage therapy, therapists who complete formal training programs and pass the national certification exam are likely to have very good job opportunities. Because referrals are a very important source of work for massage therapists, networking will increase the number of job opportunities. Joining a State or local chapter of a professional association can also help build strong contacts and further increase the likelihood of steady work.

Massage is an increasingly popular technique for relaxation and reduction of stress. As workplaces try to distinguish themselves as employee-friendly, providing professional in-office, seated massages for employees is becoming a popular on-the-job benefit.

Increased interest in alternative medicine and holistic healing will mean increased opportunities for those skilled in massage therapy. Healthcare providers and medical insurance companies are beginning to recognize massage therapy as a legitimate treatment and preventative measure for several types of injuries and illnesses. The health care industry is using massage therapy more often as a supplement to conventional medical techniques for ailments such as muscle problems, some sicknesses and diseases, and stress-related health problems. Massage therapy's growing acceptance as a medical tool, particularly by the medical provider and insurance industries, will greatly increase employment opportunities.

Older citizens who are in nursing homes or assisted living homes are also finding benefits from massage, such as increased energy levels and reduced health problems. Demand for massage therapy should grow among older age groups because they increasingly enjoy longer, more active lives and persons age 55 and older are projected to be the most rapidly growing segment of the U.S. population over the next decade. However, demand for massage therapy is presently greatest among young adults, and they are likely to continue to enjoy the benefits of massage therapy as they age.

Earnings

Median hourly earnings of massage therapists, including gratuities earned, were $15.36 in May 2004. The middle 50 percent earned between $9.78 and $23.82. The lowest 10 percent earned less than $7.16, and the highest 10 percent earned more than $32.21. Generally, massage therapists earn 15 to 20 percent of their income as gratuities. For those who work in a hospital or other clinical setting, however, tipping is not common.

Related Occupations

Other workers in the healthcare industry who provide therapy to clients include physical therapists, physical therapists' assistants and aides, chiropractors, and workers in other occupations that use touch to aid healing or relieve stress.

Sources of Additional Information

General information on becoming a massage therapist is available from State regulatory boards.

For more information on becoming a massage therapist, contact:
➤ Associated Bodywork & Massage Professionals, 1271 Sugarbush Dr., Evergreen, CO 80439.
➤ American Massage Therapy Association, 500 Davis St., Suite 900, Evanston, IL 60201. Internet: **http://www.amtamassage.org**

For a directory of schools providing accredited massage therapy training programs, contact:
➤ Commission on Massage Therapy Accreditation, 1007 Church St., Suite 302, Evanston, IL 60201. Internet: **http://www.comta.org**
➤ Accrediting Commission of Career Schools and Colleges of Technology, 2101 Wilson Blvd., Suite 302, Arlington, VA 22201. Internet: **http://www.accsct.org**

Information on national testing and national certification is available from:
➤ National Certification Board for Therapeutic Massage and Bodywork, 1901 S. Meyers Rd., Suite 240, Oakbrook Terrace, IL 60181.

Medical Assistants

(O*NET 31-9092.00)

Significant Points

- About 6 out of 10 medical assistants work in offices of physicians.

- Some medical assistants are trained on the job, but many complete 1- or 2-year programs in vocational-technical high schools, postsecondary vocational schools, and community and junior colleges.

- Medical assistants is projected to be one of the fastest growing occupations over the 2004-14 period.

- Job prospects should be best for medical assistants with formal training or experience, particularly those with certification.

Nature of the Work

Medical assistants perform administrative and clinical tasks to keep the offices of physicians, podiatrists, chiropractors, and other health practitioners running smoothly. They should not be confused with physician assistants, who examine, diagnose, and treat patients under the direct supervision of a physician. (Physician assistants are discussed elsewhere in the *Handbook*.)

The duties of medical assistants vary from office to office, depending on the location and size of the practice and the practitioner's specialty. In small practices, medical assistants usually are generalists, handling both administrative and clinical duties and reporting directly to an office manager, physician, or other health practitioner. Those in large practices tend to specialize in a particular area, under the supervision of department administrators.

Medical assistants perform many administrative duties, including answering telephones, greeting patients, updating and filing patients' medical records, filling out insurance forms, handling correspondence, scheduling appointments, arranging for hospital admission and laboratory services, and handling billing and bookkeeping.

Clinical duties vary according to State law and include taking medical histories and recording vital signs, explaining treatment procedures to patients, preparing patients for examination, and assisting the physician during the examination. Medical assistants collect and prepare laboratory specimens or perform basic laboratory tests on the premises, dispose of contaminated supplies, and sterilize medical instruments. They instruct patients about medications and special diets, prepare and administer medications as directed by a physician, authorize drug refills as directed, telephone prescriptions to a pharmacy, draw blood, prepare patients for x rays, take electrocardiograms, remove sutures, and change dressings.

Medical assistants also may arrange examining room instruments and equipment, purchase and maintain supplies and equipment, and keep waiting and examining rooms neat and clean.

Ophthalmic medical assistants and *podiatric medical assistants* are examples of specialized assistants who have additional duties. Ophthalmic medical assistants help ophthalmologists provide eye care. They conduct diagnostic tests, measure and record vision, and test eye muscle function. They also show patients how to insert, remove, and care for contact lenses, and they apply eye dressings. Under the direction of the physician, ophthalmic medical assistants may administer eye medications. They also maintain optical and surgical instruments and may assist the ophthalmologist in surgery. Podiatric medical assistants make castings of feet, expose and develop x rays, and assist podiatrists in surgery.

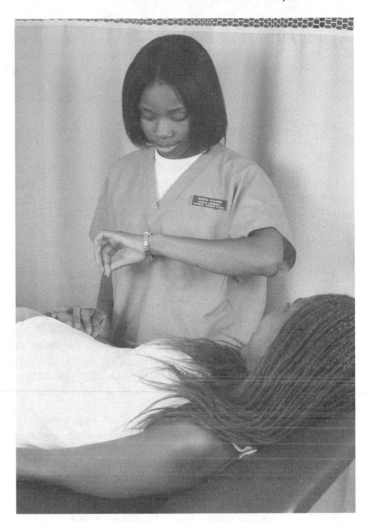

Clinical duties of medical assistants vary according to State law and include taking medical histories and recording vital signs.

Working Conditions

Medical assistants work in well-lighted, clean environments. They constantly interact with other people and may have to handle several responsibilities at once.

Most full-time medical assistants work a regular 40-hour week. Many work part time, evenings, or weekends.

Training, Other Qualifications, and Advancement

Most employers prefer graduates of formal programs in medical assisting. Such programs are offered in vocational-technical high schools, postsecondary vocational schools, and community and junior colleges. Postsecondary programs usually last either 1 year, resulting in a certificate or diploma, or 2 years, resulting in an associate degree. Courses cover anatomy, physiology, and medical terminology, as well as typing, transcription, recordkeeping, accounting, and insurance processing. Students learn laboratory techniques, clinical and diagnostic procedures, pharmaceutical principles, the administration of medications, and first aid. They study office practices, patient relations, medical law, and ethics. Accredited programs include an internship that provides practical experience in physicians' offices, hospitals, or other health care facilities.

Both the Commission on Accreditation of Allied Health Education Programs (CAAHEP) and the Accrediting Bureau of Health Education Schools (ABHES) accredit programs in medical assisting. In 2005, there were over 500 medical assisting programs accredited by CAAHEP and about 170 accredited by ABHES. The Committee on Accreditation for Ophthalmic Medical Personnel approved 17 programs in ophthalmic medical assisting and 2 programs in ophthalmic clinical assisting.

Formal training in medical assisting, while generally preferred, is not always required. Some medical assistants are trained on the job, although this practice is less common than in the past. Applicants usually need a high school diploma or the equivalent. Recommended high school courses include mathematics, health, biology, typing, bookkeeping, computers, and office skills. Volunteer experience in the health care field also is helpful.

Although medical assistants are not licensed, some States require them to take a test or a course before they can perform certain tasks, such as taking x rays or giving injections.

Employers prefer to hire experienced workers or certified applicants who have passed a national examination, indicating that the medical assistant meets certain standards of competence. The American Association of Medical Assistants awards the Certified Medical Assistant credential; American Medical Technologists awards the Registered Medical Assistant credential; the American Society of Podiatric Medical Assistants awards the Podiatric Medical Assistant, Certified credential; and the Joint Commission on Allied Health Personnel in Ophthalmology awards credentials at three levels: Certified Ophthalmic Assistant; Certified Ophthalmic Technician; and Certified Ophthalmic Medical Technologist.

Medical assistants deal with the public; therefore, they must be neat and well groomed and have a courteous, pleasant manner. Medical assistants must be able to put patients at ease and explain physicians' instructions. They must respect the confidential nature of medical information. Clinical duties require a reasonable level of manual dexterity and visual acuity.

Medical assistants may be able to advance to office manager. They may qualify for a variety of administrative support occupations or may teach medical assisting. With additional education, some enter other health occupations, such as nursing and medical technology.

Employment

Medical assistants held about 387,000 jobs in 2004. About 6 out of 10 worked in offices of physicians; about 14 percent worked in public and private hospitals, including inpatient and outpatient facilities; and 11 percent worked in offices of other health practitioners, such as chiropractors, optometrists, and podiatrists. The rest worked mostly in outpatient care centers, public and private educational services, other ambulatory health care services, State and local government agencies, employment services, medical and diagnostic laboratories, and nursing care facilities.

Job Outlook

Employment of medical assistants is expected to grow much faster than the average for all occupations through the year 2014 as the health care industry expands because of technological advances in medicine and the growth and aging of the population. Increasing utilization of medical assistants in the rapidly growing health care industry will further stimulate job growth. In fact, medical assistants is projected to be one of the fastest growing occupations over the 2004–14 period.

Employment growth will be driven by the increase in the number of group practices, clinics, and other health care facilities that need a high proportion of support personnel, particularly the flexible medical assistant who can handle both administrative and clinical duties. Medical assistants work primarily in outpatient settings, a rapidly growing sector of the health care industry.

In view of the preference of many health care employers for trained personnel, job prospects should be best for medical assistants with formal training or experience, particularly for those with certification.

Earnings

The earnings of medical assistants vary, depending on their experience, skill level, and location. Median annual earnings of medical assistants were $24,610 in May 2004. The middle 50 percent earned between $20,650 and $28,930. The lowest 10 percent earned less than $18,010, and the highest 10 percent earned more than $34,650. Median annual earnings in the industries employing the largest numbers of medical assistants in May 2004 were:

Colleges, universities, and professional schools	$27,490
Outpatient care centers	25,360
General medical and surgical hospitals	25,160
Offices of physicians	24,930
Offices of other health practitioners	21,930

Related Occupations

Workers in other medical support occupations include dental assistants, medical records and health information technicians, medical secretaries, occupational therapist assistants and aides, pharmacy aides, and physical therapist assistants and aides.

Sources of Additional Information

Information about career opportunities and the Certified Medical Assistant exam is available from:

➤ American Association of Medical Assistants, 20 North Wacker Dr., Suite 1575, Chicago, IL 60606. Internet: **http://www.aama-ntl.org**

Information about career opportunities and the Registered Medical Assistant certification exam is available from:

➤ American Medical Technologists, 710 Higgins Rd., Park Ridge, IL 60068-5765.

Information about career opportunities, training programs, and certification for ophthalmic medical personnel is available from:

➤ Joint Commission on Allied Health Personnel in Ophthalmology, 2025 Woodlane Dr., St. Paul, MN 55125-2998. Internet: **http://www.jcahpo.org/newsite/index.htm**

Information about certification for podiatric assistants is available from:

➤ American Society of Podiatric Medical Assistants, 2124 South Austin Blvd., Cicero, IL 60804. Internet: **http://www.aspma.org**

For a list of educational programs in medical assisting accredited by the Commission on Accreditation of Allied Health Education Programs, contact:

➤ Commission on Accreditation of Allied Health Education Programs, 1361 Park St., Clearwater, FL 33756. Internet: **http://www.caahep.org**

A list of ABHES-accredited educational programs in medical assisting is available from:

➤ Accrediting Bureau of Health Education Schools, 7777 Leesburg Pike, Suite 314 N, Falls Church, VA 22043. Internet: **http://www.abhes.org**

Medical Transcriptionists

(O*NET 31-9094.00)

Significant Points

● Job opportunities will be good.

● Employers prefer medical transcriptionists who have completed a postsecondary training program at a vocational school or community college.

● Many medical transcriptionists telecommute from home-based offices as employees or subcontractors for hospitals and transcription services or as self-employed, independent contractors.

● About 4 out of 10 worked in hospitals and another 3 out of 10 worked in offices of physicians.

Nature of the Work

Medical transcriptionists listen to dictated recordings made by physicians and other health care professionals and transcribe them into medical reports, correspondence, and other administrative material. They generally listen to recordings on a headset, using a foot pedal to pause the recording when necessary, and key the text into a personal computer or word processor, editing as necessary for grammar and clarity. The documents they produce include discharge summaries, history and physical examination reports, operative reports, consultation reports, autopsy reports, diagnostic imaging studies, progress notes, and referral letters. Medical transcriptionists return transcribed documents to the physicians or other health care professionals who dictated them for review and signature, or correction. These documents eventually become part of patients' permanent files.

To understand and accurately transcribe dictated reports into a format that is clear and comprehensible for the reader, medical transcriptionists must understand medical terminology, anatomy and physiology, diagnostic procedures, pharmacology, and treatment assessments. They also must be able to translate medical jargon and abbreviations into their expanded forms. To help identify terms appropriately, transcriptionists refer to standard medical reference materials—both printed and electronic; some of these are available over the Internet. Medical transcriptionists must comply with specific standards that apply to the style of medical records, in addition to the legal and ethical requirements involved with keeping patient information confidential.

Experienced transcriptionists spot mistakes or inconsistencies in a medical report and check to correct the information. Their ability to understand and correctly transcribe patient assessments and treatments reduces the chance of patients receiving ineffective or even harmful treatments and ensures high-quality patient care.

Currently, most health care providers transmit dictation to medical transcriptionists using either digital or analog dictating equipment. The Internet has grown to be a popular mode for transmitting documentation. Many transcriptionists receive dictation over the Internet and are able to quickly return transcribed documents to clients for approval. Another increasingly popular method utilizes speech recognition technology, which electronically translates sound into text and creates drafts of reports. Reports are then formatted; edited for mistakes in translation, punctuation, or grammar, and checked for consistency and any possible medical errors. Transcriptionists working in areas with standardized terminology, such as radiology or pathology, are more likely to encounter speech recognition technol-

Many medical transcriptionists receive dictation over the Internet and are able to quickly return transcribed documents to clients for approval.

ogy. However, use of speech recognition technology will become more widespread as the technology becomes more sophisticated.

Medical transcriptionists who work in physicians' offices may have other office duties, such as receiving patients, scheduling appointments, answering the telephone, and handling incoming and outgoing mail. Medical secretaries, discussed in the statement on secretaries and administrative assistants elsewhere in the *Handbook*, also may transcribe as part of their jobs. Court reporters, also discussed elsewhere in the *Handbook*, have similar duties, but with a different focus. They take verbatim reports of speeches, conversations, legal proceedings, meetings, and other events when written accounts of spoken words are necessary for correspondence, records, or legal proof.

Working Conditions

The majority of these workers are employed in comfortable settings, such as hospitals, physicians' offices, transcription service offices, clinics, laboratories, medical libraries, government medical facilities, or their own homes. Many medical transcriptionists telecommute from home-based offices as employees or subcontractors for hospitals and transcription services or as self-employed, independent contractors.

Work in this occupation presents hazards from sitting in the same position for long periods. Workers can suffer wrist, back, neck, or eye problems due to strain and risk repetitive motion injuries such as carpal tunnel syndrome. The constant pressure to be accurate and productive also can be stressful.

Many medical transcriptionists work a standard 40-hour week. Self-employed medical transcriptionists are more likely to work irregular hours—including part time, evenings, weekends, or on call at any time.

Training, Other Qualifications, and Advancement

Employers prefer to hire transcriptionists who have completed postsecondary training in medical transcription, offered by many vocational schools, community colleges, and distance-learning programs. Completion of a 2-year associate degree or 1-year certificate program—including coursework in anatomy, medical terminology, legal issues relating to health care documentation, and English grammar and punctuation—is highly recommended, but not always required. Many of these programs include supervised on-the-job experience. Some transcriptionists, especially those already familiar with medical terminology from previous experience as a nurse or medical secretary, become proficient through refresher courses and training.

The American Association for Medical Transcription (AAMT) awards the voluntary designation Certified Medical Transcriptionist (CMT), to those who earn a passing score on a certification examination. As in many other fields, certification is recognized as a sign of competence. Because medicine is constantly evolving, medical transcriptionists are encouraged to update their skills regularly. Every 3 years, CMTs must earn continuing education credits to be recertified.

In addition to understanding medical terminology, transcriptionists must have good English grammar and punctuation skills, as well as proficiency with personal computers and word processing software. Normal hearing acuity and good listening skills also are necessary. Employers require applicants to take pre-employment tests and usually prefer individuals with experience.

With experience, medical transcriptionists can advance to supervisory positions, home-based work, editing, consulting, or teaching. With additional education or training, some become medical records and health information technicians, medical coders, or medical records and health information administrators.

Employment

Medical transcriptionists held about 105,000 jobs in 2004. About 4 out of 10 worked in hospitals and another 3 out of 10 worked in offices of physicians. Others worked for business support services; medical and diagnostic laboratories; outpatient care centers; and offices of physical, occupational and speech therapists, and audiologists.

Job Outlook

Job opportunities will be good. Employment of medical transcriptionists is projected to grow faster than the average for all occupations through 2014. Demand for medical transcription services will be spurred by a growing and aging population. Older age groups receive proportionately greater numbers of medical tests, treatments, and procedures that require documentation. A high level of demand for transcription services also will be sustained by the continued need for electronic documentation that can easily be shared among providers, third-party payers, regulators, consumers, and health information systems. Growing numbers of medical transcriptionists will be needed to amend patients' records, edit documents from speech recognition systems, and identify discrepancies in medical reports.

Contracting out transcription work overseas and advancements in speech recognition technology are not expected to significantly reduce the need for well-trained medical transcriptionists. Outsourcing transcription work abroad—to countries such as India, Pakistan, Philippines, and the Caribbean—has grown more popular as transmitting confidential health information over the Internet has become more secure; however, the demand for overseas transcription services is expected only to supplement the demand for well-trained domestic medical transcriptionists. In addition, reports transcribed by overseas medical transcription services usually require editing for accuracy by domestic medical transcriptionists before they meet domestic quality standards. Speech-recognition technology allows physicians and other health professionals to dictate medical reports to a computer that immediately creates an electronic document. In spite of the advances in this technology, the software has been slow to grasp and analyze the human voice and the English language, and the medical vernacular with all its diversity. As a result, there will continue to be a need for skilled medical transcriptionists to identify and appropriately edit the inevitable errors created by speech recognition systems, and to create a final document.

Hospitals will continue to employ a large percentage of medical transcriptionists, but job growth there will not be as fast as in other industries. An increasing demand for standardized records should result in rapid employment growth in physicians' offices, especially in large group practices.

Earnings

Medical transcriptionists had median hourly earnings of $13.64 in May 2004. The middle 50 percent earned between $11.50 and $16.32. The lowest 10 percent earned less than $9.67, and the highest 10 percent earned more than $19.11. Median hourly earnings in the industries employing the largest numbers of medical transcriptionists in May 2004 were:

General medical and surgical hospitals	$13.83
Offices of physicians	13.40
Business support services	13.40

Compensation methods for medical transcriptionists vary. Some are paid based on the number of hours they work or on the number of lines they transcribe. Others receive a base pay per hour with incentives for extra production. Employees of transcription services and independent contractors almost always receive production-based pay. Independent contractors earn more than do transcriptionists who work for others, but independent contractors have higher expenses than their corporate counterparts, receive no benefits, and may face higher risk of termination than do employed transcriptionists.

Related Occupations

A number of other workers type, record information, and process paperwork. Among these are court reporters; human resources assistants, except payroll and timekeeping; receptionists and information clerks; and secretaries and administrative assistants. Other workers who provide medical support include medical assistants and medical records and health information technicians.

Sources of Additional Information

For information on a career as a medical transcriptionist, send a self-addressed, stamped envelope to:
➤ American Association for Medical Transcription, 100 Sycamore Ave., Modesto, CA 95354-0550. Internet: http://www.aamt.org

State employment service offices can provide information about job openings for medical transcriptionists.

Nursing, Psychiatric, and Home Health Aides

(O*NET 31-1011.00, 31-1012.00, 31-1013.00)

Significant Points

- Home health aides is projected to be the fastest growing occupation through 2014.

- Numerous job openings and excellent job opportunities are expected.

- Most jobs are in nursing and residential care facilities, hospitals, and home health care services.

- Modest entry requirements, low pay, high physical and emotional demands, and lack of advancement opportunities characterize this occupation.

Nature of the Work

Nursing and psychiatric aides help care for physically or mentally ill, injured, disabled, or infirm individuals confined to hospitals, nursing care facilities, and mental health settings. Home health aides have duties that are similar, but they work in patients' homes or residential care facilities.

Nursing aides—also known as nursing assistants, certified nursing assistants, geriatric aides, unlicensed assistive personnel, orderlies, or hospital attendants—perform routine tasks under the supervision of nursing and medical staff. They answer patients' call lights; deliver messages; serve meals; make beds; and help patients to eat, dress, and bathe. Aides also may provide skin care to patients; take their temperature, pulse rate, respiration rate, and blood pressure; and help them to get into and out of bed and walk. They also may escort patients to operating and examining rooms, keep patients' rooms neat, set up equipment, store and move supplies, and assist with some procedures. Aides observe patients' physical, mental, and emotional conditions and report any change to the nursing or medical staff.

Nursing aides employed in nursing care facilities often are the principal caregivers, having far more contact with residents than do other members of the staff. Because some residents may stay in a nursing care facility for months or even years, aides develop ongoing relationships with them and interact with them in a positive, caring way.

Home health aides help elderly, convalescent, or disabled persons live in their own homes instead of in a health care facility. Under the direction of nursing or medical staff, they provide health-related services, such as administering oral medications. (Personal and home care aides, who provide mainly housekeeping and routine personal care services, are discussed elsewhere in the *Handbook.*) Like nursing aides, home health aides may check patients' pulse rate, temperature, and respiration rate; help with simple prescribed exercises; keep patients' rooms neat; and help patients to move from bed, bathe, dress, and groom. Occasionally, they change nonsterile dressings, give massages and alcohol rubs, or assist with braces and artificial limbs. Experienced home health aides also may assist with medical equipment such as ventilators, which help patients breathe.

Most home health aides work with elderly or disabled persons who need more extensive care than family or friends can provide. Some help discharged hospital patients who have relatively short-term needs.

In home health agencies, a registered nurse, physical therapist, or social worker usually assigns specific duties to and supervises home health aides, who keep records of the services they perform and record each patient's condition and progress. The aides report changes in a patient's condition to the supervisor or case manager.

Psychiatric aides, also known as mental health assistants or psychiatric nursing assistants, care for mentally impaired or emotionally disturbed individuals. They work under a team that may include psychiatrists, psychologists, psychiatric nurses, social workers, and therapists.

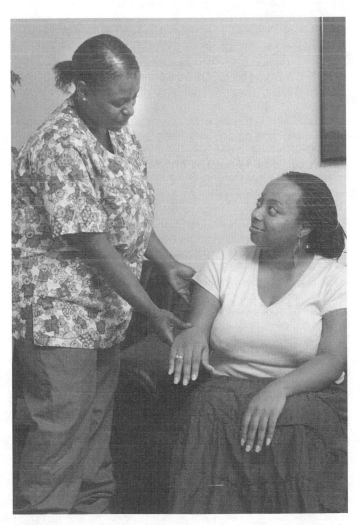

Taking a patient's pulse is one of the many routine medical tasks performed by aides.

In addition to helping patients to dress, bathe, groom themselves, and eat, psychiatric aides socialize with them and lead them in educational and recreational activities. Psychiatric aides may play games such as cards with the patients, watch television with them, or participate in group activities, such as sports or field trips. They observe patients and report any physical or behavioral signs that might be important for the professional staff to know. They accompany patients to and from examinations and treatment. Because they have such close contact with patients, psychiatric aides can have a great deal of influence on their patients' outlook and treatment.

Working Conditions

Most full-time aides work about 40 hours a week, but, because patients need care 24 hours a day, some aides work evenings, nights, weekends, and holidays. Many work part time. In 2004, 25 percent of aides worked part time compared with 16 percent of all workers. Aides spend many hours standing and walking, and they often face heavy workloads. Aides must guard against back injury because they may have to move patients into and out of bed or help them to stand or walk. Aides also may face hazards from minor infections and major diseases, such as hepatitis, but can avoid infections by following proper procedures.

Aides often have unpleasant duties, such as emptying bedpans and changing soiled bed linens. The patients they care for may be disoriented, irritable, or uncooperative. Psychiatric aides must be prepared to care for patients whose illness may cause violent behavior. While their work can be emotionally demanding, many aides gain satisfaction from assisting those in need.

Home health aides may go to the same patient's home for months or even years. However, most aides work with a number of different patients, each job lasting a few hours, days, or weeks. Home health aides often visit multiple patients on the same day.

Home health aides generally work alone, with periodic visits from their supervisor. They receive detailed instructions explaining when to visit patients and what services to perform. Aides are individually responsible for getting to patients' homes, and they may spend a good portion of the working day traveling from one patient to another. Because mechanical lifting devices available in institutional settings are seldom available in patients' homes, home health aides are particularly susceptible to injuries resulting from overexertion when they assist patients.

Training, Other Qualifications, and Advancement

In many cases, a high school diploma or equivalent is necessary for a job as a nursing or psychiatric aide. However, a high school diploma generally is not required for jobs as home health aides. Hospitals may require previous experience as a nursing aide or home health aide. Nursing care facilities often hire inexperienced workers, who must complete a minimum of 75 hours of mandatory training and pass a competency evaluation as part of a State-approved training program within 4 months of their employment. Aides who complete the program are known as certified nurse assistants (CNAs) and are placed on the State registry of nursing aides. Some States also require psychiatric aides to complete a formal training program. However, most psychiatric aides learn their skills on the job from experienced workers.

Nursing and psychiatric aide training is offered in high schools, vocational-technical centers, some nursing care facilities, and some community colleges. Courses cover body mechanics, nutrition, anatomy and physiology, infection control, communication skills, and resident rights. Personal care skills, such as how to help patients to bathe, eat, and groom themselves, also are taught.

Some employers provide classroom instruction for newly hired aides, while others rely exclusively on informal on-the-job instruction by a licensed nurse or an experienced aide. Such training may last from several days to a few months. Aides also may attend lectures, workshops, and in-service training.

The Federal Government has guidelines for home health aides whose employers receive reimbursement from Medicare. Federal law requires home health aides to pass a competency test covering a wide range of areas: communication; documentation of patient status and care provided; reading and recording of vital signs; basic infection-control procedures; basic bodily functions; maintenance of a healthy environment; emergency procedures; physical, emotional, and developmental characteristics of patients; personal hygiene and grooming; safe transfer techniques; normal range of motion and positioning; and basic nutrition.

A home health aide may receive training before taking the competency test. Federal law suggests at least 75 hours of classroom and practical training, supervised by a registered nurse. Training and testing programs may be offered by the employing agency but must meet the standards of the Center for Medicare and Medicaid Services. State regulations for training programs vary.

The National Association for Home Care offers national certification for home health aides. The certification is a voluntary demonstration that the individual has met industry standards. Some States also require aides to be licensed.

Aides must be in good health. A physical examination, including State-regulated tests such as those for tuberculosis, may be required. A criminal background check also is usually required for employment.

Applicants should be tactful, patient, understanding, emotionally stable, and dependable and should have a desire to help people. They also should be able to work as part of a team, have good communication skills, and be willing to perform repetitive, routine tasks. Home health aides should be honest and discreet, because they work in private homes. They also will need access to their own car or public transportation to reach patients' homes.

For some individuals, these occupations serve as entry-level jobs, as in the case of high school and college students who may work while also attending school. In addition, experience as an aide can help individuals decide whether to pursue a career in health care. Opportunities for advancement within these occupations are limited. Aides generally need additional formal training or education in order to enter other health occupations. The most common health care occupations for former aides are licensed practical nurse, registered nurse, and medical assistant.

Employment

Nursing, psychiatric, and home health aides held about 2.1 million jobs in 2004. Nursing aides held the most jobs—approximately 1.5 million. Home health aides held roughly 624,000 jobs and psychiatric aides held about 59,000 jobs. Around 42 percent of nursing aides worked in nursing care facilities, and another 27 percent worked in hospitals. Most home health aides—about 34 percent—were employed by home health care services. Others were employed in nursing and residential care facilities and social assistance agencies. Around 54 percent of all psychiatric aides worked in hospitals, primarily in psychiatric and substance abuse hospitals, although some also worked in the psychiatric units of general medical and surgical hospitals. Others were employed in State government agencies; residential mental retardation, mental health, and substance abuse facilities; outpatient care centers; and nursing care facilities.

Job Outlook

Numerous job openings for nursing, psychiatric, and home health aides will arise from a combination of fast employment growth and high replacement needs. High replacement needs in this large occupation reflect modest entry requirements, low pay, high physical and emotional demands, and lack of opportunities for advancement. For these same

reasons, many people are unwilling to perform the kind of work required by the occupation, limiting the number of entrants. Many aides also leave the occupation to attend training programs for other health care occupations. Therefore, persons who are interested in, and suited for, this work should have excellent job opportunities.

Overall employment of nursing, psychiatric, and home health aides is projected to grow much faster than the average for all occupations through the year 2014, although individual occupational growth rates will vary. Home health aides is expected to be the fastest growing occupation, as a result of both growing demand for home services from an aging population and efforts to contain costs by moving patients out of hospitals and nursing care facilities as quickly as possible. Consumer preference for care in the home and improvements in medical technologies for in-home treatment also will contribute to much-faster-than-average employment growth for home health aides.

Nursing aide employment will not grow as fast as home health aide employment, largely because nursing aides are concentrated in slower growing nursing care facilities and hospitals. Employment of nursing aides is expected to grow faster than the average for all occupations through 2014, in response to the long-term care needs of an increasing elderly population. Financial pressures on hospitals to discharge patients as soon as possible should boost admissions to nursing care facilities. As a result, job opportunities will be more numerous in nursing and residential care facilities than in hospitals. Modern medical technology also will drive demand for nursing aides because, as the technology saves and extends more lives, it increases the need for long-term care provided by aides.

Employment of psychiatric aides—the smallest of the three occupations—is expected to grow more slowly than the average for all occupations. Most psychiatric aides currently work in hospitals, but most job growth will be in residential mental health facilities and in home health care agencies. There is a long-term trend toward treating mental health patients outside of hospitals because it is more cost effective and allows patients to live more normal lives. Demand for psychiatric aides in residential facilities will rise in response to growth in the number of older persons—many of whom will require mental health services—but also as an increasing number of mentally disabled adults, who were formerly cared for by their elderly parents, seek care. Job growth also could be affected by changes in government funding of programs for the mentally ill.

Earnings

Median hourly earnings of nursing aides, orderlies, and attendants were $10.09 in May 2004. The middle 50 percent earned between $8.59 and $12.09 an hour. The lowest 10 percent earned less than $7.31, and the highest 10 percent earned more than $14.02 an hour. Median hourly earnings in the industries employing the largest numbers of nursing aides, orderlies, and attendants in May 2004 were as follows:

Employment services	$11.29
Local government	11.10
General medical and surgical hospitals	10.44
Nursing care facilities	9.86
Community care facilities for the elderly	9.56

Nursing and psychiatric aides in hospitals generally receive at least 1 week of paid vacation after 1 year of service. Paid holidays and sick leave, hospital and medical benefits, extra pay for late-shift work, and pension plans also are available to many hospital employees and to some nursing care facility employees.

Median hourly earnings of home health aides were $8.81 in May 2004. The middle 50 percent earned between $7.52 and $10.38 an hour. The lowest 10 percent earned less than $6.52, and the highest 10 percent earned more than $12.32 an hour. Median hourly earnings in the industries employing the largest numbers of home health aides in May 2004 were as follows:

Nursing care facilities	$9.11
Residential mental retardation, mental health and substance abuse facilities	8.97
Home health care services	8.57
Community care facilities for the elderly	8.57
Individual and family services	8.47

Home health aides receive slight pay increases with experience and added responsibility. Usually, they are paid only for the time worked in the home, not for travel time between jobs. Most employers hire only on-call hourly workers and provide no benefits.

Median hourly earnings of psychiatric aides were $11.19 in May 2004. The middle 50 percent earned between $9.09 and $14.09 an hour. The lowest 10 percent earned less than $7.63, and the highest 10 percent earned more than $16.74 an hour. Median hourly earnings in the industries employing the largest numbers of psychiatric aides in May 2004 were as follows:

General medical and surgical hospitals	$11.31
Psychiatric and substance abuse hospitals	11.06
Residential mental retardation, mental health and substance abuse facilities	9.37

Related Occupations

Nursing, psychiatric, and home health aides help people who need routine care or treatment. So do child care workers, licensed practical and licensed vocational nurses, medical assistants, occupational therapist assistants and aides, personal and home care aides, physical therapist assistants and aides, and registered nurses.

Sources of Additional Information

Information about employment opportunities may be obtained from local hospitals, nursing care facilities, home health care agencies, psychiatric facilities, State boards of nursing, and local offices of the State employment service.

Information on licensing requirements for nursing and home health aides, and lists of State-approved nursing aide programs are available from State departments of public health, departments of occupational licensing, boards of nursing, and home care associations.

Occupational Therapist Assistants and Aides

(O*NET 31-2011.00, 31-2012.00)

Significant Points

- Employment is projected to increase much faster than the average, reflecting growth in the number of individuals with disabilities or limited function who require therapeutic services.

- Occupational therapist assistants generally must complete an associate degree or a certificate program; in contrast, occupational therapist aides usually receive most of their training on the job.

- In an effort to control rising health care costs, third-party payers are expected to encourage occupational therapists to delegate more hands-on therapy work to lower-paid occupational therapist assistants and aides.

Nature of the Work

Occupational therapist assistants and aides work under the direction of occupational therapists to provide rehabilitative services to persons with mental, physical, emotional, or developmental impairments. The ultimate goal is to improve clients' quality of life and ability to perform daily activities. For example, occupational therapist assistants help injured workers re-enter the labor force by teaching them how to compensate for lost motor skills or help individuals with learning disabilities increase their independence.

Occupational therapist assistants, commonly known as *occupational therapy assistants*, help clients with rehabilitative activities and exercises outlined in a treatment plan developed in collaboration with an occupational therapist. Activities range from teaching the proper method of moving from a bed into a wheelchair to the best way to stretch and limber the muscles of the hand. Assistants monitor an individual's activities to make sure that they are performed correctly and to provide encouragement. They also record their client's progress for the occupational therapist. If the treatment is not having the intended effect, or the client is not improving as expected, the therapist may alter the treatment program in hopes of obtaining better results. In addition, occupational therapist assistants document the billing of the client's health insurance provider.

Occupational therapist aides typically prepare materials and assemble equipment used during treatment. They are responsible for a range of clerical tasks, including scheduling appointments, answering the telephone, restocking or ordering depleted supplies, and filling out insurance forms or other paperwork. Aides are not licensed, so the law does not allow them to perform as wide a range of tasks as occupational therapist assistants.

Working Conditions

The hours and days that occupational therapist assistants and aides work vary with the facility and with whether they are full- or part-time employees. Many outpatient therapy offices and clinics have evening and weekend hours, to help coincide with patients' personal schedules.

Occupational therapist assistants and aides need to have a moderate degree of strength, because of the physical exertion required in assisting patients with their treatment. For example, assistants and aides may need to lift patients. Constant kneeling, stooping, and standing for long periods also are part of the job.

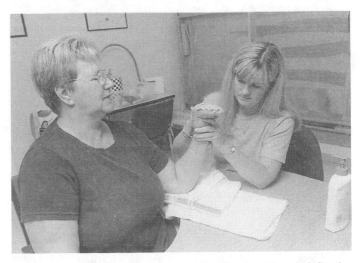

Occupational therapist assistants and aides provide rehabilitative services to persons with mental, physical, emotional, or developmental impairments.

Training, Other Qualifications, and Advancement

An associate degree or a certificate from an accredited community college or technical school is generally required to qualify for occupational therapist assistant jobs. In contrast, occupational therapist aides usually receive most of their training on the job.

There were 135 accredited occupational therapist assistant programs in 2005. The first year of study typically involves an introduction to health care, basic medical terminology, anatomy, and physiology. In the second year, courses are more rigorous and usually include occupational therapist courses in areas such as mental health, adult physical disabilities, gerontology, and pediatrics. Students also must complete 16 weeks of supervised fieldwork in a clinic or community setting. Applicants to occupational therapist assistant programs can improve their chances of admission by taking high school courses in biology and health and by performing volunteer work in nursing care facilities, occupational or physical therapists' offices, or other health care settings.

Occupational therapist assistants are regulated in most States and must pass a national certification examination after they graduate. Those who pass the test are awarded the title "Certified Occupational Therapy Assistant."

Occupational therapist aides usually receive most of their training on the job. Qualified applicants must have a high school diploma, strong interpersonal skills, and a desire to help people in need. Applicants may increase their chances of getting a job by volunteering their services, thus displaying initiative and aptitude to the employer.

Assistants and aides must be responsible, patient, and willing to take directions and work as part of a team. Furthermore, they should be caring and want to help people who are not able to help themselves.

Employment

Occupational therapist assistants and aides held about 27,000 jobs in 2004. Occupational therapist assistants held about 21,000 jobs, and occupational therapist aides held approximately 5,400. About 30 percent of jobs for assistants and aides were in hospitals, 23 percent were in offices of occupational therapists, and 18 percent were in nursing care facilities. The rest were primarily in community care facilities for the elderly, home health care services, individual and family services, and State government agencies.

Job Outlook

Employment of occupational therapist assistants and aides is expected to grow much faster than the average for all occupations through 2014. The impact of proposed Federal legislation imposing limits on reimbursement for therapy services may adversely affect the job market for occupational therapist assistants and aides in the short run. Over the long run, however, demand for occupational therapist assistants and aides will continue to rise because of the increasing number of individuals with disabilities or limited function. Job growth will result from an aging population, including the baby-boom generation, which will need more occupational therapy services. The increased prevalence of sensory disorders in children will increase the demand for occupational therapy services. Increasing demand also will result from advances in medicine that allow more people with critical problems to survive and then need rehabilitative therapy. In an effort to control rising health care costs, third-party payers are expected to encourage occupational therapists to delegate more hands-on therapy work to lower-paid occupational therapist assistants and aides.

Earnings

Median annual earnings of occupational therapist assistants were $38,430 in May 2004. The middle 50 percent earned between $31,970 and $44,390. The lowest 10 percent earned less than $25,880, and the highest 10 percent earned more than $52,700. Median annual earnings of occupational therapist assistants were $40,130 in offices of other health practitioners, which includes offices of occupational therapists.

Median annual earnings of occupational therapist aides were $23,150 in May 2004. The middle 50 percent earned between $19,080 and $31,910. The lowest 10 percent earned less than $15,820, and the highest 10 percent earned more than $41,560.

Related Occupations

Occupational therapist assistants and aides work under the supervision and direction of occupational therapists. Other workers in the health care field who work under similar supervision include dental assistants, medical assistants, pharmacy aides, pharmacy technicians, and physical therapist assistants and aides.

Sources of Additional Information

For information on a career as an occupational therapist assistant or aide, and a list of accredited programs, contact:
➤ American Occupational Therapy Association, 4720 Montgomery Lane, Bethesda, MD 20824-1220. Internet: **http://www.aota.org**

Pharmacy Aides

(O*NET 31-9095.00)

Significant Points

- Job opportunities are expected to be good for full-time and part-time work, especially for those with related work experience.

- Many pharmacy aides work evenings, weekends, and holidays.

- About 80 percent work in retail pharmacies, grocery stores, department stores, or mass retailers.

Nature of the Work

Pharmacy aides help licensed pharmacists with administrative duties in running a pharmacy. Aides often are clerks or cashiers who primarily answer telephones, handle money, stock shelves, and perform other clerical duties. They work closely with pharmacy technicians. *Pharmacy technicians* usually perform more complex tasks than do aides, although in some States the duties and titles of the jobs overlap. (See the statement on pharmacy technicians elsewhere in the *Handbook*.) Aides refer any questions regarding prescriptions, drug information, or health matters to a pharmacist. (See the statement on pharmacists elsewhere in the *Handbook*.)

Aides have several important duties that help the pharmacy to function smoothly. They may establish and maintain patient profiles, prepare insurance claim forms, and stock and take inventory of prescription and over-the-counter medications. Accurate recordkeeping is necessary to help avert dangerous drug interactions. In addition, because many people have medical insurance to help pay for prescriptions, it is essential that pharmacy aides correspond efficiently and correctly with the third-party insurance providers to obtain payment. Pharmacy

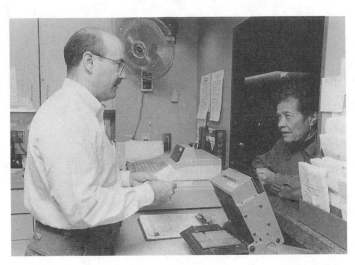

Pharmacy aides answer telephones, handle money, stock shelves, and perform other clerical duties.

aides also maintain inventory and inform the supervisor of stock needs so that the pharmacy does not run out of the vital medications that customers need. Some also clean pharmacy equipment, help with the maintenance of equipment and supplies, and manage the cash register.

Working Conditions

Pharmacy aides work in clean, organized, well-lighted, and well-ventilated areas. Most of their workday is spent on their feet. They may be required to lift heavy boxes or to use stepladders to retrieve supplies from high shelves.

Aides work the same hours that pharmacists work. These include evenings, nights, weekends, and some holidays, particularly in facilities, such as hospitals and retail pharmacies that are open 24 hours a day. There are many opportunities for part-time work in both retail and hospital settings.

Training, Other Qualifications, and Advancement

Most pharmacy aides receive informal on-the-job training, but employers favor those with at least a high school diploma. Prospective pharmacy aides with experience working as cashiers may have an advantage when applying for jobs. Employers also prefer applicants with strong customer service and communication skills, experience managing inventories, and experience using computers. Aides entering the field need strong spelling, reading, and mathematics skills.

Successful pharmacy aides are organized, dedicated, friendly, and responsible. They should be willing and able to take directions. Candidates interested in becoming pharmacy aides cannot have prior records of drug or substance abuse. Strong interpersonal and communication skills are needed because pharmacy aides interact daily with patients, coworkers, and health care professionals. Teamwork is very important because aides are often required to work with technicians and pharmacists.

Pharmacy aides almost always are trained on the job. They may begin by observing a more experienced worker. After they become familiar with the store's equipment, policies, and procedures, they begin to work on their own. Once they become experienced, aides are not likely to receive additional training, except when new equipment is introduced or when policies or procedures change.

To become a pharmacy aide, one should be able to perform repetitive work accurately. Aides need good basic mathematics skills and good manual dexterity. Pharmacy aides should be neat in appearance and able to deal pleasantly and tactfully with customers. Some employers may prefer people with experience typing, handling money, or operating specialized equipment, including computers.

Advancement usually is limited, although some aides may decide to become pharmacy technicians or to enroll in pharmacy school to become pharmacists.

Employment

Pharmacy aides held about 50,000 jobs in 2004. About 80 percent work in retail pharmacies either independently owned or part of a drug store chain, grocery store, department store, or mass retailer; the vast majority of these are in drug stores. About 10 percent work in hospitals, and the rest work in mail-order pharmacies, clinics, and pharmaceutical wholesalers.

Job Outlook

Job opportunities for full-time and part-time work are expected to be good, especially for aides with related work experience in pharmacies or as cashiers or stock clerks in other retail settings. Job openings will be created by employment growth and by the need to replace workers who transfer to other occupations or leave the labor force.

Employment of pharmacy aides is expected to grow about as fast as the average for all occupations through 2014 because of the increasing use of medication in treating patients. In addition, a greater number of middle-aged and elderly people—who use more prescription drugs than younger people—will spur demand for aides in all practice settings.

Cost-conscious insurers, pharmacies, and health systems will continue to employ aides. As a result, pharmacy aides will assume some responsibility for routine tasks previously performed by pharmacists and pharmacy technicians, thereby giving pharmacists more time to interact with patients and technicians more time to prepare medications. Employment of pharmacy aides will not grow as fast as employment of pharmacists and pharmacy technicians, however, because of legal limitations regarding aides' duties. Many smaller pharmacies that can afford only a small staff will favor pharmacy technicians because of their more extensive training and job skills.

Earnings

Median hourly wage and salary earnings of pharmacy aides were $8.86 in May 2004. The middle 50 percent earned between $7.39 and $10.96; the lowest 10 percent earned less than $6.34, and the highest 10 percent earned more than $13.79. In May 2004, median hourly earnings of pharmacy aides were $8.29 in health and personal care stores and $9.80 in grocery stores.

Related Occupations

The work of pharmacy aides is closely related to that of pharmacy technicians, cashiers, and stock clerks and order fillers. Workers in other medical support occupations include dental assistants, licensed practical and licensed vocational nurses, medical transcriptionists, medical records and health information technicians, occupational therapist assistants and aides, physical therapist assistants and aides, and surgical technologists.

Sources of Additional Information

For information on employment opportunities, contact local employers or local offices of the State employment service.

Physical Therapist Assistants and Aides

(O*NET 31-2021.00, 31-2022.00)

Significant Points

- Employment is projected to increase much faster than average; physical therapist aides may face keen competition from the large pool of qualified applicants.

- Physical therapist assistants generally have an associate degree, but physical therapist aides usually learn skills on the job.

- About 60 percent of jobs are in hospitals or offices of physical therapists.

Nature of the Work

Physical therapist assistants and aides perform components of physical therapy procedures and related tasks selected by a supervising physical therapist. These workers assist physical therapists in providing services that help improve mobility, relieve pain, and prevent or limit permanent physical disabilities of patients suffering from injuries or disease. Patients include accident victims and individuals with disabling conditions such as low-back pain, arthritis, heart disease, fractures, head injuries, and cerebral palsy.

Physical therapist assistants perform a variety of tasks. Components of treatment procedures performed by these workers, under the direction and supervision of physical therapists, involve exercises, massages, electrical stimulation, paraffin baths, hot and cold packs, traction, and ultrasound. Physical therapist assistants record the patient's responses to treatment and report the outcome of each treatment to the physical therapist.

Physical therapist aides help make therapy sessions productive, under the direct supervision of a physical therapist or physical therapist assistant. They usually are responsible for keeping the treatment area clean and organized and for preparing for each patient's therapy. When patients need assistance moving to or from a treatment area, aides push them in a wheelchair or provide them with a shoulder to lean on. Because they are not licensed, aides do not perform the clinical tasks of a physical therapist assistant.

The duties of aides include some clerical tasks, such as ordering depleted supplies, answering the phone, and filling out insurance forms and other paperwork. The extent to which an aide or an assistant performs clerical tasks depends on the size and location of the facility.

Working Conditions

The hours and days that physical therapist assistants and aides work vary with the facility and with whether they are full- or part-time employees. Many outpatient physical therapy offices and clinics have evening and weekend hours, to help coincide with patients' personal schedules. About 30 percent of all physical therapist assistants and aides work part time.

Physical therapist assistants and aides need a moderate degree of strength because of the physical exertion required in assisting patients with their treatment. In some cases, assistants and aides need to lift patients. Constant kneeling, stooping, and standing for long periods also are part of the job.

Training, Other Qualifications, and Advancement

Physical therapist aides are trained on the job, but physical therapist assistants typically earn an associate degree from an accred-

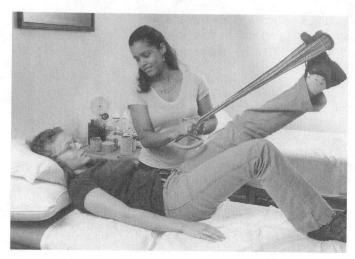

Physical therapist assistants and aides perform physical therapy procedures and related tasks.

ited physical therapist assistant program. Not all States require licensure or registration in order for the physical therapist assistant to practice. The States that require licensure stipulate specific educational and examination criteria. Complete information on practice acts and regulations can be obtained from the State licensing boards. Additional requirements may include certification in cardiopulmonary resuscitation (CPR) and other first aid and a minimum number of hours of clinical experience.

According to the American Physical Therapy Association, there were 238 accredited physical therapist assistant programs in the United States as of 2004. Accredited physical therapist assistant programs are designed to last 2 years, or 4 semesters, and culminate in an associate degree. Programs are divided into academic study and hands-on clinical experience. Academic course work includes algebra, anatomy and physiology, biology, chemistry, and psychology. Many programs require that students complete a semester of anatomy and physiology and have certifications in CPR and other first aid even before they begin their clinical field experience. Both educators and prospective employers view clinical experience as integral to ensuring that students understand the responsibilities of a physical therapist assistant.

Employers typically require physical therapist aides to have a high school diploma, strong interpersonal skills, and a desire to assist people in need. Most employers provide clinical on-the-job training.

Employment

Physical therapist assistants and aides held about 101,000 jobs in 2004. Physical therapist assistants held about 59,000 jobs, physical therapist aides approximately 43,000. Both work with physical therapists in a variety of settings. About 60 percent of jobs were in hospitals or in offices of physical therapists. Others worked primarily in nursing care facilities, offices of physicians, home health care services, and outpatient care centers.

Job Outlook

Employment of physical therapist assistants and aides is expected to grow much faster than the average for all occupations through the year 2014. The impact of proposed Federal legislation imposing limits on reimbursement for therapy services may adversely affect the short-term job outlook for physical therapist assistants and aides. However, over the long run, demand for physical therapist assistants and aides will continue to rise, in accordance with the increasing number of individuals with disabilities or limited function. The growing elderly population is particularly vulnerable to chronic and debilitating conditions that require therapeutic services. These patients often need additional assistance in their treatment, making the roles of assistants and aides vital. The large baby-boom generation is entering the prime age for heart attacks and strokes, further increasing the demand for cardiac and physical rehabilitation. In addition, future medical developments should permit an increased percentage of trauma victims to survive, creating added demand for therapy services.

Physical therapists are expected to increasingly utilize assistants to reduce the cost of physical therapy services. Once a patient is evaluated and a treatment plan is designed by the physical therapist, the physical therapist assistant can provide many aspects of treatment, as prescribed by the therapist.

Physical therapist assistants and aides with prior experience working in a physical therapy office or other health care setting will have the best job opportunities. Physical therapist aides may face keen competition from the large pool of qualified individuals with a high school diploma.

Earnings

Median annual earnings of physical therapist assistants were $37,890 in May 2004. The middle 50 percent earned between $31,060 and $44,050. The lowest 10 percent earned less than $24,110, and the highest 10 percent earned more than $52,110. Median annual earn-ings in the industries employing the largest numbers of physical therapists aides in May 2004 were:

Nursing care facilities	$40,360
General medical and surgical hospitals	37,790
Offices of other health practitioners	37,120

Median annual earnings of physical therapist aides were $21,380 in May 2004. The middle 50 percent earned between $17,990 and $26,310. The lowest 10 percent earned less than $15,380, and the highest 10 percent earned more than $33,550. Median annual earnings of physical therapist aides in May 2004 were $21,120 in general medical and surgical hospitals and $20,360 in offices of physical therapists.

Related Occupations

Physical therapist assistants and aides work under the supervision of physical therapists. Other workers in the health care field who work under similar supervision include dental assistants, medical assistants, occupational therapist assistants and aides, pharmacy aides, pharmacy technicians, and social and human service assistants.

Sources of Additional Information

Career information on physical therapist assistants and a list of schools offering accredited programs can be obtained from:
➤ The American Physical Therapy Association, 1111 North Fairfax St., Alexandria, VA 22314-1488. Internet: **http://www.apta.org**

Protective Service Occupations

Correctional Officers

(O*NET 33-1011.00, 33-3011.00, 33-3012.00)

Significant Points

- The work can be stressful and hazardous.
- Most correctional officers are employed in State and Federal prisons.
- Job opportunities are expected to be excellent.

Nature of the Work

Correctional officers are responsible for overseeing individuals who have been arrested and are awaiting trial or who have been convicted of a crime and sentenced to serve time in a jail, reformatory, or penitentiary. Correctional officers maintain security and inmate accountability to prevent disturbances, assaults, and escapes. Officers have no law enforcement responsibilities outside the institution where they work. (For more information on related occupations, see the statements on police and detectives and on probation officers and correctional treatment specialists, elsewhere in the *Handbook*.)

Police and sheriffs' departments in county and municipal jails or precinct station houses employ many correctional officers, also known as *detention officers*. Most of the approximately 3,400 jails in the United States are operated by county governments, with about three-quarters of all jails under the jurisdiction of an elected sheriff. Individuals in the jail population change constantly as some are released, some are convicted and transferred to prison, and new offenders are arrested and enter the system. Correctional

officers in local jails admit and process about 12 million people a year, with about 700,000 offenders in jail at any given time. When individuals are first arrested, the jail staff may not know their true identity or criminal record, and violent detainees may be placed in the general population. This is the most dangerous phase of the incarceration process for correctional officers.

Most correctional officers are employed in State and Federal prisons, watching over the approximately 1.4 million offenders who are incarcerated there at any given time. Other correctional officers oversee individuals being held by the U.S. Immigration and Naturalization Service pending release or deportation, or work for correctional institutions that are run by private for-profit organizations. Although both jails and prisons can be dangerous places to work, prison populations are more stable than jail populations, and correctional officers in prisons know the security and custodial requirements of the prisoners with whom they are dealing.

Regardless of the setting, correctional officers maintain order within the institution and enforce rules and regulations. To help ensure that inmates are orderly and obey rules, correctional officers monitor the activities and supervise the work assignments of inmates. Sometimes, officers must search inmates and their living quarters for contraband like weapons or drugs, settle disputes between inmates, and enforce discipline. Correctional officers periodically inspect the facilities, checking cells and other areas of the institution for unsanitary conditions, contraband, fire hazards, and any evidence of infractions of rules. In addition, they routinely inspect locks, window bars, grilles, doors, and gates for signs of tampering. Finally, officers inspect mail and visitors for prohibited items.

Correctional officers report orally and in writing on inmate conduct and on the quality and quantity of work done by inmates. Officers also report security breaches, disturbances, violations of rules, and any unusual occurrences. They usually keep a daily log or record of their activities. Correctional officers cannot show favoritism and must report any inmate who violates the rules. Should the situation arise, they help the responsible law enforcement authorities investigate crimes committed within their institution or search for escaped inmates.

In jail and prison facilities with direct supervision cellblocks, officers work unarmed. They are equipped with communications devices so that they can summon help if necessary. These officers often work in a cellblock alone, or with another officer, among the 50 to 100 inmates who reside there. The officers enforce regulations primarily through their interpersonal communications skills and through the use of progressive sanctions, such as the removal of some privileges.

In the highest security facilities, where the most dangerous inmates are housed, correctional officers often monitor the activities of prisoners from a centralized control center with closed-circuit television cameras and a computer tracking system. In such an environment, the inmates may not see anyone but officers for days or weeks at a time and may leave their cells only for showers, solitary exercise time, or visitors. Depending on the offenders' security classification within the institution, correctional officers may have to restrain inmates in handcuffs and leg irons to safely escort them to and from cells and other areas and to see authorized visitors. Officers also escort prisoners between the institution and courtrooms, medical facilities, and other destinations outside the institution.

Bailiffs, also known as *marshals* or *court officers*, are law enforcement officers who maintain safety and order in courtrooms. Their duties, which vary by location, include enforcing courtroom rules, assisting judges, guarding juries from outside contact, delivering court documents, and providing general security for courthouses.

Working Conditions

Working in a correctional institution can be stressful and hazardous. Every year, correctional officers are injured in confrontations with inmates. Correctional officers may work indoors or outdoors. Some correctional institutions are well lighted, temperature controlled, and ventilated, but others are old, overcrowded, hot, and noisy. Correctional officers usually work an 8-hour day, 5 days a week, on rotating shifts. Because prison and jail security must be provided around the clock, officers work all hours of the day and night, weekends, and holidays. In addition, officers may be required to work paid overtime.

In high security facilities, correctional officers often monitor prisoners from a centralized control center.

Training, Other Qualifications, and Advancement

Most institutions require correctional officers to be at least 18 to 21 years of age and a U.S. citizen; have a high school education or its equivalent; demonstrate job stability, usually by accumulating 2 years of work experience; and have no felony convictions. Promotion prospects may be enhanced by obtaining a postsecondary education.

The Federal Bureau of Prisons requires entry-level correctional officers to have at least a bachelor's degree; or 3 years of full-time experience in a field providing counseling, assistance, or supervision to individuals; or a combination of these two requirements.

Correctional officers must be in good health. Candidates for employment are generally required to meet formal standards of physical fitness, eyesight, and hearing. In addition, many jurisdictions use standard tests to determine applicant suitability to work in a correctional environment. Good judgment and the ability to think and act quickly are indispensable. Applicants are typically screened for drug abuse, subject to background checks, and required to pass a written examination.

Federal, State, and some local departments of corrections provide training for correctional officers based on guidelines established by the American Correctional Association and the American Jail Association. Some States have regional training academies that are available to local agencies. At the conclusion of formal instruction, all State and local correctional agencies provide on-the-job training, including training on legal restrictions and interpersonal relations. Many systems require firearms proficiency and self-defense skills. Officer trainees typically receive several weeks or months of training in an actual job setting under the supervision of an experienced officer. However, specific entry requirements and on-the-job training vary widely from agency to agency.

Academy trainees generally receive instruction in a number of subjects, including institutional policies, regulations, and operations, as well as custody and security procedures. New Federal correctional officers must undergo 200 hours of formal training within the first year of employment. They also must complete 120 hours of specialized training at the U.S. Federal Bureau of Prisons residential training center at Glynco, GA, within 60 days of their appointment. Experienced officers receive annual in-service training to keep abreast of new developments and procedures.

Some correctional officers are members of prison tactical response teams, which are trained to respond to disturbances, riots, hostage situations, forced cell moves, and other potentially dangerous confrontations. Team members practice disarming prisoners wielding weapons, protecting themselves and inmates against the effects of chemical agents, and other tactics.

With education, experience, and training, qualified officers may advance to the position of correctional sergeant. Correctional sergeants supervise correctional officers and usually are responsible for maintaining security and directing the activities of other officers during an assigned shift or in an assigned area. Ambitious and qualified correctional officers can be promoted to supervisory or administrative positions all the way up to warden. Officers sometimes transfer to related jobs, such as probation officers, parole officers, and correctional treatment specialists.

Employment

Bailiffs, correctional officers, and jailers held about 484,000 jobs in 2004. About 3 of every 5 jobs were in State correctional institutions such as prisons, prison camps, and youth correctional facilities. About 16,000 jobs for correctional officers were in Federal correctional institutions, and about 15,000 jobs were in privately owned and managed prisons.

Most of the remaining jobs were in city and county jails or in other institutions run by local governments. Some 300 of these jails, all of them in urban areas, are large: they house over 1,000 inmates. Most correctional officers who work in jails, however, work in institutions located in rural areas with smaller inmate populations.

Job Outlook

Job opportunities for correctional officers are expected to be excellent. The need to replace correctional officers who transfer to other occupations, retire, or leave the labor force, coupled with rising employment demand, will generate thousands of job openings each year. In the past, some local and State corrections agencies have experienced difficulty in attracting and keeping qualified applicants, largely because of low salaries, shift work, and the concentration of jobs in rural locations. This situation is expected to continue.

Employment of correctional officers is expected to grow more slowly than the average for all occupations through 2014. Increasing demand for correctional officers will stem from mandatory sentencing guidelines calling for longer sentences and reduced parole for inmates, and from expansion and new construction of corrections facilities. However, mandatory sentencing guidelines are being reconsidered in many States because of a combination of budgetary constraints, court decisions, and doubts about their effectiveness. Instead, there may be more emphasis on reducing sentences or putting offenders on probation or in rehabilitation programs in many States. As a result, the prison population, and employment of correctional officers, will probably grow at a slower rate than in the past. Some employment opportunities also will arise in the private sector, as public authorities contract with private companies to provide and staff corrections facilities.

Layoffs of correctional officers are rare because of increasing offender populations. While officers are allowed to join bargaining units, they are not allowed to strike.

Earnings

Median annual earnings of correctional officers and jailers were $33,600 in May 2004. The middle 50 percent earned between $26,560 and $44,200. The lowest 10 percent earned less than $22,630, and the highest 10 percent earned more than $54,820. Median annual earnings in the public sector were $44,700 in the Federal Government, $33,750 in State government, and $33,080 in local government. In the facilities support services industry, where the relatively small number of officers employed by privately operated prisons is classified, median annual earnings were $21,490. According to the Federal Bureau of Prisons, the starting salary for Federal correctional officers was about $26,747 a year in 2005. Starting Federal salaries were slightly higher in areas where prevailing local pay levels were higher.

Median annual earnings of first-line supervisors/managers of correctional officers were $44,720 in May 2004. The middle 50 percent earned between $33,070 and $60,550. The lowest 10 percent earned less than $27,770, and the highest 10 percent earned more than $70,990. Median annual earnings were $41,080 in State government and $49,470 in local government.

Median annual earnings of bailiffs were $33,870 in May 2004. The middle 50 percent earned between $24,710 and $44,240. The lowest 10 percent earned less than $17,930, and the highest 10 percent earned more than $54,770. Median annual earnings were $30,410 in local government.

In addition to typical benefits, correctional officers employed in the public sector usually are provided with uniforms or a clothing allowance to purchase their own uniforms. Civil service systems or merit boards cover officers employed by the Federal Government and most State governments. Their retirement coverage entitles correctional officers to retire at age 50 after 20 years of service or at any age with 25 years of service.

Related Occupations

A number of options are available to those interested in careers in protective services and security. Security guards and gaming surveillance officers protect people and property against theft, vandalism, illegal entry, and fire. Police and detectives maintain law and order, prevent crime, and arrest offenders. Probation officers and correctional treatment specialists monitor and counsel offenders and evaluate their progress in becoming productive members of society.

Sources of Additional Information

Further information about correctional officers is available from:
➤ American Correctional Association, 4380 Forbes Boulevard, Lanham, MD 20706. Internet: **http://www.aca.org**
➤ American Jail Association, 1135 Professional Ct., Hagerstown, MD 21740. Internet: **http://www.corrections.com/aja**

Information on entrance requirements, training, and career opportunities for correctional officers at the Federal level may be obtained from the Federal Bureau of Prisons. Internet: **http://www.bop.gov**

Information on obtaining a position as a correctional officer with the Federal Government is available from the Office of Personnel Management through USAJOBS, the Federal Government's official employment information system. This resource for locating and applying for job opportunities can be accessed through the Internet at **http://www.usajobs.opm.gov** or through an interactive voice response telephone system at (703) 724-1850 or TDD (978) 461-8404. These numbers are not tollfree, and charges may result.

Fire Fighting Occupations

(O*NET 33-1021.01, 33-1021.02, 33-2011.01, 33-2011.02, 33-2021.01, 33-2021.02, 33-2022.00)

Significant Points

● Fire fighting involves hazardous conditions and long, irregular hours.

● About 9 out of 10 fire fighting workers were employed by municipal or county fire departments.

● Applicants for municipal fire fighting jobs generally must pass written, physical, and medical examinations.

● Although employment is expected to grow faster than the average, keen competition for jobs is expected because this occupation attracts many qualified candidates.

Nature of the Work

Every year, fires and other emergencies take thousands of lives and destroy property worth billions of dollars. Fire fighters help protect the public against these dangers by rapidly responding to a variety of emergencies. They are frequently the first emergency personnel at the scene of a traffic accident or medical emergency and may be called upon to put out a fire, treat injuries, or perform other vital functions.

During duty hours, fire fighters must be prepared to respond immediately to a fire or any other emergency that arises. Because fighting fires is dangerous and complex, it requires organization and teamwork. At every emergency scene, fire fighters perform specific duties assigned by a superior officer. At fires, they connect hose lines to hydrants, operate a pump to send water to high-pressure hoses, and position ladders to enable them to deliver water to the fire. They also rescue victims, provide emergency medical attention as needed, ventilate smoke-filled areas, and attempt to salvage the contents of buildings. Their duties may change several times while the company is in action. Sometimes they remain at the site of a disaster for days at a time, rescuing trapped survivors and assisting with medical treatment.

Fire fighters work in a variety of settings, including urban and suburban areas, airports, chemical plants, other industrial sites, and rural areas like grasslands and forests. They have also assumed a range of responsibilities, including emergency medical services. In fact, most calls to which fire fighters respond involve medical emergencies, and 65 percent of all fire departments provide emergency medical service. In addition, some fire fighters work in hazardous materials units that are trained for the control, prevention, and cleanup of materials; for example, these fire fighters respond to oil spills. (For more information, see the *Handbook* statement on hazardous material removal workers.)Workers in urban and suburban areas, airports, and industrial sites typically use conventional fire fighting equipment and tactics, while forest fires and major hazardous materials spills call for different methods.

In national forests and parks, *forest fire inspectors and prevention specialists* spot fires from watchtowers and report their findings to headquarters by telephone or radio. Forest rangers patrol to ensure that travelers and campers comply with fire regulations. When fires break out, crews of fire fighters are brought in to suppress the blaze with heavy equipment, hand tools, and water hoses. Fighting forest fires, like fighting urban fires, is rigorous work. One of the most effective means of battling a blaze is creating fire lines—cutting down trees and digging out grass and all other combustible vegetation in the path of the fire— to deprive it of fuel. Elite fire fighters called smoke jumpers parachute from airplanes to reach otherwise inaccessible areas. This tactic, however, can be extremely hazardous because the crews have no way to escape if the wind shifts and causes the fire to burn toward them.

Between alarms, fire fighters clean and maintain equipment, conduct practice drills and fire inspections, and participate in physical fitness activities. They also prepare written reports on fire incidents and review fire science literature to keep abreast of technological developments and changing administrative practices and policies.

Firefighters help protect the public in the case of fires and other emergencies.

Most fire departments have a fire prevention division, usually headed by a fire marshal and staffed by *fire inspectors*. Workers in this division conduct inspections of structures to prevent fires and ensure compliance with fire codes. These fire fighters also work with developers and planners to check and approve plans for new buildings. Fire prevention personnel often speak on these subjects in schools and before public assemblies and civic organizations.

Some fire fighters become *fire investigators*, who determine the origin and causes of fires. They collect evidence, interview witnesses, and prepare reports on fires in cases where the cause may be arson or criminal negligence. They often are called upon to testify in court.

Working Conditions

Fire fighters spend much of their time at fire stations, which usually have features in common with a residential facility like a dormitory. When an alarm sounds, fire fighters respond rapidly, regardless of the weather or hour. Fire fighting involves the risk of death or injury from sudden cave-ins of floors, toppling walls, traffic accidents when responding to calls, and exposure to flames and smoke. Fire fighters also may come in contact with poisonous, flammable, or explosive gases and chemicals, as well as radioactive or other hazardous materials that may have immediate or long-term effects on their health. For these reasons, they must wear protective gear that can be very heavy and hot.

Work hours of fire fighters are longer and vary more widely than hours of most other workers. Many work more than 50 hours a week, and sometimes they may work even longer. In some agencies, fire fighters are on duty for 24 hours, then off for 48 hours, and receive an extra day off at intervals. In others, they work a day shift of 10 hours for 3 or 4 days, a night shift of 14 hours for 3 or 4 nights, have 3 or 4 days off, and then repeat the cycle. In addition, fire fighters often work extra hours at fires and other emergencies and are regularly assigned to work on holidays. Fire lieutenants and fire captains often work the same hours as the fire fighters they supervise. Duty hours include time when fire fighters study, train, and perform fire prevention duties.

Training, Other Qualifications, and Advancement

Applicants for municipal fire fighting jobs generally must pass a written exam; tests of strength, physical stamina, coordination, and agility; and a medical examination that includes drug screening. Workers may be monitored on a random basis for drug use after accepting employment. Examinations are generally open to persons who are at least 18 years of age and have a high school education or the equivalent. Those who receive the highest scores in all phases of testing have the best chances for appointment. The completion of community college courses in fire science may improve an applicant's chances for appointment. In recent years, an increasing proportion of entrants to this occupation have had some postsecondary education.

As a rule, entry-level workers in large fire departments are trained for several weeks at the department's training center or academy. Through classroom instruction and practical training, the recruits study fire fighting techniques, fire prevention, hazardous materials control, local building codes, and emergency medical procedures, including first aid and cardiopulmonary resuscitation.

They also learn how to use axes, chain saws, fire extinguishers, ladders, and other fire fighting and rescue equipment. After successfully completing this training, the recruits are assigned to a fire company, where they undergo a period of probation.

Almost all departments require fire fighters to be certified as emergency medical technicians. (For more information, see the *Handbook* statement on emergency medical technicians and paramedics.)

While most fire departments require the lowest level of certification, EMT-Basic, larger departments in major metropolitan areas are increasingly requiring paramedic certification. Some departments include this training in the fire academy, while others prefer that recruits have EMT certification beforehand, but will give them up to 1 year to become certified on their own.

A number of fire departments have accredited apprenticeship programs lasting up to 4 years. These programs combine formal, technical instruction with on-the-job training under the supervision of experienced fire fighters. Technical instruction covers subjects such as fire fighting techniques and equipment, chemical hazards associated with various combustible building materials, emergency medical procedures, and fire prevention and safety.

In addition to participating in advanced training programs conducted by local fire departments, some fire fighters attend training sessions sponsored by the U.S. National Fire Academy. These training sessions cover topics such as executive development, anti-arson techniques, disaster preparedness, hazardous materials control, and public fire safety and education. Some States also have either voluntary or mandatory fire fighter training and certification programs. In addition, a number of colleges and universities offer courses leading to 2- or 4-year degrees in fire engineering or fire science. Many fire departments offer fire fighters incentives such as tuition reimbursement or higher pay for completing advanced training.

Among the personal qualities fire fighters need are mental alertness, self-discipline, courage, mechanical aptitude, endurance, strength, and a sense of public service. Initiative and good judgment also are extremely important, because fire fighters make quick decisions in emergencies. Members of a crew live and work closely together under conditions of stress and danger for extended periods, so they must be dependable and able to get along well with others. Leadership qualities are necessary for officers, who must establish and maintain discipline and efficiency, as well as direct the activities of fire fighters in their companies.

Most experienced fire fighters continue studying to improve their job performance and prepare for promotion examinations. To progress to higher level positions, they acquire expertise in advanced fire fighting equipment and techniques, building construction, emergency medical technology, writing, public speaking, management and budgeting procedures, and public relations.

Opportunities for promotion depend upon the results of written examinations, as well as job performance, interviews, and seniority. Increasingly, fire departments are using assessment centers, which simulate a variety of actual job performance tasks, to screen for the best candidates for promotion. The line of promotion usually is to engineer, lieutenant, captain, battalion chief, assistant chief, deputy chief, and, finally, chief. For promotion to positions higher than battalion chief, many fire departments now require a bachelor's degree, preferably in fire science, public administration, or a related field. An associate's degree is required for executive fire officer certification from the National Fire Academy.

Employment

Employment figures in this *Handbook* statement include only paid career fire fighters—they do not cover volunteer fire fighters, who perform the same duties and may constitute the majority of fire fighters in a residential area. According to the U.S. Fire Administration, 70 percent of fire companies are staffed by volunteer fire fighters. In 2004, total employment in firefighting occupations was about 353,000. Fire fighters held about 282,000 jobs, first-line supervisors/managers of fire fighting and prevention workers held about 56,000, and fire inspectors held about 15,000.

About 9 out of 10 fire fighting workers were employed by municipal or county fire departments. Some large cities have thousands of career fire fighters, while many small towns have only a few. Most of the remainder worked in fire departments on Federal and State installations, including airports. Private fire fighting companies employ a small number of fire fighters and usually operate on a subscription basis.

In response to the expanding role of fire fighters, some municipalities have combined fire prevention, public fire education, safety, and emergency medical services into a single organization commonly referred to as a public safety organization. Some local and regional fire departments are being consolidated into countywide establishments in order to reduce administrative staffs, cut costs, and establish consistent training standards and work procedures.

Job Outlook

Prospective fire fighters are expected to face keen competition for available job openings. Many people are attracted to fire fighting because (1) it is challenging and provides the opportunity to perform an essential public service, (2) a high school education is usually sufficient for entry, and (3) a pension is guaranteed upon retirement after 25 years. Consequently, the number of qualified applicants in most areas exceeds the number of job openings, even though the written examination and physical requirements eliminate many applicants. This situation is expected to persist in coming years. Applicants with the best opportunities are those who are physically fit and score the highest on physical conditioning and mechanical aptitude exams. Those who have completed some fire fighter education at a community college and have EMT certification will have an additional advantage.

Employment of fire fighters is expected to grow faster than the average for all occupations through 2014. Most job growth will occur as volunteer fire fighting positions are converted to paid positions in growing suburban areas. In addition to job growth, openings are expected to result from the need to replace fire fighters who retire, stop working for other reasons, or transfer to other occupations.

Layoffs of fire fighters are uncommon. Fire protection is an essential service, and citizens are likely to exert considerable pressure on local officials to expand or at least preserve the level of fire protection. Even when budget cuts do occur, local fire departments usually trim expenses by postponing purchases of equipment or by not hiring new fire fighters, rather than through staff reductions.

Earnings

Median hourly earnings of fire fighters were $18.43 in May 2004. The middle 50 percent earned between $13.65 and $24.14. The lowest 10 percent earned less than $9.71, and the highest 10 percent earned more than $29.21. Median hourly earnings were $18.78 in local government, $17.34 in the Federal Government, and $14.94 in State government.

Median annual earnings of first-line supervisors/managers of fire fighting and prevention workers were $58,920 in May 2004. The middle 50 percent earned between $46,880 and $72,600. The lowest 10 percent earned less than $36,800, and the highest 10 percent earned more than $90,860. First-line supervisors/managers of fire fighting and prevention workers employed in local government earned about $60,800 a year.

Median annual earnings of fire inspectors and investigators were $46,340 in May 2004. The middle 50 percent earned between $36,030 and $58,260 a year. The lowest 10 percent earned less than $28,420, and the highest 10 percent earned more than $71,490. Fire inspectors and investigators employed in local government earned about $48,020 a year.

According to the International City-County Management Association, average salaries in 2004 for sworn full-time positions were as follows:

	Minimum annual base salary	Maximum annual base salary
Fire chief	$68,701	$89,928
Deputy chief	63,899	79,803
Assistant fire chief	57,860	73,713
Battalion chief	58,338	73,487
Fire captain	49,108	59,374
Fire lieutenant	44,963	53,179
Fire prevention/code inspector	43,297	54,712
Engineer	41,294	52,461

Fire fighters who average more than a certain number of hours a week are required to be paid overtime. The hours threshold is determined by the department during the fire fighter's work period, which ranges from 7 to 28 days. Fire fighters often earn overtime for working extra shifts to maintain minimum staffing levels or for special emergencies.

Fire fighters receive benefits that usually include medical and liability insurance, vacation and sick leave, and some paid holidays. Almost all fire departments provide protective clothing (helmets, boots, and coats) and breathing apparatus, and many also provide dress uniforms. Fire fighters generally are covered by pension plans, often providing retirement at half pay after 25 years of service or if the individual is disabled in the line of duty.

Related Occupations

Like fire fighters, emergency medical technicians and paramedics and police and detectives respond to emergencies and save lives.

Sources of Additional Information

Information about a career as a fire fighter may be obtained from local fire departments and from either of the following organizations:

➤ International Association of Fire Fighters, 1750 New York Ave. N.W., Washington, DC 20006. Internet: **http://www.iaff.org**

➤ U.S. Fire Administration, 16825 South Seton Ave., Emmitsburg, MD 21727. Internet: **http://www.usfa.fema.gov**

Information about professional qualifications and a list of colleges and universities offering 2- or 4-year degree programs in fire science or fire prevention may be obtained from:

➤ National Fire Academy, 16825 South Seton Ave., Emmitsburg, MD 21727. Internet: **http://www.usfa.fema.gov/nfa/index.htm**

Police and Detectives

(O*NET 33-1012.00, 33-3021.01, 33-3021.02, 33-3021.03, 33-3021.04, 33-3021.05, 33-3031.00, 33-3051.01, 33-3051.02, 33-3051.03, 33-3052.00)

Significant Points

- Police and detective work can be dangerous and stressful.

- Competition should remain keen for higher paying jobs with State and Federal agencies and police departments in affluent areas; opportunities will be better in local and special police departments that offer relatively low salaries or in urban communities where the crime rate is relatively high.

- Applicants with college training in police science or military police experience should have the best opportunities.

Nature of the Work

People depend on police officers and detectives to protect their lives and property. Law enforcement officers, some of whom are State or Federal special agents or inspectors, perform these duties in a variety of ways, depending on the size and type of their organization. In most jurisdictions, they are expected to exercise authority when necessary, whether on or off duty.

Uniformed police officers have general law enforcement duties, including maintaining regular patrols and responding to calls for service. They may direct traffic at the scene of an accident, investigate a burglary, or give first aid to an accident victim. In large police departments, officers usually are assigned to a specific type of duty. Many urban police agencies are involved in community policing—a practice in which an officer builds relationships with the citizens of local neighborhoods and mobilizes the public to help fight crime.

Police agencies are usually organized into geographic districts, with uniformed officers assigned to patrol a specific area, such as part of the business district or outlying residential neighborhoods. Officers may work alone, but, in large agencies, they often patrol with a partner. While on patrol, officers attempt to become thoroughly familiar with their patrol area and remain alert for anything unusual. Suspicious circumstances and hazards to public safety are investigated or noted, and officers are dispatched to individual calls for assistance within their district. During their shift, they may identify, pursue, and arrest suspected criminals; resolve problems within the community; and enforce traffic laws.

Public college and university police forces, public school district police, and agencies serving transportation systems and facilities are examples of special police agencies. These agencies have special geographic jurisdictions and enforcement responsibilities in the United States. Most sworn personnel in special agencies are uniformed officers; a smaller number are investigators.

Some police officers specialize in such diverse fields as chemical and microscopic analysis, training and firearms instruction, or handwriting and fingerprint identification. Others work with special units, such as horseback, bicycle, motorcycle or harbor patrol; canine corps; special weapons and tactics (SWAT); or emergency response teams. A few local and special law enforcement officers primarily perform jail-related duties or work in courts. Regardless of job duties or location, police officers and detectives at all levels must write reports and maintain meticulous records that will be needed if they testify in court.

Sheriffs and deputy sheriffs enforce the law on the county level. Sheriffs are usually elected to their posts and perform duties similar to those of a local or county police chief. Sheriffs' departments tend to be relatively small, most having fewer than 50 sworn officers. Deputy sheriffs have law enforcement duties similar to those of officers in urban police departments. Police and sheriffs' deputies who provide security in city and county courts are sometimes called bailiffs. (For information on other officers who work in jails and prisons, see correctional officers elsewhere in the *Handbook*.)

State police officers (sometimes called *State troopers* or *highway patrol officers*) arrest criminals Statewide and patrol highways to enforce motor vehicle laws and regulations. State police officers are best known for issuing traffic citations to motorists. At the scene of accidents, they may direct traffic, give first aid, and call for emergency equipment. They also write reports used to determine the cause of the accident. State police officers are frequently called upon to render assistance to other law enforcement agencies, especially those in rural areas or small towns.

State law enforcement agencies operate in every State except Hawaii. Most full-time sworn personnel are uniformed officers who regularly patrol and respond to calls for service. Others work as investigators, perform court-related duties, or carry out administrative or other assignments.

Detectives are plainclothes investigators who gather facts and collect evidence for criminal cases. Some are assigned to inter-agency task forces to combat specific types of crime. They conduct interviews, examine records, observe the activities of suspects, and participate in raids or arrests. Detectives and State and Federal agents and inspectors usually specialize in investigating one of a wide variety of violations, such as homicide or fraud. They are assigned cases on a rotating basis and work on them until an arrest and conviction occurs or until the case is dropped.

Fish and game wardens enforce fishing, hunting, and boating laws. They patrol hunting and fishing areas, conduct search and rescue operations, investigate complaints and accidents, and aid in prosecuting court cases.

The Federal Government maintains a high profile in many areas of law enforcement. *Federal Bureau of Investigation (FBI) agents* are the Government's principal investigators, responsible for investigating violations of more than 200 categories of Federal law and conducting sensitive national security investigations. Agents may conduct surveillance, monitor court-authorized wiretaps, examine business records, investigate white-collar crime, or participate in sensitive undercover assignments. The FBI investigates organized crime, public corruption, financial crime, fraud against the Government, bribery, copyright infringement, civil rights violations, bank robbery, extortion, kidnapping, air piracy, terrorism, espionage, interstate criminal activity, drug trafficking, and other violations of Federal statutes.

U.S. Drug Enforcement Administration (DEA) agents enforce laws and regulations relating to illegal drugs. Not only is the DEA the lead agency for domestic enforcement of Federal drug laws, it also has sole responsibility for coordinating and pursuing U.S. drug investigations abroad. Agents may conduct complex criminal investigations, carry out surveillance of criminals, and infiltrate illicit drug organizations using undercover techniques.

U.S. marshals and deputy marshals protect the Federal courts and ensure the effective operation of the judicial system. They provide protection for the Federal judiciary, transport Federal prisoners, protect Federal witnesses, and manage assets seized from criminal enterprises. They enjoy the widest jurisdiction of any Federal law enforcement agency and are involved to some degree in nearly all Federal law enforcement efforts. In addition, U.S. marshals pursue and arrest Federal fugitives.

Bureau of Alcohol, Tobacco, Firearms, and Explosives agents regulate and investigate violations of Federal firearms and explosives laws, as well as Federal alcohol and tobacco tax regulations.

The U.S. Department of State *Bureau of Diplomatic Security special agents* are engaged in the battle against terrorism. Overseas, they advise ambassadors on all security matters and manage a complex range of security programs designed to protect personnel, facilities, and information. In the United States, they investigate passport and visa fraud, conduct personnel security investigations, issue security clearances, and protect the Secretary of State and a number of foreign dignitaries. They also train foreign civilian police and administer a counter-terrorism reward program.

The *Department of Homeland Security* employs numerous law enforcement officers under several different agencies, including *Customs and Border Protection, Immigration and Customs Enforcement*, and the *U.S. Secret Service. U.S. Border Patrol agents* protect more than 8,000 miles of international land and water boundaries. Their missions are to detect and prevent the smuggling and unlawful entry of undocumented foreign nationals into the United States; to apprehend those persons violating the immigration laws; and to interdict contraband, such as narcotics.

Immigration inspectors interview and examine people seeking entrance to the United States and its territories. They inspect passports to determine whether people are legally eligible to enter the United States. Immigration inspectors also prepare reports, maintain records, and process applications and petitions for immigration or temporary residence in the United States.

Customs inspectors enforce laws governing imports and exports by inspecting cargo, baggage, and articles worn or carried by people, vessels, vehicles, trains, and aircraft entering or leaving the United States. These inspectors examine, count, weigh, gauge, measure, and sample commercial and noncommercial cargoes entering and leaving the United States. Customs inspectors seize prohibited or smuggled articles; intercept contraband; and apprehend, search, detain, and arrest violators of U.S. laws. *Customs agents* investigate violations, such as narcotics smuggling, money laundering, child pornography, and customs fraud, and they enforce the Arms Export Control Act. During domestic and foreign investigations, they develop and use informants; conduct physical and electronic surveillance; and examine records from importers and exporters, banks, couriers, and manufacturers. They conduct interviews, serve on joint task forces with other agencies, and get and execute search warrants.

Federal Air Marshals provide air security by fighting attacks targeting U.S. airports, passengers, and crews. They disguise themselves as ordinary passengers and board flights of U.S. air carriers to locations worldwide.

U.S. Secret Service special agents protect the President, Vice President, and their immediate families; Presidential candidates; former Presidents, and foreign dignitaries visiting the United States. Secret Service agents also investigate counterfeiting, forgery of Government checks or bonds, and fraudulent use of credit cards.

In most jurisdictions, police officers are expected to exercise arrest authority, whether they are on or off duty.

Other Federal agencies employ police and special agents with sworn arrest powers and the authority to carry firearms. These agencies include the Postal Service, the Bureau of Indian Affairs Office of Law Enforcement, the Forest Service, and the National Park Service.

Working Conditions

Police and detective work can be very dangerous and stressful. In addition to the obvious dangers of confrontations with criminals, police officers and detectives need to be constantly alert and ready to deal appropriately with a number of other threatening situations. Many law enforcement officers witness death and suffering resulting from accidents and criminal behavior. A career in law enforcement may take a toll on their private lives.

Uniformed officers, detectives, agents, and inspectors are usually scheduled to work 40-hour weeks, but paid overtime is common. Shift work is necessary because protection must be provided around the clock. Junior officers frequently work weekends, holidays, and nights. Police officers and detectives are required to work at any time their services are needed and may work long hours during investigations. In most jurisdictions, whether on or off duty, officers are expected to be armed and to exercise their authority whenever necessary.

The jobs of some Federal agents such as U.S. Secret Service and DEA special agents require extensive travel, often on very short notice. They may relocate a number of times over the course of their careers. Some special agents in agencies such as the U.S. Border Patrol work outdoors in rugged terrain for long periods and in all kinds of weather.

Training, Other Qualifications, and Advancement

Civil service regulations govern the appointment of police and detectives in most States, large municipalities, and special police agencies, as well as in many smaller jurisdictions. Candidates must be U.S. citizens, usually must be at least 20 years of age, and must meet rigorous physical and personal qualifications. Physical examinations for entrance into law enforcement often include tests of vision, hearing, strength, and agility. Eligibility for appointment usually depends on performance in competitive written examinations and previous education and experience. In larger departments, where the majority of law enforcement jobs are found, applicants usually must have at least a high school education, and some departments require a year or two of college coursework. Federal and State agencies typically require a college degree. Candidates should enjoy working with people and meeting the public.

Because personal characteristics such as honesty, sound judgment, integrity, and a sense of responsibility are especially important in law enforcement, candidates are interviewed by senior officers, and their character traits and backgrounds are investigated. In some agencies, candidates are interviewed by a psychiatrist or a psychologist or given a personality test. Most applicants are subjected to lie detector examinations or drug testing. Some agencies subject sworn personnel to random drug testing as a condition of continuing employment.

Before their first assignments, officers usually go through a period of training. In State and large local departments, recruits get training in their agency's police academy, often for 12 to 14 weeks. In small agencies, recruits often attend a regional or State academy. Training includes classroom instruction in constitutional law and civil rights, State laws and local ordinances, and accident investigation. Recruits also receive training and supervised experience in patrol, traffic control, use of firearms, self-defense, first aid, and emergency

response. Police departments in some large cities hire high school graduates who are still in their teens as police cadets or trainees. They do clerical work and attend classes, usually for 1 to 2 years, at which point they reach the minimum age requirement and may be appointed to the regular force.

Police officers usually become eligible for promotion after a probationary period ranging from 6 months to 3 years. In a large department, promotion may enable an officer to become a detective or to specialize in one type of police work, such as working with juveniles. Promotions to corporal, sergeant, lieutenant, and captain usually are made according to a candidate's position on a promotion list, as determined by scores on a written examination and on-the-job performance.

Most States require at least two years of college study to qualify as a fish and game warden. Applicants must pass written and physical examinations and vision, hearing, psychological, and drug tests similar to those taken by other law enforcement officers. Once hired, officers attend a training academy lasting from 3 to 12 months, sometimes followed by further training in the field.

To be considered for appointment as an FBI agent, an applicant must be a graduate of an accredited law school or a college graduate with one of the following: a major in accounting, electrical engineering, or information technology; fluency in a foreign language; or three years of related full-time work experience. All new agents undergo 18 weeks of training at the FBI Academy on the U.S. Marine Corps base in Quantico, Virginia.

Applicants for special agent jobs with the U.S. Secret Service and the Bureau of Alcohol, Tobacco, and Firearms must have a bachelor's degree, a minimum of three years' related work experience, or a combination of education and experience. Prospective special agents undergo 11 weeks of initial criminal investigation training at the Federal Law Enforcement Training Center in Glynco, Georgia, and another 17 weeks of specialized training with their particular agencies.

Applicants for special agent jobs with the DEA must have a college degree with at least a 2.95 grade point average or specialized skills or work experience, such as foreign language fluency, technical skills, law enforcement experience, or accounting experience. DEA special agents undergo 14 weeks of specialized training at the FBI Academy in Quantico, Virginia.

U.S. Border Patrol agents must be U.S. citizens, be younger than 37 years of age at the time of appointment, possess a valid driver's license, and pass a three-part examination on reasoning and language skills. A bachelor's degree or previous work experience that demonstrates the ability to handle stressful situations, make decisions, and take charge is required for a position as a Border Patrol agent. Applicants may qualify through a combination of education and work experience.

Postal inspectors must have a bachelor's degree and 1 year of related work experience. It is desirable that they have one of several professional certifications, such as that of certified public accountant. They also must pass a background investigation, meet certain health requirements, undergo a drug screening test, possess a valid State driver's license, and be a U.S. citizen between 21 and 36 years of age when hired.

Law enforcement agencies are encouraging applicants to take postsecondary school training in law enforcement-related subjects. Many entry-level applicants for police jobs have completed some formal postsecondary education, and a significant number are college graduates. Many junior colleges, colleges, and universities offer programs in law enforcement or administration of justice. Other courses helpful in preparing for a career in law enforcement include accounting, finance, electrical engineering, computer science, and foreign languages. Physical education and sports are helpful in developing the competitiveness, stamina, and agility needed for many law enforcement positions. Knowledge of a foreign language is an asset in many Federal agencies and urban departments.

Continuing training helps police officers, detectives, and special agents improve their job performance. Through police department academies, regional centers for public safety employees established by the States, and Federal agency training centers, instructors provide annual training in self-defense tactics, firearms, use-of-force policies, sensitivity and communications skills, crowd-control techniques, relevant legal developments, and advances in law enforcement equipment. Many agencies pay all or part of the tuition for officers to work toward degrees in criminal justice, police science, administration of justice, or public administration, and pay higher salaries to those who earn such a degree.

Employment

Police and detectives held about 842,000 jobs in 2004. About 80 percent were employed by local governments. State police agencies employed about 12 percent, and various Federal agencies employed about 6 percent. A small proportion worked for educational services, rail transportation, and contract investigation and security services.

According to the U.S. Bureau of Justice Statistics, police and detectives employed by local governments primarily worked in cities with more than 25,000 inhabitants. Some cities have very large police forces, while thousands of small communities employ fewer than 25 officers each.

Job Outlook

The opportunity for public service through law enforcement work is attractive to many because the job is challenging and involves much personal responsibility. Furthermore, law enforcement officers in many agencies may retire with a pension after 25 or 30 years of service, allowing them to pursue a second career while still in their 40s or 50s. Because of relatively attractive salaries and benefits, the number of qualified candidates exceeds the number of job openings in Federal law enforcement agencies and in most State police departments—resulting in increased hiring standards and selectivity by employers. Competition should remain keen for higher paying jobs with State and Federal agencies and police departments in more affluent areas. Opportunities will be better in local and special police departments, especially in departments that offer relatively low salaries, or in urban communities where the crime rate is relatively high. Applicants with college training in police science, military police experience, or both should have the best opportunities.

Employment of police and detectives is expected to grow about as fast as the average for all occupations through 2014. A more security-conscious society and concern about drug-related crimes should contribute to the increasing demand for police services. However, employment growth will be hindered by reductions in Federal hiring grants to local police departments and by expectations of low crime rates by the general public.

The level of government spending determines the level of employment for police and detectives. The number of job opportunities, therefore, can vary from year to year and from place to place. Layoffs, on the other hand, are rare because retirements enable most staffing cuts to be handled through attrition. Trained law enforcement officers who lose their jobs because of budget cuts usually have little difficulty finding jobs with other agencies. The need to replace workers who retire, transfer to other occupations, or stop working for other reasons will be the source of many job openings.

Earnings

Police and sheriff's patrol officers had median annual earnings of $45,210 in May 2004. The middle 50 percent earned between $34,410 and $56,360. The lowest 10 percent earned less than $26,910, and the highest 10 percent earned more than $68,880. Median annual earnings were $44,750 in Federal Government, $48,980 in State government, and $45,010 in local government.

In May 2004, median annual earnings of police and detective supervisors were $64,430. The middle 50 percent earned between $49,370 and $80,510. The lowest 10 percent earned less than $36,690, and the highest 10 percent earned more than $96,950. Median annual earnings were $86,030 in Federal Government, $62,300 in State government, and $63,590 in local government.

In May 2004, median annual earnings of detectives and criminal investigators were $53,990. The middle 50 percent earned between $40,690 and $72,280. The lowest 10 percent earned less than $32,180, and the highest 10 percent earned more than $86,010. Median annual earnings were $75,700 in Federal Government, $46,670 in State government, and $49,650 in local government.

Federal law provides special salary rates to Federal employees who serve in law enforcement. Additionally, Federal special agents and inspectors receive law enforcement availability pay (LEAP)—equal to 25 percent of the agent's grade and step—awarded because of the large amount of overtime that these agents are expected to work. For example, in 2005, FBI agents entered Federal service as GS-10 employees on the pay scale at a base salary of $42,548, yet they earned about $53,185 a year with availability pay. They could advance to the GS-13 grade level in field nonsupervisory assignments at a base salary of $64,478, which was worth $80,597 with availability pay. FBI supervisory, management, and executive positions in grades GS-14 and GS-15 paid a base salary of about $76,193 and $89,625 a year, respectively, which amounted to $95,241 or $112,031 per year including availability pay. Salaries were slightly higher in selected areas where the prevailing local pay level was higher. Because Federal agents may be eligible for a special law enforcement benefits package, applicants should ask their recruiter for more information.

According to the International City-County Management Association's annual Police and Fire Personnel, Salaries, and Expenditures Survey, average salaries for sworn full-time positions in 2004 were as follows:

	Minimum annual base salary	Maximum annual base salary
Police chief	$72,924	$92,983
Deputy chief	61,110	76,994
Police captain	60,908	75,497
Police lieutenant	56,115	67,580
Police sergeant	49,895	59,454
Police corporal	41,793	51,661

Total earnings for local, State, and special police and detectives frequently exceed the stated salary because of payments for overtime, which can be significant. In addition to the common benefits—paid vacation, sick leave, and medical and life insurance—most police and sheriffs' departments provide officers with special allowances for uniforms. Because police officers usually are covered by liberal pension plans, many retire at half-pay after 25 or 30 years of service.

Related Occupations

Police and detectives maintain law and order, collect evidence and information, and conduct investigations and surveillance. Workers in related occupations include correctional officers, private detectives and investigators, and security guards and gaming surveillance officers.

Sources of Additional Information

Information about entrance requirements may be obtained from Federal, State, and local law enforcement agencies.

For general information about sheriffs and to learn more about the National Sheriffs' Association scholarship, contact:

➤ National Sheriffs' Association, 1450 Duke St., Alexandria, VA 22314. Internet: **http://www.sheriffs.org**

Information about qualifications for employment as a FBI Special Agent is available from the nearest State FBI office. The address and phone number are listed in the local telephone directory. Internet: **http://www.fbi.gov**

Information on career opportunities, qualifications, and training for U.S. Secret Service Special Agents is available from the Secret Service Personnel Division at (202) 406-5800, (888) 813-8777, or (888) 813-USSS. Internet: **http://www.treas.gov/usss**

Information about qualifications for employment as a DEA Special Agent is available from the nearest DEA office, or call (800) DEA-4288. Internet: **http://www.usdoj.gov/dea**

Information about career opportunities, qualifications, and training to become a deputy marshal is available from:

➤ U.S. Marshals Service, Human Resources Division—Law Enforcement Recruiting, Washington, DC 20530-1000. Internet: **http://www.usmarshals.gov**

For information on operations and career opportunities in the U.S. Bureau of Alcohol, Tobacco, Firearms, and Explosives operations, contact:

➤ U.S. Bureau of Alcohol, Tobacco, Firearms, and Explosives Personnel Division, 650 Massachusetts Ave. NW., Room 4100, Washington, DC 20226. Internet: **http://www.atf.treas.gov**

Information about careers in U.S. Customs and Border Protection is available from:

➤ U.S. Customs and Border Protection, 1300 Pennsylvania Ave., NW., Washington, DC 20229. Internet: **http://www.cbp.gov**

Information about law enforcement agencies within the Department of Homeland Security is available from:

➤ U.S. Department of Homeland Security, Washington, DC 20528. Internet: **http://www.dhs.gov**

Private Detectives and Investigators

(O*Net 33-9021.00)

Significant Points

● Work hours are often irregular, and the work can be dangerous.

● About 1 in 4 are self-employed.

● Applicants typically have related experience in areas such as law enforcement, insurance, the military, or government investigative or intelligence jobs.

● Despite faster-than-average employment growth, keen competition is expected because of the large number of qualified people who are attracted to this occupation; the most opportunities will be found in entry-level jobs with detective agencies or in stores that hire detectives on a part-time basis.

Nature of the Work

Private detectives and investigators use many methods to determine the facts in a variety of matters. To carry out investigations, they may use various types of surveillance or searches. To verify facts, such as an individual's place of employment or income, they may make phone calls or visit a subject's workplace.

In other cases, especially those involving missing persons and background checks, investigators often interview people to gather as much information as possible about an individual. In all cases, private detectives and investigators assist attorneys, businesses, and the public with legal, financial, and personal problems.

Private detectives and investigators offer many services, including executive, corporate, and celebrity protection; pre-employment verification; and individual background profiles. They investigate computer crimes, such as identity theft, harassing e-mails, and illegal downloading of copyrighted material. They also provide assistance in civil liability and personal injury cases, insurance claims and fraud, child custody and protection cases, missing persons cases, and pre-marital screening. They are sometimes hired to investigate individuals to prove or disprove infidelity.

Most detectives and investigators are trained to perform physical surveillance. They may observe a site, such as the home of a subject, from an inconspicuous location or a vehicle. They continue the surveillance, which is often carried out using still and video cameras, binoculars, and a cell phone, until the desired evidence is obtained. This watching and waiting often continues for a long time.

Detectives also may perform computer database searches or work with someone who does. Computers allow investigators to quickly obtain massive amounts of information on individuals' prior arrests, convictions, and civil legal judgments; telephone numbers; motor vehicle registrations; association and club memberships; and other matters.

The duties of private detectives and investigators depend on the needs of their clients. In cases for employers that involve fraudulent workers' compensation claims, for example, investigators may carry out long-term covert observation of subjects. If an investigator observes a subject performing an activity that contradicts injuries stated in a worker's compensation claim, the investigator would take video or still photographs to document the activity and report it to the client.

Private detectives and investigators often specialize. Those who focus on intellectual property theft, for example, investigate and document acts of piracy, help clients stop illegal activity, and provide intelligence for prosecution and civil action. Other investigators specialize in developing financial profiles and asset searches. Their reports reflect information gathered through interviews, investigation and surveillance, and research, including review of public documents.

Legal investigators specialize in cases involving the courts and are normally employed by law firms or lawyers. They frequently assist in preparing criminal defenses, locating witnesses, serving legal documents, interviewing police and prospective witnesses, and gathering and reviewing evidence. Legal investigators also may collect information on the parties to the litigation, take photographs, testify in court, and assemble evidence and reports for trials.

Corporate investigators conduct internal and external investigations for corporations. In internal investigations, they may investigate drug use in the workplace, ensure that expense accounts are not abused, or determine whether employees are stealing merchandise or information. External investigations are typically done to uncover criminal schemes originating outside the corporation, such as theft of company assets through fraudulent billing of products by suppliers.

Financial investigators may be hired to develop confidential financial profiles of individuals or companies that are prospective parties to large financial transactions. These investigators often are certified public accountants (CPAs) who work closely with invest-

Some private detectives and investigators work in their offices most of the day, conducting computer searches and making phone calls.

ment bankers and other accountants. They search for assets in order to recover damages awarded by a court in fraud or theft cases.

Detectives who work for retail stores or hotels are responsible for controlling losses and protecting assets. *Store detectives*, also known as *loss prevention agents*, safeguard the assets of retail stores by apprehending anyone attempting to steal merchandise or destroy store property. They prevent theft by shoplifters, vendor representatives, delivery personnel and even store employees. Store detectives also conduct periodic inspections of stock areas, dressing rooms, and restrooms, and sometimes assist in opening and closing the store. They may prepare loss prevention and security reports for management and testify in court against persons they apprehend. *Hotel detectives* protect guests of the establishment from theft of their belongings and preserve order in hotel restaurants and bars. They also may keep undesirable individuals, such as known thieves, off the premises.

Working Conditions

Private detectives and investigators often work irregular hours because of the need to conduct surveillance and contact people who are not available during normal working hours. Early morning, evening, weekend, and holiday work is common.

Many detectives and investigators spend time away from their offices conducting interviews or doing surveillance, but some work in their office most of the day conducting computer searches and making phone calls. Those who have their own agencies and employ other investigators may work primarily in an office and have normal business hours.

When the investigator is working on a case away from the office, the environment might range from plush boardrooms to seedy bars. Store and hotel detectives work in the businesses that they protect. Investigators generally work alone, but they sometimes work with others during surveillance or when following a subject in order to avoid detection by the subject.

Some of the work involves confrontation, so the job can be stressful and dangerous. Some situations call for the investigator to be armed, such as certain bodyguard assignments for corporate or celebrity clients. Detectives and investigators who carry handguns must be licensed by the appropriate authority. In most cases, however, a weapon is not necessary, because the purpose of the work is gathering information and not law enforcement or criminal apprehension. Owners of investigative agencies have the added stress of having to deal with demanding and sometimes distraught clients.

Training, Other Qualifications, and Advancement

There are no formal education requirements for most private detective and investigator jobs, although many private detectives have college degrees. Private detectives and investigators typically have previous experience in other occupations. Some work initially for insurance or collections companies, in the private security industry, or as paralegals. Many investigators enter the field after serving in law enforcement, the military, government auditing and investigative positions, or Federal intelligence jobs.

Former law enforcement officers, military investigators, and government agents, who are frequently able to retire after 25 years of service, often become private detectives or investigators in a second career. Others enter from such diverse fields as finance, accounting, commercial credit, investigative reporting, insurance, and law. These individuals often can apply their prior work experience in a related investigative specialty. A few enter the occupation directly after graduation from college, generally with associate's or bachelor's degrees in criminal justice or police science.

The majority of States and the District of Colombia require private detectives and investigators to be licensed. Licensing requirements vary, however. Seven States—Alabama, Alaska, Colorado, Idaho, Mississippi, Missouri, and South Dakota—have no statewide licensing requirements, some States have few requirements, and many other States have stringent regulations. A growing number of States are enacting mandatory training programs for private detectives and investigators. For example, the Bureau of Security and Investigative Services of the California Department of Consumer Affairs requires private investigators to be 18 years of age or older; have a combination of education in police science, criminal law, or justice and experience equaling 3 years (6,000 hours) of investigative experience; pass a criminal history background check by the California Department of Justice and the FBI (in most States, convicted felons cannot be issued a license); and receive a qualifying score on a 2-hour written examination covering laws and regulations. There are additional requirements for a firearms permit.

For private detective and investigator jobs, most employers look for individuals with ingenuity, persistence, and assertiveness. A candidate must not be afraid of confrontation, should communicate well, and should be able to think on his or her feet. Good interviewing and interrogation skills also are important and usually are acquired in earlier careers in law enforcement or other fields. Because the courts often are the ultimate judge of a properly conducted investigation, the investigator must be able to present the facts in a manner that a jury will believe.

Training in subjects such as criminal justice and police science is helpful to aspiring private detectives and investigators. Most corporate investigators must have a bachelor's degree, preferably in a business-related field. Some corporate investigators have a master's degree in business administration or a law degree, while others are CPAs. Corporate investigators hired by large companies may receive formal training from their employers on business practices, management structure, and various finance-related topics. The screening process for potential employees typically includes a background check for a criminal history.

Some investigators receive certification from a professional organization to demonstrate competency in a field. For example, the National Association of Legal Investigators (NALI) confers the Certified Legal Investigator designation to licensed investigators who devote a majority of their practice to negligence or criminal defense investigations. To receive the designation, applicants must satisfy experience, educational, and continuing-training requirements and must pass written and oral exams administered by the NALI.

Most private-detective agencies are small, with little room for advancement. Usually, there are no defined ranks or steps, so advancement takes the form of increases in salary and assignment status. Many detectives and investigators work for detective agencies at the beginning of their careers and, after a few years, start their own firms. Corporate and legal investigators may rise to supervisor or manager of the security or investigations department.

Employment

Private detectives and investigators held about 43,000 jobs in 2004. About 26 percent were self-employed, including many who held a secondary job as a self-employed private detective. Around 27 percent of jobs were in investigation and security services, including private detective agencies, while another 15 percent were in department or other general merchandise stores. The rest worked mostly in State and local government, legal services firms, employment services companies, insurance agencies, and credit mediation establishments, including banks and other depository institutions.

Job Outlook

Keen competition is expected because private detective and investigator careers attract many qualified people, including relatively young retirees from law enforcement and military careers. The best opportunities will be in entry-level jobs with detective agencies or in stores that hire detectives on a part-time basis. The best prospects for those seeking store detective jobs will be with large chains and discount stores.

Employment of private detectives and investigators is expected to grow faster than the average for all occupations through 2014. In addition to growth, replacement of those who retire or leave the occupation for other reasons should create many job openings. Increased demand for private detectives and investigators will result from fear of crime, increased litigation, and the need to protect confidential information and property of all kinds. The proliferation of criminal activity on the Internet, such as identity theft, spamming, e-mail harassment, and illegal downloading of copyrighted materials, will increase the demand for private investigators. Employee background checks, conducted by private investigators, will become standard for an increasing number of jobs. Growing financial activity worldwide will increase the demand for investigators to control internal and external financial losses and to monitor competitors and prevent industrial spying.

Earnings

Median annual earnings of salaried private detectives and investigators were $32,110 in May 2004. The middle 50 percent earned between $24,080 and $43,260. The lowest 10 percent earned less than $19,260, and the highest 10 percent earned more than $58,470. Earnings of private detectives and investigators vary greatly by employer, specialty, and geographic area.

Related Occupations

Private detectives and investigators often collect information and protect the property and other assets of companies and individuals. Others with related duties include bill and account collectors; claims adjusters, appraisers, examiners, and investigators; police and detectives; and security guards and gaming surveillance officers. Investigators who specialize in conducting financial profiles and asset searches perform work closely related to that of accountants, auditors, financial analysts, and personal financial advisors.

Sources of Additional Information

For information on local licensing requirements, contact your State Department of Public Safety, State Division of Licensing, or local or State police headquarters.

For information on a career as a legal investigator and about the Certified Legal Investigator credential, contact:
➤ National Association of Legal Investigators, 908 21st St., Sacramento, CA 95814-3118. Internet: **http://www.nalionline.org**

Security Guards and Gaming Surveillance Officers

(O*NET 33-9031.00, 33-9032.00)

Significant Points

- Opportunities for most jobs should be favorable, but competition is expected for higher paying positions at facilities requiring longer periods of training and a high level of security, such as nuclear power plants and weapons installations.

- Because of limited formal training requirements and flexible hours, this occupation attracts many individuals seeking a second or part-time job.

- Some positions, such as those of armored car guards, are hazardous.

Nature of the Work

Guards, who are also called *security officers*, patrol and inspect property to protect against fire, theft, vandalism, terrorism, and illegal activity. These workers protect their employer's investment, enforce laws on the property, and deter criminal activity and other problems. They use radio and telephone communications to call for assistance from police, fire, or emergency medical services as the situation dictates. Security guards write comprehensive reports outlining their observations and activities during their assigned shift. They also may interview witnesses or victims, prepare case reports, and testify in court.

Although all security guards perform many of the same duties, their specific duties vary with whether the guard works in a "static" security position or on a mobile patrol. Guards assigned to static security positions usually serve the client at one location for a specified length of time. These guards must become closely acquainted with the property and people associated with it and must often monitor alarms and closed-circuit TV cameras. In contrast, guards assigned to mobile patrol duty drive or walk from location to location and conduct security checks within an assigned geographical zone. They may detain or arrest criminal violators, answer service calls concerning criminal activity or problems, and issue traffic violation warnings.

The security guard's job responsibilities also vary with the size, type, and location of the employer. In department stores, guards protect people, records, merchandise, money, and equipment. They often work with undercover store detectives to prevent theft by customers or employees, and they help apprehend shoplifting suspects prior to the arrival of the police. Some shopping centers and theaters have officers who patrol their parking lots to deter car thefts and robberies. In office buildings, banks, and hospitals, guards maintain order and protect the institutions' property, staff, and customers. At air, sea, and rail terminals and other transportation facilities, guards protect people, freight, property, and equipment. Using metal detectors and high-tech equipment, they may screen passengers and visitors for weapons and explosives, ensure that nothing is stolen while a vehicle is being loaded or unloaded, and watch for fires and criminals.

Guards who work in public buildings such as museums or art galleries protect paintings and exhibits by inspecting people and packages entering and leaving the building. In factories, laboratories, government buildings, data processing centers, and military bases, security officers protect information, products, computer codes, and defense secrets and check the credentials of people and vehicles entering and leaving the premises. Guards working at universities, parks, and sports stadiums perform crowd control, supervise parking and seating, and direct traffic. Security guards stationed at the entrance to bars and places of adult entertainment, such as nightclubs, prevent access by minors, collect cover charges at the door, maintain order among customers, and protect property and patrons.

Armored car guards protect money and valuables during transit. In addition, they protect individuals responsible for making commercial bank deposits from theft or bodily injury. When the armored car arrives at the door of a business, an armed guard enters, signs for the money, and returns to the truck with the valuables in hand. Carrying money between the truck and the business can be extremely hazardous; because of this risk, armored car guards usually wear bulletproof vests.

All security officers must show good judgment and common sense, follow directions and directives from supervisors, testify accurately in court, and follow company policy and guidelines. Guards should have a professional appearance and attitude and be able to interact with the public. They also must be able to take charge and direct others in emergencies or other dangerous incidents. In a large organization, the security manager often is in charge of a trained guard force divided into shifts; in a small organization, a single worker may be responsible for all security.

Gaming surveillance officers, also known as *surveillance agents*, and *gaming investigators* act as security agents for casino managers and patrons. Using primarily audio and video equipment in an observation room, they observe casino operations for irregular activities, such as cheating or theft, by either employees or patrons. They keep recordings that are sometimes used as evidence against alleged criminals in police investigations. Some casinos use a catwalk over one-way mirrors located above the casino floor to augment electronic surveillance equipment. Surveillance agents occasionally leave the surveillance room and walk the casino floor.

Security guards patrol and inspect property to deter crime.

Working Conditions

Most security guards and gaming surveillance officers spend considerable time on their feet, either assigned to a specific post or patrolling buildings and grounds. Guards may be stationed at a guard desk inside a building to monitor electronic security and surveillance devices or to check the credentials of persons entering or leaving the premises. They also may be stationed at a guardhouse outside the entrance to a gated facility or community and may use a portable radio or cellular telephone that allows them to be in constant contact with a central station. The work usually is routine, but guards must be constantly alert for threats to themselves and the property they are protecting. Guards who work during the day may have a great deal of contact with other employees and members of the public. Gaming surveillance often takes place behind a bank of monitors controlling several cameras in a casino and thus can cause eyestrain.

Guards usually work at least 8-hour shifts for 40 hours per week and often are on call in case an emergency arises. Some employers have three shifts, and guards rotate to divide daytime, weekend, and holiday work equally. Guards usually eat on the job instead of taking a regular break away from the site. In 2004, 16% of guards worked part time, and many individuals held a second job as a guard to supplement their primary earnings.

Training, Other Qualifications, and Advancement

Most States require that guards be licensed. To be licensed as a guard, individuals must usually be at least 18 years old, pass a background check, and complete classroom training in such subjects as property rights, emergency procedures, and detention of suspected criminals. Drug testing often is required and may be random and ongoing.

Many employers of unarmed guards do not have any specific educational requirements. For armed guards, employers usually prefer individuals who are high school graduates or who hold an equivalent certification. Many jobs require a driver's license. For positions as armed guards, employers often seek people who have had responsible experience in other occupations.

Guards who carry weapons must be licensed by the appropriate government authority, and some receive further certification as special police officers, allowing them to make limited types of arrests while on duty. Armed guard positions have more stringent background checks and entry requirements than those of unarmed guards because of greater insurance liability risks. Compared with unarmed security guards, armed guards and special police typically enjoy higher earnings and benefits, greater job security, and more potential for advancement. Usually, they also are given more training and responsibility.

Rigorous hiring and screening programs consisting of background, criminal record, and fingerprint checks are becoming the norm in the occupation. Applicants are expected to have good character references, no serious police record, and good health. They should be mentally alert, emotionally stable, and physically fit to cope with emergencies. Guards who have frequent contact with the public should communicate well.

The amount of training guards receive varies. Training requirements are higher for armed guards because their employers are legally responsible for any use of force. Armed guards receive formal training in areas such as weapons retention and laws covering the use of force.

Many employers give newly hired guards instruction before they start the job and provide on-the-job training. An increasing number of States are making ongoing training a legal requirement for retention of certification. Guards may receive training in protection, public relations, report writing, crisis deterrence, and first aid, as well as specialized training relevant to their particular assignment.

The American Society for Industrial Security International has written voluntary training guidelines that are intended to provide regulating bodies consistent minimum standards for the quality of security services. These guidelines recommend that security guards receive at least 48 hours of training within the first 100 days of employment. The guidelines also suggest that security guards be required to pass a written or performance examination covering topics such as sharing information with law enforcement, crime prevention, handling evidence, the use of force, court testimony, report writing, interpersonal and communication skills, and emergency response procedures. In addition, they recommend annual training and additional firearms training for armed officers.

Guards who are employed at establishments placing a heavy emphasis on security usually receive extensive formal training. For example, guards at nuclear power plants undergo several months of training before being placed on duty—and even then, they perform their tasks only under close supervision. They are taught to use firearms, administer first aid, operate alarm systems and electronic security equipment, and spot and deal with security problems. Guards who are authorized to carry firearms may be periodically tested in their use.

Because many people do not stay long in this occupation, opportunities for advancement are good for those who are career security officers. Most large organizations use a military type of ranking that offers the possibility of advancement in both position and salary. Some guards may advance to supervisor or security manager positions. Guards with management skills may open their own contract security guard agencies. Pay rates vary substantially with the security level of the establishment, so there is also the opportunity to move to higher paying jobs with increased experience and training.

In addition to possessing the keen observation skills required to perform their jobs, gaming surveillance officers and gaming investigators must have excellent verbal and writing abilities to document violations or suspicious behavior. They also need to be physically fit and have quick reflexes, because they sometimes must detain individuals until local law enforcement officials arrive.

Gaming surveillance officers and investigators usually need some training beyond high school, but not a bachelor's degree; previous security experience is a plus. Several educational institutes offer certification programs. Training classes usually are conducted in a casino-like atmosphere and use surveillance camera equipment. Employers prefer either individuals with significant knowledge of casino operations through work experience or those with experience conducting investigations, such as former law enforcement officers.

Employment

Security guards and gaming surveillance officers held over 1.0 million jobs in 2004. Over half of all jobs for security guards were in investigation and security services, including guard and armored car services. These organizations provide security on a contract basis, assigning their guards to buildings and other sites as needed. Most other security officers were employed directly by educational services, hospitals, food services and drinking places, traveler accommodation (hotels), department stores, manufacturing firms, lessors of real estate (residential and nonresidential buildings), and governments. Guard jobs are found throughout the country, most commonly in metropolitan areas. Gaming surveillance officers worked primarily in gambling industries; traveler accommodation, which includes casino hotels; and local government. Gaming surveillance officers were employed only in those States and on those Indian reservations where gambling has been legalized.

A significant number of law enforcement officers work as security guards when they are off duty, in order to supplement their incomes. Often working in uniform and with the official cars assigned to them,

they add a high-profile security presence to the establishment with which they have contracted. At construction sites and apartment complexes, for example, their presence often deters crime. (Police and detectives are discussed elsewhere in the *Handbook*.)

Job Outlook

Opportunities for security guards and gaming surveillance officers should be favorable. Numerous job openings will stem from employment growth attributable to the demand for increased security and from the need to replace those who leave this large occupation each year. In addition to full-time job opportunities, the limited training requirements and flexible hours attract many persons seeking part-time or second jobs. However, competition is expected for higher paying positions that require longer periods of training; these positions usually are found at facilities that require a high level of security, such as nuclear power plants or weapons installations.

Employment of security guards and gaming surveillance officers is expected to grow as fast as the average for all occupations through 2014 as concern about crime, vandalism, and terrorism continues to increase the need for security. Demand for guards also will grow as private security firms increasingly perform duties—such as providing security at public events and in residential neighborhoods—that were formerly handled by police officers. Casinos will continue to hire more surveillance officers as more States legalize gambling and as the number of casinos increases in States where gambling is already legal. In addition, casino security forces will employ more technically trained personnel as technology becomes increasingly important in thwarting casino cheating and theft.

Earnings

Median annual earnings of security guards were $20,320 in May 2004. The middle 50 percent earned between $16,640 and $25,510. The lowest 10 percent earned less than $14,390, and the highest 10 percent earned more than $33,270. Median annual earnings in the industries employing the largest numbers of security guards in May 2004 were as follows:

Elementary and secondary schools	$25,030
General medical and surgical hospitals	24,750
Local government	23,690
Traveler accommodation	21,710
Investigation and security services	19,030

Gaming surveillance officers and gaming investigators had median annual earnings of $25,840 in May 2004. The middle 50 percent earned between $20,430 and $33,790. The lowest 10 percent earned less than $17,710, and the highest 10 percent earned more than $42,420.

Related Occupations

Guards protect property, maintain security, and enforce regulations and standards of conduct in the establishments at which they work. Related security and protective service occupations include correctional officers, police and detectives, and private detectives and investigators.

Sources of Additional Information

Further information about work opportunities for guards is available from local security and guard firms and State employment service offices. Information about licensing requirements for guards may be obtained from the State licensing commission or the State police department. In States where local jurisdictions establish licensing requirements, contact a local government authority such as the sheriff, county executive, or city manager.

Food Preparation and Service Related Occupations

Chefs, Cooks, and Food Preparation Workers

(O*NET 35-1011.00, 35-2011.00, 35-2012.00, 35-2013.00, 35-2014.00, 35-2015.00, 35-2021.00)

Significant Points

- Many young people worked as cooks and food preparation workers—almost 19 percent were between 16 and 19 years old.

- More than 2 out of 5 food preparation workers were employed part time.

- Job openings are expected to be plentiful, because many of these workers transfer to other occupations with higher earnings or burn out from the fast work pace and pressure to fill orders quickly.

Nature of the Work

Chefs, cooks, and food preparation workers prepare, season, and cook a wide range of foods—from soups, snacks, and salads to entrees, side dishes, and desserts—in a variety of restaurants and other food services establishments. Chefs and cooks create recipes and prepare meals, while food preparation workers peel and cut vegetables, trim meat, prepare poultry, and perform other duties such as keeping work areas clean and monitoring temperatures of ovens and stovetops.

In general, *chefs* and *cooks* measure, mix, and cook ingredients according to recipes, using a variety of pots, pans, cutlery, and other equipment, including ovens, broilers, grills, slicers, grinders, and blenders. Chefs and head cooks also are responsible for directing the work of other kitchen workers, estimating food requirements, and ordering food supplies.

Larger restaurants and food services establishments tend to have varied menus and larger kitchen staffs. They often include several chefs and cooks, sometimes called assistant or line cooks, along with other lesser skilled kitchen workers, such as *food preparation workers*. Each chef or cook works an assigned station that is equipped with the types of stoves, grills, pans, and ingredients needed for the foods prepared at that station. Job titles often reflect the principal ingredient prepared or the type of cooking performed—*vegetable cook, fry cook, or grill cook*.

Executive chefs and *head cooks* coordinate the work of the kitchen staff and direct the preparation of meals. They determine serving sizes, plan menus, order food supplies, and oversee kitchen operations to ensure uniform quality and presentation of meals. The terms chef and cook often are used interchangeably, but generally reflect the different types of chefs and the organizational structure of the kitchen staff. For example, an *executive chef* is in charge of all food service operations and also may supervise the many kitchens of a hotel, restaurant group, or corporate dining operation. A *chef de cuisine* reports to an executive chef and is responsible for the daily operations of a single kitchen. A *sous chef*, or sub chef, is the second-in-command and runs the kitchen in the absence of the chef. Chefs tend to be more highly skilled and better trained than cooks. Many chefs earn fame both for themselves and for their kitchens because of the quality and distinctive nature of the food they serve.

The specific responsibilities of most cooks are determined by a number of factors, including the type of restaurant in which they work. *Institution and cafeteria cooks*, for example, work in the kitchens of schools, cafeterias, businesses, hospitals, and other institutions. For each meal, they prepare a large quantity of a limited number of entrees, vegetables, and desserts. *Restaurant cooks* usually prepare a wider selection of dishes, cooking most orders individually. *Short-order cooks* prepare foods in restaurants and coffee shops that emphasize fast service and quick food preparation. They grill and garnish hamburgers, prepare sandwiches, fry eggs, and cook French fries, often working on several orders at the same time. *Fast-food cooks* prepare a limited selection of menu items in fast-food restaurants. They cook and package batches of food, such as hamburgers and fried chicken, to be kept warm until served. (*Combined food preparation and service workers*, who both prepare and serve items in fast-food restaurants, are included with the material on food and beverage serving and related workers elsewhere in the *Handbook*.)

Some cooks do not work in restaurant or food service kitchens. *Private household cooks (or personal chefs)* plan and prepare meals in private homes according to the client's tastes or dietary needs. They order groceries and supplies, clean the kitchen and wash dishes and utensils. They also may serve meals. *Research chefs* combine culinary skills with knowledge of food science to develop recipes and test new formulas, experiment with flavors and eye appeal of prepared foods, and test new products and equipment for chain restaurants, food growers and processors, and manufacturers and marketers.

Food preparation workers perform routine, repetitive tasks such as readying ingredients for complex dishes, slicing and dicing vegetables, and composing salads and cold items, under the direction of chefs and cooks. They weigh and measure ingredients, go after pots and pans, and stir and strain soups and sauces. Food preparation workers may cut and grind meats, poultry, and seafood in preparation for cooking. Their responsibilities also include cleaning work areas, equipment, utensils, dishes, and silverware.

The number and types of workers employed in kitchens depends on the type of establishment. For example, fast-food establishments offer only a few items, which are prepared by fast-food cooks. Small, full-service restaurants offering casual dining often feature a limited number of easy-to-prepare items supplemented by short-order specialties and ready-made desserts. Typically, one cook prepares all the food with the help of a short-order cook and one or two other kitchen workers.

Grocery and specialty food stores employ chefs, cooks, and food preparation workers to develop recipes and prepare meals for customers to carry out. Typically, entrees, side dishes, salads, or other items are prepared in large quantities and stored at an appropriate temperature. Servers portion and package items according to customer orders for serving at home.

Working Conditions

Many restaurant and institutional kitchens have modern equipment, convenient work areas, and air conditioning, but kitchens in older and smaller eating places are often not as well designed. Kitchens must be well ventilated, appropriately lit, and properly equipped with sprinkler systems to protect against fires. Kitchen staffs invariably work in small quarters against hot stoves and ovens. They are under constant pressure to prepare meals quickly, while ensuring quality is maintained and safety and sanitation guidelines are observed.

Chefs, cooks, and food preparation workers must observe local health and sanitation standards.

Working conditions vary with the type and quantity of food prepared and the local laws governing food service operations. Workers usually must withstand the pressure and strain of standing for hours at a time, lifting heavy pots and kettles, and working near hot ovens and grills. Job hazards include slips and falls, cuts, and burns, but injuries are seldom serious.

Work hours in restaurants may include early mornings, late evenings, holidays, and weekends. Work schedules of chefs, cooks and other kitchen workers in factory and school cafeterias may be more regular. In 2004, about 40 percent of cooks and 46 percent of food preparation workers had part-time schedules, compared to 16 percent of workers throughout the economy. Work schedules in fine-dining restaurants, however, tend to be longer, because of the time required to prepare ingredients in advance. Many executive chefs regularly work 12-hour days because they oversee the delivery of foodstuffs early in the day, plan the menu, and start preparing those menu items that take the greatest amount of preparation time or skill.

The wide range in dining hours and the need for fully-staffed kitchens during all open hours creates work opportunities for individuals seeking supplemental income, flexible work hours, or variable schedules. For example, almost 19 percent of cooks and food preparation workers were 16-19 years old in 2004, and almost 11 percent had variable schedules. Kitchen workers employed by schools may work during the school year only, usually for 9 or 10 months. Similarly, resort establishments usually only offer seasonal employment.

Training, Other Qualifications, and Advancement
Most fast-food or short-order cooks and food preparation workers require little education or training; most skills are learned on the job. Training generally starts with basic sanitation and workplace safety subjects and continues with instruction on food handling, preparation, and cooking procedures.

A high school diploma is not required for beginning jobs, but it is recommended for those planning a career as a cook or chef. High school or vocational school programs may offer courses in basic food safety and handling procedures and general business and computer classes for those who want to manage or open their own place. Many school districts, in cooperation with State departments of education, provide on-the-job training and summer workshops for cafeteria kitchen workers who aspire to become cooks. Large corporations in the food services and hospitality industries also offer paid internships and summer jobs to those just starting out in the field. Internships provide valuable experience and can lead to placement in more formal chef training programs.

Executive chefs and head cooks who work in fine-dining restaurants require many years of training and experience and an intense desire to cook. Some chefs and cooks may start their training in high school or post-high school vocational programs. Others may receive formal training through independent cooking schools, professional culinary institutes, or 2- or 4-year college degree programs in hospitality or culinary arts. In addition, some large hotels and restaurants operate their own training and job-placement programs for chefs and cooks. Most formal training programs require some form of apprenticeship, internship, or out-placement program jointly offered by the school and affiliated restaurants. Professional culinary institutes, industry associations, and trade unions also may sponsor formal apprenticeship programs in coordination with the U.S. Department of Labor. Many chefs are trained on the job, receiving real work experience and training from chef mentors in the restaurants where they work.

People who have had courses in commercial food preparation may start in a cook or chef job without spending a lot of time in lower-skilled kitchen jobs. Their education may give them an advantage when looking for jobs in better restaurants. Some vocational programs in high schools may offer training, but employers usually prefer training given by trade schools, vocational centers, colleges, professional associations, or trade unions. Postsecondary courses range from a few months to 2 years or more. Degree-granting programs are open only to high school graduates. Chefs also may compete and test for certification as master chefs. Although certification is not required to enter the field, it can be a measure of accomplishment and lead to further advancement and higher-paying positions. The U.S. Armed Forces also are a good source of training and experience.

Although curricula may vary, students in formal culinary training programs spend most of their time in kitchens learning to use the appropriate equipment and to prepare meals through actual practice. They learn good knife techniques, safe food-handling procedures, and proper use and care of kitchen equipment. Training programs often include courses in nutrition, menu planning, portion control, purchasing and inventory methods, proper food storage procedures, and use of leftover food to minimize waste. Students also learn sanitation and public health rules for handling food. Training in food service management, computer accounting and inventory software, and banquet service are featured in some training programs.

The number of formal and informal culinary training programs continues to increase to meet demand. Formal programs, which may offer training leading to a certificate or a 2- or 4-year degree, are geared more for training chefs for fine-dining or upscale restaurants. They offer a wider array of training options and specialties, such as advanced cooking techniques; cooking for banquets, buffets, or parties; and cuisines and cooking styles from around the world.

The American Culinary Federation accredits more than 100 formal training programs and sponsors apprenticeship programs around the country. Typical apprenticeships last three years and combine classroom training and work experience. Accreditation is an indication that a culinary program meets recognized standards regarding course content, facilities, and quality of instruction. The American Culinary Federation also certifies pastry professionals, personal chefs, and culinary educators in addition to various levels of chefs. Certification standards are based primarily on experience and formal training.

Vocational or trade-school programs typically offer more basic training in preparing food, such as food handling and sanitation procedures, nutrition, slicing and dicing methods for various kinds of meats and vegetables, and basic cooking methods, such as baking, broiling, and grilling.

Important characteristics for chefs, cooks, and food preparation workers include working well as part of a team, having a keen sense of taste and smell, and working efficiently to turn out meals rapidly. Personal cleanliness is essential because most States require health certificates indicating that workers are free from communicable diseases. Knowledge of a foreign language can be an asset because it may improve communication with other restaurant staff, vendors, and the restaurant's clientele.

Advancement opportunities for chefs, cooks, and food preparation workers depend on their training, work experience, and ability to perform more responsible and sophisticated tasks. Many food preparation workers, for example, may move into assistant or line cook positions. Chefs and cooks who demonstrate an eagerness to learn new cooking skills and to accept greater responsibility may move up within the kitchen and take on responsibility for training or supervising newer or lesser skilled kitchen staff. Others may move from one kitchen or restaurant to another.

Some chefs and cooks go into business as caterers or personal chefs or they open their own restaurant. Others become instructors in culinary training programs. A number of cooks and chefs advance to executive chef positions or food service management positions, particularly in hotels, clubs, or larger, more elegant restaurants where they may oversee operations in a number of kitchens or restaurants. (See the statement on food service managers elsewhere in the *Handbook*.)

Employment

Chefs, cooks and food preparation workers held nearly 3.1 million jobs in 2004. The distribution of jobs among the various types of chefs, cooks, and food preparation workers was as follows:

Food preparation workers	$889,000
Cooks, restaurant	783,000
Cooks, fast food	662,000
Cooks, institution and cafeteria	424,000
Cooks, short order	230,000
Chefs and head cooks	125,000
Cooks, private household	9,200

Nearly two-thirds of all chefs, cooks, and food preparation workers were employed in restaurants and other food services and drinking places. Almost one-fifth worked in institutions such as schools, universities, hospitals, and nursing care facilities. Grocery stores, hotels, gasoline stations with convenience stores, and other organizations employed the remainder.

Job Outlook

Job openings for chefs, cooks, and food preparation workers are expected to be plentiful through 2014; however, competition should be keen for jobs in the top kitchens of higher end restaurants. While job growth will create new positions, primarily due to the expansion of family-casual dining, the overwhelming majority of job openings will stem from the need to replace workers who leave this large occupational group. Many chef, cook, and food preparation worker jobs are attractive to people seeking first-time or short-term employment, additional income, or a flexible schedule. Employers typically hire a large number of part-time workers and require minimal education and training for these lesser skilled entry-level positions. Many of these workers transfer to other occupations or stop working, creating numerous openings for those entering the field.

Overall employment of chefs, cooks, and food preparation workers is expected to increase about as fast as the average for all occupations over the 2004-14 period. Employment growth will be spurred by increases in population, household income, and leisure time that will allow people to more often dine out and take vacations. In addition, the large number of two-income households will lead more families to opt for the convenience of dining out.

Projected employment growth, however, varies by specialty. The number of higher-skilled chefs and cooks working in full-service restaurants—those that offer table service and more varied menus—is expected to increase about as fast as the average. Much of the increase in this segment, however, will come from job growth in more casual dining, rather than up-scale full-service restaurants. Dining trends suggest increasing numbers of meals eaten away from home and growth in family dining restaurants, but greater limits on expense-account meals. Similarly, employment of food preparation workers will grow faster than the average reflecting diners desires for convenience as they shop for carryout meals in a greater variety of places—full-service restaurants, limited-service eating places, or grocery stores.

Employment of fast-food cooks is expected to grow about as fast as the average. Duties of cooks in fast-food restaurants are limited; most workers are likely to be combined food preparation and serving workers, rather than fast-food cooks. Employment of short-order cooks is expected to increase about as fast as the average. Short-order cooks may work a grill or sandwich station in a full-line restaurant, but also may work in lunch counters or coffee shops that specialize in meals served quickly.

Employment of institution and cafeteria chefs and cooks will show little or no growth. Their employment will not keep pace with the rapid growth in the educational and health services industries—where their employment is concentrated. In an effort to make "institutional food" more attractive to office workers, students, staff, visitors, and patients, offices, schools and hospitals increasingly contract out their food services. Employment of cooks, private household, however, is projected to decline, reflecting the general decline in private household service employment.

Employment of chefs, cooks, and food preparation workers who prepare meals-to-go, such as those who work in the prepared foods sections of grocery or specialty food stores, should increase much faster than the average as people continue to demand quality meals and convenience. Similarly, much faster than average growth also is expected among those who work in contract food service establishments, such as those that provide catering services, and those who support employee dining rooms or staff hotel restaurants on a contract basis. These changes reflect a continuing trend among large establishments to contract out food services so they may better focus on their core business of running a hospital, hotel, factory or school. Also, there is a growing consumer desire for healthier, made-from-scratch meals without sacrificing the convenience of pre-packaged prepared foods or fast-food dining.

Earnings

Wages of chefs, cooks, and food preparation workers vary greatly according to region of the country and the type of food services establishment in which they work. Wages usually are highest in elegant restaurants and hotels, where many executive chefs are employed, and in major metropolitan areas.

Median hourly earnings of chefs and head cooks were $14.75 in May 2004. The middle 50 percent earned between $10.71 and $20.28. The lowest 10 percent earned less than $8.28, and the highest 10 percent earned more than $26.75 per hour. Median hourly earnings in the industries employing the largest number of chefs and head cooks in May 2004 were:

Other amusement and recreation industries	$19.27
Traveler accommodations	18.25
Special food services	15.06
Full-service restaurants	13.57
Limited-service eating places	12.00

Median hourly earnings of cooks, private household were $9.42 in May 2004. The middle 50 percent earned between $7.08 and $12.79.

The lowest 10 percent earned less than $6.01, and the highest 10 percent earned more than $16.55 per hour.

Median hourly earnings of restaurant cooks were $9.39 in May 2004. The middle 50 percent earned between $7.79 and $11.13. The lowest 10 percent earned less than $6.76, and the highest 10 percent earned more than $13.37 per hour. Median hourly earnings in the industries employing the largest numbers of restaurant cooks in May 2004 were:

Traveler accommodations	$10.69
Other amusement and recreation industries	10.55
Special food services	10.00
Full-service restaurants	9.34
Drinking places (alcoholic beverages)	9.27
Limited-service eating places	8.25

Median hourly earnings of institution and cafeteria cooks were $9.10 in May 2004. The middle 50 percent earned between $7.20 and $11.22. The lowest 10 percent earned less than $6.08, and the highest 10 percent earned more than $13.72 per hour. Median hourly earnings in the industries employing the largest numbers of institution and cafeteria cooks in May 2004 were:

General medical and surgical hospitals	$10.38
Special food services	10.11
Community care facilities for the elderly	9.60
Nursing care facilities	9.33
Elementary and secondary schools	8.06

Median hourly earnings of short-order cooks were $8.11 in May 2004. The middle 50 percent earned between $6.90 and $9.92. The lowest 10 percent earned less than $5.97, and the highest 10 percent earned more than $11.50 per hour. Median hourly earnings in the industries employing the largest number of short-order cooks in May 2004 were:

Full-service restaurants	$8.53
Drinking places (alcoholic beverages)	8.08
Other amusement and recreation industries	7.79
Limited-service eating places	7.21
Gasoline stations	6.99

Median hourly earnings of food preparation workers were $8.03 in May 2004. The middle 50 percent earned between $6.89 and $9.78. The lowest 10 percent earned less than $5.97, and the highest 10 percent earned more than $11.90 per hour. Median hourly earnings in the industries employing the largest number of food preparation workers in May 2004 were:

Elementary and secondary schools	$9.04
Grocery stores	8.54
Nursing care facilities	8.10
Full-service restaurants	7.94
Limited-service eating places	7.27

Median hourly earnings of fast-food cooks were $7.07 in May 2004. The middle 50 percent earned between $6.20 and $8.22. The lowest 10 percent earned less than $5.68, and the highest 10 percent earned more than $9.63 per hour. Median hourly earnings in the industries employing the largest number of fast-food cooks in May 2004 were:

Grocery stores	$8.26
Special food services	7.97
Gasoline stations	7.18
Full-service restaurants	7.16
Limited-service eating places	7.02

Some employers provide employees with uniforms and free meals, but Federal law permits employers to deduct from their employees' wages the cost or fair value of any meals or lodging provided, and some employers do so. Chefs, cooks, and food preparation workers who work full time often receive typical benefits, but part-time workers usually do not.

In some large hotels and restaurants, kitchen workers belong to unions. The principal unions are the Hotel Employees and Restaurant Employees International Union and the Service Employees International Union.

Related Occupations

Workers who perform tasks similar to those of chefs, cooks, and food preparation workers include food processing occupations, such as butchers and meat cutters, and bakers. Others who work closely with these workers include food service managers and food and beverage serving and related workers

Sources of Additional Information

Information about job opportunities may be obtained from local employers and local offices of the State employment service.

Career information about chefs, cooks, and other kitchen workers, as well as a directory of 2- and 4-year colleges that offer courses or programs that prepare persons for food service careers, is available from:

➤ National Restaurant Association, 1200 17th St. NW., Washington, DC 20036-3097. Internet: **http://www.restaurant.org**

For information on the American Culinary Federation's apprenticeship and certification programs for cooks, as well as a list of accredited culinary programs, send a self-addressed, stamped envelope to:

➤ American Culinary Federation, 180 Center Place Way, St. Augustine, FL 32095. Internet: **http://www.acfchefs.org**

For information about becoming a personal chef, contact:

➤ American Personal Chef Association, 4572 Delaware St., San Diego, CA 92116.

For general information on hospitality careers, contact:

➤ International Council on Hotel, Restaurant, and Institutional Education, 2613 North Parham Rd., 2nd Floor, Richmond, VA 23294. Internet: **http://www.chrie.org**

Food and Beverage Serving and Related Workers

(O*NET 35-3011.00, 35-3021.00, 35-3022.00, 35-3031.00, 35-3041.00, 35-9011.00, 35-9021.00, 35-9031.00, 35-9099.99)

Significant Points

● Most jobs are part time so many opportunities exist for young people—about one-fourth of these workers were 16 to 19 years old, almost six times the proportion for all workers.

● Job openings are expected to be abundant through 2014 because many of these workers transfer to other occupations or stop working, creating numerous openings.

● Tips comprise a major portion of earnings, so keen competition is expected for jobs where potential earnings from tips are greatest—bartenders, waiters and waitresses, and other jobs in popular restaurants and fine dining establishments.

Nature of the Work

Food and beverage serving and related workers are the front line of customer service in restaurants, coffee shops, and other food service establishments. These workers greet customers, escort them to seats and hand them menus, take food and drink orders, and serve food and beverages. They also answer questions, explain menu items and specials, and keep tables and dining areas clean and set for new diners. Most work as part of a team, helping coworkers to improve workflow and customer service.

Waiters and waitresses, the largest group of these workers, take customers' orders, serve food and beverages, prepare itemized checks, and sometimes accept payment. Their specific duties vary considerably, depending on the establishment. In coffee shops serving routine, straightforward fare, such as salads, soups, and sandwiches, servers are expected to provide fast, efficient, and courteous service. In fine dining restaurants, where more complicated meals are prepared and often served over several courses, waiters and waitresses provide more formal service emphasizing personal, attentive treatment and a more leisurely pace. They may recommend certain dishes and identify ingredients or explain how various items on the menu are prepared. Some prepare salads, desserts, or other menu items tableside. Additionally, they may check the identification of patrons to ensure they meet the minimum age requirement for the purchase of alcohol and tobacco products.

Waiters and waitresses sometimes perform the duties of other food and beverage service workers. These tasks may include escorting guests to tables, serving customers seated at counters, clearing and setting up tables, or operating a cash register. However, full-service restaurants frequently hire other staff, such as hosts and hostesses, cashiers, or dining room attendants, to perform these duties.

Bartenders fill drink orders either taken directly from patrons at the bar or through waiters and waitresses who place drink orders for dining room customers. Bartenders check identification of customers seated at the bar, to ensure they meet the minimum age requirement for the purchase of alcohol and tobacco products. They prepare mixed drinks, serve bottled or draught beer, and pour wine or other beverages. Bartenders must know a wide range of drink recipes and be able to mix drinks accurately, quickly, and without waste. Besides mixing and serving drinks, bartenders stock and prepare garnishes for drinks; maintain an adequate supply of ice, glasses, and other bar supplies; and keep the bar area clean for customers. They also may collect payment, operate the cash register, wash glassware and utensils, and serve food to customers seated at the bar. Bartenders usually are responsible for ordering and maintaining an inventory of liquor, mixes, and other bar supplies.

The majority of bartenders directly serve and interact with patrons. Bartenders should be friendly and enjoy talking with customers. Bartenders at service bars, on the other hand, have less contact with customers. They work in small bars often located off the kitchen in restaurants, hotels, and clubs where only waiters and waitresses place drink orders. Some establishments, especially larger, higher volume ones, use equipment that automatically measures, pours and mixes drinks at the push of a button. Bartenders who use this equipment, however, still must work quickly to handle a large volume of drink orders and be familiar with the ingredients for special drink requests. Much of a bartender's work still must be done by hand to fill each individual order.

Hosts and hostesses welcome guests and maintain reservation or waiting lists. They may direct patrons to coatrooms, restrooms, or to a place to wait until their table is ready. Hosts and hostesses assign guests to tables suitable for the size of their group, escort patrons to their seats, and provide menus. They also schedule dining reservations, arrange parties, and organize any special services that are required. In some restaurants, they act as cashiers.

Dining room and cafeteria attendants and bartender helpers assist waiters, waitresses, and bartenders by cleaning tables, removing dirty dishes, and keeping serving areas stocked with supplies. Sometimes called backwaiters or runners, they bring meals out of the kitchen and assist waiters and waitresses by distributing dishes to individual diners. They also replenish the supply of clean linens, dishes, silverware, and glasses in the dining room and keep the bar stocked with glasses, liquor, ice, and drink garnishes. Dining room attendants set tables with clean tablecloths, napkins, silverware, glasses, and dishes and serve ice water, rolls, and butter. At the conclusion of meals, they remove dirty dishes and soiled linens from tables. Cafeteria attendants stock serving tables with food, trays, dishes, and silverware and may carry trays to dining tables for patrons. *Bartender helpers* keep bar equipment clean and wash glasses. *Dishwashers* clean dishes, cutlery, and kitchen utensils and equipment.

Counter attendants take orders and serve food in cafeterias, coffee shops, and carryout eateries. In cafeterias, they serve food displayed on steam tables, carve meat, dish out vegetables, ladle sauces and soups, and fill beverage glasses. In lunchrooms and coffee shops, counter attendants take orders from customers seated at the counter, transmit orders to the kitchen, and pick up and serve food. They also fill cups with coffee, soda, and other beverages and prepare fountain specialties, such as milkshakes and ice cream sundaes. Counter attendants also take carryout orders from diners and wrap or place items in containers. They clean counters, write itemized checks, and sometimes accept payment. Some counter attendants may prepare short-order items, such as sandwiches and salads.

Some food and beverage serving workers take orders from customers at counters or drive-through windows at fast-food restaurants. They assemble orders, hand them to customers, and accept payment. Many of these are *combined food preparation and serving workers* who also cook and package food, make coffee, and fill beverage cups using drink-dispensing machines.

Other workers serve food to patrons outside of a restaurant environment, such as in hotels, hospital rooms, or cars.

Working Conditions

Food and beverage service workers are on their feet most of the time and often carry heavy trays of food, dishes, and glassware. During busy dining periods, they are under pressure to serve customers quickly and efficiently. The work is relatively safe, but care must be taken to avoid slips, falls, and burns.

Waiters and waitresses are under pressure to serve customers quickly, courteously, and efficiently during busy dining periods.

Part-time work is more common among food and beverage serving and related workers than among workers in almost any other occupation. In 2004, those on part-time schedules included half of all waiters and waitresses, and 40 percent of all bartenders.

Food service and drinking establishments typically maintain long dining hours and offer flexible and varied work opportunities. Many food and beverage serving and related workers work evenings, weekends, and holidays. Many students and teenagers seek part time or seasonal work as food and beverage serving and related workers as a first job to gain work experience or to earn spending money while in school. Around one-fourth of food and beverage serving and related workers were 16 to 19 years old—about six times the proportion for all workers.

Training, Other Qualifications, and Advancement
There are no specific educational requirements for food and beverage service jobs. Many employers prefer to hire high school graduates for waiter and waitress, bartender, and host and hostess positions, but completion of high school usually is not required for fast-food workers, counter attendants, dishwashers, and dining room attendants and bartender helpers. For many people a job as a food and beverage service worker serves as a source of immediate income, rather than a career. Many entrants to these jobs are in their late teens or early twenties and have a high school education or less. Usually, they have little or no work experience. Many are full-time students or homemakers. Food and beverage service jobs are a major source of part-time employment for high school and college students.

Restaurants rely on good food and quality customer service to retain loyal customers and succeed in a competitive industry. Food and beverage serving and related workers who exhibit excellent personal qualities—such as a neat clean appearance, a well-spoken manner, an ability to work as a member of team, and a pleasant way with patrons—will be highly sought after.

Waiters and waitresses need a good memory to avoid confusing customers' orders and to recall faces, names, and preferences of frequent patrons. These workers also should be comfortable using computers to place orders and generate customers' bills. Some may need to be quick at arithmetic so they can total bills manually. Knowledge of a foreign language is helpful to communicate with a diverse clientele and staff. Prior experience waiting on tables is preferred by restaurants and hotels that have rigid table service standards. Jobs at these establishments often offer higher wages and have greater income potential from tips, but they may also have stiffer employment requirements than other establishments, such as prior table service experience or higher education.

Usually, bartenders must be at least 21 years of age, but employers prefer to hire people who are 25 or older. Bartenders should be familiar with State and local laws concerning the sale of alcoholic beverages.

Most food and beverage serving and related workers pick up their skills on the job by observing and working with more experienced workers. Some full-service restaurants also provide new dining room employees with some form of classroom-type training that alternates with periods of actual on-the-job work experience. These training programs communicate the operating philosophy of the restaurant, help establish a personal rapport with other staff and instill a desire to work as a team. They also provide an opportunity to discuss customer service situations and the proper ways of handling unpleasant circumstances or unruly patrons with new employees. Additionally, managers, chefs and servers may meet before each shift to discuss the menu and any new items or specials, review ingredients for any potential food allergies, or talk about any food safety concerns, coordination between the kitchen and the dining room, and any customer service issues from the previous day or shift.

Some employers, particularly those in fast-food restaurants, use self-instruction or on-line programs with audiovisual presentations and instructional booklets to teach new employees food preparation and service skills. Some public and private vocational schools, restaurant associations, and large restaurant chains provide classroom training in a generalized food service curriculum. All employees receive training on safe food handling procedures and sanitation practices.

Some bartenders acquire their skills by attending a bartending or vocational and technical school. These programs often include instruction on State and local laws and regulations, cocktail recipes, proper attire and conduct, and stocking a bar. Some of these schools help their graduates find jobs. Although few employers require any minimum level of educational attainment, some specialized training is usually needed in food handling and legal issues surrounding serving alcoholic beverages and tobacco. Employers are more likely to hire and promote based on people skills and personal qualities rather than education.

Due to the relatively small size of most food-serving establishments, opportunities for promotion are limited. After gaining experience, some dining room and cafeteria attendants and bartender helpers advance to waiter, waitress, or bartender jobs. For waiters, waitresses, and bartenders, advancement usually is limited to finding a job in a busier or more expensive restaurant or bar where prospects for tip earnings are better. Some bartenders, hosts and hostesses and waiters and waitresses advance to supervisory jobs, such as dining room supervisor, maitre d'hotel, assistant manager, or restaurant general manager. A few bartenders open their own businesses. In larger restaurant chains, food and beverage service workers who excel at their work often are invited to enter the company's formal management training program. (For more information, see the *Handbook* report on food service managers.)

Employment
Food and beverage serving and related workers held 6.8 million jobs in 2004. The distribution of jobs among the various food and beverage serving workers was as follows:

Waiters and waitresses	2,252,000
Combined food preparation and serving workers, including fast food	2,150,000
Dishwashers	507,000
Bartenders	474,000
Counter attendants, cafeteria, food concession, and coffee shop	465,000
Dining room and cafeteria attendants and bartender helpers	401,000
Hosts and hostesses, restaurant, lounge, and coffee shop	328,000
Food servers, nonrestaurant	189,000
All other food preparation and serving related workers	64,000

The overwhelming majority of jobs for food and beverage serving and related workers were found in food services and drinking places, such as restaurants, coffee shops, and bars. Other jobs were found primarily in traveler accommodation (hotels); amusement, gambling, and recreation industries; educational services; grocery stores; nursing care facilities; civic and social organizations; and hospitals.

Jobs are located throughout the country but are typically plentiful in large cities and tourist areas. Vacation resorts offer seasonal employment, and some workers alternate between summer and winter resorts, instead of remaining in one area the entire year.

Job Outlook
Job openings are expected to be abundant for food and beverage serving and related workers. Overall employment of these workers

is expected to increase as fast as the average over the 2004-14 period as population, personal incomes, and employment expand. While employment growth will create many new jobs, the overwhelming majority of openings will arise from the need to replace the high proportion of workers who leave the occupations each year. There is substantial movement into and out of these occupations because education and training requirements are minimal and the predominance of part-time jobs are attractive to people seeking a short-term source of income rather than a career. However, keen competition is expected for bartender, waiter and waitress, and other food and beverage service jobs in popular restaurants and fine dining establishments, where potential earnings from tips are greatest.

Projected employment growth between 2004 and 2014 varies somewhat by type of job; however, average employment growth is expected for almost all food and beverage serving and related occupations. Employment of combined food preparation and serving workers, which includes fast-food workers, is expected to increase as fast as the average in response to the continuing fast-paced lifestyle of many Americans and the addition of healthier foods at many fast-food restaurants. Average employment growth is expected for waiters and waitresses and hosts and hostesses because increases in the number of families and the more affluent, 55-and-older population will result in more restaurants that offer table service and more varied menus. Employment of bartenders, dining room attendants, and dishwashers will grow more slowly than other food and beverage serving and related workers because diners increasingly are eating at more casual dining spots, such as coffee bars and sandwich shops, rather than at the full-service restaurants and drinking places that employ more of these workers.

Earnings

Food and beverage serving and related workers derive their earnings from a combination of hourly wages and customer tips. Earnings vary greatly, depending on the type of job and establishment. For example, fast-food workers and hosts and hostesses usually do not receive tips, so their wage rates may be higher than those of waiters and waitresses and bartenders in full-service restaurants, who typically earn more from tips than from wages. In some restaurants, workers contribute all or a portion of their tips to a tip pool, which is distributed among qualifying workers. Tip pools allow workers who don't usually receive tips directly from customers, such as dining room attendants, to feel a part of a team and to share in the rewards of good service.

In May 2004, median hourly earnings (including tips) of waiters and waitresses were $6.75. The middle 50 percent earned between $6.04 and $8.34. The lowest 10 percent earned less than $5.60, and the highest 10 percent earned more than $11.27 an hour. For most waiters and waitresses, higher earnings are primarily the result of receiving more in tips rather than higher hourly wages. Tips usually average between 10 and 20 percent of guests' checks; waiters and waitresses working in busy, expensive restaurants earn the most.

Bartenders had median hourly earnings (including tips) of $7.42 in May 2004. The middle 50 percent earned between $6.34 and $9.26. The lowest 10 percent earned less than $5.72, and the highest 10 percent earned more than $12.47 an hour. Like waiters and waitresses, bartenders employed in public bars may receive more than half of their earnings as tips. Service bartenders often are paid higher hourly wages to offset their lower tip earnings.

Median hourly earnings (including tips) of dining room and cafeteria attendants and bartender helpers were $7.10 in May 2004. The middle 50 percent earned between $6.24 and $8.25. The lowest 10 percent earned less than $5.68, and the highest 10 percent earned more than $9.88 an hour. Most received over half of their earnings as wages; the rest of their income was a share of the proceeds from tip pools.

Median hourly earnings of hosts and hostesses were $7.52 in May 2004. The middle 50 percent earned between $6.48 and $8.63. The lowest 10 percent earned less than $5.77, and the highest 10 percent earned more than $10.49 an hour. Wages comprised the majority of their earnings. In some cases, wages were supplemented by proceeds from tip pools.

Median hourly earnings of combined food preparation and serving workers, including fast food, were $7.06 in May 2004. The middle 50 percent earned between $6.18 and $8.25. The lowest 10 percent earned less than $5.65, and the highest 10 percent earned more than $9.85 an hour. Although some combined food preparation and serving workers receive a part of their earnings as tips, fast-food workers usually do not.

Median hourly earnings of counter attendants in cafeterias, food concessions, and coffee shops (including tips) were $7.53 in May 2004. The middle 50 percent earned between $6.50 and $8.59 an hour. The lowest 10 percent earned less than $5.80, and the highest 10 percent earned more than $10.38 an hour.

Median hourly earnings of dishwashers were $7.35 in May 2004. The middle 50 percent earned between $6.41 and $8.37. The lowest 10 percent earned less than $5.76, and the highest 10 percent earned more than $9.81 an hour.

Median hourly earnings of nonrestaurant food servers were $7.95 in May 2004. The middle 50 percent earned between $6.64 and $9.98. The lowest 10 percent earned less than $5.86, and the highest 10 percent earned more than $12.53 an hour.

Many beginning or inexperienced workers start earning the Federal minimum wage of $5.15 an hour. However, a few States set minimum wages higher than the Federal minimum. Also, various minimum wage exceptions apply under specific circumstances to disabled workers, full-time students, youth under age 20 in their first 90 days of employment, tipped employees, and student-learners. Tipped employees are those who customarily and regularly receive more than $30 a month in tips. The employer may consider tips as part of wages, but the employer must pay at least $2.13 an hour in direct wages. Employers also are permitted to deduct from wages the cost, or fair value, of any meals or lodging provided. Many employers, however, provide free meals and furnish uniforms. Food and beverage service workers who work full time often receive typical benefits, while part-time workers usually do not.

In some large restaurants and hotels, food and beverage serving and related workers belong to unions—principally the Hotel Employees and Restaurant Employees International Union and the Service Employees International Union.

Related Occupations

Other workers whose job involves serving customers and handling money include flight attendants, gaming services workers, and retail salespersons.

Sources of Additional Information

Information about job opportunities may be obtained from local employers and local offices of State employment services agencies.

A guide to careers in restaurants plus a list of 2- and 4-year colleges offering food service programs and related scholarship information is available from:
➤ National Restaurant Association, 1200 17th St. NW., Washington, DC 20036-3097. Internet: **http://www.restaurant.org**

For general information on hospitality careers, contact:
➤ International Council on Hotel, Restaurant, and Institutional Education, 2613 North Parham Rd., 2nd Floor, Richmond, VA 23294. Internet: **http://www.chrie.org**

Building and Grounds Cleaning and Maintenance Occupations

Building Cleaning Workers

(O*NET 37-1011.01, 37-1011.02, 37-2011.00, 37-2012.00)

Significant Points

- This very large occupation requires few skills to enter and has one of the largest numbers of job openings of any occupation each year.

- Most job openings result from the need to replace the many workers who leave these jobs because of their limited opportunities for training or advancement, low pay, and high incidence of only part-time or temporary work.

- Most new jobs will occur in businesses providing janitorial and cleaning services on a contract basis.

Nature of the Work

Building cleaning workers—including janitors, maids, housekeeping cleaners, window washers, and rug shampooers—keep office buildings, hospitals, stores, apartment houses, hotels, and residences clean, sanitary, and in good condition. Some do only cleaning, while others have a wide range of duties.

Janitors and cleaners perform a variety of heavy cleaning duties, such as cleaning floors, shampooing rugs, washing walls and glass, and removing rubbish. They may fix leaky faucets, empty trash cans, do painting and carpentry, replenish bathroom supplies, mow lawns, and see that heating and air-conditioning equipment works properly. On a typical day, janitors may wet- or dry-mop floors, clean bathrooms, vacuum carpets, dust furniture, make minor repairs, and exterminate insects and rodents. They also clean snow or debris from sidewalks in front of buildings and notify management of the need for major repairs. While janitors typically perform most of the duties mentioned, cleaners tend to work for companies that specialize in one type of cleaning activity, such as washing windows.

Maids and housekeeping cleaners perform any combination of light cleaning duties to keep private households or commercial establishments such as hotels, restaurants, hospitals, and nursing homes clean and orderly. In hotels, aside from cleaning and maintaining the premises, maids and housekeeping cleaners may deliver ironing boards, cribs, and rollaway beds to guests' rooms. In hospitals, they also may wash bed frames, brush mattresses, make beds, and disinfect and sterilize equipment and supplies with germicides and sterilizing equipment.

Janitors, maids, and cleaners use many kinds of equipment, tools, and cleaning materials. For one job they may need standard cleaning implements; another may require an electric polishing machine and a special cleaning solution. Improved building materials, chemical cleaners, and power equipment have made many tasks easier and less time consuming, but cleaning workers must learn the proper use of equipment and cleaners to avoid harming floors, fixtures, and themselves.

Cleaning supervisors coordinate, schedule, and supervise the activities of janitors and cleaners. They assign tasks and inspect building areas to see that work has been done properly; they also issue supplies and equipment and inventory stocks to ensure that supplies on hand are adequate. They also screen and hire job applicants; train new and experienced employees; and recommend promotions, transfers, or dismissals. Supervisors may prepare reports concerning the occupancy of rooms, hours worked, and department expenses. Some also perform cleaning duties.

Cleaners and servants in private households dust and polish furniture; sweep, mop, and wax floors; vacuum; and clean ovens, refrigerators, and bathrooms. They also may wash dishes, polish silver, and change and make beds. Some wash, fold, and iron clothes; a few wash windows. General houseworkers also may take clothes and laundry to the cleaners, buy groceries, and perform many other errands.

Building cleaning workers in large office and residential buildings, and more recently in large hotels, often work in teams consisting of workers who specialize in vacuuming, picking up trash, and cleaning restrooms, among other things. Supervisors conduct inspections to ensure that the building is cleaned properly and the team is functioning efficiently. In hotels, one member of the team is responsible for reporting electronically to the supervisor when rooms are cleaned.

Working Conditions

Because most office buildings are cleaned while they are empty, many cleaning workers work evening hours. Some, however, such as school and hospital custodians, work in the daytime. When there is a need for 24-hour maintenance, janitors may be assigned to shifts. Most full-time building cleaners work about 40 hours a week. Part-time cleaners usually work in the evenings and on weekends.

Building cleaning workers usually work inside heated, well-lighted buildings. However, they sometimes work outdoors, sweeping walkways, mowing lawns, or shoveling snow. Working with machines can be noisy, and some tasks, such as cleaning bathrooms and trashrooms, can be dirty and unpleasant. Janitors may suffer cuts, bruises, and burns from machines, handtools, and chemicals. They spend most of their time on their feet, sometimes lifting or pushing heavy furniture or equipment. Many tasks, such as dusting or sweeping, require constant bending, stooping, and stretching. As a result, janitors also may suffer back injuries and sprains.

Training, Other Qualifications, and Advancement

No special education is required for most janitorial or cleaning jobs, but beginners should know simple arithmetic and be able to follow

A building cleaning worker operates a compacting machine.

instructions. High school shop courses are helpful for jobs involving repair work.

Most building cleaners learn their skills on the job. Beginners usually work with an experienced cleaner, doing routine cleaning. As they gain more experience, they are assigned more complicated tasks. In some cities, programs run by unions, government agencies, or employers teach janitorial skills. Students learn how to clean buildings thoroughly and efficiently; how to select and safely use various cleansing agents; and how to operate and maintain machines, such as wet and dry vacuums, buffers, and polishers. Students learn to plan their work, to follow safety and health regulations, to interact positively with people in the buildings they clean, and to work without supervision. Instruction in minor electrical, plumbing, and other repairs also may be given. Those who come in contact with the public should have good communication skills. Employers usually look for dependable, hard-working individuals who are in good health, follow directions well, and get along with other people.

Building cleaners usually find work by answering newspaper advertisements, applying directly to organizations where they would like to work, contacting local labor unions, or contacting State employment service offices.

Advancement opportunities for workers usually are limited in organizations where they are the only maintenance worker. Where there is a large maintenance staff, however, cleaning workers can be promoted to supervisor or to area supervisor or manager. A high school diploma improves the chances for advancement. Some janitors set up their own maintenance or cleaning businesses.

Supervisors usually move up through the ranks. In many establishments, they are required to take some inservice training to improve their housekeeping techniques and procedures and to enhance their supervisory skills.

A small number of cleaning supervisors and managers are members of the International Executive Housekeepers Association, which offers two kinds of certification programs for cleaning supervisors and managers: Certified Executive Housekeeper (CEH) and Registered Executive Housekeeper (REH). The CEH designation is offered to those with a high school education, while the REH designation is offered to those who have a 4-year college degree. Both designations are earned by attending courses and passing exams, and both must be renewed every 2 years to ensure that workers keep abreast of new cleaning methods. Those with the REH designation usually oversee the cleaning services of hotels, hospitals, casinos, and other large institutions that rely on well-trained experts for their cleaning needs.

Employment
Building cleaning workers held more than 4 million jobs in 2004. More than 6 percent were self-employed.

Janitors and cleaners work in nearly every type of establishment and held about 2.4 million jobs. They accounted for more than 58 percent of all building cleaning workers. More than 29 percent worked for firms supplying building maintenance services on a contract basis, more than 20 percent were employed in public or private educational services, and 2 percent worked in hotels or motels. Other employers included hospitals; restaurants; religious institutions; manufacturing firms; government agencies; and operators of apartment buildings, office buildings, and other types of real estate.

First-line supervisors of housekeeping and janitorial workers held about 236,000 jobs. Approximately 23 percent worked in firms supplying building maintenance services on a contract basis, while approximately 13 percent were employed in hotels or motels. More than 20 percent worked for State and local governments, primarily at schools and colleges. Others worked for hospitals, nursing homes and other residential care facilities.

Maids and housekeepers held about 1.4 million jobs. Private households employed the most maids and housekeepers—almost 28 percent—while hotels, motels, and other traveler accommodations employed the second most—almost 27 percent. Hospitals, nursing homes, and other residential care facilities employed large numbers, also. Although cleaning jobs can be found in all cities and towns, most are located in highly populated areas where there are many office buildings, schools, apartment houses, nursing homes, and hospitals.

Job Outlook
Overall employment of building cleaning workers is expected to grow as fast as average for all occupations through 2014, as more office complexes, apartment houses, schools, factories, hospitals, and other buildings requiring cleaning are built to accommodate a growing population and economy. As many firms reduce costs by contracting out the cleaning and maintenance of buildings, businesses providing janitorial and cleaning services on a contract basis are expected to have the greatest number of new jobs in this field. Although there have been some improvements in productivity in the way buildings are cleaned and maintained—using teams of cleaners, for example, and better cleaning supplies—cleaning still is very much a labor-intensive job. Faster than average growth is expected among janitors and cleaners and among cleaning supervisors, but as fast as average growth is projected for maids and housekeeping cleaners. In addition to job openings arising due to growth, numerous openings should result from the need to replace those who leave this very large occupation each year. Limited promotion potential, low pay, and the fact that many jobs are part-time and temporary, induce many to leave the occupation, thereby contributing to the number of job openings and the need to replace these workers.

Much of the growth in these occupations will come from cleaning residential properties. As families become more pressed for time, they increasingly are hiring cleaning and handyman services to perform a variety of tasks in their homes. Also, as the population ages, older people will need to hire cleaners to help maintain their houses. In addition, housekeeping cleaners will be needed to clean the growing number of residential care facilities for the elderly. These facilities, including assisted-living residences, generally provide housekeeping services as part of the rent.

Earnings
Median annual earnings of janitors and cleaners, except maids and housekeeping cleaners, were $18,790 in May 2004. The middle 50 percent earned between $15,320 and $24,420. The lowest 10 percent earned less than $13,010 and the highest 10 percent earned more than $31,780. Median annual earnings in 2004 in the industries employing the largest numbers of janitors and cleaners, except maids and housekeeping cleaners, were as follows:

Elementary and secondary schools	$22,910
Local government	22,860
Colleges, universities, and professional schools	21,860
Lessors of real estate	21,050
Services to buildings and dwellings	16,820

Median annual earnings of maids and housekeepers were $16,900 in May 2004. The middle 50 percent earned between $14,570 and $20,570. The lowest 10 percent earned less than $12,530, and the highest 10 percent earned more than $25,220. Median annual earnings in 2004 in the industries employing the largest numbers of maids and housekeepers were as follows:

General medical and surgical hospitals..$18,770
Services to buildings and dwellings..17,130
Community care facilities for the elderly 17,010
Nursing care facilities...16,960
Traveler accommodation...16,250

Median annual earnings of first-line supervisors and managers of housekeeping and janitorial workers were $29,510 in May 2004. The middle 50 percent earned between $22,720 and $38,790. The lowest 10 percent earned less than $18,550, and the highest 10 percent earned more than $49,230. Median annual earnings in May 2004 in the industries employing the largest numbers of first-line supervisors and managers of housekeeping and janitorial workers were as follows:

Local government $34,780
Elementary and secondary schools 33,760
Nursing care facilities...28,370
Services to buildings and dwellings..27,760
Traveler accommodation...24,310

Related Occupations
Workers who specialize in one of the many job functions of janitors and cleaners include pest control workers; general maintenance and repair workers; and grounds maintenance workers.

Sources of Additional Information
Information about janitorial jobs may be obtained from State employment service offices.

For information on certification in executive housekeeping, contact:

➤ International Executive Housekeepers Association, Inc., 1001 Eastwind Dr., Suite 301, Westerville, OH 43081-3361. Internet: **http://www.ieha.org**

Grounds Maintenance Workers

(O*NET 37-1012.01, 37-1012.02, 37-3011.00, 37-3012.00, 37-3013.00, 37-3019.99)

Significant Points

● Opportunities should be very good, especially for workers willing to work seasonal or variable schedules, because of significant job turnover and increasing demand by landscaping services companies.

● Many beginning jobs have low earnings and are physically demanding.

● Most workers learn through short-term on-the-job training.

Nature of the Work
Attractively designed, healthy, and well-maintained lawns, gardens, and grounds create a positive first impression, establish a peaceful mood, and increase property values. Grounds maintenance workers perform the variety of tasks necessary to achieve a pleasant and functional outdoor environment. They also care for indoor gardens and plantings in commercial and public facilities, such as malls, hotels, and botanical gardens.

The duties of *landscaping workers* and *groundskeeping workers* are similar and often overlap. Landscaping workers physically install and maintain landscaped areas. They grade property, install lighting or sprinkler systems, and build walkways, terraces, patios,

decks, and fountains. In addition to initially transporting and planting new vegetation, they transplant, mulch, fertilize, and water flowering plants, trees, and shrubs and mow and water lawns. A growing number of residential and commercial clients, such as managers of office buildings, shopping malls, multiunit residential buildings, and hotels and motels, favor full-service landscape maintenance. Landscaping workers perform a range of duties, including mowing, edging, trimming, fertilizing, dethatching, and mulching for such clients on a regular basis during the growing season.

Groundskeeping workers, also called *groundskeepers*, maintain a variety of facilities, including athletic fields, golf courses, cemeteries, university campuses, and parks. In addition to caring for sod, plants, and trees, they rake and mulch leaves, clear snow from walkways and parking lots, and use irrigation methods to adjust the amount of water consumption and prevent waste. They see to the proper upkeep and repair of sidewalks, parking lots, groundskeeping equipment, pools, fountains, fences, planters, and benches.

Groundskeeping workers who care for athletic fields keep natural and artificial turf in top condition, mark out boundaries, and before events paint turf with team logos and names. They must make sure that the underlying soil on fields with natural turf has the required composition to allow proper drainage and to support the grasses used on the field. Groundskeeping workers mow, water, fertilize, and aerate the fields regularly. They also vacuum and disinfect synthetic turf after its use, in order to prevent the growth of harmful bacteria, and they remove the turf and replace the cushioning pad periodically.

Workers who maintain golf courses are called *greenskeepers*. Greenskeepers do many of the same things as other groundskeepers. In addition, greenskeepers periodically relocate the holes on putting greens to eliminate uneven wear of the turf and to add interest and challenge to the game. Greenskeepers also keep canopies, benches, ball washers, and tee markers repaired and freshly painted.

Some groundskeeping workers specialize in caring for cemeteries and memorial gardens. They dig graves to specified depths, generally using a backhoe. They mow grass regularly, apply fertilizers and other chemicals, prune shrubs and trees, plant flowers, and remove debris from graves.

Groundskeeping workers in parks and recreation facilities care for lawns, trees, and shrubs, maintain athletic fields and playgrounds, clean buildings, and keep parking lots, picnic areas, and other public spaces free of litter. They also may remove snow and ice from roads and walkways, erect and dismantle snow fences, and maintain swimming pools. These workers inspect buildings and equipment, make needed repairs, and keep everything freshly painted.

Landscaping and groundskeeping workers use handtools such as shovels, rakes, pruning and regular saws, hedge and brush trimmers, and axes, as well as power lawnmowers, chain saws, snowblowers, and electric clippers. Some use equipment such as tractors and twin-axle vehicles. Landscaping and groundskeeping workers at parks, schools, cemeteries, and golf courses may use sod cutters to harvest sod that will be replanted elsewhere.

Pesticide handlers, sprayers, and applicators, vegetation, mix pesticides, herbicides, fungicides, or insecticides and apply them through sprays, dusts, vapors into the soil, or onto trees, shrubs, lawns, or botanical crops. Those working for chemical lawn service firms are more specialized, inspecting lawns for problems and applying fertilizers , herbicides, pesticides, and other chemicals to stimulate growth and prevent or control weeds, diseases, or insect infestation. Many practice integrated pest-management techniques.

Tree trimmers and pruners cut away dead or excess branches from trees or shrubs either to maintain rights-of-way for roads, sidewalks, or utilities or to improve the appearance, health, and value of trees. Some of these workers also specialize in pruning, trimming and shaping ornamental trees and shrubs for private residences, golf courses, or other institutional grounds. Tree trimmers and pruners use handsaws, pruning hooks, shears, and clippers. When trimming near power lines, they usually use truck-mounted lifts and power pruners.

Supervisors of landscaping and groundskeeping workers perform various functions. They prepare cost estimates, schedule work for crews on the basis of weather conditions or the availability of equipment, perform spot checks to ensure the quality of the service, and suggest changes in work procedures. In addition, supervisors train workers in their tasks; keep employees' time records and record work performed; and even assist workers when deadlines are near. Supervisors who own their own business are also known as *landscape contractors*. They may also call themselves *landscape designers* if they create landscape design plans.

Supervisors of tree trimmers and pruners are often referred to as arborists. Arborists specialize in the care of individual trees and are trained and equipped to provide proper care. Some arborists plant trees, and most can recommend types of trees that are appropriate for a specific location, as the wrong tree in the wrong location could lead to future problems as a result of limited growing space, insects, diseases, or poor growth. Arborists are employed by cities to improve urban green space, utilities to maintain power distribution networks, companies to care for residential and commercial properties, as well as many other settings.

Working Conditions

Many of the jobs for grounds maintenance workers are seasonal, meaning that they are in demand mainly in the spring, summer, and fall, when most planting, mowing, trimming, and cleanup are necessary. Most of the work is performed outdoors in all kinds of weather. It can be physically demanding and repetitive, involving much bending, lifting, and shoveling. Workers in landscaping and groundskeeping may be under pressure to get the job completed, especially when they are preparing for scheduled events such as athletic competitions.

Those who work with pesticides, fertilizers, and other chemicals, as well as dangerous equipment and tools such as power lawnmowers, chain saws, and power clippers, must exercise safety precautions. Workers who use motorized equipment must take care to protect themselves against hearing damage.

Many grounds maintenance jobs are seasonal.

Training, Other Qualifications, and Advancement

There usually are no minimum educational requirements for entry-level positions in grounds maintenance, although a diploma is necessary for some jobs. In 2004, most workers had a high school education or less. Short-term on-the-job training generally is sufficient to teach new hires how to operate equipment such as mowers, trimmers, leaf blowers, and small tractors and to follow correct safety procedures. Entry-level workers must be able to follow directions and learn proper planting and maintenance procedures for their localities. They also must learn how to repair the equipment they're using. If driving is an essential part of a job, employers look for applicants with a good driving record and some experience driving a truck. Employers also look for responsible, self-motivated individuals because grounds maintenance workers often work with little supervision. Workers who deal directly with customers must get along well with people.

Laborers who demonstrate a willingness to work hard and quickly, have good communication skills, and take an interest in the business may advance to crew leader or other supervisory positions. Advancement or entry into positions such as grounds manager and landscape contractor usually requires some formal education beyond high school and several years of progressively more responsible experience.

Most States require certification for workers who apply pesticides. Certification requirements vary, but usually include passing a test on the proper and safe use and disposal of insecticides, herbicides, and fungicides. Some States require that landscape contractors be licensed.

The Professional Grounds Management Society (PGMS) offers certification to grounds managers who have a combination of 8 years of experience and formal education beyond high school and who pass an examination covering subjects such as equipment management, personnel management, environmental issues, turf care, ornamentals, and circulatory systems. The PGMS also offers certification to groundskeepers who have a high school diploma or equivalent, plus 2 years of experience in the grounds maintenance field.

The Professional Landcare Network (PLANET) offers the designations "Certified Landscape Professional" (Exterior and Interior) and "Certified Landscape Technician" (Exterior or Interior) to those who meet established education and experience standards and who pass a specific examination. The hands-on test for technicians covers areas such as the operation of maintenance equipment and the installation of plants by reading a plan. A written safety test also is administered. PLANET also offers the designations "Certified Turfgrass Professional" (CTP) and "Certified Ornamental Landscape Professional" (COLP), which require written exams.

Some workers with groundskeeping backgrounds may start their own businesses after several years of experience.

Employment

Grounds maintenance workers held about 1.5 million jobs in 2004. Employment was distributed as follows:

Landscaping and groundskeeping workers	1,177,000
First-line supervisors/managers of landscaping, lawn service, and groundskeeping workers	184,000
Tree trimmers and pruners	55,000
Pesticide handlers, sprayers, and applicators, vegetation	30,000
Grounds maintenance workers, all other	21,000

About one-third of the workers in grounds maintenance were employed in companies providing landscaping services to buildings and dwellings. Others worked for property management and real-estate development firms, lawn and garden equipment and supply stores, and amusement and recreation facilities, such as golf courses and racetracks. Some were employed by local governments, installing and maintaining landscaping for parks, schools, hospitals, and other public facilities.

Almost 1 out of every 4 grounds maintenance workers was self-employed, providing landscape maintenance directly to customers on a contract basis. About 1 of every 7 worked part time; about 8% were of school age.

Job Outlook

Those interested in grounds maintenance occupations should find plentiful job opportunities in the future. Demand for their services is growing, and because wages for beginners are low and the work is physically demanding, many employers have difficulty attracting enough workers to fill all openings, creating very good job opportunities. In addition, high turnover will generate a large number of job openings, including at the supervisory and managerial level.

More workers also will be needed to keep up with increasing demand by lawn care and landscaping companies. Employment of grounds maintenance workers is expected to grow faster than the average for all occupations through the year 2014. Expected growth in the construction of all types of buildings, from office buildings to shopping malls and residential housing, plus more highways and parks, will increase demand for grounds maintenance workers. In addition, the upkeep and renovation of existing landscaping and grounds are continuing sources of demand for grounds maintenance workers. Owners of many buildings and facilities recognize the importance of "curb appeal" in attracting business and maintaining the value of the property and are expected to use grounds maintenance services more extensively to maintain and upgrade their properties. Grounds maintenance workers working for State and local governments, however, may face budget cuts, which may affect hiring.

Homeowners are a growing source of demand for grounds maintenance workers. Many two-income households lack the time to take care of their lawn so they are increasingly hiring people to maintain it for them. They also know that a nice yard will increase the property's value. In addition, there is a growing interest by homeowners in their backyards, as well as a desire to make the yards more attractive for outdoor entertaining. With many newer homes having more and bigger windows overlooking the yard, it becomes more important to maintain and beautify the grounds. Also, as the population ages, more elderly homeowners will require lawn care services to help maintain their yards.

Job opportunities for tree trimmers and pruners should also increase as utility companies step up pruning of trees around electric lines to prevent power outages. Additionally, tree trimmers and pruners will be needed to help combat infestations caused by new species of insects from other countries. Ash trees in Michigan, for example, have been especially hurt by a pest from China.

Job opportunities for nonseasonal work are more numerous in regions with temperate climates, where landscaping and lawn services are required all year. However, opportunities may vary with local economic conditions.

Earnings

Median hourly earnings in May 2004 of grounds maintenance workers were as follows:

First-line supervisors/managers of landscaping, lawn service, and groundskeeping workers	$16.99
Tree trimmers and pruners	12.57
Pesticide handlers, sprayers, and applicators, vegetation	12.30
Landscaping and groundskeeping workers	9.82
Grounds maintenance workers, all other	9.57

Median hourly earnings in the industries employing the largest numbers of landscaping and groundskeeping workers in May 2004 were as follows:

Elementary and secondary schools	$13.25
Local government	11.25
Services to buildings and dwellings	9.78
Other amusement and recreation industries	9.14
Employment services	8.64

Related Occupations

Grounds maintenance workers perform most of their work outdoors and have some knowledge of plants and soils. Others whose jobs may require that they work outdoors are agricultural workers; farmers, ranchers, and agricultural managers; forest, conservation, and logging workers; landscape architects; and biological scientists.

Sources of Additional Information

For career and certification information on tree trimmers and pruners, contact:
➤ Tree Care Industry Association, 3 Perimeter Rd., Unit I, Manchester, NH 03103-3341. Internet: **http://www.TreeCareIndustry.org**
➤ International Society of Arboriculture, P.O. Box 3129, Champaign, IL 61826-3129. Internet: **http://www.isa-arbor.com/careersInArboriculture/careers.aspx**

For information on work as a landscaping and groundskeeping worker, contact either of the following organizations:
➤ Professional Landcare Network, 950 Herndon Parkway, Suite 450, Herndon, VA 20170-5528. Internet: **http://www.landcarenetwork.org/**
➤ Professional Grounds Management Association, 720 Light Street, Baltimore, MD 21230-3850 Internet: **http://www.pgms.org**

For information on becoming a licensed pesticide applicator, contact your State's Department of Agriculture or Department of Environmental Protection or Conservation.

Pest Control Workers

(O*NET 37-2021.00)

Significant Points

● Federal and State laws require that pest control workers be licensed.

● Training on the safe use of pest control products and a passing score on an examination are required for licensure.

● Job prospects should be favorable for qualified applicants because many people leave the occupation.

Nature of the Work

Roaches, rats, mice, spiders, termites, fleas, ants, and bees—few people welcome them into their homes or offices. Unwanted creatures that infest households, buildings, or surrounding areas are pests that can pose serious risks to human health and safety. It is a pest control worker's job to eliminate them.

Pest control workers locate, identify, destroy, control, and repel pests. They use their knowledge of pests' biology and habits, along with an arsenal of pest management techniques—applying chemicals, setting traps, operating equipment, and even modifying structures—to alleviate pest problems.

Part of pest control may require pesticide application. Pest control workers use two different types of pesticides—general use and restricted use. General use pesticides are the most widely used and are readily available; in diluted concentrations they are available

Pest control workers need extensive training to work with pest control chemicals.

to the public. Restricted use pesticides are available only to certified professionals for controlling the most severe infestations. Their registration, labeling, and application are regulated by Federal law, interpreted by the U.S. Environmental Protection Agency (EPA), because of their potential harm to pest control workers, customers, and the environment.

Pesticides are not pest control workers' only tool, however. Pest control workers increasingly use a combination of pest management techniques, known as integrated pest management. One method involves using proper sanitation and creating physical barriers, for pests cannot survive without food and will not infest a building if they cannot enter it. Another method involves using baits, some of which destroy the pests, and others that prevent them from reproducing. Yet another method involves using mechanical devices, such as traps, that remove pests from the immediate environment.

Integrated pest management is becoming popular for several reasons. First, pesticides can pose environmental and health risks. Second, some pests are becoming more resistant to pesticides in certain situations. Finally, an integrated pest management plan is more effective in the long term than use of a pesticide alone.

New technology has been introduced that allows pest control workers to conduct home inspections, mainly of termites, in much less time. The technology works by implanting microchips in baiting stations, which emit signals that can tell pest control workers if there is termite activity at one of the baiting stations. Workers pick up the signals using a device similar to a metal detector and it allows them to assess much more quickly whether termites are present.

Most pest control workers are employed as pest control technicians, applicators, or supervisors. Position titles vary by State, but the hierarchy—based on training and responsibility required—remains consistent.

Pest control technicians identify potential pest problems, conduct inspections, and design control strategies. They work directly with the customer. Some technicians require a higher level of training depending on their task. If certain products are used, the technician may be required to become a certified *applicator*.

Applicators that specialize in controlling termites are called termite control technicians. They use chemicals and modify structures to eliminate termites and prevent reinfestation. To treat infested areas, termite control technicians drill holes and cut openings into buildings to access infestations, install physical barriers, or bait systems around the structure. Some termite control technicians even repair structural damage caused by termites.

Fumigators are applicators who control pests using poisonous gases called fumigants. Fumigators pretreat infested buildings by examining, measuring, and sealing the buildings. Then, using cylinders, hoses, and valves, they fill structures with the proper amount and concentration of fumigant. They also monitor the premises during treatment for leaking gas. To prevent accidental fumigant exposure, fumigators padlock doors and post warning signs.

Pest control supervisors, also known as operators, direct service technicians and certified applicators. Supervisors are licensed to apply pesticides, but they usually are more involved in running the business. Supervisors are responsible for ensuring that employees obey rules regarding pesticide use, and they must resolve any problems that arise with regulatory officials or customers. Most States require each pest control establishment to have a supervisor; self-employed business owners usually are supervisors.

Working Conditions

Pest control workers must kneel, bend, reach, and crawl to inspect, modify, and treat structures. They work both indoors and out, in all weather conditions. During warm weather, applicators may be uncomfortable wearing the heavy protective gear—such as respirators, gloves, and goggles—required for working with pesticides.

Almost half of all pest control workers work a 40-hour week, but 25% work more hours. Pest control workers often work evenings and weekends, but many work consistent shifts.

There are health risks associated with pesticide use. Various pest control chemicals are toxic and could be harmful if not used properly. Health risks are minimized, however, by the extensive training required for certification and the use of recommended protective equipment, resulting in fewer reported cases of lost work. Because pest control workers travel to visit clients, the potential risk of motor vehicle accidents is another occupational hazard.

Training, Other Qualifications, and Advancement

A high school diploma or equivalent is the minimum qualification for most pest control jobs. Although a college degree is not required, more than 4 in 10 pest control workers have either attended college or earned a degree.

Pest control workers must have basic skills in math, chemistry, and writing, either learned at school or through an employer. Because of the extensive interaction that pest control workers have with their customers, employers prefer to hire people who have good communication and interpersonal skills. In addition, most pest control companies require their employees to have a good driving record. Pest control workers must be in good health because of the physical demands of the job, and they also must be able to withstand extreme conditions—such as the heat of climbing into an attic in the summertime or the chill of sliding into a crawlspace during winter.

Both Federal and State laws regulate pest control workers. These laws require them to be certified through training and examination, for which most pest control firms help their employees prepare. Workers may receive both formal classroom and on-the-job training, but they also must study on their own. Because the pest control industry is constantly changing, workers must attend continuing education classes to maintain their certification.

Requirements for pest control workers vary by State. Pest control workers usually begin their careers as apprentice technicians. Before performing any pest control services, apprentices must attend general training in pesticide safety and use. In addition, they must train in each pest control category in which they wish to practice. Categories may include general pest control, rodent control, termite control, fumigation, and ornamental and turf control.

In many States, training usually involves spending 10 hours in the classroom and 60 hours on the job for each category. After completing the required training, apprentices can provide supervised pest control services. To be eligible to become applicators, technicians must have a combination of experience and education and pass a test. This requirement is sometimes waived for individuals who have either a college degree in biological sciences or extensive related work experience. To become certified as applicators, technicians must pass an additional set of category exams. Depending on the State, applicators must attend additional classes every 1 to 6 years to be recertified.

Applicators with several years of experience often become supervisors. To qualify as a pest control supervisor, applicators may have to pass State-administered exams and have experience in the industry, usually a minimum of 2 years.

Employment

Pest control workers held about 68,000 jobs in 2004; about 83 percent of workers were employed in the services to buildings and dwellings industry, which includes pest control firms. Jobs are concentrated in States with warmer climates, due to the greater number of pests in these areas that thrive year round. About 12 percent of workers were self-employed.

Job Outlook

Job prospects should be favorable for qualified applicants because the nature of pest control work is not universally appealing and turnover in this occupation is relatively high. Thus, in addition to job openings arising from employment growth, opportunities will result from the need to replace workers who leave the occupation. Employment growth of pest control workers is expected to be faster than the average for all occupations through 2014. One factor limiting growth in this occupation, however, is the lack of sufficient numbers of workers willing to go into this field.

Demand for pest control workers is projected to increase for a number of reasons. Growth in the population will generate new residential and commercial buildings that will require inspections by pest control workers. Also, more people are expected to use pest control services as environmental and health concerns, greater numbers of dual-income households, and improvements in the standard of living convince more people to hire professionals rather than attempt pest control work themselves. In addition, tougher regula-

tions limiting pesticide use will demand more complex integrated pest management strategies.

Concerns about the effects of pesticide use in schools have increasingly prompted more school districts to investigate alternative means of pest control, such as integrated pest management. Furthermore, use of some newer materials for insulation around foundations has made many homes more susceptible to pest infestation. Finally, continuing population shifts to the more pest-prone sunbelt States should increase the number of households in need of pest control.

Earnings

Median hourly earnings of full-time wage and salary pest control workers were $12.61 in May 2004. The middle 50 percent earned between $10.06 and $15.97. The lowest 10 percent earned less than $8.13, and the top 10 percent earned over $20.19. Pest control supervisors usually earn the most and technicians the least, with earnings of certified applicators falling somewhere in between. Some pest control workers earn commissions based on the number of contracts for pest control services they sell. Others may earn bonuses for exceeding performance goals.

Related Occupations

Pesticide handlers also apply pesticides in a safe manner to lawns, trees, and other plants. Pest control workers visit homes and places of business to provide building services. Other workers who provide services to buildings include building cleaning workers; grounds maintenance workers; various construction trades workers, such as carpenters; and heating, air-conditioning, and refrigeration mechanics and installers.

Sources of Additional Information

Private employment agencies and State employment services offices have information about available job opportunities for pest control workers.

For information about the training and certification required in your State, contact your local office of the U.S. Department of Agriculture or your State's Environmental Protection (or Conservation) Agency.

Personal Care and Service Occupations

Animal Care and Service Workers

(O*NET 39-2011.00, 39-2021.00)

Significant Points

- Animal lovers get satisfaction in this occupation, but the work can be unpleasant, physically and emotionally demanding, and sometimes dangerous.

- Most workers are trained on the job, but employers generally prefer to hire people who have some experience with animals; some jobs require a bachelor's degree in biology, animal science, or a related field.

- Good employment opportunities are expected for most positions; however, keen competition is expected for jobs as zookeepers.

- Earnings are relatively low.

Nature of the Work

Many people like animals. But, as pet owners can attest, taking care of them is hard work. Animal care and service workers—which include animal caretakers and animal trainers—train, feed, water, groom, bathe, and exercise animals, and clean, disinfect, and repair their cages. They also play with the animals, provide companionship, and observe behavioral changes that could indicate illness or injury. Boarding kennels, animal shelters, veterinary hospitals and clinics, stables, laboratories, aquariums, and zoological parks all house animals and employ animal care and service workers. Job titles and duties vary by employment setting.

Kennel attendants care for pets while their owners are working or traveling out of town. Beginning attendants perform basic tasks, such as cleaning cages and dog runs, filling food and water dishes, and exercising animals. Experienced attendants may provide basic animal healthcare, as well as bathe animals, trim nails, and attend to other grooming needs. Attendants who work in kennels also may sell pet food and supplies, assist in obedience training, help with breeding, or prepare animals for shipping.

Animal caretakers who specialize in grooming or maintaining a pet's—usually a dog's or cat's—appearance are called *groomers*. Some groomers work in kennels, veterinary clinics, animal shelters, or pet-supply stores. Others operate their own grooming business, typically at a salon, or increasingly, by making house calls. Such mobile services are growing rapidly as it offers convenience for pet owners and flexible hours for groomers. Groomers answer telephones, schedule appointments, discuss pets' grooming needs with clients, and collect information on the pet's disposition and its veterinarian. Groomers often are the first to notice a medical problem, such as an ear or skin infection, that requires veterinary care.

Grooming the pet involves several steps: an initial brush-out is followed by an initial clipping of hair or fur using electric clippers, combs, and grooming shears; the groomer then cuts the nails, cleans the ears, bathes, and blow-dries the animal, and ends with a final clipping and styling.

Animal caretakers in animal shelters perform a variety of duties and work with a wide variety of animals. In addition to attending to the basic needs of the animals, caretakers also must keep records of the animals received and discharged and any tests or treatments done. Some vaccinate newly admitted animals under the direction of a veterinarian or veterinary technician, and euthanize (painlessly put to death) seriously ill, severely injured, or unwanted animals. Animal caretakers in animal shelters also interact with the public, answering telephone inquiries, screening applicants for animal adoption, or educating visitors on neutering and other animal health issues.

Animal caretakers who specialize in grooming or maintaining a pet's appearance are called groomers.

Caretakers in stables are called *grooms*. They saddle and unsaddle horses, give them rubdowns, and walk them to cool them off after a ride. They also feed, groom, and exercise the horses; clean out stalls and replenish bedding; polish saddles; clean and organize the tack (harness, saddle, and bridle) room; and store supplies and feed. Experienced grooms may help train horses.

In zoos, animal care and service workers, called *keepers*, prepare the diets and clean the enclosures of animals, and sometimes assist in raising them when they are very young. They watch for any signs of illness or injury, monitor eating patterns or any changes in behavior, and record their observations. Keepers also may answer questions and ensure that the visiting public behaves responsibly toward the exhibited animals. Depending on the zoo, keepers may be assigned to work with a broad group of animals such as mammals, birds, or reptiles, or they may work with a limited collection of animals such as primates, large cats, or small mammals.

Animal trainers train animals for riding, security, performance, obedience, or assisting persons with disabilities. Animal trainers do this by accustoming the animal to human voice and contact, and conditioning the animal to respond to commands. Trainers use several techniques to help them train animals. One technique, known as a bridge, is a stimulus that a trainer uses to communicate the precise moment an animal does something correctly. When the animal responds correctly, the trainer gives positive reinforcement in a variety of ways: food, toys, play, rubdowns, or speaking the word "good." Animal training takes place in small steps, and often takes months and even years of repetition. During the conditioning process, trainers provide animals mental stimulation, physical exercise, and husbandry care. In addition to their hands-on work with the animals, trainers often oversee other aspects of the animal's care, such as diet preparation. Trainers often work in competitions or shows, such as the circus or marine parks. Trainers who work in shows also may participate in educational programs for visitors and guests.

Working Conditions

People who love animals get satisfaction from working with and helping them. However, some of the work may be unpleasant, physically and emotionally demanding, and sometimes dangerous. Most animal care and service workers have to clean animal cages and lift, hold, or restrain animals, risking exposure to bites or scratches. Their work often involves kneeling, crawling, repeated bending, and lifting heavy supplies like bales of hay or bags of feed. Animal caretakers must take precautions when treating animals with germicides or insecticides. The work setting can be noisy. Caretakers of show and sports animals travel to competitions.

Animal care and service workers who witness abused animals or who assist in the euthanizing of unwanted, aged, or hopelessly injured animals may experience emotional distress. Those working for private humane societies and municipal animal shelters often deal with the public, some of whom might react with hostility to any implication that the owners are neglecting or abusing their pets. Such workers must maintain a calm and professional demeanor while they enforce the laws regarding animal care.

Animal care and service workers may work outdoors in all kinds of weather. Hours are irregular. Animals must be fed every day, so caretakers often work weekend and holiday shifts. In some animal hospitals, research facilities, and animal shelters, an attendant is on duty 24 hours a day, which means night shifts.

Training, Other Qualifications, and Advancement

Most animal care and service workers are trained on the job; however, employers generally prefer to hire people who have some experience with animals. Some training programs are available for specific types of animal caretakers, such as groomers, but formal training is usually not necessary for entry-level positions. Animal trainers often need to possess a high school diploma or GED equivalent. However, some animal training jobs may require a bachelor's degree and additional skills. For example, a marine mammal trainer usually needs a bachelor's degree in biology, marine biology, animal science, psychology, zoology, or related field, plus strong swimming skills and SCUBA certification. All animal trainers need patience, sensitivity, and experience with problem-solving and animal obedience. Certification is not mandatory for animal trainers, but several organizations offer training programs and certification for prospective animal trainers.

Most pet groomers learn their trade by completing an informal apprenticeship, usually lasting 6 to 10 weeks, under the guidance of an experienced groomer. Prospective groomers also may attend one of the 50 State-licensed grooming schools throughout the country, with programs varying in length from 2 to 18 weeks. The National Dog Groomers Association of America offers certification for master status as a groomer with a focus on four principle areas—non-sporting, sporting, terrier, and masters. The examination consists of 400 questions with a separate part testing practical skills. Beginning groomers often start by taking on one duty, such as bathing and drying the pet. They eventually assume responsibility for the entire grooming process, from the initial brush-out to the final clipping. Groomers who work in large retail establishments or kennels may, with experience, move into supervisory or managerial positions. Experienced groomers often choose to open their own salons.

Beginning animal caretakers in kennels learn on the job, and usually start by cleaning cages and feeding and watering animals. Kennel caretakers may be promoted to kennel supervisor, assistant manager, and manager, and those with enough capital and experience may open up their own kennels. The American Boarding Kennels Association (ABKA) offers a three-stage, home-study program for individuals interested in pet care. The first two stages address basic and advanced principles of animal care, while the third stage focuses on indepth animal care and good business procedures. Those who complete the third stage and pass oral and written examinations administered by the ABKA become Certified Kennel Operators (CKO).

Some zoological parks may require their caretakers to have a bachelor's degree in biology, animal science, or a related field. Most require experience with animals, preferably as a volunteer or paid keeper in a zoo. Zookeepers may advance to senior keeper, assistant head keeper, head keeper, and assistant curator, but very few openings occur, especially for the higher level positions.

Animal caretakers in animal shelters are not required to have any specialized training, but training programs and workshops are increasingly available through the Humane Society of the United States, the American Humane Association, and the National Animal Control Association. Workshop topics include cruelty investigations, appropriate methods of euthanasia for shelter animals, proper guidelines for capturing animals techniques for preventing problems with wildlife, and dealing with the general public. Because shelter workers often deal with individuals who abandon their pets, excellent communication skills, including the ability to handle emotional people, is vital. With experience and additional training, caretakers in animal shelters may become adoption coordinators, animal control officers, emergency rescue drivers, assistant shelter managers, or shelter directors.

Employment

Animal care and service workers held 172,000 jobs in 2004. Almost 3 out of 4 worked as nonfarm animal caretakers; the remainder worked as animal trainers. Nonfarm animal caretakers worked primarily in boarding kennels, animal shelters, stables, grooming shops, animal hospitals, and veterinary offices. A significant number also worked for animal humane societies, racing stables, dog and horse racetrack operators, zoos, theme parks, circuses, and other amusement and recreations services. In 2004, nearly 1 out of every 3 nonfarm animal caretakers was self-employed.

Employment of animal trainers was concentrated in animal services that specialize in training horses, pets, and other animal specialties; and in commercial sports, training racehorses and dogs. About 3 in 5 animal trainers were self-employed.

Job Outlook

Good job opportunities are expected for most positions because many workers leave this occupation each year. The need to replace workers leaving the field will create the overwhelming majority of job openings. Many animal caretaker jobs require little or no training and have flexible work schedules, attracting people seeking their first job, students, and others looking for temporary or part-time work, including retired people. The outlook for caretakers in zoos, however, is not favorable due to slow growth in zoo capacity and keen competition for the few positions. Job opportunities for animal care and service workers may vary from year to year, because the strength of the economy affects demand for these workers. Pet owners tend to spend more on animal services when the economy is strong.

In addition to replacement needs, employment of animal care and service workers is expected to grow faster than the average for all occupations through 2014. The companion pet population—which drives employment of animal caretakers in kennels, grooming shops, animal shelters, and veterinary clinics and hospitals—is expected to increase. Pet owners—including a large number of baby boomers, whose disposable income is expected to increase as they age—are expected to increasingly take advantage of grooming services, daily and overnight boarding services, training services, and veterinary services, resulting in more jobs for animal care and service workers. As many pet owners increasingly consider their pet as part of the family, their demand for luxury animal services and willingness to spend greater amounts of money on their pet will continue to grow.

Demand for animal care and service workers in animal shelters is expected to remain steady. Communities are increasingly recognizing the connection between animal abuse and abuse toward humans, and will probably continue to commit private funds to animal shelters, many of which are working hand-in-hand with social service agencies and law enforcement teams. Employment growth of personal and group animal trainers will stem from an increased number of animal owners seeking training services for their pets, including behavior modification and feline behavior training. Job openings as shelter workers will continue to be driven by high turnover as the job is extremely demanding and stressful.

Earnings

Earnings are relatively low. Median hourly earnings of nonfarm animal caretakers were $8.39 in May 2004. The middle 50 percent earned between $7.16 and $10.50. The bottom 10 percent earned less than $6.17, and the top 10 percent earned more than $13.66. Median hourly earnings in the industries employing the largest numbers of nonfarm animal caretakers in May 2004 were:

Spectator sports	$8.48
Other personal services	8.47
Social advocacy organizations	8.15
Other miscellaneous store retailers	7.95
Other professional, scientific, and technical services	7.86

Median hourly earnings of animal trainers were $10.60 in May 2004. The middle 50 percent earned between $8.10 and $15.23. The lowest 10 percent earned less than $7.07, and the top 10 percent earned more than $20.62.

Related Occupations

Others who work extensively with animals include farmers, ranchers, and agricultural managers; agricultural workers; veterinarians; veterinary technologists and technicians; veterinary assistants; biological scientists; and medical scientists.

Sources of Additional Information

For more information on jobs in animal caretaking and control, and the animal shelter and control personnel training program, write to:

➤ Humane Society of the United States, 2100 L St. NW., Washington, DC 20037-1598. Internet: **http://www.hsus.org**

For career information and information on training, certification, and earnings of animal control officers at Federal, State, and local levels, contact:

➤ National Animal Control Association, P.O. Box 1480851, Kansas City, MO 64148-0851. Internet: **www.nacanet.org**

For information on becoming an advanced pet care technician at a kennel, contact:

➤ American Boarding Kennels Association, 1702 East Pikes Peak Ave., Colorado Springs, CO 80909.

Barbers, Cosmetologists, and Other Personal Appearance Workers

(O*NET 39-5011.00, 39-5012.00, 39-5091.00, 39-5092.00, 39-5093.00, 39-5094.00)

Significant Points

● Job opportunities generally should be good, but competition is expected for jobs and clients at higher paying salons; opportunities will be best for those licensed to provide a broad range of services.

● A State license is required for barbers, cosmetologists, and most other personal appearance workers, with the exception of shampooers; qualifications vary by State.

● About 48 percent of workers are self-employed; many also work flexible schedules.

Nature of the Work

Barbers and cosmetologists, also called *hairdressers* and *hairstylists*, provide hair care services to enhance the appearance of consumers. Other personal appearance workers, such as *manicurists and pedicurists, shampooers*, and *skin care specialists* provide specialized services that help clients look and feel their best.

Barbers cut, trim, shampoo, and style hair. They also fit hairpieces and offer scalp treatments and facial shaving. In many States, barbers are licensed to color, bleach, or highlight hair and to offer permanent-wave services. Many barbers also provide skin care and nail treatments.

Hairdressers, hairstylists, and cosmetologists offer beauty services, such as shampooing, cutting, coloring, and styling hair. They may advise clients on how to care for their hair, how to straighten their hair or give it a permanent wave, or how to lighten or darken their hair color. In addition, cosmetologists may be trained to give manicures, pedicures, and scalp and facial treatments; provide makeup analysis; and clean and style wigs and hairpieces.

A number of workers offer specialized services. *Manicurists and pedicurists,* called *nail technicians* in some States, work exclusively on nails and provide manicures, pedicures, coloring, and nail extensions to clients. Another group of specialists is *skin care specialists*, or *estheticians*, who cleanse and beautify the skin by giving facials, full-body treatments, and head and neck massages and by removing hair through waxing. *Electrologists* use an electrolysis machine to remove hair. Finally, in some larger salons, *shampooers* specialize in shampooing and conditioning hair.

In addition to working with clients, personal appearance workers are expected to maintain clean work areas and sanitize all their work instruments. They may make appointments and keep records of hair color and permanent-wave formulas used by their regular clients. A growing number actively sell hair care products and other cosmetic supplies. Barbers, cosmetologists, and other personal appearance workers who operate their own salons have managerial duties that may include hiring, supervising, and firing workers, as well as keeping business and inventory records, ordering supplies, and arranging for advertising.

Working Conditions

Barbers, cosmetologists, and other personal appearance workers usually work in clean, pleasant surroundings with good lighting and ventilation. Good health and stamina are important, because these workers are on their feet for most of their shift. Prolonged exposure to some hair and nail chemicals may cause irritation, so protective clothing, such as plastic gloves or aprons, may be worn.

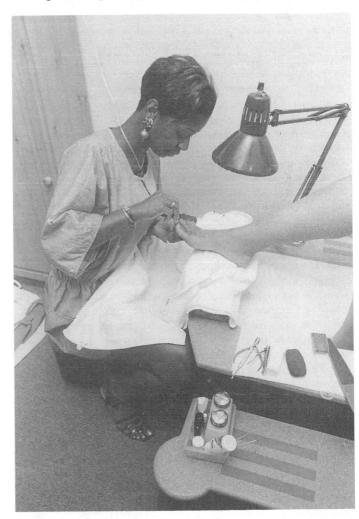

Nearly half of workers are self-employed, and many work flexible schedules.

Most full-time barbers, cosmetologists, and other personal appearance workers put in a 40-hour week, but longer hours are common, especially among self-employed workers. Work schedules may include evenings and weekends, the times when beauty salons and barbershops are busiest. Barbers and cosmetologists generally work on weekends and during lunch and evening hours; as a result, they may arrange to take breaks during less busy times. About 32 percent of cosmetologists and 17 percent of barbers work part time, and 14 percent of cosmetologists and 17 percent of barbers have variable schedules.

Training, Other Qualifications, and Advancement
All States require barbers, cosmetologists, and most other personal appearance workers, with the exception of shampooers, to be licensed; however, qualifications for a license vary by State. Generally, a person must have graduated from a State-licensed barber or cosmetology school and be at least 16 years old. A few States require applicants to pass a physical examination. Some States require graduation from high school, while others require as little as an eighth-grade education. In a few States, the completion of an apprenticeship can substitute for graduation from a school, but very few barbers or cosmetologists learn their skills in this way. Applicants for a license usually are required to pass a written test and demonstrate an ability to perform basic barbering or cosmetology services.

Some States have reciprocity agreements that allow licensed barbers and cosmetologists to obtain a license in a different State without additional formal training. Such agreements are uncommon, however, and most States do not recognize training or licenses obtained from a different State. Consequently, persons who wish to work in a particular State should review the laws of that State before entering a training program.

Public and private vocational schools offer daytime or evening classes in barbering and cosmetology. Full-time programs in barbering and cosmetology usually last 9 to 24 months, but training for manicurists and pedicurists, skin care specialists, and electrologists requires significantly less time. An apprenticeship program can last from 1 to 3 years. Shampooers generally do not need formal training or a license. Formal training programs include classroom study, demonstrations, and practical work. Students study the basic services—cutting and styling hair, chemically treating hair, shaving customers, and giving hair and scalp treatments—and, under supervision, practice on customers in school "clinics." Students attend lectures on the use and care of instruments, sanitation and hygiene, chemistry, anatomy, physiology, and the recognition of simple skin ailments. Instruction also is provided in communication, sales, and general business practices. Experienced barbers and cosmetologists may take advanced courses in hairstyling, coloring, the sale and service of wigs and hairpieces, and sales and marketing.

After graduating from a training program, students can take a State licensing examination, which consists of a written test and, in some cases, a practical test of styling skills based on established performance criteria. A few States include an oral examination in which applicants are asked to explain the procedures they are following while taking the practical test. In many States, cosmetology training may be credited toward a barbering license, and vice versa. A few States combine the two licenses into one hairstyling license. Many States require separate licensing examinations for manicurists, pedicurists, and skin care specialists.

For many barbers, cosmetologists, and other personal appearance workers, formal training and a license are only the first steps in a career that requires years of continuing education. Personal appearance workers must keep abreast of the latest fashions and beauty techniques as hairstyles change, new products are developed,

and services expand to meet clients' needs. They attend training at salons, cosmetology schools, or industry trade shows. Through workshops and demonstrations of the latest techniques, industry representatives introduce cosmetologists to a wide range of products and services. As retail sales become an increasingly important part of salons' revenue, the ability to be an effective salesperson becomes ever more vital for salon workers.

Successful personal appearance workers should have an understanding of fashion, art, and technical design. They should enjoy working with the public and be willing and able to follow clients' instructions. Communication, image, and attitude play an important role in career success. Some cosmetology schools consider "people skills" to be such an integral part of the job that they require coursework in that area. Business skills are important for those who plan to operate their own salons.

During their first months on the job, new workers are given relatively simple tasks or are assigned the simplest procedures. Once they have demonstrated their skills, they are gradually permitted to perform more complicated tasks, such as coloring hair or applying permanent waves. As they continue to work in the field, more training usually is required to learn the techniques particular to each salon and to build on the basics learned in cosmetology school.

Advancement usually takes the form of higher earnings as barbers and cosmetologists gain experience and build a steady clientele. Some barbers and cosmetologists manage large salons, lease booth space in salons, or open their own salons after several years of experience. Others teach in barber or cosmetology schools or provide training through vocational schools. Still others advance to become sales representatives, image or fashion consultants, or examiners for State licensing boards.

Employment
Barbers, cosmetologists, and other personal appearance workers held about 790,000 jobs in 2004. Of these, barbers, hairdressers, hairstylists, and cosmetologists held 670,000 jobs, manicurists and pedicurists 60,000, skin care specialists 30,000, and shampooers 27,000.

Most of these workers are employed in beauty salons or barber shops, but they also are found in nail salons, day and resort spas, department stores, nursing and other residential care homes, and drug and cosmetics stores. Nearly every town has a barbershop or beauty salon, but employment in this occupation is concentrated in the most populous cities and States.

About 48 percent of all barbers, cosmetologists, and other personal appearance workers are self-employed. Many own their own salon, but a growing number lease booth space or a chair from the salon's owner.

Job Outlook
Job opportunities generally should be good. However, competition is expected for jobs and clients at higher paying salons as applicants compete with a large pool of licensed and experienced cosmetologists for these positions. Opportunities will be best for those with previous experience and for those licensed to provide a broad range of services.

Overall employment of barbers, cosmetologists, and other personal appearance workers is projected to grow about as fast as the average for all occupations through 2014, because of an increasing population, rising incomes, and growing demand for personal appearance services. In addition to those arising from job growth, numerous job openings will come about from the need to replace workers who transfer to other occupations, retire, or leave the labor force for other reasons.

Employment trends are expected to vary among the different occupational specialties. On the one hand, slower-than-average growth is expected in employment of barbers because of the large number of retirements expected over the 2004–14 projection period and because of the relatively small number of cosmetology school graduates opting to obtain barbering licenses. On the other hand, employment of hairdressers, hairstylists, and cosmetologists should grow about as fast as the average for all workers because many now cut and style both men's and women's hair and because the demand for hair treatment by teens and aging baby boomers is expected to remain steady or even grow.

Continued growth in the number of nail salons and full-service day spas will generate numerous job openings for manicurists, pedicurists, skin care specialists, and shampooers. Employment of manicurists, pedicurists, and skin care specialists will grow faster than the average, while employment of shampooers will grow about as fast as the average. Nail salons specialize in providing manicures and pedicures. Day spas typically provide a full range of services, including beauty wraps, manicures and pedicures, facials, and massages.

Earnings

A number of factors, including the size and location of the salon, clients' tipping habits, and competition from other barber shops and salons, determine the total income of barbers, cosmetologists, and other personal appearance workers. They may receive commissions based on the price of the service, or a salary based on the number of hours worked, and many receive commissions on the products they sell. In addition, some salons pay bonuses to employees who bring in new business. A cosmetologist's or barber's initiative and ability to attract and hold regular clients also are key factors in determining his or her earnings. Earnings for entry-level workers are usually low; however, for those who stay in the profession, earnings can be considerably higher.

Although some salons offer paid vacations and medical benefits, many self-employed and part-time workers in this occupation do not enjoy such benefits.

Median annual earnings in May 2004 for salaried hairdressers, hairstylists, and cosmetologists, including tips and commission, were $19,800. The middle 50 percent earned between $15,480 and $26,600. The lowest 10 percent earned less than $12,920, and the highest 10 percent earned more than $35,990.

Median annual earnings in May 2004 for salaried barbers, including tips, were $21,200. The middle 50 percent earned between $15,380 and $30,390. The lowest 10 percent earned less than $12,950, and the highest 10 percent earned more than $43,170.

Among skin care specialists, median annual earnings, including tips, were $24,010, for manicurists and pedicurists $18,500, and for shampooers $14,610.

Related Occupations

Other workers who provide a personal service to clients and usually must be professionally licensed or certified include massage therapists and fitness workers.

Sources of Additional Information

A list of licensed training schools and licensing requirements for cosmetologists may be obtained from:
➤ National Accrediting Commission of Cosmetology Arts and Sciences, 4401 Ford Ave., Suite 1300, Alexandria, VA 22302. Internet: **http://www.naccas.org**

Information about a career in cosmetology is available from:
➤ National Cosmetology Association, 401 N. Michigan Ave., 22nd floor, Chicago, IL 60611. Internet: **http://www.ncacares.org**

For details on State licensing requirements and approved barber or cosmetology schools, contact the State boards of barber or cosmetology examiners in your State.

Child Care Workers

(O*NET 39-9011.00)

Significant Points

- About 1 out of 3 child care workers are self-employed; most of these are family child care providers.

- Training requirements vary from a high school diploma to a college degree, although a high school diploma and little or no experience are adequate for many jobs.

- Many workers leave these jobs every year, creating good job opportunities.

Nature of the Work

Child care workers nurture and care for children who have not yet entered formal schooling and also work with older children in before- and after-school situations. These workers play an important role in a child's development by caring for the child when parents are at work or away for other reasons. In addition to attending to children's basic needs, child care workers organize activities that stimulate children's physical, emotional, intellectual, and social growth. They help children explore individual interests, develop talents and independence, build self-esteem, and learn how to get along with others.

Child care workers generally are classified in three different groups, depending on the setting in which they work: Workers who care for children at the children's home, called private household workers; those who care for children in their own home, called family child care providers; and those that work at separate child care centers and centers that provide preschool services to 3- and 4-year-old children.

Private household workers who are employed on an hourly basis usually are called *babysitters*. These child care workers bathe, dress, and feed children; supervise their play; wash their clothes; and clean their rooms. Babysitters also may put children to bed and wake them, read to them, involve them in educational games, take them for doctors' visits, and discipline them. Those who are in charge of infants, sometimes called *infant nurses*, also prepare bottles and change diapers. *Nannies* work full or part time for a single family. They generally take care of children from birth to age 10 or 12, tending to the child's early education, nutrition, health, and other needs, and also may perform the duties of a housekeeper, including cleaning and laundry.

Family child care providers often work alone with a small group of children, though some work in larger settings with multiple adults. Child care centers generally have more than one adult per group of children; in groups of older children, a child care worker may assist a more experienced preschool teacher.

Most child care workers perform a combination of basic care and teaching duties, but the majority of their time is spent on caregiving activities. Workers whose primary responsibility is teaching are classified as preschool teachers, covered in the separate *Handbook* statement on teachers—preschool, kindergarten, elementary, middle, and secondary. However, many basic care activities also are opportunities for children to learn. For example, a worker who shows a child how to tie a shoelace teaches the child while also providing for that child's basic care needs. Child care programs help children learn about trust and gain a sense of security.

Child care workers spend most of their day working with children. However, they do maintain contact with parents or guardians through informal meetings or scheduled conferences to discuss each child's progress and needs. Many child care workers keep records of each child's progress and suggest ways in which parents can stimulate their child's learning and development at home. Some child care centers and before- and after-school programs actively recruit parent volunteers to work with the children and participate in administrative decisions and program planning.

Young children learn mainly through play. Child care workers recognize this and capitalize on children's play to further language development (storytelling and acting games), improve social skills (working together to build a neighborhood in a sandbox), and introduce scientific and mathematical concepts (balancing and counting blocks when building a bridge or mixing colors when painting). Often a less structured approach is used to teach young children, including small-group lessons; one-on-one instruction; and creative activities such as art, dance, and music. Child care workers play a vital role in preparing children to build the skills they will need in school.

Child care workers in child care centers or family child care homes greet young children as they arrive, help them to remove outer garments, and select an activity of interest. When caring for infants, they feed and change them. To ensure a well-balanced program, child care workers prepare daily and long-term schedules of activities. Each day's activities balance individual and group play, as well as quiet and active time. Children are given some freedom to participate in activities in which they are interested.

Concern over school-aged children being home alone before and after school has spurred many parents to seek alternative ways for their children to constructively spend their time. The purpose of before- and afterschool programs is to watch over school-aged children during the gap between school hours and their parents' work hours. These programs also may operate during the summer and on weekends. Workers in before- and after-school programs may help students with their homework or engage them in other extracurricular activities. These activities may include field trips,

Child care workers help young children learn and develop through play.

learning about computers, painting, photography, and participating in sports. Some child care workers may be responsible for taking children to school in the morning and picking them up from school in the afternoon. Before- and afterschool programs may be operated by public school systems, local community centers, or other private organizations.

Helping keep young children healthy is an important part of the job. Child care workers serve nutritious meals and snacks and teach good eating habits and personal hygiene. They ensure that children have proper rest periods. They identify children who may not feel well and, in some cases, may help parents locate programs that will provide basic health services. Child care workers also watch for children who show signs of emotional or developmental problems and discuss these matters with their supervisor and the child's parents. Early identification of children with special needs—such as those with behavioral, emotional, physical, or learning disabilities—is important to improve their future learning ability. Special education teachers often work with these preschool children to provide the individual attention they need. (Special education teachers are discussed elsewhere in the *Handbook*.)

Working Conditions

Helping children grow, learn, and gain new skills can be very rewarding. Child care workers help to improve children's communication, learning, and other personal skills. The work is sometimes routine; however, new activities and challenges mark each day. Child care can be physically and emotionally taxing, as workers constantly stand, walk, bend, stoop, and lift to attend to each child's interests and problems.

To ensure that children in child care centers receive proper supervision, State or local regulations may require a certain ratio of workers to children. The ratio varies with the age of the children. Child development experts generally recommend that a single caregiver be responsible for no more than 3 or 4 infants (less than 1 year old), 5 or 6 toddlers (1 to 2 years old), or 10 preschool-aged children (between 2 and 5 years old). In before- and afterschool programs, workers may be responsible for many school-aged children at a time.

Family child care providers work out of their own homes. While this arrangement provides convenience, it also requires that their homes be accommodating to young children. Private household workers usually work in the pleasant and comfortable homes or apartments of their employers. Most are day workers who live in their own homes and travel to work, though some live in the home of their employer, generally with their own room and bath. They often become part of their employer's family and may derive satisfaction from caring for the family.

The work hours of child care workers vary widely. Child care centers usually are open year round, with long hours so that parents can drop off and pick up their children before and after work. Some centers employ full-time and part-time staff with staggered shifts to cover the entire day. Some workers are unable to take regular breaks during the day due to limited staffing. Public and many private preschool programs operate during the typical 9- or 10-month school year, employing both full-time and part-time workers. Family child care providers have flexible hours and daily routines, but they may work long or unusual hours to fit parents' work schedules. Live-in nannies usually work longer hours than do those who have their own homes. However, although nannies may work evenings or weekends, they usually get other time off.

Training, Other Qualifications, and Advancement

The training and qualifications required of child care workers vary widely. Each State has its own licensing requirements that regulate caregiver training; these range from a high school diploma to community college courses to a college degree in child development or early childhood education. State requirements are generally higher for workers at child care centers than for family child care providers; child care workers in private settings who care for only a few children often are not regulated by States at all. Child care workers generally can obtain some form of employment with a high school diploma and little or no experience, but certain private firms and publicly funded programs have more demanding training and education requirements.

Some employers prefer to hire child care workers who have earned a nationally recognized Child Development Associate (CDA) credential or the Certified Childcare Professional designation, have taken secondary or postsecondary courses in child development and early childhood education, or have work experience in a child care setting. Other employers require their own specialized training. An increasing number of employers require an associate degree in early childhood education.

Child care workers must anticipate and prevent problems, deal with disruptive children, provide fair but firm discipline, and be enthusiastic and constantly alert. They must communicate effectively with the children and their parents, as well as with other teachers and child care workers. Workers should be mature, patient, understanding, and articulate and have energy and physical stamina. Skills in music, art, drama, and storytelling also are important. Self-employed child care workers must have business sense and management abilities.

Opportunities for advancement are limited. However, as child care workers gain experience, some may advance to supervisory or administrative positions in large child care centers or preschools. Often, these positions require additional training, such as a bachelor's or master's degree. Other workers move on to work in resource and referral agencies, consulting with parents on available child services. A few workers become involved in policy or advocacy work related to child care and early childhood education. With a bachelor's degree, workers may become preschool teachers or become certified to teach in public or private schools. Some workers set up their own child care businesses.

Employment

Child care workers held about 1.3 million jobs in 2004. Many worked part time. About 1 out of 3 child care workers were self-employed; most of these were family child care providers.

Seventeen percent of all child care workers are found in child day care services, and about 21 percent work for private households. The remainder worked primarily in local government educational services; nursing and residential care facilities; religious organizations; amusement and recreation industries; private educational services; civic and social organizations; individual and family services; and local government, excluding education and hospitals. Some child care programs are for-profit centers; some of these are affiliated with a local or national chain. Religious institutions, community agencies, school systems, and State and local governments operate nonprofit programs. A very small percentage of private industry establishments operate onsite child care centers for the children of their employees.

Job Outlook

High replacement needs should create good job opportunities for child care workers. Qualified persons who are interested in this work should have little trouble finding and keeping a job. Many child care workers must be replaced each year as they leave the occupation

temporarily to fulfill family responsibilities, to study, or for other reasons. Others leave permanently because they are interested in pursuing other occupations or because of dissatisfaction with hours, low pay and benefits, and stressful conditions.

Employment of child care workers is projected to increase about as fast as the average for all occupations through the year 2014. The number of women in the labor force of childbearing age (widely considered to be ages 15 to 44) and the number of children under 5 years of age are both expected to rise over the next 10 years. Also, the proportion of children being cared for exclusively by parents or other relatives is likely to continue to decline, spurring demand for additional child care workers. Concern about the behavior of school-aged children during nonschool hours also should increase demand for before- and afterschool programs and child care workers to staff them.

The growth in demand for child care workers will be moderated, however, by an increasing emphasis on early childhood education programs. While only a few States currently provide targeted or universal preschool programs, many more are considering or currently implementing such programs. There also is likely to be a rise in enrollment in private preschools as the value of formal education before kindergarten becomes more widely accepted. Since the majority of workers in these programs are classified as preschool teachers, this growth in preschool enrollment will mean that relatively fewer child care workers will be needed for children old enough to participate in preschool.

Earnings

Pay depends on the educational attainment of the worker and the type of establishment. Although the pay generally is very low, more education usually means higher earnings. Median hourly earnings of wage and salary child care workers were $8.06 in May 2004. The middle 50 percent earned between $6.75 and $10.01. The lowest 10 percent earned less than $5.90, and the highest 10 percent earned more than $12.34. Median hourly earnings in the industries employing the largest numbers of child care workers in 2004 were as follows:

Other residential care facilities	$9.66
Elementary and secondary schools	9.22
Civic and social organizations	7.62
Other amusement and recreation industries	7.58
Child day care services	7.34

Earnings of self-employed child care workers vary depending on the hours worked, the number and ages of the children, and the location.

Benefits vary, but are minimal for most child care workers. Many employers offer free or discounted child care to employees. Some offer a full benefits package, including health insurance and paid vacations, but others offer no benefits at all. Some employers offer seminars and workshops to help workers learn new skills. A few are willing to cover the cost of courses taken at community colleges or technical schools. Live-in nannies receive free room and board.

Related Occupations

Child care work requires patience; creativity; an ability to nurture, motivate, teach, and influence children; and leadership, organizational, and administrative skills. Others who work with children and need these qualities and skills include teacher assistants; teachers —preschool, kindergarten, elementary, middle, and secondary; and teachers—special education.

Sources of Additional Information

For an electronic question-and-answer service on child care, information on becoming a child care provider, and other resources, contact:

➤ National Child Care Information Center, 243 Church St. NW., 2nd floor, Vienna, VA 22180. Internet: **http://www.nccic.org**

For eligibility requirements and a description of the Child Development Associate credential, contact:

➤ Council for Professional Recognition, 2460 16th St. NW., Washington, DC 20009-3575. Internet: **http://www.cdacouncil.org**

For eligibility requirements and a description of the Certified Childcare Professional designation, contact:

➤ National Child Care Association, 1016 Rosser St., Conyers, GA 30012. Internet: **http://www.nccanet.org**

For information about a career as a nanny, contact:

➤ International Nanny Association, 191 Clarksville Rd., Princeton Junction, NJ 08550-3111. Telephone (tollfree): 888-878-1477. Internet: **http://www.nanny.org**

State departments of human services or social services can supply State regulations and training requirements for child care workers.

Fitness Workers

(O*NET 39-9031.00)

Significant Points

● Many group fitness and personal training jobs are part time, but many workers increase their hours by working at several different facilities or at clients' homes.

● Night and weekend working hours are common.

● Most fitness workers need to be certified.

● Employment prospects are expected to be good because of rapid growth in the fitness industry.

Nature of the Work

Fitness workers lead, instruct, and motivate individuals or groups in exercise activities, including cardiovascular exercise, strength training, and stretching. They work in commercial and nonprofit health clubs, country clubs, hospitals, universities, yoga and Pilates studios, resorts, and clients' homes. Increasingly, fitness workers also are found in workplaces, where they organize and direct health and fitness programs for employees of all ages.

Although gyms and health clubs offer a variety of exercise activities such as weightlifting, yoga, cardiovascular training, and karate, fitness workers typically specialize in only a few areas.

Personal trainers work one-on-one with clients either in a gym or in the client's home. Trainers help clients assess their level of physical fitness and set and reach fitness goals. Trainers also demonstrate various exercises and help clients improve their exercise techniques. Trainers may keep records of their clients' exercise sessions to assess clients' progress toward physical fitness.

Group exercise instructors conduct group exercise sessions that involve aerobic exercise, stretching, and muscle conditioning. Because cardiovascular conditioning classes often involve movement to music, outside of class instructors must choose and mix the music and choreograph a corresponding exercise sequence. Pilates and yoga are two increasingly popular conditioning methods taught in exercise classes. Instructors demonstrate the different moves and positions of the particular method; they also observe students and correct those who are doing the exercises improperly. Group exercise instructors are responsible for ensuring that their classes are motivating, safe, and challenging, yet not too difficult for the participants.

Fitness directors oversee the fitness-related aspects of a health club or fitness center. Their work involves creating and maintaining programs that meet the needs of the club's members, including new member orientations, fitness assessments, and workout incentive programs. They also select fitness equipment; coordinate personal training and group exercise programs; hire, train, and supervise fitness staff; and carry out administrative duties.

Fitness workers in smaller facilities with few employees may perform a variety of functions in addition to their fitness duties, such as tending the front desk, signing up new members, giving tours of the fitness center, writing newsletter articles, creating posters and flyers, and supervising the weight training and cardiovascular equipment areas. In larger commercial facilities, personal trainers are often required to sell their services to members and to make a specified number of sales. Some fitness workers may combine the duties of group exercise instructors and personal trainers, and in smaller facilities, the fitness director may teach classes and do personal training.

(Workers in a related occupation—*athletes, coaches, umpires, and related workers*—participate in organized sports; this occupation is described elsewhere in the *Handbook*.)

Working Conditions

Most fitness workers spend their time indoors at fitness centers and health clubs. Fitness directors and supervisors, however, typically spend most of their time in an office, planning programs and special events and tending to administrative issues. Those in smaller fitness centers may split their time among the office, personal training, and teaching classes. Directors and supervisors generally engage in less physical activity than do lower-level fitness workers. Nevertheless, workers at all levels risk suffering injuries during physical activities.

Since most fitness centers are open long hours, fitness workers often work nights and weekends and even occasional holidays. Some may have to travel from place to place throughout the day, to different gyms or to clients' homes, to maintain a full work schedule.

Fitness workers generally enjoy a lot of autonomy. Group exercise instructors choreograph or plan their own classes, and personal trainers have the freedom to design and implement their clients' workout routines.

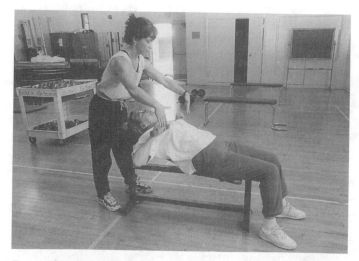

Personal trainers work one-on-one with their clients to help them achieve their fitness goals.

Training, Other Qualifications, and Advancement

Personal trainers must obtain certification in the fitness field to gain employment, while group fitness instructors do not necessarily need certification to begin working. The most important characteristic that an employer looks for in a new group fitness instructor is the ability to plan and lead a class that is motivating and safe. Group fitness instructors often get started by participating in exercise classes, and some become familiar enough to successfully audition and begin teaching class. They also may improve their skills by taking training courses or attending fitness conventions. Most organizations encourage their group instructors to become certified, and many require it.

In the fitness field, there are many organizations—some of which are listed in the last section of this statement—that offer certification. Becoming certified by one of the top certification organizations is increasingly important, especially for personal trainers. One way to ensure that a certifying organization is reputable is to see whether it is accredited or seeking accreditation by the National Commission for Certifying Agencies.

Most certifying organizations require candidates to have a high school diploma, be certified in cardiopulmonary resuscitation (CPR), and pass an exam. All certification exams have a written component, and some also have a practical component. The exams measure knowledge of human physiology, proper exercise techniques, assessment of client fitness levels, and development of appropriate exercise programs. There is no particular training program required for certifications; candidates may prepare however they prefer. Certifying organizations do offer study materials, including books, CD-ROMs, other audio and visual materials, and exam preparation workshops and seminars, but exam candidates are not required to purchase materials to sit for the exams. Certification generally is good for 2 years, after which workers must become recertified by attending continuing education classes. Some organizations offer more advanced certification, requiring an associate or bachelor's degree in an exercise-related subject for individuals interested in training athletes, working with people who are injured or ill, or advising clients on whole-life health.

Training for Pilates and yoga teachers is changing. Because interest in these forms of exercise has exploded in recent years, the demand for teachers has grown faster than the ability to train them properly. However, because inexperienced teachers have contributed to student injuries, there has been a push toward more standardized, rigorous requirements for teacher training.

Pilates and yoga teachers usually do not need group exercise certifications like the ones described above. It is more important that they have specialized training in their particular method of exercise. For Pilates, training options range from weekend-long workshops to year-long programs, but the trend is toward requiring more training. The Pilates Method Alliance has established training standards that recommend at least 200 hours of training; the group also has standards for training schools and maintains a list of training schools that meet the requirements. However, some Pilates teachers are certified group exercise instructors who go through short Pilates workshops; currently, many fitness centers hire people with minimal Pilates training if the applicants have a fitness certification and group fitness experience.

Training requirements for yoga teachers are similar to those for Pilates teachers. Training programs range from a few days to more than 2 years. Many people get their start by taking yoga; eventually, their teachers may consider them suited to assist or to substitute teach. Some students may begin teaching their own classes when their yoga teachers think they are ready; the teachers may even provide letters of recommendation. Those who wish to pursue teaching more seriously usually then pursue formal teacher training. Currently, there are many training programs through the yoga community as well as programs through the fitness industry. The Yoga Alliance has established training standards of at least 200 training hours, with a specified number of hours in areas including techniques, teaching methodology, anatomy, physiology, and philosophy. The Yoga Alliance also registers schools that train students to the standards. Because some schools may meet the standards but not be registered, prospective students should check the requirements and decide if particular schools meet them.

An increasing number of employers require fitness workers to have a bachelor's degree in a field related to health or fitness, such as exercise science or physical education. Some employers allow workers to substitute a college degree for certification, but most employers who require a bachelor's degree require both a degree and certification.

People planning fitness careers should be outgoing, good at motivating people, and sensitive to the needs of others. Excellent health and physical fitness are important due to the physical nature of the job. Those who wish to be personal trainers in a large commercial fitness center should have strong sales skills.

Fitness workers usually do not receive much on-the-job training; they are expected to know how to do their jobs when they are hired. The exception is newly certified personal trainers with no work experience, who sometimes begin by working alongside an experienced trainer before being allowed to train clients alone. Workers may receive some organizational training to learn about the operations of their new employer. They occasionally receive specialized training if they are expected to teach or lead a specific method of exercise or focus on a particular age or ability group.

A bachelor's degree, and in some cases a master's degree, in exercise science, physical education, kinesiology, or a related area, along with experience, usually is required to advance to management positions in a health club or fitness center. As in many fields, managerial skills are needed to advance to supervisory or managerial positions. College courses in management, business administration, accounting, and personnel management may be helpful for advancement to supervisory or managerial jobs, but many fitness companies have corporate universities in which they train employees for management positions.

Personal trainers may advance to head trainer, with responsibility for hiring and overseeing the personal training staff and for bringing in new personal training clients. Group fitness instructors may be promoted to group exercise director, responsible for hiring instructors and coordinating exercise classes. A next possible step is the fitness director, who manages the fitness budget and staff. The general manager's main focus is on the financial aspect of the organization, particularly setting and achieving sales goals; in a small fitness center, however, the general manager usually is involved with all aspects of running the facility.

Some workers go into business for themselves and open their own fitness centers.

Employment

Fitness workers held about 205,000 jobs in 2004. Almost all personal trainers and group exercise instructors worked in physical fitness facilities, health clubs, and fitness centers, mainly in the amusement and recreation industry or in civic and social organizations. About 7 percent of fitness workers were self-employed; many of these were personal trainers, while others were group fitness instructors working on a contract basis with fitness centers. Many fitness jobs are part time, and many workers hold multiple jobs, teaching and/or doing personal training at several different fitness centers and at clients' homes.

Job Outlook

Opportunities are expected to be good for fitness workers because of rapid growth in the fitness industry. Many job openings also will stem from the need to replace the large numbers of workers who leave these occupations each year.

Employment of fitness workers—who are concentrated in the rapidly growing arts, entertainment, and recreation industry—is expected to increase much faster than the average for all occupations through 2014. An increasing number of people spend more time and money on fitness, and more businesses are recognizing the benefits of health and fitness programs and other services such as wellness programs for their employees.

Aging baby boomers are concerned with staying healthy, physically fit, and independent. They have become the largest demographic group of health club members. The reduction of physical education programs in schools, combined with parents' growing concern about childhood obesity, has resulted in rapid increases in children's health club membership. Increasingly, athletic youth also are hiring personal trainers, and weight-training gyms for children younger than 18 are expected to continue to grow. Health club membership among young adults also has grown steadily, driven by concern with physical fitness and by rising incomes.

As health clubs strive to provide more personalized service to keep their members motivated, they will continue to offer personal training and a wide variety of group exercise classes. Participation in yoga and Pilates is expected to continue to grow, driven partly by the aging population demanding low-impact forms of exercise and relief from ailments such as arthritis.

Earnings

Median annual earnings of personal trainers and group exercise instructors in May 2004 were $25,470. The middle 50 percent earned between $17,380 and $40,030. The bottom 10 percent earned less than $14,530 while the top 10 percent earned $55,560 or more. Earnings of successful self-employed personal trainers can be much higher. Median annual earnings in the industries employing the largest numbers of fitness workers in May 2004 were as follows:

Other amusement and recreation industries	$28,670
Other schools and instruction	22,320
Civic and social organizations	20,530

Because many fitness workers work part time, they often do not receive benefits such as health insurance or retirement plans from their employers. They do get the unusual benefit of the use of fitness facilities at no cost.

Related Occupations

Occupations that focus on physical fitness, as do fitness workers, include athletes, coaches, umpires, and related workers.

Sources of Additional Information

For more information about fitness careers, and to find universities and other institutions offering programs in health and fitness, contact:

➤ IDEA Health and Fitness Association, 10455 Pacific Center Crt., San Diego, CA 92121-4339.

For information about personal trainer and group fitness instructor certifications, contact:

➤ American Council on Exercise, 4851 Paramount Dr., San Diego, CA 92123. Internet: **http://www.acefitness.org**

➤ American College of Sports Medicine, P.O. Box 1440, Indianapolis, IN 46206-1440. Internet: **http://www.acsm.org**

➤ National Academy of Sports Medicine, 26632 Agoura Rd., Calabasas, CA 91302. Internet: **http://www.nasm.org**

➤ National Strength and Conditioning Association Certification Commission, 3333 Landmark Circle, Lincoln, NE 68504. Internet: **http://www.nsca-cc.org**

For information about Pilates certification, and to find training programs, contact:

➤ Pilates Method Alliance, P.O. Box 370906, Miami, FL 33137-0906. Internet: **http://www.pilatesmethodalliance.org**

For information on yoga teacher training, and to find training programs, contact:

➤ Yoga Alliance, 7801 Old Branch Ave., Suite 400, Clinton, MD 20735. Internet: **http://www.yogaalliance.org**

To find accredited fitness certification programs, contact:

➤ National Commission for Certifying Agencies, 2025 M St., NW., Suite 800, Washington, DC 20036. Internet: **http://www.noca.org/ncca/accredorg.htm**

Flight Attendants

(O*NET 39-6031.00)

Significant Points

● Job duties are learned through formal on-the-job training.

● Competition for positions will remain strong because the opportunity for travel attracts more applicants than there are jobs, with only the most qualified being hired.

● A high school diploma is the minimum educational requirement; however, applicants with a college degree and with experience in dealing with the public are likely to have the best employment opportunities.

Nature of the Work

Major airlines are required by law to provide flight attendants for the safety of the traveling public. Although the primary job of the flight attendants is to ensure that safety regulations are followed, attendants also try to make flights comfortable and enjoyable for passengers.

At least 1 hour before each flight, attendants are briefed by the captain—the pilot in command—on such things as emergency evacuation procedures, coordination of the crew, the length of the flight, expected weather conditions, and special issues having to do with passengers. Flight attendants make sure that first-aid kits and other emergency equipment are aboard and in working order and that the passenger cabin is in order, with adequate supplies of food, beverages, and any other provided amenities. As passengers board the plane, flight attendants greet them, check their tickets, and tell them where to store carry-on items.

Before the plane takes off, flight attendants instruct all passengers in the use of emergency equipment and check to see that seatbelts are fastened, seat backs are in upright positions, and all carry-on items are properly stowed. In the air, helping passengers in the event of an emergency is the most important responsibility of a flight attendant. Safety-related actions may range from reassuring passengers during rough weather to directing passengers who must evacuate a plane following an emergency landing. Flight attendants also answer questions about the flight; distribute reading material, pillows, and blankets; and help small children, elderly or disabled persons, and any others needing assistance. They may administer first aid to passengers who become ill. Flight attendants generally serve beverages and other refreshments and, on many flights, heat and distribute precooked meals or snacks. Prior to landing, flight attendants take inventory of headsets, alcoholic beverages, and moneys collected. They also report any medical problems passengers may have had, the condition of cabin equipment, and lost and found articles.

Lead, or first, flight attendants, sometimes known as pursers, oversee the work of the other attendants aboard the aircraft, while performing most of the same duties.

Working Conditions

Because airlines operate around the clock and year round, flight attendants may work nights, holidays, and weekends. In most cases, agreements between the airline and the employees' union determine the total daily and monthly working time. Scheduled on-duty time usually is limited to 12 hours per day although some contracts provide daily actual maximums of 14 hours, with somewhat greater maximums for international flying. Attendants usually fly 65 to 90 hours a month and, in addition, generally spend about 50 hours a month on the ground preparing planes for flights, writing reports following completed flights, and waiting for planes to arrive. They may be away from their home base at least one-third of the time. During this period, the airlines provide hotel accommodations and an allowance for meal expenses.

Flight attendants are required, by law, on major airlines in order to ensure the safety of the traveling public.

Flight attendants must be flexible, reliable, and willing to relocate. However, many flight attendants elect to live in one place and commute to their assigned home base. Home bases and routes worked are bid for on a seniority basis. The longer the flight attendant has been employed, the more likely he or she is to work on chosen flights. Almost all flight attendants start out working on reserve status or on call. On small corporate airlines, flight attendants often work on an as-needed basis and must adapt to varying environments and passengers.

The combination of free time and discount airfares provides flight attendants the opportunity to travel and see new places. However, the work can be strenuous and trying. Flight attendants stand during much of the flight and must remain pleasant and efficient, regardless of how tired they are or how demanding passengers may be. Occasionally, flight attendants must deal with disruptive passengers. Also, turbulent flights can add to possible difficulties regarding service, including potential injuries to passengers.

Working in a moving aircraft leaves flight attendants susceptible to injuries. For example, back injuries and mishaps can occur when opening overhead compartments or while pushing heavy service carts. In addition, medical problems can arise from irregular sleeping and eating patterns, dealing with stressful passengers, working in a pressurized environment, and breathing recycled air.

Training, Other Qualifications, and Advancement

Airlines prefer to hire poised, tactful, and resourceful people who can interact comfortably with strangers and remain calm under duress. Applicants usually must be at least 18 to 21 years old, although some carriers may have higher minimum-age requirements. Flight attendants must have excellent health and the ability to speak clearly. All U.S. airlines require that applicants be citizens of the United States or registered aliens with legal rights to obtain employment in the United States.

Airlines usually have physical and appearance requirements. There are height requirements for reaching overhead bins, which often contain emergency equipment, and most airlines want candidates with weight proportionate to height. Vision is required to be correctable to 20/30 or better with glasses or contact lenses (uncorrected no worse than 20/200). Men must have their hair cut above the collar and be clean shaven. Airlines prefer applicants with no visible tattoos, body piercing, or unusual hairstyles or makeup.

A high school diploma is the minimum educational requirement. However, airlines increasingly prefer applicants with a college degree and with experience in dealing with the public. Applicants who attend schools and colleges that offer flight attendant training may have an advantage over other applicants. Highly desirable areas of concentration include people-oriented disciplines such as psychology and education. Flight attendants for international airlines generally must speak a foreign language fluently. For their international flights, some of the major airlines prefer candidates who can speak two major foreign languages.

In addition to education and training, airlines conduct a thorough background check as required by the FAA, which goes back as many as 10 years. Everything about an applicant is investigated, including date of birth, employment history, criminal record, school records, and gaps in employment. Employment is contingent on a successful background check. An applicant will not be offered a job or will be immediately dismissed if his or her background check shows any discrepancies.

Once hired, all candidates must undergo a period of formal training. The length of training, ranging from 3 to 8 weeks, depends on the size and type of carrier and takes place at the airline's flight training center. Airlines that do not operate training centers generally send new employees to the center of another airline. Some airlines may provide transportation to the training centers and an allowance for room, board, and school supplies, while other airlines charge individuals for training. New trainees are not considered employees of the airline until they successfully complete the training program. Trainees learn emergency procedures such as evacuating an airplane, operating emergency systems and equipment, administering first aid, and surviving in the water. In addition, trainees are taught how to deal with disruptive passengers and with hijacking and terrorist situations. New hires learn flight regulations and duties, gain knowledge of company operations and policies, and receive instruction on personal grooming and weight control. Trainees for the international routes get additional instruction in passport and customs regulations. Trainees must perform many drills and duties unaided, in front of the training staff. Throughout training, they also take tests designed to eliminate unsuccessful trainees. Toward the end of their training, students go on practice flights. Upon successful completion of training, flight attendants receive the FAA's Certificate of Demonstrated Proficiency. Flight attendants also are required to go through periodic retraining and pass an FAA safety examination to continue flying.

After completing initial training, flight attendants are assigned to one of their airline's bases. New flight attendants are placed on reserve status and are called either to staff extra flights or to fill in for crewmembers who are sick, on vacation, or rerouted. When they are not on duty, reserve flight attendants must be available to report for flights on short notice. They usually remain on reserve for at least 1 year, but, in some cities, it may take 5 to 10 years or longer to advance from reserve status. Flight attendants who no longer are on reserve bid monthly for regular assignments. Because assignments are based on seniority, usually only the most experienced attendants get their choice of assignments. Advancement takes longer today than in the past because experienced flight attendants are remaining in this career longer than they used to.

Some flight attendants become supervisors or take on additional duties such as recruiting and instructing. Their experience also may qualify them for numerous airline-related jobs involving contact with the public, such as reservation ticket agent or public-relations specialist.

Employment

Flight attendants held about 102,000 jobs in 2004. Commercial airlines employed the vast majority of flight attendants, most of whom lived in their employer's home-base city. A small number of flight attendants worked for large companies that operated aircraft for business purposes.

Job Outlook

In the long run, opportunities for persons seeking flight attendant jobs should improve as the airline industry continues to recover from the effects of September 11, 2001, and the downturn in the economy. Employment of flight attendants is expected to grow about as fast as the average for all occupations through the year 2014. Population growth and an improving economy are expected to boost the number of airline passengers. As airlines expand their capacity to meet rising demand by increasing the number and size of planes in operation, more flight attendants will be needed. Over the next decade, however, demand for flight attendants will fluctuate with the demand for air travel, which is highly sensitive to swings in the economy. During downturns, as air traffic declines, the hiring of flight attendants declines, and some experienced attendants may be laid off until traffic recovers.

Despite the improving outlook, competition is expected to be keen because this job usually attracts more applicants than there are jobs, with only the most qualified eventually being hired. College graduates who have experience dealing with the public should have the best chance of being hired. Job opportunities may be better with the faster growing regional and commuter, low-fare, and charter airlines. There also are job opportunities for professionally trained flight attendants to work for companies operating private aircraft for their executives.

The majority of job openings through the year 2014 will arise from the need to replace flight attendants who leave the labor force or transfer to other occupations, often for higher earnings or a more stable lifestyle. With the job now viewed increasingly as a profession, however, fewer flight attendants leave their jobs, and job turnover is not as high as in the past. The average job tenure of attendants is currently more than 7 years and is increasing.

Earnings

Median annual earnings of flight attendants were $43,440 in May 2004. The middle 50 percent earned between $31,310 and $67,590. The lowest 10 percent earned less than $23,450, and the highest 10 percent earned more than $95,850.

According to data from the Association of Flight Attendants, beginning attendants had median earnings of about $15,552 a year in 2004. Beginning pay scales for flight attendants vary by carrier, however. New hires usually begin at the same pay scale regardless of experience, and all flight attendants receive the same future pay increases based on an established pay scale. Flight attendants receive extra compensation for increased hours. Further, some airlines offer incentive pay for working holidays, night and international flights, or taking positions that require additional responsibility or paperwork. Most airlines guarantee a minimum of 65 to 85 flight hours per month, with the option to work additional hours. Flight attendants also receive a "per diem" allowance for meal expenses while on duty away from home. In addition, flight attendants and their immediate families are entitled to free or discounted fares on their own airline and reduced fares on most other airlines. Some airlines require that the flight attendant be with an airline for 3 to 6 months before taking advantage of this benefit. Other benefits may include medical, dental, and life insurance; 401K or other retirement plan; sick leave; paid holidays; stock options; paid vacations; and tuition reimbursement.

Flight attendants are required to purchase uniforms and wear them while on duty. The airlines usually pay for uniform replacement items, and may provide a small allowance to cover cleaning and upkeep of the uniforms.

The majority of flight attendants hold union membership, primarily with the Association of Flight Attendants. Other unions that represent flight attendants include the Transport Workers Union of America and the International Brotherhood of Teamsters.

Related Occupations

Other jobs that involve helping people as a safety professional, while requiring the ability to be calm even under trying circumstances, include emergency medical technicians and paramedics and firefighting occupations.

Sources of Additional Information

Information about job opportunities and qualifications required for work at a particular airline may be obtained by writing to the airline's human resources office.

For further information on flight attendants, contact:
➤ Association of Flight Attendants, 501 Third St. NW., Washington, DC 20001. Internet: **http://www.afanet.org**

Gaming Services Occupations

(O*NET 39-1011.00, 39-1012.00, 39-3011.00, 39-3012.00, 39-3019.99, 39-3099.99)

Gaming service workers must keep track of all the money being paid to and received from patrons.

Significant Points

- Job opportunities are available nationwide and are no longer limited to Nevada and New Jersey.

- Workers need a license issued by a regulatory agency, such as a State casino control board or commission; licensure requires proof of residency in the State in which gaming workers are employed.

- Employment is projected to grow faster than average.

- Job prospects are best for those with a degree or certification in gaming or a hospitality-related field, previous training or experience in casino gaming, and strong interpersonal and customer service skills.

Nature of the Work

Legalized gambling in the United States today includes casino gaming, State lotteries, pari-mutuel wagering on contests such as horse or dog racing, and charitable gaming. Gaming, the playing of games of chance, is a multibillion-dollar industry that is responsible for the creation of a number of unique service occupations.

The majority of all gaming services workers are employed in casinos. Their duties and titles may vary from one establishment to another. Despite differences in job title and task, however, workers perform many of the same basic functions in all casinos. Some positions are associated with oversight and direction—supervision, surveillance, and investigation—while others involve working with the games or patrons themselves, performing such activities as tending slot machines, handling money, writing and running tickets, and dealing cards or running games.

Like nearly every business establishment, casinos have workers who direct and oversee day-to-day operations. *Gaming supervisors* oversee the gaming operations and personnel in an assigned area. They circulate among the tables and observe the operations to ensure that all of the stations and games are covered for each shift. It is not uncommon for gaming supervisors to explain and interpret the operating rules of the house to patrons who may have difficulty understanding the rules. Gaming supervisors also may plan and organize activities to create a friendly atmosphere for the guests staying in their hotels or in casino hotels. Periodically, they address and adjust complaints about service.

Some gaming occupations demand specially acquired skills—dealing blackjack, for example—that are unique to casino work. Others require skills common to most businesses, such as the ability to conduct financial transactions. In both capacities, the workers in these jobs interact directly with patrons in attending to slot machines, making change, cashing or selling tokens and coins, writing and running for other games, and dealing cards at table games. Part of their responsibility is to make those interactions enjoyable.

Slot key persons coordinate and supervise the slot department and its workers. Their duties include verifying and handling payoff winnings to patrons, resetting slot machines after completing the payoff, and refilling machines with money. Slot key persons must be familiar with a variety of slot machines and be able to make minor repairs and adjustments to the machines as needed. If major repairs are required, slot key persons determine whether the slot machine should be removed from the floor. Working the floor as frontline personnel, they enforce safety rules and report hazards.

Gaming and sportsbook writers and runners assist in the operations of games such as bingo and keno, in addition to taking bets on sporting events. They scan tickets presented by patrons and calculate and distribute winnings. Some writers and runners operate the equipment that randomly selects the numbers. Others may announce numbers selected, pick up tickets from patrons, collect bets, or receive, verify, and record patrons' cash wagers.

Gaming dealers operate table games such as craps, blackjack, and roulette. Standing or sitting behind the table, dealers provide dice, dispense cards to players, or run the equipment. Some dealers also monitor the patrons for infractions of casino rules. Gaming dealers must be skilled in customer service and in executing their game. Dealers determine winners, calculate and pay winning bets, and collect losing bets. Because of the fast-paced work environment, most gaming dealers are competent in at least two games, usually blackjack and craps.

Working Conditions

The atmosphere in casinos is generally filled with fun and often considered glamorous. However, casino work can also be physically demanding. Most occupations require that workers stand for long periods; some require the lifting of heavy items. The atmosphere in casinos exposes workers to certain hazards, such as cigarette, cigar, and pipe smoke. Noise from slot machines, gaming tables, and talking workers and patrons may be distracting to some, although workers wear protective headgear in areas where loud machinery is used to count money.

Most casinos are open 24 hours a day, seven days a week and offer three staggered shifts.

Training, Other Qualifications, and Advancement

There usually are no minimum educational requirements for entry-level gaming jobs, although most employers prefer at least a high school diploma or GED. Each casino establishes its own requirements for education, training, and experience. Some of the major casinos and slot manufacturers run their own training schools, and almost all provide some form of in-house training in addition to requiring certification. The type and quantity of classes needed may vary. Many institutions of higher learning give training toward certificates in gaming, as well as offering an associate, bachelor's, or master's degree in a hospitality-related field such as hospitality management, hospitality administration, or hotel management. Some schools offer training in games, gaming supervision, slot attendant and slot repair technician work, slot department management, and surveillance and security.

Gaming services workers are required to have a license issued by a regulatory agency, such as a State casino control board or commission. Applicants for a license must provide photo identification, offer proof of residency in the State in which they anticipate working, and pay a fee. Age requirements vary by State. The licensing application process also includes a background investigation.

In addition to possessing a license, gaming services workers need superior customer service skills. Casino gaming workers provide entertainment and hospitality to patrons, and the quality of their service contributes to an establishment's success or failure. Therefore, gaming workers need good communication skills, an outgoing personality, and the ability to maintain their composure even when dealing with angry or demanding patrons. Personal integrity also is important, because workers handle large amounts of money.

Gaming services workers who manage money should have some experience handling cash or using calculators or computers. For such positions, most casinos administer a math test to assess an applicant's level of competency.

Most gaming supervisors have experience in other gaming occupations, typically as dealers, and have a broad knowledge of casino rules, regulations, procedures, and games. While an associate or bachelor's degree is beneficial, it is not a requirement for most positions. Gaming supervisors must have strong leadership, organizational, and communication skills. Excellent customer service and employee skills also are necessary.

Slot key persons do not need to meet formal educational requirements to enter the occupation, but completion of slot attendant or slot technician training is helpful. As with most other gaming workers, slot key persons receive on-the-job training during the first several weeks of employment.

Gaming and sportsbook writers and runners must have at least a high school diploma or GED. Most of these workers receive on-the-job training. Because gaming and sportsbook writers and runners work closely with patrons, they need excellent customer service skills.

Most gaming dealers acquire their skills by attending a dealer school or vocational and technical school. Most of these schools are found in Nevada and New Jersey. They teach the rules and procedures of the games as well as State and local laws and regulations. Graduation from one of these schools does not guarantee a job at many casinos, however, as most casinos require prospective dealers to also audition for open positions. During the audition, personal qualities are assessed along with knowledge of the games. Experienced dealers, who often are able to attract new or return business, have the best job prospects. Dealers with more experience are placed at the "high-roller" tables.

Advancement opportunities in casino gaming depend less on workers' previous casino duties and titles than on their ability and eagerness to learn new jobs. For example, an entry-level gaming worker eventually might advance to become a dealer or card room manager or to assume some other supervisory position.

Employment

Gaming services occupations provided 177,000 jobs in 2004. Employment by occupational specialty was distributed as follows:

Gaming dealers	83,000
Gaming supervisors	38,000
Slot key persons	23,000
Gaming and sports book writers and runners	18,000
Gaming service workers, all other	15,000

Gaming services workers are found mainly in the traveler accommodation and gaming industries. Most are employed in commercial casinos, including land-based or riverboat casinos, in 11 States: Colorado, Illinois, Indiana, Iowa, Louisiana, Michigan, Mississippi, Missouri, Nevada, New Jersey, and South Dakota. The largest number works in casinos in Nevada, and the second-largest group works in similar establishments in Atlantic City, New Jersey. Mississippi, which boasts the greatest number of riverboat casinos in operation, employs the most workers in that venue. In addition, there are 28 States with Indian casinos. Legal lotteries are held in 40 States and the District of Columbia, and pari-mutuel wagering is legal in 40 States. Forty-seven States and the District of Columbia also allow charitable gaming. Other States have recently passed legislation to permit gambling, but no casinos have been opened as of yet.

For most workers, gaming licensure requires proof of residency in the State in which gaming workers are employed. But some gaming services workers do not limit themselves to one State or even one country, finding jobs on the small number of casinos located on luxury cruise liners that travel the world. These individuals live and work aboard the vessel.

Job Outlook

With demand for gaming showing no sign of waning, employment in gaming services occupations is projected to grow faster than the average for all occupations through 2014. Even during the recent downturn in the economy, revenues at casinos have risen. In addition, the increasing popularity and prevalence of Indian casinos, particularly in California, and pari-mutuel casinos will provide substantial job openings that were not available in the past. With many States benefiting from casino gambling in the form of tax revenue or agreements with Indian tribes, additional States are reconsidering their opposition to legalized gambling and will likely approve the construction of more casinos and other gaming establishments during the next decade. Some job growth will occur in established gaming areas in Nevada and Atlantic City, New Jersey, but most of the openings in these locations will come from job turnover.

The increase in gaming reflects growth in the population and in its disposable income, both of which are expected to continue. Higher expectations for customer service among gaming patrons also should result in more jobs for gaming services workers.

Job prospects in gaming services occupations will be best for those with previous casino gaming experience, a degree or technical or vocational training in gaming or a hospitality-related field, and strong interpersonal and customer service skills. As a direct result of increasing demand for additional table games in gaming establishments, the most rapid growth is expected among gaming dealers. However, there are generally more applicants than jobs for dealers, creating keen competition for jobs. In addition to job openings arising from employment growth, opportunities will result from the need to replace workers transferring to other occupations or leaving the labor force.

Earnings

Wage earnings for gaming services workers vary according to occupation, level of experience, training, location, and size of the gaming establishment. The following were median earnings for various gaming services occupations in May 2004:

Gaming supervisors	$40,840
Slot key persons	23,010
Gaming service workers, all other	20,820
Gaming and sports book writers and runners	18,390
Gaming dealers	14,340

Gaming dealers generally receive a large portion of their earnings from tokes, which are tips in the form of tokens received from players. Earnings from tokes can vary depending on the table games the dealer operates and the personal traits of the dealer.

Related Occupations

Many other occupations provide hospitality and customer service. Some examples of related occupations are security guards and gaming surveillance officers, sales worker supervisors, cashiers, gaming change persons and booth cashiers, retail salespersons, gaming cage workers, and tellers.

Sources of Additional Information

For additional information on careers in gaming, visit your public library and your State gaming regulatory agency or casino control commission.

Information on careers in gaming also is available from:
➤ American Gaming Association, 555 13th St. NW., Suite 1010 East, Washington, DC 20004. Internet: **http://www.americangaming.org**

Personal and Home Care Aides

(O*NET 39-9021.00)

Significant Points

- Job opportunities are expected to be excellent because of rapid growth in home health care and high replacement needs.

- Skill requirements are low, as is the pay.

- About 33 percent of personal and home care aides work part time; most aides work with a number of different clients, each job lasting a few hours, days, or weeks.

Nature of the Work

Personal and home care aides help elderly, disabled, ill, and mentally disabled persons live in their own homes or in residential care facilities instead of in health facilities. Most personal and home care aides work with elderly or physically or mentally disabled clients who need more extensive personal and home care than family or friends can provide. Some aides work with families in which a parent is incapacitated and small children need care. Others help discharged hospital patients who have relatively short-term needs. (*Home health aides*—who provide health-related services, rather than mainly housekeeping and routine personal care—are discussed in the statement on nursing, psychiatric, and home health aides, elsewhere in the *Handbook.*)

Personal and home care aides—also called *homemakers, caregivers, companions,* and *personal attendants*—provide housekeeping and routine personal care services. They clean clients' houses, do laundry, and change bed linens. Aides may plan meals (including special diets), shop for food, and cook. Aides also may help clients get out of bed, bathe, dress, and groom. Some accompany clients to doctors' appointments or on other errands.

Personal and home care aides provide instruction and psychological support to their patients. They may advise families and patients on nutrition, cleanliness, and household tasks. Aides also may assist in toilet training a severely mentally handicapped child, or they may just listen to clients talk about their problems.

In home health care agencies, a registered nurse, physical therapist, or social worker assigns specific duties and supervises personal and home care aides. Aides keep records of services performed and of clients' condition and progress. They report changes in the client's condition to the supervisor or case manager. In carrying out their work, aides cooperate with health care professionals, including registered nurses, therapists, and other medical staff.

Working Conditions

The personal and home care aide's daily routine may vary. Aides may go to the same home every day for months or even years. However, most aides work with a number of different clients, each job lasting a few hours, days, or weeks. Aides often visit four or five clients on the same day.

Surroundings differ from case to case. Some homes are neat and pleasant, whereas others are untidy and depressing. Some clients are pleasant and cooperative; others are angry, abusive, depressed, or otherwise difficult.

Personal and home care aides generally work on their own, with periodic visits by their supervisor. They receive detailed instructions explaining when to visit clients and what services to perform for them. About one-third of aides work part time, and some work weekends or evenings to suit the needs of their clients.

Aides are individually responsible for getting to the client's home. They may spend a good portion of the working day traveling from one client to another. Because mechanical lifting devices that are available in institutional settings are seldom available in patients' homes, aides must be careful to avoid overexertion or injury when they assist clients.

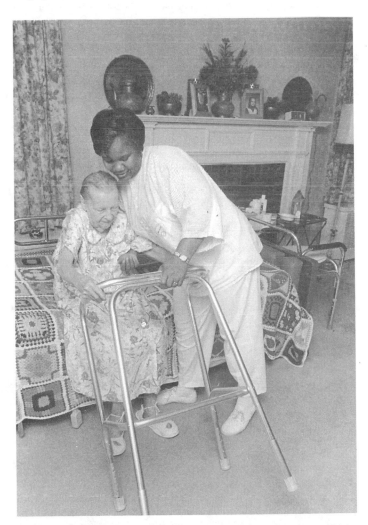

Most aides provide routine personal care and housekeeping services to elderly or disabled patients.

Training, Other Qualifications, and Advancement

In some States, the only requirement for employment is on-the-job training, which generally is provided by most employers. Other States may require formal training, which is available from community colleges, vocational schools, elder care programs, and home health care agencies. The National Association for Home Care and Hospice (NAHC) offers national certification for personal and home care aides. Certification is a voluntary demonstration that the individual has met industry standards. Certification requires the completion of a standard 75-hour course and written exam developed by NAHC. Home care aides seeking certification are evaluated on 17 different skills by a registered nurse.

Personal and home care aides should have a desire to help people and not mind hard work. They should be responsible, compassionate, emotionally stable, and cheerful. In addition, aides should be tactful, honest, and discreet because they work in private homes. Aides also must be in good health. A physical examination, including State-mandated tests such as those for tuberculosis, may be required. A criminal background check also may be required for employment. Additionally, personal and home care aides are responsible for their own transportation to reach patients' homes.

Advancement for personal and home care aides is limited. In some agencies, workers start out performing homemaker duties, such as cleaning. With experience and training, they may take on personal care duties. Some aides choose to receive additional training to become nursing and home health aides, licensed practical nurses, or registered nurses. Some experienced personal and home care aides may start their own home care agency.

Employment

Personal and home care aides held about 701,000 jobs in 2004. The majority of jobs were in home health care services; individual and family services; residential care facilities; and private households. Self-employed aides have no agency affiliation or supervision and accept clients, set fees, and arrange work schedules on their own.

Job Outlook

Excellent job opportunities are expected for this occupation, because rapid employment growth and high replacement needs are projected to produce a large number of job openings.

Employment of personal and home care aides is projected to grow much faster than the average for all occupations through the year 2014. The number of elderly people, an age group characterized by mounting health problems and requiring some assistance with daily activities, is projected to rise substantially. In addition to the elderly, other patients, such as the mentally disabled, will increasingly rely on home care. This trend reflects several developments, including efforts to contain costs by moving patients out of hospitals and nursing care facilities as quickly as possible; the realization that treatment can be more effective in familiar rather than clinical surroundings; and the development and improvement of medical technologies for in-home treatment.

In addition to job openings created by the increase in demand for these workers, replacement needs are expected to lead to many openings. The relatively low skill requirements, low pay, and high emotional demands of the work result in high replacement needs. For these same reasons, many people are reluctant to seek jobs in the occupation. Therefore, persons who are interested in and suited for this work—particularly those with experience or training as personal care, home health, or nursing aides—should have excellent job prospects.

Earnings

Median hourly earnings of personal and home care aides were $8.12 in May 2004. The middle 50 percent earned between $6.83 and $9.70 an hour. The lowest 10 percent earned less than $5.93, and the highest 10 percent earned more than $10.87 an hour. Median hourly earnings in the industries employing the largest numbers of personal and home care aides in May 2004 were as follows:

Residential mental retardation, mental health and substance abuse facilities	$9.09
Vocational rehabilitation services	8.76
Community care facilities for the elderly	8.49
Individual and family services	8.48
Home health care services	6.99

Most employers give slight pay increases with experience and added responsibility. Aides usually are paid only for the time they work in the home, not for travel time between jobs. Employers often hire on-call hourly workers and provide no benefits.

Related Occupations

Personal and home care aides combine the duties of caregivers and social service workers. Workers in related occupations that involve personal contact to help others include childcare workers; nursing, psychiatric, and home health aides; occupational therapist assistants and aides; physical therapist assistants and aides; and social and human service assistants.

Sources of Additional Information

Information about employment opportunities may be obtained from local hospitals, nursing care facilities, home health care agencies, psychiatric facilities, residential mental health facilities, social assistance agencies, and local offices of the State employment service.

Recreation Workers

(O*NET 39-9032.00)

Significant Points

- Educational requirements for recreation workers range from a high school diploma to a graduate degree.

- Competition will remain keen for full-time career positions in recreation.

- The recreation field offers an unusually large number of part-time and seasonal job opportunities.

Nature of the Work

People spend much of their leisure time participating in a wide variety of organized recreational activities, such as arts and crafts, the performing arts, camping, and sports. Recreation workers plan, organize, and direct these activities in local playgrounds and recreation areas, parks, community centers, religious organizations, camps, theme parks, and tourist attractions. Increasingly, recreation workers also are being found in workplaces, where they organize and direct leisure activities for employees.

Recreation workers hold a variety of positions at different levels of responsibility. *Recreation leaders*, who are responsible for a recreation program's daily operation, primarily organize and direct participants. They may lead and give instruction in dance, drama, crafts, games, and sports; schedule the use of facilities; keep records of equipment use; and ensure that recreation facilities and equip-

Working Conditions

Recreation workers may work in a variety of settings—for example, a cruise ship, a woodland recreational park, a summer camp, or a playground in the center of a large urban community. Regardless of the setting, most recreation workers spend much of their time outdoors and may work in a variety of weather conditions. Recreation directors and supervisors, however, typically spend most of their time in an office, planning programs and special events. Directors and supervisors generally engage in less physical activity than do lower level recreation workers. Nevertheless, recreation workers at all levels risk suffering injuries during physical activities.

Many recreation workers work about 40 hours a week. People entering this field, especially camp counselors, should expect some night and weekend work and irregular hours. Many recreation jobs are seasonal.

Training, Other Qualifications, and Advancement

Educational requirements for recreation workers range from a high school diploma—or sometimes less for those seeking many summer jobs—to graduate degrees for some administrative positions in large public recreation systems. Full-time career professional positions usually require a college degree with a major in parks and recreation or leisure studies, but a bachelor's degree in any liberal arts field may be sufficient for some jobs in the private sector. In industrial recreation, or "employee services" as it is more commonly called, companies prefer to hire those with a bachelor's degree in recreation or leisure studies and a background in business administration.

Specialized training or experience in a particular field, such as art, music, drama, or athletics, is an asset for many jobs. Some jobs also require certification. For example, a lifesaving certificate is a prerequisite for teaching or coaching water-related activities. Graduates of associate's degree programs in parks and recreation, social work, and other human services disciplines also enter some career recreation positions. High school graduates occasionally enter career positions, but this is not common. Some college students work part time as recreation workers while earning degrees.

A bachelor's degree in a recreation-related discipline and experience are preferred for most recreation supervisor jobs and are required for higher level administrative jobs. However, an increasing number of recreation workers who aspire to administrative positions are obtaining master's degrees in parks and recreation, business administration, or public administration. Certification in the recreation field may be helpful for advancement. Also, many persons in other disciplines, including social work, forestry, and resource management, pursue graduate degrees in recreation.

Programs leading to an associate's or bachelor's degree in parks and recreation, leisure studies, or related fields are offered at several hundred colleges and universities. Many also offer master's or doctoral degrees in the field. In 2004, about 100 bachelor's degree programs in parks and recreation were accredited by the National Recreation and Park Association (NRPA). Accredited programs provide broad exposure to the history, theory, and practice of park and recreation management. Courses offered include community organization; supervision and administration; recreational needs of special populations, such as the elderly or disabled; and supervised fieldwork. Students may specialize in areas such as therapeutic recreation, park management, outdoor recreation, industrial or commercial recreation, or camp management.

The NRPA certifies individuals for professional and technical jobs. Certified Park and Recreation Professionals must pass an exam; earn a bachelor's degree with a major in recreation, park resources, or leisure services from a program accredited by the NRPA and the American Association for Leisure and Recreation; or earn a bachelor's degree and have at least 5 years of relevant full-time work experience. Continuing education is necessary to remain certified.

A lifesaving certificate is a prerequisite for teaching or coaching water-related activities.

ment are used properly. Workers who provide instruction and coach groups in specialties such as art, music, drama, swimming, or tennis may be called *activity specialists. Recreation supervisors* oversee recreation leaders and plan, organize, and manage recreational activities to meet the needs of a variety of populations. These workers often serve as liaisons between the director of the park or recreation center and the recreation leaders. Recreation supervisors with more specialized responsibilities also may direct special activities or events or oversee a major activity, such as aquatics, gymnastics, or performing arts. *Directors of recreation and parks* develop and manage comprehensive recreation programs in parks, playgrounds, and other settings. Directors usually serve as technical advisors to State and local recreation and park commissions and may be responsible for recreation and park budgets. (Workers in a related occupation, *recreational therapists*, help individuals to recover from or adjust to illness, disability, or specific social problems; this occupation is described elsewhere in the *Handbook*.)

Camp counselors lead and instruct children and teenagers in outdoor-oriented forms of recreation, such as swimming, hiking, horseback riding, and camping. In addition, counselors provide campers with specialized instruction in subjects such as archery, boating, music, drama, gymnastics, tennis, and computers. In resident camps, counselors also provide guidance and supervise daily living and general socialization. *Camp directors* typically supervise camp counselors, plan camp activities or programs, and perform the various administrative functions of a camp.

Persons planning recreation careers should be outgoing, good at motivating people, and sensitive to the needs of others. Excellent health and physical fitness are often required, due to the physical nature of some jobs. Volunteer experience, part-time work during school, or a summer job can lead to a full-time career as a recreation worker. As in many fields, managerial skills are needed to advance to supervisory or managerial positions.

Employment

Recreation workers held about 310,000 jobs in 2004, and many additional workers held summer jobs in the occupation. Of those with year-round jobs as recreation workers, about 35 percent worked for local governments, primarily in park and recreation departments. Around 11 percent of recreation workers were employed in civic and social organizations, such as the Boy Scouts or Girl Scouts or the Red Cross. Another 15 percent of recreation workers were employed by nursing and other personal care facilities.

The recreation field has an unusually large number of part-time, seasonal, and volunteer jobs, including summer camp counselors, craft specialists, and afterschool and weekend recreation program leaders. In addition, many teachers and college students accept jobs as recreation workers when school is not in session. The vast majority of volunteers serve as activity leaders at local day camp programs, or in youth organizations, camps, nursing homes, hospitals, senior centers, and other settings.

Job Outlook

Competition will remain keen for career positions as recreation workers because the field attracts many applicants and because the number of career positions is limited compared with the number of lower level seasonal jobs. Opportunities for staff positions should be best for persons with formal training and experience gained in part-time or seasonal recreation jobs. Those with graduate degrees should have the best opportunities for supervisory or administrative positions. Job openings also will stem from the need to replace the large numbers of workers who leave the occupation each year.

Overall employment of recreation workers is expected to grow about as fast as the average for all occupations through 2014. People will spend more time and money on recreation, spurring growth in civic and social organizations and, to a lesser degree, State and local government. Much growth will be driven by retiring baby boomers, who, with more leisure time, high disposable income, and concern for health and fitness, are expected to increase their consumption of recreation services. Job growth also will be driven by rapidly increasing employment in nursing and residential care facilities. Employment growth may be inhibited, however, by budget constraints that local governments may face over the 2004–14 projection period.

The large number of temporary, seasonal jobs in the recreation field typically are filled by high school or college students, generally do not have formal education requirements, and are open to anyone with the desired personal qualities. Employers compete for a share of the vacationing student labor force, and although salaries in recreation often are lower than those in other fields, the nature of the work and the opportunity to work outdoors are attractive to many.

Earnings

In May 2004, median annual earnings of recreation workers who worked full time were $19,320. The middle 50 percent earned between $15,640 and $25,380. The lowest paid 10 percent earned less than $13,260, while the highest paid 10 percent earned $34,280 or more. However, earnings of recreation directors and others in supervisory or managerial positions can be substantially higher. Most public and private recreation agencies provide full-time recreation workers with typical benefits; part-time workers receive few, if any, benefits. In May 2004, median annual earnings in the industries employing the largest numbers of recreation workers were as follows:

Nursing care facilities	$20,660
Local government	19,650
Individual and family services	19,260
Other amusement and recreation industries	17,060
Civic and social organizations	16,950

Related Occupations

Recreation workers must exhibit leadership and sensitivity when dealing with people. Other occupations that require similar personal qualities include counselors, probation officers and correctional treatment specialists, psychologists, recreational therapists, and social workers.

Sources of Additional Information

For information on jobs in recreation, contact employers such as local government departments of parks and recreation, nursing and personal care facilities, the Boy Scouts or Girl Scouts, or local social or religious organizations.

For information on careers, certification, and academic programs in parks and recreation, contact:
➤ National Recreation and Park Association, Division of Professional Services, 22377 Belmont Ridge Rd., Ashburn, VA 20148-4501. Internet: **http://www.nrpa.org**

For career information about camp counselors, contact:
➤ American Camping Association, 5000 State Road 67 North, Martinsville, IN 46151-7902. Internet: **http://www.acacamps.org**

Sales and Related Occupations

Advertising Sales Agents

(O*NET 41-3011.00)

Significant Points

- Overall earnings are higher than average but can vary considerably because they are usually based on a salary plus performance-based commissions and bonuses.

- Pressure to meet monthly sales quotas can be stressful.

Nature of the Work

Advertising sales agents—often referred to as *account executives* or *advertising sales representatives*—sell or solicit advertising, including graphic art, advertising space in publications, custom-made signs, or television and radio advertising time. More than half of all advertising sales agents work in the information sector, mostly for media firms, including television and radio broadcasters, print and Internet publishers, and cable program distributors. Other agents work for firms engaged in direct mail advertising or display and outdoor advertising, such as billboards and signs. Because most revenue for magazines, newspapers, directories, and broadcasters is generated from advertising, advertising sales agents play an important role in their success.

Outside sales agents call on clients and prospects at their place of business. They may have an appointment, or they may practice "cold calling," arriving without an appointment. *Inside sales agents* work on their employer's premises and handle sales to customers who walk in or telephone the firm to inquire about advertising. Some also may make telephone sales calls—calling prospects, attempting to sell the media firm's advertising space or time, and arranging follow-up appointments between interested prospects and outside sales agents. Advertising sales agents should not be confused with *telemarketers*, whose duties are limited solely to soliciting orders for goods or services over the telephone and who work primarily in call centers that provide telemarketing services on contract.

Within the advertising and related services industry, media representative firms sell advertising space or time for media owners, including print and Internet publishers, radio and television stations, and cable systems. Media representative firms maintain offices in major cities and employ their own teams of advertising sales agents. These agents work exclusively with the executives at advertising agencies, called media buyers, who purchase advertising space for their clients. Media representative firms may represent any number of publications and radio or television stations, selling space to advertising agencies with clients who want to initiate a national advertising campaign or place advertisements outside their local market. Sales agents employed in media representation normally do not cultivate new advertisers but maintain contacts with existing advertisers through the advertising agencies. A local television or radio station or publication would have a national sales manager to promote its best interests and coordinate the efforts of all the media representative firms on its behalf.

Local sales agents are employed by local publications or radio and television stations and are responsible for sales in a local territory. For these sales agents, obtaining new accounts is an important part of the job, and they may spend much of their time traveling to and visiting prospective advertisers and current clients. During a sales call, they discuss the client's advertising needs and suggest how their products and services can meet those needs. A critical part of building a relationship with a client is to find out as much as possible about the client and its products. Sales agents inquire about the client's current customers, prospective customers, and the geographic area of the target market.

During the first meeting with a client, sales agents gather background information and explain how specific types of advertising will help promote a client's products or services most effectively. Next, the advertising sales agent prepares an advertising proposal to present to the client. This entails determining the advertising medium to be used, preparing sample advertisements, and providing clients with estimates of the cost of the proposal. Consolidation in the media industries has brought the sale of different types of advertising under one roof. Sales are increasingly made of integrated packages that include advertisements to be placed in print, online, and with a broadcast subsidiary.

After a contract has been established, advertising sales agents serve as the main contact between the client and the firm. They handle communication between the parties and assist the client in developing sample artwork or radio and television spots. They also arrange for commercial taping sessions and may accompany clients to the sessions.

Beyond selling, advertising sales agents have other duties as well. They analyze sales statistics, prepare reports, and handle the scheduling of their appointments and work hours. They read about new and existing products and monitor the sales, prices, and products of their competitors. In many firms, the advertising sales agent handles the drafting of contracts specifying the advertising work to be performed and its cost, as well as the billing and record-keeping for their customers' accounts—which may include customer service responsibilities such as answering questions or addressing any problems the client may have with the proposal. Sales agents also are responsible for developing sales tools, promotional plans, and media kits, which they use to help make the sale.

Working Conditions

Selling can be stressful work because income and job security depend directly on the agent's ability to maintain and expand clientele. Companies generally set monthly sales quotas and place considerable

Calling clients to obtain new accounts is important to an advertising sales agent's success.

pressure on advertising sales agents to meet those quotas. The added stress of rejection places more pressure on the agent.

Many advertising sales agents work more than 40 hours per week. Although the hours are long and often irregular, most have the freedom to determine their own schedule. The Internet and other electronic tools allow agents to do more work from home or while on the road, enabling them to send messages and documents to clients and coworkers, keep up with industry news, and access databases that help them target potential customers. Advertising sales agents use e-mail to conduct much of the business with their clients. Use of e-mail has considerably shortened the time it takes to negotiate a sale and place the ad. Sales agents may accomplish more in less time, but many work more hours than in the past, spending additional time on follow-up and service calls.

Training, Other Qualifications, and Advancement

Some employers prefer applicants with a college degree, particularly for sales positions that require meeting with clients. Courses in marketing, leadership, communication, business, and advertising are helpful. For those who sell over the telephone or who have a proven record of successfully selling other products, a high school degree may be sufficient. After gaining entry into the occupation, successful sales experience becomes more important than education when looking for a position. In general, smaller companies are more willing to hire unproven individuals.

Personality traits are equally important as academic background. Because they represent their employers to the executives of client organizations, advertising sales agents must have excellent interpersonal and written communication skills. Employers look for applicants who possess a pleasant personality, honesty, and a neat professional appearance. Self-motivation, organization, persistence, independence, and the ability to multitask are required because advertising sales agents set their own schedules and perform their duties without much supervision.

Training takes place mainly on the job. In most cases, an experienced sales manager instructs a newly hired advertising sales agent who lacks sales experience. In this one-on-one environment, the supervisor typically coaches the new hire and observes as she makes sales calls and contacts clients. The supervisor then advises the new hire on ways to improve. To conduct more specialized training—for example, in selling to a particular market segment, such as real estate professionals or automotive dealers—the employer may bring in a consultant.

Advancement in the occupation means taking on bigger, more important clients. Agents with proven leadership ability and a strong sales record may advance to supervisory and managerial positions such as sales supervisor, sales manager, or vice president of sales. Frequent contact with managers of other departments and people in other firms provides sales agents with leads about job openings, enhancing advancement opportunities. In small firms, where the number of supervisory and management positions is limited, advancement may come slowly. Promotion may occur more quickly in large firms.

Employment

Advertising sales agents held over 154,000 jobs in 2004. Workers were concentrated in three industries: More than 3 in 10 jobs were in newspaper, periodical, book, and directory publishers; 3 in 10 in advertising and related services; and 2 in 10 in radio and television broadcasting. A relatively small number of jobs were found in specialized design services, including industrial and graphic designers; printing and related support activities; computer systems design and related services; business support services; and cable and other program distribution.

Employment was spread around the country, but jobs in larger, well-known publications or radio and television stations were concentrated in big cities. Media representative firms also were concentrated in large cities with many advertising agencies.

Part-time employment of advertising sales agents was most common in advertising and related services and less common in publishing and radio and television broadcasting. Self-employment also was more common in advertising and related services. Overall, relatively few advertising sales agents were self-employed.

Job Outlook

Employment of advertising sales agents is expected to grow about as fast as the average for all occupations through the year 2014 because of growth in population and advertising revenue. Rising demand for advertising sales agents also will stem from fast growth in cable systems and from the expansion of firms into the growing Hispanic market.

The industries employing advertising sales agents experienced considerable consolidation in recent years, and that trend is expected to continue over the next decade, although at a slower pace. This consolidation is not expected to affect employment of advertising sales agents significantly because prospective clients still will require sales agents to create and demonstrate advertising proposals. Technology has made advertising sales agents more productive, allowing them to take on additional duties and improve the quality of the services they provide, without substantially lessening overall demand. Productivity gains have occurred mostly in the accounting, proposal creation, and customer service responsibilities of sales agents, allowing them to provide improved services.

In addition to the job openings generated by employment growth, openings will occur each year because of the need to replace sales representatives who transfer to other occupations or leave the labor force. Each year, many advertising sales agents discover they are unable to earn enough money and leave the occupation. As a result, job opportunities should be good, especially for those with a college degree or a proven sales record.

Advertising revenues are sensitive to economic downturns, which cause the industries and companies that advertise to reduce both the frequency of campaigns and the overall level of spending on advertising. Advertising sales agents must work hard to get the most out of every dollar spent on advertising under these conditions. Therefore, the number of job opportunities for advertising sales agents fluctuates with the business cycle.

Earnings

Most employers pay a combination of salaries, commissions, and bonuses. Commissions are usually based on the amount of sales, whereas bonuses may depend on individual performance, on the performance of all sales workers in the group or district, or on the company's performance. For agents covering multiple areas or regions, commissions also may be based on the difficulty in making a sale in that particular area. Sales revenue is affected by the economic conditions and business expectations facing the industries that tend to advertise. Earnings from commissions are likely to be high when these industries are doing well, low when companies decide not to advertise as frequently.

Median annual earnings for all advertising sales agents were $40,300 including commissions, in May 2004. The middle 50 percent earned between $27,740 and $59,880 a year. The lowest 10 percent earned less than $20,210, and the highest 10 percent earned more than $89,720 a year. Median annual earnings for sales agents in May 2004 in the industries employing the largest numbers of them were as follows:

Advertising and related services	$44,900
Radio and television broadcasting	38,980
Newspaper, periodical, book, and directory publishers	35,090

In addition to their earnings, advertising sales agents usually are reimbursed for expenses such as transportation costs, meals, hotels, and entertaining customers. They often receive benefits such as health and life insurance, pension plans, vacation and sick leave, personal use of a company car, and frequent flier mileage. Some companies offer incentives such as free vacation trips or gifts for outstanding sales workers.

Related Occupations
Advertising sales agents must have sales ability and knowledge of their clients' needs and businesses. Workers in other occupations requiring these skills include advertising, marketing, promotions, public relations, and sales managers; insurance sales agents; purchasing managers, buyers, and purchasing agents; real estate brokers and sales agents; sales engineers; sales representatives, wholesale and manufacturing; and securities, commodities, and financial services sales agents.

Sources of Additional Information
For information about advertising sales careers in newspaper publishing, contact:
➤ The Newspaper Association of America, 1921 Gallows Rd., Suite 600, Vienna, VA 22182. Internet: **http://www.naa.org**

Cashiers

(O*NET 41-2011.00, 41-2012.00)

Significant Points

- Cashiers are trained on the job; this occupation provides opportunities for many young people with no previous work experience.

- Nearly one-half of all cashiers work part time.

- Despite projected slower-than-average employment growth, good employment opportunities are expected because of the large number of workers who leave this occupation each year.

- Many cashiers start at minimum wage.

Nature of the Work
Supermarkets, department stores, gasoline service stations, movie theaters, restaurants, and many other businesses employ cashiers to register the sale of their merchandise. Most cashiers total bills, receive money, make change, fill out charge forms, and give receipts.

Although specific job duties vary by employer, cashiers usually are assigned to a register at the beginning of their shifts and are given drawers containing a specific amount of money with which to start—their "tills." They must count their tills to ensure that they contain the correct amount of money and adequate supplies of change. Cashiers also handle returns and exchanges. They must ensure that returned merchandise is in good condition, and determine where and when it was purchased and what type of payment was used.

After entering charges for all items and subtracting the value of any coupons or special discounts, cashiers total the customer's bill and take payment. Acceptable forms of payment include cash, personal checks, credit cards, and debit cards. Cashiers must know

the store's policies and procedures for each type of payment the store accepts. For checks and charges, they may request additional identification from the customer or call in for an authorization. They must verify the age of customers purchasing alcohol or tobacco. When the sale is complete, cashiers issue a receipt to the customer and return the appropriate change. They may also wrap or bag the purchase.

At the end of their shifts, they once again count the drawers' contents and compare the totals with sales data. An occasional shortage of small amounts may be overlooked but, in many establishments, repeated shortages are grounds for dismissal. In addition to counting the contents of their drawers at the end of their shifts, cashiers usually separate and total charge forms, return slips, coupons, and any other noncash items.

Most cashiers now use scanners and computers, but some establishments still require price and product information to be entered manually. In a store with scanners, a cashier passes a product's Universal Product Code over the scanning device, which transmits the code number to a computer. The computer identifies the item and its price. In other establishments, cashiers manually enter codes into computers, and descriptions of the items and their prices appear on the screen.

Depending on the type of establishment, cashiers may have other duties as well. In many supermarkets, for example, cashiers weigh produce and bulk food, as well as return unwanted items to the shelves. In convenience stores, cashiers may be required to know how to use a variety of machines other than cash registers, and how to furnish money orders and sell lottery tickets. Operating ticket-dispensing machines and answering customers' questions are common duties for cashiers who work at movie theaters and ticket agencies. In casinos, *gaming change persons* and *booth cashiers* exchange coins and tokens and may issue payoffs. They may also operate a booth in the slot-machine area and furnish change persons with a money bank at the start of the shift, or count and audit money in drawers.

Working Conditions
Nearly one-half of all cashiers work part time. Hours of work often vary depending on the needs of the employer. Generally, cashiers are expected to work weekends, evenings, and holidays to accommodate customers' needs. However, many employers offer flexible schedules. Because the holiday season is the busiest time for most retailers, many employers restrict the use of vacation time from Thanksgiving through the beginning of January.

Cashiers handle money and ineract with customers face-to-face.

Most cashiers work indoors, usually standing in booths or behind counters. In addition, they often are unable to leave their workstations without supervisory approval because they are responsible for large sums of money. The work of cashiers can be very repetitive, but improvements in workstation design are being made to combat problems caused by repetitive motion. In addition, the work can sometimes be dangerous; cashiers' risk from robberies and homicides is much higher than that of the total workforce, although more safety precautions are being taken to help deter robbers.

Gaming change persons and booth cashiers can expect a safer work environment than cashiers in other industries. However, casinos are not without their hazards such as exposure to fumes from cigarettes, cigars, and pipes and noise from slot machines.

Training, Other Qualifications, and Advancement

Cashier jobs tend to be entry-level positions requiring little or no previous work experience. Although there are no specific educational requirements, employers filling full-time jobs often prefer applicants with high school diplomas. Gaming change persons and booth cashiers are required to obtain a license and background check from their State's gaming board and must meet a certain age requirement, usually set at 21 years old.

Nearly all cashiers are trained on the job. In small businesses, an experienced worker often trains beginners. The trainee spends the first day observing the operation and becoming familiar with the store's equipment, policies, and procedures. After this, trainees are assigned to a register—frequently under the supervision of an experienced worker. In larger businesses, trainees spend several days in classes before being placed at cash registers. Topics typically covered in class include a description of the industry and the company, store policies and procedures, equipment operation, and security.

Training for experienced workers is not common, except when new equipment is introduced or when procedures change. In these cases, the employer or a representative of the equipment manufacturer trains workers on the job.

Persons who want to become cashiers should be able to do repetitious work accurately. They also need basic mathematics skills and good manual dexterity. Because cashiers deal constantly with the public, they should be neat in appearance and able to deal tactfully and pleasantly with customers. In addition, some businesses prefer to hire persons who can operate specialized equipment or who have business experience, such as typing, selling, or handling money. Advancement opportunities for cashiers vary. For those working part time, promotion may be to a full-time position. Others advance to head cashier or cash-office clerk. In addition, this job offers a good opportunity to learn about an employer's business and can serve as a steppingstone to a more responsible position.

Employment

Cashiers held about 3.5 million jobs in 2004. Of these, 29,000 were employed as gaming change persons and booth cashiers. Although cashiers are employed in almost every industry, 27 percent of all jobs were in food and beverage stores. Gasoline stations, department stores, other retail establishments, and restaurants also employed large numbers of these workers. Outside of retail establishments, many cashiers worked in amusement, gambling, and recreation industries, local government, and personal and laundry services. Because cashiers are needed in businesses and organizations of all types and sizes, job opportunities are found throughout the country.

Job Outlook

Opportunities for full-time and part-time cashier jobs should continue to be good, because of employment growth and the need to replace the large number of workers who transfer to other oc-

cupations or leave the labor force. There is substantial movement into and out of the occupation because education and training requirements are minimal, and the predominance of part-time jobs is attractive to people seeking a short-term source of income rather than a full-time career. Historically, workers under the age of 25 have filled many of the openings in this occupation—in 2004, almost fifty percent of all cashiers were 24 years of age or younger. Some establishments have begun hiring elderly and disabled persons to fill some of their job openings.

Cashier employment is expected to grow more slowly than the average for all occupations through the year 2014. The rising popularity of purchasing goods online may reduce the employment growth of cashiers, although many customers still prefer the traditional method of purchasing goods at stores. Also, the growing use of self-service check-out systems in retail trade, especially at grocery stores, should have an adverse effect on employment of cashiers. These self-checkout systems may outnumber checkouts with clerks in the future in many establishments. The impact on employment growth of cashiers will largely depend on the public's acceptance of the new self-service technology.

Job opportunities may vary from year to year, because the strength of the economy affects demand for cashiers. Companies tend to hire more persons for such jobs when the economy is strong. Seasonal demand for cashiers also causes fluctuations in employment.

Opportunities will be strong for gaming cashiers as more States legalize casinos and gaming becomes more popular. An increasing number of gaming venues and high turnover in this occupation will generate many job openings. However, many casinos are finding ways to use less cash in their operations, particularly the slot machines, which now generate tickets that can be accepted by other slot machines.

Earnings

Many cashiers start at the Federal minimum wage, which was $5.15 an hour in 2005. Some State laws set the minimum wage higher, and establishments must pay at least that amount. Wages tend to be higher in areas in which there is intense competition for workers.

Median hourly earnings of cashiers, except gaming in May 2004 were $7.81. The middle 50 percent earned between $6.72 and $9.10 an hour. The lowest 10 percent earned less than $5.91, and the highest 10 percent earned more than $11.30 an hour. Median hourly earnings in the industries employing the largest numbers of cashiers in May 2004 were:

Grocery stores	$7.90
Department stores	7.89
Other general merchandise stores	7.85
Health and personal care stores	7.68
Gasoline stations	7.54

Median hourly earnings for gaming cashiers in May 2004 were $9.87. The middle 50 percent earned between $8.23 and $11.74 an hour. The lowest 10 percent earned less than $7.07, and the highest 10 percent earned more than $13.51 an hour.

Benefits for full-time cashiers tend to be better than those for cashiers working part time. In addition to typical benefits, those working in retail establishments often receive discounts on purchases, and cashiers in restaurants may receive free or low-cost meals. Some employers also offer employee stock-option plans and education-reimbursement plans.

Related Occupations

Cashiers accept payment for the purchase of goods and services. Other workers with similar duties include tellers, counter and rental clerks, food and beverage serving and related workers, gaming cage workers, Postal Service workers, and retail salespersons, all of whom are discussed elsewhere in the *Handbook*.

Sources of Additional Information

General information on retailing is available from:
➤ National Retail Federation, 325 7th St. NW., Suite 1100, Washington, DC 20004.

General information on careers in grocery stores is available from:
➤ Food Marketing Institute, 655 15th St. NW., Washington, DC 20005.

For information about employment opportunities as a cashier, contact:
➤ National Association of Convenience Stores, 1605 King St., Alexandria, VA 22314-2792.
➤ United Food and Commercial Workers International Union, Education Office, 1775 K St. NW., Washington, DC 20006-1502.

Counter and Rental Clerks

(O*NET 41-2021.00)

Significant Points

- Jobs primarily are entry level and require little or no experience and minimal formal education.

- Faster-than-average employment growth is expected as businesses strive to improve customer service.

- Part-time employment opportunities should be plentiful.

Nature of the Work

Whether renting videos, air compressors, or moving vans or dropping off clothes to be drycleaned or appliances to be serviced, customers rely on counter and rental clerks to handle their transactions efficiently. Although the specific duties of these workers vary by establishment, counter and rental clerks answer questions involving product availability, cost, and rental provisions. Counter and rental clerks also take orders, calculate fees, receive payments, and accept returned merchandise. (Cashiers and retail salespersons, two occupations with similar duties, are discussed elsewhere in the *Handbook*.)

Regardless of where they work, counter and rental clerks must be knowledgeable about the company's goods and services, policies, and procedures. Depending on the type of establishment, counter and rental clerks use their special knowledge to give advice on a wide variety of products and services, ranging from hydraulic tools to shoe repair. For example, in the car rental industry, these workers inform customers about the features of different types of automobiles and about daily and weekly rental costs. They also ensure that customers meet age and other requirements for renting cars, and they indicate when and in what condition the cars must be returned. Those in the equipment rental industry have similar duties but also must know how to operate and care for the machinery rented. In drycleaning establishments, counter clerks inform customers when items will be ready and about the effects, if any, of the chemicals used on garments. In video rental stores, counter clerks advise customers about the use of video and game players and the length of a rental, scan returned movies and games, restock shelves, handle money, and log daily reports.

When taking orders, counter and rental clerks use various types of equipment. In some establishments, they write out tickets and order forms, although most use computers or barcode scanners. Most of these computer systems are user friendly, require very little data entry, and are customized for each firm. Scanners read the product

code and display a description of the item on a computer screen. However, clerks must ensure that the data on the screen pertain to the product.

Working Conditions

Firms employing counter and rental clerks usually operate nights and weekends for the convenience of their customers. As a result, many employers offer flexible schedules. Some counter and rental clerks work 40-hour weeks, but about half are on part-time schedules—usually during rush periods, such as weekends, evenings, and holidays.

Working conditions usually are pleasant; most stores and service establishments are clean, well lighted, and temperature controlled. However, clerks are on their feet much of the time and may be confined behind a small counter area or may be required to move, lift, or carry heavy machinery or other equipment. The job requires constant interaction with the public and can be stressful, especially during busy periods.

Training, Other Qualifications, and Advancement

Most counter and rental clerk jobs are entry-level positions that require little or no experience and minimal formal education. However, many employers prefer workers with at least a high school diploma.

In video rental stores, counter clerks advise customers about the use of video and game players and the length of a rental, scan returned movies and games, restock shelves, handle money, and log daily reports.

In most companies, counter and rental clerks are trained on the job, sometimes through the use of videos, brochures, and pamphlets. Clerks usually learn how to operate a firm's equipment and become familiar with the firm's policies and procedures under the observation of a more experienced worker. However, some employers have formal classroom training programs lasting from a few hours to a few weeks. Topics covered in this training include the nature of the industry, the company and its policies and procedures, operation of equipment, sales techniques, and customer service. Counter and rental clerks also must become familiar with the different products and services rented or provided by their company to give customers the best possible service.

Counter and rental clerks should enjoy working with people and should have the ability to deal tactfully with difficult customers. They also should be able to handle several tasks at once, while continuing to provide friendly service. In addition, good oral and written communication skills are essential.

Advancement opportunities depend on the size and type of company. Many establishments that employ counter or rental clerks tend to be small businesses, making advancement difficult. In larger establishments, however, jobs such as counter and rental clerks offer good opportunities for workers to learn about their company's products and business practices. These jobs can lead to more responsible positions. It is common in many establishments to promote counter and rental clerks to event planner, assistant manager, or salesperson. Workers may choose to pursue related positions, such as mechanic, or even establish their own business.

In certain industries, such as equipment repair, counter and rental jobs may be an additional or alternative source of income for workers who are unemployed or semiretired. For example, retired mechanics could prove invaluable at tool rental centers because of their knowledge of, and familiarity with, tools.

Employment
Counter and rental clerks held 451,000 jobs in 2004. About 23 percent of clerks worked in consumer goods rental, which includes video rental stores. Other large employers included drycleaning and laundry services; automotive equipment rental and leasing services; automobile dealers; amusement, gambling, and recreation industries; and grocery stores.

Counter and rental clerks are employed throughout the country, but are concentrated in metropolitan areas, where personal services and renting and leasing services are in greater demand.

Job Outlook
Employment of counter and rental clerks is expected to increase faster than the average for all occupations through the year 2014, as all types of businesses strive to improve customer service by hiring more clerks. In addition, some industries employing counter and rental clerks—for example, rental and leasing services and amusement and recreation industries—are expected to grow rapidly. Nevertheless, most job openings will arise from the need to replace experienced workers who transfer to other occupations or leave the labor force. Part-time employment opportunities are expected to be plentiful.

Earnings
Counter and rental clerks typically start at the minimum wage, which, in establishments covered by Federal law, was $5.15 an hour in 2004. In some States, the law sets the minimum wage higher, and establishments must pay at least that amount. Wages also tend to be higher in areas where there is intense competition for workers. In addition to wages, some counter and rental clerks receive

commissions, based on the number of contracts they complete or services they sell.

Median hourly earnings of counter and rental clerks in May 2004 were $8.79. The middle 50 percent earned between $7.21 and $11.99 an hour. The lowest 10 percent earned less than $6.15 an hour, and the highest 10 percent earned more than $16.79 an hour. Median hourly earnings in the industries employing the largest number of counter and rental clerks in May 2004 were as follows:

Automobile dealers	$17.87
Automotive equipment rental and leasing	10.42
Lessors of real estate	9.92
Consumer goods rental	7.78
Drycleaning and laundry services	7.62

Full-time workers typically receive health and life insurance, paid vacation, and sick leАve. Benefits for counter and rental clerks who work part time or work for independent stores tend to be significantly less than for those who work full time. Many companies offer discounts to both full-time and part-time employees on the goods or services they provide.

Related Occupations
Counter and rental clerks take orders and receive payment for services rendered. Other workers with similar duties include tellers, cashiers, food and beverage serving and related workers, gaming cage workers, Postal Service workers, and retail salespersons.

Sources of Additional Information
For general information on employment in the equipment rental industry, contact:
➤ American Rental Association, 1900 19th St., Moline, IL 61265. Internet: **http://www.ararental.org**

For more information about the work of counter clerks in drycleaning and laundry establishments, contact:
➤ International Fabricare Institute, 14700 Sweitzer Lane, Laurel, MD 20707. Internet: **http://www.ifi.org**

Demonstrators, Product Promoters, and Models

(O*NET 41-9011.00, 41-9012.00)

Significant Points

● Job openings should be plentiful for demonstrators and product promoters, but keen competition is expected for modeling jobs.

● Most jobs are part time or have variable work schedules, and many jobs require frequent travel.

● Formal training and education requirements are limited.

Nature of the Work
Demonstrators, product promoters, and models create public interest in buying products such as clothing, cosmetics, food items, and housewares. The information they provide helps consumers make educated choices among the wide variety of products and services available.

Demonstrators and product promoters create public interest in buying a product by demonstrating it to prospective customers and answering their questions. They may sell the demonstrated mer-

Models often have to travel and go on location for shoots.

chandise, or gather names of prospects to contact at a later date or to pass on to a sales staff. *Demonstrators* promote sales of a product to consumers, while *product promoters* try to induce retail stores to sell particular products and market them effectively. Product demonstration is an effective technique used by both to introduce new products or promote sales of old products because it allows face-to-face interaction with potential customers.

Demonstrators and product promoters build current and future sales of both sophisticated and simple products, ranging from computer software to mops. They attract an audience by offering samples, administering contests, distributing prizes, and using direct-mail advertising. They must greet and catch the attention of possible customers and quickly identify those who are interested and qualified. They inform and educate customers about the features of products and demonstrate their use with apparent ease to inspire confidence in the product and its manufacturer. They also distribute information, such as brochures and applications. Some demonstrations are intended to generate immediate sales through impulse buying, while others are considered an investment to generate future sales and increase brand awareness.

Demonstrations and product promotions are conducted in retail and grocery stores, shopping malls, trade shows, and outdoor fairs. Locations are selected based on both the nature of the product and the type of audience. Demonstrations at large events may require teams of demonstrators to efficiently handle large crowds. Some demonstrators promote products on videotape or on television programs, such as "infomercials" or home shopping programs.

Demonstrators and product promoters may prepare the content of a presentation and alter it to target a specific audience or to keep it current. They may participate in the design of an exhibit or customize exhibits for particular audiences. Results obtained by demonstrators and product promoters are analyzed, and presentations are adjusted to make them more effective. Demonstrators and product promoters also may be involved in transporting, assembling, and disassembling materials used in demonstrations.

A demonstrator's presentation may include visuals, models, case studies, testimonials, test results, and surveys. The equipment used for a demonstration varies with the product being demonstrated.

A food product demonstration might require the use of cooking utensils, while a software demonstration could require the use of a multimedia computer. Demonstrators must be familiar with the product to be able to relate detailed information to customers and to answer any questions that arise before, during, or after a demonstration. Therefore, they may research the product to be presented, the products of competitors, and the interests and concerns of the target audience before conducting a demonstration. Demonstrations of complex products can require practice.

Models pose for photos or as subjects for paintings or sculptures. They display clothing, such as dresses, coats, underclothing, swimwear, and suits, for a variety of audiences and in various types of media. They model accessories, such as handbags, shoes, and jewelry, and promote beauty products, including fragrances and cosmetics. The most successful models, called supermodels, hold celebrity status and often use their image to sell products such as books, calendars, and fitness videos. In addition to modeling, they may appear in movies and television shows.

Models' clients use printed publications, live modeling, and television to advertise and promote products and services. There are different categories of modeling jobs within these media, and the nature of a model's work may vary with each. Most modeling jobs are for printed publications, and models usually do a combination of editorial, commercial, and catalog work. Editorial print modeling uses still photographs of models for fashion magazine covers and to accompany feature articles, but does not include modeling for advertisements. Commercial print modeling includes work for advertisements in magazines and newspapers, and for outdoor advertisements such as billboards. Catalog models appear in department store and mail order catalogs.

During a photo shoot, a model poses to demonstrate the features of clothing and products. Models make small changes in posture and facial expression to capture the look desired by the client. As they shoot film, photographers instruct models to pose in certain positions and to interact with their physical surroundings. Models work closely with photographers, hair and clothing stylists, makeup artists, and clients to produce the desired look and to finish the photo shoot on schedule. Stylists and makeup artists prepare the model for the photo shoot, provide touchups, and change the look of models throughout the day. If stylists are not provided, models must apply their own makeup and bring their own clothing. Because the client spends time and money planning for and preparing an advertising campaign, the client usually is present to ensure that the work is satisfactory. The client also may offer suggestions.

Editorial printwork generally pays less than other types of modeling, but provides exposure for a model and can lead to commercial modeling opportunities. Often, beginning fashion models work in foreign countries where fashion magazines are more plentiful.

Live modeling is done in a variety of locations. Live models stand, turn, and walk to demonstrate clothing to a variety of audiences. At fashion shows and in showrooms, garment buyers are the primary audience. Runway models display clothes that either are intended for direct sale to consumers or are the artistic expressions of the designer. High fashion, or haute couture, runway models confidently walk a narrow runway before an audience of photographers, journalists, designers, and garment buyers. Live modeling also is done in apparel marts, department stores, and fitting rooms of clothing designers. In retail establishments, models display clothing directly for shoppers and may be required to describe the features and price of the clothing. Other models pose for sketching artists, painters, and sculptors.

Models may compete with actors and actresses for work in television and may even receive speaking parts. Television work includes commercials, cable television programs, and even game shows. However, competition for television work is intense because of the potential for high earnings and extensive exposure.

Because advertisers need to target very specific segments of the population, models may specialize in a certain area. Petite and plus-size fashions are modeled by women whose dress size is smaller or larger than that worn by the typical model. Models who are disabled may be used to model fashions or products for disabled consumers. "Parts" models have a body part, such as a hand or foot, that is particularly well-suited to model products such as fingernail polish or shoes.

Almost all models work through agents. Agents provide a link between models and clients. Clients pay models, while the agency receives a portion of the model's earnings for its services. Agents scout for new faces, advise and train new models, and promote them to clients. A typical modeling job lasts only 1 day, so modeling agencies differ from other employment agencies in that they maintain an ongoing relationship with the model. Agents find and nurture relationships with clients, arrange auditions called "go-sees," and book shoots if a model is hired. They also provide bookkeeping and billing services to models and may offer them financial planning services. Relatively short careers and variable incomes make financial planning an important issue for many models.

With the help of agents, models spend a considerable amount of time promoting and developing themselves. Models assemble and maintain portfolios, print composite cards, and travel to go-sees. A portfolio is a collection of a model's previous work that is carried to all go-sees and bookings. A composite card, or comp card, contains the best photographs from a model's portfolio, along with his or her measurements.

Models must gather information before a job. From an agent, they learn the pay, date, time, and length of the shoot. Also, models need to ask if hair, makeup, and clothing stylists will be provided. It is helpful to know what product is being promoted and what image they should project. Some models research the client and the product being modeled to prepare for a shoot. Models use a document called a voucher to record the rate of pay and the actual duration of the job. The voucher is used for billing purposes after both the client and model sign it. Once a job is completed, models must check in with their agency and plan for the next appointment.

Working Conditions

More than half of all demonstrators, product promoters, and models work part time and about 1 in 4 have variable work schedules. Many positions last 6 months or less.

Demonstrators and product promoters may work long hours while standing or walking, with little opportunity to rest. Some of them travel frequently, and night and weekend work often is required. The atmosphere of a crowded trade show or State fair is often hectic, and demonstrators and product promoters may feel pressure to influence the greatest number of consumers possible in a very limited amount of time. However, many enjoy the opportunity to interact with a variety of people.

Models work under a variety of conditions, which can often be both difficult and glamorous. The coming season's fashions may be modeled in a comfortable, climate-controlled studio or in a cold, damp outdoor location. Schedules can be demanding, and models must keep in constant touch with an agent so that they do not miss an opportunity for work. Being away from friends and family, and needing to focus on the photographer's instructions despite constant interruption for touchups, clothing, and set changes can be stressful. Yet, successful models interact with a variety of people and enjoy frequent travel. They may meet potential clients at several go-sees in one day and often travel to work in distant cities, foreign countries, and exotic locations.

Training, Other Qualifications, and Advancement

Formal training and education requirements are limited for demonstrators, product promoters, and models. Training usually is moderate term, lasting a month or more. Postsecondary education, while helpful, usually is not required: only 1 in 5 of these workers has a bachelor's degree or higher.

Demonstrators and product promoters usually receive on-the-job training. Training is primarily product oriented because a demonstrator must be familiar with the product to demonstrate it properly. The length of training varies with the complexity of the product. Experience with the product or familiarity with similar products may be required for demonstration of complex products, such as computers. During the training process, demonstrators may be introduced to the manufacturer's corporate philosophy and preferred methods for dealing with customers.

Employers look for demonstrators and product promoters with good communication skills and a pleasant appearance and personality. Demonstrators and product promoters must be comfortable with public speaking. They should be able to entertain an audience and use humor, spontaneity, and personal interest in the product as promotional tools. Foreign language skills are helpful.

While no formal training is required to begin a modeling career, models should be photogenic and have a basic knowledge of hair styling, makeup, and clothing. Some local governments require models under the age of 18 to hold a work permit. An attractive physical appearance is necessary to become a successful model. A model should have flawless skin, healthy hair, and attractive facial features. Specific requirements depend on the client, but most models must be within certain ranges for height, weight, and dress or coat size in order to meet the practical needs of fashion designers, photographers, and advertisers. Requirements may change slightly from time to time as our society's perceptions about physical beauty change; however, most fashion designers feel that their clothing looks its best on tall, thin models. Although physical requirements may be relaxed for some types of modeling jobs, opportunities are limited for those who do not meet these basic requirements.

Because a model's career depends on preservation of his or her physical characteristics, models must control their diet, exercise regularly, and get enough sleep in order to stay healthy. Haircuts, pedicures, and manicures are necessary work-related expenses for models.

In addition to being attractive, models must be photogenic. The ability to relate to the camera in order to capture the desired look on film is essential, and agents test prospective models using snapshots or professional photographs. For photographic and runway work, models must be able to move gracefully and confidently. Training in acting, voice, and dance is useful and allows a model to be considered for television work. Foreign language skills are useful because successful models travel frequently to foreign countries.

Because models must interact with a large number of people, personality plays an important role in success. Models must be professional, polite, and prompt; every contact could lead to future employment. Organizational skills are necessary to manage personal lives, financial matters, and busy work and travel schedules. Because competition for jobs is stiff and clients' needs are very specific, patience and persistence are essential.

Modeling schools provide training in posing, walking, makeup application, and other basic tasks, but attending such schools does not necessarily lead to job opportunities. In fact, many agents prefer beginning models with little or no previous experience and discourage models from attending modeling schools and purchasing professional photographs. A model's selection of an agency is an important factor for advancement in the occupation. The better the reputation and skill of the agency, the more assignments a model is likely to get. Because clients prefer to work with agents, it is very difficult for a model to pursue a freelance career.

Agents continually scout for new faces, and many of the top models are discovered in this way. Most agencies review snapshots or have "open calls", during which models are seen in person; this service usually is provided free of charge. Some agencies sponsor modeling contests and searches. Very few people who send in snapshots or attend open calls are offered contracts.

Agencies advise models on how to dress, wear makeup, and conduct themselves properly during go-sees and bookings. Because models' advancement depends on their previous work, development of a good portfolio is key to getting assignments. Models accumulate and display current tear sheets—examples of a model's editorial print work—and photographs in the portfolio. The higher the quality and currency of the photos in the portfolio, the more likely it is that the model will find work.

Demonstrators and product promoters who perform well and show leadership ability may advance to other marketing and sales occupations or open their own businesses. Because modeling careers are relatively short, most models eventually transfer to other occupations.

Employment

Demonstrators, product promoters, and models held about 120,000 jobs in 2004. Of these, models held only about 2,200 jobs in 2004. About 23 percent of all salaried jobs for demonstrators, product promoters, and models were in retail trade, especially general merchandise stores, and 14 percent were in administrative and support services—which includes employment services. Other jobs were found in advertising and related services.

Demonstrator and product promoter jobs may be found in communities throughout the Nation, but modeling jobs are concentrated in New York, Chicago, Miami, and Los Angeles.

Job Outlook

Employment of demonstrators, product promoters, and models is expected to grow about as fast as the average for all occupations through 2014. Job growth should be driven by increases in the number and size of trade shows and greater use of these workers in department stores and various retail shops for in-store promotions. Additional job openings will arise from the need to replace demonstrators, product promoters, and models that transfer to other occupations, retire, or stop working for other reasons.

Job openings should be plentiful for demonstrators and product promoters. Employers may have difficulty finding qualified demonstrators who are willing to fill part-time, short-term positions. Product demonstration is considered a very effective marketing tool. New jobs should arise as firms devote a greater percentage of marketing budgets to product demonstration.

On the other hand, modeling is considered a glamorous occupation, with limited formal entry requirements. Consequently, those who wish to pursue a modeling career can expect keen competition for jobs. The modeling profession typically attracts many more jobseekers than there are job openings available. Only models who closely meet the unique requirements of the occupation will achieve regular employment. The increasing diversification of the general population should boost demand for models more representative of diverse racial and ethnic groups. Work for male models also should increase as society becomes more receptive to the marketing of men's fashions. Because fashions change frequently, demand for a model's look may fluctuate. Most models experience periods of unemployment.

Employment of demonstrators, product promoters, and models is affected by downturns in the business cycle. Many firms tend to reduce advertising budgets during recessions.

Earnings

Demonstrators and product promoters had median hourly earnings of $9.95 in May 2004. The middle 50 percent earned between $8.18 and $13.29. The lowest 10 percent earned less than $7.25, and the highest 10 percent earned more than $20.08. Employers of demonstrators, product promoters, and models generally pay for job-related travel expenses.

Median hourly earnings of models were $10.50 in May 2004. The middle 50 percent earned between $8.44 and $14.34. The lowest 10 percent earned less than $7.16, and the highest 10 percent earned more than $17.17. Earnings vary for different types of modeling, and depend on the experience and reputation of the model. Female models typically earn more than male models for similar work. Hourly earnings can be relatively high, particularly for supermodels and others in high demand, but models may not have work every day, and jobs may last only a few hours. Models occasionally receive clothing or clothing discounts instead of, or in addition to, regular earnings. Almost all models work with agents, and pay 15 to 20 percent of their earnings in return for an agent's services. Models who do not find immediate work may receive payments, called advances, from agents to cover promotional and living expenses. Models must provide their own health and retirement benefits.

Related Occupations

Demonstrators, product promoters, and models create public interest in buying clothing, products, and services. Others who create interest in a product or service include actors, producers, and directors; insurance sales agents; real estate brokers; retail salespersons; sales representatives, wholesale and manufacturing; and reservation and transportation ticket agents and travel clerks.

Sources of Additional Information

For information about modeling schools and agencies in your area, contact a local consumer affairs organization such as the Better Business Bureau.

Insurance Sales Agents

(O*NET 41-3021.00)

Significant Points

- Agents increasingly offer comprehensive financial planning services, including retirement and estate planning; as a result, in addition to offering insurance policies, agents sell mutual funds, annuities, and securities.

- Agents must obtain a license in the States where they plan to do their selling.

- Despite slower than average growth, job opportunities should be good for college graduates who have sales ability, excellent interpersonal skills, and expertise in a wide range of insurance and financial services.

- Successful agents often have high earnings, but many beginning agents fail to earn enough from commissions to meet their income goals and eventually transfer to other careers.

Nature of the Work

Most people have their first contact with an insurance company through an insurance sales agent. These workers help individuals, families, and businesses select insurance policies that

An increasing number of insurance sales agents offer comprehensive financial planning services to their clients.

provide the best protection for their lives, health, and property. Insurance sales agents who work exclusively for one insurance company are referred to as captive agents. Independent insurance agents, or brokers, represent several companies and place insurance policies for their clients with the company that offers the best rate and coverage. In either case, agents prepare reports, maintain records, seek out new clients, and, in the event of a loss, help policyholders settle their insurance claims. Increasingly, some are also offering their clients financial analysis or advice on ways the clients can minimize risk.

Insurance sales agents, commonly referred to as "producers" in the insurance industry, sell one or more types of insurance, such as property and casualty, life, health, disability, and long-term care. Property and casualty insurance agents sell policies that protect individuals and businesses from financial loss resulting from automobile accidents, fire, theft, storms, and other events that can damage property. For businesses, property and casualty insurance can also cover injured workers' compensation, product liability claims, or medical malpractice claims.

. Life insurance agents specialize in selling policies that pay beneficiaries when a policyholder dies. Depending on the policyholder's circumstances, a cash-value policy can be designed to provide retirement income, funds for the education of children, or other benefits. Life insurance agents also sell annuities that promise a retirement income. Health insurance agents sell health insurance policies that cover the costs of medical care and loss of income due to illness or injury. They also may sell dental insurance and short-term and long-term-disability insurance policies.

An increasing number of insurance sales agents are offering comprehensive financial planning services to their clients, such as retirement planning, estate planning, or assistance in setting up pension plans for businesses. As a result, many insurance agents are involved in "cross-selling" or "total account development." Besides offering insurance, these agents may become licensed to sell mutual funds, variable annuities, and other securities. This practice is most common with life insurance agents who already sell annuities; however, property and casualty agents also sell financial products.

(See the statement on securities, commodities, and financial services sales agents elsewhere in the *Handbook*.)

Technology has greatly affected the insurance agency, making it much more efficient and giving the agent the ability to take on more clients. Agents' computers are now linked directly to the insurance carriers via the Internet, making the tasks of obtaining price quotes and processing applications and service requests faster and easier. Computers also allow agents to be better informed about new products that the insurance carriers may be offering.

The growth of the Internet in the insurance industry is gradually altering the relationship between agent and client. In the past, agents devoted much of their time to marketing and selling products to new clients, a practice that is now changing. Increasingly, clients are obtaining insurance quotes from a company's Web site and then contacting the company directly to purchase policies. This interaction gives the client a more active role in selecting a policy at the best price, while reducing the amount of time agents spend actively seeking new clients. Because insurance sales agents also obtain many new accounts through referrals, it is important that they maintain regular contact with their clients to ensure that the clients' financial needs are being met. Developing a satisfied clientele that will recommend an agent's services to other potential customers is a key to success in this field.

Increasing competition in the insurance industry has spurred carriers and agents to find new ways to keep their clients satisfied. One solution is to increase the use of call centers, which usually are accessible to clients 24 hours a day, 7 days a week. Insurance carriers and sales agents also are hiring customer service representatives to handle routine tasks such as answering questions, making changes in policies, processing claims, and selling more products to clients. The opportunity to cross-sell new products to clients will help agents' businesses grow. The use of call centers also allows agents to concentrate their efforts on seeking out new clients and maintaining relationships with old ones. (See separate *Handbook* statements on customer service representatives and on claims adjusters, appraisers, examiners, and investigators.)

Working Conditions

Most insurance sales agents are based in small offices, from which they contact clients and provide information on the policies they sell. However, much of their time may be spent outside their offices, traveling locally to meet with clients, close sales, or investigate claims. Agents usually determine their own hours of work and often schedule evening and weekend appointments for the convenience of clients. Although most agents work a 40-hour week, some work 60 hours a week or longer. Commercial sales agents, in particular, may meet with clients during business hours and then spend evenings doing paperwork and preparing presentations to prospective clients.

Training, Other Qualifications, and Advancement

For insurance sales agent jobs, most companies and independent agencies prefer to hire college graduates—especially those who have majored in business or economics. High school graduates are occasionally hired if they have proven sales ability or have been successful in other types of work. In fact, many entrants to insurance sales agent jobs transfer from other occupations. In selling commercial insurance, technical experience in a particular field can help sell policies to those in the same profession. As a result, new agents tend to be older than entrants in many other occupations.

College training may help agents grasp the technical aspects of insurance policies and the fundamentals and procedures of selling insurance. Many colleges and universities offer courses in insurance, and a few schools offer a bachelor's degree in the field.

College courses in finance, mathematics, accounting, economics, business law, marketing, and business administration enable insurance sales agents to understand how social and economic conditions relate to the insurance industry. Courses in psychology, sociology, and public speaking can prove useful in improving sales techniques. In addition, because computers provide instantaneous information on a wide variety of financial products and greatly improve agents' efficiency, familiarity with computers and popular software packages has become very important.

Insurance sales agents must obtain a license in the States where they plan to do their selling. Separate licenses are required for agents to sell life and health insurance and property and casualty insurance. In most States, licenses are issued only to applicants who complete specified prelicensing courses and who pass State examinations covering insurance fundamentals and State insurance laws. The insurance industry is increasingly moving toward uniform State licensing standards and reciprocal licensing, allowing agents who earn a license in one State to become licensed in other States upon passing the appropriate courses and examination.

A number of organizations offer professional designation programs that certify one's expertise in specialties such as life, health, and property and casualty insurance, as well as financial consulting. For example, The National Alliance for Education and Research offers a wide variety of courses in health, life and property, and casualty insurance for independent insurance agents. Although voluntary, such programs assure clients and employers that an agent has a thorough understanding of the relevant specialty. Agents are usually required to complete a specified number of hours of continuing education to retain their designation.

Employers also are placing greater emphasis on continuing professional education as the diversity of financial products sold by insurance agents increases. It is important for insurance agents to keep up to date on issues concerning clients. Changes in tax laws, government benefits programs, and other State and Federal regulations can affect the insurance needs of clients and the way in which agents conduct business. Agents can enhance their selling skills and broaden their knowledge of insurance and other financial services by taking courses at colleges and universities and by attending institutes, conferences, and seminars sponsored by insurance organizations. Most State licensing authorities also have mandatory continuing education requirements focusing on insurance laws, consumer protection, and the technical details of various insurance policies.

As the demand for financial products and financial planning increases, many insurance agents are choosing to gain the proper licensing and certification to sell securities and other financial products. Doing so, however, requires substantial study and passing an additional examination—either the Series 6 or Series 7 licensing exam, both of which are administered by the National Association of Securities Dealers (NASD). The Series 6 exam is for individuals who wish to sell only mutual funds and variable annuities, whereas the Series 7 exam is the main NASD series license that qualifies agents as general securities sales representatives. In addition, to further demonstrate competency in the area of financial planning, many agents find it worthwhile to earn the certified financial planner or chartered financial consultant designation. The Certified Financial Planner credential issued by the Certified Financial Planner Board of Standards, requires relevant experience, completion of education requirements, passing a comprehensive examination, and adherence to an enforceable code of ethics. The CFP exams test the candidate's knowledge of the financial planning process, insurance and risk management, employee benefits planning, taxes and retirement planning, and investment and estate planning. The Chartered Financial Consultant (ChFC) designation, issued by the American College in Bryn Mawr, Pennsylvania, which requires experience and the completion of an eight-course program of study. The CFP and ChFC designation and other professional designations have continuing education requirements.

Insurance sales agents should be flexible, enthusiastic, confident, disciplined, hard working, and willing to solve problems. They should communicate effectively and inspire customer confidence. Because they usually work without supervision, sales agents must be able to plan their time well and have the initiative to locate new clients.

An insurance sales agent who shows ability and leadership may become a sales manager in a local office. A few advance to agency superintendent or executive positions. However, many who have built up a good clientele prefer to remain in sales work. Some—particularly in the property and casualty field—establish their own independent agencies or brokerage firms.

Employment

Insurance sales agents held about 400,000 jobs in 2004. Most insurance sales agents employed in wage and salary positions work for insurance agencies and brokerages. A decreasing number work directly for insurance carriers. Although most insurance agents specialize in life and health insurance or property and casualty insurance, a growing number of "multiline" agents sell all lines of insurance. A small number of agents work for banks and securities brokerages as a result of the increasing integration of finance and insurance industries. Approximately 1 out of 4 insurance sales agents is self-employed.

Insurance sales agents are employed throughout the country, but most work in or near large urban centers. Some are employed in the headquarters of insurance companies, but the majority work out of local offices or independent agencies.

Job Outlook

Although employment of insurance sales agents is expected to grow more slowly than the average for all occupations through 2014, opportunities will be favorable for college graduates who have sales ability, excellent interpersonal skills, and expertise in a wide range of insurance and financial services. Multilingual agents also should be in high demand because they can serve a wider range of customers. Insurance language tends to be quite technical, so it is important for insurance sales agents to have a firm understanding of relevant technical and legal terms. Many beginning agents fail to earn enough from commissions to meet their income goals and eventually transfer to other careers. Most job openings are likely to result from the need to replace agents who leave the occupation or retire. A large number of agents are expected to retire over the next decade.

Future demand for insurance sales agents depends largely on the volume of sales of insurance and other financial products. Sales of health insurance and long-term-care insurance are expected to rise sharply as the population ages. In addition, a growing population will increase demand for insurance for automobiles, homes, and high-priced valuables and equipment. As new businesses emerge and existing firms expand their insurance coverage, sales of commercial insurance also should increase, including coverage such as product liability, workers' compensation, employee benefits, and pollution liability insurance.

Employment of agents will not keep up with the rising level of insurance sales, however. Many insurance carriers are trying to contain costs. As a result, many are shedding their captive agents—those agents working directly for insurance carriers—and are relying more on independent agents or direct marketing through the mail, by phone, or on the Internet.

Agents who incorporate new technology into their existing businesses will remain competitive. Agents who use the Internet to market their products will reach a broader client base and expand their businesses, but because most clients value their relationship with their agent, the Internet should not threaten jobs, given that many individuals still prefer discussing their policies directly with their agents, rather than through a computer. Also, the automation of policy and claims processing is allowing insurance agents to take on more clients.

Agents may face increased competition from traditional securities brokers and bankers as they begin to sell insurance policies. Because of increasing consolidation among insurance companies, banks, and brokerage firms, and due to increasing demands from clients for more comprehensive financial planning, insurance sales agents will need to expand the products and services they offer.

Agents who offer better customer service also will remain competitive. Call centers are another important way carriers and agents are offering better service to customers, because such centers provide greater access to their policies and more prompt services.

Insurance and investments are becoming more complex, and many people and businesses lack the time and expertise to buy insurance without the advice of an agent. Moreover, most individuals and businesses consider insurance a necessity, regardless of economic conditions. Therefore, agents are not likely to face unemployment because of a recession.

Earnings

The median annual earnings of wage and salary insurance sales agents were $41,720 in May 2004. The middle 50 percent earned between $29,980 and $66,160. The lowest 10 percent had earnings of $23,170 or less, while the highest 10 percent earned more than $108,800. Median annual earnings in May 2004 in the two industries employing the largest number of insurance sales agents were $42,010 for insurance carriers, and $41,840 for agencies, brokerages, and other insurance related activities.

Many independent agents are paid by commission only, whereas sales workers who are employees of an agency or an insurance carrier may be paid in one of three ways—salary only, salary plus commission, or salary plus bonus. In general, commissions are the most common form of compensation, especially for experienced agents. The amount of the commission depends on the type and amount of insurance sold and on whether the transaction is a new policy or a renewal. Bonuses usually are awarded when agents meet their sales goals or when an agency meets its profit goals. Some agents involved with financial planning receive a fee for their services, rather than a commission.

Company-paid benefits to insurance sales agents usually include continuing education, training to qualify for licensing, group insurance plans, office space, and clerical support services. Some companies also may pay for automobile and transportation expenses, attendance at conventions and meetings, promotion and marketing expenses, and retirement plans. Independent agents working for insurance agencies receive fewer benefits, but their commissions may be higher to help them pay for marketing and other expenses.

Related Occupations

Other workers who provide or sell financial products or services include real estate sales agents and brokers; securities, commodities, and financial services sales agents; financial analysts and personal financial advisors; and financial managers. Other occupations in the insurance industry include insurance underwriters; claims adjusters, examiners, and investigators.

Sources of Additional Information

Occupational information about insurance sales agents is available from the home office of many insurance companies. Information on State licensing requirements may be obtained from the department of insurance at any State capital.

For information about insurance sales careers and training, contact:

➤ Independent Insurance Agents of America, 127 S. Peyton St., Alexandria, VA 22314. Internet: **http://www.iiaa.org**
➤ Insurance Vocational Education Student Training (InVEST), 127 S. Peyton St., Alexandria, VA 22314. Internet: **http://www.investprogram.org**

For information about health insurance sales careers, contact:

➤ National Association of Health Underwriters, 2000 N. 14th St., Suite 450, Arlington, VA 22201. Internet: **http://www.nahu.org**

For general information on the property and casualty field, contact:

➤ Insurance Information Institute, 110 William St., New York, NY 10038. Internet: **http://www.iii.org**

For information about professional designation programs, contact:

➤ The American Institute for Chartered Property and Casualty Underwriters/Insurance Institute of America, 720 Providence Rd., P.O. Box 3016, Malvern, PA 19355-0716. Internet: **http://www.aicpcu.org**
➤ The American College, 270 Bryn Mawr Ave., Bryn Mawr, PA 19010-2195. Internet: **http://www.theamericancollege.edu**

Real Estate Brokers and Sales Agents

(O*NET 41-9021.00, 41-9022.00)

Significant Points

● Real estate brokers and sales agents often work evenings and weekends and usually are on call to suit the needs of clients.

● A license is required in every State and the District of Columbia.

● Although gaining a job may be relatively easy, beginning workers may face competition from well-estab lished, more experienced agents and brokers in obtaining listings and in closing an adequate number of sales.

● Employment is sensitive to swings in the economy, especially interest rates; during periods of declining economic activity and increasing interest rates, the volume of sales and the resulting demand for sales workers fall.

Nature of the Work

One of the most complex and significant financial events in peoples' lives is the purchase or sale of a home or investment property. Because of this complexity and significance, people typically seek the help of real estate brokers and sales agents when buying or selling real estate.

Real estate brokers and sales agents have a thorough knowledge of the real estate market in their communities. They know which neighborhoods will best fit clients' needs and budgets. They are familiar with local zoning and tax laws and know where to obtain financing. Agents and brokers also act as intermediaries in price negotiations between buyers and sellers.

Real estate agents usually are independent sales workers who provide their services to a licensed real estate broker on a contract basis. In return, the broker pays the agent a portion of the commission earned from the agent's sale of the property. Brokers are independent businesspeople who sell real estate owned by others; they also may rent or manage properties for a fee. When selling real estate, brokers arrange for title searches and for meetings between buyers and sellers during which the details of the transactions are agreed upon and the new owners take possession of the property. A broker may help to arrange favorable financing from a lender for the prospective buyer; often, this makes the difference between success and failure in closing a sale. In some cases, brokers and agents assume primary responsibility for closing sales; in others, lawyers or lenders do. Brokers supervise agents who may have many of the same job duties. Brokers also supervise their own offices, advertise properties, and handle other business matters. Some combine other types of work, such as selling insurance or practicing law, with their real estate business.

Besides making sales, agents and brokers must have properties to sell. Consequently, they spend a significant amount of time obtaining listings—agreements by owners to place properties for sale with the firm. When listing a property for sale, agents and brokers compare the listed property with similar properties that recently sold, in order to determine a competitive market price for the property. Once the property is sold, both the agent who sold it and the agent who obtained the listing receive a portion of the commission. Thus, agents who sell a property that they themselves have listed can increase their commission.

Most real estate brokers and sales agents sell residential property. A small number—usually employed in large or specialized firms—sell commercial, industrial, agricultural, or other types of real estate. Every specialty requires knowledge of that particular type of property and clientele. Selling or leasing business property requires an understanding of leasing practices, business trends, and the location of the property. Agents who sell or lease industrial properties must know about the region's transportation, utilities, and labor supply. Whatever the type of property, the agent or broker must know how to meet the client's particular requirements.

Before showing residential properties to potential buyers, agents meet with them to get a feeling for the type of home the buyers would like. In this prequalifying phase, the agent determines how much the buyers can afford to spend. In addition, the agent and the buyer usually sign a loyalty contract which states that the agent will be the only one to show houses to buyers. An agent or broker then generates lists of properties for sale, their location and description, and available sources of financing. In some cases, agents and brokers use computers to give buyers a virtual tour of properties in which they are interested. With a computer, buyers can view interior and exterior images or floor plans without leaving the real estate office.

Real estate brokers and sales agents have a thorough knowledge of the real estate market in their communities.

Agents may meet several times with prospective buyers to discuss and visit available properties. Agents identify and emphasize the most pertinent selling points. To a young family looking for a house, they may emphasize the convenient floor plan, the area's low crime rate, and the proximity to schools and shopping centers. To a potential investor, they may point out the tax advantages of owning a rental property and the ease of finding a renter. If bargaining over price becomes necessary, agents must follow their client's instructions carefully and may have to present counteroffers in order to get the best possible price.

Once both parties have signed the contract, the real estate broker or agent must make sure that all special terms of the contract are met before the closing date. For example, the agent must make sure that the mandated and agreed-upon inspections, including that of the home and termite and radon inspections, take place. Also, if the seller agrees to any repairs, the broker or agent must see that they are made. Increasingly, brokers and agents are handling environmental problems as well, by making sure that the properties they sell meet environmental regulations. For example, they may be responsible for dealing with lead paint on the walls. While loan officers, attorneys, or other persons handle many details, the agent must ensure that they are carried out.

Working Conditions

Advances in telecommunications and the ability to retrieve data about properties over the Internet allow many real estate brokers and sales agents to work out of their homes instead of real estate offices. Even with this convenience, much of the time of these workers is spent away from their desks—showing properties to customers, analyzing properties for sale, meeting with prospective clients, or researching the state of the market.

Agents and brokers often work more than a standard 40-hour week. They usually work evenings and weekends and are always on call to suit the needs of clients. Although the hours are long and frequently irregular, most agents and brokers have the freedom to determine their own schedule. Consequently, they can arrange their work so that they can have time off when they want it. Business usually is slower during the winter season.

Training, Other Qualifications, and Advcement

In every State and the District of Columbia, real estate brokers and sales agents must be licensed. Prospective agents must be high school graduates, be at least 18 years old, and pass a written test. The examination—more comprehensive for brokers than for agents—includes questions on basic real estate transactions and laws affecting the sale of property. Most States require candidates for the general sales license to complete between 30 and 90 hours of classroom instruction. Those seeking a broker's license need between 60 and 90 hours of formal training and a specific amount of experience selling real estate, usually 1 to 3 years. Some States waive the experience requirements for the broker's license for applicants who have a bachelor's degree in real estate.

State licenses typically must be renewed every 1 or 2 years; usually, no examination needs to be taken. However, many States require continuing education for license renewals. Prospective agents and brokers should contact the real estate licensing commission of the State in which they wish to work in order to verify the exact licensing requirements.

As real estate transactions have become more legally complex, many firms have turned to college graduates to fill positions. A large number of agents and brokers have some college training. College courses in real estate, finance, business administration, statistics, economics, law, and English are helpful. For those who intend to start their own company, business courses such as marketing and accounting are as significant as courses in real estate or finance.

Personality traits are equally as important as one's academic background. Brokers look for applicants who possess a pleasant personality, are honest, and present a neat appearance. Maturity, good judgment, trustworthiness, and enthusiasm for the job are required in order to encourage prospective customers in this highly competitive field. Agents should be well organized, be detail oriented, and have a good memory for names, faces, and business particulars.

Those interested in jobs as real estate agents often begin in their own communities. Their knowledge of local neighborhoods is a clear advantage. Under the direction of an experienced agent, beginners learn the practical aspects of the job, including the use of computers to locate or list available properties and identify sources of financing.

Many firms offer formal training programs for both beginners and experienced agents. Larger firms usually offer more extensive programs than smaller firms. More than a thousand universities, colleges, and junior colleges offer courses in real estate. At some, a student can earn an associate's or bachelor's degree with a major in real estate; several offer advanced degrees. Many local real estate associations that are members of the National Association of Realtors sponsor courses covering the fundamentals and legal aspects of the field. Advanced courses in mortgage financing, property development and management, and other subjects also are available.

Advancement opportunities for agents may take the form of higher rates of commission. As agents gain knowledge and expertise, they become more efficient in closing a greater number of transactions and increase their earnings. In many large firms, experienced agents can advance to sales manager or general manager. Persons who have received their broker's license may open their own offices. Others with experience and training in estimating property value may become real estate appraisers, and people familiar with operating and maintaining rental properties may become property managers. (See the *Handbook* statements on property, real estate, and community association managers; and appraisers and assessors of real estate.) Experienced agents and brokers with a thorough knowledge of business conditions and property values in their localities may enter mortgage financing or real estate investment counseling.

Employment

In 2004, real estate brokers and sales agents held about 460,000 jobs; real estate sales agents held approximately 24 percent of these jobs. Many worked part time, combining their real estate activities with other careers. About 6 out of 10 real estate agents and brokers were self-employed. Real estate is sold in all areas, but employment is concentrated in large urban areas and in rapidly growing communities.

Most real estate firms are relatively small; indeed, some are one-person businesses. By contrast, some large real estate firms have several hundred agents operating out of numerous branch offices. Many brokers have franchise agreements with national or regional real estate organizations. Under this type of arrangement, the broker pays a fee in exchange for the privilege of using the more widely known name of the parent organization. Although franchised brokers often receive help in training sales staff and running their offices, they bear the ultimate responsibility for the success or failure of their firms.

Real estate brokers and sales agents are older, on average, than most other workers. Historically, many homemakers and retired persons were attracted to real estate sales by the flexible and part-time work schedules characteristic of the field. These individuals could enter, leave, and later return to the occupation, depending on the strength of the real estate market, their family responsibilities, or other personal circumstances. Recently, however, the attractiveness of part-time real estate work has declined, as increasingly complex legal and technological requirements are raising startup costs associated with becoming an agent.

Job Outlook

Employment of real estate brokers and sales agents is expected to grow about as fast as the average for all occupations through the year 2014, because of the increasing housing needs of a growing population, as well as the perception that real estate is a good investment. Relatively low interest rates should continue to stimulate sales of real estate, resulting in the need for more agents and brokers. In addition, a large number of job openings will arise each year from the need to replace workers who transfer to other occupations or leave the labor force. However, job growth will be somewhat limited by the increasing use of technology, which is improving the productivity of agents and brokers. For example, prospective customers often can perform their own searches for properties that meet their criteria by accessing real estate information on the Internet. The increasing use of technology is likely to be more detrimental to part-time or temporary real estate agents than to full-time agents, because part-time agents generally are not able to compete with full-time agents who have invested in new technology. Changing legal requirements, such as disclosure laws, also may dissuade some who are not serious about practicing full time from continuing to work part time.

This occupation is relatively easy to enter and is attractive because of its flexible working conditions; the high interest in, and familiarity with, local real estate markets that entrants often have; and the potential for high earnings. Therefore, although gaining a job as a real estate agent or broker may be relatively easy, beginning agents and brokers may face competition from their well-established, more experienced counterparts in obtaining listings and in closing an adequate number of sales. Well-trained, ambitious people who enjoy selling—particularly those with extensive social and business connections in their communities—should have the best chance for success.

Employment of real estate brokers and sales agents often is sensitive to swings in the economy, especially interest rates. During periods of declining economic activity and increasing interest rates, the volume of sales and the resulting demand for sales workers falls. As a result, the earnings of agents and brokers decline, and many work fewer hours or leave the occupation altogether.

Earnings

The median annual earnings of salaried real estate sales agents, including commissions, were $35,670 in May 2004. The middle 50 percent earned between $23,500 and $58,110 a year. The lowest 10 percent earned less than $17,600, and the highest 10 percent earned more than $92,770. Median hourly earnings in the industries employing the largest number of real estate sales agents in May 2004 were as follows:

Residential building construction	$54,770
Offices of real estate agents and brokers	37,970
Activities related to real estate	32,460
Lessors of real estate	25,840

Median annual earnings of salaried real estate brokers, including commission, were $58,720 in May 2004. The middle 50 percent earned between $33,480 and $99,820 a year. Median annual earning of real estate brokers were $61,550 in offices of real estate agents and brokers and $44,920 in activities related to real estate.

Commissions on sales are the main source of earnings of real estate agents and brokers. The rate of commission varies according to whatever the agent and broker agree on, the type of property, and its value. The percentage paid on the sale of farm and commercial properties or unimproved land is typically higher than the percentage paid for selling a home.

Commissions may be divided among several agents and brokers. When the property is sold, the broker or agent who obtained the listing usually shares the commission with the broker or agent who made the sale and with the firm that employs each of them. Although an agent's share varies greatly from one firm to another, often it is about half of the total amount received by the firm. Agents who both list and sell a property maximize their commission.

Income usually increases as an agent gains experience, but individual motivation, economic conditions, and the type and location of the property also affect earnings. Sales workers who are active in community organizations and in local real estate associations can broaden their contacts and increase their earnings. A beginner's earnings often are irregular, because a few weeks or even months may go by without a sale. Although some brokers allow an agent to draw against future earnings from a special account, the practice is not common with new employees. The beginner, therefore, should have enough money to live for about 6 months or until commissions increase.

Related Occupations

Selling expensive items such as homes requires maturity, tact, and a sense of responsibility. Other sales workers who find these character traits important in their work include insurance sales agents; retail salespersons; sales representatives, wholesale and manufacturing; and securities, commodities, and financial services sales agents. Although not involving sales, the work of property, real estate, and community association managers, as well as appraisers and assessors of real estate, requires an understanding of real estate.

Sources of Additional Information

Information on licensing requirements for real estate brokers and sales agents is available from most local real estate organizations or from the State real estate commission or board.

More information about opportunities in real estate is available on the Internet site of the following organization:
➤ National Association of Realtors. Internet: **http://www.realtor.org**

Retail Salespersons

(O*NET 41-2031.00)

Significant Points

- Good employment opportunities are expected because of the need to replace the large number of workers who leave the occupation each year.

- Most salespersons work evenings and weekends, particularly during sales and other peak retail periods.

- Employers look for people who enjoy working with others and who have tact, patience, an interest in sales work, a neat appearance, and the ability to communicate clearly.

Nature of the Work

Whether selling shoes, computer equipment, or automobiles, retail salespersons assist customers in finding what they are looking for and try to interest them in buying the merchandise. They describe a product's features, demonstrate its use, or show various models and colors. For some sales jobs, particularly those involving expensive and complex items, retail salespersons need special knowledge or skills. For example, salespersons who sell automobiles must be able to explain the features of various models, the manufacturers' specifications, the types of options and financing available, and the warranty.

Consumers spend millions of dollars every day on merchandise and often form their impression of a store by evaluating its sales force. Therefore, retailers stress the importance of providing courteous and efficient service to remain competitive. For example, when a customer wants an item that is not on the sales floor, the salesperson may check the stockroom, place a special order, or call another store to locate the item.

In addition to selling, most retail salespersons—especially those who work in department and apparel stores—make out sales checks; receive cash, checks, debit, and charge payments; bag or package purchases; and give change and receipts. Depending on the hours they work, retail salespersons may have to open or close cash registers. This work may include counting the money in the register; separating charge slips, coupons, and exchange vouchers; and making deposits at the cash office. Salespersons often are held responsible for the contents of their registers, and repeated shortages are cause for dismissal in many organizations. (Cashiers, who have similar duties, are discussed elsewhere in the *Handbook*.)

Salespersons also may handle returns and exchanges of merchandise, wrap gifts, and keep their work areas neat. In addition, they may help stock shelves or racks, arrange for mailing or delivery of purchases, mark price tags, take inventory, and prepare displays.

Frequently, salespersons must be aware of special sales and promotions. They also must recognize security risks and thefts and know how to handle or prevent such situations.

Working Conditions

Most salespersons in retail trade work in clean, comfortable, well-lighted stores. However, they often stand for long periods and may need supervisory approval to leave the sales floor. They also may work outdoors if they sell items such as cars, plants, or lumber yard materials.

The Monday-through-Friday, 9-to-5 workweek is the exception rather than the rule in retail trade. Most salespersons work evenings and weekends, particularly during sales and other peak retail periods. The end-of-year holiday season is the busiest time for most retailers. As a result, many employers restrict the use of vacation time to some period other than Thanksgiving through the beginning of January.

The job can be rewarding for those who enjoy working with people. Patience and courtesy are required, especially when the work is repetitive and the customers are demanding.

Retail salespersons describe a product's features, demonstrate its use, or show various models and colors.

Training, Other Qualifications, and Advancement

There usually are no formal education requirements for this type of work, although a high school diploma or the equivalent is preferred. Employers look for people who enjoy working with others and who have the tact and patience to deal with difficult customers. Among other desirable characteristics are an interest in sales work, a neat appearance, and the ability to communicate clearly and effectively. The ability to speak more than one language may be helpful for employment in communities where people from various cultures tend to live and shop. Before hiring a salesperson, some employers may conduct a background check, especially for a job selling high-priced items.

In most small stores, an experienced employee or the proprietor instructs newly hired sales personnel in making out sales checks and operating cash registers. In large stores, training programs are more formal and are usually conducted over several days. Topics generally discussed are customer service, security, the store's policies and procedures, and how to work a cash register. Depending on the type of product they are selling, employees may be given additional specialized training by manufacturers' representatives. For example, those working in cosmetics receive instruction on the types of products the store has available and for whom the cosmetics would be most beneficial. Likewise, salespersons employed by motor vehicle dealers may be required to participate in training programs designed to provide information on the technical details of standard and optional equipment available on new vehicle models. Since providing the best possible service to customers is a high priority for many employers, employees often are given periodic training to update and refine their skills.

As salespersons gain experience and seniority, they usually move to positions of greater responsibility and may be given their choice of departments in which to work. This often means moving to areas with potentially higher earnings and commissions. The highest earnings potential usually lies in selling "big-ticket" items—such as cars, jewelry, furniture, and electronic equipment—although doing so often requires extensive knowledge of the product and an extraordinary talent for persuasion.

Opportunities for advancement vary in small stores. In some establishments, advancement is limited because one person—often the owner—does most of the managerial work. In others, some salespersons are promoted to assistant managers. Large retail businesses usually prefer to hire college graduates as management trainees, making a college education increasingly important. However, motivated and capable employees without college degrees still may advance to administrative or supervisory positions in large establishments.

Retail selling experience may be an asset when one is applying for sales positions with larger retailers or in other industries, such as financial services, wholesale trade, or manufacturing.

Employment

Retail salespersons held about 4.3 million wage and salary jobs in 2004. They worked in stores ranging from small specialty shops employing a few workers to giant department stores with hundreds of salespersons. In addition, some were self-employed representatives of direct-sales companies and mail-order houses. The largest employers of retail salespersons are department stores, clothing and clothing accessories stores, building material and garden equipment and supplies dealers, other general merchandise stores, and motor vehicle and parts dealers.

This occupation offers many opportunities for part-time work and is especially appealing to students, retirees, and others seeking to supplement their income. However, most of those selling big-ticket items work full time and have substantial experience.

Because retail stores are found in every city and town, employment is distributed geographically in much the same way as the population.

Job Outlook

As in the past, employment opportunities for retail salespersons are expected to be good because of the need to replace the large number of workers who transfer to other occupations or leave the labor force each year. In addition, many new jobs will be created for retail salespersons as businesses seek to expand operations and enhance customer service. Employment is expected to grow about as fast as the average for all occupations through the year 2014, reflecting rising retail sales stemming from a growing population. Opportunities for part-time work should be abundant, and demand will be strong for temporary workers during peak selling periods, such as the end-of-year holiday season. The availability of part-time and temporary work attracts many people seeking to supplement their income.

During economic downturns, sales volumes and the resulting demand for sales workers usually decline. Purchases of costly items, such as cars, appliances, and furniture, tend to be postponed during difficult economic times. In areas of high unemployment, sales of many types of goods decline. However, because turnover among retail salespersons is high, employers often can adjust employment levels simply by not replacing all those who leave.

Despite the growing popularity of electronic commerce, Internet sales have not decreased the need for retail salespersons. Retail stores commonly use an online presence to complement their in-store sales; there are very few Internet-only apparel and specialty stores. Retail salespersons will remain important in assuring customers that they will receive specialized service and in improving customer satisfaction, something Internet services cannot do. Therefore, the impact of electronic commerce on employment of retail salespersons is expected to be minimal.

Earnings

The starting wage for many retail sales positions is the Federal minimum wage, which was $5.15 an hour in 2004. In areas where employers have difficulty attracting and retaining workers, wages tend to be higher than the legislated minimum.

Median hourly earnings of retail salespersons, including commissions, were $8.98 in May 2004. The middle 50 percent earned between $7.46 and $12.22 an hour. The lowest 10 percent earned less than $6.38, and the highest 10 percent earned more than $17.85 an hour. Median hourly earnings in the industries employing the largest numbers of retail salespersons in May 2004 were as follows:

Automobile dealers	$18.61
Building material and supplies dealers	10.85
Department stores	8.47
Other general merchandise stores	8.36
Clothing stores	8.17

Compensation systems vary by type of establishment and merchandise sold. Salespersons receive hourly wages, commissions, or a combination thereof. Under a commission system, salespersons receive a percentage of the sales they make. This system offers sales workers the opportunity to increase their earnings considerably, but they may find that their earnings strongly depend on their ability to sell their product and on the ups and downs of the economy. Employers may use incentive programs such as awards, banquets, bonuses, and profit-sharing plans to promote teamwork among the sales staff.

Benefits may be limited in smaller stores, but benefits in large establishments usually are comparable to those offered by other employers. In addition, nearly all salespersons are able to buy their store's merchandise at a discount, with the savings depending on the type of merchandise.

Related Occupations

Salespersons use sales techniques, coupled with their knowledge of merchandise, to assist customers and encourage purchases. Workers in other occupations who use these same skills include sales representatives, wholesale and manufacturing; securities, commodities, and financial services sales agents; counter and rental clerks; real estate brokers and sales agents; purchasing managers, buyers, and purchasing agents; insurance sales agents; sales engineers; and cashiers.

Sources of Additional Information

Information on careers in retail sales may be obtained from the personnel offices of local stores or from State merchants' associations.

General information about retailing is available from:

➤ National Retail Federation, 325 7th St. NW., Suite 1100, Washington, DC 20004.

Information about retail sales employment opportunities is available from:

➤ Retail, Wholesale, and Department Store Union, 30 East 29th St., 4th Floor, New York, NY 10016.

Information about training for a career in automobile sales is available from:

➤ National Automobile Dealers Association, Public Relations Department, 8400 Westpark Dr., McLean, VA 22102-3591. Internet: **www.nada.org**

Sales Engineers

(O*NET 41-9031.00)

Significant Points

● A bachelor's degree in engineering typically is required; many sales engineers have previous work experience in an engineering specialty.

● Projected employment growth stems from the increasing number and technical nature of products and services to be sold.

● More job opportunities are expected in independent sales agencies.

● Earnings are based on a combination of salary and commissions.

Nature of the Work

Many products and services, especially those purchased by large companies and institutions, are highly complex. Sales engineers—who also may be called *manufacturers' agents, sales representatives*, or *technical sales support workers*—work with the production, engineering, or research and development departments of their companies, or with independent sales firms, to determine how products and services could be designed or modified to suit customers' needs. They also may advise customers on how best to use the products or services provided.

Selling, of course, is an important part of the job. Sales engineers use their technical skills to demonstrate to potential customers how and why the products or services they are selling would suit the customer better than competitors' products. Often, there may not be a directly competitive product. In these cases, the job of the sales engineer is to demonstrate to the customer the usefulness of the product or service—for example, how much money new production machinery would save.

Most sales engineers have a bachelor's degree in engineering, and many have previous work experience in an engineering specialty. Engineers apply the theories and principles of science and mathematics to technical problems. Their work is the link between scientific discoveries and commercial applications. Many sales engineers specialize in an area related to an engineering specialty. For example, sales engineers selling chemical products may have chemical engineering backgrounds, while those selling business software or information systems may have degrees in computer engineering. Information on engineers, including 17 engineering specialties, appears elsewhere in the *Handbook*.

Many of the duties of sales engineers are similar to those of other salespersons. They must interest the client in purchasing their products, many of which are durable manufactured products such as turbines. Sales engineers often are teamed with other salespersons who concentrate on the marketing and sales, enabling the sales engineer to concentrate on the technical aspects of the job. By working on a sales team, each member is able to focus on his or her strengths and knowledge. (Information on other sales occupations, including sales representatives, wholesale and manufacturing, appears elsewhere in the *Handbook*.)

Sales engineers tend to employ selling techniques that are different from those used by most other sales workers. They generally use a "consultative" style; that is, they focus on the client's problem and show how it could be solved or mitigated with their product or service. This selling style differs from the "benefits and features" method, whereby the salesperson describes the product and leaves the customer to decide how it would be useful.

In addition to maintaining current clients and attracting new ones, sales engineers help clients solve any problems that arise when the product is installed. Afterward, they may continue to serve as a liaison between the client and their company. Increasingly, sales engineers are asked to undertake tasks related to sales, such as market research, because of their familiarity with clients' purchasing needs. Drawing on this same familiarity, sales engineers may help identify and develop new products.

Sales engineers may work directly for manufacturers or service providers, or they may work in small independent sales firms. In an independent firm, they may sell complementary products from several different suppliers and be paid entirely on commission.

Sales engineers consult with their clients to offer them products or services that solve specific problems they may face.

Working Conditions

Many sales engineers work more than 40 hours per week to meet sales goals and their clients' needs. Selling can be stressful because sales engineers' income and job security often directly depend on their success in sales and customer service.

Some sales engineers have large territories and travel extensively. Because sales regions may cover several States, sales engineers may be away from home for several days or even weeks at a time. Others work near their home base and travel mostly by car. International travel, to secure contracts with foreign clients, is becoming more common.

Although the hours may be long and often are irregular, many sales engineers have the freedom to determine their own schedule. Consequently, they often can arrange their appointments so that they can have time off when they want it. However, most independent sales engineers do not earn any income while on vacation.

Training, Other Qualifications, and Advancement

A bachelor's degree in engineering usually is required to become a sales engineer. However, some workers with previous experience in sales combined with technical experience or training sometimes hold the title of sales engineer. Also, workers who have a degree in a science, such as chemistry, or even a degree in business with little or no previous sales experience, may be termed sales engineers.

Admissions requirements for undergraduate engineering schools include a solid background in mathematics (algebra, geometry, trigonometry, and calculus) and the physical sciences (biology, chemistry, and physics), as well as basic courses in English, social studies, humanities, and computer science. University programs vary in content, though all require the development of computer skills. For example, some programs emphasize industrial practices, preparing students for a job in industry, whereas others are more theoretical and prepare students for graduate school. Therefore, students should investigate curriculums and check accreditations carefully before making a selection. Once a university has been selected, a student must choose an area of engineering in which to specialize. Some programs offer a general engineering curriculum; students then specialize on the job or in graduate school. Most engineering degrees are granted in electrical, mechanical, or civil engineering. However, engineers trained in one branch may work in related branches.

Many sales engineers first work as engineers. For some, the engineering experience is necessary to obtain the technical background needed to sell their employers' products or services effectively. Others move into the occupation because it offers better earnings and advancement potential or because they are looking for a new challenge.

New graduates with engineering degrees may need sales experience and training before they can work directly as sales engineers. Training may involve teaming with a sales mentor who is familiar with the employer's business practices, customers, procedures, and company culture. After the training period has been completed, sales engineers may continue to partner with someone who lacks technical skills, yet excels in the art of sales.

Promotion may include a higher commission rate, larger sales territory, or elevation to the position of supervisor or marketing manager. Alternatively, sales engineers may leave their companies and form independent firms that may offer higher commissions and more freedom. Independent firms tend to be small, although relatively few sales engineers are self-employed.

It is important for sales engineers to continue their engineering and sales education throughout their careers because much of their value to their employers depends on their knowledge of the latest technology and their ability to sell that technology. Sales engi-neers in high-technology areas, such as information technology or advanced electronics, may find that technical knowledge rapidly becomes obsolete.

Employment

Sales engineers held about 74,000 jobs in 2004. About 35 percent were employed in wholesale trade and another 27 percent were employed in the manufacturing industries. Smaller numbers of sales engineers worked in information industries, such as software publishers and telecommunications; professional, scientific, and technical services, such as computer systems designs and related services and architectural, engineering, and related services; and other industries. Unlike workers in many other sales occupations, very few sales engineers are self-employed.

Job Outlook

Employment of sales engineers is expected to grow about as fast as the average for all occupations through the year 2014. Projected employment growth stems from the increasing variety and technical nature of goods and services to be sold. Competitive pressures and advancing technology will force companies to improve and update product designs more frequently and to optimize their manufacturing and sales processes. In addition to new positions created as companies expand their sales forces, some openings will arise each year from the need to replace sales engineers who transfer to other occupations or leave the labor force.

Manufacturers, especially foreign manufacturers that sell their products in the United States, are expected to continue outsourcing more of their sales functions to independent sales agencies in an attempt to control costs. This should result in more job opportunities for sales engineers in independent agencies.

In wholesale trade, both outsourcing to independent sales agencies and the use of information technology are expected to affect employment opportunities for sales engineers. Although outsourcing should lead to more jobs in independent agencies, employment growth for sales engineers in wholesale trade likely will be dampened by the increasing ability of businesses to find, order, and track shipments directly from wholesalers through the Internet, without assistance from sales engineers. Since direct purchases from wholesalers are more likely to be of commodity products, their impact on sales engineers should remain somewhat limited.

Employment opportunities and earnings may fluctuate from year to year because sales are affected by changing economic conditions, legislative issues, and consumer preferences. Prospects will be best for those with the appropriate knowledge or technical expertise, as well as the personal traits necessary for successful sales work.

Earnings

Compensation varies significantly by the type of firm and the product sold. Most employers offer a combination of salary and commission payments or a salary plus a bonus. Commissions usually are based on the amount of sales, whereas bonuses may depend on individual performance, on the performance of all workers in the group or district, or on the company's performance. Earnings from commissions and bonuses may vary greatly from year to year, depending on sales ability, the demand for the company's products or services, and the overall economy.

Median annual earnings of sales engineers, including commissions, were $70,620 in May 2004. The middle 50 percent earned between $53,270 and $91,500 a year. The lowest 10 percent earned less than $41,430, and the highest 10 percent earned more than $117,260 a year. Median annual earnings of those employed by firms in the computer systems design and related services industry were $86,980.

In addition to their earnings, sales engineers who work for manufacturers usually are reimbursed for expenses such as transportation, meals, hotels, and customer entertainment. In addition to typical benefits, sales engineers often get personal use of a company car and frequent-flyer mileage. Some companies offer incentives such as free vacation trips or gifts for outstanding performance. Sales engineers who work in independent firms may have higher but less stable earnings and, often, relatively few benefits.

Related Occupations

Sales engineers must have sales ability and knowledge of the products and services they sell, as well as technical and analytical skills. Other occupations that require similar skills include advertising, marketing, promotions, public relations, and sales managers; engineers; insurance sales agents; purchasing managers, buyers, and purchasing agents; real estate brokers and sales agents; sales representatives, wholesale and manufacturing; and securities, commodities, and financial services sales agents.

Sources of Additional Information

Information on careers for manufacturers' representatives and agents is available from:
➤ Manufacturers' Agents National Association, P.O. Box 3467, Laguna Hills, CA 92654-3467. Internet: **http://www.manaonline.org**
➤ Manufacturers' Representatives Educational Research Foundation, P.O. Box 247, Geneva, IL 60134. Internet: **http://www.mrerf.org**

Sales Representatives, Wholesale and Manufacturing

(O*NET 41-4011.01, 41-4011.02, 41-4011.03, 41-4011.04, 41-4011.05, 41-4011.06, 41-4012.00)

Significant Points

- Employment opportunities will be best for those with a college degree, the appropriate knowledge or technical expertise, and the personal traits necessary for successful selling.

- Job prospects for wholesale sales representatives will be better than those for manufacturing sales representatives, particularly in small firms.

- Earnings of sales representatives usually are based on a combination of salary and commissions.

Nature of the Work

Sales representatives are an important part of manufacturers' and wholesalers' success. Regardless of the type of product they sell, their primary duties are to interest wholesale and retail buyers and purchasing agents in their merchandise and to address clients' questions and concerns. Sales representatives represent one or several manufacturers or wholesale distributors by selling one product or a complementary line of products. Sales representatives demonstrate their products and advise clients on how using these products can reduce costs and increase sales. They market their company's products to manufacturers, wholesale and retail establishments, construction contractors, government agencies, and other institutions. (Retail salespersons, who sell directly to consumers, and sales engineers, who specialize in sales of technical products and services, are discussed elsewhere in the *Handbook*.)

Depending on where they work, sales representatives have different job titles. Those employed directly by a manufacturer or wholesaler often are called *sales representatives. Manufacturers' agents* or *manufacturers' representatives* are self-employed sales workers or independent firms who contract their services to all types of manufacturing companies. Many of these titles, however, are used interchangeably.

Sales representatives spend much of their time traveling to and visiting with prospective buyers and current clients. During a sales call, they discuss the client's needs and suggest how their merchandise or services can meet those needs. They may show samples or catalogs that describe items their company stocks and inform customers about prices, availability, and ways in which their products can save money and boost productivity. Because a vast number of manufacturers and wholesalers sell similar products, sales representatives must emphasize any unique qualities of their products and services. Manufacturers' agents or manufacturers' representatives might sell several complementary products made by different manufacturers and, thus, take a broad approach to their customers' business. Sales representatives may help install new equipment and train employees in its use. They also take orders and resolve any problems with or complaints about the merchandise.

Obtaining new accounts is an important part of the job. Sales representatives follow leads from other clients, track advertisements in trade journals, participate in trade shows and conferences, and may visit potential clients unannounced. In addition, they may spend time meeting with and entertaining prospective clients during evenings and weekends.

Sales representatives demonstrate their products and advise clients on how using these products can reduce costs and increase sales.

In a process that can take several months, sales representatives present their product to a customer and negotiate the sale. Aided by a laptop computer connected to the Internet, or other telecommunications device, they can make a persuasive audiovisual sales pitch and often can answer technical and nontechnical questions immediately.

Frequently, sales representatives who lack technical expertise work as a team with a technical expert. In this arrangement, the technical expert—sometimes a sales engineer—attends the sales presentation to explain the product and answer questions or concerns. The sales representative makes the preliminary contact with customers, introduces the company's product, and closes the sale. The representative is then able to spend more time maintaining and soliciting accounts and less time acquiring technical knowledge. After the sale, representatives may make followup visits to ensure that the equipment is functioning properly and may even help train customers' employees to operate and maintain new equipment. Those selling consumer goods often suggest how and where merchandise should be displayed. Working with retailers, they may help arrange promotional programs, store displays, and advertising.

Sales representatives have several duties beyond selling products. They analyze sales statistics; prepare reports; and handle administrative duties, such as filing expense account reports, scheduling appointments, and making travel plans. They read about new and existing products and monitor the sales, prices, and products of their competitors.

Manufacturers' agents who operate a sales agency also must manage their business. This requires organizational and general business skills, as well as knowledge of accounting, marketing, and administration.

Working Conditions

Some sales representatives have large territories and travel considerably. Because a sales region may cover several States, representatives may be away from home for several days or weeks at a time. Others work near their home base and travel mostly by car. Because of the nature of the work and the amount of travel, sales representatives may work more than 40 hours per week.

Although the hours are long and often irregular, most sales representatives have the freedom to determine their own schedule. Sales representatives often are on their feet for long periods and may carry heavy sample products, necessitating some physical stamina.

Dealing with different types of people can be stimulating but demanding. Sales representatives often face competition from representatives of other companies. Companies usually set goals or quotas that representatives are expected to meet. Because their earnings depend on commissions, manufacturers' agents are also under the added pressure to maintain and expand their clientele.

Training, Other Qualifications, and Advancement

The background needed for sales jobs varies by product line and market. Many employers hire individuals with previous sales experience who lack a college degree, but they increasingly prefer or require a bachelor's degree because job requirements have become more technical and analytical. Nevertheless, for some consumer products, factors such as sales ability, personality, and familiarity with brands are more important than educational background. On the other hand, firms selling complex, technical products may require a technical degree in addition to some sales experience. Many sales representatives attend seminars in sales techniques or take courses in marketing, economics, communication, or even a foreign language to provide the extra edge needed to make sales. In general, companies are looking for the best and brightest individuals who have the personality and desire to sell. Sales representatives need to be familiar with computer technology as computers are increasingly used in the workplace to place and track orders and to monitor inventory levels.

Many companies have formal training programs for beginning sales representatives lasting up to 2 years. However, most businesses are accelerating these programs to reduce costs and expedite the returns from training. In some programs, trainees rotate among jobs in plants and offices to learn all phases of production, installation, and distribution of the product. In others, trainees take formal classroom instruction at the plant, followed by on-the-job training under the supervision of a field sales manager.

New workers may get training by accompanying experienced workers on their sales calls. As they gain familiarity with the firm's products and clients, the new workers are given increasing responsibility until they are eventually assigned their own territory. As businesses experience greater competition, increased pressure is placed upon sales representatives to produce sales.

Sales representatives stay abreast of new products and the changing needs of their customers in a variety of ways. They attend trade shows at which new products and technologies are showcased. They also attend conferences and conventions to meet other sales representatives and clients and discuss new product developments. In addition, the entire sales force may participate in company-sponsored meetings to review sales performance, product development, sales goals, and profitability.

There are many certifications designed to raise standards and develop the skills of sales representatives, wholesale and manufacturing. A few examples are the Certified Professional Manufacturers' Representative, the Certified Sales Professional, and the Certified National Pharmaceutical Representative. Certification may involve completion of formal training and passing an examination.

Those who want to become sales representatives should be goal oriented, persuasive, and able to work well both independently and as part of a team. A pleasant personality and appearance, the ability to communicate well with people, and problem-solving skills are highly valued. Patience and perseverance also are key to completing a sale, which can take several months.

Frequently, promotion takes the form of an assignment to a larger account or territory where commissions are likely to be greater. Experienced sales representatives may move into jobs as sales trainers, who instruct new employees on selling techniques and on company policies and procedures. Those who have good sales records and leadership ability may advance to higher level positions such as sales supervisor, district manager, or vice president of sales. In addition to advancement opportunities within a firm, some manufacturers' agents go into business for themselves. Others find opportunities in purchasing, advertising, or marketing research.

Employment

Manufacturers' and wholesale sales representatives held about 1.9 million jobs in 2004. About half of all salaried representatives worked in wholesale trade. Others were employed in manufacturing, retail trade, information, and construction. Because of the diversity of products and services sold, employment opportunities are available in every part of the country in a wide range of industries.

In addition to those working directly for a firm, many sales representatives are self-employed manufacturers' agents. They often form small sales firms and work for a straight commission based on the value of their own sales. Usually, however, manufacturers' agents gain experience and recognition with a manufacturer or wholesaler before becoming self-employed.

Job Outlook

Employment of sales representatives, wholesale and manufacturing, is expected to grow about as fast as the average for all occupations through the year 2014, primarily because of continued growth in the variety and number of goods to be sold. Also, many job openings will result from the need to replace workers who transfer to other occupations or leave the labor force.

Prospective customers require sales workers to demonstrate or illustrate the particulars of a good or service. Computer technology makes sales representatives more effective and productive, for example, by allowing them to provide accurate and current information to customers during sales presentations.

Job prospects for sales representatives, wholesale and manufacturing, will be best for persons with the appropriate knowledge or technical expertise as well as the personal traits necessary for successful selling. Opportunities will be better for wholesale sales representatives than for manufacturing sales representatives because manufacturers are expected to continue contracting out sales duties to independent agents rather than using in-house or direct selling personnel. Agents are paid only if they sell, a practice that reduces the overhead cost to their clients. Also, by using an agent who usually contracts his or her services to more than one company, companies can share costs with the other companies involved with that agent. As their customers and manufacturers continue to merge with other companies, independent agents and other wholesale trade firms will, in response, also merge with each other to better serve their clients. Although the demand for independent sales agents will increase over the 2004-14 projection period, the supply is expected to remain stable, or possibly decline, because of the difficulties associated with self-employment. This factor could lead to many opportunities for sales representatives to start their own independent sales agencies.

Those interested in this occupation should keep in mind that direct selling opportunities in manufacturing are likely to be best for products for which there is strong demand. Furthermore, jobs will be most plentiful in small wholesale and manufacturing firms because a growing number of these companies will rely on agents to market their products as a way to control their costs and expand their customer base.

Employment opportunities and earnings may fluctuate from year to year because sales are affected by changing economic conditions, legislative issues, and consumer preferences.

Earnings

Compensation methods vary significantly by the type of firm and the product sold. Most employers use a combination of salary and commissions or salary plus bonus. Commissions usually are based on the amount of sales, whereas bonuses may depend on individual performance, on the performance of all sales workers in the group or district, or on the company's performance.

Median annual earnings of sales representatives, wholesale and manufacturing, technical and scientific products, were $58,580, including commissions, in May 2004. The middle 50 percent earned between $41,660 and $84,480 a year. The lowest 10 percent earned less than $30,270, and the highest 10 percent earned more than $114,540 a year. Median annual earnings in the industries employing the largest numbers of sales representatives, technical and scientific products, in May 2004 were as follows:

Computer systems design and related services	$70,220
Wholesale electronic markets and agents and brokers	65,990
Drugs and druggists' sundries merchant wholesalers	60,130
Professional and commercial equipment and	
supplies merchant wholesalers	59,080
Electrical and electronic goods merchant wholesalers	52,870

Median annual earnings of sales representatives, wholesale and manufacturing, except technical and scientific products, were

$45,400, including commission, in May 2004. The middle 50 percent earned between $32,640 and $65,260 a year. The lowest 10 percent earned less than $24,070, and the highest 10 percent earned more than $92,740 a year. Median annual earnings in the industries employing the largest numbers of sales representatives, except technical and scientific products, in May 2004 were as follows:

Wholesale electronic markets and agents and brokers	$50,680
Machinery, equipment, and supplies merchant wholesalers	46,030
Professional and commercial equipment and	
supplies merchant wholesalers	45,320
Grocery and related product wholesalers	44,210
Miscellaneous nondurable goods merchant wholesalers	40,240

In addition to their earnings, sales representatives usually are reimbursed for expenses such as transportation costs, meals, hotels, and entertaining customers. They often receive benefits such as health and life insurance, pension plan, vacation and sick leave, personal use of a company car, and frequent flyer mileage. Some companies offer incentives such as free vacation trips or gifts for outstanding sales workers.

Unlike those working directly for a manufacturer or wholesaler, manufacturers' agents are paid strictly on commission and usually are not reimbursed for expenses. Depending on the type of product or products they are selling, their experience in the field, and the number of clients they have, they can earn significantly more or less than those working in direct sales.

Related Occupations

Sales representatives, wholesale and manufacturing, must have sales ability and knowledge of the products they sell. Other occupations that require similar skills include advertising, marketing, promotions, public relations, and sales managers; insurance sales agents; purchasing managers, buyers, and purchasing agents; real estate brokers and sales agents; retail salespersons; sales engineers; and securities, commodities, and financial services sales agents.

Sources of Additional Information

Information on careers for manufacturers' representatives and agents is available from:

➤ Manufacturers' Agents National Association, One Spectrum Pointe, Suite 150, Lake Forest, CA 92630. Internet: **http://www.manaonline.org**

➤ Manufacturers' Representatives Educational Research Foundation, P.O. Box 247, Geneva, IL 60134. Internet: **http://www.mrerf.org**

Sales Worker Supervisors

(O*NET 41-1011.00, 41-1012.00)

Significant Points

- Overall employment is projected to grow more slowly than average; the number of self-employed sales worker supervisors is expected to decline.

- Applicants with retail experience should have the best job opportunities.

- In many retail establishments, managers are promoted from within the company; a postsecondary degree may speed a sales worker supervisor's advancement into management.

- Long, irregular hours, including evenings and weekends, are common.

Nature of the Work

Sales worker supervisors oversee the work of sales and related workers, such as retail salespersons; cashiers; customer service representatives; stock clerks and order fillers; sales engineers; and sales representatives, wholesale and manufacturing. Sales worker supervisors are responsible for interviewing, hiring, and training employees, as well as for preparing work schedules and assigning workers to specific duties. Many of these workers hold job titles such as *sales manager* or *department manager*. Under the occupational classification system used in the *Handbook*, however, workers with the title *manager* who mainly supervise nonsupervisory workers are called *supervisors* rather than *managers*, even though many of these workers often perform numerous managerial functions. (Related occupations discussed elsewhere in the *Handbook* are retail salespersons; cashiers; customer service representatives; stock clerks and order fillers; sales engineers; and sales representatives, wholesale and manufacturing.)

In retail establishments, sales worker supervisors ensure that customers receive satisfactory service and quality goods. They also answer customers' inquiries, deal with complaints, and sometimes handle purchasing, budgeting, and accounting. Their responsibilities vary with the size and type of establishment. As the size of retail stores and the types of goods and services increase, supervisors tend to specialize in one department or one aspect of merchandising. (Managers in eating and drinking places are discussed in the *Handbook* statement on food service managers.)

Sales worker supervisors in large retail establishments, often referred to as department managers, provide day-to-day oversight of individual departments, such as shoes, cosmetics, or housewares in large department stores; produce and meat in grocery stores; and sales in automotive dealerships. These workers establish and implement policies, goals, objectives, and procedures for their specific departments; coordinate activities with other department heads; and strive for smooth operations within their departments. They supervise employees who price and ticket goods and place them on display; clean and organize shelves, displays, and inventories in stockrooms; and inspect merchandise to ensure that nothing is

Sales worker supervisors ensure that customers receive satisfactory service and quality goods.

outdated. Sales worker supervisors also review inventory and sales records, develop merchandising techniques, and coordinate sales promotions. In addition, they may greet and assist customers and promote sales and good public relations.

Sales worker supervisors in nonretail establishments supervise and coordinate the activities of sales workers who sell industrial products, automobiles, or services such as advertising or Internet services. They may prepare budgets, make personnel decisions, devise sales-incentive programs, assign sales territories, and approve sales contracts.

In small or independent companies and retail stores, sales worker supervisors not only directly supervise sales associates, but also are responsible for the operation of the entire company or store. Some are self-employed business or store owners.

Working Conditions

Most sales worker supervisors have offices. In retail trade, their offices are within the stores, usually close to the areas they oversee. Although they spend some time in the office completing merchandise orders or arranging work schedules, a large portion of their workday is spent on the sales floor, supervising employees or selling.

Work hours of supervisors vary greatly among establishments because work schedules usually depend on customers' needs. Supervisors generally work at least 40 hours a week. Long, irregular hours are common, particularly during sales, holidays, and busy shopping hours and at times when inventory is taken. Supervisors are expected to work evenings and weekends but usually are compensated with a day off during the week. Hours can change weekly, and managers sometimes must report to work on short notice, especially when employees are absent. Independent owners often can set their own schedules, but hours must be convenient to customers.

Training, Other Qualifications, and Advancement

Sales worker supervisors usually acquire knowledge of management principles and practices—an essential requirement for a supervisory or managerial position in retail trade—through work experience. Many supervisors begin their careers on the sales floor as salespersons, cashiers, or customer service representatives. In these positions, they learn merchandising, customer service, and the basic policies and procedures of the company.

The educational backgrounds of sales worker supervisors vary widely. Regardless of the education they receive, recommended courses include accounting, marketing, management, and sales, as well as psychology, sociology, and communication. Supervisors also must be computer literate because almost all cash registers, inventory control systems, and sales quotes and contracts are computerized.

Supervisors who have postsecondary education often hold associate or bachelor's degrees in liberal arts, social sciences, business, or management. To gain experience, many college students participate in internship programs that usually are developed jointly by individual schools and firms.

The type and amount of training available to supervisors vary from company to company. Many national retail chains and companies have formal training programs for management trainees that include both classroom and on-site training. Training time may be as brief as 1 week but may also last more than 1 year in organizations that require trainees to gain experience during all sales seasons.

Ordinarily, classroom training includes topics such as interviewing and customer service skills, employee and inventory management, and scheduling. Management trainees may work in one specific department while training on the job, or they may rotate through several departments to gain a well-rounded knowledge of the company's operation. Training programs for retail franchises are generally extensive, covering all functions of the company's operation, including budgeting, marketing, management, finance, purchasing, product preparation, human resource management, and compensation. College graduates usually can enter management training programs directly.

Sales worker supervisors must get along with all types of people. They need initiative, self-discipline, good judgment, and decisiveness. Patience and a conciliatory temperament are necessary when dealing with demanding customers. Sales worker supervisors also must be able to motivate, organize, and direct the work of subordinates and communicate clearly and persuasively with customers and other supervisors.

Individuals who display leadership and team-building skills, self-confidence, motivation, and decisiveness become candidates for promotion to assistant manager or manager. A postsecondary degree may speed a sales worker supervisor's advancement into management because employers view it as a sign of motivation and maturity—qualities deemed important for promotion to more responsible positions. In many retail establishments, managers are promoted from within the company. In small retail establishments, where the number of positions is limited, advancement to a higher management position may come slowly. Large establishments often have extensive career ladder programs and may offer supervisors the opportunity to transfer to another store in the chain or to the central office if an opening occurs. Although promotions may occur more quickly in large establishments, some managers may need to relocate every several years in order to advance. Supervisors also can become advertising, marketing, promotions, public relations, and sales managers (workers who coordinate marketing plans, monitor sales, and propose advertisements and promotions) or purchasing managers, buyers, or purchasing agents (workers who purchase goods and supplies for their organization or for resale). (These occupations are covered elsewhere in the *Handbook*.)

Some supervisors who have worked in their industry for a long time open their own stores or sales firms. However, retail trade and sales occupations are highly competitive, and although many independent owners succeed, some fail to cover expenses and eventually go out of business. To prosper, owners usually need good business sense and strong customer service and public relations skills.

Employment

Sales worker supervisors held about 2.2 million jobs in 2004. Approximately 36 percent were self-employed, most of whom were store owners. About 43 percent were wage and salary sales worker supervisors employed in the retail sector; some of the largest employers were grocery stores, department stores, motor vehicle and parts dealers, and clothing and clothing accessory stores. The remaining sales worker supervisors worked in nonretail establishments.

Job Outlook

Candidates who have retail experience—as a retail salesperson, cashier, or customer service representative, for example—will have the best opportunities for jobs as sales worker supervisors. As in other fields, competition is expected for supervisory jobs, particularly those with the most attractive earnings and working conditions.

Employment of sales worker supervisors is expected to grow more slowly than the average for all occupations through the year 2014. Growth in the occupation will be restrained somewhat as retail companies hire more sales staff and increase the responsibilities of sales worker supervisors. Many job openings will occur as experienced supervisors move into higher levels of management, transfer to other occupations, or leave the labor force. However, as with other supervisory and managerial occupations, job turnover is relatively low.

The Internet and electronic commerce are creating new opportunities to reach and communicate with potential customers. Some firms are hiring Internet sales managers, who are in charge of maintaining an Internet site and answering inquiries relating to the product, to prices, and to the terms of delivery—a trend that will increase demand for these supervisors. Overall, Internet sales and electronic commerce may reduce the number of additional sales workers needed, thus reducing the number of additional supervisors required. However, the impact of electronic commerce on employment of sales worker supervisors should be minimal.

Projected employment growth of sales worker supervisors will mirror, in part, the patterns of employment growth in the industries in which they work. For example, faster-than-average employment growth is expected in many of the rapidly growing service-providing industries. In contrast, the number of self-employed sales worker supervisors is expected to decline as independent retailers face increasing competition from national chains.

Unlike mid-level and top-level managers, retail store managers generally will not be affected by the restructuring and consolidation taking place at the corporate headquarters of many retail chains.

Earnings

Salaries of sales worker supervisors vary substantially, depending on the level of responsibility the individual has; the person's length of service; and the type, size, and location of the firm.

In May 2004, median annual earnings of salaried supervisors of retail sales workers, including commissions, were $32,720. The middle 50 percent earned between $25,120 and $43,110 a year. The lowest 10 percent earned less than $20,110, and the highest 10 percent earned more than $58,400 a year. Median annual earnings in the industries employing the largest numbers of salaried supervisors of retail sales workers in May 2004 were as follows:

Building material and supplies dealers	$34,210
Grocery stores	31,360
Clothing stores	30,660
Other general merchandise stores	30,150
Gasoline stations	27,510

In May 2004, median annual earnings of salaried supervisors of nonretail sales workers, including commissions, were $59,300. The middle 50 percent earned between $43,350 and $87,580 a year. The lowest 10 percent earned less than $30,830, and the highest 10 percent earned more than $127,870 a year. Median annual earnings in the industries employing the largest numbers of salaried supervisors of nonretail sales workers in May 2004 were as follows:

Wholesale electronic markets and agents and brokers	$79,480
Professional and commercial equipment and supplies merchant wholesalers	72,320
Machinery, equipment, and supplies merchant wholesalers	61,150
Grocery and related product wholesalers	59,130
Postal Service	52,490

Compensation systems vary by type of establishment and by merchandise sold. Many supervisors receive a commission or a combination of salary and commission. Under a commission system, supervisors receive a percentage of department or store sales. Thus, supervisors have the opportunity to increase their earnings considerably, but their earnings depend on their ability to sell their product and the condition of the economy. Those who sell large amounts of merchandise or exceed sales goals often receive bonuses or other awards.

Related Occupations

Sales worker supervisors serve customers, supervise workers, and direct and coordinate the operations of an establishment. Others with similar responsibilities include financial managers, food service managers, lodging managers, and medical and health services managers.

Sources of Additional Information

Information on employment opportunities for sales worker supervisors may be obtained from the employment offices of various retail establishments or from State employment service offices.

General information on management careers in retail establishments is available from:

➤ National Retail Federation, 325 7th St. NW., Suite 1100, Washington, DC 20004.

Information on management careers in grocery stores and on schools offering related programs is available from:

➤ International Food Service Distributors Association, 201 Park Washington Ct., Falls Church, VA 22046-4521. Internet: **http://www.ifdaonline.org**

Information about management careers and training programs in the motor vehicle dealers industry is available from:

➤ National Automobile Dealers Association, Public Relations Dept., 8400 Westpark Dr., McLean, VA 22102-3591. Internet: **http://www.nada.org**

Information about management careers in convenience stores is available from:

➤ National Association of Convenience Stores, 1600 Duke St., Alexandria, VA 22314-3436.

Securities, Commodities, and Financial Services Sales Agents

(O*NET 41-3031.01, 41-3031.02)

Significant Points

- A college degree, sales ability, good interpersonal and communication skills, and a strong desire to succeed are important qualifications.

- Securities and commodities sales agents must pass licensing exams.

- Competition for entry-level jobs usually is keen, especially in larger firms; opportunities should be better in smaller firms.

- Turnover is high for beginning agents, who often are unable to establish a sizable clientele; once established, securities and commodities sales agents have a very strong attachment to their occupation because of their high earnings and considerable investment in training.

Nature of the Work

Most investors, whether they are individuals with a few hundred dollars to invest or large institutions with millions, use *securities, commodities, and financial services sales agents* when buying or selling stocks, bonds, shares in mutual funds, insurance annuities, or other financial products. In addition, many clients seek out these agents for advice on investments, insurance, tax planning, estate planning, and other financial matters.

Securities and commodities sales agents, also called brokers, stockbrokers, registered representatives, account executives, or financial consultants, perform a variety of tasks, depending on their specific job duties. When an investor wishes to buy or sell a security, for example, sales agents may relay the order through their firm's computers to the floor of a securities exchange, such as the New York Stock Exchange. There, securities and commodities sales agents known as *floor brokers* negotiate the price with other floor brokers, make the sale, and forward the purchase price to the sales agents. If a security is not traded on an exchange, as in the case of bonds and over-the-counter stocks, the broker sends the order to the firm's trading department. Here, using their own funds or those of the firm, other securities sales agents, known as *dealers*, buy and sell securities directly from other dealers, with the intention of reselling the security to customers at a profit. After the transaction has been completed, the broker notifies the customer of the final price.

Securities and commodities sales agents also provide many related services for their customers. They may explain stock market terms and trading practices, offer financial counseling or advice on the purchase or sale of particular securities, and design an individual client's financial portfolio, which could include securities, life insurance, corporate and municipal bonds, mutual funds, certificates of deposit, annuities, and other investments.

Not all customers have the same investment goals. Some individuals prefer long-term investments, for capital growth or to provide income over a number of years; others might want to invest in speculative securities, which they hope will quickly rise in price. On the basis of each customer's objectives, securities and commodities sales agents furnish information about the advantages and disadvantages of an investment. They also supply the latest price quotes on any securities, as well as information on the activities and financial positions of the corporations issuing the securities.

Most securities and commodities sales agents serve individual investors; others specialize in institutional investors, such as banks and pension funds. In institutional investing, sales agents usually concentrate on a specific financial product, such as stocks, bonds, options, annuities, or commodity futures. At other times, they may also handle the sale of new issues, such as corporate securities issued to finance the expansion of a plant.

The most important part of a sales representative's job is finding clients and building a customer base. Thus, beginning securities and commodities sales agents spend much of their time searching for customers—relying heavily on telephone solicitation. They also may meet clients through business and social contacts. Agents often join civic organizations and other social organizations to expand their networks. Many sales agents find it useful to contact potential clients by teaching adult education investment courses or by giving lectures at libraries or social clubs. Brokerage firms may give sales agents lists of people with whom the firm has done business in the past. Some agents inherit the clients of agents who have retired. After an agent is established, referrals from satisfied clients are an important source of new business.

Financial services sales agents sell a wide variety of banking and related services. They contact potential customers to explain their services and to ascertain customers' banking and other financial needs. In doing so, they discuss services such as loans, deposit accounts, lines of credit, sales or inventory financing, certificates of deposit, cash management, mutual funds, or investment services. They also may solicit businesses to participate in consumer credit card programs. Financial services sales agents who serve all the financial needs of a single affluent individual or a business often are called private bankers or relationship managers.

With deregulation of the financial services industry, the distinctions among sales agents are becoming less clear as securities firms, banks, and insurance companies venture further into each other's products and services. The agents' jobs also are becoming more important as competition between the firms intensifies.

People increasingly seek the advice and services of securities, commodities, and financial services sales agents to realize their financial goals.

Working Conditions

Most securities and commodities sales agents work in offices under fairly stressful conditions. They have access to "quote boards" or computer terminals that continually provide information on the prices of securities. When sales activity increases, due perhaps to unanticipated changes in the economy, the pace can become very hectic.

Established securities and commodities sales agents usually work a standard 40-hour week. Beginners who are seeking customers usually work longer hours. New brokers spend a great deal of time learning the firm's products and services and studying for exams in order to qualify to sell other products, such as insurance and commodities. Most securities and commodities sales agents accommodate customers by meeting with them in the evenings or on weekends.

A growing number of securities sales agents, employed mostly by discount or online brokerage firms, work in call-center environments. In these centers, hundreds of agents spend much of the day on the telephone taking orders from clients or offering advice and information on different securities. Often, such call centers operate 24 hours a day, requiring agents to work in shifts.

Financial services sales agents normally work 40 hours a week in a comfortable, less stressful office environment. They may spend considerable time outside the office, meeting with current and prospective clients, attending civic functions, and participating in trade association meetings. Some financial services sales agents work exclusively inside banks, providing service to walk-in customers.

Training, Other Qualifications, and Advancement

Because securities and commodities sales agents must be knowledgeable about economic conditions and trends, a college education is important, especially in larger securities firms. In fact, the overwhelming majority of workers in this occupation are college graduates. Although employers seldom require specialized academic training, courses in business administration, economics, and finance are helpful.

Many employers consider personal qualities and skills more important than academic training. Employers seek applicants who have considerable sales ability, good interpersonal and communication skills, and a strong desire to succeed. Some employers also make sure that applicants have a good credit history and a clean record. Self-confidence and an ability to handle frequent rejections are important ingredients for success.

Because maturity and the ability to work independently are important, many employers prefer to hire those who have achieved success in other jobs. Most firms prefer candidates with sales experience, particularly those who have worked on commission in areas such as real estate or insurance. Therefore, most entrants to this occupation transfer from other jobs. Some begin working as securities and commodities sales agents following retirement from other fields.

Securities and commodities sales agents must meet State licensing requirements, which usually include passing an examination and, in some cases, furnishing a personal bond. In addition, sales agents must register as representatives of their firm with the National Association of Securities Dealers, Inc. (NASD). Before beginners can qualify as registered representatives, they must pass the General Securities Registered Representative Examination (Series 7 exam), administered by the NASD, and be an employee of a registered firm for at least 4 months.

Most States require a second examination—the Uniform Securities Agents State Law Examination. This test measures the prospective representative's knowledge of the securities business in general, customer protection requirements, and recordkeeping procedures. Many take correspondence courses in preparation for the securities examinations. Within 2 years, brokers are encouraged to take additional licensing exams in order to sell mutual funds, insurance, and commodities.

Most employers provide on-the-job training to help securities and commodities sales agents meet the registration requirements for certification. In most firms, the training period takes about 4 months. Trainees in large firms may receive classroom instruction in securities analysis, effective speaking, and the finer points of selling; may take courses offered by business schools and associations; and may undergo a period of on-the-job training lasting up to 2 years. Many firms like to rotate their trainees among various departments, to give them a broad perspective of the securities business. In small firms, sales agents often receive training in outside institutions and on the job.

Securities and commodities sales agents must understand the basic characteristics of the wide variety of financial products offered by brokerage firms. Brokers periodically take training through their firms or outside institutions in order to keep abreast of new financial products and to improve their sales techniques. Computer training also is important, because the securities sales business is highly automated. It is mandatory for all registered securities and commodities sales agents to attend periodic continuing education classes to maintain their licenses. Courses consist of computer-based training in regulatory matters and company training on new products and services. In addition, more sales agents are taking courses to become certified financial planners. The Certified Financial Planner credential issued by the Certified Financial Planner Board of

Standards, requires relevant experience, completion of education requirements, passing a comprehensive examination, and adherence to an enforceable code of ethics. The CFP exams test the candidate's knowledge of the financial planning process, insurance and risk management, employee benefits planning, taxes and retirement planning, and investment and estate planning.

The principal form of advancement for securities and commodities sales agents is an increase in the number and size of the accounts they handle. Although beginners usually service the accounts of individual investors, they may eventually handle very large institutional accounts, such as those of banks and pension funds. After taking a series of tests, some brokers become portfolio managers and have greater authority to make investment decisions regarding an account. Some experienced sales agents become branch office managers and supervise other sales agents while continuing to provide services for their own customers. A few agents advance to top management positions or become partners in their firms.

Banks and other credit institutions prefer to hire college graduates for financial services sales jobs. A business administration degree with a specialization in finance or a liberal arts degree that includes courses in accounting, economics, and marketing serves as excellent preparation for this job. Often, financial services sales agents learn their jobs through on-the-job training under the supervision of bank officers. However, those who wish to sell mutual funds and insurance products may need to undergo formal training and pass some of the same exams required of securities sales agents.

Employment

Securities, commodities, and financial services sales agents held about 281,000 jobs in 2004. More than half of jobs were found in securities, commodity contracts, and other financial investments and related activities. One in 5 worked in depository and nondepository credit intermediation, including commercial banks, savings institutions, and credit unions. Although securities and commodities sales agents are employed by firms in all parts of the country, many work for a small number of large securities and investment banking firms headquartered in New York City. About 1 out of 8 securities, commodities, and financial services sales agents were self-employed.

Job Outlook

Employment of securities, commodities, and financial services sales agents is expected to grow about as fast as the average for all occupations through 2014. As people's incomes continue to climb, they will increasingly seek the advice and services of securities, commodities, and financial services sales agents to realize their financial goals. Growth in the volume of stocks traded over the Internet will limit job growth. Nevertheless, the overall increase in investment is expected to spur employment growth among these workers, with a majority of transactions still requiring the advice and services of securities, commodities, and financial services sales agents.

Baby boomers in their peak savings years will fuel much of this increase in investment. Saving for retirement has been made much easier by the government, which continues to offer a number of tax-favorable pension plans, such as the 401(k) and the Roth IRA. The participation of more women in the workforce also means higher household incomes and more women qualifying for pensions. Many of these pensions are self-directed, meaning that the recipient has the responsibility for investing the money. With such large amounts of money to invest, sales agents, in their role as financial advisors, will be in great demand.

Other factors that will affect the demand for brokers are the increasing number and complexity of investment products, as well as the effects of globalization. As the public and businesses become more sophisticated about investing, they are venturing into the op-

tions and futures markets. Brokers are needed to buy or sell these products, which are not traded online. Also, markets for investment are expanding with the increase in global trading of stocks and bonds. Furthermore, the New York Stock Exchange has extended its trading hours to accommodate trading in foreign stocks and compete with foreign exchanges.

Employment of sales agents is adversely affected by downturns in the stock market or the economy. Turnover is high for beginning agents, who often are unable to establish a sizable clientele even in good times. Once established, securities and commodities sales agents have a very strong attachment to their occupation because of their high earnings and considerable investment in training. Competition usually is keen, especially in larger companies with more applicants than jobs. Opportunities for beginning sales agents should be better in smaller firms.

Employment of financial services sales agents in banks will increase as banks expand their product offerings in order to compete directly with other investment firms.

Earnings

Median annual earnings of securities, commodities, and financial services sales agents were $69,200 in May 2004. The middle half earned between $40,750 and $131,290.

Median annual earnings in the industries employing the largest numbers of securities, commodities, and financial services sales agents in 2004 were:

Other financial investment activities	$94,670
Securities and commodity contracts intermediation and brokerage	85,350
Management of companies and enterprises	67,690
Nondepository credit intermediation	51,820
Depository credit intermediation	44,670

Stockbrokers, who provide personalized service and more guidance with respect to a client's investments, usually are paid a commission based on the amount of stocks, bonds, mutual funds, insurance, and other products they sell. Earnings from commissions are likely to be high when there is much buying and selling, and low when there is a slump in market activity. Most firms provide sales agents with a steady income by paying a "draw against commission"—a minimum salary based on commissions they can be expected to earn. Securities and commodities sales agents who can provide their clients with the most thorough financial services should enjoy the greatest income stability. Trainee brokers usually are paid a salary until they develop a client base. The salary gradually decreases in favor of commissions as the broker gains clients. A small, but increasing, number of full-service brokers are paid a percentage of the assets they oversee. This fee often covers a certain number of trades done for free.

Brokers who work for discount brokerage firms that promote the use of telephone and online trading services usually are paid a salary, sometimes boosted by bonuses that reflect the profitability of the office. Financial services sales agents usually are paid a salary also; however, bonuses or commissions from sales are starting to account for a larger share of their income.

Related Occupations

Other jobs requiring knowledge of finance and an ability to sell include insurance sales agents, real estate brokers and sales agents, and financial analysts and personal financial advisors.

Sources of Additional Information

For general information on the securities industry, contact:
➤ Securities Industry Association, 120 Broadway, New York, NY 10271.

For information about job opportunities for financial services sales agents in various States, contact State bankers' associations or write directly to a particular bank.

Travel Agents

(O*NET 41-3041.00)

Significant Points

- Travel benefits, such as reduced rates for transportation and lodging, attract many people to this occupation.

- Training at a postsecondary vocational school, college, or university is increasingly important.

- Travel agents increasingly specialize in specific destinations or type of travel or traveler.

- Keen competition for jobs is expected.

Nature of the Work

Constantly changing airfares and schedules, thousands of available vacation packages, and a vast amount of travel information on the Internet can make travel planning frustrating and time consuming. To sort out the many travel options, tourists and business people often turn to travel agents, who assess their needs and help them make the best possible travel arrangements. Also, many major cruise lines, resorts, and specialty travel groups use travel agents to promote travel packages to millions of people every year.

In general, travel agents give advice on destinations and make arrangements for transportation, hotel accommodations, car rentals, tours, and recreation. They also may advise on weather conditions, restaurants, and tourist attractions. For international travel, agents also provide information on customs regulations, required papers (passports, visas, and certificates of vaccination), and currency exchange rates.

Travel agents consult a variety of published and computer-based sources for information on departure and arrival times, fares, and hotel ratings and accommodations. They may visit hotels, resorts, and restaurants to evaluate comfort, cleanliness, and quality of food and service so that they can base recommendations on their own travel experiences or those of colleagues or clients.

Travel agents give advice on destinations and make arrangements for transportation, hotel accommodations, car rentals, tours, and recreation.

Travel agents also promote their services, using telemarketing, direct mail, and the Internet. They make presentations to social and special-interest groups, arrange advertising displays, and suggest company-sponsored trips to business managers. Travel agents no longer receive commission payments from domestic airlines, and agents face increasing competition from the Internet for low-cost fares. In an effort to find a niche in the market, many travel agents now specialize in travel to certain regions or for certain groups of people, such as honeymooners, grandparents, or ethnic groups.

Working Conditions

Travel agents spend most of their time behind a desk conferring with clients, completing paperwork, contacting airlines and hotels for travel arrangements, and promoting group tours. During vacation seasons and holiday periods, they may be under a great deal of pressure. Many agents, especially those who are self-employed, frequently work long hours. With advanced computer systems and telecommunication networks, it is increasingly common for travel agents to work at home.

Training, Other Qualifications, and Advancement

The minimum requirement for those interested in becoming a travel agent is a high school diploma or equivalent. Technology and computerization have increased the training needs, however, and many employers prefer applicants with more education, such as a postsecondary vocational award. Many vocational schools offer full-time travel agent programs that last several months, as well as evening and weekend programs. Travel agent courses also are offered in public adult education programs and in community and 4-year colleges. A few colleges offer bachelor's or master's degrees in travel and tourism. Although few college courses relate directly to travel or tourism, a college education sometimes is desired by employers to establish a background in fields such as computer science, geography, communication, foreign languages, and world history. Courses in accounting and business management also are important, especially for those who expect to manage or start their own travel agencies.

The American Society of Travel Agents offers a correspondence course that provides a basic understanding of the travel industry. Travel agencies also provide on-the-job training for their employees, a significant part of which consists of computer instruction. All employers require computer skills of workers whose jobs involve the operation of airline and centralized reservation systems.

Continuing education is critical, as the abundance of travel information readily available through the Internet and other sources has resulted in a more informed consumer who wants to deal with an expert when choosing a travel agent. Experienced travel agents can take advanced self-study or group-study courses from the Travel Institute, leading to the Certified Travel Counselor designation. The Travel Institute also offers marketing and sales skills development programs and destination specialist programs, which provide detailed knowledge of regions such as North America, Western Europe, the Caribbean, and the Pacific Rim. With the trend toward more specialization, these and other destination specialist courses are increasingly important.

Personal travel experience or experience as an airline reservation agent is an asset because knowledge about a city or foreign country often helps influence a client's travel plans. Patience and the ability to gain the confidence of clients also are useful qualities. Travel agents must be well-organized, accurate, and meticulous to compile information from various sources and plan and organize their clients' travel itineraries. Also, agents who specialize in business travel must work quickly and efficiently because business travel often must be arranged on short notice.

As the Internet has become an important tool for making travel arrangements, more travel agencies are using websites to provide their services to clients. This trend has increased the importance of computer skills in this occupation. Other desirable qualifications include good writing and interpersonal and sales skills.

Some employees start as reservation clerks or receptionists in travel agencies. With experience and some formal training, they can take on greater responsibilities and eventually assume travel agent duties. In agencies with many offices, travel agents may advance to office manager or to other managerial positions.

Those who start their own agencies generally have had experience in an established agency. Before they can receive commissions, these agents usually must gain formal approval from suppliers or corporations, such as airlines, ship lines, or rail lines. The Airlines Reporting Corporation and the International Airlines Travel Agency Network, for example, are the approving bodies for airlines. To gain approval, an agency must be financially sound and employ at least one experienced manager or travel agent.

There are no Federal licensing requirements for travel agents. In 2004, however, 13 States required some form of registration or certification of retail sellers of travel services. More information may be obtained by contacting the Office of the Attorney General or Department of Commerce in each State.

Employment

Travel agents held about 103,000 jobs in 2004 and are found in every part of the country. More than 3 out of 5 agents worked for travel agencies. Around 14 percent were self-employed.

Job Outlook

Employment of travel agents is expected to decline through 2014. Most openings will occur as experienced agents transfer to other occupations or leave the labor force. Because of the projected decline in employment and the fact that a number of people are attracted by the travel benefits associated with this occupation, keen competition for jobs is expected. Travel agents who specialize and can utilize the Internet to reduce their costs and better compete with other travel suppliers should have the best chance for success.

The Internet increasingly allows people to access travel information from their personal computers, enabling them to research and plan their own trips, make their own reservations and travel arrangements, and purchase their own tickets. As a result, demand will decline for travel agents who simply take orders, such as booking tickets for a specified date and time. Also, domestic airlines no longer pay commissions to travel agencies, which has reduced revenues and caused some agencies to go out of business. This change also has led many travel agents to begin charging fees for their services. To justify those fees, customers expect travel agents to provide good service and travel expertise. Opportunities may be better for agents who specialize in specific destinations, luxury travel, or particular types of travelers such as ethnic groups or groups with a special interest or hobby. Many consumers still prefer to use a professional travel agent to plan a complete trip; to deal with some of the more complex transactions; to ensure reliability; to suggest excursions or destinations that might otherwise be missed; to save time; or, in some cases, to save money.

Several factors should offset the adverse effect of Internet travel arrangement and the loss of revenues from airline bookings. For example, spending on tourism and travel is expected to increase over the next decade. With rising household incomes, smaller families,

and an increasing number of older people who are more likely to travel, more people are expected to travel on vacation—and to do so more frequently—than in the past. Business travel also should rebound from recession and terrorism-related declines as business activity expands. Business travel also should increase as U.S. businesses open more foreign operations and businesses increasingly sell their goods and services worldwide. In addition, luxury and specialty travel should increase among the growing number of Americans with the available time and money for these more expensive trips.

Another positive factor is the increasing affordability of air travel. Greater competition among airlines, especially from low-cost carriers, has brought airfares within the budgets of more people. In addition, American travel agents now organize more tours for the growing number of foreign visitors. Also, travel agents often are able to offer various travel packages at a substantial discount.

The demand for travel is sensitive to economic downturns and international political crises, when travel plans are likely to be deferred. Therefore, the number of job opportunities for travel agents fluctuates. However, the number of travelers has risen recently, possibly reflecting demand from consumers who delayed travel because of terrorism and safety concerns. Demand for travel remains volatile, though, and trends could change at any time.

Earnings

Experience, sales ability, and the size and location of the agency determine the salary of a travel agent. Median annual earnings of travel agents were $27,640 in May 2004. The middle 50 percent earned between $21,600 and $35,070. The lowest 10 percent earned less than $17,180, while the top 10 percent earned more than $44,090. Median earnings in May 2004 for travel agents employed in the travel arrangement and reservation services industry were $27,490.

Salaried agents usually enjoy standard employer-paid benefits that self-employed agents must provide for themselves. When traveling for personal reasons, agents usually get reduced rates for transportation and accommodations. In addition, agents sometimes take "familiarization" trips, at lower cost or no cost to themselves, to learn about various vacation sites. These benefits attract many people to this occupation.

Earnings of travel agents who own their agencies depend mainly on commissions from travel-related bookings and service fees they charge clients. Often it takes time to acquire a sufficient number of clients to have adequate earnings, so it is not unusual for new self-employed agents to have low earnings. Established agents may have lower earnings during economic downturns.

Related Occupations

Travel agents organize and schedule business, educational, or recreational travel or activities. Other workers with similar responsibilities include tour and travel guides, and reservation and transportation ticket agents and travel clerks.

Sources of Additional Information

For further information on training opportunities, contact:
➤ American Society of Travel Agents, Education Department, 1101 King St., Alexandria, VA 22314. Internet: **http://www.travelsense.org**

For information on training and certification qualifications, contact:
➤ The Travel Institute, 148 Linden St., Suite 305, Wellesley, MA 02482.

Office and Administrative Support Occupations

Financial Clerks

Bill and Account Collectors

(O*NET 43-3011.00)

Significant Points

- About 1 in 5 collectors works for a collection agency; others work in banks, retail stores, government, physicians' offices, hospitals, and other institutions that lend money and extend credit.

- Most jobs in this occupation require only a high school diploma, though many employers prefer workers with some postsecondary training.

- Faster-than-average employment growth is expected as companies focus more efforts on collecting unpaid debts.

Nature of the Work

Bill and account collectors, called simply *collectors*, keep track of accounts that are overdue and attempt to collect payment on them. Some are employed by third-party collection agencies, while others—known as "in-house collectors"—work directly for the original creditors, such as department stores, hospitals, or banks.

The duties of bill and account collectors are similar in the many different organizations in which they are employed. First, collectors are called upon to locate and notify customers of delinquent accounts, usually over the telephone, but sometimes by letter. When customers move without leaving a forwarding address, collectors may check with the post office, telephone companies, credit bureaus, or former neighbors to obtain the new address. The attempt to find the new address is called "skip tracing." New computer systems assist in tracing by automatically tracking when customers change their address or contact information on any of their open accounts.

Once collectors find the debtor, they inform him or her of the overdue account and solicit payment. If necessary, they review the terms of the sale, service, or credit contract with the customer. Collectors also may attempt to learn the cause of the delay in payment. Where feasible, they offer the customer advice on how to pay off the debts, such as by taking out a bill consolidation loan. However, the collector's prime objective is always to ensure that the customer pays the debt in question.

If a customer agrees to pay, collectors record this commitment and check later to verify that the payment was indeed made. Collectors may have authority to grant an extension of time if customers ask for one. If a customer fails to respond, collectors prepare a statement indicating the customer's action for the credit department of the establishment. In more extreme cases, collectors may initiate repossession proceedings, disconnect the customer's service, or hand the account over to an attorney for legal action. Most collectors handle other administrative functions for the accounts assigned to them, including recording changes of addresses and purging the records of the deceased.

Collectors use computers and a variety of automated systems to keep track of overdue accounts. Typically, collectors work at video

Bill and account collectors calculate overdue accounts and arrange repayments.

display terminals that are linked to computers. In sophisticated predictive dialer systems, a computer dials the telephone automatically, and the collector speaks only when a connection has been made. Such systems eliminate time spent calling busy or nonanswering numbers. Many collectors use regular telephones, but others wear headsets like those used by telephone operators.

Working Conditions

In-house bill and account collectors typically are employed in an office environment, while those who work for third-party collection agencies may work in a call-center environment. Workers spend most of their time on the phone tracking down and contacting people with debts. The work can be stressful as some customers can be confrontational when pressed about their debts, although some appreciate assistance in resolving their outstanding debt. Collectors may also feel pressured to meet targets for the amount of debt they are expected recover in a certain period.

Bill and account collectors often have to work evenings and weekends, when it usually is easier to reach people. As a result, it is not uncommon for workers to work part time or on flexible work schedules, though the majority work 40 hours per week.

Training, Other Qualifications, and Advancement

Most bill and account collectors are required to have at least a high school diploma. However, employers prefer workers

431

who have completed some college or who have experience in other occupations that involve contact with the public. Workers should have good communication skills and be computer literate; experience with advanced telecommunications equipment is also useful.

Once hired, workers usually receive on-the-job training. Under the guidance of a supervisor or some other senior worker, new employees learn company procedures. Some formal classroom training also may be necessary, such as training in specific computer software. Additional training topics usually include telephone techniques and negotiation skills. Workers are also instructed in the laws governing the collection of debt as mandated by the Fair Debt Collection Practices Act (FDCPA), which applies to all third party and some in-house collectors.

Workers usually advance by taking on more duties in the same occupation for higher pay or by transferring to a closely related occupation. Many companies fill supervisory positions by promoting individuals from within the organization, and workers who acquire additional skills, experience, and training improve their advancement opportunities.

Employment

Bill and account collectors held about 456,000 jobs in 2004. About 1 in 5 collectors works for a collection agency. Many others work in banks, retail stores, government, physician's offices, hospitals, and other institutions that lend money and extend credit.

Job Outlook

Employment of bill and account collectors is expected to grow faster than the average for all occupations through 2014. Cash flow is becoming increasingly important to companies, which are now placing greater emphasis on collecting unpaid debts sooner. Thus, the workload for collectors is expected to continue to increase as they seek to collect not only debts that are relatively old, but ones that are more recent. Also, as more companies in a wide range of industries get involved in lending money and issuing their own credit cards, they will need to hire collectors, because debt levels will likely continue to rise. In addition to job openings from employment growth, a significant number of openings will result from the high level of turnover in the occupation. As a result, job opportunities should be favorable.

Hospitals and physicians' offices are two of the fastest growing industries requiring collectors. With insurance reimbursements not keeping up with cost increases, the health care industry is seeking to recover more money from patients. Government agencies also are making more use of collectors to collect on everything from parking tickets to child-support payments and past-due taxes. Finally, the Internal Revenue Service (IRS) is looking into outsourcing the collection of overdue Federal taxes to third-party collection agencies. If the IRS does outsource, more collectors will be required for this large job.

Despite the increasing demand for bill collectors, employment growth may be limited due to an increased use of third party debt collectors, who are generally more efficient than in-house collectors. Also, some firms are beginning to use offshore collection agencies, whose lower cost structures allow them to collect debts that are too small for domestic collection agencies. Contrary to the pattern in most occupations, employment of bill and account collectors tends to rise during recessions, reflecting the difficulty that many people have in meeting their financial obligations. However, collectors usually have more success at getting people to repay their debts when the economy is good.

Earnings

Median hourly earnings of bill and account collectors were $13.20 in May 2004. The middle 50 percent earned between $10.87 and $16.28. The lowest 10 percent earned less than $9.22, and the highest 10 percent earned more than $20.10. In addition to a basic rate of pay, many bill and account collectors earn commissions based on the amount of debt they recover.

Related Occupations

Bill and account collectors review and collect information on accounts. Other occupations with similar responsibilities include credit authorizers, checkers, and clerks; loan officers; and interviewers.

Sources of Additional Information

Career information on bill and account collectors is available from
➤ ACA International, The Association of Credit and Collection Professionals, P.O. Box 390106, Minneapolis, MN 55439. Internet: http://www.acainternational.org

Billing and Posting Clerks and Machine Operators

(O*NET 43-3021.01, 43-3021.02, 43-3021.03)

Significant Points

● The health care industry employs 1 out of 3 workers.

● Most jobs in this occupation require only a high school diploma; however, many employers prefer to hire workers who have completed some college courses or a degree.

● Slower-than-average employment growth is expected as increased automation of billing services reduces the need for billing clerks.

Nature of the Work

Billing and posting clerks and machine operators, commonly called billing clerks, compile records of charges for services rendered or goods sold, calculate and record the amounts of these services and goods, and prepare invoices to be mailed to customers.

Billing clerks review purchase orders, sales tickets, hospital records, or charge slips to calculate the total amount due from a customer. They must take into account any applicable discounts, special rates, or credit terms. A billing clerk for a trucking company often needs to consult a rate book to determine shipping costs of machine parts, for example. A hospital's billing clerk may need to contact an insurance company to determine what items will be reimbursed and for how much. In accounting, law, consulting, and similar firms, billing clerks calculate client fees based on the actual time required to perform the task. They keep track of the accumulated hours and dollar amounts to charge to each job, the type of job performed for a customer, and the percentage of work completed.

After billing clerks review all necessary information, they compute the charges, using calculators or computers. They then prepare itemized statements, bills, or invoices used for billing and recordkeeping purposes. In one organization, the clerk might prepare a bill containing the amount due and the date and type of service; in another, the clerk would produce a detailed invoice with codes

Billing clerks review statements for errors before sending them to customers.

for all goods and services provided. This latter form might list the items sold, the terms of credit, the date of shipment or the dates services were provided, a salesperson's or doctor's identification, if necessary, and the sales total.

Computers and specialized billing software allow many clerks to calculate charges and prepare bills in one step. Computer packages prompt clerks to enter data from handwritten forms, and to manipulate the necessary entries of quantities, labor, and rates to be charged. Billing clerks verify the entry of information and check for errors before the computer prints the bill. After the bills are printed, billing clerks check them again for accuracy. Computer software also allows bills to be sent electronically if both the biller and the customer prefer not to use paper copies; this, coupled with the prevalence of electronic payment options, allows a completely paperless billing process. In offices that are not automated, *billing machine operators* run off the bill on a billing machine to send to the customer.

In addition to producing invoices, billing clerks may be asked to handle follow-up questions from customers and resolve any discrepancies or errors. Finally, all changes must be entered in the accounting records.

Working Conditions
Billing clerks typically are employed in an office environment, although a growing number—particularly medical billers—work at home. Most billing clerks work 40 hours per week during regular business hours, though about one in seven works part time. Because billing clerks use computers on a daily basis, workers may have to sit for extended periods and also may experience eye and muscle strain, backaches, headaches, and repetitive motion injuries.

Training, Other Qualifications, and Advancement
Most billing clerks need at least a high school diploma. However, many employers prefer to hire workers who have completed some college courses or a degree. Workers with an associate or bachelor's degree are likely to start at higher salaries and advance more easily than those without degrees. Employers also seek workers who are computer literate, and in particular those who have experience with billing software programs.

Billing clerks usually receive on-the-job training from their supervisor or some other senior worker. Some formal classroom training also may be necessary, such as training in the specific computer software used by the company. Workers must be careful, orderly, and detail oriented with an aptitude for working with numbers in order to avoid making errors and to recognize errors made by others. Workers also should be discreet and trustworthy, because they frequently come in contact with confidential material. Medical billers in particular need to understand and follow the regulations of the Health Insurance Portability and Accountability Act (HIPAA), which were enacted to maintain the confidentiality of patient medical records.

A number of community and career colleges offer certificate programs in medical billing. Courses typically cover basic biology, anatomy, and physiology in addition to training on coding and computer billing software.

Billing clerks usually advance by taking on more duties in the same occupation for higher pay or by transferring to a closely related occupation. Most companies fill office and administrative support supervisory and managerial positions by promoting individuals from within the organization. Workers who acquire additional skills, experience, and training improve their advancement opportunities. With appropriate experience and education, some billing clerks may become accountants, human resource specialists, or buyers.

Employment
In 2004, billing and posting clerks and machine operators held about 523,000 jobs. Although all industries employ billing clerks, the health care industry employs the most, about a third of all billing clerks. The wholesale and retail trade industries also employ a large number of billing clerks. Third-party billing companies—companies that provide billing services for other companies—are employing a growing number of billing clerks. Industries that are providing this service are the accounting, tax preparation, bookkeeping, and payroll services industry and the office administrative and business support services industries. These industries currently employ around 5 percent of the occupation, although a portion of clerks in these industries are performing the function on their own accounts. Another 3 percent—mostly medical billers—were self employed.

Job Outlook
Employment of billing and posting clerks and machine operators is expected to grow more slowly than the average for all occupations through the year 2014. Automated and electronic billing processes are greatly simplifying billing and allowing companies to send out bills faster without hiring additional workers. In addition, as the billing process becomes simplified, other people, particularly accounting and bookkeeping clerks, are taking on the billing function. Strong growth in the health care industry, which employs many billing clerks due to the complicated nature of medical billing, will generate some jobs for billing clerks in the future. Although growth will be limited, many job openings will occur as workers transfer to other occupations or leave the labor force. Turnover in the occupation is relatively high,

characteristic of an entry-level occupation that typically requires only a high school diploma.

Employment growth will occur in the expanding health care industries, but growth will be limited as more hospitals and physicians' offices use contract billing companies. Contract billing companies generally have much more sophisticated technology and software, enabling them to produce more bills per person. In all industries, including health care, the billing function is becoming increasingly automated and invoices and statements are automatically generated upon delivery of the service or shipment of goods. Bills also will increasingly be delivered electronically over the Internet, eliminating the production and mailing of paper bills.

Earnings

Median hourly earnings of billing and posting clerks and machine operators were $13.00 in May 2004. The middle 50 percent earned between $10.76 and $15.86. The lowest 10 percent earned less than $9.12, and the highest 10 percent earned more than $18.88.

Related Occupations

Billing clerks process and send records of transactions for payment; other occupations with similar responsibilities include payroll and timekeeping clerks; bookkeeping, auditing, and accounting clerks; tellers; and order clerks.

Sources of Additional Information

Information on employment opportunities for billing clerks is available from local offices of the State employment service.

Bookkeeping, Accounting, and Auditing Clerks

(O*NET 43-3031.00)

Significant Points

- Bookkeeping, accounting, and auditing clerks held more than 2 million jobs in 2004 and are employed in every industry.

- Employment is projected to grow more slowly than average as the spread of office automation lifts worker productivity.

- The large size of this occupation ensures plentiful job openings, including many opportunities for temporary and part-time work; those who can carry out a wider range of bookkeeping and accounting activities will be in greater demand than specialized clerks.

Nature of the Work

Bookkeeping, accounting, and auditing clerks are an organization's financial recordkeepers. They update and maintain one or more accounting records, including those which tabulate expenditures, receipts, accounts payable and receivable, and profit and loss. They represent a wide range of skills and knowledge from full-charge bookkeepers who can maintain an entire company's books to accounting clerks who handle specific accounts. All of these clerks make numerous computations each day and increasingly must be comfortable using computers to calculate and record data.

In small establishments, *bookkeeping clerks* handle all financial transactions and recordkeeping. They record all transactions, post debits and credits, produce financial statements, and prepare reports

Bookkeeping, accounting, and auditing clerks update and maintain accounting records.

and summaries for supervisors and managers. Bookkeepers also prepare bank deposits by compiling data from cashiers, verifying and balancing receipts, and sending cash, checks, or other forms of payment to the bank. They also may handle payroll, make purchases, prepare invoices, and keep track of overdue accounts.

In large offices and accounting departments, *accounting clerks* have more specialized tasks. Their titles, such as accounts payable clerk or accounts receivable clerk, often reflect the type of accounting they do. In addition, their responsibilities vary by level of experience. Entry-level accounting clerks post details of transactions, total accounts, and compute interest charges. They also may monitor loans and accounts to ensure that payments are up to date.

More advanced accounting clerks may total, balance, and reconcile billing vouchers; ensure the completeness and accuracy of data on accounts; and code documents according to company procedures. These workers post transactions in journals and on computer files and update the files when needed. Senior clerks also review computer printouts against manually maintained journals and make necessary corrections. They may review invoices and statements to ensure that all the information appearing on them is accurate and complete, and they may reconcile computer reports with operating reports.

Auditing clerks verify records of transactions posted by other workers. They check figures, postings, and documents to ensure that they are correct, mathematically accurate, and properly coded. They also correct or note errors for accountants or other workers to adjust.

As organizations continue to computerize their financial records, many bookkeeping, accounting, and auditing clerks are using specialized accounting software on personal computers. With manual posting to general ledgers becoming obsolete, these clerks increasingly are posting charges to accounts on computer spreadsheets and databases. They now enter information from receipts or bills into computers, and the information is then stored either electronically or as computer printouts (or both). The widespread use of computers also has enabled bookkeeping, accounting, and auditing clerks to take on additional responsibilities, such as payroll, procurement, and billing. Many of these functions require these clerks to write letters, make phone calls to customers or clients, and interact with colleagues. Therefore, good communication skills are becoming increasingly important in the occupation.

Working Conditions

Bookkeeping, accounting, and auditing clerks work in an office environment. They may experience eye and muscle strain, backaches, headaches, and repetitive motion injuries as a result of using computers on a daily basis. Clerks may have to sit for extended periods while reviewing detailed data.

Many bookkeeping, accounting, and auditing clerks work regular business hours and a standard 40-hour week. A substantial number work just part time. Full-time and part-time clerks may work some evenings and weekends. Bookkeeping, accounting, and auditing clerks may work longer hours to meet deadlines at the end of the fiscal year, during tax time, or when monthly or yearly accounting audits are performed. Those who work in hotels, restaurants, and stores may put in overtime during peak holiday and vacation seasons.

Training, Other Qualifications, and Advancement
Most bookkeeping, accounting, and auditing clerks are required to have a high school degree at a minimum. However, having some college is increasingly important and an associate degree in business or accounting is required for some positions. Although a college degree is rarely required, graduates may accept bookkeeping, accounting, and auditing clerk positions to get into a particular company or to enter the accounting or finance field with the hope of eventually being promoted to professional or managerial positions.

Experience in a related job and working in an office environment also is recommended. Employers prefer workers who are computer-literate; knowledge of word processing and spreadsheet software is especially valuable.

Once hired, bookkeeping, accounting, and auditing clerks usually receive on-the-job training. Under the guidance of a supervisor or other senior worker, new employees learn company procedures. Some formal classroom training also may be necessary, such as training in specific computer software. Bookkeeping, accounting, and auditing clerks must be careful, orderly, and detail-oriented in order to avoid making errors and to recognize errors made by others. These workers also should be discreet and trustworthy, because they frequently come in contact with confidential material. In addition, all bookkeeping, accounting, and auditing clerks should have a strong aptitude for numbers.

Bookkeepers, particularly those who handle all the recordkeeping for companies, may find it beneficial to become certified. The Certified Bookkeeper designation, awarded by the American Institute of Professional Bookkeepers, assures employers that individuals have the skills and knowledge required to carry out all the bookkeeping and accounting functions up through the adjusted trial balance, including payroll functions. For certification, candidates must have at least 2 years of bookkeeping experience, pass three tests, and adhere to a code of ethics. More than 100 colleges and universities offer a preparatory course for certification and another 150 offer a course online. The Universal Accounting Center offers the Professional Bookkeeper designation.

Bookkeeping, accounting, and auditing clerks usually advance by taking on more duties in the same occupation for higher pay or by transferring to a closely related occupation. Most companies fill office and administrative support supervisory and managerial positions by promoting individuals from within their organizations, so clerks who acquire additional skills, experience, and training improve their advancement opportunities. With appropriate experience and education, some bookkeeping, accounting, and auditing clerks may become accountants or auditors.

Employment
Bookkeeping, accounting, and auditing clerks held more than 2 million jobs in 2004. They are found in all industries and at all levels of government. Local government and the accounting, tax preparation, bookkeeping, and payroll services industry are among the individual industries employing the largest numbers of these clerks. A growing number work for employment services firms, the result of an increase in outsourcing of this occupation. About 1 out of 4 bookkeeping, accounting, and auditing clerks worked part time in 2004.

Job Outlook
Employment of bookkeeping, accounting, and auditing clerks is projected to grow more slowly than the average for all occupations through 2014. More job openings will stem from replacement needs than from job growth. Each year, numerous jobs will become available as these clerks transfer to other occupations or leave the labor force. The large size of this occupation ensures plentiful job openings, including many opportunities for temporary and part-time work.

Although a growing economy will result in more financial transactions and other activities that require these clerical workers, the continuing spread of office automation will lift worker productivity and contribute to the slower-than-average increase in employment. In addition, organizations of all sizes will continue to downsize and consolidate various recordkeeping functions, thus reducing the demand for bookkeeping, accounting, and auditing clerks. Furthermore, some work performed by these workers will be outsourced to lower-wage foreign countries. Those who can carry out a wider range of bookkeeping and accounting activities will be in greater demand than specialized clerks. Demand for full-charge bookkeepers is expected to increase, because they are called upon to do much of the work of accountants, as well as perform a wider variety of financial transactions, from payroll to billing. Certified bookkeepers and those with several years of accounting or bookkeeper experience will have the best job prospects.

Earnings
In May 2004, the median wage and salary annual earnings of bookkeeping, accounting, and auditing clerks were $28,570. The middle half of the occupation earned between $22,960 and $35,450. The top 10 percent of bookkeeping, accounting, and auditing clerks more than $43,570, and the bottom 10 percent earned less than $18,580.

Related Occupations
Bookkeeping, accounting, and auditing clerks work with financial records. Other clerks who perform similar duties include bill and account collectors; billing and posting clerks and machine operators; brokerage clerks; credit authorizers, checkers, and clerks; payroll and timekeeping clerks; procurement clerks; and tellers.

Sources of Additional Information
For information on the Certified Bookkeeper designation, contact:
➤ American Institute of Professional Bookkeepers, 6001 Montrose Rd., Suite 500, Rockville, MD 20852. Internet: **http://www.aipb.org**

Gaming Cage Workers

(O*NET 43-3041.00)

Significant Points

- Job opportunities are available nationwide and are no longer limited to Nevada and New Jersey.

- Most employers prefer applicants who have at least a high school diploma as well as experience in handling money or previous casino employment.

- Workers need a license issued by a regulatory agency, such as a State casino control board or commission; licensure requires proof of residency in the State in which gaming workers are employed and a background investigation.

Nature of the Work

Gaming cage workers, more commonly called *cage cashiers*, work in casinos and other gaming establishments. The "cage" where these workers can be found is the central depository for money, gaming chips, and paperwork necessary to support casino play.

Cage workers carry out a wide range of financial transactions and handle any paperwork that may be required. They perform credit checks and verify credit references for people who want to open a house credit account. They cash checks according to rules established by the casino. Cage workers sell gambling chips, tokens, or tickets to patrons or to other workers for resale to patrons and exchange chips and tokens for cash. They may use cash registers, adding machines, or computers to calculate and record transactions. At the end of their shift, cage cashiers must balance the books.

Because gaming establishments are closely scrutinized, cage workers must follow a number of rules and regulations related to their handling of money. For example, they monitor large cash transactions for money laundering and tax purposes, and report these transactions to the Internal Revenue Service. Also, in determining when to extend credit or cash a check, cage workers must follow detailed procedures.

Working Conditions

The atmosphere in casinos is often considered glamorous. However, casino work can also be physically demanding. This occupation requires workers to stand for long periods with constant reaching and grabbing. Sometimes cage workers may be expected to lift and carry relatively heavy items. The casino atmosphere exposes workers to certain hazards, such as cigarette, cigar, and pipe smoke. Noise from slot machines, gaming tables, and talking workers and patrons may be distracting to some, although workers wear protective headgear in areas where loud machinery is used to count money.

Most casinos are open 24 hours a day, seven days a week and offer three staggered shifts. Casinos typically require cage workers to work on nights, weekends, and holidays.

Training, Other Qualifications, and Advancement

There usually are no minimum educational requirements, although most employers prefer at least a high school diploma or the equivalent. Experience in handling money or previous casino employment also is preferred. Prospective gaming cage workers are sometimes required to pass a basic math test. Good customer

Gaming cage workers perform credit checks for patrons trying to establish house credit accounts.

service skills and computer proficiency are also necessary for this occupation. Each casino establishes its own requirements for education, training, and experience.

Once hired, gaming cage workers usually receive on-the-job training. Under the guidance of a supervisor or other senior worker, new employees learn company procedures. Some formal classroom training also may be necessary, such as training in specific gaming regulations and procedures. Gaming cage workers must be careful, orderly, and detail-oriented in order to avoid making errors and to recognize errors made by others. These workers also should be discreet and trustworthy, because they frequently come in contact with confidential material.

All gaming workers are required to have a license issued by a regulatory agency, such as a State casino control board or commission. Applicants for a license must provide photo identification, offer proof of residency in the State in which they anticipate working, and pay a fee. Age requirements vary by State. The licensing application process also includes a background investigation.

Employment

Gaming cage workers held about 20,000 jobs in 2004. All of these individuals work in establishments that offer gaming, and employment is concentrated in Nevada and Atlantic City, New Jersey. However, a growing number of States and Indian reservations have legalized gambling, and gaming establishments can now be found in many parts of the country.

Job Outlook

Employment of gaming cage workers is expected to increase about as fast as the average for all occupations through 2014. The outlook for gaming cage workers depends on the demand for gaming, which is expected to remain strong. No longer confined to Nevada and New Jersey, gaming is becoming legalized in more States that consider gaming an effective way to increase revenues. A substantial portion of this growth will come from the construction of new Indian casinos and "racinos," which are race tracks that offer casino games.

Gaming cage workers, however, will have fewer job opportunities than others in gaming establishments, as casinos find ways to reduce the amount of cash handled by employees. For example, self-serve cash-out and change machines are common along with automated teller machines. In addition, slot machines are now able to make payouts in tickets, instead of coins, which can be read by other slot machines and the amount on the ticket transferred to the new machine. These technologies reduce the amount of cash needed to play and speed up the exchange process, which means less workers are needed to handle the cage than in the past. However, a fair number of openings will result from high turnover in this occupation, due to the high level of scrutiny workers receive and the need to be accurate. Persons with good mathematics abilities, previous casino experience, some background in accounting or bookkeeping, and good customer service skills should have the best opportunities.

Earnings

Wage earnings for gaming cage workers vary according to level of experience, training, location, and size of the gaming establishment. Median hourly earnings of gaming cage workers were $10.74 in May 2004. The middle 50 percent earned between $9.24 and $12.85 an hour. The lowest 10 percent earned less than $7.91, and the highest 10 percent earned more than $14.99 an hour.

Related Occupations

Many other occupations provide hospitality and customer service. Some examples of related occupations are credit authorizers, checkers, and clerks; gaming service occupations; sales worker supervisors; cashiers; retail salespersons; and tellers.

Sources of Additional Information

Information on employment opportunities for gaming cage workers is available from local offices of the State employment service.
Information on careers in gaming also is available from:
➤ American Gaming Association, 555 13th St. NW., Suite 1010 East, Washington, DC 20004. Internet: **http://www.americangaming.org**

Payroll and Timekeeping Clerks

(O*NET 43-3051.00)

Significant Points

- Payroll and timekeeping clerks are found in every industry.
- Most employers prefer applicants with a high school diploma; computer skills are very desirable.
- Those who have completed a certification program, indicating that they can handle more complex payroll issues, will have an advantage in the job market.

Nature of the Work

Payroll and timekeeping clerks perform a vital function: ensuring that employees are paid on time and that their paychecks are accurate. If inaccuracies occur, such as monetary errors or incorrect amounts of vacation time, these workers research and correct the records. In addition, they may perform various other clerical tasks. Automated timekeeping systems that allow employees to enter the number of hours they have worked directly into a computer have eliminated much of the data entry and review by timekeepers and have elevated the job of payroll clerk. In offices that have not automated this function, however, payroll and timekeeping clerks still perform many of the traditional job functions.

The fundamental task of *timekeeping clerks* is distributing and collecting timecards each pay period. These workers review employee work charts, timesheets, and timecards to ensure that information is properly recorded and that records have the signatures of authorizing officials. In companies that bill for the time spent by staff, such as law or accounting firms, timekeeping clerks make sure that the hours recorded are charged to the correct job so that clients can be properly billed. These clerks also review computer reports listing timecards that cannot be processed because of errors, and they contact the employee or the employee's supervisor to resolve the problem. In addition, timekeeping clerks are responsible for informing managers and other employees about procedural changes in payroll policies.

Payroll clerks, also called payroll technicians, screen timecards for calculating, coding, or other errors. They compute pay by subtracting allotments, including Federal and State taxes and contributions to retirement, insurance, and savings plans, from gross earnings. Increasingly, computers are performing these calculations and alerting payroll clerks to problems or errors in the data. In small organizations or for new employees whose records are not yet entered into a computer system, clerks may perform the necessary calculations manually. In some small offices, clerks or other employees in the accounting department process payroll.

Payroll clerks record changes in employees' addresses; close out files when workers retire, resign, or transfer; and advise employees on income tax withholding and other mandatory deductions. They also issue and record adjustments to workers' pay because of previous errors or retroactive increases. Payroll clerks need to follow changes in tax and deduction laws, so they are aware of the most recent revisions. Finally, they prepare and mail earnings and tax-withholding statements for employees' use in preparing income tax returns.

In small offices, payroll and timekeeping duties are likely to be included in the duties of a general office clerk, a secretary, or an accounting clerk. However, large organizations employ specialized payroll and timekeeping clerks to perform these functions. In offices that have automated timekeeping systems, payroll clerks perform more analysis of the data, examine trends, and work with computer systems. They also spend more time answering employees' questions and processing unique data.

Working Conditions

Payroll and timekeeping clerks usually work in clean, pleasant, and comfortable office settings. Clerks usually work a standard 35- to 40-hour week; however, longer hours might be necessary during busy periods. Payroll and timekeeping clerks also may face stress at times, particularly from the pressure to meet deadlines.

Training, Other Qualifications, and Advancement

Most employers prefer applicants with a high school diploma or GED. Computer skills are very desirable. Payroll and timekeeping clerks learn their skills through a combination of on-the-job experience and informal training. Training also can be attained through programs in high schools, business schools, and community colleges. New workers receive training in payroll, timekeeping, personnel issues, workplace practices, and company policies.

Payroll and timekeeping clerks must be able to interact and communicate with individuals at all levels of the organization. In addition, clerks should demonstrate poise, tactfulness, and diplomacy, and have a high level of interpersonal skills in order to handle sensitive and confidential situations.

Most organizations specializing in payroll and timekeeping offer classes intended to enhance the marketable skills of their members. Some organizations offer certification programs; completion of a certification program indicates competence and can enhance one's advancement opportunities. For example, the American Payroll As-

Payroll and timekeeping clerks ensure that employees are paid on time and that their paychecks are accurate.

sociation offers two levels of certification, the Fundamental Payroll Certification (FPC) and the Certified Payroll Professional (CPP). The FPC is open to all individuals who wish to demonstrate basic payroll competency. The more advanced CPP is available those who have been employed in the practice of payroll for at least 3 years and who have obtained the FPC within the last 18 months. Both require experience and a passing score on a comprehensive exam.

Employment

Payroll and timekeeping clerks held about 214,000 jobs in 2004. They can be found in every industry, but a growing number work for employment services companies as temporary employees, or for accounting, tax preparation, bookkeeping, and payroll services firms, which increasingly are taking on the payroll function as a service to other companies. Approximately 18 percent of all payroll and timekeeping clerks worked part time in 2004.

Job Outlook

Employment of payroll and timekeeping clerks is expected to grow about as fast as the average for all occupations through 2014. In addition to job growth, numerous job openings will arise each year as payroll and timekeeping clerks leave the labor force or transfer to other occupations. Those who have completed a certification program, indicating that they can handle more complex payroll issues, will have an advantage in the job market.

As entering and recording payroll and timekeeping information becomes more simplified, the job itself is becoming more complex, with companies now offering a greater variety of pension, 401(k), and other investment plans to their employees. Also, the growing use of garnishment of wages for child support is adding to the complexity. These developments will fuel the demand for payroll and timekeeping clerks, who will be needed to record and monitor such information.

Firms increasingly are outsourcing the payroll function. As a result, the best employment opportunities are expected to be in companies that specialize in payroll, including companies in the employment services industry and the accounting, tax preparation, bookkeeping, and payroll services industry. Many of these companies are data processing facilities, but accounting firms also are taking on the payroll function to supplement their accounting work.

The increasing use of computers will limit employment growth of payroll and timekeeping clerks. For example, automated time clocks, which calculate employee hours, allow large organizations to centralize their timekeeping duties in one location. At individual sites, employee hours increasingly are tracked by computer and verified by managers. This information is compiled and sent to a central office to be processed by payroll clerks. In addition, the growing use of direct deposit will reduce the need to draft paychecks, because these funds are transferred automatically each pay period. Also, more organizations are allowing employees to update their payroll records electronically. In smaller organizations, payroll and timekeeping duties are being assigned to secretaries, general office clerks, or accounting clerks. Furthermore, the greater complexity of the job, coupled with the automation of records that is simplifying data entry, is resulting in payroll professionals, not payroll and timekeeping clerks, doing more of the work.

Earnings

Salaries of payroll and timekeeping clerks may vary considerably. The region of the country, size of city, and type and size of establishment all influence salary levels. Also, the level of expertise required and the complexity and uniqueness of a clerk's responsibilities may affect earnings.

Median annual earnings of payroll and timekeeping clerks in May 2004 were $30,350. The middle 50 percent earned between $24,430 and $36,930. The lowest 10 percent earned less than $19,680, and the highest 10 percent earned more than $44,270. Median annual earnings in the industries employing the largest numbers of payroll and timekeeping clerks in May 2004 were:

Management of companies and enterprises	$32,600
Elementary and secondary schools	32,390
Local government	31,620
Accounting, tax preparation, bookkeeping, and payroll services	29,040
Employment services	28,010

Some employers offer educational assistance to payroll and timekeeping clerks.

Related Occupations

Payroll and timekeeping clerks perform a vital financial function—ensuring that employees are paid on time and that their paychecks are accurate. In addition, they may perform various other office and administrative support duties. Other financial clerks include bill and account collectors; billing and posting clerks and machine operators; bookkeeping, accounting, and auditing clerks; gaming cage workers; procurement clerks; and tellers.

Sources of Additional Information

For general information about payroll and timekeeping clerks, contact:

➤ American Payroll Association, 660 North Main Ave., Suite 100, Suite 660, San Antonio, TX 78205-1217. Internet: **http://www.americanpayroll.org**
➤ WorldatWork, 14040 N. Northsight Blvd., Scottsdale, AZ 85260. Internet: **http://www.worldatwork.org**

Information on employment opportunities for payroll and timekeeping clerks is available from local offices of the State employment service.

Procurement Clerks

(O*NET 43-3061.00)

Significant Points

● About 3 in 10 procurement clerks work for Federal, State, and local governments.

● Most employers prefer applicants who have a high school diploma and who are computer-literate.

● Overall employment is expected to decline through 2014 as a result of increasing automation.

Nature of the Work

Procurement clerks compile requests for materials, prepare purchase orders, keep track of purchases and supplies, and handle inquiries about orders. Usually called *purchasing clerks* or *purchasing technicians*, they perform a variety of tasks related to the ordering of goods and supplies for an organization and make sure that what was purchased arrives on schedule and meets the purchaser's specifications.

Automation is having a profound effect on this occupation. Orders for goods now can be placed electronically when supplies are low. For example, computers integrated with cash registers at stores record purchases and automatically reorder goods when supplies reach a certain target level. However, automation is still years away for many firms, and the role of the procurement clerk is unchanged in many organizations.

Procurement clerks perform a wide range of tasks and also have a wide range of responsibilities. Some clerks act more like buyers, particularly at small to medium-size companies, while others perform strictly clerical functions. In general, procurement clerks process requests for purchases. They first determine whether there is any of the requested product left in inventory and may go through catalogs or to the Internet to find suppliers. They may prepare invitation-to-bid forms and mail them to suppliers or distribute them for public posting. Procurement clerks may interview potential suppliers by telephone or face-to-face to check on prices and specifications and thereby put together spreadsheets with price comparisons and other facts about each supplier. Upon the organization's approval of a supplier, purchase orders are prepared, mailed, and entered into computers. Procurement clerks keep track of orders and determine the causes of any delays. If the supplier has questions, clerks try to answer them and resolve any problems. When the shipment arrives, procurement clerks may reconcile the purchase order with the shipment, making sure that they match; notify the vendors when invoices are not received; and verify that the bills concur with the purchase orders.

Some purchasing departments, particularly in small companies, are responsible for overseeing the organization's inventory control system. At these organizations, procurement clerks monitor in-house inventory movement and complete inventory transfer forms for bookkeeping purposes. They may keep inventory spreadsheets and place orders when materials on hand are insufficient.

Working Conditions

Procurement clerks usually work a standard 40-hour week. Most procurement clerks work in areas that are clean, well lit, and relatively quiet. These workers sit for long periods of time in front of computer terminals, which many cause eyestrain and headaches. Workers in this occupation may sometimes be expected to work overtime or varied shifts.

Procurement clerks process requests for purchases.

Training, Other Qualifications, and Advancement

Most employers prefer applicants with a high school diploma or its equivalent or a mix of education and related experience. Most employers prefer workers who are computer-literate and have a working knowledge of word processing and spreadsheet software.

Most procurement clerks are trained on the job under close supervision of more experienced employees. Proficiency with desktop computer software is becoming increasingly important as most tasks, such as preparing purchase orders, are being filed electronically. Some procurement clerks that have more education and show a greater understanding of contracts and purchasing may be promoted to the position of purchasing agent or buyer.

Employment

In 2004, procurement clerks held about 74,000 jobs. Procurement clerks are found in every industry, including manufacturing, retail and wholesale trade, health care, and government. About 3 in 10 procurement clerks work for Federal, State, and local governments; most of these clerks work for the Federal Government.

Job Outlook

Employment of procurement clerks is expected to decline through 2014 as a result of increasing automation. The need for procurement clerks will be reduced as the use of computers to place orders directly with suppliers—called electronic data interchange—and as ordering over the Internet—known as "e-procurement"—become more commonplace. In addition, procurement authority for some purchases is now being given to employees in the departments originating the purchase. These departments may be issued procurement cards, which are similar to credit cards that enable a department to charge purchases up to a specified amount.

Although overall employment in the occupation is expected to decline, job outlook varies by industry. For example, employment will decline in manufacturing, the primary employer of procurement clerks in the goods-producing sector of the economy. In contrast, employment of procurement clerks will increase in some industries in the service-providing sector—such as retail trade, professional services, and health care—which are beginning to realize that a centralized procurement department may be more cost effective than units making purchases independently, as many service companies had been doing. However, most job openings will arise out of the need to replace workers who transfer to other occupations or leave the labor force. Persons with good writing and communication skills, along with computer skills, will have the best opportunities for employment.

Earnings

Median hourly earnings of procurement clerks in May 2004 were $14.85. The middle 50 percent earned between $11.82 and $18.11. The lowest 10 percent earned less than $9.52 and the highest 10 percent earned more than $21.03. Procurement clerks working for the Federal Government had an average annual income of $39,011 in 2005.

Related Occupations

Procurement clerks compile information and records to draw up purchase orders for materials and services. Other workers who perform similar duties are purchasing agents and buyers, order clerks, file clerks, secretaries, and receptionists and information clerks.

Sources of Additional Information

Information on employment opportunities for procurement clerks is available from local offices of the State employment service.

Tellers

(O*NET 43-3071.00)

Significant Points

- Most jobs require only a high school diploma; tellers should enjoy public contact, must feel comfortable handling large amounts of money, and should be discreet and trustworthy.

- About 3 out of 10 tellers work part time.

- Most job openings will arise from replacement needs because turnover is high.

- Although the job outlook for tellers has improved recently, employment is projected to grow more slowly than average.

Nature of the Work

The teller is the person most people associate with a bank. Tellers make up approximately one-fourth of bank employees and conduct most of a bank's routine transactions. Among the responsibilities of tellers are cashing checks, accepting deposits and loan payments, and processing withdrawals. They also may sell savings bonds, accept payment for customers' utility bills and charge cards, process necessary paperwork for certificates of deposit, and sell travelers' checks. Some tellers specialize in handling foreign currencies or commercial or business accounts.

Being a teller requires a great deal of attention to detail. Before cashing a check, a teller must verify the date, the name of the bank, the identity of the person who is to receive payment, and the legality of the document. A teller also must make sure that the written and numerical amounts agree and that the account has sufficient funds to cover the check. The teller then must carefully count cash to avoid errors. Sometimes a customer withdraws money in the form of a cashier's check, which the teller prepares and verifies. When accepting a deposit, tellers must check the accuracy of the deposit slip before processing the transaction.

Prior to starting their shifts, tellers receive and count an amount of working cash for their drawers. A supervisor—usually the head teller—verifies this amount. Tellers use this cash for payments during the day and are responsible for its safe and accurate handling. Before leaving, tellers count their cash on hand, list the currency-received tickets on a balance sheet, make sure that the accounts balance, and sort checks and deposit slips. Over the course of a workday, tellers also may process numerous mail transactions. Some tellers replenish their cash drawers and corroborate deposits and payments to automated teller machines (ATMs).

In most banks, head tellers are responsible for the teller line. They set work schedules, ensure that the proper procedures are adhered to, and act as a mentor to less experienced tellers. In addition, head tellers may perform the typical duties of a teller, as needed, and may deal with the more difficult customer problems. They may access the vault, ensure that the correct cash balance is in the vault, and oversee large cash transactions. Technology continues to play a large role in the job duties of all tellers. In most banks, for example, tellers use computer terminals to record deposits and withdrawals. These terminals often give tellers quick access to detailed information on customer accounts. Tellers can use this information to tailor the bank's services to fit a customer's needs or to recommend an appropriate bank product or service.

As banks begin to offer more and increasingly complex financial services, tellers are being trained to identify sales opportunities.

Tellers must pay attention to detail.

This task requires them to learn about the various financial products and services the bank offers so that they can briefly explain them to customers and refer interested customers to appropriate specialized sales personnel. In addition, tellers in many banks are being cross-trained to perform some of the functions of customer service representatives. (Customer service representatives are discussed separately in the *Handbook*.)

Working Conditions

Tellers work in an office environment. They may experience eye and muscle strain, backaches, headaches, and repetitive motion injuries as a result of using computers on a daily basis. Tellers may have to sit for extended periods while reviewing detailed data.

Many tellers work regular business hours and a standard 40-hour week. A substantial number work just part time. Full-time and part-time tellers may work some evenings and weekends.

Training, Other Qualifications, and Advancement

Most tellers are required to have at least a high school diploma. Some have some college training or even a bachelor's degree in business, accounting, or liberal arts. Although a degree is rarely required, graduates may accept teller positions to get into a particular company or to enter the banking field with the hope of eventually being promoted to professional or managerial positions.

Experience working in an office environment or in customer service, and particularly cash-handling experience, can be important for tellers. Regardless of experience, employers prefer workers who have good communication skills and who are computer-literate; knowledge of word processing and spreadsheet software also is valuable.

Once hired, tellers usually receive on-the-job training. Under the guidance of a supervisor or other senior worker, new employees learn company procedures. Some formal classroom training also may be necessary, such as training in specific computer software.

Tellers should enjoy contact with the public. They must have a strong aptitude for numbers and feel comfortable handling large amounts of money. They should be discreet and trustworthy, because they frequently come in contact with confidential material. Tellers also must be careful, orderly, and detail-oriented in order to avoid making errors and to recognize errors made by others.

Tellers can prepare for better jobs by taking courses offered throughout the country by banking and financial institutes, colleges and universities, and private training institutions.

Tellers usually advance by taking on more duties in the same occupation or by being promoted to head teller or to another supervisory job. Many banks and other employers fill supervisory and managerial positions by promoting individuals from within their organizations, so outstanding tellers who acquire additional skills, experience, and training improve their advancement opportunities.

Employment

Tellers held about 558,000 jobs in 2004. The overwhelming majority worked in commercial banks, savings institutions, or credit unions. The remainder worked in a variety of other finance and other industries. About 3 out of 10 worked part time.

Job Outlook

Employment prospects for tellers have improved recently. Employment is projected to grow, but more slowly than the average for all occupations through 2014. Banks are looking at their branch offices as places to attract customers for the increasing number and variety of financial products the banks sell. As recently as a few years ago, banks were closing branch offices and discouraging the use of tellers in an effort to cut costs, but in a turnaround, banks are now opening branch offices in more locations. They also are keeping them open longer during the day and on weekends, a practice that is expected to increase opportunities for tellers, particularly those who work part time. Most job openings will arise from replacement needs because turnover is high—a characteristic typical of large occupations that normally require little formal education and offer relatively low pay. Tellers who have excellent customer service skills, are knowledgeable about a variety of financial services, and can sell those services will be in greater demand in the future.

Despite the improved outlook, automation and technology will continue to reduce the need for tellers who perform only routine transactions. For example, ATMs and the increased use of direct deposit of paychecks and benefit checks have reduced the need for bank customers to interact with tellers for routine transactions. In addition, electronic banking is spreading rapidly throughout the banking industry. This type of banking, conducted over the telephone or the Internet, also will reduce the number of tellers over the long run.

Employment of tellers also is being affected by the increasing use of 24-hour telephone centers by many large banks. These centers allow a customer to interact with a bank representative at a distant location, either by telephone or by video terminal. Such centers usually are staffed by customer service representatives, who can handle a wider variety of transactions than tellers can, including applications for loans and credit cards.

Earnings

Salaries of tellers may vary with their experience and with the region of the country, size of city, and type and size of establishment. Median annual earnings of tellers were $21,120 in May 2004. The middle 50 percent earned between $18,320 and $23,900 a year. The lowest 10 percent earned less than $15,850, and the highest 10 percent earned more than $28,100 a year.

As in other occupations, part-time tellers may not enjoy the same benefits—such as vacations, health and life insurance, and pensions—as full-time workers.

Related Occupations

Tellers enter data into a computer, handle cash, and keep track of financial transactions. Other clerks who perform similar duties include bill and account collectors; billing and posting clerks and machine operators; bookkeeping, accounting, and auditing clerks; gaming cage workers; brokerage clerks; and credit authorizers, checkers, and clerks.

Sources of Additional Information

Information on employment opportunities for tellers is available from banks and other employers and local offices of the State employment service and from:
➤ Bank Administration Institute, 1 North Franklin St., Chicago, IL 60606.

Information and Record Clerks

Brokerage Clerks

(O*NET 43-4011.00)

Significant Points

● More than 9 out of 10 worked for securities and commodities, banks, and other finance industries.

● Brokerage clerks may be high school or college graduates, but positions dealing with the public, such as broker's or sales assistant and those dealing with more complicated financial records are increasingly being held by college graduates.

● Although a growing economy will result in more financial transactions that require these workers, the continuing spread of office automation and the emergence of online trading will result in slower-than-average growth in employment.

Nature of the Work

Brokerage clerks handle much of the day-to-day operations of brokerages, performing a number of different jobs with a wide range of responsibilities; all involve computing and recording data pertaining to securities transactions. Brokerage clerks also may contact customers, take orders, and inform clients of changes to their accounts. Some of these jobs are more clerical and require only a high school diploma, while others are considered entry-level positions for which a bachelor's degree is needed. Brokerage clerks, who work in the operations departments of securities firms, on trading floors, and in branch offices, also are called margin clerks, dividend clerks, transfer clerks, and broker's assistants.

The broker's assistant, also called sales assistant, is the most common type of brokerage clerk. These workers typically assist two brokers, for whom they take calls from clients, write up order tickets, process the paperwork for opening and closing accounts, record a client's purchases and sales, and inform clients of changes to their accounts. All broker's assistants must be knowledgeable about investment products so that they can communicate clearly with clients. Those with a "Series 7" license can make recommendations to clients at the instruction of the broker. This license, issued to securities and commodities sales representatives by the National Association of Securities Dealers (NASD), allows them to provide advice on securities to the public. (Securities, commodities, and financial services sales agents are discussed elsewhere in the *Handbook*.)

Brokerage clerks in the operations areas of securities firms perform many duties to facilitate the sale and purchase of stocks, bonds, commodities, and other kinds of investments. These clerks produce the necessary records of all transactions that occur in their area of the business. Job titles for many of them depend upon the type of work that they perform. Purchase-and-sale clerks, for example, match orders to buy with orders to sell. They balance and verify trades of stock by comparing the records of the selling firm with those of the buying firm. Dividend clerks ensure timely payments of stock or cash dividends to clients of a particular brokerage firm. Transfer clerks execute customer requests for changes to security registration and examine stock certificates to make sure that they adhere to banking regulations. Receive-and-deliver clerks facilitate the receipt and delivery of securities among firms and institutions. Margin clerks record and monitor activity in customers' accounts to ensure that clients make payments and stay within legal boundaries concerning their purchases of stock.

Technology is changing the nature of many of these jobs. A significant and growing number of brokerage clerks use custom-designed software programs to process transactions more quickly. Only a few customized accounts are still handled manually. Furthermore, the rapid expansion of online trading reduces the amount of paperwork because brokerage clerks are able to make trades electronically.

Working Conditions
Brokerage clerks work in offices. Usually the work flow is fairly regular; however, when sales activity increases, the pace can become hectic.

Brokerage clerks generally work a standard 40-hour week, but, they may work overtime during particularly busy periods. Most brokerage clerks work in areas that are clean and well lit, but may be noisy at times.

Training, Other Qualifications, and Advancement
Depending on the job description, brokerage clerks can be high school or college graduates. Positions dealing with the public, such as broker's or sales assistant, and those dealing with more complicated financial records are increasingly being held by college graduates.

Brokerage clerk jobs require good organizational and communication skills, as well as attention to detail. Computer skills also

Brokerage clerks record data pertaining to securities transactions.

are important in order to enter and retrieve data quickly. A Series 7 brokerage license can make a clerk more valuable to the broker because it gives the assistant the ability to answer more of a client's questions and to pass along securities recommendations from the broker. Before clerks can obtain a license, however, they must pass the General Securities Registered Representative Examination (Series 7 exam), administered by the NASD, and be an employee of a registered firm for at least 4 months.

Most new employees are trained on the job, working under the close supervision of more experienced employees. Some firms offer formal training that may include courses in telephone etiquette, computer use, and customer service skills.

Clerks may be promoted to sales representative positions or other professional positions within the securities industry. Some of the larger firms have training programs, especially for their college graduates, that provide clerks with the skills they need for advancement.

Employment
Brokerage clerks held about 75,000 jobs in 2004. More than 9 out of 10 worked for securities and commodities, banks, and other finance industries.

Job Outlook
Employment of brokerage clerks is expected to grow more slowly than the average for all occupations through the year 2014. Although a growing economy will result in more financial transactions and other activities that require these workers, the continuing spread of office automation will lift worker productivity and restrict job growth.

With people increasingly investing in securities, brokerage clerks will be required to process larger volumes of transactions. Moreover, some brokerage clerks will still be needed to update records, enter changes into customers' accounts, and verify transfers of securities. However, the emergence of online trading and widespread automation in the securities and commodities industry will limit demand for brokerage clerks in the coming decade. Some job openings will stem from the need to replace clerks who transfer to other occupations or stop working.

Earnings
Median hourly earnings of brokerage clerks were $16.94 in May 2004. The middle 50 percent earned between $13.52 and $21.60. The lowest 10 percent earned less than $11.22 and the highest 10 percent earned more than $27.11.

Related Occupations
Brokerage clerks compute and record data. Other workers who perform calculations and record data include bill and account collectors; billing and posting clerks and machine operators; bookkeeping, accounting, and auditing clerks; order clerks; and tellers.

Sources of Additional Information
State employment service offices and agencies can provide information about job openings for brokerage clerks.

Credit Authorizers, Checkers, and Clerks

(O*NET 43-4041.01, 43-4041.02)

Significant Points
- Most jobs require only a high school diploma.
- Employment is expected to decline.

Nature of the Work

Credit authorizers, checkers, and clerks review credit history and obtain the information needed to determine the creditworthiness of individuals or businesses applying for credit. They spend much of their day on the telephone or on the Internet obtaining information from credit bureaus, employers, banks, credit institutions, and other sources to determine applicants' credit history and ability to repay what they borrow or charge.

Credit authorizers, checkers, and clerks process and authorize applications for credit, including applications for credit cards. Although the distinctions among the three job titles are disappearing, some general differences remain. *Credit clerks* typically handle the processing of credit applications by verifying the information on the application, calling applicants if additional data are needed, contacting credit bureaus for a credit rating, and obtaining any other information necessary to determine applicants' creditworthiness. If clerks work in a department store or other establishment that offers instant credit, they enter the applicant's information into a computer at the point of sale. A credit rating is then transmitted from a central office within seconds to indicate whether the application should be rejected or approved.

Credit checkers investigate the credit history and current credit standing of a person or business prior to the issuance of a loan or line of credit. Credit checkers also may contact credit departments of businesses and service companies to obtain information about an applicant's credit standing. Credit reporting agencies and bureaus hire checkers to secure, update, and verify information for credit reports. These workers often are called *credit investigators* or *credit reporters.*

Credit authorizers approve charges against customers' existing accounts. Most charges are approved automatically by computer. However, when accounts are past due, overextended, or invalid, or when they show a change of address, salespersons refer the associated transactions to credit authorizers located in a central office. These authorizers evaluate the customers' computerized credit records and payment histories and quickly decide whether to approve new charges.

Working Conditions

Credit authorizers, checkers, and clerks usually work a standard 40-hour week. However, they may work overtime during particularly busy periods, such as holiday shopping seasons and store sales. Most credit authorizers, checkers, and clerks work in areas that are clean, well lit, and relatively quiet. These workers sit for long periods of time in front of computer screens, which may cause eyestrain and headaches. Part-time work is available, and temporary workers are often hired during peak workloads.

Training, Other Qualifications, and Advancement

A high school diploma or its equivalent is usually the minimum requirement for these workers. Other requirements of the job include good telephone and organizational skills and the ability to pay close attention to details and meet tight deadlines. Computer skills also are important in order to enter and retrieve data quickly.

Most new employees are trained on the job, working under close supervision of more experienced employees. Some firms offer formal training that may include courses in telephone etiquette, computer use, and customer service skills. Some credit authorizers, checkers, and clerks also take courses in credit offered by banking and credit associations, public and private vocational schools, and colleges and universities. These workers typically can advance to loan or credit department supervisor or team leader of a small group of clerks.

Employment

Credit authorizers, checkers, and clerks held about 67,000 jobs in 2004. Nearly half of these workers were employed by finance and insurance industries, mainly firms in credit intermediation and related activities, such as commercial and savings banks; credit unions; and mortgage, finance, and loan companies. Credit bureaus, collection agencies, and wholesale and retail trade establishments also employ these clerks.

Job Outlook

Employment of credit authorizers, checkers, and clerks is expected to decline through 2014. Despite a projected increase in the number of credit applications, technology will allow these applications to be processed, checked, and authorized by fewer workers than were required in the past.

Credit scoring is a major development that has improved the productivity of credit authorizers, checkers, and clerks, thus limiting employment growth in the occupation. Companies and credit bureaus now can purchase software that quickly analyzes an applicant's creditworthiness and summarizes it with a "score." Credit issuers then can easily decide whether to accept or reject an application on the basis of its score, speeding up the authorization of loans or credit. Obtaining credit ratings also has become much easier for credit checkers and authorizers because businesses now have computer systems directly linked to credit bureaus that provide immediate access to a person's credit history.

The job outlook for credit authorizers, checkers, and clerks is sensitive to overall economic activity. A downturn in the economy or a rise in interest rates usually leads to a decline in demand for

Credit authorizers process applications for credit cards.

credit. Even in slow economic times, however, job openings will arise from the need to replace workers who leave the occupation for various reasons.

Earnings
Median hourly earnings of credit authorizers, checkers, and clerks in May 2004 were $13.97. The middle 50 percent earned between $11.27 and $17.56. The lowest 10 percent earned less than $9.19, and the highest 10 percent earned more than $21.90. Median hourly earnings in nondepository credit intermediation were $13.74 in 2004, while median earnings in depository credit intermediation were $13.62.

Related Occupations
Credit authorizers, checkers, and clerks obtain and analyze credit histories. Other workers who review account information include bill and account collectors, loan officers, and insurance underwriters.

Sources of Additional Information
State employment service offices and agencies can provide information about job openings for credit authorizers, checkers, and clerks.

Customer Service Representatives

(O*NET 43-4051.01, 43-4051.02)

Significant Points

● Job prospects are expected to be excellent.

● Most jobs require only a high school diploma but educational requirements are rising.

● Strong verbal communication and listening skills are important.

Nature of the Work
Customer service representatives are employed by many different types of companies throughout the country to serve as a direct point of contact for customers. They are responsible for ensuring that their company's customers receive an adequate level of service or help with their questions and concerns. These customers may be individual consumers or other companies, and the nature of their service needs can vary considerably.

All customer service representatives interact with customers to provide information in response to inquiries about products or services and to handle and resolve complaints. They communicate with customers through a variety of means—by telephone; by e-mail, fax, or regular mail correspondence; or in person. Some customer service representatives handle general questions and complaints, whereas others specialize in a particular area.

Many customer inquiries involve routine questions and requests. For example, customer service representatives may be asked to provide a customer with their credit card balance, or to check on the status of an order that has been placed. Obtaining the answers to such questions usually requires simply looking up information on their computer. Other questions are more involved, and may call for additional research or further explanation on the part of the customer service representative. In handling customers' complaints, customer service representatives must attempt to resolve the problem according to guidelines established by the company. These procedures may involve asking questions to determine the validity of a complaint; offering possible solutions; or providing customers with

refunds, exchanges, or other offers, such as discounts or coupons. In some cases, customer service representatives are required to follow up with an individual customer until a question is answered or an issue is resolved.

Some customer service representatives help people decide what types of products or services would best suit their needs. They may even aid customers in completing purchases or transactions. Although the primary function of customer service representatives is not sales, some may spend a part of their time with customers encouraging them to purchase additional products or services. (For information on workers whose primary function is sales, see the statements on sales and related occupations elsewhere in the *Handbook*.) Customer service representatives also may make changes or updates to a customer's profile or account information. They may keep records of transactions and update and maintain databases of information.

Most customer service representatives use computers and telephones extensively in their work. Customer service representatives frequently enter information into a computer as they are speaking to customers. Often, companies have large amounts of data, such as account information, that can be pulled up on a computer screen while the representative is talking to a customer so that he or she can answer specific questions relating to the account. Customer service representatives also may have access to information such as answers to the most common customer questions, or guidelines for dealing with complaints. In the event that they encounter a question or situation to which they do not know how to respond, workers consult with a supervisor to determine the best course of action. Customer service representatives use multiline telephones systems, which often route calls directly to the most appropriate representative. However, at times, the customer service representative must transfer a call to someone who may be better able to respond to the customer's needs.

In some organizations, customer service representatives spend their entire day on the telephone. In others, they may spend part of their day answering e-mails and the remainder of the day taking calls. For some, most of their contact with the customer is face to face. Customer service representatives need to remain aware of the amount of time spent with each customer so that they can fairly distribute their time among the people who require their assistance. This is particularly important for customer service representatives whose primary activities are answering telephone calls and whose conversations often are required to be kept within set time limits. For customer service representatives working in call centers, there usually is very little time between telephone calls; as soon as representatives have finished with one call, they must move on to another. When working in call centers, customer service representatives are likely to be under close supervision. Telephone calls may be taped and reviewed by supervisors to ensure that company policies and procedures are being followed, or a supervisor may listen in on conversations.

Job responsibilities can differ, depending on the industry in which a customer service representative is employed. For example, a customer service representative working in the branch office of a bank may assume the responsibilities of other workers, such as teller or new account clerk, as needed. In insurance agencies, a customer service representative interacts with agents, insurance companies, and policyholders. These workers handle much of the paperwork related to insurance policies, such as policy applications and changes and renewals to existing policies. They answer questions regarding policy coverage, help with reporting claims, and do anything else that may need to be done. Although they must know as much as insurance agents about insurance products, and usually must have credentials equal

Customer service representatives interact with customers to provide information about products or services.

to those of an agent in order to sell products and make changes to policies, the duties of a customer service representative differ from those of an agent in that customer service representatives are not responsible for actively seeking potential customers. Customer service representatives employed by utilities and communications companies assist individuals interested in opening accounts for various utilities such as electricity and gas, or for communication services such as cable television and telephone. They explain various options and receive orders for services to be installed, turned on, turned off, or changed. They also may look into and resolve complaints about billing and service provided by utility, telephone, and cable television companies.

Working Conditions

Although customer service representatives can work in a variety of settings, most work in areas that are clean and well lit. Many work in call or customer contact centers. In this type of environment, workers generally have their own workstation or cubicle space equipped with a telephone, headset, and computer. Because many call centers are open extended hours, beyond the traditional work day, or are staffed around the clock, these positions may require workers to take on early morning, evening, or late night shifts. Weekend or holiday work also may be necessary. As a result, the occupation is well suited to flexible work schedules. Nearly 1 out of 5 customer service representatives work part time.

The occupation also offers the opportunity for seasonal work in certain industries, often through temporary help agencies.

Call centers may be crowded and noisy, and work may be repetitious and stressful, with little time between calls. Workers usually must attempt to minimize the length of each call, while still providing excellent service. To ensure that these procedures are followed, conversations may be monitored by supervisors, something that can be stressful. Also, long periods spent sitting, typing, or looking at a computer screen may cause eye and muscle strain, backaches, headaches, and repetitive motion injuries.

Customer service representatives working outside of a call center environment may interact with customers through several different means. For example, workers employed by an insurance agency or in a grocery store may have customers approach them in person or contact them by telephone, computer, mail, or fax. Many of these customer service representatives work a standard 40-hour week; however, their hours generally depend on the hours of operation of the establishment in which they are employed. Work environments outside of a call center also vary accordingly. Most customer service representatives work either in an office or at a service or help desk.

For virtually all types of customer service representatives, dealing with difficult or irate customers can be a trying task; however, the ability to resolve customers' problems has the potential to be very rewarding.

Training, Other Qualifications, and Advancement

Most customer service representative jobs require only a high school diploma. However, due to employers demanding a higher skilled workforce, many customer service jobs now require an associate or bachelor's degree. Basic to intermediate computer knowledge and good interpersonal skills also are important qualities for people who wish to be successful in the field. Because customer service representatives constantly interact with the public, good communication and problem-solving skills are a must. Verbal communication and listening skills are especially important. Additionally, for workers who communicate through e-mail, good typing, spelling, and written communication skills are necessary. High school courses in computers, English, or business are helpful in preparing for a job in customer service.

Customer service representatives play a critical role in providing an interface between customer and company, and for this reason employers seek out people who come across in a friendly and professional manner. The ability to deal patiently with problems and complaints and to remain courteous when faced with difficult or angry people is very important. Also, a customer service representative needs to be able to work independently within specified time constraints. Workers should have a clear and pleasant speaking voice and be fluent in English. However, the ability to speak a foreign language is becoming increasingly necessary, and bilingual skills are considered a plus.

Training requirements vary by industry. Almost all customer service representatives are provided with some training prior to beginning work, and training continues once on the job. This training generally covers customer service and phone skills, products and services and common customer problems with them, the use or operation of the telephone and/or computer systems, and company policies and regulations. Length of training varies, but it usually lasts at least several weeks. Because of a constant need to update skills and knowledge, most customer service representatives continue to receive instruction and training throughout their career. This is particularly true of workers in industries such as banking, in which regulations and products are continually changing.

Although some positions may require previous industry, office, or customer service experience, many customer service jobs are entry level. Customer service jobs are often good introductory positions into a company or an industry. In some cases, experienced workers can move up within the company into supervisory or managerial positions or they may move into areas such as product development, in which they can use their knowledge to improve products and services.

Within insurance agencies and brokerages, however, a customer service representative job usually is not an entry-level position. Workers must have previous experience in insurance and are often required by State regulations to be licensed like insurance sales agents. A variety of designations are available to demonstrate that a candidate has sufficient knowledge and skill, and continuing education and training are often offered through the employer. As they gain more knowledge of industry products and services, customer service representatives in insurance may advance to other, higher level positions, such as insurance sales agent.

Employment

Customer service representatives held about 2.1 million jobs in 2004. Although they were found in a variety of industries, about 1 in 4 customer service representatives worked in finance and insurance. The largest numbers were employed by insurance carriers, insurance agencies and brokerages, and banks and credit unions.

About 1 in 8 customer service representatives were employed in administrative and support services. These workers were concentrated in the business support services industry (which includes telephone call centers) and employment services (which includes temporary help services and employment placement agencies). Another 1in 8 customer service representatives were employed in retail trade establishments such as general merchandise stores, food and beverage stores, or nonstore retailers. Other industries that employ significant numbers of customer service representatives include information, particularly the telecommunications industry; manufacturing, such as printing and related support activities; and wholesale trade.

Although they are found in all States, customer service representatives who work in call centers tend to be concentrated geographically. Four States—California, Texas, Florida, and New York—employ 30 percent of customer service representatives. Delaware, Arizona, South Dakota, and Utah, have the highest concentration of workers in this occupation, with customer service representatives comprising over 2 percent of total employment in these States.

Job Outlook

Prospects for obtaining a job in this field are expected to be excellent, with more job openings than jobseekers. Bilingual jobseekers, in particular, may enjoy favorable job prospects. In addition to many new openings occurring as businesses and organizations expand, numerous job openings will result from the need to replace experienced customer service representatives who transfer to other occupations or leave the labor force. Replacement needs are expected to be significant in this large occupation because many young people work as customer service representatives before switching to other jobs. This occupation is well suited to flexible work schedules, and many opportunities for part-time work will continue to be available, particularly as organizations attempt to cut labor costs by hiring more temporary workers.

Employment of customer service representatives is expected to increase faster than the average for all occupations through the year 2014. Beyond growth stemming from expansion of the industries in which customer service representatives are employed, a need for additional customer service representatives is likely to result from

heightened reliance on these workers. Customer service is critical to the success of any organization that deals with customers, and strong customer service can build sales and visibility as companies try to distinguish themselves from competitors. In many industries, gaining a competitive edge and retaining customers will be increasingly important over the next decade. This is particularly true in industries such as financial services, communications, and utilities, which already employ numerous customer service representatives. As the trend toward consolidation in industries continues, centralized call centers will provide an effective method for delivering a high level of customer service. As a result, employment of customer service representatives may grow at a faster rate in call centers than in other areas. However, this growth may be tempered: a variety of factors, including technological improvements, make it increasingly feasible and cost-effective for call centers to be built or relocated outside of the United States.

Technology is affecting the occupation in many ways. The Internet and automated teller machines have provided customers with means of obtaining information and conducting transactions that do not entail interacting with another person. Technology also allows for a greater streamlining of processes, while at the same time increasing the productivity of workers. The use of computer software to filter e-mails, generating automatic responses or directing messages to the appropriate representative, and the use of similar systems to answer or route telephone inquiries are likely to become more prevalent in the future. Also, with rapidly improving telecommunications, some organizations have begun to position their call centers overseas.

Despite such developments, the need for customer service representatives is expected to remain strong. In many ways, technology has heightened consumers' expectations for information and services, and availability of information online seems to have generated more need for customer service representatives, particularly to respond to e-mail. Also, technology cannot replace human skills. As more sophisticated technologies are able to resolve many customers' questions and concerns, the nature of the inquiries to be handled by customer service representatives is likely to become increasingly complex.

Furthermore, the job responsibilities of customer service representatives are expanding. As companies downsize or take other measures to increase profitability, workers are being trained to perform additional duties such as opening bank accounts or cross-selling products. As a result, employers may increasingly prefer customer service representatives who have education beyond high school, such as some college or even a college degree.

While jobs in some industries, such as retail trade, may be affected by economic downturns, the customer service occupation is generally resistant to major fluctuations in employment.

Earnings

In May 2004, median annual earnings for wage and salary customer service representatives were $27,020. The middle 50 percent earned between $21,510 and $34,560. The lowest 10 percent earned less than $17,680, and the highest 10 percent earned more than $44,160.

Earnings for customer service representatives vary according to level of skill required, experience, training, location, and size of firm. Median annual earnings in the industries employing the largest numbers of these workers in May 2004 are shown below:

Insurance carriers	$29,790
Agencies, brokerages, and other insurance related activities	28,800
Depository credit intermediation	26,140
Employment services	23,100
Business support services	21,390

In addition to receiving an hourly wage, full-time customer service representatives who work evenings, nights, weekends, or holidays may receive shift differential pay. Also, because call centers are often open during extended hours, or even 24 hours a day, some customer service representatives have the benefit of being able to work a schedule that does not conform to the traditional workweek. Other benefits can include life and health insurance, pensions, bonuses, employer-provided training, and discounts on the products and services the company offers.

Related Occupations

Customer service representatives interact with customers to provide information in response to inquiries about products and services and to handle and resolve complaints. Other occupations in which workers have similar dealings with customers and the public are information and record clerks; financial clerks, such as tellers and new-account clerks; insurance sales agents; securities, commodities, and financial services sales agents; retail salespersons; computer support specialists; and gaming services workers.

Sources of Additional Information

State employment service offices can provide information about employment opportunities for customer service representatives.

File Clerks

(O*NET 43-4071.00)

Significant Points

- About 3 out of 10 file clerks work part time.
- A high school diploma or its equivalent is the most common educational requirement.
- Employment is expected to decline through the year 2014.

Nature of the Work

The amount of information generated by organizations continues to grow rapidly. File clerks classify, store, retrieve, and update this information. In many small offices, they often have additional responsibilities, such as entering data, performing word processing, sorting mail, and operating copying or fax machines. File clerks are employed across the Nation by organizations of all types.

File clerks, also called record, information, or record center clerks, examine incoming material and code it numerically, alphabetically, or by subject matter. They then store paper forms, letters, receipts, or reports or enter necessary information into other storage devices. Some clerks operate mechanized files that rotate to bring the needed records to them; others convert documents to film that is then stored on microforms, such as microfilm or microfiche. A growing number of file clerks use imaging systems that scan paper files or film and store the material on computers.

In order for records to be useful, they must be up to date and accurate. File clerks ensure that new information is added to files in a timely manner and may discard outdated file materials or transfer them to inactive storage. Clerks also check files at regular intervals to make sure that all items are correctly sequenced and placed. When records cannot be found, file clerks attempt to locate the missing material. As an organization's needs for information change, file clerks implement changes to the filing system.

When records are requested, file clerks locate them and give them to the person requesting them. A record may be a sheet of paper stored in a file cabinet or an image on microform. In the former case, the clerk retrieves the document manually and hands or forwards it to the requester. In the latter case, the clerk retrieves the microform and displays it on a microform reader. If necessary, file clerks make copies of records and distribute them. In addition, they keep track of materials removed from the files, to ensure that borrowed files are returned.

Increasingly, file clerks are using computerized filing and retrieval systems that have a variety of storage devices, such as a mainframe computer, CD-ROM, or floppy disk. To retrieve a document in these systems, the clerk enters the document's identification code, obtains the location of the document, and gets the document for the patron. Accessing files in a computer database is much quicker than locating and physically retrieving paper files. Still, even when files are stored electronically, backup paper or electronic copies usually are also kept.

Working Conditions

File clerks usually work in areas that are clean, well lit, and relatively quiet. The work is not overly strenuous but may involve a lot of standing, walking, reaching, pulling, and bending, depending on the method used to retrieve files. Prolonged exposure to computer screens may lead to eyestrain for the many file clerks who work with computers.

Training, Other Qualifications, and Advancement

Most employers prefer applicants with a high school diploma or its equivalent or a mix of education and related experience. File clerks must be able to work with others since part of the job may consist of helping fellow workers. These workers must be alert, accurate, and able to make quick decisions. Also, willingness to do routine and detailed work is important.

Most new employees are trained on the job under close supervision of more experienced employees. Proficiency with desktop computer software is becoming increasingly important as more files are now being stored electronically. These workers can advance to more senior clerical office positions such as receptionist or bookkeeping clerk.

File clerks classify, store, and retrieve large amounts of information.

Employment

File clerks held about 255,000 jobs in 2004. Although file clerk jobs are found in nearly every sector of the economy, more than 90 percent of these workers are employed in service-providing industries, including government. Healthcare establishments employed around 1 out of every 4 file clerks. About 3 out of every 10 file clerks worked part time in 2004.

Job Outlook

Employment of file clerks is expected to decline through the year 2014 largely due to productivity gains stemming from office automation and the consolidation of clerical jobs. Most files are stored digitally and can be retrieved electronically, reducing the demand for file clerks. Nonetheless, there will be some job opportunities for file clerks as a large number of workers will be needed to replace workers who leave the occupation each year. Job turnover among file clerks reflects the lack of formal training requirements, limited advancement potential, and relatively low pay. Demand for file clerks stems from the need for these workers to record and retrieve information in organizations across the economy

Jobseekers who have typing and other secretarial skills and who are familiar with a wide range of office machines, especially personal computers, should have the best job opportunities. File clerks should find opportunities for temporary or part-time work, especially during peak business periods.

Earnings

Median hourly earnings of file clerks in May 2004 were $10.11. The middle 50 percent earned between $8.22 and $12.59. The lowest 10 percent earned less than $6.97, and the highest 10 percent earned more than $15.72. Median hourly earnings in the industries employing the largest number of file clerks in May 2004 are shown below:

Local government	$11.79
General medical and surgical hospitals	10.38
Legal services	10.32
Employment services	10.06
Offices of physicians	9.07

Related Occupations

File clerks classify and retrieve files. Other workers who perform similar duties include receptionists and information clerks and stock clerks and order fillers.

Sources of Additional Information

State employment service offices and agencies can provide information about job openings for file clerks.

Hotel, Motel, and Resort Desk Clerks

(O*NET 43-4081.00)

Significant Points

- Job opportunities should be plentiful, because of substantial replacement needs.

- Evening, weekend, and part-time work hours create potential for flexible schedules.

- Professional appearance and personality are more important than formal academic training in landing a job.

Nature of the Work

Hotel, motel, and resort desk clerks perform a variety of services for guests of hotels, motels, and other lodging establishments. Regardless of the type of accommodation, most desk clerks have similar responsibilities. They register arriving guests, assign rooms, and check out guests at the end of their stay. They also keep records of room assignments and other registration-related information on computers. When guests check out, desk clerks prepare and explain the charges, as well as process payments.

Front-desk clerks always are in the public eye and typically are the first line of customer service for a lodging property. Their attitude and behavior greatly influence the public's impressions of the establishment. And as such, they always must be courteous and helpful. Desk clerks answer questions about services, checkout times, the local community, or other matters of public interest. Clerks also report problems with guest rooms or public facilities to members of the housekeeping or maintenance staff for them to correct the problems. In larger hotels or in larger cities, desk clerks may refer queries about area attractions to a concierge and may direct more complicated questions to the appropriate manager.

In some smaller hotels and motels, where smaller staffs are employed, clerks may take on a variety of additional responsibilities, such as bringing fresh linens to rooms, which usually are performed by employees in other departments of larger lodging establishments. In the smaller places, desk clerks often are responsible for all front-office operations, information, and services. For example, they may perform the work of a bookkeeper, advance reservation agent, cashier, laundry attendant, and telephone switchboard operator.

Working Conditions

Hotels are open around the clock creating the need for night and weekend work. Extended hours of operation also afford the many part-time job seekers an opportunity to find work in these establishments, especially on evenings and late-night shifts or on weekends and holidays. About half of all desk clerks work a 35 to 40 hour week—most of the rest work fewer hours—so the jobs are attractive to persons seeking part-time work or jobs with flexible schedules. Most clerks work in areas that are clean, well lit, and relatively quiet, although lobbies can become crowded and noisy when busy. Many hotels have stringent dress guidelines for desk clerks.

Desk clerks may experience particularly hectic times during check-in and check-out times or incur the pressures encountered when dealing with convention guests or large groups of tourists

Hotel, motel, and resort desk clerks answer questions about lodging services, checkout times, the local community, or other matters of public interest.

at one time. Moreover, dealing with irate guests can be stressful. Computer failures can further complicate an already busy time and add to stress levels. Hotel desk clerks may be on their feet most of the time and may occasionally be asked to lift heavy guest luggage.

Training, Other Qualifications, and Advancement
Hotel, motel, and resort desk clerks deal directly with the public, so a professional appearance and a pleasant personality are important. A clear speaking voice and fluency in English also are essential, because these employees talk directly with hotel guests and the public and frequently use the telephone or public-address systems. Good spelling and computer literacy are needed, because most of the work involves use of a computer. In addition, speaking a foreign language fluently is increasingly helpful, because of the growing international clientele of many properties.

Most hotel, motel, and resort desk clerks receive orientation and training on the job. Orientation may include an explanation of the job duties and information about the establishment, such as the arrangement of sleeping rooms, availability of additional services, such as a business or fitness center, and location of guest facilities, such as ice and vending machines, restaurants and other nearby retail stores. New employees learn job tasks through on-the-job training under the guidance of a supervisor or an experienced desk clerk. They often receive additional training on interpersonal or customer service skills and on how to use the computerized reservation, room assignment, and billing systems and equipment. Desk clerks typically continue to receive instruction on new procedures and on company policies after their initial training ends.

Formal academic training generally is not required so many students take jobs as desk clerks on evening or weekend shifts or during school vacation periods. Most employers look for people who are friendly and customer-service oriented, well groomed, and display the maturity and self confidence to demonstrate good judgment. Desk clerks, especially in high-volume and higher-end properties should be quick-thinking, show initiative, and be able to work as a member of a team. Hotel managers typically look for these personal characteristics when hiring first-time desk clerks, because it is easier to teach company policy and computer skills than personality traits.

Large hotel and motel chains may offer better opportunities for advancement than small, independently owned establishments. The large chains have more extensive career ladder programs and may offer desk clerks an opportunity to participate in a management training program. Also, the Educational Institute of the American Hotel and Motel Association offers home-study or group-study courses in lodging management, which may help some obtain promotions more rapidly.

Employment
Hotel, motel, and resort desk clerks held about 195,000 jobs in 2004. Virtually all were in hotels, motels, and other establishments in the accommodation industry. Few were self employed.

Job Outlook
Employment of hotel, motel, and resort desk clerks is expected to grow about as fast as the average for all occupations through 2014, as more hotels, motels, and other lodging establishments are built and occupancy rates rise. Job opportunities for hotel and motel desk clerks also will result from a need to replace workers, because many of these clerks either transfer to other occupations that offer better pay and advancement opportunities or simply leave the workforce altogether. Opportunities for part-time work should continue to be plentiful, because these businesses typically are staffed 24 hours a day, 7 days a week.

Employment of hotel and motel desk clerks should benefit from an increase in business and leisure travel. Shifts in preferences away from long vacations and toward long weekends and other, more frequent, shorter trips also should boost demand for these workers, because such stays increase the number of nights spent in hotels. While many lower budget and extended-stay establishments are being built to cater to families and the leisure traveler, many new luxury and resort accommodations also are opening to serve the upscale client. With the increased number of units requiring staff, employment opportunities for desk clerks should be good.

Growth of hotel, motel, and resort desk clerk jobs will be moderated by technology. Automated check-in and check-out procedures reduce the backlog of guests waiting for desk service and may reduce peak front desk staffing needs in many establishments. Nevertheless, the front desk remains the principal point of contact for guests at most properties and most will continue to have clerks on duty.

Employment of desk clerks is sensitive to cyclical swings in the economy. During recessions, vacation and business travel declines, and hotels and motels need fewer desk clerks. Similarly, employment is affected by special events, business and convention business, and seasonal fluctuations.

Earnings
Median annual earnings of hotel, motel and resort desk clerks were $17,700 in May 2004. The middle 50 percent earned between $15,190 and $21,270. The lowest 10 percent earned less than $13,040, while the highest 10 percent earned more than $25,200.

Earnings of hotel, motel and resort desk clerks vary by a number of seasonal or geographic factors, such as whether the establishment is in a major metropolitan area, a resort community, or other economic or regional characteristic. Earnings also will vary according to the size of the hotel and the level of service offered. For example, luxury hotels that offer guests more personal attention and a greater number of services typically have stricter and more demanding requirements for their desk staff. However, these higher standards of service also result in higher earnings for employees.

Related Occupations
Other positions in the hospitality industry include lodging managers. Occupations that also require workers to deal face-to-face with the public include counter and rental clerks, customer service representatives, receptionists and information clerks, and retail salespersons.

Sources of Additional Information
Information on careers in the lodging industry, as well as information about professional development and training programs, may be obtained from:
➤ Educational Institute of the American Hotel and Lodging Association, 800 N. Magnolia Ave., Suite 1800, Orlando, FL 32803. Internet: **http://www.ei-ahma.org**

Human Resources Assistants, Except Payroll and Timekeeping

(O*NET 43-4161.00)

Significant Points

- About 1 out of 4 work for Federal, State, and local governments.
- Employment will grow as human resources assistants assume more responsibilities.
- Computer, communication, and interpersonal skills are important.

Human resources assistants maintain the records of an organization's employees.

Nature of the Work

Human resources assistants maintain the human resource records of an organization's employees. These records include information such as name, address, job title, and earnings; benefits such as health and life insurance; and tax withholding. On a daily basis, these assistants record information and answer questions about employee absences and supervisory reports on employees' job performance. When an employee receives a promotion or switches health insurance plans, the human resources assistant updates the appropriate form. Human resources assistants also may prepare reports for managers elsewhere within the organization. For example, they might compile a list of employees eligible for an award.

In small organizations, some human resources assistants perform a variety of other clerical duties, including answering telephone or written inquiries from the public, sending out announcements of job openings or job examinations, and issuing application forms. When credit bureaus and finance companies request confirmation of a person's employment, the human resources assistant provides authorized information from the employee's personnel records. Assistants also may contact payroll departments and insurance companies to verify changes to records.

Some human resources assistants are involved in hiring. They screen job applicants to obtain information such as their education and work experience; administer aptitude, personality, and interest tests; explain the organization's employment policies and refer qualified applicants to the employing official; and request references from present or past employers. Also, human resources assistants inform job applicants, by telephone or letter, of their acceptance for or denial of employment.

In some job settings, human resources assistants have specific job titles. For example, *assignment clerks* notify a firm's existing employees of upcoming vacancies, identify applicants who qualify for the vacancies, and assign those who are qualified to various positions. They also keep track of vacancies that arise throughout the organization, and they complete and distribute forms advertising vacancies. When filled-out applications are returned, these clerks review and verify the information in them, using personnel records. After a selection for a position is made, they notify all of the applicants of their acceptance or rejection.

As another example, *identification clerks* are responsible for security matters at defense installations. They compile and record personal data about vendors, contractors, and civilian and military personnel and their dependents. The identification clerk's job duties include interviewing applicants; corresponding with law enforcement authorities; and preparing badges, passes, and identification cards.

Working Conditions

Human resources assistants usually work in clean, pleasant, and comfortable office settings. Assistants usually work a standard 35- to 40-hour week. Prolonged exposure to video display terminals may lead to eyestrain for assistants who work with computers.

Training, Other Qualifications, and Advancement

Most employers prefer applicants with a high school diploma or GED. Generally, training beyond high school is not required. However, training in computers, in filing and maintaining filing systems, in organizing, and in human resources practices is desirable. Proficiency using Microsoft Word, Excel, and other computer applications also is very desirable. Many of these skills can be learned in a vocational high school program aimed at office careers, and the remainder can be learned on the job.

Formal training is available at a small number of colleges, most of which offer diploma programs in office automation. Many proprietary schools also offer such programs.

Human resources assistants must be able to interact and communicate with individuals at all levels of the organization. In addition, assistants should demonstrate poise, tactfulness, diplomacy, and good interpersonal skills in order to handle sensitive and confidential situations.

Employment

Human resources assistants held about 172,000 jobs in 2004. About 1 out of 4 work for Federal, State, and local governments. Other jobs for human resources assistants were in various industries such as health care; management of companies and enterprises; finance and insurance; and administrative and support services.

Job Outlook

Employment of human resources assistants is expected to grow about as fast as the average for all occupations through 2014, as assistants assume more responsibilities. For example, workers conduct Internet research to locate resumes, they must be able to scan resumes of job candidates quickly and efficiently, and they must be increasingly sensitive to confidential information such as salaries and Social Security numbers. In a favorable job market, more emphasis is placed on human resources departments, thus increasing the demand for assistants. However, even in economic downturns there is demand for assistants, as human resources departments in all industries try to make their organizations more efficient by determining what type of employees to hire and strategically filling job openings. Human resources assistants may play an instrumental role in their organization's human resources policies. For example, they may talk to staffing firms and consulting firms, conduct other research, and then offer their ideas on issues such as whether to hire temporary contract workers or full-time staff.

As with other office and administrative support occupations, the growing use of computers in human resources departments means that much of the data entry that is done by human resources assistants can be eliminated, as employees themselves enter the data and send the electronic file to the human resources office. Such an arrangement, which is most feasible in large organizations with multiple human resources offices, could limit job growth among human resources assistants.

In addition to positions arising from job growth, replacement needs will account for many job openings for human resources assistants as they advance within the human resources department, take jobs unrelated to human resources administration, or leave the labor force.

Earnings

Median annual earnings of human resources assistants in May 2004 were $31,750. The middle 50 percent earned between $25,780 and $38,770. The lowest 10 percent earned less than $21,250 and the highest 10 percent earned more than $45,780. Median annual earnings in the industries employing the largest number of human resources assistants in May 2004 were:

Federal Government	$35,490
Elementary and secondary schools	33,030
Local government	32,460
Management of companies and enterprises	30,930
General medical and surgical hospitals	29,390

In 2005, the Federal Government typically paid salaries ranging from $20,984 to $88,103 a year. Beginning human resources assistants with a high school diploma or 6 months of experience were paid an average annual salary of $20,984. The average salary for all human resources assistants employed by the Federal Government was $36,576 in 2005.

Some employers offer educational assistance to human resources assistants.

Related Occupations

Human resources assistants maintain the personnel records of an organization's employees. On a daily basis, these assistants record information and answer questions about employee absences and supervisory reports on employees' job performance. Other workers with similar skills and expertise in interpersonal relations include bookkeeping, accounting, and auditing clerks; communications equipment operators; customer service representatives; data entry and information processing workers; order clerks; receptionists and information clerks; secretaries and administrative assistants; stock clerks and order fillers; and tellers.

Sources of Additional Information

For information about human resource careers and certification, contact:

➤ Society for Human Resource Management, 1800 Duke St., Alexandria, VA 22314. Internet: **http://www.shrm.org**

Interviewers

(O*NET 43-4061.01, 43-4061.02, 43-4111.00, 43-4131.00)

Significant Points

● A high school diploma or its equivalent is the most common educational requirement.

● The number of interviewers, except eligibility and loan, is projected to grow faster than average; however, the number of loan interviewers and clerks, and eligibility interviewers for government programs, is projected to decline.

Nature of the Work

Interviewers obtain information from individuals and business representatives who are opening bank accounts, trying to obtain loans, seeking admission to medical facilities, participating in consumer surveys, applying to receive aid from government programs, or providing data for various other purposes. By mail, by telephone, or in person, these workers solicit and verify information, create files, and perform a number of other related tasks.

The specific duties and job titles of *interviewers, except eligibility and loan*, depend upon the type of employer. In doctors' offices and other health care facilities, for example, *interviewing clerks* also are known as *admitting interviewers* or *patient representatives*. These workers obtain all preliminary information required for a patient's record or for his or her admission to a hospital, such as the patient's name, address, age, medical history, present medications, previous hospitalizations, religion, persons to notify in case of emergency, attending physician, and party responsible for payment. In some cases, interviewing clerks may be required to verify that an individual is eligible for health benefits or to work out financing options for those who might need them.

Other duties of interviewers in health care include assigning patients to rooms and summoning escorts to take patients to their rooms; sometimes, interviewers may escort patients themselves. Using the facility's computer system, interviewers schedule laboratory work, x rays, and surgeries; prepare admission and discharge records; and route these medical records to appropriate departments. They also may bill patients, receive payments, and answer the telephone. In an outpatient or office setting, interviewers schedule appointments, keep track of cancellations, and provide general information about care. In addition, the role of the admissions staff, particularly in hospitals, is expanding to include a wide range of patient services, from assisting patients with financial and medical questions to helping family members find hotel rooms.

Interviewing clerks who conduct market research surveys and polls for research firms have somewhat different responsibilities. These interviewers ask a series of prepared questions, record the responses, and forward the results to management. They may ask individuals questions about their occupation and earnings, political preferences, buying habits, satisfaction with certain goods or services sold to them, or other aspects of their lives. Although most interviews are conducted over the telephone, some are conducted in focus groups or by randomly polling people in a public place. More recently, the Internet is being used to elicit people's opinions. Almost all interviewers use computers or similar devices to enter the responses to questions.

Eligibility interviewers, government programs, determine the eligibility of individuals applying to receive government assistance, such as welfare, unemployment benefits, Social Security benefits, and public housing. These interviewers gather the relevant personal and financial information on an applicant and, on the basis of the rules and regulations of the particular government program, grant, modify, deny, or terminate an individual's eligibility for the program in question. They also help to detect fraud committed by persons who try to obtain benefits that they are not eligible to receive.

Loan interviewers and clerks review individuals' credit history and obtain the information needed to determine the creditworthiness of applicants for loans and credit cards. These workers spend much of their day on the telephone, obtaining information from credit bureaus, employers, banks, credit institutions, and other sources to determine an applicant's credit history and ability to pay back a loan or charge.

Loan clerks, also called *loan processing clerks, loan closers*, or *loan service clerks*, assemble documents pertaining to a loan, process the paperwork associated with the loan, and ensure that all information is complete and verified. Mortgage loans are the primary type of loan handled by loan clerks, who also may have to order appraisals of the property, set up escrow accounts, and secure any additional information required to transfer the property.

Interviewers ask specific questions, record answers, and may assist persons with completing applications.

The specific duties of loan clerks vary by specialty. Loan closers, for example, complete the loan process by gathering the proper documents for signature at the closing, including deeds of trust, property insurance papers, and title commitments. They set the time and place for the closing, make sure that all parties are present, and ensure that all conditions for settlement have been met. After the settlement, the loan closer records all of the documents involved and submits the final package to the owner of the loan. Loan service clerks maintain the payment records on a loan once it is issued. These clerical workers process the paperwork for payment of fees to insurance companies and tax authorities, and also may record changes in clients' addresses and ownership of a loan. When necessary, they answer calls from customers with routine inquiries as well.

Loan interviewers have duties that are similar to those of loan clerks. They interview potential borrowers; help them fill out applications for loans; investigate the applicant's background and references; verify the information on the application; and forward any findings, reports, or documents to the company's appraisal department. Finally, interviewers inform the applicant as to whether the loan has been accepted or denied.

Working Conditions
Working conditions vary for different types of interviewers, but most of these workers work in areas that are clean, well lit, and relatively quiet. Most of these workers work a standard 35 to 40 hour week, but evening and weekend work may be required in some establishments. Some interviewers may conduct surveys on the street or in shopping malls, or they may even go door to door.

Training, Other Qualifications, and Advancement
Most employers prefer applicants with a high school diploma or its equivalent or a mix of education and related experience. Because interviewers deal with the public, they must have a pleasant personality, clear speaking voice, and professional appearance. Familiarity with computers and strong interpersonal skills are very important. Fluency in a foreign language also can be beneficial.

New employees are generally trained on the job, working under the close supervision of more experienced employees, although some firms offer formal training. Some loan interviewers also take courses in credit offered by banking and credit associations, public and private vocational schools, and colleges and universities.

Experienced interviewers may advance to positions with added responsibilities or supervisory duties. Many organizations elect to fill open positions by promoting qualified individuals from within the company. Interviewers who obtain additional skills or training will have the best opportunities. For certain managerial positions, a college degree may be required.

Employment
Interviewers held about 515,000 jobs in 2004. Approximately 199,000 were interviewers, except eligibility and loan; 218,000 were loan interviewers and clerks; and 98,000 were eligibility interviewers, government programs. About 2 out of every 5 interviewers, except eligibility and loan, worked in health care and social assistance industries, while most loan interviewers and clerks worked in financial institutions. Almost all eligibility interviewers, government programs, worked in State and local government. Around 1 out of every 4 interviewers, except eligibility and loan, worked part time.

Job Outlook
Employment of interviewers is expected to grow more slowly than the average for all occupations through 2014. However, the projected change in employment varies by specialty. Most job openings should arise from the need to replace the numerous interviewers who leave the occupation or the labor force each year. Prospects for filling these openings will be best for applicants with a broad range of job skills, such as good customer service, math, and telephone skills. In addition to openings for full-time jobs, opportunities also should be available for part-time and temporary jobs.

The number of interviewers, except eligibility and loan, is projected to grow faster than average, reflecting growth in the health care and social assistance sector. This sector will hire more admissions interviewers as health care facilities consolidate staff and expand the role of the admissions staff and as an aging and growing population requires more visits to health care practitioners. In addition, an increasing use of market research will create more jobs requiring interviewers to collect data. In the future, though, more market research is expected to be conducted over the Internet, thus reducing the need for telephone interviewers to make individual calls.

The number of loan interviewers and clerks is projected to decline due to advances in technology that are making these workers more productive. Despite a projected increase in the number of applications for loans, automation will increase productivity so that fewer workers will be required to process, check, and authorize applications than in the past. The effects of automation on employment will be moderated, however, by the many interpersonal aspects of the job. Mortgage loans, for example, require loan processors to personally verify financial data on the application, and loan closers are needed to assemble documents and prepare them for settlement. Employment, however, also will be adversely affected by changes in the financial services industry. For example, significant consolidation has occurred among mortgage loan servicing companies. As a result, fewer mortgage banking companies are involved in servicing loans, making the function more efficient and reducing the need for loan service clerks.

The job outlook for loan interviewers and clerks is sensitive to overall economic activity. A downturn in the economy or a rise in interest rates usually leads to a decline in the demand for loans, particularly mortgage loans, and can result in layoffs. Even in slow economic times, however, job openings will arise from the need to replace workers who leave the occupation for various reasons.

Like that of loan interviewers and clerks, employment of eligibility interviewers for government programs also is projected to decline due to advances in technology and the transformation of government aid programs over the last decade. Automation should have a significant effect on these workers because, as with credit and loan ratings, eligibility for government aid programs can be determined instantaneously by entering information into a computer. The job outlook for eligibility interviewers, however, also is sensitive to overall economic activity; a severe slowdown in the economy will cause more people to apply for government aid programs, increasing demand for eligibility interviewers.

Earnings

Median hourly earnings of eligibility interviewers, government programs, in May 2004 were $15.92. The middle 50 percent earned between $13.04 and $19.32. The lowest 10 percent earned less than $11.19, and the highest 10 percent earned more than $21.83. Median hourly earnings of eligibility interviewers, government programs, was $15.67 in State government and $16.43 in local government in May 2004.

Median hourly earnings of loan interviewers and clerks in May 2004 were $13.94. The middle 50 percent earned between $11.45 and $17.26. The lowest 10 percent earned less than $9.48, and the highest 10 percent earned more than $21.20. Median hourly earnings of loan interviewers and clerks in depository credit intermediation was $13.13 in May 2004, while median hourly earnings in nondepository credit intermediation was $14.48.

Median hourly earnings of interviewers, except eligibility and loan, in May 2004 were $11.38. The middle 50 percent earned between $9.19 and $13.93. The lowest 10 percent earned less than $7.57, and the highest 10 percent earned more than $16.98. Median hourly earnings in the industries employing the largest number of interviewers, except eligibility and loan, in May 2004 were as follows:

State government	$16.78
Colleges, universities, and professional schools	13.55
General medical and surgical hospitals	11.94
Scientific research and development services	10.71
Other professional, scientific, and technical services	8.89

Related Occupations

Interviewers obtain information from individuals. Other workers who perform similar duties include procurement clerks, customer service representatives, and bill and account collectors.

Sources of Additional Information

State employment service offices can provide information about employment opportunities for interviewers.

For specific information on a career as a loan processor or loan closer, contact:

➤ Mortgage Bankers Association, 1919 Pennsylvania Ave. NW., Washington, DC 20006. Internet: **http://www.mortgagebankers.org**

Library Assistants, Clerical

(O*NET 43-4121.00)

Significant Points

- Minimal training requirements and flexible schedules make this occupation appealing to students, retirees, and others interested in part-time work.

- Most libraries use electronic cataloging systems so computers skills are essential.

Nature of the Work

Library assistants, clerical—sometimes referred to as *library media assistants, library aides,* or *circulation assistants*—assist librarians and library technicians in organizing library resources and making them available to users. (Librarians and library technicians are discussed elsewhere in the *Handbook.*) Library assistants register patrons so that they can borrow materials from the library and then issue a library card.

At the circulation desk, library assistants lend and collect books, periodicals, videotapes, and other materials. When an item is borrowed, assistants scan the patron's library card and the material to record the transaction in the library database; they then print a receipt with the due date or stamp the due date on the item. When an item is returned, assistants inspect returned materials for damage and enter the materials into the circulation database. Electronic circulation systems are able to automatically generate overdue notices reminding patrons that their materials are overdue, but library assistants review the record for accuracy before sending out the notice. They also answer patrons' questions and refer those they cannot answer to a librarian.

Throughout the library, assistants sort returned books, periodicals, and other items and put them on their designated shelves, in the appropriate files, or in storage areas. They locate materials to be lent, to either a patron or another library. Because nearly all card catalogues are computerized, library assistants must be familiar with computers. Before reshelving returned materials, if they notice any damage, these workers try to repair it. For example, they may use tape or paste to repair torn pages or book covers and use other specialized processes to repair more valuable materials.

Some library assistants specialize in helping patrons who have vision problems. Sometimes referred to as *library, talking-books,* or *braille-and-talking-books clerks,* they review the borrower's list of desired reading materials. They locate those materials or closely related substitutes from the library collection of large-type or braille volumes, tape cassettes, and open-reel talking books; complete the requisite paperwork; and give or mail the materials to the borrower.

Working Conditions

Library assistants who prepare library materials may sit at desks or computer terminals for long periods and can develop headaches or eyestrain from working with the terminals. Some duties can be repetitive and boring, such as shelving new or returned materials. Others can be rewarding, such as assisting patrons who are performing computer searches with the use of local and regional library networks and cooperatives. Library assistants may lift and carry books, climb ladders to reach high stacks, and bend low to shelve books on bottom shelves.

Library assistants sort and reshelve returned items.

Library assistants in school libraries work regular school hours. Those in public libraries and college and university (academic) libraries also work weekends, evenings and some holidays. About half of all library assistants work part time, making the job appealing to retirees, students, and others interested in flexible schedules.

Training, Other Qualifications, and Advancement
Training requirements for library assistants are generally minimal; most libraries prefer to hire workers with a high school diploma or GED, but little to no formal postsecondary training is expected. Some employers hire individuals with experience in other clerical jobs, while others train inexperienced workers on the job. Given the rapid spread of automation in libraries, computer skills are needed for most jobs; knowledge of databases and other library automation systems is especially useful.

Library assistants usually advance by assuming added responsibilities. Many begin by performing simple jobs such as shelving books or cataloging new books and periodicals when they arrive. After gaining experience, they may move into positions that allow them to interact with patrons, such as manning the circulation desk. Experienced aids may be able to advance into library technician positions, which involve more responsibility in providing library services to patrons.

Employment
Library assistants held about 109,000 jobs in 2004. More than half of these workers were employed by local governments in public libraries; most of the remaining employees worked in school, college, and university libraries. Opportunities for flexible schedules are abundant; nearly half of these workers were on part-time schedules.

Job Outlook
Employment of library assistants is expected to grow as fast as the average for all occupations through 2014. Efforts to contain costs in local governments and academic institutions of all types may result in more hiring of library support staff than librarians. Also, due to changing roles within libraries, library assistants are taking on more responsibility.

Many library assistants leave this relatively low-paying occupation for other jobs that offer higher pay or full-time work, so job opportunities should be good for persons interested in jobs as library assistants. The work is often attractive to retirees, students, and others who want a part-time schedule, and there is a lot of movement into and out of the occupation. Some positions become available as library assistants move within the organization. Library assistants can be promoted to library technicians and, eventually, supervisory positions in public-service or technical-service areas. Advancement opportunities are greater in large libraries.

Because most are employed by public institutions, library assistants are not directly affected by the ups and downs of the business cycle. However, some of these workers may lose their jobs if there are cuts in government budgets.

Earnings
Median hourly earnings of library assistants, clerical were $9.96 in May 2004. The middle 50 percent earned between $7.77 and $12.89. The lowest 10 percent earned less than $6.41, and the highest 10 percent earned more than $16.08.

Sources of Additional Information
Information about a career as a library assistant can be obtained from either of the following organizations:
➤ Council on Library/Media Technology, P.O. Box 42048, Mesa, AZ 85274-2048. Internet: **http://colt.ucr.edu**

➤ American Library Association, 50 East Huron St., Chicago, IL 60611. Internet: **http://www.ala.org/hrdr**

Public libraries and libraries in academic institutions also can provide information about job openings for library assistants.

Order Clerks

(O*NET 43-4151.00)

Significant Points

● Employment is expected to decline because of growth in online retailing and in business-to-business electronic commerce, and the use of automated systems that make placing orders easy and convenient.

● A high school diploma or its equivalent is the most common educational requirement.

Nature of the Work
Order clerks receive and process orders for a variety of goods or services, such as spare parts for machines, consumer appliances, gas and electric power connections, film rentals, and articles of clothing. They sometimes are called order-entry clerks, sales representatives, order processors, or order takers.

Orders for materials, merchandise, or services can come from inside or from outside of an organization. In large companies with many worksites, such as automobile manufacturers, clerks order parts and equipment from the company's warehouses. Inside order clerks receive orders from other workers employed by the same company or from salespersons in the field.

Many other order clerks, however, receive orders from outside companies or individuals. Order clerks in wholesale businesses, for instance, receive orders from retail establishments for merchandise that the retailer, in turn, sells to the public. An increasing number of order clerks are working for catalog companies and online retailers, receiving orders from individual customers by telephone, fax, regular mail, or e-mail. Order clerks dealing primarily with the public sometimes are referred to as outside order clerks.

Computers provide order clerks with ready access to information such as stock numbers, prices, and inventory. The successful filling of an order frequently depends on having the right products in stock and being able to determine which products are most appropriate for the customer's needs. Some order clerks—especially those in industrial settings—must be able to give price estimates for entire jobs, not just single parts. Others must be able to take special orders, give expected arrival dates, prepare contracts, and handle complaints.

Many order clerks receive orders directly by telephone, entering the required information as the customer places the order. However, a rapidly increasing number of orders now are received through computer systems, the Internet, faxes, and e-mail. In some cases, these orders are sent directly from the customer's terminal to the order clerk's terminal. Orders received by regular mail are sometimes scanned into a database that is instantly accessible to clerks.

Clerks review orders for completeness and clarity. They may fill in missing information or contact the customer for the information. Clerks also contact customers if the customers need additional information, such as prices or shipping dates, or if delays in filling the order are anticipated. For orders received by regular mail, clerks extract checks or money orders, sort them, and send them for processing.

After an order has been verified and entered, the customer's final cost is calculated. The clerk then routes the order to the proper

Order clerks review orders for completeness and clarity.

department—such as the warehouse—which actually sends out or delivers the item in question.

In organizations with sophisticated computer systems, inventory records are adjusted automatically, as sales are made. In less automated organizations, order clerks may adjust inventory records. Clerks also may notify other departments when inventories are low or when filling certain orders would deplete supplies.

Some order clerks must establish priorities in filling orders. For example, an order clerk in a blood bank may receive a request from a hospital for a certain type of blood. The clerk must first find out whether the request is routine or an emergency and then take appropriate action.

Working Conditions

Order clerks usually work a standard 40-hour workweek. Most order clerks work in areas that are clean, well lit, and relatively quiet. These workers sit for long periods of time in front of computer terminals, which may cause eyestrain and headaches. Order clerks in retail establishments typically work overtime during peak holiday seasons, when sales volume is high.

Training, Other Qualifications, and Advancement

Employers prefer applicants with a high school diploma or its equivalent or a mix of education and related experience. Most employers prefer workers who are computer literate and have a working knowledge of word-processing and spreadsheet software.

Most order clerks are trained on the job under the close supervision of more experienced employees. Proficiency with computer software is becoming increasingly important because most orders are being filed electronically. By taking on more duties, ambitious order clerks can receive higher pay or become eligible for advancement opportunities. Some use their experience as an order clerk to move into sales positions.

Employment

Order clerks held about 293,000 jobs in 2004. Over 50 percent of order clerks were employed in wholesale and retail trade establishments, and another 16 percent were employed in manufacturing firms. Other jobs for order clerks were in industries such as information, warehousing and storage, couriers, and business support services.

Job Outlook

Job openings for order clerks likely will be limited, as improvements in technology and office automation continue to increase worker productivity. While overall employment of order clerks is expected to decline through the year 2014, numerous openings will occur each year to replace order clerks who transfer to other occupations or leave the labor force completely. Many of these openings will be for seasonal work, especially in catalog companies or online retailers catering to holiday gift buyers.

The growth in online retailing and in business-to-business electronic commerce, and the use of automated systems that make placing orders easy and convenient, will decrease demand for order clerks. The spread of electronic data interchange, which enables computers to communicate directly with each other, allows orders within establishments to be placed with little human intervention. In addition, internal systems allowing a firm's employees to place orders directly are becoming increasingly common. Outside orders placed over the Internet often are entered directly into the computer by the customer; thus, the order clerk is not involved at all in placing the order. Some companies also use automated phone menus that are accessible with a touch-tone phone to receive orders, and others use answering machines. Developments in voice recognition technology may further reduce the demand for order clerks.

Furthermore, increased automation will allow current order clerks to be more productive, with each clerk able to handle an increasingly higher volume of orders. Sophisticated inventory control and automatic billing systems permit companies to track inventory and accounts with much less help from order clerks than in the past.

Earnings

Median hourly earnings of order clerks in May 2004 were $12.07. The middle 50 percent earned between $9.45 and $15.53. The lowest 10 percent earned less than $7.75, and the highest 10 percent earned more than $19.34. Median hourly earnings in electronic shopping and mail-order houses was $9.83 while median earnings in machinery, equipment, and supplies merchant wholesalers was $14.05 in May 2004. In business support services, median hourly earning was $9.71 in May 2004.

Related Occupations

Order clerks receive and process orders. Other workers who perform similar duties include stock clerks and order fillers as well as hotel, motel, and resort desk clerks.

Sources of Additional Information

State employment service offices and agencies can provide information about job openings for order clerks.

Receptionists and Information Clerks

(O*NET 43-4171.00)

Significant Points

- Good interpersonal skills are critical.
- A high school diploma or its equivalent is the most common educational requirement.
- Employment is expected to grow faster than average.

Nature of the Work

Receptionists and information clerks are charged with a responsibility that may have a lasting impact on the success of an organization: making a good first impression. These workers often are the first representatives of an organization that a visitor may encounter,

Receptionists answer telephones, route calls, greet visitors, and provide information about the organization.

so good interpersonal skills—being courteous, professional, and helpful—are critical. Receptionists answer telephones, route and screen calls, greet visitors, respond to inquiries from the public, and provide information about the organization. Some receptionists are responsible for the coordination of all mail into and out of the office. In addition, receptionists contribute to the security of an organization by helping to monitor the access of visitors—a function that has become increasingly important since the terrorist attacks of September 11, 2001, heightened security concerns.

Whereas some tasks are common to most receptionists and information clerks, the specific responsibilities of receptionists vary with the type of establishment in which they work. For example, receptionists in hospitals and in doctors' offices may gather patients' personal and financial information and direct them to the proper waiting rooms. In corporate headquarters, receptionists may greet visitors and manage the scheduling of the board room or common conference area. In beauty or hair salons, by contrast, receptionists arrange appointments, direct customers to the hairstylist, and may serve as cashiers. In factories, large corporations, and government offices, they may provide identification cards and arrange for escorts to take visitors to the proper office. Those working for bus and train companies respond to inquiries about departures, arrivals, stops, and other related matters.

Increasingly, receptionists use multiline telephone systems, personal computers, and fax machines. Despite the widespread use of automated answering systems or voice mail, many receptionists still take messages and inform other employees of visitors' arrivals or cancellation of an appointment. When they are not busy with callers, most receptionists are expected to perform a variety of office duties, including opening and sorting mail, collecting and distributing parcels, transmitting and delivering facsimiles, updating appointment calendars, preparing travel vouchers, and performing basic bookkeeping, word processing, and filing.

Working Conditions
Receptionists who greet customers and visitors usually work in areas that are highly visible and designed and furnished to make a good impression. Most work stations are clean, well lighted, and relatively quiet. The work performed by some receptionists and information clerks may be tiring, repetitive, and stressful as many receptionists spend all day answering continuously ringing telephones and sometimes encounter difficult or irate callers. The

work environment, however, may be very friendly and motivating for individuals who enjoy greeting customers face to face and making them feel comfortable

Training, Other Qualifications, and Advancement
Although hiring requirements for receptionists and information clerks vary by industry, a high school diploma or its equivalent is the most common educational requirement. Good interpersonal skills and being technologically proficient also are important to employers.

Receptionists and information clerks generally receive on-the-job training. However, employers often look for applicants who already possess certain skills, such as prior computer experience or answering telephones. Some employers also may prefer some formal office education or training. On the job, they learn how to operate the telephone system and computers. They also learn the proper procedures for greeting visitors and for distributing mail, faxes, and parcels.

Advancement for receptionists generally comes about either by transferring to a more responsible occupation or by being promoted to a supervisory position. Receptionists with especially strong computer skills may advance to a better paying job as a secretary or an administrative assistant.

Employment
Receptionists and information clerks held about 1.1 million jobs in 2004. More than 90 percent worked in service-providing industries. Among service-providing industries, healthcare and social assistance industries—including doctors' and dentists' offices, hospitals, nursing homes, urgent-care centers, surgical centers, and clinics—employed about one-third of all receptionists and information clerks. Manufacturing, wholesale and retail trade, government, and real estate industries also employed large numbers of receptionists and information clerks. More than 3 of every 10 receptionists and information clerks worked part time.

Job Outlook
Employment of receptionists and information clerks is expected to grow faster than the average for all occupations through 2014. This increase will result from rapid growth in service-providing industries—including physicians' offices, law firms, temporary help agencies, and consulting firms—where most are employed. In addition, turnover in this large occupation will create numerous openings as receptionists and information clerks transfer to other occupations or leave the labor force altogether. Opportunities should be best for persons with a wide range of clerical and technical skills, particularly those with related work experience.

Technology will have conflicting effects on the demand for receptionists and information clerks. The increasing use of voice mail and other telephone automation reduces the need for receptionists by allowing one receptionist to perform work that formerly required several. However, the increasing use of other technology has caused a consolidation of clerical responsibilities and growing demand for workers with diverse clerical and technical skills. Because receptionists and information clerks may perform a wide variety of clerical tasks, they should continue to be in demand. Further, they perform many tasks that are interpersonal in nature and are not easily automated, ensuring continued demand for their services in a variety of establishments.

Earnings
Median hourly earnings of receptionists and information clerks in May 2004 were $10.50. The middle 50 percent earned between $8.62 and $12.88. The lowest 10 percent earned less than $7.21,

and the highest 10 percent earned more than $15.53. Median hourly earnings in the industries employing the largest number of receptionists and information clerks in May 2004 are shown below:

Offices of dentists	$12.37
General medical and surgical hospitals	11.07
Offices of physicians	10.92
Employment services	10.28
Personal care services	8.16

In 2005, the Federal Government typically paid salaries ranging from $22,937 to $27,818 a year to beginning receptionists with a high school diploma or 6 months of experience. The average annual salary for all receptionists employed by the Federal Government was about $29,185 in 2005.

Related Occupations

Receptionists deal with the public and often direct people to others who can assist them. Other workers who perform similar duties include dispatchers, secretaries and administrative assistants, and customer service representatives.

Sources of Additional Information

State employment offices can provide information on job openings for receptionists.

Reservation and Transportation Ticket Agents and Travel Clerks

(O*NET 43-4181.01, 43-4181.02)

Significant Points

- Most jobs are found in large metropolitan airports, downtown ticket offices, large reservation centers, and train or bus stations.

- A high school diploma or its equivalent is the most common educational requirement.

- Employment is expected to grow more slowly than average because of the significant impact of technology on worker productivity.

- Applicants for jobs are likely to encounter considerable competition; those who have previous experience in the travel industry, in sales, or in customer service should have the best chances.

Nature of the Work

Each year, millions of Americans travel by plane, train, ship, bus, and automobile. Many of these travelers rely on the services of reservation and transportation ticket agents and travel clerks, who perform functions as varied as selling tickets, confirming reservations, checking baggage, and providing tourists with useful travel information.

Most *reservation agents* work for large hotel chains or airlines, helping people to plan trips and make reservations. They usually work in large reservation centers, answering telephone or e-mail inquiries and offering suggestions and information about travel arrangements, such as routes, schedules, rates, and types of accommodation. Reservation agents quote fares and room rates, provide travel information, and make and confirm transportation and hotel reservations. Most agents use proprietary networks to obtain, as quickly as possible, information needed to make, change, or cancel reservations for customers.

Transportation ticket agents are sometimes known as passenger service agents, passenger booking clerks, reservation clerks, airport service agents, ticket clerks, or ticket sellers. They work in airports, train stations, and bus stations, selling tickets, assigning seats to passengers, and checking baggage. In addition, they may answer inquiries and give directions, examine passports and visas, or check in pets. They may be required assist customers who have trouble operating self-service ticket printing machines, which also are known as kiosks. Other ticket agents, more commonly known as *gate* or *station agents*, work in airport terminals, assisting passengers boarding airplanes. These workers direct passengers to the correct boarding area, check tickets and seat assignments, make boarding announcements, and provide special assistance to young, elderly, or disabled passengers when they board or disembark.

Most *travel clerks* are employed by membership organizations, such as automobile clubs. These workers, sometimes called *member services counselors* or *travel counselors*, plan trips, calculate mileage, and offer travel suggestions, such as the best route from the point of origin to the destination, to club members. Travel clerks also may prepare an itinerary indicating points of interest, restaurants, overnight accommodations, and availability of emergency services during a trip. In some cases, they make rental car, hotel, and restaurant reservations for club members.

Reservation and transportation ticket agents and travel clerks sell tickets, confirm reservations, check baggage, and provide tourists with travel information.

Passenger rate clerks generally work for bus companies. They sell tickets for regular bus routes and arrange nonscheduled or chartered trips. They plan travel routes, compute rates, and keep customers informed of appropriate details. They also may arrange travel accommodations.

Working Conditions

Most reservation and transportation ticket agents and travel clerks work in areas that are clean and well lit. This is especially true for agents who greet customers and visitors in person. Reservation and ticket agents may spend much of their day talking on the telephone; however, they commonly work away from the public, often in large centralized reservation or phone centers. Because a large number of agents or clerks may share the same workspace, it may be crowded and noisy.

Although most reservation and transportation ticket agents and travel clerks work a standard 40-hour week, about 2 out of 10 work part time. Some high school and college students are employed part time in this occupation, working after school or during vacations. Some agents work evenings, late nights, weekends, and holidays. In general, employees with the most seniority tend to be assigned the more desirable shifts.

The work performed by reservation and transportation ticket agents and travel clerks may be repetitive and stressful. They often work under stringent time constraints or must meet quotas on the number of calls answered or reservations made. Difficult or angry customers also can create stressful situations as agents usually bear the brunt of customers' dissatisfaction. Agents may work on their feet for a large portion of their shift, and may have to lift heavy baggage. In addition, prolonged exposure to a computer monitor, which is common in this occupation, may lead to eyestrain.

Training, Other Qualifications, and Advancement

A high school diploma or its equivalent is the most common educational requirement for reservation and transportation ticket agent and travel clerk jobs. Some employers, however, prefer applicants who have completed college coursework in management or business. Experience with computers, including good typing skills, also is usually required. Some jobs require applicants to be over 18 years of age and posses a valid driver's license. Agents who handle passenger luggage must be able to lift heavy objects.

Most airline reservation and ticket agents learn their skills through formal company training programs that can last several weeks. Here, they learn company and industry policies as well as ticketing procedures. Trainees also learn to use the airline's computer system to obtain information on schedules, fares, and the availability of seats; to make reservations for passengers; and to plan passenger itineraries. In addition, they must become familiar with airport and airline code designations, regulations, and safety procedures. After completing classroom instruction, new agents work under the direct guidance of a supervisor or experienced agent. During this time the supervisors may, for example, monitor telephone conversations to improve the quality of customer service so that agents learn to provide customer service in a courteous manner, while limiting the time spent on each call.

In contrast to those who work for airlines, reservation and transportation ticket agents and travel clerks who work for automobile clubs, bus lines, and railroads are trained on the job through short in-house classes that last several days.

Many reservation and transportation ticket agents and travel clerks deal directly with the public, so a professional appearance and a pleasant personality are important. A clear speaking voice and fluency in the English language also are essential, because these employees frequently use the telephone or public-address systems.

In addition, fluency in a foreign language is becoming increasingly helpful for those seeking reservation and ticket agent jobs.

Reservation and transportation ticket agents and travel clerks may advance by being transferred to a position with more responsibilities, or by being promoted to a supervisory position. Many travel companies fill supervisory and managerial positions by promoting individuals within their organization, so those who acquire additional skills, experience, and training improve their opportunities for advancement. Some companies require that candidates for supervisory positions have an associate degree in a business-related field, such as management, business administration, or marketing. Within the airline industry, a ticket agent may advance to lead worker on the shift.

Employment

Reservation and transportation ticket agents and travel clerks held about 163,000 jobs in 2004. About 6 out of 10 are employed by airlines. Others work for automobile clubs, hotels and other lodging places, railroad companies, bus lines, and other companies that provide transportation services.

Although agents and clerks are found throughout the country, most work in large metropolitan airports, downtown ticket offices, large reservation centers, and train or bus stations. The remainder work in small, regional airports, or in small communities served only by intercity bus or railroad lines.

Job Outlook

Applicants for reservation and transportation ticket agent jobs are likely to encounter considerable competition, because the supply of qualified applicants will exceed the expected number of job openings. Entry requirements for these jobs are minimal, and many people seeking to get into the airline industry or another travel-related business often start out in such positions. The jobs provide excellent travel benefits, and many people view airline and other travel-related jobs as glamorous. Applicants who have previous experience in the travel industry, in sales, or in customer service should have the best chances.

Employment of reservation and transportation ticket agents and travel clerks is expected to grow more slowly than the average for all occupations through 2014. Although a growing population will demand additional travel services, employment of these workers will grow more slowly than this demand because of the significant impact of technology on worker productivity. Automated reservations and ticketing, as well as "ticketless" travel, for example, are reducing the need for some workers. Most train stations and airports now have self-service ticket printing machines, called kiosks, which enable passengers to make reservations, purchase tickets, and check-in for train rides and flights themselves. Many passengers also are able to check flight times and fares, make reservations, purchase tickets, and check-in for flights on the Internet. Nevertheless, not all travel-related passenger services can be fully automated, primarily for safety and security reasons. As a result, job openings will continue to become available as the occupation grows and as workers transfer to other occupations, retire, or leave the labor force altogether.

Employment of reservation and transportation ticket agents and travel clerks is sensitive to cyclical swings in the economy. During recessions, discretionary passenger travel declines, and transportation service companies are less likely to hire new workers and may even resort to layoffs.

Earnings

Median annual earnings of reservation and transportation ticket agents and travel clerks in May 2004 were $27,750. The middle 50 percent earned between $21,430 and $39,410. The lowest 10 percent earned less than $17,720, and the highest 10 percent earned more than $45,100. Many employers offer discounts on travel services to their employees. In May 2004, median annual earnings in the industries employing the larges number of agents were:

Scheduled air transportation $31,750
Travel arrangement and reservation services............................. 22,370
Traveler accommodation... 22,050

Related Occupations

Other occupations that provide travel-related services include hotel, motel, and resort desk clerks; travel agents; and flight attendants. Other occupations that make sales and provide information to customers include counter and rental clerks, order clerks, customer service representatives, and receptionists and information clerks.

Sources of Additional Information

For information about job opportunities as reservation and transportation ticket agents and travel clerks, write to the personnel manager of individual transportation companies. Addresses of airlines are available from:
➤ Air Transport Association of America, 1301 Pennsylvania Ave. NW., Suite 1100, Washington, DC 20004-1707. Internet: **http://www.airlines.org**

Material Recording, Scheduling, Dispatching, and Distributing Occupations

Cargo and Freight Agents

(O*NET 43-5011.00)

Significant Points

● Many jobs are entry level and do not require more than a high school diploma.

● Although cargo traffic is expected to grow faster than in the past, employment of cargo and freight agents will not keep pace because of technological advances.

Nature of the Work

Cargo and freight agents arrange for and track incoming and outgoing cargo and freight shipments in airline, train, or trucking terminals or on shipping docks. They expedite shipments by determining the route that shipments are to take and by preparing all necessary shipping documents. The agents take orders from customers and arrange for the pickup of freight or cargo for delivery to loading platforms. Cargo and freight agents may keep records of the cargo, such as its amount, type, weight, and dimensions. They keep a tally of missing items, record the condition of damaged items, and document any excess supplies.

Cargo and freight agents arrange cargo according to its destination. They also determine the shipping rates and other charges that can sometimes apply to the freight. For imported or exported freight, they verify that the proper customs paperwork is in order. Cargo and freight agents often track shipments electronically, using bar codes, and answer customers' inquiries on the status of their shipments.

Working Conditions

Cargo and freight agents work in a wide variety of businesses, institutions, and industries. Some work in warehouses, stockrooms, or shipping and receiving rooms that may not be temperature controlled. Others may spend time in cold storage rooms or outside on loading platforms, where they are exposed to the weather.

Most jobs for cargo and freight agents involve frequent standing, bending, walking, and stretching. Some lifting and carrying of smaller items also may be involved. Although automated devices have lessened the physical demands of this occupation, their use remains somewhat limited. The work still can be strenuous, even though mechanical material-handling equipment is employed to move heavy items.

The typical workweek is Monday through Friday; however, evening and weekend hours are common in some jobs and may be required in other jobs when large shipments are involved.

Training, Other Qualifications, and Advancement

Many jobs are entry level and do not require more than a high school diploma. Employers, however, prefer to hire those familiar with computers. Typing, filing, recordkeeping, and other clerical skills also are important.

Cargo and freight agents start out by checking items to be shipped and then attaching labels to them and making sure that the addresses are correct. Training in the use of automated equipment usually is done informally, on the job. As this occupation becomes more automated, however, workers may need longer periods of training in order to master the use of the equipment.

Advancement opportunities for cargo and freight agents vary with the place of employment.

Employment

Cargo and freight agents held about 70,000 jobs in 2004. Most jobs were in transportation. Approximately 20 percent worked in the air transportation industry and 8 percent worked in the truck transportation industry. Couriers employed another 11 percent. In addition, about 43 percent worked for firms engaged in support activities for the transportation industry.

Job Outlook

Employment of cargo and freight agents is expected to decline through 2014. Although cargo traffic is expected to grow faster than in the past, employment of cargo and freight agents will not keep pace because of technological advances. For example, the

Cargo and freight agents take orders from customers and arrange for the pickup of freight or cargo for delivery to loading platforms.

increasing use of bar codes on cargo and freight allows agents and customers to track these shipments quickly over the Internet, rather than manually tracking their location. In addition, customs and insurance paperwork now can be completed over the Internet by customers, reducing the need for cargo and freight agents.

Despite these advances in technology that dampen job growth among cargo and freight agents, job openings will continue to arise due to increases in buying over the Internet, which will result in more shipments. Jobs also will open up because of the increasing importance of same-day delivery, which expands the role of agents. In addition, many job openings will be created to replace cargo and freight agents who leave the occupation.

Earnings
Median annual earnings of cargo and freight agents in May 2004 were $34,250. The middle 50 percent earned between $25,720 and $43,250. The lowest 10 percent earned less than $20,700, and the highest 10 percent earned more than $54,480.

These workers usually receive the same benefits as most other workers. If uniforms are required, employers generally provide them or offer an allowance to purchase them.

Related Occupations
Cargo and freight agents plan and coordinate shipments of cargo by airlines, trains, and trucks. They also arrange freight pickup with customers. Others who do similar work are couriers and messengers; shipping, receiving, and traffic clerks; weighers, measurers, checkers, and samplers, recordkeeping; truck drivers and driver/sales workers; and Postal Service workers.

Sources of Additional Information
Information about job opportunities may be obtained from local employers and local offices of the State employment service.

Couriers and Messengers

(O*NET 43-5021.00)

Significant Points

- Most jobs as couriers and messengers do not require more than a high school diploma.

- Employment is expected to decline, reflecting the more widespread use of electronic information-handling technologies such as e-mail and fax.

Nature of the Work
Couriers and messengers move and distribute information, documents, and small packages for businesses, institutions, and government agencies. They pick up and deliver letters, important business documents, or packages that need to be sent or received quickly within a local area. Trucks and vans are used for larger deliveries, such as legal caseloads and conference materials. By sending an item by courier or messenger, the sender ensures that it reaches its destination the same day or even within the hour. Couriers and messengers also deliver items that the sender is unwilling to entrust to other means of delivery, such as important legal or financial documents, passports, airline tickets, or medical samples to be tested.

Couriers and messengers receive their instructions either in person—by reporting to their office—or by telephone, two-way radio, or wireless data service. Then they pick up the item and carry it to its destination. After each pickup or delivery, they check in with their dispatcher to receive instructions. Sometimes the dispatcher will

Most couriers and messengers spend much of their time outdoors or in their vehicle.

contact them while they are between stops, and they may be routed to go past a stop that recently called in a delivery. Consequently, most couriers and messengers spend much of their time outdoors or in their vehicle. They usually maintain records of deliveries and often obtain signatures from the persons receiving the items.

Most couriers and messengers deliver items within a limited geographic area, such as a city or metropolitan area. Items that need to go longer distances usually are sent by mail or by an overnight delivery service. Some couriers and messengers carry items only for their employer, which typically might be a law firm, bank, medical laboratory, or financial institution. Others may act as part of an organization's internal mail system and carry items mainly within the organization's buildings or entirely within one building. Many couriers and messengers work for messenger or courier services; for a fee, they pick up items from anyone and deliver them to specified destinations within a local area. Most are paid on a commission basis.

Couriers and messengers reach their destination by several methods. Many drive vans or cars or ride motorcycles. A few travel by foot, especially in urban areas or when making deliveries nearby. In congested urban areas, messengers often use bicycles to make deliveries. Bicycle messengers usually are employed by messenger or courier services. Although e-mail and fax machines can deliver information faster than couriers and messengers can, and although a great deal of information is available over the Internet, an electronic copy cannot substitute for the original document in many types of business transactions.

Working Conditions
Couriers and messengers spend most of their time alone, making deliveries, and usually are not closely supervised. Those who deliver by bicycle must be physically fit and are exposed to all weather conditions, as well as to the many hazards associated with heavy traffic. Car, van, and truck couriers must sometimes carry heavy loads, either manually or with the aid of a hand truck. They also have to deal with difficult parking situations, as well as traffic jams and road construction. The pressure of making as many deliveries as possible to increase one's earnings can be stressful and may lead to unsafe driving or bicycling practices. The typical workweek is Monday through Friday; however, evening and weekend hours are common.

Training, Other Qualifications, and Advancement
Most couriers and messengers are at the entry level and do not require more than a high school diploma. Employers, however, prefer to hire those familiar with computers and other electronic office and business equipment. Because communication with other people is

an integral part of some courier and messenger jobs, good oral and written communication skills are essential.

Couriers and messengers usually learn on the job, training with an experienced worker for a short time. Those who work as independent contractors for a messenger or delivery service may be required to have a valid driver's license, a registered and inspected vehicle, a good driving record, and insurance coverage. Many couriers and messengers who are employees, rather than independent contractors, also are required to provide and maintain their own vehicle. Although some companies have spare bicycles or mopeds that their riders may rent for a short period, almost all two-wheeled couriers own their own bicycle, moped, or motorcycle. A good knowledge of the geographic area in which they travel and a good sense of direction also are important.

Couriers and messengers, especially those who work for messenger or courier services, have limited advancement opportunities; a few move into the office to learn dispatching or to take service requests by phone.

Employment

Couriers and messengers together held about 147,000 jobs in 2004. Approximately 23 percent were employed in the couriers and messengers industry. About 13 percent worked in healthcare, and around 8 percent worked in the legal services industry. Another 8 percent were employed in finance and insurance firms. Technically, many messengers are self-employed independent contractors, because they provide their own vehicles and, to a certain extent, set their own schedules. In many respects, however, they are like employees, because they usually work for one company.

Job Outlook

Employment of couriers and messengers is expected to decline through 2014, despite an increasing volume of parcels, business documents, promotional materials, and other written information that must be handled and delivered as the economy expands. However, some jobs will arise out of the need to replace couriers and messengers who leave the occupation.

Employment of couriers and messengers will continue to be adversely affected by the more widespread use of electronic information-handling technologies such as e-mail and fax. Many documents, forms, and other materials that people used to have delivered by hand are now downloaded from the Internet. Many legal and financial documents, which used to be delivered by hand because they required a handwritten signature, now can be delivered electronically with online signatures. However, couriers and messengers still will be needed to transport materials that cannot be sent electronically—such as blueprints and other oversized materials, securities, and passports. Also, they still will be required by medical and dental laboratories to pick up and deliver medical samples, specimens, and other materials.

Earnings

Median annual earnings of couriers and messengers in May 2004 were $20,190. The middle 50 percent earned between $16,390 and $24,720. The lowest 10 percent earned less than $14,020, and the highest 10 percent earned more than $30,510.

These workers usually receive the same benefits as most other workers. If uniforms are required, employers generally provide them or offer an allowance to purchase them.

Related Occupations

Messengers and couriers deliver letters, parcels, and other items. They also keep accurate records of their work. Others who do similar work are Postal Service workers; truck drivers and driver/sales workers; shipping, receiving, and traffic clerks; and cargo and freight agents.

Sources of Additional Information

Information about job opportunities may be obtained from local employers and local offices of the State employment service. Persons interested in courier and messenger jobs also may contact messenger and courier services, mail-order firms, banks, printing and publishing firms, utility companies, retail stores, or other large companies.

Dispatchers

(O*NET 43-5031.00, 43-5032.00)

Significant Points

- Population growth and economic expansion are expected to spur employment growth for all types of dispatchers.

- Many dispatchers are at the entry level and do not require more than a high school diploma.

- Although there are no mandatory licensing or certification requirements, some States require public safety dispatchers to be certified.

Nature of the Work

Dispatchers schedule and dispatch workers, equipment, or service vehicles to carry materials or passengers. They keep records, logs, and schedules of the calls that they receive, the transportation vehicles that they monitor and control, and the actions that they take. They maintain information on each call and then prepare a detailed report on all activities occurring during their shifts. Many dispatchers employ computer-aided dispatch systems to accomplish these tasks. The work of dispatchers varies greatly, depending on the industry in which they work.

Regardless of where they work, all dispatchers are assigned a specific territory and have responsibility for all communications within that area. Many work in teams, especially dispatchers in large communications centers or companies. One person usually handles all dispatching calls to the response units or company drivers, while the other members of the team usually receive the incoming calls and deal with the public.

Police, fire, and ambulance dispatchers, also called public safety dispatchers, monitor the location of emergency services personnel from any one or all of the jurisdiction's emergency services departments. These workers dispatch the appropriate type and number of units in response to calls for assistance. Dispatchers, or call takers, often are the first people the public contacts when emergency assistance is required. If certified for emergency medical services, the dispatcher may provide medical instruction to those on the scene of the emergency until the medical staff arrives.

Police, fire, and ambulance dispatchers work in a variety of settings: A police station, a fire station, a hospital, or, increasingly, a centralized communications center. In many areas, the police department serves as the communications center. In these situations, all emergency calls go to the police department, where a dispatcher handles the police calls and screens the others before transferring them to the appropriate service.

When handling calls, dispatchers question each caller carefully to determine the type, seriousness, and location of the emergency. The information obtained is posted either electronically by computer or, with decreasing frequency, by hand. The request for help is communicated immediately to uniformed or supervisory personnel, who quickly decide on the priority of the incident, the kind and number of units needed, and the location of the closest and most suitable units available. Typically, a team answers calls and relays the information to be dispatched. Responsibility then shifts to the dispatchers, who send response units to the scene and monitor the activity of the public safety personnel answering the dispatched message. During the course of the shift, dispatchers may rotate these functions.

When appropriate, dispatchers stay in close contact with other service providers—for example, a police dispatcher would monitor the response of the fire department when there is a major fire. In a medical emergency, dispatchers keep in close touch not only with the dispatched units, but also with the caller. They may give extensive first-aid instructions before the emergency personnel arrive, while the caller is waiting for the ambulance. Dispatchers continuously give updates on the patient's condition to the ambulance personnel and often serve as a link between the medical staff in a hospital and the emergency medical technicians in the ambulance. (A separate statement on emergency medical technicians and paramedics appears elsewhere in the *Handbook*.)

Other dispatchers coordinate deliveries, service calls, and related activities for a variety of firms. *Truck dispatchers*, who work for local and long-distance trucking companies, coordinate the movement of trucks and freight between cities. These dispatchers direct the pickup and delivery activities of drivers, receive customers' requests for the pickup and delivery of freight, consolidate freight orders into truckloads for specific destinations, assign

Dispatchers may sit for long periods, using telephones, computers, maps, and two-way radios.

drivers and trucks, and draw up routes and pickup and delivery schedules. *Bus dispatchers* make sure that local and long-distance buses stay on schedule. They handle all problems that may disrupt service, and they dispatch other buses or arrange for repairs in order to restore service and schedules. *Train dispatchers* ensure the timely and efficient movement of trains according to orders and schedules. They must be aware of track switch positions, track maintenance areas, and the location of other trains running on the track. *Taxicab dispatchers*, or starters, dispatch taxis in response to requests for service and keep logs on all road service calls. *Tow-truck dispatchers* take calls for emergency road service. They relay the nature of the problem to a nearby service station or a tow-truck service and see to it that the road service is completed. *Gas and water service dispatchers* monitor gaslines and water mains and send out service trucks and crews to take care of emergencies.

Working Conditions

The work of dispatchers can be very hectic when many calls come in at the same time. The job of public safety dispatcher is particularly stressful because a slow or an improper response to a call can result in serious injury or further harm. Also, callers who are anxious or afraid may become excited and be unable to provide needed information; some may even become abusive. Despite provocations, dispatchers must remain calm, objective, and in control of the situation.

Dispatchers sit for long periods, using telephones, computers, and two-way radios. Much of their time is spent at video display terminals, viewing monitors and observing traffic patterns. As a result of working for long stretches with computers and other electronic equipment, dispatchers can experience significant eyestrain and back discomfort. Generally, dispatchers work a 40-hour week; however, rotating shifts and compressed work schedules are common. Alternative work schedules are necessary to accommodate evening, weekend, and holiday work, as well as 24-hour-per-day, 7-day-per-week operations.

Training, Other Qualifications, and Advancement

Many dispatchers are at the entry level and do not require more than a high school diploma. Employers, however, prefer to hire people familiar with computers and other electronic office and business equipment. Typing, filing, recordkeeping, and other clerical skills also are important.

State or local government civil service regulations usually govern police, fire, emergency medical, and ambulance dispatching jobs. Candidates for these positions may have to pass written, oral, and performance tests. Also, they may be asked to attend training classes and attain the proper certification in order to qualify for advancement.

Workers usually develop the necessary skills on the job. This informal training lasts from several days to a few months, depending on the complexity of the job. Public safety dispatchers usually require the most extensive training. While working with an experienced dispatcher, new employees monitor calls and learn how to operate a variety of communications equipment, including telephones, radios, and various wireless devices. As trainees gain confidence, they begin to handle calls themselves. In smaller operations, dispatchers sometimes act as customer service representatives, processing orders. Many public safety dispatchers also participate in structured training programs sponsored by their employer. Increasingly, public safety dispatchers receive training in stress and crisis management as well as family counseling. This training helps them to provide effective services to others;

and, at the same time, it helps them manage the stress involved in their work.

Communication skills and the ability to work under pressure are important personal qualities for dispatchers. Residency in the city or county of employment frequently is required for public safety dispatchers. Dispatchers in transportation industries must be able to deal with sudden influxes of shipments and disruptions of shipping schedules caused by bad weather, road construction, or accidents.

Although there are no mandatory licensing or certification requirements, some States require that public safety dispatchers possess a certificate to work on a State network, such as the Police Information Network. Many dispatchers participate in these programs in order to improve their prospects for career advancement.

Dispatchers who work for private firms, which usually are small, will find few opportunities for advancement. In contrast, public safety dispatchers may become a shift or divisional supervisor or chief of communications, or they may move to higher paying administrative jobs. Some become police officers or firefighters.

Employment

Dispatchers held 266,000 jobs in 2004. About 36 percent were police, fire, and ambulance dispatchers, almost all of whom worked for State and local governments—primarily local police and fire departments. About 26 percent of all dispatchers worked in the transportation and warehousing industry, and the rest worked in a wide variety of mainly service-providing industries.

Although dispatching jobs are found throughout the country, most dispatchers work in urban areas, where large communications centers and businesses are located.

Job Outlook

Employment of dispatchers is expected to grow about as fast as the average for all occupations through 2014. In addition to those positions resulting from job growth, many openings will arise from the need to replace workers who transfer to other occupations or leave the labor force.

Population growth and economic expansion are expected to spur employment growth for all types of dispatchers. The growing and aging population will increase demand for emergency services and stimulate employment growth of police, fire, and ambulance dispatchers. Many districts are consolidating their communications centers into a shared area-wide facility. Individuals with computer skills and experience will have a greater opportunity for employment as public safety dispatchers.

Employment of some dispatchers is more adversely affected by economic downturns than employment of other dispatchers. For example, when economic activity falls, demand for transportation services declines. As a result, taxicab, train, and truck dispatchers may experience layoffs or a shortened workweek, and jobseekers may have some difficulty finding entry-level jobs. Employment of tow-truck dispatchers, by contrast, is seldom affected by general economic conditions, because of the emergency nature of their business.

Earnings

Median annual earnings of dispatchers, except police, fire, and ambulance in May 2004 were $30,920. The middle 50 percent earned between $23,480 and $41,040. The lowest 10 percent earned less than $18,820, and the highest 10 percent earned more than $52,440.

Median annual earnings of police, fire, and ambulance dispatchers in 2004 were $28,930. The middle 50 percent earned between $23,060 and $35,970. The lowest 10 percent earned less than $18,710, and the highest 10 percent earned more than $44520.

Dispatchers usually receive the same benefits as most other workers.

Related Occupations

Other occupations that involve directing and controlling the movement of vehicles, freight, and personnel, as well as distributing information and messages, include air traffic controllers, communications equipment operators, customer service representatives, and reservation and transportation ticket agents and travel clerks.

Sources of Additional Information

For further information on training and certification for police, fire, and emergency dispatchers, contact:

➤ Association of Public Safety Communications Officials, International, 351 N. Williamson Blvd., Daytona Beach, FL 32114-1112. Internet: **http://www.apco911.org**

➤ International Municipal Signal Association (IMSA), PO Box 359, 165 E. Union Street, Newark, NY 14513-0539. Internet: **http://www.IMSAsafety.org**

Information on job opportunities for police, fire, and emergency dispatchers is available from personnel offices of State and local governments or police departments. Information about work opportunities for other types of dispatchers is available from local employers and State employment service offices.

Meter Readers, Utilities

(O*NET 43-5041.00)

Significant Points

- Employment is expected to decline, as a result of new automated meter reading (AMR) systems that allow meters to be monitored and billed from a central point.

- Most meter readers are employed by electric, gas, or water utilities or by local governments.

Nature of the Work

Meter readers read electric, gas, water, or steam consumption meters and record the volume used. They serve both residential and commercial consumers, either walking or driving along a designated route. Their duties include inspecting the meters and their connections for any defects or damage, supplying repair and maintenance workers with the necessary information to fix damaged meters, keeping track of the average usage, and recording reasons for any extreme fluctuations in volume.

Meter readers are constantly aware of any abnormal behavior or consumption that might indicate an unauthorized connection. They may turn off service for questionable behavior or nonpayment of charges, and they also are responsible for turning on service for new occupants. These workers usually keep records showing that the meters on which they have completed work have been serviced.

Working Conditions

Meter readers, who usually work 40 hours a week, work outdoors in all types of weather as they travel through communities and neighborhoods taking readings. The typical workweek is Monday through Friday.

Most meter readers are employed by electric, gas, or water utilities or by local governments.

Training, Other Qualifications, and Advancement

Many meter readers are at the entry level and do not require more than a high school diploma. Employers, however, prefer to hire those familiar with computers and other electronic office and business equipment. Typing, recordkeeping, and other clerical skills also are important.

Utility meter readers usually work with a more experienced meter reader until they feel comfortable doing the job on their own. They learn how to read the meters and determine the consumption rate. They also must learn the route that they need to travel to read all their customers' meters.

Advancement opportunities for meter readers vary with the place of employment.

Employment

Meter readers held about 50,000 jobs in 2004. About 44 percent were employed by electric, gas, and water utilities. Most of the rest were employed in local government, reading water meters or meters for other government-owned utilities.

Job Outlook

Employment of meter readers is expected to decline through 2014. New AMR systems allow meters to be monitored and billed from a central point, reducing the need for meter readers. However, because it will be many years before AMR systems can be implemented in all locations, there still will be some openings for meter readers, mainly to replace workers leaving the occupation.

Earnings

Median annual earnings of utility meter readers in May 2004 were $29,440. The middle 50 percent earned between $23,000 and $38,890. The lowest 10 percent earned less than $18,550, and the highest 10 percent earned more than $47,830.

These workers usually receive the same benefits as most other workers. If uniforms are required, employers generally provide them or offer an allowance to purchase them.

Related Occupations

Other workers responsible for the distribution and control of utilities include power plant operators, distributors, and dispatchers.

Sources of Additional Information

Information about job opportunities may be obtained from local employers and local offices of the State employment service.

Postal Service Workers

(O*NET 43-5051.00, 43-5052.00, 43-5053.00)

Significant Points

- Employment of Postal Service workers is expected to decline because of the increasing use of automation and electronic communication, such as the Internet.

- Keen competition is expected because the number of qualified applicants should continue to exceed the number of job openings.

- Qualification is based on an examination.

- Applicants customarily wait 1 to 2 years or more after passing the examination before being hired.

Nature of the Work

Each week, the U.S. Postal Service delivers billions of pieces of mail, including letters, bills, advertisements, and packages. To do this in an efficient and timely manner, the Postal Service employs about 619,000 individuals. Most Postal Service workers are clerks, mail carriers, or mail sorters, processors, and processing machine operators. Postal clerks wait on customers at post offices, whereas mail sorters, processors, and processing machine operators sort incoming and outgoing mail at post offices and mail processing centers. Mail carriers deliver mail to urban and rural residences and businesses throughout the United States.

Postal Service clerks, also known as window clerks, sell stamps, money orders, postal stationary, and mailing envelopes and boxes. They also weigh packages to determine postage and check that packages are in satisfactory condition for mailing. These clerks register, certify, and insure mail and answer questions about postage rates, post office boxes, mailing restrictions, and other postal matters. Window clerks also help customers file claims for damaged packages.

Postal Service mail sorters, processors, and processing machine operators prepare incoming and outgoing mail for distribution. These workers are commonly referred to as mail handlers, distribution clerks, mail processors, or mail processing clerks. They load and unload postal trucks and move mail around a mail processing center with forklifts, small electric tractors, or hand-pushed carts. They also load and operate mail processing, sorting, and canceling machinery.

Postal Service mail carriers deliver mail, once it has been processed and sorted. Although carriers are classified by their type of route—either city or rural—duties of city and rural carriers are similar. Most travel established routes, delivering and collecting mail. Mail carriers start work at the post office early in the morning, when they arrange the mail in delivery sequence. Automated equipment has reduced the time that carriers need to sort the mail, allowing them to spend more time delivering it.

Mail carriers cover their routes on foot, by vehicle, or a combination of both. On foot, they carry a heavy load of mail in a satchel or push it on a cart. In most urban and rural areas, they use a car or small truck. Although the Postal Service provides vehicles to city carriers, most rural carriers must use their own automobiles. Deliveries are made house-to-house, to roadside mailboxes, and to large buildings such as offices or apartments, which generally have all of their tenants' mailboxes in one location.

Besides delivering and collecting mail, carriers collect money for postage-due and COD (cash-on-delivery) fees and obtain signed receipts for registered, certified, and insured mail. If a customer is not

Although machines increasingly are used to sort mail, some mail still is sorted by hand.

home, the carrier leaves a notice that tells where special mail is being held. After completing their routes, carriers return to the post office with mail gathered from street collection boxes, homes, and businesses and turn in the mail, receipts, and money collected during the day.

Some city carriers may have specialized duties such as delivering only parcels or picking up mail from mail collection boxes. In contrast to city carriers, rural carriers provide a wider range of postal services, in addition to delivering and picking up mail. For example, rural carriers may sell stamps and money orders and register, certify, and insure parcels and letters. All carriers, however, must be able to answer customers' questions about postal regulations and services and provide change-of-address cards and other postal forms when requested.

Working Conditions

Window clerks usually work in the public portion of clean, well-ventilated, and well-lit buildings. They have a variety of duties and frequent contact with the public, but they rarely work at night. However, they may have to deal with upset customers, stand for long periods, and be held accountable for an assigned stock of stamps and funds. Depending on the size of the post office in which they work, they also may be required to sort mail.

Despite the use of automated equipment, the work of mail sorters, processors, and processing machine operators can be physically demanding. Workers may have to move heavy sacks of mail around a mail processing center. These workers usually are on their feet, reaching for sacks and trays of mail or placing packages and bundles into sacks and trays. Processing mail can be tiring and boring. Many sorters, processors, and machine operators work at night or on weekends, because most large post offices process mail around the clock, and the largest volume of mail is sorted during the evening and night shifts. Workers can experience stress as they process mail under tight production deadlines and quotas.

Most carriers begin work early in the morning—those with routes in a business district can start as early as 4 a.m. Overtime hours are frequently required for urban carriers. A carrier's schedule has its advantages, however. Carriers who begin work early in the morning are through by early afternoon and spend most of the day on their own, relatively free from direct supervision. Carriers spend most of their time outdoors, delivering mail in all kinds of weather. Even those who drive often must walk periodically when making deliveries and must lift heavy sacks of parcel post items when loading their vehicles. In addition, carriers must be cautious of potential hazards on their routes. Wet and icy roads and sidewalks can be treacherous, and each year dogs attack numerous carriers.

Training, Other Qualifications, and Advancement

Postal Service workers must be at least 18 years old. They must be U.S. citizens or have been granted permanent resident-alien status in the United States, and males must have registered with the Selective Service upon reaching age 18. Applicants should have a basic competency of English. Qualification is based on a written examination that measures speed and accuracy at checking names and numbers and the ability to memorize mail distribution procedures. Applicants must pass a physical examination and drug test, and may be asked to show that they can lift and handle mail sacks weighing 70 pounds. Applicants for mail carrier positions must have a driver's license and a good driving record, and must receive a passing grade on a road test.

Jobseekers should contact the post office or mail processing center where they wish to work to determine when an exam will be given. Applicants' names are listed in order of their examination scores. Five points are added to the score of an honorably discharged veteran and 10 points are added to the score of a veteran who was wounded in combat or is disabled. When a vacancy occurs, the appointing officer chooses one of the top three applicants; the rest of the names remain on the list to be considered for future openings until their eligibility expires—usually 2 years after the examination date.

Relatively few people become postal clerks or mail carriers on their first job, because of keen competition and the customary waiting period of 1 to 2 years or more after passing the examination. It is not surprising, therefore, that most entrants transfer from other occupations.

New Postal Service workers are trained on the job by experienced workers. Many post offices offer classroom instruction on safety and defensive driving. Workers receive additional instruction when new equipment or procedures are introduced. In these cases, workers usually are trained by another postal employee or a training specialist.

Postal clerks and mail carriers should be courteous and tactful when dealing with the public, especially when answering questions or receiving complaints. A good memory and the ability to read rapidly and accurately are important. Good interpersonal skills also are vital, because mail distribution clerks work closely with other postal workers, frequently under the tension and strain of meeting dispatch or transportation deadlines and quotas.

Postal Service workers often begin on a part-time, flexible basis and become regular or full time in order of seniority, as vacancies occur. Full-time workers may bid for preferred assignments, such as the day shift or a high-level nonsupervisory position. Carriers can look forward to obtaining preferred routes as their seniority increases. Postal Service workers can advance to supervisory positions on a competitive basis.

Employment

The U.S. Postal Service employed 75,000 clerks; 335,000 mail carriers; and 209,000 mail sorters, processors, and processing machine operators in 2004. Most of them worked full time. Most postal clerks provided window service at post office branches. Many mail sorters, processors, and processing machine operators sorted mail at major metropolitan post offices; others worked at mail processing centers. The majority of mail carriers worked in cities and suburbs, while the rest worked in rural areas.

Postal Service workers are classified as casual, part-time flexible, part-time regular, or full time. Casuals are hired for 90 days at a time to help process and deliver mail during peak mailing or vacation periods. Part-time flexible workers do not have a regular work schedule or weekly guarantee of hours but are called as the need arises. Part-time regulars have a set work schedule of fewer than 40 hours per week, often replacing regular full-time workers on their scheduled day off. Full-time postal employees work a 40-hour week over a 5-day period.

Job Outlook

Employment of Postal Service workers is expected to decline through 2014. Still, many jobs will become available because of the need to replace those who retire or leave the occupation. Those seeking jobs as Postal Service workers can expect to encounter keen competition. The number of applicants should continue to exceed the number of job openings because of the occupation's low entry requirements and attractive wages and benefits.

A small decline in employment is expected among window clerks over the 2004-14 projection period. Efforts by the Postal Service to provide better service may somewhat increase the demand for window clerks, but the demand for such clerks will be offset by the use of electronic communication, such as the Internet, and private delivery companies. Employment of mail sorters, processors, and processing machine operators is expected to decline because of the increasing use of automated materials handling equipment and optical character readers, barcode sorters, and other automated sorting equipment.

A small decline in employment among mail carriers is expected through 2014. Competition from alternative delivery systems and the increasing use of electronic communication are expected to influence the demand for mail carriers. In addition, the Postal Service is moving toward more centralized mail delivery, such as the use of cluster boxes, to cut down on the number of door-to-door deliveries. The best employment opportunities for mail carriers are expected to be in less urbanized areas as the number of addresses to which mail must be delivered continues to grow, especially in fast growing rural areas. However, increased use of the "delivery point sequencing" system, which allows machines to sort mail directly by the order of delivery, should reduce the amount of time that carriers spend sorting their mail, allowing them more time to handle longer routes.

The role of the Postal Service as a government-approved monopoly continues to be a topic of debate. Any legislative changes that would privatize or deregulate the Postal Service might affect employment of all its workers. Employment and schedules in the Postal Service fluctuate with the demand for its services. When mail volume is high, full-time employees work overtime, part-time workers get additional hours, and casual workers may be hired. When mail volume is low, overtime is curtailed, part-timers work fewer hours, and casual workers are discharged.

Earnings

Median annual earnings of Postal Service mail carriers were $44,450 in May 2004. The middle 50 percent earned between $37,590 and $50,580. The lowest 10 percent had earnings of less than $31,980, while the top 10 percent earned more than $54,240. Rural mail carriers are reimbursed for mileage put on their own vehicles while delivering mail.

Median annual earnings of Postal Service clerks were $40,950 in 2004. The middle 50 percent earned between $37,880 and $44,030. The lowest 10 percent had earnings of less than $36,040, while the top 10 percent earned more than $50,510.

Median annual earnings of Postal Service mail sorters, processors, and processing machine operators were $39,430 in 2004. The middle 50 percent earned between $36,240 and $42,620. The lowest 10 percent had earnings of less than $24,290, while the top 10 percent earned more than $44,540.

Postal Service workers enjoy a variety of employer-provided benefits similar to those enjoyed by Federal Government workers. The American Postal Workers Union, the National Association of Letter Carriers, the National Postal Mail Handlers Union, and the National Rural Letter Carriers Association together represent most of these workers.

Related Occupations

Other occupations with duties similar to those of Postal Service clerks include cashiers; counter and rental clerks; file clerks; and shipping, receiving, and traffic clerks. Others with duties related to those of Postal Service mail carriers include couriers and messengers, and truck drivers and driver/sales workers. Occupations whose duties are related to those of Postal Service mail sorters, processors, and processing machine operators include inspectors, testers, sorters, samplers, and weighers, and material moving occupations.

Sources of Additional Information

Local post offices and State employment service offices can supply details about entrance examinations and specific employment opportunities for Postal Service workers.

Production, Planning, and Expediting Clerks

(O*NET 43-5061.00)

Significant Points

- Many production, planning, and expediting jobs are at the entry level and do not require more than a high school diploma.

- Manufacturing firms and wholesale and retail trade establishments are the primary employers.

- Production, planning, and expediting clerks work closely with supervisors who must approve production and work schedules.

Nature of the Work

Production, planning, and expediting clerks coordinate and expedite the flow of information, work, and materials within or among offices. Most of their work is done according to production, work, or shipment schedules that are devised by supervisors who determine work progress and completion dates. Production, planning, and expediting clerks compile reports on the progress of work and on production problems. They also may schedule workers, estimate costs, schedule the shipment of parts, keep an inventory of materials, inspect and assemble materials, and write special orders for services and merchandise. In addition, they may route and deliver parts to ensure that production quotas are met and that merchandise is delivered on the date promised.

Production and planning clerks compile records and reports on various aspects of production, such as materials and parts used, products produced, machine and instrument readings, and frequency of defects. These workers prepare work tickets or other production guides and distribute them to other workers. Production and planning clerks coordinate, schedule, monitor, and chart production and its progress, either manually or with electronic equipment. They also gather information from customers' orders or other specifications and use the information to prepare a detailed production sheet that serves as a guide in assembling or manufacturing the product.

Employers prefer to hire production, planning, and expediting clerks who are familiar with computers and other electronic office and business equipment.

Expediting clerks contact vendors and shippers to ensure that merchandise, supplies, and equipment are forwarded on the specified shipping dates. They communicate with transportation companies to prevent delays in transit, and they may arrange for the distribution of materials upon their arrival. They may even visit work areas of vendors and shippers to check the status of orders. Expediting clerks locate and distribute materials to specified production areas. They may inspect products for quality and quantity to ensure their adherence to specifications. They also keep a chronological list of due dates and may move work that does not meet the production schedule to the top of the list.

Working Conditions
Production, planning, and expediting clerks work closely with supervisors who must approve production and work schedules. The typical workweek is Monday through Friday.

Training, Other Qualifications, and Advancement
Many production, planning, and expediting jobs are at the entry level and do not require more than a high school diploma. Employers, however, prefer to hire those familiar with computers and other electronic office and business equipment. Applicants who have taken business courses or have specific job-related experience may be preferred. Because communication with other people is an integral part of some jobs in the occupation, good oral and written communication skills are essential. Typing, filing, recordkeeping, and other clerical skills also are important.

Production, planning, and expediting clerks usually learn the job by doing routine tasks under close supervision. They learn how to count and mark stock, and then they start keeping records and taking inventory. Strength, stamina, good eyesight, and an ability to work at repetitive tasks, sometimes under pressure, are important characteristics. Production, planning, and expediting clerks must learn both how their company operates and the company's priorities before they can begin to write production and work schedules efficiently.

Advancement opportunities for production, planning, and expediting clerks vary with the place of employment.

Employment
In 2004, production, planning, and expediting clerks held 292,000 jobs. Jobs in manufacturing made up 42 percent. Another 14 percent were in wholesale and retail trade establishments.

Job Outlook
As increasing pressure is put on firms to manufacture and deliver their goods more quickly and efficiently, the need for production, planning, and expediting clerks will grow, although the expected decline in overall employment in manufacturing will result in slower than average employment growth for production, planning, and expediting clerks through 2014. The work of production, planning, and expediting clerks is less likely to be automated than the work of many other administrative support occupations. In addition to openings due to employment growth, job openings will arise from the need to replace production, planning, and expediting clerks who leave the labor force or transfer to other occupations.

Earnings
Median annual earnings of production, planning, and expediting clerks in May 2004 were $36,340. The middle 50 percent earned between $27,690 and $45,880. The lowest 10 percent earned less than $21,690, and the highest 10 percent earned more than $55,850.

These workers usually receive the same benefits as most other workers. If uniforms are required, employers generally provide them or offer an allowance to purchase them.

Related Occupations
Other workers who coordinate the flow of information to assist the production process include cargo and freight agents; shipping, receiving, and traffic clerks; stock clerks and order fillers; and weighers, measurers, checkers, and samplers, recordkeeping.

Sources of Additional Information
Information about job opportunities may be obtained from local employers and from local offices of the State employment service.

Shipping, Receiving, and Traffic Clerks

(O*NET 43-5071.00)

Significant Points

- Many shipping, receiving, and traffic clerk positions are at the entry level and do not require more than a high school diploma.

- Slower-than-average employment growth is expected, as a result of increasing automation and the growing use of computers to store and retrieve shipping and receiving records.

Nature of the Work
Shipping, receiving, and traffic clerks keep records of all goods shipped and received. Their duties depend on the size of the establishment they work for and the level of automation used. Larger companies typically are better able to finance the purchase of computers and other equipment to handle some or all of a clerk's responsibilities. In smaller companies, a clerk maintains records, prepares shipments, and accepts deliveries. In both environments, shipping, receiving, and traffic clerks may lift cartons of various sizes.

Shipping clerks keep records of all outgoing shipments. They prepare shipping documents and mailing labels and make sure that orders have been filled correctly. Also, they record items taken from inventory and note when orders were filled. Sometimes they fill the order themselves, obtaining merchandise from the stockroom, noting when inventories run low, and wrapping or packing the goods in shipping containers. They also address and label packages, look up and compute freight or postal rates, and record the weight and cost of each shipment. In addition, shipping clerks may prepare invoices and furnish information about shipments to other parts of the company, such as the accounting department. Once a shipment is checked and ready to go, shipping clerks may move the goods from the plant—sometimes by forklift—to the shipping dock and direct their loading.

Receiving clerks perform tasks similar to those of shipping clerks. They determine whether orders have been filled correctly by verifying incoming shipments against the original order and the accompanying bill of lading or invoice. They make a record of the shipment and the condition of its contents. In many firms, receiving clerks either use hand-held scanners to record barcodes on incoming products or manually enter the information into a computer. These data then can be transferred to the appropriate departments. The shipment is checked for any discrepancies in quantity, price, and discounts. Receiving clerks may route or move shipments to the proper department, warehouse section, or stockroom. They also may arrange for adjustments with shippers whenever merchandise is lost or damaged. Receiving clerks in small businesses may perform some duties similar to those of stock clerks. In larger establishments, receiving clerks may control all receiving platform operations, such as scheduling of trucks, recording of shipments, and handling of damaged goods.

Traffic clerks maintain records on the destination, weight, and charges on all incoming and outgoing freight. They verify rate charges by comparing the classification of materials with rate charts. In many companies, this work may be automated. Information either is scanned or is entered by hand into a computer for use by the accounting department or other departments within the company. Traffic clerks also keep a file of claims for overcharges and for damage to goods in transit.

Working Conditions

Most jobs for shipping, receiving, and traffic clerks involve frequent standing, bending, walking, and stretching. Some lifting and carrying of smaller items also may be involved. Although automated devices have lessened the physical demands of this occupation, their use remains somewhat limited. The work still can be strenuous, even though mechanical material-handling equipment is employed to move heavy items.

Due to automation and the growing use of computers to store and retrieve product information, employment of shipping and receiving clerks will grow more slowly than average.

The typical workweek is Monday through Friday; however, evening and weekend hours are common in some jobs and may be required in other jobs when large shipments are involved.

Training, Other Qualifications, and Advancement

Many shipping, receiving, and traffic clerk positions are at the entry level and do not require more than a high school diploma. Employers, however, prefer to hire those familiar with computers and other electronic office and business equipment.

Shipping, receiving, and traffic clerks usually learn the job by doing routine tasks under close supervision. They first learn how to count and mark stock, and then they start keeping records and taking inventory. Strength, stamina, good eyesight, and an ability to work at repetitive tasks, sometimes under pressure, are important characteristics. Shipping, receiving, and traffic clerks who handle jewelry, liquor, or drugs may be bonded.

Shipping, receiving, and traffic clerks check items to be shipped and attach labels to them, making sure that the addresses are correct. Training in the use of automated equipment usually is done informally, on the job. As these occupations become more automated, however, workers in them may need longer periods of training to master the use of the equipment. Advancement opportunities for shipping, receiving, and traffic clerks vary with the place of employment. Shipping, receiving, and traffic clerks are promoted to head clerk, and those with a broad understanding of shipping and receiving may enter a related field, such as industrial traffic management.

Employment

Shipping, receiving, and traffic clerks held about 751,000 jobs in 2004. Almost three out of four were employed in manufacturing or by wholesale and retail establishments. Although jobs for shipping, receiving, and traffic clerks are found throughout the country, most clerks work in urban areas, where shipping depots in factories and wholesale establishments usually are located. (For information on workers who perform duties similar to those of shipping, receiving, and traffic clerks and who are employed by the U.S. Postal Service, see the statement on Postal Service workers elsewhere in the *Handbook*.)

Job Outlook

Employment of shipping, receiving, and traffic clerks is expected to grow more slowly than the average for all occupations through 2014. Job growth will continue to be limited by automation as all but the smallest firms move to reduce labor costs by using computers to store and retrieve shipping and receiving records.

Methods of handling materials have changed significantly in recent years. Large warehouses are increasingly becoming automated, with equipment such as computerized conveyor systems, robots, computer-directed trucks, and automatic data storage and retrieval systems. Automation, coupled with the growing use of hand-held scanners and personal computers in shipping and receiving departments, has increased the productivity of shipping, receiving, and traffic clerks.

Despite technology, job openings will continue to arise because of increasing economic and trade activity and because certain tasks cannot be automated. For example, someone needs to check shipments before they go out and when they arrive, to ensure that everything is in order. In addition, openings will occur because of the need to replace shipping, receiving, and traffic clerks who leave the occupation. Because this is an entry-level occupation, many vacancies are created by a worker's normal career progression.

Earnings

Median annual earnings of shipping, receiving, and traffic clerks in May 2004 were $24,400. The middle 50 percent earned between $19,600 and $30,720. The lowest 10 percent earned less than $16,290, and the highest 10 percent earned more than $37,610.

These workers usually receive the same benefits as most other workers. If uniforms are required, employers generally provide them or offer an allowance to purchase them.

Related Occupations

Shipping, receiving, and traffic clerks record, check, and often store materials that a company receives. They also process and pack goods for shipment. Other workers who perform similar duties are stock clerks and order fillers; production, planning, and expediting clerks; cargo and freight agents; and Postal Service workers.

Sources of Additional Information

Information about job opportunities may be obtained from local employers and local offices of the State employment service.

Stock Clerks and Order Fillers

(O*NET 43-5081.01, 43-5081.02, 43-5081.03, 43-5081.04)

Significant Points

- Employers prefer to hire stock clerks and order fillers who are familiar with computers and other electronic office and business equipment.
- Employment is projected to decline, due to the use of automation in factories, warehouses, and stores.

Nature of the Work

Stock clerks and order fillers receive, unpack, check, store, and track merchandise or materials. They keep records of items entering or leaving the stockroom and inspect damaged or spoiled goods. They sort, organize, and mark items with identifying codes, such as price, stock, or inventory control codes, so that inventories can be located quickly and easily. They also may be required to lift cartons of various sizes. In larger establishments, where they may be responsible for only one task, they may be called *stock-control clerks, merchandise distributors*, or *property custodians*. In smaller firms, they also may perform tasks usually handled by shipping and receiving clerks. (A separate statement on shipping, receiving, and traffic clerks appears elsewhere in the *Handbook*.)

In many firms, stock clerks and order fillers use hand-held scanners connected to computers to keep inventories up to date. In retail stores, stock clerks bring merchandise to the sales floor and stock shelves and racks. In stockrooms and warehouses, stock clerks store materials in bins, on floors, or on shelves. Instead of putting the merchandise on the sales floor or on shelves, order fillers take customers' orders and either hold the merchandise until the customers can pick it up or send it to them.

Working Conditions

Working conditions vary considerably by employment setting. Most jobs for stock clerks and order fillers involve frequent standing, bending, walking, and stretching. Some lifting and carrying of smaller items also may be involved. Although automated devices have lessened the physical demands of this occupation, their use remains somewhat limited. Even though mechanical material-handling equipment is employed to move heavy items, the work still can be strenuous.

The typical workweek is Monday through Friday; however, evening and weekend hours are common and may be required when large shipments are involved or when inventory is taken.

Training, Other Qualifications, and Advancement

Many stock clerk and order filler positions are at the entry level and do not require more than a high school diploma. Employers, however, prefer to hire those familiar with computers and other electronic office and business equipment. Typing, filing, record-keeping, and other clerical skills also are important.

Stock clerks and order fillers usually learn the job by doing routine tasks under close supervision. They learn how to count and mark stock, and then they start keeping records and taking inventory. Strength, stamina, good eyesight, and an ability to work at repetitive tasks, sometimes under pressure, are important characteristics. Stock clerks whose sole responsibility is to bring merchandise to the sales floor to stock shelves and racks need little training. Stock clerks and order fillers who handle jewelry, liquor, or drugs may be bonded.

Training in the use of automated equipment usually is done informally, on the job. As this occupation becomes more automated, however, workers may need longer periods of training to master the use of the equipment.

Advancement opportunities for stock clerks and order fillers vary with the place of employment. With additional training, some stock clerks and order fillers advance to jobs as warehouse manager or purchasing agent.

Employment

Stock clerks and order fillers held about 1.6 million jobs in 2004. More than three out of four work in wholesale and retail trade. The greatest numbers are found in grocery stores, followed by department stores. Jobs for stock clerks are found in all parts of the country, but most work in large urban areas that have many large suburban shopping centers, warehouses, and factories.

Job Outlook

Employment of stock clerks and order fillers is projected to decline through 2014 as a result of the use of automation in factories, warehouses, and stores. Because the occupation is very large and many jobs are entry level, however, numerous job openings will occur each year to replace those who transfer to other jobs or leave the labor force.

Most jobs for stock clerks and order fillers involve frequent standing, bending, walking, and stretching.

The growing use of computers for inventory control and the installation of new, automated equipment are expected to inhibit growth in demand for stock clerks and order fillers, especially in manufacturing and wholesale trade industries, where operations are most easily automated. In addition to using computerized inventory control systems, firms in these industries are relying more on sophisticated conveyor belts and automatic high stackers to store and retrieve goods. Also, expanded use of battery-powered, driverless, automatically guided vehicles can be expected.

Employment of stock clerks and order fillers who work in grocery, general merchandise, department, apparel, and accessories stores is expected to be somewhat less affected by automation because much of their work is done manually and is difficult to automate. In addition, the increasing role of large retail outlets and warehouses, as well as catalog, mail, telephone, and Internet shopping services, should bolster employment of stock clerks and order fillers in these sectors of retail trade.

Earnings
Median annual earnings of stock clerks and order fillers in May 2004 were $20,100. The middle 50 percent earned between $16,250 and $25,910. The lowest 10 percent earned less than $13,970, and the highest 10 percent earned more than $33,420.

These workers usually receive the same benefits as most other workers. If uniforms are required, employers generally provide them or offer an allowance to purchase them.

Related Occupations
Workers who also handle, move, organize, store, and keep records of materials include shipping, receiving, and traffic clerks; production, planning, and expediting clerks; cargo and freight agents; and procurement clerks.

Sources of Additional Information
State employment service offices can provide information about job openings for stock clerks and order fillers.

Weighers, measurers, checkers, and samplers, recordkeeping

(O*NET 43-5111.00)

Significant Points

- Many jobs are at the entry level and do not require more than a high school diploma.

- Employment of weighers, measurers, checkers, and samplers is expected to decline because of the increased use of automated equipment that performs the function of these workers.

Nature of the Work
Weighers, measurers, checkers, and samplers weigh, measure, and check materials, supplies, and equipment in order to keep accurate records. Most of their duties are clerical. Using either manual or automated data-processing systems, they verify the quantity, quality, and overall value of the items they are responsible for and check the condition of items purchased, sold, or produced against records, bills, invoices, or receipts. They check the items to ensure the accuracy of the recorded data. They prepare reports on warehouse inventory levels and on use of parts. Weighers, measurers, checkers, and samplers also check for any defects in the items and record the severity of the defects they find.

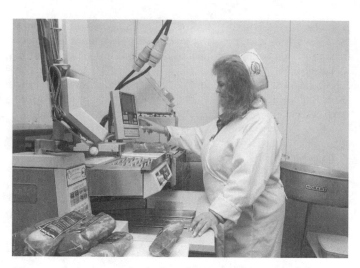

Many workers use weight scales, counting devices, tally sheets, and calculators to obtain information about products.

These workers use weight scales, counting devices, tally sheets, and calculators to obtain information about the products. They usually move objects to and from the scales with a handtruck or forklift. They issue receipts for the products when needed or requested.

Working Conditions
Working conditions vary considerably by employment setting. Weighers, measurers, checkers, and samplers work in a wide variety of businesses, institutions, and industries. Some work in warehouses, stockrooms, or shipping and receiving rooms that may not be temperature controlled. Others may spend time in cold storage rooms or on loading platforms where they are exposed to the weather.

Training, Other Qualifications, and Advancement
Many weigher, measurer, checker, and sampler jobs are at the entry level and do not require more than a high school diploma. Employers, however, prefer to hire those familiar with computers. Applicants who have specific job-related experience may be preferred. Typing, filing, recordkeeping, and other clerical skills also are important. Advancement opportunities vary with the place of employment.

Employment
Weighers, measurers, checkers, and samplers held about 88,000 jobs in 2004. Their employment is spread across many industries. Retail trade accounted for 20 percent of those jobs, manufacturing accounted for about 21 percent, and wholesale trade employed another 13 percent.

Job Outlook
Employment of weighers, measurers, checkers, and samplers is expected to decline through 2014 because of the increased use of automated equipment that performs the function of these workers. Also, many of the industries that employ these workers are expected to decrease employment. In addition to job openings resulting from job growth, openings should arise from the need to replace workers who leave the labor force or transfer to other occupations.

Earnings
Median annual earnings of weighers, measurers, checkers, and samplers in May 2004 were $24,570. The middle 50 percent earned between $19,360 and $32,560. The lowest 10 percent earned less than $16,140, and the highest 10 percent earned more than $42,190.

These workers usually receive the same benefits as most other workers. If uniforms are required, employers generally provide them or offer an allowance to purchase them.

Related Occupations
Other workers who determine and document characteristics of materials or equipment include cargo and freight agents; production, planning, and expediting clerks; shipping, receiving, and traffic clerks; stock clerks and order fillers; and procurement clerks.

Sources of Additional Information
Information about job opportunities may be obtained from local employers and local offices of the State employment service.

Other Office and Administrative Support Occupations

Communications Equipment Operators

(O*NET 43-2011.00, 43-2021.01, 43-2021.02, 43-2099.99)

Significant Points
- Switchboard operators hold 4 out of 5 jobs.
- Workers train on the job.
- Employment is expected to decline.

Nature of the Work
Most communications equipment operators work as *switchboard operators* for a wide variety of businesses, such as hospitals, hotels, telephone call centers, and government agencies. Switchboard operators use private branch exchange (PBX) or voice over Internet protocol (VoIP) switchboards to relay incoming, outgoing, and interoffice calls, usually for a single organization. They also may handle other clerical duties, such as supplying information, taking messages, and announcing visitors. Technological improvements have automated many of the tasks handled by switchboard operators. New systems automatically connect outside calls to the correct destination or automated directories, and voice-mail systems take messages without the assistance of an operator.

Some communications equipment operators work as *telephone operators*, assisting customers in making telephone calls. Although most calls are connected automatically, callers sometimes require the assistance of an operator. *Central office operators* help customers to complete local and long-distance calls, usually under special circumstances. *Directory assistance operators* provide customers with information such as telephone numbers or area codes.

When callers dial "0," they usually reach a central office operator, also known as a *local*, *long-distance*, or *call completion operator*. Most of these operators work for telephone companies, and many of their responsibilities have been automated. For example, callers can make international, collect, and credit card calls without the assistance of a central office operator. Other tasks previously handled by these operators, such as billing calls to third parties and monitoring the cost of a call, also have been automated.

Callers still need a central office operator for a limited number of tasks, including placing person-to-person calls or interrupting busy lines if an emergency warrants the disruption. When natural disasters such as storms or earthquakes occur, central office operators provide callers with emergency phone contacts. They also assist callers who are having difficulty with automated phone systems. An operator monitoring an automated system that aids a caller in placing collect calls, for example, may intervene if a caller needs assistance with the system.

Directory assistance operators provide callers with information such as telephone numbers or area codes. Most directory assistance operators work for telephone companies; increasingly, they also work for companies that provide business services. Automated systems now handle many of the responsibilities once performed by directory assistance operators. The systems prompt callers for a listing and may even connect the call after providing the telephone number. However, directory assistance operators monitor many of the calls received by automated systems. The operators listen to recordings of the customer's request and then key information into electronic directories to access the correct telephone numbers. Directory assistance operators also provide personal assistance to customers having difficulty using the automated system.

Other communications equipment operators include workers who operate satellite communications equipment, telegraph equipment, and a wide variety of other communications equipment.

Working Conditions
Most communications equipment operators work in pleasant, well-lighted surroundings. Because telephone operators spend much time seated at keyboards and video monitors, employers often provide workstations designed to decrease glare and other physical discomforts. Such improvements reduce the incidence of eyestrain, back discomfort, and injury due to repetitive motion.

Switchboard operators generally work the same hours as other clerical employees at their company. In most organizations, full-time operators work regular business hours over a 5-day workweek. Work schedules are more irregular in hotels, hospitals, and other organizations that require round-the-clock operator services. In these companies, switchboard operators may work in the evenings and on holidays and weekends.

Central office and directory assistance operators must be accessible to customers 24 hours a day; therefore, they work a variety of shifts. Some operators work split shifts, coming on duty during peak calling

Many communications equipment operators also perform clerical work.

periods in the late morning and early evening and going off duty during the intervening hours. Telephone companies normally assign shifts by seniority, allowing the most experienced operators first choice of schedules. As a result, entry-level operators may have less desirable schedules, including late evening, split-shift, and weekend work. Telephone company operators may work overtime during emergencies.

Approximately 1 in 6 communications equipment operators works part time. Because of the irregular nature of telephone operator schedules, many employers seek part-time workers for those shifts that are difficult to fill.

An operator's work may be quite repetitive and the pace hectic during peak calling periods. To maintain operators' efficiency, supervisors at telephone companies often monitor their performance, including the amount of time they spend on each call. The rapid pace of the job and frequent monitoring may cause stress.

Training, Other Qualifications, and Advancement

Switchboard operators usually receive informal on-the-job training, lasting only a few days or weeks. Because they are often the first contact with the public or client, switchboard operators often receive some training in customer service. Training may also vary by place of employment—a switchboard operator in a hospital would need training on how to handle different emergencies. Since switchboard operators' duties may include clerical work, basic computer skills training may also be required.

Entry-level central office and directory assistance operators at telecommunications companies may receive both classroom and on-the-job instruction that can last several weeks. These operators may be paired with experienced personnel who provide hands-on instruction.

New employees in both occupations are trained in the operation of their equipment and in procedures designed to maximize efficiency. They are familiarized with company policies, including the expected level of customer service. Instructors monitor both the time and quality of trainees' responses to customer requests. Supervisors may continue to monitor new employees closely after they complete their initial training session.

Employers generally require a high school diploma. Applicants should have clear speech, good hearing, and strong reading, spelling, and numerical skills. Computer literacy and typing skills also are important, and familiarity with a foreign language is helpful for some positions because of the increasing diversity of the population. Candidates for positions may be required to take an examination covering basic language and math skills. Most companies emphasize customer service and seek operators who will remain courteous to customers while working at a fast pace.

After 1 or 2 years on the job, communications equipment operators may advance to other positions within a company. Many enter clerical occupations in which their operator experience is valuable, such as customer service representative, dispatcher, and receptionist. (See the *Handbook* statements on these occupations.) Operators interested in more technical work may take training classes and advance into positions having to do with installing and repairing equipment. (See the *Handbook* statements on radio and telecommunications equipment installers and repairers, and line installers and repairers.) Promotion to supervisory positions also is possible.

Employment

Communications equipment operators held about 256,000 jobs in 2004. About 4 out of 5 worked as switchboard operators. Employment was distributed as follows:

Switchboard operators, including answering service	213,000
Telephone operators	39,000
All other communications equipment operators	4,200

Switchboard operators work in almost all industries, but are concentrated in telephone call centers, hospitals, and hotels. Many work as temporary employees in the employment services industry.

Job Outlook

Employment of communications equipment operators is projected to decline through 2014, due largely to new labor-saving communications technologies, the movement of jobs to foreign countries, and consolidation of telephone operator jobs into fewer locations, often staffed by temporary or contract workers. Virtually all job openings will result from the need to replace communications equipment operators who transfer to other occupations or leave the labor force.

Developments in communications technologies—in particular, voice recognition systems that are accessible and easy to use—will continue to have a significant impact on the demand for communications equipment operators. Voice recognition technology allows automated telephone systems to recognize human speech. Callers speak directly to the system, which interprets the speech and then connects the call. Because voice recognition systems do not require callers to input data through a telephone keypad, they are easier to use than touch-tone systems. Voice recognition systems are increasingly able to understand sophisticated vocabulary and grammatical structures; however, many companies will continue to employ operators so that those callers who do have problems can access a "live" employee if they desire.

The proliferation of cell phones has negatively affected both switchboard operators and telephone operators. By allowing for direct communication between persons, cell phones have eliminated the need for operators to transfer calls in certain situations. Cell phones have reduced the demand for directory assistance and collect calls, and have resulted in decreasing use of pay phones that often required operators to assist with the call. The increasing use of cell phones also have reduced demand for switchboard operators in hotels, because hotel guests now use in-room phones less frequently.

Electronic communication through the Internet or e-mail provides alternatives to telephone communication and requires no operators. Internet directory assistance services are reducing the need for directory assistance operators. Local telephone companies currently have the most reliable telephone directory data; however, Internet services provide information such as addresses and maps, in addition to telephone numbers. As the functions of telephones and computers converge, the convenience of Internet directory assistance is expected to attract many customers, reducing the need for telephone operators to provide this service.

As communications technologies have improved and the price of long-distance service has fallen, companies are finding other ways to reduce costs by consolidating operator jobs in low cost locations. Increasingly this has entailed the movement of telephone operator jobs offshore to other lower-wage countries in order to reduce costs.

Earnings

Median hourly earnings of switchboard operators, including answering service, were $10.38 in May 2004. The middle 50 percent earned between $8.69 and $12.64. The lowest 10 percent earned less than $7.35, and the highest 10 percent earned more than $15.13. Median hourly earnings in the industries employing the largest numbers of switchboard operators in May 2004 are:

Offices of physicians	$10.54
General medical and surgical hospitals	10.47
Traveler accommodation	10.25
Automobile dealers	9.60
Business support services	8.91

Median hourly earnings of telephone operators in May 2004 were $13.65. The middle 50 percent earned between $10.28 and $19.32. The lowest 10 percent earned less than $8.91, and the highest 10 percent earned more than $21.32.

Some telephone operators working at telephone companies are members of the Communications Workers of America or the International Brotherhood of Electrical Workers. For these operators, union contracts govern wage rates, wage increases, and the time required to advance from one pay step to the next. It normally takes 4 years to rise from the lowest paying nonsupervisory operator position to the highest. Contracts call for extra pay for work beyond the normal 6-1/2 to 7-1/2 hours a day or 5 days a week, for Sunday and holiday work, and for bilingual positions. A pay differential also is guaranteed for night work and split shifts. Many contracts provide for a 1-week vacation after 6 months of service, 2 weeks after 1 year, 3 weeks after 7 years, 4 weeks after 15 years, and 5 weeks after 25 years. Holidays range from 9 to 11 days a year.

Median hourly earnings of communication equipment operators, all other, in May 2004 were $15.23. The middle 50 percent earned between $12.27 and $18.99. The lowest 10 percent earned less than $10.23, and the highest 10 percent earned more than $22.70.

Related Occupations

Other workers who provide information to the general public include dispatchers; hotel, motel, and resort desk clerks; customer service representatives; receptionists and information clerks; and reservation and transportation ticket agents and travel clerks.

Sources of Additional Information

For more details about employment opportunities, contact a telephone company or temporary help agency, or write to either of the following unions:
➤ Communications Workers of America, 501 3rd St. NW., Washington, DC 20001.
➤ International Brotherhood of Electrical Workers, Telecommunications Department, 1125 15th St. NW., Room 807, Washington, DC 20005.

For more information on training in customer service and customer relations, contact:
➤ International Association of Administrative Professionals, 10502 NW Ambassador Dr., PO Box 20404, Kansas City, MO 64195-0404.

Computer Operators

(O*NET 43-9011.00)

Significant Points

- Computer operators rank among the most rapidly declining occupations over the 2004-14 period because advances in technology are making many of the duties traditionally performed by computer operators obsolete.

- Computer operators usually receive on-the-job training; the length of training varies with the job and the experience of the worker.

- Opportunities will be best for operators who have formal computer education, are familiar with a variety of operating systems, and keep up to date with the latest technology.

Nature of the Work

Computer operators oversee the operation of computer hardware systems, ensuring that these machines are used as efficiently and securely as possible. They may work with mainframes, minicomputers, or networks of personal computers. Computer operators must anticipate problems and take preventive action, as well as solve problems that occur during operations.

The duties of computer operators vary with the size of the installation, the type of equipment used, and the policies of the employer. Generally, operators control the console of either a mainframe digital computer or a group of minicomputers. Working from operating instructions prepared by programmers, users, or operations managers, computer operators set controls on the computer and on peripheral devices required to run a particular job.

Computer operators load equipment with tapes, disks, and paper, as needed. While the computer is running—which may be 24 hours a day for large computers—computer operators monitor the control console and respond to operating and computer messages. Messages indicate the individual specifications of each job being run. If an error message occurs, operators must locate and solve the problem or terminate the program. Operators also maintain logbooks or operating records, listing each job that is run and events, such as machine malfunctions, that occur during their shift. In addition, computer operators may help programmers and systems analysts test and debug new programs. (See the statements on computer programmers and computer systems analysts, elsewhere in the *Handbook*.)

As the number and complexity of computer networks continue to grow, a greater number of computer operators are working on personal computers (PCs) and minicomputers. In many offices, factories, and other work settings, PCs and minicomputers are connected in networks, often referred to as local area networks (LANs) or multi-user systems. Whereas users in the area operate some of these computers, many require the services of full-time operators. The tasks performed on PCs and minicomputers are very similar to those performed on large computers. This includes trying to keep computer networks secure in the face of a increasing number of cyber-attacks.

As organizations continue to look for opportunities to increase productivity, automation is expanding into additional areas of computer operations. Sophisticated software, coupled with robotics, enables a computer to perform many routine tasks formerly done by computer

Computer operators oversee the operation of computer hardware systems.

operators. Scheduling, loading and downloading programs, mounting tapes, rerouting messages, and running periodic reports can be done without the intervention of an operator. Consequently, these improvements will change what computer operators do in the future. As technology advances, the responsibilities of many computer operators are shifting to areas such as network operations, user support, and database maintenance.

Working Conditions

Computer operators generally work in well-lighted, well-ventilated, comfortable rooms. Because many organizations use their computers 24 hours a day, 7 days a week, computer operators may be required to work evening or night shifts and weekends. Shift assignments usually are made based on seniority. However, increasingly automated operations will lessen the need for shift work, because many companies can let the computer take over operations during less desirable working hours. In addition, advances in telecommuting technologies—such as faxes, modems, and e-mail—and data center automation, such as automated tape libraries, enable some operators to monitor batch processes, check systems performance, and record problems for the next shift.

Because computer operators generally spend a lot of time in front of a computer monitor, as well as performing repetitive tasks such as loading and unloading printers, they may be susceptible to eyestrain, back discomfort, and hand and wrist problems.

Training, Other Qualifications, and Advancement

Computer operators usually receive on-the-job training in order to become acquainted with their employer's equipment and routines. The length of training varies with the job and the experience of the worker. However, previous work experience is the key to obtaining an operator job in many large establishments. Employers generally look for specific, hands-on experience with the type of equipment and related operating systems they use. Additionally, formal computer training, perhaps through a community college or technical school, is recommended. Related training also can be obtained through the U.S. Armed Forces and from some computer manufacturers. As computer technology changes and data processing centers become more automated, employers will increasingly require candidates to have formal training and experience for operator jobs. And, although not required, a bachelor's degree in a computer field can be helpful when one is seeking employment as a computer operator or advancement to a managerial position.

Because computer technology changes so rapidly, operators must be adaptable and willing to learn. Analytical and technical expertise also are needed, particularly by operators who work in automated data centers, to deal with unique or high-level problems that a computer is not programmed to handle. Operators must be able to communicate well, and to work effectively with programmers, users, and other operators. Computer operators also must be able to work independently because they may have little or no direct supervision.

A few computer operators may advance to supervisory jobs, although most management positions within data processing or computer operations centers require advanced formal education, such as a bachelor's or higher degree. Through on-the-job experience and additional formal education, some computer operators may advance to jobs in areas such as network operations or support. As they gain experience in programming, some operators may advance to jobs as programmers or analysts. A move into these types of jobs is becoming much more difficult, as employers increasingly require candidates for more skilled computer jobs to possess at least a bachelor's degree.

Employment

Computer operators held about 149,000 jobs in 2004. Jobs are found in various industries such as government, health care,, manufacturing, data processing services and other information industries, and finance and insurance. A number of computer operators are employed by firms in computer systems design and related services, as more companies contract out their data processing operations.

Job Outlook

Employment of computer operators is projected to decline significantly. In fact, computer operators rank among the most rapidly declining occupations over the 2004-14 period because advances in technology are making many of the duties traditionally performed by computer operators obsolete. Experienced operators are expected to compete for the few job openings that will arise each year to replace workers who transfer to other occupations or leave the labor force. Opportunities will be best for operators who have formal computer education, are familiar with a variety of operating systems, and keep up to date with the latest technology.

Advances in technology have reduced both the size and cost of computer equipment, while increasing the capacity for data storage and processing automation. Sophisticated computer hardware and software are now used in practically every industry, in such areas as factory and office automation, telecommunications, health care, education, and government. The expanding use of software that automates computer operations gives companies the option of making systems more user-friendly, greatly reducing the need for operators. Such improvements require operators to monitor a greater number of operations at the same time and be capable of solving a broader range of problems that may arise. The result is that fewer operators will be needed to perform more highly skilled work.

Computer operators who are displaced by automation may be reassigned to support staffs that maintain personal computer networks or assist other members of the organization. Operators who keep up with changing technology, by updating their skills through additional training, should have the best prospects of moving into other areas such as network administration and technical support. Others may be retrained to perform different job duties, such as supervising an operations center, maintaining automation packages, or analyzing computer operations to recommend ways to increase productivity. In the future, operators who wish to work in the computer field will need to know more about programming, automation software, graphics interface, client/server environments, and open systems in order to take advantage of changing job opportunities.

Earnings

Median annual earnings of computer operators were $31,070 in May 2004. The middle 50 percent earned between $24,190 and $39,900 a year. The highest 10 percent earned more than $48,720, and the lowest 10 percent earned less than $19,250. Median annual earnings in the industries employing the largest numbers of computer operators in May 2004 are shown below:

Management of companies and enterprises	$34,370
Computer systems design and related services	31,780
Colleges, universities, and professional schools	28,990
Data processing, hosting, and related services	28,930
Depository credit intermediation	24,880

The average salary for computer operators employed by the Federal Government was $45,158 in 2005.

According to Robert Half International, the average starting salaries for computer operators ranged from $27,250 to $39,500 in 2005. Salaries generally are higher in large organizations than in small ones.

Related Occupations

Other occupations involving work with computers include computer software engineers; computer programmers; computer support specialists and systems administrators; computer systems analysts, and computer scientists and database administrators. Other occupations in which workers operate electronic office equipment include data entry and information processing workers, as well as secretaries and administrative assistants.

Sources of Additional Information

For information about a career as a computer operator, contact:
➤ Association for Computer Operations Management (AFCOM), 722 E. Chapman Ave., Orange, CA 92860.

For information about work opportunities in computer operations, contact establishments with large computer centers, such as banks, manufacturing firms, insurance companies, colleges and universities, and data processing service organizations. The local office of the State employment service can supply information about employment and training opportunities.

Data Entry and Information Processing Workers

(O*NET 43-9021.00, 43-9022.00)

Significant Points

- Employers generally hire high school graduates who meet company requirements for keyboarding speed; for many people, a job as a data entry and information processing worker is their first job after graduating from high school.

- Although overall employment is projected to decline, the need to replace workers who leave this large occupation each year should produce many job openings.

- Job prospects should be best for those with expertise in appropriate computer software applications.

Nature of the Work

Organizations need to process a rapidly growing amount of information. Data entry and information processing workers help ensure the smooth and efficient handling of information. By keying in text, entering data into a computer, operating a variety of office machines, and performing other clerical duties, these workers help organizations keep up with the rapid changes that are characteristic of today's "Information Age." In addition to the job titles discussed below—such as word processors, typists, and data entry keyers—data entry and information processing workers are known by various other titles, including electronic data processors, keypunch technicians, and transcribers.

Word processors usually set up and prepare reports, letters, mailing labels, and other text material. As entry-level workers, word processors may begin by keying headings on form letters, addressing envelopes, or preparing standard forms on computers. As they gain experience, they often are assigned tasks requiring a higher degree of accuracy and independent judgment. Senior word processors may work with highly technical material, plan and key complicated statistical tables, combine and rearrange materials from different sources, or prepare master copies.

Most keyboarding is now done on computers that normally are connected to a monitor, keyboard, and printer and may have "add-on" capabilities, such as optical character recognition readers. *Word processors* use this equipment to record, edit, store, and revise letters, memos, reports, statistical tables, forms, and other printed materials. Although it is becoming less common, some word processing workers are employed on centralized word processing teams that handle transcription and keying for several departments.

In addition to fulfilling the duties mentioned above, word processors often perform other office tasks, such as answering telephones, filing, and operating copiers or other office machines. Job titles of these workers frequently vary to reflect these duties. For example, administrative clerks combine word processing with filing, sorting mail, answering telephones, and other general office work. Note readers transcribe stenotyped notes of court proceedings into standard formats.

Data entry keyers usually input lists of items, numbers, or other data into computers or complete forms that appear on a computer screen. They also may manipulate existing data, edit current information, or proofread new entries into a database for accuracy. Some examples of data sources include customers' personal information, medical records, and membership lists. Usually, this information is used internally by a company and may be reformatted before other departments or customers utilize it.

Keyers use various types of equipment to enter data. Many use a machine that converts the information they type to magnetic impulses on tapes or disks for entry into a computer system. Others prepare materials for printing or publication by using data entry composing machines. Some keyers operate online terminals or personal computers. Increasingly, data entry keyers are working with nonkeyboard forms of data entry, such as scanners and electronically transmitted files. When using the new character recognition systems, data entry keyers often enter only those data which cannot be recognized by machines. In some offices, keyers also operate computer peripheral equipment such as printers and tape readers, act as tape librarians, and perform other clerical duties.

Working Conditions

Data entry and information processing workers usually work a standard 40-hour week in clean offices. They sit for long periods and

Data entry and information processing workers help ensure the smooth and efficient handling of information.

sometimes must contend with high noise levels caused by various office machines. These workers are susceptible to repetitive strain injuries such as carpal tunnel syndrome, neck and back injuries, and eyestrain. To help prevent these conditions, many offices have adopted regularly scheduled exercise breaks, ergonomically designed keyboards, and workstations that allow workers to stand or sit as they wish.

Training, Other Qualifications, and Advancement
Employers generally hire high school graduates who meet their requirements for keyboarding speed. Increasingly, employers also are expecting applicants to have training or experience in word processing or data entry tasks. Spelling, punctuation, and grammar skills are important, as is familiarity with standard office equipment and procedures.

Students acquire skills in keyboarding and in the use of word processing, spreadsheet, and database management computer software packages through high schools, community colleges, business schools, temporary help agencies, or self-teaching aids such as books, tapes, and Internet tutorials.

For many people, a job as a data entry and information processing worker is their first job after graduating from high school or after a period of full-time family responsibilities. This work frequently serves as a steppingstone to higher paying jobs with increased responsibilities. Large companies and government agencies usually have training programs to help administrative employees upgrade their skills and advance to higher level positions. It is common for data entry and information processing workers to transfer to other administrative jobs, such as secretary, administrative assistant, or statistical clerk, or to be promoted to a supervisory job in a word processing or data entry center.

Employment
Data entry and information processing workers held about 525,000 jobs in 2004 and were employed in every sector of the economy; 330,000 were data entry keyers and 194,000 were word processors. Some workers telecommute, working from their homes on personal computers linked by telephone lines to those in the main office. This arrangement enables them to key in material at home while still being able to produce printed copy in their offices.

About 1 out of 5 data entry and information processing workers held jobs in firms providing administrative and support services, including temporary help and word processing agencies, and another 1 in 5 worked for State or local government.

Job Outlook
Overall employment of data entry and information processing workers is projected to decline through 2014. Nevertheless, the need to replace those who transfer to other occupations or leave this large occupation for other reasons will produce numerous job openings each year. Job prospects will be most favorable for those with the best technical skills—in particular, expertise in appropriate computer software applications. Data entry and information processing workers must be willing to upgrade their skills continuously in order to remain marketable.

Although data entry and information processing workers are affected by productivity gains stemming from organizational restructuring and the implementation of new technologies, projected growth differs among these workers. Employment of word processors and typists is expected to decline because of the proliferation of personal computers, which allows other workers to perform duties formerly assigned to word processors and typists. Most professionals and managers, for example, now use desktop personal computers to do their own word processing. However, because technologies affecting data entry keyers tend to be costlier to implement, employment of these workers will decline less than word processors and typists.

Employment growth of data entry keyers will be dampened by productivity gains as various data-capturing technologies, such as barcode scanners, voice recognition technologies, and sophisticated character recognition readers, become more prevalent. These technologies can be applied to a variety of business transactions, such as inventory tracking, invoicing, and placing orders. Moreover, as telecommunications technology improves, many organizations will increasingly take advantage of computer networks that allow data to be transmitted electronically. These networks will permit more data to be entered automatically into computers, reducing the demand for data entry keyers.

In addition to being affected by technology, employment of data entry and information processing workers will be adversely affected by businesses that are increasingly contracting out their work. Many organizations have reduced or even eliminated permanent in-house staff—for example, in favor of temporary employment and staffing services firms. Some large data entry and information processing firms increasingly employ workers in nations with relatively lower wages. As international trade barriers continue to fall and telecommunications technology improves, this transfer of jobs will mean reduced demand for data entry keyers in the United States.

Earnings
Median annual earnings of word processors and typists in May 2004 were $28,030. The middle 50 percent earned between $22,850 and $34,900. The lowest 10 percent earned less than $18,960, while the highest 10 percent earned more than $43,190. The salaries of these workers vary by industry and by region. In May 2004, median annual earnings in the industries employing the largest numbers of word processors and typists were as follows:

Legal services	$36,890
Local government	29,190
Elementary and secondary schools	27,630
State government	27,210
Employment services	25,450

Median annual earnings of data entry keyers in May 2004 were $23,250. The middle 50 percent earned between $19,630 and $28,150. The lowest 10 percent earned less than $16,480, and the highest 10 percent earned more than $34,410. The following are median annual earnings for May 2004 in the industries employing the largest numbers of data entry keyers:

Insurance carriers	$23,980
Accounting, tax preparation, bookkeeping, and payroll services	23,120
Depository credit intermediation	21,950
Employment services	21,550
Data processing, hosting, and related services	20,750

Related Occupations
Data entry and information processing workers must transcribe information quickly. Other workers who deliver information in a timely manner are dispatchers and communications equipment operators. Data entry and information processing workers also must be comfortable working with office technology, and in this regard they are similar to court reporters, medical records and health information technicians, secretaries and administrative assistants, and computer operators.

Sources of Additional Information

For information about job opportunities for data entry and information processing workers, contact the nearest office of the State employment service.

Desktop Publishers

(O*NET 43-9031.00)

Significant Points

- About 4 out of 10 work for newspaper, periodical, book, and directory publishers, while 1 out of 4 work in printing and related support activities.

- Employment is expected to grow faster than the average for all occupations.

- Most employers prefer to hire experienced desktop publishers; among persons without experience, opportunities should be best for those with certificates or degrees in desktop publishing or graphic design.

Nature of the Work

Using computer software, desktop publishers format and combine text, numerical data, photographs, charts, and other visual graphic elements to produce publication-ready material. Depending on the nature of a particular project, desktop publishers may write and edit text, create graphics to accompany text, convert photographs and drawings into digital images and then manipulate those images, design page layouts, create proposals, develop presentations and advertising campaigns, typeset and do color separation, and translate electronic information onto film or other traditional forms. Materials produced by desktop publishers include books, business cards, calendars, magazines, newsletters and newspapers, packaging, slides, and tickets. As companies have brought the production of marketing, promotional, and other kinds of materials in-house, they increasingly have employed people who can produce such materials.

Desktop publishers use a keyboard to enter and select formatting properties, such as the size and style of type, column width, and spacing, and store them in the computer, which then displays and arranges columns of type on a video display terminal or computer monitor. An entire newspaper, catalog, or book page, complete with artwork and graphics, can be created on the screen exactly as it will appear in print. Operators transmit the pages for production either into film and then into printing plates, or directly into plates.

Desktop publishing is a rapidly changing field that encompasses a number of different kinds of jobs. Personal computers enable desktop publishers to perform publishing tasks that would otherwise require complicated equipment and extensive human effort. Advances in computer software and printing technology continue to change and enhance desktop publishing work. Instead of receiving simple typed text from customers, desktop publishers get the material over the Internet or on a computer disk. Other innovations in the occupation include digital color page makeup systems, electronic page layout systems, and off-press color proofing systems. In addition, because most materials today often are published on the Internet, desktop publishers may need to know electronic publishing technologies, such as Hypertext Markup Language (HTML) and may be responsible for converting text and graphics to an Internet-ready format.

Typesetting and page layout have been affected by the technological changes shaping desktop publishing. Increasingly, desktop publishers are using computers to do much of the typesetting and page-layout work formerly done by prepress workers, posing new challenges for the printing industry. The old "hot type" method of text composition—which used molten lead to create individual letters, paragraphs, and full pages of text—is nearly extinct. Today, composition work is done primarily with computers. Improvements in desktop-publishing software also allow customers to do much more of their own typesetting.

Desktop publishers use scanners to capture photographs, images, or art as digital data that can be either incorporated directly into electronic page layouts or further manipulated with the use of computer software. The desktop publisher then can correct mistakes or compensate for deficiencies in the original color print or transparency. Digital files are used to produce printing plates. Like photographers and multimedia artists and animators, desktop publishers also can create special effects or other visual images using film, video, computers, or other electronic media. (Separate statements on photographers and on artists and related workers appear elsewhere in the *Handbook*.)

Desktop publishers often perform writing and editing tasks as well as page layout and design. For example, in addition to laying out articles for a newsletter, desktop publishers may be responsible for editing content they receive or for writing original content themselves. A desktop publisher's writing and editing responsibilities vary widely from employer to employer. Small firms typically need desktop publishers to perform a wide range of tasks, while desktop publishers at large firms specialize in a certain part of the publishing process. (Writers and editors are discussed elsewhere in the *Handbook*.)

Depending on the establishment employing these workers, desktop publishers also may be referred to as publications specialists, electronic publishers, DTP operators, desktop publishing editors, electronic prepress technicians, electronic publishing specialists, image designers, typographers, compositors, layout artists, and Web publications designers.

Working Conditions

Desktop publishers usually work in clean, air-conditioned office areas with little noise. They generally work an 8-hour day, 5 days a week. Some workers work night shifts, weekends, and holidays.

Desktop publishers often are subject to stress and the pressures of short deadlines and tight work schedules. Like other workers who spend long hours working in front of a computer monitor, they may be susceptible to eyestrain, back discomfort, and hand and wrist problems.

Using computer software, desktop publishers capture photographs, images, or art as digital data that can be incorporated directly into electronic page layouts.

Training, Other Qualifications, and Advancement

Most workers qualify for jobs as desktop publishers by taking classes or completing certificate programs at vocational schools, universities, and colleges or through the Internet. Programs range in length, but the average certificate program takes approximately 1 year. However, some desktop publishers train on the job to develop the necessary skills. The length of on-the-job training varies by company. An internship or part-time desktop-publishing assignment is another way to gain experience as a desktop publisher.

Students interested in pursuing a career in desktop publishing may obtain an associate degree in applied science or a bachelor's degree in graphic arts, graphic communications, or graphic design. Graphic arts programs are a good way to learn about desktop publishing software used to format pages; assign type characteristics; and import text and graphics into electronic page layouts to produce printed materials such as advertisements, brochures, newsletters, and forms. Applying this knowledge of graphic arts techniques and computerized typesetting usually is intended for students who may eventually move into management positions, while 2-year associate degree programs are designed to train skilled workers. Students also develop finely tuned skills in typography, print media, packaging, branding and identity, Web site design, and motion graphics. The programs teach print and graphic design fundamentals and provide an extensive background in imaging, prepress operations, print reproduction, and emerging media. Courses in other aspects of printing also are available at vocational-technical institutes, industry-sponsored update and retraining programs, and private trade and technical schools.

Although formal training is not always required, those with certificates or degrees will have the best job opportunities. Most employers prefer to hire people who have at least a high school diploma and who possess good communication skills, basic computer skills, and a strong work ethic. Desktop publishers should be able to deal courteously with people because, in small shops, they may have to take customers' orders. They also may have to add, subtract, multiply, divide, and compute ratios to estimate job costs. Persons interested in working for firms using advanced printing technology need to know the basics of electronics and computers.

Desktop publishers need good manual dexterity, and they must be able to pay attention to detail and work independently. Good eyesight, including visual acuity, depth perception, a wide field of view, color vision, and the ability to focus quickly also are assets. Artistic ability often is a plus. Employers also seek persons who are even tempered and adaptable—important qualities for workers who often must meet deadlines and learn how to operate new equipment.

Workers with limited training and experience may start as helpers. They begin with instruction from an experienced desktop publisher and advance on the basis of their demonstrated mastery of skills at each level. All workers should expect to be retrained from time to time to handle new, improved software and equipment. As workers gain experience, they advance to positions with greater responsibility. Some move into supervisory or management positions. Other desktop publishers may start their own company or work as independent consultants, while those with more artistic talent and further education may find opportunities in graphic design or commercial art.

Employment

Desktop publishers held about 34,000 jobs in 2004. About 4 out of 10 worked for newspaper, periodical, book, and directory publishers, while 1 out of 4 worked in printing and related support activities; the rest worked in a wide variety of industries.

Firms in the publishing industry publish newspapers, periodicals, books, directory and mailing lists, and greeting cards. Printing and related support activities firms print a wide range of products—newspapers, books, labels, business cards, stationery, inserts, catalogs, pamphlets, and advertisements—while business form establishments print material such as sales receipts and business forms and perform support activities such as data imaging and bookbinding. Establishments in printing and related support activities typically perform custom composition, platemaking, and related prepress services. (A separate statement on prepress technicians and workers appears elsewhere in the *Handbook*.). Other desktop publishers print or publish materials in-house or in-plant for business services firms, government agencies, hospitals, or universities, typically in a reproduction or publications department that operates within the organization.

The printing and publishing industries are two of the most geographically dispersed industries in the United States, and desktop publishing jobs are found throughout the country. However, most jobs are in large metropolitan cities.

Job Outlook

Employment of desktop publishers is expected to grow faster than the average for all occupations through 2014, as more page layout and design work is performed in-house using computers and sophisticated publishing software. Desktop publishing is replacing much of the prepress work done by compositors and typesetters, enabling organizations to reduce costs while increasing production speeds. Many new jobs for desktop publishers are expected to emerge in commercial printing and publishing establishments. However, more companies also are turning to in-house desktop publishers, as computers with elaborate text and graphics capabilities have become common, and desktop publishing software has become cheaper and easier to use. In addition to employment growth, many job openings for desktop publishers also will result from the need to replace workers who move into managerial positions, transfer to other occupations, or leave the labor force.

Printing and publishing costs represent a significant portion of a corporation's expenses, and firms are finding it more profitable to print their own newsletters and other reports than to send them out to trade shops. Desktop publishing reduces the time needed to complete a printing job and allows commercial printers to make inroads into new markets that require fast turnaround.

Most employers prefer to hire experienced desktop publishers. As more people gain desktop-publishing experience, however, competition for jobs may increase. Among persons without experience, opportunities should be best for those with computer backgrounds who are certified or who have completed postsecondary programs in desktop publishing or graphic design. Many employers prefer graduates of these programs because the comprehensive training they receive helps them learn the page layout process and adapt more rapidly to new software and techniques.

Earnings

Earnings for desktop publishers vary according to level of experience, training, location, and size of firm. Median annual earnings of desktop publishers were $32,340 in May 2004. The middle 50 percent earned between $24,660 and $42,070. The lowest 10 percent earned less than $19,460, and the highest 10 percent earned more than $52,460 a year. Median annual earnings of desktop publishers in May 2004 were $36,040 in printing and related support services and $29,040 in newspaper, periodical, book, and directory publishers.

Related Occupations

Desktop publishers use artistic and editorial skills in their work. These skills also are essential for artists and related workers; commercial and industrial designers; news analysts, reporters, and correspondents; prepress technicians and workers; public relations specialists; and writers and editors.

Sources of Additional Information
Details about training programs may be obtained from local employers such as newspapers and printing shops or from local offices of the State employment service.

For information on careers and training in printing, desktop publishing, and graphic arts, write to:
➤ Graphic Communications Council, 1899 Preston White Dr., Reston, VA 20191-4367. Internet: **http://www.makeyourmark.org**
➤ Graphic Arts Information Network, 200 Deer Run Rd., Sewickley, PA 15143. Internet: **http://www.gain.org**

Office and Administrative Support Worker Supervisors and Managers

(O*NET 43-1011.01, 43-1011.02)

Significant Points

● Most jobs are filled by promoting office or administrative support workers from within the organization.

● Office automation will cause employment in some office and administrative support occupations to grow slowly or even decline, resulting in slower-than-average growth among supervisors and managers.

● Applicants are likely to encounter keen competition because their numbers should greatly exceed the number of job openings.

Nature of the Work
All organizations need timely and effective office and administrative support to operate efficiently. Office and administrative support supervisors and managers coordinate this support. These workers are employed in virtually every sector of the economy, working in positions as varied as teller supervisor, customer services manager, or shipping and receiving supervisor.

Although specific functions of office and administrative support supervisors and managers vary significantly, they share many common duties. For example, supervisors perform administrative tasks to ensure that their staffs can work efficiently. Equipment and machinery used in their departments must be in good working order. If the computer system goes down or a fax machine malfunctions, the supervisors must try to correct the problem or alert repair personnel. They also request new equipment or supplies for their department when necessary.

Planning the work and supervising the staff are key functions of this job. To do these effectively, the supervisor must know the strengths and weaknesses of each member of the staff, as well as the results required from and time allotted to each job. Supervisors must make allowances for unexpected staff absences and other disruptions by adjusting assignments or performing the work themselves if the situation requires it.

After allocating work assignments and issuing deadlines, office and administrative support supervisors and managers oversee the work to ensure that it is proceeding on schedule and meeting established quality standards. This may involve reviewing each person's work on a computer—as in the case of accounting clerks—or listening to how a worker deals with customers—as in the case of customer services representatives. When supervising long-term

projects, the supervisor may meet regularly with staff members to discuss their progress.

Office and administrative support supervisors and managers also evaluate each worker's performance. If a worker has done a good job, the supervisor indicates that in the employee's personnel file and may recommend a promotion or other award. Alternatively, if a worker is performing inadequately, the supervisor discusses the problem with the employee to determine the cause and helps the worker to improve his or her performance. This might require sending the employee to a training course or arranging personal counseling. If the situation does not improve, the supervisor may recommend a transfer, demotion, or dismissal.

Office and administrative support supervisors and managers usually interview and evaluate prospective employees. When new workers arrive on the job, supervisors greet them and provide orientation to acquaint them with their organization and its operating routines. Some supervisors may be actively involved in recruiting new workers—for example, by making presentations at high schools and business colleges. They also may serve as the primary liaisons between their offices and the general public through direct contact and by preparing promotional information.

Supervisors help train new employees in organization and office procedures. They may teach new employees how to use the telephone system and operate office equipment. Because most administrative support work is computerized, they also must teach new employees to use the organization's computer system. When new office equipment or updated computer software is introduced, supervisors train experienced employees to use it efficiently or, if this is not possible, arrange for their employees to receive special outside training.

Office and administrative support supervisors and managers often act as liaisons between the administrative support staff and the professional, technical, and managerial staff. This may involve implementing new company policies or restructuring the workflow in their departments. They also must keep their superiors informed of their progress and any potential problems. Often, this communication takes the form of research projects and progress reports. Because supervisors and managers have access to information such as their department's performance records, they may compile and present these data for use in planning or designing new policies.

Office and administrative support supervisors and managers also may have to resolve interpersonal conflicts among the staff. In

Office and administrative support supervisors and managers interview and evaluate prospective employees.

organizations covered by union contracts, supervisors must know the provisions of labor-management agreements and run their departments accordingly. They also may meet with union representatives to discuss work problems or grievances.

Working Conditions

Office and administrative support supervisors and managers are employed in a wide variety of work settings, but most work in clean and well-lit offices that usually are comfortable.

Most office and administrative support supervisors and managers work a standard 40-hour week. However, because some organizations operate around the clock, supervisors may have to work nights, weekends, and holidays. Sometimes, supervisors rotate among the three 8-hour shifts in a workday; in other cases, shifts are assigned on the basis of seniority.

Training, Other Qualifications, and Advancement

Most firms fill office and administrative support supervisory and managerial positions by promoting office or administrative support workers from within their organizations. To become eligible for promotion to a supervisory position, administrative support workers must prove they are capable of handling additional responsibilities. When evaluating candidates, supervisors look for strong teamwork, problem-solving, leadership, and communication skills, as well as determination, loyalty, poise, and confidence. They also look for more specific supervisory attributes, such as the ability to organize and coordinate work efficiently, to set priorities, and to motivate others. Increasingly, supervisors need a broad base of office skills coupled with personal flexibility to adapt to changes in organizational structure and move among departments when necessary.

In addition, supervisors must pay close attention to detail to identify and correct errors made by the staff they oversee. Good working knowledge of the organization's computer system also is an advantage. Many employers require postsecondary training—in some cases, an associate or even a bachelor's degree.

Administrative support workers with potential supervisory abilities may be given occasional supervisory assignments. To prepare for full-time supervisory duties, workers may attend in-house training or take courses in time management, project management, or interpersonal relations.

Some office and administrative support supervisor positions are filled with people from outside the organization. These positions may serve as entry-level training for potential higher level managers. New college graduates may rotate through departments of an organization at this level to learn the work of the organization.

Employment

Office and administrative support supervisors and managers held 1.5 million jobs in 2004. Although jobs for office and administrative support supervisors and managers are found in practically every industry, the largest number are found in organizations with a large administrative support workforce, such as banks, wholesalers, government agencies, retail establishments, business service firms, health care facilities, schools, and insurance companies. Because of most organizations' need for continuity of supervision, few office and administrative support supervisors and managers work on a temporary or part-time basis.

Job Outlook

Like those seeking other supervisory and managerial occupations, applicants for jobs as office and administrative support worker supervisors and managers are likely to encounter keen competition because the number of applicants should greatly exceed the number of job openings. Employment is expected to grow more slowly than the average for all occupations through 2014. Besides the job openings arising from growth, a large number of openings will stem from the need to replace workers who transfer to other occupations or leave this large occupation for other reasons.

Employment of office and administrative support supervisors and managers is determined largely by the demand for administrative support workers. New technology should increase office and administrative support workers' productivity and allow a wider variety of tasks to be performed by people in professional positions. These trends will cause employment in some administrative support occupations to grow slowly or even decline. As a result, supervisors will direct smaller permanent staffs—supplemented by increased use of temporary administrative support staff—and perform more professional tasks. Office and administrative support managers will coordinate the increasing amount of administrative work and make sure that the technology is applied and running properly. However, organizational restructuring should continue to reduce employment in some managerial positions, distributing more responsibility to office and administrative support supervisors.

Earnings

Median annual earnings of office and administrative support supervisors and managers were $41,030 in May 2004; the middle 50 percent earned between $31,860 and $53,110. The lowest paid 10 percent earned less than $25,190, while the highest paid 10 percent earned more than $67,800. In May 2004, median annual earnings in the industries employing the largest numbers of office and administrative support supervisors and managers were:

Insurance carriers	$49,610
Local government	42,100
State government	40,930
Offices of physicians	39,690
Depository credit intermediation	36,980

In addition to typical benefits, some office and administrative support supervisors and managers, particularly in the private sector, may receive additional compensation in the form of bonuses and stock options.

Related Occupations

Office and administrative support supervisors and managers must understand and sometimes perform the work of those whom they oversee, including bookkeeping, accounting, and auditing clerks; cashiers; communications equipment operators; customer service representatives; data entry and information processing workers; general office clerks; receptionists and information clerks; stock clerks and order fillers; order clerks; and tellers. Their supervisory and administrative duties are similar to those of other supervisors and managers.

Sources of Additional Information

For information related to a wide variety of management occupations, including educational programs and certified designations, contact:

➤ National Management Association, 2210 Arbor Blvd., Dayton, OH 45439. Internet: http://www.nma1.org

➤ International Association of Administrative Professionals, 10502 NW. Ambassador Dr., P.O. Box 20404, Kansas City, MO 64195-0404. Internet: http://www.iaap-hq.org

Office Clerks, General

(O*NET 43-9061.00)

Significant Points

- Employment growth and high replacement needs in this large occupation will result in numerous job openings.

- Prospects should be best for those with knowledge of basic computer applications and office machinery as well as good communication skills.

- Part-time and temporary positions are common.

Nature of the Work

Rather than performing a single specialized task, general office clerks have responsibilities that often change daily with the needs of the specific job and the employer. Whereas some clerks spend their days filing or keyboarding, others enter data at a computer terminal. They also can be called on to operate photocopiers, fax machines, and other office equipment; prepare mailings; proofread documents; and answer telephones and deliver messages.

The specific duties assigned to a clerk vary significantly, depending on the type of office in which he or she works. An office clerk in a doctor's office, for example, would not perform the same tasks that a clerk in a large financial institution or in the office of an auto parts wholesaler would perform. Although both may sort checks, keep payroll records, take inventory, and access information, clerks also perform duties unique to their employer, such as organizing medications, making transparencies for a presentation, or filling orders received by fax machine.

Clerks' duties also vary by level of experience. Whereas inexperienced employees make photocopies, stuff envelopes, or record inquiries, experienced clerks usually are given additional responsibilities. For example, they may maintain financial or other records, set up spreadsheets, verify statistical reports for accuracy and completeness, handle and adjust customer complaints, work with vendors, make travel arrangements, take inventory of equipment and supplies, answer questions on departmental services and functions, or help prepare invoices or budgetary requests. Senior office clerks may be expected to monitor and direct the work of lower level clerks.

Office clerks have responsibilities that often change daily with the needs of the specific job and the employer.

Working Conditions

For the most part, general office clerks work in comfortable office settings. Those on full-time schedules usually work a standard 40-hour week; however, some work shifts or overtime during busy periods. About 16 percent of clerks work part time. Many clerks also work in temporary positions.

Training, Other Qualifications, and Advancement

Although most office clerk jobs are entry-level administrative support positions, employers may prefer or require previous office or business experience. Employers usually require a high school diploma or equivalent, and some require basic computer skills, including familiarity with word processing software, as well as other general office skills.

Training for this occupation is available through business education programs offered in high schools, community and junior colleges, and postsecondary vocational schools. Courses in office practices, word processing, and other computer applications are particularly helpful.

Because general office clerks usually work with other office staff, they should be cooperative and able to work as part of a team. Employers prefer individuals who are able to perform a variety of tasks and satisfy the needs of the many departments within a company. In addition, applicants should have good communication skills, be detail oriented, and adaptable.

General office clerks who exhibit strong communication, interpersonal, and analytical skills may be promoted to supervisory positions. Others may move into different, more senior administrative jobs, such as receptionist, secretary, or administrative assistant. After gaining some work experience or specialized skills, many workers transfer to jobs with higher pay or greater advancement potential. Advancement to professional occupations within an organization normally requires additional formal education, such as a college degree.

Employment

General office clerks held about 3.1 million jobs in 2004. Most are employed in relatively small businesses. Although they work in every sector of the economy, about 46 percent worked in local government; health care and social assistance; administrative and support services; finance and insurance; or professional, scientific, and technical services industries.

Job Outlook

Employment growth and high replacement needs in this large occupation will result in numerous job openings for general office clerks. In addition to those for full-time jobs, many job openings are expected for part-time and temporary general office clerks. Prospects should be best for those who have knowledge of basic computer applications and office machinery—such as fax machines, telephone systems, and scanners—and good writing and communication skills. As general administrative support duties continue to be consolidated, employers will increasingly seek well-rounded individuals with highly developed communication skills and the ability to perform multiple tasks.

Employment of general office clerks is expected to grow more slowly than the average for all occupations through the year 2014. The employment outlook for these workers will be affected by the increasing use of technology, expanding office automation, and the consolidation of administrative support tasks. Automation has led to productivity gains, allowing a wide variety of duties to be performed by fewer office workers. However, automation also has led to a consolidation of administrative support staffs and a diversification of job responsibilities. This consolidation increases the demand for general office clerks because they perform a variety of administrative support tasks. It will become increasingly common within small businesses to find a single general office clerk in charge of all administrative support work.

Job opportunities may vary from year to year because the strength of the economy affects demand for general office clerks. Companies tend to employ more workers when the economy is strong. Industries least likely to be affected by economic fluctuations tend to be the most stable places for employment.

Earnings

Median annual earnings of general office clerks were $22,770 in May 2004; the middle 50 percent earned between $18,090 and $28,950 annually. The lowest 10 percent earned less than $14,530, and the highest 10 percent earned more than $35,810. Median annual salaries in the industries employing the largest numbers of general office clerks in May 2004 were:

Local government	$25,880
State government	24,970
Elementary and secondary schools	23,500
Colleges, universities, and professional schools	23,160
Employment services	20,910

Related Occupations

The duties of general office clerks can include a combination of bookkeeping, keyboarding, office machine operation, and filing. Other office and administrative support workers who perform similar duties include bookkeeping, accounting, and auditing clerks; communications equipment operators; customer service representatives; data entry and information processing workers; order clerks; receptionists and information clerks; secretaries and administrative assistants; stock clerks and order fillers; and tellers. Nonclerical entry-level workers include cashiers; counter and rental clerks; and food and beverage serving and related workers.

Sources of Additional Information

State employment service offices and agencies can provide information about job openings for general office clerks.

For information related to administrative occupations, including educational programs and certified designations, contact:
➤ International Association of Administrative Professionals, 10502 NW. Ambassador Dr., P.O. Box 20404, Kansas City, MO 64195-0404. Internet: **http://www.iaap-hq.org**

Secretaries and Administrative Assistants

(O*NET 43-6011.00, 43-6012.00, 43-6013.00, 43-6014.00)

Significant Points

- Numerous job openings will result from the need to replace workers who leave this very large occupation each year.

- Opportunities should be best for applicants with extensive knowledge of software applications.

- Increasing office automation and organizational restructuring will lead to slower than average growth in overall employment of secretaries and administrative assistants, but average growth is projected for legal and medical secretaries.

Nature of the Work

As the reliance on technology continues to expand in offices, the role of the office professional has greatly evolved. Office automation and organizational restructuring have led secretaries and administrative assistants to assume responsibilities once reserved for managerial and professional staff. Many secretaries and administrative assistants now provide training and orientation for new staff, conduct research on the Internet, and operate and troubleshoot new office technologies. In spite of these changes, however, the core responsibilities for secretaries and administrative assistants have remained much the same: Performing and coordinating an office's administrative activities and storing, retrieving, and integrating information for dissemination to staff and clients.

Secretaries and administrative assistants are responsible for a variety of administrative and clerical duties necessary to run an organization efficiently. They serve as information and communication managers for an office; plan and schedule meetings and appointments; organize and maintain paper and electronic files; manage projects; conduct research; and disseminate information by using the telephone, mail services, Web sites, and e-mail. They also may handle travel and guest arrangements.

Secretaries and administrative assistants are aided in these tasks by a variety of office equipment, such as fax machines, photocopiers, scanners, and videoconferencing and telephone systems. In addition, secretaries and administrative assistants often use computers to do tasks previously handled by managers and professionals: create spreadsheets; compose correspondence; manage databases; and create presentations, reports, and documents using desktop publishing software and digital graphics. They also may negotiate with vendors, maintain and examine leased equipment, purchase supplies, manage areas such as stockrooms or corporate libraries, and retrieve data from various sources. At the same time, managers and professionals have assumed many tasks traditionally assigned to secretaries and administrative assistants, such as keyboarding and answering the telephone. Because secretaries and administrative assistants often are not responsible for dictation and word processing, they have time to support more members of the executive staff. In a number of organizations, secretaries and administrative assistants work in teams to work flexibly and share their expertise.

Specific job duties vary with experience and titles. *Executive secretaries and administrative assistants*, for example, may perform

Secretaries and administrative assistants are responsible for a variety of administrative and clerical duties necessary to efficiently run an organization.

fewer clerical tasks than do secretaries. In addition to arranging conference calls and scheduling meetings, they may handle more complex responsibilities such as conducting research, preparing statistical reports, training employees, and hiring and supervising other clerical staff.

Some secretaries and administrative assistants, such as legal and medical secretaries, perform highly specialized work requiring knowledge of technical terminology and procedures. For instance, *legal secretaries* prepare correspondence and legal papers such as summonses, complaints, motions, responses, and subpoenas under the supervision of an attorney or a paralegal. They also may review legal journals and assist with legal research—for example, by verifying quotes and citations in legal briefs. *Medical secretaries* transcribe dictation, prepare correspondence, and assist physicians or medical scientists with reports, speeches, articles, and conference proceedings. They also record simple medical histories, arrange for patients to be hospitalized, and order supplies. Most medical secretaries need to be familiar with insurance rules, billing practices, and hospital or laboratory procedures. Other technical secretaries who assist engineers or scientists may prepare correspondence, maintain their organization's technical library, and gather and edit materials for scientific papers.

Working Conditions

Secretaries and administrative assistants usually work in schools, hospitals, corporate settings, government agencies, or legal and medical offices. Their jobs often involve sitting for long periods. If they spend a lot of time keyboarding, particularly at a computer monitor, they may encounter problems of eyestrain, stress, and repetitive motion ailments such as carpal tunnel syndrome.

Office work can lend itself to alternative or flexible working arrangements, such as part-time work or telecommuting—especially if the job requires extensive computer use. About 19 percent of secretaries work part time and many others work in temporary positions. A few participate in job-sharing arrangements, in which two people divide responsibility for a single job. The majority of secretaries and administrative assistants, however, are full-time employees who work a standard 40-hour week.

Training, Other Qualifications, and Advancement

High school graduates who have basic office skills may qualify for entry-level secretarial positions. However, employers increasingly require extensive knowledge of software applications, such as word processing, spreadsheets, and database management.

Secretaries and administrative assistants should be proficient in keyboarding and good at spelling, punctuation, grammar, and oral communication. Employers also look for good customer service and interpersonal skills because secretaries and administrative assistants must be tactful in their dealings with people. Discretion, good judgment, organizational or management ability, initiative, and the ability to work independently are especially important for higher level administrative positions.

As office automation continues to evolve, retraining and continuing education will remain integral parts of secretarial jobs. Changes in the office environment have increased the demand for secretaries and administrative assistants who are adaptable and versatile.

Secretaries and administrative assistants may have to attend classes or participate in online education to learn how to operate new office technologies, such as information storage systems, scanners, the Internet, or new updated software packages. They also may assist in selecting and maintaining office equipment.

Secretaries and administrative assistants acquire skills in various ways. Training ranges from high school vocational education programs that teach office skills and keyboarding to 1- and 2-year programs in office administration offered by business schools, vocational-technical institutes, and community colleges. Many temporary placement agencies also provide formal training in computer and office skills. However, many skills tend to be acquired through on-the-job instruction by other employees or by equipment and software vendors. Specialized training programs are available for students planning to become medical or legal secretaries or administrative technology specialists. Bachelor's degrees and professional certifications are becoming increasingly important as business continues to become more global.

Testing and certification for proficiency in entry-level office skills is available through organizations such as the International Association of Administrative Professionals; National Association of Legal Secretaries (NALS), Inc.; and Legal Secretaries International, Inc. As secretaries and administrative assistants gain experience, they can earn several different designations. Prominent designations include the Certified Professional Secretary (CPS) and the Certified Administrative Professional (CAP), which can be earned by meeting certain experience or educational requirements and passing an examination. Similarly, those with 1 year of experience in the legal field, or who have concluded an approved training course and who want to be certified as a legal support professional, can acquire the Accredited Legal Secretary (ALS) designation through a testing process administered by NALS. NALS offers two additional designations: Professional Legal Secretary (PLS), considered an advanced certification for legal support professionals, and a designation for proficiency as a paralegal. Legal Secretaries International confers the Certified Legal Secretary Specialist (CLSS) designation in areas such as intellectual property, criminal law, civil litigation, probate, and business law to those who have 5 years of legal experience and pass an examination. In some instances, certain requirements may be waived.

Secretaries and administrative assistants generally advance by being promoted to other administrative positions with more responsibilities. Qualified administrative assistants who broaden their knowledge of a company's operations and enhance their skills may be promoted to senior or executive secretary or administrative assistant, clerical supervisor, or office manager. Secretaries with word processing or data entry experience can advance to jobs as word processing or data entry trainers, supervisors, or managers within their own firms or in a secretarial, word processing, or data entry service bureau. Secretarial and administrative support experience also can lead to jobs such as instructor or sales representative with manufacturers of software or computer equipment. With additional training, many legal secretaries become paralegals.

Employment

Secretaries and administrative assistants held about 4.1 million jobs in 2004, ranking among the largest occupations in the U.S. economy. The following tabulation shows the distribution of employment by secretarial specialty:

Secretaries, except legal, medical, and executive	1,934,000
Executive secretaries and administrative assistants	1,547,000
Medical secretaries	373,000
Legal secretaries	272,000

Secretaries and administrative assistants are employed in organizations of every type. Around 9 out of 10 secretaries and administrative assistants are employed in service providing industries, ranging from education and health care to government and retail trade. Most of the rest work for firms engaged in manufacturing or construction.

Job Outlook

Overall employment of secretaries and administrative assistants is expected to grow more slowly than the average for all occupations over the 2004-14 period. In addition to those resulting from growth, numerous job openings will result from the need to replace workers who transfer to other occupations or leave this very large occupation for other reasons each year. Opportunities should be best for applicants with extensive knowledge of software applications, particularly experienced secretaries and administrative assistants.

Projected employment of secretaries and administrative assistants varies by occupational specialty. Employment growth in the health care and social assistance and legal services industries should lead to average growth for medical and legal secretaries. Employment of executive secretaries and administrative assistants is projected to grow average for all occupations. Growing industries—such as administrative and support services; health care and social assistance; educational services (private); and professional, scientific, and technical services—will continue to generate most new job opportunities. A decline in employment is expected for secretaries, except legal, medical, or executive; they account for about 47 percent of all secretaries and administrative assistants.

Increasing office automation and organizational restructuring will continue to make secretaries and administrative assistants more productive in coming years. Computers, e-mail, scanners, and voice message systems will allow secretaries and administrative assistants to accomplish more in the same amount of time. The use of automated equipment also is changing the distribution of work in many offices. In some cases, such traditional secretarial duties as keyboarding, filing, photocopying, and bookkeeping are being assigned to workers in other units or departments. Professionals and managers increasingly do their own word processing and data entry and handle much of their own correspondence rather than submit the work to secretaries and other support staff. Also, in some law and medical offices, paralegals and medical assistants are assuming some tasks formerly done by secretaries. As other workers assume more of these duties, there is a trend in many offices for professionals and managers to replace the traditional arrangement of one secretary per manager with secretaries and administrative assistants who support the work of systems, departments, or units. This approach often means that secretaries and administrative assistants assume added responsibilities and are seen as valuable members of a team, but it also contributes to the projected decline in the overall number of secretarial and administrative assistant positions.

Developments in office technology are certain to continue, and they will bring about further changes in the work of secretaries and administrative assistants. However, many secretarial and administrative duties are of a personal, interactive nature and, therefore, not easily automated. Responsibilities such as planning conferences, working with clients, and instructing staff require tact and communication skills. Because technology cannot substitute for these personal skills, secretaries and administrative assistants will continue to play a key role in most organizations.

Earnings

Median annual earnings of executive secretaries and administrative assistants were $34,970 in May 2004. The middle 50 percent earned between $28,500 and $43,430. The lowest 10 percent earned less than $23,810, and the highest 10 percent earned more than $53,460. Median annual earnings in the industries employing the largest numbers of executive secretaries and administrative assistants in May 2004 were:

Management of companies and enterprises	$38,950
Local government	36,940
Colleges, universities, and professional schools	34,280
Employment services	31,620
State government	30,750

Median annual earnings of legal secretaries were $36,720 in May 2004. The middle 50 percent earned between $29,070 and $46,390. The lowest 10 percent earned less than $23,270, and the highest 10 percent earned more than $56,590. Medical secretaries earned a median annual salary of $26,540 in May 2004. The middle 50 percent earned between $21,980 and $32,690. The lowest 10 percent earned less than $19,140, and the highest 10 percent earned more than $39,140. Median annual earnings of secretaries, except legal, medical, and executive, were $26,110 in May 2004.

Salaries vary a great deal, however, reflecting differences in skill, experience, and level of responsibility. Certification in this field usually is rewarded by a higher salary.

Related Occupations

Workers in a number of other occupations type, record information, and process paperwork. Among them are bookkeeping, accounting, and auditing clerks; receptionists and information clerks; communications equipment operators; court reporters; human resources assistants, except payroll and timekeeping; computer operators; data entry and information processing workers; paralegals and legal assistants; medical assistants; and medical records and health information technicians. A growing number of secretaries and administrative assistants share in managerial and human resource responsibilities. Occupations requiring these skills include office and administrative support supervisors and managers; computer and information systems managers; administrative services managers; and human resources, training, and labor relations managers and specialists.

Sources of Additional Information

State employment offices provide information about job openings for secretaries and administrative assistants.

For information on the latest trends in the profession, career development advice, and the CPS or CAP designations, contact:
➤ International Association of Administrative Professionals, 10502 NW. Ambassador Dr., P.O. Box 20404, Kansas City, MO 64195-0404. Internet: **http://www.iaap-hq.org**

Information on the CLSS designation can be obtained from:
➤ Legal Secretaries International Inc. Internet: **http://www.legalsecretaries.org**

Information on the ALS, PLS, and paralegal certifications are available from:
➤ National Association of Legal Secretaries, Inc., 314 East Third St., Suite 210, Tulsa, OK 74120. Internet: **http://www.nals.org**

Farming, Fishing, and Forestry Occupations

Agricultural Workers

(O*NET 45-2011.00, 45-2021.00, 45-2041.00, 45-2091.00, 45-2092.01, 45-2092.02, 45-2093.00, and 45-2099.99)

Significant Points

- Duties and working conditions vary widely, from raising plants in greenhouses, to harvesting crops and tending to livestock outdoors, to inspecting agricultural products at border crossings.

- Farmworkers learn through short-term on-the-job training; agricultural inspectors and animal breeders require work experience or a college degree.

- Most farmworkers receive low pay and perform strenuous work outdoors in all kinds of weather but many enjoy the rural lifestyle.

- Employment is projected to decline slightly.

Nature of the Work

Agricultural workers play a large role in getting food, plants, and other agricultural products to market. Working mostly on farms or ranches or in nurseries, slaughterhouses, or ports of entry, these workers have numerous and diverse duties. Among their activities are planting and harvesting crops, installing irrigation, delivering animals, and making sure that our food is safe.

More than 8 out of 10 agricultural workers are farmworkers and laborers. *Farmworkers and laborers, crop, nursery, and greenhouse* perform numerous activities related to growing and harvesting grains, fruits, vegetables, nuts, fiber, trees, shrubs, and other crops. Among their activities are planting and seeding, pruning, irrigating, harvesting, and packing and loading crops for shipment. Farmworkers also apply pesticides, herbicides, and fertilizers to crops; repair fences; and help with irrigation. Nursery and greenhouse workers prepare land or greenhouse beds for growing horticultural products, such as trees, plants, flowers, and sod. Their duties include planting, watering, pruning, weeding, and spraying the plants. They may cut, roll, and stack sod; stake trees; tie, wrap, and pack plants to fill orders; and dig up or move field-grown and containerized shrubs and trees.

Farmworkers, farm and ranch animals care for live farm, ranch, or aquacultural animals that may include cattle, sheep, swine, goats, horses, poultry, finfish, shellfish, and bees. The animals are usually raised to supply such products as meat, fur, skins, feathers, eggs, milk, and honey. The farmworkers' duties may include feeding, watering, herding, grazing, castrating, branding, debeaking, weighing, catching, and loading animals. On dairy farms, farmworkers operate milking machines; they also may maintain records on animals, examine animals to detect diseases and injuries, assist in delivering animals at their birth, and administer medications, vaccinations, or insecticides as appropriate. Daily duties of such farmworkers include cleaning and maintaining animal housing areas.

Other farmworkers known as *agricultural equipment operators* operate a variety of farm equipment used in plowing, sowing, maintaining, and harvesting agricultural products. The equipment may include tractors, fertilizer spreaders, haybines, raking equipment, balers, combines, and threshers, as well as trucks. These farmworkers also operate machines used in moving and treating crops after their harvest, such as conveyor belts, loading machines, separators, cleaners, and dryers. In addition, they may make adjustments and minor repairs to equipment. When not operating machines, agricultural equipment operators may perform other farm duties that are not typical of other farmworkers.

Agricultural inspectors, another type of agricultural worker, are employed by Federal and State governments to ensure compliance with laws and regulations governing the health, quality, and safety of agricultural commodities. Inspectors also make sure that the facilities and equipment used in processing the commodities meet quality standards. Meat safety is one of their prime responsibilities, and they try to ensure that the meat we eat is free of harmful ingredients or bacteria. In meat-processing facilities, inspectors may collect samples of suspected diseased animals or materials and send the samples to a laboratory for identification and analysis. They also may inspect livestock to help determine the effectiveness of medication and feeding programs. Some inspectors are stationed at export and import sites to weigh and inspect agricultural shipments leaving and entering the country to ensure the quality and quantity of the shipments. A few work at logging sites, making sure that safety regulations are enforced.

Graders and sorters of agricultural products examine agricultural commodities being prepared to be packed for market and classify them according to quality or size guidelines. They grade, sort, or classify unprocessed food and other agricultural products by size, weight, color, or condition and discard inferior or defective products. For example, graders sort eggs by color and size and also examine the fat content, or marbling, of beef, assigning a grade of "Prime," "Choice," or something else, as appropriate. The grade that is assigned determines the price at which the commodity may be sold.

Animal breeders select and breed animals using their knowledge of genetics and animal science to produce offspring with desired traits and characteristics, such as chickens that lay more eggs, pigs that produce leaner meat, and sheep with more desirable wool. Animal breeders also raise and breed animals simply to sell their offspring for money, including cats and dogs and other household pets. The larger and more expensive animals that are bred, such as horses and cattle, are usually bred through artificial insemination, which requires the taking of semen from the male and then inseminating the female with it. Using this process insures better results and also enables one prized male to sire many more offspring than through conventional mating. To know when and which animals to breed, breeders keep detailed records, including the health of the animal, its size and weight, and the amount and quality of the product produced by the animal. They also keep track of the traits of the offspring. Some breeders work as consultants for a number of farmers, while others breed and raise their own animals for eventual sale or to breed. For breeders that raise animals, they may also have to care and clean animal shelters, feed and water the animals, and oversee their day-to-day health or supervise others that perform these jobs. Additionally, animal breeders read journals and newsletters to remain current with the latest information on animal breeding and veterinary advice.

Working Conditions

Working conditions for agricultural workers vary widely. Much of the work of farmworkers and laborers on farms and ranches takes place outdoors in all kinds of weather and is physical in nature.

Many agricultural workers are found in nurseries, growing flowers and other plants.

Harvesting fruits and vegetables, for example, may require much bending, stooping, and lifting. Workers may lack adequate sanitation facilities while working in the field, and their drinking water may be limited. The year-round nature of much livestock production work means that ranch workers must be out in the heat of summer, as well as the cold of winter. While some of these workers enjoy the day-to-day variability of the work, the rural setting, working on the land, and raising animals, the work hours are generally uneven and often long, and work cannot be delayed when crops must be planted and harvested or when animals must be sheltered and fed. Weekend work is common, and farmworkers may work a 6- or 7-day week during planting and harvesting seasons. Because much of the work is seasonal in nature, many workers also obtain other jobs during slow seasons. Migrant farmworkers, who move from location to location as crops ripen, live an unsettled lifestyle, which can be stressful.

Work also is seasonal for farmworkers in nurseries; spring and summer are the busiest times of the year. Greenhouse workers enjoy relatively comfortable working conditions while tending to plants indoors. However, during the busy seasons, when landscape contractors need plants, work schedules may be more demanding, requiring weekend work. Moreover, the transition from warm weather to cold weather means that nursery workers might have to work overtime with little notice given in order to move plants indoors to protect them from a frost.

Federal meat inspectors may work in highly mechanized plants or with poultry or livestock in confined areas with extremely cold temperatures and slippery floors. The duties often require working with sharp knives, moderate lifting, and walking or standing for long periods. Many inspectors work long and often irregular hours. Inspectors may find themselves in adversarial roles when the organization or individual being inspected objects to the inspection or its potential consequences. Some inspectors travel frequently to visit farms and processing facilities. Others work at ports, inspecting cargo on the docks or on boats.

Graders and sorters may work with similar products for an entire shift, or they may be assigned a variety of items. They may be on

their feet all day and may have to lift heavy objects, whereas others may sit during most of their shift and do little strenuous work. Some graders work in clean, air-conditioned environments, suitable for carrying out controlled tests. Some may work evenings or weekends because of the perishable nature of the products. Overtime may be required to meet production goals.

Animal breeders spend most of their time outdoors around animals, but can also work in offices or in laboratories. If consulting, breeders may have to travel from farm to farm. If they need to sell the offspring, breeders may have to travel to attend shows and to meet with potential buyers. While tending to the animals, breeders may be bitten or kicked.

Farmworkers in crop production risk exposure to pesticides and other hazardous chemicals sprayed on crops or plants. However, exposure is relatively minimal if safety procedures are followed. Those who work on mechanized farms must take precautions to avoid injury when working with tools and heavy equipment. Those who work directly with animals risk being bitten or kicked.

Training, Other Qualifications, and Advancement
Farmworkers learn through short-term on-the-job training. Most do not have a high school diploma. Workers without a high school diploma are particularly common in the crop production sector, where there are more labor-intensive establishments employing migrant farmworkers.

In nurseries, entry-level workers must be able to follow directions and learn proper planting procedures. If driving is an essential part of a job, employers look for applicants with a good driving record and some experience driving a truck. Workers who deal directly with customers must get along well with people. Employers also look for responsible, self-motivated individuals, because nursery workers sometimes work with little supervision.

For graders and sorters, training requirements vary on the basis of their responsibilities. For those who perform tests on various agricultural products, a high school diploma is preferred and may be required. Simple jobs requiring mostly visual inspection may be filled by beginners provided with short-term on-the-job training.

Becoming an agricultural inspector requires relevant work experience or some college course work in a field such as biology or agricultural science. Inspectors are trained in the applicable laws or inspection procedures through some combination of classroom and on-the-job training. In general, people who want to enter this occupation should be responsible, like detailed work, and be able to communicate well. Federal Government inspectors whose job performance is satisfactory advance through a career ladder to a specified full-performance level. For positions above this level -usually supervisory positions advancement is competitive and based on agency needs and individual merit. Advancement opportunities in State and local governments and in the private sector often are similar to those in the Federal Government.

The education and training requirements for animal breeders vary with the type of breeding they do. For those whose primary activity is breeding, particularly livestock and other large or expensive animals, rather than raising animals, a bachelor's degree or higher in the animal sciences is recommended with courses in genetics, animal breeding, and animal physiology. For those with experience raising animals or those who are breeding their own animals, an associate's degree or other postsecondary training in animal breeding is recommended. Experience working around animals, especially on a farm, is helpful, even for those getting a degree.

Advancement of agricultural workers depends on motivation and experience. Farmworkers who work hard and quickly, have good communication skills, and take an interest in the business may advance to crew leader or other supervisory positions. Some agricultural workers may aspire to become farm, ranch, and other agricultural managers, or farmers or ranchers themselves. (Farmers, ranchers, and agricultural managers are discussed elsewhere in the Handbook.) In addition, their knowledge of raising and harvesting produce may provide an excellent background for becoming purchasing agents and buyers of farm products. Knowledge of working a farm as a business can help agricultural workers become farm and home management advisors. Those who earn a college degree in agricultural science could become agricultural and food scientists.

Employment

Agricultural workers held about 834,000 jobs in 2004. Of these, farmworkers were the most numerous, holding about 690,000 jobs. Graders and sorters held about 45,000 jobs, agricultural inspectors 14,000 jobs, agricultural equipment operators 60,000 jobs, and animal breeders 12,000 jobs. More than 66 percent of all agricultural workers worked for crop and livestock producers, while more than 5 percent worked for agricultural service providers, mostly farm labor contractors.

Job Outlook

Overall employment of agricultural workers is projected to decline slightly over the 2004-14 period, primarily reflecting the outlook for farmworkers in crops, nurseries, and greenhouses, who make up the large majority of all agricultural workers. Low wages, the physical demands of the work, and the large numbers of workers who leave these jobs for other occupation should result in abundant job opportunities, however.

Continued consolidation of farms and technological advancements in farm equipment that make farmworkers both more efficient and less needed will cause fewer of them to be hired. Farmworkers will increasingly work for farm labor contractors rather than being hired directly by the farm. The agriculture industry also is expected to undergo increased competition from foreign countries and rising imports, particularly from Central America, owing to the passing of a free trade agreement with that region. Nursery and greenhouse workers should experience some growth in this period, reflecting the increasing demand for landscaping services.

Slower-than-average employment growth is anticipated for agricultural inspectors. Governments at all levels are not expected to hire significant numbers of new inspectors, choosing to leave more of the routine inspection to businesses. Slower-than-average growth also is expected for graders and sorters, while employment of agricultural equipment operators is expected to decline slightly, reflecting the agriculture industry's continuing ability to produce more with fewer workers. Animal breeders also will grow more slowly than the average, as large commercial farmers continue to attempt to breed the perfect animal. However, because the occupation is so small there will be few job openings.

Earnings

Median hourly earnings in May 2004 for each of the occupations found in this statement are as follows:

Agricultural inspectors	$14.92
Animal breeders	13.55
Agricultural workers, all other	10.15
Agricultural equipment operators	8.88
Farmworkers, farm and ranch animals	8.31
Graders and sorters, agricultural products	7.90
Farmworkers and laborers, crop, nursery, and greenhouse	7.70

Few agricultural workers are members of unions.

Related Occupations

The duties of farmworkers who perform outdoor labor are related to the work of fishers and operators of fishing vessels; forest, conservation, and logging workers; and grounds maintenance workers. Farmworkers who work with farm and ranch animals perform work related to that of animal care and service workers. Animal breeders may perform some duties related to those of veterinary technologists or veterinarians.

Sources of Additional Information

Information on agricultural worker jobs is available from:
➤ National FFA Organization, The National FFA Center, Attention: Career Information Requests, P.O. Box 68690, Indianapolis, IN 46268-0960. Internet: **http://www.ffa.org**

Information on farmworker jobs is available from:
➤ Growing New Farmers Consortium, c/o New England Small Farm Institute, P.O. Box 11, Belchertown, MA 01007. Internet: **http://www.northeastnewfarmers.org**

Information on obtaining positions as an agricultural inspector with the Federal Government is available from the Office of Personnel Management through USAJOBS, the Federal Government's official employment information system. This resource for locating and applying for job opportunities can be accessed through the Internet at **http://www.usajobs.opm.gov** or through an interactive voice response telephone system at (703) 724-1850 or TDD (978) 461-8404. These numbers are not tollfree, and charges may result.

Fishers and Fishing Vessel Operators

(O*NET 45-3011.00)

Significant Points

● More than 50 percent of all workers are self-employed, among the highest proportion in the workforce.

● Many jobs require strenuous work and long hours and provide only seasonal employment.

● Employment is projected to decline, due to the depletion of fish stocks and new Federal and State laws restricting both commercial and recreational fishing.

Nature of the Work

Fishers and fishing vessel operators catch and trap various types of marine life for human consumption, animal feed, bait, and other uses. (Aquaculture the raising and harvesting, under controlled conditions, of fish and other aquatic life in ponds or confined bodies of water is covered in the *Handbook* section on farmers, ranchers, and agricultural managers.)

Fishing hundreds of miles from shore with commercial fishing vessels large boats capable of hauling a catch of tens of thousands of pounds of fish requires a crew that includes a captain, or skipper, a first mate and sometimes a second mate, a boatswain (called a deckboss on some smaller boats), and deckhands with specialized skills.

The *fishing boat captain* plans and oversees the fishing operation the fish to be sought, the location of the best fishing grounds, the method of capture, the duration of the trip, and the sale of the catch.

The captain ensures that the fishing vessel is seaworthy; oversees the purchase of supplies, gear, and equipment, such as fuel, netting, and cables; obtains the required fishing permits and licenses; and hires qualified crew members and assigns their duties. The captain plots the vessel's course using compasses, charts, and often electronic navigational equipment such as autopilots, loran systems, and satellite navigation systems. Ships also use radar to avoid obstacles and utilize depth sounders to indicate the water depth and whether there is marine life between the vessel and sea bottom. Sophisticated tracking technology allows captains to better locate and analyze schools of fish. The captain directs the fishing operation through the officers' actions and records daily activities in the ship's log. Upon returning to port, the captain arranges for the sale of the catch directly to buyers or through a fish auction and ensures that each crew member receives the prearranged portion of adjusted net proceeds from the sale of the catch. Some captains have begun buying and selling fish via the Internet, and as electronic commerce grows as a method of finding buyers for fresh catch, more captains may use computers.

The *first mate* the captain's assistant, who must be familiar with navigation requirements and the operation of all electronic equipment assumes control of the vessel when the captain is off duty. Duty shifts, called watches, usually last 6 hours. The mate's regular duty, with the help of the boatswain and under the captain's oversight, is to direct the fishing operations and sailing responsibilities of the deckhands, including the operation, maintenance, and repair of the vessel and the gathering, preservation, stowing, and unloading of the catch.

The *boatswain*, a highly experienced deckhand with supervisory responsibilities, directs the *deckhands* as they carry out the sailing and fishing operations. Before departure, the boatswain directs the deckhands to load equipment and supplies, either by hand or with hoisting equipment, and to untie lines from other boats and the dock. When necessary, boatswains repair fishing gear, equipment, nets, and accessories. They operate the fishing gear, letting out and pulling in nets and lines, and extract the catch, such as pollock, flounder, and tuna, from the nets or the lines' hooks. Deckhands use dip nets to prevent the escape of small fish and gaffs to facilitate the landing of large fish. They then wash, salt, ice, and stow away the catch. Deckhands also must ensure that decks are clear and clean at all times and that the vessel's engines and equipment are kept in good working order. Upon return to port, they secure the vessel's lines to and from the docks and other vessels. Unless "lumpers" (laborers or longshore workers) are hired, the deckhands unload the catch.

Large fishing vessels that operate in deep water generally have technologically advanced equipment, and some may have facilities on board where the fish are processed and prepared for sale. Such vessels are equipped for long stays at sea and can perform the work of several smaller boats.

Some full-time and many part-time fishers work on small boats in relatively shallow waters, often in sight of land. Navigation and communication needs are vital and constant for almost all types of boats. Crews are small usually, only one or two people collaborate on all aspects of the fishing operation, which may include placing gill nets across the mouths of rivers or inlets, entrapment nets in bays and lakes, or pots and traps for fish or shellfish such as lobsters and crabs. Dredges and scrapes are sometimes used to gather shellfish such as oysters and scallops. A very small proportion of commercial fishing is conducted as diving operations. Depending upon the water's depth, divers wearing regulation diving suits with an umbilical (air line) or a scuba outfit and equipment use spears to catch fish and use nets and other equipment to gather shellfish, coral, sea urchins, abalone, and sponges. In very shallow waters, fish are caught from small boats having an outboard motor, from rowboats, or by wading or seining from shore. Fishers use a wide variety of hand-operated equipment for example, nets, tongs, rakes, hoes, hooks, and shovels to gather fish and shellfish; catch amphibians and reptiles such as frogs and turtles; and harvest marine vegetation such as Irish moss and kelp.

Fishing vessel workers must be mechanically inclined in order to maintain their equipment.

Although most fishers are involved in commercial fishing, some captains and deckhands use their expertise in fishing for sport or recreational purposes. For this type of fishing, a group of people charter a fishing vessel, the captain, and possibly several deckhands for periods ranging from several hours to a number of days and embark upon sportfishing, socializing, and relaxation.

Working Conditions
Fishing operations are conducted under various environmental conditions, depending on the region of the country and the kind of species sought. Storms, fog, and wind may hamper fishing vessels or cause them to suspend fishing operations and return to port. Divers are affected by murky water and unexpected shifts in underwater currents. In relatively busy fisheries, smaller boats have to take care not to be hit by larger vessels.

Fishers and fishing vessel operators work under some of the most hazardous conditions of any occupation, and often help is not readily available when injuries occur. Treatment for any serious injuries may have to await transfer to a hospital. The crew must be on guard against the danger of injury from malfunctioning fishing gear, entanglement in fishing nets and gear, slippery decks resulting from fish-processing operations, ice formation in the winter, or being swept overboard a fearsome situation. Malfunctioning navigation or communication equipment may lead to collisions or shipwrecks. Divers must guard against entanglement of air lines, malfunction of scuba equipment, decompression problems, and attacks by predatory fish.

Fishers and fishing vessel operators face strenuous outdoor work and long hours. Commercial fishing trips may require a stay of several weeks or even months hundreds of miles away from one's home port. The pace of work may vary, but even during travel between the home port and the fishing grounds, deckhands on smaller boats try to finish their cleaning duties so that there are no chores remaining to be done at port. However, lookout watches are a regular responsibility, and crew members must be prepared to stand watch at prearranged times of the day or night. Although fishing gear has improved, and operations have become more mechanized, netting and processing fish are strenuous activities. Newer vessels have improved living quarters and amenities such as television and shower stalls, but crews still experience the aggravations of confined quarters, continuous close personal contact, and the absence of family.

Training, Other Qualifications, and Advancement
Fishers usually acquire their occupational skills on the job, many as members of families involved in fishing activities. No formal

academic requirements exist. Operators of large commercial fishing vessels are required to complete a Coast Guard-approved training course. Students can expedite their entrance into these occupations by enrolling in 2-year vocational-technical programs offered by secondary schools. In addition, some community colleges and universities offer fishery technology and related programs that include courses in seamanship, vessel operations, marine safety, navigation, vessel repair and maintenance, health emergencies, and fishing gear technology. Courses include hands-on experience. Secondary and postsecondary programs are normally offered in or near coastal areas.

Experienced fishers may find short-term workshops offered through various postsecondary institutions especially useful. These programs provide a good working knowledge of electronic equipment used in navigation and communication and offer information on the latest improvements in fishing gear.

Captains and mates on large fishing vessels of at least 200 gross tons must be licensed. Captains of sportfishing boats used for charter, regardless of the boats' size, must also be licensed. Crew members on certain fish-processing vessels may need a merchant mariner's document. The U.S. Coast Guard issues these documents and licenses to individuals who meet the stipulated health, physical, and academic requirements. (For information about merchant marine occupations, see the section on water transportation occupations elsewhere in the Handbook.)

Fishers must be in good health and possess physical strength. Good coordination, mechanical aptitude, and the ability to work under difficult or dangerous conditions are necessary to operate, maintain, and repair equipment and fishing gear. Fishers need stamina to work long hours at sea, often under difficult conditions. On large vessels, they must be able to work as members of a team. Fishers must be patient, yet always alert, to overcome the boredom of long watches when they are not engaged in fishing operations. The ability to assume any deckhand's functions on short notice is important. As supervisors, mates must be able to assume all duties, including the captain's, when necessary. The captain must be highly experienced, mature, and decisive and also must possess the business skills needed to run business operations.

On fishing vessels, most fishers begin as deckhands. Experienced, reliable deckhands who display supervisory qualities may become boatswains, who, in turn, may become second mates, first mates, and, finally, captains. Deckhands who acquire experience and whose interests are in ship engineering the maintenance and repair of ship engines and equipment can eventually become licensed chief engineers on large commercial vessels after meeting the Coast Guard's experience, physical, and academic requirements. Almost all captains become self-employed, and the overwhelming majority eventually own, or have an interest in, one or more fishing ships. Some may choose to run a sport or recreational fishing operation. When their seagoing days are over, experienced individuals may work in or, manage, or own stores selling fishing and marine equipment and supplies. Some captains may assume advisory or administrative positions in industry trade associations or government offices, such as harbor development commissions, or in teaching positions in industry-sponsored workshops or educational institutions. Divers with experience in fishing operations can enter a commercial diving activity for example, repairing ships or maintaining piers and marinas usually after the completion of a certified training program sponsored by an educational institution or industry association.

Employment

Fishers and fishing vessel operators held an estimated 38,000 jobs in 2004. One out of two was self-employed. Most fishing takes place off the coasts, with Alaska, Louisiana, Virginia, California, and Massachusetts bringing in the greatest volume of fish. While fishing off the New England coast has declined in recent years because of restrictions on catching certain species, it still ranks high in total value of fish caught, according to the National Marine Fisheries Service.

Job Outlook

Employment of fishers and fishing vessel operators is expected to decline through the year 2014. Some job openings will nevertheless arise from the need to replace workers who leave the occupation or retire. Fishers and fishing vessel operators depend on the natural ability of fish stocks to replenish themselves through growth and reproduction, as well as on governmental regulation to promote replenishment of fisheries. Many operations are currently at or beyond the maximum sustainable yield, partially because of habitat destruction, and the number of workers who can earn an adequate income from fishing is expected to decline. Many fishers and fishing vessel operators leave the occupation because of the strenuous and hazardous nature of the job and the lack of steady, year round income.

The use of sophisticated electronic equipment for navigation, for communication, and for locating fish has raised the efficiency of finding fish stocks. Also, improvements in fishing gear and the use of highly automated floating processors, where the catch is processed aboard the vessel, have greatly increased fish hauls. In many areas, particularly the North Atlantic and Pacific Northwest, damage to spawning grounds and excess fish harvesting capacity have adversely affected the stock of fish and, consequently, the employment opportunities for fishers. Some fisheries councils have issued various types of restrictions on harvesting, to allow stocks of fish and shellfish to naturally replenish, thereby idling many fishers. In addition, low prices for some species and rising seafood imports are adversely affecting fishing income and also causing some fishers to leave the industry. Fishers are also facing competition from farm-raised fish. Sportfishing boats, however, will continue to provide some job opportunities.

Governmental efforts to replenish stocks are having some positive results, which should increase the stock of fish in the future. Furthermore, efforts by private fishers' associations on the West Coast to increase government monitoring of the fisheries may help significantly to prevent the type of decline in fish stocks found in waters off the East Coast. Nevertheless, fewer fishers and fishing vessel operators are expected to make their living from the Nation's waters in the years ahead.

Earnings

Based on limited information, the majority of full-time wage and salary fishers earn between $322 and $775 per week. Earnings of fishers and fishing vessel operators normally are highest in the summer and fall when demand for services peaks and environmental conditions are favorable and lowest during the winter. Many full-time and most part-time workers supplement their income by working in other activities during the off-season. For example, fishers may work in seafood-processing plants, in establishments selling fishing and marine equipment, in construction, or in a number of unrelated seasonal occupations.

Earnings of fishers vary widely, depending upon their position, their ownership percentage of the vessel, the size of their ship, and the amount and value of the catch. The costs of the fishing operation the physical aspects of operating the ship, such as the fuel costs, repair and maintenance of gear and equipment, and the crew's supplies are deducted from the sale of the catch. Net proceeds are distributed among the crew members in accordance with a prearranged percentage. Generally, the ship's owner usually its captain receives half of the net proceeds. From this amount, the owner pays for depreciation, maintenance and repair, and replacement and insurance costs of the ship and its equipment; the money that remains is the owner's profit.

Related Occupations
Other occupations that involve outdoor work with fish and watercraft include water transportation occupations and fish and game wardens.

Sources of Additional Information
Names of postsecondary schools offering fishing and related marine educational programs are available from:
➤ Marine Technology Society, 5565 Sterrett Place, Suite 108, Columbia, MD 21044. Internet: **http://www.mtsociety.org**
Information on licensing of fishing vessel captains and mates and on requirements for merchant mariner documentation is available from the U.S. Coast Guard Marine Inspection Office or Marine Safety Office in your State. Or contact either of the following agencies:
➤ Office of Compliance, Commandant (G-MOC-3) 2100 Second St. SW., Washington, DC 20593. Internet:
http://www.access.gpo.gov/nara/cfr/waisidx_01/46cfr28_01.html
➤ Licensing and Evaluation Branch, National Maritime Center, 4200 Wilson Blvd., Suite 630, Arlington, VA 22203-1804.

Forest, Conservation, and Logging Workers

(O*NET 45-4011.00, 45-4021.00, 45-4022.01, 45-4023.00, 45-4029.99)

Significant Points

- Workers spend all their time outdoors, sometimes in poor weather and often in isolated areas.
- Most jobs are physically demanding and can be hazardous.
- A slight increase in overall employment is expected.

Nature of the Work
The Nation's forests are a rich natural resource, providing beauty and tranquility, varied recreational areas, and wood for commercial use. Managing and harvesting the forests and woodlands require many different kinds of workers. Forest and conservation workers

A logging equipment operator uses a feller to cut trees.

help develop, maintain, and protect the forests by growing and planting new seedlings, fighting insects and diseases that attack trees, and helping to control soil erosion. Timber-cutting and logging workers harvest thousands of acres of forests each year for the timber that provides the raw material for countless consumer and industrial products.

Forest and conservation workers perform a variety of tasks to reforest and conserve timberlands, and to maintain forest facilities, such as roads and campsites. Some forest workers, called tree planters, use digging and planting tools called "dibble bars" and "hoedads" to plant seedlings to reforest timberland areas. Forest workers also remove diseased or undesirable trees with power saws or handsaws, spray trees with insecticides and fungicides to kill insects and to protect against disease, and apply herbicides on undesirable brush and trees to reduce competing vegetation. Forest workers in private industry, usually working under the direction of professional foresters, paint boundary lines, assist with prescribed burning, aid in marking and measuring trees, and keep tallies of those trees examined and counted. Forest workers who work for State and local governments or who are under contract to the Federal Government also clear away brush and debris from camp trails, roadsides, and camping areas. Some of these workers clean kitchens and rest rooms at recreational facilities and campgrounds.

Other forest and conservation workers work in forest nurseries, sorting out tree seedlings and discarding those not meeting prescribed standards of root formation, stem development, and condition of foliage.

Some forest workers are employed on tree farms, where they plant, cultivate, and harvest many different kinds of trees. Their duties vary with the type of farm. Those who work on specialty farms, such as farms growing Christmas or ornamental trees for nurseries, are responsible for shearing treetops and limbs to control the growth of the trees under their care, to increase the density of limbs, and to improve the shapes of the trees. In addition, these workers' duties include planting the seedlings, spraying to control surrounding weed growth and insects, and harvesting the trees.

Other forest workers gather, by hand or with the use of handtools, products from the woodlands, such as decorative greens, tree cones and barks, moss, and other wild plant life. Still others tap trees for sap to make syrup or to produce chemicals.

The timber-cutting and logging process is carried out by a variety of workers who make up a logging crew. *Fallers*, commonly known as *tree fallers*, cut down trees with hand-held power chain saws or mobile felling machines. Usually using gas-powered chain saws, *buckers* trim off the tops and branches and buck (cut) the resulting logs into specified lengths.

Choke setters fasten chokers (steel cables or chains) around logs to be skidded (dragged) by tractors or forwarded by the cable-yarding system to the landing or deck area, where the logs are separated by species and type of product, such as pulpwood, saw logs, or veneer logs, and loaded onto trucks. *Rigging slingers* and *chasers* set up and dismantle the cables and guy wires of the yarding system. *Log sorters, markers, movers*, and *chippers* sort, mark, and move logs, based on species, size, and ownership, and tend machines that chip up logs.

Logging equipment operators on a logging crew perform a number of duties. They use tree harvesters to fell the trees, shear the limbs off trees, and then cut the logs into desired lengths. They drive tractors mounted on crawler tracks, called crawlers, and self-propelled machines called skidders or forwarders, which drag or transport logs from the felling site in the woods to the log landing area for loading. They also operate grapple loaders, which lift and load logs into trucks. Some logging equipment operators use tracked or wheeled equipment similar to a forklift to unload logs and pulpwood off of trucks or gondola railroad cars, usually at a sawmill or a pulp-mill woodyard. Some newer, more efficient logging equipment is now equipped with state-of-the-art computer technology, requiring more skilled operators with more training.

Log graders and *scalers* inspect logs for defects, measure logs to determine their volume, and estimate the marketable content or value of logs or pulpwood. These workers often use hand-held data collection devices to enter data about individual trees; later, the data can be downloaded or sent from the scaling area to a central computer via modem.

Other timber-cutting and logging workers have a variety of responsibilities. Some hike through forests to assess logging conditions. Some clear areas of brush and other growth to prepare for logging activities or to promote the growth of desirable species of trees.

The timber-cutting and logging industry is characterized by a large number of small crews of four to eight workers. A typical crew might consist of one or two tree fallers or one tree harvesting machine operator, one bucker, two logging skidder operators to drag cut trees to the loading deck, and one equipment operator to load the logs onto trucks. Most crews work for self-employed logging contractors who possess substantial logging experience, the capital to purchase equipment, and the skills needed to run a small business successfully. Many contractors work alongside their crews as supervisors and often operate one of the logging machines, such as the grapple loader or the tree harvester. Some manage more than one crew and function as owner-supervisors.

Although timber-cutting and logging equipment has greatly improved and operations are becoming increasingly mechanized, many logging jobs still are dangerous and very labor intensive. These jobs require various levels of skill, ranging from the unskilled task of manually moving logs, branches, and equipment to skillfully using chain saws to fell trees, and heavy equipment to skid and load logs onto trucks. To keep costs down, many timber-cutting and logging workers maintain and repair the equipment they use. A skillful, experienced logging worker is expected to handle a variety of logging operations.

Working Conditions

Forestry and logging jobs are physically demanding. Workers spend all their time outdoors, sometimes in poor weather and often in isolated areas. The increased use of enclosed machines has decreased some of the discomforts caused by inclement weather and in general made the tasks to be performed much safer. A few logging camps in Alaska and Maine house workers in bunkhouses. Workers in some sparsely populated western States, as well as northern Maine, commute long distances between their homes and logging sites. In the more densely populated eastern and southern States, commuting distances are shorter.

Most logging occupations involve lifting, climbing, and other strenuous activities, although machinery has eliminated some of the heavy labor. Loggers work under unusually hazardous conditions. Falling branches, vines, and rough terrains are constant hazards, as are the dangers associated with tree-felling and log-handling operations. Special care must be taken during strong winds, which can even halt logging operations. Slippery or muddy ground, hidden roots, or vines not only reduce efficiency, but also present a constant danger, especially in the presence of moving vehicles and machinery. Poisonous plants, brambles, insects, snakes, heat, humidity, and extreme cold are everyday occurrences where loggers work. The use of hearing protection devices is required on logging operations because the high noise level of felling and skidding operations over long periods may impair one's hearing. Experience, the exercise of caution, and the use of proper safety measures and equipment such as hardhats, eye and ear protection, and safety clothing and boots are extremely important to avoid injury.

The jobs of forest and conservation workers generally are much less hazardous than those of loggers. It may be necessary for some forestry aides or forest workers to walk long distances through densely wooded areas to accomplish their work tasks.

Training, Other Qualifications, and Advancement

Most forest, conservation, and logging workers develop skills through on-the-job training, with instruction coming primarily from experienced workers. Logging workers must familiarize themselves with the character and dangers of the forest environment and the operation of logging machinery and equipment. However, logging companies and trade associations, such as the Northeastern Loggers Association, the American Loggers Council, and the Forest Resources Association, Inc., offer training programs for workers who operate large, expensive machinery and equipment. Often, a representative of the equipment manufacturer spends several days in the field explaining and overseeing the operation of newly purchased machinery. Safety training is a vital and required part of the instruction of all logging workers.

Many State forestry or logging associations provide training sessions for tree fallers, whose job duties require more skill and experience than do other positions on the logging team. Sessions may take place in the field, where trainees, under the supervision of an experienced logger, have the opportunity to practice various felling techniques. Fallers learn how to manually cut down extremely large or expensive trees safely and with minimal damage to the felled or surrounding trees.

Training programs for loggers and foresters are common in many States. These training programs also include sessions on encouraging the health and productivity of the Nation's forests through the forest product industry's Sustainable Forest Initiative program. Logger training programs vary by State, but generally include classroom or field training in a number of areas: best management practices, environmental compliance, safety, endangered species, reforestation, and business management. Some programs lead to logger certification.

Generally, a college education is not required for most forest, conservation, and logging occupations. Many secondary schools, including vocational and technical schools and some community colleges, offer courses leading to a two-year technical degree in forestry, wildlife management, conservation, and forest harvesting, all of which are helpful in obtaining a job. A curriculum that includes field trips to observe or participate in forestry or logging activities provides a particularly good background. Generally, there are no educational requirements for forest worker jobs. Many of these workers are high school or college students who are hired on a part-time or seasonal basis to perform short-term, labor-intensive tasks, such as planting tree seedlings or conducting precommercial tree thinnings.

Experience working at a nursery or as a laborer can be useful in obtaining a job as a forest or conservation worker. Logging workers generally advance from occupations involving primarily manual labor to those involving the operation of expensive, sometimes complicated logging equipment. Inexperienced entrants usually begin as laborers, carrying tools and equipment, clearing brush, performing equipment maintenance, and loading and unloading logs and brush. For some, familiarization with logging operations may lead to jobs such as log-handling equipment operator. Further experience may lead to jobs involving the operation of more complicated machinery and yarding towers to transport, load, and unload logs. Those who have the motor skills required for the efficient use of power saws and other equipment may become fallers and buckers.

Forest, conservation, and logging workers must be in good health and able to work outdoors every day. They also must be able to work as part of a team. Many logging occupations require physical strength and stamina. Maturity and good judgment are important in making quick, intelligent decisions in dealing with hazards as they arise. Mechanical aptitude and coordination are necessary qualities for operators of machinery and equipment, who often are responsible for repair and maintenance as well. Initiative and managerial and business skills are necessary for success as a self-employed logging contractor.

Employment

Forest, conservation, and logging workers held about 92,000 jobs in 2004, distributed among the following occupations:

Logging equipment operators	43,000
Forest and conservation workers	17,000
Fallers	15,000
Log graders and scalers	9,000
Logging workers, all other	7,000

Most tree fallers, and almost half of all logging equipment operators, are employed in logging, although some work for sawmills and planing mills. Employment of log graders and scalers is concentrated largely in sawmills and planing mills.

About 45 percent of all forest and conservation workers work for government, primarily at the State and local level. Twenty one percent are employed by companies that operate timber tracts, tree farms, or forest nurseries, or for contractors that supply services to agriculture and forestry industries. Some of those employed in forestry services work on a contract basis for the U.S. Department of Agriculture's Forest Service. A small number of forest and conservation workers work in sawmills and planing mills. Although forest and conservation workers are located in every State, employment is concentrated in the West and Southeast, where many national and private forests and parks are located.

Self-employed forest, conservation, and logging workers account for more than 3 of every 10 such workers a much higher proportion of self-employment than in most other occupations.

Seasonal demand for forest, conservation, and logging workers varies by region. For example, in the northern States, winter work is common because the frozen ground facilitates logging. In the Southeast, logging and related activities occur year-round, except during periods of very wet weather.

Job Outlook

Overall employment of forest, conservation, and logging workers is expected to increase more slowly than the average for all occupations through the year 2014. Most job openings will result from replacement needs. Many logging workers transfer to other jobs that are less physically demanding and dangerous, or else they retire. In addition, some forestry workers are youths who are not committed to the occupation on a long-term basis.

Employment of forest and conservation workers is expected to grow more slowly than the average for all occupations. Setting aside more land to protect natural resources or wildlife habitats helps to create demand for more forest and conservation workers. In addition, recent Federal legislation designed to prevent destructive wildfires by thinning the forests and setting controlled burns may create more jobs for forest and conservation workers in those areas of the Nation with drier climates and higher susceptibility to forest fires.

New federal policy allowing some access to federal timberland may create some logging jobs, and job opportunities also will arise from owners of privately owned forests and tree farms. Nevertheless, domestic timber producers continue to face increasing competition from foreign producers, who can harvest the same amount of timber at lower cost. As competition increases, the logging industry is expected to continue to consolidate in order to reduce costs, thereby eliminating some jobs.

Increased mechanization of logging operations and improvements in logging equipment will continue to depress demand for many manual timber-cutting and logging workers. Employment of fallers, buckers, choke setters, and other workers whose jobs are labor intensive should decline as safer laborsaving machinery and other equipment are increasingly used. Employment of machinery and equipment operators, such as tree harvesting, skidding, and log-handling equipment operators, will be less adversely affected and should rise slightly as logging companies switch away from manual tree felling.

Weather can force the curtailment of logging operations during the muddy spring season and the cold winter months, depending on the geographic region. Changes in the level of construction, particularly residential construction, also affect logging activities in the short term. In addition, logging operations must be relocated when timber in a particular area has been harvested. During prolonged periods of inactivity, some workers may stay on the job to maintain or repair logging machinery and equipment; while others are laid off or forced to find jobs in other occupations.

Earnings

Earnings vary with the particular forestry or logging occupation and with experience. Earnings range from the minimum wage in some beginning forestry and conservation positions to about $25.46 an hour for some experienced fallers. Median hourly earnings in May 2004 for forest, conservation, and logging occupations were as follows:

Logging workers, all other	$14.29
Fallers	13.23
Logging equipment operators	13.18
Log graders and scalers	12.29
Forest and conservation workers	9.51

Earnings of logging workers vary by size of establishment and by geographic area. Workers in the largest establishments earn more than those in the smallest ones. Workers in Alaska and the Northwest earn more than those in the South, where the cost of living is generally lower.

Forest and conservation workers who work for State and local governments or for large, private firms generally enjoy more generous benefits than do workers in smaller firms. Small logging contractor firms generally offer timber-cutting and logging workers few benefits beyond vacation leAVE. However, some employers offer full-time workers basic benefits, such as medical coverage, and provide safety apparel and equipment.

Related Occupations

Other occupations concerned with the care of trees and their environment include conservation scientists and foresters, forest and conservation technicians, and grounds maintenance workers. Logging equipment operators have skills similar to material-moving operators, such as industrial truck and tractor operators, and crane and tower operators.

Sources of Additional Information

For information about timber-cutting and logging careers and about secondary and postsecondary programs offering training for logging occupations, contact:

➤ Forest Resources Association, Inc., 600 Jefferson Plaza, Suite 350, Rockville, MD 20852. Internet: **http://www.forestresources.org**

➤ American Loggers Council. P.O. Box 966, Hemphill, TX 75948. Internet: **http://www.americanloggers.org**

For information on the Sustainable Forestry Initiative training programs, contact:

➤ American Forest & Paper Association, 1111 19th St. NW., Suite 800, Washington, DC 20036. Internet: **http://www.afandpa.org**

A list of State forestry associations and other forestry-related State associations is available at most public libraries. Schools of Forestry at State land-grant colleges or universities also should be useful sources of information.

Construction Trades and Related Workers

Boilermakers

(O*NET 47-2011.00)

Significant Points

- A formal apprenticeship is the best way to learn this trade.

- Average employment growth is expected; additional openings will be created because many boilermakers are expected to retire.

- Persons with a welding certification or other welding training get priority in selection to apprenticeship programs.

Nature of the Work

Boilermakers and *boilermaker mechanics* make, install, and repair boilers, vats, and other large vessels that hold liquids and gases. Boilers supply steam to drive huge turbines in electric powerplants and to provide heat and power in buildings, factories, and ships. Tanks and vats are used to process and store chemicals, oil, beer, and hundreds of other products.

Boilers and other high-pressure vessels usually are made in sections, by casting each piece out of molten iron or steel. Manufacturers are increasingly automating this process to increase the quality of these vessels. Boiler sections are then welded together, often using automated orbital welding machines, which make more consistent welds than are possible by hand. Small boilers may be assembled in the manufacturing plant; larger boilers usually are assembled on site.

Following blueprints, boilermakers locate and mark reference points on the boiler foundation, using straightedges, squares, transits, and tape measures. Boilermakers attach rigging and signal crane operators to lift heavy frame and plate sections and other parts into place. They align sections, using plumb bobs, levels, wedges, and turnbuckles. Boilermakers use hammers, files, grinders, and cutting torches to remove irregular edges, so that edges fit properly. They then bolt or weld edges together. Boilermakers align and attach water tubes, stacks, valves, gauges, and other parts and test complete vessels for leaks or other defects. They also install refractory brick and other heat-resistant materials in fireboxes or pressure vessels. Usually, they assemble large vessels temporarily in a fabrication shop to ensure a proper fit before final assembly on the permanent site.

Because boilers last a long time—35 years or more—boilermakers regularly maintain them and update components, such as burners and boiler tubes, to increase efficiency. Boilermaker mechanics maintain and repair boilers and similar vessels. They inspect tubes, fittings, valves, controls, and auxiliary machinery and clean or supervise the cleaning of boilers using scrapers, wire brushes, and cleaning solvents. They repair or replace defective parts, using hand and power tools, gas torches, and welding equipment, and may operate metalworking machinery to repair or make parts. They also dismantle leaky boilers, patch weak spots with metal stock, replace defective sections, and strengthen joints.

Working Conditions

Boilermakers often use potentially dangerous equipment, such as acetylene torches and power grinders, handle heavy parts, and

Because boilers last a long time, boilermakers need to regularly maintain them and replace components, such as burners and boiler tubes.

work on ladders or on top of large vessels. Work is physically demanding and may be done in cramped quarters inside boilers, vats, or tanks that are often damp and poorly ventilated. In some instances, work may be done at high elevations for an extended period. To reduce the chance of injuries, boilermakers may wear hardhats, harnesses, protective clothing, safety glasses and shoes, and respirators. Boilermakers may experience extended periods of overtime when equipment is shut down for maintenance. Overtime work also may be necessary to meet construction or production deadlines. At other times there may be periods of unemployment between jobs.

Training, Other Qualifications, and Advancement

Many boilermakers learn this trade through a formal apprenticeship. Others become boilermakers through a combination of trade or technical school training and employer-provided training. Apprenticeship programs usually consist of 4 years of on-the-job training, supplemented by a minimum of 144 hours of classroom instruction each year in subjects such as set-up and assembly rigging, welding of all types, blueprint reading, and layout. Those with welding training or a welding certification will have priority in applying for apprenticeship programs. Experienced boilermakers often attend apprenticeship classes or seminars to learn about new equipment, procedures, and technology. When an apprenticeship becomes available, the local union publicizes the opportunity by notifying local vocational schools and high school vocational programs.

Some boilermakers advance to supervisory positions. Because of their broader training, apprentices usually have an advantage in promotion over those who have not gone through the full program.

Employment

Boilermakers held about 19,000 jobs in 2004. Nearly 7 out of 10 worked in the construction industry, assembling and erecting boilers and other vessels. More than 1 in 7 worked in manufacturing, primarily in boiler manufacturing shops, iron and steel plants, petroleum refineries, chemical plants, and shipyards. Some also worked for boiler repair firms or railroads.

Job Outlook

Average growth in employment of boilermakers is expected through the year 2014. Additional openings will be created by the need to replace experienced workers who are expected to retire in great numbers in the next 10 years. Unionized boilermakers are eligible to retire earlier than many other workers, partly due to the physically demanding nature of the work. Persons who have welding training or a welding certificate should have the best opportunities for being selected for boilermaker apprenticeship programs.

Growth will be limited by trends toward repairing and retrofitting, rather than replacing, existing boilers; the growing use of small boilers, which require less onsite assembly; and automation of production technologies. However, many boilers are getting older and will need replacing, which will create some demand for more boilermakers. In addition, utility companies will need to upgrade many of their boiler systems in the next few years to meet the Federal Clean Air Act. Also, as more power companies convert to coal as their primary source of fuel, additional boilers will be needed.

Most industries that purchase boilers are sensitive to economic conditions. Therefore, during economic downturns, boilermakers in the construction industry may be laid off. However, maintenance and repairs of boilers must continue even during economic downturns so boilermaker mechanics in manufacturing and other industries generally have more stable employment.

Earnings

In May 2004, the median hourly earnings of boilermakers were about $21.68. The middle 50 percent earned between $17.80 and $26.82. The lowest 10 percent earned less than $14.07, and the highest 10 percent earned more than $32.46. Apprentices generally start at about half of journey-level wages, with wages gradually increasing to the journey wage as progress is made in the apprenticeship.

About half of all boilermakers belong to labor unions. The principal union is the International Brotherhood of Boilermakers. Other boilermakers are members of the International Association of Machinists, the United Automobile Workers, or the United Steelworkers of America.

Related Occupations

Workers in a number of other occupations assemble, install, or repair metal equipment or machines. These occupations include assemblers and fabricators; machinists; industrial machinery installation, repair, and maintenance workers, except millwrights; millwrights; pipelayers, plumbers, pipefitters, and steamfitters; sheet metal workers; tool-and-die makers; and welding, soldering, and brazing workers.

Sources of Additional Information

For further information regarding boilermaking apprenticeships or other training opportunities, contact local offices of the unions previously mentioned, local construction companies and boiler manufacturers, or the local office of your State employment service.

For information on apprenticeships and the boilermaking occupation, contact:

➤ International Brotherhood of Boilermakers, Iron Ship Builders, Blacksmiths, Forgers, and Helpers, 753 State Ave., Suite 570, Kansas City, KS 66101. Internet: **http://www.boilermakers.org**

Brickmasons, Blockmasons, and Stonemasons

(O*NET 47-2021.00, 47-2022.00)

Significant Points

- Job prospects are expected to be very good.
- Most entrants learn informally on the job, but apprenticeship programs provide the most thorough training.
- The work is usually outdoors and involves lifting heavy materials and working on scaffolds.
- Nearly 1 out of 3 are self-employed.

Nature of the Work

Brickmasons, blockmasons, and stonemasons work in closely related trades creating attractive, durable surfaces and structures. The work varies in complexity, from laying a simple masonry walkway to installing an ornate exterior on a highrise building. *Brickmasons* and *blockmasons*—who often are called simply *bricklayers*—build and repair walls, floors, partitions, fireplaces, chimneys, and other structures with brick, precast masonry panels, concrete block, and other masonry materials. Some brickmasons specialize in installing firebrick linings in industrial furnaces. *Stonemasons* build stone walls, as well as set stone exteriors and floors. They work with two types of stone—natural cut stone, such as marble, granite, and limestone; and artificial stone made from concrete, marble chips, or other masonry materials. Stonemasons usually work on nonresidential structures, such as houses of worship, hotels, and office buildings, but they also work on residences.

When building a structure, brickmasons use 1 of 2 methods, either the corner lead or the corner pole. Using the corner lead method, they begin by constructing a pyramid of bricks at each corner—called a lead. After the corner leads are complete, less experienced brickmasons fill in the wall between the corners using a line from corner to corner to guide each course, or layer, of brick. Due to the precision needed, corner leads are time-consuming to erect and require the skills of experienced bricklayers.

Because of the expense associated with building corner leads, some brickmasons use corner poles, also called masonry guides, that enable them to build an entire wall at the same time. They fasten the corner poles (posts) in a plumb position to define the wall line and stretch a line between them. This line serves as a guide for each course of brick. Brickmasons then spread a bed of mortar (a cement, lime, sand, and water mixture) with a trowel (a flat, bladed metal tool with a handle), place the brick on the mortar bed, and press and tap the brick into place. Depending on blueprint specifications, brickmasons either cut bricks with a hammer and chisel or saw them to fit around windows, doors, and other openings. Mortar joints are then finished with jointing tools for a sealed, neat, uniform appearance. Although brickmasons typically use steel supports, or lintels, at window and door openings, they sometimes build brick arches, which support and enhance the beauty of the brickwork.

Stonemasons often work from a set of drawings, in which each stone has been numbered for identification. Helpers may locate and carry these prenumbered stones to the masons. A derrick operator using a hoist may be needed to lift large stone pieces into place.

When building a stone wall, masons set the first course of stones into a shallow bed of mortar. They then align the stones with wedges, plumblines, and levels, and work them into position with a hard rubber mallet. Masons continue to build the wall by alternating layers of mortar and courses of stone. As the work progresses, masons remove the wedges, fill the joints between stones, and use a pointed metal tool, called a tuck pointer, to smooth the mortar to an attractive finish. To hold large stones in place, stonemasons attach brackets to the stone and weld or bolt these brackets to anchors in the wall. Finally, masons wash the stone with a cleansing solution to remove stains and dry mortar.

When setting stone floors, which often consist of large and heavy pieces of stone, masons first use a trowel to spread a layer of damp mortar over the surface to be covered. Using crowbars and hard rubber mallets for aligning and leveling, they then set the stone in the mortar bed. To finish, workers fill the joints and clean the stone slabs.

Masons use a special hammer and chisel to cut stone. They cut stone along the grain to make various shapes and sizes, and valuable pieces often are cut with a saw that has a diamond blade. Some masons specialize in setting marble, which, in many respects, is similar to setting large pieces of stone. Brickmasons and stonemasons also repair imperfections and cracks, and replace broken or missing masonry units in walls and floors.

Most nonresidential buildings now are built with walls made of concrete block, brick veneer, stone, granite, marble, tile, or glass. In the past, masons doing nonresidential interior work mainly built block partition walls and elevator shafts, but because many types of masonry and stone are used in the interiors of today's nonresidential structures, these workers now must be more versatile. For example, some brickmasons and blockmasons now install structural insulated wall panels and masonry accessories used in many highrise buildings.

Refractory masons are brickmasons who specialize in installing firebrick and refractory tile in high-temperature boilers, furnaces, cupolas, ladles, and soaking pits in industrial establishments. Most of these workers are employed in steel mills, where molten materials flow on refractory beds from furnaces to rolling machines.

Stonemasons often work from a set of drawings in which each stone has been numbered for identification

Working Conditions

Brickmasons, blockmasons, and stonemasons usually work outdoors, but in contrast to the past when work slowed down in the winter months, new processes and materials are allowing these masons to work in a greater variety of weather conditions. Masons stand, kneel, and bend for long periods and often have to lift heavy materials. Common hazards include injuries from tools and falls from scaffolds, but these can often be avoided when proper safety equipment is used and safety practices are followed.

Training, Other Qualifications, and Advancement

Most brickmasons, blockmasons, and stonemasons pick up their skills informally, observing and learning from experienced workers. Many others receive training in vocational education schools or from industry-based programs that are common throughout the country. Another way to learn these skills is through an apprenticeship program, which generally provides the most thorough training. Knowledge of algebra, geometry, and mechanical drawing are important in this trade.

Individuals who learn the trade on the job usually start as helpers, laborers, or mason tenders. These workers carry materials, move scaffolds, and mix mortar. When the opportunity arises, they learn from experienced craftworkers how to spread mortar, lay brick and block, or set stone. As they gain experience, they make the transition to full-fledged craftworkers. The learning period on the job may last longer than if trained in an apprenticeship program. Industry-based training programs offered through construction companies usually last between 2 and 4 years.

Apprenticeships for brickmasons, blockmasons, and stonemasons usually are sponsored by local contractors, trade associations, or by local union-management committees. The apprenticeship program requires 3 years of on-the-job training, in addition to a minimum 144 hours of classroom instruction each year in subjects such as blueprint reading, mathematics, layout work, and sketching. Applicants for apprenticeships must be at least 17 years old and in good physical condition. A high school education is preferable with courses in mathematics, mechanical drawing, and shop helpful.

Apprentices often start by working with laborers, carrying materials, mixing mortar, and building scaffolds. This period generally lasts about a month and familiarizes the apprentice with job routines and materials. Next, apprentices learn to lay, align, and join brick and block. They may also learn on the job or before they are hired to work with stone and concrete, which enables them to work with more than one masonry material. .

Bricklayers who work in nonresidential construction usually work for large contractors and receive well-rounded training—normally through apprenticeship in all phases of brick or stone work. Those who work in residential construction usually work primarily for small contractors and specialize in only one or two aspects of the job.

With additional training and experience, brickmasons, blockmasons, and stonemasons may become supervisors for masonry contractors. Some eventually become owners of businesses employing many workers and may spend most of their time as managers rather than as brickmasons, blockmasons, or stonemasons. Others move into closely related areas such as construction management or building inspection.

Employment

Brickmasons, blockmasons, and stonemasons held 177,000 jobs in 2004. The vast majority were brickmasons. Workers in these crafts are employed primarily by building, specialty trade, or general contractors. Brickmasons, blockmasons, and stonemasons work throughout the country but, like the general population, are concentrated in metropolitan areas.

Nearly 1 out of 3 brickmasons, blockmasons, and stonemasons are self-employed. Many of the self-employed are contractors that work on small jobs, such as patios, walkways, and fireplaces.

Job Outlook

Job opportunities for brickmasons, blockmasons, and stonemasons are expected to be very good through 2014. A large number of masons are expected to retire over the next decade and in some areas there are not enough applicants for the skilled masonry jobs to replace those that are leaving.

Jobs for brickmasons, blockmasons, and stonemasons are also expected to increase about as fast as the average for all occupations over the 2004-14 period, as population and business growth create a need for new houses, industrial facilities, schools, hospitals, offices, and other structures. Also stimulating demand will be the need to restore a growing stock of old masonry buildings, as well as the increasing use of brick and stone for decorative work on building fronts and in lobbies and foyers. Brick exteriors should remain very popular, reflecting a growing preference for durable exterior materials requiring little maintenance.

Employment of brickmasons, blockmasons, and stonemasons, like that of many other construction workers, is sensitive to changes in the economy. When the level of construction activity falls, workers in these trades can experience periods of unemployment.

Earnings

Median hourly earnings of brickmasons and blockmasons in May 2004 were $20.07. The middle 50 percent earned between $15.34 and $25.20. The lowest 10 percent earned less than $11.68, and the highest 10 percent earned more than $30.43. Median hourly earnings in the two industries employing the largest number of brickmasons in 2004 were $22.98 in the nonresidential building construction industry and $19.95 in the foundation, structure, and building exterior contractors industry.

Median hourly earnings of stonemasons in 2004 were $16.82. The middle 50 percent earned between $12.74 and $21.45. The lowest 10 percent earned less than $9.97, and the highest 10 percent earned more than $27.23.

Earnings for workers in these trades can be reduced on occasion because poor weather and slowdowns in construction activity limit the time they can work. Apprentices or helpers usually start at about 50 percent of the wage rate paid to experienced workers. Pay increases as apprentices gain experience and learn new skills.

Some brickmasons, blockmasons, and stonemasons are members of the International Union of Bricklayers and Allied Craftsworkers.

Related Occupations

Brickmasons, blockmasons, and stonemasons combine a thorough knowledge of brick, concrete block, stone, and marble with manual skill to erect attractive, yet highly durable, structures. Workers in other occupations with similar skills include carpet, floor, and tile installers and finishers; cement masons, concrete finishers, segmental pavers, and terrazzo workers; and plasterers and stucco masons.

Sources of Additional Information

For details about apprenticeships or other work opportunities in these trades, contact local bricklaying, stonemasonry, or marble-setting contractors; the Associated Builders and Contractors; a local office of the International Union of Bricklayers and Allied Craftsworkers; a local joint union-management apprenticeship committee; or the nearest office of the State employment service or apprenticeship agency. For overall information on apprenticeship programs registered with the U.S. Department of Labor, including links to State apprenticeship sites, see Internet: **http://www.doleta.gov/atels_bat**

For information on training for brickmasons, blockmasons, and stonemasons, contact:
➤ Associated Builders and Contractors, Workforce Development Division, 4250 North Fairfax Dr., 9th Floor, Arlington, VA 22203. Internet: **http://www.trytools.org**
➤ International Union of Bricklayers and Allied Craftworkers, International Masonry Institute, The James Brice House, 42 East St., Annapolis, MD 21401. Internet: **http://www.imiweb.org**
➤ National Association of Home Builders, Home Builders Institute, 1201 15th St. NW., Washington, DC 20005. Internet: **http://www.hbi.org**
➤ National Center for Construction Education and Research, P.O. Box 141104, Gainesville, FL 32614-1104. Internet: **http://www.nccer.org**

For general information about the work of bricklayers, contact:
➤ Associated General Contractors of America, Inc., 2300 Wilson Boulevard, Suite 400, Arlington, VA 22201. Internet: **http://www.agc.org**
➤ Brick Industry Association, 11490 Commerce Park Dr., Reston, VA 22091-1525. Internet: **http://www.brickinfo.org**
➤ National Concrete Masonry Association, 13750 Sunrise Valley Dr., Herndon, VA 20171-3499. Internet: **http://www.ncma.org**

Carpenters

(O*NET 47-2031.01, 47-2031.02, 47-2031.03, 47-2031.04, 47-2031.05, 47-2031.06)

Significant Points

● About one-third of all carpenters—the largest construction trade—were self-employed.

● Job opportunities should be excellent for those with the most training and all-round skills.

● To become a skilled carpenter usually takes between 3 and 4 years of both on-the-job training and classroom instruction.

Nature of the Work

Carpenters are involved in many different kinds of construction activity, from the building of highways and bridges, to the installation of kitchen cabinets. Carpenters construct, erect, install, and repair structures and fixtures made from wood and other materials. Depending on the type of work and the employer, carpenters may specialize in one or two activities or may be required to know how to perform many different tasks. Small home builders and remodeling companies may require carpenters to learn about all aspects of building a house—framing walls and partitions, putting in doors and windows, building stairs, installing cabinets and molding, and many other tasks. Large construction contractors or specialty contractors, however, may require their carpenters to perform only a few regular tasks, such as framing walls, constructing wooden forms for pouring concrete, or erecting scaffolding. Carpenters also build tunnel bracing, or brattices, in underground passageways and mines to control the circulation of air through the passageways and to worksites.

Each carpentry task is somewhat different, but most involve the same basic steps. Working from blueprints or instructions from supervisors, carpenters first do the layout—measuring, marking, and arranging materials—in accordance with local building codes. They cut and shape wood, plastic, fiberglass, or drywall using hand and power tools, such as chisels, planes, saws, drills, and sanders. They then join the materials with nails, screws, staples, or adhesives. In the final step, carpenters check the accuracy of their work with levels, rules, plumb bobs, framing squares, or electronic versions of these tools, and make any necessary adjustments. When working with prefabricated components, such as stairs or wall panels, the carpenter's task is somewhat simpler because it does not require as

Carpenters construct, erect, install, and repair structures and fixtures made primarily of wood.

much layout work or the cutting and assembly of as many pieces. Prefabricated components are designed for easy and fast installation and generally can be installed in a single operation.

Carpenters who remodel homes and other structures need a broad range of carpentry skills because they must be able to perform any of the many different tasks these jobs may require. Since they are so well-trained, these carpenters often can switch from residential building to commercial construction or remodeling work, depending on which offers the best work opportunities.

Carpenters employed outside the construction industry perform a variety of installation and maintenance work. They may replace panes of glass, ceiling tiles, and doors, as well as repair desks, cabinets, and other furniture. Depending on the employer, carpenters install partitions, doors, and windows; change locks; and repair broken furniture. In manufacturing firms, carpenters may assist in moving or installing machinery. (For more information on workers who install machinery, see the discussion of millwrights as well as industrial machinery installation, repair, and maintenance workers, except millwrights, elsewhere in the *Handbook*.)

Working Conditions

As is true of other building trades, carpentry work is sometimes strenuous. Prolonged standing, climbing, bending, and kneeling often are necessary. Carpenters risk injury working with sharp or rough materials, using sharp tools and power equipment, and working in situations where they might slip or fall. Although many carpenters work indoors, those that work outdoors are subject to variable weather conditions.

Some carpenters change employers each time they finish a construction job. Others alternate between working for a contractor and working as contractors themselves on small jobs, depending on where the work is available.

Training, Other Qualifications, and Advancement

Carpenters learn their trade through formal and informal training programs. To become a skilled carpenter usually takes between

3 and 4 years of both classroom and on-the-job training. While there are a number of different ways to obtain this training, in general, the more formalized the process, the more skilled you will become, and the more in demand by employers. For some, this training can begin in a high school, where classes in English, algebra, geometry, physics, mechanical drawing, blueprint reading, and general shop are recommended. After high school, there are a number of different avenues that one can take to obtain the necessary training. One of the ways is to obtain a job with a contractor who will then provide on-the-job training. Entry-level workers generally start as helpers, assisting more experienced workers. During this time, the carpenter's helper may elect to attend a trade or vocational school, or community college to receive further trade-related training.

Some employers, particularly large nonresidential construction contractors with union membership, offer employees formal apprenticeships. These programs combine on-the-job training with related classroom instruction. Apprenticeship applicants usually must be at least 18 years old and meet local requirements; some union locals, for example, test an applicant's aptitude for carpentry. Apprenticeship programs are usually 3 to 4 years in length, but vary with the apprentice's skill. The number of apprenticeship programs is limited, however, so only a small proportion of carpenters learn their trade through these programs, mostly those working for commercial and industrial building contractors.

On the job, apprentices learn elementary structural design and become familiar with common carpentry jobs, such as layout, form building, rough framing, and outside and inside finishing. They also learn to use the tools, machines, equipment, and materials of the trade. Apprentices receive classroom instruction in safety, first aid, blueprint reading, freehand sketching, basic mathematics, and various carpentry techniques. Both in the classroom and on the job, they learn the relationship between carpentry and the other building trades.

Some persons aiming for carpentry careers choose to obtain their classroom training before seeking a job. There are a number of public and private vocational-technical schools and training academies affiliated with the unions and contractors that offer training to become a carpenter. Employers often look favorably upon these students and usually start them at a higher level than those without the training.

Some skills needed to become a carpenter include manual dexterity, eye-hand coordination, physical fitness, and a good sense of balance. The ability to solve arithmetic problems quickly and accurately also is required. In addition, a good work history or military service is viewed favorably by contractors.

Carpenters usually have greater opportunities than most other construction workers to become general construction supervisors because carpenters are exposed to the entire construction process. For those who would like to advance, it is increasingly important to be able to communicate in both English and Spanish in order to relay instructions and safety precautions to workers with limited understanding of English; Spanish-speaking workers make up a large part of the construction workforce in many areas. Carpenters may advance to carpentry supervisor or general construction supervisor positions. Others may become independent contractors. Supervisors and contractors need good communication skills to deal with clients and subcontractors, should be able to identify and estimate the quantity of materials needed to complete a job, and accurately estimate how long a job will take to complete and at what cost.

Employment

Carpenters are employed throughout the country in almost every community and make up the largest building trades occupation. They held about 1.3 million jobs in 2004. About one-third worked in building construction and about one-fifth worked for special trade contractors. Most of the rest of the wage and salary workers worked for manufacturing firms, government agencies, retail establishments and a wide variety of other industries. About one-third of all carpenters were self-employed.

Job Outlook

Job opportunities for carpenters are expected to be excellent over the 2004-14 period, particularly for those with the most skills. Employment of carpenters is expected to increase about as fast as average for all occupations through 2014, and turnover also creates a large number of openings each year. Contractors report having trouble finding skilled carpenters to fill many of their openings, due in part to the fact that many jobseekers are not inclined to go into construction, preferring work that is less strenuous with more comfortable working conditions. Also, many people with limited skills take jobs as carpenters but eventually leave the occupation because they dislike the work or cannot find steady employment.

The need for carpenters is expected to grow as construction activity increases in response to demand for new housing, office and retail space, and for modernizing and expanding schools and industrial plants. A strong home remodeling market also will create a large demand for carpenters.

Some of the demand for carpenters, however, will be offset by expected productivity gains resulting from the increasing use of prefabricated components and improved fasteners and tools. Prefabricated wall panels, roof assemblies and stairs and prehung doors and windows can be installed very quickly. Instead of having to be built on the worksite, prefabricated walls, partitions, and stairs can be lifted into place in one operation; beams—and, in some cases, entire roof assemblies—are lifted into place using a crane. As prefabricated components become more standardized, builders will use them more often. In addition, improved adhesives are reducing the time needed to join materials, and lightweight, cordless, and pneumatic tools—such as nailers and drills—will all continue to make carpenters more efficient. New and improved tools, equipment, techniques, and materials also have vastly increased carpenter versatility.

Carpenters with all-round skills will have better opportunities for steady work than carpenters who can perform only a few relatively simple, routine tasks. Carpenters can experience periods of unemployment because of the short-term nature of many construction projects, winter slowdowns in construction activity in northern areas, and the cyclical nature of the construction industry. During economic downturns, the number of job openings for carpenters declines. Building activity depends on many factors that vary with the state of the economy—interest rates, availability of mortgage funds, government spending, and business investment.

Job opportunities for carpenters also vary by geographic area. Construction activity parallels the movement of people and businesses and reflects differences in local economic conditions. The areas with the largest population increases will also provide the best job opportunities for carpenters and apprenticeship opportunities for persons seeking to enter carpentry.

Earnings

In May 2004, median hourly earnings of carpenters were $16.78. The middle 50 percent earned between $12.91 and $22.62. The lowest 10 percent earned less than $10.36, and the highest 10 percent earned more than $28.65. Median hourly earnings in the industries employing the largest numbers of carpenters in May 2004 were as follows:

Nonresidential building construction	$18.70
Building finishing contractors	17.51
Residential building construction	16.48
Foundation, structure, and building exterior contractors	16.40
Employment services	13.94

Earnings can be reduced on occasion, because carpenters lose worktime in bad weather and during recessions when jobs are unavailable.

Some carpenters are members of the United Brotherhood of Carpenters and Joiners of America.

Related Occupations

Carpenters are skilled construction workers. Other skilled construction occupations include brickmasons, blockmasons, and stonemasons; cement masons, concrete finishers, segmental pavers, and terrazzo workers; electricians; pipelayers, plumbers, pipefitters, and steamfitters; and plasterers and stucco masons.

Sources of Additional Information

For information about carpentry apprenticeships or other work opportunities in this trade, contact local carpentry contractors, locals of the union mentioned above, local joint union-contractor apprenticeship committees, or the nearest office of the State employment service or apprenticeship agency. You can also find information on the registered apprenticeship system with links to State apprenticeship programs on the U.S. Department of Labor's website: **http://www.doleta.gov/atels_bat**

For information on training opportunities and carpentry in general, contact:

➤ Associated Builders and Contractors, 4250 North Fairfax Dr., 9th Floor, Arlington, VA 22203. Internet: **www.trytools.org**
➤ Associated General Contractors of America, Inc., 2300 Wilson Boulevard, Suite 400, Arlington, VA 22201. Internet: **http://www.agc.org**
➤ National Center for Construction Education and Research, P.O. Box 141104, Gainesville, FL 32614-1104 Internet: **http://www.nccer.org**
➤ National Association of Home Builders, Home Builders Institute, 1201 15th St. NW., Washington, DC 20005. Internet: **http://www.hbi.org**
➤ United Brotherhood of Carpenters and Joiners of America, Carpenters Training Fund, 6801 Placid Street Las Vegas, NV 89119. Internet: **http://www.carpenters.org**

Carpet, Floor, and Tile Installers and Finishers

(O*NET 47-2041.00, 47-2042.00, 47-2043.00, 47-2044.00)

Significant Points

● Around two-fifths of all carpet, floor, and tile installers and finishers are self-employed.

● Most workers learn on the job.

● Tile installers and setters will see the fastest growth; carpet installers will have the most job openings.

● Employment of carpet, floor, and tile installers and finishers is less sensitive to fluctuations in construction activity than that of other construction trades workers.

Nature of the Work

Carpet, tile, and other types of floor coverings not only serve an important basic function in buildings, but their decorative qualities also contribute to the appeal of the buildings. Carpet, floor, and tile installers and finishers lay these floor coverings in homes, offices, hospitals, stores, restaurants, and many other types of buildings. Tile also may be installed on walls and ceilings.

Before installing carpet, *carpet installers* first inspect the surface to be covered to determine its condition and, if necessary, correct any imperfections that could show through the carpet or cause the carpet to wear unevenly. They must measure the area to be carpeted and plan the layout, keeping in mind expected traffic patterns and placement of seams for best appearance and maximum wear.

When installing wall-to-wall carpet without tacks, installers first fasten a tackless strip to the floor, next to the wall. They then install the padded cushion or underlay. Next, they roll out, measure, mark, and cut the carpet, allowing for 2 to 3 inches of extra carpet for the final fitting. Using a device called a "knee kicker," they position the carpet, stretching it to fit evenly on the floor and snugly against each wall and door threshold. They then cut off the excess carpet. Finally, using a power stretcher, they stretch the carpet, hooking it to the tackless strip to hold it in place. The installers then finish the edges using a wall trimmer.

Because most carpet comes in 12-foot widths, wall-to-wall installations require installers to join carpet sections together for large rooms. The installers join the sections using heat-taped seams—seams held together by a special plastic tape that is activated by heat.

On special upholstery work, such as stairs, carpet may be held in place with staples. Also, in commercial installations, carpet often is glued directly to the floor or to padding that has been glued to the floor.

Carpet installers use hand tools such as hammers, drills, staple guns, carpet knives, and rubber mallets. They also may use carpet-laying tools, such as carpet shears, knee kickers, wall trimmers, loop pile cutters, heat irons, and power stretchers.

Floor installers and floor layers lay floor coverings such as laminate, linoleum, vinyl, cork, and rubber for decorative purposes, or to deaden sounds, absorb shocks, or create air-tight environments. Although they also may install carpet, wood or tile, that is not their main job. Before installing the floor, floor layers inspect the surface to be covered and, if necessary, correct any imperfections in order to start with a smooth, clean foundation. They measure and cut floor covering materials according to plans or blueprints. Next, they may nail or staple a wood underlayment to the surface or may use an adhesive to cement the foundation material to the floor; the foundation helps to deaden sound and prevents the top floor covering from wearing at board joints. Finally, floor layers install the floor covering to form a tight fit.

After a carpenter installs a new hardwood floor or when a customer wants to refinish an old wood floor, *floor sanders and finishers* are called in to smooth any imperfections in the wood and apply finish coats of varnish or polyurethane. To remove imperfections and smooth the surface, they will scrape and sand wooden floors using floor-sanding machines. They then inspect the floor and remove excess glue from joints using a knife or wood chisel and may further sand the wood surfaces by hand, using sandpaper. Finally, they apply coats of finish.

Tile installers, *tilesetters*, and *marble setters* apply hard tile and marble to floors, walls, ceilings, countertops, and roof decks. Tile and marble are durable, impervious to water, and easy to clean, making them a popular building material in hospitals, tunnels, lobbies of buildings, bathrooms, and kitchens.

Prior to installation, tilesetters use measuring devices and levels to ensure that the tile is placed in a consistent manner. Tile varies in color, shape, and size, ranging in size from 1 inch to 24 or more inches on a side, so tilesetters sometimes prearrange tiles on a dry floor according to the intended design. This allows them to examine the pattern, check that they have enough of each type of tile, and determine where they will have to cut tiles to fit the design in the available space. In order to cover all exposed areas, including corners and around pipes, tubs, and wash basins, tilesetters cut tiles to fit with a machine saw or a special cutting tool. To set tile on a flat, solid surface such as drywall, concrete, plaster, or wood,

tilesetters first use a tooth-edged trowel to spread a "thin set," or thin layer, of cement adhesive or "mastic," a very sticky paste. They then properly position the tile and gently tap the surface with their trowel handle, rubber mallet, and/or a small block of wood to seat the tile evenly and firmly.

To apply tile to an area that lacks a solid surface, tilesetters nail a support of metal mesh or tile backer board to the wall or ceiling to be tiled. They use a trowel to apply a cement mortar—called a "scratch coat"—onto the metal screen, and scratch the surface of the soft mortar with a small tool similar to a rake. After the scratch coat has dried, tilesetters apply a brown coat of mortar to level the surface, and then apply mortar to the brown coat and place tile it onto the surface.

When the cement or mastic has set, tilesetters fill the joints with "grout," which is very fine cement and includes sand for joints 1/8th of an inch and larger. They then apply the grout to the surface with a rubber-edged device called a grout float or a grouting trowel to dress the joints and remove excess grout. Before the grout sets, they finish the joints with a damp sponge for a uniform appearance.

Marble setters cut and set marble slabs in floors and walls of buildings. They trim and cut marble to specified size using a power wet saw, other cutting equipment, or handtools. After setting the marble in place, they polish the marble to high luster using power tools or by hand.

Working Conditions

Carpet, floor, and tile installers and finishers generally work indoors and have regular daytime hours. However, when floor covering installers need to work in occupied stores or offices, they may work evenings and weekends to avoid disturbing customers or employees. Installers and finishers usually work under better conditions than do most other construction workers. By the time workers install carpets, flooring, or tile in a new structure, most construction has been completed and the work area is relatively clean and uncluttered. Installing these materials is labor intensive; workers spend much of

In order to cover all exposed areas, including in corners and around pipes, tilesetters use a machine saw or a special cutting tool to cut tiles to fit.

their time bending, kneeling, and reaching—activities that require endurance. Carpet installers frequently lift heavy rolls of carpet and may move heavy furniture. Safety regulations may require that they wear kneepads or safety goggles when using certain tools. Carpet and floor layers may be exposed to fumes from various kinds of glue and to fibers of certain types of carpet.

Although workers are subject to cuts from tools or materials, falls from ladders, and strained muscles, the occupation is not as hazardous as some other construction occupations.

Training, Other Qualifications, and Advancement

The vast majority of carpet, floor, and tile installers and finishers learn their trade informally on the job. A few, mostly tile setters, learn through formal apprenticeship programs taking nearly 3 years to complete, which include on-the-job training as well as related classroom instruction.

Informal training for carpet installers often is sponsored by individual contractors. Workers start as helpers, and begin with simple assignments, such as installing stripping and padding, or helping to stretch newly installed carpet. With experience, helpers take on more difficult assignments, such as measuring, cutting, and fitting.

Tile and marble setters also learn their craft mostly through on-the-job training. They start by helping carry materials and learning about the tools of the trade. They then learn to prepare the subsurface for tile or marble. As they progress they learn to cut the tile and marble to fit the job. They will also learn to apply grout and sealants used in finishing the materials to give it its final appearance. Apprenticeship programs and some contractor-sponsored programs provide comprehensive training in all phases of the tilesetting and floor layer trades.

Floor layers, except carpet, wood, and hard tile, learn on the job and begin by learning how to use the tools of the trade. They next learn to prepare surfaces to receive flooring. As they progress, they learn to cut and install the various floor coverings..

Some skills needed to become carpet, floor, and tile installers and finishers include manual dexterity, eye-hand coordination, physical fitness, and a good sense of balance and color. The ability to solve arithmetic problems quickly and accurately also is required. In addition, reliability and a good work history is viewed favorably by contractors.

Carpet, floor, and tile installers and finishers may advance to positions as supervisors or become salespersons or estimators. In these positions, they should be able to identify and estimate the quantity of materials needed to complete a job, and accurately estimate how long a job will take to complete and at what cost.

Some carpet installers may become managers for large installation firms. Many carpet, floor, and tile installers and finishers who begin working for someone else eventually go into business for themselves as independent subcontractors. Around two-fifths of all carpet, floor, and tile installers and finishers are self-employed.

For those who would like to advance, it is increasingly important to be able to communicate in both English and Spanish in order to relay instructions and safety precautions to workers with limited understanding of English; Spanish-speaking workers make up a large part of the construction workforce in many areas. Workers who want to advance supervisor jobs or become contractors need good English skills to deal with clients and subcontractors.

Employment

Carpet, floor, and tile installers and finishers held about 184,000 jobs in 2004. About 42 percent of all carpet, floor, and tile installers and finishers were self-employed, compared with 19 percent of all construction trades workers. The following tabulation shows 2004 wage and salary employment by specialty:

Tile and marble setters	44,000
Carpet installers	41,000
Floor layers, except carpet, wood, and hard tiles	16,000
Floor sanders and finishers	7,000

Many carpet installers work for flooring contractors or floor covering retailers. Most salaried tilesetters are employed by tilesetting contractors who work mainly on nonresidential construction projects, such as schools, hospitals, and office buildings. Most self-employed tilesetters work on residential projects.

Although carpet, floor, and tile installers and finishers are employed throughout the Nation, they tend to be concentrated in populated areas where there are high levels of construction activity.

Job Outlook

Employment of carpet, floor, and tile installers and finishers is expected to grow about as fast as the average for all occupations through the year 2014, reflecting the continued need to renovate and refurbish existing structures. Job growth and opportunities, however, will differ among the individual occupations. Tile and marble setters will have faster than average job growth and excellent job opportunities as demand for these workers outstrips the supply; however, because it is a small occupation, job openings will be limited. Carpet installers, the largest specialty, should have the most job openings due to high turnover in this occupation. Employment of floor sanders and finishers—a small specialty—is projected to grow more slowly than average due to the increasing use of prefinished hardwood and laminate flooring.

Carpet is expected to increasingly be used as a floor covering in nonresidential structures such as schools, offices, and hospitals. Residential homes will also continue to use carpet in many areas of the house, although other flooring types are currently more popular. Carpet is also required or highly recommended in many multifamily structures as it provides sound dampening.

Demand for tile and marble setters will stem from population and business growth, which will result in more construction of shopping malls, hospitals, schools, restaurants, and other structures in which tile is used extensively. Tile is also becoming more popular as a building material in residential structures, particularly in the growing number of more expensive homes.

Demand for floor sanders and finishers will be primarily based on growth in the residential construction and remodeling market, as homeowners increasingly choose hardwood as their flooring of choice. The need to periodically refinish older wood floors will also continue to generate demand, but growth will be slowed by the use of more prefinished hardwood and more durable finishes and laminate products that look like wood. Slow employment growth, together with the small size of this occupation, will result in relatively few job openings for these workers.

Employment of carpet, floor, and tile installers and finishers is less sensitive to changes in construction activity than most other construction occupations because much of the work involves replacing worn carpet and other flooring in existing buildings. As a result, these workers tend to be less affected by slowdowns in new construction activity.

Earnings

In May 2004, the median hourly earnings of carpet installers were $16.39. The middle 50 percent earned between $11.94 and $22.20. The lowest 10 percent earned less than $9.16, and the top 10 percent earned more than $29.27. In May 2004, median hourly earnings of carpet installers were $16.55 working for building finishing contractors, and $15.43 for home furnishings stores.

Carpet installers are paid either on an hourly basis, or by the number of yards of carpet installed. The rates vary widely depending on the geographic location and whether the installer is affiliated with a union.

Median hourly earnings of floor layers except carpet, wood, and hard tiles were $15.68 in May 2004. The middle 50 percent earned between $11.80 and $20.93. The lowest 10 percent earned less than $8.98, and the top 10 percent earned more than $28.09.

Median hourly earnings of floor sanders and finishers were $12.88 in May 2004. The middle 50 percent earned between $10.30 and $16.47. The lowest 10 percent earned less than $8.91, and the top 10 percent earned more than $21.03.

Median hourly earnings of tile and marble setters were $17.02 in May 2004. The middle 50 percent earned between $12.69 and $22.59. The lowest 10 percent earned less than $9.85, and the top 10 percent earned more than $29.35. Earnings of tile and marble setters also vary greatly by geographic location and by union membership status.

Apprentices and other trainees usually start out earning about half of what an experienced worker earns, although their wage rate increases as they advance through the training program.

Some carpet, floor, and tile installers and finishers belong to the United Brotherhood of Carpenters and Joiners of America. Some tilesetters belong to the International Union of Bricklayers and Allied Craftsmen, while some carpet installers belong to the International Brotherhood of Painters and Allied Trades.

Related Occupations

Carpet, floor, and tile installers and finishers measure, cut, and fit materials to cover a space. Workers in other occupations involving similar skills, but using different materials, include brickmasons, blockmasons, and stonemasons; carpenters; cement masons, concrete finishers, segmental pavers, and terrazzo workers; drywall installers, ceiling tile installers, and tapers; painters and paperhangers; roofers; and sheet metal workers.

Sources of Additional Information

For details about apprenticeships or work opportunities, contact local flooring or tilesetting contractors or retailers, locals of the unions previously mentioned, or the nearest office of the State apprenticeship agency or employment service.

For general information about the work of carpet installers and floor layers, contact:

➤ Floor Covering Installation Contractors Association, 7439 Milwood Dr., West Bloomfield, MI 48322.

Additional information on training for carpet installers and floor layers is available from:

➤ Joint Apprenticeship and Training Fund, International Union of Painters and Allied Trades, 1750 New York Ave. NW., Washington, DC 20006. Internet: **http://www.jatf.org**

For general information about the work of tile installers and finishers, contact:

➤ International Union of Bricklayers and Allied Craftworkers, International Masonry Institute, The James Brice House, 42 East St., Annapolis, MD 21401. Internet: **http://www.imiweb.org**

➤ National Association of Home Builders, Home Builders Institute, 1201 15th St. NW., Washington, DC 20005. Internet: **http://www.hbi.org**

For more information about tile setting and tile training, contact:

➤ National Tile Contractors Association, P.O. Box 13629, Jackson, MS 39236.

For information concerning training of carpet, floor, and tile installers and finishers, contact:

➤ United Brotherhood of Carpenters and Joiners of America, 50 F St. NW., Washington, DC 20001. Internet: **http://www.carpenters.org**

Cement Masons, Concrete Finishers, Segmental Pavers, and Terrazzo Workers

(O*NET 47-2051.00, 47-2053.00, 47-4091.00)

Significant Points

● Job opportunities are expected to be good due to a combination of job growth and a growing number of retirements.

● Most learn the job though a combination of classroom and on-the-job training that can take 3 to 4 years.

● Like many other construction trades, these workers may experience reduced earnings and layoffs during downturns in construction activity.

● Cement masons often work overtime, with premium pay, because once concrete has been placed, the job must be completed.

Nature of the Work

Cement masons, concrete finishers, and terrazzo workers all work with concrete, one of the most common and durable materials used in construction. Once set, concrete—a mixture of Portland cement, sand, gravel, and water—becomes the foundation for everything from decorative patios and floors to huge dams or miles of roadways.

Cement masons and *concrete finishers* place and finish the concrete. They also may color concrete surfaces; expose aggregate (small stones) in walls and sidewalks; or fabricate concrete beams, columns, and panels. In preparing a site for placing concrete, cement masons first set the forms for holding the concrete and properly align them. They then direct the casting of the concrete and supervise laborers who use shovels or special tools to spread it. Masons then guide a straightedge back and forth across the top of the forms to "screed," or level, the freshly placed concrete. Immediately after leveling the concrete, masons carefully smooth the concrete surface with a "bull float," a long-handled tool about 8 by 48 inches that covers the coarser materials in the concrete and brings a rich mixture of fine cement paste to the surface.

After the concrete has been leveled and floated, concrete finishers press an edger between the forms and the concrete and guide it along the edge and the surface. This produces slightly rounded edges and helps prevent chipping or cracking. Concrete finishers use a special tool called a "groover" to make joints or grooves at specific intervals that help control cracking. Next, they trowel the surface using either a powered or hand trowel, a small, smooth, rectangular metal tool.

Sometimes, cement masons perform all the steps of laying concrete, including the finishing. As the final step, they retrowel the concrete surface back and forth with powered and hand trowels to create a smooth finish. For a coarse, nonskid finish, masons brush the surface with a broom or stiff-bristled brush. For a pebble finish, they embed small gravel chips into the surface. They then wash any excess cement from the exposed chips with a mild acid solution. For color, they use colored premixed concrete. On concrete surfaces that will remain exposed after the forms are stripped, such as columns, ceilings, and wall panels, cement masons cut away high spots and loose concrete with hammer and chisel, fill any large indentations with a Portland cement paste, and smooth the surface with a carborundum stone. Finally, they coat the exposed area with a rich Portland cement mixture, using either a special tool or a coarse cloth to rub the concrete to a uniform finish.

Throughout the entire process, cement masons must monitor how the wind, heat, or cold affects the curing of the concrete. They must have a thorough knowledge of concrete characteristics so that, by using sight and touch, they can determine what is happening to the concrete and take measures to prevent defects.

Segmental pavers lay out, cut, and install pavers, which are flat pieces of masonry usually made from compacted concrete or brick. Pavers are used to pave paths, patios, playgrounds, driveways, and steps. They are manufactured in various textures and often interlock together to form an attractive pattern. Segmental pavers first prepare the site by removing the existing pavement or soil. They grade the remaining soil to the proper depth and determine the amount of base material that is needed, depending on the local soil conditions. They then install and compact the base material, a granular material that compacts easily, and lay the pavers from the center out, so that any trimmed pieces will be on the outside rather than in the center. Then, they install edging materials to prevent the pavers from shifting and fill the spaces between the pavers with dry sand.

Terrazzo workers create attractive walkways, floors, patios, and panels by exposing marble chips and other fine aggregates on the surface of finished concrete. Much of the preliminary work of terrazzo workers is similar to that of cement masons. Attractive, marble-chip terrazzo requires three layers of materials. First, cement masons or terrazzo workers build a solid, level concrete foundation that is 3 to 4 inches deep. After the forms are removed from the foundation, workers add a 1-inch layer of sandy concrete. Terrazzo workers partially embed, or attach with adhesive, metal divider strips in the concrete wherever there is to be a joint or change of color in the terrazzo. For the final layer, terrazzo workers blend and place into each of the panels a fine marble chip mixture that may be color-pigmented. While the mixture is still wet, workers add additional marble chips of various colors into each panel and roll a lightweight roller over the entire surface.

When the terrazzo is thoroughly set, helpers grind it with a terrazzo grinder, which is somewhat like a floor polisher, only much heavier. Any depressions left by the grinding are filled with a matching grout material and hand troweled for a smooth, uniform surface. Terrazzo workers then clean, polish, and seal the dry surface for a lustrous finish.

Working Conditions

Concrete, segmental paving, or terrazzo work is fast-paced and strenuous, and requires continuous physical effort. Because most finishing is done at floor level, workers must bend and kneel of-

Cement masons and concrete finishers spread the concrete, and then smooth and finish the surfaces.

ten. Many jobs are outdoors, and work is generally halted during inclement weather. The work, either indoors or outdoors, may be in areas that are muddy, dusty, or dirty. To avoid chemical burns from uncured concrete and sore knees from frequent kneeling, many workers wear kneepads. Workers usually also wear water-repellent boots while working in wet concrete.

Training, Other Qualifications, and Advancement

Most cement masons, concrete finishers, segmental pavers, and terrazzo workers learn their trades either through on-the-job training as helpers, or through 3-year or 4-year apprenticeship programs. Some workers also learn their jobs by attending trade or vocational-technical schools.

Many masons and finishers first gain experience as construction laborers. (See the section on construction laborers elsewhere in the *Handbook*.) When hiring helpers and apprentices, employers prefer high school graduates who are at least 18 years old, possess a driver's license, and are in good physical condition. The ability to get along with others is also important because cement masons frequently work in teams. High school courses in general science, mathematics, and vocational-technical subjects, such as blueprint reading and mechanical drawing provide a helpful background.

On-the-job training programs consist of informal instruction, in which experienced workers teach helpers to use the tools, equipment, machines, and materials of the trade. Trainees begin with tasks such as edging, jointing, and using a straightedge on freshly placed concrete. As training progresses, assignments become more complex, and trainees can usually do finishing work within a short time.

Apprenticeship programs usually are sponsored by local contractors, trade associations, or by local union-management committees. They provide on-the-job training in addition to the recommended minimum of 144 hours of classroom instruction each year. A written test and a physical exam may be required. In the classroom, apprentices learn applied mathematics, blueprint reading, and safety. Apprentices generally receive special instruction in layout work and cost estimation.

Cement masons, concrete finishers, segmental pavers, and terrazzo workers should enjoy doing demanding work. They should take pride in craftsmanship and be able to work without close supervision.

With additional training, cement masons, concrete finishers, segmental pavers, or terrazzo workers may become supervisors for masonry contractors, or move into construction management, building inspection, or contract estimation. Some eventually become owners of businesses, where they may spend most of their time managing rather than practicing their original trade. For those who want to own their own business, taking business classes will help to prepare workers for operating a business.

Employment

Cement masons, concrete finishers, segmental pavers, and terrazzo workers held about 209,000 jobs in 2004; segmental pavers and terrazzo workers accounted for only a small portion of the total. Most cement masons and concrete finishers worked for specialty trade contractors, primarily foundation, structure, and building exterior contractors. They also worked for contractors in residential and non-residential building construction and in heavy and civil engineering construction on projects such as highways; bridges; shopping malls; or large buildings such as factories, schools, and hospitals. A small number were employed by firms that manufacture concrete products. Most segmental pavers and terrazzo workers worked for specialty trade contractors who install decorative floors and wall panels.

Less than 5 percent of cement masons, concrete finishers, segmental pavers, and terrazzo workers were self-employed, a smaller proportion than in other building trades. Most self-employed masons specialized in small jobs, such as driveways, sidewalks, and patios.

Job Outlook

Opportunities for cement masons, concrete finishers, segmental pavers, and terrazzo workers are expected to be good, particularly for those with the most experience and skills. Employers report difficulty in finding workers with the right skills, as many qualified jobseekers often prefer work that is less strenuous and has more comfortable working conditions.

Employment of cement masons, concrete finishers, segmental pavers, and terrazzo workers is expected to grow as fast as average for all occupations through 2014. These workers will be needed to build new highways, bridges, factories, and other residential and nonresidential structures to meet the demand of a growing population. Additionally, cement masons will be needed to repair and renovate existing highways and bridges, which are deteriorating rapidly, and other aging structures. The increasing use of concrete as a building material, particularly since September 2001, will add to the demand. In addition to job growth, there are expected to be a significant number of retirements over the next decade, which will create more job openings.

Employment of cement masons, concrete finishers, segmental pavers, and terrazzo workers, like that of many other construction workers, is sensitive to the fluctuations of the economy. Workers in these trades may experience periods of unemployment when the overall level of construction falls. On the other hand, shortages of these workers may occur in some areas during peak periods of building activity.

Earnings

In May 2004, the median hourly earnings of cement masons and concrete finishers were $15.10. The middle 50 percent earned between $11.76 and $20.11. The bottom 10 percent earned less than $9.53, and the top 10 percent earned over $25.89. Median hourly earnings in the industries employing the largest numbers of cement masons and concrete finishers in May 2004 were as follows:

Residential building construction	$16.28
Nonresidential building construction	15.91
Other specialty trade contractors	15.58
Foundation, structure, and building exterior contractors	14.98
Highway, street, and bridge construction	14.86

In May 2004, the median hourly earnings of terrazzo workers and finishers were $13.45. The middle 50 percent earned between $10.44 and $19.57. The bottom 10 percent earned less than $9.07, and the top 10 percent earned over $25.72.

Like those of other construction trades workers, earnings of cement masons, concrete finishers, segmental pavers, and terrazzo workers may be reduced on occasion because poor weather and slowdowns in construction activity limit the amount of time they can work. Nonunion workers generally have lower wage rates than union workers. Apprentices usually start at 50 to 60 percent of the rate paid to experienced workers. Cement masons often work overtime, with premium pay, because once concrete has been placed, the job must be completed.

Some cement masons, concrete finishers, segmental pavers, and terrazzo workers belong to unions, mainly the Operative Plasterers' and Cement Masons' International Association of the United States and Canada and the International Union of Bricklayers and Allied Craftworkers. A few terrazzo workers belong to the United Brotherhood of Carpenters and Joiners of the United States.

Related Occupations

Cement masons, concrete finishers, segmental pavers, and terrazzo workers combine skill with knowledge of building materials to construct buildings, highways, and other structures. Other occupations involving similar skills and knowledge include brickmasons, blockmasons, and stonemasons; carpet, floor, and tile installers and finishers; drywall installers, ceiling tile installers, and tapers; and plasterers and stucco masons.

Sources of Additional Information

For general information about cement masons, concrete finishers, segmental pavers, and terrazzo workers, contact:

➤ National Concrete Masonry Association, 13750 Sunrise Valley Dr., Herndon, VA 20171-3499. Internet: **http://www.ncma.org**
➤ Associated Builders and Contractors, Workforce Development Division, 4250 North Fairfax Dr., 9th Floor, Arlington, VA 22203. Internet: **http://www.trytools.org**
➤ Associated General Contractors of America, Inc., 2300 Wilson Boulevard, Suite 400, Arlington, VA 22201. Internet: **http://www.agc.org**
➤ International Union of Bricklayers and Allied Craftworkers, International Masonry Institute, The James Brice House, 42 East St., Annapolis, MD 21401. Internet: **http://www.imiweb.org**
➤ United Brotherhood of Carpenters and Joiners, 50 F St. NW, Washington, DC 20001. Internet: **http://www.carpenters.org**
➤ Operative Plasterers' and Cement Masons' International Association of the United States and Canada, 14405 Laurel Place, Suite 300, Laurel, MD 20707. Internet: **http://www.opcmia.org**
➤ National Terrazzo and Mosaic Association, 110 E. Market St., Suite 200 A, Leesburg, VA 20176.
➤ National Center for Construction Education and Research, P.O. Box 141104, Gainesville, FL 32614-1104. Internet: **http://www.nccer.org**
➤ Portland Cement Association, 5420 Old Orchard Rd., Skokie, IL 60077. Internet: **http://www.cement.org**

For information about apprenticeships and work opportunities, contact local concrete or terrazzo contractors, locals of unions previously mentioned, a local joint union-management apprenticeship committee, or the nearest office of the State employment service or apprenticeship agency. You may also check the U.S. Department of Labor's Website for information on apprenticeships and links to State apprenticeship programs. Internet: **http://www.doleta.gov/atels_bat**

Construction and Building Inspectors

(O*NET 47-4011.00)

Significant Points

● About 45 percent of inspectors worked for local governments, primarily municipal or county building departments.

● Many home inspectors are self-employed.

● Opportunities should be best for experienced construction supervisors and craftworkers who have some college education, engineering or architectural training, or certification as construction inspectors or plan examiners.

● Home inspection has become a standard practice in the home-purchasing process, creating more opportunities for home inspectors.

Nature of the Work

Construction and building inspectors examine buildings, highways and streets, sewer and water systems, dams, bridges, and other structures to ensure that their construction, alteration, or repair complies with building codes and ordinances, zoning regulations, and contract specifications. Building codes and standards are the primary means by which building construction is regulated in the United States for the health and safety of the general public. National model building codes are published by the International Code Council (ICC), although many localities have additional ordinances and codes that modify or add to the National model codes. To monitor compliance with regulations, inspectors make an initial inspection during the first phase of construction and follow up with further inspections throughout the construction project. However, no inspection is ever exactly the same. In areas where certain types of severe weather or natural disasters—such as earthquakes or hurricanes—are more common, inspectors monitor compliance with additional safety regulations designed to protect structures and occupants during those events.

There are many types of inspectors. *Building inspectors* inspect the structural quality and general safety of buildings. Some specialize in such areas as structural steel or reinforced-concrete structures. Before construction begins, *plan examiners* determine whether the plans for the building or other structure comply with building code regulations and whether they are suited to the engineering and environmental demands of the building site. To inspect the condition of the soil and the positioning and depth of the footings, inspectors visit the worksite before the foundation is poured. Later, they return to the site to inspect the foundation after it has been completed. The size and type of structure, as well as the rate at which it proceeds toward completion, determine the number of other site visits they must make. Upon completion of the project, they make a final, comprehensive inspection.

In addition to structural characteristics, a primary concern of building inspectors is fire safety. They inspect structures' fire sprinklers, alarms, smoke control systems, fire exits. Inspectors assess the type of construction, contents of the building, adequacy of fire protection equipment, and risks posed by adjoining buildings.

Electrical inspectors examine the installation of electrical systems and equipment to ensure that they function properly and comply with electrical codes and standards. They visit worksites to inspect new and existing sound and security systems, wiring, lighting, motors, and generating equipment. They also inspect the installation of the electrical wiring for heating and air-conditioning systems, appliances, and other components.

Elevator inspectors examine lifting and conveying devices such as elevators, escalators, moving sidewalks, lifts and hoists, inclined railways, ski lifts, and amusement rides.

Home inspectors conduct inspections of newly built or previously owned homes, condominiums, town homes, manufactured homes, residential-unit living (apartments), and at times commercial buildings. Home inspection has become a standard practice in the home-purchasing process. Typically, home inspectors are hired by prospective home buyers to inspect and report on the condition of a home's systems, components, and structure. Although they look for and report violations of building codes, they do not have the power to enforce compliance with the codes. Typically, are hired either immediately prior to a purchase offer on a home or as a contingency to a sales contract. In addition to examining structural quality, home inspectors inspect all home systems and features, including roofing as well as the exterior, site, attached garage or carport, foundation, interior, plumbing, electrical, and heating and cooling systems. Some home inspections are done for homeowners who want an evaluation of their home's condition or as a way to diagnose problems.

Mechanical inspectors inspect the installation of the mechanical components of commercial kitchen appliances, heating and air-conditioning equipment, gasoline and butane tanks, gas and oil piping, and gas-fired and oil-fired appliances. Some specialize in boilers or ventilating equipment as well.

Plumbing inspectors examine plumbing systems, including private disposal systems, water supply and distribution systems, plumbing fixtures and traps, and drain, waste, and vent lines.

Public works inspectors ensure that Federal, State, and local government construction of water and sewer systems, highways, streets, bridges, and dams conforms to detailed contract specifications. They inspect excavation and fill operations, the placement of forms for concrete, concrete mixing and pouring, asphalt paving, and grading operations. They record the work and materials used so that contract payments can be calculated. Public works inspectors may specialize in highways, structural steel, reinforced concrete, or ditches. Others specialize in dredging operations required for bridges and dams or for harbors.

The owner of a building or structure under construction employs *specification inspectors* to ensure that work is done according to design specifications. Specification inspectors represent the owner's interests, not those of the general public. Insurance companies and financial institutions also may use the services of specification inspectors.

Details concerning construction projects, building and occupancy permits, and other documentation generally are stored on computers so that they can easily be retrieved, kept accurate, and be updated. For example, inspectors may use laptop computers to record their findings while inspecting a site. Most inspectors use computers to help them monitor the status of construction inspection activities and keep track of permits issued, and some can access all construction and building codes from their computers on the jobsite, decreasing the need for paper binders. However, many inspectors continue to use a paper checklist to detail their findings.

Although inspections are primarily visual, inspectors may use tape measures, survey instruments, metering devices, and equipment such as concrete strength measurers. They keep a log of their work, take photographs, and file reports. Many inspectors also use laptops or other portable electronic devices onsite to facilitate the accuracy of their written reports, as well as e-mail and fax machines to send

About 45 percent of all construction and building inspectors work for local governments, while many home inspectors are self-employed.

out the results. If necessary, they act on their findings. For example, government and construction inspectors notify the construction contractor, superintendent, or supervisor when they discover a violation of a code or ordinance or something that does not comply with the contract specifications or approved plans. If the problem is not corrected within a reasonable or otherwise specified period, government inspectors have authority to issue a "stop-work" order.

Many inspectors also investigate construction or alterations being done without proper permits. Inspectors who are employees of municipalities enforce laws pertaining to the proper design, construction, and use of buildings. They direct violators of permit laws to obtain permits and to submit to inspection.

Working Conditions

Construction and building inspectors usually work alone. However, several may be assigned to large, complex projects, particularly because inspectors tend to specialize in different areas of construction. Although they spend considerable time inspecting construction worksites, inspectors also spend time in a field office reviewing blueprints, answering letters or telephone calls, writing reports, and scheduling inspections.

Many construction sites are dirty and may be cluttered with tools, materials, or debris. Inspectors may have to climb ladders or many flights of stairs or crawl around in tight spaces. Although their work generally is not considered hazardous, inspectors, like other construction workers, wear hardhats and adhere to other safety requirements while at a construction site.

Inspectors normally work regular hours. However, they may work additional hours during periods when a lot of construction is taking place. Also, if an accident occurs at a construction site, inspectors must respond immediately and may work additional hours to complete their report. Nongovernment inspectors—especially those who are self-employed—may have a varied work schedule, at times working evenings and weekends.

Training, Other Qualifications, and Advancement

Although requirements vary considerably, depending upon where one is employed, construction and building inspectors should have a thorough knowledge of construction materials and practices in either a general area, such as structural or heavy construction, or a specialized area, such as electrical or plumbing systems, reinforced concrete, or structural steel. Home inspectors combine a knowledge of multiple specialties, so many of them have a combination of certifications, as well as previous experience in various construction trades. For example, many inspectors previously worked as carpenters, electricians, plumbers, or pipefitters.

Because inspectors must possess the right mix of technical knowledge, experience, and education, employers prefer applicants who have both formal training and experience. Most employers require at least a high school diploma or the equivalent, even for workers with considerable experience. More often, employers look for persons who have studied engineering or architecture or who have a degree from a community or junior college with courses in building inspection, home inspection, construction technology, drafting, and mathematics. Many community colleges offer certificate or associate's degree programs in building inspection technology. Courses in blueprint reading, algebra, geometry, and English also are useful. A growing number of construction and building inspectors are entering the occupation with a college degree, which often can substitute for previous experience.

Construction and building inspectors must be in good physical condition in order to walk and climb about construction and building sites. They also must have a driver's license, so that they can get to scheduled appointments.

The level of training requirements varies by type of inspector and State. In general, construction and building inspectors receive much of their training on the job, although they must learn building codes and standards on their own. Working with an experienced inspector, they learn about inspection techniques; codes, ordinances, and regulations; contract specifications; and recordkeeping and reporting duties. Supervised onsite inspections also may be a part of the training. Other requirements can include various courses and assigned reading. Some courses and instructional material are available online as well as through formal venues. An engineering or architectural degree often is required for advancement to supervisory positions.

Most States and local jurisdictions require some type of certification for employment. Even if not required, certification can enhance an inspector's opportunities for employment and advancement to more responsible positions. To become certified, inspectors with substantial experience and education must pass examinations on code requirements, construction techniques and materials, standards of practice, and codes of ethics. The International Code Council (ICC) offers multiple voluntary certifications, as do other professional associations. Many categories of certification are awarded for inspectors and plan examiners in a variety of specialties, including the Certified Building Official (CBO) certification, for code compliance, and the Residential Building Inspector (RBI) certification, for home inspectors. In a few cases, there are no education or experience prerequisites, and certification consists of passing an examination in a designated field either at a regional location or online. In addition, Federal, State, and many local governments may require inspectors to pass a civil service exam. Being a member of a nationally recognized inspection association enhances employment opportunities and may be required by some employers.

Because they advise builders and the general public on building codes, construction practices, and technical developments, construction and building inspectors must keep abreast of changes in these areas. Continuing education is imperative and is required by many States and certifying organizations. Numerous employers provide formal training to broaden inspectors' knowledge of construction materials, practices, and techniques. Inspectors who work for small agencies or firms that do not conduct their own training programs can expand their knowledge and upgrade their skills by attending State-sponsored training programs, by taking college or correspondence courses, or by attending seminars and conferences sponsored by various related organizations, such as the ICC.

Employment

Construction and building inspectors held about 94,000 jobs in 2004. Local governments—primarily municipal or county building departments—employed 45 percent. Employment of local government inspectors is concentrated in cities and in suburban areas undergoing rapid growth. Local governments employ large inspection staffs, including many plan examiners or inspectors who specialize in structural steel, reinforced concrete, and boiler, electrical, and elevator inspection.

Another 25 percent of construction and building inspectors worked for architectural and engineering services firms, conducting inspections for a fee or on a contract basis. Many of these were home inspectors working on behalf of potential real estate purchasers. Most of the remaining inspectors were employed in other service-providing industries or by State governments. About 1 in 10 construction and building inspectors was self-employed. Since many home inspectors are self-employed, it is likely that most self-employed construction and building inspectors were home inspectors.

Job Outlook

Job opportunities in construction and building inspection should be best for those highly experienced supervisors and construction craft workers who have some college education, engineering or architectural training, or certification as inspectors or plan examiners. Thorough knowledge of construction practices and skills in areas such as reading and evaluating blueprints and plans is essential.

Employment of construction and building inspectors is expected to grow faster than the average for most occupations through 2014. Concern for public safety and a desire for improvement in the quality of construction should continue to stimulate demand for construction and building inspectors in government as well as in firms specializing in architectural, engineering, and related services. Inspectors are involved in all phases of construction, including maintenance and repair work, and are therefore less likely to lose their jobs when new construction slows during recessions. In addition to openings stemming from the expected employment growth, some job openings will arise from the need to replace inspectors who transfer to other occupations or leave the labor force.

The routine practice of obtaining home inspections is a relatively recent development, causing employment of home inspectors to increase rapidly. Although employment of home inspectors is expected to continue to increase, the attention given to this specialty, combined with the desire of some construction workers to move into less strenuous and potentially higher paying work, may result in competition in some areas. In addition, increasing State regulations are starting to limit entry into the specialty only to those who have a given level of previous experience and are certified.

Earnings

Median annual earnings of construction and building inspectors were $43,670 in May 2004. The middle 50 percent earned between $34,620 and $54,970. The lowest 10 percent earned less than $27,760, and the highest 10 percent earned more than $67,380. Median annual earnings in the industries employing the largest numbers of construction and building inspectors in May 2004 were:

Local government	$43,960
Architectural, engineering, and related services	43,880
State government	39,310

Building inspectors, including plan examiners, generally earn the highest salaries. Salaries in large metropolitan areas are substantially higher than those in small jurisdictions.

Related Occupations

Because construction and building inspectors are familiar with construction principles, the most closely related occupations are construction occupations, especially carpenters, plumbers, and electricians. Construction and building inspectors also combine knowledge of construction principles and law with an ability to coordinate data, diagnose problems, and communicate with people. Workers in other occupations using a similar combination of skills include architects, except landscape and naval; appraisers and assessors of real estate; construction managers; civil engineers; cost estimators; engineering technicians; and surveyors, cartographers, photogrammetrists, and surveying technicians.

Sources of Additional Information

Information about certification and a career as a construction or building inspector is available from:
➤ International Code Council, 5203 Leesburg Pike, Suite 600, Falls Church, VA 22041. Internet: http://www.iccsafe.org

For more information about construction inspectors, contact:
➤ Association of Construction Inspectors, 1224 North Nokomis N.E., Alexandria, MN 56308. Internet: http://www.iami.org/aci/home.cfm

For more information about training and requirements for electrical inspectors, contact:
➤ International Association of Electrical Inspectors, 901 Waterfall Way, Suite 602, Richardson, TX 75080-7702. Internet: http://www.iaei.org

For information about becoming a home inspector, contact any of the following organizations:
➤ American Society of Home Inspectors, 932 Lee St., Suite 101, Des Plaines, IL 60016. Internet: http://www.ashi.org
➤ Housing Inspection Foundation, 1224 North Nokomis N.E., Alexandria, MN 56308. Internet: http://www.iami.org/hif.cfm
➤ National Association of Home Inspectors, 4248 Park Glen Rd., Minneapolis, MN 55416. Internet: http://www.nahi.org

For information about a career as a State or local government construction or building inspector, contact your State or local employment service.

Construction Equipment Operators

(O*NET 47-2071.00, 47-2072.00, 47-2073.01, 47-2073.02)

Significant Points

- Many construction equipment operators acquire their skills on the job, but formal apprenticeship programs provide more comprehensive training.
- Job opportunities are expected to be good, with employment growing about as fast as the average for all occupations.
- Hourly pay is relatively high, but some construction equipment operators cannot work in inclement weather, so total annual earnings may be reduced.

Nature of the Work

Construction equipment operators use machinery to move construction materials, earth, and other heavy materials at construction sites, mines, and sometimes your back yard. They operate equipment that clears and grades land to prepare it for construction of roads, buildings, and neighborhoods. They dig trenches to lay or repair sewer and other pipelines, and they hoist heavy construction materials. They may even work offshore constructing oil rigs. Construction equipment operators also operate machinery that applies asphalt and concrete to roads and other structures.

Operators control equipment by moving levers or foot pedals, operating switches, or turning dials. The operation of much of this equipment is becoming more complex as a result of computerized controls. Global Positioning System (GPS) technology also is being used to help with grading and leveling activities. In addition to controlling the equipment, construction equipment operators also set up and inspect the equipment, make adjustments, and perform some maintenance and minor repairs.

Construction equipment operators include: paving, surfacing, and tamping equipment operators; piledriver operators; and operating engineers and other construction equipment operators. *Operating engineers and other construction equipment operators* operate one or several types of power construction equipment. They may operate excavation and loading machines equipped with scoops, shovels, or buckets that dig sand, gravel, earth, or similar materials and load it into trucks or onto conveyors. In addition to the familiar bulldozers, they operate trench excavators, road graders, and similar equipment. Sometimes, they may drive and control industrial trucks or tractors equipped with forklifts or booms for lifting materials or with hitches for pulling trailers. They also may operate and maintain air compressors, pumps, and other power equipment at construction sites. Construction equipment operators who are classified as operating engineers are capable of operating several different types of construction equipment.

Paving and surfacing equipment operators use levers and other controls to operate machines that spread and level asphalt or spread and smooth concrete for roadways or other structures. *Asphalt paving machine operators* turn valves to regulate the temperature and flow of asphalt onto the roadbed. They must take care that the machine distributes the paving material evenly and without voids, and make sure that there is a constant flow of asphalt going into the hopper. *Concrete paving machine operators* control levers and turn handwheels to move attachments that spread, vibrate, and level wet concrete within forms. They must observe the surface of concrete to identify low spots into which workers must add concrete. They use other attachments to smooth the surface of the concrete, spray on a curing compound, and cut expansion joints. *Tamping equipment operators* operate tamping machines that compact earth and other fill materials for roadbeds. They also may operate machines with interchangeable hammers to cut or break up old pavement and drive guardrail posts into the earth.

Piledriver operators operate piledrivers—large machines, mounted on skids, barges, or cranes, that hammer piles into the ground. Piles are long heavy beams of wood or steel driven into the ground to support retaining walls, bulkheads, bridges, piers, or building foundations. Some piledriver operators work on offshore oil rigs. Piledriver operators move hand and foot levers and turn valves to activate, position, and control the pile-driving equipment.

Working Conditions

Many construction equipment operators work outdoors, in nearly every type of climate and weather condition, although in many areas of the country, some types of construction operations must be suspended in winter. Also, during periods of extremely wet weather grading and leveling activities can be difficult to perform and may be suspended. Bulldozers, scrapers, and especially tampers and piledrivers are noisy and shake or jolt the operator. Operating heavy construction equipment can be dangerous. As with most machinery, accidents generally can be avoided by observing proper operating procedures and safety practices. Construction equipment operators

Construction equipment operators use machinery to move construction materials, earth, and other heavy materials at construction sites.

are cold in the winter and hot in the summer, and often get dirty, greasy, muddy, or dusty.

Operators may have irregular hours because work on some construction projects continues around the clock or must be performed late at night or early in the morning. Some operators work in remote locations on large construction projects, such as highways and dams, or in factory or mining operations.

Training, Other Qualifications, and Advancement

Construction equipment operators usually learn their skills on the job. They may start by operating light equipment under the guidance of an experienced operator. Later, they may operate heavier equipment, such as bulldozers and cranes. However, it is generally accepted that formal training provides more comprehensive skills. Some construction equipment operators train in formal operating engineer apprenticeship programs administered by union-management committees of the International Union of Operating Engineers and the Associated General Contractors of America. Because apprentices learn to operate a wider variety of machines than do other beginners, they usually have better job opportunities. Apprenticeship programs consist of at least 3 years, or 6,000 hours, of on-the-job training and 144 hours a year of related classroom instruction.

Employers of construction equipment operators generally prefer to hire high school graduates, although some employers may train nongraduates to operate some types of equipment. Technologically advanced construction equipment has computerized controls and improved hydraulics and electronics, requiring more skill to operate. Operators of such equipment may need more training and some understanding of electronics. Mechanical aptitude and high school training in automobile mechanics are helpful because workers may perform some maintenance on their machines. Also, high school courses in science and mechanical drawing are useful. Experience operating related mobile equipment, such as farm tractors or heavy equipment, in the Armed Forces or elsewhere is an asset.

Private vocational schools offer instruction in the operation of certain types of construction equipment. Completion of such programs may help a person get a job as a trainee or apprentice. However, persons considering such training should check the school's reputation among employers in the area and find out if it offers the opportunity to work on actual machines in realistic situations.

Operators need to be in good physical condition and have a good sense of balance, the ability to judge distance, and eye-hand-foot coordination. Some operator positions require the ability to work at heights.

Employment

Construction equipment operators held about 449,000 jobs in 2004. Jobs were found in every section of the country and were distributed among various types of operators as follows:

Operating engineers and other construction equipment operators 382,000
Paving, surfacing, and tamping equipment operators 63,000
Pile-driver operators 4,400

About three out of five construction equipment operators worked in the construction industry. Many equipment operators worked in heavy construction, building highways, bridges, or railroads. About one out of five of all construction equipment operators worked in State and local government. Others—mostly grader, bulldozer, and scraper operators—worked in mining. Some also worked in manufacturing and for utility companies. Less than one in twenty construction equipment operators were self-employed.

Job Outlook

Job opportunities for construction equipment operators are expected to be good through 2014. Some potential workers may choose not to enter training programs because they prefer work that has more comfortable working conditions.

Employment of construction equipment operators is expected to increase as fast as the average for all occupations through the year 2014 even with improvements in equipment expected to continue to raise worker productivity and to moderate demand for these workers. Employment is expected to increase as population and business growth create a need for new houses, industrial facilities, schools, hospitals, offices, and other structures. More construction equipment operators also will be needed as a result of expected growth in highway, bridge, and street construction. Bridge construction is expected to grow the fastest, due to the need to repair or replace structures before they become unsafe. Highway conditions also will spur demand for highway maintenance and repair. In addition to job growth, many job openings will arise because of the need to replace experienced construction equipment operators who transfer to other occupations, retire, or leave the job for other reasons.

Like that of other construction workers, employment of construction equipment operators is sensitive to fluctuations in the economy. Workers may experience periods of unemployment when the level of construction activity falls.

Earnings

Earnings for construction equipment operators vary. In May 2004, median hourly earnings of operating engineers and other construction equipment operators were $17.00. The middle 50 percent earned between $13.19 and $23.00. The lowest 10 percent earned less than $10.98, and the highest 10 percent earned more than $29.34. Median hourly earnings in the industries employing the largest numbers of operating engineers in May 2004 were:

Highway, street, and bridge construction	$19.20
Utility system construction	18.13
Other specialty trade contractors	17.73
Local government	15.20
State government	13.52

Median hourly earnings of paving, surfacing, and tamping equipment operators were $14.42 in May 2004. The middle 50 percent earned between $11.35 and $19.30. The lowest 10 percent earned less than $9.47, and the highest 10 percent earned more than $26.51. Median hourly earnings in the industries employing the largest numbers of paving, surfacing, and tamping equipment operators in May 2004 were as follows:

Other specialty trade contractors	$15.03
Highway, street, and bridge construction	14.56
Local government	13.70

In May 2004, median hourly earnings of piledriver operators were $21.29. The middle 50 percent earned between $15.50 and $30.23. The lowest 10 percent earned less than $11.78, and the highest 10 percent earned more than $34.04.

Pay scales generally are higher in large metropolitan areas. Annual earnings of some workers may be lower than hourly rates would indicate because worktime may be limited by bad weather.

Related Occupations

Other workers who operate mechanical equipment include: agricultural equipment operators; truck drivers, heavy and tractor trailer; logging equipment operators; and a variety of material moving occupations.

Sources of Additional Information

For further information about apprenticeships or work opportunities for construction equipment operators, contact a local of the International Union of Operating Engineers, a local apprenticeship committee, or the nearest office of the State apprenticeship agency or employment service. For general information about the work of construction equipment operators, contact:

➤ National Center for Construction Education and Research, P.O. Box 141104, Gainesville, FL 32614-1104. Internet: **http://www.nccer.org**

➤ Associated General Contractors of America, 2300 Wilson Boulevard, Suite 400, Arlington, VA 22201. Internet: **http://www.agc.org**

➤ International Union of Operating Engineers, 1125 17th St. NW., Washington, DC 20036. Internet: **http://www.iuoe.org**

Construction Laborers

(O*NET 47-2061.00)

Significant Points

● Job opportunities should be good.

● With training and experience, construction laborers can move into other skilled craft occupations.

● Most construction laborers learn through informal on-the-job training, but formal apprenticeship programs provide more thorough preparation.

● Like many other construction occupations, employment opportunities are affected by the cyclical nature of the construction industry and can vary greatly by State and locality.

Nature of the Work

Construction laborers can be found on almost all construction sites performing a wide range of tasks from the very easy to the potentially hazardous. They can be found at building, highway, and heavy construction sites; tunnel and shaft excavations; and demolition sites. Many of the jobs they perform require physical strength and some training and experience. Other jobs require little skill and can be learned in a short amount of time. While most construction laborers tend to specialize in a type of construction, such as highway or tunnel construction, they are generalists who perform many different tasks during all stages of construction. However, construction laborers who work in underground construction, such as in tunnels, or in demolition are more likely to specialize in only those areas.

Construction laborers clean and prepare construction sites, which may require them to remove asbestos or lead-based paint from buildings. Laborers also remove trees and debris, tend pumps, compressors and generators, and build forms for pouring concrete. They erect and disassemble scaffolding and other temporary structures. They load, unload, identify, and distribute building materials to the appropriate location according to project plans and specifications. Laborers also tend machines; for example, they may mix concrete using a portable mixer or tend a machine that pumps concrete, grout, cement, sand, plaster, or stucco through a spray gun for application to ceilings and walls. Construction laborers often help other craftworkers, including carpenters, plasterers, operating engineers, and masons.

Construction laborers are responsible for oversight of the installation and maintenance of traffic control devices and patterns. At heavy and highway construction sites, this work may include clearing and preparing highway work zones and rights of way; installing traffic barricades, cones, and markers; and controlling traffic passing near, in, and around work zones. They also dig trenches, install sewer, water, and storm drain pipes, and place concrete and asphalt on roads. Other highly specialized tasks include operating laser guidance equipment to place pipes, operating air, electric, and pneumatic drills, and transporting and setting explosives for tunnel, shaft, and road construction.

Construction laborers operate a variety of equipment including pavement breakers; jackhammers; earth tampers; concrete, mortar, and plaster mixers; electric and hydraulic boring machines; torches; small mechanical hoists; laser beam equipment; and surveying and measuring equipment. They may use computers and other high-tech input devices to control robotic pipe cutters and cleaners. To perform their jobs effectively, construction laborers must be familiar with the duties of other craftworkers and with the materials, tools, and machinery they use.

Construction laborers often work as part of a team with other skilled craftworkers, jointly carrying out assigned construction tasks. At other times, construction laborers may work alone, reading and interpreting instructions, plans, and specifications with little or no supervision.

Working Conditions

Most laborers do physically demanding work. They may lift and carry heavy objects, and stoop, kneel, crouch, or crawl in awkward positions. Some work at great heights, or outdoors in all weather conditions. Some jobs expose workers to harmful materials or chemicals, fumes, odors, loud noise, or dangerous machinery. Some laborers may be exposed to lead-based paint, asbestos, or other hazardous substances during their work especially when working in confined spaces. To avoid injury, workers in these jobs wear safety clothing, such as gloves, hardhats, protective chemical suits, and devices to protect their eyes, respiratory system, or hearing. While working in underground construction, construction laborers must be especially alert to safely follow procedures and must deal with a variety of hazards.

Construction laborers generally work 8-hour shifts, although longer shifts are common. Overnight work may be required when working on highways. Construction laborers may work only during certain seasons in certain parts of the country. They may also experience weather-related work stoppages at any time of the year.

Construction laborers can be found on almost all construction sites performing a wide range of tasks from simple to potentially hazardous.

Training, Other Qualifications, and Advancement

Many construction laborer jobs require few skills, but others require specialized training and experience. Many workers enter the occupation with few skills by obtaining a job with a contractor who will then provide on-the-job training. Entry-level workers generally start as helpers, assisting more experienced workers. A growing route of entry is through temporary help agencies that send laborers to construction sites for short-term work. Beginning laborers perform routine tasks, such as cleaning and preparing the worksite and unloading materials. When the opportunity arises, they learn from experienced construction trades workers how to do more difficult tasks, such as operating tools and equipment. During this time, the construction laborer may elect to attend a trade or vocational school, or community college to receive further trade-related training.

The most skilled laborers usually have more formalized training. Some employers, particularly large nonresidential construction contractors with union membership, offer employees formal apprenticeships. These programs include between 2 and 4 years of classroom and on-the-job training. A core curriculum consisting of basic construction skills such as blueprint reading, the correct use of tools and equipment, and knowledge of safety and health procedures comprises the first 200 hours. The remainder of the curriculum consists of specialized skills training in three of the largest segments of the construction industry: Building construction; heavy/highway construction; and environmental remediation, such as lead or asbestos abatement, and mold or hazardous waste remediation. Workers who use dangerous equipment or handle toxic chemicals usually receive specialized training in safety awareness and procedures. Apprenticeship applicants usually must be at least 18 years old and meet local requirements. Because the number of apprenticeship programs is limited, however, only a small proportion of laborers learn their trade through these programs.

High school classes in English, mathematics, physics, mechanical drawing, blueprint reading, welding, and general shop are recommended. Laborers need manual dexterity, eye-hand coordination, good physical fitness, an ability to work as a member of a team, and a good sense of balance. The ability to solve arithmetic problems quickly and accurately also is required. In addition, a good work history or military service is viewed favorably by contractors. Computer skills also are important for advancement as construction becomes increasingly mechanized and computerized.

Through training and experience, laborers can move into other construction occupations. Laborers may also advance to become construction supervisors or general contractors. For those who would like to advance, it is increasingly important to be able to communicate in both English and Spanish in order to relay instructions and safety precautions to workers with limited understanding of English; Spanish-speaking workers make up a large part of the construction workforce in many areas. Supervisors and contractors need good English skills in order to deal with clients and subcontractors. Supervisors and contractors should be able to identify and estimate the quantity of materials needed to complete a job, and accurately estimate how long a job will take to complete and at what cost.

Employment

Construction laborers held about 1 million jobs in 2004. They worked throughout the country but, like the general population, were concentrated in metropolitan areas. Most construction laborers work in the construction industry and almost one-third work for special trade contractors. About 15 percent were self-employed in 2004.

Job Outlook

Employment of construction laborers is expected to grow more slowly than the average for all occupations through the year 2014 as the construction industry in general grows more slowly than it has in the recent past. However, job opportunities are expected to be good due to the numerous openings that rise each year as laborers leave the occupation. Opportunities will be best for those with experience and specialized skills, and for those willing to relocate to areas with new construction projects. Opportunities will also be good for laborers specializing in lead, asbestos, and other hazardous materials removal.

Although construction will continue to grow, construction laborer jobs will be adversely affected by automation as some jobs are replaced by new machines and equipment that improve productivity and quality. Also, laborers will be increasingly employed by staffing agencies that will contract laborers out to employers on a temporary basis.

Employment of construction laborers, like that of many other construction workers, can be variable or intermittent due to the limited duration of construction projects and the cyclical nature of the construction industry. Employment opportunities can vary greatly by State and locality. During economic downturns, job openings for construction laborers decrease as the level of construction activity declines.

Earnings

Median hourly earnings of construction laborers in May 2004 were $12.10. The middle 50 percent earned between $9.47 and $16.88. The lowest 10 percent earned less than $7.71, and the highest 10 percent earned more than $23.61. Median hourly earnings in the industries employing the largest number of construction laborers in May 2004 were as follows:

Highway, street, and bridge construction	$13.55
Nonresidential building construction	12.94
Other specialty trade contractors	12.43
Residential building construction	12.18
Foundation, structure, and building exterior contractors	11.90

Earnings for construction laborers can be reduced by poor weather or by downturns in construction activity, which sometimes result in layoffs. Apprentices or helpers usually start at about 50 percent of the wage rate paid to experienced workers. Pay increases as apprentices gain experience and learn new skills.

Some laborers belong to the Laborers' International Union of North America.

Related Occupations

The work of construction laborers is closely related to other construction occupations. Other workers who perform similar physical work include persons in material-moving occupations; forest, conservation, and logging workers; and grounds maintenance workers.

Sources of Additional Information

For information about jobs as construction laborers, contact local building or construction contractors, local joint labor-management apprenticeship committees, apprenticeship agencies, or the local office of your State Employment Service.

For information on education programs for laborers, contact:

➤ Laborers-AGC Education and Training Fund, 37 Deerfield Road, P.O. Box 37, Pomfret Center, CT 06259. Internet: **http://www.laborerslearn.org**

➤ National Center for Construction Education and Research, P.O. Box 141104, Gainesville, FL 32614-1104. Internet: **http://www.nccer.org**

Drywall Installers, Ceiling Tile Installers, and Tapers

(O*NET 47-2081.01, 47-2081.02, 47-2082.00)

Significant Points

- Most workers learn the trade on the job by starting as helpers to more experienced workers; additional classroom instruction may also be needed.

- Job prospects are expected to be good.

- Inclement weather seldom interrupts work, but workers may be idled when downturns in the economy slow new construction activity.

Nature of the Work

Drywall consists of a thin layer of gypsum between two layers of heavy paper. It is used for walls and ceilings in most buildings today because it is both faster and cheaper to install than plaster.

There are two kinds of drywall workers—installers and tapers—although many workers do both types of work. Installers, also called *applicators* or *hangers*, fasten drywall panels to the inside framework of residential houses and other buildings. *Tapers* or *finishers*, prepare these panels for painting by taping and finishing joints and imperfections.

Because drywall panels are manufactured in standard sizes—usually 4 feet by 8 or 12 feet—drywall installers must measure, cut, and fit some pieces around doors and windows. They also saw or cut holes in panels for electrical outlets, air-conditioning units, and plumbing. After making these alterations, installers may glue, nail, or screw the wallboard panels to the wood or metal framework. Because drywall is heavy and cumbersome, a helper generally assists the installer in positioning and securing the panel. Workers often use a lift when placing ceiling panels.

After the drywall is installed, tapers fill joints between panels with a joint compound. Using the wide, flat tip of a special trowel, they spread the compound into and along each side of the joint with brush-like strokes. They immediately use the trowel to press a paper tape—used to reinforce the drywall and to hide imperfections—into the wet compound and to smooth away excess material. Nail and screw depressions also are covered with this compound, as are imperfections caused by the installation of air-conditioning vents and other fixtures. On large projects, finishers may use automatic taping tools that apply the joint compound and tape in one step. Tapers apply second and third coats of the compound, sanding the treated areas where needed after each coat to make them as smooth as the rest of the wall surface. This results in a very smooth and almost perfect surface. Some tapers apply textured surfaces to walls and ceilings with trowels, brushes, or spray guns.

Ceiling tile installers, or *acoustical carpenters*, apply or mount acoustical tiles or blocks, strips, or sheets of shock-absorbing materials to ceilings and walls of buildings to reduce reflection of sound or to decorate rooms. First, they measure and mark the surface according to blueprints and drawings. Then, they nail or screw moldings to the wall to support and seal the joint between the ceiling tile and the wall. Finally, they mount the tile, either by applying a cement adhesive to the back of the tile and then pressing the tile into place, or by nailing, screwing, stapling, or wire-tying the lath directly to the structural framework.

Lathers also are included in this occupation. Lathers fasten metal or rockboard lath to walls, ceilings, and partitions of buildings. Lath forms the support base for plaster, fireproofing, or acoustical materials. At one time, lath was made of wooden strips. Now, lathers work

After the drywall is installed, tapers fill joints between panels with a joint compound.

mostly with wire, metal mesh, or rockboard lath. Metal lath is used where the plaster application will be exposed to weather or water or for curved or irregular surfaces for which drywall is not a practical material. Using handtools and portable power tools, lathers nail, screw, staple, or wire-tie the lath directly to the structural framework.

Working Conditions

As in many other construction trades, the work sometimes is strenuous. Drywall installers, ceiling tile installers, and tapers spend most of the day on their feet, either standing, bending, or kneeling. Some tapers use stilts to tape and finish ceiling and angle joints. Installers have to lift and maneuver heavy panels. Hazards include falls from ladders and scaffolds and injuries from power tools and from working with sharp materials. Because sanding a joint compound to a smooth finish creates a great deal of dust, some finishers wear masks for protection.

Training, Other Qualifications, and Advancement

Drywall installers, ceiling tile installers, and tapers learn their trade through formal and informal training programs. To become a skilled drywall installer, ceiling tile installer, or taper, between 3 and 4 years of both classroom and on-the-job training may be required, but many of the skills can be learned within the first year. While there are a number of different ways to obtain this training, in general the more formalized the process, the more skilled the individual becomes, and the more in demand they are by employers.

There are a number of different avenues that one can take to obtain the necessary training. The most common entry route is

to obtain a job with a contractor who will then provide on-the-job training. Entry-level workers generally start as helpers, assisting more experienced workers. During this time, employers may send the employee to a trade or vocational school, or community college to receive further classroom training.

Some employers, particularly large nonresidential construction contractors with union membership, offer employees formal apprenticeships. These programs combine on-the-job training with related classroom instruction. Usually, apprenticeship applicants must be at least 18 years old and meet local requirements. The length of the program, usually 3 to 4 years, varies with the apprentice's skill. Because the number of apprenticeship programs is limited, however, only a small proportion of drywall installers, ceiling tile installers, and tapers learn their trade through these programs.

Other jobseekers may choose to obtain their classroom training before seeking a job. There are a number of public and private vocational-technical schools and training academies affiliated with the unions and contractors that offer training to become a drywall installer, ceiling tile installer, and taper. Employers often look favorably upon these students and usually start them at a higher level than those without the training.

Installer helpers start by carrying materials, lifting and holding panels, and cleaning up debris. They also learn to use the tools, machines, equipment, and materials of the trade. Within a few weeks, they learn to measure, cut, and install materials. Eventually, they become fully experienced workers. Tapers learn their job by taping joints and touching up nail holes, scrapes, and other imperfections. They soon learn to install corner guards and to conceal openings around pipes. At the end of their training, drywall installers, ceiling tile installers, and tapers learn to estimate the cost of installing and finishing drywall.

Training for this profession can begin in a high school, where classes in English, math, mechanical drawing, blueprint reading, and general shop are recommended. Some skills needed to become a drywall installer, ceiling tile installer, and taper include manual dexterity, eye-hand coordination, good physical fitness, and a good sense of balance. The ability to solve arithmetic problems quickly and accurately also is required. In addition, a good work history or military service is viewed favorably by contractors.

Drywall installers, ceiling tile installers, and tapers may advance to carpentry supervisor or general construction supervisor positions. Others may become independent contractors. For those who would like to advance, it is increasingly important to be able to communicate in both English and Spanish in order to relay instructions and safety precautions to workers with limited understanding of English; Spanish-speaking workers make up a large part of the construction workforce in many areas. Hispanic workers who want to advance should learn English. Supervisors and contractors need good English skills in order to deal with clients and subcontractors. They also should be able to identify and estimate the quantity of materials needed to complete a job, and accurately estimate how long a job will take to complete and at what cost.

Employment

Drywall installers, ceiling tile installers, and tapers held about 196,000 jobs in 2004. Most worked for contractors specializing in drywall and ceiling tile installation; others worked for contractors doing many kinds of construction. About 43,000 were self-employed independent contractors.

Most installers and tapers are employed in populous areas. In other areas, where there may not be enough work to keep a drywall or ceiling tile installer employed full time, carpenters and painters usually do the work.

Job Outlook

Job opportunities for drywall installers, ceiling tile installers, and tapers are expected to be good. Many potential workers are not attracted to this occupation because they prefer work that is less strenuous and has more comfortable working conditions. Experienced workers will have especially favorable opportunities.

Employment is expected to increase more slowly than average for all occupations over the 2004-14 period reflecting the number of new construction and remodeling projects. In addition to jobs involving traditional interior work, drywall workers will find employment opportunities in the installation of insulated exterior wall systems, which are becoming increasingly popular.

Besides those resulting from job growth, many jobs will open up each year because of the need to replace workers who transfer to other occupations or leave the labor force. Some drywall installers, ceiling tile installers, and tapers with limited skills leave the occupation when they find that they dislike the work or fail to find steady employment.

Despite the growing use of exterior panels, most drywall installation and finishing is done indoors. Therefore, drywall workers lose less worktime because of inclement weather than do some other construction workers. Nevertheless, they may be unemployed between construction projects and during downturns in construction activity.

Earnings

In May 2004, the median hourly earnings of drywall and ceiling tile installers were $16.36. The middle 50 percent earned between $12.59 and $21.82. The lowest 10 percent earned less than $9.98, and the highest 10 percent earned more than $28.30. The median hourly earnings in the industries employing the largest numbers of drywall and ceiling tile installers in May 2004 were as follows:

Residential building construction	$17.33
Building finishing contractors	16.53
Nonresidential building construction	14.57

In May 2004, the median hourly earnings of tapers were $18.78. The middle 50 percent earned between $14.07 and $24.43. The lowest 10 percent earned less than $10.66, and the highest 10 percent earned more than $28.79.

Some contractors pay these workers according to the number of panels they install or finish per day; others pay an hourly rate. A 40-hour week is standard, but the workweek may sometimes be longer or shorter. Workers who are paid hourly rates receive premium pay for overtime. Trainees usually started at about half the rate paid to experienced workers and received wage increases as they became more highly skilled.

Related Occupations

Drywall installers, ceiling tile installers, and tapers combine strength and dexterity with precision and accuracy to make materials fit according to a plan. Other occupations that require similar abilities include carpenters; carpet, floor, and tile installers and finishers; insulation workers; and plasterers and stucco masons.

Sources of Additional Information

For information about work opportunities in drywall application and finishing and ceiling tile installation, contact local drywall installation and ceiling tile installation contractors, a local joint union-management apprenticeship committee, a State or local chapter of the Associated Builders and Contractors, or the nearest office of the State employment service or apprenticeship agency.

For details about job qualifications and training programs in drywall application and finishing and ceiling tile installation, contact:
➤ Associated Builders and Contractors, 4250 North Fairfax Dr., 9th Floor Arlington, VA 22203. Internet: **www.trytools.org**
➤ National Association of Home Builders, Home Builders Institute, 1201 15th St. NW., Washington, DC 20005. Internet: **http://www.hbi.org**
➤ Joint Apprenticeship and Training Fund, International Union of Painters and Allied Trades, 1750 New York Ave. NW., Washington, DC 20006. Internet: **http://www.jatf.org**
➤ National Center for Construction Education and Research, P.O. Box 141104, Gainesville, FL 32614-1104. Internet: **http://www.nccer.org**
➤ United Brotherhood of Carpenters and Joiners of America, Carpenters Training Fund, 6801 Placid Street, Las Vegas, NV 89119 Internet: **http://www.carpenters.org**

Electricians

(O*NET 47-2111.00)

Significant Points

● Job opportunities are expected to be good, especially for those with the right skills.

● Most electricians acquire their skills by completing an apprenticeship program lasting 4 to 5 years.

● Nearly three-fourths of electricians work for building contractors or are self-employed, but there also will be many job openings for electricians in other industries.

Nature of the Work

Electricity is essential for light, power, air-conditioning, and refrigeration. Electricians install, connect, test, and maintain electrical systems for a variety of purposes, including climate control, security, and communications. They also may install and maintain the electronic controls for machines in business and industry.

Electricians generally specialize in construction or maintenance work, although a growing number do both. Electricians specializing in construction work primarily install wiring systems into new homes, businesses, and factories, but they also rewire or upgrade existing electrical systems as needed. Electricians specializing in maintenance work primarily maintain and upgrade existing electrical systems and repair electrical equipment.

Electricians work with blueprints when they install electrical systems. Blueprints indicate the locations of circuits, outlets, load centers, panel boards, and other equipment. Electricians must follow the National Electrical Code and comply with State and local building codes when they install these systems. Regulations vary depending on the setting and require various types of installation procedures.

When electricians install wiring systems in factories and commercial settings, they first place conduit (pipe or tubing) inside partitions, walls, or other concealed areas as designated by the blueprints. They also fasten to the walls small metal or plastic boxes that will house electrical switches and outlets. They pull insulated wires or cables through the conduit to complete circuits between these boxes. In residential construction, electricians usually install plastic encased insulated wire, which does not need to be run through conduit. The gauge and number of wires installed in all settings depends upon the load and end use of that part of the electrical system. The greater the diameter of the wire, the higher the voltage and amperage that can flow through it.

Electricians connect all types of wire to circuit breakers, transformers, outlets, or other components. They join the wires in boxes

Electricians connect all types of wire to circuit breakers, transformers, outlets, or other components.

with various specially designed connectors. During installation, electricians use hand tools such as conduit benders, screwdrivers, pliers, knives, hacksaws, and wire strippers, as well as power tools such as drills and saws. After they finish installing the wiring, they use testing equipment, such as ammeters, ohmmeters, voltmeters, and oscilloscopes, to check the circuits for proper connections, ensuring electrical compatibility, and safety of components.

Maintenance work varies greatly, depending on where the electrician is employed. Electricians who specialize in residential work perform a wide variety of electrical work for homeowners. They may rewire a home and replace an old fuse box with a new circuit breaker box to accommodate additional appliances, or they may install new lighting and other electric household items, such as ceiling fans. Those who work in large factories may repair motors, transformers, generators, and electronic controllers on machine tools and industrial robots. Those in office buildings and small plants may repair all types of electrical equipment.

Maintenance electricians working in factories, hospitals, and other settings repair electric and electronic equipment when breakdowns occur and install new electrical equipment. When breakdowns occur, they must make the necessary repairs as quickly as possible in order to minimize inconvenience. They may replace items such as circuit breakers, fuses, switches, electrical and electronic components, or wire. Electricians also periodically inspect all equipment to ensure it is operating properly, and locate and correct problems before breakdowns occur. Electricians also advise management whether continued operation of equipment could be hazardous. When working with complex electronic devices, they may work with engineers, engineering technicians, line installers and repairers, or industrial machinery installation, repair, and maintenance workers. (Sections on these occupations appear elsewhere in the *Handbook*.)

Although primarily classified as work for line installers and repairers, electricians also may install low voltage wiring systems in addition to wiring a building's electrical system. Low voltage wiring involves voice, data, and video wiring systems, such as those for telephones, computers and related equipment, intercoms, and fire alarm and security systems. Electricians also may install coaxial or fiber optic cable for computers and other telecommunications equipment and electronic controls for industrial uses.

Working Conditions

Electricians work both indoors and out; at construction sites, in homes, and in businesses or factories. Work may be strenuous at times and include bending conduit, lifting heavy objects, and standing, stooping, and kneeling for long periods of time. When working outdoors, they may be subject to inclement weather conditions. Some electricians may have to travel long distances to jobsites. Electricians risk injury from electrical shock, falls, and cuts; they must follow strict safety procedures to avoid injuries.

Most electricians work a standard 40-hour week, although overtime may be required. Those in maintenance work may work nights or weekends, and be on call to go to the worksite when needed. Electricians working in industrial settings may also have periodic extended overtime during scheduled maintenance or retooling periods. Companies that operate 24 hours a day may employ three shifts of electricians.

Training, Other Qualifications, and Advancement

Most electricians learn their trade through apprenticeship programs. These programs combine on-the-job training with related classroom instruction. Apprenticeship programs may be sponsored by joint training committees made up of local unions of the International Brotherhood of Electrical Workers and local chapters of the National Electrical Contractors Association; company management committees of individual electrical contracting companies; or local chapters of the Associated Builders and Contractors and the Independent Electrical Contractors Association. Because of the comprehensive training received, those who complete apprenticeship programs qualify to do both maintenance and construction work.

Applicants for apprenticeships usually must be at least 18 years old and have a high school diploma or a G.E.D. They should have good math and English skills, since most instruction manuals are in English. They also may have to pass a test and meet other requirements. Apprenticeship programs usually last 4 years and each year include at least 144 hours of classroom instruction and 2,000 hours of on-the-job training. In the classroom, apprentices learn electrical theory and installing and maintaining electrical systems. There also take classes in blueprint reading, mathematics, electrical code requirements, and safety and first aid practices also may receive specialized training in soldering, communications, fire alarm systems, and cranes and elevators. On the job, apprentices work under the supervision of experienced electricians. At first, they drill holes, set anchors, and attach conduit. Later, they measure, fabricate, and install conduit, as well as install, connect, and test wiring, outlets, and switches. They also learn to set up and draw diagrams for entire electrical systems. To complete the apprenticeship and become electricians, apprentices must demonstrate mastery of the electrician's work

Some persons seeking to become electricians choose to obtain their classroom training before seeking a job. Training to become an electrician is offered by a number of public and private vocational-technical schools and training academies in affiliation with local unions and contractor organizations. Employers often hire students who complete these programs and usually start them at a more advanced level than those without the training. A few persons become electricians by first working as helpers, assisting electricians setting up job sites, gathering materials, and doing other nonelectrical work, before entering an apprenticeship program.

Skills needed to become an electrician include manual dexterity, eye-hand coordination, physical fitness, and a good sense of balance. The ability to solve arithmetic problems quickly and accurately also is required. Good color vision is needed because workers frequently must identify electrical wires by color. In addition, a good work history or military service is viewed favorably by apprenticeship committees and employers.

Most localities require electricians to be licensed. Although licensing requirements vary from area to area, electricians usually must pass an examination that tests their knowledge of electrical theory, the National Electrical Code, and local electric and building codes. Experienced electricians periodically take courses offered by their employer or union to keep abreast of changes in the National Electrical Code and new materials or methods of installation. For example, classes on installing low voltage voice, data, and video systems have recently become common as these systems have become more prevalent.

Experienced electricians can advance to jobs as supervisors. In construction they also may become project managers or construction superintendents. Those with sufficient capital and management skills may start their own contracting business, although this may require an electrical contractor's license. Many electricians also become electrical inspectors. Supervisors and contractors should be able to identify and estimate the correct type and quantity of materials needed to complete a job, and accurately estimate how long a job will take to complete and at what cost. For those who seek to advance, it is increasingly important to be able to communicate in both English and Spanish in order to relay instructions and safety precautions to workers with limited understanding of English; Spanish-speaking workers make up a large part of the construction workforce in many areas. Spanish-speaking workers who want to advance in this occupation need very good English skills to understand instruction presented in classes and installation instructions, which are usually written in English and are highly technical.

Employment

Electricians held about 656,000 jobs in 2004. Nearly two-thirds of wage and salary workers were employed in the construction industry; while the remainder worked as maintenance electricians in other industries. In addition, about one in ten electricians were self-employed.

Because of the widespread need for electrical services, electrician jobs are found in all parts of the country.

Job Outlook

Employment of electricians is expected to increase as fast as the average for all occupations through the year 2014. As the population and economy grow, more electricians will be needed to install and maintain electrical devices and wiring in homes, factories, offices, and other structures. New technologies also are expected to continue to stimulate the demand for these workers. For example, buildings need to increasingly accommodate the use of computers and telecommunications equipment. Also, the increasing prevalence in factories of robots and other automated manufacturing systems will require more complex wiring systems be installed and maintained. Additional jobs will be created as older structures are rehabilitated and retrofitted, which usually requires that they be brought up to meet existing electrical codes.

In addition to jobs created by the increased demand for electrical work, many openings are expected to occur over the next decade as a large number of electricians are expected to retire. This will create good job opportunities for the most qualified jobseekers. Job openings for electricians, though, will vary by area and will be greatest in the fastest growing regions of the country.

Employment of construction electricians, like that of many other construction workers, is sensitive to changes in the economy. This results from the limited duration of construction projects and the cyclical nature of the construction industry. During economic downturns, job openings for electricians are reduced as the level of construction activity declines. Apprenticeship opportunities also are less plentiful during these periods.

Although employment of maintenance electricians is steadier than that of construction electricians, those working in the automotive and other manufacturing industries that are sensitive to cyclical swings in the economy may be laid off during recessions. Also, opportunities for maintenance electricians may be limited in many industries by the increased contracting out for electrical services in an effort to reduce operating costs and increase productivity. However, increased job opportunities for electricians in electrical contracting firms should partially offset job losses in other industries.

Earnings

In May 2004, median hourly earnings of electricians were $20.33. The middle 50 percent earned between $15.43 and $26.90. The lowest 10 percent earned less than $12.18, and the highest 10 percent earned more than $33.63. Median hourly earnings in the industries employing the largest numbers of electricians in May 2004 were as follows:

Motor vehicle parts manufacturing	$30.04
Local government	22.24
Nonresidential building construction	19.99
Building equipment contractors	19.76
Employment services	15.62

Apprentices usually start at between 40 and 50 percent of the rate paid to fully trained electricians, depending on experience. As apprentices become more skilled, they receive periodic pay increases throughout the course of their training.

Some electricians are members of the International Brotherhood of Electrical Workers. Among unions representing maintenance electricians are the International Brotherhood of Electrical Workers; the International Union of Electronic, Electrical, Salaried, Machine, and Furniture Workers; the International Association of Machinists and Aerospace Workers; the International Union, United Automobile, Aircraft and Agricultural Implement Workers of America; and the United Steelworkers of America.

Related Occupations

To install and maintain electrical systems, electricians combine manual skill and knowledge of electrical materials and concepts. Workers in other occupations involving similar skills include heating, air-conditioning, and refrigeration mechanics and installers; line installers and repairers; electrical and electronics installers and repairers; electronic home entertainment equipment installers and repairers; and elevator installers and repairers.

Sources of Additional Information

For details about apprenticeships or other work opportunities in this trade, contact the offices of the State employment service, the State apprenticeship agency, local electrical contractors or firms that employ maintenance electricians, or local union-management electrician apprenticeship committees. This information also may be available from local chapters of the Independent Electrical Contractors, Inc.; the National Electrical Contractors Association; the Home Builders Institute; the Associated Builders and Contractors; and the International Brotherhood of Electrical Workers.

For information about union apprenticeship and training programs, contact:

➤ National Joint Apprenticeship Training Committee (NJATC), 301 Prince George's Blvd., Upper Marlboro, MD 20774. Internet: **http://www.njatc.org**
➤ National Electrical Contractors Association (NECA), 3 Metro Center, Suite 1100, Bethesda, MD 20814. Internet: **http://www.necanet.org**
➤ International Brotherhood of Electrical Workers (IBEW), 1125 15th St. NW., Washington, DC 20005. Internet: **http://www.ibew.org**

For information about independent apprenticeship programs, contact:

➤ Associated Builders and Contractors, Workforce Development Department, 4250 North Fairfax Dr., 9th Floor, Arlington, VA 22203. Internet: **http://www.trytools.org**

➤ Independent Electrical Contractors, Inc., 4401 Ford Ave., Suite 1100, Alexandria, VA 22302. Internet: **http://www.ieci.org**
➤ National Association of Home Builders, Home Builders Institute, 1201 15th St. NW., Washington, DC 20005. Internet: **http://www.hbi.org**
➤ National Center for Construction Education and Research, P.O. Box 141104, Gainesville, FL 32614-1104. Internet: **http://www.nccer.org**

Elevator Installers and Repairers

(O*NET 47-4021.00)

Significant Points

● Most workers belong to a union and enter the occupation through a 4-year apprenticeship program.

● High pay and good benefits, together with expected slow job growth and few separations, should result in keen competition for the few job opportunities that arise in this small occupation; prospects should be best for those with postsecondary education in electronics.

● Elevator installers and repairers are less affected by downturns in the economy and inclement weather than other construction trades workers.

Nature of the Work

Elevator installers and repairers—also called *elevator constructors* or *elevator mechanics*—assemble, install, and replace elevators, escalators, dumbwaiters, moving walkways, and similar equipment in new and old buildings. Once the equipment is in service, they maintain and repair it as well. They also are responsible for modernizing older equipment.

To install, repair, and maintain modern elevators, which are almost all electronically controlled, elevator installers and repairers must have a thorough knowledge of electronics, electricity, and hydraulics. Many elevators are controlled with microprocessors, which are programmed to analyze traffic conditions in order to dispatch elevators in the most efficient manner. With these computer controls, it is possible to get the greatest amount of service with the least number of cars.

When installing a new elevator, installers and repairers begin by studying blueprints to determine the equipment needed to install rails, machinery, car enclosures, motors, pumps, cylinders, and plunger foundations. Once this has been done, they begin equipment installation. Working on scaffolding or platforms, installers bolt or weld steel rails to the walls of the shaft to guide the elevator.

Elevator installers put in electrical wires and controls by running tubing, called conduit, along a shaft's walls from floor to floor. Once the conduit is in place, mechanics pull plastic-covered electrical wires through it. They then install electrical components and related devices required at each floor and at the main control panel in the machine room.

Installers bolt or weld together the steel frame of an elevator car at the bottom of the shaft; install the car's platform, walls, and doors; and attach guide shoes and rollers to minimize the lateral motion of the car as it travels through the shaft. They also install the outer doors and door frames at the elevator entrances on each floor.

For cabled elevators, these workers install geared or gearless machines with a traction drive wheel that guides and moves heavy steel cables connected to the elevator car and counterweight. (The counterweight moves in the opposite direction from the car and balances most of the weight of the car to reduce the weight that the elevator's motor must lift.) Elevator installers also install elevators in which a car sits on a hydraulic plunger that is driven by a pump. The plunger pushes the elevator car up from underneath, similar to a lift in an auto service station.

Elevator installers and repairers must have a thorough knowledge of electronics, electricity, and hydraulics.

Installers and repairers also install escalators. They put in place the steel framework, the electrically powered stairs and the tracks, and install associated motors and electrical wiring. In addition to elevators and escalators, installers and repairers also may install devices such as dumbwaiters and material lifts—which are similar to elevators in design—as well as moving walkways, stair lifts, and wheelchair lifts.

The most highly skilled elevator installers and repairers, called "adjusters," specialize in fine-tuning all the equipment after installation. Adjusters make sure that an elevator is working according to specifications and is stopping correctly at each floor within a specified time. Once an elevator is operating properly, it must be maintained and serviced regularly to keep it in safe working condition. Elevator installers and repairers generally do preventive maintenance—such as oiling and greasing moving parts, replacing worn parts, testing equipment with meters and gauges, and adjusting equipment for optimal performance. They also troubleshoot and may be called to do emergency repairs.

A service crew usually handles major repairs—for example, replacing cables, elevator doors, or machine bearings. This may require the use of cutting torches or rigging equipment—tools that an elevator repairer normally would not carry. Service crews also do major modernization and alteration work, such as moving and replacing electrical motors, hydraulic pumps, and control panels.

Elevator installers and repairers usually specialize in installation, maintenance, or repair work. Maintenance and repair workers generally need greater knowledge of electricity and electronics than do installers, because a large part of maintenance and repair work is troubleshooting. Similarly, adjusters need a thorough knowledge of electricity, electronics, and computers to ensure that newly installed elevators operate properly.

Working Conditions

Most elevator installers and repairers work a 40-hour week. However, overtime is required when essential elevator equipment must be repaired, and some workers are on 24-hour call. Unlike most elevator installers, workers who specialize in elevator maintenance are on their own most of the day and typically service the same elevators periodically.

Elevator installers lift and carry heavy equipment and parts, and may work in cramped spaces or awkward positions. Potential hazards include falls, electrical shock, muscle strains, and other injuries related to handling heavy equipment. Because most of their work is performed indoors in buildings under construction or in existing buildings, elevator installers and repairers lose less work time due to inclement weather than do other construction trades workers.

Training, Other Qualifications, and Advancement

Most elevator installers and repairers apply for their jobs through a local of the International Union of Elevator Constructors. Applicants for apprenticeship positions must be at least 18 years old, have a high school diploma or equivalent, and pass an aptitude test. Good physical condition and mechanical aptitude also are important.

Elevator installers and repairers learn their trade in a program administered by local joint educational committees representing the employers and the union. These programs, through which the apprentice learns everything from installation to repair, combine on-the-job training with classroom instruction in blueprint reading, electrical and electronic theory, mathematics, applications of physics, and safety. In nonunion shops, workers may complete training programs sponsored by independent contractors.

Apprentices generally must complete a 6-month probationary period. After successful completion, they work toward becoming fully qualified within 4 years. To be classified as a fully qualified elevator installer or repairer, union trainees must pass a standard examination administered by the National Elevator Industry Educational Program. Most States and cities also require elevator installers and repairers to pass a licensing examination. Both union and nonunion technicians may take the Certified Elevator Technician (CET) or the Certified Accessibility and Private Residence Lift Technician (CAT) program courses offered by the National Association of Elevator Contractors.

Most apprentices assist experienced elevator installers and repairers. Beginners carry materials and tools, bolt rails to walls, and assemble elevator cars. Eventually, apprentices learn more difficult tasks such as wiring, which requires knowledge of local and national electrical codes.

High school courses in electricity, mathematics, and physics provide a useful background. As elevators become increasingly sophisticated, workers may find it necessary to acquire more advanced formal education—for example, in a postsecondary technical school or junior college—with an emphasis on electronics. Workers with more formal education, such as an associate degree, usually advance more quickly than do their counterparts without a degree.

Many elevator installers and repairers also receive training from their employers or through manufacturers to become familiar with a particular company's equipment. Retraining is very important if a worker is to keep abreast of technological developments in elevator repair. In fact, union elevator installers and repairers typically receive continual training throughout their careers, through correspondence courses, seminars, or formal classes. Although voluntary, this training greatly improves one's chances for promotion and retention.

Some installers may receive further training in specialized areas and advance to the position of mechanic-in-charge, adjuster, supervisor, or elevator inspector. Adjusters, for example, may be picked for their position because they possess particular skills or are electronically inclined. Other workers may move into management, sales, or product design jobs.

Employment

Elevator installers and repairers held about 22,000 jobs in 2004. Most were employed by specialty trades contractors, particularly elevator maintenance and repair contractors. Others were employed by field offices of elevator manufacturers, machinery wholesalers, government agencies, or businesses that do their own elevator maintenance and repair.

Job Outlook

Workers should expect keen competition when seeking to enter this occupation. Elevator installer and repairer jobs have relatively high earnings and good benefits, involve a significant investment in training, and a large proportion are unionized. As a result, workers tend to stay in this occupation for a long time and few leave and need to be replaced, thus reducing job opportunities. Job prospects should be best for those with postsecondary education in electronics.

Employment of elevator installers and repairers is expected to increase as fast as the average for all occupations through the year 2014. Most of the demand for workers will be due to replacements. Demand for additional elevator installers depends greatly on growth in nonresidential construction, such as commercial office buildings and stores that have elevators and escalators. This sector of the construction industry is expected to grow during the decade in response to expansion of the economy. In addition, the need to continually update and repair old equipment, expand access to the disabled, and install increasingly sophisticated equipment and computerized controls also should add to the demand for elevator installers and repairers. Adding to the demand for elevator installers and repairers is a growing residential market where an increasing number of the elderly require easier access to their homes through stair lifts and residential elevators.

Elevators, escalators, lifts, moving walkways, and related equipment need to be kept in good working condition year round, so employment of elevator repairers is less affected by economic downturns and seasonality than other construction trades.

Earnings

Earnings of elevator installers and repairers are among the highest of all construction trades. Median hourly earnings of elevator installers and repairers were $28.23 in May 2004. The middle 50 percent earned between $22.96 and $33.68. The lowest 10 percent earned less than $17.36, and the top 10 percent earned more than $39.65. In May 2004, median hourly earnings in the miscellaneous special trade contractors industry were $28.68.

Three out of four elevator installers and repairers were members of unions or covered by a union contract, one of the highest proportions of all occupations. The largest numbers were members of the International Union of Elevator Constructors. In addition to free continuing education, elevator installers and repairers receive basic benefits enjoyed by most other workers.

Related Occupations

Elevator installers and repairers combine electrical and mechanical skills with construction skills, such as welding, rigging, measuring, and blueprint reading. Other occupations that require many of these skills are boilermakers; electricians; electrical and electronics installers and repairers; industrial machinery installation, repair, and maintenance workers; sheet metal workers; and structural and reinforcing iron and metal workers.

Sources of Additional Information

For further information on opportunities as an elevator installer and repairer, contact:

➤ International Union of Elevator Constructors, 7154 Columbia Gateway Dr., Columbia, MD 21046. Internet: **http://www.iuec.org**

For additional information about the Certified Elevator Technician (CET) program, contact:

➤ National Association of Elevator Contractors, 1298 Wellbrook Circle, Suite A, Conyers, GA 30012. Internet: **http://www.naec.org**

Glaziers

(O*NET 47-2121.00)

Significant Points

- Many glaziers learn the trade by working as helpers to experienced glaziers.
- Job opportunities are expected to be good.

Nature of the Work

Glass serves many uses in modern life. Insulated and specially treated glass keeps in warmed or cooled air and provides good condensation and sound control qualities, while tempered and laminated glass makes doors and windows more secure. In large commercial buildings, glass panels give office buildings a distinctive look while reducing the need for artificial lighting. The creative use of large windows, glass doors, skylights, and sunroom additions makes homes bright, airy, and inviting.

Glaziers are responsible for selecting, cutting, installing, replacing, and removing all types of glass. They generally work on one of several types of projects. Residential glazing involves work such as replacing glass in home windows; installing glass mirrors, shower doors, and bathtub enclosures; and fitting glass for tabletops and display cases. On commercial interior projects, glaziers install items such as heavy, often etched, decorative room dividers or security windows. Glazing projects also may involve replacement of storefront windows for establishments such as supermarkets, auto dealerships, or banks. In the construction of large commercial buildings, glaziers build metal framework extrusions and install glass panels or curtain walls.

Besides working with glass, glaziers also may work with plastics, granite, marble, and other similar materials used as glass substitutes, as well as films or laminates that improve the durability or safety of the glass. They may mount steel and aluminum sashes or frames and attach locks and hinges to glass doors. For most jobs, the glass is precut and mounted in frames at a factory or a contractor's shop. It arrives at the jobsite ready for glaziers to position and secure it in place. They may use a crane or hoist with suction cups to lift large, heavy pieces of glass. They then gently guide the glass into position by hand.

Once glaziers have the glass in place, they secure it with mastic, putty, or other paste-like cement, or with bolts, rubber gaskets, glazing compound, metal clips, or metal or wood moldings. When they secure glass using a rubber gasket—a thick, molded rubber half-tube with a split running its length—they first secure the gasket around the perimeter within the opening, then set the glass into the split side of the gasket, causing it to clamp to the edges and hold the glass firmly in place.

When they use metal clips and wood moldings, glaziers first secure the molding to the opening, place the glass in the molding, and then force springlike metal clips between the glass and the molding. The clips exert pressure and keep the glass firmly in place.

When a glazing compound is used, glaziers first spread it neatly against and around the edges of the molding on the inside of the opening. Next, they install the glass. Pressing it against the compound on the inside molding, workers screw or nail outside molding that loosely holds the glass in place. To hold it firmly, they pack the space between the molding and the glass with glazing compound and then trim any excess material with a glazing knife.

For some jobs, the glazier must cut the glass manually at the jobsite. To prepare the glass for cutting, glaziers rest it either on edge on a rack, or "A-frame," or flat against a cutting table. They then measure and mark the glass for the cut.

Glaziers cut glass with a special tool that has a small, very hard metal wheel. Using a straightedge as a guide, the glazier presses the cutter's wheel firmly on the glass, guiding and rolling it carefully to make a score just below the surface. To help the cutting tool move smoothly across the glass, workers brush a thin layer of oil along the line of the intended cut or dip the cutting tool in oil. Immediately after cutting, the glazier presses on the shorter end of the glass to break it cleanly along the cut.

In addition to handtools such as glasscutters, suction cups, and glazing knives, glaziers use power tools such as saws, drills, cutters, and grinders. An increasing number of glaziers use computers in the shop or at the jobsite to improve their layout work and reduce the amount of glass that is wasted.

Using a straightedge as a guide, the glazier makes a score on the surface of the glass before cutting it.

Working Conditions

Glaziers often work outdoors, sometimes in inclement weather. Their work can, at times, result in injuries as they work with sharp tools and may need to remove broken glass. They must be prepared to lift heavy glass panels and work on scaffolding, sometimes at great heights. Glaziers do a considerable amount of bending, kneeling, lifting, and standing during the installation process.

Training, Other Qualifications, and Advancement

Glaziers learn their trade through formal and informal training programs. To become a skilled glazier usually takes 3 years of both classroom and on-the-job training. There are a number of different avenues that one can take to obtain the necessary training. One of the ways is to obtain a job with a contractor who will then provide on-the-job training. Entry-level workers generally start as helpers, assisting more experienced workers. During this time, employers may send the employee to a trade or vocational school, or community college to receive further classroom training.

Some employers offer employees formal apprenticeships. These programs combine on-the-job training with related classroom instruction. Apprenticeship applicants usually must be at least 18 years old and meet local requirements. The length of the program is usually 3 years, but varies with the apprentice's skill. Because the number of apprenticeship programs is limited, however, only a small proportion of glaziers learn their trade through these programs.

On the job, apprentices or helpers, will start by carrying glass and cleaning up debris in glass shops. They often practice cutting on discarded glass. After a while, they are given an opportunity to cut glass for a job and assist experienced workers on simple installation jobs. By working with experienced glaziers, they eventually acquire the skills of a fully qualified glazier. On the job, they learn to use the tools and equipment of the trade; handle, measure, cut, and install glass and metal framing; cut and fit moldings; and install and balance glass doors. In the classroom, they are taught about glass and installation techniques as well as basic mathematics, blueprint reading and sketching, general construction techniques, safety practices and first aid.

Because most glaziers do not learn the trade through a formal apprenticeship program, some associations offer a series of written examinations that certify an individual's competency to perform glazier work at three progressively more difficult levels of proficiency. These levels include Level I Glazier; Level II Commercial Interior/Residential Glazier or Storefront/Curtainwall Glazier; and Level III Master Glazier. There also is a certification program for auto-glass repair.

Some skills needed to become a glazier include manual dexterity, eye-hand coordination, physical fitness, and a good sense of balance. The ability to solve arithmetic problems quickly and accurately also is required. In addition, a good work history or military service is viewed favorably by contractors.

Advancement generally consists of increases in pay for most glaziers; some advance to supervisory jobs or become contractors or estimators. For those who would like to advance, it is increasingly important to be able to communicate in both English and Spanish in order to relay instructions and safety precautions to workers with limited understanding of English; Spanish-speaking workers make up a large part of the construction workforce in many areas. Glaziers may advance to glazier supervisor or general construction supervisor positions. Others may become independent contractors. Supervisors and contractors need good communication skills to deal with clients and subcontractors and should be able to identify and estimate the quantity of materials needed to complete a job and accurately estimate how long a job will take to complete and at what cost.

Employment

Glaziers held 49,000 jobs in 2004. Almost two-thirds of glaziers worked for glazing contractors engaged in new construction, alteration, and repair. About 1 in 10 glaziers worked in retail glass shops that install or replace glass and for wholesale distributors of products containing glass.

Job Outlook

Job opportunities for glaziers are expected to be good as some employers report difficulty in finding qualified workers. In addition, employment is expected to grow about as fast as the average for all occupations through the year 2014.

Employment of glaziers is expected to increase as a result of growth in residential and nonresidential construction. Demand for glaziers also will be spurred by the continuing need to modernize and repair existing structures, which often involves installing new windows. Homeowners also are preferring rooms with more sunlight and are adding sunrooms and skylights to houses. Demand for specialized safety glass and glass coated with protective laminates is also growing in response to a higher need for security and the need to withstand hurricanes, particularly in many commercial and government buildings.

Like other construction trades workers, glaziers employed in the construction industry should expect to experience periods of unemployment resulting from the limited duration of construction projects and the cyclical nature of the construction industry. During bad economic times, job openings for glaziers are reduced as the level of construction declines. However, construction activity varies from area to area, so job openings fluctuate with local economic conditions. Employment opportunities should be greatest in metropolitan areas, where most glazing contractors and glass shops are located.

Earnings

In May 2004, median hourly earnings of glaziers were $15.70. The middle 50 percent earned between $12.08 and $21.58. The lowest 10 percent earned less than $9.73, and the highest 10 percent earned more than $30.36. In May 2004, median hourly earnings in the foundation, structure, and building exterior contractors industry, where most glass shops are found, were $16.10.

Glaziers covered by union contracts generally earn more than their nonunion counterparts. Apprentice wage rates usually start at 40 to 50 percent of the rate paid to experienced glaziers and increase as they gain experience in the field. Because glaziers can lose time due to weather conditions and fluctuations in construction activity, their overall earnings may be lower than their hourly wages suggest.

Some glaziers employed in construction are members of the International Union of Painters and Allied Trades.

Related Occupations

Glaziers use their knowledge of construction materials and techniques to install glass. Other construction workers whose jobs also involve skilled, custom work are brickmasons, blockmasons, and stonemasons; carpenters; carpet, floor, and tile installers and finishers; cement masons, concrete finishers, segmental pavers, and terrazzo workers; sheet metal workers; and painters and paperhangers. Other related occupations include automotive body and related repairers who install broken or damaged glass on vehicles that they repair.

Sources of Additional Information

For more information about glazier apprenticeships or work opportunities, contact local glazing or general contractors, a local of the International Union of Painters and Allied Trades, a local joint union-management apprenticeship agency, or the nearest office of the State employment service or State apprenticeship agency.

For general information about the work of glaziers, contact:
➤ International Union of Painters and Allied Trades, 1750 New York Ave. NW., Washington, DC 20006. Internet: **http://www.iupat.org**

For information concerning training for glaziers, contact:
➤ National Glass Association, Education and Training Department, 8200 Greensboro Dr., Suite 302, McLean, VA 22102-3881. Internet: **http://www.glass.org**
➤ Associated Builders and Contractors, Workforce Development Department, 4250 North Fairfax Dr., 9th Floor, Arlington, VA 22203. Internet: **www.trytools.org**

Hazardous Materials Removal Workers

(O*NET 47-4041.00)

Significant Points

- Working conditions can be hazardous, and the use of protective clothing often is required.
- Formal education beyond high school is not required, but a training program leading to a Federal license is mandatory.
- Excellent job opportunities are expected.

Nature of the Work

Increased public awareness and Federal and State regulations are resulting in the removal of hazardous materials from buildings, facilities, and the environment to prevent further contamination of natural resources and to promote public health and safety. Hazardous materials removal workers identify, remove, package, transport, and dispose of various hazardous materials, including asbestos, lead, and radioactive and nuclear materials. They also respond to emergencies where harmful substances are present. The removal of hazardous materials, or "hazmats," from public places and the environment also is called abatement, remediation, and decontamination.

Hazardous materials removal workers use a variety of tools and equipment, depending on the work at hand. Equipment ranges from brooms to personal protective suits that completely isolate workers from the hazardous material. The equipment required varies with the threat of contamination and can include disposable or reusable coveralls, gloves, hardhats, shoe covers, safety glasses or goggles, chemical-resistant clothing, face shields, and devices to protect one's hearing. Most workers also are required to wear respirators while working, to protect them from airborne particles. The respirators range from simple versions that cover only the mouth and nose to self-contained suits with their own air supply.

Asbestos and lead are two of the most common contaminants that hazardous materials removal workers encounter. In the past, asbestos was used to fireproof roofing and flooring, for heat insulation, and for a variety of other purposes. Today, asbestos is rarely used in buildings, but there still are structures that contain the material. Embedded in materials, asbestos is fairly harmless; airborne, however, it can cause several lung diseases, including lung cancer and asbestosis. Similarly, lead was a common building component found in paint and plumbing fixtures and pipes until the late 1970s. Because lead is easily absorbed into the bloodstream, often from breathing lead dust or from eating chips of paint containing lead, it can cause serious health risks, especially in children. Due to these risks, it has become necessary to remove lead-based products and asbestos from buildings and structures.

Asbestos abatement workers and *lead abatement workers* remove asbestos, lead, and other materials from buildings scheduled to be renovated or demolished. Using a variety of hand and power tools, such as vacuums and scrapers, these workers remove the asbestos and lead from surfaces. A typical residential lead abatement project involves the use of a chemical to strip the lead-based paint from the walls of the home. Lead abatement workers apply the compound with a putty knife and allow it to dry. Then they scrape the hazardous material into an impregnable container for transport and storage. They also use sandblasters and high-pressure water sprayers to remove lead from large structures. The vacuums utilized by asbestos abatement workers have special, highly efficient filters designed to trap the asbestos, which later is disposed of or stored. During the abatement, special monitors measure the amount of asbestos and lead in the air, to protect the workers; in addition, lead abatement workers wear a personal air monitor that indicates the amount of lead to which a worker has been exposed. Workers also use monitoring devices to identify the asbestos, lead, and other materials that need to be removed from the surfaces of walls and structures.

Transportation of hazardous materials is safer today than it was in the past, but accidents still occur. *Emergency and disaster response workers* clean up hazardous materials after train derailments and trucking accidents. These workers also are needed when an immediate cleanup is required, as would be the case after an attack by biological or chemical weapons.

Radioactive materials are classified as either high- or low-level wastes. High-level wastes are primarily nuclear-reactor fuels used to produce electricity. Low-level wastes include any radioactively contaminated protective clothing, tools, filters, medical equipment, and other items. *Decontamination technicians* perform duties similar to those of janitors and cleaners. They use brooms, mops, and other tools to clean exposed areas and remove exposed items for decontamination or disposal. Some of these jobs are now being done by robots controlled by persons away from the contamination site.

With experience, decontamination technicians can advance to *radiation-protection technician* jobs and use radiation survey meters to locate and evaluate materials, operate high-pressure cleaning equipment for decontamination, and package radioactive materials for transportation or disposal.

Decommissioning and decontamination workers remove and treat radioactive materials generated by nuclear facilities and power plants. With a variety of handtools, they break down contaminated items such as "gloveboxes," which are used to process radioactive materials. At decommissioning sites, the workers clean and decontaminate the facility, as well as remove any radioactive or contaminated materials.

Treatment, storage, and disposal workers transport and prepare materials for treatment or disposal. To ensure proper treatment of the materials, laws require these workers to be able to verify shipping manifests. At incinerator facilities, treatment, storage, and disposal workers transport materials from the customer or service center to the incinerator. At landfills, they follow a strict procedure for the processing and storage of hazardous materials. They organize and track the location of items in the landfill and may help change the state of a material from liquid to solid in preparation for its storage. These workers typically operate heavy machinery, such as forklifts, earthmoving machinery, and large trucks and rigs.

Mold remediation is a new and growing part of the work of some hazardous materials removal workers. Some types of mold can cause allergic reactions, especially in people who are susceptible to them. Although mold is present in almost all structures, some mold—especially the types that cause allergic reactions—can infest a building to such a degree that extensive efforts must be taken to remove it safely. Mold typically grows in damp areas, in heating and air-conditioning ducts, within walls, and in attics and basements. Although some mold remediation work is undertaken by other construction workers, mold often must be removed by hazardous materials removal workers, who take special precautions to protect themselves and surrounding areas from being contaminated.

Hazardous materials removal workers also may be required to construct scaffolding or erect containment areas prior to abatement or decontamination. In most cases, government regulation dictates that hazardous materials removal workers be closely supervised on the worksite. The standard usually is 1 supervisor to every 10 workers. The work is highly structured, sometimes planned years in advance, and team oriented. There is a great deal of cooperation among supervisors and workers. Because of the hazard presented by the materials being removed, work areas are restricted to licensed hazardous materials removal workers, thus minimizing exposure to the public.

Working Conditions
Hazardous materials removal workers function in a highly structured environment to minimize the danger they face. Each phase of an operation is planned in advance, and workers are trained to deal with safety breaches and hazardous situations. Crews and supervisors take every precaution to ensure that the worksite is safe. Whether they work with asbestos, mold, lead abatement or in radioactive decontamination, hazardous materials removal workers must stand, stoop, and kneel for long periods. Some must wear fully enclosed personal protective suits for several hours at a time; these suits may be hot and uncomfortable and may cause some individuals to experience claustrophobia.

Hazardous materials removal workers face different working conditions, depending on their area of expertise. Although many work a standard 40-hour week, overtime and shift work are common, especially in asbestos and lead abatement. Asbestos abatement and lead abatement workers are found primarily in structures such as office buildings and schools. Because they are under pressure to complete their work within certain deadlines, workers may experience fatigue. Completing projects frequently requires night and weekend work, because hazardous materials removal workers often work around the schedules of others. Treatment, storage, and disposal workers are employed primarily at facilities such as landfills, incinerators, boilers, and industrial furnaces. These facilities often are located in remote areas, due to the kinds of work being done. As a result, workers employed by treatment, storage, or disposal facilities may commute long distances to their jobs.

Hazardous materials removal workers need a license to work in this occupation.

Decommissioning and decontamination workers, decontamination technicians, and radiation protection technicians work at nuclear facilities and electric power plants. Like treatment, storage, and disposal facilities, these sites often are far from urban areas. Workers, who often perform jobs in cramped conditions, may need to use sharp tools to dismantle contaminated objects. A hazardous materials removal worker must have great self-control and a level head to cope with the daily stress associated with handling hazardous materials.

Hazardous materials removal workers may be required to travel outside their normal working areas in order to respond to emergencies, the cleanup of which sometimes takes several days or weeks to complete. During the cleanup, workers may be away from home for the entire time.

Training, Other Qualifications, and Advancement
No formal education beyond a high school diploma is required for a person to become a hazardous materials removal worker. Federal regulations require an individual to have a license to work in the occupation, although, at present, there are few laws regulating mold removal. Most employers provide technical training on the job, but a formal 32- to 40-hour training program must be completed if one is to be licensed as an asbestos abatement and lead abatement worker or a treatment, storage, and disposal worker. The program covers health hazards, personal protective equipment and clothing, site safety, recognition and identification of hazards, and decontamination. In some cases, workers discover one hazardous material while abating another. If they are not licensed to work with the newly

discovered material, they cannot continue to work with it. Many experienced workers opt to take courses in additional disciplines to avoid this situation. Some employers prefer to hire workers licensed in multiple disciplines.

For decommissioning and decontamination workers employed at nuclear facilities, training is more extensive. In addition to the standard 40-hour training course in asbestos, lead, and hazardous waste, workers must take courses dealing with regulations governing nuclear materials and radiation safety. These courses add up to approximately 3 months of training, although most are not taken consecutively. Many agencies, organizations, and companies throughout the country provide training programs that are approved by the U.S. Environmental Protection Agency, the U.S. Department of Energy, and other regulatory bodies. Workers in all fields are required to take refresher courses every year in order to maintain their license.

Workers must be able to perform basic mathematical conversions and calculations, and should have good physical strength and manual dexterity. Because of the nature of the work and the time constraints sometimes involved, employers prefer people who are dependable, prompt, and detail-oriented. Because much of the work is done in buildings, a background in construction is helpful.

Employment
Hazardous materials removal workers held about 38,000 jobs in 2004. About 8 in 10 were employed in waste management and remediation services. About 1 in 20 were employed in construction, primarily in asbestos abatement and lead abatement. A small number worked at nuclear and electric plants as decommissioning and decontamination workers and radiation safety and decontamination technicians.

Job Outlook
Job opportunities are expected to be excellent for hazardous materials removal workers. The occupation is characterized by a relatively high rate of turnover, resulting in a number of job openings each year stemming from experienced workers leaving the occupation. In addition, many potential workers are not attracted to this occupation, because they may prefer work that is less strenuous and has safer working conditions. Experienced workers will have especially favorable opportunities, particularly in the private sector, as more State and local governments contract out hazardous materials removal work to private companies.

Employment of hazardous materials removal workers is expected to grow much faster than the average for all occupations through the year 2014, reflecting increasing concern for a safe and clean environment. Special-trade contractors will have strong demand for the largest segment of these workers, namely, asbestos abatement and lead abatement workers; lead abatement should offer particularly good opportunities. Mold remediation is a growing part of the occupation at the present time, but it is unclear whether the growth will continue as builders find ways to prevent moisture from entering homes.

Employment of decontamination technicians, radiation safety technicians, and decommissioning and decontamination workers is expected to grow in response to increased pressure for safer and cleaner nuclear and electric generator facilities. Renewed interest in nuclear power production could lead to the construction of additional facilities. However, the number of older closed facilities that need decommissioning may continue to grow due to Federal legislation. These workers are less affected by economic fluctuations because the facilities in which they work must operate, regardless of the state of the economy.

Earnings

Median hourly earnings of hazardous materials removal workers were $16.02 in May 2004. The middle 50 percent earned between $12.52 and $22.27 per hour. The lowest 10 percent earned less than $10.48 per hour, and the highest 10 percent earned more than $27.25 per hour. The median hourly earnings in remediation and other waste management services, the largest industry employing hazardous materials removal workers in May 2004, were $15.46.

According to the limited data available, treatment, storage, and disposal workers usually earn slightly more than asbestos abatement and lead abatement workers. Decontamination and decommissioning workers and radiation protection technicians, though constituting the smallest group, tend to earn the highest wages.

Related Occupations

Asbestos abatement workers and lead abatement workers share skills with other construction trades workers, including painters and paperhangers; insulation workers; and sheet metal workers. Treatment, storage, and disposal workers, decommissioning and decontamination workers, and decontamination and radiation safety technicians work closely with plant and system operators, such as power-plant operators, distributors, and dispatchers and water and wastewater treatment plant operators. Police officers and firefighters also respond to emergencies and often are the first ones to respond to incidents where hazardous materials may be present.

Sources of Additional Information

For more information on hazardous materials removal workers that work in the construction industry, including information on training, contact:
➤ Laborers-AGC Education and Training Fund, 37 Deerfield Rd., P.O. Box 37, Pomfret, CT 06259. Internet: **http://www.laborerslearn.org**
➤ Heat and Frost Insulators and Asbestos Workers, 9602 M. L. King Jr. Hwy., Lanham, MD 20706 Internet: **http://www.insulators.org**

Insulation Workers

(O*NET 47-2131.00, 47-2132.00)

Significant Points

● Workers must follow strict safety guidelines to protect themselves from insulating irritants.

● Most insulation workers learn their work informally on the job; others complete formal apprenticeship programs.

● Job opportunities in the occupation are expected to be excellent.

Nature of the Work

Properly insulated buildings reduce energy consumption by keeping heat in during the winter and out in the summer. Refrigerated storage rooms, vats, tanks, vessels, boilers, and steam and hot-water pipes also are insulated to prevent the wasteful loss of heat. Insulation workers install the materials used to insulate buildings and equipment.

Insulation workers cement, staple, wire, tape, or spray insulation. When covering a steampipe, for example, insulation workers measure and cut sections of insulation to the proper length, stretch it open along a cut that runs the length of the material, and slip it over the pipe. They fasten the insulation with adhesive, staples, tape, or wire bands. Sometimes, they wrap a cover of aluminum, plastic, or canvas over the insulation and cement or band the cover in place. Insulation workers may screw on sheet metal around insulated pipes to protect the insulation from weather conditions or physical abuse.

When covering a wall or other flat surface, workers may use a hose to spray foam insulation onto a wire mesh that provides a rough surface to which the foam can cling and that adds strength to the finished surface. Workers may then install drywall or apply a final coat of plaster for a finished appearance.

In attics or exterior walls of uninsulated buildings, workers may blow in loose-fill insulation. A helper feeds a machine with fiberglass, cellulose, or rock-wool insulation, while another worker blows the insulation with a compressor hose into the space being filled.

In new construction or on major renovations, insulation workers staple fiberglass or rock-wool batts to exterior walls and ceilings before drywall, paneling, or plaster walls are put in place. In making major renovations to old buildings or when putting new insulation around pipes and industrial machinery, insulation workers often must first remove the old insulation. In the past, asbestos—now known to cause cancer in humans—was used extensively in walls and ceilings and to cover pipes, boilers, and various industrial equipment. Because of this danger, U.S. Environmental Protection Agency regulations require that asbestos be removed before a building undergoes major renovations or is demolished. When asbestos is present, specially trained workers must remove the asbestos before insulation workers can install the new insulating materials. (See the statement on hazardous materials removal workers elsewhere in the *Handbook*.)

Insulation workers use common handtools—trowels, brushes, knives, scissors, saws, pliers, and stapling guns. They may use power saws to cut insulating materials, welding machines to join sheet metal or secure clamps, and compressors to blow or spray insulation.

Working Conditions

Insulation workers generally work indoors in residential and industrial settings. They spend most of the workday on their feet, either standing, bending, or kneeling. They also work from ladders or in confined spaces. Their work usually requires more coordination than strength. In industrial settings insulation workers often must insulate pipes and vessels with temperatures that may cause burns. Minute particles from insulation materials, especially when blown, can irritate the eyes, skin, and respiratory system. Workers must follow strict safety guidelines

Insulation materials can irritate the eyes, skin, and respiratory system, requiring insulation workers to wear masks and other protective gear.

to protect themselves from insulating irritants. They keep work areas well ventilated; wear protective suits, masks, and respirators; and take decontamination showers when necessary.

Training, Other Qualifications, and Advancement
Most insulation workers learn their trade informally on the job, although some complete formal apprenticeship programs. For entry-level jobs, insulation contractors prefer high school graduates who are in good physical condition and licensed to drive. High school courses in blueprint reading, shop mathematics, science, sheet metal layout, woodworking, and general construction provide a helpful background. Applicants seeking apprenticeship positions should have a high school diploma or its equivalent and be at least 18 years old.

Trainees who learn on the job receive instruction and supervision from experienced insulation workers. Trainees begin with simple tasks, such as carrying insulation or holding material while it is fastened in place. On-the-job training can take up to 2 years, depending on the nature of the work. Installing insulation in homes generally requires less training than does learning to apply insulation in commercial and industrial settings. As they gain experience, trainees receive less supervision, more responsibility, and higher pay. A certification program has been developed by insulation contractor organizations to help all workers prove their skills and knowledge. Certification is currently limited to residential installation. Workers need at least six months of experience before they can complete certification. Certification in industrial settings is being developed

Trainees in formal apprenticeship programs receive indepth instruction in all phases of insulation. Apprenticeship programs may be provided by a joint committee of local insulation contractors and the local union of the International Association of Heat and Frost Insulators and Asbestos Workers, to which some insulation workers belong. Programs normally consist of 4 years of on-the-job training coupled with classroom instruction, and trainees must pass practical and written tests to demonstrate their knowledge of the trade.

Skilled insulation workers may advance to supervisor, shop superintendent, or insulation contract estimator, or they may set up their own insulation business.

Employment
Insulation workers held about 61,000 jobs in 2004. The construction industry employed 4 out of 5 workers; most worked for building finishing contractors. Small numbers of insulation workers held jobs in the Federal Government, in wholesale trade, and in shipbuilding and other manufacturing industries that have extensive installations for power, heating, and cooling. In less populated areas, carpenters, heating and air-conditioning installers or drywall installers may do insulation work.

Job Outlook
Job opportunities are expected to be excellent for insulation workers. Because there are no strict training requirements for entry, many people with limited skills work as insulation workers for a short time and then move on to other types of work, creating many job openings. In addition, openings will arise from the need to replace workers who retire or leave the labor force for other reasons.

In addition to the regular need to replace workers, some new jobs will arise as employment of insulation workers is expected to increase more slowly than the average for all occupations through the year 2014. In contrast to other construction workers, insulation workers work mainly on new construction, which is expected to moderate some over the next decade. Growth also will be limited by the increased efficiency of these workers and installation techniques, such as blow-in and spray-in insulation, which allows more work to be done in a shorter time and with fewer people. Insulation also is increasingly being installed by other workers in other occupations.

Some demand for insulation workers will be spurred by the continuing need for energy efficient buildings, which will generate work in existing structures as well as new construction.

Insulation workers in the construction industry may experience periods of unemployment because of the short duration of many construction projects and the cyclical nature of construction activity. Workers employed to perform industrial plant maintenance generally have more stable employment because maintenance and repair must be done on a continuing basis. Most insulation is applied after buildings are enclosed, so weather conditions have less effect on the employment of insulation workers than on that of some other construction occupations.

Earnings
In May 2004, median hourly earnings of insulation workers, floor, ceiling, and wall were $14.57. The middle 50 percent earned between $10.63 and $20.20. The lowest 10 percent earned less than $8.53, and the highest 10 percent earned more than $27.35. In May 2004, median hourly earnings of insulation workers, mechanical were $16.03. The middle 50 percent earned between $12.16 and $21.15. The lowest 10 percent earned less than $9.82, and the highest 10 percent earned more than $28.85. Median hourly earnings in the industries employing the largest numbers of insulation workers in May 2004 were:

Insulation workers, mechanical
    Building equipment contractors $15.66
    Building finishing contractors 15.55
Insulation workers, floor, ceiling, and wall
    Building finishing contractors 13.95

Union workers tend to earn more than nonunion workers. Apprentices start at about one-half of the journey worker's wage. Insulation workers doing commercial and industrial work earn substantially more than those working in residential construction, which does not require as much skill.

Related Occupations
Insulation workers combine their knowledge of insulation materials with the skills of cutting, fitting, and installing materials. Workers in occupations involving similar skills include carpenters; carpet, floor, and tile installers and finishers; drywall installers, ceiling tile installers, and tapers; roofers; and sheet metal workers.

Sources of Additional Information
For information about training programs or other work opportunities in this trade, contact a local insulation contractor, the nearest office of the State employment service or apprenticeship agency, or one of the following organizations:
➤ National Insulation Association, 99 Canal Center Plaza, Suite 222, Alexandria, VA 22314. Internet: **http://www.insulation.org**
➤ Insulation Contractors Association of America, 1321 Duke St., Suite 303, Alexandria, VA 22314. Internet: **http://www.insulate.org**

Painters and Paperhangers

(O*NET 47-2141.00, 47-2142.00)

Significant Points
- Employment prospects should be excellent due to the expected job growth, coupled with the large numbers of workers who retire or leave the occupation for other jobs.
- Most workers learn informally on the job as helpers, but training experts recommend completion of an apprenticeship program.
- Nearly one-half of all painters and paperhangers are self-employed.

Nature of the Work

Paint and wall coverings make surfaces clean, attractive, and bright. In addition, paints and other sealers protect exterior surfaces from wear caused by exposure to the weather.

Painters apply paint, stain, varnish, and other finishes to buildings and other structures. They choose the right paint or finish for the surface to be covered, taking into account durability, ease of handling, method of application, and customers' wishes. Painters first prepare the surfaces to be covered, so that the paint will adhere properly. This may require removing the old coat of paint by stripping, sanding, wire brushing, burning, or water and abrasive blasting. Painters also wash walls and trim to remove dirt and grease, fill nail holes and cracks, sandpaper rough spots, and brush off dust. On new surfaces, they apply a primer or sealer to prepare the surface for the finish coat. Painters also mix paints and match colors, relying on knowledge of paint composition and color harmony. In large paint shops or hardware stores, these functions are automated.

There are several ways to apply paint and similar coverings. Painters must be able to choose the right paint applicator for each job, depending on the surface to be covered, the characteristics of the finish, and other factors. Some jobs need only a good bristle brush with a soft, tapered edge; others require a dip or fountain pressure roller; still others can best be done using a paint sprayer. Many jobs need several types of applicators. The right tools for each job not only expedite the painter's work but also produce the most attractive surface.

When working on tall buildings, painters erect scaffolding, including "swing stages," scaffolds suspended by ropes, or cables attached to roof hooks. When painting steeples and other conical structures, they use a bosun's chair, a swing-like device.

Paperhangers cover walls and ceilings with decorative wall coverings made of paper, vinyl, or fabric. They first prepare the surface to be covered by applying "sizing," which seals the surface and makes the covering adhere better. When redecorating, they may first remove the old covering by soaking, steaming, or applying solvents. When necessary, they patch holes and take care of other imperfections before hanging the new wall covering.

After the surface has been prepared, paperhangers must prepare the paste or other adhesive. Then, they measure the area to be covered, check the covering for flaws, cut the covering into strips of the proper size, and closely examine the pattern in order to match it when the strips are hung. Much of this process can now be handled by specialized equipment.

The next step is to brush or roll the adhesive onto the back of the covering, if needed, and to then place the strips on the wall or ceiling, making sure the pattern is matched, the strips are hung straight, and the

edges are butted together to make tight, closed seams. Finally, paperhangers smooth the strips to remove bubbles and wrinkles, trim the top and bottom with a razor knife, and wipe off any excess adhesive.

Working Conditions

Most painters and paperhangers work 40 hours a week or less; about one-fourth have variable schedules or work part time. Painters and paperhangers must stand for long periods, often working from scaffolding and ladders. Their jobs also require a considerable amount of climbing and bending. These workers must have stamina, because much of the work is done with their arms raised overhead. Painters often work outdoors but seldom in wet, cold, or inclement weather. Some painting jobs can leave a worker covered with paint.

Painters and paperhangers sometimes work with materials that are hazardous or toxic, such as when they are required to remove lead-based paints. In the most dangerous situations, painters work in a sealed self-contained suit to prevent inhalation of or contact with hazardous materials.

Training, Other Qualifications, and Advancement

Painting and paperhanging is learned mostly through on-the-job training and by working as a helper to an experienced painter. However, there are a number of formal and informal training programs that provide more thorough instruction and a better career foundation. In general, the more formal the training received the more likely the individual will enter the profession at a higher level. Besides apprenticeships, some workers gain skills by attending technical schools that offer training prior to employment. These schools can take about a year to complete. Others receive training through local vocational high schools. Applicants should have good manual dexterity and color sense. There are limited opportunities for informal training for paperhangers because there are fewer paperhangers and helpers are usually not required.

If available, apprenticeships are usually the best way to enter the profession. They generally provide a mixture of classroom instruction and on-the-job training. Apprenticeships for painters and paperhangers consist of 2 to 4 years of on-the-job training, supplemented by 144 hours of related classroom instruction each year. Apprentices or helpers generally must be at least 18 years old and in good physical condition. A high school education or its equivalent, with courses in mathematics, usually is required to enter an apprenticeship program. Apprentices receive instruction in color harmony, use and care of tools and equipment, surface preparation, application techniques, paint mixing and matching, characteristics of different finishes, blueprint reading, wood finishing, and safety.

Whether a painter learns the trade through a formal apprenticeship or informally as a helper, on-the-job instruction covers similar skill areas. Under the direction of experienced workers, trainees carry supplies, erect scaffolds, and do simple painting and surface preparation tasks while they learn about paint and painting equipment. As they gain experience, trainees learn to prepare surfaces for painting and paperhanging, to mix paints, and to apply paint and wall coverings efficiently and neatly. Near the end of their training, they may learn decorating concepts, color coordination, and cost-estimating techniques. In addition to learning craft skills, painters must become familiar with safety and health regulations so that their work complies with the law.

Painters and paperhangers may advance to supervisory or estimating jobs with painting and decorating contractors. Many establish their own painting and decorating businesses. For those who would like to advance, it is increasingly important to be able to communicate in both English and Spanish in order to relay instructions and safety precautions to workers with limited English skills; Spanish speaking workers make up a large part of the construction workforce in many

Most painters start out as helpers and learn on the job.

areas. Painting contractors need good English skills in order to deal with clients and subcontractors.

Employment

Painters and paperhangers held about 486,000 jobs in 2004; most were painters. Around one-third of painters and paperhangers work for painting and wall covering contractors engaged in new construction, repair, restoration, or remodeling work. In addition, organizations that own or manage large buildings—such as apartment complexes—employ maintenance painters, as do some schools, hospitals, factories, and government agencies.

Self-employed independent painting contractors accounted for nearly one-half of all painters and paperhangers, significantly greater than the one in five of construction trades workers in general.

Job Outlook

Job prospects should be excellent because each year thousands of painters retire or leave for jobs in other occupations. There are no strict training requirements for entry into these jobs, so many people with limited skills work as painters or helpers for a short time and then move on to other types of work. Many fewer openings will arise for paperhangers because the number of these jobs is comparatively small.

In addition to the need to replace experienced workers who leave, new jobs will be created. Employment of painters is expected to grow as fast as the average for all occupations through the year 2014, reflecting increases in the level of new construction and in the stock of buildings and other structures that require maintenance and renovation. The relatively short life of exterior paints as well as changing color trends will stir demand for painters. Painting is labor-intensive and not susceptible to technological changes that might make workers more productive and slow employment growth. Paperhangers should see slower than average employment growth as easy application materials and reduced demand for paperhanging services limits growth.

Jobseekers considering these occupations should expect some periods of unemployment, especially until they gain experience. Many construction projects are of short duration, and construction activity is cyclical and seasonal in nature. Remodeling, restoration, and maintenance projects, however, often provide many jobs for painters and paperhangers even when new construction activity declines. The most versatile painters and skilled paperhangers generally are best able to keep working steadily during downturns in the economy.

Earnings

In May 2004, median hourly earnings of painters, construction and maintenance, were $14.55. The middle 50 percent earned between $11.59 and $19.04. The lowest 10 percent earned less than $9.47, and the highest 10 percent earned more than $25.11. Median hourly earnings in the industries employing the largest numbers of painters in May 2004 were as follows:

Local government	$18.36
Residential building construction	15.09
Nonresidential building construction	14.97
Building finishing contractors	14.44
Employment services	11.31

In May 2004, median earnings for paperhangers were $15.73. The middle 50 percent earned between $12.23 and $20.71. The lowest 10 percent earned less than $9.57, and the highest 10 percent earned more than $26.58.

Earnings for painters may be reduced on occasion because of bad weather and the short-term nature of many construction jobs. Hourly wage rates for apprentices usually start at 40 to 50 percent of the rate for experienced workers and increase periodically.

Some painters and paperhangers are members of the International Brotherhood of Painters and Allied Trades. Some maintenance painters are members of other unions.

Related Occupations

Painters and paperhangers apply various coverings to decorate and protect wood, drywall, metal, and other surfaces. Other construction occupations in which workers do finishing work include carpenters; carpet, floor, and tile installers and finishers; drywall installers, ceiling tile installers, and tapers; painting and coating workers, except construction and maintenance; and plasterers and stucco masons.

Sources of Additional Information

For details about painting and paperhanging apprenticeships or work opportunities, contact local painting and decorating contractors, local trade organizations, a local of the International Union of Painters and Allied Trades, a local joint union-management apprenticeship committee, or an office of the State apprenticeship agency or employment service.

For information about the work of painters and paperhangers and training opportunities, contact:

➤ International Union of Painters and Allied Trades, 1750 New York Ave. NW., Washington, DC 20006. Internet: **http://www.iupat.org**
➤ Associated Builders and Contractors, Workforce Development Department, 4250 North Fairfax Dr., 9th Floor, Arlington, VA 22203. Internet: **http://www.trytools.org**
➤ National Center for Construction Education and Research, P.O. Box 141104, Gainesville, FL 32614-1104. Internet: **http://www.nccer.org**
➤ Painting and Decorating Contractors of America, 11960 Westline Industrial Drive, Suite 201, St. Louis, MO 63146-3209. Internet: **http://www.pdca.org**

Pipelayers, Plumbers, Pipefitters, and Steamfitters

(O*NET 47-2151.00, 47-2152.01, 47-2152.02, 47-2152.03)

Significant Points

- Job opportunities should be excellent because not enough people are seeking training.

- Pipelayers, plumbers, pipefitters, and steamfitters make up one of the largest and highest paid construction occupations.

Nature of the Work

Most people are familiar with plumbers, who come to their home to unclog a drain or install an appliance. In addition to these activities, however, pipelayers, plumbers, pipefitters, and steamfitters install, maintain, and repair many different types of pipe systems. For example, some systems move water to a municipal water treatment plant and then to residential, commercial, and public buildings. Other systems dispose of waste, provide gas to stoves and furnaces, or provide for heating and cooling needs. Pipe systems in powerplants carry the steam that powers huge turbines. Pipes also are used in manufacturing plants to move material through the production process. Specialized piping systems are very important in both pharmaceutical and computer-chip manufacturing.

Although pipelaying, plumbing, pipefitting, and steamfitting sometimes are considered a single trade, workers generally specialize in one of five areas. *Pipelayers* lay clay, concrete, plastic, or cast-iron pipe for drains, sewers, water mains, and oil or gas lines. Before laying the pipe, pipelayers prepare and grade the trenches either manually or with machines. After laying the pipe, they weld, glue, cement or otherwise join the pieces together. *Plumbers* install and repair the water, waste disposal, drainage, and gas systems in homes and commercial and industrial buildings. Plumbers also install plumbing fixtures—bathtubs, showers, sinks, and toilets—and appliances such as dishwashers and water heaters. *Pipefitters* install and repair both high- and low-pressure pipe systems used in manufacturing, in the generation of electricity, and in the heating and cooling of buildings. They also install automatic controls that are increasingly being used to regulate these systems. Some pipefitters specialize in only one type of system. *Steamfitters* install pipe systems that move liquids or gases under high pressure. *Sprinklerfitters* install automatic fire sprinkler systems in buildings.

Pipelayers, plumbers, pipefitters, and steamfitters use many different materials and construction techniques, depending on the type of project. Residential water systems, for example, incorporate copper, steel, and plastic pipe that can be handled and installed by one or two plumbers. Municipal sewerage systems, on the other hand, are made of large cast-iron pipes; installation normally requires crews of pipefitters. Despite these differences, all pipelayers, plumbers, pipefitters, and steamfitters must be able to follow building plans or blueprints and instructions from supervisors, lay out the job, and work efficiently with the materials and tools of their trade. Computers and specialized software are used to create blueprints and plan layouts.

When construction plumbers install piping in a new house, for example, they work from blueprints or drawings that show the planned location of pipes, plumbing fixtures, and appliances. Recently, plumbers have become more involved in the design process. Their knowledge of codes and the operation of plumbing systems can cut costs. They first lay out the job to fit the piping into the structure of the house with the least waste of material. Then they measure and mark areas in which pipes will be installed and connected. Construction plumbers also check for obstructions such as electrical wiring and, if necessary, plan the pipe installation around the problem.

Sometimes, plumbers have to cut holes in walls, ceilings, and floors of a house. For some systems, they may hang steel supports from ceiling joists to hold the pipe in place. To assemble a system, plumbers—using saws, pipe cutters, and pipe-bending machines—cut and bend lengths of pipe. They connect lengths of pipe with fittings, using methods that depend on the type of pipe used. For plastic pipe, plumbers connect the sections and fittings with adhesives. For copper pipe, they slide a fitting over the end of the pipe and solder it in place with a torch.

After the piping is in place in the house, plumbers install the fixtures and appliances and connect the system to the outside water or sewer lines. Finally, using pressure gauges, they check the system to ensure that the plumbing works properly.

Pipelayers, plumbers, pipefitters, and steamfitters make up one of the largest and highest paid construction occupations.

Working Conditions

Pipefitters and steamfitters most often work in industrial and power plants. Plumbers work in commercial and residential settings where water and septic systems need to be installed and maintained. Pipelayers work outdoors, sometime in remote areas, as they build the pipelines that connect sources of oil, gas, and chemicals with the users of these materials. Sprinklerfitters work mostly in multistory buildings that require the use of sprinkler systems.

Because pipelayers, plumbers, pipefitters, and steamfitters frequently must lift heavy pipes, stand for long periods, and sometimes work in uncomfortable or cramped positions, they need physical strength as well as stamina. They also may have to work outdoors in inclement weather. In addition, they are subject to possible falls from ladders, cuts from sharp tools, and burns from hot pipes or soldering equipment.

Pipelayers, plumbers, pipefitters, and steamfitters engaged in construction generally work a standard 40-hour week; those involved in maintaining pipe systems, including those who provide maintenance services under contract, may have to work evening or weekend shifts, as well as be on call. These maintenance workers may spend quite a bit of time traveling to and from worksites.

Training, Other Qualifications, and Advancement

Pipelayers, plumbers, pipefitters, and steamfitters enter into the profession in a variety of ways. Most residential and industrial plumbers get their training in career and technical schools and community colleges and from on-the-job training. Pipelayers, plumbers, pipefitters, and steamfitters who work mainly for commercial enterprises are usually trained through formal apprenticeship programs.

Apprenticeship programs generally provide the most comprehensive training available for these jobs. They are administered by either union locals and their affiliated companies or by nonunion contractor organizations. Organizations that sponsor apprenticeships include: the United Association of Journeymen and Apprentices of the Plumbing and Pipefitting Industry of the United States and Canada; local employers of either the Mechanical Contractors Association of America, the National Association of Plumbing-Heating-Cooling Contractors, or the National Fire Sprinkler Association; the Associated Builders and Contractors; the National Association of Plumbing-Heating-Cooling Contractors; the American Fire Sprinkler Association, or the Home Builders Institute of the National Association of Home Builders.

Apprenticeships—both union and nonunion—consist of 4 or 5 years of on-the-job training, in addition to at least 144 hours per year of related classroom instruction. Classroom subjects include drafting and blueprint reading, mathematics, applied physics and chemistry, safety, and local plumbing codes and regulations. On the job, apprentices first learn basic skills, such as identifying grades and types of pipe, using the tools of the trade, and safely unloading materials. As apprentices gain experience, they learn how to work with various types of pipe and how to install different piping systems and plumbing fixtures. Apprenticeship gives trainees a thorough knowledge of all aspects of the trade. Although most pipelayers, plumbers, pipefitters, and steamfitters are trained through apprenticeship, some still learn their skills informally on the job.

Applicants for union or nonunion apprentice jobs must be at least 18 years old and in good physical condition. Apprenticeship committees may require applicants to have a high school diploma or its equivalent. Armed Forces training in pipelaying, plumbing, and pipefitting is considered very good preparation. In fact, persons with this background may be given credit for previous experience when entering a civilian apprenticeship program. Secondary or postsecondary courses in shop, plumbing, general mathematics, drafting, blueprint reading, computers, and physics also are good preparation.

Although there are no uniform national licensing requirements, most communities require plumbers to be licensed. Licensing requirements vary from area to area, but most localities require workers to pass an examination that tests their knowledge of the trade and of local plumbing codes.

With additional training, some pipelayers, plumbers, pipefitters, and steamfitters become supervisors for mechanical and plumbing contractors. Others, especially plumbers, go into business for themselves, often starting as a self-employed plumber working from home. Some eventually become owners of businesses employing many workers and may spend most of their time as managers rather than as plumbers. Others move into closely related areas such as construction management or building inspection.

Employment

Pipelayers, plumbers, pipefitters, and steamfitters constitute one of the largest construction occupations, holding about 561,000 jobs in 2004. About 1 in 2 worked for plumbing, heating, and air-conditioning contractors engaged in new construction, repair, modernization, or maintenance work. Others did maintenance work for a variety of industrial, commercial, and government employers. For example, pipefitters were employed as maintenance personnel in the petroleum and chemical industries, in which manufacturing operations require the moving of liquids and gases through pipes. More than 1 in 10 pipelayers, plumbers, pipefitters, and steamfitters were self-employed. Almost 1 in 3 pipelayers, plumbers, pipefitters, and steamfitters belonged to a union.

Jobs for pipelayers, plumbers, pipefitters, and steamfitters are distributed across the country in about the same proportion as the general population.

Job Outlook

Job opportunities are expected to be excellent, as demand for skilled pipelayers, plumbers, pipefitters, and steamfitters is expected to outpace the supply of workers trained in this craft. Many employers report difficulty finding potential workers with the right qualifications. In addition, many people currently working in these trades are expected to retire over the next 10 years, which will create additional job openings.

Employment of pipelayers, plumbers, pipefitters, and steamfitters is expected to grow about as fast as the average for all occupations through the year 2014. Demand for plumbers will stem from new construction and building renovation. Bath remodeling, in particular, is expected to continue to grow and create more jobs for plumbers. In addition, repair and maintenance of existing residential systems will keep plumbers employed. Demand for pipefitters and steamfitters will be driven by maintenance activities for places having extensive systems of pipes, such as powerplants, water and wastewater treatment plants, office buildings, and factories. Growth of pipelayer jobs will stem from the building of new water and sewer lines and pipelines to new oil and gas fields. Demand for sprinklerfitters will increase due to changes to State and local rules for fire protection in homes and businesses.

Traditionally, many organizations with extensive pipe systems have employed their own plumbers or pipefitters to maintain equipment and keep systems running smoothly. But, to reduce labor costs, many of these firms no longer employ full-time, in-house plumbers or pipefitters. Instead, when they need a plumber, they rely on workers provided under service contracts by plumbing and pipefitting contractors.

Construction projects generally provide only temporary employment. When a project ends, some pipelayers, plumbers, pipefitters, and steamfitters may be unemployed until they can begin work on a new project, although most companies are trying to limit these periods of unemployment in order to retain workers. In addition, the jobs of pipelayers, plumbers, pipefitters, and steamfitters are generally less sensitive to changes in economic conditions than jobs in other construction trades. Even when construction activity declines, maintenance, rehabilitation, and replacement of existing piping systems, as well as the increasing installation of fire sprinkler systems, provide many jobs for pipelayers, plumbers, pipefitters, and steamfitters.

Earnings

Pipelayers, plumbers, pipefitters, and steamfitters are among the highest paid construction occupations. In May 2004, median hourly earnings of pipelayers were $13.68. The middle 50 percent earned between $11.05 and $18.69. The lowest 10 percent earned less than $9.19, and the highest 10 percent earned more than $25.07. Also in May 2004, median hourly earnings of plumbers, pipefitters, and steamfitters were $19.85. The middle 50 percent earned between $15.01 and $26.67. The lowest 10 percent earned less than $11.62, and the highest 10 percent earned more than $33.72. Median hourly earnings in the industries employing the largest numbers of plumbers, pipefitters, and steamfitters in May 2004 were as follows:

Natural gas distribution	$23.86
Nonresidential building construction	21.55
Building equipment contractors	19.85
Utility system construction	18.29
Local government	16.30

Apprentices usually begin at about 50 percent of the wage rate paid to experienced pipelayers, plumbers, pipefitters, and steamfitters. Wages increase periodically as skills improve. After an initial waiting period, apprentices receive the same benefits as experienced pipelayers, plumbers, pipefitters, and steamfitters.

Many pipelayers, plumbers, pipefitters, and steamfitters are members of the United Association of Journeymen and Apprentices of the Plumbing and Pipefitting Industry of the United States and Canada.

Related Occupations

Other occupations in which workers install and repair mechanical systems in buildings are boilermakers; electricians; elevator installers and repairers; heating, air-conditioning, and refrigeration mechanics and installers; industrial machinery installation, repair, and maintenance workers, except millwrights; millwrights; sheet metal workers; and stationary engineers and boiler operators. Other related occupations include construction managers and construction and building inspectors.

Sources of Additional Information

For information about apprenticeships or work opportunities in pipelaying, plumbing, pipefitting, and steamfitting, contact local plumbing, heating, and air-conditioning contractors; a local or State chapter of the National Association of Plumbing, Heating, and Cooling Contractors; a local chapter of the Mechanical Contractors Association; a local chapter of the United Association of Journeymen and Apprentices of the Plumbing and Pipefitting Industry of the United States and Canada; or the nearest office of your State employment service or apprenticeship agency.

For information about apprenticeship opportunities for pipelayers, plumbers, pipefitters, and steamfitters, contact:

➤ United Association of Journeymen and Apprentices of the Plumbing and Pipefitting Industry, 901 Massachusetts Ave. NW., Washington, DC 20001. Internet: **http://www.ua.org**

For more information about training programs for pipelayers, plumbers, pipefitters, and steamfitters, contact:

➤ Associated Builders and Contractors, Workforce Development Department, 4250 North Fairfax Dr., 9th Floor, Arlington, VA 22203. Internet: **http://www.trytools.org**

➤ Home Builders Institute, National Association of Home Builders, 1201 15th St. NW., Washington, DC 20005. Internet: **http://www.hbi.org**

For general information about the work of pipelayers, plumbers, and pipefitters, contact:

➤ Mechanical Contractors Association of America, 1385 Piccard Dr., Rockville, MD 20850. Internet: **http://www.mcaa.org**

➤ Plumbing-Heating-Cooling Contractors—National Association, 180 S. Washington St, Falls Church, VA 22040. Internet: **http://www.phccweb.org**

➤ National Center for Construction Education and Research, P.O. Box 141104, Gainesville, FL 32614-1104. Internet: **http://www.nccer.org**

For general information about the work of sprinklerfitters, contact:

➤ American Fire Sprinkler Association, Inc., 9696 Skillman St., Suite 300, Dallas, TX 75243-8264. Internet: **http://www.firesprinkler.org**

➤ National Fire Sprinkler Association, P.O. Box 1000, Patterson, NY 12563. Internet: **http://www.nfsa.org**

Plasterers and Stucco Masons

(O*NET 47-2161.00)

Significant Points

● Plastering is physically demanding.

● Plastering is learned on the job, either through a formal apprenticeship program or by working as a helper.

● Job opportunities are expected to be good, particularly in the South and Southwest.

Nature of the Work

Plastering—one of the oldest crafts in the building trades—remains popular due to the relatively low cost of the material and overall durability of work. Plasterers apply plaster to interior walls and ceilings to form fire-resistant and relatively soundproof surfaces. They also apply plaster veneer over drywall to create smooth or textured abrasion-resistant finishes. In addition, plasterers install prefabricated exterior insulation systems over existing walls—for good insulation and interesting architectural effects—and cast ornamental designs in plaster. Stucco masons apply durable plasters, such as polymer-based acrylic finishes and stucco, to exterior surfaces. Plasterers and stucco masons should not be confused with drywall installers, ceiling tile installers, and tapers—discussed elsewhere in the *Handbook*—who use drywall instead of plaster when erecting interior walls and ceilings.

Plasterers can plaster either solid surfaces, such as concrete block, or supportive wire mesh called lath. When plasterers work with interior surfaces, such as concrete block and concrete, they first apply a brown coat of gypsum plaster that provides a base, which is followed by a second, or finish, coat—also called "white coat"—made of a lime-based plaster. When plastering metal lath foundations, they apply a preparatory, or "scratch," coat with a trowel. They spread this rich plaster mixture into and over the metal lath. Before the plaster sets, plasterers scratch its surface with a rake-like tool to produce ridges, so that the subsequent brown coat will bond tightly.

Helpers prepare a thick, smooth plaster for the brown coat. Plasterers spray or trowel this mixture onto the surface, then finish by smoothing it to an even, level surface.

For the finish coat, plasterers prepare a mixture of lime, plaster of paris, and water. They quickly apply this to the brown coat using a "hawk"—a light, metal plate with a handle—trowel, brush, and water. This mixture, which sets very quickly, produces a very smooth, durable finish.

Plasterers also work with a plaster material that can be finished in a single coat. This "thin-coat" or gypsum veneer plaster is made of lime and plaster of paris and is mixed with water at the jobsite This plaster provides a smooth, durable, abrasion-resistant finish on interior masonry surfaces, special gypsum baseboard, or drywall prepared with a bonding agent.

Plasterers create decorative interior surfaces as well. One way that they do this is by pressing a brush or trowel firmly against a wet plaster surface and using a circular hand motion to create decorative swirls.

For exterior work, stucco masons usually apply stucco—a mixture of Portland cement, lime, and sand—over cement, concrete, masonry, or lath. Stucco may also be applied directly to a wire lath with a scratch coat, followed by a brown coat and then a finish coat. Stucco masons may also embed marble or gravel chips into the finish coat to achieve a pebblelike, decorative finish.

When required, plasterers apply insulation to the exteriors of new and old buildings. They cover the outer wall with rigid foam insulation board and reinforcing mesh, and then trowel on a polymer-based or polymer-modified base coat. They may apply an additional coat of this material with a decorative finish.

Plasterers sometimes do complex decorative and ornamental work that requires special skill and creativity. For example, they may mold intricate wall and ceiling designs. Following an architect's blueprint, plasterers pour or spray a special plaster into a mold and allow it to set. Workers then remove the molded plaster and put it in place, according to the plan.

Working Conditions

Most plastering jobs are indoors; however, plasterers and stucco masons work outside when applying stucco or exterior wall insulation and exterior decorative finish systems. Exterior work can be greatly impacted by inclement weather as stucco must be applied when the weather permits. Plasterers work on scaffolds high above the ground.

Plastering is physically demanding, requiring considerable standing, bending, lifting, and reaching overhead. The work can be dusty and dirty, soiling shoes and clothing, and can irritate the skin and eyes, unless the proper personal protective equipment is used.

Plastering—one of the oldest crafts in the building trades—remains popular due to the relatively low cost of the material and its overall durability.

Training, Other Qualifications, and Advancement

Plasterers and stucco masons learn their trade through formal and informal training programs. Most people learn this trade informally by starting out as helpers for experienced plasterers and stucco masons. Between 2 and 3 years of on-the-job training supplemented by formal classroom training may be required to become a skilled plasterer and stucco mason.

Preparation for a career as a plasterer or stucco mason can begin in high school, where classes in mathematics, mechanical drawing, and general shop are recommended. After high school, there are a number of different avenues that one can take to obtain the necessary training. The most common way is to obtain a job with a contractor who will provide on-the-job training. Entry-level workers generally start as helpers, assisting more experienced workers. They may start by carrying materials, setting up scaffolds, and mixing plaster. Later, they learn to apply the scratch, brown, and finish coats and may also learn to replicate plaster decorations for restoration work. Employers may enroll helpers in an employer-provided training program or send the employee to a trade or vocational school, or community college to receive further classroom training.

Although most employers recommend apprenticeship as the best way to learn plastering, apprenticeships for this occupation are few. Apprenticeship programs, sponsored by local joint committees of contractors and unions, generally consist of 2 or 3 years of on-the-job training, in addition to at least 144 hours annually of classroom instruction in drafting, blueprint reading, and mathematics for layout work.

In the classroom, apprentices start with a history of the trade and the industry. They also learn about the uses of plaster, estimating materials and costs, and casting ornamental plaster designs. On the job, they learn about lath bases, plaster mixes, methods of plastering, blueprint reading, and safety. They also learn how to use various tools, such as hand and powered trowels, floats, brushes, straightedges, power tools, plaster-mixing machines, and piston-type pumps. Some apprenticeship programs allow individuals to obtain training in related occupations, such as cement masonry and bricklaying.

Applicants for apprentice or helper jobs normally must be at least 18 years old, in good physical condition, and have good manual dexterity. Applicants who have a high school education are preferred. Courses in general mathematics, mechanical drawing, and shop provide a useful background.

With additional training and experience, plasterers and stucco masons may advance to positions as supervisors, superintendents, or estimators for plastering contractors. Many become self-employed contractors. Others become building inspectors.

Employment

Plasterers and stucco masons held about 59,000 jobs in 2004. Most plasterers and stucco masons work on new construction sites. Some repair and renovate older buildings. Many plasterers and stucco masons are employed in Florida, California, and the Southwest, where exterior stucco with decorative finishes is very popular.

Most plasterers and stucco masons work for independent contractors. About 1 out of every 20 plasterers and stucco masons is self-employed.

Job Outlook

Job opportunities for plasterers and stucco masons are expected to be good through 2014. Many potential workers choose not to enter this occupation because they prefer work that is less strenuous and has more comfortable working conditions. Most job openings will be the result of plasterers and stucco masons transferring to other occupations or leaving the labor force. The best employment opportunities should continue to be in Florida, California, and the Southwest, where exterior plaster and decorative finishes are expected to remain popular. Plastering in the Northeast continues to remain in demand, especially in restoration.

Employment of plasterers and stucco masons is expected to grow more slowly than the average for all occupations through the year 2014. In past years, employment of plasterers declined as more builders switched to drywall construction. This decline has halted, however, and employment of plasterers is expected to grow as a result of the appreciation for the durability and attractiveness that troweled finishes provide. Thin-coat plastering—or veneering—in particular is gaining wide acceptance as more builders recognize its ease of application, durability, quality of finish, and sound-proofing and fire-retarding qualities, although the increased use of fire sprinklers will reduce the demand for fire-resistant plaster work. Prefabricated wall systems and new polymer-based or polymer-modified acrylic exterior insulating finishes also are gaining popularity, particularly in the South and Southwest regions of the country. This is not only because of their durability, attractiveness, and insulating properties, but also because of their relatively low cost. In addition, plasterers will be needed to renovate plasterwork in old structures and to create special architectural effects, such as curved surfaces, which are not practical with drywall materials.

Most plasterers and stucco masons work in construction, where prospects fluctuate from year to year due to changing economic conditions. Bad weather affects plastering less than other construction trades because most work is indoors. On exterior surfacing jobs, however, plasterers and stucco masons may lose time because plastering materials cannot be applied under wet or freezing conditions.

Earnings

In May 2004, median hourly earnings of plasterers and stucco masons were $15.60. The middle 50 percent earned between $12.27 and $20.32. The lowest 10 percent earned less than $9.80, and the top 10 percent earned more than $26.84.

The median hourly earnings in the largest industries employing plasterers and stucco masons in May 2004 were $15.75 in building finishing contractors, and $14.62 in foundation, structure, and building exterior contractors.

Apprentice wage rates start at about half the rate paid to experienced plasterers and stucco masons. Annual earnings for plasterers and stucco masons and apprentices can be less than the hourly rate would indicate, because poor weather and periodic declines in construction activity can limit work hours.

Related Occupations

Other construction workers who use a trowel as their primary tool include brickmasons, blockmasons, and stonemasons; cement masons, concrete finishers, segmental pavers, and terrazzo workers; and drywall installers, ceiling tile installers, and tapers.

Sources of Additional Information

For information about apprenticeships or other work opportunities, contact local plastering contractors, locals of the unions mentioned below, local joint union-management apprenticeship committees, or the nearest office of your State apprenticeship agency or employment service.

For general information about the work of plasterers and stucco masons, contact:

➤ Association of Wall and Ceiling Industries International, 803 West Broad St., Falls Church, VA 22046. Internet: **http://www.awci.org**

For information about plasterers, contact:

➤ Operative Plasterers' and Cement Masons' International Association of the United States and Canada, 14405 Laurel Place, Suite 300, Laurel, MD 20707. Internet: **http://www.opcmia.org**

For information on the training of plasterers and stucco masons, contact:

➤ International Union of Bricklayers and Allied Craftworkers, International Masonry Institute, The James Brice House, 42 East St., Annapolis, MD 21401. Internet: **http://www.imiweb.org**

Roofers

(O*NET 47-2181.00)

Significant Points

- Most roofers acquire their skills informally on the job; some roofers train through 3-year apprenticeship programs.

- Job openings for roofers should be plentiful because the work is hot, strenuous, and dirty, causing many individuals to leave for jobs in other construction trades.

- Demand for roofers is less susceptible to downturns in the economy than demand for other construction trades because most roofing work consists of repair and reroofing.

Nature of the Work

A leaky roof can damage ceilings, walls, and furnishings. To protect buildings and their contents from water damage, roofers repair and install roofs made of tar or asphalt and gravel; rubber or thermoplastic; metal; or shingles made of asphalt, slate, fiberglass, wood, tile, or other material. Repair and reroofing—replacing old roofs on existing buildings—makes up the majority of work for these workers.

There are two types of roofs—low- and steep-sloped. Roofs considered low-slope rise 4 inches per horizontal foot or less and steep-slope roofs increase more than 4 inches per horizontal foot. Most commercial, industrial, and apartment buildings have low-sloping roofs. Most houses have steep-sloped roofs. Some roofers work on both types; others specialize.

Most low-slope roofs are covered with several layers of materials. Roofers first put a layer of insulation on the roof deck. Over the insulation, they then spread a coat of molten bitumen, a tarlike substance. Next, they install partially overlapping layers of roofing felt—a fabric saturated in bitumen—over the surface. Roofers use a mop to spread hot bitumen over the surface and under the next layer. This seals the seams and makes the surface watertight. Roofers repeat these steps to build up the desired number of layers, called "plies." The top layer either is glazed to make a smooth finish or has gravel embedded in the hot bitumen to create a rough surface.

An increasing number of low-slope roofs are covered with a single-ply membrane of waterproof rubber or thermoplastic compounds. Roofers roll these sheets over the roof's insulation and seal the seams. Adhesive, mechanical fasteners, or stone ballast hold the sheets in place. The building must be of sufficient strength to hold the ballast. A small, but growing number of flat-roofed buildings are now having "green" roofs installed. A "green" roof begins with a single or multi-ply waterproof system. After it is proven to be leak free, a root barrier is placed onto it, and then layers of soil, in which trees and grass are planted. Roofers are generally responsible for making sure the roof is watertight and can withstand the weight and water needs of the plantings.

Most residential steep-slope roofs are covered with shingles. To apply shingles, roofers first lay, cut, and tack 3-foot strips of roofing felt lengthwise over the entire roof. Then, starting from the bottom edge, they staple or nail overlapping rows of shingles to the roof. Workers measure and cut the felt and shingles to fit intersecting roof surfaces and to fit around vent pipes and chimneys. Wherever two roof surfaces intersect, or shingles reach a vent pipe or chimney, roofers cement or nail flashing-strips of metal or shingle over the joints to make them watertight. Finally,

Starting from the bottom edge, roofers staple or nail overlapping rows of shingles to the roof.

roofers cover exposed nailheads with roofing cement or caulking to prevent water leakage. Roofers who use tile, metal shingles, or shakes follow a similar process.

Because of their expertise in waterproofing roofs, some roofers also waterproof and dampproof masonry and concrete walls and floors, including foundations. To prepare surfaces for waterproofing, they hammer and chisel away rough spots, or remove them with a rubbing brick, before applying a coat of liquid waterproofing compound. They also may paint or spray surfaces with a waterproofing material, or attach waterproofing membrane to surfaces. When dampproofing, they usually spray a bitumen-based coating on interior or exterior surfaces. Roofers also install equipment that requires cutting through roofs, such as ventilation ducts and attic fans.

Working Conditions

Roofing work is strenuous. It involves heavy lifting, as well as climbing, bending, and kneeling. Roofers work outdoors in all types of weather, particularly when making repairs. However, they rarely work in very cold weather as ice can be treacherous. In northern States, roofing work is generally not performed during winter months.

Workers risk slips or falls from scaffolds, ladders, or roofs, or burns from hot bitumen, but safety precautions, if followed, can eliminate most accidents. In addition, roofs can become extremely hot during the summer, causing heat-related illnesses.

Training, Other Qualifications, and Advancement

Most roofers acquire their skills informally by working as helpers for experienced roofers and by taking some employer-provided classes. Safety training is one of the first classes that a worker takes. Trainees start by carrying equipment and material, and erecting scaffolds and hoists. Within 2 or 3 months, trainees are taught to measure, cut, and fit roofing materials and, later, to lay asphalt or fiberglass shingles. Because some roofing materials are used infrequently, it can take several years to get experience working on all the various types of roofing applications.

Some roofers train through 3-year apprenticeship programs administered by local union-management committees representing roofing contractors and locals of the United Union of Roofers, Waterproofers, and Allied Workers. The apprenticeship program generally consists of a minimum of 2,000 hours of on-the-job training annually, plus a minimum of 144 hours of classroom instruction a year in subjects such as tools and their use, arithmetic, and safety. On-the-job training for apprentices is similar to that for helpers, except that the apprenticeship program is more structured. Apprentices also learn to dampproof and waterproof walls.

Good physical condition and good balance are essential for roofers, along with no fear of heights. A high school education, or its equivalent, is helpful, as are courses in mechanical drawing and basic mathematics. Most apprentices must be at least 18 years old. Experience with metal-working is helpful for workers who install metal roofing.

Roofers may advance to supervisor or estimator for a roofing contractor, or become contractors themselves.

Employment

Roofers held about 162,000 jobs in 2004. Almost all wage and salary roofers worked for roofing contractors. About 1 out of every 4 roofers was self-employed. Many self-employed roofers specialized in residential work.

Job Outlook

Job opportunities for roofers should be good through the year 2014, primarily because of the need to replace workers who leave the occupation. The proportion of roofers who leave the occupation each year is higher than in most construction trades—roofing work is hot, strenuous, and dirty, and a significant number of workers treat roofing as a temporary job until something better comes along. Some roofers leave the occupation to go into other construction trades.

Employment of roofers is expected to grow as fast as the average for all occupations through 2014. Roofs deteriorate faster and are more susceptible to weather damage than most other parts of buildings and periodically need to be repaired or replaced. Roofing has a much higher proportion of repair and replacement work than most other construction occupations. As a result, demand for roofers is less susceptible to downturns in the economy than demand for other construction trades. In addition to repair and reroofing work on the growing stock of buildings, new construction of industrial, commercial, and residential buildings will add to the demand for roofers. Jobs should be easiest to find during spring and summer when most roofing is done.

Earnings

In May 2004, median hourly earnings of roofers were $14.83. The middle 50 percent earned between $11.54 and $19.80. The lowest 10 percent earned less than $9.41, and the highest 10 percent earned more than $25.59. The median hourly earnings of roofers in the foundation, structure, and building exterior contractors industry were $14.90 in May 2004.

Apprentices usually start at about 40 percent to 50 percent of the rate paid to experienced roofers and receive periodic raises as they acquire the skills of the trade. Earnings for roofers are reduced on occasion because poor weather limits the time they can work.

Some roofers are members of the United Union of Roofers, Waterproofers, and Allied Workers.

Related Occupations

Roofers use shingles, bitumen and gravel, single-ply plastic or rubber sheets, or other materials to waterproof building surfaces. Workers in other occupations who cover surfaces with special materials for protection and decoration include carpenters; carpet, floor, and tile installers and finishers; cement masons, concrete finishers, segmental pavers, and terrazzo workers; drywall installers, ceiling tile installers, and tapers; plasterers and stucco masons; and sheet metal workers.

Sources of Additional Information

For information about apprenticeships or job opportunities in roofing, contact local roofing contractors, a local chapter of the roofers union, a local joint union-management apprenticeship committee, or the nearest office of your State employment service or apprenticeship agency.

For information about the work of roofers, contact:

➤ National Roofing Contractors Association, 10255 W. Higgins Rd., Suite 600, Rosemont, IL 60018-5607. Internet: **http://www.nrca.net**
➤ United Union of Roofers, Waterproofers, and Allied Workers, 1660 L St. NW., Suite 800, Washington, DC 20036.

Sheet Metal Workers

(O*NET 47-2211.00)

Significant Points

● Nearly two-thirds of the jobs are found in the construction industry; about one quarter are in manufacturing.

● Apprenticeship programs lasting 4 or 5 years are considered the best training.

● Job opportunities in construction should be good.

Nature of the Work

Sheet metal workers make, install, and maintain heating, ventilation, and air-conditioning duct systems; roofs; siding; rain gutters; downspouts; skylights; restaurant equipment; outdoor signs; railroad cars; tailgates; customized precision equipment; and many other products made from metal sheets. They also may work with fiberglass and plastic materials. Although some workers specialize in fabrication, installation, or maintenance, most do all three jobs. Sheet metal workers do both construction-related sheet metal work and mass production of sheet metal products in manufacturing.

Sheet metal workers first study plans and specifications to determine the kind and quantity of materials they will need. They then measure, cut, bend, shape, and fasten pieces of sheet metal to make ductwork, countertops, and other custom products. In an increasing number of shops, sheet metal workers use computerized metalworking equipment. This enables them to perform their tasks more quickly and to experiment with different layouts to find the one that results in the least waste of material. They cut, drill, and form parts with computer-controlled saws, lasers, shears, and presses.

In shops without computerized equipment, and for products that cannot be made on such equipment, sheet metal workers make the required calculations and use tapes, rulers, and other measuring devices for layout work. They then cut or stamp the parts on machine tools.

Before assembling pieces, sheet metal workers check each part for accuracy using measuring instruments such as calipers and micrometers and, if necessary, finish it by using hand, rotary, or squaring shears and hacksaws. After the parts have been inspected, workers fasten seams and joints together with welds, bolts, cement, rivets, solder, specially formed sheet metal drive clips, or other connecting devices. They then take the parts to the construction site, where they further assemble the pieces as they install them. These workers install ducts, pipes, and tubes by joining them end to end and hanging them with metal hangers secured to a ceiling or a wall. They also use shears, hammers, punches, and drills to make parts at the worksite or to alter parts made in the shop.

Some jobs are done completely at the jobsite. When installing a metal roof, for example, sheet metal workers measure and cut the roofing panels that are needed to complete the job. They secure the first panel in place and interlock and fasten the grooved edge of the next panel into the grooved edge of the first. Then, they nail or weld the free edge of the panel to the structure. This two-step process is repeated for each additional panel. Finally, the workers fasten machine-made molding at joints, along corners, and around windows and doors for a neat, finished effect.

In addition to installation, some sheet metal workers specialize in testing, balancing, adjusting, and servicing existing air-conditioning and ventilation systems to make sure they are functioning properly and to improve their energy efficiency. Properly installed duct systems are a key component to heating, ventilation, and air-condition-

Sheet metal workers make products mainly for the construction and manufacturing industries.

ing (HVAC) systems, which causes duct installers to sometimes be referred to as *HVAC technicians.* A growing activity for sheet metal workers is building commissioning, which is a complete mechanical inspection of a building's HVAC, water, and lighting systems.

Sheet metal workers in manufacturing plants make sheet metal parts for products such as aircraft or industrial equipment. Although some of the fabrication techniques used in large-scale manufacturing are similar to those used in smaller shops, the work may be highly automated and repetitive. Sheet metal workers doing such work may be responsible for reprogramming the computer control systems of the equipment they operate.

Working Conditions

Sheet metal workers usually work a 40-hour week. Those who fabricate sheet metal products work in shops that are well-lighted and well-ventilated. However, they stand for long periods and lift heavy materials and finished pieces. Sheet metal workers must follow safety practices because working around high-speed machines can be dangerous. They also are subject to cuts from sharp metal, burns from soldering and welding, and falls from ladders and scaffolds. They are often required to wear safety glasses and must not wear jewelry or loose-fitting clothing that could easily be caught in a machine. They may work at a variety of different production stations to reduce the repetitiveness of the work.

Those performing installation work do considerable bending, lifting, standing, climbing, and squatting, sometimes in close quarters or in awkward positions. Although duct systems and kitchen equipment are installed indoors, the installation of siding, roofs, and gutters involves much outdoor work, requiring sheet metal workers to be exposed to various kinds of weather.

Training, Other Qualifications, and Advancement

Sheet metal workers learn their trade through both formal and informal training programs. To become a skilled sheet metal worker usually takes between 4 and 5 years of both classroom and on-the-job training. While there are a number of different ways to obtain this training, generally the more formalized the training received by an individual, the more thoroughly skilled become, and the more are likely to be in demand by employers. For some, this training can begin in a high school, where classes in English, algebra, geometry, physics, mechanical drawing and blueprint reading, and general shop are recommended.

After high school, there are a number of different avenues that one can take to obtain the necessary training. One of the ways is to obtain a job with a contractor who will then provide training on the job. Entry-level workers generally start as helpers, assisting more experienced workers. Most begin by carrying metal and cleaning up debris in a metal shop while they learn about materials and tools and their uses. Later, they learn to operate machines that bend or cut metal. In time, helpers go out on the jobsite to learn installation. Employers may send the employee to courses at a trade or vocational school or community college to receive further formal training. Helpers may be promoted to the journey level if they show the requisite knowledge and skills. Most sheet metal workers in large-scale manufacturing receive on-the-job training, with additional class work or in-house training as necessary. The training needed to become proficient in manufacturing takes less time than the training for construction.

Some employers, particularly large nonresidential construction contractors with union membership, offer formal apprenticeships. These programs combine on-the-job training with related classroom instruction. Usually, apprenticeship applicants must be at least 18 years old and meet local requirements. The length of the program, usually 4 to 5 years, varies with the apprentice's skill. Apprenticeship programs provide comprehensive instruction in both sheet metal fabrication and installation. They may be administered by local joint committees composed of the Sheet Metal Workers' International Association and local chapters of the Sheet Metal and Air-Conditioning Contractors National Association.

On the job, apprentices learn the basics of pattern layout and how to cut, bend, fabricate, and install sheet metal. They begin by learning to install and maintain basic ductwork and gradually advance to more difficult jobs, such as making more complex ducts, commercial kitchens, and decorative pieces. They also use materials such as fiberglass, plastics, and other nonmetallic materials. Some workers may focus on exterior or architectural sheet metal installation. In the classroom, apprentices learn drafting, plan and specification reading, trigonometry and geometry applicable to layout work, the use of computerized equipment, welding, and the principles of heating, air-conditioning, and ventilating systems. Safety is stressed throughout the program. In addition, apprentices learn the relationship between sheet metal work and other construction work.

Sheet metal workers need to be in good physical condition and have mechanical and mathematical aptitude as well as good reading skills. Some additional skills needed are good eye-hand coordination, spatial and form perception, and manual dexterity also are important. Courses in algebra, trigonometry, geometry, mechanical drawing, and shop provide a helpful background for learning the trade, as does related work experience obtained in the Armed Services.

It is important for experienced sheet metal workers to keep abreast of new technological developments, such as the use of computerized layout and laser-cutting machines. Workers often take additional training, provided by the union or by their employer, to improve existing skills or to acquire new ones.

Sheet metal workers in construction may advance to supervisory jobs. Some of these workers take additional training in welding and do more specialized work. Workers who perform building and system testing are able to move into construction and building inspection. Others go into the contracting business for themselves. Because a sheet metal contractor must have a shop with equipment to fabricate products, this type of contracting business is more expensive to start than other types of construction contracting. Sheet metal workers in manufacturing may advance to positions as supervisors or quality inspectors. Some of these workers may move into other management positions.

Employment

Sheet metal workers held about 198,000 jobs in 2004. Nearly two-thirds of all sheet metal workers were found in the construction industry. Of those employed in construction, almost two-thirds worked for plumbing, heating, and air-conditioning contractors; most of the rest worked for roofing and sheet metal contractors. Some worked for other special trade contractors and for general contractors engaged in residential and commercial building. One-quarter of all sheet metal workers work outside of construction and are found in manufacturing industries, such as the fabricated metal products, machinery, and aerospace products and parts industries. Some sheet metal workers work for the Federal Government.

Compared with workers in most construction craft occupations, relatively few sheet metal workers are self-employed.

Job Outlook

Job opportunities are expected to be good for sheet metal workers in the construction industry, reflecting both employment growth and openings arising each year as experienced sheet metal workers leave the occupation. Opportunities should be particularly good for individuals who acquire apprenticeship training or who are certified welders. Job prospects in manufacturing will not be as good because

a number of manufacturing plants that employ sheet metal workers are moving to lower wage parts of the country or abroad and the ones that remain are becoming more productive.

Employment of sheet metal workers is expected to increase as fast as the average, reflecting growth in the number of industrial, commercial, and residential structures being built. The need to install energy-efficient air-conditioning, heating, and ventilation systems in older buildings as well as perform other types of renovation and maintenance work also should boost employment. In addition, the popularity of decorative sheet metal products and increased architectural restoration are expected to add to the demand for sheet metal workers.

Sheet metal workers in construction may experience periods of unemployment, particularly when construction projects end and economic conditions dampen construction activity. Nevertheless, employment of sheet metal workers is less sensitive to declines in new construction than is the employment of some other construction workers, such as carpenters. Maintenance of existing equipment—which is less affected by economic fluctuations than is new construction—makes up a large part of the work done by sheet metal workers. Installation of new air-conditioning and heating systems in existing buildings continues during construction slumps, as individuals and businesses adopt more energy-efficient equipment to cut utility bills. In addition, a large proportion of sheet metal installation and maintenance is done indoors, so sheet metal workers usually lose less worktime due to bad weather than other construction workers do.

Earnings

In May 2004, median hourly earnings of sheet metal workers were $17.09. The middle 50 percent earned between $12.49 and $23.89. The lowest 10 percent of all sheet metal workers earned less than $9.80, and the highest 10 percent earned more than $30.78. The median hourly earnings of the largest industries employing sheet metal workers in May 2004 were as follows:

Federal executive branch and United States Postal Service	$20.75
Building equipment contractors	18.04
Building finishing contractors	17.41
Foundation, structure, and building exterior contractors	15.34
Architectural and structural metals manufacturing	15.14

Apprentices normally start at about 40 to 50 percent of the rate paid to experienced workers. As apprentices acquire more skills throughout the course of their training, they receive periodic increases until their pay approaches that of experienced workers. In addition, union workers in some areas receive supplemental wages from the union when they are on layoff or shortened workweeks.

Related Occupations

To fabricate and install sheet metal products, sheet metal workers combine metalworking skills and knowledge of construction materials and techniques. Other occupations in which workers lay out and fabricate metal products include assemblers and fabricators; machinists; machine setters, operators, and tenders—metal and plastic; and tool and die makers. Construction occupations requiring similar skills and knowledge include glaziers and heating, air-conditioning, and refrigeration mechanics and installers.

Sources of Additional Information

For more information about apprenticeships or other work opportunities, contact local sheet metal contractors or heating, refrigeration, and air-conditioning contractors; a local of the Sheet Metal Workers International Association; a local of the Sheet Metal and Air-Conditioning Contractors National Association; a local joint union-management apprenticeship committee; or the nearest office of your State employment service or apprenticeship agency.

For general and training information about sheet metal workers, contact:

➤ International Training Institute for the Sheet Metal and Air-Conditioning Industry, 601 N. Fairfax St., Suite 240, Alexandria, VA 22314. Internet: **http://www.sheetmetal-iti.org**

➤ National Center for Construction Education and Research, P.O. Box 141104, Gainesville, FL 32614-1104. Internet: **http://www.nccer.org**

➤ Sheet Metal and Air-Conditioning Contractors' National Association, 4201 Lafayette Center Dr., Chantilly, VA 20151-1209. Internet: **http://www.smacna.org**

➤ Sheet Metal Workers International Association, 1750 New York Ave. NW., Washington, DC 20006. Internet: **http://www.smwia.org**

Structural and Reinforcing Iron and Metal Workers

(O*NET 47-2171.00, 47-2221.00)

Significant Points

● Earnings of structural iron and steel workers are among the highest of all construction trades.

● Most employers recommend completion of a 3- or 4-year apprenticeship.

● Workers need to be in good physical condition and not have a fear of heights.

Nature of the Work

Structural and reinforcing iron and metal workers place and install iron or steel girders, columns, and other construction materials to form buildings, bridges, and other structures. They also position and secure steel bars or mesh in concrete forms in order to reinforce the concrete used in highways, buildings, bridges, tunnels, and other structures. In addition, they repair and renovate older buildings and structures. Even though the primary metal involved in this work is steel, these workers often are known as *ironworkers*. Some ironworkers fabricate structural metal in fabricating shops, which are usually located away from the construction site. These workers are covered in the statement on assemblers and fabricators found elsewhere in the *Handbook*.

Before construction can begin, ironworkers must erect steel frames and assemble the cranes and derricks that move structural steel, reinforcing bars, buckets of concrete, lumber, and other materials and equipment around the construction site. Once this job has been completed, workers begin to connect steel columns, beams, and girders according to blueprints and instructions from supervisors and superintendents. Structural steel, reinforcing rods, and ornamental iron generally come to the construction site ready for erection—cut to the proper size, with holes drilled for bolts and numbered for assembly.

Ironworkers at the construction site unload and stack the prefabricated steel so that it can be hoisted easily when needed. To hoist the steel, ironworkers attach cables (slings) to the steel and to the crane or derrick. One worker directs the hoist operator with hand signals while another worker holds a rope (tag line) attached to the steel to prevent it from swinging. The crane or derrick hoists steel into place in the framework, whereupon two connectors position the steel with connecting bars and spud wrenches. Workers using driftpins or the handle of a spud wrench—a long wrench with a pointed handle—align the holes in the steel with the holes in the framework. Before the bolts are permanently tightened, ironworkers check vertical and horizontal alignment with plumb bobs, laser equipment, transits, or levels; then they bolt or weld the piece permanently in place.

Reinforcing iron and rebar workers set reinforcing bars (often called rebar) in the forms that hold concrete, following blueprints showing the location, size, and number of bars. They then fasten the bars together by tying wire around them with pliers. When reinforcing floors, ironworkers place spacers under the rebar to hold the bars off the deck. Although these materials usually arrive ready to use, ironworkers occasionally must cut bars with metal shears or acetylene torches, bend them by hand or machine, or weld them with arc-welding equipment. Some concrete is reinforced with welded wire fabric. Using hooked rods, workers cut and fit the fabric, and while a concrete crew places the concrete, ironworkers properly position the fabric into the concrete. Post-tensioning is another technique used in reinforcing concrete. In this technique, workers substitute cables for reinforcing bars. When the concrete is poured, the ends of the cables are left exposed. After the concrete cures, ironworkers tighten the cables with jacking equipment specially designed for the purpose. Post-tensioning allows designers to create larger open areas in a building, because supports can be placed further apart. This technique is commonly employed in parking garages and arenas.

Ornamental ironworkers install stairs, handrails, curtain walls (the nonstructural walls and window frames of many large buildings), and other miscellaneous metal after the structure of the building has been completed. As they hoist pieces into position, ornamental ironworkers make sure that the pieces are properly fitted and aligned before bolting or welding them for a secure fit.

Working Conditions

Structural and reinforcing iron and metal workers usually work outside in all kinds of weather. However, those who work at great heights do not work during wet, icy, or extremely windy conditions. Because the danger of injuries due to falls is great, ironworkers use safety devices such as safety harnesses, scaffolding, and nets to reduce risk.

Training, Other Qualifications, and Advancement

Most employers recommend a 3- or 4-year apprenticeship consisting of on-the-job training and evening classroom instruction as the best way to learn this trade. Apprenticeship programs are administered by

Because the danger of falls is great, ironworkers use safety devices such as safety belts, scaffolding, and nets to reduce risk.

committees made up of representatives of local unions of the International Association of Bridge, Structural, Ornamental and Reinforcing Iron Workers or the local chapters of contractors' associations.

Ironworkers must be at least 18 years old. A high school diploma is preferred by employers and local apprenticeship committees. High school courses in general mathematics, mechanical drawing, English, and welding are considered helpful. Because materials used in iron working are heavy and bulky, ironworkers must be in good physical condition. They also need good agility, balance, eyesight, and depth perception to work safely at great heights on narrow beams and girders. Ironworkers should not be afraid of heights or suffer from dizziness.

In the classroom, apprentices study blueprint reading; mathematics, the basics of structural erecting, rigging, reinforcing, welding, assembling, and safety training. Apprentices also study the care and safe use of tools and materials. On the job, apprentices work in all aspects of the trade, such as unloading and storing materials at the job site, rigging materials for movement by crane, connecting structural steel, and welding.

Some ironworkers learn the trade informally on the job, without completing an apprenticeship. These workers generally do not receive classroom training, although some large contractors have extensive training programs. On-the-job trainees usually begin by assisting experienced ironworkers on simple jobs, such as carrying various materials. With experience, trainees perform more difficult tasks, such as cutting and fitting different parts; however, learning through work experience alone may not provide training as complete as an apprenticeship program, and it usually takes longer.

Some experienced workers are promoted to supervisor. Others may go into the contracting business for themselves. The ability to communicate in both English and Spanish will improve opportunities for advancement.

Employment
Ironworkers held about 106,000 jobs in 2004. Structural iron and steel workers held about 73,000 jobs in 2004, while reinforcing iron and rebar workers held about 34,000 jobs. More than 4 out of 5 worked in construction, with nearly half working for foundation, structure, and building exterior contractors. Most of the remaining ironworkers worked for contractors specializing in the construction of homes; factories; commercial buildings; religious structures; schools; bridges and tunnels; and water, sewer, communications, and power lines.

Structural and reinforcing iron and metal workers are employed in all parts of the country, but most work in metropolitan areas, where the bulk of commercial and industrial construction takes place.

Job Outlook
Employment of structural and reinforcing iron and metal workers is expected to grow about as fast as average for all occupations through the year 2014, largely on the basis of projected growth in nonresidential and heavy construction. The rehabilitation, maintenance, and replacement of a growing number of older buildings, powerplants, highways, and bridges is expected to create employment opportunities. State and federal legislatures continue to support and fund the building of roads, which will secure jobs for the near future. In addition to new jobs that arise, many job openings will result from the need to replace experienced ironworkers who leave the occupation or retire.

In most areas job opportunities should be good for those with the right qualifications, although the number of job openings can fluctuate from year to year with economic conditions and the level of construction activity. During economic downturns, ironworkers can experience periods of unemployment. Similarly, job opportunities for ironworkers may vary widely by geographic area. Population growth in the South and West should create more job opportunities

than elsewhere as buildings and roads are constructed to meet the needs of the people. Job openings for ironworkers usually are more abundant during the spring and summer months, when the level of construction activity increases. Workers who are willing to relocate are often able to find work in another area.

Earnings
In May 2004, median hourly earnings of structural iron and steel workers in all industries were $20.40. The middle 50 percent earned between $14.84 and $27.21. The lowest 10 percent earned less than $11.25, and the highest 10 percent earned more than $33.53. In May 2004, median hourly earnings of reinforcing iron and rebar workers in all industries were $16.90. The middle 50 percent earned between $12.45 and $25.94. The lowest 10 percent earned less than $10.03, and the highest 10 percent earned more than $32.59.

Median hourly earnings of structural iron and steel workers in May 2004 in foundation, structure, and building exterior contractors were $21.81and in nonresidential building construction, $17.47. Reinforcing iron and rebar workers earned median hourly earnings of $16.52 in foundation, structure, and building exterior contractors in May 2004.

About half of the workers in this trade are members of the International Association of Bridge, Structural, Ornamental, and Reinforcing Iron Workers. According to the union, average hourly earnings, including benefits, for structural and reinforcing metal workers who belonged to a union and worked full time were slightly higher than the hourly earnings of nonunion workers. Structural and reinforcing iron and metal workers in New York, Boston, San Francisco, Chicago, Los Angeles, Philadelphia, and other large cities received the highest wages.

Apprentices generally start at about 50 percent to 60 percent of the rate paid to experienced journey workers. Throughout the course of the apprenticeship program, as they acquire the skills of the trade, they receive periodic increases until their pay approaches that of experienced workers.

Earnings for ironworkers may be reduced on occasion because work can be limited by bad weather, the short-term nature of construction jobs, and economic downturns.

Related Occupations
Structural and reinforcing iron and metal workers play an essential role in erecting buildings, bridges, highways, power lines, and other structures. Others who work on these construction jobs include assemblers and fabricators; boilermakers; civil engineers; cement masons; concrete finishers, segmental pavers, and terrazzo workers; construction managers; and welding, soldering, and brazing workers.

Sources of Additional Information
For more information on apprenticeships or other work opportunities, contact local general contractors; a local of the International Association of Bridge, Structural, Ornamental, and Reinforcing Iron Workers Union; a local ironworkers' joint union-management apprenticeship committee; a local or State chapter of the Associated Builders and Contractors or the Associated General Contractors; or the nearest office of your State employment service or apprenticeship agency.

For apprenticeship information, contact
➤ International Association of Bridge, Structural, Ornamental, and Reinforcing Iron Workers, Apprenticeship Department, 1750 New York Ave. NW., Suite 400, Washington, DC 20006. Internet: http//www.ironworkers.org

For general information about ironworkers, contact either of the following sources:
➤ Associated Builders and Contractors, Workforce Development Department, 4250 North Fairfax Dr., 9th Floor, Arlington, VA 22203. Internet: http//www.trytools.org
➤ Associated General Contractors of America, Inc., 2300 Wilson Boulevard, Suite 400., Arlington, VA 22201. Internet: http://www.agc.org

Installation, Maintenance, and Repair Occupations

Electrical and Electronic Equipment Mechanics, Installers, and Repairers

Computer, Automated Teller, and Office Machine Repairers

(O*NET 49-2011.01, 49-2011.02, 49-2011.03)

Significant Points

- Workers qualify for these jobs by receiving training in electronics from associate degree programs, the military, vocational schools, equipment manufacturers, or employers.

- Job growth reflects the increasing dependence of businesses and individuals on computers and other sophisticated office machines.

- Job prospects will be best for applicants with knowledge of electronics as well as repair experience.

Nature of the Work

Computer repairers, also known as *computer service technicians or data processing equipment repairers,* service mainframe, server, and personal computers; printers; and disc drives. These workers perform primarily hands-on repair, maintenance, and installation of computers and related equipment. Workers who provide technical assistance, in person or by telephone, to computer system users are known as computer support specialists or computer support technicians. (See the statement on computer support specialists and systems administrators elsewhere in the *Handbook.*)

Automated teller machines (ATMs) allow customers to carry out bank transactions without the assistance of a teller. ATMs now also provide a growing variety of other services, including stamp, phone card, and ticket sales. *Automated teller machine servicers* repair and service these machines.

Office machine and cash register servicers work on photocopiers, cash registers, mail-processing equipment, and fax machines. Newer models of office machinery include computerized components that allow them to function more effectively than earlier models.

To install large equipment, such as mainframe computers and ATMs, repairers connect the equipment to power sources and communication lines that allow the transmission of information over computer networks. For example, when an ATM dispenses cash, it transmits the withdrawal information to the customer's bank. Workers also may install operating software and peripheral equipment, checking that all components are configured to function together correctly. The installation of personal computers and other small office machines is less complex and may be handled by the purchaser.

When equipment breaks down, many repairers travel to customers' workplaces or other locations to make the necessary repairs. These workers, known as *field technicians,* often have assigned areas in which they perform preventive maintenance on a regular basis.

Bench technicians work in repair shops located in stores, factories, or service centers. In small companies, repairers may work both in repair shops and at customer locations.

Computer repairers usually replace subsystems instead of repairing them. Replacement is common because subsystems are inexpensive and businesses are reluctant to shut down their computers for time-consuming repairs. Subsystems commonly replaced by computer repairers include video cards, which transmit signals from the computer to the monitor; hard drives, which store data; and network cards, which allow communication over the network. Defective modules may be given to bench technicians, who use software programs to diagnose the problem and who may repair the modules, if possible.

When ATMs malfunction, computer networks recognize the problem and alert repairers. Common problems include worn magnetic heads on card readers, which prevent the equipment from recognizing customers' bankcards, and "pick failures," which prevent the equipment from dispensing the correct amount of cash. Field technicians travel to the locations of ATMs and usually repair equipment by removing and replacing defective components. Broken components are taken to a repair shop, where bench technicians make the necessary repairs. Field technicians perform routine maintenance on a regular basis, replacing worn parts and running diagnostic tests to ensure that the equipment functions properly.

Office machine repairers usually work on machinery at the customer's workplace; alternatively, if the machines are small enough, customers may bring them to a repair shop for maintenance. Common malfunctions include paper misfeeds caused by worn or dirty parts, and poor-quality copy resulting from problems with lamps, lenses, or mirrors. These malfunctions usually can be resolved simply by cleaning the relevant components. Breakdowns

Computer repairers repair, maintain, and install computers and related equipment.

also may result from the failure of commonly used parts. For example, heavy use of a photocopier may wear down the printhead, which applies ink to the final copy. In such cases, the repairer usually replaces the part instead of repairing it.

Workers use a variety of tools for diagnostic tests and repair. To diagnose malfunctions, they use multimeters to measure voltage, current, resistance, and other electrical properties; signal generators to provide test signals; and oscilloscopes to monitor equipment signals. To diagnose computerized equipment, repairers use software programs. To repair or adjust equipment, workers use handtools, such as pliers, screwdrivers, soldering irons, and wrenches.

Working Conditions

Repairers usually work in clean, well-lighted surroundings. Because computers and office machines are sensitive to extreme temperatures and to humidity, repair shops usually are air-conditioned and well ventilated. Field repairers must travel frequently to various locations to install, maintain, or repair customers' equipment. ATM repairers may have to perform their jobs in small, confined spaces that house the equipment.

Because computers and ATMs are critical for many organizations to function efficiently, data processing equipment repairers and ATM field technicians often work around the clock. Their schedules may include evening, weekend, and holiday shifts, sometimes assigned on the basis of seniority. Office machine and cash register servicers usually work regular business hours because the equipment they repair is not as critical.

Although their job is not strenuous, repairers must lift equipment and work in a variety of postures. Repairers of computer monitors need to discharge voltage from the equipment to avoid electrocution. Workers may have to wear protective goggles.

Training, Other Qualifications, and Advancement

Knowledge of electronics is necessary for employment as a computer, automated teller, or office machine repairer. Employers prefer workers who are certified as repairers or who have training in electronics from associate degree programs, the military, vocational schools, or equipment manufacturers. Employers generally provide some training to new repairers on specific equipment; however, workers are expected to arrive on the job with a basic understanding of equipment repair. Employers may send experienced workers to training sessions to keep up with changes in technology and service procedures.

Most office machine and ATM repairer positions require an associate degree in electronics. A basic understanding of mechanical equipment also is important, because many of the parts that fail in office machines and ATMs, such as paper loaders, are mechanical. Entry-level employees at large companies normally receive on-the-job training lasting several months. Such training may include a week of classroom instruction, followed by a period of 2 weeks to several months assisting an experienced repairer.

Field technicians work closely with customers and must have good communications skills and a neat appearance. Employers normally require that field technicians have a driver's license.

Various organizations offer certification. To receive certification, repairers must pass qualifying examinations corresponding to their level of training and experience.

Newly hired computer repairers may work on personal computers or peripheral equipment. With experience, they can advance to positions maintaining more sophisticated systems, such as networking equipment and servers. Field repairers of ATMs may advance to bench technician positions responsible for more complex repairs. Experienced workers may become specialists who help other repairers diagnose difficult problems or who work with engineers in designing equipment and developing maintenance procedures. Experienced workers also may move into management positions responsible for supervising other repairers.

Because of their familiarity with equipment, experienced repairers may move into customer service or sales positions. Some experienced workers open their own repair shops or become wholesalers or retailers of electronic equipment.

Employment

Computer, automated teller, and office machine repairers held about 168,000 jobs in 2004. Wholesale trade establishments employed about 35 percent of the workers in this occupation; most of these establishments were wholesalers of professional and commercial equipment and supplies. Many workers also were employed in electronics, appliance, and office supply stores. Others worked in electronic and precision equipment repair shops and computer systems design firms. A small number found employment with computer and peripheral equipment manufacturers, government agencies, and Internet service providers. About 15 percent of computer, automated teller, and office machine repairers were self-employed, which is more than twice the proportion for all installation, maintenance, and repair occupations.

Job Outlook

Employment of computer, automated teller, and office machine repairers is expected to grow more slowly than the average for all occupations through 2014. Limited job growth will be driven by the increasing dependence of business and individuals on computers and other sophisticated office machines. The need to maintain this equipment will create new jobs for repairers. In addition, openings will result from the need to replace repairers who retire or transfer to new occupations.

Job prospects will be best for applicants with knowledge of electronics as well as repair experience. Although computer equipment continues to become less expensive and more reliable, malfunctions still occur and can cause severe problems for users, most of whom lack the knowledge to make repairs. Computers are critical to most businesses today and will become even more so to companies that do business on the Internet and to individuals that bank, pay bills, or make purchases online.

People also are becoming increasingly reliant on ATMs. Besides offering bank and retail transactions, ATMs provide an increasing number of other services, such as employee information processing and distribution of government payments. Improvements in ATM design have increased reliability and simplified repair tasks, reducing the number and extent of repairs. However, opportunities for ATM repairers should still be available arising primarily from the need to replace workers who leave the specialty, rather than from employment growth.

Conventional office machines, such as calculators, are inexpensive, and often are replaced instead of repaired. However, digital copiers and other, newer office machines are more costly and complex. This equipment often is computerized, designed to work on a network, and capable of performing multiple functions. The growing need for repairers to service such sophisticated equipment should result in job opportunities for office machine repairers.

Earnings

Median hourly earnings of computer, automated teller, and office machine repairers were $16.90 in May 2004. The middle 50 percent earned between $13.11 and $21.36. The lowest 10 percent earned less than $10.31, and the highest 10 percent earned more than

$26.28. Median hourly earnings in the industries employing the largest numbers of computer, automated teller, and office machine repairers in May 2004 are shown below:

Professional and commercial equipment and
   supplies merchant wholesalers $18.51
Computer systems design and related services 18.08
Office supplies, stationery, and gift stores 15.69
Electronic and precision equipment repair and maintenance 14.95
Electronics and appliance stores 14.04

Related Occupations

Workers in other occupations who repair and maintain electronic equipment include broadcast and sound engineering technicians and radio operators; electronic home entertainment equipment installers and repairers; electrical and electronics installers and repairers; industrial machinery mechanics and maintenance workers; and radio and telecommunications equipment installers and repairers.

Sources of Additional Information

For information on careers and certification, contact:

➤ ACES International, 5241 Princess Anne Rd., Suite 110, Virginia Beach, VA 23462. Internet: **http://www.acesinternational.org**

➤ Electronics Technicians Association International, 5 Depot St., Greencastle, IN 46135.

➤ International Society of Certified Electronics Technicians, 3608 Pershing Ave., Fort Worth, TX 76107-4527. Internet: **http://www.iscet.org**

Electrical and Electronics Installers and Repairers

(O*NET 49-2092.01, 49-2092.02, 49-2092.03, 49-2092.04, 49-2092.05, 49-2092.06, 49-2093.00, 49-2094.00, 49-2095.00, 49-2096.00)

Significant Points

● Knowledge of electrical equipment and electronics is necessary for employment; many applicants complete 1 to 2 years at vocational schools and community colleges, although some less skilled repairers may have only a high school diploma.

● Employment is projected to grow more slowly than average, but prospects vary by occupational specialty.

● Job opportunities will be best for applicants with a thorough knowledge of electrical and electronic equipment as well as repair experience.

Nature of the Work

Businesses and other organizations depend on complex electronic equipment for a variety of functions. Industrial controls automatically monitor and direct production processes on the factory floor. Transmitters and antennae provide communication links for many organizations. Electric power companies use electronic equipment to operate and control generating plants, substations, and monitoring equipment. The Federal Government uses radar and missile control systems to provide for the national defense and to direct commercial air traffic. These complex pieces of electronic equipment are installed, maintained, and repaired by electrical and electronics installers and repairers.

Electrical equipment and electronic equipment are two distinct types of industrial equipment, although much equipment contains both electrical and electronic components. In general, electrical portions provide the power for the equipment, while electronic components control the device, although many types of equipment still are controlled with electrical devices. Electronic sensors monitor the equipment and the manufacturing process, providing feedback to the programmable logic control (PLC), which controls the equipment. The PLC processes the information provided by the sensors and makes adjustments to optimize output. To adjust the output, the PLC sends signals to the electrical, hydraulic, and pneumatic devices that power the machine—changing feed rates, pressures, and other variables in the manufacturing process. Many installers and repairers, known as *field technicians*, travel to factories or other locations to repair equipment. These workers often have assigned areas in which they perform preventive maintenance on a regular basis. When equipment breaks down, field technicians go to a customer's site to repair the equipment. *Bench technicians* work in repair shops located in factories and service centers, fixing components that cannot be repaired on the factory floor.

Some industrial electronic equipment is self-monitoring and alerts repairers to malfunctions. When equipment breaks down, repairers first check for common causes of trouble, such as loose connections or obviously defective components. If routine checks do not locate the trouble, repairers may refer to schematics and manufacturers' specifications that show connections and provide instructions on how to locate problems. Automated electronic control systems are increasing in complexity, making diagnosis more challenging. With these systems, repairers use software programs and testing equipment to diagnose malfunctions. Among their diagnostic tools are multimeters, which measure voltage, current, and resistance, and advanced multimeters, which measure capacitance, inductance, and current gain of transistors. Repairers also use signal generators, which provide test signals, and oscilloscopes, which display signals graphically. Finally, repairers use handtools such as pliers, screwdrivers, soldering irons, and wrenches to replace faulty parts and adjust equipment.

Because repairing components is a complex activity and factories cannot allow production equipment to stand idle, repairers on the factory floor usually remove and replace defective units, such as circuit boards, instead of fixing them. Defective units are discarded or returned to the manufacturer or a specialized shop for repair. Bench technicians at these locations have the training, tools, and parts needed to thoroughly diagnose and repair circuit boards or other complex components. These workers also locate and repair circuit defects, such as poorly soldered joints, blown fuses, or malfunctioning transistors.

Electrical and electronics installers often fit older manufacturing equipment with new automated control devices. Older manufacturing machines are frequently in good working order but are limited by inefficient control systems for which replacement parts are no longer available. Installers replace old electronic control units with new PLCs. Setting up and installing a new PLC involves connecting it to different sensors and electrically powered devices (electric motors, switches, and pumps) and writing a computer program to operate the PLC. Electronics installers coordinate their efforts with those of other workers who are installing and maintaining equipment. (See the statement on industrial machinery mechanics and maintenance workers elsewhere in the *Handbook.*)

Electrical and electronics installers and repairers, transportation equipment install, adjust, or maintain mobile electronic communication equipment, including sound, sonar, security, navigation, and surveillance systems on trains, watercraft, or other vehicles. *Electrical and electronics repairers, powerhouse, substation, and relay* inspect, test, maintain, or repair electrical equipment used in generating stations, substations, and in-service relays. These workers may be known as powerhouse electricians, relay technicians, or power transformer repairers. *Electric motor, power tool, and related repairers*—such as armature winders, generator mechanics, and electric golf cart repairers—specialize in installing, maintaining, and repairing electric motors, wiring, or switches.

Electronic equipment installers and repairers, motor vehicles have a significantly different job. They install, diagnose, and repair communication, sound, security, and navigation equipment in motor vehicles. Most installation work involves either new alarm or sound systems. New sound systems vary significantly in cost and complexity of installation. Replacing a head unit (radio) with a new CD player is simple, requiring the removal of a few screws and the connection of a few wires. Installing a new sound system with a subwoofer, amplifier, and fuses is far more complicated. The installer builds a fiberglass or wood box designed to hold the subwoofer and to fit inside the unique dimensions of the automobile. Installing sound-deadening material, which often is necessary with more powerful speakers, requires an installer to remove many parts of a car (for example, seats, carpeting, or interiors of doors), add sound-absorbing material in empty spaces, and reinstall the interior parts. The installer also runs new speaker and electrical cables. The new system may require additional fuses, a new electrical line to be run from the battery through a newly drilled hole in the firewall into the interior of the vehicle, or an additional or more powerful alternator or battery. Motor vehicle installers and repairers work with an increasingly complex range of electronic equipment, including DVD players, satellite navigation equipment, passive security systems, and active security systems.

Working Conditions

Many electrical and electronics installers and repairers work on factory floors, where they are subject to noise, dirt, vibration, and heat. Bench technicians work primarily in repair shops, where the surroundings are relatively quiet, comfortable, and well lighted.

Installers and repairers may have to do heavy lifting and work in a variety of positions. They must follow safety guidelines and often wear protective goggles and hardhats. When working on ladders or on elevated equipment, repairers must wear harnesses to avoid falls.

Many electrical and electronics installers and repairers diagnose, install, and repair equipment in motor vehicles.

Before repairing a piece of machinery, these workers must follow procedures to ensure that others cannot start the equipment during the repair process. They also must take precautions against electric shock by locking off power to the unit under repair.

Motor vehicle electronic equipment installers and repairers normally work indoors in well-ventilated and well-lighted repair shops. Minor cuts and bruises are common, but serious accidents usually are avoided when safety practices are observed.

Training, Other Qualifications, and Advancement

Knowledge of electrical equipment and electronics is necessary for employment. Many applicants gain this knowledge through programs lasting 1 to 2 years at vocational schools or community colleges, although some less skilled repairers may have only a high school diploma. Entry-level repairers may work closely with more experienced technicians who provide technical guidance.

Installers and repairers should have good eyesight and color perception to work with the intricate components used in electronic equipment. Field technicians work closely with customers and should have good communication skills and a neat appearance. Employers also may require that field technicians have a driver's license.

Various organizations offer certification. Repairers may specialize —in industrial electronics, for example. To receive certification, repairers must pass qualifying exams corresponding to their level of training and experience.

Experienced repairers with advanced training may become specialists or troubleshooters who help other repairers diagnose difficult problems. Workers with leadership ability may become supervisors of other repairers. Some experienced workers open their own repair shops.

Employment

Electrical and electronics installers and repairers held about 158,000 jobs in 2004. The following tabulation breaks down their employment by occupational specialty:

Electrical and electronics repairers, commercial and industrial equipment	72,000
Electric motor, power tool, and related repairers	28,000
Electrical and electronics repairers, powerhouse, substation, and relay	21,000
Electronic equipment installers and repairers, motor vehicles	19,000
Electrical and electronics installers and repairers, transportation equipment	18,000

Many repairers worked for utilities; building equipment contractors; machinery and equipment repair shops; wholesalers; the Federal Government; retailers of automotive parts and accessories; rail transportation companies; and manufacturers of electrical, electronic, and transportation equipment.

Job Outlook

Job opportunities should be best for applicants with a thorough knowledge of electrical equipment and electronics as well as with repair experience. Overall employment of electrical and electronics installers and repairers is expected to grow more slowly than the average for all occupations during the 2004–14 period, but prospects vary by occupational specialty. In addition to employment growth, the need to replace workers who transfer to other occupations or leave the labor force will result in many job openings.

Average employment growth is projected for electrical and electronics installers and repairers of commercial and industrial equipment. This equipment will become more sophisticated and will be used more frequently as businesses strive to lower costs by increasing and improving automation. Companies will install electronic controls, robots, sensors, and other equipment to automate processes such as assembly and testing. As prices decline, applications will be found across a number of industries, including services, utilities, and construction, as well as manufacturing. Improved reliability of equipment should not constrain employment growth, however: companies increasingly will rely on repairers because malfunctions that idle commercial and industrial equipment will continue to be costly.

Employment of motor vehicle electronic equipment installers and repairers also is expected to grow about as fast as the average. However, as motor vehicle manufacturers install more and better sound, security, entertainment, and navigation systems in new vehicles, and as newer electronic systems require progressively less maintenance, employment growth for aftermarket electronic equipment installers will be limited.

Employment of electric motor, power tool, and related repairers is expected to grow more slowly than average. Improvements in electrical and electronic equipment design should limit job growth by simplifying repair tasks. The design of more parts that are easily disposable will further reduce employment growth.

Employment of electrical and electronic installers and repairers of transportation equipment is also expected to grow more slowly than the average because of declining industry employment in railroad rolling stock manufacturing and shipbuilding and boatbuilding.

Employment of electrical and electronics installers and repairers, powerhouse, substation, and relay is expected to decline slightly. Consolidation and privatization in utilities industries should improve productivity, reducing employment. Newer equipment will be more reliable and easier to repair, further limiting employment.

Earnings

Median hourly earnings of electrical and electronics repairers, commercial and industrial equipment were $20.48 in May 2004. The middle 50 percent earned between $16.04 and $25.07. The lowest 10 percent earned less than $12.55, and the highest 10 percent earned more than $28.68. In May 2004, median hourly earnings were $23.79 in the Federal Government and $17.82 in building equipment contractors, the industries employing the largest numbers of electrical and electronics repairers, commercial and industrial equipment.

Median hourly earnings of electric motor, power tool, and related repairers were $15.54 in May 2004. The middle 50 percent earned between $12.12 and $19.71. The lowest 10 percent earned less than $9.48, and the highest 10 percent earned more than $23.90. In May 2004, median hourly earnings were $15.02 in commercial and industrial machinery and equipment (except automotive and electronic) repair and maintenance, the industry employing the largest number of electronic motor, power tool, and related repairers.

Median hourly earnings of electrical and electronics repairers, powerhouse, substation, and relay were $25.86 in May 2004. The middle 50 percent earned between $22.47 and $29.73. The lowest 10 percent earned less than $18.01, and the highest 10 percent earned more than $33.82. In May 2004, median hourly earnings were $26.37 in electric power generation, transmission, and distribution—the industry employing the largest number of these repairers.

Median hourly earnings of electronics installers and repairers, motor vehicles were $12.79 in May 2004. The middle 50 percent earned between $10.27 and $16.55. The lowest 10 percent earned less than $8.85, and the highest 10 percent earned more than $22.02.

Median hourly earnings of electrical and electronics repairers, transportation equipment were $19.25 in May 2004. The middle 50 percent earned between $15.06 and $23.57. The lowest 10 percent earned less than $11.86, and the highest 10 percent earned more than $27.70.

Related Occupations

Workers in other occupations who install and repair electronic equipment include broadcast and sound technicians and radio operators; computer, automated teller, and office machine repairers; electronic home entertainment equipment installers and repairers; and radio and telecommunications equipment installers and repairers. Industrial machinery mechanics and maintenance workers also install, maintain, and repair industrial machinery.

Sources of Additional Information

For information on careers and certification, contact any of the following organizations:

➤ ACES International, 5241 Princess Anne Rd., Suite 110, Virginia Beach, VA 23462. Internet: **http://www.acesinternational.org**

➤ Electronics Technicians Association International, 5 Depot St., Greencastle, IN 46135.

➤ International Society of Certified Electronics Technicians, 3608 Pershing Ave., Fort Worth, TX 76107- 4527. Internet: **http://www.iscet.org**

Electronic Home Entertainment Equipment Installers and Repairers

(O*NET 49-2097.00)

Significant Points

- Employers prefer applicants who have basic knowledge and skills in electronics; many applicants gain these skills at vocational training programs and community colleges.

- Employment is expected to grow more slowly than the average for all occupations because it often is cheaper to replace equipment than to repair it.

- Job opportunities will be best for applicants with knowledge of electronics and with related hands-on experience.

Nature of the Work

Electronic home entertainment equipment installers and repairers, also called *service technicians*, repair a variety of equipment, including televisions and radios, stereo components, video and audio disc players, video cameras, and video recorders. They also install and repair home security systems, intercom equipment, satellite television dishes, and home theater systems, which consist of large-screen televisions and sophisticated surround-sound audio components.

Customers usually bring small, portable equipment to repair shops for servicing. Repairers at these locations, known as *bench technicians*, are equipped with a full array of electronic tools and parts. When larger, less mobile equipment breaks down, customers may pay repairers to come to their homes. These repairers, known as *field technicians*, travel with a limited set of tools and parts, and attempt to complete the repair at the customer's location. If the job is complex, technicians may bring defective components back to the shop for thorough diagnosis and repair.

When equipment breaks down, repairers check for common causes of trouble, such as dirty or defective components. Many repairs consist simply of cleaning and lubricating equipment. If routine checks do not locate the trouble, repairers may refer to schematics and manufacturers' specifications that provide instructions on how to locate problems. Repairers use a variety of test equipment to diagnose and identify malfunctions. Multimeters detect short circuits, failed capacitors, and blown fuses by measuring voltage, current, and resistance. Color-bar and dot generators provide on-screen test patterns, signal generators test signals, and oscilloscopes and digital storage scopes measure complex waveforms produced by electronic equipment. Repairs may involve removing and replacing a failed capacitor, transistor, or fuse. Repairers use handtools, such as pliers, screwdrivers, soldering irons, and wrenches, to replace faulty parts. They also make adjustments to equipment, such as focusing and converging the picture of a television set or balancing the audio on a surround-sound system.

Improvements in technology have miniaturized and digitized many audio and video recording devices. Miniaturization has made repair work significantly more difficult because both the components and the acceptable tolerances are smaller. For example, an analog video camera operates at 1,800 revolutions per minute (rpm), while a digital video camera may operate at 9,000 rpm. Also, components now are mounted on the surface of circuit boards, instead of plugged into slots, requiring more precise soldering when a new part is installed. Improved technologies have lowered the price of electronic home entertainment equipment to the point where customers often replace broken equipment instead of repairing it.

Working Conditions
Most repairers work in well-lighted electrical repair shops. Field technicians, however, spend much time traveling in service vehicles and working in customers' residences.

Repairers may have to work in a variety of positions and carry heavy equipment. Although the work of repairers is comparatively safe, they must take precautions against minor burns and electric shock. Because television monitors carry high voltage even when they are turned off, repairers need to discharge the voltage before servicing such equipment.

Training, Other Qualifications, and Advancement
Employers prefer applicants who have basic knowledge and skills in electronics. Applicants should be familiar with schematics and have some hands-on experience repairing electronic equipment. Many applicants gain these skills at vocational training programs

Many electronic home entertainment equipment installers and repairers are self-employed.

and community colleges. Training programs should include both hands-on experience and theoretical education in digital consumer electronics. Entry-level repairers may work closely with more experienced technicians, who provide technical guidance.

Field technicians work closely with customers and must have good communication skills and a neat appearance. Employers also may require that field technicians have a driver's license.

Various organizations offer certification for electronic home entertainment equipment installers and repairers. Repairers may specialize in a variety of skill areas, including consumer electronics. To receive certification, repairers must pass qualifying exams corresponding to their level of training and experience.

Experienced repairers with advanced training may become specialists or troubleshooters, helping other repairers to diagnose difficult problems. Workers with leadership ability may become supervisors of other repairers. Some experienced workers open their own repair shops.

Employment
Electronic home entertainment equipment installers and repairers held about 47,000 jobs in 2004. Most repairers worked in electronics and appliance stores that sell and service electronic home entertainment products or in electronic and precision equipment repair and maintenance shops. About 1 electronic home entertainment equipment installers and repairers in 3 were self-employed, more than 4 times the proportion for all installation, maintenance, and repair occupations.

Job Outlook
Employment of electronic home entertainment equipment installers and repairers is expected to grow more slowly than average through 2014, due to decreased demand for repair work. Nevertheless, job openings will come about because of employment growth; some openings will also result from the need to replace workers who retire or who transfer to higher paying jobs in other occupations requiring electronics experience. Opportunities will be best for applicants with knowledge of electronics and with related hands-on experience.

The need for repairers is expected to grow slowly because home entertainment equipment is less expensive than in the past. As technological developments have lowered the price and improved the reliability of equipment, the demand for repair services has decreased. When malfunctions do occur, it often is cheaper for consumers to replace equipment rather than to pay for repairs.

Employment growth will be spurred somewhat by the introduction of sophisticated digital equipment, such as DVDs, high-definition digital televisions, and digital camcorders. So long as the price of such equipment remains high, purchasers will be willing to hire repairers when malfunctions occur. There also will be demand to install sophisticated home entertainment systems, such as home theaters.

Earnings
Median hourly earnings of electronic home entertainment equipment installers and repairers were $13.44 in May 2004. The middle 50 percent earned between $10.39 and $17.10. The lowest 10 percent earned less than $8.17, and the highest 10 percent earned more than $21.36. In May 2004, median hourly earnings of electronic home entertainment equipment installers and repairers were $12.86 in electronics and appliance stores and $12.28 in electronic and precision equipment repair and maintenance.

Related Occupations
Other workers who repair and maintain electronic equipment include broadcast and sound engineering technicians and radio operators;

computer, automated teller, and office machine repairers; electrical and electronics installers and repairers; and radio and telecommunications equipment installers and repairers.

Sources of Additional Information

For information on careers and certification, contact:

➤ ACES International, 5241 Princess Anne Rd., Suite 110, Virginia Beach, VA 23461. Internet: **http://www.acesinternational.org**

➤ Electronics Technicians Association International, 5 Depot St., Greencastle, IN 46135.

➤ International Society of Certified Electronics Technicians, 3608 Pershing Ave., Fort Worth, TX 76107-4527. Internet: **http://www.iscet.org**

Radio and Telecommunications Equipment Installers and Repairers

(O*NET 49-2021.00, 49-2022.01, 49-2022.02, 49-2022.03, 49-2022.04, 49-2022.05)

Significant Points

- Employment is projected to decline.

- Job opportunities will vary by specialty; for example, good opportunities should be available for central office and PBX installers and repairers experienced in current technology, while station installers and repairers can expect keen competition.

- Applicants with computer skills and postsecondary electronics training should have the best opportunities.

- Weekend and holiday hours are common; repairers may be on call around the clock in case of emergencies.

Nature of the Work

Telephones and radios depend on a variety of equipment to transmit communications signals. From electronic switches that route telephone signals to their destinations to radio transmitters and receivers that relay signals from wireless phones, the workers who set up and maintain this sophisticated equipment are called radio and telecommunications equipment installers and repairers. These workers no longer just work on equipment that transmits voice signals, but also transmissions such as data, graphics, and video.

Central office installers set up switches, cables, and other equipment in central offices. These locations are the hubs of a telecommunications network—they contain the switches and routers that direct packets of information to their destinations. Although most telephone lines connecting houses to central offices and switching stations are still copper, the lines connecting these central hubs are fiber optic. Fiber optic lines have led to a revolution in switching equipment. The greatly increased transmission capacity of each line has allowed a few fiber optic lines to replace many copper lines. Packet switching equipment is evolving rapidly, ever increasing the amount of information that a single fiber optic line can carry. These switches and routers have the ability to transmit, process, amplify, and direct a massive amount of information. Installing and maintaining this equipment requires a high level of technical knowledge.

The increasing reliability of telephone switches and routers has simplified maintenance. New self-monitoring telephone switches alert repairers to malfunctions. Some switches allow repairers to diagnose and correct problems from remote locations. When faced with a malfunction, the repairer may refer to manufacturers' manuals that provide maintenance instructions.

When problems with telecommunications equipment arise, telecommunications equipment repairers diagnose the source of the problem by testing each of the different parts of the equipment, which requires an understanding of how the software and hardware interact. Repairers often use spectrum and/or network analyzers to locate the problem. A network analyzer sends a signal through the equipment to detect any distortion in the signal. The nature of the signal distortion often directs the repairer to the source of the problem. To fix the equipment, repairers may use small handtools, including pliers and screwdrivers, to remove and replace defective components such as circuit boards or wiring. Newer equipment is easier to repair because whole boards and parts are designed to be quickly removed and replaced. Repairers also may install updated software or programs that maintain existing software.

Cable television companies employ technicians to install and maintain their distribution centers, called head ends. Their work is similar to central office installers.

PBX installers and repairers set up private branch exchange (PBX) switchboards, which relay incoming, outgoing, and interoffice calls within a single location or organization. To install switches and switchboards, installers first connect the equipment to power lines and communications cables and install frames and supports. They test the connections to ensure that adequate power is available and that the communication links function. They also install equipment such as power systems, alarms, and telephone sets. New switches and switchboards are computerized; workers install software or program the equipment to provide specific features. For example, as a cost-cutting feature, an installer may program a PBX switchboard to route calls over different lines at different times of the day. However, other workers, such as computer support specialists generally handle complex programming. (The work of computer support specialists is described in the *Handbook* statement on computer support specialists and systems administrators.) Finally, the installer performs tests to verify that the newly installed equipment functions properly. If a problem arises, PBX repairers determine whether it is located within the PBX system or originates in the telephone lines maintained by the local phone company.

Due to rapidly developing technologies, PBX installers must adapt and learn new technologies. Instead of installing PBX systems, companies are choosing to install voice-over Internet protocol (VoIP) systems. VoIP systems operate like a PBX system, but they use a company's computer wiring to run Internet access, network applications, and telephone communications. Specialized phones have their own Internet protocol (IP) addresses. The phones can be plugged into any port in the system and still use the same number.

Station installers and repairers, telephone—commonly known as *telephone installers and repairers* or *telecommunications service technicians*—install and repair telephone wiring and equipment on customers' premises. They install telephone or digital subscriber line (DSL) service by connecting customers' telephone wires to outside service lines. These lines run on telephone poles or in underground conduits. The installer may climb poles or ladders to make the connections. Once the connection is made, the line is tested. When a maintenance problem occurs, repairers test the customers' lines to determine if the problem is located in the customers' premises or in the outside service lines. When onsite procedures fail to resolve installation or maintenance problems, repairers may request support from their technical service center. Line installers and repairers, covered elsewhere in the *Handbook*, install the wires and cables that connect customers with central offices.

Radio mechanics install and maintain radio transmitting and receiving equipment. This includes stationary equipment mounted on transmission towers and mobile equipment, such as radio communications systems in service and emergency vehicles. Radio mechanics do not work on cellular communications towers and equipment. Newer radio equipment is self-monitoring and may alert mechanics to potential malfunctions. When malfunctions occur, these mechanics examine equipment for damaged components and loose or broken wires. They use electrical measuring instruments to monitor signal strength, transmission capacity, interference, and signal delay, as well as handtools to replace defective components and parts and to adjust equipment so that it performs within required specifications.

Working Conditions

Radio and telecommunications equipment installers and repairers generally work in clean, well-lighted, air-conditioned surroundings, such as a telephone company's central office, a customer's location, or an electronic repair shop or service center. Telephone installers and repairers work on rooftops, ladders, and telephone poles. Telephone, PBX, and VoIP installers must travel to a customer's location. Radio mechanics may maintain equipment located on the tops of transmissions towers. While working outdoors, these workers are subject to a variety of weather conditions.

Nearly all radio and telecommunications equipment installers and repairers work full time. Many work regular business hours to meet the demand for repair services during the workday. Schedules are more irregular at companies that need repair services 24 hours a day or where installation and maintenance must take place after business hours. At these locations, mechanics work a variety of shifts, including weekend and holiday hours. Repairers may be on call around the clock, in case of emergencies, and may have to work overtime.

The work of most repairers involves lifting, reaching, stooping, crouching, and crawling. Adherence to safety precautions is important in order to guard against work hazards. These hazards include falls, minor burns, electrical shock, and contact with hazardous materials.

Training, Other Qualifications, and Advancement

Most employers seek applicants with postsecondary training in electronics and a familiarity with computers. Training sources include 2-year and 4-year college programs in electronics or communications, trade schools, and equipment and software manufacturers. Military experience with communications equipment is valued

Radio and telecommunications equipment installers often use computers to diagnose problems with telecommunications switching equipment.

by many employers. Some equipment repairers begin working in telecommunications companies as line installers or telephone installers, before moving up to the job of central office installer and other more complex work.

Newly hired repairers usually receive some training from their employers. This may include formal classroom training in electronics, communications systems, or software and informal hands-on training assisting an experienced repairer. Large companies may send repairers to outside training sessions to keep them informed about new equipment and service procedures. As networks have become more sophisticated—often including equipment from a variety of companies—the knowledge needed for installation and maintenance also has increased.

Telecommunications equipment companies provide much of the training on specific equipment. With the rapid advances in switches, routers, and other equipment, repairers need to continually take courses and work to obtain manufacturers' certifications on the latest technology.

Repairers must be able to distinguish colors, because wires are color-coded, and they must be able to hear distinctions in the various tones on a telephone system. For positions that require climbing poles and towers, workers must be in good physical shape. Repairers who handle assignments alone at a customer's site must be able to work without close supervision. For workers who frequently contact customers, a pleasant personality, neat appearance, and good communications skills also are important.

Experienced repairers with advanced training may become specialists or troubleshooters who help other repairers diagnose difficult problems, or may work with engineers in designing equipment and developing maintenance procedures. Because of their familiarity with equipment, repairers are particularly well qualified to become manufacturers' sales workers. Workers with leadership ability also may become maintenance supervisors or service managers. Some experienced workers open their own repair services or shops, or become wholesalers or retailers of electronic equipment.

Employment

Radio and telecommunications equipment installers and repairers held about 222,000 jobs in 2004. About 215,000 were telecommunications equipment installers and repairers, except line installers, mostly working in the telecommunications industry, and the rest were radio mechanics. Radio mechanics worked in electronic and precision equipment repair and maintenance, telecommunications, electronics and appliance stores, and many other industries.

Job Outlook

Employment of radio and telecommunications equipment installers and repairers is expected to decline through 2014. Although the need for installation work will remain as companies seek to upgrade their telecommunications networks, there will be a declining need for maintenance work—performed by telecommunications equipment installers and repairers, except line installers—because of increasingly reliable self-monitoring and self-diagnosing equipment and because installation of higher capacity equipment will reduce the amount of equipment needed. The replacement of two-way radio systems with wireless systems, especially in service vehicles, will eliminate the need in many companies for onsite radio mechanics. The increased reliability of wireless equipment and the use of self-monitoring systems also will continue to lessen the need for radio mechanics. Applicants with computer skills and postsecondary electronics training should have the best opportunities for radio and telecommunications equipment installer and repairer jobs.

Job opportunities will vary by specialty. For example, good opportunities should be available for central office and PBX installers and repairers experienced in current technology, as the growing popularity of VoIP, expanded multimedia offerings such as video on demand, and other telecommunications services continue to place additional demand on telecommunications networks. These new services require high data transfer rates, which can be achieved only by installing new optical switching and routing equipment. Extending high-speed communications from central offices to customers also will require the installation of more advanced switching and routing equipment. Whereas increased reliability and automation of switching equipment will limit opportunities, these effects will be somewhat offset by the demand for installation and upgrading of switching equipment.

Station installers and repairers can expect keen competition. Prewired buildings and the increasing reliability of telephone equipment will reduce the need for installation and maintenance of customers' telephones. Upgrading internal lines in businesses and the wiring of new homes and businesses with fiber optic lines should offset some of these losses. As cellular telephones have increased in popularity, the number of pay phones is declining, which also will adversely affect employment of station installers and repairers as pay phone installation and maintenance is one of their major functions.

Earnings

In May 2004, median hourly earnings of telecommunications equipment installers and repairers, except line installers were $23.96. The middle 50 percent earned between $19.46 and $27.07. The bottom 10 percent earned less than $14.65, whereas the top 10 percent earned more than $30.85. The median hourly earnings of these workers in the wired telecommunications carriers (telephone) industry were $24.92 in May 2004.

Median hourly earnings of radio mechanics in May 2004 were $17.65. The middle 50 percent earned between $13.59 and $21.90. The bottom 10 percent earned less than $10.42, whereas the top 10 percent earned more than $27.62.

Related Occupations

Related occupations that involve work with electronic equipment include broadcast and sound engineering technicians and radio operators; computer, automated teller, and office machine repairers; electronic home entertainment equipment installers and repairers; and electrical and electronics installers and repairers. Line installers and repairers also set up and install telecommunications equipment. Engineering technicians also may repair electronic equipment as part of their duties.

Sources of Additional Information

For information on career and training opportunities, contact:
➤ International Brotherhood of Electrical Workers, Telecommunications Department, 1125 15th St. NW., Room 807, Washington, DC 20005.
➤ Communications Workers of America, 501 3rd St. NW., Washington, DC 20001.

For information on training and professional certifications for those already employed by cable telecommunications firms, contact:
➤ Society of Cable Telecommunications Engineers, Certification Department, 140 Phillips Rd., Exton, PA 19341-1318.   Internet: http://www.scte.org

Vehicle and Mobile Equipment Mechanics, Installers, and Repairers

Aircraft and Avionics Equipment Mechanics and Service Technicians

(O*NET 49-2091.00, 49-3011.01, 49-3011.02, 49-3011.03)

Significant Points

● Most workers learn their job in 1 of about 170 schools certified by the Federal Aviation Administration (FAA).

● Job opportunities should be excellent for persons who have completed an aircraft mechanic training program, but keen competition is likely for the best paying airline jobs.

● Job opportunities are likely to be the best at small commuter and regional airlines, at FAA repair stations, and in general aviation.

Nature of the Work

To keep aircraft in peak operating condition, aircraft and avionics equipment mechanics and service technicians perform scheduled maintenance, make repairs, and complete inspections required by the Federal Aviation Administration (FAA).

Many aircraft mechanics, also called airframe mechanics, power plant mechanics, and avionics technicians, specialize in preventive maintenance. They inspect aircraft engines, landing gear, instruments, pressurized sections, accessories—brakes, valves, pumps, and air-conditioning systems, for example—and other parts of the aircraft, and do the necessary maintenance and replacement of parts. They also maintain records related to the maintenance performed on the aircraft. Mechanics and technicians conduct inspections following a schedule based on the number of hours the aircraft has flown, calendar days since the last inspection, cycles of operation, or a combination of these factors. In large, sophisticated planes equipped with aircraft monitoring systems, mechanics can gather valuable diagnostic information from electronic boxes and consoles that monitor the aircraft's basic operations. In planes of all sorts, aircraft mechanics examine engines by working through specially designed openings while standing on ladders or scaffolds or by using hoists or lifts to remove the entire engine from the craft. After taking an engine apart, mechanics use precision instruments to measure parts for wear and use x-ray and magnetic inspection equipment to check for invisible cracks. They repair or replace worn or defective parts. Mechanics also may repair sheet metal or composite surfaces; measure the tension of control cables; and check for corrosion, distortion, and cracks in the fuselage, wings, and tail. After completing all repairs, they must test the equipment to ensure that it works properly.

Mechanics specializing in repair work rely on the pilot's description of a problem to find and fix faulty equipment. For example, during a preflight check, a pilot may discover that the aircraft's fuel gauge does not work. To solve the problem, mechanics may troubleshoot the electrical system, using electrical test equipment to make sure that no wires are broken or shorted out, and replace any defective electrical or electronic components. Mechanics work as fast as safety permits so that the aircraft can be put back into service quickly.

Some mechanics work on one or many different types of aircraft, such as jets, propeller-driven airplanes, and helicopters. Others specialize in one section of a particular type of aircraft, such as the engine, hydraulics, or electrical system. *Airframe mechanics* are authorized to work on any part of the aircraft except the instruments, power plants, and propellers. *Powerplant mechanics* are authorized to work on engines and do limited work on propellers. *Combination airframe-and-powerplant mechanics*—called A&P mechanics—work on all parts of the plane except the instruments. Most mechanics working on civilian aircraft today are A&P mechanics. In small, independent repair shops, mechanics usually inspect and repair many different types of aircraft.

Avionics systems are now an integral part of aircraft design and have vastly increased aircraft capability. *Avionics technicians* repair and maintain components used for aircraft navigation and radio communications, weather radar systems, and other instruments and computers that control flight, engine, and other primary functions. These duties may require additional licenses, such as a radiotelephone license issued by the U.S. Federal Communications Commission (FCC). Because of the increasing use of technology, more time is spent repairing electronic systems, such as computerized controls. Technicians also may be required to analyze and develop solutions to complex electronic problems.

Working Conditions

Mechanics usually work in hangars or in other indoor areas. When hangars are full or when repairs must be made quickly, they can work outdoors, sometimes in unpleasant weather. Mechanics often work under time pressure to maintain flight schedules or, in general aviation, to keep from inconveniencing customers. At the same time, mechanics have a tremendous responsibility to maintain safety standards, and this can cause the job to be stressful.

Frequently, mechanics must lift or pull objects weighing more than 70 pounds. They often stand, lie, or kneel in awkward positions and occasionally must work in precarious positions, such as on scaffolds or ladders. Noise and vibration are common when engines are being tested, so ear protection is necessary. Aircraft mechanics

Many aircraft mechanics specialize in preventive maintenance by inspecting aircraft engines, landing gear, instruments, pressurized sections, accessories, and other parts of the aircraft.

usually work 40 hours a week on 8-hour shifts around the clock. Overtime work is frequent.

Training, Other Qualifications, and Advancement

Most mechanics who work on civilian aircraft are certified by the FAA as an "airframe mechanic" or a "powerplant mechanic." Mechanics who also have an inspector's authorization can certify work completed by other mechanics and perform required inspections. Uncertified mechanics are supervised by those with certificates.

The FAA requires at least 18 months of work experience for an airframe or powerplant certificate. For a combined A&P certificate, at least 30 months of experience working with both engines and airframes is required. Completion of a program at an FAA-certified mechanic school can substitute for the work experience requirement. Applicants for all certificates also must pass written and oral tests and demonstrate that they can do the work authorized by the certificate. To obtain an inspector's authorization, a mechanic must have held an A&P certificate for at least 3 years, with 24 months of hands on experience. Most airlines require that mechanics have a high school diploma and an A&P certificate.

Although a few people become mechanics through on-the-job training, most learn their job in 1 of about 170 trade schools certified by the FAA. About one-third of these schools award 2-year and 4-year degrees in avionics, aviation technology, or aviation maintenance management.

FAA standards established by law require that certified mechanic schools offer students a minimum of 1,900 actual class hours. Coursework in schools normally lasts from 18 to 24 months and provides training with the tools and equipment used on the job. Aircraft trade schools are placing more emphasis on technologies such as turbine engines, composite materials—including graphite, fiberglass, and boron—and aviation electronics, which are increasingly being used in the construction of new aircraft. Additionally, employers prefer mechanics who can perform a variety of tasks.

Some aircraft mechanics in the Armed Forces acquire enough general experience to satisfy the work experience requirements for the FAA certificate. With additional study, they may pass the certifying exam. In general, however, jobs in the military services are too specialized to provide the broad experience required by the FAA. Most Armed Forces mechanics have to complete the entire training program, although a few receive some credit for the material they learned in the service. In any case, military experience is a great advantage when seeking employment; employers consider applicants with formal training to be the most desirable applicants.

Courses in mathematics, physics, chemistry, electronics, computer science, and mechanical drawing are helpful because they demonstrate many of the principles involved in the operation of aircraft, and knowledge of these principles is often necessary to make repairs. Courses that develop writing skills also are important because mechanics are often required to submit reports.

FAA regulations require current work experience to keep the A&P certificate valid. Applicants must have at least 1,000 hours of work experience in the previous 24 months or take a refresher course. As new and more complex aircraft are designed, more employers are requiring mechanics to take ongoing training to update their skills. Recent technological advances in aircraft maintenance necessitate a strong background in electronics—both for acquiring and for retaining jobs in this field. FAA certification standards also make ongoing training mandatory. Every 24 months, mechanics are required to take at least 16 hours of training to keep their certificate. Many mechanics take courses offered by manufacturers or employers, usually through outside contractors.

Aircraft mechanics must do careful and thorough work that requires a high degree of mechanical aptitude. Employers seek applicants who are self-motivated, hard working, enthusiastic, and able to diagnose and solve complex mechanical problems. Agility is important for the reaching and climbing necessary to do the job. Because they may work on the tops of wings and fuselages on large jet planes, aircraft mechanics must not be afraid of heights.

Advances in computer technology, aircraft systems, and the materials used to manufacture airplanes have made mechanics' jobs more highly technical. Aircraft mechanics must possess the skills necessary to troubleshoot and diagnose complex aircraft systems. They also must continually update their skills with and knowledge of new technology and advances in aircraft technology.

As aircraft mechanics gain experience, they may advance to lead mechanic (or crew chief), inspector, lead inspector, or shop supervisor positions. Opportunities are best for those who have an aircraft inspector's authorization. In the airlines, where promotion often is determined by examination, supervisors sometimes advance to executive positions. Those with broad experience in maintenance and overhaul might become inspectors with the FAA. With additional business and management training, some open their own aircraft maintenance facilities. Mechanics learn many different skills in their training that can be applied to other jobs, and some transfer to other skilled repairer occupations or electronics technician jobs. Mechanics with the necessary pilot licenses and flying experience may take the FAA examination for the position of flight engineer, with opportunities to become pilots.

Employment

Aircraft and avionics equipment mechanics and service technicians held about 142,000 jobs in 2004; about 5 in 6 of these workers was an aircraft mechanic and service technician. More than half of aircraft and avionics equipment mechanics and service technicians worked for air transportation companies. About 18 percent worked for the Federal Government, and about 14 percent worked for aerospace products and parts manufacturing firms. Most of the rest worked for companies that operate their own planes to transport executives and cargo. Few mechanics and technicians were self-employed.

Most airline mechanics and service technicians work at major airports near large cities. Civilian mechanics employed by the U.S. Armed Forces work at military installations. Mechanics who work for aerospace manufacturing firms typically are located in California or in Washington State. Others work for the FAA, many at the facilities in Oklahoma City, Atlantic City, Wichita, or Washington, DC. Mechanics for independent repair shops work at airports in every part of the country.

Job Outlook

Opportunities for aircraft and avionics equipment mechanics and service technicians should be excellent for who have completed aircraft mechanic training programs. Employment is expected to increase about as fast as the average for all occupations through the year 2014, and large numbers of additional job openings should arise from the need to replace experienced mechanics who retire.

Reduced passenger traffic—resulting from a weak economy and the events of September 11, 2001—forced airlines to cut back flights and take aircraft out of service. However, over the next decade passenger traffic is expected to increase as the result of an expanding economy and a growing population, and the need for aircraft mechanics and service technicians will grow accordingly. Furthermore, if the number of graduates from aircraft mechanic training programs continues to fall short of employer needs, opportunities for graduates of mechanic training programs should be excellent.

Most job openings for aircraft mechanics through the year 2014 will stem from replacement needs. Many mechanics are expected to retire over the next decade and create several thousand job openings

per year. In addition, others will leave to work in related fields, such as automobile repair, as their skills are largely transferable to other maintenance and repair occupations. Also contributing to favorable future job opportunities for mechanics is the long-term trend toward fewer students entering technical schools to learn skilled maintenance and repair trades. Many of the students who have the ability and aptitude to work on planes are choosing to go to college, work in computer-related fields, or go into other repair and maintenance occupations with better working conditions. If the trend continues, the supply of trained aviation mechanics will not be able to keep up with the needs of the air transportation industry.

Job opportunities are likely to be the best at small commuter and regional airlines, at FAA repair stations, and in general aviation. Commuter and regional airlines are the fastest growing segment of the air transportation industry, but wages in these companies tend to be lower than those in the major airlines, so they attract fewer job applicants. Also, some jobs will become available as experienced mechanics leave for higher paying jobs with the major airlines or transfer to another occupation. At the same time, general aviation aircraft are becoming increasingly sophisticated, boosting the demand for qualified mechanics. Mechanics will face more competition for jobs with large airlines because the high wages and travel benefits that these jobs offer generally attract more qualified applicants than there are openings. Also, there is an increasing trend for large airlines to outsource aircraft and avionics equipment mechanic jobs overseas; however, most airline companies prefer maintenance work done on aircraft be performed in the U.S. because of safety and regulation issues of overseas contractors.

In spite of these factors, job opportunities with the airlines are expected to be better than they have been in the past. But, in general, prospects will be best for applicants with experience. Mechanics who keep abreast of technological advances in electronics, composite materials, and other areas will be in greatest demand. Also, mechanics who are mobile and willing to relocate to smaller rural areas will have better job opportunities. The number of job openings for aircraft mechanics in the Federal Government should decline as the government increasingly contracts out service and repair functions to private repair companies.

Job opportunities for avionics technicians who are prepared to master the intricacies of the aircraft and work with A&P mechanics are expected to be good. Technicians who are cross-trained and able to work with complex aircraft systems should have the best job prospects. Additionally, technicians with licensing that enables them to work on the airplane, either removing or reinstalling equipment, are expected to be in especially high demand.

Earnings

Median hourly earnings of aircraft mechanics and service technicians were about $21.77 in May 2004. The middle 50 percent earned between $17.82 and $27.18. The lowest 10 percent earned less than $13.99, and the highest 10 percent earned more than $33.84. Median hourly earnings in the industries employing the largest numbers of aircraft mechanics and service technicians in May 2004 were:

Scheduled air transportation	$27.37
Federal Government	21.67
Nonscheduled air transportation	20.88
Aerospace product and parts manufacturing	20.60
Support activities for air transportation	18.70

Median hourly earnings of avionics technicians were about $21.30 in May 2004. The middle 50 percent earned between $18.12 and $25.12. The lowest 10 percent earned less than $14.63, and the highest 10 percent earned more than $27.85.

Mechanics who work on jets for the major airlines generally earn more than those working on other aircraft. Airline mechanics and their immediate families receive reduced-fare transportation on their own and most other airlines.

About 4 in 10 aircraft and avionics equipment mechanics and service technicians are members of unions or covered by union agreements. The principal unions are the International Association of Machinists and Aerospace Workers, and the Transport Workers Union of America. Some mechanics are represented by the International Brotherhood of Teamsters.

Related Occupations

Workers in some other occupations that involve similar mechanical and electrical work are electricians, electrical and electronics installers and repairers, and elevator installers and repairers.

Sources of Additional Information

Information about jobs with a particular airline can be obtained by writing to the personnel manager of the company.

For general information about aircraft and avionics equipment mechanics and service technicians, contact:

➤ Professional Aviation Maintenance Association, 717 Princess St., Alexandria, VA 22314. Internet: **http://www.pama.org**

For information on jobs in a particular area, contact employers at local airports or local offices of the State employment service.

Information on obtaining positions as aircraft and avionics equipment mechanics and service technicians with the Federal Government is available from the Office of Personnel Management through USA-JOBS, the Federal Government's official employment information system. This resource for locating and applying for job opportunities can be accessed through the Internet at **http://www.usajobs.opm.gov** or through an interactive voice response telephone system at (703) 724-1850 or TDD (978) 461-8404. These numbers are not tollfree, and charges may result.

Automotive Body and Related Repairers

(O*NET 49-3021.00, 49-3022.00)

Significant Points

- To become a fully skilled automotive body repairer, formal training followed by on-the-job instruction is recommended because repair of newer automobiles require more advanced skills to fix their new technologies and new body materials.

- Repairers need good reading ability and basic mathematics and computer skills in order to follow instructions and diagrams in print and computer-based technical manuals.

Nature of the Work

While running errands or driving to and from work, we sometimes observe traffic accidents. Most of the vehicle damage resulting from these collisions can be repaired and the vehicle refinished to once again look and drive like new. Automotive body repairers, also often called collision repair technicians, straighten bent bodies, remove dents, and replace crumpled parts that cannot be fixed. They repair all types of vehicles, and although some work on large trucks, buses, or tractor-trailers, most work on cars and small trucks.

Automotive body repairers use special equipment to restore damaged metal frames and body sections. Repairers chain or clamp frames and sections to alignment machines that use hydraulic pressure to align damaged components. "Unibody" vehicles—designs built without frames—must be restored to precise factory specifications for the vehicle to operate correctly. To do so, repairers use benchmark systems to make accurate measurements of how much each section is out of alignment, and hydraulic machinery to return the vehicle to its original shape.

Body repairers remove badly damaged sections of body panels with a pneumatic metal-cutting gun or by other means, and then weld in replacement sections. Repairers pull out less serious dents with a hydraulic jack or hand prying bar or knock them out with handtools or pneumatic hammers. They smooth out small dents and creases in the metal by holding a small anvil against one side of the damaged area while hammering the opposite side. Repairers also remove very small pits and dimples with pick hammers and punches in a process called metal finishing. Body repairers use plastic or solder to fill small dents that cannot be worked out of plastic or metal panels. On metal panels, they file or grind the hardened filler to the original shape and clean the surface with a media blaster before repainting the damaged portion of the vehicle.

Body repairers also repair or replace the plastic body parts that are increasingly being used on new-model vehicles. They remove damaged panels and identify the type and properties of the plastic used on the vehicle. With most types of plastic, repairers can apply heat from a hot-air welding gun or by immersion in hot water and press the softened panel back into its original shape by hand. They replace plastic parts that are badly damaged or very difficult to repair. A few body repairers specialize in repairing fiberglass car bodies.

The advent of assembly line repairs in large shops enables the establishment to move away from the one-vehicle, one-repairer method to a team approach that allows body repairers to specialize in one type of repair, such as straightening frames, repairing doors and fenders, or painting and refinishing. In most shops, automotive painters do the painting. (These workers are discussed in the section on painting and coating workers, except construction and maintenance elsewhere in the *Handbook*.) However, in small shops, workers often do both body repairing and painting. Some body repairers specialize in installing and repairing glass in automobiles and other vehicles. *Automotive glass installers and repairers* remove broken, cracked, or pitted windshields and window glass. Glass installers apply a moisture-proofing compound along the edges of the glass, place the

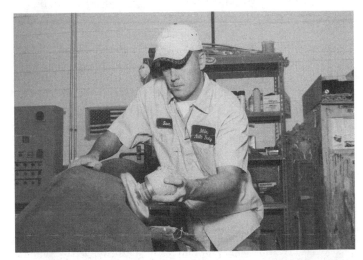

After a collision, automotive body repairers straighten, align, buff, or otherwise finish damaged parts.

glass in the vehicle, and install rubber strips around the sides of the windshield or window to make it secure and weatherproof.

Body repair work has variety and challenges: each damaged vehicle presents a different problem. Using their broad knowledge of automotive construction and repair techniques, repairers must develop appropriate methods for each job. They usually work alone, with only general directions from supervisors. In some shops, helpers or apprentices assist experienced repairers.

Working Conditions

Most automotive body repairers work a standard 40-hour week, although some, including the self-employed, work more than 40 hours a week. Repairers work indoors in body shops that are noisy with the clatters of hammers against metal and the whine of power tools. Most shops are well ventilated, in order to disperse dust and paint fumes. Body repairers often work in awkward or cramped positions, and much of their work is strenuous and dirty. Hazards include cuts from sharp metal edges, burns from torches and heated metal, injuries from power tools, and fumes from paint. However, serious accidents usually are avoided when the shop is kept clean and orderly and safety practices are observed.

Training, Other Qualifications, and Advancement

Automotive technology is rapidly increasing in sophistication, and most training authorities strongly recommend that persons seeking automotive body repair and related jobs complete a formal training program in automotive body repair or refinishing. Programs are offered in high school or in postsecondary vocational schools and community colleges, but these programs provide only a portion of the training needed to become fully skilled. Most new repairers receive primarily on-the-job training, supplemented with short-term training sessions given by vehicle, parts, and equipment manufacturers, when available. Training is necessary because advances in technology have greatly changed the structure, components, and materials used in automobiles. As a result, proficiency in new repair techniques is necessary. For example, the bodies of automobiles are usually a combination of materials—traditional steel, aluminum, and a growing variety of metal alloys and plastics. Each of these materials or composites requires the use of somewhat different techniques to reshape parts and smooth out dents and small pits.

Fully skilled automotive body repairers must have good reading ability and basic mathematics and computer skills. Restoring unibody automobiles to their original form requires body repairers to follow instructions and diagrams in technical manuals in order to make precise three-dimensional measurements of the position of one body section relative to another.

New repairers begin by assisting experienced body repairers in tasks such as removing damaged parts, sanding body panels, and installing repaired parts. Novices learn to remove small dents and to make other minor repairs. They then progress to more difficult tasks, such as straightening body parts and returning them to their correct alignment. Generally, to become skilled in all aspects of body repair requires 3 to 4 years of on-the-job training.

Certification by the National Institute for Automotive Service Excellence (ASE), although voluntary, is the recognized industry credential for automotive body repairers. Repairers may take from one to four ASE Master Collision Repair and Refinish Exams. Repairers who pass at least one exam and have 2 years of hands-on work experience earn ASE certification. The completion of a postsecondary program in automotive body repair may be substituted for 1 year of work experience. Those who pass all four exams become ASE Master Collision Repair and Refinish Technicians. Automotive body repairers must retake the examination at least every 5 years to retain their certification. While the ASE designations are

the most widely recognized, many vehicle manufacturers and paint manufacturers also have product certification programs available for body repairers.

Continuing education is required throughout a career in automotive body repair. Automotive parts, body materials, and electronics continue to change and to become more complex and technologically advanced. To keep up with the technological advances, repairers must continue to gain new skills, read technical manuals, and attend seminars and classes. Many companies within the automotive body repair industry provide ongoing training for workers.

As beginners increase their skills, learn new techniques, and complete work more rapidly, their pay increases. An experienced automotive body repairer with managerial ability may advance to shop supervisor. Some workers even open their own body repair shops. Others become automobile damage appraisers for insurance companies.

Employment

Automotive body and related repairers held about 223,000 jobs in 2004; about 1 in 10 specialized in automotive glass installation and repair. Most repairers worked for automotive repair and maintenance shops or automobile dealers. Others worked for organizations that maintain their own motor vehicles, such as trucking companies. A small number worked for wholesalers of motor vehicles, parts, and supplies. More than 1 automotive body repairer in 5 was self-employed, more than double the proportion for all installation, maintenance, and repair occupations.

Job Outlook

Employment of automotive body repairers is expected to grow as fast as average for all occupations through the year 2014. The need to replace experienced repairers who transfer to other occupations or who retire or stop working for other reasons will account for the majority of job openings. Opportunities will be best for persons with formal training in automotive body repair and refinishing. Those without formal training in automotive body refinishing or collision repair will face competition for these jobs.

Demand for qualified body repairers will increase as the number of motor vehicles in operation continues to grow in line with the Nation's population. With each rise in the number of motor vehicles in use, the number of vehicles damaged in accidents also will grow. New automobile designs increasingly have body parts made of steel alloys, aluminum, and plastics—materials that are more difficult to work with than are traditional steel body parts. In addition, new automotive designs of lighter weight are prone to greater collision damage than are older, heavier designs, so more time is consumed in repair.

However, increasing demand due to growth in the number of vehicles in operation will be somewhat tempered by improvements in the quality of vehicles and technological innovations that enhance safety and reduce the likelihood of accidents. Also, more body parts are simply being replaced rather than repaired. Larger shops also are instituting productivity enhancements, such as employing a team approach to repairs to decrease repair time and expand their volume of work. In addition, demand for automotive body repair services will be constrained as more vehicles are declared a total loss after accidents. In many such cases, the vehicles are not repaired because of the high cost of replacing the increasingly complex parts and electronic components and fixing the extensive damage that results when airbags deploy. Employment growth will continue to be concentrated in automotive body, paint, interior, and glass repair shops. Automobile dealers will employ a smaller portion of this occupation as the equipment needed for collision repair becomes more specialized and expensive to operate and maintain.

Experienced body repairers are rarely laid off during a general slowdown in the economy. Automotive repair business is not very sensitive to changes in economic conditions because major body damage must be repaired if a vehicle is to be restored to safe operating condition. However, repair of minor dents and crumpled fenders often can be deferred when drivers' budgets become tight.

Earnings

Median hourly earnings of automotive body and related repairers, including incentive pay, were $16.68 in May 2004. The middle 50 percent earned between $12.55 and $22.04 an hour. The lowest 10 percent earned less than $9.42, and the highest 10 percent earned more than $28.45 an hour. In May 2004, median hourly earnings of automotive body and related repairers were $17.73 in automobile dealers and $16.44 in automotive repair and maintenance.

Median hourly earnings of automotive glass installers and repairers, including incentive pay, were $13.45 in May 2004. The middle 50 percent earned between $10.36 and $17.04 an hour. The lowest 10 percent earned less than $8.53, and the highest 10 percent earned more than $20.63 an hour. Median hourly earnings in automotive repair and maintenance shops, the industry employing most automotive glass installers and repairers, were $13.43.

The majority of body repairers employed by independent repair shops and automotive dealers are paid on an incentive basis. Under this method, body repairers are paid a predetermined amount for various tasks, and earnings depend on the amount of work assigned to the repairer and how fast it is completed. Employers frequently guarantee workers a minimum weekly salary. Body repairers who work for trucking companies, buslines, and other organizations that maintain their own vehicles usually receive an hourly wage.

Helpers and trainees typically earn from 30 percent to 60 percent of the earnings of skilled workers. Helpers and trainees usually receive an hourly rate until they are skilled enough to be paid on an incentive basis.

Related Occupations

Repairing damaged motor vehicles often involves working on mechanical components, as well as vehicle bodies. Automotive body repairers often work closely with individuals in several related occupations, including automotive service technicians and mechanics, diesel service technicians and mechanics, auto damage insurance appraisers, and painting and coating workers, except construction and maintenance.

Sources of Additional Information

Additional details about work opportunities may be obtained from automotive body repair shops, automobile dealers, or local offices of your State employment service. State employment service offices also are a source of information about training programs.

For general information about automotive body repairer careers, contact any of the following sources:
➤ Automotive Service Association, P.O. Box 929, Bedford, Texas 76095-0929. Internet: **http://www.asashop.org**
➤ National Automobile Dealers Association, 8400 Westpark Dr., McLean, VA 22102. Internet: **http://www.nada.org**
➤ Inter-Industry Conference On Auto Collision Repair Education Foundation (I-CAR), 5125 Trillium Blvd., Hoffman Estates, IL 60192. Telephone (tollfree): 800-422-7872.
➤ Automotive Jobs Today, 8400 Westpark Drive, MS #2, McLean, VA 22102. Internet: **http://www.autojobstoday.org**
For general information about careers in automotive glass installation and repair, contact:
➤ National Glass Association. 8200 Greensboro Drive, Suite 302, McLean, VA 22102-3881. Internet: **http://www.glass.org**

For information on how to become a certified automotive body repairer, write to:
➤ National Institute for Automotive Service Excellence (ASE), 101 Blue Seal Dr. SE., Suite 101, Leesburg, VA 20175. Internet: **http://www.asecert.org**
For a directory of certified automotive body repairer programs, contact:
➤ National Automotive Technician Education Foundation, 101 Blue Seal Dr., SE., Suite 101, Leesburg, VA 20175. Internet: **http://www.natef.org**
For a directory of accredited private trade and technical schools that offer training programs in automotive body repair, contact:
➤ Accrediting Commission of Career Schools and Colleges of Technology, 2101 Wilson Blvd., Suite 302, Arlington, VA 22201. Internet: **http://www.accsct.org**

Automotive Service Technicians and Mechanics

(O*NET 49-3023.01, 49-3023.02)

Significant Points

- Formal automotive technician training is the best preparation for these challenging technology-based jobs.
- Opportunities should be very good for automotive service technicians and mechanics with diagnostic and problem-solving skills, knowledge of electronics and mathematics, and mechanical aptitude.
- Automotive service technicians and mechanics must continually adapt to changing technology and repair techniques as vehicle components and systems become increasingly sophisticated.

Nature of the Work

Anyone whose car or light truck has broken down knows the importance of the jobs of automotive service technicians and mechanics. The ability to diagnose the source of a problem quickly and accurately requires good reasoning ability and a thorough knowledge of automobiles. Many technicians consider diagnosing hard-to-find troubles one of their most challenging and satisfying duties.

The work of automotive service technicians and mechanics has evolved from mechanical repair to a high technology job. As a result, these workers are now usually called "technicians" in automotive services and the term "mechanic" is falling into disuse. Today, integrated electronic systems and complex computers run vehicles and measure their performance while on the road. Technicians must have an increasingly broad base of knowledge about how vehicles' complex components work and interact, as well as the ability to work with electronic diagnostic equipment and computer-based technical reference materials.

Automotive service technicians use their high-tech skills to inspect, maintain, and repair automobiles and light trucks that run on gasoline, ethanol and other alternative fuels, such as electricity. The increasing sophistication of automotive technology now requires workers who can use computerized shop equipment and work with electronic components while maintaining their skills with traditional hand tools. (Service technicians who work on diesel-powered trucks, buses, and equipment are discussed in the *Handbook* section on diesel service technicians and mechanics. Motorcycle technicians—who repair and service motorcycles, motor scooters, mopeds, and, occasionally, small all-terrain vehicles—are discussed in the *Handbook* section on small engine mechanics.)

When mechanical or electrical troubles occur, technicians first get a description of the symptoms from the owner or, if they work in a large shop, from the repair service estimator or service advisor who wrote the repair order. To locate the problem, technicians use a diagnostic approach. First, they test to see whether components and systems are proper and secure. Then, they isolate the components or systems that could not logically be the cause of the problem. For example, if an air-conditioner malfunctions, the technician's diagnostic approach can pinpoint a problem as simple as a low coolant level or as complex as a bad drive-train connection that has shorted out the air conditioner. Technicians may have to test drive the vehicle or use a variety of testing equipment, such as onboard and hand-held diagnostic computers or compression gauges, to identify the source of the problem. These tests may indicate whether a component is salvageable or whether a new one is required to get the vehicle back in working order.

During routine service inspections, technicians test and lubricate engines and other major components. In some cases, the technician may repair or replace worn parts before they cause breakdowns that could damage critical components of the vehicle. Technicians usually follow a checklist to ensure that they examine every critical part. Belts, hoses, plugs, brake and fuel systems, and other potentially troublesome items are among those closely watched.

Service technicians use a variety of tools in their work—power tools, such as pneumatic wrenches to remove bolts quickly; machine tools like lathes and grinding machines to rebuild brakes; welding and flame-cutting equipment to remove and repair exhaust systems, and jacks and hoists to lift cars and engines. They also use common hand tools, such as screwdrivers, pliers, and wrenches, to work on small parts and in hard-to-reach places.

Computers also have become commonplace in modern repair shops. Service technicians compare the readouts from computerized diagnostic testing devices with the benchmarked standards given by the manufacturer of the components being tested. Deviations outside of acceptable levels are an indication to the technician that further attention to an area is necessary. A shop's computerized system provides automatic updates to technical manuals and unlimited access to manufacturers' service information, technical service bulletins, and other databases that allow technicians to keep current on problem spots and to learn new procedures.

Automotive service technicians in large shops have increasingly become specialized. For example, *transmission technicians and rebuilders* work on gear trains, couplings, hydraulic pumps, and other parts of transmissions. Extensive knowledge of computer controls, the ability to diagnose electrical and hydraulic problems, and other specialized skills are needed to work on these complex components, which employ some of the most sophisticated technology used in vehicles. *Tuneup technicians* adjust the ignition timing and valves, and adjust or replace spark plugs and other parts to ensure efficient engine performance. They often use electronic testing equipment to isolate and adjust malfunctions in fuel, ignition, and emissions control systems.

Automotive air-conditioning repairers install and repair air-conditioners and service their components, such as compressors, condensers, and controls. These workers require special training in Federal and State regulations governing the handling and disposal of refrigerants. *Front-end mechanics* align and balance wheels and repair steering mechanisms and suspension systems. They frequently use special alignment equipment and wheel-balancing machines. *Brake repairers* adjust brakes, replace brake linings and pads, and make other repairs on brake systems. Some technicians specialize in both brake and front-end work. Even though electronics and electronic systems in automobiles were a specialty in the past, electronics are now so common that it is essential for all types of service technicians to be familiar with at least the basic principles of electronics.

Service technicians can specialize in several types of automotive repair, including brake repair.

Working Conditions

Nearly half of automotive service technicians work more than 40 hours a week. Some may also work evenings and weekends to satisfy customer service needs. Generally, service technicians work indoors in well-ventilated and -lighted repair shops. However, some shops are drafty and noisy. Although some problems can be fixed with simple computerized adjustments, technicians frequently work with dirty and greasy parts, and in awkward positions. They often lift heavy parts and tools. Minor cuts, burns, and bruises are common, but technicians can usually avoid serious accidents if the shop is kept clean and orderly, and safety practices are observed.

Training, Other Qualifications, and Advancement

Automotive technology is rapidly increasing in sophistication, and most training authorities strongly recommend that persons seeking automotive service technician and mechanic jobs complete a formal training program in high school, or in a postsecondary vocational school or community college. However, some service technicians still learn the trade solely by assisting and learning from experienced workers. Courses in automotive repair, electronics, physics, chemistry, English, computers, and mathematics provide a good educational background for a career as a service technician.

High school programs, while an asset, vary greatly in scope. Some aim to equip graduates with enough skills to get a job as a technician's helper or trainee technician. Other programs offer only an introduction to automotive technology and service for the future consumer or hobbyist. Some of the more extensive programs participate in Automotive Youth Education Service (AYES), which has about 500 participating schools and more than 4000 participating dealers. Students who complete these programs receive an AYES certification and upon high school graduation are better prepared to enter entry-level technician positions, or to advance their technical education.

Postsecondary automotive technician training programs vary greatly in format, but normally provide intensive career preparation through a combination of classroom instruction and hands-on practice. Some trade and technical school programs provide concentrated training for 6 months to a year, depending on how many hours the student attends each week, and award a certificate. Community college programs normally award an associate degree or certificate and usually spread the training over 2 years by supplementing the automotive training with instruction in English, basic mathematics, computers, and other subjects. Some students earn repair certificates in one particular skill and opt to leave the program to begin their career before graduation. Recently, some programs have added to their curriculums training on employability skills such as customer service and stress management. Employers find that these skills help technicians handle the additional responsibilities of dealing with the customers and parts vendors.

The various automobile manufacturers and their participating dealers sponsor 2-year associate degree programs at postsecondary schools across the Nation. The Accrediting Commission of Career Schools and Colleges of Technology (ACCSCT) currently certifies a number of automotive and diesel technology schools. Schools update their curriculums frequently to reflect changing technology and equipment. Students in these programs typically spend alternate 6- to 12-week periods attending classes full time and working full time in the service departments of sponsoring dealers. At these dealerships, students get practical experience while assigned to an experienced worker who provides hands-on instruction and timesaving tips.

The ASE certification is a nationally recognized standard for programs offered by high schools, postsecondary trade schools, technical institutes, and community colleges that train automobile service technicians. Some automotive manufacturers provide ASE-certified instruction programs with service equipment and current-model cars on which students practice new skills and learn the latest automotive technology. While ASE certification is voluntary, it does signify that the program meets uniform standards for instructional facilities, equipment, staff credentials, and curriculum. To ensure that programs keep up with ever-changing technology, repair techniques, and ASE standards, the certified programs are subjected to periodic compliance reviews and mandatory recertification, as are the ASE standards themselves. In 2004, about 2000 high school and postsecondary automotive service technician training programs had been certified by ASE.

For trainee automotive service technician jobs, employers look for people with strong communication and analytical skills. Technicians need good reading, mathematics, and computer skills to study technical manuals and to keep abreast of new technology and learn new service and repair procedures and specifications. Trainees also must possess mechanical aptitude and knowledge of how automobiles work. Most employers regard the successful completion of a vocational training program in automotive service technology as the best preparation for trainee positions. Experience working on motor vehicles in the Armed Forces or as a hobby also is valuable. Because of the complexity of new vehicles, a growing number of employers require completion of high school and additional postsecondary training.

Many new cars have several onboard computers, operating everything from the engine to the radio. Engine controls and dashboard instruments were among the first components to use electronics, but today most automotive systems, such as braking, transmission, and steering systems, are controlled primarily by computers and electronic components. Some of the more advanced vehicles have global positioning systems, Internet access, and other high-tech features integrated into the functions of the vehicle. The training in electronics is vital because electrical components, or a series of related components, account for nearly all malfunctions in modern vehicles.

In addition to electronics and computers, automotive service technicians will have to learn and understand the science behind the alternate-fuel vehicles that have begun to enter the market. The fuel for these vehicles will come from the dehydrogenization of water, electric fuel cells, natural gas, solar power, and other non-petroleum-based sources. Hybrid vehicles, for example, use the energy from braking to recharge batteries that power an electric motor, which supplements a gasoline engine. As vehicles with these new technologies become more common, technicians will need additional training to learn the science and engineering that makes them possible. Currently, the manufacturers of these alternate-fuel vehicles are providing the necessary training. However, as the warrantees begin to expire, technicians in all industries will need to be trained to service these vehicles. As the number of these automobiles on the road increases, some technicians will likely specialize in the service and repair of these vehicles.

Those new to automotive service usually start as trainee technicians, technicians' helpers, or lubrication workers, and gradually acquire and practice their skills by working with experienced mechanics and technicians. With a few months' experience, beginners perform many routine service tasks and make simple repairs. While some graduates of postsecondary automotive training programs are often able to earn promotion to the journey level after only a few months on the job, it typically takes 2 to 5 years of experience to become a journey level service technician, who is expected to quickly perform the more difficult types of routine service and repairs. An additional 1 to 2 years of experience familiarizes technicians with all types of repairs. Complex specialties, such as transmission repair, require another year or two of training and experience. In contrast, brake specialists may learn their jobs in considerably less time because they do not need a complete knowledge of automotive repair.

At work, the most important possessions of technicians are their hand tools. Technicians usually provide their own tools, and many experienced workers have thousands of dollars invested in them. Employers typically furnish expensive power tools, engine analyzers, and other diagnostic equipment, but technicians accumulate hand tools with experience. Some formal training programs have alliances with tool manufacturers that help entry-level technicians accumulate tools during their training period.

Employers increasingly send experienced automotive service technicians to manufacturer training centers to learn to repair new models or to receive special training in the repair of components, such as electronic fuel injection or air-conditioners. Motor vehicle dealers and other automotive service providers also may send promising beginners to manufacturer-sponsored technician training programs; most employers periodically send experienced technicians to manufacturer-sponsored technician training programs for additional training to maintain or upgrade employees' skills and thus increase the employees' value to the employer. Factory representatives also visit many shops to conduct short training sessions.

Voluntary certification by the National Institute for Automotive Service Excellence (ASE) has become a standard credential for automotive service technicians. Certification is available in 1 or more of 8 different areas of automotive service, such as electrical systems, engine repair, brake systems, suspension and steering, and heating and air-conditioning. For certification in each area, technicians must have at least 2 years of experience and pass the examination. Completion of an automotive training program in high school, vocational or trade school, or community or junior college may be substituted for 1 year of experience. For ASE certification as a master automobile technician, technicians must be certified in all eight areas. Technicians must retake each examination once every 5 years to maintain their certifications.

Experienced technicians who have leadership ability sometimes advance to shop supervisor or service manager. Those who work well with customers may become automotive repair service estimators. Some with sufficient funds open independent repair shops.

Employment

Automotive service technicians and mechanics held about 803,000 jobs in 2004. The majority worked for automotive repair and maintenance shops, automobile dealers, and retailers and wholesalers of automotive parts, accessories, and supplies. Others found employment in gasoline stations; home and auto supply stores; automotive equipment rental and leasing companies; Federal, State, and local governments; and other organizations. More than 16 percent of service technicians were self-employed, more than twice the proportion for all installation, maintenance, and repair occupations.

Job Outlook

Job opportunities in this occupation are expected to be very good for persons who complete automotive training programs in high school, vocational and technical schools, or community colleges as employers report difficulty in finding workers with the right skills. Persons with good diagnostic and problem-solving abilities, and whose training includes basic electronics and computer courses, should have the best opportunities. For well-prepared people with a technical background, automotive service technician careers offer an excellent opportunity for good pay and the satisfaction of highly skilled work with vehicles incorporating the latest in advanced technology. However, persons without formal automotive training are likely to face competition for entry-level jobs.

Employment of automotive service technicians and mechanics is expected to increase as fast as the average through the year 2014. Over the 2004-14 period, demand for technicians will grow as the number of vehicles in operation increases, reflecting continued growth in the number of multi-car families. Growth in demand will be offset somewhat by slowing population growth and the continuing increase in the quality and durability of automobiles, which will require less frequent service. Additional job openings will be due to the need to replace a growing number of retiring technicians, who tend to be the most experienced workers.

Most persons who enter the occupation can expect steady work, even through downturns in the economy. While car owners may postpone maintenance and repair on their vehicles when their budgets become strained, and employers of automotive technicians may cutback hiring new workers, changes in economic conditions generally have minor effects on the automotive service and repair business.

Employment growth will continue to be concentrated in automobile dealerships and independent automotive repair shops. Many new jobs also will be created in small retail operations that offer after-warranty repairs, such as oil changes, brake repair, air-conditioner service, and other minor repairs generally taking less than 4 hours to complete. Employment of automotive service technicians and mechanics in gasoline service stations will continue to decline, as fewer stations offer repair services.

Earnings

Median hourly earnings of automotive service technicians and mechanics, including commission, were $15.60 in May 2004. The middle 50 percent earned between $11.31 and $20.75 per hour. The lowest 10 percent earned less than $8.70, and the highest 10 percent earned more than $26.22 per hour. Median annual earnings in the industries employing the largest numbers of service technicians in May 2004 were as follows:

Local government	$38,160
Automobile dealers	38,060
Automotive repair and maintenance	28,810
Gasoline stations	28,030
Automotive parts, accessories, and tire stores	27,180

Many experienced technicians employed by automobile dealers and independent repair shops receive a commission related to the labor cost charged to the customer. Under this method, weekly earnings depend on the amount of work completed. Employers frequently guarantee commissioned technicians a minimum weekly salary.

Some automotive service technicians are members of labor unions such as the International Association of Machinists and Aerospace Workers; the International Union, United Automobile, Aerospace and Agricultural Implement Workers of America; the Sheet Metal Workers' International Association; and the International Brotherhood of Teamsters.

Related Occupations

Other workers who repair and service motor vehicles include automotive body and related repairers, diesel service technicians and mechanics, and small engine mechanics.

Sources of Additional Information

For more details about work opportunities, contact local automobile dealers and repair shops or local offices of the State employment service. The State employment service also may have information about training programs.

A list of certified automotive service technician training programs can be obtained from:
➤ National Automotive Technicians Education Foundation, 101 Blue Seal Dr., SE., Suite 101, Leesburg, VA 20175. Internet: **http://www.natef.org**

For a directory of accredited private trade and technical schools that offer programs in automotive service technician training, contact:
➤ Accrediting Commission of Career Schools and Colleges of Technology, 2101 Wilson Blvd., Suite 302, Arlington, VA 22201. Internet: **http://www.accsct.org**

Information on automobile manufacturer-sponsored programs in automotive service technology can be obtained from:
➤ Automotive Youth Educational Systems (AYES), 100 W. Big Beaver, Suite 300, Troy, MI 48084. Internet: **http://www.ayes.org**

Information on how to become a certified automotive service technician is available from:
➤ National Institute for Automotive Service Excellence (ASE), 101 Blue Seal Dr. SE., Suite 101, Leesburg, VA 20175. Internet: **http://www.asecert.org**

For general information about a career as an automotive service technician, contact:
➤ National Automobile Dealers Association, 8400 Westpark Dr., McLean, VA 22102. Internet: **http://www.nada.org**
➤ Automotive Retailing Today, 8400 Westpark Dr., MS #2, McLean, VA 22102. Internet: **http://www.autoretailing.org**
➤ Automotive Jobs Today, 8400 Westpark Dr., MS #2, McLean, VA 22102. Internet: **http://www.autojobstoday.org**
➤ Career Voyages, U.S. Department of Labor, 200 Constitution Ave., NW, Washington, DC 20210. Internet:
http://www.careervoyages.gov/automotive-main.cfm

Diesel Service Technicians and Mechanics

(O*NET 49-3031.00)

Significant Points

● A career as a diesel service technician or mechanic can offer relatively high wages and the challenge of skilled repair work.

● Opportunities are expected to be very good for persons who complete formal training programs.

● National certification is the recognized standard of achievement for diesel service technicians and mechanics.

Nature of the Work

The diesel engine is the workhorse powering the Nation's trucks and buses because it delivers more power, is more efficient, and is more durable than its gasoline-burning counterpart. Diesel-powered engines also are becoming more prevalent in light vehicles, including passenger vehicles, pickups, and other work trucks.

Diesel service technicians and mechanics, which includes *bus and truck mechanics* and *diesel engine specialists*, repair and maintain the diesel engines that power transportation equipment such as heavy trucks, buses, and locomotives. Some diesel technicians and mechanics also work on heavy vehicles and mobile equipment, including bulldozers, cranes, road graders, farm tractors, and combines. Other technicians repair diesel-powered passenger automobiles, light trucks, or boats. (For information on technicians and mechanics working primarily on gasoline-powered automobiles, heavy vehicles, mobile equipment, or boats, see the *Handbook* sections on automotive, heavy vehicle, and mobile equipment; and small engine service mechanics.

Technicians who work for organizations that maintain their own vehicles spend most of their time doing preventive maintenance, to ensure that equipment will operate safely. These workers also eliminate unnecessary wear on, and damage to, parts that could result in costly breakdowns. During a routine maintenance check on a vehicle, technicians follow a checklist that includes inspecting brake systems, steering mechanisms, wheel bearings, and other important parts. Following inspection, technicians repair or adjust parts that do not work properly or remove and replace parts that cannot be fixed.

Increasingly, technicians must be versatile, in order to adapt to customers' needs and new technologies. It is common for technicians to handle all kinds of repairs, from working on a vehicle's electrical system one day to doing major engine repairs the next. Diesel maintenance is becoming increasingly complex, as more electronic components are used to control the operation of an engine. For example, microprocessors now regulate and manage fuel timing, increasing the engine's efficiency. Also, new emissions standards are requiring mechanics to retrofit engines to comply with pollution regulations. In modern shops, diesel service technicians use hand-held or laptop computers to diagnose problems and adjust engine functions. Because of continual advances in automotive technology, technicians must regularly learn new techniques to repair vehicles.

Diesel service technicians use a variety of tools in their work, including power tools, such as pneumatic wrenches, to remove

Diesel technicians perform regular maintenance on engine parts to prevent unnecessary wear and save money on costly repairs.

bolts quickly; machine tools, such as lathes and grinding machines, to rebuild brakes; welding and flame-cutting equipment, to remove and repair exhaust systems; and jacks and hoists, to lift and move large parts. Common handtools—screwdrivers, pliers, and wrenches—are used to work on small parts and get at hard-to-reach places. Diesel service technicians and mechanics also use a variety of computerized testing equipment to pinpoint and analyze malfunctions in electrical systems and engines.

In large shops, technicians generally receive their assignments from shop supervisors or service managers. Most supervisors and managers are experienced technicians who also assist in diagnosing problems and maintaining quality standards. Technicians may work as a team or be assisted by an apprentice or helper when doing heavy work, such as removing engines and transmissions.

Working Conditions

Diesel technicians usually work indoors, although they occasionally make repairs to vehicles on the road. Diesel technicians may lift heavy parts and tools, handle greasy and dirty parts, and stand or lie in awkward positions to repair vehicles and equipment. Minor cuts, burns, and bruises are common, although serious accidents can usually be avoided if the shop is kept clean and orderly and if safety procedures are followed. Technicians normally work in well-lighted, heated, and ventilated areas; however, some shops are drafty and noisy. Many employers provide lockers and shower facilities.

Training, Other Qualifications, and Advancement

Although many persons qualify for diesel service technician and mechanic jobs through years of on-the-job training, authorities on diesel engines recommend the completion of a formal diesel engine training program. Employers prefer to hire graduates of formal training programs because those workers often have a head start in training and are able to advance quickly to the journey level of diesel service.

Many community colleges and trade and vocational schools offer programs in diesel repair. These programs, lasting 6 months to 2 years, lead to a certificate of completion or an associate degree. Programs vary in the degree of hands-on training they provide on equipment. Some offer about 30 hours per week on equipment, whereas others offer more lab or classroom instruction. Training provides a foundation in the latest diesel technology and instruction in the service and repair of the vehicles and equipment that technicians will encounter on the job. Training programs also improve the skills needed to interpret technical manuals and to communicate with coworkers and customers. In addition to the hands-on aspects of the training, many institutions teach communication skills, customer service, basic understanding of physics, and logical thought. Increasingly, employers work closely with representatives of training programs, providing instructors with the latest equipment, techniques, and tools and offering jobs to graduates.

Whereas most employers prefer to hire persons who have completed formal training programs, some technicians and mechanics continue to learn their skills on the job. Unskilled beginners generally are assigned tasks such as cleaning parts, fueling and lubricating vehicles, and driving vehicles into and out of the shop. Beginners usually are promoted to trainee positions as they gain experience and as vacancies become available. In some shops, beginners with experience in automobile service start as trainee technicians.

After a few months' experience, most trainees can perform routine service tasks and make minor repairs. These workers advance to increasingly difficult jobs as they prove their ability and competence. After technicians master the repair and service of diesel engines, they learn to work on related components, such as brakes, transmissions, and electrical systems. Generally, technicians with at least 3 to 4 years of on-the-job experience will qualify as journey-level diesel technicians. The completion of a formal training program speeds advancement to the journey level.

For unskilled entry-level jobs, employers usually look for applicants who have mechanical aptitude and strong problem-solving skills and who are at least 18 years of age and in good physical condition. Nearly all employers require the completion of high school. Courses in automotive repair, electronics, English, mathematics, and physics provide a strong educational background for a career as a diesel service technician or mechanic. Technicians need a State commercial driver's license to test-drive trucks or buses on public roads. Many companies also require applicants to pass a drug test. Practical experience in automobile repair at an automotive service station, in the Armed Forces, or as a hobby is valuable as well.

Employers often send experienced technicians and mechanics to special training classes conducted by manufacturers and vendors, in which workers learn the latest technology and repair techniques. Technicians constantly receive updated technical manuals and instructions outlining changes in techniques and standards for repair. It is essential for technicians to read, interpret, and comprehend service manuals in order to keep abreast of engineering changes.

Voluntary certification by the National Institute for Automotive Service Excellence (ASE) is the recognized industry credential for diesel service technicians and mechanics. Diesel service technicians may be certified as master medium/heavy truck technicians, master school bus technicians, or master truck equipment technicians. They may also be ASE-certified in specific areas of truck repair, such as gasoline engines, drivetrains, brakes, suspension and steering, electrical and electronic systems, or preventive maintenance and inspection.

For certification in each area, a technician must pass one or more of the ASE-administered exams and present proof of 2 years of relevant hands-on work experience. Two years of relevant formal training from a high school, vocational or trade school, or community or junior college program may be substituted for up to 1 year of the work experience requirement. To remain certified, technicians must be retested every 5 years. Retesting ensures that service technicians and mechanics keep up with changing technology.

The most important work possessions of technicians and mechanics are their handtools. Technicians usually provide their own tools, and many experienced workers have thousands of dollars invested in them. Employers typically furnish expensive power tools, computerized engine analyzers, and other diagnostic equipment, but individual workers ordinarily accumulate their own hand tools with experience.

Experienced diesel service technicians and mechanics with leadership ability may advance to shop supervisor or service manager. Technicians and mechanics with sales ability sometimes become sales representatives. Some open their own repair shops.

Employment

Diesel service technicians and mechanics held about 270,000 jobs in 2004. They were employed by almost every industry; in particular, those that use trucks, buses, and equipment to haul, deliver, and transport materials, goods, and people. The largest employer, the truck transportation industry, employed nearly one out of six diesel service technicians and mechanics. Slightly fewer were employed by local governments, mainly to repair school buses, waste removal trucks, and road equipment. About 1 out 10 was employed by automotive and commercial equipment repair and maintenance facilities. The rest were employed throughout the economy, including construction, manufacturing, retail and wholesale trade, and automotive leasing. A relatively small number

were self-employed. Nearly every section of the country employs diesel service technicians and mechanics, although most work in towns and cities where trucking companies, bus lines, and other fleet owners have large operations.

Job Outlook

Employment of diesel service technicians and mechanics is expected to increase about as fast as the average for all occupations through the year 2014. Besides openings resulting from employment growth, opportunities will be created by the need to replace workers who retire or transfer to other occupations.

Employment of diesel service technicians and mechanics is expected to grow as freight transportation by truck increases. Additional trucks will be needed to keep pace with the increasing volume of freight shipped nationwide. Trucks also serve as intermediaries for other forms of transportation, such as rail and air. Due to the greater durability and economy of the diesel engine relative to the gasoline engine, the number of buses, trucks, and passenger vehicles that are powered by diesel engines is expected to increase.

While diesel engines are a more efficient and powerful option, diesel engines tend to produce more pollutants than gasoline-powered engines. As governments have applied emissions-lowering standards to diesel engines, many older diesel engines must be retrofitted to comply. These new emissions control systems, such as emissions filters and catalysts, may create additional jobs for diesel service technicians and mechanics.

Careers as diesel service technicians attract many because they offer relatively high wages and the challenge of skilled repair work. Opportunities should be very good for persons who complete formal training in diesel mechanics at community and junior colleges or vocational and technical schools. Applicants without formal training may face stiffer competition for entry-level jobs.

Most persons entering this occupation can expect relatively steady work, because changes in economic conditions have less of an effect on the diesel repair business than on other sectors of the economy. During a downturn in the economy, however, some employers may lay off workers or be reluctant to hire new workers.

Earnings

Median hourly earnings of bus and truck mechanics and diesel engine specialists, including incentive pay, were $17.20 in May 2004. The middle 50 percent earned between $13.73 and $21.13 an hour. The lowest 10 percent earned less than $11.19, and the highest 10 percent earned more than $25.67 an hour. Median hourly earnings in the industries employing the largest numbers of bus and truck mechanics and diesel engine specialists in May 2004 were as follows:

Local government, excluding schools	$20.18
Motor vehicle and motor vehicle parts and supplies merchant wholesalers	17.97
Automotive repair and maintenance	16.65
General freight trucking	16.33
Elementary and secondary schools	15.73

Because many experienced technicians employed by truck fleet dealers and independent repair shops receive a commission related to the labor cost charged to the customer, weekly earnings depend on the amount of work completed. Beginners usually earn from 50 to 75 percent of the rate of skilled workers and receive increases as they become more skilled.

The majority of service technicians work a standard 40-hour week, although some work longer hours, particularly if they are self-employed. A growing number of shops have expanded their hours, either to perform repairs and routine service in a more timely fashion or as a convenience to customers. Those technicians employed by truck and bus firms providing service around the clock may work evenings, nights, and weekends, usually at a higher rate of pay than those working traditional hours.

Many diesel service technicians and mechanics are members of labor unions, including the International Association of Machinists and Aerospace Workers; the Amalgamated Transit Union; the International Union, United Automobile, Aerospace and Agricultural Implement Workers of America; the Transport Workers Union of America; the Sheet Metal Workers' International Association; and the International Brotherhood of Teamsters.

Related Occupations

Diesel service technicians and mechanics repair trucks, buses, and other diesel-powered equipment. Related technician and mechanic occupations include aircraft and avionics equipment mechanics and service technicians, automotive service technicians and mechanics, heavy vehicle and mobile equipment service technicians and mechanics, and small engine mechanics.

Sources of Additional Information

More details about work opportunities for diesel service technicians and mechanics may be obtained from local employers such as trucking companies, truck dealers, or buslines; locals of the unions previously mentioned; and local offices of your State employment service. Local State employment service offices also may have information about training programs. State boards of postsecondary career schools have information on licensed schools with training programs for diesel service technicians and mechanics.

For general information about a career as a diesel service technician or mechanic, write:

➤ Association of Diesel Specialists, 10 Laboratory Dr., PO Box 13966, Research Triangle Park, NC 27709. Internet: **http://www.diesel.org**

Information on how to become a certified diesel technician of medium to heavy-duty vehicles or a certified bus technician is available from:

➤ National Institute for Automotive Service Excellence (ASE), 101 Blue Seal Dr. SE, Suite 101, Leesburg, VA 20175. Internet: **http://www.asecert.org**

For a directory of accredited private trade and technical schools with training programs for diesel service technicians and mechanics, contact:

➤ Accrediting Commission of Career Schools and Colleges of Technology, 2101 Wilson Blvd., Suite 302, Arlington, VA 22201. Internet: **http://www.accsct.org**

➤ National Automotive Technicians Education Foundation, 101 Blue Seal Dr., SE., Suite 101, Leesburg, VA 20175. Internet: **http://www.natef.org**

Heavy Vehicle and Mobile Equipment Service Technicians and Mechanics

(O*NET 49-3041.00, 49-3042.00, 49-3043.00)

Significant Points

● Opportunities should be good for persons with formal postsecondary training in diesel or heavy equipment mechanics, especially if they also have training in basic electronics and hydraulics.

● This occupation offers relatively high wages and the challenge of skilled repair work.

● Skill in using computerized diagnostic equipment is important in this occupation.

Nature of the Work

Heavy vehicles and mobile equipment are indispensable to many industrial activities, from construction to railroads. Various types of equipment move materials, till land, lift beams, and dig earth to pave the way for development and production. *Heavy vehicle and mobile equipment service technicians and mechanics* repair and maintain engines and hydraulic, transmission, and electrical systems powering farm machinery, cranes, bulldozers, and railcars, for example. (For more detailed information on service technicians specializing in diesel engines, see the section on diesel service technicians and mechanics elsewhere in the *Handbook*.)

Service technicians perform routine maintenance checks on diesel engines and on fuel, brake, and transmission systems to ensure peak performance, safety, and longevity of the equipment. Maintenance checks and comments from equipment operators usually alert technicians to problems. With many types of modern heavy and mobile equipment, technicians can plug diagnostic computers into onboard computers to diagnose a component needing adjustment or repair. After locating the problem, these technicians rely on their training and experience to use the best possible technique to solve the problem. If necessary, they may partially dismantle the component to examine parts for damage or excessive wear. Then, using hand-held tools, they repair, replace, clean, and lubricate parts as necessary. In some cases, technicians calibrate systems by typing codes into the onboard computer. After reassembling the component and testing it for safety, they put it back into the equipment and return the equipment to the field.

Many types of heavy and mobile equipment use hydraulics, to raise and lower movable parts. When hydraulic components malfunction, technicians examine them for fluid leaks, ruptured hoses, or worn gaskets on fluid reservoirs. Occasionally, the equipment requires extensive repairs, as when a defective hydraulic pump needs replacing.

In addition to conducting routine maintenance checks, service technicians perform a variety of other repairs. They diagnose electrical problems and adjust or replace defective components. They also disassemble and repair undercarriages and track assemblies. Occasionally, technicians weld broken equipment frames and structural parts, using electric or gas welders.

It is common for technicians in large shops to specialize in one or two types of repair. For example, a shop may have individual specialists in major engine repair, transmission work, electrical systems, and suspension or brake systems. Technicians in smaller shops, on the other hand, generally perform multiple functions.

The technology used in heavy equipment is becoming more sophisticated with the increased use of electronic and computer-controlled components that run much of the equipment's functions. These onboard computers are accessed using other computers and electronic devices that are manipulated by the technician. As a result, technicians need training in electronics and the use of hand-held diagnostic computers to make engine adjustments and diagnose problems.

Service technicians use a variety of tools in their work: power tools, such as pneumatic wrenches to remove bolts quickly; machine tools, like lathes and grinding machines, to rebuild brakes; welding and flame-cutting equipment to remove and repair exhaust systems; and jacks and hoists to lift and move large parts. Service technicians also use common handtools—screwdrivers, pliers, and wrenches—to work on small parts and to get at hard-to-reach places. They may use a variety of computerized testing equipment to pinpoint and analyze malfunctions in electrical systems and other essential systems. Tachometers and dynamometers, for example, serve to locate engine malfunctions. Service technicians also use ohmmeters, ammeters, and voltmeters when working on electrical systems.

Mobile heavy equipment mechanics and service technicians keep construction and surface mining equipment, such as bulldozers, cranes, crawlers, draglines, graders, excavators, and other equipment, in working order. Typically, these workers are employed by equipment wholesale distribution and leasing firms, large construction and mining companies, local and Federal governments, and other organizations operating and maintaining heavy machinery and equipment fleets. Service technicians employed by the Federal Government may work on tanks and other armored equipment.

Farm equipment mechanics service, maintain, and repair farm equipment, as well as smaller lawn and garden tractors sold to suburban homeowners. What typically was a general repairer's job around the farm has evolved into a specialized technical career. Farmers have increasingly turned to farm equipment dealers to service and repair their equipment because the machinery has grown in complexity. Modern equipment uses more computers, electronics and hydraulics, making it difficult to perform repairs without some specialized training.

Railcar repairers specialize in servicing railroad locomotives and other rolling stock, streetcars and subway cars, or mine cars. Most work for railroads, public and private transit companies, and railcar manufacturers.

Working Conditions

Heavy vehicle and mobile equipment service technicians usually work indoors, although if repairs are needed urgently, or the machinery cannot be moved to a shop, many technicians make repairs at the worksite. To repair vehicles and equipment, technicians often lift heavy parts and tools, handle greasy and dirty parts, and stand or lie in awkward positions. Minor cuts, burns, and bruises are common; serious accidents normally are avoided when the shop is kept clean and orderly and when safety practices are observed. Technicians usually work in well-lighted, heated, and ventilated areas. However, some shops are drafty and noisy. Many employers provide uniforms, locker rooms, and shower facilities.

When heavy or mobile equipment breaks down at a construction site, it may be too difficult or expensive to bring into a repair shop, so the shop will send a field service technician to the site to make repairs. Field service technicians work outdoors and spend much of their time away from the shop. Generally, the more experienced

On-the-job repairs are usually done by the most experienced heavy vehicle technicians.

service technicians specialize in field service. They usually drive trucks specially equipped with replacement parts and tools. On occasion, they must travel many miles to reach disabled machinery. Field technicians normally earn a higher wage than their counterparts, because they are required to make on-the-spot decisions that are necessary to serve their customers.

The hours of work for farm equipment mechanics vary according to the season of the year. During the busy planting and harvesting seasons, mechanics often work 6 or 7 days a week, 10 to 12 hours daily. In slow winter months, however, mechanics may work fewer than 40 hours a week.

Training, Other Qualifications, and Advancement

Many persons qualify for service technician jobs through years of on-the-job training, but most employers prefer that applicants complete a formal diesel or heavy equipment mechanic training program after graduating from high school. They seek persons with mechanical aptitude who are knowledgeable about the fundamentals of diesel engines, transmissions, electrical systems, computers, and hydraulics. In addition, the constant change in equipment technology makes it necessary for technicians to be flexible and have the capacity to learn new skills quickly.

Many community colleges and vocational schools offer programs in diesel technology. Some tailor programs to heavy equipment mechanics. These programs educate the student in the basics of analytical and diagnostic techniques, electronics, and hydraulics. The increased use of electronics and computers makes training in the fundamentals of electronics essential for new heavy and mobile equipment mechanics. Some 1- to 2-year programs lead to a certificate of completion, whereas others lead to an associate degree in diesel or heavy equipment mechanics. These programs not only provide a foundation in the components of diesel and heavy equipment technology, but also enable trainee technicians to advance to the journey, or experienced worker, level sooner than would otherwise be possible.

A combination of formal and on-the-job training prepares trainee technicians with the knowledge to service and repair equipment typically seen by a shop. After a few months' experience, most beginners perform routine service tasks and make minor repairs. As they prove their ability and competence, they advance to harder jobs. After trainees master the repair and service of diesel engines, they learn to work on related components, such as brakes, transmissions, and electrical systems. Generally, a service technician with at least 3 to 4 years of on-the-job experience is accepted as fully qualified.

Many employers send trainee technicians to training sessions conducted by heavy equipment manufacturers. The sessions, which typically last up to 1 week, provide intensive instruction in the repair of the manufacturer's equipment. Some sessions focus on particular components found in the equipment, such as diesel engines, transmissions, axles, and electrical systems. Other sessions focus on particular types of equipment, such as crawler-loaders and crawler-dozers. As they progress, trainees may periodically attend additional training sessions. When appropriate, experienced technicians attend training sessions to gain familiarity with new technology or equipment.

High school courses in automobile repair, physics, chemistry, and mathematics provide a strong foundation for a career as a service technician or mechanic. It is also essential for technicians to be able to read and interpret service manuals in order to keep abreast of engineering changes. Experience working on diesel engines and heavy equipment acquired in the Armed Forces is valuable as well.

Voluntary certification by the National Institute for Automotive Service Excellence is the recognized industry credential for heavy vehicle and mobile equipment service technicians, who may be certified as a master medium/heavy truck technician or in a specific area of heavy-duty equipment repair, such as brakes, gasoline engines, diesel engines, drivetrains, electrical systems, or suspension and steering. For certification in each area, technicians must pass a written examination and have at least 2 years' experience. High school, vocational or trade school, or community or junior college training in gasoline or diesel engine repair may substitute for up to 1 year's experience. To remain certified, technicians must be retested every 5 years. Retesting ensures that service technicians keep up with changing technology. However, ASE currently offers no certification programs for more advanced heavy vehicle and mobile equipment repair specialties.

The most important work possessions of technicians are their handtools. Service technicians typically buy their own handtools, and many experienced technicians have thousands of dollars invested in them. Employers typically furnish expensive power tools, computerized engine analyzers, and other diagnostic equipment, but handtools are normally accumulated with experience.

Experienced technicians may advance to field service jobs, wherein they have a greater opportunity to tackle problems independently and earn additional pay. Field positions may require a commercial driver's license and a clean driving record. Technicians with leadership ability may become shop supervisors or service managers. Some technicians open their own repair shops or invest in a franchise.

Employment

Heavy vehicle and mobile equipment service technicians and mechanics held about 178,000 jobs in 2004. Approximately 125,000 were mobile heavy equipment mechanics, 33,000 were farm equipment mechanics, and 20,000 were railcar repairers. About 30 percent were employed by machinery, equipment, and supplies merchant wholesalers. More than 13 percent worked in construction, primarily for specialty trade contractors and highway, street, and bridge construction companies; another 12 percent were employed by Federal, State, and local governments. Other service technicians worked in agriculture; mining; rail transportation and support activities; and commercial and industrial machinery and equipment rental, leasing, and repair. A small number repaired equipment for machinery and railroad rolling stock manufacturers or lawn and garden equipment and supplies stores. Less than 4 percent of service technicians were self-employed.

Nearly every section of the country employs heavy and mobile equipment service technicians and mechanics, although most work in towns and cities where equipment dealers, equipment rental and leasing companies, and construction companies have repair facilities.

Job Outlook

Opportunities for heavy vehicle and mobile equipment service technicians and mechanics should be good for those who have completed formal training programs in diesel or heavy equipment mechanics. Persons without formal training are expected to encounter growing difficulty entering these jobs.

Employment of heavy vehicle and mobile equipment service technicians and mechanics is expected to grow slower than the average for all occupations through the year 2014. Most job openings will arise from the need to replace experienced repairers who retire. Employers report difficulty finding candidates with formal postsecondary training to fill available service technician positions, because many young people with mechanic training

and experience opt to take jobs as automotive service technicians, diesel service technicians, or industrial machinery repairers—jobs that offer more openings and a wider variety of locations in which to work.

Faster employment growth is expected for mobile heavy equipment mechanics than for farm equipment mechanics or railcar repairers. Increasing numbers of heavy duty and mobile equipment service technicians will be required to support growth in the construction industry, equipment dealers, and rental and leasing companies. Because of the nature of construction activity, demand for service technicians follows the Nation's economic cycle. As the economy expands, construction activity increases, resulting in the use of more mobile heavy equipment to grade construction sites, excavate basements, and lay water and sewer lines. The increased use of such equipment increases the need for periodic service and repair. In addition, the construction and repair of highways and bridges requires more technicians to service equipment. As equipment becomes more complicated, repairs increasingly must be made by specially trained technicians. Job openings for farm equipment mechanics and railcar repairers are expected to arise mostly because of replacement needs.

Construction and mining are particularly sensitive to changes in the level of economic activity; therefore, heavy and mobile equipment may be idled during downturns. In addition, winter is traditionally the slow season for construction and farming activity, particularly in cold regions. During periods when equipment is used less, few technicians may be needed, and employers may be reluctant to hire inexperienced workers. However, employers usually try to retain experienced workers during these slow periods.

Earnings

Median hourly earnings of mobile heavy equipment mechanics were $18.34 in May 2004. The middle 50 percent earned between $14.96 and $21.75. The lowest 10 percent earned less than $12.11, and the highest 10 percent earned more than $26.27. Median hourly earnings in the industries employing the largest numbers of mobile heavy equipment mechanics in May 2004 were as follows:

Federal Government	$20.41
Local government	19.22
Machinery, equipment, and supplies merchant wholesalers	18.49
Other specialty trade contractors	17.81
Highway, street, and bridge construction	17.79

Median hourly earnings of farm equipment mechanics were $13.40 in May 2004. The middle 50 percent earned between $10.77 and $16.34. The lowest 10 percent earned less than $9.08, and the highest 10 percent earned more than $19.40. In May 2004, median hourly earnings were $13.66 in machinery, equipment, and supplies merchant wholesalers, the industry employing the largest number of farm equipment mechanics.

Median hourly earnings of railcar repairers were $19.48 in May 2004. The middle 50 percent earned between $16.12 and $21.76. The lowest 10 percent earned less than $12.07, and the highest 10 percent earned more than $25.52. In May 2004, median hourly earnings were $20.38 in rail transportation, the industry employing the largest number of railcar repairers.

Many heavy vehicle and mobile equipment service technicians and mechanics are members of unions, including the International Association of Machinists and Aerospace Workers, the International Union of Operating Engineers, and the International Brotherhood of Teamsters.

Related Occupations

Workers in related repair occupations include aircraft and avionics equipment mechanics and service technicians; automotive service technicians and mechanics; diesel service technicians and mechanics; industrial machinery mechanics and maintenance workers; and small engine mechanics.

Sources of Additional Information

More details about job openings for heavy vehicle and mobile equipment service technicians and mechanics may be obtained from local heavy and mobile equipment dealers and distributors, construction contractors, and government agencies. Local offices of the State employment service also may have information on job openings and training programs.

For general information about a career as a heavy vehicle and mobile equipment service technician or mechanic, contact:

➤ The AED Foundation (Associated Equipment Dealers affiliate), 615 W. 22nd St., Oak Brook, IL 60523. Internet: **http://www.aednet.org/aed_foundation**

A list of certified diesel service technician training programs can be obtained from:

➤ National Automotive Technician Education Foundation (NATEF), 101 Blue Seal Dr., Suite 101, Leesburg, VA 20175. Internet: **http://www.natef.org**

Information on certification as a heavy-duty diesel service technician is available from:

➤ National Institute for Automotive Service Excellence (ASE), 101 Blue Seal Dr. SE., Suite 101, Leesburg, VA 20175. Internet: **http://www.asecert.org**

Small Engine Mechanics

(O*NET 49-3051.00, 49-3052.00, 49-3053.00)

Significant Points

● Employment is expected to grow as fast as the average for all occupations, and persons with formal training as a mechanic should enjoy good job prospects.

● Use of motorcycles, motorboats, and outdoor power equipment is seasonal in many areas, so mechanics may service other types of equipment or work reduced hours in the winter.

Nature of the Work

Small engines powering motorcycles, motorboats, and outdoor power equipment share many characteristics with their larger counterparts, including breakdowns. Small engine mechanics repair and service power equipment ranging from racing motorcycles to chain saws. Mechanics usually specialize in the service and repair of one type of equipment, although they may work on closely related products.

Motorcycle mechanics repair and overhaul motorcycles, motor scooters, mopeds, dirt bikes, and all-terrain vehicles. Besides repairing engines, they may work on transmissions, brakes, and ignition systems and make minor body repairs. Mechanics often service just a few makes and models of motorcycles, because most work for dealers that service only the products they sell.

Motorboat mechanics, or *marine equipment mechanics*, repair and adjust the electrical and mechanical equipment of inboard and outboard boat engines. Most small boats have portable outboard engines that are removed and brought into the repair shop. Larger craft, such as cabin cruisers and commercial fishing boats, are powered by diesel or gasoline inboard or inboard-outboard engines, which are removed only for major overhauls. Most of these repairs are performed at the docks or marinas. Motorboat mechanics also

may work on propellers, steering mechanisms, marine plumbing, and other boat equipment.

Outdoor power equipment and other small engine mechanics service and repair outdoor power equipment, such as lawnmowers, garden tractors, edge trimmers, and chain saws. They also may occasionally work on portable generators and gocarts. In addition, small engine mechanics in certain parts of the country may work on snowblowers and snowmobiles, but demand for this type of repair is both seasonal and regional.

Like large engines, small engines require periodic service to minimize the chance of breakdowns and to keep them operating at peak performance. During routine equipment maintenance, mechanics follow a checklist that includes the inspection and cleaning of brakes, electrical systems, fuel injection systems, plugs, carburetors, and other parts. Following inspection, mechanics usually repair or adjust parts that do not work properly or replace unfixable parts. Routine maintenance is normally a major part of the mechanic's work.

When a piece of equipment breaks down, mechanics use various techniques to diagnose the source and extent of the problem. The mark of a skilled mechanic is the ability to diagnose mechanical, fuel, and electrical problems and to make repairs in a minimal amount of time. Quick and accurate diagnosis requires problem-solving ability and a thorough knowledge of the equipment's operation.

In larger repair shops, mechanics may use special computerized diagnostic testing equipment as a preliminary tool in analyzing equipment. This computerized equipment provides a systematic performance report of various components to compare against normal ratings. After pinpointing the problem, the mechanic makes the needed adjustments, repairs, or replacements. Some jobs require minor adjustments or the replacement of a single item, while a complete engine overhaul requires a number of hours to disassemble the engine and replace worn valves, pistons, bearings, and other internal parts.

Small engine mechanics use common handtools, such as wrenches, pliers, and screwdrivers. They also utilize power tools,

Routine maintenance is a major part of a small engine mechanic's job.

such as drills and grinders, when customized repairs warrant their use. Computerized engine analyzers, compression gauges, ammeters and voltmeters, and other testing devices help mechanics locate faulty parts and tune engines. Some highly skilled mechanics use specialized components and the latest computerized equipment to customize and tune motorcycles and motorboats for racing.

Working Conditions

Small engine mechanics usually work in repair shops that are well lighted and ventilated, but are sometimes noisy when engines are tested. Motorboat mechanics may work outdoors at docks or marinas, as well as in all weather conditions, when making repairs aboard boats. They may work in cramped or awkward positions to reach a boat's engine.

During the winter months in the northern United States, mechanics may work fewer than 40 hours a week, because the amount of repair and service work declines when lawnmowers, motorboats, and motorcycles are not in use. Many mechanics work only during the busy spring and summer seasons. However, many schedule time-consuming engine overhauls or work on snowmobiles and snowblowers during winter downtime. Mechanics may work considerably more than 40 hours a week when demand is strong.

Training, Other Qualifications, and Advancement

Due to the increasing complexity of motorcycles and motorboats, most employers prefer to hire mechanics who have graduated from formal training programs for small engine mechanics. Because the number of these specialized postsecondary programs is limited, most mechanics learn their skills on the job or while working in related occupations. For trainee jobs, employers hire persons with mechanical aptitude who are knowledgeable about the fundamentals of small two- and four-stroke engines. Many trainees develop an interest in mechanics and acquire some basic skills through working on automobiles, motorcycles, motorboats, or outdoor power equipment as a hobby. Others may be introduced to mechanics through vocational automotive training in high school or one of many postsecondary institutions.

Trainees learn routine service tasks under the guidance of experienced mechanics by replacing ignition points and spark plugs or by taking apart, assembling, and testing new equipment. As they gain experience and proficiency, trainees progress to more difficult tasks, such as advanced computerized diagnosis and engine overhauls. Anywhere from 3 to 5 years of on-the-job training may be necessary before a novice worker becomes competent in all aspects of the repair of motorcycle and motorboat engines.

Employers often send mechanics and trainees to special courses conducted by motorcycle, motorboat, and outdoor power equipment manufacturers or distributors. These courses, which last as long as 2 weeks, upgrade workers' skills and provide information on repairing new models. They also may be used as a refresher for employees. They are usually a prerequisite for any mechanic who performs warranty work for manufacturers or insurance companies.

Most employers prefer to hire high school graduates for trainee mechanic positions, but will accept applicants with less education if they possess adequate reading, writing, and arithmetic skills. Many equipment dealers employ students part time and during the summer to help assemble new equipment and perform minor repairs. Helpful high school courses include small engine repair, automobile mechanics, science, and business arithmetic.

Knowledge of basic electronics is essential for small engine mechanics, because electronic components control an engine's performance, the vehicle's instrument displays, and a variety of other functions of motorcycles, motorboats, and outdoor power equipment.

The most important work possessions of mechanics are their handtools. Mechanics usually provide their own tools, and many experienced mechanics have invested thousands of dollars in them. Employers typically furnish expensive power tools, computerized engine analyzers, and other diagnostic equipment, but mechanics accumulate handtools with experience.

The skills used as a small engine mechanic generally transfer to other occupations, such as automobile, diesel, or heavy vehicle and mobile equipment mechanics. Experienced mechanics with leadership ability may advance to shop supervisor or service manager jobs. Mechanics with sales ability sometimes become sales representatives or open their own repair shops.

Employment

Small engine mechanics held about 73,000 jobs in 2004. Motorcycle mechanics held around 19,000 jobs. Motorboat mechanics held approximately 23,000 and outdoor power equipment and other small engine mechanics about 31,000. Almost half worked for other motor vehicle dealers, an industry that includes retail dealers of motorcycles, boats, and miscellaneous vehicles; or for retail hardware, lawn, and garden stores. Most of the remainder were employed by independent repair shops, marinas and boatyards, equipment rental companies, wholesale distributors, and landscaping services. About 20 percent were self-employed, compared to about 7 percent of workers in all installation, maintenance, and repair occupations.

Job Outlook

Employment of small engine mechanics is expected to grow about as fast as the average for all occupations through the year 2014. Most of the job openings are expected to be due to the need to replace many experienced small engine mechanics that are expected to transfer to other occupations, retire, or stop working for other reasons. Job prospects should be especially favorable for persons who complete mechanic training programs.

Motorcycle usage should continue to be popular with persons between 18 and 24 years, an age group that historically has had the greatest proportion of motorcycle enthusiasts. Motorcycles also are becoming increasingly popular with persons over the age of 40. Traditionally, this group has more disposable income to spend on recreational equipment such as motorcycles and motorboats.

Over the next decade, more people will be entering the 40-and-older age group, the group responsible for the largest segment of marine craft purchases. These potential buyers will help expand the market for motorboats, while maintaining the demand for qualified mechanics.

The construction of new single-family houses will result in an increase in the lawn and garden equipment in operation, increasing the need for mechanics. However, equipment growth will be slowed by trends toward smaller lawns and the contracting out of maintenance to lawn service firms. Small engine mechanics' growth will also be tempered by the tendency of many consumers to dispose of and replace relatively inexpensive items rather than have them repaired.

Employers will increasingly prefer mechanics to have knowledge of both two- and four-stroke engines, as well as other emissions-reducing technology, as the government increases regulation over the emissions produced by small engines. While advancements in technology will lengthen the interval between checkups, the need for qualified mechanics to perform services on motorcycles, motorboats, and lawn and garden equipment will increase.

Earnings

Median hourly earnings of motorcycle mechanics were $13.70 in May 2004. The middle 50 percent earned between $10.58 and $17.53. The lowest 10 percent earned less than $8.48, and the highest 10 percent earned more than $21.95. Median hourly earnings in May 2004 in other motor vehicle dealers, the industry employing the largest number of motorcycle mechanics, were $13.60.

Median hourly earnings of motorboat mechanics were $14.74. The middle 50 percent earned between $11.46 and $18.11. The lowest 10 percent earned less than $9.21, and the highest 10 percent earned more than $21.90. Median hourly earnings in May 2004 in other motor vehicle dealers, the industry employing the largest number of motorboat mechanics, were $14.29.

Median hourly earnings of outdoor power equipment and other small engine mechanics were $11.98 in May 2004. The middle 50 percent earned between $9.44 and $15.25. The lowest 10 percent earned less than $7.53, and the highest 10 percent earned more than $19.19. Median hourly earnings in lawn and garden equipment and supplies stores, the industry employing the largest number of outdoor power equipment and other small engine mechanics, were $11.40.

Small engine mechanics tend to receive few benefits in small shops, but those employed in larger shops often receive paid vacations, sick leave, and health insurance. Some employers also pay for work-related training and provide uniforms.

Related Occupations

Mechanics and repairers who work on mobile equipment other than small engines include automotive service technicians and mechanics, diesel service technicians and mechanics, and heavy vehicle and mobile equipment service technicians and mechanics.

Sources of Additional Information

For more details about work opportunities, contact local motorcycle, motorboat, and lawn and garden equipment dealers, boatyards, and marinas. Local offices of the State employment service also may have information about employment and training opportunities.

For a list of accredited private trade and technical schools that offer programs in small engine servicing and repair, contact:
➤ Accrediting Commission of Career Schools and Colleges of Technology, 2101 Wilson Blvd., Suite 302, Arlington, VA 22201. Internet: **http://www.accsct.org**

Other Installation, Maintenance, and Repair Occupations

Coin, Vending, and Amusement Machine Servicers and Repairers

(O*NET 49-9091.00)

Significant Points

● Most workers in this occupation learn their skills on the job.

● Opportunities should be especially good for persons with some knowledge of electronics.

Nature of the Work

Coin, vending, and amusement machines are a familiar sight in offices, schools, arcades, and casinos. These machines give out change, test our gaming skills, and dispense refreshments nearly everywhere we turn. Coin, vending, and amusement machine servicers and repairers install, service, and stock such machines and keep them in good working order.

Vending machine servicers, often called route drivers, visit machines that dispense soft drinks, candy and snacks, and other items. They collect money from the coin and cash-operated machines, restock merchandise, and change labels to indicate new selections. They also keep the machines clean and appealing.

Vending machine repairers, often called mechanics or technicians, make sure that the machines operate correctly. When checking complicated electrical and electronic machines, such as beverage dispensers, they ascertain whether the machines mix drinks properly and whether the refrigeration and heating units work correctly. If the machines are not in good working order, the mechanics repair them. On the relatively simple gravity-operated machines, repairers check the keypads, motors, and merchandise chutes. They also test coin, bill, and change-making mechanisms.

When installing machines, vending machine repairers make the necessary water and electrical connections and check the machines

for proper operation. They also make sure that the installation complies with local plumbing and electrical codes. Because many vending machines dispense food, these workers, along with vending machine servicers, must comply with State and local public health and sanitation standards.

Amusement machine servicers and repairers work on jukeboxes, video games, pinball machines, and slot machines. They make sure that the various levers, joysticks, and mechanisms function properly, so that the games remain fair and the jukebox selections are accurate. They update selections, repair or replace malfunctioning parts, and rebuild existing equipment. Those who work in the gaming industry must adhere to strict guidelines, because Federal and State agencies regulate many gaming machines.

Preventive maintenance—avoiding trouble before it starts—is a major job of repairers. For example, they periodically clean refrigeration condensers, lubricate mechanical parts, and adjust machines so that they perform properly.

If a machine breaks down, vending and amusement machine repairers inspect it for obvious problems, such as loose electrical wires, malfunctions of the coin mechanism or bill validator, and leaks. When servicing electronic machines, repairers test them with hand-held diagnostic computers that determine the extent and location of any problem. Repairers may only have to replace a circuit board or other component to fix the problem. However, if the problem cannot be readily located, these workers refer to technical manuals and wiring diagrams and use testing devices, such as electrical circuit testers, to find defective parts. Repairers decide whether they must replace a part and whether they can fix the malfunction onsite or whether they have to send the machine to the repair shop.

In the repair shop, vending and amusement machine repairers use power tools, such as grinding wheels, saws, and drills, as well as voltmeters, ohmmeters, oscilloscopes, and other testing equipment. They also use ordinary repair tools, such as screwdrivers, pliers, and wrenches.

Vending machine servicers and repairers employed by small companies may both fill and fix machines on a regular basis. These

Some vending machine repairers work in repair shops, while others repair machines on site.

combination servicers-repairers stock machines, collect money, fill coin and currency changers, and repair machines when necessary.

Servicers and repairers also do some paperwork, such as filing reports, preparing repair cost estimates, ordering parts, and keeping daily records of merchandise distributed and money collected. However, new machines with computerized inventory controls reduce the paperwork that a servicer must complete.

Working Conditions

Some vending and amusement machine repairers work primarily in company repair shops that generally are quiet, well lighted, and have adequate workspace. Others many spend substantial time on the road, visiting machines wherever they have been placed. Repairers generally work a total of 40 hours a week. However, vending and amusement machines operate around the clock, so repairers may be on call to work at night and on weekends and holidays.

Repair work is relatively safe, although servicers and repairers must take care to avoid hazards such as electrical shocks and cuts from sharp tools and other metal objects. They also must follow safe work procedures, especially when moving heavy vending and amusement machines.

Training, Other Qualifications, and Advancement

Most workers learn their skills on the job. New workers are trained informally on the job to fill and fix machines by observing, working with, and receiving instruction from experienced repairers. Employers normally hire high school graduates, and give preference to those with high school or vocational school courses in electricity, refrigeration, and machine repair. Employers usually require applicants to demonstrate mechanical ability, either through work experience or by scoring well on mechanical-aptitude tests.

Because coin, vending, and amusement machine servicers and repairers sometimes handle thousands of dollars in merchandise and cash, employers try to hire persons who are trustworthy and have no criminal records. Also, the ability to deal tactfully with people is important, because the servicers and repairers play a significant role in relaying customers' requests and concerns. A driver's license and a good driving record are essential for most vending and amusement machine servicer and repairer jobs. Some employers require their servicers to be bonded.

Electronics have become more prevalent in vending and amusement machines and employers will increasingly prefer applicants who have training in electronics. Technologically advanced machines with features such as multilevel pricing, inventory control, and scrolling messages use electronics and microchip computers extensively. Some vocational high schools and junior colleges offer 1- to 2-year training programs in basic electronics.

Beginners start training with simple jobs, such as cleaning or stocking machines. They then learn to rebuild machines by removing defective parts and repairing, adjusting, and testing the machines. Next, they accompany an experienced repairer on service calls and, finally, make visits on their own. This learning process takes from 6 months to 2 years, depending on the individual's abilities, previous education, types of machines serviced, and quality of instruction.

The National Automatic Merchandising Association has a self-study technician training program for vending machine repairers. Manuals give instruction in subjects such as customer relations, safety, electronics, and reading schematics. Upon completion of the program, repairers must pass a written test to become certified as a technician or journeyman.

To learn about new machines, repairers and servicers sometimes attend training sessions sponsored by manufacturers and distributors that may last from a few days to several weeks. Both trainees and experienced workers sometimes take evening courses in basic electricity, electronics, microwave ovens, refrigeration, and other related subjects to stay on top of new techniques and equipment. Skilled servicers and repairers may be promoted to supervisory jobs or go into business for themselves.

Employment

Coin, vending, and amusement machine servicers and repairers held about 46,000 jobs in 2004. Most repairers work for vending machine operators that sell food and other items through machines. Others work for beverage manufacturing companies that have their own machines. A growing number of servicers and repairers work for amusement, gambling, and recreation establishments that own video games, pinball machines, jukeboxes, slot machines, and similar types of amusement equipment. Although vending and amusement machine servicers and repairers are employed throughout the country, most are located in areas with large populations and, thus, many vending and amusement machines.

Job Outlook

Employment of coin, vending, and amusement machine servicers and repairers is expected to grow more slowly than the average for all occupations through the year 2014. However, opportunities should be good for persons with some formal training in electronics, which can include high school or equivalent classes in basic mechanics, electronics, circuitry, or diagnostics. Job openings for coin, vending, and amusement machine servicers and repairers will arise mostly from the need to replace experienced workers who transfer to other occupations or leave the labor force.

Establishments are likely to install additional vending machines in industrial plants, hospitals, stores, schools and prisons to meet the public demand for inexpensive snacks and other food items. The range of products dispensed by the machines is expected to increase, as vending machines continue to become increasingly automated and begin to incorporate microwave ovens, minirefrigerators, and freezers. In addition casinos and other amusement establishments are becoming an increasing source of entertainment. State and multi-State lotteries are increasingly using coin-operated machines to sell scratch-off tickets in grocery stores and other public places.

Although the number of vending machines in use is expected to increase, improved technology in newer machines will moderate employment growth because these machines require less maintenance than do older ones. The new machines also need restocking less often, and they contain computers that record sales and inventory data, reducing the amount of time-consuming paperwork that otherwise would have to be filled out. The Internet is beginning to play a large role in the monitoring of vending machines from remote locations. In addition, some new machines use wireless data transmitters to signal the vending machine company when the machine needs restocking or repairing. This allows servicers and repairers to be dispatched only when needed, instead of having to check each machine on a regular schedule.

Earnings

Median hourly earnings of coin, vending, and amusement machine servicers and repairers were $13.47 in May 2004. The middle 50 percent earned between $10.70 and $16.68 an hour. The lowest 10 percent earned less than $8.74an hour, and the highest 10 percent earned more than $20.51 an hour. Median hourly earnings were $12.66 in vending machine operators, the industry employing the largest number of coin, vending, and amusement machine servicers and repairers in May 2004.

Typically, States with some form of legalized gaming have the highest wages. Most coin, vending, and amusement machine servicers and repairers work 8 hours a day, 5 days a week, and receive premium pay for overtime. Some union contracts stipulate higher pay for night work and for emergency repair jobs on weekends and holidays than for regular hours.

Some vending machine repairers and servicers are members of the International Brotherhood of Teamsters.

Related Occupations

Other workers who repair equipment with electrical and electronic components include electrical and electronics installers and repairers; electronic home-entertainment equipment installers and repairers; heating, air-conditioning, and refrigeration mechanics and installers; and home appliance repairers.

Sources of Additional Information

Information on job opportunities in this field can be obtained from local vending machine firms and local offices of your State employment service.

For general information on vending machine servicing and repair, contact:

➤ National Automatic Merchandising Association, 20 N. Wacker Dr., Suite 3500, Chicago, IL 60606-3102. Internet: **http://www.vending.org**

➤ Vending Times, 1375 Broadway, New York, NY 10018.

➤ Automatic Merchandiser Vending Group, Cygnus Business Media, P.O. Box 803, 1233 Janesville Ave., Fort Atkinson, WI 53538-0803.

Heating, Air-Conditioning, and Refrigeration Mechanics and Installers

(O*NET 49-9021.01, 49-9021.02)

Significant Points

- Employment is projected to grow faster than average.
- Job prospects are expected to be excellent, particularly for those with training from an accredited technical school or with formal apprenticeship training.
- Obtaining certification through one of several organizations is increasingly recommended by employers and may increase advancement opportunities.

Nature of the Work

Heating and air-conditioning systems control the temperature, humidity, and the total air quality in residential, commercial, industrial, and other buildings. Refrigeration systems make it possible to store and transport food, medicine, and other perishable items. Heating, air-conditioning, and refrigeration mechanics and installers—also called technicians—install, maintain, and repair such systems. Because heating, ventilation, air-conditioning, and refrigeration systems often are referred to as HVACR systems, these workers also may be called HVACR technicians.

Heating, air-conditioning, and refrigeration systems consist of many mechanical, electrical, and electronic components, such as motors, compressors, pumps, fans, ducts, pipes, thermostats, and switches. In central forced air heating systems, for example, a furnace heats air that is distributed throughout the building via a system of metal or fiberglass ducts. Technicians must be able to maintain, diagnose, and correct problems throughout the entire system. To do this, they adjust system controls to recommended settings and test the performance of the entire system using special tools and test equipment.

Technicians often specialize in either installation or maintenance and repair, although they are trained to do both. They also may specialize in doing heating work or air-conditioning or refrigeration work. Some specialize in one type of equipment—for example, hydronics (water-based heating systems), solar panels, or commercial refrigeration. Technicians also try to sell service contracts to their clients. Service contracts provide for regular maintenance of the heating and cooling systems and they help to reduce the seasonal fluctuations of this type of work.

Technicians follow blueprints or other specifications to install oil, gas, electric, solid-fuel, and multiple-fuel heating systems and air conditioning systems. After putting the equipment in place, they install fuel and water supply lines, air ducts and vents, pumps, and other components. They may connect electrical wiring and controls and check the unit for proper operation. To ensure the proper functioning of the system, furnace installers often use combustion test equipment, such as carbon dioxide testers, carbon monoxide testers, combustion analyzers and oxygen testers.

After a furnace or air-conditioning unit has been installed, technicians often perform routine maintenance and repair work to keep the systems operating efficiently. They may adjust burners and blowers and check for leaks. If the system is not operating properly, they check the thermostat, burner nozzles, controls or other parts to diagnose and then correct the problem.

During the summer, when the heating system is not being used, heating equipment technicians do maintenance work, such as replacing filters, ducts, and other parts of the system that may accumulate dust and impurities during the operating season. During the winter, air-conditioning mechanics inspect the systems and do required maintenance, such as overhauling compressors.

Refrigeration mechanics install, service, and repair industrial and commercial refrigerating systems and a variety of refrigeration equipment. They follow blueprints, design specifications, and manufacturers' instructions to install motors, compressors, condensing units, evaporators, piping, and other components. They connect this equipment to the ductwork, refrigerant lines, and electrical power source. After making the connections, they charge the system with refrigerant, check it for proper operation, and program control systems.

When air-conditioning and refrigeration technicians service equipment, they must use care to conserve, recover, and recycle chlorofluorocarbon (CFC), hydrochlorofluorocarbon (HCFC), hydrofluorocarbon (HFC), and other refrigerants used in air-conditioning and refrigeration systems. The release of these refrigerants can be harmful to the environment. Technicians conserve the refrigerant by making sure that there are no leaks in the system; they recover it by venting the refrigerant into proper cylinders; they recycle it for reuse with special filter-dryers; or they insure that the refrigerant is properly disposed.

Heating, air-conditioning, and refrigeration mechanics and installers are adept at using a variety of tools, including hammers, wrenches, metal snips, electric drills, pipe cutters and benders, measurement gauges, and acetylene torches, to work with refrigerant lines and air ducts. They use voltmeters, thermometers, pressure gauges, manometers, and other testing devices to check airflow, refrigerant pressure, electrical circuits, burners, and other components.

Other craftworkers sometimes install or repair cooling and heating systems. For example, on a large air-conditioning installation job, especially where workers are covered by union contracts, ductwork might be done by sheet metal workers and duct installers; electrical work by electricians; and installation of piping, condensers, and other components by pipelayers, plumbers, pipefitters, and steamfitters. Home appliance repairers usually service room air-conditioners and household refrigerators. (Additional information about each of these occupations appears elsewhere in the *Handbook*.)

Working Conditions

Heating, air-conditioning, and refrigeration mechanics and installers work in homes, retail establishments, hospitals, office buildings, and factories—anywhere there is climate-control equipment. They may be assigned to specific job sites at the beginning of each day, or may be dispatched to a variety of locations if they are making service calls.

Technicians may work outside in cold or hot weather or in buildings that are uncomfortable because the air-conditioning or heating equipment is broken. In addition, technicians might have to work in awkward or cramped positions and sometimes are required to work in high places. Hazards include electrical shock, burns, muscle strains, and other injuries from handling heavy equipment. Appropriate safety equipment is necessary when handling refrigerants because contact can cause skin damage, frostbite, or blindness. Inhalation of refrigerants when working in confined spaces also is a possible hazard.

The majority of mechanics and installers work at least a 40-hour week. During peak seasons they often work overtime or irregular hours. Maintenance workers, including those who provide maintenance services under contract, often work evening or weekend shifts and are on call. Most employers try to provide a full workweek year-round by scheduling both installation and maintenance work, and many manufacturers and contractors now provide or even require service contracts. In most shops that service both heating and air-conditioning equipment, employment is stable throughout the year.

Training, Other Qualifications, and Advancement

Because of the increasing sophistication of heating, air-conditioning, and refrigeration systems, employers prefer to hire those with technical school training or those who have completed an apprenticeship. Some mechanics and installers, however, still learn the trade informally on the job.

Many secondary and postsecondary technical and trade schools, junior and community colleges, and the U.S. Armed Forces offer 6-month to 2-year programs in heating, air-conditioning, and refrigeration. Students study theory, design, and equipment construction, as well as electronics. They also learn the basics of installation, maintenance, and repair. There are three accrediting agencies that have set academic standards for HVACR programs. These accrediting bodies are HVAC Excellence, the National Center for Construction Education and Research (NCCER) and the Partnership for Air Conditioning, Heating, and Refrigeration Accreditation (PHARA). After completing these programs, new technicians generally need between an additional 6 months and 2 years of field experience before they can be considered proficient.

Apprenticeship programs frequently are run by joint committees representing local chapters of the Air-Conditioning Contractors

Heating and air-conditioning mechanics often work evenings and weekends, and can be on call if an emergency arises.

of America, the Mechanical Contractors Association of America, Plumbing-Heating-Cooling Contractors—National Association, and locals of the Sheet Metal Workers' International Association or the United Association of Journeymen and Apprentices of the Plumbing and Pipefitting Industry of the United States and Canada. Other apprenticeship programs are sponsored by local chapters of the Associated Builders and Contractors and the National Association of Home Builders. Formal apprenticeship programs normally last 3 to 5 years and combine on-the-job training with classroom instruction. Classes include subjects such as the use and care of tools, safety practices, blueprint reading, and the theory and design of heating, ventilation, air-conditioning, and refrigeration systems. Applicants for these programs must have a high school diploma or equivalent. Math and reading skills are essential. After completing an apprenticeship program, technicians are considered skilled trades workers and capable of working alone. These programs are also a pathway to certification and in some cases college credits.

Those who acquire their skills on the job usually begin by assisting experienced technicians. They may begin by performing simple tasks such as carrying materials, insulating refrigerant lines, or cleaning furnaces. In time, they move on to more difficult tasks, such as cutting and soldering pipes and sheet metal and checking electrical and electronic circuits.

Courses in shop math, mechanical drawing, applied physics and chemistry, electronics, blueprint reading, and computer applications provide a good background for those interested in entering this occupation. Some knowledge of plumbing or electrical work also is helpful. A basic understanding of electronics is becoming more important because of the increasing use of this technology in equipment controls. Because technicians frequently deal directly with the public, they should be courteous and tactful, especially when dealing with an aggravated customer. They also should be in good physical condition because they sometimes have to lift and move heavy equipment.

All technicians who purchase or work with refrigerants must be certified in their proper handling. To become certified to purchase and handle refrigerants, technicians must pass a written examination specific to the type of work in which they specialize. The three possible areas of certification are: Type I—servicing small appliances, Type II—high-pressure refrigerants, and Type III—low-pressure refrigerants. Exams are administered by organizations approved by the U.S. Environmental Protection Agency, such as trade schools, unions, contractor associations, or building groups.

Several organizations have begun to offer basic self-study, classroom, and Internet courses for individuals with limited experience. In addition to understanding how systems work, technicians also must learn about refrigerant products and the legislation and regulations that govern their use.

Throughout the learning process, job candidates may have to take a number of tests that measure their skills in the field. For those with less than 1 year of experience and taking classes, the industry has developed a series of exams to test basic competency in residential heating and cooling, light commercial heating and cooling, and commercial refrigeration. These are referred to as "Entry-level" certification exams and are commonly conducted at both secondary and postsecondary technical and trade schools. For HVACR technicians who have at least one year of experience performing installations and 2 years of experience performing maintenance and repair, they can take a number of different tests to certify their competency in working with more specific types of equipment, such as oil-burning furnaces. The tests are offered through Refrigeration Service Engineers Society (RSES), HVAC Excellence, The Carbon Monoxide Safety Association (COSA), Air Conditioning and Refrigeration Safety Coalition, and North American Technician

Excellence, Inc. (NATE), among others. Passing these tests and obtaining certification is increasingly recommended by employers and may increase advancement opportunities.

Advancement usually takes the form of higher wages. Some technicians, however, may advance to positions as supervisor or service manager. Others may move into areas such as sales and marketing. Still others may become building superintendents, cost estimators, or, with the necessary certification, teachers. Those with sufficient money and managerial skill can open their own contracting business.

Employment

Heating, air-conditioning, and refrigeration mechanics and installers held about 270,000 jobs in 2004; almost half worked for plumbing, heating, and air conditioning contractors. The remainder was employed in a variety of industries throughout the country, reflecting a widespread dependence on climate-control systems. Some worked for fuel oil dealers, refrigeration and air-conditioning service and repair shops, schools, and stores that sell heating and air-conditioning systems. Local governments, the Federal Government, hospitals, office buildings, and other organizations that operate large air-conditioning, refrigeration, or heating systems employed others. About 15 percent of mechanics and installers were self-employed.

Job Outlook

Job prospects for heating, air-conditioning, and refrigeration mechanics and installers are expected to be excellent, particularly for those with training from an accredited technical school or with formal apprenticeship training, and especially in the fastest growing areas of the country. A growing number of retirements of highly skilled technicians are expected to generate many job openings. In addition, employment of heating, air-conditioning, and refrigeration mechanics and installers is projected to increase faster than the average for all occupations through the year 2014. As the population and stock of buildings grows, so does the demand for residential, commercial, and industrial climate-control systems. The increased complexity of HVACR systems, increasing the possibility that equipment may malfunction, also will create opportunities for service technicians. Technicians who specialize in installation work may experience periods of unemployment when the level of new construction activity declines, but maintenance and repair work usually remains relatively stable. People and businesses depend on their climate-control systems and must keep them in good working order, regardless of economic conditions.

Concern for the environment has prompted the development of new energy-saving heating and air-conditioning systems. An emphasis on better energy management should lead to the replacement of older systems and the installation of newer, more efficient systems in existing homes and buildings. Also, demand for maintenance and service work should increase as businesses and homeowners strive to keep increasingly complex systems operating at peak efficiency. Regulations prohibiting the discharge and production of CFC and HCFC refrigerants should continue to result in the need to replace many existing air conditioning systems or modify them to use new environmentally safe refrigerants. The pace of replacement in the commercial and industrial sectors will quicken if Congress or individual States cut the time needed to fully depreciate the cost of new HVACR systems, which is being considered.

A growing focus on improving indoor air quality, as well as the increasing use of refrigerated equipment by a growing number of stores and gasoline stations that sell food, also should contribute to the creation of more jobs for heating, air-conditioning, and refrigeration technicians.

Earnings

Median hourly earnings of heating, air-conditioning, and refrigeration mechanics and installers were $17.43 in May 2004. The middle 50 percent earned between $13.51 and $22.21 an hour. The lowest 10 percent earned less than $10.88, and the top 10 percent earned more than $27.11. Median hourly earnings in the industries employing the largest numbers of heating, air-conditioning, and refrigeration mechanics and installers in May 2004 were:

Hardware and plumbing and heating equipment and supplies merchant wholesalers	$19.51
Direct selling establishments	17.81
Elementary and secondary schools	17.56
Commercial and industrial machinery and equipment (except automotive and electronic) repair and maintenance	17.52
Building equipment contractors	16.80

Apprentices usually begin at about 50 percent of the wage rate paid to experienced workers. As they gain experience and improve their skills, they receive periodic increases until they reach the wage rate of experienced workers.

Heating, air-conditioning, and refrigeration mechanics and installers enjoy a variety of employer-sponsored benefits. In addition to typical benefits such as health insurance and pension plans, some employers pay for work-related training and provide uniforms, company vans, and tools.

About 16 percent of heating, air-conditioning, and refrigeration mechanics and installers are members of a union. The unions to which the greatest numbers of mechanics and installers belong are the Sheet Metal Workers International Association and the United Association of Journeymen and Apprentices of the Plumbing and Pipefitting Industry of the United States and Canada.

Related Occupations

Heating, air-conditioning, and refrigeration mechanics and installers work with sheet metal and piping, and repair machinery, such as electrical motors, compressors, and burners. Other workers who have similar skills include boilermakers; home appliance repairers; electricians; sheet metal workers; and pipelayers, plumbers, pipefitters, and steamfitters.

Sources of Additional Information

For more information about opportunities for training, certification, and employment in this trade, contact local vocational and technical schools; local heating, air-conditioning, and refrigeration contractors; a local of the unions or organizations previously mentioned; a local joint union-management apprenticeship committee; or the nearest office of the State employment service or apprenticeship agency.

For information on career opportunities, training, and technician certification, contact:
➤ Air-Conditioning Contractors of America (ACCA), 2800 Shirlington Rd., Suite 300, Arlington, VA 22206. Internet: **http://www.acca.org**
➤ Refrigeration Service Engineers Society (RSES), 1666 Rand Rd., Des Plaines, IL 60016-3552. Internet: **http://www.rses.org**
➤ Plumbing-Heating-Cooling Contractors (PHCC), 180 S. Washington, St., P.O. Box 6808, Falls Church, VA 22046. Internet: **http://www.phccweb.org**
➤ Sheet Metal and Air-Conditioning Contractors National Association, 4201 Lafayette Center Dr., Chantilly, VA 20151-1209. Internet: **http://www.smacna.org**
➤ HVAC Excellence, P.O. Box 491, Mt. Prospect, IL 60056. Internet: **http://www.hvacexcellence.org**
➤ North American Technician Excellence (NATE), 4100 North Fairfax Dr., Suite 210, Arlington, VA 22203. Internet: **http://www.natex.org**
➤ Air-Conditioning and Refrigeration Institute, 4100 North Fairfax Dr., Suite 200, Arlington, VA 22203. Internet: **http://www.coolcareers.org** or **http://www.ari.org**

➤ Carbon Monoxide Safety Association, P.O. Box 669, Eastlake, CO 80614. Internet: **http://www.cosafety.org**
➤ National Occupational Competency Testing Institute. Internet: **http://www.nocti.org**
➤ Associated Builders and Contractors, Workforce Development Department, 4250 North Fairfax Dr., 9th Floor, Arlington, VA 22203. Internet: **http//www.trytools.org**
➤ Home Builders Institute, National Association of Home Builders, 1201 15th St. NW., 6th Floor, Washington, DC 20005-2800. Internet: **http://www.hbi.org**
➤ Mechanical Contractors Association of America, 1385 Piccard Dr., Rockville, MD 20850-4329. Internet: **http://www.mcaa.org**
➤ National Center for Construction Education and Research, P.O. Box 141104, Gainesville, FL 32601. Internet: **http://www.nccer.org**

Home Appliance Repairers

(O*NET 49-9031.01, 49-9031.02)

Significant Points

● Good job prospects are expected, with job openings continuing to outnumber jobseekers.

● Individuals with formal training in appliance repair and electronics should have the best opportunities.

● Overall employment is projected to grow more slowly than average, reflecting average growth among wage and salary workers and a decline among self-employed repairers.

● Repairers of small household appliances usually are trained on the job, whereas repairers of large household appliances often are trained in a formal trade school, in a community college, or directly from the appliance manufacturer.

Nature of the Work

Anyone whose washer, dryer, or refrigerator has ever broken knows the importance of a dependable repair person. Home appliance repairers, often called service technicians, keep home appliances working and help prevent unwanted breakdowns. Some repairers work specifically on small appliances such as microwaves and vacuum cleaners; others specialize in major appliances such as refrigerators, dishwashers, washers, and dryers.

Home appliance repairers visually inspect appliances and check for unusual noises, excessive vibration, leakage of fluid, or loose parts to determine why the appliances fail to operate properly. They use service manuals, troubleshooting guides, and experience to diagnose particularly difficult problems. Repairers disassemble the appliance to examine its internal parts for signs of wear or corrosion. They follow wiring diagrams and use testing devices such as ammeters, voltmeters, and wattmeters to check electrical systems for shorts and faulty connections.

After identifying problems, home appliance repairers replace or repair defective belts, motors, heating elements, switches, gears, or other items. They tighten, align, clean, and lubricate parts as necessary. Repairers use common handtools, including screwdrivers, wrenches, files, and pliers, as well as soldering guns and special tools designed for particular appliances. When repairing appliances with electronic parts, they may replace circuit boards or other electronic components.

When repairing refrigerators and window air-conditioners, repairers must take care to conserve, recover, and recycle chlorofluorocarbon (CFC) and hydrochlorofluorocarbon (HCFC) refrigerants used in the cooling systems, as is required by law. Repairers conserve the refrigerant by making sure that there are no leaks in the system; they recover the refrigerant by venting it into proper cylinders; and they recycle the refrigerant with special filter-dryers so that it can be used again. Federal regulations also require that home appliance repairers document the capture and disposal of refrigerants.

Home appliance repairers generally install household durable goods such as refrigerators, washing machines, and cooking products. They may have to install pipes in a customer's home to connect the appliances to the gas line. They measure, lay out, cut, thread, and connect pipe to a feeder line and then to the appliance. They may have to saw holes in walls or floors and hang steel supports from beams or joists in order to hold gas pipes in place. Once the gas line is in place, they turn on the gas and check for leaks. *Gas appliance repairers* check the heating unit and replace tubing, thermocouples, thermostats, valves, and indicator spindles. They also answer emergency calls about gas leaks.

Repairers also answer customers' questions about the care and use of appliances. For example, they demonstrate how to load automatic washing machines, arrange dishes in dishwashers, or sharpen chain saws to maximize their performance.

Repairers write up estimates of the cost of repairs for customers, keep records of parts used and hours worked, prepare bills, and collect payments. Self-employed repairers also deal with the original appliance manufacturers to recoup monetary claims for work performed on appliances still under warranty.

Working Conditions

Home appliance repairers who handle portable appliances usually work in repair shops that generally are quiet and adequately lighted and ventilated. Those who repair major appliances usually make service calls to customers' homes. They carry their tools and a number of commonly used parts with them in a truck or van on their service calls. Repairers may spend several hours a day driving to and from appointments and emergency calls. They may work in clean, comfortable rooms such as kitchens, but they also may work in damp, dirty, or dusty areas of homes. Repairers sometimes work in cramped and uncomfortable positions when they are replacing parts in hard-to-reach areas of appliances. Repairer jobs generally are not hazardous, but workers must exercise care and follow safety precautions to avoid electrical shocks and prevent injuries when lifting and moving large appliances. When repairing gas appliances and microwave ovens, repairers must be aware of the dangers of gas and radio-frequency energy leaks.

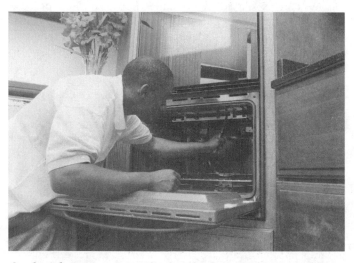

On-the-job repairs are usually done by the most experienced heavy vehicle technicians.

Home appliance repairers usually work with little or no direct supervision, a feature of the job that is appealing to many people. Many home appliance repairers work a standard 40-hour week, but may work overtime and weekend hours in the summer months, when they are in high demand to fix air-conditioners and refrigerators. Some repairers work early morning, evening, and weekend shifts and may remain on call in case of an emergency.

Training, Other Qualifications, and Advancement

Employers generally require a high school diploma for home appliance repairer jobs. Once employed, repairers of small appliances usually are trained on the job, whereas repairers of large household appliances often are trained in a formal trade school, in a community college, or directly from the appliance manufacturer. Mechanical and electrical aptitudes are desirable, and those who work in customers' homes must be courteous and tactful.

Employers prefer to hire people with formal training in appliance repair and electronics. Many repairers complete 1- or 2-year formal training programs in appliance repair and related subjects in high schools, private vocational schools, and community colleges. Courses in basic electricity and electronics are becoming increasingly important as more manufacturers install circuit boards and other electronic control systems in home appliances.

Whether their basic skills are developed through formal training or on the job, trainees usually receive additional training from their employer and from manufacturers. In shops that fix portable appliances, they work on a single type of appliance, such as a vacuum cleaner, until they master its repair. Then they move on to others, until they can repair all those handled by the shop. In companies that repair major appliances, beginners assist experienced repairers on service visits. They also may study on their own. They learn to read schematic drawings, analyze problems, determine whether to repair or replace parts, and follow proper safety procedures. Up to 3 years of on-the-job training may be needed for a technician to become skilled in all aspects of repair.

Some appliance manufacturers and department store chains have formal training programs that include home study and shop classes, in which trainees work with demonstration appliances and other training equipment. Many repairers receive supplemental instruction through 2- or 3-week seminars conducted by appliance manufacturers. Experienced repairers also often attend training classes and study service manuals. Repairers authorized for warranty work by manufacturers are required to attend periodic training sessions.

The U.S. Environmental Protection Agency (EPA) has mandated that all repairers who buy or work with refrigerants be certified in the proper handling of refrigerants. In order to become certified, a technician must pass a written examination. Exams are administered by EPA-approved organizations, such as trade schools, unions, and employer associations. There also are EPA-approved take-home certification exams. Although no formal training is required for certification, many of these organizations offer training programs designed to prepare workers for the certification examination.

In addition to earning the certification required by the EPA, home appliance repairers may exhibit their competence by passing one of several certification examinations offered by various organizations. Although voluntary, such certifications can be helpful when seeking employment. The National Appliance Service Technician Certification (NASTeC), which is administered by the International Society of Certified Electronics Technicians (ISCET), requires repairers to pass a comprehensive examination that tests their competence in the diagnosis, repair, and maintenance of major home appliances. Examinations are given in three specialty areas of appliance repair: refrigeration and air-conditioning; cooking; and laundry and dishwashing. Although the NASTeC credential does not expire, continuing education classes are available so that repairers can keep abreast of technological changes. The Professional Service Association (PSA) administers a similar certification program. Those who pass the PSA examination earn the Certified Appliance Professional (CAP) designation, which is valid for 4 years. If CAP-certified repairers complete at least 15 credit hours of instruction each year during the 4 years, they need not take the examination to become recertified. Otherwise, they must take the examination again to become recertified.

Repairers in large shops or service centers may be promoted to supervisor, assistant service manager, or service manager. Some repairers advance to managerial positions such as regional service manager or parts manager for appliance or tool manufacturers. Preference is given to those who demonstrate technical competence and show an ability to get along with other workers and customers. Experienced repairers who have sufficient funds and knowledge of small-business management may open their own repair shops.

Employment

Home appliance repairers held 50,000 jobs in 2004. About 42 percent of salaried repairers worked in retail trade establishments such as department stores and electronics and appliance stores. About 20 percent of repairers are self-employed. Almost every community in the country employs home appliance repairers; a high concentration of jobs is found in more populated areas.

Job Outlook

Good job prospects are expected, with job openings continuing to outnumber jobseekers. Many prospective workers may choose not to enter this occupation, because they prefer work that is less strenuous and that is performed under more comfortable working conditions. Individuals with formal training in appliance repair and electronics should have the best opportunities.

Overall employment of home appliance repairers is expected to increase more slowly than the average for all occupations through the year 2014. Slower-than-average employment growth is expected among wage and salary workers, while the number of self-employed home appliance repairers is projected to decline.

The number of home appliances in use is expected to increase with growth in the numbers of households and businesses. Appliances also are becoming more technologically advanced and will increasingly require a skilled technician to diagnose and fix problems. In recent years, consumers have tended to purchase new appliances when existing warranties expire rather repair old appliances. However, over the next decade, as more consumers purchase higher priced appliances designed to have much longer lives, they will be more likely to use repair services than to purchase new appliances. Employment is relatively steady during economic downturns because there is still demand for appliance repair services. In addition to new jobs created over the 2004–14 period, openings will arise as home appliance repairers retire or transfer to other occupations.

Jobs are expected to be increasingly concentrated in larger companies as the number of smaller shops and family-owned businesses declines. However, repairers who maintain strong industry relationships may still go into business for themselves.

Earnings

Median annual earnings, including commissions, of home appliance repairers were $32,180 in May 2004. The middle 50 percent earned between $23,510 and $41,090 a year. The lowest 10 percent earned less than $17,890, and the highest 10 percent earned more than $49,760 a year. Median annual earnings of home appliance repairers in May 2004 were $30,840 in electronics and appliance stores and $33,790 in personal and household goods repair and maintenance.

Earnings of home appliance repairers vary with the skill level required to fix equipment, the geographic location, and the type of equipment repaired. Because many repairers receive a commission along with their salary, earnings increase with the number of jobs a repairer can complete in a day.

Many larger dealers, manufacturers, and service stores offer typical benefits such as health insurance coverage, sick leave, and retirement and pension programs. Some home appliance repairers belong to the International Brotherhood of Electrical Workers.

Related Occupations

Other workers who repair electrical and electronic equipment include electrical and electronics installers and repairers; electronic home entertainment equipment installers and repairers; small-engine mechanics; coin, vending, and amusement machine servicers and repairers; and heating, air-conditioning, and refrigeration mechanics and installers.

Sources of Additional Information

For general information about the work of home appliance repairers, contact any of the following organizations:

➤ North American Retail Dealers Association, 10 E. 22nd St., Suite 310, Lombard, IL 60148.
➤ National Appliance Service Association, P.O. Box 2514, Kokomo, IN 46904
➤ United Servicers Association, Inc., P.O. Box 31006, Albuquerque, NM 87190.

For information on the National Appliance Service Technician Certification program, contact:

➤ International Society of Certified Electronics Technicians, 3608 Pershing Ave., Fort Worth, TX 76107. Internet: **http://www.iscet.org**

For information on the Certified Appliance Professional program, contact:

➤ Professional Service Association, 71 Columbia St., Cohoes, NY 12047.

Industrial Machinery Mechanics and Maintenance Workers

(O*NET 49-9041.00, 49-9043.00)

Significant Points

● Highly skilled mechanics usually learn their trade through a 4-year apprenticeship program, while lower skilled maintenance workers receive short-term on-the-job training.

● Employment is projected to grow more slowly than average, but applicants with broad skills in machine repair and maintenance should have favorable job prospects.

● Unlike some manufacturing occupations, these workers usually are not affected by changes in production.

Nature of the Work

A wide range of employees is required to keep sophisticated industrial machinery running smoothly—from highly skilled industrial machinery mechanics to lower skilled machinery maintenance workers who perform routine tasks. Their work is vital to the success of industrial facilities, not only because an idle machine will delay production, but also because a machine that is not properly repaired and maintained may damage the machine, the final product or injure an operator.

The most basic tasks in this process are performed by *machinery maintenance workers*. These employees are responsible for cleaning and lubricating machinery, performing basic diagnostic tests, checking performance, and testing damaged machine parts to determine whether major repairs are necessary. In carrying out these tasks, maintenance workers must follow machine specifications and adhere to maintenance schedules. Maintenance workers may perform minor repairs, but major repairs are generally left to machinery mechanics.

Industrial machinery mechanics, also called industrial machinery repairers or maintenance machinists, are highly skilled workers who maintain and repair machinery in a plant or factory. To do this effectively, they must be able to detect minor problems and correct them before they become major problems. Machinery mechanics use their understanding of the equipment, technical manuals, and careful observation to discover the cause. For example, after hearing a vibration from a machine, the mechanic must decide whether it is due to worn belts, weak motor bearings, or some other problem. Computerized diagnostic systems and vibration analysis techniques are aiding in determining the problem, but mechanics still need years of training and experience.

After diagnosing the problem, the industrial machinery mechanic disassembles the equipment to repair or replace the necessary parts. When repairing electronically controlled machinery, mechanics may work closely with electronic repairers or electricians who maintain the machine's electronic parts. (Statements on electrical and electronic installers and repairers, as well as electricians, appear elsewhere in the *Handbook*.) Increasingly, mechanics need electronic and computer skills in order to repair sophisticated equipment on their own. Once a repair is made, mechanics perform tests to ensure that the machine is running smoothly.

Primary responsibilities of industrial machinery mechanics include repair, preventive maintenance, and installation of new machinery. For example, they adjust and calibrate automated manufacturing equipment, such as industrial robots. As plants retool and invest in new equipment, they increasingly rely on mechanics to properly situate and install the machinery. In many plants, this has traditionally been the job of millwrights, but mechanics are increasingly called upon to carry out this task. (See the statement on millwrights elsewhere in the *Handbook*.)

Industrial machinery mechanics and machinery maintenance workers use a variety of tools to perform repairs and preventive maintenance. They may use a screwdriver and wrench to adjust a motor, or a hoist to lift a printing press off the ground. When replacements for broken or defective parts are not readily available, or when a machine must be quickly returned to production, mechanics may sketch a part to be fabricated by the plant's machine shop. Mechanics use catalogs to order replacement parts and often follow blueprints, technical manuals, and engineering specifications to maintain and fix equipment. By keeping complete and up-to-date records, mechanics try to anticipate trouble and service equipment before factory production is interrupted.

Working Conditions

In production facilities, these workers are subject to common shop injuries such as cuts, bruises, and strains. They also may work in awkward positions, including on top of ladders or in cramped conditions under large machinery, which exposes them to additional hazards. They often use protective equipment such as hardhats, safety glasses, steel-tipped shoes, hearing protectors, and belts.

Because factories and other facilities cannot afford to have industrial machinery out of service for long periods, mechanics may be called to the plant at night or on weekends for emergency repairs. Overtime is common among industrial machinery mechanics; about 30 percent work over 40 hours a week.

Training, Other Qualifications, and Advancement

Machinery maintenance workers typically receive short-term on-the-job training in order to perform routine tasks, such as setting

An industrial machinery mechanic adjusts a belt to reduce friction.

up, cleaning, lubricating, and starting machinery. This training may be offered by experienced workers, professional trainers, or product representatives.

Industrial machinery mechanics, on the other hand, often learn their trade through 4-year apprenticeship programs that combine classroom instruction with on-the-job-training. These programs usually are sponsored by a local trade union. Other mechanics start as helpers and learn the skills of the trade informally or by taking courses offered by machinery manufacturers and community colleges.

Mechanics learn from experienced repairers how to operate, disassemble, repair, and assemble machinery. Classroom instruction focuses on subjects such as shop mathematics, blueprint reading, welding, electronics, and computer training.

Employers prefer to hire those who have completed high school or technical school, and have taken courses in mechanical drawing, mathematics, blueprint reading, computers, and electronics. Mechanical aptitude and manual dexterity are important characteristics for workers in this trade. Good reading comprehension is also necessary to understand the technical manuals of a wide range of machines. And, in general, good physical conditioning and agility are necessary because repairers sometimes have to lift heavy objects or climb to reach equipment.

Opportunities for advancement vary by specialty. Machinery maintenance workers may gain additional skills to make more complex repairs to machinery or work as supervisors. Industrial machinery mechanics also may advance either by working with more complicated equipment or by becoming supervisors. The most highly skilled repairers can be promoted to master mechanic or can become millwrights.

Employment
Industrial machinery mechanics and maintenance workers held about 306,000 jobs in 2004. Of these, 220,000 were held by the more highly skilled industrial machinery mechanics, while machinery maintenance workers accounted for 86,000 jobs. Two out of three workers were employed in the manufacturing sector, in industries such as food processing, textile mills, chemicals, fabricated metal products, motor vehicles, and primary metals. Others worked for government agencies, public utilities, mining companies, and other establishments in which industrial machinery is used.

Job Outlook
Employment of industrial machinery mechanics and maintenance workers is projected to grow more slowly than the average for all occupations through 2014. Nevertheless, applicants with broad skills in machine repair and maintenance should have favorable job prospects. Many mechanics are expected to retire in coming years, and employers have reported difficulty in recruiting young workers with the necessary skills to be industrial machinery mechanics. Most job openings will stem from the need to replace workers who transfer to other occupations or who retire or leave the labor force for other reasons.

As more firms introduce automated production equipment, these workers will be needed to ensure that these machines are properly maintained and consistently in operation. However, many new machines are capable of self-diagnosis, increasing their reliability and somewhat reducing the need for repairers.

Industrial machinery mechanics and maintenance workers are not usually affected by changes in production. During slack periods, when some plant workers are laid off, mechanics often are retained to do major overhaul jobs and to keep expensive machinery in working order. Although these workers may face layoffs or a reduced workweek when economic conditions are particularly severe, they usually are less affected than other workers because machines have to be maintained regardless of production level.

Earnings
Median hourly earnings of industrial machinery mechanics were $18.78 in May 2004. The middle 50 percent earned between $15.09 and $22.95. The lowest 10 percent earned less than $12.14, and the highest 10 percent earned more than $27.59.

Machinery maintenance workers earned less than the higher skilled industrial machinery mechanics. Median hourly earnings of machinery maintenance workers were $15.79 in May 2004. The middle 50 percent earned between $12.21 and $20.18. The lowest 10 percent earned less than $9.60, and the highest 10 percent earned more than $24.59.

Earnings vary by industry and geographic region. Median hourly earnings in the industries employing the largest numbers of industrial machinery mechanics in May 2004 are:

Electric power generation, transmission and distribution	$25.78
Motor vehicle parts manufacturing	21.79
Plastics product manufacturing	18.04
Machinery, equipment, and supplies merchant wholesalers	17.74
Commercial and industrial machinery and equipment (except automotive and electronic) repair and maintenance	16.93

About 25 percent of industrial machinery mechanics and maintenance workers are union members. Labor unions that represent these workers include the United Steelworkers of America; the United Auto Workers; the International Association of Machinists and Aerospace Workers; the United Brotherhood of Carpenters and Joiners of America; and the International Union of Electronic, Electrical, Salaried, Machine, and Furniture Workers-Communications Workers of America.

Related Occupations
Other occupations that involve repairing and maintaining machinery include aircraft and avionics equipment mechanics and service technicians; automotive service technicians and mechanics; diesel service technicians and mechanics; elevator installers and repairers; heating, air-conditioning, and refrigeration mechanics and installers; heavy vehicle and mobile equipment service technicians and mechanics; machinists; maintenance and repair workers, general; millwrights; and small engine mechanics.

Sources of Additional Information
Information about employment and apprenticeship opportunities may be obtained from local employers, from local offices of the State employment service, or from:
➤ United Brotherhood of Carpenters and Joiners of America, 6801 Placid St., Las Vegas, NV 89119. Internet: **http://www.carpenters.org**
➤ National Tooling and Machining Association, 9300 Livingston Rd., Fort Washington, MD 20744. Internet: **http://www.ntma.org**

Line Installers and Repairers
(O*NET 49-9051.00, 49-9052.00)

Significant Points
- Line installers and repairers work outdoors; conditions can be hazardous.
- Employers prefer applicants with knowledge of electricity and electronics obtained through experience or classroom training.
- Overall employment is projected to increase more slowly than average, although a growing number of retirements should create very good job opportunities, especially for electrical powerline installers and repairers.
- Earnings are higher than in most other occupations that do not require postsecondary education.

Nature of the Work
Vast networks of wires and cables provide customers with electrical power and communications services. Networks of electrical power lines deliver electricity from generating plants to customers. Communications networks of telephone and cable television lines provide voice, video, and other communications services. These networks are constructed and maintained by *electrical powerline installers and repairers* and *telecommunications line installers and repairers*.

While the work performed by telecommunications and electrical powerline installers is quite similar, they are two distinct occupations. Working with powerlines requires specialized knowledge of transformers, electrical power distribution systems, and substations. Working with telecommunications lines requires specialized knowledge of fiber optics and telecommunications switches and routers. While both powerline and telecommunications line installers have specialized knowledge, the procedures for installing both kinds of lines are quite similar.

All line installers, or line erectors, install new lines by constructing utility poles, towers, and underground trenches to carry the wires and cables. Line erectors use a variety of construction equipment, including digger derricks, trenchers, cable plows, and borers. Digger derricks are trucks equipped with augers and cranes; workers use augers to dig holes in the ground, and cranes are used to set utility poles in place. Trenchers and cable plows are used to cut openings in the earth for the laying of underground cables. Borers, which tunnel under the earth, are used to install tubes for the wire without opening a trench in the soil.

When construction is complete, line installers string cable along the poles, towers, tunnels, and trenches. While working on poles and towers, installers first use truck-mounted buckets to reach the top of the structure or physically climb the pole or tower. Next, they pull up cable from large reels mounted on trucks. The line is then set in place and pulled so that it has the correct amount of tension. Finally, line installers attach the cable to the structure using hand and hydraulic tools. When working with electrical power lines, installers bolt or clamp insulators onto the poles before attaching the cable. Underground cable is laid directly in a trench, pulled through a tunnel, or strung through a conduit running through a trench.

Other installation duties include setting up service for customers and installing network equipment. To set up service, line installers string cable between the customers' premises and the lines running on poles or towers or in trenches. They install wiring to houses and check the connection for proper voltage readings. Line installers also may install a variety of equipment. Workers on telephone and cable television lines install amplifiers and repeaters that maintain the strength of communications transmissions. Workers on electrical powerlines install and replace transformers, circuitbreakers, switches, fuses, and other equipment to control and direct the electrical current.

In addition to installation, line installers and repairers also are responsible for maintenance of electrical, telecommunications, and cable television lines. Workers periodically travel in trucks, helicopters, and airplanes to visually inspect the wires and cables. Sensitive monitoring equipment can automatically detect malfunctions on the network, such as loss of current flow. When line repairers identify a problem, they travel to the location of the malfunction and repair or replace defective cables or equipment. Bad weather or natural disasters can cause extensive damage to networks. Line installers and repairers must respond quickly to these emergencies to restore critical utility and communications services. This can often involve working outdoors in adverse weather conditions.

Installation and repair work may require splicing, or joining together, separate pieces of cable. Each cable contains numerous individual wires; splicing the cables together requires that each wire in one piece of cable be joined to another wire in the matching piece. Line installers splice cables using small handtools, epoxy, or mechanical equipment. At each splice, they place insulation over the conductor and seal the splice with moistureproof covering. At some companies, *cable splicing technicians* perform splices on larger lines.

Communications networks are transitioning to fiber optic cables instead of conventional wire or metal cables. Fiber optic cables are made of hair-thin strands of glass, which convey pulses of light. These cables carry much more information at higher speeds than conventional cables. The higher transmission capacity of fiber optic cable has allowed communication networks to offer upgraded services, such as high-speed Internet access. Splicing fiber optic cable requires specialized equipment that carefully slices, matches, and aligns individual glass fibers. The fibers are joined by either electrical fusion (welding) or a mechanical fixture and gel (glue). More newly constructed buildings are being wired with fiber optic lines.

Line installers use safety equipment to prevent falls.

Working Conditions

Line installers and repairers must climb and maintain their balance while working on poles and towers. They lift equipment and work in a variety of positions, such as stooping or kneeling. Their work often requires that they drive utility vehicles, travel long distances, and work outdoors under a variety of weather conditions. Many line installers and repairers work a 40-hour week; however, emergencies may require overtime work. For example, when severe weather damages electrical and communications lines, line installers and repairers may work long and irregular hours to restore service.

Line installers and repairers encounter serious hazards on their jobs and must follow safety procedures to minimize potential danger. They wear safety equipment when entering utility holes and test for the presence of gas before going underground. Electric powerline workers have the more hazardous jobs. High-voltage powerlines can cause electrocution, and line installers and repairers must consequently use electrically insulated protective devices and tools when working with live cables. Powerlines are typically higher than telephone and cable television lines, increasing the risk of severe injury due to falls. To prevent these injuries, line installers and repairers must use fall-protection equipment when working on poles or towers.

Training, Other Qualifications, and Advancement

Employers of line installers and repairers usually require applicants to have at least a high school diploma. They also strongly prefer applicants with a technical knowledge of electricity or electronics, or experience obtained through vocational/technical programs, community colleges, or the Armed Forces. Programs in telecommunications, electronics, or electricity are offered by many community or technical colleges. These programs often are operated with assistance from local employers and unions. Some schools, working with local companies, offer 1-year certificate programs that emphasize hands-on field work. More advanced 2-year associate degree programs provide students with a broader knowledge of telecommunications and electrical utilities technology through courses in electricity, electronics, fiber optics, and microwave transmission. Graduates of these programs often get preferential treatment in the hiring process.

Prospective employees also should possess a basic knowledge of algebra and trigonometry, and have mechanical ability. Customer service and interpersonal skills also are important, especially for those dealing with customers. Because the work entails lifting heavy objects (many employers require applicants to be able to lift at least 50 pounds), climbing, and other physical activity, applicants should have stamina, strength, and coordination, and must be unafraid of heights. The ability to distinguish colors is necessary because wires and cables may be color-coded. A good driving record is important because workers often hold commercial driver's licenses and operate company-owned vehicles.

Line installers and repairers receive most of their training on the job. Electrical line installers and repairers often must complete formal apprenticeships or other employer training programs. These programs, which can last up to 5 years, combine on-the-job training with formal classroom courses and are sometimes administered jointly by the employer and the union representing the workers. The unions include the International Brotherhood of Electrical Workers, the Communications Workers of America, and the Utility Workers Union of America. Government safety regulations strictly define the training and education requirements for apprentice electrical line installers.

Line installers and repairers working for telephone and cable television companies receive several years of on-the-job training. They also may attend training or take online courses provided by equipment manufacturers, schools, unions, or industry training organizations. The Society of Cable Television Engineers (SCTE) provides certification programs for line installers and repairers. Applicants for certification must be employed in the cable television industry and attend training sessions at local SCTE chapters.

Entry-level line installers may be hired as ground workers, helpers, or tree trimmers, who clear branches from telephone and power lines. These workers may advance to positions stringing cable and performing service installations. With experience, they may advance to more sophisticated maintenance and repair positions responsible for increasingly larger portions of the network. Promotion to supervisory or training positions also is possible, but more advanced supervisory positions often require a college diploma.

Employment

Line installers and repairers held about 251,000 jobs in 2004. Approximately 147,000 were telecommunications line installers and repairers; the remainder were electrical powerline installers and repairers. Nearly all line installers and repairers worked for telecommunications, construction, or electric power generation, transmission, and distribution companies. Approximately 4,800 line installers and repairers were self-employed. Many of these were contractors employed by the telecommunications companies to handle customer service problems and installations.

Job Outlook

Overall employment of line installers and repairers is expected to grow more slowly than the average for all occupations through 2014. However, because many line installers and repairers are nearing retirement, job opportunities for new workers in this field should be very good, particularly for electrical powerline installers. Some companies are expanding their hiring in anticipation of increased retirements.

Employment of telecommunications line installers is projected to grow about as fast as the average for all occupations. Much of their work will involve replacing old wiring with fiber optic cable and expanding their networks to provide customers with high-speed access to data, video, and graphics. Line installers and repairers will be needed to construct and maintain the networks. However, the increasing use of wireless systems, increasingly reliable lines, and improved speeds

of data transmission over existing lines will limit employment growth. The number of households with wired telephone service is declining because of the increasing use of wireless telephones. Wireless networks do not require as many technicians to maintain and expand their systems, a characteristic that will reduce job growth. Satellite television providers are also providing strong competition. As wireless systems offer higher-speed Internet access, the number of households with wired phone or cable TV should decline further.

Very little employment growth is expected among electrical powerline installers and repairers. Despite consistently rising demand for electricity, industry deregulation is pushing companies to cut costs and maintenance, which tends to reduce employment. Most new jobs are expected to arise in the construction industry.

Earnings

Earnings for line installers and repairers are higher than those in most other occupations that do not require postsecondary education. Median hourly earnings for electrical powerline installers and repairers were $23.61 in May 2004. The middle 50 percent earned between $18.00 and $27.64. The lowest 10 percent earned less than $13.31, and the highest 10 percent earned more than $32.54. Median hourly earnings in the industries employing the largest numbers of electrical powerline installers and repairers in May 2004 are shown below:

Electric power generation, transmission and distribution	$24.96
Wired telecommunications carriers	24.15
Local government	22.25
Utility system construction	18.01
Building equipment contractors	15.77

Median hourly earnings for telecommunications line installers and repairers were $19.39 in May 2004. The middle 50 percent earned between $13.98 and $25.10. The lowest 10 percent earned less than $10.96, and the highest 10 percent earned more than $28.56. Median hourly earnings in the industries employing the largest numbers of telecommunications line installers and repairers in May 2004 are shown below:

Wired telecommunications carriers	$24.80
Cable and other subscription programming	17.36
Cable and other program distribution	16.58
Building equipment contractors	15.76
Utility system construction	14.53

Most line installers and repairers belong to unions, principally the Communications Workers of America, the International Brotherhood of Electrical Workers, and the Utility Workers Union of America. For these workers, union contracts set wage rates, wage increases, and the time needed to advance from one job level to the next.

Related Occupations

Other workers who install and repair electrical and electronic equipment include broadcast and sound engineering technicians and radio operators, electricians, and radio and telecommunications equipment installers and repairers.

Sources of Additional Information

For more details about employment opportunities, contact the telephone, cable television, or electrical power companies in your community. For general information and some educational resources on line installer and repairer jobs, write to:

➤ Communications Workers of America, 501 3rd St. NW., Washington, DC 20001.
➤ International Brotherhood of Electrical Workers, Telecommunications Department, 1125 15th St. NW., Washington, DC 20005.

Maintenance and Repair Workers, General

(O*NET 49-9042.00)

Significant Points

- General maintenance and repair workers are employed in almost every industry.

- Many workers learn their skills informally on the job; others learn by working as helpers to other repairers or to construction workers such as carpenters, electricians, or machinery repairers.

- Job opportunities should be favorable, with many openings occurring as a result of turnover in this large occupation.

Nature of the Work

Most craft workers specialize in one kind of work, such as plumbing or carpentry. General maintenance and repair workers, however, have skills in many different crafts. They repair and maintain machines, mechanical equipment, and buildings and work on plumbing, electrical, and air-conditioning and heating systems. They build partitions, make plaster or drywall repairs, and fix or paint roofs, windows, doors, floors, woodwork, and other parts of building structures. They also maintain and repair specialized equipment and machinery found in cafeterias, laundries, hospitals, stores, offices, and factories. Typical duties include troubleshooting and fixing faulty electrical switches, repairing air-conditioning motors, and unclogging drains. New buildings sometimes have computer-controlled systems that allow maintenance workers to make adjustments in building settings and monitor for problems from a central location. For example, they can remotely control light sensors that turn off lights automatically after a set amount of time or identify a broken ventilation fan that needs to be replaced.

General maintenance and repair workers inspect and diagnose problems and determine the best way to correct them, frequently checking blueprints, repair manuals, and parts catalogs. They obtain supplies and repair parts from distributors or storerooms. Using common hand and power tools such as screwdrivers, saws, drills, wrenches, and hammers, as well as specialized equipment and electronic testing devices, these workers replace or fix worn or broken parts, where necessary, or make adjustments to correct malfunctioning equipment and machines.

General maintenance and repair workers also perform routine preventive maintenance and ensure that machines continue to run smoothly, building systems operate efficiently, and the physical condition of buildings does not deteriorate. Following a checklist, they may inspect drives, motors, and belts, check fluid levels, replace filters, and perform other maintenance actions. Maintenance and repair workers keep records of their work.

Employees in small establishments, where they are often the only maintenance worker, make all repairs, except for very large or difficult jobs. In larger establishments, their duties may be limited to the general maintenance of everything in a workshop or a particular area.

Working Conditions

General maintenance and repair workers often carry out several different tasks in a single day, at any number of locations. They may work inside of a single building or in several different buildings. They may have to stand for long periods, lift heavy objects, and work

General maintenance and repair workers ensure that building equipment functions properly.

in uncomfortably hot or cold environments, in awkward and cramped positions, or on ladders. They are subject to electrical shock, burns, falls, cuts, and bruises. Most general maintenance workers work a 40-hour week. Some work evening, night, or weekend shifts or are on call for emergency repairs.

Those employed in small establishments often operate with only limited supervision. Those working in larger establishments frequently are under the direct supervision of an experienced worker.

Training, Other Qualifications, and Advancement

Many general maintenance and repair workers learn their skills informally on the job. They start as helpers, watching and learning from skilled maintenance workers. Helpers begin by doing simple jobs, such as fixing leaky faucets and replacing lightbulbs, and progress to more difficult tasks, such as overhauling machinery or building walls. Some learn their skills by working as helpers to other repair or construction workers, including carpenters, electricians, or machinery repairers.

Necessary skills also can be learned in high school shop classes and postsecondary trade or vocational schools. It generally takes from 1 to 4 years of on-the-job training or school, or a combination of both, to become fully qualified, depending on the skill level required. Because a growing number of new buildings rely on computers to control various of their systems, general maintenance and repair workers may need basic computer skills, such as how to log onto a central computer system and navigate through a series of menus. Usually, companies that install computer-controlled equipment provide on-site training for general maintenance and repair workers.

Graduation from high school is preferred for entry into this occupation. High school courses in mechanical drawing, electricity, woodworking, blueprint reading, science, mathematics, and computers are useful. Mechanical aptitude, the ability to use shop mathematics, and manual dexterity are important. Good health is necessary because the job involves much walking, standing, reaching, and heavy lifting. Difficult jobs require problem-solving ability, and many positions require the ability to work without direct supervision.

Many general maintenance and repair workers in large organizations advance to maintenance supervisor or become a craftworker such as an electrician, a heating and air-conditioning mechanic, or a plumber. Within small organizations, promotion opportunities are limited.

Employment

General maintenance and repair workers held 1.3 million jobs in 2004. They were employed in almost every industry. Around 1 in 5 worked in manufacturing industries, almost evenly distributed through all sectors, while about 1 in 6 worked for different government bodies. Others worked for wholesale and retail firms and for real estate firms that operate office and apartment buildings.

Job Outlook

Job opportunities should be favorable, especially for those with experience in maintenance or related fields. General maintenance and repair is a large occupation with significant turnover. Additionally, many job openings are expected to result from the retirement of many experienced maintenance workers over the next decade.

Employment of general maintenance and repair workers is expected to grow about as fast as average for all occupations through 2014. Employment is related to the number of buildings—for example, office and apartment buildings, stores, schools, hospitals, hotels, and factories—and the amount of equipment needing maintenance and repair. However, as machinery becomes more advanced and requires less maintenance, the need for general maintenance and repair workers diminishes. Also, as more buildings are controlled by computers, buildings can be monitored more efficiently.

Earnings

Median hourly earnings of general maintenance and repair workers were $14.76 in May 2004. The middle 50 percent earned between $11.11 and $19.17. The lowest 10 percent earned less than $8.70, and the highest 10 percent earned more than $23.40. Median hourly earnings in the industries employing the largest numbers of general maintenance and repair workers in May 2004 are shown in the following tabulation:

Local government	$15.70
Elementary and secondary schools	14.93
Activities related to real estate	12.71
Lessors of real estate	11.96
Traveler accommodation	11.19

Some general maintenance and repair workers are members of unions, including the American Federation of State, County, and Municipal Employees and the United Auto Workers.

Related Occupations

Some duties of general maintenance and repair workers are similar to those of carpenters; pipelayers, plumbers, pipefitters, and steamfitters; electricians; and heating, air-conditioning, and refrigeration mechanics. Other duties are similar to those of coin, vending, and amusement machine servicers and repairers; electrical and electronics installers and repairers; electronic home entertainment equipment installers and repairers; and radio and telecommunications equipment installers and repairers.

Sources of Additional Information

Information about job opportunities may be obtained from local employers and local offices of the State Employment Service.

Millwrights

(O*NET 49-9044.00)

Significant Points

● Training through apprenticeship programs, or through community colleges coupled with on-the-job training, generally lasts 4 years.

● Despite projected slower-than-average employment growth, skilled applicants should have good job opportunities.

● About 54 percent of millwrights belong to labor unions, one of the highest rates of membership in the economy.

Nature of the Work

Millwrights install, repair, replace, and dismantle the machinery and heavy equipment used in many industries. About half of all millwrights work in a variety of manufacturing industries; another third work for construction builders and contractors. The wide range of facilities and the development of new technologies require millwrights to continually update their skills—from blueprint reading and pouring concrete for machinery to set on to diagnosing and solving mechanical problems.

The millwright's responsibilities begin when machinery arrives at the jobsite. New equipment must be unloaded, inspected, and moved into position. To lift and move light machinery, millwrights use rigging and hoisting devices, such as pulleys and cables. With heavier equipment, they may require the assistance of hydraulic lift-truck or crane operators to position the machinery. Because millwrights often decide which device to use for moving machinery, they must know the load-bearing properties of rope, cables, hoists, and cranes.

Millwrights consult with production managers and others to determine the optimal placement of machines in a plant. When this placement requires building a new foundation, millwrights either prepare the foundation themselves or supervise its construction. As a result, they must know how to read blueprints and work with a variety of building materials.

To assemble machinery, millwrights fit bearings, align gears and wheels, attach motors, and connect belts, according to the manufacturer's blueprints and drawings. Precision leveling and alignment are important in the assembly process, so millwrights measure angles, material thickness, and small distances with tools such as squares, calipers, and micrometers. When a high level of precision is required, devices such as lasers and ultrasonic measuring and alignment tools may be used. Millwrights also work with hand and power tools, such as cutting torches, welding machines, hydraulic torque wrenches, hydraulic stud tensioners, soldering guns, and with metalworking equipment, including lathes and grinding machines.

In addition to installing and dismantling machinery, many millwrights work with mechanics and maintenance workers to repair and maintain equipment. This includes preventive maintenance, such as lubrication and fixing or replacing worn parts. (For further information on machinery maintenance, see the section on industrial machinery installation, repair, and maintenance workers, except millwrights, elsewhere in the *Handbook*.)

Increasingly sophisticated automation means more complicated machines for millwrights to install and maintain, requiring millwrights to specialize in certain machines or brand names. For example, millwrights install and maintain turbines in power plants that can weigh hundreds of tons and contain thousands

Millwrights assemble and maintain complex industrial machinery.

of parts. This machinery requires special care and knowledge, so millwrights receive additional training and are required to be certified by the manufacturer of the turbine.

Working Conditions

Working conditions vary by industry. Millwrights employed in manufacturing often work in a typical shop setting and use protective equipment to avoid common hazards. For example, protective devices, such as safety belts, protective glasses, and hardhats may be worn to prevent injuries from falling objects or machinery. Those employed in construction may work outdoors in difficult weather conditions.

Advances in some equipment, such as hydraulic wrenches and hydraulic stud tensioners, have made the work safer and eliminated the need for millwrights to use a sledge hammer to pound bolts into position. Other equipment has reduced the amount of heavy lifting and other strenuous tasks that would often cause injuries in the past.

Millwrights work independently or as part of a team. Their tasks must be performed quickly and precisely, because disabled machinery costs a company time and money. Many millwrights work overtime; about 4 in 10 millwrights report working more than 40 hours during a typical week. During power outages or other emergencies, millwrights are often assigned overtime and shift work.

Millwrights that work at construction sites may have to travel long distances to reach different worksites. For example, millwrights who specialize in turbine installation travel to wherever new power plants are being built.

Training, Other Qualifications, and Advancement

Millwrights normally receive training through 4- to 5-year apprenticeship programs that combine on-the-job training with classroom instruction, or through community college programs coupled with informal on-the-job training. These programs include training in dismantling, moving, erecting, and repairing machinery. Trainees also may work with concrete and receive instruction in related skills,

such as carpentry, welding, and sheet-metal work. Millwright apprentices attend about one week of classes every three months. Classroom instruction covers mathematics, blueprint reading, hydraulics, electricity, computers, electronics, and instruction in specific machinery.

Employers prefer applicants with a high school diploma or equivalency and some vocational training or experience. Courses in science, mathematics, mechanical drawing, computers, and machine shop practice are useful. Millwrights are expected to keep their skills up-to-date and may need additional training on technological advances, such as laser shaft alignment and vibration analysis.

Because millwrights assemble and disassemble complicated machinery, mechanical aptitude is very important. Strength and agility also are necessary for lifting and climbing. Millwrights need good interpersonal and communication skills to work as part of a team and to effectively give detailed instructions to others.

Advancement for millwrights usually takes the form of higher wages. Some advance to the position of supervisor or superintendent, while others may become self-employed contractors.

Employment

Millwrights held about 59,000 jobs in 2004. Most work in manufacturing, primarily in durable goods industries, such as motor vehicle and parts manufacturing and iron and steel mills. About 1 in 3 millwrights are employed in construction, where most work for contracting firms. Although millwrights work in every State, employment is concentrated in heavily industrialized areas.

Job Outlook

Employment of millwrights is projected to grow more slowly than the average for all occupations through the year 2014. Because millwrights will always be needed to maintain and repair existing machinery, dismantle old machinery, and install new equipment, skilled applicants should have good job opportunities. Prospects will be best for millwrights with training in installing newer production technologies. In addition to employment growth, many job openings for these workers will stem from the need to replace experienced millwrights who transfer to other occupations or retire.

Employment of millwrights has historically been cyclical, rising and falling in line with investments in automation in the Nation's factories and production facilities. To remain competitive in coming years, firms will continue to require the services of millwrights to dismantle old equipment and install new high-technology machinery. Additionally, as the services sector of the economy grows, there is an increasing number of companies in this sector employing new technology to make them more efficient, which will likely offset the loss of manufacturing work. Warehouse and distribution companies, for example, are deploying highly automated conveyor systems which are being maintained by millwrights. Employment growth from new automation will be dampened somewhat by foreign competition and the introduction of new technologies, such as hydraulic torque wrenches, ultrasonic measuring tools, and laser shaft alignment, which allow fewer millwrights to perform more work. In addition, the demand for millwrights may be adversely affected as lower paid workers, such as electronics technicians and industrial machinery mechanics and maintenance workers, assume some installation and maintenance duties.

Earnings

Median hourly earnings of millwrights were $21.02 in May 2004. The middle 50 percent earned between $16.53 and $27.07. The lowest 10 percent earned less than $13.02, and the highest 10 percent earned more than $32.17. Earnings vary by industry and geographic location. Median hourly earnings in the industries employing the largest numbers of millwrights in May 2004 were as follows:

Motor vehicle parts manufacturing $28.76
Building equipment contractors 19.88

About 54 percent of millwrights belong to labor unions, one of the highest rates of membership in the economy.

Related Occupations

To set up machinery for use in a plant, millwrights must know how to use hoisting devices and how to assemble, disassemble, and sometimes repair machinery. Other workers with similar job duties include industrial machinery installation, repair, and maintenance workers, except millwrights; tool and die makers; aircraft and avionics equipment mechanics and service technicians; structural and reinforcing iron and metal workers; assemblers and fabricators; and heavy vehicle and mobile equipment service technicians and mechanics. Millwrights also machine parts and operate computer-controlled machine tools like machinists and computer control machine tool programmers and operators. Millwrights often use welding and soldering to assemble and repair machines like welding, soldering and brazing workers.

Sources of Additional Information

For further information on apprenticeship programs, write to the Apprenticeship Council of your State's labor department, local offices of your State employment service, or local firms that employ millwrights. In addition, you may contact:

➤ United Brotherhood of Carpenters and Joiners of America, 6801 Placid St., Las Vegas, NV 89119. Internet: **http://www.carpenters.org**
➤ Associated General Contractors of America, 333 John Carlyle St., Suite 200, Alexandria, VA 22314. Internet: **http://www.agc.org**
➤ Associated Builders and Contractors, Workforce Development Dept., 2300 Wilson Blvd., Suite 400, Arlington, VA 22201. Internet: **http://www.trytools.org**
➤ National Tooling and Machining Association, 9300 Livingston Rd., Fort Washington, MD 20744. Internet: **http://www.ntma.org**

Precision Instrument and Equipment Repairers

(O*NET 49-9061.00, 49-9062.00, 49-9063.01, 49-9063.02, 49-9063.03, 49-9063.04, 49-9064.00, 49-9069.99)

Significant Points

● Training requirements include a high school diploma and, in most cases, postsecondary education, coupled with significant on-the-job training.

● Good opportunities are expected for most types of jobs.

● Overall employment is expected to grow about as fast as average, but projected growth varies by detailed occupation.

● About 1 out of 6 are self-employed.

Nature of the Work

Repairing and maintaining watches, cameras, musical instruments, medical equipment, and other precision instruments requires a high level of skill and attention to detail. For example, some devices contain tiny gears that must be manufactured to within one one-hundredth of a millimeter of design specifications, and other devices contain sophisticated electronic controls.

Camera and photographic equipment repairers work through a series of steps in fixing a camera. The first step is determining whether a repair should be attempted, because many inexpensive cameras cost more to repair than to replace. Of the problems for which repair seems worthwhile, the most complicated or expensive are referred back to the manufacturer or to a large repair center. If the repairers decide to proceed with the job themselves, they diagnose the problem, often by disassembling numerous small parts in order to reach the source. They then make needed adjustments or replace a defective part. Many problems are caused by the electronic circuits used in cameras, and fixing these circuits requires an understanding of electronics. Camera repairers also maintain cameras by removing and replacing broken or worn parts and cleaning and lubricating gears and springs. Because many of the components involved are extremely small, repairers must have a great deal of manual dexterity. Frequently, older camera parts are no longer available, requiring repairers to build replacement parts or to strip junked cameras. When machining new parts, workers often use a small lathe, a grinding wheel, and other metalworking tools.

Repairs on digital cameras are similar to those on conventional cameras, but because digital cameras have no film to wind, they have fewer moving parts. Digital cameras rely on software, so any repair to the lens requires that it be calibrated with the use of software and by connecting the camera to a personal computer.

Watch and clock repairers work almost exclusively on expensive and antique timepieces, because moderately priced timepieces are cheaper to replace than to repair. Electrically powered clocks and quartz watches and clocks function with almost no moving parts, limiting necessary maintenance to replacing the battery. Many expensive timepieces still employ old-style mechanical movements and a manual or automatic winding mechanism. This type of timepiece must be regularly adjusted and maintained. Repair and maintenance work on a mechanical timepiece requires using handtools to disassemble many fine gears and components. Each part is inspected for signs of wear. Some gears or springs may need to be replaced or machined. Exterior portions of the watch may require polishing and buffing. Specialized machines are used to clean all of the parts with ultrasonic waves and a series of baths in cleaning agents. Reassembling a watch requires lubricating key parts.

As with older cameras, replacement parts are frequently unavailable for antique watches or clocks. In such cases, watch repairers must machine their own parts. They employ small lathes and other machines in creating tiny parts.

Musical instrument repairers and tuners combine their love of music with a highly skilled craft. Often referred to as technicians, these artisans work in four specialties: Band instruments, pianos and organs, violins, and guitars. (Repairers and tuners who work on electronic organs are discussed in the *Handbook* statement on electronic home entertainment equipment installers and repairers.)

Band instrument repairers, brass and wind instrument repairers, and percussion instrument repairers focus on woodwind, brass, reed, and percussion instruments damaged through deterioration or by accident. They move mechanical parts or play scales to find problems. They may unscrew and remove rod pins, keys, worn cork pads, and pistons and remove soldered parts by means of gas torches. Using filling techniques or a mallet, they repair dents in metal and wood. These repairers use gas torches, grinding wheels, lathes, shears, mallets, and small handtools and are skilled in metalworking and woodworking. Percussion instrument repairers often must install new drumheads, which formerly were cut from animal skin, but now are made exclusively from Mylar® and other synthetic materials.

Violin and guitar repairers adjust and repair stringed instruments. Some repairers work on both stringed and band instruments. Initially, repairers play and inspect the instrument to find any defects. They replace or repair cracked or broken sections and damaged parts. They also restring the instruments and repair damage to their finish. Because the specifications of all types of instruments vary greatly, custom parts machining is considered an essential skill.

Piano tuners and repairers use similar techniques, skills, and tools. Most workers in this group are piano tuners, tuning and making minor repairs. Tuning involves tightening and loosening different strings to achieve the proper tone or pitch. Because pianos are difficult to transport, tuners normally make house calls. Some repairers specialize in restoring older pianos. Restoration is complicated work, often involving replacing many of the parts, which number more than 12,000 in some pianos. With proper maintenance and restoration, pianos often survive more than 100 years.

Pipe organ repairers do work similar to that of piano repairers, but on a larger scale. In addition, they assemble new organs. Because pipe organs are too large to transport, they must be assembled onsite. Even with repairers working in teams or with assistants, the organ assembly process can take several weeks or even months, depending upon the size of the organ.

Medical equipment repairers and *other precision instrument and equipment repairers* maintain, adjust, calibrate, and repair electronic, electromechanical, and hydraulic equipment. They use various tools, including multimeters, specialized software, and computers designed to communicate with specific pieces of hardware. Among their specialized tools is equipment designed to simulate water or air pressure. These repairers use handtools, soldering irons, and other electronic tools to repair and adjust equipment. Faulty circuit boards and other parts are normally removed and replaced. Medical equipment repairers and other precision instrument repairers must maintain careful, detailed logs of all maintenance and repair that they perform on each piece of equipment they work with.

Medical equipment repairers, often called *biomedical equipment technicians*, work on medical equipment such as defibrillators, heart monitors, medical imaging equipment (x rays, CAT scanners, and ultrasound equipment), voice-controlled operating tables, and electric wheelchairs.

Other precision instrument and equipment repairers service, repair, and replace a wide range of equipment associated with automated or instrument-controlled manufacturing processes. A precision instrument repairer working at an electric powerplant, for example, would repair and maintain instruments that monitor the operation of the plant, such as pressure and temperature gauges. Replacement parts are not always available, so repairers sometimes machine or fabricate a new part. Preventive maintenance involves regular lubrication, cleaning, and adjustment of many measuring devices. Increasingly, it also involves solving computer software problems as more control devices, such as valves, are controlled by or linked to computer networks. To adjust a control device, a technician may need to connect a laptop computer to the control device's computer and make adjustments through changes to the software commands.

Working Conditions

Camera, watch, and musical instrument repairers work under fairly similar solitary, low-stress conditions with minimal supervision. A quiet, well-lighted workshop or repair shop is typical, while a few of these repairers travel to the instrument being repaired, such as a piano, an organ, or a grandfather clock. Often, these workers can adjust their schedules, allowing for second jobs as needed. Musical instrument repairer jobs are attractive to many professional musicians because

Watch repairers use fine motor skills to perform detailed work.

the flexible hours common to repair work allow musicians to do the work while still maintaining a regular performing schedule.

Medical equipment and precision instrument and equipment repairers normally work daytime hours, but are often expected to be on call. Still, like other hospital and factory employees, some repairers work irregular hours. Precision instrument repairers work under a wide array of conditions, from hot, dirty, noisy factories, to air-conditioned workshops, to the outdoors on fieldwork. Attention to safety is essential, as the work sometimes involves dangerous machinery or toxic chemicals. Due to the individualized nature of the work, supervision is fairly minimal.

Training, Other Qualifications, and Advancement

Most employers require at least a high school diploma for beginning precision instrument and equipment repairers. Many employers prefer applicants with some postsecondary education. Much training takes place on the job. The ability to read and understand technical manuals is important. Necessary physical qualities include good fine-motor skills and acute vision. Also, precision equipment repairers must be able to pay close attention to details, enjoy problem solving, and have the desire to disassemble machines to see how they work. Most precision equipment repairers must be able to work alone with minimal supervision.

The educational background required for camera and photographic equipment repairers varies, but some knowledge of electronics is necessary. A number of workers complete postsecondary training, such as an associate degree, in electronics. The job requires the ability to read electronic schematic diagrams and comprehend other technical information, in addition to manual dexterity. New employees are trained on the job in two stages over about a year. First, they learn to repair a single product over a couple of weeks. Then, they learn to repair other products and refine their skills for 6–12 months while working under the close supervision of an experienced repairer. Finally, repairers continually teach themselves through studying manuals and attending manufacturer-sponsored seminars on the specifics of new models.

Training also varies for watch and clock repairers. Several associations, including the American Watchmakers-Clockmakers

Institute and the National Association of Watch and Clock Collectors, offer certifications. Some certifications can be completed in a few months; others require simply passing an examination; the most demanding certifications require 3,000 hours, taken over 2 years, of classroom time in technical institutes or colleges. Those who have earned the most demanding certifications are usually the most sought after by employers. Clock repairers generally require less training than do watch repairers, because watches have smaller components and require greater precision. Some repairers opt to learn through assisting a master watch repairer. Nevertheless, developing proficiency in watch or clock repair requires several years of education and experience.

For musical instrument repairers and tuners, employers prefer people with post-high school training in music repair technology. According to a Piano Technicians Guild membership survey, the overwhelming majority of respondents had completed at least some college work; most had a bachelor's or higher degree, although not always in music repair technology. Almost all repairers have a strong musical background; many are musicians themselves. Also, a basic ability to play the instruments being repaired is normally required. Courses in instrument repair are offered only at a few technical schools and colleges. Correspondence courses are common for piano tuners. Graduates of these programs normally receive additional training on the job, working with an experienced repairer. Many musical instrument repairers and tuners begin learning their trade on the job as assistants or apprentices. Trainees perform a variety of tasks around the shop. Full qualification usually requires 2 to 5 years of training and practice. Musical instrument repair and tuning requires good manual dexterity, an "ear" for pitch and tone, and good hand-eye coordination. While piano tuning requires good hearing, it can be performed by the blind.

Medical equipment repairers' training includes on-the-job training, manufacturer training classes, and associate degree programs. While an associate degree in electronics or medical technology is normally required, training varies by specialty. For those with a background in electronics, on-the-job training is more common for workers repairing less critical equipment, such as hospital beds or electric wheelchairs. An associate or even a bachelor's degree, often in medical technology or engineering, and a passing grade on a certification exam is likely to be required of persons repairing more critical equipment, such as CAT scanners and defibrillators. Some repairers are trained in the military. New repairers begin by observing and assisting an experienced worker over a period of 3 to 6 months, learning a single piece of equipment at a time. Gradually, they begin working independently, while still under close supervision. Biomedical equipment repairers are constantly learning new technologies and equipment through seminars, self-study, and certification exams.

Educational requirements for other precision instrument and equipment repair jobs also vary, but include a high school diploma, with a focus on mathematics and science courses. Because repairers need to understand blueprints, electrical schematic diagrams, and electrical, hydraulic, and electromechanical systems, most employers require an associate or sometimes a bachelor's degree in instrumentation and control, electronics, or a related engineering field. In addition to formal education, a year or two of on-the-job training is required before a repairer is considered fully qualified. Many instrument and equipment repairers begin by working in a factory in another capacity, such as repairing electrical equipment. As companies seek to improve efficiency, other types of repair workers are trained to repair precision measuring equipment. Some advancement opportunities exist, but many supervisory positions require a bachelor's degree.

Employment

Precision instrument and equipment repairers held 62,000 jobs in 2004. Employment was distributed among the detailed occupations as follows:

Medical equipment repairers	29,000
Precision instrument and equipment repairers, all other	17,000
Musical instrument repairers and tuners	6,100
Camera and photographic equipment repairers	5,100
Watch repairers	4,300

Medical equipment repairers often work for hospitals or wholesale equipment suppliers, while those in the occupation "all other precision instrument repairers" frequently work for manufacturing companies and wholesalers of durable goods. About 1 out of 6 precision instrument and equipment repairers was self-employed—they may own jewelry, camera, medical equipment, or music stores.

Job Outlook

Good opportunities are expected for most types of precision instrument and equipment repairer jobs. Overall employment growth is projected to be about as fast as the average for all occupations over the 2004–14 period; however, projected growth varies by detailed occupation.

Job growth among medical equipment repairers should be about as fast as the average for all occupations over the projection period. The rapidly expanding healthcare industry and elderly population should spark demand for increasingly sophisticated medical equipment and, in turn, create good employment opportunities in this occupation.

By contrast, employment of musical instrument repairers is expected to increase more slowly than the average. Replacement needs are expected to provide the most job opportunities as many repairers and tuners retire. School budget cuts to music programs—specifically, stringed-instrument programs—should hurt the outlook for musical repairers. With fewer new musicians, there will be a slump in instrument rentals, purchases, and repairs. Because training in the repair of musical instruments is difficult to obtain—there are only a few schools that offer training programs, and few experienced workers are willing to take on apprentices—opportunities should be good for those who receive training. Schools report that their graduates easily find employment.

Employment of camera and photographic equipment repairers is expected to decline. The popularity of inexpensive cameras adversely affects employment in this occupation, as most point-and-shoot cameras are cheaper to replace than repair. When a camera breaks, not only is replacing the camera often not much more expensive than repairing it, but the new model is also far more advanced than the old one. However, consumers are spending more on high-end digital cameras than they did on conventional cameras in the past, which should make repairing the cameras more economical.

Employment of watch repairers is expected to increase more slowly than the average. Over the past few decades, changes in technology, including the invention of digital and quartz watches that need few repairs, caused a significant decline in the demand for watch repairers. In recent years, this trend was somewhat reversed, as the growing popularity of expensive mechanical watches increased the need for these repairers. Nonetheless, few new repairers entered the field. Thus, the small number of entrants, coupled with the fact that a large proportion of watch and clock repairers are approaching retirement age, should result in very good job opportunities in this field.

The projected slower-than-average employment growth of other precision instrument and equipment repairers reflects the expected lack of employment growth in manufacturing and other industries in which they are employed. Nevertheless, good employment opportunities are expected for these workers due to the relatively small number of people entering the occupation and the need to replace repairers who retire.

Earnings
The following tabulation shows median hourly earnings for various precision instrument and equipment repairers in May 2004:

Precision instrument and equipment repairers, all other.................. $21.25
Medical equipment repairers... 17.90
Camera and photographic equipment repairers 15.54
Watch repairers 13.87
Musical instrument repairers and tuners 13.47

Earnings ranged from less than $7.94 for the lowest 10 percent of musical instrument repairers and tuners to more than $32.32 for the highest 10 percent in the occupation "all other precision instrument and equipment repairers."

Earnings within the different occupations vary significantly, depending upon skill levels. For example, a lesser skilled watch and clock repairer may simply change batteries and replace worn wrist straps, while a highly skilled watch and clock repairer with years of training and experience may rebuild and replace worn parts.

Related Occupations
Many precision instrument and equipment repairers work with precision mechanical and electronic equipment. Other workers who repair precision mechanical and electronic equipment include computer, automated teller, and office machine repairers and coin, vending, and amusement machine servicers and repairers. Other workers who make precision items include dental laboratory technicians and ophthalmic laboratory technicians. Some precision instrument and equipment repairers work with a wide array of industrial equipment.

Their work environment and responsibilities are similar to those of industrial machinery installation, maintenance, and repair workers. Much of the work of watch repairers is similar to that of jewelers and precious stone and metal workers. Camera repairers' work is similar to that of electronic home entertainment equipment installers and repairers; both occupations work with consumer electronics that are based around a circuit board, but that also involve numerous moving mechanical parts.

Sources of Additional Information
For more information about camera repair careers, contact:
➤ National Association of Photographic Equipment Technicians (NAPET), 3000 Picture Pl., Jackson, MI 49201.

For information on musical instrument repair, including schools offering training, contact:
➤ National Association of Professional Band Instrument Repair Technicians (NAPBIRT), P.O. Box 51, Normal, IL 61761. Internet: **http://www.napbirt.org**

For additional information on piano tuning and repairwork, contact:
➤ Piano Technicians Guild, 4444 Forest Ave., Kansas City, MO 66106. Internet: **http://www.ptg.org**

For information about training, mentoring programs, employers, and schools with programs in precision instrumentation, automation, and control, contact:
➤ ISA-The Instrumentation, Systems, and Automation Society, 67 Alexander Dr, Research Triangle Park, NC 27709. Internet: **http://www.isa.org**

For information about watch and clock repair and a list of schools with related programs of study, contact:
➤ American Watchmakers-Clockmakers Institute (AWI), 701 Enterprise Dr., Harrison, OH 45030-1696. Internet: **http://www.awi-net.org**

For information about medical equipment technicians and a list of schools with related programs of study, contact:
➤ Association for the Advancement of Medical Instrumentation (AAMI), 1110 North Glebe Rd., Arlington, VA 22201-4795. Internet: **http://www.aami.org**

Production Occupations

Assemblers and Fabricators

(O*NET 51-2011.01, 51-2011.02, 51-2011.03, 51-2021.00, 51-2022.00, 51-2023.00, 51-2031.00, 51-2041.01, 51-2041.02, 51-2091.00, 51-2092.00, 51-2093.00, 51-2099.99)

Significant Points

- More than half of all assemblers are team assemblers.

- Work areas may be noisy, and many assemblers may have to sit or stand for long periods.

- A high school diploma is preferred for most positions, but specialized training is required for some assembly jobs.

Nature of the Work

Assemblers and fabricators play an important role in the manufacturing process. They are responsible for putting together finished and semifinished goods, assembling the pieces of components of a product and then joining the components into a whole product. The products they produce range from entire airplanes to intricate timing devices. They fabricate and assemble household appliances, automobiles and automobile engines and parts, as well as computers and other electronic devices.

Assemblers begin by reading detailed schematics or blue prints that show how to assemble complex machines. After determining how parts should connect, they often need to use hand or power tools to trim, shim, cut, and make other adjustments to make components fit together and align properly. Once the parts are properly aligned, they connect parts with bolts and screws or by welding or soldering pieces together. Careful quality control is important throughout the assembly process, so assemblers look for both mistakes in the assembly process and faulty components. They try to help fix problems before more defective products are produced.

Changes in technology have transformed the manufacturing and assembly process. Automated manufacturing systems now use robots, computers, programmable motion control devices, and various sensing technologies. These systems change the way in which goods are made and affect the jobs of those who make them. The more advanced assemblers must be able to work with these new technologies and be comfortable using them to produce goods.

Manufacturing techniques are evolving away from traditional assembly line systems towards "lean" manufacturing systems, which is causing the nature of assemblers' work to change. Lean manufacturing involves using teams of workers within "cells" to produce entire products or components. *Team assemblers* perform all of the assembly tasks assigned to their teams, rotating through the different tasks, rather than specializing in a single task as would be done on an assembly line. The team also may decide how the work is to be assigned and how different tasks are to be performed. This worker flexibility helps companies to cover for absent workers, improves productivity, and increases their ability to respond to changes in demand by shifting labor from one product line to another. For example, if demand for a product drops, companies may reduce the number of workers involved, while individual workers perform more stages of the assembly process. Some aspects of lean production, such as rotating tasks and seeking worker input on improving the assembly process, are common to all assembly and fabrication occupations.

Although more than half of all assemblers and fabricators are classified as "team assemblers," others specialize in producing one type of product or perform the same or similar functions throughout the assembly process. These workers are classified according to the type of products they assemble or produce. *Electrical and electronic equipment assemblers* build products such as electric motors, batteries, computers, electronic control devices and sensing equipment. *Electromechanical equipment assemblers* assemble and modify electromechanical devices such as household appliances, dynamometers, actuators, or vending machines. *Coil winders, tapers, and finishers* wind wire coil used in resistors, transformers, generators, and electric motors. *Engine and other machine assemblers* construct, assemble, or rebuild engines and turbines, and machines used in almost all manufacturing industries, including agriculture, construction, mining, rolling mills, and textile, paper, and food processing. *Aircraft structure, surfaces, rigging, and systems assemblers* assemble, fit, fasten and install parts of airplanes, space vehicles, or missiles, such as the tails and wings, landing gear, and heating and ventilation systems. *Structural metal fabricators and fitters* cut, align, and fit together structural metal parts according to detailed specifications prior to welding or riveting. *Fiberglass laminators and fabricators* create products made of fiberglass, mainly boat decks and hulls and automobile body parts. *Timing device assemblers, adjusters, and calibrators* perform precision assembling or adjusting of timing devices within very narrow tolerances.

Involving assemblers and fabricators in product development has become more common. Designers and engineers consult manufacturing workers during the design stage to improve product reliability and manufacturing efficiency. For example, an assembler may tell a designer that the dash of a new car design will be too difficult to install quickly and consistently. The designer could then redesign the dash to make it easier to install.

Some experienced assemblers work with designers and engineers to build prototypes or test products. These assemblers read and interpret complex engineering specifications from text, drawings, and computer-aided drafting systems. They also may use a variety of tools and precision measuring instruments.

Working Conditions

The working conditions for assemblers and fabricators vary from plant to plant and from industry to industry. They may even vary within a plant. One consistent trend is increasingly improving working conditions. Many physically difficult tasks, such as manually tightening massive bolts or moving heavy parts in position, have been made much easier through the use hydraulic and electromechanical equipment. Most factories today are generally clean, well-lit, and well-ventilated, and depending on what type of work is being performed, they may also need to be dirt and dust-free. Electronic and electromechanical assemblers particularly must work in environments free of dust that could affect the operation of the products they build. Some assemblers may also come into contact with potentially harmful chemicals or fumes, but ventilation systems and other safety precautions normally minimize any harmful effects. Other assemblers may come in contact with oil and grease, and their working areas may be quite noisy.

Electronics assemblers work in a clean, well-lighted environment.

Most full-time assemblers work a 40-hour week, although overtime and shift work is fairly common in some industries. Work schedules of assemblers may vary at plants with more than one shift.

Training, Other Qualifications, and Advancement

New assemblers and fabricators are normally considered entry-level employees. The ability to do accurate work at a rapid pace and to follow detailed instructions are key job requirements. A high school diploma is preferred for most positions. Following detailed assembly instructions requires basic reading skills, although many instructions rely on pictures and diagrams.

Applicants need specialized training for some assembly jobs. For example, employers may require that applicants for electrical, electronic, or aircraft assembler jobs be technical school graduates or have equivalent military training. Other positions require only on-the-job training, sometimes including employer-sponsored classroom instruction, in the broad range of assembly duties that employees may be required to perform. Many new assemblers are hired as temporary workers, often through employment services firms.

Good eyesight, with or without glasses, is required for assemblers and fabricators who work with small parts. Plants that make electrical and electronic products may test applicants for color vision, because many of their products contain many differently colored wires. Manual dexterity and the ability to carry out complex, repetitive tasks quickly and methodically also are important.

As assemblers and fabricators become more experienced, they may progress to jobs that require greater skill and be given more responsibility. Experienced assemblers may become product repairers if they have learned the many assembly operations and understand the construction of a product. These workers fix assembled articles that operators or inspectors have identified as defective. Assemblers also can advance to quality control jobs or be promoted to supervisor. Experienced assemblers and fabricators also may become members of research and development teams, working with engineers and other project designers to design, develop, and build prototypes, and test new product models. In some companies, assemblers can become trainees for one of the skilled trades, such as machinist. Those with a background in math, science, and computers may advance to become programmers or operators of more highly automated production equipment.

Employment

Assemblers and fabricators held nearly 2 million jobs in 2004. They were found in almost every industry, but the vast majority, nearly

3 out of 4, were found in manufacturing. In addition, 9 percent of workers were employed by employment services firms, mostly as temporary workers. In all likelihood, many of these temporary workers were assigned to manufacturing plants. Wholesale and retail trade firms employed the next highest number of assemblers and fabricators. Team assemblers, the largest specialty, accounted for 62 percent of assembler and fabricator jobs. The distribution of employment among the various types of assemblers was as follows:

Team assemblers	1,200,000
All other assemblers and fabricators	268,000
Electrical and electronic equipment assemblers	221,000
Structural metal fabricators and fitters	90,000
Electromechanical equipment assemblers	52,000
Engine and other machine assemblers	46,000
Fiberglass laminators and fabricators	31,000
Coil winders, tapers, and finishers	28,000
Aircraft structure, surfaces, rigging, and systems assemblers	19,000
Timing device assemblers, adjusters, and calibrators	3,300

Within the manufacturing sector, assembly of transportation equipment, such as aircraft, autos, trucks, and buses, accounted for 19 percent of all jobs. Assembly of computers and electronic products accounted for another 11 percent of all jobs. Other industries that employ many assemblers and fabricators were machinery manufacturing (heating and air-conditioning equipment; agriculture, construction, and mining machinery; and engine, turbine, and power transmission equipment); electrical equipment, appliance, and component manufacturing (lighting, household appliances, and electrical equipment); and fabricated metal products.

The following tabulation shows wage and salary employment in manufacturing industries employing the most assemblers and fabricators in 2004.

Transportation equipment manufacturing	387,000
Computer and electronic product manufacturing	225,000
Machinery manufacturing	193,000
Fabricated metal product manufacturing	143,000
Electrical equipment, appliance, and component manufacturing	139,000

Job Outlook

Employment of assemblers and fabricators is expected to grow more slowly than average through the year 2014, reflecting growth in mainly nonmanufacturing industries. The largest increase in the number of assemblers and fabricators is projected to be in the employment services industry, which supplies temporary workers to the various industries. Temporary workers are gaining in importance in the manufacturing sector and elsewhere as companies strive for a more flexible workforce to meet the fluctuations in the market. There will also be more jobs for assemblers and fabricators in the wholesale and retail sectors of the economy. As more goods come unassembled from foreign countries to save on shipping costs, it is increasingly up to wholesalers and retailers to provide assembly of products to their customers.

Within the manufacturing sector, employment of assemblers and fabricators is expected to grow mainly in motor vehicle and motor vehicle parts manufacturing, furniture manufacturing, and food processing due to increasing sales of these products. In many other manufacturing industries, assemblers and fabricators have been negatively affected by increasing automation, improving productivity, and the shift of assembly to countries with lower labor costs. In addition to new jobs stemming from growth in this occupation, many job openings will result from the need to replace workers leaving this large occupational group.

The effects of automation will be felt more among some types of assemblers and fabricators than among others. Automated manufacturing systems are expensive, and a large volume of repetitive work is required to justify their purchase. Also, where the assembly parts involved are irregular in size or location, new technology only now is beginning to make inroads. For example, much assembly in the aerospace industry is done in hard-to-reach locations—inside airplane fuselages or gear boxes, for example—which are unsuited to robots; as a result, aircraft assemblers will not be easily replaced by automated processes.

The use of team production techniques has been a success in the manufacturing sector, boosting productivity and improving the quality of goods. Workers collaborate to decide how to best perform assembly tasks. Team assemblers are often consulted during the design phase of production, to make sure that the product is easy to assemble. Through continued efforts to improve the assembly process, most manufacturing companies have significantly reduced the amount of labor needed to assemble a product. By boosting productivity, companies are better able to compete with low wage companies. Thus, while the number of assemblers overall will decline in manufacturing, the number of team assemblers will remain stable.

Many producers have sent their assembly functions to countries where labor costs are lower. Decisions by American corporations to move assembly to other nations should limit employment growth for assemblers in some industries, but a free trade environment also may lead to growth in the export of goods assembled in the United States.

Earnings

Earnings vary by industry, geographic region, skill, educational level, and complexity of the machinery operated. Median hourly earnings of team assemblers were $11.42 in May 2004. The middle 50 percent earned between $9.12 and $14.60. The lowest 10 percent earned less than $7.56, and the highest 10 percent earned $18.80. Median hourly earnings in the manufacturing industries employing the largest numbers of team assemblers in May 2004 are shown below:

Motor vehicle manufacturing	$22.45
Motor vehicle parts manufacturing	12.91
Other wood product manufacturing	10.90
Plastics product manufacturing	10.54
Employment services	8.66

Median hourly earnings of electrical and electronic equipment assemblers were $11.68 in May 2004. The middle 50 percent earned between $9.54 and $14.84. The lowest 10 percent earned less than $8.01, and the highest 10 percent earned more than $18.64. Median hourly earnings in the manufacturing industries employing the largest numbers of electrical and electronic equipment assemblers in May 2004 are shown below:

Computer and peripheral equipment manufacturing	$12.80
Navigational, measuring, electromedical, and control instruments manufacturing	12.61
Electrical equipment manufacturing	12.55
Communications equipment manufacturing	11.61
Semiconductor and other electronic component manufacturing	11.02

In May 2004, other assemblers and fabricators had the following median hourly earnings:

Aircraft structure, surfaces, rigging, and systems assemblers	$17.79
Engine and other machine assemblers	16.73
Structural metal fabricators and fitters	14.34
Timing device assemblers, adjusters, and calibrators	13.76
Electromechanical equipment assemblers	12.71
Coil winders, tapers, and finishers	12.24
Fiberglass laminators and fabricators	12.18
Assemblers and fabricators, all other	11.90

Many assemblers and fabricators are members of labor unions. These unions include the International Association of Machinists and Aerospace Workers; the United Electrical, Radio and Machine Workers of America; the United Automobile, Aerospace and Agricultural Implement Workers of America; the International Brotherhood of Electrical Workers; and the United Steelworkers of America.

Related Occupations

Other occupations that involve operating machines and tools and assembling products include welding, soldering, and brazing workers; and machine setters, operators, and tenders—metal and plastic. Assemblers and fabricators also are responsible for some quality control and product testing, as is the case for inspectors, testers, sorters, samplers, and weighers.

Sources of Additional Information

Information about employment opportunities for assemblers is available from local offices of the State employment service and from locals of the unions mentioned earlier.

Food Processing Occupations

(O*NET 51-3011.01, 51-3011.02, 51-3021.00, 51-3022.00, 51-3023.00, 51-3091.00, 51-3092.00, 51-3093.00)

Significant Points

● Most employees in manual food-processing jobs require little or no training prior to being hired.

● As more jobs involving cutting and processing meat shift from retail stores to food-processing plants, job growth will be concentrated among lesser skilled workers, who are employed primarily in manufacturing.

Nature of the Work

Food processing occupations include many different types of workers who process raw food products into the finished goods sold by grocers or wholesalers, restaurants, or institutional food services. These workers perform a variety of tasks and are responsible for producing many of the food products found in every household.

Butchers as well as meat, poultry, and fish cutters and trimmers are employed at different stages in the process by which animal carcasses are converted into manageable pieces of meat, known as boxed meat, that are suitable for sale to wholesalers and retailers. Meat, poultry, and fish cutters and trimmers commonly work in animal slaughtering and processing plants, while butchers and meatcutters usually are employed in retail establishments. As a result, the nature of these jobs varies significantly.

In animal slaughtering and processing plants, *slaughterers and meatpackers* slaughter cattle, hogs, goats, and sheep and cut the carcasses into large wholesale cuts, such as rounds, loins, ribs, and chucks, to facilitate the handling, distribution, and marketing of meat. In some of these plants, slaughterers and meatpackers also further process the large parts into cuts that are ready for retail use. These workers also produce hamburger meat and meat trimmings, which are used to prepare sausages, luncheon meats, and other fabricated meat products. Slaughterers and meatpackers usually work on assembly lines, with each individual responsible for only a few of the many cuts needed to process a carcass. Depending on the type of cut, these workers use knives; cleavers; meat saws; bandsaws; or other potentially dangerous equipment.

In grocery stores, wholesale establishments that supply meat to restaurants, and institutional food service facilities, *butchers and meatcutters* separate wholesale cuts of meat into retail cuts or individually sized servings. These workers cut meat into steaks and chops, shape and tie roasts, and grind beef for sale as chopped meat. Boneless cuts are prepared with the use of knives, slicers, or power cutters, while bandsaws are required to carve bone-in pieces of meat. Butchers and meatcutters in retail food stores also may weigh, wrap, and label the cuts of meat; arrange them in refrigerated cases for display; and prepare special cuts to fill unique orders by customers.

Poultry cutters and trimmers slaughter and cut up chickens, turkeys, and other types of poultry. Although the poultry processing industry is becoming increasingly automated, many jobs, such as trimming, packing, and deboning, are still done manually. As in the animal slaughtering and processing industry, most poultry cutters and trimmers perform routine cuts on poultry as it moves along production lines.

Unlike some of the other occupations just listed, *fish cutters and trimmers*, also called *fish cleaners*, are likely to be employed in both manufacturing and retail establishments. These workers primarily scale, cut, and dress fish by removing the head, scales, and other inedible portions and cutting the fish into steaks or fillets. In retail markets, these workers may also wait on customers and clean fish to order.

Meat, poultry, and fish cutters and trimmers also prepare ready-to-heat foods. This preparation often entails filleting meat or fish; cutting it into bite-sized pieces; preparing and adding vegetables; and applying sauces, marinades, or breading.

Food processing occupations include many different types of workers, such as butchers and meatcutters, who process raw food into finished goods.

Bakers mix and bake ingredients in accordance with recipes to produce varying quantities of breads, pastries, and other baked goods. Bakers commonly are employed in grocery stores and specialty shops, and produce small quantities of breads, pastries, and other baked goods for consumption on premises or for sale as specialty baked goods. In manufacturing, bakers produce goods in large quantities, using high-volume mixing machines, ovens, and other equipment. Goods produced in large quantities usually are available for sale through distributors, grocery stores, or manufacturers' outlets.

Others in food processing occupations include *food batchmakers*, who set up and operate equipment that mixes, blends, or cooks ingredients used in the manufacture of food products, according to formulas or recipes; *food cooking machine operators and tenders*, who operate or tend to cooking equipment, such as steam-cooking vats, deep-fry cookers, pressure cookers, kettles, and boilers to prepare food products, such as meat, sugar, cheese, and grain; and *food and tobacco roasting, baking, and drying machine operators and tenders*, who use equipment to reduce the moisture content of food or tobacco products or to process food in preparation for canning. Some of the machines that are used include hearth ovens, kiln driers, roasters, char kilns, steam ovens, and vacuum drying equipment.

Working Conditions

Working conditions vary by type and size of establishment. In animal slaughtering and processing plants and large retail food establishments, butchers and meatcutters work in large meatcutting rooms equipped with power machines and conveyors. In small retail markets, the butcher or fish cleaner may work in a cramped space behind the meat or fish counter. To prevent viral and bacterial infections, work areas must be kept clean and sanitary.

Butchers and meatcutters, poultry and fish cutters and trimmers, and slaughters and meatpackers often work in cold, damp rooms. The work areas are refrigerated to prevent meat from spoiling and are damp because meat cutting generates large amounts of blood, condensation, and fat. Cool, damp floors increase the likelihood of slips and falls. In addition, cool temperatures, long periods of standing, and repetitive physical tasks make the work tiring. As a result, butchers as well as meat, poultry, and fish cutters and trimmers are more susceptible to injury than are most other workers.

Injuries include cuts and occasional amputations, which occur when knives, cleavers, or power tools are used improperly. Also, repetitive slicing and lifting often lead to cumulative trauma injuries, such as carpal tunnel syndrome. To reduce the incidence of cumulative trauma injuries, some employers have reduced employee workloads, added prescribed rest periods, redesigned jobs and tools, and promoted increased awareness of early warning signs so that steps can be taken to prevent further injury. Nevertheless, workers in the occupation still face the serious threat of disabling injuries.

Most traditional bakers work in bakeries, cake shops, hot-bread shops, hotels, restaurants, and cafeterias, and in the bakery departments of supermarkets. Bakers may work under hot and noisy conditions. Also, bakers typically work under strict order deadlines and critical time-sensitive baking requirements, both of which can induce stress. Bakers usually work in shifts and may work early mornings, evenings, weekends, and holidays. While many bakers often work as part of a team, they also may work alone when baking particular items. These workers may supervise assistants and teach apprentices and trainees. Bakers in retail establishments may be required to serve customers.

Other food processing workers—such as food batchmakers; food and tobacco roasting, baking, and drying machine operators and tenders; and food cooking machine operators and tenders—typically work in production areas that are specially designed for food preservation or processing. Food batchmakers, in particular, work in kitchen-type, assembly-line production facilities. Because this work involves food, work areas must meet governmental sanitary regulations. The ovens, as well as the motors of blenders, mixers, and other equipment, often make work areas very warm and noisy. There are some hazards, such as burns, created by the equipment that these workers use. Food batchmakers; food and tobacco roasting, baking, and drying machine operators; and food cooking machine operators and tenders spend a great deal of time on their feet and generally work a regular 40-hour week that may include evening and night shifts.

Training, Other Qualifications, and Advancement

Training varies widely among food processing occupations. However, most manual food processing workers require little or no training prior to being hired.

Most butchers as well as poultry and fish cutters and trimmers acquire their skills on the job through formal and informal training programs. The length of training varies significantly. Simple cutting operations require a few days to learn, while more complicated tasks, such as eviscerating slaughtered animals, generally require several months to learn. The training period for highly skilled butchers at the retail level may be 1 or 2 years.

Generally, on-the-job trainees begin by doing less difficult jobs, such as making simple cuts or removing bones. Under the guidance of experienced workers, trainees learn the proper use and care of tools and equipment and how to prepare various cuts of meat. After demonstrating skill with various meatcutting tools, trainees learn to divide carcasses into wholesale cuts and wholesale cuts into retail and individual portions. Trainees also may learn to roll and tie roasts, prepare sausage, and cure meat. Those employed in retail food establishments often are taught operations, such as inventory control, meat buying, and recordkeeping. In addition, growing concern about food-borne pathogens in meats has led employers to offer numerous safety seminars and extensive training in food safety to employees.

Skills that are important to meat, poultry, and fish cutters and trimmers include manual dexterity, good depth perception, color discrimination, and good hand-eye coordination. Physical strength often is needed to lift and move heavy pieces of meat. Butchers and fish cleaners who wait on customers should have a pleasant personality, a neat appearance, and the ability to communicate clearly. In some States, a health certificate is required for employment.

Bakers often start as apprentices or trainees. Apprentice bakers usually start in craft bakeries, while trainees usually begin in store bakeries, such as those in supermarkets. Bakers need to be skilled in baking, icing, and decorating. They also need to be able to follow instructions, have an eye for detail, and communicate well with others. Knowledge of bakery products and ingredients, as well as mechanical mixing and baking equipment, is important. Many apprentice bakers participate in correspondence study and may work towards a certificate in baking. Working as a baker's assistant or at other activities that involve handling food also is a useful tool for training. The complexity of the skills required for certification as a baker often is underestimated. Bakers need to know about applied chemistry; ingredients and nutrition; government health and sanitation regulations; business concepts; and production processes, including how to operate and maintain machinery. Modern food plants typically use high-speed automated equipment that often is operated by computers.

Food machine operators and tenders usually are trained on the job. They learn to run the different types of equipment by watching and helping other workers. Training can last anywhere from a month to a year, depending on the complexity of the tasks and the number of products involved. A degree in the appropriate area—dairy processing for those working in dairy product operations, for example—is helpful for advancement to a lead worker or a supervisory role. Most food batchmakers participate in on-the-job training, usually from about a month to a year. Some food batchmakers learn their trade through an approved apprenticeship program.

Food processing workers in retail or wholesale establishments may progress to supervisory jobs, such as department managers or team leaders in supermarkets. A few of these workers may become buyers for wholesalers or supermarket chains. Some food processing workers go on to open their own markets or bakeries. In processing plants, workers may advance to supervisory positions or become team leaders.

Employment

Food processing workers held 725,000 jobs in 2004. Employment among the various types of food processing occupations was distributed as follows:

Bakers	166,000
Meat, poultry, and fish cutters and trimmers	140,000
Slaughterers and meat packers	136,000
Butchers and meat cutters	134,000
Food batchmakers	87,000
Food cooking machine operators and tenders	43,000
Food and tobacco roasting, baking, and drying machine operators and tenders	18,000

Thirty-five percent of all food processing workers were employed in animal slaughtering and processing plants. Another 23 percent were employed at grocery stores. Most of the remainder worked in other food manufacturing industries. Butchers, meatcutters, and bakers are employed in almost every city and town in the Nation, while most other food processing jobs are concentrated in communities with food-processing plants.

Job Outlook

Overall employment in the food processing occupations is projected to grow about as fast as the average for all occupations through 2014. Increasingly, cheaper meat imports from abroad will have a negative effect on domestic employment in many food processing occupations. As more jobs involving cutting and processing meat shift from retail stores to food-processing plants, job growth will be concentrated among lesser skilled workers, who are employed primarily in manufacturing. Nevertheless, job opportunities should be available at all levels of the occupation due to the need to replace experienced workers who transfer to other occupations or leave the labor force.

As the Nation's population grows, the demand for meat, poultry, and seafood should continue to increase. Successful marketing by the poultry industry is likely to increase demand for chicken and ready-to-heat products. Similarly, the development of prepared food products that are lower in fat and more nutritious promises to stimulate the consumption of red meat. The trend toward preparing meat in containers at the processing level also should contribute to demand for animal slaughterers and meatpackers.

Lesser skilled meat, poultry, and fish cutters and trimmers—who work primarily in animal slaughtering and processing plants—should experience average employment growth. With the growing popularity of labor-intensive, ready-to-heat poultry products, demand for poultry workers should remain firm. Fish cutters also will be in demand, as the task of preparing ready-to-heat fish goods gradually shifts from retail stores to processing plants. Also, advances in fish farming, or "aquaculture," should help meet the growing demand for fish and produce opportunities for fish cutters.

Employment of more highly skilled butchers and meatcutters, who work primarily in retail stores, is expected to grow more slowly than average. Automation and the consolidation of the animal slaughtering and processing industries are enabling employers to transfer employment from higher paid butchers to lower wage slaughterers and meatpackers in meatpacking plants. At present, most red meat arrives at grocery stores partially cut up, but a growing share of meat is being delivered prepackaged, with additional fat removed, to wholesalers and retailers. This trend is resulting in less work and, thus, fewer jobs for retail butchers.

While high-volume production equipment limits the demand for bakers in manufacturing, overall employment of bakers is expected to increase about as fast as average due to growing numbers of large wholesale bakers in stores, specialty shops, and traditional bakeries. In addition to the growing numbers of cookie, muffin, and cinnamon roll bakeries, the numbers of specialty bread and bagel shops have been growing, spurring demand for bread and pastry bakers.

Employment of food batchmakers, food cooking machine operators and tenders, and food and tobacco cooking and roasting machine operators and tenders, is expected to grow more slowly than average. As more of this work is being done at the manufacturing level rather than at the retail level, potential employment gains will be offset by productivity gains from automated cooking and roasting equipment.

Earnings

Earnings vary by industry, skill, geographic region, and educational level. Median annual earnings of butchers and meatcutters were $25,890 in May 2004. The middle 50 percent earned between $19,780 and $34,260. The highest 10 percent earned more than $41,980 annually, while the lowest 10 percent earned less than $15,920. Butchers and meatcutters employed at the retail level typically earn more than those in manufacturing. Median annual earnings in the industries employing the largest numbers of butchers and meatcutters in May 2004 were as follows:

Other general merchandise stores	$31,900
Grocery stores	27,030
Specialty food stores	22,010
Animal slaughtering and processing	21,440

Meat, poultry, and fish cutters and trimmers typically earn less than butchers and meatcutters. In May 2004, median annual earnings for these lower skilled workers were $18,900. The middle 50 percent earned between $16,240 and $22,360. The highest 10 percent earned more than $27,430, while the lowest 10 percent earned less than $14,410. Median annual earnings in the industries employing the largest numbers of meat, poultry, and fish cutters and trimmers in May 2004 are shown in the following tabulation:

Grocery and related product wholesalers	$20,790
Grocery stores	20,650
Animal slaughtering and processing	18,660
Seafood product preparation and packaging	18,040

Median annual earnings of bakers were $21,330 in May 2004. The middle 50 percent earned between $17,070 and $27,210. The highest 10 percent earned more than $34,410, and the lowest 10 percent earned less than $14,680. Median annual earnings in the industries employing the largest numbers of bakers in May 2004 are given in the following tabulation:

Other general merchandise stores	$23,390
Bakeries and tortilla manufacturing	22,170
Grocery stores	21,340
Full-service restaurants	19,980
Limited-service eating places	18,690

Median annual earnings of food batchmakers were $22,090 in May 2004. The middle 50 percent earned between $17,010 and $28,790. The highest 10 percent earned more than $35,540, and the lowest 10 percent earned less than $14,370. Median annual earnings in the industries employing the largest numbers of food batchmakers in May 2004 are presented in the following tabulation:

Dairy product manufacturing	$26,550
Other food manufacturing	23,970
Fruit and vegetable preserving and specialty food manufacturing	23,230
Sugar and confectionery product manufacturing	21,420
Bakeries and tortilla manufacturing	20,890

In May 2004, median annual earnings for slaughterers and meatpackers were $20,860. The middle 50 percent earned between $18,120 and $23,920. The highest 10 percent earned more than $27,910, and the lowest 10 percent earned less than $15,520. Median annual earnings in animal slaughtering and processing, the industry employing the largest number of slaughterers and meatpackers, were $20,900 in May 2004.

Median annual earnings for food cooking machine operators and tenders were $20,850 in May 2004. The middle 50 percent earned between $16,680 and $26,670. The highest 10 percent earned more than $33,780, and the lowest 10 percent earned less than $13,930. Median annual earnings in fruit and vegetable preserving and specialty food manufacturing, the industry employing the largest number of food cooking machine operators and tenders, were $24,370 in May 2004.

In May 2004, median annual earnings for food and tobacco roasting, baking, and drying machine operators and tenders were $23,840. The middle 50 percent earned between $18,600 and $30,590. The highest 10 percent earned more than $37,000, and the lowest 10 percent earned less than $15,000.

Food processing workers generally received typical benefits, including pension plans for union members or those employed by grocery stores. However, poultry workers rarely earned substantial benefits. In 2004, 21 percent of all food processing workers were union members or were covered by a union contract. Many food processing workers are members of the United Food and Commercial Workers International Union.

Related Occupations

Food processing workers must be skilled at both hand and machine work and must have some knowledge of processes and techniques that are involved in handling and preparing food. Other occupations that require similar skills and knowledge include chefs, cooks, and food preparation workers.

Sources of Additional Information

State employment service offices can provide information about job openings for food processing occupations.

Metal Workers and Plastic Workers

Computer Control Programmers and Operators

(O*NET 51-4011.01, 51-4012.00)

Significant Points

- Manufacturing industries employ almost all of these workers.

- Workers learn in apprenticeship programs, informally on the job, and in secondary, vocational, or post-secondary schools; many entrants have previously worked as machinists or machine setters, operators, and tenders.

- Despite the projected decline in employment, job opportunities should be good, as employers are expected to continue to have difficulty finding qualified workers.

Nature of the Work

Computer control programmers and operators use computer numerically controlled (CNC) machines to cut and shape precision products, such as automobile parts, machine parts, and compressors. CNC machines include machining tools such as lathes, multiaxis spindles, milling machines, laser cutting, water jet cutting, and wire electrical discharge machines (EDM), but the functions formerly performed by human operators are performed by a computer control module. CNC machines cut away material from a solid block of metal, plastic, or glass—known as a workpiece—to form a finished part. Computer control programmers and operators normally produce large quantities of one part, although they may produce small batches or one of a kind items. They use their knowledge of the working properties of metals and their skill with CNC programming to design and carry out the operations needed to make machined products that meet precise specifications.

Before CNC programmers—also referred to as numerical tool and process control programmers—machine a part, they must carefully plan and prepare the operation. First, these workers review three-dimensional computer aided/automated design (CAD) blueprints of the part. Next, they calculate where to cut or bore into the workpiece, how fast to feed the metal into the machine, and how much metal to remove. They then select tools and materials for the job and plan the sequence of cutting and finishing operations.

Next, CNC programmers turn the planned machining operations into a set of instructions. These instructions are translated into a computer aided/automated manufacturing (CAM) program containing a set of commands for the machine to follow. These commands normally are a series of numbers (hence, numerical control) that describes where cuts should occur, what type of cut should be used, and the speed of the cut. CNC programmers and operators check new programs to ensure that the machinery will function properly and that the output will meet specifications. Because a problem with the program could damage costly machinery and cutting tools or simply waste valuable time and materials, computer simulations may be used to check the program instead of a trial run. If errors are found, the program must be changed and retested until the problem is resolved. In addition, growing connectivity between CAD/CAM software and CNC machine tools is raising productivity by automatically translating designs into instructions for the computer controller on the machine tool. These new CAM technologies enable programs to be easily modified for use on other jobs with similar specifications.

After the programming work is completed, CNC operators—also referred to as computer-controlled machine tool operators, metal and plastic—perform the necessary machining operations. The CNC operators transfer the commands from the server to the CNC control module using a computer network link or floppy disk. Many advanced control modules are conversational, meaning that they ask the operator a series of questions about the nature of the task. CNC operators position the metal stock on the CNC machine tool—spindle, lathe, milling machine, or other—set the controls, and let the computer make the cuts. Heavier objects may be loaded with the assistance of other workers, autoloaders, a crane, or a forklift. During the machining process, computer-control operators constantly check to see if any problems exist. Machine tools have unique characteristics, which can be problematic. During a machining operation, the operator modifies the cutting program to account for any problems encountered. Operators who make these adjustments need a basic knowledge of CNC programming. Unique, modified CNC programs are saved for every different machine that performs a task.

In order to boost productivity, manufacturers increasing prefer workers who can quickly adapt to new technology and perform a wide range of tasks. As a result, CNC operators often are required to perform many of the basic skills of a machinist and a CNC programmer. However, some manufacturers simply need CNC operators to be "button-pushers." They primarily start and stop machines, load cutting programs, and load and unload parts and tools.

Regardless of skill level, all CNC operators detect some problems by listening for specific sounds—for example, a dull cutting tool that needs changing or excessive vibration. Machine tools rotate at high speeds, which can create problems with harmonic vibrations in the workpiece. Vibrations cause the machine tools to make minor cutting errors, hurting the quality of the product. Operators listen for vibrations and then adjust the cutting speed to compensate. In older, slower machine tools, the cutting speed would be reduced to eliminate the vibrations, but the amount of time needed to finish the product would increase as a result. In newer, high-speed CNC machines, increasing the cutting speed normally eliminates the vibrations and reduces production time. CNC operators also ensure that the workpiece is being properly lubricated and cooled, because the machining of metal products generates a significant amount of heat.

Since CNC machines can operate with limited input from the operator, a single operator may monitor several machines simultaneously. Typically, an operator might monitor two machines cutting relatively simple parts cut from softer materials, while devoting most of his or her attention to a third machine cutting a much more difficult part cut from a hard metal, such as stainless steel. Operators are often expected to carefully schedule their work so that all of the machines are always operating.

Working Conditions

Most machine shops are clean, well lit, and ventilated. Most modern CNC machines are partially or totally enclosed, minimizing the

Computer control operators load programs into a machine.

exposure of workers to noise, debris, and the lubricants used to cool workpieces during machining. Nevertheless, working around machine tools presents certain dangers, and workers must follow safety precautions. Computer-controlled machine tool operators, metal and plastic, wear protective equipment, such as safety glasses to shield against bits of flying metal and earplugs to dampen machinery noise. They also must exercise caution when handling hazardous coolants and lubricants. The job requires stamina because operators stand most of the day and, at times, may need to lift moderately heavy workpieces.

Numerical tool and process control programmers work on desktop computers in offices that typically are near, but separate from, the shop floor. These work areas usually are clean, well lit, and free of machine noise. Numerical tool and process control programmers occasionally need to enter the shop floor to monitor CNC machining operations. On the shop floor, CNC programmers encounter the same hazards and exercise the same safety precautions as do CNC operators.

Most computer control programmers and operators work a 40-hour week. CNC operators increasingly work evening and weekend shifts as companies justify investments in more expensive machinery by extending hours of operation. Overtime is common during peak production periods.

Training, Other Qualifications, and Advancement

Computer control programmers and operators train in various ways—in apprenticeship programs, informally on the job, and in secondary, vocational, or postsecondary schools. In general, the more skills needed for the job, the more education and training that is needed to qualify. For example, a growing number of computer control programmers and the more skilled operators are receiving their formal training from community or technical colleges. For some specialized types of programming, such as that needed to produce complex parts for the aerospace or shipbuilding industries, employers may prefer individuals with a degree in engineering.

Less-skilled CNC operators (button-pushers) may need only a couple of weeks of on-the-job training.

Employers prefer to hire workers who have a basic knowledge of computers and electronics and experience with machine tools. In fact, many entrants to these occupations have previously worked as machinists or machine setters, operators, and tenders. Due to a shortage of applicants with the appropriate training, many employers are providing introductory courses in operating metalworking machines, safety, and blueprint reading. Persons interested in becoming computer control programmers or operators should be mechanically inclined and able to work independently and do highly accurate work.

High school or vocational school courses in mathematics (trigonometry and algebra), blueprint reading, computer programming, metalworking, and drafting are recommended. Apprenticeship programs consist of shop training and related classroom instruction. In shop training, apprentices learn filing, handtapping, and dowel fitting, as well as the operation of various machine tools. Classroom instruction includes math, physics, programming, blueprint reading, CAD software, safety, and shop practices. Skilled computer control programmers and operators need an understanding of the machining process, including the complex physics that occur at the cutting point. Thus, most training programs teach CNC operators and programmers to perform operations on manual machines prior to operating CNC machines.

To boost the skill level of all metalworkers and to create a more uniform standard of competency, a number of training facilities and colleges have recently begun implementing curriculums incorporating national skills standards developed by the National Institute of Metalworking Skills (NIMS). After completing such a curriculum and passing a performance requirement and written exam, trainees are granted a NIMS credential that provides formal recognition of competency in a metalworking field. Completion of a formal certification program provides expanded career opportunities.

Classroom training includes an introduction to computer numerical control, the basics of programming, and more complex topics, such as computer-aided manufacturing. Trainees start writing simple programs under the direction of an experienced programmer. Although machinery manufacturers are trying to standardize programming languages, there are numerous languages in use. Because of this, computer control programmers and operators should be able to learn new programming languages.

As new automation is introduced, computer control programmers and operators normally receive additional training to update their skills. This training usually is provided by a representative of the equipment manufacturer or a local technical school. Many employers offer tuition reimbursement for job-related courses.

Computer control programmers and operators can advance in several ways. Experienced CNC operators may become CNC programmers, and some are promoted to supervisory or administrative positions in their firms. A few open their own shops.

Employment

Computer control programmers and operators held about 143,000 jobs in 2004, mostly working in machine shops, plastics products manufacturing, machinery manufacturing, or transportation equipment manufacturing making mostly aerospace and automobile parts. Although computer control programmers and operators work in all parts of the country, jobs are most plentiful in the areas where manufacturing is concentrated.

Job Outlook

Computer control programmers and operators should have good job opportunities, despite the projected decline in employment. Due to the limited number of people entering training programs, employers are expected to continue to have difficulty finding workers with the necessary skills and knowledge.

Employment of both computer-controlled machine tool operators and numerical tool and process control programmers is expected to decline through 2014. While CNC machine tools will be increasingly used, advances in CNC machine tools and manufacturing technology will further automate the production process, boosting CNC operator productivity and limiting employment. The demand for computer control programmers also will be negatively affected by the increasing use of software (CAD/CAM) that automatically translates part and product designs into CNC machine tool instructions.

Employment levels of computer control programmers and operators are influenced by economic cycles—as the demand for machined goods falls, programmers and operators involved in production may be laid off or forced to work fewer hours.

Earnings

Median hourly earnings of computer-controlled machine tool operators, metal and plastic, were $14.75 in May 2004. The middle 50 percent earned between $11.65 and $18.21. The lowest 10 percent earned less than $9.47, whereas the top 10 percent earned more than $21.67. Median hourly earnings in the manufacturing industries employing the largest numbers of computer-controlled machine tool operators, metal and plastic, in May 2004 were:

Metalworking machinery manufacturing	$16.34
Other fabricated metal product manufacturing	15.62
Machine shops; turned product; and screw, nut, and bolt manufacturing	14.73
Motor vehicle parts manufacturing	13.55
Plastics product manufacturing	11.78

Median hourly earnings of numerical tool and process control programmers were $19.31 in May 2004. The middle 50 percent earned between $15.67 and $24.00. The lowest 10 percent earned less than $12.89, while the top 10 percent earned more than $28.89.

Related Occupations

Occupations most closely related to computer control programmers and operators are other metal and plastic working occupations, which include machinists; tool and die makers; machine setters, operators, and tenders—metal and plastic; and welding, soldering, and brazing workers. Numerical tool and process control programmers apply their knowledge of machining operations, metals, blueprints, and machine programming to write programs that run machine tools. Computer programmers also write detailed programs to meet precise specifications.

Sources of Additional Information

For general information about computer control programmers and operators, contact:

➤ Precision Machine Products Association, 6700 West Snowville Rd., Brecksville, OH 44141-3292. Internet: **http://www.pmpa.org**

For a list of training centers and apprenticeship programs, contact:

➤ National Tooling and Metalworking Association, 9300 Livingston Rd., Fort Washington, MD 20744. Internet: **http://www.ntma.org**

For general occupational information, including a list of training programs, contact:

➤ Precision Metalforming Association Educational Foundation, 6363 Oak Tree Blvd., Independence, OH 44131-2500. Internet: **http://www.pmaef.org**

Machinists

(O*NET 51-4041.00)

Significant Points

- Machinists learn in apprenticeship programs, informally on the job, and in vocational schools or community or technical colleges.

- Many entrants previously have worked as machine setters, operators, or tenders.

- Job opportunities are expected to be good.

Nature of the Work

Machinists use machine tools, such as lathes, milling machines, and machining centers, to produce precision metal parts. Although they may produce large quantities of one part, precision machinists often produce small batches or one-of-a-kind items. They use their knowledge of the working properties of metals and their skill with machine tools to plan and carry out the operations needed to make machined products that meet precise specifications.

Before they machine a part, machinists must carefully plan and prepare the operation. These workers first review electronic or written blueprints or specifications for a job. Next, they calculate where to cut or bore into the workpiece (the piece of steel, aluminum, titanium, plastic, silicon or any other material that is being shaped), how fast to feed the workpiece into the machine, and how much material to remove. They then select tools and materials for the job, plan the sequence of cutting and finishing operations, and mark the workpiece to show where cuts should be made.

After this layout work is completed, machinists perform the necessary machining operations. They position the workpiece on the machine tool—drill press, lathe, milling machine, or other type of machine—set the controls, and make the cuts. During the machining process, they must constantly monitor the feed rate and speed of the machine. Machinists also ensure that the workpiece is being properly lubricated and cooled, because the machining of metal products generates a significant amount of heat. The temperature of the workpiece is a key concern because most metals expand when heated; machinists must adjust the size of their cuts relative to the temperature. Some rare but increasingly popular metals, such as titanium, are machined at extremely high temperatures.

Machinists detect some problems by listening for specific sounds—for example, a dull cutting tool or excessive vibration. Dull cutting tools are removed and replaced. Cutting speeds are adjusted to compensate for harmonic vibrations, which can decrease the accuracy of cuts, particularly on newer high-speed spindles and lathes. After the work is completed, machinists use both simple and highly sophisticated measuring tools to check the accuracy of their work against blueprints.

Some machinists, often called production machinists, may produce large quantities of one part, especially parts requiring the use of complex operations and great precision. Many modern machine tools are computer numerically controlled (CNC). CNC machines, following a computer program, control the cutting tool speed, change dull tools, and perform all of the necessary cuts to create a part. Frequently, machinists work with computer control programmers to determine how the automated equipment will cut a part. (See the statement on computer control programmers and operators elsewhere in the *Handbook*.) The programmer may determine the path of the cut, while the machinist determines the type of cutting tool, the speed of the cutting tool, and the feed rate. Because most machinists train in CNC programming, they may write basic programs themselves and often set offsets (modify programs) in response to problems encountered during test runs. After the production process is designed, relatively simple and repetitive operations normally are performed by machine setters, operators, and tenders. (See the statement on machine setters, operators, and tenders—metal and plastic, elsewhere in the *Handbook*.)

Some manufacturing techniques employ automated parts loaders, automatic tool changers, and computer controls, allowing machine tools to operate without anyone present. One production machinist, working 8 hours a day, might monitor equipment, replace worn cutting tools, check the accuracy of parts being produced, adjust offsets, and perform other tasks on several CNC machines that operate 24 hours a day (lights-out manufacturing). During lights-out manufacturing, a factory may need only a few machinists to monitor the entire factory.

Other machinists do maintenance work—repairing or making new parts for existing machinery. To repair a broken part, maintenance machinists may refer to blueprints and perform the same machining operations that were needed to create the original part.

Because the technology of machining is changing rapidly, machinists must learn to operate a wide range of machines. Along with operating machines that use metal cutting tools to shape workpieces, machinists operate machines that cut with lasers, water jets, or electrified wires. While some of the computer controls may be similar, machinists must understand the unique cutting properties of these different machines. As engineers create new types of machine tools and new materials to machine, machinists must constantly learn new machining properties and techniques.

Working Conditions

Today, most machine shops are relatively clean, well lit, and ventilated. Many computer-controlled machines are partially or totally enclosed, minimizing the exposure of workers to noise, debris, and the lubricants used to cool workpieces during machining. Nevertheless, working around machine tools presents certain dangers, and workers must follow safety precautions. Machinists wear protective equipment, such as safety glasses to shield against bits of flying metal and earplugs to dampen machinery noise. They also must exercise caution when handling hazardous coolants and lubricants, although many common water-based lubricants present little hazard. The job requires stamina, because machinists stand most of the day and, at times, may need to lift moderately heavy workpieces. Modern factories extensively employ autoloaders and overhead cranes, reducing heavy lifting.

Machinists use computer controlled machine tools to make parts.

Many machinists work a 40-hour week. Evening and weekend shifts are becoming more common as companies justify investments in more expensive machinery by extending hours of operation. However, this trend is somewhat offset by the increasing use of lights-out manufacturing and the use of machine operators for less desirable shifts. Overtime is common during peak production periods.

Training, Other Qualifications, and Advancement

Machinists train in apprenticeship programs, informally on the job, and in vocational schools, or community or technical colleges. Experience with machine tools is helpful. In fact, many entrants previously have worked as machine setters, operators, or tenders. Persons interested in becoming machinists should be mechanically inclined, have good problem-solving abilities, be able to work independently, and be able to do highly accurate work (tolerances may reach 1/10,000th of an inch) that requires concentration and physical effort.

High school or vocational school courses in mathematics (especially trigonometry), blueprint reading, metalworking, and drafting are highly recommended. Apprenticeship programs consist of shop training and related classroom instruction lasting up to 4 years. In shop training, apprentices work almost full time, and are supervised by an experienced machinist while learning to operate various machine tools. Classroom instruction includes math, physics, materials science, blueprint reading, mechanical drawing, and quality and safety practices. In addition, as machine shops have increased their use of computer-controlled equipment, training in the operation and programming of CNC machine tools has become essential. Apprenticeship classes are often taught in cooperation with local community or vocational colleges. A growing number of machinists learn the trade through 2-year associate degree programs at community or technical colleges. Graduates of these programs still need significant on-the-job experience before they are fully qualified.

To boost the skill level of machinists and to create a more uniform standard of competency, a number of training facilities and colleges are implementing curriculums that incorporate national skills standards developed by the National Institute of Metalworking Skills (NIMS). After completing such a curriculum and passing a performance requirement and written exam, trainees are granted a NIMS credential, which provides formal recognition of competency in a metalworking field. Completing a recognized certification program provides a machinist with better career opportunities.

As new automation is introduced, machinists normally receive additional training to update their skills. This training usually is provided by a representative of the equipment manufacturer or a local technical school. Some employers offer tuition reimbursement for job-related courses.

Machinists can advance in several ways. Experienced machinists may become CNC programmers, tool and die makers, or mold makers, or be promoted to supervisory or administrative positions in their firms. A few open their own shops.

Employment

Machinists held about 370,000 jobs in 2004. Most machinists work in small machining shops or in manufacturing industries, such as machinery manufacturing and transportation equipment manufacturing (motor vehicle parts and aerospace products and parts). Maintenance machinists work in most industries that use production machinery.

Job Outlook

Despite relatively slow employment growth, job opportunities for machinists should continue to be good. Many young people with the necessary educational and personal qualifications needed to obtain machining skills often prefer to attend college or may not wish to enter production occupations. Therefore, the number of workers obtaining the skills and knowledge necessary to fill machinist jobs is expected to be less than the number of job openings arising each year from the need to replace experienced machinists who transfer to other occupations or retire, and from job growth.

Employment of machinists is projected to grow more slowly than the average for all occupations over the 2004-14 period because of rising productivity among these workers and strong foreign competition. Machinists will become more efficient as a result of the expanded use of and improvements in technologies such as CNC machine tools, autoloaders, and high-speed machining. This allows fewer machinists to accomplish the same amount of work previously performed by more workers. Technology is not expected to affect the employment of machinists as significantly as that of most other production occupations, however, because machinists monitor and maintain many automated systems. Due to modern production techniques, employers prefer workers, such as machinists, who have a wide range of skills and are capable of performing almost any task in a machine shop.

Employment levels in this occupation are influenced by economic cycles—as the demand for machined goods falls, machinists involved in production may be laid off or forced to work fewer hours. Employment of machinists involved in plant maintenance, however, often is more stable because proper maintenance and repair of costly equipment remain critical to manufacturing operations, even when production levels fall.

Earnings

Median hourly earnings of machinists were $16.33 in May 2004. The middle 50 percent earned between $12.84 and $20.33. The lowest 10 percent earned less than $10.08, while the top 10 percent earned more than $24.34. Median hourly earnings in the manufacturing industries employing the largest number of machinists in May 2004 were:

Aerospace product and parts manufacturing	$17.78
Motor vehicle parts manufacturing	17.46
Metalworking machinery manufacturing	17.06
Machine shops; turned product; and screw, nut, and bolt manufacturing	15.87
Employment services	11.09

Apprentices earn much less than machinists, but earnings increase quickly as they improve their skills. Also most employers pay for apprentices' training classes.

Related Occupations

Occupations most closely related to that of machinist are other machining occupations, which include tool and die makers; machine setters, operators, and tenders—metal and plastic; and computer control programmers and operators. Another occupation that requires precision and skill in working with metal is welding, soldering, and brazing workers.

Sources of Additional Information

For general information about machinists, contact:
➤ Precision Machine Products Association, 6700 West Snowville Rd., Brecksville, OH 44141-3292. Internet: **http://www.pmpa.org**

For a list of training centers and apprenticeship programs, contact:
➤ National Tooling and Machining Association, 9300 Livingston Rd., Fort Washington, MD 20744. Internet: **http://www.ntma.org**

For general occupational information and a list of training programs, contact:
➤ Precision Metalforming Association Educational Foundation, 6363 Oak Tree Blvd., Independence, OH 44131-2500. Internet: **http://www.pmaef.org**

Machine Setters, Operators, and Tenders—Metal and Plastic

(O*NET 51-4021.00, 51-4022.00, 51-4023.00, 51-4031.01, 51-4031.02, 51-4031.03, 51-4031.04, 51-4032.00, 51-4033.01, 51-4033.02, 51-4034.00, 51-4035.00, 51-4051.00, 51-4052.00, 51-4061.00, 51-4062.00, 51-4071.00, 51-4072.01, 51-4072.02, 51-4072.03, 51-4072.04, 51-4072.05, 51-4081.01, 51-4081.02, 51-4191.01, 51-4191.02, 51-4191.03, 51-4192.00, 51-4193.01, 51-4193.02, 51-4193.03, 51-4193.04, 51-4194.00, 51-4199.99)

Significant Points

- Manufacturing industries employ 10 out of 11 workers.

- A few weeks of on-the-job training is sufficient for most workers to learn basic machine operations, but a year or more is required to become a highly skilled operator or setter.

- Employment in most machine setter, operator, and tender occupations will decline over the 2004-14 period as a result of productivity improvements and competition for jobs from abroad.

Nature of the Work

Consider the parts of a toaster, such as the metal or plastic housing or the lever that lowers the toast. These parts, and many other metal and plastic products, are produced by machine setters, operators, and tenders—metal and plastic. In fact, machine tool operators in the metalworking and plastics industries play a major role in producing most of the consumer products on which we rely daily.

In general, these workers can be separated into two groups—those who set up machines for operation and those who tend the machines during production. Setup workers prepare the machines *prior* to production and may adjust the machinery during its operation. Operators and tenders primarily monitor the machinery *during* its operation, sometimes loading or unloading the machine or making minor adjustments to the controls. Many workers both set up and operate equipment. Because the setup process requires an understanding of the entire production process, setters usually have more training and are more highly skilled than those who simply operate or tend machinery. As new automation simplifies the setup process, however, less skilled workers also are increasingly able to set up machines for operation.

Setters, operators, and tenders usually are identified by the type of machine with which they work. Some examples of specific titles are drilling- and boring-machine toolsetters, milling- and planing-machine tenders, and lathe- and turning-machine tool operators. Job duties usually vary with the size of the firm and the type of machine being operated. Although some workers specialize in one or two types of machinery, many are trained to set up or operate a variety of machines. Increasing automation allows machine setters to operate multiple machines simultaneously. In addition, newer production techniques, such as team-oriented "lean" manufacturing, require machine operators to rotate between different machines. Rotating assignments result in more varied work, but also require workers to have a wider range of skills.

Machine setters, operators, and tenders—metal set up and tend machines that cut and form all types of metal parts. Setup workers plan and set up the sequence of operations according to blueprints, layouts, or other instructions. Often this involves loading a computer program with instructions into the machine's computer controls. On all machines, including those with computer controls, setup workers respond to problems during operation by adjusting the speed, feed and other variables, choosing the proper coolants and lubricants, and selecting the instruments or tools for each operation. Using micrometers, gauges, and other precision measuring instruments, they also may compare the completed work with the tolerance limits stated in the specifications.

Although there are many different types of metalworking machine tools that require specific knowledge and skills, most operators perform similar tasks. Whether tending grinding machines that remove excess material from the surface of machined products or presses that extrude metal through a die to form wire, operators usually perform simple, repetitive operations that can be learned quickly. Typically, these workers place metal stock in a machine on which the operating specifications have already been set. They may watch one or more machines and make minor adjustments according to their instructions. Regardless of the type of machine they operate, machine tenders usually depend on skilled setup workers for major adjustments when the machines are not functioning properly.

Machine setters, operators, and tenders—plastic set up and tend machines that transform plastic compounds—chemical-based products that can be produced in powder, pellet, or syrup form—into a wide variety of consumer goods such as toys, tubing, and auto parts. These products are manufactured by various methods, of which injection molding is the most common. The injection-molding machine heats and liquefies a plastic compound and forces it into a mold. After the part has cooled and hardened, the mold opens and the part is released. Many common kitchen products are produced with this method. To produce long parts such as pipes or window frames, an extruding machine usually is employed. These machines force a plastic compound through a die that contains an opening with the desired shape of the final product. Blow molding is another common plasticsworking technique. Blow-molding machines force hot air into a mold that contains a plastic tube. As the air moves into the mold, the tube is inflated to the shape of the mold, and a plastic container is formed. The familiar 2-liter soft-drink bottles are produced by this method.

Workers in three distinct specialties—setters, operators, and tenders—operate injection-molding machines. Most other types of plastic machines function in a similar manner. A typical injection-molding machine may have 25 different controls that can be adjusted. Setters or technicians set up the machines prior to their operation. These workers

A machine operator monitors a cutting and grinding machine.

are responsible for repairing any major problem. Operators monitor the many gauges on injection-molding machines, adjusting different inputs, pressures, and speeds to maintain quality. Tenders remove the cooled plastic from the mold, loading the product into boxes.

Working Conditions
Most machine setters, operators, and tenders—metal and plastic work in areas that are clean, well lit, and well ventilated. Nevertheless, many operators require stamina, because they are on their feet much of the day and may do moderately heavy lifting. Also, these workers operate powerful, high-speed machines that can be dangerous if strict safety rules are not observed. Most operators wear protective equipment, such as safety glasses and earplugs, to protect against flying particles of metal or plastic and against noise from the machines. However, many modern machines are enclosed, minimizing the exposure of workers to noise, dust, and lubricants used during machining. Other required safety equipment varies by work setting and machine. For example, those in the plastics industry who work near materials that emit dangerous fumes or dust must wear face masks or self-contained breathing apparatus.

Most workers in the occupation put in a 40-hour week, but overtime is common during periods of increased production. Because many metalworking and plastics working shops operate more than one shift daily, some operators work nights and weekends.

Training, Other Qualifications, and Advancement
Machine setters, operators, and tenders—metal and plastic learn their skills on the job. Trainees begin by observing and assisting experienced workers, sometimes in formal training programs. Under supervision, they may start as tenders, supplying materials, starting and stopping the machine, or removing finished products from it. Then they advance to the more difficult tasks performed by operators, such as adjusting feed speeds, changing cutting tools, or inspecting a finished product for defects. Eventually, they become responsible for their own machines.

The complexity of the equipment largely determines the time required to become an operator. Most operators learn the basic machine operations and functions in a few weeks, but they may need a year or more to become skilled operators or to advance to the more highly skilled job of setter. Although many operators learn on the job, some community colleges and other educational institutions offer courses and certifications in operating metal and plastics machines. In addition to providing on-the-job training, some employers send promising machine tenders to operator classes. Other employers prefer to hire workers who have completed, or currently are enrolled in, a training program.

Setters or technicians normally need a thorough knowledge of the machinery and of the products being manufactured, because they often plan the sequence of work, make the first production run, and determine which adjustments need to be made. Strong analytical abilities are particularly important for this job. Some companies have formal training programs for operators and setters; often, the programs combine classroom instruction with on-the-job training.

Although no special education is required for many jobs in the occupation, employers prefer to hire applicants with good basic skills. Many require employees to have a high school education and to read, write, and speak English. Because machinery is becoming more complex and shop-floor organization is changing, employers increasingly look for persons with good communication and interpersonal skills. Mechanical aptitude, manual dexterity, and experience working with machinery also are helpful. Those interested in becoming machine setters, operators, and tenders can improve their employment opportunities by completing high school courses in shop and blueprint reading and by gaining a working knowledge of the properties of metals and plastics. A solid math background, including courses in algebra, geometry, trigonometry, and basic statistics, also is useful. With increasing automation, experience with computers also is helpful.

Job opportunities and advancement can be enhanced as well by becoming certified in a particular machining skill. The National Institute for Metalworking Skills has developed standards for machine setters, operators, and tenders—metal. After taking a course approved by the organization and passing a written exam and performance requirement, the worker is issued a credential that signifies competence in a specific machining operation. The Society of Plastics Industry, the national trade association representing plastics manufacturers, also certifies workers in that industry. To achieve machine-operator certification, 2 years of experience operating a plastics-processing machine is recommended, and one must pass a computer-based exam.

Advancement for operators usually takes the form of higher pay, although there are some limited opportunities for operators to advance to new positions as well. For example, they can become multiple-machine operators, setup operators, or trainees for the more highly skilled position of machinist, tool and die maker, or computer-control programmer or operator. (See the statements on machinists, computer control programmers and operators, and tool and die makers elsewhere in the *Handbook*.) Some setup workers may advance to supervisory positions.

Employment

Machine setters, operators, and tenders—metal and plastic held about 1.1 million jobs in 2004. Approximately 10 of 11 jobs were found in manufacturing, primarily in fabricated metal product manufacturing, plastics and rubber products manufacturing, primary metal manufacturing, machinery manufacturing, and motor vehicle parts manufacturing. The following tabulation shows the distribution of employment of machine setters, operators, and tenders—metal and plastic by detailed occupation.

Cutting, punching, and press machine setters, operators, and tenders, metal and plastic	251,000
Molding, coremaking, and casting machine setters, operators, and tenders, metal and plastic	157,000
Grinding, lapping, polishing, and buffing machine tool setters, operators, and tenders, metal and plastic	101,000
Multiple machine tool setters, operators, and tenders, metal and plastic	97,000
Extruding and drawing machine setters, operators, and tenders, metal and plastic	89,000
Lathe and turning machine tool setters, operators, and tenders, metal and plastic	71,000
Metal workers and plastic workers, all other	55,000
Drilling and boring machine tool setters, operators, and tenders, metal and plastic	42,000
Plating and coating machine setters, operators, and tenders, metal and plastic	40,000
Forging machine setters, operators, and tenders, metal and plastic	38,000
Rolling machine setters, operators, and tenders, metal and plastic	37,000
Milling and planing machine setters, operators, and tenders, metal and plastic	31,000
Heat treating equipment setters, operators, and tenders, metal and plastic	26,000
Tool grinders, filers, and sharpeners	21,000
Metal-refining furnace operators and tenders	17,000
Foundry mold and coremakers	17,000
Pourers and casters, metal	14,000
Lay-out workers, metal and plastic	11,000
Model makers, metal and plastic	8,100
Patternmakers, metal and plastic	6,000

Job Outlook

Overall employment in the various machine setter, operator, and tender occupations is expected to decline over the 2004–14 period. In general, employment of these workers will be affected by technological advances, changing demand for the goods they produce, foreign competition, and the reorganization of production processes. Despite the overall employment decline, a large number of machine setter, operator, and tender jobs will become available due to an expected surge in retirements as some baby boomers become eligible for retirement by the end of the decade.

One of the most important factors influencing employment change in this occupation is the implementation of labor-saving machinery. In order to remain competitive by improving quality and lowering production costs, many firms are adopting new technologies, such as computer-controlled machine tools and robots. Computer-controlled equipment allows operators to tend a greater number of machines simultaneously and often makes setup easier, thereby reducing the amount of time setup workers spend on each machine. Robots are being used to load and unload parts from machines. The lower skilled manual machine tool operators and tenders are more likely to be eliminated by these new technologies, because the functions they perform are more easily automated.

The demand for machine setters, operators, and tenders—metal and plastic largely mirrors the demand for the parts they produce. The consumption of plastic products has grown as they have been substituted for metal goods in many consumer and manufactured products in recent years. The process is likely to continue and should result in stronger demand for machine operators in plastics than in metal.

Both the plastics and metal industries, however, face stiff foreign competition that is limiting the demand for domestically produced parts. One way in which larger U.S. producers have responded to this competition is by moving production operations to other countries where labor costs are lower. These moves are likely to continue and will further reduce employment opportunities for many machine operators, setters, and tenders—metal and plastic in the United States. Another way domestic manufacturers compete with low-wage foreign competition is by increasing their use of automated systems, which can make manufacturing establishments more competitive by improving their productivity. However, increased automation also limits employment growth.

Workers with a thorough background in machine operations, exposure to a variety of machines, and a good working knowledge of the properties of metals and plastics will be best able to adjust to the changing environment. In addition, new shop-floor arrangements will reward workers with good basic mathematics and reading skills, good communication skills, and the ability and willingness to learn new tasks. As workers adapt to team-oriented production methods, those who can operate multiple machines will have the best job opportunities.

Earnings

Earnings for machine operators can vary by size of the company, union or nonunion status, industry, and skill level and experience of the operator. Also, temporary employees, who are being hired in greater numbers, usually get paid less than company-employed workers. The median hourly earnings in May 2004 for a variety of machine setters, operators, and tenders—metal and plastic were:

Model makers, metal and plastic	$21.28
Patternmakers, metal and plastic...	17.86
Metal workers and plastic workers, all other...................................	16.15
Metal-refining furnace operators and tenders	15.74
Lay-out workers, metal and plastic...	15.65
Lathe and turning machine tool setters, operators, and tenders, metal and plastic	15.04
Milling and planing machine setters, operators, and tenders, metal and plastic	14.91
Tool grinders, filers, and sharpeners	14.52
Rolling machine setters, operators, and tenders, metal and plastic	14.33
Heat treating equipment setters, operators, and tenders, metal and plastic..	14.26
Multiple machine tool setters, operators, and tenders, metal and plastic..	14.06
Pourers and casters, metal...	13.92
Drilling and boring machine tool setters, operators, and tenders, metal and plastic	13.69
Foundry mold and coremakers..	13.37
Forging machine setters, operators, and tenders, metal and plastic	13.22
Grinding, lapping, polishing, and buffing machine tool setters, operators, and tenders, metal and plastic	13.19
Extruding and drawing machine setters, operators, and tenders, metal and plastic..	13.18
Plating and coating machine setters, operators, and tenders, metal and plastic..	12.96
Cutting, punching, and press machine setters, operators, and tenders, metal and plastic	12.45
Molding, coremaking, and casting machine setters, operators, and tenders, metal and plastic	11.63

Related Occupations

Workers in occupations closely related to machine setters, operators, and tenders—metal and plastic include machinists; tool and die makers; assemblers and fabricators; computer control programmers and operators; and welding, soldering, and brazing workers. Often, machine operators are responsible for checking the quality of parts being produced, work similar to that of inspectors, testers, sorters, samplers, and weighers.

Sources of Additional Information

For general information about metal machine setters, operators, and tenders, contact:
➤ National Tooling and Machining Association, 9300 Livingston Rd., Fort Washington, MD 20744. Internet: **http://www.ntma.org**
➤ Precision Metalforming Association Educational Foundation, 6363 Oak Tree Blvd., Independence, OH 44131. Internet: **http://www.pmaef.org**
➤ Precision Machine Products Association, 6700 West Snowville Rd., Brecksville, OH 44141-3292. Internet: **http://www.pmpa.org**

For information on schools and employers with training programs in plastics, contact:
➤ Society of Plastics Industry, 1667 K St. NW., Suite 1000, Washington, DC 20006. Internet: **http://www.plasticsindustry.org**

Tool and Die Makers

(O*NET 51-4111.00)

Significant Points

● Most tool and die makers train for 4 or 5 years in apprenticeships or postsecondary programs; employers typically recommend apprenticeship training.

● Employment is projected to decline because of strong foreign competition and advancements in automation.

● Excellent job opportunities are expected; employers in certain parts of the country report difficulty attracting well-trained applicants.

Nature of the Work

Tool and die makers are among the most highly skilled workers in manufacturing. These workers produce tools, dies, and special guiding and holding devices that enable machines to manufacture a variety of products we use daily—from clothing and furniture to heavy equipment and parts for aircraft.

Toolmakers craft precision tools and machines that are used to cut, shape, and form metal and other materials. They also produce jigs and fixtures (devices that hold metal while it is bored, stamped, or drilled) and gauges and other measuring devices. Die makers construct metal forms (dies) that are used to shape metal in stamping and forging operations. They also make metal molds for diecasting and for molding plastics, ceramics, and composite materials. Some tool and die makers craft prototypes of parts, and then, working with engineers and designers, determine how best to manufacture the part. In addition to developing, designing, and producing new tools and dies, these workers also may repair worn or damaged tools, dies, gauges, jigs, and fixtures.

To perform these functions, tool and die makers employ many types of machine tools and precision measuring instruments. They also must be familiar with the machining properties, such as hardness and heat tolerance, of a wide variety of common metals, alloys, plastics, ceramics, and other composite materials. As a result, tool and die makers are knowledgeable in machining operations, mathematics, and blueprint reading. In fact, tool and die makers often are considered highly specialized machinists. The main difference between tool and die makers and machinists is that machinists normally make a single part during the production process, while tool and die makers make parts and assemble and adjust machines used in the production process. (See the statement on machinists elsewhere in the *Handbook*.)

Traditionally, tool and die makers, working from blueprints, first must plan the sequence of operations necessary to manufacture the tool or die. Next, they measure and mark the pieces of metal that will be cut to form parts of the final product. At this point, tool and die makers cut, drill, or bore the part as required, checking to ensure that the final product meets specifications. Finally, these workers assemble the parts and perform finishing jobs such as filing, grinding, and polishing surfaces. While manual machining has declined, companies still employ it for some simple and low-quantity parts.

Most tool and die makers today use computer-aided design (CAD) to develop products and parts. Specifications entered into computer programs can be used to electronically develop blueprints for the required tools and dies. Numerical tool and process control programmers use computer-aided design or computer-aided manufacturing (CAD/CAM) programs to convert electronic drawings into CAM-based computer programs that contain instructions for a sequence of cutting tool operations. (See the statement on computer-control programmers and operators elsewhere in the *Handbook*.) Once these programs are developed, computer numerically controlled (CNC) machines follow the set of instructions contained in the program to produce the part. Computer-controlled machine tool operators or machinists normally operate CNC machines; however, tool and die makers are trained in both operating CNC machines and writing CNC programs, and they may perform either task. CNC programs are stored electronically for future use, saving time and increasing worker productivity.

After machining the parts, tool and die makers carefully check the accuracy of the parts using many tools, including coordinate measuring machines (CMM), which use software and sensor arms

A tool and die maker operates a manual lathe.

to compare the dimensions of the part to electronic blueprints. Next, they assemble the different parts into a functioning machine. They file, grind, shim, and adjust the different parts to properly fit them together. Finally, the tool and die makers set up a test run using the tools or dies they have made to make sure that the manufactured parts meet specifications. If problems occur, they compensate by adjusting the tools or dies.

Working Conditions

Tool and die makers usually work in toolrooms. These areas are quieter than the production floor because there are fewer machines in use at one time. They also are generally kept clean and cool to minimize heat-related expansion of metal workpieces and to accommodate the growing number of computer-operated machines. To minimize the exposure of workers to moving parts, machines have guards and shields. Most computer-controlled machines are totally enclosed, minimizing the exposure of workers to noise, dust, and the lubricants used to cool workpieces during machining. Tool and die makers also must follow safety rules and wear protective equipment, such as safety glasses to shield against bits of flying metal, earplugs to protect against noise, and gloves and masks to reduce exposure to hazardous lubricants and cleaners. These workers also need stamina because they often spend much of the day on their feet and may do moderately heavy lifting.

Companies employing tool and die makers have traditionally operated only one shift per day. Overtime and weekend work are common, especially during peak production periods.

Training, Other Qualifications, and Advancement

Most tool and die makers learn their trade through 4 or 5 years of education and training in formal apprenticeships or postsecondary programs. Apprenticeship programs include a mix of classroom instruction and on-the-job-training. According to most employers these apprenticeship programs are the best way to learn all aspects of tool and die making. A number of tool and die makers receive most of their formal classroom training from community and technical colleges, often in conjunction with an apprenticeship program.

Traditional apprenticeship programs allowed workers to advance by completing a set number of hours of on-the-job-training and successfully completing specific courses. The National Institute of Metalworking Skills (NIMS) is developing new standards that would replace the required number of hours with competency-based tests. Whether competency tests will change the length of the traditional training process will probably depend upon the apprentice's prior experience, dedication, and natural ability. However, the required training courses for a journeyman tool and die maker will continue to take 4-5 years to complete.

Even after completing the apprenticeship, tool and die makers still need years of experience to become highly skilled. Most specialize in making certain types of tools, molds, or dies.

Tool and die maker trainees learn to operate milling machines, lathes, grinders, wire electrical discharge machines, and other machine tools. They also learn to use handtools for fitting and assembling gauges, and other mechanical and metal-forming equipment. In addition, they study metalworking processes, such as heat treating and plating. Classroom training usually consists of tool designing, tool programming, blueprint reading, and, if needed, mathematics courses, including algebra, geometry, trigonometry, and basic statistics. Tool and die makers increasingly must have good computer skills to work with CAD/CAM technology, CNC machine tools, and computerized measuring machines.

Workers who become tool and die makers without completing formal apprenticeships generally acquire their skills through a combination of informal on-the-job training and classroom instruction at a vocational school or community college. They often begin as machine operators and gradually take on more difficult assignments. Many machinists become tool and die makers.

Because tools and dies must meet strict specifications—precision to one ten-thousandth of an inch is common—the work of tool and die makers requires skill with precision measuring devices and a high degree of patience and attention to detail. Good eyesight is essential. Persons entering this occupation also should be mechanically inclined, able to work and solve problems independently, have strong mathematical skills, and be capable of doing work that requires concentration and physical effort.

Employers generally look for someone with a strong educational background as an indication that the person can more easily adapt to change, which is a constant in this occupation. As automation continues to change the way tools and dies are made, workers regularly need to update their skills in order to learn how to operate new equipment. Also, as materials such as alloys, ceramics, polymers, and plastics are increasingly used, tool and die makers need to learn new machining techniques to deal with the new materials.

There are several ways for skilled workers to advance. Some move into supervisory and administrative positions in their firms or they may start their own shop. Others may take computer courses and become computer-controlled machine tool programmers. With a college degree, a tool and die maker can go into engineering or tool design.

Employment

Tool and die makers held about 103,000 jobs in 2004. Most worked in industries that manufacture metalworking machinery, transportation equipment (such as motor vehicle parts and aerospace products), and fabricated metal products, as well as plastics product manufacturing. Although they are found throughout the country, jobs are most plentiful in the Midwest, Northeast, and West, where many of the metalworking industries are located.

Job Outlook

Despite declining employment, excellent job opportunities are expected. Employers in certain parts of the country report difficulty attracting qualified applicants. The number of workers receiving training in this occupation is expected to continue to be fewer than the number of openings created each year by tool and die makers who retire or transfer to other occupations. A major factor limiting the number of people entering the occupation is that many young people who have the educational and personal qualifications necessary to learn tool and die making may prefer to attend college or may not wish to enter production occupations.

Employment of tool and die makers is projected to decline over the 2004-14 period because of strong foreign competition and advancements in automation, including CNC machine tools and computer-aided design, that should improve worker productivity. On the other hand, tool and die makers play a key role in building and maintaining advanced automated manufacturing equipment. As firms invest in new equipment, modify production techniques, and implement product design changes more rapidly, they will continue to rely heavily on skilled tool and die makers for retooling.

Earnings
Median hourly earnings of tool and die makers were $20.55 in May 2004. The middle 50 percent earned between $16.70 and $25.93. The lowest 10 percent had earnings of less than $13.57, while the top 10 percent earned more than $31.19. Median hourly earnings in the manufacturing industries employing the largest numbers of tool and die makers in May 2004 are:

Motor vehicle parts manufacturing	$26.93
Plastics product manufacturing	20.17
Forging and stamping	20.09
Metalworking machinery manufacturing	19.82
Machine shops; turned product; and screw, nut, and bolt manufacturing	18.84

Apprentice's pay is tied to their skill level. As they gain more skills and reach specific levels of performance and experience, their pay increases.

Related Occupations
The occupations most closely related to the work of tool and die makers are other machining occupations. These include machinists; computer control programmers and operators; and machine setters, operators, and tenders—metal and plastic. Another occupation that requires precision and skill in working with metal is welding, soldering, and brazing workers.

Like tool and die makers, assemblers and fabricators assemble complex machinery. When measuring parts, tool and die makers use some of the same tools and equipment that inspectors, testers, sorters, samplers, and weighers use in their jobs.

Sources of Additional Information
For career information and to have inquiries on training and employment referred to member companies, contact:
➤ Precision Machine Products Association, 6700 West Snowville Rd., Brecksville, OH 44141-3292. Internet: http://www.pmpa.org

For lists of schools and employers with tool and die apprenticeship and training programs, contact:
➤ National Tooling and Machining Association, 9300 Livingston Rd., Ft. Washington, MD 20744. Internet: http://www.ntma.org

For information on careers, education and training, earnings, and apprenticeship opportunities in metalworking, contact:
➤ Precision Metalforming Association Educational Foundation, 6363 Oak Tree Blvd., Independence, OH 44131-2500.

Welding, Soldering, and Brazing Workers

(O*NET 51-4121.01, 51-4121.02, 51-4121.03, 51-4121.04, 51-4121.05, 51-4122.01, 51-4122.02, 51-4122.03, 51-4122.04)

Significant Points
- More than 6 out of 10 jobs are found in manufacturing industries.
- Training ranges from a few weeks of school or on-the-job training for low-skilled positions to several years of combined school and on-the-job training for highly skilled jobs.
- Employment is projected to grow more slowly than average.
- Job prospects should be excellent as employers report difficulty finding enough qualified people.

Nature of the Work
Welding is the most common way of permanently joining metal parts. In this process, heat is applied to metal pieces, melting and fusing them to form a permanent bond. Because of its strength, welding is used in shipbuilding, automobile manufacturing and repair, aerospace applications, and thousands of other manufacturing activities. Welding also is used to join beams when constructing buildings, bridges, and other structures, and to join pipes in pipelines, power plants, and refineries.

Welders use many types of welding equipment set up in a variety of positions, such as flat, vertical, horizontal, and overhead. They may perform manual welding, in which the work is entirely controlled by the welder, or semiautomatic welding, in which the welder uses machinery, such as a wire feeder, to perform welding tasks.

There are about 100 different types of welding. Arc welding is the most common type. Standard arc welding involves two large metal alligator clips that carry a strong electrical current. One clip is attached to any part of the workpiece being welded. The second clip is connected to a thin welding rod. When the rod touches the workpiece, a powerful electrical circuit is created. The massive heat created by the electrical current causes both the workpiece and the steel core of the rod to melt together, cooling quickly to form a solid bond. During welding, the flux that surrounds the rod's core vaporizes, forming an inert gas that serves to protect the weld from atmospheric elements that might weaken it. Welding speed is important. Variations in speed can change the amount of flux applied, weakening the weld, or weakening the surrounding metal by increasing heat exposure.

Two common but advanced types of arc welding are Tungsten Inert Gas (TIG) and Metal Inert Gas (MIG) welding. TIG welding often is used with stainless steel or aluminum. While TIG uses welding rods, MIG uses a spool of continuously fed wire, which allows the welder to join longer stretches of metal without stopping to replace the rod. In TIG welding, the welder holds the welding rod in one hand and an electric torch in the other hand. The torch is used to simultaneously melt the rod and the workpiece. In MIG welding, the welder holds the wire feeder, which functions like the alligator clip in arc welding. Instead of using gas flux surrounding the rod, TIG and MIG protect the initial weld from the environment by blowing inert gas onto the weld.

Like arc welding, soldering and brazing use molten metal to join two pieces of metal. However, the metal added during the process has a melting point lower than that of the workpiece, so only the added metal is melted, not the workpiece. Soldering uses metals with a melting point below 800 degrees Fahrenheit; brazing uses metals with a higher melting point. Because soldering and brazing do not melt the workpiece, these processes normally do not create the distortions or weaknesses in the workpiece that can occur with welding. Soldering commonly is used to join electrical, electronic, and other small metal parts. Brazing produces a stronger joint than does soldering, and often is used to join metals other than steel, such as brass. Brazing can also be used to apply coatings to parts to reduce wear and protect against corrosion.

Skilled welding, soldering, and brazing workers generally plan work from drawings or specifications or use their knowledge of fluxes and base metals to analyze the parts to be joined. These workers then select and set up welding equipment, execute the planned welds, and examine welds to ensure that they meet standards or specifications. They are even examining the weld while they're welding. By observing problems with the weld, they compensate by adjusting the speed, voltage, amperage, or feed of the rod. Highly skilled welders often are trained to work with a wide variety of materials in addition to steel, such as titanium, aluminum, or plastics. Some welders have more limited duties, however. They perform routine jobs that already have been planned and laid out and do not require extensive knowledge of welding techniques.

Automated welding is used in an increasing number of production processes. In these instances, a machine or robot performs the welding tasks while monitored by a welding machine operator. Welding, soldering, and brazing machine setters, operators, and tenders follow specified layouts, work orders, or blueprints. Operators must load parts correctly and constantly monitor the machine to ensure that it produces the desired bond.

The work of arc, plasma, and oxy-gas cutters is closely related to that of welders. However, instead of joining metals, cutters use the heat from an electric arc, a stream of ionized gas (plasma), or burning gases to cut and trim metal objects to specific dimensions. Cutters also dismantle large objects, such as ships, railroad cars, automobiles, buildings, or aircraft. Some operate and monitor cutting machines similar to those used by welding machine operators. Plasma cutting has been increasing in popularity because, unlike other methods, it can cut a wide variety of metals, including stainless steel, aluminum, and titanium.

Working Conditions
Welding, soldering, and brazing workers often are exposed to a number of hazards, including the intense light created by the arc, poisonous fumes, and very hot materials. They wear safety shoes,

Eye protection is important during arc welding.

goggles, hoods with protective lenses, and other devices designed to prevent burns and eye injuries and to protect them from falling objects. They normally work in well-ventilated areas to limit their exposure to fumes. Automated welding, soldering, and brazing machine operators are not exposed to as many dangers, however, and a face shield or goggles usually provide adequate protection for these workers.

Welders and cutters may work outdoors, often in inclement weather, or indoors, sometimes in a confined area designed to contain sparks and glare. Outdoors, they may work on a scaffold or platform high off the ground. In addition, they may be required to lift heavy objects and work in a variety of awkward positions, while bending, stooping, or standing to perform work overhead.

Although about 52 percent of welders, solderers, and brazers work a 40-hour week, overtime is common, and some welders work up to 70 hours per week. Welders also may work in shifts as long as 12 hours. Some welders, solderers, brazers, and machine operators work in factories that operate around the clock, necessitating shift work.

Training, Other Qualifications, and Advancement
Training for welding, soldering, and brazing workers can range from a few weeks of school or on-the-job training for low-skilled positions to several years of combined school and on-the-job training for highly skilled jobs. Formal training is available in high schools, vocational schools, and postsecondary institutions, such as vocational-technical institutes, community colleges, and private welding schools. The Armed Forces operate welding schools as well. While some employers provide basic training, they prefer to hire workers with experience or more formal training. Courses in blueprint reading, shop mathematics, mechanical drawing, physics, chemistry, and metallurgy are helpful. An understanding of electricity also is very helpful and knowledge of computers is gaining importance, especially for welding, soldering, and brazing machine operators, who are becoming more responsible for the programming of computer-controlled machines, including robots.

Some welders become certified, a process whereby the employer sends a worker to an institution, such as an independent testing lab, equipment manufacturer, or technical school, to weld a test specimen according to specific codes and standards required by the employer. Testing procedures are based on the standards and codes set by industry associations with which the employer may be affiliated. If the welding inspector at the examining institution determines that the worker has performed according to the employer's guidelines, the inspector will then certify that the welder being tested is able to work with a particular welding procedure.

Welding, soldering, and brazing workers need good eyesight, hand-eye coordination, and manual dexterity. They should be able to concentrate on detailed work for long periods and be able to bend, stoop, and work in awkward positions. In addition, welders increasingly need to be willing to receive training and perform tasks in other production jobs.

Welders can advance to more skilled welding jobs with additional training and experience. For example, they may become welding technicians, supervisors, inspectors, or instructors. Some experienced welders open their own repair shops.

Employment
Welding, soldering, and brazing workers held about 429,000 jobs in 2004. Of these jobs, more than 6 of every 10 were found in manufacturing. Jobs were concentrated in fabricated metal product manufacturing, transportation equipment manufacturing (motor vehicle body and parts and ship and boat building), machinery manufacturing (agriculture, construction, and mining machinery), architectural and structural metals manufacturing, and construction. Most jobs for welding, soldering, and brazing machine setters, operators, and

tenders were found in the same manufacturing industries as skilled welding, soldering, and brazing workers.

Job Outlook

Employment of welding, soldering, and brazing workers is expected to grow more slowly than the average for all occupations over the 2004-14 period. Despite this, job prospects should be excellent as employers report difficulty finding enough qualified people. In addition, many openings are expected to arise as a large number of workers retire over the next decade.

The major factor affecting employment of welders is the health of the industries in which they work. The manufacturing sector, which employs the most welding, soldering, and brazing workers, is expected to continue to decline as more manufacturing moves overseas. Because almost every manufacturing industry uses welding at some stage of manufacturing or in the repair and maintenance of equipment, this overall decline will affect the demand for welders, although some industries will fare better than others. The construction industry is expected to have solid growth over the next decade and an increasing demand for welders. Government funding for shipbuilding as well as for infrastructure repairs and improvements are expected to generate additional welding jobs.

Pressures to improve productivity and hold down labor costs are leading many companies to invest more in automation, especially computer-controlled and robotically controlled welding machinery. This will reduce the demand for some welders, solderers, and brazers because many repetitive jobs are being automated. The growing use of automation, however, should increase demand for welding, soldering, and brazing machine setters, operators, and tenders. Welders working on construction projects or in equipment repair will not be affected by technology change to the same extent, because their jobs are often unique and not as easily automated.

Despite slower-than-average job growth, technology is creating more uses for welding in the workplace and expanding employment opportunities. For example, new ways are being developed to bond dissimilar materials and nonmetallic materials, such as plastics, composites, and new alloys. Also, laser beam and electron beam welding, new fluxes, and other new technologies and techniques are improving the results of welding, making it useful in a wider assortment of applications. Improvements in technology have also boosted welding productivity, making welding more competitive with other methods of joining materials.

Earnings

Median hourly earnings of welders, cutters, solderers, and brazers were $14.72 in May 2004. The middle 50 percent earned between $11.90 and $18.05. The lowest 10 percent had earnings of less than $9.79, while the top 10 percent earned over $22.20. The range of earnings of welders reflects the wide range of skill levels. Median hourly earnings in the industries employing the largest numbers of welders, cutters, solderers, and brazers in May 2004 were:

Motor vehicle parts manufacturing	$16.47
Agriculture, construction, and mining machinery manufacturing	14.12
Architectural and structural metals manufacturing	13.98
Commercial and industrial machinery and equipment (except automotive and electronic) repair and maintenance	13.45
Motor vehicle body and trailer manufacturing	13.45

Median hourly earnings of welding, soldering, and brazing machine setters, operators, and tenders were $14.32 in May 2004. The middle 50 percent earned between $11.73 and $17.78. The lowest 10 percent had earnings of less than $9.63, while the top 10 percent earned over $23.54. Median hourly earnings in motor vehicle parts manufacturing, the industry employing the largest numbers of welding machine operators in May 2004, were $15.43.

Many welders belong to unions. Among these are the International Association of Machinists and Aerospace Workers; the International Brotherhood of Boilermakers, Iron Ship Builders, Blacksmiths, Forgers and Helpers; the International Union, United Automobile, Aerospace and Agricultural Implement Workers of America; the United Association of Journeymen and Apprentices of the Plumbing, Pipefitting, Sprinkler Fitting Industry of the United States and Canada; and the United Electrical, Radio, and Machine Workers of America.

Related Occupations

Welding, soldering, and brazing workers are skilled metal workers. Other metal workers include machinists; machine setters, operators, and tenders—metal and plastic; computer control programmers and operators; tool and die makers; sheet metal workers; and boilermakers. Assemblers and fabricators of electrical and electronic equipment often assemble parts using soldering.

Sources of Additional Information

For information on training opportunities and jobs for welding, soldering, and brazing workers, contact local employers, the local office of the State employment service, or schools providing welding, soldering, or brazing training.

Information on careers and educational opportunities in welding is available from:
➤ American Welding Society, 550 N.W. Lejeune Rd., Miami, FL 33126. Internet: **http://www.aws.org**

Printing Occupations

Bookbinders and Bindery Workers

(O*NET 51-5011.01, 51-5011.02, 51-5012.00)

Significant Points

● Most bookbinders and bindery workers train on the job.

● Employment is expected to decline, reflecting the use of more productive machinery and the growth of imports of printed material that is already bound.

● Opportunities for hand bookbinders are limited because only a small number of establishments do this highly specialized work.

Nature of the Work

The process of combining printed sheets into finished products such as books, magazines, catalogs, folders, directories is known as "binding." Binding involves cutting, folding, gathering, gluing, stapling, stitching, trimming, sewing, wrapping, and other finishing operations. Bindery workers set up, operate, and maintain the machines that perform these various tasks.

Job duties depend on the kind of material being bound. In libraries where repair work on rare books is needed, *bookbinders* sew, stitch, or glue the assembled printed sheets, shape the book bodies with presses and trimming machines, and reinforce them with glued fabric strips. Covers are created separately, and glued, pasted, or stitched onto the book bodies. The books then undergo a variety of finishing operations, often including wrapping in paper jackets. In establishments that print new books, this work is done mechanically.

In firms that do *edition binding*, workers bind books produced in large numbers, or "runs." A small number of bookbinders work in hand binderies. These highly skilled workers design original or special bindings for limited editions, or restore and rebind rare books. *Library binders* repair books and provide other specialized binding services to libraries.

Some types of binding and finishing jobs consist of only one step. Preparing leaflets or newspaper inserts, for example, requires only folding. Binding of books and magazines, on the other hand, requires a number of steps. Workers first assemble the books and magazines from large, flat, printed sheets of paper. They then operate machines that first fold printed sheets into "signatures," which are groups of pages arranged sequentially. They then assemble the signatures in sequence and join them by means of a saddle-stitch process or perfect binding (where no stitches are used).

Bookbinders and bindery workers in small shops may perform many binding tasks, while those in large shops usually are assigned only one or a few operations, such as assembling sheets in a specified sequence, performing perfect binding, or operating laminating machinery. Others specialize as folder operators or cutter operators, and may perform adjustments and minor repairs to equipment as needed.

Working Conditions

Binderies often are noisy and jobs can be fairly strenuous, requiring considerable lifting, standing, and carrying. Binding often resembles an assembly line on which workers perform repetitive tasks. The jobs also may require stooping, kneeling, and crouching, but equipment is now widely available, such as scissor lifts, that minimize such activity out of concern for ergonomics.

Training, Other Qualifications, and Advancement

Most bookbinders and bindery workers learn the craft through on-the-job training. Inexperienced workers usually are assigned simple tasks such as moving paper from cutting machines to folding machines. They learn basic binding skills, including the characteristics of paper and how to cut large sheets of paper into different sizes with the least amount of waste. Usually, it takes 1 to 3 months to learn to operate the simpler machines but it can take up to 1 year to become completely familiar with more complex equipment, such as computerized binding machines. On letterpress equipment, as workers gain experience they advance to more difficult tasks, such as embossing and adding holograms. As workers advance, they learn to operate more types of equipment.

A bindery worker uses a machine to install a plastic spine on a document.

Formal apprenticeships are not as common as they used to be, but still are offered by some employers. Apprenticeships provide a more structured program that enables workers to acquire the high levels of specialization and skill needed for some bindery jobs.

High school students interested in bindery careers should take shop courses or attend a vocational-technical high school. Occupational skill centers also provide an introduction to a bindery career. To keep pace with changing technology, retraining is increasingly important for bindery workers. Students with computer skills and mechanical aptitude are especially in demand.

Bindery workers need basic mathematics and language skills. Bindery work requires careful attention to detail; accuracy, patience, neatness, and good eyesight also are important. Manual dexterity is essential in order to count, insert, and fold. Mechanical aptitude is needed to operate the newer, more automated equipment. Artistic ability and imagination are necessary for hand bookbinding.

Training in graphic communications also can be an asset. Vocational-technical institutes offer postsecondary programs in the graphic arts, as do some skill-updating or retraining programs and community colleges. Some updating and retraining programs require students to have bindery experience; other programs are made available by unions to their members. Four-year colleges also offer programs, but their emphasis is on preparing people for careers as graphic artists, educators, or managers in the graphic arts field.

Without additional training, advancement opportunities outside of bindery work are limited. In large binderies, experienced bookbinders or bindery workers may advance to supervisory positions.

Employment

In 2004, bookbinders and bindery workers held about 81,000 jobs, including 7,200 as skilled bookbinders and 74,000 as bindery workers. More than 3 out of 4 bindery jobs are in commercial printing plants. Traditionally, the largest employers of bindery workers were bindery trade shops, which are companies that specialize in providing binding services for printers without binderies or whose printing production exceeds their binding capabilities. However, this type of binding is now being done increasingly in-house, and is now called in-line finishing.

The publishing industry employed nearly 1 in 10 bindery workers and the advertising industry an additional number. About one in twenty work in the employment services industry, which supplies temporary workers to companies that need their services.

Job Outlook

Overall employment of bookbinders and bindery workers is expected to decline through 2014 as demand for printed material slows and productivity in printing and bindery operations increases. Contributing to this situation is the trend toward outsourcing of work to firms in foreign countries, where books and other materials with long lead times can be produced more cheaply. Most job openings, however, will result from the need to replace experienced workers who leave the occupation, many of whom will be retiring in the next decade.

Computers have caused binding to become increasingly automated. New computer-operated "in-line" equipment performs a number of operations in sequence, beginning with the presses' output and ending with a finished product. Technological advances such as automatic tabbers, counters, palletizers, and joggers have reduced labor requirements and have induced printing companies to acquire in-house binding and finishing equipment and maintain a permanent staff to operate them.

Growth in demand for specialized bindery workers who assist skilled bookbinders will be slowed as binding machinery continues to become more efficient. New technology requires a considerable investment in capital expenditures and employee training, so computer skills and mechanical aptitude are increasingly important for bindery workers.

Because the number of establishments that do hand bookbinding is small, opportunities for hand bookbinders will be limited. Though experienced workers will continue to have the best opportunities for these specialist jobs, the work done by hand bookbinders is being replaced by other activities in the binding-and-finishing field.

Earnings

Median hourly earnings of bookbinders were $13.71 in May 2004. The middle 50 percent earned between $10.22 and $18.14 an hour. The lowest 10 percent earned less than $8.67, and the highest 10 percent earned more than $21.50.

Median hourly earnings of bindery workers were $11.31 in May 2004. The middle 50 percent earned between $8.92 and $15.06 an hour. The lowest 10 percent earned less than $7.38, and the highest 10 percent earned more than $19.30. Workers covered by union contracts usually had higher earnings.

Related Occupations

Other workers who set up and operate production machinery include prepress technicians and workers; printing machine operators; machine setters, operators, and tenders—metal and plastic; and various other precision machine operators.

Sources of Additional Information

Information about apprenticeships and other training opportunities may be obtained from local printing industry associations, local bookbinding shops, local offices of the Graphic Communications International Union, or local offices of the State employment service.

For general information on bindery occupations, write to:
➤ Bindery Industries Association, International, 100 Daingerfield Road, Alexandria, VA 22314.
➤ Graphic Communications Conference of the International Brotherhood of Teamsters, 1900 L St. NW., Washington, DC 20036-5007. Internet: **http://www.gciu.org**

For information on careers and training programs in printing and the graphic arts, contact:
➤ Graphic Arts Education and Research Foundation, 1899 Preston White Dr., Reston, VA 20191-5468. Internet: **http://www.makeyourmark.org**
➤ Printing Industries of America/Graphic Arts Technical Foundation, 200 Deer Run Rd., Sewickley, PA 15143.
➤ NPES The Association for Suppliers of Printing Publishing, and Converting Technologies, 1899 Preston White Dr., Reston, VA 20191-4367. Internet: **http://www.npes.org/education/index.html**

Prepress Technicians and Workers

(O*NET 51-5021.00, 51-5022.01, 51-5022.02, 51-5022.03, 51-5022.04, 51-5022.05, 51-5022.06, 51-5022.07, 51-5022.08, 51-5022.09, 51-5022.10, 51-5022.11, 51-5022.12, 51-5022.13)

Significant Points

● Most prepress technician jobs now require formal postsecondary graphic communications training in the various types of computer software used in digital imaging.

● Employment is projected to decline as the increased use of computers in typesetting and page layout requires fewer prepress technicians.

Nature of the Work

The printing process has three stages—prepress, press, and binding or postpress. In small print shops, *job printers* are usually responsible for all three stages. They check proofs for errors and print clarity and correct mistakes, print the job, and attach each copy's pages together. In most printing firms, however, each of the stages is the responsibility of a specialized group of workers. *Prepress technicians and workers* are responsible for the first stage, preparing the material for printing presses. They perform a variety of tasks involved with transforming text and pictures into finished pages and making printing plates of the pages.

Advances in computer software and printing technology continue to change prepress work. Most customers today are able to provide printers with pages of material that look like the desired finished product they want printed and bound in volume. Using a process called "desktop publishing," customers are increasingly using their own computers to do much of the typesetting and page layout work formerly done by designers on artboards. Much of this work is now done by desktop publishers or graphic designers with knowledge of publishing software. (Sections on desktop publishers and graphic designers appear elsewhere in the *Handbook*.) It is increasingly common for prepress technicians or other printing workers to receive files from the customer on a computer disk or submitted electronically via e-mail or "file transfer protocol", known as "ftp", that contains typeset material already laid out in pages.

Prepress work is now done with the use of digital imaging technology by prepress technicians known as "preflight technicians" or production coordinators. Using this technology, these technicians take the electronic files received from customers, check it for completeness, and format it into pages using electronic page layout systems. Even though the pages may already be laid out, they still may have to be formatted to fit the dimensions of the paper stock to be used. When color printing is required, the technicians use digital color page-makeup systems to electronically produce an image of the printed pages, then use off-press color proofing systems to print a copy, or "proof," of the pages as they will appear when printed. The technician then has the proofs delivered or mailed to the customer for a final check. Once the customer gives the "OK to print," technicians use laser "imagesetters" to expose digital images of the pages directly onto thin aluminum printing plates.

Platemakers for a long time used a photographic process to make printing plates. The flat, a layout sheet onto which a negative has been attached, was placed on top of a thin metal plate coated with a light-sensitive resin. Exposure to ultraviolet light activated the chemical in parts of the plate not protected by the film's dark areas. The plate was then developed in a solution that removes the unexposed nonimage area, exposing bare metal. The chemical on areas of the plate exposed to the light hardened and became water repellent. The hardened parts of the plate form the text and images to be printed. Now, the printing industry has largely moved to technology known as "direct-to-plate", by which the prepress technicians send the data directly to a plating system, by-passing the need for stripping film onto a flat.

During the printing process, the plate is first covered with a thin coat of water. The water adheres only to the bare metal nonimage areas, and is repelled by the hardened areas that were exposed to light. Next, the plate comes in contact with a rubber roller covered with oil-based ink. Because oil and water do not mix, the ink is repelled by the water-coated area and sticks to the hardened areas. The ink covering the hardened text is transferred to paper.

The job of prepress technicians has become highly computerized.

Working Conditions

Prepress technicians and workers usually work in clean, air-conditioned areas with little noise. Some workers may develop eyestrain from working in front of a video display terminal, or musculoskeletal problems such as backaches. Those platemakers who still work with toxic chemicals face the hazard of skin irritations. Workers are often subject to stress and the pressures of short deadlines and tight work schedules.

Prepress employees usually work an 8-hour day. Some workers—particularly those employed by newspapers—work night shifts, weekends, and holidays.

Training, Other Qualifications, and Advancement

Digital imaging technology has largely replaced cold type print technology. Instead of painstakingly taping pieces of photographic negatives to flats, today's prepress technicians use computer software skills to electronically modify and lay out the material; in some cases, the first time the material appears on paper is when the final product rolls off the printing press. Traditionally, prepress technicians and workers started as helpers and were trained on the job, with some jobs requiring years of experience performing the detailed handwork to become skillful enough to perform even difficult tasks quickly. Today, persons seeking to enter prepress technician jobs require formal postsecondary graphic communications training in the various types of computer software used in digital imaging.

Postsecondary graphic communications programs are available from a variety of sources. For beginners, 2-year associate degree programs offered by community and junior colleges and technical schools, and some 4-year bachelor's degree programs in graphic design colleges teach the latest prepress skills and allow students to practice applying them. However, bachelor's programs usually are intended for students who may eventually move into management positions in printing or design jobs. Community and junior colleges, 4-year colleges and universities, vocational-technical institutes, industry-sponsored update and retraining programs, and private trade and technical schools all also offer prepress-related courses for workers who do not wish to enroll in a degree program. Many workers with experience in other printing jobs take a few college graphic communications courses to upgrade their skills and qualify for prepress jobs. Prepress training designed to train skilled workers already employed in the printing industry also is offered through unions in the printing industry. Many employers view individuals with a combination of experience in the printing industry and formal training in the new digital technology as the best candidates for prepress jobs. The experience of these applicants in printing press operator or other jobs provides them with an understanding of how printing plants operate, familiarizes them with basic prepress functions, and demonstrates their reliability and interest in advancing in the industry.

Employers prefer workers with good communication skills, both oral and written, for prepress jobs. Prepress technicians and workers should be able to deal courteously with people because, when prepress problems arise, they sometimes have to contact the customer to resolve them. Also, in small shops, they may take customer orders. Persons interested in working for firms using advanced printing technology need to know the basics of electronics and computers. Mathematical skills also are essential for operating many of the software packages used to run modern, computerized prepress equipment. At times, prepress personnel may have to perform computations in order to estimate job costs.

Prepress technicians and workers need good manual dexterity, and they must be able to pay attention to detail and work independently. Good eyesight, including visual acuity, depth perception, field of view, color vision, and the ability to focus quickly, also are needed assets. Artistic ability is often a plus. Employers also seek persons who possess an even temperament and an ability to adapt, important qualities for workers who often must meet deadlines and learn how to use new software or operate new equipment.

Employment

Prepress technicians and workers overall held about 141,000 jobs in 2004. Of these, approximately 63,000 were employed as job printers; the remainder was employed as prepress technicians and other prepress workers. Most prepress jobs are found in the printing industry, while newspaper publishing employs the second largest number of prepress technicians and workers.

The printing and publishing industries are two of the most geographically dispersed in the United States, and prepress jobs are found throughout the country. However, jobs are concentrated in large metropolitan areas such as Chicago, Los Angeles–Long Beach, New York City, Minneapolis–St. Paul, Philadelphia, Boston, and Washington, DC.

Job Outlook

Overall employment of prepress technicians and workers is expected to decline through 2014. Demand for printed material should continue to grow, spurred by rising levels of personal income, increasing school enrollments, higher levels of educational attainment, and expanding markets. But the use of computers and publishing software—often by the clients of the printing company—will result in rising productivity of prepress technicians.

Computer software now allows office workers to specify text typeface and style, and to format pages at a desktop computer terminal, shifting many prepress functions away from the traditional printing plants into advertising and public relations agencies, graphic design firms, and large corporations. Many companies are turning to in-house desktop publishing as page layout and graphic design capabilities of computer software have improved and become less expensive and more user-friendly. Some firms are finding it less costly to prepare their own newsletters and other reports than to send them out to trade shops. At newspapers, writers and editors also are doing more composition using publishing software. Rapid growth in the use of desktop publishing software already has eliminated most prepress typesetting and composition technician jobs associated with the older technologies, such as cold-type. However, opportunities will be favorable for prepress technicians with strong computer skills, such as preflight technicians, who are employed to check materials prepared by clients and adapt it for printing.

In order to compete in the desktop publishing environment, commercial printing companies are adding desktop publishing and electronic prepress work to the list of services they provide. Electronic prepress technicians, digital proofers, platemakers, and graphic designers are using new equipment and ever-changing software to design and layout publications and complete their printing more quickly. The increasing range of services offered by printing companies using new digital technologies mean that opportunities in prepress work will be best for those with computer backgrounds who have completed postsecondary programs in printing technology or graphic communications. Workers with this background will be better able to adapt to the continuing evolution of publishing and printing technology.

Earnings

Median hourly earnings of prepress technicians and workers were $15.30 in May 2004. The middle 50 percent earned between $11.69 and $20.01 an hour. The lowest 10 percent earned less than $9.06, and the highest 10 percent earned more than $24.82 an hour.

For job printers, median hourly earnings were $15.41 in May 2004. The middle 50 percent earned between $12.00 and $20.04 an hour. The lowest 10 percent earned less than $9.57, while the highest 10 percent earned more than $24.05 an hour.

Median hourly earnings in commercial printing, the industry employing the largest number of prepress technicians and workers, were $15.91 in May 2004, while the figure for these workers in the newspaper, periodical, and book publishing industry was $14.22 an hour. For job printers, median hourly earnings in commercial printing in May 2004 were $15.67, while in the newspaper, periodical, and book publishing industry median hourly earnings were $15.63.

Wage rates for prepress technicians and workers vary according to occupation, level of experience, training, location, size of firm, and union membership status.

Related Occupations

Prepress technicians and workers use artistic skills in their work. These skills also are essential for artists and related workers, graphic designers, and desktop publishers. Moreover, many of the skills used in Web site design also are employed in prepress technology.

In addition to typesetters, other workers who operate machines equipped with keyboards include data entry and information processing workers. Prepress technicians' work also is tied in closely with that of printing machine operators, including job printers.

Sources of Additional Information

Details about training programs may be obtained from local employers such as newspapers and printing shops, or from local offices of the State employment service.

For information on careers and training in printing and the graphic arts, write to:

➤ Graphic Arts Education and Research Foundation, 1899 Preston White Dr., Reston, VA 20191-5468. Internet: **http://www.makeyourmark.org**
➤ Graphic Communications Conference of the International Brotherhood of Teamsters, 1900 L St. NW., Washington, DC 20036-5007. Internet: **http://www.gciu.org**
➤ Printing Industries of America/Graphic Arts Technical Foundation, 200 Deer Run Rd., Sewickley, PA 15143-2324.

Printing Machine Operators

(O*NET 51-5023.01, 51-5023.02, 51-5023.03, 51-5023.04, 51-5023.05, 51-5023.06, 51-5023.07, 51-5023.08, 51-5023.09)

Significant Points

● Most printing machine operators are trained on the job.

● Those skilled in digital printing operations will have the best job opportunities as more printing firms convert to this printing process because of the rising demand for customized print jobs.

● The expected retirements of skilled press operators will create openings for workers with the proper training.

Nature of the Work

Printing machine operators, also known as press operators, prepare, operate, and maintain the printing presses in a pressroom. Duties of printing machine operators vary according to the type of press they operate—offset lithography, gravure, flexography, screen printing, letterpress, and digital. Offset lithography, which transfers an inked impression from a rubber-covered cylinder to paper or other material, is the dominant printing process. With gravure, the recesses on an etched plate or cylinder are inked and pressed to paper. Flexography is a form of rotary printing in which ink is applied to a surface by a flexible rubber printing plate with a raised image area. Use of flexography should increase over the next decade, but letterpress, in which an inked, raised surface is pressed against paper, remains in existence only as specialty printing. In addition to the major printing processes, plateless or nonimpact processes are coming into general use. Plateless processes—including digital, electrostatic, and ink-jet printing—are used for copying, duplicating, and document and specialty printing, usually by quick and in-house printing shops, and increasingly by commercial printers for short-run jobs and variable data printing.

To prepare presses for printing, machine operators install and adjust the printing plate, adjust pressure, ink the presses, load paper, and adjust the press to the paper size. Press operators ensure that paper and ink meet specifications, and adjust margins and the flow of ink to the inking rollers accordingly. They then feed paper through the press cylinders and adjust feed and tension controls. However, new technology becoming available skips these steps and sends the files directly to the press.

While printing presses are running, press operators monitor their operation and keep the paper feeders well stocked. They make adjustments to correct uneven ink distribution, speed, and temperatures in the drying chamber, if the press has one. If paper jams or tears and the press stops, which can happen with some offset presses, operators quickly correct the problem to minimize downtime. Similarly, operators working with other high-speed presses constantly look for problems, making quick corrections to avoid expensive losses of paper and ink. Throughout the run, operators must regularly pull sheets to check for any printing imperfections, though much of this checking for quality is now being by done computers.

In most shops, press operators also perform preventive maintenance. They oil and clean the presses and make minor repairs.

Machine operators' jobs differ from one shop to another because of differences in the kinds and sizes of presses. Small commercial shops are operated by one person and tend to have relatively small presses, which print only one or two colors at a time. Operators

Printing machine operators are increasingly using computers to operate printing presses.

who work with large presses have assistants and helpers. Large newspaper, magazine, and book printers use giant "in-line web" presses that require a crew of several press operators and press assistants. These presses are fed paper in big rolls up to 50 inches or more in width. Presses print the paper on both sides; trim, assemble, score, and fold the pages; and count the finished sections as they come off the press.

Most plants have or will soon have installed printing presses with computers and sophisticated instruments to control press operations, making it possible to set up for jobs in less time. Computers allow press operators to perform many of their tasks electronically. With this equipment, press operators monitor the printing process on a control panel or computer monitor, which allows them to adjust the press electronically.

Working Conditions

Operating a press can be physically and mentally demanding, and sometimes tedious. Printing machine operators are on their feet most of the time. Often, operators work under pressure to meet deadlines. Most printing presses are capable of high printing speeds, and adjustments must be made quickly to avoid waste. Pressrooms are noisy, and workers in certain areas wear ear protectors. Working with press machinery can be hazardous, but accidents can be avoided when press operators follow safe work practices. The threat of accidents has decreased with newer computerized presses because operators make most adjustments from a control panel. Many press operators, particularly those who work for newspapers, work weekends, nights, and holidays. They also may work overtime to meet deadlines.

Training, Other Qualifications, and Advancement

Although completion of a formal apprenticeship or a postsecondary program in printing equipment operation continues to be the best way to learn the trade, most printing machine operators are trained on the job while they work as assistants or helpers to experienced operators. Beginning press operators load, unload, and clean presses. With time and training, they may move up to become fully qualified press operators on the type of equipment on which they trained. Some operators gain experience on many kinds of printing presses during the course of their career.

Apprenticeships for press operators, once the dominant method for preparing for this occupation, are becoming less prevalent. When they are offered by the employer, they usually include on-the-job instruction and some related classroom training or correspondence school courses. Apprenticeships used to be for a fixed period of time, but now completion is based on ability to demonstrate competencies.

In contrast, formal postsecondary programs in printing equipment operation offered by technical and trade schools, community colleges, and universities are growing in importance. Some postsecondary school programs require 2 years of study and award an associate degree. Postsecondary courses in printing are increasingly important because they provide the theoretical and technical knowledge needed to operate advanced equipment.

Persons who wish to become printing machine operators need mechanical aptitude to make press adjustments and repairs. Oral and writing skills also are required. Operators should possess the mathematical skills necessary to compute percentages, weights, and measures, and to calculate the amount of ink and paper needed to do a job. Because of technical developments in the printing industry, courses in chemistry, electronics, color theory, and physics are helpful.

Technological changes have had a tremendous effect on the skills needed by printing machine operators. New presses now require operators to possess basic computer skills. Even experienced operators periodically receive retraining and skill updating. For example, printing plants that change from sheet-fed offset presses to digital presses have to retrain the entire press crew because skill requirements for the two types of presses are different.

Printing machine operators may advance in pay and responsibility by working on a more complex printing press. Through experience and demonstrated ability, for example, a one-color sheet-fed press operator may become a four-color sheet-fed press operator. Others may advance to pressroom supervisor and become responsible for an entire press crew. Press operators can also draw on their knowledge of press operations to become cost estimators, providing estimates of printing jobs to potential customers.

Employment

Printing machine operators held about 191,000 jobs in 2004. Nearly half of all operator jobs were in the printing industry. Paper manufacturers and newspaper publishers were also large employers. Additional jobs were in the "in-plant" section of organizations and businesses that do their own printing—such as banks, insurance companies, government agencies, and universities.

The printing and newspaper publishing industries are two of the most geographically dispersed in the United States, and press operators can find jobs throughout the country. However, jobs are concentrated in large printing centers such as Chicago, Los Angeles–Long Beach, New York, Minneapolis-St. Paul, Philadelphia, Boston, and Washington, DC.

Job Outlook

Employment of printing machine operators is expected to grow more slowly than average through 2014 as the output of printed materials is expected to keep going up, but increasing automation of the printing industry and the outsourcing of production to foreign countries will moderate the increase. Looming retirements of printing machine operators and the need for workers trained on increasingly computerized printing equipment will also create many job openings over the next decade, particularly for those persons who qualify for formal apprenticeship training or who complete postsecondary training programs in printing.

Demand for books and magazines will increase as school enrollments rise and information proliferates. Additional growth will also come from the increasing ability of the printing industry to profitably print shorter runs—smaller quantities—which should widen the market for printed materials as production costs decline. However, small printing jobs will increasingly be run on sophisticated high-speed digital printing equipment that requires a more complex set of operator skills, such as database management.

Demand for commercial printing also will continue to be driven by increased expenditures for print advertising materials. New market research techniques are leading advertisers to increase spending on messages targeted to specific audiences, and should continue to require the printing of a wide variety of catalogs, direct mail enclosures, newspaper inserts, and other kinds of print advertising. Newspaper printing also will continue to provide jobs.

Employment will not grow in line with output, however, because increased use of new computerized printing equipment will require fewer operators. This will especially be true with the increasing automation of the large printing presses used in the newspaper industry. In addition, more companies are having their work printed out of the country when time sensitivity of the material is not an issue. Also, new business practices within the publishing industry, such as printing-on-demand and electronic publishing, will cut into the production of printed materials. Printing-on-demand refers to the printing of materials as they are requested by customers, in contrast to printing thousands of copies of a publication prior to purchase, many of which are subsequently discarded.

Earnings
Median hourly earnings of printing machine operators were $14.38 in May 2004. The middle 50 percent earned between $10.73 and $18.83 an hour. The lowest 10 percent earned less than $8.54, and the highest 10 percent earned more than $23.06 an hour. Median hourly earnings in the industries employing the largest numbers of printing machine operators in May 2004 were:

Newspaper, periodical, book, and directory publishers	$16.46
Converted paper product manufacturing	15.72
Printing and related support activities	15.16
Plastics product manufacturing	13.76
Advertising and related services	12.68

The basic wage rate for a printing machine operator depends on the geographic area in which the work is located and on the type of press being run: pay varies by the complexity of the press and its size. Workers covered by union contracts usually have higher earnings in the newspaper industry.

Related Occupations
Other workers who set up and operate production machinery include machine setters, operators, and tenders—metal and plastic; bookbinders and bindery workers; and various precision machine operators.

Sources of Additional Information
Details about apprenticeships and other training opportunities may be obtained from local employers, such as newspapers and printing shops, local offices of the Graphic Communications Conference of the International Brotherhood of Teamsters, local affiliates of Printing Industries of America/Graphic Arts Technical Foundation, or local offices of the State employment service.

For general information about press operators, write to:
➤ Graphic Communications Conference of the International Brotherhood of Teamsters, 1900 L St. NW., Washington, DC 20036-5007. Internet: **http://www.gciu.org**

For information on careers and training in printing and the graphic arts, write to:
➤ NPES The Association for Suppliers of Printing Publishing, and Converting Technologies, 1899 Preston White Dr., Reston, VA 20191-4367. Internet: **http://www.npes.org/education/index.html**
➤ Printing Industry of America/Graphic Arts Technical Foundation, 200 Deer Run Rd., Sewickley, PA 15143.
➤ Graphic Arts Education and Research Foundation, 1899 Preston White Dr., Reston, VA 20191-5468. Internet: **http://www.makeyourmark.org**

Textile, Apparel, and Furnishings Occupations

(O*NET 51-6011.01, 51-6011.02, 51-6011.03, 51-6021.01, 51-6021.02, 51-6021.03, 51-6031.01, 51-6031.02, 51-6041.00, 51-6042.00, 51-6051.00, 51-6052.01, 51-6052.02, 51-6061.00, 51-6062.00, 51-6063.00, 51-6064.00, 51-6091.00, 51-6092.00, 51-6093.00, 51-6099.99)

Significant Points

● Most workers learn through on-the-job training.

● This group ranks among the most rapidly declining occupations because of increases in imports, offshore assembly, productivity gains from automation, and new fabrics that do not need as much processing.

● Earnings of most workers are low.

Nature of the Work
Textile, apparel, and furnishings workers produce fibers, cloth, and upholstery, and fashion them into a wide range of products that we use in our daily lives. Jobs range from those that involve computers, to those in which the worker operates large industrial machinery and smaller power equipment, to those that require substantial handwork.

Textile machine setters, operators, and tenders. Textile machine setters, operators, and tenders run machines that make

textile products from fibers. Textiles are the basis of towels, bed linens, hosiery and socks, and nearly all clothing, but they also are a key ingredient in products ranging from roofing to tires. The first step in manufacturing textiles is preparing the natural or synthetic fibers. *Extruding and forming machine operators, synthetic and glass fibers*, set up and operate machines that extrude or force liquid synthetic material such as rayon, fiberglass, or liquid polymers through small holes and draw out filaments. Other operators put natural fibers such as cotton, wool, flax, or hemp through carding and combing machines that clean and align them into short lengths collectively called "sliver." In making sliver, operators may combine different types of natural fibers and synthetics filaments to give the product a desired texture, durability, or other characteristics. *Textile winding, twisting, and drawing-out machine operators* take the sliver and draw out, twist, and wind it to produce yarn, taking care to repair any breaks.

Textile bleaching and dyeing machine operators control machines that wash, bleach, or dye either yarn or finished fabrics and other products. *Textile knitting and weaving machine operators* put the yarn on machines that weave, knit, loop, or tuft it into a product. Woven fabrics are used to make apparel and other goods, whereas some knitted products (such as hosiery) and tufted products (such as carpeting) emerge in near-finished form. Different types of machines are used for these processes, but operators perform similar tasks, repairing breaks in the yarn and monitoring the yarn supply while tending many machines at once. *Textile cutting machine operators* trim the fabric into various widths and lengths, depending on its intended use.

Apparel workers. Apparel workers cut fabric and other materials and sew it into clothing and related products. Workers in a variety of occupations fall under the heading of apparel workers. *Tailors, dressmakers, and sewers* make custom clothing and alter and repair garments for individuals. However, workers in most apparel occupations are found in manufacturing, performing specialized tasks in the production of large numbers of garments that are shipped to retail establishments for sale.

Fabric and apparel patternmakers convert a clothing designer's original model of a garment into a pattern of separate parts that can be laid out on a length of fabric. After discussing the item with the designer, these skilled workers usually use a computer to outline the parts and draw in details to indicate the positions of pleats, buttonholes, and other features. (In the past, patternmakers laid out the parts on paper, using pencils and drafting instruments such as rulers.) Patternmakers then alter the size of the pieces in the pattern to produce garments of various sizes, and they may mark the fabric to show the best layout of pattern pieces to minimize waste of material.

Once an item's pattern has been made and marked, mass production of the garment begins. Cutters and trimmers take the patterns and cut out material, paying close attention to their work because mistakes are costly. Following the outline of the pattern, they place multiple layers of material on the cutting table and use an electric knife or other tools to cut out the various pieces of the garment; delicate materials may be cut by hand. In some companies, computer-controlled machines do the cutting.

Sewing machine operators join the parts of a garment together, reinforce seams, and attach buttons, hooks, zippers, and accessories to produce clothing. After the product is sewn, other workers remove lint and loose threads and inspect and package the garments.

Shoe and leather workers. Shoe and leather workers are employed either in manufacturing or in personal services. In shoe manufacturing, *shoe machine operators and tenders* operate a variety of specialized machines that perform cutting, joining, and finishing functions. In personal services, *shoe and leather workers and repairers* perform a variety of repairs and custom leatherwork for the general public. They construct, decorate, or repair shoes, belts, purses, saddles, luggage, and other leather products. They also may repair some products made of canvas or plastic. When making custom shoes or modifying existing footwear for people with foot problems or special needs, shoe and leather workers and repairers cut pieces of leather, shape them over a form shaped like a foot, and sew them together. They then attach soles and heels, using sewing machines or cement and nails. They also dye and polish the items, utilizing a buffing wheel for a smooth surface and lustrous shine. When making luggage, they fasten leather to a frame and attach handles and other hardware. They also cut and secure linings inside the frames and sew or stamp designs onto the exterior of the luggage. In addition to performing all of the preceding steps, saddlemakers often apply leather dyes and liquid topcoats to produce a glossy finish on a saddle. They also may decorate the surface of the saddle by hand stitching or by stamping the leather with decorative patterns and designs. Shoe and leather workers and repairers who own their own shops keep records and supervise other workers.

Many upholsters reupholster old furniture.

Upholsterers. *Upholsterers* make, fix, and restore furniture that is covered with fabric. Using hammers and tack pullers, upholsterers who restore furniture remove old fabric and stuffing to get down to the springs and wooden frame. Then they reglue loose sections of the frame and refinish exposed wood. The springs sit on a cloth mat, called webbing, that is attached to the frame. Upholsterers replace torn webbing, examine the springs, and replace broken or bent ones.

Upholsterers who make new furniture start with a bare wooden frame. First, they install webbing, tacking it to one side of the frame, stretching it tight, and tacking it to the other side. Then, they tie each spring to the webbing and to its neighboring springs. Next, they cover the springs with filler, such as foam, a polyester batt, or similar fibrous batting material, to form a smooth, rounded surface. Then they measure and cut fabric for the arms, backs, seats, sides, and other surfaces, leaving as little waste as possible. Finally, sewing the fabric pieces together and attaching them to the frame with tacks, staples, or glue, they affix any ornaments, such as fringes, buttons, or rivets. Sometimes, upholsterers provide pickup and delivery of the furniture they work on. They also help customers select new coverings by providing samples of fabrics and pictures of finished pieces.

Laundry and drycleaning workers. *Laundry and drycleaning workers* clean cloth garments, linens, draperies, blankets, and other articles. They also may clean leather, suede, furs, and rugs. When necessary, they treat spots and stains on articles before laundering or drycleaning. They tend machines during cleaning and ensure that items are not lost or misplaced with those of another customer. *Pressers, textile, garment, and related materials,* shape and remove wrinkles from items after steam pressing them or ironing them by hand. Workers then assemble each customer's items, box or bag them, and prepare an itemized bill for the customer.

Working Conditions

Most people in textile, apparel, and furnishings occupations work a standard 5-day, 35- to 40-hour week. Working on evenings and weekends is common for shoe and leather workers; laundry and drycleaning workers; and tailors, dressmakers, and sewers employed in retail stores. Many textile and fiber mills often use rotating schedules of shifts so that employees do not continuously work nights or days. But these rotating shifts sometimes cause workers to have sleep disorders and stress-related problems.

Although much of the work in apparel manufacturing still is based on a piecework system that allows for little interpersonal contact, some apparel firms are placing more emphasis on teamwork and cooperation. Under this new system, individuals work closely with one another, and each team or module often governs itself, increasing the overall responsibility of each operator.

Working conditions vary by establishment and by occupation. In manufacturing, machinery in textile mills often is noisy, as are areas in which sewing and pressing are performed in apparel factories; patternmaking and spreading areas tend to be much quieter. Many older factories are cluttered, hot, and poorly lit and ventilated, but more modern facilities usually have more workspace and are well lit and ventilated. Textile machinery operators use protective glasses and masks that cover their noses and mouths to protect against airborne materials. Many machines operate at high speeds, and textile machinery workers must be careful not to wear clothing or jewelry that could get caught in moving parts. In addition, extruding and forming machine operators wear protective shoes and clothing when working with certain chemical compounds.

Work in apparel production can be physically demanding. Some workers sit for long periods, and others spend many hours on their feet, leaning over tables and operating machinery. Operators must be attentive while running sewing machines, pressers, automated cutters, and the like. A few workers wear protective devices such as gloves. In some instances, new machinery and production techniques have decreased the physical demands on workers. For example, newer pressing machines are controlled by foot pedals or by computer and do not require much strength to operate.

Laundries and drycleaning establishments often are hot and noisy; those in retail stores, however, tend to be less noisy and more comfortable. Areas in which shoe and leather workers make or repair shoes and other leather items can be noisy, and odors from leather dyes and stains frequently are present. Workers need to pay close attention when working with machines, to avoid punctures, lacerations, and abrasions.

Upholstery work is not dangerous, but upholsterers usually wear protective gloves and clothing when using sharp tools and lifting and handling furniture or springs. During most of the workday, upholsterers stand and may do a lot of bending and heavy lifting. They also may work in awkward positions for short periods.

Training, Other Qualifications, and Advancement

Most employers prefer to hire high school graduates for jobs in textile, apparel, and furnishings occupations. Entrants with postsecondary vocational training or previous work experience in apparel production usually have a better chance of getting a job and advancing to a supervisory position. Regardless of the setting, workers usually begin by performing simple tasks.

In manufacturing, textile and apparel workers need good hand-eye coordination, manual dexterity, physical stamina, and the ability to perform repetitive tasks for long periods. Machine operators usually are trained on the job by more experienced employees or by machinery manufacturers' representatives. As they gain experience, these workers are assigned more difficult operations. Further advancement is limited, however. Some production workers may become first-line supervisors, but most can advance only to more skilled operator jobs. As machinery in the industry continues to become more complex, knowledge of the basics of computers and electronics will increasingly be an asset. In addition, the trends toward cross-training of operators and working in teams will increase the time needed to become fully trained on all machines and require interpersonal skills to work effectively with others.

Retailers prefer to hire custom tailors, dressmakers, and sewers with previous experience in apparel production, design, or alteration. Knowledge of fabrics, design, and construction is very important. Custom tailors sometimes learn these skills through

courses in high school or a community college. Some experienced custom tailors open their own tailoring shop. Custom tailoring is a highly competitive field, however, and training in small-business operations can mean the difference between success and failure. Although laundries and drycleaners prefer entrants with previous work experience, they routinely hire inexperienced workers.

Precision shoe and leather workers and repairers generally learn their skills on the job. Manual dexterity and the mechanical aptitude to work with handtools and machines are important in shoe repair and leatherworking. Shoe and leather workers who produce custom goods should have artistic ability as well. Beginners start as helpers for experienced workers, but, in manufacturing, they may attend more formal in-house training programs. Beginners gradually take on more tasks until they are fully qualified workers, a process that takes about 2 years in an apprenticeship program or as a helper in a shop. In a vocational training program, it can take 6 months to a year. Learning to make saddles takes longer. Shoe repairers need to keep their skills up to date to work with the rapidly changing footwear styles and materials. Some do this by attending trade shows; others attend specialized training seminars and workshops in custom shoemaking, shoe repair, and other leatherwork sponsored by associations. Some in the shoemaking and leatherworking occupations begin as workers or repairers and advance to salaried supervisory and managerial positions. Some open their own shop, but knowledge of business practices and management and a pleasant manner when dealing with customers are needed to stay in business.

Most upholsterers learn their skills on the job, but a few do so through apprenticeships. Inexperienced persons also may take training in basic upholstery in vocational schools and some community colleges. Upholsterers should have manual dexterity, good coordination, and the strength needed to lift heavy furniture. An eye for detail, a flair for color, and the ability to use fabrics creatively also are helpful. The length of training may vary from 6 weeks to 3 years. Upholsterers who work on custom-made pieces may train for 8 to 10 years. The primary forms of advancement for upholsterers are opening their own shop or moving into management. The upholstery business is highly competitive, so operating a shop successfully is difficult. In large shops and factories, experienced or highly skilled upholsterers may become supervisors or samplemakers.

Employment

Textile, apparel, and furnishings workers held 929,000 jobs in 2004. Employment in the detailed occupations that make up this group was distributed as follows:

Sewing machine operators	256,000
Laundry and dry-cleaning workers	235,000
Tailors, dressmakers, and sewers	85,000
Pressers, textile, garment, and related materials	82,000
Upholsterers	53,000
Textile winding, twisting, and drawing out machine setters, operators, and tenders	53,000
Textile knitting and weaving machine setters, operators, and tenders	46,000
Textile cutting machine setters, operators, and tenders	28,000
All other textile, apparel, and furnishings workers	23,000
Extruding and forming machine setters, operators, and tenders, synthetic and glass fibers	23,000
Textile bleaching and dyeing machine operators and tenders	21,000
Shoe and leather workers and repairers	10,000
Fabric and apparel patternmakers	9,200
Shoe machine operators and tenders	4,600

Manufacturing jobs are concentrated in California, North Carolina, Georgia, New York, Texas, and South Carolina. Jobs in reupholstery, shoe repair and custom leatherwork, and laundry and drycleaning establishments are found in cities and towns throughout the Nation. Overall, about 11 percent of all workers in textile, apparel, and furnishings occupations were self-employed; however, 54 percent of tailors, dressmakers, and sewers and 27 percent of upholsterers were self-employed.

Job Outlook

Employment of textile, apparel, and furnishings workers is expected to decline through 2014. Apparel workers have been among the most rapidly declining occupational groups in the economy, and increasing imports, the use of offshore assembly, and greater productivity through new automation will contribute to additional job losses. Also, many new textiles require less production and processing. Employment in specialty apparel and textiles, where it may be necessary for production facilities to be close to their market, might not decrease as much as in other areas of apparel and textile production. Because of the large size of this occupation, however, job openings arise each year from the need to replace workers who transfer to other occupations, retire, or leave the occupation for other reasons.

Employment in the domestic textile and apparel industries has declined in recent years as foreign producers have gained a greater share of the U.S. market. Domestic production of apparel and textiles will continue to move abroad, and imports to the U.S. market will increase. Declines in U.S. apparel production will cause reductions in domestic textile production because the apparel industry is the largest consumer of American-made textiles. Fierce competition in the market for apparel will keep domestic apparel and textile firms under intense pressure to cut costs and produce more with fewer workers.

Although the textile industry already is highly automated, it will continue to seek to increase worker productivity through the introduction of labor-saving machinery and the invention of new fibers and fabrics that reduce production costs. Despite advances in technology, the apparel industry has had difficulty employing automated equipment extensively due to the "soft" properties of textile products. The industry produces a wide variety of apparel items that change frequently with changes in style and season. Technological developments, such as computer-aided marking and grading, computer-controlled cutters, semiautomatic sewing and pressing machines, and automated material-handling systems have increased output while reducing the need for some workers in larger firms. However, assembly continues to be the most labor-intensive step in the production of apparel, and increasing numbers of sewing machine operator jobs are expected to be lost to low-wage workers abroad. Still, improvements in productivity will allow many of the presewing functions of design, patternmaking, marking, and cutting to continue be done domestically, and employment of workers who perform these functions will not be as adversely affected.

Outside of the manufacturing sector, tailors, dressmakers, and sewers—the most skilled apparel workers—also are expected to experience declining employment. Demand for their services will continue to lessen because it is often cheaper to buy new apparel than to have clothes altered or repaired.

Employment of shoe and leather workers is expected to decline through 2014 as a result of growing imports of less expensive shoes and leather goods and increasing productivity of U.S. manufacturers. Also, buying new shoes often is cheaper than repairing worn or damaged ones. However, declines are expected to be offset somewhat as the population continues to age and more people need custom shoes for health reasons.

Employment of upholsterers is expected to decline through 2014 as new furniture and automotive seats use more durable coverings and as manufacturing firms continue to become more automated and efficient. Demand for the reupholstery of furniture also is expected to decline as the increasing manufacture of new, relatively inexpensive upholstered furniture causes many consumers simply to replace old, worn furniture. However, demand will continue to be steady for upholsterers who restore very valuable furniture. Most reupholstery work is labor intensive and not easily automated.

Earnings

Earnings of textile, apparel, and furnishings workers vary by occupation. Because many production workers in apparel manufacturing are paid according to the number of acceptable pieces they produce, their total earnings depend on skill, speed, and accuracy. Workers covered by union contracts tend to have higher earnings. Median hourly earnings by occupation in May 2004 were as follows:

Fabric and apparel patternmakers	$13.85
Extruding and forming machine setters, operators, and tenders, synthetic and glass fibers	13.37
Upholsterers	12.35
Textile knitting and weaving machine setters, operators, and tenders	11.48
Textile winding, twisting, and drawing out machine setters, operators, and tenders	10.87
Tailors, dressmakers, and custom sewers	10.79
Textile bleaching and dyeing machine operators and tenders	10.56
All other textile, apparel, and furnishings workers	10.34
Textile cutting machine setters, operators, and tenders	9.80
Shoe machine operators and tenders	9.44
Shoe and leather workers and repairers	9.29
Sewers, hand	9.13
Sewing machine operators	8.61
Pressers, textile, garment, and related materials	8.33
Laundry and dry-cleaning workers	8.28

Benefits also vary. A few large employers, for example, include childcare in their benefits package. Apparel workers in retail trade also may receive a discount on their purchases from the company for which they work. In addition, some of the larger manufacturers operate company stores from which employees can purchase apparel products at significant discounts. Some small firms, however, offer only limited benefits.

Related Occupations

Textile, apparel, and furnishings workers apply their knowledge of textiles and leathers to fashion products with use of handtools and machinery. Others who produce products using handtools, machines, and their knowledge of the materials with which they work include assemblers and fabricators; medical, dental, and ophthalmic laboratory technicians; food-processing workers; jewelers and precious stone and metal workers; and woodworkers.

Sources of Additional Information

Information about job opportunities in textile, apparel, and furnishings occupations is available from local employers and local offices of State employment services.

Woodworkers

(O*NET 51-7011.00, 51-7021.00, 51-7031.00, 51-7032.00, 51-7041.01, 51-7041.02, 51-7042.01, 51-7042.02, 51-7099.99)

Significant Points

- Most woodworkers are trained on the job; basic machine operations may be learned in a few months, but becoming a skilled woodworker often requires 2 or more years.

- Overall employment is expected to decline.

- Job prospects will be best for highly skilled woodworkers who produce customized output, which is less susceptible to automation and import competition, and for those who know how to operate computerized numerical control (CNC) machines.

- Employment is highly sensitive to economic cycles; during economic downturns, workers are subject to layoffs or reductions in hours.

Nature of the Work

Despite the development of sophisticated plastics and other materials, the demand for wood products continues unabated. Helping to meet this demand are woodworkers. Woodworkers are found in industries that produce wood, such as sawmills and plywood mills; in industries that use wood to produce furniture, kitchen cabinets, musical instruments, and other fabricated wood products; and in small shops that make architectural woodwork, furniture, and many other specialty items.

All woodworkers are employed at some stage of the process through which logs of wood are transformed into finished products. Some of these workers produce the structural elements of buildings; others mill hardwood and softwood lumber; still others assemble finished wood products. They operate machines that cut, shape, assemble, and finish raw wood to make the doors, windows, cabinets, trusses, plywood, flooring, paneling, molding, and trim that are components of most homes. Others may fashion home accessories, such as beds, sofas, tables, dressers, and chairs. In addition to these household goods, woodworkers also make sporting goods, including baseball bats and oars, as well as musical instruments, toys, caskets, tool handles, and thousands of other wooden items.

Production woodworkers set up, operate, and tend woodworking machines such as power saws, planers, sanders, lathes, jointers, and routers that cut and shape components from lumber, plywood, and other wood products. In sawmills, *sawing machine operators and tenders* set up, operate, or tend wood-sawing machines that cut logs into planks, timbers, or boards. In plants manufacturing wood products, woodworkers first determine the best method of shaping and assembling parts, working from blueprints, supervisors' instructions, or shop drawings that woodworkers themselves produce. Before cutting, they often must measure and mark the materials. They verify dimensions and may trim parts using handtools such as planes, chisels, wood files, or sanders to ensure a tight fit. *Woodworking machine operators and tenders* set up, operate, or tend specific woodworking machines, such as drill presses, lathes, shapers, routers, sanders, planers, and wood-nailing machines. Lower skilled operators may merely press a switch on a woodworking machine and monitor the automatic operation, whereas more highly skilled operators set up equipment, cut and

shape wooden parts, and verify dimensions using a template, caliper, or rule.

The next step in the manufacturing process is the production of subassemblies using fasteners and adhesives. Next, the pieces are brought together to form a complete unit. The product is then finish-sanded; stained; and, if necessary, coated with a sealer, such as lacquer or varnish. Woodworkers may perform this work in teams or be assisted by a helper.

Woodworkers have been greatly affected by the introduction of computer-controlled machinery. This technology has raised worker productivity by allowing one operator to simultaneously tend a greater number of machines. An operator can program a CNC machine to perform a sequence of operations automatically, resulting in greater precision and reliability. The integration of computers with equipment has improved production speed and capability, simplified setup and maintenance requirements, and increased the demand for workers with computer skills.

While this costly equipment has had a great effect on workers in the largest, most efficient firms, precision or custom woodworkers—who generally work in smaller firms—have continued to employ the same production techniques they have used for many years. Workers such as *cabinetmakers and bench carpenters, modelmakers and patternmakers*, and *furniture finishers* work on a customized basis, often building one-of-a-kind items. These highly skilled precision woodworkers usually perform a complete cycle of tasks—cutting, shaping, and preparing surfaces and assembling prepared parts of complex wood components into a finished wood product. For this reason, these workers normally need substantial training and an ability to work from detailed instructions and specifications. In addition, they often are required to exercise independent judgment when undertaking an assignment.

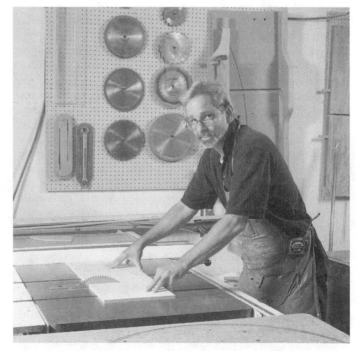

Precision or custom woodworkers often build one-of-a-kind items from start to finish.

Working Conditions

Working conditions vary by industry and specific job duties. In logging and sawmills, for example, working conditions are physically demanding because of the handling of heavy, bulky material. Workers in these industries also may encounter excessive noise, dust, and other air pollutants. However, the use of earplugs and respirators may partially alleviate these problems. Also, rigid adherence to safety precautions minimizes risk of injury from contact with rough wood stock, sharp tools, and power equipment. The risk of injury also is lowered by the installation of computer-controlled equipment, which reduces the physical labor and hands-on contact with machinery.

In furniture and kitchen cabinet manufacturing, employees who operate machinery often must wear ear and eye protection. They also must follow operating safety instructions and use safety shields or guards to prevent accidents. Those who work in the finishing area must be provided with an appropriate dust or vapor mask or a complete protective safety suit, or must work in a finishing environment that removes all vapors and dust particles from the atmosphere. Prolonged standing, lifting, and fitting of heavy objects are common characteristics of the job.

Training, Other Qualifications, and Advancement

Most woodworkers are trained on the job, picking up skills informally from experienced workers. Most woodworkers learn basic machine operations and job tasks in a few months, but becoming a skilled woodworker often requires 2 or more years.

Woodworkers increasingly acquire skills through vocational education. Some may learn by working as carpenters on construction jobs. Others may attend colleges or universities that offer training in areas including wood technology, furniture manufacturing, wood engineering, and production management. These programs prepare students for positions in production, supervision, engineering, and management and are increasingly important as woodworking technology becomes more advanced.

Beginners usually observe and help experienced machine operators. They may supply material to, or remove fabricated products from, machines. Trainees also do simple machine operating jobs while closely supervised by experienced workers, but as beginners gain experience, they perform more complex jobs with less supervision. Some may learn to read blueprints, set up machines, and plan the sequence of the work.

Employers seek applicants with a high school diploma or the equivalent because of the growing sophistication of machinery and the constant need for retraining. People seeking woodworking jobs can enhance their employment and advancement prospects by completing high school and receiving training in mathematics, science, and computer applications. Other important qualities for entrants in this occupation include mechanical ability, manual dexterity, and the ability to pay attention to detail.

Advancement opportunities often are limited and depend on education and training, seniority, and a worker's skills and initiative. Sometimes experienced woodworkers become inspectors or supervisors responsible for the work of a group of woodworkers. Production workers often can advance into these positions by assuming additional responsibilities and by attending workshops, seminars, or college programs. Those who are highly skilled may set up their own woodworking shops.

Employment

Woodworkers held about 364,000 jobs in 2004. Self-employed woodworkers, mostly cabinetmakers and furniture finishers, accounted for 14 percent of these jobs. Employment among detailed woodworking occupations was distributed as follows:

Cabinetmakers and bench carpenters	148,000
Woodworking machine setters, operators, and tenders, except sawing	92,000
Sawing machine setters, operators, and tenders, wood	58,000
Furniture finishers	34,000
Model makers, wood	3,200
Patternmakers, wood	2,500
All other woodworkers	26,000

Almost 3 out of 4 woodworkers were employed in manufacturing industries. One-third of woodworkers were found in establishments fabricating household and office furniture and fixtures, and 30 percent worked in wood product manufacturing, producing a variety of raw, intermediate, and finished woodstock. Wholesale and retail lumber dealers, furniture stores, reupholstery and furniture repair shops, and construction firms also employ woodworkers.

Woodworking jobs are found throughout the country. However, lumber and wood products-related production jobs are concentrated in the South and Northwest, close to the supply of wood, whereas furnituremakers are more prevalent in the Southeast. Custom shops can be found everywhere, but generally are concentrated in or near highly populated areas.

Job Outlook

Overall employment of woodworkers is expected to decline through 2014, although job growth and opportunities will vary by specialty. In general, opportunities for more highly skilled woodworkers will be better than for woodworkers in specialties susceptible to productivity improvements and competition from imported wood products. Despite the expected overall decline in employment of woodworkers, many job opportunities still will arise each year because of the need to replace experienced woodworkers who transfer to other occupations or leave the labor force. Firms will need woodworkers with technical skills to operate their increasingly advanced computerized machinery.

The number of new workers entering these occupations is expected to below because, as school systems face tighter budgets, the first programs to be cut often are vocational-technical programs, including those that train woodworkers. Also, interest in pursuing these jobs will continue to decline as workers question the stability of manufacturing occupations. For these reasons, competition should be mild, and opportunities should be best for woodworkers who, through vocational education or experience, develop highly specialized woodworking skills or knowledge of CNC machine tool operation.

Employment of sawing and woodworking machine setters, operators, and tenders is expected to decline through 2014. Jobs in the United States will continue to be lost as imports grow. To remain competitive with these imports, some domestic firms are expected to continue to move their production processes to foreign countries, further reducing employment. Others are using advanced technology, such as robots and CNC machinery, to reduce the number of workers needed in production. These forces will prevent employment from rising with the demand for wood products, particularly in the mills and manufacturing plants where many processes can be automated. Among woodworking machine operators, job prospects will be best for those skilled in CNC machine tool operation.

Employment of furniture finishers is expected to decline. Since furniture is largely mass-produced, it is highly susceptible to import competition; the percentage of furniture sold in the United States that is produced abroad has steadily increased over the past 10 years, a trend that is expected to continue.

Employment of bench carpenters, cabinetmakers, modelmakers, patternmakers, and other specialized woodworking occupations will grow more slowly than the average. Demand for these workers will stem from increases in population, personal income, and business expenditures, in addition to the continuing need for repair and renovation of residential and commercial properties. Therefore, opportunities should be available for those who specialize in items such as moldings, cabinets, stairs, and windows. Firms that focus on custom woodwork will be best able to compete against imports without transferring jobs offshore, so opportunities should be very good in specialized woodworking sectors, such as architectural woodworking. Modelmakers and patternmakers who know how to create and execute designs on a computer may have the best opportunities.

Employment in all woodworking specialties is highly sensitive to economic cycles. During economic downturns, workers are subject to layoffs or reductions in hours.

Earnings

Median hourly earnings of cabinetmakers and bench carpenters were $12.16 in May 2004. The middle 50 percent earned between $9.69 and $15.51. The lowest 10 percent earned less than $8.00, and the highest 10 percent earned more than $19.28. Median hourly earnings in the industries employing the largest numbers of cabinetmakers and bench carpenters in May 2004 are shown below:

Office furniture (including fixtures) manufacturing $13.42
Household and institutional furniture and
    kitchen cabinet manufacturing 11.83
Other wood product manufacturing 11.82

Median hourly earnings of sawing machine setters, operators, and tenders, wood, were $10.91 in May 2004. The middle 50 percent earned between $8.95 and $13.34. The lowest 10 percent earned less than $7.46, and the highest 10 percent earned more than $16.20. Median hourly earnings in the industries employing the largest numbers of sawing machine setters, operators, and tenders, wood, in May 2004, are shown below:

Sawmills and wood preservation $11.82
Veneer, plywood, and engineered wood product manufacturing.... 11.49
Household and institutional furniture and
    kitchen cabinet manufacturing 10.65
Other wood product manufacturing 10.49

Median hourly earnings of woodworking machine setters, operators, and tenders, except sawing, were $10.93 in May 2004.

The middle 50 percent earned between $8.93 and $13.40. The lowest 10 percent earned less than $7.55, and the highest 10 percent earned more than $16.33. Median hourly earnings in the industries employing the largest numbers of woodworking machine setters, operators, and tenders, except sawing, in May 2004, are shown below:

Office furniture (including fixtures) manufacturing $11.66
Veneer, plywood, and engineered wood product manufacturing ... 11.19
Household and institutional furniture and
    kitchen cabinet manufacturing 11.00
Sawmills and wood preservation 10.83
Other wood product manufacturing 10.47

In May 2004, median hourly earnings were $11.35 for furniture finishers and $10.16 for all other woodworkers.

Some woodworkers, such as those in logging or sawmills who are engaged in processing primary wood and building materials, are members of the International Association of Machinists. Others belong to the United Brotherhood of Carpenters and Joiners of America.

Related Occupations

Carpenters also work with wood. In addition, many woodworkers follow blueprints and drawings and use machines to shape and form raw wood into a final product. Workers who perform similar functions working with other materials include sheet metal workers, structural and reinforcing iron and metal workers, computer-control programmers and operators, machinists, and tool and die makers.

Sources of Additional Information

For information about careers, education, and training programs in woodworking, contact:
➤ WoodLINKS USA Internet: **http://www.woodlinks.com/USA/home.html**
    For information about woodworking occupations, contact local furniture manufacturers, sawmills and planing mills, cabinetmaking or millwork firms, lumber dealers, a local of one of the unions mentioned above, or the nearest office of the State employment service.

Plant and System Operators

Power Plant Operators, Distributors, and Dispatchers

(O*NET 51-8011.00, 51-8012.00, 51-8013.01, 51-8013.02)

Significant Points

- Keen competition for jobs is expected; opportunities will be best for operators with training in computers and automated equipment.

- Employment is projected to decline.

- Most entry-level workers start as helpers or laborers, and several years of training and experience are required to become fully qualified.

Nature of the Work

Electricity is vital for most everyday activities. From the moment you flip the first switch each morning, you are connecting to a huge network of people, electric lines, and generating equipment. Power plant operators control the machinery that generates electricity. Power plant distributors and dispatchers control the flow of electricity from the power plant, over a network of transmission lines, to industrial plants and substations, and, finally, over distribution lines to residential users.

Power plant operators control and monitor boilers, turbines, generators, and auxiliary equipment in power-generating plants. Operators distribute power demands among generators, combine the current from several generators, and monitor instruments to maintain voltage and regulate electricity flows from the plant. When power requirements change, these workers start or stop generators and connect or disconnect them from circuits. They often use computers to keep records of switching operations and loads on generators, lines, and transformers. Operators also may use computers to prepare reports of unusual incidents, malfunctioning equipment, or maintenance performed during their shift.

Operators in plants with automated control systems work mainly in a central control room and usually are called *control room operators* or *control room operator trainees* or *assistants*. In older plants, the controls for the equipment are not centralized, and *switchboard operators* control the flow of electricity from a central point, whereas *auxiliary equipment operators* work throughout the plant, operating and monitoring valves, switches, and gauges.

The Nuclear Regulatory Commission (NRC) licenses operators of nuclear power plants. *Reactor operators* are authorized to control equipment that affects the power of the reactor in a nuclear power plant. In addition, an NRC-licensed *senior reactor operator* must be on duty during each shift to act as the plant supervisor and supervise the operation of all controls in the control room.

Power distributors and dispatchers, also called *load dispatchers* or *systems operators*, control the flow of electricity through transmission lines to industrial plants and substations that supply residential needs for electricity. They monitor and operate current converters, voltage transformers, and circuit breakers. Dispatchers also monitor other distribution equipment and record readings at a pilot board—a map of the transmission grid system showing the status of transmission circuits and connections with substations and industrial plants.

Dispatchers also anticipate power needs, such as those caused by changes in the weather. They call control room operators to start or stop boilers and generators, in order to bring production into balance with needs. Dispatchers handle emergencies such as transformer or transmission line failures and route current around affected areas. In substations, they also operate and monitor equipment that increases or decreases voltage, and they operate

Power plant operators in plants with automated control systems usually spend most of their time in a central control room.

switchboard levers to control the flow of electricity in and out of the substations.

Working Conditions
Because electricity is provided around the clock, operators, distributors, and dispatchers usually work one of three daily 8-hour shifts or one of two 12-hour shifts on a rotating basis. Shift assignments may change periodically, so that all operators can share duty on less desirable shifts. Work on rotating shifts can be stressful and fatiguing, because of the constant change in living and sleeping patterns. Operators, distributors, and dispatchers who work in control rooms generally sit or stand at a control station. This work is not physically strenuous, but it does require constant attention. Operators who work outside the control room may be exposed to danger from electric shock, falls, and burns.

Nuclear power plant operators are subject to random drug and alcohol tests, as are most workers at such plants.

Training, Other Qualifications, and Advancement
Employers often seek high school graduates for entry-level operator, distributor, and dispatcher positions. Candidates with strong mathematics and science skills are preferred. College-level courses and prior experience in a mechanical or technical job are becoming increasingly helpful in a competitive job market. With computers now used to keep records, generate reports, and track maintenance, employers are increasingly requiring computer proficiency. Most entry-level workers start as helpers or laborers. Depending on the results of aptitude tests, their own preferences, and the availability of openings, workers may be assigned to train for one of many utility positions.

Workers selected for training as a fossil-fueled power plant operator or distributor undergo extensive on-the-job and classroom instruction. Several years of training and experience are required for a worker to become a fully qualified control room operator or power plant distributor. With further training and experience, workers may advance to shift supervisor. Utilities generally promote from within; therefore, opportunities to advance by moving to another employer are limited.

Extensive training and experience are necessary to pass the NRC examinations for reactor operators and senior reactor operators. To maintain their license, licensed reactor operators must pass an annual practical plant operation exam and a biennial written exam administered by their employers. Training may include simulator and on-the-job training, classroom instruction, and individual study. Entrants to nuclear power plant operator trainee jobs must have strong mathematics and science skills. Experience in other power plants or with Navy nuclear propulsion plants also is helpful. With further training and experience, reactor operators may advance to senior reactor operator positions.

In addition to receiving preliminary training as a power plant operator, distributor, or dispatcher, most workers are given periodic refresher training—frequently in the case of nuclear power plant operators. Refresher training usually is taken on plant simulators designed specifically to replicate procedures and situations that might be encountered at the trainee's plant.

Employment
Power plant operators, distributors, and dispatchers held about 47,000 jobs in 2004. Jobs were located throughout the country. About 64 percent of jobs were in electric power generation, transmission, and distribution. About 20 percent worked in government, mainly in local government. Others worked for manufacturing establishments that produced electricity for their own use.

Job Outlook

People who want to become power plant operators, distributors, and dispatchers are expected to encounter keen competition for these relatively high-paying jobs. While demand for electricity will increase, the slow pace of construction of new plants will limit opportunities for these workers. In addition, the increasing use of automatic controls and more computerized equipment should boost productivity and decrease the demand for operators. As a result, individuals with training in computers and automated equipment will have the best job prospects. Some job opportunities will arise from the need to replace workers who retire or leave the occupation. However, cost considerations may restrict the number of workers who are replaced, with the job duties instead being given to other workers.

A decline in employment of power plant operators, distributors, and dispatchers is projected through the year 2014, as the utilities industry continues to restructure in response to deregulation and increasing competition. Independent producers are now allowed to sell power directly to industrial and other wholesale customers. Consequently, some utilities that historically operated as regulated local monopolies have restructured their operations in order to reduce costs and compete effectively. While much of this restructuring is complete, the focus on reducing costs persists. This new focus is present in regulated utilities, as well as those that have been deregulated. As a result, the number of jobs is expected to decline.

Earnings

Median annual earnings of power plant operators were $52,530 in May 2004. The middle 50 percent earned between $43,310 and $62,030. The lowest 10 percent earned less than $34,550, and the highest 10 percent earned more than $70,330. Median annual earnings of power plant operators in May 2004 were $53,820 in electric power generation, transmission and distribution.

Median annual earnings of nuclear power reactor operators were $64,090 in May 2004. The middle 50 percent earned between $56,890 and $71,160. The lowest 10 percent earned less than $49,690, and the highest 10 percent earned more than $82,220.

Median annual earnings of power distributors and dispatchers were $57,330 in May 2004. The middle 50 percent earned between $48,010 and $69,100. The lowest 10 percent earned less than $38,220, and the highest 10 percent earned more than $83,030.

Related Occupations

Other workers who monitor and operate plant and system equipment include chemical plant and system operators; petroleum pump system operators, refinery operators, and gaugers; stationary engineers and boiler operators; and water and liquid waste treatment plant and system operators.

Sources of Additional Information

For information about employment opportunities, contact local electric utility companies, locals of unions, and State employment service offices.

For general information about power plant operators, nuclear power reactor operators, and power plant distributors and dispatchers, contact:

➤ American Public Power Association, 2301 M St. NW., Washington, DC 20037-1484. Internet: http://www.appanet.org
➤ International Brotherhood of Electrical Workers, 1125 15th St. NW., Washington, DC 20005.

Stationary Engineers and Boiler Operators

(O*NET 51-8021.01, 51-8021.02)

Significant Points

- Workers usually acquire their skills through a formal apprenticeship program or through on-the-job training supplemented by courses at a trade or technical school.

- Most States and cities have licensing requirements.

- Employment is expected to grow more slowly than the average for all occupations through the year 2014.

- Applicants may face competition for jobs; opportunities will be best for workers with training in computerized controls and instrumentation.

Nature of the Work

Heating, air-conditioning, refrigeration, and ventilation systems keep large buildings and other commercial facilities comfortable all year long. Industrial plants often have facilities to provide electrical power, steam, or other services. Stationary engineers and boiler operators operate and maintain these systems, which include boilers, air-conditioning and refrigeration equipment, diesel engines, turbines, generators, pumps, condensers, and compressors. The equipment that stationary engineers and boiler operators control is similar to equipment operated by locomotive or marine engineers, except that it is not in a moving vehicle.

Stationary engineers and boiler operators start up, regulate, repair, and shut down equipment. They ensure that the equipment operates safely, economically, and within established limits by monitoring meters, gauges, and computerized controls. Stationary engineers and boiler operators control equipment manually and, if necessary, make adjustments. They also record relevant events and facts concerning the operation and maintenance of the equipment. With regard to steam boilers, for example, they observe, control, and record the steam pressure, temperature, water level, chemistry, power output, fuel consumption, and emissions from the vessel. They watch and listen to machinery and routinely check safety devices, identifying and correcting any trouble that develops. They use hand and power tools to perform repairs and maintenance ranging from a complete overhaul to replacing defective valves, gaskets, or bearings. Servicing, troubleshooting, repairing, and monitoring modern systems all require the use of sophisticated electrical and electronic test equipment.

Stationary engineers typically use computers to operate the mechanical, electrical, and fire safety systems of new buildings and plants. Engineers monitor, adjust, and diagnose these systems from a central location, using a computer linked into the buildings' communications network.

Routine maintenance, such as lubricating moving parts, replacing filters, and removing soot and corrosion that can reduce the boiler's operating efficiency, is a regular part of the work of stationary engineers and boiler operators. They test the water in the boiler and add chemicals to prevent corrosion and harmful deposits. In most facilities, stationary engineers are responsible for the maintenance and balancing of air systems, as well as hydronic systems that heat or cool buildings by circulating fluid (such as water or water vapor) in a closed system of pipes. They also may check the air quality of the ventilation system and make adjustments to keep the operation of the boiler within mandated guidelines.

Stationary engineers and boiler operators work around hazardous machinery and must follow procedures to guard against injuries.

In a large building or industrial plant, a stationary engineer may be in charge of all mechanical systems in the building. Engineers may supervise the work of assistant stationary engineers, turbine operators, boiler tenders, and air-conditioning and refrigeration operators and mechanics. Most stationary engineers perform other maintenance duties, such as carpentry, plumbing, locksmithing, and electrical repairs. In a small building or industrial plant, there may be only one stationary engineer.

Working Conditions

Stationary engineers and boiler operators generally have steady, year-round employment. The average workweek is 40 hours. In facilities that operate around the clock, engineers and operators usually work one of three daily 8-hour shifts on a rotating basis. Weekend and holiday work often is required.

Engine rooms, power plants, boiler rooms, mechanical rooms, and electrical rooms usually are clean and well lighted. Even under the most favorable conditions, however, some stationary engineers and boiler operators are exposed to high temperatures, dust, dirt, and high noise levels from the equipment. General maintenance duties also may require contact with oil, grease, or smoke. Workers spend much of the time on their feet. They also may have to crawl inside boilers and work in crouching or kneeling positions to inspect, clean, or repair equipment.

Stationary engineers and boiler operators work around hazardous machinery, such as low- and high-pressure boilers and electrical equipment. They must follow procedures to guard against burns, electric shock, noise, danger from moving parts, and exposure to hazardous materials, such as asbestos or certain chemicals.

Training, Other Qualifications, and Advancement

Stationary engineers and boiler operators usually acquire their skills through a formal apprenticeship program or through on-the-job training supplemented by courses at a trade or technical school. In addition, valuable experience can be obtained in the Navy or the merchant marine, because marine engineering plants are similar to many stationary power and heating plants. Most employers prefer to hire persons with at least a high school diploma or the equivalent. However, continuing

education—such as college courses—is becoming increasingly important, in part because of the growing complexity of the equipment with which engineers and operators now work. Mechanical aptitude, manual dexterity, and good physical condition also are important.

The International Union of Operating Engineers sponsors apprenticeship programs and is the principal union for stationary engineers and boiler operators. In selecting apprentices, most local labor-management apprenticeship committees prefer applicants with education or training in mathematics, computers, mechanical drawing, machine shop practice, physics, and chemistry. An apprenticeship usually lasts 4 years and includes 8,000 hours of on-the-job training. In addition, apprentices receive 600 hours of classroom instruction in subjects such as boiler design and operation, elementary physics, pneumatics, refrigeration, air-conditioning, electricity, and electronics.

Those who acquire their skills on the job usually start as boiler tenders or helpers to experienced stationary engineers and boiler operators. This practical experience may be supplemented by postsecondary vocational training in computerized controls and instrumentation. However, becoming an engineer or operator without completing a formal apprenticeship program usually requires many years of work experience.

Most large and some small employers encourage and pay for skill-improvement training for their employees. Training almost always is provided when new equipment is introduced or when regulations concerning some aspect of the workers' duties change.

Most States and cities have licensing requirements for stationary engineers and boiler operators. Applicants usually must be at least 18 years of age, reside for a specified period in the State or locality in which they wish to work, meet experience requirements, and pass a written examination. A stationary engineer or boiler operator who moves from one State or city to another may have to pass an examination for a new license due to regional differences in licensing requirements.

There are several classes of stationary engineer licenses. Each class specifies the type and size of equipment the engineer is permitted to operate without supervision. A licensed first-class stationary engineer is qualified to run a large facility, supervise others, and operate equipment of all types and capacities. An applicant for this license may be required to have a high school education, apprenticeship or on-the-job training, and several years of experience. Licenses below first class limit the types or capacities of equipment the engineer may operate without supervision.

Stationary engineers and boiler operators advance by being placed in charge of larger, more powerful, or more varied equipment. Generally, engineers advance to these jobs as they obtain higher class licenses. Some stationary engineers and boiler operators advance to boiler inspectors, chief plant engineers, building and plant superintendents, or building managers. A few obtain jobs as examining engineers or technical instructors.

Employment

Stationary engineers and boiler operators held about 50,000 jobs in 2004. Jobs were dispersed throughout a variety of industries. The majority of jobs were in State and local government facilities; hospitals; educational services; electric power generation, transmission, and distribution facilities; and manufacturing firms, such as pulp, paper, and paperboard mills. Other jobs were in architectural, engineering, and related services and real estate firms. Some were employed as contractors to a building or plant.

Stationary engineers and boiler operators worked throughout the country, generally in the more heavily populated areas in which large industrial and commercial establishments are located.

Job Outlook

Applicants may face competition for jobs as stationary engineers and boiler operators. Employment opportunities will be best for those with apprenticeship training or vocational school courses covering systems that are operated by computerized controls and instrumentation.

Employment of stationary engineers and boiler operators is expected to grow more slowly than the average for all occupations through the year 2014. Continuing commercial and industrial development will increase the amount of equipment to be operated and maintained. However, automated systems and computerized controls are making newly installed equipment more efficient, thus reducing the number of jobs needed for its operation. Furthermore, relatively few job openings will arise from the need to replace experienced workers who transfer to other occupations or leave the labor force. The low replacement rate in this occupation reflects its relatively high wages.

Earnings

Median annual earnings of stationary engineers and boiler operators were $44,150 in May 2004. The middle 50 percent earned between $34,500 and $55,460. The lowest 10 percent earned less than $27,010, and the highest 10 percent earned more than $66,570. Median annual earnings of stationary engineers and boiler operators in May 2004 were $48,340 in local government and $43,710 in general medical and surgical hospitals.

Related Occupations

Workers who monitor and operate stationary machinery include chemical plant and system operators; gas plant operators; petroleum pump system operators, refinery operators, and gaugers; power plant operators, distributors, and dispatchers; and water and liquid waste treatment plant and system operators. Other workers who maintain the equipment and machinery in a building or plant are industrial machinery mechanics and maintenance workers, as well as millwrights.

Sources of Additional Information

Information about apprenticeships, vocational training, and work opportunities is available from State employment service offices, locals of the International Union of Operating Engineers, vocational schools, and State and local licensing agencies.

Specific questions about this occupation should be addressed to:

➤ International Union of Operating Engineers, 1125 17th St. NW., Washington, DC 20036. Internet: **http://www.iuoe.org**

➤ National Association of Power Engineers, Inc., 1 Springfield St., Chicopee, MA 01013.

➤ Building Owners and Managers Institute International, 1521 Ritchie Hwy., Arnold, MD 21012. Internet: **http://www.bomi-edu.org**

Water and Liquid Waste Treatment Plant and System Operators

(O*NET 51-8031.00)

Significant Points

- Employment is concentrated in local government and private water, sewage, and other systems utilities.

- Completion of an associate degree or a 1-year certificate program increases an applicant's chances for employment and promotion.

- Because the number of applicants in this field is normally low, job prospects will be good for qualified individuals, particularly those with training in all aspects of water and wastewater treatment.

Nature of the Work

Clean water is essential for everyday life. *Water treatment plant and system operators* treat water so that it is safe to drink. *Liquid waste treatment plant and system operators*, also known as wastewater treatment plant and system operators, remove harmful pollutants from domestic and industrial liquid waste so that it is safe to return to the environment.

Water is pumped from wells, rivers, streams, and reservoirs to water treatment plants, where it is treated and distributed to customers. Wastewater travels through customers' sewer pipes to wastewater treatment plants, where it is either treated and returned to streams, rivers, and oceans or reused for irrigation and landscaping. Operators in both types of plants control equipment and processes that remove or destroy harmful materials, chemical compounds, and microorganisms from the water. They also control pumps, valves, and other equipment that moves the water or wastewater through the various treatment processes, after which they dispose of the removed waste materials.

Operators read, interpret, and adjust meters and gauges to make sure that plant equipment and processes are working properly. Operators operate chemical-feeding devices, take samples of the water or wastewater, perform chemical and biological laboratory analyses, and adjust the amounts of chemicals, such as chlorine, in the water. They use a variety of instruments to sample and measure water quality and they utilize common hand and power tools to make repairs to valves, pumps, and other equipment.

Water and wastewater treatment plant and system operators increasingly rely on computers to help monitor equipment, store the results of sampling, make process-control decisions, schedule and record maintenance activities, and produce reports. When equipment malfunctions, operators also may use computers to determine the cause of the malfunction and seek its solution.

Occasionally, operators must work during emergencies. A heavy rainstorm, for example, may cause large amounts of wastewater to flow into sewers, exceeding a plant's treatment capacity. Emergencies also can be caused by conditions inside a plant, such as chlorine gas leaks or oxygen deficiencies. To handle these conditions, operators are trained to make an emergency management response and use special safety equipment and procedures to protect public health and the facility. During these periods, operators may work under extreme pressure to correct problems as quickly as possible. Because working conditions may be dangerous, operators must be extremely cautious.

The specific duties of plant operators depend on the type and size of the plant. In smaller plants, one operator may control all of the machinery, perform tests, keep records, handle complaints, and perform repairs and maintenance. A few operators may handle both a water treatment and a wastewater treatment plant. In larger plants with many employees, operators may be more specialized and monitor only one process. The staff also may include chemists, engineers, laboratory technicians, mechanics, helpers, supervisors, and a superintendent.

Water pollution standards are largely set by two major Federal environmental statutes: the Clean Water Act, which regulates the discharge of pollutants, and the Safe Drinking Water Act, which specifies standards for drinking water. Industrial facilities that send their wastes to municipal treatment plants must meet certain minimum standards to ensure that the wastes have been adequately pretreated and will not damage municipal treatment facilities. Municipal water treatment plants also must meet stringent standards for drinking water. The list of contaminants regulated by these statutes has grown over time. As a result, plant operators must be familiar with the guidelines established by Federal regulations and how they affect their plant. In addition, operators must be aware

Water and liquid waste treatment plant and system operators control equipment that treats water to make it safe for use or disposal.

of any guidelines imposed by the State or locality in which the plant operates.

Working Conditions

Water and wastewater treatment plant and system operators work both indoors and outdoors and may be exposed to noise from machinery and to unpleasant odors. Operators' work is physically demanding and often is performed in unclean locations. Operators must pay close attention to safety procedures because of the presence of hazardous conditions, such as slippery walkways, dangerous gases, and malfunctioning equipment. Plants operate 24 hours a day, 7 days a week; therefore, operators work one of three 8-hour shifts, including weekends and holidays, on a rotational basis. Operators may be required to work overtime.

Training, Other Qualifications, and Advancement

A high school diploma usually is required for an individual to become a water or wastewater treatment plant operator. Operators need mechanical aptitude and should be competent in basic mathematics, chemistry, and biology. They must have the ability to apply data to formulas prescribing treatment requirements, flow levels, and concentration levels. Some basic familiarity with computers also is necessary because of the trend toward computer-controlled equipment and more sophisticated instrumentation. Certain positions—particularly in larger cities and towns—are covered by civil service regulations. Applicants for these positions may be required to pass a written examination testing their mathematics skills, mechanical aptitude, and general intelligence.

The completion of an associate degree or a 1-year certificate program in water quality and wastewater treatment technology increases an applicant's chances for employment and promotion, because plants are becoming more complex. Offered throughout the country, these programs provide a good general knowledge of water and wastewater treatment processes, as well as basic preparation for becoming an operator.

Trainees usually start as attendants or operators-in-training and learn their skills on the job under the direction of an experienced operator. They learn by observing and doing routine tasks such as recording meter readings, taking samples of wastewater and sludge, and performing simple maintenance and repair work on pumps, electric motors, valves, and other plant equipment. Larger treatment plants generally combine this on-the-job training with formal classroom or self-paced study programs.

The Safe Drinking Water Act Amendments of 1996, enforced by the U.S. Environmental Protection Agency, specify national minimum standards for certification and recertification of operators of community and nontransient, noncommunity water systems. As a result, operators must pass an examination certifying that they are capable of overseeing wastewater treatment plant operations. There are different levels of certification, depending on the operator's experience and training. Higher levels qualify the operator for overseeing a wider variety of treatment processes. Certification requirements vary by State and by size of the treatment plant. Although relocation may mean having to become certified in a new jurisdiction, many States accept other States' certifications.

Most State drinking water and water pollution control agencies offer courses to improve operators' skills and knowledge. The courses cover principles of treatment processes and process control, laboratory procedures, maintenance, management skills, collection systems, safety, chlorination, sedimentation, biological treatment, sludge treatment and disposal, and flow measurements. Some operators take correspondence courses on subjects related to water and wastewater treatment, and some employers pay part of the tuition for related college courses in science or engineering.

As operators are promoted, they become responsible for more complex treatment processes. Some operators are promoted to plant supervisor or superintendent; others advance by transferring to a larger facility. Postsecondary training in water and wastewater treatment, coupled with increasingly responsible experience as an operator, may be sufficient to qualify a worker for becoming superintendent of a small plant, where a superintendent also serves as an operator. However, educational requirements are rising as larger, more complex treatment plants are built to meet new drinking water and water pollution control standards. With each promotion, the operator must have greater knowledge of Federal, State, and local regulations. Superintendents of large plants generally need an engineering or science degree.

A few operators get jobs as technicians with State drinking water or water pollution control agencies. In that capacity, they monitor and provide technical assistance to plants throughout the State. Vocational-technical school or community college training generally is preferred for technician jobs. Experienced operators may transfer to related jobs with industrial liquid waste treatment plants, water or liquid waste treatment equipment and chemical companies, engineering consulting firms, or vocational-technical schools.

Employment

Water and wastewater treatment plant and system operators held about 94,000 jobs in 2004. Almost 4 in 5 operators worked for local governments. Others worked primarily for private water, sewage, and other systems utilities and for private waste treatment and disposal and waste management services companies. Private firms are increasingly providing operation and management services to local governments on a contract basis.

Water and wastewater treatment plant and system operators were employed throughout the country, but most jobs were in larger towns and cities. Although nearly all operators worked full time, those in small towns may work only part time at the treatment plant, with the remainder of their time spent handling other municipal duties.

Job Outlook

Employment of water and wastewater treatment plant and system operators is expected to grow about as fast as the average for all occupations through the year 2014. Job prospects will be good for qualified individuals because the number of applicants in this field is normally low, due primarily to the unclean and physically demanding nature of the work. Workers who have training in all aspects of water and wastewater treatment and who can handle multiple duties will have the best opportunities.

The increasing population and the growth of the economy are expected to boost demand for essential water and wastewater treatment services. As new plants are constructed to meet this demand, employment of water and wastewater treatment plant and system operators will increase. In addition, many job openings will occur as experienced operators leave the labor force or transfer to other occupations.

Local governments are the largest employers of water and wastewater treatment plant and system operators. However, Federal certification requirements have increased utilities' reliance on private firms specializing in the operation and management of water and wastewater treatment facilities. As a result, employment in privately owned facilities will grow faster than the average.

Earnings

Median annual earnings of water and wastewater treatment plant and system operators were $34,960 in May 2004. The middle 50 percent earned between $27,180 and $43,720. The lowest 10 percent earned less than $21,700, and the highest 10 percent earned more than $53,540. Median annual earnings of water and liquid waste treat-

ment plant and systems operators in May 2004 were $34,990 in local government and $32,350 in water, sewage, and other systems.

In addition to their annual salaries, water and wastewater treatment plant and system operators usually receive benefits that may include health and life insurance, a retirement plan, and educational reimbursement for job-related courses.

Related Occupations

Other workers whose main activity consists of operating a system of machinery to process or produce materials include chemical plant and system operators; gas plant operators; petroleum pump system operators, refinery operators, and gaugers; power plant operators, distributors, and dispatchers; and stationary engineers and boiler operators.

Sources of Additional Information

For information on employment opportunities, contact State or local water pollution control agencies, State water and liquid waste operator associations, State environmental training centers, or local offices of the State employment service.

For information on certification, contact:

➤ Association of Boards of Certification, 208 Fifth St., Ames, IA 50010-6259. Internet: **http://www.abccert.org**

For educational information related to a career as a water or liquid waste treatment plant and system operator, contact:

➤ American Water Works Association, 6666 West Quincy Ave., Denver, CO 80235. Internet: **http://www.awwa.org**

➤ Water Environment Federation, 601 Wythe St., Alexandria, VA 22314-1994. Internet: **http://www.wef.org**

Other Production Occupations

Inspectors, Testers, Sorters, Samplers, and Weighers

(O*NET 51-9061.01, 51-9061.02, 51-9061.03, 51-9061.04, 51-9061.05)

Significant Points

- Two in three are employed in manufacturing establishments.

- While a high school diploma is sufficient for basic testing of products, complex precision-inspecting positions are filled by experienced assemblers, machine operators, or mechanics who already have a thorough knowledge of the products and production processes.

- Employment is expected to decline, reflecting the growth of automated inspection and the redistribution of quality-control responsibilities from inspectors to other production workers.

Nature of the Work

Inspectors, testers, sorters, samplers, and weighers ensure that your food will not make you sick, that your car will run properly, and that your pants will not split the first time you wear them. These workers monitor or audit quality standards for virtually all manufactured products, including foods, textiles, clothing, glassware, motor vehicles, electronic components, computers, and structural steel. As product quality becomes increasingly important to the

success of many manufacturing firms, daily duties of inspectors have changed. In some cases, the job titles of these workers also have been changed to *quality-control inspector* or a similar name, reflecting the growing importance of quality. (A separate statement on construction and building inspectors appears elsewhere in the *Handbook*.)

Regardless of title, all inspectors, testers, sorters, samplers, and weighers work to guarantee the quality of the goods their firms produce. Job duties, even within one company, vary by the type of products produced or the stage of production. Specific job duties also vary across the wide range of industries in which these workers are found. For example, materials inspectors may check products by sight, sound, feel, smell, or even taste to locate imperfections such as cuts, scratches, bubbles, missing pieces, misweaves, or crooked seams. These workers also may verify dimensions, color, weight, texture, strength, or other physical characteristics of objects. Mechanical inspectors generally verify that parts fit, move correctly, and are properly lubricated; check the pressure of gases and the level of liquids; test the flow of electricity; and do a test run to check for proper operation. Some jobs involve only a quick visual inspection; others require a longer, detailed one. Sorters may separate goods according to length, size, fabric type, or color, while samplers test or inspect a sample taken from a batch or production run for malfunctions or defects. Weighers weigh quantities of materials for use in production.

Inspectors, testers, sorters, samplers, and weighers are involved at every stage of the production process. Some inspectors examine materials received from a supplier before sending them to the production line. Others inspect components and assemblies or perform a final check on the finished product. Depending on their skill level, inspectors also may set up and test equipment, calibrate precision instruments, repair defective products, or record data.

Inspectors, testers, sorters, samplers, and weighers rely on a number of tools to perform their jobs. Although some still use hand held measurement devises such as micrometers, calipers, and alignment gauges, it is more common for them to operate electronic inspection equipment, such as coordinate measuring machines (CMMs). These machines use sensitive probes to measure a part's dimensional accuracy and allow the inspector to analyze the results using computer software. Inspectors testing electrical devices may use voltmeters, ammeters, and oscilloscopes to test insulation, current flow, and resistance. All the tools that inspectors use are maintained by calibration technicians, who ensure that they work properly and generate accurate readings.

Inspectors mark, tag, or note problems. They may reject defective items outright, send them for repair or correction, or fix minor problems themselves. If the product is acceptable, inspectors may screw a nameplate onto it, tag it, stamp it with a serial number, or certify it in some other way. Inspectors, testers, sorters, samplers, and weighers record the results of their inspections, compute the percentage of defects and other statistical measures, and prepare inspection and test reports. Some electronic inspection equipment automatically provides test reports containing these inspection results. When defects are found, inspectors notify supervisors and help to analyze and correct the production problems.

The emphasis on finding the root cause of defects is a basic tenet of modern management and production philosophies. Industrial production managers (see the statement on this occupation elsewhere in the *Handbook*) work closely with the inspectors to reduce defects and improve quality. In the past, a certain level of defects was considered acceptable because variations would always occur. Current philosophies emphasize constant quality improvement through analysis and correction of the causes of defects. The nature of inspectors' work has changed from merely checking for defects, to determining the cause of those defects.

Increased emphasis on quality control in manufacturing means that inspection is more fully integrated into the production process than in the past. Now, companies have integrated teams of inspection and production workers to jointly review and improve product quality. In addition, many companies now use self-monitoring production machines to ensure that the output is produced within quality standards. Self-monitoring machines can alert inspectors to production problems and automatically repair defects in some cases.

Some firms have completely automated inspection with the help of advanced vision inspection systems, using machinery installed at one or several points in the production process. Inspectors in these firms monitor the equipment, review output, and perform random product checks.

Testers repeatedly test existing products or prototypes under real-world conditions. For example, they may purposely abuse a machine by not changing its oil to see when failure occurs. They may devise automated machines to repeat a basic task thousands of times, such as opening and closing a car door. Through these tests, companies determine how long a product will last, what parts will break down first, and how to improve durability.

Working Conditions

Working conditions vary by industry and establishment size. As a result, some inspectors examine similar products for an entire shift, whereas others examine a variety of items. In manufacturing, it is common for most inspectors to remain at one workstation. Inspectors in some industries may be on their feet all day and may have to lift heavy objects, whereas, in other industries, they sit during most of their shift and do little strenuous work. Workers in heavy manufac-

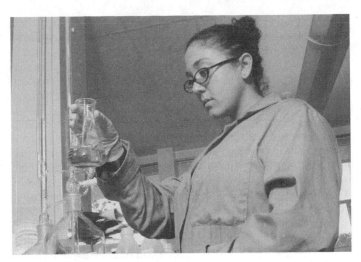

Inspectors verify that company quality control standards are being met.

turing plants may be exposed to the noise and grime of machinery; in other plants, inspectors work in clean, air-conditioned environments suitable for carrying out controlled tests. Other inspectors rarely see the products they are inspecting and instead do the majority of their work examining electronic readouts in front of a computer.

Some inspectors work evenings, nights, or weekends. Shift assignments generally are made on the basis of seniority. Overtime may be required to meet production goals.

Training, Other Qualifications, and Advancement

Training requirements vary, based on the responsibilities of the inspector, tester, sorter, sampler, or weigher. For workers who perform simple "pass/fail" tests of products, a high school diploma generally is sufficient together with basic in-house training. Training for new inspectors may cover the use of special meters, gauges, computers and other instruments; quality-control techniques; blueprint reading; safety; and reporting requirements. There are some postsecondary training programs in testing, but many employers prefer to train inspectors on the job.

Complex precision-inspecting positions are filled by experienced assemblers, machine operators, or mechanics who already have a thorough knowledge of the products and production processes. To advance to these positions, experienced workers may need training in statistical process control, new automation, or the company's quality assurance policies. As automated inspection equipment and electronic recording of results is common, computer skills are also important.

In general, inspectors, testers, sorters, samplers, and weighers need mechanical aptitude, math and communication skills, and good hand-eye coordination and vision. Advancement for these workers frequently takes the form of higher pay. They also may advance to inspector of more complex products, supervisor, or related positions such as purchaser of materials and equipment.

Employment

Inspectors, testers, sorters, samplers, and weighers held about 508,000 jobs in 2004. About 2 in 3 worked in manufacturing establishments that produced such products as motor vehicle parts, plastics products, semiconductor and other electronic components, and aerospace products and parts. Inspectors, testers, sorters, samplers, and weighers also were found in employment services, architectural, engineering, and related services, wholesale trade, and government agencies.

Job Outlook

Like that of many other occupations concentrated in manufacturing industries, employment of inspectors, testers, sorters, samplers, and weighers is expected to decline through the year 2014. The decline stems primarily from the growing use of automated inspection and the redistribution of some quality-control responsibilities from inspectors to production workers. Although numerous job openings will arise due to turnover in this large occupation, many of these jobs will be open only to experienced workers with advanced skills.

Employment of inspectors, testers, sorters, samplers, and weighers will be positively affected by the continuing focus on quality in American industry. The emphasis on improving quality and productivity has led manufacturers to invest in automated inspection equipment and to take a more systematic approach to quality inspection. Continued improvements in technologies, such as spectrophotometers and computer-assisted visual inspection systems, allow firms to effectively automate inspection tasks, increasing worker productivity and reducing the demand for inspectors. Inspectors will continue to operate these automated machines and monitor the defects they detect. Thus, while the increased emphasis on quality has increased the importance of inspection, the increased automation of inspection has limited the demand for inspectors.

Apart from automation, firms are integrating quality control into the production process. Many inspection duties are being redistributed from specialized inspectors to fabrication and assembly workers who monitor quality at every stage of the production process. In addition, the growing implementation of statistical process control is resulting in "smarter" inspection. Using this system, firms survey the sources and incidence of defects so that they can better focus their efforts on reducing production of defective products.

In some industries, however, automation is not a feasible alternative to manual inspection. Where key inspection elements are oriented toward size, such as length, width, or thickness, automation will become more important in the future. But where taste, smell, texture, appearance, fabric complexity, or product performance is important, inspection will continue to be done by workers. Employment of inspectors, testers, sorters, samplers, and weighers is expected to increase in the rapidly growing employment services industry, as more manufacturers and industrial firms hire temporary inspectors to increase the flexibility of their staffing strategies.

Earnings

Median hourly earnings of inspectors, testers, sorters, samplers, and weighers were $13.66 in May 2004. The middle 50 percent earned between $10.43 and $18.23 an hour. The lowest 10 percent earned less than $8.30 an hour, and the highest 10 percent earned more than $24.45 an hour. Median hourly earnings in the industries employing the largest numbers of inspectors, testers, sorters, samplers, and weighers in May 2004 were:

Motor vehicle parts manufacturing	$16.54
Architectural, engineering, and related services	15.59
Semiconductor and other electronic component manufacturing	12.94
Plastics product manufacturing	12.40
Employment services	10.08

Related Occupations

Other workers who conduct inspections include agricultural inspectors, construction and building inspectors, fire inspectors and investigators, occupational health and safety specialists and technicians, and transportation inspectors.

Sources of Additional Information

For general information about inspection and testing, contact:

➤ American Society for Quality, 600 North Plankinton Ave., Milwaukee, WI 53203. Internet: http://www.asq.org

Jewelers and Precious Stone and Metal Workers

(O*NET 51-9071.01, 51-9071.02, 51-9071.03, 51-9071.04, 51-9071.05, 51-9071.06)

Significant Points

- About 40 percent of all jewelers are self-employed.

- Jewelers usually learn their trade in vocational or technical schools, through distance-learning centers, or on the job.

- Prospects for new jewelers should be excellent; many employers have difficulty finding and retaining workers with the right skills to replace those who retire or who leave the occupation for other reasons.

Nature of the Work

Jewelers and precious stone and metal workers use a variety of common and specialized handtools and equipment to design and manufacture new pieces of jewelry; cut, set, and polish gem stones; repair or adjust rings, necklaces, bracelets, earrings, and other jewelry; and appraise jewelry, precious metals, and gems. Jewelers usually specialize in one or more of these areas and may work for large jewelry manufacturing firms, for small retail jewelry shops, or as owners of their own businesses. Regardless of the type of work done or the work setting, jewelers require a high degree of skill, precision, and attention to detail.

Some jewelers design or make their own jewelry. Following their own designs or those created by designers or customers, they begin by shaping the metal or by carving wax to make a model for casting the metal. The individual parts then are soldered together, and the jeweler may mount a diamond or other gem or may engrave a design into the metal. Others do finishing work, such as setting stones, polishing, or engraving. Typical repair work includes enlarging or reducing ring sizes, resetting stones, and replacing broken clasps and mountings.

In larger manufacturing businesses, jewelers usually specialize in a single operation. *Mold and model makers* create models or tools for the jewelry that is to be produced. *Assemblers* solder or fuse jewelry and their parts; they also may set stones. *Engravers* etch designs into the metal with specialized tools, and *polishers* bring a finished luster to the final product.

Jewelers typically do the handiwork required to produce a piece of jewelry, while *gemologists* and laboratory graders analyze, describe, and certify the quality and characteristics of gem stones. Gemologists may work in gemological laboratories or as quality control experts for retailers, importers, or manufacturers. After using microscopes, computerized tools, and other grading instruments to examine gem stones or finished pieces of jewelry, they write reports certifying that the items are of a particular quality. Many jewelers also study gemology in order to become familiar with the physical properties of the gem stones with which they work.

Jewelry *appraisers* carefully examine jewelry to determine its value, after which they write appraisal documents. They determine the value of a piece by researching the jewelry market, using reference books, auction catalogs, price lists, and the Internet. They may work for jewelry stores, appraisal firms, auction houses, pawnbrokers, or insurance companies. Many gemologists also become appraisers.

In small retail stores or repair shops, jewelers and appraisers may be involved in all aspects of the work. Those who own or manage stores or shops also hire and train employees; order, market, and sell merchandise; and perform other managerial duties.

New technology is helping to produce jewelry of higher quality at a reduced cost and in a shorter amount of time. For example, lasers are often used for cutting and improving the quality of stones, for applying intricate engraving or design work, and for inscribing personal messages or identification on jewelry. Jewelers also use lasers to weld metals together in milliseconds with no seams or blemishes, improving the quality and appearance of jewelry.

Some manufacturing firms use computer-aided design and manufacturing (CAD/CAM) to facilitate product design and automate some steps in the moldmaking and modelmaking process. CAD allows jewelers to create a virtual-reality model of a piece of jewelry. Using CAD, jewelers can modify the design, change the stone, or try a different setting and see the changes on a computer screen before cutting a stone or performing other costly steps. Once they are satisfied with the model, CAM produces it in a waxlike or other material. After the mold of the model is made, it is easier for manufacturing firms to produce numerous copies of a given piece of jewelry, which are then distributed to retail establishments across the country. Similar techniques may be used in the retail setting, allowing individual customers to review their jewelry designs with the jeweler and make modifications before committing themselves to the expense of a customized piece of jewelry.

Working Conditions

A jeweler's work involves a great deal of concentration and attention to detail. Working on precious stones and metals while trying to satisfy customers' and employers' demands for speed and quality can cause fatigue or stress. However, the use of more ergonomically correct jewelers' benches has eliminated most of the strain and discomfort caused by spending long periods bending over a workbench in one position.

Lasers require both careful handling to avoid injury and steady hands to direct precision tasks. In larger manufacturing plants and some smaller repair shops, chemicals, sharp or pointed tools, and jewelers' torches pose safety threats and may cause injury if proper care is not taken. Most dangerous chemicals, however, have been replaced with synthetic, less toxic products to meet safety requirements.

In repair shops, jewelers usually work alone with little supervision. In retail stores, they may talk with customers about repairs, perform custom design work, and even do some selling. Because many of their materials are valuable, jewelers must observe strict security procedures, including working behind locked doors that are opened only by a buzzer, working on the other side of barred windows, making use of burglar alarms, and, in larger jewelry establishments, working in the presence of armed guards.

Training, Other Qualifications, and Advancement

Jewelers usually learn their trade in vocational or technical schools, through distance-learning centers, or on the job. Colleges and art and design schools offer programs that can lead to the degree of bachelor of fine arts, or master of fine arts, in jewelry design. Formal training in the basic skills of the trade enhances one's employment and advancement opportunities. Many employers prefer jewelers with design, repair, and sales skills.

For those interested in working in a jewelry store or repair shop, vocational and technical training or courses offered by public and private colleges are the best sources of training. In these programs, which can vary in length from 6 months to 1 year, students learn the use and care of jewelers' tools and machines and basic jewelry-making and jewelry-repairing skills, such as designing, casting, and setting and polishing stones. Technical school courses also cover

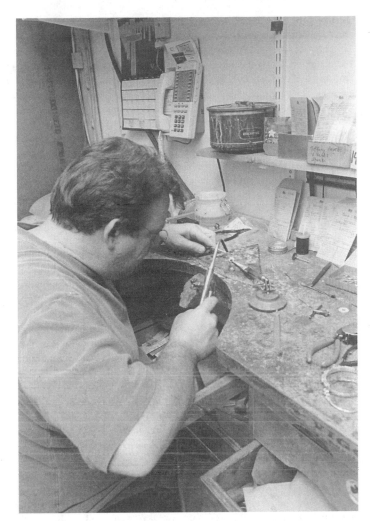

Jewelers and precious stone and metal workers use both common and specialized tools to make pieces of jewelry.

topics such as blueprint reading, math, and shop theory. To enter some technical school programs and most college programs, a high school diploma or its equivalent is required. However, some schools specializing in jewelry training do not require graduation from high school. Computer-aided design is being used increasingly in the jewelry field, and students—especially those interested in design and manufacturing—may wish to obtain training in CAD; however, most employers will provide such training.

Various institutes offer courses and programs in gemology. Programs cover a wide range of topics, including the identification and grading of diamonds and gem stones.

Most employers feel that vocational school and technical school graduates need up to a year of additional supervised on-the-job training or apprenticeship in order to refine their repair skills and learn more about the operation of the store or shop. In addition, some employers encourage workers to improve their skills by enrolling in short-term technical school courses such as fabricating, jewelry design, jewelry manufacturing, wax carving, and gemology. Employers may pay all or part of the cost of this additional training.

In jewelry manufacturing plants, workers traditionally develop their skills through informal apprenticeships and on-the-job training. The apprenticeship or training period lasts up to 1 year, depending on the difficulty of the specialty. Training usually focuses on casting, setting stones, making models, or engraving. In recent years, a growing number of technical schools have begun to offer training designed for jewelers working in manufacturing. Employers in manufacturing may prefer graduates of these programs because they are familiar with the production process, requiring less on-the-job training.

The precise and delicate nature of jewelry work requires finger and hand dexterity, good hand-eye coordination, patience, and concentration. Artistic ability and fashion consciousness are major assets, because jewelry must be stylish and attractive. Those who work in jewelry stores have frequent contact with customers and should be neat, personable, and knowledgeable about the merchandise. In addition, employers require workers of good character, because jewelers work with valuable materials.

Advancement opportunities are limited and depend greatly on an individual's skill and initiative. In manufacturing, some jewelers advance to supervisory jobs, such as master jeweler or head jeweler, but for most, advancement takes the form of higher pay for doing the same job. Jewelers who work in jewelry stores or repair shops may become managers; some open their own businesses.

Those interested in starting their own business should first establish themselves and build a reputation for their work within the jewelry trade. Once they obtain sufficient credit from jewelry suppliers and wholesalers, they can acquire the necessary inventory. Also, because the jewelry business is highly competitive, jewelers who plan to open their own store should have sales experience, as well as knowledge of marketing and business management. Courses in these areas often are available from technical schools and community colleges.

Employment

Jewelers and precious stone and metal workers held about 42,000 jobs in 2004. About 40 percent of these workers were self-employed; many operated their own store or repair shop, and some specialized in designing and creating custom jewelry.

About 1 out of 5 jobs for jewelers and precious stone and metal workers were in other miscellaneous manufacturing, which includes jewelry and silverware manufacturing. Another 3 out of 10 jobs were in retail trade, primarily in jewelry, luggage, and leather goods stores. A small number of jobs were with merchant wholesalers of miscellaneous durable goods and in repair shops providing repair and maintenance of personal and household goods. Although jewelry stores and repair shops were found in every city and in many small towns, most jobs were in larger metropolitan areas. In 2004, many jewelers employed in manufacturing worked in Rhode Island, New York, or California.

Job Outlook

Employment of jewelers and precious stone and metal workers is expected to decline slightly through 2014. Employment opportunities, however, should be excellent. New jewelers will be needed to replace those who retire or who leave the occupation for other reasons. When master jewelers retire, they take with them years of experience that require substantial time and financial resources to replace. Many employers have difficulty finding and retaining jewelers with the right skills and the necessary knowledge. Some technological advances have made jewelrymaking more efficient; however, many tasks cannot be fully automated. Jewelry work is a labor-intensive process that requires excellent handiwork.

The increasing numbers of affluent individuals, working women, double-income households, and fashion-conscious men are expected to keep jewelry sales strong. The population aged 45 and older, which accounts for a major portion of jewelry sales, also is on the rise.

Nontraditional jewelry marketers, such as discount stores, mail-order and catalogue companies, television shopping networks, and Internet retailers, have expanded the number of buying options and increased their sales volume. However, these establishments require fewer sales staff, limiting employment opportunities for jewelers and precious stone and metal workers who work mainly in sales. Because such establishments enjoy increases in sales, however, they will need highly skilled jewelers to make and repair the jewelry they sell.

Opportunities in jewelry stores and repair shops will be best for graduates from training programs for jewelers or gemologists. Despite an increase in sales by nontraditional jewelry marketers, traditional jewelers should not be affected greatly, because they have the advantage of being able to build client relationships based on trust. Many clients prefer to work directly with a jeweler, to ensure that the product is of the highest quality and meets their specifications. Many traditional jewelers expand their businesses as clients recommend their services to friends and relatives.

The jewelry industry can be cyclical. During economic downturns, demand for jewelry products and for jewelers tends to decrease. However, demand for repair workers should remain strong even during economic slowdowns, because maintaining and repairing jewelry is an ongoing process. In fact, demand for jewelry repair may increase during recessions, as people repair or restore existing pieces rather than purchase new ones. Also, many nontraditional vendors typically do not offer repair services.

Within manufacturing, increasing automation will adversely affect employment of low-skilled occupations, such as assemblers and polishers. Automation will have a lesser impact on more creative, highly skilled positions, such as moldmakers and modelmakers. Furthermore, small manufacturers, which typify the industry, will have an increasingly difficult time competing with the larger manufacturers when it comes to supplying large retailers.

Because of recent international trade agreements, exports are increasing modestly as manufacturers become more competitive in foreign markets. However, imports from foreign manufacturers are increasing more rapidly than exports, due to these same agreements. Imports compete mainly with mass-produced jewelry. Therefore, employment in luxury and custom jewelry manufacturing is least susceptible to decline caused by import competition.

Earnings

Median annual earnings for jewelers and precious stone and metal workers were $27,400 in May 2004. The middle 50 percent earned between $20,510 and $37,280. The lowest 10 percent earned less than $16,040, and the highest 10 percent earned more than $49,020. In May 2004, median annual earnings in the industries employing the largest numbers of jewelers and precious stone and metal workers were $30,530 in jewelry, luggage, and leather goods stores and $23,590 in other miscellaneous manufacturing.

Most jewelers start out with a base salary, but once they become more proficient, they may begin charging by the number of pieces completed. Jewelers who work in retail stores may earn a commission for each piece of jewelry sold. Many jewelers also enjoy a variety of benefits, including reimbursement from their employers for work-related courses and discounts on jewelry purchases.

Related Occupations

Jewelers and precious stone and metal workers do precision handwork. Other skilled workers who do similar jobs include precision instrument and equipment repairers; welding, soldering, and brazing workers; and woodworkers. Some jewelers and precious stone and metal workers create their own jewelry designs. Other occupations that require visual arts abilities include artists and related workers, and various designers—commercial and industrial, fashion, floral, graphic, and interior. Finally, some jewelers and precious stone and metal workers are involved in the buying and selling of stones, metals, or finished pieces of jewelry. Similar occupations include retail salespersons and sales representatives in wholesale trade.

Sources of Additional Information

Information on job opportunities and training programs for jewelers is available from:

➤ Gemological Institute of America, 5345 Armada Dr., Carlsbad, CA 92008. Internet: **http://www.gia.edu**

For information on the jewelry industry and on schools offering jewelry-related programs and degrees by State, contact:

➤ Manufacturing Jewelers and Suppliers of America, 45 Royal Little Dr., Providence, RI 02904.

To receive a list of accredited technical schools that have programs in gemology, contact:

➤ Accrediting Commission of Career Schools and Colleges of Technology, 2101 Wilson Blvd., Suite 302, Arlington, VA 22201. Internet: **http://www.accsct.org**

For more information about careers in the jewelry industry, including different career paths, training options, and a list of schools, contact:

➤ Jewelers of America, 52 Vanderbilt Ave., 19th Floor, New York, NY 10017. Internet: **http://www.jewelers.org**

Medical, Dental, and Ophthalmic Laboratory Technicians

(O*NET 51-9081.00, 51-9082.00, 51-9083.01, 51-9083.02)

Significant Points

- Around 3 out of 5 salaried jobs were in medical equipment and supply manufacturing laboratories, which usually are small, privately owned businesses with fewer than 5 employees.

- Most medical, dental, and ophthalmic laboratory technicians learn their craft on the job; however, many employers prefer to hire those with formal training in a related field.

- Slower-than-average employment growth is expected for dental and ophthalmic laboratory technicians, while average employment growth is expected for medical appliance technicians.

- Job opportunities should be favorable as employers have difficulty filling trainee positions.

Nature of the Work

When patients require a special appliance to see clearly, chew and speak well, or walk, their health care providers send requests to medical, dental, and ophthalmic laboratory technicians. These technicians produce a wide variety of appliances to help patients.

Medical appliance technicians construct, fit, maintain, and repair braces, artificial limbs, joints, arch supports, and other surgical and medical appliances. They read prescriptions or detailed information from orthotists, podiatrists, or prosthetists. Orthotists treat patients who need braces, supports, or corrective shoes. Podiatrists are doctors who treat foot problems and request the same appliances as orthotists. Prosthetists work with patients who need a replacement limb, such as an arm, leg, hand, or foot, due to a birth defect or an accident. The appliances are called orthoses and prostheses. Medical appliance technicians are also referred to as orthotic and prosthetic technicians.

For orthoses such as arch supports, technicians first make a wax or plastic impression of the patient's foot. Then they bend and form a material so that it conforms to prescribed contours required to fabricate structural components. If a support is mainly required to correct the balance of a patient with legs of different lengths, a rigid material is used. If the support is primarily intended to protect those with arthritic or diabetic feet, a soft material is used. Supports and braces are polished with grinding and buffing wheels. Technicians may cover arch supports with felt to make them more comfortable.

For prostheses, technicians construct or receive a plaster cast of the patient's limb to use as a pattern. Then, they lay out parts and use precision measuring instruments to measure them. Technicians may use wood, plastic, metal, or other material for the parts of the artificial limb. Next, they carve, cut, or grind the material using hand or power tools. Then, they drill holes for rivets and glue, rivet, or weld the parts together. They are able to do very precise work using common tools. Next, technicians use grinding and buffing wheels to smooth and polish artificial limbs. Lastly, they may cover or pad the limbs with rubber, leather, felt, plastic, or another material. Also, technicians may mix pigments according to formulas to match the patient's skin color and apply the mixture to the artificial limb.

After fabrication, medical appliance technicians test devices for proper alignment, movement, and biomechanical stability using meters and alignment fixtures. They also may fit the appliance on the patient and adjust them as necessary. Over time the appliance will wear down, so technicians must repair and maintain the device. They also may service and repair the machinery used for the fabrication of orthotic and prosthetic devices.

Dental laboratory technicians fill prescriptions from dentists for crowns, bridges, dentures, and other dental prosthetics. First, dentists send a specification of the item to be manufactured, along with an impression (mold) of the patient's mouth or teeth. Then, dental laboratory technicians, also called dental technicians, create a model of the patient's mouth by pouring plaster into the impression and allowing it to set. Next, they place the model on an apparatus that mimics the bite and movement of the patient's jaw. The model serves as the basis of the prosthetic device. Technicians examine the model, noting the size and shape of the adjacent teeth, as well as gaps within the gumline. Based upon these observations and the dentist's specifications, technicians build and shape a wax tooth or teeth model, using small hand instruments called wax spatulas and wax carvers. They use this wax model to cast the metal framework for the prosthetic device.

After the wax tooth has been formed, dental technicians pour the cast and form the metal and, using small hand-held tools, prepare the surface to allow the metal and porcelain to bond. They then apply porcelain in layers, to arrive at the precise shape and color of a tooth. Technicians place the tooth in a porcelain furnace to bake the porcelain onto the metal framework, and then adjust the shape and color, with subsequent grinding and addition of porcelain to achieve a sealed finish. The final product is a nearly exact replica of the lost tooth or teeth.

In some laboratories, technicians perform all stages of the work, whereas, in other labs, each technician does only a few. Dental laboratory technicians can specialize in 1 of 5 areas: orthodontic appliances, crowns and bridges, complete dentures, partial dentures, or ceramics. Job titles can reflect specialization in these areas. For example, technicians who make porcelain and acrylic restorations are called *dental ceramists*.

Ophthalmic laboratory technicians—also known as manufacturing opticians, optical mechanics, or optical goods workers—make prescription eyeglass or contact lenses. Prescription lenses are curved in such a way that light is correctly focused onto the retina of the patient's eye, improving his or her vision. Some ophthalmic laboratory technicians manufacture lenses for other optical instruments, such as telescopes and binoculars. Ophthalmic laboratory technicians cut, grind, edge, and finish lenses according to specifications provided by dispensing opticians, optometrists, or ophthalmologists and may insert lenses into frames to produce finished glasses. Although some lenses still are produced by hand, technicians are increasingly using automated equipment to make lenses.

Ophthalmic laboratory technicians should not be confused with workers in other vision care occupations. Ophthalmologists and optometrists are "eye doctors" who examine eyes, diagnose and treat vision problems, and prescribe corrective lenses. Ophthalmologists are physicians who perform eye surgery. Dispensing opticians, who also may do the work of ophthalmic laboratory technicians, help patients select frames and lenses, and adjust finished eyeglasses. (See the statement on physicians and surgeons, which includes ophthalmologists, as well as the statements on optometrists and opticians, dispensing, elsewhere in the *Handbook*.)

Ophthalmic laboratory technicians read prescription specifications, select standard glass or plastic lens blanks, and then mark them to indicate where the curves specified on the prescription should be ground. They place the lens in the lens grinder, set the dials for the prescribed curvature, and start the machine. After a minute or so, the lens is ready to be "finished" by a machine that rotates it against a fine abrasive, to grind it and smooth out rough edges. The lens is then placed in a polishing machine with an even finer abrasive, to polish it to a smooth, bright finish.

Next, the technician examines the lens through a lensometer, an instrument similar in shape to a microscope, to make sure that the degree and placement of the curve are correct. The technician then cuts the lenses and bevels the edges to fit the frame, dips each lens into dye if the prescription calls for tinted or coated lenses, polishes

Dental laboratory technicians use Bunsen burners, grinding and polishing equipment, and hand instruments, such as wax spatulas and wax carvers.

the edges, and assembles the lenses and frame parts into a finished pair of glasses.

In small laboratories, technicians usually handle every phase of the operation. In large ones, in which virtually every phase of the operation is automated, technicians may be responsible for operating computerized equipment. Technicians also inspect the final product for quality and accuracy.

Working Conditions
Medical, dental, and ophthalmic laboratory technicians generally work in clean, well-lighted, and well-ventilated laboratories. They have limited contact with the public. Salaried laboratory technicians usually work 40 hours a week, but some work part time. At times, technicians wear goggles to protect their eyes, gloves to handle hot objects, or masks to avoid inhaling dust. They may spend a great deal of time standing.

Dental technicians usually have their own workbenches, which can be equipped with Bunsen burners, grinding and polishing equipment, and hand instruments, such as wax spatulas and wax carvers. Some dental technicians have computer-aided milling equipment to assist them with creating artificial teeth.

Training, Other Qualifications, and Advancement
Most medical, dental, and ophthalmic laboratory technicians learn their craft on the job; however, many employers prefer to hire those with formal training in a related field.

Medical appliance technicians begin as a helper and gradually learn new skills as they gain experience. Formal training is also available. There are currently 4 programs actively accredited by the National Commission on Orthotic and Prosthetic Education (NCOPE). These programs offer either an associate degree for orthotics and prosthetic technicians or one-year certificate for orthotic technicians or prosthetic technicians. The programs instruct students on human anatomy and physiology, orthotic and prosthetic equipment and materials, and applied biomechanical principles to customize orthoses or prostheses. The programs also include clinical rotations to provide hands-on experience.

Voluntary certification is available through the American Board for Certification in Orthotics and Prosthetics (ABC). Applicants are eligible for an exam after completing a program accredited by NCOPE or obtaining two years of experience as a technician under the direct supervision of an ABC-certified practitioner. After successfully passing the appropriate exam, technicians receive the Registered Orthotic Technician, Registered Prosthetic Technician, or Registered Prosthetic-Orthotic Technician credential.

High school students interested in becoming medical appliance technicians should take mathematics, metal and wood shop, and drafting. With additional formal education, medical appliance technicians can advance to become orthotists or prosthetists.

Dental laboratory technicians begin with simple tasks, such as pouring plaster into an impression, and progress to more complex procedures, such as making porcelain crowns and bridges. Becoming a fully trained technician requires an average of 3 to 4 years, depending upon the individual's aptitude and ambition, but it may take a few years more to become an accomplished technician.

Training in dental laboratory technology also is available through community and junior colleges, vocational-technical institutes, and the U.S. Armed Forces. Formal training programs vary greatly both in length and in the level of skill they impart.

In 2004, 25 programs in dental laboratory technology were approved (accredited) by the Commission on Dental Accreditation in conjunction with the American Dental Association (ADA). These programs provide classroom instruction in dental materials science, oral anatomy, fabrication procedures, ethics, and related subjects. In addition, each student is given supervised practical experience in a school or an associated dental laboratory. Accredited programs normally take 2 years to complete and lead to an associate degree. A few programs take about 4 years to complete and offer a bachelor's degree in dental technology.

Graduates of 2-year training programs need additional hands-on experience to become fully qualified. Each dental laboratory owner operates in a different way, and classroom instruction does not necessarily expose students to techniques and procedures favored by individual laboratory owners. Students who have taken enough courses to learn the basics of the craft usually are considered good candidates for training, regardless of whether they have completed a formal program. Many employers will train someone without any classroom experience.

The National Board for Certification, an independent board established by the National Association of Dental Laboratories, offers certification in dental laboratory technology. Certification, which is voluntary, can be obtained in five specialty areas: crowns and bridges, ceramics, partial dentures, complete dentures, and orthodontic appliances.

In large dental laboratories, technicians may become supervisors or managers. Experienced technicians may teach or may take jobs with dental suppliers in such areas as product development, marketing, and sales. Still, for most technicians, opening one's own laboratory is the way toward advancement and higher earnings.

A high degree of manual dexterity, good vision, and the ability to recognize very fine color shadings and variations in shape are necessary. An artistic aptitude for detailed and precise work also is important. High school students interested in becoming dental laboratory technicians should take courses in art, metal and wood shop, drafting, and sciences. Courses in management and business may help those wishing to operate their own laboratories.

Ophthalmic laboratory technicians start on simple tasks if they are trained to produce lenses by hand. They may begin with marking or blocking lenses for grinding; then, they progress to grinding, cutting, edging, and beveling lenses; finally, they are trained in assembling the eyeglasses. Depending on individual aptitude, it may take up to 6 months to become proficient in all phases of the work.

Employers filling trainee jobs prefer applicants who are high school graduates. Courses in science, mathematics, and computers are valuable; manual dexterity and the ability to do precision work are essential. Technicians using automated systems will find computer skills valuable.

A very small number of ophthalmic laboratory technicians learn their trade in the Armed Forces or in the few programs in optical technology offered by vocational-technical institutes or trade schools. These programs have classes in optical theory, surfacing and lens finishing, and the reading and applying of prescriptions. Programs vary in length from 6 months to 1 year and award certificates or diplomas.

Ophthalmic laboratory technicians can become supervisors and managers. Some become dispensing opticians, although further education or training generally is required in that occupation.

Employment

Medical, dental, and ophthalmic laboratory technicians held about 87,000 jobs in 2004. Around 3 out of 5 salaried jobs were in medical equipment and supply manufacturing laboratories, which usually are small, privately owned businesses with fewer than five employees. However, some laboratories are large; a few employ more than 1,000 workers.

Employment by detailed occupation is presented in the following tabulation:

Dental laboratory technicians 50,000
Ophthalmic laboratory technicians 25,000
Medical appliance technicians 11,000

Some medical appliance technicians worked in health and personal care stores, while others worked in public and private hospitals, professional and commercial equipment and supplies merchant wholesalers, offices of physicians, or consumer goods rental centers. Some were self-employed.

Some dental laboratory technicians work in offices of dentists. Others work for hospitals providing dental services, including U.S. Department of Veterans Affairs hospitals. Some dental laboratory technicians open their own offices or work in dental laboratories in their homes.

Around 30 percent of ophthalmic laboratory technicians were in health and personal care stores, such as optical goods stores that manufacture and sell prescription glasses and contact lenses. Some were in offices of optometrists or ophthalmologists. Others worked at professional and commercial equipment and supplies merchant wholesalers. A few worked in commercial and service industry machine manufacturing firms that produce lenses for other optical instruments, such as telescopes and binoculars.

Job Outlook

Job opportunities for medical, dental, and ophthalmic laboratory technicians should be favorable, despite expected slower-than-average growth in overall employment through the year 2014. Employers have difficulty filling trainee positions, probably because entry-level salaries are relatively low and because the public is not familiar with these occupations. Most job openings will arise from the need to replace technicians who transfer to other occupations or who leave the labor force.

Medical appliance technicians will grow faster than dental and ophthalmic laboratory technicians, with employment projected to increase about as fast as the average for all occupations, due to the increasing prevalence of the two leading causes of limb loss—diabetes and cardiovascular disease. Advances in technology may spur demand for prostheses that allow for greater movement.

During the last few years, demand has arisen from an aging public that is growing increasingly interested in cosmetic prostheses. For example, many dental laboratories are filling orders for composite fillings that are the same shade of white as natural teeth to replace older, less attractive fillings. However, job growth for dental laboratory technicians will be limited. The overall dental health of the population has improved because of fluoridation of drinking water, which has reduced the incidence of dental cavities, and greater emphasis on preventive dental care since the early 1960s. As a result, full dentures will be less common, as most people will need only a bridge or crown.

Demographic trends also make it likely that many more Americans will need vision care in the years ahead. Not only will the population grow, but also, the proportion of middle-aged and older adults is projected to increase rapidly. Middle age is a time when many people use corrective lenses for the first time, and elderly persons usually require more vision care than others. However, the increasing use of automated machinery will limit job growth for ophthalmic laboratory technicians.

Earnings

Median hourly earnings of medical appliance technicians were $13.38 in May 2004. The middle 50 percent earned between $10.46 and $18.22 an hour. The lowest 10 percent earned less than $8.21, and the highest 10 percent earned more than $23.66 an hour. Median hourly earnings of medical appliance technicians in May 2004 were $13.00 in medical equipment and supplies manufacturing.

Median hourly earnings of dental laboratory technicians were $14.93 in May 2004. The middle 50 percent earned between $11.18 and $19.71 an hour. The lowest 10 percent earned less than $8.86, and the highest 10 percent earned more than $25.48 an hour. Median hourly earnings of dental laboratory technicians in May 2004 were $15.95 in offices of dentists and $14.40 in medical equipment and supplies manufacturing.

Dental technicians in large laboratories tend to specialize in a few procedures and, therefore, tend to be paid a lower wage than those employed in small laboratories who perform a variety of tasks.

Median hourly earnings of ophthalmic laboratory technicians were $11.40 in May 2004. The middle 50 percent earned between $9.33 and $14.67 an hour. The lowest 10 percent earned less than $7.89, and the highest 10 percent earned more than $17.61 an hour. Median hourly earnings of ophthalmic laboratory technicians in May 2004 were $10.88 in health and personal care stores and $10.79 in medical equipment and supplies manufacturing.

Related Occupations

Medical, dental, and ophthalmic laboratory technicians manufacture a variety of health implements, such as artificial limbs, corrective lenses, and artificial teeth, following specifications and instructions provided by health care practitioners. Other workers who make and repair medical devices or other items include dispensing opticians, orthotists and prosthetists, and precision instrument and equipment repairers.

Sources of Additional Information

For information on careers in orthotics and prosthetics, contact:
➤ American Academy of Orthotists and Prosthetists, 526 King St., Suite 201, Alexandria, VA 22314. Internet: **http://www.opcareers.org**

For a list of accredited programs for orthotic and prosthetic technicians, contact:
➤ National Commission on Orthotic and Prosthetic Education, 330 John Carlyle St., Suite 200, Alexandria, VA 22314. Internet: **http://www.ncope.org**

For a list of accredited programs in dental laboratory technology, contact:
➤ Commission on Dental Accreditation, American Dental Association, 211 E. Chicago Ave., Chicago, IL 60611. Internet: **http://www.ada.org**

For information on requirements for certification of dental laboratory technicians, contact:
➤ National Board for Certification in Dental Technology, 325 John Knox Rd., L103, Tallahassee, FL 32303. Internet: **http://www.nbccert.org**

For information on career opportunities in commercial dental laboratories, contact:
➤ National Association of Dental Laboratories, 325 John Knox Rd., L103, Tallahassee, FL 32303. Internet: **http://www.nadl.org**

For information on an accredited program in ophthalmic laboratory technology, contact:
➤ Commission on Opticianry Accreditation, 8665 Sudley Rd., #341, Manassas VA 20110.

General information on grants and scholarships is available from individual schools. State employment service offices can provide information about job openings for medical, dental, and ophthalmic laboratory technicians.

Painting and Coating Workers, Except Construction and Maintenance

(O*NET 51-9121.01, 51-9121.02, 51-9122.00, 51-9123.00)

Significant Points

● About 70 percent of jobs are in manufacturing establishments.

● Most workers acquire their skills on the job; for most operators, training lasts from a few days to several months, but becoming skilled in all aspects of automotive painting usually requires 1 to 2 years.

● Overall employment is projected to grow more slowly than average; transportation equipment painters are expected to grow about as fast as average, while coating, painting, and spraying machine setters, operators, and tenders are expected to decline.

Nature of the Work

Millions of items ranging from cars to candy are covered by paint, plastic, varnish, chocolate, or some other type of coating solution. Often, the protection provided by the paint or coating is essential to the product, as with the coating of insulating material covering wires and other electrical and electronic components. Also, many paints and coatings have dual purposes; for example, the paint finish on an automobile heightens the visual appearance of the vehicle while providing protection from corrosion.

Coating, painting, and spraying machine setters, operators, and tenders control the machinery that applies these paints and coatings to a wide range of manufactured products. Perhaps the most straightforward technique is simply dipping an item in a large vat of paint or other coating. This is the technique used by *dippers*, who immerse racks or baskets of articles in vats of paint, liquid plastic, or other solutions by means of a power hoist. Similarly, *tumbling barrel painters* deposit articles made of porous materials into a barrel of paint, varnish, or other coating; the barrel is then rotated to ensure thorough coverage.

Another familiar technique is spraying products with a solution of paint or some other coating. *Spray machine operators* use spray guns to coat metal, wood, ceramic, fabric, paper, and food products with paint and other coating solutions. Following a formula, operators fill the machine's tanks with a mixture of paints or chemicals, adding prescribed amounts of solution. Then they adjust nozzles on the guns to obtain the proper dispersion of the spray, and they hold or position the guns so as to direct the spray onto the article. Operators also check the flow and viscosity of the paint or solution and visually inspect the quality of the coating. When products are drying, these workers often must regulate the temperature and air circulation in drying ovens. Individuals who paint, coat, or decorate articles such as furniture, glass, pottery, toys, cakes, and books are known as *painting, coating, and decorating workers*.

Painting and coating workers use various types of machines to coat a range of products. Frequently, their job title reflects the specialized nature of the machine or of the coating being applied. For example, *enrobing machine operators* coat, or "enrobe," confectionery, bakery, and other food products with melted chocolate, cheese, oils, sugar, or other substances. *Paper coating machine operators* spray "size" on rolls of paper to give it its gloss or finish. *Silvering applicators* spray silver, tin, and copper solutions on glass in the manufacture of mirrors.

In response to concerns about air pollution and worker safety, manufacturers increasingly are using new types of paints and coatings, instead of high-solvent paints, on their products. Water-based paints and powder coatings are two of the most common. These compounds do not emit as many volatile organic compounds into the air and can be applied to a variety of products. Powder coatings are sprayed much as are liquid paints and then are heated to melt and cure the coating.

The adoption of new types of paints often is accompanied by a conversion to more automated painting equipment that the operator sets and monitors. When using these machines, operators position the automatic spray guns, set the nozzles, and synchronize the action of the guns with the speed of the conveyor carrying articles through the machine and drying ovens. The operator also may add solvents or water to the paint vessel, thereby preparing the paint for application. During the operation of the equipment, these workers tend painting machines, observe gauges on the control panel, and check articles for evidence of any variation from specifications. The operator then uses a spray gun to "touch up" spots where necessary.

Although the majority of painting and coating workers are employed in manufacturing, the best known group refinishes old and damaged cars, trucks, and buses in automotive body repair and paint shops. *Transportation equipment painters*, or *automotive painters*, are among the most highly skilled manual spray operators, because they perform intricate, detailed work and mix paints to match the original color, a task that is especially difficult if the color has faded.

To prepare a vehicle for painting, painters or their helpers use power sanders and sandpaper to remove the original paint or rust and then fill small dents and scratches with body filler. They also remove or mask parts they do not want to paint, such as chrome trim, headlights, windows, and mirrors. Automotive painters use a spray gun to apply several coats of paint. They apply enamel or water-based primers to vehicles with metal bodies and flexible primers to newer vehicles with plastic body parts. Controlling the spray gun by hand, they apply successive coats until the finish of the repaired sections of the vehicle matches that of the original, undamaged portions. To speed drying between coats, they may place the freshly painted vehicle under heat lamps or in a special infrared oven. After each coat of primer dries, they sand the surface to remove any irregularities and to improve the adhesion of the next coat. Final sanding of the primers may be done by hand with a fine grade of sandpaper. A sealer then is applied and allowed to dry, followed by the final topcoat.

Working Conditions

Painting and coating workers typically work indoors and may be exposed to dangerous fumes from paint and coating solutions. Although painting usually is done in special ventilated booths, operators typically wear masks or respirators that cover their noses and mouths, even in such booths. In addition, Federal legislation has led to a decrease in workers' exposure to hazardous chemicals by regulating emissions of volatile organic compounds and other hazardous air pollutants. This legislation also has led to the increasing use of more sophisticated paint booths and fresh-air systems that provide a safer work environment.

Operators have to stand for long periods, and when using a spray gun, they may have to bend, stoop, or crouch in uncomfortable positions to reach different parts of the article. Most operators work a normal 40-hour week, but self-employed automotive painters sometimes work more than 50 hours a week, depending on the number of vehicles customers want repainted.

Training, Other Qualifications, and Advancement

Most painting and coating workers acquire their skills on the job, usually by watching and helping other, more experienced workers.

To minimize exposure to harmful chemicals, painting and coating workers must wear protective masks when performing certain tasks.

For most setters, operators, and tenders, as well as for painting, coating, and decorating workers, training lasts from a few days to several months. Coating, painting, and spraying machine setters, operators, and tenders who modify the operation of computer-controlled equipment while it is running may require additional training in computer operations and minor programming.

Similarly, most transportation equipment painters start as helpers and gain their skills informally on the job. Becoming skilled in all aspects of automotive painting usually requires 1 to 2 years of on-the-job training. Beginning helpers usually remove trim, clean and sand surfaces to be painted, mask surfaces they do not want painted, and polish finished work. As helpers gain experience, they progress to more complicated tasks, such as mixing paint to achieve a good match and using spray guns to apply primer coats or final coats to small areas.

Painters should have keen eyesight and a good sense of color. The completion of high school generally is not required, but is advantageous. Additional instruction is offered at many community colleges and vocational or technical schools. Such programs enhance one's employment prospects and can speed promotion to the next level.

Some employers sponsor training programs to help their workers become more productive. Training is available from manufacturers of chemicals, paints, or equipment or from other private sources and may include safety and quality tips, as well as impart knowledge of products, equipment, and general business practices. Some automotive painters are sent to technical schools to learn the intricacies of mixing and applying different types of paint.

Voluntary certification by the National Institute for Automotive Service Excellence (ASE) is recognized as the standard of achievement for automotive painters. For certification, painters must pass a written examination and have at least 2 years of experience in the field. High school, trade or vocational school, or community or junior college training in automotive refinishing that meets ASE standards may substitute for up to 1 year of experience. To retain their certification, painters must retake the examination at least every 5 years.

Experienced painting and coating workers with leadership ability may become team leaders or supervisors. Those who acquire practical experience, college, or other formal training may become sales or technical representatives for chemical or paint companies. Eventually, some automotive painters open their own shops.

Employment

Painting and coating workers held about 186,000 jobs in 2004. Lesser skilled coating, painting, and spraying machine setters, operators, and tenders accounted for about 103,000 jobs, while more skilled transportation equipment painters constituted about 53,000. Another 29,000 jobs were held by painting, coating, and decorating workers.

Approximately 70 percent of salaried jobs were found in manufacturing establishments, where the workers applied coatings to items such as fabricated metal products, motor vehicles and related equipment, industrial machines, household and office furniture, and plastic, wood, and paper products. Outside manufacturing, workers included automotive painters employed by independent automotive repair shops and workers employed by body repair and paint shops operated by retail motor vehicle dealers. About 6 percent of painting and coating workers were self-employed.

Job Outlook

Overall employment of painting and coating workers is expected to grow more slowly than the average for all occupations through the year 2014. Employment growth for highly skilled transportation painters and automotive refinishers is projected to be faster than for painting, coating, and decorating workers. In addition to jobs arising from growth, some jobs will become available each year as employers replace experienced operators who transfer to other occupations or leave the labor force.

Despite increasing demand for manufactured goods, employment of coating, painting, and spraying machine setters, operators, and tenders is expected to decline as part of that demand will be met by products manufactured abroad. Employment will be further decreased by improvements in the automation of paint and coating applications that will raise worker productivity. For example, operators will be able to coat goods more rapidly as they use sophisticated industrial machinery that moves and aims spray guns more efficiently. Legislation has set limits on the emissions of ozone-forming volatile organic compounds and is expected to impede job growth among operators in manufacturing. As manufacturing firms switch to water-based and powder coatings to comply with the law, they will introduce more efficient automation.

Painting, coating, and decorating workers should grow more slowly than the average for all occupations. Increasing demand for hand-painted tiles and related specialty products will lead to growth among these workers. Although competition from imports should temper increases in employment, the specialized skills required by workers in this occupation should keep them from seeing as much of an impact of automation on employment.

Since the detailed work of refinishing automobiles in collision repair shops and motor vehicle dealerships does not lend itself to automation, painters employed in these establishments are projected to experience employment growth about as fast as the average for all occupations. As the demand for refinishing continues to grow, slower productivity growth among these workers will lead to employment increases that are more in line with the growing demand for their services.

The number of job openings for painting and coating workers in manufacturing industries may fluctuate from year to year due to cyclical changes in economic conditions. When demand for manufactured goods lessens, production may be suspended or reduced, and workers may be laid off or face a shortened workweek. Automotive painters, by contrast, can expect relatively steady work because automobiles damaged in accidents require repair and refinishing regardless of the state of the economy.

Earnings

Median hourly earnings of coating, painting, and spraying machine setters, operators, and tenders were $12.64 in May 2004. The middle 50 percent earned between $10.16 and $15.78 an hour. The lowest 10 percent earned less than $8.54, and the highest 10 percent earned more than $19.39 an hour.

Median hourly earnings of transportation equipment painters were $16.89 in May 2004. The middle 50 percent earned between $12.85 and $22.74 an hour. The lowest 10 percent earned less than $10.17, and the highest 10 percent earned more than $27.52 an hour. Median hourly earnings of transportation equipment painters were $16.84 in automotive repair and maintenance shops and $24.13 in motor vehicle manufacturing.

Median hourly earnings of painting, coating, and decorating workers were $10.95 in May 2004. The middle 50 percent earned between $8.76 and $13.94 an hour. The lowest 10 percent earned less than $7.44, and the highest 10 percent earned more than $18.23 an hour.

Many automotive painters employed by motor vehicle dealers and independent automotive repair shops receive a commission based on the labor cost charged to the customer. Under this method, earnings depend largely on the amount of work a painter does and how fast it is completed. Employers frequently guarantee commissioned painters a minimum weekly salary. Helpers and trainees usually receive an hourly rate until they become sufficiently skilled to work on commission. Trucking companies, bus lines, and other organizations that repair and refinish their own vehicles usually pay by the hour.

Many painting and coating machine operators belong to unions, including the International Brotherhood of Painters and Allied Trades, the Sheet Metal Workers International Association, and the International Brotherhood of Teamsters. Most union operators work for manufacturers and large motor vehicle dealers.

Related Occupations

Other occupations similar to painting and coating workers include painters and paperhangers, woodworkers, and machine setters, operators, and tenders—metal and plastic.

Sources of Additional Information

For more details about work opportunities, contact local manufacturers, automotive body repair shops, motor vehicle dealers, vocational schools, locals of unions representing painting and coating workers, or the local office of the State employment service. The State employment service also may be a source of information about training programs.

Information on how to become a certified automotive painter is available from:
➤ National Institute for Automotive Service Excellence (ASE), 101 Blue Seal Dr. S.E., Leesburg, VA 20175. Internet: **http://www.ase.com**

Photographic Process Workers and Processing Machine Operators

(O*NET 51-9131.01, 51-9131.02, 51-9131.03, 51-9131.04, 51-9132.00)

Significant Points

- A decline in employment is expected as digital photography becomes commonplace.
- Most receive on-the-job training from their companies, manufacturers' representatives, and experienced workers.
- Job opportunities will be best for individuals with experience using computers and digital technology.

Nature of the Work

Both amateur and professional photographers rely heavily on photographic process workers and processing machine operators to develop film, make prints or slides, and do related tasks, such as enlarging or retouching photographs. *Photographic processing machine operators* operate various machines, such as mounting presses and motion picture film printing, photographic printing, and film developing machines. *Photographic process workers* perform more delicate tasks, such as retouching photographic negatives, prints and images to emphasize or correct specific features.

Photographic processing machine operators often have specialized jobs. *Film process technicians* operate machines that develop exposed photographic film or sensitized paper in a series of chemical and water baths to produce negative or positive images. First, technicians mix developing and fixing solutions, following a formula. They then load the film in the machine, which immerses the exposed film in a developer solution. This brings out the latent image. The next steps include immersing the negative in a stop-bath to halt the developer action, transferring it to a hyposolution to fix the image, and then immersing it in water to remove the chemicals. The technician then dries the film. In some cases, these steps are performed by hand.

Color printer operators control equipment that produces color prints from negatives. These workers read customer instructions to determine processing requirements. They load film into color printing equipment, examine negatives to determine equipment control settings, set controls, and produce a specified number of prints. Finally, they inspect the finished prints for defects, remove any that are found, and insert the processed negatives and prints into an envelope for return to the customer.

Processing machine operators who work with digital images first load the raw images onto a computer, either directly from the camera or more commonly from a storage device such as a flash card or CD. Most processing of the images is done automatically by software, but they may also be reviewed manually by the operator, who then selects which images the customer wants printed and the quantity. Some digital processors also upload images onto a Web site so that the customer can view them from a home computer and also share them with others through the Internet.

Photographic process workers, sometimes known as *digital imaging technicians*, use computer images of conventional negatives and specialized computer software to vary the contrast of images, remove unwanted background, or combine features from different photographs. Although computers and digital technology are replacing much manual work, some photographic process workers, especially those who work in portrait studios, still perform many specialized tasks by hand directly on the photo or negative. *Airbrush artists* restore damaged and faded photographs, and may color or shade drawings to create photographic likenesses using an airbrush.

Photographic processing workers generate finished photos from film or data files.

Photographic retouchers alter photographic negatives, prints, or images to accentuate the subject. *Colorists* apply oil colors to portrait photographs to create natural, lifelike appearances. *Photographic spotters* remove imperfections on photographic prints and images.

Working Conditions

Photographic process workers and processing machine operators generally spend their work hours in clean, appropriately lighted, well-ventilated, and air-conditioned offices, photofinishing laboratories, or 1-hour minilabs. In recent years, more commercial photographic processing has been done on computers than in darkrooms, and this trend is expected to continue.

Some photographic process workers and processing machine operators are exposed to the chemicals and fumes associated with developing and printing. These workers must wear rubber gloves and aprons and take precautions against these hazards. Those who use computers for extended periods may experience back pain, eyestrain, or fatigue.

Photographic processing machine operators must do repetitive work at a rapid pace without any loss of accuracy. Photographic process workers do detailed tasks, such as airbrushing and spotting, which can contribute to eye fatigue.

Many photo laboratory employees work a 40-hour week, including evenings and weekends, and may work overtime during peak seasons. About one in four work part time.

Training, Other Qualifications, and Advancement

Most photographic process workers and processing machine operators receive on-the-job training from their companies, manufacturers' representatives, and experienced workers. New employees gradually learn to use the machines and chemicals that develop and print film as well as the computer techniques to process and print digital images.

Employers prefer applicants who are high school graduates or those who have some experience in the field. Familiarity with computers is essential for photographic processing machine operators. The ability to perform simple mathematical calculations also is helpful. Photography courses that include instruction in film processing are valuable preparation. Such courses are available through high schools, vocational-technical institutes, private trade schools, and colleges and universities.

On-the-job training in photographic processing occupations can range from just a few hours for print machine operators to several months for photographic processing workers such as airbrush artists and colorists. Some workers attend periodic training seminars to maintain a high level of skill. Manual dexterity, good hand-eye coordination, and good vision, including normal color perception, are important qualifications for photographic process workers.

Photographic process machine workers can sometimes advance from jobs as machine operators to supervisory positions in laboratories or to management positions within retail stores.

Employment

Photographic process workers held about 32,000 jobs in 2004. About three in ten photographic process workers were employed in photofinishing laboratories and one-hour minilabs. More than one in six worked for portrait studios or commercial laboratories that specialize in processing the work of professional photographers for advertising and other industries. An additional one in nine was employed by general merchandise stores, and one in ten in the printing, publishing, and motion picture industries.

Photographic processing machine operators held about 54,000 jobs in 2004. About half worked in retail establishments, primarily in general merchandise stores and drug stores. About one in three worked in photofinishing laboratories and one-hour minilabs. Small numbers were employed in the printing industry and in portrait studios and commercial laboratories that process the work of professional photographers.

Employment fluctuates somewhat over the course of the year. Typically, employment peaks during school graduation and summer vacation periods, and again during the winter holiday season.

Job Outlook

A decline in employment is expected for photographic process workers and processing machine operators through the year 2014. Some openings will still result from replacement needs, which are higher for machine operators than for photographic process workers.

In recent years, digital cameras, which use electronic memory rather than film to record images, have become standard among professional photographers and are gaining in popularity among amateur photographers as the cost of these cameras continues to fall. This will reduce the demand for traditional photographic processing machine operators. However, while many digital camera owners will choose to print their own pictures with their own equipment, a growing number of casual photographers are choosing not to acquire the needed equipment and skills to print the photos themselves. For them, self-service machines will be able to meet some of the demand, but there will still be some demand for professionals to print digital photos, as well as to develop and print photos from those who continue to use film cameras.

Digital photography also will reduce demand for photographic process workers. Using digital cameras and technology, consumers who have a personal computer and the proper software will be able to download and view pictures on their computer, as well as manipulate, correct, and retouch their own photographs. No matter what improvements occur in camera technology, though, some photographic processing tasks will still require skillful manual treatment. Moreover, not all consumers will want to invest in the software. Job opportunities will be best for individuals with experience using computers and digital technology.

Earnings

Earnings of photographic process workers vary greatly depending on skill level, experience, and geographic location. Median hourly earnings for photographic process workers were $9.63 in May 2004. The middle 50 percent earned between $7.79 and $12.97. The lowest 10 percent earned less than $6.68, and the highest 10 percent earned more than $17.99. Median hourly earnings were $10.20 in photofinishing laboratories, the largest employer of photographic process workers.

Median hourly earning for photographic processing machine operators were $9.33 in May 2004. The middle 50 percent earned between $7.78 and $11.88. The lowest 10 percent earned less than $6.84, and the highest 10 percent earned more than $15.21. Median hourly earnings in the two industries employing the largest numbers of photographic processing machine operators were $10.44 in photofinishing laboratories and $7.98 in health and personal care stores.

Related Occupations

Photographic process workers and processing machine operators need specialized knowledge of the photo developing process. Other workers who apply specialized technical knowledge include clinical laboratory technologists and technicians, computer operators, jewelers and precious stone and metal workers, prepress technicians and workers, printing machine operators, and science technicians.

Sources of Additional Information

For information about employment opportunities in photographic laboratories and schools that offer degrees in photographic technology, contact:

➤ Photo Marketing Association International, 3000 Picture Place, Jackson, MI 49201. Internet: **http://www.pmai.org**

Semiconductor Processors

(O*NET 51-9141.00)

Significant Points

- Employment is expected to decline over the next 10 years because of increasing automation of fabrication plants in this country and the building of many of the new plants abroad.

- An associate degree in a relevant curriculum is increasingly required.

Nature of the Work

Electronic semiconductors—also known as computer chips, microchips, or integrated circuits—are the miniature but powerful brains of high-technology equipment. Semiconductors are composed of a myriad of tiny aluminum or copper lines and electric switches, which manipulate the flow of electrical current. Semiconductor processors are responsible for many of the steps necessary in the manufacture of each semiconductor that goes into personal computers, missile guidance systems, and a host of other electronic equipment.

Semiconductor processors are the production workers who manufacture semiconductors in disks of varying sizes, generally eight to twelve inches wide. These disks, called wafers, are thin slices of silicon on which the circuitry of the microchips is layered. Each wafer is eventually cut into dozens or scores of individual chips.

Semiconductor processors make wafers by means of photolithography, a printing process for creating patterns from photographic images. Operating automated equipment, workers imprint precise microscopic patterns of the circuitry on the wafers, etch out the patterns with acids, and replace the patterns with metals that conduct electricity. Then, the wafers receive a chemical bath to make them smooth, and the imprint process begins again on a new layer with the next pattern. Wafers usually have from 8 to 20 such layers of microscopic, three-dimensional circuitry.

Semiconductors are produced in semiconductor-fabricating plants, or "fabs." Within fabs, the manufacturing and cutting of wafers to create semiconductors takes place in "cleanrooms"—production areas that must be kept free of any airborne matter, because even extremely small particles can damage a semiconductor. All semiconductor processors working in cleanrooms—both operators and technicians—must wear special lightweight outer garments known as "bunny suits." These garments fit over clothing to prevent lint and other particles from contaminating semiconductor-processing worksites.

Operators, who make up the majority of the workers in cleanrooms, start and monitor the sophisticated equipment that performs the various tasks during the many steps of the semiconductor production sequence. They spend a great deal of time at computer terminals, monitoring the operation of the equipment to ensure that each of the tasks in the production of the wafer is performed correctly. Operators also may transfer wafer carriers from one development station to the next; in newer fabs, the lifting of heavy wafer carriers and the constant monitoring for quality control are increasingly being automated.

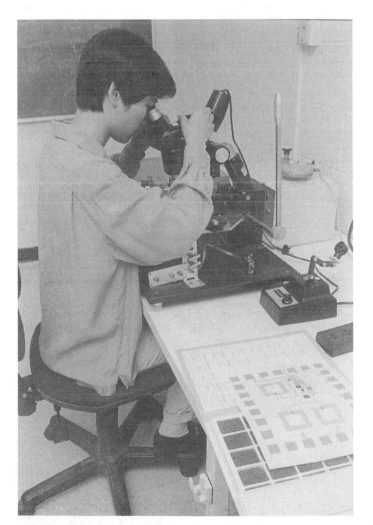

Semiconductor processing technicians use microscopes to check for flaws in semiconductor wafers.

Once begun, the production of semiconductor wafers is continuous. Operators work to the pace of the machinery that has largely automated the production process. Operators are responsible for keeping the automated machinery within proper operating parameters.

Technicians account for a smaller percentage of the workers in cleanrooms, but they troubleshoot production problems and make equipment adjustments and repairs. They also take the lead in assuring quality control and in maintaining equipment. To keep equipment repairs to a minimum, technicians perform diagnostic analyses and run computations. For example, technicians may determine if a flaw in a chip is due to contamination, and peculiar to that wafer, or if the flaw is inherent in the manufacturing process.

Working Conditions
The work pace in cleanrooms is deliberately slow. Limited movement keeps the air in cleanrooms as free as possible of dust and other particles, which can destroy semiconductors during their production. Because the machinery sets the operators' rate of work in the largely automated production process, workers maintain an easygoing pace. Although workers spend some time alone monitoring equipment, operators and technicians spend much of their time working in teams.

Technicians are on their feet most of the day, walking through the cleanroom to oversee production activities. Operators spend a great deal of time sitting or standing at workstations, monitoring computer readouts and gauges. Sometimes, they must retrieve wafers from one station and take them to another.

The temperature in the cleanrooms must be kept within a narrow range: usually, it is set at a comfortable 72 degrees Fahrenheit. Although bunny suits cover virtually the entire body, except perhaps the eyes (over which workers wear protective glasses), their lightweight fabric keeps the temperature inside fairly comfortable as well. Entry and exit of workers in bunny suits from the cleanroom are controlled to minimize contamination, and workers must be reclothed in a clean suit and decontaminated each time they return to the cleanroom.

Several highly toxic chemicals are used at various points in the process of manufacturing semiconductors. Workers who are exposed to such chemicals can be seriously harmed. However, semiconductor fabrication plants are designed with safeguards to ensure that these chemicals are handled, used, and disposed of without exposure to workers or the surrounding environment. Toxic chemicals are applied to wafers by computer-controlled machine tools in sealed chambers and there is normally little risk of workers coming into contact with them.

Semiconductor-fabricating plants operate around the clock. For this reason, night and weekend work is common. In some plants, workers maintain standard 8-hour shifts, 5 days a week. In other plants, employees are on duty for 12-hour shifts to minimize the disruption of cleanroom operations brought about by changes in shift. In some plants, managers allow workers to alternate schedules, thereby distributing the overnight shift equitably.

Training, Other Qualifications, and Advancement
People interested in becoming semiconductor processors—either operators or technicians—need a solid background in mathematics and the physical sciences. In addition to applying these disciplines to the complex manufacturing processes performed in fabs, math and science knowledge are essentials for pursuing higher education in semiconductor technology—and knowledge of both subjects is one of the best ways to advance in the semiconductor fabricating field.

Semiconductor processor workers must also be able to think analytically and critically to anticipate problems and avoid costly mistakes. Communication skills also are vital, as workers must be able to convey their thoughts and ideas both orally and in writing.

For semiconductor processor jobs, employers prefer persons who have completed associate degree programs. However, completion of a 1-year certificate program in semiconductor technology offered by some community colleges, supplemented by experience, may also be sufficient; Some semiconductor technology programs at community colleges include internships at a semiconductor fabricating plants. Others persons also may qualify by completing a degree in high-tech manufacturing, a new degree offered by some community colleges that prepares graduates to work in the semiconductor industry, as well as other industries such as pharmaceuticals, aerospace, or automotive. Degree or certificate program graduates who get hands-on training while attending school should have the best prospects.

To ensure that operators and technicians keep their skills current, many employers provide 40 hours of formal training annually. Some employers also provide financial assistance to employees who want to earn associate and bachelor's degrees to further their career or to work towards becoming a technician.

Summer and part-time employment provide another option for getting started in the field for those who are at least 18 years old and live near a semiconductor processing plant. Students often are hired to work during the summer, and some students are allowed to continue working part time during the school year. Students in summer and part-time semiconductor processor jobs learn what education they need to prosper in the field. They also gain valuable experience that may lead to full-time employment after graduation.

Some semiconductor processing technicians transfer to sales engineer jobs with suppliers of the machines that manufacture the semiconductors or become field support personnel.

Employment

Electronic semiconductor processors held approximately 45,000 jobs in 2004. Nearly all of them were employed in facilities that manufacture semiconductors and other electronic components and accessories, though a small percentage worked in plants that primarily manufacture computers and office equipment.

Job Outlook

Employment of semiconductor processors is projected to decline between 2004 and 2014. The two main reasons for this are increasing automation and the construction of many newer fabs in other countries. Semiconductor manufacturers are shifting production to larger 12" wafers, which produce twice as many chips as fabs making 8" wafers. Plants that make 12" wafers are more automated, allowing them to sharply increase production with the same number of workers. Additionally, a number of domestic companies are building more fabs overseas, where costs are lower. Imports of

semiconductors from non-U.S. companies also are growing and may continue to increase throughout the decade. In spite of the decline in employment, some jobs will open up due to the need to replace workers who leave the occupation.

Despite the expected decline in employment of semiconductor processors, the demand for semiconductor chips remains very high stemming from the many existing and future applications for semiconductors in computers, appliances, machinery, biotechnology, vehicles, cell phones and other telecommunications devices, and other equipment. Moreover, the advent of the new 64-bit microchip and "dual-core" chips is expected to provide the power of computer servers or workstations, onto desktop computers and open up a wealth of new applications, particularly in medical devices.

Industry development of semiconductors made from better materials means that semiconductors will become even smaller, more powerful, and more durable. For example, the industry has begun producing a new generation of microchips made with copper rather than aluminum wires, which will better conduct electricity. Also, technology now exists to make chips for wireless connections to the Internet possible over a range of several miles, while another company will soon be producing chips that will save massive amounts of energy in many kinds of electric products.

Job prospects will be best for people with postsecondary education in electronics or semiconductor technology.

Earnings

Median hourly earnings of electronic semiconductor processors were $13.85 in May 2004. The middle 50 percent earned between $11.44 and $16.90 an hour. The lowest 10 percent earned less than $9.53, and the top 10 percent earned more than $20.46 an hour.

Technicians with an associate degree in electronics or semiconductor technology generally start at higher salaries than those with less education. About 15 percent of all electronic semiconductor processors belonged to a union.

Related Occupations

Electronic semiconductor processors do production work that resembles the work of precision assemblers and fabricators of electrical and electronic equipment. Also, many electronic semiconductor processors have academic training in semiconductor technology, which emphasizes scientific and engineering principles. Other occupations that require some college or postsecondary vocational training emphasizing such principles are engineering technicians, electrical and electronics engineers, and science technicians.

Sources of Additional Information

For more information on semiconductor processor careers, contact:
➤ Maricopa Advanced Technology Education Center (MATEC), 2323 West 14th St., Suite 540, Tempe, AZ 85281. Internet: **http://matec.org/ops/career.shtml**

Transportation and Material Moving Occupations

Air Transportation Occupations

Aircraft Pilots and Flight Engineers

(O*NET 53-2011.00, 53-2012.00)

Significant Points

- Regional and low-fare airlines offer the best opportunities; pilots attempting to get jobs at the major airlines will face strong competition.

- Pilots usually start with smaller commuter and regional airlines to acquire the experience needed to qualify for higher paying jobs with national or major airlines.

- Many pilots have learned to fly in the military, but growing numbers have college degrees with flight training from civilian flying schools that are certified by the Federal Aviation Administration (FAA).

- Earnings of airline pilots are among the highest in the Nation.

Nature of the Work

Pilots are highly trained professionals who either fly airplanes or helicopters to carry out a wide variety of tasks. Most are *airline pilots, copilots,* and *flight engineers* who transport passengers and cargo, but 1 out of 5 pilots is a commercial pilot involved in tasks such as dusting crops, spreading seed for reforestation, testing aircraft, flying passengers and cargo to areas not served by regular airlines, directing firefighting efforts, tracking criminals, monitoring traffic, and rescuing and evacuating injured persons.

Except on small aircraft, two pilots usually make up the cockpit crew. Generally, the most experienced pilot, the *captain,* is in command and supervises all other crew members. The pilot and the copilot, often called the first officer, share flying and other duties, such as communicating with air traffic controllers and monitoring the instruments. Some large aircraft have a third pilot, the flight engineer, who assists the other pilots by monitoring and operating many of the instruments and systems, making minor in-flight repairs, and watching for other aircraft. The flight engineer also assists the pilots with the company, air traffic control, and cabin crew communications. New technology can perform many flight tasks, however, and virtually all new aircraft now fly with only two pilots, who rely more heavily on computerized controls.

Before departure, pilots plan their flights carefully. They thoroughly check their aircraft to make sure that the engines, controls, instruments, and other systems are functioning properly. They also make sure that baggage or cargo has been loaded correctly. They confer with flight dispatchers and aviation weather forecasters to find out about weather conditions en route and at their destination. Based on this information, they choose a route, altitude, and speed that will provide the safest, most economical, and smoothest flight. When flying under instrument flight rules—procedures governing the operation of the aircraft when there is poor visibility—the pilot in command, or the company dispatcher, normally files an instrument flight plan with air traffic control so that the flight can be coordinated with other air traffic.

Takeoff and landing are the most difficult parts of the flight, and require close coordination between the pilot and first officer. For example, as the plane accelerates for takeoff, the pilot concentrates on the runway while the first officer scans the instrument panel. To calculate the speed they must attain to become airborne, pilots consider the altitude of the airport, outside temperature, weight of the plane, and speed and direction of the wind. The moment the plane reaches takeoff speed, the first officer informs the pilot, who then pulls back on the controls to raise the nose of the plane. Pilots and first officers usually alternate flying each leg from takeoff to landing.

Unless the weather is bad, the flight itself is relatively routine. Airplane pilots, with the assistance of autopilot and the flight management computer, steer the plane along their planned route and are monitored by the air traffic control stations they pass along the way. They regularly scan the instrument panel to check their fuel supply; the condition of their engines; and the air-conditioning, hydraulic, and other systems. Pilots may request a change in altitude or route if circumstances dictate. For example, if the ride is rougher than expected, pilots may ask air traffic control if pilots flying at other altitudes have reported better conditions; if so, they may request an altitude change. This procedure also may be used to find a stronger tailwind or a weaker headwind to save fuel and increase speed. In contrast, because helicopters are used for short trips at relatively low altitude, helicopter pilots must be constantly on the lookout for trees, bridges, power lines, transmission towers, and other dangerous obstacles. Regardless of the type of aircraft, all pilots must monitor warning devices designed to help detect sudden shifts in wind conditions that can cause crashes.

Pilots must rely completely on their instruments when visibility is poor. On the basis of altimeter readings, they know how high above ground they are and whether they can fly safely over mountains and other obstacles. Special navigation radios give pilots precise information that, with the help of special maps, tells them their exact position. Other very sophisticated equipment provides directions to a point just above the end of a runway and enables pilots to land completely without an outside visual reference. Once on the ground, pilots must complete records on their flight and the aircraft maintenance status for their company and the FAA.

The number of nonflying duties that pilots have depends on the employment setting. Airline pilots have the services of large support staffs and, consequently, perform few nonflying duties. However, because of the large numbers of passengers, airline pilots may be called upon to coordinate handling of disgruntled or disruptive passengers. Pilots employed by other organizations, such as charter operators or businesses, have many other duties. They may load the aircraft, handle all passenger luggage to ensure a balanced load, and supervise refueling; other nonflying responsibilities include keeping records, scheduling flights, arranging for major maintenance, and performing minor aircraft maintenance and repairs.

Before departure, pilots thoroughly check their aircraft to make sure that the engines, controls, instruments, and other systems are functioning properly.

Some pilots are flight instructors. They teach their students in ground-school classes, in simulators, and in dual-controlled planes and helicopters. A few specially trained pilots are examiners or check pilots. They periodically fly with other pilots or pilot's license applicants to make sure that they are proficient.

Working Conditions

Because of FAA regulations, airline pilots flying large aircraft, cannot fly more than 100 hours a month or more than 1,000 hours a year. Most airline pilots fly an average of 75 hours a month and work an additional 75 hours a month performing nonflying duties. Most pilots have a variable work schedule, working several days on, then several days off. Most spend a considerable amount of time away from home because the majority of flights involve overnight layovers. When pilots are away from home, the airlines provide hotel accommodations, transportation between the hotel and airport, and an allowance for meals and other expenses. Airlines operate flights at all hours of the day and night, so work schedules often are irregular. Flight assignments are based on seniority. An airline seniority number is normally assigned to a pilot on completion of training. The sooner pilots are hired, the lower their seniority number and the stronger their bidding power.

Commercial pilots also may have irregular schedules, flying 30 hours one month and 90 hours the next. Because these pilots frequently have many nonflying responsibilities, they have much less free time than do airline pilots. Except for corporate flight department pilots, most commercial pilots do not remain away from home overnight. But, they may work odd hours. However, if the company owns a fleet of planes, pilots may fly a regular schedule. Flight instructors may have irregular and seasonal work schedules, depending on their students' available time and the weather. Instructors frequently work in the evening or on weekends.

Airline pilots, especially those on international routes, often experience jet lag—fatigue caused by many hours of flying through different time zones. To guard against pilot fatigue, which could result in unsafe flying conditions, the FAA requires airlines to allow pilots at least 8 hours of uninterrupted rest in the 24 hours before finishing their flight duty.

Commercial pilots face other types of job hazards. The work of test pilots, who check the flight performance of new and experimental planes, may be dangerous. Pilots who are crop-dusters may be exposed to toxic chemicals and seldom have the benefit of a regular landing strip. Helicopter pilots involved in rescue and police work may be subject to personal injury.

Although flying does not involve much physical effort, the mental stress of being responsible for a safe flight, regardless of the weather, can be tiring. Pilots must be alert and quick to react if something goes wrong, particularly during takeoff and landing.

Training, Other Qualifications, and Advancement

All pilots who are paid to transport passengers or cargo must have a commercial pilot's license with an instrument rating issued by the FAA. Helicopter pilots must hold a commercial pilot's certificate with a helicopter rating. To qualify for these licenses, applicants must be at least 18 years old and have at least 250 hours of flight experience. The experience required can be reduced through participation in certain flight school curricula approved by the FAA. Applicants also must pass a strict physical examination to make sure that they are in good health and have 20/20 vision with or without glasses, good hearing, and no physical handicaps that could impair their performance. They must pass a written test that includes questions on the principles of safe flight, navigation techniques, and FAA regulations, and must demonstrate their flying ability to FAA or designated examiners.

To fly during periods of low visibility, pilots must be rated by the FAA to fly by instruments. Pilots may qualify for this rating by having the required hours of flight experience, including 40 hours of experience in flying by instruments; they also must pass a written examination on procedures and FAA regulations covering instrument flying and demonstrate to an examiner their ability to fly by instruments. Requirements for the instrument rating vary depending on the certification level of flight school.

Airline pilots must fulfill additional requirements. Pilots must have an airline transport pilot's license. Applicants for this license must be at least 23 years old and have a minimum of 1,500 hours of flying experience, including night and instrument flying, and must pass FAA written and flight examinations. Usually, they also have one or more advanced ratings depending on the requirements of their particular job. Because pilots must be able to make quick decisions and accurate judgments under pressure, many airline companies reject applicants who do not pass required psychological and aptitude tests. All licenses are valid so long as a pilot can pass the periodic physical and eye examinations and tests of flying skills required by the FAA and company regulations.

The U.S. Armed Forces have always been an important source of trained pilots for civilian jobs. Military pilots gain valuable experience on jet aircraft and helicopters, and persons with this experience—because of the extensive flying time military pilots receive—usually are preferred for civilian pilot jobs. Those without Armed Forces training may become pilots by attending flight schools or by taking lessons from FAA-certified flight instructors. The FAA has certified about 600 civilian flying schools, including some colleges and universities that offer degree credit for pilot training. Until 2014 , trained pilots leaving the military are not expected to increase very much in number as the need for pilots grows in civilian aviation. As a result, FAA-certified schools will train a larger share of pilots than in the past.

Although some small airlines hire high school graduates, most airlines require at least 2 years of college and prefer to hire college graduates. In fact, most entrants to this occupation have a college degree. Because the number of college-educated applicants continues to increase, many employers are making a college degree an educational requirement.

Depending on the type of aircraft, new airline pilots start as first officers or flight engineers. Although some airlines favor applicants who already have a flight engineer's license, they may provide flight engineer training for those who have only the commercial license. Many pilots begin with smaller regional or commuter airlines, where they obtain experience flying passengers on scheduled flights into busy airports in all weather conditions. These jobs often lead to higher paying jobs with bigger, national or major airlines.

Initial training for airline pilots includes a week of company indoctrination; 3 to 6 weeks of ground school and simulator training; and 25 hours of initial operating experience, including a check-ride with an FAA aviation safety inspector. Once trained, pilots are required to attend recurrent training and simulator checks once or twice a year throughout their career.

Companies other than airlines usually require less flying experience. However, a commercial pilot's license is a minimum requirement, and employers prefer applicants who have experience in the type of craft they will be flying. New employees usually start as first officers, or fly less sophisticated equipment. Test pilots often are required to have an engineering degree.

Advancement for all pilots usually is limited to other flying jobs. Many pilots start as flight instructors, building up their flying hours while they earn money teaching. As they become more experienced, these pilots occasionally fly charter planes or perhaps get jobs with small air transportation firms, such as air-taxi companies. Some advance to flying corporate planes. A small number get flight engineer jobs with the airlines.

In the airlines, advancement usually depends on seniority provisions of union contracts. After 1 to 5 years, flight engineers advance according to seniority to first officer and, after 5 to 15 years, to captain. Seniority also determines which pilots get the more desirable routes. In a nonairline job, a first officer may advance to pilot and, in large companies, to chief pilot or director of aviation in charge of aircraft scheduling, maintenance, and flight procedures.

Employment

Civilian aircraft pilots and flight engineers held about 106,000 jobs in 2004. About 84,000 worked as airline pilots, copilots, and flight engineers. The remainder were commercial pilots who worked as flight instructors at local airports or for large businesses that fly company cargo and executives in their own airplanes or helicopters. Some commercial pilots flew small planes for air-taxi companies, usually to or from lightly traveled airports not served by major airlines. Others worked for a variety of businesses, performing tasks such as dusting crops, inspecting pipelines, or conducting sightseeing trips. Federal, State, and local governments also employed pilots. A few pilots were self-employed.

Pilots are located across the country, but airline pilots usually are based near major metropolitan airports or airports operating as hubs for the major airlines.

Job Outlook

The passenger airline industry is undergoing many changes, with some airlines posting increases in passenger traffic and adding routes while others are cutting back. Overall, the employment of aircraft pilots is projected to increase about as fast as average for all occupations through 2014. In the long run, demand for air travel is expected to grow along with the population and the economy. In the short run, however, employment of pilots is generally sensitive to cyclical swings in the economy. During recessions, when a decline in the demand for air travel forces airlines to curtail the number of flights, airlines may temporarily furlough some pilots.

After September 11, 2001, air travel was severely depressed. A number of the major airlines were forced to reduce schedules, lay off pilots, and even declare bankruptcy. At the same time, hiring continued at regional and low-fare airlines. Job opportunities are expected to continue to be better with the regional airlines and low-fare carriers, which are growing faster than the more well-known major airlines. Opportunities with air cargo carriers also should arise because of increasing security requirements for shipping freight on passenger airlines and growth in electronic commerce. Business and corporate travel also should provide some new jobs for pilots.

Pilots attempting to get jobs at the major airlines will face strong competition, as those firms tend to attract many more applicants than they have jobs. They also will have to compete with laid-off pilots for any available jobs. Pilots who have logged the greatest number of flying hours using sophisticated equipment typically have the best prospects. For this reason, military pilots often have an advantage over other applicants. However, prior to September 11, 2001, some airlines reported a shortage of qualified pilots to operate the most sophisticated aircraft. Thus, when hiring improves, jobseekers with the most FAA licenses will have a competitive advantage.

Fewer flight engineers will be needed as new planes requiring only two pilots replace older planes that required flight engineers. Pilots also will experience some productivity improvements as airlines switch to larger planes and adopt the low-fare carrier model that emphasizes faster turnaround times for flights, keeping more pilots in the air rather than waiting on the ground.

Earnings

Earnings of aircraft pilots and flight engineers vary greatly depending whether they work as airline or commercial pilots. Earnings of airline pilots are among the highest in the Nation, and depend on factors such as the type, size, and maximum speed of the plane and the number of hours and miles flown. For example, pilots who fly jet aircraft usually earn higher salaries than do pilots who fly turboprops. Airline pilots and flight engineers may earn extra pay for night and international flights. In May 2004, median annual earnings of airline pilots, copilots, and flight engineers were $129,250.

Median annual earnings of commercial pilots were $53,870 in May 2004. The middle 50 percent earned between $37,170 and $79,390. The lowest 10 percent earned less than $26,300, and the highest 10 percent earned more than $110,070.

Airline pilots usually are eligible for life and health insurance plans. They also receive retirement benefits and, if they fail the FAA physical examination at some point in their careers, they get disability payments. In addition, pilots receive an expense allowance, or "per diem," for every hour they are away from home. Some airlines also provide allowances to pilots for purchasing and cleaning their uniforms. As an additional benefit, pilots and their immediate families usually are entitled to free or reduced-fare transportation on their own and other airlines.

More than half of all aircraft pilots are members of unions. Most of the pilots who fly for the major airlines are members of the Airline Pilots Association, International, but those employed by one major airline are members of the Allied Pilots Association. Some flight engineers are members of the Flight Engineers' International Association.

Related Occupations

Although they are not in the cockpit, air traffic controllers and airfield operation specialists also play an important role in making sure flights are safe and on schedule, and participate in many of the decisions that pilots must make.

Sources of Additional Information

Information about job opportunities, salaries for a particular airline, and qualifications required may be obtained by writing to the personnel manager of the airline.

For information on airline pilots, contact:
➤ Air Line Pilots Association, International, 1625 Massachusetts Ave., NW., Washington, DC 20036.
➤ Air Transport Association of America, Inc., 1301 Pennsylvania Ave. NW., Suite 1100, Washington, DC 20004.
➤ Federal Aviation Administration, 800 Independence Ave. SW., Washington, DC 20591. Internet: **http://www.faa.gov**

For information on helicopter pilots, contact:
➤ Helicopter Association International, 1635 Prince St., Alexandria, VA 22314.

For information about job opportunities in companies other than airlines, consult the classified section of aviation trade magazines and apply to companies that operate aircraft at local airports.

Air Traffic Controllers

(O*NET 53-2021.00)

Significant Points

● Nearly all air traffic controllers are employed by the Federal Aviation Administration (FAA), an agency of the Federal Government.

● Replacement needs will account for most job openings, reflecting the large number of air traffic controllers who will be eligible to retire over the next decade.

● Competition to get into FAA training programs is expected to remain keen; however, graduates of these programs have good job prospects.

● Air traffic controllers earn relatively high pay and have good benefits.

Nature of the Work
The air traffic control system is a vast network of people and equipment that ensures the safe operation of commercial and private aircraft. Air traffic controllers coordinate the movement of air traffic to make certain that planes stay a safe distance apart. Their immediate concern is safety, but controllers also must direct planes efficiently to minimize delays. Some regulate airport traffic through designated airspaces; others regulate airport arrivals and departures.

Although *airport tower controllers* or *terminal controllers* watch over all planes traveling through the airport's airspace, their main responsibility is to organize the flow of aircraft into and out of the airport. Relying on radar and visual observation, they closely monitor each plane to ensure a safe distance between all aircraft and to guide pilots between the hangar or ramp and the end of the airport's airspace. In addition, controllers keep pilots informed about changes in weather conditions such as wind shear, a sudden change in the velocity or direction of the wind that can cause the pilot to lose control of the aircraft.

During arrival or departure, several controllers direct each plane. As a plane approaches an airport, the pilot radios ahead to inform the terminal of the plane's presence. The controller in the radar room, just beneath the control tower, has a copy of the plane's flight plan and already has observed the plane on radar. If the path is clear, the controller directs the pilot to a runway; if the airport is busy, the plane is fitted into a traffic pattern with other aircraft waiting to land. As the plane nears the runway, the pilot is asked to contact the tower. There, another controller, who also is watching the plane on radar, monitors the aircraft the last mile or so to the runway, delaying any departures that would interfere with the plane's landing. Once the plane has landed, a ground controller in the tower directs it along the taxiways to its assigned gate. The ground controller usually works entirely by sight, but may use radar if visibility is very poor.

The procedure is reversed for departures. The ground controller directs the plane to the proper runway. The local controller then informs the pilot about conditions at the airport, such as weather, speed and direction of wind, and visibility. The local controller also issues runway clearance for the pilot to take off. Once in the air, the plane is guided out of the airport's airspace by the departure controller.

After each plane departs, airport tower controllers notify *enroute controllers* who will next take charge. There are 20 air route traffic control centers located around the country, each employing 300 to 700 controllers, with more than 150 on duty during peak hours at the busiest facilities. Airplanes usually fly along designated routes; each center is assigned a certain airspace containing many different routes. Enroute controllers work in teams of up to three members, depending on how heavy traffic is; each team is responsible for a section of the center's airspace. A team, for example, might be responsible for all planes that are between 30 and 100 miles north of an airport and flying at an altitude between 6,000 and 18,000 feet.

To prepare for planes about to enter the team's airspace, the radar associate controller organizes flight plans coming off a printer. If two planes are scheduled to enter the team's airspace at nearly the same time, location, and altitude, this controller may arrange with the preceding control unit for one plane to change its flight path. The previous unit may have been another team at the same or an adjacent center, or a departure controller at a neighboring terminal. As a plane approaches a team's airspace, the radar controller accepts responsibility for the plane from the previous controlling unit. The controller also delegates responsibility for the plane to the next controlling unit when the plane leaves the team's airspace.

The radar controller, who is the senior team member, observes the planes in the team's airspace on radar and communicates with the pilots when necessary. Radar controllers warn pilots about nearby planes, bad weather conditions, and other potential hazards. Two planes on a collision course will be directed around each other. If a pilot wants to change altitude in search of better flying conditions, the controller will check to determine that no other planes will be along the proposed path. As the flight progresses, the team responsible for the aircraft notifies the next team in charge of the airspace

Air traffic controllers coordinate the movement of air traffic to make certain that planes stay a safe distance apart.

ahead. Through team coordination, the plane arrives safely at its destination.

Both airport tower and enroute controllers usually control several planes at a time; often, they have to make quick decisions about completely different activities. For example, a controller might direct a plane on its landing approach and at the same time provide pilots entering the airport's airspace with information about conditions at the airport. While instructing these pilots, the controller also might observe other planes in the vicinity, such as those in a holding pattern waiting for permission to land, to ensure that they remain well separated.

In addition to airport towers and enroute centers, air traffic controllers also work in flight service stations operated at more than 100 locations. These *flight service specialists* provide pilots with information on the station's particular area, including terrain, preflight and inflight weather information, suggested routes, and other information important to the safety of a flight. Flight service specialists help pilots in emergency situations and initiate and co-ordinate searches for missing or overdue aircraft. However, they are not involved in actively managing air traffic.

Some air traffic controllers work at the FAA's Air Traffic Control Systems Command Center in Herndon, VA, where they oversee the entire system. They look for situations that will create bottlenecks or other problems in the system, then respond with a management plan for traffic into and out of the troubled sector. The objective is to keep traffic levels in the trouble spots manageable for the controllers working at enroute centers.

The FAA has implemented an automated air traffic control system, called the National Airspace System (NAS) Architecture. The NAS Architecture is a long-term strategic plan that will allow controllers to more efficiently deal with the demands of increased air traffic. It encompasses the replacement of aging equipment and the introduction of new systems, technologies, and procedures to enhance safety and security and support future aviation growth. The NAS Architecture facilitates continuing discussion of modernization between the FAA and the aviation community.

Working Conditions

Controllers work a basic 40-hour week; however, they may work additional hours, for which they receive overtime, or premium, pay or equal time off. Because most control towers and centers operate 24 hours a day, 7 days a week, controllers rotate night and weekend shifts.

During busy times, controllers must work rapidly and efficiently. Total concentration is required to keep track of several planes at the same time and to make certain that all pilots receive correct instructions. The mental stress of being responsible for the safety of several aircraft and their passengers can be exhausting.

Training, Other Qualifications, and Advancement

To become an air traffic controller, a person must enroll in an FAA-approved education program and pass a pre-employment test that measures his or her ability to learn the controller's duties. Exceptions are air traffic controllers with prior experience and military veterans. The pre-employment test is currently offered only to students in the FAA Air Traffic Collegiate Training Initiative Program or the Minneapolis Community & Technical College, Air Traffic Control Training Program. The test is administered by computer and takes about 8 hours to complete. To take the test, an applicant must apply under an open advertisement for air traffic control positions and be chosen to take the examination. When there are many more applicants than available positions, applicants are selected to take the test through random selection. In addition to the pre-employment test, applicants must have 3 years of full-time work experience, have completed a full 4 years of college, or a combination of both.

In combining education and experience, 1 year of undergraduate study—30 semester or 45 quarter hours—is equivalent to 9 months of work experience. Certain kinds of aviation experience also may be substituted for these requirements.

Upon successful completion of an FAA-approved program, individuals who receive school recommendation, meet the basic qualification requirements (including being less than 31 years of age) in accordance with Federal law, and achieve a qualifying score on the FAA-authorized pre-employment test become eligible for employment as an air traffic controller. Candidates also must pass a medical exam, undergo drug screening, and obtain a security clearance before they can be hired.

Upon selection, employees attend the FAA Academy in Oklahoma City, OK, for 12 weeks of training, during which they learn the fundamentals of the airway system, FAA regulations, controller equipment, and aircraft performance characteristics, as well as more specialized tasks.

After graduation, candidates assigned to an air traffic control facility are classified as "developmental controllers" until they complete all requirements to be certified for all of the air traffic control positions within a defined area of a given facility. Generally, it takes new controllers with only initial controller training between 2 and 4 years, depending on the facility and the availability of facility staff or contractors to provide on-the-job training, to complete all the certification requirements to become certified professional controllers. Individuals who have had prior controller experience normally take less time to become fully certified. Controllers who fail to complete either the academy or the on-the-job portion of the training usually are dismissed. Controllers must pass a physical examination each year and a job performance examination twice each year. Failure to become certified in any position at a facility within a specified time also may result in dismissal. Controllers also are subject to drug screening as a condition of continuing employment.

Air traffic controllers must be articulate to give pilots directions quickly and clearly. Intelligence and a good memory also are important because controllers constantly receive information that they must immediately grasp, interpret, and remember. Decisiveness also is required because controllers often have to make quick decisions. The ability to concentrate is crucial because controllers must make these decisions in the midst of noise and other distractions.

At airports, new controllers begin by supplying pilots with basic flight data and airport information. They then advance to the position of ground controller, then local controller, departure controller, and, finally, arrival controller. At an air route traffic control center, new controllers first deliver printed flight plans to teams, gradually advancing to radar associate controller and then radar controller.

Controllers can transfer to jobs at different locations or advance to supervisory positions, including management or staff jobs, such as air traffic control data systems computer specialist, in air traffic control and top administrative jobs in the FAA. However, there are only limited opportunities for a controller to switch from a position in an enroute center to a tower.

Employment

Air traffic controllers held about 24,000 jobs in 2004. The vast majority were employed by the FAA. Air traffic controllers work at airports—in towers and flight service stations—and in air route traffic control centers. Some professional controllers conduct research at the FAA's national experimental center near Atlantic City, NJ. Others serve as instructors at the FAA Academy in Oklahoma City, OK. A small number of civilian controllers work for the U.S. Department of Defense. In addition to controllers employed by the Federal Government, some work for private air traffic control companies providing service to non-FAA towers.

Job Outlook

Employment of air traffic controllers is expected to grow about as fast as the average for all occupations through the year 2014. Increasing air traffic will require more controllers to handle the additional work. Employment growth, however, is not expected to keep pace with growth in the number of aircraft flying. New computerized systems will assist the controller by automatically making many of the routine decisions. This will allow controllers to handle more traffic, thus increasing their productivity. In addition, Federal budget constraints may limit hiring of air traffic controllers.

More job openings are expected as the result of replacement needs from workers leaving the occupation. The majority of today's air traffic controllers will be eligible to retire over the next decade, although not all are expected to do so. Nevertheless, replacement needs will result in job opportunities each year for those graduating from the FAA training programs. Despite the increasing number of jobs coming open, competition to get into the FAA training programs is expected to remain keen, as there generally are many more applicants to get into the schools than there are openings, but those who graduate have good prospects of getting a job as a controller.

Air traffic controllers who continue to meet the proficiency and medical requirements enjoy more job security than do most workers. The demand for air travel and the workloads of air traffic controllers decline during recessions, but controllers seldom are laid off.

Earnings

Air traffic controllers earn relatively high pay and have good benefits. Median annual earnings of air traffic controllers in May 2004 were $102,030. The middle 50 percent earned between $78,170 and $126,260. The lowest 10 percent earned less than $57,720, and the highest 10 percent earned more than $139,210.

The average annual salary, excluding overtime earnings, for air traffic controllers in the Federal Government—which employs 90 percent of the total—in nonsupervisory, supervisory, and managerial positions was $106,380 in May 2004. The Air Traffic Control pay system classifies each air traffic facility into one of eight levels with corresponding pay bands. Under this pay system, controllers' salaries are determined by the rating of the facility. The higher the rating, the higher the controller's salary and the greater the demand on the controller's judgment, skill, and decision making ability.

Depending on length of service, air traffic controllers receive 13 to 26 days of paid vacation and 13 days of paid sick leave each year, in addition to life insurance and health benefits. Controllers also can retire at an earlier age and with fewer years of service than other Federal employees. Air traffic controllers are eligible to retire at age 50 with 20 years of service as an active air traffic controller or after 25 years of active service at any age. There is a mandatory retirement age of 56 for controllers who manage air traffic. However, Federal law provides for exemptions to the mandatory age of 56, up to age 61, for controllers having exceptional skills and experience.

Related Occupations

Airfield operations specialists also are involved in the direction and control of traffic in air transportation.

Sources of Additional Information

For further information on how to qualify and apply for a job as an air traffic controller, contact the FAA:
➤ Federal Aviation Administration, 800 Independence Ave. SW., Washington, DC 20591. Internet: **http://www.faa.gov**

Motor Vehicle Operators

Bus Drivers

(O*NET 53-3021.00, 53-3022.00)

Significant Points

- Opportunities should be good, particularly for school bus driver jobs; applicants for higher paying public transit bus driver positions may encounter competition.

- State and Federal governments establish bus driver qualifications and standards, which include a commercial driver's license.

- Work schedules vary considerably among various types of bus drivers.

- Bus drivers must possess strong customer service skills, including communication skills and the ability to manage large groups of people with varying needs.

Nature of the Work

Bus drivers provide transportation for millions of people every year, from commuters to school children to vacationers. There are two major kinds of bus drivers: *Transit and Intercity bus drivers*, who transport people between regions of a State or of the country, along routes run within a metropolitan area or county, or on chartered excursions and tours; and *school bus drivers*, who take children to and from schools and related events.

Bus drivers pick up and drop off passengers at bus stops, stations, or—in the case of students—at regularly scheduled neighborhood locations, all according to strict time schedules. Drivers must operate vehicles safely, especially in heavy traffic. They cannot let light traffic put them ahead of schedule so that they miss passengers. Bus drivers drive a range of vehicles from 15-passenger buses to 60-foot articulated buses that can carry more than 100 passengers.

Local-transit and *intercity bus drivers* report to their assigned terminal or garage, where they stock up on tickets or transfers and prepare trip report forms. In some transportation firms, maintenance departments are responsible for keeping vehicles in good condition; in others, drivers may be expected to check their vehicle's tires, brakes, windshield wipers, lights, oil, fuel, and water supply before beginning their routes. Drivers usually verify that the bus has safety equipment, such as fire extinguishers, first aid kits, and emergency reflectors.

During the course of their shift, local-transit and intercity bus drivers collect fares; answer questions about schedules, routes, and transfer points; and sometimes announce stops. Intercity bus drivers may make only a single one-way trip to a distant city or a round trip each day. They may stop at towns just a few miles apart or only at large cities hundreds of miles apart. Local-transit bus drivers may make several trips each day over the same city and suburban streets, stopping as frequently as every few blocks.

Local-transit bus drivers submit daily trip reports with a record of trips, significant schedule delays, and mechanical problems. Intercity drivers who drive across State or national boundaries must comply with U.S. Department of Transportation regulations. These include completing vehicle inspection reports and recording distances traveled and the periods they spend driving, performing other duties, and off duty.

Some intercity drivers operate motor coaches which transport passengers on chartered trips and sightseeing tours. Drivers routinely interact with customers and tour guides to make the trip as comfortable and informative as possible. They are directly responsible for keeping to strict schedules, adhering to the guidelines of the tour's itinerary, and ensuring the overall success of the trip. These drivers act as customer service representative, tour guide, program director, and safety guide. Trips frequently last more than a day. The driver may be away for more than a week if assigned to an extended tour. As with all commercial drivers who drive across State or national boundaries, motor coach drivers must comply with U.S. Department of Transportation and State regulations.

School bus drivers usually drive the same routes each day, stopping to pick up pupils in the morning and return them to their homes in the afternoon. Some school bus drivers also transport students and teachers on field trips or to sporting events. In addition to driving, some school bus drivers work part time in the school system as janitors, mechanics, or classroom assistants when not driving buses.

Bus drivers must be alert to prevent accidents, especially in heavy traffic or in bad weather, and to avoid sudden stops or swerves that jar passengers. School bus drivers must exercise particular caution when children are getting on or off the bus. They must maintain order on their bus and enforce school safety standards by allowing only students to board. In addition, they must know and enforce the school system's rules regarding student conduct.

School bus drivers do not always have to report to an assigned terminal or garage. In some cases, they have the choice of taking their bus home or parking it in a more convenient area. School bus drivers do not collect fares. Instead, they prepare weekly reports on the number of students, trips or "runs," work hours, miles, and fuel consumption. Their supervisors set time schedules and routes for the day or week.

School bus drivers hold 7 out of 10 bus driving jobs.

Working Conditions

Driving a bus through heavy traffic while dealing with passengers is more stressful and fatiguing than physically strenuous. Many drivers enjoy the opportunity to work without direct supervision, with full responsibility for their bus and passengers. To improve working conditions and retain drivers, many buslines provide ergonomically designed seats and controls for drivers. Many bus companies use Global Positioning Systems to help dispatchers manage their bus fleets and help drivers navigate.

Intercity bus drivers may work nights, weekends, and holidays and often spend nights away from home, during which they stay in hotels at company expense. Senior drivers with regular routes have regular weekly work schedules, but others do not have regular schedules and must be prepared to report for work on short notice. They report for work only when called for a charter assignment or to drive extra buses on a regular route. Intercity bus travel and charter work tend to be seasonal. From May through August, drivers may work the maximum number of hours per week that regulations allow. During winter, junior drivers may work infrequently, except for busy holiday travel periods, and may be furloughed at times.

School bus drivers work only when school is in session. Many work 20 hours a week or less, driving one or two routes in the morning and afternoon. Drivers taking field or athletic trips, or who also have midday kindergarten routes, may work more hours a week. As more students with a variety of physical and behavioral disabilities assimilate into mainstream schools, school bus drivers must learn how to accommodate their special needs.

Regular local-transit bus drivers usually have a 5-day workweek; Saturdays and Sundays are considered regular workdays. Some drivers work evenings and after midnight. To accommodate commuters, many work "split shifts"—for example, 6 a.m. to 10 a.m. and 3 p.m. to 7 p.m., with time off in between.

Intercity bus drivers operating tour and charter buses may work any day and all hours of the day, including weekends and holidays. Their hours are dictated by the destinations, schedules, and itineraries of chartered tours. Like all commercial drivers, their weekly hours must be consistent with the Department of Transportation's rules and regulations concerning hours of service. For example, drivers may drive for 10 hours and work for up to 15 hours—including driving and nondriving duties—before having 8 hours off duty. Drivers may not drive after having worked for 60 hours in the past 7 days or 70 hours in the past 8 days. Most drivers are required to document their time in a logbook.

Training, Other Qualifications, and Advancement

Many employers prefer high school graduates and require a written test of ability to follow complex bus schedules. Many intercity and public transit bus companies prefer applicants who are at least 24 years of age; some require several years of experience driving a bus or truck. In some States, school bus drivers must pass a background investigation to uncover any criminal record or history of mental problems.

Bus driver qualifications and standards are established by State and Federal regulations. All drivers must comply with Federal regulations and with any State regulations that exceed Federal requirements. Federal regulations require drivers who operate commercial motor vehicles in excess of 26,000 pounds gross vehicle weight rating or designed to carry 16 or more persons, including the driver, to hold a commercial driver's license (CDL) with the appropriate endorsements from the State in which they live.

To qualify for a CDL, applicants must pass a knowledge test on rules and regulations and then demonstrate in a skills test that they can operate a bus safely. A national databank records all driving violations incurred by persons who hold commercial licenses, and a

State may not issue a CDL to a person who has already had a license suspended or revoked in another State. To be issued a CDL, a driver must surrender all other driver's licenses. A driver with a CDL must accompany trainees until the trainees get their own CDL. In addition to having a CDL, all bus drivers must have a "passenger" endorsement for their CDL, which requires passing a knowledge test and demonstrating the necessary skills in a vehicle of the same type as the one they would be driving in their duties. Information on how to apply for a CDL and each type of endorsement can be obtained from State motor vehicle administrations.

While many States allow those who are 18 years of age and older to drive buses within State borders, the Department of Transportation establishes minimum qualifications for bus drivers engaged in interstate commerce. Federal Motor Carrier Safety Regulations require drivers to be at least 21 years old and to pass a physical examination once every 2 years. The main physical requirements include good hearing, at least 20/40 vision with or without glasses or corrective lenses, and a 70-degree field of vision in each eye. Drivers cannot be colorblind. They must be able to hear a forced whisper in one ear at not less than 5 feet, with or without a hearing aide. Drivers must have normal blood pressure as well as normal use of their arms and legs. They may not use any controlled substances, unless prescribed by a licensed physician. Persons with epilepsy or with diabetes controlled by insulin are not permitted to be interstate bus drivers. Federal regulations also require employers to test their drivers for alcohol and drug use as a condition of employment and require periodic random tests of the drivers while they are on duty. In addition, a driver must not have been convicted of a felony involving the use of a motor vehicle, a crime involving drugs, driving under the influence of drugs or alcohol, refusing to submit to an alcohol test required by a State or its implied consent laws or regulations, leaving the scene of a crime, or causing a fatality through negligent operation of a commercial vehicle. All drivers must be able to read and speak English well enough to read road signs, prepare reports, and communicate with law enforcement officers and the public. In addition, drivers must take a written examination on the Motor Carrier Safety Regulations of the U.S. Department of Transportation.

Because bus drivers deal with passengers, they must be courteous. They need an even temperament and emotional stability because driving in heavy, fast-moving, or stop-and-go traffic and dealing with passengers can be stressful. Drivers must have strong customer service skills, including communication skills and the ability to coordinate and manage large groups of people.

Most intercity bus companies and local-transit systems give driver trainees 2 to 8 weeks of classroom and behind-the-wheel instruction. In the classroom, trainees learn Department of Transportation and company work rules, safety regulations, State and municipal driving regulations, and safe driving practices. They also learn to read schedules, determine fares, keep records, and deal courteously with passengers.

School bus drivers also are required to obtain a CDL from the State in which they live. They must additionally have a "school bus" endorsement for their CDL. To receive this endorsement, they must pass a written test and demonstrate necessary skills. The skills portion of the test is taken in a bus of the same type that they would be driving on their route. Both of these tests are specific to school buses and are in addition to the testing required to receive a CDL and the "passenger" endorsement. Many persons who become school bus drivers have never driven any vehicle larger than an automobile. They receive between 1 and 4 weeks of driving instruction and classroom training on State and local laws, regulations, and policies of operating school buses; safe driving practices; driver-pupil relations; first aid; special needs of disabled and emotionally troubled students; and emergency evacuation procedures. School bus drivers also must be aware of the school system's rules for discipline and conduct for bus drivers and the students they transport.

During training, bus drivers practice driving on set courses. They practice turns and zigzag maneuvers, backing up, and driving in narrow lanes. Then, they drive in light traffic and, eventually, on congested highways and city streets. They also make trial runs without passengers to improve their driving skills and learn the routes. Local-transit trainees memorize and drive each of the runs operating out of their assigned garage. New drivers make regularly scheduled trips with passengers, accompanied by an experienced driver who gives helpful tips, answers questions, and evaluates the new driver's performance. Most bus drivers get brief supplemental training at regular periods to keep abreast of safety issues and regulatory changes.

New intercity and local-transit drivers usually are placed on an "extra" list to drive chartered runs, extra buses on regular runs, and special runs (for example, during morning and evening rush hours and to sports events). They also substitute for regular drivers who are ill or on vacation. New drivers remain on the extra list, and may work only part time, perhaps for several years, until they have enough seniority to be given a regular run.

Senior drivers may bid for the runs that they prefer, such as those with more work hours, lighter traffic, weekends off, or—in the case of intercity bus drivers—higher earnings or fewer workdays per week.

Opportunities for promotion are generally limited. However, experienced drivers may become supervisors or dispatchers—assigning buses to drivers, checking whether drivers are on schedule, rerouting buses to avoid blocked streets or other problems, and dispatching extra vehicles and service crews to scenes of accidents and breakdowns. In transit agencies with rail systems, drivers may become train operators or station attendants. Opportunities exist for bus drivers to become either instructors of new bus drivers or master-instructors, who train new instructors. A few drivers become managers. Promotion in publicly owned bus systems is often determined by competitive civil service examination. Some motor coach drivers purchase their own equipment and open their own business.

Employment

Bus drivers held about 653,000 jobs in 2004. About 35 percent worked part time. Around 71 percent of all bus drivers were school bus drivers working primarily for school systems or for companies providing school bus services under contract. Most of the remainder worked for private and local government transit systems; some also worked for intercity and charter bus lines.

Job Outlook

Persons seeking jobs as bus drivers likely will encounter many opportunities. Individuals who have good driving records and who are willing to work a part-time or irregular schedule probably will have the best job prospects. School bus driving jobs, particularly in rapidly growing suburban areas, should be easiest to acquire because most are part-time positions with high turnover and less training required than for other bus-driving jobs. Those seeking higher paying public transit bus driver positions may encounter competition. Opportunities for intercity driving positions should be good, although employment prospects for motor coach drivers will depend on tourism which fluctuates with the cyclical nature of the economy.

Employment of bus drivers overall is expected to increase about as fast as the average for all occupations through the year 2014, primarily to meet the transportation needs of the growing general population and the school-aged population. Most job openings are expected to occur each year because of the need to replace workers who take jobs in other occupations or who retire or leave the occupation for other reasons.

The number of school bus drivers is expected to increase as fast as average over the next 10 years, although at a decreasing rate. School enrollments are projected to increase in 30 States and to decrease in 20 States. The net effect will be a slowdown in school enrollment and, therefore, in employment growth of school bus drivers. This, as well as the part-time nature of the occupation, will result in most openings for school bus drivers being to replace those who leave the occupation.

Employment growth for local-transit bus drivers is expected to be faster than the average for all occupations in 2004, and will likely be the result of the increasing popularity of mass transit due to congestion and rising fuel prices, as well as the demand for transit services in expanding portions of metropolitan areas. There may be competition for positions with more regular hours and steady driving routes.

Competition from other modes of transportation—airplane, train, or automobile—will temper job growth among intercity bus drivers. Most growth in intercity bus transportation will occur in group charters to locations not served by other modes of transportation. Like automobiles, buses have a far greater number of possible destinations than airplanes or trains. Since they offer greater cost savings and convenience over automobiles, buses usually are the most economical option for tour groups traveling to out-of-the-way destinations.

Full-time bus drivers rarely are laid off during recessions. If the number of passengers decreases, however, employers might reduce the hours of part-time local-transit and intercity bus drivers since fewer extra buses would be needed. Seasonal layoffs are common. Many intercity bus drivers with little seniority, for example, are furloughed during the winter when regularly scheduled and charter business declines, while school bus drivers seldom work during the summer or school holidays.

Earnings

Median hourly earnings of transit and intercity bus drivers were $14.30 in May 2004. The middle 50 percent earned between $10.74 and $19.31 an hour. The lowest 10 percent earned less than $8.66, and the highest 10 percent earned more than $23.53 an hour. Median hourly earnings in the industries employing the largest numbers of transit and intercity bus drivers in May 2004 were as follows:

Local government	$17.10
Interurban and rural bus transportation	15.86
Urban transit systems	13.49
Charter bus industry	10.81
Other transit and ground passenger transportation	10.74

Median hourly earnings of school bus drivers were $11.18 in May 2004. The middle 50 percent earned between $8.10 and $13.92 an hour. The lowest 10 percent earned less than $6.23, and the highest 10 percent earned more than $16.81 an hour. Median hourly earnings in the industries employing the largest numbers of school bus drivers in May 2004 were as follows:

School and employee bus transportation	$11.97
Elementary and secondary schools	10.74
Other transit and ground passenger transportation	10.62
Child day care services	9.28
Individual and family services	8.75

The benefits bus drivers receive from their employers vary greatly. Most intercity and local-transit bus drivers receive paid health and life insurance, sick leave, vacation leave, and free bus rides on any of

the regular routes of their line or system. School bus drivers receive sick leave, and many are covered by health and life insurance and pension plans. Because they generally do not work when school is not in session, they do not get vacation leave.

Many intercity and local-transit bus drivers are members of the Amalgamated Transit Union. Local-transit bus drivers in New York and several other large cities belong to the Transport Workers Union of America. Some drivers belong to the United Transportation Union or to the International Brotherhood of Teamsters.

Related Occupations

Other workers who drive vehicles on highways and city streets include taxi drivers and chauffeurs, and truck drivers and driver/sales workers.

Sources of Additional Information

For information on employment opportunities, contact local-transit systems, intercity buslines, school systems, or the local offices of the State employment service.

General information on school bus driving is available from:
➤ National School Transportation Association, 113 South West St., 4th Floor, Alexandria, VA 22314.
➤ National Association of State Directors of Pupil Transportation Services, 6298 Rock Hill Road, The Plains, VA 20198-1916.

General information on motor coach driving is available from:
➤ United Motorcoach Association, 113 South West St., 4th Floor, Alexandria, VA 22314.
➤ American Bus Association, 700 13th Street, NW., Suite 575, Washington, D.C. 20005.

Taxi Drivers and Chauffeurs

(O*NET 53-3041.00)

Significant Points

- Taxi drivers and chauffeurs may work any schedule, including full-time, part-time, night, evening, weekend, and seasonal work.
- Many taxi drivers like the independent, unsupervised work of driving their automobile.
- Local governments set license standards for driving experience and training; many taxi and limousine companies set higher standards.
- Job opportunities will be good because of the need to replace the many people who work in this occupation for short periods and then leave.

Nature of the Work

Anyone who has been in a large city knows the importance of taxi and limousine services. *Taxi drivers* and *chauffeurs* help passengers get to and from their homes, workplaces, and recreational pursuits such as dining, entertainment, and shopping, as well as to and from business-related events. These professional drivers also help out-of-town business people and tourists get around in unfamiliar surroundings. Some drivers offer sight-seeing services around their city.

At the beginning of their driving shift, taxi drivers usually report to a taxicab service or garage where they are assigned a vehicle, most frequently a large, conventional automobile modified for commercial passenger transport. They record their name, the date, and the cab's identification number on a trip sheet. Drivers check the cab's fuel and oil levels and make sure that the lights, brakes, and windshield wipers are in good working order. Drivers adjust rear and side mirrors and their seat for comfort. Any equipment or part not in good working order is reported to the dispatcher or company mechanic.

Taxi drivers pick up passengers by "cruising" for fares, prearranging pickups, and picking up passengers from taxistands in high-traffic areas. In urban areas, the majority of passengers flag down drivers cruising the streets. Customers also may prearrange a pickup by calling a cab company and giving a location, approximate pickup time, and destination. The cab company dispatcher then relays the information to a driver by two-way radio, cellular telephone, or onboard computer. Outside of urban areas, the majority of trips are dispatched in this manner. Drivers also pick up passengers waiting at cabstands or in taxi lines at airports, train stations, hotels, restaurants, and other places where people frequently seek taxis.

Some drivers transport individuals with special needs, such as those with disabilities and the elderly. These drivers, known as *paratransit drivers*, operate specially equipped vehicles designed to accommodate a variety of needs in nonemergency situations. Although special certification is not necessary, some additional training on the equipment and passenger needs may be required.

Drivers should be familiar with streets in the areas they serve so that they can use the most efficient route to destinations. They should know the locations of frequently requested destinations, such as airports, bus and railroad terminals, convention centers, hotels, and other points of interest. In case of emergency, the driver should know the location of fire and police stations as well as hospitals.

Upon reaching the destination, drivers determine the fare and announce it to their riders. Fares often consist of many parts. In many cabs, a taximeter measures the fare based on the distance covered and the amount of time the trip took. Drivers turn on the taximeter when passengers enter the cab and turn it off when they reach the final destination. The fare also may include surcharges to help cover fuel costs as well as fees for additional passengers, a fee for handling luggage, and a drop charge—an additional flat fee added for use of the cab. In some cases, fares are determined by a system of zones through which the taxi passes during a trip. Each jurisdiction determines the rate and structure of the fare system covering licensed taxis. Passengers generally add a tip or gratuity to the fare. The amount of the gratuity depends on the passengers' satisfaction with the quality and efficiency of the ride and the courtesy of the driver. Drivers issue receipts upon request by the passenger. They enter onto the trip sheet all information regarding the trip, including the place and time of pickup and dropoff and the total fee; these logs help taxi company management check drivers' activity and efficiency. Drivers also must fill out accident reports when necessary.

Chauffeurs operate limousines, vans, and private cars for limousine companies, private businesses, government agencies, and wealthy individuals. Chauffeur service differs from taxi service in that all trips are prearranged. Many chauffeurs transport customers in large vans between hotels and airports as well as bus or train terminals. Others drive luxury automobiles, such as limousines, to business events, entertainment venues, and social events. Still others provide full-time personal transportation for wealthy families and private companies.

At the beginning of the workday, chauffeurs prepare their automobiles or vans for use. They inspect the vehicle for cleanliness and, when needed, vacuum the interior and wash the exterior body, windows, and mirrors. They check fuel and oil levels and make sure the lights, tires, brakes, and windshield wipers work. Chauffeurs may perform routine maintenance and make minor repairs, such as changing tires or adding oil and other fluids when needed. If a vehicle requires a more complicated repair, they take it to a professional mechanic.

Chauffeurs cater to passengers by providing attentive customer service and paying attention to detail. They help riders into the car

by holding open doors, holding umbrellas when it is raining, and loading packages and luggage into the trunk of the car. Chauffeurs may perform errands for their employers such as delivering packages or picking up clients arriving at airports. To ensure a pleasurable ride in their limousines, many chauffeurs offer conveniences and luxuries such as newspapers, magazines, music, drinks, televisions, and telephones. Increasingly, chauffeurs work as full-service *executive assistants*, simultaneously acting as driver, secretary, and itinerary planner.

Working Conditions

Taxi drivers and chauffeurs occasionally have to load and unload heavy luggage and packages. Driving for long periods can be tiring and uncomfortable, especially in densely populated urban areas. Drivers must be alert to conditions on the road, especially in heavy and congested traffic or in bad weather. They must take precautions to prevent accidents and avoid sudden stops, turns, and other driving maneuvers that would jar passengers. Taxi drivers risk robbery because they work alone and often carry large amounts of cash.

Work hours of taxi drivers and chauffeurs vary greatly. Some jobs offer full-time or part-time employment with work hours that can change from day to day or remain the same every day. It is often necessary for drivers to report to work on short notice. Chauffeurs who work for a single employer may be on call much of the time. Evening and weekend work is common for drivers and chauffeurs employed by limousine and taxicab services.

Taxi drivers and chauffeurs may work any schedule, including full-time, part-time, night, evening, weekend, and seasonal work.

Whereas the needs of the client or employer dictate the work schedule for chauffeurs, the work of taxi drivers is much less structured. Working free of supervision, they may break for a meal or a rest whenever their vehicle is unoccupied. Many taxi drivers like the independent, unsupervised work of driving.

This occupation is attractive to individuals seeking flexible work schedules, such as college and postgraduate students, and to anyone seeking a second source of income. For example, other service workers, such as ambulance drivers and police officers, sometimes moonlight as taxi drivers or chauffeurs.

Full-time taxi drivers usually work one shift a day, which may last from 8 to 12 hours. Part-time drivers may work half a shift each day, or work a full shift once or twice a week. Drivers may work shifts at all times of the day and night because most taxi companies offer services 24 hours a day. Early morning and late night shifts are not uncommon. Drivers work long hours during holidays, weekends, and other special times when demand for their services may be heavier. Independent drivers, however, often set their own hours and schedules.

Design improvements in newer cars have reduced the stress and increased the comfort and efficiency of drivers. Many regulatory bodies overseeing taxi and chauffeur services require standard amenities such as air-conditioning and general upkeep of the vehicles. Some modern taxicabs also are equipped with sophisticated tracking devices, fare meters, and dispatching equipment. Satellites and tracking systems link many of these state-of-the-art vehicles with company headquarters. In a matter of seconds, dispatchers can deliver directions, traffic advisories, weather reports, and other important communications to drivers anywhere in the area. The satellite link also allows dispatchers to track vehicle location, fuel consumption, and engine performance. Automated dispatch systems help dispatchers locate the closest driver to a customer in order to minimize individual wait time and increase the quality of service. Drivers easily can communicate with dispatchers to discuss delivery schedules and courses of action if there are mechanical problems. When threatened with crime or violence, drivers may have special "trouble lights" to alert authorities of emergencies and guarantee that help arrives quickly.

Many municipalities and taxicab and chauffeur companies require drivers to have a neat appearance. Many chauffeurs wear formal attire, such as a tuxedo, a coat and tie, a dress, or a uniform and cap.

Training, Other Qualifications, and Advancement
Local governments set licensing standards and requirements for taxi drivers and chauffeurs which may include minimum amounts of driving experience and training. Many taxi and limousine companies set higher standards than those required by law. It is common for companies to review applicants' medical, credit, criminal, and driving records. In addition, many companies require applicants to be 21, higher than the age typically required by law. Most companies also prefer that an applicant be a high school graduate.

Persons interested in driving a taxicab or a limousine first must have a regular automobile driver's license. Usually, applicants then must acquire a taxi driver or chauffeur's license, commonly called a "hack" license. Some States require only a passenger endorsement on a driver's license; some require only that drivers be certified by their employer; while others require a Commercial Driver's License with a passenger endorsement. While States set licensing requirements, local regulatory bodies usually set other terms and conditions. These often include requirements for training, which can vary greatly. Some localities require new drivers to enroll in training programs consisting of up to 80 hours of classroom instruction before they are allowed to work. To qualify through either an exam or a training program, applicants must know local geography, motor vehicle laws, safe driving practices, and relevant regulations and display some aptitude for customer service. Some localities require an English proficiency test, usually in the form of listening comprehension; applicants who do not pass the English exam must take an English course in addition to any formal driving programs. Some classroom instruction includes route management, mapreading, and service for passengers with disabilities. Many taxicab or limousine companies sponsor applicants, giving them a temporary permit that allows them to drive before they have finished the training program and passed the test. Some jurisdictions, such as New York City, have discontinued this practice and now require driver applicants to complete the licensing process before operating a taxi or limousine.

Some taxi and limousine companies give new drivers on-the-job training. This training is typically informal and often lasts only about a week. Companies show drivers how to operate the taximeter and communications equipment and how to complete paperwork. Other topics covered may include driver safety and the best routes to popular sightseeing and entertainment destinations. Many companies have contracts with social service agencies and transportation services to transport elderly and disabled citizens in nonemergency situations. To support these services, new drivers may get special training in how to handle wheelchair lifts and other mechanical devices.

Taxi drivers and chauffeurs should be able to get along with many different types of people. They must be patient when waiting for passengers and when dealing with rude customers. It also is helpful for drivers to be tolerant and level-headed when driving in heavy and congested traffic. Drivers should be dependable since passengers expect to be picked up at a prearranged time and taken to the correct destination. To be successful, drivers must be responsible and self-motivated because they work with little supervision. Increasingly, companies encourage drivers to develop their own loyal customer base, so as to improve their business.

Many taxi drivers and chauffeurs are *lease drivers*. These drivers pay a daily, weekly, or monthly fee to the company allowing them to lease their vehicles. In the case of limousines, leasing also permits the driver access to the company's dispatch system. The fee also may include charges for vehicle maintenance, insurance, and a deposit on the vehicle. Lease drivers may take their cars home with them when they are not on duty.

Opportunities for advancement are limited for taxi drivers and chauffeurs. Experienced drivers may obtain preferred routes or shifts. Some advance to become lead drivers, who help to train new drivers, or to take dispatching and managerial positions. Many managers start their careers as drivers. Some people start their own limousine companies.

In small and medium-size communities, drivers sometimes are able to buy their own taxi, limousine, or other type of automobile and go into business for themselves. These independent owner-drivers require an additional permit allowing them to operate their vehicle as a company. Some big cities limit the number of operating permits. In these cities, drivers become owner-drivers by buying permits from owner-drivers who leave the business, or by purchasing or leasing them from the city. Although many owner-drivers are successful, some fail to cover expenses and eventually lose their permits and automobiles. For both taxi and limousine service owners, good business sense and courses in accounting, business, and business arithmetic can help an owner-driver to be successful. Knowledge of mechanics enables owner-drivers to perform their own routine maintenance and minor repairs to cut expenses.

Employment
Taxi drivers and chauffeurs held about 188,000 jobs in 2004. About 27 percent of taxi drivers and chauffeurs were self-employed.

Job Outlook

Persons seeking jobs as taxi drivers and chauffeurs should encounter good opportunities because of the need to replace the many people who work in this occupation for short periods and then transfer to other occupations or leave the labor force. Opportunities for drivers vary greatly in terms of earnings, work hours, and working conditions, depending on economic and regulatory conditions. Opportunities should be best for persons with good driving records, good customer service instincts, and the ability to work flexible schedules.

Employment of taxi drivers and chauffeurs is expected to grow faster than the average for all occupations through the year 2014, as local and suburban travel increases. Employment growth also will stem from Federal legislation requiring increased services for persons with disabilities. Rapidly growing metropolitan areas should offer the best job opportunities.

The number of job openings can fluctuate with the overall movements of the economy because the demand for taxi and limousine transportation depends on travel and tourism. During economic slowdowns, drivers seldom are laid off, but they may have to increase their work hours, and earnings may decline. When the economy is strong, job openings are numerous as many drivers transfer to other occupations. Extra drivers may be hired during holiday seasons as well as during peak travel and tourist times.

Earnings

Earnings of taxi drivers and chauffeurs vary greatly, depending on factors such as the number of hours worked, regulatory conditions, customers' tips, and geographic location. Median hourly earnings of salaried taxi drivers and chauffeurs, including tips, were $9.41 in May 2004. The middle 50 percent earned between $7.61 and $11.94 an hour. The lowest 10 percent earned less than $6.43, and the highest 10 percent earned more than $15.62 an hour. Median hourly earnings in the industries employing the largest numbers of taxi drivers and chauffeurs in May 2004 were:

Taxi and limousine service	$10.68
Other transit and ground passenger transportation	9.23
Traveler accommodation	8.48
Automobile dealers	8.45
Automotive equipment rental and leasing	8.25

Related Occupations

Other workers who have similar jobs include bus drivers and truck drivers and driver/sales workers.

Sources of Additional Information

Information on necessary permits and the registration of taxi drivers and chauffeurs is available from local government agencies that regulate taxicabs. Questions regarding licensing should be directed to your State motor vehicle administration. For information about work opportunities as a taxi driver or chauffeur, contact local taxi or limousine companies or State employment service offices.

For general information about the work of taxi drivers, chauffeurs, and paratransit drivers, contact:

➤ Taxicab, Limousine & Paratransit Association, 3849 Farragut Ave., Kensington, MD 20895.

For general information about the work of limousine drivers, contact:

➤ National Limousine Association, 49 South Maple Ave., Marlton, NJ 08053. Internet: **http://www.limo.org**

Truck Drivers and Driver/Sales Workers

(O*NET 53-3031.00, 53-3032.01, 53-3032.02, 53-3033.00)

Significant Points

- Job opportunities should be favorable.

- Competition is expected for jobs offering the highest earnings or most favorable work schedules.

- A commercial driver's license is required to operate most larger trucks.

Nature of the Work

Truck drivers are a constant presence on the Nation's highways and interstates. They deliver everything from automobiles to canned food. Firms of all kinds rely on trucks to pick up and deliver goods because no other form of transportation can deliver goods door-to-door. Even if some goods travel most of the way by ship, train, or airplane, almost everything is carried by trucks at some point in its journey.

Before leaving the terminal or warehouse, truck drivers check the fuel level and oil in their trucks. They also inspect the trucks to make sure that the brakes, windshield wipers, and lights are working and that a fire extinguisher, flares, and other safety equipment are aboard and in working order. Drivers make sure their cargo is secure and adjust the mirrors so that both sides of the truck are visible from the driver's seat. Drivers report equipment that is inoperable, missing, or loaded improperly to the dispatcher.

Once under way, drivers must be alert in order to prevent accidents. Drivers can see farther down the road because large trucks seat them higher off the ground than other vehicles. This allows them to see the road ahead and select lanes that are moving more smoothly as well as giving them warning of any dangerous road conditions ahead of them.

The duration of runs vary according to the types of cargo and the destinations. Local drivers may provide daily service for a specific route or region, while other drivers make longer, intercity and interstate deliveries. Interstate and intercity cargo tends to vary from job to job more than local cargo. A driver's responsibilities and assignments change according to the type of loads transported and their vehicle's size.

New technologies are changing the way truck drivers work, especially long-distance truck drivers. Satellites and the Global Positioning System link many trucks with their company's headquarters. Troubleshooting information, directions, weather reports, and other important communications can be instantly relayed to the truck. Drivers can easily communicate with the dispatcher to discuss delivery schedules and courses of action in the event of mechanical problems. The satellite link also allows the dispatcher to track the truck's location, fuel consumption, and engine performance. Some drivers also work with computerized inventory tracking equipment. It is important for the producer, warehouse, and customer to know their product's location at all times so they can maintain a high quality of service.

Heavy truck and tractor-trailer drivers operate trucks or vans with a capacity of at least 26,000 pounds Gross Vehicle Weight (GVW). They transport goods including cars, livestock, and other materials in liquid, loose, or packaged form. Many routes are from city to city and cover long distances. Some companies use two drivers on very long runs—one drives while the other sleeps in a berth behind the cab. These "sleeper" runs can last for days, or even weeks. Trucks on sleeper runs typically stop only for fuel, food, loading, and unloading.

Some heavy truck and tractor-trailer drivers who have regular runs transport freight to the same city on a regular basis. Other drivers perform ad hoc runs because shippers request varying service to different cities every day.

The U.S. Department of Transportation requires that drivers keep a log of their activities, the condition of the truck, and the circumstances of any accidents.

Long-distance heavy truck and tractor-trailer drivers spend most of their working time behind the wheel, but also may have to load or unload their cargo. This is especially common when drivers haul specialty cargo, because they may be the only ones at the destination familiar with procedures or certified to handle the materials. Auto-transport drivers, for example, position cars on the trailers at the manufacturing plant and remove them at the dealerships. When picking up or delivering furniture, drivers of long-distance moving vans hire local workers to help them load or unload.

Light or delivery services truck drivers operate vans and trucks weighing less than 26,000 pounds GVW. They pick up or deliver merchandise and packages within a specific area. This may include short "turnarounds" to deliver a shipment to a nearby city, pick up another loaded truck or van, and drive it back to their home base the same day. These services may require use of electronic delivery tracking systems to track the whereabouts of the merchandise or packages. Light or delivery services truck drivers usually load or unload the merchandise at the customer's place of business. They may have helpers if there are many deliveries to make during the day, or if the load requires heavy moving. Typically, before the driver arrives for work, material handlers load the trucks and arrange items for ease of delivery. Customers must sign receipts for goods and pay drivers the balance due on the merchandise if there is a cash-on-delivery arrangement. At the end of the day drivers turn in receipts, payments, records of deliveries made, and any reports on mechanical problems with their trucks.

Some local truck drivers have sales and customer service responsibilities. The primary responsibility of *driver/sales workers*, or *route drivers*, is to deliver and sell their firm's products over established routes or within an established territory. They sell goods such as food products, including restaurant takeout items, or pick up and deliver items such as laundry. Their response to customer complaints and requests can make the difference between a large order and a lost customer. Route drivers may also take orders and collect payments.

The duties of driver/sales workers vary according to their industry, the policies of their employer, and the emphasis placed on their sales responsibility. Most have wholesale routes that deliver to businesses and stores, rather than to homes. For example, wholesale bakery driver/sales workers deliver and arrange bread, cakes, rolls, and other baked goods on display racks in grocery stores. They estimate how many of each item to stock by paying close attention to what is selling. They may recommend changes in a store's order or encourage the manager to stock new bakery products. Laundries that rent linens, towels, work clothes, and other items employ driver/sales workers to visit businesses regularly to replace soiled laundry. Their duties also may include soliciting new customers along their sales route.

After completing their route, driver/sales workers place orders for their next deliveries based on product sales and customer requests.

Truck driving is an occupation well suited for those who are self-motivated and able to work with little supervision.

Working Conditions

Truck driving has become less physically demanding because most trucks now have more comfortable seats, better ventilation, and improved, ergonomically designed cabs. Although these changes make the work environment less taxing, driving for many hours at a stretch, loading and unloading cargo, and making many deliveries can be tiring. Local truck drivers, unlike long-distance drivers, usually return home in the evening. Some self-employed long-distance truck drivers who own and operate their trucks spend most of the year away from home.

Design improvements in newer trucks have reduced stress and increased the efficiency of long-distance drivers. Many newer trucks are equipped with refrigerators, televisions, and bunks.

The U.S. Department of Transportation governs work hours and other working conditions of truck drivers engaged in interstate commerce. A long-distance driver may drive for 11 hours and work for up to 14 hours—including driving and non-driving duties—after having 10 hours off-duty. A driver may not drive after having worked for 60 hours in the past 7 days or 70 hours in the past 8 days unless they have taken at least 34 consecutive hours off-duty. Most drivers are required to document their time in a logbook. Many drivers, particularly on long runs, work close to the maximum time permitted because they typically are compensated according to the number of miles or hours they drive. Drivers on long runs face boredom, loneliness, and fatigue. Drivers often travel nights, holidays, and weekends to avoid traffic delays.

Local truck drivers frequently work 50 or more hours a week. Drivers who handle food for chain grocery stores, produce markets, or bakeries typically work long hours—starting late at night or early in the morning. Although most drivers have regular routes, some have different routes each day. Many local truck drivers, particularly driver/sales workers, load and unload their own trucks. This requires considerable lifting, carrying, and walking each day.

Training, Other Qualifications, and Advancement

State and Federal regulations govern the qualifications and standards for truck drivers. All drivers must comply with Federal regulations and any State regulations that are in excess of those Federal requirements. Truck drivers must have a driver's license issued by the State in which they live, and most employers require a clean driving record. Drivers of trucks designed to carry 26,000 pounds or more—including most tractor-trailers, as well as bigger straight trucks—must obtain a commercial driver's license (CDL) from the State in which they live. All truck drivers who operate trucks transporting hazardous materials must obtain a CDL, regardless of truck size. In order to receive the hazardous materials endorsement a driver must be fingerprinted and submit to a criminal background check by the Transportation Security Administration. Federal regulations governing CDL administration allow for States to exempt farmers, emergency medical technicians, firefighters, some military drivers, and snow and ice removers from the need for a CDL at the State's discretion. In many States a regular driver's license is sufficient for driving light trucks and vans.

To qualify for a CDL an applicant must have a clean driving record, pass a written test on rules and regulations, and then demonstrate that they can operate a commercial truck safely. A national database permanently records all driving violations committed by those with a CDL. A State will check these records and deny a CDL to those who already have a license suspended or revoked in another State. Licensed drivers must accompany trainees until they get their own CDL. A person may not hold more than one license at a time and must surrender any other licenses when a CDL is issued. Information on how to apply for a CDL may be obtained from State motor vehicle administrations.

Many States allow those who are as young as 18 years old to drive trucks within their borders. To drive a commercial vehicle between States one must be 21 years of age, according to the U.S. Department of Transportation (U.S. DOT), which establishes minimum qualifications for truck drivers engaging in interstate commerce. Federal Motor Carrier Safety Regulations—published by U.S. DOT—require drivers to be at least 21 years old and to pass a physical examination once every 2 years. The main physical requirements include good hearing, at least 20/40 vision with glasses or corrective lenses, and a 70-degree field of vision in each eye. Drivers may not be colorblind. Drivers must be able to hear a forced whisper in one ear at not less than 5 feet, with a hearing aid if needed. Drivers must have normal use of arms and legs and normal blood pressure. Drivers may not use any controlled substances, unless prescribed by a licensed physician. Persons with epilepsy or diabetes controlled by insulin are not permitted to be interstate truck drivers. Federal regulations also require employers to test their drivers for alcohol and drug use as a condition of employment, and require periodic random tests of the drivers while they are on duty. A driver must not have been convicted of a felony involving the use of a motor vehicle; a crime involving drugs; driving under the influence of drugs or alcohol; refusing to submit to an alcohol test required by a State or its implied consent laws or regulations; leaving the scene of a crime; or causing a fatality through negligent operation of a motor vehicle. All drivers must be able to read and speak English well enough to read road signs, prepare reports, and communicate with law enforcement officers and the public.

Many trucking operations have higher standards than those described here. Many firms require that drivers be at least 22 years old, be able to lift heavy objects, and have driven trucks for 3 to 5 years. Many prefer to hire high school graduates and require annual physical examinations. Companies have an economic incentive to hire less risky drivers, as good drivers use less fuel and cost less to insure.

Taking driver-training courses is a desirable method of preparing for truck driving jobs and for obtaining a CDL. High school courses in driver training and automotive mechanics also may be helpful. Many private and public vocational-technical schools offer tractor-trailer driver training programs. Students learn to maneuver large vehicles on crowded streets and in highway traffic. They also learn to inspect trucks and freight for compliance with regulations. Some programs provide only a limited amount of actual driving experience. Completion of a program does not guarantee a job. Those interested in attending a driving school should check with local trucking companies to make sure the school's training is acceptable. Some States require prospective drivers to complete a training course in basic truck driving before being issued their CDL. The Professional Truck Driver Institute (PTDI), a nonprofit organization established by the trucking industry, manufacturers, and others, certifies driver training courses at truck driver training schools that meet industry standards and Federal Highway Administration guidelines for training tractor-trailer drivers.

Drivers must get along well with people because they often deal directly with customers. Employers seek driver/sales workers who speak well and have self-confidence, initiative, tact, and a neat appearance. Employers also look for responsible, self-motivated individuals who are able to work well with little supervision.

Training given to new drivers by employers is usually informal, and may consist of only a few hours of instruction from an experienced driver, sometimes on the new employee's own time. New drivers may also ride with and observe experienced drivers before getting their own assignments. Drivers receive additional training to drive special types of trucks or handle hazardous materials. Some companies give 1 to 2 days of classroom instruction covering general duties, the operation and loading of a truck, company policies, and the preparation of delivery forms and company records. Driver/sales workers also receive training on the various types of products their company carries so that they can effectively answer questions about the products and more easily market them to their customers.

Although most new truck drivers are assigned to regular driving jobs immediately, some start as extra drivers—substituting for regular drivers who are ill or on vacation. Extra drivers receive a regular assignment when an opening occurs.

New drivers sometimes start on panel trucks or other small straight trucks. As they gain experience and show competent driving skills they may advance to larger, heavier trucks and finally to tractor-trailers.

The advancement of truck drivers generally is limited to driving runs that provide increased earnings, preferred schedules, or working conditions. Local truck drivers may advance to driving heavy or specialized trucks, or transfer to long-distance truck driving. Working for companies that also employ long-distance drivers is the best way to advance to these positions. Few truck drivers become dispatchers or managers.

Some long-distance truck drivers purchase trucks and go into business for themselves. Although some of these owner-operators are successful, others fail to cover expenses and go out of business. Owner-operators should have good business sense as well as truck driving experience. Courses in accounting, business, and business mathematics are helpful. Knowledge of truck mechanics can enable owner-operators to perform their own routine maintenance and minor repairs.

Employment

Truck drivers and driver/sales workers held about 3.2 million jobs in 2004. Of these workers, 451,000 were driver/sales workers and 2.8 million were truck drivers. Most truck drivers find employment in large metropolitan areas or along major interstate roadways where trucking, retail, and wholesale companies tend to have their distribution outlets. Some drivers work in rural areas, providing specialized services such as delivering newspapers to customers.

The truck transportation industry employed 25 percent of all truck drivers and driver/sales workers in the United States. Another 25 percent worked for companies engaged in wholesale or retail trade. The remaining truck drivers and driver/sales workers were distributed across many industries, including construction and manufacturing.

Around 9 percent of all truck drivers and driver/sales workers were self-employed. Of these, a significant number were owner-operators who either served a variety of businesses independently or leased their services and trucks to a trucking company.

Job Outlook

Job opportunities should be favorable for truck drivers. In addition to growth in demand for truck drivers, numerous job openings will occur as experienced drivers leave this large occupation to transfer to other fields of work, retire, or leave the labor force for other reasons. Jobs vary greatly in terms of earnings, weekly work hours, the number of nights spent on the road, and quality of equipment. There may be competition for the jobs with the highest earnings and most favorable work schedules.

Overall employment of truck drivers and driver/sales workers is expected to increase about as fast as the average for all occupations through the year 2014, due to growth in the economy and in the amount of freight carried by truck. Competing forms of freight transportation—rail, air, and ship transportation—still require trucks to move the goods between ports, depots, airports, warehouses, retailers, and final consumers who are not connected to these other modes of transportation. Demand for long-distance drivers will remain strong because they can transport perishable and time-sensitive goods more effectively than alternate modes of transportation. Job opportunities for truck drivers with local carriers will be more competitive than those with long-distance carriers because of the more desirable working conditions of local carriers.

Job opportunities may vary from year to year, since the output of the economy dictates the amount of freight to be moved. Companies tend to hire more drivers when the economy is strong and their services are in high demand. When the economy slows, employers hire fewer drivers or may lay off some drivers. Independent owner-operators are particularly vulnerable to slowdowns. Industries least likely to be affected by economic fluctuation, such as grocery stores, tend to be the most stable employers of truck drivers and driver/sales workers.

Earnings

Median hourly earnings of heavy truck and tractor-trailer drivers were $16.11 in May 2004. The middle 50 percent earned between $12.67 and $20.09 an hour. The lowest 10 percent earned less than $10.18, and the highest 10 percent earned more than $24.07 an hour. Median hourly earnings in the industries employing the largest numbers of heavy truck and tractor-trailer drivers in May 2004 were:

General freight trucking	$17.56
Grocery and related product wholesalers	17.32
Specialized freight trucking	15.61
Employment services	14.82
Cement and concrete product manufacturing	14.47

Median hourly earnings of light or delivery services truck drivers were $11.80 in May 2004. The middle 50 percent earned between $8.96 and $16.00 an hour. The lowest 10 percent earned less than $7.20, and the highest 10 percent earned more than $20.83 an hour. Median hourly earnings in the industries employing the largest numbers of light or delivery services truck drivers in May 2004 were:

Couriers	$17.94
General freight trucking	14.79
Grocery and related product wholesalers	12.44
Building material and supplies dealers	10.85
Automotive parts, accessories, and tire stores	8.07

Median hourly earnings of driver/sales workers, including commissions, were $9.66 in May 2004. The middle 50 percent earned between $6.94 and $14.59 an hour. The lowest 10 percent earned less than $5.96, and the highest 10 percent earned more than $19.81 an hour. Median hourly earnings in the industries employing the largest numbers of driver/sales workers in May 2004 were:

Drycleaning and laundry services	$14.67
Direct selling establishments	13.55
Grocery and related product wholesalers	12.36
Limited-service eating places	6.77
Full-service restaurants	6.59

Local truck drivers tend to be paid by the hour, with extra pay for working overtime. Employers pay long-distance drivers primarily by the mile. The per-mile rate can vary greatly from employer to employer and may even depend on the type of cargo they are hauling. Some long-distance drivers are paid a percent of each load's revenue. Typically, earnings increase with mileage driven, seniority, and the size and type of truck driven. Most driver/sales workers receive commissions based on their sales in addition to their hourly wages.

Most self-employed truck drivers are primarily engaged in long-distance hauling. Many truck drivers are members of the International Brotherhood of Teamsters. Some truck drivers employed by companies outside the trucking industry are members of unions representing the plant workers of the companies for which they work.

Related Occupations

Other driving occupations include ambulance drivers and attendants, except emergency medical technicians; bus drivers; and taxi drivers and chauffeurs. Another occupation involving sales duties is sales representatives, wholesale and manufacturing.

Sources of Additional Information

Information on truck driver employment opportunities is available from local trucking companies and local offices of the State employment service.

Information on career opportunities in truck driving may be obtained from:
➤ American Trucking Associations, Inc., 2200 Mill Rd., Alexandria, VA 22314. Internet: **http://www.trucking.org**

A list of certified tractor-trailer driver training courses may be obtained from:
➤ Professional Truck Driver Institute, 2200 Mill Rd., Alexandria, VA 22314. Internet: **http://www.ptdi.org**

Information on union truck driving can be obtained from:
➤ The International Brotherhood of Teamsters, 25 Louisiana Ave., NW., Washington, DC 20001.

Rail Transportation Occupations

(O*NET 53-4011.00, 53-4012.00, 53-4013.00, 53-4021.01, 53-4013.02, 53-4031.00, 53-4041.00, 53-4099.99)

Significant Points

- Opportunities are expected to be good for qualified applicants, mainly because of the large number of workers expected to retire or leave these occupations in the next decade.

- Employment is expected to decline due to productivity increases.

- Most workers begin as yard laborers and later may have the opportunity to train for engineer or conductor jobs.

- Eight out of 10 workers are members of unions, and earnings are relatively high.

Nature of the Work

More than a century ago, freight and passenger railroads were the ties binding the Nation together and the engine driving the economy. Today, rail transportation remains a vital link in our Nation's transportation network and economy. Railroads deliver billions of tons of freight and millions of travelers per year to destinations throughout the country, while subways and light-rail systems transport millions of passengers around metropolitan areas.

Locomotive engineers are among the most experienced and skilled workers on the railroad. They operate large trains carrying cargo and passengers between stations. Most engineers run diesel-electric locomotives, although a few operate locomotives powered electrically.

Before and after each run, engineers check the mechanical condition of their locomotives, making any minor adjustments necessary. Engineers receive starting instructions from conductors. They move controls such as throttles and airbrakes to drive the locomotive. They monitor instruments that measure speed, amperage, battery charge, and air pressure, both in the brake lines and in the main reservoir.

On the open rail and in the yard, engineers confer with conductors and traffic control center personnel via two-way radio or mobile telephone to issue or receive information concerning stops, delays, and the locations of trains. They interpret and comply with orders, signals, speed limits, and railroad rules and regulations. They must have a thorough knowledge of the signaling systems, yards, and terminals on the routes over which they travel. Engineers must be constantly aware of the condition and makeup of their train, because trains react differently to acceleration, braking, and curves, depending on the grade and condition of the rail, the number of cars, the ratio of empty cars to loaded cars, and the amount of slack in the train.

Rail yard engineers operate engines within the rail yard. *Dinkey operators* drive smaller engines, mainly within industrial plants, mines and quarries, or construction projects. *Hostlers* operate engines—without attached cars—within the yard, as well as driving them to maintenance shops.

Railroad conductors coordinate the activities of freight and passenger train crews. Railroad conductors assigned to freight trains review schedules, switching orders, waybills, and shipping records to obtain loading and unloading information

regarding their cargo. In switching operations, conductors may move engines using radio control devices. Conductors assigned to passenger trains also ensure passenger safety and comfort as they go about collecting tickets and fares, making announcements for the benefit of passengers, and coordinating activities of the crew to provide passenger services.

Before a train leaves the terminal, the conductor and the engineer discuss instructions received from the dispatcher concerning the train's route, timetable, and cargo. During the run, conductors use two-way radios and mobile telephones to communicate with dispatchers, engineers, and conductors of other trains. Conductors use dispatch or electronic monitoring devices that relay information about equipment problems on the train or the rails. They may arrange for the removal of defective cars from the train for repairs at the nearest station or stop. In addition, conductors may discuss alternative routes if there is a defect in, or obstruction on, the rails.

Yardmasters coordinate the activities of workers engaged in railroad traffic operations. These activities include making up or breaking up trains and switching inbound or outbound traffic to a specific section of the line. Some cars are sent to unload their cargo on special tracks, while others are moved to different tracks to await assembly into new trains, based on their destinations. Yardmasters tell engineers where to move the cars to fit the planned train configuration. Switches—many of them operated remotely by computer—divert the locomotive or cars to the proper track for coupling and uncoupling.

Railroad brake operators act as assistants to engineers, handling the coupling and uncoupling of cars as well as operating some switches. *Signal operators* install, maintain, and repair the signals on tracks and in yards. *Switch operators* control the track switches within a rail yard.

Traditionally, freight train crews included either one or two brake operators—one in the locomotive with the engineer and another who rode with the conductor in the rear car. Brake operators worked under the direction of conductors and did the physical work involved in adding and removing cars at railroad stations and assembling and disassembling trains in railroad yards. In an effort to reduce costs, most railroads have phased out brake operators. Many modern freight trains use only an engineer and a conductor. New visual instrumentation and monitoring devices have eliminated the need for crewmembers located at the rear of the train, so the conductor is now stationed with the engineer.

In contrast to other rail transportation workers, subway and streetcar operators generally work for public transit authorities instead of railroads. *Subway operators* control trains that transport passengers through cities and their suburbs. The trains run in underground tunnels, on the surface, or on elevated tracks. Operators must stay alert to observe signals along the track that indicate when they must start, slow, or stop their train. They also make announcements to riders, may open and close the doors of the train, and ensure that passengers get on and off the subway safely.

To meet predetermined schedules, operators must control the train's speed and the amount of time spent at each station. Increasingly, however, these functions are controlled by computers and not by the operator. During breakdowns or emergencies, operators contact their dispatcher or supervisor and may have to evacuate cars.

Most workers begin as yard laborers and later may have the opportunity to train for engineer or conductor jobs.

Streetcar operators drive electric-powered streetcars, trolleys, or light-rail vehicles that transport passengers around metropolitan areas. Some tracks may be recessed in city streets or have grade crossings, so operators must observe traffic signals and cope with car and truck traffic. Operators start, slow, and stop their cars so that passengers may get on and off with ease. Operators may collect fares and issue change and transfers. They also answer questions from passengers concerning fares, schedules, and routes.

Working Conditions

Many rail transportation employees work nights, weekends, and holidays, because trains operate 24 hours a day, 7 days a week. Many work more than a 40-hour workweek. Seniority usually dictates who receives the more desirable shifts.

Many freight trains are dispatched according to the needs of customers; as a result many train crews have irregular schedules. Many workers place their names on a list and wait for their turn to work. Jobs usually are assigned on short notice and often at odd hours; working weekends is common. Those who work on trains operating between points hundreds of miles apart may spend several nights at a time away from home.

Workers on passenger trains ordinarily have regular and reliable shifts. Also, the appearance, temperature, and accommodations of passenger trains are more comfortable than those of freight trains.

Rail yard workers spend most of their time outdoors and work regardless of weather conditions. The work of conductors and engineers on local runs, on which trains frequently stop at stations to pick up and deliver cars, is physically demanding. Climbing up and down and getting off moving cars is strenuous and can be dangerous.

Training, Other Qualifications, and Advancement

Most railroad transportation workers begin as yard laborers; later they may have the opportunity to train for engineer or conductor jobs. Railroads require that applicants have a minimum of a high school diploma or its equivalent. Applicants must have good hearing, eyesight, and color vision, as well as good hand-eye coordination, manual dexterity, and mechanical aptitude. Physical stamina is required for entry-level jobs. Employers require railroad transportation job applicants to pass a physical examination, drug and alcohol screening, and a criminal background check. Federal regulation requires that the driving record of anybody applying for a job operating an engine be checked for evidence of drug or alcohol problems. Similarly, under Federal regulation, all persons licensed to operate engines are subject to random drug and alcohol testing while on duty.

Applicants for locomotive engineer jobs must be at least 21 years old. Employers almost always fill engineer positions with workers who have experience in other railroad-operating occupations. Federal regulations require beginning engineers to complete a formal engineer training program, including classroom, simulator, and hands-on instruction in locomotive operation. The instruction usually is administered by the rail company in programs approved by the Federal Railroad Administration. At the end of the training period, engineers must pass a hearing and visual acuity test, a safety conduct background check, a railroad operation knowledge test, and a skills performance test. The company issues the engineer a license after the applicant passes the examinations. Other conditions and rules may apply to entry-level engineers and usually vary with the employer.

To maintain certification, railroad companies must monitor their engineers. In addition, engineers must periodically pass an operational rules efficiency test. The test is an unannounced event requiring engineers to take active or responsive action in certain situations, such as maintaining a particular speed through a curve or yard.

Engineers undergo periodic physical examinations and drug and alcohol testing to determine their fitness to operate locomotives. In some cases, engineers who fail to meet these physical and conduct standards are restricted to yard service; in other instances, they may be disciplined, trained to perform other work, or discharged.

Conductor jobs generally are filled from the ranks of experienced rail transportation workers who have passed tests covering signals, timetables, operating rules, and related subjects. Seniority usually is the main factor in determining promotion to conductor. Entry-level conductors generally must be at least 21 years of age and are either trained by their employers or required to complete a formal conductor training program through a community college.

Newly trained engineers and conductors are placed on the "extra board" until permanent positions become available. Workers on the extras-board receive assignments only when the railroad needs substitutes for regular workers who are absent because of vacation, illness, or other reasons. Seniority rules may allow workers with greater seniority to select their type of assignment. For example, an engineer may move from an initial, regular assignment in yard service to road service.

For brake and signal operator jobs, railroad firms will train applicants either in a company program or—especially with smaller railroads—at an outside training facility. Typical training programs combine classroom and on-site training and last between 4 and 6 weeks for signal operators and between 10 and 18 weeks for brake operators.

For subway and streetcar operator jobs, subway transit systems prefer applicants with a high school education. Most transit systems that operate subways and streetcars also operate buses. In these systems, subway or streetcar operators usually start as bus drivers. Applicants must be in good health, have good communication skills, and be able to make quick, responsible judgments. New operators generally complete training programs that last from a few weeks to 6 months. At the end of the period of classroom and on-the-job training, operators usually must pass qualifying examinations covering the operating system, troubleshooting, and evacuation and emergency procedures. Some operators with sufficient seniority can advance to station manager or another supervisory position.

For yard occupations, a commercial driver's license may be required because these workers often operate trucks and other heavy vehicles. For more information on commercial driver's licenses, contact your State motor vehicle administration and see the *Handbook* statements on truck drivers and driver/sales workers or bus drivers.

Employment

Rail transportation workers held 112,000 jobs in 2004, distributed among the detailed occupations as follows:

Locomotive engineers and operators	40,000
Railroad conductors and yardmasters	38,000
Railroad brake, signal, and switch operators	17,000
Subway and streetcar operators	9,200
Rail transportation workers, all other	8,100

Most rail transportation workers are employed in either the rail transportation industry or support activities for the industry. The rest work primarily for local governments as subway and streetcar operators and for mining and manufacturing establishments that operate their own locomotives and dinkey engines to move railcars containing ore, coal, and other bulk materials.

Job Outlook

Even though employment in most railroad transportation occupations is expected to decline through the year 2014, opportunities are expected to be good for qualified applicants, due mainly to the large number of workers expected to retire or leave these occupations in the next decade. Employment is expected to decline, despite expected increases in the amount of freight carried, due to productivity increases.

Opportunities for long-distance train crews are expected to be better than those for yard jobs, because yard occupations generally require little education beyond high school and do not require as much travel. Employment of subway and streetcar operators will grow about as fast as the average for all occupations, due to increased demand for light-rail transportation systems around the country.

Demand for railroad freight service will grow as the economy and the intermodal transportation of goods expand. Intermodal systems use trucks to move shippers' sealed trailers or containers to and from terminals and employ trains—which are more fuel-efficient than trucks—to transport them over the long distances between terminals. Railroads are improving delivery times and ontime service, while reducing shipping rates, in order to compete with other modes of transportation, such as trucks, ships, and aircraft.

Growth in the number of railroad transportation workers will be adversely affected by innovations such as larger, faster, more fuel-efficient trains and computerized classification yards that make it possible to move freight more efficiently. Computers help to keep track of freight cars, match empty cars with the closest loads, and dispatch and control trains. Computer-assisted devices alert engineers to malfunctions, and work rules now allow trains to operate with two-person crews instead of the traditional three- to five-person crews.

Earnings

Median hourly earnings of rail transportation occupations in May of 2004 were relatively high, as indicated in the following tabulation:

Locomotive engineers	$24.30
Subway and streetcar operators	23.70
Railroad conductors and yardmasters	22.28
Railroad brake, signal, and switch operators	21.46

Most railroad workers are paid according to miles traveled or hours worked, whichever leads to higher earnings. Full-time employees have steadier work, more regular hours, increased opportunities for overtime work, and higher earnings than do those assigned to the extra board.

Eight out of 10 railroad transportation workers are members of unions. Many different railroad unions represent various crafts on the railroads. Most railroad engineers are members of the Brotherhood of Locomotive Engineers and Trainmen, while most other railroad transportation workers are members of the United Transportation Union. Many subway operators are members of the Amalgamated Transit Union, while others belong to the Transport Workers Union of North America.

Related Occupations

Other related transportation workers include bus drivers, truck drivers and driver/sales workers, and those working in water transportation occupations.

Sources of Additional Information

To obtain information on employment opportunities, contact either the employment offices of railroads and rail transit systems or State employment service offices.

General information about the rail transportation industry is available from:

➤ Association of American Railroads, 50 F St. N.W., Washington, DC 20001. Internet: **http://www.aar.org**

General information about career opportunities in passenger transportation is available from:

➤ American Public Transportation Association, 1666 K Street N.W., Washington, DC 20006.

General information on career opportunities as a locomotive engineer is available from:

➤ Brotherhood of Locomotive Engineers and Trainmen, 1370 Ontario St. Mezzanine, Cleveland, OH 44113. Internet: **http://www.ble.org**

General information on career opportunities as a conductor, yardmaster, or brake operator is available from:

➤ United Transportation Union, 14600 Detroit Ave., Cleveland, OH 44107. Internet: **http://www.utu.org**

Water Transportation Occupations

(O*NET 53-5011.01, 53-5011.02, 53-5021.01, 53-5021.02, 53-5021.03, 53-5022.00, 53-5031.00)

Significant Points

- Merchant mariners spend extended periods at sea.

- Entry, training, and educational requirements for most water transportation occupations are established and regulated by the U.S. Coast Guard, an agency of the U.S. Department of Homeland Security.

- Increasing global trade and tourism will generate growth in water transportation occupations.

Nature of the Work

The movement of huge amounts of cargo, as well as passengers, between nations and within our Nation depends on workers in water transportation occupations, also known on commercial ships as merchant mariners. They operate and maintain deep-sea merchant ships, tugboats, towboats, ferries, dredges, excursion vessels, and other waterborne craft on the oceans, the Great Lakes, rivers, canals, and other waterways, as well as in harbors. (Workers who operate watercraft used in commercial fishing are described in the section on fishers and fishing vessel operators elsewhere in the *Handbook*.)

Captains, mates, and pilots of water vessels command or supervise the operations of ships and water vessels, both within domestic waterways and on the deep sea. *Captains* or *masters* are in overall command of the operation of a vessel, and they supervise the work of all other officers and crew. They determine the course and speed of the vessel, maneuver to avoid hazards, and continuously monitor the vessel's position with charts and navigational aides. Captains either direct or oversee crew members who steer the vessel, determine its location, operate engines, communicate with other vessels, perform maintenance, handle lines, or operate equipment on the vessel. Captains and their department heads ensure that proper procedures and safety practices are followed, check to make sure that machinery and equipment are in good working order, and oversee the loading and discharging of cargo or passengers. They also maintain logs and other records tracking the ships' movements, efforts at controlling pollution, and cargo and passengers carried.

Deck officers or *mates* direct the routine operation of the vessel for the captain during the shifts when they are on watch. All mates stand watch for specified periods, usually 4 hours on and 8 hours off. However, on smaller vessels, there may be only one mate (called a *pilot* on some inland towing vessels), who alternates watches with the captain. The mate would assume command of the ship if the captain became incapacitated. When more than one mate is necessary aboard a ship, they typically are designated chief mate or first mate, second mate, third mate, etc. Mates also supervise and coordinate activities of the crew aboard the ship. They inspect the cargo holds during loading to ensure that the load is stowed according to specifications and regulations. Mates supervise crew members engaged in maintenance and the primary upkeep of the vessel.

Pilots guide ships in and out of harbors, through straits, and on rivers and other confined waterways where a familiarity with local water depths, winds, tides, currents, and hazards such as reefs and shoals are of prime importance. Pilots on river and canal vessels usually are regular crew members, like mates. Harbor pilots are generally independent contractors who accompany vessels while they enter or leave port. Harbor pilots may pilot many ships in a single day. *Motorboat operators* operate small, motor-driven boats that carry six of fewer passengers on fishing charters. They also take depth soundings in turning basins and serve as liaisons between ships, between ship and shore, between harbors and beaches, or on area patrol.

Ship engineers operate, maintain, and repair propulsion engines, boilers, generators, pumps, and other machinery. Merchant marine vessels usually have four engineering officers: A chief engineer and a first, second, and third assistant engineer. Assistant engineers stand periodic watches, overseeing the safe operation of engines and machinery.

Marine oilers and more experienced *qualified members of the engine department*, or QMEDs, maintain the vessel in proper running order in the engine spaces below decks, under the direction of the ship's engineering officers. These workers lubricate gears, shafts, bearings, and other moving parts of engines and motors; read pressure and temperature gauges; record data; and sometimes assist with repairs and adjust machinery.

Sailors operate the vessel and its deck equipment under the direction of the ship's officers and keep the nonengineering areas in good condition. They stand watch, looking out for other vessels and obstructions in the ship's path, as well as for navigational aids such as buoys and lighthouses. They also steer the ship, measure water depth in shallow water, and maintain and operate deck equipment such as lifeboats, anchors, and cargo-handling gear. On vessels handling liquid cargo, mariners designated as *pumpmen* hook up hoses, operate pumps, and clean tanks; on tugboats or tow vessels, they tie barges together into tow units, inspect them periodically, and disconnect them when the destination is reached. When docking or departing, they handle lines. They also perform routine maintenance chores, such as repairing lines, chipping rust, and painting and cleaning decks or other areas. Experienced sailors are designated *able seamen* on oceangoing vessels, but may be called simply *deckhands* on inland waters; larger vessels usually have a *boatswain*, or head seaman.

Studying at a maritime academy is usually the best route to becoming an officer.

A typical deep-sea merchant ship has a captain, three deck officers or mates, a chief engineer and three assistant engineers, a radio operator, plus six or more unlicensed seamen, such as able seamen, oilers, QMEDs, and cooks or food handlers. The size and service of the ship determine the number of crewmembers for a particular voyage. Small vessels operating in harbors, on rivers, or along the coast may have a crew comprising only a captain and one deckhand. The cooking responsibilities usually fall under the deckhands' duties.

On larger coastal ships, the crew may include a captain, a mate or pilot, an engineer, and seven or eight seamen. Some ships may have special unlicensed positions for entry level apprentice trainees. Unlicensed positions on a large ship may include a full-time cook, an electrician, and machinery mechanics. On cruise ships, *bedroom stewards* keep passengers' quarters clean and comfortable.

Working Conditions
Merchant mariners spend extended periods at sea. Most deep-sea mariners are hired for one or more voyages that last for several months; there is no job security after that. The length of time between voyages varies depending on job availability and personal preference.

The rate of unionization for these workers is about 36 percent, much higher than the average for all occupations. Consequently, merchant marine officers and seamen, both veterans and beginners, are hired for voyages through union hiring halls or directly by shipping companies. Hiring halls rank the candidates by the length of time the person has been out of work and fill open slots accordingly. Hiring halls typically are found in major seaports.

At sea, these workers usually stand watch for 4 hours and are off for 8 hours, 7 days a week. Those employed on Great Lakes ships work 60 days and have 30 days off, but do not work in the winter when the lakes are frozen. Workers on rivers, on canals, and in harbors are more likely to have year-round work. Some work 8-hour or 12-hour shifts and go home every day. Others work steadily for a week or a month and then have an extended period off. When working, they usually are on duty for 6 or 12 hours and off for 6 or 12 hours. Those on smaller vessels are normally assigned to one vessel and have steady employment.

People in water transportation occupations work in all weather conditions. Although merchant mariners try to avoid severe storms while at sea, working in damp and cold conditions often is inevitable. While it is uncommon nowadays for vessels to suffer disasters such as fire, explosion, or a sinking, workers face the possibility that they may have to abandon their craft on short notice if it collides with other vessels or runs aground. They also risk injury or death from falling overboard and hazards associated with working with machinery, heavy loads, and dangerous cargo. However, modern safety management procedures, advanced emergency communications, and effective international rescue systems place modern mariners in a much safer position.

Most newer vessels are air conditioned, soundproofed from noisy machinery, and equipped with comfortable living quarters. For some mariners, these amenities have helped ease the sometimes difficult circumstances of long periods away from home. Also, modern communications, especially email, link modern mariners to their families. Nevertheless, some mariners dislike the long periods away from home and the confinement aboard ship and consequently leave the occupation.

Training and Other Qualifications
Entry, training, and educational requirements for most water transportation occupations are established and regulated by the U.S. Coast Guard, an agency of the U.S. Department of Homeland Security. All officers and operators of commercially operated vessels must be licensed by the Coast Guard, which offers various kinds of licenses, depending on the position and type of vessel.

There are two ways to qualify for a deck or engineering officer's license: applicants either must accumulate sea time and meet regulatory requirements, or must graduate from the U.S. Merchant Marine Academy or one of the six State maritime academies. In both cases, applicants must pass a written examination. Federal regulations also require that an applicant pass a physical examination, a drug screening, and a National Driver Register Check before being considered. Persons without formal training can be licensed if they pass the written exam and possess sea service appropriate to the license for which they are applying. However, it is difficult to pass the examination without substantial formal schooling or independent study. Also, because seamen may work 6 or fewer months a year, it can take 5 to 8 years to accumulate the necessary experience. The academies offer a 4-year academic program leading to a bachelor-of-science degree, a license (issued only by the Coast Guard) as a third mate (deck officer) or third assistant engineer (engineering officer), and, if the person is qualified, a commission as ensign in the U.S. Naval Reserve, Merchant Marine Reserve, or Coast Guard Reserve. With experience and additional training, third officers may qualify for higher rank.

Sailors and unlicensed engineers working on U.S. flagged deep-sea and Great Lakes vessels must hold a Coast Guard-issued document. In addition, they must hold certification when working aboard liquid-carrying vessels. Able seamen also must hold government-issued certification. For employment in the merchant marine as an unlicensed seaman, a merchant mariner's document issued by the Coast Guard is needed. Most of the jobs must be filled by U.S. citizens; however, a small percentage of applicants for merchant mariner documents do not need to be U.S. citizens, but must at least be aliens legally admitted into the United States and holding a green card. A medical certificate of excellent health attesting to vision, color perception, and general physical condition is required for higher level deckhands and unlicensed engineers. While no experience or formal schooling is required, training at a union-operated school is the best source. Beginners are classified as ordinary seamen and may be assigned to any of the three unlicensed departments: Deck, engine, or steward. With experience at sea and perhaps union-sponsored training, an ordinary seaman can pass the able-seaman exam and move up with 3 years of service.

No special training or experience is needed to become a seaman or deckhand on vessels operating in harbors or on rivers or other waterways. Newly hired workers generally are given a short introductory course and then learn skills on the job. After sufficient experience, they are eligible to take a Coast Guard exam to qualify as a mate, pilot, or captain. Substantial knowledge gained through experience, courses taught at approved schools, and independent study is needed to pass the exam.

Harbor pilot training usually consists of an extended apprenticeship with a towing company or a pilots' association. Entrants may be able seamen or licensed officers.

Employment

Water transportation workers held more than 72,000 jobs in 2004. The total number who worked at some point in the year was perhaps twice as large because many merchant marine officers and seamen worked only part of the year. The following tabulation shows employment in the occupations that make up this group:

Captains, mates, and pilots of water vessels	29,000
Sailors and marine oilers	28,000
Ship engineers	12,000
Motorboat operators	3,400

About 33 percent of all workers were employed in water transportation services. About 17 percent worked in inland water transportation—primarily the Mississippi River system—while the other 16 percent were employed in water transportation on the deep seas, along the coasts, and on the Great Lakes. Another 25 percent worked in establishments related to port and harbor operations, marine cargo handling, or navigational services to shipping. The Federal government employed approximately 5 percent of all water transportation workers, most of whom worked on supply ships and are Civilian Mariners of the Department Navy's Military Sealift Command.

Job Outlook

Employment in water transportation occupations is projected to grow more slowly than the average for all occupations through the year 2014. Job growth will stem from increasing tourism and increases in shipping traffic due to rising imports that will provide greater employment in and around major port cities.

Employment in deep-sea shipping for American mariners is expected to stabilize after several years of decline. International regulations have raised shipping standards with respect to safety, training, and working conditions. Consequently, competition from ships that sail under foreign flags of convenience has lessened as the standards of operation become more uniform. This has made the costs of operating a U.S. ship more comparable to foreign-flagged ships and has modestly increased the amount of international cargo carried by U.S. ships. A fleet of deep-sea U.S.-flagged ships is also considered to be vital to the Nation's defense, so some receive Federal support through a maritime security subsidy and other provisions in laws that limit certain Federal cargoes to ships that fly the U.S. flag.

Employment growth also is expected in passenger cruise ships within U.S. waters. Vessels that operate between U.S. ports are required by law to be U.S.-flagged vessels. The building and staffing of several new cruise ships that will travel around the Hawaiian Islands will create new opportunities for employment at sea in the cruise line industry, which is composed mostly of foreign-flagged ships. In addition efforts are underway at the Federal level that could lead to greater use of ferries to handle commuter traffic around major metropolitan areas, which may cause more workers to be hired.

Moderating the growth in water transportation occupations is a projected decline in vessels operating in the Great Lakes and inland waterways. Vessels on rivers and canals and on the Great Lakes carry mostly bulk products, such as coal, iron ore, petroleum, sand and gravel, grain, and chemicals. Although ship-

ments of most of these products are expected to grow through the year 2014, imports of steel are dampening employment on the Lakes.

Job openings will also result from the need to replace those leaving the occupation. Some experienced merchant mariners may continue to go without work for varying periods. However, this situation appears to be changing, with demand for licensed and unlicensed personnel rising. Maritime academy graduates who have not found licensed shipboard jobs in the U.S. merchant marine find jobs in related industries. Because they are commissioned as ensigns in the Naval or Coast Guard Reserve, some are selected for active duty in those branches of the Service. Some find jobs as seamen on U.S.-flagged or foreign-flagged vessels, tugboats, and other watercraft or enter civilian jobs with the U.S. Navy or Coast Guard. Some take land-based jobs with shipping companies, marine insurance companies, manufacturers of boilers or related machinery, or other related jobs.

Earnings

Earnings vary widely with the particular water transportation position and the worker's experience, ranging from the minimum wage for some beginning seamen or mate positions to more than $42.02 an hour for some experienced ship engineers. Median hourly earnings of water transportation occupations in May 2004 were:

Ship engineers	$26.42
Captains, mates, and pilots of water vessels	24.20
Motorboat operators	15.39
Sailors and marine oilers	14.00

Annual pay for captains of larger vessels, such as container ships, oil tankers, or passenger ships, may exceed $100,000, but only after many years of experience. Similarly, captains of tugboats often earn more than the median reported here, with earnings dependent on the port and the nature of the cargo.

Related Occupations

Workers in other occupations who make their living on the seas and coastal waters include fishers and fishing vessel operators and some members of the Armed Forces.

Sources of Additional Information

Information on a program called "Careers Afloat", which includes a substantial listing of training and employment descriptive information and contacts in the U.S., may be obtained through:
➤ Maritime Administration, U.S. Department of Transportation, 400 7th St. SW., Room 7302, Washington, DC 20590. Internet: http://www.marad.dot.gov/acareerafloat

Information on merchant marine careers, training, and licensing requirements is available from any of the following organizations:
➤ Military Sealift Command, APMC, PO Box 120, Camp Pendleton, Virginia Beach, VA 23458-0120. Internet: http://www.sealiftcommand.com
➤ Seafarers' International Union, 5201 Auth Way, Camp Springs, MD 20746.
➤ Paul Hall Center for Maritime Training and Education, P.O. Box 75, Piney Point, MD 20674-0075. Internet: http://www.seafarers.org/phc
➤ International Organization of Masters, Mates, and Pilots, 700 Maritime Blvd., Linthicum Heights, MD 21090-1941.
➤ U.S. Coast Guard National Maritime Center, 4200 Wilson Blvd., Suite 630, Arlington, VA 22203-1804. Internet: http://www.uscg.mil/stcw/index.htm

Material Moving Occupations

(O*NET 53-1021.00, 53-7011.00, 53-7021.00, 53-7031.00, 53-7032.01, 53-7032.02, 53-7033.00, 53-7041.00, 53-7051.00, 53-7061.00, 53-7062.01, 53-7062.02, 53-7062.03, 53-7063.00, 53-7064.00, 53-7071.01, 53-7071.02, 53-7072.00, 53-7073.00, 53-7081.00, 53-7111.00, 53-7121.00, 53-7199.99)

Significant Points

- Job openings should be numerous because the occupation is very large and turnover is relatively high.

- Most jobs require little work experience or training.

- Pay is low, and the seasonal nature of the work may reduce earnings.

Nature of the Work

Material moving workers are categorized into two groups—operators and laborers. Operators use machinery to move construction materials, earth, petroleum products, and other heavy materials. Generally, they move materials over short distances—around construction sites, factories, or warehouses. Some move materials onto or off of trucks and ships. Operators control equipment by moving levers, wheels, and/or foot pedals; operating switches; or turning dials. They also may set up and inspect equipment, make adjustments, and perform minor maintenance or repairs. Laborers and hand material movers manually handle freight, stock, or other materials; clean vehicles, machinery, and other equipment; feed materials into or remove materials from machines or equipment; and pack or package products and materials.

Material moving occupations are classified by the type of equipment they operate or the goods they handle. Each piece of equipment requires different skills, as do different types of loads. (For information on *operating engineers; paving, surfacing, and tamping equipment operators; and pile-driver operators*, see the statement on construction equipment operators elsewhere in the *Handbook*.)

Industrial truck and tractor operators drive and control industrial trucks or tractors equipped to move materials around warehouses, storage yards, factories, or construction sites. A typical industrial truck, often called a forklift or lift truck, has a hydraulic lifting mechanism and forks for moving heavy and large objects. Industrial truck and tractor operators also may operate tractors that pull trailers loaded with materials, goods, or equipment within factories and warehouses or around outdoor storage areas.

Excavating and loading machine and dragline operators tend or operate machinery equipped with scoops, shovels, or buckets to dig and load sand, gravel, earth, or similar materials into trucks or onto conveyors. Construction and mining industries employ the majority of excavation and loading machine and dragline operators. *Dredge operators* excavate waterways, removing sand, gravel, rock, or other materials from harbors, lakes, rivers, and streams. Dredges are used primarily to maintain navigable channels but also are used to restore wetlands and other aquatic habitats; reclaim land; and create and maintain beaches. *Underground mining loading machine operators* use underground loading machines to load coal, ore, or rock into shuttles and mine cars or onto conveyors. Loading equipment may include power shovels, hoisting engines equipped with cable-drawn scrapers or scoops, and machines equipped with gathering arms and conveyors.

Crane and tower operators work mechanical boom and cable or tower and cable equipment to lift and move materials, machinery, and other heavy objects. Operators extend and retract horizontally mounted booms and lower and raise hooks attached to load lines. Most operators are guided by other workers using hand signals or a radio. Operators position loads from an onboard console or from a remote console at the site. While crane and tower operators are noticeable at office building and other construction sites, the biggest group works in primary metal, metal fabrication, and transportation equipment manufacturing industries that use heavy, bulky materials. *Hoist and winch operators* control movement of cables, cages, and platforms to move workers and materials for manufacturing, logging, and other industrial operations. They work in positions such as derrick operators and hydraulic boom operators. Many hoist and winch operators are found in manufacturing or construction industries.

Pump operators tend, control, and operate power-driven pumps and manifold systems that transfer gases, oil, or other materials to vessels or equipment. They maintain the equipment to regulate the flow of materials according to a schedule set up by petroleum engineers and production supervisors. *Gas compressor and gas pumping station operators* operate steam, gas, electric motor, or internal combustion engine-driven compressors. They transmit, compress, or recover gases, such as butane, nitrogen, hydrogen, and natural gas. *Wellhead pumpers* operate power pumps and auxiliary equipment to produce flows of oil or gas from extraction sites.

Tank car, truck, and ship loaders operate ship-loading and -unloading equipment, conveyors, hoists, and other specialized material-handling equipment such as railroad tank car-unloading equipment. They may gauge or sample shipping tanks and test them for leaks. *Conveyor operators and tenders* control and tend conveyor systems that move materials to or from stockpiles, processing stations, departments, or vehicles. *Shuttle car operators* run diesel or electric-powered shuttle cars in underground mines, transporting materials from the working face to mine cars or conveyors.

Laborers and hand freight, stock, and material movers manually move materials and perform other unskilled general labor. These workers move freight, stock, and other materials to and from storage and production areas, loading docks, delivery vehicles, ships, and containers. Their specific duties vary by industry and work setting. In factories, they may move raw materials or finished goods between loading docks, storage areas, and work areas, as well as sort materials and supplies and prepare them according to their work orders. Specialized workers within this group include baggage and cargo handlers, who work in transportation industries, and truck loaders and unloaders.

Hand packers and packagers manually pack, package, or wrap a variety of materials. They may inspect items for defects, label cartons, stamp information on products, keep records of items packed, and stack packages on loading docks. This group also includes order fillers, who pack materials for shipment, as well as grocery store courtesy clerks. In grocery stores, they may bag groceries, carry packages to customers' cars, and return shopping carts to designated areas.

Machine feeders and offbearers feed materials into or remove materials from automatic equipment or machines tended by other workers.

Fork lifts have hydraulic lifting mechanisms for moving heavy or large objects.

Cleaners of vehicles and equipment clean machinery, vehicles, storage tanks, pipelines, and similar equipment using water and other cleaning agents, vacuums, hoses, brushes, cloths, and other cleaning equipment.

Refuse and recyclable material collectors gather refuse and recyclables from homes and businesses into their truck for transport to a dump, landfill, or recycling center. They lift and empty garbage cans or recycling bins by hand or operate a hydraulic lift truck that picks up and empties dumpsters. They work along scheduled routes.

Working Conditions

Material moving work tends to be repetitive and physically demanding. Workers may lift and carry heavy objects and stoop, kneel, crouch, or crawl in awkward positions. Some work at great heights and some work outdoors, regardless of weather and climate. Some jobs expose workers to fumes, odors, loud noises, harmful materials and chemicals, or dangerous machinery. To protect their eyes, respiratory systems, and hearing, these workers wear safety clothing, such as gloves, hardhats, and other safety devices. These jobs have become much less dangerous as safety equipment—such as overhead guards on lift trucks—has become common. Accidents usually can be avoided by observing proper operating procedures and safety practices.

Material movers generally work 8-hour shifts, though longer shifts also are not uncommon. In industries that work around the clock, material movers may work overnight shifts. Some do this because the establishment does not want to disturb customers during normal business hours. Refuse and recyclable material collectors often work shifts starting at 5 or 6 a.m. Some material movers work only during certain seasons, such as when the weather permits construction activity.

Training, Other Qualifications, and Advancement

Little work experience or training is required for most material moving occupations. Some employers prefer applicants with a high school diploma, but most simply require workers to be at least 18 years old and physically able to perform the work. For those jobs requiring physical exertion, employers may require that applicants pass a physical exam. Some employers also require drug testing or background checks before employment. Material movers often are younger than workers in other occupations, reflecting the limited training but significant physical requirements of many of these jobs.

Material movers generally learn skills informally, on the job, from more experienced workers or their supervisors. Workers who handle toxic chemicals or use industrial trucks or other dangerous equipment must receive specialized training in safety awareness and procedures. Many of the training requirements are standardized through the U.S. Occupational Safety and Health Administration. This training is usually provided by the employer. Employers also must certify that each operator has received the training and evaluate each operator at least once every 3 years. For other operators, such as crane operators and those working with specialized loads, there are some training and apprenticeship programs, such as that offered by the International Union of Operating Engineers, as well as certifying institutions, such as the National Commission for the Certification of Crane Operators. Some employers may require crane operators to be certified. Twelve States have laws requiring crane operators to be licensed. Licensing requirements typically include a written as well as a skills test to demonstrate that the licensee can operate a crane safely.

Material moving equipment operators need a good sense of balance, the ability to judge distances, and eye-hand-foot coordination. For jobs that involve dealing with the public, such as grocery store courtesy clerks, workers should be pleasant and courteous. Most jobs require basic arithmetic skills and the ability to read procedural manuals, to understand orders, and other billing documents. Mechanical aptitude and training in automobile or diesel mechanics can be helpful because some operators may perform basic maintenance on their equipment. Experience operating mobile equipment—such as tractors on farms or heavy equipment in the Armed Forces—is an asset. As material moving equipment becomes more advanced, workers will need to be increasingly comfortable with technology.

In many of these occupations, experience may allow workers to qualify or become trainees for jobs such as construction trades workers; assemblers or other production workers; motor vehicle operators; or vehicle and mobile equipment mechanics, installers, and repairers. In many workplaces new employees gain experience in a material moving position before being promoted to a better paying and more highly skilled job. Some may eventually advance to become supervisors.

Employment

Material movers held 5.1 million jobs in 2004. They were distributed among the detailed occupations as follows:

Laborers and freight, stock, and material movers, hand	2,430,000
Packers and packagers, hand	877,000
Industrial truck and tractor operators	635,000
Cleaners of vehicles and equipment	347,000
First-line supervisors/managers of helpers, laborers, and material movers, hand	173,000
Refuse and recyclable material collectors	149,000
Machine feeders and offbearers	148,000
Excavating and loading machine and dragline operators	86,000
Conveyor operators and tenders	53,000
Crane and tower operators	44,000
Tank car, truck, and ship loaders	17,000
Wellhead pumpers	11,000
Pump operators, except wellhead pumpers	11,000
Hoist and winch operators	5,600
Gas compressor and gas pumping station operators	5,100
Loading machine operators, underground mining	4,300
Shuttle car operators	3,100
Dredge operators	2,500
All other material moving workers	58,000

About 29 percent of all material movers worked in the wholesale trade or retail trade industries. Another 22 percent worked in manufacturing; 14 percent in transportation and warehousing; 4 percent in construction and mining; and 15 percent in the employment services industry, on a temporary or contract basis. For example, companies that need workers for only a few days, to move materials or to clean up a site, may contract with temporary help agencies specializing in providing suitable workers on a short-term basis. A small proportion of material movers were self-employed.

Material movers work in every part of the country. Some work in remote locations on large construction projects such as highways and dams, while others work in factories, warehouses, or mining operations.

Job Outlook

Job openings should be numerous because the occupation is very large and turnover is relatively high—characteristic of occupations requiring little prior or formal training. Many openings will arise from the need to replace workers who transfer to other occupations or those who retire or leave the labor force for other reasons.

Employment in material moving occupations is projected to increase more slowly than the average for all occupations through 2014. Improvements in equipment, such as automated storage and retrieval systems and conveyors, will continue to raise productivity and moderate the demand for material movers.

Employment growth will stem from an expanding economy, especially in industries involved with the production, distribution, and sales of goods. Employment also will grow in the warehousing and storage industry as more firms contract out their warehousing functions to this industry. For example, a frozen food manufacturer may reduce its costs by outsourcing these functions to a refrigerated warehousing firm, which can more efficiently deal with the specialized storage needs of frozen food. Job growth for material movers depends on the growth or decline of employing industries and the type of equipment the workers operate or the materials they handle. For example, jobs in mining are expected to decline due to continued productivity increases within that industry. Job growth generally will be slower in large establishments, as they increasingly turn to automation for their material moving needs.

Both construction and manufacturing are very sensitive to changes in economic conditions, so the number of job openings in these industries will fluctuate. Although increasing automation will eliminate some routine tasks, new jobs will be created by the need to operate and maintain new equipment.

Earnings

Median hourly earnings of material moving workers in May 2004 were relatively low, as indicated by the following tabulation:

First-line supervisors/managers of helpers, laborers, and material movers, hand	$18.40
Crane and tower operators	17.99
Pump operators, except wellhead pumpers	17.04
Wellhead pumpers	16.31
Hoist and winch operators	16.19
Tank car, truck, and ship loaders	15.59
Excavating and loading machine and dragline operators	15.37
Material moving workers, all other	13.87
Industrial truck and tractor operators	12.78
Refuse and recyclable material collectors	12.38
Conveyor operators and tenders	12.23
Machine feeders and offbearers	10.68
Laborers and freight, stock, and material movers, hand	9.67
Cleaners of vehicles and equipment	8.41
Packers and packagers, hand	8.25

Wages vary according to experience and job responsibilities. Wages usually are higher in metropolitan areas. Seasonal peaks and lulls in workload can affect the number of hours scheduled and, therefore, earnings. Certified crane operators tend to have a slightly higher hourly rate than those who are not certified.

Related Occupations

Other workers who operate mechanical equipment include construction equipment operators; machine setters, operators, and tenders—metal and plastic; rail transportation workers; and truck drivers and driver/sales workers. Other entry-level workers who perform mostly physical work are agricultural workers; building cleaning workers; construction laborers; forest, conservation, and logging workers; and grounds maintenance workers.

Sources of Additional Information

For information about job opportunities and training programs, contact local State employment service offices, building or construction contractors, manufacturers, and wholesale and retail establishments.

Information on safety and training requirements is available from:
➤ U.S. Department of Labor, Occupational Safety and Health Administration (OSHA), 200 Constitution Ave., NW., Washington, DC 20210. Internet: **http://www.osha.gov**

Information on industrial truck and tractor operators is available from:
➤ Industrial Truck Association, 1750 K St., NW., Suite 460, Washington, DC 20006. Internet: **http://www.indtrk.org**

Information on training and apprenticeships for industrial truck operators is available from:
➤ International Union of Operating Engineers, 1125 17th St., NW., Washington, D.C. 20036. Internet: **http://www.iuoe.org**

Information on crane and derrick certification and licensure is available from:
➤ National Commission for the Certification of Crane Operators, 2750 Prosperity Ave., Suite 505, Fairfax, VA 22031. Internet: **http://www.nccco.org**

Job Opportunities in the Armed Forces

(O*NET 55-1011.00, 55-1012.00, 55-1013.00, 55-1014.00, 55-1015.00, 55-1016.00, 55-1017.00, 55-1019.99, 55-2011.00, 55-2012.00, 55-2013.00, 55-3011.00, 55-3012.00, 55-3013.00, 55-3014.00, 55-3015.00, 55-3016.00, 55-3017.00, 55-3018.00, 55-3019.99)

Significant Points

- Some training and duty assignments are hazardous, even in peacetime; hours and working conditions can be arduous and vary substantially.

- Enlisted personnel need at least a high school diploma or its equivalent, while officers need a bachelor's or an advanced degree.

- Opportunities should be good in all branches of the Armed Forces for applicants who meet designated standards.

Nature of the Work

Maintaining a strong national defense encompasses such diverse activities as running a hospital, commanding a tank, programming computers, operating a nuclear reactor, or repairing and maintaining a helicopter. The military provides training and work experience in these and many other fields for more than 2.6 million people. More than 1.4 million people serve in the active Army, Navy, Marine Corps, and Air Force, and more than 1.2 million serve in their Reserve components, and the Air and Army National Guard. The Coast Guard, which is also discussed in this *Handbook* statement, is now part of the U.S. Department of Homeland Security.

The military distinguishes between enlisted and officer careers. Enlisted personnel, who make up about 85 percent of the Armed Forces, carry out the fundamental operations of the military in areas such as combat, administration, construction, engineering, health care, and human services. Officers, who make up the remaining 15 percent of the Armed Forces, are the leaders of the military, supervising and managing activities in every occupational specialty of the Armed Forces.

The sections that follow discuss the major occupational groups for enlisted personnel and officers.

Enlisted occupational groups

Administrative careers include a wide variety of positions. The military must keep accurate information for planning and managing its operations. Both paper and electronic records are kept on personnel and on equipment, funds, supplies, and all other aspects of the military. Administrative personnel record information, type reports, maintain files, and review information to assist military officers. Personnel may work in a specialized area such as finance, accounting, legal affairs, maintenance, supply, or transportation.

Combat specialty occupations refer to enlisted specialties, such as infantry, artillery, and special forces, whose members operate weapons or execute special missions during combat. Persons in these occupations normally specialize by the type of weapon system or combat operation. These personnel maneuver against enemy forces and position and fire artillery, guns, and missiles to destroy enemy positions. They also may operate tanks and amphibious assault vehicles in combat or scouting missions. When the military has difficult and dangerous missions to perform, they call upon special forces teams. These elite combat forces maintain a constant state of readiness to strike anywhere in the world on a moment's notice. Team members from the special forces conduct offensive raids, demolitions, intelligence, search-and-rescue missions, and other operations from aboard aircraft, helicopters, ships, or submarines.

Construction occupations in the military include personnel who build or repair buildings, airfields, bridges, foundations, dams, bunkers, and the electrical and plumbing components of these structures. Personnel in construction occupations operate bulldozers, cranes, graders, and other heavy equipment. Construction specialists also may work with engineers and other building specialists as part of military construction teams. Some personnel specialize in areas such as plumbing or electrical wiring. Plumbers and pipefitters install and repair the plumbing and pipe systems needed in buildings and on aircraft and ships. Building electricians install and repair electrical-wiring systems in offices, airplane hangars, and other buildings on military bases.

Electronic and electrical equipment repair personnel repair and maintain electronic and electrical equipment used in the military. Repairers normally specialize by type of equipment, such as avionics, computer, optical, communications, or weapons systems. For example, electronic instrument repairers install, test, maintain, and repair a wide variety of electronic systems, including navigational controls and biomedical instruments. Weapons maintenance technicians maintain and repair weapons used by combat forces; most of these weapons have electronic components and systems that assist in locating targets and in aiming and firing the weapon.

Engineering, science, and technical personnel in the military require specific knowledge to operate technical equipment, solve complex problems, or provide and interpret information. Personnel normally specialize in one area, such as space operations, information technology, environmental health and safety, or intelligence. Space operations specialists use and repair ground-control command equipment having to do with spacecraft, including electronic systems that track the location and operation of a craft. Information technology specialists develop software programs and operate computer systems. Environmental health and safety specialists inspect military facilities and food supplies for the presence of disease, germs, or other conditions hazardous to health and the environment. Intelligence specialists gather and study information by means of aerial photographs and various types of radar and surveillance systems.

Health care personnel assist medical professionals in treating and providing services for men and women in the military. They may work as part of a patient-service team in close contact with doctors, dentists, nurses, and physical therapists to provide the necessary support functions within a hospital or clinic. Health care specialists normally specialize in a particular area—emergency medical treatment, the operation of diagnostic tools such as x-ray and ultrasound equipment, laboratory testing of tissue and blood samples, or maintaining pharmacy supplies or patients' records, among others. Dental and optical laboratory technicians construct and repair dental equipment and eyeglasses for military personnel.

Human resources development specialists recruit and place qualified personnel and provide the training programs necessary to help people perform their jobs effectively. Personnel in this career area normally specialize by activity. For example, recruiting specialists provide information about military careers to young people, parents, schools, and local communities and explain the Armed Service's employment and training opportunities, pay and benefits, and service life. Personnel specialists collect and store information about the people in the military, including information on their previous and current training, job assignments, promotions, and health. Training specialists and instructors teach classes and give demonstrations to provide military personnel with the knowledge they need to perform their jobs.

Machine operator and production personnel operate industrial equipment, machinery, and tools to fabricate and repair parts for a variety of items and structures. They may operate engines, turbines, nuclear reactors, and water pumps. Often, they specialize by type of work performed. Welders and metalworkers, for instance, work with various types of metals to repair or form the structural parts of ships, submarines, buildings, or other equipment. Survival equipment specialists inspect, maintain, and repair survival equipment such as parachutes and aircraft life support equipment.

Media and public affairs personnel deal with the public presentation and interpretation of military information and events. They take and develop photographs; film, record, and edit audio and video programs; present news and music programs; and produce graphic artwork, drawings, and other visual displays. Other public affairs specialists act as interpreters and translators to convert written or spoken foreign languages into English or other languages.

Protective service personnel include those who enforce military laws and regulations and provide emergency response to natural and human-made disasters. These personnel normally specialize by function. For example, military police control traffic, prevent crime, and respond to emergencies. Other law enforcement and security specialists investigate crimes committed on military property and guard inmates in military correctional facilities. Firefighters put out, control, and help prevent fires in buildings, on aircraft, and aboard ships.

Support service personnel provide subsistence services and support the morale and well-being of military personnel and their families. Food service specialists prepare all types of food in dining halls, hospitals, and ships. Counselors help military personnel and their families deal with personal issues. They work as part of a team that may include social workers, psychologists, medical officers, chaplains, personnel specialists, and commanders. Religious program specialists assist chaplains with religious services, religious education programs, and related administrative duties.

Transportation and material handling specialists ensure the safe transport of people and cargo. Most personnel within this occupational group are classified according to mode of transportation, such as aircraft, motor vehicle, or ship. Aircrew members operate equipment on board aircraft during operations. Vehicle drivers operate all types of heavy military vehicles, including fuel or water tank trucks, semi-trailers, heavy troop transports, and passenger buses. Quartermasters and boat operators navigate and pilot many types of small watercraft, including tugboats, gunboats, and barges. Cargo specialists load and unload military supplies, using equipment such as forklifts and cranes.

Vehicle and machinery mechanics conduct preventive and corrective maintenance on aircraft, automotive and heavy equipment, heating and cooling systems, marine engines, and powerhouse station equipment. These workers typically specialize by the type of equipment that they maintain. For example, aircraft mechanics inspect, service, and repair helicopters and airplanes. Automotive and heavy equipment mechanics maintain and repair vehicles such as humvees, trucks, tanks, self-propelled missile launchers, and other combat vehicles. They also repair bulldozers, power shovels, and other construction equipment. Heating and cooling mechanics install and repair air-conditioning, refrigeration, and heating equipment. Marine engine mechanics repair and maintain gasoline and diesel engines on ships, boats, and other watercraft. They also

The Marine Corps has many duties, including guarding U.S. embassies.

repair shipboard mechanical and electrical equipment. Powerhouse mechanics install, maintain, and repair electrical and mechanical equipment in power-generating stations.

Officer occupational groups
Combat specialty officers plan and direct military operations, oversee combat activities, and serve as combat leaders. This category includes officers in charge of tanks and other armored assault vehicles, artillery systems, special forces, and infantry. Combat specialty officers normally specialize by the type of unit that they lead. Within the unit, they may specialize by the type of weapon system. Artillery and missile system officers, for example, direct personnel as they target, launch, test, and maintain various types of missiles and artillery. Special-operations officers lead their units in offensive raids, demolitions, intelligence gathering, and search-and-rescue missions.

Engineering, science, and technical officers have a wide range of responsibilities based on their area of expertise. They lead or perform activities in areas such as space operations, environmental health and safety, and engineering. These officers may direct the operations of communications centers or the development of complex computer systems. Environmental health and safety officers study the air, ground, and water to identify and analyze sources of pollution and its effects. They also direct programs to control safety and health hazards in the workplace. Other personnel work as aerospace engineers to design and direct the development of military aircraft, missiles, and spacecraft.

Executive, administrative, and managerial officers oversee and direct military activities in key functional areas such as finance, accounting, health administration, international relations, and supply. Health services administrators, for instance, are responsible for the overall quality of care provided at the hospitals and clinics they operate. They must ensure that each department works together to provide the highest quality of care. As another example, purchasing and contracting managers negotiate and monitor contracts for the purchase of the billions of dollars worth of equipment, supplies, and services that the military buys from private industry each year.

Health care officers provide health services at military facilities, on the basis of their area of specialization. Officers who examine, diagnose, and treat patients with illness, injury, or disease include physicians, registered nurses, and dentists. Other health care officers provide therapy, rehabilitative treatment, and additional services for patients. Physical and occupational therapists plan and administer therapy to help patients adjust to disabilities, regain independence, and return to work. Speech therapists evaluate and treat patients with hearing and speech problems. Dietitians manage food service facilities and plan meals for hospital patients and for outpatients who need special diets. Pharmacists manage the purchase, storage, and dispensation of drugs and medicines. Physicians and surgeons in this occupational group provide the majority of medical services to the military and their families. Dentists treat diseases and disorders of the mouth. Optometrists treat vision problems by prescribing eyeglasses or contact lenses. Psychologists provide mental health care and also conduct research on behavior and emotions.

Human resource development officers manage recruitment, placement, and training strategies and programs in the military. They normally specialize by activity. Recruiting managers direct recruiting efforts and provide information about military careers to young people, parents, schools, and local communities. Personnel managers direct military personnel functions such as job assignment, staff promotion, and career counseling. Training and education directors identify training needs and develop and manage educational programs designed to keep military personnel current in the skills they need to perform their jobs.

Media and public affairs officers oversee the development, production, and presentation of information or events for the public. These officers may produce and direct motion pictures, videotapes, and television and radio broadcasts that are used for training, news, and entertainment. Some plan, develop, and direct the activities of military bands. Public information officers respond to inquiries about military activities and prepare news releases and reports to keep the public informed.

Protective service officers are responsible for the safety and protection of individuals and property on military bases and vessels. Emergency management officers plan and prepare for all types of natural and human-made disasters. They develop warning, control, and evacuation plans to be used in the event of a disaster. Law enforcement and security officers enforce all applicable laws on military bases and investigate crimes when the law has been broken.

Support services officers manage food service activities and perform services in support of the morale and well-being of military personnel and their families. Food services managers oversee the preparation and delivery of food services within dining facilities located on military installations and vessels. Social workers focus on improving conditions that cause social problems such as drug and alcohol abuse, racism, and sexism. Chaplains conduct worship services for military personnel and perform other spiritual duties covering the beliefs and practices of all religious faiths.

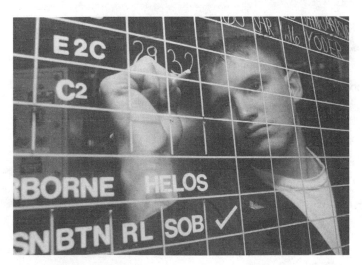

A sailor updates the status of one of the aircraft used by the Navy.

Transportation officers manage and perform activities related to the safe transport of military personnel and material by air and water. These officers normally specialize by mode of transportation or area of expertise because, in many cases, they must meet licensing and certification requirements. Pilots in the military fly various types of specialized airplanes and helicopters to carry troops and equipment and to execute combat missions. Navigators use radar, radio, and other navigation equipment to determine their position and plan their route of travel. Officers on ships and submarines work as a team to manage the various departments aboard their vessels. Ship engineers direct engineering departments aboard ships and submarines, including engine operations, maintenance, repair, heating, and power generation.

Qualifications, Training, and Advancement

Enlisted personnel. In order to join the services, enlisted personnel must sign a legal agreement called an enlistment contract, which usually involves a commitment to 8 years of service. Depending on the terms of the contract, 2 to 6 years are spent on active duty, and the balance is spent in the National Guard or Reserves. The enlistment contract obligates the service to provide the agreed-upon job, rating, pay, cash bonuses for enlistment in certain occupations, medical and other benefits, occupational training, and continuing education. In return, enlisted personnel must serve satisfactorily for the period specified.

Requirements for each service vary, but certain qualifications for enlistment are common to all branches. In order to enlist, one must be between 17 and 35 years old for active service, be a U.S. citizen or an alien holding permanent resident status, not have a felony record, and possess a birth certificate. Applicants who are aged 17 must have the consent of a parent or legal guardian before entering the service. Coast Guard enlisted personnel must enter active duty before their 28th birthday, whereas Marine Corps enlisted personnel must not be over the age of 29. Applicants must both pass a written examination—the Armed Services Vocational Aptitude Battery—and meet certain minimum physical standards, such as height, weight, vision, and overall health. All branches of the Armed Forces require high school graduation or its equivalent. In 2004, more than 9 out of 10 recruits were high school graduates.

People thinking about enlisting in the military should learn as much as they can about military life before making a decision. Doing so is especially important if you are thinking about making the military a career. Speaking to friends and relatives with military experience is a good idea. Find out what the military can offer you and what it will expect in return. Then, talk to a recruiter, who can determine whether you qualify for enlistment, explain the various enlistment options, and tell you which military occupational specialties currently have openings. Bear in mind that the recruiter's job is to recruit promising applicants into his or her branch of military service, so the information that the recruiter gives you is likely to stress the positive aspects of military life in the branch in which he or she serves.

Ask the recruiter for the branch you have chosen to assess your chances of being accepted for training in the occupation of your choice, or, better still, take the aptitude exam to see how well you score. The military uses this exam as a placement exam, and test scores largely determine an individual's chances of being accepted into a particular training program. Selection for a particular type of training depends on the needs of the service, your general and technical aptitudes, and your personal preference. Because all prospective recruits are required to take the exam, those who do so before committing themselves to enlist have the advantage of knowing in advance whether they stand a good chance of being accepted for training in a particular specialty. The recruiter can schedule you for the Armed Services Vocational Aptitude Battery without any obligation. Many high schools offer the exam as an easy way for students to explore the possibility of a military career, and the test also affords an insight into career areas in which the student has demonstrated aptitudes and interests.

If you decide to join the military, the next step is to pass the physical examination and sign an enlistment contract. Negotiating the contract involves choosing, qualifying for, and agreeing on a number of enlistment options, such as the length of active-duty time, which may vary according to the option. Most active-duty programs have first-term enlistments of 4 years, although there are some 2-, 3-, and 6-year programs. The contract also will state the date of enlistment and other options—for example, bonuses and the types of training to be received. If the service is unable to fulfill any of its obligations under the contract, such as providing a certain kind of training, the contract may become null and void.

All branches of the Armed Services offer a delayed entry program (DEP) by which an individual can delay entry into active duty for up to 1 year after enlisting. High school students can enlist during their senior year and enter a service after graduation. Others choose this program because the job training they desire is not currently available, but will be within the coming year, or because they need time to arrange their personal affairs.

Women are eligible to enter most military specialties; for example, they may become mechanics, missile maintenance technicians, heavy-equipment operators, and fighter pilots, or they may enter into medical care, administrative support, and intelligence specialties. Generally, only occupations involving direct exposure to combat are excluded.

People planning to apply the skills gained through military training to a civilian career should first determine how good the prospects are for civilian employment in jobs related to the military specialty that interests them. Second, they should know the prerequisites for the related civilian job. Because many civilian occupations require a license, certification, or minimum level of education, it is important to determine whether military training is sufficient for a person to enter the civilian equivalent or, if not, what additional training will be required. Other *Handbook* statements discuss the job outlook, training requirements, and other aspects of civilian occupations for which military training and experience are helpful. Additional information often can be obtained from school counselors.

Following enlistment, new members of the Armed Forces undergo initial-entry training, better known as "basic training" or "boot camp." Through courses in military skills and protocol recruit training provides a 6-week to 13-week introduction to military life. Days and nights are carefully structured and include rigorous physical exercise designed to improve strength and endurance and build each unit's cohesion.

Following basic training, most recruits take additional training at technical schools that prepare them for a particular military occupational specialty. The formal training period generally lasts from 10 to 20 weeks, although training for certain occupations—nuclear power plant operator, for example—may take as long as a year. Recruits not assigned to classroom instruction receive on-the-job training at their first duty assignment.

Many service people get college credit for the technical training they receive on duty, which, combined with off-duty courses, can lead to an associate degree through programs in community colleges such as the Community College of the Air Force. In addition to on-duty training, military personnel may choose from a variety of educational programs. Most military installations have tuition assistance programs for people wishing to take courses during off-duty hours. The courses may be correspondence courses or courses in degree programs offered by local colleges or universities. Tuition assistance pays up to 100 percent of college costs up to a credit-hour and annual limit. Each branch of the service provides opportunities for full-time study to a limited number of exceptional applicants. Military personnel accepted into these highly competitive programs—in law or medicine, for example—receive full pay, allowances, tuition, and related fees. In return, they must agree to serve an additional amount of time in the service. Other highly selective programs enable enlisted personnel to qualify as commissioned officers through additional military training.

Warrant officers. Warrant officers are technical and tactical leaders who specialize in a specific technical area; for example, Army aviators make up one group of warrant officers. The Army Warrant Officer Corps constitutes less than 5 percent of the total Army. Although the Corps is small in size, its level of responsibility is high. Its members receive extended career opportunities, worldwide leadership assignments, and increased pay and retirement benefits. Selection to attend the Warrant Officer Candidate School is highly competitive and restricted to those who meet rank and length-of-service requirements. The only exception is the Army aviator warrant officer, which has no prior military service requirements (table 3).

Table 1.   Military enlisted personnel by broad occupational category and branch of military service, February 2005

Occupational Group - Enlisted	Army	Air Force	Coast Guard	Marine Corps	Navy	Total, all services
Administrative occupations	14,016	25,008	2,241	9,612	25,923	76,800
Combat specialty occupations	113,689	398	851	52,256	6,264	173,458
Construction occupations	15,544	6,407	—	5,147	5,085	32,183
Electronic and electrical repair occupations	39,601	40,083	3,045	15,586	58,992	157,307
Engineering, science, and technical occupations	35,482	50,732	986	23,656	41,951	152,807
Health care occupations	27,031	17,924	682	—	26,614	72,251
Human resource development occupations	15,908	12,468	—	6,803	4,822	40,001
Machine operator and precision work occupations	4,103	7,409	1,548	2,439	12,274	27,773
Media and public affairs occupations	4,867	6,453	121	2,258	5,047	18,746
Protective service occupations	23,270	31,716	2,695	5,733	12,215	75,629
Support services occupations	13,438	1,667	1,146	2,264	10,699	29,214
Transportation and material handling occupations	53,349	34,588	10,549	22,825	42,860	164,171
Vehicle machinery mechanic occupations	48,577	50,532	5,538	18,076	50,020	172,743
Total, by service	408,875	285,385	29,402	166,655	302,766	1,193,083

SOURCE: *U.S. Department of Defense, Defense Manpower Data Center*

Table 2.   Military officer personnel by broad occupational category and branch of service, February 2005

Occupational Group - Officer	Army	Air Force	Coast Guard	Marine Corps	Navy	Total, all services
Combat specialty occupations	18,835	6,007	—	4,662	5,463	34,967
Engineering, science, and technical occupations	19,137	17,503	1,093	3,576	9,778	51,087
Executive, administrative, and managerial occupations	11,262	10,395	282	2,582	7,450	31,971
Health care occupations	9,792	9,413	43	—	6,983	26,231
Human resource development occupations	2,128	2,418	213	299	3,258	8,316
Media and public affairs occupations	224	500	20	44	282	1,070
Protective service occupations	2,237	1,410	104	309	890	4,950
Support services occupations	1,525	830	—	38	1,003	3,396
Transportation occupations	13,216	19,729	2,250	7,082	11,975	54,252
Total, by service	78,356	68,205	4,005	18,592	47,082	216,240

SOURCE: *U.S. Department of Defense, Defense Manpower Data Center*

Officers. Officer training in the Armed Forces is provided through the Federal service academies (Military, Naval, Air Force, and Coast Guard); the Reserve Officers Training Corps (ROTC) program offered at many colleges and universities; Officer Candidate School (OCS) or Officer Training School (OTS); the National Guard (State Officer Candidate School programs); the Uniformed Services University of Health Sciences; and other programs. All are highly selective and are good options for those wishing to make the military a career. Persons interested in obtaining training through the Federal service academies must be single to enter and graduate, while those seeking training through OCS, OTS, or ROTC need not be single. Single parents with one or more minor dependents are not eligible to become commissioned officers.

Federal service academies provide a 4-year college program leading to a bachelor-of-science degree. Midshipmen or cadets are provided free room and board, tuition, medical and dental care, and a monthly allowance. Graduates receive regular or reserve commissions and have a 5-year active-duty obligation, or more if they are entering flight training.

To become a candidate for appointment as a cadet or midshipman in one of the service academies, applicants are required to obtain a nomination from an authorized source, usually a member of Congress. Candidates do not need to know a member of Congress personally to request a nomination. Nominees must have an academic record of the requisite quality, college aptitude test scores above an established minimum, and recommendations from teachers or school officials; they also must pass a medical examination. Appointments are made from the list of eligible nominees. Appointments to the Coast Guard Academy, however, are based strictly on merit and do not require a nomination.

ROTC programs train students in about 575 Army, 130 Navy and Marine Corps, and 300 Air Force units at participating colleges and universities. Trainees take 3 to 5 hours of military instruction a week, in addition to regular college courses. After graduation, they may serve as officers on active duty for a stipulated period. Some may serve their obligation in the Reserves or National Guard. In the last 2 years of a ROTC program, students typically receive a monthly allowance while attending school, as well as additional pay for summer training. ROTC scholarships for 2, 3, and 4 years are available on a competitive basis. All scholarships pay for tuition and have allowances for textbooks, supplies, and other costs.

College graduates can earn a commission in the Armed Forces through OCS or OTS programs in the Army, Navy, Air Force, Marine Corps, and Coast Guard, and National Guard. These officers

generally must serve their obligation on active duty. Those with training in certain health professions may qualify for direct appointment as officers. In the case of persons studying for the health professions, financial assistance and internship opportunities are available from the military in return for specified periods of military service. Prospective medical students can apply to the Uniformed Services University of Health Sciences, which offers a salary and free tuition in a program leading to a doctor-of-medicine (M.D.) degree. In return, graduates must serve for 7 years in either the military or the U.S. Public Health Service. Direct appointments also are available for those qualified to serve in other specialty areas, such as the judge advocate general (legal) or chaplain corps. Flight training is available to commissioned officers in each branch of the Armed Forces. In addition, the Army has a direct enlistment option to become a warrant officer aviator.

Each service has different criteria for promoting personnel. Generally, the first few promotions for both enlisted and officer personnel come easily; subsequent promotions are much more competitive. Criteria for promotion may include time in service and in grade, job performance, a fitness report (supervisor's recommendation), and passing scores on written examinations. Table 3 shows the officer, warrant officer, and enlisted ranks by service.

Employment

In 2005, more than 2.6 million people served in the Armed Forces. More than 1.4 million were on active duty in the Armed Forces—about 487,000 in the Army, 350,000 in the Navy, 356,000 in the Air Force, and 185,000 in the Marine Corps. In addition, more than 1.2 million people served in their Reserve components, and the Air and Army National Guard. In addition, 33,000 individuals served in the Coast Guard, which is now part of the U.S. Department of Homeland Security. Table 1 shows the occupational composition of the 1.2 million active-duty enlisted personnel in February 2005; table 2 presents similar information for the 216,000 active-duty officers.

Military personnel are stationed throughout the United States and in many countries around the world. About half of all military jobs in the U.S. are located in California, Texas, North Carolina, Virginia, Florida, and Georgia. Approximately 169,000 service members were deployed to Operation Iraqi Freedom either in or around Iraq in June 2005. An additional 278,000 individuals were stationed outside the United States, including 21,000 assigned to ships at sea. About 106,000 were stationed in Europe, mainly in Germany, and another 81,000 were assigned to East Asia and the Pacific area, mostly in Japan and the Republic of Korea.

Table 3.   Military rank and employment for active duty personnel, January 2005

Grade	Rank and title Army	Navy	Air Force	Marine Corps	Total Employment
Commissioned officers:					
O-10	General	Admiral	General	General	34
O-9	Lieutenant General	Vice Admiral	Lieutenant General	Lieutenant General	125
O-8	Major General	Rear Admiral (U)	Major General	Major General	276
O-7	Brigadier General	Rear Admiral (L)	Brigadier General	Brigadier General	439
O-6	Colonel	Captain	Colonel	Colonel	11,483
O-5	Lieutenant Colonel	Commander	Lieutenant Colonel	Lieutenant Colonel	28,378
O-4	Major	Lieutenant Commander	Major	Major	43,846
O-3	Captain	Lieutenant	Captain	Captain	70,500
O-2	1st Lieutenant	Lieutenant (JG)	1st Lieutenant	1st Lieutenant	30,853
O-1	2nd Lieutenant	Ensign	2nd Lieutenant	2nd Lieutenant	24,948
Warrant officers:					
W-5	Chief Warrant Officer	Chief Warrant Officer	—	Chief Warrant Officer	540
W-4	Chief Warrant Officer	Chief Warrant Officer	—	Chief Warrant Officer	2,180
W-3	Chief Warrant Officer	Chief Warrant Officer	—	Chief Warrant Officer	4,618
W-2	Chief Warrant Officer	Chief Warrant Officer	—	Chief Warrant Officer	6,227
W-1	Warrant Officer	Warrant Officer	—	Warrant Officer	2,193
Enlisted personnel:					
E-9	Sergeant Major	Master Chief Petty Officer	Chief Master Sergeant	Sergeant Major/ Master Gunnery Sergeant	10,704
E-8	1st Sergeant/Master Sergeant	Senior Chief Petty Officer	Senior Master Sergeant	1st Sergeant/Master Sergeant	27,229
E-7	Sergeant First Class	Chief Petty Officer	Master Sergeant	Gunnery Sergeant	100,458
E-6	Staff Sergeant	Petty Officer 1st Class	Technical Sergeant	Staff Sergeant	174,467
E-5	Sergeant	Petty Officer 2nd Class	Staff Sergeant	Sergeant	249,816
E-4	Corporal	Petty Officer 3rd Class	Senior Airman	Corporal	260,631
E-3	Private First Class	Seaman	Airman 1st Class	Lance Corporal	216,321
E-2	Private	Seaman Apprentice	Airman	Private 1st Class	82,008
E-1	Private	Seaman Recruit	Airman Basic	Private	48,818

SOURCE: *U.S. Department of Defense*

Job Outlook

Opportunities should be good for qualified individuals in all branches of the Armed Forces through 2014. Many military personnel retire with a pension after 20 years of service, while they still are young enough to start a new career. About 170,000 personnel must be recruited each year to replace those who complete their commitment or retire. Since the end of the draft in 1973, the military has met its personnel requirements with volunteers. When the economy is good and civilian employment opportunities generally are more favorable, it is more difficult for all the services to meet their recruitment quotas. It is also more difficult to meet these goals during times of war, when recruitment goals typically rise.

America's strategic position is stronger than it has been in decades. Despite reductions in personnel due to the elimination of the threats of the Cold War, the number of active-duty personnel is expected to remain roughly constant through 2014. However, recent conflicts and the resulting strain on the Armed Forces may lead to an increasing number of active-duty personnel. The Armed Forces' current goal is to maintain a sufficient force to fight and win two major regional conflicts at the same time. Political events, however, could lead to a significant restructuring with or without an increase in size.

Educational requirements will continue to rise as military jobs become more technical and complex. High school graduates and applicants with a college background will be sought to fill the ranks of enlisted personnel, while virtually all officers will need at least a bachelor's degree and, in some cases, an advanced degree as well.

The Army has many health care specialists, including optometrists.

Earnings

The earnings structure for military personnel is shown in table 4. Most enlisted personnel started as recruits at Grade E-1 in 2004; however, those with special skills or above-average education started as high as Grade E-4. Most warrant officers had started at Grade W-1 or W-2, depending upon their occupational and academic qualifications and the branch of service of which they were a member, but warrant officer typically is not an entry-level

Air Force mechanics maintain and repair a broad range of aircraft.

occupation and, consequently, most of these individuals had previous military service. Most commissioned officers started at Grade O-1; some with advanced education started at Grade O-2, and some highly trained officers—for example, physicians and dentists—started as high as Grade O-3. Pay varies by total years of service as well as rank. Because it usually takes many years to reach the higher ranks, most personnel in higher ranks receive the higher pay rates awarded to those with many years of service.

In addition to receiving their basic pay, military personnel are provided with free room and board (or a tax-free housing and subsistence allowance), free medical and dental care, a military clothing

allowance, military supermarket and department store shopping privileges, 30 days of paid vacation a year (referred to as leave), and travel opportunities. In many duty stations, military personnel may receive a housing allowance that can be used for off-base housing. This allowance can be substantial, but varies greatly by rank and duty station. For example, in fiscal year 2005, the average housing allowance for an E-4 with dependents was $958 per month; for a comparable individual without dependents, it was $752. The allowance for an O-4 with dependents was $1,645 per month; for a comparable individual without dependents, it was $1,428. Other allowances are paid for foreign duty, hazardous duty, submarine and flight duty, and employment as a medical officer. Athletic and other facilities—such as gymnasiums, tennis courts, golf courses, bowling centers, libraries, and movie theaters—are available on many military installations. Military personnel are eligible for retirement benefits after 20 years of service.

The Veterans Administration (VA) provides numerous benefits to those who have served at least 24 months of continuous active duty in the Armed Forces. Veterans are eligible for free care in VA hospitals for all service-related disabilities, regardless of time served; those with other medical problems are eligible for free VA care if they are unable to pay the cost of hospitalization elsewhere. Admission to a VA medical center depends on the availability of beds, however. Veterans also are eligible for certain loans, including loans to purchase a home. Veterans, regardless of health, can convert a military life insurance policy to an individual policy with any participating company upon separation from the military. In addition, job counseling, testing, and placement services are available.

Veterans who participate in the Montgomery GI Bill Program receive education benefits. Under this program, Armed Forces personnel may elect to deduct up to $100 a month from their pay

Table 4.   Military basic monthly pay by grade for active duty personnel, January 2005

Grade	Years of service Less than 2	Over 4	Over 8	Over 12	Over 16	Over 20
O-10	—	—	—	—	—	$12,963.00
O-9	—	—	—	—	—	11,337.90
O-8	$8,022.30	$8,508.30	$9,089.40	$9,519.00	$9,915.30	10,742.40
O-7	6,666.00	7,233.00	7,642.50	8,113.50	9,089.40	9,714.60
O-6	4,940.70	5,784.00	6,054.90	6,087.90	7,045.50	7,763.40
O-5	4,118.70	5,021.40	5,341.80	5,799.00	6,431.10	6,793.20
O-4	3,553.80	4,449.60	4,977.60	5,582.70	5,872.20	5,933.70
O-3	3,124.50	4,168.20	4,586.70	4,962.00	5,083.20	5,083.20
O-2	2,699.40	3,660.90	3,736.20	3,736.20	3,736.20	3,736.20
O-1	2,343.60	2,948.10	2,948.10	2,948.10	2,948.10	2,948.10
W-5	—	—	—	—	—	5,548.20
W-4	3,228.60	3,671.40	4,007.10	4,341.00	4,779.00	5,117.40
W-3	2,948.40	3,238.80	3,522.30	3,918.90	4,285.50	4,509.30
W-2	2,593.50	2,965.50	3,268.20	3,564.00	3,771.30	3,977.40
W-1	2,290.20	2,684.40	3,030.90	3,275.40	3,438.30	3,659.70
E-9	—	—	—	3,989.70	4,232.40	4,575.90
E-8	—	—	3,193.50	3,422.10	3,640.50	3,949.20
E-7	2,220.00	2,638.80	2,899.50	3,084.60	3,332.40	3,458.70
E-6	1,920.30	2,296.50	2,604.30	2,779.20	2,888.70	2,908.20
E-5	1,759.50	2,060.70	2,329.80	2,450.70	2,450.70	2,450.70
E-4	1,612.80	1,877.70	1,957.80	1,957.80	1,957.80	1,957.80
E-3	1,456.20	1,641.00	1,641.00	1,641.00	1,641.00	1,641.00
E-2	1,384.50	1,384.50	1,384.50	1,384.50	1,384.50	1,384.50
E-1 4 months+	1,235.10	1,235.10	1,235.10	1,235.10	1,235.10	1,235.10
E-1 Less than 4 months	1,142.70	—	—	—	—	—

SOURCE: U.S. Department of Defense—Defense Finance and Accounting Service

The Coast Guard assists distressed vessels and protects U.S. waterways.

during the first 12 months of active duty, putting the money toward their future education. In fiscal year 2005, veterans who served on active duty for 3 or more years or who spent 2 years in active duty plus 4 years in the Selected Reserve received $1,004 a month in basic benefits for 36 months of full-time institutional training. Those who enlisted and serve less than 3 years received $816 a month for 36 months for the same. In addition, each service provides its own contributions to the enlistee's future education. The sum of the amounts from all these sources becomes the service member's educational fund. Upon separation from active duty, the fund can be used to finance educational costs at any VA-approved institution. Among those institutions which are approved by the VA are many vocational, correspondence, certification, business, technical, and flight-training schools; community and junior colleges; and colleges and universities.

Sources of Additional Information
Each of the military services publishes handbooks, fact sheets, and pamphlets describing entrance requirements, training and advancement opportunities, and other aspects of military careers. These publications are widely available at all recruiting stations, at most State employment service offices, and in high schools, colleges, and public libraries. Information on educational and other veterans' benefits is available from VA offices located throughout the country.

In addition, the Defense Manpower Data Center, an agency of the U.S. Department of Defense, publishes *Military Career Guide Online*, a compendium of military occupational, training, and career information designed for use by students and jobseekers. This information is available on the Internet: **http://www.todaysmilitary.com**

Data for Occupations Not Studied in Detail

Employment in the hundreds of occupations covered in detail in the main body of the *Handbook* accounts for more than 131 million or 90 percent of all jobs in the economy. Although occupations covering the full spectrum of work are included, those requiring lengthy education or training generally are given the most attention.

This chapter presents summary data on 129 additional occupations, for which employment projections are prepared, but for which detailed occupational information is not developed. These occupations account for about 7 percent of all jobs. For each occupation, the Occupational Information Network (O*NET) code, a brief description of the nature of the work, the number of jobs in 2004, a phrase describing the projected employment change from 2004 to 2014, and the most significant source of postsecondary education or training are presented. For a complete list of O*NET codes cited in the *Handbook*, refer to a later chapter, *Occupational Information Network (O*NET) Coverage*. For guidelines on interpreting the description of projected employment change, refer to a chapter in the front of the *Handbook*, Occupational Information Included in the *Handbook*.

The approximately 3 percent of all jobs not covered either in the detailed occupational descriptions in the main body of the *Handbook* or in the summary data presented in this chapter are mainly residual categories, such as "all other managers," for which little meaningful information could be developed.

Management, business, and financial occupations

Agents and business managers of artists, performers, and athletes
(O*NET 13-1011.00)

Represent and promote artists, performers, and athletes to prospective employers. May handle contract negotiations and other business matters for clients.

2004 employment: 21,000
Projected 2004-14 employment change: About as fast as average
Most significant source of postsecondary education or training: Bachelor's or higher degree, plus work experience

Compliance officers, except agriculture, construction, health and safety, and transportation
(O*NET 13-1041.01, 13-1041.02, 13-1041.03, 13-1041.04, 13-1041.05, 13-1041.06)

Examine, evaluate, and investigate eligibility for or conformity with laws and regulations governing contract compliance of licenses and permits, and other compliance and enforcement inspection activities not classified elsewhere. Exclude tax examiners, collectors, and revenue agents and financial examiners.

2004 employment: 177,000
Projected 2004-14 employment change: About as fast as average
Most significant source of postsecondary education or training: Long-term on-the-job training

Credit analysts
(O*NET 13-2041.00)

Analyze current credit data and financial statements of individuals or firms to determine the degree of risk involved in extending credit or lending money. Prepare reports with this credit information for use in decisionmaking.

2004 employment: 68,000
Projected 2004-14 employment change: More slowly than average
Most significant source of postsecondary education or training: Bachelor's degree

Emergency management specialists
(O*NET 13-1061.00)

Coordinate disaster response or crisis management activities, provide disaster preparedness training, and prepare emergency plans and procedures for natural (e.g. hurricanes, floods, earthquakes), wartime, or technological (e.g., nuclear power plant emergencies, hazardous materials spills) disasters or hostage situations.

2004 employment: 10,000
Projected 2004-14 employment change: Faster than average
Most significant source of postsecondary education or training: Work experience in a related occupation

Financial examiners
(O*NET 13-2061.00)

Enforce or ensure compliance with laws and regulations governing financial and securities institutions and financial and real estate transactions. May examine, verify correctness of, or establish authenticity of records.

2004 employment: 24,000
Projected 2004-14 employment change: About as fast as average
Most significant source of postsecondary education or training: Bachelor's degree

Gaming managers
(O*NET 11-9071.00)

Plan, organize, direct, control, or coordinate gaming operations in a casino. Formulate gaming policies for their area of responsibility.

2004 employment: 3,700
Projected 2004-14 employment change: Faster than average
Most significant source of postsecondary education or training: Work experience in a related occupation

Legislators
(O*NET 11-1031.00)

Develop laws and statutes at the Federal, State, or local level. Includes only elected officials.

2004 employment: 66,000
Projected 2004-14 employment change: More slowly than average
Most significant source of postsecondary education or training: Bachelor's or higher degree, plus work experience

Loan counselors

(O*NET 13-2071.00)

Provide guidance to prospective loan applicants who have problems qualifying for traditional loans. Guidance may include determining the best type of loan and explaining loan requirements or restrictions.

2004 employment: 34,000
Projected 2004-14 employment change: Faster than average
Most significant source of postsecondary education or training: Bachelor's degree

Logisticians

(O*NET 13-1081.00)

Analyze and coordinate the logistical functions of a firm or organization. Responsible for the entire life cycle of a product, including acquisition, distribution, internal allocation, delivery, and final disposal of resources.

2004 employment: 53,000
Projected 2004-14 employment change: About as fast as average
Most significant source of postsecondary education or training: Bachelor's degree

Postmasters and mail superintendents

(O*NET 11-9131.00)

Direct and coordinate operational, administrative, management, and supportive services of a U.S. post office; or coordinate activities of workers engaged in postal and related work in assigned post office.

2004 employment: 26,000
Projected 2004-14 employment change: Decline
Most significant source of postsecondary education or training: Work experience in a related occupation

Social and community service managers

(O*NET 11-9151.00)

Plan, organize, or coordinate the activities of a social service program or community outreach organization. Oversee the program or organization's budget and polices regarding participant involvement, program requirement, and benefits. Work may involve directing social workers, counselors, or probation officers.

2004 employment: 134,000
Projected 2004-14 employment change: Faster than average
Most significant source of postsecondary education or training: Bachelor's degree

Tax preparers

(O*NET 13-2082.00)

Prepare tax returns for individuals or small businesses but do not have the background or responsibilities of an accredited or certified public accountant.

2004 employment: 86,000
Projected 2004-14 employment change: About as fast as average
Most significant source of postsecondary education or training: Moderate-term on-the-job training

Transportation, storage, and distribution managers

(O*NET 11-3071.01, 11-3071.02)

Plan, direct, or coordinate transportation, storage, or distribution activities in accordance with governmental policies and regulations. Includes logistics managers.

2004 employment: 92,000
Projected 2004-14 employment change: About as fast as average
Most significant source of postsecondary education or training: Work experience in a related occupation

Professional and related occupations

Audio-visual collections specialists

(O*NET 25-9011.00)

Prepare, plan, and operate audio-visual teaching aids for use in education. May record, catalogue, and file audio-visual materials.

2004 employment: 9,300
Projected 2004-14 employment change: Faster than average
Most significant source of postsecondary education or training: Moderate-term on-the-job training

Clergy

(O*NET 21-2011.00)

Conduct religious worship and perform other spiritual functions associated with beliefs and practices of religious faith or denomination. Provide spiritual and moral guidance and assistance to members.

2004 employment: 422,000
Projected 2004-14 employment change: About as fast as average
Most significant source of postsecondary education or training: Master's degree

Dietetic technicians

(O*NET 29-2051.00)

Assist dieticians in the provision of food service and nutritional programs. Under the supervision of dieticians, may plan and produce meals based on established guidelines, teach principles of food and nutrition, or counsel individuals.

2004 employment: 25,000
Projected 2004-14 employment change: Faster than average
Most significant source of postsecondary education or training: Moderate-term on-the-job training

Directors, religious activities and education

(O*NET 21-2021.00)

Direct and coordinate activities of a denominational group to meet religious needs of students. Plan, direct, or coordinate church school programs designed to promote religious education among church membership. May provide counseling and guidance relative to marital, health, financial, or religious problems.

2004 employment: 90,000
Projected 2004-14 employment change: Faster than average
Most significant source of postsecondary education or training: Bachelor's degree

Farm and home management advisors
(O*NET 25-9021.00)

Advise, instruct, and assist individuals and families engaged in agriculture, agricultural-related processes, or home economics activities. Demonstrate procedures and apply research findings to solve problems; instruct and train in product development, sales, and the utilization of machinery and equipment to promote general welfare. Include county agricultural agents, feed and farm management advisors, home economists, and extension service advisors.

2004 employment: 16,000
Projected 2004-14 employment change: More slowly than average
Most significant source of postsecondary education or training: Bachelor's degree

Health educators
(O*NET 21-1091.00)

Promote, maintain, and improve individual and community health by assisting individuals and communities to adopt healthy behaviors. Collect and analyze data to identify community needs prior to planning, implementing, monitoring, and evaluating programs designed to encourage healthy lifestyles, policies and environments. May also serve as a resource to assist individuals, other professionals, or the community, and may administer fiscal resources for health education programs.

2004 employment: 49,000
Projected 2004-14 employment change: Faster than average
Most significant source of postsecondary education or training: Master's degree

Law clerks
(O*NET 23-2092.00)

Assist lawyers or judges by researching or preparing legal documents. May meet with clients or assist lawyers and judges in court. Excludes lawyers, and paralegal and legal assistants.

2004 employment: 51,000
Projected 2004-14 employment change: More slowly than average
Most significant source of postsecondary education or training: Bachelor's degree

Mathematical technicians
(O*NET 15-2091.00)

Apply standardized mathematical formulas, principles, and methodology to technological problems in engineering and physical sciences in relation to specific industrial and research objectives, processes, equipment, and products.

2004 employment: 1,800
Projected 2004-14 employment change: More slowly than average
Most significant source of postsecondary education or training: Master's degree

Merchandise displayers and window trimmers
(O*NET 27-1026.00)

Plan and erect commercial displays, such as those in windows and interiors of retail stores and at trade exhibitions.

2004 employment: 86,000
Projected 2004-14 employment change: About as fast as average

Most significant source of postsecondary education or training: Moderate-term on-the-job training

Orthotists and prosthetists
(O*NET 29-2091.00)

Assist patients with disabling conditions of limbs and spine or with partial or total absence of limb by fitting and preparing orthopedic braces and prostheses.

2004 employment: 6,000
Projected 2004-14 employment change: Faster than average
Most significant source of postsecondary education or training: Bachelor's degree

Psychiatric technicians
(O*NET 29-2053.00)

Care for mentally impaired or emotionally disturbed individuals, following physician instructions and hospital procedures. Monitor patients' physical and emotional well-being and report to medical staff. May participate in rehabilitation and treatment programs, help with personal hygiene, and administer oral medications and hypodermic injections.

2004 employment: 61,000
Projected 2004-14 employment change: More slowly than average
Most significant source of postsecondary education or training: Moderate-term on-the-job training

Set and exhibit designers
(O*NET 27-1027.01, 27-1027.02)

Design special exhibits and movie, television, and theater sets. May study scripts, confer with directors, and conduct research to determine appropriate architectural styles.

2004 employment: 13,000
Projected 2004-14 employment change: About as fast as average
Most significant source of postsecondary education or training: Bachelor's degree

Social science research assistants
(O*NET 19-4061.00)

Assist social scientists in laboratory, survey, and other social research. May perform publication activities, laboratory analysis, quality control, or data management. Normally these individuals work under the direct supervision of a social scientist and assist in those activities which are more routine. Excludes graduate teaching assistants, who both teach and do research.

2004 employment: 18,000
Projected 2004-14 employment change: About as fast as average
Most significant source of postsecondary education or training: Associate degree

Title examiners, abstractors, and searchers
(O*NET 23-2093.01, 23-2093.02)

Search real estate records, examine titles, or summarize pertinent legal or insurance details for a variety of purposes. May compile lists of mortgages, contracts, and other instruments pertaining to titles by searching public and private records for law firms, real estate agencies, or title insurance companies.

2004 employment: 61,000
Projected 2004-14 employment change: More slowly than average
Most significant source of postsecondary education or training:
Moderate-term on-the-job training

Service occupations

Amusement and recreation attendants
(O*NET 39-3091.00)

Perform a variety of attending duties at amusement or recreation facilities. May schedule use of recreations facilities, maintain and provide equipment to participants of sporting events or recreational pursuits, or operate amusement concessions and rides.

2004 employment: 252,000
Projected 2004-14 employment change: Much faster than average
Most significant source of postsecondary education or training:
Short-term on-the-job training

Animal control workers
(O*NET 33-9011.00)

Handle animals for the purpose of investigations of mistreatment, or control of abandoned, dangerous, or unattended animals.

2004 employment: 15,000
Projected 2004-14 employment change: About as fast as average
Most significant source of postsecondary education or training:
Moderate-term on-the-job training

Baggage porters and bellhops
(O*NET 39-6011.00)

Handle baggage for travelers at transportation terminals or for guests at hotels or similar establishments.

2004 employment: 57,000
Projected 2004-14 employment change: About as fast as average
Most significant source of postsecondary education or training:
Short-term on-the-job training

Concierges
(O*NET 39-6012.00)

Assist patrons at hotel, apartment or office building with personal services. May take messages, arrange or give advice on transportation, business services or entertainment, or monitor guest requests for housekeeping and maintenance.

2004 employment: 18,000
Projected 2004-14 employment change: About as fast as average
Most significant source of postsecondary education or training:
Moderate-term on-the-job training

Costume attendants
(O*NET 39-3092.00)

Select, fit and take care of costumes for cast members, and aid entertainers.

2004 employment: 3,500
Projected 2004-14 employment change: Faster than average
Most significant source of postsecondary education or training:
Short-term on-the-job training

Crossing guards
(O*NET 33-9091.00)

Guide or control vehicular or pedestrian traffic at such places as streets, schools, railroad crossings, or construction sites.

2004 employment: 71,000
Projected 2004-14 employment change: Faster than average
Most significant source of postsecondary education or training:
Short-term on-the-job training

Embalmers
(O*NET 39-4011.00)

Prepare bodies for interment in conformity with legal requirements.

2004 employment: 8,700
Projected 2004-14 employment change: About as fast as average
Most significant source of postsecondary education or training:
Postsecondary vocational award

First-line supervisors/managers of food preparation and serving workers
(O*NET 35-1012.00)

Supervise workers engaged in preparing and serving food.

2004 employment: 773,000
Projected 2004-14 employment change: About as fast as average
Most significant source of postsecondary education or training:
Work experience in a related occupation

First-line supervisors/managers of personal service workers
(O*NET 39-1021.00)

Supervise and coordinate activities of personal service workers, such as supervisors of flight attendants, hairdressers, or caddies.

2004 employment: 206,000
Projected 2004-14 employment change: Faster than average
Most significant source of postsecondary education or training:
Work experience in a related occupation

Funeral attendants
(O*NET 39-4021.00)

Perform a variety of tasks during a funeral, such as placing casket in parlor or chapel prior to service; arranging floral offerings or lights around casket; directing or escorting mourners; closing casket; and issuing and storing funeral equipment.

2004 employment: 30,000
Projected 2004-14 employment change: Faster than average
Most significant source of postsecondary education or training:
Short-term on-the-job training

Lifeguards, ski patrol, and other recreational protective services
(O*NET 33-9092.00)

Monitor recreational areas, such as pools, beaches, or ski slopes to provide assistance and protection to participants.

2004 employment: 113,000
Projected 2004-14 employment change: Faster than average
Most significant source of postsecondary education or training:
Short-term on-the-job-training

Locker room, coatroom and dressing room attendants
(O*NET 39-3093.00)

Provide personal items to patrons or customers in locker rooms, dressing rooms, or coatrooms.

2004 employment: 25,000
Projected 2004-14 employment change: About as fast average
Most significant source of postsecondary education or training: Short-term on-the-job training

Medical equipment preparers
(O*NET 31-9093.00)

Prepare, sterilize, install, or clean laboratory or healthcare equipment. May perform routine laboratory tasks and operate or inspect equipment.

2004 employment: 43,000
Projected 2004-14 employment change: Faster than average
Most significant source of postsecondary education or training: Short-term on-the-job training

Motion picture projectionists
(O*NET 39-3021.00)

Set up and operate motion picture projection and related sound reproduction equipment.

2004 employment: 12,000
Projected 2004-14 employment change: Decline
Most significant source of postsecondary education or training: Short-term on-the-job training

Parking enforcement workers
(O*NET 33-3041.00)

Patrol assigned area, such as public parking lot or section of city to issue tickets to overtime parking violators and illegally parked vehicles.

2004 employment: 11,000
Projected 2004-14 employment change: About as fast as average
Most significant source of postsecondary education or training: Short-term on-the-job training

Residential advisors
(O*NET 39-9041.00)

Coordinate activities for residents of boarding schools, college fraternities or sororities, college dormitories, or similar establishments. Order supplies and determine need to maintenance, repairs, and furnishings. May maintain household records and assign rooms. May refer residents to counseling resources if needed.

2004 employment: 56,000
Projected 2004-14 employment change: Much faster than average
Most significant source of postsecondary education or training: Moderate-term on-the-job training

Tour guides and escorts
(O*NET 39-6021.00)

Escort individuals or groups on sightseeing tours or through places of interest, such as industrial establishments, public buildings, and art galleries.

2004 employment: 38,000
Projected 2004-14 employment change: About as fast as average
Most significant source of postsecondary education or training: Moderate-term on-the-job training

Transportation attendants, except flight attendants and baggage porters
(O*NET 39-6032.00)

Provide services to ensure the safety and comfort of passengers aboard ships, buses, trains, or within the station or terminal. Perform duties, such as greeting passengers, explaining the use of safety equipment, serving meals or beverages, or answering questions related to travel.

2004 employment: 28,000
Projected 2004-14 employment change: About as fast as average
Most significant source of postsecondary education or training: Short-term on-the-job training

Travel guides
(O*NET 39-6022.00)

Plan, organize, and conduct long distance cruises, tours, and expeditions for individuals or groups.

2004 employment: 5,700
Projected 2004-14 employment change: About as fast as average
Most significant source of postsecondary education or training: Moderate-term on-the-job training

Ushers, lobby attendants, and ticket takers
(O*NET 39-3031.00)

Assist patrons at entertainment events by performing duties, such as collecting admission tickets and passes from patrons, assisting in finding seats, searching for lost articles, and locating such facilities as rest rooms and telephones.

2004 employment: 112,000
Projected 2004-14 employment change: About as fast as average
Most significant source of postsecondary education or training: Short-term on-the-job training

Veterinary assistants and laboratory animal caretakers
(O*NET 31-9096.00)

Feed, water, and examine pets and other nonfarm animals for signs of illness, disease, or injury in laboratories and animal hospitals and clinics. Clean and disinfect cages and work areas, and sterilize laboratory and surgical equipment. May provide routine postoperative care, administer medication orally or topically, or prepare samples for laboratory examination under the supervision of veterinary or laboratory animal technologists or technicians, veterinarians, or scientists. Excludes nonfarm animal caretakers.

2004 employment: 74,000
Projected 2004-14 employment change: Faster than average
Most significant source of postsecondary education or training: Short-term on-the-job training

Sales and related occupations

Door-to-door sales workers, news and street vendors, and related workers
(O*NET 41-9091.00)

Sell goods or services door-to-door or on the street.

2004 employment: 239,000
Projected 2004-14 employment change: Decline
Most significant source of postsecondary education or training: Short-term on-the-job training

Parts salespersons
(O*NET 41-2022.00)

Sell spare and replacement parts and equipment in repair shop or parts store.

2004 employment: 239,000
Projected 2004-14 employment change: Decline
Most significant source of postsecondary education or training: Moderate-term on-the-job training

Telemarketers
(O*NET 41-9041.00)

Solicit orders for goods and services over the telephone.

2004 employment: 415,000
Projected 2004-14 employment change: Decline
Most significant source of postsecondary education or training: Short-term on-the-job training

Office and administrative support occupations

Correspondence clerks
(O*NET 43-4021.00)

Compose letters in reply to request for merchandise, damage claims, credit and other information, delinquent accounts, incorrect billings, or unsatisfactory services. Duties may include gathering data to formulate reply and typing correspondence.

2004 employment: 23,000
Projected 2004-14 employment change: Decline
Most significant source of postsecondary education or training: Short-term-on-the-job training

Court, municipal, and license clerks
(O*NET 43-4031.01, 43-4031.02, 43-4031.03)

Perform clerical duties in courts of law, municipalities, and governmental licensing agencies and bureaus. May prepare docket of cases to be called; secure information for judges and court; prepare draft agendas or bylaws for town or city council; answer official correspondence; keep fiscal records and accounts; issue licenses or permits; record data, administer tests, or collect fees.

2004 employment: 110,000
Projected 2004-14 employment change: Faster than average
Most significant source of postsecondary education or training: Short-term-on-the-job training

Insurance claims and policy processing clerks
(O*NET 43-9041.01, 43-9041.02)

Process new insurance policies, modifications to existing policies, and claims forms. Obtain information from policyholders to verify the accuracy and completeness of information on claims forms, applications and related documents, and company records. Update existing policies and company records to reflect changes requested by policyholders

and insurance company representatives. Excludes claims adjusters, examiners, and investigators.

2004 employment: 251,000
Projected 2004-14 employment change: More slowly than average
Most significant source of postsecondary education or training: Moderate-term on-the-job training

Mail clerks and mail machine operators, except Postal Service
(O*NET 43-9051.01, 43-9051.02)

Prepare incoming and outgoing mail for distribution. Use hand or mail handling machines to time, stamp, open, read, sort, and route incoming mail; and address, seal, stamp, fold, stuff, and affix postage to outgoing mail or packages. Duties may also include keeping necessary records and completed forms.

2004 employment: 160,000
Projected 2004-14 employment change: Decline
Most significant source of postsecondary education or training: Short-term on-the-job training

New account clerks
(O*NET 43-4141.00)

Interview persons desiring to open bank accounts. Explain banking services available to prospective customers and assist them in preparing application form.

2004 employment: 98,000
Projected 2004-14 employment change: More slowly than average
Most significant source of postsecondary education or training: Work experience in a related occupation

Office machine operators, except computer
(O*NET 43-9071.01)

Operate one or more of a variety of office machines, such as photocopying, photographic, and duplicating machines, or other office machines. Excludes computer operators; mail clerks and mail machine operators; and billing and posting clerks and machine operators.

2004 employment: 100,000
Projected 2004-14 employment change: Decline
Most significant source of postsecondary education or training: Short-term on-the-job training

Proofreaders and copy markers
(O*NET 43-9081.00)

Read transcript or proof type setup to detect and mark for correction any grammatical, typographical, or compositional errors. Excludes workers whose primary duty is editing copy. Includes proofreaders of Braille.

2004 employment: 23,000
Projected 2004-14 employment change: More slowly than average
Most significant source of postsecondary education or training: Short-term on-the-job training

Statistical assistants
(O*NET 43-9111.00)

Compile and compute data according to statistical formulas for use in statistical studies. May perform actuarial computations and compile charts and graphs for use by actuaries. Includes actuarial clerks.

2004 employment: 19,000
Projected 2004-14 employment change: More slowly than average
Most significant source of postsecondary education or training: Moderate-term on-the-job training

Farming, fishing, and forestry occupations

Hunters and trappers
(O*NET 45-3021.00)

Hunt and trap wild animals for human consumption, fur, feed, bait, or other purposes.

2004 employment: 1,100
Projected 2004-14 employment change: More slowly than average
Most significant source of postsecondary education or training: Moderate-term on-the-job training

Supervisors, farming, fishing, and forestry workers
(O*NET 45-1011.01, 45-1011.02, 45-1011.03, 45-1011.04, 45-1011.05, 45-1011.06, 45-1012.00)

This broad occupation includes two detailed occupations—first-line supervisors/managers of farming, fishing, and forestry workers; and farm labor contractors. First-line supervisors/managers of farming, fishing, and forestry workers directly supervise and coordinate the activities of agricultural, forestry, aquacultural, and related workers. Farm labor contractors recruit, hire, furnish, and supervise seasonal or temporary agricultural laborers for a fee. May transport, house, and provide meals for workers. Excludes first-line supervisors/managers of landscaping, lawn service, and groundskeeping workers.

2004 employment: 61,000
Projected 2004-14 employment change: More slowly than average
Most significant source of postsecondary education or training: Work experience in a related occupation

Construction and extraction occupations

Continuous mining machine operators
(O*NET 47-5041.00)

Operate self-propelled mining machines that rip coal, metal and nonmetal ores, rock, stone, or sand form the face and load it onto conveyors or into shuttle cars in a continuous operation.

2004 employment: 8,300
Projected 2004-14 employment change: Decline
Most significant source of postsecondary education or training: Moderate-term on-the-job training

Derrick operators, oil and gas
(O*NET 47-5011.00)

Rig derrick equipment and operate pumps to circulate mud through drill hole.

2004 employment: 15,000
Projected 2004-14 employment change: Decline

Most significant source of postsecondary education or training: Moderate-term on-the-job training

Earth drillers, except oil and gas
(O*NET 47-5021.01, 47-5021.02)

Operate a variety of drills—such as rotary, churn, and pneumatic—to tap subsurface water and salt deposits, to remove core samples during mineral exploration or soil testing, and to facilitate the use of explosives in mining or construction. May use explosives. Includes horizontal and earth boring machine operators.

2004 employment: 22,000
Projected 2004-14 employment change: More slowly than average
Most significant source of postsecondary education or training: Moderate-term on-the-job training

Explosives workers, ordnance handling experts, and blasters
(O*NET 47-5031.00)

Place and detonate explosives to demolish structures or to loosen, remove, or displace earth, rock, or other materials. May perform specialized handling, storage, and accounting procedures. Includes seismograph shooters. Excludes earth drillers, except oil and gas who may also work with explosives.

2004 employment: 5,500
Projected 2004-14 employment change: More slowly than average
Most significant source of postsecondary education or training: Moderate-term on-the-job training

Fence erectors
(O*NET 47-4031.00)

Erect and repair metal and wooden fences and fence gates around highways, industrial establishments, residences, or farms, using hand and power tools.

2004 employment: 38,000
Projected 2004-14 employment change: About as fast as average
Most significant source of postsecondary education or training: Moderate-term on-the-job training

First-line supervisors/managers of construction trades and extraction workers
(O*NET 47-1011.01, 47-1011.02)

Directly supervise and coordinate activities of construction or extraction workers.

2004 employment: 750,000
Projected 2004-14 employment change: About as fast as average
Most significant source of postsecondary education or training: Work experience in a related occupation

Helpers—brickmasons, blockmasons, stonemasons, and tile and marble setters
(O*NET 47-3011.00)

Help brickmasons, blockmasons, stonemasons, or tile and marble setters by performing duties of lesser skill. Duties include using, supplying, or holding materials or tools, and cleaning work area and equipment. Excludes apprentice workers and report them with the appropriate skilled construction trade occupation. Excludes construction laborers who do not primarily assist brickmasons, blockmasons, and stonemasons or tile and marble setters.

2004 employment: 62,000
Projected 2004-14 employment change: About as fast as average
Most significant source of postsecondary education or training: Short-term on-the-job training

Helpers—carpenters
(O*NET 47-3012.00)

Help carpenters by performing duties of lesser skill. Duties include using, supplying, or holding materials or tools, and cleaning work area and equipment. Excludes apprentice workers and report them with the appropriate skilled construction trade occupation. Excludes construction laborers who do not primarily assist carpenters.

2004 employment: 109,000
Projected 2004-14 employment change: About as fast as average
Most significant source of postsecondary education or training: Short-term on-the-job training

Helpers—electricians
(O*NET 47-3013.00)

Help electricians by performing duties of lesser skill. Duties include using, supplying, or holding materials or tools, and cleaning work area and equipment. Excludes apprentice workers and report them with them the appropriate skilled construction trade occupation. Excludes construction laborers who do not primarily assist electricians.

2004 employment: 95,000
Projected 2004-14 employment change: More slowly than average
Most significant source of postsecondary education or training: Short-term on-the-job training

Helpers—extraction workers
(O*NET 47-5081.00)

Help extraction craft workers, such as earth drillers, blasters and explosives workers, derrick operators, and mining machine operators, by performing duties of lesser skill. Duties include supplying equipment or cleaning work area. Excludes apprentice workers.

2004 employment: 27,000
Projected 2004-14 employment change: Decline
Most significant source of postsecondary education or training: Short-term on-the-job training

Helpers—painters, paperhangers, plasterers, and stucco masons
(O*NET 47-3014.00)

Help painters, paperhangers, plasterers, or stucco masons by performing duties of lesser skill. Duties including using, supplying, or holding materials or tools, and cleaning work area and equipment. Excludes apprentice workers and report them with the appropriate skilled construction trade occupation. Excludes construction laborers who do not primarily assist painters, paperhangers, plasterers, or stucco masons.

2004 employment: 27,000
Projected 2004-14 employment change: About as fast as average
Most significant source of postsecondary education or training: Short-term on-the-job training

Helpers—pipelayers, plumbers, pipefitters, and steamfitters
(O*NET 47-3015.00)

Help pipelayers, plumbers, pipefitters, or steamfitters by performing duties of lesser skill. Duties including using, supplying, or holding materials or tools, and cleaning work area and equipment. Excludes apprentice workers and report them with the appropriate skilled construction trade occupation. Excludes construction laborers who do not primarily assist pipelayers, plumbers, pipefitters or steamfitters.

2004 employment: 76,000
Projected 2004-14 employment change: About as fast as average
Most significant source of postsecondary education or training: Short-term on-the-job training

Helpers—roofers
(O*NET 47-3016.00)

Help roofers by performing duties of lesser skill. Duties include using, supplying, or holding materials or tools, and cleaning work area and equipment. Excludes apprentice workers and report them with the appropriate skilled construction trade occupation. Excludes construction laborers who do not primarily assist roofers.

2004 employment: 22,000
Projected 2004-14 employment change: About as fast as average
Most significant source of postsecondary education or training: Short-term on-the-job training

Highway maintenance workers
(O*NET 47-4051.00)

Maintain highways, municipal and rural roads, airport runways, and rights-of-way. Duties include patching broken or eroded pavement, repairing guard rails, highway markers, and snow fences. May also mow or clear brush from along road or plow snow from roadway. Excludes tree trimmers and pruners.

2004 employment: 143,000
Projected 2004-14 employment change: Faster than average
Most significant source of postsecondary education or training: Moderate-term on-the-job training

Mine cutting and channeling machine operators
(O*NET 47-5042.00)

Operate machinery—such as longwall shears, plows, and cutting machines—to cut or channel along the face or seams of coal mines, stone quarries, or other mining surfaces to facilitate blasting, separating, or removing minerals or materials from mines or from the earth's surface. Includes shale planers.

2004 employment: 4,000
Projected 2004-14 employment change: Decline
Most significant source of postsecondary education or training: Moderate-term on-the-job training

Rail-track laying and maintenance equipment operators
(O*NET 47-4061.00)

Lay, repair, and maintain track for standard or narrow-gauge railroad equipment used in regular railroad service or in plant yards, quarries, sand and gravel pits, and mines. Includes ballast cleaning machine operators and railroad bed tamping machine operators.

2004 employment: 11,000
Projected 2004-14 employment change: Decline
Most significant source of postsecondary education or training:
Moderate-term on-the-job training

Rock splitters, quarry
(O*NET 47-5051.00)

Separate blocks of rough dimension stone from quarry mass using jackhammer and wedges.

2004 employment: 3,400
Projected 2004-14 employment change: More slowly than average
Most significant source of postsecondary education or training:
Moderate-term on-the-job training

Roof bolters, mining
(O*NET 47-5061.00)

Operate machinery to install roof support bolts in underground mine.

2004 employment: 4,400
Projected 2004-14 employment change: Decline
Most significant source of postsecondary education or training:
Moderate-term on-the-job training

Rotary drill operators, oil and gas
(O*NET 47-5012.00)

Set up or operate a variety of drills to remove petroleum products from the earth and to find and remove core samples for testing during oil and gas exploration.

2004 employment: 15,000
Projected 2004-14 employment change: More slowly than average
Most significant source of postsecondary education or training:
Moderate-term on-the-job training

Roustabouts, oil and gas
(O*NET 47-5071.00)

Assemble or repair oil field equipment using hand and power tools. Perform other tasks as needed.

2004 employment: 34,000
Projected 2004-14 employment change: More slowly than average
Most significant source of postsecondary education or training:
Moderate-term on-the-job training

Septic tank servicers and sewer pipe cleaners
(O*NET 47-4071.00)

Clean and repair septic tanks, sewer lines, or drains. May patch walls and partitions of tank, replace damaged drain tile, or repair breaks in underground piping.

2004 employment: 20,000
Projected 2004-14 employment change: Faster than average
Most significant source of postsecondary education or training:
Moderate-term on-the-job training

Service unit operators, oil, gas, and mining
(O*NET 47-5013.00)

Operate equipment to increase oil flow from producing wells or to remove stick pipe, casing, tools, or other obstructions from drilling wells. May also perform similar services in mining exploration operations. Includes fishing-tool technicians.

2004 employment: 17,000
Projected 2004-14 employment change: Decline
Most significant source of postsecondary education or training:
Moderate-term on-the-job training

Installation, maintenance, and repair occupations

Bicycle repairers
(O*NET 49-3091.00)

Repair and service bicycles.

2004 employment: 8,000
Projected 2004-14 employment change: About as fast as average
Most significant source of postsecondary education or training:
Moderate-term on-the-job training

Commercial divers
(O*NET 49-9092.00)

Work below surface of water, using scuba gear to inspect, repair, remove, or install equipment and structures. May use a variety of power and hand tools, such as drills, sledgehammers, torches, and welding equipment. May conduct tests or experiments, rig explosives, or photograph structures or marine life. Excludes fishers and related fishing workers, athletes and sports competitors, and police and sheriff's patrol officers.

2004 employment: 2,900
Projected 2004-14 employment change: About as fast as average
Most significant source of postsecondary education or training:
Moderate-term on-the-job training

Control and valve installers and repairers, except mechanical door
(O*NET 49-9012.01, 49-9012.02, 49-9012.03)

Install, repair, and maintain mechanical regulating and controlling devices, such as electric meters, gas regulators, thermostats, safety and flow valves, and other mechanical governors.

2004 employment: 38,000
Projected 2004-14 employment change: More slowly than average
Most significant source of postsecondary education or training:
Moderate-term on-the-job training

Fabric menders, except garment
(O*NET 49-9093.00)

Repair tears, holes, and other defects in fabrics, such as draperies, linens, parachutes, and tents.

2004 employment: 2,700
Projected 2004-14 employment change: Decline
Most significant source of postsecondary education or training:
Moderate-term on-the-job training

First-line supervisors/managers of mechanics, installers, and repairers
(O*NET 49-1011.00)

Supervise and coordinate the activities of mechanics, installers, and repairers. Excludes team or work leaders.

2004 employment: 469,000
Projected 2004-14 employment change: About as fast as average
Most significant source of postsecondary education or training:
Work experience in a related occupation

Helpers—installation, maintenance, and repair workers
(O*NET 49-9098.00)

Help installation, maintenance, and repair workers in maintenance, parts replacement, and repair of vehicles, industrial machinery, and electrical and electronic equipment. Perform duties, such as furnishing tools, materials, and supplies to other workers; cleaning work area, machines, and tools; and holding materials or tools for other workers.

2004 employment: 163,000
Projected 2004-14 employment change: About as fast as average
Most significant source of postsecondary education or training:
Short-term on-the-job training

Locksmiths and safe repairers
(O*NET 49-9094.00)

Repair and open locks; make keys; change locks and safe combinations; and install and repair safes.

2004 employment: 28,000
Projected 2004-14 employment change: About as fast as average
Most significant source of postsecondary education or training:
Moderate-term on-the-job training

Manufactured building and mobile home installers
(O*NET 49-9095.00)

Move or install mobile homes or prefabricated buildings.

2004 employment: 15,000
Projected 2004-14 employment change: More slowly than average
Most significant source of postsecondary education or training:
Moderate-term on-the-job training

Mechanical door repairers
(O*NET 49-9011.00)

Install, service, or repair opening and closing mechanisms of automatic doors and hydraulic door closers. Includes garage door mechanics.

2004 employment: 11,000
Projected 2004-14 employment change: About as fast as average
Most significant source of postsecondary education or training:
Moderate-term on-the-job training

Recreational vehicle service technicians
(O*NET 49-3092.00)

Diagnose, inspect, adjust, repair, or overhaul recreational vehicles including travel trailers. May specialize in maintaining gas, electrical, hydraulic, plumbing, or chassis/towing systems as well as repairing generators, appliances, and interior components. Includes workers who perform customized van conversions. Excludes automotive service technicians and mechanics, and bus and truck mechanics and diesel engine specialists who also work on recreation vehicles.

2004 employment: 13,000
Projected 2004-14 employment change: Faster than average
Most significant source of postsecondary education or training:
Long-term on-the-job training

Refractory materials repairers, except brickmasons
(O*NET 49-9045.00)

Build or repair furnaces, kilns, cupolas, boilers, converters, ladles, soaking pits, ovens, etc., using refractory materials.

2004 employment: 3,700
Projected 2004-14 employment change: Decline
Most significant source of postsecondary education or training:
Moderate-term on-the-job training

Riggers
(O*NET 49-9096.00)

Set up or repair rigging for construction projects, manufacturing plants, logging yards, ships and shipyards, or for the entertainment industry.

2004 employment: 13,000
Projected 2004-14 employment change: About as fast as average
Most significant source of postsecondary education or training:
Short-term on-the-job training

Security and fire alarm systems installers
(O*NET 49-2098.00)

Install, program, maintain, and repair security and fire alarm wiring and equipment. Ensure that work is in accordance with relevant codes. Excludes electricians who do a broad range of electrical wiring.

2004 employment: 47,000
Projected 2004-14 employment change: Faster than average
Most significant source of postsecondary education or training:
Postsecondary vocational award

Signal and track switch repairers
(O*NET 49-9097.00)

Install, inspect, test, maintain, or repair electric gate crossings, signals, signal equipment, track switches, section lines, or intercommunications systems within a railroad system.

2004 employment: 8,200
Projected 2004-14 employment change: More slowly than average
Most significant source of postsecondary education or training:
Moderate-term on-the-job training

Tire repairers and changers
(O*NET 49-3093.00)

Repair and replace tires.

2004 employment: 91,000
Projected 2004-14 employment change: More slowly than average
Most significant source of postsecondary education or training:
Short-term on-the-job training

Production occupations

Cementing and gluing machine operators and tenders
(O*NET 51-9191.00)

Operate or tend cementing and gluing machines to join items for further processing or to form a completed product. Processes include joining veneer sheets into plywood; gluing paper; joining rubber and rubberized fabric parts, plastic, simulated leather, or other materials. Excludes shoe machine operators and tenders.

2004 employment: 25,000
Projected 2004-14 employment change: More slowly than average
Most significant source of postsecondary education or training: Moderate-term on-the-job training

Chemical equipment operators and tenders
(O*NET 51-9011.01, 51-9011.02)

Operate or tend equipment to control chemical changes or reactions in the processing of industrial or consumer products. Equipment used includes devulcanizers, steam-jacketed kettles, and reactor vessels. Excludes chemical plant and system operators.

2004 employment: 49,000
Projected 2004-14 employment change: Decline
Most significant source of postsecondary education or training: Moderate-term on-the-job training

Chemical plant and system operators
(O*NET 51-8091.00)

Control or operate an entire chemical process or system of machines.

2004 employment: 60,000
Projected 2004-14 employment change: Decline
Most significant source of postsecondary education or training: Long-term on-the-job training

Cleaning, washing, and metal pickling equipment operators and tenders
(O*NET 51-9192.00)

Operate or tend machines to wash or clean products, such as barrels or kegs, glass items, tin plate, food, pulp, coal, plastic, or rubber, to remove impurities.

2004 employment: 18,000
Projected 2004-14 employment change: More slowly than average
Most significant source of postsecondary education or training: Moderate-term on-the-job training

Cooling and freezing equipment operators and tenders
(O*NET 51-9193.00)

Operate or tend equipment, such as cooling and freezing units, refrigerators, batch freezers, and freezing tunnels, to cool or freeze products, food, blood plasma, and chemicals.

2004 employment: 8,700
Projected 2004-14 employment change: More slowly than average
Most significant source of postsecondary education or training: Moderate-term on-the-job training

Crushing, grinding, and polishing machine setters, operators, and tenders
(O*NET 51-9021.00)

Set up, operate, or tend machines to crush, grind, or polish materials, such as coal, glass, grain, stone, food, or rubber.

2004 employment: 43,000
Projected 2004-14 employment change: More slowly than average
Most significant source of postsecondary education or training: Moderate-term on-the-job training

Cutters and trimmers, hand
(O*NET 51-9031.00)

Use hand tools or hand-held power tools to cut and trim a variety of manufactured items, such as carpet, fabric, stone, glass, or rubber.

2004 employment: 29,000
Projected 2004-14 employment change: More slowly than average
Most significant source of postsecondary education or training: Short-term on-the-job training

Cutting and slicing machine setters, operators, and tenders
(O*NET 51-9032.01, 51-9032.02, 51-9032.03, 51-9032.04)

Set up, operate, or tend machines that cut or slice materials, such as glass, stone, cork, rubber, tobacco, food, paper, or insulating material. Excludes woodworking machines setters, operators, and tenders; cutting, punching, and press machine setters, operators, and tenders, metal and plastic; and textile cutting machine setters, operators, and tenders.

2004 employment: 75,000
Projected 2004-14 employment change: Decline
Most significant source of postsecondary education or training: Moderate-term on-the-job training

Etchers and engravers
(O*NET 51-9194.01, 51-9194.02, 51-9194.03, 51-9194.04, 51-9194.05, 51-9194.06)

Engrave or etch metal, wood, rubber, or other materials for identification or decorative purposes. Includes such workers as etcher-circuit processors, pantograph engravers, and silk screen etchers. Includes photoengravers with prepress technicians and workers.

2004 employment: 12,000
Projected 2004-14 employment change: More slowly than average
Most significant source of postsecondary education or training: Long-term on-the-job training

Extruding, forming, pressing, and compacting machine setters, operators, and tenders
(O*NET 51-9041.01, 51-9041.02)

Set up, operate, or tend machines, such as glass forming machines, plodder machines, and tuber machines, to shape and form products, such as glassware, food, rubber, soap, brick, tile, clay, wax, tobacco, or cosmetics. Excludes paper goods machine setters, operators, and tenders; and shoe machine operators and tenders.

2004 employment: 74,000
Projected 2004-14 employment change: Decline
Most significant source of postsecondary education or training: Moderate-term on-the-job training

First-line supervisors/managers of production and operating workers
(O*NET 51-1011.00)

Supervise and coordinate the activities of production and operating workers, such as inspectors, precision workers, machine setters, and operators, assemblers, fabricators, and plant and system operators. Excludes team or work leaders.

2004 employment: 731,000
Projected 2004-14 employment change: More slowly than average
Most significant source of postsecondary education or training: Work experience in a related occupation

Furnace, kiln, oven, drier, and kettle operators and tenders
(O*NET 51-9051.00)

Operate or tend heating equipment other than basic metal, plastic or food processing equipment. Includes activities, such as annealing glass, drying lumber, curing rubber, removing moisture from materials, or boiling soap.

2004 employment: 30,000
Projected 2004-14 employment change: Decline
Most significant source of postsecondary education or training: Moderate-term on-the-job training

Gas plant operators
(O*NET 51-8092.01, 51-8092.02)

Distribute or process gas for utility companies and others by controlling compressors to maintain specified pressures on main pipelines.

2004 employment: 11,000
Projected 2004-14 employment change: More slowly than average
Most significant source of postsecondary education or training: Long-term on-the-job training

Grinding and polishing workers, hand
(O*NET 51-9022.00)

Grind, sand, or polish, using hand tools or hand-held power tools, a variety of metal, wood, stone, clay, plastic, or glass objects. Includes chippers, buffers, and finishers.

2004 employment: 45,000
Projected 2004-14 employment change: Decline
Most significant source of postsecondary education or training: Moderate-term on-the-job training

Helpers—production workers
(O*NET 51-9198.01, 51-9198.02)

Help production workers by performing duties of lesser skill. Duties include supplying or holding materials or tools, and cleaning work area and equipment. Excludes apprentice workers.

2004 employment: 484,000
Projected 2004-14 employment change: More slowly than average
Most significant source of postsecondary education or training: Short-term on-the-job training

Mixing and blending machine setters, operators, and tenders
(O*NET 51-9023.00)

Set up, operate, or tend machines to mix or blend materials, such as chemicals, tobacco, liquids, color pigments, or explosive ingredients. Excludes food batchmakers.

2004 employment: 120,000
Projected 2004-14 employment change: More slowly than average
Most significant source of postsecondary education or training: Moderate-term on-the-job training

Molders, shapers, and casters, except metal and plastic
(O*NET 51-9195.01, 51-9195.02, 51-9195.03, 51-9195.04, 51-9195.05, 51-9195.06, 51-9195.07)

Mold, shape, form, cast, or carve products such as food products, figurines, tile, pipes, and candles consisting of clay, glass, plaster, concrete, stone, or combinations of materials.

2004 employment: 47,000
Projected 2004-14 employment change: Decline
Most significant source of postsecondary education or training: Moderate-term on-the-job training

Packaging and filling machine operators and tenders
(O*NET 51-9111.00)

Operate or tend machines to prepare industrial or consumer products for storage or shipment. Includes cannery workers who pack food products.

2004 employment: 412,000
Projected 2004-14 employment change: More slowly than average
Most significant source of postsecondary education or training: Short-term on-the-job training

Paper goods machine setters, operators, and tenders
(O*NET 51-9196.00)

Set up, operate, or tend paper goods machines that perform a variety of functions, such as converting, sawing, corrugating, banding, wrapping, boxing, stitching, forming, or sealing paper or paperboard sheets into products.

2004 employment: 111,000
Projected 2004-14 employment change: More slowly than average
Most significant source of postsecondary education or training: Moderate-term on-the-job training

Petroleum pump system operators, refinery operators, and gaugers
(O*NET 51-8093.01, 51-8093.02, 51-8093.03)

Control the operation of petroleum refining or processing units. May specialize in controlling manifold and pumping systems, gauging or testing oil in storage tanks, or regulating the flow of oil into pipelines.

2004 employment: 43,000
Projected 2004-14 employment change: Decline
Most significant source of postsecondary education or training: Long-term on-the-job training

Separating, filtering, clarifying, precipitating, and still machine setters, operators, and tenders
(O*NET 51-9012.00)

Set up, operate, or tend continuous flow or vat-type equipment; filter presses; shaker screens; centrifuges; condenser tubes; precipitating, fermenting, or evaporating tanks; scrubbing towers; or batch stills. These machines extract, sort, or separate liquids, gases, or solids from other materials to recover a refined product. Includes dairy processing equipment operators. Excludes chemical equipment operators and tenders.

2004 employment: 38,000
Projected 2004-14 employment change: More slowly than average
Most significant source of postsecondary education or training: Moderate-term on-the-job training

Tire builders
(O*NET 51-9197.00)

Operate machines to build tires from rubber components.

2004 employment: 18,000
Projected 2004-14 employment change: Decline

Most significant source of postsecondary education or training: Moderate-term on-the-job training

Transportation and material moving occupations

Aircraft cargo handling supervisors
(O*NET 53-1011.00)

Direct ground crew in the loading, unloading, securing, and staging of aircraft cargo and baggage. Determine the quantity and orientation of cargo and compute aircraft center of gravity. May accompany aircraft as member of flight crew and monitor and handle cargo in flight, and assist and brief passengers on safety and emergency procedures. Includes loadmasters.

2004 employment: 7,700
Projected 2004-14 employment change: About as fast as average
Most significant source of postsecondary education or training: Work experience in a related occupation

Airfield operations specialists
(O*NET 53-2022.00)

Ensure the safe takeoff and landing of commercial and military aircraft. Duties include coordination between air-traffic control and maintenance personnel; dispatching; using airfield landing and navigational aids; implementing airfield safety procedures; monitoring and maintaining flight records; and applying knowledge of weather information.

2004 employment: 5,000
Projected 2004-14 employment change: About as fast as average
Most significant source of postsecondary education or training: Long-term on-the-job training

Ambulance drivers and attendants, except emergency medical technicians
(O*NET 53-3011.00)

Drive ambulance or assist ambulance drivers in transporting sick, injured, or convalescent persons. Assist in lifting patients.

2004 employment: 20,000
Projected 2004-14 employment change: Much faster than average
Most significant source of postsecondary education or training: Moderate-term on-the-job training

Bridge and lock tenders
(O*NET 53-6011.00)

Operate and tend bridges, canal locks, and lighthouses to permit marine passage on inland waterways, near shores, and at danger points in waterway passages. May supervise such operations. Includes drawbridge operators, lock tenders and operators, and slip bridge operators.

2004 employment: 3,700
Projected 2004-14 employment change: More slowly than average
Most significant source of postsecondary education or training: Short-term on-the-job training

First-line supervisors/managers of transportation and material moving machine and vehicle operators
(O*NET 53-1031.00)

Directly supervise and coordinate activities of transportation and material-moving machine and vehicle operators and helpers.

2004 employment: 228,000
Projected 2004-14 employment change: About as fast as average
Most significant source of postsecondary education or training: Work experience in a related occupation

Parking lot attendants
(O*NET 53-6021.00)

Park automobiles or issue tickets for customers in parking lot or garage. May collect fee.

2004 employment: 122,000
Projected 2004-14 employment change: Decline
Most significant source of postsecondary education or training: Short-term on-the-job training

Service station attendants
(O*NET 53-6031.00)

Service automobiles, buses, trucks, boats, and other automotive or marine vehicles with fuel, lubricants, and accessories. Collect payment for services and supplies. May lubricate vehicle, change motor oil, install antifreeze, or replace lights or other accessories, such as windshield wiper blades or fan belts. May repair or replace tires.

2004 employment: 91,000
Projected 2004-14 employment change: More slowly than average
Most significant source of postsecondary education or training: Short-term on-the-job training

Traffic technicians
(O*NET 53-6041.00)

Conduct field studies to determine traffic volume, speed, effectiveness of signals, adequacy of lighting, and other factors influencing traffic conditions, under direction of traffic engineer.

2004 employment: 6,500
Projected 2004-14 employment change: About as fast as average
Most significant source of postsecondary education or training: Short-term on-the-job training

Transportation inspectors
(O*NET 53-6051.01, 53-6051.02, 53-6051.03, 53-6051.04, 53-6051.05, 53-6051.06)

Inspect equipment or goods in connection with the safe transport of cargo or people. Includes rail transport inspectors, such as freight inspectors, car inspectors, rail inspectors, and other nonprecision inspectors of other types of transportation vehicles.

2004 employment: 26,000
Projected 2004-14 employment change: About as fast as average
Most significant source of postsecondary education or training: Work experience in a related occupation

Assumptions and Methods Used in Preparing Employment Projections

Occupational statements in the *Handbook* use 1 of 5 phrases to describe the projected change in employment between 2004 and 2014. (See page 24.) These phrases are based on numerical projections developed using the Bureau of Labor Statistics (BLS) employment projections model system. Projections of occupational employment are the sixth and final step in the system; the six steps are listed in the discussion of methods below. A full description of projections methods appears in the BLS *Handbook of Methods*. A discussion of projections methods also is accessible on the Internet at: **http://www.bls.gov/emp/empmth01.htm**. The November 2005 *Monthly Labor Review* presents a comprehensive discussion of the 2004-14 projections of the economy, labor force, and industry and occupation employment. The winter 2005-06 *Occupational Outlook Quarterly* presents the projections in a series of charts.

The projections reflect the knowledge and judgment of staff in the BLS Office of Occupational Statistics and Employment Projections and of knowledgeable people from other BLS offices, other government agencies, colleges and universities, industries, unions, professional societies, and trade associations, who furnished data and information, prepared reports, or reviewed the projections. BLS takes full responsibility, however, for the projections.

Assumptions. The information in the *Handbook* is based on an economic projection, which is characterized by a slower growth in labor force (1.0 percent annually from 2004 to 2014 compared with 1.2 percent over the past 10-year period, 1994-2004), an expected unemployment rate of 5.0 percent in 2014, a continued increase in labor productivity (2.7-percent average annual growth), and an improving but still large deficit of foreign trade. The Federal budget deficit is assumed to decline due largely to modest growth in Federal defense and nondefense expenditures. Other assumptions include consumer spending on durable goods that grows faster than consumer spending on services and nondurable goods. Within nondurable goods, a large source of consumer spending is drugs and medicines, and is assumed to grow much faster than spending on most other categories. Within services, consumer spending on medical care is expected to drive growth. Investment spending for production equipment—including communication equipment, computers, and software—will grow rapidly. Expenditures for construction of residential structures will settle down after its 2004 record high, but a still healthy 1.7-percent average annual growth is projected over the 2004-14 projection period. Spending on nonresidential construction will grow faster than the historical pace—1.3 percent annually over the projection period, compared with 0.7-percent annual growth between 1994 and 2004.

Although BLS considers these assumptions reasonable, the economy may follow a different course, resulting in a different pattern of occupational growth. Real growth also could be different because most occupations are sensitive to a much wider variety of factors than those considered in the various projections models. Unforeseen changes in consumer, business, or government spending patterns and in the ways in which goods and services are produced could greatly alter the growth of individual occupations.

Methods. This section summarizes the steps involved in BLS projections of employment by occupation. BLS uses U.S. Census Bureau projections of the population by age, gender, and race, combined with projections of labor force participation rates—the percent of the specified group of the population working or seeking work—to arrive at estimates of the civilian labor force for the projected year.

BLS projections are developed in a series of six steps, each of which is based on separate projections procedures and models and various related assumptions. These six steps, or system components, deal with:

- Size and demographic composition of the labor force
- Growth of the aggregate economy
- Final demand or gross domestic product (GDP)
- Interindustry relationships (input-output)
- Industry output and employment
- Occupational employment

These components provide the overall analytical framework needed to develop detailed employment projections. Each component is developed in order, with the results of each used as input for successive components and with some results feeding back into earlier steps. Each step is repeated a number of times to ensure internal consistency as assumptions and results are reviewed and revised.

The projections of the labor force and assumptions about other demographic variables, fiscal and monetary policies, foreign economic activity, and energy prices and availability form the input to the macroeconomic model. This model projects GDP (sales to all final consuming sectors in the economy) and the distribution of GDP by its major demand components (consumer expenditures, investment, government consumption and gross investments, and exports and imports). Estimating the intermediate flows of goods and services—for example, the steel incorporated into automobiles—is the next step in the projections process. The resulting estimates of demand for goods and services are used to project industry output of final products as well as total output by industry.

Industry output of goods and services is then converted to industry employment. Studies of trends in productivity and technology are used to estimate future output per worker hour, and regression analysis is used to estimate worker hours. These estimates, along with output projections, are used to develop the final industry employment projections.

An industry-occupation matrix, also known as the national employment matrix, is used to project employment for wage and salary workers. The matrix shows occupational staffing patterns—each occupation as a percent of employment in every industry. The matrix covering the 2004-14 period includes 336 detailed industries and 754 detailed occupations. Data for current staffing patterns in the matrix come from the BLS Occupational Employment Statistics surveys, which collect data from employers on a 3-year cycle.

The occupational staffing patterns for each industry were projected based on anticipated changes in the ways in which goods and services are produced, and were then applied to projected industry employment. The resulting employment was summed across industries to derive total wage and salary employment by occupation. Using this method, rapid employment growth is projected for health care workers while employment of rail transportation workers is expected to decline, reflecting the projected changes in the health care and railroad transportation industries, respectively.

Employment in an occupation also may grow or decline as a result of many other factors. For example, faster-than-average growth also is expected among computer support specialists as technology advances and organizations place more emphasis on network applications and on maximizing the efficiency of their computer systems. On the other hand, automation, the expanding use of computers, and developments in computer software will result in declining employment among procurement clerks, order clerks, and word processors and typists. The projected-year matrix incorporates these expected changes.

Data on self-employed workers in each occupation come from the Current Population Survey. Numbers of self-employed workers were projected separately.

Replacement needs. In most occupations, replacement needs provide more job openings than growth. Replacement openings occur as people leave occupations. Some individuals transfer to other occupations as a step up the career ladder or to change careers; some stop working temporarily, perhaps to return to school or care for a family; other workers—retirees for example—leave the labor force permanently. A discussion of replacements and the methodology used to prepare estimates is presented in *Occupational Projections and Training Data, 2006-07 Edition*, BLS Bulletin 2602.

Occupational Information Network Coverage

The *Occupational Information Network* (O*NET), which replaced the *Dictionary of Occupational Titles*, is used by public employment service offices to classify and place jobseekers. The O*NET was developed by job analysts. The information on job duties, knowledge and skills, education and training, and other occupational characteristics comes directly from workers and employers. Information on O*NET is available from O*NET Project, U.S. Department of Labor/ETA, 200 Constitution Ave. NW., Room N-5637, Washington, DC 20210-0001. Telephone (202) 693-3660. Internet: **http://www.doleta.gov/programs/onet**

The O*NET reflects the 2000 *Standard Occupational Classification* (SOC) system. With 822 detailed occupations, the SOC represents the Federal Government's most recent effort to analyze

the occupational structure in the United States and to provide a universal occupational classification system. All Federal agencies that collect occupational data adhere to the SOC. Information on the SOC, including its occupational structure, is available on the Internet: **http://www.bls.gov/soc**

Occupational statements in this 2006-07 edition of the *Handbook* list the O*NET codes that relate to or match the definitions used in the Bureau's Occupational Employment Statistics (OES) survey—the principal source of occupational employment data in the *Handbook*. All numbers listed also appear in the table below. The table is arranged by the O*NET/SOC code, followed by the O*NET/SOC title and the page on which the corresponding *Handbook* statement begins.

SOC Code	O*NET Title	Page
11-1011.01	Government service executives	67
11-1011.02	Private sector executives	67
11-1021.00	General and operations managers	67
11-1031.00	Legislators	661
11-2011.00	Advertising and promotions managers	27
11-2021.00	Marketing managers	27
11-2022.00	Sales managers	27
11-2031.00	Public relations managers	27
11-3011.00	Administrative services managers	25
11-3021.00	Computer and information systems managers	30
11-3031.01	Treasurers, controllers, and chief financial officers	42
11-3031.02	Financial managers, branch or department	42
11-3040.00	Human resources managers	50
11-3041.00	Compensation and benefits managers	50
11-3042.00	Training and development managers	50
11-3049.99	Human resources managers, all other	50
11-3051.00	Industrial production managers	54
11-3061.00	Purchasing managers	64
11-3071.01	Transportation managers	662
11-3071.02	Storage and distribution managers	662
11-9011.01	Nursery and greenhouse managers	40
11-9011.02	Agricultural crop farm managers	40
11-9011.03	Fish hatchery managers	40
11-9012.00	Farmers and ranchers	40
11-9021.00	Construction managers	32
11-9031.00	Education administrators, preschool and child care center/program	34
11-9032.00	Education administrators, elementary and secondary school	34
11-9033.00	Education administrators, postsecondary	34
11-9039.99	Education administrators, all other	34
11-9041.00	Engineering managers	38
11-9051.00	Food service managers	45
11-9061.00	Funeral directors	48
11-9071.00	Gaming managers	661
11-9081.00	Lodging managers	56
11-9111.00	Medical and health services managers	59
11-9121.00	Natural sciences managers	38
11-9131.00	Postmasters and mail superintendents	662
11-9141.00	Property, real estate, and community association managers	61
11-9151.00	Social and community service managers	662
13-1011.00	Agents and business managers of artists, performers, and athletes	661
13-1021.00	Purchasing agents and buyers, farm products	64
13-1022.00	Wholesale and retail buyers, except farm products	64
13-1023.00	Purchasing agents, except wholesale, retail, and farm products	64
13-1031.01	Claims examiners, property and casualty insurance	80
13-1031.02	Insurance adjusters, examiners, and investigators	80
13-1032.00	Insurance appraisers, auto damage	80
13-1041.01	Environmental compliance inspectors	661
13-1041.02	Licensing examiners and inspectors	661
13-1041.03	Equal opportunity representatives and officers	661
13-1041.04	Government property inspectors and investigators	661
13-1041.05	Pressure vessel inspectors	661
13-1041.06	Coroners	661
13-1051.00	Cost estimators	83
13-1061.00	Emergency management specialists	661
13-1071.01	Employment interviewers, private or public employment service	50
13-1071.02	Personnel recruiters	50
13-1072.00	Compensation, benefits, and job analysis specialists	50
13-1073.00	Training and development specialists	50
13-1079.99	Human resources, training, and labor relations specialists, all other	50
13-1081.00	Logisticians	662
13-1111.00	Management analysts	92
13-1121.00	Meeting and convention planners	95
13-2011.01	Accountants	70
13-2011.02	Auditors	70
13-2021.01	Assessors	74
13-2021.02	Appraisers, real estate	74
13-2031.00	Budget analysts	77
13-2041.00	Credit analysts	661
13-2051.00	Financial analysts	85
13-2052.00	Personal financial advisors	85
13-2053.00	Insurance underwriters	88
13-2061.00	Financial examiners	661
13-2071.00	Loan counselors	662
13-2072.00	Loan officers	90
13-2081.00	Tax examiners, collectors, and revenue agents	98
13-2082.00	Tax preparers	662
15-1011.00	Computer and information scientists, research	107
15-1021.00	Computer programmers	104
15-1031.00	Computer software engineers, applications	111
15-1032.00	Computer software engineers, systems software	111
15-1041.00	Computer support specialists	113
15-1051.00	Computer systems analysts	116
15-1061.00	Database administrators	107
15-1071.00	Network and computer systems administrators	113
15-1071.01	Computer security specialists	113
15-1081.00	Network systems and data communications analysts	107
15-1099.99	Computer specialists, all other	107
15-2011.00	Actuaries	102
15-2021.00	Mathematicians	119
15-2031.00	Operations research analysts	121
15-2041.00	Statisticians	123
15-2091.00	Mathematical technicians	663
17-1011.00	Architects, except landscape and naval	125
17-1012.00	Landscape architects	128
17-1021.00	Cartographers and photogrammetrists	130
17-1022.00	Surveyors	130
17-2011.00	Aerospace engineers	133
17-2021.00	Agricultural engineers	133
17-2031.00	Biomedical engineers	133
17-2041.00	Chemical engineers	133
17-2051.00	Civil engineers	133
17-2061.00	Computer hardware engineers	133
17-2071.00	Electrical engineers	133
17-2072.00	Electronics engineers, except computer	133
17-2081.00	Environmental engineers	133

17-2111.00	Health and safety engineers, except mining safety engineers and inspectors	135
17-2111.01	Industrial safety and health engineers	133
17-2111.02	Fire-prevention and protection engineers	133
17-2111.03	Product safety engineers	133
17-2112.00	Industrial engineers	133
17-2121.01	Marine engineers	133
17-2121.02	Marine architects	133
17-2131.00	Materials engineers	133
17-2141.00	Mechanical engineers	133
17-2151.00	Mining and geological engineers, including mining safety engineers	133
17-2161.00	Nuclear engineers	133
17-2171.00	Petroleum engineers	133
17-2199.99	Engineers, all other	133
17-3011.01	Architectural drafters	141
17-3011.02	Civil drafters	141
17-3012.01	Electronic drafters	141
17-3012.02	Electrical drafters	141
17-3013.00	Mechanical drafters	141
17-3019.99	Drafters, all other	144
17-3021.00	Aerospace engineering and operations technicians	144
17-3022.00	Civil engineering technicians	144
17-3023.01	Electronics engineering technicians	144
17-3023.02	Calibration and instrumentation technicians	144
17-3023.03	Electrical engineering technicians	144
17-3024.00	Electro-mechanical technicians	144
17-3025.00	Environmental engineering technicians	144
17-3026.00	Industrial engineering technicians	144
17-3027.00	Mechanical engineering technicians	144
17-3029.99	Engineering technicians, except drafters, all other	144
17-3031.01	Surveying technicians	130
17-3031.02	Mapping technicians	130
19-1011.00	Animal scientists	147
19-1012.00	Food scientists and technologists	147
19-1013.01	Plant scientists	147
19-1013.02	Soil scientists	147
19-1020.01	Biologists	150
19-1021.01	Biochemists	150
19-1021.02	Biophysicists	150
19-1022.00	Microbiologists	150
19-1023.00	Zoologists and wildlife biologists	150
19-1029.99	Biological scientists, all other	150
19-1031.01	Soil conservationists	153
19-1031.02	Range managers	153
19-1031.03	Park naturalists	153
19-1032.00	Foresters	153
19-1041.00	Epidemiologists	156
19-1042.00	Medical scientists, except epidemiologists	156
19-2011.00	Astronomers	170
19-2012.00	Physicists	170
19-2021.00	Atmospheric and space scientists	159
19-2031.00	Chemists	162
19-2032.00	Materials scientists	162
19-2041.00	Environmental scientists and specialists, including health	164
19-2041.00	Environmental scientists and specialists, including health	164
19-2042.01	Geologists	167
19-2042.01	Geologists	167
19-2043.00	Hydrologists	167
19-2043.00	Hydrologists	167
19-3011.00	Economists	173
19-3021.00	Market research analysts	175
19-3022.00	Survey researchers	175
19-3031.01	Educational psychologists	177
19-3031.02	Clinical psychologists	177
19-3031.03	Counseling psychologists	177
19-3032.00	Industrial-organizational psychologists	177
19-3041.00	Sociologists	182
19-3051.00	Urban and regional planners	180
19-3091.01	Anthropologists	182
19-3091.02	Archeologists	182
19-3092.00	Geographers	182
19-3093.00	Historians	182
19-3094.00	Political scientists	182
19-4011.00	Agricultural and food science technicians	185
19-4011.01	Agricultural technicians	185
19-4011.02	Food science technicians	185
19-4021.00	Biological technicians	185
19-4031.00	Chemical technicians	185
19-4041.01	Geological data technicians	185
19-4041.02	Geological sample test technicians	185
19-4051.01	Nuclear equipment operation technicians	185
19-4051.02	Nuclear monitoring technicians	185
19-4061.00	Social science research assistants	663
19-4061.01	City planning aides	350
19-4091.00	Environmental science and protection technicians, including health	185
19-4092.00	Forensic science technicians	185
19-4093.00	Forest and conservation technicians	185
21-1011.00	Substance abuse and behavioral disorder counselors	189
21-1012.00	Educational, vocational, and school counselors	189
21-1013.00	Marriage and family therapists	189
21-1014.00	Mental health counselors	189
21-1015.00	Rehabilitation counselors	189
21-1021.00	Child, family, and school social workers	196
21-1022.00	Medical and public health social workers	196
21-1023.00	Mental health and substance abuse social workers	196
21-1029.99	Social workers, all other	196
21-1091.00	Health educators	663
21-1092.00	Probation officers and correctional treatment specialists	192
21-1093.00	Social and human service assistants	194
21-2011.00	Clergy	662
21-2021.00	Directors, religious activities and education	662
23-1011.00	Lawyers	204
23-1021.00	Administrative law judges, adjudicators, and hearing officers	201
23-1022.00	Arbitrators, mediators, and conciliators	201
23-1023.00	Judges, magistrate judges, and magistrates	201
23-2011.00	Paralegals and legal assistants	207
23-2091.00	Court reporters	199
23-2092.00	Law clerks	663
23-2093.00	Title examiners, abstractors, and searchers	663
23-2093.01	Title searchers	663
23-2093.02	Title examiners and abstractors	663
25-1011.00	Business teachers, postsecondary	223
25-1021.00	Computer science teachers, postsecondary	223
25-1022.00	Mathematical science teachers, postsecondary	223
25-1031.00	Architecture teachers, postsecondary	223
25-1032.00	Engineering teachers, postsecondary	223
25-1041.00	Agricultural sciences teachers, postsecondary	223
25-1042.00	Biological science teachers, postsecondary	223
25-1043.00	Forestry and conservation science teachers, postsecondary	223
25-1051.00	Atmospheric, earth, marine, and space sciences teachers, postsecondary	223
25-1052.00	Chemistry teachers, postsecondary	223
25-1053.00	Environmental science teachers, postsecondary	223
25-1054.00	Physics teachers, postsecondary	223
25-1061.00	Anthropology and archeology teachers, postsecondary	223
25-1062.00	Area, ethnic, and cultural studies teachers, postsecondary	223
25-1063.00	Economics teachers, postsecondary	223
25-1064.00	Geography teachers, postsecondary	223
25-1065.00	Political science teachers, postsecondary	223
25-1066.00	Psychology teachers, postsecondary	223
25-1067.00	Sociology teachers, postsecondary	223
25-1069.99	Social sciences teachers, postsecondary, all other	223
25-1071.00	Health specialties teachers, postsecondary	223
25-1072.00	Nursing instructors and teachers, postsecondary	223
25-1081.00	Education teachers, postsecondary	223
25-1082.00	Library science teachers, postsecondary	223
25-1111.00	Criminal justice and law enforcement teachers, postsecondary	223
25-1112.00	Law teachers, postsecondary	223
25-1113.00	Social work teachers, postsecondary	223
25-1121.00	Art, drama, and music teachers, postsecondary	223
25-1122.00	Communications teachers, postsecondary	223
25-1123.00	English language and literature teachers, postsecondary	223
25-1124.00	Foreign language and literature teachers, postsecondary	223
25-1125.00	History teachers, postsecondary	223
25-1126.00	Philosophy and religion teachers, postsecondary	223
25-1191.00	Graduate teaching assistants	223
25-1192.00	Home economics teachers, postsecondary	223
25-1193.00	Recreation and fitness studies teachers, postsecondary	223
25-1194.00	Vocational education teachers postsecondary	223

25-1199.99	Postsecondary teachers, all other	223
25-2011.00	Preschool teachers, except special education	227
25-2012.00	Kindergarten teachers, except special education	227
25-2021.00	Elementary school teachers, except special education	227
25-2022.00	Middle school teachers, except special and vocational education	227
25-2023.00	Vocational education teachers, middle school	227
25-2031.00	Secondary school teachers, except special and vocational education	227
25-2032.00	Vocational education teachers, secondary school	227
25-2041.00	Special education teachers, preschool, kindergarten, and elementary school	232
25-2042.00	Special education teachers, middle school	232
25-2043.00	Special education teachers, secondary school	232
25-3011.00	Adult literacy, remedial education, and GED teachers and instructors	221
25-3021.00	Self-enrichment education teachers	231
25-4011.00	Archivists	210
25-4012.00	Curators	210
25-4013.00	Museum technicians and conservators	210
25-4021.00	Librarians	214
25-4031.00	Library technicians	217
25-9011.00	Audio-visual collections specialists	662
25-9021.00	Farm and home management advisors	663
25-9031.00	Instructional coordinators	213
25-9041.00	Teacher assistants	219
27-1011.00	Art directors	235
27-1012.00	Craft artists	235
27-1013.01	Painters and illustrators	235
27-1013.02	Sketch artists	235
27-1013.03	Cartoonists	235
27-1013.04	Sculptors	235
27-1014.00	Multi-media artists and animators	235
27-1019.99	Artists and related workers, all other	235
27-1021.00	Commercial and industrial designers	238
27-1022.00	Fashion designers	240
27-1023.00	Floral designers	242
27-1024.00	Graphic designers	243
27-1025.00	Interior designers	245
27-1026.00	Merchandise displayers and window trimmers	663
27-1027.01	Set designers	663
27-1027.02	Exhibit designers	663
27-2011.00	Actors	249
27-2012.01	Producers	249
27-2012.02	Directors- stage, motion pictures, television, and radio	249
27-2012.03	Program directors	249
27-2012.04	Talent directors	249
27-2012.05	Technical directors/managers	249
27-2021.00	Athletes and sports competitors	252
27-2022.00	Coaches and scouts	252
27-2023.00	Umpires, referees, and other sports officials	252
27-2031.00	Dancers	255
27-2032.00	Choreographers	255
27-2041.01	Music directors	257
27-2041.02	Music arrangers and orchestrators	257
27-2041.03	Composers	257
27-2042.01	Singers	257
27-2042.02	Musicians, instrumental	257
27-3011.00	Radio and television announcers	259
27-3012.00	Public address system and other announcers	259
27-3021.00	Broadcast news analysts	267
27-3022.00	Reporters and correspondents	267
27-3031.00	Public relations specialists	271
27-3041.00	Editors	275
27-3042.00	Technical writers	275
27-3043.01	Poets and lyricists	275
27-3043.02	Creative writers	275
27-3043.03	Caption writers	275
27-3043.04	Copy writers	275
27-3091.00	Interpreters and translators	263
27-4011.00	Audio and video equipment technicians	261
27-4012.00	Broadcast technicians	261
27-4013.00	Radio operators	261
27-4014.00	Sound engineering technicians	261
27-4021.01	Professional photographers	269
27-4021.02	Photographers, scientific	269
27-4031.00	Camera operators, television, video, and motion picture	274
27-4032.00	Film and video editors	274
29-1011.00	Chiropractors	280
29-1021.00	Dentists, general	282
29-1022.00	Oral and maxillofacial surgeons	282
29-1023.00	Orthodontists	282
29-1024.00	Prosthodontists	282
29-1029.99	Dentists, all other specialists	282
29-1031.00	Dietitians and nutritionists	284
29-1041.00	Optometrists	287
29-1051.00	Pharmacists	289
29-1061.00	Anesthesiologists	295
29-1062.00	Family and general practitioners	295
29-1063.00	Internists, general	295
29-1064.00	Obstetricians and gynecologists	295
29-1065.00	Pediatricians, general	295
29-1066.00	Psychiatrists	295
29-1067.00	Surgeons	295
29-1069.99	Physicians and surgeons, all other	295
29-1071.00	Physician assistants	293
29-1081.00	Podiatrists	298
29-1111.00	Registered nurses	303
29-1121.00	Audiologists	278
29-1122.00	Occupational therapists	285
29-1123.00	Physical therapists	292
29-1124.00	Radiation therapists	300
29-1125.00	Recreational therapists	302
29-1126.00	Respiratory therapists	307
29-1127.00	Speech-language pathologists	309
29-1131.00	Veterinarians	311
29-2011.00	Medical and clinical laboratory technologists	318
29-2012.00	Medical and clinical laboratory technicians	318
29-2021.00	Dental hygienists	320
29-2031.00	Cardiovascular technologists and technicians	316
29-2032.00	Diagnostic medical sonographers	322
29-2033.00	Nuclear medicine technologists	330
29-2034.01	Radiologic technologists	337
29-2034.02	Radiologic technicians	337
29-2041.00	Emergency medical technicians and paramedics	324
29-2051.00	Dietetic technicians	662
29-2052.00	Pharmacy technicians	336
29-2053.00	Psychiatric technicians	663
29-2054.00	Respiratory therapy technicians	307
29-2055.00	Surgical technologists	339
29-2056.00	Veterinary technologists and technicians	341
29-2061.00	Licensed practical and licensed vocational nurses	326
29-2071.00	Medical records and health information technicians	328
29-2081.00	Opticians, dispensing	334
29-2091.00	Orthotists and prosthetists	663
29-9011.00	Occupational health and safety specialists	331
29-9012.00	Occupational health and safety technicians	331
29-9091.00	Athletic trainers	314
31-1011.00	Home health aides	350
31-1012.00	Nursing aides, orderlies, and attendants	350
31-1013.00	Psychiatric aides	350
31-2011.00	Occupational therapist assistants	353
31-2012.00	Occupational therapist aides	353
31-2021.00	Physical therapist assistants	356
31-2022.00	Physical therapist aides	356
31-9011.00	Massage therapists	344
31-9091.00	Dental assistants	343
31-9092.00	Medical assistants	347
31-9093.00	Medical equipment preparers	665
31-9094.00	Medical transcriptionists	348
31-9095.00	Pharmacy aides	354
31-9096.00	Veterinary assistants and laboratory animal caretakers	665
33-1011.00	First-line supervisors/managers of correctional officers	357
33-1012.00	First-line supervisors/managers of police and detectives	362
33-1021.01	Municipal fire fighting and prevention supervisors	359
33-1021.02	Forest fire fighting and prevention supervisors	359
33-2011.01	Municipal fire fighters	359
33-2011.02	Forest fire fighters	359
33-2021.01	Fire inspectors	359
33-2021.02	Fire investigators	359
33-2022.00	Forest fire inspectors and prevention specialists	359
33-3011.00	Bailiffs	357
33-3012.00	Correctional officers and jailers	357
33-3021.01	Police detectives	362
33-3021.02	Police identification and records officers	362
33-3021.03	Criminal investigators and special agents	362
33-3021.04	Child support, missing persons, and unemployment insurance fraud investigators	362
33-3021.05	Immigration and customs inspectors	362
33-3031.00	Fish and game wardens	362
33-3041.00	Parking enforcement workers	665

33-3051.01	Police patrol officers	362
33-3051.02	Highway patrol pilots	362
33-3051.03	Sheriffs and deputy sheriffs	362
33-3052.00	Transit and railroad police	362
33-9011.00	Animal control workers	664
33-9021.00	Private detectives and investigators	366
33-9031.00	Gaming surveillance officers and gaming investigators	368
33-9032.00	Security guards	368
33-9091.00	Crossing guards	664
33-9092.00	Lifeguards, ski patrol, and other recreational protective service workers	664
35-1011.00	Chefs and head cooks	371
35-1012.00	First-line supervisors/managers of food preparation and serving workers	664
35-2011.00	Cooks, fast food	371
35-2012.00	Cooks, institution and cafeteria	371
35-2013.00	Cooks, private household	371
35-2014.00	Cooks, restaurant	371
35-2015.00	Cooks, short order	371
35-2019.99	Cooks, all other	371
35-2021.00	Food preparation workers	371
35-3011.00	Bartenders	374
35-3021.00	Combined food preparation and serving workers, including fast food	374
35-3022.00	Counter attendants, cafeteria, food concession, and coffee shop	374
35-3031.00	Waiters and waitresses	374
35-3041.00	Food servers, nonrestaurant	374
35-9011.00	Dining room and cafeteria attendants and bartender helpers	374
35-9021.00	Dishwashers	374
35-9031.00	Hosts and hostesses, restaurant, lounge, and coffee shop	374
35-9099.99	Food preparation and serving related workers, all other	374
37-1011.01	Housekeeping supervisors	378
37-1011.02	Janitorial supervisors	378
37-1012.01	Lawn service managers	380
37-1012.02	First-line supervisors and manager/supervisors — landscaping workers	380
37-2011.00	Janitors and cleaners, except maids and housekeeping cleaners	378
37-2012.00	Maids and housekeeping cleaners	378
37-2019.99	Building cleaning workers, all other	378
37-2021.00	Pest control workers	382
37-3011.00	Landscaping and groundskeeping workers	380
37-3012.00	Pesticide handlers, sprayers, and applicators, vegetation	380
37-3013.00	Tree trimmers and pruners	380
37-3019.99	Grounds maintenance workers, all other	380
39-1011.00	Gaming supervisors	397
39-1012.00	Slot key persons	397
39-1021.00	First-line supervisors/managers of personal service workers	664
39-2011.00	Animal trainers	384
39-2021.00	Nonfarm animal caretakers	384
39-3011.00	Gaming dealers	397
39-3012.00	Gaming and sports book writers and runners	397
39-3019.99	Gaming service workers, all other	397
39-3021.00	Motion picture projectionists	665
39-3031.00	Ushers, lobby attendants, and ticket takers	665
39-3091.00	Amusement and recreation attendants	664
39-3092.00	Costume attendants	664
39-3093.00	Locker room, coatroom, and dressing room attendants	665
39-4011.00	Embalmers	664
39-4021.00	Funeral attendants	664
39-5011.00	Barbers	387
39-5012.00	Hairdressers, hairstylists, and cosmetologists	387
39-5091.00	Makeup artists, theatrical and performance	387
39-5092.00	Manicurists and pedicurists	387
39-5093.00	Shampooers	387
39-5094.00	Skin care specialists	387
39-6011.00	Baggage porters and bellhops	664
39-6012.00	Concierges	664
39-6021.00	Tour guides and escorts	665
39-6022.00	Travel guides	665
39-6031.00	Flight attendants	394
39-6032.00	Transportation attendants, except flight attendants and baggage porters	665
39-9011.00	Child care workers	389
39-9021.00	Personal and home care aides	399
39-9031.00	Fitness trainers and aerobics instructors	392
39-9032.00	Recreation workers	400
39-9041.00	Residential advisors	665
41-1011.00	First-line supervisors/managers of retail sales workers	423
41-1012.00	First-line supervisors/managers of non-retail sales workers	423
41-2011.00	Cashiers	405
41-2012.00	Gaming change persons and booth cashiers	405
41-2021.00	Counter and rental clerks	407
41-2022.00	Parts salespersons	666
41-2031.00	Retail salespersons	417
41-3011.00	Advertising sales agents	403
41-3021.00	Insurance sales agents	411
41-3031.01	Sales agents, securities and commodities	426
41-3031.02	Sales agents, financial services	426
41-3041.00	Travel agents	429
41-4011.01	Sales representatives, agricultural	421
41-4011.02	Sales representatives, chemical and pharmaceutical	421
41-4011.03	Sales representatives, electrical/electronic	421
41-4011.04	Sales representatives, mechanical equipment and supplies	421
41-4011.05	Sales representatives, medical	421
41-4011.06	Sales representatives, instruments	421
41-4012.00	Sales representatives, wholesale and manufacturing, except technical and scientific products	421
41-9011.00	Demonstrators and product promoters	408
41-9012.00	Models	408
41-9021.00	Real estate brokers	414
41-9022.00	Real estate sales agents	414
41-9031.00	Sales engineers	419
41-9041.00	Telemarketers	666
41-9091.00	Door-to-door sales workers, news and street vendors, and related workers	665
43-1011.01	First-line supervisors, customer service	479
43-1011.02	First-line supervisors, administrative support	479
43-2011.00	Switchboard operators, including answering service	471
43-2021.01	Directory assistance operators	471
43-2021.02	Central office operators	471
43-2099.99	Communications equipment operators, all other	471
43-3011.00	Bill and account collectors	431
43-3021.00	Billing and posting clerks and machine operators	432
43-3021.01	Statement clerks	432
43-3021.02	Billing, cost, and rate clerks	432
43-3021.03	Billing, posting, and calculating machine operators	432
43-3031.00	Bookkeeping, accounting, and auditing clerks	434
43-3041.00	Gaming cage workers	435
43-3051.00	Payroll and timekeeping clerks	437
43-3061.00	Procurement clerks	438
43-3071.00	Tellers	440
43-4011.00	Brokerage clerks	441
43-4021.00	Correspondence clerks	666
43-4031.01	Court clerks	666
43-4031.02	Municipal clerks	666
43-4031.03	License clerks	666
43-4041.01	Credit authorizers	442
43-4041.02	Credit checkers	442
43-4051.01	Adjustment clerks	444
43-4051.02	Customer service representatives, utilities	444
43-4061.01	Claims takers, unemployment benefits	451
43-4061.02	Welfare eligibility workers and interviewers	451
43-4071.00	File clerks	447
43-4081.00	Hotel, motel, and resort desk clerks	448
43-4111.00	Interviewers, except eligibility and loan	451
43-4121.00	Library assistants, clerical	453
43-4131.00	Loan interviewers and clerks	451
43-4141.00	New accounts clerks	666
43-4151.00	Order clerks	454
43-4161.00	Human resources assistants, except payroll and timekeeping	449
43-4171.00	Receptionists and information clerks	455
43-4181.01	Travel clerks	457
43-4181.02	Reservation and transportation ticket agents	457
43-5011.00	Cargo and freight agents	459
43-5021.00	Couriers and messengers	460
43-5031.00	Police, fire, and ambulance dispatchers	461
43-5032.00	Dispatchers, except police, fire, and ambulance	461
43-5041.00	Meter readers, utilities	463
43-5051.00	Postal service clerks	464
43-5052.00	Postal service mail carriers	464
43-5053.00	Postal service mail sorters, processors, and processing machine operators	464

43-5061.00	Production, planning, and expediting clerks	466
43-5071.00	Shipping, receiving, and traffic clerks	467
43-5081.01	Stock clerks, sales floor	469
43-5081.02	Marking clerks	469
43-5081.03	Stock clerks- stockroom, warehouse, or storage yard	469
43-5081.04	Order fillers, wholesale and retail sales	469
43-5111.00	Weighers, measurers, checkers, and samplers, recordkeeping	470
43-6011.00	Executive secretaries and administrative assistants	482
43-6012.00	Legal secretaries	482
43-6013.00	Medical secretaries	482
43-6014.00	Secretaries, except legal, medical, and executive	482
43-9011.00	Computer operators	473
43-9021.00	Data entry keyers	475
43-9022.00	Word processors and typists	475
43-9031.00	Desktop publishers	477
43-9041.01	Insurance claims clerks	666
43-9041.02	Insurance policy processing clerks	666
43-9051.01	Mail machine operators, preparation and handling	666
43-9051.02	Mail clerks, except mail machine operators and postal service	666
43-9061.00	Office clerks, general	481
43-9071.00	Office machine operators, except computer	666
43-9071.01	Duplicating machine operators	666
43-9081.00	Proofreaders and copy markers	666
43-9111.00	Statistical assistants	666
45-1011.01	First-line supervisors and manager/supervisors — agricultural crop workers	667
45-1011.02	First-line supervisors and manager/supervisors — animal husbandry workers	667
45-1011.03	First-line supervisors and manager/supervisors — animal care workers, except livestock	667
45-1011.04	First-line supervisors and manager/supervisors — horticultural workers	667
45-1011.05	First-line supervisors and manager/supervisors — logging workers	667
45-1011.06	First-line supervisors and manager/supervisors — fishery workers	667
45-1012.00	Farm labor contractors	667
45-2011.00	Agricultural inspectors	485
45-2021.00	Animal breeders	485
45-2041.00	Graders and sorters, agricultural products	485
45-2091.00	Agricultural equipment operators	485
45-2092.01	Nursery workers	485
45-2092.02	General farmworkers	485
45-2093.00	Farmworkers, farm and ranch animals	485
45-2099.99	Agricultural workers, all other	485
45-3011.00	Fishers and related fishing workers	487
45-3021.00	Hunters and trappers	667
45-4011.00	Forest and conservation workers	490
45-4021.00	Fallers	490
45-4022.00	Logging equipment operators	490
45-4022.01	Logging tractor operators	490
45-4023.00	Log graders and scalers	490
45-4029.99	Logging workers, all other	490
47-1011.01	First-line supervisors and manager/supervisors — construction trades workers	667
47-1011.02	First-line supervisors and manager/supervisors — extractive workers	667
47-2011.00	Boilermakers	494
47-2021.00	Brickmasons and blockmasons	495
47-2022.00	Stonemasons	495
47-2031.01	Construction carpenters	497
47-2031.02	Rough carpenters	497
47-2031.03	Carpenter assemblers and repairers	497
47-2031.04	Ship carpenters and joiners	497
47-2031.05	Boat builders and shipwrights	497
47-2031.06	Brattice builders	497
47-2041.00	Carpet installers	499
47-2042.00	Floor layers, except carpet, wood, and hard tiles	499
47-2043.00	Floor sanders and finishers	499
47-2044.00	Tile and marble setters	499
47-2051.00	Cement masons and concrete finishers	502
47-2053.00	Terrazzo workers and finishers	502
47-2061.00	Construction laborers	509
47-2071.00	Paving, surfacing, and tamping equipment operators	507
47-2072.00	Pile-driver operators	507
47-2073.01	Grader, bulldozer, and scraper operators	507
47-2073.02	Operating engineers	507
47-2081.01	Ceiling tile installers	511
47-2081.02	Drywall installers	511
47-2082.00	Tapers	511
47-2111.00	Electricians	513
47-2121.00	Glaziers	517
47-2131.00	Insulation workers, floor, ceiling, and wall	522
47-2132.00	Insulation workers, mechanical	522
47-2141.00	Painters, construction and maintenance	523
47-2142.00	Paperhangers	523
47-2151.00	Pipelayers	525
47-2152.01	Pipe fitters	525
47-2152.02	Plumbers	525
47-2152.03	Pipelaying fitters	525
47-2161.00	Plasterers and stucco masons	528
47-2171.00	Reinforcing iron and rebar workers	534
47-2181.00	Roofers	530
47-2211.00	Sheet metal workers	531
47-2221.00	Structural iron and steel workers	534
47-3011.00	Helpers—brickmasons, blockmasons, stonemasons, and tile and marble setters	667
47-3012.00	Helpers—carpenters	668
47-3013.00	Helpers—electricians	668
47-3014.00	Helpers—painters, paperhangers, plasterers, and stucco masons	668
47-3015.00	Helpers—pipelayers, plumbers, pipefitters, and steamfitters	668
47-3016.00	Helpers—roofers	668
47-4011.00	Construction and building inspectors	504
47-4021.00	Elevator installers and repairers	516
47-4031.00	Fence erectors	667
47-4041.00	Hazardous materials removal workers	519
47-4041.01	Irradiated-fuel handlers	519
47-4051.00	Highway maintenance workers	668
47-4061.00	Rail-track laying and maintenance equipment operators	668
47-4071.00	Septic tank servicers and sewer pipe cleaners	669
47-4091.00	Segmental pavers	502
47-5011.00	Derrick operators, oil and gas	667
47-5012.00	Rotary drill operators, oil and gas	669
47-5013.00	Service unit operators, oil, gas, and mining	669
47-5021.01	Construction drillers	667
47-5021.02	Well and core drill operators	667
47-5031.00	Explosives workers, ordnance handling experts, and blasters	667
47-5041.00	Continuous mining machine operators	667
47-5042.00	Mine cutting and channeling machine operators	668
47-5051.00	Rock splitters, quarry	669
47-5061.00	Roof bolters, mining	669
47-5071.00	Roustabouts, oil and gas	669
47-5081.00	Helpers—extraction workers	668
49-1011.00	First-line supervisors/managers of mechanics, installers, and repairers	669
49-2011.01	Automatic teller machine servicers	536
49-2011.02	Data processing equipment repairers	536
49-2011.03	Office machine and cash register servicers	536
49-2021.00	Radio mechanics	542
49-2022.01	Central office and pbx installers and repairers	542
49-2022.02	Frame wirers, central office	542
49-2022.03	Communication equipment mechanics, installers, and repairers	542
49-2022.04	Telecommunications facility examiners	542
49-2022.05	Station installers and repairers, telephone	542
49-2091.00	Avionics technicians	544
49-2092.01	Electric home appliance and power tool repairers	538
49-2092.02	Electric motor and switch assemblers and repairers	538
49-2092.03	Battery repairers	538
49-2092.04	Transformer repairers	538
49-2092.05	Electrical parts reconditioners	538
49-2092.06	Hand and portable power tool repairers	538
49-2093.00	Electrical and electronics installers and repairers, transportation equipment	538
49-2094.00	Electrical and electronics repairers, commercial and industrial equipment	538
49-2095.00	Electrical and electronics repairers, powerhouse, substation, and relay	538
49-2096.00	Electronic equipment installers and repairers, motor vehicles	538
49-2097.00	Electronic home entertainment equipment installers and repairers	540
49-2098.00	Security and fire alarm systems installers	670
49-3011.01	Airframe-and-power-plant mechanics	544
49-3011.02	Aircraft engine specialists	544
49-3011.03	Aircraft body and bonded structure repairers	544
49-3021.00	Automotive body and related repairers	547
49-3022.00	Automotive glass installers and repairers	547
49-3023.01	Automotive master mechanics	549
49-3023.02	Automotive specialty technicians	549

49-3031.00 Bus and truck mechanics and diesel engine specialists 552
49-3041.00 Farm equipment mechanics 555
49-3042.00 Mobile heavy equipment mechanics, except engines 555
49-3043.00 Rail car repairers 555
49-3051.00 Motorboat mechanics 558
49-3052.00 Motorcycle mechanics 558
49-3053.00 Outdoor power equipment and other small engine mechanics 558
49-3091.00 Bicycle repairers 669
49-3092.00 Recreational vehicle service technicians 670
49-3093.00 Tire repairers and changers 670
49-9011.00 Mechanical door repairers 670
49-9012.01 Electric meter installers and repairers 669
49-9012.02 Valve and regulator repairers 669
49-9012.03 Meter mechanics 669
49-9021.01 Heating and air conditioning mechanics 562
49-9021.02 Refrigeration mechanics 562
49-9031.01 Home appliance installers 565
49-9031.02 Gas appliance repairers 565
49-9041.00 Industrial machinery mechanics 567
49-9042.00 Maintenance and repair workers, general 572
49-9043.00 Maintenance workers, machinery 567
49-9044.00 Millwrights 573
49-9045.00 Refractory materials repairers, except brickmasons 670
49-9051.00 Electrical power-line installers and repairers 569
49-9052.00 Telecommunications line installers and repairers 569
49-9061.00 Camera and photographic equipment repairers 575
49-9062.00 Medical equipment repairers 575
49-9063.01 Keyboard instrument repairers and tuners 575
49-9063.02 Stringed instrument repairers and tuners 575
49-9063.03 Reed or wind instrument repairers and tuners 575
49-9063.04 Percussion instrument repairers and tuners 575
49-9064.00 Watch repairers 575
49-9069.99 Precision instrument and equipment repairers, all other 575
49-9091.00 Coin, vending, and amusement machine servicers and repairers 560
49-9092.00 Commercial divers 669
49-9093.00 Fabric menders, except garment 669
49-9094.00 Locksmiths and safe repairers 670
49-9095.00 Manufactured building and mobile home installers 670
49-9096.00 Riggers 670
49-9097.00 Signal and track switch repairers 670
49-9098.00 Helpers—installation, maintenance, and repair workers 670
51-1011.00 First-line supervisors/managers of production and operating workers 671
51-2011.01 Aircraft structure assemblers, precision 579
51-2011.02 Aircraft systems assemblers, precision 579
51-2011.03 Aircraft rigging assemblers 579
51-2021.00 Coil winders, tapers, and finishers 579
51-2022.00 Electrical and electronic equipment assemblers 579
51-2023.00 Electromechanical equipment assemblers 579
51-2031.00 Engine and other machine assemblers 579
51-2041.01 Metal fabricators, structural metal products 579
51-2041.02 Fitters, structural metal- precision 579
51-2091.00 Fiberglass laminators and fabricators 579
51-2092.00 Team assemblers 579
51-2093.00 Timing device assemblers, adjusters, and calibrators 579
51-2099.99 Assemblers and fabricators, all other 579
51-3011.01 Bakers, bread and pastry 581
51-3011.02 Bakers, manufacturing 581
51-3021.00 Butchers and meat cutters 581
51-3022.00 Meat, poultry, and fish cutters and trimmers 581
51-3023.00 Slaughterers and meat packers 581
51-3091.00 Food and tobacco roasting, baking, and drying machine operators and tenders 581
51-3092.00 Food batchmakers 581
51-3093.00 Food cooking machine operators and tenders 581
51-4011.01 Numerical control machine tool operators and tenders, metal and plastic 585
51-4012.00 Numerical tool and process control programmers 585
51-4021.00 Extruding and drawing machine setters, operators, and tenders, metal and plastic 589
51-4022.00 Forging machine setters, operators, and tenders, metal and plastic 589
51-4023.00 Rolling machine setters, operators, and tenders, metal and plastic 589
51-4031.01 Sawing machine tool setters and set-up operators, metal and plastic 589
51-4031.02 Punching machine setters and set-up operators, metal and plastic 589
51-4031.03 Press and press brake machine setters and set-up operators, metal and plastic 589
51-4031.04 Shear and slitter machine setters and set-up operators, metal and plastic 589
51-4032.00 Drilling and boring machine tool setters, operators, and tenders, metal and plastic 589
51-4033.01 Grinding, honing, lapping, and deburring machine set-up operators 589
51-4033.02 Buffing and polishing set-up operators 589
51-4034.00 Lathe and turning machine tool setters, operators, and tenders, metal and plastic 589
51-4035.00 Milling and planing machine setters, operators, and tenders, metal and plastic 589
51-4041.00 Machinists 589
51-4051.00 Metal-refining furnace operators and tenders 589
51-4052.00 Pourers and casters, metal 589
51-4061.00 Model makers, metal and plastic 589
51-4062.00 Patternmakers, metal and plastic 589
51-4071.00 Foundry mold and coremakers 589
51-4072.01 Plastic molding and casting machine setters and set-up operators 589
51-4072.02 Plastic molding and casting machine operators and tenders 589
51-4072.03 Metal molding, coremaking, and casting machine setters and set-up operators 589
51-4072.04 Metal molding, coremaking, and casting machine operators and tenders 589
51-4072.05 Casting machine set-up operators 589
51-4081.01 Combination machine tool setters and set-up operators, metal and plastic 589
51-4081.02 Combination machine tool operators and tenders, metal and plastic 589
51-4111.00 Tool and die makers 592
51-4121.01 Welders, production 594
51-4121.02 Welders and cutters 594
51-4121.03 Welder fitters 594
51-4121.04 Solderers 594
51-4121.05 Brazers 594
51-4122.01 Welding machine setters and set-up operators 594
51-4122.02 Welding machine operators and tenders 594
51-4122.03 Soldering and brazing machine setters and set-up operators 594
51-4122.04 Soldering and brazing machine operators and tenders 594
51-4191.01 Heating equipment setters and set-up operators, metal and plastic 589
51-4191.02 Heat treating, annealing, and tempering machine operators and tenders, metal and plastic 589
51-4191.03 Heaters, metal and plastic 589
51-4192.00 Lay-out workers, metal and plastic 589
51-4193.01 Electrolytic plating and coating machine setters and set-up operators, metal and plastic 589
51-4193.02 Electrolytic plating and coating machine operators and tenders, metal and plastic 589
51-4193.03 Nonelectrolytic plating and coating machine setters and set-up operators, metal and plastic 589
51-4193.04 Nonelectrolytic plating and coating machine operators and tenders, metal and plastic 589
51-4194.00 Tool grinders, filers, and sharpeners 589
51-4199.99 Metal workers and plastic workers, all other 589
51-5011.01 Bindery machine setters and set-up operators 596
51-5011.02 Bindery machine operators and tenders 596
51-5012.00 Bookbinders 596
51-5021.00 Job printers 598
51-5022.01 Hand compositors and typesetters 598
51-5022.02 Paste-up workers 598
51-5022.03 Photoengravers 598
51-5022.04 Camera operators 598
51-5022.05 Scanner operators 598
51-5022.06 Strippers 598
51-5022.07 Platemakers 598
51-5022.08 Dot etchers 598
51-5022.09 Electronic masking system operators 598
51-5022.10 Electrotypers and stereotypers 598
51-5022.11 Plate finishers 598
51-5022.12 Typesetting and composing machine operators and tenders 598
51-5022.13 Photoengraving and lithographing machine operators and tenders 598
51-5023.01 Precision printing workers 600
51-5023.02 Offset lithographic press setters and set-up operators 600
51-5023.03 Letterpress setters and set-up operators 600

51-5023.04 Design printing machine setters and set-up operators ... 600
51-5023.05 Marking and identification printing machine setters and set-up operators ... 600
51-5023.06 Screen printing machine setters and set-up operators ... 600
51-5023.07 Embossing machine set-up operators ... 600
51-5023.08 Engraver set-up operators ... 600
51-5023.09 Printing press machine operators and tenders ... 600
51-6011.01 Spotters, dry cleaning ... 602
51-6011.02 Precision dyers ... 602
51-6011.03 Laundry and drycleaning machine operators and tenders, except pressing ... 602
51-6021.01 Pressers, delicate fabrics ... 602
51-6021.02 Pressing machine operators and tenders- textile, garment, and related materials ... 602
51-6021.03 Pressers, hand ... 602
51-6031.01 Sewing machine operators, garment ... 602
51-6031.02 Sewing machine operators, non-garment ... 602
51-6041.00 Shoe and leather workers and repairers ... 602
51-6042.00 Shoe machine operators and tenders ... 602
51-6051.00 Sewers, hand ... 602
51-6052.01 Shop and alteration tailors ... 602
51-6052.02 Custom tailors ... 602
51-6061.00 Textile bleaching and dyeing machine operators and tenders ... 602
51-6062.00 Textile cutting machine setters, operators, and tenders ... 602
51-6063.00 Textile knitting and weaving machine setters, operators, and tenders ... 602
51-6064.00 Textile winding, twisting, and drawing out machine setters, operators, and tenders ... 602
51-6091.01 Extruding and forming machine operators and tenders, synthetic or glass fibers ... 602
51-6092.00 Fabric and apparel patternmakers ... 602
51-6093.00 Upholsterers ... 602
51-6099.99 Textile, apparel, and furnishings workers, all other ... 602
51-7011.00 Cabinetmakers and bench carpenters ... 606
51-7021.00 Furniture finishers ... 606
51-7031.00 Model makers, wood ... 606
51-7032.00 Patternmakers, wood ... 606
51-7041.01 Sawing machine setters and set-up operators ... 606
51-7041.02 Sawing machine operators and tenders ... 606
51-7042.01 Woodworking machine setters and set-up operators, except sawing ... 606
51-7042.02 Woodworking machine operators and tenders, except sawing ... 606
51-7099.99 Woodworkers, all other ... 606
51-8011.00 Nuclear power reactor operators ... 608
51-8012.00 Power distributors and dispatchers ... 608
51-8013.01 Power generating plant operators, except auxiliary equipment operators ... 608
51-8013.02 Auxiliary equipment operators, power ... 608
51-8021.01 Boiler operators and tenders, low pressure ... 610
51-8021.02 Stationary engineers ... 610
51-8031.00 Water and liquid waste treatment plant and system operators ... 612
51-8091.00 Chemical plant and system operators ... 671
51-8092.01 Gas processing plant operators ... 672
51-8092.02 Gas distribution plant operators ... 672
51-8093.01 Petroleum pump system operators ... 672
51-8093.02 Petroleum refinery and control panel operators ... 672
51-8093.03 Gaugers ... 672
51-9011.01 Chemical equipment controllers and operators ... 671
51-9011.02 Chemical equipment tenders ... 671
51-9012.00 Separating, filtering, clarifying, precipitating, and still machine setters, operators, and tenders ... 672
51-9021.00 Crushing, grinding, and polishing machine setters, operators, and tenders ... 671
51-9022.00 Grinding and polishing workers, hand ... 672
51-9023.00 Mixing and blending machine setters, operators, and tenders ... 672
51-9031.00 Cutters and trimmers, hand ... 671
51-9032.01 Fiber product cutting machine setters and set-up operators ... 671
51-9032.02 Stone sawyers ... 671
51-9032.03 Glass cutting machine setters and set-up operators ... 671
51-9032.04 Cutting and slicing machine operators and tenders ... 671
51-9041.01 Extruding, forming, pressing, and compacting machine setters and set-up operators ... 671
51-9041.02 Extruding, forming, pressing, and compacting machine operators and tenders ... 671
51-9051.00 Furnace, kiln, oven, drier, and kettle operators and tenders ... 672
51-9061.01 Materials inspectors ... 614
51-9061.02 Mechanical inspectors ... 614
51-9061.03 Precision devices inspectors and testers ... 614
51-9061.04 Electrical and electronic inspectors and testers ... 614
51-9061.05 Production inspectors, testers, graders, sorters, samplers, and weighers ... 616
51-9071.01 Jewelers ... 616
51-9071.02 Silversmiths ... 616
51-9071.03 Model and mold makers, jewelry ... 616
51-9071.04 Bench workers, jewelry ... 616
51-9071.05 Pewter casters and finishers ... 616
51-9071.06 Gem and diamond workers ... 616
51-9081.00 Dental laboratory technicians ... 619
51-9082.00 Medical appliance technicians ... 619
51-9083.01 Precision lens grinders and polishers ... 619
51-9083.02 Optical instrument assemblers ... 619
51-9111.00 Packaging and filling machine operators and tenders ... 672
51-9121.01 Coating, painting, and spraying machine setters and set-up operators ... 622
51-9121.02 Coating, painting, and spraying machine operators and tenders ... 622
51-9122.00 Painters, transportation equipment ... 622
51-9123.00 Painting, coating, and decorating workers ... 622
51-9131.01 Photographic retouchers and restorers ... 625
51-9131.02 Photographic reproduction technicians ... 625
51-9131.03 Photographic hand developers ... 625
51-9131.04 Film laboratory technicians ... 625
51-9132.00 Photographic processing machine operators ... 625
51-9141.00 Semiconductor processors ... 626
51-9191.00 Cementing and gluing machine operators and tenders ... 670
51-9192.00 Cleaning, washing, and metal pickling equipment operators and tenders ... 671
51-9193.00 Cooling and freezing equipment operators and tenders ... 671
51-9194.01 Precision etchers and engravers, hand or machine ... 671
51-9194.02 Engravers/carvers ... 671
51-9194.03 Etchers ... 671
51-9194.04 Pantograph engravers ... 671
51-9194.05 Etchers, hand ... 671
51-9194.06 Engravers, hand ... 671
51-9195.01 Precision mold and pattern casters, except nonferrous metals ... 672
51-9195.02 Precision pattern and die casters, nonferrous metals ... 672
51-9195.03 Stone cutters and carvers ... 672
51-9195.04 Glass blowers, molders, benders, and finishers ... 672
51-9195.05 Potters ... 672
51-9195.06 Mold makers, hand ... 672
51-9195.07 Molding and casting workers ... 672
51-9196.00 Paper goods machine setters, operators, and tenders ... 672
51-9197.00 Tire builders ... 672
51-9198.01 Production laborers ... 672
51-9198.02 Production helpers ... 672
53-1011.00 Aircraft cargo handling supervisors ... 673
53-1021.00 First-line supervisors/managers of helpers, laborers, and material movers, hand ... 650
53-1031.00 First-line supervisors/managers of transportation and material-moving machine and vehicle operators ... 673
53-2011.00 Airline pilots, copilots, and flight engineers ... 629
53-2012.00 Commercial pilots ... 629
53-2021.00 Air traffic controllers ... 632
53-2022.00 Airfield operations specialists ... 673
53-3011.00 Ambulance drivers and attendants, except emergency medical technicians ... 673
53-3021.00 Bus drivers, transit and intercity ... 634
53-3022.00 Bus drivers, school ... 634
53-3031.00 Driver/sales workers ... 640
53-3032.01 Truck drivers, heavy ... 640
53-3032.02 Tractor-trailer truck drivers ... 640
53-3033.00 Truck drivers, light or delivery services ... 640
53-3041.00 Taxi drivers and chauffeurs ... 637
53-4011.00 Locomotive engineers ... 644
53-4012.00 Locomotive firers ... 644
53-4013.00 Rail yard engineers, dinkey operators, and hostlers ... 644
53-4021.01 Train crew members ... 644
53-4021.02 Railroad yard workers ... 644
53-4031.00 Railroad conductors and yardmasters ... 644
53-4041.00 Subway and streetcar operators ... 644
53-4099.99 Rail transportation workers, all other ... 644
53-5011.01 Able seamen ... 647
53-5011.02 Ordinary seamen and marine oilers ... 647
53-5021.01 Ship and boat captains ... 647
53-5021.02 Mates- ship, boat, and barge ... 647
53-5021.03 Pilots, ship ... 647

53-5022.00   Motorboat operators 647
53-5031.00   Ship engineers 647
53-6011.00   Bridge and lock tenders 673
53-6021.00   Parking lot attendants 673
53-6031.00   Service station attendants 673
53-6041.00   Traffic technicians 673
53-6051.01   Aviation inspectors 673
53-6051.02   Public transportation inspectors 673
53-6051.03   Marine cargo inspectors 673
53-6051.04   Railroad inspectors 673
53-6051.05   Motor vehicle inspectors 673
53-6051.06   Freight inspectors 673
53-7011.00   Conveyor operators and tenders 650
53-7021.00   Crane and tower operators.................................. 650
53-7031.00   Dredge operators 650
53-7032.01   Excavating and loading machine operators................... 650
53-7032.02   Dragline operators 650
53-7033.00   Loading machine operators, underground mining 650
53-7041.00   Hoist and winch operators.................................. 650
53-7051.00   Industrial truck and tractor operators 650
53-7061.00   Cleaners of vehicles and equipment...................... 650
53-7062.01   Stevedores, except equipment operators 650
53-7062.02   Grips and set-up workers, motion picture sets,
             studios, and stages 650
53-7062.03   Freight, stock, and material movers, hand 650
53-7063.00   Machine feeders and offbearers 650
53-7064.00   Packers and packagers, hand 650
53-7071.01   Gas pumping station operators 650
53-7071.02   Gas compressor operators 650
53-7072.00   Pump operators, except wellhead pumpers 650

53-7073.00   Wellhead pumpers 650
53-7081.00   Refuse and recyclable material collectors.................... 650
53-7111.00   Shuttle car operators.. 650
53-7121.00   Tank car, truck, and ship loaders 650
53-7199.99   Material moving workers, all other 650
55-1011.00   Air crew officers 653
55-1012.00   Aircraft launch and recovery officers.................... 653
55-1013.00   Armored assault vehicle officers 653
55-1014.00   Artillery and missile officers 653
55-1015.00   Command and control center officers 653
55-1016.00   Infantry officers 653
55-1017.00   Special forces officers 653
55-1019.99   Military officer special and tactical operations
             leaders/managers, all other 653
55-2011.00   First line supervisors/managers
             of air crew members 653
55-2012.00   First line supervisors/managers of weapons
             specialists/crew members 653
55-1013.00   First line supervisors/managers of all other
             tactical operations specialists 653
55-3011.00   Air crew members 653
55-3012.00   Aircraft launch and recovery specialists 653
55-3013.00   Armored assault vehicle crew members..................... 653
55-3014.00   Artillery and missile crew members...................... 653
55-3015.00   Command and control center specialists.................. 653
55-3016.00   Infantry 653
55-3017.00   Radar and sonar technicians 653
55-3018.00   Special forces 653
55-3019.99   Military enlisted tactical operations and air/weapons
             specialists and crew members, all other 653

Index

A

A & P mechanics, *see:* Aircraft and avionics equipment
mechanics and service technicians.................................... 544
ABE teachers, *see:* Teachers—adult literacy and remedial education ..221
Able seamen, *see:* Water transportation occupations.............................. 647
Abstractors, *see:* Medical records and health
information technicians.. 328
Abstractors, *see:* Title examiners, abstractors, and searchers............... 663
Academic deans, *see:* Education administrators.............................. 34
Account clerks, *see:* Payroll and timekeeping clerks 437
Account collectors, *see:* Bill and account collectors 431
Account executives, *see:* Advertising, marketing, promotions,
public relations, and sales managers... 27
Account executives, *see:* Advertising sales agents................................. 403
Account executives, *see:* Securities, commodities, and
financial services sales agents 426
Accountants and auditors.. 70
Accounting clerks, *see:* Bookkeeping, accounting, and
auditing clerks.. 434
Accounts payable clerks, *see:* Bookkeeping, accounting, and
auditing clerks.. 434
Accounts receivable clerks, *see:* Bookkeeping, accounting, and
auditing clerks.. 434
Acoustical carpenters, *see:* Drywall installers, ceiling tile
installers, and tapers... 511
Activity specialists, *see:* Recreation workers 400
Actors, *see:* Actors, producers, and directors 249
Actors, producers, and directors 249
Actuaries... 102
Addictions nurses, *see:* Registered nurses 303
Adjudicators, *see:* Judges, magistrates, and other judicial workers 201
Adjusters, *see:* Claims adjusters, appraisers, examiners, and
investigators 80
Administrative assistants, *see:* Secretaries and
administrative assistants... 482
Administrative assistants for human resources, *see:*
Human resources assistants, except payroll and timekeeping 449
Administrative clerks, *see:* Office clerks, general.................... 481
Administrative coordinators, *see:* Administrative services managers 25
Administrative directors, *see:* Administrative services managers........... 25
Administrative law judges, *see:* Judges, magistrates, and
other judicial workers.. 201
Administrative leaders, *see:* Office and administrative
support worker supervisors and managers............................... 479
Administrative leads, *see:* Secretaries and administrative assistants..... 482
Administrative managers, *see:* Administrative services mangers........... 25
Administrative managers, *see:* Office and administrative support
worker supervisors and managers 479
Administrative office assistants, *see:* Secretaries and
administrative assistants... 482
Administrative office assistants, officers, *see:* Administrative
services managers.. 25
Administrative office managers, *see:* Office and administrative
support worker supervisors and managers............................... 479
Administrative office managers, *see:* Secretaries and
administrative assistants... 482
Administrative office specialists, *see:* Secretaries and
administrative assistants... 482
Administrative officers, *see:* Administrative services managers 25
Administrative officers, *see:* Office and administrative
support worker supervisors and managers............................... 479
Administrative professionals, *see:* Secretaries and
administrative assistants... 482
Administrative project coordinators, *see:* Office and
administrative support worker supervisors and managers 479
Administrative services managers 25
Administrative services managers, *see:* Office and administrative
support worker supervisors and managers............................... 479
Administrative specialists, *see:* Secretaries and
administrative assistants... 482
Administrative supervisors, *see:* Office and administrative
support worker supervisors and managers............................... 479

Administrative support managers, *see:* Office and administrative
support worker supervisors and managers 479
Administrative support specialists, *see:* Secretaries and
administrative assistants... 482
Administrative technicians, *see:* Office clerks, general.................... 481
Administrative technicians, *see:* Secretaries and
administrative assistants... 482
Administrative worker supervisors, *see:* Office and
administrative support worker supervisors and managers 479
Administrators, *see:* Office and administrative support worker
supervisors and managers.. 479
Administrators, *see:* Top executives 67
Administrators, education, *see:* Education administrators 34
Administrators, medical and health services, *see:* Medical
and health services managers.. 59
Administrators, support services, *see:* Administrative
services managers.. 25
Admissions officers, *see:* Education administrators...................... 34
Admitting interviewers, *see:* Interviewers.............................. 451
Adult basic education teachers, *see:* Teachers—adult literacy and
remedial education.. 221
Adult literacy teachers, *see:* Teachers—adult literacy and
remedial education.. 221
Adult secondary education teachers, *see:* Teachers—adult literacy
and remedial education.. 221
Advertising, marketing, promotions, public relations, and
sales managers.. 27
Advertising sales agents.. 403
Advertising sales agents, *see:* Advertising, marketing,
promotions, public relations, and sales managers...................... 27
Advisors, personal financial, *see:* Financial analysts and
personal financial advisors 85
Aerobics instructors, *see:* Fitness workers............................. 392
Aeronautical drafters, *see:* Drafters 141
Aeronautical engineers, *see:* Engineers 133
Aerospace engineering and operations technicians, *see:*
Engineering technicians 144
Aerospace engineers, *see:* Engineers.................................... 133
Affirmative action coordinators, *see:* Human resources, training,
and labor relations managers and specialists 50
Agent-contract clerks, *see:* Human resources assistants,
except payroll and timekeeping 449
Agents, *see:* Real estate brokers and sales agents...................... 414
Agents, Advertising Sales, *see:* Advertising sales agents................ 403
Agents and business managers of artists, performers, and athletes 661
Agents, Bureau of Alcohol, Tobacco, and Firearms (ATF), *see:*
Police and detectives... 362
Agents, cargo and freight, *see:* Cargo and freight agents 459
Agents, customs, *see:* Police and detectives............................ 362
Agents, Drug Enforcement Administration (DEA), *see:*
Police and detectives... 362
Agents, Federal Bureau of Investigation (FBI), *see:*
Police and detectives... 362
Agents, Immigration and Naturalization Service (INS), *see:*
Police and detectives... 362
Agents, independent, *see:* Sales representatives, wholesale
and manufacturing... 421
Agents, loss prevention, *see:* Private detectives and investigators........ 366
Agents, manufacturers, *see:* Sales representatives, wholesale
and manufacturing... 421
Agents, U.S. Border Patrol, *see:* Police and detectives 362
Agents, U.S. Secret Service, *see:* Police and detectives................. 362
Agricultural and food science technicians, *see:* Science technicians 185
Agricultural and food scientists 147
Agricultural engineers, *see:* Engineers 133
Agricultural inspectors, *see:* Agricultural workers..................... 485
Agricultural managers, *see:* Farmers, ranchers, and
agricultural managers... 40
Agricultural workers... 485
Agronomists, *see:* Agricultural and food scientists 147
Aides, geriatric, *see:* Nursing, psychiatric, and home health aides 350
Aides, home care, *see:* Personal and home care aides.................... 399
Aides, home health, *see:* Nursing, psychiatric, and home health aides .350

Aides, nursing, *see:* Nursing, psychiatric, and home health aides......... 350
Aides, occupational therapist, *see:* Occupational therapist
 assistants and aides................ 353
Aides, personal care, *see:* Personal and home care aides 399
Aides, pharmacy, *see:* Pharmacy aides................ 354
Aides, physical therapist, *see:* Physical therapist assistants and aides .. 356
Aides, psychiatric, *see:* Nursing, psychiatric, and home health aides ... 350
Aides, teacher, *see:* Teacher assistants................ 219
Air Force, *see:* Job opportunities in the Armed Forces 653
Air traffic controllers................ 632
Airbrush artists, *see:* Photographic process workers and
 processing machine operators 625
Air-conditioning mechanics, *see:* Heating, air-conditioning,
 and refrigeration mechanics and installers................ 562
Aircraft and avionics equipment mechanics and service technicians.... 544
Aircraft cargo handling supervisors................ 673
Aircraft engineers, *see:* Engineers 133
Aircraft pilots, *see:* Aircraft pilots and flight engineers 629
Aircraft pilots and flight engineers 629
Aircraft structure, surfaces, rigging, and systems assemblers, *see:*
 Assemblers and fabricators 579
Airfield operations specialists 673
Airframe mechanics, *see:* Aircraft and avionics equipment
 mechanics and service technicians................ 544
Airline pilots, copilots, and flight engineers, *see:*
 Aircraft pilots and flight engineers 629
Airline stewardesses and stewards, *see:* Flight attendants................ 394
Airmen, *see:* Job opportunities in the Armed Forces................ 653
Airport service agents, *see:* Reservation and transportation
 ticket agents and travel clerks 457
Airport terminal controllers, *see:* Air traffic controllers................ 632
Airport tower controllers, *see:* Air traffic controllers 632
Allergists, *see:* Physicians and surgeons................ 295
Allopathic physicians and surgeons, *see:* Physicians and surgeons 295
Ambulance drivers and attendants, except emergency
 medical technicians 673
Ambulatory care nurses, *see:* Registered nurses................ 303
Amusement and recreation attendants 664
Amusement machine servicers and repairers, *see:*
 Coin, vending, and amusement machine servicers and repairers 560
Analysts, budget, *see:* Budget analysts................ 77
Analysts, financial, *see:* Financial analysts and
 personal financial advisors 85
Analysts, management *see:* Management analysts................ 92
Analysts, market researcher, *see:* Market and survey researchers......... 175
Analytical chemists, *see:* Chemists and materials scientists 162
Anchors, *see:* News analysts, reporters, and correspondents 267
Anesthesiologists, *see:* Physicians and surgeons................ 295
Anesthetists, certified registered nurse, *see:* Registered nurses................ 303
Animal breeders, *see:* Agricultural workers 485
Animal care and service workers 384
Animal caretakers, *see:* Veterinary assistants and laboratory
 animal caretakers................ 665
Animal control officers, *see:* Animal care and service workers 384
Animal control workers 664
Animal scientists, *see:* Agricultural and food scientists 147
Animal trainers, *see:* Animal care and service workers 384
Animators, *see:* Artists and related workers 235
Announcers 259
Anthropologists, *see:* Social scientists, other 182
Apartment house managers, *see:* Property, real estate, and
 community association managers 61
Apartment leasing agents, *see:* Real estate brokers and sales agents 414
Apartment managers, *see:* Property, real estate, and community
 association managers 61
Apartment rental agents, *see:* Real estate brokers and sales agents 414
Apparel workers, *see:* Textile, apparel, and furnishings occupations.... 602
Appellate court judges, *see:* Judges, magistrates, and
 other judicial workers................ 201
Appliance repairers, *see:* Home appliance repairers................ 565
Applications engineers, *see:* Computer software engineers 111
Applications programmers, *see:* Computer programmers 104
Applicators, *see:* Drywall installers, ceiling tile installers, and tapers .. 511
Applied mathematicians, *see:* Mathematicians................ 119
Appraisers, *see:* Claims adjusters, appraisers, examiners,
 and investigators 80

Appraisers and assessors of real estate 74
Appraisers, jewelry, *see:* Jewelers and precious stone and
 metal workers 616
Appraisers, real estate, *see:* Appraisers and assessors of real estate........ 74
Aquaculture farmers, *see:* Farmers, ranchers, and
 agricultural managers 40
Aquatic biologists, *see:* Biological scientists................ 150
Arbitrators, *see:* Human resources, training, and
 labor relations managers and specialists 50
Arbitrators, *see:* Judges, magistrates, and other judicial workers.......... 201
Arborists, *see:* Grounds maintenance workers 380
Arc cutters, *see:* Welding, soldering, and brazing workers 595
Archaeologists, *see:* Social scientists, other 182
Architects, except landscape and naval 130
Architects, landscape, *see:* Landscape architects 128
Architectural drafters, *see:* Drafters................ 141
Archivists, curators, and museum technicians................ 210
Armed forces, *see:* Job opportunities in the Armed Forces 653
Armored car guards, *see:* Security guards and
 gaming surveillance officers 368
Army, *see:* Job opportunities in the Armed Forces 653
Arrangers, music, *see:* Musicians, singers, and related workers 257
Art directors, *see:* Artists and related workers................ 235
Artificial inseminator, *see:* Agricultural workers................ 485
Artists and related workers 235
Artists, graphic, *see:* Graphic designers 243
Asbestos abatement workers, *see:*
 Hazardous materials removal workers 519
ASE teachers, *see:* Teachers—adult literacy and remedial
 education 221
Asphalt paving machine operators, *see:*
 Construction equipment operators 507
Assemblers, *see:* Jewelers and precious stone and metal workers 616
Assemblers and fabricators 579
Assessors, real estate, *see:* Appraisers and assessors of real estate 74
Asset property managers, *see:* Property, real estate, and
 community association managers 61
Assignment clerks, *see:* Human resources assistants,
 except payroll and timekeeping 449
Assignment editors, *see:* Writers and editors................ 275
Assistant cooks, *see:* Chefs, cooks, and food preparation workers 371
Assistant editors, *see:* Writers and editors................ 275
Assistant executive directors, *see:* Office and administrative
 support worker supervisors and managers 479
Assistant managers, *see:* Food service managers 45
Assistant managers, *see:* Lodging managers 56
Assistant principals, *see:* Education administrators................ 34
Assistant property managers, *see:* Property, real estate, and
 community association managers 61
Assistants, control room, *see:* Power plant operators, distributors,
 and dispatchers 608
Assistants, dental, *see:* Dental assistants 343
Assistants, legal, *see:* Paralegals and legal assistants 207
Assistants, medical, *see:* Medical assistants 347
Assistants, mental health, *see:* Nursing, psychiatric, and
 home health aides 350
Assistants, nursing, *see:* Nursing, psychiatric, and
 home health aides 350
Assistants, occupational therapist, *see:* Occupational therapist
 assistants and aides................ 353
Assistants, ophthalmic medical, *see:* Medical assistants 347
Assistants, physical therapist, *see:* Physical therapist assistants
 and aides................ 356
Assistants, physician, *see:* Physician assistants 293
Assistants, podiatric medical, *see:* Medical assistants 347
Assistants, surgeons', *see:* Physician assistants 293
Assistants, teacher, *see:* Teacher assistants................ 219
Astronautical engineers, *see:* Engineers 133
Astronomers, *see:* Physicists and astronomers 170
Athletes, coaches, umpires, and related workers 254
Athletic directors, *see:* Education administrators 34
Athletic trainers................ 314
Athletic training instructors, *see:* Athletes, coaches, umpires,
 and related workers 252
Atmospheric scientists 159
Attendance clerks, *see:* Payroll and timekeeping clerks................ 437

Attendants, hospital, *see:* Nursing, psychiatric, and home health aides 350
Attendants, personal, *see:* Personal and home care aides 399
Attorneys, *see:* Lawyers 204
Audio and video equipment operators, *see:* Broadcast and sound engineering technicians and radio operators 261
Audio control engineers, *see:* Broadcast and sound engineering technicians and radio operators 261
Audiologists 278
Audio-visual collections specialists 662
Auditing clerks, *see:* Bookkeeping, accounting, and auditing clerks 434
Auditors, *see:* Accountants and auditors 70
Authors, *see:* Writers and editors 275
Auto damage appraisers, *see:* Claims adjusters, appraisers, examiners, and investigators 81
Automated systems librarians, *see:* Librarians 214
Automated teller machine servicers, *see:* Computer, automated teller, and office machine repairers 538
Automotive air-conditioning repairers, *see:* Automotive service technicians and mechanics 549
Automotive body and related repairers 547
Automotive body repairers, *see:* Automotive body and related repairers 547
Automotive engineers, *see:* Engineers 133
Automotive glass installers and repairers, *see:* Automotive body and related repairers 548
Automotive mechanics, *see:* Automotive service technicians and mechanics 549
Automotive painters, *see:* Painting and coating workers, except construction and maintenance 622
Automotive service technicians and mechanics 549
Auxiliary equipment operators, *see:* Power plant operators, distributors, and dispatchers 608
Avionics technicians, *see:* Aircraft and avionics equipment mechanics and service technicians 544

B

Babysitters, *see:* Child care workers 389
Baggage porters and bellhops 664
Bailiffs, *see:* Correctional officers 357
Bakers, *see:* Food processing occupations 581
Ballet masters, *see:* Dancers and choreographers 255
Ballet mistresses, *see:* Dancers and choreographers 255
Bank tellers, *see:* Tellers 440
Banquet managers, *see:* Food service managers 45
Barbers, cosmetologists, and other personal appearance workers 387
Bartenders, *see:* Food and beverage serving and related workers 371
Beauty care specialists, *see:* Barbers, cosmetologists, and other personal appearance workers 371
Bedroom stewards, *see:* Water transportation occupations 647
Behavioral disorder counselors, *see:* Counselors 189
Bellhops, *see:* Baggage porters and bellhops 664
Bench carpenters, *see:* Woodworkers 606
Bench technicians, *see:* Computer, automated teller, and office machine repairers 536
Bench technicians, *see:* Electrical and electronics installers and repairers 538
Bench technicians, *see:* Electronic home entertainment equipment installers and repairers 540
Benefits administrators, *see:* Human resources, training, and labor relations managers and specialists 50
Benefits clerks, *see:* Human resources assistants, except payroll and timekeeping 449
Benefits directors, *see:* Human resources, training, and labor relations managers and specialists 50
Benefits managers, *see:* Human resources, training, and labor relations managers and specialists 50
Bibliographers, *see:* Librarians 214
Bicycle repairers 669
Bill and account collectors 431
Billing and posting clerks and machine operators 432
Billing clerks, *see:* Billing and posting clerks and machine operators 432
Billing machine operators, *see:* Billing and posting clerks and machine operators 432
Bindery machine setters, operators, and tenders, *see:* Bookbinders and bindery workers 596
Bindery workers, *see:* Bookbinders and bindery workers 596
Biochemists, *see:* Biological scientists 150
Biographers, *see:* Social scientists, other 182
Biological oceanographers, *see:* Geoscientists 167
Biological-physical anthropologists, *see:* Social scientists, other 182
Biological scientists 80
Biological technicians, *see:* Science technicians 185
Biomedical engineers, *see:* Engineers 133
Biomedical equipment technicians, *see:* Precision instrument and equipment repairers 575
Biometricians, *see:* Statisticians 123
Biophysicists, *see:* Biological scientists 150
Biostatisticians, *see:* Statisticians 123
Blankbook binding workers, *see:* Bookbinders and bindery workers 596
Blasters, *see:* Explosives workers, ordnance handling experts, and blasters 667
Bleaching and dyeing machine operators, textile, *see:* Textile, apparel, and furnishings occupations 602
Blockmasons, *see:* Brickmasons, blockmasons, and stonemasons 495
Bloggers, *see:* Writers and editors 275
Blood bank technologists, *see:* Clinical laboratory technologists and technicians 318
Boat operators, *see:* Water transportation occupations 647
Boatswains, *see:* Water transportation occupations 647
Boatswains, fishing boat, *see:* Fishers and fishing vessel operators 487
Body repairers, automotive, *see:* Automotive body and related repairers 547
Bodyguards, *see:* Security guards and gaming surveillance officers 368
Boiler mechanics, *see:* Boilermakers 494
Boiler operators, *see:* Stationary engineers and boiler operators 610
Boilermakers 494
Bonus clerks, *see:* Payroll and timekeeping clerks 437
Bookbinders and bindery workers 596
Bookkeepers, *see:* Bookkeeping, accounting, and auditing clerks 434
Bookkeepers, *see:* Payroll and timekeeping clerks 437
Bookkeeping, accounting, and auditing clerks 434
Bookmobile drivers, *see:* Library technicians 217
Booth cashiers, *see:* Cashiers 405
Border Patrol agents, *see:* Police and detectives 362
Botanists, *see:* Biological scientists 150
Brace makers, *see:* Medical, dental, and ophthalmic laboratory technicians 619
Braille clerks, *see:* Library assistants, clerical 453
Brake operators, railroad, *see:* Rail transportation occupations 644
Brake repairers, *see:* Automotive service technicians and mechanics 549
Brattice builders, *see:* Carpenters 497
Brazing workers, *see:* Welding, soldering, and brazing workers 594
Bricklayers, *see:* Brickmasons, blockmasons, and stonemasons 495
Brickmasons, blockmasons, and stonemasons 495
Bridge and lock tenders 673
Broadcast and sound engineering technicians and radio operators 261
Broadcast field supervisors, *see:* Broadcast and sound engineering technicians and radio operators 261
Broker associates, *see:* Real estate brokers and sales agents 414
Broker's assistants, *see:* Brokerage clerks 441
Brokerage clerks 441
Brokers, *see:* Insurance sales agents 411
Brokers, *see:* Sales representatives, wholesale and manufacturing 421
Brokers, *see:* Securities, commodities, and financial services sales agents 426
Brokers, real estate, *see:* Real estate brokers and sales agents 414
Buckers, *see:* Forest, conservation, and logging workers 490
Budget analysts 77
Budget managers, *see:* Budget analysts 77
Budget officers, *see:* Budget analysts 77
Building cleaning workers 378
Building construction estimators, *see:* Cost estimators 83
Building consultants, *see:* Real estate brokers and sales agents 414
Building inspectors, *see:* Construction and building inspectors 504
Building managers, *see:* Administrative services managers 25
Building managers, *see:* Property, real estate, and community association managers 61
Building superintendents, *see:* Property, real estate, and community association managers 61
Bulldozer operators, *see:* Construction equipment operators 507
Bureau of Alcohol, Tobacco, and Firearms (ATF) agents, *see:* Police and detectives 362
Bureau of Diplomatic Security special agents, *see:* Police and detectives 362

Bus dispatchers, *see:* Dispatchers 461
Bus drivers 634
Bus mechanics, *see:* Diesel service technicians and mechanics 552
Business administrators, *see:* Administrative services managers 25
Business management analysts, *see:* Management analysts 92
Business management consultants, *see:* Management analysts 92
Business managers, *see:* Agents and business managers of artists, performers, and athletes 661
Business managers, *see:* Office and administrative support worker supervisors and managers 479
Business office assistants, *see:* Secretaries and administrative assistants 482
Business office managers, *see:* Administrative services managers 25
Business support assistants, *see:* Secretaries and administrative assistants 482
Butchers and meatcutters, *see:* Food processing occupations 581
Buyers, *see:* Purchasing managers, buyers, and purchasing agents 64
Buyers' agents, *see:* Real estate brokers and sales agents 414

C

Cab drivers, *see:* Taxi drivers and chauffeurs 637
Cabinetmakers, *see:* Woodworkers 606
Cable line installers, *see:* Line installers and repairers 569
Cable splicers, *see:* Line installers and repairers 569
CAD operators, *see:* Drafters 141
Cafeteria cooks, *see:* Chefs, cooks, and food preparation workers 371
Cage cashiers, *see:* Gaming cage workers 435
Call completion operators, *see:* Communications equipment operators 471
Camera operators, television, video, and motion picture, *see:* Television, video, and motion picture camera operators and editors 274
Camera repairers, *see:* Precision instrument and equipment repairers 575
Camp counselors, *see:* Recreation workers 400
Camp directors, *see:* Recreation workers 400
Campaign managers, *see:* Public relations specialists 271
Cancer registrars, *see:* Medical records and health information technicians 328
Campaign managers, *see:* Public relations specialists 271
Captains, airline, *see:* Aircraft pilots and flight engineers 629
Captains, fishing boat, *see:* Fishers and fishing vessel operators 487
Captains, water transportation, *see:* Water transportation occupations 647
Captive agents, *see:* Insurance sales agents 411
Card puncher, *see:* Data entry and information processing workers 475
Card punching machine operator, *see:* Data entry and information processing workers 475
Cardiac and vascular nurses, *see:* Registered nurses 303
Cardiac sonographers, *see:* Cardiovascular technologists and technicians 316
Cardiographers, *see:* Cardiovascular technologists and technicians 316
Cardiographic technicians, *see:* Cardiovascular technologists and technicians 316
Cardiologists, *see:* Physicians and surgeons 295
Cardiology technologists, *see:* Cardiovascular technologists and technicians 316
Cardiopulmonary technologists, *see:* Cardiovascular technologists and technicians 316
Cardiovascular technicians, *see:* Cardiovascular technologists and technicians 316
Cardiovascular technologists and technicians 316
Career counselors, *see:* Counselors 189
Career-technical teachers, *see:* Teachers—preschool, kindergarten, elementary, middle, and secondary 227
Career-technical teachers, postsecondary, *see:* Teachers—postsecondary 223
Career-technology teachers, *see:* Teachers—preschool, kindergarten, elementary, middle, and secondary 227
Caregivers, *see:* Personal and home care aides 399
Cargo and freight agents 459
Carpenters 497
Carpet installers, *see:* Carpet, floor, and tile installers and finishers 499
Carpet, floor, and tile installers and finishers 499
Cartographers, *see:* Surveyors, cartographers, photogrammetrists, and surveying technicians 130
Cartoonists, *see:* Artists and related workers 235
Case management aides, *see:* Social and human service assistants 194
Cash managers, *see:* Financial managers 42
Cashiers 405
Cashiers, gaming, *see:* Gaming cage workers 435
Casino cage workers, *see:* Gaming cage workers 435
Casino cashiers, *see:* Gaming cage workers 435
Catering managers, *see:* Food service managers 45
Caulkers, *see:* Construction laborers 509
Ceiling tile installers, *see:* Drywall installers, ceiling tile installers, and tapers 511
Cement masons, concrete finishers, segmental pavers, and terrazzo workers 502
Cementing and gluing machine operators and tenders 670
Central office installers, *see:* Radio and telecommunications equipment installers and repairers 542
Central office operators, *see:* Communications equipment operators 471
Ceramic engineers, *see:* Engineers 133
Ceramists, dental, *see:* Medical, dental, and ophthalmic laboratory technicians 619
Certified nurse-midwives, *see:* Registered nurses 303
Certified nursing assistants, *see:* Nursing, psychiatric, and home health aides 350
Certified pest control applicators, *see:* Pest control workers 382
Certified public accountants, *see:* Accountants and auditors 70
Certified registered nurse anesthetists, *see:* Registered nurses 303
Certified respiratory therapists, *see:* Respiratory therapists 307
Chairpersons, college or university department, *see:* Education administrators 34
Chairpersons of the board, *see:* Top executives 67
Charter bus drivers, *see:* Bus drivers 634
Chauffeurs, *see:* Taxi drivers and chauffeurs 637
Checkers, *see:* Weighers, measurers, checkers, and samplers, recordkeeping 470
Chefs, cooks, and food preparation workers 371
Chemical engineering technicians, *see:* Engineering technicians 144
Chemical engineers, *see:* Engineers 133
Chemical equipment operators and tenders 671
Chemical oceanographers, *see:* Geoscientists 167
Chemical plant and system operators 671
Chemical technicians, *see:* Science technicians 185
Chemists and materials scientists 162
Chief engineers, *see:* Broadcast and sound engineering technicians and radio operators 261
Chief executive officers, *see:* Top executives 67
Chief executives, government, *see:* Top executives 67
Chief financial officers, *see:* Top executives 67
Chief information officers, *see:* Top executives 67
Chief operating officers, *see:* Top executives 67
Chief technology officers, *see:* Computer and information systems managers 30
Child care workers 389
Child protective services social workers, *see:* Social workers 196
Child welfare social workers, *see:* Social workers 196
Children's librarians, *see:* Librarians 214
Chiropractic physicians, *see:* Chiropractors 280
Chiropractors 280
Choke setters, *see:* Forest, conservation, and logging workers 490
Choreographers, *see:* Dancers and choreographers 255
Cinematographers, *see:* Television, video, and motion picture camera operators and editors 274
Circulation assistants, *see:* Library assistants, clerical 453
City planners, *see:* Urban and regional planners 180
Civil drafters, *see:* Drafters 141
Civil engineering technicians, *see:* Engineering technicians 144
Civil engineers, *see:* Engineers 133
Civil service clerks, *see:* Human resources assistants, except payroll and timekeeping 449
Claims adjusters, appraisers, examiners, and investigators 80
Claims examiners, *see:* Claims adjusters, appraisers, examiners, and investigators 80
Claims representatives, *see:* Claims adjusters, appraisers, examiners, and investigators 80
Cleaners and servants, private household, *see:* Building cleaning workers 378
Cleaners of vehicles and equipment, *see:* Material moving occupations 650
Cleaning supervisors, *see:* Building cleaning workers 378
Cleaning, washing, and metal pickling equipment operators and tenders 671

Clergy..662
Clerical assistants, *see:* Office clerks, general...................481
Clerical specialists, *see:* Secretaries and administrative assistants......482
Clerical supervisors, *see:* Secretaries and administrative assistants......482
Clerical worker supervisors, *see:* Office and administrative support
  worker supervisors and managers 479
Clerks, *see:*
  Bill and account collectors 431
  Billing and posting clerks and machine operators 432
  Bookkeeping, accounting, and auditing clerks 434
  Brokerage clerks 441
  Cargo and freight agents 459
  Communications equipment operators...............................471
  Computer operators...473
  Couriers and messengers...460
  Credit authorizers, checkers, and clerks...........................442
  Customer service representatives......................................444
  Data entry and information processing workers 475
  Desktop publishers 477
  Dispatchers..461
  File clerks 447
  Gaming cage workers..435
  Hotel, motel, and resort desk clerks 448
  Human resources assistants, except payroll and timekeeping 449
  Interviewers...451
  Library assistants, clerical...453
  Meter readers, utilities...463
  Office and administrative support worker supervisors
    and managers 479
  Office clerks, general 481
  Order clerks...454
  Payroll and timekeeping clerks 437
  Postal Service workers..464
  Procurement clerks...438
  Production, planning, and expediting clerks......................466
  Receptionists and information clerks 455
  Reservation and transportation ticket agents and travel clerks 457
  Secretaries and administrative assistants 482
  Shipping, receiving, and traffic clerks.............................467
  Stock clerks and order fillers..469
  Tellers..440
  Weighers, measurers, checkers, and samplers, recordkeeping.........469
Clerk typists, *see:* Office clerks, general 481
Climatologists , *see:* Atmospheric scientists 159
Clinical chemistry technologists, *see:* Clinical laboratory
  technologists and technicians..318
Clinical dietitians, *see:* Dietitians and nutritionists 284
Clinical laboratory scientists, *see:* Clinical laboratory technologists
  and technicians...318
Clinical laboratory technicians, *see:* Clinical laboratory
  technologists and technicians..318
Clinical laboratory technologists, *see:* Clinical laboratory
  technologists and technicians..318
Clinical laboratory technologists and technicians....................318
Clinical managers, *see:* Medical and health services managers 59
Clinical nurse specialists, *see:* Registered nurses 303
Clinical psychologists, *see:* Psychologists.........................177
Clinical social workers, *see:* Social workers 196
Clock repairers, *see:* Precision instrument and equipment
  repairers...575
Closed captioners, *see:* Court reporters 199
Closing agents, *see:* Real estate brokers and sales agents 414
Clothing designers, *see:* Fashion designers 240
CNC operators, *see:* Computer control programmers and
  operators...585
CNC programmers, *see:* Computer control programmers
  and operators 585
Coaches, *see:* Athletes, coaches, umpires, and related workers 252
Coast Guard, *see:* Job opportunities in the Armed Forces....653
Coders, *see:* Medical records and health information technicians 328
Coding specialists, *see:* Medical records and health information
  technicians...328
Coil winders, tapers, and finishers, *see:* Assemblers and
  fabricators...579
Coin, vending, and amusement machine servicers and repairers 560
Collectors, *see:* Bill and account collectors........................431
Collectors, *see:* Tax examiners, collectors, and revenue agents 98
College and university faculty, *see:* Teachers—postsecondary 223
College counselors, *see:* Counselors..................................189

Collision repair and refinish technicians, *see:* Automotive body
  and related repairers..547
Color printer operators, *see:* Photographic process workers and
  processing machine operators...625
Colorists, *see:* Barbers, cosmetologists, and other personal
  appearance workers..387
Columnists, *see:* News analysts, reporters, and correspondents............267
Combined food preparation and serving workers, *see:*
  Food and beverage serving and related workers.................374
Commentators, *see:* News analysts, reporters, and correspondents 267
Commercial and industrial designers...................................238
Commercial divers..669
Commercial loan officers, *see:* Loan officers 90
Commercial photographers, *see:* Photographers 269
Commercial pilots, *see:* Aircraft pilots and flight engineers 629
Commission clerks, *see:* Payroll and timekeeping clerks.......437
Commissioners, *see:* Top executives 67
Communications equipment operators 471
Communications specialists, *see:* Public relations specialists..............271
Community association managers, *see:* Property, real estate, and
  community association managers 61
Community dietitians, *see:* Dietitians and nutritionists 284
Community outreach workers, *see:* Social and
  human service assistants..194
Community planners, *see:* Urban and regional planners.......180
Community service managers, *see:* Social and community service
  managers..662
Community supervision officers, *see:* Probation officers and
  correctional treatment specialists.....................................192
Community support workers, *see:* Social and
  human service assistants..194
Companions, *see:* Personal and home care aides.................399
Compensation and benefits technicians, *see:* Human resources
  assistants, except payroll and timekeeping 449
Compensation, benefits, and job analysis specialists, *see:* Human
  resources, training, and labor relations managers and specialists.........50
Compensation managers, *see:* Human resources, training, and
  labor relations managers and specialists.............................50
Compliance officers, except agriculture, construction, health and
  safety, and transportation 661
Composers, *see:* Musicians, singers, and related workers.....257
Composing machine operators and tenders, *see:*
  Prepress technicians and workers 598
Compositors, *see:* Desktop publishers 477
Compositors, *see:* Prepress technicians and workers 598
Computer aides, *see:* Data entry and information
  processing workers...475
Computer and information systems managers........................30
Computer applications software engineers, *see:*
  Computer software engineers...111
Computer, automated teller, and office machine repairers....536
Computer chip processing operators, *see:*
  Semiconductor processors..626
Computer chip processing technicians, *see:*
  Semiconductor processors..626
Computer clerks, *see:* Data entry and information
  processing workers...475
Computer control operators, *see:* Computer control programmers
  and operators...585
Computer control programmers and operators 585
Computer-controlled machine tool operators, metal and plastic, *see:*
  Computer control programmers and operators 585
Computer hardware engineers, *see:* Engineers....................133
Computer operators...473
Computer programmers..104
Computer scientists and database administrators 107
Computer security specialists, *see:* Computer support specialists
  and systems administrators...113
Computer software engineers 111
Computer support specialists and systems administrators........113
Computer systems analysts..116
Computer systems software engineers, *see:*
  Computer software engineers...111
Computer technology trainers, *see:* Human resources,
  training, and labor relations managers and specialists...........50
Computer training specialists, *see:* Human resources, training,
  and labor relations managers and specialists 50
Computer typesetters, *see:* Data entry and information
  processing workers...475

Concierges 664
Conciliators, *see:* Human resources, training, and labor relations managers and specialists 50
Conciliators, *see:* Judges, magistrates, and other judicial workers 201
Concrete finishers, *see:* Cement masons, concrete finishers, segmental pavers, and terrazzo workers 502
Concrete paving machine operators, *see:* Construction equipment operators 507
Condominium association managers, *see:* Property, real estate, and community association managers 61
Conductors, music, *see:* Musicians, singers, and related workers 257
Conductors, railroad, *see:* Rail transportation occupations 644
Conference interpreters, *see:* Interpreters and translators 263
Conference planners, *see:* Meeting and convention planners 95
Conference service coordinators, *see:* Meeting and convention planners 95
Congress members, *see:* Top executives 67
Conservation scientists and foresters 153
Conservation technicians, *see:* Science technicians 185
Conservation workers, *see:* Forest, conservation, and logging workers 490
Conservators, *see:* Archivists, curators, and museum technicians 210
Construction and building inspectors 504
Construction cost estimators, *see:* Cost estimators 83
Construction electricians, *see:* Electricians 513
Construction engineers, *see:* Engineers 133
Construction equipment operators 507
Construction job cost estimators, *see:* Cost estimators 83
Construction laborers 509
Construction managers 32
Construction millwrights, *see:* Millwrights 573
Construction vehicle technicians, *see:* Heavy vehicle and mobile equipment service technicians and mechanics 555
Constructors, *see:* Construction managers 32
Consultant dietitians, *see:* Dietitians and nutritionists 284
Consultant, financial, *see:* Financial analysts and personal financial advisors 85
Content editors, *see:* Writers and editors 275
Continuous mining machine operators 667
Contract administrators, *see:* Administrative services managers 25
Contract managers, *see:* Purchasing managers, buyers, and purchasing agents 64
Contract specialists, *see:* Purchasing managers, buyers, and purchasing agents 64
Contract specialists, *see:* Real estate brokers and sales agents 414
Control and valve installers and repairers, except mechanical door 669
Control room assistants, *see:* Power plant operators, distributors, and dispatchers 608
Control room operators, *see:* Power plant operators, distributors, and dispatchers 608
Control room trainees, *see:* Power plant operators, distributors, and dispatchers 608
Control technicians, *see:* Precision instrument and equipment repairers 575
Controllers, *see:* Financial managers 42
Controllers, air traffic, *see:* Air traffic controllers
Convention managers, *see:* Meeting and convention planners 95
Convention planners, *see:* Meeting and convention planners 95
Convention services managers, *see:* Lodging managers 56
Cooking instructors, *see:* Teachers—self-enrichment education 267
Cooks, *see:* Chefs, cooks, and food preparation workers 371
Cooling and freezing equipment operators and tenders 671
Cooperative managers, *see:* Property, real estate, and community association managers 61
Coordinators, instructional, *see:* Instructional coordinators 213
Copy editors, *see:* Writers and editors 275
Copy writers, *see:* Writers and editors 275
Corporate accountants, *see:* Accountants and auditors 70
Corporate administrative assistants, *see:* Secretaries and administrative assistants 482
Corporate investigators, *see:* Private detectives and investigators 366
Corporate office services managers, *see:* Secretaries and administrative assistants 482
Corporate recruiters, *see:* Human resources, training, and labor relations managers and specialists 50
Corporate secretaries, *see:* Secretaries and administrative assistants 482
Corporate trainers, *see:* Human resources, training, and labor relations managers and specialists 50
Correctional officers 357
Correctional treatment specialists, *see:* Probation officers and correctional treatment specialists 192
Correspondence clerks 666
Correspondents, *see:* News analysts, reporters, and correspondents 267
Cosmetologists, *see:* Barbers, cosmetologists, and other personal appearance workers 387
Cost accountants, *see:* Accountants and auditors 70
Cost consultants, *see:* Cost estimators 83
Cost engineers, *see:* Cost estimators 83
Cost estimators 83
Cost/investment recovery technicians, *see:* Cost estimators 83
Costume designers, *see:* Fashion designers 240
Costume attendants 664
Counseling psychologists, *see:* Psychologists 177
Counselors 189
Counselors, loan, *see:* Loan officers 90
Counter and rental clerks 407
Counter attendants, *see:* Food and beverage serving and related workers 374
County court judges, *see:* Judges, magistrates, and other judicial workers 201
Couriers and messengers 460
Court officers, *see:* Correctional officers 357
Court reporters 199
Court, municipal, and license clerks 666
Courtesy van drivers, *see:* Taxi drivers and chauffeurs 637
CPAs, *see:* Accountants and auditors 70
Craft artists, *see:* Artists and related workers 235
Crane and tower operators, *see:* Material moving occupations 650
Creative directors, *see:* Advertising, marketing, promotions, public relations, and sales managers 27
Creative writers, *see:* Writers and editors 275
Credentials specialists, *see:* Human resources, training, and labor relations managers and specialists 50
Credit analysts 661
Credit authorizers, checkers, and clerks 442
Credit checkers, *see:* Credit authorizers, checkers, and clerks 442
Credit clerks, *see:* Credit authorizers, checkers, and clerks 442
Credit counselors, *see:* Loan officers 90
Credit investigators, *see:* Credit authorizers, checkers, and clerks 442
Credit managers, *see:* Financial managers 42
Credit reporters, *see:* Credit authorizers, checkers, and clerks 442
Criminal investigators, *see:* Police and detectives 362
Criminal lawyers, *see:* Lawyers 204
Criminologists, *see:* Social scientists, other 182
Critical care nurses, *see:* Registered nurses 303
Crop farm managers, *see:* Farmers, ranchers, and agricultural managers 40
Crop scientists, *see:* Agricultural and food scientists 147
Crossing guards 664
Cruise ship workers, *see:* Water transportation occupations 647
Crushing, grinding, and polishing machine setters, operators, and tenders 671
Cryptanalysts, *see:* Mathematicians 119
CT technologists, *see:* Radiologic technologists and technicians 337
Curators, *see:* Archivists, curators, and museum technicians 210
Curriculum specialists, *see:* Instructional coordinators 213
Customer service representatives 444
Customer service representatives, *see:* Tellers 440
Customer services managers, *see:* Office and administrative support worker supervisors and managers 479
Customs agents, *see:* Police and detectives 362
Customs inspectors, *see:* Police and detectives 362
Cutters, *see:* Welding, soldering, and brazing workers 594
Cutters and trimmers, apparel, *see:* Textile, apparel, and furnishings occupations 602
Cutters and trimmers, hand 671
Cutting and slicing machine setters, operators, and tenders 671
Cutting machine operators, textile, *see:* Textile, apparel, and furnishings occupations 602
Cutting, punching, and press machine setters, operators, and tenders, metal and plastic, *see:* Machine setters, operators, and tenders—metal and plastic 589
Cytotechnologists, *see:* Clinical laboratory technologists and technicians 318

D

Dairy farmers, *see:* Farmers, ranchers, and agricultural managers.......... 40
Dairy scientists, *see:* Agricultural and food scientists 147
Dance captains, *see:* Dancers and choreographers 255
Dancers and choreographers 255
Data coder operators, *see:* Data entry and information processing workers 475
Data entry and information processing workers 475
Data entry clerks, *see:* Data entry and information processing workers 475
Data entry clerks, *see:* Office clerks, general 481
Data entry keyers, *see:* Data entry and information processing workers 475
Data entry operators, *see:* Data entry and information processing workers 475
Data entry operators, *see:* Office clerks, general 481
Data entry technicians, *see:* Data entry and information processing workers 475
Data input clerks, *see:* Data entry and information processing workers 475
Data processing equipment repairers, *see:* Computer, automated teller, and office machine repairers 536
Data processors, *see:* Data entry and information processing workers 475
Data typists, *see:* Data entry and information processing workers 475
Database administrators, *see:* Computer scientists and database administrators 107
Dealers, *see:* Securities, commodities, and financial services sales agents 426
Dealers, gaming, *see:* Gaming services occupations 397
Deans, university, *see:* Education administrators 34
Deck officers, water transportation, *see:* Water transportation occupations 647
Deckhands, fishing boats, *see:* Fishers and fishing vessel operators 487
Decommissioning and decontamination (D&D) workers, *see:* Hazardous materials removal workers 519
Decontamination technicians, *see:* Hazardous materials removal workers 519
Decorators, interior, *see:* Interior designers 245
Defense attorneys, *see:* Lawyers 204
Delivery services truck drivers, *see:* Truck drivers and driver/sales workers 640
Demographers, *see:* Social scientists, other 182
Demographic economists, *see:* Economists 173
Demonstrators, product promoters, and models 408
Dental assistants 343
Dental ceramists, *see:* Medical, dental, and ophthalmic laboratory technicians 619
Dental hygienists 320
Dental laboratory technicians, *see:* Medical, dental, and ophthalmic laboratory technicians 619
Dental surgeons, *see:* Dentists 282
Dental technicians, *see:* Medical, dental, and ophthalmic laboratory technicians 619
Dentists 282
Department heads, college or university, *see:* Education administrators 34
Department managers, *see:* Sales worker supervisors 423
Deputy sheriffs, *see:* Police and detectives 362
Dermatologists, *see:* Physicians and surgeons 295
Dermatology nurses, *see:* Registered nurses 303
Derrick operators, oil and gas 667
Design consultants, *see:* Cost estimators 83
Design printing machine setters and set-up operators, *see:* Printing machine operators 600
Designers, *see:*
- Commercial and industrial designers 238
- Fashion designers 240
- Floral designers 242
- Graphic designers 243
- Interior designers 245

Designers, clothing, *see:* Fashion designers 240
Designers, costume, *see:* Fashion designers 240
Designers, footwear and accessory, *see:* Fashion designers 240
Design printing machine setters and set-up operators, *see:* Printing machine operators 600
Desk clerks, *see:* Hotel, motel, and resort desk clerks 448
Desktop publishers 477
Desktop publishing editors, *see:* Desktop publishers 477
Detectives and criminal investigators, *see:* Police and detectives 362
Detectives, hotel, *see:* Private detectives and investigators 366
Detectives, private, *see:* Private detectives and investigators 366
Detectives, store, *see:* Private detectives and investigators 366
Detention officers, *see:* Correctional officers 357
Development specialists, staff, *see:* Instructional coordinators 213
Developmental disabilities nurses, *see:* Registered nurses 303
Developmental psychologists, *see:* Psychologists 177
Diabetes management nurses, *see:* Registered nurses 303
Diagnostic medical sonographers 322
Die makers, *see:* Tool and die makers 592
Diesel engine specialists, *see:* Diesel service technicians and mechanics 552
Diesel engineers, *see:* Rail transportation occupations 644
Diesel mechanics, *see:* Diesel service technicians and mechanics 552
Diesel service technicians and mechanics 552
Dietetic technicians 662
Dietitians and nutritionists 284
Digital electronic prepress workers, *see:* Desktop publishers 477
Digital image processors, *see:* Desktop publishers 477
Digital imaging technicians , *see:* Photographic process workers and processing machine operators 625
Dining room and cafeteria attendants and bartender helpers, *see:* Food and beverage serving and related workers 374
Dinkey operators, *see:* Rail transportation occupations 644
Diocesan priests, *see:* Clergy 662
Dippers, *see:* Painting and coating workers, except construction and maintenance 622
Directors, *see:* Actors, producers, and directors 249
Directors of administration, *see:* Office and administrative support worker supervisors and managers 479
Directors of administrative services, *see:* Office and administrative support worker supervisors and managers 479
Directors of administrative support services, *see:* Office and administrative support worker supervisors and managers 479
Directors of admissions, *see:* Education administrators 34
Directors of human resources, *see:* Human resources, training, and labor relations managers and specialists 50
Directors of industrial relations, *see:* Human resources, training, and labor relations managers and specialists 50
Directors of instructional material, *see:* Instructional coordinators 213
Directors of operations, *see:* Administrative services managers 25
Directors of operations, *see:* Office and administrative support worker supervisors and managers 479
Directors of recreation and parks, *see:* Recreation workers 400
Directors of staff development, *see:* Human resources, training, and labor relations managers and specialists 50
Directors of student services, *see:* Education administrators 34
Directors, museum, *see:* Archivists, curators, and museum technicians 210
Directors, music, *see:* Musicians, singers, and related workers 257
Directors, religious activities and education 662
Directory assistance operators, *see:* Communications equipment operators 471
Disc jockeys, *see:* Announcers 259
Dishwashers, *see:* Food and beverage serving and related workers 374
Dispatchers 461
Dispatchers, load, *see:* Power plant operators, distributors, and dispatchers 608
Dispatchers, power, *see:* Power plant operators, distributors, and dispatchers 608
Dispensing opticians, *see:* Opticians, dispensing 334
Distribution clerks, *see:* Postal Service workers 464
Distribution managers, *see:* Transportation, storage, and distribution managers 662
Distributors, power, *see:* Power plant operators, distributors, and dispatchers 608
Dividend clerks, *see:* Brokerage clerks 441
Division secretaries, *see:* Secretaries and administrative assistants 482
DJs, *see:* Announcers 259
Doctors of dental medicine, *see:* Dentists 282
Doctors of dental surgery, *see:* Dentists 282
Doctors of optometry, *see:* Optometrists 287
Doctors, chiropractic, *see:* Chiropractors 280
Doctors, medical, *see:* Physicians and surgeons 295
Doctors, osteopathic, *see:* Physicians and surgeons 295

Doctors, podiatric, *see:* Podiatrists 298
Documentation specialists, *see:* Desktop publishers 477
Door-to-door sales workers, news and street vendors,
    and related workers 665
Dot etchers, *see:* Prepress technicians and workers 598
Drafters 141
Dredge, excavating, and loading machine operators, *see:*
    Material moving occupations 650
Dressmakers, *see:* Textile, apparel, and furnishings occupations 602
Drillers, *see:* Earth drillers, except oil and gas 667
Drilling and boring machine tool setters, operators, and tenders,
    metal and plastic, *see:* Machine setters, operators, and
    tenders—metal and plastic 589
Drill operators, *see:* Rotary drill operators, oil and gas 669
Driver-sales workers, *see:* Truck drivers and driver/sales workers 640
Drivers, bookmobile, *see:* Library technicians 217
Drivers, bus, *see:* Bus drivers 634
Drivers, cab, *see:* Taxi drivers and chauffeurs 637
Drivers, courtesy van, *see:* Taxi drivers and chauffeurs 637
Drivers, delivery services, *see:* Truck drivers and
    driver/sales workers 640
Drivers, fork lift, *see:* Material moving occupations 650
Drivers, lease, *see:* Taxi drivers and chauffeurs 637
Drivers, light truck, *see:* Truck drivers and driver/sales workers 640
Drivers, limousine, *see:* Taxi drivers and chauffeurs 637
Drivers, motor coach, *see:* Bus drivers 634
Drivers, paratransit, *see:* Taxi drivers and chauffeurs 637
Drivers, route, *see:* Truck drivers and driver/sales workers 640
Drivers, sales worker, *see:* Truck drivers and driver/sales workers 640
Drivers, school bus, *see:* Bus drivers 634
Drivers, taxi, *see:* Taxi drivers and chauffeurs 637
Drivers, tractor, *see:* Agricultural workers 485
Drivers, tractor-trailer, *see:* Truck drivers and driver/sales workers ... 640
Drivers, truck, *see:* Truck drivers and driver/sales workers 640
Drug Enforcement Administration (DEA) agents, *see:*
    Police and detectives 362
Dry-cleaning workers, *see:* Textile, apparel, and
    furnishings occupations 602
Drywall installers, ceiling tile installers, and tapers 511
DTP operators, *see:* Desktop publishers 477
Dyeing machine operators, textile, *see:* Textile, apparel, and
    furnishings occupations 602

E

Earth drillers, except oil and gas 667
Echocardiographers, *see:* Cardiovascular technologists and
    technicians 316
Ecological modelers, *see:* Environmental scientists and
    hydrologists 164
Ecologists, *see:* Biological scientists 150
Ecologists, *see:* Environmental scientists and hydrologists 164
Econometricians, *see:* Economists 173
Econometricians, *see:* Statisticians 123
Economic geographers, *see:* Social scientists, other 182
Economists 173
Edition binding workers, *see:* Bookbinders and bindery workers 596
Editors, *see:* Writers and editors 275
Education administrators 34
Education and development managers, *see:* Human resources,
    training, and labor relations managers and specialists 50
Education and training managers, *see:* Human resources, training,
    and labor relations managers and specialists 50
Education planners, *see:* Meeting and convention planners 95
Educational consultants, *see:* Instructional coordinators 213
Educational counselors, *see:* Counselors 189
EEO officers or representatives, *see:* Human resources, training, and
    labor relations managers and specialists 50
EKG technicians, *see:* Cardiovascular technologists and technicians... 316
Electric line repairers, *see:* Line installers and repairers 569
Electric motor repairers, *see:* Electrical and electronics installers
    and repairers 538
Electrical and electronic equipment assemblers, *see:*
    Assemblers and fabricators 579
Electrical and electronics engineering technicians, *see:*
    Engineering technicians 144
Electrical and electronics installers and repairers 538

Electrical drafters, *see:* Drafters 141
Electrical engineers, *see:* Engineers 133
Electrical inspectors, *see:* Construction and building inspectors 504
Electrical powerline installers and repairers, *see:*
    Line installers and repairers 569
Electricians 513
Electrocardiograph (EKG) technicians, *see:*
    Cardiovascular technologists and technicians 316
Electrologists, *see:* Barbers, cosmetologists, and
    other personal appearance workers 387
Electromechanical engineering technicians, *see:* Engineering
    technicians 144
Electromechanical equipment assemblers, *see:*
    Assemblers and fabricators 579
Electronic data processors, *see:* Data entry and information
    processing workers 475
Electronic drafters, *see:* Drafters 141
Electronic equipment installers and repairers, motor vehicles, *see:*
    Electrical and electronics installers and repairers 538
Electronic home entertainment equipment installers and repairers 540
Electronic masking system operators, *see:* Prepress technicians
    and workers 598
Electronic news gathering operators, *see:* Television, video, and
    motion picture camera operators and editors 274
Electronic prepress technicians, *see:* Desktop publishers 477
Electronic publishers, *see:* Desktop publishers 477
Electronic publishing specialists, *see:* Desktop publishers 477
Electronic reporters and transcribers, *see:* Court reporters 199
Electronic semiconductor processors, *see:*
    Semiconductor processors 626
Electronic typesetting machine operators, *see:* Data entry and
    information processing workers 475
Electronics engineers, *see:* Engineers ....
Electronics repairers, *see:* Electrical and electronics installers
    and repairers 538
Electronics technicians, *see:* Precision instrument and
    equipment repairers 576
Electrotypers and stereotypers, *see:* Prepress technicians
    and workers 598
Elementary school teachers, *see:* Teachers—preschool,
    kindergarten, elementary, middle, and secondary 287
Elevator constructors , *see:* Elevator installers and repairers 516
Elevator inspectors, *see:* Construction and building inspectors 504
Elevator installers and repairers 516
Elevator mechanics, *see:* Elevator installers and repairers 516
Eligibility interviewers, government programs, *see:* Interviewers 451
Embalmers 664
Embalmers, *see:* Funeral directors 48
Embossing machine set-up operators, *see:*
    Printing machine operators 600
Emergency and disaster response workers, *see:*
    Hazardous materials removal workers 519
Emergency care nurses, *see:* Registered nurses 303
Emergency management specialists 661
Emergency medical technicians and paramedics 324
Emergency physicians, *see:* Physicians and surgeons 295
Employee assistance plan managers, *see:* Human resources,
    training, and labor relations managers and specialists 50
Employee benefits managers and specialists, *see:* Human resources,
    training, and labor relations managers and specialists 50
Employee development managers, *see:* Human resources, training,
    and labor relations managers and specialists 50
Employee development specialists, *see:* Human resources, training,
    and labor relations managers and specialists 50
Employee placement specialists, *see:* Human resources, training,
    and labor relations managers and specialists 50
Employee relations managers, *see:* Human resources, training,
    and labor relations managers and specialists 50
Employee training specialists, *see:* Human resources, training,
    and labor relations managers and specialists 50
Employee welfare managers, *see:* Human resources, training,
    and labor relations managers and specialists 50
Employer relations representatives, *see:* Human resources, training,
    and labor relations managers and specialists 50
Employment and placement managers, *see:* Human resources,
    training, and labor relations managers and specialists 50
Employment assistants, *see:* Human resources assistants,
    except payroll and timekeeping 449

Employment clerks, *see:* Human resources assistants,
except payroll and timekeeping 449
Employment consultants, *see:* Human resources, training, and
labor relations managers and specialists 50
Employment coordinators, *see:* Human resources, training, and
labor relations managers and specialists 50
Employment counselors, *see:* Counselors 189
Employment interviewers, *see:* Human resources, training, and
labor relations managers and specialists 50
Employment managers, *see:* Human resources, training, and
· labor relations managers and specialists 50
Employment recruiters, *see:* Human resources, training, and
labor relations managers and specialists 50
Employment, recruitment, and placement specialists, *see:* Human
resources, training, and labor relations managers and specialists 50
Employment service specialists, *see:* Human resources assistants,
except payroll, training, and timekeeping 53
Employment specialists, *see:* Human resources, training, and
labor relations managers and specialists 50
EMTs, *see:* Emergency medical technicians and paramedics.............324
Encoders, *see:* Data entry and information processing workers 475
Encoding clerks, *see:* Data entry and information processing workers .. 475
Endodontists, *see:* Dentists 282
ENG operators, *see:* Television, video, and motion picture
camera operators and editors...274
Engine and other machine assemblers, *see:* Assemblers and
fabricators...579
Engineering and natural sciences managers 38
Engineering geologists, *see:* Geoscientists 167
Engineering managers, *see:* Engineering and natural
sciences managers 38
Engineering technicians 144
Engineers...133
Engineers, computer software, *see:* Computer software engineers 111
Engineers, diesel, *see:* Rail transportation occupations.................644
Engineers, locomotive, *see:* Rail transportation occupations 644
Engineers, rail yard, *see:* Rail transportation occupations.............644
Engineers, railroad, *see:* Rail transportation occupations..............644
Engineers, ship, *see:* Water transportation occupations.................647
Engineers, stationary, *see:* Stationary engineers and
boiler operators 610
English as a second language teachers, *see:* Teachers—adult literacy
and remedial education 221
English to speakers of other languages teachers, *see:*
Teachers—adult literacy and remedial education 221
Engraver set-up operators, *see:* Printing machine operators 600
Engravers, *see:* Etchers and engravers...................................671
Engravers, *see:* Jewelers and precious stone and metal workers...........616
Enlisted personnel, *see:* Job opportunities in the Armed Forces 653
Enrichment education instructors, *see:* Teachers—
self-enrichment education 231
Enrobing machine operators, *see:* Painting and coating workers,
except construction and maintenance 622
Enrollment specialists, *see:* Human resources assistants,
except payroll and timekeeping 449
Enroute controllers, air traffic, *see:* Air traffic controllers............629
Entomologists, *see:* Agricultural and food scientists....................147
Environmental chemists, *see:* Environmental scientists and
hydrologists...164
Environmental ecologists, *see:* Environmental scientists
and hydrologists 164
Environmental engineering technicians, *see:* Engineering technicians .. 144
Environmental engineers, *see:* Engineers 133
Environmental meteorologists, *see:* Atmospheric scientists 159
Environmental protection officers, *see:* Occupational health and
safety specialists and technicians 331
Environmental scientists, *see:* Environmental scientists
and hydrologists 164
Environmental scientists and hydrologists.............................164
Environmental technicians, *see:* Science technicians.................185
Epidemiologists, *see:* Medical scientists 156
Ergonomists, *see:* Occupational health and safety specialists and
technicians...331
Escort interpreters, *see:* Interpreters and translators.................263
ESL teachers, *see:* Teachers—adult literacy and remedial education.... 221
ESOL teachers, *see:* Teachers—adult literacy and remedial education. 221
Essayists, *see:* Writers and editors...................................275
Estheticians, *see:* Massage therapists 344

Estheticians, *see:* Barbers, cosmetologists, and other personal
appearance workers...387
Estimator project managers, *see:* Cost estimators 83
Estimators, *see:* Cost estimators 83
Etchers and engravers..671
Event planners, *see:* Meeting and convention planners...............95
Examiners, *see:* Claims adjusters, appraisers, examiners,
and investigators 80
Excavating and loading machine and dragline operators, *see:*
Material moving occupations...650
Executive administrative assistants, *see:* Secretaries and
administrative assistants..482
Executive administrators, *see:* Office and administrative
support worker supervisors and managers............................479
Executive administrators, *see:* Secretaries and administrative
assistants...482
Executive assistants, *see:* Secretaries and administrative assistants.....482
Executive chefs, *see:* Chefs, cooks, and food preparation workers.......371
Executive editors, *see:* Writers and editors...........................275
Executive housekeepers, *see:* Lodging managers....................56
Executive office administrators, *see:* Office and administrative
support worker supervisors and managers............................479
Executive office administrators, *see:* Secretaries and
administrative assistants..482
Executive recruiters, *see:* Human resources, training, and
labor relations managers and specialists 50
Executive secretaries, *see:* Secretaries and administrative assistants....482
Executives, *see:* Top executives......................................67
Exercise instructors, *see:* Fitness workers 392
Expediting clerks, *see:* Production, planning, and expediting clerks....466
Experimental psychologists, *see:* Psychologists....................177
Explosives workers, ordnance handling experts, and blasters..............667
Exterminators, *see:* Pest control workers.............................382
Extractive metallurgical engineers, *see:* Engineers 133
Extruding and drawing machine setters, operators, and tenders,
metal and plastic, *see:* Machine setters, operators, and tenders
—metal and plastic..589
Extruding and forming machine setters, operators, and tenders,
synthetic and glass fibers, *see:* Textile, apparel, and
furnishings occupations..602
Extruding, forming, pressing, and compacting machine setters,
operators, and tenders 671

F

Fabric and apparel patternmakers, *see:* Textile, apparel, and
furnishings occupations..602
Fabric menders, except garment 669
Fabricators, *see:* Assemblers and fabricators.......................579
Facilitators, *see:* Judges, magistrates, and other judicial workers.........201
Facilities coordinators, *see:* Administrative services managers 25
Facility coordinators, *see:* Property, real estate, and community
association managers..61
Facility managers, *see:* Administrative services managers 25
Faculty, college and university, *see:* Teachers—postsecondary 223
Fallers, *see:* Forest, conservation, and logging workers....................490
Family and general practitioners, *see:* Physicians and surgeons 295
Family child care providers, *see:* Child care workers.....................389
Family services social workers, *see:* Social workers......................196
Family therapists, *see:* Counselors 189
Farm and home management advisors....................................663
Farm equipment mechanics, *see:* Heavy vehicle and
mobile equipment service technicians and mechanics.......................555
Farmers, ranchers, and agricultural managers 40
Farmworkers, agricultural production, *see:* Agricultural workers.........485
Farmworkers, crop, nursery, and greenhouse, *see:* Agricultural
workers..485
Farmworkers, farm and ranch animals, *see:* Agricultural workers........485
Fashion designers...240
Fashion designers, *see:* Fashion designers..............................240
Fast-food cooks, *see:* Chefs, cooks, and food preparation workers.......371
FBI agents, *see:* Police and detectives................................362
Federal Bureau of Investigation agents, *see:* Police and detectives 362
Fence erectors 667
Field technicians, *see:* Broadcast and sound engineering technicians
and radio operators..261
Field technicians, *see:* Computer, automated teller, and
office machine repairers..536

Field technicians, *see:* Electrical and electronics installers
and repairers 538
Field technicians, *see:* Electronic home entertainment
equipment installers and repairers 540
File clerks 447
File clerks, *see:* Office clerks, general 481
Film and video editors, *see:* Television, video, and
motion picture camera operators and editors 274
Film processing technicians, *see:* Photographic process workers
and processing machine operators 625
Finance managers, hotels, *see:* Lodging managers 56
Finance officers, *see:* Financial managers 42
Financial aid directors, *see:* Education administrators 34
Financial analysts and personal financial advisors 85
Financial clerks, *see:*
  Bill and account collectors 431
  Billing and posting clerks and machine operators 432
  Bookkeeping, Accounting, and auditing clerks 434
  Gaming cage workers 435
  Payroll and timekeeping clerks 437
  Procurement clerks 438
  Tellers 440
Financial consultants, *see:* Financial analysts and
personal financial advisors 85
Financial consultants, *see:* Insurance sales agents 411
Financial consultants, *see:* Securities, commodities, and
financial services sales agents 426
Financial economists, *see:* Economists 173
Financial examiners 661
Financial investigators, *see:* Private detectives and investigators .. 366
Financial managers 42
Financial planners, *see:* Financial analysts and personal
financial advisors 85
Financial planners, *see:* Insurance sales agents 411
Financial planners, *see:* Securities, commodities, and
financial services sales agents 426
Financial services sales agents, *see:* Securities, commodities,
and financial services sales agents 426
Fine artists, including painters, sculptors, and illustrators,
see: Artists and related workers 235
Fine arts instructors, *see:* Teachers—self-enrichment education .. 231
Fine arts photographers, *see:* Artists and related workers ... 235
Fine arts photographers, *see:* Photographers 269
Finishers, *see:* Drywall installers, ceiling tile installers, and tapers .. 511
Fire alarm systems installers, *see:* Security and
fire alarm systems installers 670
Fire fighting occupations 359
Fire inspectors, *see:* Fire fighting occupations 359
Fire investigators, *see:* Fire fighting occupations 359
Fire prevention specialists, *see:* Fire fighting occupations .. 359
First-line supervisors/managers/contractors of farming, fishing,
and forestry workers, *see:* Supervisors, farming, fishing,
and forestry workers 667
First-line supervisors/managers of construction trades and
extraction workers 667
First-line supervisors/managers of food preparation and
serving workers 664
First-line supervisors/managers of mechanics, installers,
and repairers 669
First-line supervisors/managers of personal service workers .. 664
First-line supervisors/managers of production and
operating workers 671
First-line supervisors/managers of transportation and material
moving machine and vehicle operators 673
First mates, fishing boat, *see:* Fishers and fishing vessel operators .. 487
First responders, *see:* Emergency medical technicians
and paramedics 324
Fiscal and policy analysts, *see:* Budget analysts 77
Fiscal technicians, *see:* Payroll and timekeeping clerks 437
Fish and game wardens, *see:* Police and detectives 362
Fish cleaners, *see:* Food processing occupations 581
Fish cutters and trimmers, *see:* Food processing occupations .. 581
Fish hatchery managers, *see:* Farmers, ranchers, and
agricultural managers 40
Fishers and fishing vessel operators 487
Fitness directors, *see:* Fitness workers 392
Fitness trainers, *see:* Fitness workers 392
Fitness workers 392

Flight attendants 394
Flight engineers, *see:* Aircraft pilots and flight engineers 629
Flight service specialists, *see:* Air traffic controllers 632
Floor brokers, *see:* Securities, commodities, and
financial services sales agents 426
Floor installers, *see:* Carpet, floor, and tile installers and finishers .. 499
Floor layers, *see:* Carpet, floor, and tile installers and finishers .. 499
Floor sanders and finishers, *see:* Carpet, floor, and tile installers
and finishers 499
Floral designers 242
Florists, *see:* Floral designers 242
Food and beverage managers, *see:* Food service managers ... 45
Food and beverage managers, hotels, *see:* Lodging managers .. 56
Food and beverage serving and related workers 374
Food and tobacco roasting, baking, and drying machine operators,
see: Food processing occupations 581
Food batchmakers, *see:* Food processing occupations 581
Food cooking machine operators and tenders, *see:*
Food processing occupations 581
Food preparation workers, *see:* Chefs, cooks, and
food preparation workers 371
Food processing occupations 581
Food science technicians, *see:* Science technicians 185
Food scientists, *see:* Agricultural and food scientists 147
Food service managers 45
Food technologists, *see:* Agricultural and food scientists 147
Foot doctors, *see:* Podiatrists 298
Foot specialists, *see:* Podiatrists 298
Footwear and accessory designers, *see:* Fashion designers ... 240
Foreign language interpreters and translators, *see:*
Interpreters and translators 263
Forensic accountants, *see:* Accountants and auditors 70
Forensic nurses, *see:* Registered nurses 303
Forensic technicians, *see:* Science technicians 185
Forest and conservation technicians, *see:* Science technicians .. 185
Forest and conservation workers, *see:* Forest, conservation,
and logging workers 490
Forest, conservation, and logging workers 490
Forest fire inspectors and prevention specialists, *see:*
Fire fighting occupations 359
Foresters, *see:* Conservation scientists and foresters 153
Forging machine setters, operators, and tenders, metal and plastic, *see:*
Machine setters, operators, and tenders—metal and plastic .. 589
Fork lift operators, *see:* Material moving occupations 650
Forming machine operators, synthetic and glass fibers, *see:*
Textile, apparel, and furnishings occupations 602
Foundry mold and coremakers, *see:* Machine setters, operators,
and tenders—metal and plastic 589
Freight agents, *see:* Cargo and freight agents 459
Freight, stock, and material movers, hand, *see:*
Material moving occupations 650
Front desk clerks, *see:* Hotel, motel, and resort desk clerks .. 448
Front office managers, *see:* Lodging managers 56
Front-end mechanics, *see:* Automotive service technicians
and mechanics 549
Fry cooks, *see:* Chefs, cooks, and food preparation workers .. 371
Full-charge bookkeepers, *see:* Bookkeeping, accounting,
and auditing clerks 434
Fumigators, *see:* Pest control workers 382
Funeral attendants 664
Funeral directors 48
Funeral managers, *see:* Funeral directors 48
Furnace, kiln, oven, drier, and kettle operators and tenders ... 672
Furnace installers, *see:* Heating, air-conditioning, and
refrigeration mechanics and installers 562
Furniture finishers, *see:* Woodworkers 606

G

Game wardens, *see:* Police and detectives 362
Gaming and sports book writers and runners, *see:*
Gaming services occupations 397
Gaming cage cashiers, *see:* Gaming cage workers 435
Gaming cage workers 435
Gaming change persons, *see:* Cashiers 405
Gaming dealers, *see:* Gaming services occupations 397
Gaming investigators, *see:* Security guards and
gaming surveillance officers 368

Gaming machine servicers and repairers, *see:* Coin, vending,
and amusement machine servers and repairers 560
Gaming managers 661
Gaming services occupations 397
Gaming supervisors, *see:* Gaming services occupations 397
Gaming surveillance officers, *see:* Security guards and
gaming surveillance officers 368
Garbage collectors, *see:* Material moving occupations 650
Gas and water service dispatchers, *see:* Dispatchers 461
Gas appliance repairers, *see:* Home appliance repairers 565
Gas compressor and gas pumping station operators, *see:*
Material moving occupations 650
Gas furnace installers, *see:* Heating, air-conditioning, and
refrigeration mechanics and installers 562
Gas plant operators ....
Gas station attendants, *see:* Service station attendants 673
Gastroenterologists, *see:* Physicians and surgeons 295
Gastroenterology nurses, *see:* Registered nurses 303
Gate agents, *see:* Reservation and transportation ticket agents
and travel clerks 457
GED teachers, *see:* Teachers—adult literacy and remedial education .. 221
Gemologists, *see:* Jewelers and precious stone and metal workers 616
General and operations managers, *see:* Top executives 67
General clerks, *see:* Office clerks, general 481
General internists, *see:* Physicians and surgeons 295
General maintenance and repair workers, *see:*
Maintenance and repair workers, general 572
General managers, *see:* Administrative services managers 25
General managers, *see:* Lodging managers 56
General office clerks, *see:* Office clerks, general 481
General practitioners, *see:* Physicians and surgeons 295
General trial court judges, *see:* Judges, magistrates, and
other judicial workers 201
Genetics nurses, *see:* Registered nurses 303
Geochemists, *see:* Geoscientists 167
Geodesists, *see:* Geoscientists 167
Geodetic surveyors, *see:* Surveyors, cartographers,
photogrammetrists, and surveying technicians 130
Geographers, *see:* Social scientists, other 182
Geographic information specialists, *see:* Surveyors, cartographers,
photogrammetrists, and surveying technicians 130
Geological and geophysical oceanographers, *see:* Geoscientists 167
Geological engineers, *see:* Engineers 133
Geological technicians, *see:* Science technicians 185
Geologists, *see:* Geoscientists 167
Geomagnetists, *see:* Geoscientists 167
Geophysical prospecting surveyors, *see:* Surveyors, cartographers,
photogrammetrists, and surveying technicians 130
Geophysicists, *see:* Geoscientists 167
Geoscientists 167
Geotechnical engineers, *see:* Engineers 133
Geriatric aides, *see:* Nursing, psychiatric, and home health aides.........350
Geriatric nurses, *see:* Registered nurses 303
Gerontologists, *see:* Social scientists, other 182
Gerontology aides, *see:* Social and human service assistants 194
Gerontology social workers, *see:* Social workers 196
Geropsychologists, *see:* Psychologists 177
Glass installers, *see:* Glaziers 517
Glass installers and repairers, automotive, *see:*
Automotive body and related repairers 547
Glaziers 517
Gluing machine operators, *see:* Cementing and gluing machine
operators and tenders 670
Golf course architects, *see:* Landscape architects..................128
Government accountants and auditors, *see:* Accountants and auditors ... 70
Grader operators, *see:* Construction equipment operators.....507
Graders, agricultural products, *see:* Agricultural workers 485
Graduate TAs, *see:* Teachers—postsecondary 223
Graduate teaching assistants, *see:* Teachers—postsecondary.................223
Graphic artists, *see:* Artists and related workers 235
Graphic artists, *see:* Graphic designers..................................243
Graphic designers...243
Greenhouse managers, *see:* Farmers, ranchers, and
agricultural managers 40
Greenhouse workers, *see:* Agricultural workers 485
Greenskeepers, *see:* Grounds maintenance workers..............380
Grief counselors, *see:* Funeral directors 48
Grill cooks, *see:* Chefs, cooks, and food preparation workers 371
Grinding and polishing workers, hand.......................................672

Grinding, lapping, polishing, and buffing machine tool setters,
operators, and tenders, metal and plastic, *see:* Machine setters,
operators, and tenders—metal and plastic 589
Grips, *see:* Material moving occupations 650
Grocery baggers, *see:* Material moving occupations..............650
Groomers, *see:* Animal care and service workers 384
Grooms, *see:* Animal care and service workers.....................384
Ground controllers, *see:* Air traffic controllers 632
Grounds maintenance workers..380
Groundskeepers, *see:* Grounds maintenance workers 380
Groundskeeping workers, *see:* Grounds maintenance workers 380
Group exercise instructors, *see:* Fitness workers 392
Guards, prison, *see:* Correctional officers..............................357
Guards, security, *see:* Security guards and gaming
surveillance officers 368
Guidance counselors, *see:* Counselors...................................189
Guide interpreters, *see:* Interpreters and translators 263
Guitar repairers, *see:* Precision instrument and equipment repairers 575
Gynecologic sonographers, *see:* Diagnostic medical sonographers 322
Gynecologists, *see:* Physicians and surgeons 295
Gynecology nurses, *see:* Registered nurses 303

H

Hairdressers, *see:* Barbers, cosmetologists, and other personal
appearance workers..387
Hairstylists, *see:* Barbers, cosmetologists, and
other personal appearance workers 387
Hand compositors and typesetters, *see:* Prepress technicians
and workers 598
Hand packers and packagers, *see:* Material moving occupations..........650
Handymen, *see:* Building cleaning workers 378
Hangers, *see:* Drywall installers, ceiling tile installers, and tapers 511
Harbor pilots, *see:* Water transportation occupations 647
Hardware engineers, *see:* Engineers 133
Hazardous materials removal workers.......................................519
Head cooks, *see:* Chefs, cooks, and food preparation workers 371
Head hunters, *see:* Human resources, training, and
labor relations managers and specialists 50
Health and safety inspectors, occupational, *see:*
Occupational health and safety specialists and technicians 331
Health and safety specialists and technicians, occupational, *see:*
Occupational health and safety specialists and technicians 331
Health care administrators, *see:* Medical and health
services managers 59
Health care executives, *see:* Medical and health services managers 59
Health care interpreters and translators, *see:* Interpreters
and translators 263
Health educators...663
Health engineers, *see:* Engineers 133
Health information managers, *see:* Medical and health
services managers 59
Health information technicians, *see:* Medical records and
health information technicians 328
Health inspectors, *see:* Occupational health and safety specialists
and technicians 331
Health physicists, *see:* Occupational health and safety specialists
and technicians 331
Health psychologists, *see:* Psychologists...............................177
Health services managers, *see:* Medical and health
services managers 59
Hearing officers, *see:* Judges, magistrates, and other
judicial workers 201
Hearing therapists, *see:* Audiologists 278
Heat treating equipment setters, operators, and tenders, metal
and plastic, *see:* Machine setters, operators, and
tenders—metal and plastic 589
Heating, air-conditioning, and refrigeration engineers,
see: Engineers 133
Heating, air-conditioning, and refrigeration mechanics
and installers 562
Heating equipment technicians, *see:* Heating, air-conditioning,
and refrigeration mechanics and installers.........................562
Heavy truck and tractor-trailer drivers, *see:* Truck drivers and
driver/sales workers 640
Heavy vehicle and mobile equipment service technicians
and mechanics 555
Help-desk technicians, *see:* Computer support specialists and
systems administrators 113

Helpers—brickmasons, blockmasons, stonemasons, and tile and marble setters 667
Helpers—carpenters.............668
Helpers—cleaning, *see:* Building cleaning workers.............378
Helpers—electricians.............668
Helpers—extraction workers.............668
Helpers—installation, maintenance, and repair workers.............670
Helpers—maintenance, *see:* Building cleaning workers.............378
Helpers—painters, paperhangers, plasterers, and stucco masons.............668
Helpers—pipelayers, plumbers, pipefitters, and steamfitters, *see:* Pipelayers, plumbers, pipefitters, and steamfitters.............525
Helpers—pipelayers, plumbers, pipefitters, and steamfitters.............668
Helpers—production workers.............672
Helpers—roofers.............668
High school counselors, *see:* Counselors.............189
High school teachers, *see:* Teachers—preschool, kindergarten, elementary, middle, and secondary.............227
Highway maintenance workers.............668
Highway patrol officers, *see:* Police and detectives.............362
Histology technicians, *see:* Clinical laboratory technologists and technicians.............318
Historians, *see:* Social scientists, other.............182
HIV/AIDS nurses, *see:* Registered nurses.............303
Hoist and winch operators, *see:* Material moving occupations.............650
Holistic nurses, *see:* Registered nurses.............303
Home appliance repairers.............565
Home care aides, *see:* Personal and home care aides.............399
Home health aides, *see:* Nursing, psychiatric, and home health aides.............350
Home health nurses, *see:* Registered nurses.............303
Home inspectors, *see:* Construction and building inspectors.............504
Home management advisors, *see:* Farm and home management advisors.............663
Homemakers, *see:* Personal and home care aides.............399
Homeowner association managers, *see:* Property, real estate, and community association managers.............61
Horse breeders, *see:* Agricultural workers.............485
Horticultural specialty farmers, *see:* Farmers, ranchers, and agricultural managers.............40
Hospice nurses, *see:* Registered nurses.............303
Hospital attendants, *see:* Nursing, psychiatric, and home health aides.............350
Hostlers, *see:* Rail transportation occupations.............644
Hosts and hostesses, *see:* Food and beverage serving and related workers.............371
Hotel desk clerks, *see:* Hotel, motel, and resort desk clerks.............448
Hotel detectives, *see:* Private detectives and investigators.............366
Hotel, motel, and resort desk clerks.............448
Housekeepers, *see:* Lodging managers.............56
Housekeepers, *see:* Building cleaning workers.............378
Housing managers, *see:* Property, real estate, and community association managers.............61
Housing relocators, *see:* Property, real estate, and community association managers.............61
Human resources administrative assistants, *see:* Payroll and timekeeping clerks.............437
Human resources analysts, *see:* Human resources assistants, except payroll and timekeeping.............449
Human resources analysts, *see:* Management analysts.............92
Human resources assistants, *see:* Payroll and timekeeping clerks.............437
Human resources assistants, except payroll and timekeeping.............449
Human resources associates, *see:* Human resources assistants, except payroll and timekeeping.............449
Human resources clerks, *see:* Human resources assistants, except payroll and timekeeping.............449
Human resources consultants, *see:* Human resources, training, and labor relations managers and specialists.............50
Human resources coordinators, *see:* Human resources, training, and labor relations managers and specialists.............50
Human resources generalists, *see:* Human resources, training, and labor relations managers and specialists.............50
Human resources information system specialists, *see:* Human resources, training, and labor relations managers and specialists.............50
Human resources managers, *see:* Human resources, training, and labor relations managers and specialists.............50
Human resources recruiters, *see:* Human resources, training, and labor relations managers and specialists.............50
Human resources representatives, *see:* Payroll and timekeeping clerks.............437
Human resources supervisors, *see:* Human resources, training, and labor relations managers and specialists.............50
Human resources trainers, *see:* Human resources, training, and labor relations managers and specialists.............50
Human resources, training, and labor relations managers and specialists.............50
Human service workers, *see:* Social and human service assistants.............194
Human services managers, *see:* Human resources, training, and labor relations managers and specialists.............50
Hunters and trappers.............667
HVAC technicians, *see:* Sheet metal workers.............531
HVACR technicians, *see:* Heating, air-conditioning, and refrigeration mechanics and installers.............562
Hydraulic and pneumatic technicians, *see:* Heavy vehicle and mobile equipment service technicians and mechanics.............555
Hydrographic surveyors, *see:* Surveyors, cartographers, photogrammetrists, and surveying technicians.............130
Hydrologists, *see:* Environmental scientists and hydrologists.............164
Hygienists, dental, *see:* Dental hygienists.............320
Hygienists, industrial, *see:* Occupational health and safety specialists and technicians.............331

I

Identification clerks, *see:* Human resources assistants, except payroll and timekeeping.............449
Illustrators, *see:* Artists and related workers.............235
Image consultants, *see:* Public relations specialists.............271
Image designers, *see:* Desktop publishers.............477
Immigration and Naturalization Service (INS) agents and inspectors, *see:* Police and detectives.............362
Immigration inspectors, *see:* Police and detectives.............362
Immunohematology technologists, *see:* Clinical laboratory technologists and technicians.............318
Immunology technologists, *see:* Clinical laboratory technologists and technicians.............318
Independent adjusters, *see:* Claims adjusters, appraisers, examiners, and investigators.............80
Independent agents, *see:* Sales representatives, wholesale and manufacturing.............421
Independent insurance agents, *see:* Insurance sales agents.............411
Industrial accountants, *see:* Accountants and auditors.............70
Industrial designers, *see:* Commercial and industrial designers.............238
Industrial economists, *see:* Economists.............173
Industrial engineering technicians, *see:* Engineering technicians.............144
Industrial engineers, *see:* Engineers.............133
Industrial equipment technicians, *see:* Heavy vehicle and mobile equipment service technicians and mechanics.............555
Industrial hygienists, *see:* Occupational health and safety specialists and technicians.............331
Industrial machinery mechanics, *see:* Industrial machinery mechanics and maintenance workers.............567
Industrial machinery mechanics and maintenance workers.............567
Industrial millwrights, *see:* Millwrights.............573
Industrial-organizational psychologists, *see:* Psychologists.............177
Industrial photographers, *see:* Photographers.............269
Industrial production managers.............54
Industrial property managers, *see:* Administrative services managers.............25
Industrial relations directors, *see:* Human resources, training, and labor relations managers and specialists.............50
Industrial relations managers, *see:* Human resources, training, and labor relations managers and specialists.............50
Industrial therapists, *see:* Occupational therapists.............285
Industrial truck and tractor operators, *see:* Material moving occupations.............650
Infection control nurses, *see:* Registered nurses.............303
Information and record clerks, *see:*
    Brokerage clerks.............441
    Credit authorizers, checkers, and clerks.............442
    Customer service representatives.............444
    File clerks.............447
    Hotel, motel, and resort desk clerks.............448
    Human resources assistants, except payroll and timekeeping.............449
    Interviewers.............451
    Library assistants, clerical.............453
    Order clerks.............454
    Receptionists and information clerks.............455
    Reservation and transportation ticket agents and travel clerks.............457
Information architect librarians, *see:* Librarians.............214

Information architects, *see:* Librarians 214
Information clerks, *see:* Receptionists and information clerks 455
Information officers, *see:* Public relations specialists 271
Information processing workers, *see:* Data entry and
  information processing workers 475
Information security specialists, *see:* Computer support specialists
  and systems administrators 113
Information specialists, *see:* Public relations specialists 271
Information specialists, geographic, *see:* Surveyors, cartographers,
  photogrammetrists, and surveying technicians 130
Information systems managers, *see:* Computer and information
  systems managers 30
Information technology trainers, *see:* Human resources, training,
  and labor relations managers and specialists 50
Infusion nurses, *see:* Registered nurses 303
Inhalation therapists, *see:* Respiratory therapists 307
Inorganic chemists, *see:* Chemists and materials scientists 162
Inside order clerks, *see:* Order clerks 454
Inspectors, construction, *see:* Construction and building
  inspectors 504
Inspectors, customs, *see:* Police and detectives 362
Inspectors, farm products, *see:* Agricultural workers 485
Inspectors, fire, *see:* Fire fighting occupations 359
Inspectors, health, *see:* Occupational health and safety specialists
  and technicians 331
Inspectors, immigration, *see:* Police and detectives 362
Inspectors, occupational health and safety, *see:* Occupational health
  and safety specialists and technicians 331
Inspectors, safety, *see:* Occupational health and safety specialists
  and technicians 331
Inspectors, testers, sorters, samplers, and weighers 614
Inspectors, transportation, *see:* Transportation inspectors 673
Installers, automotive glass, *see:* Automotive body and
  related repairers 547
Institution and cafeteria cooks, *see:* Chefs, cooks, and
  food preparation workers 371
Instructional aides, *see:* Teacher assistants 219
Instructional assistants, *see:* Teacher assistants 219
Instructional coordinators 213
Instructional designers, *see:* Instructional coordinators 213
Instructional specialists, *see:* Instructional coordinators 213
Instructors, college and university, *see:* Teachers—Postsecondary ... 223
Instructors, sports, *see:* Athletes, coaches, umpires, and
  related workers 252
Instrumentation technicians, *see:* Precision instrument and
  equipment repairers 575
Insulation workers 522
Insurance adjusters, *see:* Claims adjusters, appraisers, examiners,
  and investigators 80
Insurance brokers, *see:* Insurance sales agents 411
Insurance claims and policy processing clerks 666
Insurance investigators, *see:* Claims adjusters, appraisers,
  examiners, and investigators 80
Insurance managers, *see:* Financial managers 42
Insurance sales agents 411
Insurance underwriters 88
Intercity bus drivers, *see:* Bus drivers 634
Interior decorators, *see:* Interior designers 245
Interior designers 245
Internal auditors, *see:* Accountants and auditors 70
International economists, *see:* Economists 173
International human resources managers, *see:* Human resources,
  training, and labor relations managers and specialists 50
Internet developers, *see:* Computer scientists and
  database administrators 114
Internists, general, *see:* Physicians and surgeons 295
Interpreters and translators 263
Interviewers 451
Investigators, corporate, *see:* Private detectives and investigators ... 366
Investigators, criminal, *see:* Police and detectives 362
Investigators, financial, *see:* Private detectives and investigators ... 366
Investigators, fire, *see:* Fire fighting occupations 359
Investigators, gaming, *see:* Security guards and gaming
  surveillance officers 368
Investigators, insurance, *see:* Claims Adjusters, appraisers, examiners,
  and investigators 80
Investigators, legal, *see:* Private detectives and investigators 366
Investigators, private, *see:* Private detectives and investigators 366

Investment analysts, *see:* Financial analysts and
  personal financial advisors 85
Ironworkers, *see:* Structural and reinforcing iron and
  metal workers 534

J

Jailers, *see:* Correctional officers 357
Janitors, *see:* Building cleaning workers 378
Jewelers and precious stone and metal workers 616
Job analysis managers, *see:* Human resources, training, and
  labor relations managers and specialists 50
Job analysts, *see:* Human resources, training, and
  labor relations managers and specialists 50
Job binding workers, *see:* Bookbinders and bindery workers 596
Job developers, *see:* Human resources, training, and
  labor relations managers and specialists 50
Job development specialists, *see:* Human resources, training,
  and labor relations managers and specialists 50
Job estimators, *see:* Cost estimators 83
Job opportunities in the Armed Forces 653
Job placement officers, *see:* Human resources, training, and
  labor relations managers and specialists 50
Job placement specialists, *see:* Human resources, training, and
  labor relations managers and specialists 50
Job printers, *see:* Prepress technicians and workers ....
Job service consultants, *see:* Human resources, training, and
  labor relations managers and specialists 50
Job service specialists, *see:* Human resources, training, and
  labor relations managers and specialists 50
Job training specialists, *see:* Human resources, training, and
  labor relations managers and specialists 50
Journalists, *see:* News analysts, reporters, and correspondents 267
Judges, magistrates, and other judicial workers 201
Judiciary interpreters and translators, *see:* Interpreters
  and translators 263
Junior high school teachers, *see:* Teachers—preschool, kindergarten,
  elementary, middle, and secondary 227
Justices of the peace, *see:* Judges, magistrates, and
  other judicial workers 201

K

Keepers, *see:* Animal care and service workers 384
Kennel attendants, *see:* Animal care and service workers 384
Key punch operator, *see:* Data entry and information
  processing workers 475
Keying machine operator, *see:* Data entry and
  information processing workers 475
Keypunch technicians, *see:* Data entry and
  information processing workers 475
Keypunchers, *see:* Data entry and information processing workers 475
Kindergarten teachers, *see:* Teachers—preschool,
  kindergarten, elementary, middle, and secondary 227
Knitting machine operators, textile, *see:* Textile, apparel, and
  furnishings occupations 602

L

Labor contractors, *see:* Human resources, training, and
  labor relations managers and specialists 50
Labor economists, *see:* Economists 173
Labor relations directors, *see:* Human resources, training, and
  labor relations managers and specialists 50
Labor relations managers, *see:* Human resources, training, and
  labor relations managers and specialists 50
Labor trainers, *see:* Human resources, training, and
  labor relations managers and specialists 50
Labor training managers, *see:* Human resources, training, and
  labor relations managers and specialists 50
Laboratory animal technologists and technicians, *see:*
  Veterinary technologists and technicians 341
Laboratory scientists, clinical, *see:* Clinical laboratory
  technologists and technicians 318
Laboratory technicians, clinical, *see:* Clinical laboratory
  technologists and technicians 318
Laboratory technicians, dental, *see:* Medical, dental, and
  ophthalmic laboratory technicians 619

Laboratory technicians, ophthalmic, *see:* Medical, dental, and ophthalmic laboratory technicians 619
Laboratory technologists, clinical, *see:* Clinical laboratory technologists and technicians 318
Laborers, *see:* Construction laborers 509
Laborers, agricultural, *see:* Agricultural workers 485
Laborers and freight, stock, and material movers, hand, *see:* Material moving occupations 650
LAN administrators, *see:* Computer support specialists and systems administrators 113
LAN managers, *see:* Computer and information systems managers 30
Land acquisition managers, *see:* Property, real estate, and community association managers 61
Land acquisition specialists, *see:* Property, real estate, and community association managers 61
Land agents, *see:* Property, real estate, and community association managers 61
Land agents, *see:* Real estate brokers and sales agents 414
Land surveyors, *see:* Surveyors, cartographers, photogrammetrists, and surveying technicians 130
Landlords, *see:* Property, real estate, and community association managers 61
Landscape architects 128
Landscape contractors, *see:* Grounds maintenance workers 380
Landscape designers, *see:* Grounds maintenance workers 380
Landscaping workers, *see:* Grounds maintenance workers 380
Language pathologists, *see:* Speech-language pathologists 309
Lathe and turning machine tool setters, operators, and tenders, metal and plastic, *see:* Machine setters, operators, and tenders—metal and plastic 589
Lathers, *see:* Drywall installers, ceiling tile installers, and tapers 511
Laundry and dry-cleaning workers, *see:* Textile, apparel, and furnishings occupations 602
Law clerks 663
Law librarians, *see:* Librarians 214
Lawyers 204
Layout artists, *see:* Desktop publishers 477
Lay-out workers, metal and plastic, *see:* Machine setters, operators, and tenders—metal and plastic 589
Lead abatement workers, *see:* Hazardous materials removal workers 519
Lease buyers, *see:* Property, real estate, and community association managers 61
Lease drivers, *see:* Taxi drivers and chauffeurs 637
Lease operators, *see:* Property, real estate, and community association managers 61
Leasing consultants, *see:* Real estate brokers and sales agents 414
Leasing managers, *see:* Property, real estate, and community association managers 61
Leather workers, *see:* Textile, apparel, and furnishings occupations 602
Legal assistants, *see:* Paralegals and legal assistants 207
Legal investigators, *see:* Private detectives and investigators 366
Legal nurse consultants, *see:* Registered nurses 303
Legal secretaries, *see:* Secretaries and administrative assistants 482
Legislators 661
Lens grinders and polishers, *see:* Medical, dental, and ophthalmic laboratory technician 619
Letterpress setters and set-up operators, *see:* Printing machine operators 600
Librarians 214
Library aides, *see:* Library assistants, clerical 453
Library assistants, clerical 453
Library binding workers, *see:* Bookbinders and bindery workers 596
Library clerks, *see:* Library assistants, clerical 453
Library media assistants, *see:* Library assistants, clerical 453
Library media specialists, *see:* Librarians 214
Library technical assistants, *see:* Library technicians 217
Library technicians 217
License clerks, *see:* Court, municipal, and license clerks 666
Licensed practical and licensed vocational nurses 326
Licensed vocational nurses, *see:* Licensed practical and licensed vocational nurses 326
Life skill counselors, *see:* Social and human service assistants 194
Lifeguards, ski patrol, and other recreational protective service workers 664
Lift truck operators, *see:* Material moving occupations 650
Light or delivery services truck drivers, *see:* Truck drivers and driver/sales workers 643

Limnologists, *see:* Biological scientists 150
Limousine drivers, *see:* Taxi drivers and chauffeurs 637
Line cooks, *see:* Chefs, cooks, and food preparation workers 371
Line erectors, *see:* Line installers and repairers 569
Line installers and repairers 569
Linguistic anthropologists, *see:* Social scientists, other 182
Liquid waste treatment plant and system operators, *see:* Water and liquid waste treatment plant and system operators 612
Literary interpreters, *see:* Interpreters and translators 263
Lithographers, *see:* Prepress technicians and workers 598
Livestock farmers, *see:* Farmers, ranchers, and agricultural managers 40
Load dispatchers, *see:* Power plant operators, distributors, and dispatchers 608
Loaders, tank car, truck, and ship, *see:* Material moving occupations 650
Loading machine operators, underground mining, *see:* Material moving occupations 650
Loan authorizers, *see:* Loan officers 90
Loan closers, *see:* Interviewers 451
Loan collection officers, *see:* Loan officers 90
Loan counselors 662
Loan interviewers and clerks, *see:* Interviewers 451
Loan officers 90
Loan processing clerks, *see:* Interviewers 451
Loan service clerks, *see:* Interviewers 451
Loan underwriters, *see:* Loan officers 90
Lobby attendants, *see:* Ushers, lobby attendants, and ticket takers 665
Lobbyists, *see:* Public relations specialists 271
Local account executive, *see:* Advertising sales agents 403
Local controllers, *see:* Air traffic controllers 632
Local operators, *see:* Communications equipment operators 471
Local transit bus drivers, *see:* Bus drivers 634
Local truck drivers, *see:* Truck drivers and driver/sales workers 640
Localization translators, *see:* Interpreters and translators 263
Locker room attendants, *see:* Locker room, coatroom, and dressing room attendants 665
Locksmiths and safe repairers 670
Locomotive engineers, *see:* Rail transportation occupations 644
Lodging managers 56
Log graders, *see:* Forest, conservation, and logging workers 490
Log sorters, markers, movers, debarkers, *see:* Forest, conservation, and logging workers 490
Logging equipment operators, *see:* Forest, conservation, and logging workers 490
Logisticians 662
Long distance operators, *see:* Communications equipment operators ... 471
Long haul truck drivers, *see:* Truck drivers and driver/sales workers ... 640
Longshoremen, *see:* Material moving occupations 650
Long-term care facility nurses, *see:* Registered nurses 303
Loss prevention agents, *see:* Private detectives and investigators 366
LPNs, *see:* Licensed practical and licensed vocational nurses 326
LVNs, *see:* Licensed practical and licensed vocational nurses 326
Lyricists, *see:* Writers and editors 275

M

Machine feeders and offbearers, *see:* Material moving occupations 650
Machine setters, operators, and tenders—metal and plastic 589
Machinery maintenance mechanics, *see:* Industrial machinery mechanics and maintenance workers 567
Machinists 587
Macroeconomists, *see:* Economists 173
Macromolecular chemists, *see:* Chemists and materials scientists 162
Magistrates, *see:* Judges, magistrates, and other judicial workers 201
Magnetic resonance imaging (MRI) technologists, *see:* Radiologic technologists and technicians 337
Maids and housekeeping cleaners, *see:* Building cleaning workers 378
Mail carriers, *see:* Postal Service workers 464
Mail clerks and mail machine operators, except Postal Service 666
Mail handlers, *see:* Postal Service workers 464
Mail machine operators, *see:* Mail clerks and mail machine operators, except Postal Service 666
Mail sorters, processors, and processing machine operators, *see:* Postal Service workers 464
Mail superintendents, *see:* Postmasters and mail superintendents 662
Maintenance and repair workers, general 572

Maintenance electricians, *see:* Electricians 513
Maintenance machinists, *see:* Machinists...................................587
Maintenance technicians, *see:* Broadcast and sound engineering
    technicians and radio operators 261
Maitre d's, *see:* Food and beverage serving and related workers 374
Management accountants, *see:* Accountants and auditors.....................70
Management analysts 92
Management analysts, *see:* Operations research analysts.....................121
Management assistants, *see:* Secretaries and
    administrative assistants 482
Management consultants, *see:* Management analysts 92
Management development specialists, *see:* Human resources,
    training, and labor relations managers and specialists.....................50
Management dietitians, *see:* Dietitians and nutritionists 284
Management of information systems directors, *see:* Computer
    and information systems managers 30
Management scientists, *see:* Operations research analysts...................121
Managers, *see:*
    Administrative services managers 25
    Advertising, marketing, promotions, public relations, and
      sales managers...27
    Computer and information systems managers 30
    Construction managers...32
    Engineering and natural sciences managers..............................38
    Farmers, ranchers, and agricultural managers 40
    Financial managers 42
    Food service managers 45
    Funeral directors 48
    Human resources, training, and labor relations managers
      and specialists 449
    Lodging managers...56
    Medical and health services managers 59
    Property, real estate, and community association managers................61
    Purchasing managers, buyers, and purchasing agents 64
    Top executives..67
Managers, support services, *see:* Office and administrative
    support worker supervisors and managers 479
Managing editors, *see:* Writers and editors 275
Manicurists, *see:* Barbers, cosmetologists, and other personal
    appearance workers..387
Manifold binding workers, *see:* Bookbinders and bindery workers.....596
Manpower development advisors, *see:* Human resources, training,
    and labor relations managers and specialists 50
Manpower development managers, *see:* Human resources, training,
    and labor relations managers and specialists 50
Manpower development specialists, *see:* Human resources, training,
    and labor relations managers and specialists 50
Manufactured building and mobile home installers............................670
Manufacturers' agents, *see:* Sales engineers..............................419
Manufacturers' representatives, *see:* Sales representatives,
    wholesale and manufacturing..421
Manufacturing opticians, *see:* Medical, dental, and
    ophthalmic laboratory technicians 619
Map editors, *see:* Surveyors, cartographers, photogrammetrists,
    and surveying technicians 130
Mapping technicians, *see:* Surveyors, cartographers,
    photogrammetrists, and surveying technicians 130
Marble setters, *see:* Carpet, floor, and tile installers and finishers.........499
Margin clerks, *see:* Brokerage clerks....................................441
Marine biologists, *see:* Biological scientists..............................150
Marine Corps, *see:* Job opportunities in the Armed Forces...................653
Marine equipment mechanics, *see:* Small engine mechanics...............558
Marine oilers, *see:* Water transportation occupations.......................647
Marine or hydrographic surveyors, *see:* Surveyors, cartographers,
    photogrammetrists, and surveying technicians 130
Mariners, *see:* Water transportation occupations...........................647
Marines, *see:* Job opportunities in the Armed Forces.......................653
Market and survey researchers..175
Market research analysts, *see:* Market and survey researchers 175
Market research managers, *see:* Advertising, marketing, promotions,
    public relations, and sales managers 27
Marketing coordinators, *see:* Public relations specialists....................271
Marketing managers, *see:* Advertising, marketing, promotions,
    public relations, and sales managers 27
Marketing research analysts, *see:* Market and survey researchers 175
Marketing specialists, *see:* Public relations specialists....................271
Marking and identification printing machine setters and set-up
    operators, *see:* Printing machine operators 600

Marriage and family therapists, *see:* Counselors...................189
Marshals, *see:* Correctional officers 357
Marshals and deputy marshals, U.S., *see:* Police and detectives..........362
Masons, *see:* Brickmasons, blockmasons, and stonemasons................495
Masons, *see:* Cement masons, concrete finishers,
    segmental pavers, and terrazzo workers 502
Massage therapists 344
Masseuses, *see:* Massage therapists....................................344
Masters, water transportation, *see:* Water transportation
    occupations..647
Material moving occupations...650
Material recording, scheduling, dispatching, and distributing
    occupations, except postal workers, *see:*
    Cargo and freight agents 459
    Couriers and messengers 460
    Dispatchers..461
    Meter readers, utilities..463
    Production, planning, and expediting clerks.............................466
    Shipping, receiving, and traffic clerks 467
    Stock clerks and order fillers...469
    Weighers, measurers, checkers, and samplers, recordkeeping............470
Materials engineers, *see:* Engineers....................................133
Materials scientists, *see:* Chemists and materials scientists 162
Mates, water transportation, *see:* Water transportation occupations 647
Mathematical statisticians, *see:* Statisticians...........................123
Mathematical technicians..663
Mathematicians 119
Measurers, *see:* Weighers, measurers, checkers, and
    samplers, recordkeeping...470
Meat cutters, *see:* Food processing occupations........................581
Mechanical door repairers..670
Mechanical drafters, *see:* Drafters....................................141
Mechanical engineering technicians, *see:* Engineering technicians......144
Mechanical engineers, *see:* Engineers.................................133
Mechanical inspectors, *see:* Construction and building inspectors........504
Mechanics and repairers, *see:*
    Aircraft and avionics equipment mechanics and service
      technicians...544
    Automotive body repairers and related workers 547
    Automotive service technicians and mechanics........................549
    Computer, automated teller, and office machine repairers.............536
    Diesel service technicians and mechanics 552
    Electrical and electronics installers and repairers.....................538
    Electronic home entertainment equipment installers and
      repairers...540
    Heavy vehicle and mobile equipment service technicians
      and mechanics 555
    Home appliance repairers...565
    Industrial machinery mechanics and maintenance workers............567
    Line installers and repairers..569
    Maintenance and repair workers, general 572
    Medical, dental, and ophthalmic laboratory technicians................619
    Millwrights..573
    Precision instrument and equipment repairers 575
    Radio and telecommunications equipment installers
      and repairers 542
    Small engine mechanics...558
Media aides, library, *see:* Library technicians 217
Media directors, *see:* Advertising, marketing, promotions,
    public relations, and sales managers 27
Media outreach specialists, *see:* Public relations specialists 271
Media planners, *see:* Public relations specialists 271
Media specialists, *see:* Public relations specialists.......................271
Mediators, *see:* Human resources, training, and labor relations
    managers and specialists 449
Mediators, *see:* Judges, magistrates, and other judicial workers...........201
Medical and health services managers...59
Medical appliance technicians, *see:* Medical, dental, and
    ophthalmic laboratory technicians 619
Medical assistants..347
Medical coders, *see:* Medical records and health information
    technicians..328
Medical, dental, and ophthalmic laboratory technicians 619
Medical equipment preparers...665
Medical equipment repairers, *see:* Precision instrument and
    equipment repairers 575
Medical geographers, *see:* Social scientists, other.......................182
Medical illustrators, *see:* Artists and related workers....................235

Medical interpreters and translators, *see:* Interpreters and translators 263

Medical laboratory technicians, *see:* Clinical laboratory technologists and technicians 318

Medical laboratory technologists, *see:* Clinical laboratory technologists and technicians 318

Medical record coders, *see:* Medical records and health information technicians 328

Medical records and health information technicians 328

Medical records technicians, *see:* Medical records and health information technicians 328

Medical scientists 156

Medical secretaries, *see:* Secretaries and administrative assistants 482

Medical social workers, *see:* Social workers 196

Medical technicians, *see:* Clinical laboratory technologists and technicians 318

Medical technologists, *see:* Clinical laboratory technologists and technicians 318

Medical transcriptionists 348

Medical writers, *see:* Writers and editors 275

Medical-surgical nurses, *see:* Registered nurses 303

Medicinal chemists, *see:* Chemists and materials scientists ... 162

Meeting and convention planners 95

Meeting directors, *see:* Meeting and convention planners 95

Meeting managers, *see:* Meeting and convention planners 95

Member services counselors, *see:* Reservation and transportation ticket agents and travel clerks 457

Mental health aides, *see:* Social and human service assistants 194

Mental health assistants, *see:* Nursing, psychiatric, and home health aides 350

Mental health counselors, *see:* Counselors 189

Mental health social workers, *see:* Social workers 196

Merchandise displayers and window trimmers 663

Merchandise distributors, *see:* Stock clerks and order fillers ... 469

Merchandise managers, *see:* Purchasing managers, buyers, and purchasing agents 64

Messengers, *see:* Couriers and messengers 460

Metal-refining furnace operators and tenders, *see:* Machine setters, operators, and tenders—metal and plastic 589

Metallurgical engineers, *see:* Engineers 133

Metalworking machine operators, *see:* Machine setters, operators, and tenders—metal and plastic 589

Meteorologists, *see:* Atmospheric scientists 159

Meter readers, utilities 463

Microbiologists, *see:* Biological scientists 150

Microbiology technologists, *see:* Clinical laboratory technologists and technicians 318

Microeconomists, *see:* Economists 173

Middle school teachers, *see:* Teachers—preschool, kindergarten, elementary, middle, and secondary 227

Midwives, certified nurse, *see:* Registered nurses 303

Military occupations, *see:* Job opportunities in the Armed Forces 653

Milling and planing machine setters, operators, and tenders, metal and plastic, *see:* Machine setters, operators, and tenders—metal and plastic 589

Millwrights 573

Mine cutting and channeling machine operators 668

Mine examiners, *see:* Occupational health and safety specialists and technicians 331

Mine safety engineers, *see:* Engineers 133

Mineralogists, *see:* Geoscientists 167

Mining and geological engineers, including mining safety engineers, *see:* Engineers 133

Mining machine operators, *see:* Continuous mining machine operators 667

Ministers, Protestant, *see:* Clergy 662

Mixing and blending machine setters, operators, and tenders 672

Mobile heavy equipment mechanics and service technicians, *see:* Heavy vehicle and mobile equipment service technicians and mechanics 555

Mobile home installers, *see:* Manufactured building and mobile home installers 670

Model makers and patternmakers, *see:* Woodworkers 606

Model makers, metal and plastic, *see:* Machine setters, operators, and tenders—metal and plastic 589

Models, *see:* Demonstrators, product promoters, and models 408

Mold and model makers, *see:* Jewelers and precious stone and metal workers 616

Molders, shapers, and casters, except metal and plastic 672

Molding, coremaking, and casting machine setters, operators, and tenders, metal and plastic, *see:* Machine setters, operators, and tenders—metal and plastic 589

Monetary economists, *see:* Economists 173

Mortgage bankers, *see:* Loan officers 90

Mortgage brokers, *see:* Loan officers 90

Mortgage loan officers, *see:* Loan officers 90

Morticians, *see:* Funeral directors 48

Motel desk clerks, *see:* Hotel, motel, and resort desk clerks 448

Motion picture camera operators, *see:* Television, video, and motion picture camera operators and editors 274

Motion picture projectionists 665

Motorboat mechanics, *see:* Small engine mechanics 558

Motorboat operators, *see:* Water transportation occupations 647

Motorcoach drivers, *see:* Bus drivers 634

Motorcycle mechanics, *see:* Small engine mechanics 558

Multimedia artists, *see:* Artists and related workers 235

Multiple machine tool setters, operators, and tenders, metal and plastic, *see:* Machine setters, operators, and tenders—metal and plastic 589

Municipal clerks, *see:* Court, municipal, and license clerks 666

Municipal court judges, *see:* Judges, magistrates, and other judicial workers 201

Museum directors, *see:* Archivists, curators, and museum technicians 210

Museum technicians, *see:* Archivists, curators, and museum technicians 210

Music arrangers, *see:* Musicians, singers, and related workers 257

Music conductors, *see:* Musicians, singers, and related workers 257

Music directors, *see:* Musicians, singers, and related workers 257

Music instructors, *see:* Teachers—self-enrichment education 231

Musical instrument repairers and tuners, *see:* Precision instrument and equipment repairers 575

Musicians, singers, and related workers 257

N

Nail care artists, *see:* Barbers, cosmetologists, and other personal appearance workers 387

Nail technicians, *see:* Barbers, cosmetologists, and other personal appearance workers 387

Nannies, *see:* Child care workers 389

National account executive, *see:* Advertising sales agents 403

Natural sciences managers, *see:* Engineering and natural sciences managers 38

Navy, *see:* Job opportunities in the Armed Forces 653

Neonatal nurses, *see:* Registered nurses 303

Nephrology nurses, *see:* Registered nurses 303

Network and computer systems administrators, *see:* Computer support specialists and systems administrators 113

Network systems and data communications analysts, *see:* Computer scientists and database administrators 107

Neuropsychologists, *see:* Psychologists 177

Neuroscience nurses, *see:* Registered nurses 303

Neurosonographers, *see:* Diagnostic medical sonographers 322

New account clerks 666

News analysts, reporters, and correspondents 267

News anchors, *see:* News analysts, reporters, and correspondents 267

News camera operators , *see:* Television, video, and motion picture camera operators and editors 274

News photographers , *see:* Photographers 269

News vendors, *see:* Door-to-door sales workers, news and street vendors, and related workers 665

News writers, *see:* News analysts, reporters, and correspondents 267

Newscasters, *see:* News analysts, reporters, and correspondents 267

Newsletter writers, *see:* Writers and editors 282

911 operators, *see:* Dispatchers 461

Notereaders, *see:* Data entry and information processing workers 475

Nuclear engineers, *see:* Engineers 133

Nuclear medicine technologists 330

Nuclear power reactor operators, *see:* Power plant operators, distributors, and dispatchers 608

Nuclear technicians, *see:* Science technicians 185

Numerical tool and process control programmers, *see:* Computer control programmers and operators 585

Nurse administrators, *see:* Registered nurses 303

Nurse educators, *see:* Registered nurses 303

Nurse informaticists, *see:* Registered nurses 303
Nurse practitioners, *see:* Registered nurses 303
Nurse specialists, clinical, *see:* Registered nurses 303
Nurse-midwives, certified, *see:* Registered nurses 303
Nursery and greenhouse managers, *see:* Farmers, ranchers,
    and agricultural managers 40
Nursery workers, *see:* Agricultural workers 485
Nurses, licensed practical, *see:* Licensed practical and
    licensed vocational nurses 326
Nurses, licensed vocational, *see:* Licensed practical and
    licensed vocational nurses 326
Nurses, registered, *see:* Registered nurses 303
Nursing aides, *see:* Nursing, psychiatric, and home health aides 350
Nursing assistants, *see:* Nursing, psychiatric, and home
    health aides 350
Nursing assistants, certified, *see:* Nursing, psychiatric, and
    home health aides 350
Nursing, psychiatric, and home health aides 350
Nutrition directors, *see:* Dietitians and nutritionists 284
Nutritionists, *see:* Dietitians and nutritionists 284

O

Obstetric sonographers, *see:* Diagnostic medical sonographers 322
Obstetricians and gynecologists, *see:* Physicians and surgeons 295
Occupational analysts, *see:* Human resources assistants,
    except payroll and timekeeping 449
Occupational health and safety inspectors, *see:*
    Occupational health and safety specialists and technicians 331
Occupational health and safety specialists and technicians 331
Occupational health nurses, *see:* Registered nurses 303
Occupational social workers, *see:* Social workers 196
Occupational therapist assistants and aides 353
Occupational therapists 285
Oceanographers, *see:* Geoscientists 167
ODs, *see:* Optometrists 287
Office administrative assistants, *see:* Secretaries and
    administrative assistants 482
Office administrators, *see:* Office and administrative support
    worker supervisors and managers 479
Office administrators, *see:* Secretaries and administrative
    assistants 482
Office aides, *see:* Office clerks, general 481
Office and administrative support worker supervisors and
    managers 479
Office assistants, *see:* Office clerks, general 481
Office assistants, *see:* Secretaries and administrative assistants 482
Office clerks, general 481
Office helpers, *see:* Office clerks, general 481
Office machine and cash register servicers, *see:*
    Computer, automated teller, and office machine repairers 536
Office machine operators, except computer 666
Office managers, *see:* Administrative services managers 25
Office managers, *see:* Office and administrative support
    worker supervisors and managers 479
Office managers, *see:* Secretaries and administrative assistants 482
Office specialists, *see:* Secretaries and administrative assistants 482
Office support secretaries, *see:* Secretaries and administrative
    assistants 482
Office support team leaders, *see:* Office and administrative
    support worker supervisors and managers 479
Officers, correctional, *see:* Correctional officers 357
Officers, detention, *see:* Correctional officers 357
Officers, gaming surveillance, *see:* Security guards and
    gaming surveillance officers 368
Officers, highway patrol, *see:* Police and detectives 362
Officers, loan, *see:* Loan officers 90
Officers, merchant marine, *see:* Water transportation occupations 647
Officers, military, *see:* Job opportunities in the Armed Forces 653
Officers, police, *see:* Police and detectives 362
Officers, security, *see:* Security guards and gaming surveillance
    officers 368
Officials, sports, *see:* Athletes, coaches, umpires, and
    related workers 252
Offset lithographic press setters and set-up operators, *see:*
    Printing machine operators 600
Oilers, marine, *see:* Water transportation occupations 647

Older worker specialists, *see:* Human resources, training, and
    labor relations managers and specialists 50
Oncology nurses, *see:* Registered nurses 303
Operating engineers, *see:* Construction equipment operators 507
Operating room technicians, *see:* Surgical technologists 339
Operational meteorologists, *see:* Atmospheric scientists 159
Operations analysts, *see:* Operations research analysts 121
Operations managers, *see:* Top executives 67
Operations managers, *see:* Office and administrative support
    worker supervisors and managers 479
Operations research analysts 121
Operators, auxiliary equipment, *see:* Power plant operators,
    distributors, and dispatchers 608
Operators, boiler, *see:* Stationary engineers and boiler operators 610
Operators, computer control, *see:* Computer control programmers
    and operators 585
Operators, control room, *see:* Power plant operators, distributors,
    and dispatchers 608
Operators, crane and tower, *see:* Material moving occupations 650
Operators, dinkey, *see:* Rail transportation occupations 644
Operators, dredge, excavating, and loading machine, *see:*
    Material moving occupations 650
Operators, fork lift, *see:* Material moving occupations 650
Operators, gas compressor and gas pumping station, *see:*
    Material moving occupations 650
Operators, hoist and winch, *see:* Material moving occupations 650
Operators, industrial truck and tractor, *see:* Material moving
    occupations 650
Operators, motorboat, *see:* Water transportation occupations 647
Operators, photographic processing machine, *see:*
    Photographic process workers and processing machine operators 625
Operators, power plant, *see:* Power plant operators, distributors,
    and dispatchers 608
Operators, pumping station, *see:* Material moving occupations 650
Operators, railroad brake, signal, and switch, *see:*
    Rail transportation occupations 644
Operators, reactor, *see:* Power plant operators, distributors,
    and dispatchers 608
Operators, semiconductor processing, *see:* Semiconductor
    processors 626
Operators, shuttle car, *see:* Material moving occupations 650
Operators, subway and streetcar, *see:* Rail transportation
    occupations 644
Operators, switchboard, *see:* Power plant operators, distributors,
    and dispatchers 608
Operators, systems, *see:* Power plant operators, distributors,
    and dispatchers 608
Operators, television, video, and motion picture camera, *see:*
    Television, video, and motion picture camera operators
    and editors 274
Operators, wastewater treatment plant, *see:* Water and liquid
    waste treatment plant and system operators 612
Operators, water treatment plant, *see:* Water and liquid waste
    treatment plant and system operators 612
Ophthalmic laboratory technicians, *see:* Medical, dental, and
    ophthalmic laboratory technicians 619
Ophthalmic medical assistants, *see:* Medical assistants 347
Ophthalmic nurses, *see:* Registered nurses 303
Ophthalmologic sonographers, *see:* Diagnostic medical
    sonographers 322
Ophthalmologists, *see:* Physicians and surgeons 295
Optical goods workers, *see:* Medical, dental, and ophthalmic
    laboratory technicians 619
Optical instrument assemblers, *see:* Medical, dental, and
    ophthalmic laboratory technicians 619
Optical mechanics, *see:* Medical, dental, and ophthalmic
    laboratory technicians 619
Opticians, dispensing 334
Opticians, manufacturing, *see:* Medical, dental, and
    ophthalmic laboratory technicians 619
Optometrists 287
Oral and maxillofacial radiologists, *see:* Dentists 282
Oral and maxillofacial surgeons, *see:* Dentists 282
Oral hygienists, *see:* Dental hygienists 320
Oral pathologists, *see:* Dentists 282
Order clerks 454
Order-entry clerks, *see:* Order clerks 454
Order fillers, *see:* Material moving occupations 650

Order fillers, *see:* Stock clerks and order fillers 469
Order processors, *see:* Order clerks 454
Order takers, *see:* Order clerks 454
Orderlies, *see:* Nursing, psychiatric, and home health aides 350
Ordnance handling experts, *see:* Explosives workers, ordnance handling experts, and blasters 667
Organic chemists, *see:* Chemists and materials scientists 162
Organizational development consultants, *see:* Human resources, training, and labor relations managers and specialists 50
Organizational development consultants, *see:* Management analysts 92
Organizational development managers, *see:* Human resources, training, and labor relations managers and specialists 50
Organizational economists, *see:* Economists 173
Ornamental ironworkers, *see:* Structural and reinforcing iron and metal workers 534
Orthodontists, *see:* Dentists 282
Orthopedic nurses, *see:* Registered nurses 303
Orthotics technicians, *see:* Medical, dental, and ophthalmic laboratory technicians 619
Orthotists and prosthetists 663
Osteopathic physicians and surgeons, *see:* Physicians and surgeons 295
Otorhinolaryngology nurses, *see:* Registered nurses 303
Outdoor power equipment mechanics, *see:* Small engine mechanics 558
Outside order clerks, *see:* Order clerks 454
Oxy-gas cutters, *see:* Welding, soldering, and brazing workers 594
Oxygen therapists, *see:* Respiratory therapists 307

P

Packaging and filling machine operators and tenders 672
Packers and packagers, hand, *see:* Material moving occupations 650
Painters, *see:* Artists and related workers 235
Painters and paperhangers 523
Painters, construction and maintenance, *see:* Painters and paperhangers 523
Painting and coating workers, except construction and maintenance 622
Painting, coating, and decorating workers, *see:* Painting and coating workers, except construction and maintenance 622
Painting restorers, *see:* Artists and related workers 235
Paleomagnetists, *see:* Geoscientists 167
Paleontologists, *see:* Geoscientists 167
Palliative care nurses, *see:* Registered nurses 303
Pamphlet binding workers, *see:* Bookbinders and bindery workers 596
Paper coating machine operators, *see:* Painting and coating workers, except construction and maintenance 622
Paper goods machine setters, operators, and tenders 589
Paperhangers, *see:* Painters and paperhangers 523
Paraeducators, *see:* Teacher assistants 219
Paralegals and legal assistants 209
Paramedics, *see:* Emergency medical technicians and paramedics 324
Paraprofessionals, education, *see:* Teacher assistants 219
Paratransit drivers, *see:* Taxi drivers and chauffeurs 637
Parking enforcement workers 665
Parking lot attendants 673
Parole officers, *see:* Probation officers and correctional treatment specialists 192
Parts salespersons 666
Passenger booking clerks, *see:* Reservation and transportation ticket agents and travel clerks 457
Passenger rate clerks, *see:* Reservation and transportation ticket agents and travel clerks 457
Passenger service agents, *see:* Reservation and transportation ticket agents and travel clerks 457
Paste-up workers, *see:* Prepress technicians and workers 598
Pathologists, *see:* Physicians and surgeons 295
Pathologists, oral, *see:* Dentists 282
Pathologists, speech-language, *see:* Speech-language pathologists 309
Patient representatives, *see:* Interviewers 451
Patternmakers, fabric and apparel, *see:* Textile, apparel, and furnishings occupations 602
Patternmakers, metal and plastic, *see:* Machine setters, operators, and tenders—metal and plastic 589
Paving equipment operators, *see:* Construction equipment operators 507
Paymasters, *see:* Payroll and timekeeping clerks 437
Payroll administrators, *see:* Payroll and timekeeping clerks 437
Payroll analysts, *see:* Payroll and timekeeping clerks 437
Payroll and benefits specialists, *see:* Payroll and timekeeping clerks 437
Payroll and timekeeping clerks 437
Payroll assistants, *see:* Payroll and timekeeping clerks 437
Payroll bookkeepers, *see:* Payroll and timekeeping clerks 437
Payroll clerks, *see:* Payroll and timekeeping clerks 437
Payroll coordinators, *see:* Payroll and timekeeping clerks 437
Payroll representatives, *see:* Payroll and timekeeping clerks 437
Payroll secretaries, *see:* Payroll and timekeeping clerks 437
Payroll specialists, *see:* Payroll and timekeeping clerks 437
Payroll technicians, *see:* Payroll and timekeeping clerks 437
PBX installers and repairers, *see:* Radio and telecommunications equipment installers and repairers 542
Pediatric dentists, *see:* Dentists 282
Pediatric nurses, *see:* Registered nurses 303
Pediatricians, *see:* Physicians and surgeons 295
Pedicurists, *see:* Barbers, cosmetologists, and other personal appearance workers 387
Perianesthesia nurses, *see:* Registered nurses 303
Periodontists, *see:* Dentists 282
Perioperative nurses, *see:* Registered nurses 303
Personal and home care aides 399
Personal appearance workers, *see:* Barbers, cosmetologists, and other personal appearance workers 387
Personal attendants, *see:* Personal and home care aides 399
Personal care aides, *see:* Personal and home care aides 399
Personal chefs, *see:* Chefs, cooks, and food preparation workers 371
Personal financial advisors, *see:* Financial analysts and personal financial advisors 85
Personal secretaries, *see:* Secretaries and administrative assistants 482
Personal trainers, *see:* Fitness workers 392
Personnel administrators, *see:* Human resources, training, and labor relations managers and specialists 50
Personnel analysts, *see:* Human resources assistants, except payroll and timekeeping 449
Personnel assistants, *see:* Human resources assistants, except payroll and timekeeping 449
Personnel associates, *see:* Human resources assistants, except payroll and timekeeping 449
Personnel clerks, *see:* Human resources assistants, except payroll and timekeeping 449
Personnel consultants, *see:* Human resources, training, and labor relations managers and specialists 50
Personnel coordinators, *see:* Human resources, training, and labor relations managers and specialists 50
Personnel development specialists, *see:* Human resources, training, and labor relations managers and specialists 50
Personnel directors, *see:* Human resources, training, and labor relations managers and specialists 50
Personnel managers, *see:* Human resources, training, and labor relations managers and specialists 50
Personnel officers, *see:* Human resources assistants, except payroll and timekeeping 449
Personnel officers, *see:* Human resources, training, and labor relations managers and specialists 50
Personnel recruiters, *see:* Human resources, training, and labor relations managers and specialists 50
Personnel services specialists, *see:* Human resources assistants, except payroll and timekeeping 449
Personnel technicians, *see:* Human resources assistants, except payroll and timekeeping 449
Personnel training officers, *see:* Human resources, training, and labor relations managers and specialists 50
Pest control technicians, *see:* Pest control workers 382
Pest control workers 382
Pesticide handlers, sprayers, and applicators, vegetation, *see:* Grounds maintenance workers 380
Petroleum engineers, *see:* Engineers 133
Petroleum geologists, *see:* Geoscientists 167
Petroleum pump system operators, refinery operators, and guagers 672
Petroleum technicians, *see:* Science technicians 185
Pharmacists 289
Pharmacy aides 354
Pharmacy technicians 336
Phlebotomists, *see:* Clinical laboratory technologists and technicians 318

Photoengravers, *see:* Prepress technicians and workers 598
Photogrammetrists, *see:* Surveyors, cartographers, photogrammetrists, and surveying technicians 130
Photographers 269
Photographic equipment repairers, *see:* Precision instrument and equipment repairers 575
Photographic process workers and processing machine operators 625
Photographic retouchers, *see:* Photographic process workers and processing machine operators 625
Photographic spotters, *see:* Photographic process workers and processing machine operators 625
Photojournalists, *see:* Photographers 269
Physical chemists, *see:* Chemists and materials scientists 162
Physical geographers, *see:* Social scientists, other 182
Physical metallurgical engineers, *see:* Engineers 133
Physical meteorologists, *see:* Atmospheric scientists 159
Physical oceanographers, *see:* Geoscientists 167
Physical therapist assistants and aides 356
Physical therapists 292
Physician assistants 293
Physicians and surgeons 295
Physicians, chiropractic, *see:* Chiropractors 280
Physicists and astronomers 170
Physiologists, *see:* Biological scientists 150
Piano repairers, *see:* Precision instrument and equipment repairers 575
Pilates instructors, *see:* Fitness workers 392
Pile driver operators, *see:* Construction equipment operators 507
Pilots, *see:* Aircraft pilots and flight engineers 629
Pilots, water transportation, *see:* Water transportation occupations 647
Pipe organ repairers, *see:* Precision instrument and equipment repairers 575
Pipefitters, *see:* Pipelayers, plumbers, pipefitters, and steamfitters 525
Pipelayers, plumbers, pipefitters, and steamfitters 525
Placement counselors, *see:* Human resources, training, and labor relations managers and specialists 50
Placement directors, *see:* Human resources, training, and labor relations managers and specialists 50
Placement officers, *see:* Human resources, training, and labor relations managers and specialists 50
Placement specialists, *see:* Human resources, training, and labor relations managers and specialists 50
Plan examiners, *see:* Construction and building inspectors 504
Planners, financial, *see:* Financial analysts and personal financial advisors 85
Planners, urban and regional, *see:* Urban and regional planners 180
Plant managers, *see:* Industrial production managers 54
Plant operators, wastewater treatment, *see:* Water and liquid waste treatment plant and system operators 612
Plant operators, water treatment, *see:* Water and liquid waste treatment plant and system operators 612
Plant scientists, *see:* Agricultural and food scientists 147
Plasma cutters, *see:* Welding, soldering, and brazing workers 594
Plasterers and stucco masons 528
Plastics-working machine operators, *see:* Machine setters, operators, and tenders—metal and plastic 589
Plate finishers, *see:* Prepress technicians and workers 598
Platemakers, *see:* Prepress technicians and workers 598
Plating and coating machine setters, operators, and tenders, metal and plastic, *see:* Machine setters, operators, and tenders—metal and plastic 589
Playwrights, *see:* Writers and editors 275
Plumbers, *see:* Pipelayers, plumbers, pipefitters, and steamfitters 525
Plumbing inspectors, *see:* Construction and building inspectors 504
Podiatric medical assistants, *see:* Medical assistants 347
Podiatrists 298
Poets, *see:* Writers and editors 275
Police and detectives 369
Police, fire, and ambulance dispatchers, *see:* Dispatchers 461
Police officers, *see:* Police and detectives 362
Police, transit and railroad, *see:* Police and detectives 362
Policy analysts, *see:* Operations research analysts 121
Polishers, *see:* Jewelers and precious stone and metal workers 616
Polishing workers, hand, *see:* Grinding and polishing workers, hand 672
Political analysts, *see:* Social scientists, other 182
Political geographers, *see:* Social scientists, other 182
Political scientists, *see:* Social scientists, other 182
Portrait photographers, *see:* Photographers 269
Position classifiers, *see:* Human resources, training, and labor relations managers and specialists 50
Postal Service workers 464
Postal workers, *see:* Postal Service workers 464
Posting clerks, *see:* Billing and posting clerks and machine operators 432
Postmasters and mail superintendents 662
Postsecondary career-technical teachers, *see:* Teachers—postsecondary 223
Postsecondary vocational-technical education teachers, *see:* Teachers— postsecondary 223
Poultry cutters and trimmers, *see:* Food processing occupations 581
Poultry farmers, *see:* Farmers, ranchers, and agricultural managers 40
Poultry scientists, *see:* Agricultural and food scientists 147
Pourers and casters, metal, *see:* Machine setters, operators, and tenders—metal and plastic 589
Power dispatchers, *see:* Power plant operators, distributors, and dispatchers 608
Power distributors, *see:* Power plant operators, distributors, and dispatchers 608
Power plant mechanics, *see:* Aircraft and avionics equipment mechanics and service technicians 544
Power plant operators, *see:* Power plant operators, distributors, and dispatchers 608
Power plant operators, distributors, and dispatchers 608
Power reactor operators, *see:* Power plant operators, distributors, and dispatchers 608
Power tool repairers, *see:* Electrical and electronics installers and repairers 538
Power transformer repairers, *see:* Electrical and electronics installers and repairers 538
Powerhouse electricians, *see:* Electrical and electronics installers and repairers 538
Practical nurses, licensed, *see:* Licensed practical and licensed vocational nurses 326
Practitioners, family and general, *see:* Physicians and surgeons 295
Practitioners, nurse, *see:* Registered nurses 303
Precious stone and metal workers, *see:* Jewelers and precious stone and metal workers 616
Precision instrument and equipment repairers 576
Precision printing workers, *see:* Printing machine operators 600
Prepress technicians and workers 598
Preschool teachers, *see:* Teachers—preschool, kindergarten, elementary, middle, and secondary 227
Presidents, *see:* Top executives 67
Press agents, *see:* Public relations specialists 271
Press relations specialists, *see:* Public relations specialists 271
Press secretaries, *see:* Public relations specialists 271
Pressers, textile, garment, and related materials, *see:* Textile, apparel, and furnishings occupations 602
Pretrial services officers, *see:* Probation officers and correctional treatment specialists 192
Priests, *see:* Clergy 662
Principal secretary, *see:* Secretaries and administrative assistants 482
Principals, *see:* Education administrators 34
Printing machine operators 600
Printing press machine operators and tenders, *see:* Printing machine operators 600
Printmakers, *see:* Artists and related workers 235
Prison guards, *see:* Correctional officers 357
Private accountants, *see:* Accountants and auditors 70
Private bankers, *see:* Securities, commodities, and financial services sales agents 426
Private detectives and investigators 366
Private household cooks, *see:* Chefs, cooks, and food preparation workers 371
Private investigators, *see:* Private detectives and investigators 366
Probation officers and correctional treatment specialists 192
Process metallurgical engineers, *see:* Engineers 133
Process piping or pipeline drafters, *see:* Drafters 141
Process technicians, *see:* Science technicians 185
Procurement clerks 438
Procurement technicians, *see:* Cost estimators 83
Producers, *see:* Actors, producers, and directors 249
Product designers, *see:* Commercial and industrial designers 238
Product development managers, *see:* Advertising, marketing, promotions, public relations, and sales managers 27

Product promoters, *see:* Demonstrators, product promoters, and models 408
Production and planning clerks, *see:* Production, planning, and expediting clerks 466
Production assistants, *see:* Writers and editors 275
Production cost estimators, *see:* Cost estimators 83
Production machinists, *see:* Machinists 587
Production managers, *see:* Industrial production managers 54
Production, planning, and expediting clerks 466
Professional athletes, *see:* Athletes, coaches, umpires, and related workers 252
Professional property managers, *see:* Property, real estate, and community association managers 61
Professional scouts, *see:* Athletes, coaches, umpires, and related workers 252
Professors, *see:* Teachers—postsecondary 223
Programmer-analysts, *see:* Computer programmers 104
Programmer-analysts, *see:* Computer systems analysts 116
Programmers, computer, *see:* Computer programmers 104
Programmers, computer control, *see:* Computer control programmers and operators 585
Programmers, numerical tool and process control, *see:* Computer control programmers and operators 585
Project control specialists, *see:* Cost estimators 83
Project managers, *see:* Computer and information systems managers ... 30
Project managers, *see:* Construction managers 32
Project managers, *see:* Cost estimators 83
Promoters, *see:* Public relations specialists 271
Promotions managers, *see:* Advertising, marketing, promotions, public relations, and sales managers 27
Promotions specialists, *see:* Public relations specialists 271
Proofreaders and copy markers 666
Property custodian, *see:* Stock clerks and order fillers 469
Property disposal specialists, *see:* Administrative services managers 25
Property managers, *see:* Property, real estate, and community association managers 61
Property, real estate, and community association managers 61
Prosecutors, government, *see:* Lawyers 204
Prosthetics technicians, *see:* Medical, dental, and ophthalmic laboratory technicians 619
Prosthetists, *see:* Orthotists and prosthetists 663
Prosthodontists, *see:* Dentists 282
Protestant ministers *see:* Clergy 662
Provosts, *see:* Education administrators 34
Psychiatric aides, *see:* Nursing, psychiatric, and home health aides 350
Psychiatric nurses, *see:* Registered nurses 303
Psychiatric nursing assistants, *see:* Nursing, psychiatric, and home health aides 350
Psychiatric technicians 663
Psychiatrists, *see:* Physicians and surgeons 295
Psychologists 177
Public accountants, *see:* Accountants and auditors 70
Public address system announcers, *see:* Announcers 259
Public adjusters, *see:* Claims adjusters, appraisers, examiners, and investigators 80
Public affairs specialists, *see:* Public relations specialists 271
Public defenders, *see:* Lawyers 204
Public finance economists, *see:* Economists 173
Public health dentists, *see:* Dentists 282
Public health dietitians, *see:* Dietitians and nutritionists 284
Public health social workers, *see:* Social workers 196
Public housing managers, *see:* Property, real estate, and community association managers 61
Public relations consultants, *see:* Public relations specialists 271
Public relations coordinators, *see:* Public relations specialists 271
Public relations managers, *see:* Advertising, marketing, promotions, public relations, and sales managers 27
Public relations representatives, *see:* Public relations specialists .. 271
Public relations specialists 271
Public safety dispatchers, *see:* Dispatchers 461
Public works inspectors, *see:* Construction and building inspectors .. 504
Publication assistants, *see:* Writers and editors 275
Publications specialists, *see:* Desktop publishers 477
Publicists, *see:* Public relations specialists 271
Publicity agents, *see:* Public relations specialists 271
Publicity experts, *see:* Public relations specialists 271

Publicity writers, *see:* Public relations specialists 271
Pulmonary function technologists, *see:* Cardiovascular technologists and technicians 316
Pump operators, except wellhead pumpers, *see:* Material moving occupations 650
Pumping station operators, *see:* Material moving occupations 650
Punch card operator, *see:* Data entry and information processing workers 475
Purchase-and-sales clerks, *see:* Brokerage clerks 441
Purchasing agents, *see:* Purchasing managers, buyers, and purchasing agents 64
Purchasing clerks, *see:* Procurement clerks 438
Purchasing directors, *see:* Purchasing managers, buyers, and purchasing agents 64
Purchasing managers, buyers, and purchasing agents 64
Purchasing technicians, *see:* Procurement clerks 438

Q

QMEDs, *see:* Water transportation occupations 647
Qualified members of the engine department, *see:* Water transportation occupations 647
Quality control inspectors, *see:* Inspectors, testers, sorters, samplers, and weighers 614

R

Rabbis, *see:* Clergy 662
Radar controllers, *see:* Air traffic controllers 632
Radiation protection technicians, *see:* Hazardous materials removal workers 519
Radiation therapists 300
Radio and telecommunications equipment installers and repairers 516
Radio announcers, *see:* Announcers 259
Radio mechanics, *see:* Radio and telecommunications equipment installers and repairers 542
Radio operators, *see:* Broadcast and sound engineering technicians and radio operators 261
Radiographers, *see:* Radiologic technologists and technicians 337
Radiologic nurses, *see:* Registered nurses 303
Radiologic technologists and technicians 337
Radiologists, *see:* Physicians and surgeons 295
Radiologists, oral and maxillofacial, *see:* Dentists 282
Rail-track laying and maintenance equipment operators 668
Rail transportation occupations 644
Rail yard engineers, *see:* Rail transportation occupations 644
Railcar repairers, *see:* Heavy vehicle and mobile equipment service technicians and mechanics 555
Railroad brake, signal, and switch operators, *see:* Rail transportation occupations 644
Railroad conductors, *see:* Rail transportation occupations 644
Railroad engineers, *see:* Rail transportation occupations 644
Ranchers, *see:* Farmers, ranchers, and agricultural managers 40
Range conservationists, *see:* Conservation scientists and foresters .. 153
Range ecologists, *see:* Conservation scientists and foresters 153
Range managers, *see:* Conservation scientists and foresters 153
Range scientists, *see:* Conservation scientists and foresters 153
Ratings analysts, *see:* Financial analysts and personal financial advisors 85
Re-recording mixers, *see:* Broadcast and sound engineering technicians and radio operators 261
Reactor operators, *see:* Power plant operators, distributors, and dispatchers 608
Readers, meter, *see:* Meter readers, utilities 463
Real estate agents, *see:* Real estate brokers and sales agents 414
Real estate appraisers, *see:* Appraisers and assessors of real estate .. 74
Real estate assessors, *see:* Appraisers and assessors of real estate ... 74
Real estate asset managers, *see:* Property, real estate, and community association managers 61
Real estate brokers and sales agents 414
Real estate closers, *see:* Real estate brokers and sales agents 414
Real estate managers, *see:* Property, real estate, and community association managers 61
Real estate rental agents, *see:* Real estate brokers and sales agents 414
Real property appraisers, *see:* Appraisers and assessors of real estate 74

Real property assessors, *see:* Appraisers and assessors of real estate 74
Real-time captioners, *see:* Court reporters 199
Realtors, *see:* Real estate brokers and sales agents 414
Rebuilders, transmission, *see:* Automotive service technicians and mechanics 549
Receive-and-deliver clerks, *see:* Brokerage clerks 441
Receiving clerks, *see:* Shipping, receiving, and traffic clerks 467
Receptionists and information clerks 455
Record center clerks, *see:* File clerks 447
Record clerks, *see:* File clerks 447
Recording engineers, *see:* Broadcast and sound engineering technicians and radio operators 261
Recreation attendants, *see:* Amusement and recreation attendants 664
Recreation leaders, *see:* Recreation workers 400
Recreation specialists, therapeutic, *see:* Recreational therapists 302
Recreation supervisors, *see:* Recreation workers 400
Recreation workers 400
Recreational therapists 302
Recreational vehicle service technicians 670
Recruiters, *see:* Human resources, training, and labor relations managers and specialists 50
Recruiting managers, *see:* Human resources, training, and labor relations managers and specialists 50
Recruitment consultants, *see:* Human resources, training, and labor relations managers and specialists 50
Recruitment managers, *see:* Human resources, training, and labor relations managers and specialists 50
Referees, *see:* Athletes, coaches, umpires, and related workers 252
Refractory masons, *see:* Brickmasons, blockmasons, and stonemasons 495
Refractory materials repairers, except brickmasons 670
Refrigeration mechanics, *see:* Heating, air-conditioning, and refrigeration mechanics and installers 562
Refuse and recyclable material collectors, *see:* Material moving occupations 650
Regional geographers, *see:* Social scientists, other 182
Regional planners, *see:* Urban and regional planners 180
Registered dietitians, *see:* Dietitians and nutritionists 284
Registered nurse anesthetists, certified, *see:* Registered nurses 303
Registered nurses 303
Registered representatives, *see:* Securities, commodities, and financial services sales agents 426
Registered respiratory therapists, *see:* Respiratory therapists 307
Registrars, *see:* Meeting and convention planners 95
Registrars, college or university, *see:* Education administrators 34
Registrars, tumor, *see:* Medical records and health information technicians 328
Rehabilitation counselors, *see:* Counselors 189
Rehabilitation nurses, *see:* Registered nurses 303
Reinforcing iron and rebar workers, *see:* Structural and reinforcing iron and metal workers 534
Relationship managers, *see:* Securities, commodities, and financial services sales agents 426
Relay technicians, *see:* Electrical and electronics installers and repairers 538
Religious priests, *see:* Clergy 662
Remedial education teachers, *see:* Teachers—Adult literacy and remedial education 221
Rental clerks, *see:* Counter and rental clerks 407
Rental managers, *see:* Property, real estate, and community association managers 61
Reporters, *see:* News analysts, reporters, and correspondents 267
Reporters, court, *see:* Court reporters 199
Research analysts, marketing, *see:* Market and survey researchers 175
Research chefs, *see:* Chefs, cooks, and food preparation workers 371
Research dietitians, *see:* Dietitians and nutritionists 284
Research psychologists, *see:* Psychologists 177
Researchers, survey, *see:* Market and survey researchers 175
Reservation agents, *see:* Reservation and transportation ticket agents and travel clerks 457
Reservation and transportation ticket agents and travel clerks 457
Residence leasing agents, *see:* Real estate brokers and sales agents 414
Resident managers, *see:* Lodging managers 56
Residential advisors 665
Residential electricians, *see:* Electricians 513
Resort desk clerks, *see:* Hotel, motel, and resort desk clerks 448
Respiratory care practitioners, *see:* Respiratory therapists 307

Respiratory nurses, *see:* Registered nurses 303
Respiratory therapists 307
Respiratory therapy technicians, *see:* Respiratory therapists 307
Responders, first, *see:* Emergency medical technicians and paramedics 324
Restaurant chefs, *see:* Chefs, cooks, and food preparation workers 371
Restaurant managers, *see:* Food service managers 45
Retail buyers, *see:* Purchasing managers, buyers, and purchasing agents 64
Retail managers, *see:* Sales worker supervisors 423
Retail salespersons 417
Retouchers, photographic, *see:* Photographic process workers and processing machine operators 625
Revenue agents, *see:* Tax examiners, collectors, and revenue agents 98
Revenue officers, *see:* Tax examiners, collectors, and revenue agents 98
Riggers 670
Rigging slingers and chasers, *see:* Forest, conservation, and logging workers 490
Risk and insurance managers, *see:* Financial managers 43
Risk managers, *see:* Financial managers 43
Rock splitters, quarry 669
Rolling machine setters, operators, and tenders, metal and plastic, *see:* Machine setters, operators, and tenders—metal and plastic 589
Roman Catholic priests, *see:* Clergy 662
Roof bolters, mining 669
Roofers 530
Rooms managers, *see:* Lodging managers 56
Rotary drill operators, oil and gas 669
Roustabouts, oil and gas 669
Route drivers, *see:* Truck drivers and driver/sales workers 640
Rural mail carriers, *see:* Postal Service workers 464

S

Safe repairers, *see:* Locksmiths and safe repairers 670
Safety and health practitioners, *see:* Occupational health and safety specialists and technicians 331
Safety engineers, *see:* Engineers 133
Safety inspectors, *see:* Occupational health and safety specialists and technicians 331
Safety specialists and technicians, occupational, *see:* Occupational health and safety specialists and technicians 331
Sailors, *see:* Job opportunities in the Armed Forces 653
Sailors, merchant marine, *see:* Water transportation occupations 647
Sales agents, advertising, *see:* Advertising sales agents 403
Sales agents, real estate, *see:* Real estate brokers and sales agents 414
Sales assistants, *see:* Brokerage clerks 441
Sales engineers 419
Sales engineers, *see:* Retail salespersons 417
Sales managers, *see:* Advertising, marketing, promotions, public relations, and sales managers 27
Sales representative, *see:* Advertising sales agents 403
Sales representatives, *see:* Order clerks 454
Sales representatives, *see:* Retail salespersons 417
Sales representatives, *see:* Sales engineers 419
Sales representatives, wholesale and manufacturing 422
Sales worker supervisors 423
Sales workers, *see also:*
   Cashiers 405
   Counter and rental clerks 407
   Demonstrators, product promoters, and models 408
   Insurance sales agents 411
   Real estate brokers and sales agents 414
   Retail salespersons 417
   Sales engineers 419
   Sales representatives, wholesale and manufacturing 421
   Sales worker supervisors 423
   Securities, commodities, and financial services sales agents 426
   Travel agents 429
   Truck drivers and driver/sales workers 643
Samplers, *see:* Inspectors, testers, sorters, samplers, and weighers 614
Samplers, *see:* Weighers, measurers, checkers, and samplers, recordkeeping 470
Sauce cooks, *see:* Chefs, cooks, and food preparation workers 371
Sawing machine operators and tenders, *see:* Woodworkers 606
Scalers, *see:* Forest, conservation, and logging workers 490

Scanner operators, *see:* Prepress technicians and workers 598
School and college counselors, *see:* Counselors 189
School bus drivers, *see:* Bus drivers 634
School librarians, *see:* Librarians 214
School psychologists, *see:* Psychologists 177
School social workers, *see:* Social workers 196
School superintendents, *see:* Top executives 67
School teachers, *see:* Teachers— preschool, kindergarten, elementary, middle, and secondary 227
Science technicians 185
Science writers, *see:* Writers and editors 275
Scientific illustrators, *see:* Artists and related workers 235
Scientific photographers, *see:* Photographers 269
Scouts, professional sports, *see:* Athletes, coaches, umpires, and related workers 252
Scraper operators, *see:* Construction equipment operators 507
Screen printing machine setters and set-up operators, *see:* Printing machine operators 600
Scrubs, *see:* Surgical technologists 339
Sculptors, *see:* Artists and related workers 235
Secondary school teachers, *see:* Teachers—preschool, kindergarten, elementary, middle, and secondary 227
Secret Service agents, *see:* Police and detectives 362
Secretarial assistants, *see:* Secretaries and administrative assistants 482
Secretaries, *see:* Secretaries and administrative assistants 482
Secretaries and administrative assistants 482
Securities analysts, *see:* Financial analysts and personal financial advisors 85
Securities, commodities, and financial services sales agents 426
Security and fire alarm systems installers 670
Security guards and gaming surveillance officers 369
Security officers, *see:* Security guards and gaming surveillance officers 368
Segmental pavers, *see:* Cement masons, concrete finishers, segmental pavers, and terrazzo workers 502
Seismologists, *see:* Geoscientists 167
Self enrichment teachers, *see:* Teachers—self-enrichment education 231
Semiconductor processors 626
Senators, *see:* Top executives 67
Senior administrative managers, *see:* Office and administrative support worker supervisors and managers 479
Senior administrators, *see:* Office and administrative support worker supervisors and managers 479
Senior reactor operators, *see:* Power plant operators, distributors, and dispatchers 609
Separating, filtering, clarifying, precipitating, and still machine setters, operators, and tenders 672
Septic tank servicers and sewer pipe cleaners 669
Servers, *see:* Food and beverage serving and related workers 374
Service station attendants 673
Service technicians, automotive, *see:* Automotive service technicians and mechanics 549
Service technicians, diesel, *see:* Diesel service technicians and mechanics 552
Service technicians, heavy vehicle and mobile equipment, *see:* Heavy vehicle and mobile equipment service technicians and mechanics 555
Service technicians, home appliances, *see:* Home appliance repairers 565
Service technicians, home entertainment, *see:* Electronic home entertainment equipment installers and repairers 540
Service technicians, mobile heavy equipment, *see:* Heavy vehicle and mobile equipment service technicians and mechanics 555
Service unit operators, oil, gas, and mining 669
Set and exhibit designers 663
Sewage treatment plant operators, *see:* Water and liquid waste treatment plant and system operators 612
Sewers, hand, *see:* Textile, apparel, and furnishings occupations 602
Sewing machine operators, *see:* Textile, apparel, and furnishings occupations 602
Shampooers, *see:* Barbers, cosmetologists, and other personal appearance workers 387
Sheet metal workers 531
Sheriffs and deputy sheriffs, *see:* Police and detectives 362
Ship officers, *see:* Water transportation occupations 647
Shipping-and-receiving supervisors, *see:* Office and administrative support worker supervisors and managers 479
Shipping clerks, *see:* Shipping, receiving, and traffic clerks 467
Shipping, receiving, and traffic clerks 467
Shoe and leather workers and repairers, *see:* Textile, apparel, and furnishings occupations 603
Shoe machine operators and tenders, *see:* Textile, apparel, and furnishings occupations 603
Short haul or local truck drivers, *see:* Truck drivers and driver/sales workers 640
Short-order cooks, *see:* Chefs, cooks, and food preparation workers 372
Show hosts, *see:* Announcers 259
Shuttle car operators, *see:* Material moving occupations 650
Sign language interpreters, *see:* Interpreters and translators 263
Signal and track switch repairers 670
Signal operators, railroad, *see:* Rail transportation occupations 644
Silvering applicators, *see:* Painting and coating workers, except construction and maintenance 622
Silversmiths, *see:* Jewelers and precious stone and metal workers 616
Simultaneous interpreters, *see:* Interpreters and translators 263
Singers, *see:* Musicians, singers, and related workers 257
Sketch artists, *see:* Artists and related workers 235
Skills trainers, *see:* Human resources, training, and labor relations managers and specialists 50
Skills training coordinators, *see:* Human resources, training, and labor relations managers and specialists 50
Skin care specialists, *see:* Barbers, cosmetologists, and other personal appearance workers 387
Slaughterers and meat packers, *see:* Food processing occupations 581
Slot key persons, *see:* Gaming services occupations 397
Small engine mechanics 558
Smoke jumpers, *see:* Fire fighting occupations 359
Social and community service managers 662
Social and human service assistants 194
Social psychologists, *see:* Psychologists 177
Social science research assistants 663
Social scientists, other 182
Social work assistants, *see:* Social and human service assistants 194
Social work planners and policy makers, *see:* Social workers 196
Social workers 196
Sociocultural anthropologists, *see:* Social scientists, other 182
Sociologists, *see:* Social scientists, other 182
Software engineers, *see:* Computer software engineers 111
Software quality assurance analysts, *see:* Computer systems analysts 116
Soil conservationists, *see:* Conservation scientists and foresters 153
Soil scientists, *see:* Agricultural and food scientists 147
Solderers, *see:* Welding, soldering, and brazing workers 594
Soldiers, *see:* Job opportunities in the Armed Forces 653
Songwriters, *see:* Musicians, singers, and related workers 257
Sonographers, abdominal, *see:* Diagnostic medical sonographers 322
Sonographers, cardiac, *see:* Cardiovascular technologists and technicians 316
Sonographers, diagnostic medical, *see:* Diagnostic medical sonographers 322
Sonographers, gynecologic, *see:* Diagnostic medical sonographers 322
Sonographers, obstetric, *see:* Diagnostic medical sonographers 322
Sonographers, ophthalmologic, *see:* Diagnostic medical sonographers 322
Sonographers, vascular, *see:* Cardiovascular technologists and technicians 316
Sorters, *see:* Inspectors, testers, sorters, samplers, and weighers 614
Sorters, agricultural products, *see:* Agricultural workers 485
Sound engineering technicians, *see:* Broadcast and sound engineering technicians and radio operators 261
Sound mixers, *see:* Broadcast and sound engineering technicians and radio operators 261
Sous chefs, *see:* Chefs, cooks, and food preparation workers 371
Special education teachers, *see:* Teachers—special education 232
Specialists, clinical nurse, *see:* Registered nurses 303
Specialists, diesel engine, *see:* Diesel service technicians and mechanics 552
Specialists, fire prevention, *see:* Fire fighting occupations 359
Specialists, occupational health and safety, *see:* Occupational health and safety specialists and technicians 331
Specialists, skin care, *see:* Barbers, cosmetologists, and other personal appearance workers 387
Specialists, therapeutic recreation, *see:* Recreational therapists 302
Specification inspectors, *see:* Construction and building inspectors 504

Speech-language pathologists 309
Speech therapists, *see:* Speech-language pathologists 309
Speech writers, *see:* Public relations specialists 271
Sports book writers and runners, *see:* Gaming services occupations 398
Sports competitors, *see:* Athletes, coaches, umpires, and
　related workers 252
Sports instructors, *see:* Athletes, coaches, umpires, and
　related workers 252
Sports officials, *see:* Athletes, coaches, umpires, and
　related workers 252
Sports trainers, *see:* Athletes, coaches, umpires, and
　related workers 252
Sportscasters, *see:* News analysts, reporters, and correspondents 267
Spray machine operators, *see:* Painting and coating workers,
　except construction and maintenance 622
Sprinklerfitters, *see:* Pipelayers, plumbers, pipefitters, and
　steamfitters 525
Staff assistants, *see:* Secretaries and administrative assistants 482
Staff development specialists, *see:* Instructional coordinators 213
Staff managers, *see:* Office and administrative support worker
　supervisors and managers 479
Staff training and development, managers of, *see:* Human resources,
　training, and labor relations managers and specialists 50
Staffing and assignments coordinators, *see:* Human resources
　assistants, except payroll and timekeeping 449
Staffing consultants, *see:* Human resources, training, and
　labor relations managers and specialists 50
Staffing coordinators, *see:* Human resources, training, and
　labor relations managers and specialists 50
Staffing managers, *see:* Human resources, training, and
　labor relations managers and specialists 50
Staffing specialists, *see:* Human resources, training, and
　labor relations managers and specialists 50
State police officers, *see:* Police and detectives 362
State troopers, *see:* Police and detectives 362
Station agents, *see:* Reservation and transportation ticket agents
　and travel clerks 457
Station installers and repairers, telephone, *see:* Radio and
　telecommunications equipment installers and repairers 542
Stationary engineers and boiler operators 610
Statistical assistants 666
Statisticians 123
Steadicam operators, *see:* Television, video, and motion picture
　camera operators and editors 274
Steamfitters, *see:* Pipelayers, plumbers, pipefitters, and
　steamfitters 525
Stenocaptioners, *see:* Court reporters 199
Stevedores, *see:* Material moving occupations 650
Stewardesses and stewards, airline, *see:* Flight attendants 394
Stewards, passenger ship, *see:* Water transportation occupations 647
Stock clerks and order fillers 469
Stock-control clerks, *see:* Stock clerks and order fillers 469
Stockbrokers, *see:* Securities, commodities, and
　financial services sales agents 426
Stonemasons, *see:* Brickmasons, blockmasons, and stonemasons 495
Storage managers, *see:* Transportation, storage, and
　distribution managers 662
Store detectives, *see:* Private detectives and investigators 366
Stratigraphers, *see:* Geoscientists 167
Street vendors, *see:* Door-to-door sales workers, news and
　street vendors, and related workers 665
Streetcar operators, *see:* Rail transportation occupations 644
Strength trainers, *see:* Athletes, coaches, umpires, and
　related workers 252
Structural and reinforcing iron and metal workers 534
Structural engineers, *see:* Engineers 133
Structural metal fabricators and fitters, *see:* Assemblers and
　fabricators 579
Stucco masons, *see:* Plasterers and stucco masons 528
Student affairs administrators, *see:* Education administrators 34
Studio camera operators, *see:* Television, video, and
　motion picture camera operators and editors 274
Substance abuse and behavioral disorder counselors,
　see: Counselors 189
Substance abuse social workers, *see:* Social workers 196
Subway operators, *see:* Rail transportation occupations 644
Superintendents, *see:* Top executives 67

Superintendents, general, *see:* Construction managers 32
Supervisors, farming, fishing, and forestry workers 667
Supervisors, non-retail sales workers, *see:* Sales
　worker supervisors 423
Supervisors, retail sales workers, *see:* Sales worker supervisors 423
Supply managers, *see:* Purchasing managers, buyers, and
　purchasing agents 64
Support clerks, *see:* Office clerks, general 481
Support specialists, *see:* Secretaries and administrative
　assistants 482
Support staff clerks, *see:* Office clerks, general 481
Support staff specialists, *see:* Secretaries and
　administrative assistants 482
Surfacing equipment operators, *see:* Construction equipment
　operators 507
Surgeons, *see:* Physicians and surgeons 295
Surgeons' assistants, *see:* Physician assistants 293
Surgeons, dental, *see:* Dentists 282
Surgeons, oral and maxillofacial, *see:* Dentists 282
Surgeons, podiatric, *see:* Podiatrists 298
Surgical technicians, *see:* Surgical technologists 339
Surgical technologists 339
Surveillance agents, *see:* Security guards and
　gaming surveillance officers 368
Surveillance officers, gaming, *see:* Security guards and
　gaming surveillance officers 368
Survey researchers, *see:* Market and survey researchers 175
Surveying technicians, *see:* Surveyors, cartographers,
　photogrammetrists, and surveying technicians 130
Surveyors, cartographers, photogrammetrists, and
　surveying technicians 130
Switch operators, railroad, *see:* Rail transportation
　occupations 644
Switchboard operators, *see:* Communications equipment
　operators 471
Switchboard operators, *see:* Power plant operators, distributors,
　and dispatchers 608
Synoptic meteorologists, *see:* Atmospheric scientists 159
Systems administrators, *see:* Computer support specialists
　and systems administrators 113
Systems analysts, *see:* Computer systems analysts 116
Systems analysts, *see:* Operations research analysts 121
Systems architects, *see:* Computer scientists and database
　administrators 107
Systems architects, *see:* Computer systems analysts 116
Systems developers, *see:* Computer systems analysts 116
Systems operators, *see:* Power plant operators, distributors,
　and dispatchers 608
Systems programmers, *see:* Computer programmers 104
Systems software engineers, *see:* Computer software engineers 111

T

Tailors, dressmakers, and sewers, *see:* Textile, apparel, and
　furnishings occupations 602
Talking-books clerks, *see:* Library assistants, clerical 453
Tamping equipment operators, *see:* Construction
　equipment operators 507
Tank car, truck, and ship loaders, *see:* Material moving
　occupations 74
Tapers, *see:* Drywall installers, ceiling tile installers, and tapers 512
Tax accountants, *see:* Accountants and auditors 70
Tax assessors, *see:* Appraisers and assessors of real estate 650
Tax collectors, *see:* Tax examiners, collectors, and revenue
　agents 98
Tax examiners, collectors, and revenue agents 98
Tax preparers 662
Taxi drivers and chauffeurs 637
Taxicab dispatchers, *see:* Dispatchers 461
Teacher aides, *see:* Teacher assistants 219
Teacher assistants 219
Teachers—adult literacy and remedial education 221
Teachers—postsecondary 230
Teachers—preschool, kindergarten, elementary, middle, and
　secondary 235
Teachers—self-enrichment education 267
Teachers—special education 232

Teaching assistants, graduate, *see:* Teachers—postsecondary 223
Team assemblers, *see:* Assemblers and fabricators 579
Technical education teachers, postsecondary, *see:* Teachers —postsecondary 223
Technical recruiters, *see:* Human resources, training, and labor relations managers and specialists 50
Technical sales support workers, *see:* Retail salespersons 417
Technical sales support workers, *see:* Sales engineers 419
Technical support specialists, *see:* Computer support specialists and systems administrators 113
Technical trainers, *see:* Human resources, training, and labor relations managers and specialists 50
Technical training coordinators, *see:* Human resources, training, and labor relations managers and specialists 50
Technical writers, *see:* Writers and editors 275
Technicians and technologists, *see:*
- Aircraft and avionics equipment mechanics and service technicians 644
- Archivists, curators, and museum technicians 210
- Automotive body and related repairers 548
- Automotive service technicians and mechanics 549
- Cardiovascular technologists and technicians 316
- Broadcast and sound engineering technicians and radio operators 261
- Clinical laboratory technologists and technicians 318
- Diagnostic medical sonographers 322
- Diesel service technicians and mechanics 552
- Emergency medical technicians and paramedics 324
- Engineering technicians 144
- Heavy vehicle and mobile equipment service technicians and mechanics 555
- Home appliance repairers 565
- Library technicians 217
- Medical records and health information technicians 328
- Nuclear medicine technologists 330
- Occupational health and safety specialists and technicians 331
- Pharmacy technicians 336
- Prepress technicians and workers 598
- Radiologic technologists and technicians 337
- Respiratory therapists 307
- Science technicians 185
- Semiconductor processors 626
- Surgical technologists 339
- Surveyors, cartographers, photogrammetrists, and surveying technicians 131
- Veterinary technologists and technicians 341

Technicians, dental laboratory, *see:* Medical, dental, and ophthalmic laboratory technicians 619
Technicians, medial appliance, *see:* Medical, dental, and ophthalmic laboratory technicians 619
Technicians, ophthalmic laboratory, *see:* Medical, dental, and ophthalmic laboratory technicians 619
Telecommunications equipment installers and repairers, *see:* Radio and telecommunications equipment installers and repairers 542
Telecommunications line installers, *see:* Line installers and repairers 569
Telecommunications service technicians, *see:* Radio and telecommunications equipment installers and repairers 542
Telecommunications specialists, *see:* Computer scientists and database administrators 107
Telemarketers 666
Telephone installers and repairers, *see:* Radio and telecommunications equipment installers and repairers 542
Telephone line installers, *see:* Line installers and repairers 569
Telephone operators, *see:* Communications equipment operators 471
Telephone service representatives, *see:* Customer service representatives 444
Teletype operator, *see:* Data entry and information processing workers 475
Television announcers, *see:* Announcers 259
Television, video, and motion picture camera operators and editors 274
Teller supervisors, *see:* Office and administrative support worker supervisors and managers 479
Tellers 440
Terminal controllers, air traffic, *see:* Air traffic controllers 632
Terrazzo workers, *see:* Cement masons, concrete finishers, segmental pavers, and terrazzo workers 502
Testers, *see:* Inspectors, testers, sorters, samplers, and weighers 614
Textile, apparel, and furnishings occupations 603
Textile bleaching and dyeing machine operators, *see:* Textile, apparel, and furnishings occupations 602
Textile cutting machine operators, *see:* Textile, apparel, and furnishings occupations 602
Textile knitting and weaving machine setters, operators, and tenders, *see:* Textile, apparel, and furnishings occupations 602
Textile machine operators, *see:* Textile, apparel, and furnishings occupations 602
Textile winding, twisting, and drawing out machine operators, *see:* Textile, apparel, and furnishings occupations 602
Theoretical chemists, *see:* Chemists and materials scientists 162
Theoretical mathematicians, *see:* Mathematicians 119
Therapeutic recreation specialists, *see:* Recreational therapists 302
Therapists, hearing, *see:* Audiologists 278
Therapists, industrial, *see:* Occupational therapists 285
Therapists, inhalation, *see:* Respiratory therapists 307
Therapists, marriage and family, *see:* Counselors 189
Therapists, occupational, *see:* Occupational therapists 285
Therapists, oxygen, *see:* Respiratory therapists 307
Therapists, physical, *see:* Physical therapists 292
Therapists, radiation, *see:* Radiation therapists 300
Therapists, recreational, *see:* Recreational therapists 302
Therapists, respiratory, *see:* Respiratory therapists 307
Therapists, speech, *see:* Speech-language pathologists 309
Ticket agents, *see:* Reservation and transportation ticket agents and travel clerks 457
Ticket clerks, *see:* Reservation and transportation ticket agents and travel clerks 457
Ticket sellers, *see:* Reservation and transportation ticket agents and travel clerks 457
Ticket takers, *see:* Ushers, lobby attendants, and ticket takers 665
Tile finishers, *see:* Carpet, floor, and tile installers and finishers 499
Tile installers, *see:* Carpet, floor, and tile installers and finishers 499
Tilesetters, *see:* Carpet, floor, and tile installers and finishers 499
Timber cutting and logging workers, *see:* Forest, conservation, and logging workers 490
Time and attendance clerks, *see:* Payroll and timekeeping clerks 437
Time checkers, *see:* Payroll and timekeeping clerks 437
Time clerks, *see:* Payroll and timekeeping clerks 437
Time recorders, *see:* Payroll and timekeeping clerks 437
Timekeepers, *see:* Payroll and timekeeping clerks 437
Timekeeping clerks, *see:* Payroll and timekeeping clerks 437
Tire builders 672
Tire repairers and changers 670
Title examiners, abstractors, and searchers 663
Tool and die makers 592
Tool grinders, filers, and sharpeners, *see:* Machine setters, operators, and tenders—metal and plastic 589
Toolmakers, *see:* Tool and die makers 592
Top executives 67
Tour bus drivers, *see:* Bus drivers 634
Tour guides and escorts 665
Tow truck dispatchers, *see:* Dispatchers 461
Tower controllers, air traffic, *see:* Air traffic controllers 632
Tractor-trailer drivers, *see:* Truck drivers and driver/sales workers 643
Traders, *see:* Securities, commodities, and financial services sales agents 426
Traffic clerks, *see:* Shipping, receiving, and traffic clerks 467
Traffic technicians 467
Train dispatchers, *see:* Dispatchers 461
Trainers, athletic, *see:* Athletes, coaches, umpires, and related workers 253
Trainers, athletic, *see:* Athletic trainers 314
Trainers, fitness, *see:* Fitness workers 392
Training administrators, *see:* Human resources, training, and labor relations managers and specialists 50
Training and development coordinators, *see:* Human resources, training, and labor relations managers and specialists 50
Training and development managers and specialists, *see:* Human resources, training, and labor relations managers and specialists 50
Training assistants, *see:* Human resources, training, and labor relations managers and specialists 50

Training consultants, *see:* Human resources, training, and labor relations managers and specialists 50

Training coordinators, *see:* Human resources, training, and labor relations managers and specialists 50

Training development directors, *see:* Human resources, training, and labor relations managers and specialists 50

Training directors, *see:* Human resources, training, and labor relations managers and specialists 50

Training managers, *see:* Human resources, training, and labor relations managers and specialists 50

Training specialists, *see:* Human resources, training, and labor relations managers and specialists 50

Transcribers, *see:* Data entry and information processing workers 475

Transcriptionists, medical, *see:* Medical transcriptionists ... 348

Transfer clerks, *see:* Brokerage clerks 441

Transit and railroad police, *see:* Police and detectives 364

Translators, *see:* Interpreters and translators 263

Transmission engineers, *see:* Broadcast and sound engineering technicians and radio operators 261

Transmission technicians and rebuilders, *see:* Automotive service technicians and mechanics 549

Transmitter operators, *see:* Broadcast and sound engineering technicians and radio operators 261

Transplant nurses, *see:* Registered nurses 303

Transportation attendants, *see:* Flight attendants 394

Transportation attendants, except flight attendants and baggage porters 665

Transportation engineers, *see:* Engineers 133

Transportation equipment painters, *see:* Painting and coating workers, except construction and maintenance 622

Transportation inspectors 673

Transportation, storage, and distribution managers 622

Transportation ticket agents, *see:* Reservation and transportation ticket agents and travel clerks 457

Trash collectors, *see:* Material moving occupations 650

Trauma nurses, *see:* Registered nurses 303

Travel agents 429

Travel clerks, *see:* Reservation and transportation ticket agents and travel clerks 457

Travel consultants, *see:* Travel agents 429

Travel counselors, *see:* Reservation and transportation ticket agents and travel clerks 457

Travel guides 665

Treasurers, *see:* Financial managers 43

Treatment plant and system operators, wastewater, *see:* Water and liquid waste treatment plant and system operators 612

Treatment plant and system operators, water, *see:* Water and liquid waste treatment plant and system operators 612

Treatment, storage, and disposal (TSD) workers, *see:* Hazardous materials removal workers 519

Tree planters, *see:* Forest, conservation, and logging workers 490

Tree trimmers and pruners, *see:* Grounds maintenance workers ... 380

Trial lawyers, *see:* Lawyers 204

Truck dispatchers, *see:* Dispatchers 461

Truck drivers and driver/sales workers 641

Truck mechanics, *see:* Diesel service technicians and mechanics 552

Tumbling barrel painters, *see:* Painting and coating workers, except construction and maintenance 622

Tumor registrars, *see:* Medical records and health information technicians 328

Tune-up technicians, *see:* Automotive service technicians and mechanics 549

Tuners, musical instruments, *see:* Precision instrument and equipment repairers 576

Two-stroke engine mechanics, *see:* Small engine mechanics 558

Typesetting machine operators and tenders, *see:* Prepress technicians and workers 598

Typists, *see:* Data entry and information processing workers 475

Typographers, *see:* Desktop publishers 477

U

U.S. Border Patrol agents, *see:* Police and detectives 364

U.S. Congress representatives, *see:* Top executives 67

U.S. Marshals and deputy marshals, *see:* Police and detectives 364

U.S. Secret Service special agents, *see:* Police and detectives 364

U.S. Senators, *see:* Top executives 67

Ultrasonographers, *see:* Diagnostic medical sonographers 322

Ultrasound technologists, *see:* Diagnostic medical sonographers 322

Umpires, *see:* Athletes, coaches, umpires, and related workers 252

Unclaimed property officers, *see:* Administrative services managers 25

Undertakers, *see:* Funeral directors 48

Underwriters, *see:* Insurance underwriters 88

Underwriters, loan, *see:* Loan officers 90

Uniformed police officers, *see:* Police and detectives 364

University deans, *see:* Education administrators 34

University professors, *see:* Teachers—postsecondary 223

Unlicensed assistive personnel, *see:* Nursing, psychiatric, and home health aides 350

Upholsterers, *see:* Textile, apparel, and furnishings occupations 603

Urban and regional planners 180

Urban and transportation geographers, *see:* Social scientists, other ... 182

Urology nurses, *see:* Registered nurses 303

Ushers, lobby attendants, and ticket takers 665

V

Vascular sonographers, *see:* Cardiovascular technologists and technicians 316

Vascular technologists, *see:* Cardiovascular technologists and technicians 316

Vegetable cooks, *see:* Chefs, cooks, and food preparation workers 371

Vending machine repairers, *see:* Coin, vending, and amusement machine servicers and repairers 560

Vending machine servicers, *see:* Coin, vending, and amusement machine servicers and repairers 560

Vending machine technicians, *see:* Coin, vending, and amusement machine servicers and repairers 560

Veterinarians 311

Veterinary assistants and laboratory animal caretakers 665

Veterinary technologists and technicians 341

Vice presidents, *see:* Top executives 67

Video camera operators, *see:* Television, video, and motion picture camera operators and editors 274

Video control engineers, *see:* Broadcast and sound engineering technicians and radio operators 261

Video editors, *see:* Television, video, and motion picture camera operators and editors 274

Videographers, *see:* Television, video, and motion picture camera operators and editors 274

Violin repairers, *see:* Precision instrument and equipment repairers ... 575

Vocational counselors, *see:* Counselors 189

Vocational education teachers, secondary school, *see:* Teachers—preschool, kindergarten, elementary, middle, and secondary 227

Vocational nurses, licensed, *see:* Licensed practical and licensed vocational nurses 326

Vocational-technical education teachers, postsecondary, *see:* Teachers—postsecondary 223

Voice writers, *see:* Court reporters 199

Volcanologists, *see:* Geoscientists 167

W

Wait staff, *see:* Food and beverage serving and related workers 374

Waiters and waitresses, *see:* Food and beverage serving and related workers 374

Wastewater treatment plant and system operators, *see:* Water and liquid waste treatment plant and system operators 612

Watch repairers, *see:* Precision instrument and equipment repairers 575

Water and liquid waste treatment plant and system operators 612

Water and wastewater treatment plant and system operators, *see:* Water and liquid waste treatment plant and system operators 612

Water conservationists, *see:* Conservation scientists and foresters 153

Water resources engineers, *see:* Engineers 133

Water transportation occupations 647

Water treatment plant and system operators, *see:* Water and liquid waste treatment plant and system operators 612

Weather forecasters, *see:* Atmospheric scientists 159

Weathercasters, *see:* News analysts, reporters, and correspondents 267

Weaving machine operators, textile, *see:* Textile, apparel, and furnishings occupations 602

Web designers, *see:* Computer scientists and database administrators 107

Web developers, *see:* Computer scientists and database
  administrators.. 107
Web programmers, *see:* Computer programmers 104
Web publications designers, *see:* Desktop publishers 477
Web writers, *see:* Writers and editors 275
Webmasters, *see:* Computer scientists and database administrators...... 107
Weighers, *see:* Inspectors, testers, sorters, samplers, and weighers 614
Weighers, measurers, checkers, and samplers, recordkeeping 470
Welders, *see:* Welding, soldering, and brazing workers 594
Welding machine setters, operators, and tenders, *see:* Welding,
  soldering, and brazing workers 594
Welding, soldering, and brazing workers................................ 594
Wellhead pumpers, *see:* Material moving occupations 650
Wholesale buyers, *see:* Purchasing managers, buyers, and
  purchasing agents 64
Wildlife biologists, *see:* Biological scientists 150
Wildlife officers, *see:* Police and detectives 362
Winch operators, *see:* Material moving occupations........................... 650
Window clerks, *see:* Postal Service workers 464
Window trimmers, *see:* Merchandise displayers and
  window trimmers 663
Woodworkers 606
Woodworking machine operators and tenders, *see:*
  Woodworkers 606

Word processors, *see:* Data entry and information processing
  workers... 475
Worker compensation coordinators, *see:* Human resources
  assistants, except payroll and timekeeping 449
Workforce development officers, *see:* Human resources, training,
  and labor relations managers and specialists 50
Workforce development specialists, *see:* Human resources, training,
  and labor relations managers and specialists 50
Wound, ostomy, and continence nurses, *see:* Registered nurses 303
Writers and editors 275

X

X-ray technicians, *see:* Radiologic technologists and technicians 337

Y

Yardmasters, *see:* Rail transportation occupations 646
Yoga instructors, *see:* Fitness workers.................................. 392

Z

Zookeepers, *see:* Animal care and service workers 384
Zoologists, *see:* Biological scientists.................................... 150

BLS Employment Projections Online

http://www.bls.gov/emp

Federal Government's Premier Career Guidance Publications

- Occupational Outlook Handbook
- Career Guide to Industries
- Occupational Outlook Quarterly
- Occupational Projections and Training Data

People Are Asking

- What are the fastest growing occupations and industries?
- Which occupations will add the most new jobs?

Publications

- Projections-related articles
- Special features: "Charting the projections" and "The job outlook in brief"

Searchable Databases

- Occupational Employment, Training, and Earnings
- National Employment Matrix
- Tables created by BLS

Related Links

- BLS career information for young people
- State employment projections

Contacts

- Telephone listings for industry and occupational experts at the Office of Occupational Statistics and Employment Projections

Related Publications!

Occupational Projections and Training Data

2006-07 Edition . BLS Bulletin 2602

This publication provides statistical data to support information presented in the *Occupational Outlook Handbook.* Education and training planners, career counselors, and jobseekers can compare hundreds of occupations on factors such as employment change, self-employed workers, earnings, and the most significant source of postsecondary education or training. Users also will find awards and degree data, by field of study.

Career Guide to Industries

2006-07 Edition . BLS Bulletin 2601

As a companion publication to the *Occupational Outlook Handbook,* the *Career Guide* discusses careers from an industry perspective.

The 45 industries highlighted in this bulletin account for 3 of every 4 wage and salary jobs in the Nation. The *Career Guide* describes some occupations not covered by the *Handbook,* and discusses the nature of the industry, job qualifications and advancement opportunities, industry outlook, and earnings.

Get the latest editions!

For prices and ordering information, refer to the Employment Projections Internet site. **http://www.bls.gov/emp**